Seventeenth Edition

Blue Book
of Gun Values™

By S. P. Fjestad

17th Edition
Blue Book
of Gun Values

Publisher's Note:

This book is the result of nonstop and continual firearms research obtained by attending gun shows, communicating with gun dealers and collectors throughout the country each year. This book represents an analysis of prices for which collectible firearms have actually been selling for during that period at an average retail level. Although every reasonable effort has been made to compile an accurate and reliable guide, gun prices may vary significantly depending on such factors as the locality of the sale, the number of sales we were able to consider, and economic conditions. Accordingly, no representation can be made that the guns listed may be bought or sold at prices indicated, nor shall the author or publisher be responsible for any error made in compiling and recording such prices.

All Rights Reserved
Copyright 1996, Blue Book Publications, Inc.
8009 - 34th Avenue South, Minneapolis, MN 55425
Orders Only 800-877-4867
Phone No. 612-854-5229
FAX No. 612-853-1486
e-mail: bluebook@bluebookinc.com
Website/homepage: http://www.bluebookinc.com

Published and printed in the United States of America

ISBN No. 1-886768-04-8

Library of Congress No. SV85-7287

 # Contents

Cover Details

It was hard even imagining that only last Fall, he had sworn to never grumble again over even the worst cold weather snap, after having just undergone one of the most miserably hot and woodtick-infested summers during the past three decades. The constant, late July heat had been hard on him, and several times while digging in fence posts, he had been felled by the early afternoon sun which generally had gone over the 90+ degree/90% humidity levels for weeks on end. While the transitional Indian Summer had lasted until almost the end of September, one morning while checking his mink traps, a beautiful Fall day had been canceled by a rapidly increasing cold, northwest wind that by darkness had lowered temperatures almost 50 degrees and had stripped most of the hardwoods of their vibrant colors to stark black-and-white.

He remembered that several days prior, the minnows he had carried on his back for miles and carefully placed in the deep, nearly frozen, trap encircled, water-filled animal step-holes next to a couple of sloughs had produced deadly mink sets. The morning before Summer had given way to Winter, he had caught 16 adult mink - his personal best after 20 years of packing traps.

The following months, the combination of heavy snowfall and bitter cold had changed his neatly trimmed fall beard into a visual catastrophe that now resembled a half-frozen buffalo hide. One night during his third trip into town, someone had told him the temperature had bottomed out at -60 below down South several weeks ago. Seven cords — 4 sticks at a time — through his blackened, pot-bellied wood burner had barely kept the water unfrozen in his log cabin between trapping excursions. He had even found his trusty Chesapeake frozen solid in her straw-lined doghouse one morning following a long bout of tight coughing which had developed right before Thanksgiving - probably due to heartworms.

The fresh afterbirth from his nearest neighbor's cows had been an aromatic magnet for important fur-bearing animals while it lasted - as long as the timber wolves and fox had gotten to his traps before the rest of the predators. He couldn't remember how many trapped stray dogs around the frozen birthing fluid he had shot with his short barreled, Winchester Model '94 Trapper within the past few months. While trapping had been good, lately the would-be scavengers had been starting to get recycled by an animal whose giant tracks around the grizzly, partially eaten remains suggested that this bear would have to be dealt with sooner or later.

So on this cold, March afternoon several days before Spring, the trapper had decided to bring with his Model 1886 short rifle in .45-70 just in case the big brown crossed his path between his shortened fox and beaver trap lines. As his snowshoes glided along his packed-down previous trails with some more unwanted jumbo snowflakes that seemed to be floating in mid-air, the trapper realized if he couldn't put a bullet into this unwanted meat-eater shortly, by next fall he could have trained this bear into being a trap raider. He couldn't wait to start sweating again — this time there would be no complaints, no matter how hungry and thick the mosquitoes and black flies were.

Cover Design and Final Layout — S.P. Fjestad

Art Director — Walter Horishnyk

Production Manager — Thomas Lundin

Color Separations and Image Compositing — Northwoods Color and CTS.

Printing — Worzalla located in Stevens Point, WI.

Blue Book Publications, Inc.

ORDER FORM

8009 34th Ave. S. #1391, dpt. bb17 • Minneapolis, MN 55425

800-877-4867
Domestic/Canadian orders

612-854-5229   FAX 612-853-1486
International

web site: http://www.bluebookinc.com
email: bluebook@bluebookinc.com

QUANTITY

	USA	USA	CANADA MEXICO	EUROPE/ SOUTH AMERICA	AFRICA ASIA or PACIFIC RIM	PRICE
Blue Book of Gun Values	**4th Class**	**UPS/1st Class**	All prices include s/h.			
__ 17th Edition ($27.95 retail)	$30.95	$32.95	$38.00	$40.00	$53.00	_____
__ 17th & 18th Edition	$56.95	$58.95	$76.00	$80.00	$106.00	_____
Blue Book of Guitars	**4th Class**	**UPS/1st Class**				
__ 2nd Edition ($24.95 retail)	$28.95	$30.95	$36.00	$36.00	$50.00	_____
__ 2nd & 3rd Edition	$44.95	$49.95	$72.00	$72.00	$100.00	_____
The Book of Colt Firearms	**UPS only/1st Class**					
__ 2nd Edition ($149.95 retail)	$161.00	$171.50	$177.50	$208.00	_____	
__ Deluxe Edition	$395.00	$416.00	$422.50	$454.00	_____	
__ Book Jacket 1st Ed. reprint (1st Class only)	$35.00	$37.00	$38.00	$39.00	_____	
CADA Gun Journal	**3rd Class**	**1st Class**				
__ 1 yr Subscription (12 issues)	$14.95	$29.90	$44.95	$74.95	$100.00	_____
__ 2 yr Subscription (24 issues)	$29.90	$69.90	$79.90	$89.90	$114.95	_____
__ 3 yr Subscription (36 issues)	$44.85	$104.85	$114.85	$124.85	$129.90	_____
Sporting Collectibles	**4th Class**	**1st Class**				
__ Auction Pocket Guide	$17.95	$19.00	$22.00	$26.00	$23.00	_____
__ **Mossberg - More Gun For the Money**						
	4th Class	**1st Class**				
	$29.45	$31.45	$38.50	$39.00	$47.00	_____

CALL, FAX, or MAIL your order
to the numbers and address above.
(When mailing, tear out this page,
fold & return in envelope with payment.)

MN residents add 6.5% sales tax _____
Call for expedited shipping cost _____

Total enclosed or to charge $ _____

VISA   MasterCard   DISCOVER   AMERICAN EXPRESS

Name_____

Company_____

Address_____

City_____ State_____ Zip_____

Credit Card No._____ Exp._____

Daytime Phone No._____

Signature_____

Form of Payment:
- ❑ **Personal Check**
- ❑ **Money Order**
- ❑ **Cashier's Check**
- ❑ **Visa**
- ❑ **Master Card**
- ❑ **Discover**
- ❑ **American Express**

Office Hours: 8:30am - 5:00pm CST, Monday - Friday.
Answering machine services available 5:00pm - 8:30am, Monday -Friday and weekends.
FAX 24 hours a day at 612-853-1486.
All orders are shipped within 2 working days after receiving good funds.

Blue Book Publications, Inc. • 8009 34th Ave. S. #1391, dpt. bb17 • Minneapolis, MN 55425

Acknowledgements

Many of you who have followed this project have seen the listing of names on these pages grow somewhat in proportion to the size of the book. I would like to thank all of you who have written, FAX'ed, or called me on potential revisions, additions, and corrections. This is the best tool I know of to make this publication more up-to-date and complete every year. To the people listed below, a special thanks is in order, as they have been critical in providing more information annually. So stand up and take a bow, ladies and gentlemen - all of us owe you a round of applause.

Leonardo M. Antaris, M.D.

Charles Layson

Lowell Pauli

LeRoy Merz

Richard Alexander
of Interarms

Robert Rayburn

Cpt. Mark Rendina

Richard Bauter
of Browning

Jim Spacek

Thomas Koessl

A. O. Salvo

Pat Redmond

Richard Machniak

John Kopec

Bob Jones

Gary Brown

Charles E. Carder

Brad Simpson

Karl Lippard

Roger Morris

Fred Sweeney

Rudy Etchen

Rick Crosier

Joe Prather
of Griffin & Howe

Keith Rolf

Evan Whildin

Jim Supica

James W. Whitcomb

Randy Shuman

Gurney Brown

Roy Jinks
of Smith & Wesson

Jack Heath
of Remington Arms Co.

Charles Semmer

Lynn Oliver

Syd & David M. Rachwal

Dr. Robert Beeman

Jim Jasken

Roy Marcot

Eric M. Larson

Kevin Cherry

Patrick McKune

Hal Hamilton

Dean Rinehart

John Lacy

Jeff Faintich

Don & Carol Wilkerson

Joe Gillenwater

T. Rees Day

James Goergen

Les Hovenkamp

William Larkin Moore

Tommy Rholes

Mel Neff

Martin J. Lane

Steve Engelson

David Noll

Harrison Carroll

Bruno Pardee
of U.S. Repeating Arms

Buck Dickinson

John Dougan

Gary Mingolelli

Dr. Joseph S. Eisenlauer

Felix Bedlan

John Picchietti

David Buehn

Ray Saign

Larry Del Greco

Jim Ellis

Jack Skeuse
of Parker Reproductions

Lewis Yearout

Gary Green

Larry Orr

Charlie Price

Daniel Sheil, Jr.

Gary Fadden
of Beretta U.S.A. Corp.

Larry Baer

Don Criswell

Norm Carroso

Cody Firearms Museum

R. L. Wilson

Robert White

Jim and Carol Wimer

Morris Hallowell IV

John Gyde

Kathleen Hoyt, Jeffrey Crute,
and the whole crew at Colt's
Mfg. Co., Inc.

F.E. "Pete" Wall

Mims Reed

K.W. Wheeler

Mossberg Collector's Association
and Victor & Cheryl Havlin

Ruger Collectors Association

Colt Collectors Association

Remington Society of America
and Marv Adams

Marlin Firearms Collectors
Association, Ltd.

and to

Barbara Knowles Olsen, whose 58-day stint on the cold seat while constantly watching a blue wordprocessing screen represents the longest "Bataan March" ordeal any captured employee has ever had to endure in recent memory. Her 3-D approach (discipline, dedication, and dead ditch dwellers) provided entertainment and a book without having to call a taxidermist.

Dedication

The 17th Edition Blue Book of Gun Values is dedicated to all of those people who have been nice enough to send in their comments, changes, criticism(s), compliments, and other creative criteria over the years. You may not have received an answer back, but many of you have seen your suggestions included in the next edition.

Blue Book Publications, Inc.
General Information

While many of you have probably dealt with our company for years, it may be helpful for you to know a little bit more about our operation and what we are currently publishing. As this book goes to press, we have the following publications in print (or close to it):

Blue Book of Gun Values, 17th Edition
by S.P. Fjestad

Blue Book of Guitars, 2nd/3rd Editions
edited by S.P. Fjestad

Blue Book of Pool Cues, 1st Edition
by Brad Simpson

Billiard Encyclopedia, 2nd Edition
by Victor Stein and Paul Rubino

2nd Edition *The Book of Colt Firearms*
by R.L. Wilson

Mossberg - More Gun For The Money
by Victor and Cheryl Havlin

Classic Sporting Collectibles Auction Service Catalogs
Volumes 1-4

Classic Sporting Collectibles Pocket Guide

Gun Journal
monthly firearms buy/sell magazine

In addition to publishing the above titles, we also sell many of the important firearms and other collectible related publications needed to make the right decisions and choices when buying, selling, or trading firearms or other collectibles (please refer to pages 82-89). A convenient tear-out order form is provided for re-ordering this 17th Edition and may be found between pages 24-25. Our master order form appears on page 5.

Blue Book Publications, Inc. Corporate Headquarters is located at:

Blue Book Publications, Inc.
8009 - 34th Avenue South
Minneapolis, MN 55425 U.S.A.

e-mail: bluebook@bluebookinc.com
Website/homepage: http://www.bluebookinc.com

Since we have a new phone system with voicemail, you may also wish to know extension numbers which have been provided below:

Ext. No.: 11 - Tom Stock
Ext. No.: 12 - Tom Lundin
Ext. No.: 13 - S.P. Fjestad
Ext. No.: 14 - John Allen
Ext. No.: 15 - Walter Horishnyk

Ext. No.: 16 - Lisa Winkels
Ext. No.: 17 - Jennifer Haugen
Ext. No.: 18 - Beth Marthaler
Ext. No.: 19 - Barbara Knowles Olsen
Ext. No.: 22 - DJ Pallum

Office hours are: 8:30am - 5:00pm CST, Monday - Friday
Orders Only: 800-877-4867   Phone No. 612-854-5229
FAX No. 612-853-1486 (available 24 hours a day)

Answering services (not a machine) are also available after/before normal business hours, weekends, and holidays.

We would like to thank all of you for your business in the past - you are the reason(s) we are successful. Our goal remains the same - to give you the best products, the most information for the money, and the highest level of customer service available in today's marketplace.

How to use the
Blue Book of Gun Values

The prices listed in the 17th Edition of the Blue Book of Gun Values are based on national average retail prices for both antique and modern firearms. This is not a wholesale pricing guide (I doubt if there could be such a thing). Percentages of original condition (with corresponding prices) are listed between 10%-100% for most antiques (unless configuration, rarity, and age preclude upper conditions) and 60%-100% on modern firearms since condition below 60% is seldom encountered (or purchased). Please consult our expanded color grading insert (Photo Percentage Grading System located on pages 26-64) to learn more about the condition of your firearm(s). This is the first time, to my knowledge, that color plates have been utilized to accurately illustrate the firearms percentage grading system. Since condition is the overriding factor in price evaluation, study these photos carefully to learn more about the condition of your specimen(s).

Hardcore readers may note some additional abbreviations in this newest edition (i.e., "C/B 1994, *", - some of these are due to the Brady/Crime Bills enacted during 1994.) Please refer to the Abbreviations Section for complete descriptions on these new additions. Also, the Glossary is now located on pages 95-98. Updated BATF regional information has also been provided in this edition - see page 1,342.

Since this 17th Edition is 1,360 pages, it may be easier to zero in on a particular model by referring to the extensively updated Index on pages 1,350-1,357. Hopefully, the new alphabetical tabs will also assist you in finding your section(s) faster. When looking up information in this text remember, it does not read like the Democratic platform - where another page doesn't make any difference.

For your convenience, the NRA condition standards and grading criteria have been included to make the conversion to percentages easier (see pages 22 and 23). This will especially be helpful when evaluating antiques.

For the sake of simplicity, the following organizational framework has been adopted throughout this publication.

1. Alphabetical names are located on the top of right-facing, odd-numbered pages and appear as follows:

C section

2. Trademark, manufacturer, brand name, importer, or organization is listed in bold face type alphabetically, i.e.,

SMITH & WESSON, ANSCHUTZ, MARLIN, WALTHER

3. Manufacturer information is listed directly beneath the trademark heading, i.e.,

Manufacturer located in Oberndorf/Neckar, Germany. Imported and distributed by Heckler & Koch, Inc. (U.S. headquarters) located in Sterling, VA (previously located in Chantilly, VA). In early 1991, H & K was absorbed by Royal Ordnance, a division of British Aerospace located in England.

4. Manufacturer notes may appear next under individual heading descriptions and can be differentiated by the following typeface.

As this edition went to press, Ithaca Gun remained in Chapter 11. No guns are currently being manufactured. On March 6, 1987 some assets of the Ithaca Gun Company were sold to Ithaca Acquisition Corporation.

5. Next classification is a category name (inside a screened gray box) referring mostly to a firearm's configuration, i.e.,

REVOLVERS, RIFLES, SHOTGUNS: SLIDE ACTION

6. Following a category name, a category note may follow and appears as follows:

Please refer to this heading under Colt's Firearms in the Modern Black Powder section in the back of this book for current information and values on this 2nd Generation Colt Black Powder Series (including serialization).

7. Model names appear flush left, are bold faced, and capitalized either in chronological order (normally) or alphabetical order (sometimes, the previous model name will appear at the end in parenthesis) and are grouped under category names such as PISTOLS, RIFLES, SHOTGUNS, DRILLINGS, i.e.,

AR-15, PEPPERBOX PISTOL, MODEL 1866 LEVER ACTION, MODEL 101, DHE

8. Model descriptions are denoted by the following typeface and usually include information such as,

— calibers, gauges, action type, barrel lengths, finishes, weight, and other descriptive data are further categorized adjacent to model names in this typeface. This is where most of the information is listed for each specific model including identifiable features and possibly some production data (including quantity and circa of manufacture, if known).

9. Variations within a model appear as sub-models - they are differentiated from model names by an artistic ▲ prefix, are indented, and in upper and lower case, i.e.,

▲ *Turkey Model, AR-15 9mm Carbine (R6450), Micro Buck Mark*

and are usually followed by a short description of that sub-model. These sub-model descriptions are identifiable by the following typeface,

— additional sub-model information that could include finishes, calibers, barrel lengths, special order features, and other production data specific for that sub-model.

10. Now included is yet another layer of model/information nomenclature differentiating sub-models from variations of sub-models or a lower hierarchy of sub-model information. These items are indented in from the sub-models, have the icon graphic ➤ and are in upper or upper/lower case, i.e.,

➤ **Earlier Mfg. Without Invector Choking**

A description for this level of model/information may appear next to the sub-entry and uses the following typeface,

— blued receiver with border engraving featuring Browning logo engraved on each side of the receiver.

11. Manufacturer and other notes/information appear in smaller type and should be read since they contain both important and other critical, up-to-date information, i.e.,

During 1996, this model began utilizing alloy construction on the receiver (instead of steel), and the barrel features a new barrel band at the end of the forearm incorporating a swing swivel.

12. Extra cost features/special value orders and other value added/subtracted features are placed directly under individual price lines or in some cases, category names. Add-ons or subtractions for currently manufactured guns affect 98% or better condition factors only - for most conditions 60%-95% in a currently manufactured gun, the add-ons/subtractions must be interpolated downward/upward by the condition factor. These individual lines appear bolder than other descriptive typeface, i.e.,

Add 40% for .28 or .410 ga.
100% assumes NIB condition for this model. Most of the buying/selling activity with 3rd Generation SAAs involves NIB specimens.

13. On recently discontinued models/variations, the last line that may appear under a model, sub-model, or sub-entry heading indicates the last manufacturer's suggested retail price flush right on the page, i.e.,

Last Mfg.'s Sug. Retail was $2,165.

14. Grading lines will appear at the top of each page and in the middle if pricing lines change. If you are uncertain as to how to properly grade a particular firearm, please refer to the Photo Percentage Grading System on pages 26-64 for more assistance. The most commonly encountered grading line in this text is from 100%-60%, i.e.,

Grading	100%	98%	95%	90%	80%	70%	60%
	$400	$350	$315	$260	$210	$175	$140

Antique grading lines have values listed for 100%-10%, 80%-10%, 100%-Grey, i.e.,

100%	98%	95%	90%	80%	70%	60%	50%	40%	30%	20%	10%
$12,750	$11,500	$9,950	$7,600	$6,500	$5,400	$4,400	$3,500	$2,700	$2,000	$1,600	$1,250
N/A	N/A	$575	$475	$425	$375	$340	$300	$275	$250	$220	$195

N/A indicates this particular model is not encountered enough in either 98% or 100% original condition to warrant pricing.

Grading	80%	70%	60%	50%	40%	30%	20%	10%	
	$3,150	$2,650	$2,365	$1,925	$1,650	$1,425	$1,275	$1,125

This grading line in lower condition factors includes Traces which stands for traces of blue, and Grey, which translates into a gun whose overall finish has a grayish color.

Grading	100%	95%	80%	50%	20%	Traces	Grey
	$2,000	$1,600	$1,200	$900	$700	$600	$450

Commemorative/limited edition grading and pricing lines will appear as follows:

Grading		100%	issue price
$1,225		$1,500	750

In some cases, an organization's or company's listing (i.e. Quail Unlimited, the National Wild Turkey Federation, etc.) of guns will appear as follows:

MANUFACTURER	MODEL QUANTITY	YEAR	ISSUE PRICE
Winchester	Model 12 12 ga.	800 1975	N/A
Remington	Model 1100 12 ga.	4,500 1985	Dinner Auction Gun

Grading	100%	98%	95%	90%	80%	70%	60%

15. Price line format is as follows - when the price line shown below is encountered,

Grading		100%	98%	95%	90%	80%	70%	60%
Mfg.'s Sug. Retail	$696	$625	$550	$500	$450	$400	$360	$330

it automatically indicates the gun is currently manufactured and the manufacturer's retail price is shown left of the 100% column. Following are the 100%-60% values. The 100% price is what you can typically expect to pay for that model in NIB condition (must usually melt-down to approx. whole-sale/distributor pricing, minus 10%-20%. 100% specimens without boxes, warranties, etc., that are currently manufactured must be discounted slightly (5%-15%, depending on the desirability of make and model).

16. A currently manufactured gun without a retail price published by the manufacturer/importer will appear as follows:

Grading	100%	98%	95%	90%	80%	70%	60%
No Mfg.'s Retail	$575	$500	$450	$400	$350	$300	$260

Obviously, the 100% price is the national average price a consumer will pay for a gun in new condition. The same situation for a stainless steel or limited mfg./special edition firearm without retail pricing will not have prices listed from 80%-60% as this type/configuration of firearm is almost never encountered in these lower condition factors. The price line will appear as follows:

No Mfg.'s Retail	$1,495	$1,225	$995	$795

17. A price line with 7 values listed and represented below indicates a

$495	$450	$400	$365	$330	$300	$275
N/A	$1,650	$1,400	$1,200	$1,000	$875	$750

discontinued, out of production model with values shown for 100%-60% conditions. Values are normally not listed for 50%-10% condition factors since these lower conditions are seldomly encountered on recently discontinued models. 50%-10% values however, will in many cases approximate the 60% price since any gun's shooting value will usually keep the price close to the 60% value. Obviously, no "Mfg.'s Sug. Retail" will appear in the left margin, but a last manufacturer's suggested retail price may appear flush right below the price line automatically indicating a discontinued gun, i.e.,

Last Mfg.'s Sug. Retail was $899.

18. A 4-value price line indicates a current production gun, and prices are not shown in 90% or less condition since the specimen (notice model description) is either stainless steel, a commemorative, or limited production, i.e.,

Mfg.'s Sug. Retail $475 $415 $350 $295

because these types of firearms are almost never encountered in 90% or less condition, values for lower conditions are not listed.

19. Early Winchester lever action grading and price lines incorporate price ranges on certain Winchester models which are most frequently encountered in 50% or less condition. These price range lines appear as follows:

Above Average	Average	Below Average
$1,450 - $1,175	$1,125 - $875	$825 - $450

An explanation of what to look for in these three condition ranges will precede this information in that section. The 17th Edition also includes a grading/price line that represents percentages and respective values for guns above 50% condition (photos 53-59 on pages 52-55). This grading/value line appears as follows:

95% = $1,850   90% = $1,675   80% = $995   70% = $825   60% = $695   50% = $575

Since this publication is now 1,360 pages (and Liz's diet vanished with Husband No. 8), you may want to take advantage of our new expanded Index (pages 1,350-1,357) as a speedy alternative to going through the pages. Otherwise, first look under the name of the manufacturer, importer, or brand name. Next, find the correct subdivision (either pistols, rifles, shotguns, etc.). When applicable, antiques will appear before modern guns and are subdivided like modern weapons. Once you find the correct model or sub-model under its respective subheading, determine the weapon's percentage of original condition (see the Photo Percentage Grading System starting on page 26) and find the corresponding percentage column showing the price.

Commemoratives or special/limited editions will generally appear last under a manufacturer's heading.

For those of you who would like to make notes within this publication, there may be a Notes Page at the end of each alphabetical section allowing you room for notes and miscellaneous observations.

Enlarged in the 17th Edition are sections on Trademark Index (pages 1,277-1,304), Modern Airguns (1,165-1,196), Modern Black Powder Guns (pages 1,197-1,276), and Model Serialization breakdown of major trademarks (1,305-1,335). Three or four prices will be listed for both Black Powder and Airgun Models. When using the Model Serialization section, make sure your model is listed and find the serial number within the yearly range listings.

Pieces of History

copyright 1995, Jim Supica, Old Town Station, Ltd.

A proposed rating system for historically associated firearms.

Examples # 1&3 (S&W's attributed to Theodore Roosevelt. - Photo by Paul Goodwin)

A gun with a known historical association is a tangible connection to our collective past, and such connections are rare and precious things.

Precious implies value, value implies price, and the question always arises for a collector – exactly how much is history worth? In 1993 we saw the S&W New Model Number Three which was reportedly used by Bob Ford to kill Jesse James knocked down for $163,000 on a British auction block. Late in 1994, Theodore Roosevelt's famous Holland and Holland double rifle brought a cool half million at Butterfield & Butterfield (& that was before the 10% buyers premium!) Obviously the buyers of these pieces were paying for something more than condition.

What exactly were they buying? How does one assess the "history" of a gun? An old gun accompanied by a pile of newspaper clippings, documents, and photographs can make a very impressive package. However, more than one collector has paid a handsome premium for such package, only to discover, sometimes years later, that there is nothing that really ties that particular gun to the individual or event so heavily documented in the paperwork.

Collectors have more or less agreed on a couple quantifiable systems for evaluating the "condition" of a gun. I'd like to suggest that a similar system for evaluating the historical claims of a gun might be a useful mental tool for the collector or enthusiast.

PRICES OF HISTORY

Here's how I approach it.

The value of a historically attributed gun is the sum of two figures –

1. The gun's INTRINSIC VALUE

plus

2. The gun's HISTORIC ATTRIBUTION VALUE.

The INTRINSIC VALUE is the gun's "Blue Book" value – it's worth as a gun with no story attached, as determined by make, model and condition. In this respect, it is similar to valuing collectible coins.

The HISTORIC ATTRIBUTION VALUE is the amount added to the gun's value for the story attached to the gun – it's historical ownership or usage. This is usually a far more subjective figure, and is more similar to valuing collectible historical documents.

This Historic Attribution Value is itself the product of two factors –

1. The HISTORICAL SIGNIFICANCE of the individual or event, and

2. The CREDIBILITY of the evidence supporting the gun's claim.

HISTORICAL SIGNIFICANCE

Of these two factors, HISTORICAL SIGNIFICANCE is the most subjective, and will vary from collector to collector, depending on that individual's interest in the history involved.

A gun's historical claim usually will involve either ownership by a particular individual or usage in a famous or infamous incident. Those with the highest value will have both.

What you are pricing is the fame or notoriety of the individual &/or event in question. Presidents, generals, famous lawmen and outlaws seem to rank highest. Ownership by the most famous of these can easily result in a six figure gun, especially if combined with a particular notorious event.

Ownership by lesser political or military figures, obscure lawmen, or less notorious criminals will still significantly enhance a gun's value.

Even attribution to an essentially unknown individual can add value, usually proportionate to the distance in time and the amount of information that can be dug up on the person in question.

Popular perception can certainly heavily impact the value assigned to "Historical Significance", sometimes in ways that would make an academic historian blanch. Perhaps a way to conceptualize the value of the historical significance is to look at the cumulative media & literature devoted to the individual or event. In ascending value:

* Small town newspaper clippings, family records, etc.
* Reference to individual or event can be found in library
* There has been a book published on the individual.
* Commonly recognized name.
* Portrayed on Mount Rushmnore or by Kevin Costner in recent movie.

You get the drift?

A gun traced back to someone who lived, got married, had a job and died may have a little historical value added, whereas a gun proved to have been used by a legendary character in a notorious Old West shootout may set record prices.

CREDIBILITY

The CREDIBILITY of a gun's historic claim lends itself to a more objective analysis – an analysis that a prospective buyer ignores at his own financial peril.

I tend to assign a historically attributed gun's credibility a grammar school grade – A, B, C, D, or F. Each grade represents a level of authenticity.

> A = Certain.
> B = Probable.
> C = Plausible.
> D = Questionable.
> F = Impossible.

As with school grades, each level can have a plus or minus rating.

Once a dollar value has been established for the gun's HISTORICAL SIGNIFICANCE, a factor can be applied based on the gun's CREDIBILITY rating. The following scale might serve as a guideline:

A – 100% historical attribution value.

B – 75% to 50% historical attribution value

C – 50% to 25% historical attribution value

D – 25% to 5% historical attribution value, with the caveat that a "D" gun should never go for more than double the gun's intrinsic value. In most cases, a "D" type story gun will bring only a small premium or perhaps make the gun easier to sell at its intrinsic value.

F – 0% historical attribution value. In fact, the intrinsic value of the gun may be lessened if a disproved historical name has been permanently marked on the gun.

EVALUATING CREDIBILITY

Let's take a closer look at evaluating the CREDIBILITY of a gun's historical claim:

A. To get an A rating, a gun must inspire a high degree of **Certainty** that it is what it purports to be. It must be accompanied by documentation which satisfies the following criteria:

   i. TIMELINESS – The documentation must be from the period of claimed historical association. Not from three generations later. Not from 10 years after the fact.

   ii. CERTAIN IDENTIFICATION – It must specifically identify the individual gun or group of guns in question. Most often this is done by serial number. Occasionally it may be possible to do by photograph or description of specific unique physical characteristics, but extreme caution should be used in relying on such an approach. In some cases "Provenance", discussed in B, may provide reasonably certain identification, but also should be approached with open-minded skepticism.

   iii. CREDIBILITY OF SOURCE – The identification must come from a credible source, one unlikely to intentionally or accidentally misidentify the gun. Factory records or court records are preferable. Newspaper accounts, and signed documents (preferably notarized) from credible individuals may meet this requirement.

A rated guns are very, very rare. Sort of like true "mint" guns.

B. B rated guns have a high degree of **Probability** that they are as represented. They typically are guns with strong historical documentation, but which fall a little short of the stringent criteria required for an A rating.

The most common difference between A and B guns lies in the area of Timeliness of the documentation. Often a B gun will have certain identification from a credible source, but the identification will come at some time later than the period of historical use. Often it is the case that the documentation will come from a descendant of the original user, and the gun will have been passed down within the family.

A gun that is rated "B" may also fall short of "A" status by lack of certainty of identification. This is usually a case where a stack of documentation accompanies the gun, and appears to have been with it forever. However, on close examination there is a break in the chain identifying the gun that is with the documentation as the gun referred to in the documents. This is especially common in guns lacking serial numbers or other unique identifying characteristics.

It's my contention that most of the guns which are accepted in the collecting community as "authentic" to a particular ownership are B guns. And it is here that we must address a term that is bandied about quite a bit – "Provenance".

"Provenance" seems to be something of a term of art. You find it in $40 a pop four color high end auction house catalogs, and esoteric dealer ads. It seems to mean the "pedigree" of a guns past ownership, and tends to be a document that states something like "This gun was originally owned by Mr. W who gave it to Mrs. X who sold it to Mr. Y who sold it to me, Mr. Z." A gun with superior provenance, with separate documents confirming each past owner, each meeting all the A criteria above can easily become an "A" gun.

However, often a study of a gun's provenance will reveal gaps in the documentation. For example, in the hypothetical provenance in the paragraph above, "W to X to Y to Z", the credibility of the gun is tied inextricably not only to the credibility of Mr. Z, but also the credibility and accuracy of W, X & Y.

Remember that several factors other than malfeasance can figure into the misrepresentation of a gun. Guns may be inadvertently switched. There may be errors in the recording of serial numbers or other identifying characteristics. Plus there is always room for error in intergenerational tale telling. Grandad tells seven year old Sonny how Jesse James personally gave him the old owl's head revolver in the nightstand. All the adults in the room recognize it for one of Grandad's beloved tall tales. Sixty years later, Sonny is certainly willing to draft an affidavit as to what his grandad told him.

When supporting documentation comes up short in the areas of timeliness or certainty of documentation, it is especially important to look at the credibility of the source of the information. In spite of the Grandpa & Sonny illustration above, I tend to give most credence to notarized statements from the descendants of the original owner.

I also believe that the better dealers of antique and historic arms realize that their continued success in the business rests only on their long-term reputation for veracity and fairness. A written statement from such an individual outlining the purported history of a piece can go a long way to establishing B status in my mind. The contents of any such statement must be carefully evaluated, and a conscientious dealer will make clear exactly what is known about the gun and the source of that information.

There was a recent Country & Western song, "That's my story and I'm stickin' to it." A gun can acquire something like B status in the same manner. If a particular gun establishes a particular claim and sticks to it long enough, it comes to be accepted as factual. This usually occurs through the magic of publication. If a gun is pictured in a book or magazine and represented to be a particular historic artifact, it comes to be accepted as such. The effect is magnified by repeated publication or passage of years, much in the way that it is said that old buildings and old whores establish respectability.

I must confess, I have a hard time fighting my knee jerk reaction to accept whatever appears in print. However, I try to take an extra hard look at a "B by publication" gun to see if it might fall into the D or F categories.

Some gun cranks are fond of saying that a historically attributed gun must be "Provable in a court of law." This is essentially a good perspective, but any lawyer will tell you there are varying standards of proof. An A gun is provable "beyond a reasonable doubt" while a B gun holds its claim "by a preponderance of the evidence."

Put another way, a B gun is an A gun, but less so.

C. C rated guns are **Plausible**. They "feel right" but you can't prove or disprove them. A good C gun will often be supported by some sort of documentation. There are several general types of guns that I tend to give C status:

Dealer-lettered guns – as discussed above, a thorough and well drafted report from a reputable dealer or researcher will put a gun squarely in the B or C category, depending on what the statement reveals.

To me, a blanket statement that "This gun belonged to so-and-so" raises serious questions as to the credibility. The document must state the writer's reasons for accepting the gun's history. The best ones are "Joe Friday" letters – "Just the facts, ma'am."

Stack 'o clippings guns – You've seen 'em. A gun displayed under glass with yellowed newspaper clippings, old letters, service records, tintypes, a rusty badge, etc., etc., etc. They are very impressive and nearly always fascinating. The problem is, there is nothing in writing directly connecting the specific gun in question to the individual or deed so lavishly reported.

Self-testifying guns – That is, a gun whose historic claim is based solely on a marking on the gun itself. Usually these are guns with an individual's name etched, engraved, or otherwise marked on them. Probably many are authentic, but the fact remains that, lacking other information, they cannot be proven. CAVEAT –The credibility of a "self-testifying" gun is inversely proportional to the fame of the individual in question. I.e, on a Civil War era revolver, I would give 98% credibility to a gun inscribed "To Cpl. Joe Blow from his mother" and 2% credibility to one inscribed "To Capt. G. A. Custer from Gen. U.S. Grant."

D. A "D" gun is a C gun that has a faint odor to it. Something about them makes their claim **Questionable,** but not impossible.

I tend to classify self-testifying guns with famous names inscribed on them "D" status. Also, inscribed guns where the method of inscription doesn't look quite right.

Most "story" guns which lack documentation must be considered D guns. Especially if the seller is not willing to put the story in the form of a notarized statement.

Often D guns require a sizeable leap of faith. Such as "Well, sure, most Wells Fargo guns were marked with a line stamp, but this one was probably done at a little branch office out west where they didn't have a regular stamp and couldn't spell too good...." or "Yeah, I know he said 'never trust a woman or an automatic pistol', but this is probably the 1911 that jammed on him and made him say that." All of which brings us to.....

F. For Fake. For Fraud. For Fail. For **Impossible,** no way Jose.

These are guns that are just flat wrong on their face. Most common and obvious examples are the many sixguns attributed to various Old West desperados that by serial number were made years after their death.

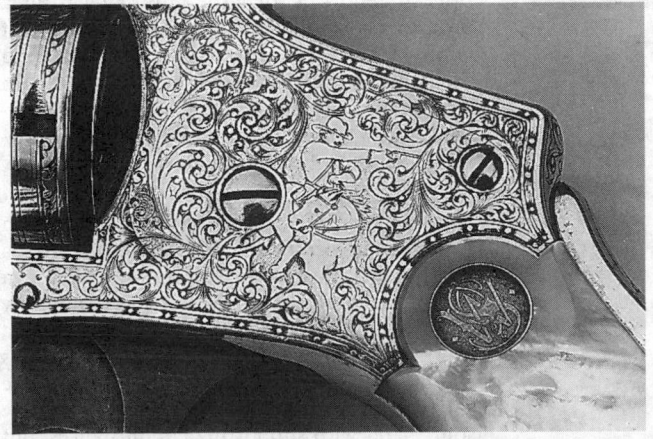

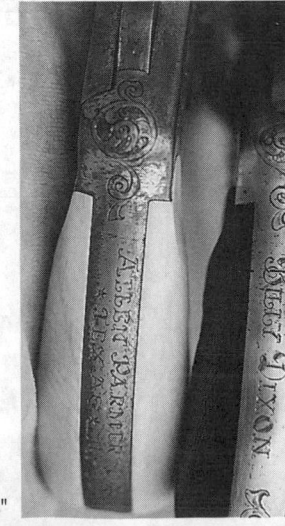

Example #1 Detail of Theodore Roosevelt
attributed S&W Lemon Squeezer
Photo by Paul Goodwin

Examples #8 "Self-testifing guns"

Example #3 Theodore Roosevelt S&W New Model #3
Photo by Paul Goodwin

TYPE OF HISTORY CLAIMED

While we've been discussing these ratings mostly in terms of association with a particular historical individual, they can also be applied to the credibility of other historical claims, such as military, police, or agency usage; period of engraving; or attribution of engraving to a particular artist.

Please note that when using this letter rating system, you must specify exactly what historical claim is being rated. In application a single gun may have different ratings for different claims.

Consider a Colt Single Action Army Cavalry model in the so-called "7th Cavalry" serial number range. Assuming the gun itself and all its markings are correct, it might be considered an "A" as a US military gun, a "B" as an Indian Wars gun, a "C" as a Little Big Horn gun, and a "D" or "F" as Gen. Custer's personal sidearm.

EXAMPLES

Let's see how this system would apply to some examples. To avoid threatening letters, we'll consider guns which are either from my personal collection, or which have been widely reported in the gun press, or where I've changed the names to protect the guilty.

We'll start out by considering four different guns associated with Theodore Roosevelt:

1. The first is a beautiful little engraved S&W lemon squeezer with pearl grips, the engraving featuring a representation of a mustachioed pistol wielding horseman bearing a passing resemblance to Theodore Roosevelt as a Rough Rider. It is accompanied by a letter from a leading West Coast gun dealer and auctioneer, reporting that the gun came from a prominent South American family, and that family legend was that it had been given to their ancestor by Roosevelt during his South American explorations. The S&W factory "letters" it as a special order gun shipped to a major distributor, further details not known.

The little gun has a good "feel" to it. It is known that TR took a S&W on his South American expedition. Roosevelt featured a hand drawn illustration of a lemon squeezer in one of his books. The revolver strives mightily for a "B" rating. However, it must remain a "C" gun, especially considering Roosevelt's prominence. It is a "story gun", with some supporting documentation from a credible source and with supporting circumstances, but sadly lacking in timeliness of its documentation. "C".

2. The next gun is a cased S&W New Model #3, acquired from a prominent East Coast gun auctioneer. It is accompanied by a letter signed by a descendent of Henry Cabot Lodge, stating that the gun had been presented to Lodge by his good friend Theodore Roosevelt. The factory letter states that there is no shipping information available on the gun. This could be consistent with a gun pulled from production for special presentation to a prominent individual, but also could have several other equally possible explanations.

Again, it sounds like a good candidate for "B" status. However the letter did not identify the gun by serial number. This problem was rectified to some degree by obtaining notarized statements from the auctioneer and intervening owner of the gun that the revolver referred to in the letter was in fact the gun in question. All told, I consider this gun to warrant a "B" rating as one owned by Henry Cabot Lodge, but a "C" rating as a Roosevelt gun.

3. The third is another New Model Number Three, this one factory engraved with target sites, chambered for the .38 service round. It is accompanied by a notarized letter from a prominent dealer stating that it was reportedly purchased from a descendant of Roosevelt's valet, corroborated by a prominent collector. The icing is a factory letter stating that the gun was shipped to Col. Roosevelt in 1898. I give this gun an "A" on strength of the factory records.

4. It might be interesting to consider the Theodore Roosevelt Holland & Holland double rifle which recently brought the record price at Butterfields. The exact and complete provenance of this gun is known from when it left the factory, specially made for TR for his African safari and commissioned by a group of prominent individuals whose names appear inside the lid of the gun case. There are photos of TR on safari with this exact gun and it's sequence of ownership is well known and documented up to present date. An "A+" gun if ever there was one.

5. Compare this to "the gun that killed Jesse James", which was also recently sold at auction. For most of the 20th century, this S&W has had the reputation of the gun used to do the wicked deed. In fact it reportedly went back to the S&W factory for engraving of the inscription on its side commemorating the event. However, a look at the supporting documentation raises some questions.

The story is that the gun was given by Bob Ford to the young son of the Marshal who briefly jailed the Ford brothers after the shooting, in appreciation for kindnesses to the imprisoned Fords by the boy. The date of the earliest documentation appears to be a 1904 affidavit and newspaper article. Yes, this is a long time ago, but it is also twenty two years after the incident in question!

The waters are muddied further by the fact that there is another gun out there with the same claim – a Colt Single Action Army mentioned by Ford in a newspaper article a month after the shooting. It helps not a bit that an 1882 newspaper account of the incident records the gun variously as a "Colt's .45" AND a "Smith & Weston" (sic).

Where does that leave us? I'd give the gun a solid "B" as a Bob Ford gun, and it certainly approaches "B by publication" status. However, given the conflicting claim, it seems to exist in some sort of schizophrenic "B/D" limbo as the gun that laid poor Jesse in his grave.

6. Consider Wyatt Earp's S&W American as another example showing that many of our greatest historic guns exist in the "B" to "D" rating range. This is the beautifully engraved gun that was used by the Franklin Mint as its model for the Wyatt Earp reproduction which graces the walls of many Old West buffs around the country. It currently resides in the outstanding Gene Autry Western Heritage Museum in Los Angeles.

The museum reports, "It is, in fact, dangerous to assume that it is a gun carried by Wyatt Earp. At one time the gun was exhibited in a small Tombstone museum with pearl grips and the name of John Clum. Those grips have disappeared and new looking walnut grips have taken their place. A number of writers have questioned this gun, others have endorsed it." Give the gun an "A" as a great Western gun, and a "C-/D+" as Earp's.

7. This might be a good point to consider the reports of incredible time-travel guns. For many years a Colt SAA has been prominently displayed in a small midwestern museum as the gun given to a local doctor by outlaw Bob Dalton in payment for medical services. Perhaps it's most intriguing characteristic is the fact that its serial number shows it was manufactured eleven years after old Bob met his final reward.

My pet theory here is alien abduction. However other explanations may occur to the thoughtful reader. "F".

8. Self-testifying guns are always intriguing, but must be approached with caution when consider-ing likelihood of authenticity. This is illustrated by an engraved pair of S&W .44 Double Action First Models which surfaced in different parts of the country, each with a semi-famous Western name engraved on the backstrap – "Billy Dixon" on one and "Allen Parmer, Texas" on the other.

Either gun by itself might rate a "C" as a self-testifying gun. However, taken together, some questions arise. The engraving is rather crude, but an identical pattern is used on each. In each case it is difficult to guess the age of the engraving.

While it is certainly possible that the same frontier engraver did both guns, the fact remains that the .44 DA is a relatively inexpensive old west six shooter which might have value enhanced considerably by fraudulent engraving & attribution.

In historical attribution, skepticism must rule, and the coincidence raises enough questions to put the guns in "D" status unless further information can be developed.

9. Which brings us to the subject of "discovered" guns – A gun whose history is not known, but is "developed" by a researcher. And here is where a potential buyer must proceed with utmost caution.

There is a gun in circulation which has been attributed to a certain very notorious Old West outlaw. The owner "discovered" the attribution by examining an old photo which may or may not have been the individual in question and deciding the grainy blob sticking out of the holster in the photo was the self same gun he happened to have. By proclaiming this association long enough, the gun began to have a life of its own and garner quite a bit of press. Without additional documentation however, it remains a "D" gun.

And it is no doubt for sale to the first reasonable offer in the mid five figures.....

FACTORY LETTERS -

"Factory letter" has come to be a generic term meaning a letter from a recognized authority based on a search of the gun's manufacturer's original records as to the disposition of a gun from the factory. It is one of the most powerful tools available to you in researching the authenticity of a gun's historical attribution.

Under optimum circumstances, it will show the purchaser of the gun from the factory (usually a distributor, sometimes an individual), the date it was shipped, the configuration of the gun (finish, barrel length, caliber, etc), and any special features. Sometimes, incomplete factory documents mean some of these elements will be missing.

Any gun that has value added for history should have a factory letter if available. At a minimum, the factory letter should not show information inconsistent with the claimed history. It's helpful if the disposition is consistent with the historical claim (i.e., gun in same configuration, shipped to same geographical area at plausible date, etc.) Under the best of circumstances, it may confirm shipment to the individual claimed.

Generally speaking, the more information you provide in your request, the more likely the researchers can find something interesting if there is something to be found. At a minimum, include positive identification of the model, serial number, caliber, and any special features.

Remember, like guns, documentation can be faked! Most factory letter sources will write a fresh letter on a gun that has already been lettered for a reduced fee in order to confirm the information in the previous letter. Also bear in mind that it is not unknown for serial numbers to be altered on guns to correspond to an historically attributed gun.

COLT – Colt Historical Dept., Kathleen Hoyt, PO Box 1868, Hartford CT 06144. $45 fee on most guns, some early guns not available due to destruction of records in a factory fire. Current turn-around time approx. 90- 120 days. Send caliber, patent dates, serial number, model if known and other details.

RUGER – I believe Ruger has a program for researching collectible Rugers. 10 Lacy Place, Southport CT 06490

SMITH & WESSON – Factory Historian Roy Jinks, PO Box 2208, Springfield MA, 01102. $20 fee. Earliest guns sometimes not available. Important that gun be correctly identified by model, best to include a photo or tracing of gun w/ all markings noted. Be sure to mention any unusual or special features (engraving, unusual barrel length, markings, special finish, etc.).

U.S. MILITARY ARMS – Springfield Research Service, PO Box 4181, Silver Spring MD 20904, does ongoing research on military arms in government records and will research individual guns for fee ranging from $10 to $50.

WINCHESTER, MARLIN, & L.C. SMITH – Buffalo Bill Historical Center, PO Box 1000, Cody, WY. $40 per letter, telephone searches available for Patron Association members. They have records for most early Winchesters after Mod. 1866 s/n 125000; for early Marlin lever action rifles; and for most L.C. Smith shotguns from 1890-1971.

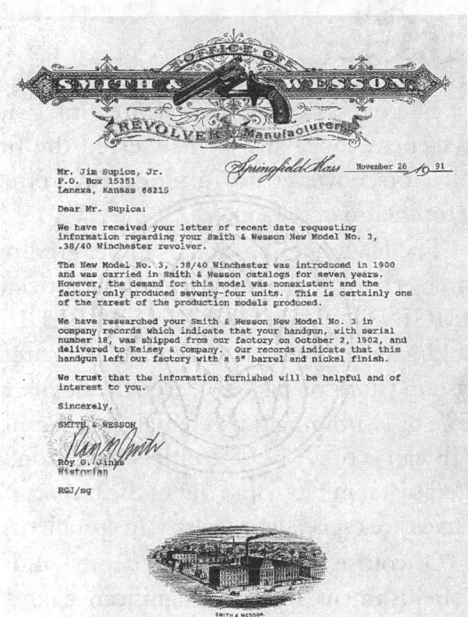

Factory Letter

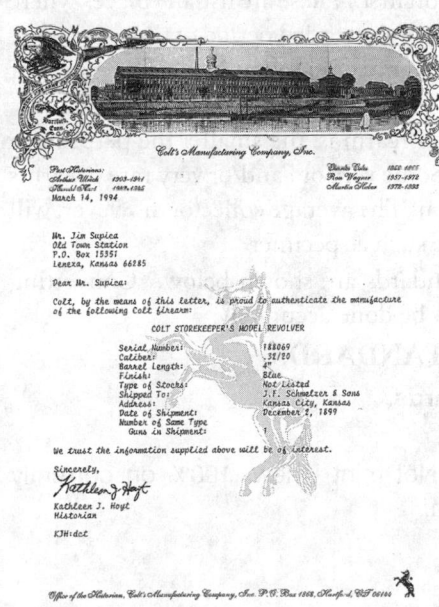

Factory Letter

ABOUT THE AUTHOR –
Jim Supica, President of Old Town Station, Ltd., Lenexa, Kansas, is a dealer, auctioneer, appraiser and collector of antique arms. He writes and publishes a quarterly catalog/journal of antique cartridge firearms called "Old Town Station Dispatch." He collects serial number one guns, S&W Model 3's, and hammerless revolvers. Comments & suggestions are welcome. POB 15351, Lenexa KS 66285 (913)492-3000

Grading Critera for Firearms

The old, NRA method of firearms grading — by relying upon adjectives such as "Excellent" or "Fair" — has served the firearms fraternity for a long time. Today's collectors, however, are turning away from such a subjective system. One man's "Fair" is another man's "Good!"

The leading professionals in the grading of firearms now utilize what is essentially an objective method for deciding the price range of a gun: THE PERCENTAGE OF ORIGINAL FACTORY FINISH BLUING REMAINING ON THE GUN. After looking critically at a few firearms, and carefully studying the Photo Percentage Grading System (starts on page 26), even the novice can soon tell whether a piece has 100%, 98%, 95%, or less bluing finish remaining. Remember, sometimes an older gun described as NIB can actually be 98% or less condition, simply because of the wear which accumulated by taking it in and out of the box and being handled too many times (commemoratives are especially prone to this problem).

Of course, factors such as "depth" and quality of the bluing finish, engraving and embellishment, historical significance, and even the condition of the stock can and do affect the price. But the basic "condition" — and therefore the price — is best determined by the percentage of original bluing finish remaining. The key word here is "original" for if anyone other than the factory has refinished the gun, its value as a collector's item is greatly diminished, with the exception of rare and historical pieces that have been properly restored. Study the photographs on pages 26-64. Note how the bluing finish in certain areas of the firearm wears off first. These are usually places where the gun rubs against the holster, hand or body over an extended period of time. A variety of firearms have been shown in four-color to guarantee that your "sampling rate" for observing finishes is as diversified as possible.

It should be noted that the older a collectible firearm is, the smaller the percentage of original bluing finish one can expect to find. Some very old and/or very rare firearms are acceptable to collectors in almost any condition! The average collector, however, will probably never have the opportunity to purchase such a specimen.

For your convenience, NRA Condition Standards are shown below. Converting from this grading system to percentages can now be done accurately.

CONVERTING TO NRA MODERN STANDARDS

When converting from NRA Modern Standards, the following rules generally apply:

New/Perfect — 100% with or without box. Not mint - new. 100% on currently manufactured firearms assumes NIB condition.

Excellent — 95%+ - 99% (typically).

Very Good — 80 - 95% - all original.

Good — 60 - 80% - all original.

Fair — 20 - 60% - May not be original (shootable, not very collectible).

Poor — Under 20%.

NRA Condition Standards

These NRA conditions listed below have been provided by the author as guidelines to assist the reader in converting and comparing condition factors to the Photo Percentage Grading System in this publication. In order to use this book correctly, the reader is urged to consult these condition standards when converting to percentages of condition. Once the gun's condition has been accurately assessed, only then can the correct values be ascertained.

MODERN CONDITIONS —

New — not previously sold at retail, in same condition as current factory production.

Perfect — in new condition in every respect.

Excellent — new condition, used but little, no noticeable marring of wood or metal, bluing perfect (except at muzzle or sharp edges).

Very Good — in perfect working condition, no appreciable wear on working surfaces, no corrosion or pitting, only minor surface dents or scratches.

Good — in safe working condition, minor wear on working surfaces, no broken parts, no corrosion or pitting that will interfere with proper functioning.

Fair — in safe working condition, but well worn, perhaps requiring replacement of minor parts or adjustments which should be indicated in advertisement, no rust, but may have corrosion pits which do not render article unsafe or inoperable.

ANTIQUE CONDITIONS —

Factory New — all original parts; 100% original finish; in perfect condition in every respect, inside and out.

Excellent — all original parts; over 80% original finish; sharp lettering, numerals and design on metal and wood; unmarred wood; fine bore.

Fine — all original parts; over 30% original finish; sharp lettering, numerals and design on metal and wood; minor marks in wood; good bore.

Very Good — all original parts; none to 30% original finish; original metal surfaces smooth with all edges sharp; clear lettering, numerals and design on metal; wood slightly scratched or bruised; bore disregarded for collectors firearms.

Good — some minor replacement parts; metal smoothly rusted or lightly pitted in places, cleaned or reblued; principal lettering, numerals and design on metal legible; wood refinished, scratched, bruised or minor cracks repaired; in good working order.

Fair — some major parts replaced; minor replacement parts may be required; metal rusted, may be lightly pitted all over, vigorously cleaned or reblued; rounded edges of metal and wood; principal lettering, numerals and design on metal partly obliterated; wood scratched, bruised, cracked or repaired where broken; in fair working order or can be easily repaired and placed in working order.

Poor — major and minor parts replaced; major replacement parts required and extensive restoration needed; metal deeply pitted; principal lettering, numerals and design obliterated, wood badly scratched, bruised, cracked or broken; mechanically inoperative, generally undesirable as a collectors firearm.

 # Grading or Graffiti?

Take a seat on the passenger's side and belt up - this time machine's going to experience enough turbulence to perhaps get out the air motion sickness bags while we return to the sleepy, pre-Mall of America western Bloomington pastures during late Fall of 1984. It had already been a full throttle year. I re-met my main high school squeeze the week after Memorial Day, was engaged by the time the fireworks flew (bigger rockets would go up later), and got married and moved over Labor Day weekend (family and friends should have thrown Minute Rice). Professionally, the 500+ page Fourth Edition of the up and coming Blue Book of Gun Values had been written, published, & half sold out, I had become manager of both Investment Rarities' Firearms and Gift divisions, and somehow also ended up as the unofficial photographer of the nation's largest gold and silver company.

Just when I thought my 200 amp fuse box was feeling a little warm from extended high energy operation, the boss called me up one afternoon in late September and unquietly leashed out "!?#@&@* it, Steve, I want to see you in my office right away". Oh no, was I going to get fired again? Whenever he sounded like that, I knew the beaters of his manure spreader were about to shower me, a faithful and dedicated employee, with legions of a young heifer's finest, thick brown latex. 3 minutes later it was "Steve, I need a way of photographing coins that would prevent some customers from sending back replaced, lower grade coins for resale that they had purportedly purchased from us a few years ago." It was a simple but expensive scam - some people were sending us back different, sub-standard coins and claiming that our company (I.R.I.) had originally sold them. I was pissed! We're talking serious upper 7-digit stuff.

So what's a mother (at this point, a potential new father was the truth) to do? Get the 35mm out and learn macro photography - real fast. Our senior numismatist (professional coin grader) at the time (and a good friend, since killed in a car accident), Dennis Wegley, didn't like my original efforts. I thought by capturing the individual scratches and striations on both sides of each coin (obverse and reverse, i.e. coin babble), I could pictorially I.D. every coin (keep in mind, some very expensive coins are less than ½ in. in diameter).

Nothing was working. I bought a lens-mounted, macro flash unit one day, burned up some more film, and was not impressed when I got the results back. I showed the color prints to Dennis and he initially shrugged "Washed out fields, Steve, pretty bad. Wow, did you notice the rim nick definition? I've never seen that before". After a little more experimentation, we determined that every coin had some discernible and identifiable rim nick wear, and properly photographed, it would serve as a veritable fingerprint to identify every coin. Hence, the world's first photo I.D. tracking system for coins was born.

But what does this have to do with the *Blue Book of Gun Values* Photo Percentage Grading System™? Keep reading. When I first toyed around with the idea of a firearms Photo Percentage Grading System™, I knew it would be successful only if the readers could equate good quality photos to a predictable percentage of original condition. Honestly, it was done more to save telecommunications time when listening to the never-ending, Rhodes scholar sounding, verbal gun description battles ("Sir, can you please hold your gun a little closer to the microphone so I can see it better?"). I never really thought it would become an industry yardstick, but I guess I'm pleasantly surprised. Hopefully, it has helped you save some time (and money) as well.

As you may be aware of, any grading system must have the human eye(s) convert what he/she sees into a definable and established grading level (this can be said about any collectible field). If this doesn't happen, an accurate grading system simply cannot be established. However, sometimes professional grading can almost attempt to define the various grades too narrowly, resulting in different opinions by various dealers/collectors on what the correct condition should be.

In the coin biz, for instance, only a handful of people (including some numismatists) will be able to look at two, top condition $5 Indian gold pieces and know the difference between the grades MS-63 and the next highest grade MS-64. (Editor's note: in the gun business grading conditions run from 100% down to 0% - in the coin business grading conditions run from MS-70, refers to Mint State 70-perfect, down to AG-03, Almost Good-03 - dog meat).

(Continued on page 25)

The problem with this coin grading structure is the price difference on the smallest grade change can add up to a whopping $47,000 difference in retail price on the right coin! In an attempt to maintain uniformity within these individual, "narrow" grades, the coin industry now mostly relies on the grading services of several successful and acknowledged coin grading companies/organizations. Most prominent today is the Professional Coin Grading Service (PCGS). To obtain the correct grade of a particular coin, it must be first sent to PCGS from an authorized PCGS dealer, after which a staff of trained experts ascertains the correct grade for each coin. Each specimen is then "slabbed" or sealed in a clear, untamperable plastic case with the grade impregnated on the outside. Prices for this grading service typically average $25 with a 15-day turnaround. These slabs are then returned to the individuals where they are bought/sold/traded by using fixed buy/sell pricing set forth in a weekly coin newsletter/price sheet referred to as the "Gray Sheet", published by *Certified Coin Dealer Newsletter*.

As you can see, this takes most of the responsibility of accurately grading coins out of the hands of established dealers/collectors and into the domain of a coin grading service. The bad news is that if you ever want to even touch or feel your coin(s) again, it must be broken out of its slab, thus losing its grade once the plastic case has been disturbed. Experienced, eagle-eyed numismatists and collectors using this system have also been known to carefully scrutinize a slabbed coin - if they think it could be regraded higher, the coin is purchased, broken out of its slab, and sent back to the coin grading service again for another paid grade evaluation. The $5 Indian coin discussed above which has been regraded 2 thin grades higher can result in a $3,145 gain (MS-62 retail is $555 while MS-64 retail is $3,700!). In other words, there is a huge monetary difference between a "98%" and "99%" coin. The real problem with this type of grading system is that even if a desirable coin has not been professionally graded, resale gets real tough.

While I doubt most gun collectors would allow their favorite firearm(s) to be slabbed in plastic even for authenticity purposes, I hope it never gets down to a professional gun grading service establishing the calculable differences between a 98-99% or 92-93% firearm. I personally see the following Photo Percentage Grading System™ as a guide to ascertain between major grades only (i.e. 98%, 95%, 90%, 80%, 40%, etc.). It was never meant or intended to delineate the subtle nuances of a "93% vs. 94%" pre-'64 Winchester Model 70. I believe there has to be a little room for interpretation/interpolation within any grading system. To be frank about it, I find verbal sparing on 92% vs. 93% condition ridiculous and a waste of my time.

As in the past, three categories of guns have been represented in the photo grading illustrations: Rifles, Shotguns, and Handguns. Older subscribers will note the inclusion of quite a few new models and variations incorporated to provide more reference material on the almost endless variations of firearms. I've always said that the final chapter on intelligence can't be written until you accumulate the additional knowledge learned after you think you know it all. The Photo Percentage Grading System™ is not intended to be "gun pornography" - some of the stuff on the following pages ain't pretty. While this isn't Disneyland, you will still find the Beauty (100%) and the Beast (0%). How can you possibly know where the middle is until you have been at both ends.

If you have any questions regarding either the photos or accompanying captions, please contact me. While no grading system is perfect, hopefully this Photo Percentage Grading System™ will enable you to ascertain the approximate grade of your individual firearms. Only after learning the correct condition of a firearm can you accurately determine its true value.

Steven P. Fjestad, Author & Publisher
Blue Book of Gun Values

P.S. I would like to thank the Great White LeRoy of the North, Richard Ellis, Patrick McKune, Robert White, Jeff Sundvall, Ward Olson and Martin Mandall for providing the iron on the following pages.
All photos in this section were taken by S.P. Fjestad and Paul Goodwin.

Photo 1 = Model 1911 Springfield Armory in 96% - 97% original condition. Notice markings and trigger wear. Also note scratch from top of trigger guard to slide stop lever indicating careless assembly. Wear on back of trigger, ordnance proofs, and diamond checkered grips are all indicative of this model.

Photo 2 = Model 1911 Springfield Armory in 60% original condition. As wear has accumulated, the metal has become a duller grayish color. Again, note martial markings next to trigger and rear of slide on both guns. Observe difference in color of front grip strap compared to Photo No. 1.

Photo 3 = Model 1911A1 manufactured by Singer for WWII contract. This pistol is ultra-rare in this condition factor - 98%. A very "crisp" specimen, considering only 500 were manufactured in 1942. In today's expensive Colt semi-auto marketplace, this all adds up to $11,500.

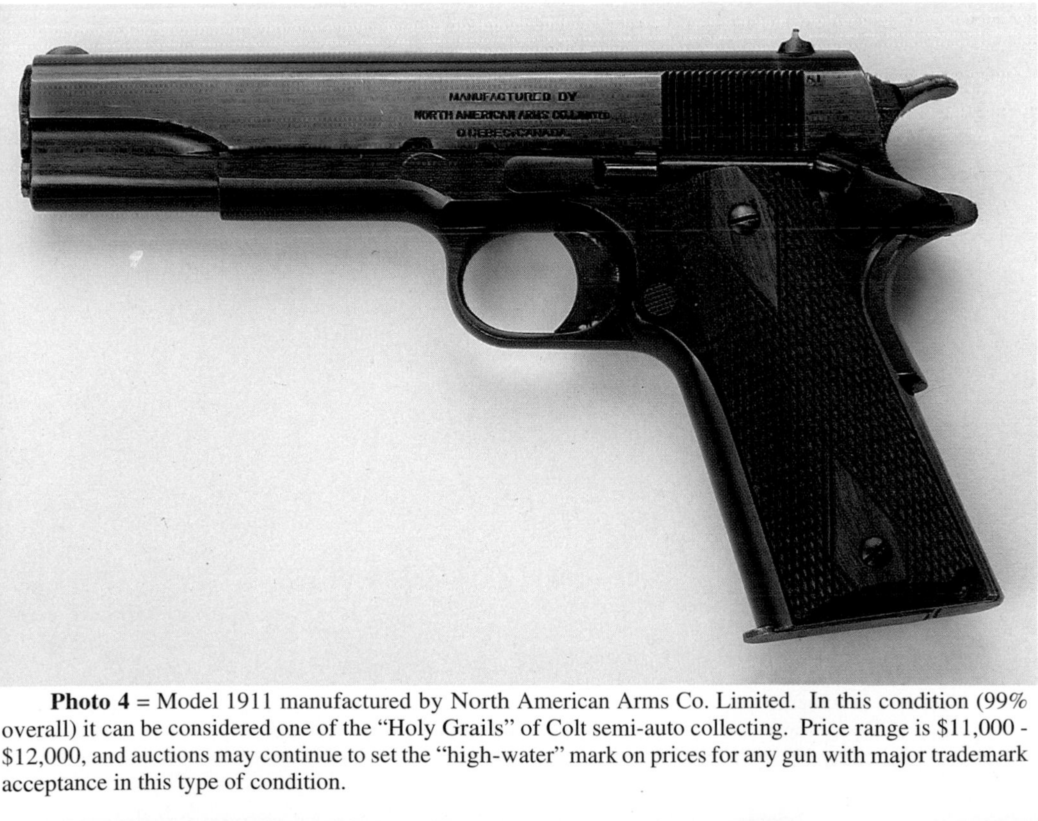

Photo 4 = Model 1911 manufactured by North American Arms Co. Limited. In this condition (99% overall) it can be considered one of the "Holy Grails" of Colt semi-auto collecting. Price range is $11,000 - $12,000, and auctions may continue to set the "high-water" mark on prices for any gun with major trademark acceptance in this type of condition.

Photo 5 = Another Model 1911 North American Arms in approximately 85% - 90% original condition Observe pitting on slide top and great condition of frame. Despite the pitting and upper slide wear, this variation's rarity still makes this specimen very desirable. Many collectors will never see a North American Arms this good.

Photo 6 = Another Model 1911 manufactured by North American Arms in approximately 75% original condition. Compare this pistol against Photo No. 5 and notice this specimen's additional wear on front grip strap and grip safety. Note different smaller 2-digit numbers on back of slide serrations on Photos 4-8.

Photo 7 = North American Arms Model 1911 in approximately 60% original condition. Again, notice the additional bluing wear compared to Photo No. 6. Bluing splotchiness on top of slide is normal once condition reaches this level.

Photo 8 = Another Model 1911 manufactured by North American Arms in approximately 20% - 30% original condition. This pistol's rarity factory, despite its condition, still make it very desirable. If you are thinking that you can buy this type of specimen for $300 - $400, not the case. $2,000 - $2,500 is more like it, because of desirability.

Photo 9 = Model 1911 manufactured under military contract by Remington U.M.C. in 98% original condition. Notice ordnance proofing, crispness of slide/frame markings, and condition of walnut grips. Overall superior condition of this specimen always guarantees a sale.

Photo 10 = Colt Model 1911 Military manufactured in 1913. This gun is in mint (99%+) condition overall as witnessed by grip condition, lack of end of barrel wear, and perfect Colt stallion on back of slide serration. Note the difference in the coloration of bluing compared to the Remington U.M.C. Model 1911 in Photo No. 9.

Photo 11 = Pre-War Colt commercial in .38 Super cal. (very desirable). This "creampuff" is in mint condition. This pristine specimen (and gun in Photo No. 10) dictate the most demand for collectors/investors. tudy this gun carefully compared to the one in Photo No. 12 - you may learn a lot.

Photo 12 = Colt Pre-War Government Model .45 that has been reblued. Note thinning of "patent legend" n slide side with slight corner rounding on bottom of slide and other originally sharp corners. There is a g difference between a rebluing job such as this and a professional restoration pictured in Photo No. 42.

Photo 13 = Colt Model 1911A1 with correct darker parkerized finish in mint condition. Observe dar plastic grips. Anybody who has ever wondered about the difference between a Model 1911A1 and a Mode 1911 will note the curved rear gripstrap as opposed to the straight one depicted in Photo No. 14.

Photo 14 = A.J. Savage slide Model 1911 with almost all the original blue finish (it's not nickel) worn off This pistol would grade approximately 5%, with no previous misuse or abuse. Even with this little blue finis remaining, it still is worth more than a 40% gun with major pitting, refinishing, or other problems.

Photos 15 & 16 = German WWII Mauser P.38 in 99% (mint) condition with typical late-war red mottled grips. This late-war variation (byf 44) shows some original machining on metal due to lack of polishing during war-time production. Unfired condition with slightest holster wear observable on slide in front of the "P.38" marking. Diagonal machining evident on frame around trigger guard (good eyes may be able to spot the "WaA135" Waffenamt proofmarking). Pretty hard to get better condition than this.

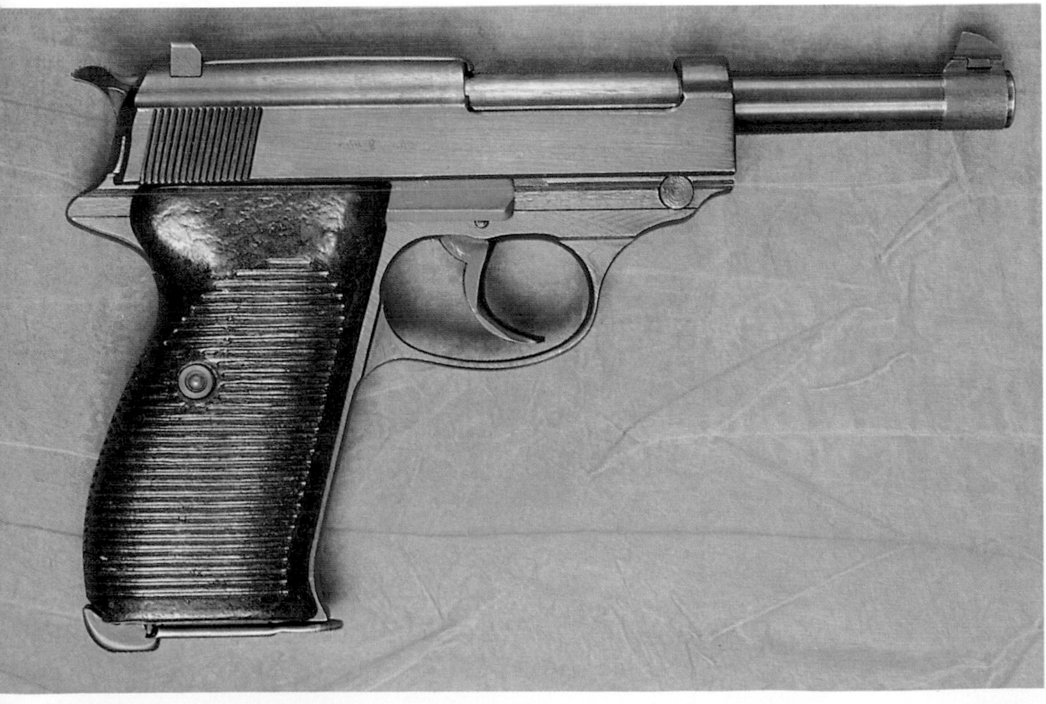

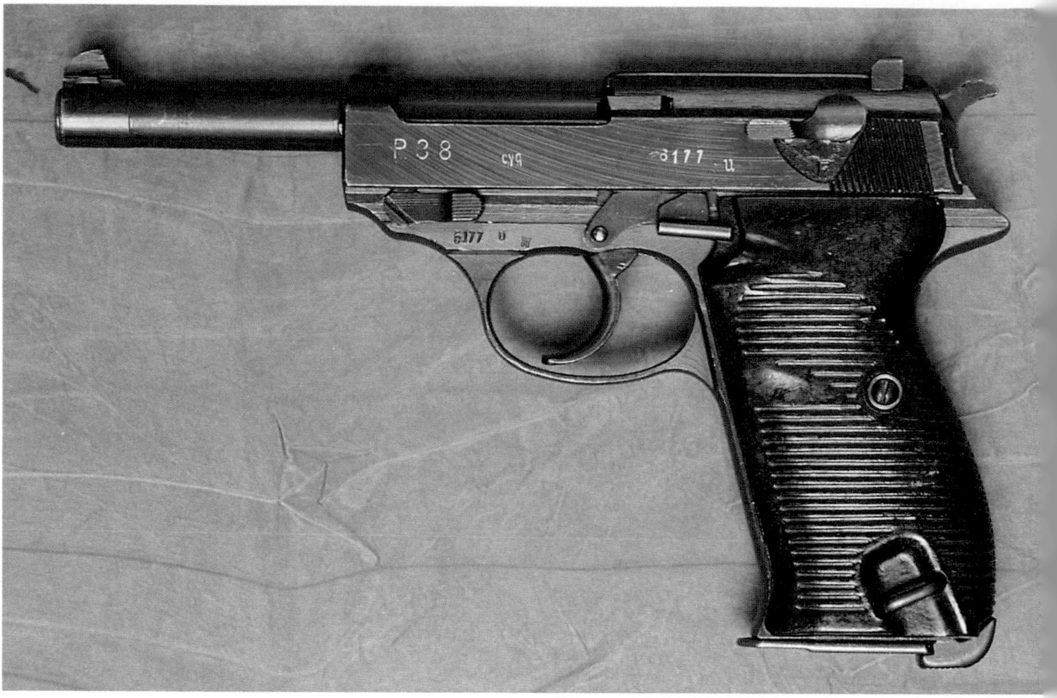

Photos 17 & 18 = Late WWII German P.38 in 99%+ original condition. "cyq" slide marking designate Spreewerke manufacture - notice visible circular machine marks indicative of most Spreewerke P.38 Initially, this factory was set up for producing railroad locomotives requiring heavy industrial machinery an tooling. When it was converted to P.38 manufacture in late war, the high cutting rates and tooling were no switched over to more delicate handgun manufacture - hence the outward rough machining appearance. Th late in the war, even the quality-conscious Germans did not have time to finish these guns to commerci specifications - over 250,000 pistols were made in less than two years.

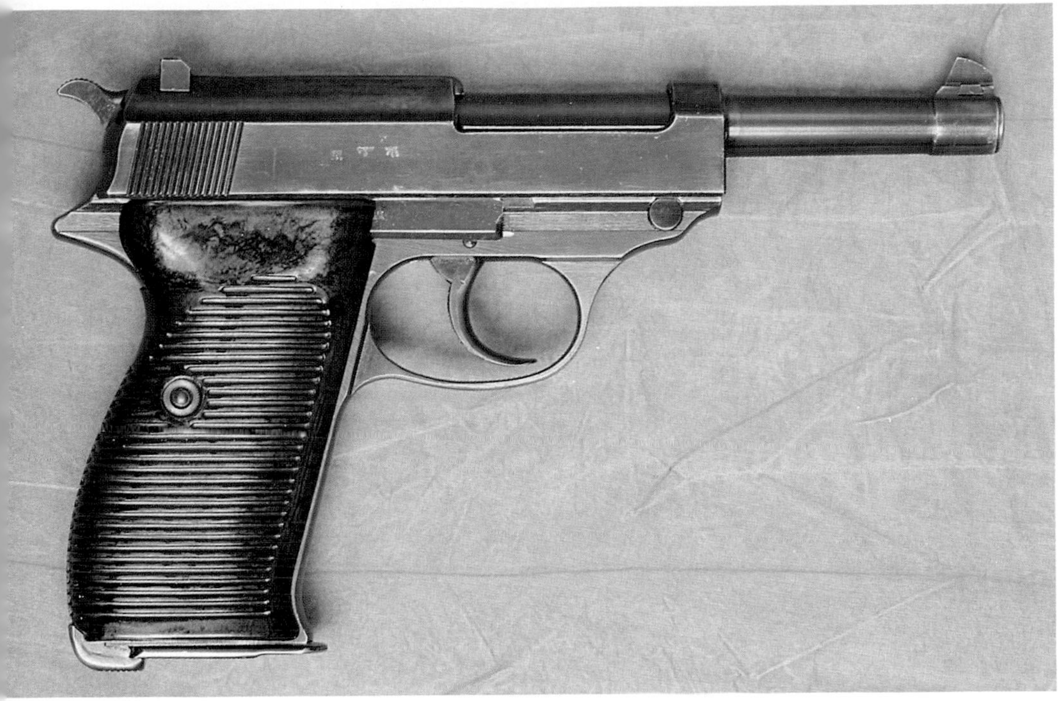

Photos 19 & 20 = German WWII Walther P.38 with rare military high polish in 97% - 98% original condition. Note how exterior frame and slide finish differ from Photos 21 and 22. Whited-in numbers and slide logo were not done at the factory, but many collectors apply this removable treatment to highlight the markings. First variation ac 41 (serial #1-4833 b) can be detected by "ac" on left trigger guard. Walther switched to rough military blue finish in third variation ac 41 (5015 I - 9573 J) for the duration of the war.

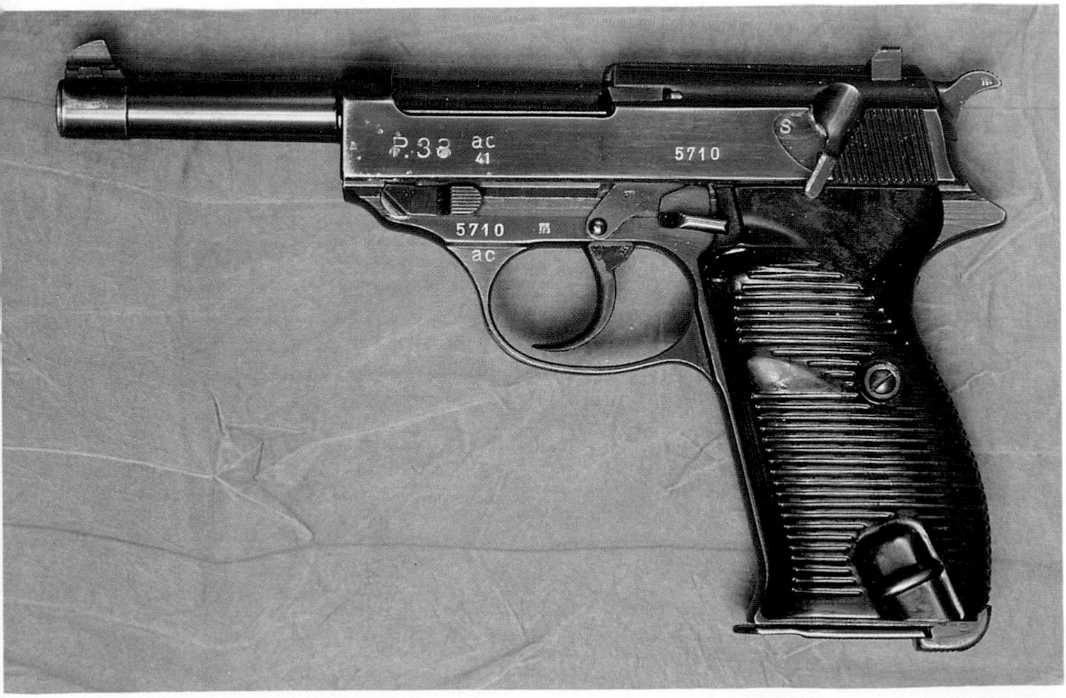

Photos 21 & 22 = German WWII Walther P.38 in 95% original condition. Typical military style finish with machine marks and finish imperfections. One-line "ac 43" slide legend indicates later mfg. as well as the Walther type dark brown grips. Front grip strap shows normal wear, as does front of slide and barrel (note shininess). Overall, a good original specimen of a common German WWII military handgun. In today's marketplace (without any additional gun legislation), this specimen retails in the $325 range.

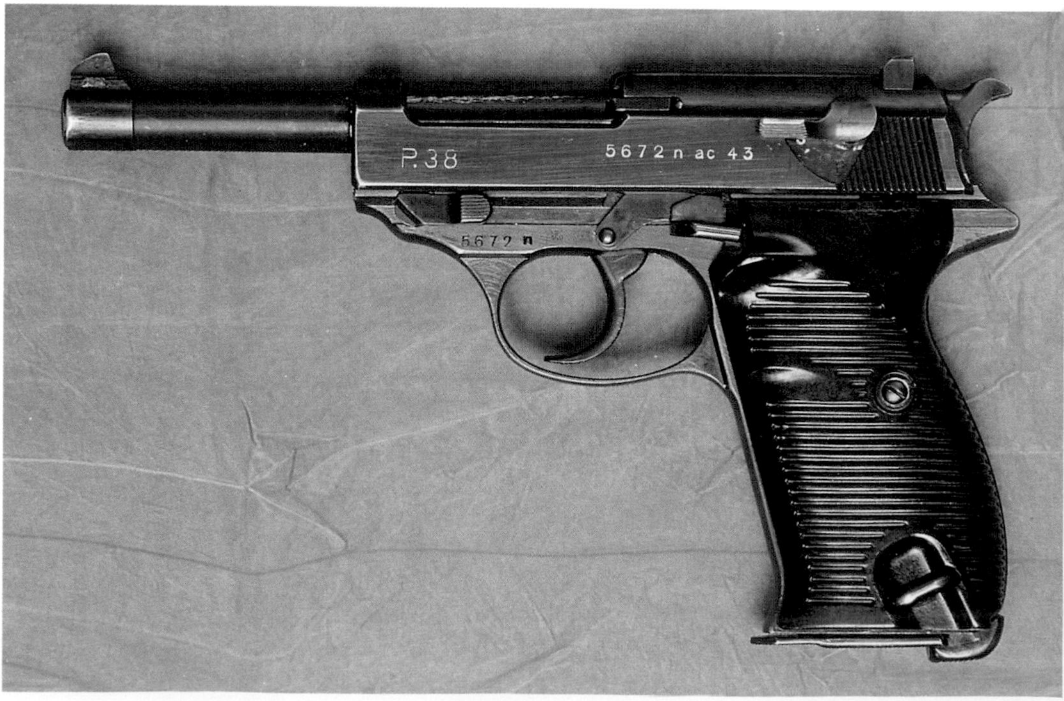

Photos 23 & 24 – Walther "O Series" P.38 (mfg. 1940) with slide banner, in 93% - 95% original condition. This series was the third variation in testing before regular military production occurred a short time later. Observe the rare high polish throughout, indicative of handmade quality manufacture. Many specimens have red paint on rear sight applied at factory, while earlier examples have black checkered grips. Good strong original gun. Anybody catch the plum colored trigger?

Photo 25 = Mauser WWII byf-43 Model in 70% original condition. This specimen shows dark areas of blotchiness from older oxidation on slide and frame. While this pistol offers little collector value (most commonly available handguns in this condition are the same), it sill maintains a minimum "spot price" as a shooter.

Photo 26 = Walther WWII ac-44 Model in 90% condition. While it appears to be original, close inspection reveals a refinished gun (note how tops of slide serial numbers and P.38 logo have disappeared when the gun was over-polished during refinishing). Because P.38's are in good supply in 90%+ original condition, this lowers the value to shooting status.

Photo 27 = Walther PPK Wartime Nazi Police Issue, 7.65 caliber - overall 80% condition. Note areas of bluing wear and rough machining marks on frame (with Nazi Eagle C marking). Plum colored trigger indicates different metal/ bluing combination, normal for this period of late war manufacture. In this condition, it is still in the $375 - $425 range.

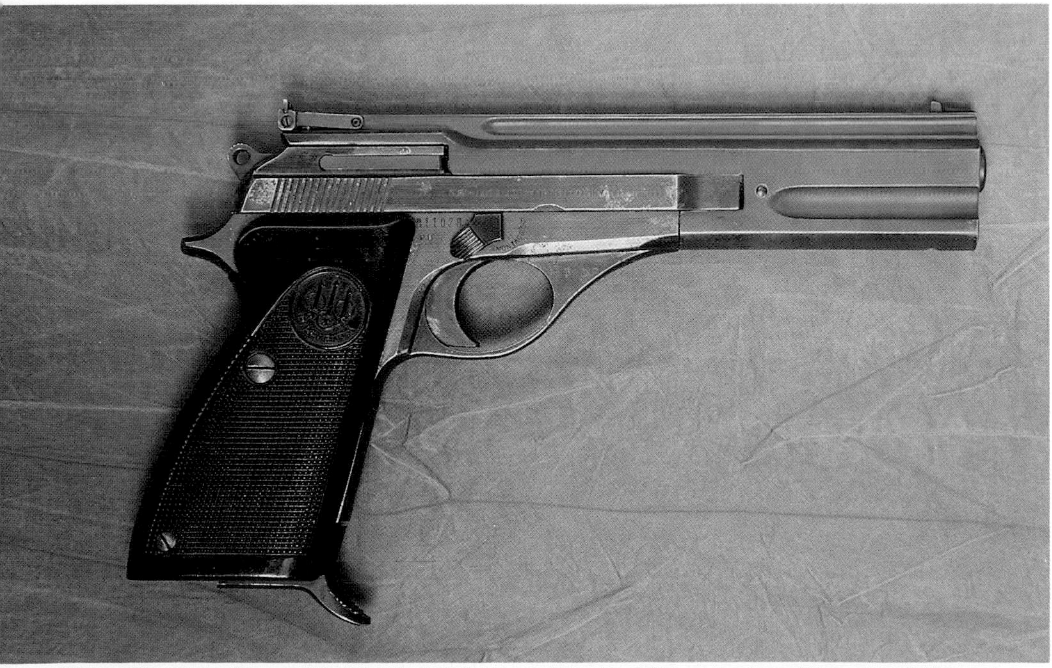

Photo 28 = Pietro Beretta Model 102 .22 LR Target Pistol in 90% original condition. Carefully studying the colors of this gun will indicate three different types of steel/alloy used in its construction. The upper barrel sleeve is a grayish color indicating a different type of pot-metal - all correct for this particular type of construction.

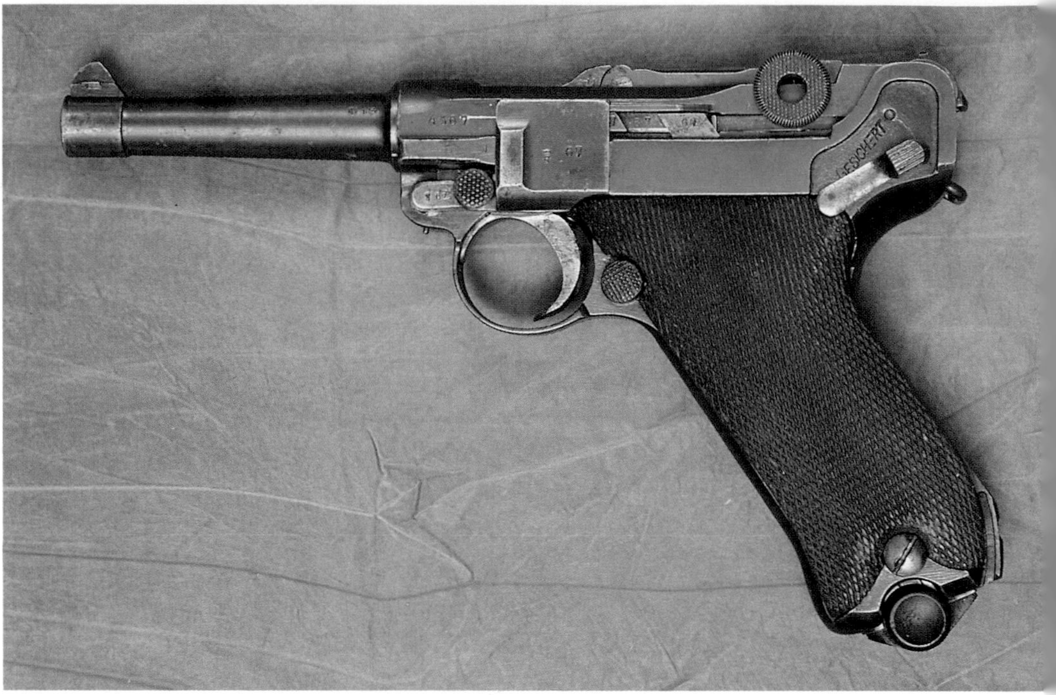

Photos 29 & 30 = 1916 dated WWI military Luger, all original and in a frequently encountered condition (80% overall). Note pitting on bottom of sideplate and "straw" freckling on safety lever, trigger, and takedown lever. Note traces of fire bluing remaining on transfer bar and that all numbers match. Careful examination reveals that grip screw has had a bad screwdriver (and careless hand) to it. Takedown reveals a very crisp bore - indicative that this gun probably was carried a lot more than it was shot. A definite plus on any WWI Luger.

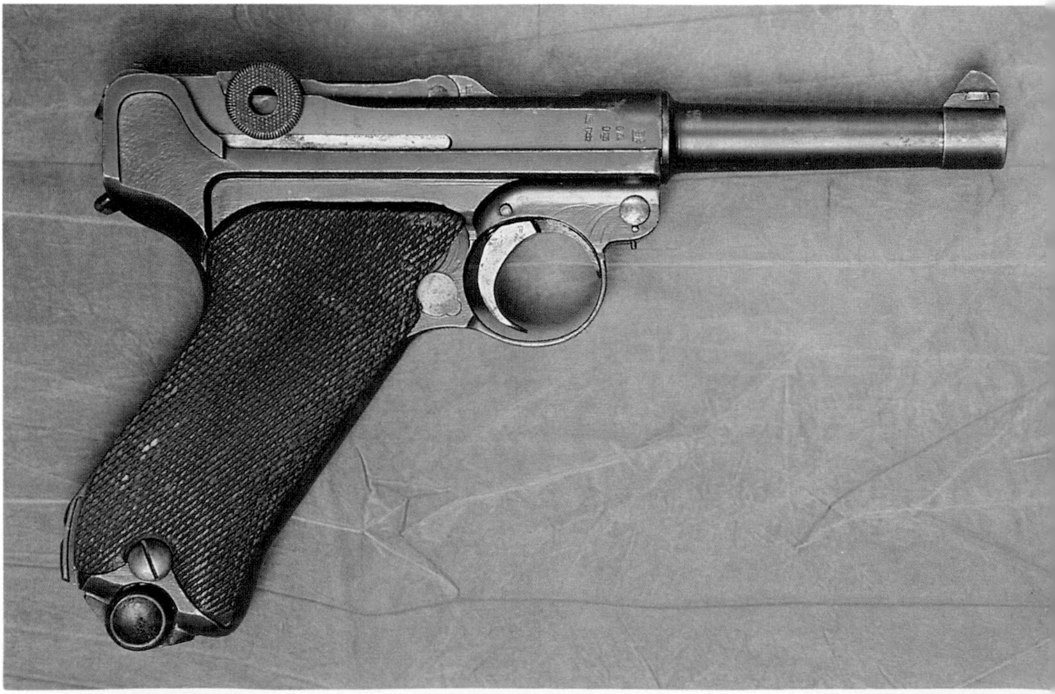

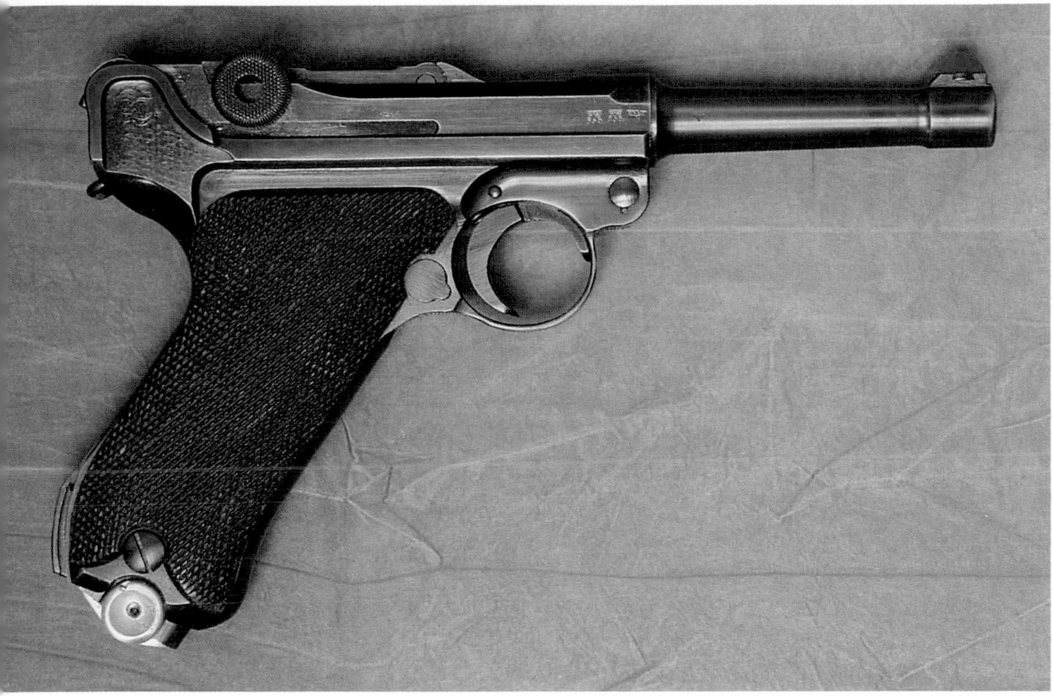

Photos 31 & 32 = 1941 dated WWII Luger in 98% original condition with matching magazine; note how sharp all corners and edges appear; nice crisp numbers on all parts. "2" appears somewhat faint on takedown lever, but is factory weak strike. Grips have nice sharp checkering, except for lower and upper left corners. Horizontal machining striations on trigger and frame metal around trigger guard are definitive signs of original finish on this variation. In today's marketplace (this gun also has a 1940 dated holster that is correct for the gun), this gun has strong collector base and would probably command $1,500.

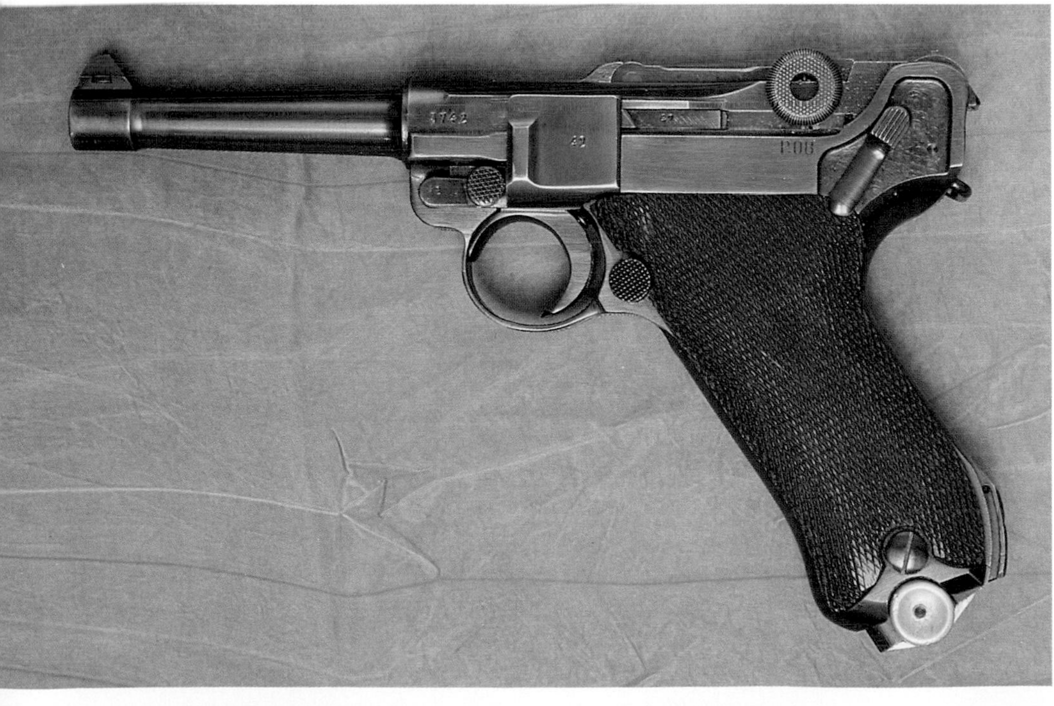

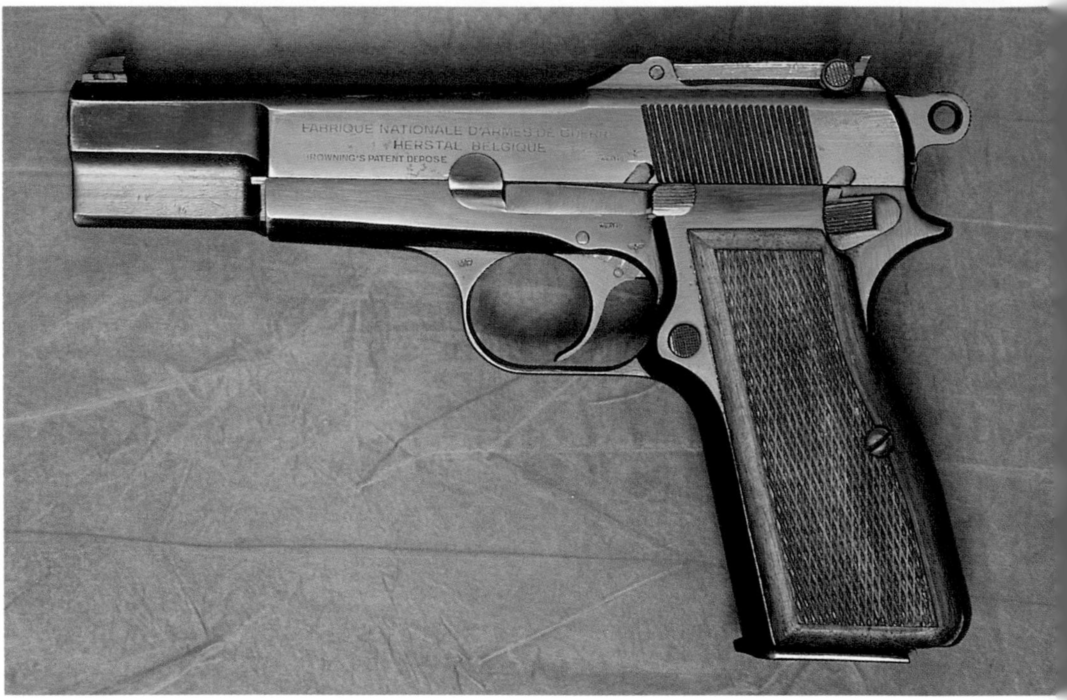

Photos 33 & 34 = Fabrique Nationale WWII Browning Hi-Power 9mm Parabellum in 98% original military finish, note Nazi Waffenamt "Wa140" markings on slide and frame. Compare slide legend to gun in Photo 36 - a beginning collector may suspect this gun has been polished a little bit too much before rebluing, thus the faint slide legend. NOT the case - military slide legends can and do look like this. The tangent rear sight makes any WWII Hi-Power in 98% original condition almost double in value (in this case, approximately $800). Unslotted rear grip strap. When finish appears better than this on some WWII military handguns, you may suspect possible refinishing.

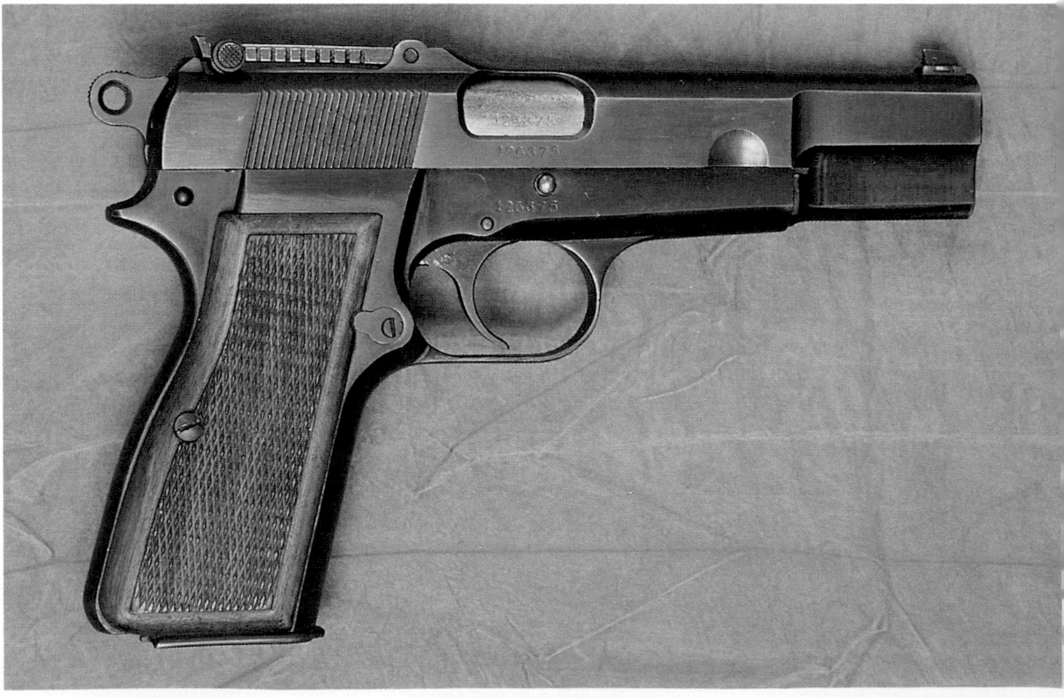

Photos 35 & 36 = Fabrique Nationale pre-war Commercial Hi-Power with tangent rear sight and slotted for shoulder stock. Approximately 95% original condition. Note how Commercial proofmarkings and slide address differ from those in Photo 33 - circled "H" marking on end of slide is correct. Also observe edge-wear on this specimen and how grips are in lower condition than in Photos 33 & 34. Overall, a nice original example of a pre-war slotted Hi-Power with tangent sight that would probably sell in the $700 range.

Photos 37 & 38 = Mauser "Flatside" Commercial Broomhandle in 7.63 Mauser caliber - 99% (near mint) original condition. Glass-like polished frame, milled-out receiver rails, and concentric ring conehammer are definitive features of this variation. Note nice original yellow strawing on trigger and fire bluing on safety lever and meter adjustment on upper 1,000-meter tangent rear sight. Bore is crisp also. With matching shoulder stock (not pictured). Condition-wise, they don't get much more pristine than this.

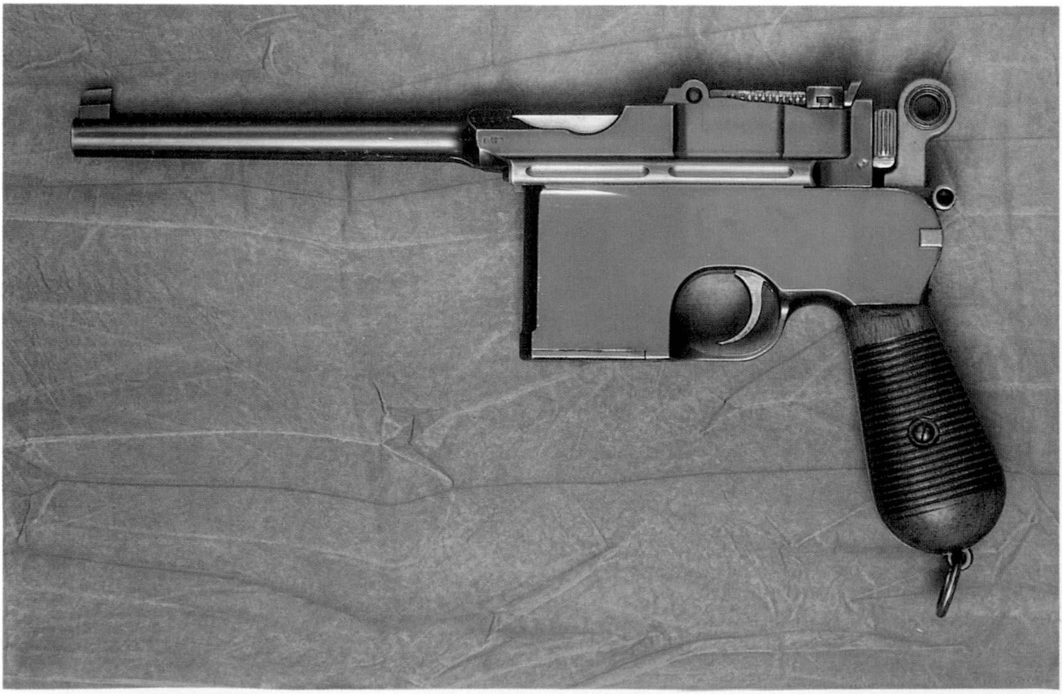

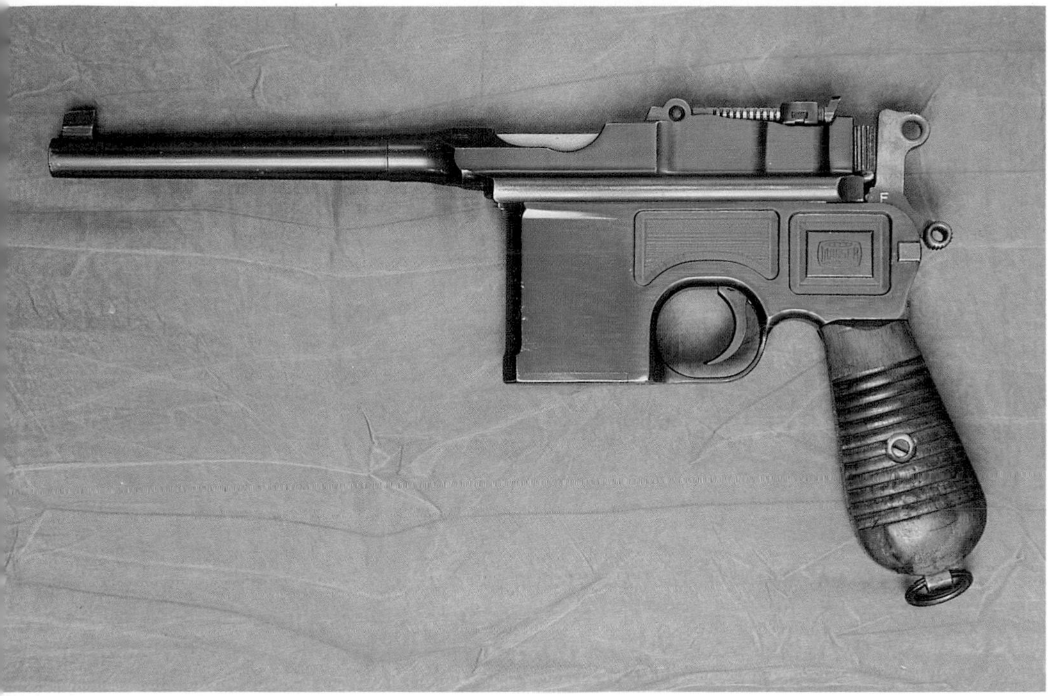

Photos 39 & 40 = Mauser 1930 Commercial Broomhandle in 98% original condition. The Mauser banner above grips on frame, solid receiver rails, 12-groove grips (somewhat worn on the bottom), and sideways "Crown U" proofmarks are all indicative of late commercial broomhandle production. This gun has a 920,000 range serial number and the end of production was approximately 921,000. A nice original gun that in the 1931 - 32 *Stoeger's Shooter's Bible* was priced at $68 (including stock). Ahhhhh - to have a time machine and go back with a few C-notes on board.

Photos 41 & 42 = Before and after photos of a rare Gabbett-Fairfax Mars Pistol manufactured in 1901 by the Mars Automatic Pistol Syndicate Ltd. Top photo reveals severe pitting on frame side just above the trigger and spring housing. The bottom photo was taken after an extensive professional restoration. Carefully observe the straw and bluing colors as opposed to before the restoration. Also, more and more professional restorations like this one are being completed with intentional slight aging to make the specimen look more natural (i.e. most collectors don't like fresh paint). While the controversy continues on restoring firearms, a quality restoration such as this will usually enhance the value of a "tired" rare and desirable specimen.

Photo 43 = Colt Pre-War New Service revolver in mint overall original condition. Notice the grip condition and barely distinguishable vertical striation between cylinder lock-up notches. A high-luster finish, near-perfect bright bluing, and mint grips all add up to a desirable, original specimen.

Photo 44 = Colt Model 1909 U.S.M.C. in 95% original condition with "light freckling". Observe polishing and coloration of bluing. Colt double action collectors should immediately key in on the fire blued screws, especially the one holding the grips in place.

Photo 45 = Colt Model 1909 U.S.M.C. in 90% overall original condition. Note holster wear on barrel tip, striations between cylinder cutouts, and shininess on frame edges. Compare grip screw coloration, muzzle wear, uniformity of Colt prancing stallion marking, and upper trigger bluing to Photo No. 44.

Photo 46 = Colt Model 1889 Double Action in approximately 60% original condition. Notice amount and location of wear, especially upper scratching in back of cylinder. This specimen's condition is about average when examining a number of similar models at a gun show. Still, an older all-original Colt.

Photo 47 = Colt Model 1851 U.S. Navy contract in approximately 90% overall condition. Note case colors remaining on frame, perfect frame screws, and brass grip straps. Cylinder scene is very crisp, and a few readers will spot the inspector cartouche on bottom of grip. A very desirable specimen.

Photo 48 = Colt Model 1851 U.S. Navy contract in approximately 70% - 80% original condition. Note the oxidized brownish splotches on barrel and areas of frame. Cylinder scene again is very sharp and screws show no tampering. In today's marketplace, still 30-40 C-notes of value.

Photo 49 = Colt Model 1851 U.S. Navy contract in 30% - 40% original condition. Note thinning and grayish patina color of bluing. Overall, a very clean original specimen showing honest wear that still deserves a proud placement in any Colt cap-and-ball aficionado's collection.

Photo 50 = Colt Antique (pre-1899 manufacture) Single Action Army (SAA) manufactured in 1875 - a third year gun. Note high luster finish and case colors on this 90% - 95% gun, also observe barrel and cylinder "freckling". If you are a Colt SAA collector, this addition would be a treasured prize.

Photo 51 = Colt 3rd Model Dragoon in approximately 80% overall condition. A beautiful specimen considering 1851 manufacture. As in some other Colt's, note the fire bluing on frame screws and trigger. Also notice the still visible cylinder scene indicating careful use. Overall, this specimen's condition is in the top 20% of its graduating class.

Photo 52 = Colt 2nd Model Dragoon with no finish remaining. While appearing original, this pistol has been artificially aged giving it an older appearance. Fakes in rarer Colt models have become more elaborate. Always get a receipt indicating condition (original or otherwise) when purchasing older Colt's in this price range.

Photo 53 = Model 71 Deluxe Rifle with 98%+ bright shiny original blue overall. Most dealers would consider this a mint specimen. Note how sharp the points of the checkering are. While this gun is not 100%, it is close. Observe the slight wear on rear hammer curvature and corners of frame. The darker appearance is normal on this model.

Photo 54 = Model 1894 Carbine with 95%+ bright shiny original receiver finish and 100% barrel/mag. bluing. Winchester collectors will recognize this as a very fine early gun by the bright vivid case colors still intact on the lever and hammer. This is an extremely desirable specimen - many dealers would call this mint, but corners of frame/loading gate and wood show a little wear. Light dings/scratches on wood are normal.

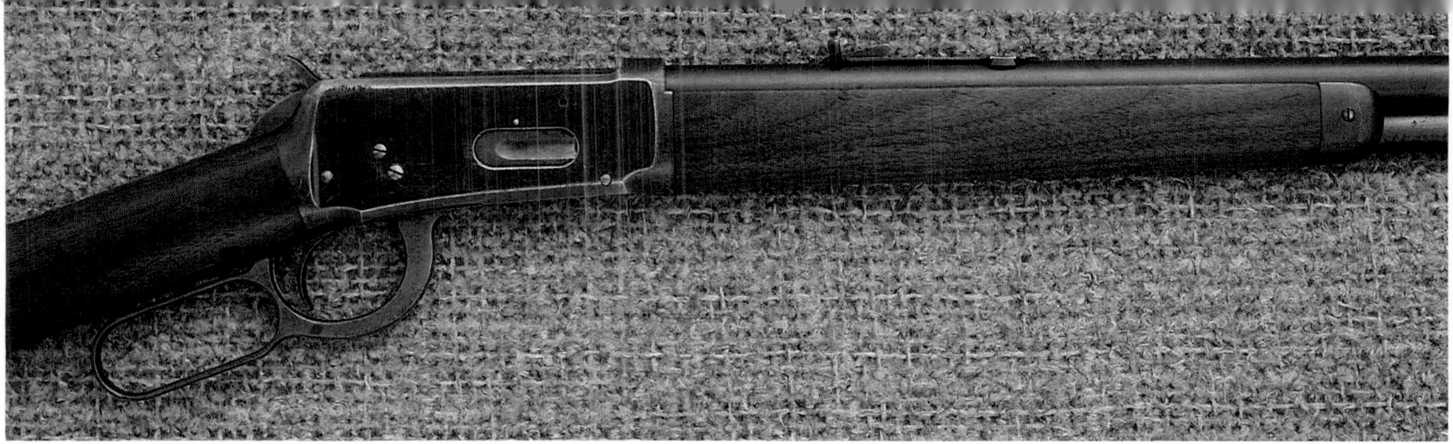

Photo 55 = Model 1894 Rifle with 90%+ bright shiny original blue on receiver and 98% barrel/mag. blue. Compare almost faded case colors on lever and hammer to Photo No. 54 - again indicating an early gun. Wood is also excellent with perfect fit to metal. A lot can be learned by concentrating on the receiver/lever corner and edge wear on Photos 54 - 63.

Photo 56 = Model 1892 Rifle with 85% - 90% original bluing with some light handling and storage marks. Note the darkness of the wood and the mostly shiny forearm cap. Also, observe the color of the bluing is turning a light patina (oxidized bluing which turns a plum-brown color after aging) compared to Photo No. 57. Overall, a nice original specimen.

Photo 57 = Model 1892 Pistol Grip Takedown Rifle with 75% - 80% original receiver bluing. This is a clean sharp gun showing no abuse - only normal wear. Notice that the checkering shows wear on the stock and forearm, and the lever has turned shiny due to use. Observe the receiver metal condition compared to Photo No. 61 - while retaining less finish this rifle is more valuable than No. 56 because of the bright bluing factor.

Photo 58 = Model 1873 Deluxe Rifle with 60% - 70% vivid receiver case colors, 95% barrel blue, and slight oxidation throughout receiver. Observe the natural color mottling on sideplate and receiver rear - also some small brown rust spots from improper storage can be seen on receiver front. Original bright case colors are extremely desirable on any older firearm.

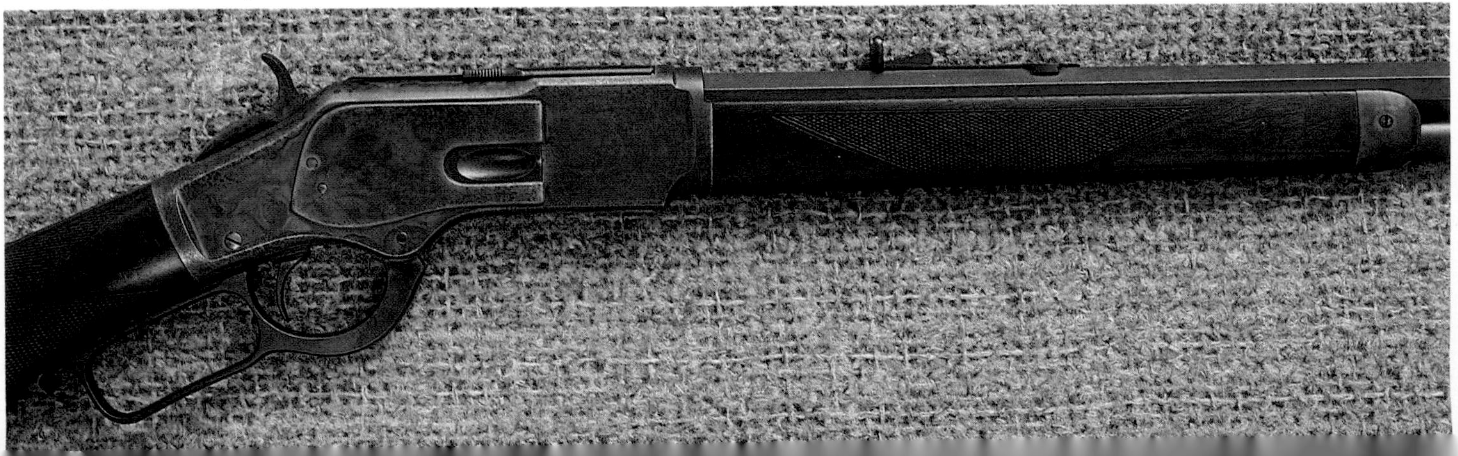

Photo 59 = Model 1892 Takedown Rifle showing approximately 60% receiver finish and 95% barrel blue. Notice that the balance of the receiver has flaked and turned brown. Also, close observation indicates that the frame screws have never been damaged by a screwdriver. Edge wear on this gun is not as prominent as it could be, probably indicating little scabbard use and mostly carrying wear.

Photo 60 = Model 55 Takedown Rifle retaining 40% - 50% of what appears to be an older reblued finish (note how frame corners are rounded due to excessive polishing compared to those on Photo No. 59). The dark wood is generally in good condition. Notice that the top frame screw shows damage and that the lever has been bent (is not flush against lower tang) due to older abuse.

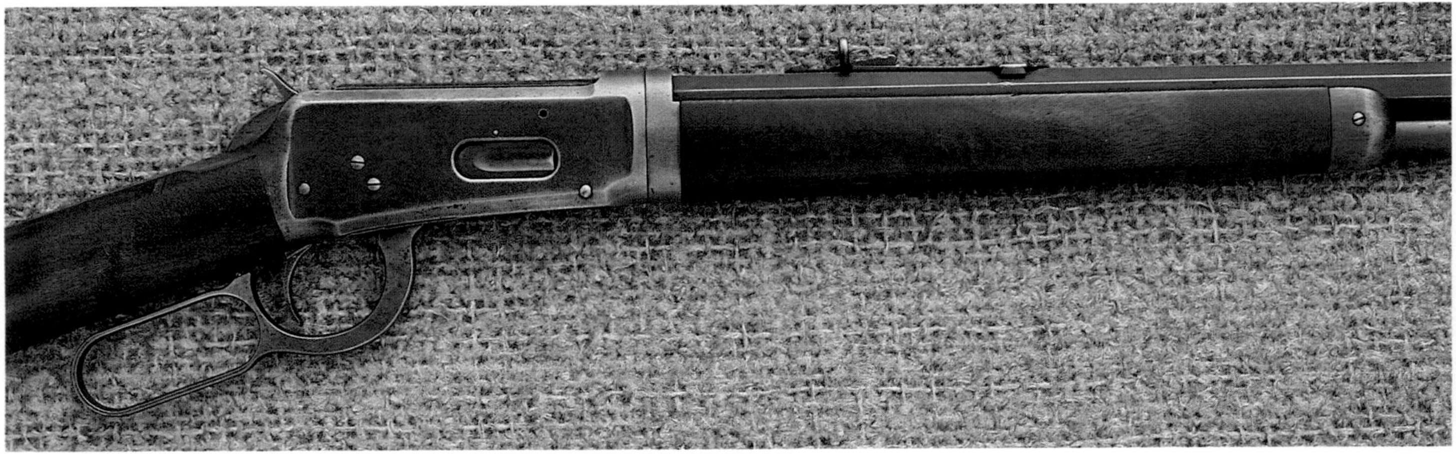

Photo 61 = Model 1894 Takedown Rifle with 40% original blue turning brown on frame and 90% barrel blue. The bottom and top of receiver and takedown ring have turned silvery from handling. This is normal wear and consistent with the rest of the gun's condition. Note that back of forearm wood sticks out next to the takedown ring indicating originality. On some refinished guns, the wood will appear lower than the receiver metal.

Photo 62 = Model 1894 Carbine depicting 20% receiver blue and 90% barrel/mag. blue. Notice the pattern of wear and how the balance of finish is turning a gun metal gray, including the barrel band. This carbine's condition is typical of many older Winchesters. A well used specimen showing no abuse. Receiver screws have been muscled-out once or twice.

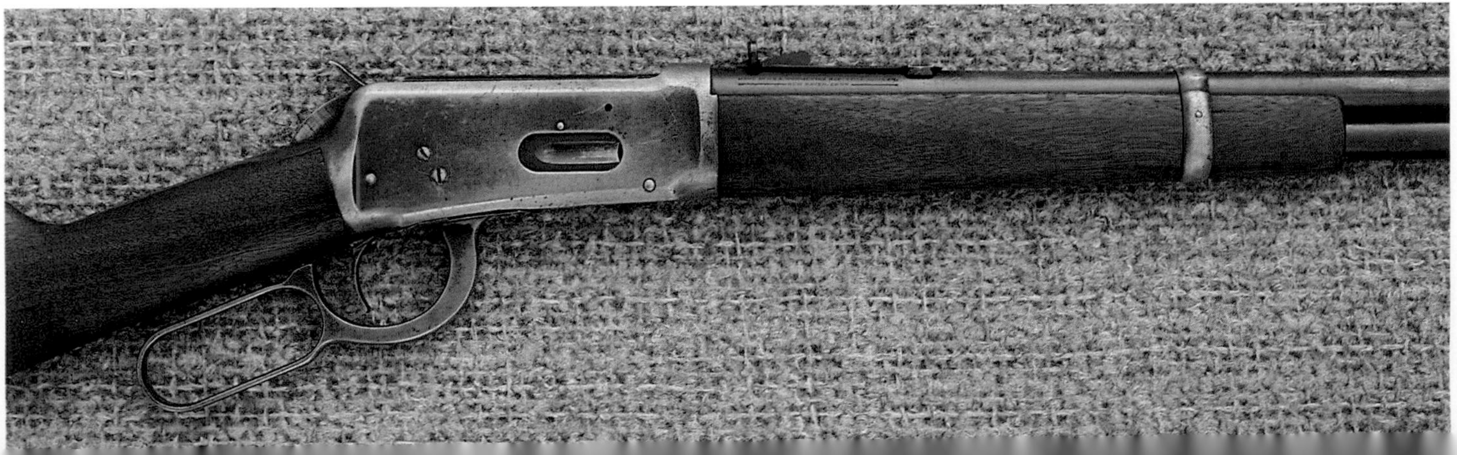

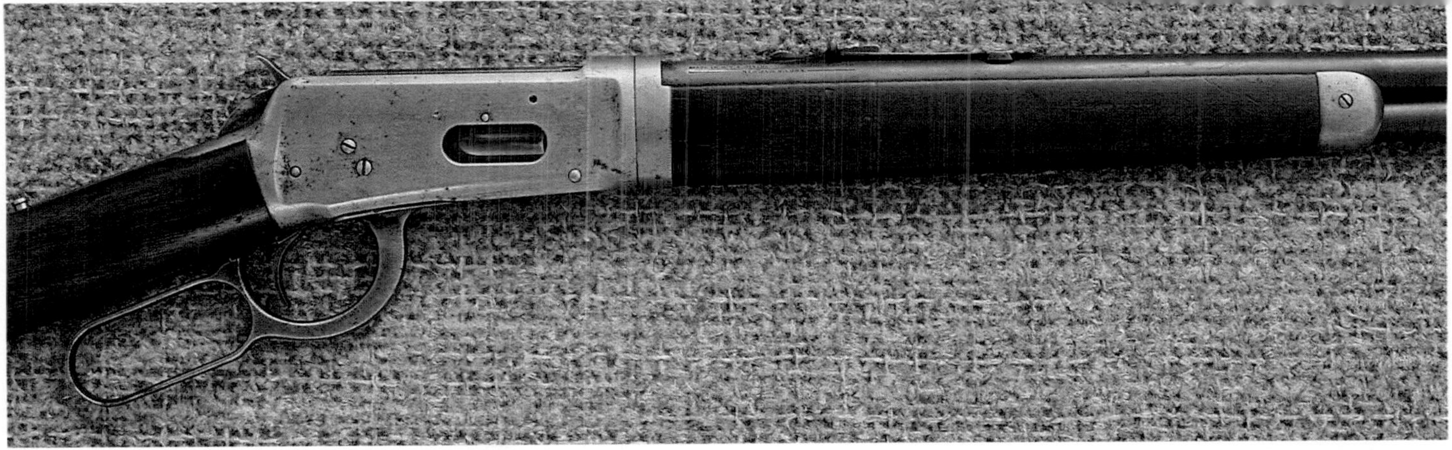

Photo 63 = Model 55 Takedown Rifle with no receiver blue remaining (it has flaked off) and 50% barrel/mag. blue. The wood is in very good condition. This is commonly referred to as a "shiny gun". While this gun appears in poor condition due to flaking, it is still a lot more desirable than the Model 1894 pictured in Photo No. 62. Loading gate bluing remains mostly intact, and frame screws indicate no wear.

Photo 64 = Model 1892 Rifle showing a lot of wear with all metal surfaces having turned a dark brown heavy patina due to much use, some abuse (note nails in front of forearm), and neglect. In the business, this is sometimes referred to (choose two only) as "brown gun", "the parts are worth this much", "decaying roadkill", "I got this much into it", "Grandpa's favorite", and is the least desirable from a condition standpoint.

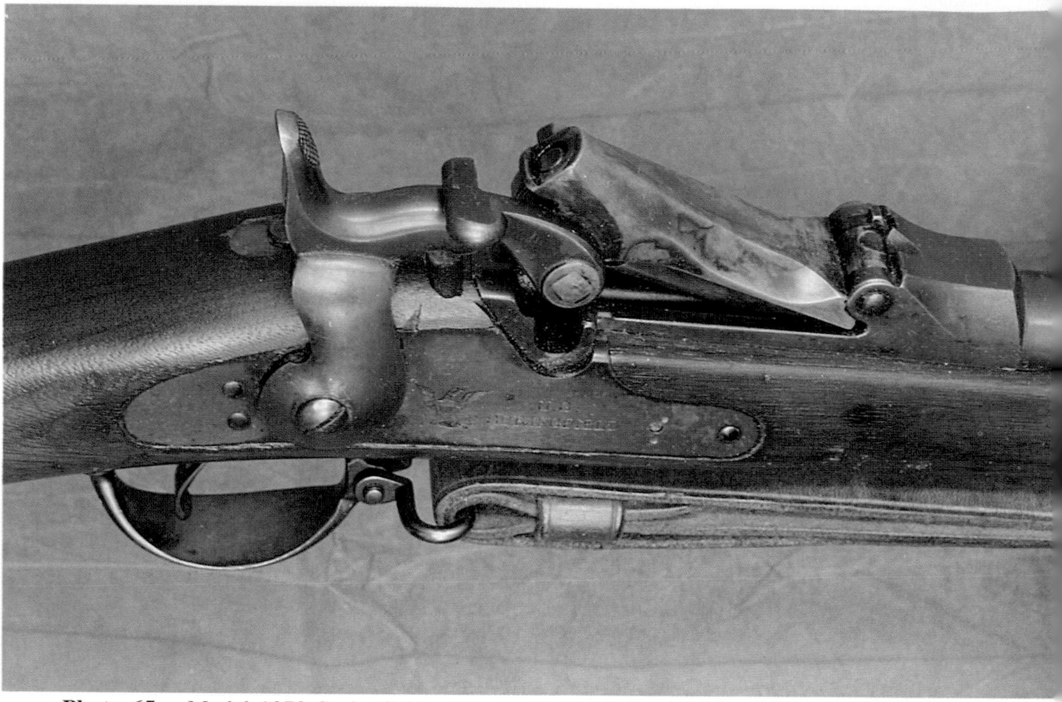

Photo 65 = Model 1873 Springfield military rifle in 98% original condition, .45-70 Govt. caliber. Observe almost perfect case colors on breech block and sideplate condition. Stock condition is also consistent with balance of gun - most of the original finish with a few slight nicks and dings. In today's marketplace, this all adds up to $1,350.

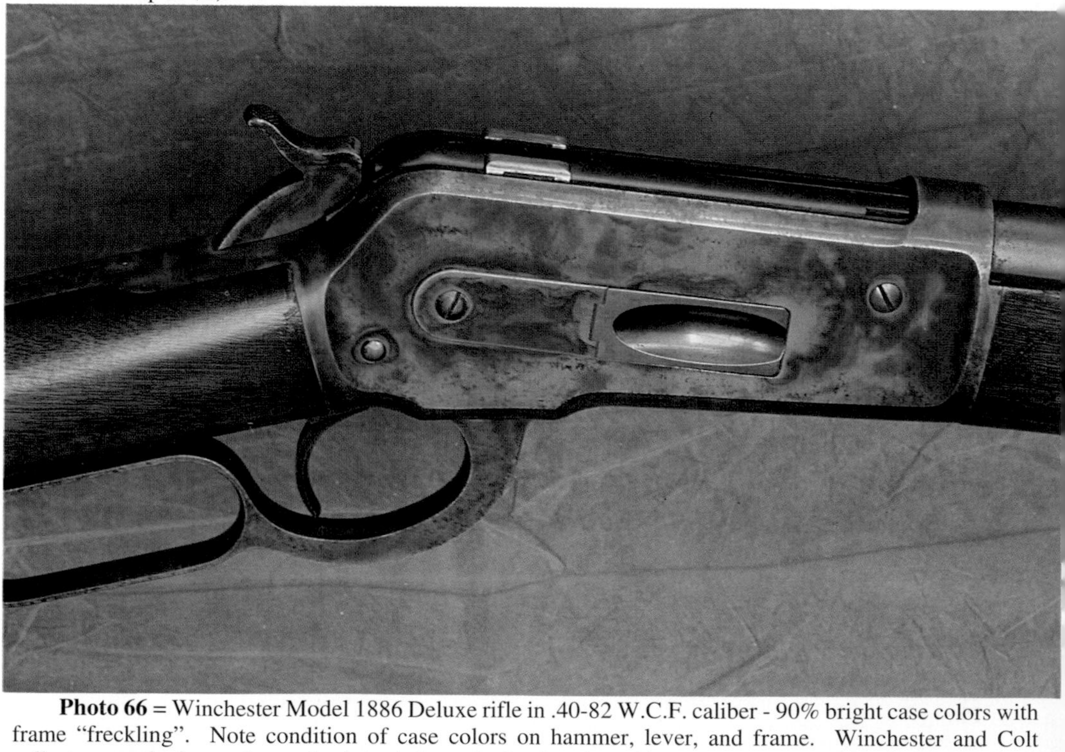

Photo 66 = Winchester Model 1886 Deluxe rifle in .40-82 W.C.F. caliber - 90% bright case colors with frame "freckling". Note condition of case colors on hammer, lever, and frame. Winchester and Colt collectors routinely reach way back in their pocketbook to buy this type of good stuff. Less than 1 out of every 1,000 Model '86s look like this!

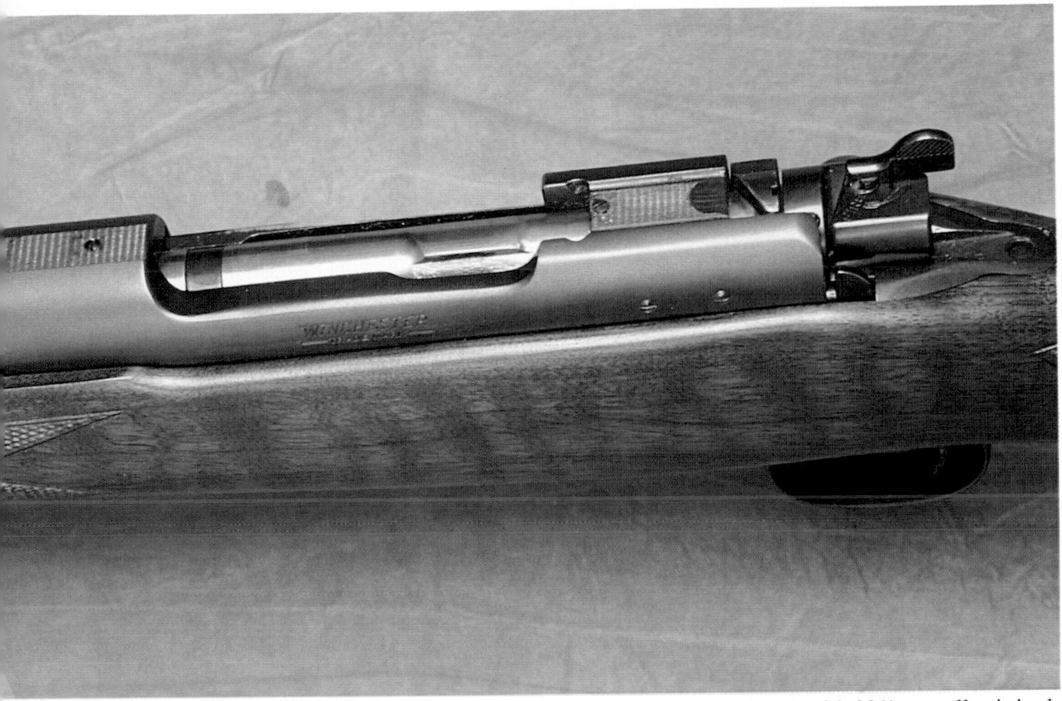

Photo 67 = Winchester Model 70 Pre-War Super Grade in .22 Hornet (rare) with 99% overall original condition. Eagle-eye readers (and Model 70 aficionados) will note the extra screw on top of rear receiver - the two in front are correct from the factory. In terms of value, it's a $500 hole (read that subtract $500).

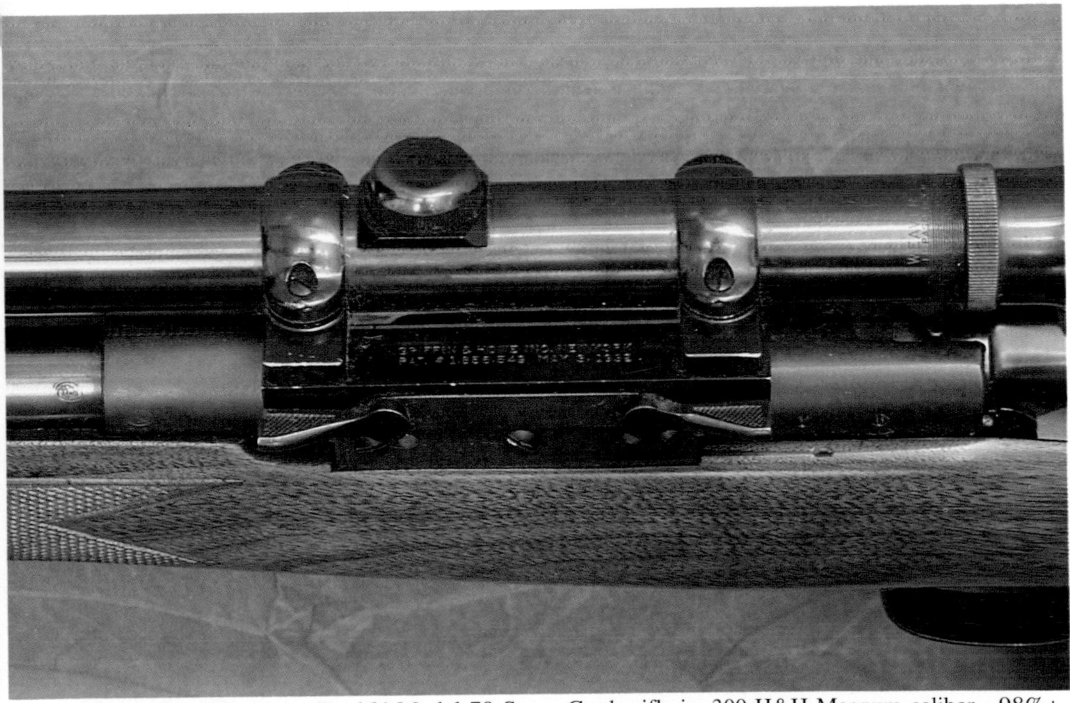

Photo 68 = Winchester Pre-'64 Model 70 Super Grade rifle in .300 H&H Magnum caliber - 98%+ original condition with non-factory Griffin & Howe scope mount, a popular option at the time. However, because Model 70 collectors don't like to see three extra screw-holes the price goes from $2,500 to $1,695.

Photo 69 = L.C. Smith Field Grade (hammerless). A mint specimen of an L.C. Smith Field Grade - unusual, since most Field guns saw heavy use while higher grades mostly saw the gun cabinet. Notice the way the case colors on frame top are mottled, wood to metal fit, and the checkering without points (common in most domestically manufactured field grade models).

Photo 70 = L.C. Smith Ideal Grade with approximately 30% original case colors remaining. This gun has been pictured from the bottom to emphasize the shininess that accumulates on the front and bottom of frame during much use. Note markings on receiver bottom, nail alterations to forearm, and visible stock cracking (adding up to a 40% decrease in value).

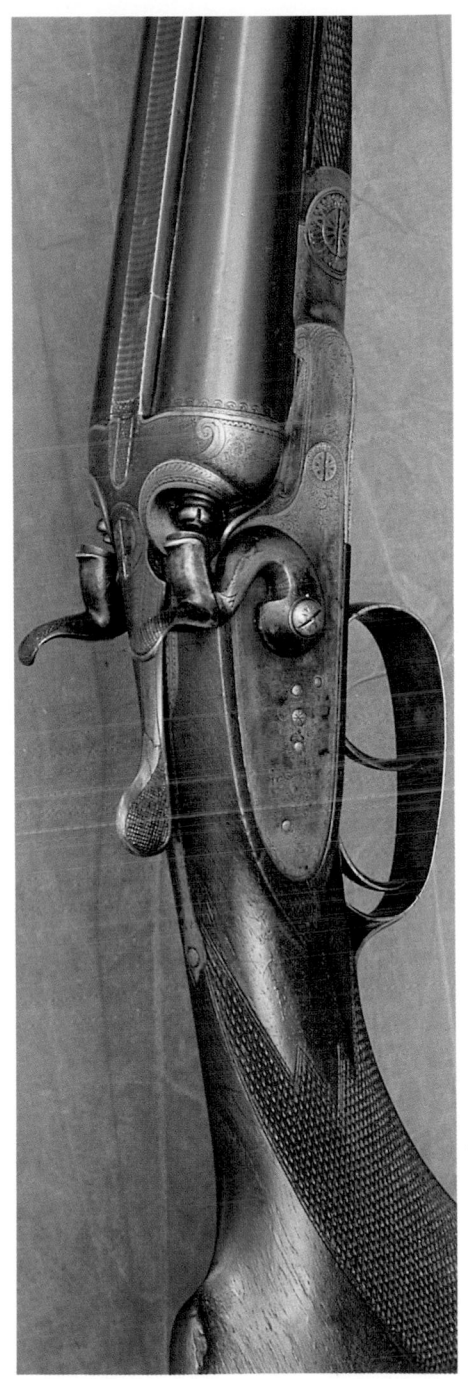

Photo 71 = Parker Brothers 20 gauge VH Grade on "0" frame that has been poorly refinished (note the incorrect color patterns on the receiver and opening lever color case hardening). Parker collectors will immediately key on the non-original case colors. Observe the difference between the redone case colors and the original L.C. Smith colors in Photo 69. If this was real - $3,250. The way it is - subtract approximately 50%.

Photo 72 = Older German 16 gauge back-action with hammers in 70% overall condition. Observe case colors centered around pins on sidelock. While most of these guns (including this one) are extremely well made with the finest of materials, domestic collector interest to date has been minimal. Typically priced at $450 - $750.

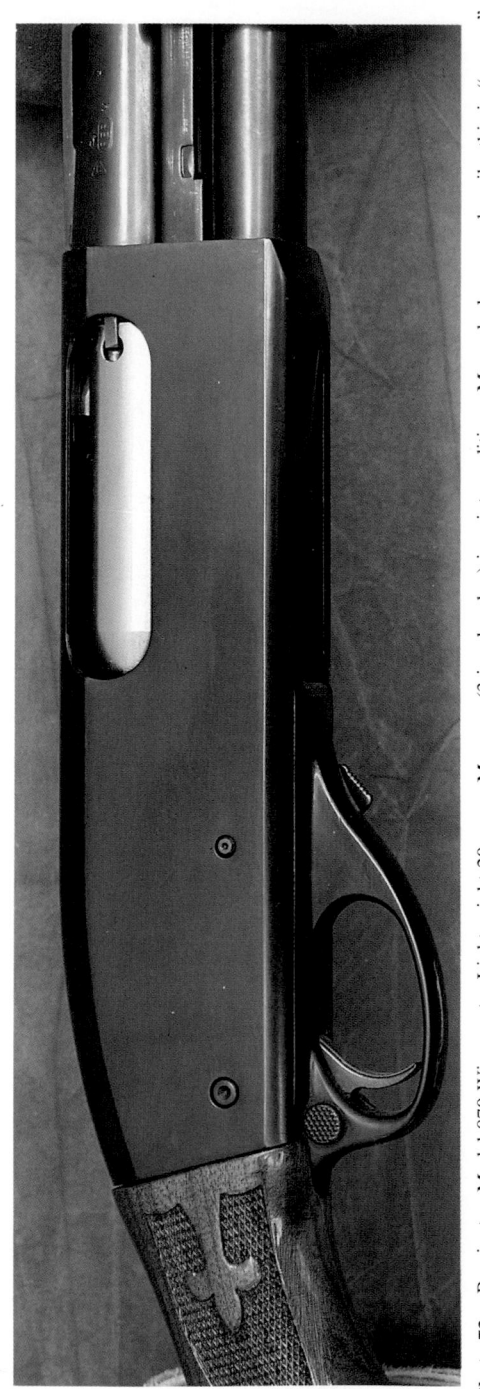

Photo 73 = Remington Model 870 Wingmaster Lightweight 20 gauge Magnum (3 in. chamber) in mint condition. Many dealers may describe this in "as new" condition. Note, however, slight wear on slide rail. Breech block also shows almost no wear with correct vertical machining striations.

Photo 74 = Remington Model 870 slide action 12 gauge in 95% condition with oxidation freckling occurring on corners of receiver bottom - the pump workhorse champion for both blue and white collar shooters for over four decades. They're not rare - they made millions. Seen priced at gun and pawn shops in the $250 range.

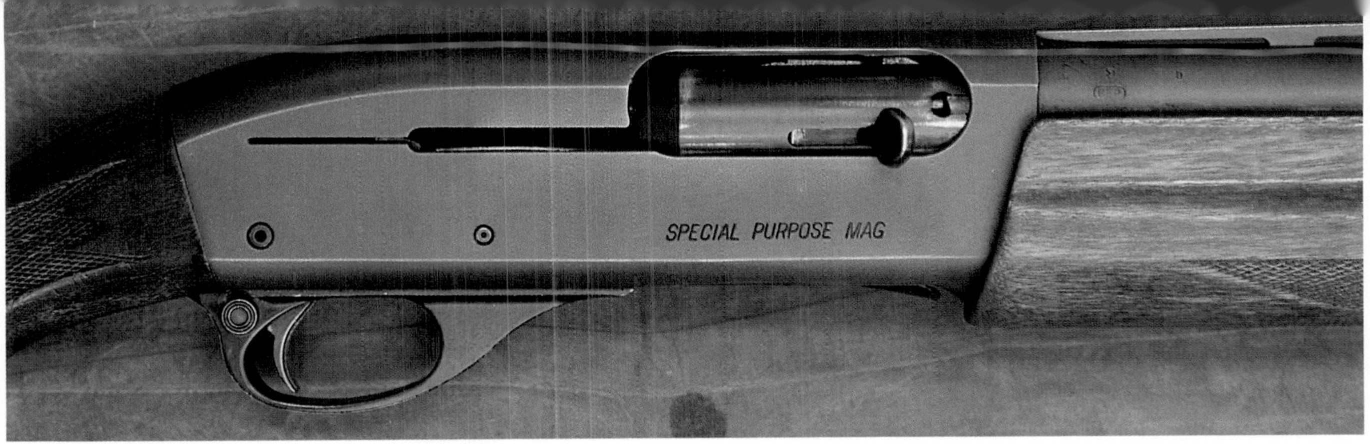

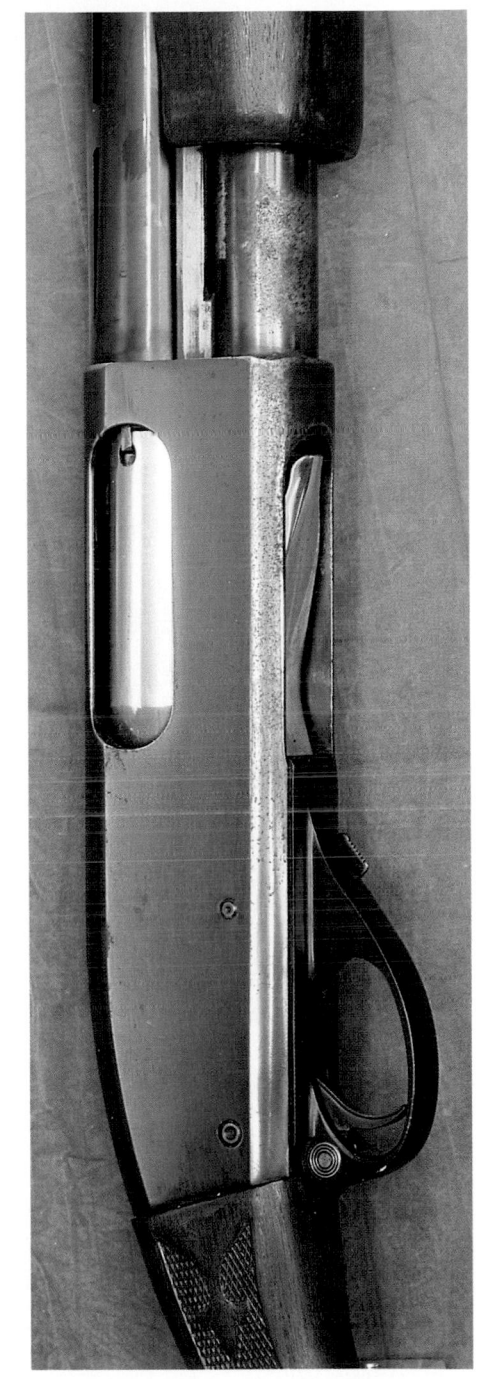

Photo 75 = Remington Model 1100 Special Purpose 12 gauge Magnum in 95% overall condition. On newer shotguns featuring this type of dull/matte finish, it can be difficult to determine how much it's been used. Observe the horizontal striations on the back of breech block - this gun's been fired more than a few times. Usually priced in the $300 range.

Photo 76 = Remington Model 870 12 gauge slide action shotgun in 75% - 80% overall condition. Pitting and shininess on front bottom of frame and magazine tube is normal, this is where the hunter carried the gun - probably without gloves since corrosive acid from hands has removed bluing.

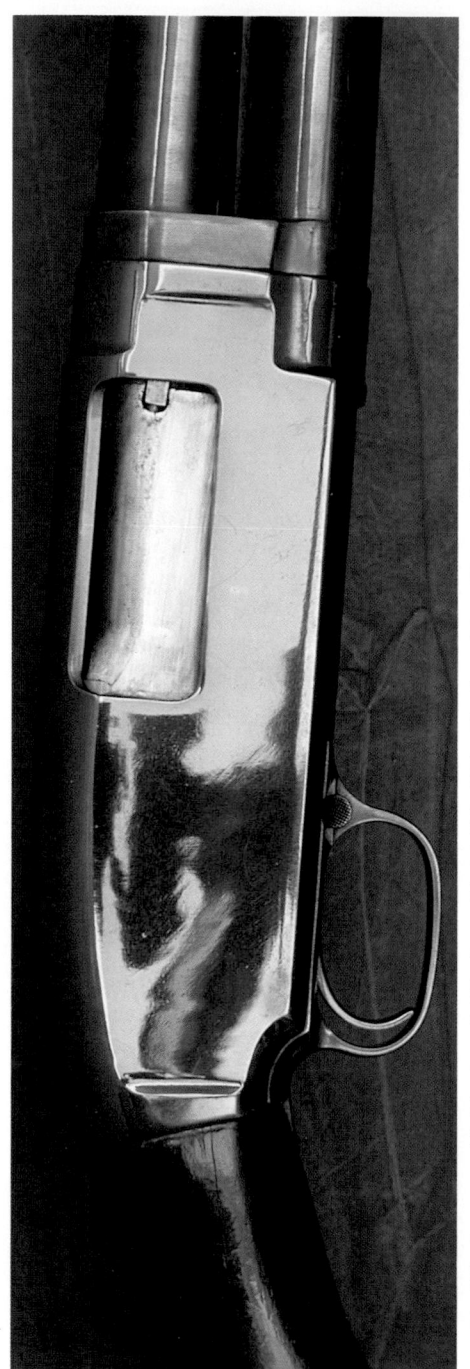

Photo 77 = What's wrong with this picture? Winchester Model 12 in 99% reblued condition. If you can't figure this out, you better put a one-year moratorium on your next Model 12 transaction until you bone up on Model 12 finishes. Probably the victim of some 1960s gunshop "$29.95 to reblue your gun - sale ends Friday!". The price tag usually reads "Normally $275 - this week only, $195!".

Photo 78 = Older Stevens 16 ga. slide action in 60% turned patina condition. Note overall grayish receiver color with brown oxidation splotching and stock crack. Screws have also been amateurly muscled out. This gun has no collector value. Figure out the shooting value and don't pay a penny more.

Firearms Associations

Listed below are the names and addresses of various firearms organizations/associations throughout the U.S. You are encouraged to join those organizations that pertain to your region and area(s) of interest. As thorough as we try to be, every year we get back quite a bit of mail for individual firearms associations that unfortunately, is undeliverable. If your club does not appear on the following pages or doesn't have a current address, please forward the correct information to us for inclusion in the next edition.

Academics for the Second Amendment (A2A)
P.O. Box 131254
St. Paul, MN 55113

Alabama Gun Collectors
P.O. Box 59606
Birmingham, AL 35259

Alaska Gun Collectors Association
c/o Wayne Anthony Ross, President
P.O. Box 101522
Anchorage, Alaska 99510

American Custom Gunmakers Guild
Jan Billeb, Executive Director
P.O. Box 812
Burlington, IA 52601
Phone/FAX No.: 319-752-6114
$60 Associate Membership Fee
$100 Commercial Associate Membership Fee

Ark - La - Tex - Gun Collectors
Thomas L. Baird, President
9601 Blom Blvd.
Shreveport, LA 71118

Bay Colony Weapons Collectors, Inc.
Ronald B. Santurjian
47 Homer Road
Belmont, MA 02178

Boardman Valley Collectors Guild
Jack Johnson, Secretary
County Road 600
Manton, MI 49663

Browning Collectors Assn.
Scherrie Brennac, Secretary
2749 Keith Dr.
Villa Ridge, MO 63089-1929
$30 - 1st Year Membership Fee
$20 Annual Membership Fee thereafter

C.A.D.A.(Collector Arms Dealer Association)
P.O. Box 427
Thomson, IL 61285

California Rifle & Pistol Association, Inc.
No Current Address Available

Central Illinois Gun Collectors Assn. Inc.
Russ Gardner, Sec./Treas.
P.O. Box 875
Jacksonville, IL 62651-0875

Central Penn Antique Arms Association
John E. Holman Jr.
978 Thistle Road
Elizabethtown, PA 17022

Chisholm Trail Antique Gun Association
E.D. Stone
1906 Richmond
Wichita, KS 67203

Civil War Round Table of North New Jersey
James F. Elliott
124 Conover Lane
Red Bank, NJ 07701

Colorado Gun Collectors Assoc.
Mr. Bud Greenwald, Secretary/Treasurer
2553 South Quitman Street
Denver, CO 80219
$25 Annual Membership Fee

Colt Collectors Association
Karen Green, Secretary
25000 Highland Way
Los Gatos, CA 95030
$35 Annual Membership Fee
$60 - Annual Membership Fee - Outside U.S.

Derringer Collectors Association
No Current Address Available

Ducks Unlimited
One Waterfowl Way
Memphis, TN 38120
Phone No.: 901-758-3825
FAX No.: 901-758-3850

The Firearms Coalition of Colorado
Bill Pittman, Chairman
P.O. Box 1454
Englewood, CO 80150-1454
Phone No.: 303-850-9342
FAX No.: 303-773-6549
$10 Annual Membership Fee

Florida Gun Collectors Association, Inc.
Betty Marquette, Show Chairman
P.O. Box 43
Branford, FL 32008

Forks of the Delaware Historical Arms Society, Inc.
97 Johnson Rd.
Bangor, PA 18013
FAX No.: 610-588-2815
$20 Annual Membership Fee

Glock Collectors Association
P.O. Box 840
Park Hills, MO 63601-0840
Phone No.: 314-431-7978
FAX No.: 314-431-7920

Golden Eagle Collectors Association
Chris Showler, Secretary
11144 Slate Creek Rd.
Grass Valley, CA 95945

Great Lakes Military Collectors Association
P.O. Box 401
Maumee, OH 43537

Gun Owners Civil Rights Alliance
Joseph E. Olson, President
P.O. Box 131254
St. Paul, MN 55113
Phone No.: 612-636-4465
$15 Annual Membership Fee

Gun Owners of America
Larry Pratt, Executive Director
8001 Forbes Pl., Suite 102
Springfield, VA 22151
$20 Annual Membership Fee

Hawaii Historic Arms Association
Box 1733
Honolulu, HI 96806

High Standard Collectors Association
540 W. 92nd St.
Indianapolis, IN 46260
$15 Annual Membership Fee

Hopkins & Allen Arms & Memorabilia Society
1309 Pamela Circle
Delphos, OH 45833

Houston Gun Collectors Association
P.O. Box 741429
Houston, TX 77274-1429

Hunter Education Association
Box 525
Draper, UT 84020
Phone No.: 801-571-9461

Indianhead Firearms Assn.
R#9 Box 186
Chippewa Falls, WI 54729

Indian Territory Gun Collectors Association
P.O. Box 33201
Tulsa, OK 74153-1201

Iroquois Arms Collectors Association
Kenneth Keller, Secretary
Susann Keller, Show Secretary
214 70th St.
Niagara Falls, NY 14304

Jersey Shore Antique Arms Collectors
Joe Sisia
P.O. Box 100
Bayville, NJ 08721-0100
$10 Annual Membership Fee

Kansas Cartridge Collectors Association
Vic Suetter
Route 1
Lincoln, KS 67455

Kentuckiana Arms Collectors Assoc.
Ginger Wilkinson, Secretary
P.O. Box 1776
Louisville, KY 40201
$20 Annual Membership Fee
502-937-1996

Kentucky Gun Collectors Association
Ruth Johnson, Executive Secretary
P.O. Box 64
Owensboro, KY 42302
Phone No.: 502-729-4197

Lancaster Muzzle Loading Rifle Association
James H. Frederick, Jr.
779 Prospect Road
Columbia, PA 17512

Long Island Antique Gun Collectors Assoc.
Frederick R. Wilkens
35 Beach Street
Farmingdale, L.I., NY 11735
$20 Annual Membership Fee

The Mannlicher Collectors Association
Don L. Henry, Executive Secretary
P.O. Box 7144
Salem, OR 97303
$20 Annual Membership Fee

Marlin Firearms Collectors Association, Ltd.
Mr. Dick Paterson, Secretary/Treasurer
407 Lincoln Bldg.
44 Main Street
Champaign, IL 61820
$5 Initiation Fee
$10 Annual Membership Fee

Maryland Arms Collectors Assoc. (MACA)
Del Kuzemchak, Secretary
33 S. Main Street P.O. Box 206
Loganville, PA 17342-0206
$25 Annual Membership Fee

Maumee Valley Gun Collectors Association
P.O. Box 492
Maumee, OH 43537

MD Licensed Firearms Dealers Assoc.
P.O. Box 2555
Silver Spring, MD 20915-2555
Phone No.: 301-942-3329

Memphis Antique Weapons Association
Lonnie Griffin 108 Clark Place
Memphis, TN 38104

Minnesota Rifle and Revolver Association
Cliff Secord
5344 Morgan Ave. N.
Brooklyn Center, MN 55430

Minnesota Weapons Collectors Association
Gail Foster, Executive Director
P.O. Box 662
Hopkins, MN 55343
$20 Annual Dues
$4 Admission - 8 shows/year

Miniature Arms Collectors/Makers Society, Ltd.
William Adrian, Membership Chairman
22 W. 071 Stratford Ct.
Glen Ellyn, IL 60137

Missouri Valley Arms Collectors Association, Inc.
L.P. Brammer, Membership Secretary
P.O. Box 33033
Kansas City, MO 64114
Phone No.: 816-333-6509
Annual Membership $20.00 — ages 21+; $10.00 — under 21

Montana Arms Collectors Association
Dean E. Yearout
1516 - 21st Ave. S.
Great Falls, MT 59405
$20 Annual Membership Fee

The Mule Deer Foundation
1005 Terminal Way, Ste. 140
Reno, NV 89502
$25 Annual Memberhsip Fee

Nat'l Automatic Pistol Collectors Assoc. (N.A.P.C.A.)
Tom Knox
Box 15738
St. Louis, MO 63163
Phone No.: 314-481-4344
$35 Annual Membership Fee - U.S. & Canada
$45 Elsewhere

National Alliance of Stocking Gun Dealers
P.O. Box 187
Havelock, NC 28532

National Mossberg Collectors Association
Victor Havlin
P.O. Box 487
Festus, MO 63028
$10 Annual Membership Fee
Phone No.: 314-937-6401

National Rifle Association (NRA)
11250 Waples Mill Rd.
Fairfax, VA 22030
Phone No.: 800-NRA-8888/703-267-1000
$35 Annual Membership Dues
$30 Annual Senior Membership (65+, also disabled vets)
$15/$30 Annual Junior Membership (20 and younger)
$10 Annual Liberty Membership
$90 for 3 years
$140 for 5 years
$750 Life Membership Dues
$375 Senior Life Membership (also disabled vets)

The National Wild Turkey Federation
P.O. Box 530
Edgefield, SC 29824
Phone No.: 1-800-843-6983
Call for membership details

New Hampshire Arms Collectors, Inc.
Warren Thayer
P.O. Box 6
Harrisville, N.H. 03450

New Mexico Gun Collectors Association
Edward C. Schmidt - Membership Chairman
P.O. Box 13687
Albuquerque, NM 87192
Phone/FAX No.: 505-836-3443
$5.00 Initiation Fee
$10.00 Annual Membership

North Eastern Arms Collectors Assoc., Inc.
Thomas J. Mulligan, President
P.O. Box 185
Amityville, NY 11701
$20 Annual Membership Fee

Northwest Montana Arms Collectors Association (NWMACA)
Paul Willis, Treasurer
P.O. Box 653
Kalispell, MT 59903-0653
Phone No.: 406-755-3580

Ohio Gun Collectors Association
John T. Snyder - Business Manager
P.O. Box 9007
Maumee, OH 43537-9007
Phone No.: 419-897-0861
FAX No.: 419-897-0860
$18.00 Annual Membership Fee
$10.00 Application Fee
Members and guests of members only.

Old Fort Gun Collectors Association
No Current Address Available

Oregon Arms Collectors, Inc.
P.O. Box 8986
Aloha, OR 97207-8986
$12 Annual Membership Fee

Pelican Arms Collectors Association
Bob Thompson
P.O. Box 747
Clinton, LA 70722

Pennsylvania Antique Gun Collectors Assoc.
Mrs. Kathleen Beyer, Secretary/Treasurer
28 Fulmer Avenue
Havertown, PA 19083
$10 Annual Membership Fee

Pheasants Forever
P.O. Box 75473
St. Paul, MN 55175
Phone No.: 612-481-7142

Potomac Arms Collectors Association
Attn: Secretary
P.O. Box 1812
Wheaton, MD 20915
$25 Annual Membership Fee

Quail Unlimited
Rt. #3 - Box 47
P.O. Box 610
Edgefield, SC 29824
Phone No.: 803-637-5731
FAX No.:803-637-0037
$25 Annual Membership includes bimonthly subscription
to Quail
Unlimited

Randall Firearms/Pistol Collector's Association
Steve Kaiser, Director
1200 Hub Tower
699 Walnut Street
Des Moines, IA 50309
Phone No.: 515-288-2646
$25 Annual Membership Fee

Randall Historian
Rick "KK" Kennerknecht
P.O. Box 903
Casper, WY 82602-0903
Phone No.: 307-234-9476
E-Mail: rekenn@trib.com
$25 - Research letter

Remington Society of America
Marv Adams, Secretary-Treasurer
130 W. South Boundary
Perrysburg, OH 43551-1754
Annual Membership $30 + $5 application fee
Life Membership $300 + $5 application fee
Phone No.: 419-874-2288

Rocky Mountain Elk Foundation
2291 W. Broadway
Missoula, MT 59802
Phone No.: 406-523-4500
FAX No.: 406-523-4581

The Ruffed Grouse Society
Ronald P. Burkert
451 McCormick Rd.
Coraopolis, PA 15108
Phone No.: 412-262-4044
$20 Annual Membership Fee
$30 Conservative Membership Fee
$100 Sustaining Membership Fee
$200+ Various Sponsor Membership Fee

Ruger Collectors Association, Inc.
P.O. Box 240
Green Farms, CT 06436
$25 Annual Membership Fee
Phone No.: 203-259-6222, Ext. 124
Safari Club International
4800 W. Gates Pass Rd.
Tucson, AZ 85745
Phone No.: 520-620-1220
$55 Annual Membership Fee USA/CAN/MEX

Sako Collectors Association, Inc.
Mims C. Reed
1725 Woodhill Lane
Bedford, TX 76021
$25 Annual Membership Fee

Santa Barbara Historical Arms Coll. Assoc.
P.O. Box 6291
Santa Barbara, CA 93160-6291
$40 Initiation
$15 Annual Membership Fee

San Bernardino Valley Arms Collectors
Robert Walter
18710 Cajon Blvd.
San Bernardino, CA 92407
Los Alamos, NM 87544

San Fernando Valley Arms Coll. Assoc.
P.O. Box 922613
Sylmar, CA 91392-2613

San Gabriel Valley Arms Collectors
Gerald C. Knight, Secretary/Treasurer
1140 Daveric Drive
Pasadena, CA 91107-1740
Phone No.: 818-351-9368
$20 Annual Dues

Second Amendment Foundation/Gun Week
12500 Northeast 10 Pl.
Bellevue, WA 98005

Smith & Wesson Collectors Association
Cally Pletl, Administrative Assistant
P.O. Box 444
Afton, NY 13730

Southern California Arms Collectors Association, Inc.
Dr. Joseph S. Eisenlauer, President
P.O. Box 7432
Thousand Oaks, CA 91359-7432

The Stark Gun Collectors, Inc.
Pat F. McDonald
602 Summerdale N.W.
Massillon, OH 44646

Tampa Bay Arms Collectors Association, Inc.
H. Allen Bounds, Secretary/Treasurer
P.O. Box 41666
St. Petersburg, FL 33743-1666
$15 Annual Membership Fee

Texas Gun Collectors Association (TGCA)
Carolyn Mims
P.O. Box 701314
San Antonio, TX 78270

The Thompson Center Association
Hilary Wright, Secretary
P.O. Box 792
Northboro, MA 01532
$25 Annual Membership Fee

Tri-State Gun Collectors, Inc.
P.O. Box 1201
Lima, OH 45801

Washington Arms Collectors, Inc.
J. Dennis Cook
P.O. Box 7335
Tacoma, WA 98407

Weapons Collectors Society of Montana
No Current Address Available

Weatherby Collectors Association, Inc.
P.O. Box 128
Moira, NY 12957
$30 - 1st Year Membership Fee
$20 Annual Membership Fee thereafter
$400 Lifetime Membership Fee

Williamette Valley Arms Collectors Association, Inc.
James Crudele, Executive Secretary
P.O. Box 5191
Eugene, OR 97405
Phone No.: 541-747-5271

Winchester Arms Collectors Association, Inc.
Richard A. Berg, Executive Secretary
P.O. Box 6754
Great Falls, MT 59406
$35 to join (includes $25 annual dues)
$400 Lifetime Membership Fee

Winchester Club of America
Larry Jones
3070 S. Wyandot
Englewood, CO 80110

Ye Connecticut Gun Guild
Robert L. Harris
U.S. Route 7-Kent Road
Cornwall Bridge, CT 06754

Zumbro Valley Arms Collectors, Inc.
Box 6621
Rochester, MN 55901

Correspondence
Inquiries/Appraisals

By the time the party favors had been passed around for this most recent New Year's Eve, we had a very good reason to celebrate - the entire backlog of correspondence had been researched, called, FAXed, and/or mailed back to the anxiously awaiting individuals.

It's a nice feeling when we finally get caught up. The trouble is, with the volume of inquiries we are getting now as compared to even five years ago, trying to play catch up ball gets to be a pretty difficult ballgame to win after awhile. Our policy regarding the evergrowing correspondence inquiries and appraisals has been changed to the following:

Correspondence that is mailed, FAXed, or E-mailed in and requires a written reply after the research has been completed will be billed at $20.00 per gun (up to five guns). At six guns, the fee drops to $15.00 per gun. Payment by check, money order, or major credit card should accompany all correspondence requesting this information/appraisal service. Correspondence sent in without payment will be returned.

Individuals requesting a photocopy of a particular page or section from this newest edition for insurance or reference purposes will be billed at $5.00 per page up to four pages and $3.50 per page thereafter.

Individuals who request a telephone appraisal(s) or additional information but do not require written documentation will also be billed at $5.00/gun. Payment can be made with most major credit cards or personal check.

Phone calls regarding firearms related questions are normally taken between 2-5 pm daily, Monday-Wednesday during most weeks, unless the responses to written correspondence preclude phone time or when we are unavailable. Voicemail messages and/or call-back slips may be returned, time permitting.

To make sure we can assist you with any correspondence, please include good quality photos of the specimen in question, any information available about that particular specimen, including caliber, barrel length, finish, stocks, barrel markings, other potentially significant gun marks that would assist us with identifying your gun, and special order features. In addition, be sure to include both your address and phone/FAX/E-mail number(s), giving us an option of how to contact you for best service. To keep up with this constant onslaught of firearms related questions, we have one of the most complete and up-to-date firearms libraries in the U.S., in addition to a large network of both dealers and collectors who can answer most of the questions we receive expeditiously.

For those of you who would like to sell a firearm(s) or have an item(s) appraised that are either difficult or impossible to try to do by written correspondence/FAX, we have made an arrangement with J & S Custom Guns located in Lakeville, MN to receive these types of guns for us. Simply call/write/FAX us or J & S Custom Guns (see page 69 for details) with the item(s) that you are wishing to have appraised or sold. Remember, even modern guns (post-1898 mfg.) sent to us for appraisal must be shipped from one FFL holder to another. In other words, modern guns sent in must be shipped from one licensed gun shop/dealer to another. If this is not convenient for you, we will try to match you up with a selected dealer from your particular area to perform this appraisal/potential sale.

In the past, we have answered thousands of gun questions at no charge. In the future, this phone service is possible only when all paid correspondence is caught up. Thank you for your patience and understanding on this matter.

All correspondence should be directed to:

Blue Book Publications, Inc.
ATTN: Research Department
8009 - 34th Ave. So.
Minneapolis, MN 55425
FAX# 612-853-1486
e-mail: guns@bluebookinc.com

SORRY - No order or request for research paid by credit card will be processed without a credit card expiration date.

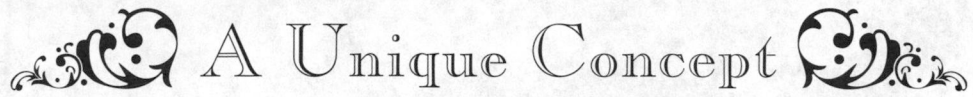

A Unique Concept

The *Blue Book of Gun Values* is the only book that:

✓ Utilizes the professionals' grading system of percentage of original finish remaining. (Eliminates confusing descriptions such as "Good", "Excellent", "Fair".)

✓ Is updated annually and expeditiously providing the freshest information available!

✓ Is based on actual selling prices. (These are the prices you can expect to pay — not artificial list prices or some "expert's" opinion.)

✓ Offers you personal consultation by mail on special questions you may have! (No book can cover everything.)

In the past I have offered one free consultation per book order. With the growth of this project (not to mention the hundreds of letters and phone calls I am already behind on), this is no longer possible. Individual appraisals and/or additional research can be provided for a fee per gun (see the "Correspondence Inquiries/Appraisals" section on page 68 for more information including prices on this service). Please include a detailed description with all pertinent information about the gun(s) in question in your letter/FAX/E-mail. Good quality photos of the receiver, special markings, etc. would also be appreciated.

BUYING OR SELLING?

Interested in buying or selling a particular firearm(s)? Or maybe hesitating because you are unsure of what a fair market price should be? Depending on what you are interested in, a referral will be made that will enable you to be sure that you are getting what you paid for (or getting paid a fair price). This service is designed to help all those people who are worried or scared about purchasing a potentially "bad gun" or getting "ripped off" when selling. We have referred hundreds of satisfied customers to the best contacts in the firearms business, based on our extensive network of dealers and collectors. There is no charge for this referral service - we are simply connecting you with the best person(s)/company possible within your field of collecting ensuring that you get a fair deal. This hybrid matchmaking can make 25%- 50% worth of difference on potentially buying or selling a gun. We have also arranged to have J & S Custom Guns located at 17400 Kenwood Trail in Lakeville, MN 55044 (Phone: 612-435-7147, FAX: 612-435-3678) receive guns for either appraisal or sale. Contact us or J & S Custom Guns directly to utilize this service. All replies are treated strictly confidential. All written correspondence/replies should be directed to:

Blue Book of Gun Values ™

Attn: John Allen
8009 34th Ave. So., Suite 1391
Minneapolis, MN 55425 USA
Phone No.: 612-854-5229
FAX NO.: 612-853-1486
e-mail: guns@bluebookinc.com

If we're not available, please leave a message.

Introductory Gunnerama

by S.P. Fjestad

Investing in firearms (or any other tangible asset for that matter) is a worthwhile effort to not only enjoy your "savings program" at home, but also to preserve value for a future date. To knowledgeably invest is always a little bit more complex than it originally appears to be. There are a lot of tracks leading out of this train station, and it's not that easy to get on the right train to get you where you want to go within a reasonable time frame. Spending money in an effort to obtain collectible firearms perhaps has more opportunities and choices today than at any time in the past. Hopefully, once you complete this article not only will you have a better perspective on how collectible firearms and other key investments have performed historically, but you will also be able to grasp today's significantly more complicated mix of supply/demand economics. Many graphs and illustrations have been provided to help you with these issues.

In an effort to provide a historical perspective in this issue, the following fictional story has been provided for your enjoyment. While the names are fictional, the facts and dates are true I will pick up the story line again at the end to provide some interesting conclusions that are very apropos when understanding the dangling price tags you see hanging from the trigger guards of today's firearms.

1875 – BUYING YOUR FIRST GUN

It's July of 1875, you're 20 years old, the temperature and humidity are unrelenting, and farm work has been responsible for too many hard hours this summer in the Ohio River valley. But today's a special day. After saving $2.00 a week for the last 30 weeks, you can finally buy that Model 1873 Winchester sporting rifle you've dreamed about ever since Bill's Hardware put it out on the rack. Even though it will cost three $20 Liberty gold pieces, the set trigger, deluxe checkered wood, and special sights are well worth the extra money. After all, Col. Colt wants $17 for a plain Peacemaker in .45 cal., expensive when other pistols are selling for under $5.00. With .44-40 shells selling for two cents each, you can only buy five boxes for now. Still, today is a day you'll remember for a long time.

1892 – MAKING A TRADE

It's 1892, farm work is just as hard, but at least your two sons are helping enough to justify that extra 160 acres you purchased from a neighbor four years ago for $640. The Winchester '73 is still in excellent shape, but now you'd like a shotgun for water fowl opportunities and a smaller caliber rifle for your growing, rambunctious boys. Besides, Bill just told you about a new Winchester lever action to be released shortly in a smaller Model 1886 frame in the same caliber as your '73, except it will be much lighter. You go back to Bill's Hardware and ask him what it'll cost "to boot" if you trade in your rifle for his Winchester Model 1887 10 gauge lever action shotgun and Model 1890 .22 cal. slide action rifle. Bill tells you that in the past 16 years the price of a new '73 like yours has gone down to $35, and that you've actually lost value on the original purchase price. After adding up $25 and $16 for the shotgun and rifle, respectively, Bill's figured it will cost you $15 to trade an allowance of just over $25 for your used rifle. After climbing back on the buckboard for a dusty ride home, you know it'll be a day your kids will remember for a long time. Yet you wonder how your '73, that was cleaned after every shooting, could lose over 50% of its value in only 16 years. Why will $20 gold pieces buy more today than they did back in 1875?

1919 – A NEW AGE

It's fall of 1919, farm work has become quite a bit easier, and only two horses are left on the homestead. New machinery makes the land more productive, and even though prices for farm products have gone up slightly, so has everything else. Your eldest son still has the 1890 Winchester on the porch at the farm while the 10 gauge lever action has sat unused in your gun cabinet for the last 15 years. Five years ago you almost traded it in for a new Model 12 pump, but after Bill's kid told you damascus guns weren't selling any more and were way down in value, you decided to purchase the Model 12 outright for $35. It's an excellent shotgun, but the newer smokeless shells kick harder than you're used to, and this new Browning semi-auto made by Remington might be the cure for hunting in three weeks. Bill's hardware has one for $45 that you'll walk over and purchase this afternoon. Yet your mind drifts back to that day in 1875 when you bought your first Winchester and you wonder why you ever traded it off. Last week Bill's kid told you the '73 was finally being discontinued by Winchester at $39, a $21 decrease after almost 40 years of manufacture! Maybe you'll special order one when you're in the store this afternoon.

1980 – TURN ON THE INFLATION

It's 1980, and since you're no longer alive, your guns have to finish this story. The Model 1890 Winchester is still on the original farm on the porch of a new house. It's in pretty tough shape now with no finish left and light pitting on the frame. The Winchester Model 1887 and 1912 shotguns are now in the possession of a great-grandson living in Pennsylvania. The lever action 10 gauge is in excellent shape since it was never used after 1910. The Remington semi-auto shotgun has been passed around and used a lot. Someone cut the stock off and put on a recoil pad, but other than that, it has over 50% original bluing remaining. Another great–grandson has the Model 1873 rifle that is still new in the box. He was certainly pleased to get the original sales receipt for the Winchester as well as an uncirculated $20 gold piece found in the owner's manual packet. Rumors have it that Great-Grandpa Frank left the gun with these items in the box before he died. Obviously, he wanted to leave his relatives something by which they could remember him for a long time.

REMINISCING OVER THE CRYSTAL BALL

It's 1995, and time to draw a few conclusions from Great-Grandpa Frank's story. Adjacent to this article is a listing of items which Frank purchased and their respective values at dates both in and out of his lifetime. While the facts speak for themselves, it is interesting to track each "purchase" chronologically. Notice that between 1875 and January of 1920 there was very little change in anything. In this 45 year interval gold fluctuated less than $1.00 total and the yearly average price of silver went from a high of $1.24 per ounce (1875) to a low of $.52 per ounce (1915). Certainly most investors today would not expect to buy and store a precious metal like silver for nearly half a century only to lose over 50% of the original purchase price when selling. During such an extended period of noninflation, it is hard for us today to rationalize a past economy in which prices remain stable and economic stability is based on preserving value by saving money rather than buying "investment vehicles" in an attempt to out-leapfrog the erosions of inflation.

After Franklin Roosevelt's unpopular executive order authorizing the public's surrender of gold in 1933, the spot price went to $35 per ounce and stayed in that range until 1971. In 1974 gold broke the $100 mark, and when deregulation occurred a year later, the double digit inflation of the late seventies set the stage for the price peaks, which went in the record book in 1980 ($750 per ounce gold and $45 per ounce silver). Collectibles also took off in this same time period with many people seeing the down side risk factor as minimal compared to the ever decreasing purchasing power of the dollar.

Tangible investments seemed to be the only way to preserve wealth when the "buy it today before it goes up tomorrow" rule seemed to be circumspect advice for storing value. It seems the phrase "short-term growth" encapsulated all the financial objectives needed to flourish during a period when some prices were changing twice a week. How quickly, even carefully laid out, long-range planning can be scrapped when value is dictated by inflation rather than normal supply and demand. While many Americans seem to agree that inflation is not beneficial to our society, few seem to understand an economy that does not allow for 10% annual increase on the price of their three bedroom rambler. A trip to Switzerland with its almost inflation proof economic system and seriously balanced budget government will quickly show how the Swiss spank the back end of America's misbehaving economic child.

INFLATIONARY EFFECT

In 1892 when Frank walked into Bill's Hardware and found out that his '73 Winchester had lost over 50% of its value in 15 years, he was disappointed, but he did not expect inflation to "pull out" or to recover his loss. In 1980 when Frank's great-grandson found out that his inherited Winchester rifle was worth $5,500, he was thankful his relative had the wisdom and insight to make such a prudent investment. How could Frank have known back then, with his limited education, that guns were about as good as anything else for long-term capital preservation?

Investment Performance Since 1875	1875	1891	1919	1955	1980	1996
Winchester Model 1873 (mfg. 1875) Oct. BBL. .44-40 Deluxe Sporting Rile in 90% original bright blue condition & case colors	$60	$35	$20	$225	$3,250	$10,250
Winchester Model 1873 Oct. BBL. .44-40 Deluxe Sporting Rifle (1919 mfg.) in 100% N.I.B. condition.	–	–	$39	$425	$5,500	$12,500
Colt S.A.A. (Peacemaker - .45Cal, mfg. 1875) 7-1/2" barrel in 90% original condition (metal turned patina)	$17	$20	$15	$125	$1,250	$3,750
Winchester Model 1887 Lever Action Shotgun 98% original condition (mfg. 1892)	–	$25	$10	$35	$450	$1,850
Winchester Model 1890 .22 cal. slide action rifle in 10% original condition	–	$16	$10	$30	$150	$235
Remington Model 11 "Autoloader Gun" 60% condition	–	–	$45	$70	$125	$120
Winchester Model 1912, Plain Barrel slide-action shotgun, 12 ga., in 90% original condition	–	–	$35	$85	$175	$300
Heckler & Koch Model SP89 Pistol (Last mfg.'s Sug. Retail was $1,325 in 1993)	–	–	–	–	–	$2,200-2,750
Gold (per ounce) annual average spot price	$20.67	$20.67	$21.92	$34.96	$613.29	$400
$20 Liberty "Double Eagle" Gold Coin in brilliant uncirculated (BU or MS-60) condition	$20	$20	$27	$75	(high) $900	$660
$20 Deposit with 3% average interest compounded annually	$20	$32.09	$73.43	$212.82	$445.59	$674
$20 Deposit with 6% average interest compounded annnually	$20	$50.81	$259.92	$2,115.92	$9,081.25	$20,531.84
W. Virginia river-bottom farm land (per acre) adjoining the Ohio River	$2 -4	$2-4	$50-75	$700-795	$1,200-1,500	$1,500-2,000

1996 – SOME CONTEMPORARY CONCLUSIONS

As you can see by looking at the performance chart provided above, there have been some significant short-term changes in the firearms' marketplace within the past several years. This in turn, has affected some long-term thinking. The real question today has become "Should I forego the proven long-term performance records of the likes of Colt SAA's, Winchester lever actions, and older antiques for some of the short-term 'baby boomers' such as AK47's, AR15's, high capacity semi auto pistols, and other victims of recent legislation which recently have been cast into the investment arena and potentially created some turbocharged price tags." In the end, it always gets down to only two factors – supply and demand. Once you fully understand every gun's unique mix of supply and demand economics, only then will you be able to intelligently make the right choices when stalking your next potential firearms purchase.

In the collectible firearm industry today, demand dictates supply. Where there is demand (read that C-notes looking for a new home), sooner or later, there will be supply. Not only does each gun model have its own blend of supply/demand factors, but each unique condition factor must also be considered when figuring out "What's the right price." I can guarantee that the demand for a re-blued 12 ga. Grade I Browning Superposed Shotgun is going to be a lot different than the same model, but in 28 ga. with NIB (new in box) condition.

To understand demand is to understand the word desirable. In my "Trash or Treasure" article that ran in Guns & Ammo's April 1993 issue, the word desirability was fully explained as it relates to "Gunneria 101." To briefly review, there are at least seven components of every gun's unique combination of desirability components. Collectively, they determine demand. Once again, these components are: 1) Trademark recognition, acceptance, and importance   2) Condition 3) Historical recognition and/or notarized provenance 4) Price 5) Rarity   6) Special Order features, embellishments, accessories, and accouterments 7) Regional demand differences.

Okay, so let's get into it. How can you accurately determine supply/demand economics one gun at a time to know what the price tags should be on today's collectible firearms? Hopefully, the following charts will enable you to better understand these unique economic principles. Most of the values below have been taken from the 17th Edition Blue Book of Gun Values.

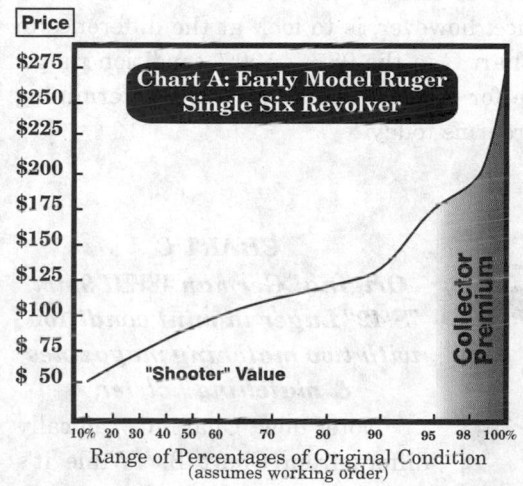

CHART A

Early Model Ruger .22 LR cal. Single Six Revolver.

If this gun could be a flavor, it would be vanilla. Many thousands were manufactured and supply & demand characteristics will not change significantly, regardless of the condition factors, throughout the country. This explains that the price line depicted above does not change that much all the way through 100% condition, as even 95% or better condition does not command that much of an additional premium over the prices under 95%. However, you can see that the last 5 percentage points of condition make the price line somewhat "more vertical," but certainly not even close to the "F15" nearly straight up performance shown in this same range in Chart C. This is because the shooting value of this particular revolver is the primary consideration for value up to approximately 95% condition, and after 95% the price line reflects the dollar premium collectors/investors will pay for this superior condition. This type of curve is typical of many of today's older, more common guns which are encountered on a regular basis.

Now let's take a look at another configuration. Actually, let's pick two different condition factors of the same gun, in this case a German WWII Military Luger, and see what happens.

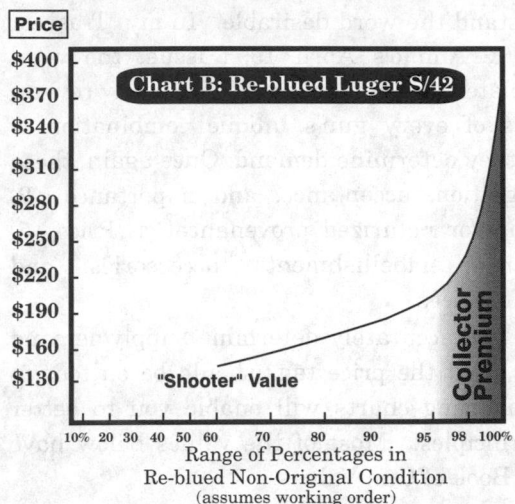

CHART B

CHART B

Re-blued German WWII 9mm "S/42" Luger.

Note how the price line differs through the various condition factors compared to Chart A. You will notice that the dollar amount range is up since even a re-blued Luger still sells for more money than an older, original 95% Ruger Single Six. Similarly, a poorly re-blued Luger isn't going to get that much more respect regardless where it pops up for sale.

Keen economic observers will also see that there isn't that much of a premium for 100% as most of the collector value has already been taken away when the gun was poorly re-blued. Of importance, however, is to look at the difference in performance between this chart and Chart C in the 98% - 100% condition range. As you can see, there is no substitute for original condition when determining overall desirability for most collector firearms today.

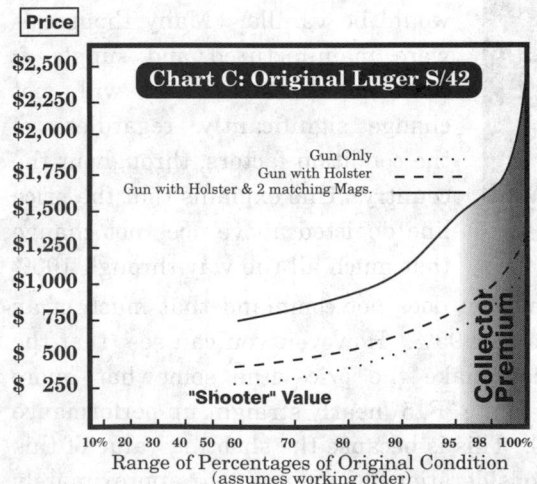

CHART C

Original German WWII 9mm "S/42" Luger in mint condition with two matching magazines & matching holster.

Note how Chart C radically differs from Chart B. While it's the same model as the gun in Chart B, look what has happened to the price. That is because at any one time there are virtually no guns in this type of rare, superior condition, not to mention the addition of the extremely desirable

accessories. Observe the almost vertical price line indicating almost no supply but a lot of serious demand. Also observe that on this particular model there are two additional entries past the 100% condition factor reflecting not only the addition of a desirable holster, but what happens when two extra matching magazines (very rare) are included. What's the price? Almost whatever the dealer wants to charge, within some limits. Typically, this is the "one phone call sale" for any savvy firearms dealer. He'll put you on the price line where he wants you. You may lower your "entry point" with slight haggling on such a premium item, but probably not much. If you don't think it's worth it, this is America after all, you can still say no (fully knowing, however, that it could be years before you may locate another similar specimen.) It can be a tough hand of poker - bluffing at this level gets expensive. In other words, pinning the tail on a donkey whose body isn't in sight can be difficult.

CHART D

Auction house sale of a ultra rare Harrington & Richardson Factory Display Board made for the 1876 Philadelphia Centennial Exhibition.

If you thought Chart C had some potential bad karma at the 95% to 100% end, study this one carefully. If you think this is fictional, you're wrong – this situation actually occurred at a

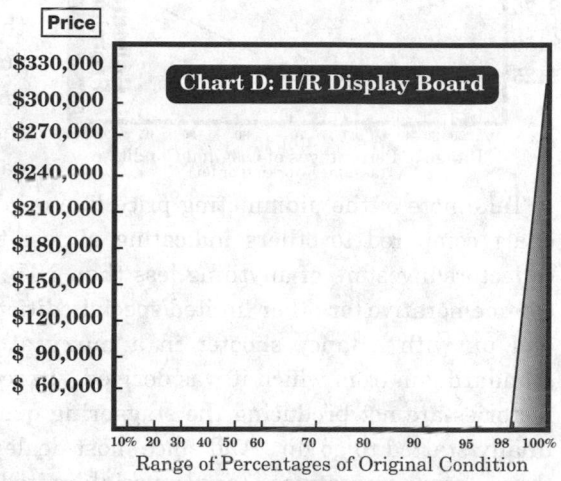

recent auction. While this is an advanced case in auction house economics, other similar cases involving fewer dollar amounts can and do exist. Note the totally vertical price line and absence of all condition factors except one since this item is literally one-of-a-kind. More unique in this scenario, however, is that the top of the price line (i.e. the winning bid) can in cases (especially this item) be totally unpredictable and completely stratospheric. On Chart C, the dealer placed you close to where he wanted you on the price line. On Chart D, the auction's job is to move you up that price line as far and as fast as possible. Serious auction bidders typically know when they want to jump off the line if the top starts appearing to resemble Mt. Everest during a bad storm. Always make sure you have enough oxygen left to get off the mountain when you want to. I have seen these slopes virtually littered with countless "economic corpses" that died while trying to go even higher. Unfortunately, these over–achievers never even considered a lower, safer base camp.

On the other side of this mountain range, you may occasionally find an auction that for one reason or another, does not have the right grouping of buyers for a particular segment or configuration of firearms. When this happens, the skillful and probable minority buyer may be treated to a bargain not seen at even most gun shows. You simply must do your homework, and take every auction gun one at a time.

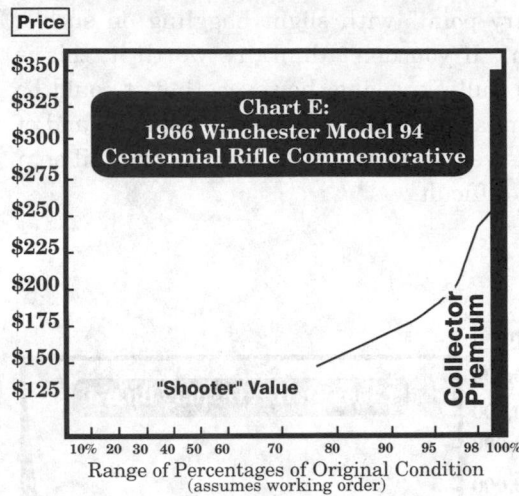

1966 Winchester Commemorative Model 94 Centennial Rifle/Carbine.

One of the characteristics of the commemorative marketplace (Chart E), is that over the years of ownership(s), most of the original mount manufactured has stayed in the same NIB condition. Thus, if supply is always constant and in one condition, demand must increase before price appreciation can occur.

Take note of the plummeting price line once you get off the 100% peg on this chart compared to others indicating almost total abandonment of demand by collectors/investors of anything less than NIB condition. This is because once a commemorative (or other limited/special editions) is no longer NIB condition, you end up with a fancy shooter in a hurry at only a small premium over the standard gun from which it was derived. In recent years, mostly because today's factories are not producing the staggering quantities of yesteryear, demand has finally started to go up. And since most dealers have no inventory remaining of these commemoratives (and special/limited editions,) the commemorative consumer is now more in charge since he/she owns the inventory. When the supply side of commemorative economics has to be purchased from knowledgeable collectors or knowing dealers and demand stays the same or increases slightly, prices have no choice but to go up. If and when the manufacturers crank up the commemorative production runs again (and it won't be like the good old days,) then the old, sluggish marketplace characteristics may reappear.

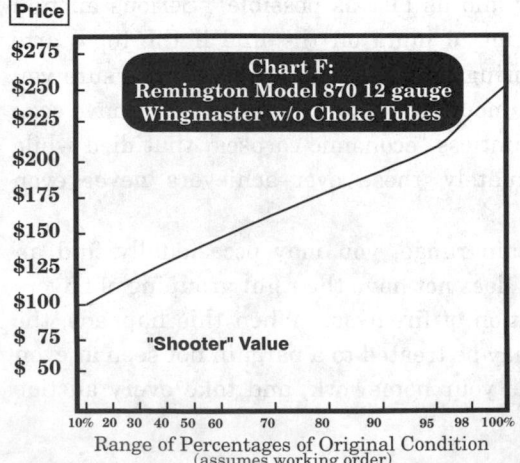

CHART F

Remington older Model 870 Field 12 ga. slide action shotgun without choke tubes.

Again, this is "vanilla" in the shotgun marketplace and there isn't that much difference between its entry level "spot price" as a shooter and what a 100% specimen will sell for. This particular shotgun has earned its reputation as the pump work house champion for both blue and white collar shooters for over four decades. Because choke tubes are now a lot more desirable on a shotgun that ever before, this configuration's overall value could be down as much as 20% compared to a similar specimen with choke tubes. The only small variable left in this chart is barrel length/choke configuration as shorter/open choked guns are somewhat more desirable than guns with longer barrels and closed choking.

CHART G

Heckler & Koch Model SP 89 paramilitary style pistol.

This particular chart has changed considerably over the past several years. With more and more federal laws focusing on this type of now banned configuration, supply/demand economics have changed drastically. Just recently, this model sold for as little as $1,500 in 100% condition. Now, some dealers are asking $3,000. The difference is that

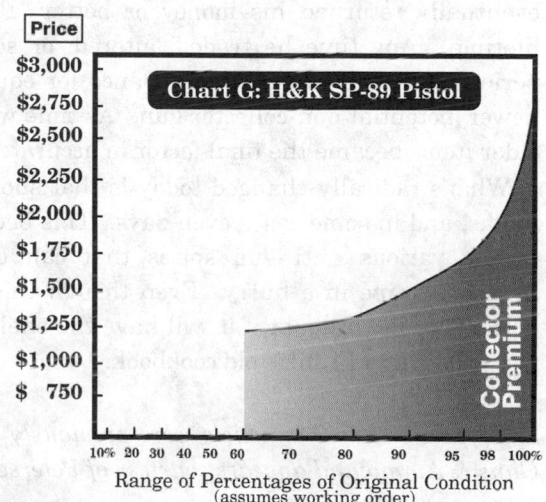

Range of Percentages of Original Condition
(assumes working order)

this configuration with its 15 shot mag., rarity factor (there are far fewer Model SP 89's floating around in today's secondary marketplace than Colt AR-15 HBar Sporter rifles), and "bad boy" image, have put it on a pedestal to those people who are attracted to this paramilitary style configuration. It's ironic that some of these folks would not have considered owning this type of gun for any price only years ago, but now they will almost gladly stand outside a gun shop in a snowstorm holding a number for service in order to pay 3X what it was priced for not that much earlier. The words speculation and risk often times describe spending money on this type of banned configuration.

OBSERVATIONS

As you have just seen, superior condition specimens of the harder to obtain major trademarks have always been at the front of the firearms pack for collectibility and price appreciation. I see no reason for this trend to be interrupted in the future unless the risk of buying an expensive, faked, or upgraded firearm flags off new investment dollars. It's no secret that "parts guns" or faked items never increase in value, regardless of what inflation does. Junk is, and will always remain, junk. Sugar coating arsenic simply doesn't retard the eventual mortality of the poison to any degree (i.e. messing around with junk only creates more junk in the end.)

In closing, the moral of this story (and article) is relatively simple. Remember, even during Frank's era, the firearms Frank bought, kept, and maintained eventually returned his money or better although not necessarily within his lifetime. Any time he traded, altered, or sold a gun outright after a holding period measured in years, his chance for equity was foregone in order to get a newer, potential non-collector gun. As time went on, the original condition of his older items became the final factor in accurately determining value.

What's radically changed today is that short-term can literally mean months, weeks, and in some cases even days. This becomes especially true when you mix in the various anti -gun spices that can drastically alter today's collectible firearms recipe in a hurry. Even though this newer gourmet effort might taste better initially, I doubt if it will have the shelf life and the ageless flavor of what you will find in Frank's old cookbook.

Some portions of this article were previously published in the Dec. 1994 issue of Guns & Ammo and appears courtesy of Petersen Publishing Co.

ADDITIONAL PUBLICATIONS
AVAILABLE FROM

Blue Book Publications, Inc.

Books - if you're serious about any area of collectibility, you really can't get along without them. The listing on the following pages represent the most complete offering of in-print collectible publications we have ever offered. And remember, these books make the perfect gift for any occasion, any time of the year.

We have decided to offer you a special bonus plan when ordering these publications. During the 17th Edition only, this premium bonus offer is in effect:

Placing
an order for:

$75 - $150	Receive a *FREE** *Classic Sporting Collectibles Pocket Guide* ($14.95 value)
$151 - $250	Receive a *FREE** *Mossberg - More Gun for the Money* ($24.95 value)
$251 - $499	Receive a *FREE** 17th Edition Deluxe Hardcover *Blue Book of Gun Values* ($45.00 value - limited quantities)
$500 - $999	Receive a *FREE** 2nd Edition of *The Book of Colt Firearms* ($149.95 value) by R.L. Wilson
$1,000 or more	Receive a *FREE** Deluxe 2nd Edition of *The Book of Colt Firearms* ($395.00 value) by R. L. Wilson

* Note! Add shipping charges for all premium bonus books.

We hope these bonus premium books will be an incentive for you to update your gun library (and maybe provide a gift for a few friends as well). As in the past, all titles contained herein were in stock at the time of this printing, but both prices and availability may change during the course of the year. Shipping charges can vary a lot depending on the weight of the book(s) and location shipped to. When you call, Fax, or mail your order in, we will inform you what the shipping charges will be on your order.

This offer expires March 1, 1997.

CALL **1-800** TO ORDER
877-4867

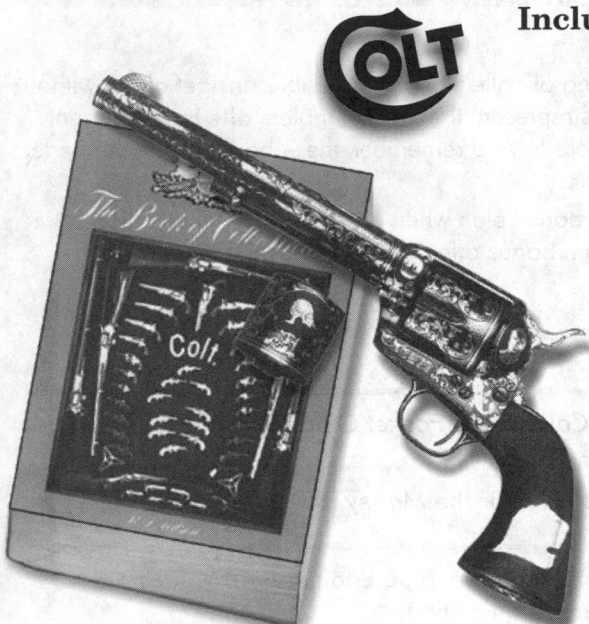

Blue Book Publications, Inc.

8009 34th Ave. S. #1391, dpt. bb17
Minneapolis, MN 55425
800-877-4867
Domestic/Canadian orders
612-854-5229   FAX 612-853-148•
International

web page: http://www.bluebookinc.com
email: bluebook@bluebookinc.com

ADDITIONAL PUBLICATIONS
—ORDER FORM—

CALL **1-800** TO ORDER
877-4867

code#	TITLE	PRICE	WEIGHT	UPS CHARGES*
C08	Classic Sporting Collectibles Pocket Guide			
M19	Mossberg - More Gun for the Money			
B05	17th Edition Deluxe Hardcover *Blue Book of Gun Values*			
C35	2nd Edition of *The Book of Colt Firearms*			
C35*	Deluxe 2nd Edition of *The Book of Colt Firearms*			

*Call us at 1-800-877-4867 for UPS charges.

Special Bonus Offer!
for Additional Publications Only:

Order $75 - $150 and receive free:
Classic Sporting Collectibles Pocket Guide

$151 - $250 and receive free:
Mossberg - More Gun for the Money

$251 - $499 and receive free:
17th Edition Deluxe Hardcover *Blue Book of Gun Values*

$500 - $999 and receive free:
2nd Edition of *The Book of Colt Firearms*

$1,000 + and receive free:
Deluxe 2nd Edition of *The Book of Colt Firearms*

	PRICE	WEIGHT	UPS CHARGES
TOTAL	$.	+	$.

TOTAL PRICE + S/H Charges $.

MN residents add 6.5% sales tax _____

Call for expedited shipping cost _____

Total enclosed or to charge $.

VISA   MasterCard   DISCOVER   ☐

Name_____

Company_____

Address_____

City_____ State_____ Zip_____

Credit Card No._____ Exp._____

Daytime Phone No._____

Signature_____

Form of Payment:
☐ **Personal Check**
☐ **Money Order**
☐ **Cashier's Check**
☐ **Visa**
☐ **Master Card**
☐ **Discover**
☐ **American Express**

CALL, FAX, or MAIL your order
to the numbers and address above.
(When mailing, tear out this page,
fold & return in envelope with payment.)

Office Hours: 8:30am - 5:00pm CST, Monday - Friday.
Answering machine services available 5:00pm - 8:30am, Monday -Friday and weekends
FAX 24 hours a day at 612-853-1486.
All orders are shipped within 2 working days after receiving good funds.

A01 AFRICAN RIFLES & CARTRIDGES by Taylor (HC) 431 pgs, Illus., 2 lbs $35.00

A02 AMERICAN GUNSMITHS by Sellers (HC) 349 pgs, 3 lbs $39.95

A03 AMERICAN KNIVES by Peterson (HC) 178 pgs, 2 lbs $24.95

A04 ASTRA AUTOMATIC PISTOLS by Antaris (HC) 248 pgs, Illus., B&W & Color photos, 4 lbs $45.00

A05 AMERICAN SOCKET BAYONETS AND SCABBARDS by Reilly (HC) 269 pgs, Illus., 3 lbs $40.00

A08 AMERICAN PREMIUM GUIDE TO KNIVES & RAZORS IDENTIFICATION AND VALUES by Sargent (SC) 474 pgs, B&W & Color photos, 3 lbs $22.95

A09 THE AMERICAN SWORD 1775-1945 by Peterson (HC) 345 pgs, Illus., 3 lbs $45.00

A10 AXIS PISTOLS by Still (HC) 360 pgs, B&W photos, 5 lbs $59.00

A11 ARSENAL OF FREEDOM, THE SPRINGFIELD ARMORY, 1890-1948, by Brophy (SC) 400 pgs, 4 lbs $29.95

A14 THE STORY OF ALLEN & WHEELOCK FIREARMS by Thomas (SC), 125 pgs, Illus., 1 lb . . $10.00

A15 AMERICAN MILITARY BELTS & RELATED EQUIPMENT by Dorsey (SC), 129 pgs, B&W photos. 3 lbs $11.95

A18 AMERICAN INDIAN TOMAHAWKS by Peterson (HC), 142 pgs, B&W photos, 2 lbs $49.95

A21 THE AMES SWORD COMPANY 1829-1935 by Hamilton, 2nd printing with some amended material (HC), 255 pgs, B&W & Color photos, 4 lbs $45.00

B01 BACKBONE OF THE WEHRMACHT, THE GERMAN K98K RIFLE, 1934-1945 by Law (Revised Edition, 1993) (HC) 367 pgs, Illus., 5 lbs $69.95

B02 THE BILLIARD ENCYCLOPEDIA by Victor Stein and Paul Rubino, 2nd Edition, (HC), 558 pgs., Illus., many color/B&W photos, avail. June 1996, 10 lbs $139.95

B03 BOOK OF THE GARAND by Hatcher (HC) 292 pgs, Illus., 2 lbs $26.95

B04 BULLARD ARMS by G. Scott Jamieson (HC) 244 pgs, Illus., 3 lbs $35.00

B05 BLUE BOOK OF GUN VALUES by Fjestad (17TH Edition) $27.95

B06 BLUE BOOK OF GUITARS Edited by S. P. Fjestad, 3rd Edition, many color/B&W photos, (SC), late Sept. release, 3 lbs. $29.95

B065 BLUE BOOK OF POOL CUES by Brad Simpson, 1st Edition, many color/B&W photos, (SC), late Sept. release, 3 lbs. $24.95

B07 BROWNING DATES OF MANUFACTURE by Madis (SC) 48 pgs, under 1 lb $5.00

B09 THE HISTORY OF BROWNING GUNS FROM 1931 by Browning (SC) under 1 lb. $14.95

B11 THE BROWNING HIGH POWER AUTOMATIC PISTOL by Stevens (HC), 297 pgs., Illus., 3 lbs $47.50

B12 THE BREECH-LOADING SINGLE-SHOT RIFLE by Roberts & Waters (SC) 333 pgs., B&W photos, 3 lbs $28.50

B13 THE BLACK RIFLE M16 RETROSPECTIVE by Stevens & Ezell (HC), 400 pgs., Illus., B&W photos, 3 lbs $59.95

B19 BEST GUNS by McIntosh (HC), 288 pgs, Color & B&W photos, 2 lbs $40.00

B20 BRITISH .22 LR TRAINING RIFLES by Petrillo (SC), 64 pgs, B&W photos, 1 lb $10.95

B21 BAYONETS from Janzen's Notebook (HC), 258 pgs, line drawings, 5 lbs $34.50

B23 BRITISH SERVICE RIFLES AND CARBINES 1888-1900 by Petrillo (SC), 72 pgs, B&W photos, 2 lbs $11.95

B24 THE BRITISH SOLDIER'S FIREARMS, From Smoothbore to Smallbore 1850-1864 by Dr. Roads (reprint) (HC), 332 pgs, B&W photos, 3 lbs . . $49.00

B26 THE BUFFALO HARVEST by Mayer & Roth (SC), 96 pgs, B&W photos, Illus., 1 lb $7.50

C01 COLT, AN AMERICAN LEGEND by Wilson (HC), 406 pgs, Illus., Color photos, 5 lbs $30.00

C02 COLT DATES OF MANUFACTURE by Wilson (SC), 61 pgs, under 1 lb. $5.00

C04 COLT PEACEMAKER ENCYCLOPEDIA, VOL I by Cochran (HC), 434 pgs, B&W photos, 4 lbs $60.00

C05 COLT PEACEMAKER BRITISH MODEL by Cochran (HC), 159 pgs, B&W photos, 2 lbs $35.00

C07 CLASSIC SPORTING COLLECTIBLES AUCTION CATALOGS by Blue Book Publications, Inc., Vols. 1-4, (SC), limited availability, 2 lbs/each $24.95/each

C08 CLASSIC SPORTING COLLECTIBLES POCKET GUIDE by Blue Book Publications, Inc., (SC), 188 pgs, 1 lb $14.95

C09 CARTRIDGES OF THE WORLD (7th Edition) by Barnes (SC), 464 pages, B&W photos, 3 lbs $23.95

C13 CIVIL WAR BREECHLOADING RIFLES by McAulay (SC), 128 pgs, Illus., 1 lb $15.00

C14 COLT'S SAA POST WAR MODELS by Garton (HC), 166 pgs, B&W photos, 2 lbs $35.00

C17 COWBOY COLLECTIBLES AND WESTERN MEMORABILIA (with price guide) by Ball and Vebell (SC), 157 pgs, Color photos, 2 lbs. $29.95

C18 COLT FIREARMS, 1836-1960, by Serven, 1991 Reprint (HC), 394 pgs, B&W photos, 4 lbs $45.00

C19 COLT PEACEMAKER ENCYCLOPEDIA, VOL II by Cochran (HC), 416 pgs, Illus., B&W photos, 3 lbs $60.00

C20 COLLECTOR'S GUIDE TO THE M1 GARAND & M1 CARBINE by Canfield (SC), 144 pgs, Illus., 2 lbs $22.00

C21 COWBOY CULTURE: The Last Frontier of American Antiques by Friedman (with price guide) (HC), 298 pgs, Color photos, 6 lbs. $79.95

C22 COLLECTING ANTIQUE BIRD DECOYS and DUCKCALLS, An Identification & Value Guide, 2nd Edition, by Luckey (SC), 232 pgs, Color & B&W photos, 2 lbs. $22.95

C23 COLT'S .38 AUTOMATIC PISTOLS by Douglas G. Sheldon (SC), 185 pgs, Illus., 1 lb $19.95

C26 CIVIL WAR PISTOLS by McAulay (SC), Illus., B&W photos, 2 lbs. $24.00

C27 COLLECTOR'S GUIDE TO UNITED STATES COMBAT SHOTGUNS by Canfield (SC), Illus., 2 lbs $24.00

C28 '51 COLT NAVIES by Swayze (HC), 243 pgs., Illus., photos, 5 lbs $59.95

C30 COLT NEW SERVICE REVOLVERS by Murphy (SC), 63 pgs, B&W photos, 1 lb $7.50

C33 CONFEDERATE EDGED WEAPONS by Albaugh III, (HC), 198 pgs., line drawings, 3 lbs $30.00

C35 THE BOOK OF COLT FIREARMS by R.L. Wilson (2nd Edition) (HC), 604 pgs, Color & B&W photos, 9 lbs $149.95

C36 COLLECTOR'S GUIDE TO COLT .45 SERVICE PISTOLS MODELS 1911 & 1911A1 by Clawson (SC), 90 pgs, B&W photos, 1 lb $19.95

C37 CARBINES OF THE CIVIL WAR, 1861-1865 by McAulay (SC), 123 pgs, line drawings, B&W photos, 2 lbs $9.95

C44 COWGIRLS: Early Images & Collectibles by Crandall (with price guide) (SC), 126 pgs, B&W & Color photos, 3 lbs $19.95

C47 COLLECTOR'S GUIDE TO AMES U.S. CONTRACT MILITARY EDGED WEAPONS: 1832-1906 by Hickox (SC), 70 pgs, Illus., 2 lbs $14.95

C48 CANES THROUGH THE AGES by Monek (HC), 320 pgs, Color photos, 7 lbs $79.95

C49 THE COLT ARMORY: History of Colt's Manufacturing Company by Grant (HC), 232 pgs, B&W & Color photos, 4 lbs $35.00

C50 COLLINS MACHETES AND BOWIES 1845-1965 by Henry (SC), 226 pgs, B&W photos, Illus., 3 lbs . . $19.95

C51 COLT'S SINGLE ACTION ARMY REVOLVER PRE-WAR POST WAR MODEL by Wilkerson (HC), B&W photos, Illus., 5 lbs $30.00

C52 COLT SCOUTS, PEACEMAKERS AND NEW FRONTIERS IN .22 CALIBER by Wilkerson, 1993, (HC), 224 pgs, B&W photos, Illus., 5 lbs. $40.00

C53 POST-WAR COLT SINGLE-ACTION REVOLVER, 1976-1986 by Wilkerson (HC), B&W photos, Illus., 5 lbs $100.00

D01 THE DERINGER IN AMERICA by Wilson & Eberhart (HC), 271 pgs, Color & B&W photos, 3 lbs. . . . $48.00

D04 DERINGER IN AMERICA, VOL. II by Eberhart & Wilson (HC) 280 pgs, Color & B&W photos, 4 lbs $65.00

D05 THE DUTCH LUGER (Parabellum), A Complete History by Martens & deVries (HC), 269 pgs, B&W photos, 352 Illus., 4 lbs. $49.95

E01 THE EAGLE ON U.S. FIREARMS by Jordan (SC), 140 pgs, B&W photos, 2 lbs. $17.50

E02 THE ILLUSTRATED ENCYCLOPEDIA OF HANDGUNS, PISTOLS AND REVOLVERS OF THE WORLD, 1870 TO PRESENT by Zhuk, (HC), 304 pgs, more than 2,500 scale drawings, 4 lbs. $49.95

F01 FLAYDERMAN'S GUIDE (6TH EDITION)(SC) 624 pgs, Illus., 3 lbs. $29.95

F02 FIREARMS & TACKLE MEMORABILIA, A COLLECTOR'S GUIDE (with price guide) by Delph (HC), 141 pgs, Color photos, 3 lbs. $39.95

F03 A.H. FOX by McIntosh (HC), 390 pgs, Illus., Color & B&W photos, 3 lb $49.50

G01 GERMAN PISTOLS AND HOLSTERS 1934/1945, MILITARY-POLICE-NSDAP Vol I by Whittington III (HC), 224 pgs, Illus., & B&W photos of pistols & holsters, 2 lbs $30.00

G02 GERMAN PISTOLS AND HOLSTERS, Vol II by Whittington III (HC), 312 pgs, Illus., & B&W photos of pistols only, 3 lbs $55.00

G03 GERMAN PISTOLS AND HOLSTERS, Vol III by Whittington III (HC), 352 pgs, Illus., & B&W photos of holsters only, 3 lbs $55.00

G06 GERMAN PISTOLS AND HOLSTERS, VOL IV by Whittington III (HC), 208 pgs, Tells where & to whom pistols & holsters were issued, 2 lbs . . . $30.00

G07 THE GUN THAT MADE THE TWENTIES ROAR by Helmer (HC), 294 pgs, Illus., 2 lbs. $24.95

G08 THE GOLDEN AGE OF SHOTGUNNING by Hinman (HC), 175 pgs, B&W photos, 2 lbs $17.95

G09 GERMAN MILITARY RIFLES AND MACHINE PISTOLS (1871-1945) by Gotz (HC), 245 pgs, Illus., & B&W photos, 4 lbs $35.00

G21 GAMBLING COLLECTIBLES, A Sure Winner (with price guide) by Schneir (SC), 158 pgs, B&W & Color photos, 3 lbs $29.95

G23 GUN ENGRAVING REVIEW by Prudhomme (HC), 1994 Printing, 168 pgs, B&W & Color photos, 3 lbs. **$60.00**

H01 HIGH STANDARD AUTOMATIC PISTOLS (1932-1950) by Petty (HC), 125 pgs, B&W photos, 1 lb . . . **$19.95**

H02 HIGH STANDARD, A COLLECTOR'S GUIDE TO THE HAMDEN & HARTFORD TARGET PISTOLS by Dance (SC), 191 pgs, Illus., & B&W photos 2 lbs **$24.00**

H03 HATCHER'S NOTEBOOK by Hatcher (HC), 640 pgs, Illus., B&W photos, 3 lbs **$39.95**

H04 HISTORY OF SMITH & WESSON by Jinks (HC), 290 pgs, Illus., 2 lbs. **$27.95**

H06 HOME GUIDE TO CARTRIDGE CONVERISON by Nonte (HC), 404 pgs, Illus., 2 lbs **$24.95**

H07 HELL, I WAS THERE by Keith (HC), 308 pgs, Illus., 3 lbs **$24.95**

H09 HUNTING WITH THE TWENTY-TWO by Landis (reprint) (HC), 429 pgs, B&W photos, 3 lbs **$45.00**

H12 THE HAMMERLESS DOUBLE RIFLE by Gray (HC), 154 pgs, B&W photos, Illus., 3 lbs. **$39.50**

H13 HOME GUNSMITHING THE COLT SINGLE ACTION REVOLVER by Smith (HC), 1995 Reprint, 119 pgs, B&W photos, Illus., 2 lbs **$24.95**

H15 HANDBOOK OF MILITARY RIFLE MARKS 1870-1950 by Hoffman & Schott (SC), 42 pgs, Illus., 2 lbs **$15.00**

H16 THE HISTORY OF SMITH AND WESSON, 1857-1945, by Neal & Jinks (1996 Reprint) (HC), 369 pgs, B&W photos, Illus., 4 lbs **$50.00**

I02 IMPERIAL LUGERS by Still (HC), 219 pgs, Color photos, 5 lbs **$59.00**

I03 IVER JOHNSON ARMS & CYCLE WORKS HANDGUNS 1871-1978 by Goforth (SC), 164 pgs, Illus., 2 lbs. **$14.95**

I07 INDIAN TRADE GUNS (Pioneer Press) (SC), 258 pgs, B&W Illus., 2 lbs **$12.00**

I08 COLLECTING INDIAN KNIVES, Identification & Value Guide by Hothem (SC), 300 pgs, B&W Illus., 2 lbs **$14.95**

J01 JAMES REID AND HIS CATSKILL KNUCKLEDUSTERS by Bowen (HC), 288 pgs, Illus., 2 lbs. **$24.95**

J02 J. STEVENS ARMS & TOOL COMPANY CATALOG 52-1908 (SC), 157 pgs, B&W photos, 2 lbs. . . **$20.00**

J04 J. STEVENS ARMS & TOOL COMPANY CATALOG 50-1902 (SC), 128 pgs, B&W photos, 2 lbs. . . **$20.00**

J05 JAPANESE RIFLES OF WORLD WAR II by McCollum (SC), 61 pgs, B&W photos, Illus., 2 lbs **$18.95**

K01 THE KRAG RIFLE by Brophy (HC), 258 pgs, Illus., 3 lbs. **$35.00**

K02 KNOW YOUR COLT .45 AUTO PISTOLS MODELS 1911 & A1 by Hoffschmidt (SC), 65 pgs, Photos, under 1 lb. **$9.95**

K03 KNOW YOUR M1 GARAND RIFLES BY Hoffschmidt (SC), 80 pgs, photos, under 1 lb **$9.95**

K04 KNOW YOUR BROOMHANDLE MAUSERS by Berger (SC), 95 pgs, Illus., under 1 lb **$9.95**

K05 KNOW YOUR WALTHER P38 PISTOLS by Hoffschmidt (SC), 77 pgs, Illus., under 1 lb **$9.95**

K06 KNOW YOUR WALTHER PP & PPK PISTOLS by Hoffschmidt (SC), 87 pgs, Illus., under 1 lb **$9.95**

K07 KNOW YOUR CZECHOSLOVAKIAN PISTOLS by Berger (SC), 96 pgs, Illus., under 1 lb **$9.95**

K08 KEITH'S RIFLES FOR LARGE GAME by Keith (HC), 406 pgs, Illus., 2 lb **$39.95**

K10 KNOW YOUR RUGER 10/22 by Workman (SC), 95 pgs, Illus., under 1 lb **$9.95**

K11 THE KENTUCKY PISTOL by Chandler & Whisker (HC), 223 pgs, B&W photos, 4 lbs **$45.00**

L01 L.C. SMITH SHOTGUNS by Brophy (HC), 244 pgs. Illus., 3 lbs. **$35.00**

L02 LUGERS AT RANDOM by Kenyon (Revised Format Edition, 1990) (HC), 416 pgs, Illus., B&W photos, 4 lbs **$49.95**

L04 LEE ENFIELD NUMBER 4 RIFLES by Petrillo (SC), 64 pgs, Illus., B&W photos, under 1 lb **$10.95**

L05 LEE ENFIELD NUMBER 1 RIFLES by Petrillo (SC), 64 pgs, Illus., B&W photos, under 1 lb **$10.95**

L06 1900 LUGER, U.S. TEST TRIALS by Reese II (SC), Illus., under 1 lb. **$6.00**

L07 LUGER TIPS by Reese II (SC), 120 pgs, Illus., under 1 lb **$12.95**

M01 MARLIN FIREARMS by Brophy (HC), 704 pgs, Illus., & B&W photos, 7 lbs. **$75.00**

M02 MORE SINGLE SHOT RIFLES by Grant (HC), 322 pgs, Illus., 2 lbs. **$29.95**

M04 MAUSER BOLT RIFLES by Olson (Third Edition, Updated 9th Printing) (HC) 360 pgs., B&W Illus., 5 lbs **$47.25**

M06 THE 336 (Marlin) by Murray (SC) 90 pgs, Illus., 1 lb **$20.00**

M08 THE HISTORY & DEVELOPMENT OF THE M16 RIFLE & CARTRIDGE by Hughes (HC) 294 pgs, Illus., B&W photos, 3 lbs **$49.95**

M10 MILITARIA, A Study of German Helmets & Uniforms (1729-1918) by Kube (HC) 235 pgs, Color & B&W photos, 3 lbs **$29.95**

M12 **THE MUZZLE-LOADING CAP LOCK RIFLE** by
Roberts (HC), 432 pgs, Illus., 2 lbs **$30.00**

M13 **MODERN SHOTGUNS AND LOADS** by Askins
(HC), 416 pgs, Illus., 2 lbs. **$30.00**

M14 **M1 CARBINE: DESIGN, DEVELOPMENT & PRO-
DUCTION** by Ruth (SC), 291 pgs, Illus., 2 lbs **$19.95**

M19 **MOSSBERG - MORE GUN FOR THE MONEY** by
V. and C. Havlin, (SC), 304 pgs, many B&W pho-
tos, 2 lbs **$24.95**

M20 **MY LAST CHANCE TO BE A BOY,** Theodore
Roosevelt's South American Expedition of 1913-
1914 by Ornig with forward by Tweed Roosevelt
(HC), 258 pgs, B&W photos, 3 lbs **$29.95**

N01 **THE NAVY LUGER** by Gortz & Walter (HC), 128
pgs, Illus., B&W photos, 2 lbs **$24.95**

N02 **THE NINETY-NINE, Revised Third Edition, a History of the Savage** by Murray (SC), Illus., 1 lb **$28.00**

N04 **L. D. NIMSCHKE FIREARMS ENGRAVER** by Wilson (reprint) (HC), 109 pages, B&W drawings, 3 lbs **$100.00**

N05 **THE NUMBER 5 JUNGLE CARBINE** by Petrillo
(SC), 32 pgs, B&W photos, 1 lbs **$7.95**

N06 **9mm PARABELLUM, A History of the World's
9mm Pistols & Ammunition** by Konig and Hugo
(HC), 301 pgs, Illus., B&W photos, 4 lbs. **$39.95**

N07 **NORTH AMERICAN INDIAN ARTIFACTS, Collector's Identification & Value Guide(5th Edition)**
by Hothem (SC), 360 pgs, B&W & Color photos, 3
lbs **$22.95**

N08 **NAUTICAL ANTIQUES** (with price guide) by Ball
(HC), 240 pgs, B&W photos, 6 lbs **$39.95**

O01 **OUTDOOR PASTIMES OF AN AMERICAN
HUNTER** by Roosevelt (SC), 369 pgs, 2 lbs **$16.95**

O03 **OLD FISHING LURES & TACKLE IDENTIFICA-
TION AND VALUES** (No.3) by Luckey (SC), 466
pgs, Illus., Color photos, 3 lbs. **$22.95**

O05 **ORDNANCE WENT UP FRONT** by Dunlap (re-
print) (HC), 417 pgs, B&W photos, 3 lbs. **$35.00**

P01 **THE PARKER GUN** by Baer (HC), 196 pgs, Illus.,
B&W photos, 3 lbs. **$35.00**

P03 **THE POWDER FLASK BOOK** by Riling (reprint)
(HC), 495 pgs, Illus., B&W photos, 5 lbs. **$69.95**

P04 **PAWNEE BILL'S HISTORIC WILD WEST, A
Photo Documentary of the 1901-1905 Show
Tours** (SC), 126 pgs., B&W photos, 2 lbs **$19.95**

P05 **THE PEACEMAKERS, Arms and Adventure in
the American West** by R.L. Wilson (HC), 391
pages, Illus., Color photos & B&W photos, 5 lbs . . . **$65.00**

P07 **THE STORY OF POPE'S BARRELS** by Smith,
(HC) 203 pgs, B&W photos, 4 lbs **$39.00**

R03 **REMINGTON ROLLING BLOCK FIREARMS** by
Schreier, Jr. (SC), 61 pgs., Illus., 1 lb. **$8.00**

R07 **THE RUGER 10/22** by Workman (SC), 320 pgs,
B&W photos, 3 lbs **$19.95**

R08 **REMINGTON FIREARMS: The Golden Age of
Collecting** by Ball (HC), 194 pgs, B&W photos, 4
lbs **$29.95**

R09 **THE REMINGTON-LEE RIFLE** by Myszkowski
(SC), 103 pgs, B&W photos, Illus., 2 lbs **$22.95**

R10 **RELOADING TOOLS, SIGHTS AND TELE-
SCOPES FOR SINGLE SHOT RIFLES** by Kelver
(SC), 182 pgs, B&W, Illus., 2 lbs **$12.50**

R11 **THE RIFLEMAN'S RIFLE, WINCHESTER MODEL
70, 1936-1963** by Rule (Reprint), (HC), 368 pgs,
B&W & Color photos, Illus., 5 lbs **$79.95**

S01 **SINGLE SHOT RIFLES** by Grant (HC), 395 pgs, Il-
lus., 4 lbs. **$29.95**

S02 **SHARPS FIREARMS** by Sellers (HC), 358 pgs, Il-
lus., 4 lbs. **$50.00**

S03 **THE SPRINGFIELD 1903 RIFLES** by Brophy
(HC), 616 pgs, Illus., B&W photos, 6 lbs **$59.95**

S07 **THE STANDARD DIRECTORY OF PROOF
MARKS** by Wirnsberger (SC), 192 pgs., Illus., 1 lb . **$14.95**

S09 **SIX GUNS, The Standard Reference Work,** by
Keith (1992) (HC), 335 pgs., Illus., 3 lbs **$35.00**

S11 **SINGLE SHOT RIFLE FINALE** by Grant (HC), 133
pgs., Illus., 2 lbs **$36.00**

S12 **SPORTING COLLECTIBLES** by Karsnitz (SC),
160 pgs, Color photos, 2 lbs. **$29.95**

S15 **SWISS VARIATIONS 1897-1947** (The Luger Pistol, Its History and Development from 1893-1947)
by Datig (SC), 88 pgs, Illus., B&W photos, 3 lbs . . . **$14.95**

S16 **SNIPING IN FRANCE** (new edition) by Hesketh-
Prichard (HC), 209 pgs, B&W photos. 3 lbs. **$25.00**

S17 **THE .45-70 SPRINGFIELD** by Royer & Riesch
(SC), 98 pgs, line drawings, 1 lb **$14.95**

S18 **SCRIMSHAW, The Whaler's Legacy** by
Lawrence (HC), 227 pgs, color photos, 5 lbs. **$69.95**

S21 **SMITH & WESSON HAND GUNS** by McHenry and
Roper (HC), 234 pgs, B&W photos, 3 lbs **$32.00**

S25 **SPENCER REPEATING FIREARMS** by Marcot
(Reprint) (HC), 316 pgs, B&W photos, Illus., 5 lbs. . **$60.00**

S27 **SHOTGUNS AND SHOOTING** by McIntosh (HC),
266 pgs, Illus., 3 lbs **$39.00**

S28 **STILL MORE SINGLE SHOT RIFLES** by Grant
(HC), 210 pgs, B&W photos, 3 lbs **$27.50**

S29 **STEEL CANVAS, The Art of American Arms** by
Wilson (HC), 384 pgs, B&W & Color photos, 6 lbs . **$65.00**

S30 **SOVIET SMALL-ARMS AND AMMUNITION** by
Bolotin (HC), 264 pgs, Illus., B&W photos, 4 lbs . . . **$49.95**

S31 **SCHUETZEN RIFLES, HISTORY AND LOAD-
INGS, Second Edition,** by Kelver (SC), 130 pgs,
B&W photos, 2 lbs **$12.50**

T01 **TRAPDOOR SPRINGFIELD** by Waite & Ernst
(HC), 213 pgs, Illus., B&W photos, 3 lbs **$39.95**

T02 **THIRD REICH LUGERS** by Still (HC), 291 pgs., Il-
lus., B&W photos, 5 lbs **$59.00**

T06 **THIRD REICH DAGGERS 1933-1945** by Bowman
(HC), 485 pgs, B&W photos, 5 lbs **$65.00**

ADDITIONAL PUBLICATIONS

T12 **THE TARGET RIFLE IN AUSTRALIA** (1860-1900) by Corcoran, 1995 Reprint (HC), 221 pgs, B&W photos, Illus, 3 lbs.... **$40.00**

U01 **U.S. MILITARY ARMS DATES OF MANUFAC-TURE** by Madis (SC), 62 pgs., under 1 lb.... **$5.00**

U04 **U.S. RIFLE M14-FROM JOHN GARAND TO THE M21** (Vol One) by Stevens (HC), 340 pgs., Illus., 3 lbs.... **$47.50**

U06 **U.S. WINCHESTER TRENCH AND RIOT GUNS** by Poyer (SC), 123 pgs, B&W Illus., 2 lbs.... **$15.95**

U07 **U.S. M1 CARBINES WARTIME PRODUCTION** by Riesch (SC), 123 pgs, B&W Illus., 2 lbs.... **$15.95**

U09 **U.S. MILITARY AUTOMATIC PISTOLS** (1894-1920) by Meadows (HC), 558 pgs, B&W & Color photos, Illus., 6 lbs.... **$79.95**

U12 **U.S. INFANTRY WEAPONS OF WORLD WAR II** by Canfield (HC), 304 pgs, B&W photos, Illus., 4 lbs **$35.00**

W01 **WINCHESTER BOOK** by Madis (HC), 654 pgo, Illus., D&W photos, 5 lbs.... **$45.00**

W02 **WINCHESTER DATES OF MANUFACTURE** by Madis (SC), 59 pgs, under 1 lb.... **$5.00**

W03 **WINCHESTER MODEL TWELVE** by Madis (HC), 174 pgs, Illus., B&W photos., 2 lbs.... **$19.95**

W04 **WINCHESTER HANDBOOK** by Madis (HC), 267 pgs, B&W photos, 2 lbs.... **$19.95**

W05 **WINCHESTER ERA** by Madis (HC), 180 pgs, Illus., 1 lb.... **$14.95**

W06 **WINCHESTER ENGRAVING** by Wilson (HC), 512 pgs, Color photos, 6 lbs **$115.00**

W08 **WINCHESTER MODEL 94** by Renneberg (HC), 208 pgs, Illus., B&W photos, 3 lbs **$34.95**

W09 **HISTORY OF WINCHESTER FIREARMS 1866-1992** (6th Edition Updated) by Henshaw (HC), 268 pgs, B&W photos, 4 lbs.... **$24.95**

W10 **WINCHESTER MODEL 42** by Schwing (HC), 160 pgs, Illus., B&W photos 3 lbs.... **$34.95**

W11 **WINCHESTER MODEL 21** by Schwing (HC), 360 pgs., Illus., Color & B&W photos, 4 lbs.... **$49.95**

W13 **WINCHESTER, AN AMERICAN LEGEND** by Wilson (HC), 404 pgs, Color photos, 5 lbs.... **$65.00**

W14 **COLLECTOR'S GUIDE TO WINCHESTER IN THE SERVICE** by Canfield (HC), 184 pgs, Illus., B&W photos, 2 lbs.... **$38.00**

W15 **THE EIGHTY-EIGHT** (Collector's Reference on the Winchester Model 88 Lever Action) by Murray (SC), 90 pgs, 1 lb.... **$23.00**

W16 **SEQUENCE OF TAKEDOWN AND ASSEMBLY FOR WINCHESTER MODEL 42** (SC), 102 pgs., drawings, 1 lb.... **$14.95**

W17 **SEQUENCE OF TAKEDOWN AND ASSEMBLY FOR WINCHESTER MODEL 70** (SC), 58 pgs., drawings, 1 lb.... **$14.95**

W18 **SEQUENCE OF TAKEDOWN AND ASSEMBLY FOR WINCHESTER MODEL 61** (SC), 94 pgs., drawings, 1 lb.... **$14.95**

W19 **SEQUENCE OF TAKEDOWN AND ASSEMBLY FOR WINCHESTER MODEL 63** (SC), 88 pgs., drawings, 1 lb.... **$14.95**

W20 **SEQUENCE OF TAKEDOWN AND ASSEMBLY FOR WINCHESTER MODEL 12** (SC), 116 pgs., drawings, 1 lb.... **$14.95**

W23 **SEQUENCE OF TAKEDOWN AND ASSEMBLY FOR WINCHESTER MODEL 94** (SC), 63 pgs, drawings, 1 lb.... **$14.95**

W24 **WAR BABY! THE U.S. CALIBER .30 CARBINE** by Larry L. Ruth (HC), 495 pgs., Illus., 4 lbs.... **$69.95**

W25 **WEATHERBY, THE MAN, THE GUN, THE LEGEND** by Gresham & Gresham (HC), 290 pgs., Illus., 3 lbs.... **$24.95**

W26 **WINCHESTER SLIDE-ACTION RIFLES, Vol. I:Model 1890 & 1906** by Schwing (HC), 400 pgs., Illus., B&W photos, 4 lbs.... **$39.95**

W28 **WAR BABY, COMES HOME, The U.S. Caliber .30 Carbine, VOL.II** by Larry Ruth (HC), 366 pgs., Illus., 3 lbs.... **$49.95**

W29 **TO THE DREAMS OF YOUTH: The .22 Caliber Single Shot Winchester Rifle** by Houze (HC), 208 pgs., Illus., B&W photos, 3 lbs.... **$34.95**

W30 **WINCHESTER SLIDE-ACTION RIFLES, VOL. II, Model 61 & 62** by Schwing (HC), 208 pgs., Illus., B&W photos, 3 lbs.... **$34.95**

W32 **WESTERN MEMORABILIA AND COLLECT-IBLES** (price guide included) by Ball (SC), 111 pgs, Color photos, 3 lbs.... **$19.95**

W35 **WEIMAR & EARLY NAZI LUGERS AND THEIR ACCESSORIES** by Still (HC), 312 pgs, B&W photos, 5 lbs.... **$59.00**

W37 **POCKET GUIDE TO WIN. MODEL 1890 RIFLE** by Tusher (SC), 52 pgs, B&W photos, 1 lb.... **$7.95**

W38 **WINCHESTER REPEATING ARMS COMPANY, Its History & Development from 1865 to 1981** by Houze (HC), 880 pgs, B&W photos, 6 lbs.... **$50.00**

W39 **WINCHESTER LEVER ACTION REPEATING FIREARMS, VOL. I, Models of 1866, 1873 & 1876** by Pirkle (SC), 202 pgs, Illus., 2 lbs.... **$19.95**

W40 **WINCHESTER SHOTGUN & SHOTSHELLS** by Stadt (Revised and Expanded Edition) (HC), 288 pgs, B&W photos, Illus., 4 lbs.... **$34.95**

W43 **THE WINCHESTER SINGLE-SHOT, A History and Analysis** by Campbell (HC), 270 pgs, B&W photos, Illus., 4 lbs.... **$55.00**

W44 **WINCHESTER: THE MODEL 12** (1912-1964), The Greatest Hammerless Repeating Shotgun Ever Built by Riffle (HC), 276 pgs, B&W & Color photos, Illus., 5 lbs.... **$49.95**

Crime Bill 1994

Aftershocks & Afterthoughts

by Thomas A. Spithaler

Not all that frequently does a firearms dealer get complaints from his customers when he lowers his prices. However, that is exactly what happened to some firearms dealers last year. This, along with the ever changing world of BATF regulations and interpretations, has made for a hectic 1995. Dealing in "assault weapons" was not the fun job or "license to steal" that it had been for the past several years.

The year that was 1995 saw just about as many changes as in 1994. It's hard to imagine but it is true. The biggest area affected, as before, is surrounding the "assault weapons" listed in the omnibus Crime Bill of 1994.

As hard as it is to accept, the prices of firearms truly are based on supply and demand (I hope I don't hear grumbling already). The people who got the best deals were the folks that had the money and time to wait around for the lowest price on their favorite AR-15, in addition to those who were of the opinion that supply and demand really do rule the firearms marketplace.

You see, as the emotions ran high after the passage of the Crime Bill, the market was awash with purchasers. People were willing to buy almost anything at any price. When a medical doctor approached me at a gun show, pointed to an AR-15 and asked, "Is this an Assault Weapon?". To which I replied, "Under the current definition, yes, it is". From this point, knowing that a person of limited knowledge is questioning me about the rifle, I figured that a few questions would come next, and then the dickering over price would begin. Well, to my surprise, the next words from the customer were "I'll take it!" This type of attitude and willingness to buy at almost any price drove prices to skyrocket.

The good doctor had no idea how to operate the rifle, what round it fired, who made it, or even what it was called. What's worse - he didn't care! He simply wanted it because the government was telling him that he soon may not be permitted to own one. As it turned out, the doctor in question was an emergency room surgeon at a local hospital. Go figure?

Situations like this overwhelmed the marketplace. We, as consumers and dealers alike, did not know what the outcome was going to be as far as the legislation went, so there were no ground rules to run by. None of us were mind readers, and even the lobbyists that I know were skeptical as to what the outcome of the Crime Bill vote would be. Well, today we all know what happened, and most of us have seen the exact wording of the rulings (or at least have access to it), and we ALL, have been affected by it. Now, it's just a matter of dealing with the results.

So now that we know what we are dealing with, let's use this time to get a few things straightened out. The laws have been established, and the market is settled. Still, however, we have a good many people who don't know what the rules are, or how the rules affect them.

How do I go about buying an assault weapon in today's marketplace? What should I look out for? Why are the prices cheaper now than before? And of course, the bottom line for everybody...am I getting a good deal?

No one likes to be "duped". Everyone likes to get the best deal possible. Here are a few simple rules to prevent yourself from being ripped off.

First, educate yourself before you begin to shop. This means have a pretty good idea ahead of time what you should expect to pay for the model that you are searching for. Talk to people who have the gun you are looking for. They will have the best idea because they have already bought the gun you want. One very important thing to remember is, you may want to call the manufacturer or importer of the firearm. No one will have more, or the most up-to-date information about the gun than these people. Good sources for locating the current value of firearms are *The Blue Book of Gun Values,* by S.P. Fjestad, a virtual "bible" of unlimited information published annually (obviously you got that one down!). *The Blue Book of Gun Values* is the standard that all dealers set their marks on. *The Gun Journal, The Gun List,* and *The Shotgun News,* are very popular alternatives, which are both published several times monthly, and are very current as to the "going rates" of firearms.

Next, let your fingers do the walking - call as many gun shops as you can to get pricing and availability. If the store you call refuses to give you the price quotes over the phone, consider them suspect. If you are a dealer, and confident that you have the best prices, why not tell people? Not giving price quotes over the phone is a fairly common business practice used to get the customer in the store. By doing this, the consumer becomes what is known as a "captive customer", and the dealers will use this tactic to push the product while you are there. As I said, you may find this is a common practice in your area, especially if there is a great deal of competition between dealers, but it is also the single most annoying practice to consumers. Dealers take note.

Prices of pre-ban firearms are coming back down. This much is obvious, but why?

After the guidelines of the Crime Bill were set, and understood, Olympic Arms released the first Post-ban AR-15 model (I'll use the AR as a standard throughout this article to relate to "assault weapons", as it is my area of expertise, and is by far the most popular assault weapon among consumers, plinkers, and competitive shooters alike). Called the PCR series, meaning "politically correct rifle", the public soon got to see that the differences between the pre and post-ban models were limited to cosmetic differences only.

A good hypothesis for decline in pre-ban sales is, while most of the general public that had a legitimate interest in these types of weapons prior to the Crime Bill either already had their rifles, or were so repulsed at the new higher prices (due directly to the very high demand and low supply) that they refused to buy. Conversely, the customers that were just beginning to have an interest in this area of firearms collecting, plinking, and/or competitive shooting, were not willing to pay the increased prices for the pre-bans, now that they had seen so little difference between the pre-ban rifles and the new "neutered" post-ban models. From this point, demand on pre-bans was reduced, the prices began to fall, and sales began to rise on the post-ban models.

The average customer now has to decide whether the cosmetic differences between the two models are worth the difference in price. To some it is worth the increased price for the pre-ban models. To most however, the sales numbers now tell us without a doubt the overwhelming answer is no, they are not worth the increased price. The post-ban versions of pre-ban "assault weapons" that are available (PCR type AR-15s as an example) are outselling pre-bans three or four to one.

Now comes the other news. To some, these two different paramilitary configurations are visibly different and further knowledge may not be deemed necessary or useful to them. However, I find in my day-to-day workings that all too many dealers still don't understand, or simply do not care to find out. This is the most disturbing fact of the post-Crime Bill world. The consumers rely on the dealer to give them the straight "poop" about what is right or wrong. After all, it is the dealer's business. All too often however, the information given out is flat-out false, or simply misleading because the dealer hasn't taken the time to educate himself on the current events that have a direct impact on his sales.

Here are some of the FAQs (Frequently Asked Questions) that the Crime Bill mess has caused:

Can I use a high capacity magazine in a post-ban firearm? The answer to this is a resounding...YES! This has been published by the BATF. A legally "grandfathered" in high capacity magazine may be used in a post-ban firearm. This is one item that BATF waffled on for some time until their new "interpretation" was released. At this time last year, all indications were no.

Can I still buy pre-ban parts? Yes, and by all means, do NOT pay a premium for them. Pre-ban parts, components, uppers, or replacement parts can still be manufactured. So, if your dealer is charging you an inflated price for a pre-ban AK-15 upper for example, don't pay it! The Crime Bill legislation only prohibits the manufacture of complete "assault weapons", not parts or components. The prices here should remain the same. Can I buy a post-ban lower, and install a pre-ban upper? Absolutely not. This would be considered the manufacture of an illegal assault weapon. Don't try to take a chance on this either. This is one area that the BATF is making a serious crack down on.

Sources from manufacturers of AR-15 type rifles tell me that serial number tracing requests from the BATF are pouring in at previously unheard of rates.

Can I put a flash suppressor on a post-ban firearm? Again, the answer is no. Not unless you remove another of the prohibited items such as a pistol grip, or bayonet lug. The Crime Bill even goes so far as to state the "threading" a muzzle for the installation of a flash suppressor is enough to get you into trouble.

This is one of the biggest gray areas of the ban. The BATF now says that the use of some "muzzle brakes" is considered legal. However, in most cases, if the unit you plan to install has slots, instead of just a series of holes, or if it has to be threaded on, it probably will not pass the BATF standards if inspected. The bottom line is a post-ban weapon can only have one of the prohibited items (flash suppressor, threaded muzzle, pistol grip, bayonet lug, collapsible or folding stock, or grenade launcher, etc.), to remain a legal firearm.

Now for the most important, and least understood of the new interpretations of the Crime Bill. This is, what qualifies as a pre-ban lower receiver? Answer, well.. not nearly as much as you may think. Here's the deal.

What the BATF has said about pre-ban lower receivers is this. Yes, the lower receiver is still considered "the core" of the firearm (which was up in the air for awhile) but it does not necessarily define an assault weapon. What this means when read carefully, is that regardless of when the receiver was manufactured, if you (the owner of the receiver) did not have ALL the parts from which to FULLY assembly a complete pre-ban firearm at the time of the passage of the Crime Bill (Sept. 14, 1994), or if it was not already at some previous time assembled into a complete working, pre-ban assault type weapon, it DOES NOT qualify as a pre-ban assault weapon. So, if you have a receiver that was manufactured in 1983, and it has been in your possession all along, and now you are going to build up the gun, it will have to be assembled as a POST-BAN configured firearm.

This is a very serious situation. Because if you build a lower receiver into a pre-ban configuration, you will need to be able to prove to the BATF, should they ever decide to check your serial number, that you had all those parts in your possession before the ban with receipts or some other means of proof. The BATF is cracking down hard on this, so double check, and make sure you are in the right.

Dealers - if you still have lowers (that is, just blank lowers) in your possession that you are selling as pre-ban lowers, unless you can prove that they are registered with the BATF as pre-ban assault weapons, you are WRONG! Not only are you endangering your customer by not supplying him with the correct information, you are in violation of the law if you sell it as a pre-ban lower and can't prove it. This is fraud!

Consumers - before you buy a "pre-ban" lower from anyone, get the serial number, and have it traced by the manufacturer. The company should be able to tell you if the lower left the factory as just a lower or a complete weapon. If it wasn't a pre-ban complete firearm, don't take the chance.

This is another difficult area to understand. If a lower was sold prior to the ban by the manufacturer as a blank lower, or actually in any other form than a complete firearm, the manufacturer has no way of identifying positively that the lower in question is legally qualified to be assembled into a pre-ban "assault weapon". Therefore, the burden of proof is going to lie in the lap of the consumer to prove that he/she had possession prior to the Crime Bill going into effect, all the parts necessary to completely assemble that lower into a pre-ban weapon. If you can't prove that, unfortunately, again, regardless of when the lower was manufactured, or how much you paid for it, it cannot be assembled into a pre-ban assault weapon - period.

If it is a legitimate pre-ban lower, and registered with the BATF as such, the BATF will know right away simply by checking their serial number list that must be provided to them (by law) by all manufacturers upon request. All pre-ban lowers, or lowers that qualify to be built into pre-ban assault weapons will be registered with the BATF.

Unfortunately, there is no quick tell solution. To the best of my knowledge, Olympic Arms is the only manufacturer that marks all their current production AR-15s with a discernible serial number system. All post-ban lowers from Olympic Arms are pre-fixed with the year of production incorporated into the serial number. In other words, the serial numbers start with 94xxxx, 95xxxx, or 96xxxx. However, because of the reasons just stated in the previous paragraph, the fact that it does not have the year of manufacture prefix does not necessarily mean that it qualifies as a pre-ban. Thoroughly confused yet?

Colt, as an alternative, is not marking its lowers in such a manner, so you must check with the manufacturer to tell. This makes it more difficult for the consumer to find out, and therefore, less desirable than other manufacturers' lowers. A bad marketing decision as far as I am concerned.

Again, your lower may very well have been manufactured before the ban, but to be built into pre-ban configuration firearm could mean becoming an unknowing felon. One quick-hint note is that PWA has never made a complete weapon, so unless someone as an individual had assembled the lower into a complete firearm, prior to the ban going into effect, it will not qualify as a pre-ban. Therefore, PWA lowers are a bad risk.

As I mentioned at the beginning of the article, things have changed quite a bit over the last year. We are getting new interpretations on the law almost daily. Things that were out of the question early in the aftermath of the Crime Bill, are now considered legal. Slip over compensators, muzzle brakes and the like are now common place. More look-alike items are on the way (such as collapsible stocks that don't really collapse) thereby, narrowing even more, the gap between the cosmetic appearances of the pre and post-ban firearms.

These new "innovations" are making the post-ban manufactured firearms more and more attractive to the average consumer. With the differences between the pre and post-ban models being totally cosmetic, and the fact that all the parts are totally interchangeable on most models, interest continues to rise in the post-ban models. This naturally, has the opposite effect on the sales of pre-ban models.

Pre-ban AR-15s are at the lowest prices they have been in two years. The competition of the post-banners is too much for the manufacturers and wholesalers that still may have some inventory left. The prices now reflect a difference of $200-$300 more to go "pre-ban". With the price differential between the two types decreasing, the sales of pre-ban guns are now at a comfortable level again. My educated guess says, wait no longer on the pre-ban purchase, the prices are not going to drop any lower.

Another area that is creating an increase in the interest of AR-15s in particular, is the fact that the AR-15 has won the DCM Championships two years running. Post-ban versions of the AR have been ruled as legal for use in Department of Civilian Marksmanship competition, and this alone has swelled interest in DCM legal super-accurate rifles. Many gunsmiths have been born working exclusively on ARs for this purpose, and the after-market manufacturers are pumping out new "accruing" accessories by the day.

It is an ever changing world for the consumer, and tough to follow the trend in pricing, so buyers beware! Use the aforementioned tips to get the best deal possible for yourself.

A couple of closing comments that should be heeded:

Dealers - know what you are talking about, don't guess! Your life is your business, so make sure you have the facts. There are a great many dealers out there (but certainly not everyone) that truly do not know the rules and how to apply them to everyday purchases and assembling of post-ban "assault weapons". There is nothing that does more harm to this industry than the spreading of misinformation. It is your responsibility to know the facts.

Consumers - don't put yourself in the position to be wrong. Once the deal, or deed is done, and you tell the BATF agent, "Honest, I didn't know", do you think he will care? Ignorance of the law is no excuse. Write your local BATF agency, or your local Federal Legislator, and get a copy of the Crime Bill and see what it truly says.

The bottom line is, you, as an individual, are the person ultimately responsible for the firearm that you own. If you are not sure the weapon you own is in a legal configuration, make sure. Don't take the chance, the penalties are too stiff.

If you ever have any questions what-so-ever that your dealer cannot answer confidently, or if you have heard rumors to the contrary, call the BATF agency closest to you, and get a clarification. I said this last year in this same publication, and it still applies, the BATF works for YOU, ask them the questions, get the agent's name, and get your answer in writing.

 Abbreviations

*	Banned due to 1994 Crime Bill		**NM**	National Match
A or X	Standard Grade Walnut		**N**	Nickel
AA or XX (2X)	Extra Grade Walnut		**NIB**	New in Box
AAA or XXX (3X)	Best Quality Walnut		**O&U**	Over and Under
ACP	Automatic Colt Pistol		**OA**	Overall
ADJ	Adjustable		**OAL**	Overall Length
AE	Automatic Ejectors		**OB**	Octagon Barrel
BR	Bench Rest		**OBFM**	Octagon Barrel w/full mag.
BPE	Black Power Express		**OBO**	Or Best Offer
B	Blue		**OCT**	Octagon
BAC	Browning Arms Company		**ODB**	Or Don't Bother
BBL	Barrel		**PG**	Pistol Grip
BOSS	Ballistic Optimizing Shooting System		**PPD**	Post Paid
BH	Butt Head, pal, not Beavis		**PRE-BAN**	Mfg. before September 13, 1994 per C/B
BP	Butt Plate		**POST-BAN**	Mfg. after September 13, 1994 per C/B
BT	Beavertail		**PRE-'89**	Paramilitary mfg. before Federal legislation in Nov. 1989
CAL	Caliber		**POST-'89**	Paramilitary mfg. after Federal legislation in Nov. 1989
CB	Crescent Buttplate		**POR/P.O.R.**	Price on Request
C/B 1994	Introduced because of 1994 Crime Bill		**QD**	Quick Detachable
CCA	Colt Collectors Association		**RB**	Round Barrel/Round Butt
CC	Case Colors		**REC**	Receiver
CF	Centerfire		**REM**	Remington
CH	Cross Hair		**RF**	Rimfire
COMP	Compensated/Competition		**RFM**	Rim Fire Magnum
CYL	Cylinder		**RK**	Round Knob
DSL	Detachable Side Locks		**RKLT**	Round Knob Long Tang
DISC	Discontinued		**RR**	Red Ramp
DA	Double Action		**SA**	Single Action
DB	Double Barrel		**SAA**	Single Action Army
DST	Double Set Triggers		**SAE**	Selective Automatic Ejectors
DTs	Double Triggers		**SB**	Shotgun Butt
DWM	DeutscheWaffen and Munitions Fabrik		**SG**	Straight Grip
EXC	Excellent		**SK**	Skeet
EXT	Extractors		**SMG**	Sub Machine Gun
F	Full Choke		**SMLE**	Short Magazine Lee Enfield Rifle
FBT	Full Beavertail Forearm		**S/N**	Serial Number
FA	Forearm		**SNT**	Single Non-Selective Trigger
F&M	Full & Modified		**SPEC**	Special
FE	Fore End		**SPG**	Semi-Pistol Grip
FFL	Federal Firearms License		**SPL**	Special
FK	Flat Knob		**SR**	Solid Rib
FKLT	Flat Knob Long Tang		**SRC**	Saddle Ring Carbine
FM	Full Mag		**SS**	Single Shot or Stainless Steel
FN	Fabrique Nationale		**SST**	Single Selective Trigger
FPS	Feet Per Second		**ST**	Single Trigger
GOVT.	Government		**S&W**	Smith & Wesson
HB	Heavy Barrel		**SxS**	Side by Side
HC	Hard Case		**TD**	Take Down
H&H	Holland & Holland		**TGT**	Target
HP	Hollow Point		**TH**	Target Hammer
IC	Improved Cylinder		**TT**	Target Trigger
IM	Improved Modified		**UMC**	Union Metallic Cartridge Co.
LC	Long Colt		**VG**	Very Good
LPI	Lines Per Inch		**VR**	Ventilated Rib
LT	Long Tang or Light		**WC**	Wad Cutter
LTRK	Long Tang Round Knob		**WD**	Wood
M	Modified Choke		**WBY**	Weatherby
Mag.	Magnum Caliber		**WIN**	Winchester
mag.	Magazine or Clip		**WCF**	Winchester Center Fire
MIL SPEC	Mfg. to Military Specifications		**WFF**	Watch For Fakes
MC	Monte Carlo		**WO**	White Outline
MFG.	Manufactured/manufacture		**W/O**	Without
MK	Mark		**WRA**	Winchester Repeating Arms Co.
M&P	Military & Police		**WRF**	Winchester Rim Fire
MR	Matted Rib		**WRM**	Winchester Rimfire Magnum
MSR	Manufacturer's Suggested Retail		**WYTL**	Would You Take less?
			WW	World War

 # Glossary

ACCOUTERMENT All equipment carried by a soldier on outside of uniform, such as buckles, belts, or canteens, but not including weapons.

ACTION The heart of the gun, receiver, bolt or breech block feeding and firearm mechanism - see Boxlock, Rolling Block, or Sidelock.

ADJUSTABLE CHOKE A device built into the muzzle of a shotgun enabling changes from one choke to another.

AIR GUN A gun which utilizes compressed air or gas to launch the projectile.

APERTURE SIGHT A rear sight assembly consisting of a hole or aperture located in an adj. rear sight through which the front sight and target are aligned.

AUTO LOADING See semi-automatic.

BACKSTRAP That part of the revolver or pistol frame that is exposed at the rear of the grip.

BARREL BAND A metal band, either fixed or adjustable, around the forend of a gun that holds the barrel to the stock.

BARREL THROAT The breech end of a revolver barrel that is chambered and somewhat funneled for passage of bullet from cartridge case mouth into barrel, also known as forcing cone.

BEAVERTAIL FOREND A wider than normal forend.

BLUING The blue or black finish of the metal parts of a gun. The process is actually one of controlled rusting and brushing and is usually created with an acid bath. Bluing minimizes light reflection, gives a "finish" to the bare metal, and protects somewhat against rust.

BORE Inside of a barrel. Also the diameter of the barrel as measured across the lands of a rifled barrel.

BOXLOCK ACTION Typified by Parker shotgun in U.S. and Westley Richards in England. Generally considered not to be as strong as the side lock. Developed by Anson & Deeley, the box lock is hammerless. It has two disadvantages: Hammer pin must be placed directly below knee of action, which is its weakest spot, and action walls must be thinned out to receive locks. These are inserted from below into large slots in action body, which is then closed with a plate. Greener crossbolt, when made correctly, overcomes many of the box lock weaknesses.

BREECH That portion of a gun which contains the action, the trigger or firing mechanism, the magazine, and the chamber portion of the barrel(s).

BUCKHORN SIGHT An open, metallic rear sight with sides that curl upward and inward.

BULL BARREL A heavier, thicker than normal barrel with little or no taper.

BUTT PLATE A protective plate (usually steel) attached to the butt.

CALIBER The diameter of the bore.

CHAMBER Rear part of the barrel that has been reamed out so that it will contain a cartridge. When the breech is closed, the cartridge is supported in the chamber, and the chamber must align the primer with the firing pin, the bullet with the bore.

CHAMBER THROAT Also called THROAT, is that area in the barrel that is directly forward of the chamber and that tapers to bore diameter.

CHARCOAL COLOR CASEHARDENING A method of hardening steel and iron while imparting colorful swirls as well as surface figure. Normally, the desired metal parts are put in a crucible packed with a mixture of charcoal and finely ground animal bone to temperatures in the 800°-900° C range, after which they are slowly cooled, and then submerged into cold water.

CHECKERING A functional decoration consisting of pointed pyramids cut into the wood generally applied to the pistol grip and forend/forearm areas affording better handling and control.

CHOKE The muzzle constriction on a shotgun to control spread of the shot.

COCKING INDICATOR Any device which the act of cocking a gun moves into a position where it may be seen or felt in order to notify the shooter that the gun is cocked. Typical examples are the pins found on some high-grade hammerless shotguns which protrude slightly when they are cocked, and also the exposed cocking knobs on bolt-action rifles. Exposed hammers found on some rifles and pistols are also considered cocking indicators.

COMB The portion of the stock on which the shooter's cheek rests.

COMBINATION GUN Generally a break-open shotgun type configuration fitted with at least one shotgun barrel and one rifle barrel. Such guns may be encountered with either two or three barrels, and less frequently with as many as four or five, and have been known to chamber for as many as four different calibers.

COMPENSATOR A recoil-reducing device which mounts on the muzzle of a gun to deflect part of the powder gases up and rearward. Also called a "muzzle brake".

CRANE In a modern solid-frame, swing-out revolver, the U-shaped yoke on which the cylinder rotates, and which holds the cylinder in the frame.

CROWNING The rounding or chamfering normally done to a barrel muzzle to insure that the mouth of the bore is square with the bore axis and that the edge is countersunk below the surface to protect it from impact damage. Traditionally, crowning was accomplished by spinning an abrasive-coated brass ball against the muzzle while moving it in a figure-eight pattern until the abrasive had cut away any irregularities and produced a uniform and square mouth.

CRYOGENIC TEMPERING Computer controlled cooling process that relieves barrel stress by subjecting the barrel to a temperature of -310 F for 22 hours.

CYLINDER A rotating cartridge container in a revolver. The cartridges are held in chambers and the cylinder turns, either to the left or the right, depending on the gun maker's design, as the hammer is cocked.

DAMASCENE The decorating of metal with another metal, either by inlaying or attaching in some fashion.

DAMASCUS BARREL A barrel made by twisting, forming and welding thin strips of steel around a mandrel.

DERRINGER Usually refers to a small, concealable pistol with one or two short barrels.

DOUBLE ACTION The principle in a revolver or auto-loading pistol wherein the hammer can be cocked and dropped by a single pull of the trigger. Most of these actions also provide capability for single action fire. In auto-loading pistols, double action normally applies only to the first shot of any series, the hammer being cocked by the slide for subsequent shots.

DOUBLE-BARRELED A gun consisting of two barrels joined either side by side or one over the other.

DOUBLE-SET TRIGGER A device which consists of two triggers one to cock the mechanism that spring-assists the other trigger, substantially lightening trigger pull.

DOVETAIL A flaring machined or hand cut slot that is also slightly tapered toward one end. Cut into the upper surface of barrels and sometimes actions, the dovetail accepts a corresponding part on which a sight is mounted. Dovetail slot blanks are used to cover the dovetail when the original sight has been removed or lost; this gives the barrel a more pleasing appearance and configuration.

DRILLING German for "triple", which is their designation for a three-barrel gun.

EJECTOR Mechanical device used to eject empty cartridges from chamber(s).

ENGINE TURNING Overlapped spots of circular polishing.

ENGLISH STOCK A very straight, slender-gripped stock.

ENGRAVING The art of engraving metal in decorative patterns. Scroll engraving is the most common type of hand engraving encountered. Much of today's factory engraving is rolled on which is done mechanically. Hand engraving requires artistry and a knowledge of metals and related materials.

ETCHING A method of decorating metal gun parts, usually done by acid etching or photo engraving.

EXTRACTOR A device which partially lifts the spent casing(s) from the breech area, allowing the empty shell(s) to be removed manually.

FALLING BLOCK A single-shot action where the breech block drops straight down when the lever is actuated.

FIT AND FINISH Terms used to describe over-all firearm workmanship.

FLOATING BARREL A barrel bedded to avoid contact with any point on the stock.

FLOOR PLATE Usually, a removable/hinged plate at the bottom of the receiver covering the magazine well.

FORCING CONE Forward part of the chamber in a shotgun where the chamber diameter is reduced to bore diameter. The forcing cone aids the passage of shot into the barrel.

FOREARM Usually a separate piece of wood in front of the receiver and under the barrel used for hand placement when shooting.

FOREND Usually, the forward portion of a one-piece rifle or shotgun stock but can also refer to a separate piece of wood.

FREE RIFLE A rifle designed for international-type target shooting. The only restriction on design is weight maximum 8 kilograms (17.6 lbs.).

FRONT STRAP That part of the revolver or pistol grip frame that faces forward and often joins with the trigger guard. In target guns, notably the .45 ACP, the front strap is often stippled to give shooter's hand a slip-proof surface.

GAUGE/GA. Terminology referring to a shotgun's bore. Determined by the amount of pure lead balls equaling the bore diameter needed to equal one pound (i.e., a 12 ga. means that 12 lead balls exactly the diameter of the bore weigh one pound). In this text, .410 is referenced as a gauge, not the correct .410 caliber (if it was a gauge, it would be a 67 ga.). Because of space considerations, however, the .410 caliber/bore is referred to as a gauge within this text.

GROOVES The spiral cuts in the bore of a rifle or handgun barrel that give the bullet its spin or rotation as it moves down the barrel.

HAMMERLESS Some "hammerless" firearms do in fact have hidden hammers, which are located in the action housing. Truly hammerless guns, such as the Savage M99, have a firing mechanism that is based on a spring-activated firing pin.

HEEL Back end of the upper edge of the buttstock at the upper edge of the buttplate or recoil pad.

LAMINATED STOCK A gunstock made of many layers of wood glued together under pressure. Together, the laminations become very strong, preventing damages from moisture, heat, and warping.

LANDS Portions of the bore left between the grooves of the rifling in the bore of a firearm. In rifling, the grooves are usually twice the width of the land. Land diameter is measured across the bore, from land to land.

MAGAZINE (mag.) The container which holds cartridges under spring pressure to be fed into the gun's chamber.

MAGNUM (Mag.) A modern cartridge with a higher-velocity load or heavier projectile than standard.

MAINSPRING The spring that delivers energy to the hammer or striker. The recoil or operating spring in semi-automatic guns is a part of the breech closing system; is not the same as the mainspring.

MANNLICHER STOCK A full-length slender stock with slender forend extending to the muzzle (full-stock) affording better barrel protection.

MICROMETER SIGHT A finely adjustable target sight.

MONTE CARLO STOCK A stock with an elevated comb used primarily for scoped rifles.

MUZZLE The forward end of the barrel where the projectile exits.

MUZZLE BRAKE A recoil-reducing device attached to the muzzle.

OVER-UNDER A two-barrel gun in which the barrels are stacked one on top of the other.

PARALLAX (Superposed) Occurs in telescopic sights when the primary image of the objective lens does not coincide with the reticle. In practice, parallax is detected in the scope when, as the viewing eye is moved laterally, the image and the reticle appear to move in relation to each other.

PARKERIZING A matted rust-resistant oxide finish, usually matte or dull gray, or black in color, found on military guns.

PEEP SIGHT A rear sight consisting of a hole or aperture through which the front sight and target are aligned.

PEPPERBOX An early form of revolving repeating pistol in which a number of barrels were bored in a circle in a single piece of metal resembling the cylinder of a modern revolver. Functioning was the same as a revolver, the entire cylinder being revolved to bring successive barrels under the hammer for firing. Though occurring as far back as the 16th century, the pepperbox did not become practical until the advent of the percussion cap in the early 1800s. Pepperboxes were made in a wide variety of sizes and styles, and reached their popularity peak during the percussion period. Few were made after the advent of practical metallic cartridges. Both single- and double-action pepperboxes were made. Single-barreled revolvers after the 1840s were more accurate and easier to handle and soon displaced the rather clumsy and muzzle-heavy pepperbox.

POPE RIB A rib integral with the barrel. Designed by Harry M. Pope, famed barrel maker and shooter, the rib made it possible to mount a target scope low over the barrel.

PROOFMARK   Proofmarks are usually applied to all parts actually tested, but normally appear on the barrel (and possibly frame), usually indicating the country of origin and circa of proof (especially on European firearms). In the U.S., there is no federalized or government proof house, only the manufacturer's in-house proofmark indicating that a firearm has passed their internal quality control standards per government specifications.

RECEIVER   That part of a rifle or shotgun (excluding hinged frame guns) that houses the bolt, firing pin, mainspring, trigger group, and magazine or ammunition feed system. The barrel is threaded into the somewhat enlarged forward part of the receiver, called the receiver ring. At the rear of the receiver, the butt or stock is fastened. In semiautomatic pistols, the frame or housing is sometimes referred to as the receiver.

RELEASE TRIGGER   A trap shooting trigger that fires the gun when the trigger is released.

RIB   A raised sighting plane affixed to the top of a barrel.

RIFLING   The spirally cut grooves in the bore of a rifle or handgun. The rifling stabilizes the bullet in flight. Rifling may rotate to the left or the right, the higher parts of the bore being called lands, the cuts or lower parts being called the grooves. Many types exist, such as oval, polygonal, button, Newton, Newton-Pope, parabolic, Haddan, Enfield, segmental rifling, etc. Most U.S.-made barrels have a right-hand twist, while British gunmakers prefer a left-hand twist. In practice, there seems to be little difference in accuracy or barrel longevity.

ROLLING BLOCK ACTION   Single shot action, designed in the U.S. and widely used in early Remington arms. Also known as the REMINGTON-RIDER action, the breech block, actuated by a lever, rotates down and back from the chamber. Firing pin is contained in block and is activated by hammer fall.

SCHNABEL FOREND   The curved/carved flared end of the forend that resembles the beak of a bird (Schnabel in German). This type of forend is common on Austrian and German guns; was popular in the U.S., but the popularity of the schnabel forend/forearm comes and goes with the seasons. A schnabel forend is often seen on custom stocks and rifles.

SHORT ACTION   A rifle action designed for shorter cartridges.

SIDELOCK   A type of action, usually long gun, where the moving parts are located on side of the lock plates, which in turn are inletted in the stock. Usually found only on better quality shotguns and rifles.

SIDE PLATES   Ornamental steel panels normally attached to a boxlock action to simulate a sidelock.

SINGLE ACTION   A firearms design which requires the hammer to be manually cocked for each shot. Also an auto-loading pistol design which requires manual cocking of the hammer for the first shot only.

SINGLE TRIGGER   One trigger on a double-barrel gun. It fires both barrels singly by successive pulls.

SLING SWIVELS   Metal loops affixed to the gun on which a carrying strap is attached.

SPUR TRIGGER   A trigger mounting system that housed the trigger in an extension of the frame in some old guns. The trigger projected only slightly from the front of the extension or spur, and no trigger guard was used on these guns.

SUICIDE SPECIAL   A mass-produced variety of inexpensive single action revolvers and derringers, usually with a spur trigger. These guns carried many fancy names; those in good condition have become true collector's items.

TAKE DOWN   A gun which can be easily taken apart in two sections for carrying or shipping.

TANG(S)   The extension straps of the receiver from which the stock is attached.

TOP STRAP   The upper part of a revolver frame, which often is either slightly grooved - the groove serving as rear sight - or which carries at its rearward end a sight that may be adjustable.

TRAP STOCK   A shotgun stock with greater length and less comb drop used for trap shooting.

TWIST BARRELS   A process in which a steel rod (called a mandrel) was wrapped with "skelps" - ribbons of iron. The skelps were then welded in a charcoal fire to form one piece of metal, after which the rod was driven out to be used again. The interior of the resulting tube then had to be laboriously bored out by hand to remove the roughness. Once polished, the outside was smoothed on big grinding wheels, usually turned by water power.

VENTILATED RIB   A sighting plane affixed along the length of a shotgun barrel with gaps or slots milled for cooling and lightweight handling.

YOUTH DIMENSIONS   Usually refers to shorter stock dimensions and/or lighter weight enabling youth/women to shoot and carry a lighter, shorter firearm.

ATTENTION GUN OWNERS

Your Firearms Are A Valuable Asset

They may be used to fund a Charitable Remainder Trust which will provide you an income for life!

or

They can be given to The NRA Foundation as assets providing you a charitable gift donation which will lower your taxes!

or

You may also give your firearms to the NRA through a designated bequest in your will!

Make sure your valuable firearms are used to the best advantage!

Help is available

The National Rifle Association's Planned Giving programs allow you to make gifts of various assets for general use or earmarked for special purposes. By taking action now, you can guarantee your firearms will benefit you in the future.

For free, confidential information about how you can receive an income for life, make a bequest, or our brochure *"How To Protect Your Rights With A Will"* please call the NRA Development Office at **1-800-672-4521** or write us at:

NRA Development Office
11250 Waples Mill Road
Fairfax, Virginia 22030

NRA MEMBERSHIP ENROLLMENT

You Can Join The NRA Today!

- For over 120 years, The National Rifle Association of America has been the leader in defending our Second Amendment right to keep and bear arms.

- We're firearms collectors dedicated to the art of gun-smithing–competitive target shooters–police officers and firearms instructors dedicated to training people in the fundamentals of personal protection and responsible firearm ownership and safety–hunters and lobbyists.

- The Constitution promises each and every American the Second Amendment right to keep and bear arms. With that right comes the obligation of safe and responsible firearm ownership.

- The NRA Institute for Legislative Action (NRA-ILA) has become the American gun owner's strongest, most effective voice in every legislative and political forum.

- NRA's competitions divisions sanctions about 12,000 shooting tournaments each year and sponsors national shooting championships including the National Matches at Camp Perry.

- By joining the NRA you'll be helping us pass laws making it illegal to harass hunters, keep hunting lands open and accessible, promote effective wildlife conservation policies and defend your right to own a firearm.

You can become a member instantly by calling 1-800-NRA 3888.

GREETINGS *from* BLUE BOOK PUBLICATIONS, INC.

Steven P. Fjestad

Beth Marthaler

Barbara K. Olsen

Lisa M. Winkels

John Allen

Rebecca Glasser

DJ Pallum

Tom Stock

Jennifer Haugen

Susanne Markgren

Walter Horishnyk

Tom Lundin

Photo from Tom Lundin's personal album.

Blue Book Publications, Inc. & the

World Wide Web

If there are some of you who have been holed up in a bunker for the last year and haven't yet heard about this thing called the Internet, it's time for a brief reality check. It seems you can't pick up a book or magazine, watch a TV show or movie, or listen to the radio without being pummeled by hyped references to "the net" and tired clichés about the information superhighway.

The Internet has been around for about twenty-five years, largely used by the government and universities as a means for researchers and scholars to share unclassified data and exchange electronic mail (e-mail). In the past couple of years, though, the growing power and ubiquity of desktop computers has made it possible for the average Joe to get on-line and "surf the net" as easily as he could run a word processing program.

You could visualize the Internet as a huge computer network that is connected to computers around the world — a vastly larger version of the Local Area Network (LAN) you might be running at the office. Your desktop computer connects by modem to a regional server (a computer branch office, if you will), which handles communications with other regional servers in neighboring cities or states. Files or messages you send from your computer to another one across the country get passed along a chain of servers until they reach their final destination. Your files may have passed through twelve different computers behind the scenes before arriving at the screen of your recipient.

The aspect of the Internet that has gained the most attention of late is the World Wide Web. Most people see the Web and the Internet as one and the same, but this isn't quite right. The Internet handles many network tasks such as electronic mail, point-to-point file transfer, and interest group file libraries. The Web is just one more thing that the Internet does. It is, however, the most visually interesting to the average computer user because it allows pages of text and graphics to be displayed on any computer that can process the files, whether IBM or Macintosh, UNIX or something else. And therein lies the reason for the Web's popularity: information that is posted on the Web (i.e., uploaded to one of the servers) can be viewed by millions of computer users regardless of the type of computer they are using.

Where does Blue Book Publications, Inc. fit into this cyberpicture? As a content provider, we have never been more blessed (or cursed) with the number of options available to us in publishing our data. We have a few irons in the fire that we feel will result in the *Blue Book of Gun Values* setting new standards for easy access to pricing information.

For instance, we're getting our feet wet in cyberspace with a Blue Book Publications home page (set your browser to **http://www.bluebookinc.com**). This page will contain brief summaries of information from material in the printed book as well as information from our other publications and links to related web sites.

Later this year we'll be starting work on a CD-ROM version of the *Blue Book of Gun Values*, completion date not yet determined. This product will contain the complete text of the pricing guide in a computer-searchable format. Our program will allow you to search out and display information by model numbers or manufacturer names, for instance, all at computer speed.

And we're continuing to revamp and improve the book in order to provide you with the most accurate, useful, information-packed printed version available. For sheer readability and convenience, nothing beats the look and feel of a good book.

What's next? Some progressive gun dealers are already advertising in cyberspace (check out our friends at http://www.gunshop.com), and it's likely that totally electronic commerce (buying and selling) isn't too far behind. Someday, you'll be able to order your *Blue Book of Gun Values* over the net, maybe using "e-cash". Is it possible that the *Blue Book of Gun Values* will one day be accessible interactively over the net? While we have no plans for it — yet — we can say one thing for sure...

We have seen the future, and it is digital.

As always, your feedback and suggestions are welcome. Please e-mail us at: **bluebook@bluebookinc.com**. Surf's up!

A section

A.A.

Previously manufactured by Azanza & Arrizablaga located in Eibar, Spain.

Grading	100%	98%	95%	90%	80%	70%	60%

A.A. — semi-auto pistol, 7.65mm, slide marked Azanza & Arrizablaga Model 1916, A.A. in oval on frame.

	$130	$105	$85	$65	$55	$50	$45

REIMS — semi-auto pistol, 6.35mm or 7.65mm, copies of M1906 Browning, marked 1914 Model.

	$120	$100	$75	$65	$55	$50	$45

A.A. ARMS INC.

Manufacturer located in Monroe, NC.

AP9 MINI-SERIES PISTOL — 9mm Para. cal., semi-auto blowback paramilitary design, phosphate/blue or nickel finish, 2 barrel lengths, 10 (C/B 1994) or 20* shot mag.

No Mfg.'s Retail	$245	$210	$185	$165	$150	$135	$125

Add $20 for nickel finish.
Add $200 for AP9 long barrel Target Model (banned 1994).

AR9 CARBINE — similar action to AP9, except has carbine length barrel and side-folding metal stock. Banned 1994.

	$750	$625	$550	$475	$400	$350	$300

A.A.A.

Previously manufactured by Aldazabal located in Spain.

M1919 — semi-auto pistol, 7.65mm.

	$110	$100	$85	$70	$65	$60	$55

A & R SALES

Previous manufacturer located in South El Monte, CA.

HANDGUN — .45 ACP cal., semi-auto patterned after Colt Model 1911 Govt., less weight than normal Colt .45.

	$225	$205	$175	$155	$145	$135	$125

RIFLE: MARK IV SPORTER — semi-auto, .308 Win., M-14 action-clip fed, adj. sights.

	$295	$260	$225	$200	$175	$155	$140

A F C

Previously manufactured by Auguste Francotte located in Liege, Belgium, 1912-1914.

SEMI-AUTO PISTOL — 6.35mm, 6 shot mag., frame marked "Francotte Liege".

	$275	$250	$220	$165	$140	$110	$85

A. J. ORDNANCE

THOMAS — .45 ACP, double action, 6 shot, 3½ in. barrel, fixed sights, checkered plastic grips, delayed blowback action, each shot double action, stainless steel barrel. Disc.

	$470	$415	$385	$360	$330	$275	$220
Chrome	$525	$470	$440	$415	$385	$330	$275

A K S (AK-47 & AKM Copies)

Select fire paramilitary design rifle originally designed in Russia (initials refer to Automat Kalashnikov, 1947). Russian mfg. select fire AK-47s have not been mfg. since the mid-50s. Semi-auto AK-47 and AKM clones are currently manufactured by several arsenals in China including Norinco and Poly Technologies, Inc. Also manufactured in other countries including Yugoslavia, Czechoslavakia, Bulgaria and Hungary. As this edition went to press, only Hungarian (imported by Sentinel Arms) and Bulgarian (imported by K.B.I) mfg. AK-47s are currently allowed to be imported with "sporterized" thumbhole stocks (see individual importer listings).

Previously, U.S. importation was discontinued for commercial sales in 1989 due to federal legislation (in original configuration with either fixed or folding stocks). "Sporterized" stock configurations have recently been responsible for this rifle to meet import regulations.

Since the Federal ban on this type of paramilitary designed rifle, demand initially surged (summer and fall of 1989). Now that the Brady and Crime bills are in effect, almost all of the interest in the "pre-ban" AK-47s has subsided, and prices continue to fall on those models/variations that were heavily imported. AK-47s are not rare - over 700 million have been manufactured in China alone since WW II.

Grading	100%	98%	95%	90%	80%	70%	60%

AK-47 & AKM MODELS

Also refer to separate listings under Poly Technologies, Inc., Norinco, Federal Ordnance, B-West, K.B.I., Sentinel Arms, American Arms, Inc., and others who have imported this configuration up until now.

AK-47 (AKM) RECENT IMPORTS — 7.62mmx39mm (former Russian M43 military cal.) or .223 cal., semi-auto Kalashnikov action, typically 16½ in. barrel, 5, 10*, or 30 (C/B 1994) shot mag., wood or synthetic stock and forearm except on folding stock model, recent importation mostly has newer "sporterized" fixed stocks with thumbholes, may be supplied with bayonet, sling, cleaning kit, patterned after former military production rifle of China and Russia. Values listed below are for generic mfg.

	$395	$360	$315	$275	$240	$220	$200

Subtract 20% for guns with "post-ban" features.
Add 10-15% for older folding stock variations.

AK-47 technically designates the original full-auto, Russian made military rifle with milled receiver. Recent semi-auto "clones" normally have stamped receivers and are technically designated AKMs. Recent mfg. AK-47 clones refer to rifles with milled receivers.

Yugoslavian, Czechoslovakian, or Hungarian manufactured AK-47s will command premiums over standard Chinese arsenal mfg. Poly Technologies,Inc., Norinco, and B-West importation (see separate listings where applicable) also will command a premium.

A M A C

See Iver Johnson section in this text. AMAC stands for American Military Arms Corporation manufactured in Jacksonville, AR. AMAC ceased operations early 1993.

A M T

Manufactured by Arcadia Machine & Tool located in Irwindale, CA. Also see Auto-Mag for discontinued models. Distributor and dealer sales.

PISTOLS: SEMI-AUTO

During late 1993, AMT changed from white outline Millet adj. sights to an adj. 3 dot (white) system mfg. by LPA in Italy.

Grading	100%	98%	95%	90%	80%	70%	60%

A

LIGHTNING — .22 LR, semi-auto, stainless steel only, 5 (bull only), 6½, 8½, 10½, or 12½ (disc. 1987) in. bull or tapered barrels, adj. sights and trigger, pistol based on semi-auto Ruger action, tapered barrels. Mfg. 1984-87.

$240 $200 $150

Last Mfg.'s Sug. Retail was $289.

This model features a frame grooved for scope mounts, Clark trigger, Millett sights, and either Pachmayr rubber or Wayland wood grips as standard equipment.

▲ *Bull's Eye Regulation Target* — similar to 6½ in. Lightning with bull barrel, except has vent. rib, wooden grips, extended rear sight. Mfg. 1986 only.

$350 $285 $220

Last Mfg.'s Sug. Retail was $436.

BABY AUTOMAG — .22 LR, semi-auto, stainless steel only, 8½ in. vent. rib barrel, Millett adj. sights, smooth walnut grips, 1,000 mfg.

$450 $400 $350

AUTOMAG II — .22 Mag., stainless steel only, 3⅜ (Compact Model), 4½, or 6 in. barrel, gas assisted action, white outline Millett adj. sights, grooved Lexan grips, 7 (Compact) or 9 shot mag., 24-32 oz. New 1987.

Mfg.'s Sug. Retail $406 $310 $235 $195

AUTOMAG III — .30 Carbine or 9mm Win. Mag. (mfg. 1993 only) cal., stainless steel, 6⅜ in. barrel, patterned after Colt Govt. Model, white outline Millett adj. sights, grooved Lexan grips, 8 shot mag., 43 oz. New 1992.

Mfg.'s Sug. Retail $470 $395 $300 $245

AUTOMAG IV — 10mm (disc. 1993) or .45 Win. Mag. cal., 6½ (.45 Win. Mag. only) or 8⅝ (disc. 1993) in. barrel, 7/8 shot mag., Millett adj. sights, stainless steel, 46 oz. New 1992.

Mfg.'s Sug. Retail $700 $570 $465 $360

AUTOMAG V — .50 AE cal., stainless steel, 6½ in. barrel, gas venting system reduces recoil, 5 shot mag., 46 oz. Mfg. 1993-95.

$815 $700 $625

Last Mfg.'s Sug. Retail was $900.

JAVELINA — 10mm cal., semi-auto, 7 in. barrel, 8 shot mag., Millett adj. sights, wraparound Neoprene grips, wide adj. trigger, long grip safety, 48 oz. Mfg. 1992 only.

$560 $460 $360

Last Mfg.'s Sug. Retail was $676.

BACKUP PISTOL — .22 LR (disc. 1987), .357 Sig. (new 1996), .380 ACP, .38 Super (new 1995), 9mm Para. (new 1995), .40 S&W (new 1995), or .45 ACP (new 1995) cal., semi-auto, choice of traditional double action (disc. 1992) or double action only (new 1992), 2½ (.22 LR or .380 ACP) or 3 in. barrel, stainless steel, Lexan grips, formerly TDE, 5 (.380 ACP or .40 S&W), 6, or 8 (.22 LR) shot mag., 18 or 23 oz. Older disc. walnut grip models are worth a slight premium.

▲ *.380 ACP*
Mfg.'s Sug. Retail $330 $235 $180 $135
.22 LR $240 $185 $140

▲ *.357 Sig., .38 Super, 9mm Para., .40 S&W, or .45 ACP cal.*
Mfg.'s Sug. Retail $450 $365 $295 $250

In 1992, AMT re-engineered this model and removed all external levers.

BACKUP PISTOL II — .380 ACP cal., single action semi-auto, stainless steel, 2½ in. barrel, 5 shot finger extension mag., black carbon fiber grips, 18 oz. New 1993.

Mfg.'s Sug. Retail $310 $225 $180 $135

Grading	100%	98%	95%	90%	80%	70%	60%

.45 ACP STANDARD GOVERNMENT MODEL — .45 ACP, similar to Colt semi-auto Govt. model, stainless steel, 5 in. barrel, fixed rear sight, loaded chamber indicator, adj. trigger, wraparound neoprene grips.

Mfg.'s Sug. Retail	$490	$390	$295	$250

HARDBALLER — .45 ACP, similar to Colt Gold Cup Model, stainless steel, 5 in. barrel, adj. Millett rear sight, serrated rib, loaded chamber indicator, adj. trigger, wraparound neoprene grips.

Mfg.'s Sug. Retail	$550	$430	$330	$275

Add $280 for 5 in. Hardballer conversion kit.

▲ *Hardballer Longslide* — similar to Hardballer, except 7 in. barrel and longer slide assembly.

Mfg.'s Sug. Retail	$596	$455	$345	$295

Add $300 for 7 in. Longslide conversion kit.

SKIPPER — similar to Hardballer, except approx. 1 in. shorter slide on pre-'84 mfg, re-released in 1991 with choice of .40 S&W or .45 ACP cal., 4¼ in. barrel, checkered walnut grips, matte finish stainless steel, Millett adj. rear sight, 7 shot mag., 33 oz. Disc. 1991.

	$350	$285	$250

Last Mfg.'s Sug. Retail was $450.

COMBAT SKIPPER — similar to Skipper, only with fixed sights. Disc. 1984.

	$375	$330	$295

BULL'S EYE TARGET MODEL — .40 S&W, similar to Hardballer with 5 in. barrel, 8 shot mag., adj. Millett sights, wraparound Neoprene grips, 38 oz. Mfg. 1991 only.

	$400	$340	$295

Last Mfg.'s Sug. Retail was $500.

"ON DUTY" DOUBLE ACTION — 9mm Para., .40 S&W, or .45 ACP (new late 1994) cal., stainless steel slide and barrel, 4½ in. barrel, 10 (C/B 1994), 15* (9mm Para.), 11* (.40 S&W), or 9 (.45 ACP) shot mag., 3-dot sighting system, anodized aluminum frame, trigger disconnect safety with inertia firing pin, carbon fiber grips, 32 oz. Mfg. 1991-94.

	$385	$295	$250

Last Mfg.'s Sug. Retail was $470.

Add $60 for .45 ACP cal.

In 1992, this model became available with either traditional double action with decocking lever or double action only with safety.

RIFLES

LIGHTNING (25/22) — .22 LR, semi-auto based on Ruger 10-22 action, stainless steel, 30 shot mag., 17½ in. bull or tapered barrel, nylon pistol grip handle and forearm, folding stock with recoil pad or youth stock, fixed sights, 6 lbs. Mfg. 1986-1993.

	$220	$175	$150

Last Mfg.'s Sug. Retail was $296.

SMALL GAME HUNTER (SGH) — .22 LR, same mechanical action as Lightning, except has matte black nylon stock with checkered forearm and grip, 22 in. barrel, 10 shot mag., no sights, removable recoil pad allows storage in stock, 6 lbs. Mfg. 1986-1993.

	$230	$190	$160

Last Mfg.'s Sug. Retail was $300.

SMALL GAME HUNTER II — similar to Small Game Hunter, except has match grade 22 in. heavyweight full-floating barrel, 10 shot rotary mag., black fiberglass nylon stock, no sights, 6 lbs. Mfg. 1993 only.

	$230	$190	$160

Last Mfg.'s Sug. Retail was $300.

Add $70 for 17½ in. stainless steel barrel.
Add $150 for 22½ in. stainless steel match grade barrel.

Grading	100%	98%	95%	90%	80%	70%	60%

CHALLENGE EDITION — .22 LR, semi-auto target variation featuring McMillan fiberglass stock, 16½ (features 6 in. barrel weight extension), 18, or 22 in. floating stainless steel bull barrel, custom designed trigger, custom order through AMT's Custom Shop. New 1994.

Mfg.'s Sug. Retail	$999	$875	$625	$550	$475	$395	$325	$275

Add $75 for 16½ in. barrel (with extension weight).

▲ **Challenge Edition With Bloop Tube** — features 16¼ in. barrel with a 6 in. bloop tube extension enabling increase bullet velocity with muzzle heavy characteristics, McMillan fiberglass STC stock. New 1996.

Mfg.'s Sug. Retail	$975		$850	$615	$535	$465	$395	$325	$275

Add $155 for compensated bloop tube.

SPORTER EDITION — .22 LR, 16½, 18, 20, or 22 in. tapered sporter barrel, McMillan fiberglass sporter stock. New 1996.

Mfg.'s Sug. Retail	$900		$800	$700	$625	$565	$500	$450	$400

HUNTER EDITION — .22 LR, 18, 20, or 22 in. regular barrel with injection molded sporter stock. New 1996.

Mfg.'s Sug. Retail	$800		$725	$650	$575	$500	$450	$400	$350

FLY SWATTER — .22 LR, 16½ in. regular barrel with injection molded sporter stock. New 1996.

Mfg.'s Sug. Retail	$700		$625	$560	$495	$450	$400	$350	$300

MAGNUM HUNTER — .22 Mag., semi-auto, 20 in. free-floating barrel, drilled and tapped, stainless steel, 10 shot straight stacked mag., w/o sights, drilled and tapped for Weaver 87-A scope base, black synthetic stock, 6 lbs. New 1995.

Mfg.'s Sug. Retail	$550		$465	$375	$275

BOLT ACTION STANDARD SINGLE SHOT — 11 various cals., post-64 push-feed action, pre-64 3-position side safety, cone breech, composite stock, cryogenic treated stainless steel barrel w/o sights, 8½ lbs. New 1996.

Mfg.'s Sug. Retail	$1,110		$975	$825	$650

▲ **Bolt Action Deluxe Single Shot** — 11 various cals., Mauser type control feeding, short, medium, or long right or left-hand action, pre-64 3-position side safety and claw type extractor, cryogenic treated stainless steel barrel w/o sights, custom Kevlar stock, approx. 8 ½ lbs. New 1996.

Mfg.'s Sug. Retail	$2,400		$2,250	$1,750	$1,450

BOLT ACTION STANDARD REPEATER — 21 various cals., post-64 push-feed action, Mauser type mag., pre-64 3-position side safety, Model 70 type trigger, composite stock, cryogenic treated stainless steel barrel w/o sights. 8½ lbs. New 1996.

Mfg.'s Sug. Retail	$1,110		$975	$825	$650

▲ **Bolt Action Deluxe Repeater** — similar features to Bolt Action Deluxe Single Shot, except has Mauser type mag. New 1996.

Mfg.'s Sug. Retail	$1,596		$1,425	$1,195	$895

A-SQUARE

Manufacturer located in Bedford, KY. Previously manufactured until 1991 in Madison, IN. Direct sales only.

A-Square also offers at extra cost different grades of walnut, different metal finishes, and various sights/scope rings. Custom calibers are also available upon special order. Values of these special order options can be obtained by contacting A-Square directly.

Grading	100%	98%	95%	90%	80%	70%	60%

RIFLES: BOLT ACTION
Add $250 for A-Grade walnut.
Add $500 for AAA-Grade fancy walnut.
Add $500 for English walnut.
Add $100 for accent package.
Add $200 for stainless steel barrel.
Add $450 for black synthetic stock.
Add $600 for weather impervious package.
Add $240 for 3-leaf steel express sights.
Add $300 for royal high gloss blue finish (disc. 1995).
Add $150 for high gloss polymer wood finish (disc. 1993).

HANNIBAL MODEL — most cals. available, bolt action built on a P-17 Enfield receiver, 22-26 in. barrel, 9 - 11¼ lbs., select walnut with pistol grip and recoil pad. New 1986.

Mfg.'s Sug. Retail	$2,995	$2,995	$2,650	$2,350	$2,100	$1,875	$1,725	$1,575

HAMILCAR MODEL — various cals. available, smaller variation of the Hannibal model featuring slimmer design gained by not needing the reinforcement for heavy Mag. cals., 4-7 shot mag., cocks on opening, 8 - 8½ lbs. Introduced 1994.

Mfg.'s Sug. Retail	$2,995	$2,995	$2,650	$2,350	$2,100	$1,875	$1,725	$1,575

CAESAR MODEL — most cals. available, bolt action built on a Remington M-700 receiver until 1993, Sako L-V actions were utilized beginning 1993, 22-26 in. barrel, select walnut with pistol grip and recoil pad, primarily a left-handed action with right-hand a special order, 9 - 10¾ lbs. New 1986.

Mfg.'s Sug. Retail	$2,995	$2,995	$2,650	$2,350	$2,100	$1,875	$1,725	$1,575

GENGHIS KHAN MODEL — .22-250 Rem., .243 Win., .25-06, or 6mm Rem. cal., features Winchester pre-64 Model 70 action, heavy taper barrel, Coil-Chek stock helps reduce recoil, designed for varmint hunting. New 1995.

Mfg.'s Sug. Retail	$2,895	$2,895	$2,550	$2,250	$2,000	$1,775	$1,625	$1,475

ATCSA
Maker: Armas De Tiro Y Casa.

COLT POCKET PISTOL COPY — revolver, .38 cal., 6 shot.

	$155	$140	$110	$100	$90	$75	$65

SINGLE SHOT REVOLVER — target pistol.

	$195	$165	$145	$110	$100	$90	$75

AYA (AGUIRRE Y ARANZABAL)
Manufacturer located in Eibar, Spain. Currently imported and marketed by Armes De Chasse (starting 1992) located in Herdford, NC. Previous manufacture was by Diarm (circa 1986-88) located in Eibar, Spain. Retail sales by importer and AYA select dealers.

AYA manufactured shotguns can be denoted by serialization. Serial numbers over 600,001 with barrel flats marked Arms de Chasse or Scotia Group are post-1988 AYA manufactured while specimens under 600,000 may have been manufactured by Diarm - Diarm manufacture is not covered by the AYA warranty, nor is the resale the same as values listed below.

SHOTGUNS: O/U
Add 10% on current models listed below if other than 12 ga.

Grading	100%	98%	95%	90%	80%	70%	60%

A

AUGUSTA — 12 ga. only, deluxe O/U sidelock, arabesque engraving in deep relief, select walnut. This model has been imported off and on during the past decade and Arms de Chasse should be contacted directly for current pricing information.

Mfg.'s Sug. Retail	$27,000	$23,500	$5,850	$4,950	$4,250	$3,500	$2,875	$2,350

CORAL "A" — 12 or 16 ga., boxlock action with Kersten cross bolt, vent. rib, ejectors, double triggers. Disc. 1985.

	$1,275	$1,050	$875	$775	$695	$625	$560

Last Mfg.'s Sug. Retail was $2,195.

CORAL "B" — similar to Coral A, except for coin-wash engraved receiver. Disc. 1985.

	$1,395	$1,100	$925	$820	$720	$650	$595

Last Mfg.'s Sug. Retail was $2,450.

MODEL 37 SUPER — 12, 16, or 20 ga., various barrel lengths and chokes, vent. rib, sidelock, auto ejector, elaborate engraving, high grade wood. Merkel style action. Prices below reflect older models. Disc.

	100%	98%	95%	90%	80%	70%	60%
12 ga.	$2,600	$2,350	$2,100	$1,900	$1,700	$1,500	$1,250
16 ga.	$2,550	$2,200	$2,000	$1,700	$1,500	$1,350	$1,150
20 ga.	$3,000	$2,500	$2,200	$1,900	$1,700	$1,600	$1,475

▲ *New Model 37 Super A* — game scene engraved, detachable sidelock action, nickel steel receiver. This model has been imported off and on during the past decade.

Mfg.'s Sug. Retail	$13,500	$12,250	$5,250	$4,300	$3,750	$3,250	$2,650	$2,175

▲ *New Model 37 Super B* — fine scroll engraved, detachable sidelock action, nickel steel receiver. Disc. 1985.

	$5,250	$4,750	$4,300	$3,720	$3,350	$2,650	$2,175

Last Mfg.'s Sug. Retail was $7,795.

79 "A" — 12 ga. only, boxlock with double locking lugs, sel. trigger, ejectors. Disc. 1985.

	$1,275	$1,075	$965	$880	$790	$705	$640

Last Mfg.'s Sug. Retail was $1,595.

79 "B" — similar to 79 "A", only more elaborate engraving. Disc. 1985.

	$1,395	$1,200	$1,085	$990	$890	$790	$695

Last Mfg.'s Sug. Retail was $1,795.

79 "C" — similar to 79 "B", only more elaborate engraving, double triggers on request. Disc. 1985.

	$2,050	$1,825	$1,605	$1,460	$1,315	$1,165	$1,000

Last Mfg.'s Sug. Retail was $2,650.

77 — 12 ga. only, Merkel style O/U sidelock with Greener crossbolt, deluxe engraving checkering. Disc. 1985.

	$3,100	$2,750	$2,500	$2,255	$2,030	$1,805	$1,600

Last Mfg.'s Sug. Retail was $4,100.

SHOTGUNS: SxS

Armes De Chasse should be contacted directly regarding special order options on the models listed below.

Values on currently imported AYA shotguns have increased considerably, while prices for used specimens (98% or less original condition) have not increased proportionately, and in some cases, have changed very little.

On current models listed below, add 10% to values if other than 12 ga.

BOLERO — similar to Matador, with non-selective single trigger and extractors. Disc. 1984.

	$440	$360	$330	$305	$275	$250	$220

IBERIA — 12 or 20 ga., 3 in., boxlock, double triggers, plain walnut. Disc. 1984.

	$566	$440	$370	$315	$285	$255	$230

A

Grading	100%	98%	95%	90%	80%	70%	60%

IBERIA II — 12 or 16 ga., 28 in. barrels, 2¾ in. chamber only, double triggers, plain walnut. Mfg. 1984-1985 only.

	$515	$430	$370	$315	$285	$255	$230

Last Mfg.'s Sug. Retail was $570.

MATADOR — 10, 12, 16, 20, 28, or .410 ga., 26, 28, or 30 in. barrel, various chokes, Anson & Deeley boxlock, auto ejectors, beavertail forearm, SST, checkered pistol grip stock. Mfg. 1955-1963.

	$475	$375	$325	$275	$225	$200	$180

Add 20% for .410 or 28 ga.

MATADOR NO. 2 —similar to Matador, with vent. rib, 12 or 20 ga. only. Disc.

	$525	$425	$360	$315	$265	$225	$200

MATADOR NO. 3A — 12 or 20 ga., 3 in. chamber in 20 ga. only, boxlock, vent. rib, ejectors, SST. Disc. 1985.

	$750	$650	$550	$495	$440	$385	$335

Last Mfg.'s Sug. Retail was $1,235.

SENIOR — 12 ga. only, self-opener, engraved sidelock action, select walnut. Top-of-the-line quality, made to special order only. Lighter up-land version also available. Disc. 1987.

	$15,500	$12,000	$10,000	$8,000	$6,500	$5,500	$4,500

Last Mfg.'s Sug. Retail was $21,000.

NO. 1 — 12 or 20 ga., full sidelock action with third lever fastener, straight grip, ejectors, DTs, elaborate fine scroll engraving. Importation disc. 1987, resumed in 1991.

Mfg.'s Sug. Retail	$7,000		$6,000	$2,925	$2,250	$1,800	$1,500	$1,200	$950

Add $2,562 for extra set of barrels.

NO. 2 — 12, 16, 20, 28 or .410 ga., 3 in. chambers, English-style sidelock, ejector, cocking indicators, DTs, third lever fastener. Importation disc. 1987, resumed 1991.

Mfg.'s Sug. Retail	$3,500		$3,000	$1,350	$950	$750	$600	$500	$425

Add $1,328 for extra set of barrels.

NO. 3-A — 12, 16, 20, 28, or .410 ga., boxlock, extractors, double triggers. Disc. 1985.

	$640	$540	$495	$450	$400	$375	$350

Last Mfg.'s Sug. Retail was $850.

Add 25%-35% for 28 or .410 ga.

NO. 4 — 12, 16 (disc. 1985), 20, 28, or .410 ga., 3 in. chambers, English-style straight stock, boxlock action, ejectors, double trigger, straight grip. Importation disc. 1987, resumed 1991.

Mfg.'s Sug. Retail	$1,800		$1,550	$625	$500	$450	$410	$365	$325

4-A DELUXE — English-style, boxlock ejector. Stock, forearm, trigger to order. Importation disc. 1985, resumed 1991.

Mfg.'s Sug. Retail	$3,100		$2,675	$1,150	$900	$800	$740	$680	$625

XXV BOXLOCK (BL) — 12 or 20 ga. only, similar to 4-A Deluxe, except 25 in. barrels, Churchill rib. Importation disc. 1986, resumed 1991.

Mfg.'s Sug. Retail	$3,000		$2,775	$1,250	$975	$875	$800	$740	$680

Add $2,013 for extra set of barrels.

XXV SIDELOCK (SL) — 12, 16, 20, 28 or .410 ga., sidelock ejector, 25 in. barrels, Churchill rib. Stock, forearm, trigger to order. Importation disc. 1986, resumed 1991.

▲ *12, 16, or 20 ga.*

Mfg.'s Sug. Retail	$4,000		$3,625	$1,700	$1,350	$975	$850	$750	$650

Add $2,097 for extra set of barrels.

Grading	100%	98%	95%	90%	80%	70%	60%

NO. 53 — 12, 16, or 20 ga., engraved sidelock ejector, sideclips, third lock. Stock, forearm, trigger to order. Importation disc. 1986, resumed 1991.

Mfg.'s Sug. Retail	$5,000	$4,625	$2,050	$1,525	$1,100	$950	$850	$750

NO. 56 — 12, 16, or 20 ga., sidelock action-engraved, ejectors, sel. trigger. Importation disc. 1985, resumed 1991.

Mfg.'s Sug. Retail	$8,000	$7,350	$3,375	$2,725	$2,300	$1,950	$1,650	$1,400

NO. 106 — 12, 16, or 20 ga., English-style boxlock, double trigger, pistol grip, 28 in. barrels. Disc. 1985.

	$530	$440	$400	$360	$320	$300	$275

Last Mfg.'s Sug. Retail was $585.

107-LI — 12 or 16 ga., English-style boxlock, double trigger, straight grip, light English scroll engraving. Disc. 1985.

	$675	$560	$520	$480	$425	$400	$360

Last Mfg.'s Sug. Retail was $745.

MODEL 116 — 12, 16, or 20 ga., 27-30 in. barrels, any choke, hand detachable H&H sidelocks, double triggers, engraved, select checkered walnut pistol grip stock. Disc. 1985.

	$1,000	$845	$795	$750	$675	$600	$500

Last Mfg.'s Sug. Retail was $1,125.

MODEL 117 — 10, 12, 16 or 20 ga., 3 in. chambers, 26-30 in. barrels, any choke, hand detachable H&H sidelocks, ejectors, SST, engraved, select checkered walnut pistol grip stock. Disc. 1986.

	$835	$715	$660	$620	$585	$545	$500

Last Mfg.'s Sug. Retail was $1,075.

QUAIL UNLIMITED MODEL 117 — 12 ga. only, 26 in. barrels choked IC/M with 3 in. chambers, upgraded wood and checkering, high gloss bluing, gold colored ST, engraved by Baron Technologies in PA, only 42 mfg. for Quail Unlimited of North America.

	$1,650	$1,400	$1,150	$975	$875	$800	$725

This model had a retail price of $1,700 but was made available to Quail Unlimited members for approx. $1,200.

MODEL 210 — 12 or 16 ga., boxlock, exposed hammers, double triggers, plain walnut, light engraving. Disc. 1985.

	$795	$675	$550	$475	$435	$395	$350

Last Mfg.'s Sug. Retail was $900.

711 BOXLOCK — 12 ga. only, boxlock, selective trigger, ejectors, vent. rib. Disc. 1984.

	$880	$680	$575	$490	$445	$395	$350

▲ **711 Sidelock** — sidelock action. Mfg. 1985 only.

	$995	$850	$775	$695	$625	$550	$475

Last Mfg.'s Sug. Retail was $1,250.

ABADIE

Maker: Several Belgian makers for Portuguese Military.

MODEL 1878 (OFFICER'S MODEL) — 9.1mm, solid frame revolver, 6 shot, ejector rod, officer's issue A.

	$220	$195	$165	$130	$120	$110	$100

MODEL 1886 (TROOPER'S MODEL) — similar to 1878, but larger, trooper issue A.

	$195	$175	$160	$120	$110	$100	$90

ABBEY, GEORGE T.

Utica, NY from 1845-1852. Chicago, IL from 1852-1874. Percussion and breechloading firearms.

100%	98%	95%	90%	80%	70%	60%	50%	40%	30%	20%	10%

PERCUSSION RIFLE

▲ *.44 cal.* — 32 in. octagon barrel.

100%	98%	95%	90%	80%	70%	60%	50%	40%	30%	20%	10%
$605	$550	$470	$415	$370	$340	$305	$275	$250	$220	$195	$165

▲ *.44 cal.* — octagon barrel, brass trimmed.

$770	$735	$695	$605	$550	$485	$450	$405	$365	$330	$275	$220

▲ *.44 cal.* — 31 in. double barrel.

$1,210	$1,100	$880	$770	$715	$650	$595	$550	$515	$475	$430	$360

▲ *.44 cal.* — double barrel O/U, brass trimmed.

$1,485	$1,295	$1,130	$990	$910	$855	$770	$715	$660	$605	$495	$330

ABBEY, F.J. & COMPANY

Chicago, IL, 1858-1878. Muzzle and breechloading shotguns and rifles.

PERCUSSION RIFLE — several variations.

$605	$550	$470	$415	$360	$305	$275	$250	$210	$175	$145	$110

PERCUSSION SHOTGUN — several variations.

$800	$715	$635	$550	$470	$415	$360	$320	$285	$250	$210	$155

ABBIATICO & SALVINELLI (FAMARS)

Manufacturer located in Gardone, Italy. Currently imported in North America by Novagun Corp. located in Phoenix, AZ. Distributed by Southwest Shooters Supply located in Phoenix, AZ.

A & S Famars manufactures some of the world's finest rifles and shotguns - only 50-60 are fabricated yearly. Values listed below are for base models with no extra embellishments or special orders. Because every A & S Famars longarm is an individual custom order, each Famars firearm must have its value ascertained on an individual appraisal basis.

Grading	100%	98%	95%	90%	80%	70%	60%

RIFLES: SxS CUSTOM MANUFACTURE

Boxlock and sidelock rifles are all best quality and range in calibers between .22 LR and .600 Nitro Express. Each gun is manufactured per individual customer special order, and values below reflect base model pricing with no additional special order features (most models can be ordered with 6 levels of engraving/ornamentation). Further information and price quotations are available by contacting the above listed distributor directly.

AFRICA EXPRESS

Mfg.'s Sug. Retail	$19,600	$18,750	$15,650	$12,000	$10,000	$8,750	$7,500	$6,250

VENUS EXPRESS PROFESSIONAL

Please contact the distributor for pricing on this model.

ROYALE DH EXPRESS SIDELOCK

Mfg.'s Sug. Retail	$36,800	$33,750	$29,500	$26,000	$22,750	$19,000	$15,750	$12,000

VENUS EXPRESS EXTRALUSSO — top-of-the-line model.

Prices are quoted per individual order.

SHOTGUNS: CUSTOM MANUFACTURE

HAMMER SHOTGUN — double barrel, SxS only, hammers, double triggers, various gauges.

Mfg.'s Sug. Retail	$19,600	$18,750	$11,750	$9,250	$8,800	$6,500	$5,500	$4,500

Grading	100%	98%	95%	90%	80%	70%	60%

BOXLOCK SHOTGUNS — SxS only, available with Anson-Deeley boxlock action, scalloped or rounded frame, various engraving patterns available.

▲ **Zeus** — 12 or 20 ga., features round action.

Mfg.'s Sug. Retail	$16,000	$14,950	$11,000	$8,950	$7,500	$6,250	$5,000	$4,750

▲ **Tribute** — 12, 20, 28, or .410 ga., scalloped back drop lock action.

Mfg.'s Sug. Retail	$18,400	$17,500	$12,600	$9,500	$8,250	$6,750	$5,750	$5,000

SxS SIDELOCK SHOTGUNS

▲ **Highline** — round body, back action.

Mfg.'s Sug. Retail	$19,600	$18,750	$15,650	$12,000	$10,000	$8,750	$7,500	$6,250

▲ **Venus** — bar action.

  Please contact the distributor for pricing on this model.

▲ **Venere** — royal back action.

Mfg.'s Sug. Retail	$22,100	$21,000	$18,000	$15,000	$12,000	$10,000	$8,500	$7,250

▲ **Royale DH** — 12, 20, 28, or .410 ga., bar action.

Mfg.'s Sug. Retail	$29,600	$27,750	$22,000	$18,000	$15,000	$12,000	$10,000	$8,500

O/U SIDELOCK SHOTGUNS

▲ **Jorema** — 12 or 20 ga.

  Please contact the distributor for pricing on this model.

▲ **Jorema Royal**

  Please contact the distributor for pricing on this model.

▲ **Royale DH** — 12, 20, 28, or .410 ga., bar action.

Mfg.'s Sug. Retail	$30,600	$28,000	$22,250	$18,500	$15,500	$12,000	$10,000	$8,500

O/U COMPETITION SHOTGUNS

▲ **RX (Excalibur)** — detachable plate lock.

Mfg.'s Sug. Retail	$7,850	$7,375	$6,650	$5,800	$4,950	$4,250	$3,600	$2,950

▲ **SX (Excalibur)** — detachable sidelocks.

Mfg.'s Sug. Retail	$13,250	$12,250	$10,000	$8,750	$7,250	$5,750	$4,950	$4,400

4-BARREL SHOTGUN

▲ **Rombo Quattrocanne** — .410 ga. only, barrels are arranged in a diamond pattern.

Mfg.'s Sug. Retail	$36,800	$33,750	$29,500	$26,000	$22,750	$19,000	$15,750	$12,000

ACCU-MATCH INTERNATIONAL INC.

Handgun and pistol parts manufacturer located in Mesa, AZ since 1995. Direct sales only.

ACCU-MATCH PISTOL — .45 ACP cal., patterned after the Colt Govt. 1911, competition pistol features stainless steel construction with 5 ½ in. match grade barrel with 3 ports, recoil reduction system, 8 shot mag., 3 dot sight system. New 1996.

Mfg.'s Sug. Retail	$840	$800	$700	$625	$550	$450	$375	$325

ACCU-TEK

Manufacturer located in Chino, CA. Distributor sales only.

Grading	100%	98%	95%	90%	80%	70%	60%

PISTOLS: SEMI-AUTO

MODEL AT-25 — .25 ACP cal., single action, 2½ in. barrel, 7 shot mag. with finger extension, similar design to AT-32, stainless steel, aluminum, or alloy construction with choice of stainless, satin aluminum, or black finish, 11 (Model AT-25AL) or 18 (Model AT-25B, disc.) oz. Mfg. 1992-95.

	$150	$125	$105	$90	$80	$70	$60

Last Mfg.'s Sug. Retail was $182.

Add $5 for satin aluminum (Model AT-25AL) or black (Model AT-25SSB, disc.) finish.

MODEL AT-32SS — .32 ACP cal., single action design, 2½ in. barrel, 5 shot mag. with finger extension, alloy (disc. 1991) or stainless steel (new 1992) construction, manual hand safety with firing pin block and trigger disconnect, side mag. release, exposed hammer, satin aluminum finish (disc. 1991), 16 oz. Mfg. in U.S. New 1990.

Mfg.'s Sug. Retail	$176	$150	$125	$110	$95	$80	$70	$60

Add $5 for black finish (Model AT-32SSB).

MODEL AT-380SS — .380 ACP cal., similar to Model AT-32, except has 2¾ in. barrel, alloy (disc. 1991) or stainless steel construction, 20 oz. New 1990.

Mfg.'s Sug. Retail	$182	$155	$135	$115	$100	$90	$80	$70

Add $5 for black finish (Model AT-380SSB).

MODEL HC-380SS — .380 ACP cal., single action semi-auto, 2½ in. barrel, 10 (C/B 1994) or 13* shot mag., manual safety with firing pin block and trigger disconnect, exposed hammer. New 1993.

Mfg.'s Sug. Retail	$230	$195	$150	$115

Add $5 for black finish (Model HC-380B, new 1995).

MODEL AT-9SS — 9mm Para. cal., double action only, 3.2 in. barrel, 8 shot mag., firing pin block with no external safeties, black or brushed stainless finish, 3 dot sights adj. for windage, 28 oz. New 1995.

Mfg.'s Sug. Retail	$317	$260	$205	$165

MODEL AT-40SS — .40 S&W cal., double action only, 3.2 in. barrel, 7 shot mag., firing pin block with no external safeties, black or brushed stainless finish, 3 dot sights adj. for windage, 28 oz. New 1995.

Mfg.'s Sug. Retail	$317	$260	$205	$165

MODEL AT-45SS — .45 ACP cal., similar to Model AT-40SS, except has 6 shot mag., stainless only, 28 oz. New 1996.

Mfg.'s Sug. Retail	$327	$265	$210	$165

ACCURACY INTERNATIONAL LTD.

Rifle manufacturer located in Hampshire, England in 1982. Distributed in the U.S. by Gunsite Training Center located in Paulden, AZ.

RIFLES: BOLT ACTION

AW MODEL — .308 Win. cal., precision bolt action featuring 26 in. 1:12 twisting stainless steel barrel with muzzle brake, 3 lug bolt, 10 shot detachable mag., synthetic thumbhole adj. stock, Parker-Hale bipod, 14 lbs. Importation began 1995.

Mfg.'s Sug. Retail	$3,295	$3,295	$2,750	$2,300	$2,000	$1,700	$1,500	$1,300

AWP MODEL — similar to AW Model, except has 24 in. barrel w/o muzzle brake, 15 lbs. Importation began 1995.

Mfg.'s Sug. Retail	$3,295	$3,295	$2,750	$2,300	$2,000	$1,700	$1,500	$1,300

Grading	100%	98%	95%	90%	80%	70%	60%

SM MODEL (SUPER MAGNUM) — .300 Win. Mag. or .338 Lapua cal., 6 lug bolt, 26 or 27 in. 1:9/1:10 twist stainless steel barrel with muzzle brake, Parker-Hale bipod, 5 shot mag., 15 ½ lbs. Importation began 1995.

Mfg.'s Sug. Retail	$3,495	$3,495	$2,875	$2,400	$2,050	$1,750	$1,550	$1,350

ACHA

Maker: Domingo Acha, Spain.

MODEL 1916 — semi-auto pistol, 7.76mm, 7 shot mag., 1903 Browning copy.

$220	$165	$100	$85	$65	$55	$45

ATLAS — semi-auto pistol, 6.35mm, 6 shot mag., slide marked ATLAS, 1906 Browning copy.

$165	$140	$125	$95	$75	$65	$50

LOOKING GLASS — semi-auto pistol, 6.35mm, 6 shot mag., blued or nickel, 1906 Browning copy, slide marked "Looking Glass", many variations.

$220	$165	$130	$100	$85	$70	$55

LOOKING GLASS — semi-auto pistol, 7.65mm, exposed hammer.

$220	$165	$140	$105	$90	$75	$65

ACME

Trade name of Davenport Arms Company Shotguns, Maltby Henley & Co. Revolvers, and Merwin Hulbert & Co. Owl Head Revolvers.

100%	98%	95%	90%	80%	70%	60%	50%	40%	30%	20%	10%

SEVEN SHOT REVOLVER — single action, .22 Short rimfire.

$360	$310	$240	$185	$165	$150	$120	$110	$100	$90	$65	$55

FIVE SHOT REVOLVER — single action, .32 Short rimfire.

$360	$320	$255	$200	$175	$160	$120	$110	$100	$90	$65	$55

ACME ARMS

Trade name for Cornwall Hardware Co., NY.

REVOLVERS

SEVEN SHOT — single action, .22 Short rimfire.

$275	$250	$210	$185	$165	$155	$140	$125	$110	$90	$85	$75

FIVE SHOT — single action, .32 Short rimfire.

$285	$255	$215	$195	$175	$165	$145	$120	$100	$90	$85	$75

SHOTGUN

SIDE-BY-SIDE — 12 ga., damascus barrel.

$275	$240	$195	$165	$145	$125	$110	$95	$65	$60	$50	$45

ACME HAMMERLESS

Maker: Hopkins & Allen, for Hulbert Brothers, 1893.

100%	98%	95%	90%	80%	70%	60%	50%	40%	30%	20%	10%

REVOLVERS

FIVE SHOT — double action, top break, .32 centerfire, non-ejecting.

$145	$125	$100	$90	$80	$70	$60	$50	$40	$30	$20	$15

Also known as Forehand Model 1891, can be hammer or hammerless.

FIVE SHOT — double action, top break, .38 centerfire, non-ejecting.

$145	$125	$100	$90	$80	$70	$60	$50	$40	$30	$20	$15

Also known as Forehand Model 1891, can be hammer or hammerless.

ACTION (M.S.)

Maker: Modesto Santos, Eibar, Spain.

Grading	100%	98%	95%	90%	80%	70%	60%

MODEL 1915 — semi-auto pistol (French Military), 7.65mm.

	$175	$145	$120	$85	$70	$60	$45

MODEL 1920 — semi-auto pistol (action), 6.35mm.

	$195	$150	$110	$85	$65	$45	$40

ACTION ARMS LTD.

Previous firearms importer and distributor until 1994. Action Arms is currently concentrating more on optics. Located in Philadelphia, PA.

Only Action Arms Models AT84S, AT88S, and the Model B Sporter will be listed under this heading. Galil, Timberwolf, and Uzi trademarks can be located in their respective sections.

CARBINES

MODEL B SPORTER — 9mm Para., patterned after the original Uzi Model B Sporter, 16.1 in. barrel, closed breech, thumbhole stock with recoil pad, 10 shot mag., adj. rear sight, 8.8 lbs. Limited importation from China 1994 only.

	$545	$475	$435	$385	$335	$295	$275

Last Mfg.'s Sug. Retail was $595.

PISTOLS

AT-84S — 9mm Para., selective double action design, patterned after the CZ-75, 4.8 in. barrel, 15 shot mag., originally introduced in 1985.

	$470	$415	$385	$360	$330	$275	$220

The AT-84S Series was mfg. in Switzerland by Industrial Technology & Machines A.G. and was sold by Action Arms between June of 1987 and 1989. Serial number range is 01201-06000. No P or H models were ever mfg. in this series (2 or 3 prototypes only).

AT-88S — 9mm or .41 Action Express (available early 1990) cal., selective double action design patterned after CZ-75, 4.8 in. barrel, 15 shot (9mm) or 10 shot (.41 AE) mag., can be "cocked and locked", fixed sights, blued metal, walnut grips, 35.3 oz. Introduced in 1987 with limited production samples being imported in 1989.

	$500	$450	$395	$360	$330	$275	$220

A very small quantity of AT-88Ss (various configurations) was made by I.T.M. of Switzerland and finishes included all blue, all chrome, or 2-tone. These pistols may exhibit both I.T.M. and A.A.L. markings. More recent manufacture was performed by Sphinx-Muller of Switzerland. These pistols are still mfg. by Sphinx-Muller, renamed the AT-2000 Series and imported by Sile Distributors.

RIFLES

TIMBERWOLF — see separate listing in T section.

ADAMS

Maker: Deane, Adams, & Deane, located in London, England.

100%	98%	95%	90%	80%	70%	60%	50%	40%	30%	20%	10%

PERCUSSION REVOLVERS

MODEL 1851 — double action, .38 cal., 4½ in. barrel.

100%	98%	95%	90%	80%	70%	60%	50%	40%	30%	20%	10%
$1,375	$1,265	$1,100	$990	$855	$745	$690	$605	$550	$440	$385	$330

MODEL 1851 — double action, .44 cal., 6 in. barrel.

$935	$880	$800	$690	$550	$495	$440	$395	$340	$305	$275	$255

MODEL 1851 — Dragoon, double action, .50 cal., 8 in. barrel.

$1,375	$1,265	$1,100	$990	$855	$715	$690	$605	$550	$385	$360	$340

MODEL 1851 — .38 cal., cased with accessories.

$1,760	$1,595	$1,375	$1,100	$990	$910	$825	$745	$660	$605	$550	$525

MODEL 1851 — .44 cal., cased with accessories.

$1,295	$1,155	$990	$880	$770	$690	$635	$550	$440	$385	$360	$330

MODEL 1851 — Dragoon, .50 cal., cased with accessories.

$1,680	$1,485	$1,210	$1,185	$990	$880	$800	$715	$635	$550	$495	$470

ADAMS, JOSEPH

Birmingham, England.

OFFICER MODEL — flintlock pistol, musket caliber .65, Brown Bess.

$2,850	$2,500	$2,250	$2,000	$1,800	$1,600	$1,400	$1,100	$900	$825	$725	$600

ADAMY, GEBRUDER

Suhl, Germany, 1920s and 1930s.

Grading	100%	98%	95%	90%	80%	70%	60%

SHOTGUN — O/U, double trigger, engraved, cased.

100%	98%	95%	90%	80%	70%	60%
$1,815	$1,650	$1,375	$1,155	$990	$880	$770

ADIRONDACK ARMS COMPANY

Plattsburgh, NY, 1870-1874.

Magazine loaded repeating rifle, .44 cal., brass or iron frame, later model, may also be marked A.S. Babbitt, Plattsburgh, N.Y., absorbed by Winchester in 1874, then disc.

This rifle was designed in 1870 and patented by Orvill M. Robinson in Upper Jay, NY. It was available in .38 and .44 cal. rimfire rifles without a wooden forend and had a high cyclic rate of fire. Original models were made in Plattsburgh, NY, at which time A.S. Babbitt became one of several additional partners. In 1872, Robinson was granted a patent for a second model rifle. It was similar to the 1870, except a wooden forend was added and the operating mechanism was changed considerably. Following these improvements, Mr. Oliver Winchester contacted Mr. Robinson and purchased the entire Robinson company, discontinuing manufacture.

100%	98%	95%	90%	80%	70%	60%	50%	40%	30%	20%	10%

EARLY MODEL — finger holds on hammer.

100%	98%	95%	90%	80%	70%	60%	50%	40%	30%	20%	10%
$2,400	$2,100	$1,750	$1,450	$1,325	$1,200	$1,075	$975	$875	$775	$675	$600

LATE MODEL — action worked by buttons top of receiver mid-section.

100%	98%	95%	90%	80%	70%	60%	50%	40%	30%	20%	10%
$2,200	$1,950	$1,675	$1,300	$1,200	$1,100	$975	$875	$775	$675	$550	$495

ADLER

Maker: Engelbrecht & Wolff located in Blasii, Germany, 1905-1907.

Grading	100%	98%	95%	90%	80%	70%	60%

SEMI-AUTO PISTOL — 7mm Adler, 8 shot mag., cocking lever on top of frame, not competitive in its price range.

100%	98%	95%	90%	80%	70%	60%
$2,200	$1,925	$1,540	$1,045	$770	$495	$330

ADVANTAGE ARMS USA, INC.

Previous manufacturer located in St. Paul, MN. Advantage Arms USA, Inc. was distributed by Wildfire Sports, Inc. also located in St. Paul.

MODEL 422 — .22 LR and Mag., 4 barrel double action derringer, rotating firing pin, this model is patterned after the Mossberg "Brownie", 2½ in. barrel, high grade alloy frame and barrel, 4 shot, available in blue, nickel, or QPQ (heat treated but appears blued) finish, 15 oz. Mfg. 1986-87 only.

$150	$135	$115	$105	$95	$85	$75

Last Mfg.'s Sug. Retail was $166.

Add $10 for .22 Mag. cal.
Add $6 for nickel finish.
Add $11 for QPQ finish.

AETNA

Previously manufactured by Harrington & Richardson located in Worchester, MA.

Type: single action revolvers, all of the same general size and configuration, solid frame, spur trigger, so called "Suicide Specials" during their day.

100%	98%	95%	90%	80%	70%	60%	50%	40%	30%	20%	10%

AETNA NO. 2 — .32 rimfire, 5 shot.

100%	98%	95%	90%	80%	70%	60%	50%	40%	30%	20%	10%
$330	$275	$215	$185	$170	$155	$145	$120	$100	$85	$75	$55

AETNA NO. 2½ — .32 rimfire, 5 shot.

$330	$275	$215	$185	$170	$155	$145	$120	$100	$85	$75	$55

MODEL 1876 — .22 rimfire, 7 shot.

$330	$275	$210	$195	$175	$165	$155	$130	$110	$95	$90	$65

MODEL 1876 — .32 rimfire, 5 shot.

$330	$275	$210	$175	$165	$155	$145	$120	$105	$90	$75	$55

MODEL 1876 — .38 rimfire, 5 shot.

$330	$275	$220	$205	$195	$175	$165	$145	$120	$105	$95	$85

AETNA ARMS COMPANY

Manufacturer located in New York, 1869-1883.

Single action pocket revolver, blued or nickel, birdshead grip, copy of S&W models 1-3, models marked ALLING are worth a slight premium.

100%	98%	95%	90%	80%	70%	60%	50%	40%	30%	20%	10%

SEVEN SHOT — .22 rimfire.

| $250 | $235 | $210 | $195 | $175 | $165 | $155 | $130 | $110 | $95 | $90 | $65 |

FIVE SHOT — .32 rimfire.

| $230 | $220 | $205 | $175 | $165 | $155 | $145 | $120 | $105 | $90 | $75 | $55 |

AGNER

Manufactured by Saxhoj Products Inc. in Denmark. Imported until 1986 by Beeman Arms, Inc. located in Santa Rosa, CA.

Grading			100%	98%	95%	90%	80%	70%	60%

PISTOL: SEMI-AUTO

MODEL M 80 — .22 LR only, stainless steel, semi-auto target pistol, new design features unique security key safety feature, adj. French walnut grips, dry fire mechanism, 5.9 in. barrel, 5 shot mag., limited production, 2.4 lbs. Imported 1981-1986.

| | | | $1,125 | $1,040 | $950 | | | | |

Last Mfg.'s Sug. Retail was $1,295.

Add $100 for left-hand action.

AIR MATCH

Previously imported by Kendall International, located in Paris, KY.

AIR MATCH 500 — .22 cal. match single shot pistol, target grips, adj. front counterweight, 10½ in. barrel. Imported 1984-86.

| | | | $550 | $495 | $450 | $425 | $395 | $360 | $330 |

Last Mfg.'s Sug. Retail was $788.

AJAX ARMY

Distributed by E.C. Meacham Co., maker unknown, circa 1880s.

100%	98%	95%	90%	80%	70%	60%	50%	40%	30%	20%	10%

SINGLE ACTION — .44 rimfire, spur trigger, solid frame.

| $550 | $440 | $360 | $315 | $275 | $255 | $230 | $210 | $185 | $170 | $155 | $140 |

AKRILL, E.

French, circa mid-1800.

FLINTLOCK RIFLE — breech loaded, .69 cal., damascus octagon barrel.

| $3,300 | $2,750 | $2,200 | $1,980 | $1,460 | $1,320 | $1,240 | $1,075 | $935 | $800 | $745 | $660 |

ALAMO RANGER

Grading			100%	98%	95%	90%	80%	70%	60%

REVOLVER — .38 cal., Spanish copy of Colt Model 1929.

| | | | $140 | $120 | $110 | $100 | $90 | $85 | $75 |

ALASKA

Maker: Hood Firearms Company, Norwich, CT, 1873-1884.

Dubbed "Suicide Specials" in their day.

100%	98%	95%	90%	80%	70%	60%	50%	40%	30%	20%	10%

REVOLVERS

SINGLE ACTION — .22 rimfire, 7 shot, spur trigger, solid frame.

$275	$220	$195	$145	$140	$125	$110	$100	$90	$75	$70	$65

FIVE SHOT — .32 Short rimfire.

$220	$195	$160	$155	$150	$140	$125	$105	$95	$85	$75	$70

ALASKAN COMMEMORATIVES

The following is a complete chronological listing of special and limited editions manufactured for the state of Alaska.

Grading	100%	Issue Price	Qty. Made

1967 ALASKAN PURCHASE CENTENNIAL WINCHESTER 94 CARBINE — see listing under Winchester Commemoratives.

1967 ALASKA PURCHASE CENTENNIAL CONTENDER — Thompson Contender with 2 barrels chambered for .22 Hornet and .357 Mag., Ser. no. C0001.

Issue price is unknown and rarity precludes accurate secondary market pricing.

1976 ALASKA PIPELINE COMMEMORATIVE — Colt SAA in .45 cal., cased with Kershaw knife.

	$1,495	$800	801

1981 ALASKA STATE TROOPER 40TH ANNIVERSARY — Smith & Wesson Model 19-5, .357 Mag., 4 in. barrel, cased with belt buckle and patch.

	$850	$500	250

1984 STATE OF ALASKA SILVER ANNIVERSARY EDITION — Smith & Wesson Model 29-3, .44 Mag., 6 in. barrel, cased with bronze brown bear and ivory grips with scrimshaw AK state seal and silver engraving.

	$12,250	$10,000	10

1984 ALASKA SILVER ANNIVERSARY — Smith & Wesson Model 29-3, .44 Mag., 6 in. barrel, cased with gold engraving.

	$1,500	$1,195	300

1984 ALASKA STATEHOOD 25TH ANNIVERSARY — Winchester Model 70XTR, .338 Win. Mag. cal., sterling silver engraving.

	$1,100	$1,080	500

1984 ALASKA 25TH ANNIVERSARY — Colt Python, .357 Mag., 6 in. barrel, engraved brown bear with gold lettering and numbers, cased.

	$1,000	$500	200

1988 IDITAROD "1 OF 1,000" — Smith & Wesson Model 629-1, .44 Mag., 6 in. barrel, cased with laser-etched box, while a thousand were planned, only 500 were mfg.

	$995	$775	500

1988 ALASKA SERIES "TOKLAT" SPECIAL — LAR mfg. Grizzly Mag., .45 Win. Mag., mfg. for Great Northern Guns in Anchorage, AK, cased with plaque.

	$1,800	$1,195	20

1990 ALASKA "GUIDE" SERIES — Freedom Arms, .454 Casull, mfg. for Great Northern Guns in Anchorage, AK, 5½ in. barrel, Custom Field Grade, engraved handle.

	$1,900	$1,300	25

Grading	100%	Issue Price	Qty. Made

1991 ALASKA "MASTER GUIDE" SERIES — Freedom Arms, .454 Casull, mfg. for Great Northern Guns in Anchorage, AK, 5½ in. barrel, Custom Premier Grade, engraved handle.

	$2,200	$1,600	26

ALDAZABAL

Maker: Aldazabal, Leturiondo & Cia.

Grading	100%	98%	95%	90%	80%	70%	60%

SEMI-AUTOMATIC PISTOL — 7.65mm, 7 shot, Eibar style.

	$195	$165	$110	$100	$90	$75	$65

ALERT

Maker: Hood Firearms Company, Norwich, CT, 1873-1881.

These revolvers were dubbed "Suicide Specials" in their day.

100%	98%	95%	90%	80%	70%	60%	50%	40%	30%	20%	10%

REVOLVERS

SINGLE ACTION — .22 rimfire, 7 shot, spur trigger, solid frame.

$220	$195	$165	$145	$130	$125	$110	$100	$90	$75	$70	$65

FIVE SHOT — .32 Short rimfire.

$170	$165	$160	$155	$150	$140	$125	$105	$95	$85	$75	$70

ALESSANDRI, LOU, AND SON

Custom rifle manufacturer located in Rehoboth, MA since 1975.

Lou Alessandri and Son are noted for their top-quality custom rifles (bolt action and side-by-side). All guns are custom built per individual specifications and a wide variety of special order options are available. In addition to building custom rifles, Lou Alessandri and Son also offer a complete line of high-quality cleaning kits and related accessories. For more information regarding both the custom firearms and accessories, please contact this company directly (see Trademark Index).

ALEXIA

Maker: Hopkins & Allen, Norwich, CT, 1867-1915.

Also known as: Blue Jacket, Captain Jack, Chichester, Defender, Dictator, Monarch, Mountain Eagle, Hopkins & Allen, Towers Police Safety, and Universal.

REVOLVERS

The revolvers listed below are single action design, solid frame, spur trigger - they were an inexpensive vest pocket pistol issued under numerous names for private companies, octagon barrel.

.22 RIMFIRE — 7 shot.

$165	$160	$155	$145	$130	$125	$110	$100	$90	$75	$70	$65

.32 SHORT RIMFIRE — 5 shot.

$170	$165	$160	$155	$150	$140	$125	$105	$95	$85	$75	$70

SINGLE ACTION .38 SHORT RIMFIRE — 5 shot.

$195	$180	$170	$165	$160	$145	$140	$120	$110	$100	$90	$85

A

100%	98%	95%	90%	80%	70%	60%	50%	40%	30%	20%	10%

.41 SHORT RIMFIRE — 5 shot.

100%	98%	95%	90%	80%	70%	60%	50%	40%	30%	20%	10%
$220	$210	$205	$195	$180	$170	$160	$145	$125	$110	$100	$90

ALFA

Maker: Armero Especialistas Reunidas, located in Eibar, Spain, circa 1920.
All revolvers are marked Alfa on grips.

Grading	100%	98%	95%	90%	80%	70%	60%

EARLY MODEL — .32, .38, or .44 cal., copies of S&W No. 2 by O. Hermanos.

100%	98%	95%	90%	80%	70%	60%
$145	$130	$120	$110	$105	$95	$75

LATE MODEL — .22 LR, .32 S&W, or .38 S&W cal., copies of Colt Police Positive and S&W Military and Police.

100%	98%	95%	90%	80%	70%	60%
$160	$150	$130	$120	$110	$100	$90

ALKARTASUNA FABRICA DE ARMAS, S.A.

Manufacturer located in Guernica, Spain.

ALKARTASUNA CARTRIDGE COUNTER — 6.35mm, 7 shot, left grip panel cartridge counter, loaded indicator, grip safety.

100%	98%	95%	90%	80%	70%	60%
$375	$325	$275	$225	$175	$150	$125

ALKARTASUNA RUBY AUTOMATIC — 7.65mm, 9 shot, $3\frac{5}{8}$ in. barrel, blue, fixed sights, checkered wood or hard rubber grips, used by French Army in WWI and WWII. Mfg. 1917-1922.

100%	98%	95%	90%	80%	70%	60%
$265	$195	$165	$110	$65	$55	$45

ALLEN & THURBER

Ethan Allen started many plants to keep up with expanding business after 1832. Listed below is a chronological order of the firms constituting the family dynasty founded by Ethan Allen.

> E. Allen — Grafton, Mass. 1832-1837
> Allen & Thurber — Grafton, Mass. 1837-1842
> Allen & Thurber — Norwich, Conn. 1842-1847
> Allen & Thurber — Worcester, Mass. 1847-1854
> Allen, Thurber, & Co. — Worcester, Mass. 1854-1856
> Allen & Wheelock — Worcester, Mass. 1856-1865
> E. Allen & Co. — Worcester, Mass. 1865-1871
> Forehand & Wadsworth — Worcester, Mass. 1871-1890
> Forehand Arms Co. — Worcester, Mass. 1890-1902

No other 19th century American firm produced a wider variety of firearms than did Ethan Allen & subsidiaries.

ALLEN FIREARMS

Previous importer located in Santa Fe, NM importing A. Uberti Firearms until early in 1987. After Allen Firearms closed, Cimarron F.A. Mfg. Co. located in Houston, TX purchased the remaining inventory (in addition to ordering new products under their name).

Allen Firearms was formerly called Western Arms and manufactured both modern and black powder reproduction firearms and accessories patterned after famous older models. Only modern cartridge guns will be shown in this section. Black powder guns will appear under Modern Black Powder Guns.

Rather than provide a complete listing of Allen Firearms models, the following rules usually apply. Since Allen Firearms imported A. Uberti firearms, the Uberti section in this text should be referenced

Grading	100%	98%	95%	90%	80%	70%	60%

for current values regarding models with similar configurations. Collectibility to date has been limited on most Allen Fireams models, and as a rule, up-to-date values on this trademark are established by current importation prices of Uberti firearms. A complete listing of older Allen Firearms models can be found in Blue Book editions Eleven and Twelve. The models listed below are provided since Uberti is not currently manufacturing them.

SHARPS/GEMMER SPORTING RIFLE — .45-70 cal. only, copy of the famous Sharps rifle. Introduced 1985.

	$575	$515	$430	$375	$320	$295	$270

Last Mfg.'s Sug. Retail was $599.

1979 JUSTIN CENTENNIAL COMMEMORATIVE — includes specially engraved 1866 sporting rifle and 1873 single action revolver (7½ in. barrel) with gold plated parts and inlay. Both guns are chambered for .44-40 cal. Also includes special hand signed pair of Justin boots, serial numbered belt buckle and presentation oak case. All serial numbers are matching.

Grading	100%	Issue Price	Qty. Made

MODEL 1873 1 of 1,000 — .44-40 cal, special wood, only 1,000 manufactured. Disc. 1985.

Grading	100%	Issue Price	Qty. Made
	$1,350	$1,500	1,000

ALPHA ARMS INC.

Previous manufacturer located in Flower Mound, TX from 1983-87.

Retail price included custom hard case.

Grading	100%	98%	95%	90%	80%	70%	60%

RIFLES: BOLT ACTION

Many special order options including an octagonal barrel, various finishes, and special sights were available at extra cost on the models listed below. These options, while not listed separately by price, will add value to the prices shown below.

ALPHA JAGUAR — available in most calibers from .222 Rem. through .338 Win., Mauser-type barreled action, Alphawood laminate stock, 20 to 24 in. barrel lengths, approx. 6 lbs. Disc. 1987.

▲ *Grade I Jaguar* — slide safety, supplied with luggage case.

	$900	$800	$700	$625	$560	$500	$425

Last Mfg.'s Sug. Retail was $995.

▲ *Grade II Jaguar* — similar to Grade I Jaguar, except has Douglas premium barrel.

	$995	$900	$800	$700	$625	$560	$500

Last Mfg.'s Sug. Retail was $1,095.

▲ *Grade III Jaguar* — similar to Grade II Jaguar, except has Model 70-type 3-position safety, honed trigger and action.

	$1,125	$995	$900	$800	$700	$625	$560

Last Mfg.'s Sug. Retail was $1,395.

▲ *Grade IV Jaguar* — similar to Grade III Jaguar, except has fully lightened action and installed swivel studs.

	$1,250	$1,050	$930	$825	$725	$640	$560

Last Mfg.'s Sug. Retail was $1,595.

ALPHA CUSTOM — available in most calibers from .222 Rem. through .338-284, many other calibers available on special order, 20 to 24 in. barrel lengths, limited production, right or left-hand, approx. 6 lbs. Mfg. 1984-1987.

	$1,525	$1,200	$975	$850	$725	$640	$560

Last Mfg.'s Sug. Retail was $1,735.

A

Grading	100%	98%	95%	90%	80%	70%	60%

ALPHA GRAND SLAM — same general specifications as the Alpha Custom, except comes standard with laminated wood stock, fluted bolt and non-glare matte finished metal parts, right or left-hand, approx., 6½ lbs. Mfg. 1985-1987.

	$1,200	$950	$875	$750	$650	$600	$525

Last Mfg.'s Sug. Retail was $1,465.

ALPHA ALASKAN — .308 Win., .350 Rem. Mag., .358 Win., or .458 Win. cal. Action is similar to Alpha Grand Slam, except barrel, receiver, bolt and safety are stainless steel, right or left-hand, approx. 6¾ - 7½ lbs. Mfg. 1985-1987.

	$1,525	$1,200	$975	$850	$725	$640	$560

Last Mfg.'s Sug. Retail was $1,735.

ALPHA BIG-FIVE — .300 H&H thru .375 H&H or .458 Win. cal., action is similar to Alpha Jaguar Grade IV, except has reinforced stock and decelerator recoil pad. Mfg. 1987 only.

	$1,575	$1,250	$1,050	$895	$750	$640	$560

Last Mfg.'s Sug. Retail was $1,795.

AMERICA REMEMBERS

An organization that privately commissions historical, limited/special editions in conjunction with various manufacturers.

America Remembers and its affiliates, the Armed Forces Commemorative Society, American Heroes and Legends, and the United States Society of Arms and Armor, issue limited edition firearms. America Remembers purchased the antique arms division of the U.S. Historical Society on April 1, 1994. Older U.S. HS firearms can be located in the U section of this text.

Grading	Most Recent Issue Price

HANDGUNS

While not specifically mentioned, the handguns listed below all have various degrees of ornamentation and other embellishments (including some inscriptions).

GENE AUTRY COWBOY EDITION SAA REVOLVER — .45 LC cal., 4¾ in. barrel, cased, 1,000 mfg.
$1,520

▲ *Gene Autry Premier Colt Edition* — .45 LC cal., Colt SAA, cased, 100 mfg.
$5,250

THE SEVENTH CAVALRY SAA TRIBUTE REVOLVER — .45 LC cal., includes buckle, cased, 500 mfg.
$1,650

JOHNNY CASH TEXAS PATERSON REVOLVER — .36 cal., cased, 1,000 mfg.
$1,500

MARINE WWII PACIFIC THEATER TRIBUTE PISTOL — .45 ACP cal., Colt mfg., includes brass medal, cased, 500 mfg.
$1,500

WWII GOLDEN ANNIVERSARY VICTORY TRIBUTE PISTOL — .45 ACP cal., Colt mfg., includes brass medal, cased, 500 mfg.
$1,575

PACIFIC NAVAL TRIBUTE PISTOL — .45 ACP cal., Auto-Ordnance mfg., includes brass medal, cased, 500 mfg.
$1,500

ARMY AIR FORCES TRIBUTE PISTOL — .45 ACP cal., Colt mfg., includes brass medal, cased, 500 mfg.
$1,500

A

Grading	Most Recent Issue Price

THE AMERICAN PATRIOT PISTOL — .45 ACP cal., Colt mfg., personalized slide, cased, unknown quantity.

$1,695

VIETNAM TRIBUTE PISTOL — .45 ACP cal., includes brass medal, cased, unknown quantity.
Working Model $995
Non-Working Model $325

THE CHUCK YEAGER TRIBUTE PISTOL — .45 ACP cal., Colt mfg., cased, 1,000 mfg.
$1,750

RIFLES

AMERICAN INDIAN TRIBUTE MODEL 94 — .45 LC cal., 16 in. carbine barrel, large loop lever style, 300 mfg. by Winchester.

$1,295

AMERICAN ARMS

Previous manufacturer located in Garden Grove, CA.

Grading	100%	98%	95%	90%	80%	70%	60%

EAGLE 380 — .380 ACP only, stainless steel semi-auto, copy of Walther PPK/S, 6 shot mag., $3\frac{1}{4}$ in. barrel, 20 oz.

			$295	$250	$215		

Last Mfg.'s Sug. Retail was $289.

Add $25 for black teflon finish (disc. 1985).

AMERICAN ARMS CO.

Manufacturer located in Boston, MA from 1870-1901 and Milwaukee, WI. from 1893-1904. American Arms Co. was acquired by Marlin in 1901.

100%	98%	95%	90%	80%	70%	60%	50%	40%	30%	20%	10%

HANDGUNS

O/U DESIGN — Wheeler Pat. Action, brass frame, spur trigger, .22 Short R.F., .32 Short R.F., .41 Short R.F.

$800	$750	$700	$650	$575	$500	$420	$360	$300	$225	$160	$110

SHOTGUNS

HAMMERLESS MODEL — 12 ga., semi-hammerless.

$600	$550	$500	$450	$350	$275	$225	$175	$150	$125	$100	$75

WHITMORE PATENT — 10 or 12 ga., hammerless, checkering, SxS. Add 10% for 10 ga. ($2\frac{7}{8}$ in. chambers).

$685	$625	$575	$520	$460	$400	$340	$270	$200	$150	$125	$100

SINGLESHOT — 12 ga., semi-hammerless, damascus barrel.

$260	$225	$200	$175	$150	$125	$90	$70	$50	$40	$30	$20

AMERICAN ARMS, INC.

Importer/manufacturer located in North Kansas City, MO. American Arms imports various Spanish shotguns (Grulla, Indesal, Lanber, Norica, and Zabala Hermanos), Italian shotguns including F. Stefano and Luigi Franchi, several European pistols and rifles, and exclusively imports Sites handguns (new

1990) mfg. in Torino, Italy. This company also manufactures several pistols in North Kansas City, MO. American Arms previously imported (1988-89 only) Norica Airguns that may be found under the Norica heading in the Modern Airguns section in the back of this publication.

American Arms also imports Franchi O/U and semi-auto shotguns which can be found under the Franchi listing in this text.

Grading	100%	98%	95%	90%	80%	70%	60%

PISTOLS

MODEL TT-9MM TOKAREV — 9mm Para., semi-auto single action, 4½ in. barrel, 9 shot mag., hammer block external safety, 31 oz. Imported 1988-89 only.

	$250	$230	$210	$195	$180	$170	$160

Last Mfg.'s Sug. Retail was $289.

This model is patterned after the Tokarev action and is made from machined steel parts in Yugoslavia.

MODEL EP-380 — .380 ACP, semi-auto double action, stainless steel, 3½ in. barrel, 7 shot mag., wood checkered grips, adj. rear sight, 25 oz. Imported 1988-90 only.

	$375	$325	$250

Last Mfg.'s Sug. Retail was $449.

This model was made in West Germany.

MODEL PK-22 CLASSIC — .22 LR, semi-auto double action, styled after Govt. .45 ACP, 3⅓ in. barrel, 8 shot finger extension mag., black polymer grips, 22 oz. New 1988.

Mfg.'s Sug. Retail	$199	$165	$140	$115	$100	$90	$80	$70

This model is made in North Kansas City, MO. It has patented safety features such as external hammer block and internal blocking of the firing pin until the trigger is pulled.

MODEL CX-22 CLASSIC — .22 LR, style patterned after Walther PPK, 3⅓ in. barrel, 8 shot finger extension mag., 22 oz. Mfg. 1990-95.

	$175	$145	$125	$110	$100	$90	$80

Last Mfg.'s Sug. Retail was $213.

This model was made in North Kansas City, MO. It has patented safety features such as external hammer block and internal blocking of the firing pin until the trigger is pulled.

▲ *CXC-22* — similar to CX-22 Classic, except has chrome slide. Mfg. in 1990 only.

	$170	$150	$125	$110	$100	$90	$80

Last Mfg.'s Sug. Retail was $189.

MODEL PX-22/25 CLASSIC — .22 LR or .25 ACP (mfg. 1991 only) cal., compact variation of the Model CX-22, 2¾ in. barrel, 7 shot finger extension mag., 15 oz. New 1989, PX-25 was mfg. 1991 only, PX-22 was disc. 1995.

	$175	$145	$125	$110	$100	$90	$80

Last Mfg.'s Sug. Retail was $206.

This model was made in North Kansas City, MO. It has patented safety features such as external hammer block and internal blocking of the firing pin until the trigger is pulled.

MODEL P-98 CLASSIC — .22 LR, semi-auto double action patterned after Walther P.38, 5 in. barrel, 8 shot mag., blue/black finish, grooved wraparound grips, 26 oz. New 1990.

Mfg.'s Sug. Retail	$209	$170	$145	$125	$110	$100	$90	$80

ESCORT — .380 ACP cal., double action only, 3⅜ in. barrel, 7 shot mag., unique thin profile, matte stainless steel, soft polymer grips, polygonal rifling, 19 oz. New 1995.

Mfg.'s Sug. Retail	$349	$285	$230	$200	$185	$170	$160	$150

SABRE — while this model was advertised, it was never mfg.

Grading	100%	98%	95%	90%	80%	70%	60%

SPECTRE — 9mm Para., .40 S&W (mfg. 1991 only), or .45 ACP (new 1993) cal., semi-auto double action, 6 in. barrel with polygonal rifling, 30 shot mag., ambidextrous safety, decocking lever, adj. sights, 4½ lbs., mfg. in Italy by Sites. Imported 1990-1993.

		$370	$325	$275	$240	$200	$185	$170

Last Mfg.'s Sug. Retail was $429.

> Add $28 for .45 ACP cal.
>
> This model was previously imported by F.I.E. located in Hialeah, FL (1989-1990).

AUSSIE SEMI-AUTO — 9mm Para. or .40 S&W cal., semi-auto double action, polymer frame with nickeled steel slide and 4 ¾ in. barrel, 10 shot mag., features 5 safeties, open slide after last shot, 23 oz. Importation from Spain began 1996.

Mfg.'s Sug. Retail	$425	$350	$250	$225	$200	$185	$170	$160

REVOLVERS: SAA

REGULATOR MODEL — .357 Mag., .44-40, or .45 LC cal., 4¾, 5½ (new 1993), or 7½ in. barrel, reproduction of the Colt Peacemaker, featuring brass trigger guard and back strap, fixed sights, half-cock and hammer block safeties, blade front, grooved rear sights, color case hardened frame, walnut grips 35 oz. Importation began 1992.

Mfg.'s Sug. Retail	$349	$290	$235	$200	$185	$170	$160	$150

> Add $50 for dual cylinder set (.44-40/.44 Spl. or .45 LC/.45 ACP).

▲ *Regulator Deluxe* — similar to Regulator Model, except .45 LC cal. only and has case hardened (pre-1993) or blued (post-1993) steel trigger guard and back strap. Importation disc. 1992, resumed 1994.

Mfg.'s Sug. Retail	$395	$320	$265	$210	$190	$170	$160	$150

> Add $30 for dual cylinder set (.44-40/.44 Spl. or .45 LC/.45 ACP). Disc. 1992.

▲ *Buckhorn* — .44 Mag cal., 4¾, 6, or 7½ in. barrel, otherwise similar to Regulator Model, 44 oz. Importation began 1993.

Mfg.'s Sug. Retail	$379	$305	$255	$205	$185	$170	$160	$150

> Add $10 for Target variation (flat top and adj. rear sight). Imported 1994 only.

UBERTI .454 SAA — .454 cal., 6 SR or 7 ½ in. top-ported barrel, hammer block safety, custom hardwood grips, wide trigger, adj. rear sight. Importation began 1996 from Italy.

Mfg.'s Sug. Retail	$869	$750	$625	$550	$495	$465	$435	$375

RIFLES

MODEL ZCY 308 — .308 cal., gas operated semi-auto AK-47 type action, Yugoslavian mfg. Imported 1988 only.

		$775	$650	$550	$450	$400	$375	$350

Last Mfg.'s Sug. Retail was $825.

MODEL AKY 39 — 7.62x39mm cal., gas operated semi-auto AK-47 type action, Teakwood fixed stock and grip, flip up Tritium night front sight and rear, Yugoslavian mfg. Imported 1988-89 only.

		$550	$495	$440	$395	$350	$300	$270

Last Mfg.'s Sug. Retail was $559.

> This model was supplied with sling and cleaning kit.

▲ *Model AKF 39 Folding Stock* — 7.62x39mm cal., folding stock variation of the Model AKY-39. Imported 1988-89 only.

		$575	$500	$450	$400	$350	$300	$270

Last Mfg.'s Sug. Retail was $589.

EXP-64 SURVIVAL RIFLE — .22 LR, semi-auto, takedown rifle stores in oversize synthetic stock compartment, 21 in. barrel, 10 shot clip mag., open sights, receiver grooved for scope mounting, cross bolt safety, 40 in. overall length, 7 lbs. Imported 1989-90 only.

		$150	$135	$125	$115	$105	$95	$85

Last Mfg.'s Sug. Retail was $169.

Grading	100%	98%	95%	90%	80%	70%	60%

MINI-MAX — .22 LR, semi-auto, 18¾ in. barrel, wood or black synthetic stock, 10 shot mag., adj. rear sight, 4⅓ lbs. Imported in 1990 only.

			$85	$75	$65	$55	$45	$40	$35

Last Mfg.'s Sug. Retail was $99.

Add $6 for wood stock.

SM 64 TD SPORTER — .22 LR, semi-auto, takedown barrel, 21 in. barrel, checkered walnut finished hardwood stock and forend, hooded front sight and adj. rear sight, 7 lbs. Imported 1989-90 only.

			$130	$115	$105	$95	$85	$75	$65

Last Mfg.'s Sug. Retail was $149.

MODEL 1860 HENRY REPLICA — .44-40 or .45 LC cal., 24¼ in. barrel, mfg. by Uberti.

Mfg.'s Sug. Retail	$996		$875	$650	$525	$425	$360	$320	$260

MODEL 1866 WINCHESTER REPLICA — .44-40 or .45 LC cal., 19 (Carbine) or 24¼ (Rifle) in. barrel, mfg. by Uberti.

Mfg.'s Sug. Retail	$829		$715	$575	$475	$375	$300	$250	$200

Subtract $32 for Carbine variation.

MODEL 1873 WINCHESTER REPLICA — .44-40 or .45 LC cal., 24¼ in. octagon barrel, case colored receiver, mfg. by Uberti.

Mfg.'s Sug. Retail	$984		$865	$650	$525	$425	$360	$320	$260

▲ *Model 1873 Deluxe Winchester Replica* — similar to Model 1873 Winchester Replica, except has better quality checkered pistol grip stock and forearm.

Mfg.'s Sug. Retail	$1,299		$1,100	$775	$625	$500	$425	$350	$275

SHOTGUNS: OVER AND UNDER

American Arms is currently importing Spanish shotguns manufactured by Zabala Hermanos, Lanber, and Indesal. Italian shotguns are also imported mfg. by Stefano Fausti (Models Silver, Waterfowl, and Turkey Special). American Arms imported Franchi Black Magic semi-auto and O/U shotguns will appear under the Franchi section in this text. Older Diarm models have been listed below.

LINCE — 12 or 20 ga., 3 in. chambers, boxlock with Greener crossbolt, various barrel lengths and chokings, available in either blue or shiny chrome finish, SST, VR, ejectors. Imported 1986 only.

			$510	$400	$380	$360	$340	$320	$300

Last Mfg.'s Sug. Retail was $610.

Add $70 for choke tubes.

SILVER MODEL — 12 or 20 ga. only, similar to Lince Model, except has brushed aluminum finished receiver, no engraving. Imported 1986-87 only.

			$495	$450	$390	$360	$330	$300	$285

Last Mfg.'s Sug. Retail was $545.

Add $50 for multi-chokes.

SILVER I — similar to Silver Model, except also available in 28 or .410 ga. (both new 1988), single selective trigger became standard in 1988, extractors, engraved frame, fixed chokes, recoil pad. New 1986.

Mfg.'s Sug. Retail	$599		$480	$395	$345	$300	$285	$270	$255

Add $26 for 28 or .410 ga.

Engraved frame became standard in 1987.

SILVER II — similar to Silver Model, except is supplied with choke tubes, deluxe walnut, and ejectors. New 1987.

Mfg.'s Sug. Retail	$699		$595	$525	$450	$395	$360	$330	$300

Add $26 for 28 or .410 ga. (fixed chokes only).

Grading	100%	98%	95%	90%	80%	70%	60%

▲ *Silver II Lite (Silver Upland Lite)* — 12, 20, or 28 ga. (disc. 1995), 3 in. chambers (except for 28 ga.), 26 in. VR barrels, with Franchoke tubes (except for 28 ga.), SST, ejectors, engraved frame with antique silver finish, checkered walnut stock and forearm, $5\frac{3}{4}$-$6\frac{1}{4}$ lbs. Importation began 1994.

Mfg.'s Sug. Retail	$899	$785	$650	$550	$485	$440	$400	$360

▲ *Small Gauge Combo* — includes 28 and .410 ga. barrels bored IC/M. Imported 1989-1993.

	$1,025	$895	$750	$625	$550	$495	$450

Last Mfg.'s Sug. Retail was $1,199.

SILVER LITE — 12 or 20 ga., $2\frac{3}{4}$ in. chambers, boxlock action, 26 in. vent. barrels with VR and choke tubes, blued alloy receiver, SST, ejectors, gold trigger, checkered walnut stock and forearm, 5 lbs. 14 oz. or 6 (12 ga.) lbs., mfg. by Lanber. Imported 1990-92.

	$625	$535	$460	$400	$360	$330	$300

Last Mfg.'s Sug. Retail was $749.

SILVER SPORTING — 12 ga. or 20 ga. (new 1996), Sporting Clay model, boxlock action, 28 or 30 (new 1993) in. ported vent. barrels with channelled broadway VR and choke tubes, nickel finished engraved receiver, SST, ejectors, figured walnut stock and forearm with handcut checkering, 7 lbs. 6 oz., mfg. by Lanber. Importation began 1990. 1993 manufacture by Pedersoli.

Mfg.'s Sug. Retail	$899	$795	$650	$550	$485	$440	$400	$360

SILVER SKEET — 12 ga. only, similar appearance to Silver Sporting, 26 or 28 (new 1993) in. ported vent. barrels with raised VR, 4 choke tubes, recoil pad, 7 lbs. 6 oz. Imported 1992-1993 only.

	$790	$685	$575	$495	$450	$400	$360

Last Mfg.'s Sug. Retail was $899.

SILVER TRAP — similar appearance to Silver Sporting, 30 in. ported barrels with raised VR, 4 choke tubes, recoil pad, trap stock dimensions, $7\frac{3}{4}$ lbs. Imported 1992-1993 only.

	$790	$685	$575	$495	$450	$400	$360

Last Mfg.'s Sug. Retail was $899.

STERLING/BRISTOL — 12 or 20 ga., 3 in. chambers, boxlock with Greener crossbolt and false side plates, various barrel lengths and choke tubes, chrome finished receiver with moderate game scene engraving, SST, VR, ejectors. Imported 1986-89.

	$695	$550	$495	$450	$400	$375	$350

Last Mfg.'s Sug. Retail was $825.

Until 1989, this model was designated the Bristol. In 1988, the engraving pattern was changed from game scene to elaborate scroll type.

SIR — 12 or 20 ga., 3 in. chambers, sidelock with Greener crossbolt, various barrel lengths and chokings, chrome finished receiver with game scene engraving, ST, VR, ejectors, deluxe checkered pistol grip stock and forearm. Imported 1986 only.

	$900	$725	$660	$610	$565	$520	$485

Last Mfg.'s Sug. Retail was $1,090.

Add $75 for choke tubes.

ROYAL — 12 or 20 ga., 3 in. chambers, sidelock with Greener crossbolt, various barrel lengths and chokings, chrome finished receiver with elaborate scroll engraving, ST, VR, ejectors, oil finished deluxe checkered pistol grip and forearm. Imported 1986-87 only.

	$1,595	$1,310	$1,080	$960	$850	$750	$675

Last Mfg.'s Sug. Retail was $1,730

Add $65 for choke tubes.

EXCELSIOR — 12 or 20 ga., 3 in. chambers, sidelock with Greener crossbolt, various barrel lengths and chokings, chrome finished receiver with elaborate deep relief engraving and multiple gold inlays, ST, VR, ejectors, oil finished deluxe checkered pistol grip and forearm. Imported 1986-87 only.

	$1,775	$1,510	$1,250	$1,100	$975	$885	$780

Last Mfg.'s Sug. Retail was $1,925.

Add $70 for choke tubes.

A

Grading	100%	98%	95%	90%	80%	70%	60%

O/U 12 WATERFOWL/TURKEY SPECIAL — 12 ga. only, Mag. chambers ($3\frac{1}{2}$ in. was added in 1989), 24 (Turkey) or 28 (Waterfowl) in. barrels with choke tubes, SST, ejectors, parkerized metal finish, matte finished stock and forearm, sling swivels, recoil pad, approx. 7 lbs. New 1987.

Mfg.'s Sug. Retail	$725	$600	$525	$450	$395	$360	$330	$300

▲ *10 ga. Waterfowl* — 10 ga. Mag., double triggers, extractors, matte finishes similar to 12 ga. Waterfowl, beavertail forearm. Imported 1988-89 only.

	$750	$625	$550	$495	$450	$390	$360

Last Mfg.'s Sug. Retail was $829.

WT-O/U10 TURKEY SPECIAL — 10 ga., $3\frac{1}{2}$ in. Mag., 26 in. barrels with choke tubes, SST (became standard in 1990), extractors, recoil pad, non-glare metal finish, 9 lbs. 10 oz. New 1988.

Mfg.'s Sug. Retail	$950	$825	$675	$550	$500	$450	$390	$360

F.S. 200 — 12 ga., trap or skeet model, 26 or 32 in. separated barrels only, SST, ejectors, boxlock with Greener crossbolt, black or chromed receiver, checkered walnut stock and forearm. Imported 1986-87 only.

	$690	$560	$500	$450	$410	$375	$350

Last Mfg.'s Sug. Retail was $835.

F.S. 300 — 12 ga., trap or skeet model, 26, 30, or 32 in. separated barrels only, SST, ejectors, boxlock with Greener crossbolt and false side plates lightly engraved, chromed receiver, checkered walnut stock and forearm. Imported 1986 only.

	$825	$675	$610	$555	$510	$470	$440

Last Mfg.'s Sug. Retail was $995.

F.S. 400 — 12 ga., trap or skeet model, 26, 30, or 32 in. separated barrels only, ST, ejectors, sidelock with Greener crossbolt, lightly engraved chromed receiver, checkered walnut stock and forearm. Imported 1986 only.

	$1,145	$945	$860	$800	$740	$680	$620

Last Mfg.'s Sug. Retail was $1,360.

F.S. 500 — same specifications as F.S. 400. Importation disc. 1985.

	$1,175	$950	$860	$795	$730	$660	$595

Last Mfg.'s Sug. Retail was $1,360.

SHOTGUNS: SIDE-BY-SIDE

American Arms is currently importing Spanish shotguns manufactured by Zabala Hermanos and Grulla. Older discontinued Diarm models will also be shown in this section.

GENTRY/YORK — 12, 16 (disc. 1990), 20, 28, or .410 ga., 3 in. chambers, boxlock, ejectors (extractors after 1986), double or SST (became standard in 1992), chromed receiver features fine scroll engraving, fixed chokes, pistol grip stock with recoil pad and beavertail forearm. New 1986.

Mfg.'s Sug. Retail	$725	$590	$450	$350	$300	$280	$260	$240

Add $32 for 28 or .410 ga.

Before 1988 this model was designated York (case coloring began 1988, silver finish began 1993). A SST is available on the 20 and 12 ga. model. DTs have been supplied with 28 or .410 ga. since 1990.

BRITTANY — 12 or 20 ga., boxlock action, 25 (20 ga.), 26, or 27 (12 ga.) in. barrels, SST, ejectors, matted solid rib, choke tubes, engraved case colored frame, checkered walnut straight grip stock with recoil pad and semi-beavertail forearm, $6\frac{1}{2}$ or 7 lbs. New 1989.

Mfg.'s Sug. Retail	$849	$685	$570	$485	$435	$400	$375	$350

The wood finish was changed in this model from oil to semi-gloss in 1991.

SHOGUN — 10 ga., $3\frac{1}{2}$ in. chambers, boxlock, ejectors, double triggers, chromed receiver features fine scroll engraving. Imported 1986 only.

	$440	$350	$325	$300	$280	$260	$240

Last Mfg.'s Sug. Retail was $525.

Grading	100%	98%	95%	90%	80%	70%	60%

DERBY — 12, 20, 28 (disc. 1991), or .410 (disc. 1991) ga., 3 in. chambers, sidelock, ejectors, double (disc. 1989) or SNT, chromed receiver features fine scroll engraving, fixed chokes, straight grip walnut stock and forearm. Imported 1986-94.

		$880	$750	$625	$500	$425	$385	$350

Last Mfg.'s Sug. Retail was $1,039.

> Add 10% for 28 or .410 ga. (disc. 1991).
> Subtract 10% for DT.
> Add approx. 50%-60% for 2-barrel set (20 and 28 ga. - approx. 300 sets mfg.) - disc. 1990.
> This model featured a case-colored receiver between 1988-90 and was changed to coin finish in late 1991. At the same time, the wood finish was changed from oil to semi-gloss.

GRULLA NO. 2 — 12, 20, 28, or .410 ga., hand fitted sidelock action, 26 or 28 in. barrels, DTs, ejectors, fixed chokes, concave rib, case colored receiver with elaborate engraving, deluxe English style straight stock and splinter forearm (checkered and hand rubbed), between $5\frac{3}{4}$ - $6\frac{1}{4}$ lbs. New 1989.

> This model is individually handcrafted with less than 800 mfg. each year. Since each gun is built per special order, American Arms should be contacted directly for a price quotation or more information (See Trademark Index). Before going to a special order basis, this model retailed for $3,099 (1994).

▲ **Small Gauge Set** — includes choice of 20/28 ga. or 28/.410 ga. barrel combination (26 in. fixed choke barrels). Imported 1989-95.

		$3,600	$3,000	$2,375	$2,000	$1,650	$1,325	$1,150

> Before going to a special order basis, this combination last retailed for $4,219 (1994/5).

WS/SS 10 WATERFOWL SPECIAL — 10 ga. only, $3\frac{1}{2}$ in. chambers, 32 in. barrels, DTs, parkerized finish, sling swivels and camouflaged sling, extractors, fixed chokes, recoil pad, 11 lbs. 3 oz. Imported 1987-1993.

		$560	$500	$440	$400	$375	$350	$325

Last Mfg.'s Sug. Retail was $639.

TS/SS 10/12 TURKEY SPECIAL — 10 (disc. 1995) or 12 ga., Mag. chambers ($3\frac{1}{2}$ in. 12 ga. introduced in 1989), 26 in. barrels only, double triggers, parkerized finish, dull finish stock and forearm, sling swivels, recoil pad, choke tubes, 7 lbs. 6 oz. or 10 lbs. 13 oz. (10 ga.). New 1987.

Mfg.'s Sug. Retail	$750	$625	$525	$450	$400	$375	$350	$325

> This model in 12 ga. is supplied with a SST.

COMBINATION GUNS

RS COMBO — choice of .222 Rem. or .308 rifle barrel under 12 ga. barrel, engraved boxlock frame with antique silver finish, DTs, 24 in. VR barrels with shotgun choke tubes, rifle sights, grooved for scope mounting, Monte Carlo stock, 7 lbs. 14 oz. Imported 1989 only.

		$675	$595	$550	$495	$450	$420	$385

Last Mfg.'s Sug. Retail was $749.

SHOTGUNS: SINGLE SHOT

SINGLE SHOT MODEL — 12, 20, or .410 ga., 3 in. Mag., non-exposed hammer, pistol grip stock, non-reflective finish. Imported 1988-89 only.

		$90	$80	$70	$60	$55	$50	$45

Last Mfg.'s Sug. Retail was $99.

▲ **Camper Special** — 12, 20, or .410 ga., 3 in. Mag., folding design, 21 in. barrel, pistol grip. Imported 1988-89 only.

		$95	$80	$70	$60	$55	$50	$45

Last Mfg.'s Sug. Retail was $107.

▲ **Slugger** — 12 or 20 ga., 24 in. Slug shotgun barrel with adj. rear sight and blade front, recoil pad. Imported 1989 only.

		$100	$85	$75	$65	$55	$50	$45

Last Mfg.'s Sug. Retail was $115.

A

▲ **Youth** — 20 or .410 ga., 26 in. barrel, 12½ in. stock dimensions, recoil pad. Imported 1989 only.

	100%	98%	95%	90%	80%	70%	60%
	$100	$85	$75	$65	$55	$50	$45

Last Mfg.'s Sug. Retail was $115.

▲ **Combo** — interchangeable rifle and shotgun barrels, choice of .22 Hornet/12 ga. with 28 in. barrel or .22 LR/20 ga. with 26 in. barrel, includes fitted hard case. Imported 1989 only.

	100%	98%	95%	90%	80%	70%	60%
	$195	$165	$130	$115	$100	$90	$80

Last Mfg.'s Sug. Retail was $235.

▲ **10 Ga. Model** — 10 ga. only, 3½ in. chambers, 26 in. multi-choke or 32 in. full fixed choke barrel, non-exposed hammer, non-reflective finish. Imported 1988-89 only.

	100%	98%	95%	90%	80%	70%	60%
	$135	$115	$95	$80	$70	$60	$55

Last Mfg.'s Sug. Retail was $149.

Add $30 for multi-chokes (26 in. barrel).

AMERICAN BARLOCK WONDER

Manufactured by Crescent Arms for Sears Roebuck & Co.

SHOTGUNS

SIDE-BY-SIDE — various gauges, hammerless or outside hammer, damascus or steel barrels. Add 15% for steel barrels, smaller gauges.

	100%	98%	95%	90%	80%	70%	60%
	$240	$225	$200	$175	$140	$100	$75

SINGLE SHOT — various gauges, hammer, steel barrel. Add 35% for smaller gauges.

	100%	98%	95%	90%	80%	70%	60%
	$125	$115	$100	$90	$75	$60	$50

AMERICAN DERRINGER CORPORATION

Manufacturer located in Waco, TX 1980-present. Distributor and dealer sales.

DERRINGERS: STAINLESS STEEL

MODEL 1 — available in over 55 cals. including .22 LR through .45-70, also 2½ in. .410 shot shell, O/U stainless steel derringer, 3 in. barrels, automatic barrel selection, "hammer block" type safety, 15 oz., spur trigger, rosewood grips. New 1980.

▲ **Regular Cals.** — most cals. between .22 LR and .38 Spl.

Mfg.'s Sug. Retail	$255		$200	$170	$130

Add approx. $150 for .22 Hornet (disc. 1989), .223 Rem., or .30-30 cal.

▲ **Larger Cals.** — typically .357 Mag. or .41 cal. and larger.

Mfg.'s Sug. Retail	$320		$270	$220	$180

Subtract approx. $65 for .357 Mag. or .45 ACP cal.
Add approx. $65 for .41 - .45 Mag. cals.
This model can be ordered with special ser. #s and other custom features at additional cost(s).

▲ **Model 1 Engraved** — limited mfg., mostly special ordered.

Mfg.'s Sug. Retail	$855		$725	$600	$495

LADY DERRINGER — .32 Mag. or .38 Spl. standard cals., also available in .22 LR (disc.), .22 Mag. (disc.), .357 Mag., .380 ACP (disc.), 9mm Para. (disc.), .45 ACP, or .45 LC/.410 shotshell cal. (disc.) at a small premium, high polished finish with synthetic ivory grips, handfitted action allowing easy cocking, cased in French styled jewelry box. New 1990.

▲ **Standard Grade** — standard model as described above, 1990 mfg. only.

	$215	$185	$160

Last Mfg.'s Sug. Retail was $250.

Grading	100%	98%	95%	90%	80%	70%	60%

▲ **Deluxe Grade** — similar to Standard Grade, except synthetic grips are scrimshawed in a cameo or rose design, choice of walnut case or French jewelry box.

Mfg.'s Sug. Retail $260 $225 $185 $160

    Add approx. $35 for .357 Mag. and $85 for .45 LC cal.

▲ **Deluxe Engraved** — similar to Deluxe Grade, except hand engraved with circa 1880 patterns. Disc. 1994.

                       $650 $515 $400

Last Mfg.'s Sug. Retail was $750.

    Mother-of-pearl grips and personalized engraving are available as extra cost options on this model.

▲ **14 KT. Gold Engraved** — entire Derringer manufactured out of a 14 KT. gold bar (contains approx. 20 oz. of 14 KT. gold and 3 oz. of stainless steel), custom engraved with diamond sights, special order only until late 1993.

                    N/A   N/A   N/A

Last Mfg.'s Sug. Retail was $100,000.

MODEL 1 TEXAS COMMEMORATIVE — .38 Spl., .44-40, or .45 LC cal., similar to Model 1 except has brass frame, stainless steel barrel, and stag grips. 500 mfg. in each cal. starting in 1986.

Grading	100%	Issue Price	Qty. Made
.44-40 cal. (current mfg.)	$295	$345	500
.45 cal. (current mfg.)	$295	$345	500
.32 Mag.	$205	$255	500+
.38 Spl. (current mfg.)	$225	$280	500
.22 LR (mfg. 1991-92)	$200	$238	500
.41 Rimfire (not shootable)	$235	$295	500
Fully engraved model	$695	$750	limited

125TH ANNIVERSARY — special edition 125th anniversary variation with pistol case. Disc. 1993.

	100%	Issue Price	Qty. Made
.44-40 or .45 cal.	$285	$320	500
.38 Spl.	$185	$225	500
Deluxe engraved model	$650	$750	limited

Grading	100%	98%	95%	90%	80%	70%	60%

MODEL 3 — .32 Mag. (new 1990 - limited availability) or .38 Spl. cal., single shot, 2½ in. barrel, 8½ oz., spur trigger, rosewood grips. Disc. 1994.

                       $95 $70 $55

Last Mfg.'s Sug. Retail was $120.

MODEL 4 — .357 Mag., .357 Max., .44 Mag., .45 ACP, or .45 LC cal. on upper barrel, 3 in. .410 shot shell lower barrel, O/U derringer combination pistol, 4¹/₁₀ in. barrel, rosewood grips, 16½ oz. New 1985.

Mfg.'s Sug. Retail $352 $310 $250 $210

    Add $30 for oversized grips.
    Add $70 for .44 Mag. cal.
    Add $143 for .45-70 cal. in both barrels.
    Add $17 for .357 Mag., .357 Max., or .45 ACP cal.

    This model is also available on special order in either .50-70 or .50 Saunders cal. (new 1989 - single shot only). Retail is $395.

▲ **Alaskan Survival Model** — similar to Model 4, except choice of .45-70 or .44 Mag. cal. upper or lower barrel.

Mfg.'s Sug. Retail $388 $340 $295 $260

Grading	100%	98%	95%	90%	80%	70%	60%

A

MODEL 6 — .22 Mag., .357 Mag., .45 LC, .45 ACP, or .45 LC/.410 ga. O/U, 6 in. barrel, 21 oz. Available in high polish, satin, or gray matte finish (standard). New 1986.
Mfg.'s Sug. Retail $300 $250 $200 $180
    Add $45 for .45 ACP cal., $63 for either .45 LC or .45 LC/.410 ga.
    Add $13 for satin finish (disc. 1994).
    Add $27 for high polish finish.
    Add $35 for oversized grips (disc. 1994).

MODEL 7 — .22 LR, .22 Mag. (new 1992), .32 Mag., .38 Spl., .38 S&W (disc. 1989), .380 ACP, or .44 Spl. cal., O/U, same basic specifications as Model 1, except ultra lightweight (7½ oz.).
Mfg.'s Sug. Retail $240 $185 $140 $115

  ▲ *.44 Special Cal.* — .44 Spl. cal. only.
Mfg.'s Sug. Retail $500 $445 $410 $350

MODEL 10 — .38 Spl. (new 1995), .45 ACP, or .45 LC/.410 ga., O/U, 3 in. stainless barrels, aluminum frame, matte finish, 10 oz. New 1988.
Mfg.'s Sug. Retail $257 $215 $175 $145
    Add $63 for .45 LC cal.
    Subtract $17 for .38 Spl. cal.

MODEL 11 — .22 LR (new 1995), .22 Mag. (new 1995), .32 Mag. (new 1995), .380 ACP (new 1995), or .38 Spl., same basic specifications as Model 1, matte gray finish, only 11 oz.
Mfg.'s Sug. Retail $225 $180 $150 $125

HIGH STANDARD DOUBLE ACTION — .22 LR or .22 Mag. cal., 3½ in. O/U barrels, double action trigger, dual extraction, hammerless, blue finish with black synthetic grips, 11 oz. Mfg. 1990-95.
             $145 $115 $95

Last Mfg.'s Sug. Retail was $170.

      This O/U Derringer duplicates the original High Standard design.

DA 38 DOUBLE ACTION — .22 LR (new 1996), .357 Mag. (new 1991), .38 Spl., 9mm Para., or .40 S&W (new 1993) cal., 3 in. O/U barrels, satin stainless steel with aluminum grip frame, double action trigger design, hammerblock thumb safety, choice of checkered rosewood, walnut, or other hardwood grips, 14.5 oz. New 1990.
Mfg.'s Sug. Retail $300 $245 $185 $150
    Add $25 for 9mm Para. cal.
    Add $50 for .357 Mag. or .40 S&W cal.
    Add $15 for Lady Derringer Model (scrimshawed synthetic ivory grips, .38 Spl. only. Mfg. 1992-94.)

MINI-COP — .22 Mag. cal., 4 shot double action design, stainless steel construction, patterned after the original Mini-Cop mfg. in Torrance, CA. Mfg. 1990-94.
             $250 $220 $185

Last Mfg.'s Sug. Retail was $313.

COP STAINLESS — .357 Mag. cal., double action, similar design to Mini-Cop. Mfg. 1991-1994.
             $315 $265 $200

Last Mfg.'s Sug. Retail was $375.

CUSTOM TARGET MODELS — .38 Spl. Wadcutter or 9mm Federal (disc.) cal., mfg. for End of Trail Derringer Match, limited production. Mfg. 1990-92.
             $695 $575 $475

Last Mfg.'s Sug. Retail was $750.

Grading	100%	98%	95%	90%	80%	70%	60%

PISTOLS: PEN DESIGN

MODEL 2 PEN PISTOL — .22 LR, .25 ACP, or .32 ACP cal., unique hinged action allows pen to be converted into a legal pistol within two seconds, folding design, 2 in. barrel, cocks on opening action, firing pin block grip safety, brushed stainless finish, 5 oz. Mfg. 1993-1994.

	100%	98%	95%
	$145	$120	$100

Last Mfg.'s Sug. Retail was $203.

Add $24 for .32 ACP cal.

PISTOLS: SEMI-AUTO

STANDARD MODEL

▲ **.25 Mag. Cal.** — .25 Mag., semi-auto single action, less than 100 manufactured in stainless steel only.

	100%	98%	95%
	$500	$400	$300

▲ **.25 ACP Cal.** — .25 ACP, semi-auto single action, less than 400 manufactured in stainless steel, less than 50 in blued steel.

	100%	98%	95%
Stainless	$400	$300	$250
Blue	$550	$400	$325

LM-4 (SEMMERLING) — while advertised, the LM-4 was never mfg. by American Derringer Corp. Refer to separate listing under Semmerling.

AMERICAN FIREARMS MANUFACTURING COMPANY, INC.

Previous manufacturer located in San Antonio, TX between 1972-1974.

AMERICAN .25 AUTOMATIC — .25 ACP cal., 8 shot, $2\frac{1}{10}$ in. barrel, smooth walnut grips, mfg. 1966-74.

	100%	98%	95%	90%	80%	70%	60%
Stainless	$195	$180	$165				
Blue	$165	$150	$140	$120	$100	$90	$85

AMERICAN .38 SPL. — .38 Spl., O/U configuration, approx. 3,000-4,000 mfg. between 1972-74.

	100%	98%	95%
	$200	$165	$135

AMERICAN .380 AUTOMATIC — .380 ACP cal., 8 shot, $3\frac{1}{2}$ in. barrel, stainless steel, smooth walnut grips. Mfg. 1972-1974.

	100%	98%	95%
	$700	$500	$300

This model is extremely rare — only 10 were manufactured. Prices hard to evaluate.

AMERICAN GUN CO.

Manufactured by Crescent Firearms Co. distributed by H. & D. Folsom Co.

HANDGUNS

REVOLVER — .32 S&W, 5 shot, double action, top break-open action.

	100%	98%	95%	90%	80%	70%	60%
	$175	$160	$140	$120	$95	$65	$50

SHOTGUNS

SxS — various gauges, hammer or hammerless, damascus or steel barrels.

	100%	98%	95%	90%	80%	70%	60%
	$240	$225	$200	$175	$140	$100	$75

Add 15% for small gauges or steel barrels.

AMERICAN FRONTIER FIREARMS CO.
Manufacturer located in Aguanga, CA since 1995. Direct sales only.

American Frontier Firearms Co. manufactures a line of older replica metallic cartridge firing revolvers (black powder or smokeless). These revolvers are manufactured in Italy and fit/finished domestically. Modern smokeless cals. include .22 LR, .32 Spl., .38 Spl., .44 Spl., or .45 LC.

Grading	100%	98%	95%	90%	80%	70%	60%

REVOLVERS

Importation on the models listed below began 1996. These revolvers are supplied with standard finish high polish blued steel parts, color case hardened hammer and/or trigger, silver-plated or blued backstrap and triggerguard, and varnished walnut grips. Special orders are also available featuring special finishes and engraving options.

1871-72 OPEN-TOP STANDARD MODEL — .38 or .44 cal., 7½ or 8 in. round barrel, non-rebated cyl.

Mfg.'s Sug. Retail	$595	$550	$450	$400	$350	$300	$275	$250

▲ *1871-72 Open-Top Tiffany Model* — similar to 1871-72 Standard Model, except has engraved gold/silver finished Tiffany grips and also available with 4¾ in. barrel.

Mfg.'s Sug. Retail	$795	$725	$575	$450	$395	$350	$300	$275

▲ *1871-72 Pocket Model* — .32 cal., 5 shot, 4¾ or 5½ in. round barrel.

Mfg.'s Sug. Retail	$350	$315	$270	$240	$210	$175	$150	$125

Add $100 for Tiffany grips.

RICHARDS 1860 ARMY CONVERSION STANDARD MODEL — .38 or .44 cal., rebated cyl., with or w/o ejector assembly, 4¾, 5½ or 7½ in. barrel.

Mfg.'s Sug. Retail	$495	$440	$375	$325	$295	$265	$235	$195

▲ *Pocket Richards Conversion Model* — .32 cal., 5 shot, rebated cyl., 4¾ or 5½ in. round barrel.

Mfg.'s Sug. Retail	$350	$315	$270	$240	$210	$175	$150	$125

Add $100 for Tiffany grips.

RICHARDS 1851 NAVY CONVERSION STANDARD MODEL — .38 or .44 cal., non-rebated cyl., 4¾, 5½ or 7½ in. barrel, w/o ejector rod assembly.

Mfg.'s Sug. Retail	$495	$440	$375	$325	$295	$265	$235	$195

RICHARDS & MASON CONVERSION 1851 NAVY STANDARD MODEL — .38 or .44 cal., features Mason ejector rod assembly and non-rebated cyl., otherwise similar to Richards 1851 Navy Conversion.

Mfg.'s Sug. Retail	$495	$440	$375	$325	$295	$265	$235	$195

▲ *Pocket Richards & Mason Navy Conversion* — .32 cal., non-rebated cyl., 5 shot.

Mfg.'s Sug. Retail	$350	$315	$270	$240	$210	$175	$150	$125

REMINGTON NEW MODEL STANDARD — .38, .44, or .45 cal., 5½ or 7½ in. barrel, with or w/o ejector rod and gate.

Mfg.'s Sug. Retail	$495	$440	$375	$325	$295	$265	$235	$195

REMINGTON NEW MODEL ARMY STANDARD — .38, .44, or .45 cal., 5½, 7½, or 8 in. barrel, supplied with ejector assembly and loading gate, includes government inspector's cartouche on left grips and sub-inspector's initialed small parts.

Mfg.'s Sug. Retail	$595	$550	$450	$400	$350	$300	$275	$250

POCKET REMINGTON — .22, .32, or .38 cal., 3½ in. barrel, with or w/o ejector rod and gate.

Mfg.'s Sug. Retail	$350	$315	$270	$240	$210	$175	$150	$125

AMERICAN HISTORICAL FOUNDATION, THE

A private organization which privately commissions historical commemoratives in conjunction with leading manufacturers and craftsmen around the world. The AHF is located in Richmond, VA. Direct retail sales only.

AHF limited edition models are not necessarily all manufactured at one time. Rather, guns are fabricated as demand dictates.

COMMEMORATIVE ISSUES

Values listed below reflect AHF's original issue prices and the last published retail price. No other values are listed since AHF limited edition firearms do not appear that frequently in the secondary marketplace. This is because the AHF has always sold to consumers directly, without involving normal gun dealers and distributors. Most AHF members are veterans, who keep these items as family collectibles and usually do not resell them. Because of this consumer direct sales program, many gun dealers do not have a working knowledge about what AHF firearms are currently selling for. The publisher suggests that those people owning AHF Commemorative Issue firearms contact the AHF (See Trademark Index) for current information, including prices as they are involved in this marketplace daily.

Grading	Most Recent Issue Price

PISTOLS

Values listed below do not include original display cases (typically priced between $85 and $180).

U.S. MARINE MUSTANG — .380 ACP cal., Colt Mustang variation with special gold slide markings and white polymer grips with Marine Corps. medallions, lockable plastic case, serial numbered MM001-MM500. 500 mfg. by Colt beginning 1994.
$695

ARMED FORCES COLT GOV'T MODEL .380 SERIES — .380 ACP cal., gold accents, smooth grips with medallions, 1,911 mfg. for each armed force beginning 1994.
$995

ARMED FORCES MODEL 1911A1 SERIES — .45 ACP cal., consists of four Model 1911A1s (one for each U.S. armed service branch), custom designed artwork with selective etchings, grips are finished in different woods and medallions, 1,911 mfg. for each branch by Auto Ordnance Corp. Original issue price was $995.
$1,095

AIRBORNE JUBILEE MODEL 1911A1 — .45 ACP cal., high polished bluing with etched commemorative inscriptions, 24 Kt. gold plated selected parts, 500 mfg. by Auto Ordnance Corp. Original issue price was $995.
$1,095

D-DAY COMMEM. M1911A1 — .45 ACP cal., serial numbered DDAY 0001 - DDAY 1,000. Introduced 1989 with issue price of $995, re-introduced 1994.
$1,095

FIVE-STAR GENERAL SERIES M1911A1 — .45 ACP cal., Auto-Ordnance M15. Ongoing series, first of series features Gen. Eisenhower, second depicts Gen. MacArthur, 500 of each mfg.
$1,295

VIETNAM WAR LIMITED EDITION M1911A1 — .45 ACP cal., ser. numbered VN001-VN2500. Issued in 1990.
$1,095

Grading	Most Recent Issue Price

WWII COLT .45 SERIES M1911A1 — .45 ACP cal., 12 variations commemorating the major campaigns of WWII, each variation is limited to 250 mfg.
$1,195
This price includes display case.
This series was originally released at $995.

WWII 50TH ANNIVERSARY M1911A1 — .45 ACP cal., gold accents, 500 mfg. of standard edition by Colt beginning 1995, 50 deluxe editions.
Standard Edition **$1,495**
Deluxe Edition **$2,995**

COLT GOLD CUP LIMITED EDITION M1911A1 — .45 ACP cal., features fully plated 24 Kt. frame and slide, smooth walnut grips with Colt medallions. 1,000 mfg. beginning 1995.
$2,195

M1911A1 AUTO-ORDNANCE MEDALS OF VALOR — .45 ACP cal., 24 Kt. gold-plated small parts and slide etching, 1,000 mfg. for each tribute (includes 6 configurations) beginning 1995.
$1,095

BERETTA M9 ARMED FORCES COMMEMORATIVE — 9mm Para. cal., 24 Kt. gold-plated small parts and etching, 1,985 mfg. for each Armed Service (Army, Navy, Air Force, Marines, Coast Guard) beginning 1995.
$1,795

GOLDEN CENTURION BERETTA .40 — .40 S&W cal., 24 Kt. gold plated with engraving, 200 mfg. by Beretta beginning 1994.
$2,195

40TH ANNIVERSARY COMMEM. RUGER MARK II — .22 LR cal., ser. numbered 40th 1-40th 950. Issued 1990. Original issue price was $995.
$1,095

ARMED FORCES RUGER — .22 LR, Ruger Govt. Model, bull barrel variation of the Ruger MK II, available in Army, Navy, Marine, and Air Force variations, high polish blue finish with 24 Kt. gold foliate motif covering barrel and receiver, various gold plated small parts, cloisonne medallion in wooden grips, 250 mfg. for each service branch.
$1,095

THE KGB MAKAROV — 9mm Makarov, Soviet mfg., polished blue finish with gold accents, supplied with holster and accessory kit, 1,000 mfg. beginning 1994.
$895

FIELD MARSHAL ROMMEL LIMITED EDITION P.38 — 9mm para. cal., blue finish with gold accents, Walther mfg. beginning 1994, 300 in Collector's Edition, 100 in Deluxe Edition.
Collector's Edition **$1,995**
Deluxe Edition **$2,995**

WWII ALLIED VICTORY P.38 TROPHY EDITION — 9mm cal., Spreewerke mfg. with updated gold accents, 250 units available beginning 1995.
$1,695

2ND AMENDMENT BROWNING HI-POWER .40 — .40 S&W, nickel plated with gold accents, 500 mfg. by BAC beginning 1994.
$1,995

ALLIED VICTORY BROWNING HI-POWER — 9mm cal., fully plated in 24 Kt. gold, 500 mfg.
$1,795

Grading	Most Recent Issue Price

A

WW II VICTORY HI-POWER — 9mm Para., 100% gold plated with etched engraving, walnut grips, 500 mfg. beginning 1995.
$1,795

CRUSADE IN EUROPE INGLIS HI-POWER — 9mm cal., 24 Kt. highlights, 500 mfg. beginning 1994.
$1,495

INGLIS SHOWCASE EDITION — 9mm cal., satin finish with polished nickel slide, 250 mfg. beginning 1995.
$1,295

GOLDEN INGLIS HIGH POWER — 9mm cal., 24 Kt. plating with engraving, 50 mfg. starting 1995.
$2,495

ETO LUGER COLLECTOR'S EDITION — 9mm cal., original WWII P.08 with gold highlights, 750 mfg.
$1,795

▲ *ETO Luger Deluxe Edition* — 10 mfg.
$3,995

MAUSER C-96 (BROOMHANDLE) SPECIAL EDITION — 7.63 Mauser, various embellishments include both engraving and gold inlays (Field Marshal Edition only), refurbished utilizing original Mauser parts. Introduced 1994.

▲ *General Officer Edition* — hand engraved with acorn and oak leaf motif, walnut grips, serial numbered GO001-GO300 on bottom of mag. well. 300 mfg. beginning 1994.
$1,995

▲ *Field Marshal Edition* — hand engraved with 24 Kt. eagle and barrel band, serial numbered FM001-FM100. 100 mfg. beginning 1994 - sold out.
$2,995

S & W TACTICAL COMPETITION — .40 S&W cal., 40 mfg. of Collector's Edition, 10 mfg. of Deluxe Edition. All are match grade.
Collector's Edition $2,795
Deluxe Edition $3,795
The Deluxe Edition is sold out.

S & W TACTICAL EDITION PC9 — 9mm Para., features red dot trigger guard mounted laser sight, top of frame is engraved, 50 mfg. beginning 1994.
$2,595

S & W SECOND AMENDMENT SIGMA .40 — .40 S&W cal., blued finish with gold etching, 250 mfg. beginning 1995.
$1,995

UZI PISTOL — 9x19mm cal., 4½ in. barrel, 100 mfg. by IMI in Israel.
$2,495
This edition is sold out.

REVOLVERS

Values listed below do not include original display cases (typically priced between $179 and $395).

TEXAS PATERSON — .36 cal., limited edition of 950, mfg. by D. Pedersoli of Italy. Original issue price was $1,495. 1st issue of the Single Colt Gold Tribute Collection.
$2,195

1847 MODEL WALKER — .44 cal., limited edition of 950, mfg. by A. Uberti, located in Italy. Original issue price was $1,895. 2nd issue of the Single Colt Gold Tribute Collection.
$2,195

Grading	Most Recent Issue Price

A

CIVIL WAR SECOND MODEL COLT DRAGOONS — .44 cal., available as either Union (hand engraved and 24 Kt. gold plating) or Confederate Model (hand engraved and silver plated). 125 mfg. of each, entire edition is sold out. Original issue price was $2,495.
$2,495

MODEL 1849 WELLS FARGO — .31 cal., patterned after the Colt 1829 Pocket, limited edition of 950, mfg. by A. Uberti. Introduced 1995.
$1,995

JEFFERSON DAVIS MODEL 1851 NAVY — .36 cal., patterned after the Colt 1851 Navy presented to J. Davis in 1858, limited edition of 250, mfg. by A. Uberti.
$2,995

GEN. ROBERT E. LEE MODEL 1851 NAVY — .36 cal., patterned after Robert E. Lee's Colt Model 1851 revolver, blued receiver with scroll engraving, silver plated grip straps and trigger guard, limited edition of 1,000 (ser. no. REL001-REL1000). Introduced 1994.
$2,195

WILD BILL HICKOCK MODEL 1851 NAVY — .36 cal., features reproduction of Wild Bill Hickock motifs, limited edition of 500, mfg. by A. Uberti.
$1,995

SAMUEL COLT GOLDEN TRIBUTE MODEL 1860 ARMY — .44 cal., gold plated with engraving, 950 mfg. beginning 1994.
$1,995

COL. J. S. MOSBY MODEL 1860 ARMY — .44 cal., limited edition of 150, mfg. by Colt Firearms, entire edition is sold out. Original issue price was $2,495.
$2,495

1862 POLICE REVOLVER — .36 cal., gold plated with engraving, 950 mfg. beginning 1993.
$1,895

J.E.B. STUART LEMAT — .44 cal., 9 shot, includes single shot .65 cal. shotgun barrel, limited edition of 500, mfg. by Navy Arms beginning 1987. Original issue price was $2,195.
$2,895

200TH CONSTITUTION COMMEMORATIVE REVOLVER — .44 Mag., Dan Wesson manufactured revolver, Collector's edition serial numbered CC001-CC950 (950 mfg.), Deluxe edition serial numbered CD001-CD500 (500 mfg.), 4 lbs. Released 1987. Original issue price for Collector's Edition was $995 (sold out), Deluxe Museum Edition was $1,595 (sold out).

Collector's Edition	$1,295
Deluxe Museum Edition	$1,595

2ND AMENDMENT COMMEM. REVOLVER — .44 Mag., 10 in. barrel, mfg. by Dan Wesson to AHF specifications, 2 different models, walnut grips with medallions. Released 1989.

▲ *Collector's Edition* — 1,500 mfg., serial numbered 2AC0001 - 2AC1500. Original issue price was $1,295.
$1,695

▲ *Deluxe Museum Edition* — 750 mfg., serial numbered 2AD001 - 2AD750. Original issue price was $1,595.
$1,895

AMERICAN DEER HUNTER COMMEMORATIVE — .44 Mag., mfg. by Dan Wesson, 10 in. barrel, 4 lbs. Issued 1990.

▲ *Sportsman's Edition* — field grade version, 750 mfg., serial numbered 001S-750S with "DEER" prefix. Original issue price was $995.
$1,095

This variation is also available in a bear, moose, elk, or sheep edition.

Grading	Most Recent Issue Price

▲ *Deluxe Trophy Edition* — 250 mfg. serial numbered 001T-250T with "DEER" prefix.
$1,995
This variation is also available in a bear, moose, elk, or sheep edition.

LEGACY EDITION COLT ANACONDA — .44 Mag., 100% plated in black and gold titanium, Legacy Edition medallions in contoured rosewood grips, 1,000 mfg. by Colt beginning 1994. Original issue price was $1,395.
$1,595

COLT PYTHON 20TH CENTURY SPECIAL EDITION — .357 Mag. cal., 8 in. barrel, gold-plated with silver cylinder, 1,000 mfg. by Colt beginning 1995.
$2,795

GENERAL PATTON SAA — .45 LC, 5½ in. barrel, 2,500 mfg. in limited edition beginning 1988, serial numbered P0001-P2500. Mfg. by A. Uberti in Italy. The entire edition is sold out. Original issue price was $1,495.
$1,895

TEDDY ROOSEVELT SAA — .44-40 cal., reproduction of Teddy Roosevelt's famous Colt engraved SAA, 750 mfg. by A. Uberti.
$1,995

HERITAGE EDITION SAA — .45 LC cal., 4¾ in. barrel, blue finish with engraving and gold accents, 250 mfg. by Colt beginning 1995.
$2,995

OLD WEST SHERIFF'S MODEL COLT — .45 LC Colt SAA, limited edition of 10, mfg. by AHF Custom Shop. This price includes display case. Edition is sold out.
$10,995

WWII BRITISH COMMANDO ENFIELD — .38 Enfield No. 2 Mark I revolver, 250 mfg. Edition is sold out.
$995
This price includes display case and Commando Knife mfg. by H.G. Long & Co.

TACTICAL EDITION F-COMP — .357 Mag., K-frame, 6 shot, 3 in. barrel with integral compensator, stainless steel, tritium night sights, engraved frame with checkered rosewood grips, 2¼ lbs., 50 total mfg. beginning 1994.
$2,795

S & W MODEL 625 BANK NOTE SPECIAL EDITION — .45 ACP cal., S & W Model 625 revolver with satin finish, combat rubber grips, polymer case, 100 mfg. starting 1995.

S & W MODEL 640 SPECIAL EDITION — .38 Spl., nickel plated with engraving, 250 mfg. beginning 1993.
$2,195

S & W .357 HUNTER SPECIAL EDITION — .357 Mag., includes special engraving, 6 in. Mag-naported barrel with integral scope, cased, 50 mfg. beginning 1994.
$3,795

RIFLES AND CARBINES

Values listed below do not include original display cases (typically priced between $249 and $499).

50 STATES HENRY — .44-40 cal., Uberti mfg. Henry repeating rifle, 100 mfg. by AHF Custom Shop, with two commemorating each state, sets are marked with state's outline and motto.
$11,995

Grading	Most Recent Issue Price

A

MODEL 1885 ELK HUNTER — .45-70 cal., Browning mfg., grayed receiver with elk panel scene engraving, 100 mfg. starting 1995.
$2,975

MODEL 1885 DEER HUNTER — .45-70 cal., Browning mfg., grayed receiver, 100 mfg. in Collector's edition, 10 mfg. in Deluxe edition, which has extensive gold inlay on blued finish.
Collector's Edition $2,975
Deluxe Edition $5,995

MODEL 81 NORTH AMERICAN BIG GAME FIVE — .308 Win. cal., Browning mfg., steel receiver with special engraving and gold etching, 250 mfg. starting 1995.
$2,495

MODEL 1861 SPRINGFIELD MUSKET — .58 cal., issued to commemorate 125th anniversary of the Civil War, 125 mfg. by Ezechiele and Rino Chiappa.
$3,495

CONSTITUTION COMMEMORATIVE HENRY — .44-40 cal., patterned after the famous Henry rifle, brass frame, hand engraved with 24 Kt. gold plating, 200 mfg. by A. Uberti. Entire edition is sold out.
$2,395

CIVIL WAR COMMEMORATIVE HENRY — similar to Constitution Commemorative Henry, choice of either Abraham Lincoln (hand engraved brass frame with gold plating and blued barrel) or Jefferson Davis (hand engraved brass frame with silver plating and brown barrel), 250 of each model mfg. by A. Uberti. Original issue price was $3,495.
$3,995

BAR BROWNING TROPHY EDITION — .30-06 cal., mfg. to commemorate the American deerhunter, grayed receiver with 24 Kt. etched motifs, 500 mfg. beginning 1993.
$2,195

WINCHESTER MODEL 94 — .30-30 cal., issued to commemorate the closing of the American West, mfg. by Winchester.
▲ *Collector's Edition* — 750 mfg. Original issue price was $1,795.
$1,895
▲ *Deluxe Museum Edition* — 250 mfg. Original issue price was $2,495.
$2,895

WINCHESTER MODEL 94 CENTENNIAL 1 OF 100 — .30-30 cal., grayed receiver with half-round/half-octagon barrel, 100 mfg. beginning 1995.
$2,495

WWII M1 GARAND RIFLE — .30-06 cal., mfg. from original WWII Garands, serial numbered WW0001-WW2500, 9½ lbs. Original issue price was $1,695.
$1,895

WWII 50TH ANNIVERSARY M1 GARAND RIFLE — .30-06 cal., mfg. from original WWII Garands, 500 units in collector edition, 50 in deluxe edition. Released 1995.
Collector Edition $3,495
Standard Edition $1,895

ARMED FORCES BASIC TRAINING COMMEMORATIVE M1 GARAND — .30-06 cal., gold accents, walnut cased, 500 mfg. for each armed force beginning 1994.
$1,395

AIRBORNE GOLDEN JUBILEE M1A1 CARBINE — .30 carbine, mfg. from original circa WWII carbines with folding stock, 500 unit limited edition.
$1,295

Grading	Most Recent Issue Price

WWII 50TH ANNIVERSARY M1 CARBINE — .30 carbine, mfg. from original circa WWII carbines, 550 in collector edition, 50 in deluxe edition beginning 1995.

Collector Edition **$1,495**
Deluxe Edition **$2,495**

VIETNAM WAR COMMEMORATIVE M1 CARBINE — .30 carbine, mfg. from original circa WWII carbines, 1,500 unit limited edition beginning 1995.

$1,495

AIRBORNE GOLDEN JUBILEE THOMPSON — .45 ACP cal., issued to commemorate 50th anniversary of the Airborne, special commemorative etchings and medallions, 500 mfg. by Auto Ordnance Corp.

$1,995

KOREAN WAR THOMPSON RIFLE — .45 ACP cal., semi-auto (also fully auto with class III license) reproduction of the famous military Thompson sub-machine gun, mfg. by Auto-Ordnance Corp., 2,000 mfg. 1984 serial numbered KW0001-KW3000. This edition is sold out.

$995

▲ *Thompson Engraved Model* — similar to above, except has full engraving coverage. 25 available within the edition limit. This edition is sold out.

$4,995

ARMED FORCES SEMI-AUTO THOMPSON — .45 ACP cal., semi-auto reproduction of the Thompson sub-machine gun, four models commemorating the four U.S. service branches (Air Force, Army, Marine Corps. and Navy), 750 manufactured for each U.S. service branch. Original issue price was $1,895.

$1,995

LAW ENFORCEMENT THOMPSON — .45 ACP cal., available in a policeman and sheriff model, 1,500 of each mfg. by Auto Ordnance Corp. Original issue price was $1,595.

$1,795

ETO/PTO THOMPSON — .45 ACP cal., 24 Kt. plated small parts, includes Cutts compensator, 500 mfg. of each theater of operation.

$1,595

SHOWCASE EDITION THOMPSON — .45 ACP cal., nickel plated with light engraving, 100 mfg. by Auto Ordnance beginning 1994.

$2,195

D-DAY 50TH ANNIVERSARY COMMEMORATIVE THOMPSON — .45 ACP cal., gold accents, 500 mfg. by Auto Ordnance beginning 1994.

$1,695

WORLD WAR II 50TH ANNIVERSARY THOMPSON — .45 ACP cal., gold accents, 500 mfg. by Auto Ordnance in standard edition, 50 deluxe beginning 1995.

Standard Edition **$2,495**
Deluxe Edition **$4,495**

VIETNAM M14 RIFLE — .308 cal., manufactured by Federal Ordnance, mfg. limited to 500 of each edition. Released 1987. Original issue price for Collector's Edition was $2,195, Deluxe Edition was $2,495. Entire edition is sold out.

Collectors Edition **$2,495**
Deluxe Museum Edition **$2,895**

M16 VIETNAM WAR COMMEMORATIVE — .223 cal., semi-auto version of the M16, includes hand engraving, 24 Kt. gold plated small parts and stock medallions, 1,500 mfg. by B.F.I., serial numbered VN0001-VN1000. This edition is sold out.

$1,995

A

Grading	Most Recent Issue Price

THE VIETNAM TRIBUTE COLT M16 SPECIAL EDITION — .223 cal., Colt Match H-bar action, includes hand engraving, 24 Kt. gold plated small parts and stock medallions, 1,500 mfg. by Colt., serial numbered VT0001-VT1500. This edition is sold out.

$1,995

ARMED FORCES M16s — four models commemorating the four U.S. service branches (Air Force, Army, Marine Corps., and Navy), hand engraved, 24 Kt. gold plated small parts, medallions in stock, bipod included, 100 mfg. for each branch. This set is now sold out.

$2,995

M16 AIRBORNE — .223 cal., carbine variation, 950 mfg. by B.F.I. Original issue price was $2,495. Entire edition is sold out.

$2,795

VIETNAM WAR TROPHY EDITION SKS — 7.62x39mm Kalashnikov, gold accents and engraving, black finish stock, cased, 1,500 mfg. beginning 1994.

$995

VIETNAM WAR AK-47 — 7.62x39mm Kalashnikov, multiple inlays on receiver, European hardwood thumbhole stock, 30 shot mag., includes walnut display case, 7¾ lbs. 1,500 mfg. by FEG in Hungary beginning 1993. Entire edition is sold out.

$1,895

AMERICAN ARMED FORCES UZI — 9mm, semi-auto, carbine variation, 1,500 were ordered in 1988, but approx. 400 were delivered by I.M.I., serial numbered UZI0001 - UZI0500, mfg. by I.M.I., includes fixed (serialized approx. UZI-001 through UZI-950) wooden stock. This model is sold out.

$2,195

> A large portion of this variation was returned to Action Arms, who in turn sold them to R.S.R. Wholesalers.

SPECIAL FORCES MAC-10 — .45 ACP, issued to commemorate 25th anniversary of the MAC-10, semi-auto, special etching and engraving, 1,500 mfg. by Military Armament Corporation. Original issue price was $1,195. Entire edition is sold out.

$1,595

WWII '03 SPRINGFIELD — .30-06 cal., 500 mfg. Original issue price was $1,495.

$1,695

SHOTGUNS

Values listed below include original display cases.

FEDERAL DUCK STAMP BROWNING EDITIONS (SUPERPOSED AND A-5) — 12 ga., 3 different grades include Citori (Japanese - 100 mfg.), B-125 (Belgium - 100 mfg.), and B-25 (Belgium - 50 mfg.), features multiple 24 Kt. gold inlays, special custom order only, 250 mfg. of A-5 Mag.

Citori	**$5,795**
B-125 (12 or 20 ga.)	**$10,495**
B-25 (12 or 20 ga.)	**$15,995**
A-5	**$2,595**

> Original issue prices were (Citori) $4,995, (B-125) $9,995, and (B-25) $14,500.

WATERFOWL CLASSIC SxS SPECIAL EDITION — 12 ga., 100 mfg. by Ugartechea from Spain beginning 1995.

$1,995

H & H UPLAND BIRD SPECIAL EDITION — 12 or 20 ga., special engraving in wood, only 10 mfg. to commemorate the discontinuance of the Cavalier deLuxe Model. Entire edition is sold out.

$19,995

Grading	Most Recent Issue Price

FRENCH REVOLUTION SHOTGUN — hand engraved, signed by Cesare Giovanelli, left side of receiver depicts the storming of Bastille, right side shows the March on Versailles, 200 mfg. by Renato Gamba. Entire edition is sold out.

$10,995

VIETNAM WAR COMBAT SHOTGUN — 12 ga., hand engraved receiver with 24 Kt. gold plated small parts, serial numbered VN001 - VN750, 750 mfg. 1988 by Savage Industries, this edition is entirely sold out.

$1,595

AMERICAN INDUSTRIES

Please refer to the Calico section in this text.

AMERICAN INTERNATIONAL

Austria.

Grading	100%	98%	95%	90%	80%	70%	60%

AMERICAN 180 AUTO CARBINE — a specialized .22 LR, designed for para military use, 177 round drum mag., 16½ in. barrel, aperture sight, high impact plastic stock.

	100%	98%	95%	90%	80%	70%	60%
	$660	$550	$440	$360	$330	$305	$275

Add $550 for Laser Lok System.
Add $125 for Extra Drum Mag. and Winder.

Note: This gun was available in a selective fire version for law enforcement only. The gun also was available with a laser assisted sighting system which, when affixed to the weapon, projects a beam to point of impact.

AMTEC 2000, INC.

Trademark incorporating Erma Werke (German) and H & R 1871 (U.S.) companies beginning 1996. Distributed exclusively by Ellett Brothers.

REVOLVERS

5 SHOT REVOLVER — .38 S&W cal., 5 shot double action, swing-out cylinder, 2 or 3 in. barrel, transfer bar safety, Pachmayr composition grips, high polish blue, matte electroless nickel, or stainless steel construction, fixed sights, approx. 25 oz. U.S. mfg. beginning 1996.

As this edition went to press, prices had yet to be established.

ANCIENS ETABLISSEMENTS PIEPER

Please refer to the Bayard section in this text for Bayard Models 1908, 1923, and 1930. In addition, Bergmann-Bayard Models 1908 and 1910 mfg. in Gaggenau, Germany will appear under the Bergman heading.

ANSCHUTZ

Manufacturer located in Ulm, Germany. Distributed by AcuSport located in Bellefontaine, OH. Previously imported and distributed until 1995 in the U.S. by Precision Sales International Inc., located in Westfield, MA.

Grading	100%	98%	95%	90%	80%	70%	60%

PISTOLS

MODEL 1416P (EXEMPLAR) — .22 LR, bolt action, Match 64 left-hand action (for right-hand shooters), approx. 7 (Silhouette Model, mfg. 1994-95) or 10 in. barrel, 5 shot mag., two-stage trigger, adj. rear sight, receiver grooved for scope, contoured grip and forestock are stippled, $3\frac{1}{3}$ lbs., also available for left-hand shooters. New 1987.

Mfg.'s Sug. Retail	$473	$415	$350	$295	$250	$225	$200	$180

This model was previously designated the Exemplar until 1996.

▲ **Exemplar Magnum** — while advertised in 1987, the .22 Mag. was never manufactured.

▲ **Exemplar XIV** — .22 LR, similar to Exemplar, except has 14 in. barrel, 4.15 lbs. Imported 1988-95.

	$450	$370	$300	$250	$225	$200	$180

Last Mfg.'s Sug. Retail was $562.

▲ **Exemplar Hornet** — .22 Hornet cal., 5 shot mag., Match 54 left hand-action, 10 in. barrel, no sights - tapped and grooved, 4.35 lbs. Imported 1988-95.

	$835	$685	$575	$525	$475	$415	$365

Last Mfg.'s Sug. Retail was $995.

RIFLES: BOLT ACTION, DISC.

Sile Distributors located in NY acted as an import agent during the early 1960s which can be identified by Sile barrel markings. Savage imported Anschutz rifles were available from 1963-1981 and also have Savage/Anschutz barrel markings. While some of those models might not be listed below, refer to models of similar caliber and quality that are listed to ascertain values.

During the period when Savage was importing Anschutz rifles, certain models in the Anschutz line were designated "Savage-Anschutz" for sales by Savage in the U.S. Conversely, certain models manufactured by Savage were designated "Anschutz-Savage" for sale by Anschutz in Europe. Some of these models did not have any modifications but others were restocked, supplied with different sights, and had other different features from their original counterparts. In most cases, the original model numbers were used.

Some "Anschutz-Savage" rifles have made their way into the U.S. While somewhat rare, these rifles are typically based on the Savage Model 110 action. They are not as desirable as those "Savage-Anschutz" marked rifles utilizing the superior Anschutz action. Anschutz also manufactured between 1,000-2,000 rifles utilizing SAKO actions in .222 Rem. cal. in the late 50s-early 60s. These guns will approximate values shown on the discontinued centerfire models listed below.

MARK 10 TARGET RIFLE — .22 LR cal., single shot, 26 in. heavy barrel, adj. sights, globe front, target stock with full pistol grip, adj. palm stop, mfg. 1963-1981.

	$350	$320	$290	$260	$230	$210	$195

MODEL 1400 — .22 LR cal., regular barrel, with sights. Disc.

	$350	$320	$290	$260	$230	$210	$195

MODEL 1407 — .22 LR cal. "I.S.U." model, heavy barrel, no sights. Disc.

	$375	$340	$300	$260	$230	$210	$195

MODEL 1408 — .22 LR cal., heavy barrel, no sights. Disc.

	$375	$340	$300	$260	$230	$210	$195

Add $150 for 1408 ED Model.

MODEL 1411 — .22 LR cal., prone position target model, heavy barrel, no sights. Disc.

	$360	$320	$290	$260	$230	$210	$195

Grading	100%	98%	95%	90%	80%	70%	60%

MODEL 1413 MATCH — .22 LR cal., adj. cheekpiece, heavy target barrel with no sights, competition model. Disc.

	$550	$475	$420	$375	$325	$285	$240

MODEL 1418 MANNLICHER — .22 LR cal., hunting model, fine checkering, clip mag.

	$650	$575	$500	$450	$365	$315	$275

MODEL 1418 — .22 LR cal., sporter variation, previous importation by Savage Arms.

	$300	$260	$225	$200	$175	$150	$125

MODEL 1450 — .22 LR cal., Sporter, 5 shot mag.

	$275	$225	$200	$175	$150	$125	$110

MODEL 1518 MANNLICHER — deluxe model of Model 1418.

	$700	$595	$540	$485	$430	$375	$325

MODEL 1574 SPORTER — .22 Mag., .222 Rem., .22-250 Rem., .223 Rem., .243 Win., or .308 Win. cal., mfg. by Krico (Kriegeskorte) located at Stuttgart and distributed by Anschutz, approx. 1,000 imported during 1970-73.

	$795	$695	$595	$540	$485	$430	$375

MODEL 153 — .222 Rem., 24 in. barrel, folding leaf rear sight, French walnut stock, rosewood forend tip and pistol grip cap. Mfg. 1963-1981.

	$550	$475	$400	$375	$350	$300	$280

MODEL 153-S — similar to Model 153, .222 Rem., 24 in. barrel, double set triggers.

	$600	$525	$450	$425	$385	$330	$305

MODEL 184 — .22 LR, 21½ in. barrel, Monte Carlo combination, checkered pistol grip, Schnabel forend, folding leaf sight. Mfg. 1963-1981.

	$350	$320	$290	$260	$230	$210	$195

MODEL 54 SPORTER — .22 LR, 5 shot clip, 24 in. round tapered barrel, Monte Carlo roll over combination, folding leaf sight, checkered pistol grip. Mfg. 1963-1981.

	$675	$595	$525	$450	$400	$360	$330

MODEL 54M — similar to Sporter, except .22 Win. Mag.

	$725	$625	$550	$475	$425	$395	$350

MODEL 141 — .22 LR, 5 shot clip, 23 in. round tapered barrel, Monte Carlo stock, folding leaf sight. Disc.

	$345	$280	$240	$200	$180	$160	$140
Model 141M (Mag.)	$400	$365	$300	$265	$225	$200	$180

MODEL 164 — .22 LR, 5 shot clip, 23 in. round tapered barrel, Monte Carlo stock, folding leaf sight. Mfg. 1963-1981.

	$380	$345	$280	$240	$200	$180	$160

MODEL 164M — similar to 164, only .22 Win. Mag.

	$400	$365	$300	$265	$225	$200	$180

SPORTER RIFLES: RECENT MANUFACTURE

KADETT — .22 LR, bolt action, youth dimensions, 22 in. barrel, 5 shot clip mag., folding leaf rear sight, single stage trigger, grooved receiver, checkered hard-wood stock, 5½ lbs. Mfg. 1987 only.

	$235	$200	$180	$165	$150	$135	$120

Last Mfg.'s Sug. Retail was $265.

A

Grading	100%	98%	95%	90%	80%	70%	60%

ACHIEVER — .22 LR, bolt action, 19½ in. barrel, single shot, folding leaf rear sight, two stage trigger, grooved receiver, stippled hard-wood stock with vented forearm and adj. length of pull, 5¼ lbs. Mfg. 1987-95.

	$340	$280	$230	$205	$185	$165	$150

Last Mfg.'s Sug. Retail was $399.

▲ **Achiever ST** — .22 cal., Mark 2000 single shot action, slide safety, two stage trigger, adj. length of pull stock, target sights, approx. 6½ lbs. Mfg. 1994-95.

	$415	$360	$315	$260	$230	$205	$185

Last Mfg.'s Sug. Retail was $485.

MODEL 1449D YOUTH — .22 LR, bolt action design, youth dimensions, 16¼ in. tapered barrel with adj. rear sight, receiver is grooved for scope mounting, 5 shot clip mag. with single shot clip adapter available, European hardwood stock, 12¼ in. trigger pull, 3½ lbs. Imported 1990-91 only.

	$210	$185	$165	$150	$135	$120	$110

Last Mfg.'s Sug. Retail was $249.

▲ **Model Woodchucker** — .22 LR, similar to Model 1449D Youth, sold exclusively by R.S.R. Wholesale.

	$210	$185	$165	$150	$135	$120	$110

MODEL 1416D LUXUS/CUSTOM — .22 LR, bolt action, 22½ in. barrel, 5 or 10 shot mag., cam cocking system on recent mfg., checkered Monte Carlo walnut stock, folding leaf sight.

Mfg.'s Sug. Retail	$674	$595	$475	$410	$350	$295	$240	$225

This model utilizes the Match 64 action, similar to the Anschutz Model 1403 Target. Until 1996, this model was designated Model 1416D Custom.

▲ **Model 1416D Fiberglass** — similar to Model 1416D Custom, except has McMillan fiberglass stock in hunter brown color and includes roll-over cheekpiece and checkered Wundhammer swell pistol grip, 5¼ lbs. Imported 1991 only.

	$755	$650	$575	$525	$475	$415	$365

Last Mfg.'s Sug. Retail was $842.

▲ **1416D Classic** — same specifications as 1416D Custom, except regular stock.

Mfg.'s Sug. Retail	$634	$560	$460	$400	$350	$295	$240	$225

Add $32 for left-hand action.

MODEL 1418D — .22 LR, Mannlicher full stock, skipline checkering, 19¾ in. barrel, same action as Model 1416D. Importation disc. 1995.

	$975	$800	$665	$550	$495	$425	$360

Last Mfg.'s Sug. Retail was $1,159.

Add $40 for set trigger (mfg. 1985-89).

MODEL 1451 SPORTER — .22 LR, 5 shot, sporter target model w/o front sight, 22 ¾ in. barrel, checkered pistol grip wood stock and forend. New 1996.

Mfg.'s Sug. Retail	$487	$420	$360	$315	$260	$230	$205	$185

MODEL 1451P — .22 LR, 5 shot, 22¾ in. barrel with front sights, grooved receiver, walnut finished hardwood stock. New 1996.

Mfg.'s Sug. Retail	$324	$285	$250	$225	$200	$185	$165	$150

MODEL 1466D REPEATER — .22 LR cal., 24 in. conically tapered barrel with open sights, grooved receiver, checkered Monte Carlo walnut stock and forend. New 1996.

Mfg.'s Sug. Retail	$766	$660	$525	$435	$375	$315	$260	$235

MODEL 1700D/1710D CUSTOM - .22 LR — .22 LR, bolt action, 5 shot mag., 24 in. barrel, iron sights, heavy barrel, Monte Carlo stock with skipline checkering, 7¼ lbs.

Mfg.'s Sug. Retail	$1,162	$1,050	$775	$650	$550	$450	$375	$325

Add $199 for Meistergrade (select walnut and gold etched trigger guard - disc. 1996).

This model was designated 1422D until 1989 when it was changed to the Model 1700D with some modifications. In 1996, model nomenclature changed from Model 1700D

A

Custom to the Model 1710D Custom. The Model 1400D Meistergrade was disc. 1987 - the last advertised retail price was $930.

The Model 1700D Custom employs the Anschutz Match 54 action.

▲ *1700D Graphite* — similar to Model 1700D Custom, except has McMillan black graphite reinforced stock with Monte Carlo roll-over cheekpiece, includes sling and swivels, 22 in. barrel, 7¼ lbs. Imported 1991-95.

	100%	98%	95%	90%	80%	70%	60%
	$1,130	$885	$760	$650	$550	$450	$375

Last Mfg.'s Sug. Retail was $1,299.

▲ *1700D Classic* — same general specifications as 1700D Custom, except smaller diameter barrel and regular stock. Disc. 1994.

	100%	98%	95%	90%	80%	70%	60%
	$1,095	$860	$750	$650	$550	$450	$375

Last Mfg.'s Sug. Retail was $1,236 on the 1700D Classic.

Add $199 for Meistergrade (select walnut and gold etched trigger guard).

This model was designated 1422DCL Classic until 1989 when it was changed to the Model 1700D Classic with some modifications. The Model 1422DCL Classic Meistergrade was disc. 1987 - the last advertised retail price was $875.

1700D FEATHERWEIGHT — similar to Model 1700D Custom, except has matte black McMillan fiberglass stock configured like the Custom Model, 22 in. barrel, no sights, 6¼ lbs. Imported 1989-95.

	100%	98%	95%	90%	80%	70%	60%
	$1,075	$895	$775	$650	$550	$450	$375

Last Mfg.'s Sug. Retail was $1,230.

▲ *1700D Featherweight Deluxe* — similar specification to the 1700D Featherweight, except has skip-line checkered Fibergrain synthetic stock with realistic wood grain. Imported 1990-95.

	100%	98%	95%	90%	80%	70%	60%
	$1,235	$1,050	$875	$775	$650	$550	$450

Last Mfg.'s Sug. Retail was $1,460.

DIE MEISTERMACHER — .22 LR, similar action and specifications as Model 1422D Custom, limited edition of 25 guns, select wood, extra polish on metal parts, hand-lapped barrel, with numerous gold inlays including Olympic wreath. Mfg. 1985.

	100%	98%	95%
	$2,500	$2,000	$1,600

Last Mfg.'s Sug. Retail was $2,475. This variation sold out in late 1988.

MODEL 1700D/1730D CUSTOM - .22 HORNET — .22 Hornet, 24 in. barrel, folding leaf sight, Monte Carlo stock with skipline checkering and rosewood grip cap, 4 shot mag., 7¾ lbs. Model 1432D was disc. 1987, and the Model 1700D was introduced 1989.

Mfg.'s Sug. Retail	$1,297	$1,130	$885	$760	$650	$550	$450	$375

Add $199 for Meistergrade variation (select walnut, disc. 1995).

This model was designated 1432D until 1987 and then reintroduced 1989 as the Model 1700D with some modifications. In 1996, model nomenclature changed from the Model 1700D Custom to the Model 1730D Custom. The Model 1432D Custom Meistergrade was disc. 1986 - the last advertised retail price was $770.

The 1700D Custom comes standard with the Anschutz Match 54 action.

▲ *1700D Graphite* — similar to Model 1700D Custom, except has McMillan black graphite reinforced stock with Monte Carlo roll-over cheekpiece, includes sling and swivels, 22 in. barrel, 7¼ lbs. Imported 1995 only.

	100%	98%	95%	90%	80%	70%	60%
	$1,235	$1,025	$840	$725	$625	$525	$425

Last Mfg.'s Sug. Retail was $1,478.

▲ *Model 1700D Classic* — same general specifications as 1700D Custom, except regular stock and 23½ (1432DCL) or 24 (1700D) in. barrel. Disc. 1994.

	100%	98%	95%	90%	80%	70%	60%
	$1,200	$995	$835	$735	$615	$500	$400

Last Mfg.'s Sug. Retail was $849 on the Model 1432DCL.

Add $199 for Meistergrade variation (select walnut).

This model was designated 1432D until 1987 and then reintroduced 1989 as the Model 1700D with some modifications. This model comes standard with the Anschutz Match 54 action.

Last Mfg.'s Sug. Retail was $1,395 on the Model 1700D Classic.

A

MODEL 1733D — .22 Hornet cal., Mannlicher full stock featuring skipline checkering, European walnut, and rosewood Schnabel tip. Mfg. 1993-95.

	$1,350	$1,100	$925	$765	$650	$550	$475

Last Mfg.'s Sug. Retail was $1,657.

MODEL 1433D — .22 Hornet, special order only, Match 54 target action, Mannlicher full stock, 4 shot mag. Set trigger new 1985 — add $15. Disc. 1986.

	$995	$840	$740	$640	$525	$425	$350

Last Mfg.'s Sug. Retail was $826.

MODEL 1516D LUXUS/CUSTOM — similar to Model 1416D, except .22 Mag., 4 shot mag.

Mfg.'s Sug. Retail	$694		$610	$485	$410	$350	$295	$240	$225

This model utilizes the Match 64 action, similar to the Anschutz Model 1403 Target. In 1996, model nomenclature changed from the Model 1516D Custom to 1516D Luxus.

▲ *1516D/DCL Classic* — same specifications as 1516D Custom, except regular stock.

Mfg.'s Sug. Retail	$654		$575	$460	$395	$350	$295	$240	$225

MODEL 1518D — .22 Mag. otherwise similar to Model 1418D (Mannlicher stock), 4 shot mag., 5½ lbs. Disc. 1995.

	$965	$775	$640	$525	$440	$375	$325

Last Mfg.'s Sug. Retail was $1,170.

Add $40 for set trigger (disc.).

MODEL 1700D CUSTOM - .22 MAG. — .22 Mag., bolt action, 5 shot mag., 24 in. barrel, iron sights, heavy barrel, Monte Carlo stock with skipline checkering, 7¼ lbs. Importation disc. 1991.

	$1,095	$895	$750	$650	$550	$450	$375

Last Mfg.'s Sug. Retail was $1,229 for Model 1700D.

Add $195 for Meistergrade variation (select walnut).

This model was designated 1522D until 1989 and then reintroduced as the Model 1700D with some modifications. The Model 1522D Custom Meistergrade was disc. 1985 - last advertised retail price was $678.

▲ *1700D Classic* — same general specifications as 1700D Custom, except smaller diameter barrel and regular stock. Importation disc. 1991.

	$1,075	$875	$725	$625	$525	$425	$350

Last Mfg.'s Sug. Retail was $1,199 for Model 1700D Classic.

Add $195 for Meistergrade variation (select walnut).

This model was designated 1522DCL until 1989 and then reintroduced as the Model 1700D with some modifications. The Model 1522DCL Classic Meistergrade was disc. 1985 - the last advertised retail price was $660.

MODEL 1700D BAVARIAN — .22 LR, .22 Mag., .22 Hornet, or .222 Rem. cal., 24 in. barrel, clip mag., checkered European style stock with European Monte Carlo cheekpiece and schnabel forend, 7½ lbs. Mfg. 1988-95.

	$1,165	$935	$775	$650	$550	$450	$375

Last Mfg.'s Sug. Retail was $1,364.

Add $170 for .22 Hornet or .222 Rem. cal.
Add $199 for Meistergrade variation (select walnut).

MODEL 1700D/1740D CUSTOM - .222 REM. — .222 Rem., otherwise similar to Model 1700D Custom, except is also available with 23.6 in. barrel.

Mfg.'s Sug. Retail	$1,298		$1,075	$895	$775	$650	$550	$450	$400

Last Mfg.'s Sug. Retail was $909 on the Model 1532D.

Add $199 for Meistergrade variation (select walnut).

This model was designated 1532D until 1987 and then reintroduced 1989 as the Model 1700D with some modifications. In 1996, model nomenclature changed from the Model 1700D Custom to the Model 1740D Custom. The Model 1532D MG Custom Meistergrade was disc. 1986 - the last advertised retail price was $770.

A

Grading	100%	98%	95%	90%	80%	70%	60%

▲ **1700D Classic** — similar to Model 1700D Custom, except regular stock. Disc. 1994.

	$1,200	$995	$835	$735	$615	$500	$400

Last Mfg.'s Sug. Retail was $849 on Model 1532DCL.

Add $199 for Meistergrade variation (select walnut).

This model was designated 1532DCL until 1987 and then reintroduced 1989 as the Model 1700D with some modifications.

Last Mfg.'s Sug. Retail was $1,395 on Model 1700D Classic.

MODEL 1533 — .222 Rem. cal., open sights, checkered walnut stock. Disc. 1994.

	$795	$725	$660	$600	$550	$475	$400

RIFLES: SINGLE SHOT SILHOUETTE

As this edition went to press, the Single Shot Silhouette rifles listed below were not being currently imported. Values reflect the most recent pricing information available.

BR-50 — .22 LR cal., single shot, 20 in. heavy barrel, no sights, black synthetic stock with adj. cheekpiece and widened forend ("ANSCHUTZ BR-50" is stenciled on sides), 11½ lbs. New 1994.

Mfg.'s Sug. Retail	$3,312	$2,775	$1,875	$1,425	$1,025	$850	$725	$625

MODEL 64S RIFLE — single shot, .22 LR, 26 in. round barrel, beavertail forearm, adj. single stage trigger, aperture sights, target stock with Wundhammer grip and adj. butt plate, checkered pistol grip, mfg. 1963-1981.

	$475	$425	$375	$325	$285	$240	$220

Subtract 15% if without sights (Model 64).

This model was available in left or right hand action.

MODEL 64MS — .22 LR, single shot silhouette target model, 21¼ in. barrel, no sights, Wundhammer swell stippled pistol grip stock, adj. trigger, 8 lbs.

Mfg.'s Sug. Retail	$987		$825	$655	$540	$450	$375	$350	$285

Add $50 for left-hand action.

This variation employs the Model 1403 action.

▲ **Model 64MS - FWT** — similar to Model 64MS, except single stage trigger, 6¼ lbs. Disc. 1988.

	$550	$475	$425	$350	$325	$260	$230

Last Mfg.'s Sug. Retail was $596.

MODEL 54.18MS — .22 LR, silhouette target model, 22 in. barrel, match 54 single shot action, walnut Wundhammer stock is stippled on pistol grip and entire forearm, no sights, 8 lbs. 6 oz.

Mfg.'s Sug. Retail	$1,579		$1,295	$1,075	$895	$760	$650	$550	$475

Add $96 for left-hand action.

This model employs the Super Match 54 action.

▲ **Model 54.18MS ED** — same action as Model 54.18MS, except has 19¼ in. barrel (⅞ in. diameter) with 14¼ in. extension tube, 3 removable muzzle weights. Disc. 1988.

	$1,075	$900	$775	$675	$575	$485	$410

Last Mfg.'s Sug. Retail was $1,215.

Add $100 for left-hand action.

MODEL 54.18MS REP — similar to Model 54.18MS, except has repeating action, 5 shot mag., thumbhole wood stock with vented forestock, 7¾ lbs. This model was introduced in 1989 with a wood stock and a retail price of $1,650. In 1990, the stock was changed to a synthetic McMillan fiberglass finished in gray.

Mfg.'s Sug. Retail	$2,066		$1,725	$1,350	$1,050	$925	$800	$695	$595

Add 10% for wood stock (1989 mfg. only).

This model features a 54 Super Match action with clip mag.

▲ **Model 54.18MS REP Deluxe** — deluxe version of the Model 54.18MS REP featuring Fibergrain McMillan stock with advanced thumbhole design and stippled checkering. New 1990.

Mfg.'s Sug. Retail	$2,450		$2,035	$1,600	$1,275	$1,025	$915	$785	$695

A

Grading	100%	98%	95%	90%	80%	70%	60%

MATCH RIFLES: BOLT ACTION - RECENT PRODUCTION

As this edition went to press, the Match rifles listed below were not being currently imported. Values reflect the most recent pricing information available.

MODEL 2000 MK — .22 LR, single shot match, 26 in. barrel, aperture sights, 7½ lbs. Disc. 1988.

	$340	$290	$250	$210	$180	$160	$145

Last Mfg.'s Sug. Retail was $400.

MODEL 1403D — .22 LR, improved Model 64S match rifle, single shot, no sights, adj. trigger, 8 lbs. 6 oz. Importation disc. in 1990.

	$600	$525	$450	$360	$300	$260	$225

Last Mfg.'s Sug. Retail was $700.

Add $50 for left-hand action (disc. 1988).

MODEL 1803D — .22 LR, Match 64 action, 25½ in. target barrel, single stage adj. trigger, blond finished wood with dark stippling on pistol grip and forearm, adj. cheekpiece and butt plate, 8.6 lbs. Imported 1987-1993.

	$850	$725	$625	$525	$430	$365	$310

Last Mfg.'s Sug. Retail was $1,012.

Add $70 for left-hand action (disc. 1989).

MODEL 1808D RT (RUNNING TARGET) — .22 LR, single shot running target model, 32½ in. barrel, adj. stock, cheekpiece, trigger, heavy beavertail forend, no sights, muzzle barrel weights, 9¼ lbs.

Mfg.'s Sug. Retail	$1,963		$1,625	$1,300	$995	$825	$725	$580	$500

Add $50 for left-hand action (disc. 1991).

This model was previously designated the Model 1808 ED Super during 1990 and earlier mfg.

MODEL 1903D — .22 LR, similar specifications to the Model 1803D, except has new improved target stock and adj. cheekpiece made from walnut finished European hardwood, color laminated stock introduced 1995, full length stippled checkering on forend and contoured pistol grip, fully adj. new style butt plate, 8.6 lbs. New 1990.

Mfg.'s Sug. Retail	$1,163		$940	$750	$640	$540	$430	$365	$310

Add $58 for left-hand action.
Add $130 for color laminated stock.

MODEL 1907 ISU — .22 LR, single shot match "I.S.U." model, 26 in. barrel, prone and position shooting, removable cheekpiece, adj. butt plate, hand stippled stock with ventilated forearm and choice of walnut, blond laminated, or color laminated (new 1995) wood, 11 lbs.

Mfg.'s Sug. Retail	$1,983		$1,660	$1,300	$1,025	$840	$700	$580	$500

Add $100 for left-hand action.
Add $156 for color laminated stock.
Add $77 for either walnut stock or shorter stock dimensions (new 1994).

This variation was designated Model 1807 before 1989.

MODEL 1910 SUPER MATCH II — .22 LR, single shot, 27¼ in. barrel, diopter sights, thumbhole stock is fully adj., 12 lbs., model down from 1813 (or 1913), special order only.

Mfg.'s Sug. Retail	$2,967		$2,415	$1,925	$1,475	$1,100	$900	$725	$625

Add $149 for left-hand action.

This variation was designated as Model 1810 before 1988.

MODEL 1911 PRONE MATCH — .22 LR, single shot match prone rifle, 27¼ in. barrel, adj. cheekpiece, butt plate, no sights.

Mfg.'s Sug. Retail	$2,325		$1,965	$1,550	$1,225	$1,025	$925	$785	$695

Add $100 for left-hand action (disc. 1993).

This variation was designated Model 1811 before 1988.

Grading	100%	98%	95%	90%	80%	70%	60%

MODEL 1913 SUPER MATCH — .22 LR single shot, top-of-the-line match rifle, every possible refinement, international diopter sights, 27$\frac{1}{4}$ in. barrel, hand and palm rest, 13.9 lbs.

Mfg.'s Sug. Retail	$3,422	$2,850	$1,925	$1,475	$1,075	$875	$725	$625

Add $170 for left-hand action.

This variation was designated Model 1813 before 1988.

MODEL 2007 ISU STANDARD — .22 LR, ISU model featuring 19$\frac{3}{4}$ in. barrel and new heavy receiver, detachable tube in front of barrel providing for different sights and counter-weights, adj. cheekpiece and rubber butt plate, grooved and vented forearm, choice of blond or walnut stock, Match 54 action, 10.8 lbs. New 1992.

Mfg.'s Sug. Retail	$2,881	$2,495	$1,900	$1,450	$1,075	$875	$725	$625

Add $134 for left-hand action (new 1993).

Add $80 for either walnut stock or shorter stock dimensions (new 1994).

This model underwent significant enigneering changes during 1994.

MODEL 2013 SUPER MATCH — .22 LR, top-of-the-line international target rifle featuring 19$\frac{3}{4}$ in. barrel with detachable front tube allowing for different sights and counter-weights, top grain walnut stock with adj. hand rest, palm rest, cheekpiece, and elaborate metal butt plate, Match 54 action, 12$\frac{1}{2}$ lbs. New 1992.

Mfg.'s Sug. Retail	$4,067	$3,500	$2,925	$2,475	$2,150	$1,900	$1,650	$1,400

Add $203 for left-hand action (new 1993).

This model underwent significant engineering changes during 1994.

BIATHLON RIFLES

As this edition went to press, the Biathlon rifles listed below were not being currently imported. Values reflect the most recent pricing information available.

MODEL 1450B — .22 LR bolt action, Mark 2000 action, 19$\frac{1}{2}$ in. barrel, European hardwood with vent. forearm and adj. butt plate, aperture sights, 5 lbs. Mfg. 1993 only.

	$650	$550	$450	$375	$300	$260	$230

Last Mfg.'s Sug. Retail was $765.

MODEL 1403B — .22 LR bolt action, Match 64 action, 21$\frac{1}{2}$ in. barrel, blonde finished European hardwood with stippled pistol grip, Biathlon design allows 4 mags. to be stored in a housing attached to the forend on right side, entry level Biathlon gun, 8$\frac{1}{2}$ lbs. Mfg. 1990-92.

	$850	$730	$660	$525	$450	$375	$335

Last Mfg.'s Sug. Retail was $998.

MODEL 1827B — .22 LR bolt action, biathlon rifle, carries four 5 shot mags. in stock, special biathlon features, 21$\frac{1}{2}$ in. barrel, limited production.

Mfg.'s Sug. Retail	$2,457	$2,050	$1,550	$1,225	$1,025	$895	$785	$695

Add $120 for left-hand action (disc. 1989).

In 1990, the stock design was changed permitting 8 mags. to be stored in two housings attached to both the stock and forend on right side.

▲ *Model 1827BT Fortner* — same general specifications as Model 1827B, except has Fortner straight pull-through bolt action, color laminated stock became available 1995, 9 lbs. New 1986.

Mfg.'s Sug. Retail	$3,722	$3,225	$2,825	$2,450	$2,275	$1,925	$1,650	$1,400

Add $368 for left-hand action.

Add $172 for color laminated stock.

In 1990, the stock design was changed permitting 8 mags. to be stored in two housings attached to both the stock and forend on right side.

RIFLES: SEMI-AUTO

MODEL 520/61 — .22 LR, semi-auto, 24 in. barrel, 10 shot mag., Monte Carlo stock, 6$\frac{1}{2}$ lbs. Disc. 1983.

	$260	$205	$185	$155	$145	$130	$120

Grading	100%	98%	95%	90%	80%	70%	60%

MARK 525 SPORTER RIFLE — .22 LR, semi-auto, 24 in. barrel, 10 shot mag., adj. rear sight, Monte Carlo stock, 6½ lbs. Imported 1984-95.

	$460	$395	$350	$295	$250	$215	$175

Last Mfg.'s Sug. Retail was $547.

▲ **Mark 525 Carbine** — similar to Mark 525 Rifle, except has 20 in. barrel. Disc. 1986.

	$400	$315	$265	$225	$200	$180	$160

ANSCHUTZ SHOTGUNS

Anschutz marked O/U shotguns that are manufactured by Miroku of Japan and are distributed in Germany only. Several grades of these shotguns are manufactured and while rarely seen in the U.S., values approximate other Miroku O/Us of similar quality and features ($650 - $1,000 assuming 95% or better condition).

APACHE

Previous importer, mfg. by Ojanguren Y Vidosa, Eibar, Spain.

HANDGUN

SEMI-AUTO — 6.35mm., clip fed.

	$190	$175	$160	$140	$120	$95	$75

ARLINGTON ORDNANCE

Importer located in Westport, CT. Previously located in Weston, CT. Distributor sales only.

M1 GARAND RIFLE — .30-06 cal., these Garands are being imported from Korea in used condition, various manufacturers, with import stamp. Importation began 1991.

No Mfg.'s Retail

	$345	$295	$250	$200	$180	$160	$140

Add $30 for stock upgrade (better wood).

▲ **Arsenal Restored M1 Garand Rifle** — .30-06 or .308 Win. cal., features new barrel, rebuilt gas system, and reinspected components. New 1994.

No Mfg.'s Retail

	$495	$385	$325	$285	$250	$200	$180

Add $20 for .308 Win. cal.

TROPHY GARAND — .308 Win. only, action is original mil-spec., includes new barrel and checkered walnut stock and forend, recoil pad. New 1994.

Mfg.'s Sug. Retail

	$695		$625	$525	$375	$325	$275	$225	$200

T26 TANKER — .30-06 or .308 Win. cal., includes new barrel and other key components, updated stock finish. New 1994.

No Mfg.'s Retail

	$550	$415	$340	$295	$265	$200	$180

.30 CAL. CARBINE — .30 Carbine, 18 in. barrel, these Carbines are being imported from Korea in used condition, various manufacturers, with import stamp. Importation began 1991.

No Mfg.'s Retail

	$225	$185	$160	$140	$125	$115	$100

Add approximately $55 for stock upgrade (better wood).

MODEL FIVE CARBINE — .30 Carbine, new mfg., 17 in. barrel, walnut finished hardwood stock with barrel band, iron sights, blue finish, features key-lockable action, 10 shot mag. New 1995.

Mfg.'s Sug. Retail

	$295		$245	$215	$185	$165	$145	$130	$115

ARMALITE, INC.

New manufacture began in 1995 in Geneseo, IL, after Eagle Arms, Inc. purchased the Armalite trademarks. Original manufacture was located in Costa Mesa, CA approx. 1959-1973.

Grading	100%	98%	95%	90%	80%	70%	60%

A

RIFLES

AR-7 EXPLORER — semi-auto, .22 LR, 16 in. aluminum barrel with steel liner, aperture sight, gun takes down and can be stored in hollow plastic stock, gun will float, mfg. 1959-1973 by Armalite, 1974-1990 by Charter Arms, and currently mfg. by Survival Arms located in Cocoa, FL from 1990-present (see Survival Arms Listing).

	$120	$100	$85	$75	$65	$55	$50

AR-7 CUSTOM — similar to AR-7 Explorer, only with custom walnut stock including cheekpiece, pistol grip. Mfg. 1964-1970.

	$175	$145	$125	$100	$90	$80	$70

AR-10 SERIES — .308 Win. cal., semi-auto paramilitary design, various configurations, with or w/o sights and carry handle, supplied with two 10 shot mags. New late 1995.

▲ *AR-10T* — features 24 in. chrome-moly 1:10 twist heavy barrel, two-stage trigger, smooth ungrooved barrel shroud, w/o sights or carry handle.

Mfg.'s Sug. Retail	$1,995	$1,795	$1,525	$1,275	$1,125	$995	$875	$750

▲ *AR-10A4* — features 20 in. chrome-lined 1:12 twist H-Bar barrel, removable front sight, w/o carry handle.

Mfg.'s Sug. Retail	$1,325	$1,195	$975	$850	$750	$675	$595	$525

Add $100 for stainless steel barrel.

▲ *AR-10A2* — features 20 in. chrome-lined 1:12 twist II-Bar barrel, includes fixed sights and carry handle.

Mfg.'s Sug. Retail	$1,325	$1,195	$975	$850	$750	$675	$595	$525

AR-180 — .223 Rem. cal., semi-auto, gas operated, 18¼ in. barrel, folding stock. Manufactured by Armalite in Costa Mesa, CA, 1969-1972, Howa Machinery Ltd., Nagoya, Japan 1972 and 1973. Since 1976 the AR-180 has been made by Sterling Armament Co. Ltd., Dagenham, Essex, England.

▲ *Sterling Mfg.*

	$850	$775	$695	$625	$550	$495	$450

▲ *Costa Mesa Mfg.*

	$995	$875	$750	$675	$600	$550	$500

▲ *Howa Mfg.*

	$1,350	$1,110	$995	$875	$795	$725	$650

M15 RIFLE/CARBINE VARIATIONS — .223 cal., various configurations, barrel lengths, sights, and other features.

▲ *M15A2 National Match Rifle* — features 20 in. stainless steel 1:8 twist heavy barrel with National Match sights and two-stage barrel, grooved barrel shroud.

Mfg.'s Sug. Retail	$1,475	$1,295	$1,050	$875	$775	$675	$595	$525

▲ *M15A2 H-Bar Rifle* — includes 20 in. chrome-lined 1:9 twist barrel, grooved barrel shroud.

Mfg.'s Sug. Retail	$895	$815	$700	$625	$550	$500	$450	$415

▲ *M15A4 Special Purpose Rifle* — includes 20 in. chrome-lined H-Bar 1:9 twist barrel with National Match sights, detachable carry handle, grooved barrel shroud.

Mfg.'s Sug. Retail	$955	$855	$730	$640	$560	$500	$450	$415

▲ *M4A1C Carbine* — features 16 in. chrome-lined 1:9 twist barrel with National Match sights and detachable carrying handle, grooved barrel shroud.

Mfg.'s Sug. Retail	$935	$840	$725	$640	$560	$500	$450	$415

▲ *M4C Carbine* — similar to M4A1C Carbine, except has non-removable carrying handle and fixed sights.

Mfg.'s Sug. Retail	$870	$785	$675	$600	$550	$500	$450	$415

Grading	100%	98%	95%	90%	80%	70%	60%

▲ *M15A4T Eagle Eye* — 24 in. stainless steel 1:8 twist heavy barrel, two-stage trigger, smooth fiberglass hand guard, Picatinny front sight rail but w/o sights and carrying handle.

Mfg.'s Sug. Retail	$1,495	$1,315	$1,050	$875	$775	$675	$595	$525

▲ *M15A4 Predator* — similar to M15A4T Eagle Eye, except has 1:12 twist barrel.

Mfg.'s Sug. Retail	$1,350	$1,215	$985	$850	$750	$675	$595	$525

▲ *M15A4 Action Master* — includes 20 in. stainless steel 1:9 twist barrel, two-stage trigger, muzzle brake, flat top design w/o sights or carrying handle.

Mfg.'s Sug. Retail	$1,200	$1,075	$925	$800	$700	$625	$565	$500

SHOTGUN

AR-17 — 12 ga., semi-auto, 24 in. barrel, interchangeable choke tubes, gas operated, high strength aluminum barrel and receiver, plastic stock and forearm, either gold anodized or black finish. Only 2000 mfg. between 1964-1965.

	$575	$460	$420	$360	$310	$260	$220

ARMAMENT TECHNOLOGY CORP.

Previous manufacturer located in Las Vegas, NV between 1972-1978.

RIFLES

In addition to the models listed below, ATC also manufactured a fully auto pistol named "Firefly II".

MODEL 4 POCKET RIFLE — .22 LR, semi-auto action (supplied by Mossberg), 5 in. barrel, shortened rifle (18½ in. overall length) with cut stock, 7 shot mag., approx. 450 mfg., approx. 3 lbs.

	$350	$295	$260	$230	$195	$175	$150

MODEL 6 — full length variation of the Model 4, Mossberg Model 453-T with ATC trademarks, approx. 12 mfg., approx. 5½ lbs.

	$125	$100	$85	$75	$65	$55	$45

M-2 FIREFLY — 9mm Para., featured a unique gas delayed blowback action, paramilitary configuration, collapsible stock, very limited mfg., 4¾ lbs.

	$475	$395	$350	$295	$250	$225	$195

ARMAS AZOR, S.A.

Manufacturer of double rifles located in Eibar, Spain. Currently imported exclusively by Armes De Chasse located in Hertford, NC beginning 1994.

RIFLES: SIDELOCK

The models listed below are English styled sidelock double rifles. Gold inlay and custom engraving prices are quoted per individual request.

AFRICA MARK I — available in most cals. between 9.3 X 74R and .375 H&H Mag., nominal engraving and select grade wood.

Retail prices range between $8,000-$10,000.

AFRICA MARK II — available in most cals. between 9.3 X 74R and .375 H&H Mag., African game scene engraving and superior grade wood.

Retail prices range between $10,000-$12,000.

AFRICA MARK III — available in most cals. between 9.3 X 74R and .470 NE Mag., intricate scroll engraving, cartridge trap, top tang, and superior quality grade wood.

Retail prices range between $13,000-$18,000.

Grading	100%	98%	95%	90%	80%	70%	60%

A

SHOTGUNS: SxS, SIDELOCK

SIDELOCK MODEL — 12-.410 ga.'s, English style sidelock game gun.

Mfg.'s Sug. Retail	$3,500	$3,275	$2,700	$2,200	$1,750	$1,500	$1,250	$995

ARMI TECNICHE OF EMILIO RIZZINI
Manufacturer located in Brescia, Italy.

This trademark has had limited importation to date and currently, there is no exclusive U.S. importer/distributor. Most Armi Tecniche of E. Rizzini O/U shotguns that have been imported recently have sold in the $475-$695 range. Please contact the factory directly (see listing in Trademark Index) for more information on this trademark or how to order directly from the manufacturer.

ARMINEX LTD.
Previous manufacturer located in Scottsdale, AZ.

TRI-FIRE — .45 ACP, 9mm Para., and .38 Super cals., single action auto, interchangeable barrels allow caliber conversion. Available in 5, 6, or 7 (disc. 1984) in. stainless barrel lengths, no grip safety, steel frame construction, ambidextrous thumb safety (on Target and Presentation only), smooth walnut grips, 38 oz. Approx. 250 mfg. between 1981-85.

	$525	$475	$425	$400	$375	$350	$325

Last Mfg.'s Sug. Retail was $396.

> Add $50 if presentation cased.
> Add approx. $130/conversion unit.

▲ *Target Model* — same specifications as Tri-Fire, except has 6 or 7 (disc. 1984) in. barrel, very limited mfg.

	$595	$550	$495	$450	$400	$360	$320

Last Mfg.'s Sug. Retail was $448.

ARMINIUS
Manufacturer located in Zella-Mehlis, Germany beginning 1922.

HANDGUNS: SINGLE SHOT

MODEL 1 — .22 LR Target, adj. sights.

	$275	$210	$195	$165	$155	$140	$110

MODEL 2 — similar to Model 1, except has set trigger.

	$340	$255	$225	$190	$170	$155	$140

HANDGUNS: REVOLVER

MODEL 3 — .25 ACP, folding trigger, hammerless.

	$175	$135	$125	$105	$100	$90	$80

MODEL 8 — .320 Revolver, folding trigger, hammerless.

	$175	$135	$125	$105	$100	$90	$80

MODEL 9 — .32 ACP.

	$185	$140	$130	$115	$105	$95	$85

MODEL 10 — .32 ACP, hammerless.

	$165	$125	$120	$100	$95	$85	$75

TARGET — .22 LR.

	$90	$70	$65	$55	$50	$45	$45

ARMITAGE INTERNATIONAL, LTD.
Previous manufacturer until 1990 located in Seneca, SC.

Grading	100%	98%	95%	90%	80%	70%	60%

SCARAB SKORPION — 9mm Para., paramilitary design patterned after the Czech Model 61, direct blow back action, 4.63 in. barrel, matte black finish, 12 shot (standard) or 32 shot (optional) mag., 3.5 lbs. Mfg. in U.S. 1989-90 only.

	$375	$330	$295	$260	$240	$220	$200

Last Mfg.'s Sug. Retail was $400.

Add $45 for threaded flash hider or imitation suppressor.
Only 602 Scarab Skorpions were manufactured during 1989-90.

ARMSCOR
Current trademark of firearms manufactured by Arms Corporation of the Philippines beginning 1995. Currently imported by K.B.I., Inc. located in Harrisburg, PA beginning 1995. Previously imported by Ruko located in Buffalo, NY until 1995 and by Armscorp Precision Inc. located in San Mateo, CA until 1991.

In 1991, the importation of Arms Corporation of the Philippines firearms was changed to Ruko Products, Inc. located in Buffalo, NY. Barrel markings on firearms imported by Ruko Products, Inc. state "Ruko-Armscor" instead of the older "Armscorp Precision" barrel markings. All Armscorp Precision, Inc. models were discontinued in 1991.

The models listed below also provide cross-referencing for older Armscorp Precision and Ruko imported models.

HANDGUNS

M-200DC REVOLVER — .38 Spl., 6 shot, double action, 2½ in. barrel, combat style rubber grips, blue only, fixed rear sight, 22 oz. New 1996.

Mfg.'s Sug. Retail	$199		$160	$125	$105	$90	$75	$65	$60

M-1911-A1 — .45 ACP cal., patterned after the Colt Govt. Model, 7 shot mag. (2 provided), 5 in. barrel, parkerized finish, skeletonized combat hammer and trigger, 38 oz. New 1996.

Mfg.'s Sug. Retail	$399		$330	$285	$260	$240	$220	$200	$185

RIFLES

M-14P — .22 LR, bolt action, 10 shot mag., 23 in. barrel, open sights, 6 lbs.

Mfg.'s Sug. Retail	$119		$95	$75	$60	$50	$45	$40	$35

A youth model is also available with shorter dimensions at no extra charge (M-14Y).

▲ **M14-D** — .22 LR, bolt action, similar to M-14P, except has adj. rear sight and rear checkered mahogany stock. Importation disc. 1995.

	$105	$85	$70	$60	$50	$45	$40

Last Mfg.'s Sug. Retail was $139.

M-1400LW — .22 LR, similar action to M-14P, except has checkered stock and Schnabel forend, 10 shot mag., hard rubber pad, 6 lbs. Imported 1990-92.

	$185	$165	$150	$135	$120	$105	$95

Last Mfg.'s Sug. Retail was $219.

▲ **M-1400S** — .22 LR, similar to M-1500(S), except has 10 shot mag., 6.7 lbs. New 1996.

Mfg.'s Sug. Retail	$189		$150	$115	$95	$75	$65	$55	$50

▲ **M-1400SC (Super Classic)** — .22 LR, otherwise similar to M-1500SC, except has 10 shot mag. and 23 in. barrel, 6 lbs. Importation began 1990.

Mfg.'s Sug. Retail	$339		$270	$210	$170	$140	$110	$95	$85

Grading	100%	98%	95%	90%	80%	70%	60%

M-1500(S) — .22 Mag., deluxe bolt action, 5 shot mag., 21½ in. barrel, checkered mahogany stock, open sights, 6½ lbs.

Mfg.'s Sug. Retail	$209	$165	$120	$95	$75	$65	$55	$50

▲ *Model 1500LW (Lightweight)* — similar to Model M-1500, except has lightweight classic European styled stock made of checkered American Walnut, with butt pad. Imported 1990-92.

	$190	$170	$150	$135	$120	$105	$95

Last Mfg.'s Sug. Retail was $229.

▲ *M-1500SC (Super Classic)* — checkered American Walnut stock with hard rubber pad and Monte Carlo cheekpiece, hardwood forend tip, engine turned bolt, 6½ lbs. Importation began 1990.

Mfg.'s Sug. Retail	$349	$280	$215	$170	$140	$110	$95	$85

M-1600 — .22 LR, semi-auto, 15 shot mag., 18 in. barrel, copy of the Armalite M16, ebony stock, 5¼ lbs.

Mfg.'s Sug. Retail	$175	$140	$110	$90	$75	$65	$55	$50

▲ *M-1600R* — similar to M-1600, except has stainless steel retractable butt stock and vent. barrel hood, 7¼ lbs. Importation disc. 1995.

	$155	$115	$95	$75	$65	$55	$50

Last Mfg.'s Sug. Retail was $199.

M-20P — .22 LR, semi-auto, 15 shot mag., 20¾ in. barrel, open sights, 5½ lbs.

Mfg.'s Sug. Retail	$119	$95	$75	$60	$50	$45	$40	$35

▲ *M-20C* — similar to Model M-20P, except has carbine style stock, barrel band, and curved steel buttplate, 16½ in. barrel, 5¼ lbs.

Mfg.'s Sug. Retail	$139	$110	$85	$70	$60	$50	$45	$40

M-1800S (CLASSIC) — .22 Hornet, bolt action, 5 shot mag., checkered hardwood stock, adj. rear sight, 6.6 lbs. New 1996.

Mfg.'s Sug. Retail	$339	$270	$210	$170	$140	$110	$95	$85

▲ *M-1800SC (Super Classic)* — similar to M-1800S, except has checkered walnut stock with forend tip, and high polish bluing. New 1996.

Mfg.'s Sug. Retail	$429	$365	$315	$255	$210	$170	$140	$110

M-2000(S) — same specifications as M-20P, except has checkered mahogany stock and adj. rear sight.

Mfg.'s Sug. Retail	$195	$110	$90	$75	$60	$55	$50	$45

▲ *M-2000SC (Super Classic)* — similar to M-2000, except has checkered American Walnut stock with cheekpiece and hardwood forend tip, engine turned bolt, 6 lbs. Importation began 1990.

Mfg.'s Sug. Retail	$319	$255	$205	$170	$140	$110	$95	$85

MODEL M-50S — .22 LR, semi-auto design, 16½ in. shrouded barrel, 25 or 30 shot mag., uncheckered mahogany stock, 6½ lbs. Disc. 1995.

	$155	$115	$95	$75	$65	$50	$45

Last Mfg.'s Sug. Retail was $209.

M-AK22(S) — .22 LR, semi-auto, copy of the famous Russian Kalashnikov AK-47 rifle, 18½ in. barrel, 10 or 15 (disc.) shot mag., mahogany stock and forearm, 7 lbs.

Mfg.'s Sug. Retail	$189	$165	$145	$125	$110	$90	$80	$75

▲ *M-AK22(F)* — similar to M-AK22, except has metal folding stock, and 30 shot mag. Disc. 1995.

	$235	$185	$160	$130	$100	$90	$80

Last Mfg.'s Sug. Retail was $299.

SHOTGUNS

MODEL M30 D or F/IC (INTERCHANGEABLE CHOKES) — 12 ga. only, 28 in. plain barrel with 3 choke tubes, 5 shot mag., uncheckered stock and forearm.

Mfg.'s Sug. Retail	$259	$220	$190	$160	$140	$120	$95	$85

A

Grading	100%	98%	95%	90%	80%	70%	60%

▲ **Model M30 D/IC (Deluxe)** — similar to Model M30 IC, except has checkered walnut stock. Importation disc.

	$235	$195	$160	$130	$110	$95	$85

Last Mfg.'s Sug. Retail was $289.

M-30 DG (DEER GUN) — 12 ga. only, law enforcement version of Model M30, 20 in. plain barrel, iron sights, 7 shot mag., about 7 lbs.

Mfg.'s Sug. Retail	$249	$215	$185	$160	$140	$120	$95	$85

M-30SAS — 12 ga. only, riot configuration with vent. barrel shroud, and Speed feed 4 shot synthetic butt stock and forearm, matte finish. New 1996.

Mfg.'s Sug. Retail	$279	$230	$195	$165	$145	$120	$95	$85

M-30F — 12 ga. only, 28 in. barrel, fixed mod. choke.

Mfg.'s Sug. Retail	$209	$165	$120	$95	$75	$65	$55	$50

M-30 R6/R8 (RIOT) — 12 ga. only, similar to Model M30DG, except has front bead sight only, 5 or 7 shot mag., cyl. bore.

Mfg.'s Sug. Retail	$199	$170	$150	$125	$110	$90	$80	$75

Add $10 for 7 shot mag.

MODEL M30 C (COMBO) — 12 ga., 20 in. barrel, 5 shot mag., unique detachable black synthetic butt stock that separates allowing pistol grip only operation. Disc. 1995.

	$210	$175	$145	$120	$100	$90	$80

Last Mfg.'s Sug. Retail was $289.

MODEL M30 RP (COMBO) — 12 ga. only, same action as M-30 DG, interchangeable black pistol grip, 18¼ in. plain barrel w/front bead sight, 6¼ lbs. Disc. 1995.

	$210	$175	$145	$120	$100	$90	$80

Last Mfg.'s Sug. Retail was $289.

ARMS CORPORATION OF THE PHILIPPINES
Please refer to the Armscor listing in this section.

ARMS RESEARCH ASSOCIATES
Previous manufacturer until 1991, located in Stone Park, IL.

KF SYSTEM — 9mm, paramilitary design carbine, 18½ in. barrel, vent. barrel shroud, 20 or 36 shot mag., matte black finish, 7½ lbs., select fire-class III transferable only.

	$395	$350	$300	$275	$250	$230	$210

Last Mfg.'s Sug. Retail was $379.

ARMS TECH LTD.
Manufacturer located in Phoenix, AZ since 1995.

SEMI-AUTO RIFLE SUPER MATCH INTERDICTION POLICE MODEL — .243 Win., .300 Win. Mag., or .308 Win. (standard) cal., features 22 in. free floating Schnieder or Douglas airgauge stainless steel barrel, gas operation, McMillan stock, and updated trigger group, detachable box mag., includes Omega mount, 13 ¼ lbs. Limited mfg. beginnning 1996.

Mfg.'s Sug. Retail	$4,800	$4,550	$4,050	$3,675	$3,300	$3,000	$2,500	$2,000

ARMSCORP USA, INC.
Manufacturer/importer located in Baltimore, MD. Dealer direct sales only.

Grading	100%	98%	95%	90%	80%	70%	60%

A

PISTOLS: SEMI-AUTO

HI POWER — 9mm, patterned after Browning design, 4⅔ in. barrel, military finish, 13 shot mag., synthetic checkered grips, spur hammer, 2 lbs. Imported 1989-90 only, mfg. in Argentina.

| | $300 | $250 | $230 | $215 | $200 | $185 | $170 |

Last Mfg.'s Sug. Retail was $450.

Add $15 for round hammer.
Add $50 for hard chrome finish w/combat grips (disc. 1989).

▲ **Compact Detective HP** — similar to Hi Power, except has 3½ in. barrel, 1.9 lbs. Mfg. 1989 only.

| | $325 | $275 | $240 | $220 | $200 | $185 | $170 |

Last Mfg.'s Sug. Retail was $475.

SD-9 — 9mm Para., double action only, blowback mechanism, 3.07 in. barrel, 6 shot mag., frame is fabricated mostly of heavy gauge sheet metal stampings, chamber indicator, Israeli mfg, 1½ lbs. Imported 1989-90 only.

| | $295 | $250 | $230 | $210 | $195 | $180 | $170 |

Last Mfg.'s Sug. Retail was $350.

This pistol has also been manufactured by Sirkis Industries - refer to their section in this text.

P22 — .22 LR, patterned after the Colt Woodsman, 4 or 6 in. barrel, 10 shot mag., checkered wooden grips, mfg. in Argentina. Imported 1989-90 only.

| | $190 | $150 | $130 | $115 | $100 | $95 | $85 |

Last Mfg.'s Sug. Retail was $225.

RIFLES: SEMI-AUTO

M-14 RIFLE (NORINCO PARTS) — .308 cal., 20 shot mag., newly mfg. M-14 using Norinco parts, wood stock. Mfg. 1991-92 only.

| | $600 | $525 | $475 | $425 | $375 | $325 | $275 |

Last Mfg.'s Sug. Retail was $688.

M-14 RIFLE (USGI PARTS) — .308 cal., 10 (C/B 1994) or 20* shot mag., newly manufactured M-14 using original excellent condition forged G.I. parts including USGI fiberglass stock with rubber recoil pad. New 1986.

| Mfg.'s Sug. Retail | $1,550 | $1,225 | $975 | $800 | $675 | $550 | $500 | $450 |

Add $25 for G.I. buttplate.
Add $45 for USGI birch stock (Model M-14RNSB).
Add $225 for new walnut stock (Model M-14RNS).

M-14 BEGINNING NATIONAL MATCH — .308 cal., mfg. from hand selected older USGI parts, except for new receiver and new USGI air gauged premium barrel, guaranteed to shoot 1¼ in. group at 100 yards. New 1993.

| Mfg.'s Sug. Retail | $1,950 | $1,625 | $1,250 | $1,000 | $875 | $795 | $695 | $600 |

M-14 NATIONAL MATCH — .308 cal., built in accordance with A.M.T.U. mil. specs., 3 different barrel weights to choose from, national match rear sight system, calibrated mag., leather sling, guaranteed 1" MOA. New 1987.

▲ **AMTU Competition Model**

| Mfg.'s Sug. Retail | $2,295 | $1,950 | $1,395 | $1,100 | $950 | $875 | $795 | $700 |

▲ **M21 Match Rifle**

| Mfg.'s Sug. Retail | $2,495 | $2,150 | $1,650 | $1,200 | $1,000 | $900 | $825 | $725 |

Grading	100%	98%	95%	90%	80%	70%	60%

T-48 FAL ISRAELI PATTERN RIFLE — .308 (7.62 NATO) cal., mfg. in the U.S. to precise original metric dimensions (parts are interchangeable with original Belgium FAL), forged receiver, hammer forged chrome lined mil.spec. 21 in. barrel (standard or heavy) with flash suppressor, adj. front sight, aperture rear sight, 10 lbs. Imported 1990-92.

	$1,075	$900	$775	$625	$525	$465	$425

Last Mfg.'s Sug. Retail was $1,244.

This model was guaranteed to shoot within 2.5 MOA with match ammunition.

▲ **T-48 FAL L1A1 Pattern** — .308 cal., fully enclosed forend with vents, 10 lbs. Imported 1992 only.

	$995	$875	$775	$625	$525	$465	$425

Last Mfg.'s Sug. Retail was $1,181.

Add $122 for wooden handguard sporter model (limited supply).

T-48 BUSH MODEL — similar to T-48 FAL, except has 18 in. barrel, 9¾ lbs. Mfg. 1990 only.

	$1,100	$925	$800	$650	$525	$465	$425

Last Mfg.'s Sug. Retail was $1,250.

FRHB — .308 (7.62 NATO) cal., Israeli mfg. with heavy barrel and bipod. Imported 1990 only.

	$1,725	$1,450	$1,150	$975	$875	$795	$725

Last Mfg.'s Sug. Retail was $1,895.

FAL — .308 cal., Armscorp forged receiver, 21 in. Argentinian rebuilt barrel, manufactured to military specs., supplied with one military 20 shot mag., aperture rear sight, 10 lbs. Mfg. 1987-89.

	$850	$750	$600	$540	$465	$420	$375

Last Mfg.'s Sug. Retail was $875.

Subtract $55 if without flash hider.
Add $75 for heavy barrel with bipod (14 lbs.).
Add $400 (last retail) for .22 LR conversion kit.
This model is guaranteed to shoot within 2.5 MOA with match ammunition.

▲ **FAL Bush Model** — similar to FAL, except has 18 in. barrel with flash suppressor, 9¾ lbs. Mfg. 1989 only.

	$875	$760	$625	$550	$465	$420	$375

Last Mfg.'s Sug. Retail was $900.

▲ **FAL Para Model** — similar to FAL Bush Model, except has metal folding stock, leaf rear sight. Mfg. 1989 only.

	$900	$775	$635	$550	$465	$420	$375

Last Mfg.'s Sug. Retail was $930.

▲ **FAL Factory Rebuilt** — factory (Argentine) rebuilt FAL without flash suppressor in excellent condition with Armscorp forged receiver, 9 lbs. 10 oz. Disc. 1989.

	$695	$625	$560	$520	$450	$400	$360

Last Mfg.'s Sug. Retail was $675.

M36 ISRAELI SNIPER RIFLE — .308 cal., gas operated semi-auto, Bullpup configuration, 22 in. free floating barrel, Armscorp M14 receiver, 20 shot mag., includes flash suppressor and bipod, 10 lbs. Civilian offering 1989 only.

	$2,900	$2,500	$2,275	$2,050	$1,900	$1,775	$1,600

Last Mfg.'s Sug. Retail was $3,000.

EXPERT MODEL — .22 LR, semi-auto, 20.9 in. barrel, 10 shot mag., wood stock with one-screw takedown, iron sights with grooved receiver, 5.1 lbs. New 1989.

	$195	$150	$125	$115	$105	$95	$85

Last Mfg.'s Sug. Retail was $225.

ARMSPORT, INC.

Current importer and distributor located in Miami, FL specializing in European manufacturers. Distributor preferred but dealer direct sales also. Beginning 1993, Armsport decided to reduce the importation of modern firearms, and has chosen to specialize instead in air rifle and black powder importation (refer

Grading	100%	98%	95%	90%	80%	70%	60%

A

to individual headings in back of book). Armsport shotguns are currently being manufactured by Sarsilmaz located in Turkey.

COMBINATION GUNS

2781 AND 2782 — 12 ga./.222 cal., O/U turkey gun, blued receiver. Model 2782 has chrome receiver. Model 2782 was imported 1985 only. Model 2782 new 1985. Disc. 1989.

	$650	$550	$495	$440	$395	$350	$300

Last Mfg.'s Sug. Retail on Model 2781 was $650.
Last Mfg.'s Sug. Retail on Model 2782 was $750 (disc. 1989).

2783 — similar to Model 2782, except is deluxe model with lateral rib. Imported 1986-1988.

	$1,350	$1,075	$925	$820	$750	$680	$600

Last Mfg.'s Sug. Retail was $1,600.

2784 — same action as Model 2783, except is chambered for .243 Win. Imported 1986-1988.

	$1,350	$1,075	$925	$820	$750	$680	$600

Last Mfg.'s Sug. Retail was $1,600.

2785 — same action as Model 2783, except is chambered for .270 Win. Imported 1986-1988.

	$1,350	$1,075	$925	$820	$750	$680	$600

Last Mfg.'s Sug. Retail was $1,600.

2786 — 20 ga./.222 cal., O/U turkey gun, otherwise same specifications as Model 2783. Mfg. 1986 only.

	$1,350	$1,075	$925	$820	$750	$680	$600

Last Mfg.'s Sug. Retail was $1,350.

2787 — similar to Model 2786, except is chambered for .243 Win. Mfg. 1986 only.

	$1,350	$1,075	$925	$820	$750	$680	$600

Last Mfg.'s Sug. Retail was $1,350.

2788 — similar to Model 2786, except is chambered for .270 Win. Mfg. 1986 only.

	$1,350	$1,075	$925	$820	$750	$680	$600

Last Mfg.'s Sug. Retail was $1,350.

4043 — 12, 16, or 20 ga./rifle O/U combination gun, choice of caliber, select walnut, 23½ in. barrels, relief engraved. Disc. 1983.

	$1,675	$1,260	$1,090	$925	$840	$755	$670

4651 — Tikka deluxe O/U shotgun/rifle, exposed hammers, combo. 12 ga./.222. 12 ga. is chambered for 3 in. shells. Disc. 1984.

	$750	$565	$490	$415	$375	$340	$300

4690 — Tikka deluxe O/U shotgun/rifle, hammerless, combo 12 ga./.222. 12 ga. is chambered for 3 in. shells. Disc. 1984.

	$1,095	$820	$750	$700	$650	$575	$500

RIFLES: BOLT-ACTION

2801 — .30-06 cal., 24 in. barrel, iron sights, checkered walnut stock and forearm. Imported 1986 only.

	$725	$600	$495	$430	$380	$335	$285

Last Mfg.'s Sug. Retail was $895.

▲ *2802* — similar to Model 2801, except chambered for .308 cal.

	$725	$600	$495	$430	$380	$335	$285

Last Mfg.'s Sug. Retail was $895.

▲ *2803* — similar to Model 2801, except chambered for .270 Win. cal.

	$725	$600	$495	$430	$380	$335	$285

Last Mfg.'s Sug. Retail was $895.

A

Grading	100%	98%	95%	90%	80%	70%	60%

▲ *2804* — similar to Model 2801, except chambered for .243 Win. cal.

	$725	$600	$495	$430	$380	$335	$285

Last Mfg.'s Sug. Retail was $895.

▲ *2805* — similar to Model 2801, except chambered for 7mm Rem. Mag.

	$725	$600	$495	$430	$380	$335	$285

Last Mfg.'s Sug. Retail was $895.

▲ *2806* — similar to Model 2801, except chambered for .300 Win. Mag.

	$725	$600	$495	$430	$380	$335	$285

4601, 4603, 4605, & 4606 — Tikka deluxe, .30-06 cal., bolt action. Model 4603 is .270 Win. Model 4605 is 7mm Rem. Model 4606 is 300 Win. Mag. Disc. 1984.

	$725	$545	$450	$380	$340	$295	$260

4602, 4604, & 4607 — Tikka deluxe .308 Win. bolt action. Model 4604 is .243 Win. Model 4607 .222 Rem. Disc. 1983.

	$675	$510	$450	$420	$390	$350	$310

RIFLES: DOUBLE & COMBINATION

4020 — Express set O/U double rifle with ejectors plus an extra set of O/U shotgun barrels. Disc. 1986.

	$3,850	$3,300	$2,860	$2,420	$2,200	$1,980	$1,760

Last Mfg.'s Sug. Retail was $4,400.

4021 — same combination as Model 4020, except rifle has extractors. Disc. 1986.

	$3,400	$2,910	$2,520	$2,135	$1,940	$1,745	$1,550

Last Mfg.'s Sug. Retail was $3,875.

4022 — Express O/U rifle only with ejectors, choice of calibers. Disc. 1986.

	$3,450	$2,945	$2,555	$2,160	$1,965	$1,770	$1,570

Last Mfg.'s Sug. Retail was $3,925.

4023 — similar to Model 4022, except has extractors. Disc. 1986.

	$2,925	$2,515	$2,180	$1,845	$1,675	$1,510	$1,340

Last Mfg.'s Sug. Retail was $3,350.

4010 — Emperor SxS, double rifle with extra set of 20 ga. barrels and forearm. Completely hand made and finished using the best materials and craftsmen, choice of caliber, leather fitted case. Disc. 1983.

	$16,300	$12,225	$10,595	$8,965	$8,150	$7,335	$6,520

4011 — similar to Model 4010, except rifle only, 9.3x74R cal. Disc. 1984.

	$12,750	$9,565	$8,290	$7,015	$6,375	$5,740	$5,100

4012 — Emperor "One-of-a-Kind" SxS rifle/shotgun set. Special engraving finishing per individual customer order, choice of gauges, calibers. Leather fitted case. Rare. Disc. 1983.

	$26,000	$19,500	$16,900	$14,300	$13,000	$11,700	$10,400

4013 — similar to Model 4012, but SxS double rifle only. Disc. 1983.

	$22,850	$17,140	$14,855	$12,570	$11,425	$10,285	$9,140

RIFLES: LEVER-ACTION

4500 & 4501 — .44-40 cal., deluxe copy of Winchester Model 1873 Rifle, engraved. Model 4501 is .357 Mag. Model 4500 (.44-40) disc. in 1984. Model 4501 (.357 Mag.) disc. 1986.

	$1,135	$975	$845	$715	$650	$585	$520

Last Mfg.'s Sug. Retail was $1,296.

4502 & 4503 — .44-40 cal., deluxe copy of Winchester Model 1873 Carbine, engraved. Model 4503 is .357 Mag. Model 4502 (.44-40) disc. in 1984. Model 4503 (.357 Mag.) disc. 1986.

	$960	$825	$715	$605	$550	$495	$440

Last Mfg.'s Sug. Retail was $1,095.

Grading	100%	98%	95%	90%	80%	70%	60%

4504 — .357 Mag., standard copy of Winchester Model 1873 carbine. Disc. 1986.

	$555	$470	$410	$345	$315	$285	$250

Last Mfg.'s Sug. Retail was $625.

RIFLES: SEMI-AUTO

2785 & 2786 — .22 LR cal., semi-auto, 10 shot mag. Model 2786 is military type with 15 shot mag. Imported 1985 only.

	$150	$125	$100	$90	$80	$70	$60

Last Mfg.'s Sug. Retail was $170.

SHOTGUNS: O/U

Armsport choking codes (on rear left of barrels) designate the following: * indicates full choke, ** identifies improved modified choking, *** refers to modified, **** is improved cylinder, ***** indicates cylinder bore.

The models listed below that have -3 suffixes indicate 1988 importation. All models listed below were discontinued in 1993, unless otherwise indicated.

2528 — 12 ga., 3 in. Mag., 28 in. barrels, single trigger with auto ejectors. Disc. 1983.

	$595	$450	$390	$330	$300	$270	$240

2626 — 20 ga., 3 in. Mag., 26 in. barrels, single trigger with auto ejectors. Disc. 1983.

	$595	$450	$390	$330	$300	$270	$240

2697 & 2698 — 10 ga., 3½ in. Mag., similar to Models 2699 & 2700 except have 3 screw-in choke tubes, Model 2698 has 32 in. barrels. New 1989.

	$1,100	$850	$675	$575	$520	$495	$475

Last Mfg.'s Sug. Retail was $1,299.

2699/2700C & 2700 — 10 ga., 3½ in. Mag., 27 (2699 - new 1989), 28 (2700C), or 32 (2700) in. barrels with 12mm vent. rib, extractors, DTs. New 1986.

	$995	$775	$625	$550	$475	$430	$395

Last Mfg.'s Sug. Retail was $1,190.

▲ **2700B** — similar to Model 2700, except has deluxe walnut (32 in. barrels only). Mfg. 1987 only.

	$660	$575	$480	$430	$395	$370	$350

Last Mfg.'s Sug. Retail was $795.

2701/2702 & 2703/2704 — 12 and 20 ga., 3 in. Mag., 26 and 28 in. barrels, double triggers, extractors. Disc. 1985, and reintroduced 1989. Current models are 2702 and 2704.

	$570	$450	$375	$295	$265	$230	$200

Last Mfg.'s Sug. Retail was $685.

2705 — .410 ga., double triggers, 26 in. barrels, bored F & F, extractors. Importation began 1986.

	$670	$525	$425	$350	$300	$275	$235

Last Mfg.'s Sug. Retail was $785.

2706 — 12 ga. only, law enforcement model, 20 in. barrels, double triggers, extractors. Imported 1986 only.

	$330	$280	$260	$240	$220	$200	$185

Last Mfg.'s Sug. Retail was $375.

2707 — 28 ga., otherwise similar to Model 2705. New 1990.

	$670	$525	$425	$350	$300	$275	$235

Last Mfg.'s Sug. Retail was $785.

2708 — 12 ga. only, slug gun, 23 in. barrels, single trigger, ejectors. Importation began 1986.

	$685	$550	$450	$385	$325	$300	$280

Last Mfg.'s Sug. Retail was $840.

A Model 2708-3 was mfg. 1986-1989. This variation had 20 in. barrels, double triggers, and extractors. Values of this earlier variation will be approx. 30-40% less than listed above.

Grading	100%	98%	95%	90%	80%	70%	60%

A

2711, 2713-3, 2721, & 2723 — 12 or 20 ga., 3 in. Mag., 26 or 28 in. barrels, extractors. Models 2721 and 2723 have ejectors and were disc. 1985. Models 2711 and 2713-3 were disc. 1989.

	$445	$385	$340	$310	$275	$250	$230

Add 25% with ejectors.

Last Mfg.'s Sug. Retail was $375 on Models 2721/2723.

Last Mfg.'s Sug. Retail was $535 on Models 2711/2713-3.

2717, 2719, 2720, & 2725 — 12 (Model 2717), 20 (Model 2719), 28 (Model 2725 - new 1990), or .410 (Model 2720) ga., 3 in. Mag. (except Model 2725), 26 or 28 in. barrels, SST.

	$645	$525	$450	$385	$325	$300	$280

Add $70 for 28 or .410 ga.

Last Mfg.'s Sug. Retail was $765.

2712, 2714-3, 2722, & 2724 — 12 or 20 ga., 3 in. Mag., 26 or 28 in. barrels. Models 2712 and 2722 are 12 ga., engraved with 12mm vent. rib. Models 2722 and 2724 have ejectors. Importation of Models 2712, 2722, and 2724 was disc. 1986. Model 2714-3 was disc. 1988.

	$500	$395	$350	$300	$275	$235	$200

Last Mfg.'s Sug. Retail was $615 on Model 2714-3.

Last Mfg.'s Sug. Retail was $395 on Models 2712/2722/2724.

2715-3 & 2716-3 — 12 ga. only, 28 in. barrels with 3 choke tubes, auto ejectors, single trigger. Imported 1988 only.

	$575	$465	$400	$350	$295	$265	$245

Last Mfg.'s Sug. Retail was $680.

2718, 2733, & 2735 — 12 and 20 ga., 3 in. Mag., 26 and 28 in. barrels, SST, extractors. Models 2733/2735 have deluxe Boss actions. Model 2718 was disc. 1985.

	$650	$540	$450	$385	$325	$300	$280

Last Mfg.'s Sug. Retail was $390 on Model 2718.

Last Mfg.'s Sug. Retail was $790 on Model 2733 and 2735.

▲ **2734 & 2736 Sporting Clays** — 12 (2734) or 20 (2736) ga., similar to Models 2733 and 2735, except has 3 choke tubes.

	$695	$560	$450	$385	$325	$300	$280

Last Mfg.'s Sug. Retail was $840.

2745, 2746 & 2747 — 12 ga., 3½ in. chambers, 24 (2745), 27/28 (2746) or 31/32 (2747) in. barrels with wide rib and 3 choke tubes, auto extractors, Boss type action. New 1989.

	$715	$575	$450	$385	$325	$300	$280

Last Mfg.'s Sug. Retail was $880.

These models were mfg. by Armi Techniche of Emilio Rizzini located in Italy.

2726, 2728, 2742, & 2744 — 12 and 20 ga., 3 in. Mag., 26 and 28 in. barrels, SST, ejectors. Models 2726 & 2728 were disc. 1985.

	$740	$595	$475	$400	$350	$315	$290

Last Mfg.'s Sug. Retail on Models 2726 & 2728 was $440.

Last Mfg.'s Sug. Retail on Models 2742 & 2744 was $930.

2727-3 & 2729-3 — 1986 designations for Models 2726 & 2728 respectively. -3 suffixes indicate 1988 designations. Importation disc. 1988.

	$550	$450	$385	$330	$295	$265	$245

Last Mfg.'s Sug. Retail was $615.

2727 & 2729 — 12 (Model 2727) or 20 (Model 2729) ga., field model, boxlock action, 26 or 28 in. barrels with wide rib and fixed chokes. New 1990.

	$660	$550	$450	$385	$325	$300	$280

Last Mfg.'s Sug. Retail was $800.

These models have evolved from Models 2726/2728 and Models 2727-3 and 2729-3.

2730 — 12 ga., skeet gun, 27 in. barrel, has six interchangeable chokes, Boss-type action.

	$775	$650	$550	$495	$450	$425	$395

Last Mfg.'s Sug. Retail was $975.

These models were mfg. by Armi Techniche of Emilio Rizzini located in Italy.

Grading	100%	98%	95%	90%	80%	70%	60%

▲ **2731** — similar to Model 2730, except is 20 ga. and has 26 in. barrels.

	$795	$675	$565	$525	$465	$435	$400

Last Mfg.'s Sug. Retail was $975.

2732 & 2732/3 — 12 ga. only, competition trap model, 30 in. barrel. New 1990.

	$930	$700	$600	$525	$470	$440	$415

Last Mfg.'s Sug. Retail was $1,165.

Add $110 for Model 2732/3 (includes choke tubes).

These two models were mfg. by Emilio Rizzini located in Italy.

2741 & 2743 — 12 (Model 2741) or 20 (Model 2743) ga., field model, 26 or 28 in. barrels with wide rib and fixed chokes, Boss type action. New 1990.

	$665	$550	$450	$385	$325	$300	$280

Last Mfg.'s Sug. Retail was $825.

These models were mfg. by Armi Techniche of Emilio Rizzini located in Italy.

2750 & 2751 — 12 (Model 2750) or 20 (Model 2751) ga., Sporting Clays configuration, 26 or 28 in. barrels with 5 choke tubes, includes engraved sideplates. New 1990.

	$830	$675	$575	$525	$475	$445	$400

Last Mfg.'s Sug. Retail was $1,050.

2760 — 12 ga., tournament trap model with choke tubes. Mfg. by Ferlib beginning 1991.

	$1,475	$1,200	$995	$800	$675	$600	$540

Last Mfg.'s Sug. Retail was $1,700.

2763 — 12 ga., sporting clays configuration, includes 5 choke tubes, mfg. by Ferlib in Italy - importation began in 1991.

	$1,525	$1,225	$1,000	$800	$675	$600	$540

Last Mfg.'s Sug. Retail was $1,775.

2765 — similar to Model 2763, except is 20 ga. with 26 in. barrels. Imported 1991 only.

	$1,700	$1,350	$1,100	$850	$700	$625	$550

Last Mfg.'s Sug. Retail was $2,000.

2791/2792 (FIELD) — 12 (2791) or 20 (2792) ga., single trigger, 26 (20 ga. only) or 28 in. VR barrels (fixed chokes). Importation began 1995.

Mfg.'s Sug. Retail	$775	$650	$565	$500	$450	$400	$350	$295

2795/2796/2797 (SPORTING CLAYS/SKEET) — 12 (2795/2797) or 20 (2796) ga., SST, ejectors, 26 (2796/2797) or 28 (2795) in. VR barrels (includes 5 choke tubes). Importation began 1995.

Mfg.'s Sug. Retail	$1,150	$950	$775	$650	$500	$425	$375	$300

2801/2802 — 12 ga., 3 in. chambers, boxlock action, single or double triggers, VR barrels. Mfg. by Sarsilmaz, importation began 1996.

Mfg.'s Sug. Retail	$475	$400	$350	$300	$275	$250	$225	$200

Add approximately $100 for ST.

2820 SPORTING CLAYS — 12 ga. only, boxlock action, SST, ejectors, deluxe model with checkered walnut stock and forearm, includes 5 choke tubes. Mfg. by E. Rizzini. Importation began late 1995.

Mfg.'s Sug. Retail	$1,200	$1,050	$850	$750	$650	$550	$450	$395

4014 — Emperor Grade SxS. Individually fitted per customer H&H type action, engraved, fitted leather case, choice of gauge, barrel lengths, etc. Completely hand finished.

	$9,175	$6,885	$5,965	$5,050	$4,590	$4,130	$3,670

Emperor Grade models are disc. Limited availability.

4015 — Emperor "One-of-a-Kind" SxS. Similar to Model 4014, except that every part of the gun is made per customer order. Specifications including style of engraving, dimensions, wood configuration, special requests, etc. No expense spared. Disc. 1984.

	$18,000	$13,500	$11,700	$9,900	$9,000	$8,100	$7,200

Grading	100%	98%	95%	90%	80%	70%	60%

4016 — Emperor SxS with outside hammers, fitted leather case, extensively engraved, any gauge. Disc. 1983.

	$4,550	$3,415	$2,960	$2,505	$2,275	$2,050	$1,820

4017 — Emperor "One-of-a-Kind" SxS with outside hammers. Flexibility of options is similar to Model 4015. Disc. 1984.

	$12,750	$9,565	$8,290	$7,015	$6,375	$5,740	$5,100

4030 & 4031 — 12 ga. SxS, Holland-style detachable locks, English walnut, ejectors, engraved. Model 4031 is 20 ga. Disc. 1983.

	$3,950	$2,965	$2,570	$2,175	$1,975	$1,780	$1,580

4032 & 4033 — 12 ga. Premier Mono Trap Gun, 32 in. barrel, ejector. Model 4033 is same, except for 34 in. barrel. Disc. 1986.

	$1,810	$1,560	$1,350	$1,145	$1,040	$935	$830

Last Mfg.'s Sug. Retail was $2,075.

4034 & 4035 — 12 ga. Premier Mono Trap Set, 32 in. single, 30 in. O/U. Model 4035 is same, except has 34 in. single, 32 in. O/U. Disc. 1986.

	$2,565	$2,215	$1,920	$1,625	$1,475	$1,330	$1,180

Last Mfg.'s Sug. Retail was $2,950.

4040 — 12 ga. Slug Special SxS, 23 in. barrels. Disc. 1984.

	$1,325	$995	$865	$730	$665	$600	$530

4046 & 4047 — 12 ga. trap gun, 34 in. barrel, extra trigger mechanism. Model 4047 is 32 in. Disc. 1986.

	$2,860	$2,460	$2,100	$1,850	$1,700	$1,500	$1,300

Last Mfg.'s Sug. Retail was $3,275.

4050 — Pigeon Grade O/U, 12 ga., engraved. Disc. 1986.

	$2,375	$2,025	$1,755	$1,485	$1,350	$1,215	$1,080

Last Mfg.'s Sug. Retail was $2,700.

4055 & 4056 — Premier Skeet 12 ga., selective trigger, ejectors, engraved, select wood. Model 4056 is 20 ga. Disc. 1983.

	$2,000	$1,500	$1,300	$1,100	$1,000	$900	$800

4061 & 4062 — .410 ga. SxS, single trigger, selective ejectors. Model 4062 is 28 ga. Disc. 1983.

	$995	$750	$650	$550	$500	$450	$400

4063 & 4064 — .410 ga. O/U, single trigger, selective ejectors. Model 4064 is 28 ga. Disc. 1983.

	$995	$750	$650	$550	$500	$450	$400

SHOTGUNS: SLIDE ACTION

2755 — 12 ga., 7 shot, Atis mfg., black anodized receiver, 24 or 28 in. barrel with VR. Mfg. 1985-87 only.

	$335	$260	$225	$195	$180	$160	$145

Last Mfg.'s Sug. Retail was $395.

▲ *2755A* — similar to Model 2755, except has 30 in. barrel. Mfg. 1986-87 only.

	$335	$260	$225	$195	$180	$160	$145

2756 — 12 ga., 28 in. VR barrel, 3 interchangeable chokes. Mfg. 1986-87 only.

	$390	$335	$280	$230	$205	$190	$175

Last Mfg.'s Sug. Retail was $465.

▲ *2756A* — similar to Model 2756, except has 30 in. vent. rib barrel. Mfg. 1986-87 only.

	$390	$335	$280	$230	$205	$190	$175

Last Mfg.'s Sug. Retail was $465.

Grading	100%	98%	95%	90%	80%	70%	60%

2757 — 12 ga. only, law enforcement model, 20 in. barrel, black receiver. Mfg. 1986-87 only.

	$310	$250	$205	$190	$175	$155	$140

Last Mfg.'s Sug. Retail was $375.

2766, 2767, & 2768 — 12 ga., Fabarms mfg., 25 in. barrel. Model 2768 has 20 in. barrel. Imported 1985 only.

	$260	$220	$200	$180	$160	$140	$120

Last Mfg.'s Sug. Retail was $300.

SHOTGUNS: SEMI-AUTO

2751 — 12 ga., 3 in. Mag., semi-auto, Atis mfg., black anodized receiver, 28 in. barrel. Mfg. 1985-87 only.

	$430	$340	$310	$285	$255	$230	$200

Last Mfg.'s Sug. Retail was $575.

▲ *2761A* — similar to Model 2751, except has 30 in. full choke barrel. Mfg. 1986-87 only.

	$430	$340	$310	$285	$255	$230	$200

Last Mfg.'s Sug. Retail was $575.

2752 — same action as Model 2751, except chrome receiver and engraving. Mfg. 1986-87 only.

	$440	$345	$310	$285	$255	$230	$200

Last Mfg.'s Sug. Retail was $600.

▲ *2752A* — similar to Model 2752, except has 30 in. barrel. Mfg. 1986-87 only.

	$440	$345	$310	$285	$255	$230	$200

Last Mfg.'s Sug. Retail was $600.

2753 — same action as Model 2751, except has 28 in. barrel with 3 interchangeable chokes. Mfg. 1986-87 only.

	$460	$355	$315	$285	$255	$230	$200

Last Mfg.'s Sug. Retail was $650.

▲ *2753A* — similar to Model 2753, except has chrome receiver and engraving. Mfg. 1986-87 only.

	$470	$365	$320	$285	$255	$230	$200

Last Mfg.'s Sug. Retail was $675.

2761 & 2762 — 12 ga., black or chrome receiver, Fabarms made, engraved action, 27 in. barrel. Add $75 for interchangeable choke tubes. Imported during 1985 only.

	$410	$360	$315	$295	$270	$245	$215

Last Mfg.'s Sug. Retail was $475.

2810/2811 — 12 ga. only, 3 in. chamber, 18¾ in. barrel, security configuration with walnut (Model 2811) or plastic (2810) full stock. Importation began 1996.

Mfg.'s Sug. Retail	$425	$365	$315	$290	$275	$250	$225	$200

Add $50 for walnut stock (Model 2811).

SHOTGUNS: SINGLE AND SIDE-BY-SIDE

1033 — 10 ga. SxS, 3½ in. Mag., 32 in. full and full chokes. Disc. 1985.

	$395	$340	$315	$275	$250	$225	$200

Last Mfg.'s Sug. Retail was $450.

1050-1 — 1986 designation for the Model 1051. -1 suffix designates 1988 and later importation.

	$650	$540	$450	$385	$325	$300	$280

Last Mfg.'s Sug. Retail was $785.

1051 & 1052 — 12 ga. SxS, 3 in. Mag., 28 in. mod. & full chokes. Model 1052 is 20 ga., 3 in. Mag., 26 in. Imp. & Mod. Disc. 1985.

	$330	$280	$260	$240	$225	$205	$180

Last Mfg.'s Sug. Retail was $375.

Grading	100%	98%	95%	90%	80%	70%	60%

1053-1 — 1986 designation for the Model 1052. -1 suffix designates 1988 and later importation.

| | $650 | $540 | $450 | $385 | $325 | $300 | $280 |

Last Mfg.'s Sug. Retail was $785.

1054-1 & 1055-1 — .410 (1054) or .28 (1055) ga. -1 suffix designates 1988 and later importation.

| | $700 | $600 | $500 | $450 | $400 | $365 | $330 |

Last Mfg.'s Sug. Retail was $860.

1055 & 1057 — 28 and .410 ga. SxS, 3 in. Mag., 26 in. barrel, Imp. and Mod. chokes. Model 1057 is 28 ga., 3 in. Mag., 26 in. Imp. & Mod. Disc. 1985.

| | $330 | $280 | $260 | $240 | $225 | $205 | $180 |

Last Mfg.'s Sug. Retail was $375.

Model 1057 was redesignated 1055 in 1985 and Model 1055 was changed to 1054.

1101, 1102, 1103, & 1104 — 12 ga., folding single barrel w/vent. rib. Model 1102 is 20 ga. Model 1103 is .410 ga. Model 1104 is 28 ga. Disc. 1985.

| | $125 | $105 | $90 | $75 | $70 | $65 | $60 |

Last Mfg.'s Sug. Retail was $140.

1107 & 1108 — 12 ga., folding single barrel 19 in., pistol grip. Model 1108 is 20 ga. Disc. 1983.

| | $135 | $105 | $95 | $85 | $75 | $70 | $65 |

1125, 1126, & 1127 — 12 or 20 ga., single barrel, 3 in. chamber, bottom lever opening, Model 1127 is 20 ga. Imported 1987-95.

| | $75 | $55 | $50 | $45 | $40 | $35 | $30 |

Last Mfg.'s Sug. Retail was $90.

The Model 1125 was disc. 1989, Models 1126/1127 were disc. 1995.

▲ *1128* — .410 ga., otherwise similar to Models 1125/1126/1127. Importation disc. 1990.

| | $75 | $55 | $50 | $45 | $40 | $35 | $30 |

Last Mfg.'s Sug. Retail was $90.

1212 & 1213 — 12 ga., SxS, outside hammers, engraved action, 20 in. barrels. Model 1213 is 20 ga. Disc. 1983.

| | $450 | $340 | $295 | $250 | $225 | $205 | $180 |

1225 — 12 ga. only, O/U configuration, folding action, top lever break. Mfg. 1986-87 only.

| | $275 | $235 | $200 | $185 | $170 | $165 | $150 |

Last Mfg.'s Sug. Retail was $345.

1226 — 20 ga. only, O/U configuration, folding action, top lever break. Mfg. 1986-87 only.

| | $275 | $235 | $200 | $185 | $170 | $165 | $150 |

Last Mfg.'s Sug. Retail was $345.

SHOTGUNS: TRI-BARREL

MODEL 2900 TRILLING — 12 ga., 3 barrel shotgun with 28 in. barrels bored F & M or choke tubes over IC/choke tubes. Importation began 1986-87 and was resumed in 1990.

| | $2,900 | $2,375 | $2,000 | $1,650 | $1,400 | $1,200 | $995 |

Last Mfg.'s Sug. Retail was $3,400.

Subtract 25% for fixed chokes (1986-87 mfg.).

This model was re-introduced in 1990 and includes choke tubes on all 3 barrels.

ARNOLD ARMS CO., INC.

Rifle manufacturer located in Arlington, WA since 1994.

A

RIFLES: BOLT ACTION

APOLLO SERIES — available in most popular cals. (including new .257, .300, and .338 Arnold Magnums) in short, long, and Magnum Apollo action featuring positive feeding bolt face insuring reliable extraction and cartridge feeding, choice of stainless steel or chrome moly action/barrel, choice of premium wood or various configurations of synthetic stocks, 3-position safety, glass-bedded receiver, one-piece bolt. New 1994.

Mfg.'s Sug. Retail	$3,285	$2,975	$2,425	$1,850	$1,425	$1,150	$975	$850

Add $21 for stainless steel construction.
Add $73 for Pacific Research stock.
Add $100 for high luster polish on metal surfaces.
Add $210 for MKII neutralizer, McMillan A2 stock.

▲ **The African Series** — available in most cals. between .243 Win. and .458 Win. Mag., Safari, African Trophy, or Grand African grade feature walnut stocks and African or Serengeti grade features synthetic stocks, 22-26 in. barrel. Series introduced 1996.

➤ **Safari Rifle** — various cals. between .243 Win. - .458 Win. Mag., No. 5 wraparound checkering pattern, 22 - 26 in. barrel w/o sights, choice of A or AA English walnut stock.

Mfg.'s Sug. Retail	$4,435	$4,100	$3,500	$3,250	$2,950	$2,650	$2,350	$2,100

Add $255 for AA grade English walnut stock.
Add $250 for stainless steel construction.

➤ **Trophy Rifle** — similar to Safari rifle, except has AAA English walnut stock with No. 9 wraparound checkering pattern.

Mfg.'s Sug. Retail	$6,098	$5,675	$4,850	$4,300	$3,950	$3,600	$3,300	$2,000

Add $157 for stainless steel construction.

➤ **Grand African Rifle** — various cals. between .338 Win. Mag. - .458 Win. Mag., exhibition grade stock with No. 10 checkering pattern, 24 or 26 in. barrel with express sights.

Mfg.'s Sug. Retail	$7,630	$7,250	$6,100	$5,350	$4,400	$3,950	$3,600	$3,300

Add $150 for stainless steel construction.

➤ **African/African Serengeti Synthetic Rifle** — similar to the African Series listed above, except has synthetic fibergrain stock with or without cheekpiece (Serengeti has Monte Carlo style), iron sights.

Mfg.'s Sug. Retail	$2,995	$2,725	$2,375	$2,050	$1,850	$1,650	$1,500	$1,350

Add $175 for stainless steel construction.

▲ **The Alaskan Series** — various cals. between .223 Rem. - .458 Win. Mag., various types of synthetic stocks, stainless or chrome moly Apollo action. Series introduced 1996.

➤ **Alaskan Rifle** — various cals. between .223 Rem. - .338 Win. Mag., black, Woodland, or artic camo. stock, scope mount only.

Mfg.'s Sug. Retail	$2,995	$2,725	$2,375	$2,050	$1,850	$1,650	$1,500	$1,350

Add $150 for stainless steel construction.

➤ **Alaskan Trophy Synthetic Rifle** — .375 H&H or larger cals., fibergrain or black synthetic stock, iron sights.

Mfg.'s Sug. Retail	$3,525	$3,200	$2,800	$2,350	$2,050	$1,775	$1,575	$1,275

Add $365 for stainless steel construction.

➤ **Alaskan Trophy Walnut Rifle** — similar to Alaskan Trophy Synthetic Rifle, except features AA walnut with No. 5 checkering, scope mount with iron sights.

Mfg.'s Sug. Retail	$5,140	$4,700	$3,850	$3,475	$2,950	$2,650	$2,350	$2,100

Add $159 for stainless steel construction.

➤ **Grand Alaskan Rifle** — various cals. between .300 Win. Mag. - .458 Win. Mag., features AAA or exhibition grade English walnut, includes scope mount and iron sights.

Mfg.'s Sug. Retail	$6,550	$6,125	$5,150	$4,600	$4,150	$3,750	$3,350	$2,000

Add $160 for stainless steel construction.

➤ **High Country Synthetic Mountain Rifle** — various cals. between .257 Roberts - .338 Win. Mag., fibergrain or black synthetic stock, scope mounts only.

Mfg.'s Sug. Retail	$2,995	$2,725	$2,375	$2,050	$1,850	$1,650	$1,500	$1,350

Add $175 for stainless steel construction.

Grading	100%	98%	95%	90%	80%	70%	60%

➤ **High Country Walnut Rifle** — similar to High Country Synthetic Mountain Rifle, except has AA English walnut stock with No. 5 checkering pattern, scope mounts only.

Mfg.'s Sug. Retail	$4,489	$4,150	$3,525	$3,250	$2,950	$2,650	$2,350	$2,100

Add $350 for stainless steel construction.

REMINGTON SERIES — various cals. between .222 Rem. - .458 Win. Mag., features Remington 700 Series action with Sako extractor, choice of walnut, McMillan, or Pacific Research stock, stainless, standard blue, or bead blasted metal finish. New 1994.

Mfg.'s Sug. Retail	$1,773	$1,600	$1,375	$1,150	$1,025	$875	$750	$625

Add $105 for stainless steel construction.
Add $190 for McMillan synthetic stock.
Add $210 for Pacific Research stock.

WINCHESTER SERIES — various cals., features Winchester pre-64 Model 70 action with claw extractor, positive feed, and integral recoil lug, choice of walnut, McMillan, or Pacific Research stock, stainless, standard blue, or bead blasted metal finish. New 1994.

Mfg.'s Sug. Retail	$1,489	$1,350	$1,075	$950	$850	$750	$650	$550

Add approx. $205 for stainless steel construction.
Add $162 for McMillan synthetic stock.
Add $259 for Pacific Research stock.

ARRIETA, S.L.

Manufacturer located in Elgoibar, Spain. Currently imported by several importers including Griffin & Howe, New England Arms, Orvis, Quality Arms, and Wingshooting Adventures.

More information can be obtained on Arrieta by either contacting the above listed importers or the factory.

RIFLES: SIDE-BY-SIDE

R-1 — 7x65R, 8x57JRS, or 9.3x74R cal., boxlock action with engraved sideplates, ejectors, quarter rib barrel with express rear sight.

Mfg.'s Sug. Retail	$8,950	$8,450	$7,000	$5,950	$5,100	$4,600	$4,000	$3,450

R-2 — similar to R-1, except has more elaborate engraving, elongated tangs, and choice of English or reinforced pistol grip with metal cap, ejectors.

Mfg.'s Sug. Retail	$12,950	$12,950	$9,950	$8,950	$7,850	$6,850	$5,900	$4,950

SHOTGUNS: CURRENT SxS

The models listed below are essentially custom ordered per individual specifications - delivery time is approx. 6 months.

All Arrieta shotguns have frames scaled to individual gauges. Various special options are available by custom order, and a few are listed below. On the models listed below, there are 4 qualities of action. Fourth quality is used on the Model 550. Third quality is used on Models 557-588. Second quality is used on Models 590 and 595 (designed for heavy use). First quality is used on Models 600-903, except for Model 900 (557 action). All Arrieta actions are self-opening except the Models 557, 570, and 578.

ADD THE FOLLOWING AMOUNTS FOR CURRENTLY MANUFACTURED SHOTGUNS.
Add 10% for small gauges (20, 28, or .410).
Add approx. $500 for single trigger depending on action.
Add 10% for matched pair.
Add 10% for rounded action on standard models.
Extra barrels are priced from $1,040-$1,570/set depending on model.

557 STANDARD — 12, 16, or 20 ga., Demi-Bloc steel barrels, detachable engraved sidelocks, double triggers, ejectors.

Mfg.'s Sug. Retail	$2,750	$2,500	$1,850	$1,425	$1,100	$900	$750	$640

Grading	100%	98%	95%	90%	80%	70%	60%

570 LIEJA — 12, 16, or 20 ga., similar to 560 (non-standard model), except has non-detachable sidelocks.
Mfg.'s Sug. Retail $3,385 $2,995 $2,250 $1,725 $1,325 $1,075 $850 $750

575 SPORT — 12, 16, or 20 ga., similar to 560, except is more elaborately engraved.
Mfg.'s Sug. Retail $3,300 $2,950 $2,200 $1,700 $1,325 $1,075 $850 $750

578 VICTORIA — 12, 16, or 20 ga., similar to 570, except is fine English scrollwork engraved.
Mfg.'s Sug. Retail $3,700 $3,450 $2,425 $1,775 $1,375 $1,100 $925 $850

585 LIRIA — 12, 16, or 20 ga., similar to 575, except has profuse engraving.
Mfg.'s Sug. Retail $4,100 $3,725 $2,775 $2,200 $1,875 $1,550 $1,250 $1,025

590 REGINA — 12, 16, or 20 ga., similar to 570, except has more profuse engraving.
Mfg.'s Sug. Retail $4,350 $3,950 $2,900 $2,400 $1,925 $1,600 $1,275 $1,050

595 PRINCIPE — all gauges, sidelock action, relief engraved hunting scenes, ejectors, DTs.
Mfg.'s Sug. Retail $6,600 $6,150 $4,700 $3,950 $3,300 $2,725 $2,275 $1,600

600 IMPERIAL — 12, 16, or 20 ga., top-of-the-line self-opening action, very ornate engraving throughout.
Mfg.'s Sug. Retail $4,990 $4,500 $3,700 $3,000 $2,500 $2,100 $1,775 $1,350

600-1 IMPERIAL — 12, 16, or 20 ga., similar to 600 Imperial, except has light border engraving around sidelocks, tangs, trigger guard. Importation disc. 1988.
$4,600 $3,825 $3,500 $3,175 $2,835 $2,460 $2,000
Last Mfg.'s Sug. Retail was $5,380.

601 IMPERIAL TIRO — all gauges, sidelock action with nickel plating, ejectors, SST, self-opening action, border engraving.
Mfg.'s Sug. Retail $5,750 $5,275 $4,825 $4,000 $3,400 $2,950 $2,500 $2,000

801 — all gauges, Holland-style detachable sidelocks, self-opening action, ejectors, coin-wash finish, finest Churchill style engraving.
Mfg.'s Sug. Retail $7,950 $7,100 $6,500 $5,850 $5,100 $4,600 $4,000 $3,450
Models 801 through 875 are also available with self-opening actions as an option — add $800.

802 — 12, 16, or 20 ga., similar to 801 only non-detachable sidelocks, finest Holland-style engraving.
Mfg.'s Sug. Retail $7,950 $7,100 $6,500 $5,850 $5,100 $4,600 $4,000 $3,450

803 — all gauges, similar to 801, finest Purdey-style engraving.
Mfg.'s Sug. Retail $5,850 $5,350 $4,875 $4,000 $3,400 $2,950 $2,500 $2,000

871 — all gauges, rounded frame sidelock action with Demi-Bloc barrels, scroll engraved, ejectors, DTs.
Mfg.'s Sug. Retail $4,290 $3,875 $3,150 $2,650 $2,150 $1,750 $1,450 $1,275

872 — all gauges, rounded frame sidelock action with Demi-Bloc barrels, elaborate scroll engraving with third lever fastener.
Mfg.'s Sug. Retail $9,790 $9,250 $8,200 $7,150 $5,950 $5,200 $4,400 $3,600

873 — all gauges, sidelock action with Demi-Bloc barrels, game scene engraving, ejectors, SST.
Mfg.'s Sug. Retail $6,850 $6,350 $4,825 $4,000 $3,400 $2,950 $2,500 $2,000

874 — all gauges, sidelock action with Demi-Bloc barrels, action is gold line engraved.
Mfg.'s Sug. Retail $7,950 $7,100 $6,500 $5,850 $5,100 $4,600 $4,000 $3,450

875 — all gauges, top-of-the-line quality, built to individual customer specs. only, elaborate engraving with gold inlays.
Mfg.'s Sug. Retail $12,950 $11,750 $9,950 $8,950 $7,850 $6,850 $5,900 $4,950

Grading	100%	98%	95%	90%	80%	70%	60%

A

931 — all gauges, self-opening action, elaborate engraving, H&H selective ejectors.
Mfg.'s Sug. Retail $14,500 $13,000 $10,500 $9,250 $8,150 $6,950 $5,950 $5,000

ARRIZABLAGA

Manufacturer located in Eibar, Spain since 1940. Currently imported and distributed by New England Arms located in Kittery Point, ME.

Arrizablaga manufactures best quality guns only, carefully made to individual customer specifications. The models listed below are essentially custom ordered per individual specifications - delivery time is approx. 9-12 months.

> ADD THE FOLLOWING AMOUNTS ON ARRIZABLAGA SHOTGUNS:
> All Arrizablaga shotguns have self-opening (assisted) actions.
> Add 10% for matched pair.
> Add $2,750 (retail) for extra barrels.
> Add $500 for 28 ga.
> Add $1,000 for .410 ga.
> Add $1,000 for single trigger.
> Add $250 for pistol grip stock.

HEAVY SCROLL MODEL — 12, 16, or 20 ga., sidelock action, elaborate engraving, deluxe oil finished stock and forearm.
Mfg.'s Sug. Retail $9,250 $9,050 $6,250 $5,400 $4,750 $4,300 $3,850 $3,325

ENGLISH SCROLL MODEL — 12, 16, or 20 ga., sidelock action, English scroll engraving, deluxe oil finished walnut stock and forearm.
Mfg.'s Sug. Retail $9,750 $9,450 $6,700 $5,650 $4,950 $4,500 $4,000 $3,450

ROUND ACTION MODEL — features English scroll engraving.
Mfg.'s Sug. Retail $10,500 $10,000 $8,150 $6,950 $5,650 $4,950 $4,500 $4,000

SPECIAL MODEL — 12, 16, or 20 ga., sidelock top of the line model, best quality wood and engraving.
Mfg.'s Sug. Retail $12,500 $12,500 $8,800 $8,200 $7,400 $6,600 $5,900 $4,950

ARSENAL, BULGARIA

Manufacturer located in Bulgaria. Imported exclusively by Sentinel Arms located in Detroit, MI since 1994.

PISTOLS

MAKAROV MODEL — 9mm Para. cal., 3⅔ in. barrel, 8 shot mag., black synthetic grips, blued finish. Importation began 1995.
No Mfg.'s Retail $195 $165 $125 $115 $105 $95 $85

RIFLES

BULGARIAN SA-93 — 7.62x39mm cal., Kalashnikov milled action with hardwood thumbhole stock, 16.3 in. barrel, 5 shot detachable mag., 9 lbs. Importation began 1995.
No Mfg.'s Retail $365 $295 $250 $215 $190 $180 $170

▲ *Bulgarian SA-93L* — 7.62x39mm cal., similar to Bulgarian SA-93 except has 20 in. barrel, with or without optics, 9 lbs. Importation began 1995.
No Mfg.'s Retail $650 $525 $450 $395 $350 $295 $250
> Add $145 with optics.

BULGARIAN SS-94 — 7.62x39mm cal., Kalashnikov action featuring single shot operation, thumbhole hardwood stock, 5 shot detachable mag., 9 lbs. Importation began 1995.
No Mfg.'s Retail $475 $375 $315 $260 $215 $190 $180

A

ASP

Customized variation of a S&W Model 39-2 semi-auto pistol (or related variations) mfg. by Armament Systems and Procedures located in Appleton, WI.

Grading	100%	98%	95%	90%	80%	70%	60%

PISTOLS

ASP — 9mm Para., compact double action semi-auto, features see-through grips with cut-away mag. making cartridges visible, Teflon coated, re-contoured lightened slide, combat trigger guard, spurless hammer, and mostly painted Guttersnipe rear sight (no front sight), supplied with 3 mag.'s, 24 oz. loaded, approx. 3,000 mfg. until 1981.

	100%	98%	95%	90%	80%	70%	60%
	$1,500	$1,275	$1,050	$875	$775	$695	$625

Add $200 for Tritium filled Guttersnipe.

This pistol is marked ASP on the magazine extension.

▲ *ASP Quest For Excellence* — special edition, marked "Quest for Excellence", included buffalo horn grips, presentation book case and letter opener, approx. 100 mfg.

	100%	98%	95%	90%	80%	70%	60%
	$3,150	$2,700	$2,400	$2,050	$1,775	$1,525	$1,275

ASP REVOLVER — .44 Spl., conversion from a Ruger Speed or Security Six, 5 shot, less than 100 mfg., unmarked.

	100%	98%	95%	90%	80%	70%	60%
	$1,275	$1,075	$950	$875	$775	$700	$650

ASPREY

While established in 1781, Asprey has been manufacturing high quality shotguns and rifles since 1990 in London, England.

RIFLES

BOLT ACTION MAGAZINE RIFLE — various cals., Mauser or Mannlicher action, ¾ rib with standard and two-folding leaf rear sight, best quality pistol grip walnut stock with traditional cheekpiece, custom order only - prices below reflect base model, leather cased with accessories.

		100%	98%	95%	90%	80%	70%	60%
Mfg.'s Sug. Retail	$14,000	$14,000	$12,000	$10,250	$8,950	$7,900	$7,200	$6,500

SxS DOUBLE RIFLE — various cals. up to .700, sidelock ejector with engraved reinforced action, pinless lockplates, best quality walnut, folding leaf rear sight on ¾ rib, custom order only - prices below reflect base models, leather cased with accessories.

▲ *Cals. up to .300*

		100%	98%	95%	90%	80%	70%	60%
Mfg.'s Sug. Retail	$56,000	$56,000	$50,000	$45,000	$40,000	$36,000	$31,000	$26,000

▲ *Cals. up to .470*

		100%	98%	95%	90%	80%	70%	60%
Mfg.'s Sug. Retail	$64,000	$64,000	$56,000	$48,500	$42,000	$37,000	$31,500	$26,000

▲ *Cals. up to .577*

		100%	98%	95%	90%	80%	70%	60%
Mfg.'s Sug. Retail	$72,000	$72,000	$62,000	$52,000	$44,500	$38,000	$32,500	$27,000

▲ *.600 and .700 Bore* — prices available by direct quotation from the factory only.

SHOTGUNS

SIDELOCK MODEL — available in 10 - .410 ga., best quality sidelock ejector model, features pinless lockplates, DTs, best quality checkered walnut, custom order only - prices below reflect base model, leather cased with accessories.

		100%	98%	95%	90%	80%	70%	60%
Mfg.'s Sug. Retail	$44,000	$44,000	$39,000	$35,000	$31,000	$27,000	$22,500	$18,000

Add $2,200 for ST.

ASTRA

Manufactured by Unceta Y Cia., Guernica, Spain. Currently imported by European American Armory located in Sharpes, FL. Previously imported until 1992 by Interarms located in Alexandria, VA. Astra pistols currently imported have a limited lifetime warranty through E.A.A.

Grading	100%	98%	95%	90%	80%	70%	60%

PISTOLS: RECENT MANUFACTURE

CONSTABLE — double action, .22 LR (10 shot, disc. in 1990.), .32 ACP (8 shot, disc. 1984), or .380 ACP (7 shot) cal., exposed hammer, 3½ in. barrel, fixed sight, blue or chrome (disc.) finish, plastic grips. Imported 1965-91.

	$295	$250	$210	$180	$165	$150	$135

Last Mfg.'s Sug. Retail was $380.

Add $10 for chrome finish or wood grips (disc. in 1990).

▲ *Constable Stainless* — .380 ACP only, stainless version of the Constable. Mfg. 1986 only.

	$350	$300	$240	$220	$200	$175	$150

Last Mfg.'s Sug. Retail was $345.

▲ *Constable Sport* — similar to Constable, except has 6 in. barrel, blue finish only, 35 oz. Mfg. 1986-87 only.

	$325	$245	$210	$180	$165	$150	$135

Last Mfg.'s Sug. Retail was $330.

▲ *Blue Engraved Constable* — blue engraved. Importation disc. 1987.

	$375	$295	$250

Last Mfg.'s Sug. Retail was $375.

Add $20 for .22 LR or checkered wood grips.

▲ *Chrome Engraved Constable* — chrome engraved. Importation disc. 1987.

	$350	$295	$250

Last Mfg.'s Sug. Retail was $390.

Add $20 for .22 LR or checkered wood grips.

CONSTABLE A-60 — .380 ACP, double action, 3½ in. barrel, 13 shot mag., ambidextrous safety, adj. rear sight, blue finish only. Imported 1986-91.

	$395	$325	$280	$245	$220	$185	$160

Last Mfg.'s Sug. Retail was $475.

MODEL A-70 — 9mm Para. or .40 S&W cal., single action, 3½ in. barrel, steel frame and slide, 7 (.40 S&W) or 8 (9mm Para.) shot mag., compact design, dual safeties, 3-dot sights, matte blue or nickel (new 1993) finish, 25¾ oz. Importation began 1991.

Mfg.'s Sug. Retail	$358	$300	$255	$225	$200	$185	$170	$160

Add $29 for nickel finish.

▲ *Model A-70 Stainless* — stainless steel variation of the A-70. Mfg. 1994 only.

	$375	$325	$275

Last Mfg.'s Sug. Retail was $435.

MODEL A-75 — 9mm Para., .40 S&W, or .45 ACP (new 1994) cal., action similar to Model A-70, except has selective double action with a decocking lever, steel or aluminum (9mm Para. only, 23½ oz.) frame. Importation began 1993.

Mfg.'s Sug. Retail	$416	$365	$305	$270	$230	$200	$180	$165

Add $29 for nickel finish.
Add $28 for .45 ACP cal.
Add $28 for Featherweight Model (9mm Para. only).

▲ *Model A-75 Stainless* — stainless steel variation of the A-75. Mfg. 1994 only.

	$435	$375	$300

Last Mfg.'s Sug. Retail was $485.

Grading	100%	98%	95%	90%	80%	70%	60%

MODEL A-80 — 9mm Para, .38 Super (disc.) or .45 ACP cal., double action, semi-auto, 15 shot mag. (9 for .45 ACP), 3¾ in. barrel. Imported 1982-89.

| | $370 | $320 | $285 | $265 | $240 | $210 | $185 |

Last Mfg.'s Sug. Retail was $425.

> Add $35 for chrome finish (disc.).
> .38 Super cal. in chrome finish will command a premium (10%-20%).

MODEL A-90 — 9mm Para. or .45 ACP cal., 1986 designation for Model A-80 with updated slide mounted safety and pushbutton mag. release, 3¾ in. barrel, 14 shot mag. (9mm), or 8 shot (.45 ACP), blue only, approx. 48 oz. Imported 1986-90, replaced by Model A-100.

| | $400 | $340 | $300 | $275 | $245 | $225 | $200 |

Last Mfg.'s Sug. Retail was $500.

MODEL A-100 — 9mm Para., .40 S&W, or .45 ACP cal., replaced the Model A-90 in 1990, with similar specifications, blue or nickel finish, re-engineered 1993 incorporating increased mag. capacity, 10 (C/B 1994), 17*/9mm, 12*/.40 S&W, or 9 shot/.45 ACP, approx. 29 oz. Importation began 1990.

| **Mfg.'s Sug. Retail** | **$444** | $375 | $325 | $275 | $250 | $225 | $200 | $185 |

> Add $38 for nickel finish.

MODEL 4000 FALCON — .22 LR, .32 ACP, or .380 ACP cal., 4 in. barrel, fixed sights, blue, plastic grips, exposed hammer. Mfg. 1956-1986.

| | $450 | $400 | $330 | $260 | $235 | $200 | $150 |

Last Mfg.'s Sug. Retail was $340.

> Add 50% for .22 cal.
> Add 100% for engraved M-4000.

▲ **Model 4000 Tri-cal. Kit** — includes frame and 3 barrels (.22 LR, .32 ACP, and .380 ACP cals.), either rust blued or salt blued finish, less than 200 mfg. Boxed.

| | $1,100 | $875 | $750 |

PISTOLS: DISC.

MODEL 1911 — .25 ACP or .32 ACP cal., semi-auto, may have external or internal hammer.

| | $295 | $225 | $165 | $135 | $115 | $100 | | $85 |

> Add 50% if with external hammer.

MODEL 1915/1916 — .32 ACP cal., semi-auto.

| | $295 | $235 | $165 | $135 | $115 | $100 | | $85 |

> Note: Models 1915/1916 were later referred to as Model 100 Special.

CAMPO GIRO 1913 — mfg. 1913.

| | $2,995 | $2,350 | $1,750 | $1,250 | $800 | $600 | $400 |

CAMPO GIRO 1913-16 — mfg. 1913-16.

| | $1,750 | $1,350 | $900 | $675 | $550 | $450 | $300 |

MODEL 200 FIRECAT AUTOMATIC PISTOL — .25 ACP cal., 2¼ in. barrel, 6 shot, blue, plastic grips, mfg. 1920-1968.

| | $240 | $190 | $165 | $145 | $125 | $110 | $100 |

> Add 50% for engraved M-200.

MODEL 300 — .32 ACP or .380 ACP cal., semi-auto.

| | $495 | $350 | $270 | $240 | $210 | $180 | $150 |

> Add 20% if Nazi-proofed.
> Add 200% for engraved M-300.

Grading	100%	98%	95%	90%	80%	70%	60%

MODEL 400 AUTOMATIC PISTOL — 9mm Bayard long, 9 shot, 6 in. barrel, blue, fixed sights, plastic grips, mfg. 1921-1945.

	$400	$325	$230	$200	$170	$135	$100

Add 200% for Navy variation.
Add 100% for Nazi accepted specimens.
Approx. serial range of Nazi accepted specimens (no markings) is S/N 92,851 - 98,850.
This particular model in "reworked" configuration has recently been imported in large quantities.

▲ **"F. Ascaso" Marked Model 400 Copies** — close copy of the Astra Model 400, produced by the Spanish Republican forces during the later part of the Spanish Civil War, F. Ascaso marked (un-numbered) mags., salt blued, estimated production is approx. 8,000, has identifying logo on slide and grip panels.

	$600	$475	$325	$250	$200	$175	$150

▲ **R.E. (Republica Espagnola) Marked Model 400 Copies** — ser. range to approx. 15,000, has identifying logo on forward slide and grip panels.

	$475	$400	$295	$240	$210	$170	$125

MODEL 600 MOD. AUTOMATIC — 9mm Luger, 8 shot, 5¼ in. barrel, blue, fixed sights, wood or plastic grips, mfg. 1944-1945.

	$300	$250	$200	$175	$155	$140	$130

Add 100% for Nazi Waffenamt proofing (serial range 1 - 10,500).

MODEL 700 SPECIAL — .32 ACP cal., semi-auto.

	$600	$500	$425	$350	$275	$215	$170

MODEL 800 CONDOR AUTOMATIC — similar to 600, except has exposed hammer, 9mm, mfg. 1958-1965.

	$1,195	$995	$895	$650	$550	$450	$350

Add 50% if NIB with accessories.

MODEL 900 — 7.63 Mauser cal., Broomhandle copy, parts non-interchangeable with Mauser. Mfg. from 1928-1936.

	$2,500	$1,850	$1,350	$850	$700	$525	$425

Add $500 for non-matching stock.
Add $750 for matching stock.
Add 50% for early Bolo grip variation.
Add 20% for specimens with Japanese characters.

MODEL 902 — 7.63 Mauser cal., semi-auto, similar to 900 except 20 shot mag.

	$13,500	$10,000	$7,500	$3,750	$2,500	$2,100	$1,700

Add $1,250 for original "booted" stock.
Deduct 60% for selective fire version.

MACHINE PISTOLS — class III, transferrable only, 10 or 20 shot detachable mag., several variations.

	$3,500	$2,750	$1,900	$1,600	$1,250	$900	$600

MODEL 3000 POCKET AUTOMATIC — .32 ACP or .380 ACP cal., 4 in. barrel, fixed sights, blue, plastic grips, mfg. 1947-1956.

	$475	$335	$240	$210	$180	$150	$120

Add 100% for engraved M3000.

MODEL 1000 OR 1000 SPECIAL — .32 ACP cal., semi-auto, extended frame to hold 12 shot mag.

	$695	$550	$400	$310	$280	$255	$225

Grading	100%	98%	95%	90%	80%	70%	60%

MODEL 2000 CUB — .22 Short or .25 ACP cal., 2¼ in. barrel, fixed sights, blue, plastic grips, also chrome finish, mfg. 1954-present, U.S. importation stopped by GCA 68. Astra also made 2000 Cubs for Colt called Jr. Model {see Colt section}.

	$200	$170	$140	$115	$95	$85	$75

Add 25% for chrome finish.
Add 50% for engraved M-2000.

MODEL 2000 CAMPER — similar to Cub, .22 Short only, with 4 in. barrel, mfg. 1955-1960.

	$350	$275	$200	$160	$125	$90	$70

REVOLVERS

ASTRA CADIX DOUBLE ACTION REVOLVER — .22 LR, 9 shot, .38 Spl., 5 shot, 4 or 6 in. barrel, adj. sights, blue, plastic grips, mfg. 1960-1968.

	$165	$155	$140	$120	$110	$85	$55

.357 D/A REVOLVER — .357 Mag., 6 shot, 3, 4, 6 or 8½ in. barrel (add $10), adj. sights, blue, checkered wood grips, mfg. 1972-1988.

	$250	$215	$185	$170	$155	$140	$125

Last Mfg.'s Sug. Retail was $295.

▲ *Stainless Steel* — 4 in. barrel only. Disc. 1987.

	$285	$245	$205				

Last Mfg.'s Sug. Retail was $330.

.44/.45 CAL. D/A REVOLVER — .41 Mag. (disc. 1985), .44 Mag. or .45 ACP (disc. 1987), 6 shot, 6 or 8½ in. (.44 Mag. only) barrels. Mfg. 1980-87.

	$280	$235	$210	$190	$180	$170	$160

Last Mfg.'s Sug. Retail was $315.

▲ *Stainless Steel* — .44 Mag. only, 6 in. barrel only, 2½ lbs. Importation disc. 1993.

	$370	$300	$265				

Last Mfg.'s Sug. Retail was $450.

CONVERTIBLE REVOLVER — 9mm with extra .357 Mag. cylinder, 6 shot, 3 in. barrel, blue only, checkered walnut grips, 2¼ lbs. Imported 1986-1993.

	$335	$275	$250	$225	$200	$180	$160

Last Mfg.'s Sug. Retail was $395.

TERMINATOR — .44 Mag. or .44 Spl. (disc.) cal., 6 shot, adj. rear sight, Roberts rubber grips, 2¾ in. shrouded barrel only. Inventories were depleted in 1989.

▲ *Blue finish*

	$250	$225	$190	$175	$160	$150	$140

Last Mfg.'s Sug. Retail was $250.

▲ *Stainless steel*

	$275	$235	$190				

Last Mfg.'s Sug. Retail was $275.

These models were distributed by Sile Distributors, Inc. located in New York, NY.

AUSTRALIAN AUTOMATIC ARMS PTY. LTD.

Manufacturer located in Tasmania, Australia. Previously imported and distributed by California Armory, Inc. located in San Bruno, CA.

SAR — .223 cal., semi-auto paramilitary design rifle, 16¼ or 20 in. (new 1989) barrel, 5 or 20 shot M-16 style mag., fiberglass stock and forearm, 7½ lbs. Imported 1986-89.

	$725	$625	$550	$510	$465	$410	$370

Last Mfg.'s Sug. Retail was $663.

Add $25 for 20 in. barrel.
Also available in fully auto version (AR).

Grading	100%	98%	95%	90%	80%	70%	60%

SAC — .223 cal., semi-auto paramilitary design carbine, 10½ in. barrel, 20 shot mag., fiberglass stock and forearm, 6.9 lbs. New 1986.

This model is available to class III dealers and law enforcement agencies only.

SAP — .223 cal., semi-auto paramilitary design pistol, 10½ in. barrel, 20 shot mag., fiberglass stock and forearm, 5.9 lbs. Imported 1986-1993.

	100%	98%	95%	90%	80%	70%	60%
	$725	$650	$575	$525	$495	$475	$450

Last Mfg.'s Sug. Retail was $799.

SP — .223 cal., semi-auto, sporting configuration, 16¼ or 20 in. barrel, wood stock and forearm, 5 or 20 shot M-16 style mag., 7.5 lbs. Imported late 1991-1993.

	100%	98%	95%	90%	80%	70%	60%
	$795	$675	$575	$525	$495	$475	$450

Last Mfg.'s Sug. Retail was $879.

Add $40 for wood stock.

AUTO MAG

Previously manufactured by Auto Mag. Corp. and TDE Corp.

Short recoil rotary bolt system made entirely of stainless steel. Most pistols were sold in .44 AMP cal. although .357 AMP was also a popular factory option. Several other calibers and variations were marketed through Lee Jurras including exotics like the .44 Condor (16 in. barrel and scoped - one of a kind). Also, a .30 cal. Cougar with 12 in. barrel and highly polished metal was a one of a kind item. Other limited Jurras variations include The Custom 100 Series (.44 cal., custom tuned, magna ported, special serialization), The Grizzly (.41 cal.), The Backpacker (.357 cal.), in addition to the Metallic Silhouette.

A unique handgun, the Auto Mag has never been a commercial success due to high manufacturing costs and initial functioning problems (mostly attributed to hand loading all the ammo - once factory ammo became available, reliability improved significantly). Initial reaction to Dirty Harry's use of this weapon in the movie "Sudden Impact" made prices escalate considerably, but most values appear to have stablized since 1986. Be aware of fakes - especially of the XP variety (re-serialized, re-stamped, location of markings, etc.). Also, the ease of barrel swapping should be considered when deciding on a potential purchase. Auto Mags were never magna ported from the factory (only The Custom 100 Series). Non-original magna porting actually detracts from the values listed below, since it is a non-factory alteration.

Serial number ranges for the various models are as follows: Pasadena mfg. - A0000 through A03700. TDE North Hollywood - mostly A02500 through A05015 although some were marked with very low ser. no.'s. TDE El Monte mfg. - A05016 through A08300. High Standard guns were originally marked with "H" prefix serial numbers (only 132 made), after which they carried standard "A0" prefix serial numbers. The "H" prefix guns remain a collectors item and command a 25% premium over values listed below. TDE/OMC marked pistols - B00001 through B00370 are known as the "B" series or solid bolt models (only 370 manufactured). This "B" series also commands collector premiums.

AMT manufactured the last two lots of Auto Mags; the first was the "C" series and was basically the same as the "B" except that only 50 guns were fabricated. The last Auto Mags made by AMT were appropriately serial numbered LAST 1 through LAST 50. These guns had the reputation of being the poorest quality but do carry collector premiums. One interesting variation is the North Hollywood "two-line" model. Also, the first .357 cal. pistols manufactured did not have the words AUTO MAG appearing on the gun. These are also collectors items.

In addition to the above calibers, a very few non-factory .22 and .25 cal. prototypes were fabricated by Kent Lomont. These specimens will usually demand a premium over the values listed below. Also, some barrels and pistols were made in Covina, CA.

Grading	100%	98%	95%	90%	80%	70%	60%

Less than 10,000 Auto Mags were produced by all manufacturers. All pistols originally had all stainless steel mags.

PISTOLS

ORIGINAL PASADENA — .44 AMP only, 6½ in. VR barrel.
$2,500 $2,300 $1,995

This model is generally regarded as having the most quality, as all components were milled from Carpenter 455 stainless steel stock.

TDE NORTH HOLLYWOOD

▲ **.44 AMP** — 6½ in. VR barrel, initial guns were mfg. from existing Pasadena parts, later mfg. required new components made by TDE.
$2,275 $1,975 $1,850

Quality on this model goes down in later mfg. (some small parts are not stainless). Because of this, higher serial numbered guns in this model are less desirable.

▲ **.357 AMP** — two line address.
$2,500 $2,300 $1,995

There are no factory records verifying this caliber.

TDE EL MONTE

▲ **.44 AMP** — 6½ VR, 8, or 10 in. tapered barrel.
$2,100 $1,800 $1,600

▲ **.357 AMP** — 6½ VR, 8, or 10 in. tapered barrel.
$1,800 $1,600 $1,500

HIGH STANDARD — "H" prefixed serial numbers, mfg. by TDE with High Standard markings.
$2,500 $2,300 $1,995

TDE/OMC "B" SERIES — 6½ VR or 10 in. barrel.
$2,500 $2,300 $1,995

AMT "C" SERIES — 6½ VR or 10 in. barrel.
$2,500 $2,300 $1,995

Add 50%+ for L.E. Jurras Custom 100 Series.
Add 10% for Jurras Lion marked models.

Lee Jurras added his Lion's head logo (from 1977 on) on TDE manufactured guns.

There were also a very limited quantity of original shoulder stocks (perhaps less than 5) - extreme rarity precludes accurate price evaluation.

Note: guns were cased (plastic attache style) with accessories. Original Auto-Mag ammo (only original mfg. by CDM in Mexico and Norma in Sweden) is currently selling for approx. $85 a box.

AUTO-ORDNANCE CORP.

Manufacturer located in West Hurley, NY. Distributor sales only.

Auto-Ordnance Corp. manufactures an exact reproduction of the original 1927 Thompson machine gun. They are currently available in semi-auto only since production ceased on fully automatic variations (Model 1928 and M1) in 1986 (mfg. 1975-1986 including 609 M1s).

CARBINES: SEMI-AUTO

Until the Crime Bill was passed in 1994, the Auto-Ordnance Thompson replicas listed below were supplied with either 15, 20, or 30 shot mags. Beginning late 1994, Auto-Ordnance began manufacturing 10 round X-drum mags. that resemble the older 50 round L-type drums - retail is approx. $110.

A

Grading	100%	98%	95%	90%	80%	70%	60%

1927 A1 STANDARD — .45 ACP, 16 in. plain barrel, solid steel construction, standard military sight, walnut stock and horizontal forearm. Disc. 1986.

			$570	$490	$430	$360	$315	$290	$270

Last Mfg.'s Sug. Retail was $575.

1927 A1 DELUXE — 10mm (mfg. 1991-93) or .45 ACP cal., 16 in. finned barrel, 10 (C/B 1994) shot mag., solid steel construction, adj. rear sight, walnut stock and hand grips.

Mfg.'s Sug. Retail	$795		$650	$530	$445	$370	$320	$295	$275

Add $190 for 50* shot drum mag. or $350 for 100 shot drum mag. (mfg. 1990-93) on this model and other 1927 variations. Also add $105 (retail) for Thompson hard case (violin type).

THOMPSON M1 CARBINE — .45 ACP, combat model, 16½ in. smooth barrel, 10 (C/B 1994) shot mag., side-cocking lever, flat black finish, walnut stock, pistol grip, and grooved forearm, 11½ lbs. New 1986.

Mfg.'s Sug. Retail	$773		$625	$515	$440	$360	$310	$285	$265

1927 A1C LIGHTWEIGHT — .45 ACP, similar to 1927 A-1 Deluxe, except receiver made of a lightweight alloy. 20% weight reduction. New 1984.

Mfg.'s Sug. Retail	$767		$625	$515	$440	$360	$310	$285	$265

1927 A5 PISTOL/CARBINE — .45 ACP, 13 in. finned barrel, alloy construction, overall length 26 in., 10 (C/B 1994) shot mag., 7 lbs. Mfg. disc. 1994.

			$625	$515	$440	$360	$305	$280	$260

Last Mfg.'s Sug. Retail was $765.

1927 A3 - .22 CAL. — .22 LR, 16 in. finned barrel, alloy frame and receiver, walnut stock, pistol grip, and forearm pistol grip, 7 lbs. Mfg. disc. 1994.

			$440	$375	$325	$285	$260	$230	$200

Last Mfg.'s Sug. Retail was $510.

PISTOLS: SEMI-AUTO

1911 A1 — .38 Super, 9mm Para., .40 S&W (mfg. 1991-93), 10mm (new 1991), or .45 ACP cal., 4½ (.40 S&W cal. only) or 5 in. barrel, 7 shot mag., single action, parts interchange with the original Colt Govt. Model, blue or nickel finish, checkered plastic grips, 39 oz.

Mfg.'s Sug. Retail	$398		$330	$280	$250	$235	$225	$215	$200

Add $39 for .40 S&W cal.
Add $30 for .38 Super, 9mm Para. cal.
Add $37 for 10mm cal.
Add $28 for satin nickel (new 1990) or $37 for duo-tone (new 1992) finish (.45 ACP only).

▲ *1911 A1 Deluxe* — .38 Super, 9mm Para., or .45 ACP cal., 5 in. barrel, 3 dot sights, wraparound grips, 39 oz. New 1991.

Mfg.'s Sug. Retail	$426		$355	$310	$260	$235	$225	$215	$200

Add 9$ for .38 Super or 9mm Para. cal.

▲ *1911 A1 General* — .38 Super (new 1996) or .45 ACP cal., 4½ in. barrel with full length recoil guide system, 7 shot mag., blued finish, 3 dot fixed Millett sights, black rubber wraparound grips, Commander styling, 37 oz. New 1992.

Mfg.'s Sug. Retail	$465		$385	$315	$255	$235	$225	$215	$200

Add $15 for .38 Super cal.

▲ *Parkerized 1911 A1* — .45 ACP cal., no frills variation of the Model 1911 A1, military parkerizing, checkered walnut grips. New 1992.

Mfg.'s Sug. Retail	$390		$325	$275	$250	$235	$225	$215	$200

This model is distributed exclusively by RSR Wholesale Guns, Inc.

▲ *Competition 1911* — .38 Super (new 1996) or .45 ACP cal., competition features include compensated barrel, commander hammer, flat mainspring housing, white 3-dot sighting system, beavertail grip safety, black textured wraparound grips. New 1993.

Mfg.'s Sug. Retail	$636		$530	$415	$375	$330	$300	$285	$270

Add $10 for .38 Super cal.

Grading	100%	98%	95%	90%	80%	70%	60%

MODEL ZG-51 "PIT BULL" — .45 ACP cal. only, compact variation of the 1911 A1, $3\frac{5}{8}$ in. barrel, 7 shot mag., 36 oz. New 1988.

Mfg.'s Sug. Retail	$455	$370	$300	$255	$235	$225	$215	$200

AUTO-POINTER

Manufactured by Yamamoto Co. Formerly imported by Sloans.

SEMI-AUTO SHOTGUN — 12 or 20 ga., gas operated. Disc.

	$275	$240	$220	$195	$180	$160	$145

A

B section

BSA GUNS LIMITED

Birmingham Small Arms, located in Birmingham, England. Manufactured 1861-current in England. Imported until 1985 by Precision Sports, from Ithaca, NY and 1986 by BSA Guns Ltd., located in Grand Prairie, TX. Imported and distributed until 1989 by Samco Global Arms, Inc., located in Miami, FL (small quantities of certain models still remain). Currently, BSA firearms are not being imported. BSA airguns may be found under the Airgun section of this text.

Grading	100%	98%	95%	90%	80%	70%	60%

RIFLES: RECENT IMPORTATION

Importation of all BSA rimfire and centerfire rifles was disc. 1987.

CF-2 ACTION — .222 R., .22-250, .243 Win., 6.5x55mm, 7x57, 7x64mm, 7mm Rem. Mag., .270 Win., .308 Win., .30-06, or .300 Win. Mag. cal., bolt action, barrel length 23-26 in., 7½-8 lbs. CF-2 nomenclature designates an action rather than a model. CF-2 actioned models are listed below. Add $70 for double set trigger option on the below listed models. Limited quantities of English mfg. models remain.

▲ *Sporter/Classic* — same cals. as above, checkered oil finished walnut stock. Imported 1986-87.

	$325	$275	$250	$225	$210	$195	$180

Last Mfg.'s Sug. Retail was $360.

    Sporter Model features Monte Carlo stock, rosewood capped forearm and pistol grip stock, and swivels.

▲ *Classic Varminter* — available in .222R-.243 W. cals. only, heavy barrel, matte finish, with swivels. Imported 1986 only.

	$325	$275	$250	$225	$210	$190	$175

Last Mfg.'s Sug. Retail was $345.

▲ *Heavy Barrel Model* — .222R, .22-250, or .243W cal., approx. 9 lbs., no sights.

	$375	$300	$260	$240	$225	$210	$180

Last Mfg.'s Sug. Retail was $410.

▲ *Carbine Model* — 20 in. barrel. Disc. 1985.

	$350	$325	$295	$270	$250	$225	$200

Last Mfg.'s Sug. Retail was $480.

▲ *Stutzen Rifle* — Mannlicher style full length stock, same general specifications as Sporter/Classic, 20½ in. barrel. Not available in 7mm Rem. Mag. or .300 Win. Mag cal.

	$450	$375	$325	$300	$275	$250	$225

Last Mfg.'s Sug. Retail was $385.

▲ *Regal Custom* — similar to Sporter Model, except has slim classic European style stock with Schnabel forend, deluxe walnut with extra checkering, ebony forend cap, engraved action and floorplate. Limited importation (1986 only).

	$875	$795	$685	$590	$550	$500	$450

Last Mfg.'s Sug. Retail was $950.

    This model was custom made by special order only.

CFT TARGET RIFLE — 7.62mm, single shot, bolt action, globe front and aperture rear sights, 26½ in. barrel, 11 lbs. Disc. 1987.

	$675	$590	$550	$500	$450	$400	$360

Last Mfg.'s Sug. Retail was $780.

RIFLES: SINGLE SHOT

NO. 12 MARTINI — .22 LR, 29 in. barrel, target sights, straight stock, pre-WWII.

	$360	$275	$250	$210	$175	$155	$130

B

Grading	100%	98%	95%	90%	80%	70%	60%

MODEL 15 — similar to 12, except pistol grip stock, better grade target sights, pre-WWII.

	100%	98%	95%	90%	80%	70%	60%
	$385	$305	$275	$240	$200	$175	$155

CENTURION MATCH RIFLE — similar to 15, except Centurion guarantee — 1½ in. grouping at 100 yards, 24 in. barrel, pre-WWII.

	100%	98%	95%	90%	80%	70%	60%
	$440	$385	$330	$275	$240	$220	$175

MATCH 12/15 — similar to 15, except made after WWII.

	100%	98%	95%	90%	80%	70%	60%
	$385	$305	$275	$240	$200	$175	$155

MODEL 12/15 — heavy barrel.

	100%	98%	95%	90%	80%	70%	60%
	$415	$330	$305	$270	$230	$195	$165

MODEL 13 — lighter version of 12.

	100%	98%	95%	90%	80%	70%	60%
	$340	$265	$235	$200	$165	$150	$125

MODEL 13 SPORTER — similar to 13, except has sport sights.

	100%	98%	95%	90%	80%	70%	60%
	$330	$240	$220	$175	$155	$140	$120
.22 Hornet	$385	$305	$275	$240	$200	$175	$155

MARTINI INTERNATIONAL MATCH — .22 LR, 29 in. heavy barrel, international sights, mfg. 1950-1953.

	100%	98%	95%	90%	80%	70%	60%
	$415	$360	$320	$275	$255	$230	$200

INTERNATIONAL LIGHT — 26 in. lightweight barrel.

	100%	98%	95%	90%	80%	70%	60%
	$415	$360	$320	$275	$255	$230	$200

INTERNATIONAL MKII — improved trigger, ejectors and stock design, mfg. 1953-1959.

	100%	98%	95%	90%	80%	70%	60%
	$425	$375	$340	$315	$285	$255	$220

INTERNATIONAL MKIII — longer action, floating barrel, mfg. 1959-1967.

	100%	98%	95%	90%	80%	70%	60%
	$495	$430	$385	$360	$330	$305	$265

INTERNATIONAL ISU — modeled to meet ISU standards, 28 in. barrel, mfg. 1968-disc.

	100%	98%	95%	90%	80%	70%	60%
	$495	$430	$385	$360	$330	$305	$265

INTERNATIONAL MARK V — similar to ISU, but heavier barrel, mfg. 1976-disc.

	100%	98%	95%	90%	80%	70%	60%
	$525	$460	$430	$375	$350	$330	$305

RIFLES: BOLT ACTION

MAJESTIC FEATHERWEIGHT DELUXE — .243, .270, .308, or .30-06 cal., bolt action, 22 in. barrel, folding sight, checkered European style stock, mfg. 1959-1965.

	100%	98%	95%	90%	80%	70%	60%
	$330	$250	$220	$195	$180	$165	$145
.458 Mag.	$445	$375	$305	$275	$220	$210	$200

MAJESTIC DELUXE — .222, .22 Hornet, .243, 7x57, .308, or .30-06 cal., heavier barrel.

	100%	98%	95%	90%	80%	70%	60%
	$330	$250	$220	$195	$180	$165	$145

MONARCH DELUXE — similar to Majestic Deluxe, but American design stock, mfg. 1965-1974.

	100%	98%	95%	90%	80%	70%	60%
	$350	$275	$250	$220	$195	$180	$165

MONARCH DELUXE VARMINT — similar to Monarch Deluxe, except .222 or .243 cal., 24 in. heavy barrel. Disc.

	100%	98%	95%	90%	80%	70%	60%
	$370	$305	$275	$250	$210	$195	$180

MARTINI ISU MATCH .22 — single shot, bolt action, .22 cal. only, similar to CFT Model. Add $100 for Mk. V.H.B. Model. Disc. 1985.

	100%	98%	95%	90%	80%	70%	60%
	$825	$700	$600	$530	$475	$435	$400

Last Mfg.'s Sug. Retail was $1,000.

B-WEST

Importer/distributor located in Tucson, AZ.

B-West imports rifles (including AK-47 clones, the Saiga, Dragunov, etc.) in addition to an IJ series .380 ACP Makarov pistol. Pre-ban AK-47 variations have recently been selling in the $395-$500 range while their current line of Makarov pistols is selling in the $130-$200 range. The Dragunov and Saiga rifles currently are priced at $1,200 and $425 respectively. To obtain more information about B-West's current line-up of imports, please contact the company directly (refer to Trademark Index).

LES BAER CUSTOM, INC.

Please refer to the L section of this text.

BAFORD ARMS, INC.

Previously manufactured by Baford Arms, Inc. located in Bristol, TN. Previously distributed by C.L. Reedy & Associates, Inc. located in Melbourne, FL.

Grading	100%	98%	95%	90%	80%	70%	60%

MODEL 35 FIRE POWER — 9mm Para., semi-auto single action, patterned after the Browning Hi-Power, total stainless steel construction, $4\frac{3}{4}$ in. barrel, combat hammer and safety, Pachmayr grips, removable barrel bushing, Millett Mk. II sights, 14 shot mag., 32 oz. Introduced late 1988 with limited mfg. until 1993.

	$500	$425	$350

Last Mfg.'s Sug. Retail was $550.

THUNDER DERRINGER — .44 Spl./.410 shotshell, single shot, tip out action, 3 in. barrel, blued steel finish, spur trigger, wood grips. Introduced late 1988 with limited mfg. until 1991, when production temporarily ceased.

	$130	$110	$95	$90	$85	$80	$75

Last Mfg.'s Sug. Retail was $130.

Add $90 for interchangeable barrel kit.

Interchangeable pistol barrels are chambered in various calibers between .22 Short and 9mm Para. There are two types: one fits flush while the other facilitates a scope mounting.

BAIKAL

Manufactured in the U.S.S.R. since approx. WWII. Currently imported by Big Bear located in Dallas, TX. Distributor and dealer sales.

Baikal shotguns have had limited importation into the U.S. 1993 marked the first year that Baikals were officially (and legally) imported into the U.S. because of Russia's previous export restrictions domestically. In prior years, however, a few O/Us have been seen for sale and have no doubt been "imported" into this country one at a time. Quality is in the intermediate level and collector interest is not particularly great. Most older O/U shotguns fall into the $400 - $1,000 range if quality is at par with other more famous trademarks.

B

Grading	100%	98%	95%	90%	80%	70%	60%

PISTOLS

IJ-70 — .380 ACP or 9x18 Makarov cal., double action semi-auto, all steel blued construction, 4 in. barrel, slide mounted safety with decocking, fully adj. target sights, choice of two 8 shot (IJ-70), two 10 (C/B 1994, Model IJ-70-HC), or two 12* shot, holster and cleaning rod, checkered plastic grips, 25 oz.

Mfg.'s Sug. Retail	$199	$175	$150	$135	$120	$105	$95	$85

Add $40 for IJ-70-HC (High Capacity).
Add $50 for .380 ACP cal.
Add $10 for nickel finish (disc.).

SHOTGUNS: RECENT IMPORTATION

IJ-18M SINGLE BARREL — 12, 16, 20, or .410 ga., 26 or 28 in. barrel.

Mfg.'s Sug. Retail	$74	$60	$50	$40	$35	$30	$30	$25

IJ-43 SxS FIELD MODEL — 12 or 20 ga., double triggers, extractors, 20, 26 (disc.), or 28 in. barrels.

Mfg.'s Sug. Retail	$299	$235	$200	$160	$130	$105	$95	$75

Add $20 for 20 in. barrels bored C/C.

IJ-27 O/U FIELD MODEL — 12 or 20 (new 1992) ga., double triggers, extractors, 26 or 28 in. barrels.

Mfg.'s Sug. Retail	$399	$330	$275	$250	$225	$195	$180	$165

Add $40 for single trigger and automatic ejectors (Model IJ-27EIC).

BAILONS GUNMAKERS LIMITED

Manufacturer and refurbisher located in Birmingham, England until 1993, when operations ceased. Inquiries regarding this trademark (including repairs) should be directed to Guthrie Consulting (see Trademark Index for listing).

HUNTING RIFLE — various cals., modified Mauser bolt action, barrel length to suit from 18 to 30 in., set triggers or match, Habicht Telescope sight (magnification and reticle to suit), engraving, and types of finishes are at optional cost, prices below reflect standard rifle with no options. Imported 1986-1993.

$2,495	$2,250	$1,995	$1,775	$1,625	$1,450	$1,300

Last Mfg.'s Sug. Retail was $2,750.

BAKER, W.H. & CO.

Manufacturer located in Syracuse, NY circa 1878-1883.

Originally started by William H. and Ellis L. Baker circa 1878. During this time, Leroy H. and Lyman C. Smith financed the new company, W.H. Baker & Co. Circa 1880, L.C. Smith bought the interest from the two Baker partners and continued production with markings reading "L. C. Smith and Co., Maker of the Baker Gun" on the rib, "Baker Pat." on the locks. Smith decided to drop the Baker name in 1883, but continued to manufacture this gun and a shotgun/rifle combination gun in Syracuse, NY until 1888. At this point, the company was sold to the Hunter Brothers and this new company, Baker Gun & Forging Co. began making both the New Baker shotguns (see separate listing below) in addition to the Ithaca gun. The company was sold to the Hunter Brothers circa 1888, and the Hunter Arms Company made L.C. Smith shotguns for approximately 60 years at which point the Marlin Firearms Company bought the business during the early 1940s.

Baker guns were originally 10 or 12 ga., and unusual in that the opening mechanism was operated by pressing forward on the front trigger. While relatively rare, most original Baker guns (including the shotgun/rifle) do not have a lot of original finish remaining. Most specimens are priced in the

$400-$850 range, assuming finish is less than 10%. If condition is better than 40%, guns have to be evaluated individually for accurate pricing.

BAKER GUN & FORGING CO.
Previous manufacturer located in Batavia, NY. 1889-1933.

B

Grading	100%	98%	95%	90%	80%	70%	60%

SHOTGUNS: SIDE BY SIDE

Note: Original damascus guns in 80% or better condition with bright case colors will approach the values of steel barrel counterparts.

THE NEW BAKER — 10 or 12 ga., exposed hammers, damascus barrels, extractors.

	100%	98%	95%	90%	80%	70%	60%
	$350	$300	$260	$225	$195	$175	$150

BATAVIA SPECIAL — 12, 16, or 20 ga., 26, 28, 30, or 32 in. barrels, any standard choke, checkered pistol grip stock, sidelock, extractors.

	100%	98%	95%	90%	80%	70%	60%
	$385	$305	$275	$260	$250	$220	$200

BATAVIA LEADER — similar to Special, except has deluxe finish.

	100%	98%	95%	90%	80%	70%	60%
	$440	$360	$335	$305	$285	$265	$220
Auto ejectors	$525	$440	$415	$385	$370	$330	$305

BLACK BEAUTY SPECIAL — similar to Leader, except has engraved, select wood.

	100%	98%	95%	90%	80%	70%	60%
	$745	$650	$615	$590	$550	$525	$495
Auto ejectors	$855	$760	$725	$700	$660	$635	$605

BATAVIA EJECTOR — similar to Leader, but finer finish.

	100%	98%	95%	90%	80%	70%	60%
	$880	$770	$745	$715	$690	$660	$635
Damascus barrels	$440	$330	$305	$275	$250	$220	$165

BAKER S GRADE — similar to Leader, but finer finish, better grade wood.

	100%	98%	95%	90%	80%	70%	60%
	$880	$775	$745	$715	$690	$650	$635
Auto ejectors	$1,100	$990	$965	$935	$910	$880	$745

BAKER R GRADE — similar to Leader, except scroll and game scene engraved, Krupp barrels, fancy wood.

	100%	98%	95%	90%	80%	70%	60%
	$1,100	$990	$965	$935	$910	$880	$745
Auto ejectors	$1,320	$1,210	$1,155	$1,100	$1,075	$1,045	$965
Damascus barrel	$550	$415	$385	$360	$330	$275	$230

PARAGON GRADE — custom order only to customer specifications.

	100%	98%	95%	90%	80%	70%	60%
	$1,650	$1,430	$1,320	$1,210	$1,155	$1,045	$770
Auto ejectors	$1,815	$1,595	$1,485	$1,375	$1,210	$1,100	$990

EXPERT GRADE — auto ejectors standard, overall finer grade wood and engraving.

	100%	98%	95%	90%	80%	70%	60%
	$2,500	$2,100	$1,850	$1,500	$1,250	$1,000	$750

DELUXE GRADE — best quality.

	100%	98%	95%	90%	80%	70%	60%
	$3,750	$3,250	$2,950	$2,650	$2,300	$2,000	$1,600

Add $200 for single trigger.

▲ **Damascus barrels** — also known as Early Paragon Grade. If condition is 50% or less subtract 50% or more. If 90% original condition or better, prices will be the same as for damascus L.C. Smith guns.

SHOTGUNS: SINGLE BARREL TRAP

Baker single barrel trap guns, although more rare than their side-by-side counterparts, are not as desirable as those models listed above. Typically, values will be 50%-75% of a side-by-side model of equal grade.

BALTIMORE ARMS COMPANY

Manufacturer of SxS shotguns located in Baltimore, MD 1895-1902.

SHOTGUNS: SxS

STYLE 1 — mfg. 1895-1900, this variation does not have the improved Hollenbeck barrel locking mechanism characterizd by the eye-shaped hole in the top rib extension.

There are 4 grades of Baltimore Arms Company shotguns: Field, Grade A, Grade B, and Grade C. Prices generally range from $295-$1,500 depending on condition and grade.

STYLE 2 — mfg. 1900-1902, this variation has the improved barrel locking mechanism and is patent date marked "FEB. 13, 1900" on the water table.

There are 4 grades of Baltimore Arms Company shotguns: Field, Grade A, Grade B, and Grade C. Prices generally range from $295-$2,000 depending on condition and grade.

BANSNER'S

Custom rifle/shotgun and related components manufacturer located in Adamstown, PA since 1995.

Bansner's produces 10 configurations of their custom rifle. There are a variety of stocks, finishes, barrels, and other special orders within these 10 models. Bansner's should be contacted directly regarding a price quotation for these rifle and/or related components (see Trademark Index).

BARRETT FIREARMS MANUFACTURING, INC.

Manufacturer located in Murfreesboro, TN. Dealer direct sales.

Grading	100%	98%	95%	90%	80%	70%	60%

MODEL 82 RIFLE — .50 Browning machine gun cartridge, semi-auto recoil operation, 33-37 in. barrel, 11 shot mag., 2,850 FPS muzzle velocity, scope sight only, parkerized finish, 35 lbs. Mfg. 1985-87.

$4,350　$3,950　$3,450　$2,700　$2,150　$1,800　$1,500
Last Mfg.'s Sug. Retail for consumers was $3,180 in 1985.

This model underwent design changes since initial production. Only 115 were mfg. starting with ser. no. 100.

MODEL 82A1 — .50 BMG, current military configuration, variant of the original Model 82, available to civilians, back-up iron sights provided, 2 mags., and fitted hard case, 29 (new late 1989) or 33 (disc. 1989) in. barrel, 10 shot mag., 32½ lbs. for 1989 and older mfg., 28½ lbs. for 1990 mfg.

Mfg.'s Sug. Retail　$6,800　　$6,375　$4,950　$4,250　$3,650　$3,150　$2,650　$2,200

Add $275 for camo backpack carrying case.
Add $1,150 for Swarovski 10X scope and mounts.

This model boasts official U.S. rifle status following government procurement during Operation Desert Storm. In 1992, a new "arrowhead" shaped muzzle brake was introduced to reduce recoil.

MODEL 90 — .50 BMG, bolt action design, 29 in. match grade barrel with muzzle brake, 5 shot detachable box mag., includes extendible bi-pod legs, Sorbothane recoil pad, scope optional, 22 lbs. Mfg. 1990-95.

$3,450　$2,950　$2,400　$2,150　$1,875　$1,600　$1,500
Last Mfg.'s Sug. Retail was $3,650.

Add $1,150 for Swarovski 10X scope and mounts.

MODEL 95 — .50 BMG, bolt action design, 29 in. match grade barrel with high efficiency muzzle brake, 5 shot detachable box mag., includes extendible bi-pod legs, Sorbothane recoil pad, scope optional, 22 lbs. New 1995.

Mfg.'s Sug. Retail　$4,000　　$3,675　$3,000　$2,425　$2,175　$1,875　$1,600　$1,500

BAR-STO

Previous manufacturer located in 29 Palms, CA.

Grading	100%	98%	95%	90%	80%	70%	60%

BAR-STO .25 ACP PISTOL — .25 ACP, patterned after the Baby Browning, brushed stainless steel finish, walnut grips, approx. 250 manufactured in circa 1974.

	$195	$165	$125

BAUER FIREARMS CORPORATION

Previous manufacturer located in Fraser, MI.

BAUER .25 ACP — .25 ACP, 2½ in. barrel, 6 shot, fixed sights, checkered walnut or pearlite grips, mfg. 1972-1984.

	$150	$130	$110	$100	$90	$80	$70

Note: These guns are identical to the Baby Browning, except stainless steel.

▲ *Bicentennial Model* — .25 ACP, engraved with buckle in display case.

	$300	$200	$150

THE RABBIT — combination gun, all metal construction, .22 cal. and .410 ga., O/U configuration. Mfg. 1982-1984.

	$125	$100	$90	$80	$70	$60	$50

BAYARD

Previously manufactured by Anciens Etablissements Pieper located in Herstal, Belgium.

Even though Bayard Models 1908, both 1923s, and 1930 were manufactured only by Anciens Etablissements Pieper of Herstal, Belgium, these pistols are listed under this heading as they are most commonly referred to by this trademark designation.

PISTOLS

.25 and .380 cals. are more rare than the .32s and will command a 20%+ premium above values listed below unless indicated differently.

MODEL 1908 POCKET AUTOMATIC — .25 ACP, .32 ACP, or .380 ACP cal., 6 shot, 2¼ in. barrel, fixed sights, blue, hard rubber grips.

	$325	$235	$165	$100	$85	$70	$55

MODEL 1923 POCKET AUTOMATIC — .25 ACP cal., 2½ in. barrel, blue, fixed sights, checkered hard rubber grips.

	$295	$225	$170	$140	$125	$95	$75

BAYARD 1923 POCKET AUTOMATIC — .32 ACP or .380 ACP cal., 6 shot, $3^5/_{16}$ in. barrel, fixed sights, blue, checkered hard rubber grips.

	$295	$225	$170	$140	$125	$95	$75

Add 100% for .380 ACP cal.

BAYARD 1930 POCKET AUTOMATIC — slight modification of 1923.

	$250	$200	$170	$145	$120	$95	$75

BEEMAN OUTDOOR SPORTS

Importer and distributor located in Santa Rosa, CA.

On April 1, 1993, Beeman Precision Arms, Inc. was split into two independent companies: Beeman Precision Airguns, division of S/R Industries (Maryland Corp.), located in Huntington Beach, CA retains worldwide distribution of Beeman airguns and accessories. Beeman Outdoor Sports, Division of

Robert's Precision Arms, Inc., located in Santa Rosa, CA had distribution of Feinwerkbau firearms until 1995.

Beeman is a large importer, primarily specializing in high quality European air rifles and pistols. Trademarks previously distributed in the U.S. are manufactured by: Agner (disc. 1986), Erma (disc. 1985), FAS (disc. 1987), Fabarm (disc. 1985), Feinwerkbau, Korth (disc. 1990), Krico (disc. 1988), Unique (disc. 1991), and Weihrauch (disc.). These trademarks appear under their respective alphabetical headings. Air rifles, pistols, and/or black powder firearms will appear under those headings in the back of the book.

The firearms listed below were manufactured to Beeman specifications, and are therefore listed under the Beeman heading.

Grading	100%	98%	95%	90%	80%	70%	60%

PISTOLS: SEMI-AUTO

BEEMAN MP-08 — .380 ACP, Luger type toggle action, 3½ in. barrel, 6 shot mag., blue, 1.4 lbs. Mfg. 1968-1990.

	$395	$335	$275	$240	$185	$145	$115

Last Mfg.'s Sug. Retail was $390.

> In 1988, Beeman took over importation of these two models (MP-08 and P-08). These revised models have new Luger style checkered walnut grips and 3½ in. barrel. Previous variations had plastic grips.

BEEMAN P-08 — .22 LR, Luger type toggle action, 8 shot mag., 3.8 in. barrel, blue, checkered walnut grips, 1.9 lbs. Mfg. 1969-1990.

	$395	$335	$275	$240	$185	$145	$115

Last Mfg.'s Sug. Retail was $390.

PISTOLS: SINGLE SHOT

MODEL SP/SPX — .22 LR cal., designed for silhouette shooting, 10 in. heavy bull barrel, blued metal parts, birchwood stocks and forearm, aperture sights, 3.9 lbs. Disc. 1994.

	$625	$550	$475	$425	$375	$330	$295

Last Mfg.'s Sug. Retail was $700.

> Only a few of these models were actually delivered.

▲ *Model SPX Deluxe* — similar to Model SPX, except has matte chrome metal finish, hand stippled walnut grips, and Anschutz rear sight. Limited mfg. 1993-94.

	$800	$725	$650	$575	$500	$425	$350

Last Mfg.'s Sug. Retail was $900.

SP STANDARD — .22 LR cal., sidelever action, 8, 10, 12, or 15 in. barrel, adj. sights and walnut grips, single shot. Made in W. Germany. Imported 1985-86 only.

	$250	$220	$180	$170	$160	$150	$140

Last Mfg.'s Sug. Retail was $250.

> Add $10 or $30 for 12 or 15 in. barrel respectively.

SP DELUXE — similar to SP Standard, except has forearm, about 3½ lbs. Made in W. Germany. Imported 1985-86 only.

	$275	$240	$200	$185	$170	$155	$145

Last Mfg.'s Sug. Retail was $300.

> Add $10 or $30 for 12 or 15 in. barrel respectively.

BEHOLLA PISTOL

Previously manufactured by Becker & Hollander located in Suhl, Germany.

BEHOLLA POCKET AUTOMATIC — .32 ACP cal., 7 shot, 2.9 in. barrel, blue, serrated wood or rubber grips, mfg. 1915-1920, from 1920-1925 the same gun was mfg. by Stenda-Werke.

	$225	$170	$150	$135	$120	$100	$90

BENELLI

Manufacturer located in Urbino, Italy. Shotguns currently imported by Heckler & Koch, Inc. located in Sterling, VA (dealer sales only). Handguns currently imported by European American Armory, located in Sharpes, FL. Previously imported by Sile Distributors, Inc., located in New York, NY until 1995 and by Saco, located in Arlington, VA.

Grading	100%	98%	95%	90%	80%	70%	60%

PISTOLS

Models B-77, B-80, and MP3S were previously imported by Sile Distributors. Models MP90S and MP95 are imported by EAA.

MODEL B-76 — 9mm Luger, selective double action, all steel, 4¼ in. barrel, 8 shot mag., 34 oz. Importation disc. in 1990.

	$390	$340	$295	$245	$225	$210	$190

Last Mfg.'s Sug. Retail was $428.

MODEL B-76S TARGET — 9mm, similar to B-76, except has 5½ in. barrel, target grips, and adj. rear sights. Importation disc. 1990.

	$475	$425	$395	$350	$325	$300	$280

Last Mfg.'s Sug. Retail was $595.

MODEL B-77 — .32 ACP, selective double action, all steel, 4¼ in. barrel, 8 shot mag. Importation disc. 1995.

	$295	$255	$225	$200	$180	$170	$160

Last Mfg.'s Sug. Retail was $385.

MODEL B-80 — .30 Luger, selective double action, all steel, 4¼ in. barrel, 8 shot mag., 34 oz. Importation disc. 1995.

	$295	$255	$225	$200	$180	$170	$160

Last Mfg.'s Sug. Retail was $385.

MODEL B-80S TARGET — similar to B-80, except has 5½ in. barrel, target grips, and adj. rear sights. Importation disc. 1995.

	$450	$375	$325	$295	$275	$250	$225

Last Mfg.'s Sug. Retail was $572.

MODEL MP3S — .32 Smith & Wesson Long Wadcutter, target variation with 5½ in. barrel, high gloss bluing, target grips, and adj. rear sights. Importation disc. 1995.

	$450	$375	$325	$295	$275	$250	$225

Last Mfg.'s Sug. Retail was $785.

MODEL MP90S — .22 S (disc.), .22 LR, or .32 WC cal., 4⅓ in. barrel, target pistol featuring forward assisted breech bolt mechanism, anatomic grips, and adj. weight, 5 shot mag., 2.4 lbs. Importation began 1992.

Mfg.'s Sug. Retail	$1,297	$1,175	$925	$800	$700	$600	$525	$450

Add $205 for .32 WC cal.

Conversion kits were previously available for this model at an extra charge. This model is imported exclusively by EAA.

MODEL MP95 — .22 LR or .32 WC cal., 4¼ in. barrel, integral Weaver style base mount, 5 or 9 shot mag., adj. trigger assembly, fully adj. sight, modular firing system, blue or chrome (.22 LR only) finish, adj. walnut grips, 2.2 lbs. New late 1994.

Mfg.'s Sug. Retail	$553		$495	$450	$415	$380	$345	$325	$300

Add $43 for chrome finish or .32 WC cal.

SHOTGUNS: SEMI-AUTO

Benelli semi-auto 3rd generation (inertia recoil) shotguns were imported starting in the late 1960s. The receivers were mfg. of light aluminum alloy - the SL-80 Model 121 had a semi-gloss, anodized black finish, the Model 123 had an ornate photo-engraved receiver, the Model Special 80 had a brushed, white nickel-plated receiver, and the Model 121 M1 had a matte finish receiver, barrel, and stock. All SL-80 Series shotguns will accept 2¾ or 3 in. shells, and all SL-80 Series 12 ga. Models have interchangeable barrels with the 4 different model receivers (121, 121 M1, 123, or Special 80). The SL-80 Series shotguns were disc. during 1985-86.

Older models (disc. before 1986) may have a parts availability problem if repairs are needed. Approx. 50,000 SL-80 series shotguns were mfg. before discontinuance - choke markings (located on side or underneath barrel) are as follows: * full choke, ** imp. mod., *** mod., **** imp. cyl. SL-80 series guns used the same action (much different than current mfg.) and all had the split receiver design. Be aware of possible wood cracking where the barrel rests on the thin area of the forend and also on the underside of the buttstock behind trigger guard.

> Subtract 5% for "SACO" marked Benelli shotguns previously imported by SACO located in Arlington, VA.

Grading	100%	98%	95%	90%	80%	70%	60%

SL-80 SERIES MODEL SL-121V — 12 ga., field grade, 26, or 28 in. fixed choke VR barrel, anodized and black semi-gloss finish on lower receiver. Disc. 1985.

	$360	$295	$260	$245	$215	$190	$175

Last Mfg.'s Sug. Retail was $397.

SL-80 SERIES MODEL SL-121/SL-122 SLUG — 12 ga., features Monte Carlo stock and flat bottom Trap Grade beavertail forearm, 21 1/16 cyl. bore barrel, fixed open ring rear iron sights and fixed front ramp, 5 shot mag., recoil pad, 7 lbs. 3 oz. Disc. 1985.

	$425	$395	$325	$275	$225	$185	$165

Last Mfg.'s Sug. Retail was $434.

SL-80 SERIES MODEL SL123V — 12 ga., stylish field grade, receiver Ergal special aluminum alloy with photo engraving, 26 or 28 in. VR barrel with various chokes, approx. 6 lbs. 13 oz. Disc. 1985.

	$425	$330	$285	$250	$225	$200	$175

Last Mfg.'s Sug. Retail was $464.

> Add $20 for trap stock, $10 for beavertail forearm and $25 for skeet barrel.

EX-L — 12 ga., similar in appearance to the Model SL123V, except has hand-engraved receiver, very limited mfg. with unpredictable premiums over Model SL123V.

SL-80 SERIES MODEL 121 M1 POLICE/MILITARY — 12 ga. only, similar in appearance to the Super 90 M1, hardwood stock, 7 shot mag., matte metal and wood finish, most stocks had adj. lateral sling attachment inside of butt stock, 18¾ in. barrel. Disc. 1985.

	$420	$365	$325	$275	$235	$200	$175

MODEL 80 SPECIAL SKEET/TRAP — 12 ga. only, 28 in. VR with mod. choke and phosphorescent bead sight, has trap/skeet Monte Carlo grade/style wood stock with recoil pad, lower receiver is nickel plated, 7lbs. 10 oz. Disc. 1986.

	$465	$375	$325	$275	$250	$225	$195

Last Mfg.'s Sug. Retail was $531.

> Trap guns should have high comb trap stock and trap grade forearm (not field grade/style wood). Trap guns should also be inspected carefully for internal wear before buying/selling.

SL-80 SERIES MODEL SL201 — 20 ga., 26 in. VR barrel bored mod., black anodized lower receiver, approx. 5 lbs. 10 oz. Disc. 1985.

	$390	$320	$275	$240	$215	$190	$165

Last Mfg.'s Sug. Retail was $399.

Grading	100%	98%	95%	90%	80%	70%	60%

BRI-BENELLI SL-80 123 SLUG GUN — 12 ga. only, premium slug gun featuring SL-80 Series action and drilled and tapped rifle bored barrel by E. R. Shaw Barrel Co., assembled by BRI in the U.S., Monte Carlo stock with beavertail forend, approx. 25 guns total mfg. 1986-1987.

	$1,395	$1,175	$995	$850	$725	$600	$495

Original issue price on this model was $750-$850. These specimens are marked "BRI-Benelli" on barrel. No warranties exist on this model.

M1 SUPER 90 SLUG — 12 ga. only, 3 in. Mag., semi-auto, incorporates improvements on the Benelli action, including rotating Montefeltro bolt system, 19¾ in. cyl. bore barrel with iron sights, 7 shot mag., fiberglass stock and forearm, 6.7 lbs. New 1986. Imported exclusively by H&K.

Mfg.'s Sug. Retail	$819	$660	$495	$360	$315	$280	$260	$240

Add $41 for ghost-ring sighting system.

M1 SUPER 90 DEFENSE — similar to Super 90 Slug, except has pistol grip stock, 7.1 lbs.

Mfg.'s Sug. Retail	$851	$685	$520	$375	$315	$280	$260	$240

Add $41 for ghost-ring sighting system.

M1 SUPER 90 TACTICAL — 12 ga. only, 18½ in. barrel, fixed rifle or ghost ring sighting system, available with synthetic pistol grip or standard butt stock, includes 3 choke tubes, 7 shot mag., 6½ lbs. New 1993.

Mfg.'s Sug. Retail	$860	$710	$540	$400	$350	$300	$270	$240

Add $42 for ghost-ring sighting system.
Add $35 for pistol grip stock.

M1 SUPER 90 ENTRY — 12 ga. only, includes 14 in. barrel, choice of pistol grip or standard stock, 5 shot mag. (2 shot extension), 6.7 lbs. New 1992.

Mfg.'s Sug. Retail	$886	$715	$540	$400	$350	$300	$270	$240

Add $42 for ghost-ring sighting system.
This model requires special licensing (Class III transfer).

M1 SUPER 90 FIELD — similar to M1 Super 90, except has 21 (new 1990), 24 (new 1990), 26, or 28 in. vent. rib barrel and 3-shot mag., includes 3 screw in choke tubes, wood (new 1994) or polymer stock and forearm, approx. 7.3 lbs.

Mfg.'s Sug. Retail	$884	$710	$475	$380	$330	$295	$275	$260

Add $16 for wood stock.
This model is available with either a short or extended magazine tube. The short tube is available on all barrel lengths - an extended mag. tube is available on 26 or 28 in. barrel only.

M1 SUPER 90 SPORTING SPECIAL — 12 ga., 18½ in. barrel, black matte finish, includes ghost ring sighting system, 6½ lbs. New 1993.

Mfg.'s Sug. Retail	$905	$725	$500	$395	$330	$295	$275	$260

MONTEFELTRO SUPER 90 STANDARD HUNTER — 12 or 20 (new 1993) ga., 3 in. chamber, 21, 24, 26, or 28 in. VR barrel with 3 choke tubes, matte black metal finish, checkered walnut stock and forearm with choice of high gloss or satin finish, 5 shot mag., 7¼ lbs. New 1988.

Mfg.'s Sug. Retail	$905	$730	$560	$410	$350	$300	$270	$240

Add $20 for left-hand action (26 or 28 in. barrel only).

▲ *Montefeltro Super 90 Limited Edition* — 20 ga. only, nickel plated lower receiver with etched gold highlights, 26 in. VR barrel. New 1995.

Mfg.'s Sug. Retail	$2,080	$1,825	$1,525	$1,225	$995	$875	$750	$625

▲ *Montefeltro Turkey Gun* — similar to Montefeltro Standard Hunter except has 24 in. VR barrel with 3 choke tubes, satin finish wood only, 7 lbs. Imported 1989 only.

	$575	$440	$370	$330	$295	$275	$260

Last Mfg.'s Sug. Retail was $675.

Grading	100%	98%	95%	90%	80%	70%	60%

▲ **Montefeltro Uplander** — similar to Montefeltro Turkey Gun except has 21 or 24 in. VR barrel with 3 choke tubes, satin finish wood only, 7 lbs. Mfg. 1989-92.

| | $650 | $450 | $375 | $330 | $295 | $275 | $260 |

Last Mfg.'s Sug. Retail was $799.

▲ **Montefeltro Slug Gun** — deer gun configuration with 19¾ in. slug barrel. Disc. 1992.

| | $650 | $450 | $375 | $330 | $295 | $275 | $260 |

Last Mfg.'s Sug. Retail was $799.

BLACK EAGLE — 12 ga., Montefeltro action, similar to Montefeltro Super 90 Standard Hunter except has black synthetic stock and forearm, 21, 24, 26, or 28 (new 1990) in. VR barrel with 3 choke tubes, right hand only. Imported 1989-90, configuration changed to competition in 1991 (see Black Eagle Competition Model).

| | $675 | $575 | $475 | $395 | $340 | $300 | $275 |

Last Mfg.'s Sug. Retail was $807.

▲ **Black Eagle Competition Model** — 12 ga. only, designed for competition shooting with action adj. for lighter loads, silver finished etched lower receiver, 26 or 28 in. VR barrel with 5 choke tubes and wrench provided, includes buttstock drop adjustment kit. New 1991.

| **Mfg.'s Sug. Retail** | **$1,205** | $985 | $780 | $635 | $500 | $395 | $340 | $300 |

▲ **Black Eagle 1994 Limited Edition** — 12 ga. only, features 26 in. VR barrel with extra fancy grade checkered walnut and gold inlays on receiver sides, 1,000 mfg. 1994-95 only with special serialization.

| | $1,775 | $1,500 | $1,225 | $995 | $875 | $750 | $625 |

Last Mfg.'s Sug. Retail was $2,000.

▲ **Black Eagle Slug Gun** — 12 ga., 24 in. rifled barrel with receiver scope mount. Imported 1990-91 only.

| | $735 | $625 | $475 | $395 | $340 | $300 | $275 |

Last Mfg.'s Sug. Retail was $859.

SUPER BLACK EAGLE — 12 ga. only, 3½ in. chamber, updated Montefeltro action accepts all 12 ga. loads, 24, 26, or 28 in. VR barrel with 5 choke tubes and wrench provided, choice of matte finish and satin stock or blued finish and high gloss wood finish (26 in. barrel only), black synthetic stock and forearm with matte metal finish became optional 1993, vent. recoil pad, includes buttstock drop adjustment kit, approx. 7.1 lbs. New 1991.

| **Mfg.'s Sug. Retail** | **$1,176** | $965 | $800 | $650 | $525 | $400 | $340 | $300 |

Add $16 for wood stock and forearm.

▲ **Super Black Eagle Custom Slug Gun** — includes 24 in. E.R. Shaw rifle barrel with matte metal finish and choice of black polymer (new 1993) or satin finished wood. New 1992.

| **Mfg.'s Sug. Retail** | **$1,220** | $1,000 | $825 | $650 | $525 | $400 | $340 | $300 |

M3 SUPER 90 — 12 ga. only, defense configuration incorporating convertible (fingertip activated) pump or semi-auto action, 19¾ in. cyl. bore barrel with rifle sights, choice of standard polymer stock or integral pistol grip, 7½ lbs. New 1989.

| **Mfg.'s Sug. Retail** | **$1,016** | $860 | $660 | $485 | $395 | $340 | $300 | $275 |

Add $99 for pistol grip stock.
Add $70 for ghost-ring sighting system.
Add $110 for folding stock (mfg. 1990-disc.) - only available as a complete gun.
Add $340 for Model 200 Laser Sight System with bracket (disc.).

EXECUTIVE SERIES BLACK EAGLE — 12 ga. only, custom order only, includes engraved receiver, select grade stock, and 5 screw-in choke tubes. Available in three grades - Type I retails for $4,550, Type II retails for $5,200, Type III retails for $6,032.

BENSON FIREARMS LTD.

Manufactured by Aldo Uberti in Italy. Previously imported and distributed from 1987-1989 by Benson Firearms Ltd. located in Seattle, WA. Benson Firearms Ltd. combined with A. Uberti USA Inc. in early 1989 and discontinued importation.

Grading	100%	98%	95%	90%	80%	70%	60%

Benson Firearms can be differentiated from other A. Uberti imports by the "Benson Firearms Seattle, WA" barrel marking. Many of the models listed below are similar to those models imported by Allen Firearms (disc. 1987) and A. Uberti USA, Inc., (current importer).

Rather than provide a complete listing of Benson Firearms models, the following rules usually apply. Since Benson Firearms imported A. Uberti firearms, the Uberti section in this text should be referenced for current values regarding models with similar configurations. Collectibility to date has been limited on most Benson Firearms models, and as a rule, up-to-date values on this trademark are established by current importation prices of Uberti firearms. A complete listing of older Benson Firearms models can be found in Blue Book editions Eleven and Twelve.

BENTON & BROWN FIREARMS, INC.
Manufacturer located in Ft. Worth Texas, beginning 1993. Dealer direct sales.

RIFLES: BOLT ACTION

MODEL 93 — available in 15 cals. between .243 Win. and .375 H&H Mag., patterned after the Model R-84 Blaser, takedown, free floating 22 or 24 in. barrels, right or left-hand action, checkered walnut stock and forearm, 7-8½ lbs. New 1993.

Mfg.'s Sug. Retail	$2,075	$1,875	$1,550	$1,225	$1,100	$995	$875	$750

Subtract $200 for fiberglass stock.
Add $450 per interchangeable barrel.

BERETTA, DR. FRANCO
Previous manufacturer located in Concesin (Brescia), Italy until 1994.

SHOTGUNS: O/U - BLACK DIAMOND SERIES

Black Diamond target guns were imported exclusively by Double M Shooting Sports until 1988.

FIELD MODEL — 12, 16, 20, 28, or .410 ga., variety of chokes, coin finish receiver.

	$595	$550	$495	$450	$395	$365	$335

Last Mfg.'s Sug. Retail was $960.

GRADE ONE — 12, 16, 20, 28, or .410 ga., variety of chokes, coin finish receiver with acid etched engraving, French walnut. Trap or skeet model also available, except in 16 ga.

	$1,020	$900	$810	$720	$630	$570	$525

Last Mfg.'s Sug. Retail was $1,440.

GRADE TWO — 12, 16, 20, 28, or .410 ga., variety of chokes, coin finish receiver with moderate engraving, French walnut. Trap or skeet model also available, except in 16 ga.

	$1,475	$1,320	$1,200	$1,080	$930	$815	$750

Last Mfg.'s Sug. Retail was $2,040.

GRADE THREE — 12, 16, 20, 28, or .410 ga., variety of chokes, coin finish receiver with scrollwork engraving, French walnut. Trap or skeet model also available, except in 16 ga.

	$2,100	$1,920	$1,775	$1,560	$1,410	$1,200	$1,035

Last Mfg.'s Sug. Retail was $3,000.

GRADE FOUR — 12, 16, 20, 28, or .410 ga., variety of chokes, coin finish receiver with elaborate engraving, French walnut. Trap or skeet model also available, except in 16 ga.

	$2,500	$2,250	$1,950	$1,650	$1,375	$1,125	$995

Last Mfg.'s Sug. Retail was $3,960.

SKEET SET — includes 12, 20, 28, and .410 ga. barrels, available in Grades One through Four.
Multiply values on Grades One - Four by 275% for 4 ga. Skeet sets.

Grading	100%	98%	95%	90%	80%	70%	60%

SHOTGUNS: O/U, S X S, & SINGLE BARREL RECENT MFG.

GAMMA STANDARD O & U — 12, 16, or 20 ga., 26 or 28 in. barrels, coin finish receiver with extensive engraving, Italian walnut. Add $83 with single trigger and ejectors. Imported 1984-1988.

	100%	98%	95%	90%	80%	70%	60%
	$400	$360	$330	$300	$275	$260	$240

Last Mfg.'s Sug. Retail was $445.

▲ *Gamma Standard* — with interchangeable choke tubes. Importation disc. 1993.

	100%	98%	95%	90%	80%	70%	60%
	$825	$695	$525	$425	$325	$250	$195

Last Mfg.'s Sug. Retail was $1,000.

> Add 20% for auto ejectors.
> Add $100 for single trigger.
> Add 36% for Gamma Trap or Skeet variation (ST).

GAMMA DELUXE O & U — 12, 16, or 20 ga., 26 or 28 in. barrels, coin finish receiver with extensive engraving, Italian walnut. Add $84 with single trigger and ejectors. Imported 1984-1988.

	100%	98%	95%	90%	80%	70%	60%
	$445	$405	$370	$350	$325	$300	$275

Last Mfg.'s Sug. Retail was $480.

▲ *Gamma Deluxe* — with interchangeable choke tubes. Importation disc. 1988.

	100%	98%	95%	90%	80%	70%	60%
	$635	$570	$530	$490	$450	$420	$390

Last Mfg.'s Sug. Retail was $685.

GAMMA TARGET O & U — 12 ga. only, SST, ejectors, Wundhammer swell pistol grip, English walnut stock and beavertail forearm. Imported 1986-1988.

	100%	98%	95%	90%	80%	70%	60%
	$550	$505	$455	$410	$370	$350	$325

Last Mfg.'s Sug. Retail was $595.

ALPHA STANDARD O & U — 12, 16, or 20 ga., 26 or 28 in. barrels, coin finish receiver with extensive engraving, Italian walnut. Imported 1984-1988, resumed 1993.

	100%	98%	95%	90%	80%	70%	60%
	$720	$650	$525	$450	$375	$300	$250

Last Mfg.'s Sug. Retail was $780.

> Add 18% for auto ejectors.
> Add $100 for single trigger.

ALPHA DELUXE O & U — 12, 16, or 20 ga., 26 or 28 in. barrels, coin finish receiver with extensive engraving, sling swivels, Italian walnut. Add $75 with single trigger and ejectors, $80 for interchangeable choke tubes (disc. 1985). Imported 1984-1988.

	100%	98%	95%	90%	80%	70%	60%
	$395	$355	$330	$300	$275	$250	$230

Last Mfg.'s Sug. Retail was $435.

AMERICA STANDARD O & U — .410 ga. only, 26 or 28 in. barrels, coin finish receiver with extensive engraving, Italian walnut. Add $85 for Deluxe model. Imported 1984-1988.

	100%	98%	95%	90%	80%	70%	60%
	$305	$280	$265	$240	$215	$205	$190

Last Mfg.'s Sug. Retail was $335.

EUROPA O & U — .410 ga. only, 26 in. barrels, coin finish receiver with some engraving, Italian walnut. Add $95 for Deluxe model (disc. 1985). Imported 1984-1988.

	100%	98%	95%	90%	80%	70%	60%
	$275	$250	$235	$220	$210	$200	$185

Last Mfg.'s Sug. Retail was $295.

FRANCIA STANDARD SxS — .410 ga. only, double triggers, extractors, checkered walnut. Imported 1986-1988. Add $19 for Deluxe Model.

	100%	98%	95%	90%	80%	70%	60%
	$235	$220	$210	$200	$185	$175	$160

Last Mfg.'s Sug. Retail was $255.

OMEGA STANDARD SxS — 12, 16, or 20 ga., 26 or 28 in. barrels, coin finish receiver with extensive engraving, Italian walnut. Imported 1984-93.

	100%	98%	95%	90%	80%	70%	60%
	$780	$695	$550	$450	$375	$300	$250

Last Mfg.'s Sug. Retail was $880.

> Add 32% for auto ejectors.
> Add 10% for single trigger (disc. 1985).

Grading	100%	98%	95%	90%	80%	70%	60%

MILANO O/U — 9mm Flobert, folding design. Imported 1993 only.

	$380	$330	$295	$250	$210	$180	$150

Last Mfg.'s Sug. Retail was $420.

VERONA/BERGAMO SxS — 9mm Flobert, folding design, Bergamo model has hammers, Verona model is hammerless. Imported 1993 only.

	$270	$225	$180	$140	$115	$95	$75

Last Mfg.'s Sug. Retail was $300.

BRESCIA SINGLE BARREL — 9mm Flobert, folding design. Imported 1993 only.

	$175	$150	$130	$110	$90	$70	$55

Last Mfg.'s Sug. Retail was $200.

BETA SINGLE BARREL — single barrel field gun, available in 12, 16, 20, 24, 28, 32, or .410 ga., VR, chrome finish receiver, folding design. Imported 1985-93.

	$215	$185	$160	$145	$135	$125	$115

Last Mfg.'s Sug. Retail was $240.

Add 10% for VR.

SHOTGUNS: SEMI-AUTO

ARIETE STANDARD — 12 ga. only, gas operated, 2¾ or 3 in. chamber, various barrel lengths, with or without choke tubes, aluminum receiver, checkered stock and forearm, approx. 6.9 lbs. Imported 1993 only.

	$995	$795	$525	$425	$325	$250	$195

Last Mfg.'s Sug. Retail was $1,180.

Add $20 for 3 in. mag. variation.

SHOTGUNS: SLIDE ACTION

ARIETE — 12 ga. only, 3 in. chamber, various barrel lengths without VR, twin action bars, matte finish, recoil pad. Imported 1993 only.

	$780	$695	$550	$450	$375	$300	$250

Last Mfg.'s Sug. Retail was $880.

BERETTA, PIETRO

Manufactured in Brescia, Italy, 1526-present and Accokeek, MD 1978 to date. Beretta U.S.A. Corp. was formed in 1977 and is located in Accokeek, MD. Beretta U.S.A. Corp. has been importing Beretta Firearms exclusively since 1980. 1970-1977 manufacture was imported exclusively by Garcia. Distributor sales only.

PISTOLS: SEMI-AUTO, DISC.

MODEL 1910 — .25 ACP cal., single action, 7 shot, fixed sights, wood grips, mfg. 1910-1934.

	$300	$275	$250	$195	$165	$145	$110

MODEL 1915 — .32 ACP, 8 shot, 3.3 in. barrel, fixed sights, blue, wood grips, mfg. 1915-1919.

	$495	$395	$275	$250	$195	$165	$110

MODEL 1915 — 9mm Glisenti, second variation - larger version, mfg. 1915.

	$525	$400	$330	$275	$220	$195	$140

9mm Para. is not interchangeable and potentially dangerous if interchanged with 9mm Glisenti.

MODEL 1923 — 9mm Glisenti, 8 shot, 4 in. barrel, fixed sights, steel grips, mfg. 1923-1935.

	$750	$600	$475	$350	$300	$250	$200

Add 25% for slotted rear grip strap.

Grading	100%	98%	95%	90%	80%	70%	60%

B

MODEL 1934 — .380 ACP (9mm Kurz), $3\frac{3}{8}$ in. barrel, fixed sights, blue, plastic grips, Italy's service weapon in WWII, military models have poorer finish, mfg. 1934-late '60s.

	100%	98%	95%	90%	80%	70%	60%
Military Model	$350	$275	$250	$195	$165	$140	$110
Commercial Model	$395	$325	$275	$220	$195	$165	$140

MODEL 1935 — .32 ACP, $3\frac{1}{2}$ in. barrel, fixed sights, blue, plastic grips, the wartime model had poor finish, mfg. 1935-1959.

	100%	98%	95%	90%	80%	70%	60%
Parkerized Military Model	$325	$265	$200	$180	$160	$140	$120
Commercial High Polish Blue	$395	$300	$215	$185	$165	$145	$125

MODEL 318 — .25 ACP, $2\frac{1}{2}$ in. barrel, fixed sights, blue, plastic grips, mfg. 1934-1939.

100%	98%	95%	90%	80%	70%	60%
$275	$250	$220	$195	$165	$140	$110

MODEL 418 — .25 ACP, fixed sights.

100%	98%	95%	90%	80%	70%	60%
$220	$190	$170	$145	$125	$110	$100

MODEL 420 — .25 ACP, chrome finish, small coverage engraving.

100%	98%	95%	90%	80%	70%	60%
$350	$300	$260	$230	$200	$175	$160

MODEL 421 — .25 ACP, gold plated, elaborate engraving.

100%	98%	95%	90%	80%	70%	60%
$475	$430	$400	$360	$320	$280	$230

PISTOLS: POST WWII MFG.

100% values on below listed models assume NIB condition.

MODEL 948 — .22 LR, $3\frac{1}{2}$ or 6 in. barrel, fixed sights, hammer.

100%	98%	95%	90%	80%	70%	60%
$175	$150	$125	$100	$75	$60	$50

MODEL 949 OLYMPIC TARGET — .22 S or LR, $8\frac{3}{4}$ in. barrel, target sights, adj. barrel weights, blue, muzzle brake, checkered wood grips with thumbrest, limited mfg. 1959-1964.

100%	98%	95%	90%	80%	70%	60%
$660	$550	$495	$385	$305	$250	$195

MODEL 950CC MINX M2 — .22 Short, hinged $2\frac{3}{8}$ in. barrel, fixed sights, blue, plastic grips. Mfg. 1955-disc.

100%	98%	95%	90%	80%	70%	60%
$135	$115	$105	$95	$85	$75	$70

MODEL 950CC SPECIAL MINX M4 — similar to M2, with 4 in. barrel.

100%	98%	95%	90%	80%	70%	60%
$135	$115	$105	$95	$85	$75	$70

MODEL 950B JETFIRE — similar to M2, in .25 ACP.

100%	98%	95%	90%	80%	70%	60%
$135	$115	$105	$95	$85	$75	$70

MODEL 951 BRIGADIER — 9mm, $4\frac{1}{2}$ in. barrel, fixed sights, blue, plastic grips, current Italian service pistol. Mfg. 1952-present.

100%	98%	95%	90%	80%	70%	60%
$250	$215	$195	$175	$150	$130	$115

Add $350 for "Brigadier" or "Israeli" Model.

MODEL 20 — .25 ACP, double action, alloy frame, 9 shot, $2\frac{1}{2}$ in. barrel, plastic or walnut grips, 10.9 oz. Disc. 1985.

100%	98%	95%	90%	80%	70%	60%
$160	$140	$125	$115	$95	$85	$75

Last Mfg.'s Sug. Retail was $214.

MODEL 70 PUMA OR COUGAR — .32 ACP or .380 ACP cal., $3\frac{1}{2}$ in. barrel, fixed or adj. sights, blue, plastic grips, .32 Puma alloy frame, .380 Cougar steel frame. Disc.

100%	98%	95%	90%	80%	70%	60%
$200	$180	$165	$150	$130	$110	$90

This model is more desirable in .380 ACP cal.

MODEL 70T — similar to 70, .32 ACP, target sights. Disc.

100%	98%	95%	90%	80%	70%	60%
$275	$250	$220	$195	$165	$150	$140

Grading	100%	98%	95%	90%	80%	70%	60%

B

MODEL 70S — .22 LR or .380 ACP cal., single action, 3½ in. barrel, 9 shot, blued finish, plastic grips, weight .22 cal. — 18 oz., .380 ACP — 23 oz., steel frame, .22 LR has adj. rear sight. Disc. 1985.

	$240	$210	$185	$170	$155	$140	$125

Last Mfg.'s Sug. Retail was $295.

MODEL 71 JAGUAR — alloy frame, .22 LR version of Model 70. Disc.

	$220	$195	$180	$160	$150	$140	$110

MODEL 72 JAGUAR — similar to 71, with 6 in. barrel. Disc.

	$220	$195	$180	$160	$150	$140	$110

MODEL 76P-76W TARGET PISTOL — .22 LR, single action, 11 shot, steel frame, 6 in. barrel, adj. sights, blued finish, thumbrest plastic grips (76-P). Disc. 1985.

	$345	$300	$275	$245	$220	$195	$170

Last Mfg.'s Sug. Retail was $395.

Add $40 for thumbrest wood grips (Model 76-W).

MODEL 80 — .22 Short cal., target pistol with limited importation into the U.S.

	$750	$675	$595	$550	$495	$450	$395

MODEL 81P-81W — .32 ACP, double action, 13 shot, 3.8 in. barrel, fixed sights, blue. Imported 1976-1984.

	$300	$250	$225	$195	$175	$155	$135

Add $90 for nickel finish.
Add $20 for wood grips (W Suffix).

MODEL 82W — .32 ACP, double action, more compact than Model 81, 10 shot, walnut grips, 17 oz. Importation disc. 1984.

	$295	$250	$225	$195	$175	$155	$135

Add $75 for nickel finish.

MODEL 84B — .380 ACP, double action, brown plastic grips, 13 shot mag., blue finish, fixed sights. Disc.

	$295	$250	$225	$195	$175	$155	$135

MODEL 84W-EL — similar to Model 84 only specially engraved, select walnut grips. Presentation case. Disc. 1984.

	$1,025	$770	$720	$615	$565	$520	$460

MODEL 86P-86W — .380 ACP only, double action, tip-up 4⅓ in. barrel, 8 shot mag., plastic or walnut grips, 23 oz. Add $80 for walnut grips (86-W). This model was advertised, but never released.

Mfg.'s Sug. Retail was $480 in 1986.

MODEL 90 DOUBLE ACTION AUTOMATIC — .32 ACP, 3⅝ in. barrel, fixed sights, blue, plastic grips. Mfg. 1969-1983.

	$275	$195	$175	$155	$130	$110	$95

MODEL 92 (FIRST SERIES) — same general specifications as current Model 92SB, originally mfg. 1976 until disc.

	$400	$350	$315	$280	$255	$240	$220

Early production Model 92s had a frame mounted safety and mag. release button at base of pistol grip in addition to a serial number suffix. The Model 92s design evolved from the Beretta Model 951.

MODEL 92S (SECOND SERIES) — similar to Model 92, except has firing pin safety. Disc.

	$375	$325	$260	$230	$200	$180	$165

Grading	100%	98%	95%	90%	80%	70%	60%

MODEL 92SB-P (THIRD SERIES) — 9mm Luger, double action, 16 shot, 4.92 in. barrel, fixed sights, alloy frame, high-polish blued finish, plastic grips (Model 92SB-P), 34½ oz. Mfg. 1980-1985.

| | $475 | $425 | $385 | $345 | $310 | $285 | $260 |

Last Mfg.'s Sug. Retail was $600.

▲ *Model 92SB-W* — similar to above, only with wooden grips. Disc. 1985.

| | $495 | $430 | $390 | $355 | $330 | $290 | $260 |

Last Mfg.'s Sug. Retail was $620.

MODEL 92SB-P COMPACT — similar to Model 92SB, except has 4.3 in. barrel, 14 shot, plastic grips (Model 92SB-P), 31 oz. Disc. 1985.

| | $500 | $440 | $385 | $345 | $310 | $285 | $260 |

Last Mfg.'s Sug. Retail was $620.

Add $60 for nickel finish.

▲ *Model 92SB-W Compact* — similar to above only with wooden grips. Disc. 1985.

| | $525 | $465 | $395 | $355 | $335 | $300 | $280 |

Last Mfg.'s Sug. Retail was $635.

MODEL 100 — .32 ACP, fixed sights. Disc.

| | $250 | $220 | $195 | $165 | $150 | $140 | $130 |

MODEL 101 — similar to 70T, in .22 LR. Disc.

| | $250 | $220 | $195 | $165 | $150 | $140 | $130 |

MODEL 102 — .22 LR, target pistol, single action, steel/alloy construction, plastic grips, 10 shot mag. with finger extension, adj. rear sight. Disc.

| | $325 | $250 | $220 | $195 | $165 | $150 | $140 |

PISTOLS: SEMI-AUTO, RECENT MFG.

On Beretta's large frame pistols, alphabetical suffixes refer to the following: F Model - double/single action system with external safety decocking lever, G Model - double/single action system with external decocking only lever, D Model - double action only without safety lever, DS Model - double action only with external safety lever.

MODEL 21(A)-W BOBCAT — .22 LR or .25 ACP, double action, alloy frame, 7 (.22 LR) or 8 (.25 ACP) shot mag., 2.4 in. barrel, walnut grips, 11½ oz.

▲ *Blue/Nickel Finish*

| Mfg.'s Sug. Retail | $244 | $195 | $155 | $140 | $130 | $115 | $95 | $85 |

Add $10 for nickel finish.
Add $50 for engraving.

▲ *Matte Finish* — matte finished metal, plastic grips. Introduced 1992.

| Mfg.'s Sug. Retail | $194 | $165 | $140 | $130 | $115 | $95 | $85 | $80 |

This model is manufactured by Beretta U.S.A. Corp. in Accokeek, MD.

▲ *Lady Beretta* — .22 LR only, similar to Model 21-W, except is specially serial numbered and has gold etching on top of frame and slide sides. Supplied with a blue velvet drawstring bag. 1990 issue.

| | $245 | $185 | $160 | $140 | $130 | $115 | $100 |

Last Mfg.'s Sug. Retail was $285.

This model was sold exclusively by Lew Horton Distributing Co.

MODEL 71 — .22 LR, single action, 8 shot, 6 in. barrel, plastic grips with thumbrest, finger extension mag. Imported 1987 only.

| | $190 | $160 | $140 | $130 | $115 | $95 | $85 |

Last Mfg.'s Sug. Retail was $215.

Grading	100%	98%	95%	90%	80%	70%	60%

MODEL 84P-84W CHEETAH — .380 ACP cal., double action semi-auto, 3.82 in. barrel, alloy frame, steel slide, 10 (C/B 1994) or 13* shot mag., firing pin block, ambidextrous manual safety (also used as a decocking lever), low dot profile sights, curved trigger guard, plastic or wood grips, blue (disc.), Bruniton, or nickel finish, 23 oz.

Mfg.'s Sug. Retail	$529	$415	$335	$300	$270	$240	$210	$190

Add $28 for wooden grips (Model 84W).
Add $70 for nickel finish (includes checkered wooden grips).

▲ *Model 84F* — similar specifications to the Model 84P-84W, except patterned after the Model 92F Govt. Model, matte black Bruniton finish, squared off trigger guard, plastic or wood grips, 23 oz. Mfg. 1990 only.

	$395	$330	$300	$270	$240	$210	$190

Last Mfg.'s Sug. Retail was $479.

MODEL 85P-85W CHEETAH — .380 ACP cal., same general specifications as the Model 84, except slimmer profile because of 8 shot straight line mag., Model 85P has plastic grips, 22 oz.

Mfg.'s Sug. Retail	$499	$390	$315	$270	$240	$210	$190	$175

Add $100 for nickel finish.
Add $31 for wooden grips (Model 85W).

▲ *Model 85F* — similar specifications to the Model 85P-85W, except patterned after the Model 92F Govt. Model, matte black Bruniton finish, squared off trigger guard, plastic or wood grips, 21.8 oz. Mfg. in 1990 only.

	$375	$300	$270	$240	$210	$190	$175

Last Mfg.'s Sug. Retail was $440.

Add $25 for wooden grips.

MODEL 86 CHEETAH — .380 ACP, double action semi-auto with 4.4 in. tip-up barrel, 8 shot mag., checkered walnut grips, matte finish, fixed sights, gold trigger, 23.3 oz. Importation began 1991.

Mfg.'s Sug. Retail	$514	$430	$350	$295	$250	$225	$190	$175

MODEL 87 CHEETAH — .22 LR, double action semi-auto, 7 shot mag., 3.82 or 6 in. target barrel with counterweight, wood grips, 20 oz. (3.82 in. barrel). Importation began 1986.

Mfg.'s Sug. Retail	$493	$400	$330	$280	$245	$210	$190	$175

▲ *Model 87 Target* — single action only target variation of the Model 87 with 6 in. barrel, 23.3 oz. Disc. 1994.

	$415	$350	$285	$245	$210	$190	$175

Last Mfg.'s Sug. Retail was $510.

MODEL 89 — .22 LR, single action target semi-auto, matte black finish on metal parts, 10 shot mag., anatomical wood grips, adj. sights, 41 oz. Importation began 1988.

Mfg.'s Sug. Retail	$736	$585	$485	$400	$350	$300	$275	$250

MODEL 92D — 9mm Para., double action only, otherwise similar to Model 92F, except does not have a manual safety lever, includes black plastic grips, 3 dot sights, 33.8 oz. Introduced 1992.

Mfg.'s Sug. Retail	$586	$460	$360	$300	$250	$210	$190	$175

Add $90 for Tritium (new 1994) sight system.
Add 10% for Trijicon (disc.) sights.

▲ *Model 92D Centurion* — 9mm Para., compact variation with 4.3 in. barrel, plastic grips only, without safety, choice of 3 dot or Tritium sights. New 1994.

Mfg.'s Sug. Retail	$586	$460	$360	$300	$250	$210	$190	$175

Add $90 for Tritium sights.

Grading	100%	98%	95%	90%	80%	70%	60%

MODEL 92F(S) — 9mm Para., official U.S. military variation of 92 Series, 4.9 in. barrel, alloy frame, steel slide, 10 (C/B 1994) or 15* shot mag., chamber loaded indicator, matte black Bruniton finish, squared off trigger guard to facilitate two-hand shooting, extended mag. base, choice of regular or 3 dot sights (new 1991). Model 92F-P has plastic grips. Model 92F-W has wood grips. New 1984.

Mfg.'s Sug. Retail	$626	$545	$445	$410	$375	$335	$300	$275

Add $21 for checkered wood grips.
Add $90 for Tritium (new 1994) sight system.
Add 10% for Trijicon (disc.) sights.
Add $164 for gold engraving/accenting (Model 92F-W only).
Add $395 for 9mm Competition Conversion Kit (new 1992).

The Model 92FS incorporates a slide retaining pin engineering change not included in the Model 92F.

Plastic grips are currently as desirable as wood, even though wood adds $25 to the retail price.

Older Italian mfg. Model 92s if in 98%+ condition are commanding slight premiums in some areas.

The U.S. military on January 15, 1985 announced that the Model 92F (M9) would replace the Colt Govt. Model .45 ACP as the standard government issue sidearm. Because of domestic political pressures, Congress requested that a new sidearm competition be conducted again in 1988. The result of this second trial was that the Department of the Army announced on May 22, 1989 that Beretta had won again. This military contract with Beretta U.S.A. Corp. involves over 320,000 Model M9 (military designation for the commercial Model 92F) being manufactured for U.S. military consumption in the 1990s. Actual delivery of commercial Model 92s began in January of 1986. Actual M9 delivery to U.S. Armed Forces has exceeded 390,000 units to date.

▲ **Model 92F(S) (Stainless)** — similar to Model 92F, except is mfg. from stainless steel, satin finish with plastic grips, 3 dot sights, initially released to law enforcement agencies only, a limited amount have found their way into the commercial market (usually with premiums being asked).

Mfg.'s Sug. Retail	$757	$625	$525	$450

Add $20 for wood grips.
Add $90 for Trijicon (1993 only) or Tritium (new 1994) sight system.

▲ **Model 92F(S) Centurion** — similar to Model 92F, except has compact barrel slide unit with full size frame, 4.3 in. barrel, choice of plastic or wood grips, 3 dot sight system, same length as Model 92F Compact, 10 (C/B 1994) or 15* shot mag., 33.2 oz. Introduced 1992.

Mfg.'s Sug. Retail	$626	$550	$450	$415	$375	$335	$300	$275

Add $21 for checkered walnut grips (Model 92F Wood).
Add $90 for Tritium sight system (new 1994).
Add 10% for Trijicon sights (disc).

▲ **Model 92F-ELS** — deluxe variation of the Model 92F featuring stainless steel finish with gold highlights on trim, frame etchings, and small parts, special ergonomic walnut grips. Mfg. 1992-94.

	$685	$550	$425

Last Mfg.'s Sug. Retail was $790.

M9 LIMITED STANDARD EDITION — commercial limited edition of the U.S. Govt. M9 military pistol, features gold inscribed slide legend "The First Decade 1985-1995", Air Force or Marine Corps emblems on right slide side, limited mfg. of 10,000 beginning late 1995.

Mfg.'s Sug. Retail	$644	$575	$475	$425

▲ **M9 Limited Deluxe Edition** — features checkered walnut grips, gold-plated hammer, grip screws, and mag. release button.

Mfg.'s Sug. Retail	$751	$650	$525	$475

▲ **Model 92F Deluxe** — deluxe model featuring gold or silver plating and elaborate engraving. New 1993.

Mfg.'s Sug. Retail	$5,429	$4,950	$3,750	$2,500

Grading	100%	98%	95%	90%	80%	70%	60%

MODEL 92F COMPACT — similar to Model 92F, except has 4.3 in. barrel and 13 shot mag., plastic or wood grips, 31½ oz. While temporarily suspended in 1986, production was resumed 1989-1993.

	$550	$450	$415	$375	$335	$300	$275

Last Mfg.'s Sug. Retail was $625.

    Add $20 for checkered walnut grips (Model 92F Wood).
    Add $65 for Trijicon sight system.

▲ *Model 92F Compact "M"* — similar to Model 92F Compact, except has 8 shot straight line mag., plastic grips only. Imported 1990-93.

	$550	$450	$415	$375	$335	$300	$275

Last Mfg.'s Sug. Retail was $625.

    Add $65 for Trijicon sight system.
    Approx. 1,200 92SBM Models were imported in the 1980s.

MODEL 92G — 9mm Para., identical to the Model 92F, except features a spring loaded decocking lever that safely lowers the hammer allowing fire-ready when unholstering the pistol. New 1990.

    The Model 92G is sold to law enforcement agencies only and prices are slightly higher than the standard Model 92FS. This pistol has been used by French Gendarmes since 1987.

MODEL 96D — double action only variation of the Model 96F, no safety, 3 dot sight system, 33.8 oz. New 1992.

Mfg.'s Sug. Retail	$607	$540	$450	$415	$375	$335	$300	$275

    Add $90 for Tritium sight system (new 1994).
    Add $65 for Trijicon sights (disc.).

▲ *Model 96D Centurion* — similar to Model 96D, except is compact variation with 4.3 in. barrel, 3 dot sights. New 1994.

Mfg.'s Sug. Retail	$607	$540	$450	$415	$375	$335	$300	$275

    Add $90 for Tritium sight system.

MODEL 96F(S) — .40 S&W cal., similar to Model 92F, 4.9 in. barrel, plastic grips only, flared grip with grip strap serrations, Bruniton matte black finish, 3 dot sight system, 10 shot mag., 33.4 oz. Introduced 1992.

Mfg.'s Sug. Retail	$643	$560	$450	$415	$375	$335	$300	$275

    Add $90 for Tritium sight system (new 1994).
    Add 10% for Trijicon sights (disc.).

▲ *Model 96F Compact* — while advertised, this model was never mfg. (suggested retail was $640).

▲ *Model 96F Centurion* — similar to Model 96F, except has 4.3 in. barrel, 33.2 oz. New 1992.

Mfg.'s Sug. Retail	$643	$560	$450	$415	$375	$335	$300	$275

    Add $90 for Tritium sight system (new 1994).

MODEL 950 BS (JETFIRE) — .22 Short (disc. 1992) or .25 ACP cal., single action, alloy frame, 8 shot (.25 cal. only) or 6 shot mag., tip-up 2½ and 4 in. (.22 only) barrel, plastic grips, thumb safety, 8-10 oz.

Mfg.'s Sug. Retail	$187	$155	$125	$110	$100	$90	$80	$70

    Add $34 for nickel finish.
    Add $80 for engraved variation.
    Subtract $30 for matte finish (new 1992), plastic grips only.
    This model is manufactured by Beretta U.S.A. Corp. in Accokeek, MD.

▲ *Model 950 EL* — same general specifications as Model 950 BS, only with wooden grips and gold plated parts. Mfg. disc. 1988.

	$190	$175	$150	$140	$130	$115	$105

Last Mfg.'s Sug. Retail was $210.

Grading	100%	98%	95%	90%	80%	70%	60%

MODEL 3000 TOMCAT — .32 ACP cal., similar to Model 21 Bobcat, except has 2.45 in. barrel, 7 shot mag., choice of matte or blue finish, plastic grips. New 1996.

Mfg.'s Sug. Retail	$240	$190	$155	$140	$130	$115	$95	$85

Add $59 for blue finish.

MODEL 8000 (COUGAR) — 9mm Para., single/double or DA only, short recoil system with 3.6 in. rotating barrel, 10 shot mag., fixed sights, anodized aluminum alloy frame, Bruniton matte black finish, 33.5 oz. New 1995.

Mfg.'s Sug. Retail	$663	$575	$465	$425	$375	$335	$300	$275

Add $36 for single/double action operation.

MODEL 8040 (COUGAR) — .40 S&W cal., single/double or DA only, short recoil system with 3.6 in. rotating barrel, 10 shot mag., fixed sights, anodized aluminum alloy frame, Bruniton matte black finish, 33.5 oz. New 1995.

Mfg.'s Sug. Retail	$663	$575	$465	$425	$375	$335	$300	$275

Add $36 for single/double action.

RIFLES: BOLT ACTION, RECENT MFG.

MODEL 500 CUSTOM — .222 Rem., .223 Rem., .243 Win., .270 Win., .30-06, or .308 Win. cal., 3 action lengths, 24 in. barrel, iron sights, checkered walnut stock with recoil pad. Importation was resumed 1988 only.

			$595	$530	$450	$395	$350	$315	$275

Last Mfg.'s Sug. Retail was $725.

▲ *Model 500S* — similar to Model 500, except is equipped with iron sights. Imported 1986 only.

			$615	$560	$460	$400	$350	$315	$275

Last Mfg.'s Sug. Retail was $700.

▲ *Model 500 DL* — same specifications as Model 500, only better walnut and light engraving. Disc. 1986.

			$1,395	$1,260	$1,000	$875	$795	$725	$650

Last Mfg.'s Sug. Retail was $1,595.

▲ *Model 500 DLS* — similar to Model 500 DL, except is equipped with iron sights. Imported 1986 only.

			$1,420	$1,285	$1,020	$875	$795	$725	$650

Last Mfg.'s Sug. Retail was $1,625.

▲ *Model 500 EELL* — same specifications as Model 500 DL, only select walnut and more engraving. Disc. 1986.

		$1,550	$1,260	$1,150	$1,000	$875	$800	$725

Last Mfg.'s Sug. Retail was $1,745.

▲ *Model 500 EELLS* — similar to Model 500 EELL, except is equipped with iron sights. Imported 1986 only.

		$1,575	$1,425	$1,200	$1,120	$875	$800	$725

Last Mfg.'s Sug. Retail was $1,785.

MODEL 501 — available in either .243 or .308 Win. cal., medium bolt action, 6 shot, 23 in. barrel, no sights, checkered walnut stock. Disc. 1986.

		$595	$530	$465	$395	$350	$315	$275

Last Mfg.'s Sug. Retail was $665.

▲ *Model 501 S* — similar to Model 501, except is equipped with iron sights. Imported 1986 only.

		$615	$560	$460	$400	$350	$315	$275

Last Mfg.'s Sug. Retail was $700.

▲ *Model 501 DL* — same specifications as Model 501, only better walnut and light engraving. Disc. 1986.

		$1,395	$1,260	$1,000	$875	$795	$725	$650

Last Mfg.'s Sug. Retail was $1,575.

▲ *Model 501 DLS* — similar to Model 501 DL, except is equipped with iron sights. Imported 1986 only.

		$1,420	$1,285	$1,020	$875	$795	$725	$650

Last Mfg.'s Sug. Retail was $1,625.

Grading	100%	98%	95%	90%	80%	70%	60%

▲ **Model 501 EELL** — same specifications as Model 501 DL, only select walnut and more engraving. Disc. 1986.

| | $1,550 | $1,260 | $1,150 | $1,000 | $875 | $800 | $725 |

Last Mfg.'s Sug. Retail was $1,745.

▲ **Model 501 EELLS** — similar to Model 501 EELL, except is equipped with iron sights. Imported 1986 only.

| | $1,575 | $1,425 | $1,200 | $1,120 | $875 | $800 | $725 |

Last Mfg.'s Sug. Retail was $1,785.

MODEL 502 — available in either .30-06, .270 or 7mm Rem. Mag. cal., long bolt action, 5 or 6 shot, 24 in. barrel, no sights, checkered walnut stock. Disc. 1986.

| | $625 | $565 | $490 | $440 | $395 | $360 | $330 |

Last Mfg.'s Sug. Retail was $710.

▲ **Model 502 S** — similar to Model 502, except is equipped with iron sights. Imported 1986 only.

| | $650 | $595 | $525 | $460 | $395 | $360 | $330 |

Last Mfg.'s Sug. Retail was $745.

▲ **Model 502 DL** — same specifications as Model 502, only better walnut and light engraving. Also available in .375 H&H Mag. Disc. 1986.

| | $1,495 | $1,310 | $1,175 | $1,025 | $900 | $775 | $695 |

Last Mfg.'s Sug. Retail was $1,640.

▲ **Model 502 DLS** — similar to Model 502, except is equipped with iron sights. Imported 1986 only.

| | $1,410 | $1,325 | $1,175 | $1,025 | $900 | $775 | $695 |

Last Mfg.'s Sug. Retail was $1,660.

▲ **Model 502 EELL** — same specifications as Model 502 DL, only select walnut and more engraving. Also available in .375 H&H Mag. Disc. 1986.

| | $1,575 | $1,425 | $1,200 | $1,120 | $875 | $800 | $725 |

Last Mfg.'s Sug. Retail was $1,785.

▲ **Model 502 EELLS** — similar to Model 502 EELL, except is equipped with iron sights. Imported 1986 only.

| | $1,575 | $1,425 | $1,200 | $1,120 | $875 | $800 | $725 |

Last Mfg.'s Sug. Retail was $1,785.

RIFLES: SEMI-AUTO, RECENT MFG.

BM-59 M-1 GARAND — with original Beretta M1 receiver, only 200 imported into the U.S.

| | $1,850 | $1,475 | $1,250 | $1,000 | $895 | $850 | $800 |

Last Mfg.'s Sug. Retail was $2,080.

BM-62 — similar to BM-59, except has flash suppressor and is Italian marked.

| | $1,850 | $1,475 | $1,250 | $1,000 | $895 | $850 | $800 |

AR-70 — .222 or .223 cal., semi-auto paramilitary design rifle, 5, 8 or 30 shot mag., diopter sights, epoxy finish, 17.72 in. barrel, 8.3 lbs.

| | $1,650 | $1,500 | $1,275 | $1,050 | $875 | $725 | $600 |

Last Mfg.'s Sug. Retail was $1,065.

1989 Federal legislation banned the importation of this model into U.S.

RIFLES: CUSTOM, RECENT MFG.

Current high grade Beretta O/U and SxS rifles are sold only by premium grade franchised Beretta dealers. For a listing of these dealers, contact a Beretta Gallery (see Trademark Index).

Add $630 for Cookleigh scope mounts or $1,400 for Zeiss 4x32mm scope on Models SS06 and 455.

MODEL S686/S689 SILVER SABLE O/U — .30-06, 9.3x74R, or .444 cal. (disc. 1995), boxlock action, double triggers. New 1995.

| Mfg.'s Sug. Retail | $3,300 | $2,995 | $2,650 | $2,175 | $1,850 | $1,550 | $1,275 | $1,050 |

Add $1,700 for Model S686/S689 Golden Eagle/Gold Sable (N/A in .444 cal.).

Grading	100%	98%	95%	90%	80%	70%	60%

MODEL S686/S689EELL DIAMOND SABLE O/U — .30-06, 9.3x74R, or .444 Marlin cal., moderate engraving. New 1995.

Mfg.'s Sug. Retail	$12,500	$11,300	$8,875	$7,800	$6,750	$5,975	$5,325	$4,700

MODEL S689 O/U — 9.3x74R or 30-06 cal., boxlock action, nickel (disc. 1985) or case hardened (new 1986) receiver, double triggers, 23 in. barrels, auto ejectors, sling swivels, 7.7 lbs. Importation disc. in 1990.

	$3,700	$2,600	$2,200	$1,850	$1,550	$1,275	$1,050

Last Mfg.'s Sug. Retail was $4,907.

Add $1,000 for scope and claw mounts.

SSO EXPRESS O/U — .375 H&H or .458 Win. Mag. cal., sidelock action, case hardened receiver, double triggers, 23 in. barrels, auto ejectors, 11 lbs., cased. Importation disc. 1989.

	$12,500	$9,500	$8,250	$6,950	$6,100	$5,600	$4,875

Last Mfg.'s Sug. Retail was $17,533.

Add $425 for claw mounts.

▲ *SSO5 EXPRESS O/U* — similar to SSO Express except has more elaborate engraving and better walnut.

	$14,250	$11,750	$8,750	$7,500	$6,750	$6,100	$5,600

Last Mfg.'s Sug. Retail was $19,600.

SSO6 EXPRESS CUSTOM SIDELOCK O/U — 9.3x74R, .375 H&H, or .458 Win. Mag. cal., next to top-of-the-line sidelock double rifle, individually built to the customer's specifications, cased. New 1990.

Mfg.'s Sug. Retail	$22,500	$20,000	$15,850	$12,500	$10,000	$8,450	$7,150	$6,000

Add $3,000 for gold inlays (SS06 Gold Custom).
Add $5,500 for extra set of barrels.

MODEL 455 SIDE-BY-SIDE — .375 H&H, .416 Rigby, .458 Win. Mag., .470 NE, or .500 3 in. NE cal., top of the line sidelock double rifle, individually built to the customer's specifications, cased. New 1990.

Mfg.'s Sug. Retail	$38,500	$34,750	$29,250	$24,000	$19,250	$16,000	$13,000	$10,000

▲ *Model 455 EELL* — similar cals. as Model 455 SxS, top-of-the-line custom sidelock double rifle featuring every refinement of the gunmaker's art, cased.

Mfg.'s Sug. Retail	$50,000	$45,000	$37,950	$33,000	$27,500	$23,000	$19,000	$16,000

SHOTGUNS: O/U, DISC.

BL-1 — 12 ga., 26, 28, or 30 in. barrels, various chokes, boxlock, extractors, double triggers, checkered pistol grip stock. Mfg. 1968-1973.

	$385	$330	$275	$220	$190	$175	$160

BL-2 — similar to BL-1, with single selective trigger, more engraving.

	$420	$385	$360	$305	$265	$225	$185

BL-2 STAKE-OUT — riot configuration with 18 in. barrels, DT, blue finish, approx. 6,000 mfg.

	$400	$340	$275	$220	$190	$175	$160

BL-2/S — similar to BL-2, with vent. rib and speed trigger. Mfg. 1974-1976.

	$440	$385	$330	$305	$265	$225	$185

BL-3 — O/U, similar to BL-2, with more engraving, vent. rib and ejectors, also available in 20 ga. Mfg. 1968-1976.

	$595	$550	$525	$470	$440	$385	$350

BL-3 SKEET

	$660	$605	$580	$525	$470	$415	$370

BL-3 TRAP

	$580	$520	$495	$450	$415	$375	$335

Grading	100%	98%	95%	90%	80%	70%	60%

BL-4 — deluxe version of BL-3, more engraving, better wood.

	$795	$715	$625	$595	$550	$495	$450

BL-4 SKEET

	$850	$745	$675	$635	$550	$495	$450

BL-4 TRAP

	$695	$625	$575	$525	$475	$425	$360

BL-5 — higher grade version of BL-4.

	$1,050	$925	$855	$775	$700	$625	$575

BL-5 SKEET

	$1,100	$960	$875	$795	$725	$650	$595

BL-5 TRAP

	$925	$850	$775	$695	$595	$525	$465

BL-6 — boxlock with scroll engraved sideplates, ejectors, SST.

	$1,450	$1,250	$1,025	$935	$850	$765	$680

BL-6 SKEET

	$1,525	$1,300	$1,075	$975	$915	$825	$715

BL-6 TRAP

	$1,295	$1,100	$950	$885	$810	$715	$650

MODEL S55B — 12 or 20 ga., O/U, 26, 28, or 30 in. barrels, various chokes, boxlock, extractors, selective trigger, checkered pistol grip stock. Disc.

	$550	$495	$440	$385	$330	$300	$280

MODEL S56 E — similar to S55B, with engraved receiver and auto ejectors. Disc.

	$605	$555	$515	$460	$415	$365	$330

MODEL S58 SKEET — similar to S56E, with 26 in. Bohler steel barrels, skeet bore, wide vent. rib, skeet.

	$770	$695	$630	$550	$495	$445	$395

MODEL S58 TRAP — similar to S58 Skeet, with 30 in. barrels, imp. mod. and full choke, Monte Carlo stock with pad.

	$700	$625	$550	$495	$450	$410	$365

SILVER SNIPE — 12 or 20 ga., 26, 28, or 30 in. barrels, boxlock, extractors, trigger optional, checkered pistol grip stock. Mfg. 1955-1967.

	$450	$415	$370	$330	$295	$265	$230

▲ *Silver Snipe SST* — with vent. rib and SST.

	$550	$495	$440	$415	$360	$330	$295

    Add 25% for ejectors.

GOLDEN SNIPE — similar to Silver Snipe, with auto ejectors and vent. rib standard.

	$660	$605	$550	$525	$470	$430	$385

▲ *Golden Snipe SST* — with SST.

	$715	$660	$605	$580	$525	$465	$410

MODEL (S)57 E — higher quality version of Golden Snipe. Mfg. 1955-1967.

	$825	$770	$660	$635	$550	$495	$450

▲ *Model (S)57 E SST* — with single selective trigger.

	$880	$825	$715	$690	$605	$540	$495

Grading	100%	98%	95%	90%	80%	70%	60%

ASEL MODEL — 12 or 20 ga., 26, 28, or 30 in. barrels, various chokes, single trigger, checkered pistol grip stock, auto ejectors. Mfg. 1947-1964.

12 ga.	$1,600	$1,375	$1,100	$990	$880	$800	$720
20 ga.	$2,750	$2,475	$2,050	$1,650	$1,375	$1,100	$895

GRADE 100 — 12 ga., 26, 28, or 30 in. barrels, any choke, sidelock, double trigger, auto ejectors, checkered pistol grip or straight stock.

$1,820	$1,550	$1,300	$1,100	$900	$775	$695

MODEL 200 — similar to 100, with chrome lined bores and action parts, higher quality engraving.

$2,310	$2,000	$1,870	$1,650	$1,375	$1,100	$875

MODEL 680 — competition trap and skeet model, 12 ga. only, boxlock, various chokes. Mono-trap model available. Silver finish receiver, hand engraved, premium walnut. Disc.

$1,215	$1,030	$870	$790	$715	$635	$550

Add $60 for 2 barrel combo. package.

SHOTGUNS: FIELD O/U, RECENT MFG.

BERETTA CHOKES AND THEIR CODES (ON REAR LEFT-SIDE OF BARREL)

*   designates full choke (F).

**   designates improved modified choke (IM).

***   designates modified choke (M).

****   designates improved cylinder choke (IC).

FK   designates skeet (SK).

***** designates cylinder bore (CYL).

MODEL 685 — 12 or 20 ga. $2\frac{3}{4}$ or 3 in. chambers, matte chromed receiver, extractors, single trigger. Disc. 1986.

$595	$525	$460	$420	$360	$320	$295

Last Mfg.'s Sug. Retail was $875.

MODEL S686 ONYX — 12 or 20 ga., 3 in. chambers, boxlock action, 26 or 28 in. barrels with multi-chokes, matte finish on metal parts, choice of standard pistol grip or English straight stock, single trigger, ejectors. New 1988.

Mfg.'s Sug. Retail	$1,473	$1,195	$895	$700	$595	$550	$480	$425

▲ *Model S686 (Onyx) Magnum* — 12 ga. only, similar to Model S686 Onyx, except has $3\frac{1}{2}$ in. chambers. Mfg. 1993, reintroduced 1996.

Mfg.'s Sug. Retail	$1,473	$1,195	$895	$700	$595	$550	$480	$425

▲ *Model 686 (Onyx) Ultralight* — 12 ga. only, $2\frac{3}{4}$ in. chambers, Ergal alloy receiver reinforced with titanium plate, matte black finish on receiver and barrels, checkered walnut stock and forearm, choke tubes, gilded lettering and logo, gold SST, ejectors, very light weight, 5 lbs. 11 oz. Importation began 1992.

Mfg.'s Sug. Retail	$1,716	$1,425	$1,050	$800	$650	$575	$525	$475

▲ *Model 686 Essential* — 12 ga. only, 3 in. chambers, 26 or 28 in. VR separated barrels with choke tubes, checkered walnut stock and forearm, matte finished metal, 6.7 lbs. New 1994.

Mfg.'s Sug. Retail	$1,186	$965	$740	$600	$550	$500	$450	$415

▲ *Model 686 (Onyx) Silver Perdiz/Silver Pigeon* — 12, 20, or 28 (new 1995) ga., 3 in. chambers (except for 28 ga.), 26 or 28 in. VR barrels with choke tubes, silvered receiver with scroll engraving, gold trigger, checkered pistol grip or straight grip walnut stock and forearm. New 1992.

Mfg.'s Sug. Retail	$1,544	$1,250	$975	$825	$725	$650	$575	$525

During 1996, the model nomenclature was changed from the Silver Perdiz to the Silver Pigeon.

▲ *Model 686 (Onyx) Silver Perdiz/Silver Pigeon Combo* — similar to Model 686 Onyx, except is supplied with 1 set each of 20 ga. (28 in.) and 28 ga. (26 in.) barrels. Introduced 1986.

Mfg.'s Sug. Retail	$2,259	$1,800	$1,375	$1,175	$975	$875	$820	$775

Grading	100%	98%	95%	90%	80%	70%	60%

MODEL 686(L) SILVER PERDIZ — 12 (disc. 1990), 20 (disc. 1990), or 28 ga., field model, boxlock action, various barrels/chokes, ejectors, single trigger, engraved silver finished receiver, special walnut, pistol or straight grip stock, fixed chokes disc. 1987. Importation disc. 1994.

	$1,100	$850	$650	$575	$525	$460	$415

Last Mfg.'s Sug. Retail was $1,355.

Subtract 10% with fixed chokes (disc.).

MODEL S686 EL GOLD PERDIZ — 12 or 20 ga., 3 in. chambers, boxlock action with floral scroll engraved sideplates, silver receiver finish, 26 or 28 VR in. barrels with choke tubes, gold SST, checkered walnut stock and forearm, cased, approx. 6.8 lbs. New 1992.

Mfg.'s Sug. Retail	$1,999	$1,650	$1,375	$1,150	$950	$875	$800	$695

MODEL S687 L (SILVER PIGEON) — 12 or 20 ga., 3 in. chambers, boxlock, various barrels/chokes, ejectors, game scene engraved nickel finished receiver, select walnut, approx. 6.8 lbs., fitted case is optional.

Mfg.'s Sug. Retail	$2,031	$1,675	$1,375	$1,150	$950	$875	$800	$695

Subtract 10% without multi-chokes (disc.).

MODEL 687 DU — 12 (1990 release), 20, 28 (1992 release) or .410 ga., mfg. for DU dinner gun auctions and membership, prices may vary significantly from region to region.

	$1,950	$1,700	$1,450	$1,175	$895	$725	$575

MODEL 687 L ONYX — 12 or 20 ga., 3 in. chambers, same game scene engraving as standard Model 687 L, except has Onyx blackened receiver, multi-chokes standard. Mfg. 1990 only.

	$1,250	$995	$825	$700	$635	$575	$525

Last Mfg.'s Sug. Retail was $1,590.

MODEL 687 GOLDEN ONYX — 12 or 20 ga., 3 in. chambers, similar to Model 686 Onyx, except has more engraving, better walnut, and several gold inlays. Imported 1988-89 only.

	$1,375	$1,075	$875	$775	$685	$635	$575

Last Mfg.'s Sug. Retail was $1,800.

MODEL S687 EL GOLD PIGEON — same general specifications as Model 687L, except also available in 28 (new 1990) or .410 (new 1990) ga., 2¾ or 3 in. chambers, boxlock with gold engraved animals on sideplates, better walnut, and more engraving, approx. 6.8 lbs, cased.

Mfg.'s Sug. Retail	$3,446	$2,875	$2,200	$1,825	$1,550	$1,350	$1,150	$1,000

Add $153 for 28 or .410 ga.

▲ *Model 687 EL DU* — small frame 28 ga., released 1992 for DU auctions and membership.

	$2,850	$2,200	$1,800	$1,550	$1,400	$1,200	$1,050

MODEL 687 EL ONYX — 12 or 20 ga., 3 in. chambers, simulated sidelock plates with classic scroll engraving. Mfg. 1990 only.

	$2,295	$2,000	$1,725	$1,500	$1,350	$1,150	$1,000

Last Mfg.'s Sug. Retail was $2,660.

MODEL S687 EELL DIAMOND PIGEON — 12, 20, or 28 ga., boxlock action, silver receiver with full sideplates and hand engraved game scenes, 3 (except 28 ga.) in. chambers and gold plated trigger, cased, multi-chokes introduced 1988, 6.8 lbs.

Mfg.'s Sug. Retail	$4,999	$4,150	$3,100	$2,450	$2,000	$1,725	$1,500	$1,250

Subtract 10% if without multi-chokes.

This model is also available with a straight grip English stock at no extra charge (20 ga. only).

▲ *Model S687 EELL Combo* — includes one set of 28 ga. (26 in. barrels with multi-chokes) and one set of 20 ga. (choice of 26 or 28 multi-choke) barrels, cased.

Mfg.'s Sug. Retail	$5,577	$4,675	$3,450	$2,675	$2,100	$1,750	$1,500	$1,250

Subtract 10% for fixed chokes.

Multi-chokes became standard in 1991.

Grading	100%	98%	95%	90%	80%	70%	60%

MODEL ASE 90 PIGEON — 12 ga. only, 28 in. fixed choke (IM/F) vent. barrels with VR, new design features nickel-chromium-molybdenum receiver with special hardening and cross bolt engaging 2 monobloc lugs, detachable trigger grouping, V-shaped main springs, cold hammered barrels, choice of silver or blued receiver with gold etching and no engraving, top quality checkered walnut stock and forearm with vent. recoil pad, choke tubes, 7 lbs. 13 oz., cased. Imported 1992-94.

	$7,100	$5,950	$4,850	$3,950	$3,300	$2,850	$2,500

Last Mfg.'s Sug. Retail was $8,070.

SHOTGUNS: SKEET O/U, RECENT MFG.

Full descriptions for the models listed below may be found under the corresponding model numbers in the Field Shotguns category.

MODEL S682 GOLD SKEET — competition skeet model, 12, 20 (disc. 1991), 28 (disc. 1988), or .410 ga. (disc. 1988), 26 or 28 in. barrels, boxlock, skeet chokes, silver finish receiver, hand engraved, premium walnut, cased. New 1984.

Mfg.'s Sug. Retail	$2,731	$2,250	$1,750	$1,350	$1,075	$950	$895	$800

▲ *Model 682 Super Skeet* — 12 ga. only, 28 in. VR barrels bored SK/SK featuring factory porting, stock has separate adj. comb cheekpiece. Mfg. 1991-95.

	$2,560	$1,925	$1,650	$1,475	$1,275	$1,050	$950

Last Mfg.'s Sug. Retail was $3,006.

▲ *Model 682 Skeet Deluxe* — similar to Model 682, except deluxe walnut and elaborate engraving. Disc. 1986.

	$2,650	$2,300	$2,100	$1,850	$1,600	$1,400	$1,200

Last Mfg.'s Sug. Retail was $3,000.

▲ *Model 682 2-Barrel Skeet Set* — 12 ga. only, two barrel set bored for skeet and sporting clays competition. Imported 1988 only.

	$4,950	$4,200	$3,675	$3,175	$2,850	$2,500	$2,175

Last Mfg.'s Sug. Retail was $6,650.

▲ *Model 682 4-Ga. Skeet Set* — four barrel skeet set comes with interchangeable barrels (28 in.) in 12, 20, 28, and 410 ga.'s. Imported 1985-95.

	$5,000	$3,995	$3,300	$2,850	$2,500	$2,175	$1,900

Last Mfg.'s Sug. Retail was $6,037.

MODEL S686 SKEET (SILVER PERDIZ) — 12 ga. only, 28 in. VR barrels bored SK/SK, checkered walnut stock and forearm, 7.6 lbs. New 1994.

Mfg.'s Sug. Retail	$1,499	$1,200	$875	$675	$595	$550	$480	$425

MODEL S687 EELL SKEET (DIAMOND PIGEON) — 12 ga. only, fixed chokes, 28 in. barrels, cased.

Mfg.'s Sug. Retail	$4,590	$3,875	$2,900	$2,450	$2,000	$1,800	$1,500	$1,250

▲ *Model S687 EELL 4-Ga. Skeet Set* — four ga. skeet set, cased. New 1988.

Mfg.'s Sug. Retail	$8,699	$7,425	$6,250	$4,850	$4,000	$3,400	$3,000	$2,700

MODEL ASE 90 GOLD SKEET — 12 ga. only, 28 in. fixed choke vent. barrels with VR, similar action and specifications as the Model ASE 90 Pigeon, 7 lbs. 13 oz., cased. New 1992.

Mfg.'s Sug. Retail	$8,737	$7,550	$6,150	$4,950	$4,000	$3,300	$2,850	$2,500

SHOTGUNS: SPORTING CLAYS O/U, RECENT MFG.

These variations have been specifically designed for sporting clay target shooting. All models listed below have 3 in. chambers, unless specified otherwise. Full descriptions for the models listed below may be found under the corresponding model numbers in the Field Shotguns category.

MODEL S682 CONTINENTAL COURSE — 12 ga. only, 2¾ in. chambers, 28 or 30 (disc. 1995) in. VR barrels with multi-chokes, designed for English Sporting Clays courses, previously was Model Super Sport with tapered rib, cased. New 1993.

Mfg.'s Sug. Retail	$2,431	$2,000	$1,600	$1,275	$1,000	$895	$795	$725

Grading	100%	98%	95%	90%	80%	70%	60%

MODEL S682 GOLD SPORTING — 12 or 20 (mfg. 1992-94) ga., similar specifications to Model 682 Skeet, $2\frac{3}{4}$ in. chambers, 28 or 30 (new 1989) in. unported or ported (new 1995) VR barrels, except over-field stock dimensions and hand engraved silver finished receiver, cased. Multi-chokes are standard.

Mfg.'s Sug. Retail	$2,789	$2,300	$1,800	$1,350	$1,075	$950	$895	$800

Add $210 for ported barrels (28 or 30 in. only).
Add $865 for extra set of 12 ga. barrels (combo. package - mfg. 1990-94).

MODEL 682 SUPER SPORTING — 12 ga. only, $2\frac{3}{4}$ in. chambers, 28 or 30 in. VR ported (new 1993) barrels with multi-chokes and tapered rib, otherwise similar to Model 682 Sporting, cased, 7.6 lbs. Imported 1989-95.

	$2,515	$1,975	$1,425	$1,050	$950	$895	$800

Last Mfg.'s Sug. Retail was $3,017.

Beginning 1993, this model featured a special fully adj. stock and length of pull.

MODEL 686 SPORTING/SPECIAL SPORTING — 12 ga. only, 3 in. chambers, deluxe checkered walnut stock and forearm with over-field dimensions, 28 or 30 (new 1991) in. barrels only, multi-chokes standard. Mfg. 1987-92.

	$1,600	$1,300	$1,050	$925	$875	$775	$695

Last Mfg.'s Sug. Retail was $1,940.

The Model 686 Special Sporting is marked "Model S686 Special", and the barrels are marked "Sporting".

▲ *Model S686 Silver Perdiz/Silver Pigeon Sporting* — 12 or 20 ga., 28 or 30 (12 ga. only) in. VR barrels with multi-chokes, 7.7 lbs. New 1993.

Mfg.'s Sug. Retail	$1,573	$1,250	$925	$700	$575	$525	$460	$415

Until 1994, this model was named the Model 686 Hunter Sport. Between 1994-95, this model was named the S686 Silver Perdiz, and beginning 1996, this model was again renamed to the 686 Silver Pigeon Sporting.

▲ *Model 686 Silver Perdiz Sporting Combo* — includes extra set of 30 in. barrels. Imported 1991-95.

	$2,250	$1,750	$1,300	$1,000	$925	$850	$775

Last Mfg.'s Sug. Retail was $2,687.

MODEL 686 COLLECTION SPORT — 12 ga. only, features multi-colored checkered wood stock and forearm, 28 in. VR barrels, 7.7 lbs. New 1996.

Mfg.'s Sug. Retail	$1,499	$1,225	$900	$695	$575	$525	$460	$415

MODEL 686 ONYX SPORTING — 12 ga. only, 28 or 30 in. vent. barrels with VR, high luster blue finish with gold lettering on receiver sides. Mfg. 1992 only.

	$1,600	$1,300	$1,050	$925	$875	$775	$695

Last Mfg.'s Sug. Retail was $1,940.

▲ *Model 686 Onyx Multi-chokes Sporting* — 12 ga. only, 28 or 30 in. VR barrels with multi-chokes. New 1993.

Mfg.'s Sug. Retail	$1,499	$1,200	$895	$695	$575	$525	$460	$415

▲ *Model 686 English Course* — 12 ga. only, features 28 in. VR barrels and special reverse tapered VR with special sighting plane designed for English courses. Mfg. 1991-92.

	$1,675	$1,350	$1,050	$925	$875	$775	$695

Last Mfg.'s Sug. Retail was $2,015.

MODEL S687 (L) SILVER PERDIZ/SILVER PIGEON SPORTING — 12 or 20 ga. only, deluxe checkered walnut stock and forearm with over-field dimensions, 28 or 30 (12 ga. only) in. barrels, multi-chokes standard. New 1987.

Mfg.'s Sug. Retail	$2,474	$2,075	$1,575	$1,200	$975	$875	$775	$675

Add $1,044 for extra set of 12 ga. barrels (combo. package - new 1991).

▲ *Model 687 English Course* — 12 ga. only, features 28 in. VR barrels and special reverse tapered VR with special sighting plane designed for English courses. Mfg. 1991-92.

	$2,225	$1,750	$1,325	$1,050	$950	$895	$800

Last Mfg.'s Sug. Retail was $2,630.

Grading	100%	98%	95%	90%	80%	70%	60%

MODEL S687 EL GOLD PIGEON SPORTING — 12 ga. only, 28 or 30 in. VR barrels with multi-chokes. New 1993.

Mfg.'s Sug. Retail	$3,489		$2,875	$2,200	$1,500	$1,100	$950	$895	$800

MODEL S687 EELL DIAMOND PIGEON SPORTING — 12 or 20 (disc. 1992) ga. only, deluxe checkered walnut stock and forearm with over-field dimensions, 28 or 30 (new 1995) in. barrels only, multi-chokes standard, cased. New 1987.

Mfg.'s Sug. Retail	$5,098		$4,250	$3,225	$2,500	$2,050	$1,725	$1,500	$1,250

Subtract $143 for 2¾ in. chambers (28 in. barrels only).
Add $875 for extra set of barrels (combo. package - 1990 mfg. only).

MODEL ASE 90 GOLD SPORTING CLAY — 12 ga. only, 28 or 30 in. vent. barrels with VR, similar action and specifications to Model ASE 90 Pigeon, 7.5 lbs., cased. New 1992.

Mfg.'s Sug. Retail	$8,815		$7,650	$6,150	$5,000	$4,050	$3,300	$2,850	$2,500

SHOTGUNS: TRAP O/U, RECENT MFG.

Full descriptions for the models listed below may be found under the corresponding model numbers in the Field Shotguns category.

MODEL S682 GOLD TRAP (GOLD X) — 12 ga. only, competition trap model, silver or Bruniton finish (matte black), 30 or 32 in. barrels with or w/o choke tubes (became standard 1996), adj. trigger, supplied with case, 8.8 lbs. New 1985.

Mfg.'s Sug. Retail	$2,789		$2,150	$1,675	$1,300	$1,175	$950	$895	$800

Subtract 10% without choke tubes.

▲ *Model 682 Mono* — single under-barrel trap model, high post vent. rib, 32 or 34 in. barrel. Imported 1985-1988.

		$1,530	$1,400	$1,200	$1,025	$925	$875	$775

Last Mfg.'s Sug. Retail was $1,890.

▲ *Model S682 Gold Live Bird (Pigeon Trap)* — 12 ga. only, includes features for international style pigeon and competition shooters including international style stock, standard or flat (new 1995) VR, and mid-rib sights, silver (new 1991) or matte black (disc.) metal finish, semi-gloss American walnut stock, light scroll engraving, sliding trigger, includes multi-chokes, cased. New 1990.

Mfg.'s Sug. Retail	$2,789		$2,200	$1,700	$1,325	$1,200	$950	$895	$800

Add $71 for tapered flat rib (disc. 1995).

▲ *Model 682 Gold X Trap Mono (Top Single)* — 12 ga. only, single over-barrel trap model, 32 or 34 in. barrel. Imported 1986-95.

		$2,275	$1,775	$1,325	$1,050	$950	$895	$800

Last Mfg.'s Sug. Retail was $2,734.

Subtract 5% if without multi-chokes.
Multi-chokes became standard in 1989.

▲ *Model 682 Unsingle* — 12 ga. only, single under barrel trap model with 32 in. high post VR, choke tubes. Imported 1992-94.

		$2,225	$1,750	$1,325	$1,050	$950	$895	$800

Last Mfg.'s Sug. Retail was $2,650.

▲ *Model 682 Mono/Top Combo (Gold X)* — 12 ga. only, supplied with mono under or upper single barrel and O/U barrel sets, multi-chokes became standard 1996. Otherwise same specifications as Model 682 Trap. Cased.

Mfg.'s Sug. Retail	$3,689		$2,950	$2,275	$1,850	$1,575	$1,375	$1,200	$1,000

Add $143 for ported barrels (30 in. barrels only, new 1995).
Subtract 5% if without multi-chokes.

MODEL S682 (GOLD X) SUPER TRAP — 12 ga. only, competition trap model, 30 in. barrels, step tapered rib, factory porting, length of pull and separate stock cheekpiece are adjustable, cased. Imported 1991-95.

		$2,300	$1,800	$1,400	$1,075	$950	$895	$800

Last Mfg.'s Sug. Retail was $2,907.

Add $69 for multi-chokes.

Grading	100%	98%	95%	90%	80%	70%	60%

▲ *Model S682 Top Mono Super Trap (Gold X)* — 12 ga. only, single over-barrel trap model, 32 or 34 in. barrel with choice of fixed or multi-chokes. Imported 1991-95.

	$2,485	**$1,850**	**$1,400**	**$1,095**	**$975**	**$900**	**$800**

Last Mfg.'s Sug. Retail was $3,083.

Add $73 for multi-chokes (32 in. barrels only) or 34 in. barrels.

▲ *Model S682 Gold Super Trap Top Combo (Gold X)* — 12 ga. only, supplied with upper single barrel and O/U barrel sets. Otherwise same specifications as Model 682 Super Trap, multi-chokes became standard 1996, cased. Imported 1991-present.

Mfg.'s Sug. Retail	**$4,190**	**$3,400**	**$2,450**	**$1,950**	**$1,650**	**$1,375**	**$1,200**	**$1,000**

Subtract 5% if without multi-chokes.

MODEL 686 INTERNATIONAL — 12 ga. only, 30 in. VR barrels bored IM/F, checkered walnut stock and forearm. Imported 1994 only.

	$1,075	**$800**	**$625**	**$550**	**$500**	**$460**	**$415**

Last Mfg.'s Sug. Retail was $1,300.

MODEL S687 EELL DIAMOND PIGEON (X TRAP) — 12 ga. only, boxlock action with engraved black (new 1992) or silver (disc. 1991) finished side plates, Monte Carlo stock with recoil pad, 30 in. barrels with choke tubes, cased.

Mfg.'s Sug. Retail	**$4,991**	**$4,200**	**$3,275**	**$2,525**	**$2,050**	**$1,725**	**$1,500**	**$1,250**

▲ *Model S687 EELL Diamond Pigeon Trap Top Mono* — 12 ga. only, single over-barrel trap model, 32 or 34 in. barrel. Imported 1988-92, resumed 1996.

Mfg.'s Sug. Retail	**$5,241**	**$4,400**	**$3,400**	**$2,625**	**$2,100**	**$1,750**	**$1,500**	**$1,250**

Add $50 for multi-chokes.

▲ *Model S687 EELL Diamond Pigeon X Bottom Mono Trap Combo* — 12 ga. only, supplied with 30 or 32 in. O/U barrels and a mono trap bottom barrel. Imported 1986-1988, resumed 1994-95.

	$4,250	**$3,300**	**$3,400**	**$3,000**	**$2,775**	**$2,550**	**$2,250**

Last Mfg.'s Sug. Retail was $4,984.

Add $53 for multi-chokes.

▲ *Model S687 EELL Diamond Pigeon X Top Mono Trap Combo* — 12 ga. only, supplied with 30 or 32 in. O/U barrels and a mono trap upper barrel, multi-chokes became standard 1995. New 1988.

Mfg.'s Sug. Retail	**$6,292**	**$5,250**	**$4,125**	**$3,375**	**$2,900**	**$2,500**	**$2,175**	**$1,900**

Subtract 5% if without multi-chokes.

MODEL ASE 90 GOLD TRAP — 12 ga. only, 30 in. vent. barrels with VR, similar action and specifications to Model ASE 90 Pigeon, 8 lbs. 6 oz., cased with extra trigger group, multi-chokes became standard 1995. New 1992.

Mfg.'s Sug. Retail	**$8,815**	**$7,650**	**$6,200**	**$4,950**	**$4,000**	**$3,350**	**$2,850**	**$2,500**

Subtract 5% if without multi-chokes.
Add $1,452 for Trap Combo package.

SHOTGUNS: CUSTOM GRADE O/U, RECENT MFG.

Current high grade Beretta O/U and SxS shotguns are sold only by premium grade franchised Beretta dealers. For a listing of these dealers, contact a Beretta Gallery (see Trademark Index).

SO-2 — 12 ga., 26-30 in. barrels, sidelock, any chokes, vent. rib, auto ejectors, SST, checkered stock in various configurations (field, skeet, or trap), grades differ in wood, engraving, and finish, cased. Mfg. 1948-present.

	$4,900	**$4,200**	**$3,000**	**$2,600**	**$2,200**	**$1,900**	**$1,675**

SO-3 — 2nd grade of the SO series. Disc. 1987.

	$7,850	**$6,800**	**$4,900**	**$4,450**	**$3,875**	**$3,400**	**$2,950**

Last Mfg.'s Sug. Retail was $8,250.

SO-3 EL — grade-up from SO-3 with better wood and engraving. Disc. 1985.

	$8,250	**$6,900**	**$6,000**	**$5,500**	**$4,450**	**$3,900**	**$3,500**

Last Mfg.'s Sug. Retail was $8,100.

Grading	100%	98%	95%	90%	80%	70%	60%

SO-3 EELL — best quality model, custom specifications, choice of engraving motifs. Disc. 1987.

	$8,995	$7,975	$6,700	$5,750	$5,000	$4,500	$3,950

Last Mfg.'s Sug. Retail was $11,625.

Add $1,375/set of O/U barrels.

SO-4 — 12 ga., sidelock, available in field, skeet, or trap configurations, custom specs., fluorescent sights, wide rib, cased. Disc. 1987.

	$8,350	$6,500	$5,900	$5,250	$4,500	$3,850	$3,250

Last Mfg.'s Sug. Retail was $8,700.

Add $2,300 for extra set of O/U barrels.

ASE90 DE LUXE — 12 ga. only, specifications furnished by customer, Competition or Field Model, cased. New 1996.

Mfg.'s Sug. Retail	$15,400	$13,100	$9,750	$8,450	$6,950	$6,000	$5,200	$4,500

SO-5 COMPETITION — best quality O/U, extensively engraved, top quality checkered walnut stock (semi-pistol grip) and forearm, available in either Trap, Skeet, or Sporting configurations, limited importation, cased.

Mfg.'s Sug. Retail	$13,900	$12,200	$9,150	$8,000	$6,750	$5,950	$5,200	$4,500

Add $5,350 for extra set of barrels.
Add $3,500 for Trap Combo set (disc.).

SO-5 EELL — next to top-of-the-line model, available in either Trap, Skeet, or Sporting Clays configuration, custom built to customer dimensions. Importation disc. 1988.

	$12,750	$10,000	$8,500	$7,500	$6,500	$5,500	$4,500

Last Mfg.'s Sug. Retail was $21,750.

SO-6 COMPETITION — 12 ga. only high quality O/U, extensively engraved, top quality checkered walnut stock (semi-pistol grip) and forearm, choice of Trap, Skeet, or Sporting Clays configuration (older mfg. included field models), built to customer specifications, limited importation, cased.

Mfg.'s Sug. Retail	$18,700	$16,800	$12,750	$10,500	$8,250	$7,250	$6,250	$5,500

Add $5,350 for extra set of barrels.

SO-6 EELL — 12 ga., current next to top-of-the-line model, field dimensions, custom built to customer specifications, cased.

Mfg.'s Sug. Retail	$30,000	$27,000	$21,750	$18,000	$14,000	$11,250	$8,750	$6,450

Add $5,350 for extra set of barrels.

SO-9 — 12, 20, 28, or .410 ga., top-of-the-line sidelock model, 1990 was the first time the SO series was offered in smaller gauges, 28 or .410 ga. models have smaller proportionate frames. New 1990.

Mfg.'s Sug. Retail	$35,000	$30,250	$23,750	$18,450	$14,500	$11,500	$8,950	$6,750

Add $5,350 for extra set of barrels.

SHOTGUNS: SxS, DISC.

MODEL 409 PB — 12, 16, 20, or 28 ga., 27, 28, and 30 in. barrels, various chokes, double triggers, plain extractors, checkered pistol grip stock. Mfg. 1934-1964.

	$770	$660	$605	$550	$495	$440	$385

MODEL 410 E — higher quality, auto ejector version of 409PB.

	$880	$770	$715	$660	$605	$550	$495

MODEL 410 — similar to 410 E, except 10 ga. Mag., 32 in. barrel, full choke, heavier construction, mfg. 1934-1981.

	$1,200	$995	$880	$795	$700	$625	$550

MODEL 411 E — similar to 409 PB, with false sideplates and finer finishing. Mfg. 1934-1964.

	$1,210	$1,100	$1,045	$990	$880	$825	$770

Grading	100%	98%	95%	90%	80%	70%	60%

MODEL 424-426 — 12 and 20 ga. (Model 426 only), 26 and 28 in. barrels, various chokes, boxlock, extractors, double triggers, light engraving, checkered straight stock. Add $115 for Model 426.

	$900	$715	$660	$635	$550	$495	$415

MODEL 426 E — similar to 424, with auto ejectors, SST, select wood and more intricate engraving, silver pigeon inlay. Disc. 1983.

	$1,115	$935	$880	$855	$770	$715	$635

MODEL 625 — 12 or 20 ga., 26-30 in. barrels, various chokes, boxlock, extractors, DTs or SST, light engraving, checkered straight stock. Imported 1984-1986.

	$795	$745	$660	$580	$530	$485	$440

Last Mfg.'s Sug. Retail was $835.

Add 15% for SST.

MODEL GR-2 — 12 and 20 ga.'s, 26 and 28 in. barrels, various chokes, boxlock, extractors, double triggers, checkered pistol grip stock. Mfg. 1968-1976.

	$660	$605	$550	$495	$385	$330	$275

MODEL GR-3 — similar to GR-2, with select wood and more engraving. Mfg. 1968-1976.

	$770	$715	$640	$560	$475	$425	$375

MODEL GR-4 — similar to GR-3, with auto ejectors. Mfg. 1968-1976.

	$880	$750	$675	$600	$500	$450	$395

SILVER HAWK — 12 ga. Mag. & 10 ga. Mag. with double triggers and extractors. Disc. 1967.

	$495	$380	$325	$275	$250	$225	$200

Add $100 for 10 ga.

SILVER HAWK FEATHERWEIGHT — 12, 16, 20, or 28 ga., 26-32 in. barrels, high solid rib, various chokes, single or double triggers, checkered pistol grip stock, beavertail forearm. Disc. 1967.

	$495	$440	$415	$385	$360	$330	$275
Single trigger	$550	$495	$440	$415	$385	$360	$330

SO-6 DOUBLE BARREL — same general specifications and embellishments as the SO series O/U guns, but SxS. Mfg. 1948-1982.

	$5,900	$5,500	$5,280	$5,060	$4,840	$4,400	$3,850

SO-7 DOUBLE BARREL — top of the line SxS, finest quality wood, more elaborate engraving. Disc.

	$8,250	$7,700	$7,150	$6,600	$6,050	$5,500	$4,620

SHOTGUNS: SxS, RECENT MFG.

MODEL 626 FIELD — 12 or 20 (disc. 1987) ga., 2$\frac{3}{4}$ in. chambers, 26 and 28 in. barrels, various chokes, boxlock, ejectors, single trigger, moderate engraving, pistol grip or straight checkered stock. Imported 1984-1988.

	$895	$800	$740	$685	$595	$540	$490

Last Mfg.'s Sug. Retail was $995.

MODEL 626 ONYX — 12 or 20 ga., 3 in. chambers, 26 or 28 (new 1990) in. VR barrels with multi-chokes, matte finished metal parts, select checkered walnut stock and forearm. Imported 1988-1993.

	$1,425	$1,125	$850	$750	$685	$595	$540

Last Mfg.'s Sug. Retail was $1,870.

▲ *Model 626 Onyx Magnum* — 12 ga. only, 3$\frac{1}{2}$ in. chambers. Mfg. 1990-92.

	$1,425	$1,175	$900	$800	$700	$600	$550

Last Mfg.'s Sug. Retail was $1,870.

Grading	100%	98%	95%	90%	80%	70%	60%

MODEL 627 EL FIELD — 12 and 20 (disc. 1987) ga., $2\frac{3}{4}$ (disc. 1990) or 3 in. (became standard in 1991) chambers, 26 and 28 in. barrels, various chokes, boxlock, ejectors, single trigger, extensive engraving, pistol grip or straight checkered stock, cased. Imported 1985-1993.

	$2,725	$2,150	$1,775	$1,500	$1,350	$1,150	$1,000

Last Mfg.'s Sug. Retail was $3,270.

Subtract 5% for fixed chokes and $2\frac{3}{4}$ in. chambers.

▲ **Model 627 EL Sport** — similar to Model 627 EL Field, except 12 ga. only, knurled rib, sporting clays dimensions. Importation disc. 1988.

	$2,725	$2,150	$1,775	$1,500	$1,350	$1,150	$1,000

Last Mfg.'s Sug. Retail was $1,995.

MODEL 627 EELL — 12 or 20 (disc. 1987) ga., $2\frac{3}{4}$ (disc.) or 3 (12 ga. only) in. chambers, 26 or 28 in. barrels, various chokes, boxlock, ejectors, single trigger, elaborate engraving, pistol grip or straight English checkered stock, cased. Imported 1985-1993.

	$4,600	$3,850	$3,300	$2,850	$2,500	$2,175	$1,900

Last Mfg.'s Sug. Retail was $5,405.

Subtract 5% if fixed chokes only.
Multi-chokes became standard in 1991.

SHOTGUNS: SxS, CUSTOM GRADE

Current high grade Beretta O/U and SxS shotguns are sold only by premium grade franchised Beretta dealers. For a listing of these dealers, contact a Beretta Gallery (see Trademark Index).

MODEL 451 SERIES — 12 ga., totally hand-made, sidelock action, ejectors, scroll engraving. Custom made to order with fitted luggage case, various grades have increasing embellishments in EL Models.

▲ **Model 451** — disc. 1987.

	$6,000	$5,200	$4,875	$4,600	$4,300	$3,995	$3,600

Last Mfg.'s Sug. Retail was $12,375.

▲ **Model 451 E** — 12 ga. only, double triggers, specifications furnished by individual customer. Imported 1989 only.

	$14,650	$10,950	$9,750	$8,500	$7,800	$6,750	$5,800

Last Mfg.'s Sug. Retail was $20,467.

Add $4,000 for extra set of barrels.
Add $750 for SST.

▲ **Model 451 EL** — disc. 1984.

	$6,450	$5,400	$4,875	$4,600	$4,300	$4,000	$3,600

▲ **Model 451 EELL** — previous top-of-the-line model, choice of engraving motifs per customer specifications. Disc. 1987, reintroduced 1989 only.

	$17,500	$12,950	$11,000	$8,500	$7,800	$6,750	$5,950

Last Mfg.'s Sug. Retail in 1989 was $24,367.
Last Mfg.'s Sug. Retail in 1987 was $14,925.

MODEL 452 — 12 ga. only, next to top-of-the-line side-by side shotgun featuring H&H style detachable locks, cased. New 1990.

Mfg.'s Sug. Retail	$24,500		$21,750	$17,750	$14,000	$10,500	$8,750	$6,650	$5,500

Add $5,500 for extra set of barrels.

▲ **Model 452 EELL** — 12 ga. only, top-of-the-line custom sidelock model featuring every refinement, cased. Importation began 1992.

Mfg.'s Sug. Retail	$35,000		$30,750	$24,500	$18,750	$14,750	$11,500	$8,950	$6,750

Add $5,500 for extra set of barrels.

Grading	100%	98%	95%	90%	80%	70%	60%

SHOTGUNS: SINGLE BARREL, DISC.

MARK II TRAP — 12 ga., 32 or 34 in. wide vent. rib, full choke, boxlock with auto ejector, Monte Carlo stock, recoil pad. Mfg. 1972-1976.

	$550	$450	$400	$360	$330	$295	$260

MODEL FS-1 SINGLE BARREL — 12, 16, 20, 28, or .410 ga., 26 or 28 in. barrels, full choke, checkered semi-pistol grip, under lever break open, folds to length of barrel (also known as Companion).

	$175	$150	$125	$110	$100	$90	$80

TR-1 TRAP — 12 ga., 32 in. full choke barrel, under lever break open, Monte Carlo pistol grip stock with pad, engraved. Mfg. 1968-1971.

	$275	$250	$220	$195	$140	$110	$100

TR-2 TRAP — similar to TR-1, with high rib, mfg. 1969-1973.

	$290	$260	$230	$205	$150	$120	$110

MODEL 412 — 12, 20, 28, or .410 ga., monobloc construction, folding action, sling swivels, checkered walnut stock and forearm, 5 lbs. Importation disc. 1988.

	$190	$170	$125	$100	$85	$70	$60

Last Mfg.'s Sug. Retail was $215.

SHOTGUNS: SLIDE ACTION, DISC.

MODEL SL-2 — 12 ga., 26, 28, or 30 in. barrels, various chokes, vent. rib, checkered pistol grip stock. Mfg. 1968-1971.

	$300	$275	$250	$220	$195	$165	$140

SILVER PIGEON — 12 ga., various chokes, light engraving.

	$250	$200	$175	$160	$150	$140	$130

GOLD PIGEON — 12 ga., various chokes, vent. rib, engraved. Add $200 for deluxe models.

	$475	$375	$310	$275	$240	$215	$195

RUBY PIGEON — 12 ga., various chokes, vent. rib, elaborately engraved, special deluxe walnut.

	$600	$475	$395	$350	$295	$260	$230

SHOTGUNS: SEMI-AUTO, DISC.

SILVER LARK — 12 ga., various chokes.

	$295	$260	$240	$220	$200	$185	$170

GOLD LARK — 12 ga., vent. rib, light scroll engraving, select walnut.

	$480	$400	$325	$260	$230	$210	$195

RUBY LARK — 12 ga., vent. rib, heavy engraving, deluxe walnut.

	$675	$550	$475	$395	$350	$295	$260

MODEL AL-1 — 12 and 20 ga., semi-auto gas operated, 26, 28, and 30 in. plain barrel, various chokes, checkered pistol grip stock. Mfg. 1971-1973.

	$385	$360	$330	$305	$250	$195	$165

MODEL AL-2 — 12 or 20 ga., 26, 28, or 30 in. barrels, vent. rib, various chokes, gas operated, checkered pistol grip stock. Mfg. 1973-1975.

	$330	$305	$275	$250	$220	$195	$165

MODEL AL-2 SKEET — similar to AL-2, with 26 in. wide rib skeet bored barrel, mfg. 1973-1975.

	$395	$360	$320	$275	$220	$200	$185

Grading	100%	98%	95%	90%	80%	70%	60%

MODEL AL-2 TRAP — similar to AL-2, with 30 in. full choke barrel, wide rib, Monte Carlo stock, with recoil pad. Mfg. 1973-1975.

	$375	$345	$315	$285	$250	$195	$165

MODEL AL-2 MAGNUM — 12 ga., 28 and 30 in. mod. or full choke, 3 in. chambers. Mfg. 1973-1975.

	$415	$385	$330	$275	$250	$230	$210

MODEL AL-3 — continuation of the AL-2 series. Mfg. 1975-1976.

	100%	98%	95%	90%	80%	70%	60%
Field grade	$395	$360	$330	$260	$240	$220	$190
Magnum grade	$425	$385	$330	$275	$250	$230	$210
Skeet grade	$400	$360	$330	$260	$240	$220	$190
Trap grade	$385	$350	$295	$250	$225	$210	$185

MODEL AL-3 DELUXE TRAP — similar to AL-3, with fully engraved receiver, premium grade wood. Mfg. 1975-1976.

	$770	$715	$660	$605	$550	$495	$440

SHOTGUNS: SEMI-AUTO, RECENT MFG.

It is possible on some of the models listed below to have production variances occur including different engraving motifs, stock configurations and specifications, finishes, etc. These have occurred when Beretta has changed from production of one model to another. Also, some European and English distributors have sold their excess inventory through Beretta U.S.A., creating additional variations/configurations that are not normally imported domestically. While sometimes rare, these specimens typically do not command premiums over Beretta's domestic models.

BERETTA CHOKES AND THEIR CODES (ON REAR LEFT-SIDE OF BARREL)

* designates full choke (F).

** designates improved modified choke (IM).

*** designates modified choke (M).

**** designates improved cylinder choke (IC).

FK designates skeet (SK).

***** designates cylinder bore (CYL).

MODEL 1200 FIELD — 12 ga., inertia recoil system, 28 in. VR barrels with multi-chokes, checkered European walnut stock and forearm (pre-1989), matte black polymer stock and forearm (starting 1989), recoil pad, 4 shot mag., approx. 8 lbs. Imported 1984-1989.

	$475	$415	$350	$295	$250	$225	$200

Last Mfg.'s Sug. Retail was $580.

▲ *Model 1200 Riot* — 12 ga. only, 2¾ or 3 in. chamber, 20 in. cyl. bore barrel with iron sights, extended mag. Imported 1989-90 only.

	$525	$425	$350	$295	$250	$225	$200

Last Mfg.'s Sug. Retail was $660.

MODEL 1201 FIELD MAGNUM — 12 ga., 3 in. chamber, 24, 26, or 28 in. VR barrel with multi-chokes (2), matte black polymer stock and forearm. Imported 1989-94.

	$500	$395	$340	$285	$250	$225	$200

Last Mfg.'s Sug. Retail was $625.

The Model 1201 can be differentiated from the Model 1200 by stock spacers to adjust length.

▲ *Model 1201 FP Riot* — 12 ga., riot configuration featuring 20 in. cylinder bore barrel, adj. rifle sights, matte finish. New 1991.

Mfg.'s Sug. Retail	$715	$565	$445	$360	$295	$250	$225	$200

Add $45 for pistol grip configuration (Model 1201 FPG3 - mfg. 1994 only).

Grading	100%	98%	95%	90%	80%	70%	60%

B

MODEL 300/301 — continuation of the AL-3 series, scroll engraved receiver. Mfg. 1977-1982.

	100%	98%	95%	90%	80%	70%	60%
Field grade	$395	$360	$330	$260	$240	$220	$190
Magnum grade	$425	$385	$330	$275	$250	$230	$210
Skeet grade	$400	$360	$330	$260	$240	$220	$190
Trap grade	$385	$350	$295	$250	$225	$210	$185

Beretta changed model nomenclature rapidly during the Model 300 Series. In approx. 10 months, the evolution of this model had progressed from the 300 to 303 Series. Beginning with the Model 303, all receivers were milled with a 3 in. ejection port window.

MODEL 301 SLUG GUN — 22 in. barrel, with sights. Disc.

	100%	98%	95%	90%	80%	70%	60%
	$395	$360	$330	$305	$265	$230	$190

MODEL 302 — 12 or 20 ga., self-compensating gas operation semi-auto, designed for both 2¾ and 3 in. shells, available with interchangeable chokes, slug barrel, trap and skeet models (disc.), VR, mag. cut-off. Mfg. 1982-1987. This model was superceded by the Model 303.

	100%	98%	95%	90%	80%	70%	60%
	$395	$365	$340	$310	$280	$255	$225

Last Mfg.'s Sug. Retail was $480.

Add $30 for multi-choke set.

▲ *Model 302 Super Lusso* — same specifications as Model A302, but includes hand engraved receiver, many gold plated parts, and stock and forearm made from presentation grade walnut. Disc. 1986.

	100%	98%	95%	90%	80%	70%	60%
	$2,150	$1,950	$1,750	$1,550	$1,300	$1,050	$895

Last Mfg.'s Sug. Retail was $2,500.

MODEL A-303 FIELD — 12 (disc. 1993) or 20 ga., 2¾ or 3 in. chambers, same gas operation as the Model 302, 26 or 28 in. VR barrel, high-strength alloy receiver, select wood with choice pistol grip or straight English stock, beavertail forearm, multi-chokes became standard 1987.

	100%	98%	95%	90%	80%	70%	60%
Mfg.'s Sug. Retail $799	$655	$465	$380	$335	$300	$270	$240

Subtract 10% without multi-chokes.
Subtract $20 for straight grip English stock.

▲ *A-303 Upland* — 12 (disc. 1993) or 20 ga., 2¾ or 3 in. chamber, 24 in. VR barrel with multi-chokes, English style straight stock, approx. 7 lbs. Importation began 1989.

	100%	98%	95%	90%	80%	70%	60%
Mfg.'s Sug. Retail $772	$640	$465	$380	$335	$300	$270	$240

▲ *A-303 Waterfowl/Turkey* — 12 ga. only, 3 in. chamber, choice of 24, 26, 28, or 30 in. VR barrel, matte finished wood and metal, multi-chokes are standard. Imported 1991 only.

	100%	98%	95%	90%	80%	70%	60%
	$540	$450	$395	$350	$300	$270	$240

Last Mfg.'s Sug. Retail was $665.

▲ *A-303 Sporting* — 12 (disc. 1994) or 20 (new 1991) ga. only, 2¾ in. chambers, sporting clay dimensions, 28 or 30 (12 ga. only) in. VR barrel with multi-chokes. New 1988.

	100%	98%	95%	90%	80%	70%	60%
Mfg.'s Sug. Retail $822	$685	$510	$445	$375	$325	$300	$275

▲ *A-303 Skeet* — 12 (disc. 1994) or 20 ga., 26 in. VR barrel with fixed skeet choking. Importation disc. 1995.

	100%	98%	95%	90%	80%	70%	60%
	$615	$440	$375	$335	$300	$270	$240

Last Mfg.'s Sug. Retail was $736.

▲ *A-303 Super Skeet* — 12 ga. only, 28 in. VR fixed choke barrel, features factory porting, adj. length of pull, and adj. separate cheekpiece on stock. Mfg. 1991-92.

	100%	98%	95%	90%	80%	70%	60%
	$975	$750	$625	$500	$425	$365	$300

Last Mfg.'s Sug. Retail was $1,160.

▲ *A-303 Trap* — 12 ga. only, 30 or 32 in. VR barrel with fixed choking or multi-chokes. Importation disc. 1994.

	100%	98%	95%	90%	80%	70%	60%
	$615	$425	$360	$325	$280	$250	$220

Last Mfg.'s Sug. Retail was $735.

Add $40 for multi-chokes (with Monte Carlo stock).

▲ *A-303 Super Trap* — 12 ga. only, 30 or 32 in. VR multi-choke barrel with step tapered rib, features factory porting, adj. length of pull, and adj. separate cheekpiece on stock. Mfg. 1991-92.

	100%	98%	95%	90%	80%	70%	60%
	$1,025	$775	$625	$500	$425	$365	$300

Last Mfg.'s Sug. Retail was $1,210.

Grading	100%	98%	95%	90%	80%	70%	60%

▲ *A-303 Slug* — 12 or 20 ga., 3 in. chamber (12 ga. only), 22 in. cylinder bore barrel, iron sights. Importation disc. 1991.

		$540	$425	$360	$325	$295	$265	$240

Last Mfg.'s Sug. Retail was $665.

▲ *A-303 Youth* — 20 ga. only, 2¾ or 3 (disc.) in. chamber, 24 in. VR barrel with multi-chokes, shortened stock, approx. 6 lbs. New 1988.

Mfg.'s Sug. Retail	$772	$640	$450	$375	$330	$300	$270	$240

MODEL A390 FIELD SILVER MALLARD — 12 ga. only, 3 in. chamber, features new gas system that will accept all 2¾ and 3 in. shotshells, single stainless steel piston with self regulating valve, mag. cut-off on left side of receiver, 22 slug (new 1994), 24, 26, 28, or 30 in. VR barrel with Mobilchoke system, standard field or matte finish (includes sling swivels) on lightly engraved receiver, adj. checkered walnut stock, gold trigger, approx. 7 lbs. New 1992.

Mfg.'s Sug. Retail	$822	$685	$495	$400	$350	$300	$270	$240

▲ *Model A390 Silver Mallard Synthetic* — 12 ga. only, 3 in. chamber, 24, 26, 28, or 30 in. barrel with multi-choke, black synthetic stock and forearm with sling swivels, matte finish, approx. 7.6 lbs. New 1996.

Mfg.'s Sug. Retail	$822	$695	$495	$395	$350	$300	$270	$240

▲ *Model A390 Silver Mallard Slug* — 12 ga. only, 3 in. chamber, 22 in. rifle barrel, gloss wood finish, adj. rear sight, approx. 7.4 lbs. New 1995.

Mfg.'s Sug. Retail	$822	$695	$495	$395	$350	$300	$270	$240

▲ *Model A390 Field Deluxe Gold Mallard* — similar to Model 390 Field, except has gold accents on receiver frame, including a gold filled snipe, setter, and P. Beretta signature, deluxe walnut. New 1993.

Mfg.'s Sug. Retail	$987	$825	$565	$450	$400	$360	$320	$285

▲ *Model A390 Sport Trap* — 12 ga. only, 3 in. chamber, 30 or 32 in. VR barrel, matte finish on wood and metal, black rubber recoil pad, 8¼ lbs. Importation began 1995.

Mfg.'s Sug. Retail	$851	$710	$500	$400	$360	$300	$270	$240

    Add $14 for multi-choke barrel (30 in. only)
    Add $100 for ported barrel.

▲ *Model A390 Sport Super Trap* — 12 ga. only, 30 or 32 in. VR multi-choke ported barrels, adj. stock comb and length of pull. New 1993.

Mfg.'s Sug. Retail	$1,258	$1,025	$800	$600	$550	$495	$460	$425

▲ *Model A390 Sport Skeet* — 12 ga. only, 3 in. chamber, 26 or 28 in. SK bored VR barrel, matte finish on wood and metal, black rubber recoil pad, 8 lbs. Importation began 1995.

Mfg.'s Sug. Retail	$849	$710	$500	$400	$350	$300	$270	$240

    Add $100 for ported barrel (28 in. only).

▲ *Model A390 Sport Super Skeet* — 12 ga. only, 28 in. skeet choke VR ported barrels, includes adj. stock comb and length of pull. New 1993.

Mfg.'s Sug. Retail	$1,199	$995	$775	$575	$525	$475	$440	$400

▲ *Model A390 Sporting* — 12 ga. only, 3 in. chamber, designed for sporting clays competition, similar to Model 390 Sport Skeet, 28 or 30 in. VR ported or unported barrel with choke tube, 8 lbs. Importation began 1995.

Mfg.'s Sug. Retail	$865	$730	$515	$400	$350	$300	$270	$240

    Add $86 for ported barrel.

MODEL PINTAIL (VICTORIA) — 12 ga., 3 in. chamber, uses Montefeltro short action, 24 or 26 in. VR barrel, matte finish, includes sling swivels, 7.3 lbs. New 1993.

Mfg.'s Sug. Retail	$743	$625	$440	$375	$325	$280	$250	$230

▲ *Vittoria Slug (Pintail)* — 12 ga. only, 24 in. slug barrel, includes rifle sights and rifle choke tubes, 7 lbs. Imported 1993-95.

		$595	$425	$360	$325	$280	$250	$230

Last Mfg.'s Sug. Retail was $700.

Grading	100%	98%	95%	90%	80%	70%	60%

COMMEMORATIVES

MODEL A-303 DUCKS UNLIMITED — 12 or 20 ga., D.U. serialization, 5,500 mfg. in 12 ga. 1986-87, 3,500 mfg. in 20 ga. 1987-88.

	100%	98%	95%
12 ga.	$575	$450	$350
20 ga.	$675	$475	$375

> These D.U. Models had no retail pricing from Beretta. Rather, they were auctioned off at D.U. dinners, and as a result, prices could vary substantially from region to region.

MODEL 687 O/U SHOTGUN TERCENTENNIAL — 12 ga., comes with S.S.T. and ejectors. Limited production, only 300 manufactured.

$2,500 $1,950 $1,400

MODEL 84 PISTOL TERCENTENNIAL — commemorative, only 300 manufactured. Fully engraved with gold inlays. Presentation case. Only 100 imported to U.S.

$1,450 $1,100 $850

BERGMANN

Manufacturer located in Gaggenau, Germany 1892-1944. Re-established in 1931 under Bergmann Erben.

100%	98%	95%	90%	80%	70%	60%	50%	40%	30%	20%	10%

SEMI-AUTO

> Prices established are for original guns with matching parts.

MODEL 1894 (ANTIQUE) — 8mm "Bergmann Schmeisser" cal. Extremely rare.

100%	98%	95%	90%	80%	70%	60%	50%	40%	30%	20%	10%
$24,500	$20,000	$18,500	$16,000	$12,000	$8,000	$7,500	$7,000	$6,500	$6,000	$5,500	$5,000

MODEL 1896-NO. 2 — 5mm, smaller type frame.

100%	98%	95%	90%	80%	70%	60%	50%	40%	30%	20%	10%
$2,250	$1,850	$1,600	$1,300	$1,100	$895	$715	$660	$610	$565	$515	$450

MODEL 1896-NO. 3 — 6.5mm - 80mm barrel.

100%	98%	95%	90%	80%	70%	60%	50%	40%	30%	20%	10%
$3,250	$2,750	$2,250	$1,800	$1,450	$925	$750	$700	$665	$630	$600	$565

MODEL 1896-NO. 4 — 8mm, military contract. Rarely seen.

100%	98%	95%	90%	80%	70%	60%	50%	40%	30%	20%	10%
$4,950	$4,250	$3,500	$3,000	$2,200	$1,500	$900	$725	$665	$630	$600	$565

MODEL 1897-NO. 5 — 7.8mm, commercial manufacture. May be fit with shoulder stock.

100%	98%	95%	90%	80%	70%	60%	50%	40%	30%	20%	10%
$5,500	$4,500	$3,500	$3,000	$2,200	$1,500	$925	$750	$700	$665	$630	$600

> Add 200% for long barrel carbine version.
> Add 100% if fit with shoulder stock.

MODEL 2 — .25 cal., small frame. Add $100 for Model 2A.

100%	98%	95%	90%	80%	70%	60%	50%	40%	30%	20%	10%
$300	$285	$260	$240	$215	$180	$160	$135	$115	$95	$80	$65

MODEL 3 — .25 cal., small frame. Add $100 for Model 3A.

100%	98%	95%	90%	80%	70%	60%	50%	40%	30%	20%	10%
$300	$285	$260	$240	$215	$180	$160	$135	$115	$95	$80	$65

ERBEN — Models I, II, and Special, .25 Cal. except Special .32 Cal.

100%	98%	95%	90%	80%	70%	60%	50%	40%	30%	20%	10%
$335	$300	$285	$260	$240	$215	$180	$160	$135	$115	$95	$80

BERGMANN-BAYARD PISTOLS

Even though the below listed Bergmann-Bayard models were manufactured only by Anciens Etablissements Pieper of Herstal, Belgium, these pistols are listed under this heading as they are most commonly referred to by this trademark designation.

100%	98%	95%	90%	80%	70%	60%	50%	40%	30%	20%	10%

MODEL 1908 STANDARD COMMERCIAL — 9mm Bergmann/Bayard, identified by a mounted knight on the left magazine housing and is without finger cuts at base of magazine housing.

| $1,850 | $1,350 | $1,000 | $750 | $600 | $500 | $400 | $360 | $335 | $310 | $285 | $260 |

Add 25% if backstrap is slotted for shoulder stock.
Add $3,000 for excellent original leather/wood shoulder stock.

MODEL 1908 SPANISH CONTRACT — 9mm Bergmann/Bayard, total contract was for 3,000 pistols, can be identified from standard commercial pistols by the Spanish military acceptance stamp struck on the receiver.

| $1,450 | $1,100 | $900 | $750 | $600 | $450 | $400 | $360 | $335 | $310 | $285 | $260 |

MODEL 1910 STANDARD COMMERCIAL — 9mm Bergmann/Bayard, mechanically similar to Model 1908 Standard Commercial except has finger cuts in bottom of magazine housing, circular grooves are present on each side of magazine base.

| $1,250 | $1,000 | $700 | $600 | $500 | $400 | $350 | $315 | $280 | $265 | $245 | $225 |

MODEL 1910 DANISH GOVERNMENT CONTRACT — 9mm Bergmann/Bayard, Trolit grips were used for the original conversion, followed later by wood replacements, total contract was for 4,840 pistols with delivery mfg. 1911-1914. This variation can be identified from the usual commercial pistols by the Danish proof mark on the left receiver side and Danish inventory number on right side of receiver.

| $1,350 | $1,100 | $900 | $750 | $600 | $450 | $400 | $360 | $335 | $310 | $285 | $260 |

Deduct 20% if converted and overstamped M.1910/21.

MODEL 1910/21 TOJHUS — 9mm Bergmann/Bayard, these pistols are marked "Haerens Tojhus" and are numbered from 1-900, original grips were black Trolit, replacement grips are either all smooth or with checkered circles above and below grip screw.

| $1,650 | $1,300 | $1,000 | $750 | $600 | $500 | $400 | $360 | $335 | $310 | $285 | $260 |

This contract was manufactured by the Danish Royal Arsenal located in Copenhagen.

MODEL 1910/21 RUSTKAMMER — 9mm Bergmann/Bayard, pistols are marked "Haerens Rustkammer", and numbered 901-2204, grip replacements are the same as noted for Haerens Tojhus.

| $1,500 | $1,200 | $900 | $750 | $600 | $450 | $400 | $360 | $335 | $310 | $285 | $260 |

This contract was manufactured by the Danish Royal Arsenal located in Copenhagen.

BERNARDELLI, VINCENZO

Manufactured since 1721 in Brescia, Italy. Currently imported and distributed by Armsport, Inc. located in Miami, FL. Previously imported and distributed by Magnum Research, Inc. located in Minneapolis, MN (1989-92), Quality Arms, Inc. located in Houston, TX, Armes De Chasse located in Chadds Ford, PA, Stoeger located in New York, NY, and Action Arms, Ltd. located in Philadelphia, PA.

There is some confusion on the Bernardelli trademark as there have been three different companies (Pietro Bernardelli, Vincenzo Bernardelli, and Santini Bernardelli) that have produced firearms. During the late 1980s, there were quite a lot of Pietro Bernardellis that were "dumped" in the American marketplace - these guns do not have the quality of Vincenzo Bernardelli and are not covered within the scope of this text. The only company that is currently manufacturing firearms is Vincenzo Bernardelli - only models from this company will be listed within this section.

Grading	100%	98%	95%	90%	80%	70%	60%

B

COMBINATION GUNS

MODEL 190 — combination rifle/shotgun chambered for 12, 16, or 20 ga. under .243, .30-06, or .308 cal., boxlock action, DTs, extractors. Imported 1989 only.

			$1,295	$1,025	$895	$800	$700	$600	$525

Last Mfg.'s Sug. Retail was $1,393.

Add $700 for extra set of 12 ga. O/U barrels.

MODEL COMB 2000 — 12, 16, or 20 ga. under choice of rifle cals., ejectors, set trigger. Importation began 1990.

Mfg.'s Sug. Retail $2,075 | $1,795 | $1,450 | $1,075 | $875 | $750 | $675 | $575

Add $621 for extra set of O/U shotgun barrels (Model COMB 2000S - disc.).

MODEL 120 — 12 ga. over choice of 12 cals., deluxe checkered walnut stock and forearm, iron sights, double triggers, vent. recoil pad, coin washed receiver with light engraving.

$1,950 | $1,585 | $1,300 | $1,050 | $850 | $760 | $650

Last Mfg.'s Sug. Retail was $2,411.

Add $130 for extra set of shotgun barrels.

PISTOLS: SEMI-AUTO, DISC.

VEST POCKET MODEL — .25 ACP cal., 2⅛ in. barrel, fixed sights, blue, bakelite grips. Mfg. 1945-1948.

$250 | $195 | $165 | $140 | $110 | $90 | $65

BABY SEMI-AUTO — .22 S or L, 2⅛ in. barrel, fixed sights, blue, bakelite grips. Mfg. 1949-1968.

$250 | $175 | $150 | $130 | $100 | $90 | $80

SPORTER MODEL — .22 LR, 6, 8, or 10 in. barrels, target sights, blue, wood grips. Mfg. 1949-1968.

$305 | $275 | $220 | $165 | $140 | $110 | $85

MODEL 60 — .22 LR, .32 ACP, or .380 ACP cal., 3½ in. barrel, fixed sights, blue, bakelite grips. Mfg. 1959-present.

$220 | $195 | $180 | $165 | $155 | $135 | $120

This model is not imported domestically.

MODEL 68 — .22 Short or .22 LR cal., vest pocket model, 6 shot, bakelite grips, 8½ oz. Current mfg.

$140 | $120 | $110 | $100 | $90 | $80 | $70

This model is not imported domestically.

PISTOLS: SEMI-AUTO, RECENT MFG.

MODEL 80 — .22 LR or .380 ACP cal., 3½ in. barrel, adj. sights, blue, thumbrest plastic grips. Imported 1968-1988.

$185 | $160 | $150 | $140 | $130 | $115 | $100

Add $5 for .380 ACP.

Note: This model was produced to conform to import regulations of GCA 1968. Importation of this model was disc. 1988.

MODEL USA — .22 LR, .32 ACP (disc.), or .380 ACP. cal., semi-auto, single action, steel frame, loaded chamber indicator, adj. sights, target bakelite grips, 7 shot (.380 ACP) or 10 shot (.22 LR) mag.

Mfg.'s Sug. Retail $425 | $380 | $295 | $250 | $215 | $185 | $165 | $145

Add $60 for chrome finish.

This model has the same technical specifications as the Model 60.

MODEL AMR — .22 LR, .32 ACP (disc.), or .380 ACP cal., similar action to USA Model except has 6 in. barrel and adj. rear sight. Disc. 1994.

$395 | $325 | $275 | $225 | $185 | $165 | $145

Last Mfg.'s Sug. Retail was $445.

Grading	100%	98%	95%	90%	80%	70%	60%

MODEL 90 SPORT TARGET — similar to Model 80, only .32 ACP or .22 LR, with 6 in. barrel. Imported 1968-1988.

| | $210 | $185 | $170 | $155 | $140 | $120 | $110 |

Last Mfg.'s Sug. Retail was $245.

MODEL 69 TARGET — .22 LR, target semi-auto, single action, 5.9 in. heavy barrel, 10 shot mag., wraparound checkered wooden grips, 38 oz.

| | $575 | $475 | $400 | $350 | $275 | $225 | $185 |

Last Mfg.'s Sug. Retail was $660.

This model was previously designated Model 100.

MODEL 100 TARGET — .22 LR, 5.9 in. barrel, adj. sight, blue, checkered wood, thumbrest grips, cased. Imported 1968-1988.

| | $395 | $325 | $295 | $260 | $225 | $190 | $175 |

Last Mfg.'s Sug. Retail was $360.

P-ONE — 9mm Para. or .40 S&W cal., double action, 10 shot mag., choice of matte black or chrome finish. Importation began 1993.

| Mfg.'s Sug. Retail | $580 | $515 | $460 | $400 | $360 | $330 | $295 | $265 |

Add $60 for chrome finish.

MODEL P010 TARGET — .22 LR, single action, 5.9 in. barrel, adj. sights and trigger, matte black finish, large anatomic walnut stippled grips with thumbrest, 10 shot mag., 40.5 oz. Imported 1989-92, re-introduced 1995.

| Mfg.'s Sug. Retail | $825 | $725 | $625 | $525 | $450 | $395 | $350 | $300 |

Add $150 for wooden case and two sets of weights.

MODEL P018 — 7.65mm (disc. 1988), .380 ACP (mfg. 1993-94), or 9mm Para., double action, semi-auto, steel construction, 4⅞ in. barrel, 10 (C/B 1994) or 16* shot mag., black plastic (standard) or walnut checkered (disc. 1992) grips, blue (disc.), black (new 1994), or chrome finish, 36 oz. Imported 1985-present.

| Mfg.'s Sug. Retail | $560 | $485 | $400 | $350 | $300 | $275 | $250 | $230 |

Add $40 for walnut grips (disc. 1992).
Add $60 for chrome finish.
Add $30 for carrying case w/combination lock (disc. 1989).

This model was extensively redesigned in 1989 and includes a "cocked and locked" feature, thumb mag. release, loaded chamber indicator, as well as other improvements.

▲ *P018 Compact* — .380 ACP or 9mm Para., similar to Model P018 except has 4 in. barrel and 10 (C/B 1994) or 14* shot mag., approx. 2 lbs. New 1989.

| Mfg.'s Sug. Retail | $610 | $545 | $430 | $375 | $310 | $275 | $250 | $230 |

Add $55 for chrome finish.

This model was also redesigned in 1989 to incorporate the same features as the Model P018.

PRACTICAL VB — 9x21mm cal., comp. gun built for IPSC competition, various configurations, black or matte chrome finish, 2, 4, or 6 port compensating system. Introduced 1993.

| Mfg.'s Sug. Retail | $1,595 | $1,395 | $1,100 | $925 | $775 | $675 | $575 | $475 |

Add $40 for 4 port compensator.
Add $65 for chrome finish.

▲ *Practical VB Customized* — state-of-the-art competition pistol featuring 4+2 port compensating system. Introduced 1993.

| Mfg.'s Sug. Retail | $2,450 | $2,025 | $1,675 | $1,325 | $1,100 | $975 | $850 | $725 |

Add $100 for chrome finish.

Grading	100%	98%	95%	90%	80%	70%	60%

DOUBLE RIFLES

EXPRESS VB — various cals., side-by-side sidelock action, ejectors, single or double triggers. Importation began 1990.

Mfg.'s Sug. Retail	$5,275	$4,675	$3,750	$3,250	$2,725	$2,275	$1,900	$1,600

Add $145 for Deluxe Model (double triggers).

EXPRESS 2000 — .30-06, 7x65R, 8x57JRS, or 9.3x74R cal., O/U boxlock design, single or double trigger, extractors, checkered walnut stock and forearm. Importation began 1994.

Mfg.'s Sug. Retail	$2,600	$2,175	$1,775	$1,550	$1,275	$1,100	$975	$875

Add $130 for single trigger.

MINERVA EXPRESS — various cals., exposed hammers, extractors, double triggers, moderate engraving. Importation began 1995.

Mfg.'s Sug. Retail	$5,850	$4,975	$3,850	$3,250	$2,725	$2,275	$1,900	$1,600

RIFLES: SEMI-AUTO

CARBINA .22 — .22 LR, blow back action. Importation began 1990.

Mfg.'s Sug. Retail	$595	$495	$350	$285	$210	$170	$150	$135

SHOTGUNS: SIDE-BY-SIDE, DISC.

MODEL 110 — 12 ga., trap or skeet model, separated barrels, high post rib.

	$2,000	$1,500	$1,300	$1,100	$1,000	$900	$800

MODEL 110 EXTRA — similar to Model 110, except engraved.

	$3,021	$2,265	$1,970	$1,665	$1,510	$1,360	$1,210

S. UBERTO 1 GAMECOCK — 12, 16, 20, or 28 ga., 25¾ in. imp. cyl. and mod., 27½ in. full and mod., hammerless, boxlock, extractors, two triggers, English style stock, checkered.

	$853	$635	$605	$550	$495	$440	$415

Add 20% for ejectors.

SHOTGUNS: SIDE-BY-SIDE, CURRENT MFG.

Bernardelli side-by-side shotguns are manufactured with straight grip, English-style stocks with pistol grip available as a special order. Importation of Bernardelli shotguns has been inconsistent in the past and current dealer inventories of older merchandise might be priced less than similar models currently imported.

A wide variety of special order options is available on these shotguns. Individual price quotations are available by contacting Armsport, Inc. located in Miami, FL.

Barrel choke markings for V. Bernardelli shotguns are as follows; Full: *, Impr. Mod: **, Mod: ***, Impr. Cyl: ****, Cylinder: CL.

BRESCIA HAMMER DOUBLE BARREL — 12, 16, or 20 ga., 25¾, 27½ and 29½ in. mod. and full, 12 ga., 25½ in. imp. cyl. and mod., sidelock, extractors, two triggers, straight English stock, splinter forearm, checkered. Importation temporarily disc.

	$2,050	$795	$600	$450	$425	$395	$350

Last Mfg.'s Sug. Retail was $2,482.

Sudden drop in values reflects desirability factor in today's marketplace.

ITALIA HAMMER DOUBLE BARREL — similar to Brescia, except higher grade engraving and wood. Importation temporarily disc.

	$2,275	$1,200	$900	$735	$650	$600	$550

Last Mfg.'s Sug. Retail was $2,844.

Sudden drop in values reflects desirability factor in today's marketplace.

Grading	100%	98%	95%	90%	80%	70%	60%

B

ITALIA EXTRA HAMMER — hammer double, 12, 16, or 20 ga. Top-of-the-line hammer model. Importation temporarily disc.

	$6,400	$3,150	$2,200	$1,650	$1,375	$1,050	$800

Last Mfg.'s Sug. Retail was $7,861.

Sudden drop in values reflects desirability factor in today's marketplace.

MODEL 112 — 12 ga., entry-level model with extractors and DTs. Imported 1989 only.

	$850	$750	$675	$625	$550	$495	$450

Last Mfg.'s Sug. Retail was $998.

Add $65 for single trigger (Model 112 M - disc.).

MODEL 112E — 12 ga., Anson & Deeley action, light engraving. Importation disc. 1989.

	$995	$850	$775	$695	$625	$550	$495

Last Mfg.'s Sug. Retail was $1,108.

MODEL 112 SI/S (EM) — similar to Model 112E, except has single or double triggers.

Mfg.'s Sug. Retail	$1,385	$1,250	$950	$825	$725	$650	$550	$450

Add $125 for ST.
Add $190 for choke tubes.

▲ *Model 112 EM - MC* — similar to Model 112 EM, except has 3 in. chambers and 5 choke tubes. Imported 1990-1992.

	$1,600	$1,000	$850	$775	$675	$575	$495

Last Mfg.'s Sug. Retail was $1,971.

▲ *Model 112 EM-MC-WF* — includes 3½ in. chambers, waterfowl model with matte finish, single trigger and 3 choke tubes. Importation disc. 1990.

	$1,275	$975	$850	$775	$675	$575	$495

Last Mfg.'s Sug. Retail was $1,444.

S. UBERTO 1 — 12, 16, 20, or 28 ga., Anson & Deeley action, Purdey locks, light engraving, case hardened receiver, double triggers, extractors.

	$1,050	$900	$800	$700	$625	$550	$495

Last Mfg.'s Sug. Retail was $1,164.

Add $65 for single trigger (Model S. Uberto 1M).

▲ *S. Uberto 1E* — similar to S. Uberto 1, except with ejectors. Importation disc. 1990.

	$1,175	$950	$850	$740	$650	$565	$495

Last Mfg.'s Sug. Retail was $1,357.

Add $65 for single trigger (Model S. Uberto 1EM).

S. UBERTO 2 — 12, 16, 20, and 28 ga.'s, Anson & Deeley action, Purdey locks, light scroll engraving, silver finished receiver, double triggers, extractors. Importation disc. 1989, resumed 1993.

Mfg.'s Sug. Retail	$1,580	$1,375	$1,150	$875	$725	$650	$550	$450

Add $35 for single trigger (Model S. Uberto 2M - disc.).

▲ *S. Uberto 2E* — similar to S. Uberto 2, except with ejectors.

Mfg.'s Sug. Retail	$1,710	$1,525	$1,300	$1,050	$875	$725	$650	$550

Add $80 for single trigger (Model S. Uberto 2EM - disc.).

S. UBERTO FS — 12, 16, 20, or 28 ga., Purdey locks, relief engraved with hunting scenes on silver finished receiver, double triggers, extractors. Importation disc. 1989, resumed 1993.

Mfg.'s Sug. Retail	$1,915	$1,695	$1,450	$1,125	$895	$750	$675	$575

Add $65 for single trigger (Model S. Uberto FSM - disc. 1989).

▲ *S. Uberto FSE* — similar to S. Uberto FS, except with ejectors. Importation disc. 1989.

	$1,375	$1,100	$975	$850	$750	$625	$550

Last Mfg.'s Sug. Retail was $1,537.

Add $65 for single trigger (Model S. Uberto FSEM).

ROMA 3 — similar to S. Uberto, double triggers, extractors, false sideplates, case hardened receiver. Importation disc. 1989, resumed 1993.

Mfg.'s Sug. Retail	$1,625	$1,425	$1,200	$895	$775	$675	$575	$475

Add $65 for single trigger (Model Roma 3M - disc.).

Grading	100%	98%	95%	90%	80%	70%	60%

B

▲ *Roma 3E* — similar to Roma 3, except with ejectors.
Mfg.'s Sug. Retail $1,770 $1,550 $1,325 $1,050 $875 $725 $650 $550
    Add $80 for single trigger (Model Roma 3EM - disc.).

ROMA 4 — more deluxe model than Roma 3, false sideplates, scroll engraved, silver finished receiver. Importation disc. 1989.

                                                   $1,250 $1,025 $900 $800 $700 $625 $550
                                  Last Mfg.'s Sug. Retail was $1,439.
    Add $65 for single trigger (Model Roma 4M).

▲ *Roma 4E* — similar to Roma 4, except with ejectors.
Mfg.'s Sug. Retail $2,000 $1,775 $1,475 $1,150 $925 $775 $675 $575
    Add $80 for single trigger (Model Roma 4EM - disc.).

ROMA 6 — 12, 16, 20, or 28 ga., fully engraved sideplates with hunting scenes, Purdey locks, silver finish receiver, single trigger, finely figured English walnut. Importation disc. 1989.

                                          $1,395 $1,150 $975 $875 $775 $675 $600
                                  Last Mfg.'s Sug. Retail was $1,619.
    Add $175 for single trigger (Model Roma 6M).

▲ *Roma 6E* — similar to Roma 6, except with ejectors, 16 ga. was disc. 1989.
Mfg.'s Sug. Retail $2,175 $1,900 $1,695 $1,475 $1,150 $925 $775 $675
    Add $80 for single trigger (Model Roma 6EM - disc.).

ROMA 7 — 12 ga., ejectors, grade up from the Roma 6. Importation began 1994.
Mfg.'s Sug. Retail $3,025 $2,600 $2,000 $1,675 $1,375 $995 $875 $750

ROMA 8 — 12 ga., ejectors, grade up from the Roma 7. Importation began 1994.
Mfg.'s Sug. Retail $3,600 $3,000 $2,425 $1,950 $1,675 $1,375 $995 $875

ROMA 9 — 12 ga., ejectors, grade up from the Roma 8. Importation began 1994.
Mfg.'s Sug. Retail $4,250 $3,550 $2,875 $2,500 $1,950 $1,675 $1,375 $995

ELIO — 12 ga. only, lightweight, extractors, fine English style scroll engraving on silver finish receiver. Importation disc. 1989.

                                          $1,125 $925 $850 $740 $650 $565 $475
                                  Last Mfg.'s Sug. Retail was $1,238.
    Add $65 for single trigger (Model Elio M).

▲ *Elio E* — similar to Elio, except with ejectors. Importation disc. 1989.
                                          $1,200 $1,000 $895 $795 $695 $595 $500
                                  Last Mfg.'s Sug. Retail was $1,353.
    Add $65 for single trigger (Model Elio EM).

SLUG GUN — 12 ga. only, 23¾ in. slug bored barrels, extractors, Anson & Deeley action, Purdey locks, lightly engraved, silver finish receiver. Importation disc. 1990.

                                          $1,325 $1,000 $895 $795 $695 $595 $500
                                  Last Mfg.'s Sug. Retail was $1,575.
    Add $65 for single trigger (Model Slug M).

SLUG LUSSO — 12 ga. only, 23¾ in. slug bored barrels, sideplates, with extensive engraving featuring hunting scenes, cheekpiece, ejectors, silver finished receiver. Importation disc. 1992.

                                          $2,325 $1,550 $1,200 $995 $875 $750 $650
                                  Last Mfg.'s Sug. Retail was $2,793.
    Add $80 for single trigger (Model Slug Lusso M).
    This model was previously designated Slug Deluxe (1988 or earlier).

HEMINGWAY — 12, 20, or 28 (new 1992) ga., boxlock action, coin finished receiver with game scene engraving, 23½ in. barrels, DTs, deluxe checkered walnut stock and forearm, 6¼ lbs.
Mfg.'s Sug. Retail $1,950 $1,625 $1,325 $1,050 $875 $750 $675 $575
    Add $70 for single trigger.
    Add $160 for single selective trigger.

Grading	100%	98%	95%	90%	80%	70%	60%

HEMINGWAY DE LUXE — similar to Hemingway, except is also available in 16 ga. and has sideplates, better wood, and more engraving.

Mfg.'s Sug. Retail	$2,200	$1,850	$1,500	$1,150	$925	$775	$675	$575

Add $80 for single trigger (Model Hemingway De Luxe M - disc.).

LAS PALOMAS PIGEON — 12 ga. live pigeon gun, single trigger, special dimensions for live pigeon shooting.

Mfg.'s Sug. Retail	$3,700	$3,125	$2,550	$2,000	$1,700	$1,375	$995	$875

Add $750 for Pigeon Model (includes single trigger).

HOLLAND V.B. LISCIO — 12 ga. only, Holland type sidelocks, light engraving, silver finish receiver, single trigger, ejectors, select walnut.

Mfg.'s Sug. Retail	$10,250	$8,450	$4,900	$4,450	$3,900	$3,350	$2,850	$2,400

HOLLAND V.B. INCISO — 12 ga. only, H&H sidelock action, Purdey locks, various barrel lengths, single trigger, ejectors, straight or pistol grip stock, 100% engraved on coin finished receiver. Importation disc. 1992.

	$10,700	$7,000	$5,500	$4,700	$4,200	$3,500	$3,000

Last Mfg.'s Sug. Retail was $12,929.

HOLLAND V.B. LUSSO — 12 ga. only, H&H sidelock action, Purdey locks, various barrel lengths, single trigger, ejectors, straight or pistol grip stock, same features as Holland V.B. Inciso, only extra select wood and game scene engraving. Importation disc. 1992.

	$8,900	$7,900	$6,500	$5,200	$4,750	$4,000	$3,450

Last Mfg.'s Sug. Retail was $14,377.

HOLLAND V.B. EXTRA — 12 ga. only, H&H style action, any barrel length and choke, double triggers, auto ejectors, straight or pistol grip stock, 100% engraved on coin finished receiver. Prices are completely dependent upon individual customer specifications. Values listed below are for engraving pattern No. 3. Importation disc. 1992.

	$13,250	$9,700	$7,450	$6,150	$5,200	$4,600	$3,950

Last Mfg.'s Sug. Retail was $16,549.

Add $1,034 for engraving pattern No. 4.
Add $4,551 for engraving pattern No. 12.
Add $8,895 for engraving pattern No. 20.
Add $621 for single trigger.

Older specimens (not custom ordered within the last 2 years) could have values considerably lower than those listed above.

HOLLAND V.B. GOLD — top-of-the-line model, made to individual order. Very limited production and ultra-rare. Importation disc. 1992.

	$47,500	$32,500	$24,000	$18,500	$13,000	$11,500	$9,950

Last Mfg.'s Sug. Retail was $57,922.

Older specimens (not custom ordered within the last 2 years) could have values considerably lower than those listed above.

SHOTGUNS: OVER & UNDER, RECENT MFG.

MODEL 115 HUNTING — 12 ga. only, boxlock action, monobloc frame, inclined plane lockings, blued receiver, single trigger, ejectors. Importation disc. 1989.

	$1,770	$1,425	$1,225	$1,000	$895	$750	$650

Last Mfg.'s Sug. Retail was $1,915.

▲ *Model 115S* — similar to 115, except moderate engraving.

	$2,150	$1,925	$1,745	$1,500	$1,250	$1,025	$950

Last Mfg.'s Sug. Retail was $2,500.

▲ *Model 115L* — similar to 115S, except extensive scroll engraving on silver finish receiver.

	$2,600	$2,375	$2,050	$1,750	$1,450	$1,100	$850

Last Mfg.'s Sug. Retail was $3,170.

Grading	100%	98%	95%	90%	80%	70%	60%

▲ **Model 115E** — sideplate, boxlock action, ejector, bulino game scene engraving.

	$4,650	$4,125	$3,600	$3,100	$2,650	$2,200	$1,800

Last Mfg.'s Sug. Retail was $5,200.

MODEL 115 TARGET — 12 ga. only, same specifications as Model 115, except trap dimensions. Importation disc. 1989.

	$1,800	$1,595	$1,375	$1,175	$1,000	$895	$750

Last Mfg.'s Sug. Retail was $2,160.

▲ **Model 115S** — same specifications as 115 Target, except light engraving. Importation disc. 1992.

	$3,275	$2,425	$1,825	$1,500	$1,250	$1,025	$895

Last Mfg.'s Sug. Retail was $3,920.

This model is available in either Pigeon, Skeet, Sporting Clays, or Trap configuration.

▲ **Model 115L** — similar to 115S, except extensive scroll engraving on silver finish receiver. Importation disc. 1990.

	$3,700	$2,995	$2,600	$2,375	$2,050	$1,750	$1,450

Last Mfg.'s Sug. Retail was $4,201.

▲ **Model 115E** — same specifications as 115S, except with extensively engraved sideplates. Importation disc. 1990.

	$5,950	$4,800	$4,125	$3,600	$3,100	$2,650	$2,200

Last Mfg.'s Sug. Retail was $6,827.

▲ **Model 115S Trap/Skeet** — 12 ga. only, available in Trap or Skeet configuration, ejectors, single trigger.

Mfg.'s Sug. Retail	$3,099		$2,750	$2,250	$1,825	$1,425	$995	$875	$725

▲ **Model 115S Sporting Clays** — 12 ga. only, SST, ejectors, choke tubes. Importation began 1995.

Mfg.'s Sug. Retail	$6,700		$5,900	$4,950	$4,450	$3,875	$3,350	$2,775	$2,100

MODEL 190 TARGET — 12 ga, SST, ejectors, engraved silver receiver, select checkered walnut stock and forearm. Imported 1986-1989.

	$1,425	$1,095	$925	$800	$700	$600	$525

Last Mfg.'s Sug. Retail was $1,572.

▲ **Model 190 MC** — similar to Model 190 Target except has Monte Carlo stock. Imported 1989 only.

	$1,000	$825	$700	$600	$525	$475	$450

Last Mfg.'s Sug. Retail was $1,155.

▲ **Model 190 Special** — 12 ga. only, similar to Model 190 Target, except has better walnut and engraving. Imported 1988-1989.

	$1,335	$1,000	$895	$800	$700	$600	$525

Last Mfg.'s Sug. Retail was $1,456.

Add $75 for single trigger (Model 190 Special MS).

These variations are hunting models.

MODEL 192 FIELD — 12 ga. only, single or double triggers, ejectors, choke tubes optional. Importation began 1995.

Mfg.'s Sug. Retail	$1,425		$1,175	$895	$750	$650	$550	$450	$375

Add $65 for single trigger.
Add $200 for choke tubes.
Add $350 for 192 Special (includes double triggers, ejectors).

MODEL 192 MS COMPETITION — 12 ga. only, ejectors, selective or non-selective triggers, multi-chokes standard on Sporting Clays Model. New 1990.

Mfg.'s Sug. Retail	$1,930		$1,725	$1,475	$1,150	$925	$775	$675	$575

Add $120 for SST.
Add $200 for choke tubes.
Add $485 for Special Sport.

This model is available in either Pigeon, Skeet, Sporting Clays, Special Sport, or Trap configuration.

Grading	100%	98%	95%	90%	80%	70%	60%

MODEL 192 MS-MC HUNTING — 12 ga. only, boxlock action with engraved coin finished receiver, 3 in. chambers, ejectors, SST, 26¾ or 28 in. VR barrels with choke tubes, steel shot compatible. Imported 1990-1992.

	$1,400	$995	$825	$700	$600	$525	$475

Last Mfg.'s Sug. Retail was $1,833.

▲ *Model 192 MS-MC-WF* — waterfowler variation which includes 3½ in. chambers, 3 choke tubes, and SST. Imported 1990 only.

	$1,275	$950	$875	$775	$675	$575	$500

Last Mfg.'s Sug. Retail was $1,444.

MODEL 200 LIGHTWEIGHT MS — 12 ga. only, silver grey finished receiver with game scene engraving, ejectors, DTs. Imported 1988-1989, resumed 1993.

Mfg.'s Sug. Retail	$1,525	$1,325	$975	$850	$725	$650	$550	$450

MODEL 220 MS HUNTING — 12 or 20 ga., silver grey finished receiver with engraving. New 1988.

Mfg.'s Sug. Retail	$1,560	$1,350	$995	$850	$725	$650	$550	$450

Add $75 for SST.
Add $180 for 12 ga. slug variation with DTs (new 1994).
Add $700 for extra set of 12 ga. barrels (disc. 1990).
This model is available with either a pistol grip or English grip (straight) stock.

MODEL LUCK — 12 ga., ejectors, boxlock action, choice of double or single trigger. Importation began 1994.

Mfg.'s Sug. Retail	$1,295	$1,100	$850	$725	$650	$550	$450	$375

Add $70 for single trigger.

SATURNO MS-MC COMPETITION — 12 ga. only, sporter configuration, boxlock action with lightly engraved side plates, ejectors, DTs. Importation began 1991.

Mfg.'s Sug. Retail	$2,100	$1,850	$1,500	$1,150	$925	$775	$675	$575

This model is available in either Pigeon, Skeet, Sporting Clays, or Trap configuration.

SATURNO MS-MC HUNTING — 12 ga. only, boxlock action with lightly engraved side plates, ejectors, SST, includes multi-chokes. Imported 1991-1992.

	$2,275	$1,525	$1,050	$875	$750	$695	$600

Last Mfg.'s Sug. Retail was $2,609.

ORIONE S — 12 ga., double Purdey lock, VR, ejectors, engraved nickel finish receiver. Importation disc. 1989.

	$1,175	$1,025	$860	$760	$650	$560	$510

Last Mfg.'s Sug. Retail was $1,425.

ORIONE L — similar to Orione S, single trigger, finer engraving, English or pistol type select walnut stock. Importation disc. 1989.

	$1,285	$1,125	$950	$840	$750	$650	$550

Last Mfg.'s Sug. Retail was $1,550.

ORIONE E — top-of-the-line, deep relief engraving. Importation disc. 1989.

	$1,375	$1,200	$1,020	$900	$820	$710	$650

Last Mfg.'s Sug. Retail was $1,660.

SHOTGUNS: SEMI-AUTO

MODEL 9MM FLOBERT — 9mm rimfire shot cartridge, 24.4 in. smooth bore barrel, 3 shot mag., steel receiver, walnut stock and forearm with sling and swivels, 5 lbs. 3 oz.

Mfg.'s Sug. Retail	$360	$295	$225	$175	$150	$125	$105	$95

SHOTGUNS: FOLDING MODELS

SINGLE BARREL — 12, 16, 20, 24, 28, 32 or .410 ga., gun folds in half. Importation disc. 1990.

	$230	$185	$150	$135	$125	$115	$100

Last Mfg.'s Sug. Retail was $265.

Grading	100%	98%	95%	90%	80%	70%	60%

DOUBLE BARREL — 12 and 16 ga., gun folds in half, double triggers. Current manufacture, but available in Europe only.

	$570	$430	$370	$315	$285	$260	$230

B

BERSA

Manufacturer located in Argentina. Currently imported and distributed exclusively by Eagle Imports, Inc. located in Wanamassa, NJ. Previously imported and distributed before 1988 by Rock Island Armory located in Geneseo, IL and Outdoor Sports Headquarters, Inc. located in Dayton, OH. Distributor sales only.

THUNDER 9 — 9mm Para., double action semi-auto, 3½ in. barrel, 10 (C/B 1994) or 14* shot mag., ambidextrous manual safety and decocking lever, automatic firing pin safety, 3-dot sights, aluminum frame, wraparound matte black polymer grips, link-free locked breech design, non-glare matte blue, satin nickel (new 1995), or duo-tone (new 1995) finish. Imported 1993-95.

	$400	$335	$295	$265	$235	$210	$190

Last Mfg.'s Sug. Retail was $475.

Add $17 for duo-tone finish.
Add $50 for satin nickel finish.

THUNDER 22 (MODEL 23) — .22 LR, double action semi-auto, 9 shot mag., 3½ in. barrel, walnut grips, 24½ oz. New 1988.

Mfg.'s Sug. Retail	$250	$220	$190	$155	$125	$115	$105	$95

Add $17 for satin nickel finish.

THUNDER 380 — .380 ACP cal., double action, 3½ in. barrel, fixed sights, 7 shot mag., deep blue, satin nickel, or duo-tone (disc. 1995) finish, rubber grips, 25¾ oz. New 1995.

Mfg.'s Sug. Retail	$250	$220	$190	$155	$125	$115	$105	$95

Add $17 for satin nickel finish.
Add $16 for duo-tone finish.

▲ *Thunder 380 Plus* — similar to Thunder 380, except has 10 shot mag. New 1995.

Mfg.'s Sug. Retail	$316	$265	$210	$165	$130	$115	$105	$95

Add $32 for satin nickel finish.
Add $17 for duo-tone finish.

MODEL 83 — .380 ACP, double action semi-auto, 3½ in. barrel, blued finish, custom walnut grips, 6 shot mag., 24½ oz. Imported 1988-94.

	$235	$180	$150	$125	$115	$105	$95

Last Mfg.'s Sug. Retail was $288.

Add $34 for satin nickel finish.

MODEL 85 — .380 ACP, similar specifications to Model 83 except has 12 shot mag., 30½ oz. Imported 1988-94.

	$285	$245	$220	$195	$170	$150	$130

Last Mfg.'s Sug. Retail was $340.

Add $47 for satin nickel finish.

MODEL 86 — .380 ACP cal., matte finish, undercover model, wraparound rubber grips, 12 shot mag. Imported 1991-94.

	$315	$265	$225	$200	$170	$150	$130

Last Mfg.'s Sug. Retail was $375.

Add $29 for nickel finish.

MODEL 90 — 9mm Para., single action, semi-auto, steel frame, checkered walnut grips, 13 shot mag., deep blue finish. Imported 1990-91 only.

	$325	$280	$250	$220	$195	$170	$150

Last Mfg.'s Sug. Retail was $384.

Grading	100%	98%	95%	90%	80%	70%	60%

SERIES 95 — .380 ACP cal., double action, 3½ in. barrel, fixed sights, 7 shot mag., matte blue or satin nickel finish, black polymer grips, 23 oz. New 1995.

Mfg.'s Sug. Retail	$225	$195	$170	$145	$125	$115	$105	$95

Add $17 for satin nickel finish.

MODEL 223 — .22 LR, single action semi-auto, 10 shot mag., 3½ in. barrel, squared-off trigger guard, nylon grips, blued action. Importation disc. 1987.

	$200	$170	$150	$125	$115	$105	$95

Last Mfg.'s Sug. Retail was $239.

MODEL 224 — similar to Model 223, except has 4 in. barrel. Imported 1987 only.

	$200	$170	$150	$125	$115	$105	$95

Last Mfg.'s Sug. Retail was $239.

MODEL 225 — similar to Model 223, except has 5 in. barrel and 10 shot mag. Disc. 1987.

	$155	$135	$125	$115	$105	$95	$85

Last Mfg.'s Sug. Retail was $170.

MODEL 226 — similar to Model 225, except has 6 in. barrel. Importation disc. 1987.

	$200	$170	$150	$125	$115	$105	$95

Last Mfg.'s Sug. Retail was $239.

MODEL 323 — .32 ACP, single action semi-auto, 8 shot mag., thumbrest plastic grips, 25 oz. Disc. 1987.

	$105	$95	$85	$75	$65	$55	$45

Last Mfg.'s Sug. Retail was $125.

MODEL 383 — .380 ACP, single action semi-auto, 3½ in. barrel, blued finish, nylon grips, 7 shot mag. Importation disc. 1988.

	$120	$95	$90	$80	$70	$60	$50

Last Mfg.'s Sug. Retail was $188.

MODEL 383 — .380 ACP, double action semi-auto, 3½ in. barrel, blued finish, custom wood grips, 7 shot mag. Importation disc. 1988.

	$135	$105	$95	$85	$75	$65	$55

Last Mfg.'s Sug. Retail was $239.

BERTUZZI

Manufacturer located in Brescia, Italy since 1886. Imported and distributed exclusively by New England Arms Co. located in Kittery Point, ME.

SHOTGUNS: S X S

MODEL ORIONE — 12 ga., scalloped Anson & Deeley boxlock action, beavertail forearm, single trigger, auto ejector. This model is available on special order only — contact the distributor listed above for availability, prices, and options. Importation disc. 1994. Retail prices started at $4,500.

BEST QUALITY SIDELOCK — various gauges, best quality sidelock model with extensive engraving. Prices start at $12,500.

HAMMER GUN — all gauges, upper tang safety, double triggers, fine quality engraving. Prices start at $12,500 with ejectors and single trigger. The self-cocking, auto-ejector mechanism is popular in this model and prices can vary between $15,000-$20,000.

SHOTGUNS: O/U

ZEUS — 12 ga., sidelock, auto ejector, deluxe engraving, deluxe wood checkering, SST. This model is available on special order only — contact the distributor listed above for availability, prices, and options. Importation disc. 1994. Retail prices generally ranged from $18,500-$27,500.

Grading	100%	98%	95%	90%	80%	70%	60%

ZEUS EXTRA LUSSO — 12 ga., sidelock, auto ejector, deluxe wood, deluxe checkering and engraving, SST. This model is available on special order only — contact the distributor listed above for availability, prices, and options. Prices generally range $25,000+.

BOSS SYSTEM — 12 or 20 ga., features Boss locking system. Importation began 1995. Prices are $32,500 for 12 ga. (no engraving) or $35,000 for 20 ga. (no engraving).

BESCHI, MARIO
Manufacturer located in Italy.

SHOTGUNS: SIDE-BY-SIDE

EXTRA LUSSO SIDELOCK — 12 or 20 ga., elaborate game scene engraving.

	100%	98%	95%	90%	80%	70%	60%
12 ga.	$20,000	$17,500	$15,250	$13,000	$11,000	$9,000	$7,000
20 ga.	$25,000	$21,750	$18,000	$15,250	$13,000	$11,000	$9,000

BOXLOCK MODEL — prices assume moderate engraving.

	100%	98%	95%	90%	80%	70%	60%
	$5,000	$4,600	$4,100	$3,600	$3,000	$2,500	$1,875

BIG BEAR
Importer located in Dallas, TX beginning 1992, specializing in the importation of both Russian military surplus and new firearms. New shotguns are currently being manufactured by the Tula Arsenal. Distributor and dealer direct sales.

PISTOLS

TOZ-35M — .22 LR, single shot, Olympic Free Pistol, adj. palm rest, firing pin cocked with cocking lever, fitted case with necessary tools. Importation began 1992.

	100%	98%	95%	90%	80%	70%	60%
Mfg.'s Sug. Retail $1,050	$850	$675	$525	$425	$350	$295	$250

IZH-70 MAKAROV — .380 ACP or 9mm Para. cal., 8 shot mag., current mfg. from Russia. Importation began 1994.

	100%	98%	95%	90%	80%	70%	60%
Mfg.'s Sug. Retail $225	$210	$165	$145	$130	$115	$100	$90

RIFLES

SAIGA SPORTER RIFLE — 7.62x39mm, semi-auto with improved Kalashnikov design, checkered hardwood stock and forearm, 10 shot mag. Importation began 1996.

	100%	98%	95%	90%	80%	70%	60%
Mfg.'s Sug. Retail $350	$300	$250	$225	$210	$195	$180	$170

Add $89 for 3.5X scope and mount.

SHOTGUNS

SAIGA SEMI-AUTO — .410 ga., 3 in. chamber, paramilitary configuration. Importation began 1996.

	100%	98%	95%	90%	80%	70%	60%
Mfg.'s Sug. Retail $399	$350	$300	$265	$235	$200	$180	$165

IJ-27 O/U — 12 ga., 2¾ in. chambers. Importation began 1995.

	100%	98%	95%	90%	80%	70%	60%
Mfg.'s Sug. Retail $399	$350	$300	$265	$235	$200	$180	$165

IJ-39E O/U — 12 ga., 2¾ in. chambers. Importation began 1995.

	100%	98%	95%	90%	80%	70%	60%
Mfg.'s Sug. Retail $695	$615	$525	$450	$400	$360	$330	$295

IJ-43 SxS — 12 ga., 2¾ in. chambers. Importation began 1995.

	100%	98%	95%	90%	80%	70%	60%
Mfg.'s Sug. Retail $299	$260	$210	$185	$170	$155	$145	$135

TOZ-87/91 — 12 ga. only, 2¾ in. chambers, nickel finish receiver, double triggers. Importation began 1995.

	100%	98%	95%	90%	80%	70%	60%
Mfg.'s Sug. Retail $650	$575	$495	$440	$395	$360	$330	$295

Grading	100%	98%	95%	90%	80%	70%	60%

TOZ-91-12-E PRESENTATION GRADE — 12 ga. only, extensive engraving with multiple game scene inlays and borders. Importation began 1995.

Mfg.'s Sug. Retail $2,200 $1,825 $1,500 $1,250 $1,000 $850 $695 $550

BIG HORN ARMS CORP.
Previous manufacturer located in Watertown, SD.

TARGET PISTOL — .22 Short only, unique action permitting auto. ejection, ambidextrous stock made of molded Tufflex with carvings, 26 oz. Approx. 1,200 mfg. Disc. in the late 60s.

                          $175 $150 $135 $125 $115 $105 $95

LIL' MAGNUM SHOTGUN — .410 diameter reloadable shot cartridge, single shot open bolt operation, included reloading equipment, approx. 2,000 mfg. in the late 60s.

                          $125 $100 $75 $65 $55 $50 $45

BIGHORN RIFLE CO.
Previous manufacturer located in Orem, UT.

BIGHORN RIFLE — Mauser action, choice of calibers, custom made bolt action of high quality, interchangeable barrels (gun is supplied with 2 barrels), adj. trigger, deluxe walnut stock, many custom options. Mfg. 1984 only.

                  $2,100 $1,800 $1,600 $1,400 $1,200 $1,000 $850

BIGHORN PISTOL — .22 LR, bolt action design, research is underway to gather more information concerning this model.

BILL HANUS BIRDGUNS
Manufactured by Armas Ugartechea in Eibar, Spain. Distributed by Bill Hanus Birdguns located in Newport, OR. Imported by Galaxy Imports located in Victoria, TX. Please refer to Ugartechea, Armas in the U section of this text.

BINGHAM, LTD.
Manufacturer located in Norcross, GA 1976-1985.

RIFLES

PPS 50 — .22 LR only, blowback action, 50 round drum mag., standard model has Beechwood stock. Add $20 for deluxe model with walnut stock. Duramil model has chrome finish and walnut stock — add $30. Disc. 1985.

                  $195 $160 $145 $135 $125 $110 $100
                                                  Last Mfg.'s Sug. Retail was $230.

This model was styled after the Soviet WWII Model PPSh Sub Machine Gun.

AK-22 — .22 LR only, blowback action, styled after AK-47, 15 shot mag. standard, 29 shot mag. available. Standard model has Beechwood stock. Deluxe model has walnut stock — add $20. Disc. 1985.

                  $225 $195 $160 $145 $135 $125 $110
                                                  Last Mfg.'s Sug. Retail was $230.

GALIL-22 — .22 LR only, patterned after Galil semi-auto paramilitary design rifle. Disc.

                  $225 $195 $160 $145 $135 $125 $110

BANTAM — .22 LR or 22 Mag., bolt action single shot, 18½ in. barrel. Disc. 1985.

                  $110 $90 $75 $65 $55 $45 $40
                                                  Last Mfg.'s Sug. Retail was $120.

Grading	100%	98%	95%	90%	80%	70%	60%

B

FG-9 — 9mm only, blowback action, semi-auto paramilitary design carbine, 20½ in. barrel. New design for 1984. While advertised this model was never manufactured.

BITTNER
Manufactured by Gustav Bittner located in Vieprty, Bohemia, (Austria, Hungary).

BITTNER MODEL 1893 — 7.7mm Bittner cal., pistol with hand activated repeater mechanism, box magazine, checkered grips, limited manufacture in circa 1893.

	100%	98%	95%	90%	80%	70%	60%
	$5,500	$4,500	$3,500	$2,700	$2,300	$1,900	$1,500

BLAND, THOMAS & SONS GUNMAKERS LTD.
English manufacturer located in England since 1840. This firm was purchased in 1990 by Woodcock Hill located in Benton, PA. Manufacturer direct sales only.

Woodcock Hill should be contacted directly (address listed in Trademark Index) for more information (including current models and prices) regarding Thomas Bland & Sons firearms. Prices will vary depending on the exchange rate between the pound/dollar.

SHOTGUNS
Both boxlock and sidelock best quality shotguns are available in all gauges with prices ranging between $9,000 - $40,000 depending upon configuration, finish, and accessories.

RIFLES
Double rifles are available in almost all calibers and specifications. Prices vary between $14,000 - $45,000 depending upon configuration, finish, and accessories. Bolt action rifles are available in any type of action, most popular calibers, and other special options. The bolt action models are not manufactured in England. Prices begin at $1,500.

BLASER
Manufactured by Blaser Jagdwaffen Gmbh in Isny/Allgau, Germany. Currently imported and distributed in the U.S. by Autumn Sales Inc. located in Fort Worth, TX. Direct sales from the importer only.

Blaser Jagdwaffen manufactures a large variety of rifles, drillings, and combination guns for the European market. The models below have been selected for domestic sales. More information is available on the European models by contacting Autumn Sales (see Trademark Index).

MODEL R-84 BOLT ACTION — .22-250 (disc. 1993), .243 Win., 6mm Rem., .25-06 Rem., .270 Win., .280 Rem., or .30-06 standard cals., .257 Wby. Mag., .264 Win. Mag., 7mm Rem. Mag., .300 Win. Mag., .300 Wby. Mag., .338 Win. Mag., or .375 H&H Magnum cal., 23 or 24 (Mag. cals. only) in. interchangeable barrel, scroll engraving on receiver, short bolt action with 60 degree rotation, checkered Turkish walnut stock and forearm, approx. 7 lbs. Mfg. 1988-94.

	100%	98%	95%	90%	80%	70%	60%
	$2,100	$1,575	$1,275	$1,050	$950	$850	$775

Last Mfg.'s Sug. Retail was $2,300.

Add $50 for left-hand action.
Add $600 per interchangeable barrel (w/scope mounts).

This model features the scope being mounted directly to the barrel (and not the receiver). Since the scope mounts are on the barrel extension, this takedown rifle is unique in that it does not require re-zeroing when the rifle is reassembled, regardless of caliber change.

B

Grading	100%	98%	95%	90%	80%	70%	60%

▲ **Model R84 Deluxe** — features a better grade of Turkish walnut with a North American game scene engraved on receiver, silver pistol grip cap with animal scene engraving.

	$2,375	$2,025	$1,650	$1,200	$1,000	$925	$825

Last Mfg.'s Sug. Retail was $2,600.

Add $50 for left hand action.

▲ **Model R84 Super Deluxe** — best grade Turkish walnut with receiver featuring African game scene engraving (animals are in gold and silver), and silver pistol grip cap with gold animal engraving.

	$2,675	$2,225	$1,775	$1,300	$1,100	$975	$895

Last Mfg.'s Sug. Retail was $2,950.

Add $50 for left hand action.

MODEL R-93 REPEATER — available in 10 domestic and 8 European calibers between .243 Win. - .416 Rem. Mag., 22, 24, or 27½ (disc.) in. barrel, unique patented rifle features straight pull bolt action (0 degree bolt lift), radial locking system, unique safety offering cartridge in chamber capability, features interchangeable barrel system and newly designed bolt, searfree trigger mechanism, non-glare "black velvet" metal finish, integrated low scope mounts, approx. 6½ - 7½ lbs. Importation began 1994.

Mfg.'s Sug. Retail	$2,800	$2,575	$2,175	$1,775	$1,300	$1,100	$975	$895

Add $550 per barrel (w/o mounts).
Add $300 for Deluxe Grade.
Add $700 for Super Deluxe Grade.

▲ **R-93 Safari** — .375 H&H or .416 Rem. cal., features 24 in. heavy barrel, open sights, large forearm, 9½ lbs. Importation began 1994.

Mfg.'s Sug. Retail	$3,300	$2,925	$2,300	$1,850	$1,450	$1,250	$1,050	$950

Add $300 for Deluxe Grade.
Add $700 for Super Deluxe Grade.

ULTIMATE BOLT ACTION — .22-250, .243, .25-06, .270, .308, .30-06, 7x57, 7x64, .264 Win. Mag., 7mm Rem. Mag., .300 Win. Mag., .338 Win. Mag., or .375 H&H cal., unique bolt action design with 60 degree bolt throw, interchangeable barrel capability, 3 locking lugs, safety lever cocks and uncocks the firing pin spring, exposed hammer, aluminum receiver, 22 or 24 in. barrel, single set trigger, silver finished receiver has light engraving, select checkered walnut stock and forearm, 6¾ lbs. Extra interchangeable barrels are $545 each, extra bolt heads are $175 each. Mfg. 1985-1989.

	$1,350	$1,100	$975	$925	$825	$750	$675

Last Mfg.'s Sug. Retail was $1,495.

All models were available in left-hand version at no extra charge.

MODEL K77 A SINGLE SHOT — .22-250, .243 Win., 6.5x55mm, .270 Win., 7x57R, 7x65R, or .30-06 standard cals., 7mm Rem. Mag., .300 Win. Mag. or .300 Wby. Magnum cal., break open action, 23 or 24 in. barrel, 3 piece take down, upper tang safety, checkered walnut stock and forearm, engraved silver finished receiver, sling swivels, 5½ lbs. Imported 1988-90.

	$2,000	$1,675	$1,475	$1,300	$1,100	$925	$800

Last Mfg.'s Sug. Retail was $2,280.

Add $50 for Mag. calibers.
Add $730-$778 per interchangeable barrel.

ULTIMATE: SPECIAL ORDER

All of the below listed models may have been ordered with a butt stock cartridge trap — add $250-$500 depending on model. Special order guns required 3 to 9 months to hand fabricate. Mfg. was disc. 1989 on all models.

▲ **Ultimate Deluxe** — similar to Ultimate, except better wood and game scene engraving.

	$1,425	$1,175	$1,000	$950	$850	$775	$700

Last Mfg.'s Sug. Retail was $1,595.

Grading	100%	98%	95%	90%	80%	70%	60%

▲ **Ultimate Deluxe Carbine** — .243 Win. or .308 Win. cal. only, 19½ in. barrel with full length forearm. New 1986.

| | $1,600 | $1,375 | $1,150 | $1,000 | $900 | $825 | $750 |

Last Mfg.'s Sug. Retail was $1,800.

▲ **Ultimate Super Deluxe** — similar to Ultimate Deluxe, except features better wood and game scene engraving. New 1986.

| | $3,750 | $3,250 | $2,900 | $2,600 | $2,300 | $2,100 | $1,850 |

Last Mfg.'s Sug. Retail was $4,030.

▲ **Ultimate Exclusive** — similar to Ultimate Super Deluxe, except features better wood and game scene engraving. New 1986.

| | $4,850 | $4,300 | $3,500 | $2,975 | $2,600 | $2,275 | $1,975 |

Last Mfg.'s Sug. Retail was $5,655.

Add $700 per interchangeable barrel.

▲ **Ultimate Super Exclusive** — similar to Ultimate Exclusive, except features better wood and game scene engraving. New 1986.

| | $7,700 | $6,800 | $5,750 | $4,700 | $3,950 | $3,450 | $2,950 |

Last Mfg.'s Sug. Retail was $8,905.

Add $950 per interchangeable barrel.

▲ **Ultimate Royal** — best quality Ultimate, featuring Bavarian cheekpiece and checkering/carving on stock and forearm, elaborate game scene engraving, gold plated hammer. New 1986.

| | $9,000 | $7,500 | $6,750 | $6,000 | $5,375 | $4,600 | $4,000 |

Last Mfg.'s Sug. Retail was $11,500.

Add $1,200 per interchangeable barrel.

BOHICA

Manufacturer and customizer located in Sedalia, CO since 1993. Direct or dealer sales only.

RIFLES: SEMI-AUTO

M16-SA — .223 Rem., .50 AE, or various custom cals., AR-15 style, 16 or 20 in. barrel, A-2 sights, standard handguard, approx. 950 mfg. through September, 1994.

| | $1,375 | $1,225 | $1,000 | $850 | $725 | $600 | $525 |

Add $100 for flat-top receiver with scope rail.
Add $65 for two-piece, free floating handguard.

In addition to the rifles listed above, Bohica also manufactured a M16-SA Match variation (retail was $2,295, approx. 10 mfg.), a pistol version of the M16-SA in both 7 and 10 in. barrel (retail was $1,095, approx. 50 mfg.), and a limited run of M16-SA in .50 AE cal. (retail was $1,695, approx. 25 mfg.).

BOITO

Manufacturer located in Brazil. Previously imported by F.I.E. Corp. located in Hialeah, FL.

Boito shotguns were inexpensive, utilitarian shotguns that are shootable, but not collectible. Because of this, prices typically range between $100 - $225, depending on the gauge and condition.

BORCHARDT

Pistol design originating in Germany circa 1894-97.

PISTOL: SEMI-AUTO

These prices are established with matching serialized parts and assume original condition.

MODEL 1893 — 7.65mm, original Luger design, 6½ in. barrel, blue finish with fire-blued small parts, checkered walnut grips, 8 shot mag., distinguished by elongated spring mechanism housing located behind the toggle assembly, may include accessories (mags., holster, stock) and/or case.

Grading	100%	98%	95%	90%	80%	70%	60%

▲ *Ludwig Loewe Mfg.* — serial numbered 1-1104.
➤ **Gun Only**

	$12,000	$10,500	$9,000	$7,500	$6,250	$4,950	$3,750

Original stocks (with attached leather holster) are priced starting at $3,500.

➤ **Cased With Accessories** — original cased gun was supplied with shoulder stock, detachable cheekpiece, leather holster, 3 regular mags. and a hold-open mag.

	$23,500	$18,000	$12,500	$10,000	$8,000	$6,500	$5,000

▲ *DWM Mfg.* — starting approx. 1895, serial numbered 1105-3000.
➤ **Gun Only**

	$11,250	$9,995	$8,500	$7,000	$5,750	$4,350	$3,250

Original stocks (with attached leather holster) are priced starting at $3,500.

➤ **Cased With Accessories** — original cased gun was supplied with shoulder stock, detachable cheekpiece, leather holster, 3 regular mags. and a hold-open mag.

	$22,500	$18,000	$12,500	$10,000	$8,000	$6,500	$5,000

BOSS & CO., LTD.

Manufacturer located in London, England 1812 to date. Direct sales from the manufacturer only.

Boss manufactures some of the world's finest shotguns and rifles (best quality guns only). Their shotguns and rifles have always been custom built per individual order. Approximately 10,000 have been manufactured to date. Listed below are the basic models (does not include special orders, optional engraving patterns, and other possible options) with current retail values computed at (1 pound = $1.57) and are for standard models only.

RIFLES: SxS OR O/U

Boss Express SxS and O/U double rifles are quoted per individual request only. Currently, the O/U rifle in .470 NE retails for $149,150. Older rifles must be appraised individually.

SHOTGUNS

BOSS SxS — all gauges (16 ga. is currently POR), barrel lengths and chokes to specifications, bar-action sidelock, easy-open action (not self-opening), square or round action, checkered stock, pistol grip (optional) or straight grip stock, single or double triggers, splinter or beavertail (optional) forearm, traditional English rose & scroll engraving.

Mfg.'s Sug. Retail	$47,100	$47,100	$33,250	$22,500	$18,750	$15,000	$13,000	$11,000

Add $3,140 for 20 ga.
Add $7,850 for 28 or .410 ga.
Add $1,490 for ST (patented "3 pull" system).
Add 10% for opening assist.

BOSS O/U — 12, 20, 28, or .410 ga. standard, barrel lengths and chokes to specifications, shell-framed sidelock, auto ejectors, double triggers or single non-selective, English straight stock standard to specifications, VR or pistol grip stock optional, traditional English rose & scroll fine engraving, limited availability.

Mfg.'s Sug. Retail	$70,650	$70,650	$52,100	$37,500	$32,500	$27,500	$22,500	$18,000

Add $3,140 for 20 ga.
Add $7,850 for 28 ga.
Individual appraisals should be secured when evaluating the .410 ga.
Add 10% for opening assist.

Note: above values represent base gun only. Any additional engraving (traditional rose and scroll) and/or special orders will add considerably to the above prices.

BOSWELL, CHARLES

Previously manufactured in London, England.

In 1988, Charles Boswell was purchased by U.S. interests and Cape Horn International (previously Cape Horn Outfitters) located in Charlotte, NC has been retained to sell and manufacture the Boswell Guns in the U.S. In addition to aquiring their entire inventory of English manufactured firearms, Charles Boswell is currently fabricating new shotguns and double rifles in the U.S. using the best materials including English lock mechanisms and will retain the Charles Boswell Co. Trademark. Every gun will be custom ordered to an individual client's requirements/specifications. Previously imported by Saxon Arms, Ltd., located in Clearwater, FL.

B

Grading	100%	98%	95%	90%	80%	70%	60%

SHOTGUNS: SIDE-BY-SIDE

Current manufacture is very limited.

BOXLOCK SxS — made to individual order, choice of engraving - including game scenes with gold, Anson & Deeley boxlock actions, select European hybrid walnut, double triggers, leather cased, currently mfg. While each shotgun is priced per individual special order, the below listed prices represent standard features and embellishments.

▲ *Best Quality*

Mfg.'s Sug. Retail	$9,500	$9,500	$7,750	$6,500	$5,650	$4,800	$4,200	$3,750

▲ *Deluxe Grade* — game scene engraved.

Mfg.'s Sug. Retail	$10,500	$10,500	$8,350	$7,250	$6,000	$5,000	$4,400	$3,750

Add $900 for single trigger.
Add $2,800 for extra set of barrels.
Add $2,200 for smaller gauges.

FEATHERWEIGHT MONARCH GRADE — lavishly engraved with gold game scenes, lightweight model, specifications per individual customer special order. Mfg. began 1989.

▲ *Boxlock Model*

Mfg.'s Sug. Retail	$12,500	$12,500	$9,750	$7,350	$6,000	$5,000	$4,400	$3,750

▲ *Sidelock Model*

Mfg.'s Sug. Retail	$25,000	$25,000	$18,750	$15,000	$12,750	$10,000	$7,950	$6,250

SIDELOCK SxS — made to individual order, choice of game scene engraving, H&H sidelock action, select European hybrid walnut, double triggers, leather cased, currently mfg. While each shotgun is priced per individual special order, the below listed values represent standard features and embellishments.

Mfg.'s Sug. Retail	$17,500	$17,500	$15,000	$12,750	$10,000	$9,000	$8,500	$7,750

Add $4,000 for smaller gauges except .410 — add $5,000.
Add $2,800 for extra set of barrels.
Add $2,800 for extra set of .410 ga. barrels.

DOUBLE RIFLES

BOXLOCK SxS RIFLE — made to individual order, .300 Express, .375 H&H, .458 Win. Mag., or .500 NE cal., choice of game scene engraving, Anson & Deeley boxlock actions, select European hybrid walnut, double triggers, leather cased.

Mfg.'s Sug. Retail	$35,000	$35,000	$27,500	$23,000	$19,000	$16,500	$15,000	$13,250

▲ *.600 Nitro Express*

This model is priced by quotation only. A recently built .600 NE sold for $123,000 in 1991.

SIDELOCK SxS RIFLE — made to individual order, .300 Express, .375 H&H, or .458 Win. Mag. cal., choice of game scene engraving, H&H sidelock action, select European hybrid walnut, double triggers, leather cased.

Mfg.'s Sug. Retail	$65,000	$65,000	$49,500	$40,000	$35,000	$31,000	$25,000	$21,500

Grading	100%	98%	95%	90%	80%	70%	60%

▲ *.600 Nitro Express*
   Mfg.'s Sug. Retail   **$125,000** $125,000 $95,000 $70,000 $54,500 $43,500 $37,500 $31,000
   Premiums are often times paid for these models due to extreme rarity and slow fabrication time.

BREDA MECCANICA BRESCIANA

Manufacturer located in Milan, Italy. Previous company name was Ernesto Breda. No current domestic importer - please refer to the Trademark Index for current factory information. Older importation was by Diana Imports Co., located in San Francisco, CA.

SHOTGUNS: SEMI-AUTO

GOLD SERIES SEMI-AUTO — 12 or 20 (lightweight) ga., semi-auto, 2¾ in., 25 or 27 in. barrels, gas operated. Current model has interchangeable choke tubes, vent. rib is standard. Add $26 for choke tubes (each).

▲ *Antares Standard* — all steel construction. Importation disc. 1988.
   $440 $375 $340 $310 $285 $260 $240
   Last Mfg.'s Sug. Retail was $495.

▲ *Argus* — lightweight standard, weighs only 6.6 lbs. Importation disc. 1988.
   $450 $380 $340 $310 $285 $260 $240
   Last Mfg.'s Sug. Retail was $510.

▲ *Aries* — Magnum, 3 in. chambers, 7.9 lbs. Importation disc. 1988.
   $460 $395 $350 $320 $295 $270 $250
   Last Mfg.'s Sug. Retail was $525.

STANDARD — 12 ga., semi-auto, 2¾ in., 25 or 27 in. barrels, recoil operated, lightly engraved. Current model has interchangeable choke tubes. Add $35 for vent. rib, $20 for choke tubes (each). Disc.
   $300 $275 $255 $230 $215 $200 $180

GRADE 1 — 12 ga., similar to standard, except with fancier wood and engraving.
   $575 $530 $485 $440 $410 $380 $350

GRADE 2 — 12 ga., exceeds Grade 1 on embellishments.
   $685 $620 $560 $500 $460 $420 $375

GRADE 3 — 12 ga., top-of-the-line semi-auto.
   $850 $790 $700 $640 $590 $540 $480

MAGNUM MODEL — 12 ga. only, chambered for 3 in. shells. Add $20 for vent. rib.
   $470 $415 $380 $350 $315 $290 $265

ALTAIR SPECIAL — 12 ga. semi-auto, 2¾ in., 25 or 27 in. barrels, gas operated, alloy construction. Current model has interchangeable choke tubes, vent. rib is standard. Add $25 for choke tubes (each). Choice of blued or chromed receiver.
   $440 $375 $340 $310 $285 $260 $240
   Last Mfg.'s Sug. Retail was $495.

SHOTGUNS: OVER AND UNDER

VEGA SPECIAL — 12 or 20 ga., boxlock action, 26 or 28 in. barrels, single trigger, ejectors, blue only.
   $575 $495 $460 $440 $400 $375 $350
   Last Mfg.'s Sug. Retail was $650.

VEGA SPECIAL TRAP — 12 ga. only, boxlock action, triggers and locks designed for competition shooting, 30 or 32 in. barrels, single trigger, ejectors, blue only.
   $885 $820 $760 $720 $675 $635 $575
   Last Mfg.'s Sug. Retail was $1,114.

Grading	100%	98%	95%	90%	80%	70%	60%

SIRIO STANDARD — 12 or 20 ga., boxlock action, 26 or 28 in. barrels, single trigger, ejectors, blue only, action extensively engraved. Also available in skeet model (28 in. barrels).

	$2,000	$1,850	$1,630	$1,480	$1,320	$1,200	$1,050

Last Mfg.'s Sug. Retail was $2,225.

SHOTGUNS: SIDE-BY-SIDE

ANDROMEDA SPECIAL — 12 ga. only, single trigger, ejectors, select checkered walnut, satin finish receiver with elaborate engraving.

	$640	$550	$480	$420	$365	$300	$250

Last Mfg.'s Sug. Retail was $685.

BREN

Manufactured 1983-86 by Dornaus & Dixon Ent., Inc., located in Huntington Beach, CA.

Bren 10 magazines played an important part in the failure of these pistols to be accepted by consumers. Originally, Bren magazines were not shipped in some cases until a year after the customer received his gun. The complications arising around manufacturing a reliable magazine domestically lead to the downfall of this company. For this reason, original Bren 10 magazines are currently selling for $150-$175 if new (watch for fakes).

PISTOLS

Note: the Bren 10 shoots a Norma factory loaded 10mm auto. cartridge. Ballistically, it is very close to a .41 Mag. Bren pistols also have unique power seal rifling, with five lands and grooves. While in production, Bren pistols underwent (4) engineering changes, the most important probably being re-designing the floorplate of the magazine, thus preventing mag. shifting while undergoing recoil.

100% values in this section assume NIB condition. Subtract 10% without box/manual.

BREN 10 STANDARD MODEL — 10mm only, semi-auto selective double action design, blue slide/silver frame finish, 5 in. barrel, 11 shot, stainless steel frame, usually supplied with two mags. although early mfg. did not include a mag. because of design problems, "83SM" scr. no. prefix. Mfg. 1984-86.

$1,550 $1,250 $975

Last Mfg.'s Sug. Retail was $500.

Add $600 for .45 conversion unit.

BREN 10 MILITARY/POLICE MODEL — 10mm only, identical to standard model, except has all black finish, "83MP" ser. no. prefix. Mfg. 1984-86.

$1,495 $1,195 $950

Last Mfg.'s Sug. Retail was $550.

BREN 10 SPECIAL FORCES MODEL — 10mm only, commercial version of the military pistol submitted to the U.S. gov't. Model D has dark finish. Model L has light finish, "SFD" ser. no. prefix on Model D, "SFL" ser. no. prefix on Model L. Disc. 1986.

Dark finish - Model D $1,595 $1,275 $975
Light finish - Model L $1,895 $1,575 $1,275

Last Mfg.'s Sug. Retail was $600.

BREN 10 DUAL-MASTER PRESENTATION MODEL — 10mm and .45 ACP, supplied with extra slide and barrel (numbered to gun) to accommodate the .45 ACP, same mags. (two) for both cals., extra fine finish, light scroll engraving, with wood presentation case, "83DM" ser. no. prefix, less than 50 mfg. Disc. 1986.

$3,800 $2,950 $2,300

Last Mfg.'s Sug. Retail was $800.

Grading	100%	98%	95%	90%	80%	70%	60%

BREN 10 JEFF COOPER COMMEMORATIVE — 10mm only, while 2,000 were annnounced for mfg., sources believe less than 30 were actually made, 22Kt. gold plated detailing, laser engraved stocks, special presentation chest. Disc. 1986.

	$4,600	$4,000	$3,700				

Last Mfg.'s Sug. Retail was $2,000.

MARKSMAN MODEL — .45 ACP, 250 mfg. (in its own ser. range) for a retail shop in Chicago called "The Marksman", action similar to Bren 10 Standard Model, "MSM" ser. no. prefix.

	$1,200	$895	$695				

Add $650 for 10mm conversion unit.
Add $100 for original nylon carrying case marked "Marksman".

BRETTON

Manufactured in Saint-Etienne, France. Imported and distributed by Mandall Shooting Supplies, Inc. located in Scottsdale, AZ.

SHOTGUNS: OVER AND UNDER

All Bretton shotguns are extremely lightweight and well balanced because of their unique design (permitting total disassembly including barrels) and use of various composition alloys.

BABY STANDARD (SPRINT MODEL) — 12 or 20 ga. only, sliding breech action allows barrels to move straight forward, 27½ in. separated barrels, double triggers, side opening lever, blued action and barrels, recoil pad, checkered walnut stock and forearm, 4.8 lbs.

Mfg.'s Sug. Retail	$995	$885	$700	$625	$575	$475	$430	$395

Available from Mandall Shooting Supply, Inc. only.

SPRINT DELUXE — 12, 16 (disc.), or 20 ga., action similar to Baby Standard, engraved coin finished receiver, 27½ in. separated barrels, deluxe checkered walnut stock and forearm, extremely lightweight, 4.8 lbs. Importation disc. 1994.

	$895	$725	$625	$575	$475	$430	$395

Last Mfg.'s Sug. Retail was $975.

Available from Quality Arms, Inc. and Mandall Shooting Supply, Inc.

FAIR PLAY MODEL — 12 or 20 ga., differs from Sprint Models in that action pivots like normal O/U, 27½ in. separated barrels, lightweight construction, 4.8 lbs.

Mfg.'s Sug. Retail	$966	$850	$675	$625	$575	$475	$430	$395

Add $64 for Fair Play Limited Model.

BRITARMS

Manufactured by Berdan Gunmakers Ltd. located in England. Previously imported and distributed until 1994 by Mandall Shooting Supplies, Inc. located in Scottsdale, AZ. Previously by Action Arms Ltd. (1982-83) located in Philadelphia, PA.

Britarms Target Pistols have had very limited importation to date in the U.S. While Britarms has manufactured other models, only the Model 2000 is listed since it has been formally imported through U.S. firms.

Model 2000 (MK II) — .22 LR, standard fire target semi-auto pistol, adj. trigger and rear sight, anatomical adj. grips, 5.82 in. barrel, 5 shot mag., 3 lbs., limited importation, including approx. 200 through Action Arms Ltd.

	$995	$825	$700	$625	$550	$495	$450

Last Mfg.'s Sug. Retail was $1,295.

This model features a bolt hold-open mechanism which serves as a manual safety to allow importation.

BRNO ARMS

Manufactured in Brno & Uherski Brod, Czechoslovakia since 1936. Brno rifles (except semi-auto), shotguns, and combination guns produced at the Brno factory are currently imported and distributed by Magnum Research Inc. located in Minneapolis, MN and Bohemia Arms located in Fountain Valley, CA. Pragotrade located in Ontario, Canada also imports this trademark for Canada currently (and exclusively). Previously imported by T.D. Arms located in New Baltimore, MI.

While little history is known about this important European trademark, the following biographical sketch will provide some information. In approximately 1916, some military personnel took over the controlling interest of the Austro-Hungarian armament shop in Brno, Czechoslovakia, renaming it The State Armament and Engineering Works. Approximately a year later, the name was changed to Czechoslovak State Armament Works. Prior to 1924, this firm was involved mainly with Mauser Model 98 type rifles (both assembly and mfg.).

In 1924, the name was again changed to Ceskoslovenska Zbrojovka A.Z. (Czechoslovakian Arms Factory Ltd.) - commonly known as the CZ firm. CZ manufactured the VZ-24 Mauser rifle for Czechoslovakia as well as other M-98 military rifles and carbines for other countries, including many which Germany used during WWII. After WWII, the name was again changed to Zbrojovka Brno (Brno Arms Works), or ZB for short.

With the iron curtain descending on Europe after WWII, communist bloc countries had little exportation to the U.S., including Czechoslovakia. In the early '50s, Brno rifles were imported by Continental Arms Corp. located in New York City. Since the sudden decline of communism in 1992, more and more products (including firearms from Czechoslovakia) will see their way into the U.S. without the 65% importation tax previously levied on goods from older communist bloc countries.

Grading	100%	98%	95%	90%	80%	70%	60%

CZ PISTOLS & RIFLES

See separate listing under CZ in this text.

RIFLES: BOLT ACTION

The Brno Lightweight Sporter was introduced in the late 1930s. A small quantity was manufactured during pre-war and WWII. Most production occured between 1946-1955. Total production of this model was approx. 40,000+ units. A design change was implemented at approximately serial number 23,000, at which time the receiver was changed to a double square bridge dovetailed to accept scope mounts.

Earlier mfg. had a rounded receiver and some had claw type scope mounts installed. These guns were referenced as Models 21 and 22 domestically, but no model designation appears on the gun. Available cals. were 6.5x57, 7x57, 7x64, 8x57, or 8x60mm. Configuration was small ring Mauser 98 receiver with double set trigger(s), butterknife bolt, checkered walnut pistol grip stock (half or full length), with cheekpiece and sling swivels, late production incorporated four variations and two barrel lengths (20.5 or 23.6 in.).

BRNO RIFLES MAY BE DATED BY THE 2-DIGIT DATE BESIDE THEIR PROOFMARKS.

HORNET SPORTER (MODEL ZKW 465) — miniature Mauser action, .22 Hornet, 22¾ in. barrel, 5 shot clip mag., 3-leaf express sight, double set trigger(s), checkered pistol grip stock, also called Z-B Mauser, serial range noted is 02,901-37,393, approx. 40,000 mfg. between 1949-1973.

$875 $700 $600 $470 $385 $305 $220

There are few examples in .218 Bee and .222 Rem. cal. - premiums can be added.

This model was redesigned with a subsequent designation of ZKB 680 Fox in approx. 1975.

B

Grading	100%	98%	95%	90%	80%	70%	60%

MODEL ZG-47 — .270 Win., .30-06, 7x57, 7x64, 8x 64S, 8x57mm, 9.3x62, or 10.75x68mm cal., large ring Mauser 98 action with 20mm dovetails on receiver ring and bridge, single trigger, hinged floorplate, rollover type safety and bolt handle designed for low scope mounting, 23½ in. barrel, checkered pistol grip walnut stock with sling swivels and Schnabel forend, approx. serial range is 0-20,000, mfg. and exported world-wide between 1956-1962 (approx.).

	$995	$875	$700	$600	$470	$385	$305

> Early specimens of this model are marked "BRNO MADE IN CZECHOSLOVAKIA". This model is generally regarded as being one of the finest rifles that Brno has manufactured.

MODEL 21H — 6.5x57, 7x57, 7x64 (scarce), or 8x57 cal., featherweight style design of the small ring Mauser type action, with (post-1949) or without 20mm dovetails on receiver ring and bridge, 20½ or 23 in. barrel, butterknife style bolt handle, double set triggers, 2-leaf rear sight, checkered pistol grip walnut stock with cheekpiece and plastic buttplate/grip cap, small Schnabel forend, sling swivels included, noted serialization is 14,410-40,098, mfg. approx. 1946-1955.

	$850	$675	$575	$470	$385	$305	$220

> This model was available in 4 different variations: short barrel/short stock, short barrel/full length stock, long barrel/short stock, long barrel/full length stock. The left receiver rail on these models is marked "ZBROJOVKA BRNO, NARODNI PODNIK".

MODEL 22F — similar to 21H, with full length stock. Disc.

	$1,050	$900	$700	$525	$440	$360	$275

MODEL 1 — .22 LR, 22¾ in. barrel, 3-leaf sight, 5 shot clip mag., checkered pistol, 6 lbs. Mfg. 1946-1957.

	$595	$540	$485	$405	$375	$320	$265

MODEL 2 — similar to Model 1, with checkered deluxe walnut stock.

	$635	$570	$515	$430	$405	$350	$295

MODEL 3 — .22 LR, target rifle model with 27½ in. heavy barrel, adj. click target sights, 5 shot clip mag., plain target style stock with large swivels, 9½ lbs. Mfg. 1949-1956.

	$635	$570	$515	$430	$405	$350	$295

MODEL 4 — similar to Model 3, except has improved trigger design and safety. Mfg. 1957-1962.

	$700	$635	$570	$515	$430	$405	$350

MODEL 5 — similar to Model 1, except has improved trigger design and safety. Mfg. 1957-1973.

	$650	$570	$515	$430	$405	$350	$295

MODEL ZKM-451 MILITARY — .22 LR. Importation began 1995.

Mfg.'s Sug. Retail	$347	$295	$250	$210	$175	$155	$135	$120

MODEL ZKM-452 — please refer to the CZ listing in this text for current information (current mfg. is by CZ).

MODEL ZKM-456 LUX SPORTER — .22 LR cal., bolt action, 5 or 10 shot mag., 24.4 in. barrel, folding rear sight, blued finish, beechwood stock with pistol grip, 6.8 lbs. Importation began 1992.

Mfg.'s Sug. Retail	$370	$315	$260	$215	$175	$155	$135	$120

> Add $18 for micrometer rear sight (ZKM-456 MI).
>
> This model and its variations are imported exclusively by Bohemia Arms International.

▲ *Model 456 L/LK Target* — .22 LR cal., Target variation of the ZKM-456 Lux featuring 25 or 28 in. barrel with adj. front and rear sights, 10.1 lbs. Importation began 1992.

Mfg.'s Sug. Retail	$358	$305	$250	$210	$170	$150	$130	$115

> Add $7 for 25 in. barrel.

▲ *Model 456 Match Single Shot* — .22 LR cal., designed for UIT competition at 50 M, features 27½ in. barrel, adj. cheekpiece and buttplate, aperture sights, 9.9 lbs. Importation began 1992.

Mfg.'s Sug. Retail	$459	$375	$335	$280	$250	$215	$175	$155

Grading	100%	98%	95%	90%	80%	70%	60%

MODEL 513 HUNTER — .22 LR, entry level bolt action, 5 shot detachable mag., beechwood stock. Imported 1994 only.

	$195	$175	$150	$125	$95	$80	$65

Last Mfg.'s Sug. Retail was $225.

B

Add $30 for Farmer Model.

This model is imported exclusively by Action Arms.

ZKK 600 — please refer to the CZ listing in this text for current information (recent mfg. is by CZ).

ZKK 601 — please refer to the CZ listing in this text for current information (recent mfg. was by CZ).

ZKK 602 — please refer to the CZ listing in this text for current information (current mfg. is by CZ).

ZKB 680 (FOX II) — .22 Hornet or .222 Rem. (disc.) cal., $23\frac{1}{2}$ in. barrel, 5 shot mag., set triggers, 5 lbs. 12 oz. Importation disc. 1991.

	$445	$380	$340	$295	$255	$230	$200

Last Mfg.'s Sug. Retail was $499.

RIFLES: SEMI-AUTO

CZ-511 — .22 LR, semi-auto, select walnut stock, adj. sights. Disc. 1986.

	$280	$250	$230	$215	$200	$190	$180

Last Mfg.'s Sug. Retail was $310.

ZKM-611 — .22 Mag. cal., $20\frac{1}{2}$ in. barrel, 6, 10 (C/B 1994), or 12* shot mag., black metal finish, beechwood (new 1996) or walnut stock and forend, grooved receiver, 6.2 lbs. Importation began 1992.

Mfg.'s Sug. Retail	$499	$415	$360	$300	$265	$230	$200	$185

Add $70 for walnut stock.

This model is imported exclusively by Magnum Research located in Minneapolis, MN.

MODEL 581 — .22 LR, semi-auto, select walnut stock, adj. sights, 5 shot mag. Disc.

	$600	$540	$495	$440	$395	$350	$295

RIFLES: O/U

SUPER EXPRESS — 7x65R, 9.3x74R, .375 H&H, or .458 Win. Mag. (disc.) cal., sidelock action with Kersten breech crossbolt, hand engraved, skipline checkering, approx. 9 lbs. Importation disc. 1992.

	$3,450	$2,875	$2,300	$1,875	$1,600	$1,375	$1,200

Last Mfg.'s Sug. Retail was $3,900.

This model previously could be ordered with 6 different types of engraving options. They were: Grade I — add $2,060, Grade II — add $1,030, Grade III — add $1,545, Grade IV — add $1,030, Grade V — add $620, Grade VI — add $660.

SUPER SAFARI — 7x64R, .375 H&H Mag., or 9.3x74R cal., action derived from the Super Express, sidelock, DT with set trigger built in, adj. point of impact, 23.6 in. barrels with open sights, deluxe skipline checkered walnut stock and forearm with vent. recoil pad, approx. 9 lbs. Importation began 1992.

No Mfg.'s Retail	$2,375	$1,975	$1,675	$1,450	$1,225	$1,000	$900

This model is imported exclusively by Bohemia Arms International.

SHOTGUNS/COMBINATIONS GUNS: O/U

The current models listed below are being imported and distributed by Bohemia Arms International located in Fountain Valley, CA unless otherwise noted.

Grading	100%	98%	95%	90%	80%	70%	60%

ZH-SERIES
> Add $25 for Monte Carlo stock (disc.).
> Add for $45 for set triggers (disc.).
>
> ZH series over and unders are unique in that they permit 8 different interchangeable barrels including rifle and shotgun sets, interrupter on double trigger, blued action, engraved, diamond checkered walnut.

ZH-300 — 12 ga. only, double triggers with rear trigger doubling as single trigger, 27½ in. barrels, 7 lbs. Imported 1986-92.

		$530	$430	$395	$360	$330	$300	$275

Last Mfg.'s Sug. Retail was $599.

> This model is available in skeet, trap, or field configuration.

ZH-301 FIELD — 12 ga. field, 27½ in. barrels, optional Monte Carlo stock (disc.).

Mfg.'s Sug. Retail	$644	$595	$495	$350	$275	$225	$195	$175

> Add $20 for Monte Carlo stock.

ZH-302 SKEET — 12 ga., skeet model, 26 in. barrels, optional Monte Carlo stock (disc.).

Mfg.'s Sug. Retail	$694	$625	$525	$375	$295	$225	$195	$175

> Add $20 for Monte Carlo stock.

ZH-303 TRAP — 12 ga., trap model, 30 in. barrels, optional Monte Carlo stock (disc.).

Mfg.'s Sug. Retail	$694	$625	$525	$375	$295	$225	$195	$175

> Add $20 for Monte Carlo stock.

ZH-304 COMBINATION GUN — 7x57Rmm x 12 ga., combination rifle/shotgun, optional adj. trigger and Monte Carlo stock. Importation disc. 1994.

		$595	$500	$450	$395	$360	$330	$300

> Add $35 for adj. trigger.
> Add $20 for Monte Carlo stock.

ZH-305 — 5.6x52Rmm x 12 ga., combination rifle/shotgun. Disc.

		$685	$640	$585	$520	$460	$415	$360

ZH-306 — 5.6x50mm Mag. x 12 ga., combination rifle/shotgun. Disc.

		$685	$640	$585	$520	$460	$415	$360

ZH-307 COMBINATION GUN — .22 Hornet x 12 ga., approx. 8 lbs. Importation began 1995.

Mfg.'s Sug. Retail	$784	$675	$550	$395	$325	$250	$195	$175

ZH-321 — 16 ga. field, 27 in. barrels. Disc. 1986.

		$570	$505	$460	$435	$410	$390	$370

Last Mfg.'s Sug. Retail was $605.

ZH-324 — 7x57Rmm x 16 ga., combination rifle/shotgun. Disc. 1986.

		$640	$570	$530	$495	$475	$450	$420

Last Mfg.'s Sug. Retail was $685.

MODEL ZH-300 COMBO SET — Model ZH-300 style engraving and features, equipped with 8 interchangeable barrels that include various O/U configurations including shotgun/shotgun and shotgun/rifle configurations in various ga.'s and cals. Imported 1986-91.

		$2,950	$2,600	$2,250	$2,000	$1,800	$1,600	$1,450

Last Mfg.'s Sug. Retail was $3,500.

MODEL 500/501 SERIES O/U SHOTGUN — 12 ga. only, 28 in. VR barrels, double or single trigger.

Mfg.'s Sug. Retail	$875	$775	$650	$550	$475	$400	$350	$295

> Add $50 for single trigger.

Grading	100%	98%	95%	90%	80%	70%	60%

B

▲ *Model 500 Combo Set* — shotgun/rifle set comprised of 4 barrels including 12 ga. over barrels with choice of 5.6x52R (disc.), 7x57R, 7x65Rmm, or 12 ga. under barrels (in either field, skeet, or trap chokings), sling swivels, set trigger on rifle/shotgun combo, chemically engraved, about 7½ lbs. Imported 1987-91.

		$1,925	$1,625	$1,400	$1,200	$1,075	$950	$825

Last Mfg.'s Sug. Retail was $2,169.

This model is available in limited quanitity.

MODEL 502 SERIES O/U COMBINATION GUN — 12 ga. only, ejectors, combination shotgun/rifle available in .222 Rem., .243 Win., .30-06, or .308 Win. cal., fixed choke, acid etched engraving, skipline checkering and cheekpiece. New 1986.

Mfg.'s Sug. Retail	$999	$875	$750	$650	$575	$500	$425	$350

BS-571/572 SHOTGUN/COMBINATION GUN — 12 ga. only, boxlock action with ejectors, 6x65R (disc.) or 7x65R rifle cal. only. Limited importation 1992-95.

		$825	$700	$600	$550	$475	$425	$375

Last Mfg.'s Sug. Retail was $995.

Add approx. $115 for rifle/shotgun (12 ga. only) combination (Model 572).

MODEL 571 SUPER SERIES — available in 12 ga. field, skeet, and trap configuration as well as combination shotgun/rifle in 12 ga. x 7x57R or 7x65R cal. Importation disc. 1991.

		$800	$700	$640	$590	$550	$515	$475

Last Mfg.'s Sug. Retail was $899.

Add $70 for single trigger or trap/skeet configuration (disc.).
Add $700 for extra set of 12 ga. field barrels.
Add $1,101 for hand engraving.

▲ *Super Combo* — 3 barrel set including 12 ga., 7x57Rmm, and 7x65R mm barrels. Imported 1987-90.

		$1,925	$1,640	$1,425	$1,250	$1,100	$1,000	$925

Last Mfg.'s Sug. Retail was $2,169.

CZ-581 — 12 ga., boxlock with Greener crossbolt, Poldi steel action, 28 in. barrels, vent. rib, ejectors, sling swivels. Importation disc. 1995.

		$585	$525	$450	$395	$355	$300	$275

Last Mfg.'s Sug. Retail was $695.

Add $30 for single trigger (disc.)

CZ-584 — 12 ga. and 7x57 Mauser rifle/shotgun combination , .222 Rem., .223 Rem. (new 1994), .243 Win. (new 1994), .30-06 (new 1994), 7mm Mauser (new 1994), and .308 Win. cals. also available, 24½ in. barrels, ejectors. Importation disc. 1986, resumed 1994 - disc. 1995.

		$750	$650	$600	$550	$500	$450	$375

Last Mfg.'s Sug. Retail was $825.

SHOTGUNS: SIDE-BY-SIDE

ZP-49 — 12 ga. only, ejectors, double triggers, true sidelock, Purdey-type top bolt, cocking indicators, walnut stock, swivels. Imported 1986-91.

		$535	$460	$420	$385	$350	$320	$290

Last Mfg.'s Sug. Retail was $589.

Add $20 for engraving.

ZP-149 — similar to ZP-49, except has game scene engraving on sideplates, choice of English or pistol grip stock. Imported began 1986.

Mfg.'s Sug. Retail	$625	$550	$475	$400	$350	$300	$250	$225

Add $45 for pistol grip stock.

ZP-349 — 12 ga. only, extractors, double triggers, true sidelock, Purdey-type top bolt, cocking indicators, walnut stock with cheek piece, beavertail forearm, swivels, 7.3 lbs. Imported 1986 only.

		$450	$390	$360	$325	$300	$270	$250

Last Mfg.'s Sug. Retail was $520.

Add $20 for engraving.

BROLIN ARMS

Handgun and custom parts manufacturer located in La Verne, CA since 1995.

Grading	100%	98%	95%	90%	80%	70%	60%

LEGEND SERIES MODEL L45 — .45 ACP, patterned after the Colt 1911 Government Model, features include throated match 5 in. barrel, polished feed ramp, flared ejection port, beveled mag. well, flat top slide, flat mainspring housing, front strap high relief cut, aluminum lightweight extended trigger, high visibility sights, 7 shot mag., commander style hammer and checkered walnut grips, 36 oz. New 1995.

Mfg.'s Sug. Retail	$449	$400	$350	$315	$295	$275	$250	$225

▲ *Legend Series Model L45C (Compact)* — similar to Model L45, except has 4 in. barrel, 32 oz. New 1995.

Mfg.'s Sug. Retail	$459	$410	$365	$320	$295	$275	$250	$225

PATRIOT SERIES MODEL P45 COMP — .45 ACP, similar to Legend Series Model L45, except has one-piece match 4 in. barrel with integral dual port compensator, 7 shot mag., test target provided, choice of blue or satin (frame only) finish, 37 oz. New 1996.

Mfg.'s Sug. Retail	$649	$585	$475	$415	$365	$325	$285	$250

Add $20 for T-tone finish (frame only).

▲ *Patriot Series Model P45C (Compact)* — .45 ACP, similar to Model P45 Comp, except has 31.4 in. barrel with integral conical lock-up system, 33 oz. New 1996.

Mfg.'s Sug. Retail	$679	$600	$485	$425	$375	$325	$285	$250

Add $20 for T-tone finish (frame only).

PRO STOCK MODEL COMPETITION PISTOL — .45 ACP, competition pistol featuring most state-of-the-art competitive improvements, 5 in. barrel, 8 shot mag., blue or satin (frame only) finish, signature wood grips, 37 oz. New 1996.

Mfg.'s Sug. Retail	$779	$685	$550	$475	$415	$360	$295	$260

Add $20 for T-tone finish (frame only).

▲ *Pro Comp Model Competition Pistol* — similar to Pro Stock Model, except has 4 in. dual port compensated heavy match barrel, blue or satin (frame only) finish, 37 oz. New 1996.

Mfg.'s Sug. Retail	$909	$795	$650	$525	$435	$375	$325	$295

Add $20 for T-tone finish (frame only).

BRONCO

Echave Y Arizmendi, Eibar, Spain.

MODEL 1918 POCKET AUTOMATIC — 7.65mm, 6 shot, $2\frac{1}{2}$ in. barrel, fixed sights, blue, hard rubber grips. Mfg. 1918-1925.

	$175	$150	$100	$80	$70	$60	$50

VEST POCKET AUTOMATIC — 6.35mm, small frame. Disc.

	$160	$125	$110	$95	$80	$60	$40

DAVID MCKAY BROWN (GUNMAKERS) LTD.

Established 1967 in Bothwell, Glasgow, Scotland. Makers of Scottish Round Action Side-by-Side and Over & Under shotguns and rifles (approx. 30 guns mfg. annually). David McKay Brown apprenticed with Alex Martin Ltd. and John Dickson & Son before establishing his own gunmaking company. All guns made to customer order on trigger plated round actions. Delivery approximately $2\frac{1}{2}$ years. Available through U.S. agent, Griffin & Howe, New York City and Bernardsville, NJ.

Prices below reflect the most recent exchange rate (1 pound = $1.57) and are for standard models only.

B

RIFLES: DOUBLE, SxS

David Mckay Brown should be contacted directly for a firm quotation on a SxS double rifle.

SHOTGUNS

Add $1,075 for single trigger.
Add $392 for Pistol/Prince of Wales grip.

SIDE-BY-SIDE SHOTGUN — 12, 16, 20, 28, or .410 ga., features rounded case colored action, double triggers, full scroll engraving, custom order only.

Mfg.'s Sug. Retail	$33,000	$33,000	$26,250	$22,750	$18,750	$15,000	$13,000	$11,000

Add $1,800 for .410 ga.

O/U SHOTGUN — 12, 16, 20, 28, or .410 ga., features rounded case colored action, double triggers, full scroll engraving, custom order only.

Mfg.'s Sug. Retail	$45,500	$45,500	$36,250	$31,000	$26,500	$22,500	$18,500	$14,750

Add $2,700 for .410 ga.

BROWN PRECISION, INC.

Manufacturer located in Los Molinos, CA since 1967.

Brown Precision Inc. manufactures primarily rifles using Remington or Winchester actions and restocks them using a combination of Kevlar, Fiberglass and Graphite (wrinkle finish) to save weight. Stock colors are green, brown, gray, black, camo brown, camo green, or camo grey.

PISTOLS

CUSTOM XP-100 HIGH COUNTRY — includes highly tuned XP-100 single shot action with Shilen stainless match grade barrel, electroless nickel or Teflon finish, fiberglass stock. New 1993.

Mfg.'s Sug. Retail	$1,690	$1,550	$1,375	$1,150	$950	$775	$650	$525

RIFLES: BOLT ACTION

STANDARD HIGH COUNTRY BOLT ACTION RIFLE — various cals. within those factory barreled actions, choice of 700 ADL/BDL, Ruger 77, or Win. Model 70 action, brown fiberglass/Kevlar stock (various colors), sling swivels and pad. Mfg. 1975-present.

Mfg.'s Sug. Retail	$1,255	$1,125	$925	$750	$625	$525	$440	$400

Add $320 for Win. Model 70 Super Grade action with controlled round feeding.
Add approx. $95 for left-hand BDL, Ruger 77, or Win. M-70 action.

▲ *Custom High Country* — similar to High Country, except many custom features can be added. Prices available per individual work order.

Mfg.'s Sug. Retail	$2,115	$1,940	$1,575	$1,400	$1,175	$950	$725	$575

HIGH COUNTRY YOUTH RIFLE — various cals., choice of Rem. Model 7 or 700 factory barreled action, fiberglass stock. New 1993.

Mfg.'s Sug. Retail	$1,340	$1,175	$975	$775	$675	$550	$495	$440

MODEL 7 SUPER LIGHT — .223, .243, 6mm, 7mm-08 Rem., or .308 Win. cal., Model 7 action, 18 in. factory barrel, no sights, 5 lbs. 4 oz. Disc. 1992.

	$995	$900	$750	$650	$575	$500	$450

Last Mfg.'s Sug. Retail was $1,059.

This model could have been special ordered with similar options from the Custom High Country Model, with the exception of left-hand action.

Grading	100%	98%	95%	90%	80%	70%	60%

LAW ENFORCEMENT SELECTIVE TARGET — .308 cal., Model 700 Varmint action with 20, 22, or 24 in. factory barrel, O.D. green camouflage treatment. Disc. 1992.

	$995	$900	$750	$650	$575	$500	$450

Last Mfg.'s Sug. Retail was $1,086.

This model could have been special ordered with similar options from the Custom High Country Model, with the exception of left-hand action.

PRO VARMINTER — various cals., includes custom tuned Rem. Model 700 ADL action, Shilen match stainless steel barrel. New 1993.

Mfg.'s Sug. Retail	$1,965	$1,750	$1,450	$1,175	$975	$775	$650	$525

Add $120 for left-hand action.
Add $485 for optional Rem. Model 40-XB action.

PRO HUNTER — available in over 25 cals., Model 700 ADL or Model 70 action, match grade stainless steel barrel, dull electroless nickel, blue, or teflon finish, express sights, synthetic stock (four different colors). New 1988.

Mfg.'s Sug. Retail	$2,670	$2,325	$1,975	$1,600	$1,375	$1,175	$995	$825

Add $120 for left-hand action.

▲ *Pro Hunter Elite* — various cals., includes many custom order features. New 1993.

Mfg.'s Sug. Retail	$3,565	$3,275	$2,750	$2,275	$1,975	$1,700	$1,525	$1,250

In late 1991, improvements were made including decelerator recoil pad, barrel band swivel, and speed lock firing pin spring.

BROWN PRECISION WINCHESTER 70 — .270 or .30-06 cal., 22 in. featherweight barrel, camo stock in four colors with black recoil pad, 6¼ lbs. Mfg. 1989-92.

	$650	$575	$475	$425	$385	$325	$300

Last Mfg.'s Sug. Retail was $750.

Add $20 for 7mm Rem. Mag. (24 in. sporter barrel).

BLASER BOLT ACTION RIFLE — standard Camex Blaser cals. and action, fiberglass stock and nickel plated barrel. Disc. 1989.

	$1,395	$1,150	$995	$875	$750	$675	$600

Last Mfg.'s Sug. Retail was $1,395.

BROWNING

Browning guns originally were manufactured in Ogden, UT, circa 1880. Current BAC headquarters (not manufacturing) are located in Morgan, UT. Browning firearms are manufactured by Fabrique Nationale in Herstal and Liege, Belgium. Since 1976, Browning has also contracted Miroku of Japan and A.T.I. in Salt Lake City, UT to manufacture both long arms and handguns. During 1992, Browning (including F.N.) was acquired by GIAT of France.

BROWNING

The Browning section in this text has been arranged in the following order — PISTOLS, RIFLES, SHOTGUNS: SEMI-AUTO, SHOTGUNS: O/U, OTHER SHOTGUNS, LIMITED EDITIONS-COMMEMORATIVES.

BROWNING HISTORY

The Browning firm, first known as J.M. Browning & Bro., was established in Ogden, Utah about 1880. Later known as Browning Brothers and Browning Arms Company (BAC), the firm actually manufactured only one gun — the Model 1878 Single Shot which was John M.'s first patent. Winchester bought the production and distribution rights to this gun in 1883, bringing it out as the Winchester M1885. From that time until 1900, Mr. Browning sold Winchester the exclusive rights to 31 rifles and 13 shotguns, of which Winchester produced only 7 rifles (M1885SS: the lever actions M1886, 1892, 1894 and 1895: and the slide action .22s M1890 and 1906) and 3 shotguns (M1887, M1893 and M1897). The other models were bought from Browning simply to keep them out of the hands of other arms makers.

John M. Browning, perhaps the greatest firearms inventor the world has ever known, was directly responsible for an estimated 80 separate firearms that evolved from his 128 patents. During his most prolific period from 1894 to 1910, Browning sold the rights to his rifles, semi-auto pistols, shotguns and machine guns to Winchester, Remington, Colt and Stevens in this country and to Fabrique Nationale for sale outside the U.S. Every Colt and FN semi-auto pistol is based on a Browning patent. In 1902, Browning broke off relations with Winchester when the company refused to negotiate a royalty arrangement for his new semi-auto shotgun(A-5). Browning took the prototype to FN where it became the most commercially successful of all his inventions. FN has produced 6 automatic pistols, 3 rifles and 2 shotguns designed by John M. Browning and is still a major producer of arms sold by Browning in the U.S. and by FN distributors worldwide.

Our American military was armed for many years with Browning designed weaponry, not the least of which is the venerable "Old Slabside" 1911 Govt. Model .45 ACP. Today, the firm that bears the Browning name still stands at the forefront with the other makers of fine sporting firearms.

BROWNING FACTS

Note: Between 1966-1971 Browning used a salt-curing process to speed the drying time needed for their walnut stock blanks. Unfortunately, the salt would be released from the wood and oxidize the metal surface(s) after a period of time. These guns, especially bolt action rifles in all grades, some BARs, Superposed shotguns, and T-bolt models should be examined carefully around the edges of the wood for signs of freckling and rust. Discount guns that show evidence of salt corrosion 15-50%, depending on how bad rusting has occurred. Check screws and wood under butt plate as well.

Since the inception and standardization of steel shot for hunting purposes, the desirability factor of shotguns has changed considerably. Any shorter barreled, open choked Belgian Browning shotgun is currently quite a bit more desirable than its 30 in., full choked barrel counterpart. Premiums do exist for this shorter barreled configuration, especially on the Belgian Superposed and A-5 Models. On newer manufacture, choke tubes have become very desirable, and specimens without choke tubes (especially guns with longer barrels) must be discounted somewhat. Browning does not recommend using steel shot in any Superposed (B-25) or older Belgian Auto-5 barrels.

BROWNING VALUES INFORMATION

Editor's Note: It is important to note the differences in values of Browning weapons manufactured in Belgium by F.N. and those made recently in Japan by Miroku. We feel that these values are somewhat higher because of collector interest in Browning guns made in Belgium and not as the result of any inferiority of the quality of Browning guns made anywhere else.

AS A FINAL NOTE: Most post-war Brownings are collectible only if in 95% or better condition as most models have relatively high mfg. and are not that old. Condition under 95% is normally very shootable, but not as collectible and values for 95% or less condition could be lower than shown in some areas.

Most 100% values in this section assume NIB condition. Subtract 10% without box/manual. Also, all add-ons or deductions in this section reflect retail pricing without any discounting. On higher grade Browning firearms that are engraved, signed specimens by FN's master engravers Funken, J. Baerten, Vrancken, and Watrin will command premiums over the values listed below.

BROWNING SERIALIZATION

In addition to the Browning serialization listed in the back of this text, the following codes will determine the year and origin of those guns made from 1975 to date. The 2 letters in the middle of the serial number are the code designations for year

Grading	100%	98%	95%	90%	80%	70%	60%

of manufacture. They represent the following: RV - 1975, RT - 1976, RR - 1977, RP - 1978, RN - 1979, PM - 1980, PZ - 1981, PY - 1982, PX - 1983, PW - 1984, PV - 1985, PT -1986, PR - 1987, PP - 1988, PN - 1989, NM - 1990, NZ - 1991, NY - 1992, NX - 1993, NW - 1994, NV - 1995, NU - 1996.

Since most Brownings use a 3-digit model identification code (appearing first on European or U.S. mfg. guns and last on Japanese mfg.), both where and when the specimen was made can easily be determined (i.e. Ser. No. 611RP2785 would be a Model B-2000 made in either Belgium or Portugal in 1978 with 2785 being the Ser. No.— Ser. No. 01479PX368 indicates a BSS 20 ga. mfg. in Japan in 1983).

PISTOLS: SEMI-AUTO, F.N. PRODUCTION UNLESS OTHERWISE NOTED

MODEL 1900-FN — 7.65mm cal., first Belgian Browning, 4 in. barrel. 724,500 mfg. 1899-1910.

	$350	$295	$240	$200	$160	$130	$100

Add 30% for early pistols with "pistol logo" grips.

MODEL 1903-FN — 9mm Browning Long cartridge, 5 in. barrel. 58,400 mfg. 1903-1939.

	$500	$425	$350	$300	$260	$220	$180

Add 50% if slotted to accept shoulder stock.

This variation was also manufactured with a detachable shoulder stock — this accessory is rare and can add as much as $2,000 to values listed above.

MODEL 1903-SWEDISH CONTRACT — 9mm cal., manufactured by Husqvarna and Swedish Arsenal (so marked), many were imported into U.S. and converted to .380 ACP from original Browning 9mm Long.

	$300	$260	$230	$200	$180	$150	$125

Deduct 25% for .380 ACP conversion.

MODEL 1905-FN (VEST POCKET) — 6.35mm (.25 ACP), dubbed "Vest Pocket" model, manufactured by Fabrique Nationale, Herstal, Belgium. 1,086,133, mfg. 1906-1959.

▲ *First Variation* — no slide lock/safety lever.

	$350	$285	$255	$225	$170	$135	$100

Add 10% for nickel finish.

▲ *Second Variation* — post 1908, with slide lock/safety lever.

	$325	$285	$255	$210	$170	$135	$100

Add 10% for nickel finish.

MODEL 1910-FN (MODEL 1955) — 7.65mm (.32 ACP) and Browning 9mm short (.380 ACP) 4 in. barrel. FN manufacture. 701,266 mfg. 1912-1980.

	$325	$300	$275	$250	$225	$195	$150

Add 20% if BAC marked and .380 ACP cal.
Add 30% if BAC marked and 7.65mm cal.

This model is also referred to as the Model 1955. BAC marked pistols were imported 1954-1968.

MODEL 1922 OR 10/22 FN — 7.65mm (.32 ACP) or .380 ACP cal., modified Model 1910 with 4½ in. barrel, longer grip frame and mag., made for commercial sale as well as military contracts. Several hundred thousand made by Nazis during the occupation of Liege, Belgium 1940-1944. Mfg. between 1912-1959.

	$240	$215	$195	$175	$150	$125	$110

Add 10% for Waffenampt proofing.
Add 20% for foreign contracts.
Add 20% if .380 ACP Waffenampt proofed.

The Model 10/22 and M1922 are the same pistol. The Model 1910 was modified by FN technicians for sale to Serbian armed forces in 1923. Also sold to France, Holland, Yugoslavia, and other countries. Also made by the German military 1940-1944.

Grading	100%	98%	95%	90%	80%	70%	60%

FN "BABY" MODEL — 6.35mm (.25 ACP) cal., lighter, smaller modification of Browning Model 1905 Vest Pocket .25, without grip safety or separate slide lock lever, imported under BAC trademark from 1954-1970 in standard blue finish, lightweight nickel and engraved Renaissance models. Mfg. 1931-1983. Total production is over 510,000.

▲ *FN Marked* — slide marked Fabrique Nationale, blued finish standard.

	$395	$350	$310	$280	$245	$225	$200

▲ *BAC Marked* — slide marked Browning Arms Co., blued finish standard.

	$300	$265	$225	$195	$180	$165	$150

▲ *Lightweight model* — nickel frame, with pearl grips.

	$395	$350	$310	$280	$245	$225	$200

▲ *Renaissance model* — engraved, satin grey finish.

	$875	$725	$550				

Add 20% if coin finished.

FN/BROWNING MODEL 10/71 — 4½ in. barrel, modified version of Model 1922 (10/22) in .380 ACP cal., grip safety, includes target sights and grips in addition to incorporating a magazine finger tip extension designed to comply with GCA of 1968. Sold in U.S. by BAC 1970-1974 as the "Standard .380", still mfg. by FN as Model 125.

	$375	$295	$250	$220	$205	$190	$160

▲ *Renaissance Model*

	$950	$750	$625				

MODEL 1935 HI-POWER — 9mm, 13 shot mag., $4^{21}/_{32}$ in. barrel, Browning's last pistol design, millions made 1927 to date in variations for commercial, military, and police use in over 68 countries, first imported under BAC trademark in 1954.

Please refer to the Fabrique Nationale section of this book for pre-1954 variations (including WWII and earlier commercial models).

HI-POWER: POST-1954 MFG. — 9mm Para. or .40 S&W (new 1995), similar to FN model 1935, has BAC slide marking, 10 (C/B 1994) or 13* shot mag., 4⅝ in. barrel, polished blue finish, checkered walnut grips, fixed sights, molded grips were introduced in 1986, ambidextrous safety was added to all models in 1989, approx. 32 (9mm Para.) or 35 (.40 S&W) oz. Mfg. 1954-present.

▲ *Polished Blue Finish* — includes fixed sights.

Mfg.'s Sug. Retail	$585	$485	$380	$330	$300	$280	$260	$240

Subtract $30 for molded grips (disc. 1990).
Add 10% for older mfg. with rounded style ring hammer.

Major identifying factors of the Hi-Power are as follows: the "Thumb-Print" feature was mfg. from the beginning (including FN mfg.) through 1959, old style internal extractors were mfg. from the beginning (including FN mfg.) through 1956, the "T" SN prefix (start visible extractor) was mfg. 1963-1972, 69C through 77C SN prefixes were mfg. 1969-1977, rounded type Ring Hammers were mfg. from the beginning (including FN mfg.) through 1972, Spur Hammers are mfg. 1970-present, and the 245 SN prefix are mfg. 1977-present.

Older specimens in original black pouches (especially with gold metal zipper) will command slight premiums over boxed guns.

▲ *Adj. sights*

Mfg.'s Sug. Retail	$636	$515	$400	$360	$330	$300	$280	$255

▲ *Mark III Matte Blue Finish* — 9mm Para. or .40 S&W (new 1994) cal., non-glare matte finish, ambidextrous safety, tapered dovetail rear fixed sight, molded grips, Mark III designation became standard in 1994, 35 oz. New 1985.

Mfg.'s Sug. Retail	$551	$480	$360	$310	$280	$260	$240	$225

Recently, Hi-Powers that appear to have a "black" finish have been noticed. These guns are painted rather than blued and some parties have been selling them as original military FNs. Do not confuse these painted specimens for original pistols and remember, original guns will be worth more than refinished pistols. Also, beware of 9mm pistols manufactured in Argentina under F.N. license.

Grading	100%	98%	95%	90%	80%	70%	60%

▲ **Silver Chrome Finish** — 9mm Para. or .40 S&W (new 1995), entire gun finished in silver chrome, includes adj. sights and Pachmayr rubber grips, 36 (9mm Para.) or 39 (.40 S&W) oz. New 1991.

Mfg.'s Sug. Retail	$651	$525	$415	$360	$330	$300	$280	$255

▲ **Practical Model** — 9mm Para. or .40 S&W (new 1995) cal., features blued slide, silver-chromed frame finish, wraparound Pachmayr rubber grips, round style serrated hammer, and choice of adj. sights (new 1993) or removable front sight, 36 (9mm Para.) or 39 (.40 S&W) oz. New 1990.

Mfg.'s Sug. Retail	$630	$515	$405	$350	$325	$300	$280	$255

Add $52 for adj. sights.

▲ **Nickel/Silver Chrome finish** — not to be confused with stainless steel (never offered in the Hi-Power). Also, this finish is different from the silver chrome finish released in 1991. Disc. 1985.

	$550	$475	$415	$375	$360	$340	$315

Last Mfg.'s Sug. Retail was $525.

▲ **.30 Luger Hi-Power** — .30 Luger cal., mfg. for European sales 1986-87 (most are marked F.N. on slide), approx. 1,500 imported late 1986-89, similar specifications as 9mm model.

	$550	$475	$415	$375	$360	$340	$315

This model was never cataloged for sale by BAC in the U.S. A few specimens have been noted with B.A.C. slide markings and are more desirable than F.N. marked pistols.

▲ **GP Competition** — 9mm, competition model with 6 in. barrel, detent adj. rear sight, rubber wraparound grips, front counterweight, improved barrel bushing, decreased trigger pull, approx. 36½ oz.

	$650	$550	$475	$425	$395	$350	$325

The original GP Competition came in a black plastic case w/accesories and is more desirable than later imported specimens which were computer serial numbered and came in a styrofoam box. Above prices are for older models — deduct 10% if newer model (computer serial numbered).

This model was never cataloged for sale by BAC in the U.S.

▲ **Tangent Rear Sight Model** — manufactured from 1965-1978. Adj. rear sight to 500 meters. A total of approx. 7,000 were imported by Browning Arms Co. Early pistols are designated by "T" prefix and were mfg. 1964-69, later pistols had spur hammers.

	$700	$600	$525	$440	$400	$370	$340

Add $100 for "T" prefix.

▲ **Capitan Polished Blue Finish** — 9mm Para. cal., features 50-500 meter tangent rear sight, blued finish with walnut grips, 32 oz. New 1993.

Mfg.'s Sug. Retail	$693	$565	$475	$385	$340	$300	$280	$260

▲ **Tangent Rear Sight Slotted** — variation with grip strap slotted to accommodate shoulder stock. Early pistols had "T" prefixes. Later pistols had spur hammers and are in the serial range 73CXXXX-74CXXXX.

	$1,100	$950	$775	$650	$525	$440	$400

Add $150 if with "T" prefix.

This variation will command a premium; beware of fakes, however (carefully examine slot milling).

BCA EDITION HI-POWER — limited edition made specifically for the Browning Collectors Association in 1980.

	$600	$495	$400

GOLD LINE HI-POWER — blued finish with gold line perimeter engraving.

	$2,250	$1,850	$1,500

RENAISSANCE HI-POWER — extensive scroll engraving on grey silver receiver, synthetic pearl grips, gold plated trigger. Disc. 1980.

Round Hammer/fixed sights	$1,350	$995	$795
Spur Hammer/fixed sights	$1,095	$895	$695

Add 5% for adj. sights.

Grading	100%	98%	95%	90%	80%	70%	60%

CASED GRADE I SET — one each .25 ACP, .380 ACP, and 9mm Para. Hi-Power Grade I Models in walnut or black vinyl case, non-matching serial numbers.
$1,500 $1,250 $895

CASED RENAISSANCE SET — one each .25 ACP, .380 ACP, and 9mm Para. Hi-Power Renaissance models in walnut or black vinyl case, non-matching serial numbers. Offered 1954-1969.
$3,500 $2,750 $2,100

Add 15% for coin finish.

CENTENNIAL MODEL HI-POWER — similar to fixed sight Hi-Power, chrome plated with inscription "Browning Centennial/1878-1978", engraved on side, cased, 3,500 mfg. in 1978. Original issue price was $495.
$695 $550 $425

CENTENNIAL MODEL HI-POWER 1 OF 100 — features extensive engraving, checkered walnut grips with border. 100 mfg. during 1989 - 34 were sold in U.S., 66 were sold in Europe.
$4,250 $3,250 $1,475

LOUIS XVI MODEL — 9mm, chemically etched throughout in leaf scroll patterns, satin finish, checkered grips, walnut case. Disc. 1984.
$895 $750 $525

Add 5% for adj. sights.

9 MM CLASSIC SERIES - PISTOL — 9mm, Hi-Power action, less than 2,500 manufactured in Classic model and under 350 manufactured in Gold Classic. Both editions feature multiple engraved scenes, and a special silver grey finish, presentation grips, cased. Mfg. 1984-86.
$850 $675 $495

Last Mfg.'s Sug. Retail was $1,000.

▲ *Gold Classic* — 5 gold inlays, select walnut grips are both checkered and carved. 500 mfg. 1984-86.
$1,800 $1,450 $1,150

Last Mfg.'s Sug. Retail was $2,000.

HI-POWER DOUBLE ACTION — this model was first listed in the Browning catalog in 1985 but was never manufactured. The proposed 1985 retail price was $494.

BDM DOUBLE ACTION — 9mm Para., new double mode design featuring slide selector allowing choice between pistol (true double action operation) or revolver mode (full hammer decocking after each shot), dual purpose decocking lever/safety, 4.73 in. barrel, 10 (C/B 1994) or 15* shot mag., matte blue finish, black molded wraparound grips, unique breech block allows visible cartridge inspection, adj. rear sight, 31 oz. New 1991-mfg. in U.S.A.

Mfg.'s Sug. Retail	$613	$510	$400	$365	$330	$300	$280	$260

This model features hammer block and firing pin block safeties.

FN DA 9 — 9mm Para., choice of double action or double action only, 4⅝ in. barrel, molded rubber grips, 10 shot mag., 31 oz. Mfg. by FN - importation began 1996.

Mfg.'s Sug. Retail	$613	$510	$400	$365	$330	$300	$280	$260

BDA-380 — .380 ACP, double action, 10 (C/B 1994) or 14* shot, 3¹³⁄₁₆ in. barrel, fixed sights, smooth walnut grips, 23 oz., introduced 1982-current production, mfg. by Beretta.

Mfg.'s Sug. Retail	$563	$445	$345	$260	$220	$175	$150	$125

▲ *Nickel finish*

Mfg.'s Sug. Retail	$607	$480	$360	$275	$230	$180	$150	$125

Grading	100%	98%	95%	90%	80%	70%	60%

BDA MODEL — 9mm (9 shot) — 2,740 mfg., .38 Super — 752 mfg., .45 ACP (7 shot), mfg. from 1977-1980 by Sig-Sauer of W. Germany (same as Sig-Sauer 220).

	100%	98%	95%	90%	80%	70%	60%
9mm	$550	$450	$375	$295	$250	$225	$200
.38 Super	$650	$575	$495	$450	$390	$350	$320
.45 ACP	$550	$450	$375	$295	$250	$225	$200

NOMAD MODEL — .22 LR, 10 shot, 4½ and 6¾ in. barrels, steel or alloy frame, adj. sights, blued finish, black plastic grips. Mfg. 1962-1974 by FN.

	100%	98%	95%	90%	80%	70%	60%
	$300	$235	$170	$140	$125	$100	$85

CHALLENGER MODEL — .22 LR, 10 shot, 4½ and 6¾ in. barrels, steel frame, adj. sights, checkered wraparound walnut grips, gold plated trigger. Mfg. 1962-1975 by FN.

	100%	98%	95%	90%	80%	70%	60%
	$350	$295	$250	$215	$190	$170	$155

▲ *Renaissance* — engraved satin nickel finish.

	100%	98%	95%
	$1,250	$875	$500

▲ *Gold Line* — blued finish, gold lining on perimeter of frame surfaces.

	100%	98%	95%
	$1,250	$875	$500

CHALLENGER II — .22 cal., Salt Lake City mfg., 6¾ in. barrel, alloy frame, plastic impregnated hardwood grips, 38 oz. Mfg. 1975-1982.

	100%	98%	95%	90%	80%	70%	60%
	$230	$180	$170	$145	$135	$120	$110

▲ *Challenger II BCA Commemorative* — mfg. to commemorate BCA's fourth anniversary.

	100%	98%	95%
	$295	$240	$175

CHALLENGER III — .22 cal., Salt Lake City mfg., 5½ in. bull barrel, 11 shot, alloy frame, adj. sights, 35 oz. Mfg. 1982-1985.

	100%	98%	95%	90%	80%	70%	60%
	$220	$190	$170	$145	$135	$120	$110

Last Mfg.'s Sug. Retail was $240.

CHALLENGER III SPORTER — similar to Challenger III, except 6¾ in. round barrel, wide trigger, 29 oz. Mfg. 1982-85.

	100%	98%	95%	90%	80%	70%	60%
	$220	$190	$170	$145	$135	$120	$110

Last Mfg.'s Sug. Retail was $240.

BUCK MARK STANDARD .22 — .22 LR, 11 shot, 5½ in. bull barrel, composite grips with skipline checkering (disc. 1990) or molded rubber grips (new 1991), adj. sights, gold trigger, matte blued finish, 36 oz. New 1985.

		100%	98%	95%	90%	80%	70%	60%
Mfg.'s Sug. Retail	$257	$190	$155	$130	$120	$110	$100	$90

Add $45 for nickel finish (new 1991).

Buck Mark models are manufactured in Salt Lake City, UT.

▲ *Micro Buck Mark* — similar to Buck Mark Standard, except has 4 in. barrel, choice of standard or nickel finish, 32 oz. New 1992.

		100%	98%	95%	90%	80%	70%	60%
Mfg.'s Sug. Retail	$257	$190	$155	$130	$120	$110	$100	$90

Add $45 for nickel finish.

▲ *Buck Mark Micro Plus* — similar to Micro Buck Mark, except has ambidextrous contoured laminated wood grips, nickel (new 1996) or blue finish.

		100%	98%	95%	90%	80%	70%	60%
Mfg.'s Sug. Retail	$314	$240	$190	$145	$135	$120	$110	$100

Add $29 for nickel finish.

▲ *Buck Mark Plus* — similar to Buck Mark, except has uncheckered laminated wooden grips and choice of nickel (new 1996) or high polish blue. New 1987.

		100%	98%	95%	90%	80%	70%	60%
Mfg.'s Sug. Retail	$314	$240	$190	$145	$135	$120	$110	$100

Add $29 for nickel finish.

Grading	100%	98%	95%	90%	80%	70%	60%

▲ *Buck Mark Bullseye Standard* — similar to Buck Mark Bullseye Target, except has molded composite grips. New 1996.

Mfg.'s Sug. Retail	$377	$290	$240	$195	$170	$150	$135	$120

▲ *Buck Mark Bullseye Target* — Bullseye model featuring 16 click per turn Pro-Target rear sight, 7 $\frac{1}{4}$ in. fluted barrel, matte blue finish, adj. trigger pull, rosewood target or 3 finger groove grips, 10 shot mag., 31 oz. New 1996.

Mfg.'s Sug. Retail	$485	$360	$280	$225	$185	$165	$140	$125

▲ *Buck Mark 5.5 Target* — same action as Buck Mark, $5\frac{1}{2}$ in. barrel with serrated top rib allowing adj. sight positioning, target sights, matte blue finish, choice of contoured walnut or walnut wraparound finger groove grips (new 1992), 35 oz. New 1990.

Mfg.'s Sug. Retail	$412	$310	$255	$215	$180	$160	$140	$125

Add $51 for nickel finish (new 1994).

▲ *Buck Mark 5.5 Gold Target* — similar to 5.5 Target, except has gold anodized frame and top rib. Introduced in 1991.

Mfg.'s Sug. Retail	$463	$345	$270	$220	$180	$160	$140	$125

▲ *Buck Mark 5.5 Field* — same action and barrel as the Target 5.5, except sights are designed for field use, anodized blue finish, contoured walnut grips, choice of contoured walnut or walnut wraparound finger groove grips (new 1992), 35½ oz. New 1991.

Mfg.'s Sug. Retail	$412	$310	$255	$215	$180	$160	$140	$125

▲ *Buck Mark Varmint* — same action as Buck Mark, $9\frac{7}{8}$ in. barrel with serrated top rib allowing adj. sight positioning, laminated wood grips, choice of contoured walnut or walnut wraparound finger groove grips (new 1992), optional detachable forearm, matte blue, 48 oz. New 1987.

Mfg.'s Sug. Retail	$391	$305	$250	$200	$175	$155	$135	$120

▲ *Buck Mark Silhouette* — silhouette variation of the Buck Mark, $9\frac{7}{8}$ in. bull barrel with serrated top rib allowing adj. sight positioning, hooded target sights, laminated wood stocks and forearm, choice of contoured walnut or walnut wraparound finger groove grips (new 1992), matte blue, 53 oz. New 1987.

Mfg.'s Sug. Retail	$435	$350	$280	$230	$195	$170	$150	$135

▲ *Buck Mark Unlimited Silhouette (Match)* — similar to Silhouette Model featuring 14 in. barrel with set back front sight, choice of contoured walnut or walnut wraparound finger groove grips (new 1992), 64 oz. New 1991.

Mfg.'s Sug. Retail	$536	$425	$330	$270	$230	$195	$170	$150

MEDALIST TARGET MODEL — .22 LR, $6\frac{3}{4}$ in. barrel, vent. rib, adj. target sights and barrel weights (3 supplied), blued finish, target walnut grips with thumbrest, dry-fire mechanism, 46 oz., cased. Mfg. 1964-1975 by FN.

	$795	$650	$575	$495	$425	$375	$325

Deduct 15% if without case and accessories.

Gold Line (407 mfg. 1963)	$1,700	$1,000	$650
Renaissance Model	$2,100	$1,400	$900

A total of 337 were mfg. by FN 1964-82.

BCA Edition Engraved (60 mfg.)	$2,350	$1,900	$1,400

INTERNATIONAL MEDALIST — target variation model manufactured 1977-80, 5.9 in. barrel, only 681 made with BAC markings and blued finish. Currently manufactured by FN in the parkerized international configuration.

	$615	$535	$475	$410	$350	$300	$275
Early Model	$735	$625	$550	$425	$360	$330	$280

RIFLES: SINGLE SHOT

100%	98%	95%	90%	80%	70%	60%	50%	40%	30%	20%	10%

MODEL 1878 STANDARD — various cals., J.M. Browning's first patent, fewer than 600 made by Browning Brothers in Ogden, Utah between 1878-1883, octagon barrel marked "Browning Bros. Ogden, Utah USA" plain wood stock and forearm with and without pistol grips, crescent steel buttplate, with or without ramrod, several receiver configurations, a very few were made in the deluxe model, seldom found in better than average used condition.

$20,000	$18,500	$15,000	$13,500	$12,000	$11,000	$10,000	$9,000	$8,000	$7,000	$6,000	$5,000

Add 50% for Deluxe Rifle (checkered stock and forearm).
Add 10% for Early Rifle with Sharps Borchardt type lever.
Add 40% for Early Rifle stamped "Ogden, U.T.".
Add 20% for any caliber other than .40-70 SS or .45-70 Govt.
Deduct 20% if stock and/or forearm have been replaced.
Deduct 20% if the original sights have been removed or replaced incorrectly.
Add 25% for Late Model with rammer rod under barrel held by two thimbles (known as "Montana Model").
Add 10% minimum for any non-standard feature, such as single or double set trigger asssemblies, removable lower stock tang, round barrel, with Ballard type stock bolts, fore-end caps of silver or pewter or other metal.

Calibers in this model are listed from rarest to most commonly encountered: .50-70 Govt., .45 Sharps, .44 Rem., .40-90 Sharps, .44-77 Sharps, .45-70 Govt., and .40-70 Sharps Straight.

This model is rare since approx. only 550 were mfg. (approx. ser. range 1-550). This patent was sold to Winchester, which became their Model 1885 single shot. To date, less than 100 original Model 1878s have been encountered indicating a high mortality rate (most remaining specimens are in poor original condition). An inherent weakness of the original design was the way the stock attached to the action - Winchester later corrected this design flaw. A few remaining examples are not serial numbered. Barter guns are rifles that have Browning stamped actions and barrels of an older gunsmith's identity.

Grading	100%	98%	95%	90%	80%	70%	60%

MODEL B-78 — .22-250, 6mm, .243, .25-06, 7mm Mag., .30-06, or .45-70 cal., 24 or 26 in. round or octagon barrel, lever activated falling block, no sights except .45-70, checkered walnut stock, approx. 24,000 mfg. 1973-1982.

	$695	$595	$465	$325	$295	$275	$250
.45-70 cal.	$795	$650	$475	$325	$295	$275	$250

The Model B-78 was reintroduced as the Model 1885 in 1985.

MODEL 1885 HIGH WALL — .22-250 Rem., .223 Rem. (disc. 1994), .270 Win., .30-06, 7mm Rem. Mag., or .45-70 cal., falling block action, sear safety, 28 in. octagonal barrel, adj. trigger, no sights, checkered walnut stock and Schnabel forearm, exposed hammer, gold trigger, 8¾ lbs. Introduced 1985.

Mfg.'s Sug. Retail	$940	$715	$560	$440	$360	$330	$295	$275

This model in .45-70 cal. is equipped with open sights.

MODEL 1885 LOW WALL — .22 Hornet, .223 Rem., or .243 Win. cal., action patterned after the Winchester Low Wall receiver, 24 in. barrel, adj. trigger, features thinner 24 in. barrel, 6¼ lbs. New 1995.

Mfg.'s Sug. Retail	$940	$715	$560	$440	$360	$330	$295	$275

MODEL BPCR (BLACK POWDER CARTRIDGE) — .40-65 (black powder only) or .45-70 (black powder or smokeless) cal., high wall action, 30 in. half-round/half-octagon barrel, checkered pistol grip stock, w/o ejector system and shell deflector, vernier tang rear sight and globe front sight with spirit level, case colored receiver, approx. 11 lbs. New 1996.

Mfg.'s Sug. Retail	$1,665	$1,525	$1,250	$1,075	$925	$800	$700	$600

Grading	100%	98%	95%	90%	80%	70%	60%

B

RIFLES: SEMI-AUTO .22 LR

GRADES I - III — .22 LR or .22 Short (disc.), takedown design, 11 shot (16 for .22 Short) tube mag. in butt stock, 19¼ in. barrel in LR, 22¼ in. barrel in short (rare), checkered pistol grip stock, semi-beavertail forearm, stock has hole machined halfway to allow partial filling of tube mag., adj. folding rear sight, grades differ in finish, amount of engraving, and grade of wood, 4¾ lbs. Mfg. 1914-1976 by FN, 1976-present by Miroku in Japan.

▲ *Grade I — FN*

	100%	98%	95%	90%	80%	70%	60%
	$475	$395	$325	$250	$195	$165	$150

Add 10-20% for "Shorts only" or thumb wheel rear sight older models if in 95% or better condition.

FN Grade I's have a lightly engraved blued steel receiver, checkered walnut, blued trigger, and a variety of rear sights.

▲ *Grade I — Miroku*

		100%	98%	95%	90%	80%	70%	60%
Mfg.'s Sug. Retail	$399	$315	$250	$210	$180	$160	$150	$140

Miroku manufactured .22s can be determined by year of manufacture in the following manner: RV suffix - 1975, RT - 1976, RR - 1977, RP - 1978, RN - 1979, PM - 1980, PZ - 1981, PY - 1982, PX - 1983, PW - 1984, PV - 1985, PT - 1986, PR - 1987, PP - 1988, PN - 1989, NM - 1990, NZ - 1991, NY - 1992, NX - 1993, NW - 1994, NV - 1995, NU - 1996.

▲ *Grade II — FN*

	100%	98%	95%	90%	80%	70%	60%
	$895	$700	$550	$400	$325	$295	$260

FN Grade II's have grey chromed receiver, deluxe wood with finer checkering, gold plated trigger, and engraving depicting two squirrels and two prairie dogs. Signed or unsigned by engraver.

▲ *Grade II — Miroku* — disc. 1984.

	100%	98%	95%	90%	80%	70%	60%
	$425	$350	$295	$225	$200	$180	$160

▲ *Grade III — FN*

	100%	98%	95%	90%	80%	70%	60%
	$1,795	$1,500	$1,150	$850	$770	$715	$605

FN Grade IIIs have coin finish or grey chromed receiver, extra deluxe walnut with skipline checkering, gold plated trigger, and more elaborate game scene engraving usually featuring a dog flushing ducks or upland game. Signed or unsigned by engraver (Funken, J. Baerten, Vrancken, and Watrin will command premiums over values listed above). A few were also special ordered with blued finish and special engraving — these command an extra premium.

▲ *Grade III — Miroku* — disc. 1983.

	100%	98%	95%	90%	80%	70%	60%
	$750	$650	$540	$495	$450	$400	$360

▲ *Grade VI — Miroku* — game scene engraved with gold plating, choice of blued or greyed receiver, deluxe walnut. New 1987.

		100%	98%	95%	90%	80%	70%	60%
Mfg.'s Sug. Retail	$819	$675	$530	$420	$365	$325	$295	$260

BAR-22 — .22 LR, 20 ¼ in. barrel, 15 shot tube mag., folding leaf sight, high polish alloy receiver, checkered pistol grip stock, 5 lbs. 13 oz. Mfg. 1977-1985 by Miroku.

	100%	98%	95%	90%	80%	70%	60%
	$275	$225	$185	$170	$155	$140	$125

Last Mfg.'s Sug. Retail was $245.

BAR-22 GRADE II — engraved model of BAR-22 featuring game scenes on silver greyed alloy receiver, select French walnut. Disc. 1985.

	100%	98%	95%	90%	80%	70%	60%
	$395	$325	$245	$210	$195	$175	$160

Last Mfg.'s Sug. Retail was $350.

RIFLES: BAR SERIES

BROWNING PATENT 1900 — .35 Rem. only, manufactured by FN from 1910-1931, only 4,913 made in standard and deluxe grades, similar to Remington Model 8 auto-loading rifle.

	100%	98%	95%	90%	80%	70%	60%
	$650	$575	$495	$440	$385	$340	$300

▲ *Deluxe model* — with checkered walnut stock and adj. sights on solid rib barrel.

	100%	98%	95%	90%	80%	70%	60%
	$750	$650	$550	$525	$470	$440	$415

Grading	100%	98%	95%	90%	80%	70%	60%

THE BAR MK II SAFARI — .243 Win., .270 Win., .30-06, .308 Win., .270 Wby. Mag. (disc. 1994), 7mm Rem. Mag., .300 Win. Mag., or .338 Win. Mag. cal., improved BAR action featuring redesigned bolt release, new gas operating system, and reduced recoil, removable trigger assembly, 22 or 24 (Mag. cals. only) in. barrel with (adj. for windage and elevation) or without sights, BOSS became optional 1994, blued finish with engraved receiver, checkered walnut stock and forearm, gold trigger, detachable box mag., approx. 7 lbs. 6 oz. except for Mag. cals. (8 lbs. 6 oz.). Mfg. by F.N. in Belgium. New 1993.

Mfg.'s Sug. Retail	$714	$610	$490	$430	$380	$350	$330	$310

Add $16 for open sights.
Add $52 for Mag. cals.

The new BAR MK II Safari does not have interchangeable magazine capability with the older pre-1993 BARs.

▲ *BAR MK II Grade III* — features Grade III engraving pattern. Mfg. by FN beginning 1996.

Mfg.'s Sug. Retail	$3,150	$2,675	$1,500	$1,150	$995	$775	$675	$575

▲ *BAR MK II Grade IV* — features Grade IV engraving pattern. Mfg. by FN beginning 1996.

Mfg.'s Sug. Retail	$3,250	$2,775	$1,600	$1,200	$995	$775	$675	$575

▲ *BAR Mark II Safari BOSS* — similar to BAR Mk II Safari, except has BOSS (ballistic optimizing shooting system) accurizing/recoil adj. assembly on barrel end, no sights. New 1994.

Mfg.'s Sug. Retail	$812	$700	$565	$485	$410	$370	$335	$310

Add $52 for Mag. cals.

BAR SEMI-AUTO — .243, .270, .280 Rem. (new 1990), .308, or .30-06 cal. available in standard model, Mag. cals. include 7mm Rem., .300 Win., and .338 Win. (reintroduced 1990), gas operated, blued receiver, 22 or 24 (Mag. only) in. barrel, rotary bolt with seven lugs, folding leaf sight, walnut stock. Grades differ in engraving, finish, and grade of wood, approx. 7 lbs. 6 oz. Mfg. 1967-present. In 1993, to celebrate the 25th Anniversary of the BAR, Browning introduced the BAR MK II Safari (See model listed above).

Add 15% for FN mfg. and assembled BARs (marked "Made in Belgium").
Add 10% for .338 Win. Mag. cal. (FN mfg. only).

Note: Original .338s were limited production, mostly seen in the deluxe Grade II only. During the last year of FN .338 production, several were delivered in a Grade I by FN. Although being rarer than the Grade II, it is not as desirable. The following prices are for Portugese assembled guns, manufactured by FN, and are so stamped on the barrel.

▲ *Grade I* — standard grade without engraving, blued finish. Ordering this model without sights became an option in 1988. Disc. 1992.

			$540	$450	$395	$350	$325	$300	$280

Last Mfg.'s Sug. Retail was $633.

Subtract $16 without sights.

FN mfg. and assembled Grade I's can be denoted by light scroll engraving on the receiver.

▲ *Grade I Magnum* — standard grade without engraving, with recoil pad, 8 lbs. 6 oz. Disc. 1992.

			$575	$495	$425	$375	$350	$330	$310

Last Mfg.'s Sug. Retail was $680.

Subtract $16 without sights.
Ordering this gun without sights became an option in 1988.

▲ *Grade II* — blued receiver, engraved with big game heads. Mfg. 1967-1974.

			$695	$595	$550	$525	$470	$440	$415

This model was previously designated Deluxe.

▲ *Grade II Magnum* — magnum version of Grade II. Mfg. 1967-1974.

			$750	$650	$595	$550	$510	$460	$430

▲ *Grade III* — features elk and sheep game scenes etched on greyed steel receiver, select checkered stock and forearm. Disc. 1984.

			$925	$800	$660	$620	$580	$560	$540

▲ *Grade III Magnum* — magnum version of Grade III. Disc. 1984.

			$1,025	$850	$700	$660	$620	$595	$580

Grading	100%	98%	95%	90%	80%	70%	60%

▲ **Grade IV** — engraved satin finish greyed receiver depicts big game animal scenes and trigger guard, carved borders on checkering. Disc. 1989.

	$1,475	$1,300	$1,150	$1,000	$900	$825	$750

Last Mfg.'s Sug. Retail was $1,670.

▲ **Grade IV Magnum** — magnum version of Grade IV. Disc. 1984.

	$1,675	$1,495	$1,225	$1,050	$950	$850	$775

Last Mfg.'s Sug. Retail was $1,720.

▲ **Grade V** — more elaborate engraving than Grade IV, with gold inlays. Mfg. 1971-1974.

	$3,000	$2,600	$2,250	$1,850	$1,600	$1,450	$1,250

▲ **Grade V Magnum** — magnum version of Grade V.

	$3,650	$2,900	$2,400	$1,950	$1,700	$1,595	$1,400

BAR NORTH AMERICAN DEER RIFLE ISSUE — .30-06 cal. only, BAR style action with silver grey finish and engraved action, 600 total production, walnut cased with accessories. Disc. 1983 but were sold through 1989.

	$2,650	$2,100	$1,700

Last Mfg.'s Sug. Retail was $3,550.

RIFLES: FAL

The following semi-auto FALs were imported by BAC in limited numbers. Current production FALs can be found under the Fabrique Nationale heading.

FAL G SERIES STANDARD — 7.62mm, paramilitary design rifle, wood butt stock, wood or nylon forearm, milled receiver.

	$3,200	$2,850	$2,300	$1,950	$1,650	$1,350	$1,040

▲ **G Series Heavy Barrel** — wood furniture, milled receiver with special bipod.

	$6,000	$5,250	$4,700	$4,160	$3,600	$3,100	$2,650

▲ **G Series Lightweight** — lightweight variation of the FAL.

	$4,000	$3,500	$3,000	$2,500	$2,100	$1,875	$1,600

The Lightweight Model had the trigger frame, magazine, and return spring tube made out of aluminum.

▲ **Browning Arms Co. Import** — milled receiver, wood or nylon furniture.

	$2,400	$2,000	$1,700	$1,550	$1,400	$1,275	$1,150

▲ **CAL Prototype** — originally imported in 1980, prototype to the current FN FNC, at first declared illegal but later given amnesty, only 20 imported.

	$6,000	$5,250	$4,700	$4,160	$3,600	$3,100	$2,650

G series FALs were imported between 1959-1962 by Browning Arms Co. This rifle was declared illegal by the GCA of 1968 and was exempted 5 years later. Total numbers exempted are: Standard model-1822, Heavy Barrel model-21, Paratrooper model-5.

RIFLES: LEVER ACTION

BL-22 GRADE I — .22 S, L, and LR, 20 in. barrel, short throw lever, folding leaf sight, 15 shot (LR) mag., exposed hammer, Western style stock and forearm, 5 lbs. Mfg. 1970-present by Miroku.

Mfg.'s Sug. Retail	$346	$275	$215	$180	$150	$125	$110	$100

▲ **BL-22 Grade II** — same general specifications as BL-22, except scroll engraved blue receiver and checkered select walnut.

Mfg.'s Sug. Retail	$396	$320	$255	$200	$170	$140	$125	$115

MODEL 53 DELUXE LIMITED EDITION — .32-20 cal. (round nose or hollow point bullets only), patterned after the original Winchester Model 53 (redesigned Model 1892), 7 shot tube mag., high polished blued metal, open sights, 22 in. tapered barrel, high grade checkered walnut stock featuring full pistol grip cap and shotgun style metal butt plate, 6½ lbs. Only 5,000 mfg. in 1990.

	$525	$425	$395

Last Mfg.'s Sug. Retail was $675.

Grading	100%	98%	95%	90%	80%	70%	60%

MODEL 65 GRADE I LIMITED EDITION — .218 Bee, patterned after the Winchester Model 65, round tapered 24 in. barrel, open sights (hooded front), blued metal finish, 7 shot tube mag., uncheckered pistol grip stock and semi-beavertail forearm, metal butt plate, 6¾ lbs. 3,500 total mfg. for Grade I in 1989 only, inventory depleted in 1990.

$475 $400 $375

Last Mfg.'s Sug. Retail was $550.

▲ *Model 65 High Grade* — greyed receiver (and lever) with scroll engraving and gold plated animals, gold plated trigger, deluxe checkered walnut stock and semi-beavertail forearm. 1,500 total mfg. in 1989, inventory depleted in 1990.

$850 $775 $700

Last Mfg.'s Sug. Retail was $850.

MODEL 71 LIMITED EDITION CARBINE — .348 Win., reproduction of the Winchester Model 71 carbine, 20 in. barrel, open sights, 4 shot mag., 8 lbs. New 1987 with inventory depleted in 1990.

▲ *Grade I* — uncheckered satin finished walnut stock and forearm. 4,000 mfg. 1986-87 only.

$450 $400 $365 $340 $320 $300 $275

Last Mfg.'s Sug. Retail was $600.

▲ *High Grade* — deluxe checkered walnut stock and forearm with high gloss finish, scroll engraved-grey receiver with gold inlays and trigger. 3,000 mfg. 1986-87 only.

$750 $600 $500

Last Mfg.'s Sug. Retail was $980.

MODEL 71 LIMITED EDITION RIFLE — .348 Win. reproduction of the Winchester Model 71 rifle, 24 in. barrel, open sights, 4 shot mag., 8 lbs. 2 oz. Mfg. 1986-87 only with inventory depleted in 1990.

▲ *Grade I* — uncheckered satin finished walnut stock and forearm. 3,000 mfg. 1986-87 only.

$495 $425 $375 $350 $325 $300 $275

Last Mfg.'s Sug. Retail was $600.

▲ *High Grade* — deluxe checkered walnut stock and forearm with high gloss finish, scroll engraved-grey receiver with gold inlays and trigger. 3,000 mfg. 1986-87 only.

$795 $625 $525

Last Mfg.'s Sug. Retail was $980.

MODEL 81 BLR SHORT ACTION — .22-250 Rem., .222 Rem. (disc. 1989), .223 Rem., .243 Win., .257 Roberts (disc. 1992), 7mm-08 Rem., .284 Win., .308 Win., or .358 Win. (disc. 1992) cal., steel receiver, rotary bolt locking lugs, 20 in. barrel with band, 3 (.284 Win. only) or 4 shot detachable mag., adj. rear sight, checkered straight grip stock, recoil pad, approx. 7 lbs, no sights optional 1988-89. 1971 mfg. in Belgium, 1972-1995 mfg. by Miroku.

$450 $365 $300 $265 $225 $195 $165

Last Mfg.'s Sug. Retail was $550.

Add 15%+ for Belgium mfg. (1971 only, designated the BLR).
Subtract $15 without sights.
.243 Win., .308 Win. and 7mm-08 Rem. cals. are the most popular in this model.

This model was also manufactured by TRW in Cleveland, OH for a very limited production in .243 and .308 cals. This variation has a 2-line legend on the right side marked "MADE IN USA" and "PATENT PENDING". While they are rare, they are not widely collected and are more of an oddity than anything else.

▲ *Model 81 BLR Long Action* — .270 Win., .30-06, or 7mm Rem Mag. cal., 22 or 24 in. barrel, approx. 8½ lbs. Mfg. 1991-95 by Miroku.

$450 $365 $300 $265 $230 $200 $170

Last Mfg.'s Sug. Retail was $580.

Grading	100%	98%	95%	90%	80%	70%	60%

NEW MODEL LIGHTNING BLR (SHORT ACTION) — .22-250 Rem., .223 Rem., .243 Win., 7mm-08 Rem., or .308 Win., cal., rotary bolt locking lugs, 20 in. barrel w/o barrel band, features aluminum alloy receiver and checkered pistol grip stock and forearm, rack and pinion geared slide, fold down hammer, trigger travels with lever, 3-5 shot detachable mag., adj. rear sight, approx. 6 ½ - 7 ¾ lbs. Mfg. by Miroku beginning late 1995.

Mfg.'s Sug. Retail	$577	$445	$350	$290	$255	$220	$195	$165

▲ **Model Lightning BLR (Long Action)** — .270 Win., .30-06, or 7mm Rem. Mag. cal., 22 or 24 in. barrel, approx. 8½ lbs. Mfg. by Miroku beginning 1995.

Mfg.'s Sug. Retail	$609	$470	$370	$310	$275	$230	$200	$170

MODEL 1886 LIMITED EDITION GRADE I RIFLE — .45-70 Govt. only, patterned after the Winchester Model 1886, blued receiver, 26 in. octagon barrel, full mag., crescent butt plate, open sights. 7,000 mfg. 1986 only.

$1,050	$895	$695

Last Mfg.'s Sug. Retail was $578.

▲ **Model 1886 Limited Edition High Grade Rifle** — same general specifications as Model 1886, except has checkered high grade walnut stock and forearm, greyed steel receiver, with game scene engraving including elk and American Bison, gold accenting with "1 of 3,000" engraved on top of barrel. 3,000 mfg. 1986 only.

$1,595	$1,200	$995

Last Mfg.'s Sug. Retail was $935.

▲ **Model 1886 Montana Centennial Rifle** — similar to Model 1886 High Grade. 2,000 mfg. 1986 only to commemorate Montana Centennial.

$1,595	$1,200	$995

Last Mfg.'s Sug. Retail was $935.

MODEL 1886 LIMITED EDITION GRADE I CARBINE — .45-70 Govt. only, saddle ring carbine, patterned after the Winchester Model 1886 Carbine, blued receiver, 22 in. round barrel, 8 shot full mag., crescent butt plate, open sights. 7,000 total mfg. 1992-1993.

$695	$575	$450

Last Mfg.'s Sug. Retail was $750.

▲ **Model 1886 Limited Edition High Grade Carbine** — same general specifications as Model 1886, except has checkered high grade walnut stock and forearm, greyed steel receiver, with game scene engraving including bear and elk, gold accenting, 3,000 total mfg. 1992-1993.

$1,095	$850	$675

Last Mfg.'s Sug. Retail was $1,175.

B-92 CARBINE — .357 Mag. or .44 Rem. Mag. cal., 20 in. barrel, patterned after the Winchester Model 92, 11 shot mag. (tubular), blued finish. Disc. 1986.

$450	$350	$275	$200	$175	$160	$150

Last Mfg.'s Sug. Retail was $342.

▲ **B-92 Centennial** — .44 Mag., 6,000 mfg. in 1978.

$450	$350	$275

Last Mfg.'s Sug. Retail was $220.

▲ **B-92 BCA Commemorative** — mfg. to commemorate BCA's third anniversary.

$450	$350	$275

MODEL 1895 LIMITED EDITION GRADE I — .30/40 Krag or .30-06 cal. only, patterned after the Winchester Model 1895, blued receiver, 24 in. barrel, 4 shot mag.(box type), select walnut, rear buckhorn sight, 8 lbs. Mfg. 1984 only.

.30/40 Krag	$550	$475	$375	$325	$300	$280	$260
.30-06	$650	$525	$400	$350	$325	$300	$280

Production totaled 6,000 in the .30-06 cal. and 2,000 in .30/40 Krag for this model.

▲ **Model 1895 Limited Edition High Grade** — same general specifications as Model 1895, except gold plated game scenes on satin finish receiver, gold trigger, and finely checkered select French walnut.

$1,095	$950	$850

Production totaled 1,000 in the .30-06 cal. and 1,000 in .30/40 Krag for this model.

Grading	100%	98%	95%	90%	80%	70%	60%

RIFLES: RIMFIRE A-BOLT SERIES BOLT ACTION

A-BOLT GRADE I RIMFIRE — .22 LR or .22 Mag. (new 1989), 60 degree bolt throw, 22 in. barrel, checkered walnut stock and forearm (approx. 170 were mfg. in 1986), or laminated stock (approx. 1,500 mfg., 390 had no sights), 5 or 15 (optional) shot mag., adj. trigger, available with or without open sights, 5 lbs. 9 oz. Mfg. 1986-96.

▲ *.22 LR cal.*
Mfg.'s Sug. Retail   **$425** $320 $255 $195 $175 $160 $145 $130
    Add $14 for open sights.
     A 15 shot mag. is also available for this model at $45 retail.

▲ *.22 Win. Mag. cal.*
Mfg.'s Sug. Retail   **$493** $375 $295 $225 $195 $175 $160 $150
    Add $21 for open sights.

A-BOLT GOLD MEDALLION RIMFIRE — .22 LR cal. only, similar to A-Bolt, except has high grade select walnut stock checkered 22 lines per inch, rosewood pistol and forend cap, high gloss finish, gold filled lettering and moderate engraving, solid recoil pad. Mfg. 1988-96.
Mfg.'s Sug. Retail   **$567** $455 $365 $310 $270 $240 $225 $210

RIFLES: CENTERFIRE A-BOLT SERIES BOLT ACTION

A-BOLT HUNTER MODEL — available in .25-06 Rem., .270 Win., .280 Rem. (new 1988), .30-06, 7mm Rem. Mag., .300 Win. Mag., or .338 Win. Mag. cal. in long action, short action available in .223 Rem. (new 1988), .22-250 Rem., .243 Win., .257 Roberts, .284 Win. (new 1989), 7mm-08 Rem., or .308 Win. cal., 3 or 4 shot mag., matte blue finish, 3 lug rotary bolt locking, 22 (short action only), 24 in. (disc. 1987), or 26 in. barrel (new 1988 - long action Mag. cals. only), 60 degree bolt throw, adj. trigger, hidden detachable mag., with or without sights, top tang thumb safety, checkered pistol grip stock, 6 lbs. 3 oz. - 7 lbs. 11oz. Mfg. 1985-1993 by Miroku. Replaced by A-Bolt Model II in 1994.

                             $415 $340 $295 $265 $240 $225 $210
                                               Last Mfg.'s Sug. Retail was $510.
    Add $65 for open sights.

▲ *Medallion Model* — same A-Bolt specifications, except also available in .375 H&H cal., features better grade walnut stock with rosewood pistol grip and forend cap, synthetic floor plate, high lustre bluing, no sights. Disc. 1993. Replaced by A-Bolt Medallion Model II in 1994.

                             $475 $385 $330 $290 $265 $250 $235
                                               Last Mfg.'s Sug. Retail was $597.
    Add $25 for left-hand action (avail. in long action cals. only).
    Add $100 for .375 H&H cal. (open sights only).
     Left hand action available in .25-06 Rem., .270 Win., .280 Rem., .30-06, 7mm Rem. Mag.,
     .300 Win. Mag., .338 Win. Mag., or .375 H&H cal.

▲ *Micro Medallion Model* — .223 Rem. (new 1988), .22-250 Rem., .243 Win., .257 Roberts, .284 Win., .308 Win., or 7mm-08 Rem. cal., scaled down variation of the A-Bolt Hunter Model, 20 in. barrel, short action only, 13⅝/16 in. length of pull, 3 shot mag., no sights, 6 lbs. 3 oz. for short action. Mfg. 1988-1993. Replaced by A-Bolt Micro Medallion Model II in 1994.

                             $475 $385 $330 $290 $265 $250 $235
                                               Last Mfg.'s Sug. Retail was $597.

▲ *Gold Medallion Model* — .270 Win., .30-06, .300 Win. Mag. (new 1993), or 7mm Rem. Mag. cal., similar to Medallion Model, except has extra select walnut stock with continental style cheekpiece, gold lettering and light engraving, no sights. Mfg. 1988-1993. Replaced by A-Bolt Gold Medallion Model II in 1994.

                             $670 $535 $430 $360 $330 $300 $265
                                               Last Mfg.'s Sug. Retail was $810.

Grading	100%	98%	95%	90%	80%	70%	60%

B

▲ **Euro-Bolt** — .22-250 Rem., .243 Win., .270 Win., .30-06, .308 Win., or 7mm Rem. Mag. cal., features European styling including Schnabel style forearm, rounded rear receiver, Mannlicher style bolt, European cheekpiece on satin finished checkered stock, low-luster bluing, hinged floor plate with removable mag., cocking indicator, upper tang thumb activated safety, 6 lbs. 14 oz. - 7 lbs. 6 oz. (Mag.). Mfg. 1993-96.

	$600	$475	$395	$350	$300	$265	$250

Last Mfg.'s Sug. Retail was $700.

▲ **Stainless Stalker** — .22-250 Rem. (left-hand only, new 1993), .25-06 Rem., .270 Win., .280 Rem., .30-06, 7mm Rem. Mag., .300 Win. Mag., .338 Win. Mag. or .375 H&H (new 1990) cal., action and barrel are stainless steel, matte black graphite fiberglass composite stock, dull stainless finish, no sights, 6 lbs. 11 oz. - 7 lbs. 3 oz. Mfg. 1987-1993. Replaced by Stainless Stalker II in 1994.

	$575	$430	$350

Last Mfg.'s Sug. Retail was $665.

Add $100 for .375 H&H cal.
Add $20 for left hand action.
Originally, this model was offered in .270 Win., .30-06, or 7mm Rem. Mag. cal. only.

▲ **Camo Stalker** - .270 Win., .30-06, or 7mm Rem. Mag. cal., laminated black and green wood stock, matte finish on metal parts, no sights. Mfg. 1987-1989.

	$400	$340	$310	$285	$250	$230	$215

Last Mfg.'s Sug. Retail was $483.

▲ **Composite Stalker** — .25-06 Rem., .270 Win., .280 Rem., .30-06, 7mm Rem. Mag., .300 Win. Mag., or .338 Win. Mag. cal., black graphite fiberglass composite stock, matte non-glare metal finish, 6 lbs. 11 oz. - 7 lbs. 3 oz. Mfg. 1988-1993. Replaced by Composite Stalker II in 1994.

	$410	$340	$295	$265	$240	$225	$210

Last Mfg.'s Sug. Retail was $525.

A-BOLT BIGHORN SHEEP ISSUE — .270 Win. only, 22 in. barrel, high grade walnut stock with gloss finish and skipline checkering, deep relief engraving on receiver barrel, floorplate, and trigger guard, two 24Kt. inlays depicting bighorn sheep. 600 mfg. 1986-87 only.

	$850	$725	$600

Last Mfg.'s Sug. Retail was $1,365.

A-BOLT PRONGHORN ISSUE — .243 Win., presentation grade walnut with skipline checkering and pearl borders, receiver and barrel engraving, multiple gold inlays on receiver top and floor plate. 500 mfg. 1987 only.

	$795	$675	$550

Last Mfg.'s Sug. Retail was $1,302.

RIFLES: CENTERFIRE A-BOLT II SERIES BOLT ACTION

The A-Bolt II Series differs from the original A-Bolt variations (disc. 1993) in that a new anti-bind bolt featuring a non-rotating bolt sleeve has been incorporated in addition to an improved trigger system. Consumers also may have their name/inscription engraved on the flat bolt-face on any A-Bolt II Series variation for an additional $25. Browning introduced the BOSS (ballistic optimizing shooting system) in 1994 as an option on A-Bolt rifles, except Micro-Medallion models and the .375 H&H caliber.

A-BOLT HUNTER SERIES (MODEL II) — cals. similar to A-Bolt series, except not available in .257 Roberts or .284 Win. cal., 22 or 26 in. barrel, available without sights, open sights, or with BOSS, 6 lbs. 7 oz. - 7 lbs. 3 oz. New 1994.

▲ **Hunter Model II** — available in 12 cals. between .22-250 Rem. - .338 Win. Mag., 22 or 26 in. barrel with or w/o open sights.

Mfg.'s Sug. Retail	$606	$480	$365	$300	$270	$240	$225	$210

Add $76 for open sights.

➤ **Hunter Model II with BOSS** — features 22 or 26 in. barrel with BOSS. New 1994.

Mfg.'s Sug. Retail	$704	$575	$475	$400	$350	$300	$275	$250

Grading	100%	98%	95%	90%	80%	70%	60%

▲ **Medallion Model II** — available in 13 cals. between .22-250 Rem. - .375 H&H, similar to Medallion Model with A-Bolt II improvements, without sights. New 1994.

| **Mfg.'s Sug. Retail** | **$707** | **$550** | **$415** | **$350** | **$300** | **$275** | **$255** | **$235** |

Add $112 for .375 H&H cal. (open sights only).
Add $28 for left-hand action.

    Left hand action available in .25-06 Rem., .270 Win., .280 Rem., .30-06, 7mm Rem. Mag., .300 Win. Mag., .338 Win. Mag., or .375 H&H cal.

➤ **Medallion Model II with BOSS** — features 22 or 26 in. barrel with BOSS. New 1994.

| **Mfg.'s Sug. Retail** | **$805** | **$650** | **$525** | **$450** | **$385** | **$325** | **$295** | **$265** |

Add $28 for left-hand action.

▲ **Micro Medallion Model II** — available in 8 cals. between .22 Hornet - .308 Win., similar to Micro Medallion Model with A-Bolt II improvements, 20 in. barrel without sights, 6 lbs. New 1994.

| **Mfg.'s Sug. Retail** | **$707** | **$550** | **$415** | **$350** | **$300** | **$275** | **$255** | **$235** |

▲ **Gold Medallion Model II** — .270 Win., .30-06, .300 Win. Mag. or 7mm Rem. Mag. cal., similar to Gold Medallion Model, except has A-Bolt II improvements, 22 or 26 in. barrel, approx. 7 ½ lbs. New 1994.

| **Mfg.'s Sug. Retail** | **$950** | **$775** | **$600** | **$450** | **$375** | **$335** | **$300** | **$265** |

➤ **Gold Medallion Model II with BOSS**

| **Mfg.'s Sug. Retail** | **$1,048** | **$850** | **$675** | **$550** | **$450** | **$375** | **$325** | **$285** |

▲ **Eclipse with BOSS** — .22-250 Rem., .243 Win., .270 Win., .30-06, .308 Win., or 7mm Rem. Mag. cal., features laminated thumbhole wood stock with cheekpiece, long action, 22 or 26 (7mm Rem. Mag. only) in. barrel with BOSS, 7 ½ - 8 lbs. New 1996.

| **Mfg.'s Sug. Retail** | **$1,025** | **$835** | **$665** | **$550** | **$450** | **$375** | **$325** | **$285** |

➤ **Eclipse Varmint with BOSS** — .22 - 250 Rem., .223 Rem., or .308 Win. cal., 26 in. heavy barrel with BOSS, 4 shot mag., otherwise similar to Eclipse Model, approx. 9 lbs. New 1996.

| **Mfg.'s Sug. Retail** | **$1,055** | **$855** | **$680** | **$560** | **$455** | **$375** | **$325** | **$285** |

▲ **Varmint II** — .22-250 Rem., .223 Rem., or .308 Win. (new 1995) cal., features A-Bolt II improvements, 22 in. heavy barrel with BOSS, blued/gloss or satin/matte (new 1995) finish, black laminated wood stock with checkering, palm swell, and solid recoil pad, without sights, 9 lbs. New 1994.

| **Mfg.'s Sug. Retail** | **$940** | **$795** | **$625** | **$495** | **$425** | **$350** | **$325** | **$285** |

▲ **Euro-Bolt II** — .243 Win., .30-06, .308 Win., or 7mm Rem. Mag. cal., similar to Euro-Bolt with A-Bolt II improvements, 22 or 26 (7mm Rem. Mag. only) in. barrel w/o sights, 6 lbs. 7 oz. - 7 lbs. 3 oz. (Mag.). New 1994.

| **Mfg.'s Sug. Retail** | **$824** | **$680** | **$510** | **$410** | **$355** | **$300** | **$265** | **$250** |

➤ **Euro-Bolt II with BOSS** — .243 Win. or .308 Win. cal., 22 in. barrel with BOSS, 6 lbs. 7 oz.

| **Mfg.'s Sug. Retail** | **$922** | **$750** | **$600** | **$500** | **$425** | **$350** | **$325** | **$295** |

▲ **Stainless Stalker II** — similar to Stainless Stalker with A-Bolt improvements, also available in .22-250 (new 1995), .223 Rem. (new 1995), .243 Win. (new 1994), or 7mm-08 Rem. (new 1995), or .308 Win. (new 1995) cal., without sights, 6 lbs. 4 oz. - 7 lbs. 3 oz. Rem. New 1994.

| **Mfg.'s Sug. Retail** | **$787** | **$650** | **$465** | **$365** | | | | |

Add $109 for .375 H&H cal. (open sights only).
Add $25 for left-hand action.

➤ **Stainless Stalker II with BOSS** — available in 13 cals. between .22-250 Rem. and .375 H&H, 22 or 26 (Mag. cals. only) in. barrel with BOSS.

| **Mfg.'s Sug. Retail** | **$910** | **$740** | **$595** | **$495** | | | | |

Add $25 for left-hand action.
Add $109 for .37 H&H cal. (open sights only).

▲ **Composite Stalker II** — similar to Composite Stalker with A-Bolt II improvements, short action also available in .223 Rem., .22-250 Rem., .243 Win., 7mm-08 Rem., or .308 Win. cal., 22 or 26 (Mag. cals. only) in. barrel without sights, 6 lbs. 4 oz. - 7 lbs. 3 oz. New 1994.

| **Mfg.'s Sug. Retail** | **$625** | **$475** | **$375** | **$315** | **$270** | **$240** | **$225** | **$210** |

Grading	100%	98%	95%	90%	80%	70%	60%

➤ **Composite Stalker II with BOSS** — available in 12 cals. between .22-250 - .338 Win. Mag., 22 or 26 (Mag. cals. only) in. barrel with BOSS.

Mfg.'s Sug. Retail	$723	$590	$485	$410	$360	$300	$275	$250

RIFLES: BOLT ACTION

MODEL 52 LIMITED EDITION — .22 LR cal., virtually identical to the original Winchester Model 52C Sporter, except for minor safety enhancements, bolt action, 24 in. drilled and tapped barrel, 5 shot detachable mag., pistol grip walnut stock with oil style finish, deep blue finish, adj. trigger, two position safety, 7 lbs. 5,000 mfg. 1991-92.

	$575	$475	$400

Last Mfg.'s Sug. Retail was $500.

MODEL BBR — .25-06, .270, .30-06, 7mm Mag., .300 or .338 Win. Mag. cal., short action available in .22-250, 243 W., 257 Roberts, 7mm-08 Rem., or 308 Win. cal., 24 in. barrel, 60 degree throw, fluted bolt, adj. trigger, hidden detachable mag., no sights, checkered pistol grip, Monte Carlo stock. Mfg. 1978-1984 by Miroku.

	$470	$360	$330	$305	$250	$220	$200

Some rare production calibers will add premiums to the values listed above (i.e., add 50% for .243 Win. cal.).

BBR RIFLE ELK ISSUE — 7mm Rem. Mag., bolt action rifle, 1,000 manufactured, deeply blued receiver which has multiple animals gold inlaid, high grade walnut stock and forearm feature skipline checkering. Disc. 1986.

	$1,195	$950	$795

Last Mfg.'s Sug. Retail was $1,395.

T-BOLT T-1 — .22 LR, straight pull bolt action, 5 shot mag., 22 in. barrel, adj. rear sight, 5½ lbs., plain pistol grip stock. Mfg. 1965-1974 by FN.

	$395	$350	$295	$255	$210	$180	$160

Add 10%-15% for left-hand model (mfg. 1969-74 only).
An aperture rear sight was standard for the first nine years of production.

T-BOLT T-2 — similar to T-1, only with select checkered walnut stock (lacquer finished), 24 in. barrel, 6 lbs.

	$500	$395	$330	$295	$240	$200	$180

Add 10%-15% for left-hand model (mfg. 1969-74 only).

▲ *Late production T-2* — features oil finished stock, plastic front sight, and Browning computerized serialization.

	$350	$295	$255	$210	$180	$160	$140

FN HIGH-POWER BOLT ACTION MODEL — .222 R. (Sako action), .22-250 (Sako action), .243 Win., .257 Roberts, .264 Win. Mag., .270, .284 Win. (Sako action), .30-06, .308 Win., 7mm Mag., .300 Win. Mag., .308 Norma Mag., .300 H&H, .338 Mag., .375 H&H, or .458 Win. Mag. cal., standard Mauser type action with either short or long (more desirable) extractor, 22 or 24 in. (heavy available) barrel, folding leaf sight (except on .222 R. and .22-250), checkered pistol grip stock. Mfg. 1959-1974 by FN.

The .243 and .308 Win. cals. were built on the small ring Mauser action prior to using the Sako medium action. The .222 Rem. Mag. was also furnished without sights.

Note: Grades differ in engraving, finish, checkering, and grade of wood. It should be noted that the salt wood problem is more common in these high powered models. Guns should be checked carefully for rust below wood surfaces.

Grading	100%	98%	95%	90%	80%	70%	60%
▲ *Safari Grade* — basic model with blued finish.							
Standard cals.	$795	$675	$550	$450	$400	$350	$325
Mag. cals.	$900	$750	$650	$595	$525	$450	$400
.257 Roberts	$1,295	$1,050	$825	$700	$600	$525	$450
.284 Win.	$1,550	$1,200	$950	$800	$700	$600	$500
.308 Norma Mag.	$1,050	$850	$700	$600	$525	$450	$400
.338 Win. Mag.	$1,150	$950	$850	$735	$650	$595	$525
.375 H&H	$1,300	$1,000	$800	$700	$600	$525	$450
.458 Win. Mag.	$1,095	$995	$895	$750	$625	$525	$450

Add 15% for Magnum long extractor models.

Between 1963 and 1974, Browning also offered short and medium barrelled actions in the Safari, Medallion and Olympian Grades. These models have Sako barrelled actions and were stocked by FN. Medium weight barrels could also be ordered.

▲ *Safari Grade - Short Sako Action* — short action, .222 Rem. or .222 Rem. Mag. cal.

	100%	98%	95%	90%	80%	70%	60%
	$800	$675	$550	$450	$400	$350	$325

▲ *Safari Grade - Medium Sako Action* — medium action, .22-250, .243, .284 or .308 cal.

	100%	98%	95%	90%	80%	70%	60%
	$800	$675	$550	$450	$400	$350	$325

Add 50% for .284 cal.

Only 192 rifles (in Safari, Medallion, and Olympian grades) were mfg. in .284 cal. between 1965-1976.

▲ *Medallion Grade* — features select figured walnut with skipline checkering, rosewood grip and forearm caps, blue/black lustre bluing, receiver and barrel portion scroll engraved, ram's head engraved on floor plate.

	100%	98%	95%	90%	80%	70%	60%
	$1,250	$995	$895	$795	$700	$600	$500

Add 10%-50% for rare calibers.
Add 15% for Mag. cals. with long extractor.

Caliber rarity is as follows: .264 Win. Mag. (least rare), .300 H&H Mag., .375 H&H long extractor, .222 Rem./.222 Rem. Mag., .284 Win. (rarest).

This model was also available with a Sako short or medium action - cals. are the same as listed for the Sako Safari.

▲ *Olympian Grade* — top-of-the-line model featuring highly figured walnut stock that is both checkered and carved. Receiver, floor plate, and trigger guard are chrome plated in a satin finish that have deep relief animal scenes engraved, as well as deep scroll work on other metal parts.

	100%	98%	95%	90%	80%	70%	60%
	$2,475	$2,150	$1,925	$1,700	$1,550	$1,350	$1,175

Add 10%-50% for rare calibers.
Add 15% for Mag. cals. with long extractor.

Caliber rarity is as follows: .264 Win. Mag. (least rare), .300 H&H Mag., .375 H&H long extractor, .222 Rem./.222 Rem. Mag., .284 Win. (rarest).

This model was also available with a Sako short or medium action - cals. are the same as listed for the Sako Safari.

RIFLES: SLIDE ACTION

BPR-22 — .22 LR or .22 Mag., short-stroke action, 20¼ in. barrel, 11 shot tube mag., mfg. 1977-1982.

	100%	98%	95%	90%	80%	70%	60%
	$275	$195	$170	$160	$140	$130	$100

▲ *BPR-22 Grade II* — similar to BPR-22, only engraved action, select walnut.

	100%	98%	95%	90%	80%	70%	60%
	$400	$350	$295	$260	$230	$200	$175

Add 10% for .22 Mag. cal.

TROMBONE MODEL — .22 LR only, slide action with tube mag., fixed sights, takedown, 24 in. barrel, hammerless, similar to Win. Model 61, with either F.N. or U.S. (rare) barrel address.

▲ *FN Barrel Address*

	100%	98%	95%	90%	80%	70%	60%
	$695	$550	$400	$350	$295	$260	$225

Grading	100%	98%	95%	90%	80%	70%	60%

▲ *BAC Barrel Markings*

	$850	$695	$495	$425	$350	$295	$250

Over 150,000 "Trombones" were mfg. by FN from 1922-1974. About 3,200 were imported by BAC in late 1960s. Very rare with factory engraving.

BCA GRADE III FN TROMBONE — only 60 manufactured for the Browning Collectors Association 1985-86, silver engraved frame with deluxe walnut.

			$2,350	$1,995	$1,600		

RIFLES: O/U

EXPRESS RIFLE — .270 Win., .30-06 cal., or 9.3x74R cal., Superposed style action. 24 in. barrels, auto ejectors, Fleur-de-lis engraving, single trigger, folding leaf rear sight, 6 lbs. 14 oz., cased. Disc. 1986.

	$2,200	$1,850	$1,600	$1,475	$1,300	$1,100	$900

Last Mfg.'s Sug. Retail was $3,125.

SHOTGUNS: SEMI-AUTO, DISC.

BROWNING CHOKES AND THEIR CODES (ON REAR LEFT-SIDE OF BARREL)

* designates full choke (F).

*- designates improved modified choke (IM).

** designates modified choke (M).

**- designates improved cylinder choke (IC).

**$ designates skeet (SK).

*** designates cylinder bore (CYL).

INV. designates barrel is threaded for Browning Invector choke tube system.

INV. PLUS designates back-bored barrels.

AUTO-5 STANDARD - 1903-1939 MFG. — 12 or 16 ga.(introduced in U.S. in 1923), 26-32 in. barrel, recoil operated, various chokes, checkered pistol grip stock, mfg. 1903-1939 and limited post-war mfg. by FN, grades differ in engraving, inlays, and grade of wood. Approx. ser. range 1-229,000 (12ga.), 1-128,000 (16 ga.).

	100%	98%	95%	90%	80%	70%	60%
Grade 1	$425	$375	$325	$285	$250	$200	$175
Solid matte rib	$495	$425	$375	$325	$275	$250	$215
With vent. rib	$550	$475	$400	$350	$300	$250	$215
Grade 2.(disc.1940)	$1,250	$1,000	$875	$750	$625	$550	$495
Solid matte rib	$1,450	$1,150	$1,000	$875	$750	$625	$575
With vent. rib	$1,625	$1,300	$1,200	$1,000	$850	$750	$650
Grade 3.(disc. 1940)	$2,500	$2,200	$1,975	$1,775	$1,500	$1,250	$995
Solid matte rib	$2,700	$2,400	$2,100	$1,850	$1,650	$1,375	$1,100
With vent. rib	$2,950	$2,550	$2,250	$2,000	$1,775	$1,500	$1,225
Grade 4.(disc.1940)	$3,995	$3,655	$3,300	$2,995	$2,550	$2,050	$1,600
Solid matte rib	$4,150	$3,885	$3,450	$3,175	$2,700	$2,200	$1,800

Early models with safety mounted in front of trigger guard are not as desirable as there are potential safety problems inherent in the design.

Pre-WWII 16 ga. A-5s could be chambered for 2⁹⁄₁₆ in. shells. These shotguns are considerably less desirable than 16 ga. A-5s chambered for 2¾ in. modern shotshells. Since some guns have been modified to 2¾ in., careful inspection is advised before purchasing or shooting. The 2⁹⁄₁₆ chambered guns can be modified by the Browning Service Dept. to accept 2¾ in. shells if so desired.

Grading	100%	98%	95%	90%	80%	70%	60%

"AMERICAN BROWNING" AUTO-5 — 12, 16, or 20 ga., Remington-produced model of the Auto-5, very similar to the Remington Model 11, except with Browning logo, mag. cut-off, and different engraving, over 45,000 mfg. in 12 ga., over 25,000 in 16 ga., and 20,000 in 20 ga., stocks have Remington style round knob pistol grips with black plastic caps. Mfg. 1940-1952 and ser. numbered approx. 229,000-346,000, 12 ga. has "B" prefix on left side of receiver, "A" denotes 16 ga., and "C" denotes 20 ga.

	$325	$275	$250	$225	$200	$180	$160

Add 10% for vent. rib and/or 20 ga.

An easy way to identify this configuration is to look for the "A", "B", or "C" prefix on the left side of receiver.

AUTO-5 STANDARDWEIGHT — 12, 20, or 16 ga., recoil operation, 26-32 in. barrels, standard production gun between 1952-1969, various chokes, checkered walnut stock and forearm, synthetic Browning marked butt plate, lacquer (until approx. 1966) or polyurethane finish, butt stock has either round knob pistol grip (1952-1976) or flat knob (introduced 1967), watch for cracked forearms on all A-5s (due to barrel recoil), between 7⅓-8 lbs.

	100%	98%	95%	90%	80%	70%	60%
Plain barrel	$425	$375	$325	$295	$270	$240	$210
Matted rib	$525	$450	$400	$350	$300	$275	$245
Vent rib	$550	$460	$410	$370	$325	$300	$265

Add 10% for NIB condition.

Barrel addresses appeared as follows: 1952-1958 "St. Louis, Missouri", 1959-1968 "St. Louis, Missouri and Montreal P.Q.", 1969-1975 "Morgan, Utah and Montreal, P.Q.". Make sure barrel address date matches year of mfg. (see listings in the back of this text). Standardweight models had H or M prefixes.

SHOTGUNS: SEMI-AUTO RECENT MFG.

Miroku manufactured A-5s can be determined by year of manufacture in the following manner: RV suffix - 1975, RT - 1976, RR - 1977, RP - 1978, RN - 1979, PM - 1980, PZ - 1981, PY - 1982, PX - 1983, PW - 1984, PV - 1985, PT - 1986, PR - 1987, PP - 1988, PN - 1989, NM - 1990, NZ - 1991, NY - 1992, NX - 1993, NW - 1994, NV - 1995, NU - 1996.

NOTE: Barrels are interchangeable between older Belgium A-5 models and recent Japanese A-5's mfg. by Miroku. A different barrel ring design might necessitate some minor sanding of the inner forearm on the older model, but otherwise, these barrels are fully interchangeable.

NOTE: The use of steel shot is recommended ONLY in those recent models manufactured in Japan incorporating the Invector choke system - NOT in the older Belgium variations.

Add 10-15% for the round knob (rounded pistol grip knob on stock) variation on FN models only.

AUTO-5 LIGHTWEIGHT (LIGHT 12) — 12 or 20 ga., recoil operated, 26, 28, and 30 in. barrels, various chokes, scroll engraved receiver, checkered pistol grip stock, approx. 10 oz. lighter than Standardweight, mfg. 1952-1976 by FN, mfg. 1976-present by Miroku in Japan. Over 2,750,000 A-5's were mfg. by FN in all configurations between 1902-1976.

	100%	98%	95%	90%	80%	70%	60%
FN model	$400	$375	$325	$295	$270	$240	$215
FN-vent. rib	$575	$450	$395	$350	$325	$295	$260

Add 10% for NIB condition.
Add 10% for 20 ga. with VR.

▲ *Light 12 Miroku* — 12 ga. only, 22, 26, 28, or 30 in. VR (became standard 1986) barrel with Invector choke system, approx. 8-8½ lbs.

		100%	98%	95%	90%	80%	70%	60%
Mfg.'s Sug. Retail	$840	$650	$485	$400	$350	$300	$280	$260

Subtract 10% without Invector chokes.

Grading	100%	98%	95%	90%	80%	70%	60%

▲ **Light 20 Miroku** — 20 ga. only, 2¾ in. chamber, similar to original Belgium Light 20, VR, 22 (new 1995), 26, or 28 in. barrel, Invector chokes standard until 1993, Invector Plus choking became standard 1994, 6 lbs. 12 oz - 7 lbs. 2 oz. New 1987.

Mfg.'s Sug. Retail	$840	$650	$495	$410	$365	$325	$295	$270

AUTO-5 MAGNUM — 12 or 20 ga., 3 in. chamber, 26, 28, 30, or 32 in. barrels, various chokes, VR, similar to Standard, 8½ - 9 lbs. Mfg. 1958-1976 by FN, mfg. 1976-present by Miroku.

	100%	98%	95%	90%	80%	70%	60%
FN model.	$550	$450	$400	$350	$320	$260	$240
FN, vent. rib.	$675	$575	$525	$480	$430	$340	$315

Add 10% for NIB condition.
Add 15% for 20 ga. with VR if NIB.

Between 1976-1985 approx. 2,000 Belgian 12 ga. A-5 Mags. were imported into the U.S. These late models can be differentiated by serialization — also, slight premiums may be asked. The 20 ga. Mag. was not introduced until 1967.

▲ **A-5 Mag. Miroku** — 12 or 20 (disc. 1996) ga., VR barrel with Invector choke system until 1993, Invector Plus choking became standard 1994, 8½ - 9 lbs.

Mfg.'s Sug. Retail	$866	$695	$540	$445	$385	$350	$325	$290

Subtract 10% without Invector chokes.

AUTO-5 STALKER — 12 ga. only, 2¾ (Light-12) or 3 (Mag. Stalker) in. chamber, 22 (Light-12 only), 26, 28, or 30, or 32 (Mag. only) in. VR barrel with Invector chokes, black matte finish graphite-fiberglass stock and forearm, matte finished metal, recoil pad, 8 lbs. 1 oz. - 8 lbs. 13 oz. New late 1992.

Mfg.'s Sug. Retail	$840	$650	$485	$410	$350	$300	$280	$260

Add $26 for Mag. Stalker.

AUTO-5 LIGHT 12 BUCK SPECIAL — similar to Standard only with 24 in. barrel, slug bore, adj. sight, mfg. 1958-1976 by FN, mfg. 1976-1984 and 1989 again by Miroku, 8 lbs. 6 oz. Between 1985-1988, Buck Special barrels were available at extra cost.

▲ *FN Mfg.*

	100%	98%	95%	90%	80%	70%	60%
	$675	$475	$410	$370	$330	$295	$240

▲ *Miroku model*

Mfg.'s Sug. Retail	$829	$645	$500	$425	$360	$320	$290	$260

Add $26 for Buck Special on 3 in. Mag. receiver.

AUTO-5 SKEET — similar to Standard Light, only with 26 or 28 in. skeet bored, vent. rib barrel. Pre-1976 mfg. by FN, 1976-1983 mfg. by Miroku.

▲ *FN Mfg.*

	100%	98%	95%	90%	80%	70%	60%
	$550	$425	$375	$325	$295	$270	$240

Add 20% for vent. rib.

▲ *Standard Miroku*

	100%	98%	95%	90%	80%	70%	60%
	$460	$420	$380	$340	$300	$270	$250

AUTO-5 TRAP MODEL — similar to Standard, 12 ga. only, 30 in. full vent. rib barrel, 8½ lbs., mfg. by FN until 1971.

	100%	98%	95%	90%	80%	70%	60%
	$595	$525	$465	$410	$335	$320	$295

AUTO-5 SWEET 16 — similar to Standardweight Model, except 16 ga. (2¾ in. chamber) only and approx. 10 oz. lighter, gold plated trigger. Mfg. 1950-1976 by Fabrique Nationale.

	100%	98%	95%	90%	80%	70%	60%
Plain Barrel	$525	$415	$350	$295	$250	$220	$195
Solid Matte Rib	$695	$575	$465	$375	$295	$250	$225
Vent. Rib	$950	$750	$575	$425	$375	$325	$275

▲ **Sweet 16 Miroku** — 16 ga. only, similar to original Belgium Sweet 16, VR, invector choke standard. Mfg. 1987-92.

	100%	98%	95%	90%	80%	70%	60%
	$580	$475	$420	$380	$340	$300	$270

Last Mfg.'s Sug. Retail was $720.

Grading	100%	98%	95%	90%	80%	70%	60%

AUTO-5 2-MILLIONTH COMMEMORATIVE — 12 ga., 2,500 mfg., 1971-74 mfg., special walnut, engraving, high-luster bluing, cased with Browning book. Issue price — $550-$700.

	$1,195	$900	$750				

A-5 CLASSIC SERIES SHOTGUN — 12 ga., 5,000 mfg. in Classic model, 500 mfg. in Gold Classic. Both editions feature game scenes, John M. Browning's profile, and other inscriptions, special silver grey finished receiver. Introduced 1984.

▲ **Classic Model** — no inlays. Factory inventories were depleted in 1987.

	$950	$750	$600				

Last Mfg.'s Sug. Retail was $1,260.

▲ **Gold Classic Model** — features 5 inlays depicting duck hunting scenes. Mfg. 1986 with inventory depleted 1989.

	$3,500	$2,750	$1,950				

Last Mfg.'s Sug. Retail was $6,500.

A-5 BCA COMMEMORATIVE — 12 ga., 3 in. Mag., round knob, Belgian mfg., issue price was $595.

	$650	$575	$450				

A-5 DU 50TH ANNIVERSARY

▲ **A-5 DU Light 12** — 12 ga. only, 5,500 mfg. in 1987 only for Ducks Unlimited chapters throughout North America. Prices will fluctuate greatly from chapter to chapter as these guns were auctioned to the highest bidder. Receiver is specially engraved and has "Fiftieth year" depicted on right side of receiver, deluxe checkered stock and forearm, high gloss blue.

	$950	$750	$600				

▲ **A-5 DU Sweet Sixteen** — 16 ga. only, companion 1988-89 DU auction gun, 4500 mfg. 1988 only.

	$950	$750	$600				

▲ **A-5 DU Light 20** — 20 ga. only, companion 1990 DU auction gun, 4500 mfg. 1990 only.

	$950	$750	$600				

DOUBLE AUTOMATIC SHOTGUN — short recoil action, 12 ga. only, 2 shot, 26, 28, or 30 in. barrel, various chokes, checkered pistol grip stock, blued steel receiver. Mfg. 1952-1971.

	$475	$400	$350	$300	$260	$220	$195
w/vent. rib	$650	$495	$420	$375	$325	$295	$245

TWELVETTE DOUBLE AUTO — similar to Double Auto, except hiduminum (aircraft alloy) frame and color anodized in blue, silver, brown, green, and black, approx. 7 lbs. without rib. Approx. 67,000 (all variations) mfg. 1952-1971.

	$475	$400	$350	$295	$250	$220	$200
w/vent. rib	$650	$495	$425	$395	$340	$280	$250

Add 20-25% for dark red, royal blue, brown, or gold colored receivers (rare).

TWENTYWEIGHT DOUBLE AUTO — similar to Twelvette, but ¾ pound lighter, 26½ in. barrel only. Mfg. 1952-1971.

	$575	$450	$375	$295	$235	$220	$200
w/vent. rib	$725	$625	$525	$450	$400	$350	$295

B/2000 STANDARD — 12 or 20 ga., 26, 28, or 30 in. barrel, various chokes, vent. rib, gas operated, checkered pistol grip stock, Belgium manufactured but assembled in Portugal, approx. 115,000 imported into the U.S. between 1974-1983.

	$360	$325	$295	$275	$250	$225	$195

B/2000 MAGNUM — similar to B/2000 Auto Shotgun, except with 3 in. chambered barrel (all receivers were the same), recoil pad, vent. rib.

	$385	$340	$310	$280	$260	$230	$200

B/2000 SKEET — similar to Standard, with 26 in. skeet bored barrel, floating vent. rib, skeet stock, pad.

	$375	$325	$295	$275	$250	$225	$195

Grading	100%	98%	95%	90%	80%	70%	60%

B/2000 TRAP — similar to Standard, with 30 or 32 in. barrel bored F or IM, floating rib, Monte Carlo trap stock.

	$375	$325	$295	$275	$250	$225	$195

B/2000 BUCK SPECIAL — 12 or 20 ga., barrel sights on 24 in. barrel.

	$375	$325	$295	$275	$250	$225	$195

1976 CANADIAN OLYMPICS B2000 — 12 ga., 100 manufactured in 1976 for Canadian sales only, high polish blue with multiple gold inlays including Olympic crest, 30 in. barrel, cased. Issue price was $1,295.

	$1,395	$995	$695

MODEL B-80 — 12 or 20 ga., 3 in. capability by changing barrel, gas operation, 4 shot, hunting models use choice of steel or aluminum receiver, anodized aluminum was used in the Superlight (12 ga. mfg. 1984 only), 6 to 8 lbs. 1 oz. Buck special disc. 1984. Components manufactured by Beretta of Italy and finished and assembled FN's plant in Portugal. Mfg. 1981-late 1988, final inventory was sold in 1991. Invector chokes became standard in 1985.

	$450	$375	$325	$295	$275	$250	$230

Last Mfg.'s Sug. Retail was $562.

Steel frames were reintroduced into production again in 1988.

▲ *Model B-80 Upland Special* — 12 or 20 ga., 2¾ in. chamber, 22 in. vent. rib barrel, straight grip stock, invector chokes. Mfg. 1986-1988.

	$475	$390	$340	$305	$280	$260	$240

Last Mfg.'s Sug. Retail was $562.

MODEL B 80 DU COMMEMORATIVE — mfg. for American DU Chapters (The Plains and others), price fluctuates greatly as collector support is sometimes limited. Unless new, this model's values approximate those of the regular Model B-80. If NIB, values recently have been in the $700-$995 range.

A-500R — 12 ga. only, 3 in. chamber, new design utilizing short recoil system with a four-lug rotary bolt design, capable of shooting all 12 gauge loads interchangeably, magazine cut off, 26, 28, or 30 in. VR barrel with Invector chokes standard, 24 in. barrel on Buck Special (fixed choke), high polished blued finish with red accents on receiver sides, gold trigger, checkered semi-pistol grip walnut stock with vent. recoil pad, 7 lbs. 11 oz. - 8 lbs. 1 oz. Mfg. 1987-1993.

	$475	$425	$375	$325	$295	$275	$250

Last Mfg.'s Sug. Retail was $560.

Add $33 for Buck Special variation (Invector chokes).

This model features fewer moving parts than many other semi-auto shotguns due to the short recoil operating system.

A-500G HUNTING — similar to A-500, except is gas operated, distinguishable by "A-500G" in gold accents on receiver, capable of shooting all 2¾ or 3 in. shells interchangeably, approx. 8 lbs. Mfg. 1990-1993.

	$555	$425	$375	$325	$295	$275	$250

Last Mfg.'s Sug. Retail was $653.

A Buck Special variation was mfg. until 1992. No premiums currently exist.

▲ *A-500G Sporting Clays* — 12 ga. only, Sporting Clays variation with 30 in. VR barrel, 8 lbs. 2 oz. Mfg. 1992-1993.

	$555	$425	$375	$325	$295	$275	$250

Last Mfg.'s Sug. Retail was $653.

GOLD HUNTER MODEL — 12 or 20 ga., 3 in. chamber, self-cleaning piston rod gas action with self-regulation, alloy receiver with non-glare black finish and "GOLD Hunter" on receiver side, 26, 28, or 30 (12 ga. only) in. VR Invector Plus (12 ga. only) or Invector (20 ga. only) choked barrel, cross-bolt safety, checkered walnut stock and forearm with recoil pad (vent on 12 ga.), 6 lbs. 12 oz. - 7 lbs. 9 oz. Parts mfg. in Belgium and final assembly in Portugal. New 1994.

Mfg.'s Sug. Retail	$735	$615	$450	$380	$325	$295	$275	$250

B

Grading	100%	98%	95%	90%	80%	70%	60%

▲ **Gold Sporting Clays Model** — similar to Gold Hunter Model, except has 2 ¾ in. chamber, 28 or 30 in. ported barrel with Invector Plus choking, approx. 7 ½ lbs. New 1996.

Mfg.'s Sug. Retail	$760	$635	$465	$395	$335	$300	$275	$250

BSA 10 — while advertised, this gun had its model nomenclature changed to the Gold 10 Ga. before mfg. started.

GOLD 10 GA. — 10 ga. Mag., 3½ in. chamber, short stroke self-cleaning gas action, 4 shot mag., steel receiver with choice of high polish (Hunting Model) or dull finish (Stalker Model) bluing, 26, 28, or 30 in. VR standard Invector choke barrel, available with either high-gloss checkered walnut (Hunting) or matte black fiberglass (Stalker) stock and forearm, vent recoil pad, approx. 10 lbs. 10 oz. Mfg. by Miroku, Japan. New 1994.

Mfg.'s Sug. Retail	$1,008	$875	$715	$600	$500	$425	$375	$325

SHOTGUNS: O/U

SUPERPOSED SHOTGUN: 1931-1976 MANUFACTURE — 12, 20, 28, or .410 ga., 26½, 28, 30, or 32 in. barrels, various chokes, boxlock, auto ejectors, SST, DT, or twin single triggers (early mfg.), checkered pistol grip stock, mfg. 1931-1940 and 1949-1976 by FN, grades differ in amount of engraving, inlay, general quality of workmanship and wood. Currently, shorter barrel (26½ in.). Superposed models are bringing a small premium over a 30 in. F & M model. Prices below assume vent. rib models, earlier matted rib guns will be 5-10% less, depending on condition.

NOTE: The use of steel shot is NOT recommended in any Superposed Series manufactured in Belgium (B-25 variations).

BROWNING CHOKES AND THEIR CODES (ON BARREL)

* designates full choke (F).

*- designates improved modified choke (IM).

** designates modified choke (M).

**- designates improved cylinder choke (IC).

**$ designates skeet (SK).

*** designates cylinder bore (CYL).

SKEET MODELS were available in every ga. and grade.

TRAP MODELS were available in every grade in 12 ga. only - deduct 5%-10% from values shown below. BROADWAY TRAP MODELS with ⅝ in. wide vent. rib were also available in every grade.
Add 10% for 20 ga. on all grades.
Add 70%-100% for 28 ga. on Grade I, 30% on higher grades.
Add 30% for .410 ga. on Grade I models only.
Add 10% for round knob, long tang stock variations.
Deduct 25% for early DT models.

▲ **Grade I Standard** — the Grade I has a blued steel frame with hand engraved scroll and rosette patterns, checkered walnut stock and forearm. Grade I Standard was disc. 1973.

	$1,395	$1,075	$925	$840	$775	$650	$550

▲ **Grade I Lightning** — similar to Grade I Standard. Disc. 1976.

	$1,650	$1,175	$975	$870	$810	$690	$600

Because of the mandatory use of steel shot in recent years, values for 12 ga. Magnum and Lightning models have gone down (these models are not compatible with steel shot).

▲ **Grade I Magnum** — 3 in. chambers with standard Browning recoil pad. Disc. 1976.

	$1,395	$1,075	$900	$825	$760	$635	$525

Because of the mandatory use of steel shot in recent years, values for 12 ga. Magnum and Lightning models have gone down (these models are not compatible with steel shot).

Grading	100%	98%	95%	90%	80%	70%	60%

▲ *Pigeon Grade* — designated Grade II after WWII and renamed Pigeon in October, 1959. This grade featured a silver grey receiver with 2 flying pigeons surrounded by fine scroll engraving on each side of the frame. The receiver bottom and tangs also exhibit fine scroll work. The Pigeon Grade was disc. 1974.

	$3,250	$2,500	$1,950	$1,825	$1,650	$1,570	$1,485

▲ *Grade III* — satin finished receiver with game scene engraving featuring pheasants and fighting cocks on receiver, receiver bottom has a retriever and pheasant. Disc. October, 1959.

	$2,500	$2,150	$2,000	$1,815	$1,650	$1,570	$1,485

▲ *Pointer Grade* — also designated Grade III, manufactured post-war only until renamed Pointer in early October, 1959. Features engraved silver grey receiver with a Pointer depicted on each frame side, select walnut. Disc. 1966, except for special orders.

	$4,250	$3,250	$2,450	$2,050	$1,850	$1,700	$1,625

▲ *Grade IV* — limited manufacture between 1950-1959, engraving usually featured a dog and bird scene in deep relief.

	$4,250	$3,250	$2,450	$2,050	$1,850	$1,700	$1,625

▲ *Diana Grade* — also designated Grade V in post-war manufacture until renamed Diana in October, 1959. Pre-WWII Grade Vs featured more delicate scroll engraving with deer adorning the right side and wild boar shown on the left. Post-WWII guns exhibit deep relief engraving with duck and pheasant game scenes on each frame side, select checkered walnut stock and forearm. Disc. 1976.

	$4,950	$4,000	$2,850	$2,150	$1,900	$1,800	$1,700

▲ *Midas Grade* — also designated Grade VI during post-war manufacture until renamed Midas in October, 1959. Pre-WWII Midas Grades featured an inlaid pigeon with outstretched wings on blued frame sides and bottom plus trigger guard. This earlier Midas also exhibited multiple gold escutcheons and gold lining. Post-war models feature deep relief scroll engraving with gold inlaid ducks and pheasants on frame sides and a quail on the bottom. Ejector trip rods, ejector hammers and firing pins are also 18Kt. gold plated. Finest checkered walnut. Disc. 1976.

	$6,250	$5,400	$3,650	$2,950	$2,600	$2,250	$1,900

▲ *Grade VI* — 12 or 20 ga. only, offered from 1955-October, 1959 only. Elaborate deep relief scroll engraved with multiple gold inlays.

	100%	98%	95%	90%	80%	70%	60%
12 ga.	$5,500	$4,500	$4,000	$3,500	$3,200	$3,000	$2,600
20 ga.	$8,250	$6,950	$5,900	$4,950	$4,250	$3,500	$2,750

SUPERPOSED WITH EXTRA BARREL(S) OR SUPER-TUBES

Could be ordered from the factory in the following combinations: 12 or 20 ga. with one extra set of barrels in same ga. 12 ga. with one extra set in 20 ga. 12 or 20 ga. with two extra barrel sets of same ga. 20 ga. with one extra set in either 28 or .410 ga. 20 ga. with both 28 and .410 ga. barrel sets. 28 ga. with extra set of .410 barrels. Super-Tubes were adaptable on 12 ga. guns only; came from the factory cased with accessories, 16½ in. long, factory installation.

Grade I extra barrel set(s) — add 40-50% of the gun's value for each extra set. Add approx. $1,500 per barrel set in higher grades.

· Super-Tubes — available for 12 ga. only, single ga. — add $250.

Super-Tube Set — 3 ga. set (20, 28 and .410 ga.'s) — add $400.

EXPOSITION/EXHIBITION MODEL

This specially manufactured Superposed saw limited production from the late '60s through 1976. This model had its own serial range (usually 3 digit) with a "C" prefix. Grades A through G ranged from fairly simple scroll designs without gold inlays up to extremely ornate designs featuring multi-colored gold inlaid game figures. Most of these guns were produced by FN for display purposes, potential production models, or potential engraving standardization. Many of these Exhibition/Exposition superposed models were consigned to Browning Arms Co. during the 1970s because of the depressed market conditions of that time. Prices are determined by the embellishments and engraving per individual gun (A Grade being the lowest, F Grade with gold being the highest). Prices usually start at around $5,000, while a F Grade with extensive gold inlays could reach 5 digits.

Grading	100%	98%	95%	90%	80%	70%	60%

B

BICENTENNIAL SUPERPOSED SUPERLIGHT SHOTGUN — specially engraved limited edition Model, 51 mfg. — one for each state and Washington, D.C. Left side has U.S. Flag, bald eagle and state emblem inlaid in gold. Right side has gold inlaid hunter and turkey. Blued receiver, fancy checkered English stock, Schnabel forend, velvet lined wood case. Made 1976 by FN.

$12,500 $9,750 $7,750

WATERFOWL SUPERPOSED SHOTGUN SERIES — 12 ga., 500 made of each issue. Gold inlays with extensive engraving, lightning action, 28 in. barrels, full-length walnut case, factory inventories were depleted on Mallard, Pintail, and Black Duck Issues in 1989.

▲ *1981 Mallard Issue*

$4,450 $3,250 $2,250

Last Mfg.'s Sug. Retail was $7,000.

This issue was sold out in 1988.

▲ *1982 Pintail Issue*

$4,450 $3,150 $2,150

Last Mfg.'s Sug. Retail was $7,000.

▲ *1983 Black Duck Issue*

$4,450 $3,150 $2,150

Last Mfg.'s Sug. Retail was $8,800.

OVER/UNDER CLASSIC SERIES SHOTGUN — 20 ga. only, 26 in. barrels, less than 2,500 manufactured in Classic model and under 350 manufactured in Gold Classic. Both editions feature multiple engraved scenes and a special silver grey finish. Select American walnut featuring oil finish. Available 1986 only.

$1,750 $1,500 $1,200

Last Mfg.'s Sug. Retail was $2,000.

▲ *Gold Classic* — 8 gold inlays, select walnut forearm and stock are both checkered and carved, many were shipped back to Belgium due to poor sales domestically. Available 1986 only.

$5,995 $4,150 $3,150

Last Mfg.'s Sug. Retail was $6,000.

SUPERPOSED SUPERLIGHT — 12 or 20 ga., 26½ in. solid or VR barrels, lightened slimmer forearm and straight grip stock. Mfg. 1967-1976 by FN.

	100%	98%	95%	90%	80%	70%	60%
12 ga.	$1,795	$1,475	$1,225	$1,110	$1,025	$925	$800
20 ga.	$2,400	$1,925	$1,575	$1,350	$1,250	$1,000	$850

For Pigeon, Diana, and Midas grade Superlight 12 ga. models use previous values on standard model high-grades and add approx. 25% (plus gauge premiums).

There is also a Quail Unlimited limited edition in the Superlight series. Values are somewhat higher but difficult to ascertain because so few are bought and sold each year.

SUPERPOSED SHOTGUN: 1983-86 MANUFACTURE — 12 or 20 ga. In 1983, Browning announced renewed production of the famous Belgium "Superposed" O/U in Grade I only. Available in Lightning or Superlight models, 3 in. chambers in Lightning 20 ga., 26½ or 28 in. barrels. Belgium manufactured from 1983-86.

▲ *Grade I* — limited mfg., not compatible with steel shot.

$1,895 $1,595 $1,395 $1,000 $800 $675 $550

Last Mfg.'s Sug. Retail was $1,995.

SUPERPOSED CONTINENTAL CENTENNIAL — 20 ga. O/U shotgun w/extra set of .30-06 O/U rifle barrels. Shotgun barrels are 26½ in., rifle barrels are 24 in., SST, ejectors, elaborate scroll engraved receiver with 2 gold inlays, special oil finish walnut, deluxe walnut full-length case. 500 mfg. 1978 only.

$3,375 $3,000 $2,600 $2,300 $2,000 $1,850 $1,650

Last Mfg.'s Sug. Retail was $6,500.

Grading	100%	98%	95%	90%	80%	70%	60%

SUPERPOSED PRESENTATION MODELS (P1-P4) — custom made versions of the Lightning Field, Super Light, Trap, and Skeet guns, specifications the same as Standard models, with differences in finish, engraving and inlay(s), and grade of wood and checkering. These guns were introduced by FN in 1977 and were disc. after 1984. Add $1,775 for extra set of barrels, add $3,600 for 2 sets of extra barrels.

    P Series Trap — deduct 10% from values listed below.
    P Series Broadway Trap — deduct 10-15% from values listed below.
    P Series Skeet 12 and 20 ga. — deduct 10-15% from values listed below.

    Since P Series Superposed were disc. 1985, collector interest will undoubtedly increase and prices might be increased somewhat. BAC has no remaining inventory of this model. Interestingly, the P series models are rarer than most of the pre-1976 high grade Superposed models.
    Add 20% for 20 ga.
    Add 30% for 28 ga.
    Add 20% for .410 ga.

▲ *Presentation 1* — silver grey or blued receiver, oak leaf and fine scroll engraved, choice of 6 different animal scenes.

                    $2,850 $2,350 $1,995 $1,750 $1,500 $1,250 $1,000

▲ *Presentation 1 w/gold inlays* — similar to Presentation 1, only with gold inlays.

                    $3,450 $2,800 $2,350 $2,050 $1,825 $1,700 $1,500

▲ *Presentation 2* — silver grey or blued receiver, high relief engraving, choice of 3 different sets of game scenes.

                    $3,400 $2,750 $2,300 $2,050 $1,825 $1,700 $1,500

▲ *Presentation 2 w/gold inlays* — similar to Presentation 2, only with gold inlays.

                    $3,950 $3,250 $2,550 $2,150 $1,925 $1,750 $1,550

▲ *Presentation 3* — silver grey or blued receiver, more elaborate high relief engraving with choice of partridges, mallards or geese depicted on frame sides in 18Kt. gold.

                    $5,450 $4,700 $4,100 $3,600 $3,200 $2,875 $2,300

▲ *Presentation 4* — features engraved side plates in either silver grey or blued finish, engraved game scenes include waterfowl on right frame side, 5 pheasants on left frame side, 2 quail on receiver bottom, and a retriever's head on trigger guard. Extra figure walnut stock and forearm.

                    $6,000 $4,950 $4,350 $3,825 $3,350 $2,950 $2,375

▲ *Presentation 4 w/gold inlays* — similar to Presentation 4, only with game scenes inlaid in 18Kt. gold.

                    $7,200 $6,500 $5,265 $4,750 $4,250 $3,650 $2,950

P SERIES SUPERLIGHT — available in various configurations including multi-barrel sets. Typically, add 20-25% onto the values listed for the regular P series as shown above. Also add 20-40% for the 28 ga.

LIEGE O/U — 12 ga., 26½, 28 or 30 in. barrels, various chokes, boxlock, auto ejectors, non-selective single trigger, vent. rib, checkered pistol grip stock. Approx. 10,000 mfg. 1973-1975 by FN.

                    $750 $625 $575 $500 $425 $400 $375

    This model is also known as the B-26.

B-26 — with BAC markings. Mfg. 1973-75.

                    $750 $625 $575 $500 $425 $400 $375

B-27 — F.N. manufactured modified B-26, imported into the U.S. in 1984, same action as Liege (B 26), blued or satin finished receiver with light engraving, no BAC markings and never cataloged.

▲ *Standard Game* — 28 in. barrels, ⁹⁄₃₂ in. vent. rib, pistol grip stock, Schnabel forearm, SST, blued receiver, choking M/F only.

                    $650 $575 $525 $475 $425 $400 $375

    Also available in Skeet model with gold "Browning" logo on blued receiver. Prices are the same.

Grading	100%	98%	95%	90%	80%	70%	60%

▲ *Deluxe Game (Grade II)* — similar to Standard Grade, except has 30 in. barrels, better wood and English scroll engraved satin finished receiver, choking M/F only.

	$875	$725	$625	$575	$510	$475	$445

▲ *Grand Deluxe Game* — 28 in. IC/IM & M/F choked barrels, game scene engraved, signed by the engraver, 90% receiver coverage.

	$1,100	$850	$775	$700	$640	$580	$520

This model was also available in a Trap configuration — values are about the same as above.

▲ *Deluxe Skeet* — similar to Deluxe, except is designed for skeet shooting.

	$850	$725	$625	$575	$510	$475	$445

International Skeet is also available at same price; hand fit pistol grip with stippling and International Type recoil pad.

▲ *Deluxe Trap* — similar to Deluxe, except is configured for trap shooting.

	$750	$650	$560	$530	$500	$475	$445

▲ *City of Liege Commemorative* — limited edition of 250 units manufactured to commemorate the 1,000th anniversary of the city of Liege, cased. Only 29 imported into the U.S.

	$1,125	$975	$910	$850	$775	$700	$600

ST-100 — 12 ga., Belgian mfg., O/U trap configuration with separated barrels and adj. point of impact, manufactured 1979-1983 for European sale mostly, floating VR, ST, deluxe checkered walnut stock and forearm, non-BAC model.

	$2,375	$1,950	$1,700	$1,400	$1,200	$975	$825

SUPERPOSED HIGH GRADES: 1985-PRESENT

Browning, in 1985, resumed production of the Superposed in Pigeon, Pointer, Diana, and Midas grades. They are available in 12 and 20 ga. only, in either a Lightning or Superlight configuration. These higher grades are custom ordered from the factory with delivery ranging from 8 to more than 12 months. Custom options can be special ordered on each grade with corresponding prices being higher than shown below. B-25 engraving patterns on these various grades will nearly duplicate those styles manufactured before 1976. Skeet models are not available.

B-25 — 12 or 20 ga. only, original Superposed Model manufactured entirely from parts fabricated in Herstal, Belgium. Also available in Superlight configuration.

▲ *Pigeon Grade*

Mfg.'s Sug. Retail	$7,875	$3,750	$2,600	$1,950	$1,825	$1,650	$1,570	$1,485

Add $2,900 for an extra set of barrels.

▲ *Pointer Grade*

Mfg.'s Sug. Retail	$9,345	$4,800	$3,350	$2,500	$2,050	$1,850	$1,700	$1,625

Add $3,100 for an extra set of barrels.

▲ *Diana Grade*

Mfg.'s Sug. Retail	$10,028	$5,800	$4,150	$2,850	$2,200	$1,900	$1,800	$1,700

Add $4,400 for an extra set of barrels.

▲ *Midas Grade*

Mfg.'s Sug. Retail	$13,808	$6,950	$5,750	$3,650	$3,000	$2,600	$2,250	$1,900

Add $5,000 for an extra set of barrels.

B-125 — 12 or 20 ga. only, retains all the features of the original Superposed, except parts are subcontracted worldwide to decrease production costs and are assembled "in the white" at Herstal's Custom Gun Shop in Belgium, choice of three different engraving styles and two receiver finishes. Introduced 1988.

▲ *Hunting Model* — available in either Hunting Lightning or Superlight configuration.

Grading	100%	98%	95%	90%	80%	70%	60%

➤ "A" Style Engraving — blued receiver with border engraving featuring Browning logo engraved on each side.
Mfg.'s Sug. Retail	$4,568	$3,925	$2,950	$2,150	$1,700	$1,450	$1,275	$1,050

➤ "B" Style Engraving — coin finished receiver with smaller game scene engravings.
Mfg.'s Sug. Retail	$4,883	$4,125	$3,150	$2,200	$1,800	$1,500	$1,300	$1,100

➤ "C" Style Engraving — coin finished receiver with elaborate scroll work and game scene engraving.
Mfg.'s Sug. Retail	$5,355	$4,450	$3,375	$2,400	$1,900	$1,600	$1,400	$1,200

▲ **Sporting Clays Model** — 12 ga. only, designed for sporting clays competition and includes Invector plus choke tube system.

➤ "A" Style Engraving — blued receiver with border engraving featuring Browning logo engraved on each side.
Mfg.'s Sug. Retail	$4,673	$3,995	$3,050	$2,150	$1,725	$1,450	$1,275	$1,050

➤ "B" Style Engraving — coin finished receiver with smaller game scene engravings.
Mfg.'s Sug. Retail	$4,988	$4,200	$3,200	$2,200	$1,775	$1,500	$1,300	$1,100

➤ "C" Style Engraving — coin finished receiver with elaborate scroll work and game scene engraving.
Mfg.'s Sug. Retail	$5,408	$4,500	$3,425	$2,425	$1,950	$1,600	$1,400	$1,200

▲ **Trap Model** — standard F-1 style engraving.
Mfg.'s Sug. Retail	$4,778	$4,075	$3,050	$2,125	$1,725	$1,450	$1,275	$1,050

SHOTGUNS: O/U CITORI HUNTING SERIES

All Citori shotguns which incorporate the Invector choke tube system may be used with steel shot.

On some Citori models, the retail value for a currently manufactured 28 or .410 ga. is less than for a 12 ga. When evaluating these smaller gauges in used condition, values will generally be higher than those listed below.

Invector Plus choke tubes are designed for back bored barrels. DO NOT USE Standard Invector choke tubes in barrels marked for the Invector Plus choking system.

CITORI HUNTING MODELS — 12, 16 (mfg. 1986-89), 20, 28 (disc. 1994) or .410 (disc. 1994) ga., 26, 28, or 30 in. barrels, various chokes, boxlock, auto ejectors, SST, vent. rib, features checkered semi-pistol grip stock with grooved semi-beavertail forearm, grades differ in amount of engraving, finish, and wood. Invector chokes became standard in 1988, Invector Plus chokes became standard 1995 on 12 or 20 ga., 6 lbs. 9 oz. - 8 lbs. 5 oz. Mfg. 1973-present by Miroku.

▲ **Grade I 12 or 20 ga.**

➤ Earlier Mfg. Without Invector Choking
		$750	$675	$575	$525	$475	$425	$395

Add 15% for 16 ga. if in 90%+ original condition.

➤ Current Mfg. — 20 ga. available with Standard Invector or Invector Plus (new 1994) choking system, Invector Plus choking standard on recently mfg. 12 ga.
Mfg.'s Sug. Retail	$1,334	$995	$725	$595	$500	$450	$395	$350

▲ **Grade I Smaller Gauges**

➤ 28 or .410 ga. — without Invector choking. Disc. 1994.
		$850	$700	$575	$495	$450	$395	$350

Last Mfg.'s Sug. Retail was $1,097.

▲ **3½ in. Magnum Model** — 12 ga., 3½ in. chambers, 28 or 30 in. VR barrels with back-bored Invector plus choke tubes, with recoil pad, 8 lbs. 9 oz. New 1989.
Mfg.'s Sug. Retail	$1,418	$1,150	$850	$775	$650	$575	$525	$475

▲ **Upland Special** — 12, 16 (mfg. 1989 only), or 20 ga., shortened checkered straight grip stock, 24 in. barrels, Invector (12 ga. disc. 1993) or Invector Plus choking, 6 lbs.-6¾ lbs. New 1984.
Mfg.'s Sug. Retail	$1,386	$1,025	$760	$600	$500	$450	$425	$395

Add 15% for 16 ga. if in 90%+ original condition.
Subtract $125 for Invector choking.

B

Grading	100%	98%	95%	90%	80%	70%	60%

B

▲ *Grade II* — 12, 20, 28, or .410 ga. Disc. 1983.

	$995	$810	$740	$685	$610	$570	$540

▲ *Grade III* — 12, 16 (mfg. 1986-89), 20, 28 (disc. 1994), or .410 (disc. 1994) ga., greyed steel receiver with engraved game scenes featuring grouse (20 ga.) and ducks (12 ga.), Invector chokes standard, Invector Plus became standard in 12 ga. in 1994. Mfg. 1985-95.

	$1,425	$1,025	$835	$725	$625	$585	$550

Last Mfg.'s Sug. Retail was $1,875.

Add 15% for 16 ga. if in 90%+ original condition.
Add 15%-25% for .410 or 28 ga. (disc. 1989).

▲ *Grade V* — 12, 20, 28, or .410 ga., extensive deep relief engraving with game scenes on satin grey receiver. Disc. 1984.

	$1,550	$1,265	$1,100	$990	$880	$795	$695

▲ *Grade VI* — 12, 16 (mfg. 1986-89), 20, 28 (disc. 1992), or .410 ga. (disc. 1989), blued or greyed receiver with extensive engraving including multiple gold inlays, Standard Invector (12 ga. disc. 1993) or Invector Plus chokes. Mfg. 1985-95.

	$2,100	$1,500	$1,225	$1,000	$895	$795	$695

Last Mfg.'s Sug. Retail was $2,715.

Add 15% for 16 ga. if in 90%+ original condition.
Add 15%-25% for 28 ga.

CITORI SUPERLIGHT MODELS — 12, 20, 28, or .410 ga., 2¾ in. chambers except for .410, English stock, oil finish, Invector chokes became standard in 1988, Invector Plus became standard 1995 for 12 or 20 ga., approx. 6 lbs.-6¾ lbs. Mfg. 1983-present.

▲ *Grade I 12 or 20 ga.*

➤ **Earlier Mfg. Without Invector Choking**

	$795	$700	$600	$550	$495	$445	$395

➤ **Current Mfg.** — 20 ga. available with Standard Invector or Invector Plus (new 1994, became standard 1995) choking system, Invector Plus choking standard on recently mfg. 12 ga.

Mfg.'s Sug. Retail	$1,386	$1,050	$750	$600	$525	$450	$395	$350

Subtract $125 for Standard Invector choking in 20 ga.

▲ *Grade I Smaller Gauges*

➤ **28 or .410 ga.** — without Invector choking until 1993, Invector choking became an option in 1994 and standard in 1995.

Mfg.'s Sug. Retail	$1,439	$1,125	$800	$675	$550	$475	$425	$375

Subtract 10% if without Invector choke tubes.

▲ *Grade III* — same gauges as Grade I, Standard Invector on 12 or 20 ga. or Invector Plus (standard in 12 ga. beginning 1994) chokes. New 1986.

Mfg.'s Sug. Retail	$2,006	$1,550	$1,150	$900	$775	$650	$585	$550

Add $236 for 28 or .410 ga.
Subtract 10% if without Invector choke tubes.

▲ *Grade V* — sideplate available. Disc. 1984.

	$1,550	$1,265	$1,100	$990	$880	$795	$695

▲ *Grade VI* — older mfg. has Invector chokes standard (option on 28 or .410 ga. beginning 1994) or Invector Plus (standard and available in 12 or 20 ga. only) chokes, choice of blue or grey (new 1996) receiver finish.

Mfg.'s Sug. Retail	$2,919	$2,200	$1,650	$1,275	$1,150	$950	$795	$695

Subtract 10% for 28 or .410 ga. without choke tubes.
Add $226 for 28 or .410 ga. with Standard Invector choking.

CITORI SPORTER MODELS — similar to Citori Superlight, except with 3 in. chambers, 26 in. barrels, various chokes, straight grip stock, Schnabel forearm. Disc. 1983.

	$875	$740	$600	$550	$495	$440	$385

Add $50 for 28 or .410 ga.

▲ *Sporter Grade II* — 12, 20, 28, or .410 ga.

	$1,250	$1,075	$1,020	$965	$880	$770	$715

Grading	100%	98%	95%	90%	80%	70%	60%

B

▲ *Sporter Grade V* — 12, 20, 28, or .410 ga.

	100%	98%	95%	90%	80%	70%	60%
	$1,575	$1,395	$1,225	$1,100	$990	$880	$825

CITORI LIGHTNING MODELS — 12, 16 (disc. 1989), 20, 28, or .410 ga., (3½ in. 12 ga. was introduced 1989), 26, 28, or 30 in. barrels, Invector chokes standard on newer mfg. smaller ga.'s, Invector Plus became standard 1995 for 12 or 20 ga., boxlock, auto ejectors, SST, vent. rib, features checkered round knob pistol grip stock and slimmer forearm, grades differ in amount of engraving, finish, and quality of wood, approx. 6¼-8 lbs. Introduced 1988.

▲ *Grade I 12, 16 or 20 ga.*
➤ **Earlier Mfg. Without Invector Choking**

	$795	$700	$600	$550	$495	$445	$395

Add 15% for 16 ga.

➤ **Current Mfg.** — 12 or 20 ga., Invector (disc. 1994) or Invector Plus choking (became standard on 12 in 1994, 20 in 1995).

Mfg.'s Sug. Retail	$1,376	$1,025	$775	$625	$550	$450	$395	$350

Subtract 10% for Standard Invector choking.

▲ *Grade I Smaller Gauges*
➤ **28 or .410 ga.** — without Invector choking until 1993, Invector choking became an option in 1994, standard in 1995.

Mfg.'s Sug. Retail	$1,418	$1,100	$825	$675	$575	$475	$425	$375

Subtract 10% if without Standard Invector choking.

▲ *Grade III* — 12, 16 (disc. 1989), 20, 28, or .410 ga., greyed steel receiver with engraved game scenes, older mfg. may or may not have Invector choking, Invector Plus choking is now standard on 12 or 20 ga. New 1988.

Mfg.'s Sug. Retail	$2,006	$1,550	$1,150	$900	$775	$650	$585	$550

Subtract 10% if without Invector choking.
Add 15% for 16 ga.

➤ **Grade III Smaller Gauges** — 28 or .410 ga., 26 in. VR barrels with or without Standard Invector choking.

Mfg.'s Sug. Retail	$2,242	$1,750	$1,300	$1,000	$850	$695	$625	$575

Subtract 10% if without Invector choking.

▲ *Grade VI* — 12, 16 (disc. 1989), 20, 28, or .410 ga., blued or greyed receiver with extensive engraving including 8 gold inlays.

Mfg.'s Sug. Retail	$2,919	$2,200	$1,625	$1,275	$1,150	$950	$795	$695

Add 15% for 16 ga.

➤ **Grade VI Smaller Gauges** — .28 or .410 ga., 26 in. VR barrels with or without Standard Invector choking.

Mfg.'s Sug. Retail	$3,145	$2,450	$1,800	$1,375	$1,200	$995	$850	$750

Subtract 10% if without Invector choke tubes.

GRAN LIGHTNING (GL) MODEL — 12, 20, 28 (new 1994), or .410 (new 1994) ga. only, 3 in. chambers, similar to Lightning Model, except has higher grade walnut stock and forearm with satin/oil finish, includes recoil pad, 26 or 28 in. barrels, Invector chokes standard on newer mfg. smaller ga.'s, Invector Plus became standard 1995 for 12 or 20 ga., 6¾ - 8 lbs. New 1990.

Mfg.'s Sug. Retail	$1,869	$1,495	$1,050	$925	$775	$650	$585	$550

➤ **Gran Lightning Smaller Gauges** — .28 or .410 ga., 26 in. VR barrels with Standard Invector choking.

Mfg.'s Sug. Retail	$1,969	$1,600	$1,150	$1,000	$825	$695	$625	$575

MICRO LIGHTNING — 20 ga. only, 2¾ in. chambers, 24 in. VR barrels, Invector or Invector Plus (new 1994) choking, 6 lbs. 3 oz. New 1991.

▲ *Grade I*

Mfg.'s Sug. Retail	$1,428	$1,075	$825	$675	$550	$450	$425	$395

Subtract 10% for standard Invector choking.

▲ *Grade III* — Invector (disc. 1993) or Invector Plus choking. Mfg. 1993-94.

	$1,415	$1,050	$850	$750	$625	$585	$550

Last Mfg.'s Sug. Retail was $1,850.

Grading	100%	98%	95%	90%	80%	70%	60%

▲ *Grade VI* — Mfg. 1993-94.

| | $2,025 | $1,575 | $1,225 | $1,025 | $895 | $795 | $695 |

Last Mfg.'s Sug. Retail was $2,680.

Subtract $267 for standard Invector choking.

SHOTGUNS: O/U CITORI SPORTING CLAYS

MODEL 325 GRADE II — 12 or 20 ga., 28, 30, or 32 (12 ga. only) in. 10mm VR barrels with Invector Plus choking, 12 ga. has ported barrels, European styling featuring checkered walnut stock and Schnabel forearm, greyed nitrous finished receiver, top tang safety, SST, ejectors, 6 lbs. 12 oz. - 7 lbs. 15 oz. Mfg. 1993-94.

| | $1,395 | $975 | $850 | $715 | $575 | $495 | $450 |

Last Mfg.'s Sug. Retail was $1,625.

▲ *Model 325 Golden Clays* — 12 or 20 ga., 28, 30, or 32 in. ported (12 ga. only) or unported (20 ga. only) VR barrels, Invector Plus choking, Model 325 Grade II features, satin grey receiver with engraving and gold inlays depicting a transitional hunting to clay pigeon scene. Mfg. 1994 only.

| | $2,425 | $1,850 | $1,450 | $1,150 | $975 | $875 | $825 |

Last Mfg.'s Sug. Retail was $3,030.

MODEL 425 GRADE I — 12 or 20 ga., 28, 30, or 32 (12 ga. only) in. 10mm VR barrels with Invector Plus choking, 12 ga. has ported barrels, with or without adj. comb, European styling featuring checkered walnut stock and Schnabel forearm, greyed nitrous finished receiver, top tang safety, SST, ejectors, solid pad, approx. 7¾ lbs. New 1995.

| Mfg.'s Sug. Retail | $1,775 | $1,495 | $1,050 | $875 | $725 | $575 | $495 | $450 |

Add $210 for adj. comb.

▲ *Model 425 Golden Clays (GC)* — 12 or 20 ga., 28, 30, or 32 in. ported (12 ga. only) or unported (20 ga. only) VR barrels, with or without adj. comb, Invector Plus choking, Model 325 Grade II features, satin grey receiver with engraving and gold inlays depicting a transitional hunting to clay pigeon scene. New 1995.

| Mfg.'s Sug. Retail | $3,308 | $2,650 | $1,950 | $1,500 | $1,175 | $975 | $875 | $825 |

Add $210 for adj. comb.

▲ *Model 425 WSSF* — 12 ga. only, special dimensions for Women's Shooting Sports Foundation, features teal finish with WSSF logo on stock, 7¼ lbs. New 1995.

| Mfg.'s Sug. Retail | $1,775 | $1,495 | $1,050 | $875 | $725 | $575 | $495 | $450 |

MODEL 802 EXTENDED SWING (ES) SPORTER — 12 ga. only, features 28 in. separated narrow (6.2mm) low post VR ported barrels which accept either Invector Plus 2 or 4 stainless steel extension tubes (extends barrels to 30 or 32 in.), adj. pull trigger, slimmer checkered and Schnabel forearm, 7 lbs. 5 oz. New 1996.

| Mfg.'s Sug. Retail | $1,880 | $1,600 | $1,100 | $925 | $750 | $600 | $525 | $475 |

GTI GRADE I — 12 ga. only, 28 or 30 in. barrel with 13mm vent. rib and barrels, red lettering on receiver during 1989 only - changed to gold lettering and borders with Browning logo in 1990, checkered stock and semi-beavertail forearm, ported barrels were introduced 1990 and became standard 1992, Invector chokes standard, back-bored Invector plus chokes became standard in 1990, approx. 8 lbs. Mfg. 1989-94.

| | $1,225 | $885 | $700 | $600 | $525 | $495 | $450 |

Last Mfg.'s Sug. Retail was $1,450.

Subtract $75 without ported barrels (disc. 1992).
Add $35 for Signature Painted Model.

The Signature Painted Model includes special paint treatment on stock and forearm featuring Browning logos and trademark - new 1993.

▲ *GTI Golden Clays* — 12 ga. only, 28, 30, or 32 in. ported VR barrels, Invector Plus choking, GTI features, satin grey receiver with Grade VI level of engraving and gold inlays depicting a transitional hunting to clay pigeon scene. Mfg. 1993-94.

| | $2,350 | $1,800 | $1,450 | $1,150 | $975 | $875 | $825 |

Last Mfg.'s Sug. Retail was $2,930.

Grading	100%	98%	95%	90%	80%	70%	60%

B

GRADE I SPECIAL SPORTING — target dimensions, high-post tapered rib, 28, 30, or 32 in. barrels, full pistol grip with palm swell, adj. comb became optional in 1994, approx. 8 lbs. 3 oz. New 1989.

Mfg.'s Sug. Retail	$1,565	$1,250	$900	$750	$625	$525	$495	$450

Add $210 for adj. comb.
Add $35 for Signature Painted Model (disc. 1994).
Subtract $75 without ported barrels (disc. 1992).
Add $800 for 2 barrel set (28 and 30 in. barrels), disc. 1990.

The Signature Painted Model includes special paint treatment on stock and forearm featuring Browning logos and trademark - mfg. 1993-94.

Ported barrels were new in 1990 and became standard in 1992.

In 1990, the Grade I designation was added to this model. Changes include back-bored barrels with Invector plus choke tubes.

▲ *Special Sporting Golden Clays (GC)* — 12 ga. only, 28, 30, or 32 in. ported barrels with high-post VR, Invector Plus choking, Special Sporting features, satin grey receiver with Grade VI level of engraving and gold inlays depicting a transitional hunting to clay pigeon scene. New 1993.

Mfg.'s Sug. Retail	$3,203	$2,575	$1,925	$1,500	$1,175	$995	$875	$825

Add $210 for adj. comb.

ULTRA SPORTER — 12 ga. only, 28 or 30 in. barrels with vent rib separating barrels, low tapered 13-10mm VR, blue or grey (new 1996) receiver with gold accents, satin finished checkered pistol grip stock and forearm, Invector Plus choking, approx. 8 lbs. New 1995.

Mfg.'s Sug. Retail	$1,722	$1,475	$1,025	$850	$725	$575	$495	$450

Add $210 for adj. comb.

This model was designated GTI until 1995.

▲ *Ultra Sporter Golden Clays (GC)* — 12 ga. only, features better wood and satin finished engraved receiver with gold inlays clay target scene. New 1995.

Mfg.'s Sug. Retail	$3,203	$2,575	$1,925	$1,500	$1,175	$995	$875	$825

Add $210 for adj. comb.

GRADE I SPECIAL SPORTING PIGEON GRADE — 12 ga. only, Vector Plus choking and ported barrels, higher grade of Special Sporting model featuring higher grade walnut and gold line receiver accents. Mfg. 1993-94.

	$1,400	$975	$850	$700	$575	$495	$450

Last Mfg.'s Sug. Retail was $1,630.

GRADE I LIGHTNING SPORTING — features 3 in. chambers, rounded pistol grip, Lightning style forearm, high or low post vent. rib, standard or adj. (new 1995) comb stock, "Lightning Sporting Clays Edition" inscribed and gold-filled on receiver, 30 in. ported or unported (disc.) barrels, approx. 8½ lbs. New 1989.

Mfg.'s Sug. Retail	$1,496	$1,250	$895	$750	$625	$525	$495	$450

Add $210 for adj. comb.
Add $69 for high-post rib.
Subtract 10% if with unported barrels.

The Signature Painted Model includes special paint treatment on stock and forearm featuring Browning logos and trademark - mfg. 1993-94.

Ported barrels were new in 1990 and became standard in 1992.

In 1990, the Grade I designation was added to this model. Changes include back-bored barrels with Invector plus choke tubes.

▲ *Lightning Sporting Golden Clays (GC)* — 12 ga. only, 28, 30, or 32 in. ported barrels with choice of low or high-post VR, standard or adj. (new 1995) comb stock, Invector Plus choking, Lightning Sporting features, satin grey receiver with Grade VI level of engraving and gold inlays depicting a transitional hunting to clay birds scene, approx. 8½ lbs. New 1993.

Mfg.'s Sug. Retail	$3,092	$2,495	$1,850	$1,475	$1,150	$995	$875	$825

Add $210 for adj. comb.
Add $111 for high-post VR.

Grading	100%	98%	95%	90%	80%	70%	60%

GRADE I LIGHTNING SPORTING PIGEON GRADE — 12 ga. only, higher grade model featuring higher grade walnut and gold line receiver accents. Mfg. 1993-94.

	$1,350	$950	$850	$700	$575	$495	$450

Last Mfg.'s Sug. Retail was $1,566.

Add $64 for high-post VR.

SHOTGUNS: O/U CITORI SKEET

CITORI SKEET MODELS — 12, 20, 28, or .410 ga., same action as Citori Field, only with high post target rib (standard 1985), 26 and 28 in. skeet barrels, recoil pad, Invector chokes became standard in 1990 in 12 and 20 ga., Invector Plus chokes with ported barrels were an option during 1992 and became standard on the 12 ga. in 1994, new Special Skeet models were introduced during 1995 with decreased weight ($\frac{1}{4}$ lb. lighter) and better swing/balance characteristics.

▲ *Grade I*

➤ **12 or 20 Ga.** — Invector Plus choking, high-post target rib, and ported barrels became standard in 1994.

Mfg.'s Sug. Retail	$1,586	$1,275	$925	$750	$625	$525	$495	$450

Add $210 for adj. comb (new 1995).
Subtract 10% if without Invector chokes.
Earlier mfg. skeet guns had a low profile, wide VR.

➤ **Smaller Gauges** — .28 or .410 ga.

Mfg.'s Sug. Retail	$1,549	$1,250	$925	$750	$650	$550	$500	$450

Subtract 10% if without Invector chokes.

▲ *Grade II* — 12, 20, 28, or .410 ga., high rib. Disc. 1983.

	$1,000	$850	$800	$740	$690	$650	$600

▲ *Grade III* — 12, 20, 28, or .410 ga., Invector chokes originally in 12 and 20 ga. and became an option on 28 and .410 ga. in 1994. New 1986.

➤ **12 or 20 Ga.** — Invector Plus choking, high-post target rib, and ported barrels became standard in 1994.

Mfg.'s Sug. Retail	$2,179	$1,675	$1,225	$925	$775	$650	$550	$495

Add $210 for adj. comb (new 1995).

➤ **Smaller Gauges** — .28 or .410 ga.

Mfg.'s Sug. Retail	$2,184	$1,695	$1,250	$950	$800	$675	$595	$550

Subtract 10% if without standard Invector choking (new 1994).

▲ *Grade V* — 12, 20, 28, or .410 ga., high rib. Disc. 1984.

	$1,495	$1,265	$1,100	$990	$880	$795	$650

▲ *Grade VI* — Skeet gauges, choice of blue or grey finished receiver with multi gold inlays, deluxe walnut. Disc. 1995.

➤ **12 Ga.** — Invector Plus choking, high-post target rib, and ported barrels became standard in 1994.

	$2,025	$1,600	$1,325	$1,100	$960	$875	$825

Last Mfg.'s Sug. Retail was $2,555.

➤ **Smaller Gauges** — 20, 28, or .410 ga., 20 ga. available with standard Invector choking, 28 and .410 ga. are choked SK/SK.

	$2,000	$1,600	$1,325	$1,100	$960	$875	$825

Last Mfg.'s Sug. Retail was $2,518.

▲ *Skeet Golden Clays (GC)* — 12, 20, 28, or .410 ga., 26 or 28 in. ported VR barrels, Invector Plus choking, Skeet features, satin grey receiver with Grade VI level of engraving and gold inlays depicting a transitional hunting to clay pigeon scene. New 1993.

➤ **12 or 20 Ga.** — Invector (disc. 1995) or Invector Plus choking, high-post target rib, and ported barrels (12 ga. only).

Mfg.'s Sug. Retail	$3,249	$2,650	$1,925	$1,575	$1,225	$1,000	$900	$825

Add $210 for adj. comb (new 1995).
Subtract approx. 10% if without Invector Plus choking.

➤ **Smaller Gauges** — 28 or .410 ga., standard Invector or fixed SK/SK choking.

Mfg.'s Sug. Retail	$3,166	$2,575	$1,950	$1,600	$1,250	$1,025	$925	$850

Subtract approx. 10% with fixed choking.

Grading	100%	98%	95%	90%	80%	70%	60%

CITORI 3 GAUGE SKEET SETS — supplied with one 20 ga. frame, 1 removable forearm, and 3 sets of barrels consisting of 20, 28 and .410 ga., cased. Mfg. 1987-96.

▲ *Grade I* — with high post target rib, standard Invector choking became standard 1994.

	$2,525	$2,075	$1,675	$1,450	$1,275	$1,050	$975

Last Mfg.'s Sug. Retail was $3,100.

▲ *Grade III* — with high post target rib, available with standard Invector choking (new 1994) or fixed SK/SK chokes.

	$3,100	$2,350	$1,875	$1,550	$1,395	$1,250	$1,125

Last Mfg.'s Sug. Retail was $3,900.

Subtract 10% for fixed SK/SK chokes.

▲ *Grade VI* — with high post target rib, fixed SK/SK chokes only. Disc. 1994.

	$3,250	$2,500	$2,000	$1,775	$1,600	$1,400	$1,275

Last Mfg.'s Sug. Retail was $3,990.

▲ *Golden Clays* — features Golden Clays accents and engraving, standard Invector choking. Mfg. 1994-95 only.

	$4,250	$3,075	$2,600	$2,100	$1,900	$1,750	$1,600

Last Mfg.'s Sug. Retail was $5,100.

CITORI 4 GAUGE SKEET SETS — supplied with one 12 ga. frame, 1 removable forearm, and 4 sets of barrels consisting of 12, 20, 28 and .410 ga.'s, cased. Imported 1985 only.

▲ *Grade I* — with high post target rib, choice of standard Invector (new 1994) or fixed SK/SK choking.

	$3,750	$2,850	$2,400	$1,975	$1,800	$1,775	$1,600

Last Mfg.'s Sug. Retail was $4,450.

Subtract 10% for fixed SK/SK choking.

▲ *Grade III* — with high post target rib, choice of standard Invector (new 1994) or fixed SK/SK choking.

	$4,575	$3,250	$2,700	$2,250	$1,950	$1,800	$1,700

Last Mfg.'s Sug. Retail was $5,450.

Subtract 10% for fixed SK/SK choking.

▲ *Grade VI* — with high post target rib, fixed SK/SK choking only. Disc. 1994.

	$4,600	$3,350	$2,775	$2,300	$2,100	$2,000	$1,900

Last Mfg.'s Sug. Retail was $5,225.

▲ *Golden Clays* — features Golden Clays accents and engraving, standard Invector choking. Mfg. 1994 only.

	$5,650	$4,100	$3,300	$2,600	$2,350	$2,100	$1,975

Last Mfg.'s Sug. Retail was $6,750.

SHOTGUNS: O/U CITORI TRAP

CITORI TRAP MODELS — similar to Standard Citori, with 12 ga., 30 and 32 in. barrels, trap chokes, Monte Carlo stock, recoil pad. Invector chokes became standard in 1988, Invector Plus chokes with ported barrels became an option in 1992, and were made standard in 1993, new Special Trap models were introduced during 1995 with decreased weight ($\frac{1}{4}$ lb. lighter) and better swing/balance characteristics.

Mfg.'s Sug. Retail	$1,586	$1,275	$925	$750	$625	$525	$495	$450

Add $210 for adj. comb (new 1995).
Subtract 10% without Invector chokes or high rib.

▲ *Trap Combination Set* — Grade I only, 32 in. O/U and 34 in. single barrel, cased. Disc.

	$1,395	$1,100	$975	$900	$825	$775	$725

▲ *Grade I Plus Trap* — features adj. rib and stock, back-bored barrels, Invector Plus choke system. Mfg. 1990-94.

	$1,560	$1,200	$940	$800	$700	$600	$500

Last Mfg.'s Sug. Retail was $2,005.

Add 5% for ported barrels.

In 1991 this model included a travel vault gun case at no extra charge. Subtract $50 for older mfg. without travel case.

Grading	100%	98%	95%	90%	80%	70%	60%

▲ *Grade I Plus Trap Combo* — includes ported barrels with Invector Plus choking and extra standard single ported barrel, luggage case. Mfg. 1992-94.

	$2,850	$2,425	$2,100	$1,900	$1,700	$1,500	$1,250

Last Mfg.'s Sug. Retail was $3,435.

▲ *Plus Trap Golden Clays* — 12 ga. only, 30 or 32 in. ported VR barrels, Invector Plus choking, Trap features, satin grey receiver with Grade VI level of engraving and gold inlays depicting a transitional hunting to clay birds scene. Mfg. 1993-94.

	$2,850	$2,275	$1,900	$1,600	$1,400	$1,200	$995

Last Mfg.'s Sug. Retail was $3,435.

▲ *Plus Trap Golden Clays Combo* — includes O/U ported barrels with Invector Plus choking and extra standard single ported barrel, luggage case. Mfg. 1993-94.

	$4,425	$3,300	$2,775	$2,250	$1,925	$1,800	$1,700

Last Mfg.'s Sug. Retail was $5,200.

▲ *Pigeon Grade* — 12 ga. only, features extra deluxe walnut, Invector Plus ported barrels, and receiver gold accents. Mfg. 1993-94.

	$1,715	$1,250	$950	$800	$700	$600	$500

Last Mfg.'s Sug. Retail was $2,225.

▲ *Signature Painted* — 12 ga. only, features painted red/black stock with Browning logos on stock and forearm, Invector Plus ported barrels. Mfg. 1993-94.

	$1,595	$1,200	$940	$800	$700	$600	$500

Last Mfg.'s Sug. Retail was $2,065.

▲ *Grade II* — high post rib. Disc. 1983.

	$1,000	$850	$800	$740	$690	$650	$600

▲ *Grade III* — 12 ga. only, high post rib, Invector Plus choking and ported barrels became standard in 1994. New 1986.

Mfg.'s Sug. Retail   **$2,179**

	$1,695	$1,200	$925	$775	$625	$550	$495

Add $210 for adj. comb. (new 1996).
Subtract 10& if without Invector Plus chokes or ported barrels.

▲ *Grade V* — high post rib. Disc. 1984.

	$1,475	$1,150	$990	$880	$795	$710	$620

▲ *Grade VI* — 12 ga. only, Invector chokes became standard in 1985, Invector Plus chokes became standard in 1994. Disc. 1994.

	$1,925	$1,525	$1,225	$1,100	$960	$875	$825

Last Mfg.'s Sug. Retail was $2,555.

Subtract $150 if without Invector Plus chokes or ported barrels.

▲ *Trap Golden Clays (GC)* — 12 ga. only, 30 or 32 in. ported VR barrels, Invector Plus choking, Trap features, Monte Carlo or regular stock, satin grey receiver with Grade VI level of engraving and gold inlays depicting a transitional hunting to clay pigeon scene. New 1993.

Mfg.'s Sug. Retail   **$3,239**

	$2,600	$1,950	$1,500	$1,200	$995	$875	$825

Add $210 for adj. comb (new 1995).

SHOTGUNS: BT-99 SINGLE BARREL

BT-99 STANDARD TRAP GUN — 12 ga., 32 or 34 in. vent. rib barrel, mod., imp. mod., or full choke, boxlock, auto ejector, checkered pistol grip with Monte Carlo or conventional style stock, beavertail forearm. Invector chokes became standard in 1986 and ported barrel with Invector Plus chokes became standard in 1992, back boring became standard in 1993. Values below assume Invector Plus choking with ported barrel. Mfg. 1968-94 by Miroku.

	$895	$700	$550	$460	$400	$360	$330

Last Mfg.'s Sug. Retail was $1,288.

Subtract $125 without Invector chokes or ported barrels.

▲ *BT-99 2 Barrel Set* — without Invector choking or barrel porting. Disc. 1983.

	$1,050	$850	$750	$700	$650	$600	$550

Grading	100%	98%	95%	90%	80%	70%	60%

▲ *BT-99 Stainless* — features all stainless construction with Invector Plus ported 32 or 34 in. black VR barrel. Mfg. 1993-94.

| | $1,325 | $995 | $850 | $700 | $575 | $495 | $450 |

Last Mfg.'s Sug. Retail was $1,738.

▲ *Pigeon Grade* — features higher grade walnut and gold receiver accents, Invector chokes and ported barrels. Mfg. 1993-94.

| | $1,225 | $895 | $715 | $600 | $525 | $495 | $450 |

Last Mfg.'s Sug. Retail was $1,505.

Older pre-1985 mfg.

| | $1,275 | $950 | $775 | $650 | $575 | $525 | $475 |

> Older Pigeon Grade guns featured a satin grey receiver with deep relief, engraved pigeons in a fleur-de-lis background.

▲ *Signature Painted* — features painted red/black stock with Browning logos on stock and forearm, Invector Plus ported barrels. Mfg. 1993-94.

| | $1,015 | $715 | $550 | $460 | $400 | $360 | $330 |

Last Mfg.'s Sug. Retail was $1,323.

▲ *BT-99 Golden Clays* — features high-grade wood and gold outline receiver and inlays depicting a transitional hunting to clay pigeon scene. Mfg. 1994 only.

| | $2,300 | $1,750 | $1,450 | $1,125 | $975 | $875 | $795 |

Last Mfg.'s Sug. Retail was $2,800.

GRADE I BT-99 PLUS — similar to BT-99, except has adj. rib to control point of impact and new recoil reduction system that reduces felt recoil by 50%, stock has adj. comb and butt plate (recoil pad), back-bored barrel, Invector chokes, 8¾ lbs. Mfg. 1989-94.

| | $1,200 | $1,000 | $875 | $775 | $675 | $595 | $550 |

Last Mfg.'s Sug. Retail was $1,835.

> Add 5% for ported barrel.
>
> In 1990, the Grade I designation was added to this model. Changes include back-bored barrels with Invector plus choke tubes. In 1991, this model was supplied with a travel vault gun case as standard equipment. Older mfg. will not have these cases as an original accessory.
>
> Beginning 1991, a Micro Plus Model was introduced that incorporates smaller dimensions (shorter stock and choice of shorter barrel). Values are the same as listed above.

▲ *BT-99 Plus Stainless* — features all stainless construction with Invector Plus ported 32 or 34 in. black VR barrel. Mfg. 1993-94.

> Beginning 1991, a Micro Plus Model was introduced that incorporates smaller dimensions (shorter stock and choice of shorter barrel). Values are the same as listed above.

| | $1,710 | $1,245 | $975 | $800 | $700 | $600 | $500 |

Last Mfg.'s Sug. Retail was $2,240.

▲ *BT-99 Plus Pigeon Grade* — features higher grade walnut and gold receiver accents, Invector chokes and ported barrels. New 1993.

| | $1,595 | $1,200 | $925 | $800 | $700 | $600 | $500 |

Last Mfg.'s Sug. Retail was $2,065.

> Beginning 1991, a Micro Plus Model was introduced that incorporates smaller dimensions (shorter stock and choice of shorter barrel). Values are the same as listed above.

▲ *BT-99 Plus Signature Painted* — features painted red/black stock with Browning logos on stock and forearm, Invector Plus ported barrels. Mfg. 1993-94.

| | $1,500 | $1,150 | $915 | $800 | $700 | $600 | $500 |

Last Mfg.'s Sug. Retail was $1,890.

> Beginning 1991, a Micro Plus Model was introduced that incorporates smaller dimensions (shorter stock and choice of shorter barrel). Values are the same as listed above.

▲ *BT-99 Plus Golden Clays* — features high-grade wood and gold outline receiver and inlays depicting a transitional hunting to clay pigeon scene. Mfg. 1994 only.

| | $2,700 | $2,350 | $2,050 | $1,850 | $1,700 | $1,550 | $1,395 |

Last Mfg.'s Sug. Retail was $3,205.

> Beginning 1991, a Micro Plus Model was introduced that incorporates smaller dimensions (shorter stock and choice of shorter barrel). Values are the same as listed above.

B

Grading	100%	98%	95%	90%	80%	70%	60%

BT-99 MAX — 12 ga. only, choice of blued steel with engraving or stainless steel barrel, receiver, and trigger guard, 32 or 34 in. high post VR ported barrel, thin forearm with finger grooves, select walnut pistol grip stock (regular or Monte Carlo) with high gloss finish, ejector/extractor selector, no safety, approx. 8 lbs. 10 oz. Mfg. 1995-96.

| | $1,250 | $925 | $725 | $600 | $525 | $495 | $450 |

Last Mfg.'s Sug. Retail was $1,496.

Add $400 for stainless steel.

SHOTGUNS: RECOILLESS SINGLE BARREL TRAP

RECOILLESS SINGLE BARREL TRAP — 12 ga., special bolt action design that eliminates 72% of felt recoil, 27 (also available in Micro Model) or 30 in. high-post vent. rib Invector Plus choked back-bored barrel, rib adjusts for 3 points of impact (3, 6 or 9 in.), stock has adj. pull (2 sizes) and comb height, anodized receiver, no safety, approx. 8½ lbs. New 1994.

| Mfg.'s Sug. Retail | $1,995 | $1,650 | $1,100 | $925 | $750 | $575 | $495 | $450 |

The Micro Model features a 27 in. barrel and shorter length of pull.

▲ *Signature Painted* — features painted red/black stock with Browning logos on stock and forearm, Invector Plus ported barrels. Mfg. 1994 only.

| | $1,580 | $1,050 | $895 | $725 | $575 | $495 | $450 |

Last Mfg.'s Sug. Retail was $1,900.

SHOTGUNS: BT-100 SINGLE BARREL

BT-100 STANDARD TRAP GUN — 12 ga. only, 32 or 34 in. steel high-post ported Invector Plus or fixed choked (F) barrel, without safety, choice of blue or stainless steel receiver, removable trigger assembly, ejector selector (either ejects or extracts) adj. comb and thumbhole stock are optional, approx. 8 lbs. 10 oz. New 1995.

| Mfg.'s Sug. Retail | $1,995 | $1,650 | $1,100 | $925 | $750 | $575 | $495 | $450 |

Add $420 for stainless steel.
Subtract $47 for fixed choke.
Add $275 for thumbhole stock (new 1995).
Add $525 for replacement trigger assembly (blue or stainless).

SHOTGUNS: A-BOLT SERIES BOLT ACTION

A-BOLT MODEL — 12 ga. only, 3 in. chamber, 2 shot mag., same bolt system as A-Bolt II Rifle, 22 or 23 in. barrel (rifled or Invector with rifled tube), available in Stalker Model with graphite fiberglass composite stock or Hunter Model with select satin finished walnut stock, dull matte finished barrel and receiver, top tang safety, choice of no sights (new 1996) or adj. rear sight, drilled and tapped receiver, approx. 7 lbs. New 1995.

▲ *Stalker Model*

| Mfg.'s Sug. Retail | $720 | $600 | $500 | $425 | $375 | $340 | $310 | $290 |

Add $25 for open sights.
Add $53 for rifled barrel.

▲ *Hunter Model*

| Mfg.'s Sug. Retail | $805 | $665 | $525 | $450 | $400 | $350 | $315 | $290 |

Add $25 for open sights.
Add $53 for rifled barrel.

SHOTGUNS: SxS, DISC.

BSS MODEL — 12 or 20 ga., 26, 28, or 30 in. barrels, various chokes, boxlock, auto ejectors, checkered pistol grip stock, beavertail forearm, selective single trigger. Mfg. 1971-1988 by Miroku.

| | $695 | $595 | $450 | $400 | $365 | $330 | $300 |

Last Mfg.'s Sug. Retail was $775.

Add 10%-15% for 20 ga.
Early guns had a single non-selective trigger (silver plated) — subtract 10%.

Grading	100%	98%	95%	90%	80%	70%	60%

▲ *Grade II* — satin greyed steel receiver featuring an engraved pheasant, duck, quail and dogs. Disc. 1983.

	$1,100	$950	$800	$700	$600	$525	$450

▲ *Sporter Model* — has straight grip stock and slim forearm, oil finish, 26 or 28 in. barrels. Disc. 1988.

	$795	$695	$550	$500	$445	$410	$370

Last Mfg.'s Sug. Retail was $775.

Add 10%-15% for 20 ga.

BSS SIDELOCK — 12 or 20 ga., engraved sidelock action in satin grey finish, ST, 26 or 28 in. barrels, English select walnut stock, splinter forend. Mfg. 1983-1988 in Miroku in Japan.

	100%	98%	95%	90%	80%	70%	60%
12 ga.	$1,995	$1,450	$1,125	$975	$825	$750	$675
20 ga.	$2,400	$1,750	$1,375	$1,100	$900	$800	$700

Last Mfg.'s Sug. Retail was $2,000.

SHOTGUNS: SLIDE ACTION

BPS MODELS — 12, 20, or 28 (new 1994) ga., gauges are chambered for Mag. ammunition. Invector option (standard for 1985) allows 6 screw-in choke tubes to be interchanged, Invector Plus chokes became standard in 1993, bottom ejection, double action bars, top tang safety, 5 shot capacity, vent. rib, all steel receiver. Mfg. by Miroku 1977-to-date.

▲ *Field/Hunting Model* — 12, 20, or 28 (new 1994) ga., 3 in. chambers, Invector or Invector Plus (new 1994 in 20 ga.) choking, various barrel lengths, Invector Plus choking became standard 1995 (except 28 ga.), 7 lbs. - 8 lbs. 3 oz.

Mfg.'s Sug. Retail	$535	$415	$330	$260	$225	$200	$185	$175

Subtract 10% if without Invector Plus choke tubes.

▲ *Stalker Model* — 12 ga. only, 3 in. chamber, all metal parts have a dull matte finish, non-glare black synthetic composite stock and forearm, approx. 7 lbs. 9 oz. New 1987.

Mfg.'s Sug. Retail	$535	$415	$330	$260	$225	$200	$185	$175

▲ *Magnum Hunting or Stalker 3½ in.* — 10 or 12 ga., 3½ in. chamber, 12 ga. 3½ in. chamber was new 1989, 24, 26 (10 ga. only), 28 or 30 in. barrel with Invector chokes and vent. rib, 4 shot mag., 8 lbs. 2 oz. - 8 lbs. 12 oz. (12 ga.) or 8 lbs. 15 oz. - 9 lbs. 8 oz. (10 ga.).

Mfg.'s Sug. Retail	$672	$555	$475	$425	$375	$340	$310	$290

In 1990, the back-bored Invector plus choke tube system became standard in 12 ga. 3½ in. chamber only.

▲ *Magnum Hunting Waterfowl* — 10 ga., 3½ in. Mag. with choice of 28 or 30 in. matte finished VR barrel with standard Invector choking, features higher grade walnut and gold trimmed receiver with Waterfowl outlined, approx. 9 lbs. 6 oz. New 1993.

Mfg.'s Sug. Retail	$861	$700	$575	$475	$400	$350	$325	$300

▲ *Pigeon Grade* — 12 ga. only, 3 in. chamber, features high grade walnut and gold trimmed receiver, 26 or 28 in. VR barrel with Invector chokes, 7 lbs. 10 oz. New 1992.

Mfg.'s Sug. Retail	$714	$580	$485	$440	$380	$340	$310	$290

▲ *Upland Special* — 12 or 20 ga., 22 in. barrel, straight grip stock with Schnabel forearm, Invector (pre-1994) or Invector Plus (new 1994, standard 1995) choking, 6½ - 7½ lbs. New 1985.

Mfg.'s Sug. Retail	$535	$415	$330	$265	$230	$200	$185	$175

Subtract 10% if without Invector Plus choke tubes.

▲ *Turkey Special* — 12 ga. only, 3 in. chamber, 20½ in. lightened barrel, non-glare walnut stock, matte finished barrel and receiver, receiver is drilled and tapped for scope base, rifle-style stock dimensions, sling swivels, new extra-full Invector choke tube, 7 lbs. 7 oz. New 1992.

Mfg.'s Sug. Retail	$572	$440	$330	$265	$230	$200	$185	$175

▲ *Youth and Ladies Model* — 20 ga. only, 22 in. vent. rib barrel, straight grip shortened stock, Invector (pre-1994) or Invector Plus (new 1994, standard 1995) choking, 6¾ lbs. New 1986.

Mfg.'s Sug. Retail	$535	$415	$330	$265	$230	$200	$185	$175

Subtract 10% if without Invector Plus choke tubes.

Grading	100%	98%	95%	90%	80%	70%	60%

▲ *Deer Special (DG or DS)* — 12 ga. only, 3 in. chamber, 20½ in. barrel with 5 in. rifled choke tube, iron sights, scope mount base, choice of gloss finish (DG) or satin finish (DS) checkered stock with recoil pad and forearm, sling swivels, polished or matte finished metal, 7 lbs. 7 oz. New 1992.

Mfg.'s Sug. Retail	$604	$465	$335	$260	$230	$200	$185	$175

▲ *Buck Special* — 12 or 20 (disc. 1984) ga., 3 in. chamber, 24 in. cyl. bore barrel, iron sights, 7 lbs. 10 oz. Reintroduced 1988.

Mfg.'s Sug. Retail	$520	$410	$325	$260	$230	$200	$185	$175

▲ *3½ in. Buck Special* — 10 or 12 (disc. 1994) ga., 3½ in. chambers, 24 in. cyl. bore barrel, 7 lbs. 10 oz. New 1990.

Mfg.'s Sug. Retail	$677	$570	$460	$410	$370	$335	$310	$290

▲ *Trap Model* — 12 ga., 30 in. barrel. Disc. 1984 but trap barrels were available separately for several years.

		$360	$300	$270	$230	$210	$190	$170

▲ *Wild Turkey Federation Commemorative* — only 500 manufactured. Disc. 1991.

		$495	$395	$325

▲ *Pacific Edition DU* — limited mfg., DU serialization, cased.

		$595	$475	$350

▲ *The Coastal DU* — limited mfg., DU serialization, cased.

		$595	$475	$350

▲ *Waterfowl Deluxe* — 12 ga. Mag., gold trigger and etching, invector chokes, limited mfg.

		$625	$525	$450

MODEL 12 LIMITED EDITION SERIES

▲ *Grade I 20 Ga.* — 20 ga. only, 2¾ in. chamber only, reproduction of the famous Winchester Model 12 with slight design improvements, 26 in. VR barrel bored modified, 5 shot mag., high post floating rib, walnut stock and forearm with semi-gloss finish, take down, 7 lbs. 1 oz. 8,000 mfg. in 1988 with inventory depleted 1990.

		$495	$400	$300

Last Mfg.'s Sug. Retail was $735.

Browning limited manufacture to 8,000 Grade I 20 Ga.'s.

▲ *Grade V 20 Ga.* — similar specifications to Grade I, except has select walnut checkered 22 lines per inch with high gloss finish, extensive game scene engraving including multiple gold inlays. Mfg. 1988 only.

		$850	$695	$575

Last Mfg.'s Sug. Retail was $1,187.

Browning Arms Company limited manufacture to 4,000 Grade V 20 Ga.'s.

▲ *Grade I 28 Ga.* — 28 ga. only, similar to Grade I 20 Ga., except in 28 ga., 26 in. VR modified choke barrel. 7,000 mfg. 1991-92.

		$495	$400	$300

Last Mfg.'s Sug. Retail was $772.

▲ *Grade V 28 ga.* — 28 ga. only, similar to Grade V 20 ga., except in 28 ga., 26 in. VR modified choke barrel. 5,000 mfg. 1991-92.

		$850	$700	$575

Last Mfg.'s Sug. Retail was $1,246.

MODEL 42 LIMITED EDITION

▲ *Model 42 Grade I* — .410 ga., 3 in. chamber, reproduction of the Winchester Model 42 with slight design improvements, 26 in. VR full choke barrel, select walnut stock, 6 lbs. 12 oz. 6,000 mfg. late 1991-1993.

		$550	$450	$350

Last Mfg.'s Sug. Retail was $800.

▲ *Model 42 Grade V* — engraving and embellishments similar to the Model 12 Grade 5 in .410 ga. 6,000 mfg. late 1991-1993.

		$900	$750	$650

Last Mfg.'s Sug. Retail was $1,360.

Grading	100%	98%	95%	90%	80%	70%	60%

LIMITED EDITION SETS INCLUDING BLACK POWDER

BICENTENNIAL 1876-1976 SET — .45-70 Model 78 rifle with specially engraved receiver, silver finish, fancy wood, cased, with engraved knife and medallion, 1,000 sets mfg. in 1976. Issue price — $1,500.

	100%	98%	95%
	$1,750	$1,300	$850

CASED GRADE I SET — one each .25 ACP, .380 ACP, and 9mm Para. Hi-Power Grade I Models in walnut or black vinyl case, non-matching serial numbers.

	$1,500	$1,250	$895

CASED RENAISSANCE SET — one each .25 ACP, .380 ACP, and 9mm Para. Hi-Power Renaissance models in walnut or black vinyl case. Mfg. 1955-1969.

	$3,500	$2,750	$2,100

Add 15% for coin finish.

JONATHAN BROWNING MOUNTAIN RIFLE — 50 cal., percussion, 30 in. octagon barrel, single set trigger, engraved lock plate, select walnut stock, cased with medallion and powder horn, 1,000 mfg. in 1978. Issue price — $650.

	$750	$595	$400

MOUNTAIN RIFLE — similar to Jonathan Browning Mountain Rifle, without Centennial embellishments, not cased. Also in .45 or .54 cal.

	$450	$375	$275	$200	$150	$135	$125

CENTENNIAL O/U RIFLE/SHOTGUN — superposed 20 ga. action fitted with .30-06, 24 in. barrels, folding leaf sight, 26½ in. mod. and full, 20 ga. barrels, auto ejectors, SST, elaborately engraved, gold inlaid, high grade checkered walnut stock, deluxe walnut case, 500 mfg. to commemorate Browning Centennial — 1878-1978.

	$4,250	$3,750	$3,000	$2,550	$2,100	$1,725	$1,500

Last Mfg.'s Sug. Retail was $7,000.

CENTENNIAL SET — complete Browning set mfg. in 1978, includes the Centennial O/U Rifle/Shotgun, 9mm Hi-Power, B92 .44 Mag., Mountain Rifle, and a set of three knives.

	$6,250	$5,000	$3,950

1 OF 50 BICENTENNIAL RIFLE — .30-06 cal., Model 78 single shot with 26 in. octagon barrel, includes special engraving by Neil Hartliep (non-factory), extra fine walnut, 4X wide angle scope, special luggage case. 50 mfg. (one for each state) during 1976 only and sold by silent mail order bidding (minimum bid was $3,100 in 1976).

As very few specimens are bought or sold each year, pricing is rather unpredictable. A few specimens have been sold in the $5,000 range recently. Remember, the work on this gun was subcontracted by Centennial Guns (division of Frigon Guns located in Clay Center, KS).

BRUCHET

Manufacturer located in Saint Etienne. Distributed exclusively from 1982-1989 by Wes Gilpin located in Dallas, TX. In 1989, Bruchet was able to get permission to use the older Darne trademark and all new manufacture will be entered under the Darne listing.

Paul Bruchet has been manufacturing his shotguns patterned after the Darne action since 1981, following his tenure at Darne as line foreman until 1979 (at which time the Darne plant closed). These new Bruchet Models were designated "A" or "B". All shotguns were totally hand made with approx. 50 guns being mfg. each year.

Since Paul Bruchet was able to retain the Darne trademark in 1989, please refer to the Darne section in this text for current manufacture.

Grading	100%	98%	95%	90%	80%	70%	60%

MODEL A — 12, 16, 20, 28, or .410 ga., small key opening, ejectors, double triggers only, basically 4 variations (1, 1A, 2, and 2A), wide assortment of customer specified special orders.

Retail values are as follows: Model 1A starts at under $2,000, the Model 2 starts at $3,000, and the Model 2A starts at $3,500. Each additional grade represents more embellishments and better grade of walnut. Magnum chambers can be ordered at a small surcharge. Importation began 1982, values represent the last published retail prices from 1989.

MODEL B — 12, 16, 20, 28, or .410 ga., large key opening, self-opening (assisted) action, ejectors, double triggers only, basically special ordered to individual customer specifications.

Retail values are as follows: Model B starts at $5,800 and includes deluxe carrying case. Each additional upgrade represents more embellishments and a better grade of walnut. Magnum chambers can be ordered at a small surcharge. Importation began 1982, values represent the last published retail prices from 1989.

BRYCO ARMS

Manufacturer located in Irvine, CA. Distributed by Jennings Firearms, Inc. located in Carson City, NV. Distributor sales only. Please refer to the Jennings Firearms, Inc. section for information on Bryco Arms manufactured pistols.

BUDISCHOWSKY

Previous manufacturer located in Mt. Clemens, MI.

PISTOLS: SEMI-AUTO

TP-70 — .22 LR, double action, 2½ in. barrel, stainless steel, fixed sights, plastic grips. Mfg. 1973-1977.

$440 $385 $330

TP-70 — similar to TP-70, except .25 ACP cal. Mfg. 1973-1977.

$330 $275 $220

Note: In 1977, Norton Arms marketed this pistol. Quality of workmanship is not on a par with the early Budischowsky and values are approx. 35% less.

SEMI-AUTO PISTOL — .223 cal., 11⅝ in. barrel, 20 or 30 shot mag., fixed sights, a novel paramilitary designed type pistol.

$470 $415 $385 $360 $305 $250 $220

RIFLES

PARAMILITARY DESIGN RIFLE — .223 cal., semi-auto, 18 in. barrel, wooden paramilitary stock.

$505 $440 $415 $385 $330 $275 $250

PARAMILITARY DESIGN RIFLE FOLDING STOCK

$525 $470 $440 $415 $360 $305 $275

BUL TRANSMARK LTD.

Manufacturer located in Tel Aviv, Israel. Exclusively imported for North America by All America Sales, Inc. located in Memphis, TN.

PISTOLS: SEMI-AUTO

M-5 frame kits only are also available at $395 retail.

Grading	100%	98%	95%	90%	80%	70%	60%

M-5 — .45 ACP, 9x19mm, or .38 Super cal., single action semi-auto, polymer frame, steel slide, aluminum speed trigger, checkered front and rear grip straps, blue finish, 10 shot mag. Importation began 1995.

	100%	98%	95%	90%	80%	70%	60%
Mfg.'s Sug. Retail $750	$625	$550	$500	$450	$400	$360	$330

B

BUSHMASTER FIREARMS

Currently manufactured by Bushmaster Firearms/Quality Parts Company located in Windham, ME. Older mfg. was by Gwinn Arms Co. located in Winston-Salem, NC 1972-1974. The Quality Parts Co. gained control in 1986.

PISTOLS: SEMI-AUTO

BUSHMASTER PISTOL — .223 Rem., semi-auto., top bolt (older models with aluminum receivers) or side bolt (current mfg.) operation, steel frame (current mfg.), 11½ in. barrel, parkerized finish, adj. sights, wood stock, 5¼ lbs.

	100%	98%	95%	90%	80%	70%	60%
	$500	$425	$350	$280	$250	$225	$180

Last Mfg.'s Sug. Retail was $375.

Add $40 for electroless nickel finish (disc. 1988).

This model uses a 30 shot M-16 mag. and the AK-47 gas system.

RIFLES: SEMI-AUTO, RECENT MFG.

BUSHMASTER RIFLE — .223 Rem., semi-auto., top bolt (older models with aluminum receivers) or side bolt (current mfg.) operation, steel frame (current mfg.), 18½ in. barrel, parkerized finish, adj. sights, wood stock, 6¼ lbs., base values are for folding stock model.

	100%	98%	95%	90%	80%	70%	60%
	$425	$325	$280	$250	$225	$180	$140

Last Mfg.'s Sug. Retail was $350.

Add $40 for electroless nickel finish (disc. 1988).
Add $65 for fixed rock maple wood stock.

This model uses a 30 shot M-16 mag. and the AK-47 gas system.

▲ **Rifle Combination System** — includes rifle with both metal folding stock and wood stock with pistol grip.

	100%	98%	95%	90%	80%	70%	60%
	$400	$360	$330	$300	$275	$250	$230

Last Mfg.'s Sug. Retail was $450.

XM15-E2 TARGET RIFLE — .223 cal., semi-auto patterned after the Colt AR-15, 20, 24, or 26 in. Govt. spec. match grade chrome lined barrel, manganese phosphate barrel finish, rear sight adj. for windage and elevation, Cage flash suppressor, mfg. started in 1989 in U.S.

	100%	98%	95%	90%	80%	70%	60%
Mfg.'s Sug. Retail $850	$775	$650	$550	$465	$430	$400	

Add $15 for 24 in. or $25 for 26 in. barrel.

▲ **XM15-E2 Carbine** — similar to above, except with telescoping buttstock and 11½ (disc. 1995), 14 (disc. 1994), or 16 in. barrel with or w/o suppressor, mfg. started in 1989.

	100%	98%	95%	90%	80%	70%	60%
Mfg.'s Sug. Retail $840	$765	$650	$550	$465	$430	$400	

Add approx. $35 for dissipator model (features lengthened handguard).

This model does not have the target rear sight system of the XM15-E2S rifle.

▲ **E2 Carbine** — .223 cal., features 16 in. match chrome barrel with new M16A2 handguard and short suppressor, choice of A1 or E2 sights. Mfg. 1994-95.

	100%	98%	95%	90%	80%	70%	60%
	$895	$825	$725	$650	$600	$550	$500

Add approx. $50 for E2 sighting system.

V MATCH RIFLE — .223 cal., top-of-the-line match/competition rifle, flat-top receiver with extended aluminum barrel shroud, choice of 20, 24, or 26 in. barrel. New 1994.

	100%	98%	95%	90%	80%	70%	60%
Mfg.'s Sug. Retail $915	$825	$695	$575	$475	$435	$400	

Add $10 for 24 in. or $20 for 26 in. barrel.

Grading	100%	98%	95%	90%	80%	70%	60%

IBUS M17S BULLPUP — .223 Rem. cal., semi-auto bullpup configuration featuring gas operated rotating bolt, 10 (C/B 1994) or 30* shot mag., 21½ plain or 22 in. barrel with flash-hider (disc.), glass composites and aluminum materials, phosphate coating. New 1992.

Mfg.'s Sug. Retail	$860	$775	$660	$555	$465	$430	$400	$365

B

C section

CETME

CETME is an abbreviation for Centro Estudios Technicos de Materiales Especiales. Previous manufacturer located in Madrid, Spain.

Grading	100%	98%	95%	90%	80%	70%	60%

AUTOLOADING RIFLE — .308 Win. cal., 17¾ in. barrel, gas operated, roller cam action, similar to HK-91 in appearance, wood military style stock, aperture rear sight.

		100%	98%	95%	90%	80%	70%	60%
		$715	$660	$605	$550	$440	$385	$330

C Z (CESKA ZBROJOVKA)

Current manufacturer located in Uhersky Brod, Czechoslovakia, 1921-current. Previous mfg. was in Strakonice, Czechoslovakia. Newly manufactured CZ firearms are currently imported exclusively by Magnum Research, Inc. located in Minneapolis, MN beginning July 1, 1994. Previously imported before 1994 by Action Arms Ltd. located in Philadelphia, PA.

While little history is known about this important European trademark, the following biographical sketch will provide some information. In approximately 1916, some military personnel took over the controlling interest of the Austro-Hungarian armament shop in Brno, Czechoslovakia, renaming it The State Armament and Engineering Works. Approximately a year later, the name was changed to Czechoslovak State Armament Works. Prior to 1924, this firm was involved mainly with Mauser Model 98 type rifles (both assembly and mfg.).

In 1924, the name was again changed to Ceskoslovenska Zbrojovka A.Z. (Czechoslovakian Arms Factory Ltd.) - commonly known as the CZ firm. CZ manufactured the VZ-24 Mauser rifle for Czechoslovakia as well as other M-98 military rifles and carbines for other countries, including many which Germany used during WWII. After WWII, the name was again changed to Zbrojovka Brno (Brno Arms Works), or ZB for short.

With the iron curtain descending on Europe after WWII, communist bloc countries including Czechoslovakia had little exportation to the U.S. Currently, CZ handguns are made at the plant in Uhersky Brod and Brno long arms are made in both Uhersky Brod and Brno. With the sudden decline in communism during the past years, more and more products (including firearms from Czechoslovakia) will see their way into the U.S. without the 65% importation tax previously levied on goods from older communist bloc countries.

PISTOLS: SEMI-AUTO, DISC.

"DUO" POCKET AUTOMATIC — .25 auto, 6 shot, 2⅛ in. barrel, fixed sights, blue or nickel, plastic grips. Mfg. 1926-present (current Z pistol by Brno).

		100%	98%	95%	90%	80%	70%	60%
		$200	$185	$170	$150	$125	$100	$75

Add 40% for WWII years.

This model was manufactured by Dushek and is similar to the Z pistol equivalent by Brno.

CZ 22 — .380 cal., derived from Mauser Nickl Pistol and manufactured under license from Mauser. Mfg. 1923 only.

		100%	98%	95%	90%	80%	70%	60%
		$400	$350	$320	$300	$275	$235	$200

CZ 24 — .380 cal.

Grading	100%	98%	95%	90%	80%	70%	60%

▲ **Standard Frame** — 8 shot mag. Over 175,000 mfg. 1924-38. Over half issued to Czech Army. Same general design as CZ 22 except no gap between trigger and frame. Add $50 if Nazi proofed. Production continued to 1941.

	$350	$320	$290	$260	$230	$195	$150

A small number were Kriegsmarine proofed. Add 200%. Beware of counterfeit markings.

▲ **Long Frame** — 9 shot mag.

	$775	$600	$500	$450	$375	$300	$225

Add $750 if fit with stock slot (either standard frame or long frame).

CZ 27 — .32 cal.

▲ **"CESKA" Slide Legend Variation** — slanted slide grooves, high polish, available as Prewar Commercial, DR proofed, or Nazi proofed. Ser. range 16,000-21,500

	$450	$400	$350	$300	$250	$200	$150

▲ **"BOHEMISCHE" Slide Legend Variation** — vertical slide grooves, high or medium polish. Ser. range 21,500-261,000. Nazi proofed.

	$225	$200	$175	$150	$135	$120	$110

Add 125% if 1941 dated.
Add 100% if 1942 or 1943 dated.
Nazi Police pistols dated 1941, 1942, or 1943 marked with Eagle/K on left trigger guard web.
A small number were Kriegsmarine proofed. Add 200%. Beware of counterfeit markings.

▲ **"fnh" Slide Legend Variation** — Medium polish or phosphate. Ser. range 261,000-476,000.

	$200	$175	$150	$125	$100	$85	$70

▲ **"Silencer Barrel" Variation** — a small number of phosphate pistols were fit with an extended barrel for silencer attachment. Usually in 450,000-460,000 Ser. range.

	$650	$600	$500	$400	$375	$350	$325

▲ **Post WWII mfg.** — dated 1945, 1946, 1947, 1948, 1949, 1950, 1951. These models will have the "NARODNI PODNIK" inscription on slide.

Currently, these variations average $250 in 95%+ condition while reworks (very common) average under $200.

VZ 38 DOUBLE ACTION AUTOMATIC — .380 auto, 9 shot, double action only, 4⅝ in. barrel, fixed sights, blue, plastic grips. Mfg. 1938-1939.

	$350	$300	$250	$200	$170	$140	$125

For Waffenampt proofed (E/WaA76 on barrel and left frame), usually phosphate finished and either unnumbered or in B291,000-B293,000 Ser. range — add $1,000.
Changed to Model 39T after 1939.

VZ 38 "BULGARIAN CONTRACT" — .380 auto, 9 shot, single or double action, prominent safety on left frame. Usually in 420,000-423,000 range.

	$1,350	$1,100	$900	$750	$600	$500	$400

MODEL 1945 DOUBLE ACTION AUTOMATIC — .25 auto, 8 shot, 2½ in. barrel, fixed sights, blue, plastic grips. Double action only. Mfg. between 1945-1952.

	$250	$200	$165	$150	$140	$130	$120

CZ HANDGUNS: RECENT MFG.

CZ-50/70 — .32 ACP cal., double action, blowback action, 3¾ in. barrel, loaded chamber indicator, 8 shot mag.

Mfg.'s Sug. Retail	$205	$165	$150	$135	$125	$115	$95	$85

This model is imported by Century International Arms, Inc. located in St. Albans, VT.

CZ-52 — 7.62 Tokarev, single action semi-auto, roller locking breech system, 4.9 in. barrel, 8 shot mag.

Mfg.'s Sug. Retail	$180	$150	$135	$125	$115	$95	$85	$75

This model is imported by Century International Arms, Inc. located in St. Albans, VT.

Grading	100%	98%	95%	90%	80%	70%	60%

CZ-70 — 7.65mm, double action, similar to Walther PP, 8 shot mag., 1 lb. 9 oz. Disc.

	$400	$350	$300	$275	$250	$225	$200

A very limited quantity of this model was imported.

CZ-75 — 9mm Para. or .40 S&W cal., Poldi steel, selective double action or double action only (.40 S&W only), thumb safety, 4¾ in. barrel, 10 (C/B 1994) or 15* shot mag., currently available in black polymer (standard), matte blue (disc. 1994), high polish blue (disc. 1994), or nickel (new 1994) finish, black plastic grips, early guns were shipped with two mags., 34.3 oz.

Mfg.'s Sug. Retail	$539	$455	$385	$350	$325	$295	$275	$250

Add $6 for .40 S&W cal.
Add $30 for nickel finish.
Add $26 for decocking safety (9mm Para. only).
Add $20 for matte blue finish.
Add $40 for high polish blue finish.
Add 15% for earlier non-import marked specimens.

"First Model" variations, mostly imported by Pragotrade of Canada, are identifiable by short slide rails, no half-cock feature, and were mostly available in high polish blue only. These early pistols sell for $1,000 if NIB condition; chrome engraved $1,500 (NIB); factory competition $1,350 (NIB)

▲ **CZ-75 Semi-Compact** — 9mm Para. only, 13 shot mag., choice of black polymer, matte, or high polish blue finish. Imported 1994 only.

	$450	$395	$360	$330	$300	$275	$250

Last Mfg.'s Sug. Retail was $519.

Add $20 for matte blue finish.
Add $40 for high polish blue finish.

▲ **CZ-75 Compact** — similar to CZ-75, except has 3.9 in. barrel, 10 (C/B 1994) or 13* shot mag., checkered walnut grips, choice of black polymer (standard), matte blue (disc. 1949), or high polish blue (disc. 1994) finish, 32 oz. New 1993.

Mfg.'s Sug. Retail	$539	$455	$385	$350	$325	$295	$275	$250

Add $20 for matte blue finish.
Add $40 for high polish blue finish.

▲ **Model CZ-75 Special Editions** — 9mm Para., similar to CZ-75, except has optional special edition finishes including all matte nickel, bright nickel frame, matte chrome, all brushed chrome, bright chrome, or gold frame, choice of matching finish slide, master blue slide, gold appointments, or master blue slide with gold appointments, price line refers to all matte nickel finish. Imported 1993 94 by Action Arms only.

	$585	$495	$415	$375	$335	$310	$285

Last Mfg.'s Sug. Retail was $699.

Subtract $10 for matte nickel frame with master blue slide.
Add $120 for matte nickel frame with master blue appts.
Add $180 for matte nickel with gold appts.
Add $180 for matte nickel frame with master blue slide and gold appts.
Add $180 for master blue with gold appts. or gold frame with master blue slide (new 1993).

CZ-82 — 9x18mm Makarov, current Czech military sidearm, recent exportation to W. Germany in Makarov chambering.

This model is similar to the CZ-83 except for cal. Prices are similar to the model CZ-83.

CZ-83 — .32 ACP (disc. 1994) or .380 ACP (new 1986) cal., modern design, 3 dot sights, 3.8 in. barrel, choice of carry modes, blue (disc. 1994) or black polymer finish, black synthetic grips, 10 (C/B 1994), 12* (.380 ACP) or 15* (.32 ACP) shot mag., 26.2 oz. Mfg. began 1985, but U.S. importation started in 1992.

Mfg.'s Sug. Retail	$409	$350	$285	$240	$210	$185	$165	$150

Grading	100%	98%	95%	90%	80%	70%	60%

▲ *CZ-83 Special Editions* — .380 ACP only, similar to CZ-83, has optional special edition finishes including all matte nickel, master high polish blue, bright nickel frame, matte chrome, all brushed chrome, bright chrome, or gold frame, choice of matching finish slide, master blue slide, gold appointments, or master blue slide with gold appointments, price line refers to all matte nickel or high polish blue finish. Importation disc. 1994.

	$490	$415	$350	$295	$250	$225	$200

Last Mfg.'s Sug. Retail was $569.

Add $90 for matte nickel frame with master blue appts.
Add $176 for matte nickel with gold appts.
Add $176 for matte nickel frame with master blue slide and gold appts.
Add $176 for master blue with gold appts. or gold frame with master blue slide (new 1993).

CZ-85 — 9mm Para. or 9x21mm (imported 1993-94 only) cal., variation of the CZ-75 with ambidextrous controls, new plastic grip design, sight rib, available in black polymer, matte blue (disc. 1994), or high-gloss blue (9mm Para. only, disc. 1994) finish, includes firing pin block and finger rest trigger, plastic grips.

Mfg.'s Sug. Retail	$549	$470	$400	$365	$330	$300	$275	$250

Add $22 for matte blue finish.
Add $44 for high polish blue.

▲ *CZ-85 Combat* — similar to CZ-85, except has fully adj. rear sight, walnut (disc. 1994) or black plastic (new 1994) grips, extended mag. release, and free dropping mag. Importation began 1992.

Mfg.'s Sug. Retail	$649	$560	$485	$395	$365	$335	$310	$285

Add $26 for matte blue finish.
Add $50 for high polish blue.

▲ *Model CZ-85 Special Editions* — 9mm Para., similar to CZ-85, has optional special edition finishes including all matte nickel, bright nickel frame, matte chrome, all brushed chrome, bright chrome, or gold frame, choice of matching finish slide, master blue slide, gold appointments, or master blue slide with gold appointments, price line refers to all matte nickel finish. Imported 1993-94 only.

	$625	$525	$435	$385	$340	$310	$285

Last Mfg.'s Sug. Retail was $749.

Subtract $60 for matte nickel frame with master blue slide.
Add $146 for matte nickel frame with master blue appts.
Add $130 for matte nickel with gold appts.
Add $130 for matte nickel frame with master blue slide and gold appts.
Add $130 for master blue with gold appts. or gold frame with master blue slide (new 1993).

▲ *Model CZ-85 Combat Special Editions* — 9mm Para., similar finishes to Model CZ-85 Special Editions, price line refers to all matte nickel finish. Limited importation 1994-95.

	$925	$825	$750	$675	$595	$525	$450

Last Mfg.'s Sug. Retail was $1,049.

Subtract $126 for matte nickel frame with master blue appts.
Add $246 for matte nickel with gold appts.
Add $246 for matte nickel frame with master blue slide and gold appts.
Add $246 for master blue with gold appts. or gold frame with master blue slide (new 1993).

CZ-100 — 9mm Para. or .40 S&W cal., double action only with firing pin block, w/o external manual safety, 3 dot sights, synthetic grips, 10 shot mag., $3\frac{3}{4}$ in. barrel, approx. 24 oz. New 1996.

Mfg.'s Sug. Retail	$489	$435	$375	$325	$285	$260	$240	$220

PAV — .22 LR, single shot, $9\frac{3}{4}$ in. barrel, all steel construction. Imported 1986 only.

	$95	$85	$75	$65	$60	$55	$50

Last Mfg.'s Sug. Retail was $105.

DRULOV 70 — .22 cal., single shot. Add $30 for set trigger. Disc. 1986.

	$105	$95	$85	$75	$70	$65	$60

Last Mfg.'s Sug. Retail was $115.

DRULOV 75 — .22 cal., single shot with set trigger & micrometer sights. Also available in left-hand. Importation disc. 1991.

	$300	$250	$215	$185	$155	$140	$120

Last Mfg.'s Sug. Retail was $349.

Grading	100%	98%	95%	90%	80%	70%	60%

DRULOV 78 — .22 cal., similar to Drulov 75. Imported 1986 only.

	$275	$240	$200	$175	$150	$130	$110

Last Mfg.'s Sug. Retail was $180.

RIFLES: COMMERCIAL

Beginning 1995, the CZ factory began producing bolt action rifles. Magnum Research, Inc. is the exclusive importer of this new line.

CZ 527 — .22 Hornet, .222 Rem., or .223 Rem. cal., Mauser style bolt action with silent safety, open sights, 5 shot detachable mag., checkered walnut stock and forearm, 6.2 lbs. Importation began 1995.

Mfg.'s Sug. Retail	$629	$555	$485	$415	$365	$330	$300	$275

CZ 537 — .243 Win., .270 Win., .30-06, .308 Win., or 7x57mm cal., detachable 4 shot (.243 and .308 Win. cals. only) or 5 shot fixed mag., choice of regular or Mannlicher (.30-06 or .308 Win. cal. only) stock, hooded ramp front sight, 7¼ lbs. Importation 1995 only.

	$575	$495	$425	$370	$330	$300	$275

Last Mfg.'s Sug. Retail was $649.

Add $60 for Mannlicher style stock.

▲ **CZ 537 Mountain Carbine** — .243 Win. only, 19 in. barrel, 5 shot detachable mag., includes ring mounts, 7.1 lbs. Imported 1994 only.

	$560	$445	$385	$340	$310	$285	$260

Last Mfg.'s Sug. Retail was $669.

CZ 550 — .243 Win., .270 Win., .30-06, .308 Win., 7x57mm (disc. 1995), .300 Win. Mag., or 7mm Rem. Mag., 4 shot detachable mag. or internal 5 shot, receiver drilled and tapped for Remington 700 style scope base, no sights, checkered stock and forearm, rubber recoil pad, 7¼ lbs. Importation began 1995.

Mfg.'s Sug. Retail	$649	$575	$495	$425	$370	$330	$300	$275

Add $30 for Mag. cals.

▲ **CZ 550 Mannlicher** — similar to CZ 550, except is available in standard cals. only, and has Mannlicher full stock. New 1996.

Mfg.'s Sug. Retail	$849	$725	$615	$525	$450	$395	$350	$310

MODEL ZKM-452 — .22 LR or .22 Win. Mag. cal., bolt action, 5, 6 (.22 Mag. only), or 10 shot mag., 24.8 in. barrel, uncheckered hardwood stock, adj. rear sight, 6.6 lbs. Importation began 1995 from CZ, earlier mfg. was by Brno.

Mfg.'s Sug. Retail	$299	$265	$220	$185	$170	$155	$140	$130

Add $80 for .22 Win. Mag. cal.

▲ **Model ZKM-452D (Deluxe)** — similar to ZKM-452 only with checkered walnut stock. Importation began 1995.

Mfg.'s Sug. Retail	$329	$275	$240	$195	$175	$160	$145	$130

Add $70 for .22 Win. Mag. cal.

ZKK 600 — .270 Win., .30-06, or 7x57mm cal., improved Mauser type action, 23½ in. barrel, checkered walnut stock, 5 shot internal mag., thumb safety, 7.2 lbs. Importation disc. 1995.

	$500	$425	$370	$330	$300	$275	$250

Last Mfg.'s Sug. Retail was $589.

ZKK 601 — .243 Win. or .308 Win. cal., otherwise similar to ZKK 600. Importation disc. 1995.

	$500	$425	$370	$330	$300	$275	$250

Last Mfg.'s Sug. Retail was $589.

ZKK 602 — .300 Win. Mag. (disc.), .375 H&H, .416 Rigby (new 1996), .416 Rem. (new 1996), 8x68mm (disc.), or .458 Win. Mag. cal., similar to ZKK 600, except has 25.2 in. barrel and 3 leaf express rear sight, 9.3 lbs.

Mfg.'s Sug. Retail	$799	$675	$575	$495	$450	$395	$350	$310

Grading	100%	98%	95%	90%	80%	70%	60%

RIFLES: MILITARY

G 33-40 — 8mm, mfg. between 1940-42, most have been sporterized.

	$350	$295	$260	$230	$200	$175	$150

This model is Brno mfg., not CZ.

CZ-M52 (1952) — 7.62x45mm Czech cal., semi-auto, 20⅔ in. barrel, 10 shot detachable mag., tangent rear sight, recently imported again by Samco Global Arms, Inc. located in Miami, FL, limited quantities.

	$350	$295	$260	$230	$200	$175	$150

CZ-M52/57 (1957) — 7.62x39mm, later variation of the CZ-M52.

	$250	$215	$185	$160	$140	$125	$110

CABANAS

Manufactured by Industrias Cabanas, S.A. in Aguilas, Mexico since 1949. Imported and retailed by Mandall Shooting Supplies, Inc. located in Scottsdale, AZ.

.22 BLANK POWERED RIFLE — shoots oversize .177 pellets/BBs powered by .22 blanks, 1,150 fps, single shot bolt action operation, iron sights, models vary in barrel lengths, stock configurations, etc. Transfer requires FFL.

▲ *Mini-82 Youth Pony*

Mfg.'s Sug. Retail	$70	$70	$65	$55	$50	$45	$40	$35

▲ *R-83 Larger Youth*

Mfg.'s Sug. Retail	$80	$80	$75	$65	$55	$45	$40	$35

▲ *Safari*

		$100	$90	$80	$70	$60	$50	$40

Last Mfg.'s Sug. Retail was $100 (disc. 1990).

▲ *Varmint*

Mfg.'s Sug. Retail	$120	$100	$90	$80	$70	$60	$50	$40

▲ *Espronceda IV*

Mfg.'s Sug. Retail	$135	$120	$110	$100	$90	$80	$70	$60

▲ *Leyre*

Mfg.'s Sug. Retail	$150	$150	$120	$110	$100	$90	$80	$70

▲ *Master* — top-of-the-line model, 19⅔ in. barrel, adj. iron sights. Disc. 1990.

	$135	$120	$110	$100	$90	$80	$70

Last Mfg.'s Sug. Retail was $150.

Blanks (6mm) and BBs (4.5mm) are available at $3.50 for 50 of each.

▲ *Phaser* — features thumb hole stock with Monte Carlo cheekpiece and finger contoured pistol grip, automatic latch, barrel weight compensator. Importation began 1991.

Mfg.'s Sug. Retail	$160	$160	$125	$110	$100	$90	$80	$70

CABELA'S INC.

Sporting goods dealer located in Sidney, NE.

In addition to the models that are listed below, Cabela's also has a wide variety of black powder muzzleloading rifles and pistols in addition to replicas of popular older Colt and Winchester firearms. Cabela's should be contacted directly (see Trademark Index) to receive a catalog on their complete model line-up.

Grading	100%	98%	95%	90%	80%	70%	60%

SHOTGUNS: SIDE BY SIDE

HEMINGWAY MODEL — mfg. for Cabela's by V. Bernardelli located in Italy, ST, ejectors. Disc. 1994.

| | $925 | $775 | $700 | $640 | $575 | $525 | $465 |

Last Mfg.'s Sug. Retail was $975.

AYA GRADE II CUSTOM — mfg. for Cabela's by AYA located in Eibar, Spain, ST, ejectors, similar to AYA Model II with Model 53 engraving and trim. Disc. and sold out.

| | $1,295 | $,1,150 | $895 | $775 | $700 | $640 | $575 |

CALICO

Manufacturer located in Bakersfield, CA. Distributor sales only.

Calico also makes select-fire machine gun pistols and carbines that are mfg. for military or law enforcement use only. These models do not appear in this publication.

A complete line of accessories is available for all Calico carbines and pistols.

CARBINES

LIBERTY 50-100 — 9mm Para., 16.1 in. barrel, downward ejection, aluminum alloy receiver, synthetic stock with pistol grip, 50 or 100 shot helical feed mag., ambidextrous safety, 7 lbs. New 1995.

| Mfg.'s Sug. Retail | $648 | $585 | $525 | $460 | $400 | $360 | $330 | $300 |

  Add $36 for 100 shot helical feed mag.

M-100 — .22 LR, semi-auto carbine, paramilitary design with folding butt stock, 100 shot helical feed mag., alloy frame, ambidextrous safety, 16.1 shrouded barrel with flash suppressor/muzzle brake, 4.2 lbs. empty. Mfg. 1986-94.

| | $265 | $225 | $195 | $175 | $160 | $150 | $140 |

Last Mfg.'s Sug. Retail was $308.

▲ **M-100 FS** — similar to M-100, except has solid stock and barrel does not have flash suppressor. New 1996.

| Mfg.'s Sug. Retail | $504 | $450 | $400 | $365 | $335 | $300 | $275 | $250 |

M-101 — while advertised, this model was never mfg.

M-105 SPORTER — similar to M-100, except has walnut distinctively styled butt stock and forend, 4¾ lbs. empty. Mfg. 1989-94.

| | $280 | $235 | $200 | $175 | $160 | $150 | $140 |

Last Mfg.'s Sug. Retail was $335.

M-106 — while advertised, this model was never mfg.

M-900 — 9mm Para., retarded blowback action, paramilitary design with collapsible butt stock, cast aluminum receiver with stainless steel bolt, static cocking handle, 16 in. barrel, fixed rear sight with adj. post front, 50 (standard) or 100 shot helical feed mag., ambidextrous safety, black polymer pistol grip and forend, 3.7 lbs. empty. Mfg. 1989-1990, reintroduced 1992-1993.

| | $560 | $475 | $350 | $300 | $285 | $270 | $255 |

Last Mfg.'s Sug. Retail was $618.

▲ **M-900S** — similar to M-900, except has non-collapsible shoulder stock. Disc. 1993.

| | $575 | $485 | $360 | $300 | $285 | $270 | $255 |

Last Mfg.'s Sug. Retail was $632.

▲ **M-901 Canada Carbine** — 9mm Para. cal., similar to M-900, except has 18½ in. barrel and sliding stock. Disc. 1992.

| | $575 | $475 | $350 | $300 | $285 | $270 | $255 |

Last Mfg.'s Sug. Retail was $643.

This model is also available with solid fixed stock (Model 901S).

Grading	100%	98%	95%	90%	80%	70%	60%

M-951 TACTICAL CARBINE — 9mm Para., 16.1 in. barrel, similar appearance to M-900 Carbine, except has muzzle brake and extra pistol grip on front of forearm, 4¾ lbs. Mfg. 1990-94.

	$475	$395	$350	$300	$275	$250	$225

Last Mfg.'s Sug. Retail was $556.

▲ *M-951S* — similar to M-951, except has synthetic buttstock. Mfg. 1991-94.

	$485	$400	$350	$300	$275	$250	$225

Last Mfg.'s Sug. Retail was $567.

PISTOLS: SEMI-AUTO

M-110 — .22 LR, same action as M-100 Carbine, 6 in. barrel with muzzle brake, 100 round helical feed mag., includes notched rear sight and adj. windage front sight, 10½ in. sight radius, ambidextrous safety, pistol grip storage compartment, 2.21 lbs. empty. New 1989.

Mfg.'s Sug. Retail	$432	$375	$325	$275	$235	$210	$195	$180

M-950 — 9mm Para., same operating mechanism as the M-900 Carbine, 6 in. barrel, 50 (standard) or 100 shot helical feed mag., 2¼ lbs. empty. Mfg. 1989-94.

	$450	$375	$325	$285	$260	$240	$225

Last Mfg.'s Sug. Retail was $518.

Many accessories were also available for this model.

CAMEX-BLASER USA, INC.

Previous importer/distributor of Blaser Jagwaffen Gmbh rifles.

Previously imported Camex-Blaser rifles can be located in the Blaser section in this text.

CAPRINUS

Previous shotgun manufacturer located in Varberg, Sweden.

SHOTGUNS: O/U

CAPRINUS SWEDEN — 12 ga., boxlock action, ejectors, ST, stainless steel receiver, unique design incorporates breaking down without forearm disassembly, 29½ in. barrels with choke tubes, limited mfg. during early 1980s.

	$3,750	$3,250	$2,850	$2,400	$2,000	$1,600	$1,200

The last manufacturer's suggested retail was approx. $5,955.

CARL GUSTAF

Manufacturer located in Eskilstuna, Sweden. No current importer. Previously imported by Hansen & Co. located in Southport, CT during 1994-95, and by Precision Sales International located in Westfield, MA during 1991-93.

RIFLES: BOLT ACTION

MODEL CG 2000 STANDARD GRADE — 6.5x55mm, 7x64mm, 9.3x62mm, .243 Win., .270 Win., .30-06, .308 Win., 7mm Rem. Mag., or .300 Win. Mag. cal., bolt action, Monte Carlo walnut stock with checkering and Wundhammer grip, 24 in. barrel, detachable 3 or 4 shot mag., with or without sights, cold-swaged barrel and receiver, 60 degree bolt, 3-way slide safety, 7½ lbs. Imported began 1991-95.

	$1,325	$1,050	$875	$725	$575	$475	$375

Last Mfg.'s Sug. Retail was $1,535.

Add $540 for Mag. cals.

This model is supplied with individual 80 meter signed test targets. This model has also been imported as the Fairfax 2000 series.

Grading	100%	98%	95%	90%	80%	70%	60%

▲ *Model 2000 Luxe Grade* — available only in .270 Win., .30-06, .308 Win., or 6.5x55mm cal., features choice of regular or Mannlicher deluxe walnut stock. Imported 1995 only.

	$1,695	$1,400	$1,200	$975	$825	$650	$475

Last Mfg.'s Sug. Retail was $1,935.

A Model 2000 Super-Luxe was also available in 6.5x55mm or .30-06 cal. - retail was $4,250.

STANDARD BOLT ACTION RIFLE — 6.5x55, 7x64, .270, 7mm Mag., .308, .30-06, or 9.3x62 cal., 24 in. barrel, folding rear sight, checkered classic style stock. Mfg. 1970-1977.

	$375	$325	$300	$275	$250	$225	$200

▲ *Monte Carlo stock*

	$450	$395	$350	$300	$275	$250	$225

GRADE II — similar to Monte Carlo Standard, in .22-250, .25-06, 6.5x55, .270, 7mm Mag., .308, .30-06, or .300 Win. Mag. cal., select stock and rosewood pistol grip cap, and forearm tip.

	$500	$425	$375	$325	$295	$275	$250

GRADE III — similar to Grade II, except fancy wood, deluxe high gloss finish.

	$575	$475	$425	$350	$325	$300	$275

DELUXE — similar to Grade III, except engraved floorplate and trigger guard, Deluxe French walnut, and jeweled bolt.

	$675	$575	$475	$400	$375	$350	$325

VARMINT TARGET MODEL — bolt action, fast lock time, .222, .22-250, .243, or 6.5 x 55 cal., 27 in. barrel, no sights, large bakelite bolt knob, target type stock. Mfg. 1970. Disc.

	$550	$495	$440	$385	$360	$320	$290

GRAND PRIX SINGLE SHOT TARGET — fastest lock time bolt action, .22 L.R, 27 in. heavy barrel with adj. weight, no sights, target stock, adj. butt plate. Mfg. 1970. Disc.

	$550	$495	$440	$385	$360	$320	$290

CARTRIDGE FIREARMS

Unknown maker.

Many models of pistols, rifles, and shotguns — antique and modern. Many poor quality copies in addition to a few high quality, nicely engraved guns. Most of these firearms that are average quality, trade in the $100-$300 area. Engraved models can add as much as 150%. Many produced.

CASARTELLI, CARLO

Manufactured in Brescia, Italy. Imported and distributed by New England Arms Co. located in Kittery Point, ME.

Casartelli rifles and shotguns are available through special order only. Virtually any custom gun can be constructed to the customer's exact specifications and requirements. More information can be obtained by writing the above importer/distributor.

RIFLES

AFRICA MODEL — BOLT ACTION — various heavy and Mag. cals., action is square bridge type Mauser, full coverage game scene engraving appropriate to caliber, takedown, limited production.

Mfg.'s Sug. Retail	$12,000	$12,000	$10,200	$7,500	$5,900	$5,300	$4,700	$4,100

SAFARI MODEL — BOLT ACTION — standard cals., regular Mauser action, full coverage game scene engraving, limited production.

Mfg.'s Sug. Retail	$8,250	$8,250	$6,250	$5,900	$5,250	$4,950	$4,150	$3,650

Grading	100%	98%	95%	90%	80%	70%	60%

KENYA — DOUBLE RIFLE — most standard and Mag. cals., sidelock action, elaborate game scene and/or scroll engraving, limited production.

Mfg.'s Sug. Retail	$35,000	$35,000	$24,250	$21,500	$17,750	$14,750	$12,000	$9,950

SHOTGUNS

SIDELOCK MODEL — various ga.'s, elaborate game scene and/or scroll engraving, limited production.

Mfg.'s Sug. Retail	$17,000	$17,000	$11,500	$9,200	$7,900	$6,500	$5,200	$4,250

CASPIAN ARMS, LTD.

Current parts manufacturer located in Hardwick, VT. Dealer direct sales only.

Caspian Arms currently fabricates both steel and alloy high quality, high capacity frames and related small parts for the Colt Government Model 1911/A1.

VIETNAM COMMEMORATIVE — .45 ACP, total production was 1,000, hand engraved by J.J. Adams, nickel plated, branch service medallion installed in grips. Limited mfg. 1986-93.

	$1,450	$995	$795

Last Mfg.'s Sug. Retail was $1,500.

Add $350 for gold plating.
Add $200 for serial numbers below RVN100.
This Vietnam Commemorative is also available in 24Kt. gold hand inlay edition for $14,000 — very limited production.

CENTURY INTERNATIONAL ARMS, INC.

Importer and distributor located in St. Albans, VT.

Century Arms imports a variety of used military rifles and pistols, including various Mauser rifle contract models, French Lebels and MAS models, Mannlichers, F.N. Model 49s, Lee Enfields, Hakims, Mosin-Nagants, Egyptian Rashids, Swedish Ljungman Model 42Bs, Chinese and Russian SKSs, M-1 carbines/Garands and various WWI and WWII used military pistols (including Mauser Broomhandles, Lugers, P.38s, Argentine mfg. M1911s, and French PA 35s). Because most of these items range in the $125-$550 price range, individual listings are not listed in this text. Most of these models are in good to new condition overall. In addition, surplus and currently manufactured ammunition is available at very competitive prices. Generally, these models offer good values to the shooter and some may be collectible. Because importation of Eastern Bloc military rifles has changed so dramatically over the past several years, Century International Arms, Inc. should be contacted directly (see Trademark Index) for a complete catalog of their currently available merchandise.

PISTOLS

HI-POWER — 9mm Para. cal., copy of the FN Browning Hi-Power, mfg. in Argentina by Fabrica Militar under license from FN, matte finish, 13 shot mag., 4.6 in barrel, 32 oz. Imported 1991-1994.

	$240	$210	$185	$160	$145	$125	$110

FP9 — 9mm Para. cal., patterned after the FN Browning Hi-Power, with 5 in. VR barrel, mfg. in Hungary, fixed sights, 14 shot mag., 2 lbs. 3 oz. Importation disc. 1994.

	$200	$175	$160	$150	$140	$120	$110

PA63 — 9mm Makarov cal., patterned after the Walther PP, aluminum frame, European mfg., 3.8 in. barrel, thumbrest grips, hammer block safety, 7 shot mag., 22 oz. Importation disc. 1994.

	$140	$125	$115	$100	$90	$85	$75

Grading	100%	98%	95%	90%	80%	70%	60%

CZECH MODEL 1952 — 7.62x25mm Tokarev or 9mm Para. cal., single action semi-auto, 8 shot mag. 2 lbs.

No Mfg.'s Retail	$165	$145	$130	$115	$100	$90	$85

Add $55 for 9mm Para. cal.

HUNGARIAN T-58 — 7.62 Tokarev or 9mm Para. cal., improved Tokarev pistol, is supplied with both 7.62 and 9mm barrels and mags., wraparound grips, thumb safety, 4½ in. barrel, 8 shot mag., 31 oz. Importation disc. 1993.

	$180	$155	$140	$125	$110	$100	$90

IJ-70 MAKROV — 9 X 18 Makrov cal., double action, 4 in. barrel, plastic grips, 25 oz. Importation began 1995.

No Mfg.'s Retail	$165	$145	$130	$115	$100	$90	$85

RUSSIAN TT PISTOL — 7.62x25mm Tokarev cal., fair condition overall, 8 shot mag., importation began 1995.

No Mfg.'s Retail	$135	$115	$100	$90	$85	$80	$75

FEG P9R — 9mm Para. cal., patterned after the FN Browning Hi-Power, except is double action and has slide mounted safety/decocking lever, all steel, 4⅔ in. barrel, 10 (C/B 1994) or 15* shot mag., 2 lbs. 3 oz.

No Mfg.'s Retail	$275	$220	$195	$175	$160	$150	$140

▲ *FEG P9RK* — compact variation of the P9R with 4⅛ in. barrel and ergonomically designed frame with contoured front grip strap, 33.6 oz. Importation began 1994.

No Mfg.'s Retail	$280	$225	$200	$180	$160	$150	$140

FEG B9R — .380 ACP cal., double action, 4 in. barrel, walnut grips, hammer drop safety, 10 (C/B 1994) or 15* shot mag., 1 lb. 9 oz.

No Mfg.'s Retail	$280	$225	$200	$180	$160	$150	$140

AP9 — .380 ACP cal., patterned after the Walther PP, developed by Hungary, alloy construction, 3.94 in. barrel, double action, thumbrest grips, 7 shot mag., 1.31 lbs. Importation disc. 1993.

	$160	$140	$125	$115	$100	$90	$85

R-61 — .380 ACP cal., patterned after the Walther PPK with aluminum alloy frame, 6 shot mag., mfg. in Hungary. Importation disc. 1993.

	$160	$140	$125	$115	$100	$90	$85

RIFLES

CBC MODEL N66 — .22 LR, semi-auto design patterned after the Remington Nylon 66, 14 shot tube mag., 19½ in. barrel. Imported 1989-91.

	$95	$80	$70	$60	$55	$50	$45

NORINCO JW-8 — .22 LR, bolt action, 5 shot mag., 23 in. barrel, sling swivels. Imported 1989-91.

	$95	$80	$70	$60	$55	$50	$45

JW-27 — .22 LR, updated JW-8, imported 1991-1993.

	$145	$110	$75	$65	$60	$55	$50

CENTURION P14 SPORTER — .300 Win. Mag., .303 British (disc.), or 7mm Rem. Mag. cal., P-14 action with sporterized stock and 24 in. barrel, checkered beechwood stock, tapped and drilled for scope mounts. New 1987.

No Mfg.'s Retail	$275	$240	$220	$190	$170	$150	$125

Beginning 1993, this model features a new fiberglass stock with steel recoil lug and recoil pad.

Grading	100%	98%	95%	90%	80%	70%	60%

CENTURION 98 SPORTER — .270 Win., .30-06, .308 Win., or 7.62x39mm (disc. 1993) cal., mfg. from military Mauser 98 actions, turned down bolt handles, black Rynite stock with integral blind mag., 22 in. barrel, 7 lbs. 6 oz.

No Mfg.'s Retail	$275	$240	$220	$190	$170	$150	$125

MAS 36 SPORTER — 7.5mm, MAS 36 action with shorter barrel, military stock has been sporterized, reblued metal, positive safety. Importation disc.

	$135	$115	$95	$85	$80	$75	$70

SWEDISH CONTRACT M96 SPORTER — 6.5x55mm, Swedish Mauser M96 with choice of synthetic or hardwood stock, 24 in. barrel, 5 shot fixed mag., 8¼ lbs.

No Mfg.'s Retail	$225	$190	$160	$135	$125	$115	$105

Add $25 for black synthetic stock.

FAL SPORTER RIFLE — .308 Win. cal., sporter version of the FAL rifle, features new black synthetic or camo thumbhole stock and new semi-auto receiver, flash hider and bayonet lug removed, 20¾ in. barrel, refurbished in matte finish, 10 lbs. 2 oz.

No Mfg.'s Retail	$600	$500	$450	$425	$375	$325	$295

ARGENTINE 1909 SPORTER — 7.65mm or .30-06 cal., sporterized version of Argentine 1909 carbine, 22¼ in. barrel, checkered beechwood European sporter stock, original military sights, 5 shot mag. Imported 1991-1993.

	$190	$170	$150	$135	$120	$110	$100

BRAZILIAN MODEL 08/34 SPORTER — .30-06, Brazilian Mauser refinished with new barrel and European Monte Carlo stock, 23 in. drilled and tapped barrel, refinished condition. Imported 1991-1993.

	$200	$180	$160	$140	$125	$110	$100

ENFIELD SPORTER NO. 4 MARK I-II — .303 British, cut down original stock to Sporter length, 25.2 in. barrel, 10 shot detach. mag.

No. Mfg.'s Retail	$110	$95	$85	$75	$65	$55	$45

Add $50 for new satin finished American walnut stock with reblued action.

TOZ-17-1 — .22 LR cal., modified TOZ-17 action, checkered pistol grip stock, rear tangent adj. sight, grooved receiver, 21 in. barrel, 5 shot detachable mag., 5.3 lbs.

No Mfg.'s Retail	$105	$85	$70	$60	$50	$40	$35

JUNGLE SPORTER NO. 5 — .303 British, 20.5 in.barrel with flash eliminator, new checkered Monte Carlo stock and forearm, detach. mag. Importation disc.

	$190	$150	$135	$125	$115	$105	$95

MAS .223 — .223 cal., civilian version of the FAMAS 5.56mm paramilitary design rifle, made by Giat in France, switchable ejection port, rubber covered cheekpiece, bullpup configuration, protected sights, with bipod, 20 shot mag. Less than 25 imported 1986-89.

	$2,750	$2,250	$1,850	$1,600	$1,400	$1,200	$1,000

This model has been banned from domestic importation due to 1989 Federal legislation.

MAK 90 — 7.62x39mm cal., AKS variation, mfg. by Norinco, thumbhole stock has recoil pad, 16½ in. barrel, two 5-shot mags.

No Mfg.'s Retail	$265	$215	$195	$180	$170	$160	$150

M-1 GARAND — .30-06, 24 in. barrel, arsenal repaired stocks, good to very good condition. Importation disc.

	$350	$275	$250	$235	$215	$200	$190

SSG SNIPER RIFLE — 5.45x39mm cal., originally mfg. during the mid '80s for East German security units, supplied with 600 rounds of ammo., includes 4X scope, 10 lbs.

No Mfg.'s Retail	$1,250	$995	$875	$750	$625	$550	$495

Grading	100%	98%	95%	90%	80%	70%	60%

M-14 SPORTER — .308 Win., sporterized M-14 with modified stock, 22 in. barrel, flash suppressor and bayonet lug have been removed, 8¼ lbs. Importation began late 1991.

No Mfg.'s Retail	$450	$375	$325	$280	$240	$200	$180

SHOTGUNS: O/U

CENTURION — 12 ga. only, boxlock action, 26 or 28 in. VR barrels, DTs, extractors, blued receiver with Century logo.

No Mfg.'s Retail	$350	$280	$240	$220	$190	$170	$150

TOZ-34P — 12 ga. only, 2¾ in. chambers, double triggers, 28 in. fixed choke VR barrels, floral or game scene engraved, extractors or ejectors.

No Mfg.'s Retail	$315	$260	$230	$190	$170	$150	$130

Add 20% for ejectors.

CENTURY MFG., INC.

Manufactured by Century Manufacturing, Inc. located in Greenfield, IN. Distributed by Century Gun Distributing Inc., located in Greenfield, IN. Consumer direct and/or dealer direct sales.

This revolver-design was originally manufactured in 1972 by Russell Wilson, who sandcasted the bronze frame (cloned after the Colt SAA configuration) in Evansville, IN. Gene Phelps purchased the manufacturing rights for this gun and formed a partnership with Earl Keller to produce a redesigned frame, also using sandcast bronze.

The original Century revolver was made in Evansville, IN beginning in 1973 (1973 was the 100th anniversary of the .45-70 Govt. cartridge - hence the term Century) and production was halted in 1976 at ser. no. 524. In late 1976, Phelps and Keller (the 2 original partners on the venture) dissolved their partnership and each began manufacturing their own version of the .45-70 revolver. Gene Phelps completely redesigned the gun's interior and began manufacturing the Heritage I, with an investment-cast steel frame, and without the Century's novel cross-bolt safety. Keller's Century Manufacturing, Inc. continued to produce the original Century, with some design refinements, and in 1985 the company was purchased by Dr. Paul Majors.

The current Century revolver features a manganese bronze frame and other components in addition to having a cross-bolt safety. They are produced in .45-70 and various other cals., in Greenfield, IN. Earl Keller died in 1986. The second series is being made in Greenfield, IN with limited production resuming in 1986. Earlier handmade "Evansville" Model 100s (disc.) are currently selling for between $2,500-$3,500, depending on the region.

REVOLVERS

Less than 1,200 Model 100s have been manufactured since 1976. Values below are for .45-70 cal. Other calibers are priced from $1,500 on up.

MODEL 100 — .30-30 (new 1987), .375 Win. (new 1986), .444 Marlin (new 1986), .45-70, .50-70 Govt. (new 1987), or .50-110 cal., single action 6 shot, manganese bronze frame, steel cylinder, 6½, 8, 10, or 12 in. round or octagon barrel, unique crossbolt safety that locks the hammer, adj. sights, walnut grips, 5 lbs. 14 oz.

Mfg.'s Sug. Retail	$1,250	$1,100	$875	$775	$675	$595	$550	$495

Add $750 for .50-70 cal.
Add $110 for normal octagon barrel.
Add $150 for stainless steel fabrication.

CHAMPLIN FIREARMS, INC.

Custom manufacturer/gunsmith located in Enid, OK. Champlin Firearms was established in 1966. Direct sales only.

Champlin Firearms, Inc. manufactures handcrafted rifles built around a patented bolt action of their own design and manufacture. Most guns are built per individual customer order and specifications. Values will vary greatly depending on the configuration, desirability, and special order specifications. All Champlin rifles are built along classic lines with best quality wood and exemplary workmanship. They have been used successfully on safaris and have shot dangerous game throughout the world.

Champlin Firearms, Inc. also inventories a wide selection of high grade, top quality shotguns and rifles (especially top trademark doubles and bolt actions). Contact George Caswell (owner) directly for a current listing (please refer to Trademark Index). Additional services include a complete gunsmithing service for all grades of English double rifles and shotguns. Custom stocks are also built to individual customer specifications. All double rifles are test fired and checked thoroughly upon completion of manufacture or repair. Again, Champlin Firearms should be contacted for consultation and quotation regarding this additional work.

Grading	100%	98%	95%	90%	80%	70%	60%

BOLT ACTION RIFLE — standard, all calibers, round or octagon barrel, adj. trigger, each rifle is built to customer specifications. Values below represent base gun with standard wood, no options, and no engraving.

Mfg.'s Sug. Retail	$8,500		$8,500	$8,000	$7,000	$6,750	$6,000	$5,250	$4,500

    Many additional special order options are available on this model and Champlin Firearms should be contacted directly for price quotations.

CHAPUIS ARMES

Manufacturer located in St. Bonnet Le Chateau, France. Currently, Chapuis Armes is exclusively imported by Chadick's, Ltd. located in Terrell, TX. Previously imported by GSI, Inc. located in Trussville, AL until 1995 and Armes De Chasse located in Chadds Ford, PA until 1993.

Chapuis rifles and shotguns are manufactured on a limited basis. Most of their emphasis is on high quality double rifles and shotguns. For further information regarding this respected French trademark, please contact the importer listed above.

RIFLES/COMBINATION GUNS

RGEX EXPRESS MODEL SxS DOUBLE RIFLE — .30-06, .300 Win. Mag., .416 Rigby, 7x65R, 8x57JRS, 8x75RS, or 9.3x74R cal., double rifle, ejectors, boxlock action, 23.6 in. barrels, deluxe checkered walnut stock with cheekpiece, full line of options are available, 7 lbs. 6 oz. Importation began 1989.

Mfg.'s Sug. Retail	$7,195		$6,675	$5,300	$4,750	$4,150	$3,650	$2,995	$2,450

Last Mfg.'s Sug. Retail was $5,938.

    Add approx. $700 for .300 Win. Mag. cal.
    Subtract approx. $300 for 8x75RS cal.
    Add approx. 60% for HGEX Express Supreme Model (engraved, not avail. in .300 Win. Mag. cal.).
    Add 110% for HGEX Express Imperial Model (scroll engraved, not avail. in .300 Win. Mag. cal.).
    Above values assume metric or .30-06 cal.

Grading	100%	98%	95%	90%	80%	70%	60%

AFRICAN P.H. (PROFESSIONAL HUNTER) GRADE SxS DOUBLE RIFLE — .30-06, .300 Win. Mag., .375 H&H Mag., .416 Rigby, 9.3x74R, or .470 NE cal., notched boxlock action with English scroll engraving, case colored receiver, selective ejectors, deluxe walnut stock with English cheekpiece.

Mfg.'s Sug. Retail	$11,995	$11,000	$8,000	$7,150	$6,250	$5,400	$4,200	$3,500

Add $3,800 for .470 NE cal.

This model was previously designated Express Agex Brousse.

EXPRESS AGEX SAVANNA SxS DOUBLE RIFLE — .300 Win. Mag., .375 H&H, .416 R Chapuis, or .470 NE cal., deluxe version of the Agex Jungle, except has hand-engraved leaves on action sides and Cape Buffalo head on floorplate of action, case colored or coin finish.

Mfg.'s Sug. Retail	$41,195	$37,995	$32,500	$27,250	$22,750	$19,250	$17,000	$15,000

Add $3,800 for .470 NE cal.

EXPRESS AGEX JUNGLE SxS DOUBLE RIFLE — .300 Win. Mag., .375 H&H, .416 R Chapuis (new 1993), or .470 NE (new 1992) cal., boxlock action, case colored or coin finish, special reinforced receiver with double underbites, 25⅝ in. barrels, fine English scroll engraving, ejectors, select French walnut with compartment in pistol grip cap.

Mfg.'s Sug. Retail	$18,295	$17,250	$13,750	$11,250	$9,000	$6,750	$5,600	$4,775

Add $2,900 for .470 NE cal.

▲ *Jungle Second Grade* — features elaborate engraving and best quality wood.

Mfg.'s Sug. Retail	$29,395	$26,000	$22,500	$19,000	$16,000	$13,000	$10,000	$8,750

Add $3,900 for .470 NE cal.

EXPRESS AGEX AFRICA SxS DOUBLE RIFLE — same cals. as AGEX Jungle, notched boxlock action, master signed scroll engraving and African game scenes, selective ejectors, cased. Importation disc. 1994.

		$19,250	$17,750	$15,250	$13,500	$11,250	$10,000	$9,000

Last Mfg.'s Sug. Retail was $20,954.

Add $2,896 for .470 NE cal.
Add $5,626 for .416 R Chapuis cal.

EXPRESS AGEX SAFARI SxS DOUBLE RIFLE — similar to AGEX Africa, except has top-of-the-line engraving and wood. Importation disc. 1994.

		$29,000	$26,550	$22,350	$19,150	$16,950	$14,000	$12,000

Last Mfg.'s Sug. Retail was $30,375.

Add $2,040 for .470 NE cal.
Add $5,134 for .416 R Chapuis cal.

SUPER ORION C15 O/U DOUBLE RIFLE — .300 Win. Mag. or .375 H&H cal., notched boxlock action with ejectors, coin finish only, 23.6 in. barrels with quarter rib, engraved action, approx. 8 lbs. Importation began 1995.

Mfg.'s Sug. Retail	$9,195	$8,250	$7,150	$6,250	$5,400	$4,200	$3,500	$3,150

Add $2,900 for .375 H&H cal.

RIFLES: SINGLE SHOT

OURAL EXEL — .270 Win., .300 Win. Mag., 7mm Rem. Mag. cal., notched boxlock action, English scroll engraving, extractors, 23⅝ in. barrel, fitted and engraved scope mounts. Importation disc. 1994.

		$4,875	$4,625	$4,150	$3,650	$2,995	$2,450	$1,950

Last Mfg.'s Sug. Retail was $5,204.

Add $281 for .300 Win. Mag. cal.
Add $854 for 7mm Rem. Mag. cal.
Add approx. 41% for Oural Luxe Model (features better engraving and wood).
Add approx. 84% for Oural Elite Model (features game scene engraving and presentation walnut).

Grading	100%	98%	95%	90%	80%	70%	60%

SHOTGUNS

Chapuis Armes is also capable of manufacturing high quality SxS and O/U shotguns. The manufacturer should be contacted directly for a price quotation regarding these configurations.

CHAPUIS, P. ARMES ET FILS

Manufacturer located in Saint-Bonnet le Chateau, France.

Paul Chapuis specializes in custom order rifles and shotguns. Currently, this manufacturer has no U.S. importer and should be contacted directly (see Trademark Index) for more model information and current pricing. This is a different company than Chapuis Armes.

CHARLES DALY

See Daly, Charles.

CHARLIN ARMS

Previously manufactured in France.

Charlin Arms previously made shotguns which were patterned after Darne firearms. Typically, they are very high quality and values seem to approximate the Darne guns. Once you have determined the comparable model in Darne, please refer to the Darne section in this book.

CHARTER ARMS

Manufactured by Charco, Inc. located in Ansonia, CT beginning 1992. Previously manufactured by Charter Arms located in Stratford, CT. Distributor and dealer sales.

As this edition went to press, Charco, Inc. was in Chapter 11 and in the process of reorganizing. While current manufacture has stopped, some distributors may still have existing inventory remaining. Values below reflect most recent pricing information.

REVOLVERS: DOUBLE ACTION

All Charter Arms revolvers have a hammer block safety system, 8 groove rifling, unbreakable beryllium copper firing pin, triple safety features, no sideplate, steel frames, and lifetime warranty to the original owner.

BONNIE & CLYDE SET — .32 H&R Mag. (Bonnie) and .38 Spl. (Clyde), matched pair, 6 shot, 2½ in. fully shrouded barrel, wood laminate grips (color coordinated), blued finish, pistols individually marked Bonnie or Clyde on barrels, supplied with gun rugs. Mfg. 1989-91.

	$425	$365	$335	$295	$260	$240	$220

LADY ON DUTY — .32 S&W or .38 Spl. cal., 5 (.38 Spl.) or 6 shot, 2 in. shrouded barrel, fixed sights, rose neoprene grips, cased. New 1995.

Mfg.'s Sug. Retail	$219		$195	$165	$145	$130	$115	$100	$85

PATHFINDER — .22 LR or .22 Mag. (disc. 1989), 6 shot, 2, 3, or 6 (disc. 1985) in. barrels, round butt, adj. sights, walnut grips, wide trigger and spur hammer. Disc. 1990.

	$185	$150	$125	$110	$90	$70	$50

▲ **Pathfinder — Square Butt** — .22 LR or .22 Mag. (disc. 1989), 6 in. barrel, square butt, otherwise similar to Pathfinder. Disc. 1990.

	$190	$155	$125	$110	$90	$70	$50

▲ **Pathfinder Stainless** — stainless variation, .22 LR or .22 Mag. (disc. 1989), 3½ in. shrouded barrel. Disc. 1990.

	$185	$150	$130

Grading	100%	98%	95%	90%	80%	70%	60%

UNDERCOVER — .32 S&W (disc. 1989) or .38 Spl. cal., 5 shot in .38 Spl., 6 shot in .32 S&W, 2 (.38 Spl.) or 3 in. barrel, wide trigger and spur hammer, fixed sights, .38 Spl. can also be ordered with pocket hammer. Disc. 1991.

	$175	$145	$115	$100	$90	$85	$80

▲ *Undercover Stainless* — 2 in. shrouded barrel only. Disc. 1994.

	$260	$195	$140

Last Mfg.'s Sug. Retail was $304.

UNDERCOVERETTE — similar to Undercover, in .32 S&W long, 6 shot, 2 in. barrel, blue. Disc.

	$155	$140	$110	$100	$90	$70	$55

BULLDOG — .44 Spl., 5 shot, 2½ or 3 (disc. 1988) in. barrels, wide trigger and spur or pocket hammer, checkered bulldog grips (walnut or neoprene), blue or electroless nickel finish. Disc. 1991, re-instated 1994.

Mfg.'s Sug. Retail	**$268**	$225	$195	$155	$125	$110	$90	$70

Add $22 for electroless nickel finish.

▲ *Bulldog Stainless* — 2½ in. bull or 3 (disc. 1989) in. regular barrel. Disc. 1991.

	$195	$155	$125

▲ *Target Bulldog* — .357 Mag. or .44 Spl. cal., 5 shot, 4 in. shrouded barrel, adj. sights, square butt only, blued finish. Mfg. 1980-1988.

	$225	$150	$125	$110	$100	$90	$80

Last Mfg.'s Sug. Retail was $255.

Subtract $10 for .357 Mag. cal.

▲ *Target Bulldog Stainless* — 9mm Federal, .357 Mag. or .44 Spl. cal., 5 shot, 5½ in. shrouded VR barrel, adj. sights, square butt target grips only, matte finished, 28 oz. Mfg. 1989-91.

	$250	$175	$125

BULLDOG PUG — .44 Spl., 5 shot, 2½ in. shrouded barrel, fixed sights, walnut or neoprene grips. Mfg. 1986-1993.

	$240	$195	$160	$130	$110	$100	$90

Last Mfg.'s Sug. Retail was $279.

▲ *Bulldog Pug Stainless* — 2½ in. shrouded barrel. Mfg. 1987-1993.

	$300	$235	$175

Last Mfg.'s Sug. Retail was $334.

BULLDOG TRACKER — .357 Mag. (.38 Spl.), 5 shot, 2½, 4 (disc. 1989), and 6 (disc. 1989) in. bull barrels, adj. sights, blue only, checkered bulldog grips, square butt on 4 or 6 in. barrel only. Disc. 1986, - reintroduced 1989-91.

	$185	$150	$125	$110	$100	$90	$80

MAGNUM PUG — .357 Mag. cal., 5 shot, fixed sights, 2.2 in. shrouded barrel, blue finish. New 1995.

Mfg.'s Sug. Retail	**$268**	$225	$195	$155	$125	$110	$90	$70

POLICE BULLDOG — .32 H&R Mag., .38 Spl. or .44 Spl. cal., 5 (.44 Spl. only) or 6 shot, fixed sights, blue only, 3½ or 4 in. barrel, Neoprene grips or square butt (.44 Spl. only). Disc. 1991.

	$175	$140	$120	$105	$95	$85	$75

Add $20 for either .44 Spl. cal or 3½ in. shrouded barrel.

▲ *Stainless Police Bulldog* — .32 Mag., .357 Mag. (new 1989), .38 Spl. (disc. 1988 - reintroduced 1990) or .44 Spl. (new 1989), 5 (.357 Mag. or .44 Spl.) or 6 (.32 Mag. or .38 Spl.) shot, square butt, 3½ or 4 in. shrouded barrel. Mfg. 1987-91.

	$195	$160	$150	$140

Add $20 for .357 Mag. or .44 Special cal.

Neoprene grips are standard on these models except for the .357 Mag. (square butt).

C

Grading		100%	98%	95%	90%	80%	70%	60%

POLICE UNDERCOVER — .32 H&R Mag. or .38 Spl. cal., 6 shot, spur or pocket hammer, 2.2 in. shrouded barrel, checkered walnut grips, fixed sights, blue or electroless nickel (new 1994) finish.

Mfg.'s Sug. Retail	$238		$205	$175	$145	$120	$100	$85	$75

Add $14 for electroless nickel finish.

▲ *Stainless Police Undercover* — similar to Police Undercover. Disc. 1993.

$240 $185 $150

Last Mfg.'s Sug. Retail was $276.

OFF DUTY — .22 LR (new 1993), .22 Mag. (new 1994), or .38 Spl. cal., 5 (.38 Spl.) or 6 (.22 LR) shot, 2 in. barrel, fixed sights, conventional or DA only, blue, matte black (disc.), or electroless nickel (new 1994) finish.

Mfg.'s Sug. Retail	$200		$170	$145	$120	$105	$90	$85	$80

Add $39 for electroless nickel finish.
Add $7 for double action only.

▲ *Stainless Off Duty* — similar to Off Duty. Disc. 1993.

$235 $180 $145

Last Mfg.'s Sug. Retail was $268.

PIT BULL — 9mm Federal, .357 Mag. (disc. 1989), or .38 Spl. (disc. 1989) cal., 5 shot, 2½, 3½, or 4 (disc. 1989) in. full shrouded barrel, Neoprene grips, approx. 26 oz. Mfg. 1989-91.

$230 $180 $150 $125 $115 $100 $90

▲ *Stainless Pit Bull* — 2½ or 3½ in. shrouded barrel. Disc. 1991.

$240 $190 $155

PISTOLS: SEMI-AUTO

MODEL 40 — .22 LR only, double action semi-auto., 3.3 in. barrel, 8 shot mag., 21½ oz., fixed sights, stainless steel. Mfg. 1984-86.

$265 $240 $220

Last Mfg.'s Sug. Retail was $319.

MODEL 79K — .32 or .380 ACP cal., double action semi-auto., 3.6 in. barrel, 7 shot mag., 24½ oz., fixed sights, stainless steel. Mfg. 1984-86.

$325 $300 $280

Last Mfg.'s Sug. Retail was $390.

EXPLORER II & S II PISTOL — .22 LR, semi-auto survival pistol, barrel unscrews, 8 shot mag., black, gold (disc.), silvertone, or camouflage finish, 6, 8, or 10 in. barrels, simulated walnut grips. Disc. 1986.

$90 $80 $70 $60 $55 $50 $45

Last Mfg.'s Sug. Retail was $109.

This model uses a modified AR-7 action.

Manufacture of this model was by Survival Arms located in Cocoa, FL.

TARGET PISTOLS

MODEL 42T (COMPETITION II TARGET) — .22 LR only, single action, 5.9 in. barrel, target model with checkered walnut grips, adj. sights, blue finish only. Mfg. 1984-1985 only.

$490 $450 $395 $350 $300 $260 $220

Last Mfg.'s Sug. Retail was $599.

Grading	100%	98%	95%	90%	80%	70%	60%

RIFLES

AR-7 EXPLORER RIFLE — .22 LR cal., takedown, barreled action stores in Cycolac synthetic stock, 8 shot mag., adj. sights, 16 in. barrel, black finish on AR-7, silvertone on AR-7S. Camouflage finish new 1986 (AR-7C). Mfg. until 1990.

	$125	$100	$85	$75	$65	$55	$50

Last Mfg.'s Sug. Retail was $146.

> In 1990, the manufacturing of this model was taken over by Survival Arms located in Cocoa, FL. Current mfg. AR-7 rifles will be found under the Survival Arms heading in the "S" section.

CHIPMUNK RIFLES

Currently manufactured by Oregon Arms, Inc. since 1988 currently located in Prospect, OR. Previously manufactured by Chipmunk Manufacturing located in Medford, OR until 1988.

CHIPMUNK SINGLE SHOT RIFLE — .22 LR or .22 Mag. (disc. 1987) cal., manually cocked single shot, $16\frac{1}{8}$ in. barrel, iron sights (adj. aperture rear), 30 in. overall length, $2\frac{1}{2}$ lbs.

Mfg.'s Sug. Retail	$185		$150	$120	$95	$80	$70	$60	$50

▲ *Deluxe Rifle* — similar to standard rifle, except has deluxe hand checkered walnut stock. New 1987.

Mfg.'s Sug. Retail	$238		$195	$165	$140	$110	$85	$75	$65

SILHOUETTE PISTOL — .22 LR, bolt action design with $14\frac{7}{8}$ in. barrel, iron sights, rear grip walnut stock. Mfg. 1984-88.

	$135	$115	$95	$80	$70	$60	$50

Last Mfg.'s Sug. Retail was $150.

CHRISTENSEN ARMS

Rifle manufacturer located in Fayette, UT since 1995. Direct sales only.

RIFLES

CARBONE ONE BOLT ACTION — most popular cals., features Remington 700 BDL short action, barrel (up to 28 in. long) features a match grade Shilen/Christensen precision stainless steel barrel liner inside a larger diameter graphite/epoxy barrel casing, black synthetic stock, Shilen trigger, approx. $6\frac{1}{2}$ lbs. New 1996.

Mfg.'s Sug. Retail	$2,750		$2,650	$2,350	$2,050	$1,800	$1,600	$1,400	$1,225

Variations include the Carbon Lite (5 lbs.), Carbon King ($7\frac{1}{2}$ lbs., .25-.338 cal.), or Carbon Cannon ($7\frac{1}{2}$ lbs., Magnum series).

CHURCHILL, E.J., (GUNMAKERS) LTD.

Previously manufactured in London, England. The company underwent various trading forms until Churchill, Atkin, Grant & Lang Ltd. closed in 1981. Currently, E.J. Churchill side by side shotguns are manufactured in Surrey, England and while they are not imported into the U.S., these models are shown with U.S. prices if purchased in England. Prices are subject to fluctuating U.S. dollar.

Churchill Guns are among the world's finest with many custom features. We will list both discontinued and current models and approximate values, but strongly urge competent appraisal if purchase or sale is contemplated.

Grading	100%	98%	95%	90%	80%	70%	60%

RIFLES

"ONE OF ONE THOUSAND RIFLE" — Mauser type bolt action, .270, 7mm Rem. Mag., .308, .30-06, .300 Win. Mag., .375 H&H Mag., or .458 Win. Mag. cal., 5 shot standard, 3 shot mag. Magnum, 24 in. barrel, classic French walnut stock, swivel recoil pad with trap, trap pistol grip cap. Mfg. 1973 for Interarms 20th Anniversary, limited, 100 mfg.

	$1,400	$1,250	$1,000	$900	$750	$700	$600

SHOTGUNS

All below models were built or finished to customer specifications pertaining to choking, chambers, barrel lengths, stock measurements, weight, engraving patterns. Standardized patterns did exist, however, for each model. The "XXV" designation referred to the 25 in. barrel length which was a Churchill specialty and was also a registered trademark.

PREMIER QUALITY SxS — all ga.'s, best quality, easy opening or standard opening, 25, 28, 30, or 32 in. barrels, any choke, sidelock, auto ejectors, standard with double triggers, engraved, checkered, straight or pistol grip stock. Also mfg. in some double rifles. Disc.

	$17,000	$15,000	$12,000	$10,000	$9,000	$7,500	$6,500

    20 ga. — add 20%.
    28 ga. — add 40%.
    SST — add $1,000.
    16 ga. — deduct 10%.
    Double rifle — add 35%.

▲ *Premier Grade* — 12 ga. only, sidelock, assisted opening, limited current mfg.

	Mfg.'s Sug. Retail	$18,750						
			$16,000	$14,000	$12,000	$10,000	$9,000	$7,500	$6,500

IMPERIAL SxS — all ga.'s, most barrel lengths, second quality sidelock model, ejectors, mostly standard opening, a few made as easy opening. Also mfg. in some double rifles. Disc.

	$13,500	$11,500	$9,500	$7,500	$6,500	$5,250	$4,000

    20 ga. — add 20%.
    28 ga. — add 40%.
    SST — add $1,000.
    16 ga. — deduct 10%.
    Double rifle — add 35%.

▲ *Imperial Grade* — 12 or 20 ga., second quality sidelock model, ejectors, standard opening, limited current mfg.

	Mfg.'s Sug. Retail	$14,250						
			$12,000	$9,950	$7,700	$6,600	$5,600	$4,500	$3,500

FIELD MODEL — 12 ga. only, most barrel lengths, third quality sidelock model. Disc.

	$9,000	$8,000	$7,000	$6,000	$5,000	$4,500	$3,500

    20 ga. — add 20%.
    28 ga. — add 40%.
    SST — add $1,000.
    16 ga. — deduct 10%.

HERCULES MODEL — all ga.'s, 25-30 in. barrels, best quality boxlock model, ejectors, easy opening or standard opening. Also made in some double rifles in .22 Hornet and similar cals.

	$9,000	$8,000	$7,000	$6,000	$5,000	$4,500	$3,500

    20 ga. — add 20%.
    28 ga. — add 40%.
    SST — add $1,000.
    16 ga. — deduct 10%.
    Double rifle — add 35%.

Grading	100%	98%	95%	90%	80%	70%	60%

UTILITY MODEL — mostly 12 ga., 25-30 in. barrels, second quality boxlock model, ejectors, checkered straight or pistol grip stock. Disc.

| | $6,250 | $4,500 | $3,500 | $3,000 | $2,500 | $2,000 | $1,800 |

20 ga. — add 20%.
28 ga. — add 40%.
.410. — add 60%.
SST — add $500.
16 ga. — deduct 10%.

CROWN MODEL — 12, 16, 20, or .410 (rare) ga., third quality boxlock model, various barrel lengths. Disc.

| | $4,500 | $3,500 | $3,000 | $2,500 | $2,000 | $1,600 | $1,200 |

20 ga. — add 20%.
28 ga. — add 40%.
.410 — add 60%.
SST — add $500.
16 ga. — deduct 10%.

REGAL — 12, 16, 20, 28, or .410 ga., second quality boxlock model introduced after WWII, released after Utility Model was disc. Premium for 28 or .410 ga.

| | $6,000 | $4,300 | $3,750 | $3,100 | $2,500 | $2,000 | $1,800 |

20 ga. — add 20%.
28 ga. — add 40%.
.410 ga. — add 60%.
SST — add $500.
16 ga. — deduct 10%.

▲ **Regal Grade** — 12, 20, 28, or .410 ga., best quality boxlock model, ejectors, standard opening, limited current production.

| Mfg.'s Sug. Retail | $5,625 | $4,800 | $4,000 | $3,500 | $3,000 | $2,500 | $2,000 | $1,800 |

PREMIER QUALITY O/U — 12, 16, or 20 ga., same barrel and bore as Premier Double, engraved, sidelock, auto ejectors, checkered pistol grip or straight stock. Disc.

| | $17,000 | $15,000 | $12,000 | $10,000 | $9,000 | $7,500 | $6,500 |

20 ga. — add 20%.
28 ga. — add 40%.
SST — add $1,000.
Vent. rib — add $500.
16 ga. — deduct 10%.

CHURCHILL

Ellett Brothers located in Chapin, SC imported and distributed Churchill shotguns until 1993. There will be no current manufacture for this trademark for 1993-94. Previously imported (until 1988) by Kassnar Imports, Inc. located in Harrisburg, PA. Not affiliated with E.J. Churchill Gunmakers, Ltd.

In late 1988, the Churchill trademark was sold to Ellett Brothers located in Chapin, SC.

RIFLES

HIGHLANDER — .25-06 Rem., .243 Win., .270 Win., .308 Win., .30-06, 7mm Rem. Mag., or .300 Win. Mag. cal., bolt action, 22 in. barrel, thumb safety, no sights, 3 or 4 shot mag., checkered walnut stock, 7½ lbs. Importation disc. 1991.

| | $395 | $350 | $330 | $300 | $270 | $240 | $215 |

Last Mfg.'s Sug. Retail was $460.

Add $30 for iron sights (disc).

Grading	100%	98%	95%	90%	80%	70%	60%

REGENT — same cals. as Highlander, deluxe checkered walnut with Monte Carlo comb and cheekpiece. Last imported by Kassner in 1988.

	$555	$455	$385	$340	$300	$280	$260

Last Mfg.'s Sug. Retail was $610.

Add $30 for iron sights.

ROTARY 22 — .22 LR, beginners rifle, bolt hold-open device, adj. rear sight, 10 shot rotary mag. Imported 1989 only.

	$120	$105	$95	$85	$75	$65	$55

Last Mfg.'s Sug. Retail was $130.

SHOTGUNS: SIDE BY SIDE

WINDSOR I — 10 (disc. 1988), 12, 16, 20, 28, or .410 ga., double barrel, 23-32 in. barrels, Anson and Deeley boxlock, antique silver finish receiver with fine scroll engraving, extractors, double triggers, checkered pistol grip and forend. Importation disc. 1991.

	$550	$465	$450	$385	$300	$250	$230

Last Mfg.'s Sug. Retail was $653.

Add $150 for 10 ga.
Add $55 for 28 or .410 ga.
Add $30 for Flyweight Models (25 in. barrels - disc. 1988).

WINDSOR II — 12 or 20 ga., double barrel, 26-30 in. barrels, Anson and Deeley boxlock, antique silver finish receiver with fine scroll engraving, ejectors, double triggers, checkered pistol grip and forend. Add $100 for 10 ga. (disc.). Importation disc. 1987.

	$595	$485	$415	$350	$315	$270	$240

Last Mfg.'s Sug. Retail was $638.

WINDSOR VI — 12 or 20 (disc.) ga., double barrel, 25 or 28 in. barrels, sidelock, antique silver finish receiver with fine scroll engraving, ejectors, double triggers, checkered pistol grip and forend. Disc. 1987.

	$840	$700	$600	$550	$510	$460	$420

Last Mfg.'s Sug. Retail was $900.

ROYAL — available in 10, 12, 20, 28, or .410 ga., DTs, extractors, checkered walnut stock and forearm, case hardened receiver. Imported late 1988-1991.

	$485	$405	$370	$310	$275	$250	$230

Last Mfg.'s Sug. Retail was $540.

Add $20 for 28 ga.
Add $74 for .410 ga.

SHOTGUNS: OVER/UNDER

MONARCH — 12, 20, 28 (disc.), or .410 (disc.) ga., 25 (disc.), 26, or 28 in. vent. rib barrels, SST, extractors, boxlock action, DT, silver finish receiver with fine scroll engraving, checkered European walnut stock and forearm, 6½-7½ lbs.

	$460	$370	$340	$300	$250	$230	$210

Last Mfg.'s Sug. Retail was $520.

Add $67 for .410 ga. with 26 in. barrels (disc.).
Deduct $40 without SST.

▲ *Monarch Turkey Gun* — 12 ga. only, 24 in. barrels with matte finish. Imported 1990-1991 only.

	$460	$370	$340	$300	$250	$230	$210

Last Mfg.'s Sug. Retail was $529.

SPORTING CLAYS MODEL — 12 ga. only, designed for sporting clays competition with 28 in. VR ported barrels with choke tubes, ejectors, raised target style VR, checkered high gloss finish stock and forearm, 7 lbs. 6 oz. Imported 1992 only.

	$800	$725	$650	$575	$500	$450	$395

Last Mfg.'s Sug. Retail was $900.

Grading	100%	98%	95%	90%	80%	70%	60%

WINDSOR III — 12, 20, or .410 ga. (disc.), double barrel, 27 or 30 in. barrels, double bottom lock, antique silver finish receiver with fine scroll engraving, extractors, SST, vent. rib, checkered pistol grip and forend. Importation disc. 1991.

	$550	$495	$450	$380	$340	$300	$280

Last Mfg.'s Sug. Retail was $625.

Add $140 for Flyweight Model or choke tubes (disc.).
Add $75 for .410 ga.

NEW WINDSOR IV — 12 or 20 ga., 3 in. chambers, boxlock action, silver receiver with full scroll engraving, 26 or 28 (12 ga. only) VR barrels with choke tubes, ejectors, SST, checkered walnut pistol grip stock with black rubber vent. recoil pad, finger grooved forearm, gloss finish, gold trigger, 5 year warranty. Mfg. 1992 only.

	$625	$525	$450	$375	$325	$295	$275

Last Mfg.'s Sug. Retail was $690.

WINDSOR IV - DISC. — 12, 20, 28, or .410 ga., double barrel, 26-30 in. barrels, double bottom lock, antique silver finish receiver with fine scroll engraving, ejectors, SST, vent. rib, checkered pistol grip and forend. Interchangeable chokes became standard in 1989. Importation disc. 1991.

	$725	$640	$530	$470	$430	$395	$360

Last Mfg.'s Sug. Retail was $852.

Deduct $52 for 28 or .410 ga.
Deduct $100 if without choke tubes.

REGENT V — 12 or 20 ga., double barrel, 27 in. barrels, double bottom lock, antique silver finish receiver with extra fine scroll engraving, ejectors, single trigger, vent. rib, checkered pistol grip and forend. Interchangeable choke tubes standard. Disc. 1986, reintroduced 1990. Limited quantities still available.

	$895	$795	$700	$620	$560	$510	$470

Last Mfg.'s Sug. Retail was $1,100.

This model was previously designated Regent VII until 1989 when it changed to the Regent V.

REGENT TRAP AND SKEET — 12 or 20 ga., double barrel, 26 or 30 in. barrels, double bottom lock, antique silver finish receiver with sideplates engraved in fine scroll, ejectors, SST, vent. rib, checkered pistol grip and forend. Importation disc. 1991.

	$795	$650	$575	$540	$485	$440	$390

Last Mfg.'s Sug. Retail was $963.

Add $40 for trap variation.

REGENT GRADE SHOTGUN/RIFLE COMBINATION — 12 ga. over either .222 Rem., .223, .243 Win. (disc.), .270 Win., .30-06, or .308 Win. cal., double barrel, 25 in. barrels, double bottom lock, antique silver finish receiver with extra fine scroll engraving, ejectors, single trigger, vent. rib, checkered pistol grip and forend. Importation disc. 1991.

	$800	$700	$635	$560	$510	$475	$440

Last Mfg.'s Sug. Retail was $927.

SHOTGUNS: SEMI-AUTO

STANDARD MODEL — 12 ga. only, gas operated and shoots different loads interchangeably without alterations, 24, 26, 28 in. VR barrel, magazine cut-off, hand checkered walnut with satin finish, matte metal finish, includes ICT choke tubes. New 1990.

	$495	$415	$375	$310	$275	$250	$230

Last Mfg.'s Sug. Retail was $550.

▲ *Turkey Model* — similar to Standard Model, except has 24 in. barrel only. New 1990.

	$510	$425	$380	$315	$275	$250	$230

Last Mfg.'s Sug. Retail was $570.

Grading	100%	98%	95%	90%	80%	70%	60%

WINDSOR GRADE — 12 ga. only, 26, 28, or 30 in. barrels, gas operation, anodized alloy receiver, vent. rib, checkered pistol grip and forend, 7½ lbs. Deluxe model includes polished receiver with etching.

	$380	$320	$300	$275	$250	$225	$200

Last Mfg.'s Sug. Retail was $420.

> Add $35 for choke tubes.
> Add $55 for Deluxe model.

REGENT GRADE — 12 ga. only, 26, 28, or 30 in. barrels, gas operation, anodized alloy receiver, vent. rib, checkered pistol grip and forend, 7½ lbs. Deluxe model includes polished receiver with etching. Disc. 1986.

	$440	$365	$340	$320	$300	$285	$270

Last Mfg.'s Sug. Retail was $495.

> Add $35 for choke tubes.
> Add $55 for Deluxe model.

SHOTGUNS: SLIDE ACTION

WINDSOR GRADE — 12 ga. only, 26, 27, 28, or 30 in. barrels, double slides, anodized alloy receiver, vent. rib, checkered pistol grip and forend, 7½ lbs. Disc. 1986.

	$385	$330	$310	$275	$250	$225	$200

Last Mfg.'s Sug. Retail was $430.

CIMARRON F.A. CO.

Importer/distributor/retailer located in Fredricksburg, TX. Currently importing Aldo Uberti, Armi San Marco, and D. Pedersoli Modern and Black Powder Firearms. Black Powder reproductions can be located in the Black Powder section under Cimarron Arms in the back of this text. Previously named Old-West Guns Co. Dealer direct sales only.

CIMARRON F.A. Cº.

REVOLVERS & CARBINES: SINGLE ACTION REPRODUCTIONS

The Cimarron Arms reproduction of the 1873 Colt Peacemaker is available in two configurations listed below. These pistols are extremely accurate reproductions of the original Colt pre-war Peacemaker and are marked (and machined) the same as the originals including serial numbers on frames, backstrap, trigger guard, and cylinder. Barrels are radiused and cylinders are beveled. Frames are color case hardened, stocks are walnut - choice of 4¾, 5½, or 7½ in. barrel. All Cimarron SAAs are barrel marked "- CIMARRON F.A. MFG. Co. HOUSTON, TX. U.S.A. -".

The "Old Model" configuration has the older style black powder frame, screw in cylinder pin retainer, and circular "bullseye" ejector head. The Standard Model includes the post-1890 style frame with spring loaded cross-pin cylinder retainer and "half-moon" ejector head.

Only the Old Model is available in the authentic old style "charcoal blue" finish (sometimes referred to as fire-bluing).

> Add $10 for charcoal blue finish.
> Add $120 for custom nickel finish.
> Add $45 for hand checkered walnut grips.
> Add $500 for "A" style engraving (30% coverage) on SAAs listed below.
> Add $575 for "B" style engraving (50% coverage) on SAAs listed below.
> Add $825 for "C" style engraving (100% coverage) on SAAs listed below.
> Add $925 for "Texas Cattlebrands" engraving pattern.

FRONTIER SIX SHOOTER — available in .22 LR (disc. 1995), .22 Mag. (disc.), .357 Mag., .38 Spl., .44-40, or .45 LC cal., 4¾, 5½, and 7½ in. barrel lengths, steel backstraps and trigger guard.

Grading		100%	98%	95%	90%	80%	70%	60%
▲ **Standard or Old Model**								
Mfg.'s Sug. Retail	$439	$375	$290	$250	$220	$195	$175	$160

Add $30 for convertible .45 ACP cylinder (4³⁄₄ or 5¹⁄₂ in. barrel only).

▲ **Sheriff's Model** — .44-40 or .45 LC cal., w/o ejector, 3 or 4 (disc. 1992) in. barrel, steel backstraps and trigger guard.

Mfg.'s Sug. Retail	$439	$375	$290	$250	$220	$195	$175	$160

▲ **New Sheriff Model** — .357 Mag., .44-40, .44 Spl., or .45 LC cal., Old Model frame only, importation began 1995.

Mfg.'s Sug. Retail	$439	$375	$290	$250	$220	$195	$175	$160

Add $35 for checkered walnut grips.

▲ **Target Model** — similar to Standard Model, except has fully adj. target rear sight, brass or steel backstrap. Importation disc. 1991.

	$355	$280	$255	$220	$195	$175	$160

Last Mfg.'s Sug. Retail was $400.

Add $40 for .357 Mag cal.

This variation is available in the Standard Model configuration only and with standard finish.

MODEL P SAA — .32-20, .38-40, .357 Mag., .44-40, .45 Spl., or .45 LC cal., features either pinched frame or pre-war configuration, standard finish only, 4³⁄₄, 5¹⁄₂, or 7¹⁄₂ in. barrel. Importation began 1996.

Mfg.'s Sug. Retail	$439	$375	$290	$250	$220	$195	$175	$160

Add $30 for convertible .45 ACP cylinder.

BUNTLINE MODEL — .357 Mag., .44-40, or .45 LC cal., 18 in. barrel, brass or steel backstrap cut for shoulder stock. Disc. 1989.

	$355	$280	$255	$220	$195	$175	$160

Last Mfg.'s Sug. Retail was $400.

Add $10 for target sights.

BUNTLINE CARBINE — similar cals. to Buntline Model, except also includes .22 LR/.22 Mag. (convertible cylinders), 18 in. barrel, includes non-detachable shoulder stock with brass hardware and finger extension trigger guard. Importation disc. 1991.

	$380	$295	$260	$225	$195	$175	$160

Last Mfg.'s Sug. Retail was $440.

Add $20 for target sights.
Add $20 for .22 LR/.22 Mag. combo.

BUCKHORN — .44 Spl. or .44 Mag., reinforced variation of the Cimarron SAA designed for more powerful cartridges, 4³⁄₄, 6 or 7¹⁄₂ in. barrel, brass or steel backstrap. Disc. 1993.

	$355	$285	$260	$220	$195	$175	$160

Last Mfg.'s Sug. Retail was $400.

▲ **Buckhorn Convertible Model** — includes .44 Mag./.44-40 cylinders, 4³⁄₄, 6 or 7¹⁄₂ in. barrel. Disc. 1989.

	$375	$295	$265	$220	$195	$175	$160

Last Mfg.'s Sug. Retail was $427.

Add $12 for target sights.

▲ **Buckhorn Target Model** — .44 Spl. or .44 Mag. cal., 4³⁄₄, 6 or 7¹⁄₂ in. barrel, adj. rear sight. Importation disc. 1991.

	$370	$290	$265	$225	$195	$175	$160

Last Mfg.'s Sug. Retail was $420.

▲ **Buckhorn Buntline** — .44-40, .44 Spl., or .44 Mag. cal., 18 in. barrel, fixed or target sights. Disc. 1989.

	$370	$285	$265	$220	$195	$175	$160

Last Mfg.'s Sug. Retail was $419.

Add $30 for target sights.

Grading	100%	98%	95%	90%	80%	70%	60%

▲ *Buckhorn Carbine* — .44-40, .44 Spl., or .44 Mag. cal., 18 in. barrel, includes non-detachable shoulder stock with brass hardware and lanyard ring. Disc. 1990.

	$375	$290	$265	$220	$195	$175	$160

Last Mfg.'s Sug. Retail was $429.

Add $30 for target sights.

NEW THUNDERER — .357 Mag., .44 Spl., .44-40, or .45 LC cal., patterned after Colt's Thunderer Model, 3½ or 4¾ in. barrel with full ejector rod housing, birdshead grips, choice of case colored or nickel finish. Importation began 1994.

Mfg.'s Sug. Retail	$449	$380	$295	$250	$220	$195	$175	$160

Add $35 for checkered walnut grips.

Add $30 for convertible .45 ACP cylinder (4¾ in. only).

SPECIAL EDITION SAAs

U.S. 7TH CAVALRY CUSTER MODEL — authentic reproduction of original Colt military cavalry contract, 7½ in. barrel, marked U.S. on lower left frame, one piece walnut grips with military cartouche.

Mfg.'s Sug. Retail	$469	$410	$345	$300	$280	$260	$240	$220

U.S. CAVALRY MODEL P (A.P. CASEY) — .45 LC only, 7½ in. barrel, Old Model frame. New 1996.

Mfg.'s Sug. Retail	$469	$410	$345	$300	$280	$260	$240	$220

U.S. ARTILLERY MODEL — Renaldo A. Carr 1895 U.S. Artillery Model Commemorative, 5½ in. barrel, limited mfg.

Mfg.'s Sug. Retail	$469	$410	$345	$300	$280	$260	$240	$220

U.S. ARTILLERY ROUGH RIDER — .45 LC only, 5½ in. barrel, Old Model frame. New 1996.

Mfg.'s Sug. Retail	$469	$410	$345	$300	$280	$260	$240	$220

7TH CAVALRY CASED SET — U.S. Cavalry Model in case with accessories. Disc. 1990.

	$695	$625	$550	$500	$460	$420	$385

Last Mfg.'s Sug. Retail was $780.

WILD BILL ELLIOT TEXAS CATTLEBRAND — .45 LC cal. New 1994.

Mfg.'s Sug. Retail	$1,395	$1,225	$1,025	$875	$750	$625	$550	$475

JUDGE ROY BEAN COMMEMORATIVE — mfg. to commemorate Judge Roy Bean's Texas cattle-brand.

Mfg.'s Sug. Retail	$1,695	$1,500	$1,175	$995	$875	$750	$625	$550

SCHOFIELD MODEL NUMBER THREE — .38 Spl., .38-40, .44 Russian/Spl., .44-40, .45 Schofield, .45 ACP, or .45 LC cal., available in 7 (Civilian or Military) or 5 (Wells Fargo only) in. barrel. New 1996.

Mfg.'s Sug. Retail	$795	$695	$625	$550	$500	$450	$400	$360

REMINGTON REPRODUCTIONS

These guns are reproductions of the Models 1875 and 1890.

Add $90 for nickel plating, $10 for charcoal blue finish on models listed below.

MODEL 1875 — available in .357 Mag., .44-40, or .45 LC cal., 7½ barrel. Disc. 1993.

	$340	$250	$200	$170	$155	$140	$120

Last Mfg.'s Sug. Retail was $390.

▲ *Model 1875 Carbine* — same cals. as Model 1875, 18 in. barrel, includes non-detachable shoulder stock with brass hardware and lanyard ring. Importation disc. 1990.

	$410	$340	$300	$265	$230	$200	$180

Last Mfg.'s Sug. Retail was $460.

MODEL 1890 — .357 Mag., .44-40, or .45 LC cal., 5½ or 7½ in. barrel. Disc. 1993.

	$340	$250	$210	$175	$160	$145	$125

Last Mfg.'s Sug. Retail was $390.

Grading	100%	98%	95%	90%	80%	70%	60%

1871 ROLLING BLOCK TARGET PISTOL — .22 LR, .22 Hornet (new 1990), .22 Mag., or .357 Mag. cal., 9½ in. barrel. Importation disc. 1990.

	$250	$200	$180	$160	$140	$125	$110

Last Mfg.'s Sug. Retail was $280.

▲ **1871 Rolling Block Baby Carbine** — same cals. as Target Pistol, has 22 in. barrel and walnut stock and forearm, brass trigger guard and butt plate. Importation disc. 1990.

	$310	$245	$205	$170	$155	$140	$120

Last Mfg.'s Sug. Retail was $340.

ROLLING BLOCK SPORTING RIFLE — .45-70 cal., 30 in. barrel, walnut stock and forearm. Imported 1989-1990 only.

	$565	$430	$395	$350	$320	$300	$275

Last Mfg.'s Sug. Retail was $620.

▲ **Deluxe Rolling Block Sporting Rifle** — similar to standard model, except has select wood. Importation disc. 1990.

	$640	$485	$450	$375	$340	$320	$295

Last Mfg.'s Sug. Retail was $720.

RIFLES: WINCHESTER REPRODUCTIONS

Add $25 for "in-the-white" or charcoal blue finish for models listed below.

HENRY RIFLE/CARBINE — .44-40, .44 Spl. (mfg. 1993-95), or .45 LC (new 1993) cal., brass frame, 24¼ in. barrel on rifle, 22 (disc. 1995, .44-40 cal. only) in. barrel on carbine.

Mfg.'s Sug. Retail	$900	$785	$575	$500	$450	$375	$325	$295

Can also be special ordered with Grade A engraving ($450 extra), Grade B engraving ($550 extra), and Grade C engraving ($725 extra).

CIVIL WAR HENRY RIFLE — .44-40 cal., 24 in. barrel, patterned after the U.S. issue original inspected by Chas. G. Chapman (C.G.C.) with military inspector's marks and cartouche. Importation began 1993.

Mfg.'s Sug. Retail	$950	$825	$625	$550	$475	$395	$350	$315

Add $25 for military sling swivels.

1866 SPORTING RIFLE (YELLOWBOY) — .22 LR (disc. 1993), .22 Mag. (disc. 1993), .38 Spl. (new 1995), .44-40, or .45 LC (new 1993) cal., brass receiver, 24 in. octagon barrel.

Mfg.'s Sug. Retail	$800	$695	$535	$425	$375	$285	$240	$200

Add $500 (retail) for A engraving, $650 for B engraving, $1,175 for C engraving.

1866 YELLOWBOY CARBINE — includes .38 Spl. (disc. 1993) cal., otherwise similar to Model 1866 Sporting Rifle, features 19 in. round barrel with 2 bands, saddle ring, uncheckered walnut stock and forearm.

Mfg.'s Sug. Retail	$790	$685	$525	$425	$375	$285	$240	$200

▲ **1866 Trapper Carbine** — .44-40 cal., 16 in. round barrel. Importation disc. 1990.

	$465	$385	$340	$320	$275	$240	$200

Last Mfg.'s Sug. Retail was $538.

▲ **1866 Yellowboy Indian Carbine** — .22 LR, .22 Mag., .38 Spl., or .44-40 cal., 19 in. round barrel. Disc. 1989.

	$575	$475	$400	$350	$300	$260	$220

Last Mfg.'s Sug. Retail was $649.

This model has a photo engraved brass frame and has brass tacks in stock and forearm.

▲ **Red Cloud Commemorative Carbine** — same cals. as Yellowboy Indian Carbine, includes special engraving representing Oglalla Indian tribe symbols, brass tacks in forearm and stock. Disc. 1989.

	$575	$475	$400	$350	$300	$260	$220

Last Mfg.'s Sug. Retail was $649.

Grading	100%	98%	95%	90%	80%	70%	60%

1873 SPORTING RIFLE — .22 LR (disc. 1993), .22 Mag. (disc. 1993), .357 Mag., .44-40, or .45 LC cal., 24 $\frac{1}{4}$ in. octagon barrel, case hardened receiver, full mag., iron sights.

Mfg.'s Sug. Retail	$880	$775	$565	$495	$450	$375	$325	$295

Add $150 for Deluxe Model with pistol grip.
Add $500 (retail) for A engraving, $650 for B engraving, $1,075 for C engraving, or $1,150 for "1 of 1000" engraving.

▲ *1873 Short Rifle* — .44-40 or .45 LC cal., features 20 in. octagon barrel, case hardened receiver, iron sights. New 1990.

Mfg.'s Sug. Retail	$880	$775	$565	$495	$450	$375	$325	$295

▲ *1873 Long Range Rifle* — .44-40 or .45 LC cal., includes 30 in. octagon barrel with full mag., case hardened receiver, iron sights. New 1990.

Mfg.'s Sug. Retail	$900	$785	$575	$500	$450	$375	$325	$295

Add $150 for Deluxe Model with pistol grip.

➤ **1873 Long Range Rifle 1 of 1,000** — .45 LC only, extensive engraving. Importation began 1995.

Mfg.'s Sug. Retail	$1,800	$1,600	$1,400	$1,150	$925	$800	$700	$600

▲ *1873 Saddle Ring Carbine* — .22 LR (disc. 1993), .22 Mag. (disc. 1993), .357 Mag., .44-40, or .45 LC cal., blued steel receiver, saddle ring, 19 in. round barrel.

Mfg.'s Sug. Retail	$880	$775	$565	$495	$450	$375	$325	$295

Add $90 for nickel plating (disc.).

▲ *1873 Trapper Carbine* — .357 Mag. (new 1990), .44-40, or .45 LC (new 1990) cal., 16 in. barrel, blue finish only. Importation disc. 1990.

	$575	$475	$400	$350	$300	$260	$220

Last Mfg.'s Sug. Retail was $650.

CLARIDGE HI-TEC INC.

Previous manufacturer located in Northridge, CA 1990-1993.

In 1990, Claridge Hi-Tec, Inc. was created - this new company took over Goncz Armament, Inc.

All Claridge Hi-Tec firearms utilized match barrels mfg. in-house that were button-rifled. The Claridge action is an original design and does not copy other actions. Claridge Hi-Tec models can be altered (Law Enforcement Companion Series) to accept Beretta 92F or Sig Model 226 magazines.

PISTOLS & CARBINES

Add $40 for polished stainless steel frame construction.

L-9 PISTOL — 9mm Para., .40 S&W, or .45 ACP cal., semi-auto paramilitary design, 7$\frac{1}{2}$ (new 1992) or 9$\frac{1}{2}$ (disc. 1991) in. shrouded barrel, aluminum receiver, choice of black matte, matte silver, or polished silver finish, one piece grip, safety locks firing pin in place, 10 (disc.), 17, or 30 shot double row mag., adj. sights, 3$\frac{3}{4}$ lbs. Mfg. 1991-1993.

	$525	$375	$300	$265	$225	$200	$175

Last Mfg.'s Sug. Retail was $598.

A trigger activated laser sighting scope is available in Models M, L, C, and T - add $395 for new mfg.

S-9 PISTOL — similar to L-9, except has 5 in. non-shrouded threaded barrel, 3 lbs. 9 oz. Disc. 1993.

	$475	$350	$280	$250	$225	$200	$175

Last Mfg.'s Sug. Retail was $535.

T-9 PISTOL — similar to L-9, except has 9$\frac{1}{2}$ in. barrel. Mfg. 1992-1993.

	$525	$375	$300	$265	$225	$200	$175

Last Mfg.'s Sug. Retail was $598.

M PISTOL — similar to L Model, except has 7$\frac{1}{2}$ in. barrel, 3 lbs. Disc. 1991.

	$500	$375	$300	$265	$225	$200	$175

Last Mfg.'s Sug. Retail was $720.

Grading	100%	98%	95%	90%	80%	70%	60%

C-9 CARBINE — same cals. as L and S Model pistols, 16.1 in. shrouded barrel, choice of composite or uncheckered walnut stock and forearm, 5 lbs. 12 oz. Mfg. 1991-1993.

	$595	$525	$450	$395	$350	$300	$275

Last Mfg.'s Sug. Retail was $675.

Add $74 for black graphite composite stock.
Add $474 for integral laser model (with graphite stock).
This model is available with either gloss walnut, dull walnut, or black graphite composite stock.

LAW ENFORCEMENT COMPANION (LEC) — 9mm, .40 S&W, or .45 ACP cal., 16¼ button rifled barrel, black graphite composition buttstock and foregrip, buttstock also provides space for an extra mag., available in either aluminum or stainless steel frame, matte black finish, available with full integral laser sighting system. Limited mfg. 1992-93.

	$650	$575	$495	$425	$375	$325	$295

Last Mfg.'s Sug. Retail was $749.

Add $400 for integral laser sighting system.

CLARK CUSTOM GUNS, INC.

Clark Custom Guns, Inc. has been customizing various configurations of both handguns and rifles since 1950. It would be impossible to list within the confines of this text the many conversions this company has performed. It is recommended to contact this company directly (see Trademark Index) for an up-to-date price sheet and catalog on their extensive line-up of high quality competition pistols that range in price from $625 - $2,285. Custom rifles are also available in addition to various competition parts, related gunsmithing services, and a firearms training facility called The Shootout.

CLASSIC DOUBLES

Previously manufactured in Tochigi City, Japan. Previously imported and distributed by Classic Doubles International, Inc. located in St. Louis, MO.

The factory closed in 1987, and all Classic Doubles remaining in inventory were sold to GU Wholesalers located in Omaha, NE in 1990. While a few models are still available through GU Wholesalers (call for availability), all values listed below reflect discontinuance of mfg. to date, there has been little collectibility in the Classic Doubles trademark. As a result, values are determined by the shooting value each model has to offer against other competing models in the same configuration. Also, in some regions of the country, 98% condition or less specimens may be priced lower than values shown in this section.

In late 1987, Winchester/Olin discontinued importation of their Japanese shotgun models (Models 101 and 23). At that point, Classic Doubles International, Inc. became the sole importer of these shotguns. There have been very few changes made during this changeover of importation. However, the new Classic Double shotguns (Models 101 and 201) do not have the Winchester trademark or definitive Winchester proofmark stamped on the barrels. The Model 201 is a new model designation.

SHOTGUNS: O/U - MODEL 101

All newly imported Classic Doubles have an interchangeable choke tube system compatible with the older Winchester manufactured models. Prices listed include a luggage style carrying case.

Values listed below for the Classic Doubles Shotguns assume NIB condition - subtract 10%-15% if without box, warranty card, and original shipping container (with packing materials).

Grading	100%	98%	95%	90%	80%	70%	60%

CLASSIC FIELD GRADE I — 12 or 20 ga., 3 in. chambers, vent. rib, 25½ or 28 in. vent. barrels with choke tubes, blued receiver with moderate scroll engraving, ejectors, checkered pistol grip or English stock and forearm, 6¼ - 7 lbs.

	$1,400	$1,250	$1,100	$1,000	$900	$825	$750

Last Mfg.'s Sug. Retail was $1,905.

C

WATERFOWL MODEL — 12 ga. only, 3 in. chambers, 30 in. barrels with vent. rib and choke tubes, matte blued receiver with moderate engraving, low gloss walnut stock with vent. recoil pad, 7 ¾ lbs.

	$1,150	$995	$895	$800	$700	$600	$500

Last Mfg.'s Sug. Retail was $1,520.

CLASSIC SPORTER — 12 ga. only, made for Sporting Clays competition, 28 or 30 in. vent. barrels and rib with choke tubes, quick detachable stock system, border engraved coin finished receiver with non-reflective matte surface on top frame and lever, checkered walnut stock and forearm, 7¾ lbs.

	$1,995	$1,500	$1,295	$1,150	$1,000	$900	$775

Last Mfg.'s Sug. Retail was $1,980.

Add $965 for extra barrel.

CLASSIC FIELD GRADE II — 12, 20, 28 or .410 ga., 28 in. VR barrels with choke tubes, deluxe walnut with round knob pistol grip stock and forearm with fine fleur-de-lis checkering, coin finished receiver (different sizes) with game scene engraving featuring hunting motifs on receiver sides and bottom, .410 ga. bored M/F only, 6¼ - 7 lbs.

	$1,795	$1,475	$1,275	$1,100	$1,000	$900	$795

Last Mfg.'s Sug. Retail was $2,190.

Add 15% for .410 ga. (baby frame).
Add 50% for 28 ga. (baby frame).
The lack of supply of the Winchester/Olin Model 101 28 ga. small frame has caused a significant in demand for the .410 or 28 ga. The Grade II .410 bore is the only round knob pistol grip produced in both Winchester and Classic Doubles manufacture.

CLASSIC FIELD GRADE II TWO BARREL SET — 12 and 20 ga. barrels, both with Winchokes, 26 in. barrels - 20 ga., 28 in. barrels - 12 ga., coin finished receiver with game scene engraving and borders, 6½ (20 ga.) or 7 (12 ga.) lbs.

	$2,695	$2,175	$1,825	$1,550	$1,375	$1,200	$1,075

Last Mfg.'s Sug. Retail was $3,420.

TARGET GUNS

CLASSIC TRAP SINGLE — 12 ga. only, over single 32 or 34 in. VR barrel with choke tubes, blued receiver with light engraving, choice of Monte Carlo or regular stock, recoil pad, 8½ lbs.

	$1,425	$1,250	$1,100	$1,000	$900	$825	$750

Last Mfg.'s Sug. Retail was $2,070.

CLASSIC TRAP O/U — 12 ga. only, 30 or 32 in. vent. barrels and rib with choke tubes, finish and engraving similar to Classic Trap Single, choice of Monte Carlo or standard stock with recoil pad, 8¾ or 9 lbs.

	$1,300	$1,125	$1,000	$900	$825	$750	$675

Last Mfg.'s Sug. Retail was $1,905.

CLASSIC TRAP COMBO — includes one set of O/U barrels (30 or 32 in.) and one over single barrel (32 or 34 in.), choke tubes, choice of Monte Carlo or standard stock, 8¾ or 9 lbs.

	$2,125	$1,875	$1,600	$1,475	$1,300	$1,175	$995

Last Mfg.'s Sug. Retail was $2,825.

CLASSIC SKEET — 12 or 20 ga., 27½ in. vent. barrels and rib, choke tubes on 12 ga. only, smaller ga.'s are bored SK/SK, similar metal finish to Classic Trap models, 7¼ or 7¾ lbs.

	$1,695	$1,375	$1,175	$1,025	$900	$825	$750

Last Mfg.'s Sug. Retail was $1,905.

Grading	100%	98%	95%	90%	80%	70%	60%

▲ **Classic Skeet 4 ga. Set** — similar to Classic Skeet except has 4 barrels (12, 20, 28, or .410 ga.), 12 ga. has choke tubes, smaller ga.'s are bored SK/SK.

	$3,900	$3,500	$3,100	$2,875	$2,600	$2,300	$1,995

Last Mfg.'s Sug. Retail was $4,765.

SHOTGUNS: SIDE BY SIDE

MODEL 201 CLASSIC — 12 or 20 ga., 3 in. chambers, forged steel monobloc with improved lug design, 26 in. choke tube barrels with vent. rib, high lustre bluing, no engraving, SST, ejectors, premium walnut stock and beavertail forearm with fancy checkering pattern, solid red rubber recoil pad, 6¾ - 7 lbs.

	$1,400	$1,200	$995	$775	$650	$575	$495

Last Mfg.'s Sug. Retail was $2,190.

Add $120 for 20 ga.

The 12 ga. could be ordered with choke tubes at no extra charge. Only 63 were mfg. with choke tubes and slight premiums are being asked.

▲ **Model 201 Classic Small Bore Set** — 28 and .410 ga. two barrel set, similar to Model 201 Classic except has smaller frame and overall dimensions, 28 in. VR barrels only bored IC/M on 28 ga. and M/F on .410 ga., very limited importation, 6 or 6½ lbs

	$4,250	$3,650	$3,250	$2,800	$2,400	$1,950	$1,475

Last Mfg.'s Sug. Retail was $3,675.

CLERKE PRODUCTS

Santa Monica, CA.

DOUBLE ACTION REVOLVER — .22 RF or .32 S&W Long cal., inexpensive double action revolvers that sold to dealers for $15 in 1971.

HI-WALL — single shot rifle, falling block replica of Winchester 1885 High Wall, lever operated, case hardened receiver, 26 in. barrel, available in most modern calibers, no sights, checkered walnut pistol grip stock, Schnabel forearm. Mfg. 1972-1974.

	$250	$225	$185	$175	$150	$140	$125

DELUXE HI-WALL — similar to Hi-Wall, except half octagon barrel, select wood and recoil pad.

	$300	$275	$235	$210	$180	$160	$145

CLIFTON ARMS

Manufacturer and retailer of custom rifles located in Medina, TX. Clifton Arms mostly specializes in composite stocks (with or without integral, retractable bipod). Manufacturer direct sales only.

Clifton Arms mostly manufactures composite, hand laminated stocks that are patterned after the Dakota 76 stock configuration. However, custom rifles can be ordered by contacting the company and specifying the type of action, caliber, barrel, stock configuration, color. Price quotations vary per individual, special order rifle.

RIFLES: BOLT ACTION

CLIFTON SCOUT RIFLE — .243 Win. (disc. 1993), .30-06, .308 Win., .350 Rem. Mag., .35 Whelen, 7mm-08 Rem. (disc. 1993), or .416 Rem. Mag. cal., choice of Dakota 76, pre-64 Winchester Model 70, or Ruger 77 MK II (standard) stainless action with bolt face altered to controlled round feeding, Shilen stainless premium match grade barrel, Clifton synthetic stock with bipod, many other special orders are available, mfg. began 1992.

Mfg.'s Sug. Retail	$2,750		$2,750	$2,150	$1,500

This model is available as a Standard Scout (.308 Win. cal. with 19 in. barrel), Pseudo Scout (.30-06 cal. with 19½ in. barrel), Super Scout (.35 Whelen or .350 Rem. Mag. with 20 in. barrel), or African Scout (.416 Rem. Mag. with 22 in. barrel).

COBRAY INDUSTRIES

See listing under S.W.D. in the S section of this text.

COGSWELL & HARRISON, LIMITED

Previous manufacture located in London, England, 1770-approx. WWII.

Grading	100%	98%	95%	90%	80%	70%	60%

C

SHOTGUNS

REGENCY — 12, 16, or 20 ga., double barrel, 26, 28, or 30 in. barrels, any choke combination, hammerless Anson & Deeley system, boxlock, double triggers, auto ejectors, straight English stock.

	$2,750	$2,500	$2,250	$2,000	$1,800	$1,600	$1,375

Last Mfg.'s Sug. Retail was $3,200.

AMBASSADOR MODEL — double barrel, same gauges and barrels as Regency, boxlock with false sideplates, auto ejectors, double triggers, engraved game scene or scroll rose motif, English stock.

	$3,650	$3,100	$2,850	$2,700	$2,500	$2,250	$1,995

Last Mfg.'s Sug. Retail was $4,000.

MARKOR — 12, 16, or 20 ga., double barrel, 27½ or 30 in. barrel and choke, boxlock, double trigger, English stock. Disc.

	$1,500	$1,350	$1,200	$1,000	$950	$825	$700
Auto ejectors	$1,750	$1,500	$1,350	$1,200	$1,100	$900	$700

HUNTIC MODEL — 12, 16, or 20 ga., double barrel, 25, 27, or 30 in. barrels, any choke, sidelock, auto ejectors, English style stock. Disc.

	$3,500	$3,200	$3,000	$2,800	$2,500	$2,175	$1,850

SST — add $400.

AVANT TOUT SERIES — 12, 16, or 20 ga., double barrel, 25, 27½, or 30 in. barrels, boxlock, false sideplates, straight English stock, auto ejectors, series disc.

	$2,250	$1,925	$1,700	$1,495	$1,350	$1,200	$1,075

REX OR AVANT TOUT III — no sideplates.

	$1,800	$1,650	$1,500	$1,350	$1,200	$1,075	$895

SANDHURST OR AVANT TOUT II

	$2,500	$2,300	$2,150	$2,000	$1,750	$1,500	$1,225

KONOR OR AVANT TOUT I

	$2,850	$2,700	$2,500	$2,250	$2,000	$1,775	$1,500

SST — add $400.
20 ga. — add 20%.
16 ga. — deduct 10%.

BEST QUALITY — 12, 16, or 20 ga.'s, double barrel, 25, 26, 28, or 30 in. barrels, any choke, hand detachable sidelock, auto ejectors, double triggers standard, English stock.

▲ *Primic Model* — disc.

	$5,750	$4,650	$4,150	$3,650	$3,050	$2,500	$1,950

▲ *Victor Model*

Mfg.'s Sug. Retail	$10,000	$8,600	$6,250	$5,000	$4,350	$3,740	$3,000	$2,375

SST — add $400.
20 ga. — add 20%.
16 ga. — deduct 10%.

Note: Degree of engraving and grade of wood are the basic differences among models.

COLT'S MANUFACTURING COMPANY, INC.

Manufacturer located in W. Hartford, CT.

Manufactured from 1836-1841 in Paterson, NJ; 1847 to 1848 in Whitneyville, CT; 1854 to 1864 in London, England; and from 1848 to date in Hartford, CT. Colt Firearms became a division of Colt Industries in 1964. In March, 1990, the Colt Firearms Division was sold to C.F. Holding Corp. located in Hartford, CT. The new company is called Colt's Manufacturing Company, Inc. The original Hartford plant was closed during 1994.

C

PERCUSSION REVOLVERS

Prices shown for percussion Colt's are for guns only. Original cased guns with accessories will bring a healthy premium over non-cased models (200-350% over a gun only is common). Be very careful when buying an "original" cased gun, as many fake cases have shown up in recent years.

If possible, it is advisable to procure a factory letter before buying/selling Models 1851 Navy, 1860 Army, or 1861 Navy. These water marked letters are available by writing Colt Firearms in Hartford, CT, with a charge of $100 per serial number (if they can research it). Include your name and address, Colt model name, serial number, and check to: COLT HISTORIAN, P.O. Box 1868, Hartford, CT 06144. Please allow 4-6 weeks for a response.

Prices shown on the following pages for extremely rare Colt's firearms might not include values in the 90%, 95%, 98%, and 100% condition columns. Prices are very hard to establish since these excellent to mint specimens are seldomly seen or sold.

100%	98%	95%	90%	80%	70%	60%	50%	40%	30%	20%	10%

POCKET MODEL PATERSON NO. 1 — also known as "Baby Paterson", .28 cal., 5 shot, 2½ in. to 4¾ in. octagon barrels, blued metal, varnished walnut grips. Serial range 1 to approx. 500. Standard bbl. marking "Patent Arms M'g Co. Paterson N.J.-Colt's Pt.". Centaur scene with four horse head trademark and "COLT" on 1 1/16 in. cylinder of round or square type. Mfg. 1837-1838.

> This and all other Paterson models have 5 shot cylinders and serial numbers are not commonly in evidence externally. Disassembly of the arm is usually necessary to determine the serial number.

> The Pocket Model Paterson No. 1 (Baby Paterson) is the first production made handgun in its Paterson, N.J. facility. It is very small in size, almost appearing as a toy or miniature.

▲ *Standard Production Model* — without attached loading lever.
N/A   N/A $31,000 $24,500 $20,000 $17,500 $15,000 $13,250 $11,750 $10,250 $9,000 $8,000

▲ *Late Production Ehlers Model* — with attached loading lever, 31/32 round back cylinder and recoil shield milled for ease of capping. Barrel marked "Patent Arms Paterson N.J.-Colt's Pt.". Approx. 500 mfg. including the Ehlers Model under Belt Model No. 2 Mfg. 1840-1843.
N/A   N/A $34,000 $27,000 $21,500 $18,000 $15,500 $13,750 $12,250 $10,750 $9,500 $8,500

BELT MODEL PATERSON NO. 2 — .31 or .34 cal., 5 shot, 2½ in. to 5½ in. octagon barrels, blued metal, varnished walnut grips. Serial range 1- approx. 850 which includes the Belt Model No. 3. All standard production Belt Models No. 2 have straight bottom style grips. Standard bbl. markings "Patent Arms M'g Co. Paterson N-J. Colt's Pt.". Centaur scene with four horse head trademark and "COLT" on cylinder of round or square backed type. Mfg 1837-1840. Somewhat heavier than the Pocket No. 1 revolver.

▲ *Standard Production Model* — without attached loading lever.
N/A   N/A $31,000 $25,000 $20,500 $18,000 $15,750 $13,750 $12,250 $11,000 $9,500 $8,500

▲ *Ehlers Model* — with attached loading lever, 1 1/16 in. round back cylinder, recoil shield milled for ease of capping. Barrel marked "Patent Arms Paterson N-J. Colt's Pt.". Approx. 500 mfg. including the Ehlers Model under Pocket Model No. 1. Mfg. 1840-1843.
N/A   N/A $37,000 $30,000 $24,500 $21,000 $18,000 $15,500 $13,500 $12,000 $10,600 $9,500

100%	98%	95%	90%	80%	70%	60%	50%	40%	30%	20%	10%

C

BELT MODEL PATERSON NO. 3

BELT MODEL PATERSON NO. 3 — .31 or .34 cal., 5 shot, 3½ in. to 5½ in. octagon barrels, blued metal, a few having case hardened hammers. Varnished walnut grips. Serial range 1- approx. 850 which includes the Belt Model No. 2. All standard production Belt Models No. 3 have the flared bottom style grips. Standard barrel markings "Patent Arms M'g Co. Paterson N-J. Colt's Pt.". The square backed cylinder is seen less often than the more common round back, both bearing the Centaur scene with four horse head trademark and "COLT". With both Belt Models, revolvers exhibiting attached loading levers are less common than those without a lever. Mfg. 1837-1840.

▲ **Standard Model W/O Lever** — without attached loading lever.

N/A	N/A	$34,000	$28,750	$23,000	$19,500	$17,000	$15,000	$13,500	$11,750	$10,500	$9,250

▲ **Standard Model With Lever** — with attached loading lever and recoil shield milled for ease of capping (scarce).

N/A	N/A	$37,400	$31,000	$25,500	$22,500	$19,750	$17,500	$15,250	$13,500	$12,000	$10,750

HOLSTER MODEL NO. 5

HOLSTER MODEL NO. 5 — also known as "Texas Paterson" - .36 cal., 5 shot, 4 in. to 12 in. octagon barrels, blued metal with case hardened frame and hammer. All cylinders bear the stage coach hold-up scene. Varnished walnut grips of flared bottom style. Serial range 1 to approx. 1,000. As with all models of Patersons, the serial number usually cannot be seen without disassembly of the revolver. Very large and heavy compared to the other Paterson models. Enjoys more popularity with collectors because of its military and frontier use. Mfg. 1838-1840.

Many specimens encountered in this variation show extreme use. Consequently, fine to mint specimens are quite rare and highly prized by collectors. Values are given for non-military marked specimens. Any specimen bearing an authenticated martial marking is truly a rarity and should be appraised individually. NOTE: Watch for fakes here. There are now many times more faked martial markings, often times on non-original Patersons, than there are originals.

▲ **Standard Production Model W/O Lever** — without attached loading lever, round or square backed cylinder.

N/A	N/A	$131,000	$98,000	$80,500	$66,500	$57,000	$49,000	$42,000	$37,000	$32,500	$28,000

▲ **Standard Production Model With Lever** — with attached loading lever, round backed cylinder and recoil shield milled for ease of capping.

N/A	N/A	$152,000	$110,500	$87,500	$73,500	$63,500	$55,000	$47,500	$41,500	$37,000	$32,500

WALKER MODEL REVOLVER

WALKER MODEL REVOLVER — .44 cal., 6 shot, 9 in. part round, part octagon barrel, blued metal with case hardened frame, lever and hammer. Cylinder left without finish, brass trigger guard. One piece walnut grips. Mfg. 1847; total production approx. 1,100. Ser. numbers beginning with no. 1 were applied for each of five different military companies (A,B,C,D, & E). The total for the military issue Walkers was approx. 1,000 revolvers; the remaining approx. 100 revolvers were produced for civilian distribution. Barrels marked "Address SamL Colt New-York City". Found on right side of barrel lug is "US" over "1847". Cylinder bears Texas Ranger/Indian fight scene. Various metal parts and walnut grips stamped with Govt. Inspectors' marks.

Because of these arms being subjected to great extremes of use, they will exhibit high degrees of wear, often to the extent that most or all markings will be worn off. Replaced parts are common and many badly worn and damaged specimens have been extensively rebuilt and restored. NOTE: Use great caution when contemplating the purchase of a Walker. A multitude of out-and-out fakes and "antiqued" reproduction Walkers have been fed into the market over the past few decades. Some of these are old enough (and have aged enough naturally) to almost resemble an authentic specimen. Enlist the services of a qualified expert before your dollars are spent. Only 10-12% of the original production of approx. 1,100 specimens have been accounted for. The acquisition of an authenticated Walker revolver is the ultimate goal of serious Colt collectors.

▲ **Standard Military Issue Model**

N/A	N/A	N/A	$235,000	$175,000	$145,000	$125,000	$90,000	$75,000	$65,000	$55,000	$50,000

100%	98%	95%	90%	80%	70%	60%	50%	40%	30%	20%	10%

▲ *Limited Civilian Issue Model* — serial range 1001 to approx. 1100. Similar to military model except Govt. inspectors' marks were not applied. Pricing is difficult on the civilian issue arms. They tend to be in considerably better condition than the much more common military specimens. The factors of scarcity and condition will often bring higher prices from the advanced collector of means, especially in the finer grades of condition. On the other hand, the collector appreciating military usage will pay more for military marked examples. This publication tries to reflect the latest trends on purchase of civilian models.

| N/A | N/A | N/A | $245,000 | $180,000 | $145,000 | $125,000 | $90,000 | $75,000 | $65,000 | $55,000 | $50,000 |

WHITNEYVILLE HARTFORD DRAGOON — .44 cal., 6 shot, 7½ in. part octagon, part round barrel, some of the left-over Walker parts were used in Dragoons, blued metal with casehardened frame, lever, hammer, brass trigger guard and steel cylinder bears Texas Ranger and Indian battle scene. Mfg. 1847. Total production approx. 240. Serial range approx. 1,100 to 1,340 in sequence following civilian Walkers.

▲ *Rear frame cut out for grips*

| N/A | N/A | $129,000 | $104,000 | $84,000 | $70,000 | $60,000 | $53,000 | $47,000 | $42,000 | $38,000 | $35,000 |

▲ *Straight rear frame*

| N/A | N/A | $95,000 | $70,000 | $50,000 | $45,000 | $35,000 | $30,000 | $25,000 | $22,000 | $20,000 | $18,500 |

FIRST MODEL DRAGOON — .44 cal., 6 shot, 7½ in. round and octagon barrel, blued metal with case hardened frame, lever, hammer, brass grip straps, silvered straps for civilian market, serial range numbered after Hartford Dragoon, 1341 to around 8000. Mfg. 1848-1850. Total production approx. 7,000. Oval cyl. slots, square back trigger guard, Texas ranger and Indian fight scene on cylinder.

▲ *Military Model*

| N/A | N/A | $44,500 | $35,000 | $25,000 | $19,000 | $16,000 | $13,500 | $10,500 | $8,750 | $7,500 | $6,500 |

▲ *Civilian Model*

| N/A | N/A | $40,000 | $26,000 | $22,000 | $17,000 | $13,000 | $10,500 | $8,000 | $6,500 | $6,000 | $5,500 |

FLUCK MODEL DRAGOON — basically a First Model Dragoon, with 7½ in. altered Walker barrels and fully martially marked, should be extensively checked over, used to replace defective Walkers. Mfg. 1848. Total production 300. Serial range approx. 2,216 to 2,515.

| N/A | N/A | $45,000 | $35,000 | $30,000 | $23,000 | $19,000 | $17,000 | $15,000 | $11,000 | $10,000 | $9,500 |

SECOND MODEL DRAGOON — .44 cal., 6 shot, 7½ in. round and octagon barrel, serial range following the First Model Dragoon 8000-10,700. Mfg. 1850-1851. Texas ranger and Indian fight scene on cylinder.

▲ *Military Model*

| N/A | N/A | $39,000 | $30,500 | $23,500 | $18,000 | $14,750 | $12,000 | $10,000 | $8,500 | $7,500 | $6,500 |

▲ *Civilian Model*

| N/A | N/A | $34,500 | $25,750 | $20,000 | $16,750 | $13,250 | $11,500 | $9,500 | $7,750 | $6,500 | $5,500 |

▲ *New Hampshire or Massachusetts* — notice state markings on front portion of trigger guard.

| N/A | N/A | $42,500 | $31,750 | $24,750 | $19,500 | $15,750 | $13,250 | $11,250 | $9,500 | $8,500 | $7,750 |

THIRD MODEL DRAGOON — .44 cal., 6 shot, 7½ in. round or octagon barrel, same basic features as earlier models, but with round trigger guard and rectangular cylinder slots, serial range approx. 10,200-19,600, some overlapping of numbers, with approx. 10,500 mfg. from 1851-1861. Texas ranger and Indian fight scene on cylinder.

▲ *Third Model Dragoon*

| N/A | N/A | $32,500 | $22,000 | $14,500 | $12,000 | $10,250 | $8,900 | $7,800 | $6,900 | $6,250 | $5,750 |

▲ *Martially marked U.S.*

| N/A | N/A | $35,000 | $25,000 | $19,500 | $14,750 | $12,750 | $11,000 | $9,500 | $8,250 | $7,250 | $6,500 |

▲ *Third Model* — 8 in. barrel.

| N/A | N/A | $37,000 | $30,000 | $27,000 | $23,000 | $19,500 | $16,500 | $14,000 | $11,500 | $9,500 | $8,000 |

100%	98%	95%	90%	80%	70%	60%	50%	40%	30%	20%	10%

▲ *First and Second variation* — shoulder stock model.

N/A	N/A	$37,500	$29,000	$23,000	$19,000	$16,350	$14,000	$11,750	$9,750	$8,250	$7,250

▲ *Third Variation*

N/A	N/A	$36,000	$28,500	$21,750	$18,500	$15,750	$13,250	$11,000	$9,000	$7,500	$6,500

▲ *C.L. Dragoon*

N/A	N/A	$48,500	$36,750	$28,000	$23,700	$20,250	$17,250	$14,750	$12,500	$10,500	$8,500

ENGLISH HARTFORD DRAGOON — basically a Third Model Dragoon, assembled at Colt's London factory, with unique serial range 1-700, some were assembled from earlier parts inventories, easy to spot with British proofs of crown over V and crown over GP, the blue was of the English type, many were engraved.

N/A	N/A	$29,000	$21,000	$15,250	$12,750	$10,500	$9,100	$8,000	$7,150	$6,500	$6,000

Recently, several 10-20% condition factory engraved English Dragoons have auctioned off at between $6,000-$8,500, depending on the amount of engraving.

1848 BABY DRAGOONS — .31 cal., 5 shot, 3, 4, 5, or 6 in. octagon barrels, most without loading lever, serial range 1-15,500, a scaled down version of the .44 caliber Dragoons, early ones with Texas Ranger scene and later ones with the holdup scene.

▲ *Type I* — left hand barrel stamping, Texas Ranger and Indian scene, approx. serial range 1-150.

N/A	N/A	$15,000	$11,750	$9,850	$8,650	$7,500	$6,500	$5,750	$5,250	$4,850	$4,350

▲ *Type II* — with Texas Ranger and Indian scene, 11,600 serial range, without loading lever.

N/A	N/A	$11,500	$8,250	$7,100	$5,750	$4,750	$3,950	$3,300	$3,000	$2,800	$2,600

▲ *Type III* — with Stagecoach scene and oval cylinder slots, serial range 10,400-12,000.

N/A	N/A	$11,500	$8,450	$6,800	$5,450	$4,500	$3,800	$3,200	$2,800	$2,500	$2,200

▲ *Type IV* — with Stagecoach holdup scene, rectangle cylinder slots, serial range 11,000-12,500.

N/A	N/A	$12,000	$9,000	$7,250	$5,900	$5,000	$4,250	$3,600	$3,250	$3,000	$2,750

▲ *Type V* — with Stagecoach holdup scene, rectangle cylinder slots and loading lever, serial range 11,600-15,500.

N/A	N/A	$11,000	$8,450	$6,800	$5,450	$4,500	$3,800	$3,200	$2,850	$2,550	$2,250

1849 POCKET MODEL — .31 cal., 5 or 6 shot, 3, 4, 5, and 6 in. octagon barrels, most with loading levers, blued metal with case hardened frame, lever and hammer, grip straps of brass (silver plated), or steel (silver plated or blued), stagecoach hold-up scene on cylinder, serial range 12,000 to 340,000. Mfg. 1850-1873.

▲ *First Type* — 4, 5, or 6 in. barrel, loading lever and small or large brass trigger guard.

N/A	N/A	$3,375	$2,625	$2,050	$1,650	$1,350	$1,000	$750	$600	$550	$475

▲ *Second Type* — 4, 5, or 6 in. barrel, loading lever and steel grip straps.

N/A	N/A	$4,075	$3,175	$2,450	$1,950	$1,650	$1,150	$850	$700	$650	$575

▲ *Wells Fargo Model* — 3 in. barrel, without loading lever and with small round trigger guard.

N/A	N/A	$10,750	$7,650	$5,350	$3,750	$2,650	$2,000	$1,700	$1,525	$1,375	$1,150

1849 LONDON POCKET MODEL — London pistols were of the same general configuration, but of better finish, serial range 1-11,000. Mfg. 1853-1857.

▲ *Early Type* — serial numbered under 1500, with small trigger guard and brass grip straps.

N/A	N/A	$5,450	$4,450	$3,650	$2,950	$2,350	$1,850	$1,450	$1,150	$1,000	$875

▲ *Late Type* — oval trigger guard and steel grip straps.

N/A	N/A	$3,500	$2,750	$2,250	$1,850	$1,475	$1,175	$950	$825	$725	$625

1851 NAVY — .36 cal., 6 shot, 7½ in. octagon barrel and loading lever, blued metal with casehardened frame, lever and hammer, one piece walnut finished grips, cylinder scene of Texas Navy battle with Mexico, serial range 1-highest recorded number was 215,348, three barrel addresses 1-74,000 (ADDRESS SAM COLT, NEW YORK CITY), 74,000-101,000 (ADDRESS SAM COLT, HARTFORD, CT.) 101,000-215,348 (ADDRESS COL. SAM COLT, NEW YORK, U.S. AMERICA). Mfg. 1850-1873.

100%	98%	95%	90%	80%	70%	60%	50%	40%	30%	20%	10%

▲ **First Model** — square back trigger guard, bottom wedge screw, serial range 1-1,250.

| N/A | N/A | $19,500 | $16,000 | $13,000 | $10,500 | $8,500 | $7,000 | $5,750 | $4,750 | $4,000 | $3,250 |

▲ **Second Model** — square back trigger guard, top wedge screw, serial range 1,250-4,000.

| N/A | N/A | $14,000 | $9,750 | $7,700 | $6,450 | $5,450 | $4,600 | $3,900 | $3,300 | $2,800 | $2,300 |

▲ **Third Model** — small round brass trigger guard, serial range 4,200-85,000.

| N/A | N/A | $6,600 | $5,250 | $4,100 | $3,400 | $2,800 | $2,300 | $1,900 | $1,550 | $1,250 | $995 |

▲ **Fourth Model** — large round brass trigger guard, serial range 85,000-215,348.

| N/A | N/A | $5,875 | $4,775 | $3,975 | $3,175 | $2,600 | $2,125 | $1,750 | $1,425 | $1,175 | $900 |

▲ **Iron Gripstrap Model** — most often seen in fourth model.

| N/A | N/A | $7,400 | $6,000 | $4,925 | $4,175 | $3,425 | $2,750 | $2,200 | $1,750 | $1,425 | $1,125 |

▲ **Martially Marked U.S. Navies** — brass or iron gripstrap.

| N/A | N/A | $10,750 | $7,500 | $6,000 | $4,750 | $3,750 | $2,900 | $2,325 | $1,875 | $1,500 | $1,200 |

▲ **Cut for shoulder stock** — first and second type (like third model Dragoon)

| N/A | N/A | $13,500 | $9,000 | $7,000 | $5,500 | $4,500 | $3,750 | $3,000 | $2,450 | $1,950 | $1,475 |

▲ **Third Type** — four screw frame.

| N/A | N/A | $8,650 | $7,250 | $6,000 | $4,850 | $3,850 | $3,100 | $2,500 | $2,000 | $1,650 | $1,325 |

51 NAVY LONDON MODEL — basically the same gun as the Hartford piece with London barrel address, with British proof marks in serial range 1-42,000. Mfg. 1853-1857.

▲ **Early First Model** — serial range below 2000, brass grip straps and small trigger guard.

| N/A | N/A | $7,500 | $6,000 | $5,025 | $4,225 | $3,475 | $2,800 | $2,250 | $1,800 | $1,475 | $1,175 |

▲ **Late Second Model** — balance of production, large round trigger guard, steel grip straps, all London parts.

| N/A | N/A | $6,925 | $5,625 | $4,725 | $3,975 | $3,275 | $2,575 | $2,000 | $1,650 | $1,375 | $1,100 |

1855 SIDEHAMMER POCKET MODEL (ROOT MODEL) — .28 cal., had 3½ in. octagon barrel, .31 cal. usually had 3½ in. or 4½ in. round barrel. Blued with case hardened lever and hammer, one piece wraparound style walnut grips.

Commonly called the "Root" Model by collectors, manufactured 1855 through 1870. The .28 cal. model serial numbered 1 through approx. 30,000. The .31 cal. round barrel model serial numbered 1 through approx. 14,000. Total production approx. 44,000.

Easily recognizable by its side mounted hammer and cylinder rotation ratchet at rear of frame.

▲ **Model 1 and 1A** — 3$\frac{7}{16}$ in. octagonal bbl., oct. load lever, .28 cal., Indian/cabin cyl. scene, Hartford barrel address. Serial range 1 to 384.

| N/A | N/A | $5,000 | $3,250 | $2,700 | $2,325 | $2,075 | $1,825 | $1,700 | $1,500 | $1,300 | $1,025 |

▲ **Model 2** — 3½ in. oct. bbl., .28 cal., Indian/cabin cyl. scene, Hartford barrel address with pointed hand. Serial range 476 to 25,000.

| N/A | N/A | $2,150 | $1,290 | $1,040 | $890 | $765 | $665 | $595 | $535 | $485 | $425 |

▲ **Model 3** — 3½ in. oct. bbl., .28 cal., full fluted cylinder, Hartford barrel address with pointed hand. Serial range 25,001 to 30,000.

| N/A | N/A | $2,175 | $1,355 | $1,105 | $955 | $830 | $730 | $650 | $585 | $535 | $485 |

▲ **Model 3A** — 3½ in. oct. bbl., .31 cal., full fluted cylinder, Hartford barrel address. Serial range 1 to 1,350.

| N/A | N/A | $2,200 | $1,250 | $1,100 | $975 | $875 | $775 | $675 | $595 | $535 | $485 |

▲ **Model 4** — 3½ in. oct. bbl., .31 cal., full fluted cylinder, Hartford barrel address. Serial range 1,351 to 2,400.

| N/A | N/A | $2,200 | $1,250 | $1,100 | $975 | $875 | $775 | $675 | $595 | $535 | $485 |

▲ **Model 5** — 3½ in. round bbl., .31 cal., full fluted cylinder, "COL. COLT NEW-YORK" barrel address. Serial range 2,401 to 8,000.

| N/A | N/A | $2,200 | $1,250 | $1,100 | $975 | $875 | $775 | $675 | $595 | $535 | $485 |

100%	98%	95%	90%	80%	70%	60%	50%	40%	30%	20%	10%

▲ *Model 5A* — 4½ in. round bbl., .31 cal., included in same serial range as Model 5.

N/A	N/A	$3,500	$2,100	$1,750	$1,350	$1,200	$1,075	$975	$875	$775	$695

▲ *Model 6* — 3½ in. round bbl., .31 cal., stage coach hold-up cylinder scene, "COL. COLT NEW-YORK" barrel address. Serial range 8,001 through 11,074.

N/A	N/A	$2,200	$1,250	$1,100	$975	$875	$775	$675	$595	$535	$485

▲ *Model 6A* — 4½ in. round bbl., .31 cal., included in same serial range as Model 6.

N/A	N/A	$2,200	$1,250	$1,100	$975	$875	$775	$675	$595	$535	$485

▲ *Model 7* — 3½ in. round bbl., .31 cal., stage coach hold-up cylinder scene, "COL. COLT NEW-YORK" barrel address. Cylinder pin retained by screw-in cylinder. Serial range 11,075 through 14,000.

N/A	N/A	$3,200	$1,750	$1,350	$1,200	$1,100	$995	$900	$800	$725	$650

▲ *Model 7A* — 4½ in. round bbl., including same cylinder scene, barrel address and serial range as Model 7.

N/A	N/A	$3,500	$1,750	$1,375	$1,250	$1,150	$1,025	$925	$825	$750	$675

1860 MODEL ARMY — .44 cal., 6 shot, 7½ and 8 in. round barrels with loading lever, blued metal with case hardened frame, lever and hammer, one piece walnut grips, normally blued steel back strap and brass trigger guard, barrel markings were (ADDRESS SAM COLT, HARTFORD, CT.) on early productions and (ADDRESS COL. SAM COLT, NEW YORK, U.S. AMERICA) on balance, serial range 1-about 200,500, Texas Navy scene on round cylinder model. Mfg. 1860-1873.

▲ *Fluted Cylinder Model* — Fluted Cylinder Model, full length cylinder flutes and no cylinder scene, 7½ or 8 in. barrel, grips of Navy (very rare) or Army size, usually 4 screw frames.

N/A	N/A	$13,000	$9,900	$7,750	$6,450	$5,400	$4,550	$3,850	$3,250	$2,750	$2,350

▲ *Round Cylinder Model* — roll engraved Texas Navy scene, some with early Hartford address, Army grips, four screw frame to about 50,000 range, most were sold to the U.S. Government and will be martially marked.

N/A	N/A	$9,700	$7,250	$6,000	$4,850	$3,850	$3,100	$2,500	$2,000	$1,650	$1,375

▲ *Civilian Model* — same general configurations as Round Cylinder Model, but with 3 screw frame, no shoulder stock cuts and better blue finish than military pieces, late New York barrel address.

N/A	N/A	$9,500	$6,625	$5,375	$4,375	$3,525	$2,825	$2,275	$1,850	$1,500	$1,225

1861 MODEL NAVY — .36 cal., 6 shot, 7½ in. round barrel with loading lever, blued metal with case hardened frame, lever and hammer, silver plated brass grip straps, the barrel address was (ADDRESS COL. SAM COLT, NEW YORK, U.S. AMERICA), serial range 1 - 38,843, cylinder scene of Texas Navy and Mexico Battle, mfg. 1861-1873.

▲ *Fluted Cylinder Navy* — in serial range 1-100, with fluted cylinder and without rolled cylinder scene.

N/A	N/A	$26,750	$19,750	$16,250	$13,250	$10,750	$8,750	$7,250	$6,250	$5,550	$4,875

▲ *Regular production model*

N/A	N/A	$9,500	$7,000	$5,750	$4,600	$3,700	$3,000	$2,450	$2,000	$1,650	$1,375

▲ *Martially Marked Navies* — will bear the U.S. stamp and inspector's marks, those marked U.S.N. on butt were of a 650 piece order for the Navy.

N/A	N/A	$12,500	$8,600	$6,600	$4,950	$4,050	$3,350	$2,775	$2,300	$1,900	$1,550

▲ *London Marked Navy* — with (ADDRESS COL. COLT, LONDON), for barrel address.

N/A	N/A	$9,450	$7,525	$5,925	$4,775	$3,900	$3,225	$2,675	$2,225	$1,850	$1,475

▲ *Shoulder Stock Cut Navy* — 4 screw frames in serial range 11,000-14,000, made for third style stock (see Dragoon stocks).

N/A	N/A	$16,500	$10,500	$8,000	$6,500	$5,500	$4,650	$3,950	$3,350	$2,850	$2,375

100%	98%	95%	90%	80%	70%	60%	50%	40%	30%	20%	10%

1862 POLICE MODEL — .36 cal., 5 shot half fluted and rebated cylinder, 4½, 5½, and 6½ in. round barrels (also 3½ in. bbl. but quite rare) and loading lever. Mfg. 1861 to 1873. Serial numbered with Model 1862 Pocket Navy, approx. 28,000 1862 Police Models were produced. Blued with case hardened frame, lever and hammer, grip straps silver plated, one piece walnut grips. Serial range 1 through approx. 47,000. Standard barrel marking "ADDRESS COL. SAML COLT NEW-YORK U.S. AMERICA". "COLTS/PATENT" on left side of frame, "PAT SEPT. 10TH 1850" stamped in cyl. flute.

Many models 1862 Police and 1862 Pocket Navy revolvers were converted to cartridge with the advent of the metallic cartridge. Consequently these models in their original cap and ball chambering are quite desirable to collectors.

▲ *Early Model* — "ADDRESS SAM COLT/HARTFORD CT" barrel address, silvered iron grip straps.

| N/A | N/A | $9,700 | $6,500 | $5,100 | $4,250 | $3,450 | $2,750 | $2,200 | $1,750 | $1,375 | $1,075 |

▲ *Early Model* — same but silvered brass grip straps.

| N/A | N/A | $9,000 | $6,150 | $4,750 | $3,850 | $3,000 | $2,300 | $1,875 | $1,535 | $1,235 | $1,000 |

▲ *Standard Production Model* — with New York barrel address.

| N/A | N/A | $8,000 | $4,200 | $3,100 | $2,400 | $1,975 | $1,675 | $1,400 | $1,175 | $925 | $775 |

▲ *Export Production Model* — with "L" below serial numbers (for export to England), steel grip straps. Most often but not always bearing British proofs.

| N/A | N/A | $8,500 | $4,470 | $3,320 | $2,585 | $2,135 | $1,810 | $1,525 | $1,275 | $1,050 | $875 |

▲ *London Marked Model* — similar to above, except with "ADDRESS, COL. COLT/LONDON" address on barrel.

| N/A | N/A | $11,500 | $8,500 | $6,500 | $5,100 | $4,050 | $3,250 | $2,750 | $2,400 | $2,150 | $1,800 |

1862 POCKET MODEL NAVY — .36 cal., 5 shot rebated cylinder, 4½ in., 5½ in., and 6½ in. octagonal barrels with loading lever. Mfg. 1861 to 1873. Serial numbered with Model 1862 Police Model, approx. 19,000 Model 1862 Pocket Navy Revolvers produced. Blued with case hardened frame, lever and hammer, grip straps silver plated brass, one piece walnut grips. Serial range 1 through approx. 47,000. Standard barrel markings "ADDRESS COL. SAML COLT NEW-YORK U.S. AMERICA". "COLTS/ PATENT" on left side of frame, stage coach hold-up scene on cylinder.

Known to collectors for many years as the Model 1853, this model has finally been correctly identified through diligent combing of factory ledgers

Because of being produced during the advent of the metallic cartridge, the number remaining in the original cap and ball state is rather few; scarce with any serial number, but particularly so in numbers over approx. 19,800.

▲ *Standard Model* — 4½, 5½ and 6½ barrel lengths.

| N/A | N/A | $8,500 | $6,175 | $4,775 | $3,850 | $3,000 | $2,300 | $1,875 | $1,535 | $1,235 | $1,000 |

▲ *Export Production Model* — with "L" below serial numbers (for export to England), steel grip straps. Often found with British proofs.

| N/A | N/A | $9,000 | $7,500 | $6,000 | $4,750 | $3,775 | $3,025 | $2,475 | $2,000 | $1,650 | $1,375 |

▲ *London Marked Model* — similar to above but "ADDRESS COL. COLT/LONDON" address on barrel.

| N/A | N/A | $14,175 | $10,650 | $8,250 | $6,550 | $5,500 | $4,650 | $3,950 | $3,350 | $2,850 | $2,375 |

2ND GENERATION BLACK POWDER SERIES

Please refer to this heading under Colt's Firearms in the Modern Black Powder section in the back of this book for current information and values on this 2nd Generation Colt Black Powder Series (including serialization).

DERRINGERS

FIRST MODEL DERRINGER — .41 rimfire, single shot, 2½ in. barrel, scroll engraving standard, blued, nickel, or silver plated barrel, downward pivoting barrel, no grips, serial numbered 1-6,500. Mfg. approx. 1870-1890.

| $3,100 | $2,350 | $2,050 | $1,825 | $1,625 | $1,425 | $1,250 | $1,075 | $875 | $750 | $675 | $650 |

100%	98%	95%	90%	80%	70%	60%	50%	40%	30%	20%	10%

SECOND MODEL DERRINGER — .41 rimfire or centerfire, single shot, 2½ in. barrel, scroll engraving standard, blued, nickel, or silver plated barrel, downward pivoting barrel, checkered and varnished walnut grips, "No 2" marked on top of barrel, serial numbered 1-9,000. Mfg. approx. 1870-1890.

100%	98%	95%	90%	80%	70%	60%	50%	40%	30%	20%	10%
$1,650	$1,400	$1,200	$1,060	$935	$835	$730	$630	$585	$535	$500	$475

.41 Centerfire — add 100%.

THIRD MODEL DERRINGER (THUER MODEL) — .41 rimfire or centerfire (rare), single shot, side pivoting 2½ in. barrel, varnished walnut grips, blued barrels, bronze frames were either nickel or silver plated, engraving optional, Colt-barrel address, spur trigger, serial numbered approx. 1-45,000. Mfg. approx. 1875-1910.

100%	98%	95%	90%	80%	70%	60%	50%	40%	30%	20%	10%
$1,400	$1,200	$890	$790	$700	$620	$550	$495	$450	$415	$385	$360

.41 centerfire is worth an additional 30-50% and early models are worth considerably more.

Grading	100%	98%	95%

FOURTH MODEL DERRINGER — .22 Short, single shot similar in appearance to the 3rd Model, 2½ in. barrel, approx. 112,000 mfg. between 1959-1963 with either D or N suffix. A few were put in books, picture frames, penholders, bookends, etc. (these will command premiums).

	100%	98%	95%
	$100	$85	$65

LORD DERRINGER — .22 Short only, side pivoting Thuer action, gold plated with black chrome barrel and walnut grips. Mfg. approx. 1959-1963 by Colt, cased.

	100%	98%	95%
	$175	$140	$100

LADY DERRINGER — .22 Short only, side pivoting Thuer action, full gold plated finish with pearlite grips. Mfg. approx. 1959-1963 by Colt, cased.

	100%	98%	95%
	$175	$140	$100

LORD & LADY CASED SET — one each of the Lord & Lady derringers or combinations, consecutive serial numbers.

	100%	98%	95%
	$350	$275	$200

LADY CASED SET — cased pair of Lady Derringers.

	100%	98%	95%
	$350	$275	$200

LORD CASED SET — cased pair of Lord Derringers.

	100%	98%	95%
	$350	$275	$200

BOOKCASE DERRINGER PAIR — includes consecutively numbered .22 Short derringers with synthetic ivory grips and nickel finish, cased inside unique hard cover "Colt Derringers" labeled book with red velvet lining, limited mfg. in early '60s.

	100%	98%	95%
	$350	$275	$200

POCKET PISTOLS

If possible, it is advisable to procure a factory letter before buying/selling this variation (open top only). These water marked letters are available by writing Colt Firearms in Hartford, CT, with a charge of $100 per serial number (if they can research it). Include your name and address, Colt model name, serial number, and check to: COLT HISTORIAN, P.O. Box 1868, Hartford, CT 06101. Please allow 4-6 weeks for a response.

100%	98%	95%	90%	80%	70%	60%	50%	40%	30%	20%	10%

CLOVERLEAF HOUSE PISTOL — .41 Short or long rimfire, cloverleaf configured 4 shot cylinder, spur trigger, $1\frac{1}{2}$ or 3 in. barrel, approx. 7,500 mfg. in ser. no. range 1-8,300 during 1871-1876.

$2,150	$1,750	$1,510	$1,310	$1,160	$1,030	$915	$815	$730	$660	$610	$575

This model is sometimes referred to as the Jim Fisk model as he was murdered by Edward Stokes with a Cloverleaf.

Add 80% for $1\frac{1}{2}$ in. barrel.

▲ **5-shot Cloverleaf** — similar to 4-shot model, except has round 5-shot cylinder and $2\frac{5}{8}$ in. barrel only, approx. 2,500 mfg. in ser. no. range 6,160-9,950 during 1871-1876.

$1,825	$1,480	$1,260	$1,085	$940	$820	$720	$640	$580	$535	$500	$475

OPEN TOP REVOLVER (OLD LINE) — .22 Short or long rimfire, $2\frac{3}{8}$ or $2\frac{7}{8}$ in. barrel, without topstrap on frame, with or without integral ejector, blued or nickel plated, varnished walnut grips, approx. 114,200 mfg. 1871-1877.

$1,175	$1,000	$900	$825	$750	$700	$600	$550	$450	$375	$325	$275

Add 120% for Early Model with ejector and high hammer spur.

NEW LINE REVOLVER AND VARIATIONS

If possible, it is advisable to procure a factory letter before buying/selling New Line Revolvers. These water marked letters are available by writing Colt Firearms in Hartford, CT, with a charge of $100 per serial number (if they can research it). Include your name and address, Colt model name, serial number, and check to: COLT HISTORIAN, P.O. Box 1868, Hartford, CT 06101. Please allow 4-6 weeks for a response.

1ST MODEL — .22, .30, .32, .38, or .41 cal. rim and centerfire, mfg. 1873-1876, 7 (.22 cal. only) or 5 shot, short cylinder flutes, cylinder stop slots cut on exterior of cylinder, $1\frac{3}{4}$, $2\frac{1}{4}$, or 4 in. barrel, full nickel or blue/case hardened finish, spur trigger, many thousands mfg. 1873-1884.

$1,150	$990	$875	$810	$740	$685	$580	$540	$425	$355	$300	$250

2ND MODEL — similar to 1st Model, except has longer cylinder flutes and cylinder stop slots are on the back of cylinder, may or may not have loading gate. Mfg. 1876-1884.

$1,050	$935	$845	$775	$705	$645	$540	$500	$390	$320	$270	$235

Caliber rarity on both models from highest mfg. to lowest is: .22, .32, .30, .41, and .38.

NEW HOUSE MODEL — .38 or .41 cal. centerfire, 5 shot, $2\frac{1}{4}$ in. barrel, spur trigger, checkered hard rubber grips. Approx. 4,000 mfg. 1880-1886 starting at ser. no. 10,300.

$1,375	$1,075	$950	$850	$760	$675	$600	$485	$425	$360	$325	$310

NEW POLICE MODEL — .32, .38, or .41 cal. centerfire, 5 shot, $2\frac{1}{4}$, $4\frac{1}{2}$, 5, or 6 in. barrel, spur trigger, with or without ejector, stamped or etched "NEW POLICE" on barrel. Approx. 4,000 mfg. 1882-1886.

$1,675	$1,425	$1,225	$1,050	$900	$785	$700	$635	$585	$550	$520	$495

PERCUSSION CONVERSIONS

Research is currently underway to categorize the many variations (including Thuer) that exist on Percussion revolvers which were converted for centerfire capability. Over 46,000 conversions were made on the following models listed in order of highest mfg. to lowest: 1862 Police and Pocket Navy, Model 1860 Army Richards, Thuer's patent conversions, Model 1851 Navy, Model 1861 Navy, Model 1860 Army Richards-Mason. Out of these, the Models 1862 Police and Pocket Navy accounted for slightly over 50%. Be wary of "2nd" generation alterations. Prices generally are in the $650-$2,500+ range with rarer variations selling for considerably more. Cased models will command 175-300%+ premiums.

"OPEN TOP" REVOLVERS

If possible, it is advisable to procure a factory letter before buying/selling this Open Top Revolver. These water marked letters are available by writing Colt Firearms in Hartford, CT, with a charge of $100 per serial number (if they can research it).

100%	98%	95%	90%	80%	70%	60%	50%	40%	30%	20%	10%

Include your name and address, Colt model name, serial number, and check to: COLT HISTORIAN, P.O. Box 1868, Hartford, CT 06101. Please allow 4-6 weeks for a response.

1871-72 OPEN TOP MODEL RIMFIRE — .44 cal. rimfire, 6 shot, 7½ in. barrel, without frame topstrap, blued metal with casehardened hammer, serial range 1-approx. 7000, barrel address (ADDRESS COL. SAM COLT, NEW YORK, U.S. AMERICA), forerunner of the single action Army, quite desirable. Mfg. 1871-1872.

▲ *Regular Production Model* — 7½ in. barrel, New York address, Navy grips.

100%	98%	95%	90%	80%	70%	60%	50%	40%	30%	20%	10%
N/A	N/A	$27,500	$22,750	$18,500	$15,000	$12,750	$8,750	$6,750	$6,000	$5,300	$4,850

▲ *Regular Production* — with Army grips.

100%	98%	95%	90%	80%	70%	60%	50%	40%	30%	20%	10%
N/A	N/A	$24,000	$18,750	$15,000	$12,500	$10,250	$7,000	$5,750	$5,000	$4,450	$4,250

▲ *Late Production* — with address (COLT PT. F. A. MANUFACTURING CO., HARTFORD, CT., U.S.A.).

100%	98%	95%	90%	80%	70%	60%	50%	40%	30%	20%	10%
N/A	N/A	$21,000	$16,000	$13,000	$10,750	$7,500	$6,000	$5,200	$4,650	$4,150	$3,700

Add 40% for models with 8 in. barrel or COLTS/PATENT frame markings.

REVOLVERS: SAA - 1873-1940 MFG. (SER. NO.'S 1 - 357,000)

Note: The Colt SAA (Single Action Army) was produced in 36 calibers with just about any special order feature or combination of special orders available directly from the factory. All of these special orders act independently and interdependently to determine a correct value for a particular Colt SAA. Single action Colt's rank at the top for revolver collectors. When contemplating a purchase in the 4 digit plus price range, several professional opinions should be secured. Caliber rarities make a major difference in pricing single actions.

It is advisable to procure a factory letter when buying or selling older or recently manufactured Colt Single Actions (hence guaranteeing authenticity and value credibility). These watermarked letters are available by writing Colt Firearms in Hartford, CT, with a charge of $55 per serial number - if Colt cannot provide you with proper documentation after conducting research, they will refund you $10. The charge is $100 per custom engraved gun ($45 for standard engraved gun) - see the Trademark Index for the address. Include your name and address, Colt model name, serial number, and check to: COLT HISTORIAN, P.O. BOX 1868, HARTFORD, CT 06144. Please allow 12-15 weeks for proper response. In addition, phone service SAA configuration validation is also provided on a premium basis on first generation SAAs ONLY through serial number 343,000 to assist in possible purchases of a critical nature. The phone number is 203-236-6311 and ask for the Historical Dept. between the hours of 1-4 P.M. EST.

Values shown below are for guns without special order features. Factory engraving, ivory grips, very rare special order barrel lengths, and special finishes would add considerably to the values shown below. One final word on single action Colts: Black Powder Colts (pre 165,000 serial range) should be scrutinized carefully for restamped serial numbers on various parts. This makes a major difference in pricing the SAA, as a true, original collector's gun differs greatly in value from a restamped "parts gun". .44-40 and .45 cals. in the pre 165,000 serial range will bring premiums over other calibers, especially in shorter barrel lengths. The .44-40 caliber is very collectible since this ammunition at inception was interchangeable with the most popular rifle/carbine of its era - the Winchester Model 1873.

EARLY MODEL SAA (PINCH FRAME) — serial range 1 - approx.160, with frame pinched to make rear sight, .45 cal., 7½ in. barrel. Mfg. 1873.

100%	98%	95%	90%	80%	70%	60%	50%	40%	30%	20%	10%
N/A	N/A	$59,500	$45,000	$30,000	$25,000	$20,000	$17,500	$15,500	$13,500	$11,500	$10,500

Watch for fakes! In this variation there are more counterfeits than original specimens.

100%	98%	95%	90%	80%	70%	60%	50%	40%	30%	20%	10%

C

MARTIALLY MARKED "U.S." SINGLE ACTION — The primary sidearm of US military forces between 1873 and 1892. Carried by all commissioned officers and mounted soldiers. Sometimes called "Cavalry Model," but issued to all branches of service. A total of 37,063 were purchased by the government at an average cost of $12.50. Specifications called for 7½ in. barrel, .45 LC cal., blue and color case hardened finish, one-piece, oil finished walnut grips. Each gun was stamped with the initials of a government inspector and with the letters "US" at the Colt plant before being approved for delivery to the National Armory at Springfield, MA.

N/A	$20,000	$18,000	$15,000	$12,000	$10,000	$8,000	$6,500	$5,750	$5,000	$4,250	$3,500

Early examples with low serial numbers and desirable inspector markings will command premiums over prices listed above. Specimens found within the "prime" Custer serial range 4,507-6,559 command high premiums - watch for fakes! Also, beware of restorations, many done in the last twenty years, in all inspector serial ranges, some of which have been skillfully "aged" to look more original. In many cases, only the serial number itself is original, the entire gun being newly fabricated. Ask for guarantee of authentication in writing, not just factory historical information.

.22 RIMFIRE SAA — .22 LR cal.

▲ *Conversion (converted from .44 cal.)*

N/A	N/A	$16,500	$12,000	$9,000	$8,000	$7,000	$6,500	$5,500	$4,500	$4,000	$3,500

▲ *Original Mfg.*

N/A	N/A	$18,000	$15,250	$13,350	$10,750	$8,725	$7,175	$6,025	$5,150	$4,475	$3,950

.44 RIMFIRE SAA — mostly in .44 Henry rimfire, 7½ in. barrel, serial numbered in own range 1-1863, mfg. 1875-1880, most specimens were shipped to Mexico and saw hard use, rare in any original condition.

N/A	N/A	$30,000	$25,000	$20,000	$17,500	$14,000	$12,000	$10,000	$8,500	$7,000	$6,000

This variation is one of the most frequently faked Colt revolvers — be careful (and get a receipt and a letter of authentication).

SINGLE ACTION ARMY (SAA) — standard commercial mfg. 1873-1940, single action, 6 shot revolver, over 30 cals., 4¾, 5½, or 7½ in. standard barrel lengths, blue with color case hardened frame or full nickel finish standard, one-piece walnut grip standard until 1884, when gutta percha (hard rubber) grips were introduced with eagle motif. Eagle-less grips standard after 1892. One piece wood available upon request until approximately 1903.

▲ *Early Civilian Mfg.* — blue and case hardened finish, italic (i.e. script) barrel address, serial range 1 to approx. 22,000 shared with early martial production 1873-1876 mfg.

N/A	$25,000	$22,500	$20,000	$16,500	$14,000	$12,000	$9,500	$7,000	$5,250	$4,000	$3,250

Subtract 40% for nickel finish.
Be wary of fake barrel addresses.

▲ *Later Civilian Mfg.* — blue and case hardened finish, black powder frames with vertical screw holding cylinder pin, serial range 22,000 - approx. 165,000, mfg. 1876-1896.

N/A	$22,000	$20,000	$17,000	$14,500	$12,000	$10,000	$8,500	$7,000	$5,000	$3,500	$2,500

Add 10% for one-piece varnished wood grips.
Add 35% for original box.
Subtract 30% for nickel finish.
Subtract 10% for plain rubber grips w/o eagle, approx. beginning serial range 143,000 in 1892.

▲ *Smokeless Powder Model* — transverse or horizontal cylinder pin latch, serial range 165,000 - 358,000, mfg. 1896-1940.

$9,000	$7,750	$6,500	$5,500	$4,500	$3,600	$2,850	$2,500	$2,250	$1,850	$1,550	$1,250

Add 30% for pre-1900 mfg.
Subtract 25% for post-1920 mfg.
Add 15% for .44-40 cal.
Subtract 25% for .32-20 cal.
Add 10% for nickel finish after 1920.
Add 30% for original box before 1920, add 20% after 1920.

It is interesting to note that while Colt began advertising their improved smokeless powder Single Action in 1896, they did not add the "VP" (verified proof) mark to the triggerguard, which is their guarantee against smokeless powder, until 1904, and that they continued

100%	98%	95%	90%	80%	70%	60%	50%	40%	30%	20%	10%

to use black powder rifling (wide grooves and narrow lands) and black powder front sights (small and low) until approximately 1910. And while they produced and sold more Single Actions in the ten years between 1899 and 1909 (serial range 200,000 - 300,000) than in any other ten year period of production, quality did not suffer.

The workmanship evident during this time was at least equal to, if not better, than before. Many collectors feel that the polish and finish work performed during the first part of the twentieth century was superior to any other period.

The date 1920 is significant to Single Action Colt collectors since that was the year the company completed changing the location of the serial numbers. Numbers on the triggerguard and backstrap were moved under the grips beginning in the 339,000 serial range (late 1919), leaving only the serial number on the frame visible, and bringing to a close the original numbering procedure which began with the percussion revolvers. Many collectors regard this as the end of the "Cowboy" period.

FACTORY ENGRAVED 1ST GENERATION SAAs — the sky is the limit here - the price range is approx. $2,500 on the low end with $250,000+ the high end (with a lot of price points between $7,500 - $25,000). The Colt Historical Department may be able to document factory engraving with a company letter.

NON-FACTORY ENGRAVED 1ST GENERATION SAAs — values of non-factory engraved SAAs are generally based upon the cost of duplication. In other words, the asking price should approximate the price of the SAA configuration (i.e., caliber, barrel length, finish, special order features, etc.), in addition to the cost of having it engraved and finished. Recognized quality by contemporary engravers may command a premium over this formula.

ARTILLERY MODEL SAA — .45 Colt, 5½ in. barrel, marked U.S. on left lower frame. With one piece walnut grips, and possibly a military cartouche. These guns are the original artillery model Colts returned to the factory or Springfield Armory. Barrels were shortened to 5½ in. and the guns were refinished and reissued to the military. Very seldom do the serial numbered parts on these guns match. Not all factory letters will indicate refurbishing as Colt did not do all of them. Mixed ser. numbers - 185-140,346.

$9,000	$7,500	$6,500	$5,750	$4,700	$3,850	$3,200	$2,750	$2,400	$2,100	$1,850	$1,650

NEW YORK STATE MILITIA SAA — in 1895, before work began on the artillery models, Colt refurbished 800 single action revolvers supplied by Springfield Armory to honor a request by the state of New York. These guns retained their 7.5 in. barrels and all original parts where possible, and were stamped on the bottom of the grip with the initials of Rinaldo A. Carr (RAC). They were given a bright, civilian finish and blued hammers. Since all other cavalry models in the government's possession were cut to 5.5 in. shortly thereafter, these 800 are quite possibly the only quantity of 7.5 in. guns remaining that could have actually seen service on the frontier. All others extant today were most likely originally issued at the time of manufacture to state militias rather than the United States Government military forces. These 800 revolvers, therefore, occupy a very significant position in the history of Colt firearms.

$15,000	$13,500	$12,000	$10,000	$9,000	$8,000	$7,000	$6,000	$5,000	$4,000	$3,000	$2,000

ETCHED BARREL .44-40 SAA — Colt Frontier, "Colt Frontier Six Shooter" acid etched into barrel instead of stamped, 45,000-128,000 ser. no. range.

N/A	$22,000	$20,000	$12,500	$9,500	$7,500	$6,500	$6,000	$5,500	$5,000	$4,000	$3,500

This variation was only mfg. from 1878-1890. Watch for fake, replaced, or re-etched barrels.

SHERIFF'S MODEL SAA — 2½ (rare), 3, 4, 4¾ (rare), or 7½ (rare) in. barrel, without ejector housing, this model's most distinguishable feature is the lack of an ejector housing. Mfg. stopped 1927. Watch For Fakes.

N/A	$17,500	$15,350	$13,600	$12,000	$10,400	$8,900	$7,400	$6,000	$4,950	$4,250	$3,750

Add 50% for black powder frame.

Fakes can be detected on this model by re-welded frames. While 2½, 4¾, or 7½ in. barrels in this variation do exist, be careful, get a second opinion, and ask for a receipt.

100%	98%	95%	90%	80%	70%	60%	50%	40%	30%	20%	10%

FLAT-TOP TARGET SAA — various calibers from .22 to .476 Eley, approx. 925 mfg., 1888-1896.

N/A	$15,000	$13,625	$11,900	$10,450	$9,000	$7,750	$6,500	$5,400	$4,550	$4,000	$3,800

Note: Different calibers make a substantial difference in pricing for this model.

BISLEY MODEL SAA — differs from single action Army by hump backed grip frame and raked hammer, approx. 44,350 mfg., 1894-1915.

▲ **.455 Eley** — mfg. for the International Revolver contests held in Bisley, England.

$5,500	$5,000	$4,750	$4,150	$3,700	$3,300	$2,900	$2,525	$2,200	$1,925	$1,675	$1,450

▲ **.45 cal.**

$4,500	$4,025	$3,675	$3,325	$3,000	$2,675	$2,350	$2,025	$1,725	$1,500	$1,425	$1,200

▲ **.44-40 cal.**

$5,350	$4,650	$4,200	$3,750	$3,300	$2,850	$2,450	$2,125	$1,850	$1,625	$1,425	$1,250

▲ **.41 cal.**

$4,250	$3,750	$3,350	$3,000	$2,675	$2,375	$2,075	$1,800	$1,550	$1,325	$1,125	$975

▲ **.38-40 cal.**

$4,150	$3,650	$3,300	$2,950	$2,625	$2,350	$2,050	$1,775	$1,525	$1,300	$1,100	$950

▲ **.32-20 cal.**

$3,950	$3,450	$3,125	$2,800	$2,500	$2,225	$1,975	$1,750	$1,475	$1,250	$1,050	$900

BISLEY TARGET FLAT-TOP — flat top frame, removable target sights, 976 mfg., 1894-1913.

Values are 200% greater than respective Standard Bisley Models.

POST-WAR 1ST GENERATION SAA — approx. 860 manufactured in various configurations after 1945. These specimens in 98%+ condition will approximate values on the pre-war models. Ser. no. range 357,000-357,860. Prices may vary, but a NIB specimen would currently be in the $4,000 range.

2ND GENERATION SINGLE ACTION ARMY: 1956-1975 MFG.

Popular demand brought back the Single Action Army in 1956 with minor modifications, most not noticeable except to experts. Serial numbers began at 0001SA and continue to 73,000SA before the "New Model" was introduced in 1976 (ser. no. 80000 SA). Premiums are paid for rare production variances if NIB condition. It should be noted that many "premium niches" exist in this model as collectors are establishing premiums paid for rarer production variances (the inter-relation of barrel length, caliber, frame type, finish quality, year of manufacture, and other special features).

The order of desirability on standard 2nd generation SAAs is as follows: $4^3/_4$ in. barrels are the most desirable, followed by $7^1/_2$ in., and then $5^1/_2$ in. Caliber desirability is as follows: .45 LC has the most demand followed by .44 Spl., .38 Spl., and then .357 Mag. It follows that desirable calibers found with desirable barrel lengths will command healthy premiums — especially if production was unusually low in a particular combination. Reference books specifically on the post-war SAA are a must when determining the rarity factors (or if they exist) on these multiple production combinations. Buntlines, Sheriff's models, and special orders through the Custom Gun Shop are in a class by themselves and have to be evaluated one at a time.

It is advisable to procure a factory letter when buying or selling older or recently manufactured Colt Single Actions (hence guaranteeing authenticity and value credibility). These watermarked letters are available by writing Colt Firearms in Hartford, CT, with a charge of $45 per serial number - if Colt cannot provide you with proper documentation after conducting research, they will refund you $10. Include your name and address, Colt model name, serial number, and check to: COLT HISTORIAN, P.O. BOX 1868, HARTFORD, CT 06144. Please allow adequate time for proper response.

Grading	100%	98%	95%	90%	80%	70%	60%

SINGLE ACTION ARMY — SA suffix, .357 Mag., .38 Special, .44 Special., or .45 LC cal., 3 (Sheriff's Model), 4¾, 5½, 7½, or 12 in. (Buntline) barrel lengths, all blue, blue/case hardened, or nickel finishes, hard rubber stocks (standard until 1970).

Because SAAs are a complex field in themselves, values below have been separated by calibers first, barrel lengths second, and finishes third (CH designates color case hardening).

▲ .357 Mag. cal.

	100%	98%	95%	90%	80%	70%	60%
4¾ in. CH frame	$1,800	$1,600	$1,325	$995	$825	$695	$625
5½ in. CH frame	$1,425	$1,200	$995	$850	$725	$595	$550
7½ in. CH frame	$1,700	$1,400	$1,100	$895	$775	$650	$575
4¾ in. Blue frame	$1,700	$1,400	$1,100	$895	$775	$650	$575
5½ in. Blue frame	$1,700	$1,400	$1,100	$895	$775	$650	$575
4¾ in. Nickel	$1,875	$1,625	$1,340	$1,025	$850	$725	$650
5½ in. Nickel	$1,775	$1,450	$1,125	$900	$775	$650	$575
7½ in. Nickel	$1,825	$1,600	$1,325	$995	$825	$695	$625

▲ .38 Spl. cal.

	100%	98%	95%	90%	80%	70%	60%
4¾ in. CH frame	$2,195	$1,825	$1,550	$1,250	$950	$825	$695
5½ in. CH frame	$1,695	$1,425	$1,200	$995	$850	$725	$595
7½ in. CH frame	$1,995	$1,700	$1,400	$1,100	$895	$775	$650
5½ in. Blue frame	$1,995	$1,700	$1,400	$1,100	$895	$775	$650
4¾ in. Nickel	$2,395	$1,950	$1,650	$1,325	$1,025	$895	$775
5½ in. Nickel	$2,395	$1,950	$1,650	$1,325	$1,025	$895	$775
7½ in. Nickel	$2,395	$1,950	$1,650	$1,325	$1,025	$895	$775

▲ .44 Spl. cal.

	100%	98%	95%	90%	80%	70%	60%
5½ in. CH frame	$1,850	$1,550	$1,300	$1,050	$875	$750	$625
7½ in. CH frame	$1,850	$1,550	$1,300	$1,050	$875	$750	$625
5½ in. Blue frame	$1,850	$1,550	$1,300	$1,050	$875	$750	$625
7½ in. Blue frame	$1,850	$1,550	$1,300	$1,050	$875	$750	$625
5½ in. Nickel	$2,395	$1,950	$1,650	$1,325	$1,025	$895	$775
7½ in. Nickel	$2,995	$2,550	$2,100	$1,775	$1,425	$1,100	$900

▲ .45 LC cal.

	100%	98%	95%	90%	80%	70%	60%
4¾ in. CH frame	$2,250	$1,850	$1,575	$1,250	$950	$825	$695
5½ in. CH frame	$1,850	$1,550	$1,300	$1,050	$875	$750	$625
7½ in. CH frame	$1,850	$1,550	$1,300	$1,050	$875	$750	$625
4¾ in. Blue frame	$1,650	$1,400	$1,200	$995	$850	$725	$595
5½ in. Blue frame	$1,650	$1,400	$1,200	$995	$850	$725	$595
7½ in. Blue frame	$1,650	$1,400	$1,200	$995	$850	$725	$595
4¾ in. Nickel	$2,250	$1,850	$1,575	$1,250	$950	$825	$695
5½ in. Nickel	$1,850	$1,550	$1,300	$1,050	$875	$750	$625
7½ in. Nickel	$1,850	$1,550	$1,300	$1,050	$875	$750	$625

Add $300+ for original ivory grips.
Add $200 for those pistols with original "black box".
100% assumes NIB condition for this model.

Earlier 2nd generations with the Rampant Colt grips (serial numbered under 50,000 approx.) are a little more desirable than those SAAs with Eagle grips (serial numbered over 50,000 approx.).

Early 2nd generation SAAs in 98%+ original condition with the black box (pre-1965) will command a premium over values listed above. "Stagecoach" boxes were used approx. 1965-1973 and are not quite as desirable as the one piece black box. Original "Stagecoach" boxes in excellent condition are currently selling for approx. $50.

Grading	100%	98%	95%	90%	80%	70%	60%

▲ **Sheriff's Model (1961 Model)** — SM suffix, .45 cal., 3 in. barrel without ejector rod housing, casehardened finish, many custom options were ordered in this variation. Approx. 500 mfg. 1961 for Centennial Arms (475 blue finish, 25 nickel finish).

	$2,150	$1,875	$1,375	$995	$800	$750	$695

Add 300% for nickel finish.
Add $200 for ivory grips.

▲ **Buntline Special** — .45 Colt only, 12 in. barrel, case hardened frame, hard rubber (rarer) or walnut grips. Over 3,900 mfg. between 1957-1975.

	$1,200	$1,000	$800	$700	$600	$575	$550

Add 50% for nickel finish (rare).

NEW FRONTIER — "NF" suffix, flat-top frame, adj. rear sight, .357 Mag., .38 Spl. (rare), .44 Spl., or .45 cal., 4¾ (rare), 5½ (rare) or 7½ (common) in. barrel, uncheckered walnut grips, case-hardened frame, over 4,200 mfg. 1961-1975.

	$950	$850	$675	$600	$550	$500	$475

Nickel or full-blue finish is very rare in this model as well as .38 Spl. in 5½ or 7½ in. barrel.

▲ **New Frontier Buntline Special** — .45 Colt only, 12 in. barrel, flat-top frame, adj. rear sight. Approx. 70 mfg. 1962-1967.

	$1,750	$1,450	$995	$850	$725	$600	$500

FACTORY ENGRAVED 2ND GENERATION SAAs — since approx. only 350 SAAs were factory engraved (with almost 90% being in .45 LC cal.), accurate pricing with this degree of rarity factor is difficult to ascertain with any degree of certainty. Prices overall will be at least 50% higher than their 3rd generation engraved counterparts. Post-war collectors and investors are picky on engraved SAAs. The rarity of the configuration in addition to the notoriety of the engraver (Albert Herbert and A.A. White are probably at the top) will make the difference on the premium(s) commanded. The Colt Historical Department may be able to document factory engraving with a company letter. The charge is $100 per engraved gun ($45 for non-engraved SAAs) - see the Trademark Index for the address.

Factory engraved 2nd generation SAAs are at least 10 times rarer than 3rd generation engraved pistols.

3RD GENERATION SINGLE ACTION ARMY: 1976-1992 MFG.

3rd model production began in 1976 with ser. no. 80000SA and reached no. 99999SA in 1978. At this point the SA suffix changed to a prefix (beginning with SA01001).

For a listing of Colt's "P-Codes" (referring to the factory's model number designations specifying caliber, finish, and barrel length), please refer to the "COLT SINGLE-ACTION MODEL NUMBERS" section in the back of this text.

The order of desirability on standard 3rd generation SAAs is as follows: 4¾ barrels are the most desirable, followed by 7½ in., and then 5½ in. Caliber desirability is as follows: .44-40 and .45 LC have the most demand followed by .44 Spl., .38 Spl., and then .357 Mag. It follows that desirable calibers found with desirable barrel lengths will command healthy premiums — especially if production was unusually low in a particular combination.

Reference books specifically on the post-war SAA are a must when determining the rarity factors (or if they exist) on these multiple production combinations. Buntlines, Sheriff's models, and special orders through the Custom Gun Shop are in a class by themselves and have to be evaluated one at a time.

Grading	100%	98%	95%	90%	80%	70%	60%

SINGLE ACTION ARMY — .357 Mag., .44 Spl., .44-40, or .45 LC cal., 3 (Sheriff's Model), 4¾, 5½, 7½, or 12 in. (Buntline) barrel lengths, all blue, blue/case hardened, or nickel finishes, walnut or rubber stocks.

It is advisable to procure a factory letter when buying or selling older or recently manufactured Colt Single Actions (hence guaranteeing authenticity and value credibility). These watermarked letters are available by writing Colt Firearms in Hartford, CT, with a charge of $45 per serial number - if Colt cannot provide you with proper documentation after conducting research, they will refund you $10. Include your name and address, Colt model name, serial number, and check to: COLT HISTORIAN, P.O. BOX 1868, HARTFORD, CT 06144. Please allow adequate time for proper response.

Because SAAs are a complex field in themselves, values below have been separated by calibers first, barrel lengths second, and finishes third (CH designates color case hardening).

▲ .357 Mag. cal.

	100%	98%	95%	90%	80%	70%	60%
4¾ in. CH frame	$850	$750	$695	$650	$600	$550	$495
5½ in. CH frame	$750	$650	$610	$575	$525	$495	$450
7½ in. CH frame	$750	$650	$610	$575	$525	$495	$450
4¾ in. Blue frame	$800	$700	$650	$620	$565	$525	$475
5½ in. Blue frame	$750	$650	$610	$575	$525	$495	$450
7½ in. Blue frame	$750	$650	$610	$575	$525	$495	$450
4¾ in. Nickel	$850	$750	$695	$650	$600	$550	$495
5½ in. Nickel	$750	$650	$610	$575	$525	$495	$450
7½ in. Nickel	$750	$650	$610	$575	$525	$495	$450

▲ .38 Spl. cal. — this cal. is hard to find in a 3rd Generation SAA.

	100%	98%	95%	90%	80%	70%	60%
4¾ in. CH frame (only 2 mfg.)	$1,495	$1,250	$1,050	$950	$825	$750	$675
5½ in. CH frame	$1,225	$1,050	$925	$825	$750	$695	$625
7½ in. CH frame	$1,225	$1,050	$925	$825	$750	$695	$625
4¾ in. Nickel	$1,425	$1,200	$1,050	$950	$825	$750	$675
5½ in. Nickel	$1,225	$1,050	$925	$825	$750	$695	$625
7½ in. Nickel	$1,225	$1,050	$925	$825	$750	$695	$625

▲ .44 Spl. cal.

	100%	98%	95%	90%	80%	70%	60%
4¾ in. CH frame	$850	$750	$695	$650	$600	$550	$495
5½ in. CH frame	$800	$700	$650	$620	$565	$525	$475
7½ in. CH frame	$750	$650	$610	$575	$525	$495	$450
4¾ in. Blue frame	$800	$700	$650	$620	$565	$525	$475
5½ in. Blue frame	$750	$650	$610	$575	$525	$495	$450
7½ in. Blue frame	$750	$650	$610	$575	$525	$495	$450
4¾ in. Nickel	$850	$750	$695	$650	$600	$550	$495
5½ in. Nickel	$800	$700	$650	$620	$565	$525	$475
7½ in. Nickel	$750	$650	$610	$575	$525	$495	$450

▲ .44-40 cal.

	100%	98%	95%	90%	80%	70%	60%
4¾ in. CH frame	$995	$895	$795	$725	$675	$595	$525
5½ in. CH frame	$995	$850	$750	$695	$650	$595	$525
7½ in. CH frame	$995	$850	$725	$675	$625	$575	$500
4¾ in. Blue frame	$950	$825	$750	$695	$650	$595	$525
5½ in. Blue frame	$895	$775	$695	$650	$600	$550	$495
7½ in. Blue frame	$895	$775	$695	$650	$600	$550	$495
4¾ in. Nickel	$995	$895	$795	$725	$675	$595	$525
5½ in. Nickel	$995	$850	$750	$695	$650	$595	$525
7½ in. Nickel	$950	$825	$725	$675	$625	$575	$500

Grading	100%	98%	95%	90%	80%	70%	60%
▲ *.45 LC*							
4¾ in. CH frame	$995	$895	$795	$725	$675	$595	$525
5½ in. CH frame	$995	$895	$800	$750	$695	$650	$575
7½ in. CH frame	$995	$895	$800	$750	$675	$625	$575
4¾ in. Blue frame	$995	$850	$750	$695	$650	$595	$525
5½ in. Blue frame	$895	$775	$695	$650	$600	$550	$495
7½ in. Blue frame	$895	$775	$695	$650	$600	$550	$495
4¾ in. Nickel	$995	$895	$795	$725	$675	$595	$525
5½ in. Nickel	$995	$895	$800	$750	$695	$650	$575
7½ in. Nickel	$995	$850	$725	$675	$625	$575	$500

Add $200 for ivory grips.
Add $100 for nickel finish.
100% assumes NIB condition for this model. Most of the buying/selling activity with 3rd Generation SAAs involves NIB specimens.

▲ *Buntline Special* — .45 Colt only, 12 in. barrel, case hardened frame.

	$795	$675	$625	$600	$575	$535	$500

Add 10% for nickel finish.

▲ *New Frontier* — "NF" suffix, flat-top frame, adj. rear sight, .44 Spl., .44-40 (rare), or .45 cal., 4¾ (rare), 5½ (rare) or 7½ (common) in. barrel, uncheckered walnut grips, case hardened frame. Mfg. 1978-1981.

	$795	$625	$475	$425	$410	$395	$380

3rd generation NF serialization can be differentiated from 2nd by 5 digits (starting with 0) followed by the NF suffix. 2nd generation guns had 4 digit numbers.

For factory engraved New Frontier Models, refer to above SAA engraved listing and subtract 25%

▲ *New Frontier Buntline Special* — .45 Colt only, 12 in. barrel, flat-top frame, adj. rear sight. Limited mfg.

	$825	$675	$500	$450	$415	$395	$380

▲ *Sheriff's Model* — .44-40 or .45 LC cal., 3 in. barrel without ejector rod housing, case hardened, nickel, or royal blue finish, approx. 4,560 guns mfg. 1980-85.

	$795	$695	$650	$575	$535	$495	$460

Add 10% for extra convertible cylinder.
Add 10% for nickel finish.
Add $200 for ivory grips.
This model was also available with two cylinders (.45 LC & .45 ACP or .44 Spl. & .44-40) — add $200. The .45 LC/.45 ACP is perhaps more desirable.

▲ *Storekeepers Model* — .45 LC cal. only, black powder frame, 4 in. barrel, without ejector rod, case hardened, royal blue, or nickel finish, approx. 280 mfg. 1984-85.

	$1,195	$900	$795	$700	$650	$575	$535

Premiums will exist for nickel finish.

FACTORY ENGRAVED 3RD GENERATION SAAs — the rarity of the SAA configuration in addition to the notoriety of the engraver will make the difference on the premium(s) commanded. Third generation factory engraved SAAs were produced in much greater numbers than their 2nd generation counterparts. As a result, pricing is also more predictable - especially on .45 LC cal. Since over 80% of all engraved 3rd generation SAAs are in .45 LC, values listed below represent this caliber. Engraved specimens encountered in other calibers (especially .44-40, approx. 2% of engraved production) will be considerably more expensive. Most specimens encountered are in 7½ in. barrel length. Pistols with 4¾ (most desirable) or 5½ in. barrels will add additional premiums (15%-30%).

Add $500 for factory ivory grips.
Add $250 for non-factory ivory grips.

Grading	100%	98%	95%	90%	80%	70%	60%

▲ *SAA Class A Engraved* — with class A engraving (25% coverage on gun).

| | $1,495 | $1,000 | $875 | $800 | $725 | $650 | $575 |

Add 10% for nickel finish.

▲ *SAA Class B Engraved* — with class B engraving (50% coverage on gun).

| | $1,750 | $1,250 | $1,050 | $975 | $880 | $760 | $650 |

Add 10% for nickel finish.

▲ *SAA Class C Engraved* — with class C engraving (75% coverage on gun).

| | $2,250 | $1,500 | $1,125 | $1,025 | $925 | $825 | $725 |

Add 10% for nickel finish.

▲ *SAA Class D Engraved* — with class D engraving (100% coverage on gun).

| | $2,750 | $1,900 | $1,400 | $1,125 | $995 | $875 | $795 |

Add 15% for nickel finish.

SINGLE ACTION ARMY: CURRENT MFG.

Most collector interest in recently manufactured SAAs is for either mint or NIB specimens.

STANDARD SINGLE ACTION ARMY — .38-40, .44-40, or .45 LC cal., 4 (disc. 1988), 4¾, 5 (disc. 1987), 5½, or 7½ in. barrel, blue (disc. 1993), royal blue (disc. 1993), color case hardened/blue (reintroduced 1989), or nickel finish, black powder frame, 3 line patent date, custom order only.
Mfg.'s Sug. Retail   **$1,213**   **$1,050**   **$895**   **$695**

Various custom order barrel lengths have been available on this model for some time.

▲ *Popular SAA Special Order Options:*
Add $185 for nickel finish.
Add $160 for royal blue finish.
Add $185 for color case hardening.
Add $383 for birdshead backstrap.
Add $129 for beveled cylinder.
Add $200 for mirror brite finish (disc.).
Add $421 for gold or silver plating.
Add $332 for stag grips.
Add $759 for plain ivory grips or $1,143 with checkering.
Add $115 for consecutive serial numbers (pair).
Add $307 for individual unique serial number.
Add $230 for custom barrel shortening.
Add $143 to modify ejector housing.
Add $100 (per set) for heat blued small parts (add $25 for screws).

Many other options are available from the Colt Custom Shop - simply contact them for availability and a price quotation.

CUSTOM ENGRAVED MODELS

▲ *European Model* — 9mm Para., nickel finish only, 4¾, 5½, or 7½ in. barrel, rosewood grips with silver medallions, 40-43 oz. Mfg. 1991-92 only.

| | $1,395 | $1,195 | $995 |

Last Mfg.'s Sug. Retail was $1,990.

▲ *U.S. Model* — .45 ACP, royal blue finish only, 4¾, 5½, or 7½ in. barrel, walnut grips, 40-43 oz. Mfg. 1991-92 only.

| | $1,295 | $1,095 | $875 |

Last Mfg.'s Sug. Retail was $1,960.

Grading	100%	98%	95%	90%	80%	70%	60%

CUSTOM SHOP ENGRAVING — Values below reflect published 1995 Custom Shop, Master Engraver (and signed) engraving options. SAA values are determined by the optional Master Engraving (Standard and Expert level engraving are also available) price scheduling shown below in addition to adding the base price of the gun (including any other special order features).

> Add $1,163 for Class "A" engraving ($\frac{1}{4}$ metal coverage).
> Add $2,324 for Class "B" engraving ($\frac{1}{2}$ metal coverage).
> Add $3,487 for Class "C" engraving ($\frac{3}{4}$ metal coverage).
> Add $4,647 for Class "D" engraving (full metal coverage).
> Add an additional 13% (approx.) for buntline engraving.
>
> Standard Engraving is performed by mostly non-recognized factory engravers and options generally include A-D style coverage but will not do gold work and the specimens are unsigned.
>
> Expert Engravers execute classic American style scroll, no gold, and may be signed.

▲ *Additional SAA Custom Order Options* — the Colt Custom Shop will perform additional work (special orders including engraving, custom stocks, non-standard barrel lengths, gold or silver plating, and other custom features) if the individual work order totals over $1,213 retail. Quotations are supplied at $25/each for these special order guns. Please contact the Colt Custom Gun Shop for this written estimate regarding these custom built SAAs. Their address is: Colt Manufacturing Company, Inc. P.O. Box 1868, Hartford, CT 06101, ATTN: Custom Shop.

SCOUT MODEL SAA

FRONTIER SCOUT (Q or F SUFFIX) — .22 LR or .22 Mag. (introduced after 1960) cal., "Q" or "F" suffix, blue with bright alloy frame, all blue, or duotone ("Q" models only) finish (rare), $4\frac{3}{4}$ or $9\frac{1}{2}$ (Buntline) barrel, available with interchangeable cylinders after 1964, black composition or walnut grips, approx. 246,000 mfg. 1957-1970.

	$400	$350	$275	$225	$175	$150	$140

> Add 10% for extra cylinder.
> Add 20% for Buntline model.
> Add 25% for "Q" suffix - mfg. 1957-58 only.

FRONTIER SCOUT (K SUFFIX) — Zamac alloy frame version of "Q" Model with "K" suffix, blue or nickel finish with walnut stocks, approx. 44,000 mfg. 1960-1970.

	$400	$350	$275	$225	$175	$150	$140

> Add 25% for nickel finish.
> This model used the alloy Zamac for manufacture (as opposed to aluminum in the "Q" and "F" suffix models), and specimens are 6 oz. heavier as a result.

FRONTIER SCOUT '62 (P SUFFIX) — blue finish version of "K" Model, except has "P" suffix, staglite grips, approx. 68,000 mfg. 1962-1970.

	$400	$350	$275	$225	$175	$150	$140

PEACEMAKER — .22 LR/.22 Mag., color casehardened steel frame, $4\frac{3}{8}$, 6, or $7\frac{1}{2}$ (nicknamed Buntline Model but may be marked Peacemaker or Buntline) in. barrel, black composition grips, furnished with interchangeable .22 LR/.22 Mag. cylinders, approx. 190,000 mfg. 1970-1977.

	$400	$350	$275	$225	$175	$150	$140

> Add 20% for $4\frac{3}{4}$ in. barrel.
> Subtract $35 if without extra cylinder.
> This model can be denoted by a "G" or "L" prefix.

Grading	100%	98%	95%	90%	80%	70%	60%

NEW FRONTIER — similar features as Peacemaker Model, except with flat top frame, ramp front and adj. rear sight, mfg. 1970-1977. Reintroduced in 1982 without convertible .22 Mag. cylinder and added cross bolt safety, available in Coltguard finish, all blue finish became standard in 1985, mfg. disc. 1986.

			$325	$275	$215	$185	$155	$140	$130

Last Mfg.'s Sug. Retail was $181.

Add 15% for Buntline model or 4¾ in. barrel.
This model can be denoted by a "G" or "L" prefix.

PISTOLS: SEMI-AUTO

Until several years ago, the Single Action Army revolver commanded the most attention among Colt handgun collectors. Since 1987, Colt Semi-Autos have been in tremendous demand and have out-accelerated many other areas of Colt collecting. Because condition and originality play such a key role in determining Colt Semi-Auto prices, many variations have had their values pushed upward to the point where it is difficult to accurately determine a realistic price - especially on those models in 98% original condition or better. As a result, some of the rarer models seldomly encountered in true 100% original condition have had their values deleted since extreme rarity precludes accurate price evaluation in this 100% condition category. As always, the hardest prices to ascertain when firearms market conditions are bullish are the 98-100% values.

MODEL 1900 — .38 ACP, 6 in. barrel, blue, sight safety, plain walnut grips - checkered hard rubber grips after S/N 2,450, high spur hammer, sight safety. Mfg. 1900-1903.

	N/A	$6,150	$4,300	$3,150	$1,850	$1,300	$1,000

Add 60%+ for USN marked.
Add 50% for US marked with inspector initials.
Deduct 30%-50% for sight safety altered (factory refinished).
This model is serial numbered approx. between 1-4,274.

MODEL 1902 SPORTING — .38 ACP, 6 in. barrel, blue, fixed sights, checkered hard rubber grips, no safety, high spur hammer and round hammer. Mfg. 1902-1908.

	N/A	$2,750	$1,850	$1,250	$850	$650	$550

This model is serial numbered approx. 4,275-11,000 and 30,000-30,190.

MODEL 1902 MILITARY — .38 ACP, 6 in. barrel, blue, similar to 1902 Sporting, hammer changed to spur type in 1908, checkered black hard rubber grips, Lanyard swivel on bottom rear of left grip. Mfg. 1902-1929.

	N/A	$2,300	$1,550	$950	$750	$625	$500

Add 30% for front slide checkering.
Add 20% with original box and instructions.
This model is serial numbered approx. 11,000-16,000 and 30,200-43,266.

MODEL 1902 MILITARY-U.S. ARMY MARKED — similar specifications to 1902 Military, only serial number range 15,001-15,200.

	N/A	$6,950	$5,250	$4,200	$3,700	$2,900	$2,250

MODEL 1903 POCKET (38 ACP) — .38 ACP, 4½ in. barrel, blue finish standard, checkered black hard rubber grips, similar to 1902 Sporting, but 4½ in. barrel, 7½ in. overall. Mfg. 1903-1929.

	$1,450	$1,150	$850	$700	$525	$475	$425

Add 10% for early round hammer.
Add 20% with original box and instructions.
This model is serial numbered approx. 16,000-47,226.

Grading	100%	98%	95%	90%	80%	70%	60%

MODEL 1903 POCKET (MODEL M 32 ACP) — .32 ACP, 4 in. barrel, wood blue, checkered hard rubber grips, hammerless, slide lock and grip safety, barrel lock bushing. Mfg. 1903-1940.

	$550	$425	$350	$300	$275	$250	$200

Add $50 for nickel finish (mostly w/pearl grips).
Add 60% for first model (Type I) mfg. 1903-1911 if in 100%-98% condition. If lower than 98%, add 20%.
Add 10% with original box and instructions.

Type I - 32 ACPs have a 4 in. barrel, barrel bushing, no magazine safety, and are serial numbered 1-71,999.

Type II - 32 ACPs still retain their barrel bushing but have a 3¾ in. barrel and were mfg. from 1908-1910. They are serial numbered 72,000-105,050.

Type III - 32 ACPs do not have a barrel bushing and were mfg. from 1910-1926. They are serial numbered 105,051-468,096.

Type IV - 32 ACPs have the added magazine safety (of which there are both the commercial and "U.S. Property" variations). They are serial numbered 468,097-554,446.

▲ *Model 1903 Parkerized* — U.S. property, 3¼ in. barrel, no barrel bushing, magazine safety, serial numbered 554,447-572,214.

	$950	$775	$625	$475	$375	$320	$275

Add 50% for blue U.S. Property S/N 554,447 - approx. 562,000.
Add 20% with original box and instructions.
The 100% value on this model assumes NIB condition.

MODEL 1905 — .45 ACP, 5 in. barrel, blue fixed sights, checkered walnut stocks, similar to 1902 .38 ACP. Mfg. 1905-1911.

	N/A	$4,350	$2,750	$1,650	$1,250	$950	$775

Add 150% for 1907 U.S. Military Contract variation (205 manufactured).
The shoulder stock option for this pistol is exceedingly rare. Depending on the condition, this accessory can add $7,500-$10,000 to the price of the gun.

MODEL 1908 POCKET (MODEL M 380 ACP) — .380 ACP, first issue, 3¾ in. barrel only, similar to Pocket Model .32 ACP (32 ACP), except chambered for .380 ACP. Mfg. 1908-1940.

	$795	$625	$425	$350	$300	$250	$225

Add 15% for Type II (see explanation below).
Add $50 for nickel finish (mostly w/pearl grips).
100% values assume NIB condition. Deduct 15% if without cardboard box. Pearl grips are normally encountered with nickel finish on this model.

Type II - 380 ACPs with barrel bushing and were mfg. 1908-1910 (6,251 mfg.). They are serial numbered 1-6,251.

Type III - 380 ACPs do not have a barrel bushing and were mfg. 1910-1926. They are serial numbered 6,252-92,893.

Type IV - 380 ACPs have the added magazine safety (of which there are both the commercial and "U.S. Property" variations). They are serial numbered 92,894-134,499.

▲ *Model 1908 "U.S. Property"* — blue finish only, U.S. property. Serial numbered 134,500-138,000.

	$2,000	$1,400	$925	$750	$650	$500	$350

VEST POCKET MODEL 1908-HAMMERLESS — .25 ACP, 2 in. barrel, fixed sights, checkered hard rubber grips on early models, walnut on later, magazine disconnect added on guns made after 1916. Mfg. 1908-1946.

	100%	98%	95%	90%	80%	70%	60%
Blue finish	$550	$425	$325	$275	$225	$200	$155
Nickel finish	$650	$475	$335	$285	$240	$215	$175

100% values assume NIB condition. Deduct 15% if without cardboard box. Pearl grips are normally encountered with nickel finish on this model.

MODEL 1909 — .45 ACP, straight handle design, 5 in. barrel, checkered walnut grips, approx. 22 mfg., ultra rare.

Extreme rarity factor precludes accurate price evaluation by individual condition factors. Specimens that are original and over 90% have sold for over $35,000 recently.

Grading	100%	98%	95%	90%	80%	70%	60%

GENERAL OFFICER'S PISTOL — issued not only to Generals, but also, many were issued to the OSS, U.S. Navy, and other government agencies, .32 U.S. Properties were blued until 1942, after which the parkerized finish became standard (most went to England and exhibit British proofmarks), .380 U.S. Properties were always blued, 1911A1 WWII specimens have standard military finish, and the Rock Island Arsenal .45s were all issued to Generals.

	100%	98%	95%	90%	80%	70%	60%
.32 cal. parkerized	$1,800	$1,550	$1,275	$1,100	$975	$875	$775
.32 cal. blue	$2,500	$2,250	$1,975	$1,725	$1,500	$1,300	$1,100
.380 ACP cal.	$2,700	$2,400	$2,100	$1,850	$1,600	$1,400	$1,200
.45 ACP cal. (WWII mfg.)	$1,500	$1,250	$1,050	$875	$775	$675	$595
M15 (Rock Island Arsenal mfg.)	$4,350	$3,750	$3,150	$2,650	$2,250	$1,850	$1,500

Values above assume issue to a General (i.e., except for the Rock Island Arsenal .45 ACP variation, there must be paperwork to link up the gun to the recipient).

GOVT. MODEL 1911 COMMERCIAL VARIATIONS

MODEL 1911 — .45 ACP, 5 in. barrel, fixed sights, 7 shot mag., flat main spring housing, polished blue finish only (commercial and original military), checkered walnut grips. Colt licensed other companies to manufacture under government contracts, 39 oz. Mfg. 1912-1925.

Most M1911 variations listed below are not as collectible if under 60% original condition. However, they are still very desirable as shooters and values (if in original condition) will approximate the 60% prices if in good mechanical condition.

Add 20% for 4-digit ser. no., 40% for 3-digit, 60%+ for 2-digit.

Colt Model 1911s are enjoying high demand as of this writing and prices have increased the most in the 95%-100% condition factors. Be careful on the 98%+ condition specimens, especially the rarer variations. Some collectors are now requiring a potential high-dollar Model 1911 to pass an X-ray examination metallurgically before purchasing.

▲ *Model 1911 Commercial* — denoted by "C" preceding serial number, approx. ser. number range C1-C138,532. Watch for fakes.

	100%	98%	95%	90%	80%	70%	60%
1912-1914 mfg.	$2,900	$1,950	$1,250	$875	$695	$550	$425
1914-1925 mfg.	$2,650	$1,675	$1,150	$850	$650	$525	$400

Deduct 15% if without cardboard box in 100% condition only.

Approx. 138,532 were mfg. between 1912-1925.

100% values assume NIB condition.

GOVT. MODEL 1911 .45 ACP MILITARY VARIATIONS

COLT MFG. MODEL 1911 MILITARY — right side of slide marked "MODEL OF 1911 U.S. ARMY", blue finish only (NOT parkerized unless reworked).

	100%	98%	95%	90%	80%	70%	60%
1912-1913 mfg.	$2,695	$1,950	$1,325	$925	$550	$475	$400
1914-1925 mfg.	$2,200	$1,600	$975	$625	$525	$425	$375

Over 2,550,000 M1911 pistols were ordered for WWI and WWII by U.S. Government but approx. 650,000 were mfg. between 1911-1925. Those pistols with a parkerized finish will indicate post-WWI reworking, usually marked with an arsenal code (ie. AA-AUGUSTA ARSENAL, SA-SPRINGFIELD ARSENAL, etc.). These reworks do not have the same values as original, unaltered specimens and prices generally are in the $295-$475 range.

NORTH AMERICAN ARMS COMPANY — less than 100 mfg. in Quebec, Ontario during 1918 only, blued finish. Be very wary of fakes as this variation is perhaps the most desirable Colt WWI Govt. semi-auto.

	100%	98%	95%	90%	80%	70%	60%
	N/A	$11,500	$9,500	$8,250	$7,150	$6,350	$5,150

Most mint/100% specimens encountered in this model have been refinished - be careful.

REMINGTON - UMC — over 21,500 mfg. (ser. numbered 1-21,676) in 1918-1919 only, blued finish.

	100%	98%	95%	90%	80%	70%	60%
	N/A	$2,450	$1,675	$950	$700	$575	$525

Most mint/100% specimens encountered in this model have been refinished - be careful.

Grading	100%	98%	95%	90%	80%	70%	60%

SPRINGFIELD ARMORY — approx. 30,000 mfg. between 1914-1915, blued finish.

	N/A	$2,150	$1,350	$875	$650	$550	$500

Serialization is 72,751-83,855, 102,597-107,596, 113,497-120,566, and 125,567-133,186.

Most mint/100% specimens encountered in this model have been refinished - be careful.

U.S. NAVY — over 31,000 mfg. for U.S. Navy contract between 1911-1914 in defined serial ranges, blued finish. Marked "MODEL OF 1911 U.S. NAVY" on right slide side.

	$4,450	$2,800	$1,950	$1,700	$1,375	$995	$750

U.S. Navy specimens are seldomly found in over 80% original condition because of the corrosive factor encountered while at sea.

U.S. MARINE CORPS. — approx. 13,500 mfg. between 1911-1913 and 1916-1918 in defined serial ranges, blued finish, right side of slide marked "MODEL OF 1911 U.S. ARMY".

	$2,975	$2,475	$1,900	$1,650	$1,200	$995	$750

WWI BRITISH SERIES — .455 cal., serialized W10001-W21000, marked "CALIBRE 455", blued finish, proofed with broad arrow British Ordnance punch. Mfg. 1915-1916.

	$2,350	$1,750	$1,100	$825	$675	$550	$475

Add 25% for variations with either Navy or Marine markings. Many WWI British-series M1911s were exported back to the U.S. following WWI and were converted to .45 ACP. Usually, a "5" has been crossed-out of the original cal. designation. These reworks are not as collectible and prices range from $350-$500.

BRITISH RAF REWORK — this variation is the WWI British series re-issued to RAF officers in the early 1920s, blued finish, differentiated by hand-stamped "RAF" or "R.A.F." on left side of frame.

	$1,250	$1,050	$825	$675	$575	$495	$460

A.J. SAVAGE MUNITIONS CO. — mfg. slides only, blued finish, marked in middle on left side of slide with flaming ordnance bomb with "S" in center.

	$1,350	$1,075	$850	$695	$600	$525	$475

NORWEGIAN TRIAL MODEL 1911 COLT — 11.25mm cal., approx. 300 mfg. with "C" prefix in 1913-14 only, usually encountered in 90% or less condition.

	$1,750	$1,250	$975	$850	$750	$595	$495

These guns were ordered for Norwegian service evaluation and were mfg. by Colt's in Hartford, CT.

NORWEGIAN MODEL 1912 11.25MM — 11.25mm cal., mfg. under license from Colt's between 1917-1919, "M1912" slide designation, approx. 500 mfg.

	$1,650	$1,300	$975	$850	$750	$595	$495

NORWEGIAN 1914 11.25MM — This model has a distinctive extended slide release, approx. 20,000 mfg. between 1919-1932.

	$1,175	$850	$695	$525	$475	$425	$375

Add 150% for Waffenamt Nazi mfg. (mfg. 1945 only).

Nazi production of the M1914 began in 1941, with serialization beginning where 1932 mfg. left off (approx. 21,000 range). Between 1941-42, approx. 7,000 pistols were mfg. without Waffenamt stampings. Nazi stamped guns (all 1945 dated) began in the mid-29,000 serial range and existing specimens indicate that approx. 1,000 were mfg. with the Nazi Eagle.

ARGENTINE CONTRACT MODEL 1916 — this Argentine variation of the Colt Model 1911 can be found under the Hispano Argentino Fabrica de Automoviles heading in the H section.

RUSSIAN CONTRACT — approx. 50,000 mfg. with frame marked "ANGLO ZAKAZIVAT", blued finish. Mfg. 1915-1917, seldomly encountered - watch for fakes.

	$2,895	$2,175	$1,850	$1,600	$1,250	$1,100	$1,000

Grading	100%	98%	95%	90%	80%	70%	60%

GOVT. MODEL 1911A1 & VARIATIONS

MODEL 1911 A1 — .45 ACP, blue or parkerized, checkered walnut grips, plastic on later military guns, checkered arched mainspring housing and longer grip safety spur. As in the Model 1911, Colt licensed other companies to produce under govt. contract during WWII. Mfg. 1925-1970.

Inspect carefully for arsenal reworks (so marked by proofing, normally on left side of frame above or behind trigger), and reparkerizing.

Most M1911 A1 variations listed below are not as collectible if under 60% original condition. However, they are still very desirable as shooters and values (if in original condition) will approximate the 60% prices if in good mechanical condition.

PRE-WWII COLT COMMERCIAL — "C" preceding serial number, mfg. 1925-1942. Approx. ser. no. range C138,533-C215,000.

	N/A	$1,495	$1,150	$850	$695	$550	$425

Add 20% with original box and instructions.

1946-1969 COLT COMMERCIAL — .45 ACP cal., 5 in. barrel, fixed sights, "C" prefix until 1950 when changed to "C" suffix, approx. 196,000 mfg. 1946-1970.

▲ *1946-1950 Mfg.* — C-Prefix with serial numbers C221,000 - C240,227.

	$1,350	$1,100	$875	$725	$660	$550	$475

▲ *1950-1970 Mfg.* — C-Suffix with serial numbers 240,228C - 336,169C.

	$850	$745	$675	$550	$475	$425	$400

Add 10% for nickel finish.

SUPER .38 AUTOMATIC PISTOL — identical to Govt. Model .45, except chambered for .38 Super automatic. Mfg. 1928-1970.

Pre-War	$2,900	$2,375	$1,750	$1,250	$1,000	$875	$750
2nd Model	$1,350	$1,100	$875	$725	$660	$550	$475
3rd Model	$1,100	$875	$725	$660	$575	$500	$435
4th Model	$895	$775	$675	$575	$500	$435	$385
CS Prefix	$850	$745	$675	$550	$475	$415	$375

Add 15% to post-war if with heavy barrel (under approx. 115,000 ser. no.).

Pre-war variations are serialized below approx. 37,000.

The 2nd Model may be differentiated by noticing the heavier barrel and Colt prancing stallion on right side. The 3rd Model has a fat barrel with Rampant Colt on left side. The 4th Model has a thin barrel and horse on left side.

SUPER MATCH .38 — similar to Super .38, but hand honed action, match grade barrel. Mfg. 1935-1946. Examine carefully for fakes.

Fixed sights	$4,950	$4,150	$3,450	$2,350	$1,575	$1,275	$1,050

Add 35% for adj. sights.

MATCH .38 AMU — .38 rimless Spl. cal. (cartridges were mfg. by Win.), this variation was mfg. by Colt from a .38 Super frame (and has .38 Super serialization) with a .38 AMU conversion kit slide, the Army took .45 frames and assembled their guns using .38 AMU kits, blued finish.

Colt mfg. (unmodified)	$2,500	$2,200	$1,900	$1,675	$1,400	$1,175	$975
Army modified	$1,400	$1,200	$995	$800	$650	$550	$495
AMU kit only	$550	$475	$425	$385	$350	$325	$295

On this configuration, the barrel, slide, and mag. were marked ".38 AMU".

SUPER MATCH .38 MS — .38 Super cal., 1961 mfg., serial numbered 101MS - 855MS, 754 total manufactured, same configuration as the .38 Midrange.

	$2,800	$2,500	$1,750	$1,495	$1,375	$1,175	$1,000

1968-1969 BB TRANSITIONAL — denoted by BB prefix on serial number.

	$950	$825	$625	$550	$495	$425	$375

C

Grading	100%	98%	95%	90%	80%	70%	60%

.45 ACP TO .22 LR CONVERSION UNIT — consists of slide assembly, barrel, bushing, floating chamber, ejector, recoil spring and guide, fitted with Stevens adj. rear sight, mfg. 1938 to 1947. Colt Master adj. sight 1947-54.

	$395	$350	$285	$195	$175	$150	$125

Add 100% for prewar mfg. (u-prefix S/N on top of slide).

.22 LR TO .45 ACP CONVERSION UNIT — converted service Ace .22 to .45 ACP. Mfg. 1938-1942. Very rare — 112 mfg.

	$3,500	$2,500	$1,750	$1,000	$800	$700	$600

These units are serial numbered on top of slide.

GOVT. MODEL 1911A1 MILITARY VARIATIONS

COLT MFG. MODEL 1911A1 MILITARY — approx. 1,643,068 mfg. between 1924-1945, ser. nos. 700,000 - on up, right side of frame marked "M1911A1 U.S. ARMY".

	$1,100	$875	$625	$485	$385	$350	$325

Add 50% for 1939 Navy variation (S/N 713,646 - 717,281).

On early 1911 A1 military models with bright blue finish — add 150% if condition is 98% or better.

A large grouping of over 7,000 Commercial 1911A1s was transferred to the U.S. government - these pistols had their commercial serial numbers crudely removed (in ser. range 860,000 - 866,000) and renumbered with a new military serial number. Some of these guns are unusual as the frames and slides have been cut for the Schwartz safety. This variation is rare, and a 20%-30% premium exists depending on the condition.

DRAKE NATIONAL MATCH — Drake made slides only for use by U.S. Army Marksmanship Unit to allow assembly of match guns.

	$1,150	$995	$850	$700	$585	$510	$450

GOVERNMENT NATIONAL MATCH REWORKS — assembled by government armorers, all parts marked "NM", parkerized finish. Most will be S.A. marked.

	$1,275	$1,075	$850	$675	$585	$510	$450

These pistols were made specifically for the U.S. shooting team at Camp Perry.

ITHACA — approx. 369,129 mfg. 1943-1945 in Ithaca, NY, ser. no. ranges 856,101 - 916,404, 1,208,674 - 1,279,673, 1,441,431 - 1,471,430, 1,816,642 - 1,890,503, and 2,619,014 - 2,693,613. Parkerized finish.

	$800	$600	$500	$450	$375	$350	$325

Add 20% with original shipping carton.

UNION SWITCH AND SIGNAL — approx. 55,000 mfg. 1943 only in Swissvale, PA, ser. no. range 1,041,405 - 1,096,404. Sandblast and blue finish.

	$1,375	$1,075	$850	$575	$495	$450	$425

REMINGTON RAND — approx. 1,086,624 mfg. 1943-1945 in Syracuse, NY, ser. no. ranges 916,405 - 1,041,404, 1,279,649 - 1,441,430, 1,471,431 - 1,609,528, 1,743,847 - 1,816,641, 1,890,504 - 2,075,103, 2,134,404 - 2,244,803, and 2,380,014 - 2,619,013. Parkerized finish.

	$750	$595	$495	$425	$375	$350	$325

Add 20% with original shipping carton.

SINGER MFG. CO. — 500 mfg. 1942 in Elizabeth, NJ, ser. no. range S800,001 - S800,500. Blued finish with plastic grips.

	N/A	$10,750	$9,350	$8,375	$7,500	$6,750	$5,875

The Singer 1911A1 variation is one of the most sought after Colt models. In recent years, values have increased significantly and as a result, many fakes have emerged. Most specimens are now recognized by ser. no. and be very cautious when contemplating a purchase. Some collectors unsure of authenticity are now requiring X-ray testing to determine originality (slide restampings, ser. no. changes, etc.).

Grading	100%	98%	95%	90%	80%	70%	60%

MEXICAN CONTRACT — mfg. approx. 1921-1927 with "C" prefix ser. nos., frames marked "EJERCITO MEXICANO", most surviving examples show much use.

	100%	98%	95%	90%	80%	70%	60%
	$1,625	$1,200	$875	$725	$625	$550	$495

BRAZILIAN CONTRACT

	100%	98%	95%	90%	80%	70%	60%
	$2,250	$1,875	$1,500	$1,250	$975	$775	$575

ARGENTINE CONTRACT MODEL 1927 — .45 ACP cal., serial numbered 1-10,000 under the mainspring housing and on the top of slide (should be matching), must have Argentine crest and "Model 1927" on right side of slide, external serial number applied to the outside of frame by the Argentine Arsenal, most have been Arsenal refinished.

	100%	98%	95%	90%	80%	70%	60%
	$1,200	$995	$825	$700	$625	$550	$495

ARGENTINE MFG. — in 1927, the Argentina Arsenal "DGFM-FMAP" began manufacturing the Model 1911A1. The slide marking is two lines and reads "EJERCITO ARGENTINO SIST.COLT.CAL. 11.25mm MOD.1927".

	100%	98%	95%	90%	80%	70%	60%
	$750	$650	$500	$450	$400	$350	$325

Add 20% for Argentine Navy "ARMADA NACIONAL" (small shipments between 1912-1948). Markings vary on different types.

ACE MODELS: PRE-WWII

COMMERCIAL ACE — .22 LR, similar to Government .45 ACP, but in .22LR cal., 4¾ in. barrel, blue, adj. sights, checkered walnut grips, almost 11,000 mfg. (ser. no. range 1-10,935) 1931-1941 and 1947.

	100%	98%	95%	90%	80%	70%	60%
	$2,125	$1,825	$1,275	$975	$775	$600	$500

Add 20% with original box and instructions.

SERVICE MODEL ACE — .22 LR, 5 in. barrel, blue or parkerized finish, similar to .45 ACP National Match except for caliber, has floating chamber to simulate .45 ACP recoil, limited mfg. 1935-1945.

	100%	98%	95%	90%	80%	70%	60%
	$2,600	$2,100	$1,800	$1,225	$875	$675	$575

Add 20% with original box and instructions.
This variation is marked "SERVICE MODEL" on left frame, serial numbers have "SM" prefix and have ranges to approx. 13,800. Parkerized finish is less desirable - subtract 10%.

PRE-WWII NATIONAL MATCH MODELS

NATIONAL MATCH — .45 ACP, similar to Government Model, except has hand honed action, match grade barrel, blue. Mfg. 1933-1941 within ser. no. range C164,800 - C215,000.
Add 10% with original box and instructions.

▲ *Fixed sights*

	100%	98%	95%	90%	80%	70%	60%
	$2,750	$2,150	$1,350	$925	$625	$550	$500

▲ *Adj. sights*

	100%	98%	95%	90%	80%	70%	60%
	$3,650	$2,950	$1,975	$1,625	$1,275	$1,075	$850

POST-WWII NATIONAL MATCH MODELS

GOLD CUP NATIONAL MATCH — .45 ACP, match grade barrel, new design bushing, flat mainspring housing, long adj. stop trigger, hand fitted slide with enlarged ejection port, adj. target sights, gold medallions in grips, "NM" suffix. Mfg. 1957-1970.

	100%	98%	95%	90%	80%	70%	60%
	$950	$800	$650	$500	$450	$425	$400

Add 10% with original box and instructions.
Note: This model was the first National Match Model manufactured following WW II.

Grading	100%	98%	95%	90%	80%	70%	60%

GOLD CUP MKIII NATIONAL MATCH — .38 Spl., similar to Gold Cup National Match, except chambered for .38 Spl., mid-range wadcutter. Mfg. 1961-1974.

	$995	$825	$695	$625	$575	$475	$435

Add 10% with original box and instructions.

MKIV/SERIES 70 GOLD CUP NATIONAL MATCH — .45 ACP, flat mainspring housing, accurizer barrel and bushing, adj. trigger, target hammer, solid rib, Colt Elliason sight. Mfg. 1970-1983.

	$775	$675	$575	$495	$450	$395	$375

MKIV/SERIES 70 GOLD CUP 75TH ANNIVERSARY NATIONAL MATCH — similar to Gold Cup except for commemorative aspect for Camp Perry, 1978, 200 made.
Add 50% to standard Mark IV/Series 70 Gold Cup prices.

GOLD CUP MKIV SERIES 80 NATIONAL MATCH — .45 ACP, 5 in. barrel, 7 or 8 (new 1992) shot mag., 39 oz., Colt-Elliason adj. rear sight, wide grooved adj. target trigger, under cut front sight, flat mainspring housing, critical internal parts are hand honed. Mfg. 1983-present.

Mfg.'s Sug. Retail	$937	$735	$575	$460	$400	$380	$350	$325

In 1992, this model was updated to accept an 8 shot mag.

▲ *Stainless Gold Cup National Match* — similar to Gold Cup, only manufactured from stainless steel, matte finish, released late in 1986.

Mfg.'s Sug. Retail	$1,003	$785	$585	$450

Add $70 for "Ultimate" bright stainless steel finish.

▲ *.38 Super Elite National Match* — two-tone gun (stainless slide and blued frame), special edition by Accu-Sports.

	$1,100	$925	$825

▲ *Bullseye National Match* — .45 ACP cal., hand built, tuned, and adjusted by Colt's custom gunsmiths for precise match accuracy, includes factory installed Bomar sights, equipped with carrying case and 2 extra mags. Mfg. 1991-92.

$1,325	$1,075	$895	$800	$725	$650	$600

Last Mfg.'s Sug. Retail was $1,500.

▲ *Presentation Gold Cup* — .45 ACP cal., similar to regular Gold Cup Series 80 National Match, except has a deep blue-mirror bright finish accented by custom jeweled hammer, trigger, and barrel hood. Supplied with oak and velvet custom case. Mfg. 1991-92.

$1,075	$895	$800	$725	$650	$600	$550

Last Mfg.'s Sug. Retail was $1,195.

PISTOLS: SEMI-AUTO - SINGLE ACTION, RECENT MFG.

The values listed below are the last published factory engraving prices - factory specified "Class A - Class D" pricing was discontinued late 1990. Beginning in 1991, factory engraving on the models listed below is done per individual price quotation. Quotations from Colt are available at $25 each (deductible from work order). These prices (disc. 1990) should be added to the cost of each engraved production gun (NIB condition only) to determine an approximate value. It should also be understood that, in most cases, the quality of the engraving and notoriety of the engraver can be as important as the amount of coverage.

SMALL FRAME ENGRAVING OPTIONS (INCLUDES MUSTANG, .380 ACP GOVERNMENT, DETECTIVE SPECIAL, AND DIAMONDBACK)

CLASS "A" ENGRAVING (¼ METAL COVERAGE) — ADD $776.
CLASS "B" ENGRAVING (½ METAL COVERAGE) — ADD $959.
CLASS "C" ENGRAVING (¾ METAL COVERAGE) — ADD $1,426.
CLASS "D" ENGRAVING (FULL METAL COVERAGE) — ADD $1,814.

MEDIUM FRAME ENGRAVING OPTIONS (INCLUDES .45 ACP GOLD CUP, GOVERNMENT MODEL, OFFICER'S ACP, PYTHON, COMBAT COMMANDER, KING COBRA, TROOPER MKV, LAWMAN MKV, AND DELTA ELITE)

Grading	100%	98%	95%	90%	80%	70%	60%

CLASS "A" ENGRAVING (¼ METAL COVERAGE) — ADD $969.
CLASS "B" ENGRAVING (½ METAL COVERAGE) — ADD $1,199.
CLASS "C" ENGRAVING (¾ METAL COVERAGE) — ADD $1,783.
CLASS "D" ENGRAVING (FULL METAL COVERAGE) — ADD $2,289.
Add 7% for 6 in. barrel, 14% for 8 in. barrel, or 25% for stainless steel construction.

Special engraving/options include inlays, seals, custom grips, lettering, prices quoted on request. Smooth ivory grips are $215 extra (1990 retail).

Beginning in 1991, Colt began shipping all models in a distinctive blue plastic carrying case/shipping container.

JUNIOR POCKET MODEL — 2¼ in. barrel, blue, checkered walnut grips, made by Astra in Spain from 1958-1968.

	100%	98%	95%	90%	80%	70%	60%
.22 Short	$350	$300	$240	$210	$180	$160	$140
.25 ACP	$300	$275	$200	$180	$150	$140	$130

Add 10% for nickel finish.

A very few conversion kits were offered for this model. They are rare and asking prices are $250-$325 if in mint condition.

COLT AUTOMATIC CALIBER .25 — .25 ACP cal., mfg. by Firearms International for Colt between 1970-1973.

	100%	98%	95%	90%	80%	70%	60%
	$300	$275	$225	$185	$150	$140	$130

COMMANDER (PRE-70 SERIES) — 9mm Para, .38 Super, or .45 ACP cal., 4¼ in. barrel, full size grips, steel or alloy (Lightweight Model) variations. Mfg. 1950-1976.

	100%	98%	95%	90%	80%	70%	60%
9mm	$595	$495	$450	$395	$365	$325	$295
.38 Super/.45 ACP	$695	$595	$525	$450	$395	$350	$300

This model has a "LW" suffix.

MKIV/SERIES 70 GOVERNMENT MODEL — .45 ACP, .38 Super, 9mm, or 9mm Steyr, 5 in. barrel, checkered walnut grips/medallion. A slight premium might be asked for the Series 70 models if NIB. Series 70 models were mfg. 1970-1983 and were serial numbered with "SM" prefixes (approx. 3,000 mfg.), "70G" prefixes 1970-1976, "G70" suffixes 1976-1980, "B70" suffixes 1979-1981, and "70B" prefixes 1981-1983.

	100%	98%	95%	90%	80%	70%	60%
Blue finish	$650	$525	$450	$400	$350	$315	$285
Nickel finish	$695	$565	$475	$415	$365	$320	$290

9mm Steyr was made for European exportation only. However, a few specimens have found their way into the United States. Prices for NIB specimens usually start in the $595+ range.

▲ *Series 70 Combat Govt.* —.45 ACP cal., bluish-black metal finish, features modifications for combat shooting, forerunner to the Combat Elite.

	100%	98%	95%	90%	80%	70%	60%
	$650	$525	$425	$395	$365	$325	$285

▲ *Series 70 Lightweight Commander* — 9mm Para, .38 Super, or .45 ACP cal., 4¼ in. barrel, full size grips, this model is denoted by a "CLW" prefix. Mfg. 1970-1983.

	100%	98%	95%	90%	80%	70%	60%
9mm	$525	$465	$415	$350	$325	$300	$275
.38 Super/.45 ACP	$575	$525	$465	$425	$375	$325	$295

▲ *Series 70 Combat Commander*

	100%	98%	95%	90%	80%	70%	60%
	$575	$500	$425	$395	$365	$325	$285

▲ *Conversion Unit* — converts .45 ACP to .22 LR, mfg. 1954-84 with either Accro adj. rear sight or fixed sight.

	100%	98%	95%	90%	80%	70%	60%
Adj. Sight	$395	$325	$275	$220	$195	$165	$140
Fixed Sight	$450	$350	$275	$225	$190	$165	$140

POST-WAR ACE SERVICE MODEL — .22 LR, similar specifications to previous Pre-WWII manufacture, "SM" prefix (most common) or "B 70" suffix, approx. 30,000 mfg. between 1978-1982.

	100%	98%	95%	90%	80%	70%	60%
	$695	$625	$550	$500	$450	$425	$395

This model is serial numbered approx. SM14,001-SM43,830.

Grading	100%	98%	95%	90%	80%	70%	60%

MKIV/SERIES 80 GOVERNMENT MODEL — .38 Super, 9mm Para. (disc. 1992), or .45 ACP cal., single action, 5 in. barrel, 7 or 8 (new 1992) shot mag. in .45 ACP, approx. 38 oz., action has firing pin safety, checkered walnut (pre-1991 mfg.) or rubber combat style grips with medallion (new 1991). Production started in 1983 with ser. no. FG01000.

▲ **Blue Finish**

Mfg.'s Sug. Retail	$735	$575	$475	$385	$340	$315	$295	$275

Add $20 for 9mm Para. (disc. 1992) cal.

▲ **Nickel Finish** — available in .45 ACP (disc. 1986) or .38 Super (disc. in 1987) cal.

$525	$465	$380	$350	$315	$285	$260

Last Mfg.'s Sug. Retail was $600.

▲ **Satin Nickel/Blue** — is supplied with Colt-Pachmayr grips. Disc. 1986.

$510	$445	$370	$345	$310	$280	$255

Last Mfg.'s Sug. Retail was $557.

▲ **Stainless Steel** — 9mm Para. (mfg. 1991-92), .38 Super (new 1990), .40 S&W (new 1992) or .45 ACP cal.

Mfg.'s Sug. Retail	$789	$625	$510	$425

Add $20 for 9mm Para. (disc. 1992) cal.

▲ **"Ultimate" Bright Stainless Steel** — .38 Super (new 1991) or .45 ACP cal., high polish stainless finish. New 1986.

Mfg.'s Sug. Retail	$863	$675	$520	$455

▲ **Limited Class Model .45 ACP** — .45 ACP cal., designed for tactical competition, includes parkerized matte finish, lightweight composite trigger, ambidextrous safety, upswept grip safety, beveled mag. well, accurized, includes signed target. New 1994.

Mfg.'s Sug. Retail	$936	$725	$575	$450	$400	$350	$325	$300

▲ **Compensated Model .45 ACP** — .45 ACP cal., designed for serious competitive shooting, blue slide with full profile BAT Compensator, Bomar rear sight, flared funnel mag. well. New 1994.

Mfg.'s Sug. Retail	$2,428	$1,900	$1,500	$1,250	$1,000	$875	$750	$625

COMBAT GOVERNMENT — .45 ACP cal., dark matte metal finish, features modifications for combat shooting, successor to the Series 70 Combat Govt. Disc.

$575	$495	$400	$345	$310	$280	$255

▲ **Special Combat Government Competition Model** — .45 ACP, competition model featuring skeletized trigger, custom tuning, polished ramp, throated barrel, flared ejection port, and cut-out hammer. Supplied with two 8 shot mags., hard chrome slide and receiver, Bomar rear and Clark dovetail front sight, flared mag. well, shipped with certified target. New 1992.

Mfg.'s Sug. Retail	$1,532	$1,275	$995	$895	$775	$650	$575	$495

▲ **Special Combat Government (Carry Model)** — similar to Special Combat Government, except has royal blue finish, bar-dot night sights, and ambidextrous safety. New 1992.

Mfg.'s Sug. Retail	$1,365	$1,125	$925	$750	$650	$575	$495	$400

▲ **Combat Elite** — .38 Super or .45 ACP cal., similar to Gold Cup, only with wraparound rubber grips, beveled magazine well, stainless steel receiver with carbon steel slide, and Accro adj. sighting system.

Mfg.'s Sug. Retail	$895	$730	$620	$455	$400	$360	$330	$300

▲ **Conversion Unit - Series 80** — converts Series 80 Govt. Model only to .22 LR or 9mm, mfg. 1984-86 with Accro adj. rear sight.

9mm Para.	$395	$295	$275	$225	$190	$175	$150
.22 LR	$525	$450	$375	$325	$250	$200	$175

Last Mfg.'s Sug. Retail was $305.

COMMANDER LIGHTWEIGHT SERIES 80 — .45 ACP, 4¼ in. barrel, similar to Government Model, except shorter and lighter alloy frame, 27½ oz., round spur hammer. Mfg. 1983-present, fixed sights.

Mfg.'s Sug. Retail	$735	$595	$485	$395	$345	$320	$300	$280

Add 10% for .38 Super or 9mm Para. (disc.) cals.

Grading	100%	98%	95%	90%	80%	70%	60%

COMBAT COMMANDER SERIES 80 — .38 Super (disc.), 9mm Para. (disc. 1992), or .45 ACP cal., similar to Lightweight, except has steel frame.

▲ *Blued Finish*

Mfg.'s Sug. Retail	$735	$575	$475	$385	$340	$315	$295	$275

Add $20 for 9mm Para. (disc.) or .38 Super (disc.) cal.

▲ *Stainless Steel* — .38 Super (new 1992) or .45 ACP cal. only. New 1990.

Mfg.'s Sug. Retail	$789	$630	$495	$430

▲ *Satin Nickel* — disc. 1986.

	$575	$475	$410	$365	$310	$275	$250

Last Mfg.'s Sug. Retail was $550.

▲ *Gold Cup Commander* — .45 ACP cal., features custom shop alterations including heavy duty adj. target sights, beveled mag. well, serrated front strap, checkered mainspring housing, wide grip safety, and Palo Alto wood grips. Mfg. 1991-1993.

$865	$715	$595	$550	$495	$440	$395

Last Mfg.'s Sug. Retail was $936

▲ *Gold Cup Commander Stainless* — stainless variation of the Gold Cup Commander. New 1992.

$870	$715	$595

Last Mfg.'s Sug. Retail was $949

OFFICER'S ACP SERIES 80 — .45 ACP only, 3½ in. barrel, 34 oz., 6 shot mag., short version of the Government Model. New 1985.

▲ *Blued Finish*

Mfg.'s Sug. Retail	$735	$575	$475	$385	$340	$315	$295	$275

▲ *Matte Blued Finish*

	$525	$440	$370	$330	$280	$250	$225

Last Mfg.'s Sug. Retail was $625 (disc. 1991).

▲ *Officer's Stainless Steel* — matte stainless steel finish. New 1986.

Mfg.'s Sug. Retail	$789	$630	$495	$430

Add $74 for "Ultimate" bright stainless steel finish (new 1987).

▲ *Officer's Lightweight* — similar to Officer's ACP, except has alloy frame and weighs 24 oz. New 1986.

Mfg.'s Sug. Retail	$735	$575	$475	$385	$340	$315	$295	$275

▲ *Officer's Satin Nickel* — disc. 1985.

	$575	$475	$450	$375	$295	$260	$235

Last Mfg.'s Sug. Retail was $513.

▲ *General Officer's Model* — bright stainless steel with rosewood grips, special edition.

Mfg.'s Sug. Retail	$750	$650	$550	$450

MKIV/SERIES 80 GOLD CUP NATIONAL MATCH — .45 ACP, flat mainspring housing, 8 shot mag., accurizer barrel and bushing, adj. trigger, target hammer, solid rib, Colt-Elliason sight, made 1983-present.

Mfg.'s Sug. Retail	$937	$735	$575	$460	$400	$380	$350	$325

In 1992, this model was updated to accept an 8 shot mag.

▲ *Stainless Gold Cup National Match* — similar to Gold Cup, only manufactured from stainless steel, matte finish, released late in 1986.

Mfg.'s Sug. Retail	$1,003	$785	$585	$475

Add $70 for "Ultimate" bright stainless steel finish.

MODEL M1991 A1 — .45 ACP only, similar to original WWII issue pistols with government issue parkerized finish, fixed sights, and black composite grips, 5 in. barrel, 7 shot mag., 38 oz., includes brown molded case. New 1991.

Mfg.'s Sug. Retail	$538	$445	$370	$330	$295	$275	$250	$225

This model is serialized consecutively with the last batch of Govt. models manufactured during 1945.

Grading	100%	98%	95%	90%	80%	70%	60%

▲ *Model M1991 Stainless Steel* — features matte stainless steel finish. New 1996.

Mfg.'s Sug. Retail	$590	$495	$435	$350			

▲ *Model M1991 A1 Officer's Compact* — similar to Model M1991 A1, except has 3½ in. barrel, 6 shot mag., 34 oz. New 1992.

Mfg.'s Sug. Retail	$538	$445	$370	$330	$295	$275	$250	$225

▲ *Model M1991 A1 Commander* — .45 ACP cal., 4¼ in. barrel, full size grip, 7 shot mag., parkerized finish, 36 oz. New 1993.

Mfg.'s Sug. Retail	$538	$445	$370	$330	$295	$275	$250	$225

DELTA ELITE — 10mm, 5 in. barrel, black neoprene grips, high profile 3 dot sights, blue finish, 8 shot mag., 38 oz. Introduced 1987.

Mfg.'s Sug. Retail	$807	$670	$515	$450	$375	$335	$300	$275

▲ *Stainless Steel* — matte stainless steel finish, new 1989.

Mfg.'s Sug. Retail	$860	$725	$550	$455			

Add $78 for "Ultimate" brite stainless steel finish (disc. 1993).

DELTA GOLD CUP STAINLESS — 10mm, target variation, includes Accro adj. rear sight and trigger (serrated also), wraparound combat grips. Mfg. 1989-1993, re-released 1995.

Mfg.'s Sug. Retail	$1,027	$875	$650	$525			

▲ *Delta Gold Cup Blue* — similar to Delta Gold Cup Stainless, except has blue finish. Mfg. 1991 only.

	$750	$600	$500	$450	$400	$360	$330

Last Mfg.'s Sug. Retail was $870.

.380 SERIES 80 GOVERNMENT MODEL — .380 ACP only, single action, 3¼ in. barrel, 7 shot mag., fixed sights, composition stocks, 21¾ oz. New 1985.

▲ *Blue Finish*

Mfg.'s Sug. Retail	$462	$355	$300	$235	$215	$200	$190	$180

▲ *Nickel Finish* — bright polish nickel finish with white composite grips. Disc. 1994.

	$405	$330	$270	$240	$220	$210	$200

Last Mfg.'s Sug. Retail was $504.

▲ *Coltguard Finish* — employs a high strength electroless matte nickel finish. Mfg. 1986-1989.

	$375	$325	$260	$235	$210	$200	$185

Last Mfg.'s Sug. Retail was $406.

▲ *Stainless Steel* — new 1989.

Mfg.'s Sug. Retail	$493	$380	$330	$270			

GOVT. POCKETLITE L.W. — similar to .380 Series 80 Govt. Model, except frame is mfg. with alloy, blue or nickel/stainless (mfg. 1992-1993) finish only, black composition grips, 14¾ oz. New 1991.

Mfg.'s Sug. Retail	$462	$370	$300	$250	$215	$200	$190	$180

Add $30 for nickel/stainless finish (disc. 1993).

MUSTANG — similar to .380 Series Govt., except has 2¾ in. barrel, 5 or 6 (new 1992) shot mag., blue finish only, 18½ oz. New 1986.

Mfg.'s Sug. Retail	$462	$370	$300	$250	$215	$200	$190	$180

▲ *Nickel finish* — bright polish nickel finish with white composite grips. Mfg. 1987-94.

	$405	$330	$270	$240	$220	$210	$200

Last Mfg.'s Sug. Retail was $504.

▲ *Stainless Steel* — stainless steel variation of the Mustang. New 1990.

Mfg.'s Sug. Retail	$493	$385	$330	$270			

▲ *Coltguard finish* — employs a high strength electroless matte nickel finish. Mfg. 1987.

	$330	$300	$260	$235	$210	$200	$185

Last Mfg.'s Sug. Retail was $406.

Grading	100%	98%	95%	90%	80%	70%	60%

MUSTANG PLUS II — .380 ACP only, 2¾ in. barrel, blued finish, black composition grips, 7 shot mag., 20 oz. New 1988.

Mfg.'s Sug. Retail	$462	$370	$300	$250	$215	$200	$190	$180

This model has the full grip length of the .380 Government Model.

▲ *Stainless Steel* — stainless steel variation of the Mustang Plus II. New 1990.

Mfg.'s Sug. Retail	$493	$385	$330	$270

MUSTANG POCKETLITE L.W. — similar to Mustang, except has aluminum alloy receiver, blue only, black composite grips, 12½ oz. Introduced 1987.

Mfg.'s Sug. Retail	$462	$370	$300	$250	$215	$200	$190	$180

▲ *Nickel/Stainless Steel Finish* — similar to Mustang Pocketlite, except has nickel finish frame and stainless steel slide. New 1991.

Mfg.'s Sug. Retail	$493	$385	$330	$270	$230	$200	$190	$180

▲ *Lady Elite* — features hard chrome receiver, blue slide with silver painted rollmark, finger extension mag., soft carrying case, limited mfg. beginning 1995.

Mfg.'s Sug. Retail	$612	$525	$450	$325	$250	$225	$200	$185

▲ *Nite Lite .380* — .380 ACP cal., features bar-dot glowing night sight, teflon coated alloy receiver with stainless slide, finger extension mag., includes carrying case. Mfg. 1994 only.

	$495	$425	$325	$250	$225	$200	$185

Last Mfg.'s Sug. Retail was $577.

PISTOLS: SEMI-AUTO, DOUBLE ACTION

DOUBLE EAGLE SERIES 90 I & II — 9mm Para. (mfg. 1991 only), .38 Super (mfg. 1991 only), .45 ACP, or 10mm (disc. 1993) cal., double action semi-auto that operates on the Browning/Colt short recoil, link pivot locking system used by the Govt. Model, 5 in. barrel, matte stainless steel only, 3 dot sighting system or Accro adj. rear sight (disc. 1994), checkered synthetic Xenoy grips, 8 shot mag. (9 shot in 9mm Para. or .38 Super cal.), decocking lever, squared off combat trigger guard, 39 oz. New 1990.

Mfg.'s Sug. Retail	$727	$610	$500	$425

Add $50 for 9mm Para. or .38 Super cal.
Add $20 for 10mm cal.

The first edition (1,000 mfg. in 1989) on this model did not have a decocking lever - retail was $916.

▲ *Double Eagle Combat Commander* — .40 S&W (new 1992) or .45 ACP cal., 4¼ in. barrel, 8 shot mag., white dot sights, 36 oz. New 1991.

Mfg.'s Sug. Retail	$727	$610	$500	$425

▲ *Officer's Model* — .45 ACP cal., 3½ in. barrel, 8 shot mag., 35 oz. New 1991.

Mfg.'s Sug. Retail	$727	$610	$500	$425

▲ *Officer's Lightweight Model* — .45 ACP cal. only, 3½ in. barrel, alloy frame with blue finish only, white dot sights, 25 oz. Mfg. 1991-1993.

	$650	$525	$450	$400	$360	$330	$295

Last Mfg.'s Sug. Retail was $696.

ALL AMERICAN MODEL 2000 — 9mm Para. only, double action semi-auto, new design features roller-bearing mounted trigger allowing double action only trigger pull every shot, utilizes a recoil operated rotary action featuring integral locking lugs similar to the military M-16 rifle, hammerless, 4½ in. barrel, matte finished steel slide and polymer receiver, 15 shot mag., 3-dot sighting system, ambidextrous mag. release, black synthetic checkered grips, internal striker block safety, checkered trigger guard and front grip strap, 29 oz. Manufacturing difficulty forced discontinuance and design and tooling were returned to Reed Knight. Mfg. 1991-1993.

Grading	100%	98%	95%	90%	80%	70%	60%

▲ **Model 2000 - Polymer Frame**

| | $425 | $375 | $325 | $275 | $250 | $225 | $200 |

Last Mfg.'s Sug. Retail was $575.

This model was also available in a 3¾ in. barrel/bushing kit allowing rapid conversion (no tools or other components were needed - $75 retail during 1993 only).

▲ **Model 2000 - Aluminum Frame** — similar to polymer Model 2000, except frame is aluminum, serial numbered RK00001-RK03000 to commemorate the designer (Reed Knight), mfg. 1993.

| | $475 | $400 | $340 | $285 | $250 | $225 | $200 |

Last Mfg.'s Sug. Retail was $575.

PISTOLS: SEMI-AUTO .22 CAL. (WOODSMAN SERIES)

The publisher wishes to express his thanks to Major Robert J. Rayburn for his generous contributions of information regarding the Colt Woodsman Series, some of which have appeared in this publication for the first time.

The Colt Woodsman was made for 62 years, and included a multitude of variations/options in models, sights, barrels, grips, markings, etc. Many of the variations are quite scarce and desirable, but generally known only to specialized collectors. The following price guidelines are for standard production models, and only for those specimens in unmodified, factory original condition.

Note: All 100% condition Woodsmans with the original serial numbered box, test target, instruction folder, hang tag, and screw driver command a 10-25% premium, depending on the model's age and rarity.

Over 690,000 Woodsmans with variations were mfg. between 1915-1977.

PRE-WOODSMAN — .22 LR, 6⅝ in. barrel. 10 shot Mag., blue only, bottom mag. release, checkered wood grips, adj. front and rear sights. Mfg. 1915-1927, production totaled about 54,000, this model was officially named "Colt Automatic Pistol, Caliber .22 Target Model", magazine base has 2-line legend "CAL .22" "COLT". Standard velocity ammo. only.

| | $995 | $775 | $525 | $425 | $325 | $275 | $250 |

This model was manufactured to use standard velocity ammunition only (not high speed). Colt did offer a conversion kit for high velocity ammo after the transition to high velocity in 1931.

Woodsmans mfg. between 1915-1922 had a lightweight pencil barrel (approx. serial range 1-31,000). The medium barrel was introduced in 1922 and was retained until the 90,000 serial range (approx. mfg. 1922-1934).

WOODSMAN 1ST SERIES — .22 LR, 10 shot Mag., blue only, bottom mag. release, checkered wood grips, marked "The Woodsman" on receiver, adj. sights, mfg. from 1927-1947, total production was approx. 112,000.

Note: Guns made prior to 1931 were designed for standard velocity .22 LR ammunition only. The new style main spring housing, designed for high velocity ammunition, began appearing at approx. ser. no. 80,000 and was completely phased in by approx. ser. no. 85,000. Later guns, INCLUDING ALL PISTOLS MADE AFTER WWII, were designed for high velocity ammunition.

Between 1934 and 1947 a tapered barrel was standard production (approx. ser. range 90,000-187,423).

▲ **Sport Model** — 4½ in. barrel, this model was introduced in 1933.

| | $1,050 | $850 | $595 | $495 | $450 | $395 | $350 |

Approx. serial range on this variation is 86,105 - 187,423 from 1933 to 1947.

▲ **Target Model** — 6⅝ in. barrel.

| | $895 | $695 | $475 | $400 | $325 | $275 | $250 |

Note: Colt discontinued the 1st series in 1947. These guns are quite different from the 2nd series started later in 1947.

Grading	100%	98%	95%	90%	80%	70%	60%

WOODSMAN 1ST SERIES MATCH TARGET — .22 LR only, 6⅝ in. heavy barrel, commonly called "Bullseye" Match Target, mfg. 1938-1944, production totaled around 16,000. Difficult to find in mint condition. Values listed assume original one-piece extended walnut grips.

	$2,000	$1,500	$995	$750	$575	$475	$400

> The correct magazine on this model has a 3-line legend "COLT WOODSMAN" "CAL. 22 L.R." "MATCH TARGET MOD.".

▲ ***"U.S. Property" Marked*** — approx. 4,000 Match Target Woodsmans were sold to the U.S. Army and U.S. Navy during WWII. Most have serial numbers above MT12500, although some were shipped out of sequence with lower numbers. The wartime guns had elongated plastic stocks and standard blue finish, although some of them are now parkerized as the result of arsenal refinishing or other non-factory modifications. They are marked with either "US PROPERTY" or the ordnance wheel with crossed cannon, as well as the initials of the govt. inspector. Some also have additional markings.

	$2,225	$1,775	$1,425	$1,150	$925	$750	$575

> Observe parkerized finish carefully on this variation as some "recent parkerizing" has been performed.

WOODSMAN 2ND SERIES — .22 LR only, slide stop and hold open, push button mag. release on this model is located on the left side of frame, Coltwood plastic grips (mfg. 1947-1950) or brown plastic grips (mfg. 1950-1955), total production on all 2nd Series was (not including the Challenger) approx. 146,000 mfg. 1947-1955.

▲ ***Sport Model*** — 4½ in. barrel.

	$750	$595	$495	$395	$350	$295	$250

▲ ***Target Model*** — 6 in. barrel.

	$650	$550	$450	$350	$325	$275	$225

▲ ***Match Target Model*** — 4½ in. heavy barrel. This variation will command a premium over the 6 in. barrel.

	$895	$795	$595	$450	$425	$400	$375

▲ ***Match Target Model*** — 6 in. heavy barrel.

	$795	$695	$500	$400	$350	$325	$300

WOODSMAN 3RD SERIES — .22 LR only, slide stop and hold open, mfg. between 1955-1977, black plastic grips (mfg. 1955-1960) or walnut grips (1960-1977), 3rd Models can be differentiated from 2nd Models by their bottom mag. release. Total production of all 3rd series Woodsman models (not including the Huntsman or Targetsman) exceeded 100,000.

▲ ***Sport Model*** — 4½ in. barrel.

	$595	$495	$395	$325	$300	$275	$250

▲ ***Target Model*** — 6 in. barrel.

	$550	$450	$350	$275	$250	$235	$225

▲ ***Match Target Model*** — 4½ in. heavy barrel.

	$795	$695	$595	$450	$400	$375	$350

▲ ***Match Target Model*** — 6 in. heavy barrel.

	$695	$595	$495	$400	$350	$325	$295

CHALLENGER MODEL — similar to Woodsman 2rd Series, only with fixed sights, without hold open, and bottom mag. release, 4½ and 6 in. barrels, mfg. between 1950-1955 with total production reaching approx. 77,000. Plastic grips.

	$450	$350	$275	$250	$225	$210	$180

HUNTSMAN MODEL — .22 LR only, fixed sights and no hold open, 4½ and 6 in. barrels, black plastic grips to serial number 141094-C - walnut grips after that cutoff, mfg. between 1955-1977 with total production reaching over 100,000.

	$350	$295	$250	$225	$200	$180	$160

> The Huntsman is very similar to the Challenger Model, except is built on a 3rd series frame.

Grading	100%	98%	95%	90%	80%	70%	60%

▲ *Huntsman Model S Master Series* — approx. 400 Model S Masters were sold in 1983. This was a parts clean up by Colt, using Huntsman frames left over from the last days of production. They were equipped with automatic slide stop and Elliason rear sight, gold etching on the slide, and a French fitted walnut case marked "1 of 400". Approx. 285 had straight, non-tapered Huntsman barrel, while the remainder had the tapered Woodsman Sport barrel with pinned front sight.

	100%	98%	95%	90%	80%	70%	60%
W/Huntsman barrel	$895	$600	$500	$425	$350	$325	$295
W/Woodsman barrel	$995	$700	$600	$500	$425	$350	$325

Above values assume original walnut case included. Values for this model in 98%-60% original condition are hard to compute, as most are mint or new.

TARGETSMAN MODEL — similar to the Huntsman, except has adj. rear sight and thumbrest on left grip, 6 in. barrel only, approx. 65,000 mfg. 1959-1977.

	100%	98%	95%	90%	80%	70%	60%
	$450	$350	$280	$260	$240	$220	$200

COLT 22 — .22 LR cal., 4½ in. VR barrel, stainless steel, fixed sights, 10 shot mag., one-piece black Pachmayr rubber grips, 33½ oz. New 1994.

	Mfg.'s Sug. Retail			
Mfg.'s Sug. Retail	$248	$225	$190	$170

▲ *Colt 22 Target* — .22 LR cal., 6 in. VR barrel with full length grooved sight rib, adj. rear sight, 40½ oz. New 1995.

Mfg.'s Sug. Retail	$377	$290	$225	$190

100%	98%	95%	90%	80%	70%	60%	50%	40%	30%	20%	10%

REVOLVERS: DOUBLE ACTION

MODEL 1877 LIGHTNING — .38 Colt or .32 Colt (very rare), 2, 2½, 3½, 4½, or 6 in. barrels without ejector. 4½, 5, 6, 7, or 7½ in. barrels with ejector, 6 shot double action, long cylinder fluting, blued finish with case hardened frame and hammer, full nickel plating also available. Over 166,000 mfg. from 1877-1910.

100%	98%	95%	90%	80%	70%	60%	50%	40%	30%	20%	10%
$1,775	$1,500	$1,200	$950	$875	$775	$700	$650	$575	$475	$350	$295

MODEL 1877 THUNDERER — .41 Colt cal. only, otherwise same general specifications as Model 1877 Lightning.

100%	98%	95%	90%	80%	70%	60%	50%	40%	30%	20%	10%
$1,800	$1,600	$1,150	$975	$875	$775	$675	$600	$525	$450	$325	$285

MODEL 1878 FRONTIER — .32-20 WCF, .38-40 WCF, .44-40 WCF, .45 Colt, or .450-.455-.476 Eley cal., 3½ or 4 in. barrels without ejector, 4¾, 5½, or 7½ in. with ejector. 6 in. is 1902 U.S. Revolver (Alaskan/Phillipines Models), 6 shot cylinder with long flutes, pinched frame, removable trigger guard, early guns have checked walnut stocks, later guns have hard black rubber. Mfg. 1878-1905. Over 51,000 made.

100%	98%	95%	90%	80%	70%	60%	50%	40%	30%	20%	10%
$3,500	$3,000	$2,500	$1,750	$1,500	$950	$850	$750	$650	$550	$435	$375

MODEL 1889 "NAVY" — .38 Short and Long Colt, and .41 Short and Long Colt, 3, 4½, and 6 in. barrel, wood or rubber grips, blue or nickel finish, the first solid frame, swing out cylinder with no visible locking latches (rotates counter-clockwise) Colt produced approx. 28,000 mfg. 1889-1894, 1st 5,000 were ordered by U.S. Navy - hence name.

▲ *Blue finish*

100%	98%	95%	90%	80%	70%	60%	50%	40%	30%	20%	10%
$1,250	$995	$895	$800	$750	$695	$650	$575	$500	$425	$350	$300

▲ *U.S. Navy Contract (S.N. 1-5,000), U.S.N. on butt - add 65%.*

MODEL 1892 "NEW ARMY & NAVY" (2ND ISSUE) — similar to 1889 Navy, but double cylinder notches, double locking bolt, and shorter flutes, square cyl. release thumb catch, .32-20 added in 1905, mfg. 1892-1907.

100%	98%	95%	90%	80%	70%	60%	50%	40%	30%	20%	10%
$895	$800	$700	$595	$475	$375	$310	$265	$235	$225	$210	$195

Add $100 for U.S.N. markings.

▲ *Models 1892, 1894, 1895, 1896, 1901.* — these were variations of the Model 1892, values will approximate those shown above.

100%	98%	95%	90%	80%	70%	60%	50%	40%	30%	20%	10%

OFFICER'S MODEL TARGET (FIRST ISSUE) — .38 Spl., 6 in. barrel, adj. front - adj. rear type sights, high luster blue, flat-top. Mfg. 1904-1908.

$1,250	$1,000	$850	$695	$595	$550	$495	$395	$295	$275	$250	$225

OFFICER'S MODEL TARGET (SECOND ISSUE) — .32 Colt or .38 Spl. cal., 4, 4½, 5, 6, or 7½ in. barrel, high luster blue through 1916, adj. front - adj. rear type sights, checkered walnut grips, deep set medallions in grips were standard from 1913-1923. Mfg. 1908-1926.

$825	$795	$600	$515	$450	$395	$330	$290	$250	$225	$210	$195

Add 60% for .32 Colt cal.

OFFICER'S MODEL TARGET (THIRD ISSUE) — similar design to the Second Issue, .22 cal. was added beginning 1930. Mfg. 1927-1949.

$675	$625	$560	$500	$450	$375	$325	$295	$265	$245	$225	$205

Add 10% for .22 LR cal. (mfg. started 1930).

MODEL 1905 MARINE CORPS — similar to New Navy Second Issue, except has a round butt, in .38 Short or Long, only 6 in. barrel. Mfg. 1905-1909 in approx. ser. no. range 10,001-10,926, about 926 mfg.

$2,650	$2,350	$2,050	$1,750	$1,625	$1,425	$1,250	$1,000	$895	$795	$695	$595

Add 30% for Military issue marked "USMC" on butt.

ARMY SPECIAL MODEL — .32-20, .38 (various), and .41 Colt, 4, 4½, 5, and 6 in. barrels, hard rubber grips standard through 1923 - checkered wood with medallions beginning 1924, fixed sights, rounded cylinder release thumb catch, has heavier frame than New Navy, approx. ser. no. range 291,000-540,000, mfg. 1908-1927.

▲ *Blue finish*

$550	$450	$375	$335	$295	$265	$245	$230	$215	$200	$185	$175

Add 15% for nickel finish.

NEW SERVICE MODEL — .38 Spl., .357 Mag., .38-40, .44-40, .44 Russian, .44 Spl., .45 ACP, .45 Colt, .450 Eley, .455 Eley, or .476 Eley, 4, 5, or 6 in. barrels in .357 Mag. and .38 Spl., 4½, 5½, and 7½ in. barrel in all others, blue or nickel finish, originally hard rubber (until approx. late '20s), with later guns having walnut grips. Mfg. 1898-1942. Rare cals. (.450 and .476 Eley cals.) will command premiums over values listed below.

▲ *Commercial*

$1,500	$1,375	$1,175	$1,000	$925	$850	$775	$650	$500	$425	$375	$295

▲ *1909 Army Model*

$1,550	$1,275	$1,125	$1,000	$925	$850	$775	$680	$590	$510	$435	$375

▲ *1909 Navy Model* — shortest production run of the Model 1909 variations.

$2,450	$2,100	$1,825	$1,450	$1,150	$1,000	$895	$775	$600	$500	$450	$395

▲ *1909 - USMC*

$2,850	$2,400	$2,100	$1,775	$1,500	$1,250	$975	$825	$700	$600	$500	$450

▲ *1917 Army*

$925	$825	$750	$670	$610	$525	$455	$390	$335	$295	$250	$200

▲ *1917 Civilian/Commercial (1917 C/CM)* — .45 ACP, 5½ in. barrel only, last patent date is OCT 5, 1926, checkered walnut grips with medallions, left side of barrel marked "Colt Model 1917 Auto Ctge." approx. 1,000 mfg. during 1932, serialized 335,000-336,000.

$1,500	$1,275	$1,050	$850	$650	$525	$450	$415	$385	$350	$325	$295

▲ *1917 Civilian/Commercial (Piece Parts Model)* — .38-40, .44-40, or .45 LC cal., 4½ or 5½ in. barrel, hard rubber grips, or checkered walnut with medallions, last patent date is July 4, 1905, approx. 1,000 mfg. serialized 336,450-337,500.

$1,200	$995	$900	$800	$625	$495	$415	$380	$360	$330	$300	$275

100%	98%	95%	90%	80%	70%	60%	50%	40%	30%	20%	10%

▲ *New Service Target* — similar to New Service Model, flat-top frame, hand-honed action and adj. front - adj. rear type sights, 6 (scarce) or 7½ in. barrel, square butt, round butt available after 1930, checkered grip straps, checkered walnut grips with medallion after 1913, blue or nickel (scarce) finish. Mfg. 1900-1940.

| $2,500 | $2,000 | $1,750 | $1,500 | $1,250 | $900 | $750 | $635 | $550 | $460 | $400 | $350 |

Add 40% for 6 in. barrel.

▲ *Shooting Master* — various cals. from 38 Spl. through .45 LC, 6 in. barrel, checkered walnut grips with Colt Medallion, machined grip straps, trigger, hammer, and ejector rod head, round or square butt, approx. ser. no. range 333,000 - 350,000.

| $1,250 | $1,100 | $975 | $900 | $825 | $755 | $665 | $575 | $500 | $435 | $395 | $375 |

Add 35% for .357 Mag.
Add 100% for .44 Spl., .45 ACP, or .45 LC cal.
The Shooting Master could be ordered with a square butt after 1933.

OFFICIAL POLICE PRE-WAR — .32-20 (disc. 1942), .41 long (disc. 1930), .38 Spl., or .22 LR (introduced 1930 - 6 in. barrel only), 6 shot, square butt, 4, 5, or 6 in. barrels, 2 in. barrel (scarce) in .38 Spl., checkered walnut grips, fixed sights. Mfg. 1927-1946.

▲ *Blue finish*

| $495 | $425 | $375 | $325 | $295 | $265 | $235 | $210 | $185 | $165 | $145 | $135 |

Add 15% for nickel finish.
Add 15% for .22 LR cal.

OFFICIAL POLICE POST-WAR — .22 LR or .38 Spl. cal., 2, 4, or 6 in. barrel, Coltwood plastic grips 1947-1954 - checkered walnut thereafter, fixed sights mfg. 1947-1969.

| $425 | $375 | $325 | $295 | $265 | $235 | $210 | $185 | $165 | $145 | $135 | $125 |

Add 15% for nickel finish.
Add 15% for .22 cal.
On this model, the 2 in. barrel in .38 Spl. cal. is scarce. .22 cal. was available with 4 or 6 in. barrel only.

MARSHAL MODEL — .38 Spl., 2 (less common) or 4 in. barrel, round butt, differentiated by "M" suffix and "COLT MARSHAL" on barrel, about 2,500 mfg. 1954-1956 in approx. ser. no. range 833350-M through 845320-M.

| $800 | $700 | $600 | $475 | $395 | $335 | $305 | $275 | $245 | $215 | $180 | $160 |

COMMANDO MODEL — .38 Spl., 2 in. (less common), 4 in. (common), or 6 in. (rare) barrel, parkerized finish, about 50,000 mfg. between 1942-1945, 32 oz., marked "COLT COMMANDO" on barrel.

| $595 | $495 | $400 | $350 | $300 | $275 | $250 | $200 | $175 | $150 | $135 | $120 |

Add 15% for 2 in. barrel.

OFFICIAL POLICE MKIII — .38 Spl., 4, 5, or 6 in. barrels. Mfg. 1969-1975.

▲ *Blue finish*

| $325 | $235 | $180 | $150 | $135 | $125 | $115 | $105 | $100 | $95 | $90 | $85 |

▲ *Nickel finish*

| $350 | $250 | $195 | $175 | $165 | $155 | $145 | $135 | $125 | $115 | $105 | $100 |

METROPOLITAN MK III — .38 Spl., similar to Official Police, except heavier and 4 in. heavy barrel only, blue finish. Mfg. 1969-1972.

| $495 | $395 | $300 | $250 | $200 | $180 | $160 | $140 | $120 | $110 | $100 | $90 |

OFFICER'S MODEL SPECIAL (FOURTH ISSUE) — .22 LR or .38 Spl., 6 in. barrel, blue, similar to Third Issue, only heavier non-tapered barrel, new style hammer and "Coltmaster Sight", checkered plastic grips. Mfg. 1949-1952.

| $575 | $500 | $450 | $375 | $325 | $295 | $265 | $245 | $225 | $205 | $190 | $175 |

Add $75 for .22 LR cal.

100%	98%	95%	90%	80%	70%	60%	50%	40%	30%	20%	10%

C

OFFICER'S MODEL MATCH (FIFTH ISSUE) — .22 LR, .22 Mag, or .38 Spl., 6 in. barrel, tapered heavy barrel, wide spur hammer, Accro sight, large target grips (walnut). Mfg. 1953-1969.

$475	$425	$375	$325	$300	$275	$250	$225	$200	$185	$170	$155

Add $75 for .22 LR cal.
Add 100% for .22 Mag. cal. (approx. 850 mfg.).
This model was also produced in "single action only" in limited numbers - add a 25%-40% premium, depending on condition.

OFFICER'S MODEL MATCH MK III (SIXTH ISSUE) — .38 Spl. only, 6 in. shrouded VR barrel, wide spur hammer, Accro sights, target grips, 496 mfg. 1969-70 only.

$1,325	$1,200	$995	$925	$850	$775	$700	$650	$600	$550	$475	$425

NEW POCKET — .32 S and LC, 2½, 3½, 5, or 6 in. barrel, rubber grips. Mfg. 1895-1905.

▲ *Blue finish*

$550	$475	$400	$335	$300	$275	$250	$215	$190	$170	$150	$140

Add 15% for nickel finish.

POCKET POSITIVE — similar to New Pocket, except has positive lock feature, also chambered for .32 Colt, .32 S&W, and .32 Colt New Police. Mfg. 1905-1940.

▲ *Blue finish*

$495	$440	$385	$350	$325	$295	$265	$235	$210	$185	$165	$145

Add 15%-20% for nickel finish.

NEW POLICE — .32 Colt and .32 Colt New Police, 2½, 4, and 6 in. barrels, fixed sights, same frame as New Pocket, except larger grips, rubber grips. Mfg. 1896-1907.

▲ *Blue finish*

$495	$395	$295	$255	$230	$215	$200	$185	$170	$160	$150	$145

Add 10% for nickel finish.

NEW POLICE TARGET — .32 cal. only, 6 in. barrel, blue, approx. 5,000 mfg. 1897-1907.

$900	$775	$650	$550	$450	$395	$350	$300	$275	$250	$225	$200

POLICE POSITIVE — .32 Colt, .32 New Police, .38 New Police, or .38 S&W, 2½ in. (.32 only), 4, 5, or 6 in. barrels, improved "positive lock" version of the New Police, hard rubber grips standard through 1923, checkered walnut grips 1924-1947. Mfg. 1907-1947.

▲ *Blue finish*

$435	$385	$335	$295	$275	$250	$225	$205	$185	$170	$160	$150

Add 15% for nickel finish.

POLICE POSITIVE TARGET MODEL — .22 LR, .22 WRF, .32 Colt, or .32 New Police, 6 in. barrel, blue, adj. sight, hard rubber grips standard through 1923, checkered walnut grips 1924-1947. Mfg. 1907-1940.

$695	$625	$575	$525	$475	$425	$390	$360	$325	$285	$250	$210

Add 40% for .32 cal.

POLICE POSITIVE SPECIAL (FIRST ISSUE) — .32-20, .32 New Police, .38 New Police, or .38 Spl., 4, 5, or 6 in. barrels, fixed sights, frame longer to permit longer cylinder, wood, rubber, or plastic grips. Mfg. 1907-1946.

$495	$450	$395	$325	$300	$275	$250	$225	$200	$185	$170	$155

CAMP PERRY MODEL — .22 LR, 8 in. (less common) or 10 in., Officer's Model frame modified to accept a flat single shot chamber. The model name was stamped on the left side of the chamber, the only single shot Colt on a revolver frame. 2,488 mfg. between 1926-1941.

$1,495	$1,250	$1,050	$900	$835	$775	$715	$645	$575	$495	$425	$365

Add 25% for 8 in. barrel.

BANKER'S SPECIAL — 2 in. barrel, blue, square butt standard through 1933, round butt standard 1934-1940. Mfg. 1926-1940.

100%	98%	95%	90%	80%	70%	60%	50%	40%	30%	20%	10%

▲ *.38 cal.*

| $1,150 | $975 | $750 | $595 | $495 | $395 | $325 | $275 | $235 | $205 | $185 | $165 |

Add 40% for nickel finish.

▲ *.22 cal.*

| $1,695 | $1,475 | $1,150 | $950 | $750 | $650 | $550 | $475 | $425 | $385 | $355 | $325 |

Add 30% for nickel finish.

COURIER — .22 S, L, & LR, .32 New Police, double action, 6 shot, 3 in. barrel, approx. 3,053 mfg. 1953-1956.

| $775 | $700 | $640 | $550 | $475 | $425 | $395 | $350 | $325 | $295 | $260 | $230 |

Add 10% for .22 cal.

Even though fewer .22 cal. Couriers were mfg. than Banker's Specials, the Banker's Specials are still more desirable as they are less frequently encountered in 95-100% condition.

AIRCREWMAN SPECIAL — .38 Spl., double action, aluminum frame, 2 in. barrel, 11 oz., fixed sights, checkered walnut grips overlapping at top of frame, inset with silver Air Force buttons, mfg. 1951 mostly.

| $3,500 | $3,100 | $2,550 | $2,100 | $1,700 | $1,350 | $1,075 | $950 | $850 | $750 | $675 | $595 |

Approx. 1,200 mfg. within ser. no. range 2,900LW - 7,775LW. Perhaps less than 25 have survived.

BORDER PATROL — .38 Spl., double action, 6 shot, 4 in. heavy barrel, 400 mfg. during 1952 only in 823,000 ser. no. range.

| $3,100 | $2,775 | $2,300 | $1,775 | $1,400 | $1,125 | $995 | $875 | $775 | $675 | $595 | $525 |

This model is built on the Official Police Model frame.

DETECTIVE SPECIAL PRE-WAR (FIRST ISSUE) — .38 Spl. cal., 2 in. barrel, blue, wood grips, square butt standard through 1933, round butt standard 1934-1936. Mfg. 1927-1946.

| $675 | $595 | $495 | $425 | $375 | $325 | $275 | $250 | $225 | $205 | $190 | $175 |

Add 15% for nickel finish.

DETECTIVE SPECIAL POST-WAR (SECOND ISSUE) — .32 New Police, .38 New Police, or .38 Spl. cal., 2 or 3 (scarce) in. barrel, plastic grips 1947-1954 - wood grips thereafter, wrap-under wood grips started in 1966. Mfg. 1947-1972.

| $445 | $385 | $325 | $250 | $225 | $200 | $185 | $170 | $160 | $150 | $140 | $120 |

Add 15% for nickel finish.
Add 15% for 3 in. barrel.

COBRA (FIRST ISSUE) — .22 LR, .32 Colt NP, .38 Colt NP, or .38 Spl. cal., first issue, 2, 3, or 4 (square butt only) in. barrel, blue or nickel finish, similar to Detective Special, only alloy frame and available in .22 LR. Mfg. began 1950.

| $445 | $385 | $325 | $250 | $225 | $200 | $185 | $170 | $160 | $150 | $140 | $120 |

Add 20% for .22 LR cal.
Add 15% for nickel finish.
Add 15% for .38 cal. with 3 in. barrel.
The .22 LR cal. is available in 3 in. barrel only.

AGENT (FIRST ISSUE) — .38 Spl., similar to Cobra first issue, except shorter grip frame. Mfg. 1955-1972.

| $425 | $375 | $295 | $235 | $200 | $180 | $160 | $145 | $130 | $120 | $110 | $100 |

AGENT L.W. — .38 Spl., similar to First Issue, except shrouded ejector rod, alloy frame, matte finish since 1982. Mfg. 1973-86.

| $375 | $325 | $275 | $215 | $175 | $160 | $145 | $135 | $125 | $115 | $105 | $100 |

Last Mfg.'s Sug. Retail was $260.

COBRA (SECOND ISSUE) — .38 Spl., similar to Cobra first issue, except shrouded ejector rod. Mfg. 1973-1981.

| $395 | $365 | $275 | $250 | $225 | $200 | $190 | $175 | $160 | $150 | $140 | $120 |

100%	98%	95%	90%	80%	70%	60%	50%	40%	30%	20%	10%

DETECTIVE SPECIAL (THIRD ISSUE) — .38 Spl., similar to Second Issue, shrouded ejector rod, 2 or 3 (scarce) in. barrel, fixed sights, wraparound wood grips. Mfg. 1973-86.

| $395 | $365 | $275 | $250 | $225 | $200 | $190 | $175 | $160 | $150 | $140 | $120 |

Last Mfg.'s Sug. Retail was $429.

Add $50 for nickel.
Add 15% for 3 in. barrel.
Also available with class A engraving - add $590 if in 98% condition or better.

COMMANDO SPECIAL — .38 Spl., similar to Detective Special with steel frame, shrouded ejector rod, 2 in. barrel, matte parkerized finish, rubber grips. Mfg. 1984-86.

| $350 | $295 | $265 | $225 | $195 | $170 | $155 | $140 | $125 | $115 | $105 | $100 |

Last Mfg.'s Sug. Retail was $260.

POLICE POSITIVE SPECIAL (SECOND ISSUE) — .38 Spl., similar to Detective Special Second Issue, except 4, 5 or 6 in. barrel. Mfg. 1947-76.

| $350 | $295 | $265 | $225 | $195 | $170 | $155 | $140 | $125 | $115 | $105 | $100 |

POLICE POSITIVE SPECIAL (THIRD ISSUE) — .38 Spl. cal., 4 in. shrouded barrel, steel frame, blue or nickel finish. Mfg. 1977-78 only.

| $395 | $350 | $300 | $220 | $185 | $170 | $150 | $135 | $125 | $115 | $105 | $100 |

Add 10% for nickel finish.

VIPER MODEL — .38 Spl., similar to Police Positive Special (Third Issue), alloy frame, 4 in. shrouded barrel. Mfg. 1977 only.

| $425 | $375 | $325 | $250 | $225 | $200 | $190 | $175 | $160 | $150 | $140 | $120 |

Add 30% for nickel finish.

DIAMONDBACK — .22 LR or .38 Spl., 2½ (scarce in .22 LR), 4, or 6 in. VR barrel, adj. sights, steel frame, checkered walnut grips. Mfg. 1966-86.

| $395 | $340 | $300 | $265 | $245 | $225 | $205 | $190 | $175 | $160 | $150 | $140 |

Last Mfg.'s Sug. Retail was $461.

Add $55 for nickel finish.
Add 20% for .22 LR cal.
Add 30% for .22 LR cal. with 2½ in. barrel.
Note: Approx. 2,200 Diamondbacks were made with 6 in. barrels and nickel finish in .22 cal. - made 1979. Add additional $150 for 100% specimens.

COLT .357 MAG — 4 in. or 6 in. barrel, heavy frame, Accro sight, blue or nickel finish, checkered walnut grips. Later guns marked Trooper. Mfg. 1953-1961.

▲ *Standard hammer*

| $450 | $375 | $325 | $295 | $275 | $265 | $255 | $245 | $230 | $220 | $210 | $200 |

▲ *Wide hammer w/target grips*

| $475 | $400 | $350 | $300 | $285 | $265 | $255 | $245 | $235 | $225 | $215 | $205 |

TROOPER — .22 LR (scarce), .357 Mag., or .38 Spl., 4 or 6 in. barrel, blue or nickel finish, quick draw ramp front sight, adj. rear sight, checkered walnut grips. Mfg. 1953-1969.

▲ *Standard hammer*

| $350 | $295 | $250 | $210 | $200 | $190 | $180 | $170 | $165 | $160 | $155 | $150 |

▲ *Wide hammer and target grips*

| $375 | $325 | $275 | $225 | $210 | $200 | $190 | $180 | $170 | $165 | $160 | $155 |

Add $75-$125 for .22 LR cal. (4 in. barrel only), depending on condition.
Add 15% for nickel finish.

Grading	100%	98%	95%	90%	80%	70%	60%

TROOPER MK III — .22 LR, .22 Mag., .357 Mag., or .38 Spl. cal., 4, 6, or 8 in. solid rib barrel, adj. sights, walnut target grips, redesigned lock work to reduce amount of hand fitting needed on earlier predecessors. Mfg. 1969-1983.

	100%	98%	95%	90%	80%	70%	60%
Blue finish	$325	$275	$190	$180	$170	$160	$150
Nickel finish	$345	$275	$200	$190	$180	$170	$160

TROOPER MK V — .357 Mag., 4 or 6 in. barrel, adj. sights, walnut target grips, improved version of Mark III action, vent. rib barrel, redesigned 1982. Disc. 1986.

▲ *Blue finish*

	100%	98%	95%	90%	80%	70%	60%
	$375	$315	$275	$215	$185	$170	$160

Last Mfg.'s Sug. Retail was $362.

▲ *Nickel finish*

	100%	98%	95%	90%	80%	70%	60%
	$400	$350	$300	$235	$200	$185	$170

Last Mfg.'s Sug. Retail was $396.

LAWMAN MK III — .357 Mag., 2 in. and 4 in. barrel, unshrouded or shrouded ejector rod for 2 in. barrel, fixed sights, checkered walnut grips. Mfg. 1969-1983.

	100%	98%	95%	90%	80%	70%	60%
Blue finish	$295	$240	$190	$180	$170	$160	$150
Nickel finish	$315	$250	$200	$190	$180	$170	$160

LAWMAN MK V — .357 Mag., 2 or 4 in. barrel, shrouded ejector rod for 2 in. barrel, fixed sights, checkered walnut grips, improved version of MK III action. Mfg. 1984 and 1985 only.

▲ *Blue finish*

	100%	98%	95%	90%	80%	70%	60%
	$295	$250	$200	$175	$160	$150	$140

Last Mfg.'s Sug. Retail was $309.

▲ *Nickel finish*

	100%	98%	95%	90%	80%	70%	60%
	$325	$280	$225	$200	$180	$170	$160

Last Mfg.'s Sug. Retail was $328.

BORDER PATROL (SECOND ISSUE) — .357 Mag., 4 in. heavy barrel, Trooper Mark III frame, limited mfg. in 1970-75.

▲ *Blue Finish* — 5,356 mfg.

	100%	98%	95%	90%	80%	70%	60%
	$525	$450	$375	$275	$235	$200	$180

▲ *Nickel Finish* — 1,152 mfg.

	100%	98%	95%	90%	80%	70%	60%
	$625	$550	$475	$375	$325	$275	$235

PEACEKEEPER — .357 Mag. cal., similar to Trooper MK V, 4 or 6 in. barrel, matte blue finish, rubber combat grips, adj. rear sight, about 42 oz. Mfg. 1985-1987.

	100%	98%	95%	90%	80%	70%	60%
	$320	$275	$245	$205	$195	$180	$165

Last Mfg.'s Sug. Retail was $330.

BOA — .357 Mag., deep blue polish, full length ejector shroud with Mark V action, 600 each mfg. in 4 and 6 in. barrel lengths. Entire production run was purchased by Lew Horton Distributing Co., Inc. located in Southboro, MA. 1985 retail was $525.

	100%	98%	95%	90%	80%	70%	60%
	$595	$525	$450	$415	$375	$350	$325

▲ *Boa Set* — 100 sets mfg. including 4 and 6 in. barrels with fully shrouded ejector rod housing, consecutive serial numbers, cases were supplied by Lew Horton. 1985 retail was $1,200.

	100%	98%	95%
	$1,450	$1,100	$875

POLICE POSITIVE (FOURTH ISSUE) — .38 Spl. cal., 6 shot, 4 in. barrel, blue finish, fixed sights, black composition grips, 25 oz. Mfg. 1994-95.

	100%	98%	95%	90%	80%	70%	60%
	$345	$290	$250	$225	$195	$180	$165

Last Mfg.'s Sug. Retail was $400.

DETECTIVE SPECIAL (FOURTH ISSUE) — .38 Spl. cal., 6 shot, 2 in. barrel, alloy frame, blue finish, black composition grips with gold medallions, 21 oz. Reintroduced 1993, disc. 1995.

	100%	98%	95%	90%	80%	70%	60%
	$345	$290	$250	$225	$195	$180	$165

Last Mfg.'s Sug. Retail was $400.

Grading	100%	98%	95%	90%	80%	70%	60%

C

▲ *Bobbed Detective Special* — .38 Spl. cal., double action only with bobbed hammer, night front sight, honed action, choice of hard chrome or standard blue finish. Mfg. 1994-95.

| | $525 | $450 | $350 | $275 | $225 | $195 | $175 |

Last Mfg.'s Sug. Retail was $599.

Add $30 for hard chrome finish.

COLT .38 SF-VI — .38 Spl. cal., 6 shot, 2 or 4 in. barrel, transfer bar safety, choice of matte (2 in.), bright polished (4 in.), or black (4 in.) finish, stainless steel, regular or bobbed (4 in. barrel only) hammer, fixed sights, black composition combat grips, 21 oz. New 1995.

| Mfg.'s Sug. Retail | $408 | $350 | $290 | $250 | $225 | $195 | $180 | $165 |

▲ *Colt Special Lady* — features 2 in. barrel, bright stainless steel finish, bobbed hammer, tuned double action trigger pull, 21 oz. New 1996.

As this edition went to press, prices had yet to be determined.

COMBAT COBRA — .357 Mag., 2½ in. barrel, special edition for Lew Horton with CC prefix and stainless steel construction.

| | $495 | $450 | $395 | $350 | $315 | $280 | $250 |

KING COBRA — .357 Mag., blued metal, black neoprene round butt grips, 2 ½ (new 1990), 4 or 6 in. solid rib barrel only, outline sights, approx. 42 oz. (4 in. barrel). Mfg. 1988-92.

| | $335 | $295 | $260 | $235 | $210 | $200 | $185 |

Last Mfg.'s Sug. Retail was $410.

KING COBRA STAINLESS — .357 Mag., stainless steel construction, black neoprene round butt grips, 2½ (mfg. 1988-94), 4, 6, or 8 (mfg. 1990-94) in. solid rib barrel, outline sights, approx. 36 oz. (2½ in. barrel). Mfg. late 1987-92, production resumed 1994.

| Mfg.'s Sug. Retail | $455 | $380 | $330 | $265 |

▲ *King Cobra "Ultimate" Bright Stainless* — similar to King Cobra, except for bright stainless steel, 2 ½ (new 1990), 4, 6, or 8 (new 1991) in. barrel. Mfg. 1988-92.

| | $400 | $340 | $280 |

Last Mfg.'s Sug. Retail was $470.

PYTHON — .357 Mag., 2½ (disc. 1994), 3 (disc., very scarce), 4, 6, or 8 in. barrel with vent rib, royal blue finish, full shrouded ejector rod, adj. rear sight, checkered walnut grips (prior to 1991), rubber Hogue monogrips (2½ or 4 in. barrel), or rubber target (6 or 8 in. barrel) grips, 38-48 oz. Mfg. 1955-present.

▲ *Blue or royal blue finish*

| Mfg.'s Sug. Retail | $815 | $580 | $450 | $375 | $325 | $300 | $275 | $250 |

Early 2½, 4 or 6 in. Pythons without letter prefix before ser. no. will bring a small premium if in 100% condition or NIB, as well as the disc. 3 in. barrel. There were also a few Pythons mfg. in .256 cal., .38 Spl., .41 Mag., and .44 Spl. The amount of premium depends on how serious the Python collector is.

Also available with Class A, B, C, or D engraving — prices are the same as the .45 ACP Government Models listed previously under the Pistols: Semi-Auto, Recent Manufacture.

▲ *Nickel finish* — available in polished or satin nickel, disc. 1985.

| | $550 | $460 | $415 | $365 | $325 | $300 | $275 |

Last Mfg.'s Sug. Retail was $693.

▲ *Stainless Steel Python* — stainless steel construction, matte finish, neoprene target or combat stocks, 2½ (disc. 1994), 4, 6 or 8 (new 1989) in. barrel. Introduced 1983.

| Mfg.'s Sug. Retail | $904 | $680 | $575 | $450 |

The 6 in. barrel includes neoprene target stocks.

▲ *"Ultimate" Bright Stainless Steel* — deluxe, highly polished stainless model, 2½ (disc.), 4, 6 or 8 in. VR barrel. New 1985.

| Mfg.'s Sug. Retail | $935 | $700 | $585 | $455 |

Grading	100%	98%	95%	90%	80%	70%	60%

ULTIMATE PYTHON — .357 Mag., specially tuned by the custom gun shop, supplied with both Elliason target and Accro white outline sighting systems, walnut and rubber grips also included, choice of Colt Royal Blue or Ultimate Stainless finish, 6 in. barrel only. Mfg. 1991-1993.

	100%	98%	95%	90%	80%	70%	60%
	$1,025	$850	$775	$695	$625	$550	$475

Last Mfg.'s Sug. Retail was $1,140.

Add $120 for Ultimate Stainless Model.

PYTHON HUNTER — .357 Mag., 8 in. barrel, includes Leupold 2X scope, Halliburton aluminum case and accessories. Mfg. 1981 only.

	100%	98%	95%	90%	80%	70%	60%
	$1,195	$1,000	$750	$650	$595	$540	$495

Last Mfg.'s Sug. Retail was $995.

PYTHON .38 SPECIAL — 8 in. barrel, blue or nickel finish. Disc.

	100%	98%	95%	90%	80%	70%	60%
	$595	$500	$425	$375	$350	$325	$300

GRIZZLY — .357 Mag. cal., 6 in. barrel, blue only, approx. 1,000 mfg.

	100%	98%	95%	90%	80%	70%	60%
	$550	$475	$425	$375	$350	$325	$295

WHITETAILER — .357 Mag. cal., 8 in. barrel, matte stainless finish, aluminum hard shell cased with 2X scope.

	100%	98%	95%	90%	80%	70%	60%
	$1,095	$950	$750	$650	$595	$540	$495

▲ *Whitetailer II* — similar to Whitetailer, except has high polish finish.

	100%	98%	95%	90%	80%	70%	60%
	$1,050	$875	$750	$650	$595	$540	$495

ANACONDA — .44 Mag. or .45 LC (new 1992) cal., double action, 4 (.44 Mag. only, new 1991), 6, or 8 (new 1991) in. VR barrel, transfer bar safety system, 6 shot, choice of matte or Realtree Grey camo (.44 Mag. with 8 in. barrel only, new 1996) metal finish, stainless steel only, black neoprene combat grips with Colt medallion, red ramp front sight, full length ejector rod housing, white outline rear adj. sight, approx. 47-59 oz. New 1990.

Mfg.'s Sug. Retail	$612		$500	$410	$355		

Add $128 for Realtree Grey camo finish.

▲ *Anaconda with scope* — .44 Mag. only, 8 in. barrel, Realtree Grey camo finish on gun and scope. New 1996.

Mfg.'s Sug. Retail	$999		$795	$625	$475		

▲ *Anaconda Hunter* — .44 Mag. cal., supplied with Leupold 2X scope, carrying case, cleaning accessories, and both walnut and rubber grips, 8 in. barrel only. Mfg. 1991-1993.

	100%	98%	95%	90%	80%	70%	60%
	$1,095	$895	$725				

Last Mfg.'s Sug. Retail was $1,200.

▲ *Custom Anaconda* — .44 Mag. cal., features 6 or 8 in. Magna-ported barrel and Elliason rear sight, contoured trigger, and Pachmayr rubber grips, brushed stainless steel. Mfg. 1992-1993, re-released 1995.

Mfg.'s Sug. Retail	$870		$695	$550	$425		

▲ *Anaconda 1st Edition* — .44 Mag. cal., ultimate high polish stainless steel, special rollmark on left side of barrel reads "Colt Anaconda First Edition", with aluminum carrying case, ser. no. range MM00001-MM01000, 1,000 mfg. 1990 only.

	$895	$750	$625				

100%	98%	95%	90%	80%	70%	60%	50%	40%	30%	20%	10%

RIFLES: DISC.

FIRST MODEL RING LEVER — .34, .36, .38, .40, or .44, 8 or 10 shot revolving cylinder, 32 in. octagon barrel, walnut stock, no forend, 200 mfg., Percussion. Mfg. 1837-1838.

▲ *Standard Model*

100%	98%	95%	90%	80%	70%	60%	50%	40%	30%	20%	10%
N/A	N/A	N/A	$37,500	$28,000	$21,500	$16,500	$13,500	$11,000	$9,000	$7,500	$6,500

▲ *Improved Model* — attached loading lever.

100%	98%	95%	90%	80%	70%	60%	50%	40%	30%	20%	10%
N/A	N/A	N/A	$41,000	$29,650	$22,750	$17,500	$14,500	$12,000	$10,000	$8,500	$7,500

100%	98%	95%	90%	80%	70%	60%	50%	40%	30%	20%	10%

SECOND MODEL RING LEVER — similar to First Model, without top strap over cylinder, .44 caliber only, Percussion, 5000 mfg., 1838-1841.

▲ *Standard Model*

100%	98%	95%	90%	80%	70%	60%	50%	40%	30%	20%	10%
N/A	N/A	N/A	$33,500	$24,500	$17,000	$13,000	$11,000	$8,780	$7,200	$6,300	$5,650

▲ *Improved Model*

| N/A | N/A | N/A | $34,750 | $26,000 | $17,750 | $13,300 | $11,200 | $8,900 | $7,325 | $6,390 | $5,725 |

MODEL 1839 CARBINE — .525 smooth bore, 6 shot cylinder, 24 in. barrel, exposed hammer for cocking, blued, walnut stock, percussion, approx. 950 mfg., 1838-1841.

▲ *Early Model*

| N/A | N/A | N/A | $38,500 | $29,000 | $22,000 | $17,500 | $14,750 | $11,500 | $9,350 | $7,750 | $6,750 |

▲ *Standard Model* — no loading lever.

| N/A | N/A | N/A | $31,000 | $22,500 | $17,000 | $13,500 | $11,250 | $9,000 | $7,500 | $6,600 | $6,000 |

MODEL 1855 REVOLVING — .36, .44, or .56 cal., various barrel lengths and stock styles, 5 or 6 shot cylinder, blued with walnut butt stock, no forend, percussion. Mfg. 1856-1864.

▲ ½ *Stock Sporter* — 24, 27, or 30 in. barrel, approx. 1500 mfg.

| N/A | N/A | N/A | $11,500 | $9,000 | $7,850 | $7,000 | $6,500 | $6,000 | $5,500 | $5,100 | $4,750 |

▲ *Full Stock Sporter* — 21, 24, 27, 30, or 31 in. barrel, approx. 2000 mfg.

| N/A | N/A | N/A | $13,500 | $11,275 | $9,150 | $8,250 | $7,500 | $6,950 | $6,500 | $6,100 | $5,750 |

▲ *Military Model, U.S.* — marked, 21-37 in. barrel, 9310 mfg.

| N/A | N/A | N/A | $17,500 | $14,650 | $11,900 | $10,500 | $9,800 | $9,050 | $8,450 | $7,900 | $7,475 |

▲ *.36 Caliber Carbine Model* — 15, 18, or 21 in. barrel, 4400 mfg.

| N/A | N/A | N/A | $17,150 | $14,350 | $11,660 | $10,525 | $9,600 | $8,875 | $8,275 | $7,750 | $7,300 |

▲ *.56 Caliber Artillery Carbine* — 5 shot, 21 in. barrel with bayonet lug and forestock, approx. 64 mfg.

| N/A | N/A | N/A | $19,000 | $16,500 | $13,500 | $10,875 | $10,125 | $3,300 | $9,450 | $9,000 | $8,400 |

▲ *Shotgun Model* — .60 or .75 cal., smooth bore, 27, 30, 33, or 36 in. barrels, 1100 mfg.

| N/A | N/A | N/A | $12,750 | $11,000 | $9,000 | $8,000 | $7,250 | $6,750 | $6,300 | $6,000 | $5,600 |

MODEL 1861 MUSKET — .58 cal., percussion, muzzle loader, 40 in. barrel, with 3 bands, metal parts, white walnut stock, 75,000 mfg., 1861-1865.

| $2,750 | $2,500 | $2,350 | $1,895 | $1,750 | $1,650 | $1,500 | $1,350 | $1,250 | $1,150 | $1,000 | $850 |

COLT-BURGESS LEVER ACTION — .44-40 cal., 25½ in. barrel, 15 shot tube mag., blue with case hardened lever and hammer, walnut stock, 6400 mfg., 1883-1885.

| $8,750 | $7,450 | $6,350 | $5,500 | $4,900 | $4,465 | $4,170 | $3,930 | $3,700 | $3,525 | $3,350 | $3,100 |

COLT-BURGESS CARBINE — similar to Rifle, with 20 in. barrel.

| $11,500 | $9,950 | $8,750 | $7,900 | $7,300 | $6,725 | $6,250 | $5,850 | $5,500 | $5,200 | $4,950 | $4,750 |

COLT-BURGESS BABY CARBINE — similar to Carbine, with lightened frame.

| $14,000 | $12,250 | $10,750 | $9,720 | $8,975 | $8,275 | $7,695 | $7,200 | $6,765 | $6,395 | $6,100 | $5,850 |

LIGHTNING SLIDE ACTION - SMALL FRAME — small frame, .22 cal., 24 in. barrel, open sights, walnut straight stock, round or octagon barrel, 90,000 mfg. Mfg. 1887-1904.

| $2,300 | $1,650 | $1,250 | $1,000 | $795 | $650 | $575 | $535 | $495 | $450 | $400 | $375 |

LIGHTNING SLIDE ACTION - MEDIUM FRAME — medium frame, similar to small frame, in .32-20, .38-40, or .44-40, with larger frame.

| $3,250 | $2,550 | $2,150 | $1,775 | $1,475 | $1,175 | $950 | $775 | $650 | $550 | $495 | $450 |

LIGHTNING CARBINE MEDIUM FRAME — similar to Rifle, with 20 in. barrel.

| $5,250 | $3,850 | $3,250 | $2,850 | $2,450 | $2,150 | $1,950 | $1,750 | $1,450 | $1,175 | $1,050 | $950 |

LIGHTNING BABY CARBINE MEDIUM FRAME — lightened version of Carbine.

| $7,000 | $5,500 | $4,750 | $4,000 | $3,450 | $2,950 | $2,450 | $2,100 | $1,850 | $1,650 | $1,425 | $1,350 |

100%	98%	95%	90%	80%	70%	60%	50%	40%	30%	20%	10%

LIGHTNING SLIDE ACTION - LARGE FRAME — large frame, .38-56, .40-60, .45-60, .45-65, .45-85, or .50-95 Express cal., large version of previously described Lightnings, 6500 mfg. Mfg. 1887-1894.

$6,250	$4,750	$3,850	$3,250	$2,750	$2,250	$1,850	$1,650	$1,450	$1,325	$1,250	$1,175

Add 25% for .50-95 Express cal.

LIGHTNING CARBINE LARGE FRAME — 22 in. barrel.

$11,500	$9,000	$7,500	$6,250	$5,350	$4,850	$4,375	$3,925	$3,625	$3,375	$3,150	$2,975

BABY CARBINE LARGE FRAME — lightened version.

$13,500	$10,750	$9,700	$8,500	$7,750	$6,850	$6,300	$5,825	$5,425	$5,075	$4,775	$4,350

Add 50% for .50-95 Express cal.

DOUBLE RIFLE SxS — Various cals. in the .45 range, hammers, very limited production between 1878-1880. Most guns were owned by friends of Caldwell Colt — Sam Colt's son, the original designer. Colt Double Rifles are extremely rare and desirable, and should be examined carefully. Prices typically range between $15,000-$25,000, if all original.

Grading	100%	98%	95%	90%	80%	70%	60%

RIFLES: .22 CAL.

COLTEER 1-22 — .22 LR and Mag., single shot bolt action, 20 or 22 in. round barrel, adj. rear sight, plain walnut stock. Approx. 50,000 mfg. 1957-1966.

	$275	$215	$175	$140	$110	$95	$80

STAGECOACH — .22 LR, semi-auto, 16½ in. barrel, 13 shot mag., deluxe walnut, saddle ring w/leather thong, roll-engraved hold-up scene. Over 25,000 mfg. 1965-mid 70's.

	$325	$275	$215	$175	$140	$110	$90

COLTEER — .22 LR, similar to Stagecoach, except 19 3/8 in. barrel, 15 shot mag., no engraving and plain walnut. Over 25,000 mfg. 1965-mid '70s.

	$275	$215	$175	$140	$110	$95	$80

COURIER — similar to Colteer semi-auto, except pistol-grip stock and enlarged forearm. Mfg. 1970-mid '70s.

	$275	$215	$175	$140	$110	$95	$80

BOLT ACTION CENTERFIRE RIFLES

COLT "57" — .243 Win. or .30-06 cal., FN Mauser action, mfg. by Jefferson Mfg. Co. in N. Haven, CT during 1957, approx. 5,000 mfg starting at ser. no. 1, checkered American Monte Carlo walnut stock, wraparound front sight.

	$550	$450	$400	$350	$300	$265	$230

This model was also available in a deluxe version with deluxe hand checkered walnut stock — add 15%.

COLTSMAN STANDARD RIFLE — .223 Rem., .243 Win., .264 Win. Mag., .30-06, .300 Win. Mag., .308 cal., mfg. by Kodiak, Mauser or Sako-action, 22 in. or 24 in.(.300 Mag.), 5 or 6 shot mag. Approx. 10,000 (both models) mfg. 1958-1966.

	$475	$400	$350	$300	$265	$230	$210

COLTSMAN CUSTOM RIFLE — deluxe variation including deluxe walnut with skipline checkering and rosewood forearm cap.

	$700	$600	$500	$450	$390	$340	$300

Grading	100%	98%	95%	90%	80%	70%	60%

COLT SAUER RIFLE (STANDARD ACTION) — non-rotating bolt action, manufactured in Germany by J. P. Sauer & Son, .25-06, .270 Win. or .30-06, 24 in. barrel, 4 round mag., no sights, checkered walnut stock with rosewood forend tip and pistol grip cap, recoil pad. Disc. 1985.

	$1,150	$975	$800	$700	$660	$620	$575

Last Mfg.'s Sug. Retail was $1,257.

COLT SAUER SHORT ACTION — similar to the standard except in .22-250, .243 Win. or .308 Win. Disc. 1985.

	$1,200	$975	$800	$700	$660	$620	$575

Last Mfg.'s Sug. Retail was $1,257.

COLT SAUER MAGNUM — similar to the standard except in 7mm Rem. Mag., 300 Win. Mag., or 300 Weatherby Mag. Disc. 1985.

	$1,250	$1,000	$800	$700	$660	$620	$575

Last Mfg.'s Sug. Retail was $1,300.

COLT SAUER GRAND ALASKAN — heavier version in .375 H&H Mag., adj. sights.

	$1,375	$1,125	$995	$900	$820	$740	$690

COLT SAUER GRAND AFRICAN — .458 Win. Mag., 4 round capacity, 9 lb. 12 oz. Disc. 1985.

	$1,450	$1,150	$995	$900	$820	$740	$690

Last Mfg.'s Sug. Retail was $1,400.

DRILLINGS

COLT SAUER DRILLING — 12 ga./.30-06 or .243 Combo gun, 25 in. barrels, engraved, 8 lbs. Disc. 1985.

	$2,950	$2,500	$2,100	$1,800	$1,500	$1,250	$1,000

Last Mfg.'s Sug. Retail was $4,228.

RIFLES: SINGLE SHOT CENTERFIRE

COLT-SHARPS RIFLE — .17 Bee, .22-250, .243, .25-06, 7mm Rem. Mag., .30-06, or .375 H&H cal., Sharps falling block action, high-gloss bluing, deluxe checkered walnut stock and forearm. Approx. 500 mfg. 1970-1977.

	$2,295	$1,950	$1,650	$1,200	$1,000	$800	$650

RIFLES: AR-15(S) AND VARIATIONS

Prices of currently manufactured models listed below automatically refer to post-ban (if any) configurations.

Rifling twists on the Colt AR-15 have changed throughout the years. They started with a 1:12 in. twist, changed to a 1:7 in. twist (to match with the new, longer .223/5.56mm SS109-type bullet), and finally changed to a 1:9 in. twist in combination with 1:7 in. twist models as a compromise for bullets in the 50-68 grain range. Current mfg. AR-15s/Match Targets have rifling twists/turns incorporated into the model descriptions.

Add $344 for Match Target 4X scope on current mfg.
Currently, older mfg. with green boxes will command a premium.

SP-1 — .223 Rem. cal., original Colt paramilitary configuration without forward bolt assist, finishes included parkerizing and electroless nickel. Mfg. 1963-84.

	$995	$850	$750	$650	$600	$550	$495

SPORTER II (R6500) — .223 Rem. cal., various configurations, disc.

	$1,150	$995	$875	$750	$675	$595	$525

Grading	100%	98%	95%	90%	80%	70%	60%

C

(SPORTER) MATCH TARGET LIGHTWEIGHT (R/MT6430, R/MT6530, or R/MT6830)** — .223
Rem. (6530, 1 turn in 7 in.), 7.62x39mm (6830, new 1992, 1 turn in 12 in.), or 9mm Para. (6430, new 1992, 1 turn in 10 in.) cal., features 16 in. barrel (non-threaded per C/B 1994), initially shorter stock and handguard, adj. rear sight for windage and elevation, includes 2 detachable 5 shot mags., approx. 7 lbs. New 1991.

	100%	98%	95%	90%	80%	70%	60%
Mfg.'s Sug. Retail $987	$825	$750	$700	$650	$600	$550	$495
Pre-ban	$975	$875	$775	$650	$600	$550	$500

Add $154 for .22 LR conversion kit (disc. 1994).

TARGET GOVT. MODEL RIFLE (R6550/R or MT6551) — .223 Rem. (5.56mm), semi-auto version of
the M-16 rifle with forward bolt assist, gas operated, 20 in. barrel (1 turn in 7 in.), straight line black nylon stock, aperture rear, post front sight, 5, 20 (disc.), or 30 (disc.) shot detachable box mag. (supplied with two 5 shot mags. starting in 1989), Model 6550 was disc. 1990, 7½ lbs.

	100%	98%	95%	90%	80%	70%	60%
Mfg.'s Sug. Retail $1,019	$865	$775	$725	$660	$600	$550	$495
Pre-ban	$895	$825	$725	$625	$575	$525	$475

Add $154 for .22 LR conversion kit (mfg. 1990-94).
Subtract $70 for older field-style rear sight assembly (pre-1987).

In 1987, Colt replaced the AR-15A2 Sporter II Rifle with the AR-15A2 Govt. Model. This new model has the 800 meter rear sighting system housed in the receiver's carrying handle (similar to the M-16 A2).

(SPORTER) COMPETITION H-BAR RIFLE (R or MT6700) — .223 Rem., features flat top upper
receiver for scope mounting, 20 in. barrel (1 turn in 9 in.), quick detachable carry handle which incorporates a 600-meter rear sighting system, counterbored muzzle, dovetailed upper receiver is grooved to accept Weaver style scope rings, supplied with two 5-shot mags., cleaning kit, and sling, matte black finish, 8½ lbs. New 1992.

	100%	98%	95%	90%	80%	70%	60%
Mfg.'s Sug. Retail $1,073	$915	$825	$775	$700	$625	$575	$525
Pre-ban	$995	$875	$750	$675	$595	$550	$495

(SPORTER) COMPETITION H-BAR RIFLE RANGE SELECTED (R6700CH) — similar to Sporter
Competition I, except has been range selected for optimal accuracy, includes Cordura nylon case, 3-9X rubber armored variable scope, and cleaning kit, 10½ lbs. Limited mfg. 1992 only.

	100%	98%	95%	90%	80%	70%	60%
Pre-ban	$1,575	$1,350	$1,200	$995	$875	$750	$675

Last Mfg.'s Sug. Retail was $1,527.

(SPORTER) MATCH TARGET H-BAR (R6600/R or MT6601) — similar to AR-15A2 Govt. Model
Rifle, except has heavy 20 in. barrel (1 turn in 7 in.), Model 6600 was disc. 1993, 8 lbs. New 1986.

	100%	98%	95%	90%	80%	70%	60%
Mfg.'s Sug. Retail $1,067	$910	$825	$775	$700	$625	$575	$525
Pre-ban	$1,050	$895	$775	$675	$625	$575	$525

Add $154 for .22 LR conversion kit (mfg. 1990-94).

▲ *(Sporter) Match Delta H-Bar (M6600DH/6601DH)* — similar to AR-15A2 H-Bar, except has 3-9X rubber armored variable scope, removable cheekpiece, adj. scope mount, and leather sling, range selected. Aluminum cased. Mfg. 1987-1991.

	100%	98%	95%	90%	80%	70%	60%
	$1,150	$995	$850	$775	$700	$625	$550

Last Mfg.'s Sug. Retail was $1,460.

Add $160 for .22 LR conversion kit (new 1990).

MATCH TARGET COMPETITION H-BAR II (MT6731) — .223 Rem., 16.1 in. barrel (1 turn in 9 in.),
matte finish, 7.1 lbs. New 1995.

	100%	98%	95%	90%	80%	70%	60%
Mfg.'s Sug. Retail $1,044	$885	$825	$775	$700	$625	$575	$525

AR-15A2 SPORTER II — standard 20 in. barrel, rear sight adj. for windage only, 7½ lbs. Disc. 1989.

	100%	98%	95%	90%	80%	70%	60%
	$995	$900	$800	$700	$600	$525	$470

Last Mfg.'s Sug. Retail was $740.

Grading	100%	98%	95%	90%	80%	70%	60%

AR-15A2 CARBINE — similar to older AR-15A2 Sporter II Rifle, except has collapsible butt stock, field sights, 16 in. barrel, shortened forearm, 5 lbs. 13 oz. Disc. 1988.

	$1,095	$950	$850	$750	$650	$575	$500

Last Mfg.'s Sug. Retail was $770.

AR-15A2 GOVT. MODEL CARBINE (R6520) — similar to AR-15A2 Govt. Model Rifle, except has collapsible butt stock, 800 meter adj. rear sight, 16 in. barrel, 5 lbs. 13 oz., shortened forearm. Mfg. 1988-1990 (civilian sales disc. because of Federal/State regulations).

	$1,250	$1,050	$925	$825	$675	$600	$575

Last Mfg.'s Sug. Retail was $880.

▲ *AR-15 9mm Carbine (R6450)* — similar to 5.56mm Carbine, except 9mm with 20 shot mag., 6 lbs. 5 oz. Mfg. 1985-86 only.

	$1,295	$1,100	$925	$850	$775	$700	$650

Last Mfg.'s Sug. Retail was $696.

AR-15 SCOPE (3X/4X) AND MOUNT — initially offered with 3X scope.

Mfg.'s Sug. Retail	$344		$245	$185	$160		

SHOTGUNS: O/U CURRENT MFG.

ARMSMEAR — 12 ga. only, 2¾ in. chambers, mfg. by Worshipful Co. Gunmakers of London, boxlock action with engraved sideplates, checkered high-grade European walnut stock and forearm, 28 (HE) or 30 (LE) in. VR barrels with screw-in chokes, choice of light (Armsmear 12 LE) or heavy (Armsmear 12 HE) engraving, 7½ lbs. New 1995.

While advertised, this model has yet to be manufactured.

100%	98%	95%	90%	80%	70%	60%	50%	40%	30%	20%	10%

SHOTGUNS: DISC.

Strong, original case colors and vivid damascus barrel patterning will make the difference when determining values on the Models 1878 and 1883. Remember, these are black powder shotguns.

MODEL 1878 HAMMER SHOTGUN SxS — 10 or 12 ga., 28-32 in. blued or browned damascus barrels, double triggers, sideplates, case hardened breech, non-automatic ejectors, semi-pistol grip stock, 22,683 mfg. between 1878-1889. Many of these guns were ordered with special features - these original guns command premiums above the prices listed below.

$3,750	$3,250	$2,950	$2,675	$2,200	$1,925	$1,650	$1,485	$1,100	$990	$880	$725

MODEL 1883 HAMMERLESS SxS — 8, 10 or 12 ga., 28-32 in. damascus barrels, many deluxe custom orders occur in this model. Mfg. from 1883-1895. Approx. serial range is No. 1-3,050 and 4,055-8,365. Seldom encountered in mint condition.

$4,250	$3,750	$3,350	$2,995	$2,675	$2,200	$1,925	$1,650	$1,485	$1,100	$990	$875

This model was generally a custom order gun with no standard grades being designated. Quality was extremely high, and the high cost of manufacture is a large reason why the gun never sold in large numbers commercially. The Model 1883 was discontinued after only 12 years of manufacture (it was one of the most expensive shotguns during its day). Values above assume moderate engraving and above average walnut.

Grading	100%	98%	95%	90%	80%	70%	60%

SxS SHOTGUN MFG. 1961-62 — 12 ga. or 16 ga., various barrel lengths, DTs, checkered stock and forearm, mfg. in France 1961-62 by Fabrication Mechanique, estimated total between 25-50 guns in serial range 467,000-469,000.

	$675	$595	$525	$450	$400	$360	$320

Grading	100%	98%	95%	90%	80%	70%	60%

STANDARD AUTO SHOTGUN — 12 or 20 ga. (also available in Mags.), mfg. by Franchi of Italy, aluminum frame, 26, 28, 30, or 32 in. plain or VR barrel, almost 5,300 mfg. (both models) 1962-1966.

	$375	$350	$325	$295	$260	$230	$200

Add $50 for VR barrel.

CUSTOM AUTO SHOTGUN — similar to Standard Model, except deluxe walnut, hand engraved receiver. Mfg. 1962-1966.

	$475	$425	$375	$350	$325	$295	$260

COLTSMAN PUMP SHOTGUN — 12, 16, or 20 ga., Franchi frame assembled by both Kodiak and Montgomery Wards, 26 or 28 in. plain barrel, aluminum frame. Approx. 2,000 mfg. 1961-1965.

	$325	$295	$260	$230	$200	$180	$165

COLT COMMEMORATIVES, SPECIAL EDITIONS, & LIMITED MFG.

During the course of a year, I receive many phone calls and letters on special editions and limited editions that do not appear in this section. It should be noted that a factory commemorative issue is a gun that has been manufactured, marketed, and sold through the auspices of the specific trademark (in this case Colt). There have literally been hundreds of special and limited editions which, although mostly made by Colt (some were subcontracted), were not marketed or retailed by Colt. These guns are NOT Colt commemoratives and for the most part, do not have the desirability factor that the factory commemoratives have. Typically, special and limited editions are made for an organization, state, special event, personality, etc. and are sold and marketed through a company/individual to those people who want to purchase them. These special editions may or may not have a retail price and oftentimes, since demand is regional, values decrease rapidly in other areas of the country. Desirability is the key to determining values on these editions. More information on these special and limited editions not listed in the following pages can be obtained by contacting Cherry's located in Greensboro, NC (see Trademark Index).

Until recently, the over-production of many factory commemoratives had created a "softness" in the commemorative marketplace. Approximately 3-5 years ago, Colt, Winchester and others decided to cut down on commemorative manufacture after perhaps too many years of over-production. Many commemorative consumers were starting to think that these "limited manufacture" guns had become more of a company marketing tool and sales gimmick rather than a legitimate vehicle for investment potential and collector support. During this 3-5 year period, both distributors and retailers saw their commemorative inventory levels gradually reach near zero - perhaps the first time in over two decades that they sold out of factory commemoratives. In other words, the commemorative "blow-out" sales were over. As this transition from distributor/dealer inventory to consumer purchases occurred, the commemorative marketplace became stronger and prices began to rise. Because the commemorative consumer is now more in charge (consumers now own most of the guns since distributor/dealer inventories are depleted) than during the 1980s, commemorative firearms are possibly as strong as they have ever been. When the supply side of commemorative economics has to be purchased from knowledgable collectors or savvy dealers and demand stays the same or increases slightly, prices have no choice but to go up. If and when the manufacturers crank up the commemorative production runs again (and it won't be like the good old days), then the old marketplace characteristics may reappear. Until then, however, the commemorative marketplace remains strong with values becoming more predictable.

As a reminder on commemoratives, I would like to repeat a few facts, especially for the beginning collector, applicable to all manufacturers of commemoratives. Commemoratives are current production guns designed as a reproduction of an historically famous gun model, or as a tie-in with historically famous persons or events. They are generally of very excellent quality and often embellished with select woods and finishes such as silver, nickel, or gold plating. Obviously, they are manufactured to be instant collectibles and to be pleasing to the eye. As with firearms in general, not all commemorative models have achieved collector status, although most enjoy an active market - especially during the past three years.Consecutive-numbered pairs as well as collections based on the same serial number will bring a premium. Remember that handguns usually are in some type of wood presentation case, and that rifles may be cased or in packaging with graphics styled to the particular theme of the collectible. The original factory packaging and papers should always accompany the firearm as they are necessary to realize full value at the time of sale. All commemorative firearms should be absolutely new, unfired, and as issued since any obvious use or wear removes it from collector status and lowers its value significantly. Many owners have allowed their commemoratives to sit in their boxes for years without inspecting them for corrosion or oxidation damage. Periodic inspection should be implemented to insure no damage occurs - this is important, since even light "freckling" created from touching the metal surfaces can reduce values significantly. A fired gun with obvious wear or without its original packaging can lose as much as 50% of its normal value - many used commemoratives get sold as "fancy shooters" with little, if any, premiums being asked.

A final note on commemoratives: One of the characteristics of commemoratives/special editions is that over the years of ownership, most of the original amount manufactured stays in the same NIB condition. Thus, if supply always is constant and in one condition, demand has to increase before price appreciation can occur. Many commemorative dealers have told me that recent changes in overseas currency rates have made domestic guns less expensive to own - for Europeans especially. For this reason, many commemoratives are being sold overseas resulting in less supply for the domestic market. This secondary demand factor has also strengthened commemorative prices. After 29 years of special edition production, many models' performance records can be accurately analyzed and the appreciation (or depreciation) can be compared against other purchases of equal vintage. You be the judge.

Grading	100%	Issue Price	Qty. Made
1961 GENESEO, ILLINOIS 125TH ANNIVERSARY DERRINGER			
	$650	$28	104
1961 SHERIFF'S MODEL — blue and case hardened, 3 in. barrel, SM suffix.			
	$1,995	$130	478
1961 SHERIFF'S MODEL — nickel, 3 in. barrel, SM suffix.			
	$5,000	$140	25
1961 125TH ANNIVERSARY MODEL SAA			
	$995	$150	7,390
1961 KANSAS STATEHOOD SCOUT			
	$350	$75	6,201
1961 PONY EXPRESS CENTENNIAL SCOUT			
	$450	$80	1,007
1961 CIVIL WAR CENTENNIAL PISTOL .22 SHORT			
	$175	$33	24,114
1962 ROCK ISLAND ARSENAL CENTENNIAL SCOUT			
	$250	$39	550
1962 COLUMBUS, OHIO SESQUICENTENNIAL SCOUT			
	$550	$100	200

Grading	100%	Issue Price	Qty. Made
1962 FORT FINDLAY, OHIO SESQUICENTENNIAL SCOUT			
	$650	$90	110
1962 FORT FINDLAY CASE PAIR — .22 LR - .22 Mag.			
	$2,500	$185	20
1962 NEW MEXICO GOLDEN ANNIVERSARY SCOUT			
	$375	$80	1,000
1962 FORT MCPHERSON, NEBRASKA CENTENNIAL DERRINGER			
	$395	$29	300
1962 WEST VIRGINIA STATEHOOD CENTENNIAL SCOUT			
	$375	$75	3,452
1963 WEST VIRGINIA STATEHOOD CENTENNIAL SAA .45			
	$1,095	$150	600
1963 ARIZONA TERRITORIAL CENTENNIAL SCOUT			
	$375	$75	5,355
1963 ARIZONA TERRITORIAL CENTENNIAL SAA .45			
	$1,095	$150	1,280
1963 CAROLINA CHARTER TERCENTENARY SCOUT			
	$395	$75	300
1963 CAROLINA CHARTER TERCENTENARY 22/45 COMBO			
	$1,495	$240	251
1963 H. COOK "1 TO 100" 22/45 COMBO			
	$1,695	$275	100
1963 FORT STEPHENSON, OHIO SESQUICENTENNIAL SCOUT			
	$550	$75	200
1963 BATTLE OF GETTYSBURG CENTENNIAL SCOUT			
	$375	$90	1,019
1963 IDAHO TERRITORIAL CENTENNIAL SCOUT			
	$375	$75	902
1963 GEN. JOHN HUNT MORGAN INDIANA RAID SCOUT			
	$650	$75	100
1964 CHERRY'S SPORTING GOODS 35TH ANNIVERSARY 22/45 COMBO			
	$1,695	$275	100
1964 NEVADA STATEHOOD CENTENNIAL SCOUT			
	$375	$75	3,984
1964 NEVADA STATEHOOD CENTENNIAL SAA .45			
	$1,095	$150	1,688
1964 NEVADA STATEHOOD CENTENNIAL 22/45 COMBO			
	$1,495	$240	189
1964 NEVADA ST. CENT. 22/45 COMBO W/EXTRA ENGR. CYLS.			
	$1,595	$350	577
1964 NEVADA "BATTLE BORN" SCOUT			
	$375	$85	981

Grading	100%	Issue Price	Qty. Made
1964 NEVADA "BATTLE BORN" SAA .45			
	$1,395	$175	80
1964 NEVADA "BATTLE BORN" 22/45 COMBO			
	$2,595	$265	20
1964 MONTANA TERRITORIAL CENTENNIAL SCOUT			
	$375	$75	2,300
1964 MONTANA TERRITORIAL CENTENNIAL SAA .45			
	$1,095	$150	851
1964 WYOMING DIAMOND JUBILEE SCOUT			
	$375	$75	2,357
1964 GENERAL HOOD CENTENNIAL SCOUT			
	$375	$75	1,503
1964 NEW JERSEY TERCENTENARY SCOUT			
	$375	$75	1,001
1964 NEW JERSEY TERCENTENARY SAA .45			
	$1,095	$150	250
1964 ST. LOUIS BICENTENNIAL SCOUT			
	$375	$75	802
1964 ST. LOUIS BICENTENNIAL SAA .45			
	$1,095	$150	200
1964 ST. LOUIS BICENTENNIAL 22/45 COMBO			
	$1,495	$240	250
1964 CALIFORNIA GOLD RUSH SCOUT			
	$375	$80	500
1964 PONY EXPRESS PRESENTATION SAA .45			
	$1,395	$250	1,004
1964 CHAMIZAL TREATY SCOUT			
	$395	$85	450
1964 CHAMIZAL TREATY SAA .45			
	$1,295	$170	50
1964 CHAMIZAL TREATY 22/45 COMBO			
	$1,995	$280	50
1964 COL. SAM COLT SESQUICENTENNIAL PRESENTATION SAA .45			
	$1,095	$225	4,750
1964 COL. SAM COLT SESQUICENTENNIAL DELUXE PRES. SAA .45			
	$1,950	$500	200
1964 COL. SAM COLT SESQUICENTENNIAL SPEC. DELUXE PRES. SAA .45			
	$2,950	$1,000	50
1964 WYATT EARP BUNTLINE SAA .45			
	$1,895	$250	150
1965 OREGON TRAIL SCOUT			
	$375	$75	1,995

Grading	100%	Issue Price	Qty. Made
1965 JOAQUIN MURIETTA 22/45 COMBO			
	$1,695	$350	100
1965 FORTY-NINER MINER SCOUT			
	$375	$85	500
1965 OLD FT. DES MOINES RECONSTRUCTION SCOUT			
	$375	$90	700
1965 OLD FT. DES MOINES RECONSTRUCTION SAA .45			
	$1,095	$170	100
1965 OLD FT. DES MOINES RECONSTRUCTION 22/45 COMBO			
	$1,695	$290	100
1965 APPOMATTOX CENTENNIAL SCOUT			
	$375	$75	1,001
1965 APPOMATTOX CENTENNIAL SAA .45			
	$1,095	$150	250
1965 APPOMATTOX CENTENNIAL 22/45 COMBO			
	$1,495	$240	250
1965 GENERAL MEADE CAMPAIGN SCOUT			
	$350	$75	1,197
1965 ST. AUGUSTINE QUADRACENTENNIAL SCOUT			
	$375	$85	500
1965 KANSAS COWTOWN SERIES — Wichita Scout.			
	$350	$85	500
1966 KANSAS COWTOWN SERIES — Dodge City Scout.			
	$350	$85	500
1966 COLORADO GOLD RUSH SCOUT			
	$375	$85	1,350
1966 OKLAHOMA DIAMOND JUBILEE			
	$375	$85	1,343
1966 DAKOTA TERRITORY SCOUT			
	$375	$85	1,000
1966 GENERAL MEADE SAA .45			
	$1,095	$165	200
1966 ABERCROMBIE & FITCH "TRAILBLAZER" — New York.			
	$1,095	$275	200
1966 KANSAS COWTOWN SERIES — Abilene Scout.			
	$350	$95	500
1966 INDIANA SESQUICENTENNIAL SCOUT			
	$375	$85	1,500
1966 PONY EXPRESS .45 SAA 4-SQUARE SET (4 GUNS)			
	$5,595	$1,400	unknown
1966 CALIFORNIA GOLD RUSH SAA .45			
	$1,295	$175	130

C

Grading	100%	Issue Price	Qty. Made
1966 ABERCROMBIE & FITCH "TRAILBLAZER" — Chicago.			
	$1,095	$275	100
1966 ABERCROMBIE & FITCH "TRAILBLAZER" — San Francisco.			
	$1,095	$275	100
1967 LAWMAN SERIES — Bat Masterson Scout.			
	$375	$90	3,000
1967 LAWMAN SERIES — Bat Masterson SAA .45.			
	$1,295	$180	500
1967 ALAMO SCOUT			
	$350	$85	4,250
1967 ALAMO SAA .45			
	$1,095	$165	750
1967 ALAMO 22/45 COMBO			
	$1,495	$265	250
1967 KANSAS COWTOWN SERIES — Coffeyville Scout.			
	$350	$95	500
1967 KANSAS TRAIL SERIES — Chisolm Trail Scout.			
	$350	$100	500
1967 WWI SERIES — Chateau Thierry .45 Auto.			
	$695	$200	7,400
1967 WWI SERIES — Chateau Thierry Deluxe.			
	$1,350	$500	75
1967 WWI SERIES — Chateau Thierry Spec. Deluxe.			
	$2,750	$1,000	25
1968 NEBRASKA CENTENNIAL SCOUT			
	$350	$100	7,001
1968 KANSAS TRAIL SERIES — Pawnee Trail Scout.			
	$350	$110	501
1968 WWI SERIES — Belleau Wood.			
	$695	$200	7,400
1968 WWI SERIES — Belleau Wood Deluxe.			
	$1,350	$500	75
1968 WWI SERIES — Belleau Wood Special Deluxe.			
	$2,750	$1,000	25
1968 LAWMAN SERIES — Pat Garrett Scout.			
	$375	$110	3,000
1968 LAWMAN SERIES — Pat Garrett .45 SAA.			
	$1,095	$220	500
1969 GEN. NATHAN BEDFORD FORREST SCOUT			
	$350	$110	3,000
1969 KANSAS TRAIL SERIES — Santa Fe Trail Scout.			
	$350	$120	501

C

Grading	100%	Issue Price	Qty. Made
1969 WWI SERIES — Battle of 2nd Marne .45 Auto.			
	$695	$220	7,400
1969 WWI SERIES — Battle of 2nd Marne Deluxe.			
	$1,350	$500	75
1969 WWI SERIES — Battle of 2nd Marne Spec. Deluxe.			
	$2,750	$1,000	25
1969 ALABAMA SESQUICENTENNIAL SCOUT			
	$350	$110	3,001
1969 ALABAMA SESQUICENTENNIAL .45 SAA			
	$15,000	unknown	1
1969 GOLDEN SPIKE SCOUT			
	$350	$135	11,000
1969 KANSAS TRAIL SERIES — Shawnee Trail Scout.			
	$350	$120	501
1969 WWI SERIES — Meuse-Argonne .45 Auto.			
	$695	$220	7,400
1969 WWI SERIES — Meuse-Argonne .45 Deluxe.			
	$1,350	$500	75
1969 WWI SERIES — Meuse-Argonne Spec. Deluxe.			
	$2,750	$1,000	25
1969 ARKANSAS TERRITORIAL SESQUICENTENNIAL SCOUT			
	$350	$110	3,500
1969 LAWMAN SERIES — .45 SAA Wild Bill Hickock.			
	$1,095	$220	500
1969 LAWMAN SERIES — Wild Bill Hickock Scout.			
	$375	$117	3,000
1969 CALIFORNIA BICENTENNIAL SCOUT			
	$350	$135	5,000
1970 KANSAS FORT SERIES — Ft. Larned Scout.			
	$350	$120	500
1970 WWII SERIES — European Theatre.			
	$695	$250	11,500
1970 WWII SERIES — Pacific Theatre.			
	$695	$250	11,500

Note: A complete set of the WWI and WWII Series standard grade models (6 guns) with matching serial numbers in NIB condition is currently selling in the $4,000 range.

1970 TEXAS RANGER SAA .45			
	$1,995	$650	1,000
1970 TEXAS RANGER GRADE II (70% ENGRAVING COVERAGE)			
	$5,000	$2,950	unknown
1970 TEXAS RANGER GRADE III (40% ENGRAVING COVERAGE)			
	$4,500	$2,250	unknown

C

Grading	100%	Issue Price	Qty. Made
1970 KANSAS FORTS — Ft. Hays Scout.			
	$350	$130	500
1970 MAINE SESQUICENTENNIAL SCOUT			
	$350	$120	3,000
1970 MISSOURI SESQUICENTENNIAL SCOUT			
	$350	$125	3,000
1970 MISSOURI SESQUICENTENNIAL .45 SAA			
	$995	$220	900
1970 KANSAS FORTS — Ft. Riley Scout.			
	$350	$130	500
1970 LAWMAN SERIES — Wyatt Earp Scout.			
	$450	$125	3,000
1970 LAWMAN SERIES — Wyatt Earp .45 SAA.			
	$1,895	$395	500
1971 NRA CENTENNIAL .45 SAA			
	$1,095	$250	5,000
1971 NRA CENTENNIAL .357 SAA			
	$850	$250	5,000
1971 NRA CENTENNIAL GOLD CUP .45 ACP			
	$850	$250	2,500
1971 1851 NAVY — U.S. Grant.			
	$595	$250	4,750
1971 1851 NAVY — Robert E. Lee.			
	$595	$250	4,750
1971 1851 NAVY — Lee-Grant Set.			
	$1,350	$500	250
1971 KANSAS SERIES — Ft. Scott Scout.			
	$350	$130	500
1972 FLORIDA TERRITORY SESQUICENTENNIAL SCOUT			
	$375	$125	2,001
1972 ARIZONA RANGER SCOUT			
	$375	$135	3,001
1975 PEACEMAKER CENTENNIAL .45			
	$1,295	$300	1,500
1975 PEACEMAKER CENTENNIAL 44.40			
	$1,295	$300	1,500
1975 PEACEMAKER CENT. CASED PAIR			
	$2,695	$625	500

USS TEXAS BATTLESHIP SPECIAL EDITION (1975) — .45 ACP, Model 1911A1 with special embellishments, nickel finish, this model is not a factory commemorative.

	$895	unknown	500

Grading	100%	Issue Price	Qty. Made

USS ARIZONA BATTLESHIP SPECIAL EDITION (1975) — .45 ACP, Model 1911A1 with special embellishments, nickel finish, this model is not a factory commemorative.

	$895	unknown	500

1976 U.S. BICENTENNIAL SET — includes SAA .45, Python .357 Mag., and black powder Dragoon in walnut display case with drawers.

	$1,895	$1,695	1,776

1976 BICENTENNIAL SAA FREEDOM COLTS — consisted of A, B, and C sets, set As were engraved, Bs had gold work and accessories, Cs were similar to Bs, but had shoulder stock. Set A prices averaged $1,500-$3,000 in 1976, set B prices varied between $3,500-$20,000, and set C prices started at $5,000. Total mfg. was 4 set As, 6 set Bs, and 1 set C. These sets in today's marketplace are too rare to accurately evaluate and pricing is literally "what the market will bear".

> These guns were all manufactured by Dwain Wright located in Applegate, OR.

1977 2ND AMENDMENT .22

	$350	$195	3,020

1977 U.S. CAVALRY 200TH ANNIVERSARY SET

	$1,250	$995	3,000

1978 STATEHOOD 3RD MODEL DRAGOON

	$6,995	$12,500	52

1979 NED BUNTLINE .45 SAA

	$795	$895	3,000

OHIO PRESIDENT'S SPECIAL EDITION (1979) — .45 ACP, Model 1911A1 with special Ohio embellishments, this is not a factory commemorative.

	$850	unknown	250

1979 TOMBSTONE CENTENNIAL .45 SAA — .45 LC cal., 7½ in. barrel, nickel finish, two-piece walnut stocks, P-1876 Model, etched with scroll engraving and Western scenes. 300 mfg. (200 singles and 50 pairs).

	$1,295	$995	300

> This model was not sold retail through the auspices of Colt.

1980 DRUG ENFORCEMENT AGENCY (DEA) .45 AUTO

	$1,100	$550	910

> This model was not sold retail through the auspices of Colt.

1980 OLYMPICS ACE MODEL SPECIAL EDITION

	$1,150	$1,000	200

> This model was not sold retail through the auspices of Colt.

1980 HERITAGE-WALKER .44 PERCUSSION

	$950	$1,475	1,847

1981 "JOHN M. BROWNING" .45 ACP SEMI-AUTO

	$795	$1,100	3,000

1980-81 .45 ACP GOVT. SIGNATURE SERIES — .45 ACP cal., blue finished Govt. slide with gold auroplated slide or nickel finish. 250 mfg. in both finishes.

	$895	$833	250

> Add $50 for blue finish.

1980-81 ACE SIGNATURE SERIES — .22 LR cal., featured Cocobolo grips with medallions, blued finish with photo engraving, cased. 1,000 mfg.

	$900	$955	1,000

Grading	100%	Issue Price	Qty. Made

1981 BUFFALO BILL SPECIAL EDITION — .44-40 cal., 7½ in. barrel, gold and silver plating, Class C engraved, ivory grips, leather cased, 250 mfg. serialized 1BB-250BB.

| | $4,975 | unknown | 250 |

This model was a special edition (not commemorative) that was made specifically for the Buffalo Bill Historical Center.

1982 JOHN WAYNE SAA STANDARD

| | $2,250 | $2,995 | 3,100 |

While advertising literature indicated 3,100 were mfg., 3,041 were sold.

1982 JOHN WAYNE SAA DELUXE

| | $7,500 | $10,000 | 500 |

While advertising literature indicated 500 were mfg., only 90 were sold.

1982 JOHN WAYNE SAA PRESENTATION

| | $12,000 | $20,000 | 100 |

While advertising literature indicated 100 were mfg., only 47 were sold.

Note: Each grade of the above John Wayne commemoratives has its own serial number range.

1983 BUFFALO BILL WILD WEST SHOW CENTENNIAL SAA .45

| | $1,250 | $1,350 | 500 |

1983 CCA LIMITED EDITION SAA — .44-40 cal., 4¾ in. barrel, nickel finish, fleur-de-lis checkered wood grips, 250 mfg. in 1983 to commemorate Colt Collector's Assn.

| | $1,295 | $825 | 250 |

This model was not sold retail through the auspices of Colt.

1983 "ARMORY MODEL" SAA .45 ACP — this model had limited production, and should not be confused as being a commemorative. So called because was shipped with extra .45 long Colt cylinder and the "Colt Armory Edition" book by E. Grant, presentation cased.

| | $1,495 | $1,125 | 500 |

Armory model commemoratives available with class A engraving — $2,062, B engraving — $2,395, C engraving — $2,995, D engraving — $3,500. 20 total available.

1983 PYTHON SILVER SNAKE SPECIAL EDITION — .357 Mag., 6 in. barrel, black chrome stainless steel, Pachmayr grips with custom shop pewter medallions, etched engraving, includes custom gun pouch.

| | $1,225 | $1,150 | 250 |

1984 1ST EDITION GOVT. MODEL .380 ACP

| | $425 | $425 | 1,000 |

Serial range RC00000-01000.

1984 JOHN WAYNE "DUKE" FRONTIER .22

| | $495 | $475 | 5,000 |

1984 COLT/WINCHESTER SET — 1 ea. of the Model 1894 Winchester carbine and Colt Peacemaker, serial numbered 1WC-4440WC, .44-40 cal., elaborate gold etching, cased. Pistol became available for sale individually in 1986 - see individual listing below for values.

Please refer to 1984 Winchester/Colt Set in the Winchester Commemorative section in this text.

WINCHESTER/COLT SAA — .44-40 cal., 7½ in. barrel, gold etching, this commemorative was originally made as part of the 1984 Winchester/Colt rifle-pistol set but now can be purchased individually. Originally mfg. 1984.

| | $895 | N/A | 4,000 |

Grading	100%	Issue Price	Qty. Made

1984 USA EDITION SAA — .44-40 cal., 7½ in. barrel, old style black powder frame, bullseye ejector rod head, 3 line patent date, high polished blue with gold line engraving. 100 guns total mfg. — 1 for each state and its capitol.

	$3,500	$4,995	100

1984 KIT CARSON .22 NEW FRONTIER — 6 in. barrel, color case hardened frame, gold artwork, serial numbered KCC0001-KCC1000, cased.

	$395	$550	1,000

1984 SECOND EDITION GOVT. MODEL .380 ACP — serial numbered 00000-01000RC.

	$495	$525	1,000

1984 OFFICER'S COMMENCEMENT ISSUE — Officer's ACP with Marine Corps emblem, rosewood grips, silver plated oak leaf scroll, cased.

	$650	$700	1,000

This model was not sold retail through the auspices of Colt.

1984 THEODORE ROOSEVELT COMMEMORATIVE SAA — .44-40 cal., 7½ in. barrel, black powder frame, case colored receiver, factory "B" hand engraving, ivory stocks, cased.

	$1,695	$1,695	500

1984 NORTH AMERICAN OILMEN SAA BUNTLINE — .45 Long Colt, 12 in. barrel, non-fluted cylinder, elaborate gold etching, ebony grips with ivory inlays, stand-up glass case, ser. nos. 1-100 mfg. for Canada, 101-200 for the U.S.

	$3,250	$3,900	200

This model was not sold retail through the auspices of Colt.

1985 TEXAS 150th SESQUICENTENNIAL SAA — .45 cal., Sheriff's model, 4 ¾ in. barrel, mirror bright blue, gold etching, 24 Kt. gold plated backstrap and trigger guard, smooth ivory grips, French fit oak presentation case. Mfg. 1985 only.

▲ *Standard Model* — 1,000 mfg.

	$1,095	$1,836	1,000

▲ *Premier Model* — elaborate engraving, 75 mfg.

	$4,995	$7,995	75

1986 150th ANNIVERSARY SAA — .45 Long Colt, 10 in. barrel, 50% engraved, royal blue finish, Goncalo Alves smooth grips, 150th anniversary logo in stocks, cherrywood case. 490 mfg. 1986 only.

	$1,595	$1,595	490

1986 150th ANNIVERSARY ENGRAVING SAMPLER SAA — various cals., 4 different engraving styles on metal surfaces, 75% coverage, ivory grips, signed by the engraver, available with either blue or nickel finish. New 1986.

	$2,500	$1,613	unknown

1986 150th ANNIVERSARY ENGRAVING SAMPLER .45 M1911 A1 — .45 ACP, 4 different engraving styles on metal surfaces, 75% coverage, ivory grips, signed by the engraver, available with either blue or nickel finish. New 1986.

	$1,095	$1,155	unknown

Add $60 for nickel.

1986 MUSTANG FIRST EDITION — .380 ACP, 1,000 manufactured serialized MU00001-MU01000 (the first thousand of production), rosewood stocks, walnut presentation case. Mfg. 1986 only.

	$450	$475	1,000

Grading	100%	Issue Price	Qty. Made

OFFICER'S ACP HEIRLOOM EDITION — .45 ACP, personalized with individual's choice for serial number (ie. John Smith 1), mirror brite bluing, jeweled barrel, hammer, and trigger, ivory grips, with historical letter and mahogany case. New 1986.

	$1,550	$1,643	open

1986 DOUBLE DIAMOND SET — set is comprised of a Python Ultimate .357 Mag. revolver and Officer's Model .45 ACP, both guns in stainless steel, smooth rosewood grips, presentation cased. 1,000 sets mfg. 1986 only, serial numbered 1-1,000 (matched).

	$1,595	$1,575	1,000

DELTA MATCH H-BAR RIFLE — AR-15 A2 H-Bar rifle selectively chosen and equipped with 3x9 variable power rubber armored scope, leather sling, shoulder stock cheekpiece, cased. Mfg. 1987.

	$1,500	$1,425	open

12TH MAN-'SPIRIT OF AGGIELAND' — .45 ACP, mfg. to commemorate Texas A & M University, serial numbered TAM001-TAM999, 24Kt gold plating including wreaths on left frame and inscription on right, cherrywood glass top presentation case, includes personalized class graduation inscription. Available 1987 only.

	$950	$950	999

This model was not sold retail through the auspices of Colt.

KLAY-COLT 1851 NAVY — .36 cal., cased reproduction of the 3rd Model 1851 Navy, special fabrication insuring old world quality, charcoal bluing, heat treated screws and accessories, cased. Introduced 1986.

▲ *Standard Edition* — no engraving.

	$1,850	$1,850	150

▲ *Engraved Edition* — choice of engraving.

	$3,150	$3,150	50

Optional engraving patterns with or without gold inlays available at extra cost.

COMBAT ELITE CUSTOM EDITION — .45 ACP, with ambidextrous thumb safety, wide grip safety, hand honed action, and carrying case, ser. numbered CG00001 - CG00500. Mfg. 1987.

	$900	$900	500

1987 SHERIFF'S EDITION — set of 5 SAA Sheriff's configuration pistols in .45 LC cal., barrel lengths include 2, 2½, 3, 4, and 5½ in., royal blue finish, smooth rosewood grips with medallions, supplied with glass top display case which displays the revolvers in a circle around a brass sheriff's badge. Serialization has 3 numeral prefix (which is the same in each set), followed by the letters "SE", followed by 1 or 2 numerals (indicating barrel length) - i.e. serial number 002SE25 indicates the second set built, Sheriff's Edition (SE), and a barrel length of 2½ inches.

	$4,250	$7,500	100 sets

1989 SNAKE EYES LIMITED EDITION — includes two Python revolvers (2½ in. barrels), one finished in brite stainless steel and the other in royal blue finish, grips are ivory like with scrimshaw "snake eyes" dice on left side and royal flush poker hand on right, includes chips and playing cards, 500 sets only of consecutive serial numbers. New 1989.

	$1,950	$2,950	500

1990 SAA HEIRLOOM II EDITION — .45 LC cal., 7 ½ in. barrel, color case hardened frame and hammer, balance of metal finished in Colt Royal Blue, one piece American Walnut grips with cartouche on lower left side, personalized inscription on backstrap, walnut cased. Available 1990 only.

	$1,395	$1,600	open

Grading	100%	Issue Price	Qty. Made

1990 JOE FOSS LIMITED EDITION .45 ACP GOVT. MODEL — .45 ACP cal., first limited edition in Colt's All American Hero Series, commemorates Joe Foss, famous American WWII Marine Fighter Pilot, gun features gold etched scenes on slide sides, smooth walnut grips, while 2,500 were advertised, only 300+ were mfg. serial numbered beginning with JF 0001. French fitted walnut presentation case, 38 oz. Mfg. 1990 only.

	$895	$1,375	300+

1911A1 50th ANNIVERSARY BATTLE OF THE BULGE — .45 ACP cal., special edition commemorating the Battle of the Bulge, silver plated with gold inlays, 300 mfg. serialized BB001-BB300.

	$1,250	$1,250	300

Add $150 for deluxe presentation case.

This special edition is sold exclusively by Cherry's located in Greensboro, NC.

COMMANDO ARMS

Manufactured previously in Knoxville, TN.

Commando Arms became the new name for Volunteer Enterprises in the late 1970s.

Grading	100%	98%	95%	90%	80%	70%	60%

MARK 45 — .45 ACP, carbine styled after the Thompson sub-machine gun, 16½ in. barrel.

	$350	$315	$280	$225	$195	$175	$160

COMPETITOR CORPORATION

Manufactured by Competitor Corporation, Inc. since 1988, and currently located in New Ipswich, NH. Previously located until 1995 in West Groton, MA. Manufacturer, dealer direct, or distributor sales.

PISTOLS

COMPETITOR — available in virtually any cal. from .17 LR - .50 AE, ranging from small rimfire to large belted Magnums, 14 in. barrel, rotary cannon action, cocks on opening, dual sliding thumb and trigger safety, rotary style ejector, click adj. sights, matte blue or optional electroless nickel finish, choice of synthetic, laminated, or natural wood grips (ambidextrous), extractor or ejector, approx. 59-70 oz. New 1988.

Mfg.'s Sug. Retail	$400	$355	$310	$275	$250	$225	$200	$185

Add $14 for ejector.
Add $40 for laminated wood stock.
Add $50 for electroless nickel finish.
Add $140 for extra 14 in. standard cal. barrel with sights.
Add $35 for 10½ - 16 in. standard cal. barrel with sights.
Add $65 for 17-23 in. barrel.
Add $60 for factory installed muzzle brake.

CONNECTICUT SHOTGUN MANUFACTURING COMPANY

Manufacturer located in New Britain, CT since 1995.

GALAZAN O/U SIDELOCK SHOTGUN — 12, 16, 20, 28, or .410 ga., features Fabbri type sidelock action with Boss-style metal reinforced forearm, top-of-the-line model utilizing best quality materials and workmanship.

Each gun is custom-built to the customer's exact specifications and priced accordingly.

CONNECTICUT VALLEY ARMS, INC.

Manufacturer located in Norcross, GA.

CVA manufactures mostly percussion/flintlock/finished and kit guns in either rifle or shotgun configurations. Black powder firearms can be found in the back of this text.

CONNECTICUT VALLEY CLASSICS, INC.

Manufacturer located in Westport, CT since 1993. Dealer direct sales.

Grading	100%	98%	95%	90%	80%	70%	60%

SHOTGUNS: O/U

The models listed below have receiver dimensions built to the exact specifications as the original Classic Doubles Model 101. The only difference is that the tang spacer has been made an integral part of the frame.

CLASSIC 101 SPORTER — 12 ga. only, boxlock action, monoblock, 28, 30, or 32 in. VR barrels with multi-chokes, SST, ejectors, nickel finished receiver with light engraving, checkered American black walnut stock and forearm with low luster finish, approx. 7¾ lbs.

	100%	98%	95%	90%	80%	70%	60%
	$1,875	$1,550	$1,225	$1,000	$825	$700	$600

Last Mfg.'s Sug. Retail was $2,195.

GRADE I CLASSIC SPORTER — 12 ga. only, boxlock action, monoblock, 28, 30, or 32 in. vented barrels with VR, lengthened forcing cones, and 2⅜ in. multi-chokes, SST, ejectors, stainless steel receiver with light engraving, checkered 20 LPI AA American black walnut stock and forearm with low luster finish, approx. 7¾ lbs.

Mfg.'s Sug. Retail	$3,195	$2,775	$2,100	$1,675	$1,250	$1,000	$825	$700

▲ *Woman's Classic Sporter* — similar to Grade I Classic Sporter, except has smaller stock dimensions and 28 in. barrels only, 7½ lbs. New 1996.

Mfg.'s Sug. Retail	$3,195	$2,775	$2,100	$1,675	$1,250	$1,000	$825	$700

This model is also available in Grade II or Grade III Woman's Classic Sporter.

▲ *Grade II Classic Sporter* — similar to Grade I Classic Sporter, except has AAA American or Claro walnut with 22 LPI hand-checkering.

Mfg.'s Sug. Retail	$3,795	$3,225	$2,350	$1,800	$1,325	$1,050	$850	$725

▲ *Grade III Classsic Sporter* — similar to Grade II Classic Sporter, except has Fleur-de-lis checkering patterns and gold accents.

Mfg.'s Sug. Retail	$4,195	$3,600	$2,750	$1,975	$1,450	$1,175	$925	$750

GRADE I CLASSIC FIELD — 12 ga. only, similar to Grade I Classic Sporter, except has solid rib and standard flush-mounted choke-tubes, 27½ in. barrels, 7½ lbs. New 1996.

Mfg.'s Sug. Retail	$3,195	$2,775	$2,100	$1,675	$1,250	$1,000	$825	$700

▲ *Classic Field Waterfowler* — 12 ga. only, 30 or 32 (disc. 1995) in. VR barrels, non-reflective surfaces, bird scene engraving, overboard barrels with lengthened forcing cones and four standard CVC chokes, 8 lbs. Introduced 1993.

Mfg.'s Sug. Retail	$2,995	$2,625	$2,000	$1,575	$1,175	$950	$775	$650

▲ *Grade II Classic Field* — similar to Grade I Classic Field, except has AAA American or Claro walnut with 22 LPI hand-checkering.

Mfg.'s Sug. Retail	$3,595	$3,100	$2,250	$1,750	$1,300	$1,050	$850	$725

▲ *Grade III Classsic Field* — similar to Grade II Classic Field, except has Fleur-de-lis checkering patterns and gold accents, choice of straight English (25½ in. VR barrels only) or pistol grip stock.

Mfg.'s Sug. Retail	$4,195	$3,600	$2,750	$1,975	$1,450	$1,175	$925	$750

CLASSIC SKEET — 12 ga. only, 29 in. vented barrels with 9mm VR, otherwise similar to Grade I Classic Sporter, 7½ lbs. New 1996.

Mfg.'s Sug. Retail	$3,195	$2,775	$2,100	$1,675	$1,250	$1,000	$825	$700

CLASSIC FLYER — 12 ga. only, live bird gun featuring AAA walnut and 22 LPI checkering, oil finish, 30 in. vented overboard barrels with 11mm tapered top rib and lengthened forcing cones, scroll engraving with pigeon scene on bottom, 8 lbs. New 1996.

Mfg.'s Sug. Retail	$3,995	$3,450	$2,650	$1,925	$1,425	$1,100	$850	$725

CONTENTO/VENTURA

Previously imported by Ventura Imports in Seal Beach, CA. Ventura also imported Bertuzzi and Piotti.

Grading	100%	98%	95%	90%	80%	70%	60%

SHOTGUNS

CONTENTO O/U — 12 ga., 32 in. barrels, boxlock, optional screw in choke tubes, high vent. rib, SST, auto ejectors, hand checkered Monte Carlo trap stock.

	100%	98%	95%	90%	80%	70%	60%
	$1,045	$990	$935	$880	$770	$690	$635

MK 2 — 2 barrel, O/U, with extra single barrel.

	$1,375	$1,320	$1,265	$1,210	$1,100	$1,020	$965

MK 2 — leather cased, combination set.

	$1,705	$1,650	$1,595	$1,540	$1,430	$1,350	$1,295

MK 3 — engraved, O/U.

	$1,650	$1,570	$1,485	$1,375	$1,295	$1,185	$1,100

MK 3 — 2 barrel, O/U, with extra single barrel.

	$2,200	$2,035	$1,925	$1,815	$1,650	$1,595	$1,515

MK 3 — leather cased, combination set.

	$2,750	$2,420	$2,200	$2,090	$1,955	$1,815	$1,760

MODEL 51 SxS — 12, 16, 20, 28, or .410 ga., 26-32 in. barrels, various chokes, extractors, boxlock, double triggers, checkered straight stock.

	$385	$360	$330	$305	$250	$220	$165
Auto ejectors	$495	$440	$385	$360	$305	$275	$220

MODEL 52 SxS — 10 ga., double triggers only, otherwise similar to 51.

	$525	$495	$470	$415	$360	$305	$250

MODEL 53 SxS — deluxe version of 51, scalloped frame, auto ejectors.

	$470	$440	$415	$385	$330	$275	$220
SST	$605	$550	$525	$495	$440	$385	$330

MODEL 61 SxS — 12 or 20 ga., 26, 27, 28, or 30 in. barrels, H&H sidelocks, various chokes, floral engraved, hand detachable locks, cocking indicators, select walnut pistol grip stock, auto ejectors.

	$880	$825	$770	$745	$690	$605	$550
SST	$1,020	$965	$910	$855	$800	$715	$660

MODEL 65 SxS — similar to 61, with elaborate engraving and quality hand finishing.

	$1,100	$1,045	$990	$965	$880	$825	$770

CONTINENTAL ARMS CORPORATION

Continental Arms imported high quality shotguns and rifles (usually Belgian) between the mid '50s and mid '70s.

RIFLES

BOLT ACTION — mostly large cals., typically custom Mauser action, makers include Defourney and Dumoulin.

Specimens should be evaluated individually due to the many configurations and embellishments encountered.

Grading	100%	98%	95%	90%	80%	70%	60%

DOUBLE RIFLE — .270, .303, .30-40, .348, .30-06, .375 H&H, .400 Jeffreys, .470, .475, .500, or .600, Nitro Express cal., 24 or 26 in. barrels, Anson & Deeley boxlock system, although some sidelocks were mfg., double triggers, checkered stock.

	$5,500	$4,620	$3,850	$3,300	$2,970	$2,750	$2,420

> Add 10% for boxlock with sideplates.
> Add 15% for ejectors.
> Add 25% for .375 H&H Magnum and larger cals.

SHOTGUNS: SxS

> Add 10% for .410 ga.
> Add 20% for 28 ga.
> Add 10% for Defourney mfg.

CENTAURE — all gauges, basic boxlock action with double triggers and extractors.

	$950	$895	$850	$700	$500	$400	$300

> Add 35% for ejectors.

CENTAURE ROYAL CROWN GRADE — all gauges, single trigger, ejectors, checkered stock and forearm, game scene engraving, can be identified by silver crown inlaid on top lever.

	$2,950	$2,700	$2,500	$2,300	$2,100	$1,950	$1,750

CENTAURE IMPERIAL CROWN GRADE — similar to Royal Crown, except gold inlay on top lever, extensive game scene engraving on receiver and barrels.

	$3,600	$3,300	$3,000	$2,750	$2,500	$2,250	$2,000

SHOTGUNS: O/U

> Add 10% for .410 ga.
> Add 20% for 28 ga.
> Add 10% for Defourney mfg.

CENTAURE BOXLOCK — 12, 20, 28, or .410 ga., ejectors, light engraving, chopper lump barrels with cross-bolt double underlocks, SST, 3-piece forearm.

	$1,750	$1,500	$1,350	$1,200	$1,025	$875	$750

CENTAURE LIEGE ROYAL CROWN GRADE — similar to Centaure Boxlock, except has game scene engraving, better figured wood and silver crown inlay.

	$2,650	$2,400	$2,150	$1,825	$1,600	$1,400	$1,200

CENTAURE IMPERIAL CROWN GRADE — similar to Royal Crown Grade, except has higher grade wood, extensive game scene engraving, oak leaf engraving on barrels, and gold inlay on top lever.

	$3,950	$3,600	$3,350	$3,150	$2,900	$2,700	$2,500

COOEY MACHINE & ARMS CO. LTD.

Previous manufacturer located in Cobourg, Ontario - Canada 1903-1961. During 1961, Cooey was sold to the Olin Corporation and placed under the supervision of the Winchester Western Division. At that point, the manufacture of Winchesters (primarily for Winchester Canada) began and continued through the mid-'70s.

Models manufactured by Cooey pre-1961 include various repeating .22 rifles, single shot shotguns (Models 84 and 840), and maybe a few others. There is limited information available on the variety of shotguns and rifles manufactured by this company (most distribution occurred in Canada). To date, there is limited collector demand for most models in this trademark and values should be based on the shooting utility rather than collector premiums due to rarity. Most values will range between $75-$150.

COOEY .22 RIFLE — .22 LR, post-WWI mfg., bolt action, open sights.

	$150	$130	$110	$95	$80	$70	$60

COONAN ARMS

Manufactured and distributed by JS Worldwide Distribution Co. located in St. Paul, MN.

Grading	100%	98%	95%	90%	80%	70%	60%

PISTOLS

COONAN .357 MAG. MODEL B — .357 Mag. only, stainless steel and alloy construction, single action, semi-auto, design based on the Colt Model 1911, 7 shot mag., 5 in. barrel, smooth walnut grips, 42 oz. New 1983.

Mfg.'s Sug. Retail	$720		$675	$530	$425

Add $35 for 6 in. barrel (new 1989).
Add $125 for Millett adj. rear sight.
Add $140 for BoMar sight.
Add $45 for .38 Spl. conversion kit (new 1986).

This model can be differentiated from the Model A in that it has an extended grip safety lever, linkless barrel system, trigger bar slot is enclosed, and recontoured rear grip strap. This model became standard in 1985.

▲ **Coonan .357 Cadet Model** — similar to .357 Mag. Model B, except is compact variation with 3.9 in. barrel and 6 shot mag., 39 oz. New 1993.

Mfg.'s Sug. Retail	$841		$775	$625	$500

▲ **Coonan .357 Cadet II** — features shorter barrel and long grip. New 1996.

Mfg.'s Sug. Retail	$841		$775	$625	$500

▲ **Model B Compensated** — 6 in. barrel with compensator, new 1990.

Mfg.'s Sug. Retail	$999		$895	$795	$650

▲ **Model Classic Compensated** — features 5 in. barrel with integral compensator, Millett white/orange outline sights, checkered black walnut grips, teflon black and matte stainless two-tone finish, 42 oz. New 1996.

Mfg.'s Sug. Retail	$1,400		$1,275	$1,025	$825	$675	$595	$525	$450

COONAN .357 MAG. MODEL A — original model without above listed improvements, special order only, inventory depleted in 1991. Serialization is under 2,000 for this model (less than 1,200 were mfg.). While discontinued, the factory has a few guns remaining in inventory.

			$1,150	$775	$550

Last Mfg.'s Sug. Retail was $625.

Add approx. $350 for early variations with engraved slide.
This variation will also shoot .38+P loads.
The first 25 Model A's were engraved on both sides of slide.

COOPER ARMS

Manufacturer located in Stevensville, MT. Dealer direct sales only.

RIFLES: BOLT ACTION

MODEL 21 VARMINT EXTREME SINGLE SHOT — .17 Rem., .17 Mach IV, .221 Fireball, .22 PPC (new 1995), .222 Rem., .222 Rem. Mag. (new 1995), .223 Rem., 6x45mm (disc. 1994), or 6x47mm (disc. 1994) cal., features heavy Varmint stainless barrel, checkered stock. New 1994.

Mfg.'s Sug. Retail	$1,675		$1,475	$1,150	$875	$700	$600	$525	$450

Add $465 for Benchrest Model with Jewell trigger (new 1995).
Add $215 for Custom Classic stock.

MODEL 22 PRO-VARMINT EXTREME SINGLE SHOT — .220 Swift, .22 BR (new 1996), .22-250 Rem., .243 Win., .25-06 Rem., .308 Win., 6mm PPC, 6.5x55mm (new 1996) or 7.62x39mm (new 1996) cal., available in either Pro-Varmint, Bench rest, or Black Jack (black synthetic stock) configuration, larger scale action of the Model 21. New 1995.

Mfg.'s Sug. Retail	$1,785		$1,525	$1,175	$900	$725	$625	$550	$475

Add $355 for Benchrest Model.

Grading	100%	98%	95%	90%	80%	70%	60%

MODEL 22 CLASSIC REPEATER — .22-250 Rem., .243 Win., .308 Win., or 7mm-08 Rem. cal., 3 shot mag. New 1996.

Mfg.'s Sug. Retail	$2,400	$2,125	$1,800	$1,525	$1,300	$1,050	$875	$650

Add $275 for Custom Classic Grade.

MODEL 36 SPORTSMAN — .22 LR, .17 CCM, or .22 Hornet cal., without Shilen barrel, standard wood with rubber recoil pad. Mfg. 1994 only.

	$675	$575	$495	$450	$400	$350	$295

Last Mfg.'s Sug. Retail was $750.

MODEL 36 MARKSMAN — .22 LR, .17 CCM, or .22 Hornet cal., 4 shot mag., 23 in. chrome moly barrel, AA Claro walnut with 22 LPI checkering, 45 degree bolt, sling swivels, hand rubbed oil finish, 7 lbs. Mfg. 1992-94.

	$975	$750	$625	$550	$495	$450	$400

Last Mfg.'s Sug. Retail was $1,125.

▲ *Model 36 Mountana Trail Blazer* — .22 LR only, lightweight field gun with sporter barrel. New 1996.

Mfg.'s Sug. Retail	$1,475	$1,300	$1,025	$775	$650	$575	$475	$425

▲ *Model 36 Classic* — .22 LR only, features choice of AAA Claro or AA French walnut with Monte Carlo cheekpiece.

Mfg.'s Sug. Retail	$1,695	$1,500	$1,175	$875	$700	$625	$525	$450

▲ *Model 36 Custom Classic* — includes Brownell No. 1 checkering pattern, ebony forend tip, and steel grip cap.

Mfg.'s Sug. Retail	$1,960	$1,700	$1,325	$1,050	$825	$700	$600	$500

▲ *Model 36 TRP-1* — target variation of the Model 36 with ISU synthetic stock and adj. cheekpiece, 23 in. Wiseman/McMillan stainless steel or chrome moly barrel, single shot, fully adj. single staged trigger, vent. forearm. Mfg. 1992-1993.

	$950	$795	$625	$525	$475	$425	$375

Last Mfg.'s Sug. Retail was $1,095.

▲ *Model MS-36 (TRP-1S)* — silhouette variation of the Model 36 TRP-1, clear epoxy finish, silhouette style stock, Pachmayr buttpad. Mfg. 1992-1993.

	$895	$725	$625	$550	$495	$450	$400

Last Mfg.'s Sug. Retail was $995.

▲ *Model 36 BR-50* — .22 LR cal., benchrest variation featuring black synthetic stock and heavy stainless barrel, Jewell trigger. New 1993.

Mfg.'s Sug. Retail	$1,850	$1,600	$1,200	$950	$750	$650	$550	$475

▲ *Model 36 IR-50* — .22 LR only, lightweight sporter style competition rifle with heavy 20 in. barrel. New 1996.

Mfg.'s Sug. Retail	$1,850	$1,600	$1,200	$950	$750	$650	$550	$475

▲ *Model 36 Featherweight* — .22 LR, .17 CCM, or .22 Hornet cal., features matte black synthetic stock and metal, Jewell trigger. New 1994.

Mfg.'s Sug. Retail	$1,850	$1,600	$1,200	$950	$750	$650	$550	$475

MODEL 38 SPORTER — .22 CCM or .17 CCM cal., 3 shot mag., 24 in. chrome moly barrel, AA Claro walnut with 22 LPI checkering, 45 degree bolt, sling swivels, hand rubbed oil finish, 8 lbs. Mfg. 1992-1993.

	$965	$750	$625	$550	$495	$450	$400

Last Mfg.'s Sug. Retail was $1,095.

Add $100 for Standard Grade (AA Claro walnut).
Add $200 for Custom Grade.
Add $300 for Custom Classic Grade.

The custom grade includes choice of AAA Claro or AA French walnut with Monte Carlo cheekpiece.

The .17 CCM and .22 CCM cartridges designate Cooper Centerfire Magnum. Basically, the .22 CCM is a centerfire derivative of the .22 Mag. cal., and the .17 CCM is simply a necked down variation.

Grading	100%	98%	95%	90%	80%	70%	60%

MODEL 40 — .17 CCM (disc. 1995), .17 Ackley Hornet, .22 CCM (disc. 1995), .22 Hornet, or .22 K Hornet cal., 3 lug action, incorporates Anschutz mag., choice of Classic, Custom Classic, or Classic Varminter configuration. New 1995.

Mfg.'s Sug. Retail	$1,825	$1,600	$1,200	$950	$750	$650	$550	$475

Add $200 for Custom Classic or Classic Varminter (disc.) Model.

COP

Previous manufacturer located in Torrance, CA.

COP DERRINGER — .357 Mag., 4 shot, 3 in. barrel, stainless steel mfg., single action, wood grips, 28 oz. COP stands for Compact Off-Duty Police. Disc.

	$350	$325	$285	$260	$240	$220	$200

COSMI, AMERICO & FIGLIO

Manufactured in Torrette, Italy since 1930. Please contact either the factory directly or New England Arms Co. for pricing and model availability (see Trademark Index).

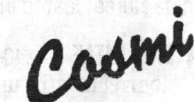

Approximately 6,900 Cosmi shotguns have been manufactured since 1930.

SEMI-AUTO SHOTGUN MODEL — 12 or 20 ga., 2¾ or 3 in. chamber, semi-auto, unique pivoting break open action loads cartridges into stock chamber from inside of receiver, 8 shot mag. with 3 shot option, Boehler Antinit steel barrel available with or without choke tubes, all internal parts are mfg. from special chrome-nickel steel, custom order gun only with dimensions specified by individual customer (approx. 6 month delivery time).

▲ *Standard Grade* — barrel and attached receiver assembly are blued, frame is chromed-nickel steel. In 1991, Cosmi introduced a new variation with solid titanium frame - more information can be obtained by contacting New England Arms Co.

Mfg.'s Sug. Retail	$6,750	$6,750	$6,000	$5,000	$4,500	$4,000	$3,500	$2,000

Add $2,000 for titanium fabrication.

Cosmi also manufactures an Extra Lusso Series with more elaborate engraving. Series C specimens start at $17,000, Series B start at $15,000, and Series A (top-of-the-line) start at $23,000.

▲ *Extra Lusso Models* — available with various styles and amounts of engraving. Prices are quoted individually and can be obtained by contacting New England Arms Co.

CRESCENT FIRE ARMS COMPANY

Manufactured 1888-1893 in Norwich, CT. Merged with N.R. Davis in the 1900's by H&D Folsom to form Crescent-Davis which was bought by J. Stevens Arms Co. in 1933. At this point, all guns and parts were moved to Chicopee Falls, MA and sold slowly as no more guns could be made with parts on hand.

Values below assume standard models with double triggers, extractors, original finish, and 100% working order. Sidelock actions were also available and will command premiums from prices listed below. Shotguns with exposed hammers can equal their hammerless counterparts if condition is 80% or better.

Grading	100%	98%	95%	90%	80%	70%	60%

SxS SHOTGUN

	100%	98%	95%	90%	80%	70%	60%
12 ga.	$195	$175	$150	$125	$100	$85	$65
16 ga.	$195	$175	$150	$125	$100	$85	$65
20 ga.	$295	$265	$230	$200	$170	$150	$125
28 ga.	$375	$325	$280	$250	$200	$150	$100
.410 ga.	$400	$350	$300	$250	$200	$150	$100

Inexpensive, but hard to duplicate at today's prices. Later bought out by Folsom and became maker of "house" guns for various companies.

AUTO & BURGLAR GUN — .410 ga., 14¼ in. double barrel, marked "NEW EMPIRE" on case colored receiver, total mfg. approximated at less than 100, must be registered.

Rarity factor precludes accurate pricing.

CUMBERLAND MOUNTAIN ARMS, INC.

Manufacturer located in Winchester, TN since early 1993.

PLATEAU RIFLE — .40-65 or .45-70 cal., patterned after the Browning Hi-wall single shot, various barrel lengths up to 32 in., manual safety, blued receiver and barrel, Marbles style buckhorn rear sight, receiver drilled for scope mounts. New 1993.

Mfg.'s Sug. Retail	$1,155	$950	$775	$650	$575	$500	$450	$400

Add approx. $200-$350 for deluxe wood.

CUSTOM GUN GUILD
Manufactured in Doraville, GA.

WOOD'S MODEL IV SINGLE SHOT — various cals., custom manufactured, falling block type single shot, lightweight, only 5½ lbs. Mfg. 1984 only.

	$2,975	$2,500	$2,250	$2,000	$1,850	$1,700	$1,050

D section

DPMS, INC.

Defense Procurement Manufacturing Services, Inc. is a manufacturer located in Becker, MN. DPMS, Inc. has been manufacturing AR-15 rifles since 1993.

Grading	100%	98%	95%	90%	80%	70%	60%

PISTOLS

▲ **Panther Pump Pistol** — .223 Rem., slide action paramilitary design, 10½ in. threaded heavy barrel, aluminum handguard incorporates slide action mechanism, pistol grip only (no stock), carrying handle with sights, 5 lbs.

Mfg.'s Sug. Retail	$1,525	$1,450	$1,200	$1,025	$925	$825	$700	$575

RIFLES

PANTHER AR-15 SERIES — .223 Rem. cal., semi-auto or slide action, paramilitary design, various barrel lengths and configurations, 10 shot mag., black synthetic stock and forearm, various weights. Introduced 1993.

▲ **Panther Classic** — 20 in. heavy barrel, semi-auto, ribbed barrel shroud, includes carrying handle with sights, 8 lbs.

Mfg.'s Sug. Retail	$999	$875	$750	$625	$550	$475	$425	$375

Add approx. $115 for left-hand variation (Southpaw Panther).

▲ **Panther Bulldog** — 20 in. stainless fluted bull barrel, semi-auto, flat-top, adj. butt stock, 11 lbs.

Mfg.'s Sug. Retail	$1,115	$995	$850	$725	$625	$550	$475	$425

▲ **Panther Carbine** — 16 in. heavy barrel, semi-auto, collapsible stock, includes carrying handle, 6½ lbs.

Mfg.'s Sug. Retail	$1,040	$900	$775	$635	$550	$475	$425	$375

D.P.M.S. also offers a pre-ban configuration in this model as well as a post-ban 16 in. free-floating barrel - contact the factory directly for more information.

▲ **Prairie Panther** — 20 in. heavy fluted barrel, semi-auto, flat-top, grooved forearm, 8¾ lbs.

Mfg.'s Sug. Retail	$1,159	$1,030	$875	$750	$635	$550	$475	$425

▲ **Panther Bull** — features 24 in. stainless bull barrel, semi-auto, flat-top, aluminum forearm, 10 lbs.

Mfg.'s Sug. Retail	$1,050	$900	$775	$635	$550	$475	$425	$375

▲ **Panther Pump** — .223 Rem., slide action paramilitary design, 20 in. threaded heavy barrel, aluminum handguard incorporates slide action mechanism, carrying handle with sights, 8½ lbs.

Mfg.'s Sug. Retail	$1,750	$1,675	$1,350	$1,150	$995	$875	$750	$625

BOLT ACTION SNIPER/VARMINT SERIES — various cals., 3 different configurations including Sniper, Informal Target Varmint, and Field Grade Varmint, features match barrel, action, and tuned trigger. Prices for the Sniper rifle start at approx. $2,400 while the Varmint guns start at approx. $1,800.

D W M

Deutsche Waffen And Munitions Fabriken. Berlin, Germany 1900-1930.

POCKET AUTOMATIC — 7.65mm, 3½ in. barrel, blue, hard rubber grips. Mfg. 1921-1931.

	$700	$630	$580	$500	$420	$380	$330

DAEWOO

Manufacturer located in Korea. Currently imported by Daewoo Precision Industries, Ltd. located in Southampton, PA.

Grading	100%	98%	95%	90%	80%	70%	60%

Exclusively distributed by Nationwide Sports Distributors beginnning in 1993. Previously imported by KBI, Inc. and Firstshot, Inc. both located in Harrisburg, PA.

Daewoo makes a variety of firearms, most of which are not imported into the U.S.

PISTOLS

DH380 — .380 ACP cal., double action design. Importation began 1995.

Mfg.'s Sug. Retail	$375	$330	$285	$260	$235	$210	$185	$165

DH40 — .40 S&W cal., otherwise similar to DP51. Importation began 1995.

Mfg.'s Sug. Retail	$450	$380	$315	$285	$250	$225	$200	$180

DP51 STANDARD (S), COMPACT (C), OR (B)— 9mm Para. cal., double action enabling lowering hammer w/o depressing trigger, 3½ (DP51 C or S) or 4 (DP51 B) in. barrel, 10 (C/B 1994), 12* (.40 S&W), or 13* (9mm Para.) shot mag., 3-dot sighting, tri-action mechanism, ambidextrous controls, alloy receiver, polished or sand-blasted black finish, 28 or 32 oz., includes lockable carrying case with accessories. Importation began 1991.

Mfg.'s Sug. Retail	$400	$350	$295	$270	$250	$225	$200	$180

Add $45 for DP51 Compact.

DP52 — .22 LR, double action, 3.8 in. barrel, alloy receiver, 10 shot mag., blue finish, 23 oz. Importation began 1994.

Mfg.'s Sug. Retail	$380	$320	$275	$225	$200	$180	$165	$150

RIFLES

MAX II (K2) — 5.56 cal. (.223), paramilitary design rifle, 18 in. barrel, gas operated rotating bolt, folding fiberglass stock, interchangeable mags. with the Colt M16, 7 lbs. Importation disc. 1986.

		$725	$650	$575	$500	$450	$415	$375

Last Mfg.'s Sug. Retail was $609.

▲ *MAX I (K1A1)* — similar to above, except has retractable stock. Importation disc. 1986.

		$725	$650	$575	$500	$450	$415	$375

Last Mfg.'s Sug. Retail was $592.

DR200 — .223 cal., paramilitary designed with sporterized stock, 10 shot mag. Importation began 1995.

Mfg.'s Sug. Retail	$535	$475	$425	$395	$375	$350	$325	$300

DAISY

Manufacturer located in Rogers, AR. Also see Daisy section under Modern Airguns. Distributor sales only.

RIFLES: DISC.

In addition to the models listed below, in 1987, Daisy assembled approximately 30,000 guns using left-over Iver Johnson parts. This model carried the Daisy trademark and was designated the '08 - it was an inexpensive bolt action single shot private labeled for Walmart. Secondary values on these rifles range from $25-$65.

V/L STANDARD RIFLE — single shot, .22 V/L, a caseless air ignited cartridge, 1,100 FPS, 18 in. barrel, plastic stock, 19,000 mfg., 1968-1969.

		$110	$90	$75	$65	$55	$45	$30

V/L PRESENTATION — similar to Collector's Kit, except does not have owner's name inscribed on butt plate, walnut stock, 4,000 mfg. for dealers.

		$165	$130	$110	$90	$70	$55	$45

Last Mfg.'s Sug. Retail was $125.

Grading	100%	98%	95%	90%	80%	70%	60%

V/L COLLECTOR'S KIT — comes with case, gun cradles, 300 rounds of ammo, and a gold plated brass butt plate with owner's name and serial number of gun, approx. 4,000 mfg., available only by direct factory order.

$275	$165	$130	$110	$90	$70	$55

Last Mfg.'s Sug. Retail was $125.

Note: The Daisy .22 V/L is the only commercial caseless ammo system. It was discontinued because the BATF ruled that the gun constituted a firearm, and since Daisy is federally licensed to manufacture air weapons only, the factory decided to discontinue manufacture.

RIFLES: RECENT MFG.

All Legacy models have a removable trigger, slings and swivels, takedown barrel, dovetail receiver for scope mounting, rifled inner steel barrel with 12 lands and grooves, and an adj. rear sight. Weight is between 6½ - 7 lbs.

MODEL 8 — .22 S or LR cal., single shot, 16 in. barrel, black synthetic stock, 30,000 mfg. for Walmart only 1987-88.

$100	$80	$70	$60	$50	$40	$35

LEGACY MODELS 2201/2211 — .22 LR cal., single shot, bolt action, plastic (2201) or walnut finished hardwood (2211) stock, models vary in features, prices range from $80-$130. Mfg. 1988-91.

LEGACY MODELS 2202/2212 — .22 LR cal., bolt action repeater, 10 shot rotary mag., plastic (2202) or walnut finished hardwood (2212) stock, models vary in features, prices range from $90-$135. Mfg. 1988-91.

Model 2202 has copolymer stock with adj. butt plate.

LEGACY MODELS 2203/2213 — .22 LR cal., semi-auto, 7 shot clip mag., models vary in features, prices range from $95-$140. Mfg. 1988-91.

Model 2203 has copolymer stock with adj. butt plate. Model 2213 has American hardwood stock.

DAKIN GUN CO.
San Francisco, CA. 1960s.

SHOTGUNS

MODEL 100 SxS — 12 or 20 ga., boxlock, engraved, double trigger.

$425	$350	$275	$240	$205	$190	$170

MODEL 147 SxS — 12 or 20 ga., boxlock, engraved, vent. rib, double trigger.

$495	$385	$300	$265	$235	$215	$195

MODEL 160 SxS — 12 or 20 ga., boxlock, single trigger, ejectors, vent. rib.

$825	$700	$595	$495	$450	$395	$360

MODEL 215 SxS — 12 or 20 ga., sidelock, heavy engraving, special walnut, single trigger, ejectors, vent. rib.

$2,250	$1,900	$1,675	$1,300	$1,100	$925	$775

MODEL 170 O&U — 12, 16, 20, or .410 ga., boxlock, light engraving, double triggers, vent rib.

$495	$400	$325	$275	$245	$220	$195

DAKOTA ARMS, INC.
Manufacturer located in Sturgis, SD. Dealer and direct sales through manufacturer only.

DAKOTA ARMS
INC

Grading	100%	98%	95%	90%	80%	70%	60%

RIFLES

Dakota Arms models listed below are also available with many custom options - please contact the factory directly for availability and pricing. Left-hand rifles are also available at no extra charge on all models. Actions (barreled or unbarreled) may also be purchased separately - please contact the manufacturer directly for individual quotations.

DAKOTA 22 RIFLE — .22 LR or .22 Hornet (disc.) cal., combines features of the Win. Model 52 Sporter and Dakota 76, full sized receiver, trigger and striker block safety similar to Dakota 76, 5 shot mag., 22 in. chrome moly barrel, checkered walnut stock, no sights, $6\frac{1}{2}$ lbs. New 1992.

Mfg.'s Sug. Retail	$1,795	$1,550	$1,150	$900	$800	$695	$625	$550

DAKOTA 76 CLASSIC GRADE — available in various cals. (short, standard, or long action), custom frame incorporating many Win. Model 70 features, 21 or 23 in. barrel, Mauser type extractor, checkered X English walnut stock, $7\frac{1}{2}$ lbs. Left-hand action available at no extra charge. New 1987.

Mfg.'s Sug. Retail	$2,850	$2,550	$1,875	$1,475	$1,200	$990	$880	$770

This Model is also available with a composite stock at no extra charge.

DAKOTA 76 VARMINT GRADE — available in 9 cals. between .17 Rem. and 6mm PPC, single shot bolt-action, heavy barrel. New 1994.

Mfg.'s Sug. Retail	$2,500	$2,275	$1,775	$1,425	$1,175	$990	$880	$770

DAKOTA 76 SAFARI GRADE — available in various cals., 23 in. barrel, one-piece drop trigger guard assembly with hinged floor plate, checkered XXX English walnut stock with ebony forearm tip. Left-hand action available at no extra charge, $8\frac{1}{2}$ lbs. New 1987.

Mfg.'s Sug. Retail	$3,750	$3,300	$2,675	$2,300	$1,925	$1,650	$1,350	$1,050

Subtract $400 (retail) if ordered with composite stock (disc.).

DAKOTA 76 AFRICAN GRADE — .404 Jeffery, .416 Dakota, .416 Rigby, or .450 Dakota cal., 4 shot mag., select wood with cross bolts in the stock, other features similar to Safari Grade Model, 24 in. barrel, "R" prefix on serial number, $9\frac{1}{2}$ lbs. New 1989.

Mfg.'s Sug. Retail	$4,275	$3,875	$3,300	$2,825	$2,400	$2,000	$1,675	$1,400

DAKOTA 76 ALPINE GRADE — .22-250, .243 Win., 6mm Rem., .250-3000, 7mm/08, .308, or .358 cal., short action variation of the Classic Grade, 21 or 23 in. barrel, lighter weight model featuring a blind 4 shot mag., checkered X English walnut slimmer stock and barrel, serial numbered with a "K" prefix, $6\frac{1}{2}$ lbs. Mfg. 1989-92.

	$1,850	$1,495	$1,300	$1,075	$925	$800	$700

Last Mfg.'s Sug. Retail was $1,995.

Other calibers were available on a special order basis.

DAKOTA 10 SINGLE SHOT MODEL — available in most rimmed and rimless commercially loaded standard and Mag. cals., standard or enlarged Magnum (new 1994) action, 23 in. round barrel, top tang safety, deluxe checkered XX English walnut stock and forearm, 6 lbs. New 1990.

Mfg.'s Sug. Retail	$2,900	$2,575	$1,975	$1,525	$1,200	$1,000	$880	$770

Add $250 for Mag. cals.

SHOTGUNS: SIDE-BY-SIDE

DAKOTA CLASSIC FIELD GRADE — 20 ga. only, case colored round boxlock action, 27 in. barrels with fixed chokes, DTs, straight grip checkered English walnut stock and splinter forearm, no engraving. New 1996.

Mfg.'s Sug. Retail	$7,950	$7,450	$6,750	$6,000	$5,400	$4,800	$4,200	$3,450

DAKOTA PREMIUM FIELD GRADE — similar to Dakota Classic Field Grade, except has exhibition grade English walnut and 50% engraving coverage.

Mfg.'s Sug. Retail	$9,950	$9,250	$7,450	$6,750	$5,950	$5,200	$4,500	$3,750

Grading	100%	98%	95%	90%	80%	70%	60%

DAKOTA AMERICAN LEGEND — 20 ga. only, fully scroll-engraved coin finish round boxlock action with gold inlays, special English walnut mfg. to customer dimensions, 27 in. barrels with concave rib, leather trunk case, 6 lbs. New 1996.

Mfg.'s Sug. Retail	$18,000	$16,000	$13,000	$11,000	$9,250	$7,500	$6,250	$5,000

  Only 100 guns are scheduled to be mfg. Also to be produced in a 12 ga. and .410/28 ga. set.

DAKOTA SINGLE ACTION REVOLVERS

Manufactured in Italy, imported and distributed by E.M.F. Co., Inc. located in Santa Ana, CA. Dealer direct sales only.

Other firearms imported by E.M.F. Co., Inc. will be found in the E section of this book.

SAA VARIATIONS

OLD MODEL — .22 LR, 32-20, .357 Mag., .38-40, .44 Spl., .44-40, or .45 LC cal., copy of the Colt S.A.A., 4⅝, 5½, or 7½ in. barrels, blue finish, case hardened frame, 1-piece walnut grips, solid brass backstrap and trigger guard. Importation disc. 1991.

	$325	$250	$200	$175	$150	$135	$120

                                                                   Last Mfg.'s Sug. Retail was $600.

  Add $100 for nickel finish (disc.).
  Add $110 for convertible cylinders.

▲ *Engraved Old Model* — .32-20, .357, .38-40, .44-40, or .45 cal., 4¾, 5½ or 7½ in. barrel. Disc. 1993, reintroduced 1996.

Mfg.'s Sug. Retail	$840	$695	$500	$425	$350	$325	$300	$275

  Add $160 for nickel finish (disc).

▲ *Cattlebrand Engraved* — .44-40 or .45 LC cal., 5½ or 7½ in. barrel, patterned after the famous Colt Cattlebrand variation (features various cattlebrands engraved on the barrel, frame and cylinder). Imported 1992-1993, reintroduced 1996.

Mfg.'s Sug. Retail	$840	$695	$500	$425	$350	$325	$300	$275

  Add $140 for silver-plating.

NEW MODEL — .357 Mag., .44-40, or .45 LC cal., features forged steel frame, black nickel backstrap and trigger guard, 4¾, 5½, or 7½ in. barrel, choice of case hardened or nickel frame, one piece walnut grips, original Colt type hammer (without transfer bar safety). Importation began 1991.

Mfg.'s Sug. Retail	$410	$325	$275	$225	$175	$150	$135	$120

  Add $125 for nickel finish.
  Add $100 for combo. cylinder.

DAKOTA PREMIER — .45 LC cal., black powder frame, initial mfg. was with 4⅝ or 5½ in. barrel, set screw cylinder pin release, steel backstrap and trigger guard, one-piece grips. This model was the predecessor to the New Hartford Model.

	$375	$295	$250	$190	$170	$160	$150

                                                                   Last Mfg.'s Sug. Retail was $520.

NEW HARTFORD MODEL — .22 LR (disc. 1992), .32-20, .357 Mag., .38-40, .44-40, .44 Spl., or .45 LC cal., features forged steel frame, backstrap, and trigger guard, exact reproduction of Colt's 1st or 2nd generation SAA, choice of black powder (with base pin frame set screw) or 2nd generation (push button cylinder pin release) frame, case hardened frame, original Colt markings, 4¾, 5½ or 7½ in. barrel. Importation began 1991.

Mfg.'s Sug. Retail	$600	$425	$350	$275	$225	$175	$150	$130

  Add $40 for .32-20, .38-40, or .44 Spl. cal.
  Add $125 for nickel finish.

▲ *Pinkerton Model* — .45 LC cal., birdshead grips, 4 in. barrel. New 1994.

Mfg.'s Sug. Retail	$700	$455	$345	$280	$220	$185	$160	$150

Grading	100%	98%	95%	90%	80%	70%	60%

▲ *Cavalry Model* — .45 LC cal., 7½ in. barrel, faithful reproduction of the original Colt Cavalry Model, one-piece walnut grips with inspector cartouche, case hardened frame and hammer. Importation began 1991.

Mfg.'s Sug. Retail	$700	$455	$345	$280	$220	$185	$160	$150

▲ *Artillery Model* — .45 LC cal., similar to Cavalry Model, except has 5½ in. barrel. Importation began 1991.

Mfg.'s Sug. Retail	$700	$455	$345	$280	$220	$185	$160	$150

▲ *Texas Sesquicentennial* — .45 LC cal., 4¾ in. barrel, 50 mfg. for Texas Sesquicentennial with special engraving, includes numbered belt buckle and presentation case. Disc. 1991.

$1,200 $925 $725

Original list price was $4,550.

▲ *Target Model* — .357 Mag., .44-40, or .45 LC cal., 5½ or 7½ in. barrel, case hardened frame, brass backstrap. Imported 1987-90.

$325 $240 $185 $150 $140 $130 $120

Last Mfg.'s Sug. Retail was $500.

▲ *Buntline Model* — 12 in. barrel, .357, .44-40, or .45 LC cal., blue only. Importation disc. 1990.

$300 $250 $175 $160 $150 $140 $130

Last Mfg.'s Sug. Retail was $520.

▲ *Buckhorn Model* — 16¼ in. barrel, otherwise similar to Buntline. Importation disc. 1987.

$295 $250 $180 $170 $160 $150 $140

Last Mfg.'s Sug. Retail was $495.

SHERIFF'S OLD/NEW MODEL — .32-20 (new), .357 Mag., .38-40 (new), .44 Spl. (new), .44-40, or .45 LC cal., 3½ in. barrel only. Importation disc. 1991, resumed 1994.

Mfg.'s Sug. Retail	$700	$455	$345	$280	$220	$185	$160	$150

U.S. ARMY — variety of cals., premium quality construction. Disc. 1985.

$300 $205 $180 $165 $155 $145 $135

Last Mfg.'s Sug. Retail was $395.

▲ *U.S. Army Commemorative* — .45 cal., 7½ in. barrel, serial numbered 1-500, blue finish, case hardened frame, steel backstrap and trigger guard, 1-piece walnut grips. Importation disc. 1987.

$350 $265 $185 $170 $160 $150 $135

Last Mfg.'s Sug. Retail was $495.

CONVERTIBLE MODEL — available with .22 LR/.22 Mag., .32-20/.32 H&R Mag., .357 Mag./9mm, or .44-40/.44 Spl. cal., .45 LC/.45 ACP double cylinders. Imported 1986-90.

$380 $310 $260 $220 $195 $170 $150

Last Mfg.'s Sug. Retail was $580.

FAST DRAW MODEL — .22 LR, .22 Mag., .32-20, .32 H&R Mag., .357 Mag., .38-40, 9mm, .44 Spl., .44-40, .45 ACP, or .45 LC cal., case hardened frame, 4⅝ in. barrel. Importation disc. 1990.

$300 $225 $165 $150 $135 $125 $110

Last Mfg.'s Sug. Retail was $480.

BISLEY MODEL — .22 LR, .22 Mag., .32-20, .32 H&R Mag., .38-40, .357 Mag., 9mm, .44 Spl., .44-40, .45 ACP, or .45 LC (current mfg.) cal., 4¾ (disc. 1994), 5½, or 7½ in. barrel lengths. Imported 1986-91, reintroduced 1993-disc. 1995.

$550 $450 $365 $275 $225 $195 $175

Last Mfg.'s Sug. Retail was $680.

Add $125 for nickel finish.
Add $112 for combo. cylinder (.45 ACP).

▲ *Engraved Bisley* — .32-20, .38-40, .357 Mag., .44-40, or .45 LC cal. (disc. 1990), 4¾, 5½ or 7½ in. barrel, action engraved throughout. Imported 1987-91.

$425 $350 $275 $250 $225 $200 $180

Last Mfg.'s Sug. Retail was $570.

Add $100 for nickel finish.

DALY, CHARLES: PRUSSIAN MFG.

Charles Daly was an importer whose goal was to give the U.S. shotgun consumer a European manufactured gun of similar quality to the premier American shotguns of the same era. In that behalf, he had various European firms fabricate shotguns with American shooting features and preferences. Many "Prussian" Dalys were built by various firms in Suhl, Germany. Importation ceased prior to WWII. These Prussian Charles Dalys utilized the finest materials and best workmanship of their time.

SHOTGUNS

In the higher grade Prussian Daly variations, there is quite a bit of difference in their manufacture, including engraving options, levels of wood embellishment, and other extra cost features at the time. H. A. Linder produced approx. 2,500 guns (ser. numbered accordingly), and many of the higher grades show a noticeable difference in the amount of engraving (from minimal to considerable game scene engraving), can be either case colored only or have gold inlaid birds and animals (the number of which can also vary), barrels can have various levels of engraving on both the breech and muzzle ends - all of these factors have considerable impact on the overall value of a particular specimen. It is estimated that it took three craftsmen one year to produce a single Diamond Regent gun.

Grading	100%	98%	95%	90%	80%	70%	60%

EMPIRE O&U — 12, 16, or 20 ga., various barrel lengths, Anson & Deeley boxlock, ejectors and double triggers, fine engraving, deluxe walnut. Disc. 1933.

	$4,000	$3,400	$2,750	$2,375	$2,000	$1,825	$1,625

DIAMOND O&U — similar to Empire model, only finer workmanship and materials.

	$5,000	$4,300	$3,475	$3,000	$2,600	$2,300	$2,000

SUPERIOR SxS — 10, 12, 20, 28, or .410 ga., Anson & Deeley boxlock, various barrel lengths, ejectors (except superior model). Disc. 1933.

	$1,050	$790	$690	$580	$525	$475	$420

EMPIRE SxS — similar to Superior, only more engraving and better wood.

	100%	98%	95%	90%	80%	70%	60%
Linder mfg.	$5,000	$4,400	$3,900	$3,500	$2,800	$2,200	$1,500
Sauer mfg.	$4,200	$3,500	$3,100	$2,800	$2,200	$1,800	$1,400

DIAMOND SxS — similar to Empire model, only more elaborate and with gold inlays.

	100%	98%	95%	90%	80%	70%	60%
Linder mfg.	$10,000	$9,000	$8,500	$8,000	$7,000	$6,000	$4,500
Sauer mfg.	$7,000	$6,200	$5,500	$5,000	$4,000	$3,000	$2,000

Deduct 20%-25% if without gold inlays.

DIAMOND REGENT SxS — top-of-the-line Prussian side-by-side and with gold inlays.

	100%	98%	95%	90%	80%	70%	60%
Linder mfg.	$16,000	$13,500	$12,000	$11,000	$8,500	$7,000	$5,000
Sauer mfg.	$8,500	$7,700	$7,000	$6,500	$5,000	$4,000	$3,000

EMPIRE SINGLE BARREL TRAP — 12 ga., 30-34 in. barrel, Anson & Deeley boxlock, ejector, vent. rib, finely engraved with select walnut, chopper lump extension, top quality. Disc. 1933.

	$2,150	$1,675	$1,375	$1,100	$960	$850	$750

SEXTUPLE SINGLE BARREL TRAP — 12 ga., 30-34 in. barrel, six locking bolts, ejector, vent. rib, elaborately engraved and checkered. Regent Diamond Model has better engraving and wood.

▲ *Empire Quality*

	$2,600	$2,100	$1,700	$1,400	$1,100	$900	$750

▲ *Regent Diamond Quality*

	$3,300	$2,850	$2,400	$1,950	$1,650	$1,350	$995

Grading	100%	98%	95%	90%	80%	70%	60%

DRILLING MODEL — 3 barrel combination gun, available in 12, 16, or 20 ga.'s and .25-20, .25-35, and .30-30 cals., extractors, double triggers, engraved action, select walnut, mfg. by both Linder and Sauer. Linder mfg. guns are extremely rare - very few specimens are to be found domestically. Sauer guns were not marked for grade, but rather had three levels of engraving which determined the grade. Most Sauer guns had a tang mounted aperture rear sight and a separate rifle cock and were sidelocks. Disc. 1933.

▲ *Superior Quality* — borderline engraving only.

Sauer mfg.	$3,000	$2,600	$2,300	$2,000	$1,700	$1,500	$1,200

▲ *Diamond Quality* — full scroll engraving.

Sauer mfg.	$5,500	$4,800	$4,400	$4,000	$3,500	$3,000	$2,200

▲ *Regent Diamond Quality* — top-of-the-line model featuring full game scene coverage.

Linder mfg.	$12,000	$11,000	$10,000	$9,000	$7,000	$6,000	$5,000
Sauer mfg.	$8,000	$7,000	$6,700	$6,000	$5,000	$4,000	$3,000

COMMANIDER O&U — 12, 16, 20, 28, or .410 ga., Anson & Deeley boxlock action, single or double triggers, ejectors. Mfg. in Belgium circa 1939.

▲ *Model 100*

	$500	$375	$325	$275	$250	$225	$200

Add $100 for single trigger.

▲ *Model 200* — similar to Model 100, except has deluxe walnut.

	$650	$490	$425	$360	$325	$300	$260

For 28 and .410 ga.'s — add 10% - 30%.

RIFLES

BOLT ACTION GRADE I — .22 Hornet, mfg. by F. Jaeger & Co. of Suhl, Germany, 5 shot mag., 24 in. barrel, miniature Mauser bolt action, deluxe walnut. Disc.

	$820	$615	$535	$455	$410	$370	$330

DALY, CHARLES: JAPANESE MFG.
Manufactured by B.C. Miroku, Japan.

SHOTGUNS: O/U

In the early sixties, C. Daly guns were manufactured by the firm of B.C. Miroku in Tokyo, Japan. This Japanese gun manufacturing company has produced guns for many companies, Browning being the biggest current customer. Miroku guns are high quality with excellent fit and finish. Many of them are highly engraved and are fine examples of the gunmaker's art. Charles Daly Miroku Guns are becoming quite collectible in some areas (smaller gauges with open chokes). Their production ceased in 1976.

O/U SHOTGUN — 12, 20, 28, or .410 ga., 26, 28, or 30 in. vent. rib barrels, various chokes, boxlock, auto ejectors, SST, select walnut checkered pistol grip stock, Superior and Diamond Grade Trap have Monte Carlo stocks, the grades differ in amount of engraving and wood. Mfg. 1963-1976 by Miroku.

Add 10% for 20 ga. on models listed below.
Add 30% for 28 ga. on models listed below.
Add 40% for .410 ga. on models listed below.
Less than 500 28 ga. guns were built on .410 frames. These guns will bring an additional 10%-15% over normal 28 ga. values.

▲ *Field Grade* — 12 or 20 ga., field gun.

	$625	$550	$525	$500	$450	$400	$375

▲ *Venture Grade*

	$550	$495	$470	$440	$415	$360	$305

Grading	100%	98%	95%	90%	80%	70%	60%
▲ *Venture Skeet* — 26 in. barrels choked skeet and skeet.							
	$575	$525	$495	$470	$440	$385	$330
▲ *Venture Trap* — 30 in. imp. mod. and full.							
	$530	$495	$470	$415	$360	$330	$300
▲ *Superior Grade*							
	$795	$715	$650	$600	$550	$495	$440
▲ *Superior Trap*							
	$700	$625	$575	$550	$500	$440	$390

This model had an optional selective ejection system enabling the shooter to deactivate the ejectors.

	100%	98%	95%	90%	80%	70%	60%
▲ *Diamond Grade Field*							
	$1,070	$990	$935	$880	$770	$715	$660
▲ *Diamond Grade Skeet*							
	$1,095	$990	$910	$800	$745	$690	$635
▲ *Diamond Grade Trap*							
	$925	$885	$800	$740	$685	$620	$560
▲ *Wide Rib Diamond Grade Flat-Top Trap*							
	$960	$920	$840	$815	$760	$700	$640
▲ *Diamond Regent Grade* — mostly 12 ga., extensive frame engraving with gold inlays, rare.							
	$2,000	$1,700	$1,425	$1,275	$1,100	$990	$880

SHOTGUNS: SxS OR SINGLE BARREL

EMPIRE DOUBLE BARREL SHOTGUN — 12, 16, or 20 ga., 26, 28, or 30 in. barrels, various chokes, boxlock, extractors, single trigger, checkered pistol grip stock. Mfg. 1968-1971.

	100%	98%	95%	90%	80%	70%	60%
	$545	$495	$470	$415	$360	$305	$250
Vent. rib	$595	$535	$500	$450	$400	$350	$300

SUPERIOR GRADE SINGLE BARREL TRAP — 12 ga., 32 or 34 in. vent. rib, full choke barrel, auto ejector, Monte Carlo stock with recoil pad. Mfg. 1968-1976.

	100%	98%	95%	90%	80%	70%	60%
	$550	$525	$495	$440	$385	$330	$305

1974 WILDLIFE COMMEMORATIVE — duck scene engraved, Diamond grade, Trap, or Skeet, limited to 500 guns. Mfg. 1974.

	100%	98%	95%	90%	80%	70%	60%
	$1,650	$1,430	$1,320	$1,100	$990	$880	$770

DALY, CHARLES: 1976 TO PRESENT

Currently imported by Outdoor Sports Headquarters, Inc. located in Dayton, OH.

The Charles Daly "Novamatic" shotguns were produced in 1968 by Breda in Italy.

SHOTGUNS: SEMI-AUTO

The Novamatic series was not imported by Outdoor Sport Headquarters, Inc.

NOVAMATIC LIGHTWEIGHT MODEL — 12 ga., 26 or 28 in. barrel, various chokes, available with quick choke interchangeable tubes, checkered pistol grip stock, similar to the Breda shotgun. Mfg. 1968 only.

	100%	98%	95%	90%	80%	70%	60%
	$305	$275	$250	$220	$195	$165	$140

Add $25 for vent. rib.
Add $15 for quick choke.

Grading	100%	98%	95%	90%	80%	70%	60%

NOVAMATIC SUPER LIGHTWEIGHT — 12 or 20 ga., similar to Lightweight, except approx. $\frac{1}{2}$ lb. lighter.

	$330	$305	$275	$250	$220	$195	$165

Add $25 for vent. rib.
Add $15 for quick choke.

NOVAMATIC MAGNUM — similar to Lightweight, with 3 in. 12 or 20 ga. chambers, 28 or 30 in. vent rib barrel, full choke.

	$330	$305	$275	$250	$220	$195	$165

NOVAMATIC TRAP — similar to Lightweight, with 30 in. full vent. rib barrel, Monte Carlo stock.

	$360	$330	$305	$275	$250	$220	$195

CHARLES DALY AUTOMATIC — 12 ga., 2¾ or 3 in. chambers, gas operation, alloy frame, pistol grip (high gloss) or English stock, vent. rib, 5 shot mag. Also available as slug gun with iron sights. Invector chokes became standard in 1986. Disc. 1988.

	$320	$275	$235	$205	$190	$170	$150

Last Mfg.'s Sug. Retail was $365.

Add $15 for oil finished English stock.

MULTI-XII — 12 ga. only, 3 in. chamber, 27 in. VR multichoke barrel, self adjusting gas operation, deluxe checkered walnut stock with recoil pad and forearm. Imported 1987-88 only.

	$425	$360	$320	$285	$250	$225	$195

Last Mfg.'s Sug. Retail was $498.

SHOTGUNS: O/U

Current O/U production is from Italy.

PRESENTATION MODEL — 12 or 20 ga., with choke tubes, Purdey double underlug locking action with decorative engraved sideplates, French walnut, single trigger, ejectors. Disc. 1986.

	$995	$840	$750	$670	$615	$560	$520

Last Mfg.'s Sug. Retail was $1,165.

FIELD MODEL — similar to Luxe Model except has fixed chokes, extractors, machine stock checkering, and blued receiver, not available in 28 or .410 ga. New 1989.

Mfg.'s Sug. Retail	$545		$440	$385	$350	$315	$285	$260	$230

DELUXE MODEL — 12, 20, 28 (disc. 1995), or .410 ga. (disc. 1995), boxlock with self adj. crossbolt, 26 or 28 in. chrome lined VR barrels with internal choke tubes, SST, ejectors, antique silver finish on receiver, deluxe hand checkered walnut stock and forearm. New 1989.

Mfg.'s Sug. Retail	$770		$650	$525	$475	$425	$400	$375	$350

SPORTING CLAYS MODEL — 12 ga. only, SST, ejectors, silver engraved receiver, checkered walnut stock and forearm, screw-in chokes, 28 (disc.) or 30 (new 1996) in. VR ported barrels. Importation began 1995.

Mfg.'s Sug. Retail	$895		$775	$700	$625	$550	$475	$395	$350

DIAMOND FIELD — 12 or 20 ga. (disc. 1986) Mag., with choke tubes. Same action as Presentation Model without sideplates, engraved, select walnut, single trigger, ejectors. Disc. 1986.

	$695	$600	$550	$510	$460	$420	$380

Last Mfg.'s Sug. Retail was $895.

▲ *Diamond Trap or Skeet* — 12 ga. only, 26 or 30 in. barrels only. Disc. 1986.

	$850	$700	$550	$500	$475	$450	$425

Last Mfg.'s Sug. Retail was $1,050.

Deduct $50 for Skeet Model.

Grading	100%	98%	95%	90%	80%	70%	60%

SUPERIOR II — 12 or 20 ga., various chokes, boxlock action, single trigger, ejectors, engraved. Disc. 1988.

	$675	$575	$475	$425	$395	$375	$350

Last Mfg.'s Sug. Retail was $875.

Add $35 for 12 ga. Mag. (disc. 1987).

FIELD III — 12 or 20 ga., various chokes, boxlock action, single trigger. Disc. 1989.

	$395	$370	$340	$315	$285	$260	$230

Last Mfg.'s Sug. Retail was $450.

SHOTGUNS: SIDE-BY-SIDE

FIELD III — 12 or 20 ga., various chokes, boxlock action, single trigger. Disc.

	$350	$315	$285	$260	$230	$210	$195

SUPERIOR — 12 or 20 ga., boxlock action, various chokes, single trigger. Disc. 1985.

	$550	$470	$405	$345	$315	$280	$250

Last Mfg.'s Sug. Retail was $624.

LUXE MODEL — 12 (disc. 1991) or 20 ga., boxlock action, SST, ejectors, 26 in. barrels with choke tubes, checkered pistol grip walnut stock with semi-beavertail forearm, recoil pad. Imported 1990-94.

	$575	$450	$395	$350	$315	$285	$260

Last Mfg.'s Sug. Retail was $650.

This model was manufactured by Hermanos located in Spain.

DAN ARMS OF AMERICA

Manufactured in Italy by Silma. Previously imported by Dan Arms of America located in Allentown, PA and by Dan Arms of North America (previously called Sportsman's Emporium Ltd.) located in Fort Washington, PA.

All shotguns listed below were discontinued in early 1988.

SHOTGUNS: O/U

LUX GRADE I — 12 or 20 ga., 3 in. Mag. chambers, 26, 28, or 30 in. barrels, vent rib, extractors, pistol grip, double trigger, European walnut.

	$280	$220	$210	$200	$190	$180	$170

Last Mfg.'s Sug. Retail was $350.

LUX GRADE II — 12 ga. only, 3 in. Mag. chambers, 26, 28, or 30 in. barrels, vent. rib, extractors, pistol grip, single trigger, European walnut.

	$320	$250	$240	$230	$215	$200	$190

Last Mfg.'s Sug. Retail was $395.

LUX GRADE III — 12 or 20 ga., 3 in. Mag. chambers, 26, 28, or 30 in. barrels, vent rib, ejectors, pistol grip, single trigger, checkered European walnut.

	$375	$300	$285	$270	$255	$240	$220

Last Mfg.'s Sug. Retail was $450.

LUX GRADE IV — 12 ga. only, 3 in. Mag. chambers, 28 in. barrels, vent. rib, ejectors, pistol grip, single trigger, checkered European walnut, multi-choked with 5 tubes.

	$460	$390	$350	$310	$285	$265	$245

Last Mfg.'s Sug. Retail was $550.

SKEET MODEL — 12 ga. only, 26½ in. barrels, 10mm vent. rib, anatomical pistol grip.

	$550	$450	$400	$355	$320	$300	$285

Last Mfg.'s Sug. Retail was $650.

TRAP MODEL — 12 ga. only, 30 in. barrels, 10mm vent. rib, anatomical pistol grip.

	$550	$450	$400	$355	$320	$300	$285

Last Mfg.'s Sug. Retail was $650.

Grading	100%	98%	95%	90%	80%	70%	60%

SILVERSNIPE — 12 or 20 ga., made to customer specifications, sideplates, select high grade walnut, name engraving upon request.

	100%	98%	95%	90%	80%	70%	60%
	$1,300	$1,200	$1,050	$900	$800	$700	$600

Last Mfg.'s Sug. Retail was $1,475.

SHOTGUNS: SIDE-BY-SIDE

FIELD MODEL — 12, 16, 20, 28, or .410 ga., double triggers, extractors, 26 or 28 in. barrels.

	100%	98%	95%	90%	80%	70%	60%
	$285	$220	$210	$200	$190	$180	$170

Last Mfg.'s Sug. Retail was $350.

DELUXE FIELD MODEL — 12 or 20 ga., single triggers, ejectors, 26 or 28 in. barrels.

	100%	98%	95%	90%	80%	70%	60%
	$440	$375	$340	$310	$290	$260	$230

Last Mfg.'s Sug. Retail was $500.

DARDICK
Previously manufactured in Hamden, CT.

PISTOLS

SERIES 1100 — .38 Dardick Tround, double action, 10 shot mag.

	100%	98%	95%	90%	80%	70%	60%
	$560	$420	$365	$310	$255	$225	$200

Dardick ammunition in itself is collectible - currently, individual rounds are selling in the $5-$10 range.

SERIES 1500 — .22, .30, or .38 Dardick Tround, double action.

	100%	98%	95%	90%	80%	70%	60%
	$875	$660	$570	$490	$440	$395	$350

Subtract $400 for .30 cal.
Note: carbine conversion units (.22 or .38 cal) add $175 — $400.

DARNE S.A.
Manufactured between 1881-1979 and 1990 to date in Saint Etienne, France. Previously imported by Wes Gilpin located in Dallas, TX until 1992. No importation since 1992.

Please refer to the Bruchet section for 1982-1990 mfg. utilizing the Darne action.

SHOTGUNS: PRE-1980 MFG.

DARNE SLIDING BREECH SHOTGUN — 12, 16, 20, or 28 ga., double barrel, SxS, unique action utilizes sliding breech lock-up, high quality mfg., 27½ in. barrel standard with other lengths available, any choke combination, either straight grip or pistol grip stock, checkered, models differ in amount of engraving and grade of wood.

▲ *Bird Hunter Model R11*

	100%	98%	95%	90%	80%	70%	60%
	$1,000	$715	$635	$550	$495	$440	$360

▲ *Pheasant Hunter Model R15*

	100%	98%	95%	90%	80%	70%	60%
	$2,300	$1,950	$1,750	$1,625	$1,500	$1,425	$1,300

▲ *Magnum Model R16*

	100%	98%	95%	90%	80%	70%	60%
	$1,650	$1,450	$1,350	$1,250	$1,125	$1,000	$900

▲ *Quail Hunter Model V19*

	100%	98%	95%	90%	80%	70%	60%
	$3,350	$2,750	$2,500	$2,250	$2,000	$1,800	$1,650

▲ *Model V22*

	100%	98%	95%	90%	80%	70%	60%
	$3,750	$3,300	$3,000	$2,600	$2,300	$2,050	$1,850

▲ *Hors Series No. 1 Model V*

	100%	98%	95%	90%	80%	70%	60%
	$4,400	$3,850	$3,575	$3,300	$3,080	$2,750	$2,200

D

Grading	100%	98%	95%	90%	80%	70%	60%

SHOTGUNS: 1989-1992 MFG.

In 1990, Paul Bruchet (the old Darne plant superintendent) obtained permission to once again use the Darne trademark. Hence, all 1990 and later mfg. has been produced by Paul Bruchet.

All new mfg. Darnes can be choked to the customer's choice. All models listed below have automatic ejectors, are oil finished by hand, and may be barreled to any length (except for Models R 11, 12, and 13). All prices are subject to change without notice. Pricing below reflects last importation pricing in 1992.

R 11 — 12 or 16 ga., half pistol grip stock, light engraving.
   $2,625 $2,175 $1,870 $1,760 $1,650 $1,375 $1,225
   Last Mfg.'s Sug. Retail was $2,875.

R 12 — similar to above, except with better engraving.
   $3,225 $2,550 $2,100 $1,870 $1,760 $1,650 $1,375
   Last Mfg.'s Sug. Retail was $4,460.

R 13 — 12, 16, or 20 ga., straight or pistol grip stock, traditional action with bouquet engraving.
   $3,675 $2,950 $2,450 $2,100 $1,870 $1,760 $1,500
   Last Mfg.'s Sug. Retail was $3,950.

R 14 — 12, 16, or 20 ga., slug gun, choice of forends, light engraving, and optional cheek rest pistol grip stock is also available.
   $3,350 $2,375 $2,100 $1,870 $1,760 $1,650 $1,375
   Last Mfg.'s Sug. Retail was $3,625.

R 15 — 12, 16, 20, 24, or 28 ga., select walnut stock and forearm with fine checkering, large scroll engraving, obturator disks.
   $3,950 $3,100 $2,575 $2,300 $2,000 $1,775 $1,475
   Last Mfg.'s Sug. Retail was $4,350.

R 17 — 12 or 20 ga., Magnum model (3 in. chambers), customer's choice of full coverage engraving, superior quality walnut and checkering.
   $4,900 $3,625 $2,950 $2,575 $2,250 $1,925 $1,600
   Last Mfg.'s Sug. Retail was $5,400.

V 19 — all gauges, easy opening large key action, top quality walnut and checkering, full coverage rose and scroll engraving with chiseled fences.
   $7,450 $6,500 $5,150 $4,700 $3,500 $2,950 $2,575
   Last Mfg.'s Sug. Retail was $8,025

V 21 — similar to V 19, except has large scroll rosace engraving and chiseled fences.
   $7,900 $6,950 $5,475 $4,950 $3,675 $3,100 $2,675
   Last Mfg.'s Sug. Retail was $8,500.

V 22 — similar to V 21, except has bulino style engraving featuring hunting scenes, ornamental borders, and gold inlays (if specified).
   $9,800 $8,250 $6,300 $5,400 $4,000 $3,475 $3,000
   Last Mfg.'s Sug. Retail was $10,750.

VHS — all gauges, top-of-the-line model incorporating customers choice of engraving style, type of inlays, and checkering pattern, best quality wood. The values below represent base prices without options.
   $11,000 $9,000 $7,000 $6,100 $4,800 $3,950 $3,375
   Last Mfg.'s Sug. Retail was $12,200.

DAVID MILLER CO.

Custom rifle manufacturer located in Tucson, AZ since 1973.

The David Miller Co. is a custom rifle maker fabricating best quality bolt action rifles only. All guns are essentially built per individual custom order and the company should be contacted directly for more information and price quotations. Currently manufactured D. Miller rifles feature the new Winchester Model 70 Super Grade action. Used rifles have to be appraised one-at-a-time to ascertain up-to-date values. Several of Mr. Miller's rifles have sold for over $100,000, and almost any feature(s) can be special ordered to produce a truly one-of-a-kind firearm.

DAVIDE PEDERSOLI & C., s.n.c.
Please refer to the Black Powder section in this text.

DAVIDSON FIREARMS
Maker: Fabrica De Armas, Eibar, Spain.

Grading	100%	98%	95%	90%	80%	70%	60%

MODEL 63B — 12, 16, 20, 28, or .410 ga., double barrel, 25, 26, 28, or 30 in. barrels, Anson & Deeley boxlock, engraved and nickel plated frame, various chokes, walnut checkered stock. Mfg. 1963-disc.

	100%	98%	95%	90%	80%	70%	60%
	$275	$260	$220	$200	$175	$165	$155

▲ *Model 63B Magnum* — similar to 63B, except 10 ga. Mag., 12, or 20 ga. Mag., 32 in. barrel.

	100%	98%	95%	90%	80%	70%	60%
12 or 20 ga.	$360	$340	$310	$275	$230	$195	$165
10 ga.	$385	$370	$340	$305	$250	$220	$195

MODEL 69SL — 12 or 20 ga., true detachable sidelock action, engraved nickel plated action, 26 in. and 28 in. barrels, imp. cyl. and mod., mod. and full, checkered walnut stock. Mfg. 1963-1976.

	100%	98%	95%	90%	80%	70%	60%
	$415	$395	$375	$340	$320	$290	$260

MODEL 73 STAGECOACH — 12 or 20 ga., detachable sidelock exposed hammers, 3 in. chambers, 20 in. mod. and full barrels, checkered walnut stock. Mfg. 1976-disc.

	100%	98%	95%	90%	80%	70%	60%
	$275	$260	$220	$200	$175	$165	$155

DAVIS INDUSTRIES
Manufacturer currently located in Chino, CA since 1995. Previously located in Mira Loma, CA until 1995. Distributor sales only.

Davis Industries provides a lifetime warranty on all products.

D-22/D-25/D-32/D-38 SERIES DERRINGER — .22 LR, .22 Mag., .25 ACP, .32 ACP, .32 H&R Mag. (new 1995), .38 Spl. (new 1992), or 9mm Para. cal., O/U steel construction, 2.4 or 2¾ (.38 Spl. only) in. vent. rib barrel, 9½ or 11½ oz., black Teflon or chrome finish.

	100%	98%	95%	90%	80%	70%	60%
Mfg.'s Sug. Retail	$75	$60	$50	$45	$40	$35	$30	$30

Add $23 for big-bore series (larger frame) in .22 Mag., .32 H&R Mag., or .38 Spl. cal.
Add $29 for big-bore 9mm Para. cal.
In this series, the .25 ACP cal. is the Model D-25 and the .32 ACP cal. is the Model D-32.

LONG BORE DERRINGER — .22 Mag., .32 H&R Mag., .38 Spl., or 9mm Para. cal., similar to D Series, except has 3¾ in. barrel, 13 oz. New 1995.

	100%	98%	95%	90%	80%	70%	60%
Mfg.'s Sug. Retail	$104	$90	$70	$60	$55	$45	$40	$35

Add $6 for 9mm Para. cal.

P-32 — .32 ACP, single action semi-auto, 6 shot mag., 2.8 in. barrel, black Teflon or chrome finish, laminated wood grips, 22 oz. New 1987.

	100%	98%	95%	90%	80%	70%	60%
Mfg.'s Sug. Retail	$79	$69	$60	$50	$45	$40	$35	$35

Grading	100%	98%	95%	90%	80%	70%	60%

P-380 — .380 ACP, single action semi-auto, similar to P-32, 5 shot mag., 2.8 in. barrel, 22 oz., bright chrome or black Teflon finish, internal shock resister for recoil, wood (disc.) or black synthetic grips. New 1989.

Mfg.'s Sug. Retail	$87	$75	$65	$55	$45	$40	$35	$35

DE FORNEY

Long gun manufacturer located in Belgium.

De Forney has specialized in both quality sidelock and boxlock (with or w/o sideplates) shotguns. Prices range from $750-$3,250 for boxlock shotguns and start in the $2,500 range for sidelock models, assuming 80% or better original condition.

DEMRO

Previous manufacturer located in Manchester, CT.

RIFLES: SEMI-AUTO

T.A.C. MODEL 1 RIFLE — .45 ACP or 9mm Luger, blow back operation, 16⅞ in. barrel, open bolt fire combination, lock-in receiver must be set to fire, also available in carbine model and fully auto.

	$595	$525	$475	$425	$395	$360	$330

XF-7 WASP CARBINE — .45 ACP or 9mm Luger, blow back operation, 16⅞ in. barrel, also available in fully auto.

	$595	$525	$475	$425	$395	$360	$330

Add $45 for case.

DESERT INDUSTRIES, INC.

Manufacturer located in Las Vegas, NV beginning 1991. Distributor and dealer direct sales. See listing under Steel City Arms, Inc. for older models.

In 1990, Desert Industries, Inc. was created - this new company took over Steel City Arms, Inc. More recently manufactured guns will have the Las Vegas slide address.

PISTOLS

THE DOUBLE DEUCE — .22 LR, double action, 2½ in. barrel, matte stainless steel construction, 6 shot mag., rosewood grips, 15 oz. New 1991.

Mfg.'s Sug. Retail	$400	$350	$295	$275	$250	$225	$200	$175

TWO BIT SPECIAL — .25 ACP, double action, 2½ in. barrel, similar to Double Deuce, except has 5 shot mag., 15 oz. New 1991.

Mfg.'s Sug. Retail	$400	$350	$295	$275	$250	$225	$200	$175

DETONICS FIREARMS INDUSTRIES

Detonics Firearms Industries was a previous manufacturer located in Bellevue, WA 1976-1988. Detonics was sold in early 1988 to the New Detonics Manufacturing Corporation, a wholly owned subsidiary of "1045 Investors Group Limited".

Please refer to the New Detonics Manufacturing Corporation in the "N" section of this text for complete model listings of both companies.

DIARM S.A.

Previous manufacturing conglomerate (25 companies) located in Deba, Spain 1986-1989. Previously imported and distributed by American Arms, Inc. located in North Kansas City, MO. Older Diarm models can be found under the American Arms, Inc. heading in this publication.

DIXIE GUN WORKS

See "Modern Black Powder Guns" Section.

DOMINGO ACHA

Manufactured in Spain.

Grading	100%	98%	95%	90%	80%	70%	60%

LOOKING GLASS — .25 and .32 cal. auto pistol.

	100%	98%	95%	90%	80%	70%	60%
	$150	$125	$105	$85	$75	$60	$50

DOMINO, IGI

Previously imported from Italy by Mandall Shooting Supplies located in Scottsdale, AZ. This firm was absorbed by FAS (see separate listing in F section) in 1990. Limited quantities of Domino pistols are still available from Mandall Shooting Supplies.

MODEL OP 601 MATCH PISTOL — .22 Short, 5 shot, 5.6 in. barrel, match sights, full target grips, vent barrel and slide to reduce recoil, adj. and removable trigger.

$1,300	$1,000	$715	$635	$550	$495	$440

Last Mfg.'s Sug. Retail was $1,495.

MODEL SP 602 MATCH PISTOL — .22 LR, 5½ in. barrel, similar to 601, but .22 LR and slightly different trigger.

$1,300	$1,100	$800	$700	$600	$550	$495

Last Mfg.'s Sug. Retail was $1,495.

DREYSE PISTOL

Manufactured by Rheinische Metallwaren and Machinenfabrik, located in Sommerda, Germany.

MODEL 1907 AUTOMATIC — 7.65mm, 8 shot, 3½ in. barrel, blue, fixed sights, hard rubber grips. Mfg. 1907-1914.

$250	$185	$150	$120	$95	$75	$50

MODEL 1910 — 9mm Para., mfg. 1912-1915. Seldomly encountered.

$4,500	$3,900	$3,300	$2,700	$2,100	$1,500	$1,000

VEST POCKET AUTOMATIC — .25 ACP, 6 shot, 2 in. barrel, blue, fixed sights, hard rubber grips. Mfg. 1912-1915.

$275	$200	$165	$130	$100	$75	$50

DRILLINGS

A Drilling is a three-barrel combination gun (two shotgun barrels and a rifle barrel, vice versa, or three shotgun barrels). Normally, two triggers fire the shotgun barrels and one of them activates the rifle barrel when the barrel selector is moved forward (usually located on the upper tang). Most well made Drillings in above average condition are surprisingly accurate when using the rifle barrel(s).

Please refer to illustrations below depicting the most commonly encountered Drilling configurations.

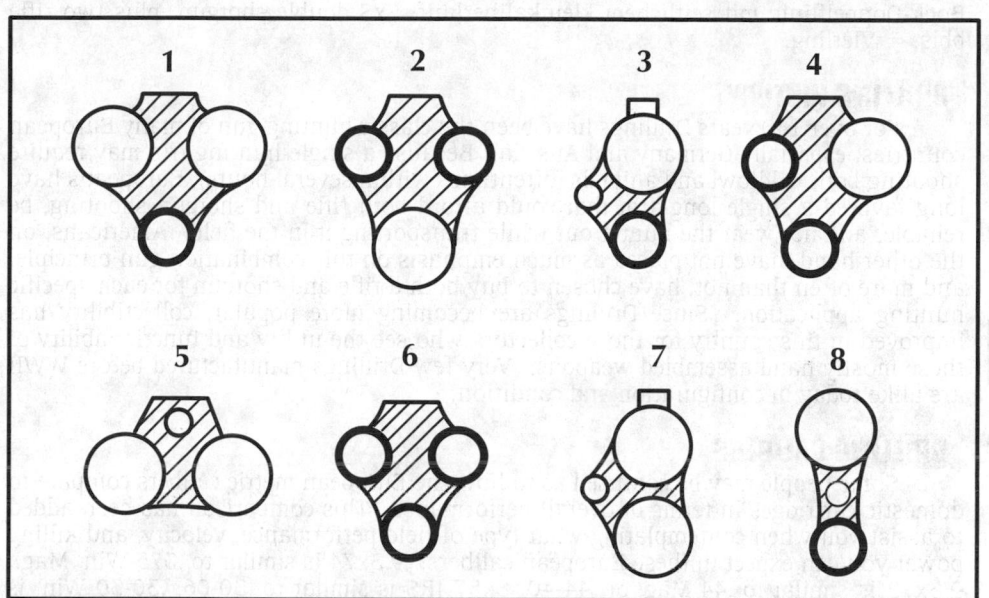

ILLUSTRATION EXPLANATIONS

Illustration No. 1 - Normal Drilling configuration with 2 shotgun barrels over a rimmed, centerfire rifle (most are 16 ga. x 16 ga. by either 9.3x72R or 8x57JR cal.).

Illustration No. 2 - Two rifle barrels over a shotgun. This configuration will normally command twice the price as No. 1. German designation is "Doppelbuchsdrilling".

Illustration No. 3 - Three barrels with no two being the same gauge or caliber. This configuration is very collectible, especially if the smallest caliber is .22 LR. Again, price will be double of No. 1.

Illustration No. 4 - Sometimes called a Bock Drilling with one shotgun and two rifle barrels. This variation brings a good premium over No. 1.

Illustration No. 5 - Rib Drilling with rifle caliber generally small (.22LR or .22 Hornet). German designation is "Schienendrilling".

Illustration No. 6 - Three shotgun barrels with the same gauge. This configuration is quite rare and healthy premiums are charged over No. 1.

Illustration No. 7 - A variation of No. 3, this configuration features shotgun O/U barrels with a rifle barrel on the side. German designation is "Bock-Doppelflinte mit seitlichem kleinkaliberlauf".

Illustration No. 8 - Very unusual - a 3-barrel drilling in vertical design - 2 rifle barrels under a shotgun barrel. This configuration is seldomly encountered.

The following German nomenclatures apply as follows: single barrel rifle = Buchse; SxS double rifle = Doppelbuchse; O/U double rifle = Bock-Doppelbuchse; SxS double shotgun = Doppelflinte; O/U double shotgun = Bock-Doppelflinte; SxS double shotgun, rifle bbl. under = Drilling; SxS double shotgun, rifle bbl. on top = Schienen- drilling; single shotgun, rifle bbl. under = Bock-Buchsflinte; single shotgun, rifle bbl. at side = Buchsflinte; single shotgun, rifle bbl. under and at side = Bock-Drilling; double rifle, shot bbl. under = Doppelbuchsdrilling; O/U double shotgun, rifle bbl. at side =

Bock-Doppelflinte mit seitlichem kleinkaliberlauf; SxS double shotgun, plus two rifle bbls. = Vierling.

DRILLING HISTORY

For over 140 years Drillings have been the classic hunting gun of many European countries, especially Germany and Austria. Because a single hunting trip may require shooting both wildfowl and animals (oftentimes within several hours), Europeans have long favored a single long-arm that could afford both rifle and shotgun shooting, be reliable, and not wear the hunter out while transporting it in the field. Americans, on the other hand, have not placed as much emphasis on this combination gun principle, and more often than not, have chosen to buy both a rifle and shotgun for each specific hunting application. Since Drillings are becoming more popular, collectibility has improved in this country for those collectors who see the utility and functionability of these mostly hand assembled weapons. Very few Drillings manufactured before WWII are alike today in configuration and condition.

DRILLING CALIBERS

Some people may be confused as to how the European metric calibers compare to domestic cartridges in terms of overall performance. This comparison has been added to assist you when contemplating what type of field performance, velocity, and killing power you can expect in these European calibers: 9.3x74 is similar to .375 Win. Mag., 9.3x72 is similar to .44 Mag. or .44-40, 8x57 JRS is similar to .30-06, .30-30 Win. is 7.62x51 R, 8x57JR is similar to .30-06, 7x65 R is similar to .280 Rem., 7x57R is similar to .257 Roberts, 6.5x57R is similar to .243 Win., 5.6x52R is a .22 Savage Hi-Power, 5.6x34R is similar to .22 Hornet.

DRILLING VALUES

Rather than list the various manufacturers of Drillings (there are hundreds), it should be noted that guns with major trademarks and established provenances (i.e. Charles Daly, Colt Sauer, Ferlach addressed, Heym, Krieghoff, J.P. Sauer, Suhl addressed, etc.) will usually be more collectible than other lesser known brands - even if the quality of worksmanship is similar. Some Drillings were assembled from manufactured parts by skilled and crafted gunsmiths and are sometimes better quality than factory specimens. Pre-war specimens are generally more desirable to collectors (even though less expensive than post-war variations) and to date, have outperformed post-war specimens in price appreciation. Many older pre-war specimens were designed for rimmed cartridges with lower breech pressures and should not be re-bored or reloaded for the "hotter" cartridges/loads available today. It should be noted that since Drillings are more complex than a typical shotgun, most of the manufacture has been done by hand - some guns have taken individual craftsmen over a year to fabricate! Ordering a new Drilling today would be a very expensive proposition, and buying a good used specimen will save you thousands of dollars (and maybe a year wait). For these reasons, many collectors feel Drillings today are under-priced since they can be purchased at a fraction of the cost for a new one (and may well be better quality also).

FEATURES THAT ADD VALUE TO DRILLINGS

Drillings with American calibers and smaller gauges will sometimes be more desirable (and expensive) than the European metric calibers (i.e. a gun configured 20 ga. x 20 ga. by .243 Win. will sell for more than a similar gun in 16 ga. x 16 ga. by 9.3 x 72R cal.). The most commonly encountered gauges and calibers are 16 ga. (most pre-war guns are chambered for 2⁹⁄₁₆ in.). In addition, a sidelock action will be more desirable than a boxlock, and a lot more expensive if the locks are also detachable.

Features and embellishments become very critical in ascertaining Drilling values also - a gun with deep relief engraving, carved stock, claw mounts w/scope, buffalo horn trigger guard and butt plate, cocking indicators, two position front sight (i.e. night sight), middle set of express sights, adj. trigger, concealed upper tang peep sight, a non-Greener safety system, lightweight (under 6½ lbs.), separate rifle cocking, shotgun barrel inserts in .22LR or .22 Mag. cal. (approx. 8 or 11 in. long), cartridge trap, etc. is going to be A LOT more collectible than a plain-Jane hammer model with a loose action.

FEATURES THAT DETRACT VALUE FROM DRILLINGS

If it isn't beautiful, it probably won't sell. Beauty sells.

OBSERVATIONS ON DRILLING COLLECTIBILITY

Condition determines whether Nitro-proofed Drillings' worth is comparable to their counterparts in black powder or damascus barrel specimens.
Drillings with original claw-mounted scopes (rail-mount or swing-off) are worth 30-40% premiums.
Many post-war variations are valued for their hunting use only, and do not have the collectibility of the pre-war guns.

CONDITION FACTORS

Condition is another major consideration - a gun that shows much use and is not operationally intact/correct may bring several thousand dollars less than another similar specimen showing little wear and excellent original finish (including the case colors). Most good boxlock Drillings in the above mentioned trademarks start in the $1,750 range and can go to $8,000 and higher if the configuration, features, and condition are all desirable. Average Drillings usually sell in the $1,000 - $2,000 range assuming worn condition, metric calibers and few features. For these reasons, Drillings have to be evaluated one at a time and a COMPETENT appraisal/evaluation should be procured before buying or selling a specimen.

DUBIEL ARMS COMPANY

Previous manufacturer located in Sherman, TX. Dubiel Arms made custom bolt action rifles from 1973-approx. 1990.

Grading	100%	98%	95%	90%	80%	70%	60%

BOLT ACTION RIFLE—custom made bolt action, .22-250-.458 Win. Mag. cals. available, barrel length and weight to order, no sights, Canjar trigger, all steel parts, custom made rifle stocks available in five styles. Disc.

	100%	98%	95%	90%	80%	70%	60%
	$2,000	$1,750	$1,500	$1,275	$1,125	$975	$825

Last Mfg.'s Sug. Retail was $2,500.

DUCKS UNLIMITED, INC.

National wildlife organization with headquarters located in Memphis, TN.

DUCKS UNLIMITED INC.

SHOTGUNS: DINNER GUNS (GUN-OF-THE-YEAR)

The makes and models listed below reflect "dinner guns" only. Dinner guns (Gun-of-the-Year) refers to those shotguns sold at the various annual banquets held by Ducks Unlimited chapters. Dinner guns do not have a retail price. Rather, banquet auction prices can vary substantially from chapter to chapter, as well as secondary market values.

MANUFACTURER	MODEL	QUANTITY	YEAR
Remington	Model 1100 12 ga.	500	1973
Remington	Model 870 12 ga.	600	1974
Winchester	Model 12 12 ga.	800	1975
Winchester	Model Super X-1 12 ga.	900	1976
Ithaca	Model 37 12 ga. (40th Ann'y)	1,125	1977

MANUFACTURER	MODEL	QUANTITY	YEAR
Ithaca	Model 51 12 ga.	1,250	1978
Weatherby	Model Patrician 12 ga.	1,600	1979
Weatherby	Model Centurion 12 ga.	2,000	1980
Remington	Model 1100 12 ga. Mag.	2,400	1981
Remington	Model 870 12 ga. Mag.	3,000	1982
Browning	Model B-80 12 ga.	3,400	1983
Browning	Model BPS 12 ga.	3,800	1984
Remington	Model 1100 12 ga.	4,500	1985
Beretta	Model A303 12 ga.	5,500	1986
Beretta	Model A303 20 ga.	3,500	1987
Browning	Model A5 12 ga. (50th Ann'y)	5,000	1987
Browning	Model A5 16 ga.	4,500	1988
Browning	Model A500 12 ga.	4,500	1989
Browning	Model A5 20 ga.	4,500	1990
Beretta	Model A390 12 ga.	4,200	1991
Franchi	Model Semi-Auto 12 ga.	4,200	1992
Winchester	Model 12 20 ga.	3,800	1993
Browning	Model A500R 12 ga.	3,300	1994
Browning	Model 12 Repro. 28 ga.	1,000	1995
Browning	Model BPS 12 ga.	3,500	1996

DUMOULIN, ERNEST

Manufacturer located in Herstal, Belgium. Imported until 1990 and retailed on a very limited basis by Midwest Gun Sport located in Zebulon, NC (formerly from Ellisville, MO.). Older importation was by Abercrombie & Fitch located in New York, NY.

Most Ernest Dumoulin rifles and shotguns are essentially custom ordered firearms with a long list of options available which, in some cases, can easily double the values of models shown below. Because of this, these options are not listed individually. To determine the exact price on a specific model with certain options, Ernest Dumoulin (see Trademark Index) should be contacted directly to obtain a firm price (dependent on the fluctuation of the U.S. dollar and other domestic and foreign regulations). Written correspondence should include a SASE (a FAX will be faster).

Grading	100%	98%	95%	90%	80%	70%	60%

RIFLES: BOLT ACTION

E. Dumoulin has had very limited importation since 1989 and all discontinued retail values reflect 1989 information.

BAVARIA DELUXE — .243 Win. through .458 Win. cals., 21½, 24, or 25½ in. octagonal barrel, French walnut stock with rosewood forend tip and pistol grip cap, no sights, custom made essentially with Sako (disc.) or Mauser action. Many engraving options available from $510-$1,900. Disc. 1985.

Series I	$995	$890	$775	$650	$575	$530	$460

Last Mfg.'s Sug. Retail was $1,080.

Add 15% for .375 H&H or .458 Win. Mag. cal.

RIFLE MOUSQUETON — .243 Win. through .338 Win. cals., 20 in. barrel, Mannlicher style, French walnut stock and pistol grip cap, no sights, custom made essentially with Sako or Mauser action. Many engraving options available from $510 - $1,900. Disc.

	$720	$620	$560	$510	$470	$420	$360

Grading	100%	98%	95%	90%	80%	70%	60%

CENTURION MODEL — .270 Win. through .458 Win. cals., 21½, 24, or 25½ in. barrels, French walnut stock with rosewood forearm tip and pistol grip cap, no sights, custom made essentially with Sako or Mauser action. Many engraving options available from $510 - $1,900. Importation disc. 1986.

	$660	$590	$535	$480	$425	$390	$360

Last Mfg.'s Sug. Retail was $740.

CENTURION CLASSIC — similar to Centurion, standard cals. only, Mauser 98 action only and has better wood.

	$1,525	$1,375	$1,175	$975	$800	$700	$600

Last Mfg.'s Sug. Retail was $1,525.

These models were also available in Mag. cals. that are divided into 4 groups — 1, 2, 3, and 4 Mag. Series. These options retailed in the $50 - $300 price range.

▲ *Diane* — grade up from Centurion Classic, 22 in. barrel, Mauser 98 action, M-70 safety, adj. steel trigger.

	$1,450	$1,250	$1,000	$825	$700	$600	$500

Last Mfg.'s Sug. Retail was $1,450.

▲ *Amazone* — grade up from Diane, 20 in. barrel, full stock.

	$1,750	$1,525	$1,325	$1,075	$865	$750	$600

Last Mfg.'s Sug. Retail was $1,750.

▲ *Bavaria Deluxe* — .243 Win. through .458 Win. cals., 21½, 24, or 25½ in. octagonal barrel, French walnut stock with rosewood forend tip and pistol grip cap, no sights, custom made essentially with Sako (disc.) or Mauser action. Many engraving options available from $510 - $1,900.

	$1,900	$1,675	$1,450	$1,200	$995	$775	$650

Last Mfg.'s Sug. Retail was $1,900.

▲ *Safari* — Mag. cals. only.

	$2,350	$1,775	$1,475	$1,200	$995	$775	$650

Last Mfg.'s Sug. Retail was $2,350.

MANNLICHER MODEL — Mauser type bolt action, various cals., full stocked. Disc. 1985.

	$730	$660	$580	$520	$470	$430	$395

Last Mfg.'s Sug. Retail was $825.

▲ *Mannlicher Classic* — similar to basic Mannlicher, except has better walnut. Disc. 1985.

	$995	$890	$775	$650	$575	$530	$460

Last Mfg.'s Sug. Retail was $1,065.

MATCH MODEL — match target rifle, adj. sights and stock. Disc. 1985.

	$1,640	$1,490	$1,300	$1,050	$900	$800	$700

Last Mfg.'s Sug. Retail was $1,860.

▲ *Match NATO* — 7.62 cal. match rifle. Disc. 1985.

	$2,640	$2,400	$2,175	$1,850	$1,595	$1,400	$1,195

Last Mfg.'s Sug. Retail was $3,000.

ST. HUBERT MODEL — Sako action, various cals. and barrel lengths. Disc. 1985.

	$1,900	$1,700	$1,495	$1,300	$1,150	$995	$850

Last Mfg.'s Sug. Retail was $2,125.

SAFARI SPORTSMAN — Mauser 98 action, .416 Rigby, .375 H&H, .505 Gibbs, or .404 Jeffreys cal., 4 shot mag., limited availability in 1986.

	$4,000	$3,550	$3,250	$2,800	$2,400	$2,000	$1,750

Last Mfg.'s Sug. Retail was $4,000.

Add $300 for .505 Gibbs cal.

AFRICAN PRO — similar to Safari Sportsman except has ebony or buffalo horn forearm tip, tilting hood for the front sight, multiple folding rear sight.

	$4,800	$4,000	$3,550	$3,250	$2,800	$2,400	$2,000

Last Mfg.'s Sug. Retail was $4,800.

Grading	100%	98%	95%	90%	80%	70%	60%

D

DOUBLE RIFLES

EUROPA I — .22 Hornet, .222 Rem., .222 Rem. Mag., 6mm Rem., .243 Win., .25-06, .30-06, 6.5x57R, 7x57R, 8x57JRS, or 9.3x74R cal., Anson & Deeley boxlock action, moderate engraving. 1989-disc.

	$4,800	$4,200	$3,800	$3,500	$3,250	$2,995	$2,700

Last Mfg.'s Sug. Retail was $4,800.

CONTINENTAL I — same calibers as Europa I, sidelock action, 12 engraving options to choose from, many options available on special order. 1989-disc.

	$8,600	$7,700	$6,995	$6,400	$5,600	$4,750	$4,150

Last Mfg.'s Sug. Retail was $8,600.

"PIONNIER" JUXTAPOSED EXPRESS RIFLES — assorted cals. from .22 Hornet through .600 Nitro Express, SxS configuration, heavily engraved, select walnut. Limited production, Anson & Deeley triple lock action, sideplates available at extra charge.

▲ *P-I and P-II* — English style scroll or bouquet (P-II) engraving.

	$7,850	$6,500	$5,825	$5,200	$4,650	$4,160	$3,700

Last Mfg.'s Sug. Retail was $7,850.

    Add $400 for P-II engraving.

▲ *P III* — English style lace engraving (tapestry style).

	$8,640	$7,750	$7,000	$6,400	$5,600	$4,750	$4,150

Last Mfg.'s Sug. Retail was $8,640.

▲ *P-IV through P-VIII* — various styles of royal engraving with or without hunting scenes.

	$9,100	$7,995	$7,450	$6,800	$6,000	$5,000	$4,350

Last Mfg.'s Sug. Retail was $9,100.

    Add $400 for gold inlays.

▲ *P-IX through P-XII* — Louis XVI style engraving.

	$9,540	$8,600	$7,800	$7,250	$6,400	$5,250	$4,500

Last Mfg.'s Sug. Retail was $9,540.

▲ *Pionnier Magnum* — .338 Win. Mag., .375 H&H, .416 Rigby, .416 Hoffman, .458 Win. Mag., .577 Nitro Express, or .600 Nitro Express. Boxlock action with Greener crossbolt.

	$10,900	$9,400	$8,650	$7,800	$7,000	$6,450	$5,825

Last Mfg.'s Sug. Retail was $10,900.

ARISTOCRATE MODEL — available in all cals. up to .375 H&H (also in 20 ga.), single shot action with low profile, exhibition oil finished walnut stock and forearm. Values below assume standard model (12 engraving options available). Imported 1987-1988 only.

	$9,100	$8,450	$7,775	$7,000	$6,450	$5,825	$5,275

Last Mfg.'s Sug. Retail was $10,400.

PRESTIGE RIFLE (SIDELOCK) — best quality sidelock, various cals., triple locking, 10 different presentation options available, values below reflect standard model without options. Custom order only, 1 year waiting period. 1986-disc.

	$17,900	$15,000	$12,500	$9,995	$8,000	$7,000	$6,000

Last Mfg.'s Sug. Retail was $17,900.

    Add $600 for Mag. cals. over .416 Rigby.

SHOTGUNS

EUROPA MODEL — 12, 20, 28, or .410 ga., Anson & Deeley boxlock action, single or double trigger, moderately engraved, oil finished stock and forearm, choice of 6 engraving options. 1989-disc.

	$3,300	$2,750	$2,350	$2,000	$1,800	$1,575	$1,400

Last Mfg.'s Sug. Retail was $3,300.

LEIGE JUXTAPOSED SHOTGUN (SxS) — 12, 16 (disc. 1986), 20, or 28 ga., Anson & Deeley locking action, elaborate engraving, deluxe walnut. 1986-disc.

Grading	100%	98%	95%	90%	80%	70%	60%

▲ **Luxe Model**

      $5,300 $4,600 $3,900 $3,300 $2,900 $2,600 $2,300
Last Mfg.'s Sug. Retail was $5,900 (disc. 1988).

▲ **Grand Luxe**

      $6,900 $6,000 $5,000 $4,300 $3,600 $3,200 $2,875
Last Mfg.'s Sug. Retail was $6,900.

Add 15% for 28 ga.
Add 15% for sideplates.
Many engraving options and other special order features can be added to the above models.

CONTINENTAL MODEL — 12, 20, 28, or .410 ga., sidelock action, double or single trigger, deluxe oil finished walnut stock, choice of 6 engraving options. 1989-disc.

      $7,400 $6,250 $5,200 $4,400 $3,700 $3,200 $2,875
Last Mfg.'s Sug. Retail was $7,400.

ETENDART JUXTAPOSED SHOTGUN (SxS) — 12, 20 and 28 ga., full sidelock, exhibition grade walnut, double triggers, top-of-the-line quality, built to special order. Values listed assume standard gun (12 engraving options available). 1987-disc.

      $14,400 $12,250 $9,995 $9,100 $8,450 $7,775 $7,000
Last Mfg.'s Sug. Retail was $14,400.

Add 6% for 28 ga.

BOSS ROYAL SUPERPOSED (O/U) — 12, 20 or 28 ga., full sidelock, exhibition grade walnut, double triggers, top-of-the-line quality, built to special order. Values listed assume standard gun (12 engraving options available). 1987-disc.

      $18,500 $16,000 $13,750 $11,000 $9,775 $8,000 $6,950
Last Mfg.'s Sug. Retail was $18,500.

Add 6% for 28 ga.

SUPERPOSED EXPRESS "INTERNATIONAL" — O/U shotgun, includes extra set of rifle barrels, 20 ga., 7 choices of rifle cals., deluxe walnut. Elaborate engraving patterns available at extra charge, limited production. Disc. 1985.

      $2,400 $2,000 $1,800 $1,575 $1,400 $1,200 $1,050
Last Mfg.'s Sug. Retail was $2,490.

COMBINATION GUNS

EAGLE MODEL — O/U configuration (shotgun barrel on bottom), 12 or 20 ga., .22 Hornet, .222 Rem., .222 Rem. Mag., 6mm Rem., .243 Win., .25-06, .30-06, 6.5x57R, 7x57R, 8x57JRS, or 9.3x74R cal., boxlock action. 1989-disc.

      $2,700 $2,400 $2,175 $1,850 $1,595 $1,400 $1,195
Last Mfg.'s Sug. Retail was $2,700.

DUMOULIN, HENRI & FILS

Manufacturer located in Herstal, Belgium. Imported and distributed by New England Arms, Co. located in Kittery Point, ME.

H. Dumoulin has manufactured quality firearms in Liege/Herstal, Belgium since 1947. They have specialized in bolt action rifles, generally built on Mauser 98 or commercial Mauser actions. The Imperial Magnum action was developed and introduced in 1987.

Grading	100%	98%	95%	90%	80%	70%	60%

RIFLES

GRAND LUXE BOLT ACTION — .300 Wby., .338 Win. Mag., .375 H&H, .378 Wby., .404 Jeffrey, .416 Rigby, .460 Wby., or .505 Gibbs cal., 24, 25.6, or 26 in. barrel, European walnut stock with ebony forend tip and pistol grip cap, folding leaf sights with hooded front, custom made on the Dumoulin Imperial Magnum double square bridge action. Many engraving options available.

Mfg.'s Sug. Retail	$7,000		$6,850	$6,200	$5,500	$4,950	$4,300	$3,600	$3,200

Add $500 for left hand action.
Add $850 for extended top and bottom tang.
Add $800 for claw mounts.
Add $700 for .505 Gibbs cal.

SOVEREIGN — available in same cals. as Grand Luxe Bolt Action, except with a higher quality finish, knurled bolt handles, gold inlayed lettering. Many engraving options available.

Pricing on this model depends on engraving, wood and other options. Imperial Magnum is also available in various stages of completion, barreled actions, actions in the white, etc. Please contact New England Arms, Co. directly for quotation.

SxS BOXLOCK RIFLE — boxlock action, best quality double rifle, highly figured European walnut, finely hand checkered with standard scroll engraving. Custom ordered to customer's dimensions. Prices start at $12,000.

SxS SIDELOCK RIFLE — sidelock action, best quality hand detachable locks, top quality European walnut, finely hand checkered with standard scroll engraving. Additional engraving or deluxe wood quoted on request. Prices start at $15,000.

SHOTGUNS

BOXLOCK MODEL — available in most ga.'s, individually built per customer special order. The importer should be contacted directly for more information and a price quotation.

SIDELOCK MODEL — available in most ga.'s, individually built per customer special order. The importer should be contacted directly for more information and a price quotation.

E section

E.M.F. CO., INC.
Current importer and distributor located in Santa Ana, CA.

Grading	100%	98%	95%	90%	80%	70%	60%

PISTOLS: REPRODUCTIONS

REMINGTON ROLLING BLOCK PISTOL — .357 Mag. cal., rolling block design. Disc. 1992.

	100%	98%	95%	90%	80%	70%	60%
	$300	$225	$185	$165	$155	$145	$135

Last Mfg.'s Sug. Retail was $395.

1875 REMINGTON OUTLAW — .357 Mag., .44-40, or .45 LC cal., copy of the Rem. Model 1875 SA, 5½ (disc.) or 7½ in. barrel only, case hardened frame, walnut grips, blue only.

Mfg.'s Sug. Retail	$550	$375	$275	$195	$165	$155	$145	$135

Add $20 for steel triggerguard.
Add $90 for nickel plating.
Add $250 for engraving.

1890 REMINGTON POLICE SINGLE ACTION — .357 Mag., .44-40, or .45 LC cal., 5½ in. barrel, lanyard ring in butt stock, blue frame, walnut grips. New 1986.

Mfg.'s Sug. Retail	$570	$390	$285	$200	$175	$155	$145	$135

Add $15 for steel triggerguard.
Add $95 for nickel plating.
Add $245 for engraving.

DERRINGERS: REPRODUCTIONS

STANDARD MODEL — .22 Short, copy of Colt Model Lord or Lady Derringer, blue, gold, or silver gold finish. Disc. 1992.

	100%	98%	95%	90%	80%	70%	60%
	$100	$80	$70	$60	$55	$50	$45

Last Mfg.'s Sug. Retail was $125.

RIFLES: MODERN REPRODUCTIONS

These models are authentic shooting reproductions mfg. in Italy.

AP 74 — .22 LR or .32 ACP cal., copy of the Colt AR-15, semi-auto, 15 shot mag., 20 in. barrel, 6¾ lbs. Importation disc. 1989.

	100%	98%	95%	90%	80%	70%	60%
	$295	$250	$200	$175	$155	$145	$135

Last Mfg.'s Sug. Retail was $295.

Add $25 for .32 cal.

▲ **Sporter Carbine** — wood sporter stock, .22 LR only. Importation disc. 1989.

	100%	98%	95%	90%	80%	70%	60%
	$320	$275	$225	$195	$175	$160	$140

Last Mfg.'s Sug. Retail was $320.

▲ **Paramilitary Paratrooper Carbine** — .22 LR only, folding wire stock, black nylon on paramilitary design model. Importation disc. 1987.

	100%	98%	95%	90%	80%	70%	60%
	$260	$190	$175	$165	$155	$145	$135

Last Mfg.'s Sug. Retail was $325.

Add $10 for wood folding stock.

▲ **"Dressed" Military Model** — with Cyclops scope, Colt bayonet, sling, and bipod. Disc. 1986.

	100%	98%	95%	90%	80%	70%	60%
	$330	$265	$240	$220	$200	$185	$170

Last Mfg.'s Sug. Retail was $450.

GALIL — .22 LR only, reproduction of the Israeli Galil, semi-auto. Importation disc. 1989.

	100%	98%	95%	90%	80%	70%	60%
	$295	$250	$200	$175	$155	$145	$135

Last Mfg.'s Sug. Retail was $295.

Grading	100%	98%	95%	90%	80%	70%	60%

KALASHNIKOV AK-47 — .22 LR only, reproduction of the Russian AK-47, semi-auto. Importation disc. 1989.

		$295	$250	$200	$175	$155	$145	$135

Last Mfg.'s Sug. Retail was $295.

FRENCH M.A.S. — .22 LR only, reproduction of the French Bull-Pup Combat Rifle, semi-auto with carrying handle, 29 shot mag. Importation disc. 1989.

	$320	$265	$240	$220	$200	$185	$170

Last Mfg.'s Sug. Retail was $320.

M1 CARBINE — .30 cal. only, copy of the U.S. Military M1 Carbine. Disc. 1985.

	$175	$150	$140	$130	$120	$110	$100

Last Mfg.'s Sug. Retail was $205.

Add $43 for Paratrooper variation.

RIFLES: REMINGTON REPRODUCTIONS

ROLLING BLOCK CARBINE — .45-70 cal., authentic reproduction of the Remington Rolling Block Carbine, 30 in. octagon barrel. Importation began 1991.

Mfg.'s Sug. Retail	$960	$725	$585	$450	$325	$250	$235	$220

BABY ROLLING BLOCK CARBINE — .357 Mag. Mfg. 1992 only.

	$395	$300	$260	$220	$185	$160	$140

Last Mfg.'s Sug. Retail was $490.

REVOLVING CARBINE — .357 Mag. (disc.), .44-40 (disc.), or .45 LC cal., 18 in. barrel, Model 1875 Army Single Action design, 5 lbs. Importation disc. 1995.

	$720	$550	$445	$325	$295	$260	$230

Last Mfg.'s Sug. Retail was $960.

TEXAS CARBINE (1858 REMINGTON) — .22 LR, action patterned after Remington revolving carbine, 21 in. octagon barrel, wood stock and forearm, brass frame. Also available with extra .22 Mag. cylinder.

Mfg.'s Sug. Retail	$400	$295	$225	$175	$150	$135	$125	$110

RIFLES: SHARPS REPRODUCTIONS

SHARPS SPORTING OR MILITARY RIFLE — .45-70 cal., copy of the Sharps Single Shot, 28 in. octagonal barrel, case hardened frame, single or double set triggers.

Mfg.'s Sug. Retail	$870	$660	$525	$425	$325	$295	$260	$230

Add $90 for blued Deluxe rifle with double set triggers.
Add $130 for browned Deluxe rifle with double set triggers.

▲ *Carbine Model* — saddle-ring carbine with 22 in. round barrel, single trigger.

Mfg.'s Sug. Retail	$870	$660	$525	$425	$325	$295	$260	$230

RIFLES: WINCHESTER REPRODUCTIONS

DELUXE 1860 HENRY RIFLE — .44-40 or .45 LC cal. only, deluxe walnut, reproduction of New Haven Arms Co.'s Henry Rifle, blued or white barrel. New 1987.

Mfg.'s Sug. Retail	$1,110	$850	$600	$450	$330	$295	$260	$230

▲ *Engraved Henry Rifle* — similar to deluxe Henry Rifle except has hand engraved receiver. Imported 1987-90.

	$1,200	$975	$700	$525	$400	$340	$295

Last Mfg.'s Sug. Retail was $1,598.

1866 YELLOWBOY CARBINE — .22 LR (disc.), .38 Spl., .44-40, or .45 LC (new 1993) cal., 19 in. barrel, saddle-ring carbine, brass frame.

Mfg.'s Sug. Retail	$825	$595	$400	$325	$250	$235	$220	$200

▲ *1866 Rifle* — same cals. as 1866 Yellowboy Carbine, 24¼ in. barrel.

Mfg.'s Sug. Retail	$848	$600	$400	$325	$250	$235	$220	$200

Grading	100%	98%	95%	90%	80%	70%	60%

▲ **Engraved Yellowboy Carbine** — .38 Spl., or .44-40 cal. only. Importation disc. 1990.

| | | $800 | $575 | $440 | $330 | $295 | $260 | $230 |

Last Mfg.'s Sug. Retail was $1,080.

1873 CARBINE — .22 Mag. (disc.), .357 Mag., .44-40, or .45 LC cal., 19 in. barrel, copy of the Winchester Model 1873, blued or case hardened receiver.

Mfg.'s Sug. Retail $1,050 $800 $600 $450 $330 $295 $260 $230

▲ **1873 Rifle** — 24¼ in. barrel, available only in .357 Mag. or .44-40 cal., case hardened receiver.

Mfg.'s Sug. Retail $1,050 $800 $600 $450 $330 $295 $260 $230

▲ **1873 "Young Boy" Carbine/Rifle** — .22 LR cal., blued steel, 19 or or 24¼ in. barrel. New 1995.

Mfg.'s Sug. Retail $1,050 $800 $600 $450 $330 $295 $260 $230

Add $50 for rifle barrel.

▲ **Engraved Rifle** — available in .357 Mag. or .44-40 cal. only. Importation disc. 1987.

| | | $895 | $635 | $500 | $450 | $400 | $360 | $325 |

Last Mfg.'s Sug. Retail was $850.

PREMIER 1873 CARBINE & RIFLE — .45 LC cal., case hardened frame, uncheckered walnut stock and forearm, full mag., rifle has 24¼ in. barrel, carbine has 19 in. barrel. Imported 1988-1989 only.

| | | $850 | $595 | $450 | $330 | $295 | $260 | $230 |

Last Mfg.'s Sug. Retail was $1,160.

Add $38 for rifle variation.

84 GUN CO.

Previous manufacturer located in Eighty Four, PA. Circa-early 1970s.

RIFLES

CLASSIC RIFLE — Bolt action, various calibers. Grades 1-4.

		100%	98%	95%	90%	80%	70%	60%
Grade 1		$420	$315	$275	$235	$210	$190	$170
Grade 2		$780	$585	$512	$430	$390	$355	$315
Grade 3		$860	$645	$560	$475	$430	$390	$345
Grade 4		$1,580	$1,185	$1,030	$870	$790	$715	$640

LOBO RIFLE — bolt action, various calibers. Grades standard, 1-4.

Standard		$415	$315	$270	$230	$210	$190	$170
Grade 1		$540	$405	$355	$300	$270	$245	$220
Grade 2		$795	$600	$520	$440	$400	$360	$320
Grade 3		$1,600	$1,200	$1,040	$880	$800	$720	$640
Grade 4		$2,350	$1,765	$1,530	$1,295	$1,175	$1,060	$940

PENNSYLVANIA RIFLE — bolt action, various calibers. Grades standard, 1-4.

Standard		$420	$315	$275	$235	$210	$190	$170
Grade 1		$540	$405	$355	$300	$270	$245	$220
Grade 2		$795	$600	$520	$440	$400	$360	$320
Grade 3		$1,600	$1,200	$1,040	$880	$800	$720	$640
Grade 4		$2,350	$1,765	$1,530	$1,295	$1,175	$1,060	$940

EAGLE ARMS, INC.

During 1995, Eagle Arms, Inc. became a division of ArmaLite, Inc. and is currently located in Geneseo, IL. Manufacture of pre-1995 Eagle Arms rifles was in Coal Valley, IL.

During 1995, Eagle Arms, Inc. reintroduced the ArmaLite trademark. The new company was organized under the ArmaLite name and Eagle Arms is now a division of ArmaLite. Currently, all post-ban rifles manufactured after this merger are part of the new ArmaLite series. Due to space

Grading	100%	98%	95%	90%	80%	70%	60%

considerations, recent ArmaLite mfg. (with the exception of the AR-10 series) appears within this section.

RIFLES

On the models listed below, E-1 accessories include collapsible carbine type buttstock (disc. per 1994 C/B) and forward bolt assist mechanism. E-2 accessories are similar, except also have national match sights.

On some of the models listed below, new ArmaLite model nomenclature will appear in front of the older Eagle Arms, Inc. model names. The A2 suffix indicates rifle is supplied with carrying handle, A3 designates a flat-top receiver, A4 designates a detachable carrying handle.

E

MODEL EA-15 E-1 RIFLE — .223 cal., patterned after the Colt AR-15A2, 20 in. barrel, forward bolt assist, 7 lbs. Mfg. 1990-1993.

	$750	$650	$575	$475	$400	$365	$325

Last Mfg.'s Sug. Retail was $800.

▲ **M4C or M15 A2/A3 Carbine (EA9025C/EA9027C)** — features collapsible (disc. per C/B 1994) or fixed (new 1994) butt stock and 16 in. barrel, 5 lbs. 14 oz. New 1990.

Mfg.'s Sug. Retail	$870	$795	$725	$600	$525	$450	$400	$375

1996 retail for the pre-ban models is $1,100-$1,165 (EA9399/EA9398).

Beginning 1993, the E-2 accessory kit became standard on this model.

▲ **M15 A2 National Match** — features 20 in. stainless steel heavy barrel with national match sights and two-stage trigger. New 1996.

Mfg.'s Sug. Retail	$1,475	$1,295	$1,050	$875	$725	$600	$525	$450

▲ **M15 A2 H-BAR Rifle (EA9040C)** — features heavy Target barrel, 8 lbs. 14 oz., includes E-2 accessories. New 1990.

Mfg.'s Sug. Retail	$895	$825	$725	$600	$525	$450	$400	$375

1996 retail for this pre-ban model is $1,100 (EA9205).

▲ **M15 A3 Eagle Spirit (EA9055S)** — includes 16 in. premium air gauge national match barrel, fixed stock, full length tubular aluminum hand guard, designed for IPSC shooting, includes match grade accessories, 8 lbs. 6 oz. Mfg. 1993-95.

	1,075	$875	$725	$600	$525	$450	$400

Last Mfg.'s Sug. Retail was $1,200.

The pre-ban variation of this model is sold out - 1995 retail was $1,475 (EA9603).

▲ **M15 A2 Golden Eagle (EA9049S)** — similar to M15 A2 H-BAR, except has (N.M.) National Match accessories, 20 in. extra heavy barrel, 12 lbs. 12 oz. New 1991.

Mfg.'s Sug. Retail	$1,200	$1,075	$875	$725	$600	$525	$450	$400

1996 retail for this pre-ban model is $1,550 (EA9500).

▲ **M15 A3/A4 Eagle Eye (EA9901)** — includes 24 in. free floating 1 in. barrel with tubular aluminum hand guard, weighted buttstock, designed for silhouette matches, 14 lbs. New 1993.

Mfg.'s Sug. Retail	$1,495	$1,325	$1,075	$875	$725	$600	$525	$450

▲ **M15 A3 Action Master (EA9052S)** — match rifle, solid aluminum handguard tube that allows for free floating 20 in. barrel with compensator, N.M. accessories, fixed stock, 8 lbs. 5 oz. New 1992.

Mfg.'s Sug. Retail	$1,200	$1,075	$875	$725	$600	$525	$450	$400

The pre-ban variation of this model is sold out - 1995 retail was $1,475 (EA5600).

▲ **M15 A3/A4 Special Purpose Rifle (SPR/EA9042C)** — 20 in. barrel, flat-top (A3) or detachable handle (A4) receiver.

Mfg.'s Sug. Retail	$955	$850	$725	$600	$525	$450	$400	$375

1996 retail for this pre-ban model is $1,165 (EA9204).

▲ **M15 A3/A4 Predator (EA9902)** — post-ban only, 18 in. barrel, National Match trigger, flat-top (A3) or detachable handle (A4) receiver. New 1995.

Mfg.'s Sug. Retail	$1,350	$1,125	$895	$725	$600	$525	$450	$400

EFFEBI SNC

Current manufacturer located in Concesio, Italy since 1994. Previously known as Dr. Franco Beretta until 1994.

To date, Effebi has limited importation into the U.S. The manufacturer should be contacted directly (see Trademark Index) for more information regarding current pricing and shotgun model availability.

EGO ARMAS, S.A.

Manufacturer located in Eibar, Spain. No current U.S. importation.

Ego Armas manufactures high quality sidelock double rifles ranging in price from $4,000-$14,000. Calibers include .375 H&H Mag. and .416 Rigby in their high quality deluxe models. Mounted scopes are also available. Boxlock and sidelock shotguns are also available ranging in price from $400-$4,000. More information, including current models and approximate U.S. pricing, can be obtained by contacting this manufacturer directly (see Trademark Index).

ENFIELD

Royal Small Arms Factory, Middlesex, England.

Grading	100%	98%	95%	90%	80%	70%	60%

NO. 2 MK. I REVOLVER — .380 British Service (based on .38 S&W with a 200 grain bullet), double action, 6 shot, 5 in. barrel, fixed sights, blue, composition grips, top break, issued to British army 1932.

| | $235 | $195 | $175 | $140 | $130 | $120 | $110 |

RIFLES

SMLE stands for Rifle, Short, Magazine, Lee-Enfield. The SMLE rifles served the British Military from 1902-1954.

NO. 1 MK. III SMLE — .303 British, bolt action, 10 shot mag., 25.2 in. barrel, open sights, long range volley sights, magazine cut-off, adopted by British Army in 1907.

| | $225 | $190 | $150 | $125 | $100 | $90 | $75 |

NO. 1 MK. III SMLE — a simplified rifle adopted by the British during WWI, volley sights and magazine cut-off deleted, the most common variation of SMLE.

| | $225 | $190 | $150 | $125 | $100 | $90 | $75 |

NO. 2 MK. IV — .22 LR cal., single shot, recently imported from Australia.

| | $495 | $425 | $375 | $315 | $260 | $215 | $160 |

NO. 3 MK. I PATTERN 14 RIFLE — modified Mauser type bolt action, .303 British, issued as substitute standard by British Army during WWI, manufactured in U.S. (the later U.S. 1917 Enfield is identical except for caliber and sights).

| | $225 | $190 | $150 | $125 | $100 | $90 | $75 |

NO. 3 MK. I — .22 cal., single shot military training model.

| | $350 | $300 | $275 | $250 | $225 | $200 | $175 |

NO. 4 MK. I — an improved SMLE with aperture rear sight, stronger receiver and more easily manufactured parts, adopted in 1939 by the British Army.

| | $215 | $185 | $145 | $120 | $95 | $75 | $55 |

This model was manufactured during WWII in Canada, England, and the U.S. To determine which armory manufactured this model, the following information should be studied. Savage-Stevens mfg. is denoted by "US Property S" with a C in ser. no., Canadian mfg.

Grading	100%	98%	95%	90%	80%	70%	60%

(Long Branch, Ontario) is indicated by "Long Branch" - no code, British mfg. was by B.S.A.; Shirley and marked "M.47C"., Royal Ordnance Factory (near Liverpool) marked "ROF(F)", or Royal Ordnance Factory (near Sheffield) marked "ROFM" or "RM" or "M".

▲ *No. 4 Mark I T Sniper Model* — with or w/o scope, with or w/o case.

	100%	98%	95%	90%	80%	70%	60%
Gun w/o scope	$575	$495	$450	$385	$315	$285	$260
Gun with scope	$1,425	$1,275	$1,075	$950	$875	$825	$750

Add $175-$225 for case, depending on condition.

NO. 5 MK. I JUNGLE CARBINE — a shorter, lighter version of the No. 4 MK. I with a 20.5 in. barrel, flash hider, recoil pad and shortened forend and hand guard, 7.2 lbs., developed during WWII.

	100%	98%	95%	90%	80%	70%	60%
	$350	$275	$200	$150	$125	$100	$85

ENFIELD AMERICA, INC.

Previous manufacturer located in Atlanta, GA.

MP-45 — .45 ACP, semi-auto paramilitary design pistol, 4½, 6, 8, 10, or 18½ in. shrouded barrel, Parkerized finish, 10, 30, 40, or 50 shot mag., 6 lbs. Mfg. 1985 only.

	100%	98%	95%	90%	80%	70%	60%
	$550	$475	$425	$350	$295	$260	$240

Last Mfg.'s Sug. Retail was $350.

ERA

Manufacturer located in Brazil.

ERA O/U SHOTGUN — 12 or 20 ga., 28 in. vent. rib barrel, full and mod., double triggers, extractors, checkered hardwood stock.

	100%	98%	95%	90%	80%	70%	60%
	$275	$250	$225	$200	$170	$150	$125
Trap version	$300	$275	$250	$225	$200	$175	$150
Skeet version	$300	$275	$250	$225	$200	$175	$150

ERA DOUBLE BARREL — 12, 20, or .410 ga., 26, 28, or 30 in. barrels, various chokes, double triggers, extractors, checkered pistol grip stock.

	100%	98%	95%	90%	80%	70%	60%
	$165	$150	$135	$125	$110	$100	$85

ERA DOUBLE RIOT MODEL — similar to Double Barrel, except 12 or 20 ga., 18 in. barrel.

	100%	98%	95%	90%	80%	70%	60%
	$185	$175	$150	$140	$125	$110	$95

ERA QUAIL MODEL — similar to Standard, except 12 or 20 ga., 20 in. barrel.

	100%	98%	95%	90%	80%	70%	60%
	$185	$175	$150	$140	$125	$110	$95

ERMA-WERKE

Manufacturer located in Dachau, Germany. Currently, pistols are imported and distributed by Precision Sales International, Inc. located in Westfield, MA, Nygord Precision Products located in La Crescenta, CA, and Mandall's Shooting Supplies, Inc. located in Scottsdale, AZ. Previously distributed by Excam located in Hialeah, FL.

Erma-Werke rifles are not currently imported into the U.S. Erma-Werke also manufactures private label handguns for American Arms Inc. (refer to their section for listings).

PISTOLS: SEMI-AUTO

MODEL LA 22 — .22 LR, semi-auto, action patterned after the Luger, mfg. 1964-1967.

	100%	98%	95%	90%	80%	70%	60%
	$395	$335	$275	$240	$200	$175	$140

Grading	100%	98%	95%	90%	80%	70%	60%

ERMA KGP68A/BEEMAN MP-08 — .32 ACP or .380 ACP cal., Luger type toggle action, 3½ (Beeman) or 4 in. barrel, 6 shot mag., blue, 1.4 lbs. Mfg. 1968-disc.

Mfg.'s Sug. Retail	$500	$450	$400	$335	$275	$240	$185	$145

This model is imported exclusively by Mandall's Shooting Supplies, Inc. located in Scottsdale, AZ. From 1988-90, Beeman took over importation of this model in .380 ACP cal. only with new Luger style checkered walnut grips and 3½ in. barrel. Previous models had plastic grips.

ERMA KGP69/BEEMAN P-08 — Luger type toggle action, .22 LR, 8 shot mag., 3¾ in. barrel, blue, plastic (disc.) or checkered walnut grips. Mfg. 1969-disc.

	$335	$275	$240	$185	$145	$115	$95

Last Mfg.'s Sug. Retail was $390.

Beeman was the sole importer of this model between 1988-90.

MODEL ESP 85A SPORT/MATCH PISTOL — .22 LR or .32 S&W Long Wadcutter, blow back semi-auto, 6 in. barrel, 5 or 8 (.32 S&W only) shot mag., choice of sporting or adj. stippled match grips with thumbrest, fully adj. and interchangeable sights, gun is supplied with 1 extra weight, extra mag., sights, disassembly tools, and attache style case ($134 option) with foam rubber cut-outs, 2½ lbs. Importation began 1989.

Mfg.'s Sug. Retail	$1,375	$1,095	$900	$775	$650	$550	$495	$450

Subtract $250 for Junior Model.
Add $165 for .32 S&W cal.
Add $80 for Match Model (with anatomical grips).
Add $775-$1,070 for conversion unit.
Add approx. $165 for chrome finish.
Add $24 for left-hand action (Match Model only - disc. 1994).
ESP 85 refers to Junior Model (new 1995). The ESP 85 series is distributed by Precision Sales International, Inc. and Mandall Shooting Supplies, Inc.

▲ *Model ESP 85A Complete Set* — includes both .22 LR and .32 S&W Long Wadcutter barrels and mags., cased with accessories, complete set was disc. 1991.

	$1,775	$1,525	$1,350	$1,125	$950	$825	$750

Last Mfg.'s Sug. Retail was $1,995.

ET-22 LUGER CARBINE — .22 LR, 11¾ in. barrel, blue rear ramp sight, checkered walnut grips and uncheckered forearm, adj. artillery type rear sight, rarely seen.

	$395	$335	$275	$240	$200	$175	$140

Add 20% for leatherette case.

REVOLVERS: DOUBLE ACTION

These models are distributed by Precision Sales International, Inc. only.

ER-772 STANDARD/MATCH — .22 LR, standard or match gun with special adj. contoured grips with stippling, 6 in. barrel, action similar to ER 777, fully adj. and extended rear sight, interchangeable front sight, 3 lbs. Imported 1990-94.

	$1,100	$875	$725	$625	$550	$495	$450

Last Mfg.'s Sug. Retail was $1,371.

ER-773 STANDARD/MATCH — .32 S&W Long, otherwise similar to ER 772 Match, 2.9 lbs. Imported 1990-95.

	$925	$825	$695	$525	$475	$425	$385

Last Mfg.'s Sug. Retail was $1,068.

ER-777 STANDARD — .357 Mag., 6 shot, 4 or 5½ in. barrel, solid rib and full barrel shroud, adj. target rear sight, blued steel, checkered sport grips, 2¾ lbs. Imported 1990-95.

	$875	$775	$650	$475	$425	$385	$350

Last Mfg.'s Sug. Retail was $1,019.

RIFLES

Models listed below are available from Mandall Shooting Supplies.

Grading	100%	98%	95%	90%	80%	70%	60%

EM1 .22 CARBINE — M1 copy .22 LR cal., 10 or 15 shot mag., 18 in. barrel, rear adj. aperature sight, 5.6 lbs. Mfg. 1966-current.

Mfg.'s Sug. Retail	$400		$365	$295	$250	$215	$190	$175	$160

EGM-1 — similar to EM1 except for unslotted butt stock, 5 shot mag.

Mfg.'s Sug. Retail	$295		$260	$230	$195	$175	$150	$125	$100

EG72 PUMP — outside hammer, .22 LR cal., 15 shot mag., 18½ in. barrel. Mfg. 1970-1976.

			$125	$95	$90	$75	$70	$65	$60

EG712 LEVER-ACTION — Win. Model 94 copy, .22 LR cal., tube mag., 18½ in. barrel. Mfg. 1976 to date.

Mfg.'s Sug. Retail	$295		$260	$230	$195	$175	$150	$125	$100

EG-73 — similar to EG712 except .22 Mag. cal., 12 shot mag. Mfg. 1973 to date.

Mfg.'s Sug. Retail	$300		$265	$230	$195	$175	$150	$125	$100

EUROPEAN AMERICAN ARMORY CORP.

Importer/distributor located in Sharpes, FL beginning late 1990.

EAA currently imports their handguns from Tanfoglio located in Italy and from H. Weihrauch located in Germany. All guns are covered by EAA's lifetime limited warranty.

PISTOLS: EUROPEAN SERIES

MODEL EA220 — .22 LR cal., 3.88 in. barrel, 10 shot mag., single action, steel frame, 26 oz., blue, chrome or blue/chrome, wooden grips. Importation disc. 1992.

				$185	$150	$120	$100	$95	$85	$75

Last Mfg.'s Sug. Retail was $225.

Add approx. $20 for chrome or blue chrome finish.

MODEL EA22-T — .22 LR cal., 6 in. barrel, 12 shot mag., single action, steel frame, target model, 40 oz. Imported 1991-1993.

				$375	$295	$260	$220	$185	$165	$150

Last Mfg.'s Sug. Retail was $450.

EUROPEAN 32 (320) — .32 ACP cal., 3.88 in. barrel, 7 shot mag., single action, steel frame, 26 oz., blue, chrome or blue/chrome, wooden grips. Importation 1991-95.

				$130	$110	$95	$85	$80	$75	$70

Last Mfg.'s Sug. Retail was $161.

Add $14 for chrome finish.

EUROPEAN 380 — .380 ACP cal., single (new 1994) or double (disc. 1994) action, 3⅞ in. barrel, blue, brushed chrome, matte blue/chrome (disc. 1993), or blue/gold plated Duo-Tone (European Lady, disc. 1995) finish, 7 shot bottom release mag., steel construction, firing pin safety, external hammer, smooth wood or ivory rose polymer (European Lady) grips, 26 oz. Importation began 1992.

Mfg.'s Sug. Retail	$161		$130	$110	$95	$85	$80	$75	$70

Add $67 for European Lady model (disc. 1995).
Add $32 for double action design (disc. 1994).
Add $14 for brushed chrome or matte blue/chrome (disc. 1993) finish.
This model employs a unique patent pending magazine gun lock system.

Grading	100%	98%	95%	90%	80%	70%	60%

PISTOLS: SEMI-AUTO - WITNESS SERIES

EA 38 SUPER SERIES — .38 Super cal., action patterned after the CZ-75, selective double action, 4½ in. barrel, steel frame, 10 (C/B 1994) or 19* shot mag., choice of stainless steel or blue, blue/chrome (disc. 1994), or brushed chrome finish, combat sights, black neoprene grips, 33 oz. Importation began 1994.

Mfg.'s Sug. Retail	$523	$465	$400	$350	$325	$295	$275	$250

Add $29 for blue/chrome or matte chrome finish.

▲ **Model EA 38 Stainless** — similar to EA 38, except is stainless steel.

Mfg.'s Sug. Retail	$595	$525	$435	$350

EA 9 SERIES — 9mm Para. cal., action patterned after the CZ-75, selective double action, 4½ in. barrel, steel frame, 10 (C/B 1994) or 16* shot mag., choice of stainless steel or blue, blue/chrome (disc. 1993), or brushed chrome finish, combat sights, black neoprene grips, 33 oz. Importation began late 1990.

Mfg.'s Sug. Retail	$408	$360	$300	$280	$250	$225	$200	$185

Add $29 for blue/chrome (disc. 1993) or brushed chrome finish.

▲ **Model EA 9 Stainless** — similar to EA 9, except is stainless steel. Importation began 1992.

Mfg.'s Sug. Retail	$480	$420	$350	$295

▲ **Model EA 9 (L) Compact** — similar to EA 9, except has 3⅝ in. barrel and 10 (C/B 1994) or 13* shot mag.

Mfg.'s Sug. Retail	$437	$375	$300	$280	$255	$225	$200	$185

Add $43 for blue/chrome (disc.) or brushed chrome finish.

EA 40 SERIES — .40 S&W cal., action patterned after the CZ-75, selective double action, 4½ in. barrel, steel frame, 10 (C/B 1994) or 12* shot mag., choice of stainless steel or blue, blue/chrome (disc.), or brushed chrome finish, combat sights, black neoprene grips, 33 oz. Importation began late 1990.

Mfg.'s Sug. Retail	$437	$375	$315	$295	$260	$230	$215	$200

Add $29 for blue/chrome (disc.) or brushed chrome finish.

▲ **Model EA 40 Stainless** — similar to EA 40, except is stainless steel. Importation began 1992.

Mfg.'s Sug. Retail	$509	$455	$365	$295

▲ **Model EA 40 (L) Compact** — similar to EA 40, except has 3⅝ in. barrel and 9 shot mag.

Mfg.'s Sug. Retail	$437	$375	$315	$295	$260	$230	$215	$200

Add $29 for blue/chrome (disc.) or brushed chrome finish.

EA 10 SUPER SERIES — 10mm cal., action patterned after the CZ-75, selective double action, 4½ in. barrel, steel frame, 12 shot mag., choice of stainless steel, blue or chrome finish, combat sights, black neoprene grips, 33 oz. Imported 1994 only.

	$450	$395	$350	$325	$295	$275	$250

Last Mfg.'s Sug. Retail was $498.

Add $27 for chrome finish.
Add $67 for stainless steel.

▲ **Model EA 10 Stainless** — similar to EA 10, except is stainless steel.

	$495	$425	$350

Last Mfg.'s Sug. Retail was $566.

EA 41 SERIES — .41 Action Express cal., action patterned after the CZ-75, selective double action, 4½ in. barrel, steel frame, 11 shot mag., blue, blue/chrome, or brushed chrome finish, combat sights, black neoprene grips, 33 oz. Importation disc. 1993.

	$450	$375	$325	$275	$250	$225	$200

Last Mfg.'s Sug. Retail was $595.

Add $40 for blue/chrome or brushed chrome finish.

Grading	100%	98%	95%	90%	80%	70%	60%

▲ *Model EA 41 Compact* — similar to EA 41, except has 3½ in. barrel and 8 shot mag.

	$495	$425	$375	$325	$295	$260	$230

Last Mfg.'s Sug. Retail was $625.

Add $40 for blue/chrome or brushed chrome finish.

EA 45 SERIES — .45 ACP cal., action patterned after the CZ-75, selective double action, 4½ in. barrel, steel frame, 10 (C/B 1994) or 11* shot mag., choice of stainless steel or blue, blue/chrome (disc. 1993), or brushed chrome finish, combat sights, walnut grips, 35 oz. Importation began late 1990.

Mfg.'s Sug. Retail	$523	$465	$400	$350	$325	$295	$275	$250

Add $29 for blue/chrome (disc. 1993) or matte chrome finish.

▲ *Model EA 45 Stainless* — similar to EA 45, except is stainless steel. Importation began 1992.

Mfg.'s Sug. Retail	$595	$510	$430	$350

▲ *Model EA 45 (L) Compact* — similar to EA 45, except has 3⅝ in. barrel and 8 shot mag.

Mfg.'s Sug. Retail	$523	$465	$400	$350	$325	$295	$275	$250

Add $29 for blue/chrome (disc.) or brushed chrome finish.

WITNESS SPORT — .38 Super, 9mm Para., .40 S&W, 10mm (disc. 1994), or .45 ACP cal., 4½ in. barrel, full size frame, standard slide length, Duo-Tone finish, extended safety and high capacity mag., target sights. Imported 1994-95.

	$535	$470	$400	$375	$350	$325	$295

Last Mfg.'s Sug. Retail was $616.

Add $86 for .38 Super, 10mm, or .45 ACP cal.

WITNESS SPORT LONG SLIDE — .38 Super, 9mm Para., .40 S&W, 10mm (disc. 1994), or .45 ACP cal., long slide variation of the EA Series, except has 4¾ in. ported or unported barrel and slide, Duo-Tone finish, extended safety and high capacity mag., competition sights, 34½ oz. Importation disc. 1995.

	$595	$500	$450	$395	$350	$325	$295

Last Mfg.'s Sug. Retail was $681.

Add $79 for .38 Super, 10mm, or .45 ACP cal.

WITNESS LIMITED CLASS — .38 Super, 9mm Para., .40 S&W, or .45 ACP cal., match frame, competition grips, high capacity mag., single action trigger, long slide with match barrel and super sight, extended safety, blue finish only. Importation began 1994.

Mfg.'s Sug. Retail	$967	$855	$715	$610	$500	$450	$400	$375

WITNESS COMBO PACKAGE — includes one built up frame and 9mm Para./.40 S&W complete conversion kits, blue, chrome, or Duo-Tone (disc. 1994) finish, full size variation with 4½ in. barrel. Importation began 1992.

Mfg.'s Sug. Retail	$588	$515	$460	$400	$375	$350	$325	$295

Add $29 for chrome or Duo-Tone finish.

▲ *Witness Combo Package (L) Compact* — similar to Witness Combo Package, except has 3⅝ in. barrels, blue only. Introduced late 1994.

Mfg.'s Sug. Retail	$588	$515	$460	$400	$375	$350	$325	$295

WITNESS MULTI-CLASS PISTOL PACKAGE — .38 Super, 9mm Para., 9x21mm, .40 S&W, or .45 ACP cal., consists of one Witness Limited Class Pistol and complete Unlimited Class top half (slide and barrel), dual chamber steel compensator, blue finish only. Imported 1994 only.

	$1,450	$1,200	$1,025	$895	$775	$650	$525

Last Mfg.'s Sug. Retail was $1,638.

WITNESS TRI-CALIBER PACKAGE — includes one built up frame and caliber conversions (9mm Para., .40 S&W, and .41 AE) that include slide, barrel, recoil guide, and spring, matte blue or chrome finish, compact or full size variations, includes carry case. Imported 1992-1993 only.

	$975	$825	$700	$575	$495	$425	$375

Last Mfg.'s Sug. Retail was $1,195.

Add $40 for chrome finish.

Grading	100%	98%	95%	90%	80%	70%	60%

WITNESS CARRY COMP GUN — .38 Super, 9mm Para., .40 S&W cal., 10mm (disc. 1994), or .45 ACP cal., full size frame with compact slide and 1 in. compensator, 10 (C/B 1994), 12* (.40 S&W), or 16* (9mm Para.) shot mag., blue or Duo-Tone (disc. 1994) finish. Importation began 1992.

Mfg.'s Sug. Retail	$552	$480	$420	$375	$325	$295	$260	$230

Add $27 for Duo-Tone finish.
Add $111 for .38 Super, 10mm, or .45 ACP cal. (blue only).

WITNESS SILVER TEAM — .38 Super, 9mm Para., 9x21mm, 10mm (disc. 1994), .40 S&W, or .45 ACP cal., dual comp. chambers, S/A trigger, super sight and drilled and tapped for scope mount, competition features include hammer, extended safety, paddle mag. release, black rubber grips, double-dip blue finish, high capacity mag. Importation began 1992.

Mfg.'s Sug. Retail	$967	$855	$710	$600	$500	$425	$375	$325

WITNESS GOLD TEAM — .38 Super, 9mm Para., 9x21mm, 10mm (disc. 1994), .40 S&W, or .45 ACP cal., triple comp. chambers, S/A trigger, super sight and drilled and tapped for scope mount, top of the line competition model featuring hand-fitted major components and 25 LPI checkering, hard chrome finish. Importation began 1992.

Mfg.'s Sug. Retail	$2,150	$1,875	$1,525	$1,250	$995	$825	$700	$575

This model is also avail. as a frame only - retail is $389.

PISTOLS: D/A WITNESS FAB 92 SERIES

F.A.B. 92 — 9mm Para. or .40 S&W cal., features hammer drop safety and decocker (Witness style), 4½ in. barrel, 16* (9mm Para.) or 12* (.40 S&W), or 10 (C/B 1994) shot mag., all steel construction, blue, chrome (disc. 1993), or Duo-Tone (disc. 1993) finish, smooth wood grips, 33 oz. Imported 1992-95.

			$335	$280	$235	$210	$190	$170	$155

Last Mfg.'s Sug. Retail was $386.

Add $40 for chrome or Duo-Tone finish.
Add $29 for .40 S&W cal.

F.A.B. designates Foreign American Brands.

▲ **F.A.B. 92 Compact** — similar to F.A.B. 92, except has 3⅝ in. barrel, 13* (9mm Para.), 10 (9mm only, C/B 1994), or 9 (.40 S&W) shot mag., 30 oz. Imported 1992-95.

			$335	$280	$235	$210	$190	$170	$155

Last Mfg.'s Sug. Retail was $386.

Add $40 for chrome or Duo-Tone finish.
Add $29 for .40 S&W cal.

REVOLVERS: SAA BOUNTY HUNTER SERIES

MODEL EASAB — .22 LR, single action revolver, 6 shot, 4¾ in. barrel, blued or chrome (disc. 1991) finish, wood grips. Importation disc. 1995.

			$70	$55	$50	$45	$40	$35	$30

Last Mfg.'s Sug. Retail was $85.

Add $20 for chrome finish.

MODEL EASAMB COMBO — includes .22 LR and .22 Mag. cylinders, 4¾ (standard), 6, or 9 in. barrel, blue finish, wood grips. Importation disc. 1995.

			$85	$75	$65	$55	$50	$45	$40

Last Mfg.'s Sug. Retail was $100.

Add $14 for 9 in. barrel.
Add $40 for gold backstrap and triggerguard (disc.).

E

Grading	100%	98%	95%	90%	80%	70%	60%

BIG BORE BOUNTY HUNTER — .357 Mag., .44 Mag., or .45 LC cal., 4½ (new 1994), 5½ (disc. 1993), or 7½ in. barrel, 6 shot, choice of blue, chrome (mfg. 1994-95), or case colored finish, gold triggerguard/backstrap (disc. 1994), or gold (disc.) finish, 32-41 oz. New 1992.

Mfg.'s Sug. Retail	$299	$260	$220	$185	$165	$150	$135	$120

Add $3 for 7½ in. barrel.
Add $45 for chrome finish (disc.).
Add $11 for case colored frame.
Add $14 for gold-plated grip strap and triggerguard.
Add approx. $100 for gold plated finish (disc.)

REVOLVERS: WINDICATOR SERIES

STANDARD GRADE — .22 LR (disc.), .22LR/.22 Mag. combo. (disc.), .22 Mag. (disc.), .32 H&R (disc. 1993), .357 Mag. (new 1994), or .38 Spl. cal., 2 (.32 H&R, .357 Mag., or .38 Spl. only), 4, or 6 (disc.) in. squared off barrel, blue or chrome (.38 Spl. only, new 1994) finish, 6 (.38 Spl.), 7 (.32 H&R), or 8 (.22 LR/.22 Mag.) shot, finger grooved rubber grips, double or single action. Importation began 1992.

Mfg.'s Sug. Retail	$179	$155	$135	$125	$115	$105	$95	$85

Add $15 for .357 Mag. cal.
Add $78 for .22 LR/.22 Mag. combo.
Add approx. $29 for longer barrel lengths.

TACTICAL GRADE — .38 Spl. only, fixed sights, 6 shot, 2 in. (bobbed hammer) or 4 in. compensated barrel, blue finish only. Imported 1992-1993.

		$220	$190	$165	$145	$130	$115	$105

Last Mfg.'s Sug. Retail was $295.

Add $80 for 4 in. compensated barrel.

TARGET GRADE — .22 LR, .357 Mag., or .38 Spl. cal., 6 or 8 (.22 LR) shot, 6 in. squared off barrel, finger grooved hardwood stocks, adj. trigger pull and rear sight, blue finish only, 3.1 lbs. Imported 1992-1993.

	$425	$325	$260	$220	$200	$185	$170

Last Mfg.'s Sug. Retail was $550.

RIFLES

EAA rifles are manufactured by Sabatti in Italy (est. 1674), Lu-Mar in Italy, and H. Weihrauch in Germany (see separate listing in the H. Weihrauch section). Importation began 1992.

SP1822 SPORTER — .22 LR, semi-auto, 18½ in. barrel, wood stock and forearm, adj. sights, 10 shot box mag., 5¼-6½ lbs. Importation began 1994.

Mfg.'s Sug. Retail	$206	$180	$145	$120	$100	$90	$80	$70

▲ *SP1822 Thumbhole* — similar to heavy barrel model, except has one-piece Bell & Carlson green synthetic thumbhole stock, without sights. Importation disc. 1995.

	$310	$260	$230	$200	$175	$150	$135

Last Mfg.'s Sug. Retail was $358.

ROVER 870 — .22-250 Rem., .243 Win., .25-06 Rem., .270 Rem., .30-06, .308 Win., 7mm Rem. Mag., .300 Win. Mag., or .338 Win. Mag. cal., bolt action rifle featuring all-steel construction with 22 in. hammer-forged rifled barrel, staggered 5 shot internal mag., open sights. Imported 1993 only.

	$795	$695	$600	$550	$495	$450	$395

Last Mfg.'s Sug. Retail was $995.

Grading	100%	98%	95%	90%	80%	70%	60%

SHOTGUNS: O/U

SCIROCCO BASIC — 12 ga. only, single trigger, extractors, 26 or 28 in. fixed choke VR barrels, boxlock action, nickel engraved receiver. Imported 1994-95.

	$425	$350	$315	$285	$260	$240	$220

Last Mfg.'s Sug. Retail was $478.

This model was mfg. by Lu-Mar located in Italy.

SCIROCCO SPORTING CLAYS — 12 ga. only, 28 or 30 in. barrels with 5 choke tubes and wide VR, SST, ejectors, Raybar front sight, nickel engraved receiver. Imported 1994-95.

	$650	$550	$495	$450	$400	$350	$315

Last Mfg.'s Sug. Retail was $734.

This model was mfg. by Lu-Mar located in Italy.

FALCON — 12, 20, or .410 ga., 3 in. chambers, 26, 28, or 30 in. fixed choke VR barrels, boxlock action, single or double trigger, extractors or ejectors, checkered pistol grip and forend. Imported 1993 only.

	$650	$525	$450	$375	$325	$295	$260

Last Mfg.'s Sug. Retail was $795.

Add $80 for .410 ga.
Add $100 for SST and ejectors.

SPORTING CLAYS PRO GOLD — 12 ga. only, 2¾ in. chambers, 28 or 30 in. screw-in choke barrels with wide VR, boxlock action, SST, ejectors, blued receiver with engraving, recoil pad with custom carry case. Imported 1993-1994.

	$850	$725	$650	$575	$525	$475	$425

Last Mfg.'s Sug. Retail was $978.

SHOTGUNS: SIDE-BY-SIDE

SABA — 12, 20, 28, or .410 ga., 3 in. chambers, boxlock action with scrolled nickel finish, DT or SST, 26 or 28 in. fixed choke barrels with raised matted rib, ejectors, checkered stock and forearm with sling swivels. Imported 1993 only.

	$950	$825	$700	$575	$495	$425	$375

Last Mfg.'s Sug. Retail was $1,195.

Add $100 for SST.

SHOTGUNS: SLIDE ACTION

MODEL PM2 — 12 ga. only, slide action, unique 7 shot detachable mag., 20 in. barrel, black wood stock and composite forearm, dual action bars, cross trigger safety, available in matte blue or chrome finish, 6.81 lbs. Imported 1992 only.

	$550	$450	$395	$335	$295	$260	$230

Last Mfg.'s Sug. Retail was $695.

Add $200 for night sights.
Add $75 for matte chrome finish.

EVANS, WILLIAM, GUN & RIFLE MAKERS

Please refer to the W section in this text.

EVOLUTION USA

Rifle manufacturer located in White Bird, ID since 1993.

RIFLES: BOLT ACTION

COYOTE — .223 Rem., .25-06 Rem., or .308 Win. cal., Rem. 700 action, Grand Master barrel with cryogenic treatment, Kevlar/graphite stock. New 1996.

Mfg.'s Sug. Retail	$1,369		$1,250	$1,025	$875	$725	$650	$575	$525

Grading	100%	98%	95%	90%	80%	70%	60%

YELLOW WOLF — .27 Gibbs, .300 Win. Mag., or 7mm Rem. Mag. cal., designed for big game, Kevlar/graphite stock. New 1996.

Mfg.'s Sug. Retail	$1,369	$1,250	$1,025	$875	$725	$650	$575	$525

RIFLES: SEMI-AUTO

WOLVERINE — .22 LR cal., Grand Master barrel, Kevlar/graphite stock. New 1996.

Mfg.'s Sug. Retail	$794	$695	$625	$550	$500	$450	$400	$360

GRENADA — .223 Rem. cal., paramilitary design based on the AR-15 with flat upper receiver, 17 in. stainless steel match barrel with integral muzzle brake, NM trigger.

Mfg.'s Sug. Retail	$1,055	$875	$750	$625	$550	$500	$450	$400

DESERT STORM — similar to Grenada, except has 21 in. match barrel.

Mfg.'s Sug. Retail	$1,037	$860	$750	$625	$550	$500	$450	$400

IWO JIMA — features carrying handle incorporating iron sights, 20 in. stainless steel match barrel, A2 HBAR action, tubular handguard.

	$1,150	$975	$850	$725	$600	$475	$425

EXCAM

Previous importer and distributor located in Hialeah, FL that went out of business late 1990. Excam distributed Dart, Erma, Tanarmi, Targa, & Warrior exclusively for the U.S. These trademarks will appear under Excam only in this book. All importation of Excam firearms ceased in 1990.

All Targa and Tanarmi pistols were manufactured in Gardone V.T., Italy. All Erma and Warrior pistols and rifles were manufactured in W. Germany. Senator O/U shotguns were manufactured by A. Zoli located in Brescia, Italy.

ERMA PISTOLS

RX 22 — .22 LR only, double action-Walther copy, 3¼ in. barrel, 8 shot mag., blue only, plastic grips, 17 oz. Assembled in the U.S. Disc. 1986.

	$140	$125	$105	$95	$90	$85	$80

Last Mfg.'s Sug. Retail was $139.

KGP 22 — .22 LR only, Luger type toggle action, 3.78 in. barrel, 8 shot mag., blue only, plastic grips, 29 oz. Importation disc. 1986.

	$220	$195	$175	$155	$135	$120	$105

Last Mfg.'s Sug. Retail was $220.

KGP 380 — .380 ACP only, Luger type toggle action, 3½ in. barrel, 5 shot mag., blue only, plastic grips, 23 oz. Disc. 1986.

	$250	$215	$185	$160	$145	$135	$125

Last Mfg.'s Sug. Retail was $230.

ERMA RIFLES

EG 712 — .22 LR only, lever action copied after the Win. Model 92, 18½ in. barrel, 15 shot, iron sights. Disc. 1985.

	$180	$160	$140	$125	$115	$100	$90

Last Mfg.'s Sug. Retail was $204.

EG 712L — .22 LR only, lever action copied after the Win. Model 92, 18½ in. octagonal barrel, deluxe walnut silver plated receiver and barrel bands, 15 shot, iron sights. Disc.

	$300	$241	$220	$180	$150	$130	$115

Grading	100%	98%	95%	90%	80%	70%	60%

EG 73 — .22 Mag. only, lever action copied after the Win. Model 92, 19¼ in. barrel, 12 shot, iron sights, blue only. Disc. 1985.

| | $205 | $185 | $160 | $140 | $130 | $120 | $105 |

Last Mfg.'s Sug. Retail was $229.

EG 722 — .22 LR only, slide action, 18½ in. barrel, 15 shot, iron sights, blue only. Disc. 1985.

| | $180 | $160 | $140 | $125 | $115 | $100 | $90 |

Last Mfg.'s Sug. Retail was $204.

EM 1 CARBINE — .22 LR or .22 Mag., gas semi-auto, copy of the original M1 carbine, 19½ in. barrel, 15 shot, iron sights, blue only. ESG 22 is 22 Mag. (12 shot) — add $100. Disc. 1985.

| | $175 | $155 | $140 | $125 | $115 | $100 | $90 |

Last Mfg.'s Sug. Retail was $195.

SENATOR OVER/UNDER SHOTGUNS

SENATOR MODEL — 12, 20, or .410 ga., 3 in. chambers, 26 or 28 in. F/M barrels, folding action, double triggers, extractors, vent. barrels and rib, checkered walnut stock and forearm, engraved silver finished receiver. Imported 1986-1987.

| | $235 | $200 | $180 | $165 | $150 | $140 | $130 |

Last Mfg.'s Sug. Retail was $275.

TANARMI HANDGUNS

MODEL TA 22 — .22 LR, 6 shot, 4¾ in. barrel, brass triggerguard and grip straps, blued finish, wood grips, 34 oz.

| | $85 | $70 | $60 | $55 | $50 | $45 | $40 |

Last Mfg.'s Sug. Retail was $99.

MODEL TA 76 S.A.A. — .22 LR, single action revolver, 4¾ in. barrel, 6 shot, blue finish only, wood grips, 32 oz.

| | $85 | $65 | $55 | $50 | $45 | $40 | $35 |

Last Mfg.'s Sug. Retail was $95.

Add $4 for chrome finish or brass backstrap and triggerguard.

▲ *Model TA 76M Combo* — includes .22 LR and .22 Mag. cylinders, 4¾ (standard), 6, or 9 in. barrel, blue finish, wood grips.

| | $95 | $75 | $65 | $60 | $55 | $50 | $45 |

Last Mfg.'s Sug. Retail was $105.

Add $6 for chrome plated finish (4¾ in. barrel only).
Add $10 for 6 (Model TA 766) or 9 (Model TA 769) in. barrel.
Add $16 for brass backstrap and triggerguard (N/A in 9 in. barrel).

TA 38SB O/U DERRINGER — .38 Spl. only, O/U Derringer-copy of Rem. Model 41, 3 in. barrels, 14 oz., with safety, blue finish only, checkered nylon grips. Importation disc. 1985.

| | $90 | $75 | $65 | $55 | $50 | $45 | $40 |

Last Mfg.'s Sug. Retail was $80.

TA 41 SERIES SEMI-AUTO — .41 Action Express cal., action similar to TA 90 Series, 11 shot mag., matte blue (Model TA 41B) or matte chrome (Model TA 41C) finish, combat sights, black neoprene grips, 38 oz. Imported 1989-90.

| | $450 | $390 | $360 | $330 | $295 | $265 | $240 |

Last Mfg.'s Sug. Retail was $490.

Add $70 for adj. target sights (Model TA 41BT).

▲ *Model TA 41C* — matte chrome finish.

| | $485 | $430 | $395 | $360 | $330 | $295 | $270 |

Last Mfg.'s Sug. Retail was $550.

Add $50 (retail) for adj. target sights (Model TA 41CT).

Grading	100%	98%	95%	90%	80%	70%	60%

▲ **Model TA 41 SS** — .41 AE, compensated variation of the Model TA 41 except has 5 in. ported barrel and slide, blue/chrome finish, competition sights, 40 oz. Import 1989-90.

	$575	$450	$420	$385	$350	$325	$300

Last Mfg.'s Sug. Retail was $650.

TA 90 SERIES SEMI-AUTO — 9mm, double action, copy of the CZ-75, 4¾ in. barrel, steel frame, 15 shot mag., matte blue (Model TA 90B) or matte chrome finish (Model TA 90C), combat sights, wood (disc. 1985) or neoprene grips, 38 oz. New 1985.

	$365	$300	$260	$225	$205	$190	$180

Last Mfg.'s Sug. Retail was $415.

Add $85 for adj. target sights (TA 90BT).

Earlier models featured a polished blue finish and nickel steel alloy frame (35 oz.).

▲ **Model TA 90C** — matte chrome finish.

	$380	$315	$270	$235	$210	$190	$180

Last Mfg.'s Sug. Retail was $430.

Add $95 for adj. target sights (TA 90CT).

▲ **Model BTA 90B and C** — 9mm, smaller version of TA 90, 3½ in. barrel, 12 shot mag., neoprene grips. Importer 1986-90.

	$380	$315	$270	$235	$210	$190	$180

Last Mfg.'s Sug. Retail was $430.

Add $20 for chrome finish (BTA 90C).

▲ **Model TA 90 SS** — 9mm, compensated variation of the Model TA 90 except has 5 in. ported barrel and slide, blue/chrome finish, competition sights, 40 oz. Import 1989-90.

	$575	$450	$420	$385	$350	$325	$300

Last Mfg.'s Sug. Retail was $650.

▲ **TA 90BK** — convertible kit including 2 barrels (9mm and .41 AE) and 2 mags. While advertised, this combination never saw production.

TARGA PISTOLS

GT 22 SERIES — .22 LR, 3.88 in. barrel, 10 shot mag., single action 26 oz., steel frame, either satin chrome (GT 22C) or standard blue (GT 22B) finish, wooden grips became standard in 1986. GT 22T is 6 in. barrel target version (12 shot mag.).

	$170	$140	$125	$110	$95	$80	$70

Last Mfg.'s Sug. Retail was $200.

Add $15 for chrome finish (Model GT 22C).

GT 26 and GT 27B OR C — .25 ACP, 2½ in. barrel, 6 shot mag., single action, 13 oz., available in standard blue alloy, satin chrome alloy (GT 27B or C), or steel frame (GT 26S), wooden grips became standard in 1986.

	$50	$45	$35	$30	$30	$25	$25

Last Mfg.'s Sug. Retail was $56.

Add $59 for steel frame (Model GT 26S).
Add $13 for chrome alloy (Model GT 27C).

GT 28 SERIES — .25 ACP, 2½ in. barrel, 5 shot mag., single action, blue alloy, wood grips. Imported 1990 only.

	$45	$35	$30	$30	$25	$25	$20

Last Mfg.'s Sug. Retail was $51.

Add $18 for chrome finish (Model GT 28C).

GT 32 SERIES — .32 ACP, 3.88 in. barrel, 7 shot mag., single action, steel frame, 26 oz., either satin chrome (GT 32C) or standard blue (GT 32B), wooden grips became standard in 1986.

	$170	$140	$125	$110	$95	$80	$70

Last Mfg.'s Sug. Retail was $200.

Add $15 for chrome finish (Model GT 32C).

Grading	100%	98%	95%	90%	80%	70%	60%

GT 380 ACP SERIES — .380 ACP, 3.88 in. barrel, 6 shot mag., single action, steel frame, 26 oz., either satin chrome (GT 380C) or standard blue (GT 380B), wooden grips became standard in 1986.

| | $175 | $145 | $135 | $125 | $115 | $105 | $95 |

Last Mfg.'s Sug. Retail was $212.

Add $8 for chrome finish (Model GT 380C).

▲ *GT 380 LW* — similar to GT 380 Series except has light alloy receiver and 3¼ in. barrel.

| | $100 | $85 | $70 | $60 | $55 | $50 | $45 |

Last Mfg.'s Sug. Retail was $119.

▲ *GT 380 BE or CE* — engraved models, either blue (BE) or chrome (CE) finish, wood grips. Importation disc. 1989.

| | $180 | $155 | $145 | $135 | $125 | $115 | $105 |

Last Mfg.'s Sug. Retail was $220.

Add $25 for chrome finish (Model GT 380 CE).

GT 380 XE — .380 ACP, 3.88 in. barrel, 11 shot mag., blue only, wood grips, 28 oz.

| | $190 | $165 | $155 | $145 | $135 | $125 | $115 |

Last Mfg.'s Sug. Retail was $235.

▲ *GT 32 XEB* — similar to GT 380 XE, only .32 ACP, 12 shot mag. Disc. 1985.

| | $165 | $145 | $135 | $125 | $115 | $100 | $95 |

Last Mfg.'s Sug. Retail was $189.

REVOLVERS

RX 38 B — .38 Spl., double action, 6 shot, 2 in. barrel, blue finish only. Importation began 1990.

| | $85 | $65 | $55 | $50 | $45 | $40 | $35 |

Last Mfg.'s Sug. Retail was $95.

UBERTI REVOLVERS

Importation of these revolvers by Excam was stopped in 1986.

ALDO UBERTI CATTLEMAN SA REVOLVER — .357 Mag., .44 Mag., or .45 LC cal., 6 shot, single action, 5½, 6, or 7½ in. barrels, target sights, wood grips, blued finish. New 1985. Disc. 1986.

| | $295 | $250 | $195 | $165 | $150 | $140 | $130 |

Last Mfg.'s Sug. Retail was $222.

Add $10 for .44 Mag. cal.

ALDO UBERTI DA INSPECTOR — .38 Spl., double action, 3 or 4 in. barrel, blue finish, wood grips, 6 shot. Disc. 1986.

| | $325 | $250 | $200 | $180 | $165 | $150 | $140 |

Last Mfg.'s Sug. Retail was $240.

Add $17 for adj. sights.

WARRIOR REVOLVERS

Importation of these revolvers by Excam was stopped in 1986.

WARRIOR DOUBLE ACTION MODEL W 722 (B) — .22 LR or .22 Mag. only, double action, 6 in. barrel, 8 shot, blue only, plastic grips, 35 oz. Disc. 1986.

| | $100 | $80 | $70 | $65 | $60 | $55 | $50 |

Last Mfg.'s Sug. Retail was $98.

Add $50 for .22 Mag. extra cyl.

WARRIOR DOUBLE ACTION MODEL W 384 (B) — .38 Spl. only, double action, 4 or 6 in. barrels, 6 shot, blue only, plastic grips, 30 oz. Vent. rib standard. Disc. 1986.

| | $135 | $110 | $100 | $90 | $80 | $70 | $65 |

Last Mfg.'s Sug. Retail was $125.

Add $5 for 6 in. barrel (W 386 B).

Grading	100%	98%	95%	90%	80%	70%	60%

WARRIOR DOUBLE ACTION MODEL W 357 — .357 Mag. only, double action, 4 or 6 in. barrels, 6 shot, blue only, plastic grips, 36 oz. Vent. rib standard. 6 in. barrel (W 3576). Disc. 1986.

	$190	$165	$145	$135	$130	$125	$120

Last Mfg.'s Sug. Retail was $185.

EXEL ARMS OF AMERICA, INC.

Previous importer located in Gardener, MA. Exel Arms previously imported Lanber (Series 100), Ugartechea (Series 200), and Laurona (Series 300) shotguns. Please refer to the appropriate sections for more information on this series.

F section

FAS

Manufacturer located in Italy. Currently imported and distributed exclusively by Nygord Precision Products located in Prescott, AZ. Previously imported by Beeman Precision Arms, Inc. located in Santa Rosa, CA and Osborne's located in Cheboygan, MI.

Grading	100%	98%	95%	90%	80%	70%	60%

PISTOLS: SEMI-AUTO

MODEL 601 — .22 Short only, semi-auto competition pistol, 5½ in. barrel, 5 shot mag., wraparound match wood grips, 41½ oz.

Mfg.'s Sug. Retail	$1,250	$1,025	$875	$695	$640	$565	$500	$450

MODEL 602 — .22 LR only, semi-auto competition pistol, 5.6 in. barrel, 5 shot mag., ergonomically designed match wood grips, 40 oz. Importation disc. 1994.

	$895	$800	$625	$600	$525	$475	$425

Last Mfg.'s Sug. Retail was $1,100.

MODEL 603 — .32 S&W Wadcutter only, semi-auto competition pistol, 5.6 in. barrel, 5 shot mag., ergonomically designed adj. or non-adj. match wood grips, 40 oz.

Mfg.'s Sug. Retail	$1,175	$975	$875	$695	$640	$565	$500	$450

MODEL 607 — .22 LR only, semi-auto competition pistol, similar to Model 602, except has removable barrel weights. Importation began 1995.

Mfg.'s Sug. Retail	$1,175	$975	$875	$695	$640	$565	$500	$450

FEG

Manufacturer located in Hungary (FEG stands for Fegyvergyar) since the turn of the century. Currently imported and distributed by KBI, Inc. located in Harrisburg, PA and Century International Arms located in St. Albans, VT (see additional listings under the Century International Arms in this text).

PISTOLS: SEMI-AUTO

All FEG pistols are supplied with two mags.

MODEL PMK-380 — .380 ACP cal., patterned after Walther PP, alloy frame, double action, 4 in. barrel, plastic grips with thumbrest, blued finish, 21 oz. Importation began 1992.

Mfg.'s Sug. Retail	$209	$195	$180	$165	$150	$135	$115	$105

MODEL SMC-380 — .380 ACP cal., double action semi-auto, patterned after Walther PPK, alloy frame, 3½ in. barrel, 6 shot mag., plastic grips with thumbrest, blue finish, 18½ oz. Importation began 1993.

Mfg.'s Sug. Retail	$259	$230	$200	$175	$160	$145	$130	$115

▲ *Model SMC-22* — .22 LR cal., 8 shot mag., otherwise similar to Model SMC-380.

Mfg.'s Sug. Retail	$259	$230	$200	$175	$160	$145	$130	$115

MODEL SMC-918 — 9x18 Makarov, double action, semi-auto, 7 shot mag., current mfg.

Mfg.'s Sug. Retail	$215	$195	$180	$165	$150	$135	$115	$105

MODEL R-9 — 9mm Para., patterned after Browning Hi-Power, double action, 13 shot mag., blued finish, steel construction, checkered wood grips. Imported 1986-87 only.

	$275	$230	$200	$180	$165	$155	$145

Last Mfg.'s Sug. Retail was $375.

Grading	100%	98%	95%	90%	80%	70%	60%

MODEL PPH — .380 ACP, patterned after Walther PP, alloy frame, double action, plastic grips with thumbrest, blued finish. Imported 1986-87 only.

| | $200 | $170 | $140 | $125 | $115 | $105 | $95 |

Last Mfg.'s Sug. Retail was $225.

MODEL MBK-9HP — 9mm Para., patterned after Browning Hi-Power, double action, 4⅔ in. barrel, 14 shot mag., blued finish, steel construction, checkered wood grips, 36 oz. Imported 1992 only.

| | $315 | $270 | $250 | $225 | $200 | $185 | $170 |

Last Mfg.'s Sug. Retail was $349.

▲ *Model MBK-9HPC* — compact variation of the Model MBK-9HP with 4 in. barrel, 34 oz. Imported 1992 only.

| | $325 | $275 | $250 | $225 | $200 | $185 | $170 |

Last Mfg.'s Sug. Retail was $359.

MODEL PJK-9HP — 9mm Para., patterned after Browning Hi-Power, all steel construction, 4¾ in. barrel, thumb safety, 10 (C/B 1994) or 13* shot mag. and cleaning rod, 32 oz. Importation began 1992.

| Mfg.'s Sug. Retail | $295 | $255 | $230 | $215 | $195 | $180 | $165 | $145 |

Add $80 for industrial hard chrome finish (Model PJK-9HPC - includes Uncle Mike's rubber grips).

MODEL GKK-92C — 9mm Para., double action semi-auto, 4 in. barrel, 14 shot mag., improved variation of MBK models, includes same accessories as PJK-9H, 34 oz. Importation disc. 1993.

| | $315 | $280 | $255 | $230 | $200 | $185 | $170 |

Last Mfg.'s Sug. Retail was $369.

MODEL GKK-40C — .40 S&W cal., 9 shot mag., otherwise similar to GKK-45. Importation began 1995.

| Mfg.'s Sug. Retail | $349 | $300 | $265 | $230 | $200 | $180 | $160 | $145 |

MODEL GKK-45 — .45 ACP cal., double action semi-auto, all steel, 4¼ in. barrel, blue (disc. 1994) or chrome (Model GKK-45C) finish checkered walnut grips, 8 shot mag., approx. 37 oz. Importation began 1993.

| Mfg.'s Sug. Retail | $349 | $300 | $265 | $230 | $200 | $180 | $160 | $145 |

RIFLES

MODEL SA-85M SEMI-AUTO — 7.62x39mm K. cal., semi-auto, sporter rifle utilizing semi-auto AKM action, 16.3 in. barrel, 6 shot detachable mag., thumb hole stock, 7 lbs. 10 oz. Importation began 1991.

| Mfg.'s Sug. Retail | $399 | $350 | $315 | $280 | $250 | $225 | $200 | $185 |

F.I.E.
Firearms import & export previously located in Hialeah, FL.

F.I.E. filed bankruptcy in November of 1990 and all models are discontinued. Parts and service for these older firearms may be obtained through Heritage Manufacturing, Inc. located in Opa Locka, FL (see Trademark Index), even though all warranties on F.I.E. guns are void.

ARMINIUS REVOLVERS: DOUBLE ACTION

All pistols under this heading were manufactured in W. Germany under the trademark Arminius. .22 cal. is 8 shot, .32 S&W is 7 shot, all others 6 shot.

MODEL 522TB — .22 LR, blue finish, 4 in. barrel, 8 shot.

| | $130 | $100 | $85 | $75 | $70 | $65 | $60 |

Last Mfg.'s Sug. Retail was $174.

Add $23 for walnut grips.

Grading	100%	98%	95%	90%	80%	70%	60%

722 SERIES — .22 LR, blue (standard) or chrome finish (disc. 1985), 6 in. barrel, 8 shot.

| | $125 | $100 | $90 | $80 | $70 | $65 | $60 |

Last Mfg.'s Sug. Retail was $161.

Add $23 for walnut grips.
Add $49 for .22 LR/.22 Mag. combo.
Add $15 for chrome finish.

STANDARD REVOLVER — .22 LR, .22 Mag., .32 Mag. or .38 Spl., 2 or 4 in. barrel, blued finish, fixed sights, without ejector assembly. U.S. mfg. 1989-90.

| | $80 | $70 | $65 | $60 | $55 | $50 | $45 |

Last Mfg.'s Sug. Retail was $101.

Add $19 for chrome finish (2 in. barrel only).
Add $38 for gold plated finish (2 in. barrel only).
Add $23 for .22 Combo package (2 cylinders - 4 in. barrel only).
Models with 4 in. barrels are available in blued finish only.

MODEL 532TB — .32 S&W, blue (standard) or chrome finish (disc. 1985), adj. sights, 4 in. barrel, 7 shot.

| | $145 | $120 | $100 | $80 | $75 | $70 | $65 |

Last Mfg.'s Sug. Retail was $183.

Add $23 for walnut grips.
Add $15 for chrome finish.

MODEL 732B — similar to Model 532TB, except has 6 in. barrel and fixed sights. Imported 1988 only.

| | $120 | $100 | $90 | $80 | $70 | $65 | $60 |

Last Mfg.'s Sug. Retail was $140.

MODEL N-38 (TITAN TIGER) — .38 Spl., blue (standard) or chrome finish (disc. 1985), 2 or 4 in. barrel, fixed sights. Disc. 1990.

| | $130 | $110 | $95 | $80 | $75 | $65 | $60 |

Last Mfg.'s Sug. Retail was $176.

Add $23 for walnut grips.
Add $15 for chrome finish.

ZEPHYR — .38 Spl., 5 shot, aluminum construction, 2 in. barrel, blue finish, checkered grips, 14 oz. Mfg. 1990 only.

| | $145 | $120 | $100 | $80 | $75 | $70 | $65 |

Last Mfg.'s Sug. Retail was $189.

▲ *Lady Zephyr* — similar to Zephyr, except has gold trimmed parts, scrimshawed red rose on ivory polymer grips, and gold case. Mfg. 1990 only.

| | $250 | $210 | $180 | $155 | $135 | $115 | $95 |

Last Mfg.'s Sug. Retail was $295.

MODEL 384TB — .38 Spl., blue (standard) or chrome finish (disc. 1985), 6 shot, 4 in. barrel.

| | $150 | $125 | $105 | $85 | $80 | $70 | $65 |

Last Mfg.'s Sug. Retail was $195.

Add $23 for walnut grips.
Add $13 for chrome finish.

MODEL 386TB — .38 Spl., blue (standard) or chrome finish (disc. 1985), 6 shot, 6 in. barrel.

| | $150 | $125 | $105 | $85 | $80 | $70 | $65 |

Last Mfg.'s Sug. Retail was $195.

Add $23 for walnut grips.
Add $13 for chrome finish.

.357 MAG. SERIES — .357 Mag., blue (standard) or chrome finish (disc. 1985), 6 shot, 3 (Model 3573TB), 4 (Model 3574TB), or 6 (Model 3576TB) in. barrels.

| | $200 | $170 | $135 | $120 | $110 | $100 | $90 |

Last Mfg.'s Sug. Retail was $255.

Add $23 for walnut grips.
Add $15 for chrome finish.

F

Grading	100%	98%	95%	90%	80%	70%	60%

REVOLVERS: DISC. SNUB-NOSE

Currently manufactured 2 in. snub-nosed revolvers are listed in the previous category under Standard Revolver, Titan Tiger, and Zephyr.

222 SERIES — .22 LR & .22 Mag. cal., blue (standard) or chrome finish, 2 in. snub-nose barrel. Disc. 1985.

	100%	98%	95%	90%	80%	70%	60%
	$135	$115	$90	$85	$75	$65	$60

Last Mfg.'s Sug. Retail was $120.

Add $15 for walnut grips.
Add $45 for .22 LR/.22 Mag. combo.

▲ *222B SERIES* — .22 LR only starting 1989, similar to 222 Series, reintroduced 1987-1989.

	$150	$120	$105	$85	$80	$70	$65

Last Mfg.'s Sug. Retail was $185.

Add $45 for .22 LR/.22 Mag. combo (disc. 1988).

232 SERIES — .32 S&W, blue (standard) or chrome finish, 2 in. barrel. Disc.

	$120	$90	$85	$75	$65	$60	$55

Add $15 for walnut grips.
Add $14 for adj. sights.
Add $28 for chrome finish.

▲ *232B SERIES* — similar to 232 Series, 2 in. barrel. Reintroduced 1987-1989.

	$150	$125	$110	$95	$85	$75	$70

Last Mfg.'s Sug. Retail was $185.

Add $5 for adj. sights.

MODEL 382TB — .38 Spl., blue (standard) or chrome finish, 2 in. barrel. Disc. 1985.

	$125	$110	$100	$90	$80	$75	$65

Last Mfg.'s Sug. Retail was $145.

Add $15 for walnut grips.
Add $16 for chrome finish.

MODEL 3572 — .357 Mag., blue (standard) or chrome finish, 2 in. barrel. Disc. 1984.

	$223	$170	$160	$135	$125	$115	$100

Add $15 for walnut grips.
Add $17 for chrome finish.

REVOLVERS: SINGLE ACTION

Combo designations on below listed models indicate 2 cylinders (.22 LR/.22 Mag.).

COWBOY — .22 LR or .22 LR/Mag. combo, 3¼ or 6 in. barrel, blued finish, square butt grip, without ejector tube, fixed sights. U.S. mfg. 1989-90.

	$75	$65	$50	$45	$40	$35	$30

Last Mfg.'s Sug. Retail was $95.

Add $23 for combo.

GOLD RUSH — .22 LR or .22 LR/Mag. combo, 3¼, 4¾, or 6½ in. barrel, round (3¼ in. barrel only) or square butt grip, gold band on barrel and cylinder, ivory-tex grips. U.S. mfg. 1989-90.

	$155	$125	$110	$95	$85	$75	$70

Last Mfg.'s Sug. Retail was $189.

Add $47 for combo.

TEXAS RANGER (TEX 22 SERIES) — .22 LR or .22 Mag. (combo only), 3¼ (new 1986), 4¾, 6½ (new 1989), 7, or 9 in. barrel, 6 shot, blue only. Mfg. U.S.

	$80	$70	$60	$50	$45	$40	$35

Last Mfg.'s Sug. Retail was $108.

Add $23 for combo.
Add $6 for 9 in. barrel.
This model with a 3¼ in. barrel is called the Little Ranger.

Grading	100%	98%	95%	90%	80%	70%	60%

BUFFALO SCOUT (E15 SERIES) — .22 LR or .22 Mag., blue (standard) or chrome finish, 4¾ in. barrel. Mfg. in Brescia, Italy - disc.

| | | $75 | $55 | $45 | $35 | $35 | $30 | $30 |

Last Mfg.'s Sug. Retail was $98.

Add $23 for walnut grips.
Add $23 for combo.
Add $9 for chrome or blue/gold finish.

▲ *The Yellow Rose Combo* — all metal parts 24 Kt. gold plated, smooth walnut grips. Mfg. 1986-90.

$130 $110 $95

Last Mfg.'s Sug. Retail was $161.

Add $151 for scrimshawed ivory polymer grips - walnut cased (new 1989).

LEGEND S.A.A. (PL-22 SERIES) — .22 LR or .22 Mag., blue only. Mfg. in Brescia, Italy. Disc. 1984.

$120 $90 $85 $75 $65 $60 $55

Add $3 for walnut grips.
Add $17 for combo.

HOMBRE MODEL — .357 Mag., .44 Mag., or .45 cal., color case hardened receiver, 5½ (disc. 1985), 6, or 7½ in. barrel, 45 oz., smooth walnut grips. Mfg. W. Germany.

$220 $180 $145 $130 $120 $110 $100

Last Mfg.'s Sug. Retail was $265.

Add $25 for brass back strap and triggerguard (disc.).

▲ *Golden Hombre* — same general specifications as Hombre, except all metal surfaces are plated in 24Kt. gold.

$300 $210 $145

Last Mfg.'s Sug. Retail was $350.

Add $65 for ivory polymer grips (new 1989).

TITAN PISTOLS: SEMI-AUTO

TITAN II (E32 SERIES) — .32 ACP (disc. 1988), or .380 ACP, single action, blue (standard) or chrome finish. Mfg. in USA - disc.

$195 $160 $135 $120 $105 $95 $85

Last Mfg.'s Sug. Retail was $220.

Add $25 for walnut grips.
Add $10 for chrome finish.

This series was redesigned in 1988 to be shorter and more compact. Older series Titans are worth approx. $50 less than values shown above.

SUPER TITAN II — .32 ACP (disc. 1988), or .380 ACP, single action, 12 shot mag. in .32 ACP, 11 for .380 cal., walnut grips, standard blue only. Mfg. U.S. - disc.

$215 $185 $155 $135 $120 $105 $95

Last Mfg.'s Sug. Retail was $260.

.22 TITAN II (E22) — .22 LR, single action, 10 shot mag., blue finish only. Walnut grips standard. Mfg. 1990 only.

$130 $105 $90 $80 $70 $65 $60

Last Mfg.'s Sug. Retail was $161.

▲ *Lady .22* — similar to .22 TITAN II except has combination blue/gold finish with scrimshawed red rose on ivory polymer grips. New 1990.

$185 $155 $130 $120 $105 $95 $85

Last Mfg.'s Sug. Retail was $208.

THE BEST (A27) — .25 ACP, single action, blue only, deluxe finish, walnut grips, steel frame, 6 shot mag. Mfg. in Spain by Astra. Importation disc. 1988.

$125 $105 $90 $80 $70 $65 $60

Last Mfg.'s Sug. Retail was $155.

Grading	100%	98%	95%	90%	80%	70%	60%

.25 TITAN (E27 SERIES) — .25 ACP, single action, blue (disc. 1989) or Dyna-chrome finish (standard 1990).

	100%	98%	95%	90%	80%	70%	60%
	$60	$50	$45	$40	$35	$30	$30

Last Mfg.'s Sug. Retail was $77.

Subtract $5 for blued finish.
Add $26 for gold trim (new 1986).
Add $62 for Misty Gold finish (1988 only).

▲ *Titan Tigress* — similar to .25 Titan except is entirely gold plated and cased, ladies pistol. Imported 1989-90 only.

	100%	98%	95%
	$130	$110	$95

Last Mfg.'s Sug. Retail was $153.

.25 TITAN (E38 SERIES) — .25 ACP, similar to E27 series except has standard blue finish. Mfg. 1990 only.

	100%	98%	95%	90%	80%	70%	60%
	$50	$45	$40	$35	$30	$30	$25

Last Mfg.'s Sug. Retail was $59.

Add $9 for Dyna-chrome finish.

SSP SERIES — .32 ACP or .380 ACP cal., single action semi-auto, $3\frac{1}{8}$ in. barrel, 5 shot mag., blue or chrome finish, composition grips, 25 oz. Mfg. in U.S. - 1990 only.

	100%	98%	95%	90%	80%	70%	60%
	$120	$95	$85	$75	$65	$60	$55

Last Mfg.'s Sug. Retail was $146.

Add $19 for chrome finish.

▲ *Lady SSP* — similar to SSP except has gold trimmed parts, scrimshawed red rose on ivory polymer grips, and gold case. Mfg. 1990 only.

	100%	98%	95%	90%	80%	70%	60%
	$210	$180	$155	$135	$120	$105	$95

Last Mfg.'s Sug. Retail was $250.

TZ-75 — 9mm Para., double action, 4.72 in. barrel, steel frame and slide, 15 shot mag., patterned after the CZ-75 action, 35 oz. Imported 1982-1989. This model was updated in 1988 (Series 88).

	100%	98%	95%	90%	80%	70%	60%
	$375	$325	$290	$270	$250	$235	$220

Last Mfg.'s Sug. Retail was $440.

Add $20 for satin chrome finish (new 1986).
Add $20 for black rubber grips.

TZ-75 SERIES 88 — 9mm Para. or .41 Action Express cal., improved TZ-75 action, 4.72 in. barrel, steel frame and slide, 11 (.41 AE) or 17 (9mm) shot mag., fixed removable rear sight, choice of matte blue, satin chrome, or blue slide/chrome frame finish, updated CZ-75 action, 35 oz. Mfg. 1988-90.

	100%	98%	95%	90%	80%	70%	60%
	$435	$360	$330	$295	$280	$260	$240

Last Mfg.'s Sug. Retail was $519.

Add $97 for .41 Action Express cal.
Add $20 for satin chrome on 9mm, $29 on .41 AE.
Add $14 for black rubber grips.

This model is also available with a blue slide/chrome frame (I.P.S.C. configuration) at no extra charge.

The TZ-75 Series 88 was re-engineered in 1988 to include: frame mounted sear locking safety (cocked and locked), Colt style firing pin safety block, improved recessed slide serrations, muzzle barrel swell, bobbed hammer design, elongated combat style slide stop, new mag. release, and removable rear sight.

▲ *TZ-75 Combo* — includes both .41 Action Express cal. and 9mm Para. barrels. Mfg. 1990 only.

	100%	98%	95%	90%	80%	70%	60%
	$615	$535	$475	$430	$395	$370	$350

Last Mfg.'s Sug. Retail was $709.

Add $29 for satin chrome or blue slide/chrome frame finish.

▲ *TZ-75 Series 88 Govt. Model* — 9mm Para. only, compact variation of the TZ-75 Series 88, $3\frac{3}{5}$ in. barrel, 12 shot mag., checkered walnut grips, $33\frac{1}{2}$ oz. Mfg. 1990 only.

	100%	98%	95%	90%	80%	70%	60%
	$435	$360	$330	$295	$280	$260	$240

Last Mfg.'s Sug. Retail was $519.

Add $20 for satin chrome or blue slide/chrome frame finish.

Grading	100%	98%	95%	90%	80%	70%	60%

▲ **TZ-75 Series 88 with ported barrel** — similar to the TZ-75 Series 88 except has 5 in. ported barrel and slide. Mfg. 1990 only.

	$615	$535	$475	$430	$395	$370	$350

Last Mfg.'s Sug. Retail was $709.

▲ **Compensated TZ-75 Series 88** — similar to the TZ-75 Series 88 except has $5\frac{3}{4}$ in. compensated barrel, 42 oz. Mfg. 1990 only.

	$700	$615	$535	$475	$430	$395	$370

Last Mfg.'s Sug. Retail was $804.

MODEL 722 TP SILHOUETTE PISTOL — .22 LR, bolt action target pistol, 10 in. free-floating barrel, 4-way adj. trigger, micro adj. rear sight, 6 or 10 shot mag., stippled pistol grip and forearm, supplied with 2-piece scope mount, 3.4 lbs. Mfg. 1990 only.

	$220	$190	$160	$140	$125	$115	$100

Last Mfg.'s Sug. Retail was $263.

SPECTRE PISTOL — 9mm Para. or .45 ACP cal., double action, unique triple action blowback system with two piece bolt, 6 in. barrel, military style configuration, adj. sights, 30 or 50 (optional with unique 4 column configuation) shot mag., 4.8 lbs. Mfg. 1989-90 only.

	$675	$600	$525	$480	$440	$400	$360

Last Mfg.'s Retail was $718.

Add $14 for mag. loading tool.

KG-99 — 9mm, paramilitary design pistol, 36 shot mag. Mini-99 also available with 20 shot mag. and 3 in. barrel. Disc. 1984.

	$550	$475	$440	$400	$365	$330	$300

This model was not manufactured but sold by F.I.E.

DERRINGERS

MODEL D38 — .38 Spl., O/U, chrome finish only, no transfer bar. Disc. 1985.

	$70	$60	$55	$45	$40	$35	$30

Last Mfg.'s Sug. Retail was $82.

Add $17 for walnut grips.

MODEL D86 — .38 Spl., single shot, 3 in. barrel, internal transfer bar safety, ammo storage compartment, blue or Dyna-chrome finish, 11 oz. New 1986.

	$80	$65	$55	$50	$45	$40	$35

Last Mfg.'s Sug. Retail was $95.

Add $9 for Dyna-chrome finish.
Add $25 for deluxe model (walnut stocks).
Add $60 for Misty Gold finish (disc.).

RIFLES: SEMI-AUTO

GR-8 BLACK BEAUTY — .22 cal. only, 14 shot, $19\frac{1}{2}$ in. barrel, 64 oz., tubular feed, black nylon stock, patterned after Rem. Nylon 66. Mfg. by C.B.C. of Brazil. F.I.E. Importation disc. 1988, now imported by K.B.I.

	$90	$75	$70	$65	$60	$55	$50

Last Mfg.'s Sug. Retail was $100.

PARA RIFLE — .22 LR, paramilitary designed rifle with case, takedown, 11 shot, matte black receiver finish. Mfg. by L. Franchi between 1979-1984. Imported into the U.S. from 1985-88.

	$225	$195	$155	$140	$130	$120	$110

Last Mfg.'s Sug. Retail was $225.

8,000 of this model were manufactured by L. Franchi. 5,000 went to the Italian Government and were used as training rifles (with German scopes). The remainder has been imported by F.I.E. (without scopes).

Grading	100%	98%	95%	90%	80%	70%	60%

SPECTRE CARBINE — 9mm Para., same action as Spectre pistol, paramilitary design carbine, collapsible metal butt stock, 30 or 50 (opt.) shot mag., adj. rear sight, with pistol and forearm grip. New 1989.

	$525	$425	$365	$300	$275	$250	$225

Last Mfg.'s Sug. Retail was $700.

RIFLES: BOLT-ACTION

MODEL 122 — .22 LR, 6 or 10 shot clip mag., 21 in. tapered barrel, Monte Carlo walnut stock, adj. sights. Mfg. by Hamilton & Hunter. New 1986.

	$100	$80	$70	$60	$55	$50	$45

Last Mfg.'s Sug. Retail was $115.

MODEL 322 — .22 LR, competition model, 26.2 in. floating barrel, adj. trigger, 6 or 10 shot mag., stippled pistol grip, 7 lbs. New 1990.

	$580	$425	$380	$340	$295	$260	$230

Last Mfg.'s Sug. Retail was $665.

MODEL 422 — similar to Model 322 except has heavy barrel, 9 lbs. New 1990.

	$580	$425	$380	$340	$295	$260	$230

Last Mfg.'s Sug. Retail was $665.

SHOTGUNS

All Franchi shotguns can be located in the Franchi section of this text.

S.O.B. — 12, 20, or .410 ga., 18½ in. single barrel, pistol grip only. Disc. 1984.

	$100	$90	$80	$70	$60	$55	$50

THE STURDY O/U — 12 or 20 ga., 3 in. chambers, 28 in. barrels, vent. rib and barrels, engraved silver finish receiver, double triggers, extractors, manufactured by Maroccini of Italy. Imported 1985-1988.

	$300	$275	$250	$235	$220	$205	$190

Last Mfg.'s Sug. Retail was $350.

▲ *Sturdy Deluxe Priti* — similar to The Sturdy model except has deluxe walnut. Importation disc. 1988.

	$325	$290	$260	$240	$225	$205	$195

Last Mfg.'s Sug. Retail was $380.

Add $70 for ejectors, SST, and choke tubes.

▲ *Model 12 Deluxe* — 12 ga. only, SST, auto ejectors, multi-choked barrels, select walnut. Imported 1988 only.

	$320	$290	$260	$240	$225	$205	$195

Last Mfg.'s Sug. Retail was $380.

THE BRUTE — 12, 20, or .410 ga., 19 in. barrels, 30 in. overall length. Side-by-side action, disc. 1984.

	$195	$150	$140	$120	$110	$100	$90

SPAS-12 — this model appears under the Franchi heading in the F section.

SAS-12 — this model appears under the Franchi heading in the F section.

LAW-12 — this model appears under the Franchi heading in the F section.

FMJ

Manufacturer located in Copperhill, TN. Dealer sales.

DERRINGERS

SINGLE BARREL DERRINGER — .45 LC x.410 (2½ in.), spur trigger, black oxide finish, 16 oz. New 1993.

Mfg.'s Sug. Retail	$70	$60	$50	$40	$35	$30	$25	$20

Grading	100%	98%	95%	90%	80%	70%	60%
.22 LR/.45 LC O/U — .22 LR x.45 LC/.410 ga. New 1995.							
Mfg.'s Sug. Retail	$90	$70	$60	$50	$40	$35	$30	$25
DOUBLE BARREL DERRINGER — .45 LC x.410 (3 in.), SxS, spur trigger, single hammer, 20 oz. New 1994.							
Mfg.'s Sug. Retail	$110	$95	$85	$70	$60	$50	$40	$35

HANDGUNS

MODEL R REVOLVER — .22 LR, 6 shot. New 1995.							
Mfg.'s Sug. Retail	$90	$70	$60	$50	$40	$35	$30	$25
MODEL MR REVOLVER — .45 LC/.410 ga., 5 shot, manual rotation. New 1996.							
Mfg.'s Sug. Retail	$140	$115	$85	$65	$55	$50	$45	$40
MODEL PP — .22 LR or .380 ACP cal., stainless construction. New 1995.							
Mfg.'s Sug. Retail	$150	$120	$90	$70				

SHOTGUNS

BEGINNERS SHOTGUN (SH) — .410 ga., 3 in. chamber, spur trigger, fixed skeleton or folding stock, 2 lbs. New 1994.							
Mfg.'s Sug. Retail	$100	$85	$70	$60	$50	$40	$35	$30
STANDARD MODEL — .410 ga., fixed or folding stock. New 1996.							
Mfg.'s Sug. Retail	$145	$120	$90	$70	$60	$55	$50	$45
Add $5 for folding stock.							

FTL

Previously manufactured by Wilkerson Arms located in Covina, CA for the FTL Marketing Corp. located in N. Hollywood, CA.

FTL AUTO NINE SEMI-AUTO PISTOL — .22 LR cal., single action, hammerless, blowback action, 8 shot mag., checkered plastic grips, fixed sights. Disc.

	$150	$125	$105	$95	$85	$75	$65

FABARM, S.p.A.

Manufacturer located in Brescia, Italy. Certain models have had limited importation by Ithaca Acquisition Corp. located in King Ferry, NY during 1993-95. Previously imported and distributed (1988-90) by St. Lawrence Sales, Inc. located in Lake Orion, MI. Previously imported until 1986 by Beeman Precision Arms, Inc. located in Santa Rosa, CA.

Fabarm guns are currently not being imported. Prices and information listed below reflect the most current information available on this trademark.

SHOTGUNS: O/U

FIELD MODEL — 12 ga. only, 29⅛ in. VR barrels, single trigger, ejectors, silver finished receiver, also available in Skeet and Trap models. Disc. 1985.

	$695	$595	$550	$500	$460	$420	$390

Last Mfg.'s Sug. Retail was $795.

Grading	100%	98%	95%	90%	80%	70%	60%

SKEET/TRAP COMBINATION SET — 12 ga. only, is supplied with both skeet and trap barrel assemblies, cased. Disc. 1986.

	$1,050	$900	$840	$780	$720	$670	$600

Last Mfg.'s Sug. Retail was $1,195.

Add $39 for high gloss wood finish.
Add $30 for auto safety.

Models below have boxlock actions with coin finished receivers and light engraving.

GAMMA FIELD — 12 or 20 (disc.) ga., SST, ejectors, 26, 28, 29, 30, or 32 in. VR barrels, fixed or innerchokes, checkered walnut stock and forearm, 6½ lbs. Importation began 1989.

Mfg.'s Sug. Retail	$1,044	$840	$715	$660	$600	$550	$450	$375

Add $28 for 5 innerchokes with wrench (3 in. chambers in 12 ga.).
Add $50 for 20 ga. (3 in. chambers).

▲ *Gamma AL Superlight* — 12 ga. only, similar to Gamma Field except receiver is made from Ergal light alloy, 6 lbs. Imported 1989-1990.

	$875	$760	$695	$625	$550	$450	$375

Last Mfg.'s Sug. Retail was $970.

Add $41 for 5 innerchokes with wrench.
Add $66 for 20 ga. with 3 in. chambers. New 1990.
This model is chambered for 2¾ in. shells only.

GAMMA SPORTING CLAYS COMPETITION — 12 ga. only, designed for sporting clays competition, SST, 28, 29, or 30 in. VR, (10mm) and barrels supplied with 5 innerchokes, special recoil pad, ejectors, checkered walnut stock and forearm. Importation began 1989.

Mfg.'s Sug. Retail	$1,175	$950	$825	$725	$650	$575	$495	$400

Add $17 for stock and forend trap (disc. - includes 28 in. barrels with 5 choke tubes).

GAMMA SKEET — 12 ga. only, 27½ or 28 in. VR barrels, SST, ejectors, supplied with 5 innerchokes, special recoil pad, checkered walnut stock and forearm, reversed Skeet chokes new 1994. Importation began 1989.

Mfg.'s Sug. Retail	$1,107	$875	$735	$695	$635	$550	$450	$375

GAMMA TRAP — 12 ga. only, 29 or 30 in. VR barrels with special trap chokes and 10mm rib, SST, ejectors, checkered Monte Carlo stock and forearm, 7½ lbs. Importation began 1989.

Mfg.'s Sug. Retail	$1,107	$875	$735	$695	$635	$550	$450	$375

GAMMA PARADOX — 12 ga. only, 25 in. VR barrels with top barrel rifled and lower barrel supplied with 3 innerchokes, SST, ejectors, checkered walnut stock and forearm, 6 lbs. 6 oz. Imported 1989-1990.

	$850	$750	$695	$625	$550	$450	$375

Last Mfg.'s Sug. Retail was $945.

▲ *Gamma Paradox AL Superlight* — similar to Gamma Paradox except receiver is made from Ergal light alloy, 5 lbs. 7 oz. Imported 1989-1990.

	$875	$760	$695	$625	$550	$450	$375

Last Mfg.'s Sug. Retail was $960.

EURALFA — 12 ga., 2¾ in. chambers, 26 or 28 in. VR barrels with fixed chokes, DT or SNT, extractors, blued receiver with photo engraving, 6½ lbs. Imported 1989-1990.

	$495	$460	$420	$390	$350	$310	$275

Last Mfg.'s Sug. Retail was $571.

▲ *Euralfa AL Superlight* — 12 ga., similar to Euralfa except receiver is made from Ergal light alloy, 6 lbs. Imported 1989-1990.

	$515	$475	$430	$400	$360	$320	$285

Last Mfg.'s Sug. Retail was $603.

▲ *Euralfa Trap* — 12 ga. only, 3 in. chambers, 30 in. barrels bored IM/F. Imported 1990.

	$550	$495	$460	$430	$400	$360	$320

Last Mfg.'s Sug. Retail was $636.

F

Grading	100%	98%	95%	90%	80%	70%	60%

▲ **Euralfa Magnum** — 12 ga., 3 in. chambers, 26, 28, or 29 in. VR (10mm wide) barrels with fixed chokes, rubber recoil pad. Imported 1989-1990.

| | $515 | $475 | $430 | $400 | $360 | $320 | $285 |

Last Mfg.'s Sug. Retail was $587.

▲ **Euralfa Innerchoke** — 12 ga. only, 3 in. chambers, 28 in. barrels. Imported 1990 only.

| | $560 | $500 | $460 | $430 | $400 | $360 | $320 |

Last Mfg.'s Sug. Retail was $652.

▲ **Euralfa Slug** — 12 ga. only, 24 in. barrels bored cyl./cyl. Imported 1990.

| | $500 | $475 | $430 | $400 | $360 | $320 | $285 |

Last Mfg.'s Sug. Retail was $571.

EURALFA PARADOX — 12 ga. only, similar to Euralfa except 25 in. VR barrels with top barrel rifled and lower barrel supplied with 3 innerchokes, 6 lbs. 6 oz. Imported 1989-1990.

| | $550 | $495 | $460 | $430 | $400 | $360 | $320 |

Last Mfg.'s Sug. Retail was $636.

▲ **Euralfa Paradox AL Superlight** — similar to Euralfa Paradox except receiver is made from Ergal light alloy, 5 lbs. 7 oz. Imported 1989-1990.

| | $550 | $495 | $460 | $430 | $400 | $360 | $320 |

Last Mfg.'s Sug. Retail was $636.

SHOTGUNS: SEMI-AUTO

The models listed below are gas operated self compensating, have 4 shot mags., aluminum receivers, twin action bars, blued receiver with photo etched game scene engraving, and checkered walnut stock and forearm. Add $25 for De Luxe engraving or camouflage wood finish.

ELLEGI STANDARD — 12 ga. only, 28 in. VR barrel with fixed choke, blued receiver, gold trigger, 6 lbs. 9 oz. Imported 1989-1990.

| | $525 | $450 | $375 | $325 | $300 | $275 | $250 |

Last Mfg.'s Sug. Retail was $619.

▲ **Ellegi Multichoke** — similar to Ellegi Standard except 5 different choke tubes extend length of barrel up to 6 in., average weight is 6 lbs. 9 oz. Imported 1989-1990.

| | $540 | $475 | $395 | $350 | $325 | $300 | $265 |

Last Mfg.'s Sug. Retail was $644.

The standard barrel length on this model is 24½ in. (30½ in. with full extra-long choke tube).

▲ **Ellegi Innerchoke** — 12 ga. only, 3 in. chamber, 28 in. VR barrel with 5 innerchokes supplied, 7 lbs. Imported 1989-1990.

| | $540 | $475 | $395 | $350 | $325 | $300 | $265 |

Last Mfg.'s Sug. Retail was $644.

▲ **Ellegi Magnum** — 12 ga. only, 3 in. chamber, 30 in. VR barrel with fixed choke, recoil pad, 7¼ lbs. Imported 1989-1990.

| | $525 | $450 | $375 | $325 | $300 | $275 | $250 |

Last Mfg.'s Sug. Retail was $619.

▲ **Ellegi Super Goose** — 12 ga. only, 3 in. chamber, 35½ in. VR (12mm wide) barrel with fixed choke, adj. rifle rear sight, supplied with rail for mounting scope rings, rubber recoil pad, designed especially for long range shooting, 7½ lbs. Imported 1989-1990.

| | $625 | $495 | $425 | $375 | $340 | $315 | $280 |

Last Mfg.'s Sug. Retail was $734.

▲ **Ellegi Slug** — 12 ga. only, 24½ in. barrel, adj. rear sight and bead front, 6 lbs. 9 oz. Imported 1989-1990.

| | $545 | $475 | $395 | $350 | $325 | $300 | $265 |

Last Mfg.'s Sug. Retail was $652.

Add $200 for combo set (includes innerchoked 28 in. barrel).

▲ **Ellegi Police** — 12 ga. only, 20 in. cylinder bored barrel, matte black receiver, non-glare stock and forearm. Imported 1989-1990.

| | $495 | $425 | $360 | $300 | $275 | $250 | $225 |

Last Mfg.'s Sug. Retail was $587.

Grading	100%	98%	95%	90%	80%	70%	60%

SHOTGUNS: SIDE X SIDE

The models listed below have boxlock actions with added sideplates.

BETA MODEL — 12 ga. only, 2¾ in. chambers, standard model with checkered walnut stock and forearm, ST, ejectors. Imported 1989 only.

	$695	$625	$550	$450	$375	$300	$250

Last Mfg.'s Sug. Retail was $920.

This model was replaced by the Beta Lux in 1990.

BETA LUX — 12 ga. only, 3 in. chambers, SST, ejectors, boxlock action, 24, 26, 28, or 30 in. barrels bored F/M, 6.6 lbs. New 1990.

Mfg.'s Sug. Retail	$1,270	$1,100	$875	$725	$625	$550	$475	$400

Add $30 for 5 Innerchokes.
Add $114 for competition trap/pigeon model (disc.)

BETA EUROPE — 12 ga. only, deluxe model with coin finished game scene engraved sideplates, 26½ or 27½ in. barrels with fixed chokes, ejectors, DT or SST, checkered English stock and splinter forearm, 6 lbs. 6 oz. Imported 1989-1990.

	$1,400	$1,100	$850	$700	$575	$495	$450

Last Mfg.'s Sug. Retail was $1,711.

Add $33 for semi-beavertail forend.
Add $130 for competition trap/pigeon model.

SHOTGUNS: SLIDE ACTION

The models listed below are variations of the same action based on a twin bar slide system, alloy receiver with anti-glare finish (including barrel), rear triggerguard safety, and 2¾ or 3 in. shell interchangeability.

Add $25 for camouflage wood finish on the models listed below.

MODEL S.D.A.S.S. — 12 ga. only, 3 in. chamber, originally designed for police and self defense use, 8 shot tube mag., 20 or 24½ in. barrel threaded for external choke tubes, approx. 6 lbs. 6 oz. Imported 1989-1990.

	$325	$285	$260	$230	$195	$160	$140

Last Mfg.'s Sug. Retail was $415.

This model with 24½ in. barrel is threaded for external multi-chokes which can add up to 6 in. to the barrel length - available for a $17 extra charge.

▲ *Special Police* — similar to Model S.D.A.S.S. except has special heavy 20 in. cylinder bored barrel VR, cooling jacket, 6 shot mag., rubber recoil pad. Imported 1989-1990.

	$340	$295	$265	$230	$195	$160	$140

Last Mfg.'s Sug. Retail was $440.

▲ *Martial* — 12 ga. only, 18, 20, 28, 30, or 35½ (disc. 1989) in. barrel, fixed sights and choke, approx. 6¼ lbs. Imported 1989-1990.

	$330	$290	$260	$225	$190	$160	$140

Last Mfg.'s Sug. Retail was $424.

Add $41 for VR.
Add $20 for 35½ (disc. 1989) in. barrel.
Add $33 for multi-choke (plain rib with 1 choke and wrench).
Add $65 for innerchoke (includes 1 choke and wrench - VR barrel only).

SHOTGUNS: SINGLE BARREL

The models listed below have receivers made out of aluminum alloy, rear triggerguard safety, and matte black finish metal surfaces.

OMEGA STANDARD — 12, 20, or .410 ga., 3 in. chamber, 26 or 28 (12 ga. only) in. barrel, checkered beech stock and forearm, approx. 5 lbs. 5 oz. Imported 1989-1990.

	$120	$95	$80	$70	$60	$55	$50

Last Mfg.'s Sug. Retail was $139.

Grading	100%	98%	95%	90%	80%	70%	60%

▲ **Goose Gun** — similar to Omega Standard except is 12 ga. only with a 35½ in. barrel, 6 lbs. Imported 1989-1990.

	$135	$115	$90	$80	$70	$60	$55

Last Mfg.'s Sug. Retail was $156.

FABBRI s.n.c.

Manufacturer located in Concesio, Italy (previously located in Gardone). No current importer - the factory should be contacted directly (see Trademark Index) for more information regarding current information and prices on the models listed below.

During 1993, the Fabbri name was changed from Armi Fabbri to Fabbri s.n.c. Fabbri manufactures approx. 20-30 guns annually.

SHOTGUNS

Fabbri shotguns are typically Tomasoni engraved. Add a large premium ($10,000+) for those guns engraved by Fracassi, A. Galeazzi, or Mimi Torcoli.

SIDE-BY-SIDE SHOTGUN — 12 or 20 ga., one of the world's best current production guns, highest-quality sidelock, ejectors, full engraving. Disc.

Currently, Fabbri SxS shotguns manufactured within the last decade and in mint condition are priced in the $35,000-$38,000 range. Deduct $15,000 for scroll engraving.

O/U SHOTGUN — 12 or 20 ga., top-of-the-line quality with any combination of engraving, wood, and other options. Current retail starts at approx. $60,000 FOB Italy.

Mint guns mfg. 1967-1983 are currently priced in the $35,000-$38,500 range, guns mfg. between 1983-1989 are priced in the $45,000 range, and mfg. within the last 7 years is currently priced in the $50,000 range.

FABRIQUE NATIONALE

Manufacturer located in Herstal and Liege, Belgium. Established a contract with John M. Browning in 1902 for exclusive manufacture of various Browning Patent Firearms. In 1992, FN was acquired by GIAT of France.

Also See: Browning Arms under Rifles, Shotguns, and Pistols.

PISTOLS: SEMI-AUTO

For FN models 1900, 1903, 1905, 1910, 1922 (10/22), Baby Model, and the Model 10/71, please refer to the Browning Pistol section in this text.

PISTOLS: HI-POWERS

The F.N. Hi-Power (also known as P-35) was Browning's last pistol design. A single action semi-auto 9mm pistol, it was the first to incorporate a staggered high capacity magazine. It has a 4²¹⁄₃₂ in. barrel, 13 shot mag., hammer and mag. safeties, a wide variety of finishes and sight options. It's probably the most widely used military pistol in the world.

PRE-WAR COMMERCIAL HP — semi-auto pistol, 9mm, blue, wood grips, fixed or tangent rear sight, slotted for stock with tangent rear sight, 13 shot mag.

	100%	98%	95%	90%	80%	70%	60%
Fixed sight	$850	$625	$500	$450	$400	$350	$300
Tangent sight	$1,750	$1,000	$750	$600	$500	$400	$375

Add $400 for original flat board stock with attached holster.

Grading	100%	98%	95%	90%	80%	70%	60%

PRE-WAR MILITARY CONTRACT — mfg. under military contract for various European countries.

	100%	98%	95%	90%	80%	70%	60%
Lithuanian Crest	$2,250	$1,650	$1,000	$750	$600	$500	$400
Latvian Contract	$2,250	$1,650	$1,100	$750	$600	$500	$400
Estonian Contract	$2,000	$1,350	$850	$700	$600	$500	$400

Since so many variations have been manufactured for military contract, the listing above represents a few of the more interesting (and collectable) models.

WWII Production: Waffenamt Proofed

There is a range of finishes during Nazi production that varies from the excellent pre-war commercial finish on early guns assembled from captured parts to the roughly milled, poorly finished specimens mfg. late in the war. Values below assume all major parts (slide, barrel, and frame) are matching.

In recent years, many Nazi production Hi-Powers have had the rear grip strap milled out and slotted to accept a shoulder stock. Careful observation is advised before purchasing a "rare" (and expensive) slotted and tangent sight specimen.

▲ *Type I: Tangent sights — slotted* — assembled from existing pre-war Belgian army parts, quality is excellent, correct ser. range is quite limited, approx. 48,000-52,000. All are proofed WaA 613.

	100%	98%	95%	90%	80%	70%	60%
	$2,950	$2,300	$1,600	$1,000	$800	$600	$500

▲ *Type II* — tangent rear sight only, approx. 50,000 mfg. with generally good quality finish.

	100%	98%	95%	90%	80%	70%	60%
	$1,350	$900	$620	$475	$450	$400	$325

▲ *Type III Standard Fixed Sights*

	100%	98%	95%	90%	80%	70%	60%
	$490	$445	$410	$350	$310	$275	$240

POST-WAR PRODUCTION — commercial mfg. began 1950, first imported with BAC markings in 1954 (see Browning HP section). Military mfg. from 1946-present, early models are identifiable by an "A" serial number prefix and are not fitted with a magazine safety. In 1947 the rear slide bushing became hardened by a new heat treatment process. Other design modifications were added in 1950 making post 1950 barrels not interchangeable with earlier frames. Many thousands manufactured under various government contracts.

Add $50 if round hammer.
Add $200 for military pistols with crests.

▲ *Tangent sight only*

	100%	98%	95%	90%	80%	70%	60%
	$700	$600	$525	$440	$400	$370	$340

▲ *Tangent sight* — slotted for stock.

	100%	98%	95%	90%	80%	70%	60%
	$1,100	$950	$775	$650	$525	$440	$400

Add $150 for "T" prefix.

▲ *Fixed sight* — ring hammer.

	100%	98%	95%	90%	80%	70%	60%
	$450	$400	$375	$350	$325	$300	$275

MUSCAT AND OMAN CONTRACT

▲ *First Model* — 9 guns.

	100%	98%	95%
	$4,500	$2,750	$1,495

▲ *Second Model* — 27 guns.

	100%	98%	95%
	$3,000	$1,700	$995

INGLIS MANUFACTURED HI-POWERS — SEE INGLIS SECTION.

RIFLES

MODEL 1949 — semi-auto, 7mm, 7.65mm, 7.92mm, or .30-06 cal., gas operated 10 shot mag., 23 in. barrel, military rifle, tangent rear sight, military stock. Mfg. 160,000.

	100%	98%	95%	90%	80%	70%	60%
	$425	$350	$275	$250	$225	$185	$155

Add 10% for .30-06 cal.
Add 100% for sniper variation.

Grading	100%	98%	95%	90%	80%	70%	60%

FN SNIPER RIFLE (MODEL 30 - BOLT ACTION) — .308 cal., this model was a Mauser actioned Sniper Rifle equipped with 20 in. extra heavy barrel, flash hider, diopter sights, Hensoldt 4X scope, hard case, bipod, and sling. 51 were imported into the U.S. with the last retail price (1988) being $2,950. When encountered today, values will range from $3,500 and higher (depending on condition).

RIFLES: FAL/LAR/FNC SERIES

After tremendous price increases between 1985-1988, Fabrique Nationale decided in 1988 to discontinue this series completely. Not only are these rifles not exported to the U.S. any longer, but all production has ceased in Belgium as well. The only way FN will produce these models again is if they are given a large military contract - in which case a "side-order" of commercial guns may be built. 1989 Federal legislation regarding this type of paramilitary design also helped push up prices to their current level. FAL rifles were also mfg. in Israel by I.M.I.

F.N. FAL — semi-auto, French designation for the FN L.A.R. (light automatic rifle), otherwise similar to LAR. See values for LAR model listed below.

F.N. L.A.R. COMPETITION (LIGHT AUTOMATIC RIFLE) — .308 Win. (7.62x51), semi-auto, competition rifle with match flash hider, 21 in. barrel, adj. 4 position fire selector on automatic models, wood stock, aperture rear sight adj. from 100-600 meters, 9.4 lbs. Mfg. 1981-83.

	$2,000	$1,750	$1,600	$1,450	$1,300	$1,175	$1,000

This model was designated by the factory as the 50.00 Model.

Mid-1987 retail on this model was $1,258. The last Mfg.'s Sug. Retail was $3,179 (this price reflected the last exchange rate and special order status of this model).

▲ *Heavy barrel rifle* — barrel is twice as heavy as standard LAR, includes wood or synthetic stock, short wood forearm, and bi-pod, 12.2 lbs. Importation disc. 1988.

	$2,500	$2,150	$1,850	$1,500	$1,350	$1,200	$1,050

Add $400 for walnut stock.

There were 2 variations of this model. The Model 50.41 had a synthetic butt stock while the Model 50.42 had a wood butt stock with steel butt plate incorporating a top extension used for either shoulder resting or inverted grenade launching.

Mid-1987 retail on this model was $1,497 (Model 50.41) or $1,654 (Model 50.42). The last Mfg.'s Sug. Retail was $3,776 (this price reflected the last exchange rate and special order status of this model).

▲ *Paratrooper rifle* — similar to LAR model, except has folding stock, 8.3 lbs. Mfg. 1950-1988.

		$1,200	$1,000	$850	$750	$650	$575	$500

There were 2 variations of the Paratrooper LAR Model. The Model 50.63 had a stationary aperture rear sight and 18 in. barrel. The Model 50.64 was supplied with a 21 in. barrel and had a rear sight calibrated for either 150 or 200 meters. Both models retailed for the same price.

Mid-1987 retail on this model was $1,310 (both the Model 50.63 and 50.64). The last Mfg.'s Sug. Retail was $3,239 (this price reflected the last exchange rate and special order status of this model).

FNC MODEL — .223 Rem. (5.56mm), lightweight combat carbine, 18½ in. barrel, NATO approved, 30 shot mag., 8.4 lbs. Disc. 1987.

		$1,100	$975	$825	$725	$625	$550	$500

Add $50 for Paratrooper model (16 or 18½ in. barrel).

While rarer, the 16 in. barrel model incorporated a flash hider that did not perform as well as the flash hider used on the standard 18½ in. barrel.

Mid-1987 retail on this model was $749 (Standard Model) and $782 (Paratrooper Model). The last Mfg.'s Sug. Retail was $2,204 (Standard Model) and $2,322 (Paratrooper Model) - these prices reflected the last exchange rate and special order status of these models.

Grading	100%	98%	95%	90%	80%	70%	60%

F.N. MAUSER SPORTER DELUXE — available in popular American and European calibers, 24 in. barrel, adj. sight, checkered pistol grip stock. Mfg. 1947-1963.

	$650	$550	$495	$460	$300	$275	$250

F.N. PRESENTATION GRADE — similar to Deluxe, except engraved and select wood.

	$1,150	$935	$855	$770	$500	$475	$450

F.N. SUPREME BOLT ACTION — .243, .270, 7mm, .308, or .30-06, 24 in. barrel, peep sight, checkered pistol grip stock. Mfg. 1957-1975.

	$650	$550	$495	$460	$300	$275	$250

F.N. SUPREME MAGNUM — similar to Bolt Action, .264 Mag., 7mm Mag., or .300 Win. Mag.

	$675	$575	$540	$495	$325	$275	$250

FAIR TECHNI-MEC

Manufacturer located in Brescia, Italy (owned by Isidoro Rizzini). Limited current importation and distribution by New England Arms Co. located in Kittery Point, ME and Mandall Shooting Supplies, Inc. located in Scottsdale, AZ.

SHOTGUNS

Techni-Mec manufactures a wide variety of shotguns including O/Us and single shots in assorted models. Some models, however, are not being imported into the U.S. at this time. For more information on the complete Techni-Mec model line-up, please contact the factory in Italy directly (please refer to the Trademark Index in the back of this text).

MODEL S 610 — 10 ga., 3½ in. Mag., O/U boxlock action, double underlug blocking, 32 in. VR barrels, SST, ejectors, checkered walnut stock and forearm. Importation began 1991.

Mfg.'s Sug. Retail	$1,000	$925	$825	$750	$675	$595	$525	$450

MODEL SPL 640 — 12, 16, 20, 28, or .410 ga., folding O/U design, DT, 26 in. VR barrels.

Mfg.'s Sug. Retail	$500	$465	$390	$325	$260	$215	$180	$160

MODEL SRL 702 — 12 ga., 2¾ in. chambers, O/U boxlock with sideplates, 30 in. barrels, standard interchangeable chokes available, black receiver with hand inlaid gold wire background. Importation began 1995.

Mfg.'s Sug. Retail	$1,750	$1,625	$1,375	$1,150	$925	$825	$750	$675

MODEL SRC 702EM — 20, 28, or .410 ga., hunting model with sideplates finished black with hand inlaid gold wire background, straight grip, SST, checkered walnut stock and schnabel forearm. Importation began 1995.

Mfg.'s Sug. Retail	$1,750	$1,625	$1,375	$1,150	$925	$825	$750	$675

MODEL SRC 902 — similar to Model SRC 702EM, except has upgraded wood and Bulino engraving on coin finished receiver, game scene engraving standard. Importation began 1995.

Mfg.'s Sug. Retail	$2,650	$2,400	$2,100	$1,825	$1,625	$1,375	$1,150	$925

FALCON FIREARMS

Previous manufacturer located in Northridge, CA from 1986-90.

PORTSIDER — .45 ACP, patterned after Colt M 1911 A-1, stainless steel, fixed sights, 5 in. barrel, 7 shot mag., available in left-hand only. Mfg. 1986-90.

	$500	$425	$375

Last Mfg.'s Sug. Retail was $580.

Grading	100%	98%	95%	90%	80%	70%	60%

▲ *Portsider Set* — features right and left-hand models with matching serial numbers. Only 100 sets mfg. 1986-1987.

$1,300 $1,100 $895

Last Mfg.'s Sug. Retail was $1,400.

GOLD FALCON — .45 ACP, machined receiver made from solid 17 Kt. gold alloy, stainless steel slide, diamond sighting system, choice of grips, standard or personalized engraving options. Only 50 mfg.

$25,000 $17,500 $11,500

Last Mfg.'s Sug. Retail was $30,500.

FAMARS, ABBIATICO & SALVINELLI

Please refer to the Abbiatico & Salvinelli listing in this text.

FAUSTI, CAV. STEFANO & FIGLIE SNC.

Manufacturer located in Marcheno, Italy.

S. Fausti manufactures shotguns in O/U, SxS, and single shot configurations. While Fausti does not have an exclusive American importer, American Arms is private labeling O/U shotguns in .410 through 10 gauge (please refer to American Arms section in this text).

FEATHER INDUSTRIES, INC.

Previous manufacturer located in Boulder, CO until 1995.

Mitchell Arms is currently manufacturing both derringers and rifles patterned after Feather Industries' designs - please refer to the M section for this newer manufacturer.

DERRINGERS

GUARDIAN ANGEL 9mm/.38 Spl. — 9mm Para., O/U design, stainless steel, double action backup derringer. Mfg. 1988-1989 only.

$130 $95 $75

Last Mfg.'s Sug. Retail was $140.

This model has interchangeable loading blocks that allow shooting 9mm Para. or .38 Spl. There is no exposed hammer and trigger is totally enclosed.

GUARDIAN ANGEL .22 LR/.22 MAG. — .22 LR or .22 Mag., design is similar to 9mm/.38 Spl. model, loading block breech, 2 in. barrel, fixed sights, 12 oz. Mfg. 1990-95.

$100 $75 $60

Last Mfg.'s Sug. Retail was $120.

Add $30 for individual extra loading blocks.

This model has interchangeable loading blocks that allow shooting .22LR or .22 Mag. There is no exposed hammer and the trigger is totally enclosed.

PISTOLS

MINI-AT — .22 LR, pistol variation of the AT-22, 5½ in. shrouded barrel, 20 shot mag., approx. 2 lbs. Mfg. 1986-1989.

$195 $165 $145 $135 $130 $125 $115

Last Mfg.'s Sug. Retail was $220.

RIFLES

AT-22 — .22 LR, semi-auto blowback action, 17 in. detachable shrouded barrel, collapsible metal stock, adj. rear sight, with sling and swivels, 20 shot mag., 3¼ lbs. Mfg. 1986-95.

$225 $175 $155 $145 $135 $125 $115

Last Mfg.'s Sug. Retail was $250.

Grading	100%	98%	95%	90%	80%	70%	60%

F2 — similar to AT-22, except is equipped with a fixed polymer buttstock. Mfg. 1992-95.

	$245	$190	$165	$150	$135	$125	$115

Last Mfg.'s Sug. Retail was $280.

AT-9 — 9mm Para., semi-auto blowback action, 16 in. barrel, paramilitary design, available with 10 (C/B 1994), 25*, 32 (disc.), or 100 (disc. 1989) mag., 5 lbs. Mfg. 1988-95.

	$440	$375	$310	$280	$260	$240	$200

Last Mfg.'s Sug. Retail was $500.

Add $80 for 100 round drum mag.

F9 — similar to AT-9, except is equipped with a fixed polymer buttstock. Mfg. 1992-95.

	$465	$385	$325	$285	$260	$240	$200

Last Mfg.'s Sug. Retail was $535.

SATURN 30 — 7.62x39mm Kalashnikov cal., semi-auto, gas operated, $19\frac{1}{2}$ in. barrel, composite stock with large thumbhole pistol grip, 5 shot detachable mag., drilled and tapped for scope mounts, adj. rear sight, $8\frac{1}{2}$ lbs. Mfg. in 1990 only.

	$695	$575	$475	$425	$375	$325	$280

Last Mfg.'s Sug. Retail was $695.

KG-9 — 9mm Para., semi-auto blowback action, 25 or 50 shot mag., paramilitary configuration. Mfg. 1989 only.

	$550	$475	$425	$375	$325	$275	$240

Last Mfg.'s Sug. Retail was $560.

SAR-180 — .22 LR, semi-auto blowback action, $17\frac{1}{2}$ in. barrel, 165 shot drum mag., fully adj. rear sight, walnut stock with combat style pistol grip and forend, $6\frac{1}{4}$ lbs. Mfg. 1989 only.

	$450	$395	$350	$295	$260	$240	$200

Last Mfg.'s Sug. Retail was $500.

Add $105 for retractable stock.
Add $395 for laser sight.

This variation was also manufactured for a limited time by ILARCO (Illinois Arms Company), previously located in Itasca, IL.

KG-22 — .22 LR, similar to KG-9 except is .22 LR and has 20 shot mag. Mfg. 1989 only.

	$295	$250	$200	$175	$155	$145	$135

Last Mfg.'s Sug. Retail was $300.

FEDERAL ENGINEERING CORPORATION

Previous manufacturer located in Chicago, IL.

RIFLES: SEMI-AUTO

XC-220 — .22 LR semi-auto paramilitary design rifle, $16\frac{5}{16}$ in. barrel length, 28 shot mag., machined steel action, $7\frac{1}{2}$ lbs. Mfg. 1984-89.

	$395	$350	$300	$275	$250	$230	$210

XC-450 — .45 ACP only, semi-auto paramilitary design carbine, $16\frac{1}{2}$ in. barrel length, 30 shot mag., fires from closed bolt, machined steel action, $8\frac{1}{2}$ lbs. Mfg. 1984-89.

	$950	$825	$750	$675	$600	$550	$500

XC-900 — 9mm only, semi-auto paramilitary design carbine, $16\frac{1}{2}$ in. barrel length, 32 shot mag., fires from closed bolt, machine steel action, 8 lbs. Mfg. 1984-89.

	$950	$825	$750	$675	$600	$550	$500

FEDERAL ORDNANCE, INC.

Previous manufacturer/importer/distributor located in South El Monte, CA from 1966-1992. Brickley Trading Co. bought the remaining assets of Federal Ordnance, Inc. in late 1992, and is currently importing various firearms from overseas.

Grading	100%	98%	95%	90%	80%	70%	60%

Federal Ordnance imported and distributed both foreign and domestic military handguns and rifles until 1992. In addition, they also fabricated firearms using mostly newer parts. Listed below are those models which were recently manufactured or remanufactured.

In addition to the models listed below, Fed. Ord. also distributed used M-1 Carbines, AK-47s, SKSs, Finnish 39s, Lee Enfields, Baby Carbines, P-14s, M-1 Garands, Hakims, Mauser 98s, and other rifles. Most of these, if they are in good to excellent overall condition, typically sell in the $165-$400 range (except the M-1 Garand), depending on the model and quality.

CARBINES

MODEL 713 DELUXE MAUSER CARBINE— 7.63 Mauser or 9mm Para. cal., 16 in. barrel, detachable stock, one 10 shot and one 20 shot detachable mag., deluxe walnut, leather case with accessories, adj. sights to 1,000 meters, 5 lbs. 1,500 mfg. 1986-92.

$1,495 $1,250 $1,050

Last Mfg.'s Sug. Retail was $1,986.

▲ **Field Grade Mauser Carbine** — 7.63 Mauser or 9mm Para. (new 1989) cal., 16 in. barrel, 10 shot fixed mag., nondetachable walnut stock. Mfg. 1987-92.

$750 $675 $600 $525 $475 $425 $400

Last Mfg.'s Sug. Retail was $1,200.

PISTOLS

In addition to the Broomhandle models listed below, Federal Ordnance also manufactured other special editions. These models include the British Model, Cut-Away, Cartridge Counter, Para La Guerra, and others. Prices are in the $800-$950 price range (retail).

MODEL 714 BROOMHANDLE — 7.63 Mauser or 9mm Para. cal., 5½ in. barrel, new frame, exterior completely refinished, 10 shot detachable mag., "fair" bore, adj. rear sight. Mfg. 1986-1991.

$550 $500 $450 $400 $350 $325 $300

Last Mfg.'s Sug. Retail was $820.

Add $100 for new barrel.

▲ **Model 714 Para La Guerra** — 7.63 Mauser or 9mm Para., remanufactured to duplicate Spanish Civil War configuration Broomhandle, includes 10 in. barrel with "Para La Guerra" engraved on side. Mfg. 1990-91 only.

$575 $525 $450 $400 $350 $325 $300

Last Mfg.'s Sug. Retail was $890.

▲ **Model 714 Bolo** — similar to Model 714 Broomhandle, except has smaller grips, 3.9 in. barrel, 10 shot mag. standard. Mfg. 1988 only.

$550 $500 $450 $400 $350 $325 $300

Last Mfg.'s Sug. Retail was $890.

STANDARD BROOMHANDLE— 7.63 Mauser or 9mm Para. cal., refurbished (new barrels, completely refinished, etc.) C-96 pistols, replaced springs, includes original Chinese shoulder/holster stock. Disc. 1991.

$525 $485 $450 $420 $390 $380 $360

Last Mfg.'s Sug. Retail was $735.

Subtract $150 without shoulder/holster stock.

▲ **Standard Bolo** — similar to Standard Broomhandle, except Bolo configuration (3.9 in. barrel and smaller grips). Includes original Chinese shoulder/holster stock. Mfg. 1990-91 only.

$480 $450 $420 $390 $380 $370 $360

Last Mfg.'s Sug. Retail was $530.

Grading	100%	98%	95%	90%	80%	70%	60%

RANGER 1911A1 GI — .45 ACP, 5 in. barrel, 7 shot mag., steel construction throughout, checkered walnut grips, 40 oz. Mfg. 1988-92.

	$385	$350	$310	$280	$260	$240	$200

Last Mfg.'s Sug. Retail was $440.

Add $20 for Ranger Extended Model (40 oz. - new 1990).
Add $40 for Ranger Ambo (ambidextrous safety, 40 oz. - new 1990).
Add $15 for lightweight Ranger Lite Model (32 oz. - new 1990).
These pistols are patterned after the Colt 1911A1 Govt. Model.

▲ *Ranger Ten* — 10mm cal., otherwise similar to regular Ranger 1911A1. Mfg. 1990-91 only.

	$675	$525	$475	$450	$420	$395	$370

Last Mfg.'s Sug. Retail was $780.

RANGER SUPERCOMP — .45 ACP or 10mm cal., compensated variation of the Ranger 1911A1 with 6 in. compensated barrel, slide, tuned trigger, and other competition features, 42 oz. Mfg. 1990-91 only.

	$1,250	$875	$775	$675	$600	$550	$495

Last Mfg.'s Sug. Retail was $1,390.

Add $10 for 10mm cal.

THE RANGER ALPHA — .38 Super, 10mm, or .45 ACP cal., 5 or 6 in. barrel, patterned after the Colt Govt. Model. Mfg. 1990-91 only.

	$895	$775	$675	$575	$475	$425	$380

Last Mfg.'s Sug. Retail was $1,000.

Add $16 for 10mm cal.
Add $16 for 6 in. barrel.
Add $9-$25 for ported 5 or 6 in. barrel depending on cal.

PETERS STAHL PS-07 — 10mm or .45 ACP cal., mfg. by Peters Stahl of W. Germany to exacting standards, 6 in. barrel with polygonal rifling, top-of-the-line competition model with compensated barrel and other advanced competition features, 45 oz. Mfg. 1990-91 only.

	$2,350	$1,800	$1,500	$1,200	$995	$825	$700

Last Mfg.'s Sug. Retail was $2,600.

Add $51 for 10mm cal.
This model was imported in very limited quantities.

RIFLES

ALL AMERICAN SPORTER — .30-06 cal., Springfield M1903 receiver, new sporter stock, drilled and tapped for scope base (included), blued finish. Mfg. late 1991-92.

	$165	$145	$120	$100	$90	$80	$75

M-14 S.A. — .308 cal., legal for private ownership (no selector), 20 shot mag., refinished original M-14 parts, available in either filled fiberglass, G.I. fiberglass, refinished wood, or new walnut stock. Mfg. 1986-91.

	$625	$550	$495	$450	$395	$335	$285

Last Mfg.'s Sug. Retail was $700.

Add $50 for filled fiberglass stock.
Add $110 for refinished wood stock.
Add $190 for new walnut stock with handguard.

TANKER GARAND — .30-06 or .308 Win. cal., original U.S. GI parts, 18 in. barrel, new hardwood stock, parkerized finish. Mfg. began late 1991.

	$675	$525	$475	$450	$420	$395	$370

CHINESE RPK 86S-7 — 7.62x39mm cal., semi-auto version of the P.R.C.-RPK light machine gun, 75 shot drum mag., 23$\frac{3}{4}$ in. barrel, with bipod. Imported 1989 only.

	$1,000	$875	$725	$650	$575	$525	$475

Last Mfg.'s Sug. Retail was $500.

FEINWERKBAU

Manufacturer located in Oberndorf, Germany. Feinwerkbau firearms are not currently imported into the U.S. and airguns (see listings in Airguns section) are imported exclusively by Beeman Precision Airguns, located in Huntington Beach, CA.

Feinwerkbau manufactures some of the world's finest quality target rifles and pistols (.22 LR rimfire and airgun).

Grading	100%	98%	95%	90%	80%	70%	60%

PISTOLS: .22 CAL. TARGET

MODEL AW-93 — .22 LR, semi-auto, Super Match pistol, top-of-the-line Target pistol. Not imported into the U.S.

RIFLES: .22 CAL. TARGET

MODEL 2000 — .22 LR only, single shot, match target bolt action rifle, fully adj. trigger, walnut stocks, four variations featuring different specifications. Importation disc. 1988.

▲ *Universal Model* — 26⅜ in. barrel, aperture sights, stippled pistol grip and forearm, 9¾ lbs.

	100%	98%	95%	90%	80%	70%	60%
	$1,150	$925	$850	$735	$650	$595	$550

Last Mfg.'s Sug. Retail was $1,395.

    Add $350 for electronic trigger.
    Add $160 for left-hand variation.

▲ *Mini 2000 (Junior)* — 22 in. barrel, aperture sights, stippled pistol grip, 9⅛ lbs.

	100%	98%	95%	90%	80%	70%	60%
	$1,025	$875	$825	$700	$625	$575	$525

Last Mfg.'s Sug. Retail was $1,225.

    Add $350 for electronic trigger.
    Add $150 for left-hand variation.

▲ *Match Model* — 26¼ in. barrel, adj. cheekpiece on stock, stippled pistol grip and forearm, aperture sights.

	100%	98%	95%	90%	80%	70%	60%
	$1,075	$895	$825	$700	$625	$575	$525

Last Mfg.'s Sug. Retail was $1,285.

    Add $390 for electronic trigger.
    Add $113 for left-hand variation.

▲ *Running Target* — adj. cheekpiece on stock, thumbhole stippled pistol grip, no sights, for running boar competition.

	100%	98%	95%	90%	80%	70%	60%
	$1,150	$925	$850	$735	$650	$595	$550

Last Mfg.'s Sug. Retail was $1,398.

    Add $142 for left-hand variation.

MODEL 2600 UNIVERSAL — .22 LR only, similar design to Model 600 air rifle, single shot, 26.3 in. barrel, aperture sights, 10.6 lbs. Imported 1986-94.

	100%	98%	95%	90%	80%	70%	60%
	$1,425	$1,125	$925	$850	$735	$650	$595

Last Mfg.'s Sug. Retail was $1,695.

    Add $160 for left-hand variation.

MODEL 2600 ULTRA MATCH FREE RIFLE — .22 LR, single shot match gun based on Model 2600 action, 26.1 in. barrel, laminate stock with thumbhole, fully adj. aperture sights, 14 lbs. 1 oz. Mfg. 1986-94.

	100%	98%	95%	90%	80%	70%	60%
	$2,175	$1,750	$1,400	$1,150	$925	$850	$735

Last Mfg.'s Sug. Retail was $2,498.

    Add $250 for electronic trigger (disc. 1988).
    Add $152 for left-hand variation.

FEMARU

Previously manufactured by Femaru-Fegyver-Es Gepgyar R.T. located in Budapest, Hungary.

Grading	100%	98%	95%	90%	80%	70%	60%

PISTOLS: SEMI-AUTO

MODEL 1910 — 7.65mm Roth/Steyr cal., rare and only infrequently encountered.

	100%	98%	95%	90%	80%	70%	60%
	$1,750	$1,550	$1,350	$1,150	$975	$850	$725

MODEL 1929 — .32 ACP or .380 ACP cal., 3.93 in. barrel, 8 shot mag., 2 piece walnut grips.

	$375	$320	$265	$215	$185	$165	$145

MODEL 1937 — .32 ACP or .380 ACP cal., 3.93 in. barrel, 8 shot mag., commercial blue finish, 2-piece walnut grips, Nazi marked jhv 41 or jhv 44.

	$325	$265	$215	$190	$175	$160	$145

Add 35% for Waffenamt proofing.
Add another 50% if with holster and 2 matching mags.

FROMMER STOP POCKET AUTO — .32 ACP, .380 ACP, 6 or 7 shot, $3\frac{7}{8}$ in. barrel, fixed sights, blue, rubber grips, locked breech, outside hammer. Mfg. 1912-1920.

	$250	$215	$180	$150	$120	$100	$80

FROMMER BABY POCKET AUTO — similar to Stop Pocket Auto, except 2 in. barrel, 5 or 6 shot.

	$250	$215	$180	$150	$115	$90	$70

FROMMER LILIPUT AUTO — blowback action, .25 auto, 6 shot, 2.14 in. barrel, blue, hard rubber grips. Mfg. in early twenties.

	$325	$250	$175	$145	$115	$90	$75

FERLACH GUNS

Includes those firearms manufactured in Ferlach, Austria from 1558 to present. Currently imported and sold by Adler Arms located in Pittsburgh, PA (a complete Ferlach catalog is available for $10 - see Adler Arms listing in the Trademark Index).

Many people are confused that Ferlach is a trademark - it is not. Rather, it is a small village in Austria where a gun guild was started as early as 1558. At that time, it was absolutely necessary that all the people involved in fabricating a firearm were located together in close proximity. This enabled the barrel maker, the stock maker, and the lock mechanism maker to work together closely to ensure that everyone was performing their task(s) correctly, effectively and efficiently. As the individual skills became better and more refined, more and more firearms were manufactured. Eventually, individual gunsmiths began to put their name on the barrel or frame of those guns which they had either manufactured solely or with the help of their fellow Ferlach craftsmen. Since all Ferlach firearms are essentially hand made per individual special order, very few are exactly alike. In the past, the gunsmiths of Ferlach have produced almost every type of shoulder arm imaginable including such modern weapons as superposed and juxtaposed rifles and shotguns, hammerless drillings, repeating rifles, 3 barrel rifles, combination guns, 4 barrel rifles/shotguns/combination guns (called Vierlings), hammer guns of every type, etc. Some of these specimens represent the highest refinement in the gunmakers trade. Because of the almost unlimited variety of Ferlach variations, it is recommended that a COMPETENT appraisal is procured before buying or selling a specimen.

As is the case with many other European weapons, those models with desirable American features will generally outperform those with European specifications (i.e. a Ferlach sidelock combination gun that is 20 ga. x .243 Win. will be more valuable than a similar specimen chambered for 16 ga. x 5.6 by 50Rmm with sling swivels). Original condition and overall beauty are the primary factors to consider when contemplating buying or selling a Ferlach longarm. Other considerations include: type of action, difficulty of fabrication (Vierlings are very complicated to construct), caliber/gauge

Grading	100%	98%	95%	90%	80%	70%	60%

desirability, notoriety of gunsmith on barrel legend, elaborateness of embellishments, condition, rarity, accessories, and any provenance a specimen might have.

Today's master gunsmiths of Ferlach carry on the old world tradition of quality in every respect. Most guns manufactured today are by individual special order with a wide range of calibers/gauges and other special features and options. As of this writing, these gunsmiths in alphabetical order are: LUDWIG BOROVNIK, FACHSCHULE, JOHANN FANZOJ, GENOSSENSCHAFT, WILFRIED GLANZNIG, JOSEF HAMBRUSCH, KARL HAUPTMANN, GOTTFRIED JUCH, JOSEF JUST, JAKOB KOSCHAT, JOHANN MICHELITSCH, WALTER OUTSCHAR, HERBERT SCHEIRING, BENEDIKT WINKLER, AND JOSEF WINKLER. Anyone wishing to contact these master gunmakers should either write to the guild or address them individually at: Ferlach, Waagplatz, 6, A-9170 Ferlach, AUSTRIA. Please allow at least 4-6 weeks for a response.

FERLIB
Manufacturer located in Gardone V.T., Italy. Distributed by Quality Arms located in Houston, TX, New England Arms Co. located in Kittery Point, ME, and Hi-Grade Imports located in Gilroy, CA.

SHOTGUNS: SIDE-BY-SIDE
Models listed below are available in 10, 12, 16, 20, 24, 28, 32, or .410 ga. Also available for an additional charge are extra quality wood and upgraded engraving.
Add 10% for 24, 28, 32, or .410 ga.
Add $250 for single trigger.
Add $650 for leather case.

HAMMER GUN — boxlock action, exposed hammers, deluxe checkered walnut stock and forearm, blued action. Disc. 1989.

$4,250	$3,500	$3,175	$2,850	$2,350	$2,100	$1,800

Last Mfg.'s Sug. Retail was $4,500.

MODEL F.VI — 12, 16, 20, 28, or .410 ga., Anson & Deeley scalloped boxlock action, ejectors, double triggers, case hardened frame, select checkered stock and forearm. Disc. 1992.

$2,950	$2,275	$1,975	$1,600	$1,250	$1,000	$750

Last Mfg.'s Sug. Retail was $3,250.

MODEL F.VII — 12, 16, 20, 28, or .410 ga., Anson & Deeley scalloped boxlock action, ejectors, double triggers, coin finish, full coverage English scroll or game scene engraving, select checkered stock and forearm.

Mfg.'s Sug. Retail	$7,500						
		$6,000	$5,250	$4,950	$4,275	$3,675	$3,000	$2,600

Add 10% for 28 or .410 ga.

MODEL F.VII/SC — 12, 16, 20, 28, or .410 ga., Anson & Deeley scalloped boxlock action, ejectors, double triggers, coin finish, game scene with scroll accent engraving with gold inlays, select checkered stock and forearm.

Mfg.'s Sug. Retail	$9,000						
		$7,200	$6,500	$5,700	$5,000	$4,350	$3,600	$3,000

Add 10% for 28 or .410 ga.

MODEL F.VII SIDEPLATE — 12, 16, 20, 28, or .410 ga., Anson & Deeley boxlock action with sideplates, ejectors, single trigger, coin finish, extensive game scene and scroll accent engraving, select checkered stock and forearm.

Mfg.'s Sug. Retail	$9,600						
		$7,700	$6,800	$6,000	$5,200	$4,450	$3,700	$3,100

Add 10% for 28 or .410 ga.

▲ *F.VII/SC Gold* — similar to F.VII Sideplate, except with gold inlays.

Mfg.'s Sug. Retail	$13,000						
		$10,400	$9,250	$8,100	$7,275	$6,350	$5,300	$4,350

Add 10% for 28 or .410 ga.

F.V. SIDELOCK — various ga.'s, full sidelock action, special order to customer specifications. Values start in the $15,000 range and go up.

FIALA OUTFITTERS INCORPORATED
New York City, NY.

Grading	100%	98%	95%	90%	80%	70%	60%

FIALA REPEATING PISTOL — .22 LR, 10 shot, 3, 7½, or 20 in. barrels, blue, plain wood grips, resembles an auto loader, but is actually hand operated by moving the slide to eject, load and cock. Mfg. 1920-1923.

	$475	$400	$340	$280	$230	$200	$175

Add 50% for 3-barrel set.
Add $150 for original case.
Add $250 for stock.
Add $300 for canvas holster stock.

FIAS
Shotgun manufacturer located in Brescia, Italy. Please contact FIAS directly (see listing in Trademark Index) to obtain current information on their models and prices.

FINNISH LION
Manufactured by Valmet (now Tikka) located in Sweden. Limited importation into the U.S by Mandall's Shooting Supplies, Inc. in Scottsdale, AZ.

RIFLES

MATCH RIFLE — .22 LR, bolt action, single shot, 29 in. barrel, extended aperture sight, globe front sight, thumbhole stock, adj. hook butt. Mfg. 1937-1972.

	$495	$415	$360	$305	$250	$210	$195

CHAMPION FREE RIFLE — .22 LR, bolt action, single shot, 29 in. barrel, double set trigger, full target stock and accessories. Mfg. 1965-1972.

	$580	$495	$440	$385	$330	$290	$265

STANDARD ISU TARGET RIFLE — .22 LR, bolt action, single shot, 27 in. barrel, full target stock and accessories. Mfg. 1966-1977.

	$330	$275	$250	$205	$180	$165	$150

TARGET RIFLE — .22 LR, target rifle with adj. stock and trigger, bolt action, single shot, aperture sights.

Mfg.'s Sug. Retail	$795	$725	$595	$495	$440	$385	$340	$295

FIOCCHI OF AMERICA, INC.
Importer and distributor located In Ozark, MO.

Fiocchi of America previously imported Pardini target pistols until 1990, and continues to manufacture a wide variety of ammunition domestically. Fiocchi also imported Antonio Zoli shotguns until 1988. These trademarks can be found in their respective sections of this text.

FIREARMS INTERNATIONAL (F I)
Previous importer/assembler located in Washington, D.C.

F.I. imported various shotguns and pistols including the Star D and Iver Johnson Pony handguns. F.I. sold less than 100 .380 ACPs that were marked Colt before the Mustang was introduced - these are rare. While some models are relatively rare, collectability to date has been minimal and most models sell in the $125-$250 range.

FORT WORTH FIREARMS
Firearms manufacturer located in Fort Worth, TX beginning 1995.

Grading	100%	98%	95%	90%	80%	70%	60%

PISTOLS: SEMI-AUTO, .22 CAL.

MATCH MASTER STANDARD — .22 LR cal., $3\frac{7}{8}$, $4\frac{1}{2}$, $5\frac{1}{2}$, $7\frac{1}{2}$, or 10 in. bull barrel, double extractors, includes upper push button and standard mag. release, beveled mag. well, angled grip, flared slide, low profile frame. New 1995.

Mfg.'s Sug. Retail	$388	$310	$265	$230	$200	$185	$170	$160

    Add $84 for 10 in. bull barrel.

▲ *Match Master Dovetail* — similar to Match Master Standard, except has $3\frac{7}{8}$, $4\frac{1}{2}$, or $5\frac{1}{2}$ barrel with dovetail rib. New 1995.

Mfg.'s Sug. Retail	$472	$385	$325	$285	$240	$215	$190	$170

▲ *Match Master Deluxe* — similar to Match Master Standard, except has Weaver rib on barrel. New 1995.

Mfg.'s Sug. Retail	$537	$450	$365	$315	$280	$240	$215	$190

    Add $92 for 10 in. barrel.

SPORT KING — .22 LR cal., $4\frac{1}{2}$ or $5\frac{1}{2}$ in. barrel, blued finish, military grips, drift sight, 10 shot mag. New 1995.

Mfg.'s Sug. Retail	$312	$275	$245	$225	$200	$185	$170	$160

CITATION — .22 LR cal., $5\frac{1}{2}$ in. bull or $7\frac{1}{4}$ in. fluted barrel, military grips, 10 shot mag. New 1995.

Mfg.'s Sug. Retail	$388	$310	$265	$230	$200	$185	$170	$160

TROPHY — .22 LR cal., $5\frac{1}{2}$ or $7\frac{1}{4}$ in. bull barrel, blued finish, military grips, 10 shot mag. New 1995.

Mfg.'s Sug. Retail	$410	$330	$285	$240	$200	$185	$170	$160

    Add $41 for left-hand action ($5\frac{1}{2}$ in. barrel only).

VICTOR — .22 LR cal., $3\frac{7}{8}$, $4\frac{1}{2}$ (VR or Weaver rib), or $5\frac{1}{2}$ (VR or Weaver rib), 8 (Weaver rib), or 10 (Weaver rib) in. barrel, blued finish, military grips, 10 shot mag. New 1995.

Mfg.'s Sug. Retail	$472	$385	$325	$285	$240	$215	$190	$170

    Add $65 for $4\frac{1}{2}$ or $5\frac{1}{2}$ in. Weaver rib barrel.
    Add approx. $148 for 8 or 10 in. Weaver rib barrel.

OLYMPIC — .22 LR or Short cal., $6\frac{3}{4}$ in. fluted barrel, blued finish, military grips, 10 shot mag. New 1995.

Mfg.'s Sug. Retail	$599	$525	$465	$415	$360	$330	$295	$265

SHARP SHOOTER — .22 LR cal., $5\frac{1}{2}$ in. bull barrel, blued finish, military grips, 10 shot mag. New 1995.

Mfg.'s Sug. Retail	$379	$300	$260	$230	$200	$185	$170	$160

RIFLES

YOUTH RIFLE — .22 LR cal., bolt action, single shot, shortened stock dimensions. New 1995.

Mfg.'s Sug. Retail	$138	$120	$105	$90	$80	$70	$60	$50

SHOTGUNS

GL 18 — 12 ga. only, security configuration with 18 in. barrel with perforated shroud, thumb operated lazer/xenon light built into end of 7 shot mag. tube, ammo storage. New 1995.

Mfg.'s Sug. Retail	$347	$295	$265	$240	$210	$190	$170	$160

F

FOX, A. H.

Originally manufactured in Philadelphia, PA 1903-1930, and in Utica, NY from 1930-approx. 1946. Manufactured by Savage 1930-1988. The A. H. Fox trademark was brought to life once again during 1993 when the Connecticut Shotgun Manufacturing Company located in New Britain, CT began producing a 20 gauge in 5 different grades.

Depending on the remaining A.H. Fox factory data, a factory letter authenticating the configuration of a particular Fox shotgun may be obtained by contacting John T. Callahan (see Trademark Index for listings and address). The charge for this service is $10.00/shotgun - please allow 2-4 weeks for an adequate response.

Mr. Ansley H. Fox first started manufacturing shotguns in circa 1896. This first company was called the Fox Gun Co. located in Baltimore, MD. Relatively few guns were made and surviving specimens today are very rare. After this venture, he was employed by the Baltimore Gun Co. for several years (circa 1900-1903). Following this period, he formed the Philadelphia Gun Co. where the predecessors to the A.H. Fox Gun Co. models were manufactured. These Philadelphia Gun Co. models (circa 1904) were the same as the newer Fox shotguns except that the hinge pin was removed. Sources indicate that the lowest grade was an "A" with the highest being an "E" (fully engraved and ultra rare). Following this tenure, Mr. Fox went on to form the A.H. Fox Gun Co. that was started approx. 1905. In addition to being an entrepreneur and trend setter, Mr. Fox also had the reputation of being an expert shot in his own right, winning more than a few events on the East Coast around the turn of the century.

The A.H. Fox Gun Company of Philadelphia, Pennsylvania, began production in 1905 and produced high quality double barrel shotguns until 1930. The Savage Arms Company, then of Utica, New York, acquired the Fox Company and produced these guns until 1942, when all but the utilitarian model B series guns were discontinued.

A.H. Fox guns are rapidly being considered an American classic comparable to L.C. Smith, Parker, and others. Collector interest is high and will undoubtedly grow. The guns do not command quite as high a price as the Smith and Parker guns, but represent a fine investment collectible value.

> The Savage made guns from 1930-1942 usually are valued at about 25% less than the early A.H. Fox guns. The recent production B series are just not in the same class and are obviously not intended to be. They are lower priced by today's standards and are designed as a utility grade hunting gun.

FOX COMPANY CHRONOLOGY

1906 - Company formed January 1906, A, B & C Grades introduced in 12 ga. only. D and F Grades introduced in 12 ga. in 1907. Ejector guns introduced in 1908. 1910 saw the introduction of the 12 ga. Sterlingworth - William H. Gough takes over as Chief of Engraving. Ansley Fox resigns in 1911 - first catalog showing Sterlingworth Model (called Model 1911). A-F Grades released in 16 and 20 ga. during 1912, as well as the addition of a 20 ga. Sterlingworth. 16 ga. Sterlingworth introduced in 1913. Fox/Kautsky single trigger introduced in 1914 - engineering transition complete. During 1915, the XE Grade was introduced. The B Grade was dropped in 1918. Single barrel trap guns (J, K, and L Grades) were introduced in 1919. 1920 saw the introduction of the M Grade single barrel trap. In 1922, both the G and HE Grades were released. Beavertail forend and vent. rib were introduced in 1927. 1929 was the Savage buy-out (November), GE Grade dropped. Company moved from Philadelphia, PA to Utica, NY in 1930. Skeeter Grade introduced in 1931 while the 20 ga. HE Grade was disc. 1932 saw the introduction of both the Trap Grade Double and SP Grade. Wildfowl Grade was introduced in 1934. 1935 was the last year of the K and L single barrel trap guns. 1937 was the last year for the J Grade single barrel trap gun. The last 16 and 12 ga. Sterlingworths were built in 1939. The outbreak of the war in 1940 saw the last FE Grade shipped, the Wildfowler Grade dropped, and the introduction of the Model B. 1942 was the last retail catalog. Factory records indicate that the last 12 ga. was shipped in 1945

Grading	100%	98%	95%	90%	80%	70%	60%

and the last 20 ga. was shipped during 1946 (SP Grade shipped in December, 1946). However, guns continued to be assembled from left-over parts and were shipped to customers as late as the 1960s.

FOX SERIAL NUMBER ASSIGNMENTS

The publisher wishes to express his thanks to Mr. Gurney Brown for providing the model serialization and years of mfg. in this section.

Ser. # range 50,000-200,000 — 12 ga. Sterlingworth — 111,556 mfg.
Ser. # range 350,000-400,000 — 16 ga. Sterlingworth — 28,481 mfg.
Ser. # range 250,000-300,000 — 20 ga. Sterlingworth — 21,304 mfg.
Ser. # range 1-50,000 — 12 ga. A-F Grades — 35,280 mfg.
Ser. # range 300,000-350,000 — 16 ga. A-F Grades — 3,875 mfg.
Ser. # range 200,000-250,000 — 20 ga. A-F Grades — 3,974 mfg.
Ser. # range 400,000-400,568 — 12 ga. Single Barrel Traps — 568 mfg.

FOX MODELS BY YEARS IN MFG.

Sterlingworth — 1910-1942 mfg. — 32 years.
Wildfowler — 1934-1940 mfg. — 6 years.
Trap Double — 1932-1942 mfg. — 10 years.
Skeeter — 1931-1942 mfg. — 11 years.
SP — 1932-1946 mfg. — 14 years.
A — 1906-1942 mfg. — 36 years.
B — 1906-1919 mfg. — 13 years.
C — 1906-1942 mfg. — 36 years.
D — 1907-1942 mfg. — 35 years.
F — 1907-1940 mfg. — 33 years.
G — 1922-1929 mfg. — 7 years.
H — 1922-1939 mfg. — 17 years.
J — 1919-1937 mfg. — 18 years.
K — 1919-1935 mfg. — 16 years.
L — 1919-1935 mfg. — 16 years.
M — 1920-1937 mfg. — 17 years.
X — 1915-1942 mfg. — 27 years.

SHOTGUNS: SxS - CURRENT MFG.

The models below are manufactured by the Connecticut Manufacturing Co. located in New Britain, CT. These finely made shotguns have the following standard features: automatic safety, auto ejectors, DTs, Chromox 26, 28, or 30 in. barrels, individual barrel chokings, 2¾ in. chambers, scalloped receiver, Turkish Circassian walnut with hand-rubbed oil finish, choice of straight, semi-pistol or full-pistol grip stock with custom dimensions, splinter forearm, ivory bead sights. Special order options are as follows: Krupp steel barrels ($200), Fox SST ($600), walnut upgrades, custom initials ($200-$250), personalized gold inlays on barrel ($500), skeleton steel buttplate ($500), beavertail forearm ($500), and traditional leather trunk case with accessories ($625). Add 25% for multi-gauge sets.

Delivery time for custom orders is currently 8-12 months, depending on gauge.

CE GRADE — 16 (new 1995), 20, 28 (new 1995), or .410 (new 1995) ga., engraved with fine scroll and game scenes, Grade I Turkish Circassian walnut. New 1993.

Mfg.'s Sug. Retail	$7,200	$7,200	$5,650	$5,050	$4,300	$3,350	$2,700	$2,100

Add $1,000 for 28 or .410 ga.
Add $2,500 for extra set of barrels.

XE GRADE — ga.'s similar to CE Grade, scroll work and engraved game scenes, Grade II Turkish Circassian walnut. New 1993.

Mfg.'s Sug. Retail	$8,500	$8,500	$7,200	$6,000	$4,850	$3,700	$3,000	$2,450

Add $1,200 for 28 or .410 ga.
Add $2,900 for extra set of barrels.

Grading	100%	98%	95%	90%	80%	70%	60%

DE GRADE — ga.'s similar to CE Grade, intricate and extensive engraving, Grade III highly figured Turkish Circassian walnut. New 1993.

Mfg.'s Sug. Retail	$12,500		$12,500	$9,950	$8,600	$7,300	$6,000	$4,850	$3,500

Add $1,300 for 28 or .410 ga.
Add $3,200 for extra set of barrels.

FE GRADE — ga.'s similar to CE Grade, gold inlays surrounded by different types of scroll work, Grade IV highly figured Turkish Circassian walnut with finest checkering. New 1993.

Mfg.'s Sug. Retail	$17,500		$17,500	$14,650	$11,750	$9,250	$7,750	$6,000	$4,250

Add $2,200 for 28 or .410 ga.
Add $4,000 for extra set of barrels.

EXHIBITION GRADE — ga.'s similar to CE Grade, individually built per customer specifications on a "cost-no-object" basis, includes best-quality leather trunk case with full accessories, Exhibition Grade Turkish Circassian walnut. New 1993.

Mfg.'s Sug. Retail	$25,000		$25,000	$20,500	$16,750	$13,500	$10,250	$8,000	$6,250

Add $4,500 for extra set of barrels.

100%	98%	95%	90%	80%	70%	60%	50%	40%	30%	20%	10%

SHOTGUNS: SxS - DISC.

STERLINGWORTH SxS — 12, 16, or 20 ga., 26, 28, or 30 in. barrels, various chokes, boxlock, extractors, double trigger, checkered pistol grip stock. Mfg. 1905-1930.

$1,495	$1,250	$1,050	$875	$750	$650	$500	$450	$400	$365	$325	$275

Add 33% for auto ejectors.
Add 50% for 20 ga.

A single trigger is a very desirable option on this model.

Ser. no. range on 12 ga. Sterlingworths is 50,000-200,000, 16 ga. is 350,000-400,000, and 20 ga. is 250,000-300,000.

STERLINGWORTH DELUXE — similar to Sterlingworth, with recoil pad and ivory bead, 32 in. barrel available.

$1,875	$1,500	$1,200	$995	$900	$825	$725	$650	$550	$475	$425	$395

Add $200 for auto ejectors.
Add 50% for 20 ga.

A single trigger was not an option on this model.

STERLINGWORTH SKEET — similar to Sterlingworth, with 26 or 28 in. skeet boring, straight grip stock.

This model is very scarce (only several are known) and the extreme rarity factor precludes accurate price evaluation.

SUPER HE GRADE — 12 ga., 2¾ (very rare) or 3 in. chambered long range gun, 30 and 32 in. full choke, auto ejectors, otherwise similar to Sterlingworth.

$4,200	$3,500	$3,000	$2,500	$2,100	$1,750	$1,600	$1,500	$1,350	$1,150	$1,000	$900

Add $300 for SST.

Original 3 in. chambered HE grades are marked "not warranteed, see instruction tag" on barrel flats. The HE grade was also manufactured in 20 ga. but is extremely rare. 2¾ in. chambers are rarer than 3 in. guns in this model.

100%	98%	95%	90%	80%	70%	60%	50%	40%	30%	20%	10%

HIGHER GRADE MODELS (A-F) — the following higher grade Fox shotguns are similar to the Sterlingworth in configuration. The grades differ in engraving and inlays, grade of wood and general workmanship. The E designation means auto ejectors.

> Early A and B grades have very little engraving and are much less desirable than later models. Values below are for later guns.
> VALUES BELOW ARE FOR 12 GA.
> Add 30% for 16 ga. (made on same frame as 20 ga.).
> Add 60% for 20 ga.
> Add $200-$1,000 for vent. rib, depending on grade.
> Add $200-$1,000 for SST, depending on grade.
> Add $200-$1,000 for beavertail forearm, depending on grade.
> Note: These guns were disc. in 1942 by Savage Arms after they mfg. them for 12 years. Pre-1930 guns were made by A.H. Fox Company.

▲ *A Grade*

100%	98%	95%	90%	80%	70%	60%	50%	40%	30%	20%	10%
$1,950	$1,675	$1,375	$1,075	$900	$825	$725	$650	$550	$475	$425	$395

▲ *AE Grade (ejectors)*

| $2,475 | $2,075 | $1,675 | $1,400 | $1,150 | $1,000 | $900 | $850 | $750 | $650 | $600 | $550 |

▲ *BE Grade (ejectors)*

| $3,800 | $3,350 | $2,675 | $2,250 | $2,000 | $1,900 | $1,700 | $1,600 | $1,500 | $1,400 | $1,300 | $1,200 |

> This model is rarely encountered.

▲ *CE Grade (ejectors)*

| $4,500 | $4,000 | $3,700 | $3,500 | $3,000 | $2,700 | $2,500 | $2,100 | $1,900 | $1,800 | $1,600 | $1,400 |

▲ *XE Grade (ejectors)*

| $7,500 | $6,000 | $5,500 | $5,000 | $4,500 | $3,800 | $3,400 | $3,000 | $2,700 | $2,400 | $2,000 | $1,800 |

▲ *DE Grade (ejectors)*

| $10,500 | $8,950 | $7,500 | $6,500 | $5,500 | $5,000 | $4,500 | $4,200 | $4,000 | $3,700 | $3,200 | $2,800 |

▲ *FE Grade (ejectors)* — top-of-the-line model, only infrequently encountered.

| $25,000 | $20,000 | $15,000 | $12,000 | $11,000 | $10,000 | $9,500 | $9,000 | $8,500 | $8,000 | $7,500 | $7,000 |

SINGLE BARREL TRAP — 12 ga., 30 or 32 in. vent. rib barrel, full choke, boxlock, auto ejector, checkered trap style stock and recoil pad. The grades differ in wood, engraving, and overall quality. ME grade is custom built and extremely high quality with gold inlays. These models were disc. 1942. 568 single barrel trap guns were mfg. between 1932-1942 and have a ser. range of 400,000-400,568, with Monte Carlo stock.

> Even though trap guns may be rarer than their SxS counterparts, to date their desirability is less since there are simply fewer collectors.

▲ *JE Grade*

| $3,500 | $3,200 | $2,800 | $2,500 | $2,100 | $1,800 | $1,500 | $1,400 | $1,300 | $1,200 | $1,100 | $900 |

▲ *KE Grade*

| $4,500 | $4,000 | $3,500 | $3,200 | $2,800 | $2,600 | $2,400 | $2,100 | $1,900 | $1,800 | $1,600 | $1,300 |

▲ *LE Grade*

| $6,500 | $5,500 | $5,000 | $4,500 | $4,000 | $3,600 | $3,200 | $2,800 | $2,400 | $2,100 | $1,800 | $1,500 |

▲ *ME Grade*

| $11,250 | $10,750 | $9,150 | $8,000 | $7,150 | $6,250 | $5,500 | $5,000 | $4,500 | $4,000 | $3,450 | $2,875 |

Grading			100%	98%	95%	90%	80%	70%	60%

MODEL B DOUBLE BARREL — 12, 16, 20, or .410 ga., 24-30 in. barrels, various chokes, vent rib on newer models, boxlock, extractors, double triggers, checkered pistol grip stock. Mfg. 1940-1986.

			100%	98%	95%	90%	80%	70%	60%
			$230	$210	$205	$185	$165	$145	$120

Last Mfg.'s Sug. Retail was $250.

MODEL B-ST — similar to model B, with single trigger. Mfg. 1955-1966.

			100%	98%	95%	90%	80%	70%	60%
			$275	$250	$220	$195	$165	$140	$120

Grading	100%	98%	95%	90%	80%	70%	60%

MODEL B-DL — similar to model B-ST, with satin chrome receiver, select wood. Mfg. 1962-1965.

| | $315 | $275 | $240 | $220 | $195 | $165 | $140 |

MODEL B-DE — similar to B-DL, with less checkering. Mfg. 1965-1966.

| | $295 | $255 | $230 | $210 | $180 | $155 | $125 |

MODEL B-SE — 12, 20, or .410 ga., single trigger, selective ejectors, vent. rib, beavertail forend, select walnut. Mfg. 1966-88.

| | $415 | $370 | $325 | $280 | $240 | $210 | $180 |

Last Mfg.'s Sug. Retail was $525.

Add 20% for .410 ga.

Even though there were multiple series designations assigned to this model, there seems to be little difference in desirability. For that reason, other designations will be priced similarly to values shown above.

FRANCHI, LUIGI

Manufacturer located in Brescia, Italy since mid-1860s. This trademark has been imported for approx. the past 30 years. Currently imported exclusively by American Arms, Inc. located in North Kansas City, MO. Some models were previously imported by FIE firearms located in Hialeah, FL.

Also see Sauer/Franchi heading in the S section.

RIFLES

CENTENNIAL SEMI-AUTO — .22 LR, 21 in. barrel, open sight to commemorate Franchi's 100th anniversary. Mfg. 1968 only.

| | $330 | $250 | $220 | $195 | $165 | $150 | $140 |

▲ *Engraved deluxe model*

| | $415 | $330 | $305 | $275 | $240 | $200 | $165 |

▲ *Gallery model*

| | $220 | $195 | $160 | $120 | $100 | $80 | $60 |

SHOTGUNS: SEMI-AUTO

BLACK MAGIC GAME — 12 ga. only, 3 in. chamber with gas metering system, interchangeable shell handling without adjustments, two-tone black alloy receiver with gold accents and trigger, 24, 26, or 28 in. VR barrel with Franchokes, checkered walnut stock and forearm, 7 lbs. Imported 1989-91.

| | $550 | $450 | $395 | $330 | $300 | $270 | $240 |

Last Mfg.'s Sug. Retail was $659.

▲ *Black Magic Skeet* — skeet variation of the Black Magic Game, 2¾ in. chamber, 26 in. ported VR barrel with fixed Tula skeet choke, skeet dimensioned stock, 7¼ lbs. Imported 1989-91.

| | $580 | $475 | $425 | $350 | $325 | $295 | $265 |

Last Mfg.'s Sug. Retail was $699.

▲ *Black Magic Trap* — trap variation of the Black Magic Game, 2¾ in. chamber, 30 in. VR barrel with Franchoke system, trap dimensioned stock, 7½ lbs. Imported 1989-91.

| | $615 | $495 | $430 | $350 | $325 | $295 | $265 |

Last Mfg.'s Sug. Retail was $739.

Grading	100%	98%	95%	90%	80%	70%	60%

STANDARD MODEL (48/AL) — 12, 20, or 28 (new 1996) ga., 24, 26, 28, or 30 (disc. in 1990) in. VR barrel, recoil operated, alloy frame, checkered pistol grip stock, VR standard,Franchokes became available in 1989, 12 ga., 6 lbs. 9 oz. and 20 ga., 5 lbs. 6 oz. Mfg. 1950-present.

Mfg.'s Sug. Retail	$649	$500	$385	$300	$270	$250	$230	$210

Add $76 for 28 ga.
Add $30 for 12 ga. 24 in. slug barrel (disc. 1994).
Subtract $50 if without Franchokes.

Starting in 1990, this model comes standard with black receiver and gold accents. Franchokes became standard in 1990.

STANDARD MAGNUM (48/AL) — similar to Standard, except 28 in. (disc. 1988) or 32 in. VR barrel, Mag. chamber, recoil pad, Mfg. 1954-1990.

	$415	$360	$300	$270	$250	$230	$210

Last Mfg.'s Sug. Retail was $482.

This model was replaced by the Combo S/T currently imported by American Arms, Inc. located in North Kansas City, MO.

COMBO S/T— while advertised, this model was never developed.

HUNTER MODEL (48/AL) — similar to Standard, except etched receiver, better wood, VR standard, Franchokes became available in 1989. Mfg. 1950-1990.

	$415	$360	$300	$270	$250	$230	$210

Last Mfg.'s Sug. Retail was $482.

Add $35 for internal Franchokes (3).
This model was imported exclusively by FIE Firearms located in Hialeah, FL.

HUNTER MAGNUM — mfg. 1954-1973.

	$430	$380	$370	$340	$315	$290	$275

PRESTIGE MODEL — 12 ga. only, gas operated, vent. rib, various barrel lengths, alloy receiver, Franchokes became available in 1989. Imported 1985-1989.

	$575	$475	$395	$325	$310	$295	$275

Last Mfg.'s Sug. Retail was $720.

Add $40 for internal Franchokes (3).
This model was imported exclusively by FIE Firearms located in Hialeah, FL.

▲ *Turkey Model* — similar to Prestige Model except has dull matte black finish, Franchokes standard. Imported 1989 only.

	$615	$515	$425	$350	$320	$300	$280

Last Mfg.'s Sug. Retail was $760.

This model was imported exclusively by FIE Firearms located in Hialeah, FL.

ELITE MODEL — same general specifications as the Prestige Model, only etched receiver, Franchokes became available in 1989. Imported 1985-1989.

	$595	$500	$425	$350	$320	$300	$280

Last Mfg.'s Sug. Retail was $740.

Add $45 for internal Franchokes (3).
This model was imported exclusively by FIE Firearms located in Hialeah, FL.

SPAS-12 — 12 ga., 2¾ in. chamber, combat shotgun that offers pump or semi-auto operation, 5 (new 1991) or 8 (disc.) shot tube mag., alloy receiver, synthetic stock with built-in pistol grip, one-button switch to change from semi-auto to slide action operation, 21½ in. barrel, 8¾ lbs. Importation disc. 1994.

	$595	$495	$410	$360	$320	$300	$280

Last Mfg.'s Sug. Retail was $769.

This model was imported exclusively by FIE Firearms located in Hialeah, FL until 1990.

Grading	100%	98%	95%	90%	80%	70%	60%

SPAS-15 — 12 ga. only, 2¾ in. chamber, operates as either semi-auto or slide action that is convertible with a one-button switch, 6 shot detachable box mag., 21½ in. barrel, lateral folding skeleton stock, carrying handle, 10 lbs. Limited importation 1989 only.

This model had very limited importation (less than 200) as the BATF disallowed further importation almost immediately. Even though the retail was in the $700 range, demand and rarity has pushed prices past the $2,000 level already.

SAS-12 — 12 ga. only, 3 in. chamber, slide action only, synthetic stock with built-in pistol grip, 8 shot tube mag., 21½ in. barrel, 6.8 lbs. Imported 1988-90 only.

	$415	$360	$300	$270	$250	$230	$210

Last Mfg.'s Sug. Retail was $473.

This model was imported exclusively by FIE Firearms located in Hialeah, FL.

LAW-12 — 12 ga. only, 2¾ in. chamber, gas operated semi-auto, synthetic stock with built-in pistol grip, 5 (new 1991) or 8 (disc.) shot tube mag., 21½ in. barrel, 6¾ lbs. Imported 1988-94.

	$570	$485	$400	$360	$320	$300	$280

Last Mfg.'s Sug. Retail was $719.

TURKEY GUN — similar to Standard Mag., 12 ga., 3 in. barrel only, turkey scene engraved. Mfg. 1963-1965.

	$415	$385	$370	$340	$315	$290	$275

SLUG GUN — 22 in. plain barrel, and rifle sights.

	$360	$330	$315	$295	$275	$255	$240

SKEET GUN — 26 in. skeet choke, vent. rib, select wood. Mfg. 1972-1974.

	$385	$370	$350	$330	$310	$285	$265

ELDORADO — fancy wood and gold filled engraved receiver. Mfg. 1954-1975.

	$450	$420	$395	$380	$360	$340	$320

CROWN GRADE — engraved hunting scene. Mfg. 1954-1975.

	$1,540	$1,320	$1,210	$1,045	$965	$910	$855

DIAMOND GRADE SILVER INLAID SCROLL — mfg. 1954-1975.

	$1,980	$1,735	$1,540	$1,430	$1,210	$1,045	$965

IMPERIAL GRADE — gold inlaid hunting scene.

	$2,420	$2,090	$1,925	$1,760	$1,595	$1,485	$1,320

Note: Standard, Skeet and Slug with steel frame mfg. 1965-1972, designated "Dynamic" 12 ga., values are the same.

MODEL 500 STANDARD — 12 ga., 26 or 28 in. barrel, various chokes, vent. rib, gas operated, checkered pistol grip stock. Mfg. 1976-disc.

	$330	$310	$305	$265	$230	$195	$165

MODEL 520 DELUXE — engraved receiver.

	$385	$365	$330	$290	$260	$220	$195

MODEL 520 ELDORADO GOLD — fine wood, engraved gold, inlaid receiver. Mfg. 1977-disc.

	$990	$770	$715	$660	$580	$525	$470

MODEL 530 AUTO TRAP — similar to 500, except 30 in. and 32 in. full, very high rib, special trap stock, pad.

	$660	$550	$525	$440	$415	$385	$330

Grading	100%	98%	95%	90%	80%	70%	60%

SHOTGUNS - O/U

DE LUXE MODEL PRITI — 12 or 20 ga., boxlock action, ST, ejectors, 26 or 28 in. VR barrels with fixed chokes. Imported 1988-1989 only.

	$395	$350	$315	$285	$240	$215	$185

Last Mfg.'s Sug. Retail was $460.

This model was imported exclusively by FIE Firearms located in Hialeah, FL.

ALCIONE MODEL — 12 ga., 28 in. barrels, less engraving than Alcione SL, separated barrels. Importation disc. 1989.

	$675	$550	$495	$460	$430	$380	$335

Last Mfg.'s Sug. Retail was $800.

Previously designated Diamond Model.

This model was imported exclusively by FIE Firearms located in Hialeah, FL.

ALCIONE SL — 12 ga., 27 or 28 in. barrels, 6 lbs. 13 oz., separated barrels, ejectors, single trigger, silver finished receiver engraved with luggage case. Importation disc. 1986.

	$1,150	$995	$875	$800	$725	$640	$550

Last Mfg.'s Sug. Retail was $1,595.

BLACK MAGIC SPORTING HUNTER — 12 ga. only, 3 in. chambers, 28 in. separated barrels with VR and Franchokes, black receiver with gold accents and trigger, SST, ejectors, checkered walnut stock and forearm, 7 lbs. Imported 1989-91.

	$995	$875	$800	$725	$650	$575	$495

Last Mfg.'s Sug. Retail was $1,249.

The Black Magic Model Series was imported exclusively by American Arms, Inc. located in North Kansas City, MO.

▲ *Black Magic Lightweight Hunter* — similar to Black Magic Sporting Hunter except 2¾ in. chambers only, 26 in. separated barrels with VR and Franchokes, alloy receiver, 6 lbs. Imported 1989-91.

	$975	$850	$775	$700	$625	$550	$475

Last Mfg.'s Sug. Retail was $1,209.

SPORTING 2000 — 12 ga. only, design for sporting clays or hunting, 28 in. vent. ported barrels with target VR and choke tubes, SST, ejectors, select walnut with checkering, solid pad, 7¾ lbs. Imported 1992-1993 only.

	$1,450	$1,250	$995	$850	$725	$650	$575

Last Mfg.'s Sug. Retail was $1,619.

ARISTOCRAT FIELD — 12 ga., 26, 28, or 30 in. barrels, various chokes, vent. rib, auto ejectors, boxlock, selective single trigger, checkered pistol grip stock. Mfg. 1960-1969.

	$660	$470	$440	$395	$375	$340	$310

ARISTOCRAT MAGNUM — similar to Field, except 32 in. barrel, 3 in. chamber, full choke, pad. Mfg. 1962-1965.

	$660	$470	$440	$395	$375	$340	$310

ARISTOCRAT SKEET — similar to Field, but 26 in. vent. rib, bored skeet no. 1 and no. 2. Mfg. 1960-1969.

	$715	$525	$495	$450	$430	$395	$365

ARISTOCRAT TRAP — 30 in. vent. rib barrel, bored mod. and full, trap stock Mfg. 1960-1969.

	$745	$550	$525	$480	$455	$415	$380

ARISTOCRAT SILVER KING — select wood, engraved coin finished receiver. Mfg. 1962-1969.

	$750	$560	$535	$485	$470	$430	$400

ARISTOCRAT DELUXE — finer wood, more engraving. Mfg. 1960-1966.

	$990	$870	$835	$810	$770	$715	$660

ARISTOCRAT SUPREME — gold inlaid game birds. Mfg. 1960-1966.

	$1,430	$1,265	$1,155	$1,075	$990	$935	$880

Grading	100%	98%	95%	90%	80%	70%	60%

ARISTOCRAT IMPERIAL — high grade wood, more engraving. Mfg. 1967-1969.

| | $2,640 | $2,200 | $2,090 | $1,925 | $1,815 | $1,650 | $1,430 |

ARISTOCRAT MONTE CARLO — highest grade wood, elaborate engraving and inlay, mfg. 1967-1969.

| | $3,520 | $3,080 | $2,915 | $2,640 | $2,420 | $2,090 | $1,870 |

FALCONET S — 12 ga., lightweight model of the Alcione SL, 27 or 28 in. barrels, 6 lbs. 1 oz., separated barrels, moderate engraving on silver finish receiver. Disc. 1985.

| | $895 | $765 | $660 | $560 | $510 | $460 | $410 |

Last Mfg.'s Sug. Retail was $1,015.

FALCONET FIELD — 12, 16, 20, 28, or .410 ga., 24-30 in. barrels, various chokes, auto ejectors, select single trigger, engraved alloy receiver, checkered walnut stock. Mfg. 1968-1975.

	100%	98%	95%	90%	80%	70%	60%
Buckskin (light)	$550	$495	$470	$440	$415	$385	$360
Ebony (black)	$550	$495	$470	$440	$415	$385	$360
Silver	$605	$550	$525	$495	$470	$415	$385

Add 25% for 28 or .410 ga.

FALCONET SKEET — 26 in. barrels, bored skeet no. 1 and no. 2, wide vent. rib, case hardened steel receiver. Mfg. 1970-1974.

| | $935 | $855 | $825 | $770 | $715 | $690 | $650 |

FALCONET INTERNATIONAL SKEET — higher grade wood, more engraving. Mfg. 1970-1974.

| | $1,045 | $935 | $865 | $825 | $770 | $745 | $700 |

FALCONET STANDARD TRAP — 12 ga., 30 in. mod. and full, wide vent. rib, trap stock, pad. Mfg. 1970-1974.

| | $935 | $855 | $825 | $770 | $715 | $690 | $650 |

FALCONET INTERNATIONAL TRAP — higher grade wood, more engraving. Mfg. 1970-1974.

| | $1,045 | $935 | $865 | $825 | $770 | $745 | $700 |

FALCONET 2000 — 12 ga. only, boxlock with alloy receiver featuring silver finish with gold plated game scenes, 26 in. separated barrels with VR and choke tubes, SST, ejectors, select checkered walnut stock and forearm, 6 lbs. Importation began 1992.

| Mfg.'s Sug. Retail | $1,419 | $1,260 | $995 | $850 | $725 | $650 | $575 | $500 |

PEREGRINE MODEL 451 — 12 ga., 26-28 in. barrels, various chokes, vent. rib, auto ejectors, alloy receiver, selective single trigger, checkered pistol grip stock. Mfg. 1975.

| | $605 | $550 | $525 | $495 | $440 | $415 | $360 |

PEREGRINE MODEL 400 — similar to 451, except steel receiver. Mfg. 1975.

| | $660 | $605 | $570 | $540 | $495 | $460 | $385 |

MODEL 2003 TRAP — 12 ga., 30 or 32 in. barrels, imp. mod. and full, or full and full, boxlock, auto ejectors, single selective trigger, high vent. rib, trap style stock, pad, cased. Mfg. 1976. Disc.

| | $1,205 | $1,090 | $1,045 | $910 | $855 | $770 | $660 |

MODEL 2004 TRAP — similar to 2003, except single barrel, cased. Mfg. 1976. Disc.

| | $1,205 | $1,090 | $1,045 | $910 | $855 | $770 | $660 |

MODEL 2005 COMBINATION TRAP — two sets of barrels, one single, one O/U, cased. Mfg. 1976. Disc.

| | $1,815 | $1,595 | $1,515 | $1,320 | $1,210 | $1,075 | $935 |

MODEL 2005/3 COMBINATION TRAP — three sets of barrels, cased. Mfg. 1976. Disc.

| | $2,420 | $2,090 | $1,980 | $1,705 | $1,515 | $1,485 | $1,320 |

Grading	100%	98%	95%	90%	80%	70%	60%

UNDERGUN MODEL 3000 — radical competition trap, very high rib separated barrels, single and O/U, set cased. Disc.

	100%	98%	95%	90%	80%	70%	60%
	$2,750	$2,530	$2,310	$2,090	$1,980	$1,870	$1,760

SHOTGUNS: SIDE-BY-SIDE

AIRONE — 12 ga., double barrel, choice of barrel length and chokes, box lock, Anson & Deeley, auto ejectors, double triggers, checkered English style stock, engraved. Mfg. 1940-1950.

	$1,320	$1,100	$935	$825	$745	$715	$660

ASTORE — double barrel, similar to Airone, except less engraving, extractors. Mfg. 1937-1960.

	$990	$910	$770	$715	$635	$580	$550

ASTORE 5 — similar to Astore, except higher grade wood, more engraving, auto ejectors. Disc.

	$2,200	$1,925	$1,650	$1,540	$1,460	$1,375	$1,320

ASTORE II — similar to Astore 5, except less elaborate, currently mfg. in Spain for Franchi.

	$1,210	$1,045	$935	$880	$800	$715	$660

SIDELOCK DOUBLE BARREL — 12, 16, or 20 ga., barrels and choke custom order, stock to order, hand detachable side lock, self-opening action, auto ejectors, six grades offered, they differ only in overall quality and ornamentation, and grade of wood used.

	100%	98%	95%	90%	80%	70%	60%
Condor	$7,700	$6,600	$6,050	$5,720	$5,500	$4,620	$3,960
Imperial	$10,450	$9,350	$8,800	$8,250	$7,480	$6,600	$5,720
Imperiales	$10,670	$9,570	$9,020	$8,470	$7,700	$6,820	$5,940

SIDE-LOCK DOUBLE BARREL

▲ *No. 5 Imperial Monte Carlo*

	$15,400	$13,200	$11,000	$9,900	$9,350	$8,250	$7,150

▲ *No. 11 Imperial Monte Carlo*

	$16,500	$14,300	$12,100	$11,000	$10,450	$9,350	$8,250

▲ *Imperial Monte Carlo Extra*

	$19,800	$17,050	$14,300	$13,200	$12,650	$11,000	$9,900

Note: Imperial Monte Carlo Extra is currently being mfg. on special order only; the other models are disc.

FRANCOTTE, AUGUSTE & CIE. S.A.

Manufacturer located in Leige, Belgium since 1805. Currently imported by Armes De Chasse located in Hertford, NC. Previously imported by VL&O between 1900-1930s, Abercrombie & Fitch until approx. 1962.

REVOLVERS

Francotte manufactured Pryse-type revolvers at the end of the previous century, and these revolvers bore the name of the well-known British retailer. Encountered only infrequently domestically, these specimens found overseas are usually priced in the $150-$650 range.

RIFLES

All newly mfg. rifles in this section are custom made to the purchaser's individual specifications.

BOLT ACTION MODEL — many calibers available between .18 Bee and .505 Gibbs Mag., select checkered walnut stock, engraved mag. floor plate, gold inlays optional, values below assume engraving.

Grading	100%	98%	95%	90%	80%	70%	60%

▲ *Short Bolt Action* — cals. with shorter cartridges.
   Mfg.'s Sug. Retail $10,600 $9,400 $7,350 $6,000 $4,950 $4,100 $3,300 $2,700
   Subtract $3,250 if without engraving.

▲ *Standard Model* — cals. with medium cartridge lengths.
   Mfg.'s Sug. Retail $8,500 $7,825 $6,100 $4,975 $4,100 $3,300 $2,700 $2,000
   Subtract $2,675 if without engraving.

▲ *Magnum Action* — cals. with longer cartridge lengths.
   Mfg.'s Sug. Retail $14,800 $13,750 $10,850 $9,350 $7,750 $6,400 $4,950 $3,950
   Subtract $7,850 if without engraving.

SINGLE SHOT MOUNTAIN RIFLE — available in a variety of cals., boxlock or sidelock action, custom order only.

▲ *Boxlock Mountain Rifle* — 6.5x50R, 7x57R, or 7x65R.
   Mfg.'s Sug. Retail $15,250 $13,900 $11,000 $9,450 $7,850 $6,500 $5,000 $4,000
   Subtract $4,800 if without engraving.
   Add 10% for optional sideplates.

▲ *Sidelock Mountain Rifle* — 7x65R or 7mm Rem. Mag. cal.
   Mfg.'s Sug. Retail $28,000 $24,800 $20,350 $16,650 $13,000 $10,500 $9,000 $8,000
   Subtract $5,725 if without engraving.

STANDARD SxS BOXLOCK RIFLE — available in a variety of cals., custom order only.
   Mfg.'s Sug. Retail $20,100 $18,650 $15,500 $11,350 $8,750 $6,950 $5,750 $5,000
   Subtract $7,600 if without engraving.
   Add $1,449 for optional sideplates.
   Add 15% for .375 H&H, .458 Win. Mag. cal., or other larger calibers upon request.

STANDARD SxS SIDELOCK RIFLE — available in a variety of cals., custom order only.
   Mfg.'s Sug. Retail $32,000 $29,450 $25,000 $20,250 $16,500 $13,000 $10,500 $9,000
   Subtract $7,000 if without engraving.

SHOTGUNS

All newly manufactured shotguns in this section are custom made to purchaser's individual specifications. Basic types listed below are also available in 24 or 32 ga. upon special order. Auguste Francotte does not manufacture guns by model - all guns are custom order.

BOXLOCK SxS — premium grade Belgium side-by-side, double triggers standard, auto ejectors. Available in 12, 16, 20, 28, or .410 ga., with English scroll engraving, Anson & Deeley boxlock action.
   Mfg.'s Sug. Retail $16,500 $15,450 $11,250 $8,000 $6,250 $5,000 $4,000 $3,250
   Subtract $5,925 if without engraving.
   Add 10% for 28 or .410 ga.
   Add $1,159 for sideplates with engraving.

▲ *Deluxe Anson & Deeley* — gold inlaid game scenes, and engraving is by customer's personal preference.
   Prices and options are quoted per individual request.

SIDELOCK SxS — true sidelock action, available in 12, 16, 20, 28, or .410 ga., Arabesque scroll engraving, various chokes and barrel lengths, custom order only.
   Mfg.'s Sug. Retail $29,300 $27,300 $22,000 $18,750 $15,150 $12,000 $9,000 $7,750
   Subtract $4,850 if without engraving.
   Add 10% for 28 or .410 ga.

▲ *Deluxe sidelock* — gold inlaid game scenes and engraving are by customer's personal preference
   Prices and options are quoted per individual request.

Grading	100%	98%	95%	90%	80%	70%	60%
JUBILEE— case colored receiver with hand engraving.							
	$2,250	$1,875	$1,525	$1,325	$1,100	$975	$850
No. 14	$2,750	$2,250	$1,975	$1,775	$1,600	$1,450	$1,150
No. 18	$2,950	$2,550	$2,250	$1,925	$1,700	$1,550	$1,225
No. 20	$3,450	$2,900	$2,575	$2,275	$1,900	$1,725	$1,375
No. 25	$4,000	$3,500	$3,000	$2,500	$2,150	$1,925	$1,575
No. 30	$5,450	$4,975	$4,500	$4,000	$3,500	$2,500	$2,200

KNOCKABOUT — disc. circa 1975.

	100%	98%	95%	90%	80%	70%	60%
	$2,350	$1,850	$1,575	$1,265	$1,100	$935	$825

> Add 75% for 20 ga.
> Add approx. 200%-250% for 28 or .410 ga.

NO. 45 EAGLE GRADE — this model can be identified by the gold eagle on frame bottom, disc. circa 1977.

	100%	98%	95%	90%	80%	70%	60%
	$7,650	$6,700	$5,850	$4,950	$4,250	$3,800	$3,000

FRASER, DANL. & CO.

Manufacturer located in Europe. Limited importation into the United States.

Danl. Fraser & Co. has been building rifles since 1873 (originally in Edinburgh, Scotland).

HIGHLANDER SINGLE SHOT — .22 LR or .22 Hornet cal., underlever falling block action (color case hardened), 24 in. (½ round, ½ octagon) barrel, folding express-style sights, pistol grip walnut stock with fine checkering. Disc.

$415	$335	$300	$280	$260	$240	$220

Last Mfg.'s Sug. Retail was $475.

▲ *Royal Highlander* — .22 LR or .22 Hornet cal., mfg. in Scotland, rose and scroll engraving with 18 Kt. inlays. Special order only — prices available upon request.

FRASER FIREARMS CORP.

Previously manufactured by R.B. Industries, Ltd. until 1990. Previously distributed by Fraser Firearms Corp. located in Fraser, MI.

FRASER 25 CAL. — .25 cal. only, copy of the Bauer semi-auto pocket model, 6 shot mag., 2¼ in. barrel, stainless steel construction.

$120	$100	$90

Last Mfg.'s Sug. Retail was $133.

> Add $17 for Model 2 (black nylon grips).
> Add $115 for Model 3 (24 Kt. gold plated).

FREEDOM ARMS

Manufacturer located in Freedom, WY.

Percussion mini-revolvers can be found in the Blackpowder Section of this text.

MINI-REVOLVERS: STAINLESS STEEL

Because Freedom Arms' manufacturing capacity has been maximized due to the success of the .454 Casull revolver, the mini-revolver series has been temporarily discontinued starting in 1989. As a result, prices have escalated on these models due to no production and normal demand.

Grading	100%	98%	95%	90%	80%	70%	60%

FA-S-22LR (PATRIOT) — .22 LR cal., 5 shot, 1, 1¾ (disc. 1988), or 3 (disc. 1988) in. barrel, Hi-Gloss finish.

$245 $200 $150

Last Mfg.'s Sug. Retail was $153.

Add $15 for 3 in. barrel model (FA-BG-22LR, Minute-Man, disc. 1988).

FA-S-22M (IRONSIDES) — .22 Mag. cal., 4 shot, 1, 1¾ (disc. 1988), or 3 in. barrel, Hi Gloss finish.

$295 $225 $185

Last Mfg.'s Sug. Retail was $177.

Add $43 for 3 in. barrel model (Bostonian).

FA-S-22-LR BUCKLE/REVOLVER COMBINATION — .22 LR, 1 in. barrel, pistol is housed in belt buckle.

$275 $225 $185

Last Mfg.'s Sug. Retail was $193.

▲ *.22 Mag. cal.*

$325 $265 $215

Last Mfg.'s Sug. Retail was $216.

F

CASULL SA REVOLVERS: STAINLESS STEEL

Freedom Arms also offers a complete line of accessories and factory installed options. The factory should be contacted directly for an up-to-date listing and prices.

MODEL 252 VARMINT — .22 LR cal., 5 shot, unique two point firing pin, choice of 7½ (Varmint Class Model with express sights, black/green laminated hardwood grips) or 10 in. (Silhouette Class Model with competition sights and black micarta grips), approx. 3¾ lbs. New 1991.

Mfg.'s Sug. Retail $1,454 $1,195 $895 $725

Add $253 for extra .22 Mag. cylinder.

▲ *Model 252 Silhouette* — silhouette shooting features, 10 in. barrel only, black micarta grips.

Mfg.'s Sug. Retail $1,509 $1,275 $940 $850

Add $23 for front sight hood.

MODEL 353 FIELD GRADE — .357 Mag., 4¾, 6, 7½, or 9 in. barrel on non-glare field grade finish, Pachmayr grips, adj. sights, 3¾ lbs. New 1992.

Mfg.'s Sug. Retail $1,253 $1,080 $875 $695

▲ *Model 353 Premier Grade* — similar to Field Grade, except has premier grade finish and laminated hardwood grips. New 1992.

Mfg.'s Sug. Retail $1,627 $1,350 $975 $750

▲ *Model 353 Silhouette* — includes silhouette competition sights, 9 in. barrel, field grade finish, Pachmayr grips and trigger overtravel screw. New 1992.

Mfg.'s Sug. Retail $1,347 $1,125 $885 $675

.44 REM. MAG. FIELD GRADE — .44 Rem. Mag., 4¾, 6, 7½, or 10 in. barrel.

Mfg.'s Sug. Retail $1,253 $1,080 $875 $695

▲ *.44 Rem. Mag. Premier Grade* — adj. sight, 4¾, 6, 7½, or 10 in. barrel.

Mfg.'s Sug. Retail $1,627 $1,350 $975 $750

Subtract $106 fixed sight.

▲ *.44 Rem. Mag. Silhouette* — field grade finish with silhouette competition sights, 10 in. barrel only, includes Pachmayr grips.

Mfg.'s Sug. Retail $1,347 $1,125 $885 $675

.454 CASULL FIELD GRADE — .454 Casull cal., 5 shot, 4¾ (fixed sight only), 6, 7½, or 10 in. barrel, stainless steel matte finish with Pachmayr presentation grips. New 1988.

Mfg.'s Sug. Retail $1,301 $1,095 $875 $695

Add $253 for extra .45 LC or .45 ACP (new 1990) cylinder.

Subtract $94 for fixed sight.

Grading	100%	98%	95%	90%	80%	70%	60%

▲ **Silhouette Model** — .454 Casull cal., includes 10 in. barrel, Pachmayr grips, field grade finish, silhouette competition sights, and trigger overtravel screw. Mfg. 1992 only.
$995 $825 $675

Last Mfg.'s Sug. Retail was $1,132.

▲ **Silhouette Pak** — .44 Mag., includes 10 in. barrel revolver, silhouette competition sight, honed action with 3 lb. trigger pull, plastic grips, locking aluminum carrying case with cleaning kit and tool. Mfg. 1990 only.
$1,000 $850 $750

Last Mfg.'s Sug. Retail was $1,180.

.454 CASULL PREMIER GRADE — .44 Rem. Mag. (disc.), .45 Win. Mag. (disc. 1989), .45 LC (disc. 1990), or .454 Casull cal., 5 shot, stainless steel with brushed finish, single action revolver, the .454 Casull shoots 225 grain bullet at over 2000 fps., 4¾, 6, 7½, 10, and 12 (disc. 1988) in. barrels, walnut (older mfg.) or laminated hardwood grips, adj. sights. Mfg. 1983-present.
Mfg.'s Sug. Retail $1,677 $1,375 $975 $775

Subtract $109 for fixed sight.

The no sights model was available in 7½ in. barrel only - receiver is drilled and tapped for scope base - mfg. 1990-91.

▲ **Silhouette Pak** — .44 Mag., includes 10 in. barrel revolver, silhouette competition sight, honed action with 3 lb. trigger pull, hardwood grips, locking aluminum carrying case with cleaning kit and tool. Mfg. 1990 only.
$1,275 $995 $850

Last Mfg.'s Sug. Retail was $1,395.

MODEL 555 FIELD GRADE — .50 AE cal., stainless steel, matte finish, Pachmayr grips, 4¾, 6, 7½, or 10 in. barrel. New 1994.
Mfg.'s Sug. Retail $1,301 $1,095 $895 $725

▲ **Model 555 Premier Grade** — adj. sights, brushed finish, impregnated hardwood grips. New 1994.
Mfg.'s Sug. Retail $1,677 $1,395 $995 $795

HUNTER PAK FIELD GRADE — .357 Mag., .44 Rem. Mag., or .454 Casull cal., 7½ in. barrel, plastic grips, field grade low profile adj. sight or no front sight base, sling and studs, locking aluminum carrying case with cleaning kit and tool. Mfg. 1990-1993.
$1,075 $925 $775

Last Mfg.'s Sug. Retail was $1,333.

Add $76 for low profile adj. sight and Pachmayr grips.

▲ **Hunter Pak Premier Grade** — .357 Mag., .44 Rem. Mag., or .454 Casull cal., 7½ in. barrel, ebony micarta grips, no sights or premier grade adj. sight, sling and studs, locking aluminum carrying case with cleaning kit and tool. Mfg. 1990-1993.
$1,395 $1,025 $850

Last Mfg.'s Sug. Retail was $1,611.

Add $100 for adj. sights.

U.S. DEPUTY MARSHALL — 3 in. barrel only with no ejector, fixed sights, U.S. Marshall medallion in left hardwood grip. Mfg. 1990-1993.
$1,325 $900 $750

Last Mfg.'s Sug. Retail was $1,558.

Add $83 for adj. sights.

SIGNATURE EDITION — .454 Casull, high polish stainless steel, 7½ in. barrel only, rosewood grips, cased with accessories, only 93 of 100 were actually mfg.
$2,300 $1,750 $1,300

Last Mfg.'s Sug. Retail was $2,684.

PRIMUS INTER PARES — 1 of every 100 guns is made in this variation, includes octagonal barrel, ivory grips, 7½ in. barrel, and cased. Disc. 1993.

FRENCH MILITARY
Manufactured in various locations in France.

Grading	100%	98%	95%	90%	80%	70%	60%

MODEL 1886 LEBEL — bolt action, 8mm Lebel, 32 in. barrel, adj. sight, military stock. Mfg. 1886 - WWII.

	$125	$100	$75	$65	$50	$40	$25

1936 MAS MILITARY RIFLE — bolt action, 7.5mm MAS, 22 in. barrel, adj. sight, military stock, bayonet in forearm. Mfg. 1936-1940.

	$125	$100	$75	$65	$50	$40	$25

MODEL 1935A AUTO PISTOL — 7.65mm long, 8 shot, 4.3 in. barrel, fixed sights, blue, checkered wood grips, French service sidearm. Mfg. 1935-1945.

	$195	$175	$150	$125	$110	$100	$90

Add 50% if Nazi proofed.

MODEL 1935S — 7.65mm French Long cal., 4⅓ in. barrel, enamel finish, Colt Govt. Model locking system, 26 oz.

	$325	$295	$260	$225	$195	$170	$150

M.A.B. MODEL C — 7.65mm, design based on FN Browning Model 1910, 6.1 in. barrel. Introduced 1933.

	$250	$220	$190	$170	$150	$125	$110

M.A.B. MODEL D — 7.65mm, 7 in barrel, single action, similar to Model C, mfg. commercially 1933-1940, many thousands mfg. for the German military during WWII (marked "Pistole MAB Kaliber 7.65mm")

	$275	$225	$200	$175	$150	$125	$110

MODEL M.A.B. PA - 15 — 9mm, single action semi-auto, 16 shot, currently used by French military.

	$550	$500	$450

MODEL M.A.B. PA - 15 TARGET — rare target variation of PA-15, adj. sight, 6 in. barrel, cased.

	$1,250	$1,000	$750

FRIGON GUNS, INC.

Previously manufactured by Marocchi in Italy. Previously imported by Frigon Guns, Inc. located in Clay Center, KS.

FT I — 12 ga. only, single barrel trap gun, blued finish, 32 or 34 in. VR barrel, quick-change stock. Mfg. 1986-94.

	$925	$675	$525	$435	$375	$350	$295

Last Mfg.'s Sug. Retail was $1,100.

FTC — 12 ga. only, quick-change stock, trap combination gun includes 1 single barrel and 1 set of O/U barrels, cased. Mfg. 1986-94.

	$1,700	$1,325	$1,050	$875	$775	$685	$620

Last Mfg.'s Sug. Retail was $1,975.

FS-4 — 4-barrel skeet set including 12, 20, 28, or .410 ga., individual forearms, quick-change stock, vent. barrels (except for .410 ga.), cased. Mfg. 1986-94.

	$2,575	$1,975	$1,675	$1,475	$1,350	$1,250	$1,150

Last Mfg.'s Sug. Retail was $2,890.

FROMMER PISTOLS

Femaru-Fegyver-Es Gepgyar R.T., Budapest, Hungary.

Please refer to the Femaru listing in this section.

FURR ARMS

Manufacturer located in Orem, UT.
Please refer to the Gatling Gun Company listing in this text.

F

F

G section

GALEF SHOTGUNS

Previous importer of Zabala Hermanos (Spanish) and Antonio Zoli (Italian) shotguns.

Grading	100%	98%	95%	90%	80%	70%	60%

COMPANION FOLDING SINGLE BARREL — 12, 16, 20, 28, or .410 ga., 28 in. barrel, full choke, 30 in. full, 12 ga. only, hammerless, underlever, checkered pistol grip stock.

	100%	98%	95%	90%	80%	70%	60%
	$125	$100	$90	$80	$70	$60	$55

MONTE CARLO TRAP — 12 ga., single barrel, 32 in. full vent. rib, hammerless, underlever, recoil pad, checkered pistol grip Monte Carlo stock, disc.

	100%	98%	95%	90%	80%	70%	60%
	$225	$185	$175	$150	$135	$125	$100

SILVER SNIPE — 12 or 20 ga., O/U, 3 in. chambers, 26, 28, or 30 in. barrels, imp. cyl. and mod. or full and mod. vent. rib, checkered pistol grip stock, boxlock, extractors, single trigger, mfg. by Angelo Zoli, disc.

	100%	98%	95%	90%	80%	70%	60%
	$450	$400	$350	$295	$275	$250	$220

GOLDEN SNIPE — O/U, similar to Silver Snipe, except has auto ejectors.

	100%	98%	95%	90%	80%	70%	60%
	$525	$475	$425	$375	$325	$300	$275

SILVER HAWK — 12 or 20 ga., SxS, 3 in. chambers, 26, 28, or 30 in. barrels, imp. cyl. and mod. or mod. and full, boxlock, extractors, checkered pistol grip and beavertail forearm. Mfg. by Angelo Zoli, 1968-1972.

	100%	98%	95%	90%	80%	70%	60%
	$425	$395	$350	$295	$255	$225	$200

GALEF ZABALA DOUBLE — 10, 12, 16, or 20 ga., SxS, 22, 26, 28, or 30 in. barrels, boxlock, extractors.

	100%	98%	95%	90%	80%	70%	60%
10 gauge	$250	$230	$200	$175	$150	$140	$125
Other gauges	$200	$175	$150	$130	$120	$110	$100

GALIL

Manufactured by Israel Military Industries (IMI). Previously imported by Action Arms, Ltd. located in Philadelphia, PA until 1994. Previously imported by Springfield Armory located in Geneseo, IL and Magnum Research, Inc., located in Minneapolis, MN.

The Models AR, ARM, Galil Sporter (disc. 1993), and Sniper Outfit have not been imported since the federal ban on this semi-auto configuration was implemented. Magnum Research importation can be denoted by a serial number prefix "MR", while Action Arms imported rifles have either "AA" or "AAL" prefixes.

RIFLES: SEMI-AUTO

Models 329, 330 (Hadar II), 331, 332, 339 (sniper system with 6/40 mounted Nimrod scope), 361, 372, 386, and 392 all refer to various configurations of the Galil rifle.

MODEL AR — .223 cal. or .308 cal., semi-auto paramilitary design rifle, gas operated - rotating bolt, 16.1 in. (.223 only) or 19 in. (.308 only) barrel, parkerized, folding stock. Flip-up Tritium night sights. 8.6 lbs.

	100%	98%	95%	90%	80%	70%	60%
	$1,795	$1,500	$1,250	$1,100	$900	$775	$650

Last Mfg.'s Sug. Retail was $950.

MODEL ARM — similar to Model AR, except includes folding bi-pod, vented hardwood handguard, and carrying handle.

	100%	98%	95%	90%	80%	70%	60%
	$2,100	$1,850	$1,575	$1,375	$1,100	$975	$825

Last Mfg.'s Sug. Retail was $1,050.

Grading	100%	98%	95%	90%	80%	70%	60%

GALIL SPORTER — similar to above, except has one-piece thumbhole stock, 4 (.308 Win.) or 5 (.223 Rem.) shot mag., choice of wood (disc.) or polymer hand guard, 8½ lbs. Imported 1991-1993.

	$875	$725	$600	$525	$475	$425	$395

Last Mfg.'s Sug. Retail was $950.

HADAR II — .308 cal., gas operated, paramilitary type configuration, 1 piece walnut thumbhole stock with pistol grip and forearm, 18½ in. barrel, adj. rear sight, recoil pad, 4 shot (standard) or 25 shot mag., 10.3 lbs. Imported 1989 only.

	$1,050	$875	$750	$675	$575	$500	$450

Last Mfg.'s Sug. Retail was $998.

SNIPER OUTFIT — .308 cal., semi-auto, limited production, sniper model built to exact I.D.F. specifications for improved accuracy, 20 in. heavy barrel, hardwood folding stock (adj. recoil pad and adj. cheekpiece) and forearm, includes Tritium night sights, bi-pod, detachable 6x40mm Nimrod scope, two 25 shot mags., carrying/storage case, 14.1 lbs. Imported 1989 only.

	$4,500	$4,000	$3,650	$3,150	$2,650	$2,150	$1,750

Last Mfg.'s Sug. Retail was $3,995.

GAMBA, RENATO

Manufacturer located in Gardone V.T., Italy. Gamba U.S.A., a subsidiary of FNGB, Corp., is the exclusive importer for Renato Gamba guns beginning late 1994. Pistols were previously imported and distributed (until 1990) by Armscorp of America, Inc. located in Baltimore, MD. Shotguns were previously (until 1992) imported by Heckler & Koch, Inc. located in Sterling, VA.

RENATO GAMBA

Filli Gamba (Gamba Brothers) was founded in 1946. G. Gamba sold his tooling to his son, Renato, in 1967 when Renato Gamba left his brothers and S.A.B. was formed. Filli Gamba closed in 1989 and the Zanotti firm was also purchsed the same year.

Renato Gamba firearms have had limited importation since 1986. In 1989, several smaller European firearms companies were purchased by R. Gamba and are now part of the Renato Gamba Group. The importation of R. Gamba guns changed in 1990 to reflect their long term interest in exporting firearms to America. Earlier imported models may be rare but have not enjoyed much collectability to date.

PISTOLS

R. Gamba pistols are currently not being imported into the U.S. Importation was discontinued in 1990.

SAB G90 STANDARD — 7.65 P (disc.), 9x18mm Ultra (disc.), or 9mm Para. cal., double action, 4.72 in. barrel, 10 (C/B 1994) or 15* shot side release mag., blue or chrome (disc.) finish, hammer drop safety on frame, smooth walnut grips, 2.2 lbs.

Mfg.'s Sug. Retail	$736		$625	$375	$325	$295	$275	$250	$225

Add $65 for chrome finish (disc.).

▲ *SAB G90 Competition* — 9mm Para., similar to SAB G90 Standard, except has adj. rear sight, "cocked and locked" operation, and checkered walnut grips. Imported 1990 only.

Mfg.'s Sug. Retail	$1,364		$1,175	$425	$375	$325	$300	$275	$250

Add $205 for stainless steel (SAB G90 Service Competition).

SAB G91 COMPACT — similar to SAB G90, except has 3.54 in. barrel, 12 shot mag., 1.87 lbs.

Mfg.'s Sug. Retail	$736		$625	$375	$325	$295	$275	$250	$225

Add $65 for chrome finish (disc.).

Grading	100%	98%	95%	90%	80%	70%	60%

▲ **SAB G91 Competition** — 9mm Para., similar to SAB G91 Compact, except has adj. rear sight, "cocked and locked" operation, and checkered walnut grips. Imported 1990 only.

	$450	**$395**	**$330**	**$300**	**$275**	**$250**	**$225**

Last Mfg.'s Sug. Retail was $575.

SAB G2001 — .380 ACP cal., double action, mfg. from forged and milled steel, high polish blue, neoprene grips, slide mount and manual safety with firing pin block, 10 shot mag. Importation began 1996.

Mfg.'s Sug. Retail	**$699**	**$615**	**$395**	**$325**	**$295**	**$275**	**$250**	**$225**

REVOLVERS

TRIDENT FAST ACTION — .32 S&W or .38 Spl. cal., 2½ or 3 in. barrel, double action, blued receiver with checkered walnut grips, 6 shot, 23 oz.

Mfg.'s Sug. Retail	**$630**	**$550**	**$425**	**$360**	**$330**	**$295**	**$270**	**$245**

TRIDENT SUPER — .32 S&W or .38 Spl. cal., 4 in. vent. rib barrel, 6 shot, double action, checkered walnut grips, 25 oz.

Mfg.'s Sug. Retail	**$683**	**$585**	**$450**	**$375**	**$340**	**$310**	**$280**	**$250**

TRIDENT MATCH 900 — .32 S&W Long W.C. or .38 Spl. cal., match gun featuring 6 in. heavy barrel and anatomically compatible checkered walnut grips, target sights, 2.2 lbs.

Mfg.'s Sug. Retail	**$895**	**$750**	**$660**	**$595**	**$525**	**$475**	**$430**	**$390**

▲ **Trident Match 901** — similar to Trident Match 900.

Mfg.'s Sug. Retail	**$895**	**$750**	**$660**	**$595**	**$525**	**$475**	**$430**	**$390**

RIFLES

SAFARI EXPRESS SxS — 7x65R, 9.3x74R, or .375 H&H cal., 25 in. barrels with open sights, underlug locking with Greener crossbolt, ejectors except on .375 H&H, coin finished receiver with scroll work and game scene engraving, DTs, deluxe checkered walnut stock with cheekpiece and recoil pad, 9.9 lbs.

	$5,685	**$4,575**	**$3,950**	**$3,575**	**$3,175**	**$2,850**	**$2,500**

Last Mfg.'s Sug. Retail was $6,630.

CONCORDE EXPRESS O/U — .30-06, 8x57LS, or 9.3x75R cal., monoblock receiver, Boss type action, ejectors, cased.

Mfg.'s Sug. Retail	**$7,540**	**$6,700**	**$5,950**	**$5,400**	**$4,900**	**$4,500**	**$4,100**	**$3,750**

Add $300 for automatic double safety system.

DAYTONA SL EXPRESS O/U — .30-06, .375 H&H, or 9.3x74R cal., monoblock receiver with Boss type improved action, detachable Gamba trigger assembly, hand engraved sideplates with game scenes and English scroll.

Mfg.'s Sug. Retail	**$20,030**	**$18,000**	**$15,950**	**$13,000**	**$10,250**	**$8,950**	**$7,950**	**$6,950**

EXPRESS MAXIM SxS — .375 H&H, .458 Win. Mag., .470 N.E., or .458 Lott (new 1995) cal., sidelock action, fine engraving with big game scenes signed by the master engraver, includes leather case.

Mfg.'s Sug. Retail	**$52,500**	**$47,750**	**$41,000**	**$34,000**	**$26,000**	**$20,500**	**$17,500**	**$13,000**

MUSTANG EXTRA SINGLE SHOT — 5.6x50 (disc.), 5.6x57R, 6.5x57R (disc.), 7x65R, .222 Rem. (disc.), .243 Win., .270 Win., or .30-06 cal., single 25½ in. barrel configuration with highly engraved sidelock action featuring triple-bite double Purdey locking system with Greener crossbolt, extra fine vine leaf Renaissance engraving (game scene upon request), double-set triggers, best quality checkered walnut stock and forearm, 6.17 lbs.

Mfg.'s Sug. Retail	**$18,500**	**$15,250**	**$12,250**	**$10,750**	**$8,950**	**$7,900**	**$6,900**	**$6,100**

G

Grading	100%	98%	95%	90%	80%	70%	60%

RGZ 1000 BOLT ACTION — 7x64, .270 Win., 7mm Rem. Mag., .300 Win. Mag., modified Mauser K-98 action, 20½ in. barrel, pistol grip stock with cheek piece, 7 lbs.

	$1,100	$885	$825	$760	$700	$640	$575

Last Mfg.'s Sug. Retail was $1,310.

▲ *RGX 1000 Express* — similar to RGZ 1000, except has 23¾ in. barrel and double set triggers, 7.7 lbs.

	$1,255	$960	$875	$795	$725	$650	$575

Last Mfg.'s Sug. Retail was $1,475.

SHOTGUNS: OVER AND UNDER

Most O/U models (except for the Daytona Trap Model) listed below were discontinued in 1990 when H&K became the exclusive importer for R. Gamba shotguns.

EUROPA 2000 — 12 ga. only, engraved, silver finished boxlock action with sideplates, vent. rib, single trigger, ejectors, deluxe checkered stock and forearm, 6.84 lbs.

	$1,250	$995	$895	$835	$775	$715	$650

Last Mfg.'s Sug. Retail was $1,475.

EDINBURGH SUPER SLUG — 12 ga. only, trap model, SST, ejectors, engraved action, deluxe checkered stock and forearm.

	$1,225	$980	$895	$835	$775	$715	$650

Last Mfg.'s Sug. Retail was $1,425.

GRIFONE SPORTING TRAP — 12 ga. only, trap model, SST, ejectors, moderately engraved action, deluxe checkered stock and forearm.

	$1,225	$980	$895	$835	$775	$715	$650

Last Mfg.'s Sug. Retail was $1,425.

GRINTA TRAP/SKEET — 12 ga. only, trap/skeet model, SST, ejectors, medium engraving coverage.

	$1,250	$995	$895	$835	$775	$715	$650

Last Mfg.'s Sug. Retail was $1,710.

VICTORY TRAP/SKEET — similar to Grinta Model, except has better walnut and more engraving.

	$1,450	$1,275	$1,050	$995	$895	$835	$775

Last Mfg.'s Sug. Retail was $1,905.

EDINBURG MATCH — similar to Victory Model, except has different style of engraving.

	$1,630	$1,300	$1,100	$995	$895	$835	$775

Last Mfg.'s Sug. Retail was $1,930.

MONTREAL MODEL 90/91 — 12 ga. only, boxlock, interchangeable trigger assembly, select walnut, vent. rib. Available in International Trap, American Skeet, Sporting, and Field models. Add $50 for adj. single barrel.

	$2,250	$1,650	$1,300	$1,100	$1,000	$900	$800

Add $200 for single selective trigger. *

The Model 90 has a flat-sided receiver, while the Model 91 has a Daytona sculpted receiver.

MONTREAL 90/91 AMERICAN TRAP COMBO — 12 ga. only, 32 in. barrels and adj. impact, single 34 in. barrel, interchangeable trigger assembly.

	$2,800	$2,100	$1,820	$1,540	$1,400	$1,260	$1,120

SINGLE BARREL TRAP-MODEL 496 — 12 ga. only, boxlock, vent. rib.

	$1,150	$865	$750	$635	$575	$520	$460

CONCORDE GAME MODEL — 12 or 20 ga., Boss type improved locking system, ejectors, 26¾ or 28 in. VR barrels. Importation began 1995.

Mfg.'s Sug. Retail	$5,650	$4,900	$4,325	$3,850	$3,400	$2,800	$2,350	$1,900

Add $520 for Sporting Clays Model.

Grading	100%	98%	95%	90%	80%	70%	60%

▲ *Grade 7* — includes engraving featuring game scenes and English scroll.

Mfg.'s Sug. Retail	$8,710	$7,800	$6,650	$5,600	$4,500	$3,750	$3,250	$2,575

Add $493 for Sporting Clays Model.

▲ *Grade 8* — features top-of-the-line English scroll engraving.

Mfg.'s Sug. Retail	$6,353	$5,675	$4,900	$4,100	$3,500	$2,895	$2,400	$2,100

Add $493 for Sporting Clays Model.

DAYTONA VARIATIONS — 12 ga. only, monolithic boxlock action, SST, ejectors, detachable trigger group, available in either Hunting, Skeet, Pigeon, Sporting Clays, Olympic Trap, or American Trap configuration, deluxe walnut with fine English scroll engraving with game scenes. Importation began 1990.

Mfg.'s Sug. Retail	$5,933	$5,100	$4,075	$3,450	$2,800	$2,350	$1,900	$1,500

Add $682 for Sporting Clays Model.
Add $1,522 for American Trap configuration.
Add $2,200 for Daytona combo package.
Add $2,620 for extra set of O/U barrels.
Add $300 for gold inlaid nomenclature.

▲ *Grade 4 Daytona Model* — most elaborately engraved Daytona model.

Mfg.'s Sug. Retail	$16,328	$13,350	$10,150	$8,350	$6,700	$5,000	$4,250	$3,750

Add $493 for Sporting Clays Model.

▲ *Grade 5 Daytona Model* — one grade below Grade 4.

Mfg.'s Sug. Retail	$14,175	$11,750	$8,950	$7,150	$5,500	$4,350	$3,750	$3,250

Add $494 for Sporting Clays Model.

▲ *Grade 6 Daytona Model* — one grade below Grade 5.

Mfg.'s Sug. Retail	$13,125	$11,150	$8,450	$6,850	$5,000	$4,250	$3,750	$3,250

Add $499 for Sporting Clays Model.

▲ *Grade 7 Daytona Model* — introductory engraved model.

Mfg.'s Sug. Retail	$10,763	$9,450	$8,175	$6,525	$4,850	$3,950	$3,350	$2,950

DAYTONA SL — deluxe variation of the Daytona Model, except has sideplates with extensive engraving, available in the same configurations as the Daytona Model, includes case. Limited importation 1990-94.

	$10,250	$8,750	$7,250	$5,400	$4,450	$3,950	$3,500

Last Mfg.'s Sug. Retail was $11,500.

Add $400 for American Trap configuration.

▲ *Grade 3* — features hand engraved sideplates with English scroll and game scenes. Importation began 1995.

Mfg.'s Sug. Retail	$18,848	$16,650	$12,950	$9,850	$8,150	$6,600	$5,000	$4,250

DAYTONA SLHH — 12 or 20 ga., H&H style sidelock action with Boss improved lock-up, top-of-the-line model, game or competition configuration, includes leather case. Importation began in 1990.

▲ *Grade 1* — similar to Grade 2, except has better engraving.

Mfg.'s Sug. Retail	$43,575	$38,000	$24,750	$20,750	$17,500	$13,000	$10,750	$8,950

Add $2,075 for gold engraving.

▲ *Grade 2* — available in either Hunting (12 ga. only), Skeet, Trap, Pigeon, or Sporting Clays configuration.

Mfg.'s Sug. Retail	$36,255	$30,450	$22,000	$18,000	$14,750	$11,000	$9,000	$7,500

▲ *One of Thousand* — top-of-the-line model with every possible refinement, individually special ordered only.

Mfg.'s Sug. Retail	$106,029	$93,500	$78,750	$69,000	$60,000	$51,000	$42,000	$33,000

BAYERN 88 COMBINATION GUN — 12 ga. over same cals. listed for Mustang Model, coin finished boxlock action with game scene engraving, double DTs, extractors, deluxe checkered walnut stock with recoil pad, 7½ lbs.

	$1,365	$1,050	$950	$860	$775	$715	$665

Last Mfg.'s Sug. Retail was $1,595.

Grading	100%	98%	95%	90%	80%	70%	60%

SHOTGUNS: SIDE X SIDE

Previous to 1989, most of the models listed below were available in 28 ga. on a 28 ga. frame by option. These 28 ga. guns will command 15%+ premiums over values listed below.

HUNTER SUPER — 12 ga. only, Anson & Deeley engraved boxlock action with silver finish, DTs, extractors, 6.84 lbs.

	$1,750	$1,275	$895	$760	$630	$575	$525

Last Mfg.'s Sug. Retail was $1,506.

PRINCIPESSA — 12 or 20 ga., similar to Hunter Super except has English straight grip stock and better engraving, 6.62 lbs. Importation disc. 1994.

	$2,750	$1,900	$1,525	$1,250	$995	$800	$625

Last Mfg.'s Sug. Retail was $2,495.

Add $200 for single trigger.

S. VINCENT 580 EXTRA DELUXE SxS — 12 ga. only, custom made to individual preferences, very high quality, sidelock action, engraving coverage 100%.

	$4,950	$4,250	$3,500	$2,750	$2,125	$1,775	$1,625

OXFORD 90 — 12 or 20 ga., boxlock action with Purdey locking system, DTs, ejectors, scroll engraving on sideplates, deluxe checkered straight grip walnut stock with recoil pad or checkered butt, 6.84 lbs.

Mfg.'s Sug. Retail	$4,300	$3,750	$3,300	$2,875	$2,475	$2,100	$1,700	$1,250

Add $525 for single trigger.

OXFORD EXTRA — 20 ga. only, includes elegantly engraved sideplates, ejectors, and better quality hand checkered stock and forearm. Importation began 1992.

Mfg.'s Sug. Retail	$5,215	$4,675	$4,000	$3,500	$3,000	$2,650	$2,100	$1,750

MODEL 624 PRINCE — 12 or 20 ga., boxlock action, ejectors, hand checkered walnut stock and forearm. Importation began 1992.

Mfg.'s Sug. Retail	$4,376	$3,800	$3,300	$2,875	$2,475	$2,100	$1,700	$1,250

Add $505 for single trigger.

MODEL 624 EXTRA — similar to Model 624 Prince, except has deep floral hand engraving.

Mfg.'s Sug. Retail	$7,575	$6,850	$5,950	$5,200	$4,500	$3,700	$3,100	$2,450

Add $500 for single trigger.

LONDON — 12 or 20 (disc.) ga., H&H side-lock system, ejectors, DT or SST, chopper lump barrels, English scroll engraving, deluxe checkered straight grip stock and forearm, 6.84 lbs.

Mfg.'s Sug. Retail	$11,613	$10,000	$8,950	$7,900	$6,900	$5,900	$4,900	$3,900

LONDON ROYAL — similar to London Model except has less extensive game scene engraving.

	$6,950	$5,750	$4,750	$3,950	$3,475	$3,050	$2,800

Last Mfg.'s Sug. Retail was $6,730.

AMBASSADOR MODEL — 12 or 20 ga., H&H side-lock system, available with either gold-line engraving on barrels and receiver with blued receiver (Gold and Black Model) or English scroll engraving (English Engraved Model), single trigger, ejectors, deluxe checkered walnut stock and forearm, cased, 6.4 lbs.

Mfg.'s Sug. Retail	$24,908	$22,000	$19,000	$15,500	$11,750	$9,000	$7,850	$6,700

This model is also available in either Field or Sporting versions upon special request.

AMBASSADOR EXECUTIVE — 12 or 20 ga. only, top-of-the-line model, made to individual order only, every possible refinement.

Mfg.'s Sug. Retail	$34,670	$30,750	$25,000	$19,995	$16,250	$12,750	$10,000	$8,750

Grading	100%	98%	95%	90%	80%	70%	60%

SHOTGUNS: SLIDE ACTION

MODEL 2100 — 12 ga. Mag., 19½ in. barrel, 7 shot mag., law enforcement configuration with matte black metal and wood, 6.62 lbs. Limited importation.

	$610	$480	$390	$330	$275	$220	$195

Last Mfg.'s Sug. Retail was $715.

GARBI, ARMAS

Manufacturer located in Eibar, Spain. Imported and distributed exclusively by W.L. Moore & Co. located in Scottsdale, AZ.

Currently, Garbi is mfg. 400-500 shotguns per year.

RIFLES: SxS

Garbi also manufactures a deluxe SxS double rifle in 7x65R, 8x57JRS, 9.3x74R, .300 H&H Mag., or .375 H&H Mag. cal. Please contact the importer or factory directly for current information (including prices) on this model.

SHOTGUNS: SxS, DISC.

MODEL 51 A — 12 ga. only, extractors, case hardened finish, straight grip.

	$450	$350	$325	$300	$280	$260	$240

MODEL 51 B — 12, 16, or 20 ga., ejectors, case hardened or coin finish receiver, straight grip.

	$850	$650	$590	$540	$500	$460	$420

MODEL 60 A — 12 ga. only, extractors, case hardened finish, true sidelock, large scroll engraving, cocking indicators, hand checkered butt, choice of grip.

	$725	$575	$530	$475	$440	$400	$360

MODEL 60 B — 12, 16, or 20 ga., ejectors, case hardened or coin finish receiver, extensive engraving, straight grip.

	$1,200	$850	$790	$735	$680	$630	$575

MODEL 62 A — 12 ga. only, extractors, case hardened finish, true sidelock, light engraving, cocking indicators, hand checkered butt, choice of grip.

	$725	$575	$530	$475	$440	$400	$360

MODEL 62 B — 12, 16, or 20 ga. only, ejectors, case hardened or coin finish receiver, extensive engraving, straight grip.

	$1,200	$850	$790	$735	$680	$630	$575

SHOTGUNS: SxS RECENT MFG.

For the following models — add 5% for 28 ga., $750 for single trigger, $120-$250 for beavertail forearm, $1,250-$2,500 per extra set of barrels (depending on grade), and $275 for Churchill style level file-cut rib.

MODEL 71 — 12, 16, or 20 ga., Holland-pattern detachable sidelock ejector double, fine English scroll engraving, oil finish, select walnut, articulated trigger. Importation disc. 1988.

	$2,250	$1,825	$1,500	$1,300	$1,075	$980	$900

Last Mfg.'s Sug. Retail was $2,600.

MODEL 100 — 12, 16, or 20 ga., Holland-pattern detachable sidelock ejector double, Purdy style scroll engraving, chopper lump barrels, oil finish, select walnut, articulated trigger.

Mfg.'s Sug. Retail	$4,500	$3,995	$2,950	$2,200	$1,650	$1,450	$1,200	$1,025

G

Grading	100%	98%	95%	90%	80%	70%	60%

MODEL 101 — 12, 16, or 20 ga., Holland-pattern sidelock ejector double with chopper lump barrels, scroll engraving, selected walnut stock.

Mfg.'s Sug. Retail	$5,800	$5,250	$3,900	$2,975	$2,350	$1,900	$1,650	$1,400

MODEL 102 — 12, 16, 20, or 28 ga., Holland-pattern sidelock ejector double with chopper lump barrels, Holland-type large scroll engraving, selected walnut stock. Importation disc. 1993.

	$5,700	$4,500	$3,450	$2,700	$2,350	$2,000	$1,750

Last Mfg.'s Sug. Retail was $7,100.

MODEL 103A — 12, 16, 20, or 28 ga., Holland-pattern sidelock ejector double with chopper lump barrels, Purdey-type fine scroll and rosette engraving, selected walnut stock.

Mfg.'s Sug. Retail	$7,100	$6,400	$4,800	$3,575	$2,750	$2,350	$2,000	$1,750

MODEL 103B — 12, 16, 20, or 28 ga., Holland-pattern sidelock ejector double with chopper lump barrels of nickel-chrome steel, H&H type easy opening mechanism, Purdey-type fine scroll and rosette engraving, well figured walnut stock.

Mfg.'s Sug. Retail	$9,800	$8,750	$6,700	$5,350	$4,350	$3,500	$2,750	$2,250

MODEL 120 — 12, 16, 20, or 28 ga., Holland-pattern sidelock ejector double with chopper lump barrels of nickel-chrome steel, H&H type easy opening mechanism, game scene engraving-3 patterns available. Well figured walnut stock. Importation disc. 1994.

	$7,500	$6,000	$4,875	$4,125	$3,375	$2,600	$2,200

Last Mfg.'s Sug. Retail was $9,400.

MODEL 200 — 12, 16, 20, or 28 ga., Holland-pattern sidelock ejector double with chopper lump barrels of nickel-chrome steel, heavy-duty locks, magnum proofed, very fine Continental style floral and scroll engraving, well figured walnut stock.

Mfg.'s Sug. Retail	$9,375	$8,350	$6,100	$4,875	$4,125	$3,375	$2,600	$2,200

SPECIAL WLM — 12, 16, 20, or 28 ga., top-of-the-line Holland-pattern sidelock ejector double with chopper lump barrels, full coverage large scroll engraving, fancy-figured walnut stock. Importation disc. 1994.

	$7,500	$6,000	$4,875	$4,125	$3,375	$2,600	$2,200

Last Mfg.'s Sug. Retail was $9,400.

SPECIAL AG — 12, 16, 20, or 28 ga., top-of-the-line Holland-pattern sidelock ejector double with chopper lump barrels, large scroll engraving patterned after Lebeau-Courally, fancy figured walnut stock. Disc.

	$8,000	$6,350	$5,200	$4,300	$3,550	$2,750	$2,300

Last Mfg.'s Sug. Retail was $9,200.

GASTINNE RENETTE

Manufacturer and retailer located in Paris, France.

Currently being manufactured with limited importation and distribution. Gastinne Renette should be contacted directly (see Trademark Index) for an up-to-date quotation or information on their current model line-up.

RIFLES: BOLT ACTION

Values listed below are base prices for each model - since all guns are made to individual order, the customer can choose the wood, level of engraving, and other special features, all at additional cost. Gastinne Renette should be contacted directly (see Trademark Index) for an individual price quotation.

STANDARD MODEL MAUSER ACTION

Mfg.'s Sug. Retail	$5,200	$5,200	$4,650	$4,150	$3,650	$3,050	$2,550	$1,900

DELUXE MAUSER ACTION

Mfg.'s Sug. Retail	$10,800	$10,800	$7,500	$6,750	$5,650	$4,800	$3,900	$2,950

Grading	100%	98%	95%	90%	80%	70%	60%

RIFLES: SINGLE SHOT

FALLING BLOCK MODEL
Mfg.'s Sug. Retail $14,000

	100%	98%	95%	90%	80%	70%	60%
	$14,000	$12,000	$9,750	$8,250	$6,750	$5,900	$5,000

SIDELOCK MODEL — features breakdown action. New 1993.
Mfg.'s Sug. Retail $34,000

	$34,000	$29,500	$25,750	$21,250	$18,000	$14,750	$11,350

RIFLES: DOUBLE SxS

BOXLOCK MODEL — variety of cals., features Anson & Deeley boxlock mechanism, color case hardened receiver. New 1993.
Mfg.'s Sug. Retail $10,000

	$10,000	$7,750	$6,950	$5,850	$4,950	$4,100	$3,200

EUROPEAN SIDELOCK
Mfg.'s Sug. Retail $36,000

	$36,000	$31,000	$27,000	$22,500	$18,750	$15,000	$12,500

AFRICAN SIDELOCK — various Mag. cals. New 1993.
Mfg.'s Sug. Retail $40,000

	$40,000	$33,000	$28,750	$23,500	$19,250	$15,500	$12,750

STANDARD TYPE G — 9.3x74R, 7.65R, .30-06, or .375 H&H cal., double bolt action, ejectors, reinforced stock, 23¾ in. barrels, bouquet style engraving with deluxe walnut stock and forearm, 7lbs. 6 oz.

	$2,995	$2,500	$2,150	$1,700	$1,560	$1,480	$1,340

DELUXE TYPE R — 9.3x74R, 7.65R, .30-06, or .375 H&H cal., double bolt action, true sideplates, ejectors, reinforced stock, 23¾ in. barrels, animal engraving with deluxe walnut stock and forearm, 7 lbs. 6 oz.

	$3,875	$3,325	$2,700	$2,175	$1,850	$1,700	$1,525

PRESIDENT TYPE PT — 9.3x74R, 7.65R, .30-06, or .375 H&H cal., double bolt action, true sideplates, ejectors, reinforced stock, 23¾ in. barrels, light engraving with gold line inlays, best quality walnut, 7 lbs. 6 oz.

	$4,250	$3,725	$3,200	$2,650	$2,250	$1,825	$1,600

SHOTGUNS: SxS

MODEL 105 — 12 or 20 ga., Anson and Deeley type triple bolt action, ejectors, double triggers, case hardened frame, 6 lbs. 8 oz.

	$2,250	$1,800	$1,400	$1,250	$1,125	$1,000	$900

MODEL 98 — 12 and 20 ga., Purdey type triple bolt action, ejectors, double triggers, case hardened frame, 6 lbs. 8 oz.

	$2,995	$2,500	$2,000	$1,850	$1,580	$1,430	$1,260

MODEL 202 — 12 or 20 ga., Purdey type triple bolt action, sidelocks, fine English engraving, first grade French walnut, ejectors, double triggers, coin finished receiver, 6 lbs. 10 oz.

	$5,250	$4,500	$3,950	$3,250	$2,500	$2,175	$1,875

MODEL 353 — 12 or 20 ga., Purdey type triple bolt action, hand detachable sidelocks, Chopper lump barrels, fine English engraving, first grade French walnut, ejectors, double triggers, case hardened receiver, best quality, 6 lbs. 10 oz.

	$19,950	$17,500	$13,650	$11,000	$8,900	$6,700	$6,250

GATLING GUN COMPANY

Manufactured since 1961 by Furr Arms located in Orem, UT. Distributed by J & G Sales, Inc. located in Prescott, AZ.

Grading	100%	98%	95%	90%	80%	70%	60%

The Gatling Gun Company manufactures high quality ⅙, ⅓, ½, ¾ and full scale brass reproductions of famous, antique machine guns and cannons. Models include the 1874 Gatling Gun on carriage (includes 225 round Broadwell feed drum and 10 exposed barrels), 1876 Camel Gun (includes 225 round Broadwell feed drum), 1883 Gatling Gun on carriage (Accles feed drum, 10 enclosed barrels), 1893 Police, British Naval Cannon, and the James Six Pounder. Prices vary according to the complexity of each model, and are available by contacting the distributor.

Except for Models 1876 Carriage Gatling (½ scale) and 1876 Camel Tripod (½ scale), all the models listed below may be purchased on a special order basis from the factory. 100% values represent the current manufacturer's suggested retail.

1874 Carriage ⅙	$5,000	$4,000	$3,500
1874 Carriage Gatling ⅓	$6,500	$5,250	$4,250
1876 Carriage Gatling ½	$12,000	$9,000	$7,500
1876 Carriage Gatling ¾	$19,000	$15,000	$12,000
1874 Camel Tripod ⅙	$4,000	$3,000	$2,500
1874 Camel Tripod ⅓	$4,500	$3,500	$2,800
1876 Camel Tripod ½	$8,000	$6,500	$5,250
1876 Camel Tripod ¾	$12,000	$9,000	$7,500
1876 Camel Tripod (Full)	$18,000	$14,500	$11,500
1893 Police Gatling ⅙	$2,500	$2,100	$1,650
1893 Police Gatling ⅓	$3,200	$2,550	$2,000
1883 Carriage Gatling ⅙	$5,000	$4,000	$3,500
1883 Carriage Gatling ⅓	$6,500	$5,250	$4,250
James Six Lb. Cannon ⅙	$900	$750	$575
James Six Lb. Cannon ⅕	$2,200	$1,850	$1,400
James Six Lb. Cannon ⅓	$3,200	$2,550	$2,000

▲ *H.M.S. Victory Naval Cannon* ⅒

$500 $375 $325

▲ *H.M.S. Victory Naval Cannon* ⅒ — this cannon is mounted on an oak ship deck section complete with planking, port lid, and working block and tackle.

$900 $750 $575

▲ *H.M.S. Victory Naval Cannon* ⅓

$3,200 $2,550 $2,000

GAUCHER

Manufacturer located in St. Etienne, France. No current importer. Previously imported and distributed by Mandall Shooting Supplies located in Scottsdale, AZ. Gaucher also manufactures double rifles - please contact the factory directly to obtain more information and current pricing.

Gaucher **Armes**

PISTOLS: TARGET

MODEL GN1 — .22 LR cal., single shot silhouette pistol featuring 10 in. barrel, adj. sights, anatomically shaped grips, monobloc lever cocking, 2.42 lbs. Limited importation.

$360 $325 $290 $260 $230 $200 $185

Last Mfg.'s Sug. Retail was $380.

MODEL GP — similar to Model GN1, except has forearm integrated into grip. Limited importation.

$300 $275 $250 $225 $200 $185 $160

Last Mfg.'s Sug. Retail was $323.

GAVAGE

Previous manufacturer located in Liege, Belgium between 1936-1943 approximately.

Grading	100%	98%	95%	90%	80%	70%	60%

GAVAGE PISTOL — 7.65mm, patterned after the "Clement", fixed barrel, limited mfg.

	100%	98%	95%	90%	80%	70%	60%
	$375	$325	$250	$200	$175	$150	$125

> This pistol is very rare if encountered with Waffenamt proofmarks - healthy premiums are being asked.

GENTRY, DAVID - CUSTOM GUNMAKER

Custom rifle gunmaker located in Belgrade, MT.

David Gentry is a current custom rifle builder who usually fabricates rifles to individual custom order requests. Current models include Gentry's Black Beauty, Mountain "70", Gray Ghost, and the Outfitter's Rifle ($2,400 base price). The Rough Rider Model was disc. 1994. David Gentry also manufactures top quality muzzle brakes, stainless steel Featherlight scope rings (1 in. and 30mm), and performs custom metal-work. Mr. Gentry should be contacted directly (see Trademark Index) for more information on options/prices.

GERMAN WWII MILITARY PISTOLS

Also See: Fabrique Nationale, Luger, Mauser, and Walther for other military pistols.

P.38 — double action, 9mm, 5 in. barrel, 8 shot mag., fixed sights, brown or black composite grips, blued finish. Many variations exhibiting a variety of metal finishes and codings, 34 oz. Over 1,000,000 manufactured during WW II.

Note: This model was adopted as the standard service pistol of the German Military in 1938. The P.38 was manufactured by Walther - code "ac" (mfg. 1939-1945), Mauser - code "byf" (mfg. Nov. of 1942-1945), and Spreewerke - code "cyq." (mfg. 1943-1945). The finish on most WWII 1942 and later P.38s is not of the same quality as the pre and early war Walther guns with the Spreewerke (cyq) models being the poorest. Pre-war Walther commercial manufactured P.38s (Models AP and Walther Banner HPs) are comparable to Zero Series - 3rd Issue values listed below.

HP "Heeres Pistole" — early Walther commercial production, high polish, hand-made, approx. 24,000 mfg. from 1938-1944.

▲ **"Swedish" HP** — experimental first production for Swedish trials, ser. range H1,001-H2,065, H prefix, rectangular firing pin and crown/N proofs.

	100%	98%	95%	90%	80%	70%	60%
	$3,500	$2,750	$2,000	$1,700	$1,400	$1,100	$900

▲ **Standard HP Production** — ser. range 2,080-approx. 24,000, high gloss finish until approx. ser. no. 20,000 - then changed to military blue (1944).

	100%	98%	95%	90%	80%	70%	60%
	$2,200	$1,600	$1,100	$900	$700	$600	$500

Add 10% for Nazi "359" military proof (scarce).
Add 10% for matching mag.

▲ **Late War HP Production** — marked "MOD P38" on left slide, rough military blue finish, some frames show heavy tool marks, ser. range 24,000-25,990, w/o matching mags.

	100%	98%	95%	90%	80%	70%	60%
	$1,600	$1,100	$900	$700	$600	$500	$450

ZERO-SERIES — with Mauser banner, high polish finish, 5-digit number w/o suffix. Mfg. 1940.
Add 10% for matching mag.

▲ **Zero Series - 1st Issue** — internal extractor, square firing pin, ser. range 01-01,000.

	100%	98%	95%	90%	80%	70%	60%
	$4,500	$3,700	$2,900	$2,100	$1,500	$1,200	$1,000

▲ **Zero Series - 2nd Issue** — external extractor, square firing pin, ser. range 01,001-03,445, more difficult to find than 1st Issue.

	100%	98%	95%	90%	80%	70%	60%
	$5,000	$4,400	$3,400	$2,500	$1,900	$1,300	$1,000

Grading	100%	98%	95%	90%	80%	70%	60%

▲ *Zero Series - 3rd Issue* — external extractor, round firing pin, 03,446-013,725, after ser. no. 10,000, some models had brown military style grips.

	$2,500	$1,625	$1,150	$850	$750	$600	$500

▲ *480 code* — "480" appears on slide, first military contract P.38, approx. 7,200 mfg. with ser. range 1-7,665, rare in any condition above 90%.

	$3,300	$2,400	$1,650	$1,150	$850	$700	$575

ac-NO DATE (UNDATED) — ac (Walther code) appears on slide without date, "ac" on triggerguard, 2,800 mfg. with ser. range 7,356-9,691, rarest military coded P.38, rarely encountered in 90% or better original condition.

	$3,400	$2,750	$2,200	$1,900	$1,500	$1,200	$950

Add 20% for matching mag.

▲ *ac-40 Surcharge* — hand-stamped "40" before regular ac-40 production, ser. range 9,691-9,978 A, 10,000 mfg., high polish, rare in any condition above 90%.

	$2,000	$1,700	$1,400	$1,050	$900	$750	$650

Add 20% for matching mag.

ac-40 CODE — indicates 1940 mfg., the 480 code was dropped in October of 1940, and the "ac" code was started, approx. 10,000 mfg. with ser. range 1B-9,900B.

	$1,775	$1,200	$850	$600	$500	$450	$400

Add 20% for matching mag.

▲ *ac-41 1st and 2nd Variation* — last military high polish guns, only 1st var. (ser. range 1-4,833 B) has "ac" on left triggerguard, 2nd var. continues to ser. no. 4,527 I.

	$900	$800	$550	$475	$400	$370	$340

Add 20% for matching mag.

ac-41 3RD VAR. or ac-42 CODE — dull military finish, ser. range (approx.) ac-41, 4,500 I to ac-42, 9,200 K. Matching magazines stop at approx. ac-42, 2,000 B.

	$850	$725	$625	$500	$425	$375	$325

Add 20% for matching mag.

"ac" or "byf" CODED 43-45 — letters are followed by two digit code corresponding to year of mfg. 1943-1945. Two line codes are more desirable than single line models. Highest P.38 production occurred in 1943 and 1944.

	$495	$425	$375	$325	$300	$260	$225

Add 10% for single-line code in ac-43 code.
Add 20% for "dual tone" (phosphate finish — byf-44 date).

"cyq" CODE AND "ac-45" MISMATCH — cyq variation typically exhibits rough machining with visible circular milling marks, mismatched slide and frame on ac-45 model.

	$425	$375	$300	$270	$250	$230	$210

LATE WAR (1945) — Zero Series with rough milled finish, ser. range 025,960-027,659.

	$1,100	$925	$795	$650	$500	$425	$350

1945 "svw" CODE — Nazi proofed only, most dual tone finish, some all blue or all gray.

	$1,000	$850	$700	$600	$500	$450	$400

Add 20% for all blue or all gray.
Deduct 50% for French production (Star proof).

1946 "svw" CODE — Mauser mfg. 1946 with French controlling production.

	$425	$365	$285	$250	$210	$190	$165

GEVARM
St. Etienne, France.

E-1 AUTOLOADING RIFLE — .22 LR, 19 in. barrel, open sights, walnut pistol grip stock.

	$165	$130	$110	$100	$85	$65	$55

GIB

Grading	100%	98%	95%	90%	80%	70%	60%

10 GAUGE MAGNUM SHOTGUN — 10 ga., 3½ in. chambers, 32 in. full choke barrel, case hardened receiver, matted rib, rubber pad, checkered pistol grip walnut stock. Disc.

	$275	$250	$235	$220	$200	$175	$150

GIBBS GUNS, INC.

Previously manufactured by Volunteer Enterprises in Knoxville, TN and previously distributed by Gibbs Guns, Inc. located in Greenback,TN.

MARK 45 CARBINE — .45 ACP only, based on TS M6 Thompson machine gun, 16½ in. barrel, 5, 15, 30, or 90 shot clip, U.S. mfg. Disc. 1988.

	$315	$275	$225	$180	$165	$155	$145

Last Mfg.'s Sug. Retail was $279.

Add $60 minimum for nickel plating.

GIBBS RIFLE COMPANY

Previous manufacturer located in Martinsburg, WV 1991-94. Gibbs Rifle Co. imported Mauser-Werke firearms until 1995.

Gibbs Rifle Co. also imports a variety of older firearms including English military rifles and handguns (both original and refurbished condition), a wide variety of used military contract pistols and rifles, in addition to other shooting products and accessories, including a bi-pod patterned after the Parker-Hale M-85.

RIFLES: BOLT ACTION

Gibbs Guns bolt action rifles utilize the Mauser K-98 action and were offered in a variety of configurations. Mfg. disc. 1994.

GIBBS ECONOMY SPORTER — 8mm Mauser, sporterized military action with good barrel and sporting sights, walnut finished checkered hardwood stock. Mfg. 1993-94.

	$185	$150	$135	$120	$100	$85	$70

Last Mfg.'s Sug. Retail was $205.

GIBBS MAUSER SPORTER — .243 Win., .270 Win., .30-06, or .308 Win. cal., features M-98 action, walnut finished checkered hardwood stock, action is drilled and tapped, flip-up rear sight and ramp front. New 1993-94.

	$250	$220	$195	$175	$150	$135	$120

Last Mfg.'s Sug. Retail was $295.

MODEL 81 CLASSIC — available in 11 cals. between .22-250 and 7mm Rem. Mag., 24 in. barrel, open sights, 4 shot mag., select checkered walnut with sling swivels, 7¾ lbs.

	$795	$595	$475	$395	$340	$300	$280

Last Mfg.'s Sug. Retail was $900.

▲ *Model 81 African* — .375 H&H or 9.3x62mm cal., similar specifications as Model 81 Classic with quarter rib and express sights, engraved action, Pachmayr recoil pad, 9 lbs.

	$925	$725	$600	$500	$425	$360	$330

Last Mfg.'s Sug. Retail was $1,050.

MODEL 85 SNIPER RIFLE — .308 cal., bolt action, 24 in. heavy barrel, 10 shot mag., camo green synthetic McMillan stock with stippling, built in adj. bi-pod and recoil pad, enlarged contoured bolt, adj. sights, 12 lbs. 6 oz.

	$1,825	$1,450	$1,275	$1,050	$875	$750	$625

Last Mfg.'s Sug. Retail was $2,050.

G

Grading	100%	98%	95%	90%	80%	70%	60%

MODEL 87 TARGET — .243, 6.5x55, .308, .30-06, or .300 Win. Mag. cal., target stock, aperture sights. Mfg. disc. 1992.

	100%	98%	95%	90%	80%	70%	60%
	$1,375	$1,100	$900	$775	$650	$550	$495

Last Mfg.'s Sug. Retail was $1,500.

MODEL 1000 STANDARD — .22-250, .243 Win., 6mm Rem., 6.5x55mm, 7x57mm, 7x64mm, .270 Win., .30-06, or .308 Win. cal., 22 in. barrel, 4 shot built in mag., checkered walnut stock with cheekpiece, open sights, 7¼ lbs.

	$425	$375	$325	$290	$260	$240	$220

Last Mfg.'s Sug. Retail was $495.

▲ *Model 1000 Clip* — similar to Model 1000 Standard, except has detachable 4 shot mag.

	$460	$395	$350	$300	$270	$240	$220

Last Mfg.'s Sug. Retail was $535.

MODEL 1100 LIGHTWEIGHT — available in 9 cals. between .22-250 and .308 Win., 22 in. barrel, open sights, 4 shot mag., 6½ lbs.

	$435	$380	$325	$290	$260	$240	$220

Last Mfg.'s Sug. Retail was $510.

▲ *Model 1100M African* — .375 H&H, or .458 Win. Mag. cal., 24 in. barrel, 4 shot mag., 9½ lbs.

	$825	$650	$575	$500	$450	$425	$400

Last Mfg.'s Sug. Retail was $930.

MODEL 1200 SUPER — bolt action, Mauser type action, .22-250, .243, 6mm, 6.5x55mm, 7 x 64mm, .270, .30-06, or .308 cal., 24 in. barrel, folding sight, skip checkered walnut stock, pad swivels, rosewood pistol grip cap and forend tip.

	$495	$400	$350	$325	$285	$270	$255

Last Mfg.'s Sug. Retail was $595.

▲ *Model 1200 Super Clip* — similar to Model 1200 Super, except has detachable 4 shot box mag.

	$525	$425	$375	$350	$300	$285	$265

Last Mfg.'s Sug. Retail was $640.

MODEL 1300S SCOUT — .243 Win. or .308 Win., 20 in. barrel with muzzle brake, internal 5 shot or detachable 5/10 shot mag., laminated checkered birchwood stock, sling swivels, 8½ lbs.

	$425	$375	$325	$290	$260	$240	$220

Last Mfg.'s Sug. Retail was $495.

Add $30 for detachable mag. (Model 1300C)

MODEL 1500S SURVIVOR — .308 Win. cal., bolt action, matte stainless construction, black composite (Kevlar/fiberglass) stock, 22 in. barrel, 4 shot mag., 7 lbs. Mfg. began 1993.

	$395	$350	$300	$270	$240	$210	$185

Last Mfg.'s Sug. Retail was $450.

Add $30 for detachable clip (Model 1500C).
This model is made for the Gibbs Rifle Co. by Bell & Carlson, Inc.

RIFLES: MIDLAND BOLT ACTION SERIES

MODEL 2100 MIDLAND DELUXE — similar to Model 2600 Midland, except has checkered walnut stock and pistol grip cap.

	$335	$280	$235	$210	$190	$180	$170

Last Mfg.'s Sug. Retail was $390.

MODEL 2600 MIDLAND — .22-250, .243 Win., 6mm Rem., 6.5x55mm, 7x57mm, 7x64mm, .270 Win., .30-06, or .308 Win. cal., 22 in. barrel, 4 shot mag., checkered hardwood stock with Monte Carlo cheekpiece, open sights, drilled and tapped action, 7 lbs.

	$320	$270	$225	$200	$180	$165	$150

Last Mfg.'s Sug. Retail was $375.

Grading	100%	98%	95%	90%	80%	70%	60%

MIDLAND 2700 LIGHTWEIGHT — lightweight variation of the Model 2100 Midland Deluxe featuring tapered barrel, anodized aluminum trigger housing and lightened stock with full pistol grip and recoil pad, Schnabel forend, 6½ lbs.

	$350	$285	$245	$225	$200	$190	$180

Last Mfg.'s Sug. Retail was $415.

MIDLAND 2800 — similar to Model 2600 Midland, except has laminate birchwood stock, 7 lbs.

	$340	$280	$240	$210	$190	$180	$170

Last Mfg.'s Sug. Retail was $405.

SHOTGUNS

MIDLAND STALKER — 12 ga., trigger bar safety, unique squeeze break open action and cocking system, 28½ in. barrel bored F, hardwood stock and forearm, 6 lbs.

	$90	$65	$55	$45	$35	$30	$25

Last Mfg.'s Sug. Retail was $110.

GLOCK

Manufactured by Glock Ges.m.b.H. in Austria since 1983. Exclusively imported and distributed by Glock, Inc., located in Smyrna, GA.

All Glock pistols have a "safe action" safety system (double action only) which includes trigger safety, firing pin safety, and drop safety. Glock pistols have only 35 parts for reliability and simplicity in operation.

PISTOLS: SEMI-AUTO

Most of the models below are available in a cutaway configuration for sale to law enforcement agencies.

MODEL 17 SPORT/SERVICE — 9mm, double action, polymer frame, mag., trigger and other pistol parts. Steel barrel, slide, and springs, 10 (C/B 1994), 17*, or 19* shot mag., 4.49 in. barrel with hexagonal rifling, adj. (Sport Model) or fixed (Service Model) rear sight, hammerless, includes extra mag., case, and spare rear sight, 24 oz. empty. Importation began late 1985.

Mfg.'s Sug. Retail	$606	$510	$395	$300

Add $28 for adj. rear sight.
Add $72 for fixed meprolight sight.
Add $90 for fixed trijicon sight.

▲ *Model 17L Competition Model* — competition version of the Model 17, includes internally compensated 6.02 in. barrel, recalibrated trigger pull (3½ lb. pull), adj. rear sight, 25.4 oz. New 1988.

Mfg.'s Sug. Retail	$790	$670	$545	$425

Add $28 for adj. sight.

▲ *Glock 17 Desert Storm Commemorative* — 9mm Para., features coalition forces listing on top of barrel, inscription on side of slide "NEW WORLD ORDER", 1,000 mfg. in 1991 only.

	$995	$825	$600

Last Mfg.'s Sug. Retail was $795.

MODEL 19 COMPACT SPORT/SERVICE — similar to Model 17, except has scaled down dimensions with 4.02 in. barrel and serrated grip straps, 10 (C/B 1994), 15*, or 17* shot mag., fixed (Service Model) or adj. (Sport Model) rear sight, 23 oz. New 1988.

Mfg.'s Sug. Retail	$606	$510	$395	$300

Add $28 for adj. rear sight.
Add $72 for fixed meprolight sight.
Add $90 for fixed trijicon sight.

Grading	100%	98%	95%	90%	80%	70%	60%

MODEL 20 SPORT/SERVICE — 10mm Norma cal., similar action to Model 17, features 4.6 in. barrel, 10 (C/B 1994) or 15* shot mag., thicker triggerguard, fixed (Service Model) or adj. (Sport Model) rear sight, 28.4 oz. New 1990.

Mfg.'s Sug. Retail	$658	$570	$475	$415

Add $29 for adj. rear sight.
Add $73 for fixed meprolight sight.
Add $90 for fixed trijicon sight.

MODEL 21 SPORT/SERVICE — .45 ACP cal., otherwise similar to Model 20, 10 (C/B 1994) or 13* shot mag., 27.2 oz. Introduced May, 1991.

Mfg.'s Sug. Retail	$658	$570	$475	$415

Add $29 for adj. rear sight.
Add $73 for fixed meprolight sight.
Add $90 for fixed trijicon sight.

MODEL 22 SPORT/SERVICE — .40 S&W cal., similar to Model 20, except has 4.49 in. barrel, 10 (C/B 1994) or 15* shot mag., 24 oz. Introduced 1990.

Mfg.'s Sug. Retail	$606	$510	$395	$300

Add $28 for adj. rear sight.
Add $72 for fixed meprolight sight.
Add $90 for fixed trijicon sight.

200 Model 22s were originally shipped with serial numbers beginning with "NY-1". Somehow, they probably were erroneously numbered at the factory (probably thinking that they somehow were part of the New York State Troopers shipment of Model 17s) during 1990. Premiums will occur on this variation.

MODEL 23 COMPACT SPORT/SERVICE — compact variation of the Model 22 with 4.02 in. barrel and 10 (C/B 1994) 13* shot mag., 22.4 oz. New 1990.

Mfg.'s Sug. Retail	$606	$510	$395	$300

Add $28 for adj. rear sight.
Add $72 for fixed meprolight sight.
Add $90 for fixed trijicon sight.

MODEL 24 — similar to Model 17L Competition, except in .40 S&W cal., choice of standard or compensated barrel and fixed or adj. rear sight. New 1994.

Mfg.'s Sug. Retail	$790	$660	$525	$415

Add $40 for compensated barrel.
Add $28 for adj. rear sight.

MODEL 26 — sub-compact variation of the Model 19, except has shortened grip, 3½ in. barrel, 10 shot mag., approx. 22 oz. New 1995.

Mfg.'s Sug. Retail	$606	$510	$395	$300

Add $28 for adj. rear sight.
Add $72 for fixed meprolight sight.
Add $90 for fixed trijicon sight.

MODEL 27 — sub-compact variation of the Model 23, except has shortened grip, 3½ in. barrel, 9 shot mag., approx. 22 oz. New 1995.

Mfg.'s Sug. Retail	$606	$510	$395	$300

Add $28 for adj. rear sight.
Add $72 for fixed meprolight sight.
Add $90 for fixed trijicon sight.

GOLAN
See KSN Industries Ltd. listing.

GOLDEN EAGLE
Trademark of rifles/shotguns produced by Nikko Limited located in Tochigi, Japan.

Please refer to the Nikko Firearms Limited listing in this text for a complete chronological history of Nikko - Japan's previous long gun manufacturer.

Grading	100%	98%	95%	90%	80%	70%	60%

RIFLES

MODEL 7000 GRADE I — bolt action, all popular American calibers, including .270, and .300 Wby., 24 or 26 in. barrels, select skipline checkered walnut stock, rosewood forend tip, golden eagle head engraved in pistol grip cap, recoil pad. Mfg. 1976-1981.

	100%	98%	95%	90%	80%	70%	60%
	$600	$550	$525	$450	$375	$340	$290

MODEL 7000 GRADE I AFRICAN — similar to 7000, except .375 H&H and .458 Win. Mag., open sights.

	100%	98%	95%	90%	80%	70%	60%
	$650	$590	$555	$480	$400	$365	$315

MODEL 7000 GRADE II — scroll engraving, better grade wood.

	100%	98%	95%	90%	80%	70%	60%
	$690	$625	$590	$510	$430	$395	$340

SHOTGUNS

MODEL 5000 GRADE I — O/U shotgun, 12 or 20 ga., 26, 28, or 30 in. barrels, various chokes, vent. rib, engraved receiver, gold eagle head inlay, auto ejectors, SST, checkered pistol grip beavertail stock. Mfg. 1975 1981.

	100%	98%	95%	90%	80%	70%	60%
	$850	$775	$700	$625	$560	$510	$440

MODEL 5000 GRADE I SKEET — similar to 5000, except 26 or 28 in. skeet bored, wide rib.

	100%	98%	95%	90%	80%	70%	60%
	$875	$800	$725	$650	$580	$510	$440

MODEL 5000 GRADE I TRAP — similar to Field, except 30 or 32 in. barrel, mod. and full, imp. mod. and full, or full and full choke, wide rib, trap stock with pad.

	100%	98%	95%	90%	80%	70%	60%
	$875	$800	$725	$650	$580	$510	$440

MODEL 5000 GRADE II — available in Field, Trap, and Skeet, more engraving, better grade wood, with screaming eagle on receiver in gold.

	100%	98%	95%	90%	80%	70%	60%
	$950	$875	$790	$710	$630	$540	$460
Skeet	$975	$895	$810	$725	$640	$540	$460
Trap	$975	$895	$810	$725	$640	$540	$460

GRANDEE GRADE III — similar to 5000 Grade II, except elaborate engraving, inlays, and better grade wood.

	100%	98%	95%	90%	80%	70%	60%
	$2,500	$2,200	$1,900	$1,575	$1,250	$1,000	$850

G

GOLDEN STATE ARMS

Previous importer located in Pasadena, CA. Golden State Arms imported and subcontracted various firearms constructed by European and Japanese manufacturers - achieving private label status on some guns. Most firearms previously imported by Golden State Arms (including private labels) are not that collectible. In many cases, the shooting value will determine the price of a specimen. In some models or configurations which are currently desirable, however, premiums may exist.

GONCZ ARMAMENT, INC.

Previous owner/manufacturer located in North Hollywood, CA 1984-1990.

While advertised, records indicate very few Goncz pistols or carbines were actually produced. All of these guns were prototypes or individually hand-built and none were ever mass produced through normal fabrication techniques.

In 1990, Claridge Hi-Tec, Inc. purchased Goncz Armament, Inc.

GRANGER, G.

Manufacturer located in Saint Etienne, France since 1902.

G. Granger manufactures high quality, limited production side-by-side boxlock and sidelock shotguns in 12, 16, or 20 ga. All guns are made on a custom order basis with prices ranging between $20,000 - $37,800. Prices will vary per customer specifications and appointments. G. Granger should be contacted directly (see Trademark Index) regarding up-to-date model information (including current pricing).

GRANT, STEPHEN

Previously manufactured in London, England.

Manufacturer specializing in custom order only SxS rifles and shotguns. Shotguns (12, 16, or 20 ga.) can be top or side lever and are equipped with sidelocks and a self-opening mechanism. Very limited production making values hard to establish. Prices are at par with similar quality H&H firearms.

GREAT WESTERN ARMS COMPANY

Great Western Arms Co. was located at 9001-9007 Miner Street, Los Angeles, CA. Founded through the efforts of Mr. Hy Hunter, with William R. Wilson as President.

Originated probably in early 1953. When Colt Firearms Company ceased production of what is known today as "First Generation Single Action Army Revolvers," Mr. Hunter could see the public's continued demand of such a revolver. After several trips to the Colt factory to ascertain Colt's intent of reviving their production of the S.A. Army, and being assured it would never be revived, he founded the G.W. Arms Co. The main change between the Colt S.A. and the G.W. Frontier was removing the firing pin from the hammer and the design of a rebounding firing pin inserted in the revolver frame. This firm also redesigned the Remington 2 shot derringer and designed a derringer in 2 cals., .38 S&W and .38 S&W Special. Approx. 2,000 of these were mfg. Production of the Frontier probably did not exceed 23,000. When the Colt Company resumed production of their 2nd Generation S.A. 1873 Revolver, it rang the death knell of Great Western Arms Co. products, and the G.W. Arms Co. soon disappeared with its last sales of their "Frontier" being sold as unassembled "Kit Guns" to be assembled by the purchaser.

100%	98%	95%	90%	80%	70%	60%	50%	40%	30%	20%	10%

SINGLE ACTION REVOLVER: FRONTIER— .45 Colt, .44-40, .44 Mag., .44 Spl., .357 Atomic, .357 Mag., .38 S&W Spl., .32-20 WCF, or .22 Rimfire cal., 7½, 5½, or 3½ in. barrel, blue with casehardened colors on frame, gate and hammer, all blue, satin blue, nickel, black nickel, copper plated black oxide, gold, silver, gold and silver and parkerizing, grips were imitation stag (plastic), wood, pearl, ivory and sterling silver on special order. Unfinished "Kit Guns" were also sold, allowing buyer to assemble and finish.

$650	$625	$600	$575	$550	$500	$450	$350	$325	$295	$270	$250

Add 50% for Special .22 Target Model with micro sights.
Add 100% for Fast Draw Model.
Add 25% for electroplated barrels.
Add 25% for electroplated cylinder.
Add minimum 5% for any finish other than parkerized or blue with casehardened frame.
Add 20% for consecutive ser. no. sets.
Add 50% if with factory original presentation case.
Add 60% if with factory original letter.
Add 25% for .44 Mag. or .357 Atomic cal.
Add 50% for factory original cals. not listed above.
Add 60% for Sheriff Model (called Deputy Model).
Add 80% for any barrel length above 7½ in.
Add minimum 100% for original factory engraving.
Add minimum 300% for original factory engraving with silver and gold.
Add 75% for factory sterling silver grips.
Add 20% for factory pearl or ivory grips.
Add 10% for factory wood grips.
Add 30% for any gun with a longer than factory standard or shorter than standard barrel.
Deduct 25% for assembled kit guns.
Values for unassembled kit gun in original box are same as above.

GREAT WESTERN DERRINGER — .38 S&W or .38 S&W Spl. cal. (not interchangeable). Basically an improved version of the Remington 2 shot derringer frame.

$395	$375	$350	$325	$300	$250	$200	$175	$150	$125	$100	$90

Add 10% for consecutive ser. no. sets.
Add 20% for factory pearl or ivory grips.
Add 25% for factory original casing.
Add minimum 200% for factory original engraving.

GREENER, W.W., LIMITED

Manufacturer located in Birmingham, England since 1829. W.W. Greener does not have current importation into the U.S. Until 1994, Gibbs Rifle Co. located in Martinsburg, WV was the U.S. agent.

RIFLES: SxS - CURRENT MFG.

Boxlock and sidelock rifle quotations may be obtained by writing the company directly (see Trademark Index). A complete choice of calibers, engraving options, and walnut selection are available on a special order basis only.

Grading	100%	98%	95%	90%	80%	70%	60%

SHOTGUNS: SINGLE SHOT

GP MK II — 12 ga. only, famed general purpose (GP) English shotgun configuration featuring Greener Martini action, 28 or 30 in. barrel, walnut stock and forearm. Mfg. resumed in 1991.

	Mfg.'s Sug. Retail	$522		$522	$450	$400	$350	$300	$250	$195

Grading	100%	98%	95%	90%	80%	70%	60%

SHOTGUNS: SxS - CURRENT MFG.

Various hard and soft cases are available for the models listed below with prices ranging from $500 up to $3,200.

NO. 5 NEEDHAM EJECTOR—12, 16, 20, or .410 ga., scalloped boxlock action, DT, any barrel length.

Mfg.'s Sug. Retail	$4,470	$4,470	$3,750	$3,175	$2,750	$2,250	$1,825	$1,475

This model has been re-introduced to commemorate the takeover of J. V. Needham by W.W. Greener in 1874.

DH 40—similar to No. 5 Needham Ejector, except has better engraving and deluxe walnut stock and forearm.

Mfg.'s Sug. Retail	$6,705	$6,705	$5,900	$5,000	$4,250	$3,500	$2,850	$2,100

DH 75—12 ga. only, 2¾ in. chambers, Greener "Facile Princeps" scalloped boxlock action 27, 28, or 30 in. barrels, case hardened receiver, choice of engraving (game scene or fine scroll work).

Mfg.'s Sug. Retail	$11,175	$11,175	$9,950	$8,450	$7,250	$6,000	$4,950	$3,875

DOH 90—12, 16, 20, or .410 ga., 2½, 2¾ or 3 in. Mag. chambers, best boxlock featuring Anson & Deeley scalloped boxlock action with Greener easy-opening device, French walnut stock, DT.

Mfg.'s Sug. Retail	$14,900	$14,900	$12,500	$9,750	$8,250	$7,000	$5,850	$4,675

L 120—12, 16, 20, or .410 ga., best sidelock ejector model with dovetail lump barrels, fine scroll engraving with choice of bright or color case hardened frame finish.

Mfg.'s Sug. Retail	$22,350	$22,350	$19,500	$16,000	$13,000	$10,000	$7,850	$6,000

L 150—12, 16, 20, or .410 ga., 2½ or 3 in. chambers, very best sidelock ejector model with chopper lump barrels and easy-opening device, bright or color case hardened frame finish.

Mfg.'s Sug. Retail	$29,800	$29,800	$24,000	$21,000	$17,000	$14,000	$11,000	$8,500

L 500—12, 16, 20, or .410 ga., new St. George sidelock ejector model incorporating top-of-the-line carved engraving, walnut, and workmanship.

Because this model is entirely custom ordered per individual choice, a price quotation is necessary on every order.

SHOTGUNS: DISC.

FARKILLER GRADE F35 — double barrel, 12 ga., 28, 30, or 32 in. barrels, hammerless boxlock, checkered straight or semi-pistol grip stock.

	$2,420	$2,200	$2,090	$1,870	$1,760	$1,650	$1,540
Auto ejectors	$3,300	$3,025	$2,750	$2,475	$2,035	$1,925	$1,650

FARKILLER GRADE F35 LARGE BORE — similar to F35 above, except 8 or 10 ga.

	$2,750	$2,585	$2,310	$2,090	$1,980	$1,815	$1,650
Auto ejectors	$3,575	$3,300	$3,080	$2,860	$2,640	$2,090	$1,925

HAMMERLESS EJECTOR MODELS—12, 16, 20, 28, or .410 ga., 26, 28, or 30 in. barrels supplied with any choke combination, auto ejectors, single or double triggers, straight or semi-pistol grip stock, grades differ as follows:

▲ *Jubilee Grade DH35*

	$2,420	$2,255	$2,090	$1,925	$1,650	$1,540	$1,375

▲ *Sovereign Grade DH40*

	$2,860	$2,695	$2,420	$2,200	$1,980	$1,815	$1,595

▲ *Crown Grade DH55*

	$3,300	$3,080	$2,915	$2,750	$2,420	$2,035	$1,760

▲ *Royal Grade DH75*

	$4,400	$4,180	$3,850	$3,300	$3,080	$2,915	$2,640

Add $400 for SST.

Note: Degree of engraving and grade of wood are the basic differences between models.

Grading	100%	98%	95%	90%	80%	70%	60%

EMPIRE — double barrel, 12 ga. only, 2¾ or 3 in., any choke, 28, 30, or 32 in. barrel, hammerless, boxlock, straight stock or semi pistol grip.

	$1,760	$1,540	$1,320	$1,100	$935	$825	$770
Auto ejectors	$1,980	$1,760	$1,540	$1,320	$1,155	$1,045	$990

EMPIRE DELUXE — double barrel, similar to Empire, only better grade wood.

	$1,980	$1,760	$1,540	$1,320	$1,155	$1,045	$990
Auto ejectors	$2,200	$1,980	$1,760	$1,540	$1,375	$1,265	$1,100

GENERAL PURPOSE — 12 ga., improved Martini action, single shot, 26, 30, or 32 in. barrel, full or mod., auto ejectors, straight checkered stock.

$330	$305	$275	$220	$195	$165	$160

GREIFELT AND COMPANY

Previously manufactured in Suhl, E. Germany.

SHOTGUNS: SIDE-BY-SIDE

MODEL 22 — 12 or 20 ga., 28 or 30 in. mod. and full, hammerless, boxlock, false sideplates, extractors, checkered pistol grip or English style stock, post-WWII.

$2,200	$1,760	$1,595	$1,320	$1,100	$990	$825

MODEL 22E — similar to Model 22, except has auto ejectors.

$2,750	$2,200	$1,980	$1,760	$1,540	$1,430	$1,265

MODEL 103 — 12 or 16 ga., 28 or 30 in. mod. and full, extractors, double triggers, checkered pistol grip or English stock, post-war.

$1,980	$1,650	$1,485	$1,210	$990	$880	$715

MODEL 103E — similar to Model 103, except has auto ejectors.

$2,200	$1,760	$1,595	$1,320	$1,100	$990	$825

SHOTGUNS: OVER/UNDER & DRILLING

GRADE NO. 1 — O/U, 12, 16, 20, 28, or .410 ga., any barrel 26-32 in., choke, vent. or solid rib, Anson & Deeley boxlock, auto ejectors, checkered pistol grip or English stock, pre-war.

12 or 20 ga.	$3,600	$3,200	$2,850	$2,500	$2,100	$1,750	$1,500

    Deduct 10% for 16 ga.
    Add 30% for 28 or .410 ga.
    Add $300 for vent. rib.
    Add $400 for SST.

GRADE NO. 3 — similar to No. 1, except less elaborate engraving, pre-WWII.

12 ga.	$2,850	$2,500	$2,200	$2,000	$1,650	$1,350	$1,200

    Deduct 10% for 16 ga.
    Add 20% for 28 or .410 ga.
    Add $300 for vent. rib.
    Add $400 for SST.

MODEL 143E — O/U, similar to model 1, except not as high quality as pre-war model, not available in 28 or .410 ga. Mfg. post-WWII.

$2,400	$2,150	$1,850	$1,550	$1,350	$1,175	$1,000

    Add 10% for vent. rib and SST.

G

Grading	100%	98%	95%	90%	80%	70%	60%

O/U COMBINATION GUN — 12, 16, 20, 28, or .410 ga., shotgun barrel, rifle in any rimmed caliber, 24 or 26 in. solid rib barrel, pre-WWII.

	$5,200	$4,800	$4,400	$4,000	$3,600	$3,150	$2,800

Add $700 for auto ejectors.
Deduct 10% for 16 ga.
Add 20% for 28 or .410 ga.
Deduct 40-50% for obsolete rifle caliber.
Above values for 12 or 20 ga. over obtainable rifle cartridge.

DRILLING — 12, 16, or 20 ga., SxS over any rimmed rifle caliber, 26 in. barrels, boxlock, extractors, double triggers, rifle sight activated by barrel selector, pre-WWII.

	$3,500	$3,000	$2,750	$2,550	$2,300	$2,000	$1,750

Deduct 10% for 16 ga.
Deduct 40-50% for obsolete cals.
Previous values for 12 and 20 ga. over available caliber.

GRENDEL, INC.

Previous manufacturer located in Rockledge, FL until 1995.

PISTOLS

G

MODEL P-10 SERIES — .380 ACP, semi-auto, blowback double action, 10 shot mag., small dimensions, hammerless, matte blue finish, 15 oz. Mfg. disc. 1991.

	$140	$125	$115	$105	$95	$90	$85

Last Mfg.'s Sug. Retail was $155.

Add $15 for electroless nickel finish.
Add $15 for nickel green finish.
Green finish was available at no extra charge.

MODEL P-12 — .380 ACP, semi-auto, double action only, 3 in. barrel, steel construction with polymer grip area, no external safety, 11 shot Zytel mag., blue or electroless nickel finish, 11 lb. trigger pull, 13 oz. Mfg. 1992-95.

	$155	$135	$120	$110	$100	$90	$80

Last Mfg.'s Sug. Retail was $175.

Add $20 for nickel finish.
Add $50 for threaded barrel with muzzle brake parts option.

MODEL P-30 — .22 Mag. cal., blowback similar action to P-12, 5 in. barrel, hammerless, matte black finish, 10 (C/B 1994) or 30* shot mag., 21 oz. Mfg. 1990-95.

	$200	$175	$155	$140	$125	$115	$105

Last Mfg.'s Sug. Retail was $225.

Add $25 for electroless nickel finish (disc. 1991).
Add $35 for scope mount (Weaver base).

▲ *Model P-30M* — similar to Model P-30, except has 5.6 in. barrel with removable muzzle brake. Mfg. 1990-95.

	$205	$180	$160	$140	$125	$115	$105

Last Mfg.'s Sug. Retail was $235.

Add $25 for electroless nickel finish (disc. 1991).

MODEL P-30L — similar to Model P-30, except has 8 in. barrel with removable muzzle brake, 22 oz. Mfg. 1991-92.

	$240	$200	$180	$160	$140	$125	$110

Last Mfg.'s Sug. Retail was $280.

Add $15 for Model P-30LM that allows for fitting various accessories.

MODEL P-31 — .22 Mag., same action as P-30, except has 11 in. barrel, enclosed synthetic barrel shroud and flash hider, 48 oz. Mfg. 1990-95.

	$285	$240	$215	$185	$160	$145	$130

Last Mfg.'s Sug. Retail was $345.

Grading	100%	98%	95%	90%	80%	70%	60%

RIFLES/CARBINES

MODEL R-31 — similar design to Model P-31, except has 16 in. barrel and telescoping stock, 64 oz. Mfg. 1991-95.

	$315	$260	$235	$210	$185	$165	$150

Last Mfg.'s Sug. Retail was $385.

SRT-20F COMPACT — .243 Win. or .308 cal., bolt action based on the Sako A-2 action, 20 in. match grade finned barrel with muzzle brake, folding synthetic stock, integrated bi-pod rest, no sights, 9 shot mag., 6.7 lbs. Disc. 1989.

	$575	$525	$475	$395	$365	$340	$320

Last Mfg.'s Sug. Retail was $525.

Grendel previously manufactured the SRT-16F, SRT-20L, and SRT-24 - all were disc. 1988. Values are approx. the same as the SRT-20F.

GRIFFIN & HOWE

Custom gunsmith/manufacturer located in New York, NY **Griffin & Howe** and Bernardsville, NJ.

Founded in 1923 by Seymour Griffin and James Howe, Griffin & Howe continues to build its custom rifles as well as providing the full spectrum of gunsmithing services and importation of fine English guns.

Griffin & Howe has been building custom rifles since 1923. They also perform a variety of custom gunsmithing services. Prices may vary greatly depending on configuration, desirability, condition and special features. Most used Griffin & Howe Custom Rifles in average condition and without special engraving start at $3,150+ and rise according to condition and nature of the individual gun. Since 1923, fewer than 2,800 have been made. In 1930, Griffin & Howe became a subsidiary of Abercrombie & Fitch and remained with them until 1976 when it became a privately held company. Because all Griffin & Howe rifles are essentially special ordered, accurate pricing can be ascertained only by examining each individual gun. Elaborate specimens by this maker trademark will command over $10,000. Engraving by Joseph Fugger, Winston Churchill, Bob Swartley or Kornbrath will add considerably to the value.

Pricing on new custom rifles, with a wide selection of options, is available directly from Griffin & Howe.

RIFLES

Values below represent a base gun with normal wood and no options.

G&H CLASSIC FRENCH WALNUT STOCK — custom honed action with lapped lugs, Douglas premium barrel, hand engraving, French walnut sporter stock with ebony forend tip, G&H pistol grip cap, "Griffin & Howe, New York" barrel address, custom order.

Mfg.'s Sug. Retail	$5,500	$5,500	$4,350	$3,550	$3,150	$2,750	$2,500	$2,250

G&H PRE-'64 MODEL 70 CLASSIC SYNTHETIC STOCK — features glass bedded synthetic classic sporter stock in black or woodgrain finish, Douglas premium barrel, "Griffin & Howe, New York" barrel address, custom order.

Mfg.'s Sug. Retail	$2,250	$2,250	$1,900	$1,650	$1,400	$1,175	$995	$850

WIN M70 STANDARD ACTION — for .243, .270, .30-06, or .308 cal.

	$5,000	$4,250	$3,450	$3,150	$2,750	$2,500	$2,250

WIN M70 MEDIUM — for .300, 7mm, or .338 cal.

	$5,300	$4,500	$3,600	$3,350	$2,950	$2,750	$2,350

Grading	100%	98%	95%	90%	80%	70%	60%

WIN M70 MAGNUM — for .375, or .416 Rem. cal.

	100%	98%	95%	90%	80%	70%	60%
	$5,500	$4,750	$3,850	$3,500	$3,000	$2,850	$2,450

WIN M52 — for .22 LR cal.

	$2,500	$2,250	$1,750	$1,650	$1,450	$1,300	$1,150

WIN HIGHWALL

	$1,850	$1,650	$1,250	$1,150	$1,000	$950	$850

SPRINGFIELD 1903

	$2,450	$2,150	$1,750	$1,550	$1,350	$1,250	$1,100

SPRINGFIELD 1922

	$2,450	$2,150	$1,750	$1,550	$1,350	$1,250	$1,100

MAUSER STANDARD

	$3,200	$2,850	$2,250	$2,000	$1,750	$1,650	$1,450

MAUSER MAGNUM

	$7,500	$6,500	$5,250	$4,750	$4,250	$3,850	$3,350

SAVAGE 99

	$1,850	$1,650	$1,250	$1,150	$1,025	$950	$850

SHOTGUNS: SIDE-BY-SIDE

ROUND BODY GAME GUN — 12, 16, 20, 28, or .410 ga., features case colored round frame with sidelock action and 3rd fastener, H&H style selective ejectors, 26, 28, or 30 in. barrels, double triggers, checkered straight grip stock and splinter forearm, mfg. by Arrieta.

Mfg.'s Sug. Retail	$5,750	$5,300	$4,600	$4,100	$3,500	$2,900	$2,400	$1,850

Add $200 for 28 or .410 ga.

GRULLA ARMAS

Manufacturer located in Eibar, Spain since 1932. Currently imported by Gunsport, Ltd. Inc. since 1994. Grulla Armas manufactures a complete line of quality SxS shotguns in addition to both SxS and bolt action rifles.

RIFLES

C-95 BOLT ACTION — .338 Win. Mag. or .375 H&H cal., deluxe bolt action featuring extensively scroll engraved square bridge receiver with elongated upper tang, octagon barrel with quarter rib and express sights, deluxe checkered wood with ebony forend, custom made per individual order. New 1996.

Mfg.'s Sug. Retail	$7,500	$6,950	$6,400	$5,750	$4,950	$4,300	$3,600	$2,750

E-95 SxS DOUBLE RIFLE — 9.3x74R or .375 H&H cal., top-of-the-line double rifle utilizing H&H type sidelocks with scroll engraving, skeleton steel buttplate, regulated barrels, beavertail forend, custom made per individual order. New 1996.

Mfg.'s Sug. Retail	$20,000	$18,000	$15,750	$13,250	$11,750	$9,650	$8,500	$7,250

SHOTGUNS: SIDE-BY-SIDE, SIDELOCK

The models listed below are currently available in 12, 16, 20, 28, or .410 ga. All guns have double triggers with hinged front, selective auto-ejectors, and straight grip stock with splinter forearm. Values represent standard models with no options.

MODEL 209 - HOLLAND — coin finished receiver with scroll engraving.

Mfg.'s Sug. Retail	$3,295	$2,850	$2,475	$2,100	$1,800	$1,500	$1,325	$1,100

Grading		100%	98%	95%	90%	80%	70%	60%

MODEL 215 — similar to Model 209, except has rose and scroll engraving with 3rd lever fastener and better wood.

Mfg.'s Sug. Retail	$3,895		$3,500	$2,950	$2,475	$2,100	$1,800	$1,500	$1,325

MODEL 216 — features delicate scroll engraving with border designs.

Mfg.'s Sug. Retail	$4,395		$3,900	$3,500	$2,950	$2,475	$2,100	$1,800	$1,500

MODEL 219 — Similar to Model 216, except has more elaborate engraving and better wood.

Mfg.'s Sug. Retail	$5,795		$5,175	$4,550	$3,950	$3,500	$2,950	$2,475	$1,995

CONSORT — features easy-opening H&H style action, scroll engraving with border fences.

Mfg.'s Sug. Retail	$6,325		$5,750	$5,100	$4,550	$3,850	$3,275	$2,650	$2,200

WINDSOR — similar to Consort Model, except has more engraving.

Mfg.'s Sug. Retail	$6,825		$6,100	$5,550	$4,950	$4,350	$3,750	$3,000	$2,400

MODEL 219-P

Mfg.'s Sug. Retail	$7,425		$6,825	$6,100	$5,550	$4,850	$4,100	$3,200	$2,600

SUPER MH — features Boss style fine engraving with rosettes.

Mfg.'s Sug. Retail	$12,150		$11,250	$9,500	$8,475	$7,425	$6,200	$5,000	$4,150

NUMBER 1 — next to the top-of-the-line gun with best quality features.

Mfg.'s Sug. Retail	$14,925		$12,750	$10,400	$8,750	$7,575	$6,350	$5,150	$4,200

ROYAL — top-of-the-line model with H&H style scroll engraving.

Mfg.'s Sug. Retail	$16,695		$14,950	$12,750	$10,400	$8,750	$7,575	$6,350	$5,150

GUN WORKS, LTD.

Previously manufactured and distributed in Buffalo, NY. Early guns were made in Tonawanda, NY.

X-CALIBER — .44 Mag., single shot, tip up pistol, 8 in. barrel, matte type blue finish, ergonomic hardwood grips, probably used older Sterling Arms parts and restamped the barrel address. Limited mfg.

	$350	$300	$260	$230	$200	$175	$150

MODEL 9 — O/U derringer, .357 Mag., 9mm or .38 Super, or .38 Spl. cal., electroless nickel finish, 2½ in. barrel, wood grips, Millett sights, 15 oz. Disc. 1986.

	$135	$120	$105	$95	$65	$55	$50

Last Mfg.'s Sug. Retail was $149.

GUSTAF, CARL

See listing under Carl Gustaf.

GYROJET

See MBA Gyrojet listing in the M Section of this text.

G

G

H section

HHF

Manufacturer located in Huglu, Turkey. Imported by Turkish Firearms Corp. located in Manassas Park, VA since 1993. HHF designates Huglu Hunting Firearms.

Grading	100%	98%	95%	90%	80%	70%	60%

SHOTGUNS

All 12 and 20 ga. shotguns listed below are supplied with five choke tubes. All 12, 16, and 20 ga. shotguns are equipped with automatic ejectors - extractors are available for $200 less.

HHF also has a special order line with delivery time taking approx. 6 months - please contact the importer directly (see Trademark Index) for current pricing and availability for these special order shotguns.

MODEL 101B O/U — 12 ga. only, trap configuration, 30 or 32 in. separated VR barrels, coin finished receiver with moderate engraving. New 1993.
Mfg.'s Sug. Retail	$1,720		$1,535	$1,225	$975	$775	$650	$525	$475
Add $545 for extra top-single barrel (Model 101 B AT-DT).

MODEL 103D FIELD O/U — 12, 16, 20, 28, or .410 ga., 26 or 28 in. vented barrels with VR, coin finished receiver with light engraving. New 1994.
Mfg.'s Sug. Retail	$1,700		$1,515	$1,225	$975	$775	$650	$525	$475
Add $55 for 28 or .410 ga.

▲ **Model 103C O/U** — 12 or 20 ga., skeet model, features 27 or 28 in. separated barrels with VR, blued receiver with light engraving and gold inlays. New 1996.
Mfg.'s Sug. Retail	$1,700		$1,515	$1,225	$975	$775	$650	$525	$475

▲ **Model 103F O/U** — 12 or 20 ga., sporting clays configuration, 28 or 30 in. vented barrels with VR, engraved coin finished receiver with engraved blued side plates. New 1996.
Mfg.'s Sug. Retail	$1,875		$1,650	$1,300	$1,025	$795	$650	$525	$475

MODEL 200A FIELD SxS — 12, 16, 20, 28, or .410 ga., engraved coin finished scalloped boxlock action, SST, 26 or 28 in. SR barrels, checkered walnut stock with cheekpiece and beavertail forearm. New 1995.
Mfg.'s Sug. Retail	$1,150		$975	$825	$700	$600	$500	$400	$300

MODEL 201A FIELD SxS — 12, 16, or 20 ga., 28 in. SR barrels only, coin finished boxlock receiver with engraving on side plates. New 1995.
Mfg.'s Sug. Retail	$1,700		$1,515	$1,225	$975	$775	$650	$525	$475

MODEL 202A FIELD SxS — 12, 16, or 20 ga., features coin finished boxlock with Greener crossbolt, DTs, splinter forearm, 28 in. SR barrels only. New 1995.
Mfg.'s Sug. Retail	$1,285		$1,075	$875	$750	$625	$525	$400	$300

HJS ARMS, INC.

Manufacturer located in Brownsville, TX. Distributor and dealer sales.

DERRINGERS

FRONTIER FOUR MODEL A01 — .22 LR cal., 4 barrels with rotating firing pin, stainless steel, 2 in. barrels, spur trigger, plastic grips, 5½ oz. New 1993.
Mfg.'s Sug. Retail	$170		$145	$125	$115

Grading	100%	98%	95%	90%	80%	70%	60%

FRONTIER FOUR MODEL A03 — similar to Model A01, except has brass frame and blue barrel. New 1995.

Mfg.'s Sug. Retail	$185	$165	$135	$120			

LONE STAR MODEL A10 — .38 S&W or .380 ACP cal., single shot, stainless steel, 2 in. barrels, spur trigger, rotating firing pin blocker, plastic grips, 6 oz. New 1993.

Mfg.'s Sug. Retail	$190	$165	$135	$120			

H.J.S. INDUSTRIES, INC.
Brownsville, TX.

FRONTIER FOUR DERRINGER — 4 shot derringer, .22 LR cal. only, stainless steel construction, 5½ oz.

$115	$90	$80

LONE STAR DERRINGER — single shot derringer, .38 S&W only, stainless steel construction, 6 oz.

$137	$105	$95

H & R 1871, INC. (Harrington & Richardson)

Holding company located in Gardner, MA since 1991.

H & R 1871 Inc. is a new company utilizing the older H & R trademark and does not accept warranty work for older (pre-1986 mfg.) Harrington & Richardson, Inc. firearms. Distributor sales only.

The use of the original Harrington & Richardson trademark was permitted during 1991. All new manufacture will use this trademark, but older H & Rs manufactured by Harrington & Richardson, Inc. are not the responsibility of H & R 1871, Inc.

REVOLVERS

Additional revolvers using the New England Firearms trademark may be located in the N section of this text.

929 SIDEKICK — .22 LR cal., 9 shot, blued metal, swing-out cylinder, 4 in. heavy barrel, square butt with brown laminate grips, 30 oz. New 1996.

Mfg.'s Sug. Retail	$160	$140	$110	$95	$85	$75	$65	$55

▲ **929 Sidekick Trapper Edition** — similar to 929 Sidekick, except has gray laminate grips and special barrel markings, limited mfg. 1996 only.

Mfg.'s Sug. Retail	$175	$150	$115	$95	$85	$75	$65	$55

939 PREMIER (WESTERN 939) — .22 LR cal., 9 shot, blued metal, swing-out cylinder, target model with ribbed 6 in. heavy barrel and adj. rear sight, hardwood grips, 36 oz. New 1995.

Mfg.'s Sug. Retail	$185	$145	$125	$105	$90	$75	$65	$55

FOURTY-NINER (WESTERN 949) — .22 LR cal., 9 shot fixed cylinder, case colored receiver, 5½ or 7½ in. barrel, hardwood grips, fixed sights, approx. 37 oz. New 1995.

Mfg.'s Sug. Retail	$185	$145	$125	$105	$90	$75	$65	$55

SPORTSMAN 999 — .22 LR cal., single or double action, 9 shot, 4 or 6 in. barrel with fluted solid rib, top break action with auto shell ejection, smooth hardwood stocks, transfer bar safety, blue finish, adj. sights, 30-34 oz. Mfg. began 1991.

Mfg.'s Sug. Retail	$280	$225	$180	$145	$125	$115	$100	$90

Grading	100%	98%	95%	90%	80%	70%	60%

RIFLES

ULTRA SINGLE SHOT — .22-250 Rem. (disc. 1994), .223 Rem., .25-06 Rem. (new 1995), .308 Win. (new 1995), or .357 Rem. Max. (new 1996) cal, single shot break-open action, side-lever release, heavy 22 (.22-250 Rem. or .223 Rem.), 22 normal (.308 Win.), or 26 (.25-06) in. barrel with scope mount rail, checkered curly maple (disc. 1994) or laminated hardwood Monte Carlo stock with black lined recoil pad, sling swivel studs, 7-8 lbs. New 1993.

Mfg.'s Sug. Retail	$250	$210	$170	$135	$115	$105	$95	$85

This model features a scope rail on .25-06 Rem. and .308 Win. cals.

▲ *Rocky Mountain Elk Foundation Commemorative* — .280 Rem. cal., 26 in. blue barrel, features RMEF medallion in stock, high gloss bluing, 7-8 lbs. New 1995.

Mfg.'s Sug. Retail	$270	$220	$175	$135

WESSON & HARRINGTON BUFFALO CLASSIC — .45-70 cal., Topper style break-open action, 32 in. barrel, case hardened frame, checkered walnut stock and forearm, 8 lbs. Introduced 1995.

Mfg.'s Sug. Retail	$329	$285	$230	$195

SHOTGUNS: SINGLE SHOT

TOPPER 098 — 12, 16 (new 1992), 20, 28 (mfg. 1992-95), or .410 ga., 3 in. chamber, 26 or 28 in. barrel, break open side lever release action, transfer bar safety, ejector, satin nickel frame with blue barrel, black finish hardwood stock with full pistol grip and forearm, 5-6 lbs. Mfg. began 1991.

Mfg.'s Sug. Retail	$115	$95	$80	$70	$60	$50	$40	$35

▲ *Topper Deluxe* — 12 ga. only, 3½ in. chamber, satin nickel frame with blue barrel, 28 in. barrel with 1 choke tube, black finish hardwood stock (with recoil pad) and forearm, 5-6 lbs. New 1991.

Mfg.'s Sug. Retail	$135	$110	$90	$80	$70	$60	$50	$40

▲ *Topper Deluxe Rifled Slug Gun* — 12 ga. only, 24 in. compensated barrel, rifle sights, dark American hardwood stock and forearm, satin nickel frame, approx. 5½ lbs. New 1996.

Mfg.'s Sug. Retail	$170	$150	$115	$95	$85	$75	$65	$55

▲ *H & R NWTF Turkey Mag.* — 10 (new 1996) or 12 (mfg. 1991-95) ga., 3½ in. chamber, 24 in. drilled and tapped barrel with 1 choke tube, entire gun is covered in mossy oak camo, includes sling and swivels, 6 lbs. Introduced 1991.

Mfg.'s Sug. Retail	$180	$145	$120	$100	$85	$75	$65	$55

This model is part of the National Wild Turkey Federation (NWTF) sponsorship program.

▲ *Topper Jr.* — 20 or .410 ga., smaller variation of the Topper 098 with youth dimensions including 22 in. barrel and shortened stock with recoil pad, satin nickel frame with blue barrel, 5-6 lbs. Mfg. began 1991.

Mfg.'s Sug. Retail	$120	$100	$85	$70	$60	$50	$40	$35

▲ *Topper Classic Youth (Limited Edition)* — 20, 28, or .410 ga., 22 in. barrel, checkered American black walnut stock and forearm, recoil pad. Mfg. began 1991.

Mfg.'s Sug. Retail	$145	$120	$95	$80	$70	$60	$50	$40

▲ *1994 NWTF Youth Turkey Gun* — 20 ga., 3 in. chamber, 22 in. full choke barrel, features Realtree camo finish and sling, limited mfg. 1994-95.

	$140	$110	$95	$85	$75	$65	$55

Last Mfg.'s Sug. Retail was $160.

THE TAMER — .410 ga., 3 in. chamber, synthetic thumbhole stock is designed to hold 4 shells, transfer bar safety, 20 in. full choke barrel, electroless nickel finish. New 1994.

Mfg.'s Sug. Retail	$125	$100	$90	$80	$70	$60	$50	$40

980 ULTRA SLUG HUNTER — 12 or 20 ga., 3 in. chamber, 22 (20 ga., Youth Model) or 24 in. fully rifled heavy barrel, side-release lever, Monte Carlo hardwood stock with recoil pad, matte finished receiver, 9 lbs. New 1995.

Mfg.'s Sug. Retail	$210	$180	$145	$120	$100	$85	$75	$65

H-S PRECISION, INC.

Custom rifle manufacturer located in Rapid City, SD. H-S Precision, Inc. also manufactures synthetic stocks and custom machine barrels as well.

In addition to the models listed below, H-S Precision, Inc. will also build rifles using a customer's action (Remington 700 ADL or 700 BDL, Sako, Weatherby, or Winchester). These models will be approx. 16% less expensive than values listed below (not available in Sniper Model).

Grading	100%	98%	95%	90%	80%	70%	60%

RIFLES: BOLT ACTION - CUSTOM MFG.

All H-S Precision rifles feature Kevlar/graphite laminate stocks, cut rifle barrels, and other high tech innovations including a molded in aluminum bedding block system.

PRO SERIES SPORTER/VARMINT — .223 Rem., .22 PPC, .22-250 Rem., .243 Win., 6mm PPC, 7mm-08 Rem., or .308 Win. cal. are available in short action, .270 Win., .30-06, 7mm Rem. Mag., .300 Win. Mag., or .338 Win. Mag. cal. are available in long action, Remington ADL action only, each rifle is built per individual specifications. New 1990.

	Mfg.'s Sug. Retail	$1,850		$1,850	$1,425	$1,200	$895	$750	$650	$575

Add $150 for left-hand action.
Add $880 for extra stainless barrel (disc.).

PRO SERIES LONG RANGE (TACTICAL MARKSMAN) — .223 Rem., .243 Win., .30-06, .308, 7mm Rem. Mag., or .300 Win. Mag. cal., stainless fluted barrel standard, Remington BDL action. New 1990.

	Mfg.'s Sug. Retail	$1,950		$1,950	$1,500	$1,250	$925	$775	$675	$575

Add $150 for left-hand action.

TAKEDOWN PRO SERIES SPORTER/VARMINT — .22-250, .243 Win., 7mm-08 Rem., or .308 Win. cal. in short action, .25-06 Rem., .270 Win., .30-06, 7mm Rem. Mag., .300 Win. Mag., or .338 Win. Mag. cal. in long action, stainless steel barrel, Remington BDL takedown action, matte blue finish. New 1990.

	Mfg.'s Sug. Retail	$2,640		$2,640	$2,000	$1,570	$1,225	$900	$800	$700

Add $1,000 for extra barrel.

TAKEDOWN PRO SERIES LONG RANGE (TACTICAL MARKSMAN) — .223 Rem., .243 Win., .30-06, .308 Win., 7mm Rem. Mag., .300 Win. Mag., or .338 Win. Mag. cal., includes "kwik klip" and stainless fluted barrel. New 1990.

	Mfg.'s Sug. Retail	$2,920		$2,920	$2,225	$1,675	$1,350	$995	$850	$750

A complete rifle package consisting of 2 calibers (.308 Win. and .300 Win. Mag.), scope and fitted case is available for $5,200 retail.

HWP INDUSTRIES

Previous manufacturer located in Milwaukee, WI.

THE SLEDGEHAMMER — .500 HWP Mag. cal., 5 shot revolver, double action, stainless steel, full shrouded 4 in. barrel (quick change), Pachmayr grips. Limited mfg. 1989 only.

	$1,150	$895	$750

Last Mfg.'s Sug. Retail was $1,295.

HAENEL, C.G.

Previous manufacturer located in Suhl, Germany. Mfg. between 1925-1940.

Grading	100%	98%	95%	90%	80%	70%	60%

RIFLES

MAUSER-MANNLICHER SPORTING RIFLE — M/88 Mauser type action, 7x57, 8x57, or 9x57 cal., 22 or 24 in. octagon barrel, Mannlicher box mag., double set triggers, raised rib on barrel leaf sight, sporter stock.

	$440	$360	$330	$275	$250	$220	$165

88 MAUSER SPORTER — similar to Mauser-Mannlicher, with Mauser 5 shot mag.

	$525	$450	$375	$325	$275	$240	$200

PISTOLS

SCHMEISSER MODEL 1 & 2 — .25 ACP cal., similar to Baby Browning.

	$385	$340	$300	$275	$230	$200	$180

MODELS 200-205 — See Hammerli-Walther

HAMBRUSCH JAGDWAFFEN GmbH

Manufacturer located in Ferlach, Austria since 1782. Currently imported and distributed by CONCO Arms, located in Emmaus, PA, since 1993.

Hambrusch Jagdwaffen manufactures many types of high-grade long arms including SxS shotguns, combination guns, drillings, double rifles, and single shot rifles. The combinations of these above configurations are almost endless - please contact CONCO Arms directly (see Trademark Index) for current model information and price quotations. Please allow 4-6 weeks for a reply.

HAMMERLI

Manufacturer located in Lenzburg, Switzerland. Currently imported and distributed by Sigarms Inc. located in Exeter, NH. Previously imported until 1995 by Hammerli Pistols USA, located in Groveland, CA. Previously imported by Mandall Shooting Supplies, Inc. located in Scottsdale, AZ and Beeman Precision Arms located in Santa Rosa, CA.

PISTOLS

MODEL 100 FREE PISTOL — .22 LR cal., 11½ in. octagon barrel, blue, martini action single shot, set trigger, micro rear sight, walnut stock and forearm. Mfg. 1933-1949.

	$880	$660	$605	$550	$470	$440	$385

▲ *Deluxe model* — carved stock.

	$990	$770	$715	$660	$580	$550	$495

MODEL 101 — similar to Model 100, but heavy round barrel, improved action and sights, matte finish. Mfg. 1956-1960.

	$880	$660	$605	$550	$470	$440	$385

MODEL 102 — similar to Model 101, except high polished finish. Mfg. 1956-1960.

	$880	$660	$605	$550	$470	$440	$385
Deluxe model.	$990	$770	$715	$660	$580	$550	$495

MODEL 103 FREE PISTOL — similar to Model 101, except lighter octagon polished barrel. Mfg. 1956-1960.

	$935	$715	$660	$605	$580	$550	$495

Grading	100%	98%	95%	90%	80%	70%	60%

MODEL 104 MATCH PISTOL — similar to Model 103, except lighter round barrel, redesigned stock, mfg. 1961-1965.

	$760	$660	$550	$495	$470	$440	$385

MODEL 105 MATCH PISTOL — similar to Model 103, except redesigned action and stock, octagon barrel. Mfg. 1962-1965.

	$935	$715	$660	$605	$580	$550	$495

MODEL 106 MATCH PISTOL — similar to Model 105, except improved trigger.

	$910	$690	$580	$525	$495	$470	$415

MODEL 107 MATCH PISTOL — similar to Model 105, except improved trigger.

	$990	$770	$660	$550	$525	$495	$440

▲ *Deluxe model* — engraved and carved wood.

	$1,320	$990	$880	$660	$635	$605	$550

MODEL 120-1 SINGLE SHOT FREE PISTOL — .22 LR cal., bolt action, 9.9 in. barrel, blue barrel and receiver, side lever operated, anodized aluminum lever and frame, walnut checkered grips.

	$440	$360	$305	$275	$220	$200	$175

MODEL 120-2 — similar to 120-1, except stocks hand contoured.

	$470	$385	$330	$305	$250	$220	$195

MODEL 120 HEAVY BARREL — similar to 120-1, with 5.7 in. bull barrel.

MODEL 150 FREE PISTOL — .22 LR cal., 11.3 in. barrel, improved Martini-type action, set trigger, innovative design incorporating many unusual features. Disc. 1989.

	$1,850	$1,495	$1,275	$1,120	$980	$900	$850

Last Mfg.'s Sug. Retail was $1,980.

Add $113 for left-hand variation.
The Model 150 was replaced by the Model 160.

MODEL 151 FREE PISTOL — replacement for the Model 150 Free Pistol. Imported 1990-1993.

	$1,850	$1,495	$1,275	$1,120	$995	$900	$800

Last Mfg.'s Sug. Retail was $1,980.

MODEL 152 FREE PISTOL — .22 LR cal., 11.3 in. barrel. improved Martini-type action, electronic trigger release, innovative design incorporating many unusual features. State of the art target pistol. Disc. 1992.

	$1,995	$1,600	$1,350	$1,195	$1,090	$990	$895

Last Mfg.'s Sug. Retail was $2,105.

Add $57 for left-hand variation.

MODEL 160 FREE PISTOL — .22 LR cal., similar to Model 150, except has poly-carbon fiber grips and forend, includes carrying case. New 1993.

Mfg.'s Sug. Retail	$2,085	$1,895	$1,495	$1,150	$900	$800	$700	$595

Add $290 for smaller adj. grips.

MODEL 162 FREE PISTOL — .22 LR cal., replacement for the Model 152 Free Pistol, includes poly-carbon fiber grips and forend, includes carrying case. New 1993.

Mfg.'s Sug. Retail	$2,295	$2,045	$1,650	$1,350	$1,125	$900	$800	$700

Add $290 for smaller adj. grips.

MODELS 200-205 — See Hammerli-Walther

INTERNATIONAL MODEL 206 — .22 LR cal., .22 S, semi-auto, $7\frac{1}{16}$ in. barrel with muzzle brake, adj. sights, walnut grips, blue. Mfg. 1962-1969.

	$690	$605	$495	$470	$385	$360	$330

INTERNATIONAL MODEL 207 — similar to 206, except adj. grip heel.

	$705	$635	$505	$480	$395	$370	$340

Grading	100%	98%	95%	90%	80%	70%	60%

INTERNATIONAL MODEL 208 — .22 LR cal., semi-auto, 9 shot, 6 in. barrel, blue, adj. sights, checkered walnut grips with adj. heel. Mfg. 1966-1988.

| | $1,600 | $1,300 | $1,050 | $950 | $880 | $835 | $770 |

Last Mfg.'s Sug. Retail was $1,755.

This model was replaced by the Model 208S.

▲ *Model 208S* — similar to Model 208, except has redesigned triggerguard and interchangeable rear sight element. Importation started 1988.

| Mfg.'s Sug. Retail | $1,925 | $1,695 | $1,225 | $975 | $875 | $775 | $675 | $575 |

Add $125 for factory scope mount.
Add $180 for smaller adj. grips.

▲ *Model 208 Deluxe* — similar to Model 208, except has carved grips and elaborate engraving. Importation disc. 1988.

| | $2,995 | $2,500 | $1,995 |

Last Mfg.'s Sug. Retail was $3,250.

▲ *Model 208C (Commemorative)* — limited edition commemorative. Disc 1987.

| | $2,100 | $1,750 | $1,400 |

Last Mfg.'s Sug. Retail was $2,225.

INTERNATIONAL MODEL 209 — .22 Short, semi-auto, 5 shot, 4¾ in. barrel, muzzle brake, adj. sights, blue, walnut stock. Mfg. 1966-1970.

| | $800 | $690 | $635 | $550 | $525 | $485 | $440 |

INTERNATIONAL MODEL 210 — similar to 209, but grips have adj. heel. Mfg. 1966-1970.

| | $800 | $715 | $660 | $590 | $540 | $525 | $495 |

MODEL 211 — .22 LR cal., semi-auto, 9 shot, 6 in. barrel, adj. sights, blue, similar to Model 208 except non-adj. walnut stocks. Importation disc. 1990.

| | $1,550 | $1,275 | $1,050 | $950 | $880 | $835 | $770 |

Last Mfg.'s Sug. Retail was $1,669.

MODEL 212 HUNTER — .22 LR cal., semi-auto, hunter's pistol, 9 shot, 5 in. barrel, adj. sights, blue, walnut stocks. Importation disc. 1993.

| | $1,250 | $1,000 | $875 | $775 | $675 | $575 | $475 |

Last Mfg.'s Sug. Retail was $1,395.

MODEL 215 — .22 LR cal., semi-auto, Model 208 specs on commercial target model, 9 shot, 5 in. barrel, adj. sights, blue, walnut stocks. Importation disc. 1990.

| | $1,395 | $1,050 | $895 | $775 | $695 | $650 | $600 |

Last Mfg.'s Sug. Retail was $1,505.

MODEL 230 RAPID FIRE PISTOL — .22 S cal., semi-auto, 5 shot, 6.3 in. barrel, blue, adj. sights, smooth walnut grips. Mfg. 1970-1983.

| | $705 | $635 | $580 | $530 | $485 | $450 | $415 |

MODEL 230-2 — similar to 230, except checkered grips with adj. heel. Mfg. 1970-1983.

| | $735 | $655 | $605 | $570 | $515 | $485 | $470 |

MODEL 232-1 RAPID FIRE PISTOL — .22 S cal., semi-auto, 6 shot, 5.1 in. barrel, blue, adj. sights, contoured walnut grips. Importation disc. 1993.

| | $1,395 | $1,125 | $950 | $850 | $750 | $700 | $650 |

Last Mfg.'s Sug. Retail was $1,505.

Add $25 for wraparound grips sizes S-M-LG (Model 232-2).

H

Grading	100%	98%	95%	90%	80%	70%	60%

MODEL 280 — .22 LR or .32 S&W Long cal., new modular pistol design utilizing carbon fiber synthetic material to replace frame and other critical parts, adj. grips, trigger, and rear sight, 4.6 in. barrel, 5 or 6 shot mag., approx. 2.2 lbs. New 1988.

Mfg.'s Sug. Retail	$1,565	$1,365	$1,050	$875	$775	$675	$575	$475

Add $200 for .32 S&W Long cal.
Add $765 (.22 LR) or $965 (.32 S&W Long) for conversion kit.
Add $200 for smaller adj. grips.
A package is also available with both calibers, magazines, and hard case for $2,595.

MODEL P-240 — see S.I.G.- HAMMERLI for this model.

RIFLES: TARGET

OLYMPIC 300 METER — .30-06 cal., bolt action, single shot free rifle, U.S.A. import, 7x57mm overseas, 20½ in. heavy barrel, double set trigger, aperture rear sight, globe front, free rifle stock with thumbhole pistol grip, beavertail forearm, Swiss style target butt. Mfg. 1945-1959.

	$880	$745	$605	$550	$470	$440	$415

HAMMERLI-TANNER 300 METER FREE RIFLE — similar to Olympic 300 , except 7.5mm standard, can be ordered in other calibers. Mfg. 1962-disc.

	$895	$825	$770	$715	$660	$580	$520

Last Mfg.'s Sug. Retail was $935.

MODEL 45 SMALLBORE MATCH RIFLE — .22 LR cal., bolt action, single shot, 27½ in. heavy barrel, same sights and stock type as Hammerli-Tanner. Mfg. 1945-1957.

	$660	$550	$470	$440	$385	$360	$330

MODEL 54 SMALLBORE MATCH RIFLE — similar to 45 Smallbore, except adj. butt. Mfg. 1954-1957.

	$670	$560	$480	$450	$395	$370	$340

MODEL 503 SMALLBORE FREE RIFLE — similar to 54 Smallbore, except free style stock.

	$660	$550	$470	$440	$385	$360	$330

MODEL 505 MATCH RIFLE — match stock with aperture sights.

	$690	$580	$495	$470	$415	$385	$360

MODEL 506 SMALLBORE MATCH RIFLE — similar to 503 Smallbore. Mfg. 1963-1966.

	$690	$580	$495	$470	$415	$385	$360

SPORTING RIFLE — various calibers, set triggers, Mauser repeating action.

	$725	$650	$490	$425	$360	$325	$300

HAMMERLI-WALTHER

Target Pistols manufactured under joint effort.

PISTOLS: SEMI-AUTO

MODEL 200 OLYMPIA — .22 Short or LR cal., 7½ in. barrel, 1952 type, adj. sights, barrel weight, blue, checkered walnut grips. Mfg. 1952-1958.

	$660	$605	$550	$440	$415	$385	$360

MODEL 200 OLYMPIA — 1958 type, similar to 1952 type, except has muzzle brake. Mfg. 1958-1963.

	$715	$605	$550	$495	$470	$415	$385

MODEL 201 — similar to 200, 1952 type, except 9½ in. barrel. Mfg. 1955-1957.

	$660	$605	$550	$440	$415	$385	$360

MODEL 202 — similar to 201, except adj. heel grips. Mfg. 1955-1957.

	$715	$605	$550	$495	$470	$415	$385

MODEL 203 — similar to 200, except has adj. heel grip.

Grading	100%	98%	95%	90%	80%	70%	60%
▲ *1955 Type* — no muzzle brake.							
	$715	$605	$550	$495	$470	$415	$385
▲ *1958 Type* — muzzle brake.							
	$770	$660	$605	$550	$525	$470	$440

MODEL 204 — similar to 200, except .22 LR cal. only.

	100%	98%	95%	90%	80%	70%	60%
▲ *1956 Type* — no muzzle brake.							
	$745	$635	$580	$525	$495	$470	$440
▲ *1958 Type* — muzzle brake.							
	$800	$690	$635	$550	$525	$495	$470

MODEL 205 — .22 LR cal., similar to 204, except adj. heel grips.

	100%	98%	95%	90%	80%	70%	60%
1956 type	$800	$690	$635	$550	$525	$495	$470
1958 type, M.B.	$855	$745	$715	$635	$580	$525	$495

HARRINGTON & RICHARDSON, INC.

Previous manufacturer located in Gardner, MA - formerly from Worchester, MA. Successors to Wesson & Harrington, manufactured from 1871 until January 24, 1986. In 1991, H & R 1871, Inc. was fomed (see their listing in the front of this section) and several new Topper shotgun models and the Sportsman 999 revolver were reintroduced. H & R 1871, Inc. is not responsible for the warranties or safety of older pre-1986 H & R firearms.

A manufacturer of utilitarian firearms for over 115 years, H & R ceased operation on January 24, 1986. Even though new manufacture (under H & R 1871, Inc.) is utilizing the H & R trademark, the discontinuance of older models in either NIB or mint condition may command slight asking premiums, but probably will not affect values on those handguns only recently discontinued. Most H & R firearms are still purchased for their shooting value rather than collecting potential.

Please refer to H & R listing in the Serialization section for alphabetical suffix information on how to determine year of manufacture for most H & R firearms between 1940-82.

PISTOLS: PRE-1942

MODEL 4 — .32 S&W Long 6 shot, or .38 S&W Long 5 shot, (1904), double action, 2½, 4½, and 6 in. barrels, blued or nickel, hard rubber grips, solid frame, fixed sights.

	100%	98%	95%	90%	80%	70%	60%
	$95	$85	$70	$55	$45	$35	$30

MODEL 5 — .32 S&W Long, 5 shot only, (1905), double action, same as Model 4.

	$95	$85	$70	$55	$45	$35	$30

MODEL 6 — .22 LR, 7 shot only, (1906), double action, similar to Model 4.

	$95	$85	$70	$55	$45	$35	$30

AMERICAN — .32 S&W, 6 shot, .38 S&W, 5 shot, double action, 2½, 4, or 6 in. barrels, fixed sights, blue or nickel.

	$95	$85	$70	$55	$45	$35	$30

YOUNG AMERICAN — .22 Long, 7 shot, .32 S&W, 5 shot, double action, 2, 4½, or 6 in. barrel, fixed sights, blue or nickel.

	$95	$85	$70	$55	$45	$35	$30

VEST POCKET — double action, 1⅛ in. barrel, blue or nickel, solid frame, spurless hammer.

	$95	$85	$70	$55	$45	$35	$30

HUNTER — .22 LR, double action, 10 in. octagon barrel, 9 shot, checkered walnut grips.

	$140	$110	$100	$85	$65	$55	$45

Grading	100%	98%	95%	90%	80%	70%	60%

TRAPPER — .22 LR cal., double action, 7 shot, 6 in. octagon barrel, checkered walnut stocks.

| | $140 | $120 | $100 | $85 | $65 | $55 | $45 |

MODEL 922 — .22 LR cal., first issue, 9 shot, 10 in. octagon barrel on early models, 6 in. round barrel on later models, checkered walnut grips.

| | $140 | $120 | $100 | $85 | $65 | $55 | $45 |

AUTOMATIC EJECTING — .32 S&W cal., 6 shot, .38 S&W, 5 shot, double action, 3¼, 4, 5, or 6 in. barrels, hinged break open, blue or nickel finish, fixed sights, black rubber grips.

| | $160 | $150 | $105 | $90 | $75 | $65 | $55 |

PREMIER — .22 LR cal., 7 shot, .32 S&W, 5 shot, double action, break open, small frame.

| | $95 | $85 | $70 | $55 | $45 | $35 | $30 |

HAMMERLESS — .22 LR cal., 7 shot, .32 S&W, 5 shot, double action, 2, 3, 4, 5, or 6 in. barrels, small frame, break open, blue or nickel, black rubber grips.

| | $125 | $110 | $100 | $85 | $65 | $55 | $45 |

HAMMERLESS — .32 S&W cal., 6 shot, .38 S&W, 5 shot, double action, 3¼, 4, 5, or 6 in. barrels, large frame, break open.

| | $125 | $110 | $100 | $85 | $65 | $55 | $45 |

TARGET MODEL — .22 LR cal., .22 WRF cal., 7 shot, double action, 6 in. barrel, fixed sights, break open, small frame, blue only, walnut grips.

| | $140 | $120 | $100 | $85 | $70 | $60 | $50 |

.22 SPECIAL — .22 LR cal., .22 WRF cal., 7 shot, double action, 6 in. barrel, break open, large frame, blue only, gold plated front sight, walnut grips.

| | $165 | $140 | $120 | $100 | $85 | $70 | $60 |

EXPERT — double action, similar to .22 Special, except 10 in. barrel.

| | $150 | $140 | $120 | $100 | $85 | $70 | $60 |

SPORTSMAN NO. 199 — .22 LR cal., 9 shot, single action, 6 in. barrel, adj. target sights, break open, blue only, checkered walnut grips.

| | $195 | $165 | $140 | $110 | $90 | $75 | $65 |

DEFENDER — .38 S&W cal., double action, 4 or 6 in. barrel, fixed sights, blue, break open, black plastic grips, made during WWII for police reserves and major corporation guards.

| | $140 | $120 | $110 | $100 | $85 | $65 | $55 |

ULTRA SPORTSMAN — .22 LR cal., 9 shot, single action, 6 in. barrel, blue, break open, adj. sights, walnut grips, short cylinder action, wide hammer spur.

| | $220 | $200 | $180 | $150 | $120 | $100 | $85 |

NEW DEFENDER — .22 LR cal., 9 shot, double action, 2 in. barrel, break open, adj. sights, blue, round butt, checkered walnut grip.

| | $220 | $200 | $180 | $150 | $120 | $100 | $85 |

USRA SINGLE SHOT TARGET — .22 LR cal., 7, 8, or 10 in. barrel, blue, hinged break open, adj. sights, walnut grips. Mfg. 1928-1941.

| | $440 | $415 | $385 | $330 | $290 | $250 | $195 |

Add 10% for nickel finish.

.25 CAL. SELF LOADING PISTOL — .25 ACP cal., 6 shot, 2 in. barrel, blue, black rubber grips.

| | $330 | $305 | $250 | $195 | $165 | $140 | $110 |

Grading	100%	98%	95%	90%	80%	70%	60%

.32 CAL. SELF LOADING PISTOL — .32 ACP cal., 8 shot, 3½ in. barrel, fixed sights, black rubber grips.

	$330	$305	$250	$195	$165	$140	$110

Add 20% for type I models if in 90%+ original condition.

Type I models with 12 slide pull grooves are serialized 1-3,025. Type II (more common) are serialized 3,026 - 35,000.

HANDY GUN — shotgun (mfg. 1920-1934) or rifle (mfg. 1931-1933) pistol mfg. between 1921-1933, available in either 8 or 12¼ in. choked or unchoked shotgun barrel, in either .410 or 28 ga., 12¼ in. barrel for rifle, rifle cals. (.22 LR or .32-20) also were available, although not as common. Guns were either case hardened (in Tiger stripe colors), or blued. Case hardened frames have "Handy Gun" stamped on side. Serial numbers on barrel lug and back of frame-numbers should match. .410 ga. in 12¼ in. barrel length is most common. These guns had to be registered during the Amnesty period pre-1968 or became illegal and are now subject to seizure. The legality of the Handy Gun may be obtained by contacting a regional BATF branch.

	100%	98%	95%	90%	80%	70%	60%
Shotgun	$495	$450	$400	$350	$295	$250	$200
Rifle, .32-20 cal.	$1,200	$1,000	$800	$650	$550	$500	$450
Rifle, .22 cal.	$900	$750	$650	$550	$500	$450	$350

Values above refer to the most commonly encountered variation (.410 ga. with 12¼ in. barrel). Premiums are added for rarer variations.

Add $50-75 for original box or $75-175 for original H & R holster.

The serialization range of the H & R Handy Gun is approximatley 1-53,637.

A detachable wire stock was available on the rifles and optional on the shotguns. Most shotgun models were not drilled for a shoulder stock. In 1934, a .410 model with an 18 in. choke barrel was mfg. These are extremely rare with no more than 50 being mfg.

REVOLVERS: RECENT PRODUCTION

MODEL 504 SQUARE BUTT — .32 H&R Mag., 5 shot, 4 or 6 in. bull barrels, adj. rear sight, swing out cylinder, blue, black plastic and walnut grips. Mfg. 1984 and 1985.

	$165	$145	$135	$120	$110	$100	$90

Last Mfg.'s Sug. Retail was $185.

▲ *Model 504 Round Butt* — compact design available with 3 or 4 in. barrel only. Disc. 1985.

	$165	$145	$135	$120	$110	$100	$90

Last Mfg.'s Sug. Retail was $185.

MODEL 532 — .32 H&R Mag., 5 shot, 2½ and 4 in. barrels, solid frame revolver, blue, pull pin cylinder, black plastic and walnut grips. Mfg. 1984 and 1985.

	$100	$90	$80	$70	$60	$50	$45

Last Mfg.'s Sug. Retail was $115.

MODEL 586 — .32 H&R Mag., 5 shot, Western-style revolver, double action, 4½, 5½, 7½, or 10 in. barrels, adj. rear sight, fixed cylinder, antique finish, black plastic or walnut grips. Made 1984 and 1985.

	$175	$155	$135	$120	$110	$100	$90

Last Mfg.'s Sug. Retail was $195.

MODEL 603 — .22 Mag. cal., 6 in. barrel, double action. Disc.

	$159	$120	$110	$95	$90	$80	$70

MODEL 604 — same specifications as the Model 603, only has 6 in. bull barrel.

	$170	$130	$115	$95	$90	$80	$70

MODEL 622 — .22 Short, Long, or LR cal., solid frame, 6 shot, 2½, 4, or 6 in. barrels, blue, plastic grips. Mfg. 1957-1985.

	$95	$82	$70	$60	$55	$50	$45

Last Mfg.'s Sug. Retail was $104.

Grading	100%	98%	95%	90%	80%	70%	60%

MODEL 623 — same basic specifications as the Model 622, only nickel finish. Disc.

| | $115 | $95 | $75 | $60 | $55 | $50 | $45 |

MODEL 632 GUARDSMAN — .32 S&W cal., 6 shot, 2½ or 4 in. barrel, solid frame, checkered tenite grips, blue. Mfg. 1953-1984.

| | $104 | $82 | $70 | $60 | $55 | $50 | $45 |

MODEL 633 — same basic specifications as the Model 632, only nickel finish. Disc.

| | $115 | $95 | $75 | $60 | $55 | $50 | $45 |

MODEL 642 — .22 Mag cal., 2½ or 4 in. barrel. Disc.

| | $95 | $70 | $65 | $60 | $50 | $45 | $40 |

MODEL 649 CONVERTIBLE — .22 LR or .22 Mag. cal., furnished with extra cylinder, Western style, double action, side loading, 5½ or 7½ in. barrel, 6 shot, walnut grips, blued finish. Mfg. 1976-1985.

| | $140 | $120 | $110 | $95 | $90 | $80 | $70 |

Last Mfg.'s Sug. Retail was $160.

MODEL 650 CONVERTIBLE — similar to Model 649, except with nickel finish and only available with 5½ in. barrel. Disc. 1985.

| | $150 | $130 | $115 | $100 | $90 | $80 | $70 |

Last Mfg.'s Sug. Retail was $175.

MODEL 666 — .22 LR or .22 Win. Mag. cal., 6 shot, 6 in. barrel, blue, plastic grips, convertible. Mfg. 1976-1982.

| | $100 | $90 | $70 | $50 | $45 | $35 | $30 |

MODEL 676 — .22 LR or .22 Win. Mag. cal., 6 shot, 4½, 5½, 7½, or 12 in. barrel, side load and eject, convertible (includes .22 LR/.22 Mag. cylinders), blue, case hardened frame, one piece walnut stock. Mfg. 1976-1982.

| | $140 | $120 | $100 | $85 | $60 | $45 | $35 |

MODEL 686 CONVERTIBLE — .22 LR or .22 Mag. cal., furnished with extra cylinder, Western style, double action, side loading, 5½, 7½, 10 or 12 in. barrel, 6 shot, walnut grips, color case hardened frame, adj. rear sight, 12 in. barrel. Disc. 1984.

| | $185 | $160 | $140 | $125 | $110 | $90 | $80 |

MODEL 732 — .32 S&W or .32 H&R Mag. cal., 6 shot, 2½ and 4 in. barrels, fixed sights, swing out cylinder, blue, black plastic grips. Add $15 for .32 H&R Mag. cal. Mfg. 1958-disc.

| | $127 | $100 | $85 | $75 | $65 | $55 | $45 |

MODEL 733 — same specifications as the Model 732, only nickel finish and available only with 2½ in. barrel. Add $15 for .32 H&R Mag. cal.

| | $140 | $125 | $110 | $85 | $75 | $60 | $50 |

MODEL 900 — .22 S, L, or LR cal., 9 shot, 2½, 4, or 6 in. barrels, snap out cylinder, blue, black plastic grips. Mfg. 1962-1973.

| | $90 | $85 | $70 | $55 | $50 | $40 | $30 |

MODEL 901 — similar to 900, but chrome with white tenite grips. Mfg. 1962-1963.

| | $110 | $100 | $90 | $70 | $50 | $40 | $30 |

MODEL 904 — .22 cal., double action, 4 or 6 in. bull barrel, target grade, 9 shot. Disc. 1985.

| | $150 | $135 | $120 | $105 | $95 | $85 | $70 |

Last Mfg.'s Sug. Retail was $168.

MODEL 905 — similar to Model 904, except with nickel finish and 4 in. barrel only. Disc. 1985.

| | $160 | $140 | $125 | $105 | $95 | $80 | $70 |

Last Mfg.'s Sug. Retail was $185.

Grading	100%	98%	95%	90%	80%	70%	60%

MODEL 922 — Second Issue, .22 LR cal., 9 shot, 2½, 4, or 6 in. barrels, solid frame, blue, plastic grips. Mfg. 1950-1982.

	$85	$70	$60	$45	$40	$30	$25

MODEL 923 — similar to 922, only nickel.

	$90	$75	$65	$50	$45	$35	$30

MODEL 925 DEFENDER — .38 S&W cal., 5 shot, 2½ in. barrel, blue, break open, adj. sight, wraparound one piece grip. Mfg. 1964-1984.

	$130	$120	$100	$85	$70	$60	$50

▲ *Model 935* — similar to Model 925, except with nickel finish.

	$145	$135	$115	$100	$70	$60	$50

MODEL 926 — .22 LR cal., 9 shot, or .38 S&W, 5 shot, 4 in. barrel, blue, adj. rear sight, break open, walnut grips. Mfg. 1968-1982.

	$130	$120	$100	$85	$70	$60	$50

▲ *Model 926 Abilene Kansas Centennial* — .22 LR cal., barrel is marked "Abilene Kansas" and "1869 Centennial 1969", mfg. 1969 only.

	$175	$155	$125	$105	$90	$80	$70

MODEL 929 SIDEKICK — .22 LR cal., 9 shot, 2½, 4, or 6 in. barrels, swing out cylinder, plastic grips, blue. Mfg. 1956-1985.

	$115	$100	$70	$55	$45	$35	$30

Last Mfg.'s Sug. Retail was $127.

MODEL 930 SIDEKICK — similar to 929 Sidekick, only nickel finish and not available with 6 in. barrel. Disc. 1985.

	$125	$110	$80	$65	$55	$45	$40

Last Mfg.'s Sug. Retail was $140.

MODEL 939 ULTRA SIDEKICK — .22 S, L, or LR, 9 shot, 6 in. barrel, swing out cylinder, vent rib, adj. sights, blue. Mfg. 1958-1982.

	$110	$100	$85	$70	$55	$45	$30

MODEL 940 ULTRA SIDEKICK — similar to 939, only round barrel. Disc.

	$105	$95	$75	$65	$50	$40	$30

MODEL 949 "FORTY NINER" — .22 S, L, or LR, 5½ in. barrel, double action, solid frame, 9 shot, side load and Western style ejection, adj. rear sight, walnut grips. Mfg. 1960-1985.

	$115	$100	$85	$70	$55	$50	$45

Last Mfg.'s Sug. Retail was $127.

MODEL 950 — similar to Model 949, except with nickel finish. Disc. 1985.

	$125	$105	$90	$70	$55	$50	$45

Last Mfg.'s Sug. Retail was $145.

MODEL 976 — similar to 949, only color case hardened frame. Disc.

	$100	$90	$85	$70	$60	$50	$35

MODEL 999 SPORTSMAN — Second Issue, .22 LR cal., 9 shot, 4 or 6 in. vent. rib barrel, top-break action, adj. sights, walnut grips. Mfg. 1950-1985.

	$195	$170	$155	$140	$125	$110	$95

This model was also made in a Sportsman Centennial Commemorative. Add 15%-25% if NIB.

MODEL 999 ENGRAVED — similar to 999, only engraved throughout, 6 in. barrel only. Disc. 1985.

	$425	$375	$300	$260	$225	$190	$175

Last Mfg.'s Sug. Retail was $525.

H

Grading	100%	98%	95%	90%	80%	70%	60%

RIFLES

REISING MODEL 60 — semi-auto, .45 ACP cal., 12 or 20 shot, 18¼ in. barrel, detachable mag. Mfg. 1944-1946.

	$360	$340	$310	$275	$220	$200	$175

MODEL 65 MILITARY — .22 LR cal., 10 shot mag., 23 in. barrel, Redfield aperture rear sight. Mfg. 1944-1946 for USMC.

	$250	$230	$200	$165	$145	$130	$110

MODEL 150 — semi-auto, .22 LR cal., 5 shot. Mfg. 1949-1953.

	$95	$85	$70	$55	$40	$35	$30

MODEL 155 — single shot, .44 Mag. or .45-70 cal., break open. Mfg. 1972-disc.

	$150	$130	$115	$95	$75	$55	$45

MODEL 157 — single shot, .22 Mag., .22 Hornet, or .30-30 cal., break open. Mfg. 1976-disc.

	$135	$110	$100	$80	$65	$45	$35

MODEL 158 — .22 Jet, .22 Hornet, .30-30, .357 Mag or .44 Mag. cal., single shot break open, 22 in. barrel, side or top lever action release, ejector, case hardened frame. Disc. 1985.

	$120	$105	$90	$80	$60	$50	$40

Last Mfg.'s Sug. Retail was $115.

▲ *Model 158 Combination* — supplied with rifle barrel and 20 ga., 26 in. barrel. Disc. 1985.

	$195	$175	$150	$135	$115	$100	$90

Last Mfg.'s Sug. Retail was $145.

MODEL 165 — .22 LR, 10 shot. Mfg. 1945-1961.

	$120	$110	$95	$85	$70	$55	$50

MODEL 171 — .45-70 Model 1873 Trapdoor copy, 22 in. barrel, Model 174 is the deluxe model. Disc.

	$350	$300	$270	$250	$230	$210	$195

MODEL 171-DL — single shot, .45-70 govt. cal., Springfield copy, 22 in. barrel. Mfg. 1984 and 1985.

	$400	$350	$295	$250	$225	$200	$185

Last Mfg.'s Sug. Retail was $385.

MODEL 174

	$400	$375	$325	$300	$250	$210	$195

MODEL 300 ULTRA — bolt action, .22-250, .243 Win., .270 Win., .30-06, .308 Win., 7mm Mag., or .300 Win. Mag. cal., 22 or 24 in. barrel. Mfg. 1965-1978.

	$440	$415	$360	$305	$250	$210	$195

MODEL 301 CARBINE — similar to 300, but 18 in. barrel, full length Mannlicher stock, N/A .22-250.

	$440	$415	$360	$305	$250	$220	$195

MODEL 317 ULTRA WILDCAT — short action Sako, .17 Rem., .17-223, .222 Rem., or .223 Rem. cal., 20 in. barrel, no sights. Mfg. 1968-1976.

	$485	$440	$415	$360	$305	$275	$220

MODEL 317P PRESENTATION — similar to 317, but deluxe wood basketweave checkering. Mfg. 1968-1976.

	$625	$550	$495	$440	$400	$360	$305

MODEL 333 — similar to 300, in 7mm Mag. cal., plainer version. Mfg. 1974 only.

	$250	$230	$215	$180	$160	$140	$120

MODEL 340 — .243 Win., .270 Win., .30-06, .308 Win., 7mm Mauser cal., bolt action, 5 shot, 22 in. barrel, checkered walnut. Mfg. 1982-1984.

	$395	$300	$275	$240	$220	$200	$180

Grading	100%	98%	95%	90%	80%	70%	60%

MODEL 360 ULTRA AUTOMATIC — .243 Win. or .308 Win. cal., 3 shot, 22 in. barrel. Mfg. 1965-1978.

	$350	$330	$315	$275	$240	$220	$200

MODEL 370 ULTRA MEDALIST TARGET — Varmint Rifle, .22-250, .243 Win., or 6mm Rem. cal., 24 in. varmint weight barrel, semi-beavertail forearm. Mfg. 1968-1973.

	$440	$415	$360	$305	$275	$220	$195

MODEL 422 — slide action, .22 S, L, or LR cal. Mfg. 1956-1958.

	$110	$100	$85	$65	$45	$40	$30

Model 450 — similar to Model 451 Medalist, only no sights.

	$150	$140	$120	$110	$95	$70	$55

MODEL 451 MEDALIST — bolt action, .22 LR cal., 5 shot, 26 in. barrel. Mfg. 1948-1961.

	$165	$150	$140	$110	$100	$85	$55

MODEL 700 — .22 Win. Mag. cal., semi-auto, 5 shot, clip mag., 22 in. barrel. Mfg. 1977-1985.

	$200	$175	$150	$130	$110	$90	$75

Last Mfg.'s Sug. Retail was $210.

MODEL 700DL — similar to Model 700, except deluxe checkered walnut. 4-power scope is standard, recoil pad. Disc. 1985.

	$315	$270	$230	$195	$175	$150	$135

Last Mfg.'s Sug. Retail was $360.

MODEL 750 — .22 cal. single shot bolt action, 22 in. barrel, open sights, youth stock dimensions. Disc. 1985.

	$85	$75	$60	$50	$45	$40	$35

Last Mfg.'s Sug. Retail was $95.

MODEL 865 — .22 cal. bolt action, 5 shot mag., 22 in. barrel. Disc. 1985.

	$90	$80	$65	$55	$50	$45	$40

Last Mfg.'s Sug. Retail was $105.

MODEL 5200 TARGET — .22 cal. target rifle, heavy 28 in. barrel, adj. trigger, no sights, single shot. 11 lbs. Disc. 1985.

	$475	$450	$400	$350	$300	$275	$250

Last Mfg.'s Sug. Retail was $450.

MODEL 5200 SPORTER — .22 cal., bolt action, 5 shot, 24 in. barrel, adj. sights, checkered walnut. Disc. 1983.

	$525	$495	$450	$400	$350	$325	$295

SHOTGUNS

HARRICH NO. 1 — single barrel Trap Gun, 12 ga., 32 or 34 in. full choke, high quality, engraved, vent. rib. Mfg. by Ferlach of Austria from 1971-1975.

	$1,650	$1,595	$1,485	$1,320	$1,100	$880	$770

MODEL 3 HAMMERLESS — similar to Model 8, but no visible external hammer. Mfg. 1908-1942.

	$85	$75	$70	$55	$45	$40	$30

MODEL 5 LIGHTWEIGHT — 24, 28, or .410 ga. only. Mfg. 1908-1942.

	$95	$90	$75	$65	$55	$40	$35

MODEL 6 HEAVY BREECH — similar to Model 8, only 10 ga. - 20 ga., heavier barrels. Mfg. 1908-1942.

	$95	$85	$75	$60	$50	$45	$35

MODEL 7 OR 9 BAY STATE — similar to Model 8, only 12, 16, 20 or .410 ga., rounded pistol grip. Mfg. 1908-1942.

	$85	$75	$70	$55	$45	$40	$30

Grading	100%	98%	95%	90%	80%	70%	60%

MODEL 8 STANDARD — single shot, 12, 16, 20, 24, 28, or .410 ga., 26-32 in. barrels, plain pistol grip stock, auto ejector, break open. Mfg. 1908-1942.

	$150	$125	$95	$75	$65	$60	$55

Add 100% for 28 or .410 ga.

FOLDING GUN — 12, 16, 20, 28, or .410 ga., hinged frame, barrel folds against stock. Mfg. 1908-1942.

	$165	$150	$135	$100	$85	$60	$50

Add 75% for 28 or .410 ga.

TOPPER — 12, 16, 20, or .410 ga., single shot, top or side lever break open action, 10 different variations of this shotgun, all are very similar and values run too close to differentiate, with ejector. Mfg. 1946-disc.

	$145	$125	$100	$85	$70	$55	$45

Add 15% for Topper Deluxe (Model 488, chrome finish).
This model was also designated the Model 48, Model 158 (not in 28 ga.), Model 162 Buck gun with open sights, and Model 198 (28 or .410 ga. only).

MODEL 088 — 12, 16, 20, 28, or .410 ga., single shot, hammer model, ejector, top or side lever break open action, blue barrel finish with case hardened frame, Disc. 1985.

	$85	$75	$55	$50	$45	$40	$35

Last Mfg.'s Sug. Retail was $95.

MODEL 099 — 12, 16, 20, or .410 ga., similar to Model 088, only electroless nickel finish, ejector, top or side lever break open action. Disc. 1984.

	$95	$80	$60	$55	$50	$45	$40

MODEL 162 — 12 or 20 ga., single shot, 24 in. slug barrel with rifle sights, case hardened frame, top or side lever break open action. Disc. 1984.

	$115	$105	$90	$80	$65	$55	$45

MODEL 176 — 10 (3½ in.), 12, or 20 ga., Mag., single shot, 32-36 in. heavy barrel, top or side lever break open action. Mfg. 1977-1985.

	$110	$95	$80	$70	$60	$50	$45

Last Mfg.'s Sug. Retail was $125.

MODELS 348/349 BOLT ACTION — 12 or 16 ga., 3 shot tube mag., 28 in. barrel (Model 349 has adj. vari-choke), walnut stock, 7½ lbs. Disc.

	$115	$90	$75	$60	$50	$45	$40

MODEL 400 PUMP ACTION — 12, 16, or 20 ga., 28 in. full choke. Mfg. 1955-1967.

	$155	$145	$125	$110	$90	$75	$55

MODEL 401 PUMP — similar to 400, but H&R variable choke. Mfg. 1956-1963.

	$165	$155	$140	$120	$100	$90	$65

MODEL 402 PUMP — similar to 400, only .410 ga., lightweight. Mfg. 1959-1967.

	$175	$165	$150	$140	$110	$100	$85

MODEL 403 AUTOLOADER — .410 ga., 26 in. full choke, takedown. Mfg. 1964 only.

	$195	$180	$165	$155	$120	$100	$85

MODEL 404 — double barrel, SxS, 12, 20, or .410 ga., 26 or 28 in. barrel, boxlock, extractors, double triggers. Mfg. by Rossi of Brazil 1969-1972.

	$185	$175	$165	$145	$110	$90	$70

MODEL 404C — similar to 404, only checkered stock.

	$200	$185	$175	$155	$120	$100	$85

MODEL 440 — pump action, 12, 16, or 20 ga., 26, 28, or 30 in. barrels, available in various chokes, plain pistol grip and slide. Mfg. 1968-1973.

	$145	$130	$110	$100	$85	$70	$55

H

Grading	100%	98%	95%	90%	80%	70%	60%

MODEL 442 — pump action, similar to 440, only vent. rib, checkered stock. Mfg. 1969-1973.

	$175	$165	$155	$140	$100	$85	$65

MODEL 490 — 20 or .410 ga., made for junior shooters, Greenwing finish — add $10. Disc. 1984.

	$85	$65	$60	$50	$45	$40	$40

MODEL 1212 — O/U, Field, 12 ga., 2¾ in., 28 in. vent. rib barrels, various chokes, checkered walnut stocks. Mfg. by Lanber Arms, Spain, from 1976-disc.

	$310	$295	$275	$250	$200	$175	$155

MODEL 1212 WATERFOWL — similar to Model 1212, except 3 in. 12 ga., 30 in. barrel.

	$320	$310	$285	$260	$210	$185	$165

SINGLE SHOT COMBINATION GUNS

MODEL 058 — 20 ga./.30-30, .22 Rem. Jet, .22 Hornet, .44 Mag., .357 Mag. combination — 2 separate barrels supplied, blue only. Disc. 1985.

	$155	$130	$110	$95	$85	$75	$65

Last Mfg.'s Sug. Retail was $145.

MODEL 258 COMBINATION HANDY GUN II — supplied with 20 ga., 22 in. barrel and 22 in. rifle barrel in .22 Hornet, .30-30 Win., or .357 Mag. cal., electroless, matte nickel finish, side lever action release, cased, 6½ lbs. Disc. 1985.

	$175	$155	$140	$130	$120	$100	$95

Last Mfg.'s Sug. Retail was $195.

COMMEMORATIVES & REPLICAS

ABILENE ANNIVERSARY .22 REVOLVER — 300 mfg. 1967.

	$150	$115	$75

Last Mfg.'s Sug. Retail $83.50 (1967).

H&R 100TH ANNIVERSARY OFFICER'S MODEL — 1871-1971, Commemorative Officer's Model, Springfield 1873 Replica, Trapdoor, .45-70 cal., engraved metal work, 26 in. barrel, anniversary plaque on stock, 10,000 mfg. in 1971.

	$475	$425	$350

Last Mfg.'s Sug. Retail was $250 (1971).

MODEL 171 AND 171 DELUXE — listed in previous rifle section.

MODEL 173 RIFLE — .45-70, similar to Officer's Model, no plaque on stock. Mfg. 1972-1983.

	$495	$425	$325

MODEL 174 CARBINE (LITTLE BIG HORN) — .45-70, Little Big Horn Commercial Carbine. Quantity unknown.

	$395	$325	$250

Last Mfg.'s Sug. Retail was $220 (1972).

MODEL 178 — .45-70, Infantry Musket Replica, 32 in. barrel. Mfg. 1973-1984.

	$375	$325	$250

1873 SPRINGFIELD TRAPDOOR — .45-70 cal., unknown quantities mfg. 1973.

	$450	$350	$275

Last Mfg.'s Sug. Retail was $250.

CUSTER MEMORIAL ISSUE — .45-70 cal., limited production, deluxe walnut stock, highly engraved, gold inlaid, mahogany display case and two volumes on Custer history. Each weapon bears the name of one who fell at Little Big Horn.

▲ *Officer's Model* — 25 mfg., must be new with original box/accessories.

	$3,995	$3,150	$2,400

Last Mfg.'s Sug. Retail was $3,000 (1973).

Grading	100%	98%	95%	90%	80%	70%	60%

▲ *Enlisted Men's Model* — 243 mfg., must be new with original box/accessories.

	$1,995	**$1,400**	**$900**				

Last Mfg.'s Sug. Retail was $2,000 (1973).

HARRIS GUNWORKS

Current manufacturer located in Phoenix, AZ since 1995. Previously named Harris-McMillan Gunworks and G. McMillan and Co., Inc. (please refer to the M section for more information on these two Trademarks).

RIFLES: BOLT ACTION

BENCHREST COMPETITOR — .222 Rem., 6mm PPC, 6mm BR, or .308 Win. cal., benchrest configuration. New 1993.

Mfg.'s Sug. Retail	$2,600	$2,375	$1,925	$1,675	$1,425	$1,200	$1,025	$875

NATIONAL MATCH COMPETITOR — .308 Win. cal. New 1993.

Mfg.'s Sug. Retail	$2,600	$2,375	$1,925	$1,675	$1,425	$1,200	$1,025	$875

LONG RANGE TARGET MODEL — .300 Win. Mag. cal., black synthetic fully adj. stock, w/o sights, gray barrel finish. New 1996.

Mfg.'s Sug. Retail	$2,600	$2,375	$1,925	$1,675	$1,425	$1,200	$1,025	$875

TALON SPORTER — available in various cals. between .22-250 and .416 Rem., receiver available in either 4340 chrome molybdenum or 17-4 stainless steel, drilled and tapped, match grade barrel. New 1992.

Mfg.'s Sug. Retail	$2,600	$2,375	$1,950	$1,650	$1,325	$1,000	$895	$800

> The Talon action is patterned after the Winchester pre-64 Model 70. It features a cone breech, controlled feed, claw extractor, and 3 position safety.

SIGNATURE CLASSIC SPORTER — various cals. available between .22-250 and .416 Rem., premium wood stock, matte metal finish, buttoning used on rifling for 22 or 24 in. stainless steel barrel, McMillan action made from 4340 chrome moly steel (either left or right-handed), 3 or 4 shot mag. supplied with 5 shot test target. New 1988.

Mfg.'s Sug. Retail	$2,600	$2,375	$1,950	$1,650	$1,325	$1,000	$895	$800

SIGNATURE VARMINTER — similar to Signature Model, except is available in 10 cals. between .22-250 and .350 Rem. Mag., hand bedded fiberglass stock, adj. trigger, 26 in. heavily contoured barrel. New 1988.

Mfg.'s Sug. Retail	$2,600	$2,375	$1,950	$1,650	$1,325	$1,000	$895	$800

SIGNATURE TITANIUM MOUNTAIN RIFLE — .270 Win., .280 Rem., .30-06, .300 Win. Mag., .338 Win. Mag., or 7mm Rem. Mag. cal., lighter weight variation with shorter barrel. New 1990.

Mfg.'s Sug. Retail	$2,600	$2,375	$1,950	$1,650	$1,325	$1,000	$895	$800

> Add $600 for titanium alloy receiver.

SIGNATURE ALASKAN — available in 11 cals. between .270 Win. and .416 Rem. New 1990.

Mfg.'s Sug. Retail	$3,300	$3,050	$2,475	$2,100	$1,575	$1,200	$1,000	$900

TALON SAFARI — available in 15 cals. between .300 Win. Mag. and .460 Weatherby, hand bedded fiberglass stock, 4 shot mag., 24 in. stainless steel barrel, matte black finish, 9 ½ lbs. New 1988.

Mfg.'s Sug. Retail	$3,500	$3,225	$2,650	$2,300	$1,675	$1,300	$1,100	$950

> Add $300 for .300 Phoenix, .30/416 Imp., .30/378 Wby., .338 Lapua, .378 Wby., .416 Wby. or Rigby, or .460 Wby. cal.

> The Talon action is patterned after the Winchester pre-64 Model 70. It features a cone breech, controlled feed, claw extractor, and 3 position safety. Older Signature action rifles do not have this new Talon action.

Grading	100%	98%	95%	90%	80%	70%	60%

M-40 SNIPER RIFLE — .308 Win., Remington action with McMillan match grade heavy contour barrel, fiberglass stock with recoil pad, 4 shot mag., 9 lbs. New 1990.
Mfg.'s Sug. Retail $2,000 $1,825 $1,450 $1,125 $925 $800 $700 $600

M-86 SNIPER RIFLE — .300 Phoenix, .30-06 (new 1989), .300 Win. Mag. or .308 cal., fiberglass stock, variety of optical sights. New 1988.
Mfg.'s Sug. Retail $2,000 $1,825 $1,450 $1,125 $925 $800 $700 $600
    Add $300 for .300 Phoenix cal. with Harris action.
    Add $200 for takedown feature (new 1993).

M-87 LONG RANGE SNIPER RIFLE — .50 BMG, stainless steel bolt action, 29 in. barrel with muzzle brake, single shot, camo synthetic stock, accurate to 1500 meters, 21 lbs. New 1988.
Mfg.'s Sug. Retail $3,735 $3,350 $2,750 $2,350 $2,000 $1,850 $1,700 $1,575

 ▲ *M-87R* — same specs. as Model 87, except has 5 shot fixed box mag. New 1990.
Mfg.'s Sug. Retail $4,000 $3,750 $2,950 $2,550 $2,200 $2,000 $1,850 $1,700

M-89 SNIPER RIFLE — .308 Win., 28 in. barrel with suppressor (also available without), fiberglass stock adj. for length and recoil pad, 15¼ lbs. New 1990.
Mfg.'s Sug. Retail $2,700 $2,375 $1,895 $1,475 $1,100 $950 $800 $700
    Add $425 for muzzle suppressor.

M-92 BULL PUP — .50 BMG cal., bullpup configuration with shorter barrel. New 1993.
Mfg.'s Sug. Retail $4,000 $3,750 $2,950 $2,550 $2,200 $2,000 $1,850 $1,700

M-93SN — .50 BMG cal., similar to M-87, except has folding stock and detachable 5 or 10 shot box mag. New 1993.
Mfg.'s Sug. Retail $4,150 $3,800 $3,250 $2,750 $2,300 $2,000 $1,850 $1,700

HARTFORD ARMS & EQUIPMENT COMPANY
Hartford Arms was the forerunner of High Standard Arms Co., who acquired them in 1932.

HARTFORD AUTOMATIC TARGET — .22 LR, 10 shot, 6¾ in. barrel, blue, black rubber grips. Mfg. 1929-1930.
     $650 $575 $500 $450 $375 $300 $275

HARTFORD REPEATING PISTOL — .22 cal., similar in appearance to Automatic, except a hand operated repeater. Mfg. 1929-1930.
     $495 $425 $360 $310 $260 $250 $225

HARTFORD SINGLE SHOT TARGET — similar in appearance to Automatic, .22 LR cal., 6¾ in. barrel, target sights, case colored frame and slide, blue barrel, rubber or wood grips. Mfg. 1929-1930.
     $475 $390 $350 $310 $260 $250 $225

HASKELL MANUFACTURING
Manufacturer located in Lima, OH. Distributed by MKS Supply located in Mansfield, OH. Distributor sales only.
Refer to listing under Hi-Point Firearms.

HATFIELD GUN CO., INC.
Manufacture by Hatfield Gun Co., Inc. (designated Hatfield Rifle Works until 1986) located in St. Joseph, MO.
    Hatfield also manufactures flintlock and percussion black powder rifles which can be located in the Modern Black Powder Guns section of this text.

H

Grading	100%	98%	95%	90%	80%	70%	60%

SHOTGUNS: SxS

In addition to Grades I and II listed below, Hatfield also offers custom order shotguns built per individual special order - prices start at $3,000.

GRADE I UPLANDER — 20 or 28 ga., 3 in. chambers, 26 in. IC/M, matted rib barrels, case hardened boxlock action, single trigger, ejectors, deluxe checkered straight grip maple stock and forearm, 5¾ lbs, cased. New 1987.

Mfg.'s Sug. Retail	$2,249	$1,975	$1,700	$1,500	$1,325	$1,150	$900	$725

Add $800 for extra 28 ga. barrels.

▲ *Collector's Grade I* — mfg. 1990-92.

	$1,475	$1,200	$1,000	$875	$700	$550	$475

Last Mfg.'s Sug. Retail was $1,625.

Add $400 for extra 28 ga. barrels.

GRADE II PIGEON — similar to Grade I, except has scroll engraving on top lever, sides, floor plate, and triggerguard, cased. New 1987.

Mfg.'s Sug. Retail	$2,995	$2,650	$2,250	$1,825	$1,475	$1,100	$900	$775

Add $995 for extra 28 ga. barrels.

▲ *Collector's Grade II* — mfg. 1990-92.

	$2,675	$2,000	$1,600	$1,250	$1,050	$875	$775

Last Mfg.'s Sug. Retail was $3,025.

Add $400 for extra 28 ga. barrels.

GRADE III SUPER PIGEON — includes heavy relief scroll engraving (total coverage) on frame, top lever, floor plate, and triggerguard, leather cased. Mfg. 1987-disc.

	$2,350	$1,900	$1,495	$1,200	$1,025	$900	$775

Last Mfg.'s Sug. Retail was $3,500.

Add $900 for extra 28 ga. barrels.

▲ *Collector's Grade III* — mfg. 1990-disc.

	$3,000	$2,500	$2,000	$1,750	$1,400	$1,175	$995

Last Mfg.'s Sug. Retail was $4,375.

Add $900 for extra 28 ga. barrels.

GRADE IV GOLDEN QUAIL — more extensive engraving including six 24 Kt. gold inlays on frame and floor plate, 2 gold barrel bands, leather cased. Mfg. 1987-disc.

	$3,995	$3,575	$2,900	$2,350	$1,900	$1,600	$1,300

Last Mfg.'s Sug. Retail was $5,500.

Add $900 for extra 28 ga. barrels.

▲ *Collector's Grade IV* — mfg. 1990-disc.

	$4,475	$3,900	$3,300	$2,650	$2,175	$1,800	$1,500

Last Mfg.'s Sug. Retail was $6,625.

Add $1,350 for extra 28 ga. barrels.

GRADE V WOODCOCK — previous top-of-the-line model with best quality engraving and multiple gold inlays, leather cased. Mfg. 1987-disc.

	$4,600	$4,400	$3,350	$2,700	$2,175	$1,800	$1,500

Last Mfg.'s Sug. Retail was $6,900.

Add $1,500 for extra 28 ga. barrels.

▲ *Collector's Grade V* — mfg. 1990-disc.

	$6,200	$5,700	$4,475	$3,900	$3,300	$2,650	$2,200

Last Mfg.'s Sug. Retail was $8,500.

Add $2,000 for extra 28 ga. barrels.

GRADE VI BLACK WIDOW — mfg. 1990-disc.

	$5,200	$4,875	$3,700	$3,000	$2,500	$2,100	$1,800

Last Mfg.'s Sug. Retail was $7,900.

Grading	100%	98%	95%	90%	80%	70%	60%

GRADE VII ROYALE — mfg. 1990-disc.

	100%	98%	95%	90%	80%	70%	60%
	$5,200	$4,875	$3,700	$3,000	$2,500	$2,100	$1,800

Last Mfg.'s Sug. Retail was $7,900.

GRADE VIII TOP HAT — top-of-the-line model with best quality wood and extensive engraving with gold inlays. Built to individual customer specifications. Mfg. 1990-disc.

	100%	98%	95%	90%	80%	70%	60%
	$12,000	$9,750	$8,750	$7,500	$6,500	$5,500	$4,500

Last Mfg.'s Sug. Retail was $17,500.

SIDELOCK MODEL — 20 ga. only, satin gray finished receiver, full engraving. New 1995.

Mfg.'s Sug. Retail	$12,000	$10,750	$8,750	$7,500	$6,250	$5,000	$4,850	$3,600

▲ *Grade II Sidelock* — features high relief full coverage engraving, color case hardened receiver, multiple gold and silver inlays.

Mfg.'s Sug. Retail	$17,500	$15,000	$12,000	$10,750	$8,750	$7,000	$5,750	$4,650

SHOTGUNS: O/U

BOXLOCK O/U — 20 ga. only, boxlock action with satin gray finished receiver, maple stock. New 1995.

Mfg.'s Sug. Retail	$3,749	$3,350	$2,950	$2,550	$2,175	$1,725	$1,450	$1,100

Add $1,425 for extra 28 ga. barrels.

HAWES FIREARMS

Previously manufactured by J.P. Sauer & Sohn in Eckernförde, Germany. Previously imported by Hawes Firearms in Van Nuys, CA.

Rather than give an individual listing of the various single action revolvers that have been imported, a generalized price range is as follows: centerfire single actions usually are in the $130 - $250 range while .22 rimfire models are typically valued between $60 - $140.

HECKLER & KOCH

Manufacturer located in Oberndorf/Neckar, Germany. Imported and distributed by Heckler & Koch, Inc. (U.S. headquarters) located in Sterling, VA (previously located in Chantilly, VA). In early 1991, H & K was absorbed by Royal Ordnance, a division of British Aerospace located in England.

PISTOLS: SEMI-AUTO, RECENT MFG.

HK4 — double action auto, .380, .32 auto, .25 auto, and .22 LR, available with all caliber conversion units, 3⅓ in. barrel, blue, plastic grips. In recent years, used HK 4s have been imported into the U.S. at discount prices - thus affecting used HK 4 prices. Disc. 1984.

	100%	98%	95%	90%	80%	70%	60%
.25 or .32 ACP cal.	$295	$260	$230	$215	$180	$150	$130
.22 or .380 cal.	$430	$345	$300	$250	$195	$160	$140

▲ *.380 with .22 conversion*

		98%	95%	90%	80%	70%	60%
	$480	$385	$350	$325	$310	$290	$280

▲ *.380 with all conversions*

		98%	95%	90%	80%	70%	60%
	$590	$475	$450	$420	$390	$375	$360

This model was also mfg. in a French model in .22 LR and/or .32 ACP (about 500 imported).

P9S — .45 ACP or 9mm Para., double action combat model, 4 in. barrel, phosphated finish, sculptured plastic grips, fixed sights. Although production ceased in 1984, limited quantities were available until 1989.

		98%	95%	90%	80%	70%	60%
	$650	$525	$400	$360	$320	$290	$265

Last Mfg.'s Sug. Retail was $1,299.

Grading	100%	98%	95%	90%	80%	70%	60%

P9S TARGET — .45 ACP or 9mm Para., 4 in. barrel, phosphated finish, adj. sights and trigger. Although production ceased in 1984, limited quantities were available until 1989.

| | $1,100 | $850 | $600 | $540 | $500 | $465 | $430 |

Last Mfg.'s Sug. Retail was $1,382.

P9S COMPETITION KIT — 9mm Para only, similar to P9S Target, except extra $5\frac{1}{2}$ in. barrel and weight, competition walnut grip, 2 slides. Disc. 1984.

| | $1,150 | $950 | $875 | $800 | $720 | $640 | $550 |

Last Mfg.'s Sug. Retail was $2,250.

P7 PSP — 9mm Para., older variation of the P7 M8, without extended triggerguard, ambidextrous mag. release (European style), or heat shield. Standard production ceased 1986. A re-issue of this model was mfg. in 1990 with approx. 150 mfg.

| | | $865 | $650 | $525 | $460 | $410 | $390 | $370 |

Last Mfg.'s Sug. Retail was $1,135.

P7 M8 — 9mm Para., unique squeeze cocking single action, extended square combat type triggerguard with heat shield, 4.13 in. fixed barrel with polygonal rifling, 8 shot mag., ambidextrous mag. release, fixed 3-dot sighting system, stippled black plastic grips, black phosphate or nickel (new 1992) finish, includes 2 mags., 28 oz.

| **Mfg.'s Sug. Retail** | **$1,187** | $900 | $745 | $650 | $550 | $450 | $410 | $390 |

Add $92 for Tritium sights (various colors, new 1993).
Add $566 for .22 LR conversion kit (barrel, slide, and two mags.).

P7 M13 — similar to P7 M8, only with staggered 13 shot mag., 30 oz. Disc. 1994.

| | $975 | $785 | $700 | $630 | $580 | $530 | $480 |

Last Mfg.'s Sug. Retail was $1,330.

Add $85 for Tritium sights (various colors, new 1993).

P7 M10 — .40 S&W cal., similar specifications as P7 M13, except has 10 shot mag., 39 oz. Mfg. 1991-94.

| | $975 | $800 | $725 | $650 | $600 | $550 | $495 |

Last Mfg.'s Sug. Retail was $1,315.

Add $85 for Tritium sights (various colors, new 1993).

P7 K3 — .22 LR or .380 ACP cal., uses unique oil-filled buffer to decrease recoil, 3.8 in. barrel, 8 shot mag. (includes 2), $26\frac{1}{2}$ oz. Mfg. 1988-94.

| | $840 | $715 | $600 | $525 | $450 | $410 | $390 |

Last Mfg.'s Sug. Retail was $1,100.

Add $525 for .22 LR conversion kit.
Add $228 for .32 ACP conversion kit.
Add $85 for Tritium sights (various colors, new 1993).

USP 9 — 9mm Para., semi-auto, available in regular DA/SA mode or DA only (9 variants), 4.13 in. barrel, Browning-type action with H&K recoil reduction system, polymer frame, all metal surfaces specially treated, can be carried cocked and locked, stippled synthetic grips, bobbed hammer, 3-dot sighting system, multiple safeties, 10 (C/B 1994) or 16* shot polymer mag., $26\frac{1}{2}$ oz. New 1993.

| **Mfg.'s Sug. Retail** | **$636** | $565 | $475 | $425 | $385 | $350 | $325 | $295 |

Add $20 for control lever (safety/decocking lever on right side).
Add $88 for Tritium sights (various colors, new 1993).

▲ *USP 9 Stainless* — similar to USP 9, except has satin finished stainless steel slide. New 1996.

| **Mfg.'s Sug. Retail** | **$681** | $595 | $485 | $430 |

Add $20 for control lever (safety/decocking lever on right side).

USP 40 — .40 S&W, similar to USP 9, 9 variants of DA/SA/DAO, 10 (C/B 1994) or 13* shot mag., $27\frac{3}{4}$ oz. New 1993.

| **Mfg.'s Sug. Retail** | **$636** | $565 | $475 | $425 | $385 | $350 | $325 | $295 |

Add $20 for control lever (safety/decocking lever on right side).
Add $88 for Tritium sights (various colors, new 1993).

Grading	100%	98%	95%	90%	80%	70%	60%

▲ **USP 40 Stainless** — similar to USP 40, except has satin finished stainless steel slide. New 1996.
Mfg.'s Sug. Retail   **$681**   **$595**   **$485**   **$430**
    Add $20 for control lever (safety/decocking lever on right side).

USP 45 — .45 ACP cal., similar to USP 9, 9 variants of DA/SA/DAO, 10 (C/B 1994) or 13* shot mag., 27¾ oz. New 1995.
Mfg.'s Sug. Retail   **$696**   **$615**   **$500**   **$440**   **$385**   **$350**   **$325**   **$295**
    Add $20 for control lever (safety/decocking lever on right side).
    Add $88 for Tritium sights (various colors, new 1993).

▲ **USP 45 Stainless** — similar to USP 45, except has satin finished stainless steel slide. New 1996.
Mfg.'s Sug. Retail   **$741**   **$660**   **$535**   **$475**
    Add $20 for control lever (safety/decocking lever on right side).

MARK 23 — .45 ACP cal., 5.87 in. barrel, polymer frame and integral grips, 3-dot sighting, 10 shot mag., squared off triggerguard, 2.6 lbs., limited availability. New 1996.
Mfg.'s Sug. Retail   **$1,995**   **$1,775**   **$1,575**   **$1,325**   **$1,075**   **$900**   **$775**   **$650**

SP 89 — 9mm Para., semi-auto, recoil operated delayed roller-locked bolt system, 4.5 in. barrel, 15 shot mag., rotated aperture adj. rear sight (accepts HK claw-lock scope mounts), 4.4 lbs. Mfg. 1990-1993.

  $2,495   **$2,150**   **$1,800**   **$1,300**   **$1,100**   **$975**   **$875**
                                  Last Mfg.'s Sug. Retail was $1,325.

    Add $129 for adj. target grip.

VP 70Z — 9mm, 18 shot, double action only, 4½ in. barrel, parkerized finish, plastic receiver/grip assembly. Disc. 1984.

  $425   **$375**   **$325**   **$275**   **$250**   **$230**   **$210**

    Add 100% if frame cut for shoulder stock (Model VP 70M).

RIFLES: SEMI-AUTO

The models listed below, being of a paramilitary design, were disc. 1989 due to Federal legislation as a result of the controversy with this type of firearms configuration.

In 1991, the HK-91, HK-93, and HK-94 were discontinued. Last published retail prices (1991) were $999 for fixed stock models and $1,199 for retractable stock models.

In the early '70s, S.A.C.O. importers located in Virginia sold the Models 41 and 43 which were the predecessors to the Model 91 and 93, respectively. Values for these earlier variations will be higher than values listed below.

SR-9 — .308 cal. (7.62mm), semi-auto sporting rifle, 19.7 in. barrel, Kevlar reinforced fiberglass thumbhole stock and forearm, 5 shot mag., diopter adj. rear sight, accepts HK claw-lock scope mounts. Mfg. 1990-1993.

  $1,775   **$1,450**   **$1,150**   **$995**   **$850**   **$725**   **$650**
                                  Last Mfg.'s Sug. Retail was $1,369.

SR-9T — .308 cal., precision target rifle with adj. MSG 90 buttstock and PSG-1 trigger group, 5 shot mag. Mfg. 1992-1993.

  $2,495   **$2,100**   **$1,800**   **$1,550**   **$1,150**   **$995**   **$850**
                                  Last Mfg.'s Sug. Retail was $1,799.

SR-9TC — .308 cal., similar to SR-9T, except has PSG-1 adj. buttstock. Mfg. 1993 only.
  $2,995   **$2,600**   **$2,300**   **$2,000**   **$1,675**   **$1,250**   **$1,050**
                                  Last Mfg.'s Sug. Retail was $1,946.

PSG-1 — .308 cal. only, high precision marksman's rifle, 5 shot mag., adj. buttstock, includes accessories and case (Hensholdt illuminated 6 x 42 power scope), 17.8 lbs.
Mfg.'s Sug. Retail   **$10,497**   **$9,250**   **$8,150**   **$6,975**   **$5,950**   **$5,100**   **$4,500**   **$3,850**

Grading	100%	98%	95%	90%	80%	70%	60%

MODEL 41 — 7.62mm cal., predecessor to the Model 91 A-2, originally imported by Golden State Arms.

	$1,200	$1,050	$950	$850	$750	$650	$550

MODEL 91 A-2 — .308 cal. (7.62mm), semi-auto paramilitary design rifle, delayed roller lock bolt system, antennuated recoil, black cycolac stock, 17.7 in. barrel, 20 shot mag., 9.7 lbs. Importation disc. 1989.

▲ *Fixed stock model*

	$1,695	$1,375	$1,150	$995	$895	$795	$695

Last Mfg.'s Sug. Retail was $999.

Add $200 for desert camo finish.
Add $275 for NATO black finish.

▲ *Model 91 A-3* — with retractable metal stock.

	$2,150	$1,825	$1,500	$1,275	$1,075	$950	$850

Last Mfg.'s Sug. Retail was $1,114.

Add $775 for .22 LR conversion kit.

▲ *Model 91 A-2 Package* — includes A.R.M.S. mount, B-Square rings, Leupold 3x9 compact scope with matte finish. Importation disc. 1988.

	$2,450	$2,150	$1,750	$1,395	$1,175	$995	$875

Last Mfg.'s Sug. Retail was $1,285.

Add $300 for retractable stock.

MODEL 93 A-2 — .223 cal. (5.56mm), smaller version of the H&K 91, 25 shot mag., 16.14 in. barrel, 8 lbs.

▲ *Fixed stock model*

	$1,575	$1,425	$1,200	$1,050	$925	$825	$750

Last Mfg.'s Sug. Retail was $946.

Add $200 for desert camo finish.
Add $275 for NATO black finish.

▲ *Model 93 A-3* — with retractable metal stock.

	$1,850	$1,675	$1,450	$1,250	$1,075	$975	$850

Last Mfg.'s Sug. Retail was $1,114.

▲ *Model 93 A-2 Package* — includes A.R.M.S. mount, B-Square rings, Leupold 3x9 compact scope with matte finish. Importation disc. 1988.

	$2,450	$2,150	$1,700	$1,400	$1,200	$1,050	$950

Last Mfg.'s Sug. Retail was $1,285.

Add $300 for retractable stock.

MODEL 94 CARBINE A-2 — 9mm, semi-auto carbine, 16.54 in. barrel, aperture rear sight, 15 shot mag. New 1983.

▲ *Fixed stock model*

	$2,450	$2,150	$1,700	$1,400	$1,200	$1,050	$950

Last Mfg.'s Sug. Retail was $946.

▲ *Model 94 Carbine A-3* — retractable metal stock.

	$2,750	$2,400	$2,000	$1,700	$1,475	$1,275	$1,000

Last Mfg.'s Sug. Retail was $1,114.

▲ *Model 94 A-2 Package* — includes A.R.M.S. mount, B-Square rings, Leupold 3x9 compact scope with matte finish. Importation disc. 1988.

	$3,000	$2,625	$2,150	$1,900	$1,675	$1,350	$1,100

Last Mfg.'s Sug. Retail was $1,285.

Add $300 for retractable stock.

▲ *Model 94 SGI* — 9mm, semi-auto, target rifle, aluminum alloy bi-pod, Leupold 6X scope, 15 or 30 shot mag. Imported 1986 only.

	$2,595	$2,250	$1,900	$1,675	$1,475	$1,275	$1,000

Last Mfg.'s Sug. Retail was $1,340.

Grading	100%	98%	95%	90%	80%	70%	60%

MODEL 270 — .22 LR cal. semi-auto, sporting rifle, 19.7 in. barrel with standard or polygonal rifling, 5 or 20 shot mag., high luster blue, plain walnut stock, approx. 5.7 lbs. Disc. 1985.

	$475	$400	$350	$300	$275	$250	$225

Last Mfg.'s Sug. Retail was $200.

MODEL 300 — .22 Mag. cal., semi-auto, 5 or 15 shot, polygonal rifling standard, otherwise similar to H&K 270 with checkered walnut stock. Importation disc. 1989.

	$675	$575	$525	$450	$400	$375	$350

Last Mfg.'s Sug. Retail was $608.

Add $175-$225 for factory H&K scope mount system.

▲ *Model 300 Package* — includes A.R.M.S. mount, B-Square rings, Leupold 3x9 compact scope with matte finish. Importation disc. 1988.

	$895	$785	$700	$650	$600	$550	$500

Last Mfg.'s Sug. Retail was $689.

MODEL 630 — .223 cal., semi-auto, delayed roller lock bolt system, 17.7 in. barrel, reduced recoil, checkered walnut, 4 or 10 shot mag., 7.04 lbs. Importation disc. 1986.

	$795	$725	$650	$550	$495	$460	$430

Last Mfg.'s Sug. Retail was $784.

Add $175-$225 for factory H&K scope mount system.

The .222 Rem. cal. was also available in this model. Most were French contracts.

MODEL 770 — .308 cal., 3 or 10 shot mag., 19.7 in. barrel, 7.92 lbs., otherwise similar to model 630. Importation disc. 1986.

	$775	$695	$625	$530	$485	$450	$420

Last Mfg.'s Sug. Retail was $797.

Add $175-$225 for factory H&K scope mount system.

Significant price increases stopped the importation of this model.

Approx. 6 Model 770s were imported in .243 Win. cal. during 1984. Values for the .243 cal. will be considerably higher than listed above for the .308 cal.

MODEL 940 — .30-06 cal., 21.6 in. barrel, 8.62 lbs., otherwise same as Model 770. Importation disc. 1986.

	$895	$825	$725	$625	$565	$500	$465

Last Mfg.'s Sug. Retail was $917.

Add $175-$225 for factory H&K scope mount system.

Cals. 7x64mm and 9.3x62mm were also available in this model.

Significant price increases stopped the importation of this model.

▲ *Model 940K* – similar to Model 940, except has 16 in. barrel and higher cheekpiece. Two imported 1984 only.

Rarity precludes accurate price evaluation.

MODELS SL6 & SL7 CARBINE — .223 or .308 cal., 17.71 in. barrel, semi-auto, delayed roller lock bolt system, reduced recoil, vent. wooden hand guard, 3 or 4 shot mag., 8.36 lbs., matte black metal finish, HK-SL6 is .223 cal., HK-SL7 is .308 cal. Disc. in 1986.

	$725	$650	$550	$495	$460	$430	$400

Add $175-$225 for factory H&K scope mount system.

RIFLES: BOLT ACTION

BASR — .22, .22-250, 6mm PPC, .300 Win. Mag., .30-06, or .308 cal., Kevlar stock, stainless steel barrel, limited production. Special order only. Mfg. 1986 only.

	$5,750	$5,000	$4,500	$4,000	$3,650	$3,300	$2,600

Last Mfg.'s Sug. Retail was $2,199.

Less than 135 of this variation were manufactured and they are extremely rare. Contractual disputes with the U.S. supplier stopped H&K from receiving any BASR models.

SHOTGUNS

H & K imported Benelli shotguns can be found under their own heading.

Grading	100%	98%	95%	90%	80%	70%	60%

MODEL 512 SEMI-AUTO — 12 ga. only, mfg. by Franchi for German military contract, rifle sights, matte finished metal, walnut stock, fixed choke pattern diverter giving rectangular shot pattern. Importation disc. 1991.

	$1,500	$1,300	$1,100	$925	$800	$700	$600

Last Mfg.'s Wholesale was $1,895.

HELWAN

Previously imported by Navy Arms Co. and Interarms until 1995.

BRIGADIER — 9mm Para., single action, 4.5 in. barrel, all steel construction, 8 shot mag. with finger extension, black plastic grips, 32.6 oz. Imported 1988-94.

	$195	$150	$125	$115	$105	$95	$85

Last Mfg.'s Sug. Retail was $260.

This model is patterned after the Beretta Model 1952. They were manufactured at the Helwan arsenal in Egypt.

HENDRY, RAMSAY & WILCOX

Manufacturer located in Perth, Scotland.

Hendry, Ramsay & Wilcox manufacture top quality shotguns and rifles and are priced per individual quotation. Please contact the factory directly (see Trademark Index) for more information on this trademark.

HENRY RIFLE

Please refer to the Winchester section in this text.

HERITAGE MANUFACTURING, INC.

Manufacturer located in Opa Locka, FL since 1993. Dealer and distributor sales.

REVOLVERS

ROUGH RIDER SAA SERIES — .22 LR or .22 LR/.22 Mag. combo, SAA design with hammer block safety, blue or nickel (available in combo package only) finish, 2 ¾ (birdshead grips only), 3 (disc. 1994, included birdshead grips), 3¾ (new 1995, birdshead grips only), 4¾, 6½, or 9 in. barrel, choice of traditional or birdshead (3¾ or 4¾ in. only) smooth wood grips. New 1993.

Mfg.'s Sug. Retail	**$110**	$95	$70	$60	$50	$45	$40	$35

Add $20 for combo package.
Add $40 for nickel finish (combo package only).
Add $20 for birdshead grips.
Add $30 for 9 in. barrel.

SENTRY D/A SERIES — .22 Mag., .32 Mag., .38 Spl., or 9mm cal., snubnose design, with 2 or 4 (.22 LR or .38 Spl.) in. barrel, 6 (centerfire) or 8 (rimfire) shot, transfer bar safety, blue or nickel finish, black polymer grips, ramp front sight. New 1993.

Mfg.'s Sug. Retail	**$130**	$110	$85	$70	$55	$50	$45	$40

Add $10 for nickel finish.

PISTOLS: SEMI-AUTO

H-25S/B — .25 ACP cal., 6 shot mag. with finger extension, single action, choice of blue or blue/gold (disc. 1995) finish. New 1993.

Mfg.'s Sug. Retail	**$150**	$125	$95	$80	$65	$55	$50	$45

Add $10 for nickel steel.
Add $10 for Model H-25G (blue/gold finish with checkered grips).

Grading	100%	98%	95%	90%	80%	70%	60%

STEALTH COMPACT — 9mm para. or .40 S&W cal., double action only, stainless steel slide and 3.9 in. barrel, black polymer frame, 10 shot mag. with finger extension, fixed sights, black synthetic grips, choice of stainless slide, two-tone stainless slide, or black finish, 20 oz. New 1996.

Mfg.'s Sug. Retail	$300	$260	$220	$190	$170	$150	$135	$110

HEROLD RIFLE

Franz Jaeger, Suhl, Germany.

BOLT ACTION SPORTING RIFLE — miniature Mauser action, .22 Hornet, 24 in. barrel, leaf sight, double set trigger, select checkered stock, imported by Daly & Stoeger, pre-WWII.

	$990	$880	$825	$770	$660	$550	$495

HERTERS

Previous importer/distributor/retailer headquartered in Waseca, MN from early 1960s - 1979.

Herters subcontracted various manufacturers (mostly European) to fabricate Powermag revolvers, U-9/J-9 rifles, and shotguns which were mostly patterned after more famous original models. Most of these copies were designed to undersell the competition at the time and while quality in most cases was quite good, consumer sales were not strong enough to continue production. While many Herters models are relatively rare, collectibility to date has been minimal. Herters model values are usually under the original trademarks from which they were derived and to date have been based more on the shooting utility than the collector potential.

HEYM, FRIEDRICH WILH.

Originally founded in 1865 by F.H. Heym with location in Suhl. Currently manufactured in Muennerstadt, Germany. Previously imported by Jager-Sport, Ltd. located in Cranston, RI 1993-94 only. Previously imported and distributed by Heckler & Koch, Inc. (until 1993) located in Sterling, VA. Previously imported and distributed by Heym America, Inc. (subsidiary of F.W. Heym of W. Germany) located in Fort Wayne, IN.

Pre-war guns will bring a premium over values listed below.

OVER AND UNDERS

MODEL 22 S2 — rifle/shotgun combination, 12, 16, or 20 ga. (3 in.), under rifle (17 cals. available), single set trigger, takedown feature (standard 1990), coin finish with engraving, 5½ lbs.

	$3,675	$3,000	$2,450	$1,875	$1,575	$1,325	$1,100

Last Mfg.'s Sug. Retail was $4,125.

Subtract $380 without engraving.

This model features a dampened rifle barrel which prevents the "climbing" of groups, thereby enhancing accuracy.

MODEL 55 BF — rifle/shotgun combination, popular U.S. and European cals., shotgun barrels interchangeable in 12 (disc.), 16, or 20 ga., 25 or 28 in. barrels, boxlock, auto ejectors, silver finish, fine German engraving, folding leaf sight, checkered pistol grip stock. Extra barrels — add $3,250 for O/U rifle and $2,250 for O/U shotgun or shotgun/rifle combination.

	$6,500	$5,400	$4,950	$4,525	$3,950	$3,615	$3,210

Last Mfg.'s Sug. Retail was $7,485.

▲ *Model 55 B* — O/U rifle only, various cals., engraving similar to Model 55 BF. Importation disc. 1994.

	$9,250	$7,800	$7,000	$6,000	$5,150	$4,700	$4,000

Last Mfg.'s Sug. Retail was $10,800.

Add $5,715 for extra set of interchangeable barrels.

Grading	100%	98%	95%	90%	80%	70%	60%

▲ *Model 55 BS* — O/U rifle only with different caliber for each barrel, double set triggers, "Bergstutzen" design.

$9,000 $7,750 $6,950 $5,950 $5,125 $4,650 $3,975
Last Mfg.'s Sug. Retail was $10,435.

▲ *Model 55 F* — O/U shotgun, ejectors, 20 or 16 ga., engraved, 6.6 lbs. Importation disc. 1992.

$5,100 $4,525 $3,950 $3,615 $3,200 $2,775 $2,300
Last Mfg.'s Sug. Retail was $5,500.

▲ *Model 55 SS* — sidelock version of Model 55 F, large engraved hunting scenes.

$4,500 $3,825 $3,300 $2,850 $2,400 $2,000 $1,700
Last Mfg.'s Sug. Retail was $4,890.

MODEL 200 — 20 ga., 3 in. chambers, boxlock action, DTs, 28 in. VR barrels, light engraving, previous importation.

$895 $795 $700 $650 $600 $550 $500

DRILLINGS

MODEL 33 BOXLOCK STANDARD — 16 or 20 ga., boxlock, Arabesque engraving, shotgun barrels over popular European cals., and .222, .243, .270, .308, and .30-06 rifle barrel, 25 in. full and mod. barrels, set trigger on rifle, checkered pistol grip stock.

$7,400 $5,950 $4,950 $4,525 $3,950 $3,615 $3,210
Last Mfg.'s Sug. Retail was $8,700.

▲ *Model 33 Deluxe* — same specifications as Standard Model, only hunting scene engraved.

$7,600 $6,000 $5,000 $4,600 $4,025 $3,700 $3,300
Last Mfg.'s Sug. Retail was $9,080.

MODEL 37 SIDELOCK STANDARD — shotgun barrels (12, 16, or 20 ga.) over rifle, detachable sidelocks, select French walnut, border engraving, 8 lbs.

$10,400 $8,800 $7,750 $6,650 $5,700 $4,900 $3,950
Last Mfg.'s Sug. Retail was $11,815.

▲ *Model 37 Deluxe* — similar to Model 37 Standard, except has large engraved hunting scenes.

$12,000 $9,950 $8,200 $7,475 $6,500 $5,650 $4,600
Last Mfg.'s Sug. Retail was $13,750.

MODEL 37 B STANDARD — rifle barrels over shotgun (20 ga.), sidelock, border engraved, about 8.6 lbs.

$13,250 $10,875 $9,500 $8,400 $7,550 $6,500 $5,650
Last Mfg.'s Sug. Retail was $15,065.

▲ *Model 37 B Deluxe* — similar to Model 37 B Standard, except has large hunting scene engraving.

$15,600 $12,750 $10,700 $9,450 $8,200 $7,050 $5,750
Last Mfg.'s Sug. Retail was $17,620.

RIFLES: BOLT ACTION

On the models listed below, a "N" suffix in the model denotes standard calibers whereas "G" refers to Mag. cals.

MODEL SR 20N CLASSIC SPORTER — available in 18 cals., Mauser type bolt action, single trigger, French walnut, 24 in. Krupp steel barrel except Mag. (25 in.).

$1,825 $1,425 $1,100 $900 $800 $700 $600
Last Mfg.'s Sug. Retail was $2,120.

Subtract $70 without iron sights.
Add $430 for left-hand variation.
Add $115 for Mag. cals. (G suffix).

▲ *Model SR 20 Hunter* — similar to Model SR 20N, except has classic style fiberglass stock with either matte blue or parkerized metal finish. Imported 1988-90.

$1,500 $1,225 $1,050 $900 $800 $700 $600
Last Mfg.'s Sug. Retail was $1,750.

Grading	100%	98%	95%	90%	80%	70%	60%

▲ **Model SR 20L** — Mannlicher style stock, European configuration, 18 in. barrel, 7 lbs.

	$1,475	$1,225	$985	$895	$785	$720	$650

Last Mfg.'s Sug. Retail was $1,700.

SR 20 TROPHY — available in all SR 20 cals., bolt action, 22 or 24 (Mag. cals. only) in. octagonal barrel, classic stock configuration with cheekpiece and recoil pad. Importation began 1989.

	$2,550	$2,100	$1,800	$1,500	$1,250	$985	$895

Last Mfg.'s Sug. Retail was $2,815.

Add $120 for Mag. cals.

This model is available with either right hand or left-hand action.

SR 20G CLASSIC SPORTER — available in various cals., bolt action, 22 or 24 in. round barrel, steel grip cap. Importation began 1989.

	$1,875	$1,600	$1,300	$1,050	$900	$785	$720

Last Mfg.'s Sug. Retail was $2,235.

Subtract $70 without iron sights.

This model is available with either right hand or left-hand action.

SR 20 ALPINE — available in standard cals. between .243 Win. and 9.3x62, mountain style rifle with Mannlicher forend and classic buttstock, supplied with mounted open sights. Importation began 1989.

	$1,900	$1,650	$1,325	$1,075	$925	$800	$750

Last Mfg.'s Sug. Retail was $2,165.

This model is available with either right hand or left-hand action.

SR 20 MATCH — .308 cal. only, 24 in. heavy barrel, target stock with accessory rail, large bolt handle, supplied without sights, 9 lbs. New 1991.

	$1,860	$1,600	$1,300	$1,050	$900	$785	$720

Last Mfg.'s Sug. Retail was $2,200.

SR 20 CLASSIC SAFARI — .375 H&H, .404 Jeffries (disc.), .425 Express, or .458 Win. Mag., 24 in. barrel only, express rear sight and large front post sights, tight grained walnut. Importation began 1989.

	$2,150	$1,650	$1,250	$1,050	$875	$800	$700

Last Mfg.'s Sug. Retail was $2,530.

This model is available with either right hand or left-hand action.

EXPRESS SERIES RIFLE — .338 Lapua Mag., .375 H&H, .378 Wby. Mag., .404 rimless Jeffries (disc. 1992), .416 Rigby, .450 Ackley, .460 Wby. Mag., .500 NE (new 1994), or .500 A-Square, express sights, Timney single trigger. Imported 1989-94.

	$5,750	$4,500	$3,825	$3,000	$2,350	$2,000	$1,750

Last Mfg.'s Sug. Retail was $6,550.

Add $375 for muzzle brake (includes installation).

Add $555 for left-hand action (disc. 1992).

▲ **.600 NE Rifle** — .600 NE cal., 24 in. barrel, reinforced action, 2 shot mag. Imported 1991-94.

	$9,950	$8,150	$7,150	$6,000	$5,125	$4,650	$3,975

Last Mfg.'s Sug. Retail was $11,350.

RIFLES: SINGLE SHOT

MODEL HR 30N SINGLE SHOT — available in many cals., Ruger No. 1 falling block action, 24 in. barrel, French walnut with Bavarian cheekpiece, round barrel, Sporter or full length carbine style French walnut stock, engraved coin finished receiver, 6.6 lbs.

	$3,500	$2,975	$2,350	$1,950	$1,675	$1,350	$1,175

Last Mfg.'s Sug. Retail was $4,040.

Add $440 for Mag. cals.

Add $1,710 for Mannlicher stocked Carbine Model.

Add $850 for hunting scene engraving (minimum extra charge).

Grading	100%	98%	95%	90%	80%	70%	60%

MODEL HR 38 N — available in many cals., Ruger No. 1 falling block action 24 in. barrel, octagon barrel, French walnut with Bavarian cheekpiece, Sporter or full length carbine style French walnut stock, engraved coin finished receiver, 6.6 lbs.

$4,150 $3,450 $2,875 $2,300 $1,950 $1,675 $1,350
Last Mfg.'s Sug. Retail was $4,835.

Add $235 for Mag. cals.
Add $2,400 for sideplates with engraved large game hunting scenes.

SIDELOCK RIFLE SHOTGUN

MODEL 35 STANDARD — 3 barrels, (two rifle and one shotgun), choice of cals. with top barrel either 16 or 20 ga., light border engraving, 8¼ lbs.

$13,650 $11,000 $9,250 $8,000 $6,850 $5,700 $4,600
Last Mfg.'s Sug. Retail was $15,100.

Add $2,430 for hunting scene engraving.

RIFLES: SIDE-BY-SIDE

MODEL 88 B — available in various cals. up to .375 H&H, SxS double rifle, boxlock action, Krupp steel barrels, double underlocking lugs with Greener crossbolt, ejectors, checkered circassian walnut, built to customer specifications, 7½ lbs. Importation disc. 1994.

$10,750 $9,600 $8,575 $7,100 $6,125 $5,420 $4,575
Last Mfg.'s Sug. Retail was $12,500.

Add $1,950 for .375 H&H cal.

▲ *Model 88 BSS* — sidelock model with interceptor sears. Importation disc. 1994.

$14,350 $11,925 $10,250 $8,750 $7,425 $6,300 $5,175
Last Mfg.'s Sug. Retail was $16,600.

▲ *Model 88 B Safari* — available in .375 H&H, .458 Win. Mag., .470 Nitro Express, or .500 Nitro Express cal., 24 in. barrels, 9.9 lbs. Importation disc. 1994.

$14,150 $11,825 $10,000 $8,650 $7,400 $6,300 $5,175
Last Mfg.'s Sug. Retail was $16,400.

Add $5,870 for extra pair of interchangeable rifle barrels.
Add $3,150 for extra pair of interchangeable 20 ga. shotgun barrels.

MODEL 88 BF RIFLE-SHOTGUN — 2 barrel set with 20 ga. barrels and an extra set of rifle barrels available in cals. .375 H&H Mag., .458 Win. Mag., .470 N.E., or .500 N.E.

$13,100 $10,750 $9,600 $8,150 $6,900 $5,850 $4,850
Last Mfg.'s Sug. Retail was $15,060.

This model is a larger frame variation of the Model 88 B.

▲ *Model 88B/F Safari* — includes set of rifle and shotgun barrels, choice of .375 H&H, .458 Win. Mag., .470 NE, or .500 NE cal. and extra set of 20 ga. 3 in. chamber barrels.

$16,150 $14,100 $11,950 $10,250 $8,950 $6,750 $5,250
Last Mfg.'s Sug. Retail was $18,530.

MODEL 88 F SIDE-BY-SIDE SHOTGUN — available in cals. 20 ga. with 2¾ or 3 in. chambers.

$13,300 $11,250 $10,100 $9,400 $8,000 $6,950 $5,800
Last Mfg.'s Sug. Retail was $14,650.

HI-POINT FIREARMS

Distributed by MKS Supply, Inc. located in Mansfield, Ohio.

Prior to 1993, trademarks sold by MKS Supply, Inc. (including Beemiller, Inc., Haskell Manufacturing, Inc., Iberia Firearms, Inc., and Stallard Arms, Inc.) had their own separate manufacturers' markings. Beginning in 1993, Hi-Point Firearms eliminated these individualized markings and chose instead to have currently manufactured guns labelled Hi-Point Firearms.

HI-POINT FIREARMS

Grading	100%	98%	95%	90%	80%	70%	60%

PISTOLS: SEMI-AUTO

MODEL 380 POLYMER — .380 ACP cal., semi-auto single action, $3\frac{1}{2}$ in. barrel, polymer frame, 3-dot sights, 8 shot mag. with thumb activated release, 3-dot sights, satin black finish. New 1995.

Mfg.'s Sug. Retail	$80	$70	$65	$60	$55	$50	$45	$40

JS-9 — 9mm Para. cal., semi-auto single action, $4\frac{1}{2}$ in. barrel, thumb safety, fixed sights, 8 shot mag., non-glare military blue finish (early mfg.) or satin black finish (new 1991), copolymer synthetic grips, 41 oz. New 1990.

Mfg.'s Sug. Retail	$140	$125	$100	$85	$75	$70	$65	$60

Add $10 for nickel finish (disc.).

This model is manufactured by Stallard Arms, Inc. located in Mansfield, OH.

▲ *JS-9 Compact* — compact variation of the Model JS-9 with $3\frac{1}{2}$ in. barrel and 8 shot mag., choice of regular or polymer (new 1994) frame, 3-dot or adj. (mfg. 1995 only) sights, 32 (polymer) or 35 oz. New 1993.

Mfg.'s Sug. Retail	$125	$100	$85	$75	$70	$65	$60	$55

Add $8 for adj. sights (disc.).

This model is manufactured by Beemiller, Inc. located in Mansfield, OH.

JS-40 — .40 S&W cal., semi-auto single action, black finish, $4\frac{3}{4}$ in. barrel, 8 shot mag., 44 oz. New 1992.

Mfg.'s Sug. Retail	$149	$135	$110	$100	$90	$80	$75	$70

Add $7 for nickel finish (disc. 1994).

This model is manufactured by Iberia Firearms, Inc. located in Iberia, OH.

JS-45 — .45 ACP cal., semi-auto single action, similar to Stallard Arms JS-9mm, except has 7 shot mag. and $4\frac{3}{4}$ in. barrel, 44 oz. New 1991.

Mfg.'s Sug. Retail	$149	$135	$110	$100	$90	$80	$75	$70

Add $10 for nickel finish (disc. 1994).

This model is manufactured by Haskell Mfg., Inc. located in Lima, OH.

RIFLES: SEMI-AUTO

9MM CARBINE — 9mm para. cal., $16\frac{1}{2}$ in. barrel, one-piece black polymer stock features pistol grip, 10 shot mag., aperture rear sight, parkerized or chrome finish. New 1996.

Mfg.'s Sug. Retail	$169	$150	$120	$105	$95	$85	$75	$70

HIGGINS, J.C.

Trademark used on Sears & Roebuck rifles and shotguns manufactured between 1946-1962.

The J.C. Higgins trademark has appeared literally on hundreds of various models (shotguns and rifles) sold through the Sears & Roebuck retail network. Most of these models were manufactured through subcontracts with both domestic and international firearms manufacturers. Typically, they were "spec." guns made to sell at a specific price to undersell the competition. Most of these models were derivatives of existing factory models with less expensive wood and perhaps missing the features found on those models from which they were derived.

To date, there has been very little interest in collecting J.C. Higgins guns, regardless of rarity. Rather than list J.C. Higgins models, a general guideline is that values generally are under those of their "1st generation relatives". The Ranger trademark was also used by Sears & Roebuck - it is not any more desirable than those guns marked J.C. Higgins. As a result, prices are ascertained by the shooting value of the gun, rather than its collector value.

HIGH STANDARD

High Standard Mfg. Co. was founded in 1926. They purchased Hartford Arms and Equipment Co. in 1932. The original plant was located in New Haven, CT from 1932-1952 until they moved to a larger facility at Hamden, CT from 1951-1976. High Standard also operated another Hamden, CT plant between 1940-1949. A final move was made to East Hartford, CT in 1977 where they remained until the doors were closed in January, 1984.

High Standard values have risen dramatically over the past several years. Many collectors have realized the rarity and quality factors this trademark has earned (Models C, A, D, E, H-D, H-E, H-A, H-B First Model, G-380, GB, GD, GE, GO - 13 different variations had a total production of less than 43,000 pistols). For these reasons, top condition High Standard pistols are getting more difficult to find each year.

Note catalog numbers did not always change with design series and in 1966/1967 changed with accessories offered and not design series.

> The approx. ser. number cut-off for New Haven, CT marked guns is 43X,XXX.
> The approx. ser. number cut-off for Hamden, CT manufacture is 44X,XXX - 2,495,000 and G or ML 010000 - G or ML 25,000.
> The approx. ser. number range for E. Hartford, CT manufacture is ML 25,000 - ML 87,000 and SH 10,000 and SH 35,000.

Grading	100%	98%	95%	90%	80%	70%	60%

SEMI-AUTO PISTOLS

Pre-war High Standard Semi-Automatic pistols had 3 different takedown types.

TYPE I-A MFG. 1932-38. Takedown lever on left side of frame next to safety. Round retracting rod on rear of slide. This takedown was used on Models B & C.

TYPE I-B MFG. 1938. Similar to I-A Type except has strengthened rectangular rod on rear of slide.

TYPE II MFG. 1939. Takedown lever located on right side of frame. Round pick-up rod on top of slide.

HAMMERLESS FIXED BARREL SERIES

This series consists of the 5 original pistols mfg. in 1932-1942. All serial numbers are located on forestrap of frame. This series is also sometimes referred to as the "Letter Models".

MODEL B — original High Standard pistol, basically the same gun as Hartford Arms 1925 Automatic, .22 LR, small frame, 4½ or 6¾ in. light weight barrel, fixed Patridge type front and rear sights, checkered hard rubber grips with or without H.S. monogram, 10 shot mag. Beginning ser. no. 5,000. Approx. 65,000 mfg. 1932-42.

	$675	$575	$450	$325	$250	$200	$150

> Add $75 for I-B Type takedown.
> Less than 14,000 pistols with this takedown were mfg.

MODEL S — essentially a Model B with a 6¾ in. smooth bore barrel only without choke, chambered for .22 LR shot shell cartridge, left side of slide is stamped "HI-STANDARD MODEL S .22 LR SHOT ONLY", this variation was never a production model with approx. 5-10 guns mfg. total, 10 shot mag., a second variation using Model C slides was called the Model C/S - also not a production model with approx. 5 mfg. Mfg. 1939 only.

> Because of the extreme rarity factory of this model, a specimen in almost any condition will bring $3,000 - $5,000. This model was used primarily for pest control.

Grading	100%	98%	95%	90%	80%	70%	60%

MODEL C — identical to Model B in appearance, except .22 Short only, small frame, $4\frac{1}{2}$ or $6\frac{3}{4}$ in. light weight barrel, fixed rear sight, checkered hard rubber grips with or without H.S. monogram, this action was adapted for the decreased power of the .22 Short cartridge. Beginning ser. no. 500 to 31XX, later beginning ser. no. 42XXX. Approx. 4,700 mfg. 1936-42.

	$950	$795	$550	$375	$275	$230	$200

Add $100 for I-A takedown.
Add $250 for I-B takedown.
This model was used primarily for plinking and gallery shooting. The Model C was made in all 3 variations of takedowns - I-A, I-B, and Type 2 (but less than 100 were mfg. in I-B).

MODEL A — similar to Model B, except enlarged frame, squared-off butt, .22 LR, $4\frac{1}{2}$ or $6\frac{3}{4}$ in. light weight barrel, adj. rear sight, checkered walnut grips, automatic slide lock, trigger stop, 10 shot mag. Beginning ser. no. 33XXX. Approx. 7,300 mfg. 1938-42.

	$850	$695	$495	$360	$260	$220	$200

Add $250 for I-B takedown.

MODEL D — identical to Model A except $4\frac{1}{2}$ or $6\frac{3}{4}$ in. medium weight barrel, .22 LR, adj. sights, walnut grips, slide lock trigger stop, 10 shot mag. Beginning ser. no. 33XXX. Approx. 2,500 mfg. 1938-42.

	$950	$775	$550	$400	$300	$250	$215

Add $250 for I-B takedown.

MODEL E — high quality, deluxe model of the hammerless series, .22 LR, adj. sight, $4\frac{1}{2}$ or $6\frac{3}{4}$ in. heavy bull barrel, checkered walnut target grips with thumbrest, automatic slide lock, 10 shot mag. Beginning ser. no. 34XXX. Approx. 2,600 mfg. 1938-42.

	$1,275	$1,045	$800	$575	$440	$360	$300

Add $250 for I-B takedown.

EXPOSED HAMMER — FIXED BARREL SERIES

This series consists of 4 pistols that were introduced in 1940. Frame and slide modified to accommodate external hammer. All ser. no.'s located on forestrap of frame. Prefix "H" added to standard model designation with the exception of Model C. Mfg. 1940-42. This series has very low production numbers. May also be referred to as the "Hammer Letter Models".

MODEL H-D — first exposed hammer model, similar to Model D, .22 LR, $4\frac{1}{2}$ or $6\frac{3}{4}$ in. medium weight barrel, adj. sight, target or standard walnut grips, no external safety, 10 shot mag. High quality pistol. Beginning ser. no. 45,463. Approx. 2,000 mfg. 1940-42.

	$1,650	$1,350	$1,275	$900	$695	$565	$475

This variation is infrequently encountered.

MODEL H-E — high quality, deluxe model of exposed hammer series, .22 LR, $4\frac{1}{2}$ or $6\frac{3}{4}$ in. heavy barrel, adj. sight, deluxe hand checkered walnut grips with thumbrests, no external safety, 10 shot mag. Rarest of the H.S. pistols. Beginning ser. no. 51,802. Approx 1,000 mfg. 1941-42.

	$2,275	$1,875	$1,300	$950	$725	$600	$500

MODEL H-A — similar to Model A, .22 LR, $4\frac{1}{2}$ or $6\frac{3}{4}$ in. light weight barrel, adj. sight, plain checkered walnut grips, no external safety, 10 shot mag. Very rare gun. Beginning ser. no. 53,176. Approx. 1,000 mfg. 1940-42.

	$1,050	$865	$665	$475	$365	$295	$250

MODEL H-B — duplicate of Model B with external hammer, .22 LR, $4\frac{1}{2}$ or $6\frac{3}{4}$ in. light weight barrel, fixed sight, checkered hard rubber grips with or without H.S. monogram, no external safety, 10 shot mag. This first Model H-B had beginning ser. no. 52,405. Approx. 2,200 mfg. 1940-42.

	$850	$695	$495	$355	$275	$235	$200

H

Grading	100%	98%	95%	90%	80%	70%	60%

▲ *Model H-B Second Model* — H.S. reintroduced a H-B second model similar to first model, except with external safety. Beginning ser. no. 308XXX. Approx. 25,000 mfg. 1949-1954.

	$750	$595	$435	$310	$235	$200	$170

U.S. MILITARY SERIES

These models are earlier H.S. pistols adapted as training guns during WWII. They were the sole suppliers of the .22 cal. pistol for military training. Ser. no.'s located on forestrap of frame.

MODEL B-US — adapted Model B with minor changes, .22 LR, available in 4½ in. barrel only, checkered hard rubber grips, fixed sight, marked "Property of U.S." on right side of frame and on top of barrel. Ordnance acceptance crossed cannon stamped on right side of frame above triggerguard, 10 shot mag. Beginning ser. no. 95XXX. Approx. 14,000 mfg. 1942-43.

	$875	$725	$495	$350	$275	$235	$195

MODEL USA-HD — the government needed a training pistol similar to the Colt Model 1911 .45 ACP. The result was a Model HD with external safety and fixed sight, 4½ in. medium weight barrel, .22 LR only. The barrel is marked "Property of USA", black checkered hard rubber grips. First models mfg. had high gloss blue finish, changed to a Parkerized finish near ser. no. 130XXX. Beginning ser. no. 109XXX-153XXX. Approx. 44,000 mfg. 1943-46.

	$775	$625	$445	$320	$250	$200	$170

Add 20% for early blue finish.

MODEL USA-HD-MS — variation of the Model USA-HD with attached silencer, mfg. for U.S. Government covert operations, original ownership required NFA transfer, approx. 2,000 mfg.

	$3,850	$3,350	$2,900	$2,500	$2,250	$1,995	$1,750

MODEL H-D MILITARY — though called H-D Military, this model was not mfg. for the government. Essentially a USA-HD with the addition of adj. sights, .22 LR, 4½ or 6¾ in. barrel, checkered walnut grips, external safety, 10 shot mag. Beginning ser. no. 147XXX. Approx. 150,000 mfg. 1946-55.

	$695	$575	$395	$295	$225	$190	$160

Add 20% for all-blue finish.

MODEL G-380 — this is H.S.'s only in-house production of a center-fire pistol. A transition model to the G-series using a lever takedown. Has exposed hammer, fixed sights, .380 cal., checkered black plastic grips, external safety, 5 in. barrel only, 6 shot mag. Beginning ser. no. 100. Approx. 7,400 mfg. 1947-50.

	$775	$635	$445	$325	$245	$210	$180

THE G-SERIES

This series is hammerless with interchangeable target barrel, 6¾ in. and plinking barrel, 4½ in., consists of 4 pistols, all using lever takedown. An adaptation of the G-380 design. Ser. no.'s on right side of slide and rear right side of frame. Mfg. 1949-50.

MODEL GB — similar to Model B with light barrel, small frame, .22 LR, external safety, fixed sight, checkered brown plastic grips, interchangeable 4½ or 6¾ in. barrel with lever takedown, 10 shot mag. Beginning ser. no. 311XXX. Approx. 4,900 mfg. 1949-50.

	$650	$535	$410	$295	$225	$185	$155

Add 15-20% for both barrels.

Grading	100%	98%	95%	90%	80%	70%	60%

MODEL GD — large frame with medium weight with interchangeable $4\frac{1}{2}$ or $6\frac{3}{4}$ in. barrel with lever takedown, .22 LR, featured new adj. "Davis" sight, named for designer G.F. Davis. Grips avail. in plain checkered walnut or deluxe with thumbrest grips, 10 shot mag. Beginning ser. no. 311XXX. Approx. 3,300 mfg. 1949-50.

	$925	$750	$535	$385	$295	$245	$205

Add 15-20% for both barrels.

This sight is adjustable for both windage and elevation.

MODEL GE — deluxe top-of-the-line quality .22 LR pistol, large frame with interchangeable $4\frac{1}{2}$ or $6\frac{3}{4}$ in. heavy "bull" barrel with lever takedown, "Davis" sight adj. sight, deluxe walnut hand checkered grips with thumbrest, 10 shot mag. Beginning ser. no. 312XXX. Approx. 2,900 mfg. 1949-50.

	$1,345	$1,095	$775	$555	$425	$360	$300

Add 15-20% for both barrels.

MODEL G-O — also known as First Model Olympic. First fired in Olympic competition in 1948. Adaptation of Model GE in .22 cal. short. Deluxe top-of-the-line quality, interchangeable $4\frac{1}{2}$ or $6\frac{3}{4}$ in. heavy "bull" barrel with lever takedown, "Davis" adj. sight, deluxe hand checkered walnut grips with thumbrests. First High Standard large production gun with aluminum slide. Has unique curved magazine, flat milled surface on top of barrel. Rare. Beginning ser. no. 307XXX. Approx. 1,200 mfg. 1949-50.

	$1,595	$1,295	$950	$625	$475	$395	$345

Add 15-20% for both barrels.

This model has a grooved fore and rear strap.

THE SUPERMATIC SERIES

All of this series were mfg. at the New Haven, CT plant from 1951-53. Consisted of 4 guns, featuring the lever takedown introduced in the G-Series. Hammerless, new positive lock safety, use of one screw to attach grips, no production figures available. Approximate serial range of this series is 340,000- 440,000.

SPORT-KING (FIRST MODEL) — .22 LR, 10 shot mag., similar to Field-King but has fixed sight and light weight interchangeable $4\frac{1}{2}$ or $6\frac{3}{4}$ in. barrel featuring lever takedown.

	$600	$495	$355	$255	$195	$160	$135

Add 10-15% for extra barrel.
Add $50 w/o slide lock.

This model was available with or without slide lock.

The High Standard catalog number for this model was 9080-81, while both barrels were numbered 9082.

FIELD-KING (FIRST MODEL) — plain version of Supermatic, .22 LR, 10 shot mag., interchangeable $4\frac{1}{2}$ or $6\frac{3}{4}$ in. barrels with lever takedown, "Davis" adj. sight, 10 shot mag.

	$850	$695	$485	$350	$275	$235	$195

Add 10-15% for both barrels.

The High Standard catalog number for this model was 9090-91, while both barrels were numbered 9092.

SUPERMATIC (FIRST MODEL) — .22 LR, 10 shot mag., $4\frac{1}{2}$ or $6\frac{3}{4}$ in. interchangeable barrel with lever takedown, "Davis" adj. sight, slide lock, front and back straps grooved, serrated rib between front and rear sight, adj. 2 oz. and 3 oz. weights which dovetail into and beneath barrel.

	$895	$750	$525	$370	$280	$225	$195

Add 15-20% for both barrels.

The High Standard catalog numbers for this model were 9070-71, while both barrels were numbered 9072.

H

Grading	100%	98%	95%	90%	80%	70%	60%

OLYMPIC (SECOND MODEL) — .22 cal. short, identical in all respects to the Supermatic, except has aluminum slide for rapid recoil, interchangeable 4½ or 6¾ in. barrel with lever takedown, "Davis" adj. sight, adj. 2 oz. and 3 oz. weights, 10 shot mag.

	$1,175	$950	$675	$485	$375	$315	$265

Add 15-20% for both barrels.

The High Standard catalog numbers for this model were 9043-44, while both barrels were numbered 9045.

QUICK CHANGE CONVERSION KIT — avail. in 1951 to let you shoot both .22 LR or .22 Short in the Supermatic, Olympic, or Field-King models. Featured factory fitted barrel, slide, barrel weights and magazine included in this kit.

	$500	$400	$350

This kit featured all components fitted neatly into a small maroon and yellow box.

Cat. # 9150 Supermatic/Field King to 22 short, 4½ Bbl.

Cat. # 9151 Supermatic/Field King to 22 short, 6¾ Bbl.

Cat. # 9152 Olympic to Supermatic 22 L.R., 4½ Bbl.

Cat. # 9153 Olympic to Supermatic 22 L.R., 6¾ Bbl.

Cat. # 9154 Olympic to Field King 22 L.R., 4½ Bbl.

Cat. # 9155 Olympic to Field King 22 L.R., 6¾ Bbl.

THE M-100 AND M-101 SERIES

All of this series were mfg. at the Hamden, CT plant from 1954-57. Hammerless design consisting of 5 pistols featuring a new push-button type takedown. The beginning ser. no. for .22 LR pistols only in this series was 443,611. This series featured slanted plastic grips as standard issue. The serial range for this series was 443,XXX-770,XXX. Conversion unit factory nomenclature for this series is as follows:

Cat. # 9150 Supermatic/Field King to 22 short, 4½ Bbl.

Cat. # 9151 Supermatic/Field King to 22 short, 6¾ Bbl.

Cat. # 9152 Olympic to Supermatic 22 L.R., 4½ Bbl.

Cat. # 9153 Olympic to Supermatic 22 L.R., 6¾ Bbl.

Cat. # 9154 Olympic to Field King 22 L.R., 4½ Bbl.

Cat. # 9155 Olympic to Field King 22 L.R., 6¾ Bbl.

M-100/M-101 Conversion unit pricing is similar to the M-102, M-103, and M-104 Conversion units (please refer to that section).

DURA-MATIC — .22 LR, 4½ or 6¾ in. barrels, fixed sight, oversized plastic grips. M-100 or M-101 stamped on right side of slide. Mfg. 1954-70. The Duramatic was sold by Sears Roebuck & Co. as the J. C. Higgins Model 80. This Sears variation had some minor exterior differences, but mechanically it was the same. Unique thumb screw takedown, push-button mag. release and oversized triggerguard.

	$365	$295	$225	$160	$125	$105	$90

Add 20% for extra barrel.

Add 10% for M-100 (has push button to release thumb screw).

The High Standard catalog number for this model was 9124-25, while both barrels were numbered 9126.

SPORT-KING (SECOND MODEL) — SK 100 or SK 101 (questions remain about this configuration) stamped on right side of slide, .22 LR, similar to Flite-King but with steel slide and frame, front and rear grip straps on this model are smooth. This model was also avail. in nickel. Fixed rear sight.

	$450	$375	$260	$185	$140	$120	$100

Add 15-20% for both barrels.

Add 20% for nickel finish.

The High Standard catalog number for this model was 9100-01, while both barrels were numbered 9102.

Grading	100%	98%	95%	90%	80%	70%	60%

SPORT-KING LIGHTWEIGHT — .22 LR, similar to standard Sport-King, except has forged aluminum alloy frame. The word "Lightweight" is inscribed in script on the left side of frame. Also avail. in nickel. Mfg. 1956-64.

	$530	$450	$315	$225	$175	$150	$125

Add 20% for nickel finish (H.S. number 9166-67, both barrels - 9168).
Add 15 - 20% for both barrels.
The High Standard catalog number for this model was 9156-57, while both barrels were numbered 9158.

FLITE-KING (FIRST MODEL) — LW 100 or LW 101 (questions remain about this configuration) stamped on right side of slide, .22 Short, 10 shot mag., 4½ or 6¾ in. interchangeable light weight barrel with push-button takedown, alloy slide, front and rear grip straps on this model are smooth. First commercial use of aluminum alloy for frame. Fixed rear sight. Mfg. until 1960.

	$600	$495	$380	$275	$210	$175	$150

Add 15-20% for both barrels.
The High Standard catalog number for this model was 9103-04, while both barrels were numbered 9105.

FIELD-KING (SECOND MODEL) — FK 100 or FK 101 stamped on right side of slide, .22 LR, 10 shot mag. 4½ or 6¾ in. interchangeable barrel with push-button takedown, front and rear grip straps on this model are smooth. Slotted stabilizer 6¾ in. target barrel was an option. Adj. rear sight.

	$750	$615	$475	$345	$265	$215	$180

Add $75 for Models marked FK100.
The High Standard catalog number for this model was 9115-16, while both barrels were numbered 9117.

SUPERMATIC (SECOND MODEL) — S 100 or S 101 stamped on right side of slide, .22 LR, 10 shot mag., 4½ or 6¾ in. interchangeable barrel with push-button takedown, adj. 2 oz. or 3 oz. weights. Integral slotted stabilizer with 6¾ in. target barrel was an option. Adj. rear sight.

	$850	$695	$475	$350	$275	$230	$195

The High Standard catalog number for this model was 9118-19, while both barrels were numbered 9120.

OLYMPIC (THIRD MODEL) — O-100 or O-101 stamped on right side of alloy slide, .22 Short, 10 shot mag., 4½ or 6¾ in. interchangeable barrel with push-button takedown, adj. 2 oz. or 3 oz. weights. Integral slotted stabilizer 6¾ in. target barrel was an option. Adj. rear sight.

	$1,025	$825	$595	$425	$325	$275	$235

The High Standard catalog number for this model was 9121-22, while both barrels were numbered 9123.

MODEL 102 AND 103 SERIES

This series included the following and were mfg. in Hamden, CT. The words "Model 102" or "Model 103" and the serial number were inscribed on the right side of slide, and the serial number was duplicated on the right side of the new and longer frame. A new and larger push-button takedown enabling easier use was another improvement. A grooved and wider trigger in addition to a new rear sight were also added on the target models. The 102 Series was mfg. from 1957-1960 and the serial range was approx. 770,XXX-1,100,XXX. The 103 Series was mfg. between 1960-1963 and the approximate serial range was 1,100,XXX-1,330,XXX. Plastic grips were standard and checkered walnut grips with thumbrest were optional.

Original cased 102/103 Series Trophy's, Olympic Trophy's, Olympic Citation's, and Special Presentation combinations in 98%+ condition are currently bringing premiums with asking prices in the $1,700-$2,000 range.

Grading	100%	98%	95%	90%	80%	70%	60%

SPORT-KING — similar to the Series 100/101, but stamped Model 102 or Model 103, nickel finish was available 1974-77, the 100/101 lightweight Sport King was still available but was disc. in 1964, this basic Sport-King was mfg. from 1958-77.

	$395	$325	$230	$165	$125	$100	$85

Add 50% for nickel finish.
Add 20% for 102 Models.
Add 25% for Sport King Lightweight.

The High Standard catalog number for this model was 9200-9201, while both barrels - (102 only) were numbered 9202.

FLITE-KING — similar to Series 100/101, this variation of the Flite-King featured an all steel frame with an alloy slide. Mfg. 1958-1965.

	$550	$450	$345	$265	$215	$175	$150

Add 10% for 102 Models.

The High Standard catalog number for this model was 9220-21, while both barrels (102 only) were numbered 9222.

SUPERMATIC TOURNAMENT — .22 LR, 10 shot, 4½, 5½ bull (avail. 1963), or 6¾ in. straight barrel, brown diamond checkered plastic slant grips, adj. sight, push-button takedown, this model featured smooth front and back grip straps. The govt. ordered a quantity of Mod. 102 Tournament for training. These were marked "US" on right side of frame. Mfg. 1958-1965.

	$750	$615	$475	$345	$265	$220	$185

The High Standard catalog number for this model was 9270-71, while both barrels were numbered 9272.

103 series pistols were numbered 9271-9275, (5½).

SHARPSHOOTER — .22 LR cal., 10 shot, 5½ in. bull barrel. Introduced 1969.

	$650	$535	$415	$300	$230	$190	$160

Add $100 for Sport King frame.

The High Standard catalog no. was 9205. First Models used a Sport King frame - Model 103 only.

SUPERMATIC CITATION — .22 LR cal., 10 shot, 6¾, 8, and 10 in. tapered barrels, diamond checkered plastic slant grips, adj. sight, push-button takedown, one grade above Tournament. Grooved front and back grip straps. Sight located on 8 and 10 in. barrel (a 5½ in. target bull barrel became avail. in 1962). Detachable stabilizer and 2 or 3 oz. barrel weights available. Mfg. 1958-65.

	$925	$760	$530	$380	$290	$245	$210

The High Standard catalog number for this model was 9260-61-62. 8 in. and 10 in. barrel set, 9262-8, 5½ bull barrel, 103 only - 9263. The govt. ordered a quantity of Mod. 102 Citations for training and are marked "U.S." on left side of frame.
Add $125 for 8 in. barrel.
Add $225 for 10 in. barrel.

SUPERMATIC TROPHY — .22 LR, 10 shot, 6¾ in., 8 in. and 10 in. tapered barrels, 5½ bull and 7¼ in. fluted barrels became avail. in 1962, detachable barrel weights and stabilizer were also available, walnut checkered grips. Features gold trigger, gold safety button and gold inlaid lettering, adj. sight and push-button takedown. Mfg. 1958-63.

	$1,050	$860	$660	$475	$365	$300	$255

Add $150 for 8 in. barrel.
Add $250 for 10 in. barrel.

This variation was High Standards Top-of-the-Line Target pistol.

The High Standard catalog number for this model was 9250-51-52. 8 in. and 10 in. barrel set, 9252-8, 5½ bull barrel (103 only) - 9254, 7¼ fluted barrel (103 only) - 9255.

Grading	100%	98%	95%	90%	80%	70%	60%

ISU OLYMPIC — This is the model which brought the 33rd Gold Medal in the Rome Olympics in 1960. .22 Short, 10 shot, 6¾ in. barrel with integral stabilizer, checkered walnut grips, high luster finish, alloy slide. Top-of-the-line Olympic model. Complies with all rapid-fire International Shooting Union regulations. Mfg. 1961-66.

	$1,150	**$925**	**$600**	**$430**	**$330**	**$280**	**$240**

Add $500 for Model 9289 marked "Olympic Trophy"
The High Standard catalog number for this model was 9289-9299, 9289 (103 only).

OLYMPIC — same basic gun as Citation in .22 Short, but it is of lesser quality finish. Adj. sight located on 8 in. barrel. Mfg. 1958-65.

	$1,075	**$895**	**$550**	**$395**	**$315**	**$265**	**$225**

Add $350 for Model 9280-81-82 marked "OLYMPIC CITATION".
Add $150 for 8 in. barrel.
Add $250 for 10 in. barrel.
This model has also been observed with markings "OLYMPIC CITATION". Numbering was 9200-01-82, 8 in. and 10 in. barrel set 9282-8, 5½ bull barrel (Model 103, 1963 only) - 9294.

MODEL 104 SERIES

This series was mfg. from 1964-1972. This is the last series to feature the slant grip trophy pistol. Serial No. range is approx. 1,330,000-2,330,000.

SUPERMATIC TOURNAMENT — similar to Model 102/103 series. Mfg. 1964-65.

	$895	**$725**	**$525**	**$375**	**$290**	**$245**	**$210**

The High Standard catalog number for this model was 9271-9275.
The 104 Tournament is quite rare.

SHARPSHOOTER — .22 LR cal., 10 shot, 5½ in. bull barrel. Mfg. 1969-72 (numbered 104) and 1973 (unnumbered).

	$895	**$725**	**$525**	**$375**	**$290**	**$245**	**$210**

The High Standard catalog number for this model was 9205. The 104 Sharpshooter is very rare.

SUPERMATIC CITATION — similar to Model 102/103 series, brown plastic grips or walnut checkered grips, grooved front and back straps.

	$975	**$825**	**$575**	**$375**	**$295**	**$245**	**$210**

Add $150 for 8 in. barrel.
Add $250 for 10 in. barrel.
The 5½ in. bull barrel, 9263 - disc. 1966 (supplied with extra mag). The 5½ in. bull barrel, 9244 - available 1966. The 6¾ in. tapered barrel, 9260 - disc. 1965. The 8 in. tapered barrel, 9261 - disc. 1965. The 10 in. tapered barrel, 9262 - disc. 1965.

SUPERMATIC TROPHY — similar to Model 102/103 series, Top-of-the-line target, 5½ in. bull, 7¼ in. fluted barrel available, extra mag., muzzle brake and weights were supplied with gun, grooved front and back straps, checkered walnut grips. Mfg. 1964-65.

	$1,095	**$895**	**$595**	**$425**	**$325**	**$275**	**$235**

Add $50 for high blue finish.
The High Standard catalog number for this model was 9254-55.

OLYMPIC — similar to Model 102/103, grooved front and back straps, checkered walnut grips were optional.

	$1,095	**$895**	**$595**	**$425**	**$330**	**$280**	**$240**

Add $100 for catalog number 9295.
Add $150 for 8 in. barrel.
The 5½ in. bull barrel, 9294 - disc. 1964. The 5½ in. bull barrel, 9295 - avail. 1964-65, was supplied with muzzle brake and weights. The 8 in. tapered barrel, 9281 - disc. 1964.

Grading	100%	98%	95%	90%	80%	70%	60%

ISU OLYMPIC — .22 Short, similar to Model 102/103 Olympic series, grooved front and back straps, 6¾ in. barrel with det. muzzle brake & wts. avail., brown plastic grips standard or walnut checkered grips optional.

	$1,150	$950	$595	$430	$330	$280	$240

The High Standard catalog number for this model was 9237-9299.

CONVERSION KITS MODEL 102/103/104 — Cat. # 9263 Olympic to Supermatic Citation, 6¾ Bbl., Cat. # 9264 Olympic to Supermatic Citation, 8 Bbl., Cat. # 9265 Olympic to Supermatic Citation, 10 Bbl., Cat. # 9283 Supermatic Citation to Olympic, 6¾ Bbl., Cat. # 9284 Supermatic Citation to Olympic, 8 Bbl., Cat. # 9285 Supermatic Citation to Olympic, 10 Bbl., Cat. # 9286 Supermatic Trophy to Olympic, 6¾ Bbl., Cat. # 9287 Supermatic Trophy to Olympic, 8 Bbl., Cat. # 9288 Supermatic Trophy to Olympic, 10 Bbl.

	$500	$450	$400	$325	$275	$225	$195

Add $100 for Trophy Conversions.
Add $125 for 8 in. barrel.
Add $225 for 10 in. barrel.

HIGH STANDARD DID NOT HAVE A MODEL 105 SERIES

MILITARY MODEL 106 SERIES

This series was mfg. 1965-1968. This new military model features a walnut checkered grip and a frame that has the exact heft and feel of the famous Military 45. This military model features a new slide and a new adj. rear bridge or saddle type sight, permanently fixed to the frame. Front and rear grip straps are stippled and a new design magazine has an extension foot. Removable stabilizer and wts. available on all models. Beginning serial no. for 106 series was approx. 1,436,000-2,030,000.

SUPERMATIC TOURNAMENT MILITARY — bottom of the line .22 long rifle target pistol, smooth front & back straps, slide mounted rear sight instead of bridge sight, 5½ in. bull or 6¾ in. straight barrel with military grips.

	$595	$490	$375	$275	$215	$180	$155

Add $100 for 9230-31.
The High Standard catalog no. 9230-31 was disc. early 1966 (supplied with extra mag). 9232-33 became available 1966.

SUPERMATIC CITATION MILITARY — middle of the line .22 long rifle target pistol, stippled front & back straps, 5½ in. bull barrel or 7¼ in. fluted barrel, new rear bridge or saddle type sight.

	$825	$695	$475	$350	$270	$230	$195

Add $150 for 9240-41.
The High Standard catalog no. 9240-41 was disc. early 1966, (supplied with extra mag., muzzle brake, and weights). 9242-43 became available 1966.

SUPERMATIC TROPHY MILITARY — top-of-the-line .22 LR target pistol, stippled front and back straps, 5½ bull or 7¼ in. fluted barrel avail., gold plated trigger, safety and magazine release, gold filled lettering.

	$995	$825	$575	$425	$325	$275	$235

Add $200 for 9245-46.
The High Standard catalog number for this model 9245-46 was disc. early 1966, (supplied with extra mag., muzzle brake, weights, wrench and cleaning tool). 9247-48 became available 1966.

OLYMPIC MILITARY — .22 Short target pistol, 5½ in. bull barrel, back & front straps, stippled alloy slide, bridge rear sight, military grips, supplied with extra mag. and weights. Disc. early 1966.

	$1,095	$895	$575	$425	$325	$275	$235

The High Standard catalog number for this model was 9235.

Grading	100%	98%	95%	90%	80%	70%	60%

OLYMPIC ISU MILITARY — .22 Short target pistol, 6¾ in. tapered barrel with integral stabilizer and wts., front and back straps stippled, rear bridge or saddle type sight, military grips, supplied with extra mag. and weights. Disc. 1966.

| | $1,150 | $950 | $575 | $425 | $325 | $275 | $235 |

Add $150 for 9236.

The High Standard catalog number for this model was 9236. The Model 9238 became available 1966.

MODEL 107 SERIES

The Military 107 Series was mfg. 1968-1972. However, 107 unmarked variations were mfg. 1973-75. ML prefix variations were mfg. 1975 - mid-1981 are also covered within this grouping. The 107 series is basically identical to the Military Model 106 Series. Serial no. range is approx. 2,030,000-2,300,000. In 1968 the company was sold to the Leisure Group, Inc.

SUPERMATIC TOURNAMENT — similar to Model 106 series, this was the last of the Tournament pistols, adj. sight replace the bridge sight, 5½ bull or 6¾ in. tapered barrel. Disc. 1971.

| | $595 | $495 | $375 | $275 | $215 | $180 | $155 |

The High Standard catalog number for this model was 9232-33.

SUPERMATIC CITATION — similar to Model 106 series, middle of the line target pistol, 7¼ fluted and 5½ in. bull barrel available.

| | $825 | $695 | $475 | $340 | $260 | $220 | $185 |

The High Standard catalog number for this model was 9242-43.

SUPERMATIC TROPHY — similar to Model 106 series, Top-of-the-Line target pistol.

| | $950 | $775 | $595 | $425 | $325 | $265 | $225 |

The High Standard catalog number for this model was 9247-48.

OLYMPIC ISU — .22 short target pistol for Olympic Style Rapid Fire Events. 6¾ in. fluted barrel with integral stabilizer & two det. wts.

| | $1,150 | $950 | $550 | $395 | $325 | $265 | $225 |

The High Standard catalog number for this model was 9238.

THE VICTOR — introduced 1972, newest and most expensive production target pistol, all steel vented rib running length of barrel until 1974 when it changed to an alloy VR/SR, early adj. sight located on rear of barrel on rib., .22 long rifle built on a military frame, walnut grips, available in 4½ or 5½ in. barrel, push-button takedown, stippled front and rear straps, 10 shot mag., barrel slab sided, wts. are rectangular. Mfg. in Hamden, CT. Stamped "THE VICTOR" on left side of barrel.

| | $825 | $675 | $520 | $375 | $295 | $235 | $200 |

Add $100 for 4½ in. barrel.

The High Standard catalog number for the vent. rib model was catalog number 9216-17.

NUMBERED SERIES

In 1973, High Standard stopped marking the series numbers (either 104 or 107) on the guns. These guns just carry the normal seven digit serial number and are sometimes referred to as "NUMBERED SERIES" or "UNNUMBERED SERIES" or "SEVEN- NUMBER SERIES". These pistols include the following - the Sport King, Sharpshooter, Supermatic Citation, Supermatic Trophy, The Victor, and the ISU Olympic (in both military and slant grip models). The serial number range for these guns is 2,330,000 to 2,500,000.

H

Grading	100%	98%	95%	90%	80%	70%	60%

PLINKER — .22 long rifle, introduced in 1970-73. Successor to Duramatic and identical in almost all aspects. Thumb screw takedown.

| | $365 | $295 | $225 | $160 | $115 | $100 | $85 |

Early guns were marked M-101, R.H. slide 1970-71.
The High Standard catalog number for this model was 9214-15.

SPORT KING — similar to Series 102/103, 4½ or 4¾ in. barrel.

| | $365 | $295 | $240 | $170 | $130 | $115 | $100 |

The High Standard catalog number for this Model was 9200-01.

SPORT KING (NICKEL PLATED) — .22 LR, this was a nickel plated Sport King with black slanted plastic grips with silver medallion insert on grip. Mfg. 1974-77.

| | $415 | $345 | $275 | $195 | $145 | $125 | $105 |

The High Standard catalog number for this Model was 9208-09.

SHARPSHOOTER — .22 LR, successor to the Tournament, introduced in 1969 as part of the Model 103 Series, new model using the slant model grip frame, 5½ in. bull barrel only.

| | $575 | $450 | $325 | $250 | $195 | $165 | $140 |

The High Standard catalog number for this Model was 9205.

SUPERMATIC CITATION — identical to 104 Series, 5½ in. bull barrel only.

| | $875 | $725 | $525 | $375 | $290 | $245 | $210 |

The High Standard catalog number for this Model was 9244.

SUPERMATIC CITATION MILITARY — .22 LR, similar to 107 Series.

| | $795 | $625 | $450 | $325 | $255 | $215 | $185 |

The High Standard catalog number for this Model was 9242-43.

SUPERMATIC TROPHY MILITARY — .22 LR, similar to 107 Series.

| | $950 | $795 | $550 | $395 | $325 | $265 | $225 |

The High Standard catalog number for this Model was 9247-48.

ISU OLYMPIC — identical to 104 Series, 6¾ in. barrel.

| | $1,150 | $950 | $550 | $395 | $325 | $265 | $225 |

The High Standard catalog number for this Model was 9237.

ISU OLYMPIC MILITARY — .22 Short cal., otherwise identical to 107 series.

| | $1,150 | $950 | $550 | $395 | $325 | $265 | $225 |

The High Standard catalog number for this Model was 9238.

THE VICTOR — slant grip, mfg. 1973-74.

| | $2,750 | $2,250 | $1,600 | $1,150 | $885 | $725 | $615 |

Add $75 for early steel rib.
Add $200 for solid rib.
Add $150 for 4½ in. barrel.
The High Standard catalog numbers for this model were: 4½ vent. rib, 9218 mfg. 1973-74.
5½ vent. rib, 9219 mfg. 1973-74. 4½ solid rib, 9226 mfg. 1974 only. 5½ solid rib, 9229
mfg. 1974 only.

THE VICTOR — .22 LR cal., similar to 107 series, Hamden mfg., military grips, in 1974, an aluminum vent. rib was used to lighten this variation, a solid rib was also available.

| | $795 | $675 | $475 | $350 | $270 | $230 | $195 |

Add $150 for solid rib.
Add $75 for steel rib.
Add $100 for 4½ in. barrel.
The High Standard catalog number for the solid rib with military grips was 9206-11. The
vent. rib model was catalog number 9216-17.

Grading	100%	98%	95%	90%	80%	70%	60%

G PREFIX SERIES

Identical to 103/104 series (most models retained the same HS catalog no.) Due to the GCA of 1968, High Standard decided to serialize their rifles and shotguns beginning with ser. no. 3,000,000. In 1975, handgun serialization (pistols, revolvers, and derringers) was up to ser. no. 2,500,000 and High Standard felt they needed an alternate serial number system before handgun serialization reached 3,000,000. They decided to use the following prefixes - G for slant grip pistols, ML for military grip pistols, R for revolvers, and D for derringers. These prefixes were followed by the 5 digit ser. no. This is the last of the slant grip pistols.

SPORT KING — identical to 102/103 series, $4\frac{1}{2}$ or $6\frac{3}{4}$ in. barrel. Disc. 1977.

		$365	$295	$215	$165	$140	$120	$100

The High Standard catalog numbers for this model were 9200-01.

SPORT KING (NICKEL PLATED) — identical to 102/103 series, nickel plated, $4\frac{1}{2}$ or $6\frac{3}{4}$ in. barrel. Disc. 1977.

		$425	$350	$260	$190	$145	$125	$105

The High Standard catalog numbers for this model were 9208-09.

SHARPSHOOTER — identical to 103 series, $5\frac{1}{2}$ in. bull barrel only. Disc. 1977.

		$525	$400	$325	$250	$195	$165	$140

The High Standard catalog number for this Model was 9205.

SUPERMATIC CITATION — identical to numbered series, $5\frac{1}{2}$ in. bull barrel only. Disc. 1976.

		$775	$650	$450	$335	$225	$215	$185

The High Standard catalog number for this model was 9244.

OLYMPIC ISU — identical to numbered series, $6\frac{3}{4}$ in. tapered barrel. Disc. 1977.

		$1,150	$950	$550	$425	$315	$270	$230

The High Standard catalog no. for this Model was 9237.

ML PREFIX SERIES

As mentioned in the G Prefix section, High Standard revised their serial numbering system in 1975 from a 7 digit serial number to a five digit serial number with an ML prefix. These guns are basically identical to the guns listed in the 107 series category, but are listed here for chronological and value reasons. Mfg. mid-1975 through 1981. Guns with serial numbers between ML1,000 and ML24,999 were manufactured in Hamden, CT. Guns with serial numbers between ML25,000 and ML87,000 were manufactured in East Hartford, CT.

SPORT KING — .22 LR cal., similar to previous Sport Kings, but they now use military grips. Some of these Sport Kings were labeled "SPORT KING-M". Mfg. 1977-1981 in East Hartford only.

		$365	$295	$215	$155	$120	$100	$85

The High Standard catalog number for this model was 9258-59.

SHARPSHOOTER — .22 LR, some of the Sharpshooters with military grips were labeled "SHARPSHOOTER-M". Mfg. 1979-1981 in East Hartford only.

		$525	$415	$315	$225	$175	$150	$130

The High Standard catalog number for this model was 9210.

▲ *Sharpshooter Survival Pack* — introduced 1981, includes Sharpshooter –M– pistol, electroless nickel, push-button take down, packaged in canvas carrying case with extra nickel magazine, $5\frac{1}{2}$ in. bull barrel.

		$695	$550	$415	$300	$230	$195	$165

The High Standard catalog number for this model was 9424.

Grading	100%	98%	95%	90%	80%	70%	60%

SUPERMATIC CITATION MILITARY — .22 LR cal., similar to previous model.

	100%	98%	95%	90%	80%	70%	60%
	$750	$650	$425	$325	$245	$210	$180

Deduct 10% for East Hartford model.
The High Standard catalog number for this model was 9242-43.

SUPERMATIC TROPHY MILITARY — .22 LR cal., similar to previous series.

	100%	98%	95%	90%	80%	70%	60%
	$950	$795	$525	$385	$295	$255	$215

Deduct 10% for East Hartford model.
The High Standard catalog number for this model was 9247-48.

SUPERMATIC ISU OLYMPIC MILITARY — .22 Short target pistol, similar to previous model. Disc. 1981.

	100%	98%	95%	90%	80%	70%	60%
	$1,150	$950	$525	$395	$300	$255	$215

Deduct 10% for East Hartford model.
The High Standard catalog number for this model was 9238 (disc. 1977).

THE VICTOR — .22 LR, similar to previous model, military grip, vent. or solid rib. Last solid rib mfg. in 1977. Later Victors in this series were stamped simply "VICTOR" above triggerguard.

	100%	98%	95%	90%	80%	70%	60%
	$795	$675	$475	$340	$260	$220	$185

Add $150 for solid rib models.
Add $100 for 4½ in. barrel length.
Deduct 10% for East Hartford models.
The High Standard catalog number for this model was 9216-17, catalog number for the solid rib model was 9206-9211 (disc. 1977).

10-X — specifically designed for top flight shooting, 5½ in. bull barrel, push-button takedown. This model used hand-picked parts and was precisely assembled by a High Standard Master Gunsmith (with his initials under the left grip of each gun). Black matte finish, black painted walnut grips, stippled front and back straps. Mfg. 1980 in East Hartford.

▲ *Push Button Barrel Release*

	100%	98%	95%	90%	80%	70%	60%
	$2,750	$2,275	$1,625	$1,195	$925	$715	$595

The High Standard catalog number for this model was 9372.

SH SERIES

This was the last series of High Standard pistols and can be differentiated 107/Unnumbered/ML series by the mechanical differences within the frame assembly. Mfg. from mid 1981-1984. Serial No. range was approx. 10,000-35,000 and is prefixed "SH". Features a new barrel release in place of the push button takedown. An allenhead screw attached the frame to the barrel. A few guns were mfg. with push-button takedown from parts left over from the previous series. Also, some guns in this series have a "V" suffix.

SPORT KING — similar to ML series, except has allen screw take down, 4½ or 6¾ in. barrel.

	100%	98%	95%	90%	80%	70%	60%
	$335	$265	$195	$145	$110	$95	$80

The High Standard catalog number for this model was 9258-59 (disc. 1983).

SPORT KING — .22 LR, SH prefix serial no. with allen screw takedown, military grips with new electroless nickel model available. Mfg. 1982-84.

	100%	98%	95%	90%	80%	70%	60%
	$395	$350	$245	$175	$135	$115	$100

This model was also called the "SPORT KING-M".
The High Standard catalog number for this model was 9450-51.

SHARPSHOOTER — .22 , SH prefix serial no. with allen screw takedown, military grips. Mfg. 1982.

	100%	98%	95%	90%	80%	70%	60%
	$450	$375	$295	$215	$170	$145	$125

This model was also sometimes called "SHARPSHOOTER-M".
The High Standard catalog number for this model was 9210 (disc. 1982).

Grading	100%	98%	95%	90%	80%	70%	60%

SUPERMATIC CITATION MILITARY — .22 LR, SH prefix, similar to previous Citation model with allen screw takedown, military grips. Disc. May 1982.

| | $550 | $450 | $385 | $280 | $215 | $185 | $160 |

The High Standard catalog number for this model was 9242-43.

CITATION II — .22 LR, 10 shot, new variation of the Supermatic Citation, 5½ and 7¼ in. barrels, checkered military-type wood grips, allen screw takedown, SH prefix serial no., slabbed sided barrel, electroless nickel model also available, this model replaced the Sharpshooter. Mfg. 1983-84.

| | $595 | $495 | $400 | $290 | $225 | $190 | $165 |

The High Standard catalog number for this model was 9348-49.

SUPERMATIC TROPHY MILITARY — .22 LR, similar to previous Trophy Model with SH prefix, allen screw takedown, military grips.

| | $625 | $550 | $425 | $350 | $275 | $235 | $195 |

The High Standard catalog number for this model was 9247-48.

VICTOR — .22 LR, similar to previous Victor, new allen screw takedown, SH prefix, military grips, 5½ in. vent. barrel only mfg. in this Victor Series, some Victor serial no.'s had a "V" suffix.

| | $650 | $550 | $425 | $300 | $235 | $195 | $165 |

The High Standard catalog number for this model was 9217.

10X — .22 LR, high quality gun similar to previous 10X, but with allen screw takedown, a High Standard 10X Victor was also offered. These had a 5½ in. vented victor rib; only a few were mfg., limited mfg. also in 7¼ in. fluted barrel.

▲ *Allen Screw Barrel Release*

| | $2,350 | $1,900 | $1,425 | $995 | $795 | $675 | $575 |

Add $1,250 for Victor VR model.

Add $1,000 for fluted barrel.

The High Standard catalog number for this model was 9234-9249-9372.

SURVIVAL PACK — Sharpshooter "M" or Citation II electroless nickel, allen screw takedown, packaged in canvas carrying case with extra nickel magazine. Disc. 1984.

| | $575 | $475 | $395 | $275 | $215 | $185 | $160 |

The High Standard catalog number for this model was 9424.

COMMEMORATIVE MODELS

1972 OLYMPIC COMMEMORATIVE — a highly engraved version of a Supermatic Trophy Military, Model 107, in .22 LR, has 5 Olympic gold rings on right side of receiver, Ser. no. has a "T" prefix, high polish blue finish, 5½ in. bull barrel, lined presentation case avail. Limited edition of 1,000 guns, but it is believed only about 175-200 of these pistols were manufactured due to their high price, issue price was $550. Mfg. 1972-1974 only.

| | $3,850 | $2,950 | $1,750 |

1974 retail on this model was $605. Early models were marked "MODEL 107", and were not hi-polished.

The High Standard catalog number for this model was 9207.

1980 OLYMPIC COMMEMORATIVE — .22 Short, an ISU Olympic Military with 6¾ in. tapered barrel with integral stabilizer and weights. Has 5 Olympic gold rings on right side of receiver. Produced in a limited edition of 1,000 guns. Ser. no. has a "USA" prefix, blue finish, lined presentation case avail. Mfg. 1980 only.

| | $1,395 | $900 | $600 |

The High Standard catalog number for this model was 9239.

Grading	100%	98%	95%	90%	80%	70%	60%

CONVERSION KITS

These kits convert .22 LR to .22 Short, contain an alloy slide with vent. rib, barrel weight, and two Short mags., kit comes in "gun size box" set in styrofoam. These kits were designated either #9370 or #9371 when mfg., depending on the pistol to be converted.

VICTOR KIT — this model was designated #9370 when in mfg.

	$550	$450	$350

TROPHY/CITATION KIT — this kit also includes a stabilizer. This model was designated #9371 when in mfg.

	$550	$450	$350

DERRINGERS

FIRST MODEL — double action only O/U, .22 S, L, or LR, or .22 WMR, 2 shot, 3½ in. barrels, blue or nickel. Black or white grips. D-100, D-101, DM-101 appears on left side of gun. The first derringer was mfg. about 1962 in Hamden, CT.

	$225	$195	$175	$145	$125	$100	$90

Add $30 for nickel finish.

LATE MODELS — double action only O/U, .22 S, L, or LR, or .22 WMR 2 shot, 3½ in. barrels, blue or nickel, plastic grips. Mfg. in E. Hartford 1978-84.

▲ *Blue Finish* — .22 LR or .22 Mag. This model was designated #9193 and #9194 when in mfg.

	$225	$195	$175	$145	$125	$100	$90

▲ *Nickel Finish* — .22 Mag.

	$250	$220	$195	$170	$140	$110	$100

▲ *Electroless Nickel* — included walnut grips. This model was designated #9420-21.

	$295	$250	$185

▲ *Silver plated* — includes presentation case. 500 mfg. This model was designated #9341. Ser. no. has "SP" prefix.

	$495	$450	$300

▲ *Gold plated* — introduced in 1965. Includes presentation case. This model was designated #9195 Ser. No. has "GP" prefix. Mfg. 1964-65.

	$495	$450	$300

Add 120% for a cased, matched set with consecutive serial numbers (mfg. 1965 only).

REVOLVERS

Add 20% for extra convertible cylinder (.22 LR/.22 Mag.) on those models listed below that apply.

SENTINEL — .22 LR, 9 shot, swing out cylinder, 3, 4, or 6 in. barrel, aluminum frame, made 1955-1956.

	100%	98%	95%	90%	80%	70%	60%
Blue finish	$120	$110	$100	$95	$85	$70	$55
Nickel finish	$130	$120	$110	$105	$95	$85	$65
Pink finish	$295	$265	$230	$200	$180	$160	$140
Yellow finish	$295	$265	$230	$200	$180	$160	$140

SENTINEL IMPERIAL — similar to Sentinel, with adj. sights, walnut grips, made 1962-1965.

	100%	98%	95%	90%	80%	70%	60%
Blue finish	$140	$125	$115	$110	$100	$90	$75
Nickel finish	$150	$140	$125	$120	$110	$100	$90

SENTINEL DELUXE — similar to Sentinel, except adj. sights, wide trigger, 4 and 6 in. barrel, square butt, made 1957-1974.

	100%	98%	95%	90%	80%	70%	60%
Blue finish	$140	$125	$115	$110	$100	$90	$75
Nickel finish	$150	$140	$115	$120	$110	$100	$90

H

Grading	100%	98%	95%	90%	80%	70%	60%

SENTINEL SNUB — similar to Deluxe, except checkered bird's-head grip, 2⅜ in. barrel.

Blue finish	$145	$140	$130	$120	$110	$90	$85
Nickel finish	$155	$150	$145	$130	$120	$100	$95

DURANGO — .22 LR, double action, steel frame, 4½ and 5½ in. barrel, wood grips, made 1971-1973.

Blue finish	$145	$130	$120	$95	$85	$70	$55
Nickel finish	$150	$140	$125	$105	$95	$85	$65

HOMBRE DOUBLE ACTION — similar to Double Nine steel frame, but no ejector rod housing, 4½ in. barrel, made 1971-1973.

Blue finish	$125	$120	$110	$105	$95	$85	$65
Nickel finish	$140	$130	$120	$115	$105	$95	$75

LONGHORN STEEL FRAME — similar to Double Nine, except 9½ in. barrel.

Fixed sights	$210	$170	$150	$120	$110	$105	$85
Adj. sights	$165	$155	$150	$130	$120	$115	$95

HIGH SIERRA — similar to Double Nine steel frame, except 7 in. octagon barrel, gold plated grip frame. Discontinued in 1984. Add $10 for adj. sights.

Fixed sights	$235	$175	$150	$130	$120	$105	$90

KIT GUN — .22 LR, swing out cylinder, 9 shot, 4 in. barrel, adj. sights, blue, walnut grips, made 1970-1973.

	$155	$145	$140	$125	$115	$105	$85

DOUBLE NINE — .22 LR, Western style double action, 5½ in. barrel, aluminum frame, simulated stag, ebony or ivory grips, made 1959-1984.

Blue finish	$235	$180	$160	$140	$120	$105	$90
Nickel finish (disc. 1982)	$245	$190	$170	$150	$130	$115	$100

POSSE — similar to Double Nine aluminum, except 3½ in. barrel, blue, brass grip frame, walnut grips, made 1961-1966.

	$120	$110	$95	$90	$85	$70	$55

NATCHEZ — similar to Double Nine aluminum, except has bird's-head grip, made 1961-1966.

	$120	$110	$100	$90	$85	$70	$55

LONGHORN ALUMINUM FRAME — similar to Natchez, but 4½, 5½, and 9½ in. barrel, longhorn hammer spur, made 1961-1966.

	$145	$130	$110	$100	$85	$70	$55

▲ *9½ in. model* — Discontinued in 1984.

	$250	$190	$160	$140	$120	$100	$90

CAMP GUN DOUBLE ACTION — .22 LR or .22 Win. Mag., 6 in. barrel, blue, adj. rear sight, checkered walnut grips, made 1976-1984.

	$250	$185	$165	$145	$125	$110	$100

SENTINEL 1 DOUBLE ACTION — .22 LR, 2, 3, and 4 in. barrel, 9 shot, smooth walnut grips, made 1974-1984.

Blue finish	$235	$180	$160	$140	$120	$105	$90
Nickel finish	$250	$195	$175	$150	$130	$110	$95

Blue w/adj. sights — add $15 to above prices.

SENTINEL MARK IV DOUBLE ACTION — similar to Sentinel 1, except .22 WRM.

Blue finish	$145	$140	$125	$120	$115	$95	$90
Nickel finish	$155	$150	$140	$130	$125	$105	$100

▲ *Adj. sights*

	$160	$155	$150	$145	$125	$115	$100

H

Grading	100%	98%	95%	90%	80%	70%	60%

SENTINEL MARK II DOUBLE ACTION — .357 Mag., 6 shot, double action, 2½, 4, and 6 in. barrel, blue, fixed sights, wood grips, made 1974-1976.

	100%	98%	95%	90%	80%	70%	60%
	$225	$190	$165	$155	$150	$140	$130

SENTINEL MARK III DOUBLE ACTION — similar to Mark II, except adj. sights.

	100%	98%	95%	90%	80%	70%	60%
	$250	$220	$185	$175	$170	$160	$150

CRUSADER — .357 Mag., .44 Mag. or .45 LC, double action employing gear assembly, swing-out cylinder, unique action, adj. sights, limited mfg. starting 1976 because of expensive fabrication.

	100%	98%	95%	90%	80%	70%	60%
	$575	$495	$440	$395	$360	$320	$295

Add 10% for NIB condition.

LIMITED EDITIONS

GRISWOLD & GUNNISON — copy of Confederate Revolver, 7½ in. barrel, 500 mfg. in 1974.

$250 $195 $150

Last Mfg.'s Sug. Retail was $175.

LEECH & RIGDON — black powder commemorative, 500 mfg. in 1974.

$250 $195 $150

Last Mfg.'s Sug. Retail was $175.

PRESIDENTIAL DERRINGER — limited mfg. in 1974-77. Cased.

$500 $400 $295

Last Mfg.'s Sug. Retail was $150.

SCHNEIDER & GLASSICK — 1,000 mfg. in 1975 only.

$325 $250 $175

Last Mfg.'s Sug. Retail was $325.

CRUSADER 50TH ANNIVERSARY — .44 Mag. or .45 LC cal., approx. 50 mfg. for each cal. in 8⅜ in. barrel with ⅓ coverage engraving (ser. no. 1-50). Also, advertising materials at the time listed 450 revolvers of each cal. in a 6 in. barrel (ser. no. 51-500). Cased. Mfg. in 1977 only.

Standard Model w/o engraving $1,550 $1,250 $975

Limited availability might affect asking prices considerably. Two gun sets with matching serial numbers were also available - current asking prices are over $3,250.

BICENTENNIAL BLACK POWDER — .36 cal., 1776-1976 bicentennial edition with belt buckle. Cased.

$525 $395 $300

RIFLES

SPORT KING FIELD MODEL — .22 S (hi-speed), .22 L, .22 LR, semi-auto, tube mag., 22 in. barrel, open sight, plain pistol grip stock, made 1960-1966.

	100%	98%	95%	90%	80%	70%	60%
	$100	$90	$85	$75	$65	$55	$45

SPORT KING SPECIAL — similar to Field, except beavertail forearm and Monte Carlo stock.

	100%	98%	95%	90%	80%	70%	60%
	$140	$120	$95	$90	$75	$65	$55

SPORT KING CARBINE — similar to Field, except 18 in. barrel, straight grip, barrel band and sling, made 1964-1973.

	100%	98%	95%	90%	80%	70%	60%
	$170	$150	$120	$110	$100	$90	$85

SPORT KING DELUXE — similar to Special, but stock checkered, made 1966-1975.

	100%	98%	95%	90%	80%	70%	60%
	$185	$160	$140	$115	$90	$75	$65

HI-POWER FIELD BOLT ACTION — Mauser type action, .270, .30-06, 4 shot mag., 22 in. barrel, folding rear sight, plain stock, made 1962-1966.

	100%	98%	95%	90%	80%	70%	60%
	$295	$230	$210	$195	$180	$165	$150

Grading	100%	98%	95%	90%	80%	70%	60%

HI-POWER DELUXE — similar to Field, except checkered Monte Carlo stock, swivels, made 1962-1966.

	$350	$285	$240	$220	$205	$195	$165

FLITE KING SLIDE ACTION — .22 S, L, or LR, 24 in. barrel, tube mag., hammerless, patridge sight, Monte Carlo stock with pistol grip, semi beavertail forearm, made 1962-1975.

	$120	$105	$95	$85	$65	$60	$50

SHOTGUNS

SUPERMATIC FIELD GRADE — 12 ga., 28 and 30 in. barrel, mod. or full, gas operated semi-auto, plain pistol grip stock, made 1960-1966.

	$205	$185	$175	$160	$145	$140	$120

SUPERMATIC SPECIAL — 12 ga., similar to Field, 27 in. barrel, adj. choke, made 1960-1966.

	$210	$195	$180	$165	$150	$145	$125

SUPERMATIC DELUXE — similar to Field, except vent. rib, checkered stock and forearm, made 1961-1966.

	$265	$225	$200	$175	$160	$155	$140

SUPERMATIC TROPHY — similar to Deluxe, except 27 in. barrel, adj. choke.

	$235	$215	$205	$180	$165	$160	$145

SUPERMATIC DUCK — similar to Field, except 3 in. Mag., 30 in. full barrel, recoil pad, made 1961-1966.

	$275	$235	$190	$160	$145	$125	$110

SUPERMATIC DUCK VENT RIB — similar to Duck, vent. rib, checkered stock and forearm, made 1961-1966.

	$295	$250	$210	$175	$150	$130	$115

SUPERMATIC DEER GUN — similar to Field, except 22 in. cylinder bore barrel, rifle sights, checkered stock and forearm, recoil pad, made 1965.

	$230	$210	$200	$185	$165	$155	$140

SUPERMATIC SKEET — similar to Deluxe Rib, except 26 in. barrel, skeet bore, made 1962-1966.

	$300	$260	$225	$195	$175	$160	$150

SUPERMATIC TRAP — similar to Skeet, except 30 in. full barrel, trap stock with pad, made 1962-1966.

	$245	$230	$220	$205	$185	$170	$160

Note: All preceding models, except Deer and Trap, chambered only for 20 ga., 3 in. Mag. values are $10 higher.

High Standard restyled the Supermatic Autoloader in 1966. The new model Supermatics are recognized by the new checkering pattern and jeweled bolt. All models previously listed were offered, 12 and 20 ga. values are $25 higher per model. All are considered deluxe models. They were discontinued in 1975.

FLITE KING PUMP FIELD GRADE — 12, 20, 28, or .410 ga., slide action, 26, 28, or 30 in. barrel, imp. cyl., mod., or full choke, plain pistol grip stock and slide, made 1960-1966.

	$165	$150	$140	$130	$120	$110	$100

FLITE KING SPECIAL — 12, 20, 28, or .410 ga., similar to Pump Field, except 27 in. barrel, adj. choke, made 1960-1966.

	$155	$130	$120	$110	$100	$90	$80

FLITE KING DELUXE RIB — 12, 20, 28, or .410 ga., similar to Pump Special, except vent. rib, checkered stock, made 1961-1966.

	$195	$175	$170	$165	$155	$140	$125

H

Grading	100%	98%	95%	90%	80%	70%	60%

FLITE KING TROPHY — 12, 20, 28, or .410 ga., similar to Deluxe Rib, except 27 in. vent. rib barrel, adj. choke, made 1960-1966.

	$200	$180	$175	$170	$160	$145	$130

FLITE KING BRUSH — 12 ga. only, similar to Field, except 18 or 20 in. cylinder bore barrel, rifle sights, made 1962-1964.

	$185	$170	$165	$160	$150	$140	$120

FLITE KING BRUSH DELUXE — 12 ga. only, similar to Brush, except adj. aperture rear sight, checkered stock, recoil pad, swivels and sling, 20 in. barrel only, made 1964-1966.

	$265	$230	$195	$170	$155	$145	$130

FLITE KING SKEET — 12, 20, 28, or .410 ga. only, similar to Deluxe Rib, except 26 in. vent. rib, skeet bore, made 1962-1966.

	$265	$230	$195	$170	$155	$145	$130

Add 35% for 28 or .410 ga.

FLITE KING TRAP — 12 ga. only, similar to Deluxe Rib, except 30 in. vent. rib, full choke and pad, made 1962-1966.

	$250	$220	$195	$165	$150	$140	$125

Note: Flite King is available in 16 ga. also, except for the Brush, Skeet, and Trap models. Values are about $20 less per model. A .410 bore was offered in all models that were offered in 20 ga., except the Special and Trophy models. Values are generally the same per model.

High Standard restyled the Flite King in 1966. The new models have a jeweled bolt and new checkering pattern. These new guns were available as Deluxe, Deluxe Rib, Brush, Brush Deluxe, Skeet Deluxe, and Trap Deluxe. Their values are about $20 higher per model.

The new redesigned Flite King was also offered in Deluxe, Deluxe Rib, and Deluxe Skeet, in 20, 28, and .410 ga.'s.

MODEL 10B — 12 ga. combat shotgun, 18 in. barrel, semi-auto, unique design incorporates raked pistol grip in front of receiver and metal shoulder pad attached directly to rear of receiver, black cycolac plastic shroud and pistol grip, folding carrying handle, provisions made for attaching a small flashlight to receiver top, extended blade front sight, very compact size (28 in. overall). Discontinued.

	$650	$575	$500	$425	$375	$325	$275

The predecessor to this model was the 10A. This variation had the flashlight built in.

RIOT SHOTGUN — 18 or 20 in. barrel, police riot gun was also offered until 1975. This was a reliable weapon available with or without rifle sights, 12 ga. only on the Flite King Action.

	$195	$165	$155	$140	$130	$120	$115

SUPERMATIC INDY O/U — this model was mfg. in Japan by Nikko and imported in 1974 and 1975, boxlock, fully engraved receiver, selective auto ejectors and single trigger, 12 ga., $27\frac{1}{2}$ sk & sk, $29\frac{1}{2}$ imp. mod. and full, or full and full, trap air flow aluminum vent. rib, checkered (skipline) pistol grip stock with pad and vent. forearm.

	$925	$830	$760	$700	$645	$590	$530

SUPERMATIC SHADOW SEVEN O/U — similar to Indy O/U, except less elaborate engraving, unvented forearm, standard vent. rib, regular checkering, no recoil pad, imported 1974-1975.

	$760	$685	$615	$540	$490	$440	$400

SUPERMATIC SHADOW AUTO — 12 and 20 ga., $2\frac{3}{4}$ or 3 in. chambers in 12 ga., air flow rib, 26 in. imp. cyl. or skeet, 28 in. mod., imp. mod. or full and 30 in. full or trap, checkered walnut stock, gas operated, imported 1974-1975.

	$390	$340	$290	$260	$225	$195	$165

HIGH STANDARD MANUFACTURING COMPANY, INC.

Manufacturer located in Houston, TX.

This new company was formed during 1993, utilizing many of the same employees and original material vendors that the original High Standard company used during their period of manufacture (1926-1984).

Grading	100%	98%	95%	90%	80%	70%	60%

PISTOLS

SPORT KING — .22 LR cal., 4½ or 6¾ in. barrel, blued finish, military grips, 10 shot mag. New late 1996.

As this edition went to press, prices for this model had yet to be established.

SUPERMATIC CITATION — .22 LR cal., 5½ or 7¼ (disc. 1995) in. barrel, matte blue or parkerized finish, military grips, 10 shot mag. New 1994.

Mfg.'s Sug. Retail	$446	$385	$310	$255	$225	$200	$185	$170

Subtract $30 for universal mount instead of open-sight rib.
Add $309 for .22 Short conversion kit (includes VR barrel, slide, and 2 mags.).

SUPERMATIC TOURNAMENT — .22 LR cal., choice of 4½ (disc. 1995), 5½, or 6¾ (disc. 1995) in. barrel, matte blue, non-adj. trigger, approx. 44 oz. New 1995.

Mfg.'s Sug. Retail	$399	$355	$290	$245	$210	$190	$170	$150

SUPERMATIC TROPHY — .22 LR cal., 5½ or 7¼ in. barrel, blued finish, military grips, 10 shot mag. New 1994.

Mfg.'s Sug. Retail	$516	$450	$350	$295	$250	$200	$185	$170

Add $20 for 7¼ in. barrel.
Add $309 for .22 Short conversion kit (includes VR barrel, slide, and 2 mags.).

VICTOR — .22 LR cal., 4½ or 5½ in. barrel, blue or parkerized (new 1995) finish, military grips, with open sight rib or universal mount (IISUM, blue only, new 1996), 10 shot mag., 45 oz. New 1994.

Mfg.'s Sug. Retail	$532	$465	$360	$300	$250	$200	$185	$170

Subtract $53 for universal mount (no open sight rib).
Add $397 for .22 Short conversion kit (includes VR barrel, slide, and 2 mags.).

▲ *Victor 10X* — parkerized finish, 5½ in. barrel only, built by Bob Shea, 45 oz. New 1996.

Mfg.'s Sug. Retail	$1,195	$1,075	$925	$825	$750	$625	$550	$495

CITATION MS — .22 LR cal., 10 in. barrel with (new 1996) or w/o RPM sights, matte blue finish, military grips, 10 shot mag., 49 oz. New 1994.

Mfg.'s Sug. Retail	$695	$615	$525	$450	$395	$335	$285	$225

Subtract $135 if w/o RPM sights.

OLYMPIC I.S.U. — .22 Short cal., 6¾ in. fluted barrel with integral muzzle brake, blued finish, military grips, 10 shot mag. Mfg. 1994-95 only.

	$550	$450	$385	$315	$250	$200	$185

Last Mfg.'s Sug. Retail was $625.

OLYMPIC MILITARY — .22 Short cal., 5½ in. fluted bull barrel with removable stabilizer, aluminum alloy slide with steel frame. New 1995.

Mfg.'s Sug. Retail	$536	$470	$365	$300	$250	$200	$185	$170

OLYMPIC RAPID FIRE — .22 Short cal., 4 in. VR barrel with integral muzzle brake and forward mounted compensator, gold-plated small parts, matte finish, special grips with rear support, adj. trigger, 46 oz. New 1996.

Mfg.'s Sug. Retail	$1,995	$1,800	$1,575	$1,300	$1,025	$875	$750	$625

10X — .22 LR cal., 5½ in. barrel, blued finish, military grips, High Standard's most accurate pistol, choice of either factory or Shea custom tuning, 10 shot mag., approx. 45 oz. New late 1994.

Grading		100%	98%	95%	90%	80%	70%	60%
▲ *Houston Mfg. 10X*								
Mfg.'s Sug. Retail	$869	$745	$625	$545	$465	$400	$325	$275
▲ *Custon Shea 10X* — limited mfg. (approx. 150 pistols annually), hand-built by Bob Shea. New 1995.								
Mfg.'s Sug. Retail	$1,095	$975	$875	$775	$675	$550	$495	$450

HISPANO ARGENTINO FABRICA DE AUTOMOVILES SA (HAFDASA)

Manufacturer located in Buenos Aires, Brazil.

This company manufactured both commercial and military contracts, including the Argentine Contract Model 1916 listed below (patterned after the Colt Government Model 1911).

ARGENTINE CONTRACT MODEL 1916 PISTOL — mfg. 1915, ser. nos. are in C20,001-C21,000 (1,000 pistols), marked with Argentine seal on top of the slide.

		$1,400	$1,000	$725	$575	$450	$410	$350

> This variation is not to be confused with the Ballester Molina Model (mfg. by Hispano Argentino Fabrica de Automoviles SA, Buenos Aires, Brazil - also known as the Hafdasa) with integral grip safety and mainspring housing (.45 ACP) that resembles a Colt 1911, but was not licensed or mfg. by Colt.

HOFER-JAGDWAFFEN, PETER

Master gunsmith located in Ferlach, Austria. Custom order only, best quality rifles (over 100 cals. available) and shotguns (O/U and SxS) made per individual order — prices typically start at $20,000+. Information can be obtained by writing to Mr. Hofer directly at: Peter Hofer-Jagdwaffen, Kirchgasse 24, A-9170 Ferlach, Austria, or FAXing him at: 0011-434227/3683/30.

HOLLAND & HOLLAND LTD.

Manufacturer located in London, England since 1835. All H&H long guns are built per individual special order. Orders may be placed directly with their recently opened office located in New York, NY or directly with the factory in England. Please refer to these listings in the Trademark Index for address, telephone, or FAX information.

HOLLAND & HOLLAND
Established 1835

Holland & Holland over the years has justly earned the reputation of producing some of the finest firearms ever manufactured. Their double rifles chambered for the black powder express cartridges are still among the most powerful rifles ever made, while exhibiting outstanding quality and superior craftsmanship. Most of these fine arms were made to order for the famous, wealthy, or royalty of their day. Because of the individual nature of each firearm, these early guns, as with any high grade item, must be individually appraised.

The early double rifles were proofed and regulated with the black powder guns of their day. These exposed hammer rifles were almost exclusively sold cased with accessories by Holland & Holland. They are seldom found on the market, and then not in the best of condition. Purchase of these as well as any high grade firearm should include trusted appraisal.

RIFLES: MODERN

ROOK RIFLE — .250, .295/.300, .360, .380 black powder cals., single shot, break-open action, various levels of embellishment - Royal Models were made but most Rook rifles were base models with few extra features. Values today range from $295 (average condition, small cal.) to $995 (larger cal., better wood, perhaps cased). Disc.

Grading	100%	98%	95%	90%	80%	70%	60%

BEST QUALITY MAGAZINE RIFLE — Mauser 98 (current mfg.) or Enfield (disc.) action, various cals., incl. .300 H&H Mag., .375 H&H Mag., 4 shot mag., 24 in. barrel, folding leaf sight, checkered French walnut stock available in traditional configuration or with Monte Carlo pattern.

Mfg.'s Sug. Retail	$20,800		$20,800	$15,700	$11,150	$7,500	$5,300	$4,250	$3,600

The values above represent the standard model without additional options (of which there are a wide array). Mfg. to customer specifications.

DE LUXE MAGAZINE RIFLE — similar to Best Quality, except with deluxe grade walnut and various engraving options, very limited mfg.

There is no standard base price on this model - rather, individual options are custom ordered and are individually priced.

NO. 2 MODEL DOUBLE RIFLE SxS — various British and American cals., 24-28 in. barrels, sidelock, folding leaf sight, checkered French walnut stock, auto ejectors.

	$15,000	$13,000	$11,000	$10,000	$9,000	$7,000	$6,500

ROYAL DOUBLE SxS RIFLE — available in most popular cals. between .250 and .577, similar to No. 2, except has deluxe finish and more engraving. Values listed below reflect most recent factory information.

▲ *.300 or .375 cal.*

Mfg.'s Sug. Retail	$73,740		$73,740	$47,350	$31,500	$25,500	$19,000	$16,000	$13,500

▲ *.465 cal.*

Mfg.'s Sug. Retail	$77,120		$77,120	$49,650	$33,000	$26,000	$20,000	$17,000	$14,000

▲ *.577 cal.*

Mfg.'s Sug. Retail	$84,200		$84,000	$55,000	$35,750	$27,000	$21,500	$18,000	$15,000

ROYAL DE LUXE SxS RIFLE — same cals. as the Royal Double SxS, top-of-the-line model, every refinement, built to individual order only with almost any option possible.

▲ *.240 H&H, 7mm H&H, or 8mm cal.*

Mfg.'s Sug. Retail	$93,000		$93,000	$63,750	$46,000	$40,000	$35,000	$30,000	$25,000

▲ *.275 H&H, .300 H&H, or 9.3mm cal.*

Mfg.'s Sug. Retail	$97,300		$97,300	$67,500	$48,000	$41,000	$35,000	$30,000	$25,000

▲ *.375 H&H or .465 H&H cal.*

Mfg.'s Sug. Retail	$101,700		$101,700	$70,500	$50,000	$42,350	$36,000	$31,000	$26,000

▲ *.577 NE or .600 NE cal.*

Mfg.'s Sug. Retail	$111,200		$111,200	$84,200	$55,000	$45,000	$39,500	$32,500	$27,250

H&H .700 BORE DOUBLE RIFLE — .700 H&H cal., 1,000 grain jacketed bullet, approx. 19 lbs. with 26 in. barrels chambered 3½ in. This is the largest caliber rifle available in the world today.

▲ *Royal Model*

Mfg.'s Sug. Retail	$115,920		$115,920	$98,500	$86,750	$78,500	$70,000	$62,500	$55,000

▲ *Royal De Luxe Model*

Mfg.'s Sug. Retail	$153,000		$153,000	$115,000	$93,500

SHOTGUNS: SINGLE SHOT AND SIDE BY SIDE

Holland & Holland currently manufactures the Royal De Luxe Game Gun and Royal Game Gun models in sidelock configuration (and are listed below). In addition to the sidelock models, H&H also manufactures the boxlock models Cavalier, Cavalier De Luxe, Northwood, and Northwood De Luxe. The values below assume standard model with double triggers, game rib, standard walnut, or casing. Additional special order features will add considerable value to the price of a new custom order.

In 1988, Holland & Holland absorbed W & C Scott and manufactured the Chatsworth, Bowood, and Kinmount boxlock models until they were discontinued in

Grading	100%	98%	95%	90%	80%	70%	60%

late 1990. H&H has phased this trademark out, and more information can be found in the W & C Scott section of this text.

SINGLE BARREL TRAP GUN — 12 ga., 30 or 32 in. full choke barrel, vent. rib, boxlock, auto ejector, Monte Carlo pistol grip stock, pad. Disc.

	$20,000	$15,000	$12,000	$10,000	$8,750	$6,750	$4,950

Last Mfg.'s Sug. Retail was $28,420.

▲ *Trap Guns - Older Mfg.*

	100%	98%	95%	90%	80%	70%	60%
Standard Grade	$5,000	$4,500	$4,000	$3,250	$2,500	$2,250	$2,000
De Luxe Grade	$8,250	$7,000	$6,250	$5,000	$4,500	$3,750	$3,000
Exhibition Grade	$10,500	$8,950	$7,500	$6,000	$5,500	$5,000	$4,250

NORTHWOOD SxS BOXLOCK — 12, 16 (disc. 1992), 20, or 28 (disc. 1992) ga., 28 or 30 in. barrels, scalloped-case colored receiver, boxlock, auto ejectors, double triggers, border engraving, checkered pistol grip or straight stock. The values shown below are for standard model. Disc. 1993.

	$5,950	$5,200	$4,450	$3,850	$3,300	$2,800	$2,300

Last Mfg.'s Sug. Retail was $6,705.

Add approx. 10% for 28 ga.

▲ *Northwood De Luxe* — 12, 16, 20, or 28 ga., scalloped-case colored receiver with moderate engraving and select walnut, double triggers. Disc. 1993.

	$6,375	$5,450	$4,600	$3,950	$3,350	$2,850	$2,400

Last Mfg.'s Sug. Retail was $7,450.

Add approx. 10% for 28 ga.

CAVALIER SxS BOXLOCK — 12, 20, or 28 (disc. 1992) ga., best quality model boxlock with scalloped frame, double triggers, ejectors, and case colored receiver. Disc.

	$9,500	$7,750	$6,350	$5,500	$4,850	$4,100	$3,500

Last Mfg.'s Sug. Retail was $11,175.

Add approx. 10% for 28 ga.

▲ *Cavalier De Luxe* — similar to Cavalier Model, except has deluxe walnut and better engraving. Disc. 1993.

	$9,950	$8,000	$6,500	$5,600	$4,950	$4,200	$3,600

Last Mfg.'s Sug. Retail was $11,920.

Add approx. 10% for 28 ga.

DOMINION GAME GUN — 12, 16, or 20 ga., 25-30 in. barrels, any choke, sidelock, auto ejectors, double triggers, checkered straight grip stock. Disc. 1990.

	$5,650	$4,750	$4,150	$3,650	$3,250	$2,850	$2,425

Add 20% for 20 gauge.

ROYAL HAMMERLESS EJECTOR SIDELOCK (NON-SELF OPENING) — 12, 16, 20, 28, or .410 ga., non-self opening, customer specifications as to barrel length and chokes, hand detachable sidelocks, stocked in pistol grip or straight style to specifications. Mfg. 1885-disc.

	$17,500	$14,750	$10,750	$9,000	$7,950	$6,950	$6,350

Add 20% for 20 gauge.
Add 40% for 28 gauge.
Add 60% for .410 gauge.
Subtract $1,000 without SST.
Above values are for older, previously manufactured specimens.

ROYAL GAME GUN — 12, 16, 20, 28 or .410 ga., best quality sidelock self opening game gun. Mfg. per individual customer specifications. Values below reflect most recent factory information. Mfg. 1922 to date.

Mfg.'s Sug. Retail	$48,050	$48,050	$31,500	$22,500	$17,500	$12,750	$10,500	$9,000

Add $5,070 for 28 or .410 ga.
Add $4,470 for ST.
Add $3,100 for VR (disc.).

ROYAL DE LUXE GAME GUN — 12, 16, 20, 28, or .410 ga., top-of-the-line sidelock self opening shotgun. Mfg. per individual customer specifications. Current production.

▲ *12, 16, or 20 ga.*

	Mfg.'s Sug. Retail	$63,500	$63,500	$38,000	$25,750	$18,500	$14,000	$11,250	$9,000

▲ *28 or .410 ga.*

	Mfg.'s Sug. Retail	$70,100	$70,100	$43,000	$29,250	$22,750	$17,500	$14,500	$9,950

Add $6,600 for 28 or .410 ga.
Add $4,470 for ST.
Add $3,100 for VR (disc.).

Older mfg. is sometimes referred to as the De Luxe Model.

BADMINTON SIDELOCK — similar to Royal model, without self opening action. Disc.

	$10,500	$9,000	$8,000	$7,000	$6,000	$5,000	$4,000

Add 20% for 20 gauge.
Add 40% for 28 gauge.
Add 60% for .410 gauge.
Add $1,000 for SST.

Above values are for older, previously manufactured specimens.

▲ *Badminton Game Gun* — 12 or 20 ga., double or single trigger. Disc. 1988.

	$20,000	$17,000	$14,500	$12,250	$10,000	$8,500	$6,750

Last Mfg.'s Sug. Retail was $28,000.

RIVIERA SIDELOCK — similar to Badminton model, with two sets of barrels. Mfg. until 1967.

	$15,000	$11,500	$9,500	$7,950	$7,100	$6,350	$5,600

Add 20% for 20 gauge.
Add 40% for 28 gauge.
Add 60% for .410 gauge.

CENTENARY SIDELOCK — 12 ga., 2 in. chambers, lightened version of Royal, Badminton, and Dominion grades. The values would be the same as for the standard models, mfg. until 1962.

SHOTGUNS: O/U

H&H has finalized the design elements of their new O/U shotguns. The descriptions and prices listed below reflect the most current information on these new models.

ROYAL MODEL O/U SHOTGUN OLD MODEL — 12 ga., customer specifications as to barrel length and choke, hand detachable sidelocks, auto ejectors, checkered straight grip stock. Mfg. until 1951. Very rare, very few mfg.

	$37,500	$32,000	$28,000	$23,500	$20,000	$18,000	$16,500

Add 5% for single trigger.

ROYAL NEW MODEL O/U — similar to Old Model, with improved narrow action. Mfg. until 1960, fewer than 30 mfg.

	$36,000	$31,000	$27,000	$22,500	$19,000	$17,000	$15,500

ROYAL O/U SIDELOCK GAME GUN — 12 or 20 ga., somewhat similar to New Model, with improved cocking, striking and ejection, slimmer action body, DT, 25 to 30 in. game or VR barrels, 2¾ in. chambers, finest checkered walnut straight hand or pistol grip stock, scroll engraved receiver with color case hardened or bright finish, prototype testing has finished and guns are available for demonstration, 5 lbs. 1 oz - 7 lbs. 8 oz. Written quotations on this re-released model are available by contacting H&H directly (see Trademark Index). Values listed below are for base models only and reflect the most recent factory information.

	Mfg.'s Sug. Retail	$60,375	$60,375	$32,750	$26,000	$21,750	$19,500	$18,250	$16,000

Add $4,470 for single trigger.

28 and .410 ga. variations are scheduled for release in 1997. Estimated retail as this edition goes to press is $67,220.

Grading		100%	98%	95%	90%	80%	70%	60%

ROYAL DE LUXE MODEL — similar to Royal O/U Sidelock Game Gun, except choice of more elaborate engraving and exhibition wood.

▲ *12 or 20 ga.*
Mfg.'s Sug. Retail $79,700 $79,700 $49,000 $37,500 $29,250 $23,500 $20,000 $18,000
   Add $4,470 for single trigger.

▲ *28 or .410 ga.*
Mfg.'s Sug. Retail $88,700 $88,700 $55,000 $41,000 $32,000 $25,500 $22,500 $19,500

SPORTING O/U MODEL — 12 ga. only, 2¾ in. chambers, designed with a trigger plate action, Game or Sporting Clays configuration featuring detachable SST mechanism, 28 to 32 in. game or VR barrels. Options on specifications to include screw-in chokes, 12 ga. - 7½-8 lbs., 20 ga. - 6 lbs. 6 oz. New 1993. Values below reflect most recent factory information.

▲ *12 or 16 ga.*
Mfg.'s Sug. Retail $29,380 $29,380 $23,750 $19,500 $15,250 $12,750 $10,750 $8,750

SPORTING DE LUXE MODEL — similar to Sporting O/U Model, except with choice of more elaborate engraving and exhibition wood. New 1993.
Mfg.'s Sug. Retail $38,800 $38,800 $28,250 $22,750 $17,750 $13,950 $11,000 $9,000
   Add $1,900 for 20 or 28 ga.

HOLLOWAY & NAUGHTON

Company trade name which has been manufacturing guns since the late 1800s.

Please contact the factory directly (see Trademark Index) for more information including individual quotations.

SHOTGUNS: O/U

O/U MODEL — all gauges, features shallow coin finish sidelock action, SST, exhibition grade wood, engraving per customer specifications, special order only.
Mfg.'s Sug. Retail $39,250 $39,250 $34,000 $29,500 $23,000 $17,750 $13,750 $10,250

HOLLOWAY ARMS CO.

Previous manufacturer located in Fort Worth, TX.

Holloway firearms did not make many rifles or carbines before operations ceased.

RIFLES/CARBINES: SEMI-AUTO

HAC MODEL 7 — 7.62mm NATO (.308), gas operated semi-auto paramilitary design rifle, 20 in. barrel, adj. front and rear sights, 20 shot mag., side folding stock. Mfg. 1984-1985 only. Also available in fully auto (class III dealers only) — add $80. Add $50 for left-hand variation.
                $995 $895 $795 $695 $595 $525 $465
                                                  Last Mfg.'s Sug. Retail was $675.

▲ *Model 7C* — 16 in. carbine, same general specifications as Model 7. Disc. 1985.
                $995 $895 $795 $695 $595 $525 $465
                                                  Last Mfg.'s Sug. Retail was $675.

   Also available from the manufacturer were the models 7S and 7M (Sniper and Match models).

HOLMES FIREARMS

Previous manufacturer located in Wheeler, AR. Distributed by D.B. Distributing, Fayetteville, AR.

These pistols were mfg. in very limited numbers, most were in prototype configuration and exhibit changes from gun to gun. These models were open bolt and subject to 1988 federal legislation regulations.

Grading	100%	98%	95%	90%	80%	70%	60%

PISTOLS: SEMI-AUTO

MP-83 — 9mm or .45 ACP cal., paramilitary design pistol, 6 in. barrel, walnut stock and forearm, blued finish, 3½ lbs. Add $75 for deluxe package and $220 for conversion kit. Mfg. 1985 only.

	100%	98%	95%	90%	80%	70%	60%
	$595	$550	$500	$450	$400	$375	$350

Last Mfg.'s Sug. Retail was $450.

MP-22 — .22 LR cal., 2½ lbs., steel and aluminum construction, 6 in. barrel, similar appearance to MP-83. Mfg. 1985 only.

	100%	98%	95%	90%	80%	70%	60%
	$395	$360	$320	$285	$250	$230	$210

Last Mfg.'s Sug. Retail was $400.

SHOTGUNS

COMBAT 12 — 12 ga., riot configuration, cylinder bore barrel. Disc. 1983.

	100%	98%	95%	90%	80%	70%	60%
	$795	$720	$650	$595	$550	$500	$450

Last Mfg.'s Sug. Retail was $750.

HOPKINS & ALLEN ARMS COMPANY, 1902-1914

H&A started their firearms business in 1867, manufacturing percussion revolvers. Before 1870, they were producing rimfire cartridge guns and eventually centerfire handguns and long guns. Prior to 1896, H&A guns were marked "HOPKINS & ALLEN MANUFG. CO. NORWICH CONN." or other private tradenames, including Merwin, Hulbert & Company. Hopkins & Allen guns are about equally priced with Stevens, N.R. Davis, Crescent Firearms Co., etc. There are many exceptions due to the numerous limited production guns, examples are the AA GRADE double shotgun and the "PARROT BEAK" Derringer. Hopkins & Allen also manufactured firearms which were not described in their catalogs.

Compiled from Hopkins & Allen catalogs by Charles E. Carder.

HANDGUNS

Most H&A handguns are nickel plated, with blue finish costing $.50 extra, grips are hard rubber, wood or pearl. Some have engraving from low to very good quality. Revolver barrel lengths vary from 1¾-6 in. Calibers are .22 rimfire to .38 centerfire.

FOREHAND MODEL — breaktop, double action, five shot, .32 caliber. Values range from $60-$150.

FOREHAND MODEL — similar to above except hammerless. (This model was offered in large and small frame). Values range from $60-$150.

FOREHAND MODEL — large frame as above in .32 and .38 centerfire with full hammer or "bobbed" hammer. Values range from $60-$150.

FOREHAND MODEL — solid frame and hard rubber grips, otherwise as above in small frame. Values range from $50-$135.

FOREHAND MODEL — similar to above models, with "folding hammer". .22 rimfires were seven shot, while .32 and .38 centerfires were five shot. By 1909, the Forehand logo was dropped from these revolvers. Values range from $50-$135.

H&A NEW MODEL AUTOMATIC HAMMER REVOLVER — similar to breaktop with hammer, produced in small and large frame, in .22 rimfire, .32 and .38 centerfire. Values range from $50-$135.

H&A SOLID FRAME — .32 and .38 centerfire, five shot, double action, hammer or "bobbed" hammer. Values range from $40-$140.

H&A XL MODEL — similar to above in .22, .32 and .38 calibers. Values range from $40-$140.

H

H&A RANGE MODEL — .22, .32 and .38 caliber, solid frame, loading gate on right side, wood target style grips, single or double action. (Two models, large and small frames.) Values range from $50-$165.

H&A TRIPLE ACTION SAFETY POLICE REVOLVER — breaktop with newly design locking mechanism, .22, .32 and .38 caliber, hard rubber or pearl grips. (Considered to be one of the best designed breaktops on the market. Other options for this model, include hammerless, engraved, wood target or pearl grips.) Values range from $70-$190.

H&A NEW VEST POCKET DERRINGER — .22 short rimfire, single shot, tip up, single action, 3½ in. overall length, folding trigger, blue or nickel finish, wood or pearl grips with golden monograms. This model was first listed about 1910 and known as the "Parrot Beak". An estimate of less than one thousand were produced and they are very rare. Values range from $550-$1900.

H&A NEW MODEL TARGET PISTOL — .22 rimfire, single shot breaktop with the same new locking mechanism as the Safety Police Revolver, wood target grips with golden monograms, blue finish and 6, 8 or 10 in. barrels. Values range from $200-$450.

H&A NEW MODEL SKELETON STOCK TARGET PISTOL — similar to above, with rounded hard rubber grips with logo, detachable "skeleton metal stock", 18 in. barrel and blue finish. Values range from $250-$525.

RIFLES

Hopkins & Allen started building "falling block" rifles circa 1887-1914 with the buy-out of the Baystate Arms Company. Most commonly seen is the "Junior" model, known after 1902 as 922, 925, and 932. These numbers were in reference to the catalog numbers, not model numbers. In the very late 1890s or early 1900s, the Number 722, 822 and 832 rifles were added. In 1906, a "bolt action" repeater was added to their line, followed in 1909 by a "bolt action" single shot "military". Lyman tang sights were an option for many H&A rifles - add $60-$75.

Grading	100%	98%	95%	90%	80%	70%	60%
NUMBER 922 — falling block, lever operated, .22 cal. rimfire, with round bbl.							
	$195	$165	$125	$110	$90	$75	$60
NUMBER 925 — similar to above in .25 cal. rimfire.							
	$195	$150	$110	$95	$80	$70	$60
NUMBER 932 — similar to above in .32 cal. rimfire.							
	$195	$150	$110	$95	$80	$70	$60
NUMBER 938 — similar to above in .38 S&W centerfire.							
	$225	$200	$175	$150	$125	$100	$75
NUMBER 1922 — similar to above in .22 cal. with octagon bbl.							
	$200	$180	$165	$150	$125	$100	$75
NUMBER 1932 — similar to above in .32 cal.							
	$200	$165	$125	$110	$90	$75	$65
NUMBER 2922 — similar to above in .22 cal., with checkering.							
	$265	$225	$195	$175	$150	$125	$100
NUMBER 2932 — similar to above in .32 caliber.							
	$265	$225	$195	$175	$150	$125	$100
NUMBER 3922 — similar to above in .22 rimfire, " SCHUETZEN RIFLE", nickeled Swiss butt plate, octagon barrel. (Schuetzen rifles in good cond. are somewhat rare.)							
	$495	$450	$400	$365	$325	$275	$200

H

NUMBER 3925 — similar to above in .25-20 centerfire. (This caliber rifle is more rare than the .22 rimfire).

	100%	98%	95%	90%	80%	70%	60%
	$650	$600	$550	$500	$450	$350	$250

NUMBER 44XL — similar to Number 922, except has smooth bore, chambered for the 44XL shotshell. (Referred to as, "TAXIDERMIST'S" or "LADIES GUN").

	$350	$325	$275	$235	$200	$175	$140

NUMBER 722 — rolling block, thumb operated, .22 cal. rimfire.

	$195	$1655	$125	$110	$90	$75	$60

SCOUT MILITARY RIFLE — similar to above with military style stock and a "Bonneted Indian" stamped on the left side of frame. (These are somewhat rare).

	$325	$285	$250	$200	$175	$150	$135

NUMBER 822 — rolling block, lever operated, .22 cal. rimfire.

	$195	$175	$150	$125	$100	$85	$75

NUMBER 832 — similar to above in .32 cal. rimfire. (This model was offered first with "pig tail" type levers and later with "loop" type levers. The "loop levers" are somewhat rare.)

	$225	$200	$175	$150	$125	$100	$75

NUMBER 4922 — .22 rimfire cal., bolt action, repeater.

	$135	$120	$100	$80	$70	$60	$50

NUMBER 5022 — similar to above with deluxe checkering.

	$175	$150	$135	$100	$85	$75	$60

MILITARY RIFLE — similar to above, except single shot with military style stock and sling. (In good condition, these are somewhat rare.)

	$250	$225	$200	$185	$165	$140	$125

NOISELESS — .22 rimfire, similar to the Number 922, except for checkered wood and the addition of a noise suppressor attached to the muzzle, by means of mating threads inside of suppressor and outside of barrel. The job is so well fitted, that it is difficult to recognize the suppressor. The front sight is attached to a dovetail slot in the suppressor. (These rifles are listed under the National Firearms Act of 1934 and must have proper licensing. Very rare.) Values range from $250-$550.

SHOTGUNS: SxS

Hopkins & Allen purchased Forehand Arms Co. and continued to produce their line of firearms and after a few years, dropped the Forehand name. In 1902, they offered the Forehand double boxlocks with or without outside hammers. Most models were offered in 12, 16 & 20 gauge. Sidelocks were added 1906-09. In 1902, the AA GRADE, a very high quality boxlock, was offered for $100 to $125. It had fine Damascus barrels, straight grip, plain or automatic ejectors, fine wood and engraving and was competitive with some Remingtons, L.C. Smiths, Bakers and other fine guns of that era. This gun was very short lived and today is rare. One feature found on all H&A double barrel guns is the "rib extension" or "doll's head".

BOXLOCK — Anson & Deeley type frame, damascus, twist, and steel barrels. Values range from $75-$250.

BOXLOCK — similar to above, except with outside hammers. Values range from $75-$250.

SIDELOCK — hammerless, damascus, twist, and steel barrels. Values range from $90-$250.

SIDELOCK — similar to above, except with outside hammers. Values range from $75-$250.

H

SINGLE BARREL SHOTGUNS

H&A produced a "falling block" shotgun in most gauges circa 1887 - early 1900s. Falling Blocks (FBs) in 12 ga. were built on heavy frames with the 20 and 16 gauges sharing a medium frame. Prior to 1902, some FBs were chambered for .45-70 shotshells and, today, these are rare if in good condition. From the 1890s through 1914, 38XL, 44XL shotshell guns were periodically offered in the Junior frame. After 1902, "tip-over" single shotguns were offered in Forehand designs and, later, the Davenport designs.

FALLING BLOCK — lever operated, outside hammer. Values range from $100-$275.

BOXLOCK — with outside hammer, damascus, twist, and steel barrels. Values range from $65-$150.

BOXLOCK — hammerless, top safety. Values range from $65-$150.

GOOSE GUNS — outside hammer, 8, 10, or 12 ga., were offered with barrels up to 40 inches long. Values range from $90-$200.

"SAFETY SINGLE GUN" — engraved with outside hammer and top safety. (Was offered in 1911 and recommended for trap shooting for $15.00). Values range from $100-$200.

HORTON, LEW, DIST. CO.
See Lew Horton Dist. Co. listing.

HOWA
Manufacturer located in Tokyo, Japan beginning 1967.

Recently, Howa rifles have been imported by Weatherby (Vanguard Series), Smith & Wesson (pre-1985), and Mossberg (1986-87). Currently, Howa sporting rifles are being imported by Interarms and this trademark will appear in the Interarms section in this text.

HUNTER ARMS COMPANY
Manufacturer located in Fulton, NY between 1891 and 1945.

The Hunter Arms Company was formed to manufacture L.C. Smith shotguns. Please refer to the L.C. Smith section in this text for further information regarding this manufacturer (including Fulton, Fulton Special, and Hunter Special models.)

HUSQVARNA
Previous manufacturer located in Husqvarna, Sweden.

Also see: Lahti Pistols

Grading	100%	98%	95%	90%	80%	70%	60%

RIFLE: BOLT ACTION

HI-POWER — Mauser type action, .220 Swift, .270, or .30-06 cal., open sight, checkered beech wood. Mfg. 1946-1951, early models found in 6.5x55, 8x57, 9.3 x 57 cals.

	100%	98%	95%	90%	80%	70%	60%
	$395	$365	$330	$295	$265	$235	$200

MODEL 1951 — similar to Hi-Power, except high profile stock.

	100%	98%	95%	90%	80%	70%	60%
	$425	$385	$340	$300	$270	$240	$210

SERIES 1100 DELUXE — similar to Model 1951, except has European walnut and jeweled bolt. Mfg. 1952-1956.

	100%	98%	95%	90%	80%	70%	60%
	$440	$360	$330	$310	$290	$275	$250

Grading	100%	98%	95%	90%	80%	70%	60%

SERIES 1000 SUPER GRADE — similar to Model 1951, has walnut Monte Carlo stock. Mfg. 1952-1956.

	$440	$360	$330	$310	$290	$275	$250

SERIES 3100 CROWN GRADE — improved HVA Mauser action, .243, .270, .30-06, 7mm, or .308 cal., 24 in. barrel, walnut stock, black forend tip and pistol grip cap. Mfg. 1954-1972.

	$470	$385	$360	$330	$315	$305	$275

SERIES 3000 CROWN GRADE — similar to 3100, except has Monte Carlo stock.

	$470	$385	$360	$330	$315	$305	$275

SERIES 4100 LIGHTWEIGHT — HVA Mauser action, calibers same as 3100, $20\frac{1}{2}$ in. barrel, open sights, lightweight walnut stock, pistol grip, Schnabel forend. Mfg. 1954-1972.

	$470	$385	$360	$330	$315	$305	$275

SERIES 4000 LIGHTWEIGHT — similar to 4100, except has Monte Carlo stock, no sights.

	$470	$385	$360	$330	$315	$305	$275

MODEL 456 LIGHTWEIGHT — similar to 4000/4100, except full length stock. Mfg. 1959-1970.

	$495	$415	$385	$360	$330	$310	$290

SERIES 6000 IMPERIAL GRADE — similar to 3100, except has select wood, 3 leaf folding sight. Mfg. 1968-1970.

	$580	$495	$470	$440	$395	$365	$330

SERIES 6000 IMPERIAL LIGHTWEIGHT — similar to 6000 Imperial, except $20\frac{1}{2}$ in. barrel, lightweight stock.

	$580	$495	$470	$440	$395	$365	$330

SERIES P-3000 PRESENTATION — similar to Crown, except engraved action, special wood. Mfg. 1968-1970.

	$770	$660	$635	$605	$550	$510	$485

MODEL 9000 CROWN GRADE — Husqvarna action, .300 Win. Mag. added to line, $23\frac{1}{2}$ in. barrel, adj. trigger, adj. sight, walnut stock. Mfg. 1971-1972.

	$470	$385	$360	$330	$315	$305	$275

MODEL 8000 IMPERIAL — similar to 9000, but jeweled bolt, engraved floor plate, no sights and deluxe stock. Mfg. 1971-1972.

	$605	$525	$495	$470	$415	$385	$350

HY-HUNTER INC. FIREARMS MANUFACTURING CO.

Previous manufacturer located in W. Germany, imported by Hy-Hunter Inc.

Previous importer of single action revolvers in various calibers. Typically, prices are determined by their shooting value rather than their collector value. Prices generally range from $100-$175 depending on caliber and finish.

HYPER

Previous manufacturer located in Jenks, OK.

SINGLE SHOT RIFLE — all calibers, all standard lengths and contours, falling block triggerguard lever activated, adj. trigger, no sights, stocked to customer specifications, in AA grade walnut. Disc. 1984.

	$2,200	$1,980	$1,925	$1,870	$1,650	$1,540	$1,375

Add $75 for stainless barrel.
Add $85 for octagon barrel.

▌section

I A B SHOTGUNS

Manufactured by Industria Armi Bresciane, Italy. Previously distributed by Sporting Arms International, Inc. located in Indianola, MS.

I A B manufactures high quality competition (O/U and single barrel trap or skeet) shotguns in various styles and configurations including combo sets. These guns employ a boxlock action, have ejectors, and various amounts of engraving. Prices for 100% condition usually start in the $550-$900 price range. I A B shotguns are not being imported currently - values for older models will be determined by the prices shooters, not collectors, are willing to pay for them.

I A I

Please refer to the Irwindale Arms, Inc. heading in this section

I A R

Importer/distributor located in San Juan Capistrano, CA.

IAR imports and distributes "cowboy" type firearms including exposed hammer shotguns (price range $1,199-$1,466), and a .22 LR SAA revolver (price range $270-$351). Please contact IAR for more information (see Trademark Index listing) on these models.

I G A SHOTGUNS

Manufacturer located in Veranopolis, Brazil. Currently imported by Stoeger Industries, Inc. located in Wayne, NJ.

Grading	100%	98%	95%	90%	80%	70%	60%

UPLANDER SxS — 12, 16 (new 1996), 20, 28, or .410 ga., 3 in. chambers, underlug lockup, checkered pistol grip or straight English (20 or .410 ga. only) stock, Youth Model also available in .410 ga., double triggers, extractors.

Mfg.'s Sug. Retail	$398	$295	$210	$170	$145	$130	$115	$100

    Add $44 for choke tubes (12 or 20 ga.).
    Add $10 for Youth Model (.410 ga. with 24 in. barrels and shortened stock).
    Add $52 for Ladies Model (20 ga. with 24 in. barrels and shortened stock).

COACH GUN SxS — 12, 20, or .410 (new 1991) ga., choice of blue or nickel (new 1996) finish, only 20 in. barrels.

Mfg.'s Sug. Retail	$382	$280	$195	$165	$140	$125	$110	$100

    Add $42 for nickel finish.
    Add $30 for engraved stagecoach scene on receiver (new 1996).

CONDOR O/U — 12 ga. only, single trigger, ejectors, presentation walnut, chrome lined bores. Disc. 1985.

		$580	$500	$450	$410	$375	$350	$325

                                                     Last Mfg.'s Sug. Retail was $667.

CONDOR I SINGLE TRIGGER O/U — 12 or 20 ga., 3 in. chambers, sliding underlug action, VR, deluxe checkered walnut, separated barrels.

Mfg.'s Sug. Retail	$500	$375	$325	$250	$225	$210	$195	$180

    Choke tubes became standard 1992.

CONDOR II DOUBLE TRIGGER O/U — 12 or 20 (disc.) ga., sliding underlug action, VR, checkered walnut, separated barrels.

Mfg.'s Sug. Retail	$415	$325	$275	$250	$225	$195	$170	$150

Grading	100%	98%	95%	90%	80%	70%	60%

CONDOR SUPREME — 12 or 20 ga., boxlock action, single trigger, ejectors, 26 or 28 in. VR barrels with choke tubes. Importation began 1995.

Mfg.'s Sug. Retail	$599		$515	$465	$415	$360	$320	$280	$240

ERA 2000 — 12 ga. only, 26 or 28 in. VR barrels with choke tubes, single trigger. Imported 1992-94.

			$585	$375	$315	$250	$215	$195	$180

Last Mfg.'s Sug. Retail was $710.

REUNA SINGLE BARREL — 12, 20, or .410 ga., exposed hammer with half-cock, extractor.

Mfg.'s Sug. Retail	$120		$95	$70	$60	$50	$45	$40	$35

Add $22 for choke tubes (12 ga. new 1992, 20 ga. new 1993).

▲ *Reuna Single Barrel Youth* — 20 or .410 ga., 22 in. barrel, features rubber recoil pad. Importation began 1993.

Mfg.'s Sug. Retail	$132		$100	$75	$60	$50	$45	$40	$35

IBERIA FIREARMS

Manufacturer located in Iberia, OH. Distributed by MKS Supply located in Mansfield, OH. Distributor sales only.

Please refer to the Hi-Point section in this text.

IMPERIAL GUN CO. LTD

Manufacturer located in Surrey, Great Britain beginning 1992.

To date, the Imperial Gun Co. Ltd. has had limited importation into the U.S. Please contact the factory directly (see Trademark Index) for more information on their current model lineup and pricing.

INDIAN ARMS

Previously manufactured by Indian Arms Corporation located in Detroit, MI.

INDIAN ARMS .380 SEMI-AUTO — .380 ACP, patterned after Walther PPK, stainless steel, 3¼ in. barrel, 6 shot mag., natural or blue finish, with (early specimens) or without key lock safety, with or without VR barrel, walnut grips, 20 oz. Mfg. 1975-1977.

			$350	$275	$225

This model had limited manufacture with approx. 1,000 guns being made.

INDUSTRIA ARMI GALESI

Previous manufacturer located in Brescia, Italy.

PISTOL: SEMI-AUTO

GALESI MODEL 6 POCKET AUTO — .22 LR, .25 ACP, 6 shot, 2¼ in. barrel blue, fixed sights, plastic grips. Mfg. 1930-disc.

			$130	$120	$105	$90	$75	$65	$55

GALESI MODEL 9 POCKET AUTO — .22 LR, .32 ACP, .380 ACP, 8 shot, 3¼ in. barrel, blue, fixed sights, plastic grips. Mfg. 1930-disc.

			$140	$125	$110	$100	$85	$65	$55

INFALLIBLE

Mfg. by Warner Arms Corp. located in Norwich, CT and Davis-Warner Arms Corp. located in Assonet, MA.

INFALLIBLE PISTOL — .32 ACP cal., 3.2 in. barrel, 7 shot mag., 24.7 oz.

Grading	100%	98%	95%	90%	80%	70%	60%

▲ **Type I** — mfg. and marked "Warner Arms Corp., Norwich, Conn.", serial range is 501-2,299.

	$325	$295	$270	$250	$225	$200	$180

▲ **Type II** — marked "Davis-Warner Arms Corporation, Assonet, Massachusetts", serial range is 2,300-5,299.

	$295	$270	$250	$225	$195	$170	$150

▲ **Type III** — marked "Warner Arms Corporation, Norwich, Connecticut", serial range is 5,300-7,400.

	$295	$270	$250	$225	$195	$170	$150

INFINITY

Manufactured by Strayer-Voight Inc. located in Grand Prairie, TX since 1994.

PISTOLS: SEMI-AUTO

STANDARD MODEL — .38 Super, .40 S&W, .45 ACP, 9x23mm, or 9x25mm cal., competition pistol featuring lightweight hardened frame, 5 in. barrel, Novak fixed rear sight, 10 shot mag., and other competition features. New 1994.

Mfg.'s Sug. Retail	$1,465	$1,375	$1,250	$1,025	$900	$775	$650	$525

Add $157 for extended beavertail grip safety.

COMPETITION MODEL — same cals. as Standard Model, features 6 port compensated barrel, nickel finished slide and upper frame. New 1994.

Mfg.'s Sug. Retail	$1,910	$1,775	$1,525	$1,300	$1,100	$925	$775	$625

INGLIS HI-POWERS

Manufactured by John Inglis Co. Limited of Toronto, Canada. Over 151,000 Inglis Hi-Powers were manufactured between February 1944 and September 1945 under military contractual agreement.

CHINESE CONTRACT PATTERN 35

▲ **Chinese No. 1** — large Chinese characters (6) on left slide, slotted for stock and tangent sights.

	$2,500	$1,800	$1,350	$995	$900	$800	$700

Add $300 for wooden holster stock.

CH SERIES CANADIAN MILITARY

▲ **MK 1-No. 1 Inglis** — tangent sight, slotted.

	$1,150	$975	$850	$725	$650	$550	$450

Add $300 for wooden holster stock.
This model has been recently imported again.

T SERIES CANADIAN MILITARY

▲ **MK 1-No. 2 Inglis** — fixed sight, without slot.

	100%	98%	95%	90%	80%	70%	60%
0 T	$775	$675	$595	$550	$530	$460	$395
1 T	$725	$600	$550	$500	$450	$400	$350
2 T	$600	$500	$450	$395	$345	$295	$275
3 T	$550	$450	$400	$350	$300	$260	$240
4 T	$550	$450	$400	$350	$300	$260	$240
5 T	$550	$450	$400	$350	$300	$260	$240
6 T	$550	$450	$400	$350	$300	$260	$240
7 T	$550	$450	$400	$350	$300	$260	$240
8 T	$800	$695	$595	$550	$530	$460	$395
9 T	$860	$750	$650	$550	$530	$460	$395
10 T	$825	$725	$625	$525	$510	$460	$395

▲ **Inglis "diamond logo"** — - refers to Inglis trademark in diamond shaped logo on left side of slide, mfg. 1946-47 for commercial sales to stay solvent.

	$550	$450	$400	$350	$300	$260	$240

Grading	100%	98%	95%	90%	80%	70%	60%
▲ *MK 1-No. 2 Inglis* — fixed sight, slotted. Inspect slot carefully.	$1,150	$975	$850	$725	$650	$550	$450

Add $200 for wooden holster stock.

INGRAM

Military Armament Corp. (Mac), previously located in Atlanta, GA. Disc. late 1982.

MAC 10 — .45 ACP or 9mm cal., semi-auto, open bolt, pistol version of the sub machine gun, 16 and 32 shot mag., compact construction, all metal construction, rear aperture and front blade sight. Disc. 1982.

	$850	$775	$700	$650	$600	$550	$495

Add approx. $160 for accessories (barrel extension, case, and extra mag).

MAC 10A1 — similar to MAC 10 except fires from a closed bolt.

	$295	$275	$250	$230	$215	$200	$190

MAC 11 — similar to MAC 10 except in .380 ACP cal.

	$650	$595	$550	$525	$500	$480	$460

INTERARMS

Manufacturer/importer/distributor located in Alexandria, VA.

Interarms has imported a multitude of trademarks and models since the early 1960s. Most of the models shown below are recent imports, and specific information on older, limited import models can be obtained by contacting Interarms directly. The Astra, Rossi, Star, and Walther trademarks will be found in their own sections listed alphabetically in this text.

HELWAN PISTOLS

Please refer to the Helwan section in this text.

VIRGINIAN REVOLVERS: SINGLE ACTION

Virginian Revolvers were previously imported from Europe by various manufacturers (including Hammerli of Switzerland). They were also manufactured in Midland, VA from 1976-1984. Older models with exceptional quality (including Hammerli guns) are worth a premium over values listed below.

VIRGINIAN DRAGOON STANDARD — improved action patterned after Colt S.A. design, 6 shot, .44 Mag. cal. only, 6, 7½, 8⅜, or 12 (Buntline) in. barrel, blue finish, smooth walnut grips, adj. rear sight, 51 oz. with 7½ in. barrel.

	$255	$225	$205	$190	$180	$170	$160

Last Mfg.'s Sug. Retail was $315.

Add 15% for Buntline Model.

▲ *Dragoon Standard Stainless* — .44 Mag. or .45 LC cal., 6 (disc.), 7½ (disc.), or 8⅜ in. barrel, same general specifications as Standard Dragoon.

	$265	$230	$210

Last Mfg.'s Sug. Retail was $315.

DRAGOON SILHOUETTE — .357 or .44 Mag. cal., stainless steel, 7½, 8⅜, or 10½ in. (standard on .357 Mag.) barrel, special sights and grips.

	$365	$320	$275

Last Mfg.'s Sug. Retail was $425.

DRAGOON ENGRAVED — .44 Mag. only, choice of stainless steel or blue finish, 6 or 7½ in. barrel.

	$545	$470	$430	$395	$360	$320	$285

Last Mfg.'s Sug. Retail was $625.

Add $75 for presentation case.

Grading	100%	98%	95%	90%	80%	70%	60%

DRAGOON "DEPUTY" — .357 or .44 Mag. cal., blued barrel, case hardened frame, 5 in. barrel only.

| | $250 | $215 | $195 | $180 | $165 | $155 | $145 |

Last Mfg.'s Sug. Retail was $295.

▲ **Stainless Deputy** — similar to above, except .44 Mag. available in 6 in. barrel only, stainless steel.

| | $255 | $225 | $205 |

Last Mfg.'s Sug. Retail was $295.

VIRGINIAN .22 CONVERTIBLE — .22 LR/.22 Mag. cylinders, 5½ in. barrel only, adj. rear sight, 38 oz.

| | $185 | $155 | $145 | $135 | $125 | $115 | $105 |

Last Mfg.'s Sug. Retail was $219.

▲ **Virginian .22 Convertible Stainless** — stainless steel fabrication, otherwise similar to above.

| | $200 | $170 | $155 |

Last Mfg.'s Sug. Retail was $239.

RIFLES: HOWA MFG.

MODEL 1500 HUNTER — .22-250, .223, .243, .270, .308, .30-06, .300 Win. Mag., or 7mm Rem. Mag. cal., 3 (Mag. cals. only) or 5 shot, 22 or 24 in. barrel, adj. rear sight and trigger, checkered walnut stock. Importation with Interarms 1988 only.

| | $360 | $310 | $285 | $260 | $240 | $225 | $205 |

Last Mfg.'s Sug. Retail was $440.

Add $15 for 7mm Rem. Mag./.300 Win. Mag. cal.

▲ **Model 1500 Lightning** — .270, .30-06, .300 Win. Mag., or 7mm Rem. Mag. cal., lightweight variation of the Model 1500 Hunter featuring lightweight Carbolite (synthetic) stock, 7 lbs. Imported 1988-91.

| | $415 | $335 | $290 | $260 | $240 | $225 | $205 |

Last Mfg.'s Sug. Retail was $539.

Add $20 for Mag. cals.

MODEL 1500 TROPHY — .22-250, .223, .243, .270, .308, .30-06, .300 Win. Mag., .338 Win. Mag. or 7mm Rem. Mag. cal., 3 (Mag. cals. only) or 5 shot, 22 or 24 in. barrel, adj. rear sight and trigger, select Monte Carlo stock with skipline checkering. Imported 1988-92.

| | $528 | $410 | $335 | $290 | $260 | $240 | $225 |

Last Mfg.'s Sug. Retail was $528.

Add $20 for Mag. cals.

▲ **Model 1500 Varmint** — .22-250, .223, or .308 (new 1990) cal., 24 in. heavy barrel without sights, 5 shot mag., 7 lbs. 1 oz. Imported 1988-92.

| | $435 | $350 | $300 | $275 | $255 | $230 | $210 |

Last Mfg.'s Sug. Retail was $565.

LIGHTNING RIFLE — .22-250, .223, .243, .270, .30-06, .308, 7mm Mag., .300 Win. Mag., or .338 Win. Mag. cal., 22 or 24 in. barrel, black synthetic Carbelite stock with cheekpiece and pressed checkering, no sights, 3 or 5 shot mag., high luster bluing, approx. 7½ lbs. Importation began 1993.

| Mfg.'s Sug. Retail | $425 | $330 | $285 | $245 | $220 | $195 | $175 | $160 |

Add $20 for Mag. cals.

LIGHTNING WOODGRAIN — .243 Win., .270 Win., .30-06, .308, or 7mm Rem. Mag. cal., features lightweight Carbelite synthetic stock with simulated wood grain and checkering, 22 in. barrel, 5 shot mag., no sights, 7.5 lbs. Imported 1994 only.

| | $450 | $395 | $365 | $320 | $275 | $250 | $225 |

Last Mfg.'s Sug. Retail was $537.

Add $19 for 7mm Rem. Mag. cal.

REALTREE CAMO RIFLE — .270 or .30-06 (disc. 1993) cal., 22 in. barrel, 5 shot mag., monobloc receiver, drilled and tapped, thumb safety, entire rifle is coated with a Realtree brown leaf camo pattern, no sights, 8 lbs. Imported 1993-94.

| | $495 | $400 | $350 | $325 | $300 | $280 | $260 |

Last Mfg.'s Sug. Retail was $620.

Grading	100%	98%	95%	90%	80%	70%	60%

RIFLES: MAUSER ACTIONS

Whitworth rifles are mfg. in England. Mark X rifles are currently mfg. in Yugoslavia by Zastava Arms.

MARK X VISCOUNT — .22-250 (disc. 1993), .243 (disc. 1993), .25-06 (disc. 1993), .270 (disc. 1993), 7x57mm (disc. 1993), 7mm Rem. Mag. (disc. 1994), .308 (disc. 1994), .30-06, or .300 Win. Mag. (disc. 1994) cal., 5 shot, 3 shot mag., 24 in. barrel, adj. rear sight and trigger, classic style Monte Carlo stock. Disc. 1983, re-introduced 1985.

Mfg.'s Sug. Retail	$471	$375	$300	$265	$240	$225	$205	$190

Add $15 for 7mm Rem. Mag. or .300 Win. Mag. cal.

This model is often referred to as the Viscount. Early manufacture was done in Manchester, England. Recent manufacture is in Yugoslavia. Earlier Manchester guns (before approx. 1980) will bring a slight premium over the values listed above.

▲ *Mini Mark X* — .223 or 7.62x39mm (new in 1990) cal., miniature M98 Mauser System action, 20 in. barrel with iron sights, checkered hardwood stock, 5 shot mag., adj. trigger, 6.35 lbs. Imported 1987-94.

	$360	$295	$265	$240	$225	$205	$190

Last Mfg.'s Sug. Retail was $455.

▲ *Lightweight Mark X* — .22-250 (new 1994), .270 (disc.), .30-06 (disc. 1994), or 7mm Rem. Mag. (disc.) cal., similar to Mark X Viscount, except has Carbolite (synthetic) stock and 20 in. barrel, 7 lbs. Imported 1988-90, reintroduced 1994.

Mfg.'s Sug. Retail	$438	$350	$290	$265	$240	$225	$205	$190

MARK X REALTREE — .270 Win. or .30-06 cal., features Realtree Camo finish. New 1994.

Mfg.'s Sug. Retail	$549	$460	$390	$365	$320	$275	$250	$225

MARK X WHITWORTH — current cals. include .270 Win., .30-06, and .300 Win. Mag., Mauser action, 24 in. barrel, open sights, 5 shot mag. (.300 Win. Mag. is only 3), checkered deluxe walnut with ebony forearm tip, thumb safety with sling swivels, adj. trigger, rubber recoil butt plate, 7 lbs. Imported since 1984.

Mfg.'s Sug. Retail	$565	$475	$400	$365	$320	$275	$250	$225

Add $19 for 7mm Rem. Mag. (disc.) or .300 Win. Mag. cal.

This model was the Whitworth American Field Series until 1987. Early manufacture was done in Manchester, England. Recent manufacture is by Zastava located in Yugoslavia. Earlier Manchester guns (before approx. 1980) will bring a slight premium over the values listed above.

WHITWORTH MANNLICHER STYLE CARBINE — .243, .270, .308, 7x57mm, or .30-06 cal., bolt action with full length walnut Mannlicher style stock, open sights, sling swivels, thumb safety, 20 in. barrel, 5 shot mag., 7 lbs. Imported 1984-87.

	$570	$495	$455	$410	$375	$340	$310

Last Mfg.'s Sug. Retail was $675.

WHITWORTH EXPRESS RIFLE — .375 H&H (disc. 1993) or .458 Win. Mag. cal., 3 shot, 24 in. barrel, 3 leaf express sight, English style stock of walnut, checkered pistol grip forearm, 8½ lbs. Mfg. 1974-present.

Mfg.'s Sug. Retail	$703	$600	$540	$465	$425	$395	$375	$350

RIFLES: BOLT ACTION

MODEL JW-15 — .22 LR, 5 shot detachable mag., 23.8 in. barrel, open sights, blued finish, Model 70 style safety, patterned after the Brno Model ZKM, 5.5 lbs. Importation began 1990.

Mfg.'s Sug. Retail	$109	$85	$70	$60	$50	$40	$35	$30

This model is mfg. by Norinco in China.

ENFIELD NO. 4 — .303 British cal., genuine British Commonwealth issue, 25¼ in. barrel, 10 shot box mag., 9 lbs.

Mfg.'s Sug. Retail	$86	$75	$60	$50	$40	$35	$35	$35

Grading	100%	98%	95%	90%	80%	70%	60%

RIFLES: SEMI-AUTO

22-ATD — .22 LR only, patterned after the Browning Semi-Auto, 19.4 in. barrel, 11 shot mag. in stock, blued finish, checkered hardwood stock, take-down design, adj. rear sight, 4.6 lbs. New 1987.

Mfg.'s Sug. Retail $150	$130	$105	$95	$90	$80	$75	$70

    Add $16 for camo case (disc.).

    This model is mfg. by Norinco in China.

RIFLES: DISC.

CAVALIER — similar to Viscount, except modern style stock, roll-over cheekpiece, rosewood pistol grip cap and forend tip, recoil pad. Disc.

	$365	$330	$305	$290	$265	$230	$195

MANNLICHER STYLE CARBINE — similar to Cavalier, except 20 in. barrel, full length stock, no Magnum or varmint calibers. Disc.

	$365	$330	$305	$290	$265	$230	$195

CONTINENTAL CARBINE — similar to Mannlicher Style, except with double set trigger. Disc.

	$395	$365	$330	$310	$285	$255	$220

THE MARQUIS — .243, .270, .308, 7x57mm, or .30-06 cal., 20 in. barrel, adj. trigger. Mannlicher style carbine. Disc. 1984.

	$430	$325	$300	$275	$250	$230	$215

ALASKAN — similar to Mark X, except .375 H&H or .458 Win. Mag. cal., recoil pad and extra stock crossbolt. Disc. 1984.

	$460	$350	$330	$310	$290	$250	$210

INTERDYNAMIC OF AMERICA, INC.

Distributor located in Miami, FL 1981-84.

KG-9 — 9mm Para., 3 in. barrel, open bolt, semi-auto paramilitary design pistol. Disc. approx. 1982.

	$750	$700	$650	$600	$575	$550	$525

KG-99 — 9mm Para., 3 in. barrel, semi-auto paramilitary design pistol, closed bolt, 36 shot mag., 5 in. vent. shroud barrel, blue only, a stainless steel version of the KG-9. Mfg. by Interdynamic 1984 only.

	$260	$200	$180	$160	$145	$130	$120
KG-99M, mini pistol	$213	$165	$155	$145	$135	$125	$115

INTRATEC

Manufacturer located in Miami, FL. Distributor sales only.

DERRINGERS

TEC-38 DERRINGER — .38 Spl., O/U, derringer, 3 in. barrel, blue frame, double action, 13 oz. Mfg. 1986-1988.

	$110	$95	$85	$75	$65	$60	$55

    Last Mfg.'s Sug. Retail was $125.

Grading			100%	98%	95%	90%	80%	70%	60%

PROTECTOR SERIES PISTOLS

PROTEC-22 — .22 LR cal., double action semi-auto, 2½ in. barrel, 10 shot mag., fixed sights, choice of black, satin, or Tec-Kote finish, black, gray, or driftwood colored wraparound grips, 13 oz. New 1993.

Mfg.'s Sug. Retail	$112	$90	$70	$55	$40	$35	$30	$25

Add $5 for satin, Tec-Kote finish, or black slide/frame finish.

PROTEC-25 — .25 ACP., double action only semi-auto, 2½ in. barrel, 8 shot mag., otherwise similar to Protec-22. New 1991.

Mfg.'s Sug. Retail	$112	$90	$70	$55	$40	$35	$30	$25

Add $5 for satin, Tec-Kote finish, or black slide/frame finish.

TEC-SERIES PISTOLS

CAT-9 — 9mm Para. New 1995.

Mfg.'s Sug. Retail	$255	$215	$180	$160	$135	$120	$110	$100

CAT-45 — .45 ACP. New 1995.

Mfg.'s Sug. Retail	$255	$215	$180	$160	$135	$120	$110	$100

TEC-DC9 — 9mm Para., semi-auto paramilitary design pistol, 5 in. shrouded barrel, matte black finish, 10 (C/B 1994) or 32* shot mag. Mfg. 1985-94.

	$245	$175	$155	$140	$130	$120	$110

Last Mfg.'s Sug. Retail was $269.

▲ *TEC-9DCK* — similar to TEC-9, except has new durable Tec-Kote finish with better protection than hard chrome. Mfg. 1991-94.

	$250	$185	$160	$140	$130	$120	$110

Last Mfg.'s Sug. Retail was $297.

▲ *TEC-DC9S* — matte stainless version of the TEC-9. Disc. 1994.

	$300	$240	$185

Last Mfg.'s Sug. Retail was $362.

Add $203 for above TEC-9 with accessory package (deluxe case, 3-32 shot mags., paramilitary design grip, and recoil compensator).

TEC-DC9M — mini version of the Model TEC-9, including 3 in. barrel and 20 shot mag. Disc. 1994.

	$245	$175	$155	$140	$130	$120	$110

Last Mfg.'s Sug. Retail was $245.

▲ *TEC-DC9MK* — similar to TEC-9M, except has Tec-Kote rust resistant finish. Mfg. 1991-1994.

	$255	$185	$155	$140	$130	$120	$110

Last Mfg.'s Sug. Retail was $277.

▲ *TEC-DC9MS* — matte stainless version of the TEC-9M. Disc. 1994.

	$275	$225	$180

Last Mfg.'s Sug. Retail was $339.

TEC-9C — 9mm, carbine variation with 16½ in. barrel, 36 shot mag. Only 1 gun mfg. 1987 - extreme rarity precludes pricing.

TEC-22 "SCORPION" — .22 LR, semi-auto pistol, paramilitary design, 4 in. barrel, ambidextrous safety, military matte finish, or electroless nickel, 30 shot mag., adj. sights, 30 oz. Mfg. 1988-90.

	$190	$165	$150	$135	$120	$100	$90

Last Mfg.'s Sug. Retail was $202.

Add $20 for TEC-Kote finish.

▲ *TEC-22N* — similar to TEC-22, except has nickel finish. Mfg. 1990 only.

	$200	$175	$160	$140	$125	$105	$95

Last Mfg.'s Sug. Retail was $226.

Add $16 for threaded barrel (Model TEC-22TN).

Grading	100%	98%	95%	90%	80%	70%	60%

TEC-22T — threaded barrel variation of the TEC-22 "Scorpion". Mfg 1991-94.

		$145	$125	$110	$100	$90	$80	$70

Last Mfg.'s Sug. Retail was $161.

Add $23 for Tec-Kote finish.

SPORT-22 — 4 in. barrel, 10 shot Ruger styled rotary mag., adj. rear sight, 28 oz. New 1995.

Mfg.'s Sug. Retail	$130	$110	$90	$80	$70	$60	$50	$45

PISTOLS: DOUBLE ACTION

This series is designed by N. Sirkis of Israel.

CATEGORY 9/40/45 — .380 ACP (new 1995), 9mm Para., .40 S&W (new 1994), or .45 ACP (new 1994) cal., double action only, black finish, polymer frame with top sight channel, only 27 parts, blowback action on 9mm Para., locked breech on .45 ACP or .40 S&W, 6 (.45 ACP cal.), 7 (.40 S&W), or 7 (9mm Para.) shot mag., 3 or 3¼ in. barrel, 18-21 oz. New 1993.

Mfg.'s Sug. Retail	$210	$185	$165	$145	$130	$115	$100	$90

Add $15 for 9mm Para. cal.
Add $45 for .40 S&W or .45 ACP cal.

IRWINDALE ARMS, INC. (IAI)

Previous manufacturer located in Irwindale, CA 1988-1991.

PISTOLS

In June, 1991, AMT retained manufacture of all IAI models. Please refer to the AMT section for current models.

AUTOMAG III — .30 Carbine or 9mm Win. Mag. (mfg. 1990-92), stainless steel only, 6⅜ in. barrel, patterned after Colt Govt. Model, Millett adj. sights with white outline, grooved Lexan grips, 8 shot mag., 43 oz. Mfg. 1989-91.

		$550	$475	$395

Last Mfg.'s Sug. Retail was $606.

AUTOMAG IV — .45 Win. Mag., or 10mm cal., semi-auto, 6½ or 8⅝ (mfg. 1991) in. barrel, 7 shot mag., Millett adj. sights, stainless steel only, 46 oz. Mfg. 1990-91.

		$565	$485	$500

Last Mfg.'s Sug. Retail was $630.

JAVELINA — 10mm, semi-auto, 5 (disc. 1991) or 7 in. barrel, 8 shot mag., Millett adj. sights, wraparound Neoprene grips, stainless steel, wide adj. trigger, long grip safety, 48 oz. Mfg. 1990-91.

		$525	$450	$375

Last Mfg.'s Sug. Retail was $570.

BACKUP PISTOL — .380 ACP cal., semi-auto action, 2½ in. barrel, stainless steel, Lexan grips, 5 shot mag. in .380, 18 oz. Older disc. walnut grip models are worth a slight premium. Disc. 1989.

		$200	$165	$135

Last Mfg.'s Sug. Retail was $243.

ISRAEL ARMS LTD.

Please refer to the KSN Industries Ltd. listing in this text.

ISRAELI MILITARY INDUSTRIES (IMI)

Manufacturer located in Israel.

IMI manufactured guns (including Galil, Jericho, Magnum Research, Timberwolf, Uzi, and others) can be located in their respective sections of this text.

ITALIAN MILITARY ARMS

Grading	100%	98%	95%	90%	80%	70%	60%

MODEL 1891 MANNLICHER-CARCANO — bolt action, 6.5mm, 6 shot, 31 in. barrel, straight handle, adj. sight, military stock.

	$120	$100	$85	$70	$55	$40	$30

MODEL 38 TERNI MILITARY RIFLE — 7.35mm, similar to 1891, except turned down bolt handle, 21 in. barrel and folding bayonet.

	$120	$100	$85	$70	$55	$40	$30

GLISENTI MODEL 1910 — 9mm Glisenti cal., 4 in. barrel, 7 shot mag., checkered wooden grips, official Italian service pistol of both WWI and WWII, 32 oz.

	$675	$525	$375	$300	$225	$200	$185

Warning: 9mm Parabellum ammunition cannot be used in this pistol - only 9mm Glisenti, as it is approx. 25% less powerful than the 9mm Para.

BRIXIA — similar to Glisenti Model 1910, except utilizes simplified mfg. techniques, mostly sold to civilians.

	$795	$600	$400	$300	$215	$190	$175

ITHACA GUN

Manufacture of Ithaca Guns ceased August, 1995. Manufactured in Ithaca, NY, 1883 to Nov. of 1986. In early 1987, production was resumed until August, 1995 as Ithaca Acquisition Corp. using the old trademark. On March 6, 1987 some assets of the Ithaca Gun Company were sold to Ithaca Acquisition Corporation. In the past, Ithaca also absorbed companies including Syracuse Arms Co., Lefever Arms Co., Union Fire Arms Co., Wilkes-Barre Gun Co., as well as others.

As this edition went to press, Ithaca Gun remained in Chapter 11 since August, 1995. No guns are currently being manufactured, but Ithaca is trying to resolve its financial matters so that it may resume production shortly.

COMBINATION GUNS

LSA-55 TURKEY GUN — O/U shotgun-rifle combo, 12 ga., .222 Rem., 24½ in. ribbed barrel, exposed hammer, folding rear sight, checkered Monte Carlo stock. Mfg. by Tikka, Finland 1970-1981.

	$605	$550	$415	$495	$425	$385	$330

HANDGUNS

X-CALIBER SINGLE SHOT — .22 LR or .44 Mag. cal., break open action with contoured wooden grip and forearm, 8, 10 or 15 in. barrel, unique dual firing pin detonates both rimfire and centerfire cartridges. Model 20 is target model (blued finish with Goncalo Alves wood grips), or Model 30 Hunting (sandblasted teflon finish with American walnut grips). Frames and barrels can be purchased separately. While advertised in 1988, this gun was only manufactured in .22 cal. with approx. 300 units being produced before production ceased due to unsolvable production problems. Mfg.'s Sug. Retail was $270.

ITHACA 50TH ANNIVERSARY MODEL — .45 ACP cal., 5 in. match barrel with bushing, blue polished or tactical matte finish, checkered diamond pattern walnut grips, extended beavertail grip safety, includes plastic case and certificate, only 2,500 mfg. with special serialization beginning 1995.

Mfg.'s Sug. Retail	$795	$695	$625	$550	$500	$450	$400	$360

This model is offered exclusively by All American Sales, Inc. located in Memphis, TN.

Grading	100%	98%	95%	90%	80%	70%	60%

MODEL 20 — consists of one .22 LR and one .44 Mag. 10 or 12 in. barrel, single shot design, frame and barrels have sandblasted matte blue finish, ambidextrous walnut grip and forend. Introduced June, 1994.

Mfg.'s Sug. Retail	$349	$295	$250	$225	$200	$180	$160	$145

RIFLES: BOLT ACTION

LSA-55 STANDARD — Mauser type action, .222, .22-250, 6mm, .243, or .308 cal., 22 in. barrel, leaf sight, 3 shot clip mag., checkered Monte Carlo stock. Mfg. in Finland by Tikka from 1969 to 1977.

	$400	$375	$350	$310	$275	$250	$230

LSA-55 DELUXE — similar to Standard, except rollover cheekpiece, rosewood pistol grip cap and forend tip, skipline checkering, no sights, scope mounts furnished.

	$475	$415	$385	$350	$300	$280	$260

LSA-55 HEAVY BARREL — similar to LSA-55, except .222 or .22-250 only, target heavy barrel, special beavertail stock 8½ lbs.

	$450	$400	$375	$340	$295	$275	$255

LSA-65 — similar to LSA-55, except long action for calibers .25-06, .270, or .30-06. Mfg. 1969 to 1977.

	$400	$375	$350	$310	$275	$250	$230

LSA-65 DELUXE — similar to LSA-55 Deluxe, except .25-06, .270, or .30-06.

	$475	$415	$385	$350	$300	$280	$260

RIFLES: LEVER ACTION

MODEL 49 SADDLEGUN — .22 LR cal., lever action, single shot. Mfg. 1961-1978. Martini-style action .22 Mag. — add $15; deluxe model — add $45.

	$125	$110	$100	$75	$65	$50	$40

MODEL 49 PRESENTATION — like model 49, except gold-plated trigger, hammer, engraved receiver, fancy walnut. Mfg. 1962-1974.

	$220	$165	$155	$130	$120	$110	$100

MODEL 49 ST. LOUIS BICENTENNIAL — like deluxe model 49, except inscription on receiver, 200 mfg. 1964.

	$195	$160	$125				

Last Mfg.'s Sug. Retail was $35.

MODEL 72 SADDLEGUN — .22 or .22 Mag., lever action, 18½ in. barrel, hooded front sight. Mfg. 1973-1978 by Erma Werke, W. Germany.

	$185	$140	$130	$110	$100	$90	$85

MODEL 72 DELUXE — similar to Model 72, except has silver finished engraved receiver, deluxe walnut, octagon barrel. Mfg. 1974-1976.

	$260	$195	$185	$155	$145	$130	$120

RIFLES: SEMI-AUTO

MODEL X5-C — .22 LR cal., 7 shot Mag., semi-auto action. Mfg. 1958-1964. Model X5-T has tube mag.

	$150	$125	$100	$80	$70	$60	$55

MODEL X-15 — .22 LR cal., similar to X5-C only forearm is not grooved. Mfg. 1964-1967.

	$150	$125	$100	$80	$70	$60	$55

Grading	100%	98%	95%	90%	80%	70%	60%

RIFLES: SINGLE SHOT

MODEL 89 — .243 Win., .30-06, .375 H&H, .416 Rigby, or 7mm cal., falling block action, 26 or 28 in. Shilen barrel, full-length uncheckered walnut stock. New 1994.

Mfg.'s Sug. Retail	$658	$585	$520	$460	$400	$360	$330	$295

SHOTGUNS: SIDE x SIDE - EARLY MFG.

ITHACA HAMMERLESS DOUBLE BARREL — 12, 16, 20, 28 or .410 ga., 26-32 in. fluid steel or damascus barrels, boxlock, extractors, double triggers, any standard choke, checkered pistol grip stock and forearm, grades shown differ in overall quality, ornamentation, grade of wood, and style of checkering. In 1925, the rotary bolt and stronger frame were adapted (ser. no.'s after 400,000 - commonly referred to as NID or New Ithaca Double). Values are the same as for pre-400,000 serial range shotguns.

> Values below are for guns mfg. between 1925-1948. Newer models can be found later in this section.
> Add $200 for SST.
> Add $150 for SNT.
> Add $350 for VR on Grades 4, 5, 7, and $2,000 Grade.
> Add $200 for VR - lower grades.
> Add $175 for beavertail forearm.
> Add 33% for auto ejectors on Grades No. 1, 2, and 3.
> Subtract 33% if without ejectors on Grades 4E-7E.
> Early hammer doubles in average condition are approx. valued between $175-$450. However, if 60% condition remains (including original case colors), values can approximate those listed below.

100%	98%	95%	90%	80%	70%	60%	50%	40%	30%	20%	10%

FIELD GRADE

▲ *10 ga. Mag.*

$2,000	$1,800	$1,500	$1,400	$1,300	$1,200	$1,100	$950	$825	$775	$675	$600

> 3½ in. chambered 10 ga. Mags. are serial numbered over 500,000. Total mfg. was approx. 850 guns for all grades. 2⅞ in. chambered 10 ga.'s are priced the same as a 12 ga. A 12 ga., 3 in. model was also made on the 10 ga. frame - only 87 were mfg. and specimens are noted in the 500,000 serial range.

▲ *12 ga.*

$1,000	$800	$600	$550	$500	$450	$415	$380	$350	$325	$300	$265

▲ *16 ga.*

$1,100	$900	$800	$750	$700	$650	$600	$550	$500	$425	$375	$325

▲ *20 ga.*

$1,400	$1,200	$1,000	$900	$850	$800	$750	$700	$600	$550	$500	$400

▲ *28 ga.*

$3,000	$2,700	$2,500	$2,200	$2,000	$1,800	$1,700	$1,600	$1,500	$1,400	$1,200	$1,000

▲ *.410 ga.*

$3,000	$2,700	$2,500	$2,200	$2,000	$1,800	$1,700	$1,600	$1,500	$1,400	$1,200	$1,000

GRADE NO. 1 — manufactured in both Fleus and NID models, similar to Field Grade.

▲ *12 ga.*

$1,225	$1,000	$800	$600	$550	$500	$450	$415	$380	$350	$325	$300

▲ *16 ga.*

$1,375	$1,150	$925	$825	$750	$700	$650	$600	$550	$500	$425	$375

▲ *20 ga.*

$1,700	$1,400	$1,200	$1,000	$900	$850	$800	$750	$700	$600	$550	$500

▲ *28 ga.*

$3,500	$2,795	$2,400	$2,200	$2,000	$1,800	$1,700	$1,600	$1,500	$1,400	$1,200	$1,075

100%	98%	95%	90%	80%	70%	60%	50%	40%	30%	20%	10%

▲ .410 ga.

| $3,700 | $2,895 | $2,450 | $2,250 | $2,000 | $1,800 | $1,700 | $1,600 | $1,500 | $1,400 | $1,200 | $1,075 |

GRADE NO. 2

▲ 10 ga. Mag.

| $2,400 | $2,000 | $1,800 | $1,600 | $1,400 | $1,300 | $1,200 | $1,100 | $950 | $900 | $800 | $700 |

3½ in. chambered 10 ga. Mags. are serial numbered over 500,000. Total mfg. was approx. 850 guns for all grades. 2⅞ in. chambered 10 ga.'s are priced the same as a 12 ga.

▲ 12 ga.

| $1,500 | $1,200 | $1,000 | $800 | $600 | $550 | $500 | $450 | $415 | $380 | $350 | $325 |

▲ 16 ga.

| $1,500 | $1,200 | $1,000 | $900 | $800 | $750 | $700 | $650 | $600 | $550 | $500 | $450 |

▲ 20 ga.

| $1,800 | $1,500 | $1,200 | $1,100 | $1,000 | $900 | $850 | $800 | $750 | $700 | $650 | $550 |

▲ 28 ga.

| $4,000 | $3,000 | $2,600 | $2,200 | $1,900 | $1,800 | $1,700 | $1,600 | $1,500 | $1,400 | $1,300 | $1,200 |

▲ .410 ga.

| $4,000 | $3,000 | $2,700 | $2,400 | $2,200 | $2,000 | $1,900 | $1,800 | $1,700 | $1,600 | $1,500 | $1,400 |

GRADE NO. 3

▲ 10 ga. Mag.

| $3,000 | $2,500 | $2,100 | $1,800 | $1,600 | $1,400 | $1,300 | $1,200 | $1,100 | $950 | $825 | $700 |

3½ in. chambered 10 ga. Mags. are serial numbered over 500,000. Total mfg. was approx. 850 guns for all grades. 2⅞ in. chambered 10 ga.'s are priced the same as a 12 ga.

▲ 12 ga.

| $1,850 | $1,500 | $1,200 | $1,000 | $800 | $750 | $700 | $650 | $600 | $550 | $500 | $450 |

▲ 16 ga.

| $1,850 | $1,500 | $1,200 | $1,000 | $900 | $850 | $800 | $750 | $700 | $650 | $600 | $550 |

▲ 20 ga.

| $2,400 | $1,800 | $1,500 | $1,300 | $1,200 | $1,100 | $1,000 | $900 | $850 | $800 | $750 | $700 |

▲ 28 ga. — only 5 mfg.

Extreme rarity factor precludes accurate pricing evaluation.

▲ .410 ga. — only 7 mfg.

Extreme rarity factor precludes accurate pricing evaluation.

GRADE NO. 4E — auto ejectors.

▲ 10 ga. Mag.

| $4,000 | $3,500 | $3,000 | $2,500 | $2,100 | $1,800 | $1,700 | $1,600 | $1,500 | $1,400 | $1,300 | $1,200 |

3½ in. chambered 10 ga. Mags. are serial numbered over 500,000. Total mfg. was approx. 850 guns for all grades. 2⅞ in. chambered 10 ga.'s are priced the same as a 12 ga.

▲ 12 ga.

| $3,500 | $3,000 | $2,500 | $2,100 | $1,700 | $1,400 | $1,200 | $1,100 | $1,000 | $900 | $800 | $700 |

▲ 16 ga.

| $4,000 | $3,700 | $3,000 | $2,400 | $2,000 | $1,700 | $1,500 | $1,400 | $1,300 | $1,200 | $1,100 | $900 |

▲ 20 ga.

| $4,500 | $4,000 | $3,700 | $3,500 | $3,300 | $3,000 | $2,800 | $2,500 | $2,100 | $1,800 | $1,500 | $1,200 |

▲ 28 ga.

Extreme rarity factor precludes accurate pricing evaluation.

100%	98%	95%	90%	80%	70%	60%	50%	40%	30%	20%	10%

▲ *.410 ga.*
> Extreme rarity factor precludes accurate pricing evaluation.

GRADE NO. 5E — auto ejectors.

▲ *10 ga.* — only 9 mfg.
> Extreme rarity factor precludes accurate pricing evaluation.

▲ *12 ga.*

100%	98%	95%	90%	80%	70%	60%	50%	40%	30%	20%	10%
$4,250	$3,500	$3,200	$3,000	$2,700	$2,200	$1,700	$1,500	$1,200	$1,100	$1,000	$900

▲ *16 ga.*

100%	98%	95%	90%	80%	70%	60%	50%	40%	30%	20%	10%
$4,250	$3,500	$2,800	$2,500	$2,200	$1,800	$1,600	$1,400	$1,300	$1,200	$1,100	$1,000

▲ *20 ga.*

100%	98%	95%	90%	80%	70%	60%	50%	40%	30%	20%	10%
$5,500	$4,500	$4,000	$3,700	$3,300	$3,000	$2,700	$2,400	$2,100	$1,900	$1,700	$1,500

▲ *28 ga.*
> Extreme rarity factor precludes accurate pricing evaluation.

▲ *.410 ga.*
> Extreme rarity factor precludes accurate pricing evaluation.

GRADE NO. 7E — auto ejectors, only 22 mfg. in all gauges.
> Extreme rarity factor precludes accurate pricing evaluation on this model.

$2,000 GRADE — 12 ga., top-of-the-line model, auto ejectors, single selective trigger.

100%	98%	95%	90%	80%	70%	60%	50%	40%	30%	20%	10%
$11,000	$9,500	$8,450	$7,400	$6,500	$5,650	$4,750	$4,000	$3,250	$2,600	$2,100	$1,600

> Rarity on 16 or 20 ga. precludes accurate pricing.

PRE-WAR $1,000 GRADE — 12 ga., top-of-the-line models, auto ejectors, single selective trigger.

100%	98%	95%	90%	80%	70%	60%	50%	40%	30%	20%
$13,000	$11,000	$9,500	$8,450	$7,400	$6,500	$5,650	$4,750	$4,000	$3,250	$2,600	$2,100

> Rarity on 16 or 20 ga. precludes accurate pricing.

SOUSA GRADE — has mermaids on triggerguard in gold, only 11 manufactured (including one .410 ga.). This model is very rare and prices are hard to establish. Recently, the price range has been approx. $15,000-$40,000, depending on original condition.
> This model had help in development by the famous band director and composer, John Phillip Sousa.

Grading	100%	98%	95%	90%	80%	70%	60%

SHOTGUNS: SINGLE BARREL TRAP

CENTURY TRAP — 12 ga., 32 or 34 in. VR barrel, engraved, auto ejector, full choke, checkered walnut stock. Mfg. 1973 and 1976 by SKB.

100%	98%	95%	90%	80%	70%	60%
$550	$525	$470	$440	$385	$360	$320

CENTURY II TRAP — improved trap stock version of Century, Monte Carlo stock.

100%	98%	95%	90%	80%	70%	60%
$600	$550	$495	$470	$415	$385	$350

SINGLE BARREL TRAP — 12 ga., 30, 32, or 34 in. barrels, VR, boxlock, auto ejector, checkered pistol grip and forearm, grades differ in engraving, overall workmanship, and grade or wood and checkering. Values on these models sometimes vary greatly depending on originality of finish, customer alterations, and other variations trap shooters might use to alter dimensions for their particular shooting requirements. Below values represent trap guns in original, unaltered condition.

> Note: Flues model mfg. prior to 1921 with serial numbers under 400,000 generally have better engraving than NID (New Ithaca Double) models over serial number 400,000 (also referred to as Knick models).

> Trap guns under 60% original condition will be within 25% of the value shown in the 60% column.

Grading	100%	98%	95%	90%	80%	70%	60%

▲ *Victory Grade* — disc. 1938.

	$995	$850	$775	$675	$575	$495	$440

▲ *No. 4E* — disc. 1976.

	$1,500	$1,200	$1,000	$875	$750	$650	$595

▲ *No. 5E* — 12 ga., 32 or 34 in. barrel, custom order only, elaborate engraving, quality worksmanship throughout. Originally mfg. 1925-1986, mfg. resumed 1988-91.

	$2,950	$2,550	$2,175	$1,900	$1,725	$1,495	$1,300

Last Mfg.'s Sug. Retail was $7,500.

▲ *No. 6E* — this model was available by special order only. Rarity factor precludes accurate pricing.

▲ *No. 7E* — disc. 1964.

	$5,500	$4,700	$4,000	$3,500	$3,000	$2,500	$2,200

▲ *Dollar Grade* — 12 ga., 32 or 34 in. barrel. Top-of-the-line model custom built to customer specifications. Original mfg. was stopped 1986 and resumed 1988-91.

	$5,950	$5,200	$4,600	$3,850	$3,250	$2,775	$2,250

Last Mfg.'s Sug. Retail was $10,000.

▲ *$5,000 Grade* — similar to Pre-War $1,000 grade.

	$9,500	$8,900	$8,175	$7,650	$6,725	$5,825	$4,950

▲ *Sousa Grade* — extremely rare.

Extreme rarity factor precludes accurate pricing evaluation. Prices will be higher than the $5,000 Grade.

SHOTGUNS: MISCELLANEOUS

AUTO & BURGLAR SxS — 20 ga., 10 or 14 in. barrels, with or without cocking indicators, blue finish, pistol grip, classified as Curio (short barreled shotgun status) in 1977 - must be registered, offered in Model A (has grip spur on back of pistol grip) or B (squared grips). Approx. 4,500 mfg. 1922-1933.

▲ *Model A* — serial no. range is 343,336-398,365.

	$1,850	$1,450	$1,200	$975	$775	$675	$575

▲ *Model B* — serial no. range is 425,000 464,699.

	$1,450	$1,200	$975	$775	$675	$575	$465

Add $300-$500 for original holster (very scarce).

These models were manufactured in production lots of approx. 100 (as demand dictated).

MODEL 66 LEVER ACTION — 12, 20, or .410 ga. single shot lever action, field gun only. Mfg. 1963-1978.

	$125	$95	$90	$75	$70	$65	$55

Add 33% to .410 ga.
Add 25% for VRs that were also available on special order.

▲ *Model 66 RS* — 20 ga. slug gun with 22 in. barrel and rifle type sights, recoil pad.

	$150	$130	$110	$90	$80	$70	$60

Note: Ventilated ribs were also available on special order — add 25%.

SHOTGUNS: O/U

Please refer to the Fabarm section in this text for those models previously imported by Ithaca (imported 1994-95).

SKB SHOTGUNS: PREVIOUSLY IMPORTED BY ITHACA

Note: Can be found under SKB heading.

SHOTGUNS: SLIDE ACTION

In 1987, Ithaca Acquisition Corp. reintroduced the Model 37 as the Model 87. New Model 87s are listed below and also include pre-1986 mfg. (Model 37s). Unless a

Grading	100%	98%	95%	90%	80%	70%	60%

particular Model 37 specimen has rare features, special wood, or was a deluxe order, values will approximate most older models as well.

Even though Ithaca has ceased production on the slide action shotguns listed below, manufacturer's suggested retail prices have been intentionally included to give the reader the most recent factory information.

MODEL 37 TRENCH AND RIOT GUNS — see separate listing under Trench Guns in the T Section.

MODEL 37 DS POLICE SPECIAL — 12 ga. only, 18½ in. barrel with rifle sights, Parkerized finish on metal, oil finished stock, typically subcontracted by police departments or law enforcement agencies, with or without unit code markings.

	$295	$250	$225	$200	$185	$170	$160

MODEL 37 FEATHERLIGHT STANDARD — 12, 16, or 20 ga., bottom ejection, 4 shot mag., 26, 28, or 30 in. barrel, hammerless, take down, any standard choke. Mfg. 1937-disc.

	$245	$225	$195	$175	$160	$140	$125

MODEL 37V — similar to 37, except VR. Mfg. 1962-disc.

	$315	$260	$240	$195	$180	$170	$165

All currently manufactured Model 37s have the Featherlight designation. Prices above are for older manufactured Model 37's.

MODEL 37D — similar to 37, except recoil pad, beavertail forearm, checkered. Mfg. 1954-1981.

	$295	$275	$235	$200	$185	$175	$160

MODEL 37DV — similar to 37D, except VR. Mfg. 1962-1981.

	$350	$295	$250	$225	$200	$185	$170

MODEL 37 FIELD GRADE MAGNUM — 12 or 20 ga., 3 in. chambers, VR, walnut stock and corncob forearm, supplied with three choke tubes. Mfg. 1984-1986.

	$300	$240	$195	$180	$170	$165	$150

Last Mfg.'s Sug. Retail was $428.

MODEL 37 FIELD GRADE STANDARD — 12 or 20 ga., economy model, corncob forearm, 26, 28, or 30 in. barrel. Mfg. 1983-1985 only.

	$245	$225	$195	$175	$160	$140	$120

Last Mfg.'s Sug. Retail was $298.

MODEL 37 ENGLISH ULTRALITE — 12 or 20 ga., 25 or 26 in. barrels, world's lightest pump, 20 ga. weighs 4¾ lb., 12 ga. weighs 5½ lbs., checkered straight stock. Mfg. 1983-1986.

	$375	$325	$295	$250	$225	$200	$180

Last Mfg.'s Sug. Retail was $522.

MODEL 37R — solid rib. Mfg. 1937-1967.

Plain stock	$295	$200	$175	$145	$130	$110	$90
Checkered stock	$335	$245	$200	$175	$165	$145	$120

MODEL 37R DELUXE — similar to 37R, except fancy wood. Mfg. 1937-1955.

	$395	$325	$265	$230	$210	$195	$165

MODEL 37 SUPREME — 12 ga. only, deluxe checkered walnut stock and forearm, 28 or 30 in. VR barrel, engraved receiver, approx. 7¾ lbs. Disc.

	$650	$575	$495	$425	$375	$325	$295

MODEL 37S SKEET GRADE — similar to 37, except Knicker VR, large forearm, fancy wood. Mfg. 1937-1955.

	$475	$425	$375	$335	$300	$275	$250

Grading	100%	98%	95%	90%	80%	70%	60%

MODEL 37T TRAP GRADE — similar to 37S, except trap stock, select walnut, recoil pad. Mfg. 1937-1955.

	$475	$425	$375	$325	$295	$275	$250

Add 20% for early models with Fleur-de-lis checkering.

MODEL 37T TARGET GRADE — replaced 37S and 37T. Mfg. from 1955-1961.

	$475	$425	$375	$325	$295	$275	$250

MODEL 37 SUPER DELUXE DEERSLAYER — similar to Model 37 (87) Deerslayer, except fancy wood. Mfg. 1962-1985.

	$390	$335	$300	$270	$235	$210	$185

Last Mfg.'s Sug. Retail was $447.

MODEL 37 BICENTENNIAL — 12 ga., engraved, fancy wood, cased with pewter buckle, 1,776 mfg. 1976, 100% value assumes NIB condition with case and belt buckle.

	$425	$375	$340	$315	$295	$270	$250

MODEL 37 2500 SERIES CENTENNIAL — 12 ga., customized version of the Model 37 commemorating Ithaca's 100th year anniversary, silver plated, etched antique finish receiver, deluxe walnut. Mfg. 1980-1984.

	$850	$690	$600	$505	$460	$415	$370

Last Mfg.'s Sug. Retail was $919.

MODEL 37 PRESENTATION — 12 ga., blued, engraved, gold mounted receiver with extra-fancy walnut, cased, limited production. Mfg. 1981-86.

	$1,475	$1,245	$1,080	$915	$830	$745	$665

Last Mfg.'s Sug. Retail was $1,658.

MODEL 37 DUCKS UNLIMITED — 12 ga., VR.

	$385	$305	$275				

MODEL 37 $1000 GRADE — all gauges, deluxe engraving and checkering, gold inlaid, select figured walnut, hand-finished parts. Mfg. 1937-1940.

	$5,750	$5,200	$4,750	$4,250	$3,750	$3,250	$2,650

MODEL 37 $5000 GRADE — similar to $1000 Grade, post-war designation. Mfg. 1947-1967.

	$5,250	$4,850	$4,250	$3,850	$3,250	$2,850	$2,250

MODEL 87 FIELD (BASIC) — 12 or 20 ga., 3 in. chamber, economy model, walnut stock and forearm with pressed checkering, 26, 28, or 30 (disc.) in. barrel with 3 choke tubes standard. Reintroduced 1987.

Mfg.'s Sug. Retail	$477		$360	$290	$240	$195	$170	$160	$145

▲ *Model 87 Basic Field Combo* — 12 or 20 ga., includes 20/25 in. deer barrel with special bore and 28 in. VR multi-choke field barrel, unckeckered walnut stock and corncob forearm, 7 lbs. Mfg. 1989-92.

	$400	$315	$275	$235	$210	$190	$170

Last Mfg.'s Sug. Retail was $459.

Add $32 for rifled bore barrel.
Add $104 for laminated wood (includes rifle bored barrel).

▲ *Model 87 Camo Field* — 12 ga. only, 3 in. chamber, 24, 26, or 28 in. VR barrel, camo-seal rust resistant finish on exterior parts. Available in either green or brown camo finish. Mfg. began 1986, resumed 1988.

Mfg.'s Sug. Retail	$542		$425	$315	$260	$200	$175	$160	$145

▲ *Model 87 Turkey Field* — 12 ga. only, 24 in. VR barrel with choice of fixed full choke or full choke tube, camo or matte blue finish. New 1989.

Mfg.'s Sug. Retail	$466		$365	$285	$235	$190	$170	$160	$145

Add $85 for camo finish.
Add $43 for full choke tube.

Grading	100%	98%	95%	90%	80%	70%	60%

MODEL 87 ULTRALITE FIELD — 12 or 20 ga., 3 in. chamber, aluminum receiver, 20 (disc. 1988), 24, 25 (disc. 1988), or 26 in. barrel. 20 ga. weighs 5 lbs., 12 ga. weighs 5¾ lbs, multi-chokes (3) became standard in 1989. Originally mfg. 1985-86, reintroduced 1988-90.

			$400	$340	$285	$240	$210	$190	$170

Last Mfg.'s Sug. Retail was $481.

Add $50 for slim grip model (12½ in. stock - disc. 1985).
Subtract $42 if without multiple choke feature.
The 20 and 25 in. barrels were disc. when mfg. was resumed 1988.

▲ *Model 87 Ultra Deluxe* — similar to Ultralite Field except has cut checkering, high gloss lacquer finish, and gold trigger. Mfg 1989-91.

	$425	$360	$300	$250	$220	$190	$170

Last Mfg.'s Sug. Retail was $514.

MODEL ENGLISH 87 — 20 ga. only, 3 in. chamber, 24 or 26 in. VR barrel with 3 choke tubes, steel receiver, checkered walnut stock and forearm, recoil pad, 6¾ lbs. New 1991.

Mfg.'s Sug. Retail	$545	$425	$315	$260	$200	$175	$160	$145

MODEL 87 DELUXE — similar to Model 87 Field Grade except has cut checkering, 26, 28, or 30 in. VR barrel, high gloss lacquer finish, and gold trigger, newer mfg. includes 3 choke tubes. New 1989.

Mfg.'s Sug. Retail	$533	$415	$310	$255	$200	$175	$160	$145

Add $54 for combo package (includes 20 in. special bore deer barrel, disc. 1992).
Add $87 for combo package with 20 or 25 in. rifled bore deer barrel, disc. 1992.

▲ *Model 87 Deluxe Magnum* — 12 or 20 ga., 3 in. chambers, VR, deluxe wood with checkered forearm. Mfg. 1981-1986, production resumed 1988 only.

	$320	$270	$230	$210	$200	$185	$165

Last Mfg.'s Sug. Retail was $395.

Add $77 for Combo package (extra 28 in. barrel).
New mfg. 20 ga. shotguns were available with a 25 in. barrel only (with choke tubes).

MODEL 87 SUPREME GRADE — 12 or 20 ga., presentation walnut, high luster blue, limited production, previously available in either trap, skeet, or field models, fixed chokes. Originally manufactured 1967-86, reintroduced 1988.

Mfg.'s Sug. Retail	$809	$640	$475	$395	$325	$295	$270	$250

BASIC DEERSLAYER — 12 ga. only, 20 or 25 in. special bore or rifled barrel, oil finished stock and corncob forearm with no checkering, iron sights, matte metal finish, 7 lbs. New 1989.

Mfg.'s Sug. Retail	$425	$345	$280	$240	$195	$175	$160	$145

Add $40 for rifled barrel.

MODEL 87 FIELD DEERSLAYER — 12 or 20 ga., rifle slug barrel, 20 or 25 in. special bore barrel, open sights. Mfg. 1959-86, reintroduced 1988-1993.

	$300	$250	$210	$180	$160	$150	$140

Last Mfg.'s Sug. Retail was $364.

MODEL 87 DELUXE DEERSLAYER — similar to Field Deerslayer except has cut checkering, high gloss lacquer finish, and gold trigger. New 1989.

Mfg.'s Sug. Retail	$465	$365	$285	$235	$190	$170	$160	$145

Add $34 for rifled bore.
Add $120 for combo package (28 in. multi-choke barrel).

▲ *Model 87 Ultra Deerslayer* — similar to Deluxe Deerslayer except has aluminum frame. Mfg. 1989-90 only.

	$350	$285	$245	$200	$175	$160	$145

Last Mfg.'s Sug. Retail was $444.

MONTE CARLO DEERSLAYER II — 12 ga. only, 20 or 25 in. barrel with rifling, Monte Carlo stock and forearm with cut checkering, receiver is drilled and tapped for scope mounting, 7 lbs. New 1989.

Mfg.'s Sug. Retail	$567	$445	$335	$270	$210	$175	$160	$145

Grading	100%	98%	95%	90%	80%	70%	60%

DEERSLAYER II FAST TWIST — 12 ga. only, 25 in. rifled permanently fixed barrel, Monte Carlo stock with checkering, receiver is drilled and tapped. Mfg. 1992-1993.

		$440	$385	$325	$275	$235	$200	$180

Last Mfg.'s Sug. Retail was $550.

MODEL 87 MILITARY & POLICE — 12 or 20 (new 1989) ga., short barrel Model 37 w/normal stock or pistol grip only, 18½ or 20 in. barrel, 5 or 8 shot. Originally disc. 1983, reintroduced 1989-1993.

		$265	$230	$200	$180	$170	$160	$150

Last Mfg.'s Sug. Retail was $323.

> Add $104 for nickel finish (mfg. 1991-92 only).
> Subtract $35 without parkerizing (disc.).

SHOTGUNS: SEMI-AUTO

DEER GUN — 12 ga. only, 3 in. chamber, 24 in. rifled barrel with front and rear rifle sights, 5 shot mag., 7 lbs. Importation begun 1994.

Mfg.'s Sug. Retail	$775	$695	$475	$425	$375	$325	$300	$285

MODEL 51A FEATHERLIGHT STANDARD — 12 or 20 ga., 30 in. full, 28 in. full or mod., 26 in. imp. cyl., gas operated, autoloading, checkered pistol grip stock. Mfg. 1970-1985. Vent. rib became standard during late production.

	100%	98%	95%	90%	80%	70%	60%
Older models (no VR)	$250	$230	$200	$180	$165	$150	$130
Recent production (w/VR)	$285	$265	$235	$210	$190	$175	$165

Last Mfg.'s Sug. Retail with VR was $477.

MODEL 51A MAGNUM — similar to 51 Standard, except 3 in. shells only, blue finish, recoil pad, VR became standard in 1984. Disc. for 1985.

	100%	98%	95%	90%	80%	70%	60%
Older models w/o VR	$265	$235	$220	$205	$180	$165	$150
Vent. rib	$295	$275	$250	$225	$200	$185	$170

MODEL 51A MAGNUM WATERFOWLER — similar to 51 Standard, except 3 in. shells only, matte finished metal & flat finished walnut, recoil pad. Vent. rib standard. Mfg. 1984-1986.

		$325	$295	$275	$250	$230	$200	$180

Last Mfg.'s Sug. Retail was $625.

> Add $40 for camouflaged exterior finish (mfg. 1986 only).

MODEL 51A SUPREME TRAP — similar to 51 Standard, except 12 ga. only, 30 in. barrel, 7 post rib, full choke, select wood, pad, trap style stock. Add $36 for Monte Carlo. Mfg. 1970-1986.

		$425	$365	$315	$295	$270	$250	$230

Last Mfg.'s Sug. Retail was $869.

MODEL 51A SUPREME SKEET — similar to 51 Standard, except 26 in. VR barrel, skeet choke, select wood. Mfg. 1970-present. 20 ga. was available 1983. Disc. 1986.

		$465	$395	$340	$300	$280	$260	$240

Last Mfg.'s Sug. Retail was $858.

MODEL 51A DEERSLAYER — similar to 51 Standard, with 24 in. slug barrel, rifle sights, recoil pad, no rib. Mfg. 1972-1983.

		$350	$300	$260	$230	$195	$180	$165

Last Mfg.'s Sug. Retail was $477.

MODEL 51A TURKEY GUN — .12 ga. Mag. only, 26 in. barrel, matte finish, sling and swivels included. Mfg. 1984-1986.

		$360	$305	$275	$265	$250	$230	$210

Last Mfg.'s Sug. Retail was $625.

MODEL 51 DUCKS UNLIMITED — similar to 51 Deluxe, with D/U emblem on receiver.

		$425	$375	$335	$300	$280	$260	$230

Grading	100%	98%	95%	90%	80%	70%	60%

MODEL 51 PRESENTATION — 12 ga., blued, engraved, gold engraved receiver with deluxe walnut. Mfg. 1984-1986.

	$1,250	$1,000	$875	$700	$575	$450	$325

Last Mfg.'s Sug. Retail was $1,658.

MODEL XL 300 — 12 or 20 ga., gas operated, various barrel lengths with or w/o VR, mfg. 1973-76.

	$250	$230	$200	$180	$165	$150	$130

Add 15% for VR barrel.

MODEL XL 900 — 12 or 20 ga., gas operated, various barrel lengths with VR, mfg. 1973-78.

	$295	$275	$245	$210	$185	$170	$150

Add 10% for skeet, trap, or slug variations.

SEMI-AUTO: MAG-10 SEMI-AUTO

All Ithaca Mag-10s were disc. 1986.

MAG-10 — 10 ga., 3½ in. Mag., semi-auto, various barrel lengths, stainless steel breech block assembly, gas operated, various chokes, plain barrel, 11 lb. Mfg. 1975-1986.
100% values assume NIB condition - if without, subtract 10%.

▲ *Standard Grade* — no checkering, ribless barrel, dull finished wood.

	$600	$550	$500	$460	$430	$395	$375

Last Mfg.'s Sug. Retail was $726.

▲ *Standard Grade with VR* — available in 22, 26, 28, or 32 in. barrel lengths - otherwise similar to Standard Grade.

	$595	$550	$495	$450	$400	$360	$330

Last Mfg.'s Sug. Retail was $781.

Add $60 for camouflaged exterior finish.
Add $60 for interchangeable choke tubes (3) - became available in 1986.

▲ *Deluxe Vent* — select checkered walnut stock and forearm, 22, 26, 28, or 32 in. barrels, high lustre wood finish.

	$675	$600	$550	$495	$450	$400	$350

Last Mfg.'s Sug. Retail was $924.

▲ *Supreme Grade* — extra-select checkered walnut stock and forearm, otherwise similar to Deluxe Vent.

	$795	$725	$675	$595	$550	$495	$450

Last Mfg.'s Sug. Retail was $1,124.

▲ *Mag. 10 Roadblocker* — 22 in. cylinder bored ribless barrel, parkerized finish.

	$625	$575	$500	$460	$430	$400	$375

Last Mfg.'s Sug. Retail was $741.

▲ *National Wild Turkey Fed. Special Edition* — mfg. in 1985 only.

	$950	$795	$625

MAG-10 PRESENTATION OR CENTENNIAL — 10 ga. Mag., blued, engraved, gold inlaid receiver, extra fancy walnut. Limited production. Approx. 200 mfg. in Presentation Grade 1983-1986.

	$1,875	$1,550	$1,300	$1,050	$915	$830	$745

Last Mfg.'s Sug. Retail was $1,727.

PERAZZI SHOTGUNS

NOTE: Ithaca was sole importer for Perazzi in the '70s. All new and used models will be in the P section under Perazzi. Perazzi today distributes their own firearms.

IVER JOHNSON ARMS, INC.

Manufactured in Fitchburg, MA, 1883-1984 and Jacksonville, AR 1984-1993. Formerly Johnson Bye & Co. 1871-1883. Renamed Iver Johnson & Co. in 1871 until 1891. Renamed Iver Johnson's Arms & Cycle Works in 1891 with manufacturing moving to Fitchburg, MA. In 1975 the name changed to Iver Johnson's Arms, Inc., and two years later, company facilities were moved to Middlesex, MA. In 1982,

Grading	100%	98%	95%	90%	80%	70%	60%

production was moved to Jacksonville, AR under the trade name Iver Johnson Arms, Inc. In 1983, Universal Firearms, Inc. was acquired by Iver Johnson Arms, Inc.

Iver Johnson Arms was sold in March of 1987 and was acquired by American Military Arms Corporation (AMAC). AMAC ceased operations in early 1993.

REVOLVERS

MODEL 1900 — .22, .32 S&W, or .38 S&W cal., double action, 2½, 4½, or 6 in. barrel, fixed sights, blue or nickel, rubber grips. Mfg. 1900-1947.

	$125	$80	$70	$60	$55	$45	$40

MODEL 1900 TARGET — .22 LR, 6 shot, 6 or 9½ in. barrel, blue, fixed sights. Mfg. 1925-1942.

	$140	$90	$80	$70	$65	$55	$50

TARGET SEALED 8 — .22 LR, 8 shot, 6 or 10 in. barrel, blue, fixed sights, rubber grips. Mfg. 1931-1957.

	$150	$100	$95	$80	$75	$65	$60

TARGET 9 SHOT — similar to Target Sealed 8, except 9 shot. Mfg. 1929-1946.

	$145	$90	$80	$70	$65	$55	$50

SAFETY HAMMER MODEL — .22 LR, .32 S&W, or .38 S&W cal., 2 or 3 in. barrel standard, 4, 5, or 6 in. available at extra cost, fixed sights, blue (standard) or nickel, break open. Mfg. 1892-1950.

	$125	$80	$70	$60	$55	$45	$40

SAFETY HAMMERLESS — .32 S&W or .38 S&W cal., 2, 3 (.32 only), 3¼, 4, 5, or 6 in. barrel, double action only, break open, fixed sights, rubber grips, blue or nickel. Mfg. 1895-1950.

	$125	$100	$95	$80	$75	$65	$60

.22 SUPERSHOT — .22 LR, 6 in. barrel, blue, fixed sights, checkered wood grips, break open, no counterbore. Mfg. 1929-1949.

	$150	$80	$70	$60	$55	$45	$40

TRIGGER COCKING SINGLE ACTION — .22 LR, 8 shot, 6 in. barrel, break open, counterbored, blue, checkered wood grips, first pull on trigger cocks, second fires. Mfg. 1940-1947. Rare in 100% condition.

	$175	$120	$110	$95	$80	$75	$65

.22 TARGET SINGLE ACTION — .22 LR, 8 shot, 6 in. barrel, break open, counterbored, checkered wood, adj. grips and sights. Mfg. 1938-1948.

	$160	$120	$110	$95	$80	$75	$65

SUPERSHOT SEALED 8 — .22 LR, 8 shot, break open, blue, adj. sights, checkered wood grips. Mfg. 1931-1957.

	$175	$130	$120	$110	$90	$85	$75

SUPERSHOT 9 — similar to Sealed 8, only 9 shot, not counterbored. Mfg. 1929-1949.

	$135	$90	$80	$75	$60	$50	$40

PROTECTOR SEALED 8 — .22 LR, 8 shot, 2½ in. barrel, break open, fixed sights, blue, wood grips. Mfg. 1933-1949.

	$175	$135	$125	$110	$90	$80	$75

SUPERSHOT MODEL 844 — .22 LR, 8 shot, 4½ or 6 in. barrel, adj. sights, break open, blue, wood grips. Mfg. 1955-1956.

	$100	$90	$85	$80	$75	$60	$50

ARMSWORTH MODEL 855 — .22 LR, single action, 8 shot, 6 in. barrel, break open, blue, adj. sights, wood grips, adj. finger rest. Mfg. 1955-1957.

	$135	$125	$120	$110	$90	$80	$75

Grading	100%	98%	95%	90%	80%	70%	60%

MODEL 55A TARGET — .22 LR, 8 shot, 4½ or 6 in. barrel, solid frame, blue, fixed sights, wood grips, loading gate. Mfg. 1955-1984.

	$75	$65	$55	$45	$35	$30	$15

CADET — .22 LR, .22 WRM, .32 S&W, .38 S&W, or .38 Spl. cal., 2½ in. barrel, blue, fixed sights, plastic grips. Mfg. 1955-1984.

	$110	$90	$80	$75	$65	$55	$50

MODEL 57A TARGET — .22 LR, 8 shot, 4½ or 6 in. barrel, solid frame, blue, adj. sights, wood grips. Mfg. 1955-1975.

	$100	$80	$75	$65	$55	$45	$40

MODEL 66 TRAILSMAN — .22 LR, 6 in. barrel, break open, blue, adj. sights, rebounding hammer, wood grips. Mfg. 1958-1975.

	$110	$90	$85	$75	$65	$55	$50

SIDEWINDER — .22 LR, 6 or 8 shot, 4¾ or 6 in. barrel, solid frame, blue, nickel, or case hardened plastic grips, wood on case color model. Mfg. 1961-disc. 8 shot pre-1975.

	$110	$90	$85	$75	$65	$55	$50

SIDEWINDER S — similar to Sidewinder, except .22 WMR, interchangeable cylinder.

	$125	$100	$95	$85	$75	$65	$60

MODEL 67 VIKING — .22 LR, 8 shot, 4½ or 6 in. barrel, break open, blue, adj. sights, wood grips with thumbrest. Mfg. 1964-1975.

	$135	$110	$100	$95	$85	$75	$65

MODEL 67S VIKING — .22 LR, .32 S&W, or .38 S&W cal., 8 shot in .22, 5 shot in .32 or .38, 2¾ in. barrel, break open, adj. sights, plastic grips. Mfg. 1964-1975.

	$130	$100	$95	$85	$75	$60	$50

AMERICAN BULLDOG — .22 LR, .22 WRM, or .38 Spl. cal., 6 shot in .22, 5 shot in .38, 2½ or 4 in. barrel, blue or nickel, adj. sights, plastic grips. Mfg. 1974-1976.

	$135	$110	$100	$90	$80	$65	$60

ROOKIE — .38 Spl., 5 shot, 4 in. barrel, solid frame, blue or nickel, plastic grips. Mfg. 1975-1984.

	$100	$80	$75	$65	$55	$45	$35

SPORTSMAN — .22 LR, 6 shot, 4¾ or 6 in. barrel, solid frame, blue, fixed sights, plastic grips. Mfg. 1974-1976.

	$100	$80	$75	$65	$55	$45	$35

DELUXE TARGET — similar to Sportsman, adj. sights. Mfg. 1975-1976.

	$110	$90	$85	$75	$65	$55	$40

SWING OUT — .22 LR, .22 WRM, .32 S&W, or .38 S&W cal., 6 shot in .22, 5 shot in .32 or .38, 2, 3, or 4 in. barrel, VR, 4 or 6 in., blue or nickel, fixed or adj. sights. Mfg. 1977-1984.

	$130	$110	$100	$90	$80	$75	$65

▲ *VR Barrel* — 4 or 6 in. VR barrel, adj. sights.

	$170	$150	$140	$130	$125	$120	$100

PISTOLS: SEMI-AUTO

AMAC also manufactured a Super Enforcer .30 cal., Delta 786 9mm (disc. 1989), and a M-2 machine gun which are not listed in this text.

Grading	100%	98%	95%	90%	80%	70%	60%

TRAILSMEN PISTOL — .22 LR only, semi-auto, all steel construction, 4½ or 6 in. barrel, blue finish, black checkered composition grips, 10 shot mag., approx. 30 oz. Mfg. 1985-86 and reintroduced 1990 only.

	$200	$165	$145	$130	$120	$110	$100

Last Mfg.'s Sug. Retail was $230.

Add $20 for hardwood stocks and high polish blue (disc. 1990).

PONY PISTOL (PO380 SERIES) — .380 ACP only, semi-auto single action, 3 in. barrel, 6 shot mag., all steel construction, blue or matte blue finish, 20 oz. Mfg. 1985-1986 (by Firearms International) and reintroduced 1990 only.

	$290	$245	$210	$185	$170	$155	$140

Last Mfg.'s Sug. Retail was $330.

▲ **Pony .380 Stainless** — similar to Pony Pistol, except is stainless steel construction. New 1990 only.

	$315	$280	$240				

Last Mfg.'s Sug. Retail was $365.

▲ **Nickel Pony** — with nickel finish. Mfg. 1985 only.

	$260	$230	$215	$200	$185	$170	$160

Last Mfg.'s Sug. Retail was $290 for nickel finish.

POCKET PISTOL (TP SERIES) — .22 LR or .25 ACP cal., semi-auto, double action, 3 in. barrel, 7 shot finger tip extension mag., black plastic grips, fixed sights, blue or matte finish, 15 oz. Previously mfg. 1985-86, reintroduced 1988-90.

	$145	$125	$110	$100	$90	$80	$70

Last Mfg.'s Sug. Retail was $165.

Add $15 for nickel finish (disc. 1989).

AMAC-22/25 COMPACT — .22 Short (disc.) or .25 ACP cal., semi-auto, single action, 5 shot mag., 2 in. barrel, all steel construction, plastic grips, 9.3 oz. Disc. 1993.

	$165	$135	$115	$100	$90	$80	$70

Last Mfg.'s Sug. Retail was $200.

Add $10 for nickel finish (disc. 1990).

▲ **Compact Elite Engraved** — similar to .25 ACP Compact, except has extensive engraving. Mfg. 1991-93.

	$850	$600	$475				

Last Mfg.'s Sug. Retail was $1,000.

SILVER HAWK — .22 LR or .25 ACP cal., double action semi-auto, similar to TP-22 Series, except is stainless steel. Mfg. 1990-93.

	$215	$185	$160				

Last Mfg.'s Sug. Retail was $250.

SUPER ENFORCER (MODEL 3000) — .30 cal. only, pistol version of the Carbine with 11 in. shrouded barrel. Add $40 for stainless steel (disc. for 1986). Mfg. 1985-1986 only.

	$285	$250	$225	$200	$175	$160	$145

Last Mfg.'s Sug. Retail was $255.

▲ **Enforcer** — similar to Super Enforcer model, except has 10½ in. barrel. Reintroduced 1988-disc. 1993.

	$325	$275	$240	$200	$175	$160	$145

Last Mfg.'s Sug. Retail was $417.

CATTLEMAN MAGNUM — .357 Mag., .44 Mag., or .45 Colt, single action, 6 shot, Colt replica, 4¾, 5½, or 7½ in. barrel, case color frame, blue barrel, and brass grip frame, smooth walnut grips, fixed sights. Disc. 1984.

	$190	$175	$150	$140	$130	$125	$110
.44 Mag.	$220	$190	$175	$165	$145	$135	$125

BUCKHORN MAGNUM — similar to Cattleman, except flat top, adj. sights.

	$210	$190	$175	$165	$145	$140	$125

Grading	100%	98%	95%	90%	80%	70%	60%

BUNTLINE BUCKHORN MAGNUM — similar to Buckhorn, only 18 in. barrel, detachable stock.

	$345	$310	$295	$275	$260	$250	$225
.44 Mag.	$375	$325	$310	$295	$280	$275	$250

TRAIL BLAZER — .22 LR, or .22 Mag. cal., interchangeable cylinder, 5½ or 6½ in. barrel, blue.

	$175	$145	$130	$120	$110	$100	$80

RIFLES

MODEL X — .22 Short, Long, or LR, bolt action, single shot, 22 in. barrel, open sight, pistol grip with knob forend. Mfg. 1928-1932.

	$90	$60	$50	$40	$35	$30	$25

MODEL 2X — improved Model X, 24 in. heavy barrel larger stock, adj. sights. Mfg. 1932-1955.

	$120	$95	$75	$50	$40	$35	$30

LI'L CHAMP — .22 LR only, single shot bolt action, 16¼ in. barrel, black molded stock, nickel plated bolt, youth dimensions, (32½ in. overall length), 3 lbs. Introduced 1986, reintroduced 1988 only.

	$75	$60	$50	$45	$40	$35	$35

Last Mfg.'s Sug. Retail was $92.

LONG RANGE RIFLE — .308 (new 1991) or .50 BMG cal., bolt action design, single shot, 29 in. stainless steel fluted barrel with muzzle brake, adj. trigger pull, built in bipod, adj. rail stock, includes Leupold M-1 Ultra 20X scope, 36 lbs. Limited mfg. between 1988-1993.

	$4,350	$3,500	$3,150	$2,750	$2,400	$2,100	$1,800

Last Mfg.'s Sug. Retail was $5,000.

9MM CARBINE (JJ9MM SERIES) — 9mm only, copy of U.S. military M1, 16 in. barrel, blue finish only, 20 shot mag. Mfg. 1985-86 only.

▲ *Hardwood Stock Model* — disc. 1986.

	$230	$200	$180	$170	$160	$150	$140

Last Mfg.'s Sug. Retail was $255.

▲ *Standard Model* — with plastic stock. Disc. 1985.

	$225	$200	$180	$170	$160	$150	$140

Last Mfg.'s Sug. Retail was $250.

▲ *Folding Plastic Stock Model* — disc. 1985.

	$255	$225	$200	$180	$170	$160	$150

Last Mfg.'s Sug. Retail was $281.

DELTA-786 CARBINE — 9mm Para., semi-auto, patterned after the U.S. military M1 Carbine, 16 in. barrel, matte black finish. Mfg. 1989 only.

	$575	$425	$360	$325	$295	$260	$230

Last Mfg.'s Sug. Retail was $665.

.30 CAL. CARBINE — .30 M1 or 9mm Para. (new 1991) cal., semi-auto, 18 or 20 (new 1991) in. barrel, available in various stock configurations, hardwood stock. Mfg. 1985-1986, reintroduced 1988-disc. 1993.

	$285	$215	$190	$165	$150	$140	$130

Last Mfg.'s Sug. Retail was $350.

Add $16 for 9mm Para. cal.
Add $35 for walnut stock, Parkerized finish (disc. 1990), or 20 in. barrel (new 1991).

▲ *Paratrooper Model* — similar to standard model, except has folding synthetic stock. Disc. 1993.

	$345	$270	$225	$195	$165	$150	$140

Last Mfg.'s Sug. Retail was $433.

▲ *Stainless Steel Variation* — disc. 1985.

	$230	$200	$180

Last Mfg.'s Sug. Retail was $250.

Grading	100%	98%	95%	90%	80%	70%	60%

▲ *5.7mm Johnson (Spitfire) Cal.* — remilled, add $30 for stainless steel.

	$195	$175	$165	$155	$145	$135	$125

Last Mfg.'s Sug. Retail was $219.

.22 CAL. U.S. CARBINE — .22 LR or .22 Mag. cal., 18½ in. barrel, except for Mag. (19.3 in.), 5.8 lbs., 15 shot mag., sling swivels. Mfg. 1985-1986, reintroduced 1988 only.

	$150	$120	$110	$100	$90	$85	$80

Last Mfg.'s Sug. Retail was $183 for .22 Mag. cal.

Add $120 for .22 Mag. model (gas operated — disc. 1986).

Last Mfg.'s Sug. Retail was $166 for .22 LR cal.

TARGETMASTER SLIDE ACTION — .22 LR or Mag. (disc. 1986) cal., 18½ in. barrel, 12 shot (LR) tube mag., 5¾ lbs. Mfg. 1985 only, reintroduced 1988-90.

	$175	$140	$125	$115	$100	$90	$80

Last Mfg.'s Sug. Retail was $209.

This model was designated EW.22 HBP previously.

MODEL EW.22 HBL LEVER ACTION (WAGONMASTER) — .22 S, L, and LR or .22 Mag. cal., 18½ in. barrel, walnut finish, hardwood stock, blue finish, 5¾ lbs., grooved for scope mounts. Mfg. 1985-1986, reintroduced 1988-90.

	$175	$140	$125	$115	$100	$90	$80

Last Mfg.'s Sug. Retail was $209.

Add $23 for .22 Mag. cal. (19 in. barrel).
This model was designated EW.22 HBL previously. It was also available in a Junior model featuring smaller dimensions; values same as listed above.

TRAIL BLAZER SEMI-AUTO (MODEL IJ.22 HB) — .22 LR only, 10 shot clip mag., 18½ in. barrel, 5.8 lbs. Mfg. 1985 only.

	$115	$100	$90	$85	$80	$75	$70

Last Mfg.'s Sug. Retail was $125.

SHOTGUNS

CHAMPION — 10, 12, 16, 20, 24, 28, 32, or .410 ga., also available in .44, .45, 12mm, or 14mm rifle cal., single barrel shotgun or rifle, 26-32 in. full barrel, exposed hammer, auto ejector, plain pistol grip stock. Mfg. 1909-1956.

	$145	$100	$80	$60	$40	$35	$25

Values on both smaller gauge shotguns and rifles would be considerably higher than those listed above. A mint .32 ga. might command 400% more than the above values. Rifles will also bring premiums over values listed above.

MATTED RIB GRADE — similar to Champion, except in 12, 16, or 20 ga. only, solid rib, checkered stock. Mfg. 1909-1948.

	$165	$115	$95	$70	$50	$45	$40

This model has either a semi-octagon (with top matted) or jacketed breech.

TRAP GRADE — similar to Matted Rib, except 32 in. full barrel, 12 ga., vent rib. Mfg. 1909-1942.

	$275	$165	$140	$120	$100	$90	$80

HERCULES GRADE — 12, 16, 20, 28, or .410 ga., double barrel, 26-32 in. barrels, hammerless, boxlock, various chokes, extractors and double triggers standard, checkered pistol grip or straight stock. Mfg. 1918-1943.

	$600	$400	$375	$365	$335	$310	$290

Add $100 for auto ejectors.
Add $100 for SST.
Add 10% for 16 ga.
Add 20% for 20 ga.
Add 200% for 28 ga.
Add 100% for .410 ga.

The Hercules Model was mfg. in both USA and Canada. The Hercules name was dropped in 1936 and became known as the "Iver Johnson Hammerless" until the end of production.

Grading	100%	98%	95%	90%	80%	70%	60%

Case colored frames were standard until 1936, blued frames were standard 1937-1943. A special run of Hercules Doubles was built in the 1930s for Montgomery Ward under the "Western Field" name. All Western Field guns had a beavertail forearm, twin ivory sights, and recoil pad. Hercules 28 ga. SxS's are extremely rare.

SKEET-ER MODEL — 12, 16, 20, 28, or .410 ga., similar to Hercules Model, except has blued receiver, super select wood and beavertail forearm, many Skeet-ers were special order guns with options including selective or non-selective Miller trigger, custom stock, barrel chokes, chamber lengths, checkering and wood finishes, sling swivels, recoil pad, checkered butt, VR, and various engraving patterns. Approx. 1,800 mfg. 1933-1942.

	$1,095	$800	$600	$525	$450	$410	$390

Add 20% for auto ejectors.
Add 20% for SST.
Add 50% for factory VR.
Add 20% for 16 or 20 ga.
Add 100% for 28 or .410 ga.
Add 200% for rare factory engraving.

.410 ga. is the most commonly encountered gun and was made on a special small frame. This model was probably responsible for more Skeet records than any other American .410 ga. SxS shotgun.

SUPER TRAP — 12 ga. only, 32 in. full VR, boxlock, extractors, checkered pistol grip stock, beavertail forend and recoil pad. Mfg. until 1942. Scarce.

	$1,095	$750	$550	$475	$415	$395	$370

Add $100 for auto ejectors.
Add $100 for SST.

SILVER SHADOW — O/U, 12 ga., 26 or 28 in. barrels, various chokes, extractors, vent rib, checkered pistol grip stock, Italian mfg. Disc.

	$375	$325	$300	$275	$225	$185	$175

Add $100 for ST.

J section

J.O. ARMS
Please refer to the KSN Industries Ltd. listing in this text.

JP ENTERPRISES, INC.
Manufacturer/customizer located in Shoreview, MN since 1995.

Grading	100%	98%	95%	90%	80%	70%	60%

PISTOLS: SEMI-AUTO

LEVEL I CUSTOM — .45 ACP cal., features Springfield 1911A1 in blue or stainless finish, lapped slide and frame. New 1995.

Mfg.'s Sug. Retail	$599	$550	$495	$450	$400	$360	$330	$300

Add $43 for stainless steel construction.

LEVEL II CUSTOM — similar to Level I Custom, except has JP complete comp kit, reworked trigger, coco bolo grips. New 1995.

Mfg.'s Sug. Retail	$999	$875	$750	$650	$550	$500	$450	$400

Add $51 for stainless steel construction.

RIFLES: SEMI-AUTO

A-2 MATCH — .223 Rem. cal., AR-15 style configuration, includes JP fire control system, composite ambidextrous thumbhole stock with pistol grip, Mil-Spec A-2 upper assembly with match rear sight. New 1995.

Mfg.'s Sug. Retail	$1,085	$995	$875	$750	$625	$550	$475	$415

A-2 FLAT TOP — .223 Rem. cal., features Eagle Arms lower and International Flat Top upper free floating tube, 16 or 20 SGW heavy match barrel with JP recoil eliminator, adj. gas system. New 1995.

Mfg.'s Sug. Retail	$1,295	$1,125	$975	$875	$750	$625	$550	$475

THE EDGE — .223 Rem. cal., match upper/lower receiver system, 2-piece free floating forend, standard or laminated thumbhole wood stock, 16 or 20 in. barrel with recoil eliminator, includes Harris bi-pod. New 1996.

Mfg.'s Sug. Retail	$2,595	$2,375	$2,025	$1,700	$1,425	$1,150	$875	$750

Add $299 for laminated thumbhole stock (when ordered with gun).

JSL (HEREFORD)
Manufacturer located in Hereford, England. Imported until 1994 by Specialty Shooters Supply, Inc. located in Fort Lauderdale, FL. Direct sales only.

SPITFIRE (G1) — 9mm Para. or 9x21mm cal., patterned after the Czech CZ-75/85, 3.7 in. barrel, ambidextrous safety, commander style hammer, black non-slip rubberized grip panels, investment cast stainless steel fabrication, 10 (C/B 1994) or 15* shot mag., 2.2 lbs. Imported 1992-94.

▲ *Spitfire Standard* — includes fixed rear sight, 2 mags., presentation case, and allen key.

Mfg.'s Sug. Retail	$1,332	$1,332	$1,100	$925

Add $81 for adj. rear sight (Sterling Model).

To date, the manufacture of Spitfire variations has been very limited, and as a result, they are not incorporated into this section.

JACKSON HOLE FIREARMS

Previous manufacturer located in Jackson Hole, WY during the mid-70s.

Grading	100%	98%	95%	90%	80%	70%	60%

RIFLES

BOLT ACTION RIFLE—various cals., Mauser 98 action utilizing patented system for interchangeable barrels, checkered walnut stock.

	100%	98%	95%	90%	80%	70%	60%
	$1,050	$875	$800	$725	$650	$575	$495

Jackson Hole Firearms manufactured a limited quantity of their unique interchangeable barrel bolt action rifles. Collectibility to date has been minimal, and values are affected by the J.P. Sauer Models 90 and 200 which also feature the interchangeable barrel design.

JAGD-UND SPORTWAFFEN SUHL GmbH

Manufacturer located in Suhl, Germany since 1535.

Currently, the famous Merkel trademark (mfg. by Jagd-Und Sportwaffen Suhl GmbH) is imported by Gun South Inc. located in Trussville, AL. Please refer to the Merkel listing in this text for current information regarding this older European trademark. See the Trademark Index in this text for current factory information.

JAPANESE MILITARY RIFLES

Manufactured during WWII in Japan.

RIFLES: MILITARY

Subtract 20% if National Crest (chrysanthemum flower) has been ground off front receiver ring.
Subtract 20% if serial numbers are not matching.
Subtract 10%-40% for training rifles of each type.

MODEL 38 ARISAKA RIFLE — Jap. Mauser type action, 6.5mm, 31 in. barrel, adj. sight, adapted 1905.

	100%	98%	95%	90%	80%	70%	60%
	$165	$135	$105	$95	$75	$65	$50

Add 50%+ for short barrel.
Add 50% for sniper variation.

MODEL 38 CAVALRY CARBINE — similar to T38 Rifle, except shorter barrel. Mfg. 1911.

	100%	98%	95%	90%	80%	70%	60%
	$175	$140	$110	$100	$80	$70	$55

Add 300% for paratrooper variation with hinged stock.

MODEL 44 CAVALRY ARISAKA CARBINE — similar to T38 Carbine, 6.5mm with 19 in. barrel, folding bayonet.

	100%	98%	95%	90%	80%	70%	60%
	$275	$235	$210	$190	$170	$155	$135

MODEL 99 SERVICE RIFLE — WWII version of 38, 7.7mm.

	100%	98%	95%	90%	80%	70%	60%
	$165	$135	$110	$100	$80	$70	$55

Add 20% for monopod.
Add 50% for sniper variation.
Add 50%+ for long barrel.

PARATROOPER TAKEDOWN VERSION — adopted 1940, crossbolt barrel lock.

Type 2	100%	98%	95%	90%	80%	70%	60%
	$425	$350	$275	$225	$190	$165	$135

NAMBU PISTOLS — See Nambu section in this text.

JARRETT RIFLES, INC.

Manufacturer located in Jackson, SC since 1979. Direct custom order sales only.

Grading	100%	98%	95%	90%	80%	70%	60%

PISTOLS

CUSTOM XP-1 HUNTER — various cals., re-machined Remington XP-100 action, Jarrett match grade stainless steel barrel, McMillan fiberglass stock, various options.

Mfg.'s Sug. Retail	$2,450	$2,450	$2,100	$1,800	$1,500	$1,250	$995	$850

ULTIMATE REDHAWK — .44 Mag., features Hogue grips and muzzle brake. New 1995.

Mfg.'s Sug. Retail	$950	$950	$875	$750	$625	$550	$500	$450

RIFLES: BOLT ACTION

A wide variety of options is available for Jarrett custom rifles (holders of 16 world records in rifle accuracy). The factory should be contacted directly (see Trademark Index for info.) for pricing and availability regarding these special order options. Custom gunsmithing services are also available and again, the manufacturer should be contacted directly for gunsmith quotations. Custom gunsmithing requires individuals to supply receivers.

Values listed below for Jarrett firearms assume the customer supplies the company with an action - Jarrett then blueprints every action for proper dimensioning and rigid tolerances.

JARRETT CUSTOM RIFLE — various cals., Remington Model 700 right-hand or left-hand action, McMillan fiberglass stock, blued receiver, Jarrett satin finish match grade barrel, sling studs and leather sling, rings and base, weights vary.

Mfg.'s Sug. Retail	$2,850	$2,850	$2,300	$1,850	$1,500	$1,250	$995	$850

WALKABOUT — various cals. in short action only, features Remington Model 7 action (left-hand utilizes Rem. Model 700 short action), weights vary. New 1995.

Mfg.'s Sug. Retail	$2,850	$2,850	$2,300	$1,850	$1,500	$1,250	$995	$850

COUP de GRACE — various cals. New 1996.

Mfg.'s Sug. Retail	$3,495	$3,495	$2,750	$2,300	$1,800	$1,500	$1,250	$995

PROFESSIONAL HUNTER — Mag. cals. to customer's specifications, features Winchester controlled round feed Model 70 action with claw extractor and 3 position bolt shroud safety, Jarrett match grade stainless steel barrel, McMillan stock, quarter rib with iron sights, includes 2 sets of detachable rings and two 1.5X-5X Leupold scopes, takedown action.

Mfg.'s Sug. Retail	$6,000	$6,000	$5,000	$4,250	$3,500	$2,850	$2,300	$1,850

CLASSIC SERIES — only various cals., 100 mfg. 1989 only.

		$3,195	$2,650	$2,100	$1,650	$1,375	$1,150	$875

INVESTOR SERIES — only various cals., 100 mfg. 1989 only.

		$3,195	$2,650	$2,100	$1,650	$1,375	$1,150	$875

ACCURACY LEGEND SERIES — similar to Jarrett Custom Rifle, except has many accuracy tune-ups incorporated as well as muzzle brake. 100 mfg. 1993 only.

		$3,495	$2,850	$2,300	$1,850	$1,500	$1,250	$995

Last Mfg.'s Sug. Retail was $3,495.

COUP de MAIM — various cals., similar to the Jarrett Custom Rifle, includes muzzle brake, matte black or olive drab finish, Model 70 style bolt release. 100 mfg. 1995 only.

		$2,750	$2,300	$1,800	$1,500	$1,250	$995	$775

Last Mfg.'s Sug. Retail was $3,495.

PRIVATE COLLECTION — similar quality as the Jarrett Custom Rifle, except many extra cost special order options are included, ser. numbered 1-100. Mfg. 1994 only.

		$3,495	$2,850	$2,300	$1,850	$1,500	$1,250	$995

Last Mfg.'s Sug. Retail was $3,495.

J

Grading	100%	98%	95%	90%	80%	70%	60%

SILENT PARTNER SERIES — only various cals., only 10 mfg. 1994 only.

	100%	98%	95%	90%	80%	70%	60%
	$3,495	$2,850	$2,300	$1,850	$1,500	$1,250	$995

ULTIMATE HUNTER SERIES — only various cals., 100 mfg. 1989 only.

	100%	98%	95%	90%	80%	70%	60%
	$3,495	$2,850	$2,300	$1,850	$1,500	$1,250	$995

SHOTGUNS

Value changes below reflect customer supplied action.

JARRETT ULTIMATE SHOTGUN — 12 ga., Remington Model 870 action with 21 in. hand lapped barrel with interchangeable chokes, 8 shot mag. extension, matte black or olive drab green finish.

	Mfg.'s Sug. Retail						
	$800	$800	$675	$575	$500	$425	$350	$295

JEFFERY, W.J. & CO. LTD

Previously manufactured in London, England.

In addition to making a complete line of their own shotguns and rifles, W.J. Jeffery also was subcontracted by many other exporters, distributors, and retailers (including London's famous Army & Navy department store). Many models were produced and rather than list them individually, a generalized format has been adopted for determining values on both rifles and shotguns.

RIFLES

SINGLE SHOT — various cals., falling block action, checkered walnut stock and forearm, usually multiple folding leaves rear sight (also tangent), excellent quality. Prices start in the $600 range for poor condition specimens in obsolete or undesirable cals. and can go up to $5,000 for 100% condition in .600 Nitro Express.

Subtract substantially for the Martini action variation.

BOXLOCK DOUBLE RIFLE — many cals., various engraving patterns, top or under (usually large cals.) lever opening, multiple folding leaves rear sight, checkered walnut stock and forearm. Prices usually start in the $1,500 range for poor condition in undesirable cals. and can exceed $8,000 if encountered with elaborate engraving in .475 Express or larger cals.

Subtract approx. 40% if with hammers, over 50% if with damascus barrels.

SIDELOCK DOUBLE RIFLE — various cals., available in No. 1 or No. 2 grade, top-lever opening, best quality engraving, deluxe checkered walnut stock and forearm, almost any custom order could be filled. Prices start in the $3,250 range for 60% condition in smaller cals. and can easily go to $12,000+ when found in excellent condition in the larger cals.

Subtract approx. 40% if with hammers, over 50% if with damascus barrels.

SHOTGUNS

BOXLOCK SHOTGUN — most ga.'s, many combinations of options available, top-lever opening, many ranges of engraving, high quality and worksmanship. Values usually start in the $650 range if in poor condition and can go to $4,500+ if in a small ga. in near new condition ($1,750 for 12 ga.).

Subtract approx. 40% if with hammers, over 50% if with damascus barrels.

SIDELOCK SHOTGUN — most ga.'s, many combinations of options available, top-lever opening, many ranges of engraving, high quality and worksmanship. Values usually start in the $1,250 range if in poor condition and can go to $8,500+ if in a small ga. in near new condition ($3,950 for 12 ga.).

JENNINGS FIREARMS, INC.

Previously manufactured until 1995, by Bryco Arms located in Irvine, CA. Previously distributed by Jennings Firearms, Inc. in Carson City, NV. Previously manufactured by Calwestco located in Chino, CA. Distributor sales only.

Grading	100%	98%	95%	90%	80%	70%	60%

PISTOLS: SEMI-AUTO

All pistols listed below are single action and were disc. approx. 1995.

MODEL J-22 — .22 LR cal., 6 shot, semi-auto single action, 2½ in. barrel, positive safety locks sear, satin nickel, bright chrome or black teflon finish, 13 oz. Disc. 1995.

	$65	$50	$40	$35	$30	$30	$30

Last Mfg.'s Sug. Retail was $79.

MODEL J-25 — .25 cal., aluminum alloy frame, 2.5 in. barrel, single action, synthetic ivory, walnut, or black combat grips, positive safety, 11 oz. Mfg. 1988-95.

	$60	$50	$45	$40	$35	$30	$30

Last Mfg.'s Sug. Retail was $70.

This model is available in either satin nickel, bright chrome, or black teflon finish.

MODEL M-38 — .22 LR, .32 ACP, or .380 ACP cal., semi-auto single action, 2.8 in. barrel, pressure cast fabrication using non-ferrous alloy, chrome or blue finish, black combat grips, 16 oz. Mfg. 1991-95.

	$100	$75	$65	$50	$40	$35	$30

Last Mfg.'s Sug. Retail was $115.

Add $20 for .380 ACP cal.

MODEL M-48 — .22 LR, .32 ACP, or .380 ACP cal., semi-auto single action, 4 in. barrel, larger frame variation of the M-38, chrome or blue finish, black combat grips, 24 oz. Mfg. 1991-95.

	$110	$95	$85	$75	$70	$65	$60

Last Mfg.'s Sug. Retail was $129.

MODEL M-58 — .380 ACP or 9mm Para. cal., 3¼ in. barrel, 10 shot mag., blue or nickel finish, black synthetic grips, 36 oz. Disc. 1995.

	$110	$95	$85	$75	$70	$65	$60

Last Mfg.'s Sug. Retail was $129.

Add $30 for 9mm Para. cal.

MODEL M-59 — .380 ACP or 9mm Para. cal., 4 in. barrel, 10 shot mag., blue or nickel finish, black synthetic grips, 36 oz. Disc. 1995.

	$110	$95	$85	$75	$70	$65	$60

Last Mfg.'s Sug. Retail was $129.

Add $30 for 9mm Para. cal.

JERICHO

Trademark of Israeli Military Industries (I.M.I.). Previously imported by K.B.I., Inc. located in Harrisburg, PA.

JERICHO 941 — 9mm Para., .41 Action Express (by conversion only), or .40 S&W cal. (new 1991), semi-auto double action or single action, 4.72 in. barrel with polygonal rifling, all steel fabrication, 3 dot Tritium sights, 11 or 16 (9mm) shot mag., ambidextrous safety, polymer grips, decocking lever, 38½ oz. Imported 1990-92.

	$550	$475	$425	$375	$325	$295	$260

Last Mfg.'s Sug. Retail was $649.

Add $299 for .41 AE conversion kit.

Industrial hard chrome or nickel finishes were also available for all Jericho pistols.

J

Grading	100%	98%	95%	90%	80%	70%	60%

▲ *Jericho 941 Pistol Package* — includes 9mm Para. and .40 S&W barrels, also includes .41 AE conversion kit, cased with accessories. Mfg. 1990-91 only.

	$695	$625	$550	$495	$450	$400	$360

Last Mfg.'s Sug. Retail was $775.

JOHNSON AUTOMATICS, INC.

Previous manufacturer located in Providence, RI. Johnson Automatics, Inc. moved many times during its history, often with slight name changes. M.M. Johnson, Jr. died in 1965, and the company continued production at 104 Audubon Street in New Haven, CT as Johnson Arms, Inc. mostly specializing in sporter semi-auto rifles in .270 Win. or 30-06.

MODEL 1941 — .30-06 or 7mm cal., semi-auto, 22 in. removable air cooled barrel, recoil operated, perforated metal handguard, aperture sight, military stock. Most were made for Dutch military, some used by U.S. Marine Paratroopers, during WWII all .30-06 and 7mm were ordered by South American governments.

	$1,850	$1,575	$1,250	$995	$850	$750	$675

Subtract $50 for 7mm cal.
Subtract 10% if serial no.'s don't match.

JURRAS

Previous custom pistolsmith located in Prescott, AZ. Previously distributed by J & G Sales located in Prescott, AZ.

Ammunition for Jurras pistols was manufactured by Robert Davis, Jr. located in Athens, TN.

PISTOLS

Lee E. Jurras manufactures custom pistols in larger calibers. Almost any caliber is available by special order and the listings below represent a few of his more standard items. Special order inquiries may be directed to Mr. Jurras, in Prescott, AZ.

HOWDAH — available in .375, .416, .460, .475, .500, or .577 cal., action based on Thompson/Center Contender receiver, 12 in. bull barrel, nitex finish, adj. rear sights, limited mfg. (100).

▲ *Custom Grade*

	$1,150	$925	$800	$725	$650	$575	$500

▲ *Presentation Grade* — .375 Jurras or .460 Jurras, deluxe Claro walnut stock and forearm.

	$2,000	$1,750	$1,500	$1,250	$1,050	$950	$825

.416, .475, .500, or .577 calibers command a premium on this model.

J

K section

K.B.I., INC.

Importer/manufacturer located in Harrisburg, PA. Distributor and dealer sales.

K.B.I., Inc. imports Armscor (Arms Corp. of the Philippines) and C.B.C. from Brazil. K.B.I. previously imported the Jericho pistol manufactured by I.M.I. from Israel. The Jericho pistol may be found under its own heading in this text.

Grading	100%	98%	95%	90%	80%	70%	60%

FEG PISTOLS

Please refer to the FEG section in this text.

RIFLES

KBI, Inc. also imports several Russian curios and relics, including the Simonov semi-auto carbine ($229 retail, $249 with laminated wood stock) and the Dragunov Sniper Rifle ($5,995 retail).

KASSNAR BOLT ACTION GRADE I — available in 9 cals., thumb safety that locks trigger, with or w/o deluxe sights, 22 in. barrel, 3 or 4 shot mag., includes swivel posts and oil finished standard grade European walnut with recoil pad, 7½ lbs. Imported 1989-1993.

		$445	$385	$325	$275	$225	$195	$175

Last Mfg.'s Sug. Retail was $499.

NYLON 66 — .22 LR, patterned after the Remington Nylon 66. Imported until 1990 from C.B.C. in Brazil, South America.

		$125	$110	$95	$85	$75	$70	$65

Last Mfg.'s Sug. Retail was $134.

MODEL 122 — .22 LR, bolt action design with clip mag. Imported from South America until 1990.

		$125	$110	$95	$85	$75	$70	$65

Last Mfg.'s Sug. Retail was $136.

MODEL 522 — .22 LR, bolt action design with tube mag. Imported from South America until 1990.

		$130	$115	$100	$85	$75	$70	$65

Last Mfg.'s Sug. Retail was $142.

BANTAM SINGLE SHOT — .22 LR, youth dimensions. Imported 1989-90 only.

		$110	$90	$85	$75	$70	$65	$60

Last Mfg.'s Sug. Retail was $120.

SHOTGUNS

GRADE I O/U — 12, 20, 28, or .410 ga., gold plated SST, extractors, vent. rib, checkered walnut stock and forearm. Imported 1989-1993.

		$525	$425	$350	$295	$265	$240	$220

Last Mfg.'s Sug. Retail was $599.

Add $70 for 28 or .410 ga.
Add $50 for choke tubes (12 and 20 ga. only).
Add $150 for automatic ejectors (with choke tubes only).

K

Grading	100%	98%	95%	90%	80%	70%	60%

GRADE II SxS — 10, 12, 16, 20, 28, or .410 ga., boxlock action, case hardened receiver, English style checkered European walnut stock with splinter forearm, chrome barrels with concave rib, extractors, double hinged triggers. Imported 1989-90 only.

	$515	$435	$375	$325	$275	$250	$225

Last Mfg.'s Sug. Retail was $575.

Add $95 for 28 or .410 ga.
Add $85 for 10 ga.

KDF, INC.

Previous manufacturer/current customizer and rifle parts supplier located in Sequin, TX. Previously mfg. from Mauser K-15 actions imported from Oberndorf, Germany. Previously, KDF rifles were manufactured by Voere (until 1986) in Vohrenbach, W. Germany. Manufacture in 1987 was absorbed by Mauser-Werke in Oberndorf, Germany.

Older KDF rifles were private labeled by Voere and were marked KDF. Since Voere was absorbed by Mauser-Werke in 1987, model designations changed. Mauser-Werke does not private label (i.e. newer guns are marked Mauser-Werke), and these rifles can be found under the Mauser-Werke heading in this text.

RIFLES: U.S. MFG.

In 1989, KDF announced the release of a new American built redesigned Model K15 with many improvements. While advertised, approximately only 25 were manufactured in various cals.

K15 — .22-250 (disc. 1992), .243 Win., 6mm Rem., .25-06 Rem., .270 Win., .280 Rem., .30-06 cal. or .308 Win. cal., 60 degree short lift bolt action with 3 lugs, Kevlar composite or laminate walnut stock, adj. single stage competition trigger, box magazine, thumb activated slide safety, satin blue finish, 24 in. match grade barrel, deluxe checkered walnut stock with ebony accents and Pachmayr Decelerator recoil pad, approx. 8 lbs. Limited mfg. in U.S. starting 1989.

	$1,750	$1,375	$1,150	$950	$750	$650	$575

Last Mfg.'s Sug. Retail was $1,950.

▲ *K15 Magnum* — .270 Wby., .300 Win. Mag. (disc.), .300 Wby., 7mm Rem. Mag., .338 Win. Mag., .340 Wby. (disc.), .375 H&H, .411 KDF, .416 Rem. Mag. (disc.), or .458 Win. Mag. cal., similar to K15, except has 26 in. barrel. Mfg. in U.S. starting in 1989.

	$1,795	$1,400	$1,175	$975	$775	$675	$600

Last Mfg.'s Sug. Retail was $2,000.

KDF CLASSIC — cals. similar to K15, custom tuned Remington 700 action, bench rest barrel, Brown Precision stock, KDF accurizing, Arnold jewell custom trigger, matte blue finish, Pachmayr Decelerator pad, includes rings and bases.

	$1,750	$1,375	$1,150	$950	$750	$650	$575

Last Mfg.'s Sug. Retail was $1,950.

Add $50 for Mag. cals.

KDF FRONTIER — cals. similar to KDF Classic, custom tuned Winchester Model 70 action, bench rest barrel, Brown Precision stock, KDF accurizing, Arnold jewell custom trigger, matte blue finish, Pachmayr Decelerator pad, includes rings and bases.

	$1,750	$1,375	$1,150	$950	$750	$650	$575

Last Mfg.'s Sug. Retail was $1,950.

Add $50 for Mag. cals.
Add $150 for action with positive feeding claw extractor.

K

Grading	100%	98%	95%	90%	80%	70%	60%

KDF VARMINT — varmint cals., custom tuned Remington 700 or XP action, bench rest heavy contour barrel, Brown Precision stock, KDF accurizing, Arnold jewell custom trigger, matte blue finish, Pachmayr Decelerator pad, includes rings and bases.

| | $2,000 | $1,725 | $1,425 | $1,200 | $950 | $750 | $650 |

Last Mfg.'s Sug. Retail was $2,250.

Add $250 for Rem. XP action.

RIFLES: OLDER VOERE MFG. (PRE-1988)

TITAN SPORTER SERIES — various cals., bolt action, 24 or 26 in. barrel length, select walnut, pistol grip stock.

This series is available with either European Monte Carlo high-luster stock or in classic featherweight configuration with Schnabel forend — add $50-$200.

▲ *Titan Menor* — .222 or .223 cal. Importation disc. 1987.

| | $675 | $615 | $560 | $495 | $450 | $395 | $350 |

Last Mfg.'s Sug. Retail was $765.

Add $100 for Match or Competition model (.223 cal.).

▲ *Titan II Standard* — many cals., between .243 and .30-06. Disc. 1988.

| | $950 | $825 | $725 | $625 | $550 | $500 | $450 |

Last Mfg.'s Sug. Retail was $1,075.

Add $100 for Match or Competition model (.308 cal.).

▲ *Titan II Magnum* — available in cals. between 7mm Rem. and .375 H&H. Disc. 1988.

| | $995 | $875 | $750 | $650 | $575 | $520 | $475 |

Last Mfg.'s Sug. Retail was $1,125.

▲ *Titan .411 KDF Mag.* — .411 KDF cal., 26 in. barrel with recoil arrestor, 3 shot mag., blue or electroless nickel finish, 9¼ lbs. Imported 1986-1988.

| | $1,175 | $965 | $810 | $725 | $650 | $575 | $520 |

Last Mfg.'s Sug. Retail was $1,300.

MODEL 2005 — .22 LR only, semi-auto, 19½ in. barrel, Monte Carlo stock, 5 shot clip mag., iron sights, 6 lbs. Imported 1986 only.

| | $135 | $115 | $100 | $90 | $85 | $80 | $75 |

Last Mfg.'s Sug. Retail was $165.

This model was ruled no longer importable by the BATF.

▲ *Model 2005 Deluxe* — similar to Model 2005, except has deluxe checkered walnut. Mfg. 1986-87 only.

| | $160 | $135 | $110 | $95 | $85 | $80 | $75 |

Last Mfg.'s Sug. Retail was $185.

MODEL 2107 — .22 LR or .22 Mag. cal., bolt action, 19½ in. barrel, 5 shot clip mag., adj. iron sights, 6 lbs. Imported 1986-87 only.

| | $175 | $150 | $125 | $105 | $95 | $85 | $80 |

Last Mfg.'s Sug. Retail was $197.

Add $42 for .22 Mag. cal.

▲ *Model 2107 Deluxe (Mauser 107)* — similar to Model 2107, except has deluxe checkered walnut. Imported 1986-1988.

| | $185 | $165 | $140 | $125 | $110 | $105 | $100 |

Last Mfg.'s Sug. Retail was $219.

Add $50 for .22 Mag. cal.

This model has been redesignated KDF-Mauser Model 107 since current distributor/dealer inventories have been depleted.

MODEL 2112 — .22 LR or .22 Mag. cal., similar to Model 2107, except has extra select walnut. Imported 1988 only.

| | $235 | $200 | $180 | $160 | $145 | $135 | $125 |

Last Mfg.'s Sug. Retail was $279.

Add $50 for .22 Mag. cal.

Grading	100%	98%	95%	90%	80%	70%	60%

K-14 INSTA FIRE RIFLE — .22-250, .270, .300 Wby. Mag., or .458 Win. Mag. cal., 24 or 26 in. barrel, no sights, ultra fast lock time, hidden detachable mag., checkered Monte Carlo stock, recoil pad.

	$725	$650	$575	$525	$475	$425	$375
K15 (.22 cal.)	$235	$205	$175	$150	$135	$120	$105

K-15 (MODEL 225) — available in 13 cals. between .243 Win. and .300 Wby. Mag., bolt action, 60 degree bolt lift with 3 locking lugs, ultra fast lock time, adj. trigger, 24 or 26 (Mag. only) in. barrel, 3 or 5 shot mag., no sights, guaranteed ½ in. accuracy at 100 yards, many stock options available at extra cost. Left-handed action available in certain cals. at a $50 charge.

▲ *Deluxe Standard Sporter* — standard model available in 6 regular cals. and 9 Mag. cals. Disc. 1988.

	$1,075	$950	$810	$700	$625	$550	$495

Last Mfg.'s Sug. Retail was $1,275.

Add $50 for Magnum action.
Add $525 for .411 KDF cal.

In addition to the 15 regular cals., it is also possible to order various other factory cals. as a $200 option.

This model has been redesignated KDF-Mauser Model 225 (standard cals.) since current distributor/dealer inventories have been depleted.

▲ *K-15 Fiberstock Pro-hunter* — similar to the K-15, except is supplied with fiberglass stock (various colors), choice of parkerized, matte blue, or electroless nickel metal finish, and recoil arrestor installed. Imported 1986-1988.

	$1,420	$1,200	$950

Last Mfg.'s Sug. Retail was $1,680.

Add $50 for Magnum action.

This model has been redesignated KDF-Mauser Model 225 (standard cals.) since current distributor/dealer inventories have been depleted.

▲ *K-15 Dangerous Game* — .411 KDF Mag. (new cartridge 1985), choice of finishes, oil finished deluxe American walnut stock. Imported 1986-1988.

	$1,895	$1,500	$1,150

Last Mfg.'s Sug. Retail was $2,100.

This model has been redesignated KDF-Mauser Model 225 since current distributor/dealer inventories have been depleted.

▲ *K-15 Swat Rifle* — .308 cal. standard, 24 or 26 in. barrel, parkerized metal, oil finished target walnut stock, 3 or 4 shot detachable mag., 10 lbs. Importation disc. 1988.

	$1,475	$1,250	$1,000	$850	$725	$650	$575

Last Mfg.'s Sug. Retail was $1,725.

K-16 — available in 6 standard cals. between .243 Win. and .300 Win. Mag. in addition to optional cals., modified Remington Model 700 action, standard features include KDF accurizing and Insta Fire ignition, single stage adj. trigger, Dupont Rynite stock (camel or gray), choice of finishes (high-gloss blue standard), recoil pad and quick detachable sling swivels, many options available. Imported 1988 only.

	$765	$675	$615	$560	$495	$450	$395

Last Mfg.'s Sug. Retail was $876.

Add $120 for KDF muzzle brake.
Add $250 for optional cals.
Add $350 for .411 KDF Mag. cal.

K-22 (MAUSER 201) — .22 LR cal., bolt action, free floating 21 in. barrel, clip 5 shot mag., adj. trigger, scaled down version of the K-15, unusual action incorporates two front-located locking lugs on bolt face that engage Stellite inserts on the front receiver portion, guaranteed 1 in. groupings at 100 yards, blue only, no sights, select walnut stock with cheekpiece, standard model disc. 1987.

	$310	$285	$260	$240	$225	$210	$195

Last Mfg.'s Sug. Retail was $345.

Add $50 for .22 Mag. cal.

K

Grading	100%	98%	95%	90%	80%	70%	60%

▲ **K-22 Deluxe (Mauser 201)** — better walnut and stock options. Model notation changed in 1988.

| | $410 | $360 | $295 | $275 | $250 | $235 | $210 |

Last Mfg.'s Sug. Retail was $495.

Add $50 for .22 Mag. cal.

This model has been redesignated KDF-Mauser Model 201 since current distributor/dealer inventories have been depleted.

▲ **K-22 Deluxe Custom** — richly layered walnut and stock options. Importation disc. 1987.

| | $655 | $595 | $550 | $495 | $450 | $395 | $350 |

Last Mfg.'s Sug. Retail was $725.

Add $50 for .22 Mag. cal.

▲ **K-22 Deluxe Special Select** — top-of-the-line bolt action, double set triggers. Importation disc. 1987.

| | $1,060 | $950 | $850 | $750 | $695 | $650 | $595 |

Last Mfg.'s Sug. Retail was $1,225.

Add $50 for .22 Mag. cal.

SHOTGUNS

CONDOR O/U — 12 ga., 28 in. barrel, various chokes, selective single trigger, auto ejectors, wide VR, boxlock, checkered pistol grip stock, Italian made.

| | $660 | $635 | $605 | $580 | $525 | $470 | $415 |

BRESCIA S X S — 12 ga., 28 in. barrel, full and mod., double triggers, engraved, checkered pistol grip stock.

| | $330 | $305 | $275 | $250 | $195 | $165 | $140 |

K.F.C.

Formerly manufactured by Kawaguchiya Firearms Co., Ltd. Previously imported and distributed by La Paloma Marketing, Inc. located in Tucson, AZ.

SHOTGUNS

MODEL 250 — 12 ga. only, semi-auto incorporating a patented, cushioned piston assembly, 26, 28, or 30 in. barrel, matte blue finish, vent. rib standard, checkered premium walnut, 7 lbs. Manufactured 1980-86.

| | $360 | $290 | $270 | $250 | $235 | $220 | $205 |

Last Mfg.'s Sug. Retail was $485.

Add $60 for multi-chokes.

▲ **Model 250 Deluxe** — same specifications as Model 250, except has scrolled acid etching panels on both sides of normally black receiver. Disc. 1986.

| | $395 | $310 | $290 | $270 | $250 | $225 | $210 |

Last Mfg.'s Sug. Retail was $520.

FIELD GUN O/U — 12 ga. only, VR, premium grade walnut, semi pistol grip stock, F&IC chokes. Disc. 1986.

| | $645 | $565 | $530 | $495 | $470 | $445 | $410 |

Last Mfg.'s Sug. Retail was $748.

E-1 TRAP OR SKEET O/U — 12 ga. only, VR, oil finished premium grade walnut, semi pistol grip stock, engraved. Disc. 1986.

| | $935 | $800 | $750 | $700 | $625 | $550 | $495 |

Last Mfg.'s Sug. Retail was $1,070.

E-2 TRAP OR SKEET O/U — 12 ga. only, VR, oil finished premium grade walnut, semi pistol grip stock, detailed engraving. Disc. 1986.

| | $1,450 | $1,250 | $1,075 | $950 | $850 | $750 | $650 |

Last Mfg. Sug. Retail was $1,660.

K

KSN INDUSTRIES LTD.

Manufacturer located in Kfar Saba, Israel. Imported exclusively by J.O. Arms, Inc. located in Houston, TX, and marketed exclusively by All America Sales, Inc. located in Memphis, TN.

Grading	100%	98%	95%	90%	80%	70%	60%

KAREEN MK II — 9mm Para. or .40 S&W (new late 1994), semi-auto single action, 3.85 (Compact) or 4.64 (Standard) in. barrel, two-tone finish, rubberized grips, regular or Meprolite sights, 10 (C/B 1994), 13*, or 15* shot mag., 33 oz. New 1993.

Mfg.'s Sug. Retail	$411	$360	$305	$255	$225	$200	$185	$170

Add approx. $160 for two-tone finish with Meprolite sights.

▲ *Kareen Mk II Compact* — compact variation with 3.85 in. barrel.

Mfg.'s Sug. Retail	$497	$415	$360	$315	$255	$225	$200	$185

GOLAN MODEL — 9mm Para. or .40 S&W cal., single or double action, ambidextrous safety with decocking feature, steel slide with alloy frame, $3\frac{7}{8}$ in. barrel, matte black finish, 29 oz. New 1994.

Mfg.'s Sug. Retail	$650	$565	$515	$460	$410	$360	$330	$295

Add $35 for .40 S&W cal.

KAHR ARMS

Manufacturer located in Blauvelt, NY since 1993. Distributor and dealer sales.

PISTOLS

THE KAHR K9 — 9mm Para., trigger cocking, double action only, locked breech with Browning type recoil lug, steel construction, firing pin block safety, $3\frac{1}{2}$ in. barrel, 7 shot mag., wraparound black polymer grips, matte or electroless nickel (new 1996) finish, 25 oz. New 1993.

Mfg.'s Sug. Retail	$595	$540	$475	$425	$365	$315	$285	$250

Add $83 for electroless nickel finish.
Add $97 for night sights (new 1996).

KASSNAR IMPORTS, INC.

Previous importer and distributor (operations ceased April, 1989) located in Harrisburg, PA.

Kassnar also imported Omega shotguns which can be found in their individual section.

PISTOLS

PJK-9HP — 9mm, single action, patterned after the Browning Hi-Power, $4\frac{3}{4}$ in. barrel, 13 shot mag., cone hammer, checkered walnut grips, 32 oz.

$225	$200	$185	$175	$165	$155	$145

Add $15 for VR barrel.

This pistol was imported from Hungary. Approx. 18,000 (including the MBK-9HP) were imported until importation was disc. because of Federal ramifications.

MBK-9HP — 9mm, double action, patterned after the Browning Hi-Power, $4\frac{2}{3}$ in. barrel, spur hammer, blued metal, checkered walnut grips, 14 shot mag., 36 oz. Limited importation was stopped in late 1985.

$295	$260	$230	$190	$175	$165	$155

Grading	100%	98%	95%	90%	80%	70%	60%

PMK-380 — .380 ACP, double action, patterned after the Walther PP, plastic grips with thumbrest, 4 in barrel, 7 shot mag., 21 oz. Limited importation.

	$275	$235	$200	$185	$175	$165	$155

This model was imported in very limited quantities before Interarms began exclusive importation.

KEBERST INTERNATIONAL
Previously manufactured and distributed by Kendall International located in Paris, KY.

KEBERST MODEL 1A — .338 Lapua Mag., .338-416 Rigby, or .338-06 cal., bolt action, muzzle brake and unique recoil pad, camouflaged synthetic stock, package includes 3-9 power Leupold scope, stainless steel cleaning rod, custom designed case, built to special order only. Mfg. 1987-1988 only.

	$3,475	$2,850	$2,475	$2,100	$1,750	$1,400	$1,150

Last Mfg.'s Sug. Retail was $3,750.

Add $275 for 10X Ultra scope.

KEL-TEC CNC INDUSTRIES, INC.
Manufacturer located in Cocoa, FL since 1994.

PISTOLS: SEMI-AUTO

P-11 — 9mm Para., double action only, locked breech design, 3.1 in. barrel, aluminum frame with steel slide, transfer bar safety, matte blue or electroless nickel (disc. 1995) finish, black, gray, or green synthetic grips, 10 shot double column mag., 14 oz. New 1995.

Mfg.'s Sug. Retail	$309		$260	$200	$180	$165	$150	$135	$125

Add $10 for gray or green synthetic grips.
Add $30 for electroless nickel finish (disc. 1995).

▲ *P-11 Stainless* — similar to P-11, except is stainless steel, available with black (P-11SB), gray (P-11SGY), or green (P-11SGN) grips. New 1996.

Mfg.'s Sug. Retail	$408		$350	$275	$230

KEMEN
Competition shotgun manufacturer located in Elgoibar, Spain since 1989. Exclusively imported in the U.S. by Puglisi Gun Emporium located in Duluth, MN, and distributed in the U.S. by Kemen America located in Duluth, MN.

SHOTGUNS: O/U

Kemen shotguns are built to individual custom specifications. Their unique metal finish makes them almost impervious to any type of oxidation or rust.

KM-4 STANDARD GRADE — 12 or 20 ga., competition shotgun with 32 in. vent. or separated barrels with VR and Briley choke tubes, detachable trigger group, blued receiver with gold accents, checkered walnut Monte Carlo stock and forearm, cased, 8-8½ lbs.

Mfg.'s Sug. Retail	$4,995		$4,675	$4,200	$3,850	$3,375	$2,850	$2,375	$2,100

Add $1,000 for 20 ga.

KM-4 LUXE A/B — similar to KM-4 Standard Grade, except has nickel finished receiver with choice of fine scroll or game scene engraving.

Mfg.'s Sug. Retail	$8,595		$7,950	$7,375	$6,800	$6,275	$5,600	$4,950	$4,250

Add $500 for 20 ga.

K

Grading	100%	98%	95%	90%	80%	70%	60%

KM-4 SUPERLUXE — similar to KM-4 Luxe A/B, except has nickel finished receiver with more elaborate game scene engraving.

    Mfg.'s Sug. Retail $9,795 $9,100 $8,450 $7,350 $6,450 $5,700 $4,950 $4,250

      Add $600 for 20 ga.

KM-4 EXTRALUXE A/B — similar to KM-4 Superluxe, except has nickel finished receiver with choice of Purdey style fine scroll or extra fine game scene engraving.

    Mfg.'s Sug. Retail $10,995 $10,100 $9,150 $8,250 $7,250 $6,200 $5,400 $4,500

      Add $1,900 for Extraluxe B (game scene) engraving.
      Add $600 for 20 ga.

KM-4 EXTRA GOLD — features engraved sideplate action with multiple gold inlays, select wood.

    Mfg.'s Sug. Retail $14,895 $13,500 $11,000 $9,450 $7,950 $6,850 $5,750 $4,650

      Add $800 for 20 ga.

KM-4 SUPREMA — top-of-the-line model, custom ordered to individual specifications.

    Mfg.'s Sug. Retail $27,995 $24,950 $22,000 $18,500 $15,000 $12,500 $10,250 $8,700

      Add $1,500 for 20 ga.

KENDALL INTERNATIONAL

Previous importer/distributor located in Paris, KY. Kendall International also imported Australian Automatic Arms, the Keberst Rifle, and several air rifles that can be found in their respective sections in this text.

KEPPELER + FRITZ GmbH

Manufacturer located in Fichtenberg, Germany. No current importer.

Keppeler manufactures many types of top quality rifles which are typically centerfire and target configured (UIT-CISM, Prone, Free, and Sniper Bullpup). Both metric and domestic calibers are available as well as a variety of special order options. Please contact the factory directly for more information and current pricing (see Trademark Index).

KEPPLINGER, ING. HANNES

Manufacturer located in Kufstein, Austria. No current importer.

RIFLES

    Kepplinger rifles are essentially built per individual order. In addition to his unique bolt action, he also makes other bolt action designs and O/U rifles as well. It is recommended that Mr. Kepplinger of Kufsteiner Waffenstube be contacted for more information, including price quotations on his quality, custom order rifles (please refer to the Trademark Index).

3-S SYSTEM RIFLE — various cals., unique short action allows for straight on cartridge loading, high strength alloy main parts, grip safety on lower pistol grip, unique uncocking device allowing manual cocking/decocking of the firing pin spring, 23.6 in. standard barrel, 3 shot detachable mag., iron sights, receiver drilled for scope mounts, best quality wood, available in either Schnabel forearm or Mannlicher configuration, many styles of engraving are optional, 7.14 lbs.

      This model is currently priced at approx. $4,650 FOB Austria.

KESSLER ARMS CORPORATION

Manufacturer located in Silver Creek, NY.

Grading	100%	98%	95%	90%	80%	70%	60%

LEVERMATIC SHOTGUN — lever action, 12, 16, or 20 ga., 26 or 28 in. full choke, takedown, plain pistol grip stock. Disc. 1953.

	$150	$125	$100	$85	$65	$55	$50

BOLT ACTION SHOTGUN — 12, 16, or 20 ga., 26 or 28 in. full, takedown, plain stock. Mfg. 1951-1953.

	$90	$65	$50	$45	$35	$35	$35

J. KIMBALL ARMS CO.

Previous manufacturer located in Detroit, MI.

AUTOMATIC PISTOL — .30 U.S. Carbine or .22 Hornet (very rare) cal., semi-auto, 7 shot, 3 in.(Combat Model) or 5 in. (Target Model) barrel, approx. 32 oz. Less than 300 mfg. in 1958 only.

	$950	$850	$725	$600	$500	$395	$300

Functional weaknesses of this pistol caused discontinuance. Surviving specimens should be checked carefully for slide failures and other potential problems. Values above assume no operational damage to the pistol. .22 Hornet cal. rarity factor precludes accurate price evaluation.

KIMBER OF AMERICA, INC.

Manufacturer located in Oregon beginning 1993. Exclusively distributed by Nationwide Sports Distributors, Inc. located in South Hampton and Tyrone, PA and Sparks, NV.

PISTOLS

CLASSIC .45 — .45 ACP cal., patterned after the Colt Government Model 1911, 5 in. barrel, various finishes, 8 shot mag., high beavertail grip safety, forged frame, steel construction, choice of grips, 38 oz. New 1995.

▲ *Custom Model* — features matte black oxide or royal finish (stainless steel is optional), black synthetic or checkered walnut (custom royal finish only) grips.

Mfg.'s Sug. Retail	$575	$500	$450	$400	$360	$330	$300	$275

Add $75 for stainless contruction.
Add $140 for custom royal finish.

▲ *Gold Match* — features Bo-Mar sights, 8 or 10 shot mag., and fancy walnut checkered diamond grips.

Mfg.'s Sug. Retail	$925	$825	$725	$625	$550	$475	$400	$350

A Gold Match first edition (only 500 mfg.) is also available.

RIFLES: BOLT ACTION

MODEL 82C CLASSIC — .22 LR, 22 in. drilled and tapped barrel, 4 shot mag., A Claro checkered walnut stock, polished and blued metal, 6½ lbs. New 1993.

Mfg.'s Sug. Retail	$785	$675	$575	$515	$460	$400	$360	$330

This model is available in either right or left-hand action.

MODEL 82C SUPER AMERICA — .22 LR, 22 in. drilled and tapped barrel, 4 shot mag., AAA Claro checkered walnut stock with skeletonized pistol grip cap, polished and blued metal, 6½ lbs. New 1993.

Mfg.'s Sug. Retail	$1,175	$1,025	$925	$825	$725	$650	$575	$475

CUSTOM MATCH — .22 LR, features AA french walnut with 22 LPI wraparound checkering, matte rust blue finish. New 1995.

Mfg.'s Sug. Retail	$1,850	$1,675	$1,400	$1,175	$925	$775	$650	$525

SUPER CLASSIC — .22 LR, features AAA Claro walnut with 18 LPI side panel checkering, polished and blued metal. New 1995.

Mfg.'s Sug. Retail	$1,090	$975	$875	$775	$675	$600	$550	$450

This model is available in either right or left-hand action.

K

Grading	100%	98%	95%	90%	80%	70%	60%

VARMINT — .22 LR, features 25 in. fluted stainless steel barrel, A Claro walnut with 18 LPI side panel checkering. New 1995.

Mfg.'s Sug. Retail	$885	$750	$625	$550	$495	$445	$395	$350

RIFLES: SPORTERIZED SWEDISH MAUSER 96 RIFLES

Beginning 1995, Kimber began sporterizing the Swedish Mauser Model 96 military surplus rifles. They feature stainless steel fluted barrels and a black synthetic Ramline stock, receivers are drilled and tapped to accept Weaver scope mounts, bead blasted bluing, and original reprofiled military bolt. The Sporter configuration includes .243 Win., 6.5x55mm, or .308 Win. cal., while the heavy fluted barrel models are available in .22-250 Rem. or .308 Win. (Varmint or Heavy Barrel). Prices range from $325-$495, depending on the configuration. Sporters are also available as a combo package with scope and hardshell case. For more information, please contact Nationwide Sports Distributors directly (see Trademark Index).

KIMBER OF OREGON, INC.

Previous manufacturer located in Clackamas, OR between 1980-1991.

Kimber of Oregon had its final sale in 1991, and is now out of business. Rare models are starting to attract premiums already. In some models, magazines for these fine quality rifles are getting extremely hard to find with healthy premiums being asked. Once "B" suffix models were introduced, older manufacturer started being referred to as "A" models.

RIFLES: BOLT ACTION

Note: No suffix in Kimber models denotes pre-1986 action design, "B" suffix models incorporate the new action with improved cocking system, faster lock time, swept-back bolt design, improved recoil lug, and are right-handed.

> Extra fancy walnut on any Kimber will always command a premium.
> Add $175 for skeleton grip cap on models listed below.
> Add $275 for skeleton buttplate on models listed below.
> Add $100 for checkered bolt handle on models listed below.
> Add $300 for raised quarter rib.
> Add $100 for forend tip.
> Extra fancy walnut on any Kimber will always command a premium.

MODEL 82 .22 CAL. SERIES

STANDARD MODEL 82 — .22 LR, .22 Mag., or .22 Hornet cal., Mauser type rear locking bolt action, 3 (.22 Hornet), 4 (.22 Mag.), or 5 (.22 LR) shot mag., 22 in. (Sporter) or 24 in. (Varmint) barrel, deluxe claro walnut, steel butt plate, rocker style safety, 6½ lbs. Add $100-$200 for .22 Hornet or .22 Mag. cal., depending on the variation.

▲ *Classic Model* — disc. 1988.

$850	$725	$625	$525	$450	$375	$335

Last Mfg.'s Sug. Retail was $750.

> Add $55 for disc. Cascade Model (Monte Carlo cheekpiece).
> There were 34 custom Cascades mfg.

▲ *Custom Classic Model* — higher grade claro walnut, ebony forearm tip, Niedner style steel butt plate. Disc. 1988.

$925	$775	$650	$550	$475	$400	$350

Last Mfg.'s Sug. Retail was $995.

Also previously available in the .218 Bee (approx. 130 standard mfg., 36 Mashburn mfg.) or .25-20 (approx. 200 mfg. single shot only) cals. These cals. may bring a slight premium. Mfg. 1985 only (retail price was $695).

Grading	100%	98%	95%	90%	80%	70%	60%

▲ *Deluxe Grade* — .22 LR only, similar to Custom Classic Model, AA walnut, 5 or 10 (optional) shot mag., 6½ lbs. Mfg. 1989-90 only.

| | $995 | $895 | $700 | $595 | $525 | $450 | $395 |

Last Mfg.'s Sug. Retail was $1,195.

A left-hand variation was also available at no extra charge, but had limited mfg. in 1990.

SPORTER MODEL — .17 Ackley Hornet (approx. 9 mfg.), .17 K. Hornet (approx. 88 mfg.), or .22 LR cal., includes Model 82A action, 22 in. sporter weight barrel, 4 shot mag., round top receiver with bases, checkered stock and forend, 6½ lbs. Mfg. 1991 only.

| | $895 | $750 | $650 | $550 | $495 | $450 | $395 |

Last Mfg.'s Sug. Retail was $995.

RIMFIRE VARMINTER — .22 LR only, Model 82A action, free floating 25 in. medium heavy barrel, laminated stock, 5 or optional 10 shot mag., rubber butt pad, 8¼ lbs. Mfg. 1990-91 only.

| | $795 | $675 | $550 | $475 | $425 | $375 | $325 |

Last Mfg.'s Sug. Retail was $795.

HUNTER GRADE — .22 LR only, similar to Rimfire Varminter with Super America configured barrel and action with low glare metal finish. Mfg. 1990 only.

| | $750 | $600 | $525 | $450 | $395 | $340 | $295 |

Last Mfg.'s Sug. Retail was $895.

MINI CLASSIC — .22 LR only, Model 82 action, 18 in. barrel, steel butt plate, sling swivels. Mfg. 1988 only.

| | $550 | $475 | $415 | $375 | $340 | $300 | $275 |

Last Mfg.'s Sug. Retail was $795.

GOVERNMENT MODEL 82A TARGET — .22 LR only, specifically designed for U.S. Army training, 25 in. heavy target barrel including scope blocks, oversized stock, some rifles are "star" marked indicating an accuracy guarantee, 10¾ lbs. Mfg. 1987-91.

| | $695 | $575 | $500 | $450 | $400 | $350 | $325 |

Last Mfg.'s Sug. Retail was $595.

20,000 rifles were mfg. 1987-1989 to fill the initial U.S. government contract. U.S. property marked guns do exist in private hands - all within a low serial number range (watch markings carefully). Commercial guns were manufactured for the private sector with values listed above.

ALL AMERICAN MATCH — .22 LR only, precision rifled 25 in. free floating target grade barrel, stock is adj. both vertically and for length of pull, fully adj. single stage trigger, approx. 9 lbs. Mfg. 1990-91 only.

| | $750 | $600 | $525 | $450 | $395 | $340 | $295 |

Last Mfg.'s Sug. Retail was $895.

CONTINENTAL — .22 LR, .22 Mag., or .22 Hornet cal., Sporter action only, full length Mannlicher stock, open sights, deluxe walnut. Add $200 for .22 Mag. or .22 Hornet cal. New 1987.

This model was only available as a special order with prices on request from the factory.

▲ *Super Continental* — similar to Continental, except has AAA claro walnut with 22 lines/in. checkering. Mfg. 1987-1988.

| | $1,395 | $1,250 | $1,000 | $875 | $795 | $700 | $625 |

Last Mfg.'s Sug. Retail was $1,465.

Three laminated stock variations with cheekpieces were mfg.

SUPER AMERICA — top-of-the-line model, includes detachable scope mounts, Niedner checkered steel butt plate and best quality walnut, available in Sporter configuration only. This model was disc. 1988, and reintroduced 1990-91.

| | $1,075 | $950 | $775 | $625 | $550 | $475 | $425 |

Last Mfg.'s Sug. Retail was $1,295.

▲ *Super Grade* — similar to Super America, AAA walnut, beaded cheekpiece, 5 or 10 (optional) shot mag., 6½ lbs. Mfg. 1989 only.

| | $1,075 | $950 | $775 | $625 | $550 | $475 | $425 |

Last Mfg.'s Sug. Retail was $1,295.

K

Grading	100%	98%	95%	90%	80%	70%	60%

CUSTOM MATCH — .22 LR or .22 Mag. cal., limited edition of 217 rifles, match dimension chamber, french walnut stock with 22 L.P.I. checkering, rust blued finish, other custom rifle features. Introduced 1984.

	$1,675	$1,350	$1,000	$875	$795	$725	$650

Add $200 for .22 Mag. cal.

BROWNELL — .22 LR, only 500 mfg. to commemorate the late Leonard Brownell, Mannlicher style extra deluxe claro walnut stock. Mfg. 1986 only.

	$1,475	$1,175	$825

Last Mfg.'s Sug. Retail was $1,500.

CENTENNIAL — .22 LR only, limited edition (100 rifles) to commemorate centennial of .22 LR cal., includes hand-picked checkered walnut, moderate engraving, special Wilson Arms match barrel, skeleton butt plate and other refinements, serial numbered C1-C100. Mfg. 1987 only.

	$2,600	$2,350	$1,900

Last Mfg.'s Sug. Retail was $2,950.

TENTH ANNIVERSARY ISSUE — .22 LR, limited edition, french walnut stock featuring slim forend design with shadowed cheekpiece, Neidner steel buttplate and other refinements. Mfg. 1989 only.

	$1,495	$1,200	$975

Add $100 for matte finish.

MODEL 84 CENTERFIRE SERIES

Add $75 for forend tip - option A.
Add $300 for iron sights - option B.
Add $100 for checkered bolt handle - option C.
Add $200 for skeleton grip cap - option D.
Add $300 for skeleton buttplate - option G.
Add $250-$300 for 3-position safety in this series.

STANDARD MODEL 84 — .17 Rem., .17 Mach IV (disc. 1987), 6x45 or 47mm (disc. 1987), 5.6x50mm (disc. 1987), .221 Fireball, .222 Rem., .222 Rem. Mag. (disc. 1987), or .223 Rem. cal., "Mini-Mauser" type head locking bolt action, 5 shot mag., 22 (Sporter) or 24 (Varmint) in. barrel, deluxe claro walnut, steel buttplate, rocker style safety, 6½ lbs.

▲ *Classic Model* — disc. 1988.

	$950	$775	$625	$550	$475	$425	$375

Last Mfg.'s Sug. Retail was $885.

Add $55 for disc. Cascade Model (Monte Carlo cheekpiece).
Also available in left-hand action in .22 Hornet, .222 Rem., .223 Rem., 6x45mm, 6x47mm, .17 Rem., and .17 Mach IV (very limited mfg.).

CUSTOM CLASSIC MODEL — higher grade claro walnut, ebony forearm tip, Niedner style steel butt plate. Disc. 1988.

	$1,150	$975	$795	$650	$550	$475	$425

Last Mfg.'s Sug. Retail was $1,130.

▲ *Deluxe Grade Sporter* — .17 Rem., .221 Rem., or .223 Rem. cal., Mauser action, AA walnut, similar to Custom Classic Model, 6¼ lbs. Mfg. 1989-90.

	$1,075	$950	$775	$625	$550	$475	$425

Last Mfg.'s Sug. Retail was $1,295.

Also available in left-hand action (.223 cal. only), limited mfg.

CONTINENTAL — .221 Fireball (extremely rare, mfg. 1988 only) .222 Rem. or .223 Rem. cal., Sporter action only, full length Mannlicher stock, open sights, deluxe walnut. New 1987.

This model was only available as a special order with prices on request from the factory.

K

Grading	100%	98%	95%	90%	80%	70%	60%

▲ **Super Continental** — similar to Continental (same cals.), except has AAA claro walnut with 22 lines/in. checkering. Mfg. 1987-1988.

| | $1,495 | $1,250 | $950 | $850 | $775 | $695 | $625 |

Last Mfg.'s Sug. Retail was $1,600.

Three laminated stocks were mfg. in .223 Rem. cal.

HUNTER GRADE — .17 Rem., .222 Rem., or .223 Rem. cal., laminated stock, Super America configured action and barrel with low glare metal finish. Mfg. 1990 only.

| | $825 | $650 | $550 | $475 | $425 | $375 | $325 |

Last Mfg.'s Sug. Retail was $995.

SPORTER — .17 Rem., .22 Hornet, .222 Rem., .22-250 Rem., or .223 cal., 22 in. sporter weight barrel, "A" grade Claro walnut, round top receiver with bases, 4 shot mag., hand checkering. Mfg. 1991 only.

| | $975 | $800 | $700 | $600 | $550 | $500 | $495 |

Last Mfg.'s Sug. Retail was $1,095.

This model was available in either right or left-hand action.

▲ **Big Bore Sporter** — .250 Savage or .35 Rem. cal., similar action to Sporter Model, except has ¾ in. red Pachmayr Decelerator recoil pad. Mfg. 1991 only.

Extreme rarity precludes accurate price evaluation - consult an expert when buying/selling this model. This model was available in either right or left-hand action.

Last Mfg.'s Sug. Retail was $1,095.

SUPER AMERICA/SUPER GRADE — .17 Rem., .17 MK IV, .221, .22 Hornet, .222 Rem., .222 Mag., .22-250 Rem., .223 Rem., 5.6x56mm, or 6x47mm, cal., 22 in. sporter weight barrel, top-of-the-line, with detachable scopemounts, available in Sporter configuration only, 4 shot mag., right or left-hand action. Disc. 1988, reintroduced 1990-91.

| | $1,425 | $1,195 | $925 | $850 | $775 | $695 | $625 |

Last Mfg.'s Sug. Retail was $1,495.

Be careful when buying rare cals. and/or options on this model.

▲ **Big Bore Super America** — .250 Savage or .35 Rem., similar action to Super America Model, except has ¾ in. red Pachmayr Decelerator recoil pad. Mfg. 1991 only.

| | $2,100 | $1,775 | $1,425 | $1,125 | $925 | $800 | $700 |

Last Mfg.'s Sug. Retail was $1,495.

CUSTOM MATCH — .222 Rem. or .223 Rem. cal., limited edition of 200 rifles, match dimension chamber, french walnut stock with 22 L.P.I. checkering, rust blued finish, other custom rifle features. Introduced 1986.

| | $2,050 | $1,600 | $1,350 | $995 | $850 | $750 | $650 |

TENTH ANNIVERSARY ISSUE — .223 Rem. cal., limited edition, french walnut stock featuring slim forend design with shadowed cheekpiece, 22 in. barrel, roundtop receiver with mounts, Neidner steel buttplate and other refinements. Mfg. 1989 only.

| | $1,850 | $1,550 | $1,200 |

Add $100 for matte finish.

ULTRA VARMINTER — .17 Rem., .22 Hornet (rare, new 1991), .221 Rem. (disc. 1990), .222 Rem., .22-250 Rem. (rare), or .223 Rem. cal., 24 in. medium weight stainless steel barrel, laminated birch stock, plain butt stock, right or left-hand action, 7¾ lbs. Mfg. 1989-91 only.

| | $1,295 | $1,075 | $925 | $775 | $650 | $550 | $475 |

Last Mfg.'s Sug. Retail was $1,295.

▲ **Super Varminter** — similar to Ultra Varminter except has steel barrel, AAA walnut stock with beaded cheekpiece, 7¼ lbs. Mfg. 1989-91 only.

| | $1,475 | $1,250 | $975 | $850 | $725 | $600 | $500 |

Last Mfg.'s Sug. Retail was $1,495.

MODEL 89 BIG GAME RIFLE SERIES

Fewer than 5,000 Model 89 BGRs were mfg.

Grading	100%	98%	95%	90%	80%	70%	60%

MODEL 89 BGR — .270 Win., .280 Rem., 7mm Rem. Mag., .30-06, .300 Win. Mag., .338 Win. Mag., or .375 H&H cal., new action incorporates features from both Mauser 98 and Win. pre-64 Model 70, three position safety, 22 or 24 in. barrel, matte blue finish will command a premium. Introduced late 1988.

▲ *Classic Model* — deluxe claro walnut checkered 18 lines/in. with steel butt plate. Disc. 1988.

	$790	$675	$550	$475	$395	$340	$295

Last Mfg.'s Sug. Retail was $985.

Add $200 for .375 H&H cal.
Add $100 for matte finish.

▲ *Custom Classic Model* — higher grade claro walnut, ebony forearm tip, Niedner style steel butt plate. Disc. 1988.

	$1,025	$865	$750	$625	$500	$440	$365

Last Mfg.'s Sug. Retail was $1,230.

Add $200 for .375 H&H cal.

DELUXE GRADE — similar to Custom Classic Model, round top receiver with Model 70 scope mount hole configuration, AA walnut stock with ebony forend tip and rubber recoil pad (no cheekpiece), 22 or 24 in. barrel, $7\frac{1}{2}$-$8\frac{1}{2}$ lbs. New 1989.

▲ *Featherweight Barrel Model* — .257 Roberts (rare), .25-06 Rem., 7x57mm (rare, disc. 1990), .270 Win., .280 Rem., or .30-06 cal., 5 shot mag., 22 in. Featherweight barrel, right-hand action only, $7\frac{1}{2}$ lbs. Disc. 1990.

	$1,525	$1,175	$975	$825	$700	$600	$525

Last Mfg.'s Sug. Retail was $1,795.

Add $470 for Super America Grade with square bridge, dovetail receiver.
Add $100 for matte finish.
The Super America Grade will accept Kimber double lever scope mounts and has one grade better wood than the Deluxe Grade with beaded cheekpiece.

▲ *Medium-weight Barrel Model* — .300 Win. Mag., .300 H&H (rare, disc. 1990), .300 Wby. (very rare, new 1991), .338 Win. Mag., .35 Whelen (rare, disc. 1990), or 7mm Rem. Mag. cal., 3 shot mag., 24 in. medium-weight barrel, right-hand action only, $7\frac{3}{4}$-$8\frac{1}{2}$ lbs. Disc. 1990.

	$1,600	$1,225	$1,000	$850	$725	$625	$550

Last Mfg.'s Sug. Retail was $1,895.

Add $495 for Super America Grade with square bridge, dovetail receiver.
Add $100 for matte finish.
The Super America Grade will accept Kimber double lever scope mounts and has one grade better wood than the Deluxe Grade with beaded cheekpiece.

▲ *Heavy-weight Barrel Model* — .375 H&H Mag. cal., 3 shot mag., 24 in. heavy-weight barrel, right-hand action only, 9 lbs. Disc. 1990.

	$1,700	$1,275	$1,050	$900	$775	$700	$650

Last Mfg.'s Sug. Retail was $1,995.

Add $495 for Super America Grade with square bridge, dovetail receiver.
Add $100 for matte finish.
The Super America Grade will accept Kimber double lever scope mounts and has one grade better wood than the Deluxe Grade with beaded cheekpiece.

SPORTER MODEL — same cals. as Deluxe/Super America Models, 22 in. featherweight or 24 in. medium or heavy barrel, double square bridge dovetail receiver, "A" grade Claro walnut stock with $\frac{3}{4}$ in. red Pachmayr Decelerator recoil pad (Mag. cals. only with 24 in. barrel). Mfg. 1991 only.

	$1,325	$1,000	$875	$750	$625	$500	$450

Last Mfg.'s Sug. Retail was $1,595.

Add $100 for medium magnum action.
Add $200 for heavy magnum action (.375 H&H and .458 Win. Mag. cals.).

K

Grading	100%	98%	95%	90%	80%	70%	60%

HUNTER GRADE — .270 Win., .30-06, .300 Win. Mag., .338 Win. Mag., or 7mm Rem. Mag. cal., laminated stock, Super America configured action and barrel with low glare metal finish. Mfg. 1990-91 only.

	$1,250	$975	$850	$725	$600	$500	$450

Last Mfg.'s Sug. Retail was $1,495.

   Add $100 for Mag. cals.

SUPER GRADE — similar to Super America Model, square top frame, AAA walnut, 22 or 24 in. barrel, plain butt stock, 7½-8½ lbs. Mfg. 1989 only.

	$1,500	$1,275	$995	$825	$695	$550	$500

Last Mfg.'s Sug. Retail was $1,495.

   Add $100 for .375 H&H cal.
   Add $100 for matte blue metal finish.
   The 24 in. barrel was available in Mag. cals. only.

LIMITED WILDLIFE EDITION SERIES — series of 5 guns, includes .257 Roberts (Whitetail Deer Edition), .270 Win. (Mule Deer Edition), .338 Win. Mag. (Rocky Mt. Elk Edition), 7mm Rem. Mag. (Big Horn Sheep Edition), and .375 H&H (Grizzly Bear Edition) cals. included, hand select walnut, special Shilen Rifle barrel, gold plated trigger, receivers are stamped "Wildlife Edition", special prefix serialization, only 25 sets were to be manufactured in 1991 only, includes rings, swivels, and hard case.

   While advertised, only one .270 Win. Mule Deer model was mfg.   Retail price was scheduled to be $3,595.

MODEL 89 AFRICAN SERIES

MODEL 89 AFRICAN — .375 H&H (rare), .416 Rigby (most common) cal., or .505 Gibbs (rare) cal., Magnum action, 24 in. heavy barrel, AA English walnut stock with beaded cheekpiece and rubber recoil pad, includes twin recoil cross bolts, express sights on quarter rib, drop box magazine, 10-10½ lbs. Mfg. 1990-91 only.

	$4,250	$3,750	$3,250	$2,575	$2,050	$1,725	$1,525

Last Mfg.'s Sug. Retail was $3,595.

   .375 H&H or .505 Gibbs cal. will command a premium.

PISTOLS

PREDATOR MODEL — .221 Fireball, .223 Rem., 6mm TCU (disc. 1987), 7mm TCU, or 6x45mm (disc. 1987) cal., single shot Model 84 action with shortened 14⅞ in. barrel, scope use only, one piece deluxe walnut stock with contoured pistol grip, 5¼ lbs., rare cals. will command a premium. Approx. 200 mfg. 1987-1988 only.

▲ *Hunter Grade* — AA claro walnut without checkering. Disc. 1988.

	$1,675	$1,450	$1,250	$1,000	$875	$750	$675

Last Mfg.'s Sug. Retail was $995.

▲ *Super Grade* — similar to Hunter Grade, except has select French walnut with ebony forend tip and 22 lines/in. checkering. Disc. 1988.

	$2,275	$1,950	$1,750	$1,500	$1,300	$1,100	$950

Last Mfg.'s Sug. Retail was $1,195.

KIMEL INDUSTRIES, INC.

Previously manufactured until late 1994, by AAArms located in Monroe, NC. Previously distributed by Kimel Industries, Inc. located in Matthews, NC.

K

Grading	100%	98%	95%	90%	80%	70%	60%

PISTOLS

AP-9 PISTOL — 9mm Para., semi-auto paramilitary design, blowback action with bolt knob on left side of receiver, 5 in. barrel with vent. shroud, front mounted 10 (C/B 1994) or 20* shot detachable mag., black matte finish, adj. front sight, 3 lbs. 7 oz. Mfg. 1989-94.

	$245	$185	$155	$135	$120	$110	$100

Last Mfg.'s Sug. Retail was $279.

Add $10 for nickel finish.

▲ **Mini AP-9** — compact variation of the AP-9 Model with 3 in. barrel, blue or nickel finish. Mfg. 1991-94.

	$240	$180	$155	$135	$120	$110	$100

Last Mfg.'s Sug. Retail was $273.

Add $10 for nickel finish.

▲ **Target AP-9** — target variation of the AP-9 with 12 in. match barrel with shroud, blue finish only. Mfg. 1991-94.

	$255	$190	$160	$140	$120	$110	$100

Last Mfg.'s Sug. Retail was $294.

▲ **P-95** — similar to AP-9, except without barrel shroud and is supplied with 5 shot mag., parts are interchangeable with AP-9. Mfg. 1990-91 only.

	$225	$175	$155	$135	$120	$110	$100

Last Mfg.'s Sug. Retail was $250.

AR-9 Carbine — 9mm Para., carbine variation of the AP-9 with 16½ in. barrel, 20 shot mag., and steel rod folding stock. Mfg. 1991-94.

	$335	$255	$220	$195	$175	$155	$135

Last Mfg.'s Sug. Retail was $384.

KLEINGUENTHER FIREARMS CO.

Manufacturer located in Seguin, TX. The original KDF Co. was started by Mr. Robert Kleinguenther and sold in the early 1980s. At this juncture, Mr. Kleinguenther started a new company called **KLEINGUENTHER®** Kleinguenther Firearms Co. Direct custom order sales only.

RIFLES: BOLT ACTION

Values listed below are for base model only with no additional customer special order options.

BOLT ACTION RIFLE — various cals., individual customer special order rifle with a variety of options, guns are guaranteed to shoot ½ M.O.A., choice of actions, various weights. Currently, the manufacturer does not have availability on either the Winchester Model 70 Custom or the Mauser K-15 action.

▲ **Winchester Model 70 Custom**

	$975	$800	$675	$575	$500	$450	$400

Last Mfg.'s Sug. Retail was $975.

▲ **Sako Action** — various cals., newer guns feature the ballistic recoil muzzle brake system (60-70% recoil reduction), most newer stocks are mfg. out of high density, warp-free, wood panel material.

Mfg.'s Sug. Retail	$1,650	$1,650	$1,375	$1,175	$1,025	$925	$825	$750

Add $155 for ballistic recoil muzzle brake system.

▲ **K-15**

	$1,375	$1,100	$950	$800	$675	$575	$500

Last Mfg.'s Sug. Retail was $1,375.

KNIGHT'S MANUFACTURING COMPANY

Manufactured by Knight's Manufacturing Company located in Vero Beach, FL. Dealer and consumer direct sales.

Grading	100%	98%	95%	90%	80%	70%	60%

RIFLES: SEMI-AUTO

Some of the models listed below were also available in pre-ban configurations. Currently, premiums are being asked but are unpredictable.

SR-25 SPORTER — .308 Win. cal., 20 in. lightweight barrel, AR-15 configuration with carrying handle, 5, 10, or 20 (disc. per C/B 1994) shot detachable mag., less than 2 MOA guaranteed, non-glare finish, 8.8 lbs. New 1993.

Mfg.'s Sug. Retail	$2,995		$2,795	$2,250	$1,900	$1,600	$1,300	$1,000	$850

▲ *SR-25 Carbine* — 16 in. free floating barrel, grooved non-slip handguard, removable carrying handle, 7¾ lbs. New 1995.

Mfg.'s Sug. Retail	$2,995		$2,795	$2,250	$1,900	$1,600	$1,300	$1,000	$850

SR-25 MATCH — similar to SR-25 Standard, except has 24 in. free floating match barrel and flattop receiver, less than 1 MOA guaranteed, 10¾ lbs. New 1993.

Mfg.'s Sug. Retail	$2,995		$2,795	$2,250	$1,900	$1,600	$1,300	$1,000	$850

▲ *SR-25 Lightweight Match* — features 20 in. medium contour free floating barrel, 9½ lbs. New 1995.

Mfg.'s Sug. Retail	$2,995		$2,795	$2,250	$1,900	$1,600	$1,300	$1,000	$850

SR-50 — .50 BMG cal., semi-auto, features high strength materials and lightweight design, fully locked breech and two lug breech bolt, horizontal 10 shot box mag., tubular receiver supports a removable barrel, approx. 32 lbs. (includes scope and mount). New 1996.

Mfg.'s Sug. Retail	$4,994		$4,500	$3,850	$3,500	$3,150	$2,700	$2,300	$1,995

KODIAK CO.

Previous manufacture located in North Haven, CT - circa 1965.

Kodiak Co. was in business for only a short time in the mid-1960s. They produced the first .22 Mag. semi-auto rifle (Model 260), as well as a center fire bolt action (Model 158 Deluxe), and a slide action shotgun (Model 458). While Kodiak long guns are rare and extremely well made, collectability to date has been minimal with most specimens selling at a slight premium over similar quality trade name counterparts of that era. Kodiak Firearms prior to 1963, were marketed under the trade name of Jefferson.

KOLIBRI

Manufactured 1914-1925 by H. Grabner located in Krems/Donau, Austria.

KOLIBRI SEMI-AUTO PISTOL — 2.7 or 3mm centerfire, unrifled barrel, 5 shot box mag., world's smallest semi-auto centerfire pistol.

		$1,200	$1,000	$875	$740	$600	$520	$440

Individual rounds of 2.7 or 3mm (rarer) ammunition are currently trading in the $75 range as it has the distinction of being the world's smallest centerfire shell (shooting a 3 grain bullet).

KONGSBERG

Manufacturer located in Norway. Currently imported and distributed beginning 1996, by Kongsberg America L.L.C. located in Fairfield, CT. Previously imported until 1996 by Lew Horton Distributing Co., Inc., located in Westboro, MA.

Grading	100%	98%	95%	90%	80%	70%	60%

RIFLES: BOLT ACTION

Add $50 for iron sights on models listed below.

393 SERIES — .22-250 Rem., .243 Win., .270 Win., .30-06, .308 Win., 6.5x55 Swedish, 7mm Rem. Mag., .300 Win. Mag. or .338 Win. Mag. cal., available in either Classic, De Luxe, Thumbhole (.22-250 Rem. or 308 Win. only), or Select (Standard) configuration, checkered pistol grip, forend mounted recoil lug which connects to stock, 3-position rear safety, fixed rotary mag., fully adj. trigger. Importation began 1994.

▲ *Classic Model*

Mfg.'s Sug. Retail	$995	$875	$750	$675	$575	$495	$440	$385

Add $114 for Mag. cals.
Add $138 for left-hand action.

▲ *Select Model (Standard Model in Europe)*

Mfg.'s Sug. Retail	$980	$860	$735	$660	$560	$495	$440	$385

Add $113 for Mag. cals.
Add $138 for left-hand action.

▲ *De Luxe Model*

Mfg.'s Sug. Retail	$1,124	$940	$795	$700	$595	$515	$450	$395

Add $112 for Mag. cals.
Add $137 for left-hand action.

▲ *Thumbhole Model* — .22-250 Rem. or .308 Win. cal., features thumbhole stock. New 1996.

Mfg.'s Sug. Retail	$1,580	$1,350	$1,175	$1,000	$875	$750	$625	$500

Add $138 for left-hand action.

KORRIPHILA

Previous manufacturer located in Germany. Previously imported and distributed by Osborne's located in Cheboygan, MI.

This trademark had very limited U.S. importation, and the information listed below reflects the last information received (1988).

HSP 701 TYPE I — 7.65 Luger, .38 Spl., 9mm Luger, 9mm Police, 9mm Steyr, .45 ACP, or 10mm auto cal., semi-auto, double action, 40% stainless steel parts, 4 in. barrel, blue or satin finish, very limited production.

	$2,000	$1,675	$1,375	$1,100	$995	$820	$740

Last Mfg.'s Sug. Retail was $2,395.

▲ *Type II* — similar to Type I, except has 5 in. barrel.

	$2,150	$1,750	$1,475	$1,200	$1,075	$850	$760

Last Mfg.'s Sug. Retail was $2,615.

▲ *Type III* — similar to Type II, except single action trigger.

	$2,200	$1,800	$1,550	$1,200	$1,075	$850	$760

Last Mfg.'s Sug. Retail was $2,785.

KORTH

Manufacturer located in Ratzeburg, Germany. Currently imported in limited quantities by Mandall Shooting Supplies, Inc. located in Scottsdale, AZ. Previously imported by Beeman Precision Arms, located in Santa Rosa, CA and by Osborne's in Cheboygan, MI.

Korth handguns are very high quality and are literally manufactured one-at-a-time, resulting in limited mfg. and importation.

REVOLVERS

Currently, Mandall Shooting Supplies, Inc. is stocking these guns with extra cylinders (.22 LR/.22 Mag. or .357 Mag./9mm Para.). This is because both cylinders are cut from the same billet of steel, and for metallurgical reasons, once a gun is made with

Grading	100%	98%	95%	90%	80%	70%	60%

a single cylinder, the extra convertible cylinder cannot be ordered at a later date. Probably the world's most expensive revolver.

SPORT/COMBAT RIMFIRE — .22 LR or .22 Mag. cal., 3, 4 (Combat only), 5¼, or 6 in. barrel (VR available on 4 in. or longer barrel only) , 6 shot, micro adj. sights (Sport), Combat sights fully adj., full length shrouded ejector rod, adj. trigger, checkered and oil finished walnut grips, 2.6 lbs. Introduced 1967.

Mfg.'s Sug. Retail	$3,300	$3,100	$2,250	$1,850	$1,600	$1,325	$1,050	$925

Add $400 for stainless steel (limited mfg.).
Add $200 for ISU Match Model.
Add $670 for special order 8 in. barrel.
Subtract $475 if without extra .22 LR cylinder.

SPORT/COMBAT CENTERFIRE — .22 Rem. Jet, .32 S&W Long, .32 H&R Mag., .38 Spl., .357 Mag., or 9mm Para. cal., 2½ (scarce), 3, 4 (Combat only), 5¼ or 6 in. barrel, 5 (1st Model) or 6 shot, otherwise similar specs. as Sport/Combat Rimfire Model, 2.1-2.6 lbs.

Mfg.'s Sug. Retail	$3,500	$3,300	$2,350	$1,850	$1,600	$1,325	$1,050	$925

Add $400 for stainless steel (limited mfg.).
Add $200 for ISU Match Model.
Add $200 for .22 Rem. Jet.
Add $670 for special order 8 in. barrel.
Subtract $475 if without extra 9mm Para. cylinder.

This model is available in additional rimmed and rimless calibers on special order. Most importation has occurred in either .357 Mag. or 9mm Para. cal.

PRESENTATION MODEL — deluxe variation of the Sport/Target Model.

This variation is available with etching, engraving, and other special options that are priced per individual quotation from the importer.

PISTOLS: SEMI-AUTO

KORTH SEMI-AUTO — 9mm Para. or 9x21mm IMI (special order only), double action, 4, 5, or 6 in. barrel, all steel construction, 10 shot mag., adj. sights, checkered walnut stocks, very limited production and special order only. Introduced 1986 with first guns shipped 1988.

Mfg.'s Sug. Retail	$3,295	$2,995	$2,250	$1,750

Add $500+ for interchangeable barrels.

KRAG-JORGENSEN

U.S. magazine military rifle. First U.S. (.30-40) military repeating rifle to shoot smokeless powder ammunition. Manufactured 1892-1902.

There have been many conversions of Krag-Jorgensen rifles - many of which are hard to identify. As a rule, these conversions are not as desirable as these specific models listed below.

M1892-DATED 1894 — Springfield Armory, with cleaning rod. Note: designated Type I, has wide, solid upper barrel band.

$4,180	$3,960	$3,740	$3,575	$3,300	$3,000	$2,600

▲ *Dated 1894 or 1895* — designated Type II. Upper band has double strap instead of being solid as in Type I.

$1,870	$1,705	$1,540	$1,210	$880	$720	$595

ARSENAL-ALTERED TO M1896 STYLE

$250	$220	$195	$165	$140	$125	$105

M1896 — Dated 1896, 1897, 1898, Springfield Armory.

$470	$440	$330	$250	$220	$185	$155

M1896 CARBINE

$660	$580	$495	$385	$360	$320	$280

K

Grading	100%	98%	95%	90%	80%	70%	60%

M1895 CARBINE — This is a variant that was dated 1895 and 1896 and omits the word "Model".

	$880	$800	$660	$550	$440	$385	$330

M1896 CADET RIFLE

	$3,025	$2,750	$2,530	$2,200	$1,815	$1,500	$1,200

M1898 RIFLE

	$575	$495	$440	$360	$330	$250	$220

M1898 CARBINE

	$1,450	$1,225	$950	$800	$660	$580	$525

M1899 CARBINE

	$635	$525	$495	$470	$440	$395	$360

M1899 CARBINE, PHILIPPINE CONSTABULARY

	$1,100	$990	$825	$715	$550	$480	$400

Watch yourself - many counterfeits have surfaced in recent years.

KRICO

Manufactured in Furth-Stadeln, Germany by Sportwaffenfabrik Kri-egeskorte Gmbh. Currently imported by Mandall Shooting Supplies, Inc. located in Scottsdale, AZ. Previously imported (until 1988) by Beeman Precision Firearms Inc. located in Santa Rosa, CA.

Between 1983-86, Krico was imported/distributed by over ten U.S. companies/individuals. Beeman Precision Arms imported these rifles 1986-1988 in limited quantities. Krico manufactures a high quality rifle and to date, has had limited domestic distribution.

RIFLES: BOLT ACTION

SPORTING RIFLE — .22 Hornet or .222 Rem. cal., miniature Mauser action, 4 shot, 22, 24, or 26 in. barrel, single or double set triggers, open sights, checkered walnut stock, pistol grip. Mfg. 1956-1962.

	$605	$550	$495	$440	$400	$360	$305

CARBINE — similar to Sporting Rifle, except 20 or 22 in. barrel, full length stock.

	$635	$580	$415	$470	$420	$375	$320

SPECIAL VARMINT RIFLE — similar to Sporting Rifle, except heavy barrel, no sights.

	$605	$550	$495	$440	$400	$360	$300

MODEL 300 SPORTER — .22 LR, .22 Mag., or .22 Hornet cal., select walnut with straight, checkered stock and fuller forearm, $23\frac{1}{2}$ in. barrel, 5 shot mag., grooved receiver, $6\frac{1}{2}$ lbs.

Mfg.'s Sug. Retail	$595	$550	$495	$450	$410	$380	$350	$320

Add $30 for .22 Mag. cal.
Add $155 for .22 Hornet cal.
This model was designated Model 302 Sporter until 1986.

▲ *Model 300 Deluxe* — similar to Model 300 Standard, except has deluxe wood and checkering. Importation began 1991.

Mfg.'s Sug. Retail	$695	$625	$550	$480	$430	$385	$350	$320

Add $25 for .22 Mag. cal.
Add $200 for .22 Hornet cal.

MODEL 311 SMALL BORE RIFLE — .22 LR only, bolt action, 5 or 10 shot, 22 in. barrel, single or double set trigger, open sights, checkered stock. Disc.

	$330	$275	$250	$220	$195	$165	$155

Add 30% for Kaps $2\frac{1}{2}$ power scope.

Grading	100%	98%	95%	90%	80%	70%	60%

MODEL 320 MANNLICHER SPORTER — .22 LR, .22 Mag., or .22 Hornet cal., full stock sporter, 19½ in. barrel, 5 shot mag., double set triggers, 6 lbs.

Mfg.'s Sug. Retail $750	$650	$575	$500	$460	$430	$395	$370

Add $25 for .22 Mag. cal.
Add $150 for .22 Hornet cal.

This model was designated Model 304 Mannlicher Sporter until 1986. In 1991 it was redesignated the Model 320 Stutzen.

MODEL 340 S ST — .22 LR only, silhouette model, 21 in. bull barrel, match trigger, no sights, 5 shot mag., stippled pistol grip and forearm, 7½ lbs.

Mfg.'s Sug. Retail $795	$750	$625	$550	$500	$450	$375	$325

▲ *Model 340 Kricotronic* — similar to above, except with Krico electronic trigger. Importation disc. 1988.

$1,295	$995	$900	$800	$690	$600	$550

Last Mfg.'s Sug. Retail was $1,450.

▲ *Model 340 Mini-Sniper* — non-glare wood and metal finish, military style barrel with muzzle brake, vent. forearm, no sights, match trigger (interchangeable), 5 shot, raised cheekpiece. Importation disc. 1988.

$1,050	$825	$725	$600	$550	$500	$450

Last Mfg.'s Sug. Retail was $1,200.

BIATHLON MODEL 360 S — .22 LR cal., standard biathlon configuration with conventional straight pull bolt.

Mfg.'s Sug. Retail $1,695	$1,375	$1,075	$925	$750	$625	$550	$500

BIATHLON MODEL 360 S2 — .22 LR cal., biathlon competition rifle featuring unique pistol grip operated rapid fire action, includes 5 mags., aperture sights, snow guards, and black stock.

Mfg.'s Sug. Retail $1,595	$1,300	$1,050	$900	$750	$625	$550	$500

MODEL 400 SPORTER — .22 LR or .22 Hornet cal., 23½ in. barrel, select checkered walnut with European style curved cheekpiece, 5 shot mag., open sights, 6.8 lbs.

Mfg.'s Sug. Retail $895	$840	$750	$625	$550	$500	$450	$375

Add $55 for .22 Hornet cal.

▲ *Model 400 Match Single Shot* — .22 LR only, match rifle configuration.

Mfg.'s Sug. Retail $950	$875	$750	$625	$550	$500	$450	$375

▲ *Model 400 Silhouette* — .22 LR only, designed for silhouette shooting, no sights.

Mfg.'s Sug. Retail $775	$725	$615	$550	$500	$450	$375	$325

MODEL 420 L ST MANNLICHER SPORTER — .22 Hornet only, full stock sporter, 19½ in. barrel, double set triggers, 5 shot, 6½ lbs.

$875	$750	$625	$550	$500	$450	$375

MODEL 440 — .22 Hornet, otherwise similar to Model 340. Importation disc. 1988.

$900	$725	$575	$525	$450	$400	$360

Last Mfg.'s Sug. Retail was $1,025.

MODEL 600 HUNTING — .222 Rem., .223 Rem., .22-250 Rem., .243 Win., .308 Win., or 5.6x50 Mag. cal., 23½ in. barrel, select checkered walnut with curved European style cheekpiece and vent. forend, 3 or 4 shot mag., open sights, single set trigger, 7 lbs.

Mfg.'s Sug. Retail $1,295	$1,100	$975	$850	$750	$625	$550	$500

Add $55 for Model 600 SC.
Add $300 for Model 600 Benchrest.
Add $355 for Model 600 in sniper configuration.

This model is also available in single shot configuration at no extra charge as well as in a Match Model Group I & II - add $100 for Group II.

K

Grading	100%	98%	95%	90%	80%	70%	60%

MODEL 620 MANNLICHER SPORTER — same cals. as Model 600, full stock sporter, 20¾ in. barrel, double set triggers, 3 shot mag., 6.8 lbs. Importation disc. 1988.

	$1,165	$965	$875	$760	$695	$650	$590

Last Mfg.'s Sug. Retail was $1,300.

MODEL 640 S ST VARMINT — .22-250, .222 Rem., or .223 Rem. cal., 23¾ in. heavy barrel, high Monte Carlo comb and full cheekpiece, rosewood forearm tip and grip cap, Wundhammer hand swell, double set triggers, 4 shot mag., 9.6 lbs. Importation disc. 1990.

	$875	$750	$625	$550	$500	$450	$375

Last Mfg.'s Sug. Retail was $950.

▲ *Model 640 Sniper* — similar to Model 640, except has non-adj. cheekpiece. Importation disc. 1988.

	$1,325	$1,075	$965	$875	$760	$695	$650

Last Mfg.'s Sug. Retail was $1,500.

MODEL 640 DELUXE/SUPER SNIPER — .223 Rem. or .308 Win., 23 in. barrel, select walnut stock has stippled hand grip, adj. cheekpiece and vent. forearm, engine turned bolt assembly, 3 shot mag., match trigger, 10 lbs. Importation disc. 1988.

	$1,495	$1,175	$1,025	$875	$760	$695	$650

Last Mfg.'s Sug. Retail was $1,725.

This model was known as the 650 Sniper/Match until 1986.

MODEL 700A ECONOMY — .222 Rem., .243 Win., or .308 Win. cal. (Group I) or 6.5x55mm, 7x64mm, .270 Win., or .30-06 cal. (Group II), without sights, single trigger. Importation began 1991.

Mfg.'s Sug. Retail	$995	$900	$775	$650	$550	$500	$450	$375

Add $70 for Group II cals.

MODEL 700 SERIES — .17 Rem., .22-250 Rem., .222 Rem., .222 Rem. Mag., .223 Rem., 5.6x50mm Mag., .243 Win., .308 Win., or 5.6x57 RWS cal. (Group I), 6.5x55mm, 7x57mm, .270 Win., 7x64mm, .30-06, or 9.3x72 cal. (Group II), or 6.5x68mm, 7mm Rem. Mag., .300 Win. Mag., 8x68S, 7.5mm Swiss, or 6x62mm Freres (Group III), matte black metal finish, open sights, approx. 7 lbs. Importation began 1991.

▲ *Model 700 Hunting* — available in Group I or II cals. only, walnut hunting stock with Bavarian cheekpiece, recoil pad, and palm swell grip.

Mfg.'s Sug. Retail	$1,249	$1,075	$950	$850	$750	$625	$550	$500

Add $50 for Group II cals.

▲ *Model 700 DeLuxe* — similar to Model 700 Hunting, except has better grade walnut and is available in Group III cals. also.

Mfg.'s Sug. Retail	$1,379	$1,150	$1,000	$875	$750	$625	$550	$500

Add $20 for Group II cals.
Add $71 for Group III cals.
Add $150 for left-hand action.
Add $346-$516 for repeating variation in Groups I-III.

▲ *Model 700 Stutzen* — full stock variation (Mannlicher) of the Model 700 DeLuxe.

Mfg.'s Sug. Retail	$1,450	$1,200	$1,025	$895	$750	$625	$550	$500

Add $39 for Group II cals.
Add $160 for Group III cals.
Add $275 for DeLuxe variation (includes better wood and finish).

MODEL 700 DL R SPORTER — .270 or .30-06 cal., 23½ in. barrel, curved European cheekpiece, select walnut, 3 shot Mag., single set trigger, open sights, 7 lbs. Importation disc. 1990.

	$925	$800	$650	$575	$500	$450	$375

Last Mfg.'s Sug. Retail was $1,025.

Subtract $30 for Model 700 DM ST.
Add $470 for Model 700 DLM.

MODEL 720 MANNLICHER SPORTER — similar to Model 700, only has 20¾ in. barrel, double set triggers, 6.8 lbs. Importation disc. 1990.

	$1,100	$975	$850	$750	$625	$550	$500

Last Mfg.'s Sug. Retail was $1,295.

K

Grading	100%	98%	95%	90%	80%	70%	60%

▲ *Model 720 Limited Edition* — .270 cal. only, 24Kt. gold scroll work on bolt handle, receiver, barrel and mounts. Trigger and front side are gold plated. Serial numbered in gold. Disc. 1986.

	$2,310	$1,990	$1,700	$1,450	$1,200	$1,050	$950

Last Mfg.'s Sug. Retail was $2,659.

RIFLES: SEMI-AUTO

MODEL 260 SPORTER — .22 LR only, semi-auto action, standard features. Importation began 1991.

Mfg.'s Sug. Retail	$595	$550	$495	$450	$410	$380	$350	$320

H. KRIEGHOFF GUN CO. (SHOTGUNS OF ULM)

Current manufacturer located in Ulm, Germany. Previous manufacture was in Suhl, Germany, 1886-1948. Currently imported and distributed by Krieghoff International Inc. located in Ottsville, PA. Dealer direct sales only.

WWII Krieghoff Lugers appear in the Luger section of this text.

SHOTGUNS: OVER AND UNDER

Subtract 20%-50% for shotguns mfg. before 1960.

MODEL 32 STANDARD — O/U, 12, 20, 28, or .410 ga., 28-32 in. high rib barrels, ejectors, boxlock, single trigger, select wood. Disc. 1983.

	$2,475	$2,200	$1,900	$1,400	$1,175	$895	$775

▲ *Low Rib* — 28 or .410 ga., two-barrel set, 50% premium.

	$3,520	$2,860	$2,640	$2,200	$1,980	$1,870	$1,540

Allem's Guncraft, Inc. located in Zionsville, PA, still has limited quantities of original Model 32s (both O/U and single barrel) with a choice of 30 or 32 in. barrels (Vandalia or Low Rib). The current retail is $4,495. A limited supply of original Model 32 barrels (O/U and Single) is also available - retail price is $1,895.

MODEL 32 4-BARREL SKEET SET — O/U, 12, 20, 28, or .410 ga., matched barrels in case, grades differ in engraving and wood quality, available as follows:

	100%	98%	95%	90%	80%	70%	60%
Standard	$11,250	$9,950	$8,650	$7,450	$6,200	$4,950	$3,700
Munchen Grade	$13,250	$11,250	$9,500	$8,300	$6,600	$5,775	$5,225
San Remo Grade (unmarked)	$16,995	$13,750	$11,000	$9,000	$7,800	$6,600	$6,325
Monte Carlo (Silver Crown, 50 mfg.)	$18,750	$16,000	$13,750	$11,000	$9,000	$7,800	$6,600
Crown Grade (400 mfg.)	$24,995	$21,000	$17,750	$14,750	$12,100	$10,350	$9,650
Super Crown Grade (48 mfg.)	$29,995	$25,750	$20,750	$16,750	$14,775	$12,650	$10,350

MODEL 32 SINGLE BARREL TRAP — same action as O/U, 12 ga., 32-34 in. barrel, VR, mod., imp. mod., or full choke.

	$1,850	$1,400	$1,200	$1,000	$895	$795	$695

KS-5 SINGLE BARREL TRAP — 12 ga. only, 32 or 34 in. barrel, adj. point of impact, innovative trigger configuration, optional choke tubes, redesigned streamlined receiver (new 1993). New 1985.

Mfg.'s Sug. Retail	$3,675	$3,175	$2,775	$2,475	$2,125	$1,875	$1,625	$1,400

Add $2,100 per additional barrel.
Add $425 for screw-in choke option.
Add $395 for factory adj. comb stock.
Add $425 for aluminum case.

Adj. point of impact on this model is achieved by means of different, optional fronthangers.

K

Grading	100%	98%	95%	90%	80%	70%	60%

▲ *KS-5 Special* — 12 ga. only, 32 or 34 in. barrel, features adj. rib and comb stock, cased. New 1990.

Mfg.'s Sug. Retail	$4,695	$4,100	$3,550	$2,975	$2,475	$2,050	$1,750	$1,500

Add $2,750 per additional barrel.

Add $425 for screw-in choke option.

Adj. point of impact on this model is achieved by an adj. rib and comb stock at no extra charge.

K-80 TRAP — 12 ga. only, available in O/U, Unsingle, Top Single (single top barrel), and Combo (O/U with extra trap barrel) configurations, standard model has silver finished receiver, adj. rib allowing variable points of impact (new 1993). In O/U configuration the barrels are separated, about 8½ lbs. A wide variety of custom order options can be ordered on this model.

For the Model K-80 Trap, extra barrels cost $2,900 for O/Us, $2,950 for top single, and $3,575 for unsingle barrel.

$650 for O/U screw-in chokes (5 tubes).

Add $425 for 3 screw-in chokes (single barrel guns only).

Add $425 for single release trigger or $750 for double release trigger.

▲ *Standard Model O/U* — special order only for Top Single, add 9% for Unsingle, or 40% for Combo Standard K-80 variations.

Mfg.'s Sug. Retail	$7,375	$6,200	$5,025	$4,250	$3,550	$3,000	$2,600	$2,295

▲ *Bavaria Model O/U* — game scene engraved silver receiver with light scroll perimeter scroll work, select walnut. Special order only for Top Single, add 5% for Unsingle, or 24% for Combo Bavaria variations.

Mfg.'s Sug. Retail	$12,525	$10,575	$7,800	$6,375	$5,000	$4,375	$3,950	$3,300

▲ *Danube Model O/U* — fine English scrollwork on receiver sides and floor plate. Special order only for Top Single, add 4.5% for Unsingle, or 20% for Combo Danube variations.

Mfg.'s Sug. Retail	$23,625	$19,325	$13,950	$10,750	$9,000	$7,150	$6,570	$5,850

▲ *Gold Target Model* — deep chiseled scroll engraving with gold line accents, 100% coverage finest quality walnut. Special order only for Top Single, add 3% for Unsingle, and 14% for Combo Gold Target variations.

Mfg.'s Sug. Retail	$27,170	$22,000	$15,500	$12,750	$9,500	$7,750	$7,000	$6,650

▲ *Centennial Model* — 12 ga. only, available in combo configuration only, 100 only mfg. 1986 to commemorate Krieghoff's centennial year, ser. no. 14501-14600. H. Krieghoff's signature inlaid in gold on frame sides. Add $150 for screw-in interchangeable chokes, $1,755 for 4-barrel set.

				$6,000	$5,000	$4,400

Last Mfg.'s Sug. Retail was $5,995.

K-80 SKEET O/U — 12 ga. only, available in Lightweight (8mm rib), Standardweight (8mm rib), or International (12mm rib) configurations, factory porting on both barrels, 28 in. barrels only, 8.2 lbs.

For the Model K-80 Skeet, add $925 for International Model (Tula choking/even choking became standard in 1996), $675 for Skeet Special (choke tubes & tapered flat rib).

International Skeet models are supplied with hard case. Standardweight and Lightweight models include soft case.

▲ *Standard Model* — available with either lightweight (Dural aluminum) or standardweight frame. Hard case optional.

Mfg.'s Sug. Retail	$6,900	$5,850	$4,475	$3,375	$2,850	$2,450	$2,125	$1,900

▲ *Bavaria Model O/U* — game scene engraved silver receiver with light perimeter scroll work, select walnut. Available in either Standardweight or Lightweight (disc. 1995) configuration.

Mfg.'s Sug. Retail	$12,050	$10,050	$6,700	$5,700	$5,000	$4,375	$3,950	$3,300

▲ *Danube Model O/U* — fine English scrollwork on receiver sides and floorplate. Available in either standardweight or lightweight (disc. 1995) configuration.

Mfg.'s Sug. Retail	$23,150	$18,475	$14,000	$10,650	$9,000	$7,150	$6,570	$5,850

▲ *Gold Target Model* — deep chiseled scroll engraving with gold line accents, 100% coverage finest quality walnut. This model is available in standardweight frame only.

Mfg.'s Sug. Retail	$26,695	$21,650	$15,350	$12,850	$9,550	$7,750	$7,000	$6,650

K

Grading	100%	98%	95%	90%	80%	70%	60%

▲ **Centennial Skeet** — available in skeet configuration — special features as noted above on Centennial Model description listed under K-80 Trap. Mfg. 1986 only.

$3,675 $3,150 $2,700

Last Mfg.'s Sug. Retail was $3,980.

K-80 2-BARREL LIGHTWEIGHT SKEET SET — 12 ga. Tula and tubing barrel, 8mm rib, hard case standard. New 1988.

▲ *Standard Grade*
Mfg.'s Sug. Retail	$11,840		$9,400	$7,000	$5,150	$4,300	$3,875	$3,300	$3,000

Subtract $1,845 for heavy barrel variation, which does not include sub-gauge tubes.
Retail price for 2 barrel heavy set with choke tubes is $9,995.

▲ *Bavaria Model O/U* — game scene engraved silver receiver with light perimeter scroll work, select walnut. Importation began 1988.
Mfg.'s Sug. Retail	$16,990		$14,975	$11,250	$8,575	$7,200	$6,200	$5,250	$4,800

Subtract $1,845 for heavy barrel variation, which does not include sub-gauge tubes.
Retail price for 2 barrel heavy set with choke tubes is $15,115.

▲ *Danube Model O/U* — fine English scroll work on receiver sides and floorplate. Importation began 1988.
Mfg.'s Sug. Retail	$28,090		$22,945	$15,250	$17,750	$9,400	$7,750	$7,000	$6,650

Subtract $1,845 for heavy barrel variation, which does not include sub-gauge tubes.
Retail price for 2 barrel heavy set with choke tubes is $26,245.

▲ *Gold Target Model* — deep chiseled scroll engraving with gold line accents, 100% coverage finest quality walnut.
Mfg.'s Sug. Retail	$31,635		$25,975	$20,500	$15,950	$12,375	$9,950	$8,700	$7,500

Subtract $1,845 for heavy barrel variation.
Retail price for 2 barrel heavy set with choke tubes is $28,064.

K-80 4-BARREL SKEET SET — 1 barrel each of 12, 20, 28, and .410 ga., 12 ga. is Tula choked (even patterning), 8mm tapered flat or standard VR, includes hard case. Since most shooters prefer different gauge insert tubes (Briley, etc.) rather than barrel sets, values have gone down considerably recently for these 4 gauge sets.

▲ *Standard Grade* — satin finished receiver with skeet scroll engraving.
Mfg.'s Sug. Retail	$16,950		$13,150	$7,625	$6,275	$5,350	$4,500	$4,000	$3,650

▲ *Bavaria Model O/U* — game scene engraved silver receiver with light perimeter scrollwork, select walnut.
Mfg.'s Sug. Retail	$22,100		$18,200	$12,500	$9,750	$8,250	$6,900	$5,400	$4,350

▲ *Danube Model O/U* — fine English scroll work on receiver sides and floorplate.
Mfg.'s Sug. Retail	$33,200		$26,100	$17,000	$13,000	$10,500	$8,700	$7,500	$6,250

▲ *Gold Target Model* — deep chiseled scroll engraving with gold line accents, 100% coverage finest quality walnut.
Mfg.'s Sug. Retail	$36,745		$29,650	$17,350	$13,000	$10,500	$8,700	$7,500	$6,250

K-80 PIGEON O/U — 12 ga. only, available with 28, 29, or 30 in. barrels, standard tapered step rib, IM/SF choking, available in Lightweight or Standardweight configuration (no extra charge).

Beginning 1992, the K-80 Pigeon Model is available by special order only. Rather than list the various Pigeon models separately, their current values will be approximately the same as the corresponding K-80 Trap/Skeet Models listed above.

K-80 SPORTING CLAYS O/U — 12 ga. only, 28, 30 (new 1991), or 32 (new 1993) in. barrels with 5 choke tubes, choice of 8mm VR skeet, tapered flat (broadway) or step rib (special order), sporting clay stock dimensions. New 1988.

Add $3,195 for extra set of O/U barrels with 5 choke tubes.
Add $2,800 for extra set of O/U barrels with 1 choke tube.

▲ *Standard Grade* — satin finished receiver with sporting scroll engraving.
Mfg.'s Sug. Retail	$8,150		$6,750	$5,425	$4,500	$3,650	$3,000	$2,600	$2,100

Grading	100%	98%	95%	90%	80%	70%	60%

▲ *Bavaria Model O/U* — game scene engraved silver receiver with light scroll perimeter scroll work, select walnut.

Mfg.'s Sug. Retail $13,300		$10,800	$8,200	$6,600	$5,350	$4,450	$3,950	$3,300

▲ *Danube Model O/U* — fine English scroll work on receiver sides and floorplate.

Mfg.'s Sug. Retail $24,400		$19,000	$13,750	$10,750	$8,350	$7,000	$5,950	$4,950

▲ *Gold Target Model* — deep chiseled scroll engraving with gold line accents, 100% coverage finest quality walnut.

Mfg.'s Sug. Retail $27,945		$22,350	$16,150	$13,350	$9,700	$7,875	$7,000	$6,650

ULM-P LIVE PIGEON — 12 ga. only, live pigeon gun with hand detachable sidelocks, 28 or 30 in. VR barrels, standard grade has light scrollwork engraving.

Mfg.'s Sug. Retail $22,500		$17,500	$12,000	$9,175	$7,700	$6,000	$5,450	$4,995

▲ *Bavaria Grade* — similar to Ulm-P, only with elaborate game scene engraving.

Mfg.'s Sug. Retail $29,500		$22,000	$14,750	$11,450	$8,750	$6,750	$5,700	$5,300

KS-2 SERIES — any ga., full H&H type sidelocks, priced by individual special order. Prices start at $24,000. Custom order only with substantial wait.

O/U SHOTGUN OR COMBINATION GUN

Add $695 for hand detachable sidelocks (Ulm only).
Add $1,290 for 4-claw scope mount system.

TECK MODEL — O/U shotgun or rifle/shotgun combo., 12 and 16 ga., various cals. (7x57R, 7x64mm, 7x65R, .30-06, or .308 Win.), boxlock action, Kersten double crossbolt, auto ejectors, 7½ lbs.

Mfg.'s Sug. Retail $7,750		$6,650	$5,100	$4,400	$3,550	$3,000	$2,600	$2,295

▲ *Teck Dural* — Dural aluminum frame variation of the Teck, 6.8 lbs.

Mfg.'s Sug. Retail $7,750		$6,625	$5,100	$4,400	$3,550	$3,000	$2,600	$2,295

ULM   — similar to Teck, except sidelock and fully engraved with leaf arabesques.

Mfg.'s Sug. Retail $14,500		$11,700	$8,975	$7,600	$6,350	$5,250	$4,400	$3,500

▲ *Ulm Dural* — Dural aluminum frame variation of the Ulm.

Mfg.'s Sug. Retail $14,500		$11,700	$8,975	$7,600	$6,350	$5,250	$4,400	$3,500

ULM PRIMUS — similar to Ulm, except game scene engraved with English arabesques.

Mfg.'s Sug. Retail $22,850		$18,100	$12,850	$9,000	$7,000	$5,975	$5,450	$4,995

▲ *Ulm Primus Dural* — Dural aluminum frame variation of the Ulm Primus.

Mfg.'s Sug. Retail $22,850		$18,100	$12,850	$9,000	$7,000	$5,975	$5,450	$4,995

ULTRA — combination O/U, 12 ga. only, various calibers (lower barrel), 25 in. barrels, "Kickspannar" mechanism allows manual cocking from thumb safety, satin finish receiver, VR, 6 lbs. New 1985.

Mfg.'s Sug. Retail $4,950		$3,975	$2,575	$1,850	$1,400	$1,200	$1,050	$900

▲ *Ultra-B* — similar to Ultra, except features a selector to switch the front set trigger to the top shotgun barrel. Disc. 1995.

	$4,050	$2,675	$1,925	$1,550	$1,350	$1,150	$1,000

Last Mfg.'s Sug. Retail was $4,990.

DOUBLE RIFLES

Various grades differ in style and amount of engraving, choice of walnut and various options that can be special ordered.

Add $1,500-$2,500 for 4-claw scope mount (standard or European).

K

Grading	100%	98%	95%	90%	80%	70%	60%

TECK O/U — .30-06, .300 Win. Mag. (disc. 1994), .308 Win., 7x56R (disc. 1994), 7x65R (new 1995), 8x57JRS, 8x75RS (new 1995), 9.3x74R, .375 H&H (disc. 1988), or .458 Win. Mag. cal., 25 in. barrels, boxlock action, cocking indicators, hard case included.

Mfg.'s Sug. Retail	$10,500	$8,725	$6,475	$5,200	$4,300	$3,650	$3,300	$3,000

Add $1,400 for .375 H&H or .458 Win. Mag. cal.
Add $990 for DTs with front set trigger.

▲ **Teck-Handspanner** — manual cocking, 7x65R, .30-06, or .308 Win. on 16 ga. receiver frame.

Mfg.'s Sug. Retail	$12,500	$10,200	$7,950	$6,675	$5,175	$4,375	$3,950	$3,200

ULTRA O/U — various cals. up to 9.3x74R, features unique manual cocking/self cocking device and interchangeable muzzle wedge for adjustable point of impact. New 1993.

Mfg.'s Sug. Retail	$6,970	$6,300	$5,625	$4,950	$4,250	$3,500	$2,950	$2,250

CLASSIC O/U — same standard cals. as Teck O/U, boxlock action, light engraving. New 1995.

Mfg.'s Sug. Retail	$7,850	$6,975	$5,900	$5,150	$4,300	$3,500	$2,950	$2,250

▲ **Classic O/U Big Bore** — .375 H&H, .416 Rigby, .458 Win Mag., .470 NE, or .500 NE cal. New 1995.

Mfg.'s Sug. Retail	$9,450	$8,250	$6,925	$5,950	$5,000	$4,150	$3,350	$3,150

ULM O/U — similar to Teck Double Rifle, except has any combination of cals., with sidelocks and more elaborate engraving.

Mfg.'s Sug. Retail	$17,900	$14,300	$10,350	$8,550	$6,900	$6,100	$5,500	$4,950

Add $695 for hand detachable sidelocks.
Add $1,775 with single/double trigger.

▲ **Ulm Dekor** — sidelock with light scroll engraving. Importation disc. 1991.

	$10,450	$9,150	$8,000	$6,750	$5,600	$5,000	$4,400

Last Mfg.'s Sug. Retail was $12,500.

▲ **Ulm Primus** — deluxe sidelock.

Mfg.'s Sug. Retail	$26,000	$19,750	$13,000	$10,250	$8,100	$6,550	$5,700	$5,300

TRUMPF SxS — boxlock action, similar to Teck model, except in .30-06, 8x57JRS, or 9.3x74R cal. Disc. 1994.

	$13,200	$9,700	$8,350	$6,900	$6,100	$5,500	$4,950

Last Mfg.'s Sug. Retail was $16,150.

CLASSIC SxS STANDARD — same standard cals. as Teck O/U, boxlock action, 21½ (optional) or 23½ in. regulated barrels, DTs, manual cocking device, removable wedge and integrated front sight in cals. up to .375 H&H, extractors, choice of standard or bavarian style stock, light engraving, with or w/o side plates, various engraving options, 7½-11 lbs. New 1995.

Mfg.'s Sug. Retail	$7,850	$6,950	$5,950	$5,150	$4,350	$3,500	$2,950	$2,250

Add $2,995 for a set of 20 ga./3 in. barrels.
Add $1,950 for side plates with standard scroll engraving.

▲ **Classic SxS Big Five (Big Bore)** — .375 H&H, .375 Flanged Mag. NE (new 1996), .416 Rigby, .458 Win. Mag., .470 NE, .500/.416 NE (new 1996) or .500 NE cal. New 1995.

Mfg.'s Sug. Retail	$9,450	$8,300	$6,975	$5,975	$5,000	$4,150	$3,350	$3,150

Add $2,995 for a set of 20 ga./3 in. barrels.
Add $1,950 for side plates with standard scroll engraving.

NEPTUN SxS — sidelock double rifle, same features as the Ulm model. Importation disc. 1991.

	$12,750	$10,400	$8,700	$7,350	$6,000	$5,450	$4,995

Last Mfg.'s Sug. Retail was $15,500.

DRILLINGS

H. Krieghoff drillings can be ordered with a variety of cals. (.222 Rem., .243 Win., .270 Win., or .30-06) and special order features. Prices shown below are for standard guns with no options. Better models will have a finer grade walnut and exhibit more elaborate deep relief engraving.

K

Grading	100%	98%	95%	90%	80%	70%	60%

Add $450 for free floating rifle barrels on Trumpf and Neptun Models listed below (both regular steel frame and Dural variations).
Add $1,290 for 3-claw scope mount system.

PLUS MODEL — 12 or 20 ga. over rifle barrel (.222 Rem., .243 Win., .270 Win., or .30-06 cal.), boxlock action, light engraving. New 1988.

Mfg.'s Sug. Retail	$5,955	$4,875	$3,525	$2,750	$2,175	$1,825	$1,525	$1,200

TRUMPF MODEL — 12, 16, or 20 ga. O/U, or rifle shotgun combo., various cals., boxlock, 25 in. barrels, 7½ lbs.

Mfg.'s Sug. Retail	$9,950	$8,300	$6,300	$5,350	$4,250	$3,300	$2,750	$2,200

Add $1,850 for single trigger.

▲ *Trumpf Dural* — Dural aluminum frame variation of the Trumpf, 6.8 lbs., cased.

Mfg.'s Sug. Retail	$9,950	$8,300	$6,300	$5,350	$4,250	$3,300	$2,750	$2,200

NEPTUN MODEL — 12 or 20 ga., variety of cals., elaborate engraving, sidelocks.

Mfg.'s Sug. Retail	$16,500	$13,250	$10,400	$9,000	$7,550	$6,200	$5,100	$4,150

▲ *Neptun Dural* — Dural aluminum frame variation of the Neptun, cased.

Mfg.'s Sug. Retail	$16,500	$13,250	$10,400	$9,000	$7,550	$6,200	$5,100	$4,150

NEPTUN PRIMUS MODEL — similar to Neptun Model, only hand detachable sidelocks and elaborate deep relief engraving.

Mfg.'s Sug. Retail	$24,000	$18,200	$13,550	$10,450	$8,400	$7,100	$5,850	$4,950

▲ *Neptun Primus Dural* — Dural aluminum frame variation available at no extra charge.

Mfg.'s Sug. Retail	$24,000	$18,200	$13,550	$10,450	$8,400	$7,100	$5,850	$4,950

K

L section

L.A.R. MANUFACTURING, INC.

Manufacturer located in West Jordan, UT.

Grading	100%	98%	95%	90%	80%	70%	60%

PISTOLS

GRIZZLY WIN. MAG. MARK I — .357 Mag., .357/.45 Grizzly Win. Mag. (new 1990), .45 ACP, 10mm, or .45 Win. Mag., single action, semi-auto based on the Colt 1911 design, 5.4 in. (new 1986), 6½ in., 8 in. (new 1987), or 10 in. (new 1987) barrel, parkerized finish, 7 shot mag., ambidextrous safeties, checkered rubber grips, adj. sights, 48 oz. empty. Also can be converted to .45 ACP, 10mm (new 1988), .357 Mag., or .30 Mauser (disc.). New 1984.

▲ *Short Barrel Lengths* — 5.4 or 6.5 in. barrel.

	100%	98%	95%	90%	80%	70%	60%
Mfg.'s Sug. Retail $1,000	$875	$675	$625	$525	$495	$475	$450

Add $14 for .357 Mag. cal.
Add $150 for hard chrome or nickel frame.
Add $260 for full hard chrome or nickel frame.
Add $233-$248 for cal. conversion units.
Conversion units include .357 Mag., 10mm, 40 S&W (1991-1993 only), and .45 ACP cals.

▲ *Long Barrel Lengths* — .357 Mag., .45 Win. Mag., or .357/.45 Grizzly Win. Mag. (new 1990), 8 or 10 in. barrel, extended slides. Disc. 1995.

	100%	98%	95%	90%	80%	70%	60%
	$1,195	$975	$895	$800	$725	$650	$575

Last Mfg.'s Sug. Retail was $1,313.

Add $62 for 10 in. barrel.
Add $24 for .357 Mag.
Add $143 for scope mounts (disc.).
Add $110 for muzzle compensator.

GRIZZLY .44 MAG. MARK 4 — .44 Mag., choice of lusterless blue, parkerized, chrome, or nickel finish, 5⁴⁄₁₀ or 6½ in. barrel, adj. sights. New 1991.

	100%	98%	95%	90%	80%	70%	60%
Mfg.'s Sug. Retail $1,014	$875	$715	$635	$550	$495	$475	$450

GRIZZLY .50 MARK 5 — .50 Action Express, single action semi-auto, 5⁴⁄₁₀ or 6½ in. barrel, 6 shot mag., checkered walnut grips, 56 oz. New 1993.

	100%	98%	95%	90%	80%	70%	60%
Mfg.'s Sug. Retail $1,152	$1,025	$865	$720	$615	$525	$495	$475

GRIZZLY WIN. MAG. MARK II — similar to Mark I, except has fixed sights, standard safeties, and different metal finish. Mfg. 1986 only.

	100%	98%	95%	90%	80%	70%	60%
	$625	$550	$525	$495	$475	$450	$425

Last Mfg.'s Sug. Retail was $550.

Add $25 for .357 Mag.

RIFLES

BIG BOAR COMPETITOR RIFLE — .50 BMG, single shot, bolt action design in bullpup configuration, alloy steel receiver and bolt, 36 in. heavy barrel with compensator, thumb safety, 28.4 lbs. New 1994.

	100%	98%	95%	90%	80%	70%	60%
Mfg.'s Sug. Retail $2,570	$2,295	$1,925	$1,600	$1,275	$1,100	$995	$895

Add $100 for parkerizing.
Add $250 for nickel frame.
Add $350 for full nickel frame.

L E S INCORPORATED

Previous manufacturer located in Morton Grove, IL.

L

Grading	100%	98%	95%	90%	80%	70%	60%

PISTOL: SEMI-AUTO

This pistol was patterned after the Steyr Model GB.

P-18 ROGAK DOUBLE ACTION — 9mm Para., double action, 18 shot, $5\frac{1}{2}$ in. barrel, stainless steel, black plastic grips with partial thumb rest. Disc.

				$350	$295	$265	

▲ *High polish finish*

				$395	$330	$295	

Approx. 2,300 P-18s were mfg. before being disc.

LABANU INCORPORATED

Manufactured by Norinco in China, and imported exclusively by Labanu Inc. located in Ronkonkoma, NY.

SKS - SPORTER RIFLE — 7.62x39mm, sporterized variation of the SKS with thumbhole stock, 16 $\frac{1}{2}$ in. barrel, includes accessories, 5 lbs. Importation began 1995.

Mfg.'s Sug. Retail	$189	$165	$150	$135	$120	$110	$95	$85

LAHTI PISTOL

Previous manufacturer located in Husqvarna, Sweden & Vkt (state rifle factory in Jyvaskyla), Finland.

SWEDISH MODEL 40 — 9mm Para., $4\frac{3}{4}$ in. barrel, blued finish, fixed sights, plastic grips, mfg. 1940-1944.

$395	$350	$300	$275	$260	$250	$240

Add 10% for Holster-Rig.

Note: It is important to note that there are diversely marked variations of this pistol, such as RPLT (Danish State Police); such police markings reduce value by about 10%.

FINNISH L-35 — mfg. 1935-1944.

$1,050	$900	$825	$760	$680	$620	$575

Add 100% for earlier pistols with shoulder stock lug.

LAKE FIELD ARMS LTD.

Manufacturer located in Ontario, Canada. Lake Field Arms Ltd. was acquired by Savage Arms, Inc. during late 1994. Distributor sales only through most major U.S. distributors.

Lake Field rifles manufactured after the Savage acquisition are marked Savage - please refer to the Savage section for current mfg.

L

RIFLES: .22 RIMFIRE

MARK I — .22 LR, single shot bolt action, $20\frac{3}{4}$ in. rifled or smooth bore barrel, adj. rear sight, thumb rotary safety, walnut finish hardwood stock, $5\frac{1}{2}$ lbs. Disc.

$110	$75	$65	$55	$50	$40	$30

Last Mfg.'s Sug. Retail was $135.

Add $14 for left-hand variation.

This model is also available in youth dimensions (19 in. barrel) at no extra charge (Model Mark I-Y).

Grading	100%	98%	95%	90%	80%	70%	60%

MARK II — .22 LR, bolt action, 10 shot clip mag., 20¾ in. barrel, adj. rear sight, thumb rotary safety, walnut finish hardwood stock, 5½ lbs. Disc.

	$120	$80	$70	$60	$50	$40	$30

Last Mfg.'s Sug. Retail was $140.

Add $15 for left-hand variation (mfg. 1993-95).

This model is also available in youth dimensions (19 in. barrel) at no extra charge (Model Mark II-Y).

MODEL 64B — .22 LR, semi-auto, side ejection, 10 shot clip mag., 20¼ in. barrel, adj. rear sight, thumb rotary safety, walnut finish hardwood stock, 5½ lbs. Disc.

	$120	$85	$75	$65	$55	$45	$40

Last Mfg.'s Sug. Retail was $143.

MODEL 90B (BIATHLON) — .22 LR, biathlon rifle, includes five 5-shot mags., 21 in. barrel, aperture sights, one-piece natural finish hardwood stock, 8¼ lbs. Mfg. 1991-95.

	$430	$300	$225	$195	$170	$150	$130

Last Mfg.'s Sug. Retail was $570.

Add $55 for left-hand variation (new 1993).

MODEL 91T — .22 LR, target rifle, single shot, 25 in. barrel with aperture sights, dark hardwood finished stock, 8 lbs. Mfg. 1991-95.

	$340	$255	$215	$175	$150	$135	$115

Last Mfg.'s Sug. Retail was $455.

Add $45 for left-hand variation (mfg. 1993-95).

▲ *Model 91TR* — repeater version of the Model 91T, 5 shot mag. Mfg. 1993-95.

	$360	$265	$215	$175	$150	$135	$115

Last Mfg.'s Sug. Retail was $485.

Add $45 for left-hand variation (mfg. 1993-95).

MODEL 92S — .22 LR, 5 shot detachable mag., 21 in. barrel, hardwood stock with Monte Carlo cheekpiece, 8 lbs. Mfg. 1993-95.

	$300	$240	$200	$175	$160	$150	$135

Last Mfg.'s Sug. Retail was $388.

Add $37 for left-hand variation.

MODEL 93M — .22 Mag. cal., 5 shot clip mag., thumb operated rotary safety, 20¾ in. barrel, hardwood stock, 5¾ lbs. Mfg. 1995 only.

	$140	$120	$100	$85	$75	$65	$55

Last Mfg.'s Sug. Retail was $168.

LAMES

Previous manufacturer located In Italy.

SHOTGUNS

FIELD MODEL O/U — 12 ga., 26, 28, or 30 in. barrels, various chokes, VR, engraving, SST, auto ejectors, checkered pistol grip stock with pad.

	$400	$380	$365	$350	$325	$300	$275

▲ *Separated barrels*

	$500	$480	$465	$450	$425	$400	$375

STANDARD TRAP O/U — similar to Field, 30 or 32 in. various trap bore barrels, with wide VR, trap style Monte Carlo stock.

	$600	$575	$550	$525	$425	$400	$450

CALIFORNIA TRAP O/U — similar to Standard Trap, with separated barrels.

	$700	$675	$650	$625	$525	$500	$450

Grading	100%	98%	95%	90%	80%	70%	60%

SKEET MODEL — similar to Field, with 26 in. skeet bore barrels, skeet stock and separated barrels.

	$600	$575	$550	$525	$425	$400	$350

LANBER SHOTGUNS

Manufacturer located in Zaldibar, Spain. Previously imported and distributed until 1994, by Eagle Imports, Inc. located in Wanamassa, NJ. Previously imported by Exel Arms of America, Inc., located in Gardener, MA, and by Lanber Arms of America located in Adrian, MI.

Lanber makes a wide range of quality O/U and semi-auto shotguns. Currently, there is no domestic importer, and the factory must be contacted directly for more information and current pricing (please refer to Trademark Index).

LANBER SHOTGUNS: OVER AND UNDER

The last Mfg.'s Sug. Retail on all models listed below reflects 1987 pricing, the last year they were imported. Any future importation could reflect pricing changes.

EXEL SERIES 100: MODELS 101 THROUGH 104 — 12 ga., boxlock action, vent. rib, extractors, single trigger. Add $16 for 103 Mag., $92 for ejectors (Model 104 only).

	$400	$350	$310	$270	$240	$225	$200

Last Mfg.'s Sug. Retail was $451.

These models were previously designated the 844ST Series.

EXEL MODEL 105 — 12 ga., boxlock action, single trigger, ejectors, Lanber screw-in chokes, deluxe wood, engraved satin finish action.

	$575	$495	$440	$405	$370	$345	$310

Last Mfg.'s Sug. Retail was $644.

This model was previously designated the Model 2004LCH.

EXEL MODELS 106 AND 107 — 12 ga., similar to 105, only more deluxe version with vent. barrels and rib, blued receiver only, interchangeable Lanber screw-in chokes. Trap model is Model 107.

	$725	$625	$550	$500	$475	$450	$425

Last Mfg.'s Sug. Retail was $845.

These models were previously designated 2008LCH and 2009LCH respectively.

The following models were imported by Lanber Arms of America, Inc. located in Adrian, MI until business ceased in late 1986.

844 ST — 12 ga. only, boxlock, 26 or 28 in. barrels, choked IC/IM, extractors, SST, automatic safety, VR, European walnut with hand checkering, blued finish with engraved receiver, 7⅛ lbs. Importation disc. 1986.

	$395	$340	$320	$300	$285	$270	$255

Last Mfg.'s Sug. Retail was $450.

▲ *844 MST* — 12 ga. only, 3 in. chambers, 30 in. F & M barrels, otherwise similar to 844 ST. Importation disc. 1986.

	$405	$350	$335	$320	$310	$300	$295

Last Mfg.'s Sug. Retail was $470.

2004 LCH — 12 ga. only, boxlock action, 28 in. barrels, SST, ejectors, supplied with 5 screw-in choke tubes, engraved satin finish receiver, checkered European walnut, 7⅜ lbs. Importation disc. 1986.

	$575	$485	$460	$440	$420	$395	$380

Last Mfg.'s Sug. Retail was $650.

L

Grading	100%	98%	95%	90%	80%	70%	60%

2004 LCH SKEET — 12 ga. only, 28 in. barrels supplied with 5 choke tubes, blued finish, moderately engraved, select checkered walnut, $7\frac{3}{8}$ lbs. Importation disc. 1986.

| | $740 | $635 | $585 | $560 | $540 | $520 | $495 |

Last Mfg.'s Sug. Retail was $845.

2004 LCH TRAP — 12 ga. only, 30 in. barrels supplied with 3 choke tubes, European walnut has trap dimensions, blued finish. Importation disc. 1986.

| | $675 | $625 | $585 | $560 | $540 | $520 | $495 |

Last Mfg.'s Sug. Retail was $845.

MODEL 82 FIELD GRADE — 12 or 20 ga., 3 in. chambers, boxlock action, SST, ejectors, 26 or 28 in. VR barrels with fixed chokes, checkered walnut stock and forearm. Limited importation 1994 only.

| | $500 | $425 | $395 | $360 | $330 | $295 | $275 |

Last Mfg.'s Sug. Retail was $585.

MODEL 87 DELUXE FIELD GRADE — 12 or 20 ga., better quality walnut stock and forearm. 26 (20 ga. only) or 28 in. VR barrels with choke tubes. Limited importation 1994 only.

| | $800 | $675 | $575 | $500 | $425 | $350 | $295 |

Last Mfg.'s Sug. Retail was $915.

MODEL 97 SPORTING CLAYS — 12 ga. only, Sporting Clays configuration featuring 28 in. barrels with choke tubes. Limited importation 1994 only.

| | $835 | $695 | $585 | $500 | $425 | $350 | $295 |

Last Mfg.'s Sug. Retail was $965.

LASALLE

Previous manufacturer located in France.

SLIDE ACTION SHOTGUN — 12 or 20 ga., 26, 28, or 30 in. barrels, various chokes, alloy frame, checkered pistol grip stock.

| | $250 | $225 | $200 | $175 | $150 | $125 | $100 |

AUTOMATIC SHOTGUN — 12 ga., 26, 28, or 30 in. barrels, various chokes, gas operated, checkered pistol grip stock.

| | $300 | $275 | $250 | $225 | $200 | $175 | $150 |

LASERAIM ARMS, INC.

Manufactured in Thermopolis, WY. Marketed and distributed by Laseraim Arms, Inc. located in Little Rock, AR, a division of Emerging Technologies, Inc. Direct or limited dealer sales only.

PISTOLS: STAINLESS STEEL

Add approx. $30 for adj. sights.
Add approx. $150 for standard laser sight.
Add approx. $180 for clip laser sight.
Add approx. $225 for hotdot laser.

SERIES I — .40 S&W (disc. 1994), .45 ACP, or 10mm cal., semi-auto single action, $3\frac{3}{8}$ (Compact Model, .45 ACP only), $5\frac{1}{2}$ (disc. 1994), or 6 in. barrel with compensator, Millett adj. sights, ambidextrous safety, all metal parts Teflon coated, beveled mag. well, integral accessory mounts, 7 (.45 ACP) or 8 (10mm or .40 S&W) shot mag., 46 or 52 oz. New 1993.

| **Mfg.'s Sug. Retail** | $750 | | $650 | $525 | $445 |

Series I Illusion and Dream Team variations were made during 1993-94. Retail prices respectively were $650 and $695.

L

Grading	100%	98%	95%	90%	80%	70%	60%

SERIES II — .40 S&W (disc. 1994), .45 ACP, or 10mm cal., similar technical specs. as the Series I, except has non-reflective stainless steel finish, fixed or adj. sights, and 3 ⅜ (Compact Model, .45 ACP only), 5, or 7 (.45 ACP only) in. non-compensated barrel, 37 or 43 oz. New 1993.

Mfg.'s Sug. Retail	$550	$485	$385	$300			

    Series II Illusion and Dream Team variations were made during 1993-94. Retail prices respectively were $500 and $545.

SERIES III — .45 ACP cal., 5 in. ported barrel, serrated slide, Hogue grips. New 1994.

Mfg.'s Sug. Retail	$675	$595	$465	$415	$375	$345	$310	$275

SERIES IV — .45 ACP cal., 3⅜ (Compact Model) or 5 in. ported barrel, serrated slide, diamond checkered wood grips. New 1994.

Mfg.'s Sug. Retail	$625	$550	$450	$400	$360	$330	$300	$265

LAURONA

Manufacturer located in Eibar, Spain. Currently imported by Galaxy Imports located in Victoria, TX.

Laurona manufactures high quality O/U shotguns and O/U express rifles/combination guns. Beginning 1992, Laurona switched from a one-piece, demi-block type of fabrication to a monobloc system which has improved strength characteristics while reducing weight in their X-Series line of shotguns and express rifles.

Laurona long guns come standard with a black chrome metal finish that is extremely resistant to oxidation. Left hand stocks are available for the 83 MG Super Game, 85 MS Super Game, Trap, and Super Skeet, Silhouette Trap models, and Silhouette Sporting Clays.

Suffix designations on Laurona shotguns refer to the following: G - twin single triggers, S - selective single trigger, M - multi-chokes, T - Tulip, BV - beavertail.

All Super Game Models were available with a deluxe package which includes a recoil pad, mid-bead sight, and select wood for an additional $250. Special order dull matte finished barrels (with multi-chokes) were available for an additional $200 - extra barrels were priced between $635 (20 ga.) or $800 (12 ga.) per set.

If more information is required on an older Laurona model not listed in this publication, it is advisable to do the following. Please send/FAX an accurate description of your specimen (including Laurona model name, serial number, and other pertinent data - include photos if possible) to Galaxy Imports located at P.O. Box 3661, Victoria, TX 77903, phone: 512-573-4867, FAX: 512-576-9622. The charge for this service is $25 per serial number.

RIFLES: O/U CURRENT MFG.

MODEL 2000X EXPRESS RIFLE — .30-06, 8x57 JRS, 8x75 RS, 9.3x74 R, or .375 H&H Mag. cal., monobloc construction, 24 in. separated barrels featuring quarter rib sight and convergency adjustment at muzzle, matte black chrome finish, open sights, ejectors or extractors, SST or DT, approx. 8.1 lbs. New 1992.

    This model must be custom ordered - please contact Galaxy Imports for more information.

    This model accepts Leupold or European styled ring mounts.

  ▲ *Model 2000X Combo* — includes choice of cals. listed above, except for .375 H&H Mag. with 12 ga. under-barrel. New 1992.

    This model must be custom ordered - please contact Galaxy Imports for more information.

SHOTGUNS: O/U DISC. MFG.

    Laurona shotguns are no longer being imported by Exel Arms of America, Inc. Laurona shotguns were imported until 1991 by Galaxy Imports located in Victoria, TX,

Grading	100%	98%	95%	90%	80%	70%	60%

and these recent models can be located in the Laurona section of this text.   Model nomenclature has changed from the discontinued Exel 300 Series below.

EXEL 300 SERIES — These over and unders are available in 12 or 20 ga. only. Model 301 is basic gun with 310 being the highest grade.

▲ *Models 301 and 302* — 12 ga., double selective trigger system, ejectors, pistol grip, vent. rib, lightly engraved chrome finish receiver, various chokes and barrel lengths. Importation disc. 1986.

	$485	$415	$380	$340	$300	$275	$250

Last Mfg.'s Sug. Retail was $553.

▲ *Models 303 and 304* — 12 ga., similar to 301/302, except has better engraving on coin finish receiver, vent. barrels. Importation disc. 1987.

	$545	$470	$430	$385	$340	$315	$270

Last Mfg.'s Sug. Retail was $623.

Previously designated Model 82G Super.

▲ *Models 305(A) and 306(A)* — 12 or 20 ga., similar to 303/304, except has better engraving on coin finish receiver, screw-in choke tubes. Importation disc. 1987.

	$625	$535	$470	$430	$390	$350	$315

Last Mfg.'s Sug. Retail was $711.

Previously designated Models 83MG and 85MS.

▲ *Models 307 and 308* — 12 ga., trap model, 29 in. barrels, extensive engraving, Monte Carlo stock. Importation disc. 1987.

	$580	$500	$460	$420	$380	$340	$300

Last Mfg.'s Sug. Retail was $668.

Previously designated Model 82U Trap.

▲ *Models 309 and 310* — super trap model, 29 in. vent. barrels, more extensive engraving than Models 307/308. Importation disc. 1987.

	$630	$545	$495	$460	$415	$385	$340

Last Mfg.'s Sug. Retail was $726.

Previously designated Model 82 S. Trap.

▲ *Model 82* — double selective trigger system, ejectors, pistol grip, vent. rib, various chokes and barrel lengths. Disc.

	$549	$410	$380	$340	$300	$275	$250

SHOTGUNS: O/U RECENT MFG.

While no current Laurona shotguns are listed, Galaxy Imports should be contacted (see listing in Trademark Index) regarding Laurona's newer models and pricing since importation will once again resume.

MODEL 82 — double selective trigger system, ejectors, pistol grip, vent rib, various chokes and barrel lengths. Disc.

	$549	$410	$380	$340	$300	$275	$250

This model was imported by Exel Arms of America, Inc.

SUPER GAME MODELS — 12 or 20 ga., boxlock, 28 in. barrels, unique twin single triggers, ejectors, extensive fine scroll engraving on a satin finished receiver, anti-rust black chrome barrel finish, VR, elongated forcing cones, checkered walnut stock and forearm.

Twin single triggers can function as conventional double triggers in addition to either trigger functioning as a non-selective single trigger. For example, each trigger can fire both barrels - the back trigger fires from top to bottom and the front trigger uses the bottom to top sequence.

▲ *82 G Super Game* — new designation for 82 Super Game, with T forend, 2¾ in. chambers, 28 in. separated barrels choked F/M or IC/IM with 8mm VR, twin single triggers. Importation disc. 1989.

	$975	$875	$795	$675	$625	$550	$495

Last Mfg.'s Sug. Retail was $1,100.

This model was previously designated 82 Super Game.

L

Grading	100%	98%	95%	90%	80%	70%	60%

▲ *82 Pigeon Competition* — similar to 82 Trap Competition, except 28 in. barrels with different chokings. Importation disc. 1986.

	$545	$465	$440	$420	$405	$390	$375

Last Mfg.'s Sug. Retail was $630.

▲ *82 Trap Combo* — trap model, 8mm VR, non-selective single trigger. Importation disc. 1986.

	$485	$390	$375	$360	$350	$340	$330

Last Mfg.'s Sug. Retail was $566.

▲ *82 Trap Competition* — 29 in. barrels, oil finished Monte Carlo stock, 13mm VR, non-selective single trigger, motif engraving, rubber recoil pad, 8.1 lbs. Importation disc. 1986.

	$540	$460	$435	$420	$405	$390	$375

Last Mfg.'s Sug. Retail was $625.

83 MG SUPER GAME — 12 or 20 ga., similar to 82 G Super Game except has multi-chokes, 2¾ or 3 in. Mag. chambers.

	$1,275	$1,025	$895	$795	$675	$625	$550

Last Mfg.'s Sug. Retail was $1,540.

▲ *83 MG Super Game 2 Barrel Set* — includes 2 sets of barrels (12 and 20 ga.).

	$1,775	$1,500	$1,275	$1,000	$875	$775	$700

Last Mfg.'s Sug. Retail was $2,180.

▲ *83 M Puma Hunting* — importation disc. 1986.

	$485	$445	$425	$410	$395	$380	$375

Last Mfg.'s Sug. Retail was $529.

84 S SUPER GAME — similar to 82 G Super Game except has SST and available with 3 in. Mag. chambers. Importation disc. 1989.

	$925	$840	$775	$675	$625	$550	$495

Last Mfg.'s Sug. Retail was $1,100.

84 S SUPER TRAP — 29 in. barrels, extensive fine scroll engraving, separated barrels with 13mm aluminum VR, rubber recoil pad, full pistol grip stock with orthopedic grip, beavertail forearm, single selective trigger, elongated forcing cones, choked IM/F or M/F, 7¾ lbs.

	$1,650	$1,250	$995	$875	$750	$625	$495

Last Mfg.'s Sug. Retail was $1,920.

85 MS SUPER GAME — available in 12 or 20 ga., similar to 83 MG Super Game, except has SST.

	$1,295	$1,025	$895	$795	$675	$625	$550

Last Mfg.'s Sug. Retail was $1,575.

▲ *85 MS Super Game 2 Barrel Set* — includes 2 sets of barrels (12 and 20 ga.).

	$1,800	$1,500	$1,275	$1,000	$875	$775	$700

Last Mfg.'s Sug. Retail was $2,215.

85 MS SUPER TRAP — similar to 84 S Super Trap, except chokes are full over multi-choke.

	$1,675	$1,250	$995	$875	$750	$625	$495

Last Mfg.'s Sug. Retail was $1,970.

▲ *85 MS Super Pigeon* — similar to 85 Super Trap, except choked IM/choke tube with 28 in. barrels and 13mm aluminum rib, stocked for live pigeon shooting, 7¼ lbs.

	$1,625	$1,250	$995	$875	$750	$625	$495

Last Mfg.'s Sug. Retail was $1,890.

Add $60 for left-hand stock.

85 S SUPER SKEET — 12 ga. only, 28 in. barrels, 2¾ in. chambers with elongated forcing cones, extensive fine scroll engraving, rust resistant black chrome finish, separated barrels, 13mm aluminum VR, mechanical triggers with 5 lb. pull, 7¼ lbs.

	$1,550	$1,225	$995	$875	$750	$625	$495

Last Mfg.'s Sug. Retail was $1,810.

▲ *85 MS Special Sporting* — 12 ga. only, similar to 85 MS Super Pigeon except with field stock designed for upland game, SST, 28 in. barrels choked IM over multi-choke, 7¼ lbs. Imported 1988-90.

	$1,575	$1,225	$995	$875	$750	$625	$500

Last Mfg.'s Sug. Retail was $1,850.

Grading	100%	98%	95%	90%	80%	70%	60%

GTO/GTU TRAP COMBO SILHOUETTE SERIES — 12 ga. only, $2\frac{3}{4}$ in. chamber, features black and silver striped receiver, 29 in. O/U barrels with multi-F chokes and 34 in. top single barrel with multi-F chokes. Import 1990 only.

	$2,175	$1,650	$1,300	$1,050	$900	$800	$725

Last Mfg.'s Sug. Retail was $2,660.

Add $110 for GTU Model (bottom single barrel).

SILHOUETTE GAME — 12 ga. only, 3 in. chambers, 28 in. barrels, multi-K chokes. Although advertised, this model was never imported (similar specifications as the Model 85 MS Super Game).

SILHOUETTE 300 SPORTING CLAYS — 12 ga. only, 3 in. chambers, 28 in. barrels with 11mm VR, field stock with special recoil pad designed for dropped stock style shooting, $7\frac{1}{4}$ lbs. Imported 1988-90.

	$1,495	$1,200	$975	$875	$750	$625	$500

Last Mfg.'s Sug. Retail was $1,760.

Available with either flush or knurled multi-chokes.

SILHOUETTE 300 TRAP — 12 ga. only, similar to 85 MS Super Trap except has 29 in. steel barrels with 11mm VR, flush or knurled multi-chokes, black chrome finish, distinctive silver striped receiver (similar to Silver Sporting Clays), 8 lbs. Imported 1988-90.

	$1,525	$1,200	$975	$875	$750	$625	$500

Last Mfg.'s Sug. Retail was $1,790.

SILHOUETTE SINGLE BARREL TRAP — 34 in. barrel only with $7/16$ in. VR, choice of either top single or bottom single barrel. Imported 1991 only.

	$1,725	$1,275	$995	$875	$750	$625	$495

Last Mfg.'s Sug. Retail was $2,030.

Add $110 for bottom single barrel.

SILHOUETTE ULTRA-MAGNUM — 12 ga., $3\frac{1}{2}$ in. chamber, 28 in. barrels, single trigger, ejectors, checkered walnut stock and forearm. Imported 1990-91 only.

	$1,495	$1,200	$975	$875	$750	$625	$500

Last Mfg.'s Sug. Retail was $1,760.

▲ *Waterfowler Ultra-Magnum* — similar to Silhouette Ultra-Magnum, except has non-glare finish and 29 in. barrels. Imported 1990-91 only.

	$1,495	$1,200	$975	$875	$750	$625	$500

Last Mfg.'s Sug. Retail was $1,760.

LAW ENFORCEMENT ORDNANCE CORPORATION

Previous manufacturer located in Ridgway, PA until 1990.

STRIKER-12 — 12 ga. Mag., paramilitary design shotgun featuring 12 shot rotary mag., $18\frac{1}{4}$ in. barrel, semi-auto, alloy shrouded barrel with PG extension, folding or fixed paramilitary design stock, 9.2 lbs., limited mfg. 1986-1990.

	$595	$550	$500	$450	$425	$395	$375

Last Mfg.'s Sug. Retail was $725.

Add $150 for folding stock.
Add $100 for Marine variation ("Metal Life" finish).

Earlier variations were imported and available to law enforcement agencies only. In 1987, manufacture was started in PA and these firearms could be sold to individuals (18 in. barrel only). This design was originally developed in South Rhodesia.

LAZZERONI ARMS COMPANY

Manufacturer located in Tucson, AZ since 1995. Direct/dealer sales.

L

Grading	100%	98%	95%	90%	80%	70%	60%

RIFLES: BOLT ACTION

MODEL 2000 — .257 Scramjet, .284 Firehawk, .308 Warbird, or .338 Titan, bolt action design, features precision machined receiver, helically fluted bolt with heavy duty extractor, stainless steel match barrel with integral muzzle brake, adj. benchrest trigger, matte finish metal, various stock configurations. New 1996.

▲ *Model L2000ST-F* — features 27 in. barrel with conventional fiberglass stock.

Mfg.'s Sug. Retail	$3,695	$3,400	$3,150	$2,800	$2,500	$2,250	$1,975	$1,725

▲ *Model L2000ST-W* — features 27 in. barrel with conventional black wood laminate stock.

Mfg.'s Sug. Retail	$4,795	$4,400	$4,050	$3,600	$3,200	$2,800	$2,400	$2,000

▲ *L2000ST-FW Package* — features 27 in. barrel with one conventional fiberglass and one black wood laminate stock.

Mfg.'s Sug. Retail	$5,295	$4,875	$4,450	$4,050	$3,600	$3,200	$2,800	$2,400

▲ *L2000SLR* — features 28 in. extra heavy fluted barrel and conventional fiberglass stock, not chambered in .338 Titan.

Mfg.'s Sug. Retail	$3,895	$3,575	$3,250	$2,875	$2,550	$2,250	$1,975	$1,725

▲ *L2000SP-F* — 23 in. barrel, thumbhole fiberglass stock.

Mfg.'s Sug. Retail	$3,695	$3,400	$3,150	$2,800	$2,500	$2,250	$1,975	$1,725

▲ *L2000SP-W* — 23 in. barrel, thumbhole black wood laminate stock.

Mfg.'s Sug. Retail	$4,795	$4,400	$4,050	$3,600	$3,200	$2,800	$2,400	$2,000

▲ *L2000SP-FW Package* — features 23 in. barrel with one thumbhole fiberglass and one black wood laminate thumbhole stock.

Mfg.'s Sug. Retail	$5,295	$4,875	$4,450	$4,050	$3,600	$3,200	$2,800	$2,400

LEBEAU-COURALLY

Manufactured since 1865 in Liege, Belgium. Currently imported by New England Arms Co. located in Kittery Point, ME.

Lebeau-Courally manufactures only best quality rifles and shotguns. Approximately 50 are manufactured annually.

RIFLES: SINGLE SHOT

SINGLE SHOT — 6.5x57 R, 7x65 R, or other metric cals., best quality, boxlock or sidelock action.

The importers should be contacted directly (see Trademark Index) for current information and prices regarding this model.

RIFLES: SIDE-BY-SIDE

BOXLOCK EJECTOR — 8x57 JRS or 9.3x74 R cal., Anson & Deeley boxlock, ejectors, select French walnut stock, quarter rib with ramp front sight, about 8 lbs. Importation disc. 1988, resumed 1993.

Mfg.'s Sug. Retail	$19,100	$17,500	$15,750	$13,250	$11,500	$9,250	$7,500	$6,250

Add $1,400 for standard cals.

SIDELOCK EJECTOR — 7x65 R, 8x57 JRS, 9.3x74 R, .30-06, .375 H&H, .458 Win. Mag., .470 NE (new 1991), or .577 NE (new 1992), chopper lump barrels, reinforced action, select French walnut stock, quarter rib with ramp front sight, approx. 8 lbs.

Mfg.'s Sug. Retail	$38,000	$34,000	$29,000	$24,500	$20,750	$17,500	$14,500	$11,850

SHOTGUNS

For currently manufactured shotguns — add $2,250 for single trigger. Older mfg. Lebeau-Courally shotguns have a completely different action and locking system than the newer models. These older models are typically seen priced in the $750-$2,500 range.

Grading	100%	98%	95%	90%	80%	70%	60%

SOLOGNE SxS — 12, 16, or 20 ga., Anson & Deeley boxlock action, various chokes and barrel lengths, select walnut, no engraving. Add $850 for false sideplates.

Mfg.'s Sug. Retail	$14,650	$13,250	$11,250	$9,350	$7,500	$6,250	$5,150	$4,350

GRAND RUSSE MODEL — grade up from Sologne Model.

Mfg.'s Sug. Retail	$18,820	$16,480	$13,000	$10,750	$8,475	$7,375	$5,250	$4,450

BOXLOCK EJECTOR SxS — 12, 16, or 20 ga., choice of classic or rounded action, with or without sideplates, select French walnut stock, choice of numerous engraving patterns (optional), 26, 28, or 30 in. barrels, double trigger.

Mfg.'s Sug. Retail	$14,650	$13,250	$11,250	$9,350	$7,500	$6,250	$5,150	$4,350

▲ *Boxlock with sideplates*

Mfg.'s Sug. Retail	$15,500	$13,850	$11,650	$9,650	$7,700	$6,250	$5,150	$4,350

SIDELOCK EJECTOR SxS — 12, 16, 20, 28, or .410 ga., choice of classic or rounded action, chopper lump barrels, select French walnut stock, choice of numerous engraving patterns (optional), 26, 28, or 30 in. barrels, double triggers.

Mfg.'s Sug. Retail	$31,100	$26,500	$22,750	$18,750	$14,750	$11,000	$8,750	$7,000

Add 10% for 28 or .410 ga.

SIDELOCK O/U — 12, 20, or 28 ga., Greener locking system.

Mfg.'s Sug. Retail	$37,600	$33,800	$29,000	$24,500	$20,750	$17,500	$14,500	$11,850

BOSS MODEL O/U — 12 or 20 ga., Boss pattern sidelock with low profile action, top-of-the-line O/U individually made to customer specifications.

Mfg.'s Sug. Retail	$60,500	$54,000	$48,000	$39,500	$31,750	$24,500	$16,500	$12,000

LEFEVER ARMS COMPANY

Previous manufacturer located in Syracuse, NY.

SHOTGUNS

The Lefever was the first commercially successful hammerless double barrel shotgun made in America. They were made in Syracuse, NY from 1885-1916, at which time the company was acquired by Ithaca Gun Company. Ithaca made the Lefever after 1916. In 1921, the Box Lock Nitro Special was introduced and in 1934, the Lefever Grade A was introduced. Production of Lefever guns ceased in 1948.

The following is a percentage breakdown of gauges made between 1885-1916 (totaling 100%): 8 ga.—½%, 10 ga.—25%, 12 ga.—60%, 14 ga.—½%, 16 ga.—8%, 20 ga.—6%. Total manufacture was approx. 72,000 during this period. Damascus specimens of this trademark are worth approximately the same if in 60% or better original condition as their fluid steel barrel counterparts because of the rarity and desirability factors. Subtract 10%-30% on values with respective condition factors 50%-10%. Prices shown below for 90% and up condition are very difficult to evaluate and are meant as a guide only - any Lefever shotgun is rare and hard to evaluate if in over 95%.

100%	98%	95%	90%	80%	70%	60%	50%	40%	30%	20%	10%

SIDELOCK DOUBLE BARREL SHOTGUN — 10, 12, 16, or 20 ga., 26-32 in. barrels, any choke, boxlock action (even though model nomenclature referred to sidelock model), cocking indicators on all but DS and DSE grades, double triggers standard, checkered straight or pistol grip stock, auto ejectors designated by letter E after grade. Mfg. 1885-1919.

Add 50% for 16 ga.
Add 100% for 20 ga.
Add 10% for SST.

▲ *I Grade*

$1,250	$1,150	$1,025	$925	$850	$775	$700	$630	$565	$500	$425	$350

100%	98%	95%	90%	80%	70%	60%	50%	40%	30%	20%	10%
▲ *DS Grade*											
$1,250	$1,150	$1,025	$925	$850	$775	$700	$630	$565	$500	$425	$350
▲ *DSE Grade*											
$1,650	$1,400	$1,250	$1,100	$950	$850	$775	$715	$650	$600	$540	$475
▲ *H Grade*											
$1,800	$1,500	$1,300	$1,200	$1,100	$1,000	$950	$900	$800	$750	$650	$550
▲ *HE Grade*											
$2,500	$2,200	$1,800	$1,600	$1,400	$1,250	$1,100	$1,000	$900	$850	$800	$700
▲ *G Grade*											
$2,000	$1,800	$1,600	$1,500	$1,400	$1,300	$1,200	$1,100	$1,000	$900	$800	$600
▲ *GE Grade*											
$2,800	$2,600	$2,200	$1,800	$1,700	$1,500	$1,400	$1,300	$1,200	$1,100	$1,000	$900
▲ *F Grade*											
$2,200	$1,900	$1,700	$1,600	$1,500	$1,400	$1,100	$1,000	$900	$800	$700	$650
▲ *FE Grade*											
$3,000	$2,700	$2,400	$2,000	$1,800	$1,600	$1,400	$1,300	$1,100	$1,000	$900	$800
▲ *E Grade*											
$3,000	$2,500	$2,300	$2,100	$1,900	$1,800	$1,600	$1,400	$1,200	$1,100	$900	$800
▲ *EE Grade*											
$4,000	$3,500	$3,200	$3,000	$2,700	$2,500	$2,300	$2,100	$1,900	$1,800	$1,600	$1,500
▲ *D Grade*											
$3,500	$3,000	$2,500	$2,200	$2,000	$1,800	$1,600	$1,500	$1,400	$1,200	$1,100	$1,000
▲ *DE Grade*											
$5,000	$4,500	$4,000	$3,700	$3,200	$2,700	$2,200	$2,000	$1,800	$1,600	$1,400	$1,200
▲ *C Grade*											
$5,000	$4,500	$4,000	$3,200	$2,700	$2,400	$2,200	$2,000	$1,900	$1,800	$1,600	$1,300
▲ *CE Grade*											
$8,000	$7,500	$7,000	$5,500	$4,700	$4,200	$4,000	$3,400	$3,000	$2,500	$2,100	$1,750
▲ *B Grade*											
$5,750	$5,275	$4,850	$4,425	$4,050	$3,675	$3,175	$$2,750	$2,600	$2,400	$2,200	$2,000
▲ *BE Grade*											
$10,000	$9,000	$8,250	$7,500	$6,750	$5,950	$5,100	$4,400	$3,700	$3,500	$3,200	$3,000
▲ *A grade* — auto ejectors standard.											
$20,000	$17,750	$15,500	$13,750	$11,250	$9,250	$8,150	$7,200	$6,300	$5,400	$4,700	$4,200
▲ *AA grade* — auto ejectors standard.											
$30,000	$26,250	$21,750	$18,750	$15,500	$12,750	$10,250	$8,250	$7,150	$6,500	$6,000	$5,500

▲ *Optimus Grade* — auto ejectors standard. Extreme rarity precludes accurate percentage pricing.

▲ *Thousand Dollar Grade* — auto ejectors standard. Extreme rarity precludes accurate percentage pricing.

Grading	100%	98%	95%	90%	80%	70%	60%

NITRO SPECIAL DOUBLE BARREL SHOTGUN — 12, 16, 20, or .410 ga., 26-32 in. barrels, various chokes, boxlock, extractors, checkered pistol grip stock. Mfg. 1921-1948.

	100%	98%	95%	90%	80%	70%	60%
	$450	$395	$350	$300	$250	$225	$200

Add $75 for ST.
Add 20% for 16 ga.
Add 50% for 20 ga.
Add 200% for .410 ga.

Grading	100%	98%	95%	90%	80%	70%	60%

GRADE A DOUBLE BARREL SHOTGUN — 12, 16, 20, or .410 ga., 26-32 in. barrels, various chokes, boxlock, checkered pistol grip stock. Mfg. 1934-1942.

	100%	98%	95%	90%	80%	70%	60%
	$880	$770	$715	$660	$550	$495	$440

> Add 33% for auto ejectors.
> Add $75 for ST.
> Add $75 for beavertail forearm.
> Add 20% for 16 ga.
> Add 50% for 20 ga.
> Add 200% for .410 ga.

GRADE A SKEET MODEL — similar to Grade A, with 26 in. skeet bore barrels, auto ejector, single trigger and beavertail forearm standard.

	100%	98%	95%	90%	80%	70%	60%
	$1,155	$1,045	$990	$935	$825	$770	$715

> Add 50% for 16 ga.
> Add 100% for 20 ga.
> Add 200% for .410 ga.

SINGLE BARREL TRAP GUN — 12 ga. only, 30 or 32 in. VR barrel, full choke, boxlock, auto ejector, checkered pistol grip stock. Disc. 1942.

	100%	98%	95%	90%	80%	70%	60%
	$550	$440	$385	$330	$275	$250	$195

LONG RANGE SINGLE BARREL FIELD — 12, 16, 20, or .410 ga., 26-32 in. barrel, boxlock, extractor, checkered pistol grip stock. Disc. 1942.

	100%	98%	95%	90%	80%	70%	60%
	$330	$275	$250	$220	$165	$140	$120

LEFEVER, D.M. & SON

Previous manufacturer located in Bowling Green, OH.

SHOTGUNS

"Uncle Dan" Lefever, founder of Lefever Arms, designed and manufactured the first breech loading double hammerless shotgun made in the U.S. Production started in 1872 and continued in the Syracuse, NY plant until he sold his interest in the Lefever Arms Company during the early 1900s. He then moved to Ohio and started another factory under the name D.M. Lefever & Son. After his death a few years later the Ohio factory was closed, while his old company (Lefever Arms Co.) continued manufacturing Lefevers until being sold to Ithaca Gun Company in the early 1920s. From that point, Lefever Arms Co. was a branch of Ithaca and continued to make shotguns until shortly after WWII.

Total production on D.M. Lefever shotguns between 1901-1904 totaled less than 1,200. Because of their inherent rarity, values listed below show only 10%-80% condition specimens. D.M. Lefever specimens are so rare in 80%+ condition that prices cannot be accurately ascertained.

L

Grading	80%	70%	60%	50%	40%	30%	20%	10%

NEW LEFEVER DOUBLE BARREL SHOTGUN — 12, 16, or 20 ga., boxlock action, any length barrel and choke on order, auto ejectors standard on all grades except O Excelsior, double triggers standard on all except Uncle Dan grade, optional single triggers available, checkered walnut pistol grip or straight stock, grades differ as to engraving, wood, checkering and overall quality. Mfg. 1904-1906.

> Add 50% for 16 ga.
> Add 10% for SST.

▲ *O Excelsior Grade*

	80%	70%	60%	50%	40%	30%	20%	10%
	$2,365	$1,925	$1,650	$1,475	$1,350	$1,175	$950	$750

Grading	80%	70%	60%	50%	40%	30%	20%	10%
▲ *Excelsior Grade w/ejectors*								
	$2,640	$2,310	$1,925	$1,595	$1,450	$1,300	$1,045	$825
▲ *F Grade, No. 9*								
	$3,000	$2,640	$2,310	$1,925	$1,725	$1,575	$1,300	$1,000
▲ *E Grade, No. 8*								
	$4,000	$3,350	$2,875	$2,300	$2,075	$1,800	$1,575	$1,250
▲ *D Grade, No. 7*								
	$4,400	$4,125	$3,850	$3,375	$2,975	$2,750	$2,500	$1,925
▲ *C Grade, No. 6*								
	$4,950	$4,400	$4,125	$3,850	$3,575	$3,175	$2,750	$2,420
▲ *B Grade, No. 5*								
	$6,600	$5,500	$4,600	$4,275	$3,975	$3,750	$3,450	$3,100
▲ *AA Grade, No. 4*								
	$8,800	$7,700	$6,600	$5,500	$4,850	$4,400	$3,700	$3,350

UNCLE DAN GRADE — too rare to accurately determine values.

SINGLE BARREL TRAP GUN — 12 ga., 26-32 in. full choke, auto ejector, boxlock, checkered pistol grip stock. Mfg. 1904-1906. Too rare to accurately determine values.

LE FORGERON

Manufacturer located in Belgium. Previously imported and distributed by Midwest Gun Sport in Zebulon, NC.

SHOTGUNS

Prices below reflect circa 1989 information as this was the last year they were formally imported.

Grading	100%	98%	95%	90%	80%	70%	60%
BOXLOCK EJECTOR SxS — 20 or 28 ga. only, with or without sideplates, select French walnut stock, choice of engraving patterns (optional), single trigger.							
	$3,975	$3,650	$3,325	$2,995	$2,600	$2,250	$1,900

Last Mfg.'s Sug. Retail was $4,400.

Add $1,000 for sideplates.

SIDELOCK EJECTOR SxS — 20 or 28 ga. only, select French walnut stock, choice of engraving patterns (optional), rounded action, single trigger.

	$10,200	$9,250	$8,500	$7,900	$7,100	$6,300	$5,500

Last Mfg.'s Sug. Retail was $11,600.

RIFLES

MODEL 6020 — 9.3x74R cal., boxlock action, beavertail forearm, pistol grip stock.

	$4,450	$4,025	$3,750	$3,475	$3,100	$2,800	$2,550

Last Mfg.'s Sug. Retail was $4,900.

Add $700 for sideplates (Model 6040).

MODEL 6030 — sidelock action, engraved action with deluxe French walnut stock and forearm.

	$8,475	$7,900	$7,100	$6,300	$5,500	$4,700	$4,000

Last Mfg.'s Sug. Retail was $8,950.

LE FRANCAIS PISTOLS

Manufactured by Francais D'armes Et Cycles located in Ste. Etienne, France.

Grading	100%	98%	95%	90%	80%	70%	60%

STAFF OFFICER MODEL AUTOMATIC — .25 auto, 2½ in. barrel, blue, fixed sights, rubber grips, no visible cocking piece. Mfg. 1914-disc.

	100%	98%	95%	90%	80%	70%	60%
	$275	$230	$200	$165	$140	$115	$80

POLICEMAN MODEL AUTOMATIC — .32 auto, double action, 7 shot, 3½ in. barrel, hinged finned barrel, blue, fixed sights, rubber grips. Mfg. 1950s.

	100%	98%	95%	90%	80%	70%	60%
	$850	$800	$700	$575	$435	$350	$275

ARMY MODEL AUTOMATIC — 9mm Browning, 8 shot, 5 in. barrel, blue, fixed sights, checkered walnut grips. Mfg. 1928-1938. Early model with tapered barrel, later model with finned barrel.

	100%	98%	95%	90%	80%	70%	60%
	$1,400	$1,100	$850	$700	$550	$425	$350

LES BAER CUSTOM, INC.

Pistol/rifle customizer located in Hillsdale, IL.

Les Baer has been customizing both 1911 type pistols and select rifles for many years. The company should be contacted directly (see Trademark Index) for an up-to-date price sheet and catalog on their extensive line-up of high quality competition pistols that range in price from $1,180 - $2,820. Competition parts and related gunsmithing services are also available.

LEW HORTON DIST. CO.

Firearms distributor located in Westboro, MA. While Lew Horton is not a manufacturer or an importer, since 1983 this company has been responsible for many special and limited editions that are listed below with quanities but without prices since they may vary greatly from region to region.

SPECIAL/LIMITED EDITIONS

Grading	Qty. Made	Year Issue	Retail Price
COLT MODELS			
SAA Horse Pistol	100	1983	$1,100
Presidential - Gold SAA & Det. Spec. w/Gold Eye	600	1985	$525
Colt Boa (includes complete production run of 4 & 6 in. barrel)	600	1985	$525
Ultimate Officer's .45 ACP	500	1989	$777
Lt. Commander .45 ACP	800	1985	$590
Combat Cobra 2½ in.	1,000	1987	$500
Lady Colt (MK IV .380 ACP)	1,000	1989	$547
Night Commander .45 ACP	250	1989	$725
El Presidente .38 Super Govt.	350	1990	$800
El Comandante .38 Super Govt.	500	1991	$800
El General .38 Super Govt.	500	1991	$850
El Capitan .38 Super	500	1991	$875
Detective Special	100	1992	$430
Elite Ten/Forty	100	1992	$900
El Patron	500	1992	$850
El Jefe	500	1992	$849
El Dorado	750	1992	$1,099
El Teniente	400	1992	$1,037
El Coronel	750	1993	$900
Classic Gold Cup	300	1993	$1,285
Classic Single Action	180	1993	$680
Night Officer	350	1993	$680

L

Grading	Qty. Made	Year	Issue	Retail Price
El Presidente Premier Edition	10	1993		$3,000
Classic Government	300	1993		$965
Night Government	300	1993		$705
El Caballero	500	1994		$986
El Potro	500	1994		1,025
Frontier Six Shooter	100	1994		$1,849
McCormick Factory Racer	500	1994		$1,149
Springfield Armory Bicentennial Edition	400	1994		$1,000
Springfield Armory Premier Bicentennial	200	1994		$1,213

BERETTA
Lady Beretta	100	1985		$285

H&R 1871, INC.
999 Premier Edition	100 pr.	1993		$345

SMITH & WESSON
Model 25-3 Lew Horton Special	100	-		$500
Model 29-3 Lew Horton Special	5,000	-		$425
Model 629-3 Lew Horton Special	5,000	-		$400
Model 24-3 Lew Horton Special	5,000	1983-84		$380
Model 686 Lew Horton Special	-	1984		$450
Model 657-3 Lew Horton Special	5,000	1986		$410
Model 624-2 Lew Horton Special	7,000	1986-87		$395
Model 640 Carry Comp	250	1991		$750
.40 Compensated	150	1992		$1,699
.40 Tactical	200	1992		$1,499
Shorty Forty	-	1992		$950
Model 629 Hunter	200	1992		$1,234
Model 629 Carry Comp	300	1992		$1,000
Model 686 Carry Comp 4 in.	300	1992		$1,000
Model 657 Classic Hunter	350	1993		$545
Shorty 356	-	1993		$999
356 Tactical	-	1993		$1,350
Model 629 Hunter II	200	1993		$1,234
Model 629 Carry Comp II	100	1993		$1,000
Model 686 Carry Comp 3 in.	300	1993		$1,000
686 Competitor	400	1993		$1,100
686 Hunter	200	1993		$1,153
Model 5906 Shorty Nine	200	1993		$999
Model 60 Carry Comp	300	1993		$800
Model 629 Unfluted	300	1993		$1,234
Model 629 Hunter III	300	1994		$1,234
Springfield Armory Bicentennial Edition	500	1994		$775
Paxton Quigley Model 640	250	1994		$800
Model 625 Classic Snub	300	1994		$603
Model 629 Classic Hunter	500	1994		$1,234
Model 629 Quad-magnaported .44 Mag.	150	1994		$900
Shorty Forty Mark II	150	1995		$999

MOSSBERG
Night Persuader Special Edition	300	1990		not listed

REMINGTON
Model 541J Curley Maple	500	1994		$500

Grading	Qty. Made	Year Issue	Retail Price
TAURUS			
Model PT-92AF	250	1990	not listed
Model 85 3 in. Ported Blue	500	1995	$229
Model 85 3 in. Ported Stainless	500	1995	$349

In addition to the special/limited editions listed above, Lew Horton also subcontracted special editions that were sold from company flyers and other promotional materials. They include the following Smith & Wesson Models - Classic Hunter M29 (500 mfg. 1989), Model 63 2 in. (500 mfg. 1989), Model 36 2nd Amendment (200 mfg. 1989), Model 60 25th Anniversary (100 mfg. 1989), Model 629 Classic Hunter (mfg. 1986), Model 5967 (500 mfg. 1990), and the Model 3914 (200 mfg. 1990). There are two Remington models - the M1100 Special Field (200 mfg. 1987-88) and the M700 BDL .257 Roberts cal. (500 mfg. 1990). There are three Colt models - the Combat Python (750 mfg. 1987-88), the Pocketlite (350 mfg. 1989), and the Custom Cobra Stainless Sets (2 sizes, mfg. 1989).

LIBERATOR

Manufactured by the Guide Lamp Corporation (division of General Motors) in 1942 only.

Grading	100%	98%	95%	90%	80%	70%	60%

LIBERATOR PISTOL — .45 ACP cal., single shot, simplistic design and action utilizing nonstrategic WWII materials, mfg. for European resistance movement during WWII (most were issued or air-dropped in Europe), each gun was individually packaged in a paraffin-coated cardboard box which included the gun, a graphics only (no English) instruction sheet, wooden ram rod, and 10 rounds of .45 ACP ammo stored in the gun's butt, 4 in. smooth bore barrel, sheet steel stamping mfg. with welds, 1 million mfg. 1942 only.

	100%	98%	95%	90%	80%	70%	60%
	$650	$525	$465	$415	$380	$340	$300

Even though 1 million of these pistols were mfg., remaining specimens brought into the U.S. with the above listed accessories are rare since all were delivered overseas. While the Liberator's appearance is crude, remember that the entire production run (1 million) was mfg. and ready for overseas shipment in 13 weeks.

LIBERTY ARMS WORKS, INC.

Manufacturer located in West Chester, PA. Dealer direct sales only.

L.A.W. ENFORCER — .22 LR, 9mm Para., 10mm, .40 S&W (new 1994), or .45 ACP cal., patterned after the Ingram MAC 10, single action semi-auto, 6¼ in. threaded barrel, closed bolt operation, manual safety, 10 (C/B 1994) or 30* shot mag., 5 lbs. 1 oz. New 1991.

Mfg.'s Sug. Retail	$545	$495	$450	$415	$385	$335	$295	$275

LIEGEOISE D'ARMES

Manufacturer located in Belgium.

Small manufacturer specializing in boxlock shotguns, normally engraved and with ejectors. Prices usually start in the $600+ range.

LIGNOSE (BERGMAN)

Manufacturer located in Suhl, Germany.

EINHAND MODEL 2A POCKET AUTOMATIC — .25 auto, 6 shot, 2 in. barrel, blue, rubber grips, can be cocked by rearward pressure on triggerguard.

	$220	$205	$195	$165	$140	$110	$85

MODEL 3 POCKET AUTOMATIC — similar to 3A, except without one hand cocking trigger guard.

	$220	$205	$195	$165	$140	$110	$85

Grading	100%	98%	95%	90%	80%	70%	60%

MODEL 3A POCKET AUTOMATIC — similar to 2A, except longer grip, 9 shot capacity.

	$220	$205	$195	$165	$140	$110	$85

MODEL 2 POCKET AUTOMATIC — similar to 2A, without one hand cocking triggerguard.

	$165	$155	$140	$110	$90	$75	$55

LILIPUT

Previous mfg. by August Menz, located in Suhl, Germany.

PISTOLS: SEMI-AUTO

4.25mm CAL. — 4.25mm centerfire Liliput cal. (shoots 12 grain bullet), blue or nickel finish, limited 1920s mfg.

	$550	$495	$425	$385	$340	$300	$280

6.35mm CAL. — .25 ACP cal., mfg. in large quantities pre-WWII.

	$165	$155	$140	$110	$90	$75	$55

LJUNGMAN

Previously manufactured by Carl Gustaf, located in Eskilstuna, Sweden.

AG 42 — semi-auto rifle, 6.5mm, 10 shot mag., wood stock, tangent rear sight, hooded front, bayonet lug, designed in 1941. This was the first mass produced, direct gas operated rifle. This weapon was also used by the Egyptian armed forces and was known as the Hakim.

	$850	$700	$600	$495	$450	$400	$365

LJUTIC INDUSTRIES, INC.

Manufacturer located in Yakima, WA. Dealer direct sales only.

Prior to 1960, Ljutic Industries, Inc. was doing business as Ljutic Gun Co.

TRAP SHOTGUNS

To date approx. 12,500 target shotguns have been manufactured total (all models).

DYNATRAP SINGLE BARREL SHOTGUN — 12 ga., 33 in. barrel, full choke, push button opening, extractor, trap stock.

	$2,500	$2,150	$1,600	$1,475	$1,300	$1,200	$1,100

Add $300 for release trigger.
Add $400 for extra release trigger.
Add $250 for extra pull trigger.

MODEL X-73 SINGLE BARREL — 12 ga., 33 in. full, push button opening, high rib fancy Monte Carlo stock.

	$2,500	$2,250	$2,000	$1,850	$1,700	$1,600	$1,500

Add $300 for extra pull trigger.
Add $500 for extra release trigger.

MONO GUN SINGLE BARREL — 12 ga., 34 in. barrel, custom choked, custom stocked, pull or release trigger, a "built to customers specifications" trap gun. Also known as Standard Rib or Medium Rib.

L

Grading	100%	98%	95%	90%	80%	70%	60%

▲ **Standard, Medium, or Olympic Rib Model**
Mfg.'s Sug. Retail $4,595 $4,595 $3,500 $2,950 $2,775 $2,500 $2,200 $1,900

    Add $200 for screw-in choke tubes.
    Add $1,400 for stainless steel construction.
    Add $3,400 for stainless steel SLE Pro Model.
    Add $900 for SLE Pro Package (includes Laib adj. comb, adj. alum. base plate with 2 pads, and Pro barrel with special bore).
    Approximately 3,000 Mono Guns have been manufactured to date.

▲ **LTX (Deluxe Mono Trap)** — similar to Mono Gun except has 33 in. medium rib barrel and exhibition wood and checkering.
Mfg.'s Sug. Retail $5,795 $5,795 $4,350 $3,750 $3,300 $2,950 $2,500 $2,250

    Add $500 for extra pull trigger.
    Add $400 if with release trigger.
    Add $200 for choke tube barrel with 2 chokes.
    Add $750 for extra release trigger.
    Add $2,195 for extra standard rib barrel.
    Add $1,200 for stainless steel LTX or LTX Pro Package (includes Laib adj. comb, adj. alum. base plate with 2 pads, and Pro barrel with special bore).

SPACE GUN — 12 ga. only, single barrel, unusual design permits in-line round stock with recoil pad, circular forearm wraps around barrel, high post rib on muzzle half of barrel.
Mfg.'s Sug. Retail $4,995 $4,995 $3,600 $3,100 $2,600 $2,200 $1,950 $1,750

LM 6 O/U — 12 ga. only, supplied with one set of O/U barrels, deluxe wood and checkering, separated barrels on O/U.
Mfg.'s Sug. Retail $14,995 $14,995 $12,000 $9,250 $8,000 $6,950 $6,250 $5,600

    Add $5,000 for extra set of O/U barrels.
    Add $7,000 for top single barrel (includes 2 pull trigger groups, and 2 forearms).

BI MATIC AUTO LOADER — 12 ga., 2 shot, 26-32 in. barrels, low recoil, trap or skeet models available, stock and choking to customer specifications. Limited mfg.
Mfg.'s Sug. Retail $5,995 $5,995 $4,450 $2,500 $2,100 $1,750 $1,250 $900

    Add $2,000 for extra barrel.
    Add $750 for extra release trigger.

LLAMA - Gabilondo y Cia, S.A.

Manufacturer located in Vitoria, Spain. Currently imported by Import Sports Inc. located in Wanamassa, NJ. Previously imported and distributed by Stoeger Industries, Inc. located in South Hackensack, NJ until 1993.

PISTOLS: SEMI-AUTO

MODEL IIIA — .380 auto, 7 shot, 3 in. barrel, adj. sights, blue, plastic grips. Mfg. 1951-disc.
    $235 $200 $180 $160 $140 $120 $110

MODEL XA — similar to Model IIIA, except .32 auto.
    $235 $200 $180 $160 $140 $120 $110

MODEL XV — similar to Model XA, except .22 LR.
    $235 $200 $180 $160 $140 $120 $110

MODELS C-IIIA, C-XA, C-XV — similar to Model C, except engraved chrome.
    $305 $260 $230 $205 $180 $155 $140

MODELS BE-IIIA, BE-XA, BE-XV — similar to Model CE, except engraved, blue.
    $290 $250 $220 $195 $165 $140 $125

    Deluxe Models, all blue or chrome engraved with simulated pearl grips, add $20.

MODEL G-IIIA — similar to IIIA, except gold engraved, simulated pearl grips.
    $1,515 $880 $825 $660 $550 $440 $330

L

Grading	100%	98%	95%	90%	80%	70%	60%

MODEL VIII — .38 Super, 9 shot, 5 in. barrel, fixed sights, wood grips. Mfg. 1952-disc.

	100%	98%	95%	90%	80%	70%	60%
	$305	$255	$220	$195	$180	$165	$140

MODEL IXA — similar to Model VIII, except .45 ACP.

	100%	98%	95%	90%	80%	70%	60%
	$305	$255	$220	$195	$180	$165	$140

MODEL XI — similar to Model IXA, except 9mm.

	100%	98%	95%	90%	80%	70%	60%
	$305	$255	$220	$195	$180	$165	$140

MODELS C-VIII, C-IXA, C-XI — similar to Model VIII, except satin chrome.

	100%	98%	95%	90%	80%	70%	60%
	$360	$315	$285	$260	$220	$195	$165

MODELS CE-VIII, CE-IXA, CE-XI

	100%	98%	95%	90%	80%	70%	60%
	$425	$350	$310	$285	$265	$220	$195

MODELS BE-VIII, BE-IXA, BE-XI — similar to Model CE, except blue, engraving.

	100%	98%	95%	90%	80%	70%	60%
	$425	$350	$295	$275	$250	$210	$180

Deluxe Models, similar to above, except simulated pearl grips - add $20.

OMNI — .45 ACP or 9mm, double action, all steel construction, 2 sear bars, 3 safeties, $4\frac{1}{4}$ in. barrel, 7 shot mag. in .45 cal., 13 shot mag. in 9mm, blue finish. Importation disc. 1986.

	100%	98%	95%	90%	80%	70%	60%
9mm Para.	$440	$380	$330	$295	$260	$225	$200

Last Mfg.'s Sug. Retail was $546.

	100%	98%	95%	90%	80%	70%	60%
.45 ACP Caliber	$395	$360	$320	$285	$250	$220	$195

Last Mfg.'s Sug. Retail was $500.

SMALL FRAME MODEL — .22 LR (disc. 1994), .32 ACP (disc. 1993), or .380 ACP cal., Colt 1911 A1 design, semi-auto, single action, $3\frac{11}{16}$ in. barrel, 7 shot mag., 23 oz. Also available in satin chrome, optional engraving patterns.

		100%	98%	95%	90%	80%	70%	60%
Mfg.'s Sug. Retail	$249	$215	$175	$155	$135	$120	$110	$100

Add $60 for duo-tone finish (.380 ACP only, mfg. 1991-1993).
Add $43 for satin chrome finish (not avail. in .32 ACP cal.).

COMPACT FRAME MODEL (IX-D) — 9mm (disc.) or .45 ACP cal., scaled down variation of the Large Frame Model, $4\frac{1}{4}$ in. barrel, 7 or 9 shot mag., 34 or 37 oz. New 1986.

		100%	98%	95%	90%	80%	70%	60%
Mfg.'s Sug. Retail	$400	$320	$250	$200	$180	$160	$155	$150

Add $25 for satin chrome finish.
Add $90 for duo-tone finish (mfg. 1990-1993).

GOVERNMENT MODEL (IX-C) — 9mm (disc.), .38 Super (new 1988), or .45 ACP cal., similar to Small Frame Model, $5\frac{1}{8}$ in. barrel, 36 oz., 9 shot mag. in 9mm, 7 shot mag. in .45 ACP. Engraved and deluxe models available also.

		100%	98%	95%	90%	80%	70%	60%
Mfg.'s Sug. Retail	$400	$320	$250	$200	$180	$160	$150	$140

Add $25 for satin chrome finish (.45 ACP only).
Add $90 for duo-tone finish (.45 ACP only, mfg. 1991-1993).

MINI-MAX — 9mm Para., .40 S&W, or .45 ACP cal., mini-compact variation featuring 6-8 shot mag., choice of matte, satin chrome, duo-tone (.45 ACP only), or stainless steel finish/construction. New 1996.

		100%	98%	95%	90%	80%	70%	60%
Mfg.'s Sug. Retail	$367	$295	$245	$200	$180	$160	$150	$140

Add $42 for satin chrome finish.
Add $16 for duo-tone finish.
Add $66 for stainless steel construction.

MAX-I MODEL — 9mm Para. or .45 ACP cal., patterned after the Colt Govt. Model, single action only, $4\frac{1}{4}$ (Compact Model) or $5\frac{1}{2}$ in. barrel, 3-dot combat sights, 7 (.45 ACP) or 9 (9mm Para.) shot mag., matte blue finish, rubber grips, 34 or 36 oz. New 1995.

		100%	98%	95%	90%	80%	70%	60%
Mfg.'s Sug. Retail	$350	$290	$245	$200	$180	$160	$150	$140

Add $17 for duo-tone finish (.45 ACP cal. only).
Add $50 for satin chrome finish (new 1996).

L

Grading	100%	98%	95%	90%	80%	70%	60%

▲ *Max-I Compensated* — .45 ACP only, 7 or 10 shot mag., features compensated barrel.

Mfg.'s Sug. Retail $492	$445	$385	$330	$250	$200	$180	$160

Add $25 for 10 shot model.

MODEL 82 — 9mm Para., double action, 4¼ in. barrel, blue finish, 3-dot sighting system, 15 shot mag., ambidextrous safety, loaded chamber indicator, black polymer grips, 39 oz. Imported 1988-1993.

	$850	$675	$550	$495	$450	$395	$365

Last Mfg.'s Sug. Retail was $975.

MODEL 87 COMPETITION — 9mm Para., competition variation of the Model 82, includes built in ported compensator, oversize magazine and safety release, fixed barrel bushing, beveled rapid load magazine well, 14 shot mag., extended and serrated triggerguard, and adj. trigger. Imported 1989-1993.

	$1,275	$995	$850	$750	$650	$575	$500

Last Mfg.'s Sug. Retail was $1,450.

REVOLVERS

MARTIAL DOUBLE ACTION REVOLVER — .22 LR, .38 Spl., 6 shot, 4 and 6 in. barrels, target sights, blue, checkered wood grips. Mfg. 1969-1976.

	$220	$200	$180	$165	$140	$120	$100

DELUXE MARTIAL — similar to Martial, except finish as follows:

Satin chrome	$275	$250	$220	$195	$165	$140	$120
Chrome, engraved	$305	$275	$250	$220	$195	$165	$140
Blue, engraved	$290	$265	$235	$210	$180	$155	$120
Gold, engraved	$1,430	$880	$770	$660	$550	$495	$415

COMANCHE I — similar to Martial .22, double action. Mfg. 1977-1982.

	$255	$220	$195	$165	$155	$140	$110

COMANCHE II — similar to Martial .38, double action. Mfg. 1977-1982 and 1986 in .22 LR and .22 Mag. only.

	$240	$220	$195	$165	$155	$140	$110

Last Mfg.'s Sug. Retail was $272.

COMANCHE III — .22 LR (disc.) or .357 Mag., double action, 6 shot, 4, 6, or 8½ (disc. 1986) in. barrel, blue, adj. sights, checkered walnut grips. Mfg. 1975-95. Before 1977, it was called "Comanche".

	$280	$245	$200	$165	$155	$140	$130

Last Mfg.'s Sug. Retail was $339.

▲ *Satin Chrome Finish (disc.)*

	$330	$270	$230	$205	$185	$170	$160

Last Mfg.'s Sug. Retail was $395.

▲ *Gold Finish (disc.)*

	$1,100	$880	$825	$660	$550	$440	$330

SUPER COMANCHE IV — .44 Mag., double action, 6 or 8½ in. VR barrel, adj. sights, blue only.

Mfg.'s Sug. Retail $440	$350	$285	$235	$220	$205	$185	$175

SUPER COMANCHE V — .357 Mag., double action, 6 shot, 4, 6, or 8½ in. VR barrel, adj. sights, blue only. Importation disc. 1988.

	$335	$275	$230	$210	$200	$190	$180

Last Mfg.'s Sug. Retail was $414.

LORCIN ENGINEERING CO., INC.

Manufacturer located in Mira Loma, CA. Distributor sales only.

Grading	100%	98%	95%	90%	80%	70%	60%

DERRINGERS

STAINLESS MODEL O/U — .357 Mag. or .45 LC cal., 3½ in. barrel, synthetic grips, tip-up action, rebounding hammer, fixed sights. New 1996.

Mfg.'s Sug. Retail	$110		$95	$80	$65		

PISTOLS: SEMI-AUTO

L-22 MODEL — .22 LR cal., similar to L-25 Model, except 2.55 in. barrel and 9 shot mag., black or chrome finish, 16 oz. New 1992.

Mfg.'s Sug. Retail	$89	$75	$60	$50	$45	$40	$35	$35

L-25 MODEL — .25 ACP cal., semi-auto single action, 6 shot mag., 2.4 in. barrel, anatomically designed grips to fit hand better, choice of black and gold, chrome and pearl, satin chrome and pearl, teflon camo finish (new 1992), or black and pearl finish, 13.5 oz. New 1989.

Mfg.'s Sug. Retail	$79	$65	$50	$45	$40	$35	$35	$35

Add $20 for lightweight frame (Model LT 25, new in 1990).

▲ *Lady Lorcin* — same specifications as the L-25 Model, except is available in chrome, satin chrome, or black exterior finish with pink grips. New 1990.

Mfg.'s Sug. Retail	$79	$70	$60	$50	$45	$40	$35	$35

L-32 — .32 ACP cal., semi-auto single action, 7 shot mag., 3.5 in. barrel, available in black or chrome finish, 23 oz. New 1992.

Mfg.'s Sug. Retail	$89	$80	$70	$60	$50	$45	$40	$35

L-380 — .380 ACP cal., semi-auto single action, 7 or 10 (new 1995) shot mag., 3.5 in. barrel, available in black or chrome finish, 23 oz. New 1992.

Mfg.'s Sug. Retail	$100	$85	$75	$65	$55	$50	$45	$40

Add $29 for 10 shot mag. variation.

L9MM — 9mm Para., semi-auto single action, 10 (C/B 1994) or 13* shot mag., 4½ in. barrel, grip safety, black finish, 3-dot sights, 36 oz. New 1994.

Mfg.'s Sug. Retail	$149	$125	$115	$100	$90	$85	$80	$75

Add $20 for disc. 13 shot mag. variation.

LUCCHINI, SANDRO

Manufacturer located in Sarezzo (Brescia), Italy.

Lucchini manufactures high quality double rifles and shotguns, many of which have elaborate gold inlay work. Please contact the manufacturer directly (see Trademark Index) for more information.

LUCIANO, BOSIS

Manufacturer located in Travagliato, Italy. Imported by New England Arms, Co. located in Kittery Point, ME.

All Luciano guns are manufactured on a custom order basis only. Annual production is approx. 25 guns. Please contact the importer directly for more information.

SHOTGUNS

MICHAELANGELO O/U — Boss style sidelock action, chopper lump barrels.

Prices start in the $30,000 range and go up according to special orders.

QUEEN SxS — Holland & Holland type sidelock action, chopper lump barrels.

Prices start in the $20,000 range and go up according to special orders.

COUNTRY SxS — Anson & Deely type boxlock action, chopper lump barrels.

Prices start in the $12,500 range and go up according to special orders.

LUGERS WITH VARIATIONS

Note: The Luger section in this book is arranged chronologically by year of manufacture (1900 models to Post-War production), under individual manufacturer headings.

Often times, year of production can be hard to nail down, especially on commercial models. An easier way to initially identify your Luger is to categorize by toggle marking first - then by chamber marking within groups (chronologically for dated chambers). Once you know period of manufacture, simply refer to the appropriate subheading in this section. While some rare variations will be excluded in this generalized overview, it will be very helpful to establish correct, basic knowledge about your particular Luger.

While many recently imported Lugers would make workable shooters, they have in no way lowered prices on 90%+ condition specimens due to normal collector activity in top quality only pistols. Recently imported Lugers should have the importer's name visibly stamped on an exterior surface. Most of these imports are in the 9mm - 4 in. barrel configuration.

Every year more and more reblued, restrawed, regripped, reframed, rebarreled Lugers are sold to unknowing military handgun collectors as rare variations. On any expensive contract variation, careful inspection on all parts must be made before potentially purchasing. If in doubt, secure 2 or 3 additional appraisals/observations from qualified individuals. Lugers are a field in themselves and an experienced Winchester dealer would not be qualified to guesstimate the originality of these German handguns.

A final note on Lugers: Original pistols in 95%-100% condition have not been affected by the influx of recent imports as these newly imported guns are usually in 80% and lower condition or have been reblued.

It seems that every year the prices of top quality (98%+ condition) original Lugers get more expensive and less predictable - FOR THIS REASON, THE 100% VALUES ON SOME VINTAGE LUGERS HAVE BEEN OMITTED INTENTIONALLY SINCE RARITY PRECLUDES ACCURATE PRICE EVALUATION IN THIS CONDITION FACTOR. Please contact this publication for current estimated 100% values on Lugers.

REFERENCE GUIDE BY TOGGLE MARKING

DWM TOGGLE IDENTIFICATION

L

DWM MODELS — mfg. from 1900 to 1930 in Berlin, Germany.
- ▲ *1900 Models* — grip safety and "Dished" Toggles, ser. nos. 1-24,999.
- ▲ *1906 Models* — grip safety, many chamber markings, ser. nos. 25,000-74,000.
- ▲ *1908 Commercial Models* — no grip safety, 9mm, ser. nos. 39,000-74,000.
- ▲ *1908 Military Models* — no stock lug.
- ▲ *1914 Military Models* — stock lug, dated 1913-1918.
- ▲ *1920 Commercial Models* — no grip safety, usually 3⅞ in. barrel. Most common Luger, undated chamber, 7.65mm or 9mm.
    Note: Lugers with 4 inch barrels are most frequently encountered in military and commercial models. 6 in. barrels usually denote "Navy" models. 8 in. barrels usually denote "Artillery" models. Guns with barrels over 8 inches are rare and should be checked carefully for originality.

DWM COMMERCIAL LUGERS

DWM MEANS DEUTSCHE WAFFEN & MUNITIONS FABRIKEN

These are models manufactured from 1900-1923 found in the five digit serial range.

MODEL 1900 — ser. range 1-20,000. Configuration: 4¾ in. x .30 Commercial, American Eagle, Swiss.

MODEL 1900 — ser. range 20,001-21,000. Configuration: 4¾ in. x .30 Bulgarian.

MODEL 1902 — ser. range 21,001-25,000. Configuration: 9mmx4 in. "fat barrels" and 11¾ in. x .30 Carbine models, intermixed with 4¾ x .30 American Eagles and Commercials.

MODEL 1906 — ser. range 25,001-39,000. Configuration: Commercial American Eagle, Navy Commercial and Swiss, both 4¾ in. x .30 and 9mm x 4 in. grip safety models.

MODEL 1908 — ser. range 39,001-71,000. Configuration: First 9mm x 4 in. without grip safety, M1908 Commercials were interspersed with .30 and 9mm Eagles, Commercials, Navy Commercials, and a few Carbines and Swiss.

MODEL 1914 — ser. range 71,001-74,000. Configuration: Last pre-WWI Commercial Lugers, made with stock lug, with a few 9mm Commercials mixed in.

MODEL 1920 — ser. range 2,000i-9,999u. Configuration: Post-WWI Commercials, mostly 3⅞ in. x .30 cal.

MODEL 1923 — ser. range 89,001-91,000. Configuration: The last thousand or so made have "safe" on lever and "loaded" on the extractor, 3⅞ in. x .30 barrels.

ERFURT TOGGLE IDENTIFICATION

ERFURT MODELS

Produced from 1911-1914 and 1916-1918 in Erfurt, Germany. Military Model - Chamber dated 1911-1914 and 1916-1918. Erfurt models exhibit the most proof marks and individual parts numbering. Walnut grips.

SIMSON & CO. TOGGLE IDENTIFICATION

SIMSON & CO.

Manufactured 1922 to 1934 in Suhl, Germany. Most Simson Lugers are military models (9mm - 4 in. barrels). During this 10 year period, Simson supplied the German Army Lugers exclusively. Can be dated 1925-1928. Many reworks of WWI DWM Military Lugers were refurbished by Simson, and can be detected by the Simson "Eagle-over-6" proof on repaired parts. A very few Simsons made in 1934 have just an "S" on the toggle (very rare).

SWISS TOGGLE IDENTIFICATION

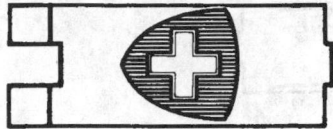 

SWISS

Manufactured 1924 to 1929 by WAFFENFABRIK Bern, Switzerland. Relatively rare - these Swiss models have "improved" changes (flat and curved front grip strap), 4¾ in. barrels, walnut or plastic grips, grip safety. 1929 model has Geneva Cross in shield on front link.

MAUSER TOGGLE IDENTIFICATION

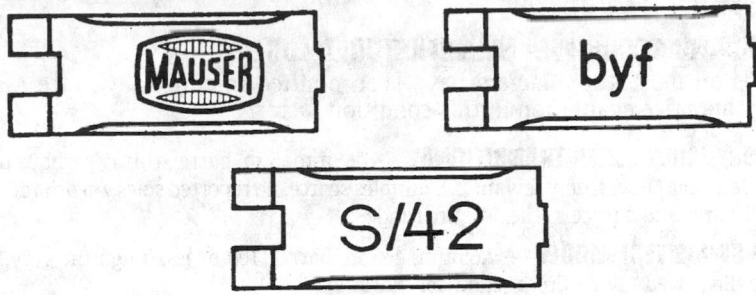

MAUSER VARIATIONS

Manufactured 1934-1942 in Oberndorf, Germany. Between 1930 and 1934 Mauser Werke was primarily engaged in reworking older Lugers, since transfer of machinery and personnel to the DWM plant in Berlin was completed in 1931. Mauser "Banner" models were made from 1934 to 1942, many are dated from 1939-1942 on the chamber. S/42 models are MOSTLY MILITARY contract guns manufactured between 1934 and 1940, usually chamber marked. "42" toggle marked guns (Mauser code) were mfg. 1939 and 1940 and are dated. "byf" marked toggles indicate guns made for German military use after 1940 and are more common than other military models. The Mauser Werke trademark also appears on those Lugers made in the 1970s.

KRIEGHOFF TOGGLE IDENTIFICATION

KRIEGHOFF MODELS

Manufactured between 1934-1946 in Suhl, Germany. Early Krieghoffs are side frame inscribed. The German Luftwaffe contracted with Krieghoff for military guns in 1935. Early military Krieghoffs have "S" marked chambers, most are chamber dated between 1936 and 1945. Krieghoff Lugers are prized for their quality fit and finish and command higher prices because of their rarity factor.

L

VICKERS TOGGLE IDENTIFICATION

VICKERS

Manufactured by Vickers, Ltd., circa 1921, in England from DWM parts for military contract sale to the Netherlands. Added barrel date is a date of arsenal refinish or refurbishing. Distinguishable by Vickers toggle and "rust" marked safety. Serial range is 1-10,100. Grips can be finely checkered with shallow contour or very coarsely checkered. Configuration is 9mm, 4 in. barrel, and grip safety.

Grading	100%	98%	95%	90%	80%	70%	60%

PRE-1900 AND 1900 DWM MANUFACTURED LUGERS

Values on most 100% Lugers have been omitted intentionally since rarity precludes accurate price evaluation in this condition factor.

1898/99 BORCHARDT LUGER TRANSITIONAL — 7.65mm, 5 in. barrel, this is perhaps one of the most desirable Lugers, only few mfg. Examples scarce, no reported sales, an original example would command a price in the 5-figure range.

1899/1900 SWISS TEST MODEL — 7.65mm, 4¾ in. barrel, 100 or less mfg., the very first true Luger. Engraved "Swiss Cross" chamber marking.

	N/A	$15,000	$10,000	$7,500	$6,500	$6,000	$5,000

This variation is serial numbered in the 1-50 range approx.

1900 COMMERCIAL DWM — 7.65mm, 4¾ in. barrel, 5,500 mfg.

	N/A	$2,600	$1,600	$1,000	$750	$600	$500

1900 SWISS COMMERCIAL DWM — 7.65mm, 4¾ in. barrel, 2,000 commercially mfg. and 3000 military mfg.

	N/A	$3,500	$2,000	$1,200	$800	$600	$500

Add 15% for wide trigger (found only in ser. no. range 4,000).

1900 AMERICAN EAGLE DWM — 7.65mm, 4¾ in. barrel, approx. 12,000 mfg.

	N/A	$2,750	$1,500	$1,000	$700	$600	$500

Add 30% for U.S. Test Model (approx. ser. no. range 6,100-7,100).

1900 BULGARIAN DWM — 7.65mm, 4¾ in. barrel, 1,000 mfg., very rare in U.S., most often seen in the 60% and lower condition.

	N/A	$7,500	$4,500	$3,500	$2,700	$2,200	$1,800

Deduct 30% if rebarreled.

LUGERS: 1902-DWM MFG.

1902 COMMERCIAL — 9mm, 4 in. barrel, serial number range 22,300-22,400 and 22,900-23,500 (500-600 mfg.). Commonly called "Fat Barrel" model.

	N/A	$6,750	$4,650	$3,400	$3,000	$2,500	$2,000

1902 AMERICAN EAGLE — 9mm, 4 in. barrel, 600-700 mfg., commonly called the "fat barrel". Same ser. range as 1902 Commercial Model.

	N/A	$7,350	$5,500	$4,000	$3,000	$2,500	$2,000

Grading	100%	98%	95%	90%	80%	70%	60%

1902 CARTRIDGE COUNTER AMERICAN EAGLE — 9mm, only 50 mfg. with the Powell Indication Device; be extremely wary of fakes. ser. no. range 22,401-22,450.

| | N/A | $20,000 | $13,500 | $9,500 | $7,500 | $6,000 | $5,000 |

1902 DANZIG TEST — 7.65 or 9mm, blank toggle, 4 in. barrel, Crown D proofs.

| | N/A | $4,600 | $3,700 | $3,000 | $2,200 | $1,800 | $1,500 |

1902 CARBINE — 7.65mm, 11¾ in. barrel, approx. 2500 mfg.

| Gun w/matching stock | N/A | $11,350 | $9,250 | $5,750 | $4,250 | $3,000 | $2,000 |
| Gun only | N/A | $7,500 | $5,950 | $3,500 | $2,700 | $2,200 | $1,800 |

Add approx. 40% for American Eagle variation.
Subtract 20% for non-matching stock.

1902/06 TRANSITIONAL CARBINE — 11¾ in. barrel, 50-100 mfg., may have new model frame. Ser. nos. start at 50,000.

| | N/A | $9,000 | $6,250 | $4,500 | $4,200 | $4,000 | $3,800 |

Deduct 30% if without matching stock.

1903 COMMERCIAL — 7.65mm, 4 in. barrel, 50 mfg., extractor marked "charge". Ser. range 25,000-25,050, with 90 degree toggle checkering.

| | N/A | $6,500 | $6,000 | $5,500 | $5,000 | $3,000 | $2,500 |

LUGERS: 1904-DWM MFG.

1904 NAVY DWM — 9mm, 6 in. barrel, limited mfg., a Transitional Navy, fat barrel with 90 degree toggle checkering and toggle lock, should have 2-digit ser. no.

Extreme rarity precludes accurate price evaluation. Most of these pistols available for sale are fakes - buyer beware.

LUGERS: 1906-DWM MFG.

1906 COMMERCIAL 7.65mm W/"GESICHERT" MARKED SAFETY — 7.65mm, 4¾ in. barrel, "GESICHERT" marked safety, long frame. Approx. 750 mfg.

| | N/A | $1,700 | $1,300 | $1,100 | $900 | $750 | $600 |

1906 COMMERCIAL 9mm PARA. — 9mm, 4 in. barrel, 3,500-4,000 mfg. Scarcer than 7.65mm.

| | N/A | $1,900 | $1,400 | $1,000 | $800 | $650 | $500 |

1906 COMMERCIAL 7.65mm — 7.65mm, 4¾ in. barrel, area under safety polished bright, 5000 mfg.

| | N/A | $1,700 | $1,250 | $800 | $600 | $500 | $400 |

1906 AMERICAN EAGLE - 9MM — 9mm, 4 in. barrel, American Eagle stamped in front of breech, 3,000 mfg.

| | N/A | $2,350 | $1,500 | $1,100 | $700 | $550 | $450 |

1906 AMERICAN EAGLE - 7.65MM — 7.65mm, 4¾ in. barrel, 7,500-8,000 mfg. Add 40% for long frame.

| | N/A | $1,900 | $1,400 | $750 | $600 | $475 | $400 |

1906 NAVY COMMERCIAL — 9mm, 6 in. barrel, approx. 2,500 mfg. Add 50% for 7.65 cal. with 6 in. barrel.

| | N/A | $3,400 | $2,600 | $1,800 | $1,600 | $1,200 | $950 |

1906 NAVY MILITARY FIRST ISSUE — 9mm, 6 in. barrel, first issue, 19,000 mfg., mostly altered safety marking - "GESICHERT" in lower position. Ser. no. range 1-9,000a.

Add 10% for Navy unit markings.
Add 25% for unaltered safety variation.

| | N/A | $3,000 | $2,250 | $1,600 | $1,200 | $875 | $600 |

L

Grading	100%	98%	95%	90%	80%	70%	60%

1906 NAVY MILITARY SECOND ISSUE — 9mm, 6 in. barrel, second issue, 2,000 mfg. Ser. range 9,000a-1,000b.

	N/A	$3,250	$2,500	$1,725	$1,400	$1,100	$900

Add 10% for Navy unit markings.

LUGERS: 1906-1918 DWM AND ERFURT MFG.

Most common variations in good supply within this section in 50% or less condition will approximate the 60% value. This reflects its value as a representative shooter rather than a higher priced collector's gun.

1906 SWISS COMMERCIAL — 7.65 or 9mm, 4¾ in. barrel, less than 1,000 mfg., Swiss "Cross in Sunburst," short frame.

	N/A	$2,400	$1,750	$1,500	$1,350	$1,200	$1,100

Add 20% for "Cross in Shield".

1906 SWISS MILITARY — 7.65mm, 4¾ in. barrel, long frame, Swiss Police has Cross in Shield. Either "Cross in Shield" or "Cross in Sunburst".

	N/A	$2,400	$1,600	$1,200	$900	$800	$700

1906/23 DUTCH — 9mm, 4 in. barrel, approx. 4,000 mfg., often seen as arsenal rework.

	N/A	$1,600	$1,400	$900	$750	$600	$525

Add 200% for original finish and barrel.

1906 BRAZILIAN — 7.65mm, 4¾ in. barrel, 5,000 mfg., extremely rare in fine condition.

	N/A	$2,500	$1,800	$1,000	$800	$700	$650

1906 BULGARIAN — 7.65mm, 4¾ in. barrel, 1,500 mfg., most rebarrelled to 9mm (deduct 60%).

	N/A	$4,200	$3,500	$3,500	$2,000	$1,850	$1,450

This is the rarest Bulgarian - most are fakes or have been restored.

1908 BULGARIAN — 9mm, 4 in. barrel, DWM on chamber, 10,000 mfg., extremely rare in mint condition.

	N/A	$2,500	$1,800	$1,000	$825	$750	$675

1906 PORTUGUESE ARMY — 7.65mm, 4¾ in. barrel, Manuel II crest on chamber. Approx. 5,000 mfg.

	N/A	$1,450	$950	$600	$525	$450	$350

1906 ROYAL PORTUGUESE NAVY — 9mm, 4 in. barrel, Anchor & Crown on chamber, very rare. Most are fakes.

	N/A	$9,500	$6,000	$4,000	$2,500	$2,000	$1,500

1906 REPUBLIC OF PORTUGAL NAVY — Anchor R.P. on chamber, very rare. Most are fakes.

	N/A	$9,500	$6,000	$4,000	$2,500	$2,000	$1,500

1906 RUSSIAN — 9mm, 4 in. barrel, approx. 1,000 mfg., only 6 reported.

	N/A	$12,000	$9,500	$6,000	$3,200	$2,600	$2,000

1906 VICKERS DUTCH — 9mm, 4 in. barrel, approx. 10,000 assembled by Vickers Ltd. from DWM supplied parts.

	N/A	N/A	N/A	N/A	N/A	N/A	$895

1906 FRENCH COMMERCIAL — 7.65mm, 4¾ in. barrel.

	N/A	$2,350	$1,800	$1,575	$1,400	$1,200	$995

Add 100% if cased with accessories.

1908 COMMERCIAL AND MILITARY — DWM, 9mm, 4 in. barrel, Test/Acceptance Model, approx. 500 mfg. Ser. no. range 69,000-71,200.

	N/A	$1,200	$800	$700	$575	$475	$400

L

Grading	100%	98%	95%	90%	80%	70%	60%

1908 NAVY COMMERCIAL — 9mm, 6 in. barrel. Add 50% for 7.65mm with 6 in. barrel.

	N/A	$3,750	$2,800	$2,200	$1,800	$1,500	$1,300

1908 DWM MILITARY — 9mm, 4 in. barrel, approx. 95,000 mfg. Each year, undated 1st issue or dated 1910-1913, no stock lug, except for a few late 1913 mfg. guns.

	N/A	$795	$650	$450	$400	$350	$300

Add 20%+ for Imperial unit markings (depends on history of unit).
Add 20% for undated or for 1913 date w/stock lug.

Approx. 25,000 1st issue pistols were mfg., 20,000 dated 1910, 15,000 dated 1911, 10,000 dated 1912, 25,000 dated 1913.

1908 DWM COMMERCIAL — 9mm, 4 in. barrel, no stock lug or hold open, blank chamber.

	N/A	$800	$600	$450	$400	$350	$300

1910-1914 DATED 1908 ERFURT MILITARY — 9mm, 4 in. barrel (dated 1910-1914), 1911, 1912, and most 1913 chamber dates do not have stock lugs.

	N/A	$800	$625	$525	$400	$350	$295

Add 20%+ for Imperial unit markings (depends on history of unit).
Add 20% for 1913 chamber date with stock lug.

WWI ERFURT MILITARY SERIAL RANGES

CHAMBER DATE	OBSERVED LOW SERIAL	OBSERVED HIGH SERIAL	APPROXIMATE QTY. MADE
1911	575	9548	10,000
1912	255	866b	22,000
1913	575	2563b	25,000
1914	2137	539A	25,000
1915	none observed		
1916	13	5764b	80,000
1917	844	2854n	150,000
1918	304	5816s	180,000

Production data appears courtesy of Jan C. Still.

1908 NAVY — 9mm, 6 in. barrel, scarce. Ser. No. range 1,000B-10,000B, 9,000 mfg.

	N/A	$3,250	$2,200	$1,600	$1,200	$1,000	$895

1908 BOLIVIAN CONTRACT — 9mm, 4 in. barrel.

	N/A	$3,000	$2,500	$1,700	$1,300	$1,100	$900

1913 COMMERCIAL DWM — 9mm, 4 in. barrel, grip safety and stock lug, horizontal "N" proof mark, 71,000 ser. no. range, rare.

	N/A	$2,250	$1,500	$1,050	$900	$780	$700

1914 COMMERCIAL DWM — 9mm, 4 in. barrel, undated, stock lug, horizontal crown-N proofed.

	N/A	$1,000	$800	$550	$450	$400	$350

1914 NAVY — 9mm, 6 in. barrel, scarce. Dated 1916 and 1917.

	N/A	$3,000	$2,250	$1,600	$1,200	$1,000	$900

Add 20% for 16 date.

Watch for fakes made from 1920 Commercials with new barrels and rear toggles added. Crown M proofs and date will look "fresh" (16 date usually encountered).

L

Grading	100%	98%	95%	90%	80%	70%	60%

1916-1918 DATED ERFURT MILITARY — 9mm, 4 in. barrel, dated 1916-1918 - there are no known 1915 chamber dated Erfurts.

	N/A	$795	$595	$475	$400	$350	$300

Add 20% for 1914 date.
Add $75 for original holster in average+ condition.
Add 10% for matching mag.
Add 50% for 2 matching mags.
Add 20%+ for Imperial unit markings (depends on history of unit).

Note: Date stamped on top frame is date of production; thus dates could be 1914, 1915, 1916, 1917, or 1918. All are Military P.08s, however. 99%-100% Erfurts are rare.

1914 ERFURT ARTILLERY — 9mm, 1914 date is only one seen, 8 in. barrel.

	N/A	$2,250	$1,600	$1,000	$900	$800	$700

Add 20%+ for Imperial unit markings (depends on history of unit).

1912-1918 DATED WWI DWM MILITARY — 9mm, 4 in. barrel. 1912-1918 dated. Most frequently encountered WWI military Luger, stock lug.

	N/A	$850	$595	$475	$400	$350	$295

Add $75 for original holster in average+ condition.
Add 20% for matching mag.
Add 100% for 2 matching mags.
Add 20%+ for Imperial unit markings (depends on history of unit).

Note: Date stamped on top frame is date of production; thus dates could be 1914, 1915, 1916, 1917, or 1918. All are Military P.08s, however.

WWI DWM MILITARY SERIAL RANGES

CHAMBER DATE	OBSERVED LOW SERIAL	OBSERVED HIGH SERIAL	APPROXIMATE QTY. MADE
1908	(undated) 34	2636b	25,000
1910	5095b	5358d	20,000
1911	1524c	4825e	13,000
1912	599	9974	10,000
1913	2617	3850d	25,000
1914	282	6212c	40,000
1915	1398	2557d	100,000
1916	287	5438q	180,000
1917	587	3521m	60,000
1918	3690	9018n	190,000

Production data appears courtesy of Jan C. Still.

1914-1918 DATED DWM ARTILLERY — 9mm, 8 in. barrel. Dated 1914-1918.

	N/A	$1,675	$1,100	$800	$600	$500	$400

Add $350 for matching stock.
Add $200 for proper non-matching stock.
Add $200 for original leather holster with shoulder strap.
Add 40% for rare 1914 chamber date.
Add 20%+ for Imperial unit markings (depends on history of unit).

LUGERS: 1920-1930 DWM

Most common variations in good supply within this section in 50% or less condition will approximate the 60% value. This reflects its value as a representative shooter rather than a higher priced collector's gun.

Grading	100%	98%	95%	90%	80%	70%	60%

1920 DWM OR ERFURT — 9mm, 4 in. barrel, military and police, reworked and issued to police units, many thousand reworked, double date also, 1920 and 1921 dated.

	N/A	$700	$540	$450	$375	$300	$250

1920 COMMERCIAL — 7.65mm or 9mm cal., 3⅞-4 in. barrel, many thousand produced.

	$1,000	$700	$450	$385	$335	$285	$250

Add 25% for 9mm cal.

1920 NAVY COMMERCIAL — 9mm, 6 in. barrel, very rare rework, Navy rear sight. Add 20% for 7.65mm with 6 in. barrel.

	N/A	$2,000	$1,400	$1,000	$900	$800	$700

1920 COMMERCIAL ARTILLERY — 9mm, 8 in. barrel, very rare rework.

	N/A	$1,350	$950	$800	$600	$500	$400

While this variation is undoubtedly rarer than the 1914-1918 military Artillery models, it is less desirable.

1920 "LONG BARREL" COMMERCIAL — 7.65mm or 9mm, 10-20 in. barrel, extremely rare.

	N/A	$1,400	$1,100	$1,000	$750	$655	$600

Watch for fakes - these guns have to be evaluated one at a time. Barrel should have matching nos. and Crown N proof.

1920 NAVY CARBINE — 7.65mm, 11¾ in. barrel, long frame (if short frame, be wary of fakes, very few produced). Navy rear sight, no forearm under barrel.

	N/A	$2,000	$1,600	$1,100	$1,025	$950	$850

1920 CARBINE — 7.65mm, 11¾ in. barrel, very rare.

		100%	98%	95%	90%	80%	70%	60%
Gun only		N/A	$5,450	$4,750	$4,000	$3,000	$2,500	$2,000
Gun with stock		N/A	$9,250	$7,250	$6,400	$5,500	$4,650	$3,650

1920 SWISS REWORK — 7.65mm 3⅝-6 in. barrel, several hundred produced.

	N/A	$1,400	$1,100	$1,000	$750	$655	$600

ABERCROMBIE & FITCH COMMERCIAL — 7.65mm or 9mm, long frame, 4¾ in. barrel, 100 mfg., total for both cals. A few 6 in. barrels - add 30%.

	N/A	$4,250	$3,500	$3,000	$2,500	$2,100	$1,850

Inspect barrel legend very carefully (as in beware of fakes) - must have reinforced frame (look for rib in rear frame well).

1920/21-DWM — 9mm, 4 in. barrel.

	N/A	$700	$600	$450	$400	$350	$300

Deduct 20% if arsenal reworked.

1920/23 STOEGER AMERICAN EAGLE — 7.65mm or 9mm, 3⅝-24 in. barrels, less than 1,000 mfg., made by DWM for Stoeger, sold in USA, longer barrel models have higher value.

		100%	98%	95%	90%	80%	70%	60%
3⅞ - 6 in. barrels		N/A	$2,500	$1,450	$1,200	$1,050	$950	$825
8 in. barrel		N/A	$4,500	$2,300	$2,000	$1,650	$1,200	$995

Add 50% for Mauser mfg., safe and loaded extractor, or V ser. no. suffix.

Be extremely careful when examining the frame markings on this variation as there are many fakes in the marketplace.

1923 DWM COMMERCIAL — 7.65mm, 3⅝ in. barrel, 14,000 mfg. (ser. range 74,000-89,000).

	$1,000	$700	$450	$385	$335	$285	$250

1923 DWM "SAFE AND LOADED" COMMERCIAL — "safe and loaded" marked on frame and ejector, 7.65mm, 3⅞ in. barrel, safety and extractor marked in English, 2,000 mfg. (ser. range 89,000-91,000).

	N/A	$1,375	$1,000	$850	$600	$500	$420

L

Grading	100%	98%	95%	90%	80%	70%	60%

1923 FINNISH LUGER — 7.65mm, approx. 5,000-7,000 units made for Finnish military contract (Army and Navy), marked "SA" surrounded by a rectangle, most have been recently imported into the U.S.

	N/A	$550	$450	$375	$325	$300	$275

LUGERS: KRIEGHOFF MFG.

Add 20% for matching mag. on Krieghoff Models listed below.

1923 DWM/KRIEGHOFF COMMERCIAL — 7.65mm x 3⅞ in. or 9mm x 4 in. barrels, few made, reworked by Krieghoff, chamber dated 1921 or unmarked, most in "in" range, Krieghoff stamped on back-frame. Be wary of fakes.

	N/A	$1,650	$1,300	$1,100	$880	$770	$660

DWM/KRIEGHOFF COMMERCIAL — 7.65mm or 9mm, 4 in. barrel, a few hundred made, side frame marked Krieghoff. Most are fake.

	N/A	$2,700	$2,000	$1,650	$1,300	$1,000	$800

KRIEGHOFF COMMERCIAL SIDE FRAME — 7.65mm or 9mm, 4 or 6 in. barrel, 1500 mfg., 1,000 with side frame marked, and 500 without. "P" prefix ser. nos.

	N/A	$2,400	$2,000	$1,600	$995	$800	$700

Add 30% for side frame marked 7.65mm.

KRIEGHOFF S CODE EARLY — 9mm, 4 in. barrel, 1,800 mfg., German Luftwaffe. Has fat walnut grips, "H-K Suhl" toggle.

	N/A	$2,500	$1,900	$1,500	$995	$895	$775

KRIEGHOFF S CODE MID SERIES — 9mm, 4 in. barrel, 500-700 mfg., Luftwaffe, ser. no. range 1600-2500, fine-checkered plastic grips.

	N/A	$2,650	$1,950	$1,500	$995	$800	$700

KRIEGHOFF S CODE LATE — 9mm, 4 in. barrel, 1,800 mfg., Luftwaffe, ser. no. range 2300-4200.

	N/A	$2,500	$1,800	$1,200	$750	$600	$500

KRIEGHOFF GRIP SAFETY — 9mm, 4 in. barrel, extremely rare, test trial gun.

	$3,800	$3,500	$3,000

KRIEGHOFF 36 DATE — 9mm, 4 in. barrel, 500-700 made, Luftwaffe military, 2 digit date, coarse checkered plastic grips.

	N/A	$2,800	$2,000	$1,650	$1,300	$1,000	$800

KRIEGHOFF 1936-1945 DATED — 9mm, 4 in. barrel, approx. 9,000 mfg., 4 digit chamber date, 1936, 1937 and 1940 most common; 1938 and 1941 through 1944 dates command 70-200% premiums. 1945 is extremely rare - add 500%.

	N/A	$2,500	$1,825	$1,550	$1,320	$1,225	$1,100

The 1941 "large date" is very rare - watch for fakes (re-dated frames) on this model in general.

POST-WAR KRIEGHOFF TYPE I — 9mm, 4 in. barrel, 150 mfg. for occupation forces, H-K marked toggle link.

	N/A	$1,800	$1,300	$1,200	$1,100	$995	$875

POST-WAR KRIEGHOFF TYPE II — 9mm, 4 in. barrel, 150 mfg., unmarked toggle link, many parts proofed "Eagle-over-2".

	N/A	$1,200	$1,100	$1,000	$900	$800	$775

POST-WAR KRIEGHOFF COMMERCIAL — 7.65mm, 4 in. barrel, 100-200 mfg., unmarked toggle, many parts proofed "Eagle-over-2".

	N/A	$1,200	$1,100	$1,000	$900	$800	$775

Grading	100%	98%	95%	90%	80%	70%	60%

LUGERS: MAUSER MFG.

Most common variations in good supply within this section in 50% or less condition will approximate the 60% value. This reflects its value as a representative shooter rather than a higher priced collector's gun.

1935-06 PORTUGUESE GNR — 7.65mm, 4¾ in. barrel, 564 mfg., GNR on chamber, Portuguese marked safety and extractor.

	N/A	$1,950	$1,400	$1,000	$700	$650	$425

1934/06 MAUSER SWISS COMMERCIAL — 7.65mm, 4¾ in. barrel, a few hundred produced, "Cross in Sunburst" or blank chamber, grip safety.

	N/A	$2,800	$2,400	$2,000	$1,500	$1,250	$850

1934 MAUSER BANNER COMMERCIAL — 7.65mm or 9mm, 4 in. barrel, hundreds produced, unmarked chamber, "v" suffix to ser. no.

	N/A	$1,800	$1,600	$1,400	$1,150	$950	$725

Add 15% for "Kal. 7.65" barrel marking.

S/42 K DATE — mfg. 1934 only, 9mm, 4 in. barrel, approx. 10,000 mfg., military.

	N/A	$2,450	$1,800	$900	$800	$700	$550

Add 50% for "large eagle over M Navy" proofmark.

S/42 G DATE — mfg. 1935 only, 9mm, 4 in. barrel, many thousand produced.

	N/A	$1,150	$875	$650	$450	$400	$375

Add 20% for Navy markings.

S/42 DATED CHAMBER — 9mm, 4 in. barrel, many thousands produced, "S/42" stamped rear toggle, chamber dated 1936-1940. One of the most frequently encountered WWII military Lugers.

	N/A	$875	$675	$525	$425	$375	$350

Add $100 for original holster in average+ condition.
Add 25% for matching mag.
Add 100% for 2 matching mags.
Add 75% for Navy markings.
Add 20% for 1936 date.
Add 30% for "strawed" 1937 date.
The last regular production S/42 Models were mfg. approx. April of 1939.

MAUSER PERSIAN (IRANIAN) CONTRACT — 9mm, 4 and 8 in. barrels, 1,000 — 8 in. mfg., and 1,000 — 4 in. mfg., Farsi numerals.

		100%	98%	95%	90%	80%	70%	60%
4 in. barrel		N/A	$3,750	$3,200	$2,750	$2,250	$2,000	$1,750
Artillery (8 in.)		N/A	$2,400	$2,000	$1,800	$1,650	$1,475	$1,200

Add 50% for Artillery with matching rig.
This variation became less desirable after the U.S. hostage situation occurred in Iran.

1936-1942 DATED MAUSER BANNER — 9mm, 4 in. barrel, over 1,000 mfg., commercial and contract sales. No sear safety, often have strawed small parts.

	N/A	$1,500	$1,050	$800	$700	$600	$500

MAUSER BANNER DUTCH CONTRACT — 9mm, 4 in. barrel, 1,000 mfg., safety marked "Rust". Dated 1936-1940.

	N/A	$2,100	$1,500	$1,000	$600	$500	$400

Add 25% for 1936, 1937, 1938, or 1939 chamber date.

MAUSER BANNER SWEDISH CONTRACT — 275 mfg. in 9mm, 4¾ in. barrels, dated 1938, 25 mfg. in 9mm, dated 1939, 30 mfg. in 7.65mm, dated 1939, very rare in 7.65mm dated 1940.

	N/A	$2,700	$1,800	$1,200	$695	$600	$500

Add 15% for 7.65mm cal. (4$E3/4 in. barrel).

L

Grading	100%	98%	95%	90%	80%	70%	60%

CODE "S/42" COMMERCIAL CONTRACT — 9mm, 4 in. barrel, a few hundred produced, dated 1938. Commercial proof marks only.

	N/A	$1,200	$975	$750	$650	$550	$500

CODE "42" — 9mm, 4 in. barrels, dated 1939-1940, rear toggle marked "42". One of the most frequently encountered WWII military Lugers. Add 40% for Navy markings.

	N/A	$750	$550	$375	$325	$275	$250

Add $100+ for original holster in average+ condition.

MAUSER BANNER POLICE — approx. 30,000 mfg., dated 1939-1942, police contract, have sear safeties, blued small parts. A few observed dated 1938.

	N/A	$1,500	$1,000	$600	$500	$400	$350

Add 30% with 1938 chamber date (rare).

CODE "41-42" — 9mm, 4 in. barrel, 2-digit date, approx. 7,000 mfg. in January of 1941, "41" dated chamber, "42" code, most 42 dates are reworks.

	N/A	$1,350	$950	$650	$425	$375	$350

Add $125+ for original holster in average+ condition.

CODE "byf" — 9mm, 4 in. barrel, thousands made, chamber dated 41 and 42. Rear toggle is stamped "byf", standard magazine was "fxo" marked and had an un-numbered plastic bottom. One of the most frequently encountered WWII military Lugers.

	N/A	$925	$775	$575	$450	$375	$350

Add 20% for original black bakelite grips.
Add $125 for original holster in average+ condition.
Code "byf" Lugers with black bakelite grips are referred to as the "Black Widow" variation.

AUSTRIAN BUNDES HEER — 9mm, 4 in. barrel, several hundred produced, Austrian Federal Army, no serial letter suffix-same ser. placement as KU. Rarely encountered in mint condition.

	N/A	$1,400	$1,000	$950	$825	$750	$650

MAUSER 1934 CODE BYF, S/42 AND 42 KU — 3,500 mfg. Post-1942 Luftwaffe subcontract.

	N/A	$1,700	$1,300	$950	$825	$750	$650

LUGER: REWORKS

DEATH'S HEAD REWORK — 9mm, 4 in. barrel, very rare, possible early SS unit issue. Most are fakes.

	N/A	$1,800	$995	$850	$700	$600	$450

SIMSON REWORK — 9mm, 4 in. barrel, DWM toggles, Simpson Eagle proofs on reworked parts.

	N/A	$750	$550	$450	$375	$325	$295

DOUBLE DATED DWM/ERFURT — 9mm, 4 or 8 in. barrel, very scarce. 1920 over 1910-1918 chamber dates. Often with sear safety and mag. safety remnant.

	N/A	$795	$500	$300	$275	$250	$225

Add 75% for intact mag. safety.
Add 40% for 8 in. barrel.

KONZENTRATION LUGER REWORK — 9mm, 4 in. barrel, 200-300 marked "KI 1933" and issued to guards working in the first concentration camps - most went to Dachau. Most are fakes.

	N/A	$1,100	$850	$600	$475	$400	$350

LUGERS: SIMSON MFG.

SIMSON & COMPANY — 7.65mm or 9mm, $3\frac{7}{8}$ or 4 in. barrel, military and limited commercial sales, many thousands produced, but rarely found.

	N/A	$1,300	$800	$650	$500	$450	$375

L

Grading	100%	98%	95%	90%	80%	70%	60%

SIMSON MILITARY DATED — 9mm, 4 in. barrel, 2,000 mfg., dated 1925.

| | N/A | $2,000 | $1,500 | $1,000 | $800 | $675 | $550 |

This model is most commonly encountered with a 1925 chamber date.

SIMSON S CODE — 9mm, 4 in. barrel, less than 1,000 mfg. Rare.

| | N/A | $1,600 | $1,200 | $975 | $675 | $550 | $475 |

LUGERS: SWISS BERN

1906 BERN — 7.65mm, 4¾ in. barrel, "Waffenfabrik Bern" on toggle, Swiss military, bordered checkered walnut grips, exactly 17,874 mfg.

| | N/A | $2,075 | $1,400 | $1,000 | $800 | $600 | $500 |

1929 SWISS BERN — 7.65mm, 4¾ in. barrel, 29,857 mfg., many machining changes to simplify production, straight front grip strap, P prefix designates commercial model, brown or black plastic grips.

| | N/A | $1,775 | $1,100 | $900 | $800 | $600 | $500 |

Add 20% for ribbed plastic grips and mag. bottom.

LUGERS: KDF, INTERARMS, STOEGER, & RECENT IMPORT

Note: Post-WWII Lugers have been manufactured by Mauser Werke in Oberndorf, W. Germany during the 1970s, and by both Stoeger Industries and Mitchell Arms (see separate listing under Mitchell Arms) in recent years. Currently, the Stoeger Luger is the only Luger available for sale domestically. Earlier Mauser importation was by Precision Imports, Inc. located in San Antonio, TX and Interarms of Alexandria, VA (and so marked on these guns).

Prices below for 100% condition Lugers assume NIB status. If without box and accessories, deduct 25%.

INTERARMS MAUSER P.08 — 7.65 and 9mm, 4 or 6 in. barrel, fully-contoured front grip strap.

| | $795 | $525 | $450 | $400 | $375 | $350 | $300 |

INTERARMS "SWISS-STYLE" MAUSER EAGLE — 9mm or 7.65mm, "straight" front grip strap, American eagle logo on top of frame.

| | $695 | $475 | $425 | $375 | $350 | $325 | $275 |

Add 10% for 6 in. barrel in 9mm.

STOEGER .22 CAL. LUGER — .22 LR cal., toggle action, all steel construction, 4½ in. barrel, 10 shot mag. capacity, previously mfg. in the U.S. until 1985.

| | $150 | $125 | $100 | $85 | $70 | $60 | $50 |

Last Mfg.'s Sug. Retail was $200.

▲ *"1 of 1,000"* — 1,000 mfg. in 1984-85, includes wooden box and extra mag.

| | $295 | $225 | $175 | | | | |

STOEGER LUGER — 9mm Para., choice of 4 or 6 (Navy) in. barrel, stainless steel construction, choice of polished stainless or matte black (new 1996) upper frame finish, American eagle engraved on top of frame, curved front grip strap, 7 shot mag., plastic mag. bottom, approx. 30 oz. New 1994.

| Mfg.'s Sug. Retail | $695 | $625 | $550 | $495 | | | |

Add $65 for matte black finish.

NEW MODEL CARBINE WITH STOCK — 9mm Para., authentic reproduction of the original Luger Carbine complete with matching stock, accessories, and case.

| Mfg.'s Sug. Retail | $7,431 | $4,995 | $3,850 | $2,000 | | | |

Manufacture has been disc. but limited quantities are still available through Interarms.

L

Grading	100%	98%	95%	90%	80%	70%	60%

CARTRIDGE COUNTER — left grip is slotted and contains a numbered metal strip. Introduced 1983.

| Mfg.'s Sug. Retail | $3,865 | $2,650 | $1,550 | $950 |

Manufacture has been disc. but limited quantities are still available through Interarms.

COMMEMORATIVE BULGARIAN — 100 available on U.S. market.

$1,800 $1,200 $800

COMMEMORATIVE RUSSIAN — 100 available on U.S. market.

$1,800 $1,200 $800

▲ *Matched pair of each*

$4,000 $2,550 $1,850

MAUSER SPORT PARABELLUM — 10 each, 7.65mm and 9mm, imported target barrel and adj. sights.

$2,500 $2,000 $1,250

MAUSER SPORT PARABELLUM

▲ *Consecutive pair* — 7.65mm or 9mm.

$4,250 $3,175 $1,950

LUGERS: SPECIAL INTEREST

SPANDAU LUGER — 200 mfg. as prototype in 1918, 10 known. Controversial.

Prices vary substantially on this "variation" and are not predictable.

M04/05 G.L. BABY LUGER — 7.65mm or 9mm, 3¼ in. barrel, G.L. proofed, hand-made under Georg Luger's supervision, two known to exist. Made with shortened barrel, mag., and grip frame.

BABY LUGER 1925/26 — Prototype, .380/.32 ACP, 4 mfg., only 1 known is .380. Only Luger documented by the manufacturer.

VONO REWORK — 7.65mm or 9mm, 4 in. barrel, commercial, rework by W.P. Von Nordheim, extremely rare variation.

$1,500 $1,275 $1,050 $900 $800 $700 $600

1900 DWM CARBINE — 7.65mm, 11¾ in. barrel, 100 mfg., only one known to exist. Characterized by "Ski slope" sight on rear toggle.

1907 U.S. ARMY TEST TRIAL — .45 cal., at least four mfg., three known to exist. BIG bucks.

CONVERSIONS: JOHN MARTZ — John Martz of Lincoln, CA has converted P.38s and WWI or WWII Lugers into various configurations since 1968. These conversions are known for their quality workmanship and functional accuracy. Below is a generalized listing of variations he has fabricated and their values to date with production totals.

▲ *.380 ACP Baby Luger* — 6 mfg. (disc.).

$5,500 $3,200 $2,400

▲ *7.65mm Baby Luger (Grip Safety)* — 16 mfg.

$4,500 $3,750 $3,000

▲ *9mm Baby Luger* — 127 mfg., 2 to 3 in. barrel.

$2,500 $2,000 $1,500

▲ *Standard .45 ACP Luger* — 48 mfg., .45 ACP, fixed sights, 2¾ - 8 in. barrel.

$5,500 $3,750 $3,000

▲ *Navy Model* — .45 ACP, 6 or 8 in. barrel, adj. rear Navy sight, 48 mfg. total (disc.).

$5,000 $3,950 $3,100

Add 10% for Navy Model with 100-200 meter rear sight.

▲ *Navy Model Ltd. Edition* — .38 Super, 6 in. barrel, adj. rear Navy sight, 10 mfg. (disc.).

$5,550 $4,250 $3,250

Subtract 10% for fixed rear sight (standard model with 4 in. barrel).

L

Grading	100%	98%	95%	90%	80%	70%	60%

▲ *Standard Model* — .38 Super, 4 to 8 in. barrel, fixed sight, 2 mfg.

	100%	98%	95%
	$5,500	$3,750	$3,000

▲ *Target Luger* — .22 Mag., 6 or 8 in. barrel, fixed sight, 5 mfg. (disc.).

	100%	98%	95%
	$6,750	$4,250	$3,200

▲ *Luger Carbines (with shoulder stock)* .22 Mag. (disc.), 7.65mm Para., 9mm Para., or .38 Super cal., 11-18 in. barrel with adj. rear sights. Disc.

	100%	98%	95%
	$6,950	$4,350	$3,200

    Add 20% for .22 Mag. cal. (2 mfg.).

    81 Luger carbines with 16 in. barrels were mfg. with shoulder stocks.

    31 Luger carbines with 12 in. barrels were mfg. w/o shoulder stocks.

▲ *Experimental Lugers* — experimental pistols have been made in .40 S&W (disc.), .41 AE (disc.), and .357 Mag. Most have 8 in. barrels (except for .40 S&W cal., disc.). Extreme rarity (and not for sale status) precludes accurate price evaluation.

LUGERS: ACCESSORIES

.22 CALIBER CONVERSION UNITS:

ERMA — (POSTWAR-GREEN CARD BOARD BOX)

	100%	98%	95%	90%	80%	70%	60%
	$350	$320	$295	$275	$250	$225	$200

ERMA-PREWAR IN WOODEN BOX — Pre-war in wooden box - deduct 20% for mismatched. Add 20% for Nazi Navy property numbered.

	100%	98%	95%	90%	80%	70%	60%
	$825	$750	$650	$550	$550	$430	$400

DETACHABLE STOCKS:

ARTILLERY TYPE FLAT BOARD

	100%	98%	95%	90%	80%	70%	60%
	$325	$250	$200	$165	$135	$120	$110

NAVAL-TYPE FLAT BOARD

	100%	98%	95%	90%	80%	70%	60%
	$1,250	$995	$750	$600	$450	$410	$350

CARBINE CONTOURED (ORIGINAL)

	100%	98%	95%	90%	80%	70%	60%
	$2,250	$1,775	$1,200	$900	$850	$750	$700

HOLLOW ARTILLERY HOLSTER TYPE — hollow wood broomhandle type-very rare (watch for fakes).

	100%	98%	95%	90%	80%	70%	60%
	$6,750	$6,000	$5,500	$5,000	$4,500	$4,000	$3,500

IDEAL TELESCOPING WITH GRIPS — mfg. U.S. by Ideal Corp.

	100%	98%	95%	90%	80%	70%	60%
	$1,600	$1,200	$800	$700	$600	$550	$500

"SNAIL" DRUM MAGAZINE:

1ST ISSUE

	100%	98%	95%
	$875	$700	$500

2ND ISSUE

	100%	98%	95%
	$700	$625	$475

LOADING TOOL

	100%	98%	95%
	$550	$500	$450

ARTILLERY HOLSTER RIG, COMPLETE

	100%	98%	95%
	$925	$775	$575

    Subtract 20% if shoulder strap is missing.

NAVAL HOLSTER RIG, COMPLETE

	100%	98%	95%	90%	80%	70%	60%
	$3,500	$3,000	$2,500	$2,000	$1,500	$1,200	$1,000

L

LUNA

Previous manufacturer located in Germany.

Grading	100%	98%	95%	90%	80%	70%	60%

SINGLE SHOT

SINGLE SHOT TARGET RIFLE — falling block action, .22 LR and .22 Hornet, 20 in. barrel, adj. sights, target type stocks, pre-WWII.

	100%	98%	95%	90%	80%	70%	60%
	$990	$880	$800	$690	$605	$550	$495

MODEL 200 FREE PISTOL — .22 LR, 11 in. barrel, blue, target sights, checkered target grips, pre-WWII.

	100%	98%	95%	90%	80%	70%	60%
	$1,100	$990	$855	$770	$660	$605	$525

L

M section

MAC (MILITARY ARMAMENT CORP.)

Please refer to FMJ and Ingram sections in this text. MAC is located in Copperhill, TN (please refer to the FMJ listing in the Trademark Index for current information).

MAS

Manufacture D'Armes St. Etienne (MAS) located in France.
Please refer to the French Military heading in this text.

MBA GYROJET

Previous manufacturer (1966-1969) located in San Ramon, CA.

Grading	100%	98%	95%	90%	80%	70%	60%

MARK I GYROJET PISTOL — 12mm or 13mm (no cartridge case), uses spin-stabilized rocket projectiles that accelerate to 1,250 FPS in .12 seconds, 2 in. (rare) or 5 in. barrel, 6 shot semi-auto action drives rocket projectile (primer activated) into fixed firing pin, smooth walnut grips, black, antique nickel, or gold-plated finish, 13 or 16 oz., "A" prefix until ser. no. 49, "B" prefixes followed, there are also other variations and experimental models in addition to the production models listed below. Not particularly accurate.

> The rocket ammunition for this model is rare and reports of $20+/round are not uncommon.

▲ *Mark I Model A Cased* — 13mm, black finish, smooth walnut grips, walnut cased with 10 rounds and medal.

	100%	98%	95%	90%	80%	70%	60%
	$1,450	$1,300	$1,100	$950	$875	$795	$700

▲ *Mark I Model B Cased* — 13mm, black, nickel, satin, or green finish, many variations with different grips, casings, and barrel lengths, wood cased.

	100%	98%	95%	90%	80%	70%	60%
	$1,150	$1,000	$900	$800	$700	$600	$500

> Add approx. 25% for satin finish.

▲ *Mark I Model B Uncased or Cardboard* — either with cardboard case or no case, black finish.

	100%	98%	95%	90%	80%	70%	60%
	$595	$525	$450	$400	$360	$330	$300

▲ *Mark II Model C Uncased or Cardboard* — 12mm, black finish, walnut grips.

	100%	98%	95%	90%	80%	70%	60%
	$595	$525	$450	$400	$360	$330	$300

> This variation was manufactured in 12mm to conform with the 1968 GCA, since any caliber over .50 was classified as a destructive device (i.e., 12mm = .49 cal. and 13mm - .51 cal.). In 1982, the 13mm guns were reclassified as curios and relics.

▲ *Mark I Presentation Model* — cased with 10 dummy/live rounds and bronze medal honoring rocket pioneers Robert H. Goddard and Joseph J. Stubbs.

	100%	98%	95%
	$2,250	$1,600	$995

MARK I MODEL A or B CARBINE — 13mm, same action as Mark I pistol, black (Model A) or satin (Model B) finish, full stock with pistol grip extension, 18 in. barrel, nickel finish, 4½ lbs. Limited mfg.

	100%	98%	95%	90%	80%	70%	60%
Model A	$1,695	$1,600	S$1,475	$1,350	$1,225	$1,100	$1,000
Model B	$1,050	$850	$750	$650	$595	$550	$500

MK ARMS INC.

Previous manufacturer located in Irvine, CA until approx. 1992.

M

Grading	100%	98%	95%	90%	80%	70%	60%

RIFLES: SEMI-AUTO

MK 760 — 9mm Para., semi-auto, paramilitary design carbine configuration, steel frame, 16 in. shrouded barrel, fires from closed bolt, 14, 24, or 36 shot mag., parkerized finish, folding metal stock, fixed sights. Mfg. 1983-approx. 1992.

	$575	$525	$475	$415	$375	$340	$310

Last Mfg.'s Sug. Retail was $575.

MKE

Manufacturer located in Ankara, Turkey. Previously distributed by Mandall Shooting Supplies, Inc., located in Scottsdale, AZ.

KIRIKKALE DOUBLE ACTION AUTOMATIC — 7.65mm (disc.) or .380 ACP, 7 shot, blue, fixed sights, checkered plastic grips, this is a close copy of Walther's PP and the Turkish Army's standard service pistol. Disc. 1987.

	$365	$295	$240	$215	$185	$170	$155

Last Mfg.'s Sug. Retail was $395.

Although disc. by the Turkish Government in 1987, Mandall Shooting Supplies still has limited amounts of inventory on this model.

M.O.A. CORPORATION

Manufacturer located in Eaton, OH. Dealer direct sales only.

PISTOLS

Approx. 500-600 Maximum pistols are produced annually.

MAXIMUM — available in 28 standard chamberings between .22 Rimfire and .44 Mag., additional custom calibers are also available upon special order, single shot lever action pistol, falling block action, Chromoly receiver (disc. 1991), Armoloy coated Chromoly (disc. late 1992), or stainless steel (new 1991, standard 1992) receiver, 8¾ (new 1989), 10¾, or 14 in. interchangeable barrel, transfer bar safety, adj. open sights, walnut grips and forearm. New 1986.

Mfg.'s Sug. Retail	$653		$585	$510	$460	$430	$395	$375	$350

Add $52 for scope mounts.
Subtract $85 for steel receiver.
Add $58 for stainless steel barrel on either receiver.
Add $125 for muzzle brake.
Add $164 per extra steel barrel.
Add $222 per extra stainless steel barrel.

Barrels must be fitted to individual receivers at the factory initially. Afterwards, they can be changed by the customer with the spanner wrench (included with extra barrels).

▲ *Carbine Model* — cals. up to .250 Sav., stainless receiver, otherwise similar to Maximum, except has 18 in. barrel. Mfg. 1986-87, reintroduced 1994.

Mfg.'s Sug. Retail	$827		$750	$640	$530	$440	$375	$330	$300

Add $50 for stainless steel barrel.

MAGNUM RESEARCH, INC.

MAGNUM RESEARCH, INC.

Centerfire pistols (Desert Eagle Series) are mfg. by Saco Defense located in Saco, ME beginning late 1995. Previous manufacture was by TAAS/IMI (Israeli Military Industries). .22 Rimfire semi-auto pistols (Mountain Eagle) were previously manufactured by Ram-Line. Single shot pistols (Lone Eagle) are manufactured by Magnum Research sub-contractors. Distributed by Magnum Research, Inc., in Minneapolis, MN. Dealer and distributor sales.

Grading	100%	98%	95%	90%	80%	70%	60%

In addition to the models listed below, Magnum Research can also provide a variety of special order options through their custom shop including a choice of seven different finishes in addition to various sight systems. Prices can be obtained by contacting Magnum Research directly.

PISTOLS

THE MOUNTAIN EAGLE — .22 LR cal., semi-auto single action, 6 (new 1995) or 6½ (disc. 1994) in. polymer and steel barrel, features alloy receiver and polymer technology, matte black finish, adj. rear sight, 15 or 20 shot mag. 21 oz. New 1992.

Mfg.'s Sug. Retail	$239	$185	$155	$135	$115	$100	$85	$75

▲ *Mountain Eagle Compact Edition* — similar to Mountain Eagle, except has 4½ in. barrel with shortened grips, adj. rear sight, 10 or 15 shot mag., plastic case, 19.3 oz. New 1996.

Mfg.'s Sug. Retail	$199	$165	$135	$120	$105	$95	$80	$70

▲ *Mountain Eagle Target Edition* — .22 LR cal., Target variation of the Mountain Eagle, featuring 8 in. accurized barrel, 2-stage target trigger, jeweled bolt, adj. sights with interchangeable blades, 23 oz. New 1994.

Mfg.'s Sug. Retail	$279	$235	$185	$150	$135	$120	$105	$95

PISTOLS: DESERT EAGLE SERIES

Magnum Research also offers a Collector's Edition Presentation Series. Special models include a Gold Edition (serial numbered 1-100), a Silver Edition (serial numbered 101-500), and a Bronze Edition (serial numbered 501-1,000). Each pistol from this series is supplied with a walnut presentation case, 2 sided medallion, and certificate of authenticity. Prices are available upon request by contacting Magnum Research directly.

Alloy frames on the Desert Eagle Series of Pistols were discontinued in 1992. However, if sufficient demand warrants, these models will once again be available to consumers at the same price as the steel frames.

Beginning late 1995, the Desert Eagle frame assembly for the .357 Mag., .44 Mag., and .50 AE cals. is based on the .50 caliber frame. Externally, all three pistols are now identical in size. This new platform called the Desert Eagle Pistol Mark XIX Component System enables .44 Mag. and .50 AE conversions to consist of simply a barrel and a magazine - conversions to or from the .357 Mag. also include a bolt. In addition, the new Desert Eagle also features standard Hogue soft rubber grips.

> Add $195 for custom shop finishes including polished chrome, matte chrome, brushed chrome, bright nickel, satin nickel, polished blue, or polished blue with gold accents. Gold plating is also available for an additional $500.

THE BABY EAGLE — 9mm Para., .40 S&W, or .41 AE cal., double action, all steel construction, 3.62 (9mm Para. only, new 1993) or 4.72 in. barrel, short barrel recoil operation, polygonal rifling, combat styled triggerguard, decocking slide safety or frame mounted safety (Model 9mmF), blued (disc. 1995), standard black (new 1996), or chrome finish, 10 (C/B 1994), 16* (9mm Para.), 11* (.41 AE), or 10 (.40 S&W) shot mag., 38½ oz. Model 9mmFS is short barrel with frame mounted safety. New 1991.

Mfg.'s Sug. Retail	$569	$495	$425	$375	$335	$300	$275	$250

> Add $90 for chrome finish (9mm only beginning 1996).
> Add $239 for conversion kit (9mm to .41 AE or .41 AE to 9mm, includes barrel, spring, and mag.).

MARK XIX .357 MAG. DESERT EAGLE — features .50 cal. frame, standard black finish, 6 or 10 in. barrel, mfg. by Saco beginning late 1995.

Mfg.'s Sug. Retail	$979	$850	$750	$650	$550	$475	$400	$350

> Add $50 for 10 in. barrel.

M

Grading	100%	98%	95%	90%	80%	70%	60%

MARK VII .357 MAG. DESERT EAGLE — .357 Mag., gas operated, semi-auto pistol, 6, 10, or 14 in. barrel lengths, steel (58.3 oz.) or alloy (47.8 oz.) frame, adaptable to .44 Mag. with optional kit, 9 shot mag. (8 for .44 Mag.). Mark VII mfg. 1983-95.

	$685	$575	$500	$455	$415	$380	$355

Last Mfg.'s Sug. Retail was $789.

Add approx. $150 for 10 or 14 in. barrel.
Add $495 for .357 Mag. to .41 Mag./.44 Mag. conversion kit (6 in. barrel).
Add approx. $685 for .357 Mag. to .44 Mag. conversion kit (10 or 14 in. barrel).

▲ *Whitetail Special .357 Mag.* — 14 in. barrel, includes scope mount, target walnut grips, and Desert Eagle premiums. Mfg. 1990-1992.

	$925	$750	$650	$550	$450	$400	$375

Last Mfg.'s Sug. Retail was $1,088.

Add $50 for stainless steel frame.

▲ *Stainless Steel .357 Mag.* — similar to .357 Mag. Desert Eagle, except has stainless steel frame, 58.3 oz. Mfg. 1987-95.

	$750	$650	$550				

Last Mfg.'s Sug. Retail was $839.

Add approx. $150 for 10 or 14 in. barrel.

MARK VII .41 MAG. DESERT EAGLE — .41 Mag., similar to .357 Desert Eagle, 6 in. barrel only, 8 shot mag., steel (62.8 oz.) or alloy (52.3 oz.) frame. Mfg. 1988-95.

	$785	$675	$565	$500	$465	$420	$390

Last Mfg.'s Sug. Retail was $899.

Add $395 for .41 Mag. to .44 Mag. conversion kit (6 in. barrel only).

▲ *Stainless Steel .41 Mag.* — similar to .41 Mag. Desert Eagle, except has stainless steel frame, 58.3 oz. Mfg. 1988-95.

	$825	$700	$550				

Last Mfg.'s Sug. Retail was $949.

MARK XIX .44 MAG. DESERT EAGLE — features .50 cal. frame, standard black finish, 6 or 10 in. barrel, mfg. by Saco beginning late 1995.

Mfg.'s Sug. Retail	$999	$865	$765	$650	$550	$475	$400	$350

Add $50 for 10 in. barrel.

MARK VII .44 MAG. DESERT EAGLE — .44 Mag., similar to .357 Desert Eagle, 8 shot mag., steel (62.8 oz.) or alloy (52.3 oz.) frame. Mfg. 1986-95.

	$785	$675	$565	$500	$465	$420	$390

Last Mfg.'s Sug. Retail was $899.

Add approx. $200 for 10 or 14 in. barrel.
Add $475 for .44 Mag. to .357 Mag. conversion kit (6 in. barrel).
Add $675 for .44 Mag. to .357 Mag. conversion kit (10 or 14 in. barrel).
Add $395 for .44 Mag. to .41 Mag. conversion kit (6 in. barrel).

▲ *Stainless Steel .44 Mag.* — similar to .44 Mag. Desert Eagle, except has stainless steel frame, 58.3 oz. Mfg. 1987-95.

	$825	$700	$550				

Last Mfg.'s Sug. Retail was $949.

Add approx. $210 for 10 or 14 in. barrel.

HUNTER EDITION MARK VII — .357 or .44 Mag., 6 in. barrel with extra 14 in. hunting barrel, includes Leupold 2X EER scope, scope mount. Mfg. late 1987-1993.

	$1,200	$975	$825	$675	$550	$475	$425

Last Mfg.'s Sug. Retail was $1,350.

Add $110 for .44 Mag. cal.

MARK XIX .50 MAG. DESERT EAGLE — features .50 cal. frame, standard black finish, 6 or 10 in. barrel, mfg. by Saco beginning late 1995.

Mfg.'s Sug. Retail	$1,049	$895	$775	$675	$575	$475	$400	$350

Add $50 for 10 in. barrel.

Grading	100%	98%	95%	90%	80%	70%	60%

MARK VII .50 MAG. DESERT EAGLE — .50 AE cal., 6 in. barrel, steel only, black standard finish, 7 shot mag., 72.4 oz. Mfg. 1991-95.

	$1,125	$950	$825	$675	$550	$475	$425

Last Mfg.'s Sug. Retail was $1,249.

> This new cartridge utilizes the same rim dimensions as the .44 Mag. and is available with a 300 grain bullet. The .50 Mag. Action Express cal. has 60% more stopping power than the .44 Mag., with a minimal increase in felt recoil.

PISTOLS: SINGLE SHOT

LONE EAGLE (SSP-91) — .22 LR (disc. 1992), .22 Win. Mag. (disc. 1992), .22 Hornet, .22-250, .223, .243, .30-30, .30-06, .308, 6mmBR (disc. 1992), 7mm-08, 7mmBR, .35 Rem., .357 Max., .358 Win., .44 Mag., .444 Marlin, or 7.62x39mm (new 1996) cal., circular rear breech action, quick change 14 in. barrels (drilled and tapped), black synthetic Valox stock with pistol grip, 4 lbs. 3 oz. - 4 lbs. 7 oz. New in 1991.

Mfg.'s Sug. Retail	$308	$265	$225	$185	$155	$135	$120	$110

Add $35 for adj. hunting sights.
Add $110 for integral muzzle brake on barrel (.30-06, .308 Win., or 7mm-08 cal. only).

RIFLES: BOLT-ACTION

MOUNTAIN EAGLE RIFLE — .270 Win., .280 Rem., .30-06, .300 Win. Mag., .300 Wby. Mag., .338 Win. Mag., .340 Wby. Mag., 7mm Rem. Mag., .375 H&H, or .416 Rem. Mag. cal., Sako action, adj. trigger, 4 or 5 shot mag., match grade Krieger barrel with cut rifling, H-S Precision composite stock with aluminum bedding block, includes carrying case. New 1994.

Mfg.'s Sug. Retail	$1,369	$1,225	$1,025	$875	$750	$625	$550	$495

Add $90 for left-hand action.
Add $300 for .375 H&H or .416 Rem. Mag. cal.

▲ **Varmint Mountain Eagle** — .222 Rem. or .223 Rem. cal., 26 in. stainless steel heavy fluted barrel, w/o sights, approx. 9¾ lbs. New 1996.

Mfg.'s Sug. Retail	$1,429	$1,275	$1,050	$895

MAGTECH

Importer/distributor located in Las Vegas, NV. Manufactured by CBC located in Brazil. Distributor sales only.

RIFLES

MODEL 122 — .22 LR, bolt action, 6 shot detachable clip, safety lever disconnects trigger from firing mechanism, uncheckered hardwood stock, 5.7 lbs. Imported 1992 only.

	$115	$95	$80	$70	$60	$50	$40

Last Mfg.'s Sug. Retail was $131.

SHOTGUNS

MODEL 151 SINGLE SHOT — 12, 16, 20, or .410 ga., 26, 28, or 30 in. barrel, exposed hammer, ejector, front triggerguard opening mechanism, 5 - 6½ lbs. Imported 1992 only.

	$95	$80	$70	$60	$50	$40	$35

Last Mfg.'s Sug. Retail was $109.

MODEL MT-586-2 — 12 ga. only, 3 in. chamber, standard Field model shotgun, 28 in. barrel with fixed chokes, hardwood stock and forearm, double slide bars. Importation began 1993.

Mfg.'s Sug. Retail	$229	$190	$175	$160	$140	$130	$120	$110

The Model MT-586 preceded the MT-586-2, the MT-586 was disc. 1994.

▲ **Model MT-586-2-VR** — similar to Model MT-586, except has choice of 26 or 28 in. VR barrel with interchangeable chokes. Importation began 1993.

Mfg.'s Sug. Retail	$259	$220	$185	$170	$155	$140	$130	$120

M

Grading	100%	98%	95%	90%	80%	70%	60%

MODEL MT-586 SLUG — 12 ga. only, slug gun featuring 24 in. cylinder bore barrel with rifle sights, matte finished metal parts, and special Monte Carlo stock. Imported 1993-95.

	$195	$180	$165	$145	$130	$120	$110

Last Mfg.'s Sug. Retail was $239.

MODEL MT-586.2P — 12 ga. only, 3 in. chamber, slide action, 19 in. cylinder bored barrel, 7 shot mag., double slide bars, steel construction, hardwood stock, 7.3 lbs. Importation began 1992.

Mfg.'s Sug. Retail	$219	$185	$170	$155	$140	$130	$120	$110

MAKAROV

Pistol design originating from Russia. Russian mfg. Makarovs may be found under "Russian Service Pistol and Rifle" heading in this text. Pistols listed below have recently been imported by Century International Arms, Inc. located in St. Albans, VT.

PISTOLS

CHINESE AND GERMAN MAKAROV — 9mm Makarov cal., patterned after the Soviet PM pistol and made in E. Germany by state factories, double action semi-auto, blowback design, all steel, slide mounted safety that doubles as a decocking lever, 3.6 in. barrel, 8 shot mag., 25 oz.

No Mfg.'s Retail	$185	$145	$125	$105	$95	$85	$75

The importation of this type of pistol has been increased beginning 1992, since import restrictions have been lowered due to changes in eastern bloc politics and domestic import laws regarding previous communist bloc countries.

MALIN, F.E.

Previous manufacturer located in England. Previously imported by Saxon Arms, Inc. located in Clearwater, FL. Charles Boswell purchased Malin shortly before manufacture stopped.

SHOTGUNS: O/U AND SxS

BOXLOCK — made to individual order, choice of game scene engraving, Anson & Deeley boxlock actions, select European hybrid walnut, double triggers, leather cased, current manufacture. Prices start at $3,750 and each shotgun is priced per individual special order.

SIDELOCK — made to individual order, choice of game scene engraving, H&H sidelock action, select European hybrid walnut, double triggers, leather cased, current manufacture. Prices start at $5,000 and each shotgun is priced per individual special order.

MAMBA

Previously mfg. by Viper Mfg. Co. (a division of Sandock Austral Boksburg) located in South Africa.

AUTO PISTOL — 9mm Para., less than 80 imported into the U.S.

Rarity factor precludes accurate pricing, values vary greatly in different regions.

MANCHESTER ARMS INC.

Previous manufacturer located in Lenoir, TN.

COMMANDO MARK 45 — .45 ACP cal., paramilitary type design with detachable mag., wood pistol grip, 5 in. barrel with muzzle brake. Disc.

	$450	$395	$350	$300	$265	$235	$200

MANDALL SHOOTING SUPPLIES, INC.

Importer/distributor/retailer located in Scottsdale, AZ.

Mandall Shooting Supplies distributes/imports various firearms including pistols, revolvers, rifles, shotguns, as well as other models. Most of these firearms can be located under their individual trademark headings and include Bretton, Britarms, Cabanas, Erma-Werke, FAS, Gaucher, Hammerli, Domino, Korth,

Grading	100%	98%	95%	90%	80%	70%	60%

Krico rifles, Mandall private label shotguns, Sig, Sig-Hammerli, Tanner rifles, Techni-Mec, Zanardini, and A. Zoli shotguns and rifles.

Due to the fluctuation of the U.S. dollar against the currencies of other countries, the above trademarks can change price during the course of a year. For this reason, Mandall Shooting Supplies, Inc. should be contacted directly for current pricing and special order questions.

COACH SHOTGUN — 12, 16, or 20 ga., SxS sidelock shotgun with either external hammers or hammerless, 18, 26, 28, or 30 in. barrels, DT, sling swivels, mfg. in Spain.

	100%	98%	95%	90%	80%	70%	60%
Mfg.'s Sug. Retail $500	$465	$390	$365	$330	$300	$270	$240

MANNLICHER SCHOENAUER SPORTING RIFLES

Manufactured by Steyr, Daimler, Puch, in Austria from 1850s-present. Please refer to Steyr-Mannlicher in this text for current manufactured rifles.

RIFLES: PRE-WWII BOLT ACTIONS

Add approx. $175-$200 for all takedown pre-war models listed below.

MODEL 1903 CARBINE — 6.5x54mm Mannlicher Schoenauer cal., bolt action, 5 shot, 17.7 in. barrel, rotary mag., two leaf rear sight, double set trigger, full length stock.

	100%	98%	95%	90%	80%	70%	60%
	$1,050	$875	$770	$550	$470	$385	$330

This caliber may also be referred to as 6.5x53mm.

This model is normally encountered in poor condition.

MODEL 1905 CARBINE — similar to Model 1903, except 9x56mm Mannlicher Schoenauer cal. only, 19.7 in. barrel.

	100%	98%	95%	90%	80%	70%	60%
	$900	$775	$500	$395	$295	$220	$200

This model is normally encountered in poor condition. It is perhaps the least desirable of pre-war models because of the wide variation in bore diameters.

MODEL 1908 CARBINE — similar to Model 1905, except in 8x56mm Mannlicher Schoenauer cal. only.

	100%	98%	95%	90%	80%	70%	60%
	$900	$700	$550	$350	$310	$250	$200

This model is frequently noticed in better condition factors. Some exceptional takedown variations also exist within this model.

MODEL 1910 CARBINE — similar design to the Model 1905, except originally chambered for 9.5x56mm Mannlicher, .375 Express, or 9.5x57mm Mauser, this model was the predecessor of the post-war Model 1924.

	100%	98%	95%	90%	80%	70%	60%
	$1,050	$875	$770	$550	$470	$385	$330

MODEL 1924 CARBINE — similar to 1905, except .30-06.

	100%	98%	95%	90%	80%	70%	60%
	$995	$795	$695	$550	$450	$300	$200

HIGH VELOCITY SPORTING RIFLE — bolt action, 7x64 Brenneke, .30-06, 8x60 Mag., 9.3x62mm, 10.75x68mm, 23.6 in. barrel, 3 leaf sight, half stock.

	100%	98%	95%	90%	80%	70%	60%
	$1,050	$850	$650	$475	$400	$325	$200

Add $200 for 10.75x68mm, 7x64, or 8x60 cal.

RIFLES: POST-WWII BOLT ACTION

Values below represent standard models with no engraving. Original engraving will add at least $200 to prices listed below with some heavily engraved "Alpine" models selling for large premiums. A variation of the 1950-1952 Series is called the "GK" because of its traditionally styled European stock - which is a variant of the pre-war style and approaches the design of the Model 1961 MCA. Of the calibers listed below for post-WWII models, the 6.5x54mm is considered one of the most desirable, as well as the 9.3x62mm.

In 1951, Steyr (at Stoeger's request) made the following changes to the Model 1950 (named Improved Model 1950). These include: an ebony tip and fuller forend were added in addition to a left-side dummy plate cuts for side mount, left-side of

M

Grading	100%	98%	95%	90%	80%	70%	60%

receiver was flattened to facilitate side scope mount, flatter bolt handle requiring slot inside of stock.

In 1952, changes included a carved cheekpiece, change from ¾ in. sling swivels to 1 in., swept back bolt handle, wood on left-side of stock over the dummy sideplate cutout thickened to strengthen the stock with a side mount in place, and removal of loading ears and clip guides, thereby streamlining the receiver and enabling lower scope mounting.

At one time Stoeger listed 18 versions of the M1950-52 family defined as #S-1 through #S-18 with three major differences existing within each block of Model 1950, Improved Model 1950, and Model 1952. The differences were: single and double set triggers (DST), rifle or carbine style, 6.5mm Carbine, single trigger or DST.

MODEL 1950 — various cals. including .244 Rem., .257 Roberts, .270 Win., .280 Rem., .30-06, .358 Win., 6.5x54mm (very desirable), 7x57mm, 8x57mm Mauser, or 9.3x62mm Mauser, bolt action, 5 shot rotary mag., 24 in. barrel, low bolt handle, half length stock, ebony forearm. Mfg. 1950-1952.

	$800	$675	$600	$450	$395	$350	$300

MODEL 1950 CARBINE — similar to Model 1950, except has 20 in. barrel, full length stock. Mfg. 1950-1952.

	$800	$675	$600	$450	$395	$350	$300

MODEL 1950 CARBINE 6.5 — similar to Model 1950 Carbine, except 6.5x54mm cal., 18½ in. barrel. Mfg. 1950-1952.

	$895	$675	$600	$500	$425	$375	$295

Deduct 50% if encountered with oversized bore (over .265 in.).

IMPROVED MODEL 1952 — same specifications as Model 1950, except swept back bolt handle. Mfg. 1952-1956.

	$725	$625	$550	$475	$425	$375	$295

IMPROVED MODEL 1952 CARBINE — .257 Roberts, .270 Win., 7x57mm, or .30-06 cal., swept bolt handle, otherwise similar to Model 1950 Carbine.

	$800	$675	$600	$450	$395	$350	$300

IMPROVED MODEL 1952 6.5 CARBINE — similar to Model 1952 Carbine, except 6.5mm, 18½ in. barrel. Mfg. 1952-1956.

	$900	$750	$575	$500	$450	$425	$385

MODEL 1956 RIFLE — similar to Improved Model 1952, except .243 and .30-06 cals., new high comb stock design, 22 in. barrel, half length stock. Mfg. 1956-1960.

	$625	$540	$450	$400	$350	$325	$295

▲ *Model 1956 Magnum* — includes .257 Wby., .458 Win. Mag., 6.5x68mm, or 8x68mm cal.

	$875	$800	$750	$650	$575	$500	$460

MODEL 1956 CARBINE — similar to Model 1956 Rifle, except .243, 6.5x53mm, .257 Roberts, .270, 7mm, .30-06, or .308 cal., 20 in. barrel, full length stock. Mfg. 1956-1960.

	$800	$675	$600	$450	$395	$350	$300

MODEL 1961 MCA RIFLE — similar to Model 1956 Rifle, except Monte Carlo stock. Mfg. 1961-1971.

	$775	$650	$550	$450	$395	$350	$295

MODEL 1961 MCA CARBINE — similar to Model 1956 Carbine, except Monte Carlo stock. Mfg. 1961-1971.

	$800	$700	$575	$495	$450	$395	$350

RIFLES: CURRENT MANUFACTURE

Current production guns are now called Steyr-Mannlicher models and can be located under this trademark in the S section.

MANUFRANCE

Manufacturer located in St. Etienne, France since 1902.

Manufrance currently manufactures many models in both rifles and shotguns that are not being imported in the U.S. at this time. Those models are not covered in this book.

Grading	100%	98%	95%	90%	80%	70%	60%

AUTO SHOTGUN — 12 ga., 26, 28, or 30 in. imp. cyl., mod. and full, 2¾ or 3 in. chamber, gas operated, walnut stock, black matte receiver, VR.

	100%	98%	95%	90%	80%	70%	60%
	$330	$305	$290	$275	$255	$240	$220

FALCOR — O/U, 12 ga., VR, 26 in. imp. cyl. and mod., 28 in. mod. and full, SST, auto ejector, chrome lined barrel, walnut checkered stock.

	100%	98%	95%	90%	80%	70%	60%
	$715	$665	$635	$605	$550	$495	$470

MANURHIN

Manufactured by Manurhin Equipment since 1972, located in Mulhouse, France. Previously owned by Matra Manurhin Defense. Currently imported and distributed by Sphinx U.S.A. located in Meriden, CT and on a special order only basis by ABO Industries located in San Diego, CA (previously Atlantic Business Organization located in New York, NY until 1992). Previously imported (1984-86) directly by Matra-Manurhin International, Inc., located in Fort Lauderdale, FL.

Manurhin in France has been manufacturing models PP, PPK, and PPK/S since 1952. Previously, they were imported by Interarms out of Alexandria, VA. In 1984, Manurhin imported their new models directly and they were marked Manurhin on the left front slide assembly. This differs from the previous Walther stamped guns. Also, no Interarms logo appears on the right side.

HANDGUNS: CURRENT IMPORTATION

MODEL PP — .380 ACP cal., 3⅛ in. barrel, 7 shot mag., blue only, 24 oz., all steel construction, double action with positive steel hammer block safety. Importation resumed 1988.

Mfg.'s Sug. Retail	$495	$425	$360	$320	$275	$230	$205	$185

This model is imported by ABO Industries located in San Diego, CA.

MODEL PPK/S — .380 ACP cal., 3¼ in. barrel, 7 shot mag., blue only, all steel construction, double action with positive steel hammer block safety, 23 oz. Importation resumed 1988.

Mfg.'s Sug. Retail	$495	$425	$360	$320	$275	$230	$205	$185

This model is imported by ABO Industries located in San Diego, CA.

MODEL 73 DEFENSE REVOLVER — .357 Mag./.38 Spl., 6 shot, 2½, 3, or 4 in. barrel, checkered wood stocks, mfg. to precise tolerances, 31-33½ oz. Importation began 1988.

Mfg.'s Sug. Retail	$1,340	$1,200	$1,000	$850	$725	$600	$500	$425

MODEL 73 GENDARMERIE — .357 Mag./.38 Spl., 6 shot, similar to Model 73 Defense except has adj. sighting components and also is offered in 5¼, 6, or 8 in. barrel lengths. Manufactured for police requirements. Importation began 1988.

Mfg.'s Sug. Retail	$1,885	$1,675	$1,125	$900	$750	$625	$525	$450

MODEL 73 SPORT — .357 Mag./.38 Spl., 6 shot, sport shooting features include minimized hammer stroke, micrometer rear sight, and free release trigger with fitted adj. sights. Importation began 1988.

Mfg.'s Sug. Retail	$1,885	$1,675	$1,125	$900	$750	$625	$525	$450

MODEL 73 CONVERTIBLE — includes choice of .22 LR/.38 Spl. or .22 LR/.32 cal. cylinders and barrels (5¾ in. for .38 Spl. and 6 in. for .22 LR/.32). Imported 1988-95.

	$1,925	$1,675	$1,325	$1,125	$950	$800	$700

Last Mfg.'s Sug. Retail was $2,200.

▲ *3 Cylinder Model 73 Convertible* — similar to Model 73 Convertible except includes 3 calibers (.22 LR, .32, and .38 Spl.). Imported 1988-95.

	$2,375	$1,950	$1,700	$1,375	$1,150	$975	$850

Last Mfg.'s Sug. Retail was $2,690.

M

Grading	100%	98%	95%	90%	80%	70%	60%

MODEL 73 SILHOUETTE — .22 LR or .357 Mag. cal., Silhouette variation with fully adj. rear sight and either 10 (.22 LR) or 10¾ (.357 Mag.) in. heavy barrel with full shroud, contoured wooden target grips, approx. 4 lbs. Importation began 1988.

Mfg.'s Sug. Retail	$1,975	$1,750	$1,175	$925	$750	$625	$525	$450

Add $13 for .357 Mag. cal.

MODEL MR 88 — .357 Mag. cal., stainless steel, 4, 5, or 6 in. barrel, fixed sights, rubber grips. Importation began 1996.

Mfg.'s Sug. Retail	$878	$775	$625	$450

MODEL MR 96 — .357 Mag. cal., black finish, 3, 4, 5, or 6 in. VR barrel, adj. rear sight, ergonomic rubber grips. Importation began 1996.

Mfg.'s Sug. Retail	$858	$750	$615	$425	$375	$350	$325	$295

This model allows the user to unlock, swing the cylinder out, and eject the cases with one movement of the hand.

PISTOLS: PREVIOUS IMPORTATION

P-1 — 9mm, similar to W. German P-38, double action, 5 in. barrel.

$440	$380	$325	$275	$230	$205	$185

MODEL P4 — 9mm, P.38 variation issued to the French Police when in Berlin during post-WWII.

$495	$440	$380	$325	$275	$230	$200

MODEL PP — .22 LR, .32 ACP, or .380 ACP cal., 3⅞ in. barrel, 10 shot mag.-.22 LR, 8 shot mag.-.32 ACP, 7 shot mag.-.380 ACP, blue only, all steel construction, double action with positive steel hammer block safety, 24 oz. Add $10 for .22 LR cal., $46 for Durgarde finish. Imported 1984-86.

$360	$320	$275	$230	$205	$185	$170

Last Mfg.'s Sug. Retail was $419.

▲ *Collector Model* — blue finish, special engraving. Imported 1986 only.

$465	$415	$350

Last Mfg.'s Sug. Retail was $529.

▲ *Presentation Model* — blue finish, special ornamentation. Imported 1986 only.

$720	$650	$500

Last Mfg.'s Sug. Retail was $819.

Also available with various engraving options in either blue, nickel, or gold finish - prices range from $222 - $540.

MODEL PPK/S — .22 LR, .32 ACP, or .380 ACP cal., 3¼ in. barrel, 10 shot mag.-.22 LR, 8 shot mag.-.32 ACP, 7 shot mag.-.380 ACP, blue only, all steel construction, double action with positive steel hammer block safety, 23 oz. Add $10 for .22 LR cal. Imported 1984-86.

$360	$320	$275	$230	$205	$185	$170

Last Mfg.'s Sug. Retail was $419.

▲ *PPK/S Durgarde* — similar to above, only with bonded brushed chrome finish. Add $14 for .22 LR cal.

$410	$365	$325	$290	$265	$250	$240

Last Mfg.'s Sug. Retail was $465.

▲ *Collector Model* — blue finish, special engraving. Imported 1986 only.

$465	$415	$350

Last Mfg.'s Sug. Retail was $529.

▲ *Presentation Model* — blue finish, special ornamentation. Imported 1986 only.

$720	$650	$500

Last Mfg.'s Sug. Retail was $819.

Also available with various engraving options in either blue, nickel, or gold finish - prices range from $222-$540.

PP SPORT — .22 LR cal. only, double action, 6.1 or 8.1 in. barrel, blue finish only, precision adj. sights, contoured plastic grips with thumb rest, 25 oz. New Manurhin design for 1985. Imported 1984-86.

$545	$485	$430	$385	$325	$290	$270

Last Mfg.'s Sug. Retail was $635.

M

Grading	100%	98%	95%	90%	80%	70%	60%

▲ **PP Sport-C** — similar to PP Sport, except has single action with softened trigger.

	$540	$475	$415	$370	$310	$280	$260

Last Mfg.'s Sug. Retail was $635.

MARATHON PRODUCTS, INC.

Previously manufactured by Santa Barbara Armaments exclusively for Marathon Products, Inc. Most of the below listed models were also available in kit form but are not shown in this book.

.22 FIRST SHOT — .22 cal., single shot bolt action, 16½ in. barrel, hardwood stock, open sights, 31 in. total length, 3.8 lbs. Mfg. 1985-87.

	$55	$45	$40	$35	$35	$30	$30

Last Mfg.'s Sug. Retail was $60.

▲ **.22 Super Shot** — similar to First Shot, except with 24 in. barrel and regular dimension stock. Mfg. 1985-87.

	$55	$45	$40	$35	$35	$30	$30

Last Mfg.'s Sug. Retail was $60.

▲ **.22 Hot Shot Pistol** — .22 LR only, bolt action, single shot, fixed sights, 14¾ in. barrel, hardwood stock with target grip configuration. Mfg. 1986-87.

	$55	$45	$40	$35	$35	$30	$30

Last Mfg.'s Sug. Retail was $60.

CENTERFIRE MODEL — .243, .270 Win., 7x57, 7mm Rem. Mag., .30-06, .300 Win. Mag., or .308 Mag. cal., Mauser type bolt action, 5 shot fixed box mag., 24 in. barrel, select walnut with recoil pad, adj. trigger, open sights, 7.9 lbs. Available 1985-86 only.

	$295	$240	$215	$195	$180	$170	$160

Last Mfg.'s Sug. Retail was $320.

MARBLE ARMS & MFG. CO.

Manufacturer located in Gladstone, MI.

In addition to axes and compasses, Marble Arms & Mfg. Co. also manufactured their Game Getter O/U combination gun from approx. 1907 to the late 1920s. During this period of production, the gun underwent quite a few changes including sights (an aperture sight mounted on the rear backstrap was standard until changed to a top frame sight), different configuration folding metal stock, and other changes.

GAME GETTER MODELS — .22 S, L, or LR cal., upper rifled barrel over choice of .44-40 Game Getter/.410 ga. (2 in.) or .410 ga. (2½ in.) smooth bore lower barrel (a few were also mfg. with both barrels bored for .22 LR cal.), choice of 12, 15, or 18 in. separated barrels, folding steel skeleton attached stock, pivoting hammer striker mechanically selects upper or lower barrel, tip-up barrels are opened by pulling triggerguard back, gutta percha or walnut stocks, approx. 3½ lbs.

▲ **Model 1908** — ser. no. range approx. 700-9,999.

	$1,550	$1,400	$1,250	$1,000	$875	$750	$625

▲ **Model 1921** — ser. no. range approx. 10,000-approx. 20,000.

	$1,050	$895	$650	$600	$550	$520	$480

Add $100 for original leather holster in good condition.

There were two Marble's models - the Model 1908 and the Model 1921. The Model 1908 also had a 1908A variation which utilized the Marble's flexible tang sight and a 1908B Model which utilized a filler blank in place of the tang sight. Serialization on the 1908 model was approx. 700-9,999. The grip plates on the Model 1908 were hard rubber with fleur-de-lis design and Marble's logo - the last gun was mfg. May of 1914.

In 1921, a new model was introduced in similar barrel lengths as the Model 1908. Serialization began at 10,001 and went to approx. 20,000. Currently, the 1908 is more desirable since it is a better built gun. The Model 1908 was chambered .22 LR upper barrel and 2 in. .410 ga. or .44 shot or .44 ball bottom barrel. The Model 1921 was chambered similarly, had walnut or plastic grips - also, a few were chambered for 2½ in. A few 1908s were mfg. with bottom barrels in .25-20, .32-20, or .38-40 cal., but specimens are very rare.

Above values assume 18 in. barrels or correct registration on 12 or 15 in. models. Those 12 or 15 in. barreled Game Getters not registered during the 1968 BATF amnesty program

M

are not legally transferable today. If not a legal configuration, values will drop considerably since they are basically a black market item and subject to BATF confiscation.

The lower barrel of this model was capable of shooting .410 ga. 2 in. paper or brass shotshells, .410 ga. 2½ in. paper shotshell (standard configuration), and .410 or .44 cal. round ball cartridges.

MARGOLIN

Russian Target Pistol manufacturer located in the U.S.S.R.

TARGET MODEL — .22 LR, semi-auto, manufactured to precise tolerances, used by some members of the Russian shooting team, basically individually made to shooters specifications, seldomly encountered in the U.S.A., while rare, desirability to date has been limited, current mfg.

Margolin pistols are typically priced in the $475-$750 range, depending on features and assuming 95%+ original condition. While currently imported Chinese copies are considerably less expensive, they do not have the quality (or accuracy) of the Russian Margolins.

MARLIN FIREARMS COMPANY

Marlin has been manufacturing firearms since 1870. From 1969- present manufacture has been located in North Haven, CT. Previously, Marlin was manufactured (1870-1969) in New Haven, CT. Distributor sales only.

PISTOLS: DERRINGERS AND REVOLVERS

Research is underway to gather more information on the variety of derringers and revolvers that Marlin mfg. between 1863-1901. While many of these variations sell in the $150-$250 range (average condition), rarer specimens with 90% original condition will be priced higher.

100%	98%	95%	90%	80%	70%	60%	50%	40%	30%	20%	10%

RIFLES: ANTIQUE MANUFACTURE

Values below are for standard models only without special order features.

MODEL 1881 LEVER ACTION — .32-40, .38-55, .40-60, .45-70, or .45-85 cal., tube mag., 28 in. octagonal barrel standard, top ejection, blued finish with case hardened hammer, lever, and butt plate. First models (pre ser. no. 600) are rare, add 200-300% premium. Approx. 20,000 mfg. between 1881-1892.

$1,950	$1,700	$1,450	$1,175	$900	$825	$725	$625	$550	$500	$450	$400

This model came in 3 frame styles for various calibers.
Add approx. 15% for .45-70 cal.

MODEL 1888 LEVER ACTION — .32-20, .38-40, or .44-40 cal., 24 in. octagonal barrel most frequently encountered, top ejection, blued finish with case hardened hammer, lever, and butt plate, short throw lever action principle. Approx. 4,800 mfg. between 1888-1889. Ser. range approx. 19,560 - 27,850.

$2,650	$2,375	$2,075	$1,825	$1,625	$1,400	$1,200	$1,000	$875	$750	$625	$500

MODEL 1889 LEVER ACTION — .25-20 (very rare), .32-20, .38-40, or .44-40 cal., 24 in. octagonal barrel most frequently encountered, side ejection with solid top frame, blued finish with case hardened hammer, lever, and butt plate, short throw lever action principle. Approx. 55,000 mfg. between 1889-1899. Ser. range approx. 25,000-100,000.

$995	$875	$700	$550	$465	$425	$385	$340	$295	$260	$230	$200

Also available as Carbine with either a 15 in. (only 367 mfg.) or 20 in. (approx. 10,000 mfg.) barrel or Musket (30 in. barrel - add 300-500%, very rare).

MODEL 1891 LEVER ACTION — .22 Rimfire and .32 Rimfire/Centerfire, 24 in. octagonal barrel most often encountered, choice of side loading (1st variation) or tube loading (2nd variation), blued finish with case hardened hammer, lever, and butt plate, sear safety system on lever action. Approx. 18,650 mfg. between 1891-1897. Ser. No. range is approx. 37,500-118,000.

$1,800	$1,625	$1,450	$1,150	$995	$925	$850	$775	$695	$625	$550	$475

Add 50% for deluxe, pistol grip checkered model.
Subtract 40% for tube loading model (.32 Centerfire).
Add $100 each for special sights (including correct Lyman, Marbles, Beeches combo, etc.).

M

100%	98%	95%	90%	80%	70%	60%	50%	40%	30%	20%	10%

MODEL 1892 LEVER ACTION — .22 S, L, or LR, .32 S or L, 16, 24, 26, or 28 in. barrel, tubular mag., open sight, plain straight stock. Mfg. 1892-1916.

| $1,575 | $1,350 | $1,175 | $875 | $725 | $675 | $600 | $525 | $475 | $425 | $385 | $340 |

    Add 10% for .22 cal.
    Subtract 10% for .32 cal.
    Add $100 each for special sights (including correct Lyman, Marbles, Beeches combo, etc.).
    .22 cals. will bring a premium in this model.

MODEL 1893 LEVER ACTION — .25-36 Marlin, .30-30, .32 Spl., .32-40, or .38-55 cal., 20-32 in. round or octagonal barrels, case colored receiver, 10 shot tube mag., straight grip stock. Mfg. 1893-1936. Musket model also mfg. - 30 in. barrel and military style forearm.

| $1,795 | $1,525 | $1,300 | $1,100 | $950 | $800 | $600 | $450 | $400 | $375 | $350 | $325 |

    Add 15%-20% for .30-30 or .32 Spl. cal.
    Add approx. 40% for special lightweight model.

    Later production guns were marked "Model'93" and have less value. This model had two barrel variations - one was marked "special smokeless steel" while the other was marked "for Black Powder".

MODEL 1893 CARBINE — .30-30, .32 Spl., .32-40 cal., or .38-55 cal., 15 (only 61 mfg.) or 20 in. round barrel, case colored receiver, 7 shot tube mag., straight or pistol grip stock. Mfg. 1893-1936.

| $1,950 | $1,725 | $1,525 | $1,300 | $1,100 | $950 | $800 | $600 | $450 | $400 | $375 | $350 |

MODEL 1894 LEVER ACTION — .25-20, .32-20, .38-40, or .44-40 cal., case colored receiver, 10 shot tube mag., 24 in. round or octagon barrel, straight or pistol grip stock. Mfg. 1894-1934.

| $1,850 | $1,550 | $1,325 | $1,100 | $950 | $800 | $600 | $450 | $400 | $375 | $350 | $325 |

    Later production guns were marked "Model '94" and have less value. This model was also available in both a Carbine and Musket variation.

MODEL 1895 LEVER ACTION — .33 WCF, .38-56, .40-65, .40-70, .40-82, or .45-70 cal., case colored receiver, 9 shot tube mag., 24 or 26 in. round or octagon barrel standard, other lengths were available, open sights, plain straight or pistol grip stock. Mfg. 1895-1915.

| $2,250 | $1,800 | $1,550 | $1,300 | $1,000 | $850 | $750 | $700 | $650 | $600 | $550 | $525 |

    Premiums exist for .40-70 (approx. 60 mfg.), .45-70, and .45-90 cal.

    In 1912, a lightweight variation was introduced with hard rubber butt plate and half-magazine, cals. were .33 CF and .45-70 (commands a premium), and round barrels were either 22 or 24 in. A Carbine variation was also offered with approx. 200 mfg. - premiums may run as high as 150% over rifle values listed above.

MODEL 1897 LEVER ACTION — .22 S, L, or LR, tube mag., 16, 24, 26, or 28 in. barrel, case colored receiver, takedown, open sights, plain straight or pistol grip stock. Mfg. 1897-1922.

| $1,850 | $1,550 | $1,325 | $1,100 | $950 | $800 | $600 | $450 | $400 | $375 | $350 | $325 |

    16 in. barrel "Bicycle Rifles" will bring a premium of 100%.
    Add $100 each for special sights (including correct Lyman, Marbles, Beeches combo, etc.).

RIFLES: MODERN PRODUCTION

Year of manufacture can be determined from 1946-1968 by the following letter prefix: 1946-C, 1947-D, 1948-E, 1949-F, 1950-G, 1951-H, 1952-J, 1953-K, 1954-L, 1955-M, 1956-N, 1957-P, 1958-R, 1959-S, 1960-T, 1961-U, 1962-V, 1963-W, 1964-Y,Z, 1965-AA, 1966-AB, 1967-AC, 1968-AD.

The models below are listed in numerical sequence to assist quick access.

M

Grading		100%	98%	95%	90%	80%	70%	60%

MODEL MR-7 BOLT ACTION — .270 Win. or 30-06 cal., 4 shot box mag. with removable hinged floorplate, 3 position safety, adj. 3-6 lb. trigger, 22 in. barrel, checkered American walnut stock, cocking indicator, forged receiver, damascened bolt, includes sling swivels, with or without sights, approx. 7 ½ lbs. New 1996.

| Mfg.'s Sug. Retail | $571 | | $475 | $425 | $365 | $315 | $275 | $240 | $215 |

    Add $40 for open sights.

Grading	100%	98%	95%	90%	80%	70%	60%

MODEL 9 CAMP CARBINE SEMI-AUTO — 9mm only, 16½ in. barrel, 12 or 20 shot mag. (disc. 1989), 4 shot clip mag. became standard in 1990, sand blasted steel receiver, open sights, last shot automatic hold-open, 6¾ lbs. New 1985.

Mfg.'s Sug. Retail	$424	$325	$225	$170	$150	$140	$130	$125

Add 10% for nickel plating (mfg. 1991-94, Model 9N).

A new high visibility orange front sight post with cutaway hood was added in 1989.

MODEL 18 SLIDE ACTION — .22 S, L, or LR, tube mag., 20 in. round or octagon barrel, open sight, exposed hammer, plain straight grip stock. Mfg. 1906-1909.

	$330	$250	$195	$165	$125	$100	$85

MODEL 20 SLIDE ACTION — .22 S, L, or LR, 24 in. octagon barrel, open sight, exposed hammer, takedown, plain straight grip stock. Mfg. 1907-1922.

	$300	$250	$195	$165	$125	$100	$85

MODEL 25 SLIDE ACTION — .22 Short, tube mag., 23 in. barrel, open sight, exposed hammer, takedown, plain straight grip stock. Mfg. 1909-1910.

	$360	$275	$220	$185	$150	$120	$95

MODEL 25MB — .22 Mag. cal., bolt action, 16¼ in. micro-groove barrel, 7 shot clip mag., hardwood stock, takedown action, 6 lbs. Mfg. 1987-88 only.

	$145	$115	$95	$85	$75	$70	$65

Last Mfg.'s Sug. Retail was $173.

This model included both a scope and gun case.

MODEL 25MN — .22 Mag. cal., bolt action, 7 shot clip mag., 22 in. barrel, walnut finished hardwood stock (pressed checkering became standard 1994), grooved receiver, adj. rear sight (new 1995), 6 lbs. New 1989.

Mfg.'s Sug. Retail	$198	$155	$115	$90	$80	$75	$70	$65

Add $6 for 4X scope.

MODEL 27 SLIDE ACTION — .25RF, .25-20, or .32-20 cal., ⅔ tube mag., 7 shot, 24 in. octagon barrel, open sight, plain straight grip stock. Mfg. 1910-1916.

	$330	$250	$225	$200	$165	$140	$125

Subtract 15% for .25RF cal.

MODEL 27S — similar to 27, with round or octagonal barrel.

	$330	$250	$195	$140	$110	$100	$85

MODEL 29 SLIDE ACTION — similar to Model 20, with 23 in. round barrel, ½ tube mag. Mfg. 1913-1916.

	$330	$250	$195	$140	$110	$100	$85

MODEL 30/30A LEVER ACTION — .30-30 cal., 20 in. barrel, promotional model mfg. 1964-1983.

	$220	$185	$160	$135	$120	$110	$100

MODEL 30 AS LEVER ACTION — .30-30 cal. only, 20 in. barrel, walnut finish hardwood stock (pressed checkering became standard 1995), open sights (adj. rear sight became standard 1995), no frills version of the 336 CS, 7 lbs. New 1985.

Mfg.'s Sug. Retail	$377	$275	$210	$145	$130	$125	$120	$115

Add $57 for 4X scope.

MODEL 32 SLIDE ACTION — .22 S, L, or LR, ⅔ tube mag., 24 in. octagon barrel, open sight, plain pistol grip stock, hammerless. Mfg. 1914-1915.

	$330	$250	$195	$165	$125	$100	$85

MODEL 1936 RIFLE/CARBINE LEVER ACTION — .30-30 or .32 Spl. cal., 6 shot, 20 or 24 in. barrel, tubular mag., open sights, pistol grip stock, barrel band. Mfg. 1936-1937.

	$350	$300	$275	$250	$200	$175	$150

MODEL 36A RIFLE — similar to Model 1936 Rifle, 24 in. barrel, ⅔ tube mag. Mfg. 1938-1947.

	$275	$250	$200	$165	$150	$125	$110

M

Grading	100%	98%	95%	90%	80%	70%	60%

MODEL 36A-DL — similar to Model 36A, with deluxe checkered stock, sling and swivels. Mfg. 1940-1947.

	$325	$300	$275	$250	$200	$175	$150

MODEL 36RC — .30-30 or .32 Spl. cal., regular carbine variation with 20 in. barrel. Mfg. 1938-1947.

	$275	$220	$195	$165	$140	$110	$95

MODEL 36SC — similar to Model 36RC, except has ⅔ length magazine tube. Mfg. 1938-1947.

	$275	$250	$195	$165	$140	$125	$110

MODEL 37 SLIDE ACTION — similar to Model 29, with 24 in. barrel, full length tube mag. Mfg. 1913-1916.

	$330	$250	$195	$165	$125	$100	$85

MODEL 38 SLIDE ACTION — .22 S, L, or LR, ⅔ tube mag., 24 in. octagon barrel, open sights, hammerless, takedown, plain pistol grip stock. Mfg. 1920-1930.

	$330	$250	$195	$165	$125	$100	$85

MODEL 39 LEVER ACTION — .22 S, L, or LR, 24 in. octagon barrel with tube mag., open sights, takedown, case hardened receiver and lever, S-shaped pistol grip stock, bluing on barrel, forend tip, mag. tube, bolt, hammer, and screws, various qualities of walnut (X, 2X, or 3X), hard rubber buttplate. Approx. 40-50,000 mfg. 1922-1938.

	N/A	N/A	$1,995	$1,575	$1,150	$900	$625

Early models with fancy 2X-3X wood will bring a considerable premium.

Excellent original condition in this model is extremely hard to find since most specimens were well used due to the 16/25 shell mag. capacity, reliability, and the fact that the balance point of the gun (the receiver) normally wore first due to carrying wear. Earlier guns without a prefix or with an S prefix are noted for their superior workmanship and fine finish. Later HS prefix (High Speed) are not quite as valuable as these earlier guns.

MODEL 39A — similar to Model 39, with blued or color case hardened receiver (mfg. 1939-1941, includes first and second variations), round barrel. Introduced 1939.

	100%	98%	95%	90%	80%	70%	60%
Case Hardened Finish	$1,275	$1,050	$875	$650	$495	$425	$375
Blue Finish	$475	$425	$375	$335	$295	$250	$200

Add approx. 75% for third and fourth variations with blue finish.
Add approx. 40% for the fifth variation.

The first variation of the Model 39A mfg. in 1939 is distinguishable by a buttstock and lever similar to those on earlier Model 39s. The second variation mfg. 1940-41 has a rounded lever like current production and no "S" shape to bottom of pistol grip. The third variation has a blued receiver beginning in 1945, no flutes in buttstock comb, a new ramp front sight, hard rubber buttplate, and continued ballard rifling. The fourth variation is similar except for flute in buttstock comb. In 1951, the fifth variation was introduced adding a white plastic spacer to the buttplate. Through 1953, they still maintained the deep ballard rifling.

GOLDEN 39A — similar to Model 39A, with gold-plated trigger, sling swivels. Mfg. 1960-1987.

	$225	$195	$175	$150	$135	$115	$90

MODEL 39A "MOUNTIE" — straight grip stock, slim forearm, otherwise similar to 39A. Mfg. 1953-1972.

	$225	$195	$175	$150	$135	$115	$90

▲ **Model 39A "MOUNTIE" with K prefix** — 24 in. barrel and slender forearm. Mfg. 1953 only.

	$595	$550	$475	$425	$360	$295	$250

90TH ANNIVERSARY 39A — similar to Model 39A, with chrome barrel and action, select checkered walnut stock, carved squirrel on side of butt stock. 500 mfg. in 1961.

	$795	$695	$550	$400	$350	$300	$250

Last Mfg.'s Sug. Retail was $100.

90TH ANNIVERSARY MODEL 39M MOUNTIE CARBINE — similar to 90th Anniversary Model 39A, except 20 in. barrel, straight stock. 500 mfg. in 1960.

	$795	$695	$550	$400	$350	$300	$250

Last Mfg.'s Sug. Retail was $100.

M

Grading	100%	98%	95%	90%	80%	70%	60%

MODEL 39A-DL — similar to 90th Anniversary, with blue barrel and action, regular production. Mfg. 1960-1963.

	$250	$195	$165	$140	$110	$100	$85

MODEL 39A OCTAGON — similar to Golden 39A, with octagon barrel, no pistol grip cap, 2,551 rifles and 2,140 carbines were produced. Mfg. 1973.

	$595	$550	$475	$425	$360	$295	$250

MODEL 39 CARBINE — similar to 39M, with light barrel, ¾ tube mag. Mfg. 1963-1967.

	$225	$195	$175	$150	$135	$115	$90

MODEL 39D — similar to 39M, with pistol grip stock. Mfg. 1971-1973.

	$225	$195	$175	$150	$135	$115	$90

MODEL 39AS — .22 LR cal., current production model, lever action, tube mag., 19 shot, 24 in. barrel, walnut stock (cut checkering became standard 1994), open sights, gold trigger, takedown, 6½ lbs.

Mfg.'s Sug. Retail	$445	$345	$240	$165	$145	$130	$110	$100

This model was previously designated the Model 39A. In 1988, the Model 39AS became the standard production model and included a rebounding hammer and hammer block safety.

MODEL 39TDS — .22 LR cal., carbine variation of the Model 39AS, 16½ in. barrel with open sights, 5¼ lbs. Mfg. 1988-95.

	$345	$240	$175	$155	$135	$120	$110

Last Mfg.'s Sug. Retail was $443.

MODEL 39M — carbine version of Model 39A, 20 in. lightweight barrel, 16 shot tube mag., squared finger lever, 6 lbs. Disc. 1987.

	$225	$180	$155	$145	$130	$110	$100

Last Mfg.'s Sug. Retail was $304.

MODEL 39M OCTAGON — similar to Model 39M, with octagon barrel. Mfg. 1973.

	$595	$550	$475	$425	$360	$295	$250

MODEL 39 CENTURY LTD — Marlin Centennial 1870-1970 Commemorative, 20 in. octagon barrel, select walnut straight stock, brass forearm cap and butt plate, name plate in butt. 35,388 mfg. 1970.

	$395	$340	$275	$195	$180	$155	$140

MODEL 39A ARTICLE II — NRA Centennial Commemorative 1871-1971, "Right to Bear Arms" medallion in receiver, 24 in. octagon barrel, fancy pistol grip stock, brass butt plate and forearm cap. Mfg. 6,244 1971.

	$320	$295	$260	$260	$215	$190	$170

MODEL 39M ARTICLE II CARBINE — similar to 39A Article II, with 20 in. barrel, straight grip stock. Mfg. 3,824.

	$285	$225	$200	$185	$160	$150	$140

MODEL 45 CARBINE — .45 ACP only, 7 shot clip mag., sandblasted steel receiver, 16½ in. barrel, last shot hold open device, adj. rear sight, 6¾ lbs. New 1986.

Mfg.'s Sug. Retail	$424	$325	$225	$170	$150	$140	$130	$125

A new high visibility orange front sight post with cutaway hood was added in 1989.

MODEL 56 — similar to Model 57 Levermatic, with clip mag. Mfg. 1955-1964.

	$175	$150	$125	$100	$85	$75	$65

MODEL 57 LEVERMATIC — .22 S, L, or LR, tube mag., 22 in. barrel, open sight, Monte Carlo pistol grip stock. Mfg. 1959-1965.

	$185	$160	$145	$130	$110	$100	$80

MODEL 57M — Mag. version of Model 57 Levermatic.

	$225	$200	$165	$150	$135	$125	$110

M

Grading	100%	98%	95%	90%	80%	70%	60%

MODEL 60SS SEMI-AUTO STAINLESS — .22 LR, 14 shot tube mag., stainless steel construction with laminated black/gray birch stock with Monte Carlo cheekpiece, Mar-Shield finish, 22 in. barrel, open sights with adj. rear, 5½ lbs. New 1993.

Mfg.'s Sug. Retail	$244	$195	$160	$145			

MODEL 62 LEVERMATIC — .256 Mag. or .30 Carbine cal., 4 shot clip mag., 23 in. barrel, open sight, pistol grip Monte Carlo stock. Mfg. 1963-1969.

.256 Mag.	$325	$300	$275	$235	$200	$175	$150
.30 Carbine	$235	$200	$180	$165	$150	$135	$120

MODEL 70P (PAPOOSE) — .22 LR cal. only, semi-auto, takedown carbine with 16¼ in. barrel, 7 shot clip mag., rustproof receiver, bolt hold open, is supplied with floating nylon carrying case. Mfg. 1986-94.

$170	$125	$90	$75	$65	$60	$55

Last Mfg.'s Sug. Retail was $225.

Subtract $25 if without 4X scope (became standard 1993).

▲ *Model 70PSS* — similar to Model 70P, except has stainless steel breech bolt and barrel, black checkered synthetic stock with swing swivels, last shot hold-open became standard in 1996, 3¼ lbs. New 1995.

Mfg.'s Sug. Retail	$255	$195	$160	$135			

MODEL 78C — .22 LR cal., semi-auto, takedown carbine with 16¼ in. barrel. Mfg. 1990-95.

$185	$155	$130	$120	$110	$100	$90

MODEL 322 BOLT ACTION VARMINT — Sako Mauser type action, .222 Rem., 3 shot clip mag., 24 in. medium weight barrel, 2 position aperture sight, checkered stock. Mfg. 1954-1957.

$395	$365	$325	$275	$235	$200	$185

MODEL 336A RIFLE — improved 36A, .30-30, .35 Rem., or .32 Spl. cal., round breech bolt, 24 in. barrel with ⅔ mag. Mfg. 1948-1962, re-introduced 1973-1980.

$250	$230	$210	$190	$180	$165	$145

Add 10%-15% for pre-62 mfg.

The .35 Rem. cal. was added in 1953, .32 Spl. was disc. in 1962.

▲ *Model 336ADL Rifle* — similar to Model 336A Rifle, except has deluxe checkered walnut stock and forearm. Mfg. 1948-1962.

$475	$425	$375	$325	$275	$230	$200

MODEL 336 RC CARBINE — .30-30, .32 Spl., or .35 Rem. cal., standard model carbine. Mfg. 1948-68.

$240	$220	$195	$165	$155	$140	$120

MODEL 336C CARBINE — .30-30, .32 Spl., or .35 Rem. cal., standard model carbine with 20 in. barrel. Mfg. 1969-1983.

$235	$210	$185	$160	$150	$135	$115

MODEL 336SC SPORTING CARBINE — similar to Model 336C, with 20 in. barrel and ⅔ length mag. tube. Mfg. 1948-1963.

$250	$235	$210	$190	$180	$165	$145

MODEL 336SC .219 ZIPPER — similar to Model 336SC, in .219 Zipper cal., 5 shot mag. Mfg. 1955-1960.

$495	$415	$360	$330	$275	$250	$220

MODEL 336SD CARBINE — .30-30, .32 Spl., or .35 Rem. cal., deluxe sporting carbine with 20 in. barrel. Mfg. 1954-1962.

$275	$250	$235	$215	$200	$185	$165

MODEL 336 CS CARBINE LEVER ACTION — .30-30 Win., or .35 Rem. cal., 6 shot tube mag., 20 in. barrel, hammer block safety, American black walnut pistol grip stock (cut checkering became standard 1994), 7 lbs. Introduced 1984.

Mfg.'s Sug. Retail	$444	$345	$240	$200	$185	$175	$165	$150

M

Grading	100%	98%	95%	90%	80%	70%	60%

MODEL 336 LTS CARBINE — .30-30 cal. only, 16¼ in. barrel, 5 shot tube mag., 6½ lbs. Mfg. 1988-89 only.

	$275	$225	$200	$185	$175	$165	$150

Last Mfg.'s Sug. Retail was $346.

MODEL 336 ER (EXTRA RANGE) — .307 (disc. 1984) or .356 Win. cal., 5 shot tube mag., 20 in. barrel, walnut pistol grip stock, open sights, 7 lbs. Mfg. 1983-86.

	$325	$300	$250	$225	$200	$175	$150

Last Mfg.'s Sug. Retail was $350.

MODEL 336T CARBINE "TEXAN" — .30-30, .35 Rem., or .44 Mag. cal., similar to 336C, with straight stock, 18½ (1983 only) or 20 in. barrel. Mfg. 1954-1983.

	$275	$220	$195	$165	$155	$140	$120

Add 15% for .44 Mag. cal.

MODEL 336DT CARBINE "TEXAN" — select stock version of 336T, longhorn and map of Texas carved on butt stock. Mfg. 1962-1963.

	$400	$350	$275	$225	$175	$150	$135

MODEL 336 TS TEXAN — similar to 336 CS, except is .30-30 cal., 18½ in. barrel, straight grip stock and squared finger lever, crossbolt safety. Mfg. 1984-87.

	$240	$185	$160	$150	$140	$130	$120

Last Mfg.'s Sug. Retail was $314.

MODEL 336 OCTAGON RIFLE — .30-30 cal. only, with 22 in. octagon barrel, standard model. Mfg. 1973.

	$350	$300	$250	$225	$200	$175	$150

MODEL 336 MARAUDER CARBINE — .30-30 or .35 Rem. cal., 16¼ in. barrel. Mfg. 1963-1964.

	$375	$325	$300	$265	$235	$210	$185

Be careful for re-barreled examples of this model.

MODEL 336 MAGNUM CARBINE — .44 Mag. cal., 20 in. standard carbine configuration. Mfg. 1963-1967.

	$285	$250	$225	$200	$175	$160	$150

MODEL 336 ZANE GREY CENTURY CARBINE — .30-30 cal., similar to 336 Octagon, 22 in. octagon barrel, Zane Grey medallion inlaid in receiver, select walnut stock, pistol grip, brass butt plate and forearm cap. Approx. 10,000 mfg. in 1971.

	$295	$250	$220				

This model was mfg. to commemorate the 100th anniversary of the birth of Zane Grey.

MODEL 336 PRESENTATION RIFLE — .30-30 cal., 22 in. octagon barrel, engraved action, sold with Model 39 Presentation. Mfg. 1970 only.

	$550	$475	$400				

MARLIN CENTENNIAL MATCHED PAIR — Model 336 and Model 39 serial numbered the same, .30-30 or .22 LR cal., engraved, deluxe wood, inlaid medallions, cased. 1,000 mfg. sets in 1971.

	$1,150	$875	$695				

Last Mfg.'s Sug. Retail was $750.

MODEL 375 — similar to Model 336 CS, except is .375 Win. cal. Mfg. 1980-83.

	$265	$245	$225	$200	$175	$160	$150

MODEL 444 LEVER ACTION — .444 Marlin cal., 4 shot tube mag., 24 in. barrel, open sights, straight grip, Monte Carlo stock, recoil pad, swivels, sling. Mfg. 1965-1971.

	$325	$300	$245	$225	$200	$185	$160

▲ *Model 444 S* — similar to Model 444, except has pistol grip stock. Mfg. 1972-1983.

	$265	$240	$225	$200	$185	$165	$150

MODEL 444 SS SPORTER — similar to Model 444, with 22 in. barrel and hammer block safety, pistol grip stock without Monte Carlo configuration (cut checkering became standard 1994), 7½ lbs. Mfg. 1984-present.

Mfg.'s Sug. Retail	$527	$420	$340	$275	$230	$195	$180	$170

M

Grading	100%	98%	95%	90%	80%	70%	60%

MODEL 455 BOLT ACTION SPORTER — FN Mauser action with Sako trigger, .30-06, or .308 cal., 24 in. barrel, stainless steel barrel, Lyman aperture sight, checkered Monte Carlo pistol grip stock. Mfg. 1957-1959.

	$415	$330	$305	$250	$220	$195	$165

MODELS 780, 781, 782, and 783 BOLT ACTION — .22 LR or .22 Mag. (Models 782 and 783) cal., tube or clip mag., 22 in. barrel. Disc. 1988.

	$110	$85	$75	$70	$65	$55	$50

Last Mfg.'s Sug. Retail was $162.

Add $17-$25 for Models 782 and 783.

MODELS 880/881 BOLT ACTION — .22 LR or .22 Mag. cal., replacements for Models 780, 781, Model 880 is .22 LR with 7 shot clip mag. and 22 in. barrel, (cut checkering became standard 1994), Model 881 is .22 LR with 17 shot tube mag. and 22 in. barrel, 6 lbs. New 1989.

Mfg.'s Sug. Retail	$240	$180	$140	$100	$85	$75	$70	$65

Add $10 for Model 881.

▲ *Model 880SS* — similar to Model 880, except is stainless steel, black fiberglass synthetic stock. New 1994.

Mfg.'s Sug. Retail	$257	$200	$150	$110

▲ *Model 880SQ* — similar to Model 880, except has black fiberglass filled synthetic stock with checkering and heavy 22 in. barrel, without sights and grooved receiver, matte finish, 7 lbs. New 1996.

Mfg.'s Sug. Retail	$264	$195	$155	$110	$95	$80	$70	$65

MODELS 882/883 BOLT ACTION — .22 Win. Mag., 7 shot clip (Model 882) or 12 shot tube mag. (Model 883), checkered (cut checkering became standard 1994), black walnut Monte Carlo stock with Mar-Shield finish, adj. semi-buckhorn rear sight and hooded front, thumb safety, 6 lbs. New 1989.

Mfg.'s Sug. Retail	$265	$200	$155	$110	$95	$85	$75	$70

Add $16 for Model 883.
Add $35 for nickel finish on Model 883N (disc. 1993).
The Models 882 and 883 are the replacements for Models 782 and 783.

▲ *Model 882SS* — .22 Win. Mag., similar to Model 882, except is stainless steel and stock is black synthetic with molded-in checkering. New 1995.

Mfg.'s Sug. Retail	$283	$210	$165	$125

▲ *Model 882L* — similar to Model 882, except has laminated hardwood stock. New 1992.

Mfg.'s Sug. Retail	$281	$210	$160	$115	$95	$85	$75	$70

▲ *Model 883SS* — .22 Win. Mag., similar to Model 883, except is stainless steel and stock is laminated two-tone brown birch with Monte Carlo cheekpiece. New 1993.

Mfg.'s Sug. Retail	$292	$225	$170	$120

MODEL 922M SEMI-AUTO — .22 Win. Mag. cal., 7 shot detachable mag., 20½ in. barrel, Garand style safety, alloy receiver, hold-open device, uncheckered or checkered (became standard 1994) walnut stock with solid pad, blued steel (hard coated on receiver), 6½ lbs. New 1993.

Mfg.'s Sug. Retail	$411	$325	$280	$230	$200	$185	$175	$165

MODEL 990 SEMI-AUTO — .22 LR cal. only, 18 shot tube mag., 22 in. barrel, last shot automatic bolt hold-open, Monte Carlo American black walnut stock with pistol grip, 5½ lbs. Disc. 1987.

	$115	$90	$75	$65	$60	$55	$50

Last Mfg.'s Sug. Retail was $159.

MODEL 990L SEMI-AUTO — .22 LR cal., 14 shot tube mag., 22 in. barrel, laminated two-tone brown Monte Carlo stock, gold trigger, adj. rear sight, grooved receiver, 5¾ lbs. Mfg. 1993-94.

	$180	$160	$145	$130	$120	$110	$100

Last Mfg.'s Sug. Retail was $223.

MODEL 995 SEMI-AUTO — .22 LR cal., 7 shot clip mag., 18 in. barrel, Monte Carlo walnut stock, 5 lbs. Disc. 1994.

	$160	$125	$85	$70	$65	$60	$55

Last Mfg.'s Sug. Retail was $206.

M

Grading	100%	98%	95%	90%	80%	70%	60%

▲ *Model 995SS* — .22 LR cal., stainless steel barrel and nickel-plated small parts, black fiberglass stock with molded-in checkering, adj. rear sight, last shot hold-open new 1996, 5 lbs. New 1995.

Mfg.'s Sug. Retail	$238	$185	$140	$110			

MODEL 1894 — .44 Spl. or .44 Mag. cal., 20 in. bbl., 10 shot tube mag., adj. sights, straight grip walnut stock and forearm, 6 lbs. Mfg. 1969-1984.

	$400	$300	$250	$195	$165	$145	$130

MODEL 1894 C — without hammer block safety, mfg. 1979-1984.

	$375	$275	$225	$180	$160	$145	$130

MODEL 1894 SPORTER — .44 Mag. only, 6 shot half mag. tube, crescent shaped hard rubber buttplate, 1,398 mfg. 1973 only.

	$475	$425	$360	$300	$250	$200	$175

MODEL 1894 CS (CARBINE) — copy of original Model 1894, .357 Mag./.38 Spl., 9 shot mag., 18½ in. round barrel, open sights, straight grip stock (cut checkering became standard 1994), squared finger lever, 6 lbs. Mfg. 1984-present.

Mfg.'s Sug. Retail	$459	$365	$265	$195	$170	$150	$140	$130

MODEL 1894 BAT MASTERSON COMMEMORATIVE CARBINE — .44 Mag., features gold-plated receiver with Giovanelli engraving, checkered walnut stock and forearm, 500 mfg. beginning 1995.

Mfg.'s Sug. Retail	$895	$895	$725	$475			

This model is available exclusively from Cherry's located in NC.

MODEL 1894 S (SPORTER) — .41 Mag. (disc. 1991), .44 Mag./.44 Spl., or .45 LC (mfg. 1988-91) cal., Model 1894 with addition of hammer block safety, 20 in. barrel, 10 shot tube mag., adj. sights, 6 lbs., straight grip walnut stock and forearm (cut checkering became standard 1994).

Mfg.'s Sug. Retail	$459	$365	$265	$195	$170	$150	$140	$130

MODEL 1894 COWBOY — .45 LC cal., 10 shot tube mag., incorporates "cowboy shooter" features, straight grip stock with checkering, adj. Marbles-type rear sight, blued finish, 24 in. barrel, 7 ½ lbs. New 1996.

Mfg.'s Sug. Retail	$668	$525	$425	$350	$295	$250	$225	$195

MODEL 1894 M (.22 MAG.) — .22 Mag. cal., with 20 in. barrel, 11 shot tube mag., straight grip walnut stock and forearm, 6¼ lbs. Disc. 1989.

	$275	$210	$180	$150	$135	$125	$115

Last Mfg.'s Sug. Retail was $358.

MODEL 1894 CL — .218 Bee (new 1990), .25-20 or .32-20 cal., 6 shot (two-thirds length) tube mag., 22 in. barrel, 6¼ lbs. Mfg. 1988-94.

	$385	$290	$210	$175	$155	$140	$130

Last Mfg.'s Sug. Retail was $502.

▲ *Model 1894 CL Limited Edition* — features gold inlaid Marlin horse and rider logo. 100 mfg. 1995 only.

	$850	$625	$450				

MODEL 1894 CENTURY LIMITED — .44-40 cal., limited edition commemorative mfg. to celebrate the Model 1894's 100th Anniversary, 24 in. tapered octagon barrel with full 12 shot tube mag., features Giovanelli engraved receiver, bolt, and lever, receiver is case colored using traditional methods, checkered straight grip stock and forearm, crescent butt plate, 6½ lbs. 2,500 mfg. 1994 only.

	$950	$700	$475				

Last Mfg.'s Sug. Retail was $1,088.

MODEL 1894 OCTAGON — similar to 1894 Carbine, with octagon barrel. Mfg. 1973.

	$325	$300	$275	$250	$225	$200	$185

MODEL 1895 LEVER ACTION — .45-70 Govt., 4 shot tube mag., 22 in. barrel, open sights, straight grip stock with curved buttplate, forearm cap, sling and swivels. Mfg. 1972-1984.

	$295	$250	$225	$200	$185	$165	$140

Early new Model 1895 Marlins had cut rifling suitable for cast bullets, while later mfg. was switched to Marlins "Micro Groove" shallow rifling. Changes were also made from a

Grading	100%	98%	95%	90%	80%	70%	60%

straight stock to a pistol grip stock and from a traditional receiver to one with the newer hammer-block, push-button safety. Early guns with a straight grip stock, traditional receiver, and cut rifling command premiums over later mfg. The most recent guns with pistol grip, Micro Groove rifling, and hammer-block safety are the least desirable from a collector's standpoint.

▲ **Model 1895 S** — similar to Model 1895, except has pistol grip stock and straight buttpad.

	100%	98%	95%	90%	80%	70%	60%
	$265	$225	$200	$175	$165	$150	$140

MODEL 1895 SS — similar to Model 1895 S only with hammer block safety, cut checkering became standard 1994. New 1983.

Mfg.'s Sug. Retail	$523	$410	$315	$225	$175	$155	$140	$130

▲ **Model 1895 SS Cody Stampede 75th Anniversary** — .45-70 cal., includes semi-fancy checkered walnut stock with medallion, serial numbered CS-001 - CS-200, 200 mfg. 1994 only.

	$650	$395	$275

Last Mfg.'s Sug. Retail was $695.

MODEL 1895 CENTURY LIMITED (CLTD) — .45-70 cal., commemorates Marlin's 125th Anniversary, 24 in. half-round half-octagonal barrel, crescent buttplate, satin finished engraved receiver, checkered walnut stock and forearm. Approx. 2,500 mfg. 1995 only.

	$995	$700	$475

Last Mfg.'s Sug. Retail was $1,104.

▲ **Model 1895 CLTD Marlin Collectors Association Standard Rifle** — .45-70 cal., 70 mfg. late 1995 for Marlin Firearms Collectors Association.

	$625	$550	$450

Last Mfg.'s Sug. Retail was $700.

MODEL 2000 TARGET BOLT ACTION — .22 LR cal., single shot (can be converted), 22 in. heavy barrel with Lyman adj. sights, 2 stage target trigger, molded synthetic stock made from fiberglass and Kevlar with twice baked blue enamel, adj. buttplate, aluminum forearm rail, 8 lbs. Mfg. 1991-95.

	$495	$410	$350	$300	$275	$250	$225

Last Mfg.'s Sug. Retail was $602.

Add $34 for 5-shot clip conversion unit (for summer biathlon competition).

▲ **Model 2000A Target** — similar to Model 2000 Target, except has adj. comb, ambidextrous pistol grip, and molded-in logo. Mfg. 1994 only.

	$525	$425	$365	$315	$290	$260	$230

Last Mfg.'s Sug. Retail was $625.

▲ **Model 2000L** — .22 LR cal., updated version of the Model 2000, featuring gray/black laminated stock, adj. aperature rear and aperature insert front sight, double bedding screws, 8 lbs. New 1996.

Mfg.'s Sug. Retail	$602	$500	$415	$350	$300	$275	$250	$225

MARLIN PROMOTIONAL MODELS — Models 15 (disc.), 15Y (disc.), 15YN (Youth Model - new 1989, 1996 MSR $172), 25 (disc.), 25M (disc.), 25N (new 1989, 1996 MSR $173), 60 (1996 MSR $158), 70 (disc.), 70HC (mfg. 1989-95, last 1995 MSR was $167), and 75C (disc.) are inexpensive, utilitarian .22 LR or .22 Mag. cal. (Model 25M only), rifles designed for inexpensive shooting.

Series 15 and 25 Models designate bolt action, Series 60 and 70 designate semi-auto design.

RIFLES: BOLT ACTION, SINGLE SHOT

Between 1930 to date, Marlin has made a number of .22 cal. rimfire rifles, bolt action single shots, bolt action repeaters and auto loaders. These have normally been good quality, inexpensive weapons. In 1960, the name Glenfield was also used in connection with these guns. We will list these models for reference purposes with price ranges appearing at the end of each listing.

M

Grading	100%	98%	95%	90%	80%	70%	60%

Model 65 — 1932-1938. Price Range $35 - $65.
Model 65E — 1932-1938. Price Range $45 - $75.
Model 100 — 1936-1941. Price Range $45 - $75.
Model 100S Tom Mix Special — disc. Price Range $125 - $250.
Model 100SB — 1936-1941. Price Range $50 - $85.
Model 101 — 1951-disc. Price Range $45 - $75.
Model 101 DL — disc. Price Range $60 - $90.
Model 101G — 1960-1965, Marlin Glenfield. Price Range $40 - $70.
Model 10 — 1966-disc., Marlin Glenfield. Price Range $40 - $65.
Model 122 — 1966-disc. Price Range $40 - $65.

BOLT ACTION: REPEATING RIFLES
Model 80 — 1934-1939. Price Range $45 - $85.
Model 80E — 1934-1940. Price Range $50 - $90.
Model 80C — 1940-1970. Price Range $50 - $90.
Model 80DL — 1940-1965. Price Range $60 - $95.
Model 80G — 1960-1965, Marlin Glenfield. Price Range $40 - $70.
Model 20 — 1966-disc., Marlin Glenfield. Price Range $40 - $70.
Model 780 — 1971-1988. Price Range $45 - $75.
Model 781 — 1971-1988. Price Range $45 - $75.
Model 782 — 1971-1988, .22 WRM. Price Range $65 - $100.
Model 783 — 1971-1988, .22 WRM. Price Range $65 - $100.
Model 980 — 1962-1970, .22 WRM. Price Range $65 - $100.
Model 81 — 1937-1940. Price Range $25 - $50.
Model 81E — 1937-1940. Price Range $60 - $85.
Model 81C — 1940-1970. Price Range $60 - $85.
Model 81DL — 1940-1965. Price Range $65 - $90.
Model 81G — 1960-1965 Marlin Glenfield. Price Range $50 - $75.

AUTOLOADING RIFLES
Model 50 — 1931-1935. Price Range $75 - $125.
Model 50E — 1931-1934. Price Range $75 - $135.
Model A-1 — 1936-1940. Price Range $75 - $125.
Model A-1E — 1935-1946. Price Range $75 - $135.
Model A-1C — 1941-1946. Price Range $65 - $125.
Model A-1DL — 1941-1946. Price Range $65 - $135.
Model 88-C — 1948-1956. Price Range $65 - $135.
Model 88-DL — 1953-1956. Price Range $65 - $135.
Model 89-C — 1948-1961. Price Range $65 - $135.
Model 89-DL — 1950-1961. Price Range $65 - $135.
Model 98 — 1957-1959. Price Range $65 - $135.
Model 99 — 1959-1960. Price Range $65 - $135.
Model 99C — 1961-1978. Price Range $65 - $135.
Model 99G — 1960-1965, Marlin Glenfield. Price Range $65 - $135.
Model 60 — 1960-present, Marlin Glenfield (1996 MSR $158).
Model 99DL — 1960-1964. Price Range $65 - $135.
Model 49 — 1968-1970. Price Range $65 - $135.
Model 49DL — 1971-1978. Price Range $65 - $135.
Model 99M1 — 1964-1978. Price Range $65 - $135.
Model 989M2 — 1966-disc. Price Range $65 - $135.
Model 989 — 1962-1965. Price Range $65 - $135.
Model 70 (HC) — 1966-1995, Marlin Glenfield. Price Range $75 - $145.
Model 989G — 1962-1964, Marlin Glenfield. Price Range $65 - $135.
Model 990 — disc. Price Range $65 - $135.

SHOTGUNS

MODEL 1898 SLIDE ACTION — 12 ga., 5 shot tube mag., 26-32 in. barrels, various chokes, exposed hammer, pistol grip stock, grades differ in quality of wood and engraving on C and D. Mfg. 1898-1905.

	100%	98%	95%	90%	80%	70%	60%
Grade A	$325	$275	$225	$200	$165	$150	$140
Grade B	$580	$495	$440	$415	$360	$305	$275
Grade C	$880	$715	$635	$580	$525	$495	$440
Grade D	$1,760	$1,540	$1,320	$1,210	$1,045	$965	$880

Grading	100%	98%	95%	90%	80%	70%	60%

MODEL 16 — 16 ga. only, 26 or 28 in. barrel, various chokes, takedown, pistol grip stock. Mfg. 1904-1910.

	100%	98%	95%	90%	80%	70%	60%
Grade A	$325	$275	$225	$200	$165	$150	$140
Grade B	$495	$415	$360	$330	$305	$275	$250
Grade C	$635	$525	$495	$440	$415	$385	$330
Grade D	$1,320	$1,100	$990	$825	$715	$635	$550

MODEL 17 SLIDE ACTION — 12 ga., 30 or 32 in. full choke barrel, solid frame, straight stock. Mfg. 1906-1908.

	100%	98%	95%	90%	80%	70%	60%
	$335	$275	$235	$200	$165	$150	$140

MODEL 17 BRUSH GUN — similar to Model 17, with 26 in. cylinder bore barrel. Mfg. 1906-1908.

	100%	98%	95%	90%	80%	70%	60%
	$325	$275	$235	$200	$165	$150	$140

MODEL 17 RIOT GUN — similar to Model 17, with 20 in. barrel. Mfg. 1906-1908.

	100%	98%	95%	90%	80%	70%	60%
	$325	$275	$235	$200	$165	$150	$140

MODEL 19 SLIDE ACTION — improved lightened version of Model 1898, matte top surface on barrel Mfg. 1906-1907.

	100%	98%	95%	90%	80%	70%	60%
Grade A	$325	$275	$235	$200	$165	$150	$140
Grade B	$495	$415	$360	$330	$305	$275	$250
Grade C	$635	$525	$495	$440	$415	$385	$330
Grade D	$1,320	$1,100	$990	$825	$715	$635	$550

MODEL 21 SLIDE ACTION — straight grip version of Model 19.

	100%	98%	95%	90%	80%	70%	60%
Grade A	$325	$275	$235	$200	$165	$150	$140
Grade B	$495	$415	$360	$330	$305	$275	$250
Grade C	$635	$525	$495	$440	$415	$385	$330
Grade D	$1,320	$1,100	$990	$825	$715	$635	$550

MODEL 24 — improved 21, takedown, automatic recoil lock on slide, solid matte rib. Mfg. 1908-1915.

	100%	98%	95%	90%	80%	70%	60%
Grade A	$325	$275	$235	$200	$165	$150	$140
Grade B	$525	$440	$385	$360	$330	$305	$275
Grade C	$660	$550	$525	$470	$440	$415	$360
Grade D	$1,375	$1,155	$1,045	$880	$770	$660	$580

MODEL 26 — similar to Model 24 Grade A, with solid frame, 30 or 32 in. full choke barrel. Mfg. 1909-1915.

	100%	98%	95%	90%	80%	70%	60%
	$275	$230	$210	$195	$165	$150	$140

MODEL 26 BRUSH GUN — 26 in. cylinder bore barrel. Mfg. 1909-1915.

	100%	98%	95%	90%	80%	70%	60%
	$275	$230	$210	$195	$165	$150	$140

MODEL 26 RIOT GUN — 20 in. cylinder bore barrel. Mfg. 1909-1915.

	100%	98%	95%	90%	80%	70%	60%
	$250	$195	$180	$165	$150	$140	$120

MODEL 28 HAMMERLESS — 12 ga., 26-32 in. barrels, various chokes, takedown, matte top barrel, pistol grip stock. Mfg. 1913-1922.

	100%	98%	95%	90%	80%	70%	60%
Grade A	$295	$265	$235	$200	$165	$150	$140
Grade B	$495	$415	$360	$330	$305	$275	$250
Grade C	$635	$525	$495	$440	$415	$385	$330
Grade D	$1,320	$1,100	$990	$825	$715	$635	$550

MODEL 28TS TRAP GUN — similar to Model 28, with 30 in. matte rib barrel, full choke, high comb straight grip stock. Mfg. 1915.

	100%	98%	95%	90%	80%	70%	60%
	$415	$330	$275	$250	$220	$195	$165

MODEL 28T — similar to Model 28TS, with fancy wood, checkering, better finish. Mfg. 1915.

	100%	98%	95%	90%	80%	70%	60%
	$605	$525	$495	$470	$415	$360	$305

M

Grading	100%	98%	95%	90%	80%	70%	60%

MODEL 30 — similar to Model 16, with automatic recoil lock on slide, also mfg. in 20 ga. 1915-1917 (Model 30-20). Mfg. 1910-1914.

	100%	98%	95%	90%	80%	70%	60%
Grade A	$325	$275	$235	$200	$165	$150	$140
Grade B	$495	$415	$360	$330	$305	$275	$250
Grade C	$635	$525	$495	$440	$415	$385	$330
Grade D	$1,320	$1,100	$990	$825	$715	$635	$550

MODEL 30 FIELD GRADE — similar to Model 30 Grade B, with 25 in. mod. barrel, straight stock. Mfg. 1913-1917.

	100%	98%	95%	90%	80%	70%	60%
	$335	$275	$220	$180	$160	$130	$115

MODEL 31 — scaled down small ga. (16 and 20 ga.) version of the Model 28, has 26 and 28 in. barrels, various chokes, Model 31-16 was mfg. 1914-1917, Model 31-20 was mfg. 1911-1923.

	100%	98%	95%	90%	80%	70%	60%
Grade A	$385	$305	$250	$220	$195	$165	$140
Grade B	$495	$415	$360	$330	$305	$275	$250
Grade C	$636	$525	$495	$440	$415	$385	$330
Grade D	$1,320	$1,100	$990	$825	$715	$635	$550

MODEL 31F FIELD GUN — 25 in. mod. barrel. Mfg. 1915-1917.

	100%	98%	95%	90%	80%	70%	60%
	$395	$350	$325	$295	$265	$225	$200

MODEL 42A — similar to Model 24, but lesser quality finishing. Mfg. 1922-1934.

	100%	98%	95%	90%	80%	70%	60%
	$250	$220	$195	$165	$140	$120	$100

MODEL 43 HAMMERLESS — similar to Model 28, with lesser quality finish. Mfg. 1923-1930.

	100%	98%	95%	90%	80%	70%	60%
	$275	$225	$200	$175	$150	$125	$100

MODEL 43TS — similar to Model 28T, lower quality.

	100%	98%	95%	90%	80%	70%	60%
	$525	$440	$415	$385	$360	$305	$275

MODEL 44A — similar to Model 31 Grade A, 20 ga. only. Mfg. 1923-1935.

	100%	98%	95%	90%	80%	70%	60%
	$360	$275	$250	$220	$195	$165	$140

MODEL 44S — select checkered stock.

	100%	98%	95%	90%	80%	70%	60%
	$470	$385	$360	$330	$195	$165	$140

MODEL 49 — lower priced version of Model 42A. They were given to purchasers of 4 shares of Marlin stock. 3,000 mfg. in 1925-1928.

	100%	98%	95%	90%	80%	70%	60%
	$440	$360	$305	$275	$220	$195	$165

MODEL 53 — similar to Model 43 Hammerless. Mfg. 1929-1930.

	100%	98%	95%	90%	80%	70%	60%
	$330	$275	$250	$220	$195	$165	$140

MODEL 63 — similar to Model 43 Hammerless, later model. Mfg. 1931-1935.

	100%	98%	95%	90%	80%	70%	60%
	$330	$250	$220	$195	$165	$140	$110

MODEL 63TS — similar to Model 43TS, with trap style stock.

	100%	98%	95%	90%	80%	70%	60%
	$385	$305	$250	$220	$195	$165	$140

M

MODEL .410 LEVER ACTION — .410 ga., 22 or 26 in. barrel, full choke, lever action, similar to 1893, exposed hammer, plain pistol grip stock. Mfg. 1929-1932 as a stockholders promotional firearm.

	100%	98%	95%	90%	80%	70%	60%
	$750	$650	$550	$500	$475	$425	$350

▲ *Model .410 Deluxe* — includes deluxe checkered walnut stock and forearm.

	100%	98%	95%	90%	80%	70%	60%
	$895	$795	$695	$650	$575	$525	$500

MODEL 60 SINGLE BARREL — 12 ga., 30 or 32 in. barrel, full choke, top lever, break open, exposed hammer, pistol grip stock. Approx. 3,000 mfg.

	100%	98%	95%	90%	80%	70%	60%
	$195	$165	$140	$120	$110	$100	$90

Grading	100%	98%	95%	90%	80%	70%	60%

MODEL 90 O/U — 12, 16, 20, or .410 ga. shotgun or combination gun configuration (12 ga. over .30/30 barrels), 26, 28, or 30 in. barrels, boxlock, extractors, checkered pistol grip stock. Mfg. 1937-1958. Guns made from 1937-1949 had vent. separated barrels, after 1949, solid barrels.

	$450	$385	$360	$330	$290	$265	$230

Add 50% for combination gun configuration.

▲ *With single trigger*

	$550	$495	$470	$440	$400	$375	$340

Add 25% for .410 ga.

MODEL 120 MAGNUM — slide action, 12 ga., 3 in. chamber, 26-38 in. barrel, takedown, various chokes, checkered pistol grip stock. Mfg. 1971-1985.

	$290	$225	$215	$205	$195	$180	$165

Last Mfg.'s Sug. Retail was $370.

Subtract $35 if without VR.

MODEL 778 — 12 ga. Mag. slide action, 20-38 in. barrels, 7¾ lbs. Disc. 1984.

	$225	$190	$175	$155	$140	$125	$110

PREMIER MARK I SLIDE ACTION — 12 ga. only, aluminum receiver, takedown, manufactured in France for Marlin.

	$200	$180	$160	$150	$140	$120	$95

PREMIER MARK II — similar to Mark I, except with engraved receiver and checkering. Mfg. 1960-1963 in France.

	$275	$235	$200	$175	$150	$125	$100

PREMIER MARK IV — similar to Mark II, only deluxe grade with better wood, more engraving. Mfg. 1960-1963 in France.

	$305	$250	$220	$195	$165	$140	$110
With VR	$330	$275	$250	$220	$195	$165	$140

SHOTGUNS: BOLT ACTION

MODEL 55 — 12, 16, or 20 ga., 2 shot detachable mag., 26 and 28 in. full choke barrel, plain pistol grip stock. Mfg. 1950-1965.

	$90	$70	$55	$40	$35	$30	$25
With adj. choke	$100	$85	$65	$50	$45	$40	$30

MODEL 55 GOOSE GUN — similar to Model 55, except 12 ga. only, 36 in. full choke barrel, 3 in. chamber, 2 shot clip mag., leather carrying strap and detachable swivels, rubber recoil pad, 8 lbs. Mfg. 1962-present.

Mfg.'s Sug. Retail	$308	$235	$185	$145	$125	$115	$100	$90

MODEL 55 SWAMP GUN — similar to Model 55, 12 ga., 20 in. adj. choke barrel, 3 in. mag. Mfg. 1963-1965.

	$105	$90	$70	$55	$50	$45	$35

MODEL 55S SLUG GUN — 24 in. barrel, cylinder bore, rifle sights. Mfg. 1974-1983.

	$140	$120	$110	$95	$85	$55	$40

MODEL 512 SLUGMASTER — 12 ga., 3 in. chamber, bolt action, 2 shot box mag., 21 in. rifled barrel, adj. rear sight, receiver is drilled and tapped for scope mount (included), walnut finished birch stock with pressed checkering and vent. recoil pad, 8 lbs. New 1994.

Mfg.'s Sug. Retail	$386	$315	$230	$200	$180	$160	$145	$130

MODEL 5510 — 10 ga., 3½ in. mag., 2 shot clip mag., 34 in. barrel, leather carrying strap and detachable swivels, rubber recoil pad, 10½ lbs. Mfg. 1976-1985.

	$220	$170	$160	$150	$140	$130	$120

Last Mfg.'s Sug. Retail was $282.

M

MAROCCHI

Manufactured since 1922 by Armi Marocchi in Brescia, Italy. Currently **ARMI ⚙ MAROCCHI** imported and distributed by Precision Sales International, Inc. located in Westfield, MA.

Marocchi makes a wide variety of quality shotguns and O/U rifles. Many of their models however, are not being imported currently. Discontinued Frigon guns (manufactured by Marocchi) appear under the F section in this text.

Grading	100%	98%	95%	90%	80%	70%	60%

SHOTGUNS: AVANZA SERIES

This model was imported exclusively by Precision Sales International, Inc.

AVANZA — 12 or 20 (disc. 1993) ga., 3 in. chambers, monobloc boxlock action, 26 or 28 in. vent. barrels with VR (with or without choke tubes), SST, ejectors, deluxe checkered walnut stock and forearm with vent. recoil pad, high polish bluing with gold accents, all steel lightweight mfg., 6 lbs. 5 oz. - 6 lbs. 13 oz. Imported 1990-95.

	100%	98%	95%	90%	80%	70%	60%
	$725	$595	$525	$475	$425	$375	$325

Last Mfg.'s Sug. Retail was $829.

Add $45 for 20 ga. (disc. 1993).
Subtract 10% if without choke tubes (3).

▲ *Avanza Sporting Clays* — 12 ga. only, 3 in. chambers, built on 20 ga. frame, 28 in. vent. barrels with VR and choke tubes, select checkered walnut stock with deluxe recoil pad and forearm, gold-plated trigger, 7 lbs. Mfg. 1991-95.

	100%	98%	95%	90%	80%	70%	60%
	$780	$620	$560	$500	$450	$400	$350

Last Mfg.'s Sug. Retail was $889.

Add $99 for Premier Grade (disc., included select walnut and gold etched triggerguard).
This model features a trigger that is adjustable for length and pull without special tools.

SHOTGUNS: CONQUISTA SERIES

This model is imported exclusively by Precision Sales International, Inc.

CONQUISTA SPORTING CLAYS — 12 ga. only, boxlock action with brushed coin finish, SST, ejectors, adj. trigger, choice of 28, 30, or 32 in. 10mm VR barrels with choke tubes, right or left-hand (Grade I only) action, checkered walnut stock and forearm with recoil pad, 7⅞ lbs. New 1994.

▲ *Grade I* — features coin finished receiver with perimeter line engraving.

		100%	98%	95%	90%	80%	70%	60%
Mfg.'s Sug. Retail	$1,895	$1,650	$1,425	$1,200	$1,000	$850	$700	$550

Add $50 for left-hand variation.

▲ *Lady Sport* — 12 ga. only, features lighter weight specialized stock designed to fit women, cased, 7½ lbs. New 1995.

		100%	98%	95%	90%	80%	70%	60%
Mfg.'s Sug. Retail	$1,945	$1,675	$1,425	$1,200	$1,000	$850	$700	$550

Add $50 for left-hand variation.
Add $50 for Lady Sport Spectrum (partially colored receiver).

▲ *Grade II* — features better walnut and game scene engraving on receiver.

		100%	98%	95%	90%	80%	70%	60%
Mfg.'s Sug. Retail	$2,285	$1,950	$1,650	$1,425	$1,200	$1,000	$850	$700

Add $50 for left-hand variation.

▲ *Grade III* — features more elaborate game scene engraving on receiver sides and fine scrollwork throughout rest of action, includes hard gun case and stock wrench.

		100%	98%	95%	90%	80%	70%	60%
Mfg.'s Sug. Retail	$3,250	$2,975	$2,450	$2,150	$1,825	$1,625	$1,400	$1,175

CONQUISTA TRAP MODEL — 12 ga. only, Trap configuration, 30 or 32 in. 10mm VR barrels with fixed chokes, 8¼ lbs. New 1994.

▲ *Grade I* — features coin finished receiver with perimeter line engraving.

		100%	98%	95%	90%	80%	70%	60%
Mfg.'s Sug. Retail	$1,895	$1,650	$1,425	$1,200	$1,000	$850	$700	$550

▲ *Grade II* — features better walnut and game scene engraving on receiver.

		100%	98%	95%	90%	80%	70%	60%
Mfg.'s Sug. Retail	$2,285	$1,950	$1,650	$1,425	$1,200	$1,000	$850	$700

M

Grading	100%	98%	95%	90%	80%	70%	60%

▲ **Grade III** — features more elaborate game scene engraving on receiver sides and fine scrollwork throughout rest of action, includes hard gun case and stock wrench.

Mfg.'s Sug. Retail	$3,250	$2,975	$2,450	$2,150	$1,825	$1,625	$1,400	$1,175

CONQUISTA SKEET MODEL — 12 ga. only, Skeet configuration, 28 in. 10mm VR barrels with fixed Skeet chokes, 7¾ lbs. New 1994.

▲ **Grade I** — features coin finished receiver with perimeter line engraving.

Mfg.'s Sug. Retail	$1,895	$1,650	$1,425	$1,200	$1,000	$850	$700	$550

▲ **Grade II** — features better walnut and game scene engraving on receiver.

Mfg.'s Sug. Retail	$2,285	$1,950	$1,650	$1,425	$1,200	$1,000	$850	$700

▲ **Grade III** — features more elaborate game scene engraving on receiver sides and fine scrollwork throughout rest of action, includes hard gun case and stock wrench.

Mfg.'s Sug. Retail	$3,250	$2,975	$2,450	$2,150	$1,825	$1,625	$1,400	$1,175

CLASSIC DOUBLES MODEL 92 — 12 ga. only, 3 in. chambers, sporting clays configuration featuring 30 in. vented barrels with VR, back-boring, elongated forcing cones, and three screw-in chokes, low profile blued receiver, checkered walnut stock, and Schnabel forearm, adj. trigger, gold receiver accents and trigger. New 1996.

Mfg.'s Sug. Retail	$1,500	$1,375	$1,125	$925	$850	$775	$700	$650

SHOTGUNS & COMBO GUNS

The following models were imported exclusively by Sile Distributors, Inc. until 1994. Other Marocchi models were also imported by Sile Distributors on a limited basis.

FIELD MASTER I O/U — 12 ga. only, 26 or 28 in. VR barrels and rib with choke tubes, engraved coin finished receiver, extractors, SNT, checkered walnut stock and forearm. Disc. 1994.

	$455	$395	$325	$275	$240	$215	$200

Last Mfg.'s Sug. Retail was $530.

▲ **Field Master II** — similar to Field Master I except has SST and choke tubes. Disc. 1994.

	$475	$350	$295	$260	$225	$210	$190

Last Mfg.'s Sug. Retail was $550.

SKEET MODEL — 12 ga. only, 26 in. barrels bored SK/SK. Disc. 1994.

	$445	$395	$325	$275	$240	$215	$200

Last Mfg.'s Sug. Retail was $520.

TRAP MODEL — 12 ga. only, 30 in. barrels bored M/F, ejectors. Disc. 1994.

	$560	$485	$415	$360	$300	$260	$230

Last Mfg.'s Sug. Retail was $630.

MODEL 2000 SINGLE SHOT — 12 ga. only, 3 in. chamber, hammer, 28 in. barrel, ejector, lightly engraved receiver. Importation disc. 1991.

	$80	$70	$60	$50	$45	$40	$35

Last Mfg.'s Sug. Retail was $94.

VALLEY COMBO — 12 ga. over .222 Rem. cal., 23½ in. separated barrels with VR, 3 in. chamber, fold down rear sight and will accept claw scope mounts, fixed cylinder choke, DTs, engraved silver receiver, satin finish walnut Monte Carlo stock with checkering and recoil pad, 8¼ lbs. Disc. 1994.

	$585	$480	$415	$375	$325	$295	$275

Last Mfg.'s Sug. Retail was $700.

M

MASQUELIER S.A.

Manufacturer located in Belgium. Previously distributed (until 1986) by Ambel Ltd., Inc. located in Sugar Land, TX.

Grading	100%	98%	95%	90%	80%	70%	60%

SHOTGUNS

BOXLOCK SxS — 12 ga. only, $2\frac{3}{4}$ in. chambers, Anson & Deeley boxlock action, ejectors, fine scroll engraving with French walnut. Importation disc. 1986.

$4,400 $4,000 $3,650 $3,300 $2,995 $2,600 $2,200
Last Mfg.'s Sug. Retail was $4,780.

SIDELOCK SxS — 12 ga. only, $2\frac{3}{4}$ in. chambers, H&H style sidelocks, auto ejectors, English style fine scroll engraving with French walnut. Importation disc. 1986.

$12,500 $10,000 $8,750 $7,600 $6,700 $5,800 $5,000
Last Mfg.'s Sug. Retail was $15,850.

RIFLES

CARPATHE — .243, .270, .30-06, 7x57R, or 7x65R cal., single shot, hair trigger, push-down cocking system. Importation disc. 1986.

$3,500 $3,200 $2,900 $2,600 $2,300 $2,100 $1,850
Last Mfg.'s Sug. Retail was $3,850.

EXPRESS — .270, .30-06, 8x57JRS, or 9.3x74R cal., O/U configuration, SST, ejectors. Add $800 for extra set of 20 ga. barrels. Importation disc. 1986.

$3,300 $3,000 $2,800 $2,600 $2,300 $2,100 $1,850
Last Mfg.'s Sug. Retail was $3,600.

ARDENNES MODEL — top-of-the-line model, custom order only. Importation disc. 1986.

$6,600 $6,000 $5,400 $4,800 $4,300 $3,900 $3,450
Last Mfg.'s Sug. Retail was $7,250.

MATIBA

Manufactured by Macchine Termo Balistiche located in Italy. To date, this trademark has had little importation domestically.

REVOLVERS

MATIBA REVOLVER — various cals., 6, 7, or 8 shot, unique design permits barrel to fire lowest shell in cylinder (6 o'clock position), mechanism to rear of cylinder, interchangeable barrels.

Depending on features, standard variations of this model usually sell in the $300-$650 range.

MATRA MANURHIN DEFENSE

Please refer to the Manurhin heading in this section.

MAUSER-WERKE OBERNDORF WAFFENSYSTEME GmbH

Manufacturer located in Oberndorf, Germany 1812 to date. During 1994, the name was changed from Mauser-Werke to Mauser-Werke Oberndorf Waffensysteme GmbH. In 1996, GSI located in Trussville, AL became the importer for select rifle models only. Previously imported by Gibb's Rifle Co., Inc. until 1995, Precision Imports, Inc. located in San Antonio, TX until 1993, and KDF located in Seguin, TX (1987-89).

PISTOLS: SEMI-AUTO

The Models 1906-08, 1912-14, and HSv are very rare and only infrequently encountered. A competent appraisal is advisable before buying or selling these models.

MODEL 1906-08 — 9mm Export (9x25mm), detachable mag., incorporates features of both the pocket pistols and Model 1896 Broomhandle. Ser. range 1-100 (est.).

$39,500 $35,000 $29,500 $25,000 $19,500 $15,000 $9,950

Grading	100%	98%	95%	90%	80%	70%	60%

MODEL 1912-14 — generally chambered for 9mm Para., similar to pocket pistol configuration, but considerably larger, earliest specimens have inscribed slide legend. Those under serial number 100 (approx.) are not slotted for shoulder stock while those over 100 are generally slotted. Ser. range 1-175 (est.).

	$25,000	$20,000	$16,000	$12,000	$10,000	$8,000	$6,000

Add 50% if slotted with matching shoulder stock.
This variation is very rare in .45 ACP cal. or with a tangent rear sight.

WTP MODEL I VEST POCKET AUTOMATIC — 6.35mm, 6 shot, 2½ in. barrel, blue, rubber grips. Mfg. 1922-1937.

	$495	$325	$250	$200	$160	$140	$100

WTP MODEL II — similar to Model I, but 2 in. barrel. Mfg. 1938-1940.

	$650	$525	$450	$350	$250	$200	$150

POCKET MODEL 1910 — 6.35mm or 7.65mm, 9 shot, 3 in. barrel, blue fixed sights, checkered walnut or hard rubber grips. Mfg. 1910-1934.

	$395	$275	$180	$165	$150	$140	$130

POCKET MODEL 1914 — similar to Model 1910, but 7.65mm, 3.4 in. barrel. Mfg. 1914-1934.

	$395	$275	$175	$165	$150	$145	$135

Add 10% for Eagle WWI proofs.
Add 500% for the "humpback" model.

POCKET MODEL 1934 — similar to Model 1914, but one-piece grip. Mfg. 1934-1939.

	$450	$325	$210	$175	$160	$150	$140

Add 15% for Waffenamt.
Add 100% for Nazi Navy marked.

MODEL HSv — 9mm Para. cal., limited mfg., similar features to Model HSc, except has larger dimensions.

	$19,500	$15,000	$10,000	$8,500	$7,000	$6,500	$5,500

PISTOLS: HSc MODEL & VARIATIONS

MODEL HSc DOUBLE ACTION — 7.65mm (8 shot) or .380 ACP (7 shot), 3.4 in. barrel, blue or nickel, fixed sights, checkered walnut grips. Mfg. 1938-present (current mfg. is by R. Gamba in Italy).

▲ *Early Commercial* — standard pre-war Commercial Model. Most frequently encountered variation.

	$450	$340	$300	$265	$225	$200	$185

▲ *Transitional* — exhibits features of both early and late models.

	$425	$320	$290	$250	$215	$195	$175

HSc WWII MILITARY VARIATIONS

▲ *Early Nazi Army* — proofed 655 and 135.

	$425	$340	$300	$265	$225	$200	$185

▲ *Early Nazi Navy* — marked on front grip strap.

	$750	$595	$540	$500	$440	$395	$350

▲ *Early Nazi Police* — Eagle L proof only.

	$475	$395	$360	$320	$285	$245	$200

▲ *Wartime Nazi Army* — proof 135 and WaA 135. Eagle N proofed also.

	$375	$325	$290	$250	$200	$180	$150

▲ *Wartime Nazi Navy* — proofed on left side of triggerguard.

	$550	$450	$400	$340	$295	$260	$230

▲ *Wartime Nazi Police* — proofed Eagle L. Add 10% if Eagle F.

	$475	$395	$360	$320	$285	$245	$200

▲ *Wartime Commercial* — standard WWII Commercial Model.

	$375	$325	$290	$265	$200	$180	$150

M

Grading	100%	98%	95%	90%	80%	70%	60%

▲ **Swiss Commercial** — ser. range 800,000-900,000. Very rare.

	$1,400	$1,250	$1,125	$995	$900	$850	$600

▲ **Low Grip Screw** — very rare, less than 2,000 mfg.

	$3,000	$2,300	$1,600	$1,200	$1,000	$800	$650

Add 20% if Navy marked.

▲ **Cutaways** — mfg. to visibly show mechanism. Should not be proofed.

	$1,495	$1,000	$900	$850	$800	$750	$700

HSc POST-WWII VARIATIONS

▲ **French Manufacture** — frequently encountered in poor condition — post-WWII production.

	$325	$275	$245	$220	$180	$155	$130

▲ **Mauser Production** — .32 or .380 cal., 15 shot, mfg. 1968-1981.

	$350	$295	$260	$225	$180	$150	$130

Deduct 20% if not boxed or in .32 cal.

▲ **Interarms Import** — imported by Interarms from 1983-1985 (Italian mfg. by Gamba).

	$325	$275	$250	$220	$180	$150	$125

Last Mfg.'s Sug. Retail was $415.

▲ **One of Five Thousand Edition** — American Eagle edition (marked on gun), 5,000 total mfg. (serial numbered 1-5000).

	$375	$300	$250				

▲ **Armes de Chasse Import** — previously imported by Armes De Chasse located in Chadds Ford, PA on a limited basis. For G15 variation (9 shot) add $58.

	$475	$425	$330	$300	$260	$240	$220

Last Mfg.'s Sug. Retail was $695.

Add $195 for Limited Series.

▲ **E.A.A. Import** — imported by European American Armory, distributed by RSR Wholesale.

	$225	$195	$175	$150	$125	$110	$95

▲ **Current Gamba Mfg.** — .32 ACP or .380 ACP cal., steel construction, double action, double safety, stippled walnut grips, currently imported by Gamba, USA.

Mfg.'s Sug. Retail	$699	$595	$425	$330	$300	$260	$240	$220

MAUSER LUGERS

The original Mauser Luger P.08 is currently being imported by Gibbs Rifle Company, Inc. located in Martinsburg, WV since 1994 - pricing is upon request only. Both pre-war and post-war Mauser manufactured Lugers will be found in the Luger section of this book.

PISTOLS: RECENT MFG.

The pistols listed below are manufactured by FEG located in Hungary.

MODEL 80 SA — .380 ACP or 9mm Para., semi-auto single action patterned after the Browning Hi-power, 4²/₃ in. barrel, blue finish with checkered walnut grips, round hammer, steel construction, 10 (C/B 1994) or 13* shot mag., 1.95 lbs. Importation began 1992.

Mfg.'s Sug. Retail	$520	$450	$325	$275	$240	$215	$185	$165

MODEL 90 DA — similar to Model 80 SA, except is double action, spur hammer, and has 10 (C/B 1994) or 14* shot mag., 2.15 lbs. Importation began 1992.

Mfg.'s Sug. Retail	$516	$445	$325	$275	$240	$215	$185	$165

▲ **Model 90 DAC** — similar to Model 90 DA, except is compact model with 4⅛ in. barrel, 2.05 lbs. Importation began 1992.

Mfg.'s Sug. Retail	$520	$450	$325	$275	$240	$215	$185	$165

MODEL 1896 BROOMHANDLES

Note: Manufactured in Oberndorf, Germany between 1897 & 1938.

Grading	100%	98%	95%	90%	80%	70%	60%

While many variations of the famous 1896 Broomhandle exist, most common Broomhandles are pre-war Commercials, Model 1930 Commercials, Red 9s, and Bolos. They can be found in chronological order in this section. Holster stocks are a very popular accessory in this model. Commercial stocks may be matching or may not be serial numbered to gun (proper stock). Add $300+ for stock depending on overall original condition and if matching/non-matching.

In 1984, Federal legislation once again allowed importation of non-domestic WWI and WWII military handguns. While many of these newer imports would make workable shooters, they have in no way lowered prices on 90%+ condition specimens due to normal collector activity in top quality only pistols. Recently imported Broomhandles should have the importer's name visibly stamped on an exterior surface.

CONEHAMMER VARIATIONS

STANDARD CONEHAMMER — 7.63 Mauser, distinguishable by circular machined upper hammer with concentric rings. 5.5 in. barrel, 23 groove wooden grips, rear adjustable sight available in 1-10, 50-500, 100-300, 50-300, 50-700 meter configurations, 10 shot mag.

	$3,200	$2,500	$1,850	$1,200	$1,050	$925	$700

Add 40% for matching stock.

FIXED SIGHT CONEHAMMER — 7.63 Mauser, similar to Standard Conehammer, except has fixed rear sight.

	$4,200	$3,000	$1,800	$1,300	$1,100	$925	$700

6 SHOT CONEHAMMER - FIXED SIGHT — 7.63 Mauser, 4¾ in. barrel, 6 shot mag., rare.

	$7,500	$6,000	$4,500	$3,500	$3,000	$2,500	$2,000

▲ *6 Shot Conehammer w/adjustable sight* — 7.63 Mauser, 5.5 in. barrel, very rare.

	$11,000	$8,500	$6,000	$5,000	$4,000	$3,000	$2,500

Sales of this variation are extremely limited.

TURKISH CONEHAMMER — 7.63 Mauser, 5.5 in. barrel, 10 shot mag. Approx. 1,000 mfg. for Turkey in 1898, Farsi serial numbers.

	$6,500	$4,500	$3,000	$2,400	$2,100	$1,800	$1,500

"SYSTEM MAUSER" CONEHAMMER — 7.63 Mauser, "SYSTEM MAUSER" marked on top of chamber, improved 5.5 in. tapered barrel, 10 shot mag.

	$13,500	$10,000	$6,000	$5,000	$4,000	$3,500	$3,000

▲ *Stepped barrel variation* — similar to System Mauser variation, except has older 5.5 in. stepped barrel with no taper.

	$20,000	$15,000	$10,000	$8,000	$7,000	$6,000	$5,000

Add 40% for "SYSTEM MAUSER" stock.

20 SHOT CONEHAMMER — 7.63 Mauser, 20 shot non-detachable mag., frame can either be flatside or have milled panels, 5.5 in. tapered barrel, extremely rare.

	$30,000	$25,000	$15,000	$12,000	$9,000	$8,000	$7,000

Add 20% for milled panel variation.
Add 40% for matching stock cut for 20 shot mag.
At least several Large Ring Hammer variations of this model have been reported - extreme rarity precludes accurate price evaluation.

EARLY TRANSITIONAL LARGE RING HAMMER — 7.63 Mauser, distinguishable by large, open centered ring, 10 shot mag., 5.5 in. barrel.

	$3,000	$2,250	$1,550	$1,200	$1,050	$925	$700

This variation is normally found in the 12,000-15,000 serial range only.

FLATSIDE VARIATIONS

Add approximately $500 for a matching shoulder stock on the following models, $350 for non-matching.

M

Grading	100%	98%	95%	90%	80%	70%	60%

ITALIAN CONTRACT FLATSIDE — 7.63 Mauser, distinguishable by flatside frame and DV/AV proofmarks, 10 shot mag., 5.5 in. barrel.

	100%	98%	95%	90%	80%	70%	60%
	$3,500	$2,500	$1,600	$1,300	$1,100	$900	$700

This variation is found in the 1-5,000 serial range only.

FLATSIDE COMMERCIAL — 7.63 Mauser, 5.5 in. barrel, 23 groove walnut grips, adj. rear sight typically marked 1-10 or 50-1,000.

	100%	98%	95%	90%	80%	70%	60%
	$2,700	$2,000	$1,500	$1,000	$800	$600	$400

Early specimens may have pinned rear sights. Found in serial range 20,000-30,000.

POST 1900 VARIATIONS

Add approximately $400 for a matching shoulder stock on the following models, $325 for non-matching. This assumes excellent condition - exceptions are noted.

PRE-WAR LARGE RING BOLO — 7.63 Mauser, 3.9 in. barrel, floral grips, usually found in 29,000 and 40,000 serial range.

	100%	98%	95%	90%	80%	70%	60%
	$4,250	$3,000	$2,000	$1,450	$1,000	$700	$450

Add $850 for short pre-war bolo stock, $1,500 if stock matches pistol.

LARGE RING SHALLOW MILLING — 7.63 Mauser, 5.5 in. barrel, 23 groove walnut or hard rubber grips, normally found in the 30,000-33,000 ser. range.

	100%	98%	95%	90%	80%	70%	60%
	$2,500	$1,600	$1,000	$750	$625	$500	$400

LARGE RING DEEP MILLING — 7.63 Mauser, 5.5 in. barrel, 35 groove walnut or hard rubber grips, normally found in the 34,000 ser. range.

	100%	98%	95%	90%	80%	70%	60%
	$2,650	$1,650	$1,000	$750	$625	$500	$400

PRE-WAR SMALL RING BOLO — 7.63 Mauser, 3.9 in. barrel, floral/checkered rubber or 31-36 groove walnut grips, usually found in 40,000-44,000 serial range.

	100%	98%	95%	90%	80%	70%	60%
	$3,250	$2,300	$1,600	$1,200	$800	$575	$400

Add $850 for short pre-war bolo stock, $1,500 if stock matches pistol.

6-SHOT BOLO — 7.63 Mauser, distinctive 6 shot mag., 3.9 in. barrel, either fixed rear sight (more common) or adjustable, could have either large ring or small ring hammer.

	100%	98%	95%	90%	80%	70%	60%
	$6,500	$5,000	$3,500	$3,000	$2,600	$2,200	$1,500

Add $850 for short pre-war bolo stock, $1,500 if stock matches pistol.

STANDARD PRE-WAR COMMERCIAL — 7.63 Mauser, 5.5 in. barrel, 10 shot mag., 34 groove walnut or checkered black rubber grips, typically 50-1,000 meter adj. rear sight.

	100%	98%	95%	90%	80%	70%	60%
	$1,600	$1,200	$850	$725	$600	$500	$400

This variation is the most commonly encountered of all M1896 broomhandles. It can be encountered in the 39,000-274,000 serial range. Early guns below serial no. 100,000 are often Von Lengerke and Detmold marked and can be encountered with hard rubber grips. Rifling changed from 4 groove to 6 groove at approx. serial no. 100,000.

Note: This model is once again being imported by domestic distributors/dealers. Condition is somewhat poor, and prices usually start in the $250 range. These specimens usually have been reblued in addition to other reworking because the original condition has generally been very poor.

MAUSER BANNER CHAMBER MARKED — 7.63 Mauser or 9mm Export/9mm Mauser (rare), 5.5 in. barrel, distinguishable by Mauser banner trademark on top of chamber, 32 groove walnut grips. Approx. 10,000 mfg. in serial range 84,000-94,000.

	100%	98%	95%	90%	80%	70%	60%
	$2,700	$1,900	$1,250	$850	$725	$600	$500

This model is very similar in appearance to the Pre-War Commercial.

PERSIAN CONTRACT — 7.63 Mauser, 5.5 in. barrel, distinguished by Persian lion crest in left rear frame panel, must be in the 154,000 serial range, 50-1,000 meter adj. rear sight.

	100%	98%	95%	90%	80%	70%	60%
	$3,750	$2,800	$2,200	$1,600	$1,100	$850	$700

This variation is frequently faked - pay close attention to serial no. and Persian crest.

Grading	100%	98%	95%	90%	80%	70%	60%

STANDARD WARTIME COMMERCIAL — 7.63 Mauser, 5.5 in. barrel, 10 shot mag., 30 groove walnut grips, adj. 50-1,000 meter rear sight.

	100%	98%	95%	90%	80%	70%	60%
	$1,400	$1,000	$750	$650	$550	$450	$350

This variation is encountered almost as frequently as the Standard Pre-War Commercial. It is usually found in the 290,000-440,000 serial range. It was the first model to utilize the "new safety" design, and can be noticed by the "NS" marking on the back of hammer. Similar features as the Pre-War Commercial, except finish and polishing exhibit more machine and tooling marks.

Note: This model is once again being imported by domestic distributors/dealers. Condition is somewhat poor, and prices usually start in the $250 range. These specimens usually have been reblued in addition to other reworking because the original condition has generally been very poor.

RED-9 ADJ. SIGHT — 9mm P, 5.5 in. barrel, 10 shot mag., 24 groove walnut grips usually marked with large red no. 9, adj. 50-500 meter rear sight, standard WWI military contract model with separate serial range 1-150,000, generally poorly finished. Mfg. 1916-1918.

	100%	98%	95%	90%	80%	70%	60%
	$1,650	$1,250	$1,000	$850	$750	$650	$550

Add $600 for matching stock.
Add $350 for non-matching stock.
Add $200 for original leather.
Add 10% if Prussian Eagle proofed on front of magazine well.

Note: Be cautious for originality since metal refinishing is prevalent in this model. The last 10,000 guns of this German military contract are not military proofed, are better polished, and will command a slight premium.

RED-9 FIXED SIGHT — 9mm P, 3.9 in. barrel, this is a 1920 commercial rework of the Red-9 military, may be dated 1920 and/or have police markings on front grip strap.

	100%	98%	95%	90%	80%	70%	60%
	$925	$750	$650	$550	$475	$400	$350

Because of the Treaty of Versailles following WWI, barrels had to be shortened to less than 4 inches and the adj. rear sight removed.

FRENCH GENDARME — 7.63 Mauser, 3.9 in. barrel, distinguished by Bolo barrel length on large frame, hard rubber or walnut (rare) grips, found in the serial range 431,000-434,000, adj. 50-500 meter rear sight.

	100%	98%	95%	90%	80%	70%	60%
	$2,850	$2,000	$1,250	$850	$700	$550	$400

EARLY POST-WAR BOLO — 7.63 Mauser, 3.9 in. barrel, shot extractor, small ring hammer, usually found in the 440,000-500,000 serial range. Fit with full-size stock.

	100%	98%	95%	90%	80%	70%	60%
	$2,350	$1,650	$925	$725	$600	$500	$375

Add 50% for long barrel Bolos in approx. the 475,000 serial range.

LATE POST-WAR BOLO — 7.63 Mauser, 3.9 in. barrel, similar features of Early Post-War Bolo except has Mauser banner trademark on left rear frame panel, usually encountered in the 500,000-700,000+ serial range. Fit with full-size stock.

	100%	98%	95%	90%	80%	70%	60%
	$2,600	$1,750	$1,250	$800	$625	$500	$375

Add 10% for late pistols with high polish salt blue finish.

POST 1930 VARIATIONS

Add approximately $500 for a matching shoulder stock on the following models, $350 for non-matching.

EARLY MODEL 1930 COMMERCIAL — 7.63 Mauser, 5.2 (common) or 5.5 in. stepped barrel, 12 groove walnut grips, adj. 50-1,000 meter rear sight, usually found in the 800,000-890,000 serial range.

	100%	98%	95%	90%	80%	70%	60%
	$2,100	$1,500	$950	$750	$625	$500	$375

This broomhandle variation had a high polish, salt blue finish. Small parts are still fire blued and milling grooves were machined in receiver rails.

LATE MODEL 1930 COMMERCIAL — 7.63 Mauser, 5.5 in. stepped barrel, similar appearance to early 1930 Commercial except has solid receiver rails and various small parts are salt blued. Ser. range 890,000-921,000 with production ending in late 1930s.

	100%	98%	95%	90%	80%	70%	60%
	$2,000	$1,400	$950	$750	$625	$500	$375

This model is serial numbered on rear top of breech bolt assembly.

Grading	100%	98%	95%	90%	80%	70%	60%

MODEL 1930 REMOVABLE MAG. — 7.63 Mauser, 5.5 in. stepped barrel, 12 groove walnut grips, adj. 50-1,000 meter rear sight, very rare.

	$15,000	$13,000	$9,000	$5,000	$4,000	$3,200	$2,500

Original specimens of this variation have frames without the extra cuts required for the selector switch. Fakes are usually welded up Schnellfeuers made to look original. Only a very few are known in the 84,000-88,000 serial range. They are not slotted for the shoulder stock. Also known as the Model 711.

SCHNELLFEUER (MODEL 712) — 7.63 Mauser, 5.5 in. stepped barrel, 12 groove walnut grips, adj. 50-1,000 meter rear sight, switchable full auto variation generally with selector switch, separate serial range 1-100,000, 10 or 20 shot detachable mag. 712 stock is internally grooved for selector switch.

	$3,750	$3,150	$2,600	$2,200	$1,800	$1,500	$1,200

Add $750 for correct stock.
Deduct 60% if Class III transferable only (dealer sample).
The Model 712 is classified as a machine gun and is subject to registration and payment of a $200 transfer tax.

BROOMHANDLE CARBINES: SEMI-AUTO

FLUTED BARREL MODEL — marked "July 1897".

	$28,000	$16,000	$12,000	$8,000	$6,000	$5,000	$4,000

FLATSIDE CONE HAMMER — 7.63mm, 11¾ in. barrel, experimental variation.

	$20,000	$17,500	$12,250	$7,000	$6,000	$5,000	$4,000

FLATSIDE TRANSITIONAL — 7.63mm, 11¾ in. barrel.

	$17,500	$13,250	$9,000	$7,000	$6,000	$5,000	$4,000

LARGE RING HAMMER TRANSITIONAL — 7.63mm, 11¾ in. barrel.

	$15,000	$12,000	$9,000	$7,000	$6,000	$5,000	$4,000

LARGE RING HAMMER — 7.63mm, 14½ in. barrel.

	$15,000	$12,000	$9,000	$8,000	$7,000	$6,000	$5,000

SMALL RING HAMMER — 7.63mm, 14½ in. barrel.

	$14,000	$11,000	$8,500	$8,000	$7,000	$6,000	$5,000

BROOMHANDLE COPIES FROM OTHER COUNTRIES

These pistols are Chinese manufactured copies of the original German design.

HAND-MADE MAUSER CHINESE MARKED AND OTHERS — very poorly made Mauser copies, many thousands made.

	$650	$550	$475	$400	$300	$250	$235

HAND-MADE UNMARKED — poor quality.

	$650	$550	$475	$400	$300	$250	$235

ASIATIC FLATSIDE UNMARKED — better quality, not exceedingly rare.

	$1,200	$950	$740	$680	$600	$500	$400

TAKU-NAVAL DOCKYARD FLATSIDE — machine-made, better quality, not exceedingly rare, approx. 6,000 mfg.

	$1,500	$1,100	$740	$680	$600	$500	$400

Add 30% with correct stock.
Add 5% if with holster.

Grading	100%	98%	95%	90%	80%	70%	60%

SHANSEI ARSENAL .45 CAL. — .45 ACP cal., approx. 8,500 mfg., scarce and desirable in excellent condition.

	$5,500	$4,500	$3,500	$2,100	$1,700	$1,600	$1,475

Recently, a small number of currently manufactured pistols have been marketed as "restorations". Buyer beware! These restorations are priced in the $1,500-$2,000 range. Also, fake stocks have recently surfaced.

SPANISH COPIES OF MAUSER BROOMHANDLES

VERY EARLY ASTRA-900 — Bolo grips, frame has single-line address, approx. 1,200 mfg.

	$2,750	$2,500	$2,200	$2,000	$1,750	$1,600	$1,475

EARLY ASTRA-900 — single-line address, approx. ser. range 1,200-12,000.

	$2,500	$2,000	$1,350	$850	$700	$525	$425

LATE ASTRA-900 — two and three-line address, two-line address ser. range is approx. 12,000-20,000, three-line address ser. range is approx. 20,000-34,400.

	$2,350	$1,850	$1,350	$850	$700	$525	$425

Add 20% for Japanese character variation in the 27,000 serial range or if in Nazi procurement range.

ROYAL SEMI-AUTO — early Royals are mostly seen in semi-auto with round bolts.

	$3,000	$2,450	$1,900	$1,300	$850	$700	$600

There were many variations of the Royals and above values assume standard variation.

ROYAL SELECTIVE FIRE — 7.63mm, most of approx. 25,000 Royals manufactured were selective fire, several variations, transferable only. Add 20% if detachable mag., 100% if equipped with pneumatic rate retarder.

Class III	$2,500	$2,200	$2,000	$1,800	$1,700	$1,600	$1,475

This model had either a fixed mag., detachable mag., or pneumatic rate retarder.

MILITARY RIFLES

Subtract 30% if bolt is not matching or contract crests have been removed.

ARGENTINA

	100%	98%	95%	90%	80%	70%	60%
Model 1891 Rifle Argentine pattern	$350	$295	$250	$200	$140	$110	$85
Model 1891 Carbine	$395	$320	$250	$210	$145	$115	$90
Model 1909 Rifle	$375	$315	$240	$205	$145	$115	$90
Model 1909 Cavalry Carbine	$350	$295	$250	$200	$140	$110	$85
Model 1909 Mountain Carbine	$395	$320	$250	$210	$145	$115	$90
FN Mle 24 Short Rifle	$295	$275	$215	$185	$125	$100	$80
FN Mle 30 Short Rifle	$295	$275	$215	$185	$125	$100	$80

AUSTRIA

	100%	98%	95%	90%	80%	70%	60%
Model 1914 Rifle	N/A	N/A	$895	$695	$495	$350	$295

BELGIUM

	100%	98%	95%	90%	80%	70%	60%
Model 1889 Rifle	$350	$295	$250	$200	$140	$110	$85
Model 1889 Carbine	$350	$295	$250	$200	$140	$110	$85
Model 1889 Carbine with "yataghan"	$350	$295	$250	$200	$140	$110	$85
Model 1889 Carbine Lightened	$350	$295	$250	$200	$140	$110	$85
Model 1916 Carbine	$325	$285	$220	$190	$135	$110	$85
Model 1935 Short Rifle	$375	$315	$240	$205	$145	$115	$90
Model 1889/36 Short Rifle	$295	$275	$215	$185	$125	$100	$80
Model 35/46 & 50 SH. Rifles .30-06 cal.	$325	$285	$220	$190	$135	$110	$85

M

Grading	100%	98%	95%	90%	80%	70%	60%
BOLIVIA							
Model 1895 Rifle, Argentine Pattern	$195	$175	$125	$90	$70	$60	$55
Model 1907 Rifle	$295	$275	$215	$185	$125	$100	$80
Model 1907 Short Rifle	$295	$275	$215	$185	$125	$100	$80
Czech marked Model VZ 24 Short Rifle	$295	$275	$215	$185	$125	$100	$80
Standard Modell Mauser Banner Short Rifle	$295	$275	$215	$185	$125	$100	$80
Model 1950 Rifle Series B-50	$275	$250	$210	$180	$120	$95	$75
BRAZIL							
Model 1894 Rifle	$225	$195	$175	$125	$90	$70	$60
Model 1894 Carbine	$250	$225	$190	$145	$110	$85	$65
Model 1904 Mauser Vergueiro Rifle	$295	$275	$215	$185	$125	$100	$80
Model 1904 Rifle	$295	$275	$215	$185	$125	$100	$80
Model 1907 Carbine	$295	$275	$215	$185	$125	$100	$80
Model 1908 Rifle	$325	$285	$220	$190	$135	$110	$85
Model 1908 Short Rifle	$295	$275	$215	$185	$125	$100	$80
Model 1922 Carbine	$295	$275	$215	$185	$125	$100	$80
Model 1924 VZ 24 Carbine	$250	$225	$190	$145	$110	$85	$65
Model 1924/34 Czech Carbine	$295	$275	$215	$185	$125	$100	$80
Model 1908/34 Rifle .30-06 cal.	$275	$250	$210	$180	$120	$95	$75
Model 1935 Mauser Banner Rifle	$350	$295	$250	$200	$140	$110	$85
Model 1935 Mauser Banner Carbine	$350	$295	$250	$200	$140	$110	$85
Model M954 Rifle .30-06 cal.	$275	$250	$210	$180	$120	$95	$75
CHILE							
Model 1893 Rifle - Bent bolt handle	$350	$295	$250	$200	$140	$110	$85
Model 1895 Rifle - Army	$285	$250	$210	$180	$120	$95	$75
Model 1895 Rifle - Anchor crest	$295	$275	$215	$185	$125	$100	$80
Model 1895 Short Rifle	$295	$275	$215	$185	$125	$100	$80
Model 1895 Carbine	$350	$295	$250	$200	$140	$110	$85
Model 1912 Rifle	$295	$275	$215	$185	$125	$100	$80
Model 1912 Short Rifle	$295	$275	$215	$185	$125	$100	$80
Model 1935 Carbine - Mauser Banner	$495	$450	$395	$325	$275	$225	$150
CHINA							
Gew 1871 Rifle - Chinese marked	$450	$395	$350	$325	$295	$275	$250
Kar 1871 Carbine - Chinese marked	$495	$450	$395	$325	$275	$225	$150
Model 1907 Rifle - China contract	$495	$450	$395	$325	$275	$225	$150
Model 98/22 Rifle	$395	$320	$250	$210	$145	$115	$90
Model 24/30 FN Short Rifles	$275	$250	$210	$180	$120	$95	$75
Model 21 Chinese-made VZ 24	$395	$320	$250	$210	$145	$115	$90
Std. Modell 1933 Mauser Banner Rifle	$395	$320	$250	$210	$145	$115	$90
Std. Modell 1933 Mauser Banner Carbine	$395	$320	$250	$210	$145	$115	$90
Chiang Kai-Shek Rifle - Chinese copy	$295	$275	$215	$185	$125	$100	$80
Chinese VZ 24 P prefix - "1937" SH. Rifle	$395	$320	$250	$210	$145	$115	$90
Chinese copy VZ 24 w/Jap. folding byt.	$595	$550	$495	$450	$395	$325	$275
COLOMBIA							
Model 1891 Rifle - Argentine pattern	$195	$175	$125	$90	$70	$60	$55
Model 1912 Rifle - Steyr	$395	$320	$250	$210	$145	$115	$90
Model 1912 Short Rifle - Steyr	$450	$395	$350	$325	$295	$275	$250
Model 24 FN Short Rifle	$295	$275	$215	$185	$125	$100	$80
Model 30 FN Short Rifle	$295	$275	$215	$185	$125	$100	$80
Model 29 Short Rifle - Steyr	$395	$320	$250	$210	$145	$115	$90
Model 1950 Rifle - FN .30-06 cal.	$295	$275	$215	$185	$125	$100	$80

M

Grading	100%	98%	95%	90%	80%	70%	60%
COSTA RICA							
Model 1895 Rifle	$295	$275	$215	$185	$125	$100	$80
Model 1910 Rifle	$450	$395	$350	$325	$295	$275	$250
Model 24 FN Short Rifle	$350	$295	$250	$200	$140	$110	$85
CZECHOSLOVAKIA							
Model 1919 Mauser - Jelen Rifle	N/A	N/A	$2,500	$2,250	$2,000	$1,800	$1,600
Model 1921 Mauser - Jelen Rifle	N/A	N/A	$2,400	$2,100	$1,950	$1,775	$1,550
Model 98/22 Rifle	$395	$320	$250	$210	$145	$115	$90
Model VZ 23 Short Rifle	$395	$320	$250	$210	$145	$115	$90
Model VZ 23A Short Rifle	$395	$320	$250	$210	$145	$115	$90
Model VZ 24 Short Rifle	$295	$275	$215	$185	$125	$100	$80
Model 98/29 Rifle	$395	$320	$250	$210	$145	$115	$90
Model VZ 08/33 Carbine	$295	$275	$215	$185	$125	$100	$80
Model VZ 12/33 Carbine - light VZ 24	$295	$275	$215	$185	$125	$100	$80
Model VZ 16/33	$450	$395	$350	$325	$295	$275	$250
Model "JC" Short Rifle	$595	$550	$495	$450	$395	$325	$275
Model "L" SH. Rifle cal., .303, Lithuania	N/A	$1,200	$895	$775	$675	$595	$550
DOMINICAN REPUBLIC							
M1953 Rifle - Ex-Brazil M1908	$250	$225	$190	$145	$110	$85	$65
M1953 SH. Rifle - Ex-Brazil M1908 SHR.	$250	$225	$190	$145	$110	$85	$65
ECUADOR							
Model 1891 Rifle - Argentine pattern	$350	$295	$250	$200	$140	$110	$85
Model 1907 Rifle	$395	$320	$250	$210	$145	$115	$90
Model VZ 24 Short Rifle	$350	$295	$250	$200	$140	$110	$85
Model VZ 12/33 Carbine	$250	$225	$190	$145	$110	$85	$65
Model 24/30 FN Short Rifle	$295	$275	$215	$185	$125	$100	$80
EL SALVADOR							
Model 1895 Rifle - Chilean pattern	$295	$275	$215	$185	$125	$100	$80
Model VZ 12/33 Carbine	$250	$225	$190	$145	$110	$85	$65
ESTONIA							
Czech Model "L" Short Rifle - .303 cal.	N/A	$1,200	$895	$775	$675	$595	$550
ETHIOPIA							
Model 24 FN Short Rifle	$595	$550	$495	$450	$395	$325	$275
Model 24 FN Carbine	$595	$550	$495	$450	$395	$325	$275
Model 1933 Standard Modell Rifle	$595	$550	$495	$450	$395	$325	$275
FRANCE							
svw MB I ☆ Modified 98K Carbine - Hex. stacking rod	$295	$275	$215	$185	$125	$100	$80
GERMANY							
Model 1871 Rifle - Gew 71	$595	$550	$495	$450	$395	$325	$275
Model 1871 Carbine - Kar 71	$595	$550	$495	$450	$395	$325	$275
Model 1871 Short Rifle - Jaeger 71	$695	$625	$575	$495	$450	$395	$325
Model 1871/84 Rifle	$395	$320	$250	$210	$145	$115	$90
Model 1888 Commission Rifle	$250	$225	$190	$145	$110	$85	$65
Model 1888/05 Commission Rifle	$250	$225	$190	$145	$110	$85	$65
Model 1888/14 Commission Rifle	$250	$225	$190	$145	$110	$85	$65
Model 1888 Commission Carbine	$295	$275	$215	$185	$125	$100	$80
Model 1891 Comm. Carbine w/stacking hook	$350	$295	$250	$200	$140	$110	$85
Model 1888/97 Rifle	N/A	N/A	N/A	$4,000	$3,500	$3,200	$2,800
Model 1898 Rifle - Gew 98	$350	$295	$250	$200	$140	$110	$85
Model 1898 Carbine - Kar. 98, 16.9 in. bbl.	N/A	N/A	$4,500	$4,000	$3,500	$3,200	$2,800

M

Grading	100%	98%	95%	90%	80%	70%	60%
Model 1898/17 Rifle	N/A	N/A	N/A	$4,200	$3,600	$3,200	$2,800
Model 1898/18 Rifle	N/A	N/A	N/A	$4,200	$3,600	$3,200	$2,800
Model 1909 Self Loading Carbine	N/A	N/A	$5,000	$4,500	$4,200	$3,800	$3,500
Model 1898A Carbine	$350	$295	$250	$200	$140	$110	$85
Model 1898AZ Carbine (also Model 98a)	$325	$285	$220	$190	$135	$110	$85
Model 1898b Carbine	$495	$450	$395	$325	$275	$225	$150
Model Gew. 98 (Transitional)	$295	$275	$215	$185	$125	$100	$80
Model K98k Carbine (1936-45, coded mfg.)	$495	$450	$395	$325	$275	$225	$150
Model K98k, Para-troop model	$1,800	$1,500	$1,300	$1,100	$900	$800	$700
Model K98k "Kriegs-modell"	$350	$295	$250	$200	$140	$110	$85
Model 33/40 Carbine ("DOT" 1941-43)	$800	$750	$600	$500	$400	$350	$300
Model 24 (T) Rifle	$450	$395	$350	$325	$295	$275	$250
Model 98/40	$450	$395	$350	$325	$295	$275	$250
Model 29 (O) Rifle L/W issue	$800	$700	$650	$600	$550	$500	$460
Model VG-1	N/A	NA/	N/A	$800	$700	$600	$500
G 43 Semi-Automatic Rifle	$1,100	$1,000	$900	$750	$700	$600	$500
G 41M Semi-Automatic Rifle	$3,500	$3,300	$3,000	$2,800	$2,600	$2,300	$2,000
G 41W Semi-Automatic Rifle	$2,800	$2,500	$2,200	$1,800	$1,600	$1,400	$1,200

GREECE

	100%	98%	95%	90%	80%	70%	60%
Model 1930 FN Short Rifle	$395	$320	$250	$210	$145	$115	$90

GUATEMALA

	100%	98%	95%	90%	80%	70%	60%
Czech VZ 24 Short Rifle	$350	$295	$250	$200	$140	$110	$85

HAITI

	100%	98%	95%	90%	80%	70%	60%
Model 1930 FN Short Rifle	N/A	N/A	$275	$225	$175	$125	$90

IRAN (PERSIA)

	100%	98%	95%	90%	80%	70%	60%
Model 98/29 Rifle	$395	$320	$250	$210	$145	$115	$90
Model 98/29 Short Rifle	$395	$320	$250	$210	$145	$115	$90
Model 49 Carbine	$395	$320	$250	$210	$145	$115	$90

IRAQ

	100%	98%	95%	90%	80%	70%	60%
Model 1948 98k Carbine	$295	$275	$215	$185	$125	$100	$80

ISRAEL

	100%	98%	95%	90%	80%	70%	60%
German 98k with Israeli marks	$295	$275	$215	$185	$125	$100	$80
Czech 98k w/large triggerguard	$250	$225	$190	$145	$110	$85	$65
Model 1950 FN Rifle (7.62mm)	$250	$225	$190	$145	$110	$85	$65

LATVIA

	100%	98%	95%	90%	80%	70%	60%
Czech VZ 24 Short Rifle	N/A	N/A	$395	$325	$275	$225	$160

LIBERIA

	100%	98%	95%	90%	80%	70%	60%
Model 24 FN Short Rifle	N/A	N/A	$395	$325	$275	$225	$160

LITHUANIA

	100%	98%	95%	90%	80%	70%	60%
Czech "L" Model Short Rifle (.303)	N/A	N/A	$775	$675	$600	$550	$500
Model VZ 24 Short Rifle	N/A	N/A	$700	$650	$575	$495	$425
Model 30 FN Short Rifle	N/A	N/A	$700	$650	$575	$495	$425
Model 1900 Rifle	$595	$550	$495	$450	$395	$325	$275

Grading	100%	98%	95%	90%	80%	70%	60%
MANCHURIA							
Mukden Arsenal Rifle	$1,000	$900	$850	$775	$700	$600	$500
MEXICO							
Model 1895 Rifle	$250	$225	$190	$145	$110	$85	$65
Model 1895 Carbine	$250	$225	$190	$145	$110	$85	$65
Model 1902 Rifle	$350	$295	$250	$200	$140	$110	$85
Model 1907 Rifle	$395	$320	$250	$210	$145	$115	$90
Model 1910 Rifle	$350	$295	$250	$200	$140	$110	$85
Model 1912 Rifle	$350	$295	$250	$200	$140	$110	$85
Model 1924 FN Short Rifle	$295	$275	$215	$185	$125	$100	$80
Model 1924 Carbine	$250	$225	$190	$145	$110	$85	$65
Model 1936 Short Rifle	$295	$275	$215	$185	$125	$100	$80
Model 1954 Short Rifle	$295	$275	$215	$185	$125	$100	$80
NETHERLANDS							
Model 1950 Carbine "W"or"J" crest	$450	$395	$350	$325	$295	$275	$250
NICARAGUA							
Model VZ 12/33 Short Rifle	N/A	N/A	$195	$175	$125	$90	$70
ORANGE FREE STATE							
Model 1896 Rifle (OVS marked), DWM	N/A	$375	$325	$290	$250	$175	$125
Model 1896 Rifle (OVS marked), Loewe & Sons	N/A	$375	$325	$290	$250	$175	$125
Model 1896 Rifle, Chile overmark	$325	$285	$220	$190	$135	$110	$85
Model 1895 Short Rifle	$325	$285	$220	$190	$135	$110	$85
PARAGUAY							
Model 1895 Rifle	$295	$275	$215	$185	$125	$100	$80
Model 1907 Rifle (DWM)	$325	$285	$220	$190	$135	$110	$85
Model 1907 Carbine (Full-stocked)	$350	$295	$250	$200	$140	$110	$85
Model 1927 Rifle (Oviedo)	$295	$275	$215	$185	$125	$100	$80
Model 1927 Short Rifle	$295	$275	$215	$185	$125	$100	$80
Model 1927 Carbine (Full-stocked)	$325	$285	$220	$190	$135	$110	$85
Model 1933 Standard Modell Rifle	$295	$275	$215	$185	$125	$100	$80
M24 "Model 1935" FN Short Rifle	$350	$295	$250	$200	$140	$110	$85
PERU							
Model 1891 Rifle (Lange sight)	$295	$275	$215	$185	$125	$100	$80
Model 1891 Carbine (Lange sight)	$295	$275	$215	$185	$125	$100	$80
Model 1909 Rifle	$395	$320	$250	$210	$145	$115	$90
Model VZ 24 Short Rifle (Model 32)	$295	$275	$215	$185	$125	$100	$80
Model VZ 32 Short Rifle (Model 32)	$295	$275	$215	$185	$125	$100	$80
Model 1935 FN Short Rifle (7.65mm/.30-06)	$350	$295	$250	$200	$140	$110	$85
POLAND							
Model 1898 Rifle	$395	$320	$250	$210	$145	$115	$90
Model 1898 Carbine (Kar 98a)	$295	$275	$215	$185	$125	$100	$80
Model 1929 Short Rifle (Wz 29)	$295	$275	$215	$185	$125	$100	$80

M

Grading	100%	98%	95%	90%	80%	70%	60%
PORTUGAL							
Model 1904 Mauser-Verguiero Rifle	$250	$225	$190	$145	$110	$85	$65
Model 1937 Short Rifle	$395	$320	$250	$210	$145	$115	$90
Model 937a Short Rifle	$395	$320	$250	$210	$145	$115	$90
ROMANIA							
Model VZ 24 Short Rifle, "M" or "C" Crest	$395	$320	$250	$210	$145	$115	$90
SAUDI ARABIA							
Model 1930 FN Short Rifle	N/A	N/A	$230	$160	$125	$90	$65
SERBIA							
Model 1878/80 Rifle	N/A	$495	$450	$395	$325	$275	$225
Model 1885 Cavalry Carbine	N/A	$495	$450	$395	$325	$275	$225
Models 1886/6C and 1880/7C	N/A	$495	$450	$395	$325	$275	$225
Model 1899 Rifle	$350	$295	$250	$200	$140	$110	$85
Model 1889/07 Rifle	$350	$295	$250	$200	$140	$110	$85
Model 1899/08 Rifle	$350	$295	$250	$200	$140	$110	$85
Model 1899C Short Rifle	$250	$225	$190	$145	$110	$85	$65
Model 1899/08 Carbine	$350	$295	$250	$200	$140	$110	$85
Model 1910 Rifle	$350	$295	$250	$200	$140	$110	$85
SIAM (THAILAND)							
Model 1902 Rifle (Type 45)	$250	$225	$190	$145	$110	$85	$65
Model 1923 Short Rifle (Type 66)	$250	$225	$190	$145	$110	$85	$65
SLOVAK REPUBLIC							
Model VZ 24 Short Rifle	N/A	$450	$395	$350	$325	$295	$275
SOUTH AFRICAN REPUBLIC							
Model 1896 Rifle "ZAR" marked	N/A	$315	$295	$225	$175	$150	$120
SPAIN							
Model 1891 Rifle	$295	$275	$215	$185	$125	$100	$80
Model 1892 Rifle	$295	$275	$215	$185	$125	$100	$80
Model 1892 Carbine	$295	$275	$215	$185	$125	$100	$80
Model 1893 Rifle	$250	$225	$190	$145	$110	$85	$65
Model 1895 Carbine (Full-stocked)	$250	$225	$190	$145	$110	$85	$65
Model 1916 Short Rifle	$195	$175	$125	$90	$70	$60	$55
Model 1943 Short Rifle	$225	$195	$175	$125	$90	$70	$60
SWEDEN							
Model 1894 Carbine	$325	$285	$220	$190	$135	$110	$85
Model 1896 Rifle	$295	$275	$185	$150	$100	$65	$50
Model 1938 Short Rifle	$275	$250	$210	$180	$120	$95	$75
Model 1940 Short Rifle (8mm)	$595	$550	$495	$450	$395	$325	$275
SYRIA							
Model 1948 Carbine	$275	$250	$210	$180	$120	$95	$75

M

Grading	100%	98%	95%	90%	80%	70%	60%
TURKEY							
Model 1887 Rifle	$495	$450	$395	$325	$275	$225	$150
Model 1887 Carbine	$550	$500	$450	$375	$325	$260	$200
Model 1890 Rifle	$325	$285	$220	$190	$135	$110	$85
Model 1893 Rifle	$295	$275	$215	$185	$125	$100	$80
Model 1903 Rifle	$250	$225	$190	$145	$110	$85	$65
Model 1905 Carbine	$375	$315	$240	$205	$145	$115	$90
Model VZ 98/22 Rifle	$295	$275	$215	$185	$125	$100	$80
Model 1888 Rifle (Turkish marked)	$195	$175	$125	$90	$70	$60	$55
Model 1888/38 Rifle (improved)	$195	$175	$125	$90	$70	$60	$55
Model 1938 Rifle	$195	$175	$125	$90	$70	$60	$55
Model 1938 Short Rifle	$195	$175	$125	$90	$70	$60	$55
URUGUAY							
Model 1895 Rifle	$495	$450	$395	$325	$275	$225	$150
Model 1904 Rifle	$525	$495	$450	$395	$325	$260	$210
Czech VZ 32 Short Rifle (Model 1934)	$375	$315	$240	$205	$145	$115	$90
Mle 24 FN Short Rifle	$450	$400	$350	$300	$250	$200	$150
VENEZUELA							
Model 1910 Rifle	$350	$295	$250	$200	$140	$110	$85
Czech VZ 24/26 Short Rifle	$350	$295	$250	$200	$140	$110	$85
Mle 24/30 FN Short Rifle	$350	$295	$250	$200	$140	$110	$85
Mle 24/30 FN Carbine	$350	$295	$250	$200	$140	$110	$85
YEMEN							
Mle 30 Short Rifle (Markings unknown)	N/A	N/A	$285	$260	$210	$175	$150
YUGOSLAVIA							
M90T Short Rifle (ex-Turkish M1890)	N/A	$250	$225	$190	$145	$110	$85
Model M24B Rifle (ex-Mexican M1912)	N/A	N/A	$275	$250	$210	$180	$120
Mle 22 FN Short Rifle	$295	$275	$215	$185	$125	$100	$80
Mle 24 FN Short Rifle	$295	$275	$215	$185	$125	$100	$80
Czech VZ 24 Short Rifle	$325	$285	$220	$190	$135	$110	$85
Model 1924 Short Rifle (Kragujevac)	$325	$285	$220	$190	$135	$110	$85
Model 30 FN Short Rifle	$295	$275	$215	$185	$125	$100	$80
Model 30 FN Carbine	$295	$275	$215	$185	$125	$100	$80

MAUSER OBERNDORF SPORTERS

Approx. 125,000 commercial sporting Mausers were built between 1898 and 1946. Three action lengths; overall measurements: Short (Kurz) 8¼ in., Standard 8¾ in., and Magnum 9¼ in. Optional squarebridge receiver rings for custom sight mounting. Innumerable variations of triggers, barrels, sights and checkering.

Add $350-$550 for conversion unit.
Add 50% for single squarebridge action.
Add 100% for double squarebridge action.
Add 100% for Short (Kurz) action, except on Type K below.
Add 100% for Magnum action, except on African Type below.

SPECIAL RIFLE, TYPE A — expressly made for English market, superior finish, with round tapered barrel, silver-bead front sight on sleeved-on block with matted surface, hinged floorplate, pear shaped bolt knob, horn forend tip and PG cap, sling eyes.

	100%	98%	95%	90%	80%	70%	60%
	$3,000	$2,400	$2,000	$1,500	$1,000	$750	$575

NORMAL RIFLE, TYPE B — 24 in. barrel, steel-capped PG, Schnabel forend, sling swivels, pear shaped bolt knob, hinged floorplate.

	100%	98%	95%	90%	80%	70%	60%
	$2,000	$1,600	$1,400	$1,200	$900	$600	$475

M

Grading	100%	98%	95%	90%	80%	70%	60%

LIGHT SHORT RIFLE, TYPE K — 6.5x54 Mauser, 8x51, or .250-300 Savage, Kurz action, 22 in. barrel, steel PG cap, sling swivels, pear shaped bolt knob, hinged floorplate, hard rubber buttplate.

	$4,000	$3,500	$3,000	$2,500	$1,500	$1,250	$1,250

CARBINE, TYPE S — 20 or 24 in. barrel stocked to muzzle, steel PG cap, horn buttplate, sling swivels, pear shaped bolt knob, hinged floorplate.

	$2,500	$2,000	$1,750	$1,400	$1,000	$750	$575

CARBINE, TYPE M — 20 in. barrel stocked to muzzle with steel forend cap, steel PG cap, trapdoor steel buttplate holding sectional cleaning rod, butterknife bolt handle, hinged floorplate.

	$2,500	$2,000	$1,750	$1,400	$1,000	$750	$575

MILITARY SPORTING RIFLE, TYPE C — stepped round barrel, round bolt knob, half grip, banner Mauser imprint in side of buttstock.

	$750	$600	$500	$450	$400	$350	$295

AFRICAN TYPE — 28 in. round barrel, stocked to 4 in. from muzzle, Magnum action, pear shaped bolt knob.

	$5,000	$4,000	$3,000	$2,500	$2,250	$2,000	$2,000

RIFLES: BOLT-ACTION, RECENT MFG.

Currently, Mauser-Werke is currently being imported by GSI located in Trussville, AL beginning 1996. Gibbs Rifle Company, Inc. imported Mauser 1994-95. Previously imported by Precision Imports located in San Antonio, TX (until 1993), and KDF Inc. located in Seguin, TX (until 1989).

Add $150 for double set triggers on all current models listed below.

MODEL 66A — similar to Model 66S except has American configured laminate stock (wood grain), cals., action, and features are the same as the Model 66S. Imported 1988-89 only.

▲ *Standard Calibers*

	$1,900	$1,425	$1,150	$925	$800	$700	$650

Last Mfg.'s Sug. Retail was $2,100.

Add $630 per interchangeable barrel.

The A suffix on this model denotes American.

▲ *Magnum Calibers* — includes Weatherby Mag. cals. also.

	$2,050	$1,500	$1,200	$975	$825	$700	$650

Last Mfg.'s Sug. Retail was $2,270.

Add $670 per interchangeable barrel.

▲ *Big Game Calibers* — includes most popular Mag. cals. up to .458 Win. Mag.

	$2,350	$1,900	$1,425	$1,150	$950	$825	$750

Last Mfg.'s Sug. Retail was $2,700.

MODEL 66S STANDARD — telescoping short action, 5.6x57mm, 6.5x57mm, 7x57mm Mauser (disc. 1992), 7x64mm, 9.3x62mm, .243 Win., .270 Win., .30-06, or .308 Win. cal., 24 in. barrel, standard interchangeable barrels, single or double set triggers, adj. and detachable sights, Monte Carlo walnut stock with checkering, swivels, new safety, rosewood tipped forearm and pistol grip, rubber recoil pad, 7½ lbs. Mfg. 1974-1995.

	$2,350	$1,275	$995	$875	$775	$695	$625

Last Mfg.'s Sug. Retail was $2,722.

▲ *Model 66 Magnum* — 28 in. barrel, 6.5x68mm, 8x68S, 9.3x64mm, 7mm Rem. Mag., .300 Win. Mag., or .300 Wby. Mag. cal., 7.9 lbs. Disc. 1995.

	$2,500	$1,325	$1,050	$900	$795	$695	$625

Last Mfg.'s Sug. Retail was $2,925.

▲ *Model 66 Carbine (Stutzen-Mannlicher)* — current cals. include .243 Win., .270 Win., .30-06, 7x64mm, or 9.3x62mm, 21 in. barrel, full-stock (Mannlicher only) and half-stock (disc. in 1989), double or single triggers, 7.5 lbs. Disc. 1995.

	$2,500	$1,325	$1,050	$900	$795	$695	$625

Last Mfg.'s Sug. Retail was $2,925.

This model was available in a half-stock "Ultra" variation until 1989. Values are similar to those listed above.

Grading	100%	98%	95%	90%	80%	70%	60%

▲ *Model 66S Diplomat* — similar cals. as the Model 66S Standard, except not available in 5.6x57mm, similar features, except includes selected walnut and special engraving including deer and wild boar game scenes. Disc. 1995.

$4,650 $3,850 $3,350 $2,750 $2,250 $1,850 $1,400
Last Mfg.'s Sug. Retail was $5,317.

Add $390 for Mag. cals. (similar to Model 66S Magnum).

▲ *Safari/Big Game Model 66* — .375 H&H Mag. or .458 Win. Mag. cal., single trigger, 9.3 lbs. Disc. 1995.

$2,950 $1,850 $1,350 $1,025 $875 $775 $650
Last Mfg.'s Sug. Retail was $3,487.

MODEL 66 SM — telescoping short action, .243 Win. (disc.), .270 Win., 7x57mm Mauser (disc.), 7x64, .308 Win., .30-06, or 6.5x57 cal. (disc.), 24 in. barrel, standard interchangeable barrels, set trigger, adj. and detachable sights, Monte Carlo walnut stock with checkering, swivels, new safety, anatomical gripped select walnut stock with Mauser-nose, cocking lever on tang, rubber recoil pad, 7¼ lbs. Importation 1981-95.

$2,875 $1,800 $1,375 $1,025 $875 $775 $650
Last Mfg.'s Sug. Retail was $3,398.

▲ *Model 66 SM Ultra* — all standard cals., 21 in. barrel, 7¼ lbs.

$1,625 $1,325 $1,140 $920 $760 $650 $550
Last Mfg.'s Sug. Retail was $1,903.

▲ *Model 66SM Magnum* — cals. similar to Model 66 S Magnum, except not available in 9.3x64mm cal., 26 in. barrel, 8.4 lbs. Disc. 1995.

$3,025 $1,925 $1,375 $1,025 $875 $775 $650
Last Mfg.'s Sug. Retail was $3,578.

▲ *Model 66SM Diplomat* — similar cals. as the Model 66SM Standard, similar features, except includes selected walnut and special engraving including deer and wild boar game scenes. Disc. 1995.

$5,075 $3,975 $3,450 $2,775 $2,250 $1,850 $1,400
Last Mfg.'s Sug. Retail was $5,943.

Add $382 for Mag. cals. (similar to Model 66SM Magnum).

▲ *Model 66SM Carbine (Mannlicher type full stock)* — .30-06 cal. only currently, 21 in. barrel, 7 lbs. Disc. 1995.

$3,025 $1,925 $1,375 $1,025 $875 $775 $650
Last Mfg.'s Sug. Retail was $3,578.

These models were previously available on a custom order only basis through KDF, Inc. located in Seguin, TX.

MODEL 66 SL — similar to Model 66 SM, except features extra select walnut with special graining, 7¼ lbs. Disc. 1985.

$1,370 $1,275 $890 $720 $580 $475 $420
Last Mfg.'s Sug. Retail was $1,470.

▲ *Model 66 SL Ultra* — 7x64 or .30-06 cal., 21 in. barrel, 7¼ lbs. Disc. 1985.

$1,475 $1,325 $940 $750 $600 $450 $400
Last Mfg.'s Sug. Retail was $1,520.

▲ *Magnum Calibers* — similar to Model 66 S, 8.4 lbs. Disc. 1985.

$1,475 $1,325 $940 $750 $600 $450 $400
Last Mfg.'s Sug. Retail was $1,520.

▲ *Mannlicher Type Full Stock* — 21 in. barrel, 7 lbs. Disc. 1985.

$1,475 $1,325 $940 $750 $600 $450 $400
Last Mfg.'s Sug. Retail was $1,520.

MODEL 66SL DIPLOMAT — same specifications as Model 66 SM, except includes selected walnut and special engraving including deer and wild boar game scenes.

Add $93 for Mannlicher full-stock (21 in. barrel).
Add $387 for Mag. cals.

This model was available on an individual custom order basis only. The last published retail price (1988) for a standard model without options was $3,167.

MODEL 660 — U.S. designation of 66S. Imported 1971-1973.

$925 $820 $720 $600 $500 $450 $400

M

Grading	100%	98%	95%	90%	80%	70%	60%

MODEL 66S DELUXE — special order engraved and inlaid, select wood. Priced per individual customer order. All guns are custom made only.

MODEL 66P — imported 1995 only.

	$4,250	$3,575	$3,075	$2,600	$2,075	$1,700	$1,375

Last Mfg.'s Sug. Retail was $4,888.

MODEL 66SP SUPER MATCH — .300 Win. Mag. or .308 Win. cal., telescoping short action, 27½ in. heavy barrel with muzzle brake, no sights, match trigger, 3 shot mag., select European walnut stock with stippling and thumbhole, adj. cheekpiece and butt plate, includes premium scope, 12 lbs. Not currently imported.

Mfg.'s Sug. Retail	$4,737	$4,150	$3,500	$3,050	$2,600	$2,075	$1,700	$1,375

Values above reflect most recent U.S. prices.

MODEL 77 — .243 Win., .270 Win., 6.5x57, 7x64, .308 Win., or .30-06 cal., 24 in. barrel, set trigger on tang, adj. and detachable sights, walnut stock with European cheekpiece and hand checkering, swivels, new safety, steel detachable box mag., rubber recoil pad, 7¼ lbs. Disc.

	$1,130	$950	$875	$810	$750	$675	$595

Last Mfg.'s Sug. Retail was $1,331.

▲ *Model 77 Ultra* — 6.5x57, 7x64 or .30-06 cal., 20 in. barrel, 7.7 lbs. Disc.

	$1,175	$975	$895	$835	$760	$675	$595

Last Mfg.'s Sug. Retail was $1,394.

▲ *Magnum Calibers* — similar to Model 66S, 8⅛ lbs. Disc.

	$1,175	$975	$895	$835	$760	$675	$595

Last Mfg.'s Sug. Retail was $1,394.

▲ *Mannlicher type full stock* — 20 in. barrel, Mauser-set trigger, 7.7 lbs. Disc.

	$1,175	$975	$895	$835	$760	$675	$595

Last Mfg.'s Sug. Retail was $1,394.

▲ *Big Game Model* — .375 H&H Mag. cal., 26 in. barrel, 8⅛ lbs. Disc.

	$1,075	$1,000	$900	$795	$675	$575	$475

Last Mfg.'s Sug. Retail was $1,150.

MODEL 77 SPORTSMAN — .243 or .308 Win. cal., sports version of the Model 77, set trigger on the tang, no sights, 24 in. barrel, 9 lbs. Disc.

	$1,495	$1,230	$1,075	$985	$895	$820	$740

Last Mfg.'s Sug. Retail was $1,754.

Add $430 for Zeiss 2½-10X scope and mounts.

MODEL 83 MATCH SINGLE SHOT — .308 Win. cals. only, cylinder locking action with 3 locking lugs in rear, match trigger, anatomical match stock with select walnut, adj. comb and butt plate. Disc.

	$2,170	$1,815	$1,660	$1,545	$1,400	$1,195	$925

Last Mfg.'s Sug. Retail was $2,594.

This model is a UIT standard rifle at 300 meters.

MODEL 83 MATCH UIT FREE RIFLE — .308 Win. cals. only, cylinder locking action with 3 locking lugs in rear, match trigger, anatomical match stock with select walnut, adj. comb and butt plate. Disc.

	$2,320	$1,940	$1,760	$1,600	$1,430	$1,195	$925

Last Mfg.'s Sug. Retail was $2,771.

M

MODEL 83 STANDARD RIFLE — similar to Model 83 Match, except has removable 10 shot steel mag., 26 in. barrel. Disc.

	$2,320	$1,950	$1,800	$1,625	$1,460	$1,250	$1,000

Last Mfg.'s Sug. Retail was $2,766.

MODEL 86 LAMINATED/FIBERGLASS (SR) — .308 cal., updated version of the Model 83 action, 25.6 in. fluted barrel with muzzle brake, laminate wood or fiberglass stock with rail in forearm, adj. trigger, 9 shot detachable mag., cased, 10.8 lbs. Limited importation 1989-95.

	$4,250	$3,675	$3,075	$2,600	$2,075	$1,700	$1,375

Last Mfg.'s Sug. Retail was $4,888.

Add $224 for match thumbhole wood stock (disc.).
Add $318 for fiberglass stock.

Grading	100%	98%	95%	90%	80%	70%	60%

MODEL SR 93 — .300 Win. Mag., .308 Win., or .338 Lapua Mag. cal., precision rifle employing skeletonized cast magnesium/aluminum stock, adj. ergonomics, 27 in. fluted barrel with muzzle brake, integrated bi-pod, 4 or 5 shot mag., approx. 13 lbs. without accessories.

> While advertised, this model has not been produced to date.

MODEL 94 — .243 Win., .270 Win., .30-06, .308 Win., .300 Win. Mag., 7x64mm, 7mm Rem. Mag., 8x68S, 9.3x62 Mag. cal., 22 or 24 in. interchangeable barrel, aluminum block in stock bedding system, 60 degree bolt, 6 lug locking system, checkered walnut stock and forearm, 3 or 4 shot mag., lateral slide safety, approx. 7¼ lbs. Mfg. began 1994, U.S. importation was disc. 1995.

	$1,550	$1,325	$1,100	$925	$850	$775	$700

Last Mfg.'s Sug. Retail was $1,795.

> Add $180 for Mag. cals.

MODEL 96 — .270 Win. or .30-06 cal., 16 lug bolt slides straight back allowing for low scope mounts, safety mechanism in bolt in addition to rear tang safety, checkered walnut stock, 5 shot mag., w/o sights, 22 in. barrel, 6¼ lbs. New 1996.

Mfg.'s Sug. Retail	$699		$625	$550	$500	$450	$400	$360	$330

> This model is distributed exclusively by RSR Distributing.

MODEL 98 COMMERCIAL — various cals., features original breech mechanisms refurbished to new condition, barrel, trigger system, and stock are new from factory. Importation began late 1995.

> While advertised, this model has not been imported into the U.S. due to legalities.

MODEL 99 — 5.6x57mm, 6.5x57mm, 7x57mm, 7x64mm, .243 Win., .25-06, .270 Win., .30-06 or .308 Win. cal., bolt action with 60 degree throw, 24 in. free-floating barrel, jeweled bolt, available in either hand-rubbed oil or high-luster lacquer finish for stock, mini-claw extractor, adj. single stage trigger, 4 shot detachable mag., no sights, 8 lbs. Imported 1989-disc.

▲ *Classic Lacquer Finish* — high-luster lacquer finish for stock.

	$1,110	$925	$850	$775	$700	$625	$550

Last Mfg.'s Sug. Retail was $1,272.

> This model is available with either a Schnabel forearm with regular stock or rosewood capped forearm with American Monte Carlo stock.

▲ *Classic Oil Finish* — hand-rubbed oil finish for stock. Disc.

	$1,130	$995	$875	$775	$700	$625	$550

Last Mfg.'s Sug. Retail was $1,130.

> This model is available with either a Schnabel forearm with regular stock or rosewood capped forearm with American Monte Carlo stock.

MODEL 99 MAGNUM — 8x68S, 9.3x64mm, 7mm Rem. Mag., .257 Wby., .270 Wby., .300 Wby., .300 Win. Mag., .338 Win. Mag., or .375 H&H cal., similar specifications as Model 99, except has 26 in. barrel and 3 shot mag. Imported 1989-disc.

▲ *Classic Lacquer Finish* — high-luster lacquer finish for stock.

	$1,135	$950	$875	$775	$700	$625	$550

Last Mfg.'s Sug. Retail was $1,322.

> This model is available with either a Schnabel forearm with regular stock or rosewood capped forearm with American Monte Carlo stock.

▲ *Classic Oil Finish* — hand-rubbed oil finish for stock.

	$1,025	$895	$795	$725	$625	$550	$495

Last Mfg.'s Sug. Retail was $1,180.

> This model is available with either a Schnabel forearm with regular stock or rosewood capped forearm with American Monte Carlo stock.

MODEL 225 — available in 13 cals. between .243 Win. and .300 Wby. Mag., bolt action, 60 degree bolt lift with 3 locking lugs, ultra fast lock time, adj. trigger, 24 or 26 (Mag. only) in. barrel, 3 or 5 shot mag., no sights, guaranteed ½ in. accuracy at 100 yards, many stock options available at extra cost.

M

Grading	100%	98%	95%	90%	80%	70%	60%

▲ **Deluxe Standard Sporter** — standard model available in 6 regular cals. and 9 Mag. cals. Importation disc. 1989.

| | $1,275 | $1,000 | $875 | $750 | $625 | $550 | $495 |

Last Mfg.'s Sug. Retail was $1,400.

Add $90 for Mag. cals.

This model was formerly the KDF Model K-15.

MODEL 226 — left-handed variation of the Model 225 with slight changes. Disc. 1989.

| | $1,275 | $1,000 | $875 | $750 | $625 | $550 | $495 |

Last Mfg.'s Sug. Retail was $1,400.

MODEL 2000 BOLT ACTION — .270 Win., .308 Win., or .30-06 cal., 5 shot mag., 24 in. barrel, leaf rear sight, checkered walnut stock. Mfg. by F.W. Heym for Mauser, 1969-1971.

| | $305 | $290 | $275 | $220 | $175 | $155 | $140 |

MODEL 3000 — bolt action, .243 Win., .270 Win., .308 Win., or .30-06 cal., 5 shot mag., 22 in. barrel, no sights, walnut Monte Carlo style stock, rosewood forearm and pistol grip, skipline checkering, recoil pad and swivels. Mfg. 1971-1974.

| | $500 | $450 | $425 | $400 | $375 | $325 | $275 |

MODEL 3000 MAGNUM — similar to 3000, except 7mm Rem. Mag., .300 Win. Mag., or .375 H&H Mag. cal., 3 shot mag., 26 in. barrel.

| | $550 | $500 | $450 | $425 | $375 | $350 | $325 |

This model was mfg. by Heym for Mauser.

MODEL 4000 VARMINT RIFLE — similar to 3000, except smaller action, .222 Rem. or .223 Rem. cal., folding leaf rear sight, rubber butt plate.

| | $425 | $400 | $375 | $350 | $300 | $260 | $225 |

This model was mfg. by Heym for Mauser.

RIFLES: .22 CAL.

MODEL 105 STANDARD — .22 LR only, semi-auto, 10 shot mag., approx. 5 lbs. Importation began 1995.

| Mfg.'s Sug. Retail | $330 | $285 | $250 | $205 | $180 | $170 | $155 | $140 |

MODEL 107 STANDARD — .22 LR only, bolt action, 19½ in. barrel, 5 shot clip mag., adj. iron sights, 6 lbs. Imported 1988-89, reintroduced 1993 only.

| | $300 | $260 | $215 | $185 | $170 | $155 | $140 |

Last Mfg.'s Sug. Retail was $356.

This model is the same as KDF's previous Model 2107 mfg. by Voere.

▲ **Model 107 Deluxe** — .22 LR or .22 Mag. cal., similar to Model 2107, except has deluxe checkered walnut. Imported 1988-89 only.

| | $290 | $240 | $210 | $175 | $150 | $135 | $120 |

Last Mfg.'s Sug. Retail was $320.

Add $90 for .22 Mag. cal.

This model is the same as KDF's previous Model 2107 Deluxe mfg. by Voere.

M

MODEL 201 — .22 LR or .22 Mag. cal., bolt action, free-floating 21 in. barrel, clip 5 shot mag., adj. trigger, scaled-down version of the K-15, unusual action incorporates two front-located locking lugs on bolt face that engage Stellite inserts on the front receiver portion, blue only, no sights, beechwood stock with cheekpiece, 6½ lbs.

| Mfg.'s Sug. Retail | $716 | $635 | $515 | $465 | $415 | $365 | $315 | $260 |

Add $19 for sights (disc.).
Add $77 for .22 Mag. cal. (Model 201-SM).

This model is the same as KDF's disc. Model K-22 mfg. by Voere. Before 1989, this model came standard with a walnut stock.

▲ **Model 201 Luxus** — similar to the Model 201 except has walnut stock with rosewood forend.

| Mfg.'s Sug. Retail | $809 | $710 | $650 | $550 | $475 | $425 | $375 | $295 |

Add $27 for sights (disc.).
Add $67 for .22 Mag. cal.

This model is the same as KDF's previous Model K-22 Deluxe mfg. by Voere.

Grading	100%	98%	95%	90%	80%	70%	60%

MODEL DSM34 — .22 LR, bolt action, 25.98 in. barrel. "Deutches Sportmodell" lightweight trainer, side sling, no bayonet lug.

	$625	$375	$325	$300	$260	$225	$200

MODEL MS 420B — .22 LR Sporter, bolt action, pre-war, 5 shot clip mag.

	$1,200	$725	$650	$550	$495	$450	$395

Add 15%-25% for double set triggers (rare).

MODEL ES340 — .22 LR, single shot, bolt action, 25½ in. barrel, adj. sights, checkered pistol grip, grooved forearm, pre-1935.

	$725	$425	$350	$325	$295	$260	$230

MODEL ES350 — .22 LR, single shot, bolt action, 27½ in. barrel, championship rifle, micrometer rear sight, ramp front sight, checkered full target stock, swivels, pre-1935.

	$925	$550	$500	$460	$430	$400	$375

Add 15%-25% for double set triggers (rare).

MODEL M410 — .22 LR, bolt action, repeating, 5 shot detachable mag., 23½ in. barrel, adj. sights, sporter stock, checkered pistol grip, swivels, pre-1935.

	$1,200	$725	$650	$550	$495	$450	$395

Add 15%-25% for double set triggers (rare).

MODEL M420 — .22 LR, bolt action, repeating, 5 shot detachable mag., 25½ in. barrel, adj. sights, sporter stock, checkered pistol grip, swivels, pre-1935.

	$1,200	$725	$650	$550	$495	$450	$395

Add 15%-25% for double set triggers (rare).

MODEL EN310 — .22 LR, single shot, bolt action, 19¾ in. barrel, fixed sights, plain pistol grip stock, pre-1935.

	$625	$365	$315	$280	$260	$225	$200

MODEL EL320 — .22 LR, single shot, bolt action, 23½ in. barrel, fixed sights, checkered pistol grip stock.

	$695	$395	$330	$295	$275	$250	$225

MODEL KKW — .22 LR, single shot, bolt action, target, 26 in. barrel, tangent rear sight, military style stock with bayonet lug. This weapon was also produced by Walther, Gustloff, and Anschutz. It was used as a training rifle in addition to commercial sales. Deduct 15% for 4mm KKW Models.

	$625	$375	$325	$300	$260	$225	$200

MODEL MS350B — .22 LR, bolt action, repeating, 5 shot mag., 26¾ in. barrel, grooved receiver for scope or sight, micrometer rear sight, ramp front sight, target stock, checkered pistol grip and forearm, swivels.

	$1,200	$725	$650	$550	$495	$450	$395

MODEL ES350B — .22 LR, bolt action, single shot, 5 shot mag., 26¾ in. barrel, grooved receiver for scope or sight, micrometer rear sight, ramp front sight, target stock, checkered pistol grip and forearm, swivels.

	$750	$425	$350	$325	$295	$260	$230

MODEL ES340B — .22 LR, bolt action, single shot, 26¾ in. barrel, adj. sight, plain pistol grip stock.

	$650	$375	$325	$300	$260	$225	$200

MODEL MM410BN — .22 LR, bolt action sporter, 5 shot mag., 23½ in. barrel, adj. sights, lightweight stock, checkered pistol grip, swivels.

	$1,100	$650	$575	$500	$450	$400	$365

MODEL MS420B — .22 LR, bolt action target, 5 shot mag., 26¾ in. barrel, adj. sights, target style stock, checkered pistol grip, swivels.

	$1,100	$650	$575	$500	$450	$400	$365

M

Grading	100%	98%	95%	90%	80%	70%	60%

SHOTGUNS

Mauser shotguns were sub-contracted to various European firms and were made in various O/U (including field and target), SxS (both boxlock and sidelock), and single shot configurations. While they are relatively rare (these shotguns had limited importation into the U.S. by Bauer located in Michigan - models included the 496 single shot, 496 SxS, 580 SxS, 610 O/U, 620 O/U, 71E O/U, and others), collectability to date has been minimal. Values will depend on the grade, configuration, features, engraving, and overall desirability. Most of these shotguns have been priced in the $395-$1,350 range, depending on the configuration's desirability.

MAVERICK ARMS, INC.

Currently manufactured by Maverick Arms, Inc. located in Eagle Pass, TX. Administrative offices are at O.F. Mossberg & Sons, located in North Haven, CT. Distributor sales only.

SHOTGUNS

Beginning 1992, all Maverick slide action shotguns incorporate twin slide rails in the operating mechanism.

MODEL 60 SEMI-AUTO — while advertised, this model was never manufactured.

MODEL 88 FIELD MODEL SLIDE ACTION — 12 ga. only, 3 in. chamber, slide-action, 24 (Deer Model with iron sights), 28, or 30 in. plain or VR barrel, wood (disc.) or black synthetic stock and forearm with recoil pad, fixed or Accu-chokes, aluminum alloy receiver, crossbolt safety, approx. $7\frac{1}{4}$ lbs. New 1989.

Mfg.'s Sug. Retail	$221	$185	$145	$125	$115	$110	$105	$100

Add $14 for VR.
Add $14 for Deer Model (24 in. cyl. bore barrel).
Add $18 for choke tube barrel (one choke supplied).

▲ *Model 88 Deer Combos* — includes various combinations of extra Deer barrels with rifle sights, 28 in. plain or VR barrel, or extra $18\frac{1}{2}$ in. cyl. bore barrel. Mfg. 1990-95.

	$245	$190	$160	$130	$120	$110	$105

Last Mfg.'s Sug. Retail was $294.

Add $10 for VR barrel.
Add $17 for Accu choke barrel.
Add $29 for wood stock and forearm (mfg. 1992 only).

▲ *Model 88 Security* — 12 ga., $18\frac{1}{2}$ in. barrel with cyl. bore choke, regular or pistol grip synthetic stock, 6 or 8 shot, plain synthetic forearm. New 1993.

Mfg.'s Sug. Retail	$213	$180	$145	$125	$115	$110	$105	$100

Add $18 for 8 shot model.
Add $18 with pistol grip stock.
Add $98 for Bullpup configuration (6 or 9 shot) (disc. 1994).
Add $47-$65 for combo package.

▲ *Model 88 Combat* — 12 ga. only, combat design featuring pistol grip stock and forearm, black synthetic stock is extension of receiver, $18\frac{1}{2}$ in. cyl. bore barrel with vented shroud with built-in carrying handle, open sights. Mfg. 1990-92.

	$240	$215	$190	$175	$160	$150	$140

Last Mfg.'s Sug. Retail was $282.

MODEL 91 SLIDE ACTION — 12 ga. only, $3\frac{1}{2}$ in. chamber, $18\frac{1}{2}$ cyl. bore or 28 in. VR barrel with 1 choke tube, otherwise similar to Model 88. Mfg. 1991-95.

	$230	$190	$170	$160	$150	$140	$130

Last Mfg.'s Sug. Retail was $269.

Add $2 for VR barrel.

Grading	100%	98%	95%	90%	80%	70%	60%

MODEL 95 BOLT ACTION — 12 ga. only, 3 in. chamber, synthetic stock with recoil pad, 25 in. barrel bored mod., cross-bolt triggerguard safety. New mid-1995.

Mfg.'s Sug. Retail	$184	$155	$135	$115	$100	$90	$80	$70

McBROS RIFLES

Manufacturer located in Phoenix, AZ since 1993. Dealer sales only.

RIFLES: BOLT ACTION

AMERICAN HUNTER — available in 16 cals. between .22-250 Rem. and .416 Rem. Mag., camouflaged fiberglass stock, match grade stainless steel barrel, choice of MCRT (Rem. Model 700 custom type action mfg. to aerospace standards) or MCR (Rem. Model 700 BDL action that has been trued). New 1993.

Mfg.'s Sug. Retail	$1,875	$1,725	$1,500	$1,225	$1,025	$900	$775	$650

Add $425 for MCRT action.

▲ **Yukon Hunter** — available in 7 Mag. cals. between .300 Win. Mag. and .416 Rem. Mag., built to aerospace tolerances for any hunting situation, barrel band sling swivel, folding leaf sight, black synthetic stock. New 1993.

Mfg.'s Sug. Retail	$2,150	$1,925	$1,650	$1,375	$1,175	$1,000	$850	$750

Add $425 for MCRT action.

▲ **Outdoorsman** — .30-378 Wby. or .338-378 Wby. cal., Wby. action only. New 1996.

Mfg.'s Sug. Retail	$2,400	$2,195	$1,750	$1,475	$1,225	$1,025	$900	$775

MCR SNIPER MODEL — .308 Win. or .300 Win. Mag. cal. New 1993.

Mfg.'s Sug. Retail	$1,925	$1,800	$1,525	$1,250	$1,025	$900	$775	$650

▲ **MCRT Sniper Model** — same cals. as MCR Sniper Model. New 1993.

Mfg.'s Sug. Retail	$2,375	$2,175	$1,750	$1,475	$1,225	$1,025	$900	$775

BENCHREST COMPETITOR — .222 Rem., 6mm PPC, 6mm BR (disc. 1995), 7mm BR, or .308 Win. cal., benchrest configuration. New 1993.

Mfg.'s Sug. Retail	$2,450	$2,250	$1,875	$1,650	$1,425	$1,200	$1,025	$875

1000 YARD BENCHREST (NATIONAL MATCH COMPETITOR) — .300 Win. Mag. (new 1996), .30-378 Wby. (new 1996), 7.82 Warbird (new 1996), .308 Win. (disc. 1995) or .338-378 Wby. (new 1996) cal. New 1993.

Mfg.'s Sug. Retail	$2,500	$2,275	$1,900	$1,650	$1,425	$1,200	$1,025	$875

BOOMER — .50 BMG cal., available as either single shot sporter, repeater sporter, light benchrest, or heavy benchrest variation. New 1993.

Mfg.'s Sug. Retail	$3,250	$2,975	$2,525	$2,175	$1,875	$1,650	$1,375	$1,100

Add $300 for repeating action.
Add $175 for heavy benchrest variation.

McMILLAN, G. & CO. INC.

Previous trademark established circa 1988, located in Phoenix, AZ.

G. McMillan & Co. Inc. had various barrel markings from 1988-95 including G. McMillan, Harris - McMillan, and Harris Gunworks (currently manufactured) - please refer to the Harris Gunworks section in this text for current information.

HANDGUNS

WOLVERINE — available in 9mm Para., 10mm, .38 Super, .38 Wad Cutter, .40 S&W, .45 ACP, or .45 Italian cal., interchangeable barrels, competition ready handgun patterned after the Colt 1911. Imported 1992-95.

▲ **Combat Wolverine** — combat features including 5½ in. compensated barrel.

	$1,600	$1,350	$1,025	$875	$750	$625	$550

Last Mfg.'s Sug. Retail was $1,700.

M

Grading	100%	98%	95%	90%	80%	70%	60%

▲ **Competition Match Wolverine** — competition features including 6 in. non-compensated barrel.

$1,600 $1,350 $1,025 $875 $750 $625 $550

Last Mfg.'s Sug. Retail was $1,700.

SIGNATURE JR. BOLT ACTION — available in a variety of cals., utilizes Signature benchrest short action, choice of stainless steel barrel lengths, right or left-hand action, single shot or repeater, McMillan design fiberglass stock, choice of electroless nickel or teflon finish, 5 lbs. Mfg. 1992-95.

$2,175 $1,775 $1,350 $995 $895 $800 $700

Last Mfg.'s Sug. Retail was $2,400.

This model was also available in all titanium.

RIFLES: BOLT ACTION

The models listed below were also available with custom wood stocks at varying prices. McMillan also manufactured a custom rifle from a supplied action - features included new barreling, a fiberglass stock, matte black finish, and range testing to guarantee ¾ M.O.A. Prices started at $1,400.

Add $150 for stainless steel receiver on most models listed below.

TALON SPORTER — available in various cals. between .22-250 and .416 Rem., receiver available in either 4340 chrome molybdenum or 17-4 stainless steel, drilled and tapped, match grade barrel. Mfg. 1992-95.

$2,375 $1,950 $1,650 $1,325 $1,000 $895 $800

Last Mfg.'s Sug. Retail was $2,600.

The Talon action is patterned after the Winchester pre-64 Model 70. It features a cone breech, controlled feed, claw extractor, and 3 position safety.

SIGNATURE CLASSIC SPORTER — various cals. available between .22-250 and .416 Rem., premium wood stock, matte metal finish, buttoning used on rifling for 22 or 24 in. stainless steel barrel, McMillan action made from 4340 chrome moly steel (either left or right-handed), 3 or 4 shot mag. supplied with 5 shot test target. Mfg. 1988-95.

$2,250 $1,850 $1,350 $950 $850 $750 $675

Last Mfg.'s Sug. Retail was $2,400.

SIGNATURE VARMINTER — similar to Signature Model, except is available in 10 cals. between .22-250 and .350 Rem. Mag., hand bedded fiberglass stock, adj. trigger, 26 in. heavily contoured barrel. Mfg. 1988-95.

$2,250 $1,850 $1,350 $995 $895 $800 $700

Last Mfg.'s Sug. Retail was $2,400.

SIGNATURE TITANIUM MOUNTAIN RIFLE — .270 Win., .280 Rem., .30-06, .300 Win. Mag., .338 Win. Mag., or 7mm Rem. Mag. cal., lighter weight variation with shorter barrel. Mfg. 1990-95.

$2,750 $2,195 $1,850 $1,450 $1,100 $925 $825

Last Mfg.'s Sug. Retail was $3,000.

Add $605 for titanium alloy light contour match grade barrel.

SIGNATURE ALASKAN — available in 11 cals. between .270 Win. and .416 Rem. Mfg. 1990-95.

$3,050 $2,475 $2,100 $1,575 $1,200 $1,000 $900

Last Mfg.'s Sug. Retail was $3,300.

TALON SAFARI — available in 15 cals. between .300 Win. Mag. and .460 Weatherby, hand-bedded fiberglass stock, 4 shot mag., 24 in. stainless steel barrel, matte black finish, 9 ½ lbs. Mfg. 1988-95.

$3,275 $2,675 $2,300 $1,675 $1,300 $1,100 $950

Last Mfg.'s Sug. Retail was $3,600.

Add $600 for .300 Phoenix, .338 Lapua, .378 Wby., .416 Wby. or Rigby, or .460 Wby. cal.

The Talon action is patterned after the Winchester pre-64 Model 70. It featured a cone breech, controlled feed, claw extractor, and 3-position safety. Older Signature action rifles did not have this new Talon action.

M-40 SNIPER RIFLE — .308 Win., Remington action with McMillan match grade heavy contour barrel, fiberglass stock with recoil pad, 4 shot mag., 9 lbs. Mfg. 1990-95.

$1,675 $1,375 $1,050 $895 $800 $700 $600

Last Mfg.'s Sug. Retail was $1,800.

Grading	100%	98%	95%	90%	80%	70%	60%

M-86 SNIPER RIFLE — .300 Phoenix, .30-06 (new 1989), .300 Win. Mag. or .308 cal., fiberglass stock, variety of optical sights. Mfg. 1988-95.

	$1,725	$1,400	$1,075	$925	$825	$725	$625

Last Mfg.'s Sug. Retail was $1,900.

> Add $550 for .300 Phoenix cal.
> Add $200 for takedown feature (new 1993).

▲ **M-86 Sniper System** — includes Model 86 Sniper Rifle, bipod, Ultra scope, rings, and bases. Cased. Mfg. 1988-92.

	$2,460	$2,050	$1,825	$1,600	$1,350	$1,100	$950

Last Mfg.'s Sug. Retail was $2,665.

M-87 LONG RANGE SNIPER RIFLE — .50 BMG, stainless steel bolt action, 29 in. barrel with muzzle brake, single shot, camo synthetic stock, accurate to 1500 meters, 21 lbs. Mfg. 1988-95.

	$3,350	$2,750	$2,350	$2,000	$1,850	$1,700	$1,575

Last Mfg.'s Sug. Retail was $3,735.

▲ **M-87 Sniper System** — includes Model 87 Sniper Rifle, bipod, 20X Ultra scope, rings, and bases. Cased. Mfg 1988-92.

	$3,950	$3,400	$3,000	$2,750	$2,450	$2,200	$2,000

Last Mfg.'s Sug. Retail was $4,200.

▲ **M-87R** — same specs. as Model 87, except has 5 shot fixed box mag. Mfg. 1990-95.

	$3,750	$2,950	$2,550	$2,200	$2,000	$1,850	$1,700

Last Mfg.'s Sug. Retail was $4,000.

> Add $300 for Combo option.

M-89 SNIPER RIFLE — .308 Win., 28 in. barrel with suppressor (also available without), fiberglass stock adj. for length and recoil pad, 15¼ lbs. Mfg. 1990-95.

	$2,075	$1,675	$1,375	$1,050	$895	$800	$700

Last Mfg.'s Sug. Retail was $2,300.

> Add $425 for muzzle suppressor.

M-92 BULLPUP — .50 BMG cal., bullpup configuration with shorter barrel. Mfg. 1993-95.

	$3,750	$2,950	$2,550	$2,200	$2,000	$1,850	$1,700

Last Mfg.'s Sug. Retail was $4,000.

M-93SN — .50 BMG cal., similar to M-87, except has folding stock and detachable 5 or 10 shot box mag. Mfg. 1993-95.

	$3,950	$3,250	$2,750	$2,300	$2,000	$1,850	$1,700

Last Mfg.'s Sug. Retail was $4,300.

.300 PHOENIX LONG RANGE RIFLE — .300 Phoenix cal., special fiberglass stock featuring adj. cheekpieces to accommodate night vision optics, adj. buttplate, 29 in. barrel, conventional box mag., 12½ lbs. Mfg. 1992 only.

	$2,700	$2,195	$1,850	$1,450	$1,100	$925	$825

Last Mfg.'s Sug. Retail was $3,000.

> .300 Phoenix is a new cartridge developed to function at ranges in excess of 800 yards. It produces muzzle velocities of 3100 ft. per second with a 250 grain bullet.

COMPETITION MODELS — available in Metallic Silhouette (.308 or 7mm/08 cal. - disc. 1989), National Match (.308 cal. only), Long Range (.300 Win. Mag. only), or Bench Rest (shooter's choice). Each model made specifically for individual competition events. Mfg. 1988-95.

Mfg.'s Sug. Retail	$2,600	$2,325	$1,775	$1,450	$1,100	$895	$800	$700

Last Mfg.'s Sug. Retail was $2,600.

> Add $200 for Benchrest Model.
> Subtract $300 for Metallic Silhouette model (disc. 1989).

MENZ, AUGUST

Previous manufacturer located in Suhl, Germany.

Please refer to listings in the Liliput section of this text.

M

MERCURY

Previous importer of Spanish mfg. shotguns.

Grading	100%	98%	95%	90%	80%	70%	60%

MAGNUM DOUBLE BARREL — 10, 12, or 20 ga. Mag., 28 and 32 in. barrels, full and mod., boxlock, extractors, double triggers, engraved frame, checkered pistol grip stock.

	100%	98%	95%	90%	80%	70%	60%
	$300	$275	$250	$225	$200	$180	$150
10 gauge	$400	$375	$325	$300	$275	$225	$200

MERCURY

Previous manufacturer located in Belgium.

MERCURY SEMI-AUTO — .22 LR, 7 shot mag., steel frame, fixed sights.

	100%	98%	95%	90%	80%	70%	60%
	$400	$375	$325	$300	$275	$225	$200

MERKEL, GEBRUDER

Manufacturer located in Suhl, Germany since 1535. Currently imported exclusively by GSI, Inc. located in Trussville, AL. Previously imported (until 1992) by Armes de Chasse located in Chadds Ford, PA 19317.

For many years Merkel shotguns had a unfair disadvantage in this country because of the politics of importing firearms from communist bloc countries (goods were subject to a 65% non-favored nation tax). With the reunification of Germany in 1991, this trademark has become more competitive domestically. Merkel continues to manufacture high quality guns. Recently manufactured guns beginning 1995 employ an alpha numeric date code for year of manufacture, making it difficult to determine year of manufacture by serial number. Higher grade models (including the 300 Series) continue to be manufactured one at a time by hand, with less than 30 being mfg. annually.

DRILLINGS

Current Merkel Drillings include a choice of 12, 16, or 20 ga. for the shotgun barrels with the rifle barrel being bored in most popular U.S. and metric cals. between .22 Hornet and 9.3x74R. All current models are boxlocks with extractors. Presently, there are four Drilling models available (Models 90 - disc. 1994, 90S, 90K, 95 - disc. 1994, 95S, and 95K) ranging in value from $5,995 (Model 90S), $6,495 (Model 90K), $7,195 (Model 95S), and $7,695 (Model 95K). Models differ in amount of engraving, cocking systems, and quality of wood - please contact the importer for more information on these individual models.

MERKEL ANSON DRILLING — usually 2 shotguns over rifle, although 2 rifles over shotgun have been noted, 12, 16, or 20 ga., calibers 7x57R, 8x57JR, and 9.3x74R cals. most common, others noted, 25.6 in. or 21.6 in. barrels, boxlock, Anson & Deeley system, double triggers, extractors, checkered pistol grip stock, pre-WWII.

MODEL 142 — engraved.

	100%	98%	95%	90%	80%	70%	60%
	$5,000	$4,000	$3,000	$2,750	$2,500	$2,200	$2,000

MODEL 142 — less ornamentation.

	100%	98%	95%	90%	80%	70%	60%
	$4,000	$3,500	$3,000	$2,500	$2,250	$2,100	$2,000

MODEL 145 — least ornamentation.

	100%	98%	95%	90%	80%	70%	60%
	$3,000	$2,800	$2,700	$2,600	$2,500	$2,100	$1,900

RIFLES AND COMBINATION GUNS

Models and values listed below reflect 1993 information (with the economic integration of previous Eastern bloc countries into the free marketplace, Merkel is once again manufacturing a more complete line-up of firearms).

M

Grading	100%	98%	95%	90%	80%	70%	60%

O/U COMBINATION GUN — 12, 16, or 20 ga., over 5.6x50R, 5.6x52R, 6.5x55, 6.5x57R, 7x57R, 7x65R, 8x57JRS, 9.3x74R, .22 Hornet, .222 Rem., .243 Win., .30-06, .308 Win., or .375 H&H Mag. (disc. 1994) cal., 25.6 in. barrels, various chokes.

▲ **Model 210E**

Mfg.'s Sug. Retail $6,195	$5,700	$4,600	$3,700	$3,150	$2,600	$2,100	$1,800

▲ **Model 211E**

Mfg.'s Sug. Retail $6,995	$6,300	$4,550	$3,750	$3,250	$2,775	$2,275	$1,925

▲ **Model 213E**

Mfg.'s Sug. Retail $13,595	$12,150	$10,250	$7,950	$6,850	$5,725	$4,600	$3,550

▲ **Model 313E**

Mfg.'s Sug. Retail $20,695	$17,750	$14,250	$12,000	$9,750	$8,250	$7,000	$5,800

SxS COMBINATION GUN — similar gauges and cals. to O/U Combination Gun, boxlock models include 8EI and 9EI, 10EI is a sidelock, boxlock models range in price from $5,500-$7,000 and the Model 10EI is $9,500. Importation disc. 1990.

O/U DOUBLE RIFLE — same cals. as the O/U Combination Gun, various actions, engraving options, and other special orders.

▲ **Model 220E Boxlock** — boxlock blitz action, scroll engraved case hardened receiver, DTs, pistol grip with cheekpiece. Importation disc. 1994.

$9,575	$8,250	$7,150	$6,100	$5,100	$4,250	$3,500

Last Mfg.'s Sug. Retail was $10,795.

▲ **Model 221E Boxlock** — similar to 220E, except has silver grayed receiver with hunting scene engraving.

Mfg.'s Sug. Retail $9,995	$9,350	$8,200	$7,350	$6,250	$5,100	$4,250	$3,350

▲ **Model 223E Sidelock** — sidelock action with arabesque engraving featuring large scrolls, sideplates removed without tools.

Mfg.'s Sug. Retail $16,295	$14,950	$12,750	$10,500	$9,500	$8,350	$7,350	$6,250

▲ **Model 323E Sidelock** — similar to 223E Sidelock, except has medium scrollwork engraving, top-of-the-line O/U double rifle.

Mfg.'s Sug. Retail $24,595	$21,500	$19,150	$16,500	$13,250	$11,000	$9,750	$8,350

SxS DOUBLE RIFLE — same cals. as listed for the O/U Combination Gun.

▲ **Model 140-1** — Anson & Deeley boxlock action with cocking indicators, double triggers, engraved case hardened receiver. Importation began 1994.

Mfg.'s Sug. Retail $5,295	$4,625	$3,625	$2,900	$2,350	$1,975	$1,825	$1,675

Add $200 for set front trigger.
Add $700 for engraved hunting scenes on silver/gray receiver (Model 140-1.1).

▲ **Model 150-1** — Anson & Deeley boxlock action with cocking indicators and sideplates, double triggers, silver grayed receiver with Arabesque engraving. Importation began 1994.

Mfg.'s Sug. Retail $6,795	$6,050	$5,075	$4,250	$3,700	$3,250	$2,675	$2,100

Add $200 for set front trigger.
Add $1,100 for hunting scene engraving (Model 150-1.1).

▲ **Model 160S-1** — sidelock action with Greener crossbolt featuring fine Arabesque engraving, H&H ejectors, DTs, pistol grip stock with cheekpiece.

Mfg.'s Sug. Retail $11,995	$10,475	$8,750	$7,375	$6,350	$5,200	$4,350	$3,550

Add $500 for set front trigger.
Add $1,000 for single non-selective trigger.
Add $1,300 for engraved hunting scenes on silver/gray receiver (Model 160S-1.1).

SHOTGUNS: DISC.

MODEL 100 O/U — 12, 16, or 20 ga., various barrel lengths and chokes, boxlock, Greener cross bolt, double triggers, extractors, checkered pistol grip or English style stock, pre-WWII.

Plain	$1,450	$1,250	$1,000	$925	$850	$675	$550
Ribbed	$1,550	$1,300	$1,050	$950	$875	$700	$575

M

Grading	100%	98%	95%	90%	80%	70%	60%

MODEL 101 — similar to 100, except selective extractors, rib barrel, some English style scroll engraving, pre-WWII.

	$1,600	$1,325	$1,100	$1,000	$900	$750	$600

MODEL 101E — similar to 100, except auto ejectors, pre-WWII.

	$1,750	$1,425	$1,250	$1,150	$1,000	$875	$750

MODEL 400 — similar to 101, except arabesque engraving and Kersten double cross bolt, pre-WWII.

	$1,650	$1,350	$1,200	$1,100	$975	$825	$675

MODEL 400E — similar to 400, except auto ejector, pre-WWII.

	$1,800	$1,450	$1,325	$1,175	$1,025	$925	$775

MODEL 410 — similar to 400, except more engraving and fancier wood, pre-WWII.

	$1,750	$1,425	$1,250	$1,150	$1,000	$875	$750

MODEL 410E — similar to 410, except auto ejectors, pre-WWII.

	$1,900	$1,600	$1,450	$1,225	$1,100	$995	$875

MODEL 200 O/U — 12, 16, 20, 24, 28, or 32 ga., ribbed barrels in various lengths, Kersten double cross bolt, scalloped frame, boxlock, double triggers, extractors, cocking indicators, either pistol grip or English style checkered stock.

	$1,700	$1,350	$1,100	$990	$770	$660	$635

MODEL 210 — similar to 200, except engraved and better grade wood, pre-WWII.

	$1,900	$1,500	$1,300	$1,075	$895	$800	$725

MODEL 201 O/U — 12, 16, or 20 ga., Greener crossbolt, hunting engraving or fine arabesque, dark walnut.

	$2,000	$1,600	$1,425	$1,200	$995	$900	$800

MODEL 201E — similar to 201, except with auto ejectors, pre-WWII.

	$2,400	$1,825	$1,600	$1,400	$1,200	$1,075	$950

MODEL 202 — similar to 201, except with false sideplates, higher quality wood, more profuse engraving, pre-WWII.

	$2,800	$2,400	$2,035	$1,700	$1,450	$1,200	$1,050

MODEL 202E — similar to 202, with auto ejectors, pre-WWII.

	$3,200	$2,800	$2,485	$2,050	$1,700	$1,425	$1,200

MODEL 203E O/U — similar to 202E, except better engraving and wood.

	$4,000	$3,400	$2,900	$2,500	$2,100	$1,800	$1,425

MODEL 204E O/U — similar to 203E, but fine English scroll engraving and Merkel sidelocks, ejectors, pre-WWII.

	$5,650	$4,900	$4,300	$3,850	$3,300	$2,750	$2,100

MODEL 300 O/U — 12, 16, 20, 24, 28, or 32 ga., various lengths and choke ribbed barrels, Merkel-Anson boxlock, Kersten double cross bolt, two underlugs, scalloped frame, either English or pistol grip style stock, cocking indicators, pre-WWII.

	$2,100	$1,900	$1,700	$1,550	$1,375	$1,200	$1,050

This model is usually encountered without engraving and has standard wood.

MODEL 300E — similar to 300, with auto ejectors, pre-WWII.

	$2,500	$2,250	$1,900	$1,750	$1,500	$1,350	$1,175

This model is usually encountered without engraving and has standard wood.

MODEL 301 — similar to 300, but more profusely engraved and better grade wood pre-WWII.

	$5,250	$4,250	$3,995	$3,500	$3,000	$2,600	$2,150

MODEL 310E — similar to 300, with auto ejectors, pre-WWII.

	$6,250	$5,300	$4,450	$3,900	$3,400	$3,000	$2,550

Grading	100%	98%	95%	90%	80%	70%	60%

MODEL 302 — similar to 301, but has auto ejectors and more elaborate ornamentation, false sideplates and better grade wood.

	$10,500	$8,500	$6,500	$5,750	$4,900	$4,150	$3,400

MODEL 304E O/U — special order version of 303E, higher quality and more ornamentation, top of Merkel O/U line.

	$16,500	$12,000	$10,500	$8,750	$7,500	$6,250	$5,000

MODEL 130 SxS — all standard gauges, barrel lengths and chokes, Anson & Deeley action with false side plates, boxlock, auto ejectors, English style or pistol grip stock, elaborate game scenes and arabesque engraving, pre-WWII.

	$12,000	$9,500	$7,500	$6,350	$5,400	$4,600	$3,950

MODEL 127 SxS — all standard gauges, barrel lengths and chokes, H&H style hand detachable sidelocks, auto ejectors, double triggers, pistol or English style stock elaborately engraved, this is a best grade gun, pre-WWII.

	$21,500	$16,500	$12,500	$10,000	$8,800	$7,000	$5,750

SHOTGUNS: SxS RECENT IMPORTATION

MODEL 8 — 12, 16 (disc.), or 20 ga., case hardened scalloped boxlock action with light engraving, Greener crossbolt with chopper lump extension, extractors, SST (current) or DT, standard walnut with checkering, pistol grip or English style stock, sling swivels (disc. 1992). Disc. 1994.

	$1,150	$950	$795	$700	$625	$550	$475

Last Mfg.'s Sug. Retail was $1,695.

While discontinued, limited quantities of this model are still available.

MODEL 47E — 12, 16, or 20 ga., case hardened scalloped boxlock action with chopper lump extension and Greener crossbolt, 26 (disc.), 26¾, or 28 in. barrels, SST (current) or DT, ejectors, deluxe checkered walnut, pistol grip or English style stock, sling swivels (disc. 1992), 6-7 lbs.

Mfg.'s Sug. Retail	$2,295	$1,895	$1,475	$1,200	$975	$850	$750	$650

MODEL 47S — 12, 16, 20, 28 (disc.), or .410 (disc.) ga., coin finished sidelock action with scroll engraving, Greener crossbolt, ST (current) or DT, deluxe walnut stock (with cheekpiece) and forearm, sling swivels (disc. 1992).

Mfg.'s Sug. Retail	$4,895	$4,375	$3,875	$3,300	$2,750	$2,300	$1,975	$1,625

Add $995 for 28 or .410 ga. (mfg. 1992 only).

MODEL 76E — top-of-the-line boxlock shotgun. Importation disc. 1992.

	$2,600	$2,100	$1,850	$1,600	$1,325	$995	$775

Last Mfg.'s Sug. Retail was $3,500.

MODEL 147 — 12, 16, 20, or 28 (new 1995, 147E only) ga., 26¾ or 28 in. barrels, Anson & Deeley boxlock, any choke, SST (current) or DT, extractors, straight or pistol grip stock, hunting scene engraved.

Mfg.'s Sug. Retail	$2,595	$2,100	$1,675	$1,325	$1,050	$875	$750	$650

Add $200 for H&H style auto ejectors (Model 147E).
Add $1,000 for 28 ga (Model 147E only).

MODEL 122 — 12, 16, or 20 ga., Anson & Deeley boxlock action with silver grayed false sideplates, H&H ejectors, SST or DT, fine hunting scenes with arabesque engraving, pistol grip or English style stock. Importation began 1993.

Mfg.'s Sug. Retail	$4,595	$4,000	$3,575	$3,125	$2,550	$2,050	$1,725	$1,375

Subtract $100 for 20 ga.

MODEL 122E — 12, 16, or 20 ga., coin finished sidelock action with Greener crossbolt and chopper lump extension, cocking indicators, ejectors, DTs, deluxe game scene engraving. Importation disc. 1991.

	$3,200	$2,800	$2,250	$1,950	$1,650	$1,375	$995

Last Mfg.'s Sug. Retail was $3,500.

M

Grading	100%	98%	95%	90%	80%	70%	60%

MODEL 147S — 12, 16, 20, 28, or .410 (disc.) ga., coin finished sidelock action with Greener crossbolt and chopper lump extension, 25½ (disc.), 26 (disc.), 26¾, or 28 in. barrels, ejectors, ST (current) or DT, deluxe game scene engraving, 6-7 lbs.

Mfg.'s Sug. Retail $6,195 $5,700 $4,950 $4,250 $3,750 $3,000 $2,500 $2,100

   Add $300 for 28 ga. or $750 for .410 ga. (mfg. 1992 only).

MODEL 247S — 12, 16, or 20 ga., similar to Model 147S, except has deluxe scroll engraving. Importation disc. 1991, resumed 1993.

Mfg.'s Sug. Retail $6,895 $6,375 $4,450 $3,650 $3,150 $2,625 $2,175 $1,850

MODEL 347S — 12, 16, or 20 ga., similar to Model 247S, except has more elaborate engraving and better walnut. Importation disc. 1991, resumed 1993.

Mfg.'s Sug. Retail $7,895 $7,000 $4,850 $3,950 $3,350 $2,775 $2,275 $1,925

MODEL 447S — similar to Model 347S, except has smaller type of scroll engraving. Importation disc. 1991, resumed 1993.

Mfg.'s Sug. Retail $8,995 $7,750 $5,350 $4,250 $3,550 $2,900 $2,400 $2,000

SHOTGUNS: O/U CURRENT IMPORTATION

MODEL 200E BOXLOCK — 12, 16, or 20 ga., case hardened scalloped boxlock action with minor scroll engraving, 26 (disc.), 26¾, or 28 in. barrels, checkered European walnut stock and forearm, ejectors, SST or DT, pistol grip or English style stock, solid rib, 6-7 lbs. Importation disc. 1994.

   $3,000 $2,500 $2,050 $1,850 $1,600 $1,300 $1,100

Last Mfg.'s Sug. Retail was $3,695.

   While discontinued, limited quantities of this model are still available.

▲ *Model 200ES Skeet* — 12 ga. only, 26¾ in. VR barrels bored skeet/skeet. Imported 1993-94.

   $4,550 $3,950 $3,500 $3,000 $2,500 $2,100 $1,625

Last Mfg.'s Sug. Retail was $4,995.

▲ *Model 200ET Trap* — 12 ga. only, 30 in. VR barrels bored full/full (other choke configurations available upon request). Importation disc. 1994.

   $4,400 $3,750 $3,300 $2,800 $2,300 $2,000 $1,550

Last Mfg.'s Sug. Retail was $5,195.

   While discontinued, limited quantities of this model are still available.

MODEL 201E — 12, 16, 20, or 28 (new 1995) ga., similar to Model 200E, except has coin finished action with light game scene engraving.

Mfg.'s Sug. Retail $5,495 $4,895 $4,150 $3,350 $2,700 $2,150 $1,775 $1,425

   Add $500 for 28 ga.

▲ *Model 201ES Skeet* — 12 ga. only, 26¾ in. VR barrels bored skeet/skeet. Importation began 1993.

Mfg.'s Sug. Retail $8,195 $7,650 $6,575 $5,350 $4,300 $3,450 $2,900 $2,250

▲ *Model 201ET Trap* — 12 ga. only, 30 in. VR barrels bored full/full (other choke configurations available upon request).

Mfg.'s Sug. Retail $8,195 $7,650 $6,575 $5,350 $4,300 $3,450 $2,900 $2,250

MODEL 202E — similar to 201E, except has fine hunting scenes with arabesque engraving on silver false sideplates, not available in 28 ga. Importation began 1993.

Mfg.'s Sug. Retail $9,295 $8,125 $6,850 $5,175 $4,400 $3,700 $3,350 $2,850

MODEL 203E SIDELOCK — 12, 16, or 20 ga. (24, 28, and 32 ga.'s were once available but are now disc.), 26 (disc.), 26¾, or 28 in. barrels, VR, H&H ejectors, SST (current) or DT, elaborate scroll engraving on coin finished receiver, sidelock screws are H&H style but the removable sidelocks are not, choice of English or pistol grip stock, 6-7 lbs.

Mfg.'s Sug. Retail $11,295 $9,300 $6,150 $4,775 $3,800 $3,350 $2,500 $2,150

▲ *Model 203ES Skeet* — 12 ga. only, 26¾ in. VR barrels bored skeet/skeet. Importation began 1993.

Mfg.'s Sug. Retail $13,995 $11,650 $8,800 $7,100 $5,875 $4,900 $3,950 $3,500

▲ *Model 203ET Trap* — 12 ga. only, 30 in. VR barrels bored full/full (other choke configurations available upon request).

Mfg.'s Sug. Retail $13,995 $11,650 $8,800 $7,100 $5,875 $4,900 $3,950 $3,500

Grading	100%	98%	95%	90%	80%	70%	60%

MODEL 303E — similar to 203E, except H&H type with hidden thumbnail detachable sidelocks, double underlugs, more ornamentation and better wood.

Mfg.'s Sug. Retail	$18,995	$15,750	$13,500	$11,250	$9,350	$8,000	$7,000	$5,800

MODEL 304E (LUXUS GRADE) — available in SxS, O/U, Drilling, or Combo configuration, top-of-the-line Merkel with extensive engraving and typically stock carving (with or without inlays).

Values generally start at $16,500 and go up according to engraving and stock work.

Luxus variations are also encountered in the 201 and 203 series in addition to older pre-war models.

SHOTGUNS: SPORTING CLAYS COMPETITION

MODEL 47LSC SxS SPORTING CLAYS — 12 ga. only, features Anson & Deeley boxlock action with scroll engraved case hardened receiver, 28 in. barrels with Briley screw-in chokes, H&H style ejectors, SST adj. for length of pull, select grade checkered walnut stock with pistol grip and beavertail forearm, competition recoil pad. Disc. 1994.

		$2,725	$2,400	$2,050	$1,725	$1,450	$1,125	$925

Last Mfg.'s Sug. Retail was $2,995.

MODEL 200SC O/U SPORTING CLAYS — 12 ga. only, 3 in. chambers, 30 in. VR fixed choke barrels with lengthened forcing cones, Kersten double cross-bolt lock, color case hardened receiver, Blitz action, SST, fitted luggage case. New 1995.

Mfg.'s Sug. Retail	$7,495	$6,750	$4,600	$3,750	$3,200	$2,625	$2,175	$1,850

Add $500 for Briley choke tubes (5 total).

MERRILL

Originally designed by Jim Rock, currently with R.P.M.

A newer variation of the Sportsman, now designated the XL and Hunter Model XL is currently being offered by R.P.M. Please refer to the R.P.M. listing for more information.

SPORTSMAN SINGLE-SHOT PISTOL — .22 S, L, or LR, .22 WMR, .22 Rem. Jet., .22 Hornet, 30 Herrett, .38 Spl., .357 Mag., .256 Win. Mag., .45 Colt, .44 Mag., or .30-30 cal., 9 in. barrel, hinged break open available, smooth walnut grips.

		$650	$575	$525	$450	$395	$350	$300

Add $70 for interchangeable barrels.
Add $25 for wrist support.

MERWIN HULBERT & CO.

Merwin Hulbert & Co. headquarters were located in New York, NY from 1874-1891. Manufactured at the Hopkins & Allen Manufacturing Co. (not by Hopkins & Allen) factory utilizing their own workforce and equipment which at the time was state-of-the-art.

Merwin Hulbert & Co. were designers and promoters who created a revolver that had such advanced features as an automatic ejection system, streamlined appearance, and ease of shooting.

Grading	100%	95%	80%	50%	20%	Traces	Grey

REVOLVERS

FIRST MODEL — .44-40 cal. various barrel lengths.

	$2,000	$1,600	$1,200	$900	$700	$600	$450

ENGRAVED .44-40 CALS.

	$7,000	$6,000	$5,000	$4,000	$3,000	$2,000	$1,000

SECOND MODEL

	$1,800	$1,400	$1,000	$800	$600	$500	$450

ENGRAVED

	$7,000	$6,000	$5,000	$4,000	$3,000	$2,000	$1,000

Grading	100%	95%	80%	50%	20%	Traces	Grey
THIRD MODEL S.A.							
	$1,500	$1,200	$900	$700	$600	$500	$450
THIRD MODEL D.A.							
	$1,400	$1,100	$800	$600	$500	$400	$400
ENGRAVED							
	$6,000	$5,500	$4,500	$3,500	$2,500	$1,500	$1,000

This model is rare and only infrequently encountered.

Grading	100%	95%	80%	50%	20%	Traces	Grey
FOURTH MODEL S.A. — 7 in. barrel.							
	$10,000	$8,000	$6,000	$4,000	$3,000	$2,000	$1,000

This model is rare and only infrequently encountered.

Grading	100%	95%	80%	50%	20%	Traces	Grey
FOURTH MODEL S.A. — 5½ in. barrel.							
	$4,000	$3,200	$2,500	$2,000	$1,500	$1,100	$800

This model is rare and only infrequently encountered.

Grading	100%	95%	80%	50%	20%	Traces	Grey
FOURTH MODEL D.A. — 5½ in. barrel.							
	$3,000	$2,500	$2,000	$1,500	$1,000	$800	$600

This model is rare and only infrequently encountered.

Grading	100%	95%	80%	50%	20%	Traces	Grey
FOURTH MODEL D.A. — 7 in. barrel.							
	$9,000	$7,500	$5,500	$3,500	$2,500	$1,000	$800

This model is rare and only infrequently encountered.

Grading	100%	95%	80%	50%	20%	Traces	Grey
FOURTH MODEL S.A. — 3½ in. barrel.							
	$10,000	$8,000	$6,000	$4,000	$3,000	$2,000	$1,000

This model is rare and only infrequently encountered.

Grading	100%	95%	80%	50%	20%	Traces	Grey
FOURTH MODEL D.A. — 3½ in. barrel.							
	$9,000	$7,500	$5,500	$3,500	$2,500	$1,500	$800

This model is rare and only infrequently encountered.

POCKET PISTOLS

Add 25% for blued finish.
Add 25% for extra matching barrel.
Add $300 for pearl, ivory, or mottled grips.

Grading	100%	95%	80%	50%	20%	Traces	Grey
POCKET ARMY S.A. SECOND MODEL							
	$1,800	$1,400	$1,000	$800	$600	$500	$450
POCKET ARMY S.A. THIRD MODEL							
	$1,550	$1,175	$900	$725	$575	$475	$425
POCKET ARMY D.A.							
	$1,500	$1,200	$900	$750	$550	$450	$400
POCKET ARMY FOURTH MODEL							
	$9,000	$7,500	$5,500	$3,500	$2,500	$1,500	$800

This model is rare and only infrequently encountered.

Grading	100%	95%	80%	50%	20%	Traces	Grey
.38 BIRDSHEAD GRIP							
	$1,000	$800	$600	$500	$450	$350	$300

This model is rare and only infrequently encountered.

Grading	100%	95%	80%	50%	20%	Traces	Grey
.38 SAW HANDLE							
	$800	$600	$500	$400	$300	$250	$200
.38 SINGLE ACTION							
	$2,000	$1,700	$1,400	$1,000	$700	$500	$300

This model is rare and only infrequently encountered.

Grading	100%	95%	80%	50%	20%	Traces	Grey

1ST MODEL .38 CAL. 5 SHOT

▲ *Spur Trigger Birdshead*

| | $1,000 | $800 | $600 | $500 | $450 | $350 | $300 |

This model is rare and only infrequently encountered.

▲ *Spur Trigger Saw Handle*

| | $800 | $600 | $500 | $400 | $300 | $250 | $200 |

2ND AND 3RD MODELS .38 CAL. 5 SHOT

▲ *Birdshead Grips*

| | $1,000 | $800 | $600 | $500 | $450 | $350 | $300 |

This model is rare and only infrequently encountered.

▲ *Saw Handle Double Action*

| | $800 | $600 | $500 | $400 | $300 | $250 | $200 |

.32 CAL. LONG ON .38 CAL. FRAME 7 SHOT

| | $1,200 | $1,000 | $900 | $800 | $700 | $500 | $400 |

This model is rare and only infrequently encountered.

.32 S&W 5 SHOT

| | $600 | $550 | $400 | $350 | $300 | $250 | $200 |

.22 CAL. 7 SHOT

| | $500 | $450 | $350 | $250 | $200 | $150 | $100 |

Add approx. 200% for engraved model.

FOREIGN S.A. .44 CAL.

▲ *Frontier Army*

| | $1,800 | $1,400 | $1,000 | $800 | $600 | $400 | $300 |

▲ *Frontier Army D.A.*

| | $1,600 | $1,200 | $900 | $700 | $500 | $400 | $300 |

FOREIGN S.A. .44 CAL. 7 IN.

| | $1,500 | $1,200 | $800 | $600 | $500 | $450 | $400 |

FOREIGN S.A. .44 CAL. 3½ IN.

| | $1,100 | $700 | $500 | $400 | $300 | $250 | $200 |

Grading	100%	98%	95%	90%	80%	70%	60%

MICHIGAN ARMAMENT

Previous manufacturer located in Michigan until circa 1981.

PISTOLS: SEMI-AUTO

GUARDIAN - SS — .380 ACP cal., patterned after the Walther PPK, bears close resemblance to the Indian Arms .380 semi-auto, 3¼ in. barrel, checkered walnut grips with medallion, 6 shot finger extension mag., fixed sights. Disc.

| | $350 | $275 | $225 | $210 | $190 | $170 | $150 |

MIIDA

Manufactured by Nikko Firearms, Ltd. in Tochigi, Japan. Imported by Marubeni America Corp. located in New york, NY 1972-1974.

MODEL 612 FIELD — O/U shotgun, 12 ga., 26 or 28 in. barrels, VR, various chokes, boxlock, auto ejectors, single selective trigger, checkered pistol grip stock. Mfg. 1972-1974.

| | $800 | $725 | $650 | $575 | $510 | $440 | $400 |

M

Grading	100%	98%	95%	90%	80%	70%	60%

MODEL 2100 SKEET GUN — similar to Model 612, with 27 in. VR, skeet bore barrels, more elaborate engraving. Mfg. 1972-1974.

	$875	$775	$700	$615	$550	$465	$425

MODEL 2200T TRAP GUN — similar to Model 2100, except with 29¾ in. imp. mod. and full choke barrels, wide VR, 60% engraved coverage and select wood. Mfg. 1972-1974.

	$925	$825	$750	$665	$595	$500	$450

MODEL 2200S SKEET GUN — similar to Model 2200T, except with 27 in. skeet bore barrels.

	$925	$825	$750	$665	$595	$500	$450

MODEL 2300 SERIES TRAP OR SKEET — similar to Model 2200 Trap/Skeet but with more engraving. Mfg. 1972-1974.

	$975	$875	$800	$715	$630	$550	$500

MODEL GRT GRANDEE TRAP GUN — 12 ga., 29¾ in. full choke barrels, single selective trigger, auto ejector, boxlock with side plates, receiver fully engraved as well as breech ends of barrel, triggerguard and locking lever, gold inlaid, extensive silver line inlays, high grade select walnut stock. Mfg. 1972-1974.

	$2,500	$2,200	$1,900	$1,575	$1,250	$1,000	$850

MODEL GRS GRANDEE SKEET GUN — similar to Model GRT, with 27 in. skeet bored barrels.

	$2,500	$2,200	$1,900	$1,575	$1,250	$1,000	$850

MIL-SPEC INDUSTRIES CORP.

Handgun importer located in Roslyn Heights, NY since 1995. Manufactured by Transmark Ltd. located in Tel-Aviv, Israel.

M-5 1911A1 (BUL 1911-A1) — 9mm Para., 9x21mm, 9x22mm, .40 S&W, .45 HP, or .45 ACP cal., high tech polymer and stainless steel frame, beavertail grip safety, aluminum trigger, 4¼ (Commander) or 5 (Standard) in. barrel, approx. 28 oz. New 1995.

Mfg.'s Sug. Retail	$690		$625	$550	$500	$450	$400	$360	$330

Add $5 for parkerized finish.
Add $45 for electroless nickel finish.
Add $50 for hard chrome finish.

MILLER, DAVID CO.

See David Miller Co. listing.

MIROKU FIREARMS MFG. CO.

Manufacturer located in Miroku, Japan since 1893. Miroku currently manufactures long arms for Browning and Winchester (please refer to individual sections), in addition to their own line of firearms mostly distributed in Europe.

Shotguns marked Miroku only without another trademark listing represent that period of manufacture before Miroku began manufacturing shotguns for other companies (i.e. Charles Daly, SKB, Browning, and others). Most guns marked Miroku only were made on a limited basis and although somewhat rare, collector desirability to date has been minimal. Since model notations were not specified in most instances (many shotguns were made to test market demand), a model rundown is virtually impossible. Values can be approx. ascertained by comparing a Miroku shotgun of similar gauge, features, engraving/wood, and condition to an equivalent Japanese Charles Daly model. Miroku also manufactured revolvers up until approx. 1964 which may be designated Liberty Chief - limited importation into the U.S.

MITCHELL ARMS, INC.

Manufacturer, importer and distributor located in Santa Ana, CA. Distributor sales only.

Grading	100%	98%	95%	90%	80%	70%	60%

DERRINGERS: O/U

GUARDIAN ANGEL — .22 LR or .22 Mag. cal., double action, hammerless, choice of blue, satin, nickel, or gold finish. New 1996.

Mfg.'s Sug. Retail	$143	$125	$105	$95	$85	$80	$75	$70

    Add $10 for .22 Mag. cal.
    Add $20 for blue or nickel finish.
    Add $40 for gold finish.
    Add $7 for Deluxe Model with case and angel charm.

PISTOLS

AMERICAN EAGLE LUGER — 9mm Para., 4 in. barrel, stainless steel with toggle action, checkered American walnut grips, American Eagle version, contoured front grip strap. Disc. 1994.

		$590	$475	$400	$350	$300	$260	$230

Last Mfg.'s Sug. Retail was $695.

ROLLING BLOCK PISTOL — .22 LR, .22 Mag., .223, .357 Mag., or .45 LC cal., reproduction of the Remington Rolling Block design, 10 in. barrel. Mfg. 1991-92 only.

		$340	$285	$240	$210	$185	$170	$150

Last Mfg.'s Sug. Retail was $395.

PISTOLS: HIGH STANDARD AND MITCHELL TARGET

    Mitchell Arms manufactured High Standard marked pistols during 1993-94. Due to litigation, the High Standard logo was dropped in 1994, and High Standard model nomenclature was dropped in 1996. These guns feature push button barrel takedown and usually, a choice between stainless steel or royal blue steel construction. Mitchell Arms is not responsible, nor do they have spare parts, for the older High Standard pistols manufactured in New Haven and East Hartford, CT.

MONARCH (CITATION II) — .22 LR, 5½ or 7¼ in. fluted barrel, frame mounted bridge rear sight, checkered walnut grips with thumb rest, push button take down, stippled front and rear grip straps, adj. trigger, travel, and weight. Available in stainless or royal blue steel. Mfg. began 1993.

Mfg.'s Sug. Retail	$489	$395	$295	$245	$215	$190	$170	$150

MEDALIST (OLYMPIC I.S.U.) — .22 S or LR (new 1994), military grip style, 6¾ in. special barrel with internal stabilizer, adj. barrel weights, other features similar to Citation II, stainless steel or blue finish. Mfg. began 1993.

Mfg.'s Sug. Retail	$599	$500	$425	$375	$325	$275	$225	$195

BARON (SHARPSHOOTER II) — .22 LR, 5½ in. bull barrel, standard trigger, adj. rear sight, smooth grip frame, stainless steel or blue finish. Mfg. began 1993.

Mfg.'s Sug. Retail	$395	$315	$280	$240	$210	$185	$160	$135

SPORTSTER (SPORT KING II) — .22 LR, 4½ or 6¾ in. tapered barrel, military black checkered plastic grips, stainless steel only, adj. rear sight. Mfg. began 1993.

Mfg.'s Sug. Retail	$325	$265	$220	$185	$160	$135	$120	$110

MEDALLION (TROPHY II) — .22 LR, 5½ or 7¼ in. fluted barrel, military grips with full checkering and thumb rest, bridge rear sight, gold-plated trigger safety and mag. release, stippled front and rear grip straps, stainless steel or royal blue finish. New 1993.

Mfg.'s Sug. Retail	$498	$400	$300	$250	$220	$190	$170	$150

SOVEREIGN (VICTOR II) — .22 LR, 4½ or 5½ in. full length VR or black rib barrel, checkered walnut grips with thumb rest, gold-plated trigger, safety, mag. release, and side lock, rib mounted sights. New 1993.

Mfg.'s Sug. Retail	$595	$495	$425	$375	$325	$275	$225	$195

    Add $80 for Weaver style base built into VR.

M

Grading	100%	98%	95%	90%	80%	70%	60%

HIGH STANDARD COLLECTORS ASSOCIATION SPECIAL EDITIONS

▲ *HSCA-SE Trophy II* — .22 LR, 100 mfg. 1993 only, cased.

	$450	$375	$300

▲ *HSCA-SE Victor II*

	$495	$400	$325

▲ *HSCA-SE Citation II*

	$435	$365	$285

▲ *HSCA-SE Three Gun Set* — includes Trophy II, Olympic II, and Victor II.

	$1,495	$1,295	$1,050

▲ *HSCA-SE Six Gun Set* — includes 6¾ in. I.S.U. Olympic (.22 Short), 4½ in. Victor, 7¼ in. Citation, 5½ in. Sharpshooter, 4½ in. Sport King, and Trophy Model. Special engraving, cased, HSCA prefix with 2-digit serial number, 19 sets total mfg. 1994 only.

Mfg.'s Sug. Retail	$2,995	$2,550	$2,100	$1,675

PISTOLS: SEMI-AUTO, GOLD & ALPHA SERIES

1911 GOLD/SIGNATURE SERIES (STANDARD) — .45 ACP, features new tapered barrel slide lock-up, wide body except staggered mag., full length guide rod recoil buffer assembly, beveled mag. well, blue (disc. 1995) or stainless steel, 8 shot mag., walnut checkered grips, fixed or adj. sights. New 1994.

▲ *Blue Finish*

	$465	$395	$350	$325	$295	$270	$250

Last Mfg.'s Sug. Retail was $535.

▲ *Stainless Steel*

Mfg.'s Sug. Retail	$675	$585	$525	$475

▲ *Tactical Model* — stainless steel, features elongated grip safety and serrated front slide, fixed or adj. rear sight. New 1996.

Mfg.'s Sug. Retail	$735	$640	$550	$500

Add $40 for adj. rear sight.

▲ *Bullseye Model* — similar to Tactical Model, except has fully adj. rear sight. New 1996.

Mfg.'s Sug. Retail	$950	$850	$700	$575

▲ *IPSC Limited Model* — choice of ghost ring or adj. rear sight. New 1996.

Mfg.'s Sug. Retail	$1,195	$1,075	$875	$675

Add $45 for ghost ring sight.

1911 GOLD/SIGNATURE SERIES (WIDE BODY) — .45 ACP, features new tapered barrel slide lock-up, full length guide rod recoil buffer assembly, beveled mag. well, blue (disc. 1995) or stainless steel, 10 (C/B 1994) or 13* shot mag., walnut checkered grips, fixed or adj. sights. New 1994.

▲ *Blue Finish*

	$595	$525	$475	$425	$375	$335	$295

Last Mfg.'s Sug. Retail was $685.

▲ *Standard Model* — stainless steel, fixed sights, smooth grips. New 1996.

Mfg.'s Sug. Retail	$840	$765	$650	$550

▲ *Tactical Model* — stainless steel, features elongated grip safety and serrated front slide, adj. rear sight. New 1996.

Mfg.'s Sug. Retail	$895	$795	$675	$575

MITCHELL .44 — .44 Mag., 5½ in. barrel, blue finish, 7 shot mag., checkered walnut grips, adj. rear sight. New 1996.

Mfg.'s Sug. Retail	$1,190	$1,050	$900	$800	$725	$650	$575	$495

JEFF COOPER SIGNATURE/COMMEMORATIVE MODEL — .45 ACP cal., blue finish. New 1996.

▲ *Signature Model*

Mfg.'s Sug. Retail	$795	$725	$625	$560	$500	$450	$415	$375

M

Grading	100%	98%	95%	90%	80%	70%	60%

▲ **Commemorative Model** — 1,000 mfg. beginning 1996.

Mfg.'s Sug. Retail	$1,895	$1,650	$1,400	$1,200	$1,000	$800	$675	$550

ALPHA SERIES — .45 ACP cal., interchangeable sideplate module allows SA, DA only, or dual action configuration, low profile rib, combat hammer, extended tang, full wraparound rubber grips, ambidextrous mag. release, 5 in. barrel, adj. rear sight.

> While advertised in 1995, production will not begin until 1997.

▲ **Alpha X Series** — similar to Alpha Series, except has 14 shot mag., available to police, military, and export only.

> While advertised in 1995, production will not begin until 1997.

PISTOLS: TOKAREV DESIGN

The models listed below are imported from Yugoslavia.

Because of recent firearms legislation/laws, demand for the models listed below has escalated considerably. Because of this, premiums may be asked over 90%-100% values listed below.

MODEL 57A — .30 Mauser, single action semi-auto, 9 shot mag., hammer block and mag. safety, all steel construction. Imported 1990 only.

	$240	$215	$180	$160	$145	$135	$120

Last Mfg.'s Sug. Retail was $280.

MODEL 70A — 9mm Para., otherwise similar to Model 57A. Imported 1990 only.

	$240	$215	$180	$160	$145	$135	$120

Last Mfg.'s Sug. Retail was $280.

88A OFFICERS MODEL — 9mm Para., newer slenderized variation issued to the Officers Corps., short slide and frame, finger extension mag. Imported 1990 only.

	$255	$225	$190	$165	$145	$135	$120

Last Mfg.'s Sug. Retail was $300.

SKORPION — .32 ACP only, single action, $4\frac{5}{8}$ in. barrel, 20 or 30 shot mag., blue finish only. Mfg. Yugoslavia. Imported 1990 only.

	$615	$520	$480	$440	$395	$360	$330

Last Mfg.'s Sug. Retail was $740.

SPECTRE — 9mm, single action, 8 in. shrouded barrel, unique frame/barrel cooling system, 30 or 50 shot mag., approx. 4 lbs. Imported 1987-1988 only.

	$675	$600	$525	$480	$440	$400	$360

Last Mfg.'s Sug. Retail was $670.

▲ **Spectre Carbine** — 9mm, carbine model with folding butt stock. Imported 1988 only.

	$675	$600	$525	$480	$440	$400	$360

Last Mfg.'s Sug. Retail was $680.

REVOLVERS: SINGLE ACTION

SINGLE ACTION ARMY — .22 LR (disc.), .357 Mag., .44 Mag. (disc.), .45 ACP (disc.), or .45 LC cal., $4\frac{3}{4}$, $5\frac{1}{2}$, 6 (disc. 1993), or $7\frac{1}{2}$ in. barrel lengths, hammer block safety mechanism, steel construction, case hardened frame, one-piece walnut stock. Add $20 for adj. sights on some older models. Imported 1986-94.

▲ **Cowboy Model** — .357 Mag., .44-40 (disc.), .45 ACP (disc.), or .45 LC cal., $4\frac{3}{4}$ in. barrel.

	$300	$230	$195	$170	$155	$145	$135

Last Mfg.'s Sug. Retail was $399.

> Add $40 for nickel finish.
> Add $50 for adj. rear sight (disc.).
> Add $95 for steel back strap and triggerguard.

▲ **U.S. Army Model** — similar to Cowboy Model, except has $5\frac{1}{2}$ in. barrel.

	$300	$230	$195	$170	$155	$145	$135

Last Mfg.'s Sug. Retail was $399.

> Add $40 for nickel finish.

M

Grading	100%	98%	95%	90%	80%	70%	60%

▲ *U.S. Cavalry Model* — similar to Cowboy Model, except has 7½ in. barrel.

	100%	98%	95%	90%	80%	70%	60%
	$300	$230	$195	$170	$155	$145	$135

Last Mfg.'s Sug. Retail was $399.

> Add $40 for nickel finish.

▲ *.44 Mag.* — .44 Mag. cal., fully adj. target sights. Disc. 1992.

	$425	$350	$295	$250	$200	$180	$165

Last Mfg.'s Sug. Retail was $495.

▲ *Rimfire Model* — .22 LR cal. Importation disc. 1989.

	$230	$200	$180	$160	$145	$130	$120

Last Mfg.'s Sug. Retail was $280.

> Add $30 for adj. rear sight.

▲ *Silhouette Model* — available with 10, 12, or 18 in. barrel in .44 Mag. or .45 LC cal. Importation disc. 1991.

	$395	$325	$260	$220	$195	$170	$155

Last Mfg.'s Sug. Retail was $450.

> Add $175 for shoulder stock (available with 18 in. barrel only).
> The shoulder stock is available with .44 Mag./.44-40 cals. only.

▲ *Dual Cylinder* — available in either .22 LR/.22 Mag. (disc.), .22 LR/.22 Mag. stainless (disc. 1988), .357 Mag./9mm Para. (disc. 1993), .44 Mag./.44-40 (disc. 1991), or .45 LC/.45 ACP (new 1990). Imported 1986-94.

	$475	$415	$365	$335	$300	$275	$250

Last Mfg.'s Sug. Retail was $549.

> Add $50 for adj. rear sight (disc.).
> Add $39 for nickel finish.
> Add $93 for for steel backstrap.

▲ *Stainless Model* — available in .22 LR or .357 Mag. (disc. 1987) only, adj. sights. Imported 1986-1988 only.

	$260	$225	$195				

Last Mfg.'s Sug. Retail was $301.

> Add $25 for .357 Mag.

BAT MASTERSON MODEL — .45 LC cal., 4¾ , 5½ or 7½ in. barrel with full ejector rod housing, nickel-plated, one-piece walnut stocks, hammer-block safety, rear sight is square notch in frame, two-piece backstrap. Imported 1989-94.

	$375	$285	$240	$210	$185	$170	$150

Last Mfg.'s Sug. Retail was $439.

> Add $156 for extra .45 ACP cylinder.

MODEL 1875 REMINGTON — .357 Mag. or .45 LC cal., royal blue finish with color case hardened frame, walnut grips. Imported 1990-91.

	$345	$285	$245	$210	$185	$170	$150

Last Mfg.'s Sug. Retail was $399.

> Add $76 for nickel finish.
> Add $51 for extra convertible .45 ACP cylinder.

REVOLVERS: DOUBLE ACTION

TITAN II — .357 Mag. cal., 6 shot, 2, 4, or 6 in. barrel, blue or stainless, fixed sights, shrouded eject or rod, target hammer. Mfg. 1995 only.

	$285	$250	$220	$190	$170	$150	$135

Last Mfg.'s Sug. Retail was $339.

TITAN III — similar to Titan II, except has adj. rear sight. Mfg. 1995 only.

	$340	$285	$245	$200	$175	$150	$135

Last Mfg.'s Sug. Retail was $429.

GUARDIAN II — .38 spl., 6 shot, 3 or 4 in. barrel, fixed sights, blue only, target or combat grips. Mfg. 1995 only.

	$240	$215	$185	$165	$145	$130	$120

Last Mfg.'s Sug. Retail was $275.

Grading	100%	98%	95%	90%	80%	70%	60%

GUARDIAN III — similar to Guardian II, except has adj. rear sight, and 6 in. barrel. Mfg. 1995 only.

	$260	$230	$195	$175	$155	$140	$130

Last Mfg.'s Sug. Retail was $305.

RIFLES: MODERN

MODEL 15/22 OR 20/22 SEMI-AUTO CARBINE — .22 LR, semi-auto, American walnut stock, high polish blue, detachable 10 shot mag. Mfg. 1994-95.

	$155	$125	$105	$95	$85	$75	$65

Last Mfg.'s Sug. Retail was $179.

Subtract $40 for 20/22 Special.
Add $20 for Deluxe model (includes deluxe walnut, rosewood accents, and fine line checkering).

LW22 SEMI-AUTO — .22 LR, semi-auto, 10 shot mag., composite or skeleton stock, patterned after Feather Industries semi-auto. New 1996.

Mfg.'s Sug. Retail	$275	$240	$220	$195	$175	$160	$145	$130

Add $30 for composite stock.

LW9 SEMI-AUTO — 9mm Para., semi-auto, blowback action, composite or skeleton stock, patterned after Feather Industries 9mm semi-auto. New 1996.

Mfg.'s Sug. Retail	$500	$450	$395	$360	$330	$300	$270	$240

Add $35 for composite stock.

MODEL 9303/9304/9305 STANDARD BOLT ACTION — .22 LR (9303) or .22 Mag. (9304, new 1995), standard or deluxe variation, 10 shot mag. Mfg. 1994-95.

	$240	$195	$180	$160	$145	$130	$120

Last Mfg.'s Sug. Retail was $275.

Add $14 for .22 Mag. cal.
Subtract $76 for special bolt action (9305).

MODEL 9301/9302 DELUXE BOLT ACTION — similar to 9304/9305, except includes deluxe walnut, rosewood accents, and fine line checkering. Mfg. 1994-95.

	$265	$220	$190	$170	$150	$135	$125

Last Mfg.'s Sug. Retail was $313.

Add $12 for .22 Mag. cal.

M-16A3 — .22 LR, .22 Mag. (disc. 1987), or .32 ACP cal., patterned after Colt's AR-15. Mfg. 1987-94.

	$235	$195	$175	$160	$145	$130	$120

Last Mfg.'s Sug. Retail was $266.

Add $100 for .22 Mag. cal. or .32 ACP (disc. 1988).

CAR-15/22 — .22 LR, carbine variation of M-16 with shorter barrel and collapsible stock. Mfg. 1990-94.

	$235	$195	$175	$160	$145	$130	$120

Last Mfg.'s Sug. Retail was $266.

GALIL — .22 LR or .22 Mag. cal., patterned after Galil semi-auto paramilitary design rifle, choice of wood stock or folding stock (new 1992). Mfg. 1987-1993.

	$285	$240	$195	$160	$150	$140	$130

Last Mfg.'s Sug. Retail was $359.

MAS — .22 LR or .22 Mag. cal., patterned after French MAS rifle. Mfg. 1987-1993.

	$285	$240	$195	$160	$150	$140	$130

Last Mfg.'s Sug. Retail was $359.

Add $75 for .22 Mag. cal. (disc. 1988).

PPS-30/50 — .22 LR cal., patterned after the Russian WWII PPS military rifle, full length barrel shroud, 20 shot banana clip, adj. rear sight, walnut stock. Mfg. 1989-94.

	$235	$195	$175	$160	$145	$130	$120

Last Mfg.'s Sug. Retail was $266.

Add $100 for 50 shot drum magazine.

M

Grading	100%	98%	95%	90%	80%	70%	60%

AK-22 — .22 LR or .22 Mag. (new 1988) cal., copy of the famous Russian AK-47, fully adj. sights, built in cleaning rod, high quality European walnut or folding stock, 20 shot clip mag. Mfg. 1985-94.

| | $235 | $195 | $175 | $160 | $145 | $130 | $120 |

Last Mfg.'s Sug. Retail was $266.

Add $40 for folding stock.

AK-47 — 7.62x39 cal., copy of the original SKS AK-47, semi-auto, teak stock and forend, 30 shot steel mag., last shot hold open. Mfg. Yugoslavia. Imported 1986-1989.

| | $595 | $550 | $495 | $450 | $400 | $360 | $310 |

Last Mfg.'s Sug. Retail was $675.

Add $23 for steel folding butt stock.
Add $150 for 75 shot steel drum mag.

▲ ***.308 NATO AK-47 (M77B1)*** — .308 (7.62 NATO) cal., milled receiver, adj. gas port, otherwise similar to AK-47 except has scope rail, day/night Tritium sights, and 20 shot mag. Imported 1989 only.

| | $900 | $800 | $700 | $595 | $525 | $475 | $425 |

Last Mfg.'s Sug. Retail was $775.

Add $600 for military issue sniper scope and rings.

M76 — similar to AK-47, except is 7.92mm cal. and has longer barrel and frame set up for scope mount, counter sniper design, 10 shot mag., mfg. to mil. specs. Imported 1986-1989.

| | $1,725 | $1,535 | $1,350 | $1,100 | $900 | $820 | $760 |

Last Mfg.'s Sug. Retail was $1,995.

SKS-M59 — 7.62x39 cal., copy of the SKS-M59 standard rifle, full walnut stock, fully adj. sights, gas operated. Mfg. in Yugoslavia. Imported 1986-1989.

| | $610 | $525 | $465 | $410 | $360 | $315 | $260 |

Last Mfg.'s Sug. Retail was $699.

R.P.K. — 7.62x39mm or .308 Win. cal., forged heavy barrel with cooling fins, teak stock, detachable bipod, mil. specs. Importation disc. 1992.

| | $1,050 | $875 | $725 | $650 | $575 | $525 | $475 |

Last Mfg.'s Sug. Retail was $1,150.

Add $845 for .308 Win. cal.

MODEL M-90 — 7.62x39mm or .308 Win. cal., AK-47 type action, in various configurations (heavy barrel, folding or fixed stock, finned barrel, etc.), plastic thumbhole stock, 5 shot mag., limited importation from Yugoslavia 1991-92.

| | $750 | $650 | $550 | $495 | $450 | $395 | $350 |

Last Mfg.'s Sug. Retail was $829.

Add $31 for folding stock.
Add $69 for .308 Win. cal. (wood stock only).

RIFLES: REPRODUCTIONS

HENRY RIFLE — .44-40 cal., polished brass frame, octagonal barrel, original loading system. Imported 1990.

| | $840 | $650 | $585 | $520 | $465 | $415 | $375 |

Last Mfg.'s Sug. Retail was $999.

M

Iron frame also available at extra charge.

MODEL 1866 — .22 LR (disc.), .38 Spl. (disc.), or .44-40 cal., patterned after the Winchester Model 1866 rifle, solid brass frame, octagon barrel. Imported 1990-1993.

| | $715 | $535 | $465 | $415 | $375 | $335 | $295 |

Last Mfg.'s Sug. Retail was $829.

This model is also available in a carbine variation.

MODEL 1873 — .22 LR (disc.), .38 Spl.(disc), .357 Mag. (disc.), .44-40 (disc.), or .45 LC cal., patterned after the Winchester 1873 rifle, octagon barrel, solid steel frame. Imported 1990-1993.

| | $810 | $640 | $550 | $515 | $465 | $415 | $375 |

Last Mfg.'s Sug. Retail was $950.

This model was also available in a carbine variation until 1992.

Grading	100%	98%	95%	90%	80%	70%	60%

SHOTGUNS: SLIDE ACTION

MODEL 9104/9105 — 12 ga. only, features 20 in. barrel with bead sights, 5 shot mag. tube, uncheckered walnut stock and forearm. New 1994.

Mfg.'s Sug. Retail	$279		$240	$195	$175	$160	$145	$130	$120

Add $20 for adj. rear rifle sight (Model 9105).
Add $20 for interchangeable choke tube (Model 9104 only).

MODEL 9108/9109 — 12 ga. only, all-purpose protection featuring 20 in. barrel with 7 shot mag., choice of military green (special order), brown walnut, or black regular or pistol grip stock and forearm. New 1994.

Mfg.'s Sug. Retail	$279		$240	$195	$175	$160	$145	$130	$120

Add $20 for adj. rear rifle sight (Model 9109).
Add $20 for interchangeable choke tube (Model 9108 only).

MODEL 9111/9113 — 12 ga. only, 18½ in. barrel with bead sights, 6 shot mag., choice of brown or green synthetic (special order), brown walnut or black regular or pistol grip stock and forearm. New 1994.

Mfg.'s Sug. Retail	$279		$240	$195	$175	$160	$145	$130	$120

Add $20 for adj. rear rifle sight (Model 9113).
Add $20 for interchangeable choke tube (Model 9111 only).

MODEL 9114 — 12 ga. only, designed for police and riot control, choice of synthetic pistol grip or top folding (disc. 1994) buttstock, 20 in. barrel with iron sights, 6 shot mag. New 1994.

Mfg.'s Sug. Retail	$349		$295	$255	$210	$180	$160	$145	$130

MODEL 9115 — 12 ga. only, design based on Special Air Services riot gun, 18½ in. barrel with vent. heat shield, parkerized finish, 6 shot mag., stealth gray stock featuring 4 shell storage. New 1994.

Mfg.'s Sug. Retail	$349		$295	$255	$210	$180	$160	$145	$130

Add $20 for interchangeable choke tube.

MONTANA ARMORY, INC.

Manufactured by C. Sharps Arms Company, Inc. located in Big Timber, MT. Distributed by Montana Arms located in Big Timber, MT.

Montana Armory, Inc. currently distributes smokeless powder replicas of C. Sharps rifles/carbines and the Winchester Model 1885 single shot. They are able to shoot both smokeless and black powder loads. Most models are available in the following cals.: .40-50, .40-70, .40-90, .45-70, .45-90, .45-100, .45-110, .45-120, .50-70, .50-90, .50-100, and .50-140. All models are authentically reproduced and high quality.

RIFLES: BLACK POWDER CARTRIDGE

Currently, Montana Armory is experiencing a back order situation on some of their models. New Models 1875 and 1885 are experiencing a 6-18 month wait while the New Model 1874 is currently running over 2+ years for delivery.

MODEL 1874 LONG RANGE EXPRESS

			$895	$825	$750	$650	$550	$475	$410

Last Mfg.'s Sug. Retail was $995.

NEW MODEL 1874 SPORTING

Mfg.'s Sug. Retail	$1,075		N/A	N/A	N/A	N/A	$750	$650	$550

In addition to the 1874 Sporting Model, a custom long range target rifle or Scheutzen short range target rifle is available in this model. Because of the extended back order situation on this model, premiums will probably exist for those people who would rather pay a premium than wait.

NEW MODEL 1874 BOSS — features 34 in. No. 1 heavy tapered octagon barrel, vernier tang sight, straight grip stock with cheekrest and steel shotgun butt.

Base price is $3,675 and custom order only. Please contact the factory to obtain a custom quotation on this model.

M

Grading	100%	98%	95%	90%	80%	70%	60%

NEW MODEL 1875 SPORTING RIFLE — similar to New Model 1875 Classic, except has receiver with round crown.

Mfg.'s Sug. Retail	$935	$850	$795	$725	$650	$575	$495	$395

NEW MODEL 1875 CLASSIC RIFLE — receiver with octagon top, 26, 28, or 30 in. tapered full octagon barrel, straight grip stock with steel toe plate, 9½ lbs. New 1992.

Mfg.'s Sug. Retail	$1,185	$1,050	$950	$825	$675	$550	$475	$410

NEW MODEL 1875 CARBINE — features 24 in. tapered round barrel. New 1996.

Mfg.'s Sug. Retail	$810	$750	$675	$600	$500	$450	$375	$325

NEW MODEL 1875 SADDLE RIFLE — receiver with octagon top, 26 in. barrel only.

Mfg.'s Sug. Retail	$910	$835	$760	$685	$625	$550	$460	$365

NEW MODEL 1875 BUSINESS RIFLE — receiver with round top, 28 in. heavy tapered round barrel.

Mfg.'s Sug. Retail	$810	$750	$675	$600	$500	$450	$375	$325

Add $50 for barrel sights.

NEW MODEL 1885 HIGHWALL — .22 LR, .22 Hornet, .219 Zipper, .30-40 Krag, .32-40, .38-55, .40-65, or .45-70 cal., patterned after the Winchester Model 1885 single shot, falling block action, case colored receiver and small parts, 26-30 in. octagon barrel. New 1992.

Mfg.'s Sug. Retail	$1,095	$975	$850	$750	$650	$550	$475	$410

MONTGOMERY WARD

Catalog sales/retailer that has subcontracted various domestic and international manufacturers to private label various brand names under the Montgomery Ward conglomerate.

Montgomery Ward shotguns and rifles have appeared under various labels and endorsers, including Western Field and others. There have literally been hundreds of various models (shotguns and rifles) sold through the Montgomery Ward retail network. Most of these models were manufactured through subcontracts with both domestic and international firearms manufacturers. Typically, they were "spec." guns made to sell at a specific price to undersell the competition. Most of these models were derivatives of existing factory models with less expensive wood and perhaps missing the features found on those models from which they were derived.

To date, there has been very little interest in collecting Montgomery Ward guns, regardless of rarity. Rather than list Montgomery Ward models, a general guideline is that values generally are under those of their "1st generation relatives". As a result, prices are ascertained by the shooting value of the gun, rather than its collector value.

MORINI

Target Pistol Manufacturer located in Switzerland. Currently imported by Nygord Precision Products located in La Crescenta, CA and Mandall Shooting Supplies located in Scottsdale, AZ. Previously imported and distributed by Osborne's, located in Cheboygan, MI.

M

PISTOLS: COMPETITION

CM-80 STANDARD — .22 LR only, single shot, adj. grips, frame, and sights. Importation disc. 1989.

		$925	$825	$725	$650	$585	$520	$465

Last Mfg.'s Sug. Retail was $1,015.

Add $50 for left-hand model.

▲ **CM-80 Super Competition** — similar to CM-80 Standard, except has deluxe finish, and unique plexiglass front sighting system. Importation disc. 1989.

		$1,085	$920	$800	$690	$590	$520	$450

Last Mfg.'s Sug. Retail was $1,196.

Add $50 for left-hand model.

CM-84E FREE PISTOL — .22 LR, single shot, anatomical grips, electric trigger.

Mfg.'s Sug. Retail	$1,495	$1,325	$1,100	$925	$800	$675	$575	$495

Grading	100%	98%	95%	90%	80%	70%	60%

MODEL CM-102E — .22 LR cal., advanced rapid fire competition pistol featuring updated ergonomic grips and flared triggerguard. New 1992.

Mfg.'s Sug. Retail	$1,695	$1,525	$1,250	$995	$895	$795	$695	$595

MOSSBERG, O.F. & SONS, INC.

Manufactured 1919-1964 in New Haven, CT, 1964-present in North Haven, CT. Oscar Mossberg developed an early reputation as a designer and inventor for the Iver Johnson, Marlin-Rockwell, Stevens and Shattuck Arms companies. In 1915, he began producing a 4- shot, .22 palm pistol known as the "Novelty," with revolving firing pin. After producing approx. 600 of these pistols, he sold the patent to C. S. Shattuck, which continued to manufacture under the name  "Unique." The first 600 had no markings except serial numbers, and were destined for export to South America. Very few of these original "Novelty" pistols survived in this country, and are extremely rare specimens.

Since 1985, O.F. Mossberg & Sons, Inc. has produced only shotguns and accessories. The publisher wishes to express thanks for the valuable Mossberg contributions provided by Victor and Cheryl Havlin, founders of the National Mossberg Collectors Association, and NMCA director Joseph S. Eisenlauer (specializing in .22 smoothbore rifles). More information about the NMCA (including membership info.) can be found in the Firearms Associations section of this text.

PISTOLS: DISC.

BROWNIE — .22 long rifle, top break open action, rotating firing pin, 4-bbl. derringer, double action, 4-shot, approx. 32,000 mfg. 1919-1932.

	$350	$300	$275	$250	$205	$175	$150

RIFLES: DISC.

MODEL K — .22 S, L and LR, tube mag., hammerless, 22 in. bbl., takedown, open sights, plain straight stock. Mfg. 1922-1931.

	$250	$225	$200	$175	$150	$100	$85

MODEL M — similar to Model K, except has 24 in. octagonal bbl. Mfg. 1928-1931.

	$285	$250	$200	$175	$150	$100	$85

MODEL S — similar to Model K, except has shorter mag. tube and 19¾ in. bbl., very rare. Mfg. 1927-1931.

	$350	$275	$225	$200	$175	$150	$135

MODEL L — .22 S, L and LR, falling block action, single shot, 24 in. takedown bbl., open sights, pistol grip stock. Mfg. 1929-1932.

	$450	$350	$300	$275	$200	$185	$165

MODEL L-1 — rare target version of Model L with Lyman 2A tang sight and factory sling.
Add $50 to Model L values.

MODEL R — .22 S, L and LR, bolt action, 24 in. round bbl., first tube feed, ivory bead front sight, open sporting bbl. sight. Mfg. 1930-1932.

	$250	$225	$200	$175	$150	$100	$85

MODEL B — .22 S, L and LR single shot, bolt action, 22 in. round tapered bbl. Mfg. 1930-1932.

	$165	$125	$100	$75	$60	$50	$35

MODEL C — .22 S, L and LR single shot, 24 in. bbl., ivory bead front sight, open sporting rear sight. Mfg. 1931-1932.

	$165	$125	$100	$75	$60	$50	$35

MODEL C-1 — target version of Model C, Lyman front and rear sights, leather sling and swivels, special walnut stock, rare.
Add $50 to Model C values.

Grading	100%	98%	95%	90%	80%	70%	60%

MODELS 10, 14, 20, 21, 25, 25A, 125 — .22 S, L and LR, single shot models. Mfg. 1933-1938.

| | $165 | $125 | $100 | $75 | $60 | $50 | $35 |

Add 25% to prices above for models equipped with aperture sights.

MODEL 26B — .22 S, L and LR, entirely new design in single shot rifles, easily identified by bolt handle at extreme rear of bolt, 26 in. tapered bbl., hooded ramp front sight, No. 4 rear peep, open bbl. sight, swivels. Mfg. 1938-1941.

| | $165 | $125 | $100 | $75 | $60 | $50 | $35 |

MODEL 26-C — similar to Model 26B with less expensive sights. Mfg. 1938-1941.

| | $140 | $100 | $85 | $70 | $55 | $45 | $35 |

MODEL 26M (OR B26M) — rare version of 26 series model with two-piece Mannlicher-style stock. Mfg. 1938.

| | $185 | $140 | $125 | $100 | $85 | $70 | $55 |

MODEL 30 — .22 S, L and LR, single shot, 24 in. bbl., rear peep and ramp front sights, swivels. Mfg. 1933-1935.

| | $140 | $100 | $90 | $75 | $65 | $55 | $45 |

MODEL 34 — similar to Model 30, except with heavy stock, target style. Mfg. 1934-1935.

| | $150 | $110 | $100 | $85 | $70 | $55 | $45 |

MODEL 35 — .22 single shot, first full target model, 26 in. heavy target bbl., walnut stock, hooded front ramp, No. 4 rear peep with adj. aperture, approx. $9\frac{1}{2}$ lbs. Mfg. 1935-1937.

| | $275 | $225 | $200 | $175 | $150 | $125 | $90 |

MODEL 35A — revised version of Model 35, with all-new "master action," approx. $8\frac{1}{4}$ lbs. Mfg. 1937.

| | $275 | $235 | $210 | $185 | $160 | $135 | $110 |

Add 25% for Model 35A-LS with Lyman sights.

MODEL 40 — .22 S, L, and LR, repeater with tube mag., 16 shot, 24 in. bbl., No. 3 Mossberg aperture sight, hooded ramp front sight, swivels, approx. 5 lbs. Mfg. 1933-1935.

| | $125 | $100 | $90 | $80 | $70 | $65 | $60 |

MODEL 44 — similar to Model 40, but with heavier target stock, approx. 6 lbs. Mfg. 1934-1935.

| | $150 | $125 | $100 | $90 | $80 | $70 | $65 |

MODEL 42 — .22 S, L, and LR, first model with 7 rd. magazine, 24 in. bbl., front ramp, sporting bbl., rear aperture sights, 42 in. overall length, approx. 5 lbs. Mfg. 1935-1937.

| | $125 | $100 | $90 | $80 | $70 | $65 | $60 |

MODEL 42A — redesign of Model 42, new master action with shorter bolt and receiver. Mfg. 1937-1938.

| | $150 | $125 | $100 | $90 | $80 | $70 | $65 |

MODEL 42B — same basic specs. as Model 42A, approx. 6 lbs. Mfg. 1938-1941.

| | $150 | $125 | $100 | $90 | $80 | $70 | $65 |

MODEL 42C — similar to Model 42B, with open bbl. and bead front sights. Mfg. 1938-1941.

| | $110 | $100 | $90 | $80 | $65 | $55 | $45 |

MODEL 42M — .22 S, L and LR, 7-shot magazine, bolt action, two-piece Mannlicher-style stock, 23 in. bbl., 40 in. overall length, $6\frac{3}{4}$ lb., front ramp, open bbl., receiver aperture sights, trapdoor buttplate for extra mag. in butt stock. Mfg. 1940-1944.

| | $175 | $150 | $135 | $110 | $100 | $75 | $50 |

Add $40 for extra magazine in butt stock.

MODEL 42M(a), 42M(b), 42M(c) — similar to Model 42M with minor changes in extractors and sights. Mfg. 1944-1950.

| | $175 | $150 | $135 | $110 | $100 | $75 | $50 |

Grading	100%	98%	95%	90%	80%	70%	60%

MODEL 42MB — military version of the Model 42M, approx. 50,000 mfg. for US and British troops as a training rifle. US Property marked with serial number, usually found w/o bbl. sight. Mfg. 1942-1943.

| | $200 | $175 | $150 | $135 | $110 | $100 | $75 |

Add $50 for Lend-Lease models with British proofs.

MODEL L42A — left-handed version of Model 42A with true left handed aperture sight, walnut stock, 1¼ in. swivels. Mfg. 1937-1938.

| | $225 | $200 | $175 | $150 | $135 | $125 | $100 |

MODEL 43 — .22 S, L and LR, target rifle, 7-round magazine, external trigger adjustment, 13/16 in. diameter barrel, 26 in. long walnut stock with four-position 1¼ in. swivels in front, Lyman 17A front sight, Lyman 57 MS receiver peep sight, rare. Mfg. 1937-1938.

| | $250 | $225 | $200 | $185 | $175 | $150 | $135 |

MODEL L43 — left-handed version of Model 43 target rifle with left-handed Lyman 57 MS rear aperture sight, rare. Mfg. 1937-1938.

| | $350 | $335 | $300 | $275 | $250 | $225 | $200 |

Add $75 for models with true left-handed Mossberg scope.

MODEL 44B — .22 cal. target model, clip fed, 26 in. heavy bbl., 43 in. overall length, approx. 8 lbs., front ramp and No. 4 receiver aperture sights, four-position front swivels, walnut stock. Mfg. 1938-1941.

| | $250 | $225 | $200 | $185 | $175 | $150 | $135 |

MODEL 44US — .22 cal. target model, 7 round magazine, bolt action, 26 in. heavy bbl., overall length 43 in., approx. 8½ lbs., ramp front sight with hood, rear aperture sight, detachable swivels. Mfg. 1943-45.

| | $200 | $185 | $175 | $165 | $150 | $135 | $125 |

MODEL 44US (US PROPERTY MARKED) — used by all branches of military for target training, approx. 53,000 mfg. 1943-1944.

| | $320 | $295 | $260 | $230 | $215 | $190 | $170 |

MODEL 44US(a), 44US(b), 44US(c), 44US(d) — same rifle as 44US with minor changes in sights and extractors. Mfg. 1944-1949.

| | $200 | $185 | $175 | $165 | $150 | $135 | $125 |

MODEL 45 — .22 cal. S, L and LR, tube fed, bolt action, 24 in. heavy target bbl., overall length 42½ in., approx. 6¾ lbs., hooded front sight, sporting bbl. sight, receiver aperture sight. Mfg. 1935-1937.

| | $175 | $150 | $135 | $125 | $100 | $85 | $65 |

MODEL 45-A — similar to Model 45 with newer, master action. Mfg. 1937-38.

| | $175 | $150 | $135 | $125 | $100 | $85 | $65 |

MODEL L45-A — similar to Model 45-A, true left-handed version. Mfg. 1937-1938.

| | $225 | $200 | $175 | $150 | $135 | $125 | $100 |

MODEL 46 — .22 S, L and LR, tube fed, bolt action, 26 in. heavy bbl., overall 44½ in., beavertail walnut stock, hooded ramp front, rear aperture sight, 7½ lbs. Mfg. 1935-1937.

| | $175 | $150 | $135 | $125 | $100 | $85 | $65 |

MODEL 46T — similar to Model 46 with heavier bbl. and stock. Mfg. 1936-1937.

| | $200 | $175 | $150 | $135 | $125 | $100 | $75 |

MODEL 46A — similar to Model 46 with master action. Mfg. 1937-1938.

| | $175 | $150 | $135 | $125 | $100 | $85 | $65 |

MODEL 46-ALS — similar to Model 46-A with Lyman 17A front sight and 57-MS rear aperture, rare. Mfg. 1937-1938.

| | $225 | $200 | $175 | $150 | $125 | $110 | $100 |

MODEL L46-ALS — similar to Model 46-ALS with true left-handed action and left-handed Lyman rear sight, very rare. Mfg. 1937-1938.

| | $325 | $300 | $275 | $250 | $225 | $200 | $175 |

M

Grading	100%	98%	95%	90%	80%	70%	60%

MODEL 46B — .22 S, L and LR, tube fed, new streamlined design, 43⅓ in. overall, walnut stock, 7 lbs. Mfg. 1938-1945.

| | $150 | $135 | $110 | $100 | $85 | $75 | $65 |

MODEL 46B-T — heavy barrel and stock, target version of Model 46-B, rare. Mfg. 1938.

| | $200 | $175 | $150 | $135 | $110 | $95 | $85 |

MODEL 46M — .22 S, L and LR, bolt action, tube fed, with two-piece Mannlicher-style walnut stock, 23 in. bbl., overall 40 in., hooded front, sporting bbl., rear aperture sight, 7 lbs. Mfg. 1940-1945.

| | $185 | $150 | $135 | $125 | $110 | $95 | $80 |

MODEL 46M(a), 46M(b) — similar to Model 46M with minor changes in sights. Mfg. 1945-1952.

| | $185 | $150 | $135 | $125 | $110 | $95 | $80 |

MODEL 50 — .22 cal. semi-auto, tube fed through butt stock, 24 in. bbl., overall 43¾ in., hooded front sight, open bbl. sight, no swivels, 6¾ lbs. Mfg. 1939-1942.

| | $165 | $150 | $135 | $125 | $110 | $85 | $65 |

MODEL 51 — similar to Model 50 with receiver aperture sight, heavier, beavertail stock, q.d. swivels, 7¼ lbs. Mfg. 1939.

| | $165 | $150 | $135 | $125 | $110 | $85 | $65 |

MODEL 51M — similar to Model 51 with two-piece Mannlicher style walnut stock, 20 in. bbl, 40 in. overall, front ramp, rear aperture, sporting bbl. sights, 7 lbs. Mfg. 1939-1946.

| | $185 | $150 | $135 | $125 | $110 | $95 | $80 |

MODEL 140B — .22 S, L and LR, bolt action, clip fed, 24½ in. bbl., 42 in. overall, walnut stock, front ramp, sporting bbl., rear aperture sight, 5¾ lbs. Mfg. 1957-1958.

| | $165 | $150 | $135 | $125 | $110 | $85 | $65 |

MODEL 140K — similar to Model 140B with post front and no aperture sight. Mfg. 1955-1958.

| | $135 | $100 | $90 | $80 | $70 | $60 | $50 |

MODEL 142A — .22 S, L and LR, bolt action, 7 round clip, carbine model with fold down forearm, walnut stock with sling, 18 in. bbl., 27 in. overall length, rear aperture sight and military front sight, no bbl. sight, early models had "T" shaped bolt handles and wood forearms, later models had round knob bolt handle and black plastic forearm, 5 lbs. Mfg. 1949-1957.

| | $165 | $150 | $135 | $125 | $110 | $85 | $65 |

MODEL 142K — similar to Model 142A with less expensive sights, sporting barrel and post front type. No aperture sight. Mfg. 1953-1957.

| | $125 | $110 | $100 | $90 | $80 | $75 | $55 |

MODEL 144 — .22 caliber, full target rifle, heavy 26 in. bbl., 43 in. overall length, 8 lbs., q.d. swivels, four-position front swivels, rear aperture, front ramp sights, "T" shaped bolt handle. Mfg. 1949-1954.

| | $200 | $185 | $165 | $150 | $135 | $125 | $110 |

MODEL 144LS — similar to Model 144, with round knob handle, Lyman 57-MS aperture and 17-A front sight. Mfg. 1954-1960.

| | $250 | $235 | $220 | $200 | $185 | $165 | $150 |

MODEL 144LS-A — similar to Model 144LS, with Mossberg S-130 rear aperture in place of Lyman 57-MS. Mfg. 1960-1979.

| | $200 | $185 | $165 | $150 | $135 | $125 | $110 |

MODEL 144LS-B — last generation of 144 series, 27 in. bbl., 15/16 in. diameter, 44 in. overall length, new Mossberg S-331 aperture, Lyman 17-A front sight, 8½ lbs. Mfg. 1979-1985.

| | $275 | $250 | $235 | $210 | $190 | $175 | $165 |

MODEL 146-B — .22 S, L and LR, bolt action, tube fed, capacity of 30S, 23L, 20LR, 26 in. bbl., overall length 43¼ in., ramp front sight, leaf bbl. and rear aperture sight, walnut Monte Carlo stock with cheekpiece, QD swivels, adj. trigger, Schnabel forend, 7 lbs. Mfg. 1949-1954.

| | $180 | $150 | $135 | $125 | $100 | $85 | $65 |

M

Grading	100%	98%	95%	90%	80%	70%	60%

MODEL 146B-A — similar to Model 146-B, with different bbl. sight. Mfg. 1954-1958.

	$180	$150	$135	$125	$100	$85	$65

MODEL 151-K — .22 caliber semi-auto, butt fed, 24 in. bbl., overall 44 in., open sights, walnut Monte Carlo stock with cheekpiece and Schnabel forend, 6 lbs. Mfg. 1950-1951.

	$160	$135	$110	$90	$80	$70	$60

MODEL 151(M) — .22 caliber semi-auto butt fed, capacity 15LR, 20 in. bbl., overall 40 in., two-piece Mannlicher-style walnut stock, QD swivels, steel butt plate, hooded ramp front, sporting rear, micro-click aperture sights, 7 lbs. Mfg. 1946-1947.

	$175	$150	$135	$125	$100	$85	$65

MODELS 151M(a), 151M(b), 151M(c) — similar to Model 151M with minor changes in butt plate and sights. Mfg. 1947-1958.

	$175	$150	$135	$125	$100	$85	$65

MODEL 152 — .22 caliber semi-auto, clip fed with 7 round capacity, carbine model with hinged, fold-down forend, Monte Carlo stock with adj. sling, 18 in. bbl., 27 in. overall, receiver aperture and military post front sights, 5 lbs. Mfg. 1948-1952.

	$175	$150	$135	$125	$100	$85	$65

MODEL 152K — similar to Model 152 with open sights. Mfg. 1950-1957.

	$150	$125	$110	$100	$90	$75	$50

MODEL 320B — .22 caliber single shot, junior target model, bolt action, new closed breech design, 24 in. bbl., overall 43½ in., 5¾ lbs., walnut finish Monte Carlo stock with swivels and pistol grip, front ramp, rear aperture and sporting bbl. sights. Mfg. 1960-1971.

	$165	$140	$125	$110	$85	$75	$55

MODELS 320K, 320K-A — similar to Model 320B with open sights, no swivels, later models marked 321, 321K. Mfg. 1960-1980.

	$105	$95	$80	$70	$60	$55	$50

MODELS 340B, 340B-A — .22 S, L, LR, bolt action, 7 round clip magazine, 24 in. bbl., 43½ in. overall length, walnut, Monte Carlo stock with cheekpiece and pistol grip, front ramp, sporting bbl., rear aperture sights, 6½ lbs. Mfg. 1958-1980.

	$165	$140	$125	$110	$85	$75	$55

MODELS 340K, 340K-A — similar to Model 340B with open sights, later models marked 341. Mfg. 1958-1980.

	$105	$95	$80	$70	$60	$55	$50

MODEL 340M — .22 caliber bolt action, clip fed, same operating design as other 340 series, with one-piece, walnut Mannlicher-style Monte Carlo stock with pistol grip and swivels, 18½ in. bbl., 38½ in. overall, open rear and bead front sights, rare, 5¼ lbs. Mfg. 1970-1972.

	$250	$235	$210	$200	$185	$175	$165

MODEL 342 — .22 S, L and LR, bolt action, clip fed, carbine model with hinged, black plastic, fold-down forend, walnut Monte Carlo stock with swivels and sling, 18 in. bbl., 38 in. overall, military post front and rear aperture sight, 5 lbs. Mfg. 1957-1959.

	$165	$140	$125	$110	$85	$75	$55

MODELS 342K, 342K-A — similar to Model 342 with open sights. Mfg. 1958-1971.

	$105	$95	$80	$70	$60	$55	$50

MODEL 344, 344K — .22 caliber bolt action, clip fed, walnut finish, checkered stock, 344K is carbine length. Mfg. 1985.

	$165	$140	$125	$110	$85	$75	$55

MODEL 346B — .22 S, L, and LR, bolt action tube feed, closed-breech design, walnut Monte Carlo stock with cheekpiece, QD swivels, capacity 25S, 20L, 18LR, 24 in. bbl., 42½ in. overall, rear aperture, sporting bbl., hooded front ramp sights, 6½ lbs. Mfg. 1958-1960.

	$165	$140	$125	$110	$85	$75	$55

M

Grading	100%	98%	95%	90%	80%	70%	60%

MODEL 346K, 346K-A — similar to Model 346B w/ open sights. Mfg. 1958-1968.

| | $135 | $120 | $110 | $100 | $80 | $70 | $55 |

MODEL 350K — .22 caliber semi-auto, LR only, clip fed, walnut Monte Carlo stock with pistol grip and cheekpiece, 23½ in. bbl., overall 43½ in., open sights, 6 lbs. Mfg. 1958-1960.

| | $95 | $85 | $75 | $65 | $60 | $50 | $40 |

MODEL 350 K-A — similar to Model 350K with dovetail bbl. sight. Mfg. 1960-1968.

| | $95 | $85 | $75 | $65 | $60 | $50 | $40 |

MODEL 351K — .22 LR semi-auto, tube fed through stock, walnut, Monte Carlo stock with pistol grip, 24 in. bbl., 43 in. overall, 6 lbs. Mfg. 1958-1960.

| | $95 | $85 | $75 | $65 | $60 | $50 | $40 |

MODEL 351K-A — similar to Model 351K with dovetail bbl. sight. Mfg. 1960-68.

| | $95 | $85 | $75 | $65 | $60 | $50 | $40 |

MODEL 352 — .22 LR, clip fed, carbine model with fold-down black plastic forend, walnut Monte Carlo stock, pistol grip, swivels, web strap, 18 in. bbl., overall 38 in., rear peep, post front sights, 5 lbs. Mfg. 1957-1959.

| | $135 | $120 | $100 | $85 | $75 | $65 | $55 |

MODELS 352K, 352 K-A, 352K-B — similar to Model 352 with open sights. Mfg. 1960-1971.

| | $110 | $95 | $85 | $75 | $70 | $65 | $55 |

MODEL 377, "PLINKSTER" — .22 LR, semi-auto, tube fed, synthetic stock with "thumb hole," capacity 15 rds., 20 in. bbl., overall 40 in., 6.25 lbs., equipped with 4X scope. Mfg. 1977-1979.

| | $175 | $150 | $135 | $100 | $85 | $75 | $65 |

MODELS 380, 380S — same basic design as Model 377, only with solid, wood stock, open sights. Model 480 same in 1985. Mfg. 1980-1985.

| | $135 | $115 | $100 | $85 | $75 | $65 | $55 |

MODEL 400 "PALAMINO" — .22 S, L and LR, lever action, tube fed, walnut, beaver tail stock and forearm, cross bolt safety, 24 in. bbl., overall length, 41 in., bead front, open rear sights, 5½ lbs. Mfg. 1959-1964.

| | $225 | $195 | $170 | $150 | $135 | $100 | $85 |

Model 400-A similar to above in specs and value, dovetail.

MODEL 402 — carbine version of Model 400, bbl. 20 in. Mfg. 1961-1971.

| | $225 | $195 | $170 | $150 | $135 | $100 | $85 |

MODEL 430 — .22 LR semi-auto, tubular mag. under bbl. with capacity of 18 LR, walnut checkered Monte Carlo stock and checkered forend, 24 in. bbl., overall length 43½ in., open sights, 6.25 lbs. Mfg. 1970-1971.

| | $135 | $115 | $100 | $85 | $75 | $65 | $55 |

MODEL 432 — similar to Model 430 above with 20 in. bbl., straight grip, smooth stock and forend, walnut finish. Mfg. 1970-1971.

| | $115 | $100 | $85 | $75 | $65 | $60 | $50 |

MODEL 472 — .30-30 or .35 Rem. cal., lever action carbine, 20 in. barrel, open sights, pistol grip or straight stock, saddle ring on straight model. Mfg. 1972-disc.

| | $180 | $155 | $145 | $130 | $120 | $110 | $90 |

MODEL 472 RIFLE — similar to Carbine, except 24 in. barrel, pistol grip stock. Mfg. 1974-1976.

| | $195 | $165 | $155 | $145 | $130 | $120 | $100 |

MODEL 472 BRUSH GUN — similar to Carbine, except 18 in. barrel, straight stock only. Mfg. 1974-1976.

| | $195 | $165 | $155 | $145 | $130 | $120 | $100 |

MODEL 472 ONE IN FIVE THOUSAND — similar to Brush Gun, except Indian scene etched on receiver, brass butt plate, saddle ring and barrel bands, select stock, only 5,000 mfg., 1974.

| | $415 | $210 | $195 | $175 | $165 | $145 | $120 |

Grading	100%	98%	95%	90%	80%	70%	60%

MODEL 479 PCA — .30-30 lever action, 20 in. barrel, 6 shot capacity.

	$195	$135	$120	$110	$95	$85	$75

MODEL 479 RR — limited edition "Roy Rogers" signature model, gold trigger, barrel bands, 5,000 total mfg. New 1983.

	$350	$275	$215				

MODEL 479 — .30-30 cal. only, lever action, 6 shot tube mag., 20 in. barrel with adj. sights, 7 lbs. Mfg. 1985 only.

	$190	$175	$160	$150	$145	$140	$135

Last Mfg.'s Sug. Retail was $232.

Mossberg also has made several .22 bolt action and semi-auto sporters that are in the $115 - $130 price range. While they are good shooting models, they are not covered in this section as they are not collectible.

MODEL 620K — .22 WMR Magnum, single shot, bolt action, walnut Monte Carlo stock, pistol grip, cheekpiece, sling swivels, 24 in. bbl., overall 44¾ in., open rear, post front sights, 6 lbs. Mfg. 1959-1960.

	$150	$135	$115	$100	$85	$75	$65

MODEL 620K-A — similar to Model 620K with change in bbl. sight. Mfg. 1960-1968.

	$150	$135	$115	$100	$85	$75	$65

MODELS 640K, 640K-S — similar to 620 series, but 5 shot clip repeater. Mfg. 1959-1984.

	$195	$150	$135	$125	$105	$90	$75

MODEL 640KS — similar to Model 640K with deluxe checkered stock and gold trigger. Mfg. 1960-1968.

	$225	$200	$185	$150	$135	$120	$110

MODEL 640M — full length, Mannlicher-styled stock, version of 640, checkered stock, Monte Carlo, cheekpiece, pistol grip, swivels and leather strap, heavy receiver, jeweled bolt, 20 in. bbl., overall 40¾ in., open rear sights, bead front, 6 lbs. Mfg. 1971.

	$250	$225	$200	$185	$175	$165	$150

MODEL 642K — .22 mag. WMR, carbine style, bolt action, 5 rd. clip, fold-down forend, walnut stock with web sling, 18 in. bbl., overall 38¼ in., open bbl. and bead front sights, 5 lbs. Mfg. 1960-1968.

	$225	$200	$185	$150	$135	$120	$110

MODEL 800 — .222, .22-250, .243, or .308 cal., bolt action, 22 in. barrel, folding sight, checkered pistol grip stock. Mfg. 1967-disc.

	$220	$195	$165	$110	$85	$55	$45

MODEL 800VT — similar to 800, except .222, .22-250, or .243 cal., 24 in. heavy barrel, no sights. Mfg. 1968-disc.

	$220	$195	$165	$110	$85	$55	$45

MODEL 800M — similar to 800, except 20 in. barrel, full length stock, spoon bolt handle. Mfg. 1969-1972.

	$275	$240	$220	$205	$175	$160	$145

MODEL 800D — similar to 800, with roll-over combination and cheekpiece, checkered stock with rosewood forearm tip and pistol cap, no .222 available. Mfg. 1970-1973.

	$325	$300	$275	$250	$225	$200	$165

MODEL 810 — .270, .30-06, 6.5mm Rem. Mag., or .338 Win. Mag. cal., bolt action, 22 or 24 in. barrel, leaf sight, checkered Monte Carlo stock. Mfg. 1970-disc.

	$300	$275	$250	$225	$200	$175	$150

RIFLES: RECENT MFG.

In 1985, Mossberg purchased the parts inventory and importing rights for those rifles that Smith & Wesson imported from Howa of Japan. These new models were identical to those models which S&W disc.

M

Grading	100%	98%	95%	90%	80%	70%	60%

MODEL 1500 MOUNTAINEER GRADE I — .223, .243, .270, 30-06, or 7mm Mag. cal., bolt action, 22 or 24 (7mm Mag. only) in. barrel, 5 or 6 shot mag., available with or without sights, hardwood stock is satin finished, blued finish, about 7 lbs. 10 oz. Imported 1986-87 only. Add $15 for 7mm Rem. Mag. cal., $25 for iron sights.

	$285	$250	$225	$195	$180	$165	$150

Last Mfg.'s Sug. Retail was $335.

▲ *Model 1500 Varmint* — .22-250, .223, or .308 cal., similar to Model 1500 Grade I, except has 24 in. heavy barrel only, Monte Carlo stock. Imported 1986-87 only. Add $10 for parkerized finish (oil finished stock with swivels — not available in .22-250 cal.).

	$360	$300	$270	$235	$205	$190	$175

Last Mfg.'s Sug. Retail was $457.

Blued finish and high gloss wood finish available with .22-250 or .223 cal. only. Parkerized variation is available in .223 or .308 cal. only (matte wood finish, includes swivels).

MODEL 1500 MOUNTAINEER GRADE II — similar to Grade I Mountaineer, except has select checkered American walnut stock. Also available in .300 or .338 Win. Mag. cal. Imported 1986-87 only.

	$315	$270	$235	$205	$190	$175	$160

Last Mfg.'s Sug. Retail was $368.

Add $15 for Mag. cals.
Add $25 for iron sights.

MODEL 1550 — similar to Model 1500, except has detachable mag. and available in standard cals. (.243, .270, or .30-06), with or without sights. Imported 1986-87 only. Add $24 for iron sights.

	$330	$280	$245	$210	$190	$175	$160

Last Mfg.'s Sug. Retail was $391.

MODEL 1700 LS — .243, .270, or .30-06 cal., no sights, jeweled bolt body and knurled bolt handle, detachable mag., Schnabel forend, deluxe checkering, 7 lbs. Imported 1986-87 only.

	$405	$365	$310	$275	$240	$205	$190

Last Mfg.'s Sug. Retail was $492.

"TARGO" SHOTGUN/RIFLES

These dual-purpose smoothbore rifles were designed to fire both .22 RF bullets and shotshell ammunition. Targo barrels are threaded either externally (Models 26T, 42TR, 42T, B42T) or internally (Models 320TR, 340TR) at the muzzle for attachment of rifled and smoothbore adapters which enable the shooter to use the gun as a standard rifle, or (with the smoothbore adapter installed) as a miniature shotgun. Mossberg produced a line of Targo accessories including a barrel-mounted miniature clay target launcher, a pistol grip hand trap frame, a hand thrower, a target carrier, clay targets, hard rubber "practice" targets, and a target catching net. The presence of one or more of these accessories augments the value of any model Targo gun. Prices quoted below are for guns with all listed features exclusive of Targo accessories.

MODEL 26-T SINGLE SHOT — single-shot, bolt action, thumb lever safety located at rear of bolt, black plastic buttplate and contoured black plastic triggerguard (#R413), rifle-style open rear sight with screw adjustments for windage and elevation, shotgun style elevated front bead sight with removable sight hood, smoothbore and rifled screw-on barrel adapters and spanner wrench for adapter removal and installation, stock generally provided with sling swivels, forend necks down toward muzzle, takedown screw has retaining bail to facilitate removal by hand. Manufactured 1940-42 (only 873 mfg.).

	$600	$450	$375	$335	$280	$245	$220

100% price is estimated since an example would be extremely rare.

MODEL 42T BOLT ACTION REPEATER — box magazine (7-round) fitted with adapter screw to enable firing of .22 Short cartridges, same safety, buttplate, optional stock swivels, and shotgun style front sight as Model 26T, #R145 contoured black plastic triggerguard, supplied with the smoothbore barrel adapter only (rifled adapter, open rear sight, and front sight hood were not provided), produced 1940-42 (906 guns made), examples in 95% or better condition are uncommon.

	$440	$325	$310	$295	$260	$235	$200

M

Grading	100%	98%	95%	90%	80%	70%	60%

MODEL 42TR BOLT ACTION REPEATER — produced before and after WWII until roughly 1949. Pre-War (1940-42) guns identical to Model 42T except rifled adapter, open rear sight, and front sight hood were provided, and no stock swivels. The earliest pre-War 42TRs were marked using a 42T barrel stamp and a separate "R" (stamped to the right of the "T"). Post-War (1946-49) guns have slotted takedown screw, magazine plate, shorter unnecked forend, and (frequently) a blued bolt knob. The most common of all Targo guns. A total of 6,577 guns were produced during the period 1940-42 (post-War production figures are not available). Both early and late versions of this model are comparably priced.

	$415	$345	$295	$280	$245	$190	$175

Add $250 for cased gun with clay targets and Targo accessories.

Note: A very small number of 42TRs were supplied with fitted cases and Targo accessories and were used as dealer displays. The pre-War 42TR display guns came in a hard (plywood) luggage case. The post-War guns were supplied in a semi-hard (fiberboard) luggage case. Less than a dozen cased 42TRs are known to exist, though others may surface in the future.

MODEL B42T BOLT ACTION REPEATER — identical to the Model 42TR, except stock has sling swivels and metal buttplate with trapdoor for magazine storage. Gun was supplied with extended 15-round box magazine in addition to the standard 7-round clip. A comparatively scarce model marketed exclusively through mail order stores (e.g., Spiegel) in the early 1940s. According to factory records, only 250 guns were made, all in 1940.

	$465	$385	$350	$325	$285	$250	$210

MODEL 320TR SINGLE SHOT BOLT ACTION — automatic safety with thumb lever located on right side of receiver, black plastic buttplate and contoured black plastic triggerguard. Rifle-style ("U" notch) rear sight adjustable for elevation (via sliding wedge) and windage (by deflecting sight arm laterally by hand). Sporting type vertical blade front sight. Gun supplied with rifled and smooth-bore screw-in barrel adapters. A wire target carrier and a hand thrower for launching miniature clay targets were included with each gun. Mfg. 1961-62.

	$320	$240	$225	$190	$150	$135	$115

MODEL 340TR BOLT ACTION REPEATER — 7-round box magazine featuring adjustable top bar to accommodate feeding of .22 S, L, and LR cartridges. Two known variations of thumb lever safety markings (words "OFF"/"ON" and red dot). Other features identical to Model 320TR. Mfg. 1961-62.

	$345	$265	$240	$215	$165	$145	$125

SHOTGUNS: BOLT ACTION - DISC.

MODELS G-4, 70, 73, 73B — .410 ga., single shot, mfg. 1932-1940.

	$110	$100	$85	$70	$60	$50	$40

MODELS 80, 83, 83B, 83D — .410 ga., 3 or 4 shot, internal top-loading mag., mfg. 1933-1946.

	$135	$110	$95	$75	$60	$50	$40

MODELS 75, 75A, 75B — 20 ga., bolt action, single shot, mfg. 1933-1940.

	$110	$100	$85	$70	$60	$50	$40

MODELS 85, 85A, 85B, 85D — 20 ga., 2 or 3 shot mag., mfg. 1934-1940.

	$110	$100	$85	$70	$60	$50	$40

MODELS 173, 173A, 173Y — .410 ga., single shot, "Y" designates youth model, mfg. 1957-1973.

	$110	$100	$85	$70	$60	$50	$40

MODELS 183, 183D, 283D(a), 183D-B, 183D-C, 183D-D, 183D-E, 183D-F, 183K, 183K-B, 183K-C, 183T, 184T, 184TY, 283T, 284T, 284TY — .410 ga., bolt action shotgun, 2 or 3 shot mag., various screw-on or C-Lect choke on some models, mfg. 1948-1985.

	$125	$110	$95	$75	$60	$55	$50

MODELS 185, 185D, 185D-A, 185D-B, 185D-C, 185K, 185K-A, 185K-B — 20 ga., 2 shot 2¾ in. mag., various screw-on or C-Lect chokes, mfg. 1947-1959.

	$125	$110	$95	$75	$60	$55	$50

M

Grading	100%	98%	95%	90%	80%	70%	60%

MODELS 190, 190D, 190D-A, 190K-A, 190K-B — 16 ga., bolt action, 2 shot 2¾ in. mag., various screw-on or C-Lect choke, mfg. 1955-1958.

	$125	$110	$95	$75	$60	$55	$50

MODELS 195, 195A, 195K-A, 195D — same as model 185 Series above, only .12 ga. version, mfg. 1954-1968.

	$125	$110	$95	$75	$60	$55	$50

MODELS 385, 385K, 385KA, 385T, 485A, 485B — 20 ga., bolt action, 3 in. capacity chamber, detachable box mag., mfg. 1960-1986.

	$125	$110	$95	$75	$60	$55	$50

MODELS 390, 390K-A, 390K-B, 490A — 16 ga., 3 in. capacity chamber, detachable box mag., mfg. 1971-1976.

	$125	$110	$95	$75	$60	$55	$50

MODELS 395, 395K, 395KA, 395S, 395 SPL., 495A, 495B — 12 ga., 3 in. capacity chamber, detachable box mag., mfg. 1963-1983.

	$125	$110	$95	$75	$60	$55	$50

Add $40 for slug barrel ("S" designation) or 38 in. barrel (spl.).

MODELS 595, 595K — 12 ga., bolt action, special police stock, 4 shot mag., mfg. 1983-1985.

	$175	$150	$135	$110	$95	$85	$75

Add $40 for 38 in. barrel (spl.).

SHOTGUNS

In 1985, Mossberg purchased the parts inventory and manufacturing rights for the shotguns that Smith & Wesson discontinued in 1984. These new models (manufactured in Japan) are identical to those models which S&W discontinued. Parts and warranties are not interchangeable.

During 1994, to celebrate their 75th anniversary, Mossberg released a new Crown Grade variation within most models, including the 500 and 835 Series, which can be differentiated from previous manufacture by cut checkering, redesigned walnut or American hardwood stocks and forearms, screw-in choke tubes, and 4 different camo patterns.

MODEL 200K SLIDE ACTION — slide action shotgun, 12 ga., 28 in., select choke, plain pistol grip stock, black nylon slide handle. Mfg. 1955-1959.

	$130	$110	$100	$90	$65	$55	$40

MODEL 200D — similar to 200K, except interchangeable choke tubes (2). Mfg. 1955-1959.

	$130	$110	$100	$90	$65	$55	$40

HOME SECURITY SLIDE ACTION — 20 (new 1996) or .410 ga., 18½ in. barrel with spreader choke, Model 500 slide-action, 5 shot mag., blued metal finish, synthetic field stock with pistol grip forearm, 6¼ lbs. New 1990.

Mfg.'s Sug. Retail	$293	$250	$210	$190	$165	$145	$125	$110

▲ *Laser Home Security .410* — includes laser sighting device in right front of forearm. Mfg. 1990-1993.

	$400	$350	$315	$280	$250	$225	$195

Last Mfg.'s Sug. Retail was $451.

MODEL 500 SLIDE ACTION REGAL SERIES — 12 or 20 ga., slide action, 26 or 28 in. barrel, select checkered walnut, VR. Add $19 for Accu-choke. Disc. 1987.

	$240	$195	$175	$165	$155	$145	$135

Last Mfg.'s Sug. Retail was $286.

Add $39 for Combo pack (includes 1 extra 24 in. slugster barrel).

Grading	100%	98%	95%	90%	80%	70%	60%

MODEL 500 SLIDE ACTION FIELD GRADE — 12, 20, or .410 ga., slide action, 24 in. (with rifle sights) or 20-28 in. barrel (with various chokes), upper receiver slide safety, C Lect (disc.) & Accu choke (became standard 1994) choke system, checkered hardwood pistol grip stock after 1973. Mfg. 1962-present.

Mfg.'s Sug. Retail	$278	$230	$185	$155	$135	$120	$110	$100

Add $6 for .410 ga. (fixed choke only).
Subtract 10% if without VR (disc.).
Subtract 10% for fixed choke barrel in 12 or 20 ga.

▲ *Model 500 Slugster* — 12 or 20 ga., 24 in. cyl. or rifled bore barrel, choice of sights, walnut finished hardwood stock and forearm.

Mfg.'s Sug. Retail	$285	$230	$190	$155	$135	$120	$110	$100

Add $39 for rifled bore barrel (12 ga. only).
Add $64 for rifled bore barrel with scope base and dual comb stock (disc.).

▲ *Model 500 Bantam* — 20 or .410 ga. (new 1991) only, 22 in. (20 ga.), 24 in. fixed choke barrel (.410 ga.), or 26 in. VR barrel with Accu-choke(s), blue or blue matte (Bantam Jake with Realtree Camo finish in 20 ga./22 in. VR barrel only), 20 ga. has walnut finish stock and .410 ga. has synthetic stock (both stocks are tailored for youth dimensions), 6.9 lbs. New 1990.

Mfg.'s Sug. Retail	$281	$230	$185	$155	$135	$120	$110	$100

Add $4 for .410 ga.
Add $45 for Bantam Jake configuration (disc. 1993).

▲ *Model 500 Turkey* — 12 or 20 (new 1995) ga., 22 (20 ga. only) or 24 in. barrel, Woodlands metal/wood camo finish.

Mfg.'s Sug. Retail	$324	$265	$195	$150

Subtract $15 for 20 ga.
Add $60 for 24 in. VR barrel with Ghost Ring Sight (12 ga. only).

▲ *Model 500 Camo* — 12 ga. only, parkerized camo, OFM Camo (became standard late 1991), or Woodlands (new 1995) metal and stock finish, 24-30 in. VR barrel (choice of cylinder bore with rifle sights or Accu-II chokes), includes swivels, camo sling, and drilled and tapped receiver, older Speedfeed stock (disc. 1990) holds 4 extra shells. New 1986.

Mfg.'s Sug. Retail	$296	$240	$185	$140

Subtract 10% if without Accu-II choke system.
Add $30 for speedfeed in synthetic stock (disc. 1990).
Add $29 for complete set of 5 choke tubes.
Accu-chokes became standard in 1991. Current models are supplied with 2 choke tubes.

▲ *Model 500 Camo Combo* — 12 or 20 ga., includes a wide variety of extra barrel combinations including slug barrel options, prices vary slightly depending on the configuration (gauge/barrel/choke set-up). Rifled bores, VR barrels, and Accu-chokes became standard in the combo package late 1994.

Mfg.'s Sug. Retail	$379	$330	$275	$235	$200	$180	$160	$145

Add $45 for dual-comb stock (new 1996).

▲ *Model 500 Muzzleloader Combo* — 12 ga. only, includes 24 in. (rifled bore only, new 1993) or 28 in. VR Accu-choke barrel and additional 24 in. .50 cal. muzzleloader conversion barrel with rifled bore and iron sights, walnut finished hardwood stock and forearm, 7.2 lbs. New 1991.

Mfg.'s Sug. Retail	$385	$335	$280	$240	$200	$180	$160	$145

▲ *Model 500 Quail Unlimited* — 20 ga. only, 26 in. VR barrel with Accu-II chokes (3), engraved receiver and hand selected stock and forearm, 3,500 mfg. in 1991 to commemorate the 10th anniversary of Quail Unlimited.

	$295	$240	$195

Last Mfg.'s Sug. Retail was $359.

▲ *Model 500 Sporting Steel Shot* — 12 ga. only, 3 in. chamber, 28 in. VR Accu-choke barrel with special Accu-steel tube for shooting steel shot. Mfg. 1987-90.

	$250	$200	$175	$165	$155	$145	$135

Add $29 for camo stock (disc. 1989).
This model was phased out of production in 1990 since all Mossberg shotguns currently manufactured are capable of shooting steel shot safely. The last mfg.'s sug. retail was $295.

M

Grading	100%	98%	95%	90%	80%	70%	60%

MODEL 500 VIKING SLIDE ACTION — 12 or 20 ga., 24 (12 ga. only, with rifled barrel and sights), 26 (20 ga. only) or 28 (12 ga. only) in. VR barrel with one Accu Choke and twin bead sights, matte finish with green synthetic stock and forearm, approx. 7 lbs. New 1996.

Mfg.'s Sug. Retail	$266	$220	$185	$155	$135	$120	$110	$100

Add $48 for 12 ga. rifled barrel.

MODEL 500 SPORTING CROWN GRADE SLIDE ACTION — 12, 20 (Bantam), or .410 (Bantam) ga., 22 (20 ga. only), 24, 26, or 28 in. VR (unless with rifle sights) barrel, blue finish, walnut finished stock, safety on back of receiver top, Accu chokes except for .410 ga., supplied with 1 Accu choke.

Mfg.'s Sug. Retail	$281	$230	$185	$155	$135	$120	$110	$100

Add $4 for rifle sights (Turkey Model with matte finish, 12 ga. only).
Add $4-$6 for .410 ga. with plain or VR barrel.
Add approx. $22-$91 for 10 various combo packages.

▲ *Model 500 Slugster Crown Grade* — 12 or 20 ga., 24 in. barrel only with choice of cyl. or rifled bore, blue or Marinecote (new 1995) finish.

Mfg.'s Sug. Retail	$288	$235	$185	$155	$135	$120	$110	$100

Add $127 for Marinecote finish (with synthetic stock).
Add $38 for rifled bore barrel.
Add $66 for rifled bore barrel with trophy scope base and dual-comb stock.

MODEL 500 PERSUADER SLIDE ACTION — 12 or 20 (new 1995) ga., 6 or 8 shot, 18½ in. plain barrel, cyl. bore or Accu (new 1995) chokes, optional rifle sights (12 ga./20 in. cyl. bore barrel only), blue or parkerized (12 ga. only) finish, speedfeed stock was disc. 1990, optional bayonet lug, plain pistol grip wood or synthetic stock.

Mfg.'s Sug. Retail	$281	$235	$185	$160	$145	$130	$115	$100

Add $23 for rifle sights (12 ga. only).
Add $34 for parkerized finish (includes synthetic stock and forearm).
Add $40 for combo with pistol grip (disc.).

▲ *Night Persuader Special Edition* — 12 ga. only, includes synthetic stock and factory installed Mepro-Light night sight bead sight, only 300 mfg. for Lew Horton Distributing in 1990 only.

	$295	$250	$200	$175	$150	$130	$115

Last Mfg.'s Sug. Retail was $296.

MODEL 500 SPECIAL PURPOSE SLIDE ACTION — 12 ga. only, 14 in. barrel bored cyl., choice of blue or parkerized finish, synthetic stock with or without speedfeed.

Mfg.'s Sug. Retail	$378	$330	$270	$240	$220	$200	$175	$160

Add $21 for speedfeed stock.
Add $76 for Ghost Ring sight (parkerized finish only).

MODEL 500 CRUISER SLIDE ACTION — 12, 20, or .410 (new 1993) ga., 14 (12 ga. only, disc. 1995), 18½, 20, or 21 (20 ga. only - new 1995) in. cylinder bore barrel with shroud, 6 or 8 shot mag., pistol grip forearm only. New 1989.

Mfg.'s Sug. Retail	$272	$205	$185	$170	$155	$145	$135	$120

Add $7 for .410 ga.
Add $96 for 14 in. barrel (disc.).
Add approx. $34 for camper case (new 1993).

MODEL 500 MARINER SLIDE ACTION — 12 ga. only, 18½ or 20 in. cyl. bore barrel, 6 or 9 shot, Marinecote finish on all metal parts (more rust-resistant than stainless steel), synthetic stock and forearm, fixed or Ghost Ring (new 1995) sights.

Mfg.'s Sug. Retail	$403	$345	$265	$210			

Add $12 for 9 shot model.
Add $56 for Ghost Ring sights.
Add $23 for speedfeed stock (mini-combo only - disc.).

MODEL 500 CAMPER — 12, 20, or .410 ga. only, 18½ in. barrel, synthetic pistol grip (no stock), camo carrying case optional, blued finish. Mfg. 1986-90 only.

	$235	$190	$175	$165	$155	$145	$135

Last Mfg.'s Sug. Retail was $276.

Add $25 for .410 ga.
Add $30 for camo case.

Grading	100%	98%	95%	90%	80%	70%	60%

MODEL 500 HI-RIB TRAP — 12 ga. only, high post trap rib, 28 or 30 in. barrel. Add $20 for Accu-choke. Disc. 1986.

	$285	$250	$230	$200	$175	$155	$140

Last Mfg.'s Sug. Retail was $334.

MODEL 500 SUPER GRADE — similar to Model 500 Field, except VR and checkered, no 16 ga. Mfg. 1965-1976.

	$250	$215	$180	$170	$160	$140	$130

MODEL 500 ATR SUPER GRADE — similar to Model 500 Field, except 12 ga., VR, 30 in. full, checkered Monte Carlo. Mfg. 1968-1971.

	$295	$260	$230	$200	$175	$155	$140

MODEL 500 PIGEON GRADE — similar to 500 Super Grade, except etched and scroll engraving, select wood, floating VR. Mfg. 1971-1975.

	$385	$330	$305	$250	$210	$185	$165

MODEL 500 APTR PIGEON GRADE TRAP — similar to 500 ATR, except trap style stock. Mfg. 1971-1975.

	$440	$415	$330	$250	$220	$200	$175

MODEL 500 DSPR DUCK STAMP COMMERCIAL — similar to Pigeon Grade, except wood duck etching. 1,000 mfg. 1975.

	$525	$330	$310	$285	$260	$220	$195

MODEL 500L SERIES — similar to 500 Field Grade, except no 16 ga., etched receiver, new style stock and slide. Mfg. 1977-1983.

	$250	$220	$210	$200	$175	$165	$140

MODEL 500 BULLPUP — 12 ga. only, 18½ (6 shot) or 20 (9 shot) in. barrel, bullpup configuration, 6 or 9 shot mag., includes shrouded barrel, carrying handle, ejection port in stock, employs high impact materials. Mfg. 1986-1990 by Mossberg, currently mfg. under the Maverick trademark.

	$350	$300	$255				

Last Mfg.'s Sug. Retail was $425.

Add $15 for 8 shot mag. (disc.).

MODEL 500 GHOST RING SIGHT SLIDE ACTION — 12 ga. only, 3 in. chamber, 18½ or 20 in. cyl. bore or Accu choke (20 in. only - new 1995) barrel, 6 or 9 shot tube mag., blue or parkerized finish, synthetic field stock, includes ghost ring sighting device. New 1990.

Mfg.'s Sug. Retail	$331	$265	$225	$180	$160	$150	$140	$130

Add $53 for parkerized finish.
Add $48 for 9 shot mag. (20 in. barrel only).
Add $123 for Accu choke barrel (parkerized finish only).
Add $134 for speedfeed stock (new 1994 - 9 shot, 20 in. barrel only).

MODEL 500/590 INTIMIDATOR LASER — 12 ga. only, 3 in. chamber, 18½ (Model 500) or 20 (Model 590) in. cyl. bore barrel, 6 (Model 500) or 9 (Model 590) shot tube mag., blue or parkerized finish, synthetic field stock, includes laser sighting device. Mfg. 1990-1993.

▲ *Model 500 Intimidator*

	$440	$375	$340	$295	$260	$230	$195

Last Mfg.'s Sug. Retail was $505.

Add $22 for parkerized finish.

▲ *Model 590 Intimidator*

	$495	$440	$375	$340	$295	$260	$230

Last Mfg.'s Sug. Retail was $556.

Add $45 for parkerized finish.

SPECIAL PURPOSE 590 SLIDE ACTION — similar to Model 500, except has 9 shot mag., 20 in. cyl. bore barrel with ¾ shroud, and bayonet lug, blued or parkerized finish. New 1987.

Mfg.'s Sug. Retail	$329	$285	$240	$200	$185	$165	$145	$125

Add $50 for parkerized finish.
Add $33 for speedfeed (blue) or $83 for speedfeed (parkerized) stock.

M

Grading	100%	98%	95%	90%	80%	70%	60%

▲ *Model 590 Mariner* — similar to Model 500 Mariner except is 9 shot and has 20 in. barrel. Mfg. 1989-1993.

| | $310 | $250 | $200 | $185 | $165 | $145 | $125 |

Last Mfg.'s Sug. Retail was $353.

Add $17 for speedfeed stock (disc. 1990).
Add $15 for pistol grip adapter (mini combo - disc.).

▲ *Model 590 Bullpup* — similar to Model 500 Bullpup except is 9 shot and has 20 in. barrel. Mfg. 1989-90 only.

| | $425 | $360 | $300 | $250 | $225 | $195 | $175 |

Last Mfg.'s Sug. Retail was $497.

MODEL 695 BOLT ACTION — 12 ga. only, bolt action with detachable 2 shot mag., 22 in. barrel with choice of fully rifled and ported or Accu Choke barrel, black synthetic with polished blue (Slug Model with rifle sights) or Woodlands camo finish (Turkey Model with bead sights) on both metal and synthetic stock. New 1996.

| Mfg.'s Sug. Retail | $276 | $230 | $190 | $160 | $140 | $130 | $120 | $115 |

Add $17 for Slug Model.

MODEL 712 SEMI-AUTO — 12 ga. only, semi-auto, gas operated, shoots 2¾ and 3 in. shells interchangeably, plain barrel or VR, top of receiver safety, checkered hardwood stock, rubber recoil pad, fixed or Accu Choke II choking. Mfg. 1986-1988 only.

| | $285 | $250 | $220 | $200 | $190 | $175 | $160 |

Last Mfg.'s Sug. Retail was $345.

Subtract $25 without Accu II choking.
Add $90 for combo pack (includes 1 extra 24 in. slugster barrel).

▲ *Model 712 Steel Shot* — similar to Model 712, except has Accu-Steel choking system for steel shot, 28 in. VR barrel. Mfg. 1988 only.

| | $290 | $250 | $220 | $200 | $190 | $175 | $160 |

Last Mfg.'s Sug. Retail was $349.

▲ *Model 712 Camo/Speedfeed* — 12 ga. only, similar to Model 712, except has camo finished metal parts, stock, and forearm, 24 or 28 in. barrel. Add $20 for Accu II choke. Mfg. 1986-87 only.

| | $340 | $295 | $240 | | | | |

Last Mfg.'s Sug. Retail was $390.

MODEL 712 REGAL SEMI-AUTO — 12 or 20 ga., action same as Model 712, special bright bluing, VR only, deluxe checkered walnut stock and forearm, gold trigger, inlaid medallion on receiver, top of receiver safety. Add $20 for Accu II choke. Mfg. 1986-87 only.

| | $310 | $280 | $250 | $225 | $200 | $185 | $170 |

Last Mfg.'s Sug. Retail was $366.

NEW HAVEN BRAND — similar to previous models, except plainer finish. Disc.
Values are 20% less per model.

MODEL 835 ULTI-MAG SLIDE ACTION — 12 ga. with 3½ in. chamber (new 1988), slide action, 24 (Turkey Model - new 1990) or 28 in. VR barrel with Accu-Mag choke tubes, 6 shot mag., safety on top rear of receiver, choice of camo synthetic or checkered hardwood stock. Introduced late 1988, disc. 1991.

| | $375 | $310 | $265 | $220 | $190 | $165 | $150 |

Last Mfg.'s Sug. Retail was $430.

Add $30 for synthetic camo field stock.
Various Combo packages were available in this model with prices ranging from $469-$534 depending on barrel chokings and scope base options.
This model was followed by the 835 Regal Series introduced in late 1991.

ULTI-MAG 835 FIELD GRADE SLIDE ACTION — 12 ga. only, 3½ in. chamber, 24 in. cyl. bore, 24 in. VR (Turkey Special, disc. 1993), or 28 in. VR barrel with 1 Accu-Mag choke, walnut finish stock and forearm (pressed checkering became standard 1994), blued finish, approx. 7½ lbs.

| Mfg.'s Sug. Retail | $313 | $260 | $220 | $200 | $185 | $165 | $145 | $125 |

Add $40 for combo package (disc. 1993).

M

Grading	100%	98%	95%	90%	80%	70%	60%

ULTI-MAG 835 CROWN GRADE SLIDE ACTION — similar to Field Grade, except has gold trigger and cut checkering on walnut finished hardwood stock, blue or OFM Woodland camo (24 in. Turkey only) finish. New 1994.

Mfg.'s Sug. Retail	$316	$265	$225	$205	$185	$165	$145	$125

   Add $53 for combo package (includes 24 in. cylinder bore barrel).

MODEL 835 VIKING SLIDE ACTION — 12 ga. only, 28 in. VR barrel with one Accu Choke and twin bead sights, matte blue finish with green synthetic stock and forearm, 7.7 lbs. New 1996.

Mfg.'s Sug. Retail	$301	$250	$220	$200	$185	$165	$145	$125

MODEL 835 CAMO SLIDE ACTION — 12 ga. only, 3½ in. chamber, OFM Woodland Camo (all-purpose camo), Realtree (new 1993), Realtree AP (all purpose gray, new 1996), or Mossy Oak (new 1994) finish, 24 (Turkey Special) or 28 in. VR barrel with 6 choke tubes, dual comb (disc. 1995) or synthetic stock, 7.7 lbs. New 1991.

Mfg.'s Sug. Retail	$493	$405	$325	$275	$235	$200	$175	$160

   Subtract $41 for OFM Marsh finish (disc.).
   Subtract $52 for Woodlands finish.
   Add $108 for hard case.
   Add $22 for combo package.
   OFM Marsh finish on this model includes a dual comb stock.

MODEL 835 WALNUT ULTI-MAG (REGAL) SLIDE ACTION — 12 ga., 3½ in. chamber, 28 in. VR barrel with Accu-Mag chokes or 24 in. rifled slug barrel, single (new 1993) or dual comb (2 comb inserts are provided for the stock affording different shooting positions), aluminum receiver, back-bored barrel, double slide bars, high gloss walnut stock with recoil pad, approx. 7½ lbs. New late 1991.

Mfg.'s Sug. Retail	$404	$350	$290	$260	$230	$200	$175	$160

   Add $8 for dual comb stock.
   Add $30 for 24 in. slug barrel with trophy scope base and dual comb stock.
   Add $72-$83 for combo package (includes extra slug barrel with choice of sights).

MODEL 835 WILD TURKEY FED. LIMITED EDITION — 12 ga. with 3½ in. chamber, 24 in. VR barrel with Accu-Mag. chokes, camo finish, includes camo sling, medallion in stock, and 10-pack of Federal Turkey loads. Mfg. 1989 only.

				$425	$360	$295		

Last Mfg.'s Sug. Retail was $477.

MODEL 835 NWTF SPECIAL EDITION — 12 ga. only, 24 in. VR barrel with Accu-Mag chokes, features Realtree camo finish, drilled and tapped receiver, 7½ lbs. Mfg. 1991 only to commemorate the National Wild Turkey Federation.

				$380	$300	$225		

Last Mfg.'s Sug. Retail was $436.

MODEL 835 WATERFOWL LIMITED EDITION — 12 ga. with 3½ in. chamber, 28 in. VR barrel with Accu-Mag. chokes, camo finish, synthetic stock, camo sling. Mfg. 1990 only.

				$425	$360	$295		

Last Mfg.'s Sug. Retail was $480.

MODEL 1000 SEMI-AUTO — 12 or 20 ga., gas semi-auto, 2¾ in. chamber, scroll engraved aluminum alloy receiver, plain or VR barrel, also available in trap and skeet configuration, checkered walnut stock and forearm. Imported 1986-87 only. VR became standard in 1987.

			$410	$345	$300	$270	$245	$220	$200

Last Mfg.'s Sug. Retail was $472.

   Add $28 for multi-choke II.
   Deduct $50 if without VR.
   Model 1000 barrels are not interchangeable with Model 1000 Super barrels.

▲ ***Model 1000 Junior*** — similar to Model 1000, except 20 ga. only, shortened stock, and 22 in. VR multi-choke barrel. Imported 1986-87 only.

			$425	$355	$310	$275	$250	$220	$200

Last Mfg.'s Sug. Retail was $499.

▲ ***Model 1000 Slug*** — 12 or 20 ga., 22 in. barrel with rifle sights, recoil pad. Imported 1986-87 only.

			$405	$340	$295	$270	$245	$220	$200

Last Mfg.'s Sug. Retail was $464.

M

Grading	100%	98%	95%	90%	80%	70%	60%

▲ *Model 1000 Skeet* — 12 or 20 ga., steel receiver, 26 in. VR barrel bored skeet. Mfg. 1986 only.

	$395	$335	$295	$270	$245	$220	$200

Last Mfg.'s Sug. Retail was $439.

MODEL 1000 SUPER SEMI-AUTO — 12 or 20(Super 20) ga., gas semi-auto, 3 in. chambers, shoots 2¾ and 3 in. shells interchangeably, steel receiver, vent. recoil pad, select checkered walnut stock and forearm, multi-choke II is standard (except on slug barrel). Slug models are approx. the same price as values listed directly below. Imported 1986-87 only.

	$495	$405	$365	$330	$295	$270	$245

Last Mfg.'s Sug. Retail was $577.

Model 1000 Super barrels are not interchangeable with Model 1000 barrels.

▲ *Model 1000 Super Waterfowler* — 12 ga. only, matte finished wood and metal, includes swivels and camouflaged sling, 28 in. multi-choke barrel. Imported 1986-87 only.

	$510	$430	$370

Last Mfg.'s Sug. Retail was $605.

▲ *Model 1000 Super Skeet* — 12 or 20 ga., 25 in. barrel, jug choking. Imported 1986-87 only.

	$575	$495	$450	$410	$375	$330	$295

Last Mfg.'s Sug. Retail was $658.

▲ *Model 1000 Super Trap* — 12 ga. only, 30 in. multi-choke II barrel with high VR, Monte Carlo stock, recoil pad. Mfg. 1986 only.

	$470	$380	$345	$320	$285	$270	$250

Last Mfg.'s Sug. Retail was $560.

MODEL 3000 SLIDE ACTION — 12 or 20 ga. only, 3 in. chamber, slide action, steel receiver, double action bars, various chokes and VR barrel lengths, checkered walnut stock and forearm, vent. recoil pad. Add $25 for multi-choke II. This model was introduced in 1986 and the field version was disc. in 1987.

	$325	$275	$250	$220	$200	$185	$170

Last Mfg.'s Sug. Retail was $360.

▲ *Model 3000 Waterfowler* — 12 ga. only, similar to Model 3000, except has dull matte finish on wood and metal, includes swivels and camouflaged sling, VR only. Add $30 for multi-choke II option, $70 for camo/speedfeed stock. Mfg. 1986 only.

	$340	$295	$265

Last Mfg.'s Sug. Retail was $386.

▲ *Model 3000 Law Enforcement* — 12 or 20 ga. only, 18½ or 20 in. cylinder bore only, rifle or bead sights. Mfg. 1986-87 only.

	$325	$275	$250	$220	$200	$185	$170

Last Mfg.'s Sug. Retail was $362.

Add $25 for rifle sights.
Add $33 for black speedfeed stock.

MODEL 5500 SEMI-AUTO — 12 ga., 2¾ or 3 in. mag., gas operated, 18½ - 30 in. barrels. Add $20 for VR. Disc. 1985.

	$250	$235	$205	$185	$170	$155	$140

Last Mfg.'s Sug. Retail was $307.

▲ *Model 5500 Mag.* — 12 ga. only, 3 in. chamber, 30 in. VR barrel. Disc. 1985.

	$275	$250	$225	$205	$190	$175	$160

Last Mfg.'s Sug. Retail was $325.

MODEL 5500 MKII SEMI-AUTO — 12 ga. only, supplied with 2 VR barrels - 26 in./2¾ in. chamber or 28 in./3 in. chamber VR barrel, includes choice of Accu-II choke tubes (lead shot only) or Accu-Steel choke tubes, blue or camo finish (new 1990), checkered hardwood stock and forearm, top receiver safety, recoil pad, 7½ lbs. Mfg. 1989-92.

	$260	$225	$200	$180	$160	$140	$125

Last Mfg.'s Sug. Retail was $294.

Add $10 for 24 in. rifled bore barrel.
Add $43 for camo metal finish and synthetic stock.
Add $30 for Turkey Model (24 in. barrel, camo finish, and synthetic stock).

This model is also available with different Combo options. Prices vary between $463-$484, depending on configuration of barrel choking.

M

Grading	100%	98%	95%	90%	80%	70%	60%

▲ **Model 5500 U.S. Shooting Team** — 2¾ in. chamber, 26 in. non-Mag. barrel with VR and Accu-II chokes, blue finish, checkered walnut stock and forearm, 7½ lbs. Mfg. 1991-92.

	$325	$250	$225	$200	$185	$170	$160

Last Mfg.'s Sug. Retail was $376.

▲ **NWTF Special Edition** — 12 ga. only, 3 in. chamber, 24 in. VR barrel with 1 choke tube, Mossy Oak Camo finish with synthetic stock and forearm, 7.3 lbs. Mfg. 1991-92.

	$365	$300	$265	$235	$200	$175	$160

Last Mfg.'s Sug. Retail was $428.

MODEL 6000 SEMI-AUTO — 12 ga. only, 2¾ or 3 in. chamber 28 in. VR barrel with Accu-choke, economical model with walnut finish stock, blue finish, 7.7 lbs. Mfg. 1993 only.

	$280	$240	$215	$200	$185	$165	$145

Last Mfg.'s Sug. Retail was $321.

MODEL 9200 SEMI-AUTO — 12 ga. only, 3 in. chamber, gas operated semi-auto, shoots any shell interchangeably, 18½ (SP only), 22 (Bantam only), 24 in. rifled, 24 (Turkey), 26 (U.S. Shooting Team variation, new 1993), or 28 in. VR barrel with 3 Accu-chokes, engraved aluminum receiver, synthetic (18½ in. barrel only) or walnut stained hard wood stock (1 in. shorter on Bantam Model) and forearm, top tang safety, approx. 7½ lbs. New 1992.

Mfg.'s Sug. Retail	$478	$390	$285	$240	$215	$190	$170	$160

Add approx. $68-$85 for combo pack.
Add $22 for 24 in. rifled bore barrel with trophy scope base.
Subtract $88 for synthetic stock (Special Purpose with matte blue finish, 18½ in. barrel).

▲ **Model 9200 Viking** — 12 ga. only, 28 in. VR barrel with one Accu Choke and twin bead sights, matte finish with green synthetic stock and forearm, 7.7 lbs. New 1996.

Mfg.'s Sug. Retail	$404	$350	$295	$260	$230	$200	$175	$160

▲ **Model 9200 Camo** — similar to Model 9200, except is supplied with OFM, Mossy Oak, Realtree (mfg. 1994-95), Realtree AP (new 1996) or Woodlands (new 1995) camo finish, 24 (Turkey) or 28 (OFM Marsh or Woodlands camo) in. VR barrel. New 1992.

Mfg.'s Sug. Retail	$463	$380	$275	$235	$210	$190	$170	$160

Add $99 for Turkey Model.
Add $72 for combo pack.
Subtract $31 for one choke tube only (Turkey Model).

MOUNTAIN RIFLES INC.

Rifle manufacturer located in Palmer, AK since 1995.

RIFLES: BOLT ACTION

MOUNTAINEER — various cals., choice of M-700 Rem. or M-70 Win. action, Chrome Moly barrel with ultra muzzle brake, Timney trigger, parkerized finish, fiberglass stock with decelerator pad, 5½ lbs. New 1995.

Mfg.'s Sug. Retail	$2,295	$2,095	$1,800	$1,400	$1,050	$875	$750	$675

SUPER MOUNTAINEER — similar to the Mountaineer, except has Kevlar epoxy bedded stock with steel cross-bolts on Mag. cals., 4¼ lbs. New 1995.

Mfg.'s Sug. Retail	$2,395	$2,225	$1,850	$1,450	$1,075	$875	$750	$675

PRO MOUNTAINEER — various cals., Winchester M-70 controlled feed action, choice of fiberglass pillar eboxy bedded, Kevlar, or KSDB (Kevlar Stock Drop Box mag.) stock with decelerator pad, parkerized finish. 6 lbs. New 1995.

Mfg.'s Sug. Retail	$2,295	$2,095	$1,800	$1,400	$1,050	$875	$750	$675

Add $100 for Kevlar stock (Pro Mountaineer KS).
Add $500 for KSDB stock with drop mag.

PRO SAFARI MOUNTAINEER — various cals., Winchester M-70 controlled feed action, high gloss bluing, exhibition grade English walnut with decelerator pad, 4 shot detachable mag. 7-9 lbs. New 1995.

Mfg.'s Sug. Retail	$3,995		$3,795	$3,350	$2,875	$2,350	$1,775	$1,450	$1,200

M

Grading	100%	98%	95%	90%	80%	70%	60%

MUSGRAVE

Manufacturer located in the Republic of South Africa since 1951.

Currently, this manufacturer has no importation into the U.S. (due to Federal regulations) and listings below represent older models. Newer models manufactured by Musgrave (imported into Austria and Switzerland) include the Model 90 (features Musgrave action) Standard Rifle, Model 90 Light Rifle, Mini-90, Model 90 Varmint, Model 90 De Luxe Rifle, Magnum Rifle in addition to the same series in the Mauser 98 action. More information can be obtained (including prices and availability) by writing this manufacturer directly at: MUSGRAVE MANUFACTURERS & DISTRIBUTORS LTD., P.O. Box 183, Bloemfontein 9300, Jagersfontein Road, Republic of South Africa.

VALIANT BOLT ACTION RIFLE — .243, .270, .30-06, .308, or 7mm Mag. cal., 24 in. barrel, leaf sight, skip checkered straight stock, pistol grip. Mfg. 1971-1976.

	$375	$325	$275	$250	$220	$195	$175

PREMIER — similar to Valiant, with 26 in. barrel, select Monte Carlo stock, rosewood pistol grip cap and forearm tip.

	$425	$365	$315	$275	$250	$225	$200

RSA SINGLE SHOT TARGET RIFLE — .308 cal. only, 26 in. heavy barrel, target sights and stock. Mfg. 1971-1976.

	$425	$365	$315	$275	$250	$225	$200

MUSKETEER RIFLES

Firearms International Company, Washington, D.C.

SPORTER — .243, .25-06, .270, .265 Mag., .308, .30-06, 7mm Mag., or .300 Win. Mag. cal., bolt action, FN Mauser action, 24 in. barrel, no sights, checkered Monte Carlo stock. Mfg. 1963-1972.

	$375	$325	$275	$250	$220	$195	$175

SPORTER DELUXE — adj. trigger, select wood, tear drop pistol grip, skipline checkering.

	$425	$365	$315	$275	$250	$225	$200

CARBINE — similar to Sporter, except 20 in. barrel and full length stock.

	$375	$325	$275	$250	$220	$195	$175

N section

NS FIREARMS CORP.
Division of KFS, Inc. located in Atlanta, GA. Mfg. in China.

Grading	100%	98%	95%	90%	80%	70%	60%

RIFLES: BOLT ACTION

MODEL 522 SPORTER — .22 LR cal., 21 in. cold hammer forged barrel, 5 shot detachable mag., grooved receiver, checkered walnut stock, 7¾ lbs. New 1994.

	Mfg.'s Sug. Retail	$299	$250	$215	$185	$165	$145	$125	$110

NAMBU PISTOLS
Manufacturer located in Japan for the Japanese Military between 1902-1945.

TYPE 14 — 8mm, semi-auto pistol, recoil operated, 4.7 in. barrel, blued, wood grips, 8 shot mag., a simply designed pistol used by Japanese armed forces from 1925-1945.

> Type 14 Nambus have a 3 or 4-digit number just forward of the lanyard ring on the right side of frame (on back of grip). To determine year and month of manufacture add "1925" to the first two digits and the last number will indicate the month (i.e. code 13.3 indicates a gun built in March of 1938).
> Add 10% for matching mag. on models listed below.

▲ *1925-1930 Mfg.*

	$500	$420	$360	$320	$295	$260	$230

▲ *1930-1935 Mfg.* — small triggerguard.

	$450	$350	$260	$220	$200	$180	$165

▲ *1935-1945 Mfg.* — large triggerguard.

	$295	$260	$215	$195	$180	$165	$150

Add 10% for strawed trigger and safety.

TYPE 94 — 8mm, semi-auto, recoil operated, 3.8 in. barrel, blued, and bakelite wood grips, 6 shot mag. Mfg. 1934-1945.

	$275	$225	$185	$160	$150	$135	$120

Add 20% for pre-WWII commercial.
Add 20% for late square back.

HAMADA NAMBU — .32 ACP cal., semi-auto, available with rough (early production, mostly prototypes) or polished (production) finish, very rare.

	$2,850	$2,575	$2,300	$2,000	$1,800	$1,600	$1,475

BABY NAMBU — 7mm Nambu, semi-auto, 3¼ in. barrel, blued, wood grips, grip safety, one of the most desirable Japanese handguns.

	$2,300	$2,000	$1,800	$1,600	$1,475	$1,300	$1,050

Add 10% for matching mag.
Add 50% for chamber marked "TGE" (Tokyo Gas & Electric).

PAPA NAMBU (MODEL 1904) — 8mm, semi-auto, 4.7 in. barrel, wood grips, grip safety, 8 shot mag., essentially the same action as the Baby, but a larger version. Mfg. 1904-1925.

	$1,450	$1,250	$1,100	$900	$700	$600	$500

Add 10% for matching mag.
Add 50% for chamber marked "TGE" (Tokyo Gas & Electric).

N

Grading	100%	98%	95%	90%	80%	70%	60%

GRANDPA NAMBU—8mm, similar to Papa Nambu, except has smaller triggerguard and fixed lanyard ring, cherry wood based mag., issued with 2 matching mags. Early Tokyo arsenal or later Thai issue, all Grandpa frames are slotted.

	$5,000	$3,950	$2,950	$2,600	$2,150	$1,850	$1,500

Add 100% for matching shoulder stock.
Add $3,000 for spare stock alone.
Add 10% for second matching mag.
Original stocks are rare and expensive (selling in the $2,500-$3,500 range).

1893 REVOLVER (MODEL 26) — 9mm, double action only, 4.7 in. barrel, blued, wood grips. Mfg. 1893-1925.

	$350	$300	$250	$200	$150	$135	$120

Subtract 25% for arsenal rework.

NATIONAL WILD TURKEY FEDERATION

National organization located in Edgefield, SC.

Although the National Wild Turkey Federation is not a manufacturer or importer, this organization has been responsible for many special and limited editions that are listed below with quanities but without prices since they may vary greatly from region to region. NWTF suffix after model name indicates National Wild Turkey Federation gun of the year. Some of the models (and current values) may be listed under manufacturer listings in this text.

MANUFACTURER	MODEL	QUANTITY	YEAR	ISSUE PRICE
Navy Arms	Black Powder 12 ga. NWTF	500	1983	$350
Winchester	Model 23	300	1985	$1,895
Browning	BPS 12 ga. NWTF	500	1986	$495
American Arms	SxS 10 ga. 3½ in.	150	1985/86	$695
Winchester	Model 1300 Win-Cam 12 ga.	500	1987/88	$449
Winchester	Model 1300 12 ga. Trade Gun	-	-	$458
Beretta	Model A-303 12 ga. NWTF	500	1988/89	$695
Winchester	Model 1300 12 ga. Win-Cam NWTF	500	1989	$479
Winchester	Model 1300 12 ga. Trade Gun	-	-	$458
Browning	Model A5 12 ga. NWTF	500	1990	$925
Mossberg	Model 835 12 ga. Auction	500	1991	$567
Mossberg	Model 835 12 ga. Trade Gun	-	-	$436
Remington	Model 11-87 12 ga. Auction	500	1992	-
Remington	Model 11-87 12 ga. Trade Gun	-	-	$698
Winchester	Model 1300 12 ga. Auction	500	1993	$671
New England Firearms	SxS 20 ga. Auction	-	-	$167
New England Firearms	SxS 12 ga. Trade Gun	-	-	$200
New England Firearms	SxS 10 ga. Trade Gun	-	-	$240
American Arms	Model Turkey 12 ga. Auction	300	1993	-
Mossberg	Model 9200 12 ga. Auction	600	1994	$690
Mossberg	Model 9200 12 ga. Trade	-	1994	-
Luigi Franchi	Model 610 12 ga. Auction	600	1995	-
Fausti	O/U 12 ga. Auction	720	1996	-
Mossberg	Model 500 Camo 12 ga. Auction	-	1996	-
New England Firearms	Topper Jr. 20 ga. Auction	-	1996	-

NAVY ARMS COMPANY

Importers since 1958 located in Ridgefield, NJ. Navy Arms firearms are fabricated by various manufacturers including the Italian companies Davide Pedersoli & Co., Pietta & Co., and Uberti & Co.

N

Grading	100%	98%	95%	90%	80%	70%	60%

PISTOLS

TU-711 MAUSER — 9mm Para. cal., patterned after Mauser 711 (semi-auto version of the Model 712 Schnellfeuer), $5\frac{1}{4}$ in. barrel, 712 upper receiver that has been converted to 9mm Para. and mounted on new lower receiver, supplied with 10 and 20 shot detachable mag., mfg. in China, 2 lbs. 11 oz. Imported 1992 only.

	$575	$475	$425	$375	$325	$295	$275

Last Mfg.'s Sug. Retail was $650.

TT-OLYMPIA — .22 LR cal., patterned after the Walther Olympia that won 1936 Olympics, $4\frac{5}{8}$ in. barrel, checkered walnut grips, mfg. in China, 27 oz. Importation began 1992.

Mfg.'s Sug. Retail	$290	$255	$225	$195	$175	$160	$150	$140

TU-90 PISTOL — .30 Tokarev or 9mm Para. cal., patterned after the rare Tokagypt variation (improved TT-33 Tokarev), $4\frac{1}{2}$ in. barrel, single action, wraparound synthetic grips, unique forward motion safety, mfg. in China, 30 oz. Importation began 1992.

Mfg.'s Sug. Retail	$130	$115	$100	$90	$80	$70	$60	$50

   Add $15 for 9mm Para. cal.
   Add $40 for pistol combo (includes both cals.).

LUGER MODEL — .22 LR cal. only, 10 shot mag., Luger toggle type action, available in blued or matte finish, 4, 6, or 8 in. barrel, checkered walnut stocks. Mfg. in U.S. 1986-87 only.

	$140	$120	$95	$85	$75	$70	$65

Last Mfg.'s Sug. Retail was $165.

GRAND PRIX SILHOUETTE — .30-30, 7mm Spl., .44 Mag., or .45-70 cal., $13\frac{3}{4}$ in. barrel, non-glare matte blue finish, walnut forearm and grips, adj. heat dispersing aluminum rib, adj. target sights, 4 lbs. Mfg. 1985 only.

	$320	$280	$240	$220	$195	$175	$150

Last Mfg.'s Sug. Retail was $375.

REVOLVERS: RECENT MFG.

1873 SINGLE ACTION ARMY — .44-40 or .45 LC cal., reproduction of the Colt SAA, case hardened frame with blue or nickel finish, 3 (Sheriff's Model - new 1992), $4\frac{3}{4}$, $5\frac{1}{2}$, or $7\frac{1}{2}$ in. barrel, approx. 36 oz.

Mfg.'s Sug. Retail	$390	$330	$265	$210	$180	$160	$145	$130

   Add $65 for nickel finish.
   Subtract $20 for brass triggerguard and backstrap.

   ▲ *1873 SAA Economy* — .44-40 or .45 LC cal., 3, $4\frac{3}{4}$, $5\frac{1}{2}$, or $7\frac{1}{2}$ in. barrel, brass triggerguard and backstrap, 2-piece walnut grips. Imported 1993-95.

	$295	$230	$185	$160	$145	$130	$120

Last Mfg.'s Sug. Retail was $345.

   ▲ *1873 SAA Cavalry Model* — .45 LC cal. only, exact replica of the original U.S. Government issue SAA, $7\frac{1}{2}$ in. barrel, arsenal stampings, inspector's cartouche on walnut stocks.

Mfg.'s Sug. Retail	$480	$425	$345	$295	$260	$230	$200	$175

   ▲ *1895 SAA Artillery Model* — similar specifications to the Cavalry Model, except has $5\frac{1}{2}$ in barrel.

Mfg.'s Sug. Retail	$480	$425	$345	$295	$260	$230	$200	$175

1875 REMINGTON REVOLVER — .44-40 or .45 LC cal., reproduction of the 1875 Remington revolver, $7\frac{1}{2}$ in. barrel, case colored frame, 41 oz. Importation disc. 1991, resumed 1994.

Mfg.'s Sug. Retail	$435	$360	$295	$260	$230	$200	$175	$150

1890 REMINGTON REVOLVER — .44-40 LC or .45 LC cal., reproduction of the 1890 Remington revolver, $5\frac{1}{2}$ in. barrel, brass triggerguard and lanyard loop, 39 oz. Importation disc. 1991, resumed 1994.

Mfg.'s Sug. Retail	$445	$370	$295	$260	$230	$200	$175	$150

1875 SCHOFIELD CAVALRY MODEL — .44-40 or .45 LC cal., patterned after the original Schofield Cavalry Model, $7\frac{1}{2}$ in. barrel. New 1994.

Mfg.'s Sug. Retail	$795	$695	$575	$475	$400	$325	$250	$195

N

Grading	100%	98%	95%	90%	80%	70%	60%

1875 SCHOFIELD WELLS FARGO MODEL — .44-40 or .45 LC cal., 5½ in. barrel. New 1994.

Mfg.'s Sug. Retail	$795	$695	$575	$475	$400	$325	$250	$195

RIFLES: REPLICA MFG.

REVOLVING CARBINE — .357 Mag., .44-40, or .45 Colt cal., 6 shot cylinder, 20 in. barrel, case hardened frame, straight stock. Mfg. 1968-1984.

	$575	$475	$425	$375	$325	$275	$225

REMINGTON ROLLING BLOCK BUFFALO RIFLE — .444 Marlin (disc.), .45-70, or .50-70 (disc.) cal., replica of Remington Rolling Block, 26 or 30 in. heavy octagon or ½ round/½ octagon barrel, open sight, straight grip stock. Mfg. 1971-present.

Mfg.'s Sug. Retail	$650	$500	$375	$295	$230	$180	$160	$140

Add $60 for long or short Creedmoor sight.
Add $55 for 50x3¼ Sharps cal. (disc.).

BUFFALO CARBINE — similar to Rifle, with 18 in. barrel. Disc. 1985.

	$385	$325	$280	$230	$180	$160	$140

Last Mfg.'s Sug. Retail was $375.

ROLLING BLOCK BABY CARBINE — .22 LR, .22 Hornet, .357 Mag., or .44-40 cal., replica of small frame Remington, 20 in. octagon or 22 in. round barrel, open sight, straight stock. Mfg. 1968-1984.

	$215	$175	$140	$110	$90	$65	$55

ROLLING BLOCK NO. 2 CREEDMOOR TARGET — similar to Buffalo Rifle, in .45-70 or .50-70 (disc.) cal., with Creedmoor tang sight, color case hardened receiver, checkered walnut.

Mfg.'s Sug. Retail	$875	$695	$525	$400	$285	$195	$175	$150

SHARPS SPORTING RIFLE/CARBINE — .45-70 or .54 (black powder) cal., reproduction of Sharps sporting rifle and carbine, 22 or 28½ (rifle) in. barrel, case colored frame and hammer, fixed rear sight. Disc. 1994.

	$615	$475	$365	$275	$195	$175	$150

Last Mfg.'s Sug. Retail was $775.

SHARPS PLAINS RIFLE — .45-70 cal., 32 in. octagon barrel, case hardened receiver, checkered stock and forearm, double set triggers, 9½ lbs. New 1996.

Mfg.'s Sug. Retail	$1,050	$925	$850	$775	$700	$625	$575	$525

Add $65 for vernier rear tang sight.

SHARPS BUFFALO RIFLE — .45-70 or .45-90 cal., 28 in. octagon heavy barrel, case colored receiver, checkered stock, 10 lbs. 10 oz. New 1996.

Mfg.'s Sug. Retail	$1,080	$940	$865	$785	$700	$625	$575	$525

Add $65 for vernier rear tang sight.

1874 SHARPS SNIPER/INFANTRY RIFLE — .45-70 cal., patterned after the 3-band military sniper rifle, 30 in. barrel, color case hardened frame, hammer, and furniture, ST or DST (Sniper rifle, disc. 1995). New 1994.

Mfg.'s Sug. Retail	$1,055	$895	$780	$650	$475	$395	$350	$325

Add $55 for DST.
Subtract $65 for single trigger (Infantry rifle).

1874 SHARPS CAVALRY CARBINE — .45-70 cal., patterned after Sharps Cavalry carbine, 22 in. barrel, color case hardened frame, hammer, patchbox, and furniture. New 1994.

Mfg.'s Sug. Retail	$935	$735	$535	$395	$280	$195	$175	$150

KODIAK MARK IV DOUBLE RIFLE — .45-70 cal., patterned after the Colt Double rifle, semi-regulated barrels, hammers, folding leaf rear sight, 24 in. barrels, color cased hardened receiver, 10 lbs. 3 oz. New 1996.

Mfg.'s Sug. Retail	$3,125	$2,800	$2,400	$2,250	$2,000	$1,800	$1,600	$1,400

▲ *Deluxe Kodiak Mark IV* — similar to Kodiak Mark IV Double rifle, except has brown barrels and hand-engraved satin finished receiver. New 1996.

Mfg.'s Sug. Retail	$4,000	$3,700	$3,150	$2,850	$2,600	$2,375	$2,000	$1,750

N

Grading	100%	98%	95%	90%	80%	70%	60%

HENRY RIFLE — .44-40 or .44 Rimfire (disc. 1989) cal., reproduction of Winchester's famous Henry Rifle, brass or iron frame. New for 1985.
> Add $370 for "A" pattern engraving (25% coverage).
> Add $585 for "B" pattern engraving (35% coverage).
> Add $975 for "C" pattern engraving (50% coverage).
> The above special order engraving patterns usually require 30-60 days.

▲ *Military Rifle* — 24 in. barrel, brass frame, blued barrel, walnut stock, original style sling swivels, 9¼ lbs. New for 1985.

Mfg.'s Sug. Retail $895	$700	$550	$450	$350	$275	$225	$195

▲ *Union Pacific Railroad Commemorative* — .44-40 cal., only 100 mfg.

$795	$575	$475	

Last Mfg.'s Sug. Retail was $695.

▲ *Engraved Rifle* — limited mfg., extensive engraving on brass frame. Disc. 1988.

$1,510	$1,275	$1,100	$900	$750	$650	$550

Last Mfg.'s Sug. Retail was $1,850.

> Add $100 for steel frame.

▲ *Carbine* — 24 in. barrel, limited edition of 1,000 units including 50 engraved specimens, no swivels, 8¼ lbs.

Mfg.'s Sug. Retail $875	$685	$540	$450	$350	$275	$225	$195

▲ *Engraved Carbine* — limited production, only 50 mfg. Disc. 1988.

$1,450	$1,225	$1,075	$900	$750	$650	$550

Last Mfg.'s Sug. Retail was $1,750.

▲ *Trapper Model* — 16½ in. barrel, 7¼ lbs., 34¼ in. overall length.

Mfg.'s Sug. Retail $875	$685	$540	$450	$350	$275	$225	$195

▲ *Iron Frame Model* — with steel frame and butt plate, 24 in. blued barrel, select walnut, 9¼ lbs.

Mfg.'s Sug. Retail $945	$760	$665	$560	$485	$430	$360	$295

> This model is available with either blued or color case hardened receiver.

MODEL 1866 YELLOWBOY CARBINE/RIFLE — .22 LR (disc.), .357 Mag. (disc.), or .44-40 cal. only, choice of rifle (24 in. octagon barrel) or carbine (19 in. round barrel), case hardened receiver, replica of the Winchester Model 1866. Mfg. 1972-1984, re-introduced.

Mfg.'s Sug. Retail $670	$545	$450	$350	$250	$195	$175	$150

> Add $10 for rifle variation.

YELLOWBOY TRAPPER — .44-40 cal., 16½ in. barrel.

$575	$475	$425	$375	$325	$275	$225

MODEL 1873 STANDARD RIFLE/CARBINE — .44-40 or .45 LC cal., choice of rifle (24 in. octagon barrel) or carbine (19 in. round barrel), replica of the Winchester Model 1873.

Mfg.'s Sug. Retail $800	$695	$600	$515	$425	$350	$295	$250

> Add $20 for rifle variation.

▲ *Model 1873 Trapper* — .44-40 cal., similar to Carbine, with 16½ in. barrel.

$575	$475	$425	$375	$325	$275	$225

▲ *Model 1873 Deluxe Sporting Rifle* — deluxe variation of the Model 1873 featuring case hardened receiver, checkered pistol grip stock, and choice of 24 (carbine) or 30 (rifle) in. barrel, 8 lbs. 14 oz. New 1992.

Mfg.'s Sug. Retail $930	$820	$695	$550	$425	$325	$275	$225

> Add $30 for rifle variation.

▲ *Model 1873 1 of 1,000* — only 1,000 mfg., deluxe wood, special engraving.

$1,000	$775	$550	

RIFLES: MODERN MFG.

In addition to the models listed below, Navy Arms in late 1990 purchased the manufacturing rights to the English firm, Parker-Hale. In 1991, Navy Arms built a manufacturing facility located in Martinsburg, WV to produce these rifles domestically.

N

Grading	100%	98%	95%	90%	80%	70%	60%

The name of this new company is Gibbs Rifle Co. and their section should be consulted for current models and values.

TU-KKW TRAINING RIFLE — .22 LR cal., replica of the German "KKW" Gewehr training rifle, full sized Mauser 98K action with military sights, 26 in. barrel, detachable 5 shot mag., mfg. in China, 8 lbs. Imported 1992-94.

	$210	$180	$150	$135	$120	$105	$90

Last Mfg.'s Sug. Retail was $310.

Add $125 for 2¾ power Type 89 quick mount scope (Sniper Trainer).

TU-33/40 CARBINE — .22 LR or 7.62x39mm cal., based on WWII Mauser G33/40 mountain carbine, 20¾ in. barrel, includes sling, adj. rear sight, mfg. in China, 7 lbs. 7 oz. Imported 1992-94.

	$180	$150	$135	$120	$105	$90	$75

Last Mfg.'s Sug. Retail was $210.

7.62x39mm cal. is POR from Navy Arms in this model.

JW-15 RIFLE — .22 LR cal., sporter bolt action based on Brno Model 5 action, 24 in. barrel, detachable 5 shot mag., receiver top is dove-tailed, mfg. in China, 5 lbs. 12 oz. Imported 1992-94.

	$85	$70	$60	$50	$40	$35	$30

Last Mfg.'s Sug. Retail was $100.

MARTINI TARGET RIFLE — .444, or .45-70 cal., single shot, 26 or 30 in. octagon barrel, tang sight, pistol grip stock. Mfg. 1972-1984.

	$480	$420	$350	$250	$195	$175	$150

RPKS-74 — .223 or 7.62x39mm (new 1989) cal., semi-automatic version of the Chinese RPK Squad Automatic Weapon, Kalashnikov action, 19 in. barrel, integral folding bipod, 9½ lbs. Imported 1988-1989 only.

	$525	$445	$350	$250	$195	$175	$150

Last Mfg.'s Sug. Retail was $649.

USED MILITARY FIREARMS

Navy Arms sells a wide variety of original military firearms in used condition. Handguns include the Mauser Broomhandle, Japanese Nambu, Colt 1911 Government Model, Tokarev, Browning Hi-Power, S & W Model 1917, and others. Rifles include Mauser contract models, Japanese Type 38s, Enfields, FNs, Nagants, M1 Carbines, M1 Garands, Chinese SKSs, Egyptian Rashids, French MAS Model 1936s, among others. Most of these firearms are priced in the $75-$500 price range depending on desirability of model and condition. Navy Arms should be contacted directly regarding specific prices for these models.

SHOTGUNS: RECENT IMPORTATION

Importation of the models listed below was disc. in 1990.

MODEL 83 O/U — 12 or 20 ga., manufactured in Italy by R. Luciano, 3 in. chambers, extractors, double triggers, engraved chrome receiver, vent. barrels (bored M/F or IC/M) and rib. Introduced 1985.

	$280	$240	$215	$195	$170	$160	$150

Last Mfg.'s Sug. Retail was $320.

MODEL 93 O/U — 12 or 20 ga., manufactured in Italy by R. Luciano, 3 in. chambers, ejectors, double triggers, engraved chrome receiver, vent. barrels (bored M/F or IC/M) and rib. Introduced 1985.

	$325	$285	$250	$220	$200	$185	$160

Last Mfg.'s Sug. Retail was $380.

MODEL 95 O/U — similar to Model 93, except with single trigger and multi-chokes (includes 5 tubes), extractors.

	$375	$330	$295	$265	$235	$210	$190

Last Mfg.'s Sug. Retail was $420.

N

Grading	100%	98%	95%	90%	80%	70%	60%

MODEL 96 SPORTSMAN O/U — 12 ga. only, 3 in. chambers, vent. barrels and rib, engraved chrome receiver, gold-plated receiver, multi-choked with 5 choke tubes, ejectors. Introduced 1985.

| | $470 | $425 | $375 | $330 | $295 | $260 | $230 |

Last Mfg.'s Sug. Retail was $530.

MODEL 100 O/U — 12, 20, 28, or .410 ga., 3 in. chambers, 26 in. VR barrels, photo-engraved hard chrome receiver, single trigger, extractors, checkered walnut stock and forearm, approx. 6¼ lbs. Introduced 1985.

| | $225 | $205 | $190 | $170 | $160 | $150 | $140 |

Last Mfg.'s Sug. Retail was $250.

MODEL 100 SxS — 12 or 20 ga., 3 in. chambers, 27½ in. barrels, checkered European walnut, double triggers, extractors, 6½ or 7 lbs. Imported 1985-1987 only.

| | $380 | $330 | $290 | $260 | $230 | $200 | $170 |

Last Mfg.'s Sug. Retail was $475.

MODEL 150 SxS — similar to Model 100, except with ejectors. Imported 1985-1987 only.

| | $455 | $395 | $350 | $310 | $280 | $250 | $220 |

Last Mfg.'s Sug. Retail was $574.

MODEL 105 SINGLE BARREL — 12, 20, or .410 ga., 26 or 28 in. full choke barrel only, folding action, engraved chrome receiver, checkered hardwood stock and forearm. New 1985.

| | $80 | $70 | $65 | $60 | $55 | $50 | $45 |

Last Mfg.'s Sug. Retail was $90.

This model was designated the Model 600 before 1988.

▲ *Model 105 Deluxe* — similar to Model 105, except has European walnut stock and VR.

| | $95 | $85 | $75 | $65 | $60 | $55 | $50 |

Last Mfg.'s Sug. Retail was $105.

This model was designated the Model 600 Deluxe before 1988.

P.V. NELSON, (GUNMAKERS)

Manufacturer located in Bucks, England (factory is located in London).

P.V. Nelson manufactures best quality shotguns and double rifles per individual customer order. Double rifles feature back action locks, and bolsters for extra strength. Side-by-side and over/under shotguns are available in most gauges, with a choice of rounded or regular action. Please contact the factory directly (see Trademark Index) to find out more information about this quality English manufacturer. P.V. Nelson manufactures 10-20 guns annually.

NEW DETONICS MANUFACTURING CORPORATION

Previous manufacturer located in Phoenix, AZ 1989-1992. Formerly named Detonics Firearms Industries (previous manufacturer located in Bellevue, WA 1976-1988). Detonics was sold in early 1988 to the New Detonics Manufacturing Corporation, a wholly owned subsidiary of "1045 Investors Group Limited".

PISTOLS: STAINLESS STEEL

MARK I — .45 ACP cal., matte blue. Disc. 1981.

| | $550 | $450 | $395 |

MARK II — .45 ACP cal., satin nickel finish. Disc. 1979.

| | $495 | $375 | $300 |

MARK III — .45 ACP cal., hard chrome finish. Disc. 1979.

| | $520 | $390 | $325 |

MARK IV — .45 ACP cal., polished blue. Disc. 1981.

| | $539 | $410 | $360 |

N

Grading	100%	98%	95%	90%	80%	70%	60%

COMBATMASTER MC1 (FORMERLY MARK I) — .45 ACP, 9mm, or .38 Super cal., 3½ in. barrel, two-tone (slide is non-glare blue and frame is matte stainless) finish, 6 shot mag., fixed sights, 28 oz. Disc. 1992.

$775 $575 $450

Last Mfg.'s Sug. Retail was $920.

Add $15 for OM-3 model (polished slide - disc. 1983).
Add $100 for 9mm or .38 Super cal. (disc. 1990).
This model was originally the MC1, then changed to the Mark I, then changed back to the MC1.

COMBATMASTER MARK V — .45 ACP, 9mm, or .38 Super cal., matte stainless finish, fixed sights, 6 shot mag. in .45 ACP, 7 shot in 9mm and .38 Super, 3½ in. barrel, 29 oz. empty. This model was disc. 1985.

$620 $550 $495

Last Mfg.'s Sug. Retail was $689.

Add $100 for 9mm or .38 Super cal.

COMBATMASTER MARK VI — .45 ACP, 9mm, or .38 Super cal., 3½ in. barrel, 6 shot mag., adj. sights and polished stainless slide sides. Disc. 1989.

$685 $575 $450

Last Mfg.'s Sug. Retail was $795.

Add $100 for 9mm or .38 Super cal.

▲ *.451 Detonics Mag. Cal.* — limited mfg. 1,000. Disc. 1985.

$1,000 $900 $775

Last Mfg.'s Sug. Retail was $1,165.

COMBATMASTER MARK VII — similar to Mark VI, only no sights, special order only, 25 oz.

$895 $775 $600

Add $100 for 9mm or .38 Super cal.
Add $350 for .451 Detonics Mag., (disc. 1982).

MILITARY COMBAT MC2 — .45 ACP, 9mm, or .38 Super cal., dull, non-glare combat finish, fixed sights. Comes with camouflaged pile-lined wallet, and Pachmayr grips. Disc. 1984.

$621 $560 $500

Add $55 for 9mm or .38 Super.

O.S. MODEL — .45 ACP cal. only, emergency backup pistol, similar to Combatmaster, 6 shot mag., choice of satin stainless or all black finish. 2 mfg. 1991 only.
Extreme rarity precludes accurate price evaluation.

SCOREMASTER — .45 ACP or .451 Mag. cal., match gun with closer tolerances, 5 or 6 in. barrel. Millett adj. sights, grip safety, 7 or 8 shot mag., 42 oz. Disc. 1992.

$995 $850 $695

Last Mfg.'s Sug. Retail was $1,178.

Add $40 for 6 in. barrel.

COMPMASTER — .45 ACP cal. only, similar to Scoremaster, except is fully compensated. Mfg. 1988-92.

$1,995 $1,575 $1,250

Last Mfg.'s Sug. Retail was $1,550.

This model was called the Janus Competition Scoremaster in 1988-1989.

COMPETITION MASTER T.F. — .45 ACP cal., competition model with dual port compensator, rotational torque compensating vents, patented cone barrel system, hand tuned trigger, includes all competition modifications. Disc. 1992.

$1,995 $1,575 $1,250

Last Mfg.'s Sug. Retail was $1,550.

SERVICEMASTER — .45 ACP cal. only, shortened version of the Scoremaster, non-glare combat finish, 4¼ in. barrel, coned barrel system, 8 shot mag., interchangeable front and adj. rear sights, 39 oz. Disc. 1986.

$825 $675 $575

Last Mfg.'s Sug. Retail was $686.

Grading				100%	98%	95%	90%	80%	70%	60%

▲ **Servicemaster II** — similar to Servicemaster, except has polished stainless steel finish. Mfg. 1986-92.

$925 $750 $625

Last Mfg.'s Sug. Retail was $998.

LADIES ESCORT SERIES

This series is designed specifically to suit a woman's shooting requirements.

ROYAL ESCORT — .45 ACP cal., action similar to Combatmaster, 3½ in. barrel, 6 shot mag., black frame, slide and grips are iridescent purple, hammer and trigger are 24 Kt. gold-plated. Mfg. 1990-92.

$860 $675 $525

Last Mfg.'s Sug. Retail was $990.

MIDNIGHT ESCORT — similar to Royal Escort, except is stainless with a black slide and smooth black grips. Mfg. 1990-92.

$965 $725 $580

Last Mfg.'s Sug. Retail was $1,090.

JADE ESCORT — similar to Midnight Escort, except has stainless frame, jade colored slide and grips. Mfg. 1990 only.

$825 $650 $525

Last Mfg.'s Sug. Retail was $918. Less than 25 of this color were mfg.

POCKET 9 — 9mm, double action, 3 in. barrel, 6 shot mag., soft matte sheen finish, 26 oz. Mfg. 1985-86 only.

$425 $385 $325

Last Mfg.'s Sug. Retail was $458.

The entire Pocket 9 series was disc. 1986.

▲ **Pocket 9 LS** — similar to Pocket 9, except has 4 in. barrel. Mfg. 1986 only.

$410 $370 $325

Last Mfg.'s Sug. Retail was $458.

▲ **Pocket .380** — similar to Pocket 9, except is .380 ACP cal., 23 oz. Mfg. 1986 only.

$410 $370 $325

Last Mfg.'s Sug. Retail was $458.

POWER 9 — 9mm, similar to Pocket 9, except has polished slide sides and is supplied with 2 mags. Disc. 1986.

$455 $410 $350

Last Mfg.'s Sug. Retail was $509.

NEW ENGLAND ARMS CO.

Importer/distributor/retailer located in Kittery Point, ME.

New England Arms Co. imports, distributes, or retails the following trademarks: Beretta Premium Grades, Bertuzzi, Luciano Bosis, Carlo Casartelli, Americo Cosmi, Henri Dumoulin, Ferlib, Lebeau-Courally, Westley Richards, F.lli Rizzini, B. Rizzini, Fabio Zanotti, and Webley & Scott. These trademarks may be found under their own headings in this text. For further information regarding any one of these manufacturers, please contact New England Arms, Co. directly. New England Arms also offers quality restoration services on best quality shotguns and rifles executed by trained European craftsmen, in addition to performing firearms appraisals and evaluation work.

NEW ENGLAND FIREARMS

Manufacturer located in Gardner, MA. Distributor sales only.

All NEF firearms utilize a transfer bar safety and have a $10 service plan which guarantees life-time warranty.

REVOLVERS: D/A

Ultra Models listed below are available in blue finish only. Beginning 1993, all Ultras include lockable storage case.

Grading	100%	98%	95%	90%	80%	70%	60%

STANDARD REVOLVER .22 (MODEL R92) — .22 LR cal., 9 shot, swing out cylinder, 2½ or 4 in. barrel, blue or nickel finish, hardwood stocks, fixed rear sight, 25-28 oz. New 1988.

Mfg.'s Sug. Retail	$135	$120	$95	$80	$70	$60	$55	$40

   Add $10 for nickel finish.

▲ *Standard Revolver .32 H&R Mag. (Model R73)* — .32 H&R Mag. cal. similar to Standard Revolver .22, except has 5 shot cylinder, 2½ or 4 in. barrel, choice of blue or nickel (2½ barrel in. only), 23-26 oz. New 1988.

Mfg.'s Sug. Retail	$135	$125	$95	$80	$70	$60	$55	$40

   Add $10 for nickel finish (2½ in. barrel only).

ULTRA MODEL — .22 LR cal., 9 shot, swing-out cylinder, 4 or 6 in. solid rib target-grade barrel with rebated muzzle and fully adj. rear sight, blue finish, smooth hardwood grips, 36 oz.

Mfg.'s Sug. Retail	$170	$145	$110	$95	$80	$70	$60	$55

ULTRA MAG (MODEL R22) — .22 Mag. cal., 6 shot, 4 or 6 in. solid rib barrel, adj. rear sight, swing-out cylinder, blue finish, 36 oz. New 1988.

Mfg.'s Sug. Retail	$170	$145	$110	$95	$80	$70	$60	$55

LADY ULTRA — .32 H&R Mag. cal., swing-out cylinder, 5 shot, blue finish, 3 in. barrel with rib, adj. sights, thinner contoured grips, 31 oz. New 1991.

Mfg.'s Sug. Retail	$170	$145	$110	$95	$80	$70	$60	$55

   New England Firearms Co. also manufactures blank starter revolvers (.22 or .32 cal.) which are variations of this model.

SHOTGUNS/COMBINATION GUNS

PARDNER — 12, 16 (new 1989), 20, 28 (new 1991), or .410 ga., 2¾ or 3 in. chamber (12 and 20 ga.), single shot, break open action, safety transfer bar mechanism on hammer, side lever release, color case hardened receiver, 24 (disc.), 26, 28, or 32 in. fixed choke barrel, extractor, walnut stained hardwood stock and forearm, 5-6 lbs. New 1987.

Mfg.'s Sug. Retail	$100		$90	$80	$70	$60	$50	$45	$40

   Add $5 for 32 in. barrel (12 ga. only).

▲ *Pardner Youth Model* — 20, 28, or .410 ga., similar to Pardner, except has 22 in. barrel.

Mfg.'s Sug. Retail	$110		$95	$80	$70	$60	$50	$45	$40

▲ *Pardner Special Purpose 10 ga.* — 10 ga. only, 3½ in. chamber, 24 (Turkey full choke with matte black finish, new 1996), 28, or 32 (new 1996) in. barrel, blue or camo paint finish, recoil pad, 9½ lbs. New 1988.

Mfg.'s Sug. Retail	$150	$130	$110	$90	$75	$65	$55	$45

   Add $10 for camo finish, swivels, and swing.
   Add $30 for 32 in. barrel with camo finish, swivels, and sling.
   Add $35 for 24 in. Turkey full choke variation.

▲ *National Wild Turkey Federation (NWTF)* — 10 or 20 (new 1993) ga., Mag. chamber, 22 (20 ga. only) or 24 in. barrel with full screw-in choke, full mossy oak camo treatment, includes swivels and sling. New 1992.

Mfg.'s Sug. Retail	$230	$190	$160	$135	$110	$95	$80	$70

   Subtract $80 for 20 ga.
   This model has been drilled and tapped for scope mounts.

SURVIVAL SERIES — 12, 20, or .410/.45 LC (new 1995) ga., 3 in. chamber, 20 (.410/.45 LC) or 22 in. barrel with Mod. choke, blue or electroless nickel finish, synthetic thumbhole designed hollow stock with pistol grip, removable forend holds additional ammo, sling swivels, and black nylon sling, 6 lbs. Mfg. 1992-93, re-instated 1995.

Mfg.'s Sug. Retail	$130		$110	$90	$70	$60	$50	$45	$40

   Add $16 for electroless nickel finish.
   Add $16 for .410/.45 LC ga.

TRACKER SLUG MODEL — 10 ga. x 3½ in. (mfg. 1994 only), 12, or 20 ga., 24 in. cylinder bore barrel, case colored receiver, includes recoil pad and adj. sights, 6 lbs. New 1992.

Mfg.'s Sug. Retail	$130		$110	$85	$70	$60	$50	$45	$40

Grading	100%	98%	95%	90%	80%	70%	60%

▲ **Tracker II** — 12 or 20 ga., 3 in. chamber, similar to Tracker Slug Model except has 24 in. rifled bore barrel. New 1995.

Mfg.'s Sug. Retail	$140	$115	$90	$70	$60	$50	$45	$40

RIFLES

HANDI-RIFLE — .22 Hornet, .22-250 Rem. (mfg. 1992-94), .223 Rem., .243 Win. (new 1992), .270 Win. (new 1993), .280 Rem. (new 1996), .30-30, .30-06 (new 1992), .44 Rem. Mag. (new 1996), or .45-70 cal., break open single shot action, 22 or 26 (.280 Rem. only) in. bull or regular barrel, blued receiver, walnut stained hardwood stock, scope mount rail or ramp front and adj. folding rear sights, sling swivels, 7 lbs. New 1989.

Mfg.'s Sug. Retail	$210	$175	$140	$115	$95	$80	$70	$60

Add $5 for .280 Rem. cal.

This model in .22-250 Rem. or .223 Rem. cal. is supplied with heavy barrel, scope mount, and no sights.

SURVIVOR RIFLE — .223 Rem. or .357 Mag. cal., similar in design to the Survival Series shotgun, 22 in. barrel, blue or nickel finish, .357 Mag. cal. has open sights, .223 Rem. cal. has integral scope rail, 6 lbs. New 1996.

Mfg.'s Sug. Retail	$220	$185	$150	$120	$95	$80	$70	$60

Add $15 for nickel finish.

NEWTON ARMS CO.

Previous manufacturer located in Buffalo, NY 1913-1932. Also named Charles Newton Rifle Corp. and Buffalo Newton Rifle Co.

NEWTON-MAUSER RIFLE — Oberndorf bolt action, .256 Newton cal., 24 in. barrel, double set triggers, checkered pistol grip stock. Pre-WWI mfg.

	$800	$650	$550	$440	$385	$330	$275

FIRST TYPE STANDARD RIFLE — Newton bolt action, .22, .256, .280, .30, .33, .35 Newton, and .30-06 cals., 24 in. barrel, double set triggers, open or aperture sights, checkered pistol grip stock. Mfg. 1916-1918 by Newton Arms.

	$1,150	$925	$750	$625	$500	$440	$385

SECOND TYPE STANDARD RIFLE — improved Newton action, has Enfield type bolt handle, .256, .30, .35 Newton, and .30-06 cals., open sights, checkered pistol grip stock. Mfg. post-WWI by Charles Newton Rifle Corporation.

	$1,000	$825	$660	$600	$500	$440	$385

BUFFALO NEWTON RIFLE — similar to Second Type. Mfg. 1922-1932 by Buffalo Newton Rifle company.

	$1,000	$825	$660	$600	$500	$440	$385

SPRINGFIELD NEWTON — kit consisting of a Newton barrel and sporter stock, barrels were chambered for Newton calibers, kits were available to adapt Springfield rifles into Newton calibers in the 1920s when the NRA made the Springfields available to its membership.

	$595	$540	$495	$450	$410	$375	$330

NIKKO FIREARMS CO. LTD.

Previous manufacturer located in Tochigi, Japan circa 1958-1989.

The publisher wishes to thank the Golden Eagle Collectors Association located at 11144 Slate Creek Road, Grass Valley, CA 95945 for providing this publication with the information listed below. Please refer to the Golden Eagle heading in this text for information on Nikko manufactured Golden Eagle firearms.

Both Nikko Firearms Co., Ltd. and Nikko Arms Co., Ltd. were trade names used by the Kodensha Co., Ltd. of Tochigi, Japan on products they manufactured and distributed worldwide. Nikko is the name of the Prefecture, or district, in which Tochigi City is located, about 50 miles north of Tokyo. The word Nikko translates to English as "sunshine". Kodensha first manufactured or distributed under the Nikko name

N

in April 1955, and exported out of Japan beginning in August 1958. Nothing is known of the origin of the Kodensha Co.

Kodensha first approached the American shotgun market in about 1958 or '59 using the Japanese export marketing firm of Kyowa-Boeki-Bussan. They contacted various US distributors, and in about 1959 or '60, Continental Arms Co. of New York City began importing the Nikko "Grade 5". Continental imported these Nikko over/unders, in various models and configurations, until about 1972.

In 1962, the Kodensha Co. Ltd. formed a joint venture with Olin/Winchester of New Haven, CT to produce the Winchester Model 101 over/under shotgun. This venture was known as the Olin-Kodensha Co. Ltd. Added a little later was the side-by-side Model 23, and the Model 96 Xpert (a budget priced 101). The "pre-Olin" Kodensha factory was considerably outdated, and the joint venture began a complete modernization process, with the financial and technical assistance of Olin. Millions of dollars of machinery and technology were brought in, and the entire manufacturing process was upgraded to the then current standards.

One of the conditions of the joint venture was that Kodensha restrict their own products (made in the same factory, but recorded separately from the joint venture) to sale in Japan only. At the outset of the 25 years that the joint venture existed, Kodensha was probably amenable to this, as they were reaping huge financial and technical benefits from Olin. But, by the mid '60s, when the factory was in place and running smoothly, Kodensha essentially ignored that condition of the agreement, leaving Olin at somewhat of a disadvantage, not wanting to jeopardize their investment or production source. Additionally, Olin/Winchester was allowed only 2 permanent personnel, hardly enough to monitor the activities of a factory which employed up to 400 people. As an example, when walnut stock blanks arrived from France, Kodensha took first pick, and Olin got what was left over.

Kodensha converted an existing building near the manufacturing plant into an assembly area for Nikko, and other brands of guns. This building was probably the "true" Nikko Firearms Co. Ltd. Manufactured components from the Olin-Kodensha factory were carted to the Nikko plant for final assembly and fitting. This "dual-factory" arrangement continued until the mid-1980s. In 1981, for an unknown reason, the Olin-Kodensha name was changed to OK Firearms Co. Ltd. In October 1987, Olin/Winchester sold their interest in OK Firearms to Classic Doubles International, which continued making the 101 style shotgun under their own name. For reasons unknown, Classic Doubles went out of business in December 1988. Shortly thereafter, the entire factory was torn down, and all that remains today is a vacant lot.

During the "dual-factory" days, Nikko produced firearms for the following distributors or retailers: 1) Kanematsu Gosho of Arlington Heights, IL approx. 1974-1982 - distributed Nikko brand shotguns, Golden Eagle brand shotguns and rifles (1975 through March 1977 only); 2) Golden Eagle Firearms, Houston, TX March 1977 through early 1981 - Golden Eagle shotguns and rifles; 3) Tradewinds, Inc. of Tacoma, WA exported from Japan by Caspoll International, Tokyo January 1971 through December 1972 - Shadow Seven; Shadow Indy (Model 707); Gold, Silver, and Black Shadow over/under shotguns; 4) Marubeni America, Inc. of New York City 1972-1974 - Miida brand over/under shotguns; 5) Winchester GMBH of West Germany, manufactured by Olin-Kodensha (dates unknown - early '80s) - Winchester Model 777 rifle (Golden Eagle look-alike); 6) Parker Reproduction shotguns, distributed in the US by Reagent Chemical & Research, Inc. 1984-1988; 7) International Star Commerce Corp. (ISCC) of Salt Lake City, Utah approx. 1982 - distributor of Nikko brand shotguns; 8) Moore Supply Co. of Salt Lake City, UT beginning mid-1981 - distributor of Nikko brand shotguns; 9) USA Nikko, Inc. of Los Angeles, CA (factory reps and distributors of Nikko shotguns), initial date unknown, through December 1981; 10) Weatherby, Inc. of Los Angeles, CA May 1972 to 1981. Centurion semi-auto and Patrician pump shotguns, some Mark 22 rifles. Olympian O/U shotgun and possibly other O/Us from 1978-81. Model 82 semi-auto and Model 92 pump shotguns; 11) Savage Industries of Hamden, CT 1981-1982 - Savage/Fox FA-1 and FP-1 shotguns; 12) Charles Daly. "Automatic" distributed by Sloan's (Japanese made only) mid-1980s; 13) Sears, Roebuck Co. Ted Williams Model 400 and possibly others; 14) Churchill semi-auto, imported by Kassnar mid-1980s; 15) High Standard of Hamden, CT 1974-75 - Supermatic Shadow Indy (Model 707, an O/U), Supermatic Shadow Seven (also O/U), and Supermatic Shadow semi-auto.

NOTE: ALL of the semi-auto shotguns used essentially the same design. Each distributor may have made a few cosmetic or dimensional embellishments to differentiate their gun. Differences exist in barrel/breech fit, magazine caps, pistol grip caps, checkering pattern, piston size, ejector location, fluted bolt. Use caution if interchanging parts. Generally, the same statement can be made about the pump versions also.

NOBLE MFG. CO.

Previous manufacturer located in Haydenville, MA between 1950-1970.

Nobel manufactured both semi-auto, lever, and slide action rifles in addition to both slide action and SxS shotguns. While most models were relatively inexpensive, good working, utilitarian guns, there has been little collectibility to date and most rifles are seen priced in the $35-$85 price range while the shotguns are priced in the $65-$175 range.

NORINCO

Manufacturer located in China. Various importers have included: Century International Arms, Inc. located in St. Albans, VT; China Sports, Inc. located in Ontario, CA; Interarms located in Alexandria, VA; KBI, Inc. located in Harrisburg, PA; and others. Distributor sales only.

Norinco pistols, rifles, and shotguns are manufactured in the People's Republic of China by Northern China Industries Corp. (Norinco has over 100 factories). Due to current legislation, Chinese firearms are not allowed to be imported in the U.S.

Grading	100%	98%	95%	90%	80%	70%	60%

PISTOLS

The models below have been discontinued this year as they are currently no longer being imported.

MODEL 213 — 9mm Para. cal., single action, satin blue finish. Imported 1988 only.

	100%	98%	95%	90%	80%	70%	60%
	$185	$150	$135	$125	$115	$105	$100

Last Mfg.'s Sug. Retail was $200.

TYPE 54-1 TOKAREV STANDARD — 7.62x25mm or .38 Super cal., single action semi-auto, 4.5 in. barrel, 8 shot mag., fixed sights, blue finish, 29 oz. Imported 1989-95.

	100%	98%	95%	90%	80%	70%	60%
	$125	$100	$80	$70	$65	$60	$55

Last Mfg.'s Sug. Retail was $145.

▲ **Type 54-1 Double Column** — similar to Standard Model, except is also available in 9mm Para. cal. and has 10 (C/B 1994) or 13* shot mag., 35 oz. Imported 1991-95.

	100%	98%	95%	90%	80%	70%	60%
	$155	$135	$120	$110	$100	$90	$80

Last Mfg.'s Sug. Retail was $185.

▲ **Type 54-1 Compact** — .38 Super, 9mm Para., or 7.62x25mm cal., 3.8 in. barrel, 8 shot mag., 27 oz. Imported 1991-95.

	100%	98%	95%	90%	80%	70%	60%
	$155	$135	$120	$110	$100	$90	$80

Last Mfg.'s Sug. Retail was $185.

TYPE 59 MAKAROV — 9x18mm Makarov or .380 ACP cal., double action semi-auto, 3.5 in. barrel, 8 shot bottom release mag., checkered plastic grips, PPK design with additional features, adj. rear sight, 24 oz. Imported 1989-95.

	100%	98%	95%	90%	80%	70%	60%
	$150	$135	$125	$115	$95	$85	$75

Last Mfg.'s Sug. Retail was $185.

TYPE 77B — 9mm Para. cal., semi-auto single action, action patterned after the older German Lignose (unique design permits one handed operation utilizing "triggerguard cocking" enabling the slide to be moved backward cocking the hammer), 5 in. barrel, 8 shot mag., adj. rear sight, 34 oz. Imported 1991-95.

	100%	98%	95%	90%	80%	70%	60%
	$235	$200	$180	$160	$140	$120	$100

Last Mfg.'s Sug. Retail was $285.

MODEL 1911 A1 — .45 ACP cal. only, patterned after the Colt 1911 A1, 5 in. barrel, 7 shot mag., fixed sights, blue or parkerized finish, wood grips, 39 oz. Imported 1991-95.

	100%	98%	95%	90%	80%	70%	60%
	$275	$245	$220	$195	$180	$165	$150

Last Mfg.'s Sug. Retail was $320.

N

PARAMILITARY DESIGN CARBINES & RIFLES

The models below have been discontinued this year as they are currently no longer being imported.

Grading	100%	98%	95%	90%	80%	70%	60%

TYPE 84S AK RIFLE — .223 cal., semi-auto Kalashnikov action, 16.34 in. barrel, hardwood stock and pistol grip, 30 shot mag., 1,000 meter adj. rear sight, includes bayonet and sheath, 8.87 lbs. Imported 1988-1989 only.

	$495	$450	$400	$360	$330	$300	$285

Last Mfg.'s Sug. Retail was $350.

▲ *Type 84S-1* — similar to Type 84S AK except has under-folding metal stock. Imported 1989 only.

	$525	$475	$425	$385	$350	$325	$300

Last Mfg.'s Sug. Retail was $350.

▲ *Type 84S-3* — similar to Type 84S AK except has composite fiber stock (1½ in. longer than wood stock). Imported 1989 only.

	$550	$500	$450	$400	$375	$350	$325

Last Mfg.'s Sug. Retail was $365.

▲ *Type 84S-5* — similar to Type 84S AK except has side-folding metal stock. Imported 1989 only.

	$525	$475	$425	$385	$350	$325	$300

Last Mfg.'s Sug. Retail was $350.

AK-47 THUMBHOLE — .223 Rem. or 7.62x39mm cal., features new thumbhole stock for legalized import, 5 shot mag. Imported 1991-1993, configuration was restyled and renamed NHM-90/91 in 1994.

	$450	$400	$360	$330	$285	$250	$225

Last Mfg.'s Sug. Retail was $375.

Add $8 for .223 Rem. cal.

MODEL B THUMBHOLE — 9x19mm, patterned after the Uzi, features sporterized thumbhole wood stock, 10 shot mag. Importation 1995 only.

	$550	$485	$440	$400	$360	$330	$295

Last Mfg.'s Sug. Retail was $625.

R.P.K. RIFLE — 7.62mm cal., includes bipod. Importation disc. 1993.

	$600	$550	$495	$425	$395	$375	$325

Last Mfg.'s Sug. Retail was $600.

TYPE SKS — .223 or 7.62x39mm cal., SKS action, 20.47 in. barrel, 10 (C/B 1994) or 30* shot clip mag., 1,000 meter adj. rear sight, hardwood stock, new design accepts standard AK mag., with or w/o folding bayonet, 8.8 lbs. Imported 1988-1989, re-introduced 1992 with Sporter configuration stock. Short term demand could dictate limited supplies with this model. Importation disc. 1995.

	$125	$110	$100	$90	$80	$75	$70

Last Mfg.'s Sug. Retail was $150.

Add $100 for synthetic stock and bayonet.
Subtract 15% if refinished.

TYPE 81S AK RIFLE — 7.62x39mm cal., semi-auto Kalashnikov action, 17.5 in. barrel, 5, 30, or 40 shot clip mag., 500 meter adj. rear sight, fixed wood stock, hold open device after last shot, 8 lbs. Imported 1988-1989.

	$495	$450	$400	$360	$330	$300	$285

Last Mfg.'s Sug. Retail was $385.

▲ *Type 81S-1* — similar to Type 81S AK except has under-folding metal stock. Imported 1988-1989.

	$525	$475	$425	$385	$350	$325	$300

Last Mfg.'s Sug. Retail was $385.

TYPE 56S-2 — 7.62x39mm cal., older Kalashnikov design with side-folding metal stock. Importation disc. 1989.

	$495	$450	$400	$360	$330	$300	$285

Last Mfg.'s Sug. Retail was $350.

TYPE 86S-7 RPK RIFLE — 7.62x39mm cal., AK action, 23.27 in. heavy barrel with built-in bipod, in-line butt stock, 11.02 lbs. Imported 1988-1989.

	$850	$775	$700	$640	$595	$550	$500

Last Mfg.'s Sug. Retail was $425.

N

Grading	100%	98%	95%	90%	80%	70%	60%

TYPE 86S BULLPUP RIFLE — 7.62x39mm cal., bullpup configuration with AK action, under-folding metal stock, 17¼ in. barrel, ambidextrous cocking design, folding front handle, 7 lbs. Imported 1989 only.

| | $725 | $650 | $575 | $525 | $460 | $410 | $350 |

Last Mfg.'s Sug. Retail was $400.

DRAGUNOV (MODEL 350 NDM-86 OR SVD) — 7.62x54mm cal., sniper variation of the AK-47, features 24 in. barrel with muzzle brake, special laminated skeletonized wood stock with vent. forearm, detachable 10 shot mag., 8 lbs. 9 oz. Importation disc. 1995.

| | $2,775 | $2,350 | $1,925 | $1,575 | $1,275 | $1,050 | $900 |

Last Mfg.'s Sug. Retail was $3,080.

This model is also imported by Gibbs Rifle Co. located in Martinsburg, WV.

▲ **Dragunov Carbine** — similar to Dragunov rifle, except shorter barrel, various accessories including a lighted scope were also offered.

| | $1,700 | $1,500 | $1,300 | $1,100 | $995 | $875 | $750 |

OFFICERS NINE — 9mm cal., 16.1 in. barrel, action patterned after the IMI Uzi, 32 shot mag., black military finish, 8.4 lbs. Limited 1988-1989.

| | $550 | $475 | $415 | $375 | $335 | $300 | $275 |

Last Mfg.'s Sug. Retail was $450.

SPORTING RIFLES

MODEL EM-321 — .22 LR cal., slide action, 19.5 in. barrel, 10 shot tube mag., hardwood stock and forearm, fixed sights, 6 lbs. Importation began 1989-90, resumed 1994.

| **No Mfg.'s Retail** | $135 | $115 | $95 | $85 | $75 | $65 | $55 |

TYPE EM-332 — .22 LR cal., bolt action, 18½ in. barrel with adj. rear sight, mag. holder on stock holds two extra 5 shot mags., Monte Carlo stock with cheekpiece and recoil pad, 4½ lbs. Imported 1991-1993.

| | $225 | $195 | $165 | $140 | $120 | $95 | $80 |

NHM-90/91 SPORT — 7.62x39mm cal., choice of 16.34 (NHM-90) or 23.27 (NHM-91) in. barrel, hardwood thumbhole stock, NHM-91 has bipod, 5 shot mag., 9-11 lbs. Imported 1994-95.

| | $350 | $300 | $265 | $225 | $200 | $185 | $150 |

The .223 Rem. cal. is also available for the Model NHM-90. Each Model NHM-90/91 is supplied with three 5 shot mags., sling, and cleaning kit.

SHOTGUNS

TYPE HL12-203 O/U — 12 ga. only, 2¾ in. chambers, boxlock action, ejectors, 30 in. vent. barrels and rib, single trigger, multi-chokes, checkered stock and forearm, 7½ lbs. Imported 1989-1993.

| | $400 | $350 | $300 | $265 | $225 | $200 | $185 |

TYPE HL12-102 PUMP — 12 ga. only, 2¾ in. chamber, 28.4 in. barrel, 3 shot mag., crossbolt safety on rear triggerguard, fixed chokes, 9.3 lbs. Imported 1989-1993.

| | $230 | $200 | $175 | $165 | $150 | $135 | $120 |

NORTH AMERICAN ARMS, INC.

Manufactured by North American Arms, Inc. located in Provo, UT. This company is owned by Teleflex Defense Systems, also located in Spanish Fork, UT. Distributor and dealer sales.

MINI REVOLVERS

All mini revolvers are manufactured to highest quality control standards and have half-way notches cut on the front cylinder face allowing the hammer to lock up the cylinder between cartridges. This allows the gun to be carried fully loaded without the danger of accidental discharge.

Grading	100%	98%	95%	90%	80%	70%	60%

NAA .22 LR — .22 Short (new 1994) or .22 LR cal., 5 shot, single action, spur trigger, 1⅛, 1⅝, or 2½ (disc.) in. barrel, stainless steel, plastic (disc.) or laminated rosewood grips, approx. 4½ oz. Mfg. 1975-present.

Mfg.'s Sug. Retail	$157	$130	$105	$85

Add $15 for 2½ in. barrel (disc.).
Add $31 for holster grip accessory.
The optional holster grip allows the pistol to fold forward allowing concealability, safety, and a clip which allows it to be attached to a belt.

▲ **Viper Belt Buckle Option** — belt buckle with built in 1⅛ or 1⅝ in. barrel revolver (.22 LR cal.), disc. 1990, reintroduced 1993.

Mfg.'s Sug. Retail	$194	$170	$145	$125

NAA .22 MAGNUM — similar to .22 LR, except in .22 Mag. cal.

Mfg.'s Sug. Retail	$178	$150	$120	$100

Add $18 for 2½ in. barrel (disc.).

NAA .22 MAGNUM CONVERTIBLE — similar to NAA .22 Mag., except has extra LR cylinder in pouch.

Mfg.'s Sug. Retail	$210	$180	$155	$115

Add $18 for 2½ in. barrel (disc.).

MINI-MASTER TARGET REVOLVER — .22 LR or .22 Mag. cal., 5 shot, 4 in. heavy vent. barrel, unfluted bull cylinder, spur trigger, fixed or adj. white outline rear sight, oversize black rubber Mini-master grip, 10.7 oz. New 1990.

Mfg.'s Sug. Retail	$264	$230	$190	$170

Add $38 for extra combo cylinder.
Add $15 for adj. rear sight (elevation only).
This model was also available in hot fuschia colored oversized grips.

MINI-MASTER BLACK WIDOW — .22 LR or .22 Mag. cal., 2 in. heavy VR barrel, full size black rubber grip, fixed or adj. rear sight, unfluted cylinder, 8.8 oz. New 1991.

Mfg.'s Sug. Retail	$235	$200	$165	$130

Add $35 for extra combo cylinder.
Add $14 for adj. rear sight (elevation only).
This model was also available in hot fuschia colored oversized grips.

NAA STANDARD SET — 3 gun set (.22 Short, .22 LR, and .22 Mag. cals.) in walnut display case with matching serial numbers, high polish finish with matte contours.

Mfg.'s Sug. Retail	$675	$500	$435	$360

NAA DELUXE SET — 3 gun set (.22 Short, .22 LR, and .22 Mag. cals.) in walnut display case with matching serial numbers, high polish finish on entire gun.

Mfg.'s Sug. Retail	$727	$625	$525	$400

CASED .22 MAG. — includes .22 Mag. cal. model in walnut display case with high polish finish with matte contours.

Mfg.'s Sug. Retail	$323	$275	$215	$175

REVOLVERS

NAA SINGLE ACTION REVOLVER — .45 Win. Mag. or .450 Mag. Express cal., polished stainless steel, transfer bar safety inside the hammer, 5 shot, 7½ in. barrel, walnut grips, includes presentation case.

Matte finish	$1,200	$950	$700
High polish finish	$1,400	$1,100	$850
Both cylinders	$1,650	$1,275	$975

Last Mfg.'s Sug. Retail was $650.

Also available by special order with 10½ in. barrel and optional scope. Extra cylinders are also available at $75-$100 extra and must be fitted to the gun. A set including 2 cylinders can also be ordered.

NORTH AMERICAN SAFARI EXPRESS

Trademark for those rifles (SxS) assembled by A. Francotte of Belgium for exclusive importation by Armes De Chasse located in Chadds Ford, PA.

N

N

O section

O.D.I. (OMEGA DEFENSIVE INDUSTRIES)

Previously manufactured in Midland Park, NJ from approximately 1981-1982. Essex Arms located in Island Pond, VT has acquired the remaining O.D.I. Viking inventory of parts for the Viking pistol (see Trademark Index). Previously, Randco Manufacturing located in Monrovia, CA was providing service (and had parts) for these older O.D.I. Pistols.

Grading	100%	98%	95%	90%	80%	70%	60%

VIKING & VIKING COMBAT — .45 ACP or 9mm cal., Viking Model is Government size and the Combat Model is Commander size. All stainless steel construction, the design utilizes the Seecamp double action, teakwood grips. 9mm advertised but never saw production. 5 in. barrel on the Viking Model and 4 1/4 in. barrel on the Viking Combat Model, 7 shot mag., 39 oz. Approx. 200-300 Viking Combat Models were made from kits.

$475 $375 $295

Last Mfg.'s Retail was $579.

OBREGON

Manufactured previously by Fabrica de Armas Mexico located in Mexico City, Mexico.

OBREGON — 11.35mm cal., patterned somewhat after the Colt Model 1911A1, features tubular slide and Savage/Steyr type action, limited mfg. in Mexico for commercial sale during and after WWII, slide marked "Sistema Obregon Cal 11.35mm".

Extreme rarity factor precludes accurate price evaluation on this model.

OLD-WEST GUN CO.

Importer and distributor that took over the inventory of Allen Firearms after they went out of business in early 1987. Old-West Gun Co. in late 1987 changed their name to Cimarron Arms. Refer to Cimarron Arms in this text for approximate prices on similar models from Old-West Gun Co.

OLYMPIC ARMS, INC.

Manufacturer located in Olympia, WA. Dealer direct sales.

In late 1987, Olympic Arms, Inc. acquired Safari Arms of Phoenix, AZ.

PISTOLS: SEMI-AUTO

There is no post-ban OA-93 pistol.

OA-93 PISTOL — .223 Rem. (most common) or 7.62x39mm (very limited mfg.) cal., semi-auto, gas operated without buffer tube stock, or charging handle, 6 (most common), 9, or 14 in. free-floated match barrel, upper receiver utilizes integral scope mount base, 30 shot mag., 4 lbs. 3 oz., approx. 500 mfg. before Crime Bill discontinued mfg. Mfg. 1993-94 only.

$2,450 $2,200 $1,925 $1,700 $1,500 $1,300 $1,100

Last Mfg.'s Sug. Retail was $2,700.

Add $800 for 7.62x39mm cal.

RIFLES: BOLT ACTION

In 1993, Olympic Arms purchased the rights, jigs, fixtures, and machining templates for the Bauska Big Bore Magnum Mauser action. Please contact Olympic Arms (see Trademark Index) for more information regarding Bauska actions both with or without fluted barrels.

ULTRA MAG BBK-01 — various cals. between .300 Win. Mag.-.505 Gibbs, custom order rifle available with many barrel options and other special order features, price on request from the factory.

This model was formerly the Bauska BBK-02.

O

Grading	100%	98%	95%	90%	80%	70%	60%

BOLT ACTION SAKO — various cals. between .17 Rem.-.416 Rem. Mag., 26 in. fluted barrel, various stock configurations, values below represent base price with no options.

Mfg.'s Sug. Retail	$715	$650	$575	$500	$450	$400	$360	$330

ULTRA CSR TACTICAL RIFLE — .308 Win. cal., Sako action, 26 in. broach cut heavy barrel, Bell & Carlson black or synthetic stock with aluminum bedding, Harris bipod, carrying case. New 1996.

Mfg.'s Sug. Retail	$1,235	$1,075	$875	$725	$625	$550	$500	$450

RIFLES: SEMI-AUTO

On the models listed below, the PCR variations refer to those guns manufactured after the Crime Bill was implemented in September, 1994. PCR rifles have smooth barrels (no flash suppressor), a 10 shot mag., and fixed stocks. Older, discontinued named models refer to the original, pre-ban model nomenclature. Limited quantities remain on pre-ban rifles.

COMPETITOR RIFLE — .22 LR, Ruger 10/22 action with 20 in. barrel featuring button cut rifling, Bell & Carlson thumbhole fiberglass stock, black finish and matte stainless fluted barrel, includes bipod, 6.9 lbs. New 1996.

Mfg.'s Sug. Retail	$635	$575	$500	$450	$400	$360	$330	$300

ULTRAMATCH/PCR-1 — .223 cal., AR-15 action with modifications, 20 or 24 in. match stainless steel barrel, handle removed, Williams set trigger, scope mounts, 10 lbs. 3 oz. New 1985.

➤ PCR-1

Mfg.'s Sug. Retail	$1,100	$995	$825	$725	$600	$550	$500	$460

➤ ULTRAMATCH

Mfg.'s Sug. Retail	$1,515	$1,400	$1,200	$1,000	$875	$775	$675	$550

INTERCONTINENTAL — .223 cal., features synthetic wood-grained thumbhole butt stock and aluminum handguard, 20 in. ultra match barrel (free floating). Mfg. 1992-93.

$1,650	$1,350	$1,050	$875	$750	$600	$550

Last Mfg.'s Sug. Retail was $1,371.

INTERNATIONAL MATCH — .223 cal., similar to Ultramatch, except has custom aperture sights. Mfg. 1991-93.

$1,475	$1,150	$950	$800	$675	$575	$525

Last Mfg.'s Sug. Retail was $1,240.

SERVICE MATCH/PCR SERVICE MATCH — .223 cal., AR-15 action with modifications, 20 in. SS Ultramatch barrel, carrying handle, standard trigger, choice of A1 or A2 flash suppressor (Service Match only), 8¾ lbs.

➤ PCR SERVICE MATCH

Mfg.'s Sug. Retail	$1,135	$1,025	$825	$695	$595	$530	$495	$450

➤ SERVICE MATCH

Mfg.'s Sug. Retail	$1,200	$1,075	$875	$725	$625	$550	$500	$450

MULTIMATCH ML-1/PCR-2 — .223 cal., tactical short range rifle, 16 in. Ultramatch barrel, aluminum collapsible (Multimatch ML-1) or fixed (PCR-2) stock, carrying handle, stealth vortex flash suppressor (Multimatch ML-1 only), 5 lbs. 14 oz. New 1991.

➤ PCR-2

Mfg.'s Sug. Retail	$1,025	$950	$860	$775	$650	$575	$495	$450

➤ MULTIMATCH ML-1

Mfg.'s Sug. Retail	$1,200	$1,075	$875	$725	$625	$550	$500	$450

MULTIMATCH ML-2/PCR-3 — .223 cal., features International Match upper receiver with SS 16 in. Ultramatch barrel, carrying handle, 5 lbs. 14 oz. New 1991.

➤ PCR-3

Mfg.'s Sug. Retail	$1,025	$950	$860	$775	$650	$575	$495	$450

➤ MULTIMATCH ML-2

Mfg.'s Sug. Retail	$1,200	$1,075	$875	$725	$625	$550	$500	$450

O

Grading	100%	98%	95%	90%	80%	70%	60%

AR-15 MATCH/PCR-4 — .223 cal., patterned after the AR-15 with 20 in. barrel and solid synthetic stock, 8 lbs. 5 oz. New 1975.

   ➤ **PCR-4**

Mfg.'s Sug. Retail	$810	$715	$650	$575	$500	$475	$425	$395

   ➤ **AR-15 MATCH**

Mfg.'s Sug. Retail	$1,075	$995	$875	$775	$650	$575	$495	$450

CAR-15/PCR-5 — modified AR-15 with choice of 11½ (disc. 1993) or 16 in. barrel, stow-away pistol grip and collapsible stock (CAR-15 only), 7 lbs. New 1975.

   ➤ **PCR-5** — .223, 9mm Para. (new 1996), .40 S&W (new 1996), or .45 ACP (new 1996) cal.

Mfg.'s Sug. Retail	$775	$685	$625	$550	$475	$450	$400	$375

   Add $45 for 9mm Para., .40 S&W, or .45 ACP cal.

   ➤ **CAR-15** — .223, 9mm Para., .40 S&W, .45 ACP, or 7.62x39mm cal.

Mfg.'s Sug. Retail	$1,030	$960	$860	$775	$650	$575	$495	$450

   Add $170 for pistol cals.

PCR-8 — 7.62x39mm cal., 16 in. barrel, post-ban only, A-2 stowaway stock, carrying handle, 7 lbs. New 1995.

Mfg.'s Sug. Retail	$835	$725	$650	$565	$475	$450	$400	$375

OA-93 CARBINE — .223 cal., 16 in. barrel, design based on OA-93 pistol, aluminum folding stock, flat-top receiver, Vortex flash suppressor, 7½ lbs. New 1995.

Mfg.'s Sug. Retail	$1,550	$1,400	$1,200	$1,000	$875	$775	$675	$550

COUNTER SNIPER RIFLE — .308 cal., bolt action utilizing M-14 mags., 26 in. heavy barrel, camo-fiberglass stock, 10½ lbs. Disc. 1987.

	$1,100	$900	$775	$695	$550	$440	$410

Last Mfg.'s Sug. Retail was $1,225.

SURVIVOR I CONVERSION UNIT — .223 or .45 ACP cal., converts M1911 variations into carbine, bolt action, collapsible stock, 16¼ in. barrel, 5 lbs.

	$275	$225	$195

This kit is also available for S&W and Browning Hi-Power models.

OMEGA

Maker: Armero Specialistas Reunidas, Eibar, Spain, 1920s.

SEMI AUTOMATIC PISTOL — "Eibar" type, marked Omega on slide, 6 shot mag.

6.35 cal.	$125	$115	$100	$80	$70	$55	$40
7.65 cal.	$130	$120	$105	$90	$80	$70	$55

OMEGA FIREARMS

Previously manufactured in Flower Mound, TX.

SINGLE SHOT BOLT ACTION RIFLE — various cals., premium walnut. Disc. late 1960s.

	$775	$650	$575	$495	$425	$360	$295

OMEGA PISTOL

Previously manufactured and distributed by Springfield Armory located in Geneseo, IL. Omega conversion kits only are currently mfg. by Safari Arms located in Olympia, WA under license from Peters-Stahl in Germany. See the Safari Arms section in this text for more information.

O

Grading	100%	98%	95%	90%	80%	70%	60%

PISTOLS: SEMI-AUTO

OMEGA — .38 Super, 10mm Norma, or .45 ACP cal., single action, ported slide, 5 or 6 in. interchangeable ported or unported barrel with Polygon rifling, special lock-up system eliminates normal barrel link and bushing, Pachmayr grips, dual extractors, adj. rear sight. Mfg. 1987-90.

	100%	98%	95%	90%	80%	70%	60%
	$625	$560	$495	$425	$360	$295	$265

Last Mfg.'s Sug. Retail was $849.

Add $663 for interchangeable conversion units.
Add $336 for interchangeable 5 or 6 in. barrel (including factory installation).

Each conversion unit includes an entire slide assembly, one mag., 5 or 6 in barrel, recoil spring guide mechanism assembly, and factory fitting.

OMEGA RIFLES/SHOTGUNS

Omega was the trademark of select rifles/shotguns previously imported by K.B.I., Inc. located in Harrisburg, PA, until 1994.

RIFLES

To date, there has been little collector interest for Omega rifles. Values are mostly determined by the shooting value rather than collector value.

SHOTGUNS

STANDARD O/U — 12, 20 (disc.), 28 (disc.), or .410 (disc) ga., boxlock action, folding design, SNT, 26 or 28 in. VR barrels, extractors, checkered walnut stock and forearm, 5½-7 lbs. Disc. 1994.

	$425	$330	$295	$260	$230	$200	$180

▲ *Deluxe O/U* — 12 ga. only, similar to Standard Model except has better walnut. Importation disc. 1990.

	$335	$290	$255	$220	$185	$160	$140

Last Mfg.'s Sug. Retail was $379.

STANDARD SxS — 20, 28, or .410 ga., boxlock action, folding design, double triggers, hardwood stock and forearm, 26 in. barrels, extractors, 5½ lbs. Disc. 1989.

	$190	$165	$140	$120	$110	$100	$90

Last Mfg.'s Sug. Retail was $229.

Add $40 for 28 or .410 ga.

▲ *Deluxe SxS* — .410 ga. only, similar to Standard Model except has better walnut. Disc. 1989.

	$200	$185	$170	$155	$140	$130	$120

Last Mfg.'s Sug. Retail was $249.

SINGLE BARREL — 12, 20, or .410 ga., various barrel lengths, matte blue finish, extractor. Importation disc. 1987.

	$85	$75	$65	$55	$45	$40	$35

Last Mfg.'s Sug. Retail was $95.

STANDARD FOLDING SINGLE BARREL — 12, 16, 20, 28, or .410 ga., 28 or 30 in. barrel, checkered hardwood stock, matte chrome receiver, approx. 5½ lbs. Importation disc. 1987.

	$160	$135	$115	$100	$85	$70	$65

Last Mfg.'s Sug. Retail was $180.

DELUXE FOLDING SINGLE BARREL — 12, 16, 20, 28, or .410 ga., similar to Standard Model, except has checkered walnut stock and forearm, blued receiver. Importation disc. 1987.

	$195	$160	$135	$115	$100	$85	$70

Last Mfg.'s Sug. Retail was $220.

O

OMNI

Manufacturer located in Riverside, CA since 1995.

Grading	100%	98%	95%	90%	80%	70%	60%

BOLT ACTION RIFLE — .50 BMG cal., competition single shot, 34 or 36 in. barrel with muzzle brake, synthetic thumbhole stock, includes Leupold Mark 4 scope, designed for FCSA competition shooting. New 1996.

| Mfg.'s Sug. Retail | $3,800 | | $3,600 | $3,200 | $2,800 | $2,500 | $2,150 | $1,800 | $1,500 |

    Add $400 for painted stock.

OPUS SPORTING ARMS, INC.

Previous manufacturer located in Long Beach, CA.

OPUS ONE — .243, .270, or .30-06 cal., U.S.R.A. Co. Model 70 action, 24 in. barrel, deluxe checkered walnut stock with ebony forend cap, guaranteed 100 yard accuracy, 6¾ lbs., Halliburton cased. Mfg. 1987-1988 only.

    $2,350 $1,995 $1,675 $1,250 $1,000 $875 $795
        Last Mfg.'s Sug. Retail was $2,700.

OPUS TWO — similar to Opus One, except in 7mm Rem. Mag. or .300 Win. Mag. cal., 7¼ lbs., cased. Mfg. 1987-1988 only.

    $2,350 $2,050 $1,705 $1,300 $1,000 $875 $795
        Last Mfg.'s Sug. Retail was $2,700.

OPUS THREE — similar to Opus Two, except in .375 H&H or .458 Win. Mag. cal., 10¼ lbs., cased. Mfg. 1987-1988 only.

    $2,600 $2,275 $1,800 $1,375 $1,050 $900 $825
        Last Mfg.'s Sug. Retail was $2,850.

OREGON ARMS

Please refer to the Chipmunk Manufacturing Inc. section.

ORTGIES PISTOLS

Previously manufactured by Deutsche Werke A.G. located in Erfurt, Germany.

VEST POCKET AUTOMATIC — .25 ACP cal., 6 shot, 2¾ in. barrel, blue or nickel finish, fixed sights, wood grips, post-WWI.

    $275 $200 $165 $145 $125 $110 $100

POCKET AUTOMATIC — .32 ACP cal. (8 shot) or .380 ACP cal. (7 shot), 3¼ in. barrel, blue or nickel finish, fixed sights, wood grips.

    $300 $225 $175 $150 $130 $115 $105

    Add 20% for .380 ACP cal. or double safety variation.

ORVIS

Retailer/importer of private label subcontracted rifles/shotguns located in Dallas, Houston, TX and many other locations.

Orvis imports various rifles and shotguns under subcontract with various international manufacturers. Typical custom order delivery time is 6-8 months. Most of these private label models will approximate the values of the equivalent model manufactured by the subcontractor unless there are additional features and/or options which will add to the value.

SHOTGUNS: OVER/UNDER

SKB GREEN MOUNTAIN UPLANDER (MODEL 555) — 12, 20, 28, or .410 ga., 25-27 in. barrels, blued frame, straight stock with leather covered recoil pad. Disc.

    $750 $675 $600 $550 $500 $450 $400
        Last Mfg.'s Sug. Retail was $995.

    Add 15% for 28 or .410 ga.

O

Grading	100%	98%	95%	90%	80%	70%	60%

UPLANDER SERIES — 12, 20, or 28 ga., boxlock action, 26 in. barrels with choke tubes (except 28 ga.), SST, straight grip, select American black walnut with 24 LPI checkering, leather covered recoil pad since 1992, 6-7 lbs. Mfg. by P. Beretta of Italy.

Mfg.'s Sug. Retail	$2,950	$2,950	$2,300	$1,900	$1,500	$1,175	$995	$875

    Add $950 for combo 28/20 ga.

WATERFOWLER — 12 ga. only, 3 in. chambers, matte metal finish, 28 in. barrels with choke tubes, steel shot compatible, 7½ lbs. Mfg. by P. Beretta of Italy.

Mfg.'s Sug. Retail	$2,950	$2,950	$2,300	$1,900	$1,500	$1,175	$995	$875

SPORTING CLAYS — 12 ga. only, 30 in. vented barrels with VR and choke tubes, adj. trigger, oil finished checkered walnut stock and forearm. New 1994.

Mfg.'s Sug. Retail	$3,300	$3,300	$2,550	$2,000	$1,550	$1,175	$995	$875

    This model is also available in a women's configuration in 20 ga. with lightweight frame - includes carrying case.

SUPER FIELD — 12 or 20 ga., 26 (Uplander 20 ga. only), 28 (All Rounder), or 30 (Sporting Clays) in. VR barrels, configurations include Uplander 20 ga. with straight grip stock, All Rounder 12 ga. with 28 in. barrels and pistol grip stock, and Sporting Clays 12 ga. with 30 in. barrels, wide rib, and pistol grip stock, blued receiver, choke tubes, mfg. in Italy. Limited importation 1995 only.

		$1,495	$1,250	$1,000	$875	$750	$625	$500

Last Mfg.'s Sug. Retail was $2,150.

PREMIER GRADE — 12 or 20 ga., 3 in. chambers, 20 ga. features 28 in. barrels with straight grip stock, 12 ga. features pistol grip stock, select oil-finished European stock and forearm, choke tubes, blued frame with scrolled engraving, adj. trigger cased, mfg. in Belgium. New 1995.

Mfg.'s Sug. Retail	$6,450	$6,450	$5,875	$5,250	$4,675	$4,000	$3,450	$2,675

    Add $100 for Premier Grade Sporting.

    This model is also available as a 20 ga. Superlight with straight grip stock and 26 in. barrels.

ORVIS DELUXE GRADE — similar to Uplander and Waterfowler, except has engraved bird scenes and scroll work on antique coin-finished receiver, deluxe checkered walnut stock and forearm, case. Imported 1993-94 only.

		$4,250	$3,575	$2,950	$2,300	$1,900	$1,500	$1,275

Last Mfg.'s Sug. Retail was $4,950.

RUGER/ORVIS MODEL — 12 or 20 ga., 3 in. chambers, Red Label Ruger action with customized Orvis features including blued receiver and straight grip English checkered stock. Importation disc. 1993.

		$1,295	$975	$850	$725	$600	$495	$450

Last Mfg.'s Sug. Retail was $1,295.

SHOTGUNS: SxS

WATERFOWLER — 12 ga. only, 3 in. chambers, matte metal finish, 28 in. barrels with choke tubes, 7¾ lbs. Mfg. by P. Beretta of Italy until 1993.

		$1,950	$1,725	$1,475	$1,125	$950	$825	$700

Last Mfg.'s Sug. Retail was $1,950.

CUSTOM UPLANDER — 12, 16, 20, 28, or .410 ga., custom ordered gun, 25 or 27 in. barrels only, sidelock action, DT, mfg. by Arrieta located in Spain.

Mfg.'s Sug. Retail	$3,450	$3,450	$2,750	$2,275	$1,800	$1,400	$995	$725

    Add $950 for SNT.
    Add $1,200 for extra set of barrels (same ga.).

FINE GRADE — 12, 16, 20, 28, or .410 ga., custom ordered gun, custom order barrel lengths, sidelock action, DT, mfg. by Arrieta located in Spain.

Mfg.'s Sug. Retail	$4,850	$4,850	$3,950	$3,250	$2,550	$1,995	$1,500	$1,150

    Add $950 for SNT.
    Add $1,950 for extra set of barrels (same ga.).

O

Grading	100%	98%	95%	90%	80%	70%	60%

ROUNDED ACTION — similar to Fine Grade, except sidelock action has rounded corners and finer engraving and wood upgrade, leather cased, mfg. by Arrieta located in Spain.

Mfg.'s Sug. Retail	$6,550	$6,550	$5,000	$4,050	$3,300	$2,550	$1,995	$1,500

0

P section

P.A.F.

Pretoria Arms Company. Previous manufacturer located in S. Africa.

Grading	100%	98%	95%	90%	80%	70%	60%

.25 ACP PISTOL — .25 ACP cal., patterned after the Baby Browning, blued finish. Approx. 10,000 mfg.

	100%	98%	95%	90%	80%	70%	60%
	$375	$300	$275	$250	$225	$200	$180

P.A.W.S., INC.

Manufacturer located in the U.S. Dealer direct sales. Previously distributed by Sile Distributors, Inc. located in New York, NY.

ZX6/ZX8 CARBINE — 9mm Para. or .45 ACP cal., semi-auto paramilitary design carbine, 16 in. barrel, 10 or 32* shot mag., folding metal stock, matte black finish, aperture rear sight, partial barrel shroud, 7½ lbs. New 1989.

Mfg.'s Sug. Retail	$700	$615	$535	$450	$400	$360	$330	$295

The ZX6 is chambered for 9mm Para., while the ZX8 is chambered for .45 ACP.

P.S.M.G. GUN COMPANY

Previous manufacturer located in Arlington, MA.

SIX IN ONE SUPREME — .22 LR, .30 Luger, .38 Super, .38 Spl., 9mm, or .45 ACP cal., single action semi-auto, 3¼, 5, or 7½ in. barrel with solid cooling rib, adj. rear sight, limited mfg. Mfg. 1988-89.

	$700	$600	$500	$450	$400	$365	$330

Last Mfg.'s Sug. Retail was $895.

Add $20-$55 for caliber options.
Add $25 for 7½ in. barrel.
Add $35 for satin nickel plating.
Add $225 per extra barrel.
Add $450 per individual conversion unit.

P.V. NELSON, (GUNMAKERS)

Please refer to the N section for this manufacturer.

PTK INTERNATIONAL, INC.

Distributor located in Atlanta, GA.

Please refer to listing under Poly-Technologies in this section.

P.38s

Standard German military 9mm handgun beginning 1938. On older WWII German mfg., please refer to the German WWII Military Pistols section of this text.

P.38: JOHN MARTZ CONVERSIONS

▲ *Baby P.38* — 9mm Para. cal., shortened barrel (3 in.) grip, and two 7 shot mags., 47 mfg.

	$2,500	$2,000	$1,500

▲ *P.38* — .38 Super or .45 ACP cal., various barrel lengths.

	$5,500	$3,250	$2,500

▲ *P.38 Carbine* — 9mm Para. cal., 16 in. barrel, adj. rear sight, 27 mfg.

	$5,500	$3,850	$2,650

PARAMOUNT

Previous manufacture by Imperial Gun Co., Ltd. located in Surrey, England. Actions were previously imported by O.K. Weber, Inc. located in Eugene, OR and Olympic Arms, Inc. located in Olympia, WA.

Grading	100%	98%	95%	90%	80%	70%	60%

THE IMPERIAL — .308 cal., single shot target rifle featuring thumbhole stock and CPE aperture rear sight, fully adj. trigger, vent. forearm. Disc. 1994.

| | $3,250 | $2,700 | $2,250 | $1,850 | $1,400 | $1,000 | $795 |

Last Mfg.'s Sug. Retail was $3,400.

RANGEMASTER — various cals., single shot design, steel frame, contoured walnut grips, satin chrome finish, 8½ lbs. Limited importation 1992-94.

| | $1,600 | $1,400 | $1,200 | $995 | $895 | $795 | $695 |

Last Mfg.'s Sug. Retail was $1,800.

PARA-ORDNANCE MFG. INC.

Manufacturer located in Scarborough, Ontario, Canada. Various U.S. distributors. Distributor sales only.

Para-Ordnance also manufactures the Model 85 full or semi-auto paint-shell carbine (styled after the Ingram). This model retails for $300.

PISTOLS: SEMI-AUTO

P14 — .45 ACP cal., patterned after the Colt Model 1911A1 except has choice of alloy, steel, or stainless steel frame that has been widened slightly for extra shot capacity (13* shot), 10 shot (C/B 1994) mag., single action, 3-dot sight system, rounded combat hammer, 5 in. ramped barrel, 38 oz. with steel frame or 28 oz. with alloy frame. Introduced 1990.

| Mfg.'s Sug. Retail | $705 | | $600 | $485 | $425 | $385 | $350 | $325 | $295 |

Add $45 for steel frame.

P13 — similar to P14, except has 10 (C/B 1994) or 12* shot mag., 4¼ in. barrel, and satin nickel finished slide, 35 oz. with steel frame or 25 oz. with alloy frame. New 1993.

| Mfg.'s Sug. Retail | $705 | | $600 | $485 | $425 | $385 | $350 | $325 | $295 |

Add $45 for steel frame.

P12 — compact variation of the P14 featuring 10 (C/B 1994) or 11* shot mag. and 3½ in. barrel, 33 oz. with steel frame or 24 oz. with alloy frame. New 1990.

| Mfg.'s Sug. Retail | $705 | | $600 | $485 | $425 | $385 | $350 | $325 | $295 |

Add $45 for steel frame.

P16 — .40 S&W cal., otherwise similar to P14, steel frame only. New 1995.

| Mfg.'s Sug. Retail | $750 | | $640 | $515 | $435 | $385 | $350 | $325 | $295 |

PARDINI

Manufacturer located in Lu, Italy. Currently imported by Nygord Precision Products located in Phoenix, AZ and Mo's Competitor Supplies & Range, Inc. located in Brookfield, CT. Previously imported and distributed by Fiocchi of America, Inc., located in Ozark, MO until 1990.

PISTOLS

Pardini pistols have always been known for their technological improvements developed from ongoing design research. During 1991, the entire Pardini pistol line was modified both internally and externally to improve function and reliability - these changes included the addition of grooves on the barrel shroud to accept scope mounts directly. Pardini air pistols may be found in the Airgun section of this text.

Grading	100%	98%	95%	90%	80%	70%	60%

MODEL SP (STANDARD PISTOL) — .22 LR only, target grips, adj. sights, 4.92 in. barrel, interchangeable grips, detachable mag. New 1991.

Mfg.'s Sug. Retail $995		$875	$715	$575	$475	$425	$395	$375

LADIES PISTOL — similar to Standard Pistol, except grips are suitable for smaller hands. Imported 1986-90 only.

	$850	$700	$600	$520	$460	$410	$380

Last Mfg.'s Sug. Retail was $955.

This variation is imported in limited quantities only.

MODEL GP (RAPID FIRE PISTOL) — .22 Short, features enclosed style grip assembly, adj. sights, 5.12 in. barrel. New 1991.

Mfg.'s Sug. Retail $1,050		$925	$750	$600	$500	$450	$420	$395

Add $400 for "Schumann" Model (special muzzle ports, sights, etc.)

MODEL HP (CENTERFIRE PISTOL) — .32 S&W Long cal., otherwise similar to Standard Pistol, 4.92 in. barrel. New 1991.

Mfg.'s Sug. Retail $1,095		$995	$840	$715	$575	$500	$440	$415

MODEL K50 (FREE PISTOL) — .22 LR, single shot, sliding rotating bolt, 9.06 in. barrel, tilted anatomical grip, top-of-the-line match pistol. New 1991.

Mfg.'s Sug. Retail $1,050		$925	$750	$600	$500	$450	$420	$395

PARKER BROTHERS

Originally manufactured in Meriden, CT from 1866-1934. Remington took over production in 1934, and in 1938, the plant was moved to Ilion, NY. Over 4,500 "Transition Guns" (exhibiting Meriden and Ilion characteristics) were produced in Meriden between 1934-1937 and about 4,500 Parkers were manufactured at the Ilion location before production stopped. Total production reached approx. 242,387.

95% of the original Parkers bought and sold each year are in 30% or less condition (referring to original case colors). Percentages on following pages refer to the amount of original case colors remaining on frame.

SHOTGUNS: DAMASCUS BARRELS

Parker damascus barreled shotguns (hammer or hammerless) are very collectible if original condition is over 40%. Specimens in 90% or better condition with strong case colors can approximate values of the steel barrel models if the bores are in excellent condition also (no pitting). Values for under 40% specimens fall off rapidly and are no longer comparable to steel barrel guns. As an example, a steel "D" Grade (without ejectors) might range from $1,500 to $7,000 (10%-100%) with a rather even downward progression of values in between the high and low values. A 100% damascus "D" Grade could have a $3,500+ price tag hanging from the triggerguard while 5%-15% condition specimen is typically seen priced in the $375-$550 range. Remember, the guns are not rare but their condition is.

SHOTGUNS: FLUID STEEL BARRELS

Values listed below in the 95%-100% condition columns can vary immensely as there is almost no supply for these high demand items, always a prerequisite for unpredictable prices.

Note: Values are for non-ejector guns through the CH grade, ejectors assumed on BHE and better models. Add 15% - 30% for vent. ribs. Skeet model has beavertail forearm and single selective trigger valued at approx. 50%-75% higher than values shown. Higher grade guns typically had ejectors, and will not make as much difference percentage-wise in the overall value as those lower grades with ejectors. Ejectors typically will add 50% more value to a Parker in common grades. Also, lower condition high grade models sometimes have their values established by the potential gain in refurbishing these specimens.

P

Due to the extremely high value of Parker Guns, extreme care should be taken in their purchase. There are many upgraded and refinished guns represented as original; expert advice should always be sought. Many collectors would rather own a specimen with 30% original case colors than a refinished gun that is 100% (regardless who did the work). Many advanced collectors will discount a refinished Parker's value 40%-60% of the price for an original gun. Misrepresentation of refinished or upgraded Parkers is rampant today - especially case colors. Believe it or not, also beware of fake boxes and hanging tags - if the box and Parker shotgun are an original "pair", the value is enhanced tremendously. If the box/hanging tag is fake, you could pay as much as $1,500 to learn this lesson! In other words, do your homework, be careful, shop carefully, and above all, get a receipt for exactly what you are purchasing.

Frame size on Parker shotguns is determined by the number on the bottom of the barrel lug on breech. Frame sizes (from largest to smallest) include 7, 6, 5, 4, 3, 2, 1½, 1, ½, 0, 00, and 000. 8 ga. guns typically are framed 5, 6, or 7. 10 ga. guns typically are 3 or 4. 12 ga. guns typically range from 2 through 1 (more desirable). "½" frame 12 ga. guns are very rare and desirable. 20 and 16 ga.'s range from 2 through 0 (more desirable). 28 ga. guns are either 0 or 00 (more desirable and twice as expensive). .410 ga. shotguns are 0, 00, or 000 (most common and most desirable). 8 and 10 ga. steel barreled shotguns are very rare, and prices can equate .410 ga. values if the original condition is there.

The grade on Parker shotguns is a number or initials located on the water table of the frame. An alphabetical designation would indicate the grade immediately. For numerals, a "2" would indicate a GH, while an "8" would specify an A-1 Special - interpolate for the others (numbers 3 through 7). Parker shotguns manufactured by Remington will have date codes stamped on left barrel flat that corresponds to the month and the year (see Remington serialization in the Serialization Section). Also, if a Parker gun was returned to Remington for repair, alteration, or refinishing, it will usually have the date code stamped with a suffix of 3 (i.e. OK3 represents some type of rework completed in either July of 1941 or 1963). There is some ambiguity with the year as the year codes repeat.

A note about Parker condition: Percentages of condition indicate the amount of original case colors remaining on the frame, but sometimes these colors are faded and the rest of the gun is excellent - hence, all the separate condition factors must be considered when determining overall condition.

A Parker IS NOT 60% if the barrel bluing and stock/forearm varnish are 60% but case colors are only 10%. Typically, a 60% case color Parker shotgun will have 90%+ blue and varnish, yet this does not mean the gun is 90% overall. Similarly, a 20% case color Parker will probably have 90% barrel bluing remaining.

Strong, original case colors are the key in determining Parker condition and subsequent values.

▲ *PREMIUMS FOR PARKER SHOTGUNS:*
    Add 50% for ejectors (except AAH).
    Add 20% for SST.
    Add 20% for beavertail forearm.
    Add 20%-50% for VR (rare on smaller gauges).
    Add 20% for straight English stock.
    Add 20% for skeleton steel butt plate.
    Add 20% for short barrels (26 in. with open chokes).

	100%	98%	95%	90%	80%	70%	60%	50%	40%	30%	20%	10%

P

TROJAN — Parker's lowest-priced gun, single or double triggers, but no auto ejectors available, very rarely found in mint condition because they were used a lot, a genuine utility gun, introduced 1912-13 with approx. 48,000 total mfg.

▲ *12 ga.*

| $2,200 | $1,800 | $1,500 | $1,175 | $950 | $850 | $750 | $650 | $600 | $575 | $525 | $500 |

▲ *16 ga.*

| $3,000 | $2,500 | $2,000 | $1,750 | $1,500 | $1,200 | $1,050 | $950 | $750 | $700 | $650 | $600 |

▲ *20 ga.*

| $3,500 | $3,000 | $2,500 | $1,800 | $1,700 | $1,600 | $1,500 | $1,775 | $1,300 | $1,100 | $1,000 | $800 |

VH — Parker's biggest selling model, offered with all options, the most commonly found Parker. Approx. 60,000 mfg. 10 ga. is very rare in this model.
      Add 50% for ejectors (VHE Model).

▲ *12 ga.*

| $3,250 | $2,750 | $2,200 | $1,750 | $1,450 | $1,200 | $1,100 | $1,000 | $900 | $800 | $750 | $700 |

▲ *16 ga.*

| $3,250 | $2,750 | $2,200 | $1,750 | $1,450 | $1,200 | $1,100 | $1,000 | $925 | $850 | $775 | $700 |

▲ *20 ga.*

| $3,950 | $3,750 | $3,500 | $3,200 | $3,000 | $2,800 | $2,400 | $2,200 | $2,000 | $1,800 | $1,600 | $1,400 |

▲ *28 ga.*

| $6,500 | $6,250 | $5,750 | $5,150 | $4,600 | $3,900 | $3,220 | $2,875 | $2,645 | $2,500 | $2,300 | $2,200 |

▲ *.410 ga.*

| $18,500 | $16,100 | $14,000 | $12,250 | $10,000 | $8,750 | $7,900 | $6,900 | $6,250 | $5,750 | $5,350 | $4,775 |

PH — offered for a very short time, most had damascus barrels, prices here are for fluid steel barrels only. Approx. 8,500 mfg. A very few .410 ga.'s were mfg. 10 ga. is very rare in this model.
      Add 50% for ejectors (PHE Model).

▲ *12 ga.*

| $3,150 | $2,850 | $2,600 | $2,350 | $2,100 | $1,850 | $1,625 | $1,400 | $1,150 | $995 | $900 | $825 |

▲ *16 ga.*

| $3,150 | $2,850 | $2,600 | $2,350 | $2,100 | $1,850 | $1,625 | $1,400 | $1,150 | $995 | $900 | $825 |

▲ *20 ga.*

| $4,600 | $4,300 | $4,000 | $3,750 | $3,350 | $2,950 | $2,600 | $2,350 | $2,175 | $1,900 | $1,650 | $1,400 |

▲ *28 ga.*

| $8,100 | $7,800 | $7,400 | $7,000 | $6,500 | $6,000 | $5,750 | $5,500 | $5,000 | $4,500 | $3,750 | $3,000 |

GH — very popular model, barrels marked Parker, special steel, engraved moderately with all options available. Approx. 28,500 mfg. 10 ga. is very rare in this model.
      Add 50% for ejectors (GHE Model).

▲ *12 ga.*

| $3,950 | $3,500 | $3,150 | $2,475 | $1,850 | $1,625 | $1,500 | $1,300 | $1,100 | $950 | $900 | $800 |

▲ *16 ga.*

| $4,250 | $3,750 | $3,350 | $2,600 | $2,175 | $1,850 | $1,650 | $1,350 | $1,150 | $1,050 | $950 | $900 |

▲ *20 ga.*

| $4,600 | $4,000 | $3,700 | $3,400 | $3,100 | $2,800 | $2,500 | $2,300 | $2,200 | $1,800 | $1,600 | $1,500 |

▲ *28 ga.*

| $7,000 | $6,375 | $5,750 | $5,125 | $4,550 | $4,200 | $3,800 | $3,300 | $3,000 | $2,700 | $2,500 | $2,400 |

▲ *.410 ga.*

| $20,000 | $17,250 | $15,350 | $12,850 | $10,500 | $8,525 | $8,000 | $7,500 | $7,000 | $6,500 | $6,000 | $5,500 |

DH — the most popular higher grade gun, very tastefully engraved and flawlessly finished. Approx. 48,000 mfg. 10 ga. specimens were mfg. by Remington in the over-238,000 serial range, have $3\frac{1}{2}$ in. chambers, and while relatively rare, premiums are minimal.
      Add 40% for ejectors (DHE Model).

P

	100%	98%	95%	90%	80%	70%	60%	50%	40%	30%	20%	10%

▲ *12 ga.*
$5,500 $4,850 $4,100 $3,450 $2,675 $2,175 $1,850 $1,625 $1,400 $1,200 $1,050 $900

▲ *16 ga.*
$5,800 $4,925 $4,200 $3,500 $2,675 $2,175 $1,850 $1,625 $1,400 $1,250 $1,100 $1,000

▲ *20 ga.*
$6,375 $5,750 $5,500 $5,300 $5,000 $4,800 $4,000 $3,500 $3,000 $2,500 $2,000 $1,500

▲ *28 ga.*
$10,500 $9,250 $8,175 $7,800 $7,500 $7,000 $6,700 $6,500 $6,200 $6,000 $5,500 $5,000

▲ *.410 ga.*
$40,500 $35,250 $28,250 $22,000 $18,950 $16,350 $14,000 $12,750 $10,650 $9,100 $8,000 $7,250

CH — scarce because they were only slightly more decorative than the DH, Acme steel barrels. Approx. 5,000 mfg. 10 ga. is very rare in this model.
Add 33% for ejectors (CHE Model).

▲ *12 ga.*
$6,250 $5,575 $4,775 $4,000 $3,350 $2,600 $2,400 $2,200 $2,000 $1,800 $1,500 $1,300

▲ *16 ga.*
$6,575 $5,700 $4,850 $4,050 $3,350 $3,000 $2,700 $2,600 $2,400 $2,200 $1,800 $1,500

▲ *20 ga.*
$8,450 $7,425 $6,375 $5,550 $4,950 $4,500 $4,300 $4,000 $3,800 $3,500 $3,000 $2,500

▲ *28 ga.*
$21,000 $17,500 $13,850 $10,500 $9,250 $8,175 $7,000 $6,375 $5,750 $5,125 $4,550 $3,895

▲ *.410 ga.* — very rare, approx. 6 are known to exist.
N/A N/A $35,250 $28,250 $23,250 $19,950 $17,250 $14,450 $12,950 $11,000 $9,950 $8,950

BH — quite popular and decorative, 4 styles of engraving available, Acme steel barrels. Approx. 13,000 mfg. 10 ga. is very rare in this model.
Add 25% for ejectors (BHE Model).

▲ *12 ga.*
$9,500 $8,450 $7,425 $6,375 $5,550 $4,950 $4,300 $3,750 $3,100 $2,800 $2,500 $2,000

▲ *16 ga.*
$9,950 $8,650 $7,600 $6,400 $5,550 $4,950 $4,300 $3,750 $3,100 $2,800 $2,500 $2,000

▲ *20 ga.*
$17,500 $14,500 $12,000 $10,250 $9,300 $8,275 $7,100 $6,375 $5,650 $5,200 $4,700 $4,000

▲ *28 ga.*
N/A N/A N/A $17,500 $13,850 $10,500 $9,250 $8,175 $7,000 $6,275 $5,350 $4,550

▲ *.410 ga.* — only 2 guns are known in this gauge, the BHE .410 is also the highest grade .410 ga. known to have been made. Extreme rarity precludes accurate price evaluation, but will be VERY expensive.

AHE — a scarce gun, extremely decorative and flawlessly executed, Acme steel barrels. Approx. 5,500 mfg. 10 ga. is very rare in this model.
Subtract 25% if without ejectors (AH Model).

▲ *12 ga.*
$23,000 $19,550 $16,100 $12,250 $9,250 $8,000 $7,150 $6,500 $6,000 $5,500 $5,000 $4,500

▲ *16 ga.*
$26,000 $21,000 $17,000 $13,000 $9,375 $8,100 $7,500 $7,000 $6,500 $6,000 $5,500 $5,000

▲ *20 ga.*
$32,500 $27,650 $21,000 $17,500 $13,850 $10,500 $9,250 $8,500 $8,000 $7,500 $7,000 $6,500

▲ *28 ga.*
N/A N/A N/A $31,500 $23,750 $18,975 $16,000 $14,000 $12,250 $10,750 $9,000 $8,250

▲ *.410 ga.* — no original guns known to exist.

100%	98%	95%	90%	80%	70%	60%	50%	40%	30%	20%	10%

AAHE — very elaborate model, early AAs have Whitworth barrels, late ones have Peerless. Approx. 340 mfg.
 Subtract 20% if without ejectors (AAH Model).

▲ *12 ga.*

100%	98%	95%	90%	80%	70%	60%	50%	40%	30%	20%	10%
$35,000	$32,000	$28,500	$26,000	$23,000	$21,000	$19,000	$17,000	$15,500	$13,750	$12,000	$10,500

▲ *16 ga.*

$39,000	$35,000	$32,000	$28,500	$26,000	$23,000	$21,000	$19,000	$17,000	$15,500	$13,750	$12,000

▲ *20 ga.*

$57,500	$54,000	$50,000	$45,000	$40,250	$35,000	$31,050	$28,000	$24,750	$21,000	$19,550	$17,250

▲ *28 ga.*

N/A	N/A	N/A	$68,500	$63,250	$58,750	$53,475	$46,000	$39,500	$33,925	$28,175	$25,875

A-1 SPECIAL GRADE — 100% engraved, all were special ordered, each one inspected by the company president before being shipped. Approx. 320 mfg.

▲ *12 ga.*

$75,000	$67,500	$61,000	$57,000	$51,750	$46,250	$40,250	$36,175	$31,050	$28,500	$26,450	$22,000

▲ *16 ga.*

$75,000	$67,500	$61,000	$57,000	$51,750	$46,250	$40,250	$36,175	$31,050	$28,500	$26,450	$22,000

▲ *20 ga.*

N/A	N/A	N/A	$90,000	$82,000	$76,000	$70,000	$64,000	$57,500	$53,000	$46,500

▲ *28 ga.* — extreme rarity and desirability factors preclude accurate price evaluation by condition factors. 70% original condition A-1 Specials HAVE sold for over $90,000.

SINGLE BARREL TRAP GUNS

 12 ga. only, 30 (rare), 32, and 34 (rare) in. barrels, any boring is available, as is stock configuration, boxlock, auto ejector. The grades differ only in engraving, checkering and wood finish.

 It should be noted that single barrel trap guns cannot be compared to the SxS models as they are not as desirable even though they are rarer. Most side by side collectors are not that interested in single barrel trap models and very few collectors specialize in single barrels.

 Add 15% for 30 or 34 in. barrel.

S.C. GRADE

$3,750	$3,475	$3,100	$2,700	$2,350	$1,875	$1,625	$1,400	$1,150	$995	$900	$825

S.B. GRADE

$4,475	$4,100	$3,750	$3,475	$3,100	$2,700	$2,350	$1,875	$1,625	$1,400	$1,150	$995

S.A. GRADE

$5,250	$4,825	$4,375	$3,875	$3,425	$3,050	$2,675	$2,275	$1,875	$1,550	$1,200	$1,050

S.A.A. GRADE

N/A	N/A	$5,500	$4,750	$4,000	$3,575	$3,050	$2,675	$2,375	$1,850	$1,575	$1,350

S.A.-1 SPECIAL GRADE

N/A	N/A	N/A	$13,000	$10,000	$9,150	$8,350	$7,425	$6,375	$5,550	$4,950	$4,300

PARKER PISTOLS
Refer to the Wyoming Arms section in this text.

P

PARKER REPRODUCTIONS

Previously imported by the Parker Reproduction Division of Reagent Chemical & Research, Inc., located in Middlesex, NJ. Previously distributed by Parker Reproductions located in Webb City, MO. These shotguns were manufactured in Japan to original Parker specifications by Winchester until the factory closed in January, 1989.

In 1984 Winchester was contracted by Reagent Chemical & Research, Inc. to manufacture a new Parker shotgun. The new SxS was a DHE model, available in 20 and 28 ga. initially. These models were fabricated in Japan to original Parker specifications, and the reproduction is so authentic that most parts are interchangeable with original Parker guns. Mfg. 1984-89. In 1993, a 16/20 ga. combo was introduced in some models.

Grading	100%	98%	95%	90%	80%	70%	60%

SHOTGUNS: SIDE BY SIDE

Models listed below with Mfg.'s Sug. Retail indicates limited existing inventory as this edition goes to press. Because of the high quality and limited mfg. of these reproductions, they are becoming quite collectible.

DHE GRADE — 12 (new 1986), 20, or 28 (new 1984) ga., boxlock action, ejectors, single selective or double triggers, beavertail or splinter forend, straight or pistol grip stock, skeleton steel butt plate, engraving in original DH style, case hardened frame, rust blued barrels. Supplied with leather trunk case, canvas and leather cover, and snap caps.

Mfg.'s Sug. Retail	$3,370	$2,525	$2,325	$2,175	$1,950	$1,750	$1,550	$1,375

Add $150 for beavertail forend.
Add $650 for Sporting Clays Model w/choke tubes.
Add $800 per extra set of barrels, depending on gauge.

Quantities mfg. for this model are as follows: 12 ga. - 2,137 mfg., 20 ga. - 6,050 mfg., 28 ga. - 4,203 mfg.

▲ *DHE Steel Shot Special* — similar to 12 ga. D Grade, except has strengthened No. 1½ barrels, 3 in. chambers, and 28 in. chrome lined barrels, 7¼-7½ lbs. Approx. 250 mfg. 1987-89.

	$2,900	$2,500	$2,200	$1,950	$1,750	$1,550	$1,375

Last Mfg.'s Sug. Retail was $3,120.

Add $100 for beavertail forend.

▲ *DHE Small Gauge Combo* — available in either 28/.410 ga. (disc.) or 16/20 ga. (new 1993) combo with 2 barrels and 2 forends. Less than 160 mfg. of the 28/.410 combo.

➤ **28/.410 ga. Combo**

	$6,500	$5,750	$4,500	$4,000	$3,625	$3,150	$2,900

Last Mfg.'s Sug. Retail was $4,970.

➤ **16/20 ga. Combo** — new 1994.

Mfg.'s Sug. Retail	$4,870	$4,600	$4,200	$3,800	$3,500	$3,300	$2,950	$2,600

▲ *DHE 3-Barrel Set* — includes 28, and .410 ga. barrels, cased.

Mfg.'s Sug. Retail	$5,630	$5,350	$4,800	$4,400	$4,100	$3,850	$3,600	$3,400

BHE GRADE LIMITED EDITION — 12, 20, or 28 ga., original Parker BH specifications, single selective or double trigger(s), straight or pistol grip stock, engraved skeleton butt plate, bank note scroll engraving around game scenes, cased. Only 100 manufactured in each gauge — mfg. began late 1987-89.

	$4,875	$4,400	$3,950	$3,500	$2,650	$2,150	$1,800

Last Mfg.'s Sug. Retail was $3,970.

Add $4,000 for 28 or .410 ga.
Add $1,000 for extra set of barrels.
Add $150 for beavertail forend.

A 28/.410 ga. combo was also available with 2 forends. Only seven 28 ga.'s were mfg. in this model.

Grading	100%	98%	95%	90%	80%	70%	60%

A-1 SPECIAL — 12, 16/20 ga. combo (new 1993), 20, or 28 (sold out) ga., original Parker A-1 specifications, single selective or double trigger(s), fine scroll engraving with game scenes, 32 lines/in. checkering, cased with accessories. Limited mfg. 1988-89.

Mfg.'s Sug. Retail	**$11,200**	**$10,500**	**$8,500**	**$7,250**	**$6,000**	**$5,475**	**$4,800**	**$4,350**

    Add $3,000+ for 28 ga. (sold out).
    Add $1,000 for extra set of barrels.
    Add $200 for beavertail forend.
    Add $1,700 for 16 ga. barrel (splinter model only).

▲ *A-1 Special Custom Engraved* — custom (per individual special order) engraving, available with two sets of barrels only, cased with accessories. Limited mfg. 1988-89. Prices start at $11,000 and go up according to individualized special features.

▲ *Federal Duck Stamp Collector's Series* — available in 12 or 20 ga., A-1 Special specifications, authorized by U.S. Department of Interior. Mfg. was limited to 10 per year in 1988-89 only.

	$13,500	**$10,000**	**$8,000**

Last Mfg.'s Sug. Retail was $14.000.

This model includes special case and 2 barrels per buyer's specifications.

PARKER-HALE LIMITED

Previous manufacturer located in Birmingham, England. Rifles were manufactured in England until 1991 when Navy Arms purchased the manufacturing rights and built a plant in West Virginia for fabrication. This new company is called Gibbs Rifle Company and they manufactured models very similar to older Parker-Hale rifles during 1992-94. Shotguns were manufactured in Spain and imported by Precision Sports, a division of Cortland Line Company, Inc. located in Cortland, NY until 1993.

RIFLES: BOLT ACTION

All Parker rifle importation was discontinued in 1991. Parker-Hale bolt action rifles utilize the Mauser K-98 action and were offered in a variety of configurations. A single set trigger option was introduced in 1984 on most models which allows either "hair trigger" or conventional single stage operation - add $85.

MODEL 81 CLASSIC — available in 11 cals. between .22-250 and 7mm Rem. Mag., 24 in. barrel, open sights, 4 shot mag., select checkered walnut with sling swivels, 7¾ lbs. New 1985.

		$715	**$565**	**$475**	**$395**	**$340**	**$300**	**$280**

Last Mfg.'s Sug. Retail was $860.

▲ *Model 81 African* — .375 H&H or 9.3x62mm cal., similar specifications as Model 81 Classic and has engraved action. New 1986.

		$875	**$700**	**$600**	**$500**	**$425**	**$360**	**$330**

Last Mfg.'s Sug. Retail was $1,110.

MODEL 84 TARGET — 7.62mm, match rifle with special sights, adj. cheekpiece on stock. Importation disc. 1990.

		$1,080	**$875**	**$760**	**$680**	**$610**	**$530**	**$465**

Last Mfg.'s Sug. Retail was $1.300.

MODEL 85 SNIPER RIFLE — .308 cal., bolt action, extended heavy barrel, 10 shot mag., camo green synthetic stock with stippling, built in adj. bipod, enlarged contoured bolt, adj. recoil pad. Importation began 1989.

		$1,750	**$1,425**	**$1,275**	**$1,050**	**$875**	**$750**	**$625**

Last Mfg.'s Sug. Retail was $1.975.

MODEL 86 TARGET — 7.62mm, 27½ in. barrel, 5 shot mag., stippled stock and forend, aperture front and rear sights, 11¼ lbs. Distributed 1986 only by North American Precision.

		$980	**$830**	**$760**	**$690**	**$610**	**$530**	**$465**

Last Mfg.'s Sug. Retail was $1.149.

Grading	100%	98%	95%	90%	80%	70%	60%

MODEL 87 TARGET — .243, 6.5x55, .308, .30-06, or .300 Win. Mag. cal., target stock, aperture sights. Importation began 1987.

	$1,375	$1,100	$900	$775	$650	$550	$495

Last Mfg.'s Sug. Retail was $1,525.

MODEL 1000 STANDARD — available in 9 cals. between .22-250 and .308 Win., 22 in. barrel, 4 shot mag., walnut stock with cheekpiece, 7¼ lbs. Disc. 1988.

	$400	$330	$285	$255	$230	$215	$195

Last Mfg.'s Sug. Retail was $500.

MODEL 1100 LIGHTWEIGHT — available in 9 cals. between .22-250 and .30-06, 22 in. barrel, open sights, 4 shot mag., 6½ lbs. New 1985.

	$495	$400	$350	$325	$285	$270	$255

Last Mfg.'s Sug. Retail was $595.

▲ *Model 1100M African* — .375 H&H, .404 Jeffery, or .458 Win. Mag. cal., 24 in. barrel, 4 shot mag., 9½ lbs.

	$800	$650	$575	$500	$450	$425	$400

Last Mfg.'s Sug. Retail was $960.

MODEL 1200 SUPER — bolt action, Mauser type action, .22-250, .243, 6mm, .25-06, .270, .30-06, .300 Win. Mag., 7mm Rem., or .308 cal., 24 in. barrel, folding sight, skip checkered walnut stock, pad swivels, rosewood pistol grip cap and forend tip. Mfg. 1968-present.

	$540	$450	$375	$330	$295	$275	$260

Last Mfg.'s Sug. Retail was $680.

This model in Magnum cals. is called the 1200 M Super Magnum.

▲ *Model 1200 C (Super Clip)* — similar to Model 1200 Super, except has detachable 4 shot box mag.

	$590	$500	$400	$350	$300	$280	$265

Last Mfg.'s Sug. Retail was $740.

MODEL 1200P PRESENTATION — similar to 1200, except .243 or .30-06 cal., scroll engraved, no sights. Mfg. 1969-1975.

	$495	$425	$395	$340	$315	$305	$275

MODEL 1200 SUPER VARMINT — similar to 1200, except .22-250, 6mm, .25-06, or .243 cal., 24 in. heavy barrel, no sights. Disc. 1988.

	$525	$425	$365	$325	$285	$270	$255

Last Mfg.'s Sug. Retail was $660.

MODEL 1300 C SCOUT — shorter barrel variation.

	$695	$550	$450	$385	$330	$300	$275

Last Mfg.'s Sug. Retail was $785.

MODEL 2100 MIDLAND (HYBRID ACTION) — available in 11 cals. between .22-250 or .300 Win. Mag. cal., 22 in. barrel, 4 shot mag., open sights, 7 lbs.

	$325	$270	$230	$200	$190	$180	$170

Last Mfg.'s Sug. Retail was $365.

▲ *Model 2100 Midland Magnum* — .300 Win. Mag., or 7mm Rem. Mag. cal., 24 in. barrel, 4 shot mag., 9½ lbs. Imported 1989-90 only.

	$380	$325	$295	$270	$260	$250	$240

Last Mfg.'s Sug. Retail was $430.

MODEL 2600 MIDLAND SPECIAL — .243 Win., .270 Win., .308 Win., or .30-06 cal., Midland Gun Co. action, iron sights. New 1989.

	$295	$250	$225	$200	$190	$180	$170

Last Mfg.'s Sug. Retail was $330.

MIDLAND 2700 LIGHTWEIGHT — lightweight variation of the Model 2600.

	$340	$285	$240	$200	$190	$180	$170

Last Mfg.'s Sug. Retail was $390.

Grading	100%	98%	95%	90%	80%	70%	60%

SHOTGUNS: SIDE-BY-SIDE

Parker-Hale shotguns were manufactured by Ugartechea in Eibar, Spain and imported as Parker-Hale models by Precision Sports located in Cortland, NY until 1994. Please refer to the Ugartechea section of this text.

PASTUSEK INDUSTRIES

Manufacturer located in Fort Worth, TX since 1993. Distributed by Fort Worth Firearms located in Fort Worth, TX.

PISTOLS

HSK (SPORT KING) — .22 LR, 4½ or 5½ in. barrel. New 1995.

Mfg.'s Sug. Retail	$312	$275	$250	$225	$195	$175	$150	$135

HSS (SHARPSHOOTER) — .22 LR, 5½ in. bull barrel. New 1995.

Mfg.'s Sug. Retail	$379	$315	$275	$240	$210	$190	$165	$150

HSC (SUPERMATIC CITATION) — .22 LR, 5½ bull or 7¼ in. fluted barrel. New 1995.

Mfg.'s Sug. Retail	$388	$340	$295	$265	$230	$210	$180	$165

Add $22 for 7¼ in. fluted barrel.
This model is also available with an 8, 10, or 12 in. bull barrel.

HST (SUPERMATIC TROPHY) — .22 LR, 5½ bull or 7¼ in. fluted barrel. New 1995.

Mfg.'s Sug. Retail	$494	$400	$340	$275	$240	$220	$180	$165

This model is also available with an 8, 10, or 12 in. bull barrel. Left-hand ejection is also an option on this model.

HSV (VICTOR) — .22 LR, 3⅞, 4½, 5½, 8 (optional), or 10 (optional) in. VR barrel. New 1995.

Mfg.'s Sug. Retail	$569	$475	$375	$300	$250	$230	$185	$165

Add $30 for dove tail rib on 5½ in. barrel only.
Add $79 for weaver rib on 5½ in. barrel only.

HSO (OLYMPIC) — .22 S or .22 LR, 6¾ in. barrel only. New 1995.

Mfg.'s Sug. Retail	$599	$495	$395	$325	$265	$245	$195	$170

PAUZA SPECIALTIES

Manufactured by Pauza Specialties since 1991, located in Baytown, TX. Distributed by U.S. General Technologies, Inc. located in South San Francisco, CA. Dealer sales only.

RIFLE/CARBINE

P50 SEMI-AUTO — .50 BMG cal., semi-auto, 24 (carbine) or 29 (rifle) in. match grade barrel, 5 shot detachable mag., one-piece receiver, 3-stage gas system, takedown action, all exterior parts Teflon coated, with aluminum bipod, 25 or 30 lbs. New 1992.

Mfg.'s Sug. Retail	$6,495	$5,950	$5,250	$4,600	$4,100	$3,650	$3,200	$2,800

PEDERSEN CUSTOM GUNS

Previously a division of O.F. Mossberg, North Haven, CT. Manufactured between 1973-1975.

RIFLES

MODEL 3000 — bolt action rifle, Mossberg Model 810 action, .270, .30-06, 7mm Mag., or .338 Mag. cal., 22 and 24 in. barrel, open sight, checkered Monte Carlo stock.

▲ *Grade III* — no engraving.

	$550	$495	$470	$440	$420	$385	$330

P

Grading	100%	98%	95%	90%	80%	70%	60%
▲ *Grade II* — moderately engraved.							
	$660	$580	$525	$495	$440	$420	$385
▲ *Grade I* — heavily engraved and inlaid, with select wood.							
	$990	$770	$745	$690	$635	$560	$495
▲ *Presentation Model* — top-of-the-line model.							
	$1,250	$1,000	$895	$800	$745	$690	$635

MODEL 4700 — custom deluxe lever action, (Model 472 Mossberg), .30-30 or .35 Rem. cal., 5 shot, tube mag., 24 in. barrel, open sight, black walnut stock.

	100%	98%	95%	90%	80%	70%	60%
	$250	$195	$165	$155	$145	$130	$120

SHOTGUNS

MODEL 4000 SLIDE ACTION SHOTGUN — custom Mossberg Model 500, 12, 20, or .410 ga., 3 in. chamber, 26 in. imp. cyl. or skeet, 28 in. full or mod., 30 in. full, vent. rib, floral engraved, checkered select walnut stock. Mfg. 1975.

	100%	98%	95%	90%	80%	70%	60%
	$460	$375	$330	$305	$265	$230	$220

MODEL 4000 TRAP — similar to 4000, except 12 ga., 30 in. full, Monte Carlo trap stock and pad. Mfg. 1975.

	100%	98%	95%	90%	80%	70%	60%
	$485	$395	$350	$325	$285	$255	$240

MODEL 4500 — similar to 4000, less engraving.

	100%	98%	95%	90%	80%	70%	60%
	$420	$330	$305	$275	$240	$200	$175

MODEL 4500 TRAP — similar to 4000 Trap, less engraving.

	100%	98%	95%	90%	80%	70%	60%
	$440	$350	$310	$280	$240	$210	$200

MODEL 1500 O/U HUNTING GUN — 12 ga., 2¾ or 3 in. chambers, 26 in. imp. cyl. and mod., 28 in. mod. and full, 30 in. mod. and full, boxlock, auto ejectors, selective or non-selective single trigger, checkered pistol grip stock. Mfg. 1973-1975.

	100%	98%	95%	90%	80%	70%	60%
	$700	$575	$500	$440	$415	$385	$365

MODEL 1500 SKEET — similar to Hunting Gun, except 27 in. skeet, skeet stock. Mfg. 1973-1975.

	100%	98%	95%	90%	80%	70%	60%
	$725	$600	$525	$450	$425	$400	$385

MODEL 1500 TRAP — similar to Hunting Gun, except 30 and 32 in. full barrels, trap Monte Carlo stock. Mfg. 1973-1975.

	100%	98%	95%	90%	80%	70%	60%
	$650	$550	$475	$435	$410	$375	$350

MODEL 1000 O/U HUNTING GUN — 12 or 20 ga., 26, 28, or 30 in. barrels, various chokes, boxlock, auto ejectors, SST, checkered select walnut stock, silver inlays, more engraving. Mfg. 1973-1975.

	100%	98%	95%	90%	80%	70%	60%
Grade I	$2,200	$1,980	$1,870	$1,700	$1,540	$1,460	$1,375
Grade II	$1,815	$1,540	$1,430	$1,265	$1,185	$1,100	$1,045

MODEL 1000 TRAP GUN — similar to Hunting Gun, but 12 ga., 30 or 32 in. mod. and full barrels, Monte Carlo trap stock. Mfg. 1973-1975.

	100%	98%	95%	90%	80%	70%	60%
Grade I	$2,100	$1,800	$1,650	$1,500	$1,350	$1,200	$995
Grade II	$1,650	$1,500	$1,375	$1,200	$1,050	$900	$725

MODEL 1000 SKEET — similar to Hunting Gun, except 26 or 28 in. barrels, bored skeet. Mfg. 1973-1975.

	100%	98%	95%	90%	80%	70%	60%
Grade I	$2,255	$2,145	$2,035	$1,870	$1,705	$1,625	$1,540
Grade II	$1,980	$1,705	$1,595	$1,430	$1,350	$1,265	$1,210

MODEL 200 S X S — 12 or 20 ga., 26 in. imp. cyl. and mod., 28 in. mod. and full, 30 in. mod. and full, boxlock, auto ejectors, SST. Mfg. 1973-1974.

	100%	98%	95%	90%	80%	70%	60%
Grade I	$2,420	$2,175	$2,090	$1,955	$1,790	$1,705	$1,625
Grade II	$2,200	$1,955	$1,815	$1,735	$1,625	$1,540	$1,485

MODEL 2500 DOUBLE BARREL — 12 or 20 ga., 26 in. imp. cyl. and mod., 28 in. mod. and full, auto ejectors, boxlock, checkered pistol grip stock and forearm.

	100%	98%	95%	90%	80%	70%	60%
	$470	$385	$360	$305	$275	$260	$240

PEDERSOLI, DAVIDE & C. s.n.c.

Manufacturer of modern, black powder, and older historically significant firearms located in Brescia, Italy.
D. Pedersoli manufactures top quality black powder replicas and other high quality reproductions. Most of their production domestically is subcontracted by other U.S. firms. Please refer to the Black Powder listing in the back of this text for more information.

Grading	100%	98%	95%	90%	80%	70%	60%

DELUXE CREEDMOOR 45/70 SINGLE SHOT RIFLE — .45/70 cal., case colored receiver w/o engraving, 34 in. part round/part octagon barrel, checkered walnut stock, long venier tang sight, metal butt plate, 12 lbs. 2 oz. Limited mfg. beginning 1995.

Mfg.'s Sug. Retail	$1,095	$1,050	$850	$625			

PENTHENY de PENTHENY

Current manufacturer and gunsmith located in Santa Rosa, CA. Established in 1987.

RIFLES

The rifles listed below include ebony forend tips, old English style black recoil pads, steel skeleton grip caps, four panels of 22 LPI checkering, and other custom features. These models are built on a U.S.R.A. company Model 70 action.

THE INVADER — small and medium bore cals., classic styled Claro walnut stock, blued finish.

Mfg.'s Sug. Retail	$3,750	$3,750	$2,900	$2,350	$1,950	$1,500	$1,150	$875

THE NORMAN — Mag. cals., classic styled English walnut stock, blued finish.

Mfg.'s Sug. Retail	$3,750	$3,750	$2,900	$2,350	$1,950	$1,500	$1,150	$875

THE CONQUEROR — large bore cals., classic styled English walnut stock, blued finish, rifle has secondary recoil lug, dual steel reinforcing bolts, and express sights including fixed and folding leaves.

Mfg.'s Sug. Retail	$4,500	$4,500	$3,500	$2,900	$2,350	$1,950	$1,500	$1,150

PERAZZI

Manufacturer located in Brescia, Italy since 1952. Imported and distributed by Perazzi USA, Inc. located in Monrovia, CA (previously located in Rome, NY).

Note: Previously, Perazzi shotguns were imported by both Winchester and Ithaca during the 1960s and 1970s. The company now has its own distribution network and its current model line-up is extensive. Perazzi shotguns are well known for their quality control standards and reliability in clay target championships and in-field conditions.

Because of the devaluation of the U.S. dollar since 1984, Perazzi shotguns have gone up in value substantially.

SHOTGUNS: DISC.

Perazzi shotguns have incorporated many improvements during their manufacture. One of the most important changes has been the modification of the forearm design. Basically, there have been 4 different types: Type 1 has a serial range of 30,000 - 33,250, Type 2 is serial numbered 33,251 - 35,450, Type 3 has a range of 35,451 - 51,242, Type 4 started at 51,243 and is still current as of this writing. Differences include changes in the forearm iron and barrel lug attachment. Because of these forearm changes (and other parts modifications), the desirability factor on a Type 4 forearm shotgun as opposed to a Type 1 is much greater. Competition shooters prefer Types 3 or 4 as they are the current design. If a Type 1 or 2 competition gun develops problems, they are automatically retrofitted to the Type 4 design - and these modifications are expensive. For these reasons, the serial number of a Perazzi competition gun will determine its type. Since Types 1 through 3 are discontinued, Types 1 and 2 will be less desirable (and less expensive) than the values listed below for Type 3.

Grading	100%	98%	95%	90%	80%	70%	60%

As a final note on older Perazzi shotguns, the most collectable models will be those specimens which exhibit the highest quality and are equally rare. Older SCO grades on small frames with older style "V" springs are at the top for desirability. Also, any older SPECIAL GUNS were all custom made - usually engraved by master engravers with Angelo Galeazzi being considered the best. These models are exceedingly rare, with prices going over the $40,000 level in today's marketplace.

COMPETITION ONE TRAP GRADE — single shot, 12 ga., auto ejector, VR, cased.

	$2,500	$2,150	$1,875	$1,650	$1,450	$1,300	$1,175

COMPETITION ONE O/U TRAP — similar to Competition, except O/U double.

	$4,500	$3,950	$3,500	$3,000	$2,500	$2,150	$1,850

COMPETITION ONE SKEET

	$4,250	$3,750	$3,200	$2,700	$2,350	$2,000	$1,750

SINGLE BARREL TRAP — 12 ga., 34 in. VR, full choke barrel, boxlock, auto ejector, checkered pistol grip stock, recoil pad. Mfg. 1971-1972.

	$2,350	$2,050	$1,800	$1,600	$1,450	$1,300	$1,175

LIGHT GAME MODEL O/U FIELD — 12 ga., 27½ in. VR barrels, mod. and full or imp. cyl. and mod., boxlock, auto ejectors, field stock. Mfg. 1972-1974.

	$4,995	$4,500	$3,900	$3,300	$2,800	$2,400	$2,050

MT-6 GRADE — 12 ga., VR, auto ejector, cased, five interchangeable choke tubes. Disc. 1983.

	$4,500	$3,750	$3,250	$2,800	$2,500	$2,200	$1,900

This model was also manufactured in DHO and SHO models as well. Please refer to those models listed in the current manufacture section for approximate values.

CURRENTLY MFG. TRAP, SKEET, AND HUNTING SHOTGUNS

Not until 1988 did most single barrel trap guns have a "Special" option package which includes an adjustable trigger group (designated P4). This P4 trigger is now standard. Non-adj. trigger is a special order. Values below assume shotguns with the "Special" designation (became standard in 1988).

Models listed in the following sections assume a Type 4 forearm attachment design and are serial numbered 51,243 and above. Models that are serial numbered below 51,243 are an older design and will be priced less than the newer Type 4 models (see explanation under SHOTGUNS: DISC.).

Rather than describe all the following models individually, descriptions will appear only once and are listed below. This is because the various grades have similar features and engraving (i.e., an SCO Grade Sideplate in American Skeet would appear similar to an American Trap SCO Grade Sideplate, except for stock dimensions of course).

Older SHO (Type 3s) and DHO models with rebounding hammers (disc.) are perhaps the most collectable Perazzi shotguns currently.

Beginning with this edition, SC3 and other higher grade models have not been listed due to space consideration. The 14th edition does include all pertinent information (including 1993 pricing) pertaining to Perazzi higher grade models.

PERAZZI GRADES WITH DESCRIPTIONS

Due to space considerations and relative low manufacture, the higher grade Perazzis have been described but not individually priced. Please contact Perazzi, USA for more information and prices on these higher grades (see Trademark Index).

▲ *Special Model* — introductory level model with high polished blue on barrels and receiver, normally listing model name on lower frame sides in gold letters and numerals. Checkered walnut stock (interchangeable) and forearm, all have adjustable trigger assembly.

P

▲ **Gold Outline Model** — similar to Standard Model, except has gold line engraving around perimeter of frame, also features better grade of walnut. This configuration is very rare.

▲ **SC3 Model** — features coin finished receiver with two different styles of scroll engraving and four different patterns of game scene engraving (snipe, grouse, pointing bird dog, or woodcock). Better grade of walnut than the Gold Outline Model.

▲ **SCO Model** — more elaborate than SC3 Model in that it features two different styles of scroll engraving (deep relief "gargoyles" or fine English scroll) and four different game scene engraving patterns (two different styles of ducks, grouse, or woodcock). Again, a better grade of walnut (in addition to finer checkering) is utilized.

▲ **SCO Gold Grade Model** — differentiated from SCO Model in that it has six engraving patterns featuring multiple gold inlays on receiver sides (including two different duck scenes, two separate grouse scenes, one woodcock, and one deep relief "gargoyle").

▲ **SCO Grade Sideplate Model** — includes coin finished receiver with game scene engraved sideplates (with boxlock action). Game scene engraving choices include three different duck scenes, one grouse, one "Chisel" relief scroll, and a Diana Goddess of the Hunt pattern.

▲ **SCO Gold Grade Sideplate Model** — similar to SCO Grade Sideplate Model, except has game figures on sideplates in relief gold. Patterns include three different grouse scenes, two separate ducks patterns, and dogs flushing upland game. This model can also be ordered with detachment lever for sideplates.

▲ **Extra Grade Model** — denoted by top-of-the-line fine bank note style game scene engraving with elaborate scroll and relief work on metal perimeters. Game scene choices include two different dog scenes, one grouse, and one duck. Top quality Circassian walnut finely checkered.

▲ **Extra Gold Grade Model** — top-of-the-line boxlock model that differs from Extra Grade Model in that birds/dogs are in gold relief. This model can also be ordered with detachment lever for sideplates.

▲ **SHO Over & Under Model** — features sidelock action with coin finished receiver and intricate bank note game scene engraving with choices including three different duck patterns and one pheasant. Top quality walnut and checkering. Type One SHOs have non-rebounding firing pins, while Type Two guns have rebounding firing pins (since 1985).

> This model is individually hand made per customer's specifications. Currently, no orders are being taken for this series.

▲ **SHO Gold Over & Under Model** — similar to SHO Over & Under Model, except features game scene of wildlife in relief gold. This model is the best sidelock special order grade that Perazzi currently offers for sale.

> This model is individually hand made per customer's specifications. Currently, no orders are being taken for this series.

▲ **DHO Side-by-Side Models** — top-of-the-line sidelock model in 12 ga. only for DHO and DHO Gold grades. DHO Extra and DHO Gold Extra grades have similar engraving to Extra Grade and Extra Gold Grade models and are available in all gauges. The DHO Gold Extra is the most elaborate, highly finished side-by-side shotgun (and expensive - current retail is $82,000) that an individual can currently special order from any company. The DHO model is exceedingly rare, and specimens should be appraised individually.

> This model is entirely hand made per customer's specifications. Currently, no orders are being taken for this series.

Some descriptions on the Standard Models listed below have not been duplicated into the other Perazzi sections because of space consideration.

AMERICAN TRAP SHOTGUNS: SINGLE BARREL

12 ga. only, 32 or 34 in. barrel, high post rib, select walnut, more expensive models vary in the amount of engraving, grade of walnut, and other special order features.

NOTE: Combination guns (Combo Models) listed below include either a 32 or 34 in. single barrel and a set of either 29½ or 31½ in. O/U barrels. Current combination guns (Combo Models) include MX6, MX7, MX11, MX14, MX8 Special, DB81 Special, and MX10.

Subtract $600 for shotguns without the "Special" model designation (pre-1988).

P

Grading	100%	98%	95%	90%	80%	70%	60%

STANDARD GRADE MODELS
Add 35%-43% for Combo Models depending on model variation.

▲ *TM1 Special* — features normal trap rib. Disc. 1995.

	$5,150	$3,675	$3,100	$2,350	$2,150	$1,850	$1,675

Last Mfg.'s Sug. Retail was $6,150.

▲ *TMX Special* — features high post trap rib.
Mfg.'s Sug. Retail $6,590 $5,400 $3,875 $3,200 $2,400 $2,150 $1,850 $1,675

▲ *MX3 Special* — features rib similar to TM1 Special. Disc. 1992.

	$5,200	$3,700	$3,250	$2,450	$2,200	$1,900	$1,700

Last Mfg.'s Sug. Retail was $6,150.

▲ *MX6* — removable trigger group, 32 or 34 in. barrel. New 1995.
Mfg.'s Sug. Retail $6,270 $4,250 $3,450 $2,575 $2,200 $1,900 $1,700 $1,475

▲ *MX7* — non-removable trigger group, barrel selector, 32 or 34 in. barrel. Mfg. 1995 only.

	$4,850	$3,600	$3,050	$2,350	$2,150	$1,850	$1,675

Last Mfg.'s Sug. Retail was $5,650.

▲ *MX8 Special* — has tapered stepped rib and adj. trigger. Disc. 1994.

	$8,570	$7,350	$6,200	$4,350	$3,600	$3,200	$2,875

Last Mfg.'s Sug. Retail was $7,300.

▲ *MX9* — 12 ga., 32 or 34 in. barrel with choke tubes, unique VR on vent. barrel features removable center inserts significantly changing the point of shot pattern impact, fully adj. cheekpiece. Mfg. 1993-94.

	$6,500	$5,700	$4,400	$3,700	$3,250	$2,900	$2,625

Last Mfg.'s Sug. Retail was $9,200.

▲ *MX9 Combo* — includes a set O/U barrels and top single trap barrel, features new rib design with interchangeable middle bead inserts to change point of impact. Mfg. 1992-94.

	$9,500	$8,750	$7,600	$6,500	$5,600	$4,500	$4,000

Last Mfg.'s Sug. Retail was $12,800.

This model is available with or without choke tubes. Choke tubes include 5 chokes and 5 rib inserts (3 in. pattern per insert).

▲ *MX10* — 12 ga., 32 or 34 in. barrel featuring center-pivoting VR allowing for adj. point of impact, fixed chokes, fully adj. cheekpiece, removable trigger. Mfg. 1993-94.

	$9,200	$8,500	$7,650	$6,300	$4,400	$3,700	$3,250

Last Mfg.'s Sug. Retail was $9,450.

▲ *MX11* — removable trigger group, adj. comb, 32 or 34 in. barrel. New 1995.
Mfg.'s Sug. Retail $7,620 $6,150 $3,950 $3,550 $3,200 $2,875 $2,600 $2,375

▲ *MX14* — removable trigger group, adj. comb, unsingle configuration, 32 or 34 in. barrel. New 1995.
Mfg.'s Sug. Retail $7,030 $5,950 $3,950 $3,550 $3,200 $2,875 $2,600 $2,375

▲ *Grand American 88 Special* — features MX3 high ramped rib and grooved forearm. Mfg. 1988-92.

	$6,000	$4,250	$3,600	$3,200	$2,875	$2,600	$2,375

Last Mfg.'s Sug. Retail was $7,000.

▲ *DB81 Special* — features ultra high ramped rib. Disc. 1994.

	$7,950	$6,375	$4,500	$3,700	$3,250	$2,900	$2,625

Last Mfg.'s Sug. Retail was $7,600.

INTERNATIONAL/OLYMPIC TRAP SHOTGUNS: O/U

12 ga. only, unless indicated otherwise. Current barrel lengths include 29½, 30¾, or 31½ in.

STANDARD GRADE MODELS

The MX2/MX2L configuration is available mainly for the European marketplace. Values for this model represent recent pricing - Perazzi U.S.A. should be contacted directly for an up-to-date price quotation.

Models with "Special" nomenclature feature Perazzi's new, adjustable (4 positions) trigger group introduced on certain models beginning 1988.

Grading	100%	98%	95%	90%	80%	70%	60%

▲ **MX3 Special** — includes 6.4mm high ramped rib and separated barrels. Disc. 1992.

| | | $5,525 | $4,050 | $3,400 | $2,950 | $2,675 | $2,350 | $1,975 |

Last Mfg.'s Sug. Retail was $6,500.

   Add $380 for MX3C Model (includes choke tubes).

▲ **MX6** — removable trigger group. New 1995.
Mfg.'s Sug. Retail   **$5,700** $4,900 $3,650 $3,050 $2,350 $2,150 $1,850 $1,675

▲ **MX7C** — 29½ or 31½ in. barrels, features fixed coil spring trigger mechanism, safety incorporates selector switch, non-removable trigger group. New 1993.
Mfg.'s Sug. Retail   **$6,100** $5,000 $4,250 $3,550 $2,950 $2,625 $2,300 $2,000

▲ **Mirage MX8** — denoted by low profile rib, vent. barrels and grooved forearm.
Mfg.'s Sug. Retail   **$8,090** $6,450 $4,500 $3,700 $3,250 $2,875 $2,600 $2,375
   This model is also available with standard triggers.

▲ **MX8 Special** — similar to MX8, except four position adj. trigger (P4S).
Mfg.'s Sug. Retail   **$8,570** $6,775 $4,650 $3,825 $3,325 $2,900 $2,625 $2,400

▲ **MX8/20** — 20 ga., 29½ in. barrels with fixed chokes, flat VR with removable trigger group. New 1993.
Mfg.'s Sug. Retail   **$8,020** $6,450 $4,500 $3,700 $3,250 $2,875 $2,600 $2,375

▲ **MX9** — 29½ or 31½ in. barrels with choke tubes, unique VR on vent. barrels features removable center inserts significantly changing the point of shot pattern impact, fully adj. cheekpiece, removable trigger. Mfg. 1993-94.

| | | $7,825 | $6,350 | $5,500 | $4,950 | $4,200 | $3,800 | $3,650 |

Last Mfg.'s Sug. Retail was $9,600.

▲ **MX10** — 12 or 20 ga., 29½ in. barrels featuring center-pivoting VR allowing for adj. point of impact, fixed chokes, fully adj. cheekpiece, removable trigger. New 1993.
Mfg.'s Sug. Retail   **$10,300** $8,550 $7,500 $6,400 $5,500 $4,950 $4,200 $3,800

▲ **MX11** — removable trigger group and adj. comb. New 1995.
Mfg.'s Sug. Retail   **$7,620** $6,150 $4,300 $3,600 $3,200 $2,875 $2,600 $2,375

▲ **Grand American 88 Special** — features high ramped rib, separated barrels, and grooved forearm. Disc. 1992.

| | | $6,225 | $4,400 | $3,700 | $3,250 | $2,900 | $2,625 | $2,400 |

Last Mfg.'s Sug. Retail was $7,400.

▲ **DB81 Special** — features ultra high ramped rib and vent. barrels.
Mfg.'s Sug. Retail   **$8,810** $6,950 $4,700 $3,875 $3,350 $2,950 $2,650 $2,450

▲ **MX2/MX2L** — denoted by 8.2mm high rib, Monte Carlo stock, and vented side ribs. Model MX2L designates light weight model and has no side ribs. Disc. 1992.

| | | $4,550 | $3,700 | $3,400 | $3,050 | $2,750 | $2,500 | $2,275 |

Last Mfg.'s Sug. Retail was $5,510.

OVER/UNDER SIDELOCK MODELS — older models without rebounding hammers are not as desirable.
The most desirable configurations in this model are the Skeet, Pigeon, and Sporting variations (pricing follows new SHO Gold values). All SHO sidelock models were disc. 1992.

▲ **SHO Older Mfg.**

| | | $19,000 | $16,750 | $12,250 | $9,500 | $8,500 | $7,600 | $6,800 |

   Add $6,000 for game scene engraving.

▲ **SHO Newer Mfg.**

| | | $35,000 | $27,750 | $25,750 | $23,750 | $21,750 | $19,750 | $17,750 |

Last Mfg.'s Sug. Retail was $43,000.

▲ **SHO Gold Older Mfg.**

| | | $25,000 | $21,000 | $18,000 | $15,000 | $13,000 | $11,000 | $9,250 |

▲ **SHO Gold Newer Mfg.**

| | | $65,000 | $55,000 | $49,500 | $45,500 | $40,000 | $35,500 | $30,000 |

Last Mfg.'s Sug. Retail was $48,000.

▲ **SHO Extra** — while advertised, none were sold.

Last Mfg.'s Sug. Retail was $80,000.

Grading	100%	98%	95%	90%	80%	70%	60%

▲ *SHO Gold Extra* — while advertised, none were sold.

Last Mfg.'s Sug. Retail was $86,000.

AMERICAN SKEET SHOTGUNS: O/U

12 ga. only, 26, 27⅝ (standard and most common), or 28⅜ in. separated barrels, select walnut, more expensive models vary in the amount of engraving, grade of walnut, and other special order features.

STANDARD GRADE MODELS

▲ *MX3 Special* — introductory skeet model, detachable and adj. four position P4S trigger, flat rib. Barrel lockup is same as MX8. Disc. 1992.

	$5,400	$4,100	$3,400	$2,950	$2,675	$2,350	$1,975

Last Mfg.'s Sug. Retail was $6,500.

Previous to 1988, this model was designated the MX3. It did not have the P4 adj. selective trigger group.

▲ *MX6* — removable trigger group. New 1995.

Mfg.'s Sug. Retail	$6,270	$4,900	$3,650	$3,050	$2,350	$2,150	$1,850	$1,675

▲ *MX7C* — 27⅝ or 28⅜ in. barrels with choke tubes, features fixed coil spring trigger mechanism, safety incorporates selector switch, non-removable trigger group. Mfg. 1993-95.

	$5,700	$4,950	$4,250	$3,550	$2,950	$2,625	$2,300

Last Mfg.'s Sug. Retail was $6,100.

▲ *MX8 Mirage* — 12 or 20 ga., 27⅝ in. barrels bored SK/SK, flat VR with removable trigger group. New 1993.

Mfg.'s Sug. Retail	$8,090	$6,375	$4,400	$3,600	$3,100	$2,700	$2,500	$2,300

▲ *Mirage Special* — evolved from Olympic Skeet Model, features detachable and adj. four position trigger.

Mfg.'s Sug. Retail	$8,570	$6,775	$4,650	$3,825	$3,325	$2,900	$2,625	$2,400

▲ *MX10* — removable trigger group, adj. rib and comb. New 1995.

Mfg.'s Sug. Retail	$10,300	$8,550	$7,500	$6,400	$5,500	$4,950	$4,200	$3,800

▲ *MX11* — removable trigger group, adj. comb. New 1995.

Mfg.'s Sug. Retail	$7,620	$6,150	$4,300	$3,600	$3,200	$2,875	$2,600	$2,375

AMERICAN SKEET O/U SHOTGUNS: 4-GAUGE SETS

STANDARD GRADE MODELS

▲ *MX3 Special*

	$10,500	$9,150	$8,230	$7,500	$6,750	$6,000	$5,300

Last Mfg.'s Sug. Retail was $15,400.

▲ *Mirage Special* — disc. 1994.

	$11,000	$9,750	$8,475	$7,700	$6,950	$6,100	$5,300

Last Mfg.'s Sug. Retail was $17,500.

INTERNATIONAL/OLYMPIC SKEET SHOTGUNS: O/U

Available in 12 ga. only. Usually supplied with 29½ in. barrels.

Since the international skeet variations are similar to the American skeet models, rather than duplicating these models (with the exception of the Mirage MX8), please refer to pricing in the American Skeet Shotguns section for corresponding values and information. Only the Model MX8 remains below, since there is no similar American model.

STANDARD GRADE MODELS

Older Mirage Models (without the "Special" designation) do not have the adjustable 4 position trigger. Subtract $250-$500 on values listed below for these older variations.

P

Grading	100%	98%	95%	90%	80%	70%	60%

▲ *Mirage MX8* — developed especially for Olympic Skeet Competition featuring vent. barrels with optional muzzle brakes on sides, grooved forearm, interchangeable trigger groupings with non-adj. trigger.

Mfg.'s Sug. Retail $8,090	$6,375	$4,400	$3,600	$3,100	$2,700	$2,500	$2,300

OVER/UNDER SIDELOCK MODELS — older models without rebounding hammers are not as desirable.

▲ *SHO Older Mfg.*

	$18,000	$15,750	$12,000	$9,500	$8,500	$7,600	$6,800

▲ *SHO Newer Mfg.*

	$35,850	$30,000	$25,000	$20,000	$17,000	$14,500	$12,750

Last Mfg.'s Sug. Retail was $43,000.

▲ *SHO Gold Older Mfg.*

	$18,000	$15,750	$12,000	$9,500	$8,500	$7,600	$6,800

▲ *SHO Gold Newer Mfg.*

	$45,000	$34,500	$27,250	$22,000	$18,500	$15,950	$13,750

Last Mfg.'s Sug. Retail was $48,000.

▲ *SHO Extra* — imported 1985-1992.

	$68,750	$54,700	$38,100	$32,000	$26,500	$21,250	$18,000

Last Mfg.'s Sug. Retail was $80,000.

▲ *SHO Gold Extra* — similar to SHO Extra, except has gold inlays. Imported 1992 only.

	$72,750	$56,500	$39,500	$33,000	$27,000	$22,000	$18,500

Last Mfg.'s Sug. Retail was $86,000.

COMPETITION SPORTING SHOTGUNS: O/U

12 ga. only, unless indicated otherwise, designed for sporting clays competition.

The Mirage Sporting Classic Models listed below replace the Mirage Special Sporting and incorporate several new improvements.

STANDARD GRADE MODELS

The MX1/MX1B configuration is available mainly for the European marketplace. Values for this model represent recent pricing - Perazzi USA should be contacted directly for an up-to-date price quotation.

Choke tubes became standard on Perazzi's Sporting shotguns beginning in 1992. Subtract $400 - $500 for older variations without choke tubes (Models without the "C" suffix nomenclature). Older specimens without the "Special" designation do not have adjustable 4 position trigger group - subtract $400 from values below without this feature.

▲ *MX3C Special Sporting* — features VR and barrels, includes adj. four position trigger, and 5 interchangeable choke tubes. Disc. 1992.

	$5,000	$4,275	$3,600	$3,200	$2,875	$2,600	$2,375

Last Mfg.'s Sug. Retail was $6,880.

▲ *MX6* — removable trigger group, external selector, 7 chokes. New 1995.

Mfg.'s Sug. Retail $6,740	$6,075	$5,125	$4,350	$3,550	$2,950	$2,625	$2,300

▲ *MX7C Sporting* — sporting configuration, includes 5 choke tubes. Imported 1992-95.

	$4,500	$4,100	$3,550	$2,950	$2,625	$2,300	$2,100

Last Mfg.'s Sug. Retail was $6,670.

▲ *MX8 Mirage* — 12 or 20 ga., $27\frac{5}{8}$, $28\frac{3}{8}$, or $29\frac{1}{2}$ in. barrels with fixed or screw-in chokes. New 1993.

Mfg.'s Sug. Retail $9,160	$7,500	$5,400	$4,150	$3,650	$3,150	$2,900	$2,600

▲ *MX10* — 12 or 20 ga., $27\frac{5}{8}$ in. barrels with fixed chokes. New 1993.

Mfg.'s Sug. Retail $11,340	$9,150	$7,850	$6,500	$5,500	$4,950	$4,200	$3,600

▲ *MX11* — removable trigger group, adj. comb, external selector, 7 chokes. New 1995.

Mfg.'s Sug. Retail $8,690	$6,825	$4,675	$3,825	$3,325	$2,900	$2,625	$2,400

▲ *Mirage Special Sporting* — $28\frac{3}{8}$ in. barrels with choke tubes, external SST (non-adj.), special sporting dimension stock and forend, Schnabel forearm.

Mfg.'s Sug. Retail $9,160	$6,775	$4,650	$3,825	$3,325	$2,900	$2,625	$2,400

Grading	100%	98%	95%	90%	80%	70%	60%

▲ *Mirage Special Sporting Classic* — similar to Mirage Sporting, except has engraving package, SC3 quality wood, and SST.

Mfg.'s Sug. Retail $10,200	$8,200	$5,900	$4,375	$3,750	$3,150	$2,900	$2,600

▲ *MX1/MX1B Sporting* — 12 ga. only, MX1 has high tapered ramped rib and separated barrels. MX1B has lower profile flat rib.

Mfg.'s Sug. Retail $8,090	$5,000	$3,700	$3,400	$3,050	$2,750	$2,500	$2,275

COMPETITION PIGEON-ELECTROCIBLES CONFIGURATION: O/U

12 ga. only.

STANDARD GRADE MODELS

This configuration specifically made for pigeon/electrocibles competition shooting and is currently available in the MX1B, Mirage, Mirage Special, MX10, and MX11 Models. Subtract $1,000 for 27½ in. barrels, or $500 for 28⅜ in. barrels.

▲ *MX1B* — removable trigger group, 27½ in. barrels. New 1995.

Mfg.'s Sug. Retail $8,090	$4,500	$4,100	$3,600	$3,100	$2,700	$2,500	$2,300

▲ *Mirage* — removable trigger group, 27½, 28⅜, 29½, or 31½ in. barrels. New 1995.

Mfg.'s Sug. Retail $7,850	$6,375	$4,400	$3,600	$3,100	$2,700	$2,500	$2,300

▲ *Mirage Special* — removable trigger group, adj. trigger, 28⅜, 29½, or 31½ in. barrels. New 1995.

Mfg.'s Sug. Retail $8,570	$6,775	$4,650	$3,825	$3,325	$2,900	$2,625	$2,400

▲ *MX10* — removable trigger group, adj. rib and comb, 27½ or 29½ in. barrels. New 1995.

Mfg.'s Sug. Retail $10,300	$8,550	$7,500	$6,400	$5,500	$4,950	$4,200	$3,800

▲ *MX11* — removable trigger group, adj. comb., 27½ in. barrels. New 1995.

Mfg.'s Sug. Retail $7,620	$6,150	$4,300	$3,600	$3,200	$2,875	$2,600	$2,375

HUNTING SHOTGUNS: O/U BOXLOCK ACTION

12, 20, 28, or .410 ga., 26 (disc. on MX8/12 ga. and MX12 1994), 26¾, or 27½ in. barrels only, choice of chokes. These small frame shotguns are available in 20, 28, or .410 ga. but choke tubes (MX20C designation) are optional only in 20 ga.

STANDARD GRADE MODELS

▲ *MX8* — 12 or 20 ga., removable trigger group, separated barrels with fixed or screw-in chokes. New 1993.

Mfg.'s Sug. Retail $8,090	$6,000	$4,400	$3,600	$3,100	$2,700	$2,500	$2,300

▲ *MX12* — 12 ga. only, 2¾ in. chambers only, separated barrels with VR, coil springs, SST (fixed trigger group), Schnabel forearm, light receiver border engraving.

Mfg.'s Sug. Retail $8,090	$6,000	$4,400	$3,600	$3,100	$2,700	$2,500	$2,300

Vented side rib guns with flushed chokes are available beginning 1993.

▲ *MX20* — similar to MX12, except 20, 28, or .410 ga. on smaller frame, 2¾ or 3 in. chambers.

Mfg.'s Sug. Retail $8,090	$5,500	$4,400	$3,600	$3,100	$2,700	$2,500	$2,300

▲ *MX28/MX410* — 28 or .410 ga., small frame, 3 in. chambers on .410 ga., flat VR barrels with fixed chokes, fixed trigger (non-removable), straight grip, satin nickel receiver. New 1993.

Mfg.'s Sug. Retail $16,170	$13,650	$10,500	$7,750	$5,950	$4,560	$4,175	$3,800

HUNTING SHOTGUNS: O/U SIDELOCK MODELS

All SHO models were disc. in 1992 (they were available through special order only).

▲ *SHO Older Mfg.* — older models without rebounding hammers are not as desirable.

	$18,000	$15,750	$12,000	$9,500	$8,500	$7,600	$6,800

▲ *SHO Newer Mfg.* — 12 ga. only, introductory sidelock O/U model with bank note game scene engraving on coin finished receiver.

	$35,500	$29,950	$25,000	$20,000	$17,000	$14,500	$12,750

Last Mfg.'s Sug. Retail was $43,000.

P

▲ **SHO Gold Older Mfg.** — older models without rebounding hammers are not as desirable.

	$18,000	$15,750	$12,000	$9,500	$8,500	$7,600	$6,800

▲ **SHO Gold Newer Mfg.** — similar to SHO, except has game scenes in gold relief.

	$38,650	$31,500	$26,500	$21,250	$18,000	$15,500	$13,750

Last Mfg.'s Sug. Retail was $48,000.

▲ **SHO Extra** — importation began 1992.

	$68,750	$54,700	$38,100	$32,000	$26,500	$21,250	$18,000

Last Mfg.'s Sug. Retail was $80,000.

▲ **SHO Gold Extra** — similar to SHO Extra, except has gold inlays. Importation began 1992.

	$72,750	$56,500	$39,500	$33,000	$27,000	$22,000	$18,500

Last Mfg.'s Sug. Retail was $86,000.

HUNTING SHOTGUNS: SxS SIDELOCK MODELS

DHO Models have not been included within the scope of this text due to the extreme rarity factor. Please contact Perazzi, USA for more information on these models and current pricing.

Deduct 40% without rebounding hammers on older DHO models.

PEREGRINE INDUSTRIES, INC.

Manufacturer located in Huntington Beach, CA beginning 1991. Dealer direct sales only.

While advertised, Peregrine has yet to manufacture the Falcon Model.

PERUGINI-VISINI

Manufacturer located in Brescia, Italy. Rifles were previously imported and distributed until 1992 by W.L. Moore, located in Westlake Village, CA. All other models listed below were previously imported and distributed by Armes De Chasse located in Chadds Ford, PA until 1988.

As this edition went to press, Perugini-Visini did not have an importer for the U.S. Please contact the factory directly for more information (see listing in Trademark Index).

RIFLES

STANDARD MODEL: BOLT ACTION — available in most U.S. and metric cals., Mauser 98K action, 24 or 26 in. barrel, 3 shot mag.(non-detachable), matte finished European walnut, high polish bluing, no sights. Importation disc. 1987.

	$4,250	$3,800	$3,400	$2,950	$2,500	$2,000	$1,800

Last Mfg.'s Sug. Retail was $4,250.

DELUXE MODEL: BOLT ACTION — similar to Standard Model, except has finely checkered oil finished walnut stock, sights, knurled bolt handle, and is cased. Importation disc. 1987.

	$4,250	$3,800	$3,400	$2,950	$2,500	$2,000	$1,800

Last Mfg.'s Sug. Retail was $4,250.

MODEL EAGLE: SINGLE SHOT — available in most U.S. and metric cals., Anson & Deeley type action, ejector, sights, adj. trigger, oil finished finely checkered European walnut stock, 24 or 26 in. Hammerli barrel. Importation disc. 1987.

	$5,255	$4,500	$3,800	$3,400	$2,950	$2,500	$2,000

Last Mfg.'s Sug. Retail was $5,255.

MODEL VICTORIA M SxS — .30-06 (disc.), 7x57R, 7x65R, or 9.3x74R cal., Anson & Deeley type boxlock action, border engraving, ejectors, folding leaf rear sight, DTs, 24 or 26 in. monobloc barrels with chopper lumps, leather cased. Importation disc. 1992.

	$7,000	$5,700	$4,600	$3,500	$2,950	$2,500	$2,000

Last Mfg.'s Sug. Retail was $7,900.

▲ **Model Victoria D Mag. SxS** — similar to Model Victoria, except in .375 H&H, .458 Win., .470 NE, or .500-3 in. NE cal., demi-bloc barrels, and has elaborate engraving. Importation disc. 1992.

	$10,950	$9,150	$8,200	$7,400	$6,600	$5,800	$5,100

Last Mfg.'s Sug. Retail was $13,750.

Grading	100%	98%	95%	90%	80%	70%	60%

MODEL SELOUS SxS — 9.3x74R, .375 H&H, .458 Win. Mag., .470 NE, or .500 3 in. NE cal., H&H style detachable sidelock action, ejectors, folding leaf rear sight, border engraving with best quality checkered walnut, top-of-the-line model, leather cased. Importation disc. 1992.

	$23,000	$18,500	$15,000	$12,000	$10,000	$9,000	$8,150

Last Mfg.'s Sug. Retail was $26,000.

BOXLOCK EXPRESS SxS — .444 Marlin or 9.3x74R cal., Anson & Deeley boxlock action, ejectors, color case hardened frame, iron sights. Importation disc. 1989.

	$3,150	$2,800	$2,500	$2,200	$1,950	$1,700	$1,475

Last Mfg.'s Sug. Retail was $3,500.

BOXLOCK MAGNUM O/U — .270 Win., .375 H&H, or .458 Win. Mag. cal., Anson & Deeley boxlock action, ejectors, monobloc barrels, select walnut. Importation disc. 1989.

	$5,500	$4,900	$4,300	$3,750	$3,100	$2,600	$2,200

Last Mfg.'s Sug. Retail was $6,100.

SIDELOCK SUPER EXPRESS SxS — choice of 9 different cals. including .470 Nitro Express, H&H patterned sidelocks, chopper lump barrels, third lever fastener, multi-leaf express sights, coin finished or case hardened receiver, engraving patterns optional. Importation disc. 1989.

	$9,500	$8,400	$7,400	$6,850	$6,100	$5,600	$5,000

Last Mfg.'s Sug. Retail was $10,500.

SHOTGUNS

LIBERTY MODEL — 12, 20, 28, or .410 ga., Anson & Deeley type engraved action, 28 in. chopper lump barrels, double Purdey-type lock, ejectors, leather cased. Importation disc. 1989.

	$5,255	$4,500	$3,800	$3,400	$2,950	$2,500	$2,000

Last Mfg.'s Sug. Retail was $5,255.

CLASSIC MODEL — 12 or 20 ga., H&H style scroll engraved sidelock action, 28 in. chopper lump barrels, double Purdey-type lock, best quality checkered walnut stock and forearm, top-of-the-line model, leather cased. Importation disc. 1989.

	$10,970	$8,650	$7,500	$6,925	$6,200	$5,675	$5,050

Last Mfg.'s Sug. Retail was $10,970.

PETERS STAHL GmbH

Manufacturer located in Paderborn, Germany.

Peters Stahl manufactures high quality semi-auto pistols based on the Model 1911 design but to date, has had little domestic importation. In the past, Peters Stahl has manufactured guns for Federal Ordnance, Omega, Schuetzen Pistol Works, and Springfield Armory.

PHELPS MFG. CO.

Current manufacturer located in Evansville, IN.

Phelps Manufacturing Company began shipping guns in early 1978. Phelps guns are investment-cast in 4140 steel, with basic single-action simplicity, using a transfer bar in the action. Currently, Phelps Mfg. Co. has limited quantities remaining of the pistols listed below.

HERITAGE I — .45-70 cal., single action revolver, incorporates transfer bar hammer safety, blue finish (standard), nickel (optional), adj. rear sight, 8 in. barrel standard, other barrel lengths up to 20 in. available, 6 lbs.

Mfg.'s Sug. Retail	$2,250		$2,050	$1,675	$1,425

Add $20 for each additional in. of barrel.

EAGLE I — .444 Marlin cal., single action revolver, blue finish, adj. rear sight, barrel options same as Heritage I, 6 lbs.

Mfg.'s Sug. Retail	$2,250		$2,050	$1,675	$1,425

PATRIOT — .375 Win. cal., single action revolver, blue finish, adj. rear sight, barrel options are the same as Heritage I. Limited mfg. 1993-94.

	$1,925	$1,550	$1,350

Last Mfg.'s Sug. Retail was $2,225.

Grading	100%	98%	95%	90%	80%	70%	60%

GRIZZLY .50-70 — .50-70 cal., otherwise similar to Heritage I. New 1992.
   Mfg.'s Sug. Retail $2,580 $2,300 $1,875 $1,500
      Add $20 for each additional in. of barrel.

PHILLIPS & ROGERS, INC.
Manufacturer located in Conroe, TX since 1992. Dealer direct sales.

In addition to manufacturing the firearms listed below, Phillips & Rogers also makes a multi-caliber conversion cylinder for all Ruger, .357 Mag., new model Blackhawk revolvers - the retail price is $145. Multi-caliber conversion cylinders are also available for the Ruger new Model Blackhawk (allows shooting .45 LC, .45 Win. Mag., or .45 ACP - retail price is $185) and the Ruger Super Blackhawk (converts .44 Mag. to .50 AE - $550).

MEDUSA MODEL 47 REVOLVER — multi-caliber, over 25 cals. in the .355 - .380 diameter range (including .357 Mag., .38 Super, .38 Spl., 9mm Para., etc.), unique design utilizes no half-moon clips or cylinder/barrel changes, 2½, 4, 5, 6, or 8 in. barrel, 6 shot, double action, matte blue finish, rubber or wood grips. New 1993.
   Mfg.'s Sug. Retail $899 $795 $695 $595 $550 $495 $450 $400

UNDERCOVER MODEL — similar cals. as the Medusa Model 47, with the exception of 9mm Win. Mag., 5 shot 2 or 2½ in. barrel, stainless steel or blued finish, rubber grips.
      While advertised, this model has yet to be manufactured.

PHOENIX ARMS
Manufacturer located in Ontario, CA since 1992. Distributor sales only.

PISTOLS: SEMI-AUTO

RAVEN — .25 ACP cal., single action semi-auto, 2⁷⁄₁₆ in. barrel, 6 shot mag., alloy frame, choice of finishes and grips.
   Mfg.'s Sug. Retail $79 $69 $50 $45 $40 $35 $30 $25
      This model is supplied with a magazine disconnect lock.

HP MODEL — .22 LR or .25 ACP cal., single action semi-auto, 3 in. VR barrel, 10 (.25 ACP) or 11 (.22 LR) shot staggered mag., alloy frame, firing pin block safety, adj. rear sight, choice of polished blue or satin nickel finish, mag. lock, 20 oz. New 1994.
   Mfg.'s Sug. Retail $100 $85 $65 $50 $45 $40 $35 $30
      Add $45 for extended 5 in. barrel and mag. conversion kit.

PHOENIX ARMS CO.
Previous importer located in Lowell, MA.

PHOENIX — .25 ACP cal., Belgian semi-auto, previously manufactured by Robar et DeKerkhove located in Liege, Belgium.
      This trademark is rarely encountered - values would start at $350 and go up according to original condition.

PIETTA, F.LLI
Manufacturer located in Gussago, Italy.

Pietta manufactures black powder and modern firearms reproductions in many configurations for various American companies including Navy Arms, Dixie Gun Works, Mitchell Arms, K.B.I., and others. Please refer to the individual company headings in the Black Powder section of this text for more information on Pietta manufactured firearms, or contact the factory directly for a comprehensive catalog listing of the wide assortment of firearms this company manufactures (see Trademark Index).

P

PIOTTI

Manufacturer located in Brescia, Italy. Currently imported and distributed exclusively by W.L. Moore & Co. located in Westlake Village, CA.

Fratelli Piotti is one of Italy's premier gunmakers. These shotguns meet the highest British standards of craftsmanship and are made to customer specifications. Variety of gauges, engraving, styles, chokes, etc.

> For the following models — add $1,400 for single trigger, $600 for hand-detachable locks, approx. $850 for leather case, $600 for 16 or 20 ga., $800 for 28 or .410 ga. boxlock, $1,600 for 28 or .410 ga. sidelock.

Grading	100%	98%	95%	90%	80%	70%	60%

SHOTGUNS

PIUMA (BSEE) SxS — 12, 16, 20, 28, or .410 ga., Anson & Deeley boxlock ejector double with chopper double barrels, level file-cut rib, light scroll and rosette engraving, scalloped frame.
Mfg.'s Sug. Retail $11,800 $10,250 $8,950 $7,800 $6,700 $5,600 $4,500 $3,400

WESTLAKE SxS — 12, 16, 20, 28, or .410 ga., H&H sidelock action, moderate scroll engraving. Mfg. disc. 1989.
$8,500 $7,500 $6,050 $5,300 $4,700 $4,200 $3,750
Last Mfg.'s Sug. Retail was $8,400.

MONTE CARLO SxS — 12, 16, 20, 28, or .410 ga., best-quality H&H pattern sidelock ejector double with chopper lump barrels, Purdey style scroll and rosette engraving. Importation disc. 1990.
$10,500 $9,250 $8,200 $7,100 $6,000 $5,000 $4,500
Last Mfg.'s Sug. Retail was $11,400.

KING NUMBER 1 SxS — 12, 16, 20, 28, or .410 ga., best-quality H&H pattern sidelock ejector double with chopper lump barrels, level file-cut rib, very fine, full coverage scroll engraving with small floral bouquets, gold crest in forearm, gold crown in top lever, name in gold and finely figured wood.
Mfg.'s Sug. Retail $20,600 $17,750 $14,750 $11,750 $9,250 $7,650 $6,600 $5,500

LUNIK SxS — 12, 16, 20, 28, or .410 ga., best-quality H&H pattern sidelock ejector double with lump (demi-bloc) barrels, level, file-cut rib, Renaissance style large scroll engraving in relief, gold crown in top lever, gold name, and gold crest in forearm, finely figured wood.
Mfg.'s Sug. Retail $22,200 $19,000 $15,750 $12,500 $9,750 $8,000 $6,900 $5,850

KING EXTRA SxS — 12, 16, 20, 28, or .410 ga., best-quality H&H pattern sidelock ejector double with chopper lump barrels, level file-cut rib, choice of either bulino game scene engraving or game scene engraving with gold inlays, engraved and signed by a master engraver, exhibition grade wood.
Mfg.'s Sug. Retail $22,500 $20,000 $16,750 $13,750 $9,950 $8,250 $7,000 $5,850

MONACO NUMBER 1 OR 2 SxS — 12, 16, 20, 28, or .410 ga., best-quality H&H pattern sidelock ejector double with lump (demi-bloc) barrels, level, file-cut rib, Renaissance style large scroll engraving in relief, gold crown in top lever, gold name, and gold crest in forearm, finely figured wood.
Mfg.'s Sug. Retail $29,300 $25,250 $20,750 $17,000 $14,250 $11,750 $9,950 $8,450

MONACO NUMBER 4 SxS — top-of-the-line model with every refinement incorporated. Custom order only and extremely rare.
Mfg.'s Sug. Retail $40,000 $35,000 $28,000 $23,000 $18,750 $15,000 $11,750 $9,950

PIOTTI O/U — 12 or 20 ga., 3 in. chambers, 26-32 in. barrels, single or double triggers, Turkish Circassian walnut, various engraving patterns, 6 lbs - 20 ga., approx. 7½ 12 ga. New 1995.
Mfg.'s Sug. Retail $35,600 $29,000 $23,500 $19,250 $15,750 $12,750 $10,000 $9,100

BOSS O/U — 12 or 20 ga. New 1992.
Mfg.'s Sug. Retail $35,600 $29,000 $23,500 $19,250 $15,750 $12,750 $10,000 $9,100

PIRANHA

Manufactured by Ultima Technologies, Inc. located in Phoenix, AZ beginning late 1996.

Grading	100%	98%	95%	90%	80%	70%	60%

While advertised in the past, the Piranha pistol may be produced later this year. Please contact the factory directly (see Trademark Index) for more information on this pistol.

PIRANHA SEMI-AUTO — .30 Luger, 9mm Para., or 9mm Largo cal., semi-auto, various barrel lengths, caliber changes with barrel change, unique action removes 85% of recoil, 2.7 lbs. Mfg. to begin late 1996.

While retail has yet to be established, the 1996 MSR is projected at approx. $600.

POLY TECHNOLOGIES, INC.

Distributed by PTK International, Inc. located in Atlanta, GA. Previously imported by Keng's Firearms Specialty, Inc., located in Riverdale, GA. Manufactured in China by Poly Technologies, Inc.

Poly Technologies commercial firearms are made to Chinese military specifications and have excellent quality control.

These models have been banned from domestic importation due to 1989 Federal legislation.

RIFLES/CARBINES: SEMI-AUTO

POLY TECH AKS-762 — 7.62x39mm K or .223 Rem. cal., 16¼ in. barrel, semi-auto version of the Chinese AKM (Type 56) paramilitary design rifle, 8.4 lbs., wood stock. Imported 1988-89.

	100%	98%	95%	90%	80%	70%	60%
	$525	$460	$415	$365	$300	$250	$230

Last Mfg.'s Sug. Retail was $400.

Add $25 for side-fold plastic stock.

This model was also available with a downward folding stock at no extra charge.

CHINESE SKS — 7.62x39mm Soviet military, 20⁹⁄₂₀ in. barrel, full wood stock, machine steel parts to Chinese military specifications, 7.9 lbs. Imported 1988-89.

	100%	98%	95%	90%	80%	70%	60%
	$295	$270	$230	$200	$175	$140	$130

Last Mfg.'s Sug. Retail was $200.

RUSSIAN AK-47/S (LEGEND) — 7.62x39mm Soviet military, 16³⁄₈ in. barrel, semi-auto configuration of the original AK-47, fixed, side-folding, or under-folding stock, with or w/o spike bayonet, 8.2 lbs. Imported 1988-89.

	100%	98%	95%	90%	80%	70%	60%
	$875	$775	$700	$650	$600	$525	$450

Last Mfg.'s Sug. Retail was $550.

The S suffix in this variation designates third model specifications.

▲ *National Match Legend* — utilizes match parts in fabrication.

	100%	98%	95%	90%	80%	70%	60%
	$975	$850	$725	$650	$600	$525	$450

U.S. M-14/S — .308 cal., semi-auto, 22 in. barrel, forged receiver, patterned after the famous M-14, 9.2 lbs. Imported 1988-89.

	100%	98%	95%	90%	80%	70%	60%
	$675	$625	$550	$495	$420	$385	$360

Last Mfg.'s Sug. Retail was $700.

POWELL, WILLIAM & SON (GUNMAKERS) LTD.

Please refer to the W Section for this Trademark.

PRANDELLI-GASPERINI

Previous manufacturer located in Brescia, Italy. Previously imported by Richland Arms located in Blissfield, MI.

Prandelli-Gasperini made both O/U and S X S shotguns in either sidelock or boxlock. Currently, older boxlock models start at approx. $550 (assuming 80% or better original condition). Sidelock models in similar condition usually start at $1,650, depending on gauge, embellishments, and condition.

Approx. 250 specimens of this trademark were imported during Richland Arms importation.

P

PRECISION SMALL ARMS

Manufactured in Charlottesville, VA under F.N. license in the U.S by Precision Small Arms located in Beverly Hills, CA. Dealer and Distributor sales.

Grading	100%	98%	95%	90%	80%	70%	60%

PSP-25 PISTOL — .25 ACP, semi-auto, single action, patterned after the Baby Browning, 2.2 ⅛ in. barrel, 6 shot mag., black polymer grips, all steel construction with high polish finish, dual safety system, wt. 9.5 oz. New 1989.

Mfg.'s Sug. Retail	$249	$220	$190	$175	$160	$150	$140	$130

Add $52 for industrial chrome/brushed chrome satin finish.

This pistol is mfg. in the U.S. under license from Fabrique Nationale.

▲ *PSP-25 Stainless Steel* — features stainless steel construction. New 1996.

Mfg.'s Sug. Retail	$327	$285	$230	$195

▲ *PSP-25 Featherweight* — features aircraft aluminum frame with chromed slide and mag., gold-plated trigger. New 1996.

Mfg.'s Sug. Retail	$375	$315	$250	$225	$200	$185	$170	$160

▲ *PSP-25 Renaissance* — features chrome receiver with full coverage scroll engraving. New 1996.

Mfg.'s Sug. Retail	$925	$825	$675	$500

▲ *PSP Signature Editions* — similar to above, except has "Michael B. Kassnar" signature on left slide top in gold. Mfg. 1989-91.

	$325	$295	$260	$230	$200	$175	$160

Last Mfg.'s Sug. Retail was $385.

There were also two limited editions (less than 10 mfg.) which retailed for $1,458 and approx. $2,150.

PREMIER

Previously manufactured in Italy and Spain.

SHOTGUNS: SIDE-BY-SIDE

REGENT DOUBLE BARREL SHOTGUN — 12, 16, 20, 28, or .410 ga., 26, 28, or 30 in. barrels, various chokes, checkered pistol grip stock and beavertail forearm. Mfg. 1955-disc.

	$275	$250	$220	$195	$140	$110	$100

REGENT MAGNUM EXPRESS — 12 ga., 3 in. chambers only, 30 in. full, recoil pad. Mfg. 1957-disc.

	$305	$275	$250	$220	$165	$140	$110

REGENT 10 GAUGE MAGNUM — similar to 12 ga. Mag., but 10 ga., 3½ in. chamber, 32 in. full and full. Mfg. 1975-disc.

	$330	$305	$275	$250	$195	$165	$140

BRUSH KING — 12 or 20 ga., 22 in. imp. cyl. and mod. barrels, straight grip stock. Mfg. 1959-disc.

	$275	$250	$220	$195	$140	$110	$100

MONARCH SUPREME GRADE — 12 or 20 ga., 26 or 28 in. barrels, various chokes, boxlock, auto ejectors, select stock. Mfg. 1959-disc.

	$440	$385	$360	$330	$275	$250	$200

PRESENTATION CUSTOM GRADE — custom made, gold and silver game scene. Mfg. 1959-disc.

	$1,100	$990	$880	$825	$715	$605	$495

AMBASSADOR MODEL — 12, 16, 20, or .410 ga., 26 or 28 in. barrels, mod. and full choke, checkered pistol grip stock. Mfg. 1957-disc.

	$385	$360	$330	$305	$250	$220	$195

Note: The Premier is a trade name for guns that have been produced in both Spain and Italy for various importers.

PRINZ

Manufacturer of bolt action rifles, single shot rifles, and combination guns. Previously imported and distributed by Helmut Hofmann Inc. located in Placitas, NM.

Grading	100%	98%	95%	90%	80%	70%	60%

GRADE 1 BOLT ACTION — .243 Win., .30-06, .308 Win., .300 Win. Mag. or 7mm Rem. Mag. cal., single or double set trigger(s), oil finished walnut stock.

	100%	98%	95%	90%	80%	70%	60%
	$495	$440	$385	$360	$330	$275	$250

▲ *Grade 1 Carbine* — similar to Grade 1 except has carbine barrel.

	$570	$495	$435	$390	$360	$330	$275

GRADE 2 BOLT ACTION — similar to Grade 1 except has rosewood forend cap.

	$545	$485	$425	$385	$360	$330	$275

TIP UP RIFLE — available in 8 cals. between .222 Rem. and .30-06, high quality and limited mfg. Importation began 1989.

	$2,175	$1,900	$1,675	$1,375	$1,100	$950	$775

PRINCESS MODEL 85 — combination gun available in 12 ga. (2¾ in. chamber) and choice of 8 cals. between .222 Rem. and .30-06.

	$1,450	$1,275	$1,100	$925	$800	$775	$650

This model comes standard with a leather case.

PURDEY, JAMES & SONS, LTD.

Manufacturer located in London, England. Purdey has been making top quality firearms since 1814 - annual production is approximately 55 guns.

Purdey guns have long been regarded as among the finest in the world. They have typically been made to customer specifications, and as such, should be appraised individually for purposes of evaluation. Values vary with gauge, barrel length, chamber length and age. Listed below are the modern models and approximate values for reference purposes - including currently mfg. models computed at an exchange rate of 1 pound = $1.57 Please secure several qualified appraisals before buying or selling Purdey long guns.

RIFLES

Prices listed below for rifles are for new guns only, with standard fine engraving.

PURDEY DOUBLE RIFLE — various English Nitro Express cals., 25½ in. barrels, folding leaf sight, checkered pistol grip stock, recoil pad, sidelock, auto ejectors. Mfg. pre-WWII and post-war.

▲ *Smaller calibers.* — .300 H&H or .375 H&H cal.

		100%	98%	95%	90%	80%	70%	60%
Mfg.'s Sug. Retail	$75,753	$75,753	$54,750	$42,250	$31,650	$26,500	$21,500	$16,950

▲ *Large calibers.*
➤ .470 NE

		100%	98%	95%	90%	80%	70%	60%
Mfg.'s Sug. Retail	$78,893	$78,893	$64,250	$46,750	$37,500	$30,250	$26,500	$22,750

➤ .577 NE

		100%	98%	95%	90%	80%	70%	60%
Mfg.'s Sug. Retail	$88,705	$88,705	$77,385	$64,250	$46,750	$37,500	$30,250	$26,500

➤ .600 NE

		100%	98%	95%	90%	80%	70%	60%
Mfg.'s Sug. Retail	$90,275	$90,275	$78,500	$65,750	$46,750	$37,500	$30,250	$26,500

The above values represent guidelines only for this trademark. Since each Purdey is basically a special order, new gun pricing is calculated per individual customer work order.

MAGAZINE RIFLE — Mauser type bolt action, 7x57mm, .300 H&H Mag., or 10.75x73mm cal., 24 in. barrel, folding leaf sight, checkered pistol grip stock.

	$6,875	$5,750	$4,500	$3,800	$3,500	$3,000	$2,500

Add a premium for large cals.

Grading	100%	98%	95%	90%	80%	70%	60%

SHOTGUNS

BEST QUALITY GAME GUN SxS — 12, 16, or 20 ga., 26-30 in. barrels, any choke and style of rib, checkered straight or pistol grip stock. Mfg. 1880-present, auto ejector gun, best quality only.

		100%	98%	95%	90%	80%	70%	60%
Mfg.'s Sug. Retail	$45,138	$45,138	$36,750	$29,250	$27,350	$19,500	$17,000	$14,250

Add $1,962 for 28 or .410 ga. on new mfg.
Add approx. $10,520 for extra set of barrels depending on gauge.

▲ *Older mfg.*

	100%	98%	95%	90%	80%	70%	60%
Game gun	$23,450	$19,000	$15,750	$13,500	$11,000	$9,500	$8,750
Heavy Duck gun	$20,500	$17,000	$14,000	$11,000	$9,500	$8,750	$8,000

Add 50% for 20 ga.
Add 35%-50% for 28 or .410 ga.
Deduct 10% if not cased with accessories.
Add $1,000 for SST.

O/U GUN — 12, 16, 20, or 28 ga., 26-30 in. barrels, any choke, sidelock, auto ejectors, ST, checkered straight or pistol grip stock. Since WWII, Purdey has taken over the Woodward Company, and later guns have the Woodward O/U action. Very few early actions; early guns - ⅓ less.

		100%	98%	95%	90%	80%	70%	60%
Mfg.'s Sug. Retail	$57,305	$57,305	$42,650	$35,000	$28,750	$23,650	$19,950	$17,000

Add $3,140 for 28 or .410 ga.
Add $15,465 for extra set of barrels.

▲ *Older mfg.*

	100%	98%	95%	90%	80%	70%	60%
	$37,500	$33,000	$30,000	$26,000	$21,500	$17,750	$15,000

Add $3,000 for Woodward action.
Add 25% for 20 ga.
Add 60%+ for 28 ga.
Add 10% for SST.

SINGLE BARREL TRAP GUN — 12 ga. Purdey action only, similar to O/U specifications. Mfg. prior to WWII.

	100%	98%	95%	90%	80%	70%	60%
	$11,250	$10,000	$8,750	$7,900	$7,200	$6,750	$5,950

Q section

QFI (QUALITY FIREARMS INC.)
Previous manufacturer located in Opa Locka, FL December, 1990-1992.

Grading	100%	98%	95%	90%	80%	70%	60%

PISTOLS: SEMI-AUTO

MODEL LA380 — .380 ACP cal., single action semi-auto, 6-shot, magazine disconnect, hammer, trigger, and firing pin block safety, 3¼ in. barrel, blue or chrome finish. Mfg. 1991-1992.

	100%	98%	95%	90%	80%	70%	60%
	$125	$100	$90	$80	$70	$60	$55

Last Mfg.'s Sug. Retail was $147.

Add $23 for chrome finish.

▲ **Model LA380SS** — stainless steel variation of the Model LA380. Mfg. 1992 only.

	100%	98%	95%
	$195	$165	$135

Last Mfg.'s Sug. Retail was $220.

MODEL SA 25 — .25 ACP cal., semi-auto single action, 2½ in. barrel, 6-shot, includes inertial firing pin, external exposed hammer with half cock, and trigger blocking thumb safety, blue, dynachrome, or blue/gold finish, smooth walnut grips. Mfg. 1991 only.

	100%	98%	95%	90%	80%	70%	60%
	$55	$45	$40	$35	$30	$25	$25

Last Mfg.'s Sug. Retail was $55.

Add $50 for blue/gold finish.
Add $10 for chrome finish with pearlite plastic grips.

TIGRESS MODEL — .25 ACP or .380 ACP cal., semi-auto single action, 2½ (.25 ACP) or 3¼ (.380 ACP) in. barrel, blue frame with gold-plated slide, 6-shot with finger extension on mag., white polymer grips with a red rose scrimshawed on both sides, designed for women, supplied with zippered gold pouch, 14 or 25 oz. Mfg. 1991 only.

	100%	98%	95%	90%	80%	70%	60%
	$130	$100	$90	$80	$70	$60	$55

Last Mfg.'s Sug. Retail was $155.

Add $85 for .380 ACP cal.

REVOLVERS: DOUBLE ACTION
All pistols under this heading are 6-shot.

RP SERIES STANDARD REVOLVER — .22 LR, .22 Mag., .32 S&W Long, .32 Mag. or .38 Spl., 2 or 4 in. barrel, blued or chrome finish, fixed sights, hammer block safety, without ejector assembly, composition grips. Mfg. in U.S. 1990-disc.

	100%	98%	95%	90%	80%	70%	60%
	$85	$70	$65	$60	$55	$50	$45

Last Mfg.'s Sug. Retail was $105.

Add $15-20 for chrome finish.
Add approx. $5 for 4 in. barrel.

MODEL SO 38 — .38 Spl., swing out cylinder, 6-shot, 2 in. SR or 4 in. VR barrel, hammer block safety, composition grips. Mfg. 1991 only.

	100%	98%	95%	90%	80%	70%	60%
	$175	$135	$115	$95	$80	$75	$65

Last Mfg.'s Sug. Retail was $175.

REVOLVERS: SINGLE ACTION

SAA WESTERN RANGER — .22 LR cal., 6-shot, 3, 4 (disc. 1991), 4¾ (new 1992), 6 (disc. 1991), 6½ (new 1992), 7 (disc. 1991), or 9 in. barrel, blue finish with gold accenting, walnut grips. Mfg. 1991-1992.

	100%	98%	95%	90%	80%	70%	60%
	$85	$70	$65	$60	$55	$50	$45

Last Mfg.'s Sug. Retail was $105.

Add approx. $5 for 7 (disc.) or $7 for 9 in. barrel.
Add approx. $15-35 for .22 Mag. extra cylinder (combo).

Grading	100%	98%	95%	90%	80%	70%	60%

SAA PLAINS RIDER — similar to Western Ranger, except has black composition grips and no gold accenting. Mfg. 1991-1992.

| | $80 | $65 | $55 | $50 | $45 | $40 | $35 |

Last Mfg.'s Sug. Retail was $100.

　　　Add $11 for 9 in. barrel.
　　　Add approx. $26 for .22 Mag. extra cylinder (combo).

SAA HORSEMAN SERIES — .357 Mag., .44 Mag., or .45 LC cal., 6-shot, 6½ or 7½ in. barrel, color case hardened or blue (Dark Horseman only) finish, walnut or black composition grips, hammer block safety. Mfg. 1991 only.

| | $250 | $220 | $190 | $170 | $150 | $130 | $115 |

Last Mfg.'s Sug. Retail was $250.

　　　The Dark Horseman has an extended grip frame with black composition grips and an adj. rear sight.

QUAIL UNLIMITED, INC.

National hunting organization with national headquarters located in Edgefield, SC.

Although Quail Unlimited, Inc. is not a manufacturer or importer, this organization has been responsible for many special and limited editions that are listed below with quanities but without secondary market prices since they may vary greatly from region to region. Some of the models (and current values) may be listed under manufacturer listings in this text. Because of the relatively low quantities involved with these special editions, most of the models listed below have premiums currently being asked over issue prices - the amount will vary with the region and acceptance by Quail Unlimited members. Quail Unlimited designated their special editions as follows: 1986 - Grand Slam I - Bobwhite Edition, 1987 - Grand Slam II - California Edition, 1988 - Grand Slam III - Gambel Edition, 1989 - Grand Slam IV - Mountain Quail Edition, 1990 - Grand Slam V - Scaled Quail Edition, 1992 - Gun Dog I - Pointer Edition, 1993 - Gun Dog II - Setter Edition, 1994 - Gun Dog III - Brittany Edition, the Golden Covey Series was also available in the Full Covey Edition (I) and the Bobwhite Edition (II).

MANUFACTURER	MODEL	QUANTITY	YEAR	ISSUE PRICE
Browning	Superposed 20 ga.	100	1986	$2,850
Winchester	Model 101 28 ga.	100	1987	$2,195
Browning	Sweet 16 16 ga.	100	1988	$1,895
Winchester	Model 23 12 ga.	100	1989	$2,885
Browning	Citori Lightning .410 ga.	100	1990	$2,295

Add $500 to issue price for silver finish (standard finish was nickel).
Add $700 to issue price for gold finish (standard finish was nickel).

Browning	Model A-5 20 ga.	100	1992	$1,795
Browning	Citori Lightning 28 ga.	100	1993	$2,395
Browning	Model A-5 12 ga.	100	1993	$1,795
Browning	Model A-5 20 ga.	100	1994	$1,895
Browning	Citori Lightning .410 ga.	100	1994	$2,395
Browning	Model A-5 20 ga.	100	1995	$1,895
Belgian Browning	Model A-5 20 ga. 3 in. GRIII	75	1996 (15th Anniv.)	$2,195
Belgian Browning	Model A-5 20 ga. 3 in. GRV	25	1996 (15th Anniv.)	$3,995
Rizzini	SxS 20 ga.	100	1996 (15th Anniv.)	$2,850
Rizzini	SxS 20 ga. (Gold)	15	1996 (15th Anniv.)	$4,250

QUALITY ARMS, INC.

Importer and sales agent located in Houston, TX.

Quality Arms currently imports Arrieta and Ferlib shotguns in addition to other quality European trademarks. They will also act as an import agent for those individuals who would like to special order a non-domestic trademark with a minimum of dealer mark-up. See the Trademark Index for more information.

QUALITY PARTS CO./BUSHMASTER

A division of Bushmaster Firearms, Inc. located in Windham, ME that manufactures paramilitary rifles patterned after the AR-15. Distributor and dealer sales. Please refer to the Bushmaster section in this text for model listings and values.

Q

Q

R section

RAF

Manufacturer of shotguns and rifles located in St. Etienne France beginning 1994.

RAF manufactures both superposed rifles, shotguns, combination guns, and semi-auto rimfire rifles. To obtain more information about a current line-up of RAF firearms, please contact the factory directly (see Trademark Index).

RND MANUFACTURING

Manufacturer located in Longmont, CO. Distributed by Mesa Sportsmen's Association, L.L.C. located in Delta, CO.

THE EDGE — .223 Rem. or .308 Win. cal., semi-auto patterned after the AR-15, CNC machined, 18, 20, or 24 in. barrel, choice of synthetic (Grade I), hand-made laminated thumbhole (Grade II), or custom laminated thumbhole with fluted barrel (Grade III) stock, vented aluminum shroud, approx. 8-10 lbs. New 1996.

Mfg.'s Sug. Retail	$2,495	$2,325	$2,150	$1,800	$1,575	$1,375	$1,200	$1,075

Add $355 for Grade II.
Add $504 for Grade III or .308 Win. cal.

R.G. INDUSTRIES

Importers located in Miami, FL. Operations ceased in January of 1986.

Grading	100%	98%	95%	90%	80%	70%	60%

HANDGUNS

R.G. Industries manufactured and imported plain utilitarian revolvers and semi-auto pistols. Unfortunately, because of the current product liability situation, R.G. Industries was litigated out of business. Whereas their models represent good values, they are not collectible, and a generalized listing is provided below.

RG 14 S, RG 23, RG 31 — prices vary from $61 to $100 retail.

RG 40, RG 74, & HIGHNOON S.A. — prices vary from $125 to $150 retail.

RG 26 SEMI-AUTO — .25 auto, 6 shot mag., 2¼ in. barrel, plastic grips, single action, 12 oz.

	$65	$55	$50	$40	$35	$30	$25

Last Mfg.'s Sug. Retail was $66.

RPM

Manufacturer located in Tucson, AZ. Direct sales only.

PISTOLS: SINGLE SHOT

XL PISTOL — many cals., 8, 10¾, 12, or 14 in. barrel, tip-up action, right or left-hand action.

Mfg.'s Sug. Retail	$925	$875	$825	$750	$675	$600	$550	$500

XL HUNTER — many cals., stainless steel frame, 5¹⁄₁₆ in. under-lug, 12 or 14 in. Douglas barrel, ISGW rear and Patridge front sight, external positive extractor. New 1995.

Mfg.'s Sug. Retail	$1,195	$1,100	$900	$700

Subtract $100 if w/o positive extractor.

RWS

RWS is a trademark of Dynamit Nobel which has been manufacturing firearms in Nuremberg Stadeln, Germany since 1865. RWS firearms were imported until 1995 by Dynamit Nobel of America, Inc. located in

Grading	100%	98%	95%	90%	80%	70%	60%

Closter, NJ. Other trademarks currently being distributed by Dynamit Nobel can be located under individual heading names in this text.

RIFLES: MATCH TARGET

MODEL 820 L — .22 LR only, 24 (disc.) or 26 in. barrel, no. 100 aperture sight, oil polished stock for 3 position match, stippled pistol grip and forearm, recoil pad, adj. trigger, 10.6 lbs. Disc. 1994.

	$1,275	$1,000	$850	$700	$575	$475	$400

Last Mfg.'s Sug. Retail was $1,500.

Previous to 1986 this model was designated the 820 S and was supplied with a no. 75 aperture rear sight.

▲ *Model 820 S* — with Model 82 aperture sight.

	$1,100	$895	$795	$650	$560	$480	$420

Last Mfg.'s Sug. Retail was $995.

MODEL 820 F MATCH — similar to Model 820 L, except has heavy match barrel, 15.4 lbs. Disc. 1994.

	$1,750	$1,400	$1,275	$1,000	$850	$700	$575

Last Mfg.'s Sug. Retail was $2,000.

▲ *Model 820 SF* — with Model 82 aperture sight. Disc.

	$1,125	$900	$795	$650	$560	$480	$420

Last Mfg.'s Sug. Retail was $1,010.

MODEL 820 K — .22 LR only, made for running boar competition, 24 in. barrel, stock similar to Model 820 SF, no sights, 9½ lbs. without barrel weight or scope. Importation disc. 1986.

	$900	$775	$695	$615	$540	$470	$420

Last Mfg.'s Sug. Retail was $870.

RADOM

Polish Arsenal, located in Radom, Poland.

RADOM REVOLVER — Nagant design, dated 1931-1936.

	$1,100	$850	$700	$550	$400	$300	$200

P-35 AUTOMATIC — 9mm, 8 shot, 4¾ in. barrel, blue, fixed sights, plastic grips. Mfg. 1935-WWII.

▲ *Polish Eagle* — dated 1936, 1937 (scarcest date), 1938, or 1939.

	$1,850	$1,425	$1,000	$700	$500	$400	$300

▲ *Polish Eagle Nazi Capture*

	$2,500	$1,825	$1,200	$900	$700	$600	$500

▲ *Nazi Type I Slotted*

	$550	$450	$350	$295	$230	$180	$150

▲ *Nazi Type II No Slot w/Takedown Lever*

	$400	$325	$275	$225	$200	$185	$150

▲ *Nazi Type III No Slot, No Takedown Lever*

	$315	$275	$240	$200	$180	$160	$140

▲ *Nazi Type III* — parkerized with wood grips, small parts blued.

	$600	$475	$350	$295	$230	$200	$175

Note: Certain Radoms with German acceptance marks will bring a premium.

RAM-LINE, INC.

Previous manufacturer located in Grand Junction, CO until 1995.

In addition to the Ram-Tech pistol, Ram-Line, Inc. also manufactured a complete line of synthetic and woodstocks for a variety of firearms. Ram-Line also manufactured a complete line of magazines for most popular pistols and rifles.

Grading	100%	98%	95%	90%	80%	70%	60%

EXACTOR PISTOL — .22 LR cal., single action semi-auto, aircraft alloy receiver with 5½ in. polymer VR barrel and steel liner, unique two-motion safety featuring blocks on hammer, trigger, and sear, 15 shot mag., matte finish, easy disassembly, injected molded grip, fixed sight, 20.3 oz., supplied with case. Mfg. 1990-93.

	$195	$165	$135

Last Mfg.'s Sug. Retail was $225.

▲ *Target Exactor* — similar to above, except has 7½ in. barrel, 23 oz. Disc. 1993.

	$265	$230	$195

Last Mfg.'s Sug. Retail was $300.

RAM-TECH PISTOL — similar to Exactor pistol, except 4½ in. barrel w/o VR. Mfg. 1994-95.

	$175	$145	$125

Last Mfg.'s Sug. Retail was $200.

RANDALL FIREARMS COMPANY

Previously manufactured in Sun Valley, CA. Manufactured between June 7, 1983 and December 15, 1984 - final plant closing was June 15, 1985.

Before manufacturing ceased in May of 1985, 24 models with 12 variations in 3 different calibers had been produced. In some instances, production on certain models was very limited and premiums for these low volume niches are starting to develop. Between June of 1983 and May of 1984, 9,968 handguns were manufactured with 75% of all 9mm cals. being exported to Europe, and 35% of 9mm production employing a 10 groove barrel. Models manufactured after 1984 came equipped with an extended slide stop, long trigger and beavertail grip safety. Production ser. no.'s started at 02000 for right hand models and 02100 for left hand models. All but the first 200 (approx.) serial numbers started with "RF" and ended with "C" or "W". A few rare mis-marks are in circulation. Total mfg. for all models and variations was 9,968. Randall prototype serialization starts with a "T" — less than 45 were manufactured and these specimens command up to a 50% premium. In addition, 78 serial numbers under 2,000 were manufactured by special order.

Models below are generally described with values per specific variations listed afterward.

PISTOLS: SEMI-AUTO

The following is a complete listing for Randall Firearms variations including production statistics. Values shown below represent recent aftermarket prices, but it should be noted regional interest can change these prices significantly. Despite being discontinued a relatively short time ago, Randall pistols are currently enjoying good demand.

All original Randall pistols had no blued parts. Only the front and rear sights were finished in black oxide.

Add 10%-20% for original factory boxes and paperwork.
Add 50% for prototypes with "T" serial numbers.

COMBAT MODEL — same size as Service Model, ribbed top fixed sight slide, Pachmayr grips on right hand model only, left hand models had Herrett walnut grips. While this model was advertised as having a flat mainspring housing, it was never produced.

Last Mfg.'s Sug. Retail was $549.

RAIDER/SERVICE MODEL-C — 9mm or .45 ACP cal., Colt Commander Model design, 4¼ in. barrel, 36 oz., total stainless steel construction. Add $130 for adj. sights/ribbed slide, available in either right-hand or left-hand (only 2 mfg.) model. Roll-marked Service Model-C in 1983 and Raider in 1984.

Last Mfg.'s Sug. Retail was $460.

▲ *Raider/Service Model-C Featherweight* — .45 ACP only, alloy receiver, stainless steel slide, roll-marked Service Model-C, T-type serial numbers, 29 oz. Disc. 1984, only 4 mfg.

FULL SIZE SERVICE MODEL — .38 Super, 9mm, or .45 ACP cal., Colt Model 1911 A1 design, 5 in. barrel, total stainless steel construction, 38 oz. Available in either right-hand or left-hand model.

Last Mfg.'s Sug. Retail was $460.

Grading	100%	98%	95%	90%	80%	70%	60%

CURTIS E. LEMAY 4-STAR MODEL — 9mm or .45 ACP cal., Gen. Curtis E. LeMay design, 4¼ in. barrel, 6 (.45 ACP) or 7 (9mm) shot mag., total stainless steel construction, 35 oz. Available in either right-hand or left-hand model, left hand models are a true mirror image with over 17 major parts changes.

Last Mfg.'s Sug. Retail was $533.

This model was ½ in. shorter in magazine well and had a cast, squared off triggerguard compared to the Colt 1911A1 design.

▲ *Curtis E. LeMay Featherweight Model* — .45 ACP cal. only, alloy receiver, stainless steel slide, T-type serial numbers, 28 oz. Disc. 1984 (only one mfg.).

RANDALL MATCHED SETS — .45 ACP cal. only, each set consisted of a right-hand and a left-hand Service Model with matching serial numbers. Only 4 sets were mfg. on a special order basis. A111/B111 model configuration.

Last Mfg.'s Sug. Retail was $1,250.

RANDALL VARIATIONS

IDENTIFYING RANDALL MODELS:

Randall pistols are denoted by a four-character model notation, starting with an alphabetical prefix followed by three digits. The alphabetical prefix will be either A, B, or C — A designates right-hand configuration only, B designates left-hand configuration only, and C designates right-hand lightweight model. The first digit will be 1, 2, or 3 — 1 denotes Service Model, 2 denotes Service Model-C or Raider, 3 represents the C.E. LeMay Model. The second digit again will be either 1, 2, or 3 — 1 designates round top and fixed sight slide, 2 denotes flat top fixed sight slide, and 3 represents adj. sights, flat top frame. The third digit again, is either 1, 2, or 3 — 1 denotes .45 ACP cal., 2 designates 9mm Para., and 3 represents .38 Super. Hence, if you had a left-hand Randall in the service model size with a flat top adj. sight slide, and in .45 ACP cal., your model would be a B131. These model codes are not marked on the pistols.

▲ *A111* — 3,421 mfg.

	$680	$595	$510	$465

Five A111s were mfg. with Austrian proof marks with premiums existing (one NIB specimen recently sold for $3,000).

▲ *A112* — 301 mfg.

	$895	$795	$650	$525

▲ *A121* — 1067 mfg.

	$700	$625	$510	$465

▲ *A122* — 19 mfg.

	$1,325	$1,125	$940	$795

▲ *A131* — 2083 mfg.

	$725	$640	$535	$495

▲ *A211* — 992 mfg.

	$750	$660	$535	$480

▲ *A212* — 76 mfg.

	$925	$815	$600	$500

▲ *A231* — 574 mfg.

	$850	$750	$535	$505

▲ *A232* — 5 mfg.

	$1,500	$1,075	$990	$775

▲ *A311* — 361 mfg.

	$1,100	$950	$725	$575

Most LeMay models (4¼ in. barrel) were shipped in gunrugs without a factory box. Original factory LeMay boxes are rare — add 10% premium. Beware of Randall LeMay and service model pistols made from parts kits. There were 226 LeMay receivers and 322 service model receivers (all right hand) sold that could be parts guns. Accordingly, values are less for parts guns. A parts gun listing is available for $20.

Grading	100%	98%	95%	90%	80%	70%	60%

▲ **A312** — 1 mfg.
Too rare to evaluate.

▲ **A331** — 293 mfg.

	100%	98%	95%	90%
	$1,200	$1,075	$700	$595

The note that appears for the Model A311 also applies to this variation.

▲ **A332** — 9 mfg.

	100%	98%	95%	90%
	$1,450	$1,275	$975	$825

▲ **B111** — 297 mfg.

	100%	98%	95%	90%
	$1,250	$1,100	$850	$750

▲ **B121** — 110 mfg.

	100%	98%	95%	90%
	$1,500	$1,325	$1,075	$895

▲ **B122** — 2 mfg.
Extreme rarity precludes accurate price evaluation.

▲ **B123** — 2 mfg.
Extreme rarity precludes accurate price evaluation.

▲ **B131** — 225 mfg.

	100%	98%	95%	90%
	$1,450	$1,250	$925	$775

▲ **B311** — 52 mfg.

	100%	98%	95%	90%
	$1,575	$1,325	$895	$750

▲ **B312 w/.45 ACP factory conversion** — 1 mfg.
Rarity precludes accurate price evaluation.

▲ **B312** — 9 mfg.

	100%	98%	95%	90%
	$2,750	$2,300	$1,800	$1,550

▲ **B321** — 1 mfg.
Rarity precludes accurate price evaluation. The B321 was the only factory 3-slide set. It was fitted with the 3 different LH LeMay slides available (B311, B321, & B331). This model was mirror polished, engraved, and had ivory grips with the Randall logo.

▲ **B331** — 45 mfg.

	100%	98%	95%	90%
	$1,775	$1,495	$1,050	$875

▲ **B2/321** — 1 mfg.
Rarity precludes accurate price evaluation. This was the only factory model variation to leave Randall Firearms. This was a Left-hand Raider with the C.E. LeMay slide.

▲ **C211** — 5 mfg.
Rarity precludes accurate price evaluation.

▲ **C331** — 1 mfg.
Too rare to evaluate.

▲ **C332** — 4 mfg.
Rarity precludes accurate price evaluation.

▲ **Matched Sets** — large premiums exist for different models with the same serial number if NIB condition. Only 4 were mfg.

RANGER ARMS INC.

Previous manufacturer located in Gainesville, TX until the early 1970s.

Ranger Arms Inc. manufactured good quality, bolt action rifles in various calibers and configurations. Although somewhat rare in that there were not a large number manufactured, collectibility to date has been limited with specimens in 90%+ condition, typically priced in the $375-$500 range.

RAVELL

Manufacturer located in Barcelona, Spain. Currently, Ravell has no single U.S. importer and values below represent guns purchased directly from Spain without import duty/shipping.

Grading	100%	98%	95%	90%	80%	70%	60%

MAXIM DOUBLE RIFLE — .375 H&H or 9.3x74R cal., H&H type sidelock action with automatic ejectors, Purdey scroll engraving, 23 in. barrels, deluxe walnut with full pistol grip and rubber butt plate, double articulated triggers.

	100%	98%	95%	90%	80%	70%	60%
Mfg.'s Sug. Retail $7,000	$6,600	$6,100	$5,000	$4,000	$3,500	$2,950	$2,600

Add $460 for .375 H&H Mag. cal.

RAVEN ARMS

Previous manufacturer located in Industry, CA 1970-1991. Approximately 2 million were mfg.

P-25 — .25 cal., single action semi-auto, 2⁷⁄₁₆ in. barrel, 6 shot mag., walnut grips, available in nickel, blue, or chrome finish, 15 oz. Disc. 1984.

$70	$60	$50	$40	$30	$25	$25

MP-25 — similar to Model P-25, except die-cast slide serrations are slightly different. Disc. 1992.

$60	$50	$45	$40	$35	$30	$25

Last Mfg.'s Sug. Retail was $70.

Walnut, slotted plastic, or ivory colored grips are available for this model. In 1987, a new sear-block safety was incorporated into manufacture.

RECORD-MATCH

Manufactured by Anschutz, located in Zella-Mehlis, Germany.

MODEL 210 FREE PISTOL — .22 LR, Martini action, 11 in. barrel, single shot, blue, carved and checkered walnut grips and forearm, set trigger (button release), micrometer rear sight, deluxe target pistol, pre-WWII.

$1,320	$1,265	$1,210	$1,100	$880	$745	$550

MODEL 210A — similar to 210, but alloy frame.

$1,265	$1,210	$1,155	$1,045	$825	$690	$495

MODEL 200 FREE PISTOL — similar to 210, but less deluxe features and spur trigger guard, pre-WWII.

$990	$935	$770	$660	$525	$440	$360

REISING ARMS COMPANY

Manufacturer originally located in Hartford, CT and later in New York, NY.

TARGET AUTOMATIC PISTOL — .22 LR, 12 shot, 6½ in. barrel, blue, hard rubber grips, hinged frame, outside hammer. Mfg. 1921-1924.

$450	$395	$340	$315	$265	$220	$195

This model was mfg. in Hartford, CT from serial number 1,001-4,000. The New York, NY address occurs in the serial range 10,000-12,000.

Warning: This pistol's slide may crack if modern high speed .22 ammo is used.

REMINGTON ARMS COMPANY

Originally E. Remington, Litchfield, Herkimer County, NY 1816-1828; moved to Ilion, NY in 1828. Manufactured in Ilion, NY to date.

Remington®

100%	98%	95%	90%	80%	70%	60%	50%	40%	30%	20%	10%

REMINGTON TRADEMARKS - 1816-PRESENT

1816-1847 — Remington (mostly barrel and lock markings)
1847-1856 — E. Remington & Son
1856-1888 — E. Remington & Sons
1888-1910 — Remington Arms Company
1910-1920 — Remington Arms U.M.C. Company
1920 to date — Remington Arms Company, Inc.

HANDGUNS: 1857-1945 MFG.

BEALS' FIRST MODEL POCKET REVOLVER — percussion .31 cal., 5 shot, smooth cylinder, 3 in. octagon barrel, blue finish, 1-piece Gutta Percha grips, brass or iron trigger guard. Approx. 5,000 produced, 1857-1858.

N/A	N/A	$795	$700	$635	$585	$535	$500	$475	$450	$425	$395

BEALS' SECOND MODEL POCKET REVOLVER — percussion .31 cal., 5 shot, smooth cylinder, 3 in. octagon barrel, blue finish, 2-piece Gutta Percha grips, spur trigger. Approx. 1,000 produced 1858-1860.

N/A	N/A	$5,000	$4,500	$4,050	$3,650	$3,250	$2,850	$2,500	$2,250	$2,000	$1,850

BEALS' THIRD MODEL POCKET REVOLVER — percussion .31 cal., 5 shot, smooth cylinder, 4 in. octagon barrel, blue finish, 2-piece Gutta Percha grips, spur trigger, first Remington revolver with loading lever. Approx. 1,000 produced.

N/A	N/A	$1,125	$1,025	$925	$850	$775	$700	$625	$550	$500	$450

BEALS' NAVY REVOLVER — percussion .36 cal., 6 shot, smooth cylinder, 7½ in. octagon barrel, blue finish, 2-piece walnut grips, some martially marked with inspector's initials and cartouche on grips. Approx. 15,000 produced, 1860-1862. Barrel address is "Beals' Patent, Sept. 14, 1858 - Manufactured by Remingtons', Ilion, N.Y."

▲ *Commercial Model* — single wing base pin (very rare), less than 400 mfg. Serial range under 200.

N/A	N/A	$3,175	$2,850	$2,550	$2,250	$2,000	$1,825	$1,675	$1,550	$1,450	$1,375

▲ *Commercial Model* — several variations with serialization 1-15,500, most were purchased by military but were not inspected.

N/A	N/A	$2,500	$2,250	$2,025	$1,800	$1,575	$1,350	$1,150	$950	$750	$575

Subtract 20% for cartridge conversion.

▲ *Martially marked* — serial range 13,500-15,500.

N/A	N/A	$2,800	$2,450	$2,100	$1,900	$1,750	$1,625	$1,500	$1,375	$1,250	$1,150

BEALS' ARMY REVOLVER — percussion .44 cal., 6 shot, smooth cylinder, 8 in. octagon barrel, blue finish, 2-piece walnut grips. Barrel address is "Beals' Patent, Sept. 14, 1858 - Manufactured by Remingtons', Ilion, N.Y."

$3,750	$3,100	$2,800	$2,550	$2,325	$2,125	$1,900	$1,700	$1,500	$1,300	$1,100	$975

Subtract 20% for cartridge conversions.

▲ *Martially marked* — serial range is 850-1,900 inspected by "WAT" or "CGC".

N/A	N/A	$5,850	$5,000	$4,350	$3,750	$3,250	$2,850	$2,500	$2,150	$1,800	$1,450

RIDER'S DOUBLE-ACTION POCKET REVOLVER — percussion .31 cal., 5 shot, unusual "mushroom-shaped" cylinder, 3 in. octagon barrel, blue finish, 2-piece Gutta Percha grips, brass triggerguard, no loading lever. One of the earliest double-action handguns produced. Approx. 20,000 produced, 1860-1888.

N/A	N/A	$725	$625	$575	$525	$485	$450	$425	$400	$375	$350

Subtract 30% for cartridge conversion.

RIDER'S SINGLE-SHOT DERRINGER — percussion .17 cal., all brass construction, grips included. Less than 1,000 produced, 1860-1863. MANY FAKES, caveat emptor.

N/A	N/A	$5,150	$4,600	$4,150	$3,750	$3,400	$3,100	$2,800	$2,500	$2,300	$2,100

100%	98%	95%	90%	80%	70%	60%	50%	40%	30%	20%	10%

R

MODEL OF 1861 NAVY REVOLVER — percussion .36 cal., 6 shot, unfluted cylinder, 7½ in. octagon barrel, blue finish, 2-piece walnut grips. Loading lever has slot allowing cylinder pin to be pulled forward without lowering lever. Approx. 6,000 produced 1862-1863 in serial range 15,000-21,000. Barrel address "Patented Dec. 17, 1861, 1858 - Manufactured by Remingtons', Ilion, N.Y.".

▲ *Commercial Model*

N/A	N/A	$1,950	$1,700	$1,450	$1,250	$1,050	$950	$825	$725	$600	$500

Subtract 30% for cartridge conversion.

▲ *Martially Marked* — over 4,000 martially inspected "CGC".

N/A	N/A	$2,450	$2,200	$1,950	$1,700	$1,450	$1,200	$1,000	$850	$700	$575

MODEL OF 1861 ARMY REVOLVER — percussion .44 cal., 6 shot, unfluted cylinder, 8 in. octagon barrel, blue finish, 2-piece walnut grips. Majority are martially inspected "CGC". Loading lever has slot allowing cylinder pin to be pulled forward without lowering lever. Approx. 10,000 produced 1862-1863 in serial range 1,900-12,000. Barrel address "Patented Dec. 17, 1861, 1858 - Manufactured by Remingtons', Ilion, N.Y.".

N/A	N/A	$2,250	$2,000	$1,750	$1,500	$1,250	$1,050	$900	$800	$675	$550

Subtract 30% for cartridge conversion.

NEW MODEL ARMY REVOLVER — percussion .44 cal., 6 shot, unfluted cylinder, 8 in. octagon barrel, blue finish, 2-piece walnut grips. Approx. 135,000 produced 1863-1888 in serial range 12,000-148,000. Barrel address "Patented Sept. 14, 1858 - Manufactured by Remingtons', Ilion, N.Y. - New Model". Early models lack "New Model" markings on barrel and have transition features from "1861" model.

N/A	N/A	$1,400	$1,250	$1,100	$1,000	$900	$800	$700	$600	$500	$425

Add 25% for cartridge conversion (most are in .44 rimfire).
Add 25% for martially inspected.

NEW MODEL NAVY REVOLVER — percussion .36 cal., 6 shot, unfluted cylinder, 7½ in. octagon barrel, blue finish, 2-piece walnut grips. Approx. 18,000 produced in percussion from 1863-1878 with serial range 21,000-48,000. None were martially marked at time of mfg. Approx. 4,000 were purchased by U.S. Navy during 1863-1865 in serial range 21,000-32,000. Barrel address "Patented Sept. 14, 1858 - Manufactured by Remingtons', Ilion, N.Y. - New Model". Early specimens lack "New Model" markings on barrel and have transition features from "1861" model.

N/A	N/A	$2,550	$2,250	$1,950	$1,650	$1,350	$1,125	$975	$825	$675	$550

Subtract 20% for cartridge conversion if in less than 50%+ original condition.
No premium for martial markings.

NEW MODEL BELT REVOLVER, SINGLE ACTION — percussion .36 cal., 6 shot, unfluted or fluted cylinder, 6½ in. octagon barrel, blue or nickel finish, 2-piece walnut grips. Approx. 5,000 produced 1863-1888.

N/A	N/A	$1,325	$1,150	$1,000	$900	$800	$725	$650	$575	$525	$475

Add 50% for fluted cylinder (cylinder numbered to the gun).
Subtract 30% for cartridge conversion.

NEW MODEL BELT REVOLVER, DOUBLE ACTION — percussion .36 cal., 6 shot, smooth or fluted cylinder, 6½ in. octagon barrel, blue or nickel finish, 2-piece walnut grips. Approx. 2,500 produced 1863-1888.

N/A	N/A	$1,025	$900	$800	$700	$625	$575	$525	$475	$425	$400

Add 100% for fluted cylinder (most not numbered to the gun).
Subtract 30% for cartridge conversion.

NEW MODEL POLICE REVOLVER — percussion .36 cal., 5 shot, smooth cylinder, 3 to 6½ in. octagon barrels, blue or nickel finish, 2-piece walnut grips. Approx. 18,000 produced 1863-1888.

N/A	N/A	$950	$875	$815	$750	$700	$650	$600	$550	$510	$475

Add 10% for 6½ in. barrel.
Subtract 40% for cartridge conversion.

100%	98%	95%	90%	80%	70%	60%	50%	40%	30%	20%	10%

R

NEW MODEL POCKET REVOLVER — percussion .31 cal., 5 shot, smooth cylinder, spur trigger, 3 to 4½ in. octagon barrel, blue or nickel finish, 2-piece walnut grips. Approx. 25,000 produced, 1863-1888.

N/A	N/A	$900	$825	$750	$700	$650	$600	$550	$475	$425	$390

Add 25%-50% for brass frame and/or trigger sheath.
Subtract 40% for cartridge conversion.

ZIG-ZAG DERRINGER — cartridge .22 cal., 6 shot, 6 barrel cluster (rotating), ring trigger, 3 in. barrel cluster, blue finish, 2-piece hard rubber grips. Less than 1,000 produced, 1861-1863. Reputed to be Remington's first cartridge handgun.

N/A	N/A	$2,275	$2,025	$1,775	$1,525	$1,325	$1,175	$1,050	$950	$850	$765

ELLIOT'S FIVE SHOT DERRINGER — cartridge .22 cal., 5 shot, 5 barrel cluster (fixed), 3 in. barrel cluster, blue and/or nickel finish, 2-piece hard rubber, walnut, ivory or pearl grips, ring trigger. Approx. 25,000 produced (combined production total with .32 cal.).

N/A	N/A	$1,250	$1,125	$1,025	$900	$800	$700	$600	$525	$475	$425

ELLIOT'S FOUR SHOT DERRINGER — cartridge .32 cal., 4 shot, 4 barrel cluster (fixed), ring trigger, 3⅜ in. barrel cluster, blue and/or nickel finish, 2-piece hard rubber, walnut, ivory or pearl grips. Approx. 25,000 produced (combined production with .22 cal.).

N/A	N/A	$950	$850	$775	$700	$625	$575	$515	$455	$400	$365

VEST POCKET DERRINGER — cartridge .22, .30, .32, or .41 cal., single shot, various barrel lengths, blue or nickel finish, 2-piece walnut grips, spur trigger.

▲ **.22 Rimfire** — approx. 25,000 produced, 1865-1888.

N/A	N/A	$765	$685	$635	$575	$525	$475	$425	$375	$325	$275

Subtract 25% for guns lacking company name.

▲ **.30 or .32 Rimfire** — number produced unknown, 1865-1888.

N/A	N/A	$1,050	$950	$850	$725	$600	$550	$500	$450	$400	$350

▲ **.41 Rimfire** — approx. 25,000 produced, 1865-1888.

N/A	N/A	$950	$850	$750	$650	$575	$525	$475	$425	$375	$325

OVER AND UNDER DERRINGER — cartridge .41 Rimfire cal., 2 shot, 3 in. superimposed barrels, oscillating firing pin, spur trigger, blue and/or nickel finish, hard rubber, walnut, ivory or pearl 2-piece grips. Approx. 150,000 produced, 1866-1934. A.K.A. Double Derringer or Model 95.

▲ **Type One, Early Variation** — maker's name and patent data stamped between the barrels, made without extractor. 1866-1888.

N/A	N/A	$1,250	$1,150	$1,025	$900	$800	$700	$625	$550	$475	$425

▲ **Type One, Late Variation** — maker's name and patent data stamped between the barrels, made with extractor. 1866-1888.

N/A	N/A	$1,325	$1,200	$1,100	$1,025	$950	$875	$800	$750	$700	$650

▲ **Type Two** — two line markings atop barrels, maker's name and patent data. 1866-1888.

N/A	N/A	$775	$650	$575	$525	$475	$425	$375	$325	$275	$225

▲ **Type Three** — marked on top of barrel, single line, "REMINGTON ARMS CO., ILION, N.Y." 1888-1911.

N/A	N/A	$750	$650	$525	$450	$400	$350	$300	$250	$225	$200

▲ **Type Four** — marked on top of barrel, single line, "REMINGTON ARMS-U.M.C. CO. ILION, N.Y."

N/A	N/A	$650	$575	$500	$425	$375	$325	$290	$255	$225	$195

MODEL 1866 NAVY ROLLING BLOCK PISTOL — cartridge .50 Rimfire cal., single shot, 8½ in. round barrel, spur trigger, walnut grip and forearm, blue finish. Approx. 6,500 produced, 1866-1875. Erroneously designated as, "Model of 1865 Navy".

▲ **Martially Marked**

N/A	N/A	$3,100	$2,600	$2,350	$2,150	$1,950	$1,750	$1,550	$1,400	$1,275	$1,175

Subtract 30% if not martially marked (Commercial Model mfg. 1866-1875).
Subtract 15% for centerfire breech block.
Less than 150 remain in original condition.

100%	98%	95%	90%	80%	70%	60%	50%	40%	30%	20%	10%

R

MODEL 1870 NAVY ROLLING BLOCK PISTOL — cartridge .50 Centerfire cal., single shot, 7 in. round barrel, standard trigger with triggerguard, walnut grip and forearm, blue finish. Approx. 6,400 produced 1870-1875. Modified by Remington for the Navy from the Model 1866.

| N/A | N/A | $1,750 | $1,550 | $1,350 | $1,200 | $1,075 | $975 | $875 | $800 | $725 | $750 |

Add approx. 20% for 8 in. commercial version (approx. 200-400 mfg.) without inspector's marks.

MODEL 1871 ARMY ROLLING BLOCK PISTOL — cartridge .50 Centerfire cal., single shot, 8 in. round barrel, standard trigger with triggerguard, walnut grip and forearm, blue finish. Approx. 5,000 produced, 1871-1872.

| N/A | N/A | $1,575 | $1,375 | $1,200 | $1,075 | $975 | $875 | $775 | $675 | $600 | $550 |

Subtract 10% for Commercial Model.

Pistols produced between 1871-1872 are martially marked.

MODEL 1887 TARGET ROLLING BLOCK PISTOL — cartridge .22, .25 Rimfire and .32, .50 Centerfire cals., single shot, 8 in. round barrel, standard trigger with triggerguard, walnut grip and forearm, blue finish. Approx. 900 produced 1887-1891. A.K.A. "Plinker Model of 1887".

| N/A | N/A | $1,535 | $1,325 | $1,175 | $1,050 | $950 | $850 | $750 | $650 | $575 | $525 |

Add 10% for Navy framed.

Navy framed 1887s are discernible by military proofs on right side of frame, Remington altered from original Navy Model 1870. Estimated mfg. of 100.

MODEL 1891 TARGET MODEL ROLLING BLOCK PISTOL — cartridge .22, .25 Rimfire and .32 Centerfire cals., single shot, 10 in. part octagon, part round barrel, standard trigger with triggerguard, smooth walnut grip and forearm, blue finish. Approx. 100 produced 1891-1900.

| N/A | N/A | $1,750 | $1,535 | $1,325 | $1,175 | $1,050 | $950 | $850 | $750 | $675 | $625 |

MODEL 1901 TARGET ROLLING BLOCK PISTOL — cartridge .22 S and L, .25 Rimfire, .32 Centerfire, or .44 S&W Russian cal., single shot, 10 in. part octagon, part round barrel, standard trigger with triggerguard, checkered walnut grip and forearm, blue finish. Approx. 800 produced 1900-1909.

| N/A | N/A | $1,750 | $1,535 | $1,325 | $1,175 | $1,050 | $950 | $850 | $750 | $675 | $625 |

Add $100 for S&W Russian.

RIDER'S MAGAZINE PISTOL — cartridge .32 cal., 5 shot, 3 in. octagon barrel, spur trigger, walnut, rosewood, ivory or pearl grips. Approx. 10,000 produced, 1871-1888.

| N/A | N/A | $1,325 | $1,225 | $1,100 | $1,000 | $900 | $800 | $700 | $625 | $575 | $525 |

Add 50% with case hardened magazine.

ELLIOT'S SINGLE SHOT DERRINGER — cartridge .41 Rimfire cal., single shot, 2½ in. round barrel, spur trigger, walnut 2-piece grips, blue and/or nickel finish. Approx. 10,000 produced, 1867-1888. A.K.A. "Mississippi Derringer".

| N/A | N/A | $1,000 | $875 | $775 | $675 | $600 | $550 | $500 | $450 | $400 | $350 |

NUMBER ONE (SMOOT PATENT) REVOLVER — cartridge .30 Rimfire cal., 5 shot, 2¾ in. octagon barrel, spur trigger, walnut, hard rubber, pearl or ivory 2-piece grips. Number produced debatable, 1873-1888.

| N/A | N/A | $465 | $430 | $395 | $360 | $325 | $290 | $265 | $240 | $215 | $190 |

Add 100% on early #1s with revolving recoil shield.

On Number One through Number Four Revolvers, ivory grips refer to Remington Celluloid, not genuine ivory. Only in rare instances does ivory appear.

NUMBER TWO (SMOOT PATENT) REVOLVER — cartridge .30 or .32 Rimfire cal., 5 shot, 2¾ in. octagon barrel, spur trigger, hard rubber, pearl or ivory 2-piece grips. Number produced debatable, 1873-1888.

| N/A | N/A | $450 | $425 | $400 | $375 | $350 | $300 | $275 | $250 | $225 | $200 |

100%	98%	95%	90%	80%	70%	60%	50%	40%	30%	20%	10%

NUMBER THREE (SMOOT PATENT) REVOLVER — cartridge .38 Rimfire or .38 Centerfire cal., 3¾ in. octagon barrel with or without barrel rib, spur trigger, hard rubber, ivory or pearl 2-piece grips, "Bird-Head and SawHandle" grip frame with Remington logo "R" on the "saw-handle" hard rubber grips, Bird-Head referred to models with or without a barrel rib. Number produced debatable, 1875-1888.

N/A	N/A	$500	$475	$450	$425	$400	$350	$325	$300	$275	$250

Add small premiums on Centerfire Number 3s.

NUMBER FOUR REVOLVER — cartridge .38 and .41 Rimfire or .38 and .41 Centerfire cals., 5 shot, 2½ in. round barrel, hard rubber, pearl or ivory 2-piece grips. Number produced debatable, 1877-1888.

N/A	N/A	$550	$525	$500	$475	$450	$400	$375	$350	$325	$300

Add small premiums on Centerfire Number 4's.

IROQUOIS REVOLVER — cartridge .22 Rimfire cal., 7 shot, 2¼ in. round barrel, spur trigger hard rubber, pearl or ivory 2-piece grips, fluted or non-fluted cylinder. Approx. 10,000 produced between, 1878-1888.

N/A	N/A	$475	$440	$410	$385	$345	$300	$275	$250	$225	$200

Subtract 33% if unmarked.
Add 20% for fluted cylinder.

MODEL 1875 SINGLE ACTION REVOLVER — cartridge .44 or .45 Centerfire cal., 6 shot, 7½ or 5¾ in. round barrel, standard trigger with triggerguard, blue or nickel finish, walnut, ivory, or pearl 2-piece grips. Approx. 25,000 produced, 1875-1888.

N/A	N/A	$4,250	$3,750	$3,250	$2,750	$2,450	$2,150	$1,850	$1,675	$1,475	$1,100

Add 25% for blue finish.
Add 10% for government markings.
Add 50% for .45 cal.
There is some debate over originality of the 5¾ in. barrel.

MODEL 1888 SINGLE ACTION REVOLVER — cartridge .44 Centerfire cal., resembles 1890 SA, has "E. Remington & Sons" barrel address, 5¾ in. barrel, nickel finish with walnut grips, perhaps mfg. during Remington's period of bankruptcy and receivership (circa late 1880s).

N/A	N/A	$3,250	$2,800	$2,400	$2,000	$1,650	$1,275	$950	$850	$725	$625

MODEL 1890 SINGLE ACTION REVOLVER — cartridge .44 Centerfire cal., 6 shot, 7½ or 5¾ in. round barrel, standard trigger with triggerguard, hard rubber 2-piece grips with Remington monogram, ivory or pearl grips on special order, blue or nickel finish. Approx. 2,000 produced, 1891-1894.

➤ Blue finish

N/A	N/A	$7,750	$6,950	$6,300	$5,600	$4,875	$4,100	$3,400	$2,575	$1,775	$1,100

➤ Nickel finish

N/A	N/A	$6,400	$5,800	$5,200	$4,500	$4,000	$3,500	$2,950	$2,000	$1,400	$900

MODEL 51 SEMI-AUTO — cartridge .32 or .380 Centerfire cal., 8 shot (7 in mag., 1 in chamber), hard rubber 2-piece grips with company's name. Approx. 65,000 produced, 1918-1934.

N/A	N/A	$500	$475	$450	$425	$400	$350	$325	$300	$275	$250

Add 10% for .32 ACP cal.
Note: .380 cal. much more numerous than .32 cal.

REMINGTON - UMC — over 21,500 mfg. (ser. numbered 1-21,676) in 1918-1919 only, blued finish.

N/A	$1,950	$1,625	$950	$700	$575	$525	$475	$425	$375	$325	$275

The cut-off serial number for 1918 mfg. is 13,152.

MARK III SIGNAL PISTOL — 10 ga., single shot, brass frame, 9 in. round steel barrel, spur trigger, walnut 2-piece grips. Approx. 25,000 produced, 1915-1918.

N/A	N/A	$300	$265	$230	$210	$190	$175	$160	$145	$130	$110

HANDGUNS: POST-WWII MFG.

Please contact the Remington Custom Shop for current information and pricing on the XP-100 series of pistols (see Trademark Index).

Grading	100%	98%	95%	90%	80%	70%	60%

MODEL XP-100 VARMINT SPECIAL — single shot bolt action pistol, .221 Rem. Fireball (disc. 1985-1986) 10½ in. barrel) or .223 Rem. (new 1986) cal., 14½ in. barrel, adj. sights (.221 cal. only), drilled and tapped for scope, one-piece pistol grip nylon stock, 4⅜ lbs. Mfg. 1963-1992.

		$335	$295	$230	$195	$165	$150	$140

Last Mfg.'s Sug. Retail was $419.

Add $100 for original hard zipper case.

XP-SILHOUETTE — .35 Rem. (mfg. 1987-1993) or 7mm BR cal., bench rest model, 10½ (new 1993) or 14½ (disc. 1992) in. barrel, target sights became standard 1993, older models had no sights but were drilled and tapped, nylon (disc. 1992) or walnut (new 1993) stock, 3⅞ lbs.

Mfg.'s Sug. Retail	$625	$535	$455	$400	$360	$330	$270	$220

Add $15 for .35 Rem. cal.

MODEL XP-100 HUNTER — .223 Rem., 7mm BR Rem., 7mm-.08 Rem., or .35 Rem. cal., 14½ in. barrel, no sights, laminated wood stock, 4⅜ lbs. New 1993.

Mfg.'s Sug. Retail	$548	$460	$380	$330	$270	$220	$200	$180

XP-100R KS — .22-250 (new 1992), .223 Rem., .250 Savage, 7mm-08 Rem., .308 (new 1992), .35 Rem., or .350 Rem. Mag. cal., repeater variation, Kevlar synthetic stock, right hand action only, open sights (except for .223 Rem. and .250 Savage) 4⅛ lbs.

Mfg.'s Sug. Retail	$840	$735	$600	$540	$495	$450	$400	$365

This model is available through Remington's Custom Shop only.

XP-100 CUSTOM — .22-250 (new 1992), .223 Rem., .250 Savage, 6mm BR, 7mm BR, .308 (new 1992), .35 Rem., or 7mm-08 Rem. cal., choice of standard or heavy barrel, available through custom gun shop only, choice of right or left hand action, wood stock with contoured pistol grip, without sights. New 1986.

Mfg.'s Sug. Retail	$945	$825	$735	$660	$575	$525	$450	$400

Also available, on special order only, is the .458x2 in. caliber.

100%	98%	95%	90%	80%	70%	60%	50%	40%	30%	20%	10%

RIFLES: DISC. MFG.

REVOLVING PERCUSSION RIFLE — .36 or .44 cal., 6 shot unfluted cylinder, 24 or 28 in. octagon barrel, walnut stock with crescent butt, scroll triggerguard, blue with case hardened frame. Less than 1,000 mfg., 1866-1879.

▲ *.36 Caliber*

N/A	N/A	$2,900	$2,640	$2,475	$2,310	$2,200	$2,090	$1,980	$1,925	$1,815	$1,760

▲ *.44 Caliber* — very rare.

N/A	N/A	$9,875	$8,700	$6,000	$4,250	$3,750	$3,250	$2,875	$2,600	$2,300	$1,975

Due to poor percussion sales, most of the remaining factory stock was converted to .38 R.F., factory conversions will be serial numbered similarly on the recoil plate and cylinder.

MODEL 1862 "ZOUAVE RIFLE" — .58 cal., muzzle loading percussion, 33 in. round barrel, two barrel bands, blue barrel, case hardened lock, brass furniture. Mfg. 12,501, 1862-1865.

N/A	N/A	$3,000	$2,600	$2,250	$1,800	$1,575	$1,300	$1,050	$850	$650	$450

U.S. NAVY ROLLING BLOCK CARBINE — .50-70 cal., 23¼ in. barrel, open sight, blue with case hardened frame, bar and ring on frame, walnut straight grip stock. Mfg. 5,000, 1868-1869.

N/A	N/A	$1,750	$1,350	$1,250	$950	$800	$750	$625	$515	$450	$395

LONG RANGE "CREEDMOOR" — rolling block, .44-90, .44-100, or .44-70, cal., barrel ⅓ octagon, long range tang sight, globe front sight, checkered pistol grip stock, blue. Approx. 500 mfg., 1873-1886.

N/A	N/A	$9,800	$8,825	$6,250	$4,475	$3,875	$3,175	$2,700	$2,475	$2,150	$1,800

100%	98%	95%	90%	80%	70%	60%	50%	40%	30%	20%	10%

R

NO. 1 SPORTING RIFLE — rolling block, .40-50, .40-70, .44-70, .44-77, .45-70, .50-45, or .50-70 centerfire or .46 rimfire cal., 28 or 30 in. octagon barrels, folding leaf sight, straight or pistol grip stock. Approx. 10,000 mfg., 1868-1902.

| N/A | N/A | $1,000 | $875 | $775 | $650 | $550 | $450 | $375 | $330 | $275 | $220 |

Subtract 15% for rimfire cals.
Add 10% for .44-77, .45-70, or .50-70 cal. (primary buffalo hunting cals.).

NO. 1½ SPORTING RIFLE — .22, .25 Stevens, .25 Long, .32, and .38 Long & Extra Long rimfire, also in .32-20, .38-40, and .44-40 in centerfire, 24-28 in. octagon medium weight barrel, straight grip walnut stock, somewhat lighter than the No. 1 Sporting. Several thousand mfg., 1888-1897.

| N/A | N/A | $875 | $775 | $675 | $575 | $500 | $450 | $400 | $350 | $275 | $200 |

Subtract 15% for rimfire cals.

NO. 2 SPORTING RIFLE — available in many rimfire cals. between .22 and .38 as well as centerfire cals. between .22 to .38-40, blued finish with case hardened frame, perch belly style walnut stock, many special orders available, smaller size action than the No.1 and rear of frame is curved, mfg. 1873-1909.

| N/A | N/A | $600 | $560 | $520 | $460 | $410 | $360 | $300 | $250 | $200 | $150 |

Subtract 15% for rimfire cals.

LIGHT BABY CARBINE — rolling block, .44-40 cal., 20 in. lightweight round barrel with band, straight stock. Few thousand mfg., 1892-1902.

| N/A | N/A | $2,500 | $2,000 | $1,650 | $1,375 | $1,500 | $895 | $775 | $700 | $640 | $575 |

Add 25% for blued barrel with color case hardened receiver.

REMINGTON — HEPBURN NO. 3 — falling block, single shot, side lever actuated, blue barrel, case hardened actions, patented 1879, first introduced 1880, many custom features were offered, variations as follows:

NO. 3 SPORTING & TARGET — various cals. from .22 Win. to .50-90 Sharps, 26, 28, or 30 in. round or octagon barrel, open sight, semi-pistol grip stock. Mfg. 1883-1907.

| N/A | N/A | $1,150 | $1,045 | $935 | $880 | $770 | $660 | $550 | $495 | $440 | $385 |

NO. 3 MATCH RIFLE A QUALITY — similar to Sporting and Target, with target match sights (tang), and Schuetzen stock. Less than 1,000 mfg., 1883-1907.

| N/A | N/A | $1,400 | $1,150 | $1,045 | $960 | $880 | $825 | $715 | $605 | $550 | $495 |

▲ *B Quality* — select grade wood.

| N/A | N/A | $1,825 | $1,525 | $1,200 | $1,045 | $935 | $880 | $770 | $715 | $605 | $550 |

NO. 3 LONG RANGE CREEDMOOR — .44 cal., 32 or 34 in. octagon barrel, tang sight, otherwise similar to Target Model. A few hundred mfg., 1880-1907.

| N/A | N/A | $2,000 | $1,675 | $1,400 | $1,225 | $1,100 | $1,045 | $935 | $880 | $770 | $715 |

NO. 3 MID RANGE CREEDMOOR — similar to Long Range, in .40-65 cal., 28 in. barrel.

| N/A | N/A | $2,000 | $1,700 | $1,400 | $1,045 | $935 | $880 | $770 | $715 | $660 | $605 |

NO. 3 LONG RANGE MILITARY — similar to Creedmoor, with 34 in. full musket stock, in .44-75-520 Rem. cal., military sights, 1880s.

| N/A | N/A | $2,625 | $2,250 | $1,925 | $1,700 | $1,540 | $1,430 | $1,320 | $1,100 | $990 | $825 |

NO. 3 SCHUETZEN MATCH — under lever actuated, 30 or 32 in. barrel, tang sight, palm rest, target stock, approx. 23 mfg. in 1903, perhaps the rarest single shot American rifle.

Extreme rarity factor precludes accurate price evaluation but a few have been observed with price tags in the $5,000-$20,000+ range, depending on condition.

▲ *With False Muzzle*

Even rarer than above - add a premium according to condition.

100%	98%	95%	90%	80%	70%	60%	50%	40%	30%	20%	10%

R

NO. 4 ROLLING BLOCK RIFLE — .22 S-L-LR, .25 Stevens (barrels marked "25-10"), or .32 Short or Long cal., 22½ octagon barrel standard with round barrels available late in the series, blued finish with case hardened frame, solid frame initially followed by takedown in 2 different types (lever - most common, or knob), this model was Remington's smallest rolling block. Approx. 350,000 mfg. 1890-1933.

$550	$475	$395	$350	$300	$260	$230	$200	$165	$130	$115	$100

Add 25% for smooth bore barrel.

Solid frame variations will command a premium, especially if over 50% original condition.

▲ *Model 4-S "Boy Scout"*

N/A	N/A	$1,100	$975	$850	$750	$650	$550	$450	$350	$275	$225

▲ *Model 4-S Military* — .22 S-L-LR, either marked "MILITARY MODEL" (most common) or "AMERICAN BOY SCOUT" (rare), 28 in. round barrel with musket type forend (1 barrel band), thought to have been used by military academies to train their young cadets.

N/A	N/A	$825	$725	$625	$550	$480	$410	$340	$285	$240	$200

Bayonets are an extremely rare accessory for this model.

NO. 6 ROLLING BLOCK RIFLE — .22 S-L-LR or .32 Short or Long rimfire cal., 20 in. round barrel, boy's gun with small dimensions, takedown action, case hardened (early mfg.) or blue finish, also available in smooth bore, 497,000 mfg. 1902-1933.

$275	$235	$190	$160	$150	$140	$130	$120	$110	$100	$90	$75

Add 25% for smooth bore barrel.

Original case colors will bring a premium on this model.

REMINGTON KEENE MAGAZINE BOLT RIFLE — .45-70 Govt., .40, or .43 cal. Approx. 5,000 mfg. 1880-1888.

▲ *Frontier Model* — made for U.S. Dept. of Interior (Indian Police), marked U.S.I.D.

N/A	$1,150	$900	$800	$725	$650	$575	$500	$425	$350	$275	$200

▲ *Carbine Model* — 22 in. full stock.

N/A	$975	$850	$750	$650	$550	$475	$400	$325	$275	$225	$175

▲ *Army Rifle* — 32½ in. barrel, full stock.

N/A	$975	$850	$750	$650	$550	$475	$400	$325	$275	$225	$175

▲ *Sporter Rifle* — ½ oct. barrel, full or "BUTTON" mag. Add for pistol grip and select wood variations.

N/A	$975	$850	$750	$650	$550	$475	$400	$325	$275	$225	$175

▲ *Navy Rifle* — 29½ in. barrel, full stock.

N/A	$975	$850	$750	$650	$550	$475	$400	$325	$275	$225	$175

Grading		100%	98%	95%	90%	80%	70%	60%

RIFLES: CENTERFIRE - SEMI-AUTO & SLIDE ACTION

The models below have been listed in numerical sequence for quick reference.

MODEL FOUR SEMI-AUTO — 6mm Rem., .243 Win., .270 Win., .280 Rem., .30-06, .308 Win. (disc. 1984) or 7mm Express Rem. (early mfg. barrel marking) cal., gas operation with metering system, 22 in. barrel, 4 shot detachable mag., deluxe Monte Carlo stock and forend, detachable sights. Mfg. 1982-1987.

$395	$360	$325	$275	$250	$225	$195

Last Mfg.'s Sug. Retail was $475.

▲ *Model Four Diamond Anniversary* — .30-06 only, less than 1,500 mfg. in 1981 to commemorate 75th anniversary of the Model 8, custom shop engraved with premium checkered walnut stock and forearm.

$1,000	$795	$600

▲ *D Peerless Grade*

$1,975	$1,870	$1,200

Last Mfg.'s Sug. Retail was $2,291.

Grading	100%	98%	95%	90%	80%	70%	60%

▲ *F Premier Grade*

              $4,150 $3,835 $2,650

Last Mfg.'s Sug. Retail was $4,720.

▲ *F Premier Gold Grade* — with gold inlays.

              $6,420 $5,735 $4,000

Last Mfg.'s Sug. Retail was $7,079.

MODEL SIX SLIDE ACTION — 6mm Rem. (disc. 1984), .243 Win., .270 Win., .30-06, or .308 Win. (disc. 1984) cal., pump action, detachable sights, 4 shot mag. Mfg. 1981-1987.

      $400 $360 $290 $265 $235 $215 $195

Last Mfg.'s Sug. Retail was $439.

▲ *D Peerless Grade*

              $1,975 $1,870 $1,200

Last Mfg.'s Sug. Retail was $2,291.

▲ *F Premier Grade*

              $4,150 $3,835 $2,650

Last Mfg.'s Sug. Retail was $4,720.

▲ *F Premier Gold Grade* — with gold inlays.

              $6,420 $5,735 $4,000

Last Mfg.'s Sug. Retail was $7,079.

MODEL 8 AUTOLOADING RIFLE — .25, .30, .32, or .35 Rem. cal., 22 in. barrel, open sights, 5 shot non-detachable box mag., plain stock. Approx. 60,000 mfg. 1906-1936. Also made in higher grades C through F — add premiums.

      $400 $320 $270 $220 $195 $165 $140

    Add 15% for .25 cal.

MODEL 14/14A SLIDE ACTION — .25, .30, .32, or .35 cal., 22 in. barrel, open sight, plain pistol grip stock. Mfg. 1912-1935.

      $350 $285 $230 $195 $165 $130 $110

MODEL 14R CARBINE — similar to 14A, with 18½ in. barrel, straight grip stock.

      $400 $325 $285 $260 $220 $195 $165

MODEL 14½ RIFLE — similar to 14A, with 22½ in. barrel, .38-40 or .44-40 cal. Mfg. 1912-1934.

      $600 $550 $475 $425 $350 $300 $275

    Add 100% for "fingernail" safety.

    Quantities mfg. of this model are unknown as serial numbers were intermixed with the Model 14.

MODEL 14½R CARBINE — similar to 14½ Rifle, with 18½ in. barrel.

      $675 $600 $525 $475 $425 $375 $325

MODEL 25/25A SLIDE ACTION — .25-20 or .32-20 cal., 24 in. barrel, open sight, tube mag., plain pistol grip stock. Mfg. 1923-1936.

      $375 $325 $300 $250 $200 $175 $150

MODEL 25R CARBINE — similar to 25A, with 18 in. barrel and straight stock.

      $495 $425 $350 $275 $225 $200 $175

MODEL 74 SPORTSMAN SEMI-AUTO — .30-06 only, 22 in. barrel, 4 shot mag., uncheckered hardwood stock and forearm, open sights, 7½ lbs. Mfg. 1985-1987.

      $295 $260 $235 $210 $190 $175 $160

Last Mfg.'s Sug. Retail was $353.

MODEL 76 SPORTSMAN SLIDE ACTION — .30-06 cal. only, 22 in. barrel, 4 shot mag., uncheckered hardwood stock and forearm, open sights, 7½ lbs. Mfg. 1985-1987.

      $255 $225 $195 $180 $170 $160 $150

Last Mfg.'s Sug. Retail was $319.

Grading	100%	98%	95%	90%	80%	70%	60%

MODEL 81 "WOODSMASTER" SEMI-AUTO — .30, .32, .35 Rem., or .300 Savage cal., semi-auto, takedown action, 5 shot, non-detachable box mag., 22 in. round barrel, notched elevator rear sight. An improvement of the Model 8 is available in 5 grades. Better grades bring higher prices. 56,091 mfg. 1936-1950.

	$400	$350	$300	$250	$200	$175	$150

Add 20% for .25 cal.

The .32 Rem. cal. was dropped after WWII and the .300 Savage was added in 1940. While a few specimens have been observed in .25 cal., it is probably the result of part swapping as the Remington Co. cannot verify this cal.

MODEL 141/141A SLIDE ACTION — .30, .32, or .35 Rem. cal., 24 in. barrel, takedown, open sight, plain pistol grip stock. Mfg. 1936-1950.

	$395	$305	$250	$220	$195	$165	$140

MODEL 740 WOODMASTER & 740A AUTOLOADER — .280 (marked 7mm Express, mfg. 1957-58), .30-06 or .308 cal., 22 in. barrel, open sight, box mag., gas operated, plain pistol grip stock. Mfg. 1955-1960.

	100%	98%	95%	90%	80%	70%	60%
.30-06 cal.	$315	$250	$225	$210	$200	$190	$180
.308 cal.	$340	$300	$265	$250	$235	$220	$200

Add 15% for carbine version.

MODEL 740ADL — similar to 740A, with checkered stock, grip cap and swivels. Mfg. 1955-1960.

	100%	98%	95%	90%	80%	70%	60%
.30-06 cal.	$375	$325	$280	$250	$225	$200	$180
.308 cal.	$415	$350	$300	$275	$250	$225	$200

Add 15% for carbine version.

MODEL 740BDL — similar to 740ADL, with select wood.

	100%	98%	95%	90%	80%	70%	60%
.30-06 cal.	$395	$340	$295	$250	$225	$200	$180
.308 cal.	$425	$375	$350	$325	$275	$225	$200

Add 15% for carbine version.

MODEL 742 (A) "WOODSMASTER" SEMI-AUTO — 6mm Rem., .243, .280 (marked 7mm Express 1979-82), .30-06, or .308 cal., 22 in. barrel, open sights, 4 shot box mag., gas operated, checkered pistol grip stock. Mfg. 1960-1980.

	$325	$290	$275	$250	$235	$210	$185

Add 10% for .280 Rem. cal.

MODEL 742ADL DELUXE — similar to the Model 742A, except has fine checkering, sling swivels and engraved game scenes on receiver.

	$350	$300	$275	$260	$235	$215	$195

MODEL 742 CARBINE — similar to 742, except .280 (marked 7mmExpress 1979-82), .30-06, or .308 cal. only, 18½ in. barrel. Mfg. 1961-1980.

	$350	$300	$275	$260	$235	$215	$195

MODEL 742BDL — similar to 742, except .30-06 or .308 cal. only, Monte Carlo basket weave stock and forend, black pistol grip cap and forend tip. Mfg. 1966-1980.

	$350	$300	$275	$260	$235	$215	$195

MODEL 742D PEERLESS GRADE — similar to 742, with scroll engraving and fancy wood. Mfg. 1961-1980.

	$2,000	$1,870	$1,200

MODEL 742F PREMIER GRADE — similar to 742, with extensive game scenes and scroll engraving, best grade wood.

	$4,200	$3,860	$2,650

MODEL 742F PREMIER GRADE (WITH INLAYS) — gold inlaid model.

	$6,500	$5,785	$4,180

MODEL 742 150TH YEAR ANNIVERSARY — .30-06 only. Mfg. 1966 only.

	$395	$325	$300

Grading	100%	98%	95%	90%	80%	70%	60%

MODEL 742 CANADIAN CENTENNIAL — 1,000 mfg. in 1967. Issue price was $200.

	100%	98%	95%
	$395	$325	$300

REMINGTON/RUGER CANADIAN CENTENNIAL SET — Please refer to the Sturm Ruger section of this text.

MODEL 742 BICENTENNIAL — similar to 742, with inscription on receiver. Mfg. 1976 only.

	100%	98%	95%	90%	80%	70%	60%
	$400	$325	$300	$275	$225	$200	$185

R

MODEL 760 SLIDE ACTION "GAMEMASTER" RIFLE — .222, .223, 6mm, .243, .257 Roberts, .270, .280 (marked 7mmExpress 1979-82), .30-06, .300 Sav., .308 or .35 Rem. cal., 22 in. barrel, detachable mag., uncheckered pistol grip stock. Mfg. 1952-1982.

	100%	98%	95%	90%	80%	70%	60%
	$375	$325	$275	$250	$225	$200	$175
.222 cal.	$1,150	$900	$800	$725	$650	$575	$500
.223 cal.	$1,350	$995	$850	$775	$700	$625	$575
.257 Roberts cal.	$850	$695	$575	$450	$400	$350	$300

Add 10% for .300 Savage or .35 Rem. cal.

The Model 760 seems to have regional pricing differences in the rare calibers. Values in the Eastern U.S. seem to be quite a bit higher than prices encountered in the Midwest and West. Hence, values on the .222, .223, and .257 R cals. reflect a nationalized average rather than one region's high or another's low. A few Model 760s were also mfg. in .244 cal. (before going to 6mm) — very rare with pricing unpredictable.

MODEL 760 CARBINE — .270, .280 (marked 7mmExpress 1979-82), .30-06, .308, or .35 Rem. cal., 18½ in. barrel.

	100%	98%	95%	90%	80%	70%	60%
	$450	$400	$375	$325	$300	$275	$250

Subtract 10% for .30-06 cal.

MODEL 760D PEERLESS GRADE — similar to 760, with engraving and fancy wood. Mfg. 1953-1982.

	100%	98%	95%	90%	80%	70%	60%
	$1,100	$935	$825	$770	$690	$605	$525

MODEL 760F — similar to 760, with extensive engraved game scenes, best grade wood.

	100%	98%	95%	90%	80%	70%	60%
	$2,420	$1,980	$1,760	$1,650	$1,485	$1,375	$1,100

▲ *Gold Inlaid Model*

	100%	98%	95%	90%	80%	70%	60%
	$5,500	$4,675	$4,180	$3,960	$3,300	$2,750	$2,200

MODEL 760 150 YEAR ANNIVERSARY — .30-06 only. Mfg. 1966 only.

	100%	98%	95%	90%	80%	70%	60%
	$395	$325	$300	$275	$225	$200	$185

MODEL 760 BICENTENNIAL — similar to 760, with commemorative inscription engraved on receiver. Mfg. 1976 only.

	100%	98%	95%	90%	80%	70%	60%
	$395	$325	$300	$275	$225	$200	$185

MODEL 760ADL — similar to 760, except with checkered pistol grip deluxe wood and sling swivels. Mfg. 1953-1963.

	100%	98%	95%	90%	80%	70%	60%
	$395	$350	$325	$300	$275	$250	$225

MODEL 760BDL — similar to 760, except .270, .30-06, or .308 cal. only, basket weave checkering pattern became standard mid-'70s, Monte Carlo stock, black pistol grip and forend tip. Mfg. 1953-1982.

	100%	98%	95%	90%	80%	70%	60%
	$300	$275	$250	$225	$210	$200	$175

MODEL 7400 SEMI-AUTO RIFLE — 6mm Rem. (disc. 1987), .243 Win., .270 Win., .280 Rem., .30-06, .308 Win., or .35 Whelen (disc. 1995) cal., same action as 742, gas operation, 22 in. barrel, 4 shot detachable mag., pressed checkered Monte Carlo walnut stock, 7½ lbs. Mfg. 1982 to date.

		100%	98%	95%	90%	80%	70%	60%
Mfg.'s Sug. Retail	$573	$460	$380	$300	$255	$230	$210	$185

Beginning in 1990, a high gloss wood finish became available in cals. .270 and .30-06 (Model 7400 High Gloss).

▲ *Model 7400 SP (Special Purpose)* — .270 Win. or .30-06 cal., similar to Model 7400, except has non-reflective matte finish on both wood and metalwork. Mfg. 1993-94.

	100%	98%	95%	90%	80%	70%	60%
	$435	$370	$300	$255	$230	$210	$185

Last Mfg.'s Sug. Retail was $524.

Grading	100%	98%	95%	90%	80%	70%	60%

▲ *Model 7400 Carbine* — .30-06 cal. only, similar to Model 7400 Rifle, except has 18½ in. barrel, 7¼ lbs. New 1988.

Mfg.'s Sug. Retail	$534	$460	$380	$300	$255	$230	$210	$185

▲ *Model 7400 175th Anniversary* — .30-06 cal. only, Anniversary Model with light engraving and high gloss finish. Mfg. in 1991 only.

		$435	$365	$300

Last Mfg.'s Sug. Retail was $515.

▲ *Model 7400 Engraved* — the below listed engraved Model 7400s were introduced 1988.

▲ *D Peerless Grade*

Mfg.'s Sug. Retail	$2,610		$2,100	$1,650	$1,200

▲ *F Premier Grade*

Mfg.'s Sug. Retail	$5,377		$4,495	$3,550	$2,500

▲ *F Premier Gold Grade* — with gold inlays.

Mfg.'s Sug. Retail	$8,062		$7,125	$4,050	$3,000

MODEL 7600 SLIDE ACTION RIFLE — 6mm Rem. (disc. 1984), .243 Win., .270 Win., .280 Rem. (new 1988), .30-06, .308 Win., or .35 Whelen (new 1988) cal., modified 760 action, 22 in. barrel, detachable mag., pressed checkered pistol grip stock and forearm, 7½ lbs. Mfg. 1981 to date.

Mfg.'s Sug. Retail	$540	$440	$375	$285	$230	$205	$185	$165

Beginning in 1990, a high gloss wood finish became available in cals. .270 and .30-06 (Model 7600 High Gloss).

▲ *Model 7600 Carbine* — .30-06 cal. only, similar to Model 7600 Rifle, except has 18½ in. barrel, 7¼ lbs.

Mfg.'s Sug. Retail	$540	$440	$375	$285	$230	$205	$185	$165

▲ *Model 7600 SP (Special Purpose)* — .270 Win. or .30-06 cal., similar to Model 7600, except has non-reflective matte finish on wood and metalwork. Mfg. 1993-94.

		$420	$360	$280	$230	$205	$185	$165

Last Mfg.'s Sug. Retail was $496.

▲ *Model 7600 Engraved* — the below listed engraved Model 7600s were introduced 1988.

▲ *D Peerless Grade*

Mfg.'s Sug. Retail	$2,610		$2,100	$1,650	$1,200

▲ *F Premier Grade*

Mfg.'s Sug. Retail	$5,377		$4,495	$3,550	$2,500

▲ *F Premier Gold Grade* — with gold inlays.

Mfg.'s Sug. Retail	$8,062		$7,125	$4,050	$3,000

RIFLES: RIMFIRE

From 1930-1960 Remington produced a number of bolt action .22 cal. Rimfire rifles, both single shot and repeaters. They were good quality, serviceable weapons with many slight variations upon a basic design.

Model 33	$200	$150	$125	$100	$85	$75	$60
Model 33 NRA	$300	$225	$200	$175	$150	$125	$100

263,557 of the Model 33 were mfg. 1932-1935.

Model 34	$200	$150	$125	$100	$85	$75	$60
Model 34 NRA	$300	$225	$200	$175	$150	$125	$100

162,941 of the Model 34 were mfg. 1932-1936.

Model 341 A	$150	$125	$100	$85	$75	$65	$55
Model 341 P	$175	$150	$125	$100	$85	$75	$70
Model 341 SB	$275	$235	$200	$175	$140	$125	$110

131,604 of the Model 341 "Sportsmaster" were mfg. 1936-1940.

Model 41 A	$150	$125	$100	$75	$65	$60	$55
Model 41 AS	$200	$175	$160	$150	$140	$125	$110
Model 41 P	$150	$125	$100	$85	$65	$60	$55
Model 41 SB	$235	$195	$175	$160	$140	$125	$110

306,880 of the Model 41 "Targetmaster" were produced 1936-1940.

Grading	100%	98%	95%	90%	80%	70%	60%
Model 411	$400	$375	$350	$300	$250	$225	$200

The Model 411 is similar to the Model 41 single shot, but in CB Cap or .22 Short and without safety on rear of bolt. Eye screw for gallery use. 1,316 mfg. 1937- 1939 (although never cataloged). Add 50% premium for .22 Short.

	100%	98%	95%	90%	80%	70%	60%
Model 510 A	$125	$110	$90	$75	$65	$60	$55
Model 510 C (Carbine)	$175	$150	$95	$85	$75	$65	$60
Model 510 P	$135	$125	$95	$85	$75	$65	$60
Model 510 Routledge/Smoothbore	$200	$165	$150	$120	$110	$100	$90

Add 15% for Model Skeet-O Bore

	100%	98%	95%	90%	80%	70%	60%
Model 510 SB	$200	$150	$125	$120	$110	$100	$90

These models were mfg. 1939-1962.

	100%	98%	95%	90%	80%	70%	60%
Model 511 A	$150	$135	$120	$100	$75	$60	$55
Model 511 P	$175	$150	$125	$100	$75	$60	$55

These models were mfg. 1939-1962.

	100%	98%	95%	90%	80%	70%	60%
Model 512 A	$150	$135	$120	$100	$75	$60	$55
Model 512 P	$175	$150	$125	$100	$75	$60	$55

These models were mfg. 1940-1962.

	100%	98%	95%	90%	80%	70%	60%
Model 510-X	$140	$125	$110	$90	$80	$70	$60
Model 510-X SB	$200	$175	$150	$135	$125	$120	$110
Model 511-X	$155	$125	$110	$100	$90	$80	$70
Model 512-X	$155	$125	$110	$100	$90	$80	$70

These models were mfg. 1964-1966.

	100%	98%	95%	90%	80%	70%	60%
Model 514 (1948-1970)	$135	$110	$90	$75	$65	$55	$40
Model 514 P (disc. 1971)	$175	$165	$145	$120	$85	$75	$65
Model 514 BC (disc. 1971)	$155	$135	$120	$100	$85	$75	$65
Model 514 Routledge/Smoothbore	$170	$145	$120	$110	$100	$90	$80

MODEL 12A SLIDE ACTION RIFLE — .22 S, L, and LR, hammerless, 22 in. barrel, open sights, tube mag., plain grip stock. Mfg. 1909-1936.

	100%	98%	95%	90%	80%	70%	60%
	$325	$275	$225	$175	$120	$95	$85

Originally designated Model 12.

MODEL 12B (GALLERY SPECIAL) — similar to 12C, except .22 Short, all had octagon barrels.

	100%	98%	95%	90%	80%	70%	60%
	$475	$435	$400	$300	$250	$200	$150

Add 15% for extended mag. tube.

MODEL 12C — similar to 12A, except 24 in. octagon barrel. Also mfg. in grades D, E, and F — add premiums.

	100%	98%	95%	90%	80%	70%	60%
	$450	$365	$325	$250	$185	$140	$110

MODEL 12C NRA TARGET — limited manufacture.

	100%	98%	95%	90%	80%	70%	60%
	$600	$500	$400	$350	$300	$220	$140

MODEL 12CS — similar to 12C, chambered for .22 Rem. Spl. (.22 WRF).

	100%	98%	95%	90%	80%	70%	60%
	$400	$300	$250	$200	$120	$95	$85

MODEL 16/16A AUTOLOADING RIFLE — .22 autoloading cal., 22 in. barrel, open sight, tube mag. in butt stock, straight stock. Mfg. 1914-1928. Also mfg. in grades C, D, and F — add premiums.

	100%	98%	95%	90%	80%	70%	60%
	$400	$350	$250	$200	$140	$110	$90

MODEL 24/24A AUTOLOADING RIFLE — .22 S or LR, 19 in. barrel, open sights, Browning semi-auto design, bottom ejection, tube mag. through butt stock, takedown, plain pistol grip stock. Approx. 131,000 mfg. 1922-1935. Also, mfg. in Grades C Special, D Peerless, E Expert, and F Premier.

	100%	98%	95%	90%	80%	70%	60%
	$400	$300	$250	$170	$140	$110	$90

MODEL 37 "RANGEMASTER" BOLT ACTION — .22 LR, 5 shot with single shot adapter, 28 in. barrel, target sight and scope bases, target stock. Mfg. 1937-1940.

	100%	98%	95%	90%	80%	70%	60%
	$600	$475	$400	$350	$300	$250	$225

MODEL 37 - 1940 — improved trigger and stock design. Mfg. 1940-1954.

	100%	98%	95%	90%	80%	70%	60%
	$450	$400	$350	$305	$275	$220	$195

Total manufacture of the Model 37 was 12,198.

R

Grading	100%	98%	95%	90%	80%	70%	60%

MODEL 121A SLIDE ACTION RIFLE — hammerless, .22 S, L, or LR, 24 in. round barrel, tube mag., plain pistol grip stock. Mfg. 1936-1954.

	$400	$300	$250	$200	$175	$160	$150

Originally designated Model 121.

MODEL 121S — similar to 121A, except chambered for .22 Rem. Spl. (rare).

	$450	$375	$315	$260	$215	$175	$150

MODEL 121SB/ROUTLEDGE — similar to 121A, except smooth bore for .22 shot. at least 5 different chamberings and barrel markings.

	$600	$500	$350	$275	$240	$200	$165

MODEL 241/241A SPEEDMASTER — .22 S or LR, 24 in. barrel, replaced the Model 24, open sights, takedown, tube mag. through stock, non-checkered walnut stock and forearm. Approx. 56,000 mfg. 1935-1949.

	$360	$275	$250	$195	$150	$120	$100

This model was also available in a Special, Peerless, Expert, and Premier Grade - add premiums.

MODEL 513TR "MATCHMASTER" BOLT ACTION — .22 LR, 27 in. barrel, Redfield aperture sight, target stock, 6 shot, sling swivels. Mfg. 1940-1969.

	$350	$275	$220	$180	$140	$115	$95

MODEL 513S — similar to 513TR, with Marbles open sight and checkered sporter stock. Mfg. 1941-1956.

	$495	$450	$350	$290	$260	$230	$210

MODEL 521TL JR. BOLT ACTION — .22 LR, 25 in. barrel, Lyman target sights, takedown, 6 shot mag., target stock. Mfg. 1947-1969.

	$275	$250	$175	$150	$125	$100	$90

MODEL 522 VIPER — .22 LR, semi-auto blowback action, 20 in. barrel, full-length black synthetic resin stock with beavertail fore-end, 10 shot mag., cocking indicator, adj. rear sight, grooved synthetic receiver, $4\frac{5}{8}$ lbs. New 1993.

Mfg.'s Sug. Retail	$165	$145	$120	$100	$90	$80	$70	$60

MODEL 541S CUSTOM — .22 S, L, or LR, bolt action, 24 in. barrel, no sights, 5 shot, scroll engraved receiver and triggerguard, checkered walnut stock with rosewood pistol grip cap and forend tip. Mfg. 1972-1984.

	$400	$350	$300	$275	$250	$225	$200

MODEL 541T — .22 LR only, 5 shot clip mag., 24 in. standard or heavy (new 1993) barrel, checkered American walnut stock with satin finish, barrel is drilled and tapped, $5\frac{7}{8}$ lbs. New 1986.

Mfg.'s Sug. Retail	$455	$375	$290	$235	$200	$180	$165	$150

Add $26 for heavy barrel.

MODEL 550A AUTOLOADER — .22 S, L, or LR interchangeably, 24 in. barrel, open sight, shell deflector, 2 extractors, tube mag., plain one piece pistol stock. Approx. 220,000 mfg., 1941-1946.

	$195	$150	$110	$90	$80	$70	$60

This model replaced the Model 241.

MODEL 550-1 — similar to 550A, except has single extractor, mfg. 1946-1971.

	$135	$115	$100	$85	$75	$65	$55

MODEL 550P — similar to 550-1, with aperture sight.

	$190	$150	$125	$105	$85	$75	$65

MODEL 550-2G — similar to 550-1, except 22 in. barrel and eye screw for counter chain in shooting gallery.

	$200	$175	$150	$130	$110	$100	$85

Grading	100%	98%	95%	90%	80%	70%	60%

MODEL 552A SPEEDMASTER — .22 S, L, or LR, 23 in. barrel, semi-auto open sight, tube mag., pistol grip stock. Mfg. 1957-disc.

	$160	$135	$120	$100	$85	$75	$65

This model was also mfg. in a 150th Anniversary Model (1966 only). Slight premiums are being asked if condition is 98% or better.

MODEL 552C — similar to 552A, with 21 in. barrel. Mfg. 1961-1977.

	$170	$145	$130	$110	$95	$85	$75

▲ *Model 552 BDL Deluxe Speedmaster* — similar to Model 552, except checkered walnut Monte Carlo stock and forearm. Mfg. 1966 to date.

Mfg.'s Sug. Retail	$340	$265	$190	$155	$125	$105	$90	$75

MODEL 572 LIGHTWEIGHT (4 LBS.) — .22 S,L, LR, slide action, anodized alloy receiver and barrel, steel sleeved, checkered "Sun-Grain" stock and forend. Offered in 3 colors. Approx. 34,785 mfg., 1958-1962.

	100%	98%	95%	90%	80%	70%	60%
Buckskin Tan	$225	$200	$150	$130	$120	$110	$100
Crow-Wing Black	$375	$345	$295	$195	$150	$125	$100
Teal-Wing Blue	$575	$500	$400	$250	$195	$175	$150

MODEL 572SB/ROUTLEDGE — similar to 572A, except smooth bore.

	$350	$275	$225	$175	$140	$120	$100

MODEL 572(A) FIELDMASTER — .22 S, L, or LR, slide action, 21 in. barrel, walnut stock and forearm, tube mag., 5½ lbs. Mfg. 1955-1988.

	$160	$145	$125	$105	$90	$75	$65

Last Mfg.'s Sug. Retail was $176.

This model was also mfg. in a 150th Anniversary Model (1966 only). 20% premiums if condition is 98% or better

▲ *Model 572 BDL Deluxe Fieldmaster* — similar to Model 572, except with checkered walnut Monte Carlo stock and forearm. Mfg. 1966 to date.

Mfg.'s Sug. Retail	$353	$275	$200	$160	$125	$105	$90	$75

MODEL 580 SINGLE SHOT — .22 S, L or LR, bolt action, 24 in. barrel, open sights, Monte Carlo stock. Mfg. 1968-1978.

	$125	$115	$105	$100	$90	$80	$75

MODEL 580BR — Boy's Model, 1 in. shorter stock. Mfg. 1971-1978.

	$150	$120	$100	$85	$70	$65	$50

MODEL 581 — .22 LR cal., bolt action, 6 shot clip mag., converts to single shot. Mfg. 1967-1983.

	$150	$115	$110	$100	$90	$70	$60

MODEL 581 SPORTSMAN — .22 LR cal., bolt action, 5 shot clip mag., 24 in. barrel, hardwood uncheckered stock, 4¾ lbs. New 1986.

Mfg.'s Sug. Retail	$239	$200	$170	$145	$125	$105	$90	$75

MODEL 582 — similar to 581, with tube mag. Mfg. 1967-1983.

	$150	$110	$100	$90	$70	$65	$60

MODEL 591 BOLT ACTION — 5mm Rimfire Mag., 24 in. barrel, open sight, 5 shot clip mag., Monte Carlo stock. Approx. 25,000 mfg. 1970-1974.

	$195	$125	$100	$85	$75	$65	$50

5mm Rimfire ammo has been disc. for some time, and as a result, collectability on this model is mostly for 100% condition since there is no shooter utility in lower conditions. Original 5mm ammo is selling for $35-$50 per box.

MODEL 592 — similar to 591, with tube mag. Approx. 7,000 mfg. 1970-1974.

	$195	$125	$100	$85	$75	$65	$50

Grading	100%	98%	95%	90%	80%	70%	60%

RIFLES: RIMFIRE - "NYLON SERIES"

NYLON 10 SINGLE SHOT — .22 S, L, or LR, bolt action. Mfg. 1962-1964.

	$275	$210	$160	$120	$60	$50	$40

▲ **Nylon 10-SB** — similar to Nylon 10, except smooth bore barrel used for .22 shot cartridges.

	$500	$400	$250	$175	$150	$140	$125

This model is infrequently encountered.

MODEL 10-C — similar to Model 77, renamed after changing to a 10 shot mag. Mfg. 1971-1978.

	$110	$85	$70	$65	$60	$55	$50

MODEL 11 NYLON — bolt action repeater, clip fed, 6 or 10 shot mag., 4½ lbs. Mfg. 1962-1964.

	$250	$200	$150	$110	$75	$50	$40

MODEL 12 NYLON — similar to 11, with tube mag. Mfg. 1962-1964.

	$250	$200	$150	$110	$75	$50	$40

NYLON 66 AUTOLOADER — .22 LR, 19⅝ in. barrel, open sights, butt stock tube mag. holds 14 shells, 4 lbs. Stock made from Zytel plastic in black, brown, or green. Mfg. 1959-1987.

	$140	$115	$95	$80	$70	$60	$50

Add 25% for Black Diamond.
Add 30% for Apache black.
Add 50% for Seneca green.

Chrome Finish	$185	$150	$120	$95	$75	$65	$55

Last Mfg.'s Sug. Retail was $124.

NYLON 66 150TH ANNIVERSARY — mfg. in 1966 only with 150th Anniversary Remington logo on receiver.

	$200	$185	$150	$100	$85	$70	$60

NYLON 66 BICENTENNIAL — inscription on receiver. Mfg. 1976 only, brown nylon stock only.

	$200	$185	$150	$100	$85	$70	$60

NYLON 76 LEVER ACTION — similar appearance to Nylon 66 with brown or black stock, short throw lever action. Mfg. 1962-1964 only.

	$220	$180	$145	$100	$70	$60	$55

The Nylon 76 "Trail Rider" is the only lever action repeating rifle ever mfg. by Remington.

NYLON 77 — similar to Nylon 66, except with 5 shot clip mag. Mfg. 1970-1971 only.

	$140	$125	$100	$75	$65	$55	$45

NYLON APACHE 77 — similar to Model 10-C, but bright green stock. Mfg. for K-Mart in 1987.

	$135	$100	$65	$55	$50	$45	$40

RIFLES: BOLT ACTION CENTERFIRE

The models in this section have been listed in numerical sequence for quick reference.

MODEL SEVEN LIGHTWEIGHT — compact bolt action available in .17 Rem. (mfg. 1993-95), .222 Rem. (disc.), .223 Rem., .243 Win., 6mm Rem. (disc. 1995), 7mm-08 Rem., or .308 Win. cal., 18½ in. barrel, 6¼ lbs., 4 or 5 shot mag., individually test fired, oil finished American walnut, adj. rear and ramp front sight (without sights on .17 Rem.), mfg. 1982-present.

Mfg.'s Sug. Retail	$569	$465	$365	$275	$225	$205	$180	$165

Add $27 for .17 Rem. cal.
Add 10% for .222 Rem. cal.

All steel Model Sevens (including floor plate and triggerguard) are currently commanding a small premium.

▲ **Model Seven SS** — .243 Win., .308 Win., or 7mm-08 Rem. cal., features stainless steel construction, 20 in. barrel w/o sights, and synthetic stock. New 1994.

Mfg.'s Sug. Retail	$623	$495	$385	$295	$235	$205	$180	$165

Grading	100%	98%	95%	90%	80%	70%	60%

▲ *Model Seven Custom MS (Mannlicher Stock)* — .222 Rem., .22-250 Rem., .223 Rem., .243 Win., .250 Savage, .257 Roberts, .308 Win., .35 Rem., .350 Rem. Mag., 6mm Rem., or 7mm-08 Rem. cal., features 20 in. custom shop barrel with Model 7 action bedded to a Mannlicher style laminate full stock. New 1994.

| Mfg.'s Sug. Retail | $1,093 | $935 | $725 | $535 | $475 | $425 | $385 | $340 |

▲ *Model Seven Youth* — .243 Win., 6mm Rem.(disc. 1995), .308 Win. (disc.), or 7mm-08 (new 1994) cal., uncheckered hardwood stock shortened 1 in., 6 lbs. New 1993.

| Mfg.'s Sug. Retail | $465 | $380 | $340 | $285 | $225 | $205 | $180 | $165 |

▲ *Model Seven FS* — .243 Win., 7mm-08 Rem., or .308 Win. cal., 18½ in. parkerized blue barrel, gray or gray camo Kevlar fiberglass stock, adj. rear sight, 5¼ lbs. Mfg. 1987-89 only.

| | $525 | $455 | $415 | $375 | $335 | $310 | $285 |

Last Mfg.'s Sug. Retail was $600.

▲ *Model Seven Custom KS* — .223 Rem. (new 1989), 7mm BR (mfg. 1989-1993), 7mm-08 Rem. (new 1989), .308 Win. (new 1991), .35 Rem. or .350 Rem. Mag., 20 in. barrel, synthetic Kevlar stock with solid recoil pad. New 1987.

| Mfg.'s Sug. Retail | $1,089 | $935 | $715 | $535 | $475 | $425 | $385 | $340 |

This model is available from the Custom Shop only (special order).

MODEL 30A BOLT ACTION RIFLE — Enfield M/1917 type action, 7mm, .30-06, .25, .30, .32, or .35 Rem. cal., 22 in. barrel, checkered pistol grip stock. Mfg. 1921-1940.

| | $550 | $475 | $400 | $350 | $300 | $260 | $200 |

MODEL 30R CARBINE — similar to 30A, with 20 in. barrel.

| | $575 | $500 | $450 | $375 | $325 | $275 | $225 |

MODEL 30S — deluxe version of Model 30A, .257 Robts., 7mm, or .30-06 cal., 24 in. barrel, Lyman receiver sight, special stock. Mfg. 1930-1940.

| | $625 | $550 | $500 | $450 | $375 | $300 | $250 |

MODEL 78 SPORTSMAN BOLT ACTION — .223 Rem., .243 Win., .270 Win., .30-06, or .308 Win. cal., 22 in. barrel, 4 shot mag., uncheckered hardwood stock, open sights, 7 lbs. Mfg. 1985-89.

| | $270 | $235 | $210 | $190 | $170 | $160 | $150 |

Last Mfg.'s Sug. Retail was $333.

MODEL 600 BOLT ACTION — .222, .223 (very rare), 6mm, .243, .308, or .35 Rem. cal., 18½ in. VR barrel, dog leg bolt handle, checkered pistol grip stock. 94,086 were mfg. 1964-1968.

Reg. cals.	$400	$325	$275	$210	$195	$175	$155
.35 Rem.	$475	$410	$350	$320	$295	$270	$250
.222 cal.	$450	$395	$350	$320	$295	$270	$250
.223 cal.	$925	$800	$700	$500	$400	$350	$325

315 Model 600s in .223 cal. were mfg.

▲ *Model 600 Montana Centennial* — 6mm Rem., 1,020 mfg. in 1964 only.

| | $850 | $700 | $450 |

Last Mfg.'s Sug. Retail was $125.

MODEL 600 MAGNUM — 6.5mm Rem. Mag. or .350 Rem. Mag. cal., walnut (limited mfg. 1964 only) laminated walnut/beech stock with or without recoil pad (early mfg. walnut stocks did not have recoil pad). Mfg. 1965-1968.

| | $750 | $650 | $550 | $500 | $460 | $440 | $420 |

During 1964, early guns had a non-laminated walnut stock without recoil pad, with barrel markings ".350 Rem. Magnum".

MODEL 600 MOHAWK — .222 Rem., 6mm Rem. (only 14,000 mfg.), .243 Win., or .308 Win. cal., this variation was a promotional model, 18½ in. barrel with no rib. 94,920 were mfg. in 1971-1980.

| | $325 | $300 | $285 | $265 | $240 | $225 | $200 |

MODEL 660 BOLT ACTION — .222, 6mm, .243, or .308 cal., 20 in. barrel, open sight, dog leg bolt handle, checkered pistol grip stock, black pistol grip cap and forend tip. 50,536 were mfg. 1968-1971.

| | $400 | $350 | $275 | $225 | $200 | $185 | $175 |

Add 10% for .222 Rem. cal.

Grading	100%	98%	95%	90%	80%	70%	60%

▲ *.223 cal.* — 227 total mfg. This cal. was never listed in a Remington catalog.

	$1,100	$875	$725	$600	$500	$400	$350

MODEL 660 MAGNUM — 6.5 Mag. or .350 Mag. cal., laminated stock and recoil pad.

	$750	$650	$550	$450	$400	$350	$300

MODEL 720A BOLT ACTION — Enfield type action, .257 Robts., .270, or .30-06 cal., 22 in. barrel, open sights, 5 shot, checkered pistol grip stock, 2,500 mfg. 1941-1944.

	$1,150	$975	$850	$700	$600	$500	$400

Add 50%+ for .270 Win. cal.
Add 100%+ for .257 Robts. cal.

Most of the Model 720As were purchased by the military and used as trophies - these are discernible by crossed cannon proofs on wood.

Most of this model was chambered for .30-06 cal. Approx. 100 were chambered for .270 Win. and 20 or less were chambered for the .257 Robts.

MODEL 720R — similar to 720A, except with 20 in. barrel.

	$1,250	$1,050	$900	$750	$650	$550	$450

This is the rarest variation in the Model 720 Series.

MODEL 720S — similar to 720A, except with 24 in. barrel.

	$1,200	$1,000	$850	$700	$600	$500	$400

MODEL 721(A) BOLT ACTION — .270 Win., .280 Rem., or .30-06 cal., 24 in. barrel, open sights, 4 shot, plain pistol grip stock. Mfg. 1948-1962.

	$350	$275	$225	$200	$165	$155	$145

.280 Rem. (688 mfg.) and .264 Win. Mag. (1,115 mfg.) are rare in this model. 100% condition on these calibers could bring $700+.

MODEL 721ADL — similar to Model 721A, except has deluxe checkered stock.

	$415	$375	$350	$300	$250	$200	$175

The above model suffix does not appear on the gun. ADL features will determine the model.

MODEL 721BDL — similar to 721ADL, except has extra select wood.

	$550	$500	$425	$375	$325	$300	$275

The above model suffix does not appear on the gun. BDL features will determine the model.

MODEL 721A MAGNUM — .264 Win. Mag. or .300 H&H cal., 26 in. heavy barrel, recoil pad, 3 shot mag., 8¼ lbs.

	$450	$400	$360	$320	$295	$275	$260

MODEL 721ADL MAGNUM — similar to 721A Mag., checkered.

	$495	$450	$400	$350	$315	$290	$275

MODEL 721BDL MAGNUM — similar to 721ADL Mag., select wood.

	$595	$540	$465	$425	$385	$360	$330

MODEL 722(A) — short action version of 721A, .222 Rem., .222 Rem. Mag., .223 Rem., .243 Win., .244 Rem., .257 Roberts, .264 Win. Mag., .300 Savage, or .308 Win. cal., 7 lbs. Mfg. 1948-1962.

	$325	$265	$220	$200	$165	$155	$145

Subtract 10% for .300 Savage cal.
Add 10% for .257 Roberts or .308 Win. cal.

.222 Rem. Mag. (3,803 mfg.) and .243 Win. (2,186 mfg.) are rare in this model. Add approx. 25% to above values for these cals.

MODEL 722ADL — similar to Model 722(A), except with deluxe checkered wood.

	$400	$375	$350	$300	$250	$200	$175

The above model suffix does not appear on the gun. ADL features will determine the model.

Grading	100%	98%	95%	90%	80%	70%	60%

MODEL 722BDL — similar to Model 722ADL, except features extra select wood.

	100%	98%	95%	90%	80%	70%	60%
	$500	$450	$375	$325	$280	$265	$245

The above model suffix does not appear on the gun. BDL features will determine the model.

MODEL 725ADL BOLT ACTION — .222, .243, .244, .270,, .280, or .30-06 cal., 22 in. barrel, open sights, 4 shot, checkered Monte Carlo stock. 16,635 mfg. 1958-1961.

	100%	98%	95%	90%	80%	70%	60%
.30-06 cal.	$500	$425	$375	$350	$325	$300	$280
.270 Win.	$550	$500	$450	$400	$375	$350	$325
.280 Rem.	$650	$575	$500	$450	$400	$350	$325
.222 Rem.	$650	$525	$475	$425	$375	$350	$325
.244 Rem.	$650	$525	$475	$425	$375	$350	$325
.243 Win.	$650	$525	$475	$425	$375	$350	$325

Caliber mfg. breakdown is as follows: 7,657 in .30-06; 2,784 in .280 Rem.; 2,818 in .270 Win.; 840 in .244 Rem.; 1,478 in .222 Rem.; 998 in .243 Win.

MODEL 725 KODIAK — .375 H&H Mag. or .458 Win. Mag. cal., 26 in. barrel, 3 shot, recoil reducer in muzzle, deluxe checkered Monte Carlo stock, black pistol grip cap and forend tip. 52 mfg. 1961 only.

	100%	98%	95%	90%	80%	70%	60%
	$3,000	$2,700	$2,500	$2,250	$2,000	$1,800	$1,650

Only 24 rifles in .458 Win. Mag. were mfg. and 28 rifles in .375 H&H Mag.

MODEL 788 BOLT ACTION — .222, .22-250, .223, 6mm, .243, .308, .30-30, 7mm-08, or .44 Mag. cal., 18½ (Carbine), 22, or 24 in. barrel, open sight, plain pistol grip Monte Carlo stock. Mfg. 1967-1984.

	100%	98%	95%	90%	80%	70%	60%
Rifle	$325	$275	$250	$225	$210	$200	$185
Carbine (18½ in. barrel)	$325	$275	$250	$225	$210	$200	$185

Add 15% for 7mm-08 Rem. cal.
Add 30 for .44 Mag. cal.

RIFLES: MODEL 700 & VARIATIONS

MODEL 700ADL DELUXE BOLT ACTION — .22-250 (disc. 1991), .222 Rem. Mag. (disc.), .25-06 (disc. 1991), 6mm (disc.), .243, .270, .280 Rem. (marked 7mmExpress 1979-82), .30-06, .308, or 7mm Rem. Mag. cal., 20 (carbine), 22, or 24 in. barrel, open sights, 4 shot mag., checkered Monte Carlo stock or brown laminated stock (new 1988). Mfg. 1962-present.

		100%	98%	95%	90%	80%	70%	60%
Mfg.'s Sug. Retail	$472	$380	$320	$260	$210	$175	$165	$155

Add $27 for 7mm Rem. Mag. cal.
Add 20% for 20 in. carbine model.
Add 50% for .222 Rem. Mag. or .280 Rem. cal. in carbine variation.
Add 15% for 7mm Rem. Mag., .264 Win. Mag., or .300 Win. Mag. cal. with stainless steel barrel (mfg. 1962-1970).

Remington, in 1987-89, introduced a Model 700 Gun Kit that enabled the owner to assemble the stock to the barreled action. All metal work is completely finished and wood finishing is all that is required. This kit was available in most popular cals. - last mfg.'s sug. retail price was $333 (1989). Add $20 for 7mm Rem. Mag. cal.

▲ **Model 700ADL Synthetic** — same cals. as Model 700ADL Deluxe, features fiberglass reinforced synthetic stock with positive checkering, black matte finish on metal/wood, open sights. Approx. 7⅜ lbs. New 1996.

		100%	98%	95%
Mfg.'s Sug. Retail	$412	$335	$265	$225

Add $27 for 7mm Rem. Mag. cal.

▲ **Model 700ADL/LS** — .243 Win. (new 1989), .270 Win. (new 1989), .30-06, or 7mm Rem. Mag. cal., brown laminate stock with checkering. Mfg. 1988-1993.

	100%	98%	95%	90%	80%	70%
	$400	$345	$275	$230	$210	$195	$165

Last Mfg.'s Sug. Retail was $485.

Add $27 for 7mm Rem. Mag. cal.

Grading	100%	98%	95%	90%	80%	70%	60%

MODEL 700BDL CUSTOM DELUXE — similar to 700ADL Deluxe, except with hinged floorplate, cut skipline checkering, black pistol grip cap and forend tip, .17 Rem., .22-250, .222 Rem., .223 Rem., .243 Win., .25-06, .264 Mag. (disc.), .270 Win., .280 Rem. (mfg. 1992-95), .300 Savage (mfg. 1992 only), .30-06, .308 Win. (disc. 1995), .35 Whelen (mfg. 1989-94), 6mm Rem. (disc. 1994), 7mm Rem. Mag., 7mm-08 Rem. (disc. 1994), .300 Win. Mag., .338 Win. Mag. (mfg. 1988-94), or 8mm Mag. (disc.) cal. Supplied with iron sights first year.

Mfg.'s Sug. Retail	$576	$465	$385	$325	$280	$250	$220	$195
.222 Rem. Mag.		$525	$475	$400	$340	$300	$280	$260
.350 Rem. Mag.		$625	$525	$425	$350	$325	$300	$275
6.5mm Rem. Mag.		$625	$525	$425	$350	$325	$300	$275

Add $40 for left-hand model (available in certain cals. only).
Add $27 for .17 Rem., 7mm Rem. Mag., .300 Win. Mag., .35 Whelen or .338 Win. Mag. cal.
Add 15% for 7mm Rem. Mag., .264 Win. Mag., or .300 Win. Mag. cal. with stainless steel barrel (mfg. 1962-1970).

Remington mfg. the Model 700BDL in .350 Rem. Mag. and 6.5mm Rem. Mag. Approx. 1,500 were assembled in 1969 only. The .350 Rem. Mag. mfg. in 1969 is 3 times rarer than the 1985 Model 700 Classic chambered for .350 Rem. Mag.

▲ *Model 700BDL DM* — .243 Win., .25-06 Rem., .270 Win., .280 Rem., 6mm Rem., 7mm Rem. Mag., 7mm-08 Rem., .30-06, .308 Win., .300 Win. Mag., or .338 Win. Mag. cal., Monte Carlo walnut stock with 20 LPI skip-line checkering, high polish bluing, black forend cap, open sights, 3-4 shot detachable mag. New 1995.

Mfg.'s Sug. Retail	$629	$515	$435	$355	$315	$285	$265	$250

Add $27 for Mag. cals.
Add $40 for left-hand model (available in certain cals. only).

▲ *Model 700BDL Lew Horton Special Edition* — .257 Roberts cal., 500 mfg. in 1990 only, first time the 700BDL has been offered in .257 Roberts cal.

	$575	$525	$450	$395	$360	$325	$280

Last Mfg.'s Sug. Retail was $580.

MODEL 700 MUZZLE LOADER (ML/MLS) — .50 or .54 cal., inline black powder bolt action design, please refer to listing in the Black Powder section.

MODEL 700BDL EUROPEAN — .243 Win., .270 Win., .280 Rem., 7mm-08 Rem., 7mm Rem. Mag., .30-06, or .308 cal., Monte Carlo stock with hand-rubbed oil finish, 22 or 24 (Mag. cals. only) in. barrel, hinged floorplate, iron sights, approx. 7¼ lbs. Disc. 1994

	$445	$375	$325	$280	$250	$220	$195

Last Mfg.'s Sug. Retail was $532.

Add $27 for 7mm Rem. Mag. cal.

MODEL 700BDL MOUNTAIN RIFLE (FIXED MAG.) — .243 Win. (new 1988), .25-06 (new 1992), .257 Roberts (new 1991), .270 Win., 7mm-08 Rem. (new 1988), .280 Rem., .30-06, .308 (new 1988), or 7x57mm Mauser (new 1990) cal., 22 in. tapered barrel, checkered satin finished American walnut stock with cheekpiece and ebony forend, 4 shot mag., without sights, 6¾ lbs. Mfg. 1986-94.

	$445	$380	$315	$275	$250	$220	$195

Last Mfg.'s Sug. Retail was $532.

▲ *Model 700BDL Mountain Stainless* — .25-06, .270 Win., .280 Rem., or .30-06 cal., 22 in. barrel, black synthetic stock with pressed checkering, blind mag., 7¼ lbs. Mfg. 1993 only.

	$450	$385	$315

Last Mfg.'s Sug. Retail was $532.

MODEL 700 MOUNTAIN RIFLE DM — .243 Win., .25-06 Rem., .270 Win., .280 Rem., 7mm-08 Rem., or .30-06 cal., detachable mag., satin finished American walnut stock, satin bluing, without sights, 6¾ lbs. New 1995.

Mfg.'s Sug. Retail	$629	$515	$440	$355	$315	$285	$265	$250

Grading	100%	98%	95%	90%	80%	70%	60%

MODEL 700 CUSTOM KS MOUNTAIN RIFLE — .270 Win., .280 Rem., .300 Win. Mag., .300 Wby. Mag. (new 1989), .30-06, .338 Win. Mag. (new 1986), .35 Whelen (new 1989), 7mm Rem. Mag., 8mm Rem. Mag. (new 1986), or .375 H&H Mag. cal., 22 in. barrel, features extra lightweight Kevlar fiber-reinforced stock — available in either right or left-hand action. New 1986.

Mfg.'s Sug. Retail	$1,089	$885	$750	$565	$465	$415	$385	$350

    Add $67 for left-hand action.

    This model is available from the Custom Shop only (special order).

▲ *Model 700 Custom KS Mountain Stainless Rifle* — similar to Model 700 Custom KS Mountain Rifle, except in stainless steel, not available in .35 Whelen or 8mm Rem. Mag. cal., not available in left-hand action. New 1995.

Mfg.'s Sug. Retail	$1,241	$1,080	$895	$700

MODEL 700 SENDERO SPECIAL — .25-06 Rem., .270 Win., .300 Win. Mag., or 7mm Rem. Mag. cal., similar to Model 700 VS, except has long action for Mag. cals., 24 (non-cataloged) or 26 in. barrel, 9 lbs. New 1994.

Mfg.'s Sug. Retail	$686	$565	$465	$395	$325	$295	$265	$250

    Add $27 for Mag. cals.
    Add $100 for fluted barrel (not cataloged).

▲ *Model 700 Sendero SF (Stainless Fluted)* — .25-06 Rem., .300 Win. Mag., or 7mm Rem. Mag. cal., 26 in. varmint type flued barrel, approx. 8½ lbs. New 1996.

Mfg.'s Sug. Retail	$826	$700	$575	$450

    Add $27 for Mag. cals.

MODEL 700 CAMO SYNTHETIC — .22-250 (disc. 1993), .243 Win., .270 Win. (disc. 1993), .280 Rem. (disc. 1993), 7mm-08 Rem. (disc. 1993), 7mm Rem. Mag., .30-06, .308 (disc. 1993), or .300 Wby. Mag. (disc. 1993) cal., 22 or 24 (Mag. only) in. barrel, features synthetic stock and is fully camouflaged in Mossy Oak Bottomland pattern, iron sights, approx. 7¼ lbs. Mfg. 1992-94.

	$490	$425	$350	$315	$285	$265	$250

Last Mfg.'s Sug. Retail was $581.

    Add $27 for Mag. cals.

MODEL 700BDL SS (STAINLESS SYNTHETIC) — .223 Rem. (mfg. 1993-94), .243 Win. (mfg. 1993-94), .25-06 (disc. 1994), .270 Win., .280 Rem. (disc. 1995), .30-06, .308 (disc. 1994), 7mm Rem. (mfg. 1993-94), 7mm-08 Rem. (mfg. 1993-94), .300 Win. Mag. (new 1993), .300 Wby. Mag. (mfg. 1993-94), .338 Win. Mag. (mfg. 1993-94), 7mm Rem. Mag., or 7mm Wby. Mag. (disc. 1994) cal., features matte finished 416 stainless steel barrel, receiver, and bolt, black synthetic stock with checkering, drilled and tapped, hinged floorplate mag., 24 in. barrel, no sights, 6¼ - 7 lbs. New 1992.

Mfg.'s Sug. Retail	$623	$515	$435	$350

    Add $26 for Mag. cals.

▲ *Model 700LSS* — .300 Win. Mag. or 7mm Rem. Mag. cal., stainless steel barreled action, gray tinted laminate Monte Carlo wood stock, 24 in. barrel, w/o sights, 7½ lbs. New 1996.

Mfg.'s Sug. Retail	$676	$550	$450	$360

▲ *Model 700BDL SS DM* — .243 Win., .25-06 Rem., .270 Win., .280 Rem., 6mm Rem. (disc. 1995), 7mm Rem. Mag., 7mm-08 Rem., .30-06, .308 Win., .300 Win. Mag., .300 Wby. Mag., or .338 Win. Mag. cal., features 3-4 shot detachable mag., stainless steel, 24 in. barrel, satin finish metalwork, black non-reflective stock with checkering, without sights. New 1995.

Mfg.'s Sug. Retail	$676	$550	$450	$360

    Add $26 for Mag. cals.
    Add $86 for muzzle brake (Model 700BDL SS DM-B, new 1996, Mag. cals. only).

MODEL 700BDL VARMINT SPECIAL — .22-250, .222, .223, .25-06 (disc.), 6mm, .243, .308 Win., or 7mm-08 cal., 24 in. heavy barrel, checkered walnut stock, no sights. Mfg. 1967-1994.

	$480	$420	$350	$315	$285	$265	$250

Last Mfg.'s Sug. Retail was $565.

▲ *Model 700VS (Varmint Synthetic)* — .220 Swift, .22-250, .223 Rem., or .308 Win. cal., composite, textured black and gray synthetic stock features Kevlar, fiberglass, and graphite, matte metal finish, 26 in. barrel w/o sights, 9 lbs. New 1992.

Mfg.'s Sug. Retail	$686	$565	$415	$395	$325	$295	$265	$250

Grading	100%	98%	95%	90%	80%	70%	60%

▲ *Model 700VS SF (Varmint Synthetic Stainless Fluted)* — .220 Swift, .22-250 Rem., .223 Rem., or .308 Win. cal., stainless steel action with 26 in. barrel with flutes. New 1994.

Mfg.'s Sug. Retail	$826	$695	$550	$450			

▲ *Model 700 VLS (Varmint Laminated Stock)* — .222 Rem. (mfg. 1995 only), .22-250 Rem., .223 Rem., .243 Win., or .308 Win. cal., 26 in. heavy barrel, blued metalwork, w/o sights, brown laminated stock with skip line checkering, 9⅜ lbs. New 1995.

Mfg.'s Sug. Retail	$609	$510	$435	$355	$315	$285	$265	$250

MODEL 700 SAFARI GRADE — heavier 700BDL, in .375 H&H, 8mm Rem. Mag. (new 1986), .416 Rem. Mag. (new 1989), or .458 Win. Mag. cal., 3 shot mag., 24 in. barrel, available with either Classic or Monte Carlo stock configuration, Custom Shop special order only, 9 lbs. Mfg. 1962-present.

Mfg.'s Sug. Retail	$1,093	$915	$750	$560	$440	$415	$385	$330

Add $67 for left-hand stock (Classic stock only).

▲ *Model 700 Custom KS Safari Grade* — 8mm Rem. Mag., .375 H&H, .416 Rem. Mag., or .458 Win. Mag., stock made from extra lightweight Kevlar fiber, 24 in. barrel. New 1989.

Mfg.'s Sug. Retail	$1,326	$1,135	$895	$725	$640	$560	$485	$430

Add $68 for left-hand stock.

▲ *Model 700 Custom KS Safari Stainless* — .375 H&H, .416 Rem. Mag., or .458 Win. Mag. cal., features Kevlar stock and stainless steel action. New 1993.

Mfg.'s Sug. Retail	$1,405	$1,200	$1,050	$875			

▲ *Model 700 Mountain Rifle Custom KS Wood Grained Kevlar* — similar to Model 700 Custom KS Safari Grade, except has wood grained Kevlar stock. Mfg. 1992-1993.

	$1,000	$875	$750	$650	$550	$485	$430

Last Mfg.'s Sug. Retail was $1,109.

Add $63 for left-hand action.

MODEL 700 APR (AFRICAN PLAINS RIFLE) — .300 Win. Mag., .300 Wby. Mag., .338 Win. Mag., .375 H&H, or 7mm Rem. Mag, custom shop variation with 26 in. custom shop barrel, satin finish metal and brown, pressure laminated, checkered wood stock with satin finish and butt pad. New 1994.

Mfg.'s Sug. Retail	$1,466	$1,250	$1,025	$895	$750	$650	$550	$485

MODEL 700 ALASKAN WILDERNESS RIFLE — .300 Win. Mag., .300 Wby. Mag., .338 Win. Mag., .375 H&H, or 7mm Rem. Mag., black synthetic Kevlar stock, stainless steel action plated with satin finished black chrome. New 1994.

Mfg.'s Sug. Retail	$1,318	$1,125	$950	$750			

MODEL 700BDL CLASSIC — similar to 700BDL, except classic straight stock, high polish bluing, has been offered in .220 Swift, .222 Rem., .22-250, .250 Savage (250/3000), 6.5x55mm Swedish, 6mm, 7x57mm Mauser, .243, .25-06 Rem., .257 Roberts, .264 Win. Mag., .270, .300 Win. Mag., .300 Wby. Mag., .30-06, 7mm Wby. Mag., .338 Win. Mag., .350 Rem. Mag., .35 Whelen, .300 H&H, or .375 H&H cal.

Mfg.'s Sug. Retail	$623	$500	$395	$315	$265	$250	$220	$195

This model is produced in limited quantities of a different caliber each year. Add premiums for several older calibers in NIB condition only (including 7x57mm Mauser, .257 Roberts, .300 H&H, and .375 H&H).

The following is a list of annual Limited Classic calibers offered previously with year of manufacture: 7x57mm (1981), .257 Roberts (1982), .300 H&H (1983), .250 Savage (1984), .350 Rem. Mag. (1985), .264 Win. Mag. (1986), .338 Win. Mag. (1987), .35 Whelen (1988), .300 Wby. Mag. (1989), .25-06 Rem. (1990), 7mm Wby. Mag. (1991), .220 Swift (1992), and .222 Rem. (1993), 6.5x55mm Swedish (new 1994), .300 Win. Mag. (1995), .375 H&H (1996).

MODEL 700 AS — .22-250, .243 Win., .270 Win., .280 Rem., .30-06, .308 Win., 7mm Rem. Mag., or .300 Wby. Mag. cal., synthetic stock is made from Arylon resin, matte black finished stock and metal, 22 or 24 in. barrel, 6½ lbs. Mfg. 1989-91 only.

	$445	$370	$310	$275	$250	$220	$195

Last Mfg.'s Sug. Retail was $528.

Add $21 for 7mm Rem. Mag. or .300 Wby. Mag. cal.

Grading	100%	98%	95%	90%	80%	70%	60%

MODEL 700 RS — .270 Win., .280 Rem., or .30-06 cal., 22 in. polished blue barrel, gray or gray camo DuPont Rynite synthetic stock with smooth cheekpiece and solid recoil pad, iron sights, $7\frac{1}{4}$ lbs. Mfg. 1987-1988 only.

	$490	$440	$405	$370	$335	$310	$285

Last Mfg.'s Sug. Retail was $547.

Add 10% for .280 Rem. cal.

In 1987 approx. 1,000 rifles were dual barrel marked - 7mm EXP REM .280 REM. These specimens will command a 40% premium.

MODEL 700 FS — .243 Win., .270 Win., .30-06, .308 Win., or 7mm Rem. Mag. cal., 22 in. polished blue barrel, gray or gray camo Kevlar fiberglass stock with solid recoil pad, iron sights, $6\frac{1}{4}$ lbs. Mfg. 1987-1988 only.

	$530	$460	$415	$375	$335	$310	$285

Last Mfg.'s Sug. Retail was $613.

Add $20 for 7mm Rem. Mag. cal. (24 in. barrel).

MODEL 700C GRADE — from custom shop, no engraving, deluxe checkered wood with rosewood forearm cap. Mfg 1964-1983.

	$850	$775	$695	$635	$510	$440	$400

MODEL 700D PEERLESS GRADE — scroll engraving, best wood. Mfg. 1962-1983.

	$1,650	$1,400	$1,200	$1,000	$880	$825	$690

MODEL 700F PREMIER GRADE — elaborate engraving, best wood. Mfg. 1962-1983.

	$3,250	$2,750	$2,420	$2,200	$2,035	$1,870	$1,760

MODEL 700 CUSTOM GRADE — special order only, grades differ in amount of engraving and type of walnut. Available as a custom order only through Remington. Values below reflect 1991 information. The Remington Custom Shop should be contacted for a current price quotation and the availability of options.

Special order Model 700s mfg. between early '60s - 1982 were designated C Grade, D Grade, or F Grade. Values will approximate Custom Grade Models I-III listed below. In 1991, Remington discontinued Custom Grade Model designations.

▲ *Custom Grade Model I* — mfg. 1983-1991.

	$1,100	$925	$795

Last Mfg.'s Sug. Retail was $1,314.

▲ *Custom Grade Model II* — mfg. 1983-1991.

	$1,995	$1,675	$1,295

Last Mfg.'s Sug. Retail was $2,335.

▲ *Custom Grade Model III* — mfg. 1983-1991.

	$2,900	$2,150	$1,750

Last Mfg.'s Sug. Retail was $3,650.

▲ *Custom Grade Model IV* — mfg. 1983-1991.

	$4,875	$4,100	$2,950

Last Mfg.'s Sug. Retail was $5,695.

MODEL 700 CUSTOM RIFLE — the Remington Custom Shop should be contacted directly (see Trademark Index) for current information regarding this model. New 1992.

Mfg.'s Sug. Retail	$2,507	$2,050	$1,725	$1,275	$1,025	$875	$750	$625

Beginning 1992, Remington stopped Custom Grade Model designations in favor of individualized quotations per work order. The Custom Shop should be contacted directly regarding special order pricing (see Trademark Index).

RIFLES: TARGET BOLT ACTION

MODEL 40X SPORTER — .22 LR only, sporterized version of the 40X Target Rifle, 5 shot clip, custom 700 stock, a special order only gun from the factory. Rare, less than 700 mfg. 1969-1977, parts clean-up to 1980.

	$1,850	$1,325	$925	$800	$720	$650	$595

This model was last listed in the 1977 Remington catalog — retail was $525.

Grading	100%	98%	95%	90%	80%	70%	60%

MODEL 40X TARGET RIFLE — bolt action single shot, .22 LR, 28 in. heavy barrel, Redfield Olympic sights, scope bases, target stock, rubber butt, 12¾ lbs. Mfg. 1955-1964.

	100%	98%	95%	90%	80%	70%	60%
	$495	$395	$325	$260	$220	$190	$175
No sights	$450	$360	$295	$240	$200	$180	$165

MODEL 40X STANDARD BARREL — similar to 40X Target Rifle, with lighter barrel, 10¾ lbs.

	100%	98%	95%	90%	80%	70%	60%
	$475	$380	$310	$250	$220	$190	$175
No sights	$450	$360	$295	$240	$200	$180	$165

MODEL 40X CENTERFIRE — similar to Model 40X Rim Fire, except in .222, .222 Mag., .30-06, or .308 cal. Mfg. 1961-1964.

	100%	98%	95%	90%	80%	70%	60%
	$475	$380	$310	$250	$220	$190	$175
No sights	$450	$360	$295	$240	$200	$180	$165

MODEL 40XB RANGEMASTER RIMFIRE — .22 LR, bolt action single shot, 28 in. light or heavy barrel, no sights, target stock with guide rail, rubber butt. Mfg. 1964-1974.

	100%	98%	95%	90%	80%	70%	60%
	$525	$420	$335	$275	$220	$195	$165

Add a premium for this model equipped with a mag.

MODEL 40-XB RANGE MASTER CENTERFIRE — over 12 cals., custom made, 27½ in. barrel (current model is stainless), single shot or repeater, walnut stock, test fired, 10½ - 11 lbs.. Mfg. 1964-present.

Mfg.'s Sug. Retail	$1,333	$1,095	$900	$660	$500	$410	$370	$315

Add $100 for repeater model.
Add $62 for left-hand action (disc. 1994)

An International Free Rifle was also offered - only 107 were mfg. with premiums being paid.

MODEL 40-XB KS (KEVLAR STOCK) — .220 Swift, 27¼ in. bright finished stainless steel barrel, single shot, black finish Kevlar stock, no sights, 9¾ lbs. New 1987.

Mfg.'s Sug. Retail	$1,504	$1,250	$935	$700

Subtract $20 for bench rest model (Model 40-XBBR KS).
Add $100 for repeater model.
Add $168 for 2 oz. trigger.

MODEL 40-XB REPEATER — similar to 40XB Centerfire, with 5 shot mag. Disc.

	$870	$770	$625	$500	$420	$370	$315

MODEL 40-XC KS — .223 Rem. (new 1995) or 7.62 Nato cal., National Match Course rifle, adj. trigger pull, wood (disc. 1989) or Kevlar (standard 1990) stock.

Mfg.'s Sug. Retail	$1,484	$1,240	$925	$695

Subtract $120 for wood stock.

MODEL 40-XR KS RIMFIRE SINGLE SHOT — .22 LR, single shot bolt action, 24 in. heavy barrel, no sights, adj. butt plate and palm stop, target wood (disc. 1989) or Kevlar (standard 1990) stock. Mfg. 1974-present.

Mfg.'s Sug. Retail	$1,381	$1,165	$875	$675

Subtract $120 for wood stock.
Add $89 for benchrest model (Model 40-XR BR).

MODEL 40-XR KS SPORTER — .22 LR, Model 40-XR action, match chambered, custom sporter contoured 24 in. barrel, drilled and tapped receiver, w/o sights, special order. New 1994.

Mfg.'s Sug. Retail	$1,428	$1,195	$950	$700	$600	$500	$425	$375

MODEL 40-XR CUSTOM SPORTER — the Remington Custom Shop should be contacted directly (see Trademark Index) for current information on this model.

Mfg.'s Sug. Retail	$2,507	$2,050	$1,700	$1,250	$1,025	$875	$750	$625

Beginning 1992, Remington stopped Custom Grade Model designations in favor of individualized quotations per work order. The Custom Shop should be contacted directly regarding special order pricing (see Trademark Index).

Grading	100%	98%	95%	90%	80%	70%	60%

MODEL 40XR CUSTOM SPORTER — .22 cal. only, single shot, available on special order from Remington's Custom Shop only, Grades I-IV (disc. 1991) increase by amount of engraving, quality of wood, and other special order options/features. Mfg. 1986-1991.

Values for Custom Grades listed below reflect 1991 (the year of discontinuance) price information. The Remington Custom Shop should be contacted directly regarding current values and options.

▲ *Custom Grade Model I* — mfg. 1986-1991.

	$1,100	$925	$795

Last Mfg.'s Sug. Retail was $1,314.

▲ *Custom Grade Model II* — mfg. 1986-1991.

	$1,995	$1,675	$1,295

Last Mfg.'s Sug. Retail was $2,335.

▲ *Custom Grade Model III* — mfg. 1986-1991.

	$2,900	$2,150	$1,750

Last Mfg.'s Sug. Retail was $3,650.

▲ *Custom Grade Model IV* — mfg. 1986-1991.

	$4,875	$4,100	$2,950

Last Mfg.'s Sug. Retail was $5,695.

MODEL 540X RIMFIRE — .22 LR, single shot bolt action, 26 in. heavy barrel, no sights, target stock, adj. butt. Mfg. 1969-1974.

	$325	$285	$250	$225	$200	$175	$150

MODEL 540XR — similar to 540X, with large position style stock with adj. butt plate. Mfg. 1974-1983.

	$350	$300	$275	$225	$200	$185	$175

RIFLES: FLINTLOCK

Please refer to the Black Powder section in the back of this book for more information.

100%	98%	95%	90%	80%	70%	60%	50%	40%	30%	20%	10%

SHOTGUNS: SxS

It may be helpful to consult the "NRA Antique Condition Standards" in this text to convert to the Percentage Grading System listed below.

MODEL 1873 SxS HAMMER — includes Models 1875, 1876, 1878, and 1879, also known as Whitmore Hammer Lifter or Whitmore Lifter, 10 or 12 ga., 28 or 30 in. decarbonized or damascus barrels, top "thumb-lever" action activated by pushing upward on opening lever, rib top marked "E. REMINGTON & SONS, ILION. N.Y.", patented "AUG.8.1871, APRIL 16.1872", made in various models and grades, high grade models are damascus barreled, pistol grip was optional. Approx. 13,000 mfg. of all Whitmore models combined, mfg. 1873-1882.

▲ *Decarbonized Steel Barrels, Grade 1*

$1,350	$1,000	$850	$650	$550	$450	$400	$350	$300	$275	$250	$225

There were also a very few double rifles and combination guns (shotgun/rifle barrel) made in this model - they are very rare. Above values represent standard Grade 1 decarbonized steel barrel model without checkering or engraving.

MODEL 1882 SxS HAMMER — includes the rare Model 1883, 10 or 12 ga., 28, 30, or 32 in. decarbonized, twist, or damascus steel barrels, rib marked "E. REMINGTON & SONS, ILION, N.Y.", checkered pistol grip stock, decarbonized steel barrels were lowest grade, higher grade examples are damascus barreled and will bring premiums. Approx. 16,000 Model 1882s, and possibly 1,000 Model 1883s were mfg., produced from 1882-1888.

▲ *Decarbonized Steel Barrels, Grade 1*

$1,275	$1,075	$995	$895	$825	$725	$625	$525	$425	$325	$275	$225

R

100%	98%	95%	90%	80%	70%	60%	50%	40%	30%	20%	10%

▲ *Damascus Barrels, Grade 2*

$1,150	$1,025	$800	$650	$550	$450	$400	$350	$300	$275	$250	$225

Add 15% for Model 1883 variation to above values.
Add 15% for optional auxiliary rifle barrel inserts.

MODEL 1885/1887 SxS HAMMER — 10, 12, or 16 ga., slightly improved variation of the Model 1882, 28, 30, or 32 in. decarbonized, twist, or damascus steel barrels, top of rib marked "E. REMINGTON & SONS, ILION, N.Y.", higher grades are damascus barreled and bring premiums, approx. 7,000 mfg. 1885-1889.

▲ *Decarbonized Steel Barrels, Grade 1*

$1,550	$1,300	$1,075	$995	$895	$825	$725	$625	$525	$425	$325	$275

▲ *Damascus Barrels, Grade 2*

$1,400	$1,150	$950	$850	$750	$650	$550	$450	$350	$300	$275	$250

MODEL 1889 SxS HAMMER — 10, 12 or 16 ga., 28, 30, or 32 in. decarbonized, twist, or damascus barrels, exposed "circular" hammers, rib top marked "REMINGTON ARMS CO. ILION N.Y. U.S.A.", checkered pistol grip stock, grade number is stamped on water table left of the serial number, higher grades are damascus barreled and will bring premiums. 134,200 mfg. 1889-1908.

▲ *Decarbonized Steel Barrels, Grade 1*

$1,300	$1,200	$1,000	$900	$850	$775	$650	$550	$425	$375	$295	$225

▲ *Twist Steel Barrels, Grade 2*

$1,250	$1,050	$950	$850	$750	$650	$550	$450	$350	$300	$275	$225

Grades range from No. 1 - No. 7, No. 7 being the highest. Decarbonized steel was never offered on higher grades. No. 3 - No. 7 are various grades of damascus steel barrels. Grades 4-7 are engraved.

MODEL 1894 SxS HAMMERLESS — 10, 12, or 16 ga., 26-32 in. "Remington", "Ordnance", or damascus steel barrels, auto ejectors, hammerless, boxlock, double triggers, checkered pistol grip or straight stock. 41,194 mfg. 1894-1910 in the 100,000 block serial range.

$1,300	$1,200	$1,000	$900	$850	$775	$650	$550	$425	$375	$325	$295

Deduct 10% for non-ejector guns.

Grades offered range from "A" (lowest) to "E" and "Special" (highest). Large premiums exist for higher grade models in excellent condition. Trap model was named either "F.E." or "C.E.O.". Values above assume "A" model (most frequently encountered specimen). Engraving begins with Grade "B".

MODEL 1900 SxS HAMMERLESS — 12 or 16 ga., 28 or 30 in. Remington or damascus steel barrels, lower priced to meet market competition, quality is a cut below the Model 1894. 98,475 mfg. 1900-1910 in the 300,000 block serial range.

$1,000	$900	$775	$700	$625	$500	$450	$350	$250	$200	$185	$150

Deduct 10% for non-ejector guns.

Grades ranged from "K", "K.E.", or damascus "K.D." and "K.E.D.". Both steel and damascus barrels were guaranteed for nitro powder, mechanically the same as Model 1894. No engraving was offered on this model.

PARKER AHE — while advertised, the Remington re-issue of the original Parker AHE Model was never mfg. due to product liability considerations. Older Remington manufactured Parkers may be found in the Parker section of this text.

Grading	100%	98%	95%	90%	80%	70%	60%

SHOTGUNS: SLIDE ACTION & SEMI-AUTO

MODEL 1908 SLIDE ACTION — 12 ga., hammerless, bottom ejection, takedown, plain barrel only, blue finish, sight notch on receiver top, marked "REMINGTON ARMS CO." with February 3rd, 1903 and May 18th, 1905 patent dates, walnut pistol grip stock and short forearm, hard rubber buttplate, 7½ lbs., approx. 10,000 mfg. 1908-1910.

	100%	98%	95%	90%	80%	70%	60%
	$350	$275	$225	$175	$160	$135	$110

There were 7 grades of this model (No.'s 0-6) that were originally priced from $27 to approx. $140. This model was renamed the Model 10 in 1911.

MODEL 10A SLIDE ACTION — 12 ga., 26-32 in. barrels, various chokes, takedown, plain pistol grip stock. Mfg. 1907-1929. Add 10% for 32 in. full choke barrel.

	100%	98%	95%	90%	80%	70%	60%
	$350	$275	$225	$175	$160	$135	$110

REMINGTON AUTOLOADING GUN (PRE-MODEL 11) — 12 ga. only, original Remington mfg. of the Browning A-5, various grades, 20 (riot), 26, or 28 in. plain or matted rib barrel. Mfg. 1905-1910.

	100%	98%	95%	90%	80%	70%	60%
	$350	$275	$225	$175	$160	$135	$110

Add 20% for matted rib.

MODEL 11A AUTOLOADER 5-SHOT — 12, 16, or 20 ga., 26-32 in. barrels, takedown, various chokes, Browning type, checkered pistol stock. Approx. 300,000 mfg., 1911-1948.

	100%	98%	95%	90%	80%	70%	60%
Plain barrel	$295	$240	$215	$185	$165	$150	$120
Solid rib	$395	$315	$235	$200	$185	$165	$140
Vent. rib	$440	$360	$335	$305	$275	$220	$165

This model was mfg. under "A - 5" patent agreements (including royalties) with Fabrique Nationale in Herstal, Belgium.

MODEL 11B SPECIAL — higher grade wood, engraved.

	100%	98%	95%	90%	80%	70%	60%
	$525	$440	$385	$360	$305	$250	$195

MODEL 11D TOURNAMENT

	100%	98%	95%	90%	80%	70%	60%
	$950	$850	$725	$550	$495	$470	$440

MODEL 11E EXPERT

	100%	98%	95%	90%	80%	70%	60%
	$1,175	$975	$875	$775	$675	$595	$525

MODEL 11F PREMIER

	100%	98%	95%	90%	80%	70%	60%
	$1,850	$1,550	$1,375	$1,100	$975	$850	$750

Note: Grades differ in quality, grade of wood, and amount of engraving.

SPORTSMAN MODEL — 12, 16, or 20 ga., 26 in. barrel, skeet choke, beavertail forend. Mfg. 1931-1949.

	100%	98%	95%	90%	80%	70%	60%
Plain barrel	$325	$275	$250	$195	$165	$140	$120
Solid rib	$400	$350	$300	$250	$200	$180	$150
Vent. rib	$470	$415	$360	$330	$275	$250	$220

This model was manufactured in Field, Riot, and Skeet configurations.

MODEL 17A SLIDE ACTION — 20 ga., 26-32 in. barrel, various chokes, takedown, bottom ejection, 4 shot mag., plain grip stock. Approx. 48,000 mfg., 1917-1933.

	100%	98%	95%	90%	80%	70%	60%
Plain barrel	$300	$250	$220	$195	$165	$140	$110
Solid. rib	$395	$360	$325	$290	$270	$250	$210

Grades range from A - F in suffix form, F being the highest. Large premiums are paid for mint condition, higher grade models.

MODEL 29A SLIDE ACTION — 12 ga., 26-32 in. barrel, bottom ejection, various chokes, takedown, 5 shot mag., checkered pistol grip stock. Approx. 24,000 mfg., 1929-1933. Add 15% for solid rib, 25% for VR.

	100%	98%	95%	90%	80%	70%	60%
	$325	$265	$235	$200	$150	$120	$100

▲ *32 in. barrel*

	100%	98%	95%	90%	80%	70%	60%
	$525	$475	$425	$350	$250	$200	$180

Grades range from A - C and TA - TF, lowest to highest. Premiums exist for finer condition upper grades. The Model 29 was similar in appearance to the Model 10.

Grading	100%	98%	95%	90%	80%	70%	60%

MODEL 29S — "Trap Special" with trap style straight grip stock, matted rib.

	100%	98%	95%	90%	80%	70%	60%
	$500	$450	$425	$375	$350	$325	$300

MODEL 31A SLIDE ACTION — 12, 16, or 20 ga., side ejection, 2 or 4 shot mag., 26-32 in. barrels, various chokes, takedown, pistol grip stock. Approx. 160,000 mfg., 1931-1949.

	100%	98%	95%	90%	80%	70%	60%
Plain barrel	$395	$345	$300	$265	$225	$185	$150
Solid rib	$455	$385	$345	$300	$270	$230	$190
Vent. rib	$475	$415	$375	$320	$290	$250	$210

Grades range from A - F suffixes. Higher grades will bring considerable premiums in excellent condition. TC suffix is Target Model. A Model 31L (lightweight) was mfg. 1948-1950 and while rare, demand dictates to subtract 10% for this variation. Early models will command a small premium in this model.

MODEL 31 SPECIAL — higher grade wood and engraving.

	100%	98%	95%	90%	80%	70%	60%
	$650	$550	$440	$385	$360	$305	$275

MODEL 31 TOURNAMENT

	100%	98%	95%	90%	80%	70%	60%
	$1,100	$880	$715	$580	$525	$495	$470

MODEL 31E EXPERT

	100%	98%	95%	90%	80%	70%	60%
	$1,320	$1,100	$935	$880	$770	$660	$605

MODEL 31F PREMIER

	100%	98%	95%	90%	80%	70%	60%
	$2,420	$1,980	$1,760	$1,540	$1,320	$1,100	$880

Note: Grades differ in quality, grade of wood, and amount of engraving.

MODEL 31TC TRAP — similar to 31A, with 12 ga. only, 30 or 32 in. barrel, vent. rib, full choke, trap stock and beavertail forend, pad.

	100%	98%	95%	90%	80%	70%	60%
	$660	$550	$495	$470	$415	$385	$305

Subtract 10% for lightweight receiver.

MODEL 31S TRAP — solid rib barrel, plainer wood.

	100%	98%	95%	90%	80%	70%	60%
	$495	$415	$385	$330	$275	$250	$220

MODEL 31H HUNTER — similar to 31S, with sporter stock.

	100%	98%	95%	90%	80%	70%	60%
	$470	$385	$360	$305	$250	$220	$195

MODEL 31 SKEET — similar to 31A, with 26 in. skeet bored barrel, standard solid rib, beavertail forend.

	100%	98%	95%	90%	80%	70%	60%
Plain barrel	$495	$415	$385	$330	$275	$250	$220
Vent. rib	$605	$495	$445	$415	$360	$305	$275

Subtract 10% for lightweight receiver.

SHOTGUNS: MODEL 870 & VARIATIONS

3 in. shells (12 or 20 ga.) may be shot in Magnum receivers only regardless of what the barrel markings may indicate (the ejection port is larger in these Magnum models with M suffix serialization).

MODEL 870AP SLIDE ACTION — "Wingmaster", 12, 16, or 20 ga., 26, 28, or 30 in. barrel, 5 shot, various chokes, plain pistol grip stock. Mfg. 1950-1963.

	100%	98%	95%	90%	80%	70%	60%
Plain barrel	$220	$195	$175	$165	$140	$120	$110
Vent. rib	$250	$220	$200	$195	$165	$150	$140

Add 15% for "Sun Grain" blonde wood (optional beginning 1959).

MODEL 870DL — deluxe checkered version of 870AP. Mfg. 1950-1963.

	100%	98%	95%	90%	80%	70%	60%
Plain barrel	$250	$220	$200	$180	$165	$140	$120
Matted top barrel	$275	$250	$220	$210	$195	$165	$140
Vent. rib	$300	$275	$250	$225	$200	$175	$150

MODEL 870BDL — select walnut stock.

	100%	98%	95%	90%	80%	70%	60%
Plain barrel	$275	$250	$220	$200	$180	$165	$140
Vent. rib	$315	$290	$260	$240	$210	$195	$165

Grading	100%	98%	95%	90%	80%	70%	60%

SPORTSMAN 12 PUMP — 12 ga. only (3 in. chamber), 28 or 30 in. barrel, recoil pad, VR standard, hardwood stock and forearm, Model 870 type action, 7½ lbs. Mfg. 1985-86 only.

| | $225 | $195 | $180 | $165 | $150 | $140 | $130 |

Last Mfg.'s Sug. Retail was $270.

Add $35 for Rem. chokes

MODEL 870 EXPRESS — 12, 20 (new 1991), 28, or .410 ga., 3 in. chamber, 20, 21 (Turkey Express only), 25 (28 or .410 ga. only), 26, or 28 in. VR Rem. choked (12 or 20 ga., supplied with Mod. Rem. choke) barrel, parkerized metal, matte finished hardwood stock and forearm, solid recoil pad, 7¼ lbs. New 1987.

Mfg.'s Sug. Retail $292 | $240 | $195 | $165 | $150 | $140 | $130 | $125

Add $15 for 28 or .410 ga.
Add $13 for Turkey Express Model.
Add $103 for Combo package (extra 20 in. IC barrel, 12 or 20 ga.).

▲ *Model 870 Synthetic Express* — 12 ga. only, 26 in. VR barrel with 1 Rem. choke, features black synthetic stock and forearm. New 1994.

Mfg.'s Sug. Retail $299 | $245 | $195 | $165 | $150 | $140 | $130 | $125

▲ *Model 870 Express Deer Gun* — 12 ga. only, 20 in. IC choked barrel or fully rifled barrel with rifle sights, Monte Carlo stock. Introduced in 1991.

Mfg.'s Sug. Retail $287 | $235 | $195 | $165 | $150 | $140 | $130 | $125

Add $38 for fully rifled deer barrel.
Add $78 for cantilever scope system and IC Rem. choke (disc. 1991).

▲ *Model 870 Youth* — 20 ga. only, 21 in. VR barrel with Rem. choke, 13 in. LOP with recoil pad, 6 lbs.

Mfg.'s Sug. Retail $292 | $240 | $195 | $165 | $150 | $140 | $130 | $125

Add $33 for Youth Deer Gun (fully rifled 20 in. barrel). New 1994.

▲ *Model 870 Express Synthetic HD (Home Defense)* — 12 ga. only, 18 in. cyl. choked barrel with bead sights, synthetic stock and forend. Introduced 1991.

Mfg.'s Sug. Retail $292 | $235 | $195 | $165 | $150 | $140 | $130 | $125

MODEL 870 FIELD WINGMASTER — 12, 16 (disc. 1980), 20, 28 (mfg. temporarily disc. late 1994), or .410 (mfg. temporarily disc. late 1994) ga., various barrel lengths, incorporates twin slide rails, 3 in. chambers became standard in 1985, Rem. chokes became standard in 1987, lightweight frame on 20 ga. was introduced 1972, checkered walnut stock and forearm, a choice of high gloss or satin wood finish became available in 1991. Mfg. 1964-present.

Plain barrel | $250 | $225 | $205 | $190 | $175 | $160 | $150

▲ *Vent. rib* — became standard in 1985.

Mfg.'s Sug. Retail $505 | $360 | $285 | $245 | $200 | $185 | $170 | $160

Subtract $13 for 20 ga.
Subtract 10% without Rem. chokes.
Add $48 for left-hand model (12 ga. only, disc. 1994).
Add $80 for 20 in. fully rifled Cantilever deer barrel (12 ga. - new 1992 or 20 ga. - mfg. 1992-95).

▲ *Small Gauge Model 870* — scaled down 870 on lightweight smaller frame, in 28 or .410 ga., 25 in. fixed choke (F or M) barrel, 6-6½ lbs. Mfg. 1969-temporarily disc. VR became standard 1984.

| | $415 | $350 | $295 | $240 | $200 | $185 | $170 |

Last Mfg.'s Sug. Retail was $504.

Subtract $40 without VR.

MODEL 870 MAGNUM DUCK GUN — 3 in. chamber, 12 or 20 ga., 26, 28, or 30 in. full or mod. barrel, recoil pad. Mfg. 1964-present. 3 in. chambers became standard on all Model 870s starting in 1985. Rem. chokes became standard 1987 (introduced 1986 as $40 option).

Please refer to Model 870 Field Wingmaster prices.

MODEL 870 SPECIAL PURPOSE — 12 ga. only, differs only in that metal parts are sand blasted, choice of Mossy Oak Camo (new 1992), black synthetic, or checkered wood stock with low luster finish, 21 (Turkey barrel), 26, or 28 in. VR barrel. Rem. chokes were introduced 1986.

Add $75 for wood stock and forearm (disc. 1992).
Subtract 10% without Rem. chokes.

Grading	100%	98%	95%	90%	80%	70%	60%

▲ *Model 870 Special Purpose Synthetic Camo* — 12 ga. only, 26 or 28 (disc. 1995) in. VR barrel with Rem. choke, available in either Mossy Oak (disc. 1995) or Bottomland finish. New 1994.

Mfg.'s Sug. Retail	$483	$370	$300	$235	$200	$170	$150	$130

▲ *Model 870 SPS-BG Camo (Special Purpose Synthetic Big Game)* — 12 ga. only, 20 in. plain barrel with rifle sights and Rem. choke. Mfg. 1994 only.

		$350	$285	$235	$200	$170	$150	$130

Last Mfg.'s Sug. Retail was $442.

▲ *Model 870 Special Purpose Turkey (SPS-T)* — 12 ga. only, 21 in. VR barrel with Rem. choke, available in flat black, Mossy Oak, or Greenleaf finish.

Mfg.'s Sug. Retail	$412	$310	$280	$230	$200	$170	$150	$130

Add $85 for either Camo finish.

▲ *Model 870 Special Purpose Deer Gun (SPS-Deer)* — 12 ga. only, 3 in. chamber, 20 in. Rem. choke barrel (disc. 1992) or fully rifled barrel with iron sights (new 1993), satin finished (disc. 1992) or black synthetic (new 1993) stock and forearm, matte black metal, 7¼ lbs. New 1989.

Mfg.'s Sug. Retail	$423	$335	$270	$225	$195	$175	$160	$145

Add $28 for Cantilever deer barrel with Rem. choke.
Add $60 for fully rifled Cantilever deer barrel.
Add $65 for Cantilever scope mount system (disc. 1992).

MODEL 870 LIGHTWEIGHT — 20 ga. only, lighter and shorter mahogany stock than model listed below, 23 in. barrel. Mfg. 1972-1983.

		$270	$230	$210	$190	$175	$165	$155

Add $30 for VR.

MODEL 870 LIGHTWEIGHT (MAGNUM) — 20 ga., 3 in. chamber, 26 or 28 in. barrel, 6 lbs. Mfg. 1972-1994. Rem. chokes became standard 1987.

		$365	$320	$260	$225	$200	$175	$160

Last Mfg.'s Sug. Retail was $460.

Subtract 10% without Rem. chokes.
Subtract $40 without VR.

MODEL 870 SPECIAL FIELD — 12 or 20 (LW-20) ga., lighter straight grip stock with solid recoil pad, 21 (disc. 1993) or 23 (new 1994) in. VR barrel, 6¼ or 7 lbs. New 1984. Rem. chokes became standard 1987 (introduced 1986 as $40 option). Disc. 1995.

		$380	$320	$265	$230	$210	$190	$175

Last Mfg.'s Sug. Retail was $473.

Subtract 10% without Rem. chokes.

MODEL 870 BRUSHMASTER — 12 or 20 (disc.) ga., 20 in. barrel with imp. cyl. (disc.) or Rem. choke and rifle sights, 3 in. chamber standard for 1985, normal bluing with satin finished wood. Disc. 1994.

		$355	$310	$255	$225	$200	$175	$160

Last Mfg.'s Sug. Retail was $452.

Add $43 for left-hand model.

MODEL 870 MARINE MAGNUM — 12 ga. only, 18 in. barrel, features electroless nickel plating on all metal parts, supplied with 7 shot mag., sling swivels and Cordura sling, 7½ lbs.

Mfg.'s Sug. Retail	$500	$385	$325	$255	$225	$200	$175	$160

MODEL 870 POLICE — 12 ga. only, 18 or 20 in. plain barrel, choice of blue or parkerized finish, bead or rifled (disc. 1995, 20 in. barrel only) sights, Police cylinder or IC choke. New 1994.

Mfg.'s Sug. Retail	$411	$320	$275	$220	$195	$175	$160	$145

Add $13 for parkerized finish.
Add $44 for rifled sights.

MODEL 870 RIOT — 12 ga. only, 18 or 20 in. barrel, choice of blue or parkerized metal finish. Disc. 1991.

		$295	$265	$225	$200	$170	$150	$130

Last Mfg.'s Sug. Retail was $355.

Add $19 for police rifle sights (20 in. barrel only).

MODEL 870 D-GRADE (TOURNAMENT) — custom order only, any gauge. Mfg. 1950-present.

Mfg.'s Sug. Retail	$2,610	$2,100	$1,650	$1,200

Grading	100%	98%	95%	90%	80%	70%	60%

MODEL 870 F-GRADE (PREMIER) — custom order only, any gauge. Mfg. 1950-present.
Mfg.'s Sug. Retail $5,377 $4,495 $3,550 $2,500

MODEL 870 F-GRADE W/GOLD (GOLD PREMIER) — with gold inlays, custom order only. Mfg.
1950-present.
Mfg.'s Sug. Retail $8,062 $7,125 $4,050 $3,000
> Note: Grades differ in quality, grade of wood, and amount of engraving.

MODEL 870 DUCKS UNLIMITED — "DU" in serial number, disc.
$335 $270 $195

> Remington has offered many variations of the Model 870 specifically manufactured according to individual DU chapter specifications. The price of a DU 870 varies substantially from the "DU point of purchase" to real market conditions. When contemplating a DU gun it is always important to know how many of that particular variation were manufactured. The Remington factory normally has this information unless the special DU work was subcontracted elsewhere.

> While most DU guns are good vehicles for fund raising, their collectability to date has been minimal. Actual market conditions indicate that unless production is truly limited, most DU firearms sell very close to the model it was derived from. Also, any collectability that does exist is for 100% guns new in the box with warranty papers. Used DU guns have values comparable to the standard model from which they are derived.

> In addition to regular DU guns, Remington has also produced special editions including the 1982 Mississippi Edition (dinner gun) and a 1974 DU (dinner gun — first 500 mfg.). These were rarer DU shotguns, and current values could vary significantly.

MODEL 870 BICENTENNIAL — 12 ga. only, configurations include Trap, Skeet, and Trade, mfg. to commemorate U.S. Bicentennial (1776-1976).
Trap or Skeet $425 $350 $295
Trade $375 $295 $225
> In 1976, the 870 Bicentennial Trap retailed for $255 (add $10 for Monte Carlo stock), and the Skeet retailed for $220.

MODEL 870 SKEET — 12, 20, 28, or .410 ga., 26 in. VR skeet bore barrel. Mfg. 1950-1981.
$295 $260 $230 $215 $200 $185 $170

MODEL 870 SKEET MATCHED PAIR — .410 or 28 ga., 1,503 cased sets mfg. 1969 only.
$995 $850 $700 $650 $620 $575 $530

MODEL 870 TA TRAP — 12 ga. trap model, deluxe walnut, VR. Add $15 for Monte Carlo stock. Disc. 1986.
$365 $345 $280 $240 $220 $200 $180
Last Mfg.'s Sug. Retail was $430.

MODEL 870 TB TRAP — similar to 870, with 28 or 30 in. VR full choke barrel, trap stock, recoil pad. Mfg. 1950-1981.
$395 $355 $285 $245 $220 $200 $185

MODEL 870 TC TRAP — higher grade walnut and special VR, Rem. chokes became standard 1987. Mfg. 1950-1979, reintroduced 1996.
Mfg.'s Sug. Retail $632 $565 $450 $350 $275 $240 $220 $200
Add $15 for Monte Carlo stock.
Early Model 870 TC Trap guns had hand cut checkering.

COMPETITION TRAP — 12 ga. competition model, reduced recoil, special checkered walnut, VR. Mfg. 1980-1986.
$500 $450 $385 $325 $280 $240 $210
Last Mfg.'s Sug. Retail was $680.

MODEL 870 ALL AMERICAN TRAP — 30 in. full choke barrel, engraved receiver, triggerguard and barrel, deluxe trap stock. Approx. 1,000 mfg., 1972-1976.
$795 $700 $650 $605 $495 $440 $385

Grading	100%	98%	95%	90%	80%	70%	60%

SHOTGUNS: SEMI-AUTO

MODEL 48 SPORTSMAN SEMI-AUTO — 12, 16, or 20 ga., 26, 28, or 32 in. barrels, 3 shot, mechanical (solid breech) ejection system, various chokes, rounded receiver, checkered pistol grip stock with cap. Approx. 275,000 mfg., 1949-1959.

	100%	98%	95%	90%	80%	70%	60%
	$300	$225	$200	$185	$175	$165	$140
VR barrel	$325	$275	$250	$200	$175	$165	$140

MODEL 48B SELECT

	100%	98%	95%	90%	80%	70%	60%
	$420	$360	$310	$290	$245	$220	$195

MODEL 48D TOURNAMENT

	100%	98%	95%	90%	80%	70%	60%
	$1,100	$825	$715	$660	$605	$440	$415

MODEL 48F PREMIER

	100%	98%	95%	90%	80%	70%	60%
	$2,420	$2,035	$1,540	$1,210	$990	$770	$715

MODEL 48A RIOT GUN — 12 ga. only, 20 in. plain barrel.

	100%	98%	95%	90%	80%	70%	60%
	$275	$220	$195	$165	$150	$140	$110

MODEL 48SA SKEET — 26 in. barrel, skeet bore, ivory bead. Mfg. 1949-1960.

	100%	98%	95%	90%	80%	70%	60%
	$305	$275	$255	$230	$210	$195	$165
With VR barrel	$360	$310	$285	$260	$230	$210	$195

MODEL 48SC TARGET

	100%	98%	95%	90%	80%	70%	60%
	$385	$360	$330	$305	$275	$250	$220

MODEL 48SD TOURNAMENT

	100%	98%	95%	90%	80%	70%	60%
	$1,100	$825	$715	$660	$605	$440	$415

MODEL 48SF PREMIER

	100%	98%	95%	90%	80%	70%	60%
	$2,200	$1,925	$1,650	$1,210	$990	$770	$715

MODEL 11-48 SEMI-AUTO — 12, 16, 20, 28 (introduced 1952), or .410 (introduced 1954) ga., recoil operated action, walnut stock. Approx. 429,000 mfg., 1949-1968.

	100%	98%	95%	90%	80%	70%	60%
Plain barrel	$300	$225	$200	$185	$175	$165	$140
VR barrel	$325	$275	$250	$200	$175	$165	$140

Add 15% - 40% for 28 or .410 ga.

MODEL 58ADL "SPORTSMAN - 58" SEMI-AUTO — 12, 16, or 20 ga., 26, 28, or 30 in. barrel, gas operation, various chokes, 3 shot, checkered pistol grip stock, scroll game scene engraved. Approx. 271,000 mfg., 1956-1963.

	100%	98%	95%	90%	80%	70%	60%
Plain barrel	$275	$250	$220	$195	$140	$120	$110
VR barrel	$360	$305	$275	$250	$220	$165	$140

Add 5% for Magnum in 12 ga.

MODEL 58BDL — similar to 58ADL, with select wood.

	100%	98%	95%	90%	80%	70%	60%
Plain barrel	$325	$275	$250	$225	$210	$195	$165
VR barrel	$365	$325	$300	$275	$250	$200	$175

MODEL 58SA SKEET GUN — similar to 58ADL, with 26 in. skeet bore VR barrel, skeet stock.

	98%	95%	90%	80%	70%	60%
	$360	$330	$305	$275	$250	$200	$175

MODEL 58SC TARGET

	100%	98%	95%	90%	80%	70%	60%
	$495	$440	$415	$385	$330	$305	$275

MODEL 58D TOURNAMENT

	100%	98%	95%	90%	80%	70%	60%
	$825	$715	$635	$580	$525	$470	$440

MODEL 58SF PREMIER

	100%	98%	95%	90%	80%	70%	60%
	$1,650	$1,375	$1,210	$1,045	$965	$880	$800

Note: Models differ in grade of wood, and amount of engraving.

Grading	100%	98%	95%	90%	80%	70%	60%

MODEL 878A "AUTOMASTER" — 12 ga. gas operated semi-auto, 26, 28, or 30 in. barrels, action similar to Model 58. Approx. 62,000 mfg., 1959-1962. Add 15% for VR.

	$235	$200	$185	$170	$160	$150	$135

> Barrels on this model are interchangeable with those on the Model 58.

MODEL SP-10 — 10 ga., 3½ in. chamber, semi-auto stainless steel gas system operation, lighter recoil than most 12 ga. Mags., 26 or 30 in. barrel with ⅜ in. VR and Rem. chokes (2), checkered stock and forearm with low gloss satin finish, matte metal finish, crossbolt safety, recoil pad, supplied with camo sling, approx. 11 lbs. Introduced 1989.

Mfg.'s Sug. Retail	$1,033	$895	$765	$650	$595	$525	$450	$395

> The first 5,000 SP-10s were assigned special serialization (LE89 prefix) and will no doubt command premiums shortly.
>
> This model is NOT a re-designed Ithaca Mag-10 and the parts are NOT interchangeable. The SP-10 is a new design.

▲ **Model SP-10 Camo** — 23 in. VR barrel, choice of Mossy Oak or Bottomland (new 1994) Camo finish. New 1993.

Mfg.'s Sug. Retail	$1,121	$965	$875	$750	$675	$625	$550	$475

▲ **Model SP-10 Turkey Combo** — includes choice of either 26 or 30 VR regular barrel and extra 22 in. deer barrel with rifle sights. Mfg. 1991-94.

	$1,000	$870	$750	$675	$625	$550	$475

> Last Mfg.'s Sug. Retail was $1,132.

SHOTGUNS: MODEL 1100 & VARIATIONS

3 in. shells (12 or 20 ga.) may be shot in Magnum receivers only, regardless of what the barrel markings may indicate (the ejection port is larger in these Magnum models with M suffix serialization).

MODEL 1100 SEMI-AUTO FIELD — 12 (disc. 1987), 16 (disc.), or 20 ga., 26, 28, or 30 in. barrels, various chokes, gas operated, checkered pistol grip stock, Rem. chokes became standard 1987 (introduced 1986 as $40 option), VRs became standard in 1985 on this model, 20 ga. lightweight frame became standard 1972, prices below assume VR and Rem. chokes. Mfg. 1963-1988.

	$325	$280	$250	$220	$200	$180	$165

> Last Mfg.'s Sug. Retail was $545.

> Subtract $40 if without VR.
> Subtract $45 if without Rem. chokes.
> This model is currently produced only in a Lightweight or Mag. 20 (3 in. chamber), 28, or .410 ga., since the release of the Model 11-87.

SPORTSMAN 12 AUTO — 12 ga. only, 2¾ in. chamber, 28 or 30 in. barrel, similar to Model 1100 action, VR standard, hardwood stock and forearm, 7¾ lbs. Mfg. 1985-86 only. Add $40 for Rem. chokes (new 1986).

	$300	$260	$220	$195	$170	$160	$150

> Last Mfg.'s Sug. Retail was $405.

MODEL 1100 SPECIAL FIELD — 12, 20 (LT-20), or .410 (limited mfg.) ga., 21 (disc. 1993) or 23 (new 1994) in. VR barrel, various chokes, gas operated, checkered straight grip stock, VR standard, high gloss wood finish (1991 only) or satin wood finish. New 1984. Rem. chokes became standard in 1987.

Mfg.'s Sug. Retail	$625	$480	$395	$325	$265	$230	$210	$180

> Subtract 10% if without Rem. chokes.
> Add 15%-20% for .410 ga.
> Two hundred .410 ga.'s were mfg. for National Shooting Supplies in Houston, TX.

MODEL 1100 SMALL GAUGE — 28 or .410 ga., 25 in. barrel, scaled down receiver, skeet and field fixed choke, VR standard. Mfg. 1969-temporarily disc. 1994.

	$495	$425	$350	$285	$250	$225	$200

> Last Mfg.'s Sug. Retail was $647.

Grading	100%	98%	95%	90%	80%	70%	60%

MODEL 1100 LT-20 — similar to 1100, 20 ga. only, 2¾ in. chamber, with mahogany stock and lightened receiver, 26, or 28 in. barrel, VR became standard 1985, hi-gloss or satin finish, 6½ lbs. Mfg. 1970-present.

Mfg.'s Sug. Retail	$625	$480	$395	$325	$265	$225	$200	$180

Subtract $40 if without VR.

MODEL 1100 YOUTH — similar to Model 1100 Lightweight, except stock is 1 in. shorter and 21 in. barrel only.

Mfg.'s Sug. Retail	$625	$480	$395	$325	$265	$225	$200	$180

MODEL 1100 LIGHTWEIGHT MAGNUM (LT-20 MAG.) — chambered for 3 in. 20 ga. Mag., 20, 26, or 28 in. barrel, Rem. chokes became standard 1987. Introduced 1977.

Mfg.'s Sug. Retail	$625	$480	$395	$325	$265	$225	$200	$180

Subtract 10% if without VR.

MODEL 1100 MAGNUM DUCK GUN — similar to 1100, in 12 (disc. 1987) or 20 ga., 3 in. chamber, recoil pad, VR became standard 1984. Mfg. 1963-1988. Rem. chokes became standard 1987.

		$400	$325	$280	$260	$220	$200	$180

Last Mfg.'s Sug. Retail was $533.

Add $80 for left-hand model (disc. 1986).
Subtract $40 if without VR.
Subtract $45 if without Rem. chokes.

▲ *Model 1100 Magnum Special Purpose (SP)* — 12 ga. only, low luster finish on stock and forearm, sand blasted metal parts. Mfg. 1985-86 only. Add $40 for Rem. chokes (new 1986).

		$365	$300	$275	$255	$220	$200	$180

Last Mfg.'s Sug. Retail was $550.

MODEL 1100 SYNTHETIC — 12 or 20 ga., 2¾ in. chamber, 26 (20 ga. only) or 28 (12 ga. only) in. VR barrel with Rem. choke, checkered black synthetic stock and forearm, matte metal finish, 7-7½ lbs. New 1996.

Mfg.'s Sug. Retail	$492	$395	$320	$265

MODEL 1100 "1 OF 3,000" FIELD — 12 ga. only, limited edition, serial numbered 1-3,000, deluxe walnut, gold washed etched hunting scenes on receiver, 28 in. modified VR barrel. Mfg. 1980.

		$1,100	$900	$600	$500	$425	$350	$300

MODEL 1100 DEER GUN — 12 (disc. 1987) or 20 ga., 20 (disc.), 21 in. (20 ga. only) or 22 (disc.) in. imp. cyl. barrel with rifle sights.

Mfg.'s Sug. Retail	$584	$435	$345	$270	$225	$200	$185	$165

Add $80 for left-hand model (disc. 1986).
Add $117 for 21 in. fully rifled Cantilever deer barrel.

▲ *Model 1100 Special Purpose Deer (SP)* — similar to Model 1100 Deer Gun, except has low luster finish on stock and forearm, sandblasted metal parts. Mfg. 1986 only.

		$335	$295	$275	$255	$220	$200	$180

Last Mfg.'s Sug. Retail was $495.

MODEL 1100 LT-20 (TOURNAMENT SKEET) — 12 or 20 (LT-20) ga., 26 in. skeet bored barrel, optional Cutts Compensator. Mfg. 1963-1994, reintroduced 1996.

Mfg.'s Sug. Retail	$710	$595	$495	$440	$375	$325	$275	$225

Add $40 for left-hand model (disc. 1986).

MODEL 1100 SMALL GAUGE SKEET — 28 or .410 ga., 25 or 26 (disc.) in. VR barrel, 6½-7¼ lbs. Mfg. 1969-temporarily disc. 1994.

		$525	$430	$375	$325	$275	$225	$200

Last Mfg.'s Sug. Retail was $692.

2½ in. chamber is standard on the .410 ga.

MODEL 1100 SKEET MATCHED PAIR — 28 and .410 ga.'s, walnut stock and forearm. 5,067 cased Skeet sets were mfg. 1969 and 1970 only.

		$1,125	$950	$800	$725	$675	$630	$600

Grading	100%	98%	95%	90%	80%	70%	60%

MODEL 1100 SPORTING — 28 ga. only, 25 in. VR barrel with Rem. chokes, high gloss checkered walnut stock and forearm, 6½ lbs. New 1996.

Mfg.'s Sug. Retail $725	$615	$500	$450	$375	$325	$275	$225

MODEL 1100 TA TRAP — 12 ga., 30 in. barrel, recoil pad on regular stock, available in left or right-hand. Mfg. 1979-86.

	$410	$330	$295	$270	$230	$210	$190

Last Mfg.'s Sug. Retail was $570.

Add $15 for Monte Carlo stock.
Add $50 for left-hand model.

MODEL 1100 TB TRAP — 12 ga., 30 in. VR full choke barrel, special trap stock, select wood. Mfg. 1963-1981.

	$435	$350	$300	$270	$230	$210	$190
Monte Carlo stock	$450	$360	$310	$280	$235	$220	$195

MODEL 1100 TOURNAMENT TRAP — 12 ga., 30 in. VR full choke barrel, special trap stock, extra select wood. Mfg. 1979-86.

	$540	$480	$390	$345	$295	$255	$210

Last Mfg.'s Sug. Retail was $675.

Add $15 for Monte Carlo stock.

MODEL 1100 150TH ANNIVERSARY — limited mfg. in 1966 only.

	$400	$340	$290

MODEL 1100 BICENTENNIAL — 12 ga. only, configurations include Trap, Skeet, and Trade, mfg. to commemorate U.S. Bicentennial (1776-1976).

Trap or Skeet	$425	$350	$295
Trade	$375	$295	$225

In 1976, the 1100 Bicentennial Trap retailed for $320 (add $10 for Monte Carlo stock), the Skeet retailed for $285, and the Trade retailed for $270.

MODEL 1100 DUCKS UNLIMITED — "DU" in serial number.

Remington has offered many variations of the Model 1100 specifically manufactured according to individual DU chapter specifications. The price of a DU 1100 varies substantially from the "DU point of purchase" to real market conditions. When contemplating a DU gun it is always important to know how many of that particular variation were manufactured. The Remington factory normally has this information unless the special DU work was subcontracted elsewhere.

While most DU guns are good vehicles for fund raising, their collectability to date has been minimal. Actual market conditions indicate that unless production is truly limited, most DU firearms sell very close to the model it was derived from. Also, any collectability that does exist is for 100% guns new in the box with warranty papers. Used DU guns have values comparable to the standard model from which they are derived.

In addition to regular DU guns, Remington has also produced special editions including the 1982 Atlantic Flyway (dinner gun) and a 1981 DU Lt. 20 ga. and 12 ga. (dinner gun — 2,400 mfg. each), and a 1973 dinner gun (600 mfg.). These were rarer DU shotguns, and current values could vary significantly.

MODEL 1100 D-GRADE (TOURNAMENT) — custom order only, any gauge. Mfg. 1963-present.

Mfg.'s Sug. Retail	$2,610	$2,100	$1,650	$1,200

MODEL 1100 F-GRADE (PREMIER) — custom order only, any gauge. Mfg. 1963-present.

Mfg.'s Sug. Retail	$5,377	$4,495	$3,550	$2,500

MODEL 1100 F-GRADE W/GOLD (GOLD PREMIER) — with gold inlay, custom order only. Mfg. 1963-present.

Mfg.'s Sug. Retail	$8,062	$7,125	$4,050	$3,000

Note: Grades differ in quality, grade of wood, and amount of engraving.

Grading	100%	98%	95%	90%	80%	70%	60%

SHOTGUNS: MODEL 11-87 & VARIATIONS

MODEL 11-87 PREMIER — 12 ga. only (3 in. chamber), 26, 28, or 32 in. VR Rem. choked barrel, successor to Model 1100, gas compensating action adaptable to all loads, stainless steel magazine tube, polished blue finish, satin finished and checkered walnut stock and forearm, a high gloss wood finish option became available in 1991 at N/C, solid recoil pad, $8\frac{1}{8}$-$8\frac{3}{8}$ lbs. Introduced 1987.

Mfg.'s Sug. Retail	$670	$535	$425	$335	$285	$240	$220	$200

    Add $50 for left-hand action.
    Add $64 for fully rifled 21 in. Cantilever deer barrel.
    Note: Model 11-87 Premier barrels are not interchangeable with Model 1100 barrels.

MODEL 11-87 SP (SPECIAL PURPOSE) — see individual sub-models listed below.

▲ *Model 11-87 SP 3 in. Magnum* — 12 ga. only (3 in. chamber), 26, 28, or 30 (disc.) in. VR Rem. choked barrel, parkerized metal with satin finish wood stock and forearm, vent. recoil pad, included camouflaged nylon sling, $8\frac{1}{4}$ lbs. New 1987.

Mfg.'s Sug. Retail	$644	$515	$430	$340	$285	$240	$220	$200

    Subtract $20 for 21 in. Deer barrel with rifle sights.

▲ *Model 11-87 SPS 3 in. Magnum* — similar to Model 11-87 SP 3 in. Mag., except is supplied with black synthetic stock and forearm.

Mfg.'s Sug. Retail	$644	$515	$430	$340	$285	$240	$220	$200

▲ *Model 11-87 SPS Camo (Special Purpose Synthetic Camo)* — 12 ga. only, 26 or 28 in. VR barrel with Rem. choke, available in Mossy Oak Bottomland finish. New 1994.

Mfg.'s Sug. Retail	$730	$580	$430	$350	$290	$250	$225	$200

▲ *Model 11-87 SPS-BG Camo (Special Purpose Synthetic Big Game)* — 12 ga. only, 21 in. plain barrel with rifle sights and Rem. choke. Mfg. 1994 only.

		$555	$425	$350	$290	$250	$225	$200

    Last Mfg.'s Sug. Retail was $692.

▲ *Model 11-87 SPS (Special Purpose Deer Gun)* — 12 ga. only (3 in. chamber), 21 in. IC or Rem. choked (new 1989) or fully rifled (new 1993) barrel with iron sights, parkerized metal with matte finished wood or black synthetic (new 1993) stock and forearm, vent. recoil pad, includes camouflaged nylon sling, $7\frac{1}{4}$ lbs. New 1987.

Mfg.'s Sug. Retail	$665	$525	$430	$340	$285	$240	$220	$200

    Add $18 for Cantilevered deer barrel with Rem. choke.
    Add $60 for fully rifled Cantilever deer barrel.
    Add $54 for Cantilever scope mount system.
    Subtract 10% for fixed choke barrel.
    Rem. chokes became standard on this model in 1989.

▲ *Model 11-87 SPS-T (Special Purpose Turkey)* — 12 ga. only, 21 in. VR barrel with Rem. choke, available in flat black, Mossy Oak, or Greenleaf finish.

Mfg.'s Sug. Retail	$657	$525	$425	$335	$285	$240	$220	$200

    Add $87 for either Camo finish.

MODEL 11-87 SPORTING CLAYS — 12 ga. only, 26 or 28 in. VR barrel with extended Rem. chokes (knurled extension chokes allow for no-wrench field changes), specially balanced, satin finished walnut, top metal surfaces have been fine matte finished, radiused recoil pad, twin bead sights on $\frac{5}{16}$ wide VR, $7\frac{1}{2}$ lbs. New 1992.

Mfg.'s Sug. Retail	$732	$630	$525	$425	$375	$325	$295	$260

MODEL 11-87 PREMIER SKEET — 12 ga. only, 26 in. VR Rem. choked barrel, deluxe walnut with quality cut checkering, $7\frac{3}{4}$ lbs. New 1987.

Mfg.'s Sug. Retail	$718	$560	$460	$350	$295	$250	$225	$200

    Add $72 for left-hand action (26 in. barrel only).
    Subtract 10% if without Rem. chokes.

Grading	100%	98%	95%	90%	80%	70%	60%

MODEL 11-87 PREMIER TRAP — 12 ga. only, 30 in. raised VR Rem. choked barrel, deluxe walnut with quality cut checkering, 8¼ lbs. New 1987.

Mfg.'s Sug. Retail	$725		$575	$465	$375	$325	$285	$240	$215

 Add $16 for Monte Carlo stock.
 Add $37 for left-hand action (disc. 1994).
 Subtract 10% if without Rem. chokes.

MODEL 11-87 175TH ANNIVERSARY — 12 ga. only, 28 in. barrel with Rem-chokes, 175th Anniversary Model (1816-1991) with light engraving and high gloss wood finish. 1991 mfg. only.

           $515 $425 $335

Last Mfg.'s Sug. Retail was $618.

MODEL 11-87 D-GRADE (TOURNAMENT) — custom order only, any gauge. Mfg. 1963-present.

Mfg.'s Sug. Retail	$2,610		$2,100	$1,650	$1,200

MODEL 11-87 F-GRADE (PREMIER) — custom order only, any gauge. Mfg. 1963-present.

Mfg.'s Sug. Retail	$5,377		$4,495	$3,550	$2,500

MODEL 11-87 F-GRADE W/GOLD (GOLD PREMIER) — with gold inlay, custom order only. Mfg. 1963-present.

Mfg.'s Sug. Retail	$8,062		$7,125	$4,050	$3,000

 Note: Grades differ in quality, grade of wood, and amount of engraving.

100%	98%	95%	90%	80%	70%	60%	50%	40%	30%	20%	10%

SHOTGUNS: SINGLE BARREL

MODEL NO. 3 RIDER SINGLE BARREL — 10, 12, 16, 20, 24, or 28 ga., single barrel, 30 or 32 in. barrels, top lever break open, plain pistol grip stock. Approx. 25,000 mfg. 1893-1905.

$325	$290	$260	$230	$200	$170	$140	$110	$85	$65	$50	$35

MODEL NO. 9 RIDER SINGLE BARREL — similar to No. 3, with auto ejector. Mfg. 1902-1910.

$375	$325	$290	$260	$230	$200	$170	$140	$110	$85	$65	$50

Grading	100%	98%	95%	90%	80%	70%	60%

MODEL 90-T (TRAP) — 12 ga., 32 (disc. 1993) or 34 in. full choke VR barrel with fixed full choke, matte black receiver and wood around tang area, deluxe checkered stock and forearm, short throw top-lever release, elongated forcing cone, approx. 8¾ lbs. New 1992.

Mfg.'s Sug. Retail	$3,199		$2,775	$2,350	$1,975	$1,650	$1,375	$1,150	$975

 ▲ *Model 90-T High Post w/adj. Rib* — features high post, adj. rib. New 1994.

Mfg.'s Sug. Retail	$3,992		$3,400	$2,750	$2,350	$1,975	$1,650	$1,375	$1,150

MODEL 310 SKEET — .32 Rimfire case loaded with No. 12 leadshot, breakopen single shot, .310 bore shotgun mfg. at Remington's Brazilian plant, used in conjunction with a self-operated trap set which threw half-size clay targets, entire set-up included gun, shooting booth, ammunition, and trap thrower, 5½ lbs., mfg. circa late '50s - early '60s.

Gun only			$375	$325	$275	$225	$195	$175	$150

 Add 25%-75% depending on the amount of original accessories included.

 This model was never mass produced, but test marketed for approx. 5 years in CT, NJ, and TX primarily at amusement parks. It failed commercially due to lack of sales.

SHOTGUNS: O/U

 Values listed below for Model 3200s assume NIB condition - subtract 10%-15% if without box, warranty card, and original shipping container (with packing materials).

Grading	100%	98%	95%	90%	80%	70%	60%

MODEL 32 — 12 ga., double lock action, SST, separated barrels, 26, 28, or 30 in. barrels without rib, SR, or VR. Approx. 6,050 mfg. (ser. range approx. 0001-6,053) 1931-1947. There is a discrepancy as to when serialization started on this model.

	100%	98%	95%	90%	80%	70%	60%
	$1,800	$1,550	$1,300	$1,100	$1,000	$900	$800

Add 10% for SST.
Add 10% for vent. or solid rib.
Add 20% for VR on 28 in. barrels.

MODEL 32 SERIALIZATION IS AS FOLLOWS: 1931 - 0001-1,009; 1932 - 1,010-1,903; 1933 - 1,904-1,948; 1934 - 1,949-2,727; 1935 - 2,728-3,610; 1936 - 3,611-4,259; 1937 - 4,260-4,755; 1938 - 4,756-4,958; 1939 - 4,959-5,202; 1940 - 5,203-5,425; 1941 - 5,426-5,741; 1942 - 5,742-6,020; 1943 - 6,021-6,031; 1944 - 6,032-6,049; 1945 to 1947 - 6,050-6,053.

MODEL 32D TOURNAMENT

	100%	98%	95%	90%	80%	70%	60%
	$3,500	$2,950	$2,400	$2,100	$1,750	$1,400	$1,175

MODEL 32E EXPERT — less than 35 mfg.

	100%	98%	95%	90%	80%	70%	60%
	$5,000	$4,450	$3,850	$3,350	$2,650	$2,200	$1,875

MODEL 32F PREMIER

	100%	98%	95%	90%	80%	70%	60%
	$6,500	$5,750	$5,000	$4,400	$3,520	$2,750	$2,300

Note: Grades differ in quality, grade of wood, and amount of engraving.

MODEL 32 SKEET — similar to 32A, with 26 or 28 in. skeet bored barrels, SST. Mfg. 1932-1942.

	100%	98%	95%	90%	80%	70%	60%
	$2,100	$1,700	$1,500	$1,200	$1,000	$900	$800

Add 10% for VR.
Add 20% for VR on 28 in. barrels.

MODEL 32TC TARGET — similar to 32A, with 30 or 32 in. VR full choke barrels, trap style stock. Mfg. 1932-1942.

	100%	98%	95%	90%	80%	70%	60%
	$3,500	$2,800	$2,400	$2,000	$1,650	$1,450	$1,250

Add 10% for 30 in. VR barrels.
Add 28% for 28 in. VR barrels.

MODEL 396 SKEET/SPORTING CLAYS — 12 ga. only, satin finished boxlock action with engraved sideplates, 28 or 30 in. barrels with 10mm VR and Rem. chokes, select checkered walnut stock and target style forend, Sporting Clays Model has ported barrels, SST, ejectors, approx. 7½ lbs. New 1996.

		100%	98%	95%	90%	80%	70%	60%
Mfg.'s Sug. Retail	$2,526	$2,175	$1,850	$1,600	$1,400	$1,200	$1,050	$900

Add $130 for Sporting Clays Model.

MODEL 3200 FIELD — 12 ga., 26, 28, or 30 in. barrels, VR, various chokes, boxlock, auto ejectors, single selective trigger, checkered pistol grip stock, separated barrels. Mfg. 1972-1984.

	100%	98%	95%	90%	80%	70%	60%
	$1,100	$1,000	$950	$900	$850	$800	$750

Model 3200s with shorter barrels (26 or 28 in.) and open choking are more desirable than 30 in. tubes bored F/M.

MODEL 3200 SERIALIZATION IS AS FOLLOWS: 1973 - 4,200-16,667; 1974 - 16,668-27,393; 1975 - 27,394-35,303; 1976 - 35,304-39,216; 1977 - 39,217-41,432; 1978 - 41,433-42,813; 1979 - 42,814-44,278; 1980 - 44,279-45,504; 1981 - 45,505-45,974; 1982 - 45,975-47,200; 1983 - 47,201-47,308.

MODEL 3200 MAGNUM — 12 ga., 3 in. chambers, 30 in. heavy wall barrels (steel shot compatible), less than 1,000 mfg. 1975-1980.

	100%	98%	95%	90%	80%	70%	60%
	$1,495	$1,175	$950	$800	$715	$650	$575

MODEL 3200 SKEET — similar to 3200 Field, with 26 or 28 in. skeet bored barrels, skeet style stock. Mfg. 1973-1980.

	100%	98%	95%	90%	80%	70%	60%
	$1,295	$1,050	$950	$850	$750	$650	$575

28 in. barrels will command a premium on this model.

This model was also mfg. in a 28 in. IM/F configuration with gold pigeon on bottom for live pigeon shooting. Since less than 300 were mfg., prices in the $2,300 range are being asked if NIB condition. This model generally had a trap style rib, but there have been

Grading	100%	98%	95%	90%	80%	70%	60%

some field ribs as well. Originally, it was called the "Competition Live Pigeon" and was mfg. with a competition receiver and trap grade style wood.

▲ *Model 3200 Competition Skeet Four Ga. Set* — includes 12, 20, 28, or .410 ga., cased.

	100%	98%	95%	90%	80%	70%	60%
	$6,000	$5,500	$5,000	$4,600	$4,200	$4,000	$3,800

28 in. barrels will command a premium on this model.

MODEL 3200 COMPETITION SKEET — similar to 3200 Skeet, with scroll engraved frame and trigger guard, select wood. Mfg. 1973-1983.

	$1,695	$1,375	$1,075	$925	$850	$750	$675

Add 20% for 28 in. VR barrels.

MODEL 3200 TRAP — similar as 3200 Field, with 30 or 32 in. barrels choked IM/F or F/F, stock and rib. Mfg. 1973-1980.

	$1,200	$1,000	$900	$850	$750	$725	$700

MODEL 3200 SPECIAL TRAP — similar to 3200 Trap, except fancy wood. Mfg. 1973-1981.

	$1,200	$1,200	$1,000	$900	$800	$750	$700

MODEL 3200 COMPETITION TRAP — similar to 3200 Trap, with scroll engraving. Mfg. 1973-1981.

	$2,125	$1,650	$1,450	$1,250	$995	$800	$700

Add 25% for "Pigeon" Grade (gold pigeon on receiver bottom - approx. 250 mfg.).

There was a special production of this model during 1991-92 which was limited to approx. 100 guns.

MODEL 3200 PREMIER — 12 ga., sold through Remington's International Division, 500 mfg. 1975 only, patterned after "One of 1000" series, regular or Monte Carlo stock, 116 were engraved in Belgium — add 25%+.

	$2,900	$2,500	$2,150	$1,800	$1,500	$1,200	$1,025

MODEL 3200 "ONE OF 1000" — limited edition, elaborate engraving, fancy wood, supplied with hard case, made in both skeet and trap models. Mfg. 1,000 each model mfg. 1973 (Trap) and 1974 (Skeet).

	100%	98%	95%	90%	80%	70%	60%
Trap (30 IM/F or F/F)	$2,150	$1,750	$1,475	$1,325	$1,200	$1,075	$875
Skeet (26 or 28 in. SK/SK)	$2,150	$1,750	$1,475	$1,325	$1,200	$1,075	$875

Add 20% for 28 in. barrels on the Skeet Model.

PEERLESS FIELD GRADE — 12 ga. only, 3 in. chambers, 26, 28, or 30 in. VR barrels with Rem. chokes, boxlock with engraved sideplates, SST, ejectors, high-gloss checkered walnut stock and forearm with vent. recoil pad, 3.28 milliseconds lock time, blued metal, approx. 7½ lbs. New 1993.

Mfg.'s Sug. Retail	$1,225	$1,050	$925	$750	$675	$600	$550	$495

This model is an entirely new design not sharing any parts with either the Models 32 or 3200.

RENATO GAMBA
Please refer to the Gamba section in this text.

RENETTE, GASTINNE
Please refer to the Gastinne Renette section of this text.

RHODE ISLAND ARMS COMPANY
Previous manufacturer located in Hope Valley, RI.

MORRONE O/U — 12 or 20 ga., 26 or 28 in. plain barrels, boxlock, extractors, single trigger, checkered straight or pistol grip stock. Mfg. 1949-1953, only 500 of these guns were mfg., 450 in 12 ga., and 50 in 20 ga., very few with VR, they are quite rare although collector interest is not overwhelming.

	$1,100	$880	$770	$660	$550	$495	$440

Add 20% for 20 gauge.
Add 20% for VR.

RICHLAND ARMS COMPANY

Previous importer (until 1986) located in Blissfield, MI. The models listed below were made by various manufacturers located in either Italy or Spain.

Grading	100%	98%	95%	90%	80%	70%	60%

R

SHOTGUNS

MODEL 80 LS SINGLE SHOT — 12, 20, or .410 ga., 26 or 28 in. full choke barrel. Mfg. 1986 only.

	$140	$120	$110	$100	$90	$80	$70

Last Mfg.'s Sug. Retail was $162.

MODEL 711 MAGNUM SxS — 10 ga., 3½ in. chamber, 12 ga., 3 in. chamber, 32 in. full and full, 30 in. full and full, 20, 28, and .410 ga.'s also available on special order, hammerless, boxlock, extractors, checkered, walnut stock, recoil pad. Mfg. 1963-1985 in Spain.

	100%	98%	95%	90%	80%	70%	60%
10 gauge	$400	$325	$275	$250	$230	$210	$190
12 gauge	$340	$295	$265	$250	$230	$210	$190
20 gauge	$450	$340	$295	$260	$230	$210	$195

MODEL 707 DELUXE SxS — 12 or 20 ga., 3 in. chambers, 26, 28, or 30 in. barrels, various chokes, boxlock, extractors, double triggers, checkered stock and forend. Mfg. 1963-1972 in Spain.

	$330	$305	$290	$275	$250	$230	$210

MODEL 200 FIELD GRADE SxS — 12, 16, 20, 28, or .410 ga., 22, 26, and 28 in. barrels, various chokes, Anson & Deeley boxlock, extractors, double triggers, checkered stock, 6 lbs. 2 oz. - 7 lbs. 4 oz. Mfg. 1963-1985 in Spain.

	$320	$285	$255	$225	$195	$175	$150

Last Mfg.'s Sug. Retail was $379.

MODEL 202 ALL PURPOSE — similar to Field, except 2 sets of barrels, 12 and 20 ga. only. Mfg. 1963-disc. in Spain.

	$305	$260	$230	$220	$195	$165	$150

MODEL 41 ULTRA O/U — 20, 28, or .410 ga., 3 in. chambers (.410 ga. only), single non-selective trigger, 26 or 28 in. barrels, extractors, VR, engraved silver finished receiver, select checkered walnut stock and forearm, 6 lbs. 2 oz. Importation disc. 1986.

	$265	$220	$210	$200	$190	$180	$170

Last Mfg.'s Sug. Retail was $298.

MODEL 747 O/U — 12 or 20 ga. only, 3 in. chambers, Greener crossbolt, boxlock action, VR and barrels, SST, extractors. Importation disc. 1986.

	$420	$350	$325	$310	$295	$280	$265

Last Mfg.'s Sug. Retail was $464.

MODEL 757 O/U — 12 ga., 3 in. chambers, boxlock action with Greener crossbolt, vent. barrels and rib, double triggers, extractors, walnut stock and forearm, 7 lbs. 4 oz. New 1986. Add $70 for multi-chokes (Model 7570). Importation disc. 1986.

	$290	$260	$230	$215	$200	$185	$170

Last Mfg.'s Sug. Retail was $325.

MODEL 787 O/U — 12 ga. only, 3 in. chambers, boxlock action with silver finish, single trigger, vent. barrels and rib, extractors, walnut stock with recoil pad, is supplied with 5 interchangeable choke tubes, 7¼ lbs. Made 1986 only.

	$435	$375	$340	$310	$295	$280	$265

Last Mfg.'s Sug. Retail was $471.

MODEL 808 O/U — 12 ga., 26, 28, or 30 in. barrels, various chokes, boxlock, extractors, checkered stock. Mfg. 1963-1968 in Italy.

	$420	$360	$330	$315	$290	$270	$230

MODEL 810 O/U — 10 ga., 3½ in. chambers, ST, extractors.

	$600	$550	$500	$460	$430	$395	$360

Grading	100%	98%	95%	90%	80%	70%	60%

MODEL 828 O/U — 28 ga., single non-selective trigger, extractors, engraved, only 250 imported.

	100%	98%	95%	90%	80%	70%	60%
	$550	$500	$450	$400	$350	$325	$300

RIEDL RIFLE COMPANY

SINGLE SHOT RIFLE — available in any caliber, 22-30 in. barrel, rack and pinion action, lever trigger-guard activated, fully adj. trigger, select walnut stock, basically custom made.

	100%	98%	95%	90%	80%	70%	60%
	$495	$470	$440	$415	$385	$330	$305
▲ *Stainless barrel*	$560	$535	$505	$480	$450	$395	$370

RIFLES, INC.

Manufacturer located in Cedar City, UT. Dealer or direct sales.

RIFLES: BOLT ACTION

CLASSIC various cals., features Remington or Winchester stainless steel control-round action, stainless lapped barrel, matte stainless finish, laminated fiberglass stock with pillar glass bedding, approx. 6½ lbs. New 1996.

Mfg.'s Sug. Retail	$1,550		$1,550	$1,275	$1,000

LIGHTWEIGHT STRATA STAINLESS — various cals., lightened stainless Remington action, match grade barrel with slimbrake, matte stainless finish, 4¾ lbs. New 1996.

Mfg.'s Sug. Retail	$2,150		$2,150	$1,800	$1,500

SAFARI — various cals., features Winchester Model 70 control-round feeding, match grade barrel with slimbrake, matte stainless or black Teflon finish. New 1996.

Mfg.'s Sug. Retail	$1,950		$1,950	$1,600	$1,325

RIGBY, JOHN & CO. (GUNMAKERS), LTD.

Manufacture began in Dublin, Ireland in 1735. Current manufacture is in London, England. Griffin & Howe is the U.S. agent/importer for J. Rigby (see Trademark Index).

The first London Branch of J. Rigby was opened in 1865 and the Dublin Premises were closed during 1895. The firm became a company in 1900, and has been responsible for many of the large caliber developments in both rifles and ammunition.

Rigby is one of the world's finest weapons makers. A good portion of the guns they manufacture were custom built to customer specifications. They were chambered for the large black powder express cartridges used for dangerous game in Africa and Asia. The modern Rigby guns follow this same tradition.

We will list the modern Rigby Guns with approximate values but strongly urge that if purchase or sale is contemplated, professional appraisal be utilized.

RIFLES

.350 MAGNUM MAGAZINE RIFLE — .350 Magnum cal. originally most were rechambered to .375 H&H Mag. cal.

	100%	98%	95%	90%	80%	70%	60%
	$3,995	$3,400	$2,950	$2,600	$2,300	$2,000	$1,700

Values assume out of production models.

SINGLE SHOT FALLING BLOCK — Farquharson lever actuated action, various English and European cals., 24 in. barrel, ejector, checkered pistol grip stock, deluxe finish and engraving.

	100%	98%	95%	90%	80%	70%	60%
	$4,100	$3,400	$2,800	$2,400	$2,000	$1,600	$1,250

This model can also be ordered new from the factory with prices starting at approx. $18,000. Values above refer to older specimens that were not custom ordered.

Grading	100%	98%	95%	90%	80%	70%	60%

RIGBY MAGAZINE RIFLE — Mauser action (pre-1939), bolt action, various standard cals. including .243 Win., .270, .275 Rigby, 7x57mm, .30-06, .300 H&H, .300 Win. Mag., .308, 7mm Rem. Mag., or .375 H&H, 3-5 shot mag., 20-25 in. barrel, checkered half pistol grip stock, includes non-detachable scope mounts.

> New Rigby Magazine Rifles start in price at $9,950.
> Add $500 for .375 H&H, .404 Rigby, or .458 Win. Mag. cal.
> Add $1,920 for express sights.
> Add approx. $500 for Mag. cals.
> Above values are minimums for the Standard Rigby bolt action rifle. The factory quotes a price range of $5,760-$11,520 depending on alternate type of action (Brno, Dumoulin, Heym, or Mauser Magnum), the grade of wood, engraving, telescopic sight, case, or other details.

LIGHTWEIGHT MAGAZINE RIFLE — similar to Standard, with 24 in. barrel.

> New Rigby Magazine Rifles start in price at $9,950.
> Add $500 for .375 H&H, .404 Rigby, or .458 Win. Mag. cal.

.416 RIGBY BIG GAME MAGAZINE RIFLE — similar to Standard Rigby rifle, except is available in .375 H&H, .404 (disc.), .416 Rigby, .416 Rem. Mag., .458 Win. Mag., or .505 cal. only, modified Brno square bridge magnum action, 4 shot mag., 21-24 in. barrel, approx. 10 lbs.

> New Rigby Magazine Rifles start in price at $12,760.
> Add $680 for .505 cal.

▲ **.416 Rigby Deluxe Model** — same cals. as Big Game Rifle, includes extra quality wood and special engraving.

> New .416 Rigby Magazine Rifles start at $14,850, depending on options.
> Add $6,800 for Hartmann & Weiss action.

.450 MAGNUM RIMLESS RIGBY RIFLE — .450 Mag. cal., Mauser square-bridge Magnum action, 4 shot mag., 3 position safety, 21 or 24 in. barrel with quarter rib, folding express sights, select walnut, 10-11 lbs. New 1995.

> New .450 Rigby Magazine Rifles start at $12,670, depending on options.

▲ **.450 Magnum Deluxe Model** — includes extra quality wood and special engraving.

> New .450 Deluxe Rigby Magazine Rifles start at $14,850, depending on options.

BEST QUALITY SIDELOCK EJECTOR DOUBLE RIFLE — .22 LR, .275 Mag., .350 Mag., .416, .458 Win. Mag., .465, or .470 Nitro Express cal., 24-28 in. barrels, sidelocks, folding express rear sight, checkered pistol grip stock, deluxe finish and engraving.

Mfg.'s Sug. Retail	$63,350	$63,350	$47,500	$38,000	$29,000	$24,000	$20,000	$17,500

> Add $8,200 for .577 cal.
> Add $18,000 for .600 NE cal.
> Subtract 35% without ejectors.
> Rigby sidelock double rifles can instantly be recognized by their contoured sideplates.

SECOND QUALITY BOXLOCK EJECTOR DOUBLE RIFLE — .470 cal., 22-26 in. barrel, similar to Best Quality, except has boxlock action.

> New 2nd Quality Double Rifles start at $18,200, depending on options.
> Subtract 35% without ejectors.
> Values above are for larger calibers, smaller cals. could have less value than listed.

THIRD QUALITY BOXLOCK EJECTOR DOUBLE RIFLE — similar to Second Quality, with plainer wood and less engraving.

	$12,750	$10,750	$9,750	$8,750	$7,350	$6,350	$5,000

> Subtract 35% without ejectors.
> Values above are for larger calibers, smaller cals. could have less value than listed.

SHOTGUNS: SxS

The sidelock models listed below have an approximate delivery period of 1 - 2½ years.

Grading	100%	98%	95%	90%	80%	70%	60%

BEST QUALITY SIDELOCK — 12 or 20 ga. only, features DTs, elaborate fine English scroll engraving with border scroll on frame. Values below do not include value added tax (VAT) from England.

Mfg.'s Sug. Retail $31,400	$31,400	$24,500	$19,500	$14,000	$11,000	$8,750	$7,500

Add $3,140 for self-opening system.

▲ *Sidelock Matched Pair*

Mfg.'s Sug. Retail $64,370	$64,370	$48,000	$40,000	$33,000	$26,000	$21,000	$15,750

BOXLOCK DOUBLE BARREL SHOTGUN — all ga.'s, barrel lengths and chokes to order, checkered stock to order, auto ejectors, double triggers.

▲ *Chatsworth Grade*

$4,500	$3,500	$3,000	$2,500	$2,000	$1,600	$1,200

▲ *Sackville Grade* — deluxe engraved.

$5,900	$5,000	$4,500	$3,750	$3,100	$2,650	$2,200

Add 20% for 20 ga.
Add 40% for 28 ga.
Add 60% for .410 ga.

▲ *Boxlock Game Gun* — 12, 20, or 28 ga., traditional deep scroll engraving, current mfg.

This is John Rigby's only current production boxlock shotgun. The factory should be contacted directly (see Trademark Index) for a price quotation on this model.

SIDELOCK DOUBLE BARREL SHOTGUN — all ga.'s, barrel lengths and chokes to specifications, double triggers, auto ejectors stocked to order.

▲ *Sandringham Grade*

$9,500	$7,500	$6,000	$5,000	$4,450	$3,775	$2,950

▲ *Regal Grade* — deluxe engraved.

$12,500	$10,000	$8,750	$7,500	$6,400	$5,250	$4,250

Add 20% for 20 ga.
Add 40% for 28 ga.
Add 60% for .410 ga.

▲ *Sidelock Game Gun* — 12 or 20 ga., engraving similar to Best Quality SxS rifle, current mfg.

New Sidelock Game Guns start at $35,500, depending on options.
Add $3,225 for self-opening system.
A matched pair of the Sidelock Game Guns starts at $73,000.

RIZZINI, BATTISTA

Manufacturer located in Marcheno, Italy since 1965. Imported in the U.S. by W.L. Moore & Co. located in Scottsdale, AZ and New England Arms Company located in Kittery Point, ME.

Rizzini®B.
GUN MAKERS

RIFLES: O/U

EXPRESS 90 — various cals., ST, ejectors, deluxe wood and features.

Mfg.'s Sug. Retail $3,975	$3,600	$3,300	$2,950	$2,600	$2,300	$1,950	$1,625

Add $430 for upgraded wood (Model Express 90 L).

EXPRESS 92 — similar to Express 90, except has sideplates with more elaborate engraving.

Mfg.'s Sug. Retail $5,875	$5,325	$4,875	$4,150	$3,500	$3,000	$2,500	$1,900

SHOTGUNS

AURUM O/U — 12, 16, or 20 ga., boxlock action, light engraving, cased. New 1996.

Mfg.'s Sug. Retail $1,625	$1,475	$1,300	$1,125	$900	$775	$650	$525

ARTEMIS O/U — similar to Aurum, except has better engraving and wood, cased. New 1996.

Mfg.'s Sug. Retail $1,850	$1,650	$1,475	$1,300	$1,125	$900	$775	$650

R

Grading	100%	98%	95%	90%	80%	70%	60%

ARTEMIS EL O/U — top-of-the-line gun with elaborate engraving and best quality walnut, Nizzoli cased. New 1996.

Mfg.'s Sug. Retail	$12,500	$10,750	$9,650	$8,200	$6,875	$5,900	$4,850	$4,250

780 FIELD SERIES O/U — 10, 12, or 16 ga., boxlock action, DTs, extractors, checkered walnut stock and forearm.

Mfg.'s Sug. Retail	$1,225	$1,075	$875	$750	$675	$595	$525	$450

Add $550 for 10 ga.
Add $150 for ejectors (Model S780 E).
Add $200 for SST with ejectors (Model S780 EM).
Add $350 for SST, ejectors, and upgraded wood (Model S780 EML).
A Model S780 EMEL is also available that is entirely hand-finished and engraved for $5,995.

▲ **780 Competition Series** — includes Skeet, Trap, and Sporting Clays configuration.

Mfg.'s Sug. Retail	$1,600	$1,375	$1,050	$925	$825	$725	$625	$525

▲ **780 Small Gauge Series** — includes 20, 28, or 36 ga., DTs, ejectors.

Mfg.'s Sug. Retail	$1,500	$1,275	$975	$875	$800	$725	$625	$525

Add $50 for SST (Model 780 EM).

782 EM FIELD SERIES O/U — 12 or 16 ga., boxlock action with sideplates, SST ejectors, extractors, checkered walnut stock and forearm.

Mfg.'s Sug. Retail	$1,700	$1,450	$1,150	$995	$875	$750	$675	$550

Add $450 for Slug variation (Model 782 EM Slug).
Add $350 for better engraving and wood (Model 782 EML).
A Model S7820 EMEL is also available that is entirely hand-finished and engraved for $12,000.

▲ **S 782 EMEL Deluxe** — three ga. (20, 28, and .410), 27½ in. VR barrels with choke tubes (except .410 ga.), coin finished receiver with side plates featuring elaborate Bulino game scene engraving with gold inlays and fine scroll borders, deluxe English walnut, Nizzoli hard case. Importation began 1994.

Mfg.'s Sug. Retail	$10,250	$8,900	$8,175	$7,000	$6,200	$5,350	$4,800	$3,950

790 SERIES O/U COMPETITION — 12 or 20 ga., choice of Trap, Skeet, or Sporting Clays configuration, features black frame outlined with gold line engraving.

Mfg.'s Sug. Retail	$2,275	$1,975	$1,575	$1,300	$1,050	$925	$825	$695

Subtract $150 for 20 ga. Trap.
Subtract $50 for 20 ga. Skeet.
Add $1,050 for 20 ga. Sporting (includes sideplates and quick detachable stock).
A Model 790 Trap EL is also available that is entirely hand-finished with 18 Kt. gold and hand engraving - prices begin at $5,650 in 12 ga., $5,200 in 20 ga.

▲ **790 Small Gauge Series** — similar to 790 Competition Series, except in 20, 28, or 36 ga., SST and ejectors standard.

Mfg.'s Sug. Retail	$1,750	$1,475	$1,150	$995	$875	$750	$675	$550

A Model 790 EMEL is also available that is entirely hand-finished with 18 Kt. gold and hand engraving - prices begin at $6,995.

▲ **S 790 EMEL Deluxe** — three ga. (20, 28, and .410), 27½ in. VR barrels with choke tubes (except .410 ga.), color case hardened receiver with ornate ornamental engraving and Rizzini crest, deluxe English walnut, Nizzoli hard case. Importation began 1994.

Mfg.'s Sug. Retail	$8,750	$8,200	$7,450	$6,700	$6,000	$5,350	$4,800	$3,950

792 SMALL GAUGE MAG. SERIES O/U — 20, 28, or 36 ga., Mag. chambers, SST, ejectors, includes engraved sideplates.

Mfg.'s Sug. Retail	$2,000	$1,700	$1,275	$1,050	$895	$750	$675	$595

A Model 792 EMEL is also available that is entirely hand-finished with 18 Kt. gold and hand engraving - prices begin at $6,995.

▲ **S 792 EMEL Deluxe** — three ga. (20, 28, and .410), 27½ in. VR barrels with choke tubes (except .410 ga.), coin finished receiver with side plates featuring upgraded Bulino game scene engraving and fine scroll borders, deluxe English walnut, Nizzoli hard case. Importation began 1994.

Mfg.'s Sug. Retail	$8,750	$8,200	$7,450	$6,700	$6,000	$5,350	$4,800	$3,950

Grading	100%	98%	95%	90%	80%	70%	60%

MODEL 2000 O/U TRAP — 12 ga. only, includes nickel finished receiver with sideplates, gold trigger, VR barrels and rib.

Mfg.'s Sug. Retail	$2,200	$1,900	$1,500	$1,275	$1,025	$925	$825	$695

A Model 2000 Trap EL is also available that is entirely hand finished with 18 Kt. gold and hand-engraving - prices begin at $5,290.

MODEL 2000-SP — 12 ga. only, 26, 28, 30, or 32 in. overbored barrels with choke tubes, includes engraved sideplates, semi-fancy select walnut with quick detachable stock, cased. Importation began 1994.

Mfg.'s Sug. Retail	$3,650	$3,250	$2,800	$2,400	$1,975	$1,600	$1,300	$1,000

PREMIER SPORTING — 12 or 20 ga., 29½ in. multi-choke (5 chokes) barrels, cased. Importation began 1994.

Mfg.'s Sug. Retail	$3,060	$2,600	$2,475	$2,200	$1,950	$1,675	$1,500	$1,375

UPLAND EL — three ga. (20, 28, and .410), 27½ in. VR barrels with choke tubes (except .410 ga.), case hardened receiver, deluxe walnut, hard case. Importation began 1994.

Mfg.'s Sug. Retail	$3,060	$2,725	$2,475	$2,200	$1,950	$1,675	$1,500	$1,375

MODEL MC SINGLE BARREL — 12, 16, 20, 24, 28, 32, 36, or .410 ga., 27½ in. single barrel with VR, sling swivels, checkered hardwood stock.

Mfg.'s Sug. Retail	$440	$375	$285	$240	$200	$175	$160	$145

RIZZINI, F.LLI

Manufacturer located in Magno di Gardone V.T., Italy. Currently imported and distributed by W.L. Moore & Co. located in West Lake Village, CA and New England Arms, Co. located in Kittery Point, ME.

In the past, this manufacturer collaborated with Antonio Zoli to make "spec" guns that were usually imported by Abercrombie & Fitch or Von Lengerke & Detmold. These guns are normally marked on the water table "Zoli-Rizzini" or "F.lli Rizzini" (in the latter case, most of the time these guns have the Abercrombie & Fitch, etc. logo as well). These guns are not to be confused with the quality of current Rizzini F.lli mfg. Normally, these older Field Grade models (non-ejector, boxlock actions in 12, 16, 20, 28, or .410 ga.) sell in the $395-$800 range, with a 25% premium for 28 or .410 ga. Deluxe Field Models with a scalloped boxlock action and ejectors are currently valued in the $600-$1,200 range, with a 25% premium for 28 or .410 ga. The Extra Lusso Model (top-of-the-line) currently sell in the $2,500 range in 12 ga., $3,850 in 20 ga., $4,000 in 28 ga., and $4,250 in .410 ga. - deduct $250 for double triggers or plain wood.

Rizzini shotguns are made to individual custom order only (about 25 are made a year). Prices below do not include engraving (prices range from $8,700-$21,700) and are subject to fluctuation in exchange rates.

SHOTGUNS

Add approx. $6,800-$8,400 for fine English scroll or ornamental engraving.
Add approx. $15,600-$19,600 for Fracassi style ornamental engraving.

R2-E BOXLOCK EJECTOR — 12, 16, or 20 ga., select walnut, detachable bottom inspection plate, various barrel lengths, without engraving.

Mfg.'s Sug. Retail	$25,000	$22,500	$15,250	$12,250	$9,950	$8,850	$7,100	$6,200

▲ **28 or .410 ga.** — otherwise similar to above.

Mfg.'s Sug. Retail	$27,500	$24,500	$16,750	$13,000	$10,000	$8,950	$7,300	$6,300

R1-E SIDELOCK EJECTOR — 12, 16, or 20 ga., H&H patterned sidelocks, select Circassian walnut, various barrel lengths, without engraving.

Mfg.'s Sug. Retail	$43,700	$38,950	$25,000	$19,250	$15,700	$12,500	$10,400	$9,150

▲ **28 or .410 ga.** — otherwise similar to above.

Mfg.'s Sug. Retail	$48,700	$43,250	$29,750	$23,000	$16,750	$13,250	$11,200	$9,875

THE ROBAR COMPANIES, INC.
Manufacturer located in Phoenix, AZ.

Robar manufactures a complete line of semi-auto, .45 ACP pistols and various configurations including the Deluxe Pistol Package, Robar Combat Master, Thunder Ranch pistol, or new .45 Super. These guns are built up from other makers including Springfield and Colt to provide the configuration/modifications necessary. Robar also manufactures a complete line of rifles including the SR60, SR90, QR2, Robar 50 BMG, Hunter, Precision Hunter, Varminter, and Thunder Ranch Precision Rifle. Defensive shotguns are also manufactured and include the Thunder Ranch model. Please contact Robar directly (see Trademark Index) for more information including current prices on their lineup of firearms including custom metal and wood finishes.

ROCKY MOUNTAIN ARMS, INC.
Manufacturer located in Longmont, CO since 1990.

Rocky Mountain Arms is a quality specialty manufacturer of rifles and pistols. All firearms are finished in Dupont Teflon-S industrial coatings. Direct sales only (see listing in Trademark Index for more information).

Grading	100%	98%	95%	90%	80%	70%	60%

PISTOLS: SEMI-AUTO

BAP (BOLT ACTION PISTOL) — .308 Win., 7.62x39mm, or 10mm Rocky Mountain Thunderer (10x51mm) cal., features 14 in. heavy fluted Douglas Match barrel, Kevlar/graphite pistol grip stock, supplied with Harris bipod and black nylon case. Mfg. 1993 only.

	100%	98%	95%	90%	80%	70%	60%
	$1,425	$1,275	$1,100	$950	$825	$700	$575

Last Mfg.'s Sug. Retail was $1,595.

1911A1-LH — .40 S&W or .45 ACP cal., specifically designed for left-handed shooters, featuring left side ejection port and right side controls, gold cup size, stainless steel construction, hand fitted parts, integral ramp barrel, Millett adj. sights, test target. Mfg. 1991-93.

	100%	98%	95%
	$1,295	$995	$750

Last Mfg.'s Sug. Retail was $1,395.

Add $100 for Bomar sights.

BACKUP PLUS — .45 ACP, hand tuned AMT Back-up pistol, black DuPont Teflon-S finish, Tritium front nite sight. New 1995.

		100%	98%	95%	90%	80%	70%	60%
Mfg.'s Sug. Retail	$650	$575	$515	$450	$400	$360	$330	$300

22K PISTOLS — .22 LR, AR style pistols featuring 7 in. barrel, choice of matte black or NATO Green Teflon-S finish, will use Colt conversion kit, choice of carrying handle or flat-top upper receiver, 10 or 30 shot mag., includes black nylon case. Mfg. 1993 only.

	100%	98%	95%	90%	80%	70%	60%
	$475	$425	$375	$350	$325	$295	$275

Last Mfg.'s Sug. Retail was $525.

Add $50 for flat-top receiver with Weaver style bases.

PATRIOT PISTOL — .223 Rem. cal., AR style pistol featuring 7 in. match barrel with integral Max Dynamic muzzle brake, 21 in. overall, available with either carrying handle upper receiver with fixed sights or flat-top receiver with Weaver style bases, fluted upper receiver became an option in 1994, accepts standard AR-15 mags, 5 lbs. Mfg. 1993-94 (per C/B).

	100%	98%	95%	90%	80%	70%	60%
	$2,295	$1,975	$1,625	$1,425	$1,250	$1,075	$950

Last Mfg.'s Sug. Retail was $1,795.

Add $200 for black milled upper and lower receiver w/o carrying handle.

KOMRADE — 7.62x39mm cal., includes carrying handle upper receiver with fixed sights, floating 7 in. barrel, teflon red or black finish, 5 lbs., 5 shot mag. Mfg. 1994-95.

	100%	98%	95%	90%	80%	70%	60%
	$1,825	$1,650	$1,425	$1,200	$975	$850	$775

Last Mfg.'s Sug. Retail was $1,995.

Grading	100%	98%	95%	90%	80%	70%	60%

RIFLES: BOLT ACTION

PROFESSIONAL SERIES — .223 Rem., .30-06, .308 Win., or .300 Win. Mag. cal., bolt action rifle utilizing modified Mauser action, fluted 26 in. Douglas premium heavy match barrel with integral muzzle brake, custom Kevlar-Graphite stock with off-set thumbhole, test target. Mfg. 1991-95.

	100%	98%	95%	90%	80%	70%	60%
	$2,050	$1,650	$1,275	$995	$850	$725	$600

Last Mfg.'s Sug. Retail was $2,200.

Add $100 for .300 Win. Mag. cal.
Add $300 for left-hand action.

POLICE MARKSMAN — .308 Win. or .300 Win. Mag. cal., similar to Professional Series, except has 40X-C stock featuring adj. cheekpiece and buttplate, target rail, Buehler micro-dial scope mounting system. Mfg. 1991-95.

	100%	98%	95%	90%	80%	70%	60%
	$2,325	$1,995	$1,650	$1,325	$1,100	$900	$700

Last Mfg.'s Sug. Retail was $2,500.

Add $100 for .300 Win. Mag. cal.
Add $400 for left-hand action.
Add $400 for illuminated dot scope (4X-12X x 56mm).

NINJA SCOUT RIFLE — .22 Mag., takedown rifle based on Marlin action, black stock, 16½ in. match grade crowned barrel, forward mounted Weaver style scope base, adj. rear sight, 7 shot mag. Mfg. 1991-95.

	100%	98%	95%	90%	80%	70%	60%
	$640	$575	$525	$460	$430	$390	$360

Last Mfg.'s Sug. Retail was $695.

Add $200 for illuminated dot scope (1.5X-4X) w/ extended eye relief.

SCOUT SEMI-AUTO — .22 Mag., patterned after Marlin action. Mfg. 1993-95.

	100%	98%	95%	90%	80%	70%	60%
	$650	$575	$495	$395	$350	$295	$260

Last Mfg.'s Sug. Retail was $725.

Add $200 for illuminated dot scope (1.5X-4X) w/ extended eye relief.

RIFLES: SEMI-AUTO

M-SHORTEEN — .308 Win. cal., compact highly modified M1-A featuring 17" match crowned barrel, custom front sight, mod. gas system, hand honed action & trigger, custom muzzle brake. Mfg. 1991-94.

	100%	98%	95%	90%	80%	70%	60%
	$1,650	$1,425	$1,175	$995	$850	$725	$600

Last Mfg.'s Sug. Retail was $1,895.

Add $200 for Woodland/Desert camo.

VARMINTER — .223 Rem. cal. only, AR-15 styled rifle with 20 in. fluted heavy match barrel, flat-top receiver with Weaver style bases, round metal National Match hand guard with floating barrel, choice of NATO green or matte black Teflon-S finish, supplied with case and factory test target (sub-MOA). Mfg. 1993-94.

	100%	98%	95%	90%	80%	70%	60%
	$2,195	$1,800	$1,600	$1,400	$1,200	$1,000	$875

Last Mfg.'s Sug. Retail was $2,495.

PATRIOT MATCH RIFLE — .223 Rem., 20 in. Bull Match barrel, regular or milled upper and lower receivers, two-piece machined aluminum hand guard, choice of DuPont Teflon finish in black or Nato green, 1/2 MOA, hard case. New 1995.

		100%	98%	95%	90%	80%	70%	60%
Mfg.'s Sug. Retail	$2,500	$2,375	$1,975	$1,650	$1,400	$1,200	$1,000	$895

Add approx. $325 for milled upper receiver.
Add approx. $650 for milled upper and lower receivers.

SHOTGUNS: SLIDE ACTION

870 COMPETATOR — 12 ga., 3 in. chamber, security configuration with synthetic stock, hand-honed action, ghost ring adj. sights, "bear coat" finish, high visibility follower. New 1996.

		100%	98%	95%	90%	80%	70%	60%
Mfg.'s Sug. Retail	$795	$695	$625	$550	$500	$450	$400	$360

ROCKY MOUNTAIN ELK FOUNDATION

National hunting organization with national headquarters located in Missoula, MT.

Grading	100%	98%	95%	90%	80%	70%	60%

RUGER NO. 1-A LIGHT SPORTER — .35 Whelen cal., features gold inlaid elk on right side of receiver and mountain scene with gold accents on left side, engraved by Adams & Son, blue finish, deluxe wood, 50 mfg. 1995 only.
Mfg.'s Sug. Retail $2,395 $2,395 $1,850 $1,475

ROGAK

Please refer to the L E S Incorporated listing in this text for more information on the Rogak Pistol.

ROHM

Manufacturer located in Sontheim, Germany. Limited importation into the U.S.

DERRINGER — .22 LR, blued, copy of Remington O/U derringer. Excellently made, but half-cock safety is old design and could fail if dropped. No longer imported.

	$150	$115	$95	$85	$75	$65	$55

ROCHE, CHRISTIAN

Manufacturer located in Veauche, France.

Christian Roche manufactures quality side by side shotguns and double rifles. Since all orders are per individual specifications, the factory must be contacted directly to obtain a current price quotation and information (see Trademark Index).

ROSS RIFLE COMPANY

Quebec, Canada.

CANADIAN 1907 MARK II — .303 Brit. cal., bolt action, straight pull, 28 in. barrel, pre-WWII.

$295	$250	$200	$180	$160	$140	$120

MODEL 1910 SPORTING RIFLE — similar action as 1907, .280 Ross or .303 Brit. cal., checkered Sporter stock, leaf sights. Mfg. 1910-1920.

$275	$225	$200	$180	$160	$140	$120

Note: Many experts state this rifle is unsafe to fire.

ROSSI

Manufactured by Amadeo Rossi S.A., located in S. Leopoldo, Brazil. Currently imported by Interarms, located in Alexandria, VA.

REVOLVERS: DOUBLE ACTION

MODEL 31 — .38 Spl., 5 shot, 4 in. medium barrel, target trigger and hammer, 22 oz. Disc. 1985. Add $5 for nickel.

$120	$105	$95	$85	$75	$70	$65

Last Mfg.'s Sug. Retail was $139.

MODEL 51 — .22 LR, 6 shot, 6 in. barrel, blue only, adj. sights. Disc. 1985.

$125	$110	$100	$90	$85	$80	$75

Last Mfg.'s Sug. Retail was $149.

▲ *Sportsman 511 Stainless* — .22 LR only, stainless steel, 4 in. barrel, with matted rib, adj. rear sight, 6 shot, hardwood stocks, 30 oz. Imported 1986-90 only.

$190	$160	$125

Last Mfg.'s Sug. Retail was $235.

Grading	100%	98%	95%	90%	80%	70%	60%

MODEL 68 — .38 Spl., 5 shot, 2 or 3 in. barrel, blue or nickel (3 in. barrel only), choice of wood or rubber grips with 2 in. barrel.

Mfg.'s Sug. Retail	$225	$165	$135	$100	$90	$80	$70	$65

MODEL 69 — .32 S&W, 6 shot, 3 in. barrel, walnut grips. Disc. 1985. Add $5 for nickel.

		$120	$105	$95	$85	$75	$70	$65

Last Mfg.'s Sug. Retail was $139.

MODEL 70 — .22 cal, 6 shot, 3 in. barrel. Disc. 1985. Add $5 for nickel.

		$120	$105	$95	$85	$75	$70	$65

Last Mfg.'s Sug. Retail was $139.

MODEL 84 STAINLESS — .38 Spl., 6 shot, 3 or 4 in. solid raised rib barrel, standard service sights, checkered hardwood grips, 27½ oz. Imported 1985-86 only.

	$190	$155	$125

Last Mfg.'s Sug. Retail was $205.

MODEL 515(M) STAINLESS — .22 LR or .22 Mag. (Model 515M) cal., double action, 6 shot, classic kit gun design, stainless steel with shrouded ejector rod, adj. rear sights, checkered custom wood grips, 4 in. barrel, 30 oz. Imported 1992 only.

	$195	$145	$110

Last Mfg.'s Sug. Retail was $248.

MODEL 515 STAINLESS — .22 Mag., similar to 515(M), supplied with 2 pairs of grips (checkered wood and rubber wraparound). Importation began 1994.

Mfg.'s Sug. Retail	$270	$210	$165	$140

MODEL 518 STAINLESS — .22 LR, otherwise similar to Model 515 Stainless.

Mfg.'s Sug. Retail	$255	$195	$155	$135

MODEL 720 STAINLESS — .44 Spl. cal., choice of hammer or hammerless (new 1994) design, 3 in. ribbed barrel, double action, 5 shot with unfluted cylinder, full ejector rod shroud, adj. rear sight, rubber combat grips, stainless, 27½ oz. Importation began 1992.

Mfg.'s Sug. Retail	$290	$220	$180	$155

MODEL 851 STAINLESS — .38 Spl., 3 (disc. 1994) or 4 in. VR barrel, 6 shot, walnut grips, adj. rear sight, 27½ oz. New 1985.

Mfg.'s Sug. Retail	$255	$195	$155	$135

This model was previously the Model 85 Stainless.

MODEL 877 STAINLESS — .357 Mag. cal., 6 shot, small frame, 2 in. barrel with full ejector rod housing, rubber combat grips, 26 oz. New 1996.

Mfg.'s Sug. Retail	$290	$220	$175	$150

MODEL 88 STAINLESS — .38 Spl., 5 shot, stainless steel construction, 2 or 3 in. barrel, hardwood or rubber (2 in. barrel only) grips, 21 oz.

Mfg.'s Sug. Retail	$255	$195	$145	$110

▲ **Model 88 Lady Rossi** — .380 Spl., 2 in. barrel, stainless steel, slim round grips. Importation began 1995.

Mfg.'s Sug. Retail	$285	$215	$175	$150

MODEL 89 STAINLESS — .32 S&W cal. only, 6 shot, 3 in. barrel. Imported 1985-86. Reintroduced 1989-90.

	$175	$135	$115

Last Mfg.'s Sug. Retail was $215.

MODEL 94 — .38 Spl., 6 shot, 3 or 4 in. barrel, blued finish only, 27½ oz. Imported 1985-1988.

	$160	$140	$120	$110	$95	$85	$75

Last Mfg.'s Sug. Retail was $185.

MODEL 951 — .38 Spl., 6 shot, 3 or 4 in. VR barrel, blued finish only, 27½ oz. Imported 1985-90.

	$190	$155	$135	$120	$110	$100	$90

Last Mfg.'s Sug. Retail was $233.

This model was previously designated the Model 95.

Grading	100%	98%	95%	90%	80%	70%	60%

MODEL 971 — .357 Mag., 4 in. solid rib barrel with internal ejector shroud, 6 shot, adj. rear sight, blue only, hardwood grips, 36 oz. Importation began 1988.

Mfg.'s Sug. Retail	$255	$200	$160	$145	$135	$125	$115	$105

▲ *Model 971 Stainless* — .357 Mag., 2½ (new 1992), 4, or 6 in. solid rib barrel with full shroud, 6 shot, combat style rubber grips, adj. rear sight, 35.4-40.5 oz. Importation began 1989.

Mfg.'s Sug. Retail	$290		$220	$175	$145

▲ *Model 971 Compensated* — .357 Mag. cal., stainless steel, 3¼ in. compensated barrel, 32 oz. Importation began 1993.

Mfg.'s Sug. Retail	$290		$220	$175	$145

MODEL 971 VRC STAINLESS — .357 Mag. cal., stainless steel, 6 shot, choice of 2½, 4, or 6 in. barrel with 8-port vented rib compensator and full-length ejector shroud, combat rubber grips, adj. rear sight, 30-39 oz. New 1996.

Mfg.'s Sug. Retail	$340		$295	$220	$175

RIFLES

MODEL 65/92 SRC LEVER ACTION — .38 Spl./.357 Mag., .44 Spl./.44 Mag., .44-40 (new 1995), or .45 LC (new 1995) cal., patterned after Win. Model 92, 16 (.38 Spl./.357 Mag. only) or 20 in. round barrel, 5-5¾ lbs. Also available in matte blue finish at no extra charge.

Mfg.'s Sug. Retail	$360	$285	$220	$165	$125	$110	$100	$90

This model in .44 Spl./.44 Mag., .44-40, or .45 LC cal. sometimes is also known as the Model 65.

▲ *Blue Engraved* — with etched engraving and special wood. Disc. 1989.

	$275	$225	$175

Last Mfg.'s Sug. Retail was $327.

▲ *Gold or Chrome Engraved* — either gold (disc. 1987) or chrome (disc.) finish with special wood.

	$280	$230	$185	$150	$130	$120	$110

Last Mfg.'s Sug. Retail was $330.

MODEL 62 SA SLIDE ACTION — .22 LR cal., copy of Win. 1890 "gallery" model, rifle (23 in. barrel) or carbine (16½ in. barrel) available, takedown action, round or octagon barrel, 12 or 13 shot tube mag.

Mfg.'s Sug. Retail	$240	$185	$145	$115	$95	$85	$80	$75

Add $10 for nickel finish.
Add $10 for octagon barrel.

▲ *Model 62 SA Carbine (C)* — similar to Model 62 SA, except has 16½ in. carbine barrel with full length mag. tube (12 shot), 4¼ lbs. Importation began 1988.

Mfg.'s Sug. Retail	$240	$185	$145	$115	$95	$85	$80	$75

Add $10 for nickel finish.

▲ *Model 62 SA Stainless* — similar to regular model, except is stainless steel. Imported 1986 only.

	$165	$145	$120

Last Mfg.'s Sug. Retail was $192.

MODEL 59 — .22 Mag. version of Model 62 SA, 10 shot mag., 5.5 lbs.

Mfg.'s Sug. Retail	$280	$220	$170	$130	$120	$110	$100	$90

SHOTGUNS

OVERLUND SxS — 12, 20, or .410 ga., exposed hammers, 20 (Coach Model), 26, or 28 in. barrels, double triggers. Importation disc. 1988.

	$275	$230	$185	$155	$140	$125	$115

Last Mfg.'s Sug. Retail was $332.

Add $5 for .410 ga.

Grading	100%	98%	95%	90%	80%	70%	60%

SQUIRE SxS — 12, 20, or .410 ga., hammerless, 20, 26 or 28 in. barrels, double triggers, raised matted rib, beavertail forearm, pistol grip, hardwood stock, 3 in. chambers. Imported 1985-90.

			$300	$245	$195	$160	$150	$140	$130

Last Mfg.'s Sug. Retail was $350.

    Add $10 for .410 ga.

ROTTWEIL

R

Manufacturer located in Rottweil, Germany. Currently imported by Dynamit Nobel-RWS Inc. located in Closter, NJ.

SHOTGUNS

PARAGON — 12 ga. only, new design featuring boxlock action, 11 different stock configurations, detachable and interchangeable trigger action, trigger and sear safety, ejectors (switchable to extractors), various barrel lengths and rib combinations, cased. Importation began 1993.

Mfg.'s Sug. Retail	$6,995	$6,500	$5,750	$4,850	$3,950	$3,000	$2,500	$2,250

MODEL 650 FIELD O/U — 12 ga. only, 28 in. barrels with VR, ejectors, single trigger, select checkered walnut, multi-choked with 6 choke tubes, lightly engraved, coin finished receiver. Importation disc. 1986.

	$750	$650	$595	$550	$500	$460	$435

Last Mfg.'s Sug. Retail was $850.

MODEL 72 FIELD O/U — 12 ga. only, 28 in. vent. barrels and rib, sand blasted receiver, select walnut with checkered stock and forearm, single trigger, ejectors. Importation disc. 1987.

	$1,850	$1,650	$1,450	$1,200	$1,000	$850	$700

Last Mfg.'s Sug. Retail was $2,295.

MODEL 72 AMERICAN SKEET O/U — 12 ga. only, 26¾ in. barrels, VR, ejectors, select French walnut, marginal engraving on sand blasted receiver, single trigger, 7½ lbs. Importation disc. 1987.

	$1,850	$1,650	$1,450	$1,200	$1,000	$850	$700

Last Mfg.'s Sug. Retail was $2,295.

    This model was distributed exclusively by Paxton Arms, located in Dallas, TX.

MODEL 72 AAT SINGLE BARREL TRAP — 12 ga. only, adj. American trap (AAT), barrel features adj. point of impact, 34 in. barrel bored full, high VR. Importation disc. 1986.

	$1,400	$1,200	$1,000	$850	$700	$650	$600

Last Mfg.'s Sug. Retail was $2,295.

MODEL 72 AT O/U — 12 ga. only, 32 in. IM & F barrels, VR and barrels, sand blasted receiver, checkered select walnut stock and forearm, non-adj. point of impact, single trigger ejectors. Importation disc. 1987.

	$1,850	$1,650	$1,450	$1,200	$1,000	$850	$700

Last Mfg.'s Sug. Retail was $2,295.

MODEL 72 AAT COMBINATION — 12 ga. only, comes with 2 single barrels (32 and 34 in.) that have adj. impacts. Importation disc. 1986.

	$2,450	$2,100	$1,850	$1,600	$1,450	$1,250	$995

Last Mfg.'s Sug. Retail was $2,850.

    ▲ *72 AAT Combination* — supplied with 1 single adj. barrel and 32 in. O/U barrels.

	$2,450	$2,100	$1,850	$1,600	$1,450	$1,250	$995

Last Mfg.'s Sug. Retail was $2,850.

MODEL 72 AAT 3-BARREL SET — 12 ga. only, supplied with 2 single barrels (32 and 34 in.) with adj. impact and 1 set of 32 in. O/U barrels bored IM & F. Importation disc. 1986.

	$2,850	$2,600	$2,300	$2,000	$1,800	$1,600	$1,400

Last Mfg.'s Sug. Retail was $3,250.

MODEL 72 INTERNATIONAL TRAP — 12 ga. only, O/U 30 in. barrels bored IM & F with extra high rib. Importation disc. 1987.

	$1,850	$1,650	$1,450	$1,200	$1,000	$850	$700

Last Mfg.'s Sug. Retail was $2,295.

Grading	100%	98%	95%	90%	80%	70%	60%

MODEL 72 INTERNATIONAL SKEET — 12 ga. only, 26¾ in. barrels, VR, select walnut stock and forearm. Importation disc. 1987.

	$1,850	$1,650	$1,450	$1,200	$1,000	$850	$700

Last Mfg.'s Sug. Retail was $2,295.

ROYAL AMERICAN SHOTGUNS

Previously imported by Royal Arms International, located in Woodland Hills, CA.

SHOTGUNS

MODEL 100 O/U — 12 or 20 ga., 2¾ in. chambers, double triggers, extractors, vent. rib and barrels. Imported 1985-87 only.

	$325	$265	$240	$220	$200	$180	$170

Last Mfg.'s Sug. Retail was $390.

Add $40 for above model with 3 in. chambers, single trigger, and auto ejectors.

MODEL 600 BOXLOCK SxS — 12, 20, 28, or .410 ga., sideplates, silver finished receiver, 3 in. chambers, single trigger, auto ejectors. Imported 1985-87 only.

	$365	$295	$265	$235	$210	$195	$180

Last Mfg.'s Sug. Retail was $420.

Subtract 25% for double triggers and 2¾ in. chambers.

MODEL 800 SIDELOCK SxS — 12, 20, 28, or .410 ga., sidelocks with sideplates, silver finished receiver, 3 in. chambers, single trigger, checkered straight grip stock with select walnut, auto ejectors. Imported 1985-87 only.

	$775	$650	$595	$550	$500	$460	$435

Last Mfg.'s Sug. Retail was $899.

RUBY

Manufacturer located in Eibar, Spain.

MILITARY TYPE — trade name for Spanish auto pistol fashioned after Colt's M1903, cal. 7.65mm, mag. release at bottom of grip, fixed sights. No longer mfg.

	$200	$150	$100	$75	$70	$65	$60

RUGER

See Sturm, Ruger, & Co. section in this text.

RUKO SPORTING GOODS, INC.

Importer (non-exclusive) located in Buffalo, NY that imported Arms Corp. of the Philippines firearms 1990-95. Ruko Sporting Goods, Inc. (previously Ruko Products) firearms were manufactured by the Arms Corporation of the Philippines. In 1991, Ruko Products, Inc. became the exclusive domestic importer for arms manufactured by Arms Corp. of the Philippines. These firearms were marked "Ruko-Armscor" on the barrels.

Please refer to the Armscor section for current importation, as well as previous importation by Armscorp Precision, Inc. and Ruko Products, Inc.

RUSSIAN SERVICE PISTOLS AND RIFLES

Manufactured at various Russian military arsenals (including Tula).

Because of what has happened during the recent collapse of Communism (and resultant influx of capitalism dealing with exporting both Russian military handguns and longarms), many domestic importers are now importing Russian guns on a major basis. While it is true that even five years ago it was hard to obtain any type of a Russian military weapon in the U.S., now the dime-a-dozen rule applies. Most Russian pistols and rifles currently imported are no longer rare, and for the most part, their shooting value must be considered to be the most important factor in pricing.

Grading	100%	98%	95%	90%	80%	70%	60%

MODEL TT30 & TT33 TOKAREV AUTOMATIC — 7.62mm Russian cal., design borrowed from Colt 1911 Petter-type unitized trigger/hammer assembly, 8 shot, $4\frac{1}{2}$ in. barrel, blue. Mfg. 1930-1954.

	$325	$290	$250	$225	$165	$145	$110

Add 20% for matching mag.
Add 50% for TT30 Model.
Values listed above assume original condition - no recent imports.

▲ *TT Recent Import* — 7.62x25mm Tokarev cal., must be stamped by importer, state Russian mfg., currently imported by Century Arms International, Inc. and others.

No Mfg.'s Retail	$140	$110	$90	$80	$70	$60	$50

NAGANT REVOLVER — 7 shot, cylinder comes forward to seal barrel. Add 10% for pre-communist Imperial marked.

	$260	$225	$185	$165	$135	$115	$100

"GRU" marked gun (State Police) has shorter barrel and grip frame. While rarer, there is a slight premium being asked.

MAKAROV MD — 9mm, clip fed double action, post-war manufacture.

	$450	$400	$350	$300	$250	$200	$150

Subtract 60% for recent imports or commercial models with adj. rear sight.

TOKAREV M38 & M40 RIFLE — semi-auto Russian issue bolt action. Add 20% for M38, 100% for scoped sniper.

	$365	$310	$270	$250	$230	$210	$195

RUTTEN HERSTAL

Manufacturer of O/U shotguns located in Herstal, Belgium. Currently imported by Labanu, Inc. located in Ronkonkoma, NY.

SHOTGUNS: O/U

MODEL RM 100 — 12 ga., 3 in. chambers, VR multi-choke barrels, ejectors, checkered walnut stock and forearm, hard case. Importation began 1995.

Mfg.'s Sug. Retail	$1,095		$875	$775	$675	$575	$500	$450

MODEL RM 285 — similar to Model RM 100, except has engraved side plates and silver engraved receiver, select walnut with Schnabel forearm, hard case. Importation began 1995.

Mfg.'s Sug. Retail	$1,295	$1,025	$850	$725	$600	$500	$450

R

S section

S.A.C.M.

S.A.C.M. stands for Societe Alasacienne de Construction Mechanique. Previously manufactured in Cholet, France.

Grading	100%	98%	95%	90%	80%	70%	60%

FRENCH MODEL 1935A — semi-auto, 7.65mm long, 8 shot, 4.3 in. barrel, blue, fixed sights, checkered stocks, used by French troops in WWII and Indo-China 1945-1954. Mfg. 1935-1945.

	100%	98%	95%	90%	80%	70%	60%
	$250	$220	$205	$180	$165	$150	$140

Add 50% for Nazi WWII mfg. (Waffenamt proofed).

SAE

Spain America Enterprises Inc. (SAE) Previous importer of Felix Sarasqueta Shotguns from Spain. SAE was located in Miami, FL.

SHOTGUNS: O/U

MODEL 70 — 12 or 20 ga., 3 in. chambers, boxlock action, single trigger, ejectors, 26 in. VR barrel, European checkered walnut stock and forearm, standard finish is blue, Model 70 multi-choke has silver finished action with Florentine engraving and low gloss stock finish. Imported 1988 only.

	$400	$275	$260	$245	$230	$215	$195

Last Mfg.'s Sug. Retail was $598.

Add $120 for multi-chokes (27 in. barrel).

MODEL 66C — 12 ga. only, 26 in. Skeet or 30 in. F&M VR barrels, boxlock with engraved sideplates including 24Kt. inlays, Monte Carlo deluxe stock and beavertail forearm. Imported 1988 only.

	$950	$725	$650	$575	$495	$450	$395

Last Mfg.'s Sug. Retail was $1,544.

SHOTGUNS: SxS

MODEL 210S — 12, 20, or .410 ga., 3 in. chambers, boxlock action, double triggers, extractors, silver finished receiver with light engraving, approx. 7 lbs. Imported 1988 only.

	$420	$280	$260	$245	$230	$215	$195

Last Mfg.'s Sug. Retail was $638.

MODEL 340X — 12 or 20 ga., sidelock action, 26 in. barrels with $2\frac{3}{4}$ in. chambers, H&H boxlock action, case hardened finish with moderate scroll engraving, straight grip select walnut stock and forearm with high gloss finish. Imported 1988 only.

	$700	$550	$495	$460	$430	$395	$375

Last Mfg.'s Sug. Retail was $1,170.

MODEL 209E — 12, 20, or .410 ga., H&H type sidelock action, 26 or 28 in. barrels with $2\frac{3}{4}$ in. chambers, hand engraved coin finished receiver, select checkered walnut stock and forearm, double triggers. Imported 1988 only.

	$925	$700	$650	$575	$495	$450	$395

Last Mfg.'s Sug. Retail was $1,490.

S K B ARMS COMPANY

Manufacturer located in Tokyo, Japan by the new S K B Arms Company. Currently imported and distributed by G.U. Inc. located in Omaha, NE. SKB has been manufacturing firearms since 1855. Distributor and dealer sales.

Grading	100%	98%	95%	90%	80%	70%	60%

Formerly imported by Ithaca. In 1987, importation resumed on most SKB models. While the model numbers have changed, quality is similar to those models imported previously by Ithaca. In most cases, the newer models are derived closely from their previous counterparts. Listings below will differentiate older disc. models from currently imported models.

SHOTGUNS: O/U AND SINGLE SHOT

MODEL 500 — 12, 20, 28, or .410 ga., field grade, VR, selective ejector, 26 in. imp. cyl. and mod., 28 in. full and mod., and 30 in. full and mod., checkered stock. Mfg. in Japan by SKB 1966-1979.

	$525	$440	$395	$365	$330	$300	$275

Add 15% for 20 ga.
Add 25% for 28 or .410 ga.

▲ *Model 500 Magnum* — 12 ga., 3 in. Mag., field grade, similar to 500, except 3 in. Mag. chambers.

	$625	$455	$410	$385	$355	$320	$290

MODEL 505 DELUXE FIELD O/U — 12, 20, or 28 (disc.) ga., silver nitride engraved receiver, 3 in. chambers, 26 or 28 in. barrels (supplied with choke tubes), single selective trigger, ejectors, checkered walnut stock with recoil pad and forearm. Importation disc. 1992, but limited quantities of 12 or 20 ga. remain.

Mfg.'s Sug. Retail	$999	$910	$760	$675	$575	$500	$460	$420

Last Mfg.'s Sug. Retail was $995.

Add $500 for combo package (disc.).
The combo package includes either 12/20 ga. barrels with inter-chokes or 28/.410 ga. barrels.

▲ *Model 505 Trap* — 12 ga., 30 or 32 in. choke tube barrels with or without Monte Carlo stock, high rib.

	$875	$725	$650	$525	$475	$430	$395

Last Mfg.'s Sug. Retail was $995.

Add $400 for O/U Trap Combo.
The above Combo includes one set of O/U Trap barrels and a top single Trap barrel.

▲ *Model 505 Trap Single Barrel* — 12 ga., 32 or 34 in. barrel with multi-chokes, regular or Monte Carlo stock.

	$875	$725	$650	$525	$475	$430	$395

Last Mfg.'s Sug. Retail was $995.

▲ *Model 505 Skeet* — 12, 20, 28, or .410 ga., 28 in. barrels with multi-chokes.

	$875	$725	$650	$525	$475	$430	$395

Last Mfg.'s Sug. Retail was $995.

▲ *Model 505 3-Ga. Skeet Set* — includes 20, 28, and .410 ga. extra Skeet barrels, aluminum case.

$1,925	$1,575	$1,350	$1,200	$1,125	$950	$875

Last Mfg.'s Sug. Retail was $2,195.

▲ *Model 505 Sporting Clay* — 28 or 30 in. multi-choke barrels, dimensioned for Sporting Clay competition.

	$885	$725	$650	$525	$475	$430	$395

Last Mfg.'s Sug. Retail was $1,045.

MODEL 585 DELUXE FIELD O/U — 12, 20, 28, or .410 (new 1995) ga., silver nitride engraved receiver, 3 in. chambers, 26 or 28 in. barrels (supplied with choke tubes), similar to 505 Series, except has .735 diameter bore on 12 ga. models and includes lengthened forcing cones with extended length "Competition Series" Inter-Choke System designed to improve shot patterns and reduce recoil, SST, ejectors, checkered walnut stock with recoil pad and forearm (Youth model is also available with shortened dimensions), 6 lbs. 10 oz. - 7 lbs. 11 oz. Importation began 1992.

Mfg.'s Sug. Retail	$1,249	$1,050	$825	$675	$575	$500	$460	$420

Add $50 for 28 or .410 ga.

Grading	100%	98%	95%	90%	80%	70%	60%

▲ **Model 585 Field Set** — includes 12/20, 20/28, 28/.410 ga. 26 or 28 (new 1994) in. VR barrels with SKB inter-choke system (on 12 and 20 ga.), silver nitride receiver with finely engraved scroll game scenes, low profile receiver, cross bolt locking system, SST, ejectors, manual safety, checkered high gloss American walnut stock and forearm.

Mfg.'s Sug. Retail	$1,999	$1,800	$1,550	$1,300	$1,100	$995	$895	$800

Add $50 for 20/28 ga. set or 28/.410 ga. set.

▲ **Model 585 Trap** — 12 ga., 30 or 32 in. choke tube barrels with or without Monte Carlo stock, high rib.

Mfg.'s Sug. Retail	$1,349	$1,100	$850	$700	$525	$475	$430	$395

Add $650 for O/U Trap Combo.

The above Combo includes one set of O/U Trap barrels and a top single Trap barrel.

▲ **Model 585 Skeet** — 12, 20, 28, or .410 ga., 28 or 30 (12 ga. only - new 1994) in. barrels with multi-chokes.

Mfg.'s Sug. Retail	$1,349	$1,100	$850	$700	$525	$475	$430	$395

Add $50 for 28 or .410 ga.

▲ **Model 585 3-Ga. Skeet Set** — includes 20, 28, and .410 ga. extra Skeet barrels, aluminum case.

Mfg.'s Sug. Retail	$3,149	$2,695	$2,175	$1,800	$1,575	$1,475	$1,375	$1,275

▲ **Model 585 Sporting Clays** — 12, 20, or 28 ga., 28 in. (all gauges), 30 in. (12 ga. only), or 32 in. (12 ga. only) multi-choke barrels, dimensioned for Sporting Clay competition, narrow rib ⅜ in. became available 1994.

Mfg.'s Sug. Retail	$1,399	$1,175	$875	$725	$550	$475	$430	$395

Add $50 for 28 ga.

➤ **Model 585 Sporting Clays Set** — includes 2 sets of barrels (12 ga.-30 in., 20 ga.-28 in.), cased. New 1996.

Mfg.'s Sug. Retail	$1,999	$1,800	$1,550	$1,300	$1,100	$995	$895	$800

▲ **Model 585 Waterfowler** — 12 ga. only, 3½ in. chambers, matte blue finish. Imported 1995 only.

		$1,125	$850	$700	$525	$475	$430	$395

Last Mfg.'s Sug. Retail was $1,329.

▲ **Model 585 Youth/Ladies** — 12 or 20 ga., 26 or 28 (12 ga. only) in. VR barrels, features 13½" LOP, barrels have .735 in. bores with lengthened forcing cones. New 1994.

Mfg.'s Sug. Retail	$1,249	$1,150	$795	$675	$525	$475	$430	$395

MODEL 600 FIELD GRADE — similar to Model 500, except silver-plated frame and select wood.

			$700	$495	$465	$440	$375	$345	$325

Add 20% for 20 ga.

An unknown quantity of Model 600s were mfg. with blued receivers - a small premium may be asked.

MODEL 600 MAGNUM — similar to Model 600 Field, except chambered for 3 in. Mag., 12 ga. Mfg. 1969-1972 by SKB.

			$720	$510	$480	$455	$415	$390	$355

MODEL 600 TRAP GRADE — similar to Model 600, except 12 ga. only, trap stock, recoil pad, select wood.

			$675	$555	$520	$485	$445	$410	$385

MODEL 600 DOUBLES GUN — similar to Model 600 Trap, except choked for 21 yd. and 30 yd. targets. Mfg. 1973-1975.

			$675	$555	$520	$485	$445	$410	$385

MODEL 600 SKEET GRADE — 12, 20, 28, or .410 ga., 26 or 28 in. barrels, bored S&S, otherwise similar to 600 Trap.

			$700	$540	$510	$475	$430	$400	$370
28 or .410 ga.			$850	$740	$620	$560	$485	$440	$420

MODEL 600 SKEET GRADE COMBO SET — similar to Model 600 Skeet, except fitted with matched set of 20, 28, and .410 ga. barrels, in fitted case.

			$2,000	$1,430	$1,265	$1,155	$935	$770	$660

Grading	100%	98%	95%	90%	80%	70%	60%

MODEL 605 FIELD O/U — similar to Model 505 Deluxe Field except has silver finished engraved receiver with better walnut. Importation disc. 1992.

	$1,075	$850	$750	$675	$575	$500	$450

Last Mfg.'s Sug. Retail was $1,195.

Add $500 for extra set of barrels (Combo).

▲ *Model 605 Trap* — 12 ga., 30 or 32 in. choke tube barrel with or without Monte Carlo stock, high rib.

	$1,075	$850	$750	$675	$575	$500	$450

Last Mfg.'s Sug. Retail was $1,195.

Add $400 for O/U Trap Combo.

The above Combo includes one set of O/U Trap barrels and a top single Trap barrel.

▲ *Model 605 Trap Single Barrel* — 12 ga., 32 or 34 in. barrel with multi-chokes.

	$1,075	$850	$750	$675	$575	$500	$450

Last Mfg.'s Sug. Retail was $1,195.

▲ *Model 605 Skeet* — 12, 20, 28, or .410 ga., 28 in. barrels with multi-chokes.

	$1,100	$850	$750	$675	$575	$500	$450

Last Mfg.'s Sug. Retail was $1,195.

▲ *Model 605 3-Ga. Skeet Set* — includes 20, 28, and .410 ga. extra Skeet barrels, aluminum case.

	$2,175	$1,650	$1,400	$1,250	$1,125	$950	$875

Last Mfg.'s Sug. Retail was $2,395.

▲ *Model 605 Sporting Clay* — 28 or 30 in. multi-choke barrels, dimensioned for Sporting Clay competition.

	$1,110	$850	$750	$675	$575	$500	$450

Last Mfg.'s Sug. Retail was $1,245.

▲ *Model 605 DU Sponsor Gun* — mfg. for DU chapters - dinner auction gun, 850 mfg. in 12 ga. (1990) and 850 mfg. in 20 ga. (1991). Features gold inlays and presentation case.

DU sponsor gun values are usually hard to ascertain in the secondary marketplace. Currently, prices seem to range between $1,200-$1,700.

MODEL 680 ENGLISH — similar to Model 600 Field, except English style stock, select walnut and fine scroll engraving. Mfg. 1973-1976.

	$725	$640	$600	$555	$520	$495	$445

Add 20% for 20 ga.

MODEL 685 FIELD O/U — similar to Model 585 Deluxe Field, except has silver finished engraved receiver with gold inlays and better walnut, engine turned interior metal parts.

	$1,325	$950	$795	$675	$575	$500	$450

Last Mfg.'s Sug. Retail was $1,549.

▲ *Model 685 Field Set* — includes 12/20, 20/28, 28/.410 ga. 26 or 28 (new 1994) in. VR barrels with SKB inter-choke system (on 12 and 20 ga.), silver nitride receiver with finely engraved scroll game scenes, low profile receiver, cross bolt locking system, SST, ejectors, manual safety, checkered high gloss American walnut stock and forearm.

	$1,850	$1,650	$1,500	$1,350	$1,275	$1,100	$1,000

Last Mfg.'s Sug. Retail was $2,149.

▲ *Model 685 Trap* — 12 ga., 30 or 32 in. choke tube barrel with or without Monte Carlo stock, high rib.

	$1,365	$975	$825	$700	$600	$525	$450

Last Mfg.'s Sug. Retail was $1,595.

Add $600 for O/U Trap Combo.

The above Combo includes one set of O/U Trap barrels and a top single Trap barrel.

▲ *Model 685 Skeet* — 12, 20, 28, or .410 ga., 28 or 30 (12 ga. only - new 1994) in. barrels with multi-chokes.

	$1,365	$975	$825	$700	$600	$525	$450

Last Mfg.'s Sug. Retail was $1,595.

▲ *Model 685 3-Ga. Skeet Set* — includes 20, 28, and .410 ga. extra Skeet barrels, aluminum case.

	$2,550	$2,175	$1,875	$1,675	$1,450	$1,275	$1,125

Last Mfg.'s Sug. Retail was $2,949.

Grading	100%	98%	95%	90%	80%	70%	60%

▲ **Model 685 Sporting Clay** — 28 (all gauges), 30 (12 ga. only), or 32 (12 ga. only) in. multi-choke barrels, dimensioned for Sporting Clay competition, narrow rib ⅜ in. became available 1994. Importation disc. 1995.

	$1,365	$975	$825	$700	$600	$525	$450

Last Mfg.'s Sug. Retail was $1,595.

▲ **Model 685 Sporting Clay Set** — includes one set of 12 ga. (28, 30, or 32 in. VR barrels) and 20 ga. (28 in. only) or one set of 32 and 28 in. barrels in 12 ga only. Imported 1994-95.

	$2,000	$1,675	$1,500	$1,350	$1,200	$1,025	$895

Last Mfg.'s Sug. Retail was $2,295.

▲ **Model 685 DU Sponsor Gun** — mfg. for DU chapters - dinner auction gun, 850 mfg. in 12 ga. (1990) and 850 mfg. in 20 ga. (1991). Features gold inlays and presentation case.

DU sponsor gun values are usually hard to ascertain in the secondary marketplace. Currently, prices seem to range between $1,200-$1,700.

MODEL 700 TRAP GRADE — 12 ga., similar to Model 600 Trap, except more engraving, better grade wood, wide rib. Mfg. 1969-1975.

$820	$770	$740	$685	$630	$595	$565

MODEL 700 DOUBLES GUN — 12 ga., similar to Model 700 Trap, except choked for 21 yd. and 30 yd. targets. Mfg. 1973-1975.

$795	$770	$740	$685	$630	$595	$565

MODEL 700 SKEET GRADE — 12 ga., similar to Model 700 Doubles, only bored S&S, available in 12 or 20 ga.

$840	$770	$740	$685	$620	$585	$555

MODEL 785 DELUXE FIELD O/U — 12, 20, 28, or .410 ga., silver nitride engraved receiver, 3 in. chambers, 26 or 28 in. barrels (supplied with choke tubes), similar to 505 Series, except has .735 diameter bore on 12 ga. models and includes lengthened forcing cones with extended length "Competition Series" Inter-Choke System designed to improve shot patterns and reduce recoil, SST, ejectors, checkered walnut stock with recoil pad and forearm (Youth model is also available with shortened dimensions), 6 lbs. 10 oz. - 7 lbs. 11 oz. Importation began 1995.

Mfg.'s Sug. Retail	$1,899	$1,735	$1,525	$1,300	$1,100	$995	$895	$800

Add $50 for 28 or .410 ga.

▲ **Model 785 Field Set** — includes 12/20, 20/28, 28/.410 ga., 26 or 28 in. VR barrels with SKB inter-choke system (on 12 and 20 ga.), silver nitride receiver with finely engraved scroll game scenes, low profile receiver, cross bolt locking system, SST, ejectors, manual safety, checkered high gloss American walnut stock and forearm.

Mfg.'s Sug. Retail	$2,749	$2,450	$2,150	$1,850	$1,575	$1,475	$1,375	$1,275

Add $70 for 20/28 ga. set or 28/.410 ga. set.

▲ **Model 785 Trap** — 12 ga., 30 or 32 in. choke tube barrels with or without Monte Carlo stock, high rib.

Mfg.'s Sug. Retail	$1,949	$1,765	$1,525	$1,300	$1,100	$995	$895	$800

Add $770 for O/U Trap Combo.

The above Combo includes one set of O/U Trap barrels and a top single Trap barrel.

▲ **Model 785 Skeet** — 12, 20, 28, or .410 ga., 28 or 30 (12 ga. only) in. barrels with multi-chokes.

Mfg.'s Sug. Retail	$1,949	$1,765	$1,525	$1,300	$1,100	$995	$895	$800

Add $50 for 28 or .410 ga.

▲ **Model 785 3-Ga. Skeet Set** — includes 20, 28, and .410 ga. extra Skeet barrels, aluminum case.

Mfg.'s Sug. Retail	$3,929	$3,450	$2,750	$2,250	$1,825	$1,575	$1,400	$1,295

▲ **Model 785 Sporting Clays** — 12, 20, or 28 ga., 28 in. (all gauges), 30 in. (12 ga. only), or 32 in. (12 ga. only) multi-choke barrels, dimensioned for Sporting Clay competition with ⅜ in. narrow rib.

Mfg.'s Sug. Retail	$2,029	$1,830	$1,550	$1,325	$1,100	$995	$895	$800

Add $50 for 28 ga.

➤ **Model 785 Sporting Clays Set** — includes 2 sets of barrels (12 ga.-30 in., 20 ga.-28 in.), cased. New 1996.

Mfg.'s Sug. Retail	$2,889	$2,575	$2,300	$2,050	$1,800	$1,600	$1,400	$1,200

Grading	100%	98%	95%	90%	80%	70%	60%

MODEL 800 TRAP GRADE — 12 ga., similar to Model 700 Trap, except more engraving, better grade wood, wide rib. Mfg. 1969-1975.

| | $1,150 | $875 | $775 | $675 | $575 | $500 | $425 |

MODEL 800 SKEET GRADE — 12 or 20 ga., skeet chokes. Mfg. 1969-1975.

| | $1,200 | $1,000 | $895 | $795 | $680 | $595 | $565 |

MODEL 880 CROWN GRADE — 12, 20, 28, or .410 ga., coin finished receiver, extensively engraved with sideplates, SST, ejectors, select walnut with fleur-de-lis scroll style checkering, double cross bolt action. Disc. 1980.

| | $1,650 | $1,300 | $1,150 | $975 | $890 | $835 | $750 |

Add 25% for 28 or .410 ga.

MODEL 885 O/U — available in either Field, Skeet, or Trap configuration, coin finished receiver featuring fine scroll engraving with game scenes, boxlock action with sideplates, beginning 1992, the Model 885 Series in 12 ga. features lengthened forcing cones, .735 bore, and a competition series of extended length multi-chokes. Imported 1988-94.

▲ *Model 885 Field* — 12, 20, 28, or .410 ga., field dimensions, barrels include choke tubes. Imported 1989-94.

| | $1,600 | $1,200 | $975 | $825 | $725 | $650 | $595 |

Last Mfg.'s Sug. Retail was $1,895.

▲ *Model 885 Trap* — 12 ga., 30 or 32 in. barrels with multi-chokes, standard or Monte Carlo stock.

| | $1,650 | $1,200 | $975 | $850 | $750 | $650 | $595 |

Last Mfg.'s Sug. Retail was $1,949.

Add $700 for O/U Trap Combo.
The above Combo includes one set of O/U Trap barrels and a top single Trap barrel.

▲ *Model 885 Skeet* — 12, 20, 28, or .410 ga., 28 or 30 (12 ga. only - new 1994) in. barrels with multi-chokes.

| | $1,650 | $1,200 | $975 | $850 | $750 | $650 | $595 |

Last Mfg.'s Sug. Retail was $1,949.

▲ *Model 885 Field Set* — includes 12/20, 20/28, 28/.410 ga. 26 or 28 (new 1994) in. VR barrels with SKB inter-choke system (on 12 and 20 ga.), silver nitride receiver with finely engraved scroll game scenes, low profile receiver, cross bolt locking system, SST, ejectors, manual safety, checkered high gloss American walnut stock and forearm.

| | $2,450 | $2,150 | $1,750 | $1,500 | $1,250 | $1,075 | $925 |

▲ *Model 885 3-Ga. Skeet Set* — includes 20, 28, and .410 ga. extra Skeet barrels, aluminum case.

| | $3,200 | $2,700 | $2,300 | $1,975 | $1,725 | $1,500 | $1,400 |

Last Mfg.'s Sug. Retail was $3,595.

▲ *Model 885 Sporting Clay* — 28 (all gauges), 30 (12 ga. only), or 32 (12 ga. only) in. multi-choke barrels, dimensioned for Sporting Clay competition, narrow rib ⅜ in. became available 1994.

| | $1,650 | $1,200 | $975 | $850 | $750 | $650 | $595 |

Last Mfg.'s Sug. Retail was $1,949.

MODEL 5600 — 12 ga. only, available as Trap or Skeet model only, VR (Trap only) and vent. barrels (Skeet only), no engraving, select walnut. Disc. 1980.

| | $575 | $495 | $450 | $420 | $390 | $360 | $330 |

▲ *Model 5700* — available as Trap or Skeet model only, light engraving, select walnut, VR. Disc. 1980.

| | $750 | $625 | $540 | $495 | $460 | $430 | $400 |

▲ *Model 5800* — available as Trap or Skeet model only, more deluxe engraving, select walnut. Disc. 1980.

| | $950 | $800 | $695 | $595 | $500 | $450 | $425 |

SHOTGUNS: SxS

Models 100, 150, 200, 280, 300, 400, 480 — 12 and 20 ga. only, 25-30 in. barrels, all boxlock actions, more expensive models differ in the amount of engraving, grade of walnut, and style of checkering, beavertail forend, 6¼ - 7 lbs. Disc. 1980.

Grading	100%	98%	95%	90%	80%	70%	60%

MODEL 100 — 12 or 20 ga., Mag. model also, SST, AE, blue only.

	$485	$425	$380	$340	$310	$275	$250

MODEL 150 — similar to Model 100, except scroll engraving, beavertail forearm. Mfg. 1972-1974 by SKB.

	$520	$435	$385	$345	$310	$275	$250

MODEL 200 — 12 or 20 ga., Mag. model also, SST, AE, boxlock, scalloped frame, lightly engraved coin finished receiver.

	$550	$475	$410	$375	$340	$310	$280

MODEL 200 (NEW MFG.) — similar to original Model 200, SST, ejectors, recoil pad. Imported 1987-1988 only.

	$725	$525	$425	$420	$375	$345	$325

Last Mfg.'s Sug. Retail was $895.

S

> Add 25% for choke-tubes.
>
> This model was supplied with 3 factory choke-tubes during 1988 - only 400 were mfg. (retail was $995).

▲ *Model 200E (English)* — similar to New Model 200, except has straight grip stock. Importation disc. 1988.

	$725	$525	$425	$420	$375	$345	$325

Last Mfg.'s Sug. Retail was $895.

MODEL 280 ENGLISH — 12 or 20 ga., Mag. model also, SST, AE, lightly engraved blue receiver, straight grip.

	$850	$775	$625	$525	$440	$410	$375

MODEL 300 — 12 or 20 ga., Mag. model also, SST, AE, lightly engraved coin finished receiver.

	$750	$650	$575	$485	$440	$410	$375

MODEL 385 — 20 or 28 ga., boxlock action with silver nitride receiver, engraved scroll and game scene designs, SST, ejectors, automatic safety, semi-fancy American walnut, English or pistol grip stock, limited quantities, importation began 1992.

Mfg.'s Sug. Retail	$1,695	$1,475	$1,250	$925	$800	$700	$600	$525

▲ *Model 385 DU Commemorative* — features gold inlaid mallards on both receiver sides and gold inlaid DU duck head on receiver bottom, includes hard shell case, and signed letter from SKB president, DU proofmarks, limited mfg. - 200 sets in 1992.

Mfg.'s Sug. Retail	$5,000	$4,500	$3,650	$2,800

> This model is not a DU dinner gun.

MODEL 400 — 12 or 20 ga., Mag. model also, boxlock, SST, AE, moderately engraved coin finished receiver with sideplates.

	$695	$600	$510	$460	$430	$410	$385

MODEL 400 (RECENT MFG.) — similar to original Model 400, SST, ejectors, recoil pad. Imported 1987-1988 only.

	$975	$850	$780	$690	$595	$525	$475

Last Mfg.'s Sug. Retail was $1,195.

▲ *Model 400E (English)* — similar to New Model 400, except has engraved sideplates and straight grip stock. Importation disc. 1989.

	$975	$850	$780	$690	$595	$525	$475

Last Mfg.'s Sug. Retail was $1,195.

MODEL 480 ENGLISH — 12 or 20 ga., Mag. model also, SST, AE, moderately engraved coin finished receiver, straight grip.

	$1,250	$1,000	$825	$725	$625	$525	$475

Grading	100%	98%	95%	90%	80%	70%	60%

SHOTGUNS: SEMI-AUTO

MODEL 300 STANDARD — 12 or 20 ga., 3 in. chamber, 26 in. imp. cyl., 28 in. mod. or full, 30 in. full, recoil operated, autoloading, checkered pistol grip stock. Mfg. 1968-1972.

	100%	98%	95%	90%	80%	70%	60%
	$295	$255	$205	$165	$155	$145	$140
Vent. rib model	$320	$275	$220	$195	$165	$155	$150

MODEL 1300 UPLAND — 12 or 20 ga., 3 in. chamber, 22, 26, or 28 in. VR barrel with multi-chokes, matte black receiver, checkered walnut stock and forearm. Importation resumed 1988.

		100%	98%	95%	90%	80%	70%	60%
Mfg.'s Sug. Retail	$495	$450	$385	$340	$300	$270	$240	$210

This model was previously designated the Model 300. The new Model 1300 is also available in Slug configuration with 22 in. barrel/iron sights at no extra charge. New Model 1300s have a magazine cutoff system on front left side of frame.

XL 900 MR — 12 ga. only, gas operated semi-auto, 26-30 in. barrels, 5 shot, alloy receiver, etched game bird scroll work on receiver, shoots both $2\frac{3}{4}$ and 3 in. shells by interchanging barrels. Disc. 1980.

	100%	98%	95%	90%	80%	70%	60%
	$325	$280	$260	$240	$225	$190	$175

▲ *XL 900* — similar to XL 900 MR, only in 20 ga. and no recoil pad, $6\frac{1}{4}$ lbs.

	100%	98%	95%	90%	80%	70%	60%
	$360	$315	$275	$250	$230	$190	$175

XL 900 TRAP GRADE — similar to XL 900 MR, 12 ga. only, scroll engraved black chrome receiver, 30 in. imp. mod. or full, trap style stock, straight or Monte Carlo, recoil pad. Mfg. 1980-disc.

	100%	98%	95%	90%	80%	70%	60%
	$395	$350	$320	$305	$275	$265	$260

XL 900 SKEET GRADE — similar to XL 900 MR, except scroll engraved black chrome receiver, 26 in. barrel, skeet stock. Mfg. 1972-disc.

	100%	98%	95%	90%	80%	70%	60%
	$400	$350	$320	$305	$275	$265	$260

XL 900 SLUG GUN — similar to XL 900 MR, except 24 in. slug barrel, rifle sights, no rib. Mfg. 1972-disc.

	100%	98%	95%	90%	80%	70%	60%
	$350	$310	$280	$265	$250	$220	$200

MODEL 1900 — 12 or 20 ga., 3 in. chamber, 22, 26, or 28 in. VR barrel with multi-chokes, deluxe outdoor field scene etched on receiver, gold trigger, approx. 1,000-2,000 mfg. per year.

		100%	98%	95%	90%	80%	70%	60%
Mfg.'s Sug. Retail	$545	$485	$430	$395	$360	$330	$295	$260

This model was previously designated the Model 900. The new Model 1900 is also available in Slug configuration with 22 in. barrel and iron sights or Trap Model at no extra charge. New Model 1900s have a magazine cutoff system on front left side of frame.

MODEL 3000 — 12 or 20 ga., 3 in. chamber, gas semi-auto (shoots both $2\frac{3}{4}$ and 3 in. shells interchangeably) with semi-squareback styling, elaborate game scenes etched on both sides of receiver, deluxe checkered walnut stock and forearm. Imported 1988-90.

	100%	98%	95%	90%	80%	70%	60%
	$545	$475	$415	$380	$350	$315	$285

Last Mfg.'s Sug. Retail was $597.

Add $125 for Trap model ($2\frac{3}{4}$ in. chamber).

This model has not previously been imported in this configuration.

SHOTGUNS: SLIDE ACTION

MODEL 7300 — 12 or 20 ga., $2\frac{3}{4}$ or 3 in. chambers, blue only, French walnut stock-hand checkered, twin action slide bars. Disc. 1980.

	100%	98%	95%	90%	80%	70%	60%
	$295	$250	$225	$200	$180	$165	$150

MODEL 7900 — trap or skeet variation of the Model 7300.

	100%	98%	95%	90%	80%	70%	60%
	$350	$310	$265	$235	$200	$180	$160

SKS

Designates a semi-auto rifle design originally developed by the Russian military. Currently manufactured in Russia, China, Yugoslavia, and many other countries.

Over 600 million SKS models have been manufactured in China alone. This configuration has been the best-selling semi-auto rifle in America (and other countries) for several years now. Fear that upcoming gun legislation could outlaw this model is perhaps the largest single element of the additional demand factor.

Grading	100%	98%	95%	90%	80%	70%	60%

SKS — 7.62x39mm Russian, semi-auto rifle, Soviet designed, original Soviet mfg. as well as copies mfg. in China, Russia, Yugoslavia, and other countries, gas operated weapon, 10 shot fixed mag., wood stock (thumbhole design on newer mfg.), with or w/o (newer mfg.) permanently attached folding bayonet, on recent tangent rear and hooded front sight.

No Mfg.'s Retail	$155	$135	$120	$100	$90	$85	$80

This model may also be listed under those importers/distributors who import this model and are listed in this text.

SSK INDUSTRIES

Class II manufacturer located in Wintersville, OH.

SSK Industries uses Thompson Center flatside frames and applies an industrial hard chrome finish. Most SSK handguns and rifles are extensively customized in exotic calibers, finishes, and various engraving options. Receivers and barrels may be purchased separately - values below are for complete assembled pistol.

SSK has also manufactured various limited editions including the Handgun Hunters International (HHI) Models 1, 2, and 3. Issue price on these guns was $1,100 (Model 3), $1,200 (Model 2), and $1,300 (Model 1). Only 50 were mfg. total in 1987. SSK also customizes a Ruger Super Redhawk (.44 Mag. or .45 LC cal.). This variation comes with either a scoped 7½ in. octagon barrel (Beauty Model) or a 6 in. bull barrel with muzzle brake (Beast Model). Prices start at $1,430 - add $245 for .45 LC cal.

PISTOLS

Values listed below are for basic models with no options or special features.

SSK-CONTENDER — over 150 cals. available from .17 Bee to .50-70, various custom barrels available, basically, this is a custom order gun only.

Mfg.'s Sug. Retail	$1,100	$1,100	$875	$795	$675	$600	$550	$495

Individual barrels are available starting at $268.
An arrestor muzzle brake is available on special order.
This model includes barrel, frame, stocks, and sights as standard equipment.

SSK-XP100 — various cals. between .17 and .50, includes TSOB mount and rings.

Mfg.'s Sug. Retail	$1,200	$1,200	$975	$850	$725	$650	$575	$500

The .50 cal. XP100 (12.9 X 50.8 JDJ) comes with SSK muzzle brake, scope, dies and new reinforced fiberglass stock - retail price is $1,700.

RIFLES

Values listed below are for basic models with no options or special features. In addition, SSK also custom manufactures a bolt action rifle available in almost any caliber and configuration - prices start at $1,800 and can go as high as $6,000, depending on the customer's individual special orders. SSK also has developed a 6.5mm, 7mm, or .30 cal. upper unit conversion for AR-15s and M-16s utilizing heavy sub-sonic bullets - $1,000 (whispers).

Grading	100%	98%	95%	90%	80%	70%	60%

SSK TCR 87 — .14 through .600 cals., any Nitro Express cals. are also available, features Thompson Center TRC 87 receiver, and SSK custom barrels, muzzle brakes and exotic finishes are available at extra cost.

	100%	98%	95%	90%	80%	70%	60%
Mfg.'s Sug. Retail $1,000	$1,000	$850	$700	$600	$550	$500	$450

SSK RUGER NO. 1 — many cals. including .577 NE (optional), custom order rifle based on a Ruger No. 1 frame.

	100%	98%	95%	90%	80%	70%	60%
Mfg.'s Sug. Retail $1,400	$1,400	$1,125	$850	$725	$650	$575	$500

Add $700 for .577 NE

S   STI INTERNATIONAL

Manufacturer located in Austin, TX since 1993.

PISTOLS: SEMI-AUTO

EAGLE 5.5 COMP — .38 Super, .40 S&W, or .45 ACP cal., features modular frame, 5½ in. compensated barrel.

	100%	98%	95%	90%	80%	70%	60%
Mfg.'s Sug. Retail $2,149	$1,875	$1,625	$1,400	$1,200	$1,000	$825	$700

EAGLE 5.1 — .38 Super, .40 S&W, or .45 ACP cal., 5.1 in. barrel, govt. model full-size, adj. rear sight.

	100%	98%	95%	90%	80%	70%	60%
Mfg.'s Sug. Retail $1,549	$1,350	$1,150	$950	$825	$700	$575	$475

HAWK 4.3 — similar to Eagle 5.1, except size is comparable to Commander Model.

	100%	98%	95%	90%	80%	70%	60%
Mfg.'s Sug. Retail $1,549	$1,350	$1,150	$950	$825	$700	$575	$475

FALCON 3.9 — .38 Super, .40 S&W, or .45 ACP cal., 3.9 in. barrel, size is comparable to Officers Model, adj. rear sight.

	100%	98%	95%	90%	80%	70%	60%
Mfg.'s Sug. Retail $1,649	$1,425	$1,175	$975	$850	$700	$575	$475

S.W.D., INC.

Previously manufactured in Atlanta, GA. Similar models have previously been manufactured by R.P.B. Industries, Inc. (1979-82), and were met with B.A.T.F. disapproval because of convertibility into fully automatic operation. "Cobray" is a trademark for the M11/9 semi-automatic pistol. Dealer sales.

COBRAY PISTOLS

M-11/NINE mm SEMI-AUTO PISTOL — 9mm Para., fires from closed bolt, 3rd generation design, stamped steel frame, 32 shot mag., parkerized finish, similar in appearance to Ingram Mac 10.

	100%	98%	95%	90%	80%	70%	60%
	$245	$225	$200	$175	$160	$150	$140

This model is also available in a fully-auto variation, class III transferable only.

CARBINES

SEMI-AUTO CARBINE — 9mm, same mechanism as M11, 16¼ in. shrouded barrel, telescoping stock.

	100%	98%	95%	90%	80%	70%	60%
	$295	$265	$230	$195	$170	$160	$150

REVOLVERS

LADIES HOME COMPANION — .45-70 cal., double action design utilizing spring wound 12 shot rotary mag., 12 in. barrel, steel barrel and frame, 9 lbs. 6 oz. Mfg. 1990-94.

	100%	98%	95%	90%	80%	70%	60%
	$650	$525	$400	$360	$335	$310	$290

Grading	100%	98%	95%	90%	80%	70%	60%

SHOTGUNS

TERMINATOR — 12 or 20 ga., single shot paramilitary design shotgun with 18 in. cylinder bore barrel, parkerized finish, ejector. Mfg. 1986-1988 only.

	$95	$80	$70	$60	$55	$50	$45

Last Mfg.'s Sug. Retail was $110.

SABATTI S.r.l.

Manufacturer located in Gardone, Italy with history tracing back to 1674. Some models are currently imported by European American Armory located in Sharpes, FL. In 1960, the sons of Antonio Sabatti formed the current company, and manufacture currently includes O/U and SxS shotguns, O/U combination and double rifles, bolt action rifles, and single shot shotguns.

SAFARI ARMS

Manufacturer located in Olympia, WA. Schuetzen Pistol Works is the custom shop division of Safari Arms. M-S Safari Arms was started in 1978 and was a division of M-S Safari Outfitters. In 1987, Safari Arms was absorbed by Olympic Arms.

Safari Arms previously made the Phoenix, Special Forces, Camp Perry, and Royal Order of Jesters commemoratives in various configurations and quantities. Prices average in the $1,500 range except for the Royal Order of Jesters ($2,000).

PISTOLS: SAFARI ARMS

Safari Arms currently manufactures mostly single action, semi-auto pistols derived from the Browning M1911 design with modifications.

ENFORCER — .45 ACP, 3.8 in. barrel, 6 shot mag., shortened grip, available with max hard finish aluminum frame, parkerized, electroless nickel or lightweight anodized finishes, flat or arched mainspring housing, adj. sights, ambidextrous safety, neoprene or checkered walnut grips, 27 oz. (lightweight model).

Mfg.'s Sug. Retail	$740	$670	$555	$500	$450	$425	$400	$375

This model was originally called the Black Widow. After Safari Arms became Schuetzen Pistol Works, this model was changed extensively to include stainless construction, beavertail grip safety, and combat style hammer.

MATCHMASTER — similar to the Enforcer, except has 5 or 6 in. barrel and 7 shot mag., approx. 40 oz.

Mfg.'s Sug. Retail	$715	$645	$530	$485	$450	$425	$400	$375

Add $129 for 6 in. barrel.

GI SAFARI — .45 ACP cal., patterned after the Colt Model 1911, Safari frame, beavertail grip safety and commander hammer, parkerized matte black finish, 39.9 oz. New 1991.

Mfg.'s Sug. Retail	$585	$535	$450	$395	$350	$295	$275	$250

COHORT PISTOL — .45 ACP cal., features Enforcer slide and MatchMaster frame, 3.8 in. stainless steel barrel, beavertail grip safety, extended thumb safety and slide release, commander style hammer, smooth walnut grips with laser etched Black Widow logo, 37 oz. New 1995.

Mfg.'s Sug. Retail	$780	$695	$575	$515	$460	$425	$400	$375

PISTOLS: SAFARI ARMS, DISC.

BLACK WIDOW — .45 ACP cal., 3.9 in. barrel, hand-contoured front grip strap, schrimshawed ivory Micarta grips with Black Widow emblem, 6 shot mag., 27 oz. Inventory was depleted 1988.

	$565	$510	$460	$430	$400	$375	$350

Last Mfg.'s Sug. Retail was $595.

Grading	100%	98%	95%	90%	80%	70%	60%

BILL OF RIGHTS BICENTENNIAL MATCHED SET—includes the MatchMaster Pistol and Service-Match Rifle, features beryllium receivers and special engraving. Disc.

$8,950 $6,500 $4,750

Last Mfg.'s Sug. Retail was $7,400.

PARTNER—.22 LR, formerly the Whitney Wolverine, 8 shot mag., black plastic grips, non-adj. sights. New late 1995.

Mfg.'s Sug. Retail $315 $275 $250 $225 $200 $185 $170 $155

TARGET PISTOLS

MODEL 81 — .38 Spl. or .45 ACP, 5 in. barrel, hand-contoured front grip strap, 2 lbs. 10 oz. Disc. 1987.

$775 $695 $550 $440 $410 $375 $350

Last Mfg.'s Sug. Retail was $875.

Add $50 for Deluxe Model (with Herrett adj. grips).

▲ *Model 81L* — .38 Spl. or .45 ACP, 6 in. barrel, 2 lbs. 13 oz. Disc. 1987.

$850 $775 $695 $550 $440 $410 $375

Last Mfg.'s Sug. Retail was $975.

Add $50 for Deluxe Model (with Herrett adj. grips).

▲ *Model 81 NM* — .38 Spl. or .45 ACP, similar frame as Model 81, except has flat front grip strap, 5 in. barrel, 2 lbs. 5 oz. Disc. 1987.

$775 $695 $550 $440 $410 $375 $350

Last Mfg.'s Sug. Retail was $875.

▲ *Model 81BP* — .38 Spl. or .45 ACP, 6 in barrel, contoured front grip strap, faster cycle time, 2 lbs. 9 oz. Disc. 1987.

$875 $775 $695 $550 $440 $410 $375

Last Mfg.'s Sug. Retail was $995.

▲ *Silueta* — .45 ACP or .38/.45 Wildcat, 10 in. extended barrel, designed for silhouette shooting, 2 lbs. 14 oz. Disc. 1987.

$875 $775 $695 $550 $440 $410 $375

Last Mfg.'s Sug. Retail was $1,050.

ULTIMATE/UNLIMITED — various cals., bolt action target pistol, single shot, 14^{15}/$_{16}$ in. barrel, black finished metal, laminate stock. Disc. 1987.

$850 $775 $695 $550 $440 $410 $375

Last Mfg.'s Sug. Retail was $975.

OMEGA CONVERSION KITS

OMEGA — 9mm Para., 9x21mm, .38 Super, .40 S&W, or .45 ACP cal., linkless multi-caliber system mfg. in the U.S. under license from Peters-Stahl of Germany, conversion unit only - customer must supply 1911 frame for complete gun. Mfg. 1993-94.

$750 $650 $550

Last Mfg.'s Sug. Retail was $845.

Add $165 per individual barrel.
Add $25 each per individual mag.

SCHUETZEN PISTOL WORKS

CARRYCOMP — similar to MatchMaster, except utilizes W. Schuemann designed hybrid compensator system, 5 in. barrel, available in stainless steel or steel, 38 oz. New 1993.

Mfg.'s Sug. Retail $1,150 $1,025 $875 $750 $600 $500 $425 $375

▲ *Enforcer CarryComp* — similar to Enforcer, except utilizes W. Schuemann designed hybrid compensator system, available in stainless steel or steel, 36 oz. New 1993.

Mfg.'s Sug. Retail $1,300 $1,175 $1,025 $875 $750 $600 $500 $425

Grading	100%	98%	95%	90%	80%	70%	60%

RENEGADE — .45 ACP cal., left-hand action (port on left side), 4½ (4-star, disc. 1996) or 5 (new 1994) in. barrel, 6 shot mag., adj. sights, stainless steel construction, 36-39 oz. New 1993.

Mfg.'s Sug. Retail	$1,075	$950	$800	$700	$600	$525	$450	$395

Add $60 for 4-star (4½ in. barrel).

RELIABLE — similar to Renegade, except has right-hand action. New 1993.

Mfg.'s Sug. Retail	$815	$725	$615	$525	$450	$425	$400	$375

Add $60 for 4-star (4½ in. barrel).

GRIFFON PISTOL — .45 ACP cal., 5 in. stainless steel barrel, 10 shot mag., standard govt. size with beavertail grip safety, full-length recoil spring guide, commander style hammer, smooth walnut grips, 40½ oz.

Mfg.'s Sug. Retail	$910	$850	$725	$650	$575	$500	$450	$395

BIG DEUCE — .45 ACP cal., 6 in. longslide version of the MatchMaster, matte black slide with satin stainless steel frame, smooth walnut grips, 40.3 oz. New 1995.

Mfg.'s Sug. Retail	$844	$750	$650	$575	$500	$450	$400	$350

SAKO

Manufacturer located in Riihimaki, Finland. Current models are presently being imported by Stoeger Industries, Inc. located in Wayne, NJ. Previously imported by Garcia and Rymac.

RIFLES: DISC.

Add 10%-15% for popular Mag. cals. on rifles listed below.
Note: Prices below are for pre-1972 Garcia and Rymac imported rifles unless stated otherwise.
Pre-Garcia Sakos utilize the L61R action.
Subtract approx. 25% for post-1972 models.

DELUXE — various cals., Monte Carlo stock, skipline checkering, long, medium, or short actions, contrasting pistol grip cap and forend tip, engraved floorplate.

$895	$825	$750	$600	$440	$410	$375

STANDARD SPORTER — long, medium, and short actions.

$695	$650	$595	$475	$440	$410	$375

HEAVY BARREL MODEL — long, medium, and short actions.

$695	$650	$595	$475	$440	$410	$375

FULL STOCK MODELS — 20 in. carbine barrel (all actions), 23½ in. barrel on rifle (short & medium actions).

▲ *Finnbear* — long action.

$895	$850	$725	$650	$500	$425	$375

▲ *Forester* — medium action.

$850	$800	$725	$600	$475	$425	$375

▲ *Vixen* — short action.

$850	$800	$725	$600	$475	$425	$375

Early short action pre-Vixen Sakos had detachable mags.

MAUSER ACTION (FN) — .270 Win. or .30-06 cal., long action. Mfg. 1950-1957.

$550	$500	$400	$345	$310	$280	$260

MAGNUM MAUSER (FN) — 8x60S, 8.2x57mm, .300 H&H, or .375 H&H cal.

$695	$635	$580	$495	$450	$410	$375

MODEL 74 — various cals.

$560	$495	$440	$375	$340	$320	$290

Grading	100%	98%	95%	90%	80%	70%	60%

FINNWOLF — .243 Win. or .308 Win. cal., lever action, 4 shot clip early model, 3 shot clip later model. Mfg. 1962-1974.

		$775	$675	$550	$500	$440	$410	$375

Add 10% for early model.

ANNIVERSARY MODEL — 7mm Rem. Mag. only, 1,000 mfg.

		$1,995	$1,250	$850

The 100% value on this model refers to NIB condition.

RIFLES: RECENT MFG.

All Sako left-handed models are available in medium or long action only.

FINNFIRE — .22 LR cal., 22 in. regular or heavy (new 1996) cold-hammer forged free floating barrel, single stage adj. trigger, 50 degree bolt lift, 2 position safety, European walnut stock, cocking indicator, 5 or 10 shot mag., integral 11mm dovetail (for scope mounting), with (new 1996) or w/o open sights, $5\frac{1}{4}$ lbs. Importation began 1994.

Mfg.'s Sug. Retail	$732	$625	$545	$475	$425	$385	$350	$325

Add $65 for heavy barrel.

HUNTER LIGHTWEIGHT RIFLE — available in short action (AI) in .17 Rem., .222 Rem., or .223 Rem. cal., medium action (AII) in .22-250 Rem., .243 Win., .308 Win., or 7mm-08 Rem. cal., or long action (AIII) in .25-06 Rem., .270 Win., .280 Rem., .30-06, .270 Wby. Mag., 7mm Wby. Mag., 7mm Rem. Mag., .300 Win. Mag., .300 Wby. Mag., .338 Win. Mag., .340 Wby. Mag., .375 H&H, or .416 Rem. Mag. (new 1991) cal., $21\frac{1}{4}$, $21\frac{3}{4}$, or 22 in. barrel, classic styled stock with choice of oil or lacquer finish, finely checkered French walnut.

Mfg.'s Sug. Retail	$1,050	$850	$685	$550	$490	$460	$430	$410

Add $35 for long action.
Add $50-$70 for Mag. cals.
Add approx. $80 for left-hand action (available in all Mag. cals. - new 1994).

▲ **Hunter Carbine (Handy)** — available in medium action in .22-250 Rem. (disc. 1990), .243 Win. (new 1991), .308 Win. (new 1991) cal. or long action in .25-06 Rem. (disc. 1990), 7mm Rem. Mag. (disc. 1990), .338 Win. Mag. cal., or .375 H&H Mag. (new 1990) cal., $18\frac{1}{2}$ in. barrel with iron sights, oil or lacquer finished deluxe walnut stock with checkering, approx. 7 lbs. Mfg. 1986-91.

		$725	$650	$600	$490	$460	$430	$410

Last Mfg.'s Sug. Retail was $945.

Add $50-$65 for long action (Mag. cals.).

LONG RANGE HUNTING MODEL — available in long action in .25-06 Rem., .270 Win., .300 Win. Mag., or 7mm Rem. Mag. cal., 26 in. heavy barrel only w/o sights. New 1996.

Mfg.'s Sug. Retail	$1,275	$1,030	$785	$625	$545	$495	$465	$440

FIBERCLASS MODEL — available in medium action (disc. 1992) in .22-250 Rem., .243 Win., .308 Win., or 7mm-08 cal., or long action in .25-06 Rem., .270 Win., .280 Rem., .30-06, 7mm Rem. Mag., .300 Win. Mag., .338 Win. Mag., .375 H&H, or .416 Rem. Mag. (new 1991) cal., has black fiberglass stock.

Mfg.'s Sug. Retail	$1,388	$1,170	$930	$785	$725	$630	$560	$510

Add $17-$37 for Mag. cals.
Subtract $40 for medium action cals. (disc. 1992).
Add $80 for left-hand action (disc. 1989).

▲ **FiberClass Carbine (Handy)** — available in medium action in .243 Win. or .308 Win. cal. and long action in .25-06 Rem. (disc.), .270 Win. (disc.), .30-06, 7mm Rem. Mag. (disc.), .300 Win. Mag. (disc.), .338 Win. Mag., or .375 H&H (new 1991) cal., $18\frac{1}{2}$ in. barrel with fiberglass stock. Mfg. 1986-91.

		$995	$895	$775	$725	$630	$560	$510

Last Mfg.'s Sug. Retail was $1,239.

Add $50-$65 for Mag. cals.

Grading	100%	98%	95%	90%	80%	70%	60%

LAMINATED RIFLE — available in short action (disc. 1989), medium action in .22-250 Rem., .243 Win., .308 Win., or 7mm-08 Rem. cal., or long action in .25-06 Rem., .270 Win., .280 Rem., .30-06, 7mm Rem. Mag., .300 Win. Mag., .338 Win. Mag., .375 H&H, or .416 Rem. Mag. (new 1991) cal., features laminated wood stock. Mfg. 1988-95.

	100%	98%	95%	90%	80%	70%	60%
	$985	$790	$635	$550	$495	$460	$430

Last Mfg.'s Sug. Retail was $1,200.

Add $35 for short action.
Add $55 for long action.
Add $75-$95 for Mag. cals.
Add approx. $100 for left-hand action (disc.).
The left-handed action was available in .270 Win., .280 Rem., .30-06, 7mm Rem. Mag., .300 Win. Mag., .338 Win. Mag., .375 H&H, or .416 Rem. Mag. cal.

MODEL TRG-21 — .308 Win. cal., bolt action, 25¾ in. barrel, new design features modular synthetic stock construction with adj. cheekpiece and buttplate, stainless steel barrel, cold hammer forged receiver, and resistance free bolt, 10 shot detachable mag., 10½ lbs. Importation began 1993.

	100%	98%	95%	90%	80%	70%	60%
Mfg.'s Sug. Retail $4,265	$3,825	$3,225	$2,650	$2,250	$1,750	$1,450	$1,250

MODEL TRG-41 — .338 Lapua Mag., similar to Model TRG-21, except has long action and 27⅛ in. barrel, 7¾ lbs. Importation began 1994.

	100%	98%	95%	90%	80%	70%	60%
Mfg.'s Sug. Retail $4,825	$4,275	$3,400	$2,750	$2,300	$1,750	$1,450	$1,250

MODEL TRG-S — available in medium action (disc. 1993) in .243 Win. or 7mm-08 cal., or long action in .25-06 Rem. (new 1994), .270 Win., 6.5x55Smm, .30-06, .308 Win. (disc. 1995), .270 Wby. Mag., 7mm Wby. Mag., 7mm Rem. Mag., .300 Win. Mag., .300 Wby. Mag. (new 1994), .338 Win. Mag., .338 Lapua Mag. (new 1994), .340 Wby. Mag., 7 STW (26 in. barrel only), .375 H&H Mag., or .416 Rem. Mag. cal., Sporter variation derived from the Model TRG-21, 22 or 24 (Mag. cals. only) in. barrel, 5 shot detachable mag., fully adj. trigger, 60 degree bolt-lift, matte finish, 7¾ lbs. Importation began 1993.

	100%	98%	95%	90%	80%	70%	60%
Mfg.'s Sug. Retail $790	$685	$560	$490	$460	$430	$410	$380

Add $40 for Mag. cals.

MANNLICHER CARBINE — available in short action (disc. 1989), medium action in .243 Win. or .308 Win. cal., or long action in .25-06 Rem. (disc. 1991), .270 Win., .30-06, 7mm Rem. Mag. (disc. 1991), .300 Win. Mag. (disc. 1991), .338 Win. Mag., or .375 H&H cal., 18½ in. barrel, two-piece full Mannlicher style stock, open sights.

	100%	98%	95%	90%	80%	70%	60%
Mfg.'s Sug. Retail $1,275	$1,030	$785	$625	$545	$495	$465	$440

Add $35 for long action.
Add $60-$75 for Mag. cals.

PPC MODEL — 22 PPC or 6 PPC cal., 21¾ or 23¾ (Benchrest Model) in. barrel, single shot in Benchrest Model, 4 shot mag. in Hunter or Deluxe Model, checkered walnut stock, Deluxe Model has rosewood pistol grip and forearm caps plus skip line checkering, matte lacquer finish on Hunter and Deluxe, oiled finish on Benchrest, 6¼ or 8¾ (Benchrest Model with heavy barrel) lbs. Importation began 1989.

	100%	98%	95%	90%	80%	70%	60%
Mfg.'s Sug. Retail $1,475	$1,195	$900	$725	$650	$590	$540	$500

Add $320 for Deluxe Hunter Model (disc. 1993).
Add $85 for Benchrest Model (disc. 1993).

VARMINT RIFLE — available in short action (AI) in .17 Rem., .222 Rem., or .223 Rem., and medium action (AII) .22-250 Rem., .243 Win., .308 Win., or 7mm-08 cal., 22¾ in. heavy barrel, no sights.

	100%	98%	95%	90%	80%	70%	60%
Mfg.'s Sug. Retail $1,240	$1,025	$795	$615	$545	$475	$430	$400

Also available in single shot configuration (6mm PPC or .22 PPC only) — subtract $110 (disc. 1989).

Grading	100%	98%	95%	90%	80%	70%	60%

CLASSIC GRADE — currently available in .243 Win., .270 Win., .30-06, or 7mm Rem. Mag. cal., short (AI, disc. 1992), medium (AII), or long (AIII) action, classic styled stock, finely checkered French walnut with matte lacquer finish. Disc. 1985, reintroduced 1992.

Mfg.'s Sug. Retail	$1,050	$895	$745	$600	$545	$475	$430	$400

Add $50 for Mag. cal.
Add $35 for long action.
Add $120-$135 for left hand action (disc. 1994) (.270 Win. or 7mm Rem. Mag cal. only).

In 1992, the Classic Grade was once again imported into the U.S. in .243 Win., .270 Win., .30-06, or 7mm Rem. Mag. cal.

DELUXE LIGHTWEIGHT RIFLE — available in short action (AI) in .17 Rem., .222 Rem., or .223 Rem. cal., medium action (AII) in .22-250 Rem., .243 Win., .308 Win., or 7mm-08 Rem. cal., or long action (AIII) in .25-06 Rem., .270 Win., .280 Rem., .30-06, 7mm Rem. Mag., .300 Win. Mag., .300 Wby. Mag., .338 Win. Mag., .375 H&H, or .416 Rem. Mag. (new 1991) cal., 21¼, 21¾, or 22 in. barrel, deluxe quality skipline checkered walnut stock with rosewood forend tip.

Mfg.'s Sug. Retail	$1,475	$1,185	$965	$750	$650	$595	$540	$500

Add $35 for long action.
Add $50-$70 for Mag. cals.
Add $150-$175 for left-hand action (disc. 1994) (available in long action only).

SAFARI GRADE — available in long (AIII) action only, .300 Win. Mag. (disc. 1989), .338 Win. Mag., .375 H&H Mag., or .416 Rem. Mag. (new 1991) cal., deluxe walnut with sculptured cheekpiece, 22 in. barrel, 4 shot mag., open sights, sling swivels.

Mfg.'s Sug. Retail	$2,765	$2,235	$1,785	$1,475	$1,250	$1,050	$900	$795

SUPER DELUXE — a limited edition rifle available on special order only, various cals. are available in the short (AI), medium (AII), and long (AIII) actions, presentation grade walnut with both checkering and carving, rosewood forend tip.

Mfg.'s Sug. Retail	$3,100	$2,400	$1,825	$1,475	$1,250	$1,050	$900	$795

MODEL 78 — .22 LR, .22 Mag., or .22 Hornet cal., clip mag., same size as short action Standard Model. Importation disc. 1986.

	$480	$395	$340	$310	$280	$265	$250

Last Mfg.'s Sug. Retail was $647.

Add $30 for .22 Hornet cal.

FINSPORT MODEL 2700 — available in long (AIII) action only, .270 Win., .300 Win. Mag. cals., select checkered walnut. Disc. 1985.

	$795	$680	$600	$560	$510	$475	$430

Last Mfg.'s Sug. Retail was $910.

PISTOLS

Less than 200 Triace pistols were imported into the United States.

TRIACE — .22 Short, .22 LR or .32 S&W Wadcutter cals., target pistol incorporating unique action, competition walnut grips with thumb rest and adj. heel, blued finish with chrome accents. Imported 1985-86 only.

	$1,300	$1,150	$950	$825	$700	$600	$500

Last Mfg.'s Sug. Retail was $1,395.

▲ *Triace Pistol Kit* — consists of Triace frame, .22 Short, .22 LR, and .32 S&W barrels. Cased with accessories. Imported 1985-86 only.

	$2,500	$2,200	$2,000	$1,500	$1,300	$1,175	$1,025

Last Mfg.'s Sug. Retail was $2,385.

SAMCO GLOBAL ARMS, INC.

Importer/distributor located in Miami, FL. Dealer sales.

Samco Global Arms currently imports a variety of foreign and domestic surplus military rifles (including various contract Mausers, Loewe, Steyr, Czech, Lee Enfield, etc.). Most of these guns are in the $60-$250 range and they offer excellent values to both shooters and collectors. Samco also sells newly remanufactured sporting rifles (German or Spanish) in .308 Win. or 7x57mm cal. These sporters range in value from approx. $195-$250.

SARASQUETA, FELIX

Manufacturer located in Eibar, Spain. Previously imported and distributed by SAE (Spain America Enterprises), Inc. located in Miami, FL.

Current information including pricing can be obtained by contacting the factory directly (please refer to the Trademark Index).

Grading	100%	98%	95%	90%	80%	70%	60%

SHOTGUNS

MODEL MERKE O/U — 12 ga. only, boxlock action, 22 or 27 in. separated barrels, single non-selective trigger, blue only, extractors, recoil pad. Imported 1986 only.

	100%	98%	95%	90%	80%	70%	60%
	$255	$215	$200	$190	$180	$170	$160

Last Mfg.'s Sug. Retail was $291.

SARASQUETA, J.J.

Manufacturer located in Eibar, Spain. Imported until 1984 by American Arms, Inc. located in Overland Park, KS.

SHOTGUNS: SxS

MODEL 107 E — 12, 16, or 20 ga., ejectors, various barrel lengths, checkered walnut stock and forearm, double triggers.

	100%	98%	95%	90%	80%	70%	60%
	$360	$290	$270	$255	$240	$215	$200

Last Mfg.'s Sug. Retail was $435.

MODELS 119E-132E-1882E — more deluxe versions of Model 107E.

	100%	98%	95%	90%	80%	70%	60%
	$470	$375	$340	$315	$285	$255	$230

Last Mfg.'s Sug. Retail was $570.

MODEL 130 E — more deluxe version of Model 119 E.

	100%	98%	95%	90%	80%	70%	60%
	$800	$635	$590	$555	$515	$480	$450

Last Mfg.'s Sug. Retail was $960.

MODEL 131 E — action similar to Model 107 E, except has deluxe engraving.

	100%	98%	95%	90%	80%	70%	60%
	$1,050	$845	$770	$710	$665	$620	$585

Last Mfg.'s Sug. Retail was $1,250.

MODEL 1882 E LUXE — double triggers, moderate engraving, otherwise similar to Model 107 E.

	100%	98%	95%	90%	80%	70%	60%
	$825	$660	$615	$565	$520	$480	$450

Last Mfg.'s Sug. Retail was $990.

▲ *Model 1882 E Luxe w/gold inlays* — SST, extensive engraving.

	100%	98%	95%	90%	80%	70%	60%
	$1,120	$920	$850	$790	$740	$695	$650

Last Mfg.'s Sug. Retail was $1,320.

▲ *Model 1882 E Luxe w/silver inlays* — SST, extensive engraving.

	100%	98%	95%	90%	80%	70%	60%
	$1,055	$855	$795	$740	$700	$660	$630

Last Mfg.'s Sug. Retail was $1,260.

Grading	100%	98%	95%	90%	80%	70%	60%

MODEL 150 E — 12 or 16 ga., single trigger, ejectors, select walnut and extensive engraving.

	100%	98%	95%	90%	80%	70%	60%
	$1,285	$1,035	$960	$895	$835	$770	$695

Last Mfg.'s Sug. Retail was $1,500.

▲ *Model 150 E Trap* — similar to Model 150 E, except trap dimensions on stock.

	100%	98%	95%	90%	80%	70%	60%
	$1,360	$1,125	$1,010	$940	$875	$790	$720

Last Mfg.'s Sug. Retail was $1,600.

SARASQUETA, VICTOR

Previous manufacturer located in Eibar, Spain. Trademark is currently owned by Diarm S.A.

SHOTGUNS

MODEL 3 SxS — 12, 16, or 20 ga., all standard barrel lengths and chokes, boxlock, double triggers, checkered English style stock and forend.

	100%	98%	95%	90%	80%	70%	60%
Extractors	$445	$395	$350	$295	$250	$215	$185
Auto ejectors	$575	$515	$450	$375	$300	$250	$225

HAMMERLESS SIDELOCK — 12, 16, 20, 28, or .410 ga., SxS, barrel length and choke to order, straight English style stock, models differ as to amount of engraving, grade of wood, and overall quality as follows:

    Add 25% for 28 ga.
    Add 30% for .410 ga.

MODEL 4 — extractors.

	100%	98%	95%	90%	80%	70%	60%
	$620	$550	$525	$495	$450	$415	$360

MODEL 4E — auto ejectors.

	100%	98%	95%	90%	80%	70%	60%
	$680	$605	$580	$550	$505	$470	$415

MODEL 203 — extractors.

	100%	98%	95%	90%	80%	70%	60%
	$650	$570	$545	$515	$475	$435	$380

MODEL 203E — auto ejectors.

	100%	98%	95%	90%	80%	70%	60%
	$710	$625	$600	$570	$530	$490	$435

MODEL 6E

	100%	98%	95%	90%	80%	70%	60%
	$800	$715	$690	$660	$615	$580	$525

MODEL 7E

	100%	98%	95%	90%	80%	70%	60%
	$855	$770	$745	$715	$670	$635	$580

MODEL 10E

	100%	98%	95%	90%	80%	70%	60%
	$1,735	$1,595	$1,485	$1,405	$1,320	$1,240	$1,100

MODEL 11E

	100%	98%	95%	90%	80%	70%	60%
	$1,870	$1,680	$1,595	$1,515	$1,430	$1,350	$1,265

MODEL 12E

	100%	98%	95%	90%	80%	70%	60%
	$2,145	$1,900	$1,790	$1,705	$1,570	$1,430	$1,375

SARDIUS

Manufacturer located in Israel. Previously imported and distributed by Armscorp of America, Inc. located in Baltimore, MD.

SD-9 — 9mm Para., semi-auto double action, compact design, 3.07 in. barrel, matte black finish, 6 shot mag., 3 dot sighting system, 1.54 lbs. Imported 1988-90 only.

	100%	98%	95%	90%	80%	70%	60%
	$315	$280	$260	$240	$220	$200	$185

Last Mfg.'s Sug. Retail was $350.

SARRIUGARTE, FRANCISO S.A.

Manufacturer located in Elgoibar, Spain. Previously part of the Diarm S.A. Group which was imported and distributed by American Arms, Inc. located in North Kansas City, MO.

SAUER, J.P. & SOHN

Manufactured since 1751 in Germany (originally Prussia). Previously located in Suhl - currently headquartered in Eckernforde, W. Germany. Currently imported by Sigarms located in Exeter, NH since 1995. Previously imported by the Paul Company Inc. located in Wellsville, KS until 1995 and by G.U., Inc. located in Omaha, NE until 1994. In 1972, J.P. Sauer & Sohn formed a cooperation with the Sig Swiss Industrial Company which is presently the parent house of Sauer & Sohn.

S

Grading	100%	98%	95%	90%	80%	70%	60%

PISTOLS

MODEL 1913 POCKET AUTOMATIC — .32 auto, 7 shot, 3 in. barrel, fixed sights, blue, black rubber grips. Mfg. 1913-1930.

	100%	98%	95%	90%	80%	70%	60%
	$295	$225	$185	$165	$155	$145	$135

MODEL 1913 25 AUTOMATIC — .25 auto, 7 shot, 2½ in. barrel, fixed sights, blue, black rubber grips. Mfg. 1913-1930.

	$325	$250	$200	$175	$150	$140	$135

MODEL 28 — .25 ACP, 7 shot, 3 in. barrel, fixed sights, blue, black rubber grips. Mfg. 1930-1938.

	$300	$240	$185	$170	$155	$145	$135

BEHORDEN (SERVICE) MODEL — .32 ACP, 3 in. barrel, blue only, black plastic grips.

	$325	$240	$200	$175	$150	$145	$135

MODEL 38 H DOUBLE ACTION AUTOMATIC — .22 LR (extremely rare), .32 ACP, or .380 ACP (rare) cal., 3¼ in. barrel, fixed sights, blue, plastic grips. Mfg. 1938-1945.

	100%	98%	95%	90%	80%	70%	60%
.32 ACP	$395	$325	$240	$205	$185	$165	$150
.380 ACP	$3,000	$2,500	$2,000	$1,500	$1,250	$995	$775
.22 LR	$3,500	$2,750	$2,200	$1,600	$1,250	$995	$775

Add 10% for Waffenamt proofing.
Add 15% for police markings.
Add 60% for alloy frame.

RIFLES: BOLT ACTION

SAUER PRE-WWII BOLT ACTION RIFLE — most popular European cals. and .30-06, 22 or 24 in. barrel, raised solid rib, Krupp steel, double set triggers, folding 3 leaf express sight, checkered sporter stock. Mfg. pre-WWII.

	$715	$550	$495	$440	$360	$330	$305

MODEL 200 BOLT ACTION — available in 15 cals. between .243 Win. and .375 H&H Mag., short and medium actions only, 23.62 in. unique interchangeable barrels, 6 lug bolt, easily detachable stock and forearm, optional set trigger, detachable mag. with hidden release button, 7.7 lbs. Importation disc. 1993.

	$1,225	$925	$800	$700	$600	$525	$450

Last Mfg.'s Sug. Retail was $1,395.

Add $100 for 7mm Rem. Mag. or .300 Win. Mag. cal.
Add $300 for extra interchangeable barrel.

During 1986-1989, Sauer exported to Sigarms 4,170 Model 200 rifles, 1,370 of these were in Mag. cals.

Grading	100%	98%	95%	90%	80%	70%	60%

▲ *Model 200 Lightweight* — similar to Model 200, only with alloy receiver, 6.6 lbs.

	$1,225	$925	$800	$700	$600	$525	$450

Last Mfg.'s Sug. Retail was $1,395.

Add $150 for left-hand version.

▲ *Model 200 Lux* — similar to Model 200, except has deluxe walnut, rosewood forend tip and pistol grip cap, marmorized bolt and gold trigger.

	$1,395	$1,175	$925	$800	$700	$600	$525

Last Mfg.'s Sug. Retail was $1,595.

▲ *American 200 Lux* — similar to Model 200 Lux, except has high gloss Monte Carlo stock, 24 in. barrel, jeweled bolt, and gold trigger.

	$1,395	$1,175	$925	$800	$700	$600	$525

Last Mfg.'s Sug. Retail was $1,595.

Add $150 for left-hand version.

▲ *European 200 Lux* — similar to Model 200 Lux, except has European configured stock with Schnabel forearm, 26 in. barrel.

	$1,395	$1,175	$925	$800	$700	$600	$525

Last Mfg.'s Sug. Retail was $1,595.

Add $95 for left-hand version.

▲ *Model 200 Carbon Fiber* — similar to Model 200, except has carbon fiber stock. Imported 1987-88 only.

	$800	$700	$625	$565	$500	$465	$430

Last Mfg.'s Sug. Retail was $1,200.

MODEL 200 TR TARGET — 6.5x55mm or .308 Win. cal., true left hand variation, 200 meter diopter sights, modular design allows changing single components including caliber, free floating barrel with vent. forearm, 5 shot mag., interchangeable barrel systems, 12.1 lbs. Importation began 1994.

Mfg.'s Sug. Retail	$1,900	$1,775	$1,575	$1,400	$1,250	$1,100	$950	$825

MODEL 202 MEDIUM STANDARD — .243 Win., .270 Win., .30-06, .308 Win., 6.5x55mm, or 7x64mm cal., choice of machine steel or light alloy receiver, modular design allowing barrel change within 2 minutes, dual saftey, 2 piece figured walnut stock, cocking indicator, detachable 3-5 shot mag., takedown with interchangeable barrels, right or left hand action. Importation began 1994.

Mfg.'s Sug. Retail	$899	$815	$725	$650	$600	$550	$495	$435

▲ *Model 202 Standard Magnum* — .300 Win. Mag., .300 Wby. Mag., .338 Win. Mag., .375 H&H, 7mm Rem. Mag., 6.5x68mm, or 8x68mm cal., converts to 7 cals. Importation began 1994.

Mfg.'s Sug. Retail	$949	$850	$775	$675	$625	$550	$495	$435

▲ *Model 202 Super Grade* — similar to Model 202 Medium Standard except has Claro walnut, wood upgrade with rosewood forend and pistol grip caps, jeweled and polished bolt, high-luster epoxy finish. Importation began 1994.

Mfg.'s Sug. Retail	$1,020	$900	$800	$700	$625	$550	$495	$435

Add $40 for Mag. cals.
Add $165 for .375 H&H cal.

MODEL 202 HUNTER MATCH — 6.5x55mm or .308 Win. cal., match grade 28 in. barrel, matte black metal, French walnut stock, includes target style alloy rail in forend, 10.1 lbs. Importation began 1994.

Mfg.'s Sug. Retail	$1,495	$1,300	$1,025	$900	$795	$600	$475	$425

MODEL 202 ALASKA — .300 Win. Mag., .300 Wby. Mag., or .375 H&H cal., 26 in. barrel, matte metal finish, epoxy fiberglass/beechwood laminated stock. Importation began 1994.

Mfg.'s Sug. Retail	$1,335	$1,175	$995	$875	$775	$600	$475	$425

Add $115 for .375 H&H.

Grading	100%	98%	95%	90%	80%	70%	60%

MODEL 90 BOLT ACTION — available in 16 cals. between .222 Rem. and .458 Win. Mag., short, medium and long actions, 22.44 or 26 in. barrel, 3 or 4 shot detachable mag., deluxe checkered walnut stock, approx. 7½ lbs. (except .458 Win. Mag.). Importation disc. 1989.

	$775	$675	$600	$550	$500	$465	$430

Last Mfg.'s Sug. Retail was $1,175.

During 1985-1989, Sauer exported to Sigarms 2,300 Model 90 rifles, 1,100 of these were in Mag. cals.

▲ *Model 90 Stutzen* — Mannlicher style full stock, not available in European or Mag. cals. Importation disc. 1989.

	$800	$700	$600	$550	$500	$465	$430

Last Mfg.'s Sug. Retail was $1,225.

▲ *Safari Model* — .458 Win. Mag, 23.62 in. barrel, 10½ lbs. Imported 1986-1988 only.

	$1,250	$950	$850	$750	$650	$575	$500

Last Mfg.'s Sug. Retail was $1,675.

MODEL 90 LUX — .300 Win. Mag., .300 Wby., .338 Win. Mag, or .375 H&H cal., similar to Model 90, except has deluxe oil finished walnut stock with rosewood forearm tip and pistol grip cap, recoil pad, gold trigger.

Mfg.'s Sug. Retail	$1,495	$1,300	$1,025	$900	$795	$585	$465	$430

▲ *Model 90 Stutzen Lux* — Mannlicher style full stock, not available in European or Mag. cals. Importation disc. 1990.

	$1,200	$1,020	$900	$795	$585	$465	$430

Last Mfg.'s Sug. Retail was $1,325.

MODEL 90 SUPREME — .25-06 Rem., .270 Win., .30-06, .300 Win. Mag., .300 Wby., 7mm Rem. Mag., .338 Win. Mag., or .375 H&H cal., similar to Model 90 Lux, except has high gloss lacquer stock with Monte Carlo cheekpiece, jeweled bolt, and gold trigger. New 1987.

Mfg.'s Sug. Retail	$1,395	$1,275	$1,025	$900	$795	$585	$465	$430

On Models 90 Lux and Supreme add 69% for Grade I engraving, 105% for Grade II, 128% for Grade III, and 164% for Grade IV.
Add $54 for mag. cals.

▲ *Safari Model Lux* — .458 Win. Mag., 23.62 in. barrel, 10½ lbs., Bugina oil finished stock, rosewood forearm and pistol grip cap, Williams sights, recoil pad, gold trigger.

Mfg.'s Sug. Retail	$1,795	$1,650	$1,400	$1,100	$950	$895	$700	$600

RIFLES: DRILLINGS — O/U COMBINATION GUNS

SAUER MODEL 3000 DRILLING — available in either 16 ga./.30-06, 6.5x57R, 7x57R, 7x65R or 12 ga./.222 Rem. (disc.), .243 Win., .30-06, 6.5x57R, 7x57R, 7x65R, 9.3x74R, Greener cross-bolt and double barrel lug locking, cocking indicators, front set trigger, automatic sight, walnut pistol grip stock with hog-back and cheekpiece, grade III scroll engraving, 7¼ lbs.

Mfg.'s Sug. Retail	$4,600	$4,300	$3,600	$3,100	$2,675	$2,200	$1,800	$1,400

This model was also previously imported by Weatherby and Colt - please refer to separate listings for more information.

▲ *Luxury Grade* — similar to Model 3000 standard, except select root timber and extensive engraving featuring two animals.

Mfg.'s Sug. Retail	$6,100	$5,550	$4,875	$4,400	$3,875	$3,475	$3,000	$2,575

COMBO BBF 54 O/U — standard grade combination gun, 16 ga./.222 Rem., .243 Win., 6.5x57R, 7x57R, 7x65R, and .30-06 cals., ejectors, double triggers with front set trigger, moderate engraving on coin finished receiver, Greener cross-bolt with double barrel lugs, 6 lbs. Importation disc. 1986.

	$2,200	$2,060	$1,760	$1,565	$1,380	$1,250	$1,125

Last Mfg.'s Sug. Retail was $2,495.

▲ *Luxury Grade* — similar to Combo BBF 54, except game scene engraved and deluxe crotch walnut.

	$2,450	$2,200	$2,000	$1,785	$1,600	$1,475	$1,300

Last Mfg.'s Sug. Retail was $2,745.

S

Grading	100%	98%	95%	90%	80%	70%	60%

LUFTWAFFE SURVIVAL DRILLING — 12 or 16 ga. (65mm) SxS over 9.3x74 R, 28 in. barrels, large eagle swastika on stock and breech end of right barrel. Originally mfg. for Luftwaffe pilots during WWII.

	$4,500	$4,000	$3,600	$3,200	$2,600	$2,400	$2,200

Add 20% for original aluminum case and accessories.

SAUER MODEL 3000E DRILLING — see listing under Colt Sauer Drilling.

SNIPER RIFLE — very accurate, special order only Sniper Rifle, built to customer specifications.

	$4,845	$3,655	$3,200	$2,850	$2,500	$2,275	$2,000

S

SHOTGUNS

MODEL 60 — various ga.'s, boxlock action, DT, extractors, checkered walnut stock and forearm, this model was the standard model of its period.

	$975	$875	$750	$650	$550	$450	$395

Add 20% for 20 ga.

ROYAL DOUBLE BARREL SHOTGUN — 12, 16 or 20 ga., 26, 28, or 30 in. barrels, various chokes, boxlock, scalloped engraved frame, cocking indicators, SST, auto ejectors, Krupp steel barrel, checkered pistol grip stock. Mfg. 1955-1977.

	$1,650	$1,375	$1,210	$1,100	$880	$770	$660

Add 20% for 20 ga.

ARTEMIS — 12 ga., 28 in. barrels, mod. and full choke, H&H type sidelock, SST, auto ejector, Krupp steel, checkered pistol grip stock. Mfg. 1966-1977.

▲ *Grade I* — fine line engraved.

	$5,500	$4,620	$3,850	$3,520	$3,080	$2,640	$2,200

▲ *Grade II* — extensive engraving.

	$6,600	$5,500	$4,840	$4,235	$3,850	$3,300	$3,080

GRADE 380

	$4,500	$4,000	$3,500	$3,000	$2,500	$2,200	$1,500

GRADE F-40

Rarity factor precludes accurate price evaluation.

MODEL F-45

	$12,000	$10,500	$9,000	$8,000	$6,500	$5,000	$3,200

MODEL F-60

	$23,000	$20,000	$17,000	$14,000	$12,000	$9,000	$5,000

MODEL 66 O/U FIELD GUN — 12 ga., 28 in. mod. and full, Krupp steel barrels, H&H type sidelocks, SST, auto ejectors, checkered pistol grip stock, available in three grades of engraving. Mfg. 1966-1975.

	100%	98%	95%	90%	80%	70%	60%
Grade I	$2,200	$1,760	$1,540	$1,320	$1,100	$880	$770
Grade II	$3,080	$2,420	$1,980	$1,650	$1,430	$1,210	$990
Grade III	$3,850	$3,300	$2,860	$2,420	$1,980	$1,650	$1,320

MODEL 66 O/U SKEET GUN — similar to Field Gun, with 26 in. VR skeet bored barrel and vent. forearm. Mfg. 1966-1975.

MODEL 66 O/U TRAP GUN — similar to 66 Skeet, with 30 in. barrels, full and full, or mod. and full choke, trap style stock.

	100%	98%	95%	90%	80%	70%	60%
Grade I	$2,090	$1,760	$1,540	$1,320	$1,100	$880	$770
Grade II	$3,080	$2,420	$1,980	$1,650	$1,430	$1,210	$880
Grade III	$3,850	$3,300	$2,860	$2,420	$1,980	$1,650	$1,320

Grading	100%	98%	95%	90%	80%	70%	60%

SAUER/FRANCHI STANDARD GRADE O/U — 12 ga. only, double triggers, checkered walnut stock and forearm, SST, blued finish only, sling swivels, VR. Importation disc. 1986.

	$375	$340	$315	$290	$275	$260	$245

Last Mfg.'s Sug. Retail was $785.

▲ *Regent Grade* — similar to Standard grade, except has single trigger and lightly engraved silver finished receiver. Importation disc. 1986.

	$475	$395	$350	$310	$290	$275	$265

Last Mfg.'s Sug. Retail was $825.

▲ *Favorit Grade* — similar to Regent Grade, except has elaborate scroll engraving on coin finished receiver, gold-plated trigger. Importation disc. 1986.

	$550	$495	$450	$420	$385	$350	$300

Last Mfg.'s Sug. Retail was $875.

▲ *Diplomat Grade* — similar to Favorit Grade, except has more elaborate scroll engraving and with model name gold filled on receiver sides and barrel, extra grain French walnut, cased.

	$875	$750	$625	$550	$495	$460	$435

Last Mfg.'s Sug. Retail was $1,520.

SAUER/FRANCHI SPORTING S O/U — 12 ga. only, 28 in. barrels, ejectors, SST, select European walnut with checkered stock and forearm, 10mm VR, plain silver finished receiver with model name gold filled on both sides. Importation disc. 1986.

	$800	$700	$600	$500	$450	$420	$395

Last Mfg.'s Sug. Retail was $1,375.

SAUER/FRANCHI MODEL TRAP O/U — similar to Sporting S, except has 29 in. barrels, trap chokes and stock dimensions. Importation disc. 1986.

	$875	$750	$625	$550	$495	$460	$435

Last Mfg.'s Sug. Retail was $1,375.

SAUER/FRANCHI MODEL SKEET O/U — similar to Sporting S, except has skeet chokes. Importation disc. 1986.

	$875	$750	$625	$550	$495	$460	$435

Last Mfg.'s Sug. Retail was $1,375.

SAVAGE ARMS, INC.

Initially manufactured in Utica, NY. Later manufacture was in Chicopee Falls, MA. Currently manufactured in Westfield, MA since 1959. Distributor sales only.

This company originally started in Utica, NY in 1895. The Model 1895 was initially manufactured by Marlin between 1895-1899. The company was renamed Savage Arms Co. in 1899. After WWI, the name was again changed to the Savage Arms Corporation. Savage moved to Chicopee Falls, MA circa 1946 (to its J. Stevens Arms Co. plants). In the mid-1960s the company became The Savage Arms Division of American Hardware Corp., which later became The Emhart Corporation. This division was sold in September 1981, and became Savage Industries, Inc. located in Westfield, MA (since the move in circa 1959). On November 1, 1989, Savage Arms Inc. acquired the majority of assets of Savage Industries, Inc.

Savage Arms, Inc. will offer service and parts on their current line of firearms only (those manufactured after Nov. 1, 1989). These models include the 24, 99, and 110 plus the importation of the Model 312. Warranty and repair claims for products not acquired by Savage Arms, Inc. will remain the responsibility of Savage Industries. For information regarding the repair and/or parts of Savage Industries firearms, please refer to the Trademark Index in the back of this text. Parts for pre-1981 Savage Industries firearms may be obtained by contacting the Gun Parts Corporation located in West Hurley, NY (listed in Trademark Index). Savage Arms, Inc. has older records/info. on pistols, the Model 24, older mfg. Model 99s, and Model 110 only. A factory letter authenticating the configuration of a particular specimen may be obtained by contacting Mr. John Callahan (see Trademark Index for

Grading	100%	98%	95%	90%	80%	70%	60%

listings and address). The charge for this service is $10.00/gun - please allow 2-4 weeks for an adequate response.

PISTOLS

MODEL 1907 AUTO PISTOL — .32 ACP or .380 ACP cal., 9 (.380 ACP) or 10 (.32 ACP) shot mag., $3^{13}/_{16}$ (.32 ACP) or $4^{5}/_{16}$ (.380 ACP) in. barrel, blue, fixed sights, metal (early mfg. on .32 ACP only until serial no. 10,980) or hard rubber grips, exposed cocking piece. Mfg. 1910-1917.

	100%	98%	95%	90%	80%	70%	60%
.32 ACP	$350	$250	$175	$150	$125	$115	$100
.380 ACP	$465	$415	$355	$300	$250	$200	$150

Add large premiums for factory nickel, silver, or gold finish (rare).

There were three different types of pearl grips: the early variation was a snap-on with an S/A logo, screw-on with an indianhead logo, and the flared 1917 with no logo. Asking prices for the grips alone are in the $250-$1,000 range (this also applied to the Model 1915 Hammerless and Model 1917 Automatic).

MODEL 1915 HAMMERLESS — similar to Model 1907, with grip safety and no visible cocking piece. Mfg. 1915-1917.

	100%	98%	95%	90%	80%	70%	60%
.32 ACP	$475	$425	$375	$300	$250	$225	$200
.380 ACP	$595	$550	$500	$400	$300	$250	$200

Add 10% with original box and instruction manual.

MODEL 1917 AUTOMATIC — similar to Model 1907, with spur cocking piece and trapezoidal grips. Mfg. 1920-1928.

	100%	98%	95%	90%	80%	70%	60%
.32 ACP	$275	$225	$175	$145	$130	$110	$100
.380 ACP	$445	$400	$350	$300	$250	$200	$150

Add 10% with original box and instruction manual.

M1907 U.S. ARMY TEST TRIAL .45 ACP — .45 ACP, large version of Model 1910, exposed hammer. Approx. 400 mfg. 1907-1911 for military trials.

	100%	98%	95%	90%	80%	70%	60%
	$5,500	$4,400	$3,300	$2,800	$2,400	$2,000	$1,800

Add 250% for experimental M1910 and M1911.

Most pistols were repurchased from the government, reconditioned (many reblued), and resold to the public as commercial models. Add 100% if in original condition.

MODEL 101 SINGLE SHOT — single action, .22 cal., $5^{1}/_{2}$ in. barrel, adj. sight, swing out barrel, blue, wood grips. Mfg. 1960-1968.

	100%	98%	95%	90%	80%	70%	60%
	$150	$120	$95	$80	$70	$60	$50

COMBINATION GUNS

All Model 24s are under the domain of Savage Arms, Inc.

MODEL 24 O/U COMBINATION GUN — .22 over .410, 24 in. separated barrels, open rifle sight, visible hammer, break open, plain pistol grip stock. Mfg. 1950-1965.

	100%	98%	95%	90%	80%	70%	60%
	$160	$130	$110	$100	$85	$70	$55

MODEL 24B-DL

	100%	98%	95%	90%	80%	70%	60%
	$185	$155	$135	$120	$100	$90	$80

MODEL 24S — similar to Model 24, with 20 ga. or .410 barrel, sidelever, dovetail for scope. Mfg. 1965-1971.

	100%	98%	95%	90%	80%	70%	60%
	$185	$155	$135	$120	$100	$90	$80

MODEL 24MS — similar to Model 24S, with .22 WRM barrel. Mfg. 1965-1971.

	100%	98%	95%	90%	80%	70%	60%
	$170	$140	$120	$110	$90	$85	$70

MODEL 24DL — similar to Model 24S, with top lever, satin chrome frame and checkered stock. Mfg. 1965-1969.

	100%	98%	95%	90%	80%	70%	60%
	$170	$140	$120	$110	$90	$85	$70

Grading	100%	98%	95%	90%	80%	70%	60%

MODEL 24MDL — similar to Model 24DL, with .22 WRM barrel. Mfg. 1965-1969.

	$175	$145	$125	$115	$95	$85	$70

MODEL 24FG — similar to Model 24S, with top lever. Mfg. 1972-disc.

	$165	$130	$110	$90	$85	$65	$55

MODEL 24 FIELD — .22 LR or .22 Mag. over 20 or .410 ga., lightweight field version, 24 in. separated barrels, 3 in. chambers, 6¾ lbs. Disc. 1989.

	$185	$150	$120	$100	$85	$80	$70

Last Mfg.'s Sug. Retail was $209.

MODEL 24F PREDATOR — choice of .22 LR, .22 Hornet, .222 Rem. (disc. 1989), .223 Rem., or .30-30 cal. over 12 or 20 ga., 3 in. chamber, 24 in. barrels, wood (disc.) or matte black Dupont Rynite synthetic, hammer block safety, DTs, approx. 8 lbs. New 1989.

Mfg.'s Sug. Retail	$400	$375	$325	$275	$240	$210	$180	$165

Add $14 for Camo Rynite stock (disc., Model 24F-T, Turkey Model-12 ga./.22 Hornet or .223 Rem. cal. only).

The .22 LR cal. is available with 20 ga. barrel only.

MODEL 24V — similar to Model 24, with .22 Hornet (disc. 1984), .222 Rem., .223 Rem., .30-30, .357 Max., or .357 Mag.(disc.), over 24 in. 20 ga. (3 in.) barrel, single trigger, 7 lbs. Mfg. 1971-89.

	$300	$265	$230	$200	$175	$150	$130

MODEL 24D — .22 LR or .22 Mag. over .410 or 20 ga., black or case hardened frame, game scene decoration was eliminated in 1974, forearm not checkered after 1976.

	$250	$220	$185	$150	$130	$115	$105

MODEL 24C CAMPER'S COMPANION — nickel finish, .22 LR over 20 ga., 20 in. barrel cylinder bore, buttplate opens to store ten .22 LR cartridges and one 20 ga. shell in buttstock, carrying case, 5¾ lbs. Mfg. 1972-1988.

	$200	$165	$130	$115	$105	$95	$80

Last Mfg.'s Retail was $239.

Add 10% for nickel finish (Model 24CS - shipped with pistol grip stock also).

MODEL 24 VS — similar to Model 24CS, only .357 Mag. over 20 ga., nickel finish, accessory pistol grip stock is included.

	$250	$210	$185	$160	$145	$135	$120

MODEL 389 — 12 ga. with 3 in. chamber over choice of .308 Win. or .222 Rem., choke tubes standard, hammerless, double triggers, checkered walnut stock and forearm with recoil pad. Mfg. 1988-90 only.

	$800	$640	$550	$495	$435	$365	$300

Last Mfg.'s Sug. Retail was $919.

RIFLES

Savage made a wide variety of inexpensive, utilitarian rifles that to date have attracted mostly shooting interest, but little collector interest. A listing of these models may be found in the back of this text under "Serialization".

MODEL 1895 — .303 Savage only, lever action, mfg. in either carbine (22 in.), rifle (26 in.), or musket (30 in.) variations, round (scarce) or octagon barrel that has Marlin proofmark under the forend, closed top, solid breech, side ejecting, 5 shot rotating box mag., unfired shots indicator. Originally mfg. by Marlin, marked "Savage Repeating Arms Co. Utica, N.Y. U.S.A. Pat. Feb. 7, 1893.", approx. 6,000 mfg. 1895-1899, early models had hole in top of bolt — later ones were smooth.

	$1,500	$1,250	$995	$880	$770	$660	$495

Values assume rifle configuration — add premiums for the carbine (rare) and musket.

Grading	100%	98%	95%	90%	80%	70%	60%

MODEL 1899 — .25-35, .30-30, .303 Savage, .32-40, or .38-55 cal., improvement of Model 1895, 20 in. round (carbine), 22 in. (round), or 26 in. (round, half-octagon or full octagon) barrel marked "Savage Arms Company, Utica, N.Y. Pat. Feb. 7, 1893.", over 75,000 mfg. 1899-1917, approx. 7½ lbs. Older "perch-belly stocks" and high-gloss bluing will command a 10%-15% premium on this variation.

	$695	$575	$500	$450	$375	$300	$225

Add 25% for takedown (added 1909).
Add 10% for .25-35, .32-40, or .38-55 cal.

In 1905 Savage broadened the variety of this model and added the 1899A2, CD, BC, AB, Excelsior, Leader, Crescent, Victor, Rival, Premier, and Monarch (top-of-the-line model). Prices at the time ranged from $21 to $250 — quite a range of prices. Any factory engraved Savage 99 is rare (less than 1,000 mfg. to date) with values having to be computed one gun at a time. Recently, a collection of older, engraved Model 99s was sold with prices ranging from $2,000 to over $40,000. Because of this, the above values assume standard rifle with no engraving options (Grades A through G).

All Model 99s fall within the domain of Savage Arms, Inc.

▲ *Model 1899-D Military Rifle (Musket)* — .30-30 or .303 cal., 28 or 30 in. round barrel with two barrel bands, straight grip stock with bayonet lug.

	$3,500	$3,200	$2,800	$2,400	$2,000	$1,600	$1,200

▲ *Model 1899-F Carbine* — various cals., 3 different variations, the first variation was made approx. 1899-1905 with small barrel band and receiver ring (scarce), the second and third variations are not quite as desirable.

	$1,500	$1,275	$1,100	$925	$800	$700	$600

Add approx. 40% for .25-35, .32-40, or .38-55 cal.

MODEL 99A — .30-30, .300 Sav., or .303 Sav. cal., lever action, 24 in. barrel, open sight, hammerless, straight grip stock, crescent butt. Mfg. 1920-1936.

	$550	$440	$330	$275	$180	$165	$150

MODEL 99A RECENT MFG. — similar to original, with .243 Win., .250 Sav., .300 Sav., .308 Win. or .375 Win. cal., 20 or 22 in. barrel, tang safety, conventional butt. Mfg. 1971-1981.

	$375	$340	$310	$275	$250	$225	$200

Approx. 1,000 rifles were made in .375 Win. cal. - add 150%-200% to values listed.

MODEL 99B — takedown version of original 99A, 24 (introduced 1926-27) or 26 (initial standard barrel length) in. barrel. Mfg. 1920-1934.

	$650	$600	$550	$495	$330	$250	$195

MODEL 99H CARBINE — .250-3000, .30-30, .300 Sav. (scarce) or .303 cal., solid frame, carbine type stock. Mfg. 1931-1942.

	$440	$330	$275	$220	$180	$165	$150

There were four variations of this model - the latter three had barrel bands. This variation did not have a saddle ring.

MODEL 99E — .22 Hi Power, .250-3000, .30-30, .300 Sav., or .303 Sav. cal., 22 in. barrel, cross-checked trigger. Mfg. 1920-1936.

	$475	$350	$275	$220	$180	$165	$150

Add 15% for .22 Hi Power cal.

MODEL 99E CARBINE — .243 Win., .250 Sav., .300 Sav., or .308 Win. cal., 22 in. barrel, checkered pistol grip stock, 5 shot rotary mag. Mfg. 1960-1982.

	$320	$260	$230	$200	$180	$165	$150

Last Mfg.'s Sug. Retail was $343.

MODEL 99F FEATHERWEIGHT — similar to pre-war 99E, except takedown and ½ pound lighter, also mfg. with .410 shotgun barrel. Mfg. 1920-1942.

	$440	$330	$275	$220	$195	$175	$160

Add 50% for .410 shotgun barrel.

Grading	100%	98%	95%	90%	80%	70%	60%

MODEL 99F — .243 Win., .250-3000, .284 Win., .300 Sav., .308 Win., or .358 Win. cal., solid frame, checkered pistol grip stock. Disc. 1970.

| | $350 | $310 | $285 | $260 | $230 | $210 | $190 |

Add 10% for .358 Win. cal.
Add 15% for .284 Win. cal.
This model had the receiver marked "99M".

MODEL 99G — similar to 99E pre-war, with checkered stock and takedown. Mfg. 1920-1942.

| | $660 | $565 | $475 | $350 | $275 | $235 | $200 |

MODEL 99EG — similar to 99G, with solid frame and no checkering. Mfg. 1936-1941.

| | $550 | $440 | $330 | $260 | $230 | $210 | $190 |

MODEL 99EG POST-WAR — .243 Win., .250 Sav., .300 Sav., .308 Win., or .358 Win. cal., checkered stock. Mfg. 1946-1960.

| | $350 | $310 | $285 | $260 | $230 | $210 | $190 |

Add 10% for .358 Win. cal.

MODEL 99R PRE-WAR — .250-3000 or .300 Sav. cal., 22 or 24 in. barrel, large pistol grip stock and forearm. Mfg. 1936-1942.

| | $495 | $440 | $305 | $275 | $250 | $220 | $195 |

MODEL 99R POST-WAR — similar to Pre-War, .300 Sav., .308 Win., .358 Win., or .243 Win. cal., 24 in. barrel only, swivel studs. Mfg. 1946-1960.

| | $350 | $310 | $285 | $260 | $230 | $210 | $190 |

Add 10% for .358 Win. cal.

MODEL 99RS PRE-WAR — similar to 99R Pre-War, with Lyman aperture sight, swivels and sling. Mfg. 1936-1942.

| | $605 | $550 | $440 | $330 | $275 | $250 | $220 |

MODEL 99RS POST-WAR — similar to 99R Post-War, with Redfield receiver sight. Mfg. 1946-1958.

| | $350 | $330 | $285 | $250 | $225 | $200 | $180 |

MODEL 99T — 20 or 22 in. barrel, solid frame, lightweight, checkered pistol grip stock. Mfg. 1936-1942.

| | $440 | $330 | $275 | $205 | $180 | $165 | $150 |

MODEL 99K — engraved receiver and fancy wood stock, Lyman aperture sight and folding middle sight. Mfg. 1931-1942.

| | $2,200 | $1,870 | $1,210 | $880 | $770 | $550 | $440 |

MODEL 99DL — .243 Win., .250-3000, .284 Win., .300 Savage, .308 Win., or .358 Win. cal., Monte Carlo stock and sling swivels. Post-war mfg. 1960-1973.

| | $350 | $310 | $285 | $260 | $230 | $210 | $185 |

Add 10% for .358 Win. cal.

MODEL 99C — similar to Model 99F Post-War, available in .22-250 Rem. (rare), .243 Win., .284 Win. (disc.), 7mm-08 (disc.), or .308 Win. cal., 22 in. barrel, Monte Carlo stock with cut checkering and recoil pad, top tang safety, cocking indicator, open sights, detachable 4 shot mag., 7¾ lbs. Mfg. 1965-temporarily disc. until late 1995.

| | $525 | $430 | $365 | $300 | $260 | $230 | $200 |

Last Mfg.'s Sug. Retail was $629 (1994).

Add 10% for .22-250 cal.

MODEL 99CD — similar to Model 99C, with Monte Carlo cheekpiece stock. Mfg. 1980-1981.

| | $525 | $450 | $375 | $325 | $295 | $260 | $230 |

MODEL 99-358 — .358 Win. cal., recoil pad. Mfg. 1977-1980.

| | $450 | $400 | $350 | $325 | $295 | $260 | $230 |

Grading	100%	98%	95%	90%	80%	70%	60%

MODEL 99PE — elaborately engraved and plated receiver, tang, and lever, fancy wood with hand cut checkering. Mfg. 1966-1970.

| | $1,320 | $990 | $740 | $500 | $375 | $300 | $260 |

This model had the receiver marked "99M".

MODEL 99DE CITATION — similar to Model 99PE, except with less engraving and pressed checkering. Mfg. 1968-1970.

| | $885 | $660 | $495 | $330 | $250 | $220 | $195 |

This model had the receiver marked "99M".

MODEL 99M — while the receivers on Models 99F, 99PE, and 99DE were marked "99M" this is not a model designation. Rather, the "M" barrel designation indicated Monte Carlo stock.

SAVAGE 1895 ANNIVERSARY — a replica of the original M1895, .308 Win. cal., 24 in. octagon barrel, engraved receiver, brass-plated lever, straight stock, Schnabel forend, medallion in stock, brass crescent butt plate. Mfg. 9,999 in 1970 only, to commemorate Savage's 75th year.

| | $450 | $350 | $275 |

Last Mfg.'s Sug. Retail was $195 and mfg. by Savage Industries, Inc.

MODEL 1903 SLIDE ACTION — .22 S, L, or LR, 24 in. barrel, open sights, box mag., pistol grip stock. Mfg. 1903-1921.

| | $275 | $220 | $110 | $90 | $75 | $65 | $45 |

MODEL 1909 SLIDE ACTION — similar to Model 1903, with 20 in. round barrel. Mfg. 1909-1915.

| | $220 | $140 | $110 | $90 | $75 | $65 | $45 |

MODEL 1904 SINGLE SHOT — .22 S, L, or LR, bolt action, 18 in. barrel, straight stock. Mfg. 1904-1917.

| | $140 | $85 | $55 | $45 | $35 | $30 | $30 |

MODEL 1905 SINGLE SHOT — similar to Model 1904, except 24 in. barrel, takedown. Mfg. 1905-1919.

| | $140 | $85 | $55 | $45 | $35 | $30 | $30 |

MODEL 1912 AUTOLOADER — .22 LR, 20 in. barrel, takedown, straight stock. Mfg. 1912-1916.

| | $295 | $235 | $195 | $150 | $115 | $75 | $65 |

MODEL 1914 SLIDE ACTION — .22 S, L, and LR, 24 in. octagon barrel, plain pistol grip stock. Mfg. 1914-1924.

| | $250 | $225 | $195 | $135 | $110 | $75 | $65 |

MODEL 19 NRA BOLT ACTION — .22 LR, 25 in. barrel, adj. aperture sight, 5 shot military stock. Approx. 50,000 mfg. 1919-1937.

| | $220 | $140 | $110 | $100 | $90 | $75 | $65 |

Between 1943-1945 approx. 6,000 Model 19s were made under military contract — add 15%.

MODEL 10 BOLT ACTION TARGET (1933 NRA MODEL) — .22 LR, 25 in. barrel, speed lock, adj. aperture sight, target stock. Mfg. 1933-1946.

| | $250 | $165 | $140 | $110 | $100 | $90 | $70 |

MODEL 19L — similar to Model 19, with Lyman receiver sight. Mfg. 1933-1942.

| | $330 | $275 | $195 | $140 | $120 | $110 | $100 |

MODEL 19M — similar to Model 19, with 28 in. heavy barrel and scope bases. Mfg. 1933-1942.

| | $330 | $275 | $195 | $165 | $140 | $120 | $110 |

MODEL 19H — similar to Model 19, except .22 Hornet. Mfg. 1933-1942.

| | $550 | $495 | $330 | $220 | $175 | $165 | $155 |

Grading	100%	98%	95%	90%	80%	70%	60%

MODEL 1920 BOLT ACTION — Mauser type action, .250-3000 or .300 Sav. cal., 22 or 24 in. barrel, open sights, 5 shot, checkered pistol grip, Schnabel forend. Mfg. 1920-1926.

	$330	$250	$220	$200	$175	$165	$155

Add 10% for .250-3000 cal.

MODEL 1920-1926 — similar to Model 1920, with 24 in. barrel, Lyman aperture sight, Mfg. 1926-1927.

	$330	$250	$220	$200	$175	$165	$155

MODEL 23A BOLT ACTION RIFLE — .22 LR, 23 in. barrel, open sights, plain pistol grip stock, Schnabel forend. Mfg. 1923-1933.

	$220	$165	$140	$110	$95	$85	$70

MODEL 23AA — improved version of Model 23A, with speedlock and checkered stock. Mfg. 1933-1942.

	$275	$195	$165	$130	$110	$100	$85

MODEL 23B — same configuration as Model 23A, with .25-20 cal., 25 in. barrel, full forearm. Mfg. 1923-1942.

	$220	$140	$110	$100	$90	$75	$65

MODEL 23C — similar to Model 23B, with .32-20. Mfg. 1923-1942.

	$220	$140	$110	$100	$90	$75	$65

MODEL 23D — similar to Model 23B, with .22 Hornet. Mfg. 1933-1947.

	$305	$250	$220	$195	$165	$140	$110

MODEL 25 SLIDE ACTION — .22 S, L, or LR, 24 in. octagon barrel, open sight, takedown, hammerless, tube mag., plain pistol grip stock. Mfg. 1925-1929.

	$275	$235	$200	$150	$125	$75	$65

MODEL 40 BOLT ACTION RIFLE — .250-3000, .300 Sav., .30-30, or .30-06 cal., 22 or 24 in. barrel, open sight, 4 shot mag., plain pistol grip stock, Schnabel forend. Mfg. 1928-1940.

	$330	$220	$195	$165	$155	$140	$120

Add 10% for .250-3000 cal.

MODEL 45 SUPER — similar to Model 40, with Lyman receiver sight and checkered stock. Mfg. 1928-1940.

	$385	$275	$250	$200	$175	$165	$140

MODEL 29 SLIDE ACTION — .22 S, L, or LR, 22 in. barrel, octagon until 1940, round on post-WWII, open sights, checkered pistol grip stock on pre-war, plain on late model. Mfg. 1929-1967.

	$235	$200	$165	$100	$90	$75	$65
Pre-war	$295	$250	$195	$120	$110	$100	$90

MODEL 3 SINGLE SHOT — .22 S, L, or LR, bolt action, 26 in. barrel, 24 in. barrel on post-war, open sights, plain grip stock. Mfg. 1933-1952.

	$85	$65	$55	$40	$30	$30	$30

MODEL 3S — similar to Model 3, with aperture sight. Mfg. 1933-1942.

	$100	$85	$70	$55	$40	$30	$30

MODEL 3ST — similar to Model 3S, with swivels and sling. Mfg. 1933-1942.

	$110	$90	$85	$70	$45	$35	$30

MODEL 4 BOLT ACTION REPEATER — .22 S, L, or LR, 24 in. barrel, open sight, takedown, 5 shot, checkered pistol grip stock on pre-war, plain stock on post-war. Mfg. 1933-1965.

	$110	$85	$70	$55	$40	$30	$30
Pre-war	$120	$95	$85	$65	$50	$40	$30

Grading	100%	98%	95%	90%	80%	70%	60%

MODEL 4S — similar to Model 4, with aperture sight. Mfg. 1933-1942.

	100%	98%	95%	90%	80%	70%	60%
	$120	$90	$75	$65	$55	$40	$30

MODEL 4M — similar to Model 4, except .22 WRM.

	100%	98%	95%	90%	80%	70%	60%
	$110	$85	$70	$55	$45	$30	$30

MODEL 5 — similar to Model 4, with tubular mag. Mfg. 1936-1961.

	100%	98%	95%	90%	80%	70%	60%
	$110	$85	$70	$55	$45	$30	$30

MODEL 5S — similar to Model 5, with aperture sight. Mfg. 1936-1942.

	100%	98%	95%	90%	80%	70%	60%
	$120	$95	$85	$65	$55	$40	$30

MODEL 6 AUTOLOADER — .22 S, L, or LR, 24 in. barrel, tubular mag., takedown, checkered pistol grip stock on pre-war, plain stock on post-war. Mfg. 1938-1968.

	100%	98%	95%	90%	80%	70%	60%
	$140	$110	$95	$85	$65	$55	$40
Pre-war	$150	$120	$105	$95	$75	$65	$50

MODEL 6S — similar to Model 6, with aperture sight. Mfg. 1938-1942.

	100%	98%	95%	90%	80%	70%	60%
	$150	$120	$105	$95	$75	$65	$45

MODEL 7 AUTOLOADER — similar to Model 6, with box mag. Mfg. 1939-1951.

	100%	98%	95%	90%	80%	70%	60%
	$140	$110	$95	$65	$55	$55	$40
Pre-war	$150	$120	$105	$95	$75	$65	$50

MODEL 7S — similar to Model 7, with aperture sight. Mfg. 1938-1942.

	100%	98%	95%	90%	80%	70%	60%
	$150	$120	$105	$95	$75	$65	$45

MODEL 60 AUTOLOADER — .22 LR, 20 in. barrel, leaf sight, tubular mag., checkered Monte Carlo stock. Mfg. 1969-1972.

	100%	98%	95%	90%	80%	70%	60%
		$95	$85	$70	$55	$45	$35	$30

MODEL 90 AUTOLOADING CARBINE — similar to Model 60, with 16½ in. barrel, plain carbine stock, with barrel band.

	100%	98%	95%	90%	80%	70%	60%
		$95	$85	$70	$55	$45	$35	$30

MODEL 88 AUTOLOADER — similar to Model 60, except has walnut finished hardwood stock. Mfg. 1969-1972.

	100%	98%	95%	90%	80%	70%	60%
		$85	$65	$55	$45	$40	$35	$30

MODEL 63/63K SINGLE SHOT — .22 S, L, or LR, bolt action, 18 in. barrel, open sights, trigger locks with key, full length pistol grip stock, Model 63s were mfg. 1964-69, Model 63Ks were mfg. 1970-1972.

	100%	98%	95%	90%	80%	70%	60%
		$80	$65	$55	$45	$40	$35	$30

MODEL 63KM — similar to Model 63K, except .22 WRM.

	100%	98%	95%	90%	80%	70%	60%
		$90	$70	$65	$55	$45	$40	$35

MODEL 219 SINGLE SHOT — .22 Hornet, .25-20, .32-20, or .30-30 cal., 26 in. barrel, open sight, hammerless, break open, top lever, plain pistol grip stock. Mfg. 1938-1965.

	100%	98%	95%	90%	80%	70%	60%
.30-30 cal.	$140	$125	$110	$100	$90	$80	$70

Add 15% for all other cals.

MODEL 219L — similar to Model 219, with side lever. Mfg. 1965-1967.

	100%	98%	95%	90%	80%	70%	60%
	$100	$85	$70	$55	$45	$35	$30

MODELS 221, 222, 223, 227, 228, AND 229 — single shot, similar to Model 219, only supplied with additional shotgun barrel, interchangeable, different model numbers are for different cals., ga.'s, and barrel lengths, all have been disc.

	100%	98%	95%	90%	80%	70%	60%
	$130	$100	$85	$65	$55	$45	$30

SAVAGE/STEVENS MODEL 65 — please refer to listing under Stevens section.

Grading	100%	98%	95%	90%	80%	70%	60%

MODEL 34M — similar to Model 34, chambered for .22 WRM. Mfg. 1969-1973.

	$90	$70	$55	$45	$35	$30	$30

MODEL 35 — .22 LR, bolt action, 22 in. barrel, 5 shot clip mag., open sights, hardwood Monte Carlo stock. Disc. 1985.

	$90	$80	$65	$50	$35	$30	$30

Last Mfg.'s Sug. Retail was $100.

MODEL 46 — similar to Model 34, with tubular mag. Mfg. 1969-1973.

	$90	$70	$55	$45	$35	$30	$30

MODEL 65M — similar to Model 65, in .22 WRM.

	$95	$75	$65	$55	$45	$35	$30

SAVAGE/STEVENS MODEL 72 "CRACKSHOT" — please refer to listing under Stevens section.

SAVAGE/STEVENS MODEL 89 SINGLE SHOT — please refer to listing under Stevens section.

MODEL 340 BOLT ACTION — .22 Hornet, .222 Rem., .223 Rem., or .30-30 cal., 22 and 24 in. barrel, open sights, 4 or 5 shot mag., 7½ lbs., plain pistol grip stock. Mfg. 1950-1985.

	$225	$195	$170	$160	$150	$140	$130

Last Mfg.'s Sug. Retail was $257.

EL 340C — similar to Model 340, with aperture sight, checkered stock and sling swivels. Mfg. 1952-1960.

	$235	$205	$180	$165	$155	$145	$135

MODEL 340V — .225 Win., varmint configuration, 24 in. barrel. Limited mfg. in late 1960s.

	$295	$265	$235	$205	$180	$165	$150

MODEL 340S DELUXE — similar to Model 340, with aperture sight, checkered stock, sling swivels. Mfg. 1952-1960.

	$260	$225	$205	$190	$175	$160	$150

MODEL 342 AND 342S — similar to Model 340, .22 Hornet designation. Mfg. 1950-1955.

	$250	$215	$200	$185	$170	$160	$150

RIFLES: RECENT MFG.

The 110 Series was first produced in 1958. Beginning in 1992, Savage Arms, Inc. began supplying this model with a master trigger lock, earmuffs, shooting glasses (disc. 1992), and test target.

Beginning 1994, all Savage rifles employ a laser etched bolt featuring the Savage logo. During 1996, Savage began using pillar bedded stocks for many of their rifles. Savage introduced a new line of Rimfire rifles during 1996.

Recent Savage nomenclature usually involves alphabetical suffixes which mean the following: B - Brown laminated wood stock, C - detachable box mag., F - composite/synthetic stock, G - hardwood stock, K - standard muzzle brake, AK - adj. muzzle brake with fluted barrel, L - left-hand, NS - no sights, P - police (tactical) rifle, SE - safari express, SS - stainless steel, SS-S - stainless steel single shot, T - Target, U - high luster blued metal finish and/or stock finish, V - Long Range (Varmint), XP - package gun (scope, sling, and rings/base), Y - Youth/Ladies Model. Hence, the Model 116-FCSAK designates a 116 series firearm with composite stock, detachable stainless steel mag., and adj. muzzle brake on barrel.

Grading	100%	98%	95%	90%	80%	70%	60%

MARK I-G SERIES BOLT ACTION RIMFIRE — .22 S, L, LR, or LRS cal., single shot, self-cocking, 19 (Mark I-GY) or 20¾ in. barrel, checkered hardwood stock, approx. 5 lbs. New 1996.

Mfg.'s Sug. Retail	$119	$105	$90	$80	$75	$70	$65	$60

This Model is also available with left-hand action (Mark I-GL) or with smooth bore barrel (Mark I-GSB) at no extra charge.

MARK II-G SERIES BOLT ACTION RIMFIRE — .22 LR cal., similar to Mark I-G Series, except has detachable 10 shot mag., approx. 5 lbs. New 1996.

Mfg.'s Sug. Retail	$126	$110	$95	$85	$75	$70	$65	$60

This Model is also available with left-hand action (Mark II-GL) or in Youth Model (Mark II-GY).
Add $5 for Mark II-GXP package (includes 4x15mm scope).

MODEL 64-G SEMI-AUTO RIMFIRE — .22 LR cal., semi-auto, 20¼ in. barrel with adj. rear sight, 10 shot detachable mag., checkered hardwood stock, thumb operated rotary safety, 5½ lbs. New 1996.

Mfg.'s Sug. Retail	$123	$110	$95	$85	$75	$70	$65	$60

Add $6 for Model 64-GXP package (includes 4x15mm scope).

MODEL 93-G MAGNUM BOLT ACTION — .22 Win. Mag. cal., 20¾ in. barrel with adj. rear sight, 5 shot detachable mag., checkered hardwood Monte Carlo stock, 5¾ lbs. New 1996.

Mfg.'s Sug. Retail	$145	$125	$110	$95	$85	$75	$70	$65

MODEL 99-C LEVER ACTION — .243 Win. or .308 Win. cal., detachable box mag., checkered Monte Carlo stock and forearm, high gloss bluing, 22 in. barrel with adj. rear sight, drilled and tapped, 7¾ lbs. New 1996.

Mfg.'s Sug. Retail	$650	$575	$495	$450	$400	$360	$330	$300

MODEL 99-CE (CENTENNIAL EDITION) — .300 Savage cal. only, limited edition featuring fully engraved nickel receiver and lever, 24 Kt. gold-plated receiver figures, trigger, and safety, deluxe hand checkered walnut stock and forearm, 1,000 mfg. 1996 only, serial numbered AS0001-AS1000. New 1996.

Mfg.'s Sug. Retail	$1,660	$1,500	$1,100	$750

MODEL 110 SPORTER BOLT ACTION — .243 Win., .270 Win., .308 Win., or .30-06 cal., 22 in. barrel, open sight, 4 shot, checkered pistol grip stock. Mfg. 1958-1963.

	$175	$145	$120	$110	$95	$85	$55

MODEL 110-MC — similar to Model 110, with Monte Carlo stock. Mfg. 1959-1969.

	$195	$160	$140	$120	$110	$95	$85

MODEL 110-M — similar to Model 110MC, except 7mm Rem. Mag., .264 Win. Mag., .300 Win. Mag., or .338 Win. Mag. cal., recoil pad. Mfg. 1963-1969.

	$275	$220	$195	$150	$140	$125	$110

MODEL 110-C/CL — various cals., push-button detachable mag., walnut stock. Mfg. 1966-disc.

	$300	$265	$230	$200	$185	$170	$160

MODEL 110-D — .22-250 Rem. (disc.), .223 Rem., .243 Win., .25-06 Rem. (disc.), .270 Win., .308 Win. (disc.), .30-06, 7mm Rem. Mag., .300 Win. Mag. (disc.), or .338 Win. Mag. cal., similar to Model 110B, hinged floorplate, checkered walnut stock, removable and adj. rear sight, 7½ lbs. Mfg. 1966-1988.

	$340	$290	$260	$240	$215	$190	$170

Last Mfg.'s Sug. Retail was $409.

Add $80 for left-hand version.

Grading	100%	98%	95%	90%	80%	70%	60%

MODEL 110-E — .22-250 Rem., .223 Rem., .243 Win., .270 Win., 7mm Rem. Mag., .308 Win., or .30-06 cal., 22 or 24 (Mag. only) in. barrel, open sights, uncheckered hardwood Monte Carlo stock, blind internal floorplate, 7 lbs. Mfg. 1963-1988.

	$260	$230	$190	$175	$165	$155	$145

Last Mfg.'s Sug. Retail was $325.

Subtract $16 without sights.

MODEL 110-F — .22-250 Rem., .223 Rem., .243 Win., .250 Sav. (new 1993), .25-06 Rem. (new 1993), .308 Win., .30-06, .270 Win., 7mm-08 Rem. (new 1993), 7mm Rem. Mag., .300 Sav. (new 1993), .300 Win. Mag., .338 Win. Mag. (new 1991) cal., 22 or 24 (Magnum) in. barrel, black DuPont Rynite stock with swivel studs and recoil pad, adj. rear sight, drilled and tapped for scope mounts, 4 or 5 shot mag., 6¾ lbs. Mfg. 1989-1993.

	$335	$300	$265	$235	$210	$195	$180

All Model 110 mfg. is in the domain of Savage Arms, Inc.

▲ **Model 110-FNS** — similar to Model 110-F, except has no sights. Mfg. 1991-1993.

	$325	$285	$250	$225	$200	$190	$175

▲ **Model 110-FXP3** — .22-250 Rem. (new 1992), .223 Rem. (new 1992), .243 Win., .270 Win., .30-06, .308 Win. (new 1992), 7mm Rem. Mag., or .300 Win. Mag. cal., similar to Model 110-F except is without sights and has integral Weaver type scope bases. Mfg. 1989-1993.

	$415	$370	$325	$285	$250	$225	$195

MODEL 110-CY — .223 Rem. (new 1993), .243 Win., .270 Win. (new 1994), .300 Savage (disc. 1995), or .308 Win. (new 1994) cal., 22 in. barrel, youth/ladies variation with shortened classic stock, open sights, 6½ lbs. Mfg. starting 1991.

Mfg.'s Sug. Retail	$358	$325	$290	$250	$220	$195	$175	$160

MODEL 110-WLE — .250-3000 Savage, .300 Savage, or 7x57mm Mauser cal. Mfg. 1991-1993.

	$425	$390	$360	$320	$280	$250	$225

1,000 of each cal. will be mfg. in this model.

▲ **Model 110-WLE 1 of 1,000** — 7x57mm Mauser, features select walnut stock with Monte Carlo cheekpiece, high luster blue finish with laser etched Savage logo on bolt body, drilled and tapped, 1,000 mfg. beginning 1992, 7¾ lbs. Mfg. 1992-1993 only.

	$415	$370	$325	$285	$250	$225	$195

MODEL 110-FM SIERRA LIGHT WEIGHT — .243 Win., .270 Win., .30-06, or .308 Win. cal., features 20 in. high gloss barrel w/o sights, black graphite/fiberglass-filled stock with non-glare finish, drilled and tapped, 6¼ lbs. New 1996.

Mfg.'s Sug. Retail	$410	$355	$310	$260	$230	$205	$175	$160

MODEL 110-FP TACTICAL POLICE RIFLE — .223 Rem., .25-06 Rem. (new 1995), .300 Win. Mag. (new 1995), .30-06 (new 1996), .308 Win., or 7mm Rem. Mag. (new 1995) cal., 24 in. heavy pillar bedded barrel tactical rifle, all metal parts are non-reflective, 4 shot internal mag., black Dupont Rynite stock, right or left-hand (new 1996) action, tapped for scope mounts, 8½ lbs. New 1990.

Mfg.'s Sug. Retail	$429	$375	$320	$270	$240	$210	$175	$160

Also available in left-hand action at no additional charge (new 1996, Model 110-FLP).

MODEL 110-G — .22-250 Rem., .223 Rem., .243 Win., .250 Sav. (new 1992), .25-06 Rem. (new 1992), .300 Sav. (new 1993), .308 Win., .30-06, .270 Win., 7mm-08 Rem. (new 1992), 7mm Rem. Mag., or .300 Win. Mag. cal., top loading internal box mag., 22 or 24 in. barrel, adj. iron sights, checkered hardwood stock, approx. 7 lbs. Mfg. 1989-1993.

	$325	$285	$250	$225	$200	$190	$175

Subtract $10-$20 if without sights (Model 110-GNS).

Grading	100%	98%	95%	90%	80%	70%	60%

▲ *Model 110-GC* — .270 Win., .30-06, 7mm Rem. Mag., or .300 Win. Mag. cal., features detachable 3 or 4 shot mag., 22 or 24 in. barrel, checkered hardwood stock, adj. sights, 6¾ lbs. Mfg. 1992-1993.

	$410	$325	$275	$240	$210	$180	$165

Add $20 for Mag. cals.

▲ *Model 110-GXP3 Package* — .22-250 Rem., .223 Rem., .243 Win., .250 Savage (disc. 1995), .25-06, .270 Win., .300 Savage (disc. 1995), .30-06, .308 Win., 7mm-08 Rem. (disc. 1995), 7mm Rem. Mag., or .300 Win. Mag. cal., similar to Model 110-G, except has no sights, includes 3x9x32 scope, rings, bases, QD swivels, and deluxe rifle sling, includes integral Weaver type scope bases. New 1989.

Mfg.'s Sug. Retail	$418	$370	$320	$275	$240	$210	$175	$160

Also available in left-hand action at no additional charge (Model 110-GLXP3).

▲ *Model 110-GCXP3 Package* — .270 Win., .30-06, .300 Win. Mag., or 7mm Rem. Mag. cal., 22 or 24 in. barrel, checkered hardwood stock, detachable box mag., package includes 3x9x32 scope, rings, bases, QD swivels, and deluxe rifle sling, 7¼ lbs.

Mfg.'s Sug. Retail	$482	$420	$360	$310	$275	$235	$190	$175

Also available in left-hand action at no additional charge (Model 110-GLCXP3).

▲ *Model 110-GL* — .30-06, .270 Win., or 7mm Rem. Mag. cal., left hand variation of the Model 110-G. Mfg. 1989-1993.

	$325	$265	$225	$200	$180	$165	$150

▲ *Model 110-GLNS* — similar to Model 110-GL, except has no sights. Mfg. 1991-1993.

	$320	$260	$220	$200	$180	$165	$150

MODEL 110-K — .243 Win., .270 Win., or .30-06 cal., incorporates laminated camouflage stock. Mfg. 1986-1988.

	$335	$280	$240

Last Mfg.'s Sug. Retail was $399.

MODEL 110-S — .308 Win. & 7mm-08 Rem. (disc.) cals., silhouette model, 22 in. heavy barrel, Wundhammer swell pistol grip with stippling, no sights, 4 shot mag., 8 lbs. 10 oz. Disc. 1985.

	$340	$290	$255	$225	$205	$190	$175

Last Mfg.'s Sug. Retail was $385.

MODEL 110-V — .22-250 Rem. or .223 Rem. cal. only, varmint model, 26 in. heavy barrel, no sights, 5 shot mag., stippled walnut Wundhammer pistol grip stock, 9¼ lbs. Disc. 1989.

	$370	$315	$265	$230	$205	$190	$175

Last Mfg.'s Sug. Retail was $439.

MODEL 110-GV — .22-250 Rem. or .223 Rem. cal., varmint variation, 24 in. medium barrel, no sights, checkered hardwood stock with rubber rifle pad, drilled and tapped for scope, 8¼ lbs. Mfg. 1989-1993.

	$380	$285	$250	$225	$200	$190	$175

MODEL 110-B — similar to Model 110E, select stock and pistol grip cap on previous manufacture. Mfg. 1976-1979. Reintroduced 1989 with laminate stock (Model 110-B Laminate).

	$360	$300	$265	$235	$205	$190	$175

MODEL 110-B LAMINATE — similar to Model 110-B, except is available in .300 Win. Mag. or .338 Win. Mag. also, has brown laminate hardwood stock with iron sights, approx. 7½ lbs. Mfg. 1989-91.

	$385	$310	$250	$225	$200	$190	$180

Last Mfg.'s Sug. Retail was $477.

MODEL 110-P PREMIER GRADE — similar to Model 110B, with select French walnut stock, skip checkered, rosewood forend and pistol grip cap, sling swivels, 7mm Mag. has recoil pad. Mfg. 1964-1970.

	$440	$330	$310	$275	$250	$220	$195
7mm Mag.	$460	$350	$330	$305	$275	$240	$220

Grading	100%	98%	95%	90%	80%	70%	60%

MODEL 110-PE PRESENTATION GRADE — similar to Model 110P, with engraved receiver, floorplate and triggerguard. Mfg. 1968-1970.

	100%	98%	95%	90%	80%	70%	60%
	$660	$550	$525	$470	$440	$415	$385
7mm Mag.	$690	$580	$550	$495	$470	$440	$415

MODEL 111 CHIEFTAIN ACTION — .243 Win., .270 Win., 7x57mm, 7mm Mag., or .30-06 cal., 22 in. barrel, 24 in. barrel (Mag. cals.), leaf sight, 4 shot detachable mag., checkered walnut Monte Carlo stock, pistol grip cap, sling swivels. Mfg. 1974-1978.

	100%	98%	95%	90%	80%	70%	60%
	$375	$350	$300	$250	$225	$200	$175
Magnum	$395	$375	$325	$295	$275	$225	$195

MODEL 111-F — similar to Model 111-G, except has black graphite/fiberglass stock (with non-glare finish) and also available in .338 Win. Mag. cal., solid recoil pad. New 1994.

		100%	98%	95%	90%	80%	70%	60%
Mfg.'s Sug. Retail	$376	$340	$300	$260	$230	$195	$175	$160

Subtract $8 if without sights (Model 111-FNS).

This model is also available in left-hand (Model 111-FL) or without sights (Model 111-FNS).

▲ *Model 111-FC* — .270 Win., .30-06, .300 Win. Mag., or 7mm Rem. Mag. cal., 22 or 24 in. barrel, detachable box mag., black graphite/fiberglass stock. New 1994.

		100%	98%	95%	90%	80%	70%	60%
Mfg.'s Sug. Retail	$418	$370	$325	$275	$230	$195	$175	$160

This model is also available with left-hand action (Model 111-FLC).

MODEL 111-FAK EXPRESS — .270 Win., .30-06, .300 Win. Mag., .338 Win. Mag., or 7mm Rem. Mag. cal., 22 in. barrel with adj. muzzle brake, black or black matte graphite/fiberglass-filled stock, w/o sights, 6¾ lbs. New 1996.

		100%	98%	95%	90%	80%	70%	60%
Mfg.'s Sug. Retail	$450	$390	$340	$285	$240	$200	$180	$165

MODEL 111-FCXP3 PACKAGE — .270 Win., .30-06, .300 Win. Mag., or 7mm Rem. Mag. cal., detachable box mag., 22 or 24 in. barrel, package includes bore sighted 3x9x32 scope, rings, bases, QD swivels, and deluxe rifle sling, 7¼ lbs. New 1994.

		100%	98%	95%	90%	80%	70%	60%
Mfg.'s Sug. Retail	$489	$440	$390	$345	$300	$270	$230	$200

This model is also available with left-hand action (Model 111-FLCXP3).

MODEL 111-FXP3 PACKAGE — .22-250 Rem., .223 Rem., .243 Win., .250 Savage (disc. 1996), .25-06 Rem., .270 Win., .300 Savage (disc. 1996), .30-06, .308 Win., .300 Win. Mag., .338 Win. Mag., 7mm Rem. Mag., or 7mm-08 Rem. (disc. 1996) cal., 22 or 24 in. barrel, black graphite/fiberglass composite stock, non-glare finish, package consists of bore sighted 3x9x32 scope, rings, bases, QD swivels, and deluxe rifle sling, approx. 7¼ lbs. New 1994.

		100%	98%	95%	90%	80%	70%	60%
Mfg.'s Sug. Retail	$447	$390	$340	$285	$240	$200	$180	$165

This model is also available with left hand action (Model 111-FLXP3).

MODEL 111-G — .22-250 Rem., .223 Rem., .243 Win., .250 Savage (disc. 1996), .25-06 Rem., .270 Win., .300 Savage (disc. 1996), .30-06, .308 Win., .300 Win. Mag., .338 Win. Mag. (disc. 1993 - not available with wood stock), 7mm-08 Rem. (disc. 1996), or 7mm Rem. Mag. cal., walnut finished hardwood stock with cut checkering and vent. recoil pad, open sights, top tang safety with red dot indicator, drilled and tapped, 6⅜ or 7 lbs. New 1994.

		100%	98%	95%	90%	80%	70%	60%
Mfg.'s Sug. Retail	$358	$330	$290	$250	$225	$195	$175	$160

Subtract $5 without sights.

This model is also available in left-hand (Model 111-GL) or without sights (Model 111-GNS).

▲ *Model 111-GC* — .270 Win., .30-06, .300 Win. Mag., or 7mm Rem. Mag. cal., 22 or 24 in. barrel, detachable box mag., walnut finished hardwood stock with cut checkering and vent. recoil pad. New 1994.

		100%	98%	95%	90%	80%	70%	60%
Mfg.'s Sug. Retail	$407	$365	$315	$270	$240	$210	$175	$160

This model is also available with left hand action (Model 111-GLC).

Grading	100%	98%	95%	90%	80%	70%	60%

MODEL 112V VARMINT RIFLE — .220 Swift, .222 Rem., .223 Rem., .225 Win., .22-250 Rem., .243 Win., or .25-06 Rem. cal., single shot, bolt action, 26 in. heavy barrel, no sights, heavy select walnut stock, checkered, swivels. Mfg. 1975-1978.

	$350	$325	$300	$275	$250	$235	$225

MODEL 112 R — .22-250 Rem., .25-06 Rem., or .243 cal., similar to Model 112V, except has 4 shot mag. Disc. 1980.

	$340	$305	$275	$250	$230	$210	$175

MODEL 112-BV — .22-250 Rem. or .223 Rem. cal., alloy steel construction, 26 in. barrel with recessed muzzle, 4 shot mag., brown laminate stock with ambidextrous Wundhammer style pistol grip, 9½ lbs. Mfg. 1993 only.

	$475	$430	$365	$315	$285	$250	$215

MODEL 112-BVSS LONG RANGE — .22-250 Rem., .223 Rem., .25-06 (new 1996), .30-06 (new 1996), .308 Win. (new 1996), .300 Win. Mag. (new 1996), or 7mm Rem. Mag. (new 1996) cal., 4 shot, pillar bedded laminate wood with Wundhammer palm swell, 26 in. stainless steel fluted barrel, bolt handle and triggerguard, recessed muzzle, 10½ lbs. New 1994.

Mfg.'s Sug. Retail	$535	$470	$400	$350	$300	$270	$230	$200

▲ *Model 112-BVSS-S* — .220 Swift, .223 Rem., .22-250 Rem., or .300 Win. Mag. (new 1996) cal., single shot, 26 in. stainless steel fluted barrel, with target features, 10½ lbs. New 1994.

Mfg.'s Sug. Retail	$535	$470	$400	$350	$300	$270	$230	$200

MODEL 112-BT COMPETITION GRADE — .223 Rem. or .308 Win. cal., laminated pillar bedded wood stock with adj. cheek rest and Wundhammer palm swell, vent. forend, alloy steel receiver with 26 in. matte black finished heavy stainless steel barrel w/o sights, drilled and tapped receiver, approx. 10⅞ lbs. New 1994.

Mfg.'s Sug. Retail	$1,000	$895	$795	$695	$625	$550	$495	$400

▲ *Model 112-BT-S* — .300 Win. Mag. cal., otherwise similar to Model 112-BT Competition Grade. New 1995.

Mfg.'s Sug. Retail	$1,000	$895	$795	$695	$625	$550	$495	$400

MODEL 112-FV — .22-250 Rem. or .223 Rem. cal., varmint variation with 26 in. heavy barrel, with or w/o iron sights, 4-shot mag., black Rynite synthetic stock with recoil pad, 8⅞ lbs. New 1991.

Mfg.'s Sug. Retail	$400	$355	$300	$260	$235	$200	$175	$160

▲ *Model 112-FVS* — similar to Model 112-FV, except is single shot with solid bottom receiver and is available in .220 Swift (new 1993) cal. Mfg. 1992-93 only.

	$375	$340	$295	$265	$235	$210	$195

▲ *Model 112-FVSS LONG RANGE* — .22-250 Rem., .223 Rem., .25-06 (new 1995), .30-06 (new 1996), .308 Win. (new 1996), .300 Win. Mag. (new 1995), or 7mm Rem. Mag. (new 1995) cal., alloy receiver with 26 in. fluted stainless steel barrel, 4 shot mag., black synthetic pillar bedded sporter stock w/o sights, 8⅞ lbs. New 1993.

Mfg.'s Sug. Retail	$510	$450	$395	$350	$300	$270	$230	$200

This model is also available with left hand action (Model 112-FLVSS, new 1996).

▲ *Model 112-FVSS-S* — .220 Swift, .22-250 Rem., .223 Rem., or .300 Win. Mag. (new 1996) cal., single shot variation, pillar bedded stock, 8⅞ lbs. New 1994.

Mfg.'s Sug. Retail	$510	$450	$395	$350	$300	$270	$230	$200

MODEL 114-C (CLASSIC) 114-CU (CLASSIC ULTRA) — .270 Win., .30-06, .300 Win. Mag., or 7mm Rem. Mag. cal., 22 or 24 in. barrel, features high gloss classic American black walnut stock with cut checkering, fitted grip cap, and recoil pad, removable 3 or 4 shot staggered box mag., available with deluxe adj. sights (Model 114-CU, disc. 1995) or w/o sights (Model 114-C, new 1996), approx. 7⅛ lbs. New 1991.

Mfg.'s Sug. Retail	$525	$465	$400	$350	$300	$270	$230	$200

Grading	100%	98%	95%	90%	80%	70%	60%

MODEL 114-CE (CLASSIC EUROPEAN) — same cals. as the Model 114-C, features oil finished stock with Schnabel forend and skip-line checkering, high luster bluing, 22 or 24 in. barrel with adj. rear sight, 7⅛ lbs. New 1996.

Mfg.'s Sug. Retail	$600	$525	$465	$400	$350	$300	$270	$230

MODEL 116-FSS — .22-250 Rem. (mfg. 1992 only), .223 Rem. (new 1992), .243 Win. (new 1993), .270 Win., .30-06, .308 Win., 7mm Rem. Mag., .300 Win. Mag., or .338 Win. Mag., features black Dupont Rynite synthetic stock, stainless steel metal parts, drilled and tapped for scope mounting, 22 or 24 in. barrel, 3 or 4 shot mag., 6¾ lbs. New 1991.

Mfg.'s Sug. Retail	$491	$440	$390	$350	$300	$270	$230	$200

This model is also available with left-hand action (Model 116-FLSS).

▲ *Model 116-FCS* — .270 Win., .30-06, 7mm Rem. Mag., or .300 Win. Mag. cal., otherwise similar to Model 116-FSS, except has removable 3 or 4 shot mag. with recessed push button release, 22 or 24 in. barrel, 6½ lbs. New 1992.

Mfg.'s Sug. Retail	$554	$485	$425	$370	$325	$290	$260	$230

This model is also available with left-hand action (Model 116-FLCS).

▲ *Model 116-FSK (Kodiak)* — similar cals. as Model 116-FCS, except also available in .338 Win Mag. cal., stainless steel construction, 22 in. barrel with recoil arrester, cocking indicator, 3 shot mag., black synthetic sporter stock, no sights, 6½ lbs. New 1993.

Mfg.'s Sug. Retail	$554	$485	$425	$370	$325	$290	$260	$230

This model is also available with left-hand action (Model 116-FLSK).

MODEL 116-US (ULTRA STAINLESS) — .270 Win., .30-06, 7mm Rem. Mag., or .300 Win. Mag. cal., 24 in. barrel, checkered walnut stock and forearm with ebony tip, no sights, 7⅛ lbs. New 1995.

Mfg.'s Sug. Retail	$700	$625	$550	$500	$450	$400	$360	$330

MODEL 116-SE (SAFARI EXPRESS) — .300 Win. Mag., .338 Win. Mag., .425 Express (mfg. 1995 only), or .458 Win. Mag. cal., stainless steel receiver and 24 in. barrel with adj. muzzle brake, controlled round feeding, select grade checkered walnut stock with solid recoil pad and ebony forend, 3-leaf express sights, 8½ lbs. New 1994.

Mfg.'s Sug. Retail	$900	$800	$725	$660	$610	$570	$530	$475

MODEL 116-FSAK — .270 Win., .30-06, .300 Win. Mag., .338 Win. Mag., or 7mm Rem. Mag. cal., features 22 in. fluted stainless steel barrel with adj. muzzle brake, 6½ lbs. New 1994.

Mfg.'s Sug. Retail	$581	$500	$440	$380	$335	$295	$265	$235

This model is also available with left-hand action (Model 116-FLSAK).

MODEL 116-FCSAK — .270 Win., .30-06, .300 Win. Mag., or 7mm Rem. Mag. cal., features push button activated detachable box mag., 22 in. fluted barrel with adj. muzzle brake, 6½ lbs. New 1994.

Mfg.'s Sug. Retail	$644	$575	$500	$430	$365	$315	$275	$245

This model is also available with left-hand action (Model 116-FLCSAK).

MODEL 170 PUMP RIFLE — .30-30 or .35 Rem. cal., 22 in. barrel, folding leaf sight, 3 shot tube mag., checkered pistol grip stock. Mfg. 1970-1981.

		$180	$155	$140	$110	$90	$65	$55

This model was mfg. by Savage Industries, Inc.

MODEL 170C — similar to 170, .30-30 only, 18½ in. barrel. Mfg. 1974-1981.

		$195	$170	$150	$115	$90	$65	$55

SERIES 900 — .22 LR cal., single (Target/Silhouette Model) or 5 shot (Biathlon Model), 21 or 25 (Target Model) in. free floated barrel, uncheckered hardwood stock, right or left-hand action, approx. 8 lbs. New 1996.

Grading	100%	98%	95%	90%	80%	70%	60%

▲ *900B Biathlon* — blonde stock, supplied with five 5-shot mags., includes shooting rail and barrel snow cover, aperture rear sight.

Mfg.'s Sug. Retail	$498	$445	$395	$350	$300	$265	$230	$200

▲ *900S Silhouette* — brown hardwood stock, heavy 21 in. barrel with muzzle crown, scope bases installed, w/o sights.

Mfg.'s Sug. Retail	$346	$300	$265	$230	$200	$180	$160	$140

▲ *900TR Target* — features aperture sights, shooting rail with hand stop.

Mfg.'s Sug. Retail	$415	$375	$315	$275	$235	$200	$180	$160

SHOTGUNS

Most Savage shotguns (except the Model 312 Series) fall under the domain of Savage Industries, Inc.

Savage made a wide variety of inexpensive, utilitarian shotguns that to date have attracted mostly shooting interest, but little collector interest. A listing of these models may be found in the back of this text under "Serialization".

MODEL 420 O/U — 12, 16, or 20 ga., 26-30 in. barrel, various chokes, boxlock, double trigger, extractors, plain pistol grip stock. Mfg. 1938-1942.

	$385	$305	$275	$250	$210	$195	$155
Single trigger	$440	$360	$330	$305	$265	$220	$195

MODEL 430 — similar to Model 420, with checkered stock and solid rib, recoil pad.

	$440	$360	$305	$275	$240	$220	$195
Single trigger	$495	$415	$360	$320	$285	$265	$220

MODEL 220 SINGLE BARREL — 12, 16, 20, 28 or .410 ga., 26-32 in. barrel, various chokes, hammerless, plain pistol grip stock. Mfg. 1938-1965.

	$125	$100	$85	$75	$65	$50	$40

MODEL 220P — similar to Model 220, with poly choke, not made in .410.

	$90	$65	$55	$45	$35	$30	$30

MODEL 220 AC — similar to Model 220, with Savage adj. choke.

	$100	$85	$65	$55	$45	$35	$30

MODEL 220L — similar to Model 220, with sidelever. Mfg. 1965-1972.

	$90	$65	$55	$45	$35	$30	$30

MODEL 720 AUTOLOADER STANDARD — 12 or 16 ga., Browning A-5 style action, 26-32 in. barrels, various chokes, checkered pistol grip stock. Mfg. 1930-1949.

	$225	$180	$165	$155	$140	$120	$110

MODEL 720 RIOT — see the "Trench/Riot Shotgun" category in the T section for more information and prices.

MODEL 726 UPLAND SPORTER — similar to Model 720, except 2 shell mag. Mfg. 1931-1949.

	$275	$195	$165	$155	$140	$120	$110

MODEL 740C SKEET GUN — similar to Model 726, with Cutts Compensator and skeet stock, 24½ in. barrel. Mfg. 1936-1949.

	$305	$230	$200	$175	$155	$140	$120

MODEL 745 LIGHTWEIGHT — similar to Model 720, with alloy receiver, 12 ga. only, 28 in. barrel. Mfg. 1940-1949.

	$275	$195	$165	$155	$140	$120	$110

MODEL 755 STANDARD SEMI-AUTO — 12 or 16 ga., 26, 28, or 30 in. barrel, various chokes, rounded off receiver, checkered pistol grip stock. Mfg. 1949-1958.

	$265	$180	$160	$150	$140	$120	$110

Grading	100%	98%	95%	90%	80%	70%	60%

MODEL 755SC — similar to Model 755, with Savage Super Choke.

	$275	$195	$165	$155	$140	$120	$110

MODEL 775 LIGHTWEIGHT — similar to Model 755, with alloy receiver. Mfg. 1950-1965.

	$275	$195	$180	$165	$150	$140	$120

MODEL 775SC — similar to Model 775, with Savage Super Choke.

	$285	$205	$195	$175	$160	$150	$130

MODEL 750 SEMI-AUTO — 12 ga., Browning patterned semi-auto, 26 or 28 in. barrels, various chokes, checkered pistol grip stock. Mfg. 1960-1967.

	$275	$195	$165	$155	$140	$120	$110

MODEL 750SC — similar to Model 750, with Savage Super Choke.

	$285	$205	$175	$165	$150	$130	$120

MODEL 750AC — similar to Model 750, with poly choke.

	$285	$205	$175	$165	$150	$130	$120

MODEL 28 SLIDE ACTION — 12, 16, or 20 ga., patterned after the Winchester Model 12. Disc.

	$300	$265	$235	$190	$165	$150	$130

This model was available in either standard configuration (Models 28A and 28B), Riot (28C), Trap (28D), Special (28S).

MODEL 30 SLIDE ACTION — 12, 16, 20, or .410 ga., 26, 28, or 30 in. barrels, various chokes, VR, plain pistol grip stock. Mfg. 1958-1970.

	$220	$175	$155	$140	$120	$100	$85
Checkered Late Model	$230	$185	$165	$150	$130	$110	$95

MODEL 30AC — similar to Model 30, with adj. choke, checkered wood, 12 ga. only. Mfg. 1959-1970.

	$240	$200	$175	$160	$145	$120	$100

MODEL 30T TRAP AND DUCK GUN — similar to Model 30, with 30 in. full, 12 ga. only, Monte Carlo stock and pad. Mfg. 1963-1970.

	$230	$185	$165	$150	$130	$110	$90

MODEL 30FG TAKEDOWN ACTION — 12, 20, or .410 ga., 26, 28, or 30 in., barrel, various chokes, checkered pistol grip stock. Mfg. 1970-1975.

	$175	$155	$130	$110	$95	$85	$70

MODEL 30T TAKEDOWN TRAP — 12 ga. only, 30 in. full, Monte Carlo stock with pad. Mfg. 1970-1973.

	$195	$175	$155	$140	$110	$100	$85

MODEL 30AC TAKEDOWN — similar to Model 30FG, with adj. choke, 12 or 20 ga., 26 in. barrel. Mfg. 1971-1972.

	$200	$180	$165	$150	$120	$110	$90

MODEL 30 TAKEDOWN SLUG GUN — similar to Model 30FG, with 32 in. cylinder bore barrel, rifle sights. Mfg. 1971-disc.

	$195	$175	$160	$140	$110	$100	$85

MODEL 30D TAKEDOWN — similar to Model 30FG, with VR, engraved receiver and pad. Mfg. 1971-disc.

	$200	$180	$165	$150	$120	$110	$90

MODEL 67 SLIDE ACTION — see listing under Stevens Section.

FOX MODELS B, B-SE, AND STEVENS 311 — see listing under Stevens Section.

Grading	100%	98%	95%	90%	80%	70%	60%

MODEL 242 O/U — .410 ga., single exposed hammer, single trigger, barrel selector lever, full chokes. Mfg. 1977-1981.

	$350	$300	$260	$230	$200	$175	$150

MODEL 440 O/U — 12 or 20 ga., 26, 28, or 30 in. barrels, various chokes, boxlock, SST, extractors, checkered pistol grip stock, VR. Imported from Italy 1968-1972.

	$495	$440	$415	$385	$330	$305	$250

MODEL 440T — similar to Model 440, 12 ga., 30 in. only, imp mod. or full choke, wide VR, trap style stock, pad. Mfg. 1969-1972.

	$550	$470	$440	$415	$385	$360	$330

MODEL 444 DELUXE — similar to Model 440, with auto ejectors, select walnut. Mfg. 1969-1972.

	$550	$470	$440	$415	$385	$360	$330

MODEL 550 SxS — 12 or 20 ga., 26, 28, or 30 in. barrels (made by Valmet - rare), various chokes, boxlock, auto ejectors, single trigger, checkered pistol grip stock. Mfg. 1971-1973.

	$275	$220	$195	$165	$150	$130	$110

MODEL 312 SERIES O/U — 12 ga. only, boxlock action, 3 in. chambers, vent. barrels, satin chrome finished receiver, checkered walnut stock and forearm, SST, choke tubes, approx. 7 lbs. Mfg. 1990-93.

The Model 312 Series falls under the domain of Savage Arms, Inc.

▲ *312 Field* — 26 or 28 in. VR barrels with choke tubes.

	$585	$520	$485	$435	$395	$360	$330

▲ *312 Trap* — 30 in. barrels only, Monte Carlo stock with recoil pad.

	$615	$550	$500	$460	$415	$375	$330

▲ *312 Sporting Clays* — 28 in. barrels only with 7 choke tubes provided, recoil pad.

	$595	$530	$485	$435	$395	$360	$320

MODEL 330 O/U — 12 or 20 ga., 26, 28, or 30 in. barrels, various chokes, boxlock, SST, extractors, checkered pistol grip stock. Mfg. by Valmet between 1969-1980.

	$495	$440	$385	$335	$275	$250	$220

Add 25% for extra set of barrels.

MODEL 333T — similar to Model 330, with 30 in. VR barrels bored imp. mod. and full choke, trap stock with pad. Mfg. by Valmet between 1972-1980.

	$550	$470	$415	$385	$360	$305	$275

MODEL 333 O/U — 12 or 20 ga., 26, 28, or 30 in. barrels, various chokes, boxlock, SST, auto ejectors, checkered pistol grip stock. Mfg. by Valmet between 1973-1980.

	$580	$525	$470	$440	$400	$375	$330

Add 25% for extra set of barrels.

MODEL 2400 O/U COMBINATION GUN — 12 ga. full choke barrel over .222 or .308 rifle barrel, 23½ in. barrels, folding leaf sight, solid rib, dovetailed for scope mount, checkered Monte Carlo stock. Mfg. by Valmet between 1975-1980.

	$605	$550	$525	$495	$440	$415	$385

SCATTERGUN TECHNOLOGIES INC. (S.G.T.)

Manufacturer located in Nashville, TN since 1991. Distributor, dealer, and consumer sales.

S.G.T. manufactures practical defense and combat shotguns in 12 ga. only, utilizing Remington Models 870 and 11-87 actions in various configurations as listed below. All shotguns feature 3 in. chamber capacity and parkerized finish.

Grading	100%	98%	95%	90%	80%	70%	60%

SHOTGUNS: SLIDE ACTION

STANDARD MODEL — 18 in. barrel, adj. ghost ring rear sight, 7 shot mag., side saddle, synthetic buttstock and forearm with 11,000 CP flashlight.
Mfg.'s Sug. Retail $735 $640 $500 $395

PROFESSIONAL MODEL — similar to Standard Model, except has 14 in. barrel and 6 shot mag.
Mfg.'s Sug. Retail $735 $640 $500 $395

ENTRY MODEL — 12½ in. barrel with fixed choke, adj. ghost ring sight, 5 shot mag., side saddle, synthetic buttstock and nylon strap assisted forearm with 5,000 CP flashlight.
Mfg.'s Sug. Retail $695 $625 $500 $395

COMPACT MODEL — 12½ in. barrel with fixed choke, adj. ghost ring sight, 5 shot mag., synthetic butt stock and forearm. New 1994.
Mfg.'s Sug. Retail $575 $510 $420 $315

PRACTICAL TURKEY MODEL — 20 in. barrel with extra full choke, adj. ghost ring rear sight, 5 shot mag. for 3 in. shells, synthetic buttstock and forearm. New 1995.
Mfg.'s Sug. Retail $625 $565 $515 $465 $430 $395 $360 $330

LOUIS AWERBUCK SIGNATURE MODEL — 18 in. barrel with fixed choke, adj. ghost ring sight, 5 shot mag., side saddle, wood butt stock with recoil reducer and forearm. New 1994.
Mfg.'s Sug. Retail $665 $600 $475 $380

F.B.I.MODEL — similar to Standard Model, except has 5 shot mag.
Mfg.'s Sug. Retail $705 $625 $490 $385

PATROL MODEL — 18 in. barrel, adj. ghost ring sight, 5 shot mag., synthetic butt stock and forearm.
Mfg.'s Sug. Retail $545 $485 $400 $295

BORDER PATROL MODEL 20 — similar to Patrol Model, except has 7 shot mag.
Mfg.'s Sug. Retail $575 $510 $420 $315

BORDER PATROL MODEL 21 — similar to Border Patrol Model 20, except has 14 in. barrel and 6 shot mag.
Mfg.'s Sug. Retail $575 $510 $420 $315

CONCEALMENT MODEL 00 — 12½ in. barrel with fixed choke, 5 shot mag., bead sight, grooved wood forearm and pistol grip.
Mfg.'s Sug. Retail $530 $475 $385 $275

CONCEALMENT MODEL 01 — similar to Concealment Model 00, except has synthetic finger-grooved combat forearm and pistol grip. Disc. 1993.
$475 $395 $295

Last Mfg.'s Sug. Retail was $525.

CONCEALMENT MODEL 02 — similar to Concealment Model 00, except has Pachmayr forearm and pistol grip. Disc. 1993.
$495 $415 $315

Last Mfg.'s Sug. Retail was $555.

CONCEALMENT MODEL 03 — similar to Concealment Model 01, except has synthetic nylon strap assisted forearm with 5,000 CP flashlight. Disc. 1993.
$550 $455 $350

Last Mfg.'s Sug. Retail was $625.

BREACHING MODEL — similar to Concealment Model 00, except has standoff device.
Mfg.'s Sug. Retail $435 $390 $340 $275

Grading	100%	98%	95%	90%	80%	70%	60%

SHOTGUNS: SEMI-AUTO

K-9 MODEL — 18 in. barrel, adj. ghost ring sight, 7 shot mag., side saddle, synthetic buttstock and forearm.

Mfg.'s Sug. Retail	$795	$700	$560	$450			

SWAT MODEL — similar to K-9 Model, except has 14 in. barrel and forearm with 11,000 CP flashlight.

Mfg.'s Sug. Retail	$965	$850	$680	$540			

URBAN SNIPER MODEL — 18 in. rifled barrel, scout optics, 7 shot mag., side saddle, synthetic butt stock, forearm and bipod.

Mfg.'s Sug. Retail	$1,050	$920	$760	$525			

SCHALL

Previous manufacturer located in Hartford, CT.

REPEATING HANDGUN — .22 LR only, target pistol, mag. fed manual repeating action. Unusual.

	$425	$360	$320	$270	$220	$180	$150

SCHELLER - SPEZIALWAFFEN

Manufacturer located in Suhl, Germany specializing in bolt action rifles.

For more information regarding this manufacturer (including current model information and U.S. prices) please contact this company directly (see Trademark Index).

SCHULTZ & LARSEN

Manufacturer located in Otterup, Denmark since 1911.

NO. 47 MATCH RIFLE — .22 LR, bolt action, single shot, 28 in. heavy barrel, target sights, set trigger, free rifle stock.

	$660	$550	$495	$440	$385	$360	$330

M61 MATCH RIFLE — .22 LR, bolt action, single shot, 28 in. heavy barrel, target sights, set trigger, free rifle stock, palm rest.

	$895	$825	$740	$680	$600	$550	$500

M62 MATCH RIFLE — various cals., bolt action, single shot, 28 in. heavy barrel, target sights, set trigger, free rifle stock, palm rest.

	$995	$875	$780	$700	$620	$550	$500

MODEL 54 FREE RIFLE — any American centerfire standard caliber, plus 6.5x55mm, 27 in. heavy barrel, target sights, free rifle stock.

	$825	$745	$690	$605	$550	$495	$440

MODEL 54J SPORTING RIFLE — .270 Win., .30-06, 7x61 Sharpe and Hart cal., bolt action, 3 shot, 24 in. barrel, checkered Monte Carlo stock, no sights.

	$650	$550	$470	$415	$360	$330	$300

MODEL 68 DL — .22-250 Rem., .243 Win., 6mm Rem., .264 Win. Mag., .270 Win., .30-06, .308 Win., 7x61 S&H, 7mm Rem. Mag., 8x57 JS, .300 Win. Mag., .308 Norma Mag., .338 Win. Mag., .358 Norma Mag., or .458 Win. Mag. cal., bolt action, 24 in. barrel, Bofors Steel receiver, bolt has 4 rear locking lugs, select French walnut, adj. trigger, no sights except for .458 Mag.

	$725	$650	$575	$525	$495	$460	$430

SCHUETZEN PISTOL WORKS

Schuetzen Pistol Works is the custom shop for Safari Arms - please refer to the Schuetzen Pistol Works catagory under the Safari Arms Listing for more information.

SCHUETZEN RIFLES

A Schuetzen Rifle is a special single shot target rifle. During the time span 1875-1945 this target configuration rifle was very popular for competition shooters. Many of these guns had elaborate locking systems, top quality sights, double set triggers, heavy barrels, palm and thumb rests, sculptured cheekpiece, Swiss style butt plate, etc. Rather than list all the various domestic and European makers (there are hundreds), it should be noted that since there are so many combinations of options for this configuration that most guns have to be examined and appraised individually. Most non-major trademarks sell in the $550-$1,500 range, depending on features and condition. Schuetzen Rifles are a field in themselves and a knowledgeable dealer/collector should be consulted before buying or selling one of these guns.

SCOTT, W.C., LTD.

Established in 1834 by William Scott, located in Birmingham, England, and remained in the family until 1897. At this time, Scott merged with P. Webley & Son to form Webley & Scott Revolver and Arms Co., Ltd. (later changed to Webley & Scott Ltd.). Even though Scott family members were no longer associated with this new company, the Scott gun-line was continued with the trademark intact until 1935. Thereafter, only a few guns were marked Scott. In 1979, Webley & Scott ceased manufacture of all firearms. A new company, W. & C. Scott, was formed in 1980 utilizing mostly employees of Webley & Scott. W. & C. Scott remained part of its parent company, Harris & Sheldon (also had controlling interest in Hardy and Churchill trademarks), until 1985 when Scott was purchased by Holland & Holland. Manufacture of Scott guns decreased substantially after the merger, and in September 1991, W. & C. Scott ceased operation all together. During its 157 years of production, Scott and Webley & Scott produced approximately, 150,00 double guns, 10,000 rifles (either double or bolt-action) and thousands of single guns and single rifles.

Grading	100%	98%	95%	90%	80%	70%	60%

SHOTGUNS: SxS

All W.C. Scott Shotguns were discontinued in 1990. W.C. Scott also manufactured many hammer guns that vary in price from $250-$2,500, depending on grade and original condition.

KINMOUNT — 12, 16, 20, or 28 ga., double barrel boxlock action, ejectors, deluxe checkered walnut, scroll engraving.

	100%	98%	95%	90%	80%	70%	60%
	$6,500	$5,750	$5,000	$4,500	$4,000	$3,000	$2,500

Last Mfg.'s Sug. Retail was $11,000.

Add 20% for 28 or .410 ga.
Add 10% for SNT.

BOWOOD — 12, 16, 20, or 28 ga., double barrel boxlock action, ejectors, deluxe checkered walnut, extensive scroll engraving.

	100%	98%	95%	90%	80%	70%	60%
	$7,500	$6,500	$5,750	$5,000	$4,500	$4,000	$3,500

Last Mfg.'s Sug. Retail was $12,500.

Add 20% for 28 or .410 ga.
Add 10% for SNT.

Grading	100%	98%	95%	90%	80%	70%	60%

CHATSWORTH — 12, 16, 20, or 28 ga., top-of-the-line boxlock action, ejectors, deluxe checkered walnut, extensive scroll engraving.

	$8,750	$7,500	$6,500	$5,750	$5,000	$4,500	$4,000

Last Mfg.'s Sug. Retail was $14,000.

Add 20% for 28 or .410 ga.
Add 10% for SNT.

BLENHEIM — 12 bore only, upgraded models, custom made to individual specifications, originally priced per individual order.

Specimen rarity precludes percentage grading pricing. Individual appraisals have to be secured on this model.

SECURITY INDUSTRIES
Previous manufacturer located in Little Ferry, NJ.

MODEL PSS 38 DOUBLE ACTION — .38 Spl. 5 shot cylinder, 2 in. barrel, stainless steel, fixed sights, wood grips. Mfg. 1973-1978.

	$175	$150	$140	$130	$125	$110	$100

MODEL PM357 — similar to Model PSS 38, except .357 Mag., 2½ in. barrel. Mfg. 1975-disc.

	$225	$175	$165	$150	$140	$125	$110

MODEL PPM 357 — .357 Mag., 5 shot, 2 in. barrel, spurless hammer until 1977, new models have spur. Mfg. 1965-disc.

	$225	$175	$165	$150	$140	$125	$110

SEDCO INDUSTRIES, INC.
Previous manufacturer located in Lake Elsinore, CA until 1991.

MODEL SP-22 — .22 LR cal., semi-auto single action, 2½ in. barrel, rotary safety, serrated slide, nickel, satin nickel (new 1990), or black metal finish, simulated pearl grips in white, blue, gray, or pink, 11 oz. Mfg. 1989-90 only.

		$60	$55	$50	$45	$40	$35	$35

Last Mfg.'s Sug. Retail was $69.

SEDGLEY, R.F., INC.
Previous manufacturer located in Philadelphia, PA.

SPRINGFIELD SPORTING RIFLE — '03 Springfield bolt action, .220 Swift, .218 Bee, .22-3000, .22-4000, .22 Hornet, .25-35, .250-3000, .257 Roberts, .270 Win., 7mm, or .30-06 cal., 24 in. barrel, Lyman receiver sight, checkered pistol grip stock, pre-WWII.

	$1,250	$1,125	$995	$875	$750	$625	$495

SPRINGFIELD CARBINE SPORTER — similar to Rifle, with 20 in. barrel, and full length stock.

	$1,450	$1,250	$1,125	$995	$875	$750	$625

SEECAMP, L.W. CO., INC.
Manufacturer located in Milford, CT. Dealer direct sales only.

All Seecamp pistols are hand machined and hand fitted from stainless steel. Manufacture has always emphasized quality over quantity - this explains why values often exceed the company's retail prices. There is simply more demand than supply. Currently, approx. 100 pistols (LWS 32 Model) per month are being fabricated.

Grading	100%	98%	95%	90%	80%	70%	60%

LWS .25 ACP MODEL — .25 ACP, double action, semi-auto, 2 in. barrel, 7 shot mag., stainless steel, matte finish, 12 oz. Approx. 5,000 mfg. 1982-1985.

	$340	$295	$260	$235	$220	$210	$200

Last Mfg.'s Sug. Retail was $275.

LWS 32 MODEL — .32 ACP Silvertip, double action, semi-auto, 2 in. barrel, stainless steel, 6 shot mag., 12½ oz., extreme backorder situation coupled with high demand has resulted in elevated 100% values.

Mfg.'s Sug. Retail	$425	$795	$725	$650	$575	$495	$450	$425

This model is available in either a matte or polished finish. The polished finish carries a slight premium.

MATCHED PAIR — includes both .25 ACP and .32 ACP pistols with the same serial number, approx. 200 sets were mfg. before the BATF stopped this practice.

	$950	$800	$700

This set contains a matte finished .25 ACP and a polished .32 ACP.

SEITZ

SINGLE BARREL TRAP GUN — 12 ga. only, single barrel, various barrel lengths, pull or release trigger, only 45 guns mfg.

	$18,500	$16,000	$13,000	$10,000	$8,500	$7,700	$6,950

SEMMERLING

Previously manufactured by Semmerling Corporation, located in Boston, MA from 1978-82.

Less than 600 LM-4 pistols have been mfg. While advertised by the American Derringer Corporation, this model was never manufactured.

LM-4 PISTOL — .45 ACP cal., 2 in. barrel, blue, smallest .45 ACP repeater available, slide is worked manually with thumb on serrated slide-top, extremely high quality, hand fitted and choice of finishes include chrome, electroless nickel, or high polish blue.

Chrome	$2,950	$2,600	$2,300	$2,100	$1,950	$1,725	$1,600
Electroless nickel	$3,200	$2,950	$2,600	$2,300	$2,100	$1,950	$1,725
High polish blue	$4,950	$4,500	$4,000	$3,600	$3,200	$2,800	$2,500

The original U.S. Army contract pistol sold for $5,000. Earlier mfg. by Lichtman will also command a premium over values listed above.

▲ *Stainless Steel* — matte finish stainless steel variation of the LM-4, combat gray, satin, high polish finish, rosewood grips.

While advertised by the American Derringer Corporation, this model was never manufactured.

SENTINEL ARMS

Exclusive importers of Arsenal, Bulgaria, pistols and rifles. Please refer to listing under Arsenal, Bulgaria.

SHARPS, C., ARMS CO. INC.

Manufacturer of Sharps reproductions for Montana Armory, Inc. Please refer to the Montana Armory, Inc. section.

SHARPS, CHRISTIAN

Manufactured in Windsor, VT under Sharps Rifle Manufacturing Company between 1851-1855. Manufactured in Hartford, CT under same name between 1855-1874. Reorganized as Sharps Rifle Company in 1876 with production resuming in Hartford (1876 only) and Bridgeport, CT. from 1877-1881.

100%	98%	95%	90%	80%	70%	60%	50%	40%	30%	20%	10%

REVOLVER, PERCUSSION — made 1850s in Philadelphia, production about 2000, 3 in. octagonal tip-up barrel with rib, .25 caliber, 6 shot.

| $1,950 | $1,750 | $1,500 | $1,275 | $1,100 | $1,000 | $900 | $800 | $700 | $600 | $500 | $400 |

PEPPERBOX PISTOL — also marked Sharps and Hankins, 4-shot breech-loading, .32, .30, or .22 rimfire cal., firing pin rotates, brass frame with silver plating, or case-hardening on iron frame.

▲ *First Model* — 5 variations, 2½ in. barrel. Scarcer variations can be worth up to 150% more.

| $595 | $550 | $500 | $465 | $430 | $400 | $360 | $330 | $300 | $275 | $250 | $225 |

▲ *Second Model* — 5 variations, 3 in. barrel. Scarcer variations can be worth up to 150% more.

| $595 | $550 | $500 | $465 | $430 | $400 | $360 | $330 | $300 | $275 | $250 | $225 |

▲ *Third Model* — Sharps and Hankins markings, .32 rimfire short, 4 variations, 3½ in. barrel. Premium for scarcer variations.

| $750 | $700 | $650 | $600 | $560 | $520 | $480 | $440 | $400 | $360 | $320 | $280 |

▲ *Fourth Model* — 4 variations, 2½, 3, or 3½ in. barrel, birds head grip, .32 rimfire long. Premium for scarcer variations.

| $650 | $575 | $525 | $475 | $430 | $400 | $360 | $330 | $300 | $275 | $250 | $225 |

RIFLES: BREECH LOADING

The Model 1863 Carbine was one of the highest production rifles of the Civil War with production totaling over 100,000. During a period after the Civil War, the Model 1874 was loosely dubbed "Buffalo Rifle" because of its involvement on the western plains.

MODEL 1851 CARBINE — .52-caliber percussion, breech-loading, Maynard tape primer, U.S. military markings. Deduct 40% for non-martial sporting rifle version.

| $7,500 | $6,950 | $6,500 | $5,500 | $4,950 | $4,450 | $3,950 | $3,450 | $2,875 | $2,350 | $1,975 | $1,600 |

MODEL 1852 CARBINE — slanting breech, approx. 4500 mfg. 1853-1855, caliber .52 with Sharps' patented pellet primer built into lockplate. Add 50% for U.S. martial markings. Also sporting rifles in .52, .44, or .36 cal.

| $3,000 | $2,750 | $2,500 | $2,250 | $2,000 | $1,825 | $1,675 | $1,495 | $1,300 | $1,100 | $995 | $800 |

MODEL 1853 CARBINE — mfg. 1854-1858 in quantity of some 10,350, caliber .52 with Sharps' patented pellet primer feed. Deduct 10% for sporting-rifle version.

| $3,000 | $2,750 | $2,500 | $2,250 | $2,000 | $1,825 | $1,675 | $1,495 | $1,300 | $1,100 | $995 | $800 |

MODEL 1855 CARBINE — U.S. martial model in .52 caliber, breech-loading, Maynard tape primer system, sling ring is mounted on left side.

| $6,000 | $5,500 | $5,150 | $4,775 | $4,500 | $4,125 | $3,600 | $3,150 | $2,500 | $2,050 | $1,800 | $1,400 |

STRAIGHT-BREECH RIFLES AND CARBINES, 1859, 1863, 1865 — breech-loading caliber .52 with Sharps' patented pellet-priming system in lockplate. (Prices listed are for models that are original and have not been converted). The Model 1859 is worth a slight premium.

| $7,000 | $6,500 | $5,500 | $4,500 | $3,500 | $3,250 | $2,750 | $2,300 | $2,000 | $1,625 | $1,300 | $1,000 |

Over 32,000 carbines (majority) and rifles were converted to .50-70 centerfire. Can be detected by additional "DFC" ribbon cartouche on left center of stock. These converted specimens (mostly Model 1863s) are worth approx. 70% of values listed above.

COFFEE-MILL MODEL — built-in coffee-grinding mill in stock for cavalry use. Easy to fake.

| $20,000 | $17,750 | $15,250 | $13,000 | $10,750 | $9,000 | $7,750 | $6,900 | $6,250 | $5,500 | $4,825 | $4,300 |

MODEL 1874 RIFLE — mfg. from 1871 until 1881, known as the "Buffalo Rifle" in its day. Many variations, cals., and accessories. Research should be done before purchasing.

▲ *Sporting Rifle* — .50, .45, .44, or .40 cal. Heavier barrels are worth more. Approx. 6,500 mfg.

| $15,000 | $14,000 | $12,500 | $10,000 | $8,000 | $6,250 | $4,750 | $4,000 | $3,150 | $2,675 | $2,175 | $1,700 |

100%	98%	95%	90%	80%	70%	60%	50%	40%	30%	20%	10%

▲ *Business Rifle* — .45 or .50 cal., basically a no-frills version of the Model 1874 Rifle with round barrel, double triggers, and open sights.

| $9,000 | $8,500 | $7,750 | $7,350 | $6,950 | $6,500 | $5,950 | $5,450 | $4,850 | $4,000 | $2,850 | $1,950 |

▲ *Meacham Type* — mfg. from spare parts and parts converted from Civil War carbines by various firms, including Sharps.

| $8,000 | $7,500 | $7,000 | $6,000 | $5,000 | $4,250 | $3,500 | $2,750 | $2,000 | $1,750 | $1,500 | $1,250 |

▲ *Military Rifle* — mostly in .50-70 or .45-70 cal., 30 in. barrel with three bands. Approx. 1700 mfg.

| $5,000 | $4,650 | $4,400 | $3,900 | $3,475 | $3,400 | $2,750 | $2,300 | $2,000 | $1,625 | $1,300 | $1,000 |

▲ *Military Carbine* — mostly .50-70 cal. Fewer than 500 mfg.

| $6,000 | $5,500 | $5,150 | $4,775 | $4,500 | $4,125 | $3,600 | $3,150 | $2,500 | $2,050 | $1,800 | $1,400 |

CREEDMOOR, MID-RANGE, & LONG-RANGE — these have a basically common look, though there are many differences and variations among them.

| $15,000 | $13,750 | $11,250 | $10,250 | $8,650 | $7,475 | $6,175 | $5,250 | $4,750 | $3,950 | $3,450 | $2,950 |

SCHUETZEN RIFLE — .40-50 cal., 30 in. octagonal barrel. Only 70 mfg.

| $12,000 | $11,250 | $9,250 | $8,150 | $6,950 | $5,550 | $4,600 | $3,750 | $3,150 | $2,675 | $2,175 | $1,700 |

SHERIDAN PRODUCTS INCORPORATED
Previous manufacturer located in Racine, WI.

Grading			100%	98%	95%	90%	80%	70%	60%

PISTOL

KNOCKABOUT — .22 S or L, single shot, 5 in. barrel, checkered plastic grips, fixed sights. Mfg. 1953-1960.

			$110	$100	$85	$75	$60	$50	$40

SHILEN RIFLES, INCORPORATED
Previous manufacturer located in Enis, TX.

RIFLES: BOLT ACTION

Older Shilen rifles have become very desirable for target shooters and other accuracy enthusiasts. Because of their limited mfg. (only 600-800 are guesstimated to have been mfg.) and new found demand, prices have gone up considerably on this trademark.

DGA SPORTER — .17 Rem., .223 Rem., .22-250 Rem., .220 Swift, 6mm Rem., .243 Win., .250 Savage, .257 Roberts, .284 Win., .308 Win., or .358 Win. cal., 3 shot mag., 24 in. barrel, no sights, claro walnut stock.

			$1,475	$1,175	$950	$800	$675	$575	$495

DGA VARMINTER — similar to Sporter, except 25 in. medium heavy barrel.

			$1,395	$1,100	$900	$775	$650	$575	$495

DGA SILHOUETTE RIFLE — similar to Varminter, .308 Win. cal. only.

			$1,395	$1,100	$900	$775	$650	$575	$495

DGA BENCHREST RIFLE — single shot, choice of cals., 26 in. heavy barrel or medium barrel, no sights, choice of fiberglass or walnut stock, thumbhole available.

			$1,450	$1,200	$950	$800	$650	$575	$495

SHILOH RIFLE MFG. CO.

Manufacturer located in Big Timber, MT. Dealer direct sales.

The Shiloh Rifle Mfg. Company is currently manufacturing replicas of Sharps rifles and carbines. They are available as black powder or modern cartridge rifles. Most models are available in the following cals.: .40-50, .40-65 Win., .40-70, .40-90, .45-70, .45-90, .45-100, .45-110, .45-120, .50-70, .50-90 (disc.), .50-100, and .50-140 (disc.). Percussion Rifles also are available in .54 cal. and are breech loading. All models are authentically reproduced and are high quality.

Grading	100%	98%	95%	90%	80%	70%	60%

S

RIFLES: BLACK POWDER CARTRIDGE

Currently, Shiloh is experiencing a back order situation with deliveries taking longer than some consumers are willing to wait. Because of this type of market (when demand is greater than supply), secondary market prices can become very unpredictable and explains why N/A has replaced many prices on the listings below. Some dealers and shooters are currently getting over $2,000 for a #3 Sporter in NIB condition!

Values below are without special orders or features. Shiloh Rifle Mfg. Co. should be contacted (see Trademark Index) regarding their long list of custom features (including engraving).

MODEL 1874 LONG RANGE EXPRESS

Mfg.'s Sug. Retail $1,174	N/A	N/A	N/A	N/A	$475	$410	$350

MODEL 1874 NO. 1 SPORTING

Mfg.'s Sug. Retail $1,148	N/A	N/A	N/A	N/A	$450	$395	$325

MODEL 1874 NO. 2 SPORTING

	N/A	N/A	N/A	N/A	$320	$285	$270

MODEL 1874 NO. 3 SPORTING

Mfg.'s Sug. Retail $1,044	N/A	N/A	N/A	N/A	$380	$320	$295

MODEL 1874 BUSINESS RIFLE

Mfg.'s Sug. Retail $1,050	N/A	N/A	N/A	N/A	$380	$320	$295

MODEL 1874 HUNTER'S RIFLE

	N/A	N/A	N/A	N/A	$450	$400	$375

MODEL 1874 HARTFORD — features Hartford collar between receiver and barrel assembly. New 1989.

Mfg.'s Sug. Retail $1,214	N/A	N/A	N/A	N/A	$475	$410	$350

MODEL 1874 MILITARY RIFLE

	N/A	N/A	N/A	N/A	$475	$410	$350

Last Mfg.'s Sug. Retail was $995.

MODEL 1874 MILITARY CARBINE

	N/A	N/A	N/A	N/A	$380	$320	$295

Last Mfg.'s Sug. Retail was $925.

MODEL 1874 CARBINE "CIVILIAN"

	N/A	N/A	N/A	N/A	$380	$320	$295

Last Mfg.'s Sug. Retail was $895.

MODEL 1874 SADDLE RIFLE

Mfg.'s Sug. Retail $1,102	N/A	N/A	N/A	N/A	$380	$320	$295

Grading	100%	98%	95%	90%	80%	70%	60%

MODEL 1874 ROUGHRIDER
Mfg.'s Sug. Retail $1,044

	100%	98%	95%	90%	80%	70%	60%
	N/A	N/A	N/A	N/A	$380	$320	$295

Add $84 for semi-fancy walnut.

MODEL 1874 JAEGER HUNTING RIFLE — hunting rifle with lightweight half-octagon/half-round barrel. Mfg. 1987-92.

	N/A	N/A	N/A	N/A	$320	$295	$270

Last Mfg.'s Sug. Retail was $835.

MODEL 1874 CREEDMOOR TARGET RIFLE — includes fancy wood, AA finish, 32 in. half-round/half-octagon barrel, pewter forearm cap, Creedmoor sights, 10 lbs. New 1996.
Mfg.'s Sug. Retail $1,908

	N/A	N/A	N/A	N/A	$890	$720	$650

MODEL 1874 MIDRANGE RIFLE — 30 in. octagon barrel, extra fancy wood, pewter forearm cap, buckhorn blade sight, AA finish. New 1996.
Mfg.'s Sug. Retail $2,064

	N/A	N/A	N/A	N/A	$970	$860	$770

MODEL 1874 SCHUETZEN RIFLE — 28 in. half-round/half-octagon, semi-fancy wood, Schuetzen style buttplate, sporting style forearm, limited mfg.
Mfg.'s Sug. Retail $1,902

	N/A	N/A	N/A	N/A	$975	$890	$730

NUMBER 2 CREEDMOOR SILHOUETTE — special order cal., 30 in. round tapered barrel, extra fancy checkered wood, single trigger, polished barrel and small parts, w/o cheekpiece, limited mfg.
Mfg.'s Sug. Retail $2,214

	N/A	N/A	N/A	N/A	$900	$750	$600

"QUIGLEY" SHARPS BUFFALO RIFLE — .45-70 or .45-110 cal., 34 in. heavy barrel, military stock with patch box, vernier aperture rear sight with globe front, mfg. for the motion picture "Quigley Down Under", approx. 13 lbs. New 1990.
Mfg.'s Sug. Retail $2,660

	N/A	N/A	N/A	N/A	$1,050	$825	$700

RIFLES: PERCUSSION-BREECH LOADING

Models 1863 Sporting, 1863 Military Rifle and Carbine models listed below have prices available through special request only. Last retail prices shown below indicate 1992 information as Shiloh is currently concentrating their production efforts on black powder cartridge rifles.

MODEL 1863 SPORTING

	$735	$675	$575	$450	$380	$320	$295

Last Mfg.'s Sug. Retail was $785.

MODEL 1863 NO. 2 SPORTING

	$600	$550	$470	$415	$360	$300	$275

MODEL 1863 NO. 3 SPORTING

	$575	$525	$440	$385	$340	$290	$270

MODEL 1863 MILITARY RIFLE

	$850	$800	$650	$550	$475	$410	$350

Last Mfg.'s Sug. Retail was $895.

MODEL 1863 MILITARY CARBINE

	$740	$690	$550	$450	$380	$320	$295

Last Mfg.'s Sug. Retail was $795.

MODEL 1859 MILITARY CARBINE

	$490	$440	$360	$305	$275	$220	$165

MODEL 1862 ROBINSON CONFEDERATE CARBINE

	$855	$805	$650	$550	$475	$410	$350

Last Mfg.'s Sug. Retail was $915.

Grading	100%	98%	95%	90%	80%	70%	60%

MONTANA CENTENNIAL RIFLE SERIES — mfg. to commemorate Montana's 100th Centennial (1889-1989), limited manufacture. Mfg. 1988-90.

▲ *Creedmoor Rifle* — .45-70 cal., extra fancy rifle with engraving, 32 in. barrel, walnut cased. 100 mfg. only ser. numbered 1-101.

$3,750 $2,500 $1,950

Last Mfg.'s Sug. Retail was $3,750.

▲ *Hartford Rifle* — .45-70 cal, 30 in. barrel, case colored receiver with pewter forearm cap, 12 lbs. Serial numbered 102-902.

$1,375 $995 $750

Last Mfg.'s Sug. Retail was $1,375.

▲ *Bridgeport Rifle* — .45-70, 30 in. barrel, similar to Hartford rifle without Pewter forearm cap, 12 lbs.

$1,075 $775 $575

Last Mfg.'s Sug. Retail was $1,075.

SIDEWINDER

Manufactured by D-Max, Inc. located in Bagley, MN beginning 1993. Dealer or consumer sales.

SIDEWINDER — .45 LC or 2½/3 in. .410 shotshells/slugs, 6 shot, stainless steel construction, 6½ or 7½ in. bull barrel (muzzle end bored for choke), Pachmayr grips, hammer bar safety, adj. rear sight, unique design permits one cylinder to shoot above listed loads, cased with choke tube, 3.8 lbs. New 1993.

Mfg.'s Sug. Retail $775 $695 $575 $475

SIG

Manufactured by Sig Swiss Industrial Company since 1860 in Neuhausen, Switzerland. P 210 pistols are currently imported and distributed by Sigarms Located in Exeter, NH (refer to the Sig Sauer section).

RIFLES

PE-57 — 7.5 Swiss cal. only, semi-auto version of the Swiss military rifle, 24 in. barrel, includes 24 shot mag., leather sling, bipod and maintenance kit. Importation disc. 1988.

$3,250 $2,850 $2,500 $2,250 $2,000 $1,800 $1,600

Last Mfg.'s Sug. Retail was $1,745.

The PE-57 was previously distributed in limited quantities by Osborne's located in Cheboygan, MI.

SIG-AMT SEMI-AUTO RIFLE — semi-auto version of SG510-4 auto paramilitary design rifle, roller delayed blowback action, .308 Win., 5, 10, or 20 shot mag., 18¾ in. barrel, wood stock, folding bipod. Mfg. 1960-present. Importation disc. 1988.

$2,500 $2,250 $2,000 $1,850 $1,700 $1,550 $1,400

Last Mfg.'s Sug. Retail was $1,795.

SG 550/551 — .223 Rem. cal. with heavier bullet, Swiss Army's semi-auto version of its newest paramilitary design rifle (SIG 90), 20.8 (SG 550) or 16 in. (SG 551 Carbine) barrel, some synthetics used to save weight, 20 shot mag., diopter night sights, built-in folding bipod, 7.7 or 9 lbs.

$4,250 $3,875 $3,500 $3,250 $2,995 $2,700 $2,500

Last Mfg.'s Sug. Retail was $1,950.

Add $250 for case.

This model has been banned from domestic importation due to 1989 Federal legislation.

SIG-HAMMERLI

Previously manufactured by Hammerli Ltd. in Lenzburg, Switzerland.

Grading	100%	98%	95%	90%	80%	70%	60%

P240 TARGET PISTOL — .32 S&W Long Wadcutter or .38 (disc.) cal., single action, 5 shot mag., 5.9 in. barrel, blued finish, thumb rest walnut grips, adj. sights and trigger, 3 lbs. Add $100 for Morini adj. grips. Importation mostly disc. 1986.

		$1,475	$1,225	$1,000	$875	$775	$700	$660

Last Mfg.'s Sug. Retail was $1,350.

.38 Mid-range cal. is very desirable in this model - healthy premiums (and inconsistent) are being asked.

.22 CONVERSION UNIT

	$550	$495	$400

Last Mfg.'s Sug. Retail was $595.

SIG SAUER

Manufacturer located in Germany. Currently imported, manufactured, and distributed by Sigarms located in Exeter, NH.

PISTOLS: SEMI-AUTO

P 210 — 9mm or 7.65 Para., single action, 4¾ in. barrel, 8 shot mag., standard weapon of the Swiss Army, 2 lbs.

Originally mfg. in 1947, this pistol was first designated the SP 47/8 and became the standard military pistol of the Swiss Army in 1949. Later designated the P 210, this handgun has been mfg. continuously for over 40 years.

▲ **P 210-1** — polished finish, walnut grips, special hammer, fixed sights. Importation disc. 1986.

	$2,000	$1,675	$1,400	$1,195	$975	$850	$750

Last Mfg.'s Sug. Retail was $1,861.

▲ **P 210-2** — matte finish, field sights, plastic grips. Importation disc. 1987.

	$1,775	$1,325	$1,000	$875	$750	$625	$550

Last Mfg.'s Sug. Retail was $1,350.

▲ **P 210-5** — matte finish, micrometer sights, 150mm or 180mm (rare) extended barrel, hard rubber grips, special order only, very limited mfg. Importation disc. 1987.

	$1,950	$1,600	$1,400	$1,195	$975	$825	$725

Last Mfg.'s Sug. Retail was $1,795.

▲ **P 210-6** — matte finish, fixed (current importation) or micrometer sights, 120mm barrel, hard rubber grips. Limited importation.

Mfg.'s Sug. Retail	$2,300	$2,100	$1,425	$1,000	$950	$775	$650	$575

Add $600 for .22 LR conversion kit.

▲ **P 210-7** — .22 LR or 9mm Para., regular or target long barrel, limited importation.

	$3,375	$2,950	$2,600	$2,300	$1,950	$1,600	$1,275

▲ **P 210 Deluxe Models** — various models differ in the amount of engraving, gold inlays, carved wooden grips, presentation cases, and other special order features available from the factory. Prices start at $3,500 and can go up to $5,500, depending on the amount of special orders executed.

MODEL P220 — .22 LR (disc.), .38 Super, 7.65mm (disc.), 9mm Luger (disc 1991), or .45 ACP cal., 7 (.45 ACP) or 9 shot mag., regular double action or double action (.45 ACP cal. only), 4.4 in. barrel, decocking lever safety, matte blue, lightweight alloy frame, black plastic grips, (action is same as Browning BDA), values are for .45 ACP cal. and assume American side mag. release (standard 1986), 28.2 oz. Mfg. 1976-present.

Mfg.'s Sug. Retail	$805	$690	$610	$495	$440	$395	$350	$310

Add $100 for Siglite night sights.
Add $45 for factory K-Kote finish.
Add $45 for nickel finished slide (new 1992).
Add $70 for electroless nickel finish (disc. 1991).
Add $680 for .22 LR conversion kit (disc.).
Subtract 10% for "European" Model (bottom mag. release - includes 9mm and .38 Super cals.).

Grading	100%	98%	95%	90%	80%	70%	60%

MODEL P225 — 9mm Para., regular double action or double action only, similar to P220, shorter dimensions, 3.85 in. barrel, 8 shot, thumb actuated button release mag., fully adj. sights, 28.8 oz.

Mfg.'s Sug. Retail	$780	$675	$600	$500	$450	$400	$350	$310

    Add $70 for factory K-Kote finish.
    Add $100 for Siglite night sights.
    Add $70 for nickel finished slide (new 1992).
    Add $70 for electroless nickel finish (disc. 1991).

MODEL P226 — .357 SIG (new 1995) or 9mm Para. cal., compact variation, choice of traditional double action or double action only (new 1992) operation, 10 (C/B 1994), 15*, or 20* shot mag., 4.4 in. barrel, alloy frame, high contrast sights, 29.9 oz. New 1983.

Mfg.'s Sug. Retail	$825	$735	$630	$525	$475	$415	$360	$310

    Add $50 for .357 SIG cal.
    Add $100 for Siglite night sights.
    Add $50 for K-Kote (Polymer) finish (9mm Para. only).
    Add $50 for nickel finished slide (new 1992, 9mm Para. only).
    Add $70 for electroless nickel finish (disc. 1991).
    This model is also available in double action only (all finishes) at no extra charge.

▲ *Model P226 Jubilee* — limited edition commemorating SIG's 125th anniversary, features gold-plated small parts, carved select walnut grips, special slide markings, cased. Mfg. 1985 only.

$1,495 $1,175 $950

Last Mfg.'s Sug. Retail was $2,000.

MODEL P228 — 9mm Para., choice of traditional double action or double action only (new 1992) operation, compact design, 3.86 (compact) or 4.41 in. barrel, 10 (C/B 1994) or 13* shot mag., automatic firing pin lock safety, 3 dot sighting system, alloy frame, choice of blue, nickel slide (new 1991), or K-Kote finish, 29.3 oz. New 1990.

Mfg.'s Sug. Retail	$825	$735	$630	$525	$475	$415	$360	$310

    Add $100 for Siglite night sights.
    Add $50 for K-Kote (Polymer) finish.
    Add $50 for nickel finished slide (new 1992).
    Add $70 for electroless nickel finish (disc. 1991).
    This model is also available in double action only (all finishes) at no extra charge.

MODEL P229 — .357 SIG (new 1995), 9mm Para. (new 1994), or .40 S&W cal., similar to Model P228, except has blackened stainless steel or nickel slide with aluminum alloy frame, 10 (C/B 1994) or 12* shot mag., includes lockable carrying case, 30½oz. New 1991.

Mfg.'s Sug. Retail	$875	$775	$650	$550	$475	$415	$360	$310

    Add $100 for Siglite night sights.
    Add $25 for nickel slide (new 1996).
    This model is also available in double action only at no extra charge.

MODEL P230 — .22 LR (disc.)-10 shot, .32 ACP-8 shot, .380 ACP-7 shot, or 9mm Ultra (disc.)-7 shot, 3.6 in. barrel, regular double action or double action only, blue, wood grips, 17.6 oz. Mfg. 1976-present.

Mfg.'s Sug. Retail	$510	$425	$375	$300	$270	$240	$215	$190

    Add $35 for stainless slide (.380 ACP only).

▲ *Model P230 SL Stainless* — similar to Model P230, except stainless steel construction, 22.4 oz.

Mfg.'s Sug. Retail	$595	$480	$425	$350

MODEL P239 — .357 SIG or 9mm Para. cal., regular double action or double action only, blackened stainless slide and aluminum alloy frame, firing pin lock safety, 3.6 in. barrel, 8 shot mag., fixed sights, 27½ oz. New 1996.

Mfg.'s Sug. Retail	$575	$475	$415	$325	$285	$255	$220	$195

    Add $100 for Siglite night sights.

Grading	100%	98%	95%	90%	80%	70%	60%

RIFLES

MODEL SSG 2000 — available in .223, 7.5mm Swiss, .300 Wby. Mag., or .308 (standard) cal., bolt action, 4 shot mag., no sights, deluxe sniper rifle featuring thumbhole style walnut stock with stippling and thumbwheel adj. cheekpiece, 13 lbs. Importation disc. 1986.

	$2,480	$2,260	$1,950	$1,700	$1,500	$1,300	$1,100

Last Mfg.'s Sug. Retail was $2,850.

This model was available in .223, .300 Wby. Mag., or 7.5mm cal. by special order only.

SILE DISTRIBUTORS

Distributor/importer/manufacturer located in New York, NY.

In addition to distributing a wide variety of firearms and related accessories (including the mfg. of stocks and grips), Sile Distributors also has had some firearms "private labeled" to their specifications.

SILMA SPORTING GUNS

Manufacturer located in Brescia, Italy since 1949. Currently, Silma does not have a domestic importer. To date, there has been limited importation into the U.S. All Silma Shotguns are high quality and utilize premium materials in their manufacture.

Rather than list the various shotgun models and options separately, the following information will help you in ascertaining correct values. Models 70 and 80 are O/U hunting models available in either 12, 20, or .410 ga. They are available with double triggers standard, extractors or ejectors (extra cost), with or without sideplates, or in superlight configuration - retail values range between $500-$1,000. Competition models (including T.J. 70, T.S. 81, Cobra T1, T2, or T3) are also available for trap, skeet, or sporting clays events. Values range between $1,000-$6,200 (with T.J. 70 being the least expensive, and Cobra T2 the most expensive). Two side by side models (AS/70 N and AS/70 FJ) are also available.

For further information regarding Silma's current model line-up, please contact either the Blue Book of Gun Values or the factory. To order a shotgun directly from the manufacturer, please contact them by FAX (refer to the Trademark Index) for more information and a firm price quotation.

SIRKIS INDUSTRIES, LTD.

Manufacturer located in Ramat-Gan, Israel. Previously imported and distributed by Armscorp of America, Inc. located in Baltimore, MD.

PISTOLS: SEMI-AUTO

S.D. 9 — 9mm Para., double action mechanism, frame is constructed mostly of heavy gauge sheet metal stampings, 3.07 in. barrel, parkerized finish, loaded chamber indicator, 7 shot mag., plastic grips, 24½ oz. Imported under this trademark between 1986-1988.

	$300	$250	$225	$200	$190	$180	$170

Last Mfg.'s Sug. Retail was $330.

This pistol is now listed under the Sardius heading in this section.

RIFLES

MODEL 35 MATCH RIFLE — .22 LR only, single shot bolt action, 26 in. full floating barrel, select walnut, match trigger, micrometer sights. Disc. 1985.

	$650	$625	$595	$550	$510	$460	$420

Last Mfg.'s Sug. Retail was $690.

Grading	100%	98%	95%	90%	80%	70%	60%

MODEL 36 SNIPER RIFLE — 7.62mm only, gas operated action, carbon fiber stock, 22 in. barrel, flash suppressor, free range sights. Disc. 1985.

	100%	98%	95%	90%	80%	70%	60%
	$670	$580	$520	$475	$430	$390	$350

Last Mfg.'s Sug. Retail was $760.

SKORPION

Please refer to Armitage International, Ltd. in the "A" section of this text.

SMITH, L.C.

Manufactured from 1880-1888 in Syracuse, NY. Manufactured in Fulton, NY 1890-1945 by Hunter Arms Company.

The L.C. Smith shotgun was made from 1890-1945 by the Hunter Arms Company in Fulton, New York. In 1946, the company was acquired by Marlin Firearms Company. Production continued until 1951 when it ceased for a period of 17 years. In 1968, Marlin brought the L.C. Smith back to life for a period of 5 years. Production stopped in 1973. The L.C. Smith is one of the finest American made shotguns and collector interest is very high. All values shown are for hammerless shotguns.

HAMMERLESS SHOTGUNS 1890-1913

All prices listed below are for guns with fluid steel barrels (except A-1 grade).

It is important to note that damascus barreled guns with hammers in 90% original condition or better are very collectible and values can approximate those of steel barrel models if the bore is excellent with no pitting. Damascus specimens below 90% condition are not as collectible, however, and values fall off rapidly if under 90%. Prices shown below for 90% and up condition are very difficult to evaluate and are meant as a guide only. L.C. Smith shotguns are rare and hard to evaluate if over 95% condition in the higher grades.

100%	98%	95%	90%	80%	70%	60%	50%	40%	30%	20%	10%

00 GRADE — 12, 16, or 20 ga. Approx. 60,000 mfg.

100%	98%	95%	90%	80%	70%	60%	50%	40%	30%	20%	10%
$1,500	$1,200	$800	$600	$500	$465	$430	$395	$375	$350	$325	$295

Add 33% for auto ejectors.
Add 50% for 20 ga.

O GRADE — 10, 12, 16, or 20 ga. Approx. 30,000 mfg.

100%	98%	95%	90%	80%	70%	60%	50%	40%	30%	20%	10%
$1,600	$1,400	$1,000	$775	$675	$600	$550	$515	$460	$400	$350	$300

Add 50% for 20 ga.

NO. 1 GRADE — 10, 12, 16, or 20 ga. Approx. 10,000 mfg.

100%	98%	95%	90%	80%	70%	60%	50%	40%	30%	20%	10%
$2,400	$1,950	$1,425	$995	$850	$750	$700	$625	$550	$495	$450	$400

Add 33% for auto ejectors.
Add 50% for 20 ga.
Add $200 for SST.

NO. 2 GRADE — 10, 12, 16, or 20 ga. Approx. 13,000 mfg.

100%	98%	95%	90%	80%	70%	60%	50%	40%	30%	20%	10%
$2,900	$2,275	$1,700	$1,400	$1,200	$1,000	$825	$750	$675	$600	$550	$500

Add 33% for auto ejectors.
Add 75% for 20 ga.
Add $200 for SST.

NO. 3 GRADE — 10, 12, 16, or 20 ga. Approx. 4,000 mfg.

100%	98%	95%	90%	80%	70%	60%	50%	40%	30%	20%	10%
$3,475	$2,950	$2,400	$1,850	$1,500	$1,300	$1,100	$995	$875	$775	$625	$500

Add 25% for auto ejectors.
Add 75% for 20 ga.
Add $200 for SST.

100%	98%	95%	90%	80%	70%	60%	50%	40%	30%	20%	10%

PIGEON GRADE — 10, 12, 16, or 20 ga. Approx. 1,200 mfg.

100%	98%	95%	90%	80%	70%	60%	50%	40%	30%	20%	10%
$3,475	$2,950	$2,400	$1,850	$1,500	$1,300	$1,100	$995	$875	$775	$625	$500

Add 25% for auto ejectors.
Add 75% for 20 ga.
Add $200 for SST.

NO. 4 GRADE — 10, 12, 16, or 20 ga. Approx. 500 mfg., seldomly encountered.

$10,000	$8,000	$5,750	$4,500	$3,500	$2,650	$2,000	$1,775	$1,500	$1,375	$1,200	$1,095

Add 25% for auto ejectors.
Add 75% for 20 ga.
Add $200 for SST.

A-1 GRADE — 10, 12, or 16 ga. Approx. 700 mfg. Damascus barrels only.

$4,850	$3,700	$3,000	$2,200	$1,850	$1,725	$1,425	$1,175	$995	$800	$700	$600

Auto ejectors standard.
Add $200 for SST.

NO. 5 GRADE — 10, 12, 16, or 20 ga. Approx. 500 mfg.

$9,000	$7,000	$4,950	$4,500	$4,000	$3,500	$3,150	$2,700	$2,450	$2,200	$1,995	$1,800

Auto ejectors standard.
Add $200 for SST.
Add 75% for 20 ga., extremely rare.

MONOGRAM GRADE — 10, 12, 16, or 20 ga. Approx. 100 mfg.

$10,750	$9,475	$7,400	$6,000	$5,500	$5,000	$4,600	$4,100	$3,800	$3,500	$3,250	$3,000

Auto ejectors standard.
Add 50% for 20 ga., extremely rare.

A-2 GRADE — 10, 12, 16, or 20 ga. Approx. 200 mfg.

$15,000	$11,000	$8,000	$7,000	$6,000	$5,200	$4,700	$4,200	$3,850	$3,500	$3,250	$3,000

Auto ejectors standard.
20 ga. — only 6 mfg.

A-3 GRADE — 10, 12, 16, or 20 ga. Approx. 20 mfg. Rarity precludes accurate pricing on this model.
Auto ejectors standard.
20 ga. — only 2 mfg.

SHOTGUNS: 1914-1951 MFG.

Fulton trademarked shotguns mfg. by Hunter Arms Co. were inexpensive, utilitarian shotguns designed for a price point rather than quality. Models Fulton and Fulton Special were supplied in 12, 16, 20, or .410 ga. (rare). When encountered today, values usually are in the $100-$300 range. The Hunter Special, although not an L.C. Smith shotgun, did employ the rotary locking bolt system. This was also a low priced gun in its day and prices today are usually in the $125-$350 range. These models had nothing in common with the L.C. Smith shotguns of that time.

L.C. SMITH DOUBLE BARREL SHOTGUN — 12, 16, 20, or .410 ga., any choke, sidelock, auto ejectors standard from Crown Grade up, extractors on lower grades, double or single triggers, straight, ½ pistol grip, or pistol grip stock, grade specifications differ in grade of wood, degree of engraving, and overall quality. Featherweight models were also manufactured on a regular basis and are so marked - values will approximate those listed below for standard models.

STANDARD FIELD GRADE

$1,250	$1,000	$775	$675	$600	$500	$465	$435	$395	$375	$340	$295

Add 33% for auto ejectors.
Add $200 for SST.
Add 30% for 20 ga.
Add 300% for .410 ga.

	100%	98%	95%	90%	80%	70%	60%	50%	40%	30%	20%	10%

IDEAL GRADE STANDARD
$1,600	$1,400	$1,100	$900	$825	$750	$700	$650	$595	$550	$530	$495

Add 33% for auto ejectors.
Add $200 for SST.
Add 30% for 20 ga.
Add 400% for .410 ga.

TRAP GRADE
$2,000	$1,500	$1,200	$1,100	$1,000	$925	$850	$775	$675	$600	$550	$500

Auto ejectors — add 33%.
Add $200 for SST.
Add 50% for 20 ga.
Add 400% for .410 ga.

SPECIALTY GRADE
$2,950	$2,450	$1,800	$1,375	$1,100	$1,000	$925	$875	$825	$775	$695	$625

Add $200 for SST.
Add 50% for 20 ga.
Add 400% for .410 ga.
Add 33% for auto ejectors.

EAGLE GRADE
$4,750	$4,250	$3,500	$2,900	$2,350	$1,850	$1,500	$1,400	$1,300	$1,200	$1,100	$1,000

Add $200 for SST.
Add 50% for 20 ga.

SKEET SPECIAL GRADE
$3,100	$2,600	$1,650	$1,200	$1,100	$925	$875	$825	$775	$725	$675	$600

Add $200 for SST.
Add 50% for 20 ga.
Add 400% for .410 ga.
Add 33% for auto ejectors.

PREMIER SKEET GRADE
$3,100	$2,600	$1,650	$1,200	$1,100	$925	$875	$825	$775	$725	$675	$600

Add $200 for SST.
Add 50% for 20 ga.
Add 400% for .410 ga.
Add 33% for auto ejectors.

CROWN GRADE
$5,750	$4,950	$4,250	$4,000	$3,500	$3,100	$2,700	$2,450	$2,225	$2,000	$1,900	$1,800

Add $200 for SST.
20 gauge — very rare.
.410 — rare and very expensive, only 6 mfg.

MONOGRAM GRADE
$12,000	$9,750	$7,750	$6,400	$5,650	$5,100	$4,650	$4,150	$3,775	$3,500	$3,250	$3,000

Add 50% for 20 ga.

PREMIER GRADE — very limited mfg., rarity precludes accurate pricing on this model.

DELUXE GRADE — very limited mfg., rarity precludes accurate pricing on this model.

SINGLE BARREL TRAP GUN — 12 ga. only, 32 or 34 in. VR barrel, boxlock, auto ejector, checkered pistol grip stock, recoil pad. Approx. 2,650 mfg. 1917-1951.

▲ *Olympic Grade*
$1,650	$1,400	$1,200	$1,100	$1,000	$900	$800	$725	$675	$625	$575	$550

▲ *Specialty Grade*
$1,950	$1,700	$1,500	$1,400	$1,300	$1,200	$1,125	$1,075	$1,000	$925	$875	$800

▲ *Crown Grade*
$3,450	$3,125	$2,750	$2,350	$2,100	$2,000	$1,900	$1,800	$1,700	$1,600	$1,500	$1,400

100%	98%	95%	90%	80%	70%	60%	50%	40%	30%	20%	10%
▲ *Monogram Grade*											
$6,000	$5,000	$4,250	$3,700	$3,150	$2,750	$2,400	$2,150	$2,000	$1,850	$1,700	$1,525
▲ *Premier Grade*											
$9,750	$8,350	$6,400	$5,275	$3,850	$3,300	$2,900	$2,600	$2,350	$2,100	$1,900	$1,750
▲ *Deluxe Grade*											
$13,950	$12,000	$9,995	$7,850	$6,000	$5,000	$4,500	$3,995	$3,375	$2,900	$2,500	$2,150

Grading					100%	98%	95%	90%	80%	70%	60%

1968-1973 MFG.

1968 SxS MODEL — 12 ga., 28 in. VR barrel, full and mod. choke, sidelock, extractors, double triggers, checkered pistol grip stock. Mfg. 1968-1973 by Marlin.

$725	$600	$550	$495	$425	$350	$275

1968 SxS DELUXE MODEL — similar to Standard, with Simmons floating rib, beavertail forearm. Mfg. 1971-1973 by Marlin.

$995	$825	$725	$600	$495	$400	$350

SMITH & WESSON

Manufacturer located in Springfield, MA 1857 to date. S & W became a subsidiary of Bangor-Punta from 1957-1983. Between 1983-1987 Smith & Wesson was owned by the Lear Siegler Co. On May 22, 1987 Smith & Wesson was sold to Tompkins, an English holding company.

In this 17th Edition, the Smith & Wesson section format has been revised - hopefully, for easier use. Smith & Wessons have been classified into the following groups - TIP-UPS, TOP-BREAKS, SINGLE SHOTS, EARLY HAND EJECTORS (Named Models), NUMBERED MODEL REVOLVERS (Modern Hand Ejectors), SEMI-AUTOS, RIFLES, and SHOTGUNS.

Each category is fairly self-explanatory. Among the early revolvers, Tip-ups have barrels that tip up so the cylinder can be removed for loading or unloading, whereas Top-breaks have barrels & cylinders that tip down with automatic ejection.

Hand Ejectors are the modern type revolvers with swing out cylinders. In 1958 S&W began a system of numbering all models they made. Accordingly, the Hand Ejectors have been divided into two sections - the Early Hand Ejectors include the named models introduced prior to 1958. The Numbered Model Revolvers are the models introduced or continued after that date, and are easily identified by the model number stamped on the front of the frame, visible when the cylinder is open. Editor's note: Jim Supica is to be thanked for this new format on Smith & Wesson information.

TIP-UPS

Spur-trigger rimfires, these include the earliest S&W revolvers, made 1857-1881. A latch at the bottom front of the frame allows the hinged barrel to be tipped up and the cylinder removed for loading and unloading. These pistols are listed in order of model number (1, 1½, 2).

100%	98%	95%	90%	80%	70%	60%	50%	40%	30%	20%	10%

MODEL NO. 1 FIRST ISSUE TIP-UP — .22 Short, single action, 7 shot non-fluted cylinder, 3³⁄₁₆ in. octagon barrel, bottom break, spur trigger, silver-plated brass frame, blue barrel and cylinder, square rosewood grips, circular sideplate, cross-section of frame is oval with rounded frame sides. 11,671 mfg. 1857-1860.

▲ *First Type* — serial range approx. 1-200.

$7,000	$6,450	$5,650	$4,750	$4,150	$3,875	$3,625	$3,275	$2,925	$2,500	$1,950	$1,650

S

100%	98%	95%	90%	80%	70%	60%	50%	40%	30%	20%	10%

▲ *Second Type* — serial range approx. 200-1130.

| $6,000 | $5,450 | $4,500 | $3,500 | $2,750 | $2,100 | $1,900 | $1,750 | $1,600 | $1,450 | $1,300 | $1,150 |

▲ *Third Type* — serial range approx. 1130-3000.

| $2,950 | $2,600 | $2,275 | $1,925 | $1,750 | $1,600 | $1,500 | $1,400 | $1,300 | $1,200 | $1,100 | $1,025 |

▲ *Fourth Type* — serial range approx. 3000-4200.

| $2,300 | $1,850 | $1,700 | $1,600 | $1,450 | $1,300 | $1,200 | $1,125 | $1,050 | $975 | $925 | $900 |

▲ *Fifth Type* — serial range approx. 4200-5500.

| $2,300 | $1,950 | $1,700 | $1,600 | $1,450 | $1,300 | $1,200 | $1,125 | $1,050 | $975 | $925 | $900 |

▲ *Sixth Type* — serial range approx. 5500-11,671.

| $2,150 | $1,800 | $1,550 | $1,450 | $1,300 | $1,175 | $1,075 | $1,000 | $925 | $875 | 8215 | $800 |

MODEL NO. 1 SECOND ISSUE TIP-UP — similar to First Issue, except flat sided frame and irregular shaped sideplate. 117,000 mfg. 1860-1868. Serial range approx. 11,672- approx. 128,000.

| $950 | $875 | $825 | $795 | $755 | $700 | $625 | $575 | $525 | $475 | $425 | $390 |

▲ *Second Quality* — is marked on approx. 4,402 revolvers.

| $1,250 | $1,100 | $1,000 | $925 | $850 | $775 | $700 | $625 | $575 | $525 | $475 | $435 |

MODEL NO. 1 THIRD ISSUE TIP-UP — similar to Second Issue, except fluted cylinder, round barrel, and birdshead grip. 131,163 mfg. 1868-1881. This model has its own serial range no. 1-131,163.

▲ $3\frac{3}{16}$ *in. barrel Model.* — will have markings on top of barrel.

| $475 | $435 | $400 | $375 | $350 | $325 | $300 | $275 | $250 | $225 | $200 | $175 |

▲ *Short barrels* $2^{11}\!/_{16}$ - $2\frac{3}{4}$ *in.* — will have markings on side of barrel.

| $900 | $850 | $775 | $720 | $680 | $640 | $600 | $560 | $520 | $480 | $440 | $400 |

MODEL NO. 1½ FIRST ISSUE TIP-UP — .32 rimfire, single action, 3½ or 4 (rare) in. octagon barrel, 5 shot non-fluted cylinder, bottom break, spur trigger, blue or nickel, rosewood grips, square butt. 26,300 mfg. 1865-1868. Serial range 1- approx. 26,300.

| $575 | $500 | $435 | $375 | $325 | $300 | $275 | $250 | $225 | $210 | $195 | $185 |

▲ *4 in. barrel*

| $3,500 | $3,150 | $2,750 | $2,300 | $1,950 | $1,650 | $1,450 | 1,250 | $1,050 | $900 | $775 | $650 |

Watch for fakes (i.e. stretched barrels).

MODEL NO. 1½ SECOND ISSUE TIP-UP — similar to First Issue, with birdshead grips and round barrel. 100,700 mfg. 1868-1875. Serial range 26,301-127,100.

▲ *2½ in. barrel model* — barrel markings on side, length varies from 2½-2¾ in. (scarce).

| $600 | $525 | $450 | $385 | $365 | $335 | $305 | $275 | $250 | $225 | $200 | $180 |

▲ *3½ in. barrel model*

| $425 | $385 | $335 | $300 | $275 | $250 | $225 | $200 | $180 | $165 | $150 | $135 |

▲ *Transitional Model* — octagon barrel with birdshead grips, serial range 27,200-28,800, rare.

| $2,000 | $1,750 | $1,525 | $1,425 | $1,350 | $1,275 | $1,200 | $1,125 | $1,075 | $1,000 | $950 | $900 |

MODEL NO. 2 ARMY TIP-UP — .32 rimfire long, similar in appearance to No. 1½ First Issue, except 6 shot cylinder, different barrel lengths, used as a sidearm during Civil War. 77,155 mfg. 1861-1874. Serial number range 1-77,155.

▲ *5 or 6 in. Early Model* — referred to as 2-pin variation, serial range 1-3,000.

| $1,950 | $1,750 | $1,550 | $1,375 | $1,225 | $1,125 | $1,025 | $925 | $825 | $750 | $675 | $600 |

▲ *5 or 6 in. Standard Model* — remainder of serial range.

| $1,375 | $1,225 | $1,100 | $1,000 | $900 | $800 | $700 | $625 | $525 | $450 | $400 | $375 |

▲ *4 in. Barrel Model*

| $2,750 | $2,500 | $2,150 | $1,850 | $1,650 | $1,550 | $1,450 | $1,350 | $1,250 | $1,100 | $975 | $875 |

Note: Watch for fakes on 4 in. model.

100%	98%	95%	90%	80%	70%	60%	50%	40%	30%	20%	10%

TOP-BREAKS

These revolvers have a latch just in front of the hammer, and the barrel & cylinder tip down, with an automatic extractor ejecting the shells when the gun is opened. Mfg 1870-1940, they include single action (spur-trigger or triggerguard), double action, and safety hammerless designs. They are listed in order of frame size. Model 1-1/2 is the smallest or .32 cal. sized frame; Model 2 is the medium or .38 cal. sized frame; Model 3 is the large or .44 cal. frame. Within each frame size, they are listed by action type - SA, DA, or "Hammerless", as may be applicable.

.32 SINGLE ACTION — .32 S&W, spur trigger, top break, rebounding hammer, auto extraction. 97,574 mfg. 1878-1892. Serial range 1-97,574.

▲ *Early Model* — without strain screw, serial range 1-6,500.

100%	98%	95%	90%	80%	70%	60%	50%	40%	30%	20%	10%
$435	$390	$350	$315	$285	$255	$225	$195	$170	$145	$125	$110

▲ *Later Model* — with strain screw, remainder of serial range.

100%	98%	95%	90%	80%	70%	60%	50%	40%	30%	20%	10%
$375	$330	$295	$265	$230	$205	$180	$155	$135	$125	$115	$100

▲ *8 or 10 in. barrel* — mfg. circa 1887-88, very rare.

100%	98%	95%	90%	80%	70%	60%	50%	40%	30%	20%	10%
$3,000	$2,600	$2,200	$1,800	$1,600	$1,475	$1,350	$1,225	$1,000	$1,000	$900	$800

.32 DOUBLE ACTION FIRST MODEL TOP BREAK — .32 S&W, 5 shot fluted cylinder, 3 in. round barrel, square edged side plate, blue or nickel finish, black rubber grips, one of the rarest of all S&Ws. Only 30 mfg. 1880. Serial range 1-30.

100%	98%	95%	90%	80%	70%	60%	50%	40%	30%	20%	10%
$5,500	$5,000	$4,350	$3,800	$3,400	$3,100	$2,800	$2,550	$2,350	$2,100	$1,900	$1,750

.32 DOUBLE ACTION SECOND MODEL — similar to First Model, except irregular shaped sideplate, 3, 3¼, 4, 5, or 6 in. barrel, 22,142 mfg. 1880-1882. Serial range 31-22,172.

100%	98%	95%	90%	80%	70%	60%	50%	40%	30%	20%	10%
$475	$425	$380	$340	$300	$260	$220	$180	$150	$120	$100	$90

.32 DOUBLE ACTION THIRD MODEL — similar to Second Model, except without groove around cylinder. 22,232 mfg. 1882-1883. Serial range 22,173-43,405.

100%	98%	95%	90%	80%	70%	60%	50%	40%	30%	20%	10%
$475	$425	$380	$340	$300	$260	$220	$180	$150	$120	$100	$90

.32 DOUBLE ACTION FOURTH MODEL — similar to Third Model, except rounded triggerguard. 239,600 mfg. 1883-1909. Serial range 43,406-approx. 282,999.

100%	98%	95%	90%	80%	70%	60%	50%	40%	30%	20%	10%
$345	$305	$270	$240	$210	$185	$160	$135	$115	$100	$90	$85

An 8 or 10 in. on this model will command a premium.

.32 DOUBLE ACTION FIFTH MODEL — similar to Fourth Model, except integral front sight. 44,641 mfg. 1909-1919. Serial range approx. 28,300-327,641.

100%	98%	95%	90%	80%	70%	60%	50%	40%	30%	20%	10%
$375	$335	$300	$270	$240	$215	$190	$165	$135	$120	$105	$90

.32 SAFETY HAMMERLESS FIRST MODEL (LEMON SQUEEZER) TOP BREAK — .32 S&W cal., 5 shot fluted cylinder, 2, 3 (most common), 3½, or 6 (rare) in. round barrel, blue or nickel, black rubber grips. This model was dubbed New Departure at the time. 91,417 mfg. 1888-1902. Serial range 1-91,417.

Short 2 in. barrel versions known as "Bicycle model" will bring 25% to 50% premium on all Lemon Squeezers. Six inch barrels will bring a premium as well.

▲ *Standard Model* — 2, 3, or 3½ in. barrel.

100%	98%	95%	90%	80%	70%	60%	50%	40%	30%	20%	10%
$500	$475	$450	$425	$400	$375	$350	$325	$275	$235	$185	$150

.32 SAFETY HAMMERLESS SECOND MODEL — 2, 3, 3½, or 6 in. barrel. 78,500 mfg. 1902-1909. Serial range 91,418-170,000.

100%	98%	95%	90%	80%	70%	60%	50%	40%	30%	20%	10%
$450	$425	$400	$375	$350	$325	$300	$275	$235	$200	$165	$130

.32 SAFETY HAMMERLESS THIRD MODEL — 2 (Bicycle Model), 3, 3½, or 6 in. barrel. 73,000 mfg. 1909-1937. Serial range 163,082-242,981 (with some overlap from the Second Model).

100%	98%	95%	90%	80%	70%	60%	50%	40%	30%	20%	10%
$450	$425	$400	$375	$350	$325	$300	$275	$235	$200	$165	$130

100%	98%	95%	90%	80%	70%	60%	50%	40%	30%	20%	10%

.38 SINGLE ACTION FIRST MODEL (BABY RUSSIAN) TOP BREAK SPUR TRIGGER — .38 S&W cal., 5 shot fluted cylinder, $3\frac{1}{4}$ or 4 in. barrel, blue with wood grips, nickel with "S&W" monogram hard rubber grips. 25,548 mfg. 1876-1877. Serial range 1-25,548.

▲ *Standard Model*

| $625 | $525 | $450 | $400 | $365 | $330 | $295 | $260 | $235 | $200 | $185 | $150 |

▲ *Very Early Model* — with early hammer style safety latch (up to approx. ser. no. 100).

| $2,500 | $2,250 | $2,000 | $1,750 | $1,450 | $1,150 | $950 | $800 | $700 | $600 | $500 | $400 |

This type of hammer configuration is called the "Aldrich" model.

▲ *Early Model* — having two screws to hold sideplate (up to approx. ser. no. 2,550).

| $735 | $625 | $550 | $500 | $465 | $425 | $390 | $355 | $320 | $285 | $250 | $235 |

.38 SINGLE ACTION SECOND MODEL — similar to above, except very short ejector housing under barrel, cal. and cylinder same as above, $3\frac{1}{4}$, 4, 5, 6, 8, or 10 in. barrel, grips same as above. 108,225 mfg. 1877-1891. Serial range 1-108,255.

▲ *Standard Model*

| $335 | $275 | $235 | $200 | $185 | $160 | $150 | $140 | $130 | $125 | $120 | $115 |

▲ *8 or 10 in. Barrel*

| $2,500 | $2,200 | $1,800 | $1,575 | $1,375 | $1,200 | $1,050 | $950 | $850 | $775 | $700 | $650 |

.38 SINGLE ACTION THIRD MODEL (MODEL OF 1891) — similar to above, except has trigger-guard, cal. and cylinder same as above, also accepts the single shot barrel, $3\frac{1}{2}$, 4, 5, or 6 in. barrel, blue or nickel finish with "S&W" monogram, hard rubber grips. 26,850 mfg. 1891-1911. Serial range 1-28,107 which also includes the serial number range of the Single Shot First Model in .38 S&W cal. and the .38 S.A. Mexican Model described below. Barrel marked "Model of 1891".

| $1,800 | $1,650 | $1,425 | $1,250 | $1,075 | $950 | $850 | $775 | $700 | $625 | $550 | $475 |

Add 50%-75% for single shot barrel with matching serial number.

.38 SINGLE ACTION MEXICAN MODEL — essentially same as above, except has spur trigger, .38 S&W cal., 5 shot fluted cylinder, $3\frac{1}{4}$, 4, 5, or 6 in. barrel, blue or nickel finish, "S&W" monogram checkered hard rubber or walnut grips. Features unique to this model are flat sided hammer half cock notch and "inserted" spur trigger assembly (not integral with frame). This model would also accept the single shot barrel, limited mfg. 1891-1911. Serial range described above. Watch out for fakes!

| $2,875 | $2,550 | $2,250 | $2,000 | $1,750 | $1,550 | $1,400 | $1,250 | $1,150 | $1,050 | $975 | $950 |

Add 50%-75% for single shot barrel with matching serial number.

.38 DOUBLE ACTION FIRST MODEL TOP BREAK — .38 S&W cal., 5 shot fluted cylinder, $3\frac{1}{4}$ or 4 in. barrel, blue or nickel finish, "S&W" monogram checkered hard rubber grips. 4,000 mfg. 1880. Serial range 1-4,000.

| $900 | $850 | $750 | $650 | $550 | $475 | $400 | $325 | $250 | $200 | $150 | $125 |

.38 DOUBLE ACTION SECOND MODEL — .38 S&W cal., cylinder same as above, $3\frac{1}{4}$, 4, 5, or 6 in. barrel, blue or nickel finish, "S&W" monogram checkered hard rubber grips in black or red. 115,000 mfg. 1880-1884. Serial range approx. 4,001-approx. 119,000.

| $350 | $275 | $235 | $200 | $175 | $155 | $135 | $120 | $110 | $100 | $90 | $85 |

A 2 in. variation, while extremely rare, was manufactured in this Second Model, Third Model, Fourth Model, Fifth Model, and Perfected Models listed below. Large premiums do exist ($850-$1,500) - watch for fakes!

.38 DOUBLE ACTION THIRD MODEL — .38 S&W cal., cylinder same as above, $3\frac{1}{4}$, 4, 5, 6, 8, or 10 in. barrel, blue or nickel finish, "S&W" monogram hard rubber grips. 203,700 mfg. 1884-1895. Serial range approx. 119,001-322,700.

| $325 | $265 | $225 | $190 | $170 | $150 | $135 | $120 | $110 | $100 | $90 | $85 |

▲ *8 or 10 in. Barrel*

| $2,150 | $1,850 | $1,600 | $1,400 | $1,250 | $1,125 | $1,000 | $900 | $800 | $700 | $600 | $535 |

100%	98%	95%	90%	80%	70%	60%	50%	40%	30%	20%	10%

.38 DOUBLE ACTION FOURTH MODEL — .38 S&W cal., cylinder same as above, 3¼, 4, 5, or 6 in. barrel, blue or nickel finish, "S&W" monogram checkered hard rubber grips, also offered in an extended square butt target style. 216,300 mfg. 1895-1901. Serial range 322,701-539,000.

$325	$270	$230	$200	$175	$155	$135	$120	$110	$100	$90	$85

.38 DOUBLE ACTION FIFTH MODEL — .38 S&W cal., cylinder, barrel, and grip specifications same as above with the additional availability of an extended square butt target style walnut grip as an option. 15,000 mfg. 1909-1911. Serial range approx. 539,001-554,077.

$500	$465	$425	$375	$325	$285	$250	$225	$200	$180	$150	$125

.38 DOUBLE ACTION PERFECTED MODEL TOP BREAK — .38 S&W cal., cylinder, barrel and grip specifications same as above, triggerguard is integral part of frame, and side plate is on right side - not left side. The last of the S&W break open revolvers. 59,400 mfg. 1909-1920. Serial range 1-59,400. Identified by having both top latch and side latch.

$500	$465	$425	$375	$325	$285	$250	$225	$200	$180	$150	$125

This model was mfg. with 2 latches (side latch and top latch).

▲ **.38 Double Action Perfected Model Top Latch Only** — as above, except no side latch - rare.

$1,250	$1,125	$975	$850	$750	$650	$550	$440	$350	$275	$235	$200

.38 SAFETY HAMMERLESS FIRST MODEL (.38 NEW DEPARTURE) OR "LEMON SQUEEZER" TOP BREAK — .38 S&W cal., 5 shot fluted cylinder, 3¼, 4, 5, or 6 in. barrel, blue or nickel finish, "S&W" monogram checkered hard rubber grips. Approx. 5,125 mfg. in 1887. Serial range 1-5,250 which reflects an overlap with the .38 Safety Second Model D.A.

$750	$685	$615	$550	$485	$435	$375	$325	$275	$250	$225	$150

Add 25% for blue finish.

▲ **6 in. Barrel**

$1,450	$1,200	$1,025	$900	$790	$675	$565	$490	$425	$375	$340	$310

.38 SAFETY HAMMERLESS SECOND MODEL — .38 S&W cal., cylinder same as above, 3¼, 4, or 5 in. barrel, finish and grips same as above. 37,350 mfg. 1887-1890. Serial range approx. 5,001-42,483 which reflects some overlap from the First Model listed above.

$500	$465	$425	$375	$325	$285	$250	$225	$200	$180	$150	$125

U.S. MARTIALLY MARKED — 100 purchased by Govt. in 1890, serial range 41,333-41,470.

$5,000	$4,650	$4,400	$4,050	$3,750	$3,500	$3,300	$3,150	$2,950	$2,750	$2,550	$2,350

Beware of fakes!

.38 SAFETY HAMMERLESS THIRD MODEL — .38 S&W cal., cylinder same as above, 3¼, 4, 5, or 6 in. barrel, finish and grips same as above. 73,500 mfg. 1890-1898. Serial range 24,284-116,002.

$400	$375	$330	$300	$275	$250	$225	$200	$175	$150	$135	$110

.38 SAFETY HAMMERLESS FOURTH MODEL — .38 S&W cal., cylinder, barrel lengths, finishes and grips same as above. 104,000 mfg. 1898-1907. Serial range 116,003 to approx. 220,000 reflecting some overlap with the Fifth Model from approx. 216,500- 223,100.

$340	$280	$240	$205	$190	$165	$155	$145	$135	$125	$115	$100

A 2 in. barrel in this variation is rare (Bicycle Model).

.38 SAFETY HAMMERLESS FIFTH MODEL — .38 S&W cal., cylinder same as above, 2, 3¼, 4, 5, or 6 in. barrel, blue or nickel finish, "S&W" monogram checkered hard rubber or checkered walnut grips. 41,500 mfg. 1907-1940. Serial range 220,000-261,493 reflecting some overlap with Fourth Model listed above from 216,500-223,100.

$340	$280	$240	$205	$190	$165	$155	$145	$135	$125	$115	$100

▲ **2 in. Barrel**

$825	$750	$670	$635	$575	$540	$505	$480	$455	$432	$410	$390

100%	98%	95%	90%	80%	70%	60%	50%	40%	30%	20%	10%

MODEL 3 AMERICAN FIRST MODEL

MODEL 3 AMERICAN FIRST MODEL — .44 S&W or .44 rimfire Henry cal., single action, 6 shot fluted cylinder, 6, 7, or 8 in. round barrel, blue or nickel finish, walnut grips. 8,000 mfg. 1870-1872. Serial range 1-approx. 8,000.

▲ *Standard Model* — vent. hole in extractor housing, first 1,500 mfg.

	100%	98%	95%	90%	80%	70%	60%	50%	40%	30%	20%	10%
	N/A	$6,000	$5,000	$4,250	$3,700	$3,175	$2,750	$2,500	$2,250	$2,000	$1,750	$1,500

▲ *Standard Model* — without hole in extractor.

	N/A	$4,000	$3,450	$2,975	$2,550	$2,250	$2,150	$1,850	$1,650	$1,450	$1,250	$1,100

▲ *Transitional Model* — includes locking notch on hammer, shorter cylinder, serial range 6,700-8,000.

	N/A	$4,500	$4,000	$3,525	$3,050	$2,650	$2,250	$2,150	$1,850	$1,650	$1,450	$1,200

▲ *.44 Rimfire Henry* — limited mfg. Watch for fakes!

	N/A	$6,000	$5,000	$4,000	$3,750	$3,500	$3,250	$3,000	$2,750	$2,500	$2,250	$2,000

▲ *U.S. Marked* — approx. 1,000 mfg.

	N/A	$12,000	$10,750	$9,100	$8,100	$7,250	$6,500	$5,900	$5,375	$4,850	$4,450	$4,000

▲ *Nashville Police* — very rare, only 32 manufactured. Scarcity precludes accurate pricing.

MODEL 3 SECOND MODEL AMERICAN

MODEL 3 SECOND MODEL AMERICAN — .44 S&W or .44 rimfire Henry cal., single action, 6 shot fluted cylinder, 5½, 6, 6½, 7, or 8 in. barrel, blue or nickel, walnut grips. 20,735 mfg. 1872-1874, serial range approx. 8,000-32,800 which includes commercial version of Model 3 Russian First Model.

▲ *Standard Model* — .44 S&W, American cal., 8 in. barrel.

	N/A	$4,000	$3,450	$2,975	$2,550	$2,250	$2,150	$1,850	$1,650	$1,450	$1,250	$1,100

Add 35% for 5½, 6, 6½, or 7 in. barrel.

▲ *Standard Model .44 Rimfire Henry* — 6, 7, or 8 in. barrel, 3,014 mfg.

	N/A	$5,000	$4,500	$4,000	$3,525	$3,050	$2,650	$2,250	$2,150	$1,850	$1,650	$1,450

MODEL 3 RUSSIAN FIRST MODEL (OLD OLD RUSSIAN)

MODEL 3 RUSSIAN FIRST MODEL (OLD OLD RUSSIAN) — .44 S&W Russian, 5½, 6, 7, or 8 in. barrel, Russian contract 8 in., blue or nickel finish, walnut grips, looks similar to First and Second Model American. 5,165 mfg. 1871-1874 for commercial sale and 20,014 for Russian Contract. Serial range 6,000-32,800, see Model 3 Second Model American.

▲ *Commercial Version* — 4,665 mfg.

$3,000	$2,750	$2,550	$2,350	$2,100	$1,900	$1,700	$1,500	$1,375	$1,275	$1,175	$1,075

▲ *Reject Russian Contract* — 500 mfg. Serial range 1-approx. 2,000.

$3,500	$3,250	$2,975	$2,750	$2,450	$2,275	$2,000	$1,850	$1,775	$1,675	$1,595	$1,500

▲ *Russian Contract* — 20,014 mfg., rare, most sent to Russia, cryllic marked. Serial range 1-approx. 20,014.

	N/A	N/A	$6,750	$5,975	$5,125	$4,450	$3,800	$3,350	$2,950	$2,600	$2,250	$2,000

MODEL 3 RUSSIAN SECOND MODEL (OLD RUSSIAN)

MODEL 3 RUSSIAN SECOND MODEL (OLD RUSSIAN) — 2nd and 3rd Model Russians have an extreme knuckle at the top of backstrap and triggerguard spur, 85,200 mfg. in all variations between 1873-78, 7 in. barrel, small screw in top-strap of frame, features longer ejector housing.

▲ *Commercial Version* — 6,200 mfg.

	N/A	$2,750	$2,500	$2,250	$2,000	$1,750	$1,500	$1,300	$1,000	$925	$800	$700

▲ *.44 Rimfire Henry* — approx. 500 mfg.

	N/A	$5,000	$4,500	$4,000	$3,525	$3,050	$2,650	$2,250	$2,150	$1,850	$1,650	$1,500

▲ *Russian Contract* — approx. 70,000 mfg. for Russian Military contract, cryllic marked, rare in U.S.

	N/A	N/A	$3,150	$2,850	$2,525	$2,275	$2,100	$1,950	$1,800	$1,650	$1,500	$1,350

▲ *Turkish Model* — 1,000 mfg. in their own serial number range in .44 Rimfire. This is probably the rarest and most valuable variation.

	N/A	N/A	$5,000	$4,500	$4,000	$3,600	$3,250	$2,900	$2,675	$2,475	$2,250	$2,000

▲ *Japanese Contract* — marked with an anchor.

	N/A	N/A	$2,925	$2,600	$2,300	$2,050	$1,825	$1,650	$1,500	$1,375	$1,250	$1,175

100%	98%	95%	90%	80%	70%	60%	50%	40%	30%	20%	10%

MODEL 3 RUSSIAN THIRD MODEL — commonly called the "New Model Russian" and is similar to old model, except has shorter extractor housing, 6½ in. barrel, large knurled screw in top-strap of frame, shorter ejector housing, approx. 60,600 mfg. between 1874 and 1878. Values are similar to old model for comparable variations. In addition, the Tula Arsenal in Russia also mfg. 300,000-400,000 pistols for domestic use and Ludwig Loewe in Germany mfg. 100,000.

▲ *Commercial Version* — approx. 13,500 mfg.

| N/A | $2,750 | $2,500 | $2,250 | $2,000 | $1,750 | $1,500 | $1,300 | $1,050 | $900 | $795 | $675 |

▲ *.44 Rimfire Henry*

| N/A | $5,000 | $4,500 | $4,000 | $3,525 | $3,050 | $2,650 | $2,250 | $2,150 | $1,850 | $1,650 | $1,500 |

▲ *Russian Contract* — 41,138 mfg. Cyrillic lettering.

| N/A | $3,500 | $3,200 | $2,900 | $2,650 | $2,400 | $2,200 | $2,000 | $1,775 | $1,575 | $1,325 | $1,100 |

▲ *Ludwig & Loewe, & Tula Copies* — copies mfg. for the Russian government.

| N/A | $2,800 | $2,500 | $2,250 | $2,000 | $1,800 | $1,625 | $1,475 | $1,350 | $1,225 | $1,100 | $950 |

Add 50% for Tula copies.

▲ *Turkish Contract* — 5,000 mfg., utilizes .44 Russian cylinder - chambered for .44 Rimfire.

| N/A | $4,000 | $3,700 | $3,425 | $3,100 | $2,850 | $2,575 | $2,325 | $2,025 | $1,700 | $1,425 | $1,200 |

▲ *Japanese Contract* — 1,000 made.

| N/A | $2,600 | $2,300 | $2,000 | $1,800 | $1,625 | $1,475 | $1,350 | $1,225 | $1,100 | $950 | $800 |

NEW MODEL NO. 3 — features very short extractor housing under the barrel, knuckle on backstrap is less pronounced than 2nd and 3rd Models, 35,796 mfg. between 1878-1912.

▲ *Commercial Version* — 3½, 4, 5, 6, 6½, 7, or 8 in. barrel, .44 Russian cal.

| $9,950 | $9,250 | $8,675 | $8,000 | $7,150 | $6,300 | $5,400 | $4,600 | $3,800 | $2,900 | $1,900 | $875 |

Add 10% if cut for shoulder stock.
Add 40% for shoulder stock.
Add 50% for factory target sights.

Early model has rack and gear extractor and will bring a premium over the later mfg. Also, premiums do exist for all but 6 and 6½ in. barrel lengths; premiums for unusual chamberings.

▲ *Japanese Navy Model* — anchor on frame or butt, several marking variations exist.

| $2,950 | $2,650 | $2,300 | $2,000 | $1,800 | $1,625 | $1,475 | $1,325 | $1,175 | $900 | $775 | $650 |

▲ *Australian Model* — 7 in. barrel, detachable stock, for Australian Colonial Police, broad arrow marking, 200 mfg.

| $3,350 | $2,975 | $2,625 | $2,350 | $2,250 | $2,150 | $2,050 | $1,950 | $1,850 | $1,750 | $1,650 | $1,575 |

▲ *Argentine Model* — 2,000 mfg., marked "Ejercito Argentina" (very rare).

| $5,000 | $4,675 | $4,350 | $4,050 | $3,750 | $3,450 | $3,150 | $2,850 | $2,550 | $2,375 | $2,175 | $2,000 |

▲ *State of Maryland Model* — U.S. marked, serial number range 7,126-7,405.

| $6,000 | $5,500 | $5,000 | $4,600 | $4,150 | $3,850 | $3,600 | $3,250 | $2,900 | $2,675 | $2,475 | $2,250 |

NEW MODEL NO. 3 FRONTIER — .44-40 cal., single action, 4, 5, or 6½ in. barrel, blue or nickel finish, walnut or hard rubber grips. 2,072 mfg. 1885-1908.

▲ *Japanese Purchase* — 786 converted to .44 Russian cal., cylinder should measure 1 9/16 in., in the Frontier serial range of 1-2,072.

| $2,500 | $2,200 | $1,100 | $1,750 | $1,550 | $1,375 | $1,200 | $1,050 | $900 | $775 | $675 | $600 |

▲ *Standard Model* — .44-40.

| $3,500 | $3,200 | $2,975 | $2,725 | $2,500 | $2,250 | $2,000 | $1,750 | $1,500 | $1,275 | $1,125 | $1,000 |

NEW MODEL NO. 3 - .38 WIN. — separate ser. range, only 74 mfg., ser. no. 1-74.

| N/A | N/A | $6,000 | $5,500 | $4,950 | $4,575 | $3,925 | $3,500 | $3,150 | $2,750 | $2,375 | $2,000 |

NEW MODEL NO. 3 TARGET MODEL — .32-44 S&W or .38-44 S&W, 4,333 mfg. between 1887-1910.

| $3,150 | $2,800 | $2,475 | $2,175 | $1,925 | $1,700 | $1,500 | $1,350 | $1,200 | $1,050 | $900 | $775 |

100%	98%	95%	90%	80%	70%	60%	50%	40%	30%	20%	10%

NEW MODEL NO. 3 TURKISH — .44 rimfire, 5,461 mfg. between 1879-1888, in separate serial number series.

$5,400	$5,025	$4,675	$4,350	$4,050	$3,750	$3,450	$3,150	$2,850	$2,550	$2,275	$1,950

MODEL 3 SCHOFIELD FIRST MODEL — .45 S&W, single action, 7 in. barrel, 6 shot fluted cylinder, blue finish only, walnut grips, 3,035 mfg. 1875.

▲ *U.S. Issue* — 3,000 mfg.

N/A	N/A	$4,700	$4,325	$3,875	$3,650	$3,350	$3,050	$2,750	$2,450	$2,150	$1,850

▲ *Commercial Model (not U.S. marked)* — 35 were produced without U.S. markings, very rare - beware of fakes - there could be more phony ones than real ones.

$15,000	$14,150	$13,250	$12,000	$10,500	$8,950	$7,500	$6,150	$5,350	$4,900	$4,500	$4,000

▲ *Wells Fargo and Company* — barrel cut to approx. 5 in. with Wells Fargo markings.

$15,000	$14,150	$13,250	$12,000	$10,500	$8,950	$7,500	$6,150	$5,350	$4,900	$4,500	$4,000

Beware of fakes, although most fakes are poor quality and easy to spot.

Many Schofields are found with cut 5 in. barrels and no Wells Fargo marking - these will bring approx. 66% of uncut values or if they have fake WF markings their value is ½ of the uncut values.

MODEL 3 SCHOFIELD SECOND MODEL — improved version of First Model.

▲ *Standard Model* — U.S. on butt.

N/A	N/A	$4,250	$3,875	$3,525	$3,250	$3,000	$2,750	$2,500	$2,250	$2,000	$1,750

▲ *Commercial Model* — blue or nickel finish, nickel finish was done at a later date by the factory, 650 mfg.

N/A	N/A	$4,700	$4,325	$3,875	$3,650	$3,350	$3,050	$2,750	$2,450	$2,150	$1,850

▲ *Wells Fargo and Company* — barrel cut to 5 in. with Wells Fargo markings.

$15,000	$14,150	$13,250	$12,000	$10,500	$8,950	$7,500	$6,150	$5,350	$4,900	$4,500	$4,000

Beware of fakes, although most fakes are poor quality and easy to spot.

Many Schofields are found with cut 5 in. barrels and no Wells Fargo marking - these will bring approx. 66% of uncut values or if they have fake WF markings their value is ½ of the uncut values.

.44 DOUBLE ACTION FIRST MODEL — .44 S&W Russian cal. 6 shot fluted cylinder, 4, 5, 6, or 6½ in. barrel, blue or nickel finish, "S&W" monogram checkered hard rubber or walnut grips. Walnut grips with "S&W" inlays will be found after 1900. 53,668 mfg. 1881-1913. Serial range 1-54,668.

▲ *Standard Model* — all barrel lengths and $1^7/_{16}$ in. cylinder.

$1,800	$1,600	$1,450	$1,275	$1,000	$925	$825	$725	$625	$500	$375	$250

▲ *Standard Model* — similar to above, except has $1^9/_{16}$ in. late production cylinder.

$1,800	$1,600	$1,450	$1,275	$1,000	$925	$825	$725	$625	$500	$375	$250

▲ *.44 Double Action Wesson Favorite* — as standard model above but in 5 in. barrel only, blue or nickel finish, patent markings are on the cylinder rather than on the barrel, grooved barrel rib, external and internal lighning cuts to reduce weight. Approx. 1,000 mfg. 1882-1883. Ser. range included with .44 Double Action First Model, between approx. 8,900-10,100.

$7,600	$6,670	$5,995	$5,360	$4,750	$4,170	$3,600	$3,200	$2,825	$2,500	$2,275	$2,000

Add 30-40% for blue finish.

.38 WIN. DOUBLE ACTION — .38-40 cal., 4, 5, 6, or 6½ in. barrel, only 276 mfg. in separate ser. range 1-276.

$3,550	$3,155	$2,780	$2,200	$1,970	$1,825	$1,700	$1,500	$1,400	$1,300	$1,225	$1,125

.44 DOUBLE ACTION FRONTIER — .44-40 cal., 4, 5, 6, or 6½ in. barrel, only 15,340 mfg. in separate ser. range 1-15,340.

$1,900	$1,700	$1,450	$1,225	$1,050	$900	$750	$550	$400	$350	$275	$250

Add 100% for factory target sights.

100%	98%	95%	90%	80%	70%	60%	50%	40%	30%	20%	10%

SINGLE SHOTS

FIRST MODEL — .22 LR, .32 S&W, or .38 S&W cal., 6, 8, or 10 in. barrel, blue or nickel, hard rubber grips. 1,251 mfg. 1893-1905, ser. range (same as Third Model 38 Single Action) 1-28,107.

▲ *.22 LR* — 862 mfg.

100%	98%	95%	90%	80%	70%	60%	50%	40%	30%	20%	10%
$800	$700	$625	$575	$525	$475	$425	$375	$350	$325	$300	$285

▲ *.32 S&W* — 229 mfg.

100%	98%	95%	90%	80%	70%	60%	50%	40%	30%	20%	10%
$950	$850	$775	$700	$650	$600	$550	$500	$450	$400	$350	$335

▲ *.38 S&W* — 160 mfg.

100%	98%	95%	90%	80%	70%	60%	50%	40%	30%	20%	10%
$1,075	$950	$850	$775	$725	$675	$625	$575	$525	$475	$425	$395

SECOND MODEL .22 LR — similar to First Model, but will not accommodate a revolver cylinder, flatsided frame (does not have recoil shield) 10 in. barrel only, 4,617 mfg. 1905-1909. Ser. range 1-4,617.

100%	98%	95%	90%	80%	70%	60%	50%	40%	30%	20%	10%
$750	$675	$625	$575	$525	$475	$425	$375	$325	$280	$250	$225

THIRD MODEL .22 S (OLYMPIC MODEL) OR LR — similar to Second Model, except is built on "I" solid frame with integral triggerguard, side plate on right side, made both single or double action. 6,949 mfg. 1909-1923. Serial range 4,618-11,641.

100%	98%	95%	90%	80%	70%	60%	50%	40%	30%	20%	10%
$725	$650	$600	$550	$500	$450	$400	$350	$300	$265	$235	$210

Add 30% for Olympic Model in .22 Short (approx. 1,600 mfg.).

STRAIGHT LINE TARGET SINGLE SHOT —.22 LR, single shot, 10 in. barrel, sideswing barrel, blue, target sights, smooth walnut grips, shaped like an autoloader. 1,870 mfg. 1925-1936. Ser. range 1-1,870. Values below assume case.

100%	98%	95%	90%	80%	70%	60%	50%	40%	30%	20%	10%
$1,275	$1,100	$950	$850	$750	$650	$550	$450	$415	$350	$335	$315

Deduct 30% w/o case.

EARLY HAND EJECTORS (NAMED MODELS)

Named Models. 1896-1958. Listed in order of caliber, except where newer mfg. might also include model number. These will NOT have any model number stamped on the frame. Several were continued after 1958 as Numbered Models, so be sure to check that section as well.

.22/.32 HAND EJECTOR (ALSO KNOWN AS .22/32 BEKEART MODEL) — .22 LR cal., 6 shot fluted cylinder, 6 in. barrel, blued, checkered walnut grips with "S&W" medallions, extension style square butt, there were several hundred thousand of the standard .22/.32 Hand Ejector mfg., but only those guns with a separate identification number on the bottom of the wooden grips are classified as true Bekeart Models.

▲ *Bekeart Model* — will be found with separate identification number on bottom of wooden grip. Serial range for early Bekeart Model is 138,226-139,275.

100%	98%	95%	90%	80%	70%	60%	50%	40%	30%	20%	10%
$1,075	$875	$750	$650	$550	$450	$350	$275	$200	$150	$135	$110

This model was specifically mfg. for a San Francisco retailer, Phil Bekeart. Originally, Mr. Bekeart ordered 1,000 guns to his specifications, S&W mfg. 3,000, but only 292 were delivered.

▲ *Standard .22/.32 Hand Ejector Model* — over 100,000 mfg. between approx. 1913-1953.

100%	98%	95%	90%	80%	70%	60%	50%	40%	30%	20%	10%
$850	$675	$550	$450	$375	$325	$275	$225	$175	$135	$115	$100

MODEL .22 HAND EJECTOR (LADYSMITH) — originally chambered for .22 S&W (same as .22 Long), 7 shot fluted cylinder, small frame, available in blue or nickel finish, dubbed "Ladysmith" because many women (including Ladies of the Night) liked them as a personal defense weapon due to the diminutive size. Over 26,000 mfg. between 1902-1921.

S

100%	98%	95%	90%	80%	70%	60%	50%	40%	30%	20%	10%

▲ *First Model* — .22 L, 3, or 3½ in. barrel length, serial numbered 1-4,575, checkered hard rubber grips, round butt. 4,575 mfg. 1902-1906. Serial range 1-4,575. Identifiable by frame mounted cylinder release lever.

| $1,575 | $1,350 | $1,150 | $1,000 | $850 | $750 | $650 | $550 | $475 | $435 | $390 | $350 |

▲ *Second Model* — .22 L, 3, or 3½ in. barrel, distinguishable from first model in that cylinder locking device was placed on barrel bottom, locking both ends. 9,400 mfg. 1906-1910. S.N. 4,576-13,950.

| $1,500 | $1,300 | $1,100 | $950 | $800 | $700 | $600 | $525 | $475 | $425 | $375 | $325 |

▲ *Third Model* — .22 L, 2½, 3, 3½, or 6 in. barrel, smooth walnut grips with S&W medallion inlays, square butt. Ivory or pearl grips will command a premium. 12,200 mfg. 1910-1921. Serial range 13,951-26,154.

| $1,450 | $1,225 | $1,050 | $900 | $750 | $650 | $550 | $475 | $425 | $375 | $325 | $325 |

Add 85% for 6 in. barrel with target sights.
Add 95% for 6 in. barrel with plain sights.

.32 HAND EJECTOR FIRST MODEL (MODEL OF 1896) — .32 S&W long cal., 6 shot fluted cylinder, 3¼, 4¼ or 6 in. barrel, blue or nickel, black rubber grips, round or square butt, cylinder stock is mounted in frame top-strap, patent markings are on cylinder, rather than on barrel, extension target grip. 19,712 mfg. 1896-1903. Serial range 1-19,712.

| $535 | $475 | $425 | $375 | $335 | $300 | $275 | $250 | $225 | $200 | $175 | $150 |

.32 HAND EJECTOR (MODEL OF 1903) .32 S&W long cal., 6 shot fluted cylinder, 3¼, 4¼ or 6 in. barrel, blue or nickel, black rubber grips. 19,425 mfg. 1903-1904. Serial range 1-19,425.

| $400 | $340 | $300 | $275 | $250 | $225 | $200 | $175 | $150 | $130 | $115 | $100 |

▲ *.32 Hand Ejector (Model of 1903 - 1st Change)* — rubber or walnut grips. 31,700 mfg. 1904-1906. Serial range 19,426-51,126.

| $395 | $340 | $300 | $275 | $250 | $225 | $200 | $175 | $150 | $130 | $115 | $100 |

▲ *.32 Hand Ejector (Model of 1903 - 2nd Change)* — rubber or walnut grips. 44,373 mfg. 1906-1909. Serial range 51,127-95,500.

| $395 | $340 | $300 | $275 | $250 | $225 | $200 | $175 | $150 | $130 | $115 | $100 |

▲ *.32 Hand Ejector (Model of 1903 - 3rd Change)* — rubber or walnut grips. 624 mfg. 1909-1910. Serial range 95,501-96,125.

| $525 | $475 | $420 | $385 | $350 | $320 | $290 | $265 | $240 | $220 | $205 | $190 |

▲ *.32 Hand Ejector (Model of 1903 - 4th Change)* — rubber or walnut grips. 6,374 mfg. 1910. Serial range 96,126-102,500.

| $400 | $340 | $300 | $275 | $250 | $225 | $200 | $175 | $150 | $130 | $115 | $100 |

▲ *.32 Hand Ejector (Model of 1903 - 5th Change)* — rubber or walnut grips.

| $355 | $315 | $280 | $250 | $225 | $200 | $175 | $150 | $125 | $110 | $100 | $90 |

.32 HAND EJECTOR THIRD MODEL — .32 S&W long caliber, 6 shot fluted cylinder, 3¼, 4¼ or 6 in. barrel, blue or nickel finish, grips of checkered hard rubber with "S&W" monogram, round butt. 271,531 mfg. 1911-1942. Serial range approx. 263,001-534,532.

| $350 | $310 | $275 | $250 | $225 | $200 | $175 | $150 | $125 | $110 | $100 | $90 |

.32-20 HAND EJECTOR FIRST MODEL — .32-20 Winchester caliber, 6 shot fluted cylinder, 4, 5, 6, or 6½ in. barrel, blue or nickel, case hardened trigger and hammer, grips of hard rubber with "S&W" monogram or walnut, round butt style.

| $650 | $575 | $520 | $475 | $450 | $425 | $400 | $375 | $350 | $325 | $305 | $290 |

.32-20 HAND EJECTOR SECOND MODEL (MODEL OF 1902) — .32-20 caliber, 6 shot fluted cylinder, 4, 5, or 6½ in. barrel, blue or nickel, grips of hard rubber with "S&W" monogram or walnut, round butt style. 4,499 mfg. 1902-1905. Serial range 5,312-9,811.

| $725 | $575 | $475 | $400 | $350 | $300 | $250 | $200 | $150 | $125 | $110 | $95 |

▲ *.32-20 Hand Ejector Second Model (Model of 1902 - 1st Change)* — grip also available in checkered walnut with square butt. 8,313 mfg. 1903-1905. Serial range 9,812-18,125.

| $710 | $565 | $465 | $390 | $340 | $290 | $240 | $190 | $140 | $120 | $105 | $90 |

S

100%	98%	95%	90%	80%	70%	60%	50%	40%	30%	20%	10%

.32-20 HAND EJECTOR (MODEL OF 1905) — caliber, cylinder, barrel and grip specifications same as above. 4,300 mfg. 1905-1906. Serial range 18,126-22,426.

$725	$575	$475	$400	$350	$300	$250	$200	$150	$125	$110	$95

▲ *.32-20 Hand Ejector (Model of 1905 - 1st Change)* — 4, 5, 6, or 6½ barrel, blue or nickel, grips same as above, round or square butt. 11,073 mfg. 1906-1907. Serial range 22,427 to approx. 33,500.

$710	$565	$465	$390	$340	$290	$240	$190	$140	$120	$105	$90

▲ *.32-20 Hand Ejector (Model of 1905 - 2nd Change)* — caliber, cylinder, barrel and grip specifications same as above. 11,699 mfg. 1906-1907. Serial range 33,501-45,200.

$710	$565	$465	$390	$340	$290	$240	$190	$140	$120	$105	$90

▲ *.32-20 Hand Ejector (Model of 1905 - 3rd Change)* — caliber and cylinder same as above, 4 or 6 in. barrel, finish and grips same as above. 20,499 mfg. 1909-1915. Serial range approx. 45,201-65,700.

$700	$550	$455	$380	$330	$280	$230	$180	$140	$120	$105	$90

▲ *.32-20 Hand Ejector (Model of 1905 - 4th Change)* — caliber and cylinder same as above, 4, 5, or 6 in. barrel, finish and grips same as above. 78,983 mfg. 1915-1940. Serial range 65,701-144,684.

$575	$450	$375	$325	$280	$235	$200	$175	$135	$115	$100	$85

.38 MILITARY & POLICE FIRST MODEL (MODEL OF 1899) — .38 S&W Special cal., early models were marked .38 United States Service, these models are also referred to as .38 Hand Ejectors, 6 shot fluted cylinder, 4, 5, 6, or 6½ in. barrel, blue or nickel finish, "S&W" monogram checkered hard rubber or checkered walnut grips with walnut grips exhibiting an impressed circle at top, left plain for civilian issue, marked with inspector's initials for military issue. 20,975 mfg. 1899-1902. Serial range 1-20,975.

On these models, fixed sights are referred to as Military & Police models while target sights are referred to as .38 Hand Ejectors.

▲ *Standard Model - Civilian Issue*

$650	$550	$475	$425	$375	$325	$275	$240	$205	$190	$180	$170

▲ *U.S. Navy Model* — 1,000 revolvers in .38 United States Service cal. with 6 in. barrel, blued, checkered walnut grips, delivered in 1900. Stamped on butt "U.S.N." with an anchor and inspector's initials. All in S&W serial range 5,001-6,000. U.S. Navy serial range 1-1,000.

$1,900	$1,600	$1,375	$1,200	$1,050	$925	$825	$725	$625	$525	$435	$375

▲ *U.S. Army Model* — 1,000 revolvers in .38 United States Service cal. with 6 in. barrel, blued, checkered walnut grips, inspector's initials "K.S.M." on right grip panel with "J.T.T.1901" on left grip panel. Stamped on butt "U.S. ARMY/MODEL 1899". S&W serial range 13,001-14,000.

.38 MILITARY & POLICE SECOND MODEL (MODEL OF 1902) — .38 S&W Special and .38 United States Service cal., 6 shot fluted cylinder, 4, 5, 6, and 6½ in. barrels, blue or nickel, "S&W" monogram checkered hard rubber or checkered walnut grips. 12,827 mfg. 1902-1903. Serial range 20,976-33,803.

▲ *Standard Model* — civilian issue, all in .38 S&W Special cal. (barrel is marked .38 United States Service cal.).

$545	$470	$425	$390	$335	$320	$290	$260	$235	$210	$200	$185

▲ *U.S. Navy Model* — 1,000 revolvers in .38 United States Service caliber with 6 in. barrel, delivered in 1902. Stamped on butt "U.S.N." with "J.A.B.", anchor, and arrow through horizontal "S" and "No." (Naval Ser. No. designation).

$1,800	$1,575	$1,400	$1,250	$1,125	$1,000	$900	$800	$750	$700	$650	$610

.38 MILITARY & POLICE SECOND MODEL - 1ST CHANGE — .38 S&W Special cal., 6 shot fluted cylinder, 4, 5, or 6½ in. barrel, blue or nickel, "S&W" monogram checkered hard rubber or checkered walnut grips, rounded butt style, checkered walnut grips of square butt style available after the 58,000 serial range. 28,645 mfg. 1903-1905. Serial range 33,804-62,449.

▲ *Standard Model* — hard rubber grips, round butt.

$395	$345	$310	$275	$250	$210	$175	$150	$135	$125	$115	$100

100%	98%	95%	90%	80%	70%	60%	50%	40%	30%	20%	10%

▲ *Standard Model* — checkered walnut grips or square butt to frame style. All will have serial numbers over the 58,000 range.

100%	98%	95%	90%	80%	70%	60%	50%	40%	30%	20%	10%
$410	$355	$335	$300	$275	$235	$200	$175	$160	$145	$130	$115

.38 MILITARY & POLICE (MODEL OF 1905) — .38 S&W Special cal., 6 shot fluted cylinder, 4, 5, or 6½ in. barrel, blue or nickel finish, "S&W" monogram checkered hard rubber (round butt) or checkered walnut (square butt) grips. 10,800 mfg. 1905-1906. Serial range 62,450-73,250.

100%	98%	95%	90%	80%	70%	60%	50%	40%	30%	20%	10%
$440	$385	$345	$310	$275	$240	$205	$175	$150	$125	$110	$100

.38 MILITARY & POLICE (MODEL OF 1905 - 1ST CHANGE) — .38 S&W Special cal., 6 shot fluted cylinder, 4, 5, 6, or 6½ in. barrel, blue or nickel finish, grips same as above. 73,648 mfg. (including Model 1905 2nd change), exact quantity of both models has not been determined. The first change mfg. in 1906-1908. Serial range 73,251-unknown.

100%	98%	95%	90%	80%	70%	60%	50%	40%	30%	20%	10%
$310	$275	$250	$225	$200	$175	$155	$135	$115	$100	$90	$80

.38 MILITARY & POLICE (MODEL OF 1905 - 2ND CHANGE) — .38 S&W Special cal., cylinder barrel lengths, finishes and grip styles same as above. 73,648 (including Model 1905 1st change) mfg. Exact quantity unknown. The second change mfg. in 1908-1909. Serial range unknown-146,899.

100%	98%	95%	90%	80%	70%	60%	50%	40%	30%	20%	10%
$310	$275	$250	$225	$200	$175	$155	$135	$115	$100	$90	$80

.38 MILITARY & POLICE (MODEL OF 1905 - 3RD CHANGE) — .38 S&W Special cal., 6 shot fluted cylinder, 4, 5, or 6 in. barrel, finishes and grip styles same as above. 94,803 mfg. 1909-1915. Serial range 146,900-241,703.

100%	98%	95%	90%	80%	70%	60%	50%	40%	30%	20%	10%
$310	$275	$250	$225	$200	$175	$155	$135	$115	$100	$90	$80

.38 MILITARY & POLICE (MODEL OF 1905 - 4TH CHANGE) — .38 S&W Special cal., 6 shot fluted cylinder, 2, 4, 5, or 6 in. barrel, finishes and grip styles same as above. 458,296 mfg. 1915-1942. Serial range 241,704 - approx. 700,000.

100%	98%	95%	90%	80%	70%	60%	50%	40%	30%	20%	10%
$295	$255	$230	$205	$180	$165	$140	$125	$110	$100	$90	$80

.44 HAND EJECTOR FIRST MODEL (.44 HAND EJECTOR NEW CENTURY OR .44 TRIPLE LOCK) — .44 S&W Special cal. (standard), .44-40 W.C.F., .44 S&W Russian, .45 LC, .450 Eley, or .455 Mark II cal., 4, 5, 6½, or 7½ in. barrel, checkered walnut grips and square butt, gold monogram inlay on later production walnut grips. 15,375 mfg. 1908-1915. Serial range 1-5,375 (with respect to .455 Mark II).

▲ *Standard Model* — in .44 Russian, .44-40, .45 Colt (marking), or .450 Eley cal.

100%	98%	95%	90%	80%	70%	60%	50%	40%	30%	20%	10%
N/A	$2,275	$1,875	$1,650	$1,450	$1,275	$1,130	$985	$840	$695	$550	$365

25% of this model's production was in .45 Colt.

▲ *Conversion Model* — .455 Mark II cal.

100%	98%	95%	90%	80%	70%	60%	50%	40%	30%	20%	10%
$885	$765	$675	$600	$540	$480	$420	$360	$300	$250	$235	$225

Only 808 factory conversions of .44 Special to .455 cal. were mfg.

▲ *Standard Model* — .44 S&W Special cal.

100%	98%	95%	90%	80%	70%	60%	50%	40%	30%	20%	10%
$1,182	$1,037	$910	$800	$715	$630	$545	$460	$375	$310	$225	$215

Add 100% for factory target sights.

▲ *British Target Model Triple Lock* — .455 cal., 6½ or 7½ in. barrel, with drift adj. sights (not screw operated) for shooting at Bisley, England.

100%	98%	95%	90%	80%	70%	60%	50%	40%	30%	20%	10%
$3,200	$2,950	$2,675	$2,350	$1,875	$1,650	$1,450	$1,275	$1,130	$985	$840	$695

.44 HAND EJECTOR 2ND MODEL — .44 S&W Special cal. as standard, .38-40, .44-40, or .45 LC cal., 4, 5, 6, or 6½ in. barrel, blue or nickel finish, checkered walnut grips of square butt style, with or w/o "S&W" monogram inlays. 34,624 mfg. 1915-1937. Ser. range 15,376-approx. 50,000.

▲ *Standard Caliber* — .44 S&W Special cal.

100%	98%	95%	90%	80%	70%	60%	50%	40%	30%	20%	10%
$675	$595	$530	$475	$430	$385	$340	$295	$250	$210	$175	$145

Add 50% for factory target sights.

100%	98%	95%	90%	80%	70%	60%	50%	40%	30%	20%	10%

▲ *Special Calibers* — .38-40, .44-40, or .45 LC cal.

100%	98%	95%	90%	80%	70%	60%	50%	40%	30%	20%	10%
$2,450	$2,150	$1,800	$1,600	$1,400	$1,200	$1,000	$895	$795	$700	$575	$475

.44 HAND EJECTOR THIRD MODEL (MODEL 1926 HAND EJECTOR THIRD MODEL) — .44 S&W

Special cal., very rare in .44-40 or .45 LC cal., 6 shot fluted cylinder, 4, 5, or 6½ in. barrel, finishes and grips same as above. Approx. 33,054 mfg. 1926-1949. Ser. range 28,358-S62,489.

▲ *Standard Model* — .44 S&W Special Cal.

100%	98%	95%	90%	80%	70%	60%	50%	40%	30%	20%	10%
$825	$715	$625	$550	$490	$430	$370	$310	$225	$175	$150	$125

There is also a Post-War variation of this model mfg. 1946-49 in the ser. range S62,490-S74,000. These transitional guns have safety hammer blocks but long actions. The values are similar to those listed above.

▲ *.44 Hand Ejector 1926 Target Model* — target sight, blue only, otherwise same as above. Mfg. 1926-1941.

100%	98%	95%	90%	80%	70%	60%	50%	40%	30%	20%	10%
$3,950	$3,250	$2,800	$1,950	$1,725	$1,600	$1,500	$1,400	$1,250	$1,100	$975	$925

There is also a Post-War variation of this model mfg. 1946-49 in the ser. range S62,490-S74,000. These transitional guns have safety hammer blocks but long actions. The Post-War Target Model has a barrel rib and 1950s style micrometer rear sight. The values are similar to those listed above.

.455 HAND EJECTOR FIRST MODEL — .455 Mark II cal., ser. range 1-5,000 in its own range, English or Canadian proofed.

100%	98%	95%	90%	80%	70%	60%	50%	40%	30%	20%	10%
$885	$765	$675	$600	$540	$480	$420	$360	$300	$250	$235	$225

Subtract 20%-40% for conversion to American caliber.

.455 HAND EJECTOR SECOND MODEL — ser. range 5,001-74,755, generally British or Canadian proofed.

100%	98%	95%	90%	80%	70%	60%	50%	40%	30%	20%	10%
$550	$480	$420	$360	$300	$250	$235	$225	$215	$200	$185	$150

Subtract 20%-40% for conversion to American caliber.

Grading	100%	98%	95%	90%	80%	70%	60%

.32 HAND EJECTOR (MODEL 30) — .32 S&W Long, 6 shot, 2, 3, 4, or 6 in. barrel, blue or nickel, fixed sights, walnut or rubber grips. Mfg. 1908-1976.

100%	98%	95%	90%	80%	70%	60%
$275	$220	$165	$140	$110	$105	$100

This model was designated Model 30 after 1958.

.45 HAND EJECTOR (MODEL OF 1917) — .45 Auto Rim or .45 ACP in half moon clip, 6 shot, 5½ in. barrel, fixed sights, satin blue on military - high gloss blue on commercial, smooth walnut on military, checkered walnut on commercial.

▲ *Military* — 175,000 mfg., 1917-1919.

100%	98%	95%	90%	80%	70%	60%
$800	$600	$475	$350	$220	$195	$165

▲ *Commercial* — mfg. 1919-1941.

100%	98%	95%	90%	80%	70%	60%
$650	$500	$395	$370	$320	$285	$185

Add 200% for factory target sights.

▲ *Brazilian Contract of 1937* — Brazilian shield on right side, 14,000 recently imported.

100%	98%	95%	90%	80%	70%	60%
$175	$150	$125	$110	$100	$90	$80

Add 100% for older "non-import".

REGULATION POLICE — .32 S&W, 6 shot, 2, 3, 4, or 6 in. barrel in .32 cal., square butt, walnut grips, fixed sights, blue or nickel. Mfg. 1917-1957.

100%	98%	95%	90%	80%	70%	60%
$325	$275	$225	$170	$145	$135	$125

Add 100% for Regulation Police Target (6 in. barrel only, blue).

VICTORY MODEL — .38 S&W Spl. cal., mfg. in accordance to British/American lend-lease agreement of WWII, parkerized finish, mfg. 1942-1944.

100%	98%	95%	90%	80%	70%	60%
$425	$375	$325	$275	$225	$200	$175

Grading	100%	98%	95%	90%	80%	70%	60%

K-22 OUTDOORSMAN — K frame, .22 LR, 6 shot, 6 in. round barrel, blue, adj. target sights, walnut grips. Mfg. 1931-1940.

	$575	$500	$450	$375	$330	$285	$250

K-22 MASTERPIECE — similar to K-22 Outdoorsman, but has micro click rear sight, short action, round barrel w/o rib. 1,067 mfg. in 1940 only with serial range 682,420-696,952 in .38 Hand Ejector range.

	$1,200	$1,050	$875	$750	$675	$600	$550

.22/32 KIT GUN — similar to Standard .22/32 Hand Ejector Model, except has 2 or 4 in. barrels, round or square butt. Mfg. 1935-1953.

	$800	$700	$575	$500	$450	$400	$350

Add 50% for pre-war mfg.

U.S. AIR FORCE LIGHTWEIGHT (MARKED M 13) — .38 Spl., aluminum cylinder and frame. Most were destroyed by the Government. Perhaps S&W's most faked revolver!

	$800	$725	$675	$525	$475	$425	$350

This model was purchased in large quantities during 1953 and early 1954 only. While S&W never assigned a model number to this variation, M 13 is marked on the top strap and thus retains the Model 13 designation. In 1954, a conventional steel cylinder replaced the aluminum cylinder because of cracking.

This model was based on the S&W .38 Military & Police Airweight (later became the Model 12).

.357 MAGNUM FACTORY REGISTERED — This model was mfg. 1935-1938. It could be custom ordered with any barrel length from $3\frac{1}{2}$ - $8\frac{3}{4}$ in., adj. sights, checkered walnut grips. The gun was hand fitted and registered to the buyer by a number found on the inside of the yoke. This practice was disc. 1938 (approx. 5,500 were mfg.) due to the tremendous demand for the .357 Mag. revolver.

	$1,500	$1,275	$1,025	$875	$675	$575	$500

Add 20% for non-standard barrel lengths.
Common barrel lengths were $3\frac{1}{2}$, 4, 5, and $6\frac{1}{2}$ in.

.357 MAGNUM PRE-WAR NON-REGISTERED — similar to above, but not registered. 1,142 mfg. 1938-1941.

	$1,000	$850	$725	$650	$525	$470	$385

.44 MAGNUM (5 SCREW) — .44 Mag. 5 screw, can be discerned by 4 exposed screws on right sideplate, 1 in front of the triggerguard. Approx. 6,500 mfg. during 1956-1957. Disc.

	$850	$750	$650	$575	$560	$450	$400

▲ **4 in. barrel** — 500 mfg. in 1957-58 only.

	$1,800	$1,600	$1,395				

A rare variation in this model is a 5 in. barrel. Only 500 were mfg. in 1956-57 with bright blue finish, diamond target stocks, and wood case. In NIB condition the value is $2,800 - add 25% for nickel finish.

NUMBERED MODEL REVOLVERS (MODERN HAND EJECTORS)

Modern Hand Ejectors. 1957-present. Beginning in 1957, each S&W revolver is identified by a Model Number stamped on the front of the frame, visible when the cylinder is opened. They are listed in order of model number. See previous section for earlier hand ejectors without model numbers.

To determine which variation a particular revolver is in the following section, simply swing the cylinder out to the loading position and notice the model number inside the yoke. A two-digit number followed by a dash and another number designates which engineering change was underway when the gun was manufactured. Hence, a 48-3 is a Model 48 in its 3rd engineering change (and should be designated when ordering parts). Usually, earlier variations are the most desirable to collectors

Grading	100%	98%	95%	90%	80%	70%	60%

unless a particular improvement is rare. The same rule applies to semi-auto pistols and the model designation is usually marked on the outside of the gun.

Beginning 1994, S&W started providing synthetic grips and drilled/tapped receiver for scope mounting on certain models.

ADD 10%-15% FOR THOSE MODELS LISTED BELOW THAT ARE PINNED AND RECESSED (PRE-1981 MFG.).

MODEL 10 M & P — .38 Spl., 6 shot, round or square butt (4 in. bbl. only starting 1992), fixed sights, 2, 3 (disc.), 4 (standard or heavy), 5 (disc.), or 6 (disc.) in. barrels.

Mfg.'s Sug. Retail	$383	$290	$220	$160	$140	$130	$115	$100

Add $7 for 4 in. barrel.
Add $12 for nickel finish (disc. 1991, 4 in. only).

The Model 10 is currently available in 2 or 4 in. barrel only (a 4 in. heavy barrel nickel square butt variation was disc. in 1992).

MODEL 12 M & P AIRWEIGHT — similar to Model 10, only alloy frame, 2 or 4 in. barrel. Disc. 1986.

	$280	$245	$210	$200	$185	$175	$150

Last Mfg.'s Sug. Retail was $320.

Add $40 for nickel finish (disc.).

MODEL 13 M & P — .357 Mag., fixed sights, 3 (round butt) or 4 (square butt) in. heavy barrel.

Mfg.'s Sug. Retail	$394	$290	$225	$165	$145	$135	$125	$120

Add $20 for nickel finish (disc. 1986).

▲ *Model 13 - N.Y. State Police* — .357 Mag., 4 in. barrel, blued, fixed sights, 1200 were mfg. for the N.Y. State Police and are so marked. All 1200 were recalled by S&W and exchanged for Model 28s.

	$375	$300	$250	$200	$175	$150	$140

MODEL 14 K-38 — .38 Spl., target model, blue only. Disc. 1981.

	$300	$250	$215	$200	$185	$175	$160

Add $20 for 6 in. barrel single action.

MODEL 14 K-38 MASTERPIECE — .38 Spl., 6 in. full lug barrel, adj. rear sight, combat style Morado wood square butt grips, blue finish, 47 oz.

Mfg.'s Sug. Retail	$465	$360	$300	$255	$225	$200	$185	$165

MODEL 15 COMBAT MASTERPIECE — .38 Spl., adj. sights, 6 shot, square butt, 2 (disc.), 4, 6 (disc. 1991), or 8⅜ (disc.) in. barrel (6 and 8⅜ new 1986).

Mfg.'s Sug. Retail	$419	$315	$250	$210	$190	$180	$160	$150

Add $31 for TT or TH (disc. 1991).
Add $11 for 8⅜ in. barrel (disc.).
Add $20 for nickel finish (disc. 1987).

K-32 MASTERPIECE (MODEL 16) — .32 S&W long, 6 in. barrel, adj. sights, checkered walnut, blue. Only 3630 mfg., 1947-1974.

	$1,350	$1,150	$995	$875	$750	$625	$525

▲ *Pre-War K-32 (Model 16)* — only 104 mfg. pre-war, scarce.

	$2,250	$1,950	$1,700	$1,475	$1,250	$1,050	$875

MODEL 16 — .32 cal./.32 Mag., 6 shot, 4 (mfg. 1990-91 only), 6, or 8⅜ (disc. 1991) in. barrel, square butt, blue finish only, TH and TT. Mfg. 1990-92.

	$335	$280	$225	$210	$200	$190	$180

Last Mfg.'s Sug. Retail was $419.

Add 5%-10% for 8⅜ in. barrel.

MODEL 17 K-22 MASTERPIECE — .22 LR, blue only, 4 (mfg. 1986-93), 6 (current mfg.), or 8⅜ (disc. 1992) in. barrel. Disc. 1993, reintroduced 1996.

Mfg.'s Sug. Retail	$490	$375	$275	$240	$215	$200	$185	$175

Add $39 for full lug 6 in. long barrel (w/TT & TH, disc.).
Add $50 for full lug 8⅜ in. long barrel (w/TT & TH, disc. 1992).

Grading	100%	98%	95%	90%	80%	70%	60%

MODEL 17-2 PROTOTYPE MERCOX DART PROJECTILE GUN — .530 Dart Projectile, .22 Ramset blank gas generator, 12 in. barrel, blue finish only, 25 prototype units mfg. 1966 only.

	$6,950	**$6,750**	**$3,750**				

Add $500 for handmade Safariland holster.
Add $100-$500 depending on variation of projectile (six known).

MODEL 18 .22 COMBAT MASTERPIECE — .22 LR, combat style adj. sights, 4 in. barrel, blue only. Disc. 1985.

	$305	**$270**	**$225**	**$200**	**$180**	**$175**	**$165**

Last Mfg.'s Sug. Retail was $352.

Add $30 for TT and TH.

MODEL 19 .357 COMBAT MAGNUM — K frame, .357 Mag., adj. sights, 2½ (round butt), 4 (square butt), or 6 (square butt) in. barrel, bright blue or nickel (disc. 1992) finish, drilled/tapped receiver and synthetic grips became standard 1994.

Mfg.'s Sug. Retail	**$416**	**$320**	**$255**	**$205**	**$190**	**$180**	**$170**	**$160**

Add $10 for 4 in. or $14 for 6 in. barrel.
Add $35 for white outline rear sight (disc. 1994).
Add $20 for nickel finish - disc. 1991 (4 or 6 in. only).
Add $60 for TS, TT, TH, RR, and WO - disc. 1991 (6 in. barrel only).

This model is supplied with a round butt on 2½ in. barrel. Nickel finish is available with a 4 or 6 in. barrel only. The 2½ and 6 in. barrels (blue finish) were disc. in 1991 along with the 4 and 6 in. nickel variations.

.38/44 HEAVY DUTY (MODEL 20) — .38 cal., 6 shot, 4, 5, or 6½ in. barrel lengths, fixed sights, walnut grips, blue or nickel, walnut grips. Mfg. 1930-1941 and re-introduced 1946 (with S prefix starting at serial 62,940). The 38/44 Heavy Duty became the Model 20 in 1957.

	$595	**$490**	**$450**	**$415**	**$385**	**$340**	**$300**

Add 40% for 6½ in. barrel.
Early post-war models had long action (ser. range S62,489-approx. S74,000).

MODEL 20 — .38 Spl. or .44 cal., 6 shot, 4, 5, or 6½ in. barrel, fixed sights, blue or nickel finish, checkered walnut grips. Mfg. 1957-1967.

	$350	**$285**	**$260**	**$220**	**$195**	**$145**	**$125**

.44 HAND EJECTOR FOURTH MODEL - MODEL OF 1950 MILITARY (MODEL 21) — .44 S&W, 6 shot, 4, 5, or 6½ in. large frame, blue, walnut grips, fixed sights, 1,200 mfg. scattered throughout serial range S75,000-S263,000. Mfg. 1950-1966.

	$1,750	**$1,575**	**$1,350**	**$1,100**	**$875**	**$650**	**$550**

Add 50% for 6½ in. (rare).

.45 HAND EJECTOR MODEL OF 1950 MILITARY (MODEL 22) — .45 auto rim or .45 ACP, same specifications as 1917 Army, except redesigned hammer, short action, fixed sights. Approx. 1,200 mfg. 1950-1964.

	$1,500	**$1,275**	**$1,050**	**$875**	**$725**	**$650**	**$525**

.44 HAND EJECTOR FOURTH MODEL - 1950 TARGET (MODEL 24) — redesigned hammer, short action, 6½ in. ribbed barrel standard, satin blue or bright blue micrometer sights, serialization begins at approx. S75,000. Mfg. 1950-1967.

	$695	**$575**	**$500**	**$400**	**$375**	**$350**	**$320**

Add 20% for bright blue.
Add 40% for 4 in. barrel.
Add 50% for 5 in. barrel.

.45 HAND EJECTOR MODEL OF 1950 TARGET (MODEL 26) — adj. sights, thin ribbed barrel.

	$770	**$660**	**$550**	**$440**	**$275**	**$200**	**$150**

Add 100% for .45 Colt cal. (200 mfg.).

Grading	100%	98%	95%	90%	80%	70%	60%

.38-44 OUTDOORSMAN (MODEL 23) — .38 Spl., similar to Model 20 in .38 Spl., except with adj. sights, blue only, pre-war guns had plain barrels, post-war mfg. featured ribbed 6½ in. barrel standard. Mfg. 1930-1967.

	$650	$550	$450	$375	$300	$280	$270

Add 20% for post-war transitional variation.

Early post-war models had long action (ser. range S62,489-approx. S74,000). There were 4,761 pre-war revolvers, 2,326 post-war, and 6,039 styled after the 1950 model.

The 44 in this model's nomenclature refers to the size frame, not the caliber. This variation became designated the Model 23 after 1958.

MODEL 24-3 — .44 Spl., 4 or 6½ in. barrel, bright blue only, checkered Goncalo Alves target grips (without speedloader cutout), barrel and frame not pinned, 7,500 mfg. 1983 only.

▲ *4 in. barrel.* — 2,625 mfg.

	$450	$425	$400	$375	$325	$275	$225

▲ *6½ in. barrel.* — 4,875 mfg.

	$400	$375	$350	$325	$275	$225	$175

Last Mfg.'s Sug. Retail was $359.

▲ *Model 24 Lew Horton Special* — .44 Spl., 3 in. barrel, round butt, adj. sights, blue finish, includes special fitted holster.

	$380	$325	$250

Deduct 10% without holster.

MODEL 25-2 .45 ACP (1955 TARGET MODEL) — N frame, blue finish only, target grips, 6 (later mfg.) or 6½ (earlier mfg.) in. barrel. Disc. approx. 1985.

	$450	$400	$350	$300	$235	$200	$190

Last Mfg.'s Sug. Retail was $347.

Add $150 for 6½ in. barrel (older mfg. with pinned barrel).

This model also accepts the .45 Auto Rim Cartridge.

▲ *Model 25 Lew Horton Special* — .45 ACP, 3 in. barrel, adj. sights, blue finish, only 100 mfg.

	$500	$450	$375

MODEL 25-5 — .45 Long Colt cal., 4, 6, or 8⅜ in. barrel, blue or nickel finish (no extra charge - disc. 1987). Disc. 1991.

	$375	$315	$250	$215	$200	$190	$180

Last Mfg.'s Sug. Retail was $429.

Add 5%-10% for 8⅜ in. barrel.

MODEL 27 — .357 Mag., N-frame, 3½ (disc.), 4 (disc. 1991), 5 (disc.), 6, or 8⅜ (disc. 1991) in. barrel, blue or nickel (disc. 1987) finish. Disc. 1994.

	$380	$300	$235	$220	$205	$190	$180

Last Mfg.'s Sug. Retail was $486.

Add $28 for white outlined rear sight -(disc. 1991).
Add $8 for 8⅜ in. barrel - (disc. 1991).
Add 20% for 3½ or 5 in. barrel (disc.).

▲ *3½ and 5 in. barrel* — disc.

	$425	$365	$275	$265	$240	$230	$180

MODEL 28 HIGHWAY PATROLMAN — .357 Mag., "Highway Patrol" utility model, dull finish, adj. sights, standard grips, blue only, 4 or 6 in. barrel. Disc. 1986.

	$270	$235	$210	$200	$190	$180	$150

Last Mfg.'s Sug. Retail was $306.

Add $20 for TS.

MODEL 29 .44 MAGNUM (4 SCREW) — .44 Mag., 4 screw, can be discerned by 3 exposed screws on lower right side plate (eliminated top screw on sideplate). Mfg. began 1957 after approx. ser. no. S175,000 and was disc. 1961.

	$695	$650	$600	$550	$475	$425	$375

MODEL 29 (3 SCREW) — .44 mag., 4, 6½, or 8⅜ in. barrel, eliminated top screw on sideplate and 1 screw in front of triggerguard. Disc.

	$650	$550	$500	$400	$300	$275	$250

> Subtract $40 if without case.
>
> The S serial number prefix was used on this model until 1968, at which time the law required a new numbering system, and the serial number prefix was changed to N. The S prefix designates the hammer block safety.

MODEL 29 — .44 Mag., 6 shot, similar to Model 25-5, except .44 Mag., 4 (disc. 1992), 6, or 8⅜ in. barrel, blue or nickel (disc. 1991) finish.

Mfg.'s Sug. Retail	$554	$390	$325	$285	$265	$255	$245	$210

> Add $12 for 8⅜ in. barrel (disc. 1995).
> Add $11 for nickel finish (disc. 1991).
> Add $45 for combat grips with scope mount - disc. 1991 (8⅜ in. barrel only).
>
> Older Model 29 mfg. (including 4 and 5 screw variations) will appear under the previous subheading: "REVOLVERS: MODERN DISC."

▲ *Model 29 Lew Horton Special* — similar to Model 29, except has 3 in. barrel, round butt, adj. sights.

	$425	$350	$295

MODEL 29 CLASSIC — .44 Mag., 5, 6½, or 8⅜ in. full lug barrel, blue only, round butt with Hogue conversion square butt grips, interchangeable front sights with white outline rear sight, frame is drilled and tapped to accept scope mounts, blue finish only. Mfg. 1990-94.

	$475	$375	$295	$280	$260	$240	$225

Last Mfg.'s Sug. Retail was $591.

> Add $8 for 8⅜ in. barrel.

MODEL 29 SILHOUETTE — .44 Mag., 10⅝ in. barrel, adj. front and rear sights, bright blue only, Goncalo Alves target stocks. Mfg. 1983-91.

	$550	$475	$395	$335	$290	$260	$240

Last Mfg.'s Sug. Retail was $536.

MODEL 29 MAGNACLASSIC — .44 Mag., 7½ in. full lug, ported barrel, high bright bluing, round butt, interchangeable front sight, supplied with cherry wood display case mfg. in England, 3,000 mfg. in 1990 only.

	$850	$725	$600	$500	$450	$395	$360

Last Mfg.'s Sug. Retail was $999.

MODEL 31 — .32 S&W Long, fixed sights, 2, 3 or 4 (disc.) in. barrel, blue only. Disc. 1991.

	$290	$235	$195	$185	$175	$165	$150

Last Mfg.'s Sug. Retail was $365.

> Add 25% for early flatlatch models.

.38 TERRIER (MODEL 32) — .38 S&W, 5 shot, 2 in. barrel, walnut or rubber grips, blue or nickel, fixed sights, built on .32 frame. Mfg. 1936-1974.

	$330	$220	$175	$150	$135	$125	$115

> This variation was designated the Model 32 after 1958.

MODEL 33 — .38 S&W, 5 shot, 2, 3, 4 in. barrel, square butt, walnut grips, fixed sights, blue or nickel finish. Mfg. 1958-74.

	$325	$275	$225	$170	$145	$135	$125

MODEL 34 — .22 LR or .32 cal. (disc.), adj. sights, J frame, 6 shot, 2 or 4 in. barrel, round or square butt, blue or nickel (disc. 1986) finish. Disc. 1991. This model was re-issued for 2-3 years.

	$300	$235	$195	$185	$175	$165	$150

Last Mfg.'s Sug. Retail was $366.

> Add $25 for nickel finish.
> Add 25% for early flatlatch models.

Grading	100%	98%	95%	90%	80%	70%	60%

.22/32 TARGET MODEL OF 1953 (MODEL 35) — similar to Standard .22/.32 Hand Ejector Model, except micrometer rear sight, magna target grips. Mfg. 1953-1974.

| | | $425 | $300 | $265 | $230 | $200 | $180 | $160 |

MODEL 35 .22/.32 TARGET

| | | $300 | $250 | $195 | $165 | $130 | $110 | $90 |

MODEL 36 (CHIEF'S SPECIAL) — .38 Spl., 5 shot, J frame, round or square (disc. 1991) butt, 2 in. regular or 3 in. (heavy only, disc. 1994) barrel, blue or nickel (disc. 1992) finish.

Mfg.'s Sug. Retail $377 $275 $220 $175 $165 $155 $150 $145

Add $12 for nickel finish (disc., round butt - 2 in. barrel only).

Note: 1st models with high polish blue and diamond grips will bring premiums when mint in original box.

MODEL 36 LADYSMITH — .38 S&W Special, 5 shot, 2 in. regular or 3 (disc. 1991) in. heavy barrel, blue finish only, grips are anatomically designed for women (round butt on 2 in., wood combat grips on 3 in.), fixed sights, redesigned double action, 20-23 oz., Morocco grained (disc. 1991) or soft side case. New 1990.

Mfg.'s Sug. Retail $408 $310 $235 $195 $185 $175 $165 $150

MODEL 37 CHIEF'S SPECIAL AIRWEIGHT — similar to Model 36 Chief's Special, except alloy frame and 2 in. barrel only, blue or nickel (disc. 1995) finish.

Mfg.'s Sug. Retail $412 $320 $240 $195 $185 $175 $165 $150

Add $16 for nickel finish (disc.).

MODEL 38 BODYGUARD AIRWEIGHT — .38 S&W Spl., 5 shot, alloy frame, round butt, shrouded hammer, 2 in. barrel, blue or nickel finish.

Mfg.'s Sug. Retail $444 $335 $255 $205 $190 $180 $170 $150

Add $16 for nickel finish.

CENTENNIAL MODEL 40 — .38 Spl., 2 in. barrel double action only, fully concealed hammer, grip safety, checkered walnut grips, blue or nickel. Mfg. 1953-1974.

| | | $475 | $425 | $345 | $290 | $260 | $240 | $220 |

This model commands a premium for the first series with no letter prefix.

CENTENNIAL AIRWEIGHT MODEL 42 — .38 S&W Spl., aluminum variation of Model 40 Centennial, mfg. began 1953. Disc.

Blue $475 $425 $395 $325 $300 $265 $240
Nickel $1,100 $950 $875 $775 $675 $550 $475

MODEL 42 — .38 Spl., blue finish only. Disc.

| | | $450 | $400 | $360 | $320 | $295 | $270 | $250 |

.22/32 KIT GUN AIRWEIGHT (MODEL 43) — .22 LR, 3½ in. barrel, round or square butt, adj. sights, aluminum frame and cylinder, mfg. 1955-1974.

| | | $425 | $350 | $275 | $240 | $185 | $165 | $150 |

.22 MILITARY & POLICE (MODEL 45) — .22 LR only, originally mfg. as training gun between 1931-1957, also mfg. 500 in 1963 (Model 45).

Pre-War N/A N/A $1,900 $1,600 $1,350 $1,250 $950
Post-War $650 $550 $450 $375 $300 $280 $270

MODEL 48 K-22 MASTERPIECE — .22 Mag, 4, 6 or 8⅜ in. barrel, blue only. Disc. 1986.

| | | $275 | $245 | $200 | $185 | $175 | $165 | $150 |

Last Mfg.'s Sug. Retail was $320.

Add $15 for 8⅜ in. barrel.
Add $15 for TT, TH, and TS (disc.).

Grading	100%	98%	95%	90%	80%	70%	60%

MODEL 49 BODYGUARD — similar to Model 38, only steel frame, 2 in. barrel, blue or nickel (disc.) finish.

Mfg.'s Sug. Retail	$409	$300	$260	$180	$170	$160	$150	$145

Add $25 for nickel finish (disc.).

.38 CHIEFS SPECIAL TARGET (MODEL 50) — .38 Special cal., Chiefs Special Target, mfg. from 1955 in 2 in. or 3 (mfg. began mid '70s) in. barrels, target sights, most were unmarked for model number, approx. 1,100 mfg. The other variation was designated Model 36.

	$795	$700	$625	$550	$475	$400	$350

MODEL 51 — .22 Mag. only, .22/32 kit gun, 3½ in. barrel, 6 shot, adj. rear sight, blue or nickel, walnut stocks. Disc.

	$400	$350	$300	$275	$250	$225	$200

MODEL 53 .22 REM. JET — .22 S, L, or LR inserts, 6 shot, 4, 6, or 8⅜ in. barrel, blue, walnut grips, adj. sights. Mfg. 1960-1974.

	$735	$650	$550	$470	$385	$360	$330

Add 10% for 8⅜ in. barrel.

MODEL 57 — .41 Mag., similar to Model 29, except for cal., 4 (disc. 1991), 6 or 8⅜ (disc. 1991) in. barrel, blue or nickel (disc.) finish. Disc. 1993.

	$350	$255	$225	$205	$190	$175	$165

Last Mfg.'s Sug. Retail was $466.

Add 10%-20% for S prefix serialization.
Add 10% for nickel finish if NIB.
Add $20 for 8⅜ in. barrel.

MODEL 58 — .41 Mag, M&P, fixed sights, 4 in. barrel, blue or nickel finish. Disc.

	$495	$450	$385	$340	$315	$290	$260

Add $25 for nickel finish or "S" serial number prefix.

MODEL 60 CHIEF'S SPECIAL — .38 Spl., stainless version of Chief's Special, 2 (disc. 1995) or 3 in. full lug barrel.

Mfg.'s Sug. Retail	$458	$335	$250	$195

Subtract $25 for 2 in. barrel.
Add 30% for early Model 60s without letter prefix and bright satin finish.
The full lug barrel option began in 1990 with limited mfg. It has been tested for +P+ ammo and features an adj. rear sight - 24½ oz.

▲ *Model 60 .357 Mag. Chief's Special* — .357 Mag. cal., 2⅛ in. barrel, round butt, synthetic grips. New 1996.

Mfg.'s Sug. Retail	$431	$325	$250	$195

MODEL 60 LADYSMITH — .38 S&W Special, 5 shot, 2 in. regular or 3 in. heavy barrel (disc. 1991), frosted stainless steel finish, grips are anatomically designed for women (round butt on 2 in., wood combat grips on 3 in.), fixed sights, redesigned double action, 20-23 oz, Morocco grained (disc. 1991) or soft side case. New 1990.

Mfg.'s Sug. Retail	$461	$345	$245	$195

MODEL 63 .22/32 KIT GUN — .22 LR/.32, stainless kit gun, 2 or 4 in. barrel, 19 oz.

Mfg.'s Sug. Retail	$458	$350	$240	$195

Add $4 for 4 in. barrel.

MODEL 64 M & P — .38 S&W, stainless Model 10, has 2, 3, or 4 in. barrel. 3 (square butt disc. 1992) 4 in. (square butt only) barrels are heavy.

Mfg.'s Sug. Retail	$415	$310	$220	$185

Add $8 for 3 or 4 in. barrel.

Grading	100%	98%	95%	90%	80%	70%	60%

MODEL 65 — .357 Mag., stainless version of Model 13, has 3 (round butt) or 4 (square butt) in. heavy barrels.

Mfg.'s Sug. Retail	$427	$315	$225	$185			

Add $35 for TT, TH, and TS (disc.).

MODEL 65 LADYSMITH — .357 Mag., 3 in. barrel with round butt, glass beaded stainless finish, soft side case. New 1992.

Mfg.'s Sug. Retail	$461	$355	$250	$195			

MODEL 66 — .357 Mag., stainless version of model 19, has 2½, 3 (only 2,500 mfg.), 4, or 6 in. barrel.

Mfg.'s Sug. Retail	$466	$370	$270	$195			

Add $5 for 4 or 6 in. barrel.
Add $48 for TH and TT with 4 (disc. 1991) or 6 in. barrel only.

Note: Several models of the Model 66 were made — such features as an all-stainless steel rear sight and a recessed cylinder will bring a slight premium if NIB.

MODEL 67 COMBAT MASTERPIECE — .38 S&W, stainless version of Model 15, has 4 in. barrel. Disc. 1988, reintroduced 1991.

Mfg.'s Sug. Retail	$467	$345	$250	$195			

1991 mfg. includes square butt and red ramp front sight insert.

MODEL 68 — .38 Spl. cal., similar in appearance to the Model 66, except is in .38 Spl. cal., 4 or 6 in. barrel, approx. 7,500 mfg.

			$750	$625	$495		

This model was originally ordered by CA Highway Patrol. Add 10% for CHP markings.

MODEL 442 CENTENNIAL AIRWEIGHT — .38 S&W Spl. cal., 2 in. barrel only, blue or nickel (disc. 1995) finish, round butt. New 1993.

Mfg.'s Sug. Retail	$427	$325	$250	$205	$190	$180	$170	$150

Add $15 for nickel finish (disc.).

MODEL 520 — .357 Mag., 4 in. barrel, fixed sights, N frame, originally ordered for N.Y. State Police but never purchased. Approx. 3,000 mfg. with box.

		$325	$275	$240	$210	$185	$175	$165

MODEL 547 M & P — 9mm, 3 or 4 in. heavy barrel, 6 shot, round (3 in. barrel) or square (4 in. barrel) butt, blue only, 32 oz. Disc. 1985.

		$295	$265	$240	$210	$195	$185	$175

Last Mfg.'s Sug. Retail was $317.

MODEL 581 — .357 Mag., L-Frame, 4 in. barrel, 6 shot, blue or nickel finish, 38 oz. Disc. 1992.

		$275	$225	$180	$170	$160	$150	$145

Last Mfg.'s Sug. Retail was $335.

Add $20 for nickel (disc. 1987).
This model was disc. 1985-86, and reintroduced 1987-92.

MODEL 586 (DISTINGUISHED COMBAT MAGNUM) — .357 Mag., L-Frame, 4, 6, or 8⅜ (disc. 1991) in. barrel, fixed or adj. sights, blue or nickel (disc. 1991) finish.

Mfg.'s Sug. Retail	$461	$345	$275	$210	$195	$185	$175	$165

Add 5%-10% for nickel finish (disc.).
Add $4 for white outlined rear sight (disc. 1994).
Add $5 for 6 in. barrel.
Add $22 for 8⅜ in. barrel (disc. 1991).
Add $35 for adj. front sight - disc. 1991 (6 in. barrel only, new 1986).

▲ **1985 Model 586 Iowa Highway State Patrol** — mfg. to commemorate 50th anniversary, gold etching, 4 in. barrel. Mfg. 1985 only.

			$375	$250	$225		

S

Grading	100%	98%	95%	90%	80%	70%	60%

MODEL 610 — 10mm cal., 6 shot, 5 or 6½ in. full lug barrel, round butt, target hammer optional, approx. 5,000 mfg. 1990 only.

| | | | $550 | $450 | $375 |

Last Mfg.'s Sug. Retail was $510.

MODEL 617 — .22 LR cal., stainless steel variation of the Model 17 (K-22 Masterpiece), 6 shot, 4, 6, or 8⅜ in. barrel, straight backstrap grip, combat trigger and grips, semi-target. New 1990.
Mfg.'s Sug. Retail $460 $345 $250 $195

> Add $30 for 6 in. barrel with TT and TH.
> Add $41 for 8⅜ in. barrel with TT and TH.

MODEL 624 .44 TARGET — .44 S&W Spl., 6 shot, 4 or 6½ in. barrel, 42 oz. Mfg. 1986-87 only.
$340 $250 $225

Last Mfg.'s Sug. Retail was $449.

> Add $14 for 6½ in. barrel.

▲ *Model 624-2 Lew Horton Special* — .44 Spl., 3 in. barrel with round butt, adj. sights, includes special fitted holster.
$395 $350 $295

> Deduct 10% if without holster.

MODEL 625 — .45 ACP, stainless variation of the Model 25-2, 6 shot, 3 (disc. 1991), 4 (disc. 1991), or 5 in. barrel, round butt, full lug barrel, Pachmayr grips. New 1988.
Mfg.'s Sug. Retail $597 $485 $385 $300

> This variation has the frame stamped "625-2", roll engraved barrel with ".45 CAL MODEL OF 1988" barrel inscription.

MODEL 627 — .357 Mag. cal., also known as "Model of 1989" (stamped on barrel), N-frame, round butt, unfluted cylinder, full underlug 5½ in. barrel. Disc.
$545 $425 $325

MODEL 629 — .44 Mag., similar to Model 29. Available with 4, 6, or 8⅜ in. barrel.
Mfg.'s Sug. Retail $587 $490 $390 $300

> Add $5 for 6 in. barrel or $19 for 8⅜ in. barrel.
> Add $52 for combat grips with scope mount - disc. 1991 (8⅜ in. barrel only).
> During 1978, approx. 100 revolvers were made with pinned barrels and recessed cylinders, serial range is 629,XXX-866,XXX, includes wood box. Prices range from $650-$750, depending on condition.

▲ *Model 629 Classic* — stainless steel variation of the Model 29 Classic, 5, 6½, or 8⅜ in. barrel. New in 1990.
Mfg.'s Sug. Retail $629 $500 $400 $315

> Add $21 for 8⅜ in. barrel.

▲ *Model 629 Classic DX* — .44 Mag., similar to Classic, except is supplied with 2 sets of grips (Hogue combat square and Morado wood round butt stocks), 6½ or 8⅜ in. barrel, 5 interchangeable front sights, numbered test target, 51-54 oz. New 1992.
Mfg.'s Sug. Retail $811 $660 $565 $480

> Add $27 for 8⅜ in. barrel.

▲ *Model 629 Magna Classic* — .44 Mag., similar to Model 29, 3,000 mfg. during 1990 only.
$900 $825 $750

Last Mfg.'s Sug. Retail was $999.

▲ *Model 629 Lew Horton Special* — .44 Mag., 3 in. barrel with round butt, adj. sights.
$400 $350 $295

MODEL 631 — .32 Mag., 6 shot, 2 or 4 in. barrel, combat stocks, round butt only, approx. 5,500 mfg. 1990-92.
$340 $275 $200

Last Mfg.'s Sug. Retail was $386.

Grading	100%	98%	95%	90%	80%	70%	60%

▲ **631 Ladysmith** — 2 in. barrel only, rose stocks.

$365 $295 $225

Last Mfg.'s Sug. Retail was $400.

MODEL 632 CENTENNIAL — .32 Mag., 2 or 3 (disc. 1991) in. barrel, stainless/alloy construction, fully concealed hammer, small frame, Santoprene combat grips, fixed sights, 15.5 oz. Mfg. 1991-1992.

$315 $240 $195

Last Mfg.'s Sug. Retail was $410.

MODEL 637 CHIEF'S SPECIAL AIRWEIGHT — .38 S&W Spl., 5 shot, alloy frame, 2 in. barrel, stainless steel cylinder and barrel. 560 mfg. during 1991, reintroduced 1996.

Mfg.'s Sug. Retail $428 $315 $225 $185

MODEL 638 BODYGUARD AIRWEIGHT — .38 S&W Spl., 5 shot, alloy frame, 2 in. barrel, shrouded hammer, round butt, stainless steel barrel and cylinder, 1,200 mfg. during 1990 only.

$310 $250 $210

Last Mfg.'s Sug. Retail was $395.

MODEL 640 CENTENNIAL — .38 S&W, 5 shot, 2⅛ (new 1991) or 3 (disc. 1992) in. barrel, fully concealed hammer, round butt, tested for +P+ ammo, 22½ oz. New in 1991.

Mfg.'s Sug. Retail $469 $350 $250 $195

MODEL 642 CENTENNIAL AIRWEIGHT — .38 Spl, 5 shot, 2 or 3 (disc. 1991) in. barrel, alloy frame with stainless steel cylinder and barrel, combat grips, concealed hammer, fixed rear sight, approx. 16 oz. Mfg. 1990-1992, reintroduced 1996.

Mfg.'s Sug. Retail $442 $325 $250 $195

▲ **Model 642 LadySmith Airweight** — smooth wood grips, includes soft side carry case. New 1996.

Mfg.'s Sug. Retail $461 $355 $265 $200

MODEL 648 — .22 Mag., 6 in. full lug barrel, combat grips, square butt, combat trigger, semi-target hammer. Mfg. 1990-94.

$350 $250 $195

Last Mfg.'s Sug. Retail was $464.

MODEL 649 BODYGUARD — similar to Model 49 Bodyguard, except in stainless steel, 2 in. barrel. New 1986.

Mfg.'s Sug. Retail $469 $350 $250 $195

MODEL 650 — .22 Mag., service kit gun, 3½ in. heavy barrel, J-Frame, fixed sights. Mfg. 1983-87.

$250 $200 $185

Last Mfg.'s Sug. Retail was $305.

MODEL 651 KIT GUN — .22 Mag., target kit gun, 4 in. barrel, J-Frame, adj. sights (same as old Model 51). Mfg. 1983-87, re-released in late 1990.

Mfg.'s Sug. Retail $460 $340 $245 $195

This model could be ordered with a factory fitted optional .22 LR cylinder until 1987 (last mfg. sug. retail was $295 for the cylinder alone). This variation with the extra cylinder is very desirable.

MODEL 657 — .41 Mag., 4 (disc.), 6, or 8⅜ (disc. 1992) in. barrel. New 1986.

Mfg.'s Sug. Retail $528 $410 $315 $260

Add $17 for 8⅜ in. barrel (disc. 1992).

▲ **Model 657-3 Lew Horton Special** — .41 Mag., 3 in. barrel with round butt, adj. sights.

$410 $360 $300

MODEL 681 DISTINGUISHED SERVICE — .357 Mag., 4 in. barrel, L-Frame. Disc. 1988, reintroduced 1991-1992.

$320 $235 $195

Last Mfg.'s Sug. Retail was $412.

1991 mfg. includes square butt.

Grading	100%	98%	95%	90%	80%	70%	60%

MODEL 686 DISTINGUISHED COMBAT — .357 Mag., similar to Model 586, except 2½ (new 1990), 4, 6, or 8⅜ in. barrel, adj. sights, L-Frame.

Mfg.'s Sug. Retail	$481		$385	$265	$225		

    Add $10 for 4 in. or $14 for 6 in. barrel.
    Add $34 for 8⅜ in. barrel.
    Add $14 for white outline rear sight (disc. 1994).
    Add $47 for adj. front sight with 6 or 8⅜ (disc. 1991) in. barrel only - new 1986.

▲ *Model 686 Plus* — .357 Mag. cal., 7 shot, 2½, 4, or 6 in. barrel, synthetic grips, combat trigger, round (2½ in. barrel only) or square butt, white outline rear sight on 4 or 6 in. barrel. New 1996.

Mfg.'s Sug. Retail	$498		$395	$275	$225		

  ▲ *1984 Model 686 Lew Horton Edition* — 2½ in. barrel only, limited mfg.

			$450	$275	$225		

MODEL 940 CENTENNIAL — 9mm Para. cal., fully concealed hammer, 2 or 3 (disc. 1992) in. barrel, fixed rear sight, Santoprene combat grips, 23-25 oz. New 1991.

Mfg.'s Sug. Retail	$474		$375	$260	$220		

PISTOLS: SEMI-AUTO

Listed in order of model number (except .32 and .35 Automatic Pistols). Alphabetical models will appear at the end of this section.

To understand S&W 3rd generation model nomenclature, the following rules apply. The first two digits (of the four digit model number) specify caliber. Numbers 39, 59, and 69 refer to 9mm Para. cal. The third digit refers to the model type. 0 means standard model, 1 is for compact, 2 is for standard model with decocking lever, 3 is for compact variation with decocking lever, 4 is for standard with double action only, 5 designates a compact model in double action only, 6 indicates a non-standard barrel length, 7 is a non-standard barrel length with decocking lever, 8 refers to non-standard barrel length in double action only. The fourth digit refers to the material(s) used in the fabrication of the pistol. 3 refers to an aluminum alloy frame with stainless steel slide, 4 designates an aluminum alloy frame with carbon steel slide, 5 is for carbon steel frame and slide, 6 is a stainless steel frame and slide, and 7 refers to a stainless steel frame and carbon steel slide. Hence, a Model 4053 refers to a pistol in .40 S&W cal. configured in compact version with double action only and fabricated with an aluminum alloy frame and stainless steel slide. This model nomenclature does not apply to 2 or 3 digit model numbers (i.e., Rimfire Models and the Model 52).

100%	98%	95%	90%	80%	70%	60%	50%	40%	30%	20%	10%

.32 AUTOMATIC PISTOL — .32 ACP cal., 7 shot mag., 3½ in. barrel, blued with "S&W" monogram inlayed plain walnut grip. 957 mfg. 1924-1936. Serial range starting with S.N. 1.

$3,250	$2,800	$2,500	$2,250	$2,000	$1,750	$1,500	$1,250	$1,100	$1,000	$950	$900

.35 AUTOMATIC PISTOL (MODEL 1913) — .35 S&W Auto. cal., 7 shot mag., 3½ in. barrel, blue or nickel w/"S&W" monogram inlayed in plain walnut grips. 8,350 mfg. 1913-1921. Serial range starting with No. 1.

$775	$625	$525	$450	$375	$325	$275	$235	$200	$185	$175	$165

    A slight premium might exist for the first model (up to ser. no. 3,125).

Grading	100%	98%	95%	90%	80%	70%	60%

MODEL 39 STEEL FRAME — 9mm Para., 8 shot, 4 in. barrel, walnut stocks, blue, adj. rear windage only sight, double action, walnut grips, 927 mfg. 1954-1966.

			$1,100	$875	$775	$675	$600	$500	$425

    First commercially mfg. 9mm double action semi-auto in the U.S.

Grading	100%	98%	95%	90%	80%	70%	60%

MODEL 39 ALLOY FRAME — 9mm, double action, 8 shot mag., 4 in. barrel, checkered walnut grips, adj. sight, alloy frame. Disc. 1982.

	$360	$325	$260	$240	$220	$200	$195

Add $35 for nickel finish.

MODEL 41 .22 RF (Field) — .22 S (disc.) or LR, match target pistol, single action, 10 shot mag., adj. sights, walnut grips, 5½ or 7 in. heavy barrel, blue only. Mfg. 1957-present.

Mfg.'s Sug. Retail	$753	$535	$465	$375	$300	$260	$240	$220

Add $60 for 5 or 5½ in. barrel with extended sight (disc.).
Add $35 for 7⅜ in. barrel with muzzle brake (disc.).
Add 125% for .22 Short cal. with counterweight and muzzle brake (disc.).

Earlier variations (A series guns with cocking indicator, Model 41-1, etc.) will command substantial premiums over values listed above.

Note: there are several disc. barrels on the Model 41. They are the 5 in. standard weight with extended sight, 7⅜ in. with muzzle brake, and 5½ in. heavy barrel with extended sight.

MODEL 44 — 9mm Para. cal., single action design, S&W's rarest semi-auto pistol, approx. 10 mfg.
Extreme rarity precludes accurate price evaluation.

MODEL 46 — .22 LR, 5, 5½, or 7 in. barrel, blue, nylon grips, adj. sights. Mfg. 4000, 1957-1966.

	$450	$335	$300	$260	$225	$200	$195

This model is similar to the Model 41, except has double action, and does not have high polish bluing.

MODEL 52-A — .38 AMU, same action as Model 39, 4 in. barrel. Originally mfg. for U.S. Army Marksman Training Unit, 87 mfg.

	$3,000	$2,500	$2,200	$1,950	$1,600	$1,300	$1,000

MODEL 52 — .38 Spl. Wad Cutter only, similar action to Model 39, except incorporates a set screw locking out the double action, 5 in. barrel, 5 shot mag. Approx. 3,500 mfg. 1961-1963.

	$875	$775	$675	$575	$475	$395	$360

MODEL 52-1 — .38 Spl. Wad Cutter only, 5 shot mag., 5 in. barrel, single action trigger and hammer, bright blue only. Mfg. 1963-1971.

	$500	$460	$385	$350	$325	$300	$295

MODEL 52-2 — .38 Spl. Mid Range Wad Cutter only, single action semi-auto, 5 in. barrel, adj. sights, checkered walnut grips, blue only, 5 shot mag. Mfg. 1971-1993.

	$675	$556	$450	$400	$350	$295	$265

Last Mfg.'s Sug. Retail was $908.

MODEL 59 — similar to Model 39, except has 14 shot mag., black nylon grips. Disc. 1981.

	$385	$340	$270	$250	$225	$215	$200

Add $35 for nickel finish.

MODEL 61 ESCORT — .22 LR, 5 shot, semi-auto, blue or nickel, 2½ in. barrel, plastic grips, mfg. 1970-1974.

Blue finish	$250	$210	$165	$150	$140	$110	$95
Nickel finish	$275	$230	$165	$150	$140	$110	$95

MODEL 147-A — 9mm Para., 14 shot, steel frame, 4 in. barrel, black plastic grips, adj. sights for windage only, similar to Model 59, except has steel frame, 112 mfg. in 1979 only.

	$1,050	$875	$800	$725	$650	$575	$495

MODEL 410 — .40 S&W cal., double action, steel slide with alloy frame, blue finish, 4 in. barrel, 10 shot mag., single side safety, 3 dot sights, straight backstrap with synthetic grips, 29.4 oz. New 1996.

Mfg.'s Sug. Retail	$490	$390	$290	$230	$205	$190	$175	$165

Grading	100%	98%	95%	90%	80%	70%	60%

MODEL 411 — .40 S&W cal., 4 in. barrel, 11 shot mag., fixed sights, blue finish, aluminum alloy frame, manual safety. Mfg. 1993-95.

	$440	$375	$335	$310	$295	$280	$265

Last Mfg.'s Sug. Retail was $525.

MODEL 422 .22 RF (FIELD) — .22 LR, single action, $4\frac{1}{2}$ or 6 in. barrel, aluminum frame with steel slide, 10 shot mag., fixed sights, black plastic or wood grips, matte blue finish, 22 oz. New 1987.

Mfg.'s Sug. Retail	$235	$185	$150	$115	$110	$105	$100	$95

▲ *Model 422 Target* — .22 LR, single action, $4\frac{1}{2}$ or 6 in. barrel, aluminum frame with steel slide, 10 shot mag., adj. rear sight, checkered walnut grips, matte blue finish, 22 oz. New 1987.

Mfg.'s Sug. Retail	$290	$225	$175	$140	$115	$110	$105	$95

MODEL 439 — 9mm, double action, 4 in. barrel, blue or nickel finish, alloy frame, 8 shot mag., checkered walnut grips, 30 oz. Disc. 1988.

	$385	$315	$255	$240	$225	$210	$200

Last Mfg.'s Sug. Retail was $472.

Add $34 for nickel finish (disc. 1986).
Add $26 for adj. sights.

MODEL 457 COMPACT — .45 ACP cal., traditional double action, alloy frame and steel slide, $3\frac{3}{4}$ in. barrel, single side safety, 3 dot sights, 7 shot mag., straight grips backstrap, blue finish only, black synthetic grips, 29 oz. New 1996.

Mfg.'s Sug. Retail	$490	$390	$290	$230	$205	$190	$175	$165

MODEL 459 — 9mm, 14 shot version of Model 439, checkered nylon stocks, limited mfg. with squared-off triggerguard with serrations. Disc. 1988.

	$410	$345	$290	$270	$255	$240	$210

Last Mfg.'s Sug. Retail was $501.

Add $26 for adj. sights.
Add $44 for nickel finish (disc. 1986).

▲ *Model 459 Brushed Finish* — 9mm Para., 14 shot, 4 in. barrel, dull finish, fixed sights, special grips made to F.B.I. or Police specs., 803 mfg.

	$650	$600	$550	$440	$385	$330	$300

MODEL 469 "MINI" — 9mm, double action, alloy frame, 12 shot finger extension mag., short frame, bobbed hammer, $3\frac{1}{2}$ in. barrel, sandblast blue or satin nickel finish, ambidextrous safety standard (1986), molded Delrin black Grips, 26 oz. Disc. 1988.

	$370	$320	$265	$250	$235	$220	$210

Last Mfg.'s Sug. Retail was $478.

MODEL 539 — 9mm, double action, steel frame, 8 shot, 4 in. barrel, blue or nickel. Disc. 1983.

	$450	$395	$375	$350	$325	$300	$275

Add $35 for nickel finish.
Add $30 for adj. rear sight.

MODEL 559 — 9mm, double action, steel frame, 12 shot, 4 in. barrel, blue or nickel. Disc. 1983.

	$485	$435	$375	$275	$250	$225	$200

Add $35 for nickel finish.
Add $30 for adj. rear sight.

MODEL 622 .22 RF (Field) — .22 LR, single action, $4\frac{1}{2}$ or 6 in. barrel, stainless/ alloy construction, 10 shot mag., fixed sights, black plastic grips, $21\frac{1}{2}$ or $23\frac{1}{2}$ oz. New 1990.

Mfg.'s Sug. Retail	$284	$220	$175	$160

▲ *Model 622 Target* — .22 LR, single action, $4\frac{1}{2}$ or 6 in. barrel, stainless steel construction, 10 shot mag., adj. rear sight, checkered walnut grips, $21\frac{1}{2}$ or $23\frac{1}{2}$ oz. New 1990.

Mfg.'s Sug. Retail	$337	$275	$225	$175

Subtract $27 for VR barrel (new 1996).

Grading	100%	98%	95%	90%	80%	70%	60%

MODEL 639 STAINLESS — 9mm, similar to Model 439-only stainless steel, 8 shot mag., ambidextrous safety became standard 1986, 36 oz. Disc. 1988.

$420 $300 $275

Last Mfg.'s Sug. Retail was $523.

> Add $27 for adj. sights.

MODEL 645 STAINLESS — .45 ACP only, 5 in. barrel, 8 shot mag., squared off trigger guard, black molded nylon grips, ambidextrous safety, fixed sights, $37\frac{1}{2}$ oz. New 1986. Disc. 1988.

$475 $365 $300

Last Mfg.'s Sug. Retail was $622.

> Add $27 for adj. sight.
> Approx. 150 Model 645 "Interim" pistols were mfg. in 1988 only. Add $120 to values listed above.

MODEL 659 STAINLESS — 9mm, similar to Model 459-only stainless steel, 14 shot mag., ambidextrous safety became standard 1986, $39\frac{1}{2}$ oz. Disc. 1988.

$445 $335 $300

Last Mfg.'s Sug. Retail was $553.

> Add $27 for adj. sights.
> Approx. 150 Model 659 "Interim" pistols were mfg. in 1988 only. Add $150 to values listed above.

MODEL 669 STAINLESS — 9mm, smaller version of Model 659 with 12 shot finger extension mag., $3\frac{1}{2}$ in. barrel, fixed sights, molded Delrin grips, ambidextrous safety standard, 26 oz. Mfg. 1986-1988 only.

$425 $305 $275

Last Mfg.'s Sug. Retail was $522.

> Approx. 150 Model 669 "Interim" pistols were mfg. in 1988 only. Add $150 to values listed above.

MODEL 745 IPSC — .45 ACP, single action, 5 in. barrel, stainless steel frame with steel slide, hammer, and trigger, checkered walnut stocks, fixed rear sight, $38\frac{3}{4}$ oz. Mfg. 1987-90.

$575 $440 $335

Last Mfg.'s Sug. Retail was $699.

> Early guns had optional "IPSC" markings. Later, these markings became standard.

MODEL 908 — 9mm Para., compact variation of the Model 909/910, $3\frac{1}{2}$ in. barrel, 3 dot sights, 8 shot mag., straight backstrap, 26 oz. New 1996.

Mfg.'s Sug. Retail	$443	$360	$275	$225	$205	$190	$175	$165

MODEL 909 — 9mm Para. cal., 4 in. barrel, traditional double action, 9 shot mag., fixed sights, single side safety, alloy frame and steel slide, curved backstrap with black synthetic grips, 27 oz. New 1994.

Mfg.'s Sug. Retail	$443	$360	$275	$225	$205	$190	$175	$165

MODEL 910 — similar to Model 909, except has 10 shot mag., 28 oz. New 1994.

Mfg.'s Sug. Retail	$443	$360	$275	$225	$205	$190	$175	$165

MODEL 915 — 9mm Para. cal., 4 in. barrel, fixed sights, 10 (C/B 1994) or 15* shot mag., manual safety, aluminum alloy frame, blue finish. Mfg. 1993-94.

	$350	$255	$225	$205	$190	$175	$165

Last Mfg.'s Sug. Retail was $467.

MODEL 1006 STAINLESS — 10mm, double action semi-auto, stainless steel construction, 5 in. barrel, exposed hammer, 9 shot mag., fixed or adj. sights, ambidextrous safety. Mfg. 1990-1993.

$635 $530 $400

Last Mfg.'s Sug. Retail was $769.

> Add $27 for adj. rear sight.

Grading	100%	98%	95%	90%	80%	70%	60%

MODEL 1026 STAINLESS — 10mm, 5 in. barrel, traditional double action, features frame mounted decocking lever, 9 shot mag., straight backstrap. Mfg. 1990-91 only.

$630 $525 $400

Last Mfg.'s Sug. Retail was $755.

MODEL 1046 STAINLESS — 10mm, 5 in. barrel, fixed sights, double action only, 9 shot mag., straight backstrap. Mfg. 1991 only.

$620 $515 $400

Last Mfg.'s Sug. Retail was $747.

MODEL 1066 STAINLESS — 10mm, 4¼ in. barrel, 9 shot mag., straight backstrap, ambidextrous safety, traditional double action, fixed sights. Mfg. 1990-1992.

$610 $515 $395

Last Mfg.'s Sug. Retail was $730.

Add $40 for Tritium night sights - disc. 1991 (Model 1066-NS).
Only 1,000 Model 1066-NSs were manufactured.

MODEL 1076 STAINLESS — similar to Model 1026 Stainless, except has 4¼ in. barrel. Mfg. 1990-1993.

$645 $530 $400

Last Mfg.'s Sug. Retail was $778.

MODEL 1086 STAINLESS — similar to Model 1066 Stainless, except is double action only.

$710 $515 $395

Last Mfg.'s Sug. Retail was $730.

MODEL 2206 STAINLESS .22 RF (FIELD) — .22 LR cal., similar to Model 622 Field, except is all stainless steel with black plastic grips, 6 in. barrel with standard (disc. 1995) or adj. rear sight, 35 or 39 oz. New 1990.

Mfg.'s Sug. Retail $385 $290 $225 $175

Subtract $58 if w/o adj. sights.

▲ *Model 2206 Stainless Target* — similar to Model 2206 Stainless, except has adj. target sight, target stocks, and is drilled and tapped. New 1994.

Mfg.'s Sug. Retail $433 $360 $275 $225

MODEL 2213 STAINLESS .22 RF "SPORTSMAN" — .22 LR cal., single action, 3 in. barrel, alloy frame with stainless steel slide, 8 shot mag., 2 dot fixed rear sight, black plastic molded grips, 18 oz., includes holster/carry case. New 1992.

Mfg.'s Sug. Retail $314 $235 $195 $160

MODEL 2214 .22 RF "SPORTSMAN" — .22 LR cal., similar to Model 2213, except has alloy frame with blue carbon steel slide with matte black finish, and no case. New in 1991.

Mfg.'s Sug. Retail $269 $210 $175 $160 $150 $140 $130 $120

MODEL 3904 — 9mm Para., double action semi-auto, aluminum alloy frame, 4 in. barrel with fixed bushing, 8 shot mag., Delrin one piece wraparound grips, exposed hammer, ambidextrous safety, beveled magazine well, extended squared off triggerguard, adj. or fixed rear sight, 3 dot sighting system, 28 oz. Mfg. 1989-91.

$450 $385 $350 $325 $300 $280 $265

Last Mfg.'s Sug. Retail was $541.

Add $25 for adj. rear sight.

MODEL 3906 STAINLESS — stainless steel variation of the Model 3904, 35½ oz. Mfg. 1989-91.

$510 $435 $375

Last Mfg.'s Sug. Retail was $604.

Add $28 for adj. rear sight.

MODEL 3913 COMPACT STAINLESS — stainless steel variation of the Model 3914, 25 oz. New 1990.

Mfg.'s Sug. Retail $622 $510 $425 $365

Grading	100%	98%	95%	90%	80%	70%	60%

▲ *Model 3913NL* — similar to Model 3913 Ladysmith, except does not have Ladysmith on the slide. Disc. 1994.

| | **$510** | **$425** | **$365** | | | | |

Last Mfg.'s Sug. Retail was $622.

▲ *Model 3913 LadySmith* — similar to Model 3913 Stainless, except has white Delrin grips and mag. does not have finger extension, 25 oz. New in 1990.

| **Mfg.'s Sug. Retail** | **$640** | **$530** | **$435** | **$365** | | | |

MODEL 3914 COMPACT — 9mm Para., double action semi-auto, aluminum alloy frame, 3½ in. barrel, hammerless, 8 shot finger extension mag., fixed sights only, ambidextrous safety, blue finish, straight backstrap grip, 25 oz. Mfg. 1990-95.

| | **$465** | **$385** | **$340** | **$320** | **$295** | **$280** | **$265** |

Last Mfg.'s Sug. Retail was $562.

This model is also available with a single side manual safety at no extra charge - disc. 1991 (Model 3914NL).

▲ *Model 3914 LadySmith* — similar to Model 3914, except has Delrin grips, 25 oz. Mfg. 1990-91 only.

| | **$485** | **$415** | **$365** | | | | |

Last Mfg.'s Sug. Retail was $568.

MODEL 3953 COMPACT STAINLESS — 9mm Para., double action only, aluminum alloy frame with stainless steel slide, compact model with 3½ in. barrel, 8 shot mag. New in 1990.

| **Mfg.'s Sug. Retail** | **$622** | **$510** | **$425** | **$365** | | | |

MODEL 3954 — similar to Model 3953, except has blue steel slide. Mfg. 1990-1992.

| | **$445** | **$380** | **$340** | **$320** | **$295** | **$280** | **$265** |

Last Mfg.'s Sug. Retail was $528.

MODEL 4003 STAINLESS — .40 S&W cal., traditional double action, 4 in. barrel, 11 shot mag., white dot fixed sights, ambidextrous safety, aluminum alloy frame with stainless steel slide, one piece Xenoy wraparound grips, straight gripstrap, 28 oz. Mfg. 1991-1993.

| | **$585** | **$495** | **$395** | | | | |

Last Mfg.'s Sug. Retail was $698.

MODEL 4004 — .40 S&W cal., similar to Model 4003, except has aluminum alloy frame with blue carbon steel slide. Mfg. 1991-1992.

| | **$540** | **$460** | **$375** | **$325** | **$295** | **$280** | **$265** |

Last Mfg.'s Sug. Retail was $643.

MODEL 4006 STAINLESS — .40 S&W cal., 3½ (Shorty Forty) or 4 in. barrel, 10 (C/B 1994) or 11* shot mag., satin stainless finish, exposed hammer, Delrin one piece wraparound grips, 3 dot sights, 38½ oz. New in 1990.

| **Mfg.'s Sug. Retail** | **$745** | **$625** | **$525** | **$400** | | | |

Add $30 for adj. rear sight.
Add $80 for fixed Tritium night sights (new 1992).
The bobbed hammer option on this model was disc. in 1991.

MODEL 4013 COMPACT STAINLESS — .40 S&W cal., semi-auto, standard double action, 3½ in. barrel, 8 shot mag., fixed sights, ambidextrous safety, alloy frame. New 1991.

| **Mfg.'s Sug. Retail** | **$722** | **$595** | **$485** | **$385** | **$330** | **$295** | **$280** | **$265** |

MODEL 4014 COMPACT — similar to Model 4013, except is steel with blue finish. Mfg. 1991-1993.

| | **$510** | **$425** | **$375** | **$330** | **$300** | **$275** | **$250** |

Last Mfg.'s Sug. Retail was $635.

MODEL 4026 STAINLESS — .40 S&W cal., traditional double action with frame mounted decocking lever, 10 (C/B 1994) or 11* shot mag., fixed sights, curved backstrap, 36 oz. Mfg. 1991-1993.

| | **$620** | **$520** | **$400** | | | | |

Last Mfg.'s Sug. Retail was $731.

Grading	100%	98%	95%	90%	80%	70%	60%

MODEL 4043 STAINLESS — .40 S&W cal., double action only, aluminum alloy frame with stainless steel slide, 4 in. barrel, 10 (C/B 1994) or 11* shot mag., one piece Xenoy wraparound grips, straight backstrap, white dot fixed sights, 30 oz. New 1991.

Mfg.'s Sug. Retail	$727	$600	$485	$385

MODEL 4044 — .40 S&W cal., similar to Model 4043, except has carbon steel slide. Mfg. 1991-1992.

$540	$460	$375	$325	$295	$280	$265

Last Mfg.'s Sug. Retail was $643.

MODEL 4046 STAINLESS — similar to Model 4006 Stainless, except is double action only, 4 in. barrel only. New in 1991.

Mfg.'s Sug. Retail	$745	$625	$520	$400

Add $110 for Tritium night sights (new 1992).

MODEL 4053 COMPACT STAINLESS — double action only variation of the Model 4013. New 1991.

Mfg.'s Sug. Retail	$722	$595	$485	$380

MODEL 4054 — double action only variation of the Model 4014. Mfg. 1991-1992.

$510	$425	$375

Last Mfg.'s Sug. Retail was $629.

MODEL 4505 — .45 ACP, carbon steel variation of the Model 4506, fixed or adj. rear sight. 1,200 mfg. 1991 only.

$575	$500	$450	$400	$350	$300	$265

Last Mfg.'s Sug. Retail was $660.

Add $27 for adj. rear sight.

MODEL 4506 STAINLESS — .45 ACP, 5 in. barrel, 8 shot mag., combat triggerguard, exposed hammer, fixed or adj. rear sight, straight backstrap (curved is optional), Delrin one-piece grips, $38\frac{1}{2}$ oz. New in 1990.

Mfg.'s Sug. Retail	$774	$645	$530	$400

Add $32 for adj. rear sight.

Approx. 100 Model 4506s left the factory mismarked Model 645 on the frame. In NIB condition they are worth $700.

MODEL 4516 COMPACT STAINLESS — .45 ACP, hammerless compact variation of the Model 4506, $3\frac{3}{4}$ in. barrel, 7 shot mag., ambidexterous safety, fixed rear sight only, 34 oz. New 1990.

Mfg.'s Sug. Retail	$774	$640	$530	$400

Original model is marked 4516 while later mfg. changed slide legend to read 4516-1. Original mfg. is more collectible and slight premiums are being asked.

MODEL 4526 STAINLESS — similar to Model 4506 Stainless, except has frame mounted decocking lever. Mfg. 1990-91 only.

$635	$530	$400

Last Mfg.'s Sug. Retail was $762.

MODEL 4536 STAINLESS — similar to Model 4516 Compact, except has frame mounted decocking lever only. Mfg. 1990-91 only.

$635	$530	$400

Last Mfg.'s Sug. Retail was $762.

MODEL 4546 STAINLESS — similar to Model 4506 Stainless, except is double action only. Mfg. 1990-91 only.

$620	$520	$400

Last Mfg.'s Sug. Retail was $735.

MODEL 4556 STAINLESS — .45 ACP, features double action only, $3\frac{3}{4}$ in. barrel, 7 shot mag., fixed sights. Mfg. 1991 only.

$620	$520	$400

Last Mfg.'s Sug. Retail was $735.

Grading	100%	98%	95%	90%	80%	70%	60%

MODEL 4566 STAINLESS — .45 ACP, traditional double action with ambidextrous safety, 4¼ in. barrel, 8 shot mag. New in 1990.

Mfg.'s Sug. Retail	$774	$640	$530	$400			

MODEL 4567-NS STAINLESS — similar to Model 4566 Stainless, except has Tritium night sights, stainless steel frame and carbon steel slide. 2,500 mfg. in 1991 only.

		$620	$520	$400			

Last Mfg.'s Sug. Retail was $735.

MODEL 4576 STAINLESS — .45 ACP, features 4¼ in. barrel, frame mounted decocking lever, fixed sights. Mfg. 1990-1992.

		$635	$535	$410			

Last Mfg.'s Sug. Retail was $762.

MODEL 4586 STAINLESS — .45 ACP, 4¼ in. barrel, double action only, 8 shot mag. New in 1990.

Mfg.'s Sug. Retail	$774	$640	$525	$400			

MODEL 5903 — 9mm Para., double action semi-auto, 4 in. barrel, stainless steel slide and alloy frame, exposed hammer, 10 (C/B 1994) or 15" shot mag., adj. (disc. 1993) or fixed rear sight, ambidextrous safety. New 1990.

Mfg.'s Sug. Retail	$690	$570	$470	$395	$365	$325	$300	$285

Add $30 for adj. rear sight (disc).

MODEL 5904 — similar to Model 5903, except has steel slide and blue finish, 26½ oz. New 1989.

Mfg.'s Sug. Retail	$642	$520	$440	$360	$330	$300	$280	$265

Add $30 for adj. rear sight (disc. 1993).

MODEL 5905 — 9mm Para., similar to Model 5904, except has carbon steel frame and slide. Approx. 5,000 mfg. 1990-91 only.

More research is underway regarding this model.

	$650	$575	$500	$440	$375	$335	$300

MODEL 5906 STAINLESS — stainless steel variation of the Model 5904, 37½ oz. New 1989.

Mfg.'s Sug. Retail	$707	$590	$480	$395			

Add $35 for adj. rear sight.
Add $110 for Tritium night sights.

MODEL 5924 — 9mm Para., 4 in. barrel, features frame mounted decocking lever, 15 shot mag., 37½ oz. Mfg. 1990-91 only.

	$515	$440	$365	$330	$300	$280	$265

Last Mfg.'s Sug. Retail was $635.

MODEL 5926 STAINLESS — stainless variation of the Model 5924. Disc. 1992.

	$580	$480	$395			

Last Mfg.'s Sug. Retail was $697.

MODEL 5943 STAINLESS — 9mm Para., double action only, 4 in. barrel, aluminum alloy frame with stainless steel slide, straight backstrap, 15 shot mag. Mfg. 1990-91 only.

	$550	$465	$390			

Last Mfg.'s Sug. Retail was $655.

▲ **Model 5943-SSV Stainless** — similar to Model 5943 Stainless, except has 3½ in. barrel, Tritium night sights. Mfg. 1990-91 only.

	$580	$485	$395			

Last Mfg.'s Sug. Retail was $690.

MODEL 5944 — similar to Model 5943 Stainless, except has blue finish slide. Mfg. 1990-91 only.

	$510	$435	$360	$330	$300	$280	$265

Last Mfg.'s Sug. Retail was $610.

MODEL 5946 STAINLESS — double action only, one piece Xenoy wraparound grips, all stainless steel variation of the Model 5943, 39½ oz. New in 1990.

Mfg.'s Sug. Retail	$707	$590	$475	$390			

Grading	100%	98%	95%	90%	80%	70%	60%

MODEL 6904 COMPACT — compact variation of the Model 5904, 3½ in. barrel, 10 (C/B 1994) or 12* shot finger extension mag., fixed rear sight, 26½ oz. New 1989.

Mfg.'s Sug. Retail	$614	$500	$405	$350	$325	$300	$280	$265

MODEL 6906 COMPACT STAINLESS — stainless steel variation of the Model 6904, 26½ oz. New 1989.

Mfg.'s Sug. Retail	$677	$555	$455	$375

   Add $111 for Tritium night sights (new 1992).

MODEL 6926 STAINLESS — 9mm Para., 3½ in. barrel, standard double action, features frame mounted decocking lever, aluminum alloy frame with stainless slide, 12 shot mag. Mfg. 1990-91 only.

	$550	$455	$375

Last Mfg.'s Sug. Retail was $663.

MODEL 6944 — 9mm Para., double action only, 3½ in. barrel, 12 shot mag., aluminum alloy frame with blue steel slide. Mfg. 1990-91 only.

	$480	$400	$350	$325	$300	$280	$265

Last Mfg.'s Sug. Retail was $578.

MODEL 6946 STAINLESS — similar to Model 6944, except has stainless steel slide, semi-bobbed hammer, 26½ oz. New in 1990.

Mfg.'s Sug. Retail	$677	$550	$450	$375

SIGMA MODEL SW380 — .380 ACP cal., double action only, 3 in. barrel, fixed sights, polymer frame and steel slide, striker firing system, blue finish only, 6 shot mag., shortened grip, 14 oz. New 1996.

Mfg.'s Sug. Retail	$308	$255	$225	$205	$190	$180	$170	$160

SIGMA MODEL SW9F — 9mm Para. cal., double action only, 4½ in. barrel, fixed sights, polymer frame and steel slide, striker firing system, blue finish only, 10 (C/B 1994) or 17* shot mag., 26 oz. New 1994.

Mfg.'s Sug. Retail	$593	$485	$390	$345	$320	$295	$280	$265

   Add $104 for Tritium night sights.

▲ *Compact Sigma Model SW9C* — similar to Sigma Model SW9F, except has 4 in. barrel, 26 oz. New 1996.

Mfg.'s Sug. Retail	$593	$485	$390	$345	$320	$295	$280	$265

SIGMA MODEL SW40F — .40 S&W cal., double action only, 4½ in. barrel, fixed sights, polymer frame, blue finish only, 10 (C/B 1994) or 15* shot mag., 26 oz. New 1994.

Mfg.'s Sug. Retail	$593	$485	$390	$345	$320	$295	$280	$265

   Add $104 for Tritium night sights.

▲ *Compact Sigma Model SW40F* — similar to Sigma Model SW40F, except has 4 in. barrel, 26 oz. New 1996.

Mfg.'s Sug. Retail	$593	$485	$390	$345	$320	$295	$280	$265

ENGRAVING OPTIONS FOR CURRENTLY MFG. HANDGUNS

The prices listed below are for original factory finished guns with no extra engraving. The listings below show 1993 factory engraving costs. These prices should be added to the cost of each engraved production gun to determine the correct value.

CLASS "C" ENGRAVING—1/3 METAL COVERAGE

   Pistols — add $1,025.
   For J Frame — add $810.
   10⅝ in. N Frame — add $1,242.
   2-5 in. K, L, or N Frame — add $1,045.
   6-8⅜ in. K, L, or N Frame — add $1,188.

CLASS "B" ENGRAVING — ⅔ METAL COVERAGE
Pistols — add $1,339.
For J Frame — add $1,322.
10⅝ in. N Frame — add $1,546.
2-5 in. K, L, or N Frame — add $1,366.
6-8⅜ in. K, L, or N Frame — add $1,478.

CLASS "A" ENGRAVING — FULL COVERAGE
Pistols — add $1,629.
For J Frame — add $1,388.
2-5 in. K, L, or N Frame — add $1,677.
6-8⅜ in. K, L, or N Frame — add $1,774.
10⅝ in. N Frame — add $1,855.

SPECIAL ENGRAVING — Also available: inlays, seals, game scenes, lettering, prices quoted on request.

LASERSMITH ENGRAVING — laser etching was available 1989-1990 only. This process involved a digitally controlled laser producing a variety of designs, logos, commemorative messages, or autograph on the metal surface(s). Some of these designs were made exclusively for major firearms distributors. Others were custom designed for clubs or organizations. Retail prices started at just under $18 and can go as high as $150+, depending on the amount and complexity of the laser etching. To date, premiums are not being paid for these "rarer" variations.

S&W COMMEMORATIVES/SPECIAL EDITIONS

During the course of a year, I receive many phone calls and letters on special editions and limited editions that do not appear in this section. It should be noted that a commemorative issue is a gun that has been manufactured, marketed, and sold through the auspices of the specific trademark (in this case S&W). During the past several decades, hundreds of limited editions have been ordered through various police agencies, state highway patrol units, and other law enforcement organizations. Many of these variations do not have the special suffix serialization (and may not have had a retail price when issued). Since most of these special editions/commemoratives were made for a specific organization, regional demand has a lot to do with determining values (a Model 66 Montana HP Commemorative will not sell for a premium in Alabama). For this reason, most of these guns will not appear in this section and you should contact the factory to learn more about the provenance of these special editions. Remember - values on these models can vary A LOT from one region to another and an averaged "national" single price is almost impossible. While these guns do have special interest, they do not have the collectability or desirability of many of the standard models listed below.

The variations listed below represent the only five factory S&W Commemoratives manufactured to date. Anything else will be a special or limited edition made for a organization, company, or special event.

Grading	100%	Issue Price	Qty. Made
MODEL 19 TEXAS RANGER — .357 Mag., with or without knife, approx. 8,000 with knife, approx. 2,000 without, cased. Mfg. 1973 only.			
	$595	$250	10,000
▲ *Model 19 Texas Ranger Deluxe* — approx. 50 mfg. with a serial numbers divisible by 10, cased.			
	N/A	N/A	50
125TH ANNIVERSARY COMMEMORATIVE — .45 LC cal., plain variation was called Model 25-3, 10,000 mfg. total in 1977, cased with nickel silver medallion, and Roy Jinks's book, "125th Anniversary of Smith & Wesson".			
	$450	$350	10,000

Grading	100%	Issue Price	Qty. Made

▲ *125th Anniversary Commemorative Deluxe* — Model 25-4, approx. 50 mfg. with S&W prefix serial numbers divisible by 10, cased, sterling silver medallion, and a leather bound "History of Smith & Wesson" book by Roy Jinks.

	N/A	N/A	50

MODEL 29 ELMER KEITH COMMEMORATIVE — .44 Mag. cal., 4 in. barrel, standard and deluxe editions, approx. 2,000 total mfg.

	$850	N/A	2,000

50TH ANNIVERSARY OF THE .357 MAGNUM — Model 27, both standard and deluxe editions, 1987 mfg.

	$450	N/A	N/A

MODEL 544 TEXAS WAGON TRAIN COMMEMORATIVE — .44-40 cal. only, 6 shot, 5 in. barrel, bright blue finish, adj. sights, 7,800 mfg. 1986 to commemorate the Texas Sesquicentennial (1836-1986). Special markings on frame and barrel, smooth Goncalo commemorative grips, ser. no. TWT001 - TWT7800 (estimated). Made 1986 only.

	$450	N/A	7,800

100%	98%	95%	90%	80%	70%	60%	50%	40%	30%	20%	10%

RIFLES

S&W in 1984 disc. importation of all Howa manufactured rifles. Mossberg continued importation utilizing both leftover S&W parts in addition to fabricating their own.

MODEL 320 REVOLVING RIFLE — .320 S&W, 6 shot cylinder, 16, 18, or 20 in. round barrel, hard rubber grips, detachable shoulder stock, blue or nickel (rare, add a premium) finish. 977 mfg. 1879-1887.

▲ *16 or 20 in. barrel Model* — 239 mfg. with 16 in., and 224 with 20 in. barrel.

$9,750	$9,350	$8,700	$8,100	$7,675	$7,000	$6,375	$5,600	$4,800	$3,850	$2,950	$1,950

▲ *18 in. barrel Model* — 514 mfg.

$9,750	$9,350	$8,700	$8,100	$7,675	$7,000	$6,375	$5,600	$4,800	$3,850	$2,950	$1,950

Grading	100%	98%	95%	90%	80%	70%	60%

MODEL A BOLT ACTION RIFLE — .22-250 Rem., .243 Win., .270 Win., .308 Win., .30-06, 7mm Mag., or .300 Win. Mag. cal., 23¾ in. barrel, folding leaf sight, checkered Monte Carlo stock with rosewood forend tip and pistol grip cap. Mfg. 1969-1972.

	$385	$330	$305	$275	$220	$195	$165

MODEL B — similar to Model A, in .243 Win., .270 Win., or .30-06 cal., 20¾ in. barrel, Schnabel forend.

	$425	$305	$275	$250	$195	$165	$140

MODEL C — similar to Model B, with cheekpiece.

	$425	$305	$275	$250	$195	$165	$140

MODEL D — similar to Model C, with full length stock.

	$550	$385	$360	$305	$250	$220	$195

MODEL E — similar to Model D, with no cheekpiece.

	$550	$385	$360	$305	$250	$220	$195

Note: These rifles were made for S&W by Husqvarna in Sweden.

Grading	100%	98%	95%	90%	80%	70%	60%

MODEL 1500 MOUNTAINEER — .222 Rem., .22-250 Rem., .223 Rem, .243 Win, .25-06 Rem, .270 Win, .30-06, or .308 Win. cal., bolt action, 22 in. barrel 5-6 shot mag., no sights, walnut stock and forend, approx. 7 lbs. 10 oz. New 1983.

| | | $300 | $250 | $245 | $210 | $195 | $175 | $160 |

Add $27 for sights.

▲ *Model 1500 Mountaineer Magnum* — 7mm Rem. Mag. or .300 Win. Mag. cal.

| | | $325 | $275 | $260 | $225 | $200 | $180 | $160 |

MODEL 1500 DELUXE — same cals. as standard 1500, Monte Carlo stock, skip-line checkering, select walnut, no sights. New 1983.

| | | $350 | $300 | $260 | $220 | $200 | $180 | $160 |

Add $20 for 7mm Mag. and .300 Win. Mag.

MODEL 1500 DELUXE VARMINT — .222 Rem, .22-250 Rem., or .223 Rem. cal., heavy 24 in. barrel, skip-line checkering, no sights. New 1983.

| | | $350 | $275 | $315 | $275 | $215 | $195 | $170 |

Add $15 for parkerized finish.

MODEL 1700 LS "CLASSIC HUNTER" — .243 Win, 270 Win, or .30-06 cal., 22 in. barrel, removable 5 shot mag., solid recoil pad, no sights, Schnabel forend, finely checkered. New 1983.

| | | $400 | $350 | $315 | $265 | $240 | $220 | $195 |

SHOTGUNS

S&W in 1984 disc. importation of all Howa manufactured shotguns. Mossberg continued importation utilizing both leftover S&W parts in addition to fabricating their own.

MODEL 916 SLIDE ACTION SHOTGUN — 12, 16, or 20 ga., 20, 26, 28, or 30 in. barrels, various chokes, plain pistol grip stock, solid frame. Mfg. 1972-disc.

| | | $175 | $150 | $140 | $130 | $120 | $110 | $100 |

▲ *Vent. rib and pad*

| | | $200 | $175 | $155 | $145 | $135 | $130 | $120 |

MODEL 916T SLIDE ACTION — similar to 916, except barrels can be interchanged.

| | | $195 | $170 | $155 | $145 | $135 | $130 | $125 |

▲ *Vent. rib and pad*

| | | $225 | $200 | $180 | $170 | $155 | $145 | $135 |

MODEL 96 SLIDE ACTION — various cals., ga.'s, disc.

| | | $125 | $110 | $100 | $90 | $75 | $70 | $65 |

MODEL 1000 P SLIDE ACTION — 12 ga, various barrel lengths, chokes, VR.

| | | $350 | $305 | $270 | $230 | $210 | $190 | $170 |

This model is the same as the Model 3000.

MODEL 3000 SLIDE ACTION — 12 or 20 ga., 3 in. chambers, 22-30 in. barrels, walnut stock and forend, 6¼-7½ lbs.

| | | $350 | $305 | $270 | $230 | $210 | $190 | $170 |

Add $30 for multi-choke insertion tubes.
Subtract $40 for slug gun (rifle sights on 22 in. barrel).
This model was also available in a "Waterfowler" variation - values are approx. the same as listed above.

MODEL 3000 POLICE — 12 ga. only, blue or parkerized finish, many combinations of finishes, stock types, and other combat accessories were available for this model, 18 or 20 in. barrel.

| | | $332 | $255 | $215 | $185 | $170 | $155 | $140 |

Add $70 for folding stock.

Grading	100%	98%	95%	90%	80%	70%	60%

MODEL 1000 AUTOLOADER — 12 or 20 ga., 22-30 in. barrels, various chokes, gas operated, vent rib, engraved alloy receiver, checkered pistol grip stock. Mfg. 1972-1984.

	$350	$325	$295	$260	$240	$220	$200

Add $30 for multi-choke tubes.
Add approx. $125 for slug barrel.

▲ *12 and 20 gauge* — Magnum 28 or 30 in. barrel, multi-chokes, steel receiver, "M" suffix.

	$375	$340	$310	$275	$255	$235	$215

▲ *Model 1000 Super 12* — handles all loads interchangeably, top-of-the-line model during its time.

	$500	$450	$400	$360	$330	$300	$280

Add $50 for multi-choke.

MODEL 1000 TARGET — 12 or 20 ga., skeet, super skeet and trap models available. Super skeet has 15 barrel muzzle vents to reduce recoil. Trap model has multi-choke tubes, Monte Carlo select walnut stock and forend. Both alloy and steel receivers available in Skeet model, Trap is steel only.

	100%	98%	95%	90%	80%	70%	60%
Skeet/Super Skeet	$400	$390	$335	$260	$235	$215	$190
Trap (Model 1000T)	$595	$525	$450	$375	$325	$285	$235

Note: Shotguns made for S&W by Howa Machinery, Ltd., Japan.

SNAKE CHARMER

Manufactured by Sporting Arms Manufacturing, Inc. located in Littlefield, TX. Distributor sales only.

SNAKE CHARMER II — .410 ga. only, stainless steel, break open single shot, molded plastic stock and forend, shell holder in stock, 3½ lbs. Also available as Night Charmer (disc. 1988) and Sea Charmer (disc. 1988).

Mfg.'s Sug. Retail	$149		$125	$100	$85		

Add $10 for Night Charmer.
Add $18 for Sea Charmer.
Subtract $10 for black carbon steel barrel (New Generation Model).

SOCIETA SIDERURGICA GLISENTI

Manufacturer located in Brescia, Italy.

GLISENTI MODEL 1910 — 9mm Glisenti, 7 shot, 4 in. barrel, fixed sights, blue, checkered wood, rubber or plastic grips, Italian service pistol. Mfg. 1910-WWII.

Warning: While some Glisentis may chamber and fire the 9mm Luger cartridge, it is extremely dangerous to do so.

	$550	$400	$285	$250	$225	$200	$185

SODIA, FRANZ

Manufacturer located in Ferlach, Austria until 1992.

Sodia arms are superb and are often excellently engraved and inlaid. Professional appraisal should be sought before purchase, since prices are high. Sodia is famous for double-barrel shotguns as well as two and three barrel combinations of rifles and shotguns.

BOCHDRILLING — various cals., top quality workmanship.

	$7,000	$6,500	$6,000	$5,000	$4,000	$3,000	$2,500

DOPPLEBUSCHE — various cals., top quality workmanship.

	$5,000	$4,500	$4,000	$3,000	$2,000	$1,800	$1,600

RIFLE, OVER/UNDER — various cals., top quality workmanship.

	$4,500	$4,250	$4,000	$3,500	$3,000	$2,000	$1,800

Grading	100%	98%	95%	90%	80%	70%	60%

TRAP SHOTGUN — 12 ga. only, boxlock action, various degrees of engraving and ornamentation.

	100%	98%	95%	90%	80%	70%	60%
	$2,500	$1,850	$1,475	$1,100	$900	$750	$600

SOKOLOVSKY CORPORATION SPORT ARMS (SCSA)

Previous manufacturer until 1990 located in Sunnyvale, CA.

SOKOLOVSKY .45 AUTOMASTER — .45 ACP only, stainless steel, single action, 6 in. barrel, 6 shot mag., adj. Millet sights, unique action, is free of external devices, 55 oz. Mfg. 1984-90.

	100%	98%	95%
	$2,700	$2,200	$1,850

Last Mfg.'s Sug. Retail was $3,300.

Total production on this model is 50 pistols.

S

SPENCER REPEATING FIREARMS

Manufactured by Spencer Repeating Rifle Company located in Boston, MA between 1860-1868. Spencer manufactured approximately 144,000 rimfire rifles and carbines, of which approximately 107,000 were contracted to the United States Government during the Civil War.

The brainchild of young Christopher Miner Spencer, more than 13,500 Spencer M1860 Army rifles, 800 M1860 Navy rifles, and 48,000 M1860 Army carbines saw action during the Civil War.

In late 1864, the Chief of Ordnance directed modifications, including reducing the bore from .52 to .50 caliber, and shortening the barrel from 22 inches to 20 inches. The new carbine was designated a Spencer M1865 carbine. Nearly 19,000 were produced by the Spencer Repeating Rifle Company, and another 30,500 by the Burnside Rifle Company, although all were delivered too late to see action in the Civil war. Model 1865 carbines and re-furbished M1860 carbines became the mainstay of America's troops on the Western Frontier until replaced by "Trap-Door" Springfield carbines after 1873.

The author wishes to express his thanks to Mr. Roy Marcot for providing most of the information listed below.

100%	98%	95%	90%	80%	70%	60%	50%	40%	30%	20%	10%

SMALL-FRAME MILITARY CARBINES AND SPORTING RIFLES — fewer than four dozen prototype small-frame .38 cal. sporting rifles and .44 cal. military carbines were made by Christopher Spencer in Hartford between 1860 and 1861. They are exceedingly rare, and only a few are in private hands.

100%	98%	95%	90%	80%	70%	60%	50%	40%	30%	20%	10%
N/A	$12,000	$11,000	$10,000	$8,900	$8,000	$7,000	$6,000	$5,250	$4,250	$3,250	$2,250

MODEL 1860 NAVY RIFLES — the rarest of production Spencer firearms, 803 Spencer Model 1860 Navy rifles with sword-type bayonets were produced for the U.S. Navy Bureau of Ordnance between 1862 and 1863.

100%	98%	95%	90%	80%	70%	60%	50%	40%	30%	20%	10%
N/A	$9,000	$7,950	$6,850	$5,850	$4,850	$3,950	$3,450	$2,900	$2,500	$2,000	$1,500

Add $350-$750 for sword-type bayonets.

MODEL 1860 ARMY RIFLES — between 1863 and 1864, the Spencer factory in Boston produced 11,471 Spencer M1860 Army rifles for the Federal Ordnance Department, another 200 for the U.S. Navy, and approximately 2,000 for private purchase. All were issued with Pattern M1855 angular bayonets which fit only these rifles.

100%	98%	95%	90%	80%	70%	60%	50%	40%	30%	20%	10%
N/A	$6,000	$5,000	$4,000	$3,250	$2,450	$2,150	$1,900	$1,700	$1,500	$1,250	$1,100

Add $200-$450 for angular bayonets.

100%	98%	95%	90%	80%	70%	60%	50%	40%	30%	20%	10%

S

MODEL 1860 CARBINES — beginning in October 1863, the Spencer factory began delivering the first of 45,733 Spencer M1860 carbines to the Ordnance Department for use by Federal cavalrymen. As many as 3,000 additional M1860 carbines went to private purchasers, and also saw action in the war. Because Spencer carbines were so important to the Federal war effort, nearly all saw hard use during the last 18 months of fighting. This resulted in very few weapons available today in excellent condition, and fewer yet with case colors remaining on the receiver.

100%	98%	95%	90%	80%	70%	60%	50%	40%	30%	20%	10%
N/A	$7,500	$6,750	$6,000	$3,250	$2,250	$1,950	$1,750	$1,500	$1,200	$875	$700

Subtract 25% for Springfield Armory reconditioned Spencer Model 1860 carbines (after the war).

MODEL 1865 CARBINES — in 1865 and 1866, the Spencer factory delivered 18,959 Spencer M1865 carbines to the Federal Ordnance Department. Concurrently, the Burnside Rifle Company of Providence, Rhode Island manufactured and delivered 30,502 Spencer M1865 carbines to the Ordnance Department.

100%	98%	95%	90%	80%	70%	60%	50%	40%	30%	20%	10%
N/A	$4,500	$3,975	$3,500	$2,600	$1,850	$1,650	$1,475	$1,275	$1,000	$875	$700

MODEL 1865 ARMY RIFLES — as many as 3,000 Spencer M1865 Army rifles were made by the Spencer factory in 1865. While none were ordered by the U.S. Army Ordnance Department, 2,000 went to the Commonwealth of Massachusetts National Guard, and another 1,000 went to Canadian troops and to private purchasers.

100%	98%	95%	90%	80%	70%	60%	50%	40%	30%	20%	10%
N/A	$3,500	$2,600	$1,850	$1,650	$1,475	$1,275	$1,000	$875	$775	$650	$550

SPRINGFIELD ARMORY RIFLE MUSKET CONVERSION OF SPENCER CARBINES — in 1871, General Dyer, Chief of Ordnance, directed that 1,109 Spencer M1865 carbines be converted to two-band muskets. Each was fitted with Springfield .50 calber barrels which held standard M1855 pattern bayonet.

100%	98%	95%	90%	80%	70%	60%	50%	40%	30%	20%	10%
N/A	$3,975	$3,500	$2,950	$2,550	$2,325	$2,175	$1,975	$1,750	$1,500	$1,000	$875

MODEL 1867 ARMY RIFLES AND CARBINES — in 1867, the Spencer factory produced approx. 1,000 M1867 Army rifles and 12,000 carbines. All were intended for private domestic or foreign military sales.

100%	98%	95%	90%	80%	70%	60%	50%	40%	30%	20%	10%
N/A	$2,950	$2,500	$1,950	$1,500	$1,300	$1,100	$900	$800	$700	$600	$500

NEW MODEL ARMY RIFLES AND CARBINES — in their final year of production, 1868, the Spencer Repeating Rifle Company produced approx. 1,000 Army rifles and 5,000 carbines. These too, were intended for private domestic or foreign military sales.

100%	98%	95%	90%	80%	70%	60%	50%	40%	30%	20%	10%
N/A	$2,950	$2,500	$1,950	$1,500	$1,300	$1,100	$900	$800	$700	$600	$500

SPORTING RIFLES — between 1864 and 1868, the Spencer factory produced approximately 2,000 sporting rifles for the civilian trade. The initial 200 or so were made from surplus military M1860 Army rifle receivers. Thereafter, approximatley 1,800 sporting rifles were made expressly as such. The majority chambered the Spencer 56-46 bottleneck rimfire cartridge, but a small number were produced in .50 caliber, chambering 56-50 and the 56-52 cartridges. Spencer sporting rifles missing the rear tang sight are worth approximately 25% less than those listed below.

100%	98%	95%	90%	80%	70%	60%	50%	40%	30%	20%	10%
N/A	$3,975	$3,500	$2,950	$2,550	$2,225	$1,975	$1,750	$1,350	$1,000	$800	$675

SPHINX

Manufactured by Sphinx Engineering S.A. located in Switzerland. Currently imported by Sphinx U.S.A., located in Meriden, CT. Previously imported by Sile Distributors located in New York, NY.

Grading	100%	98%	95%	90%	80%	70%	60%

PISTOLS

MODEL AT-380 — .380 ACP cal., semi-auto double action only, 3.27 in. barrel, stainless steel frame, two-tone finish, 10 shot mag. with finger extension, checkered walnut grips.

Mfg.'s Sug. Retail	$494	$435	$375	$350	$325	$295	$275	$250

Add $20 for black finish.
Add $71 for N/Pall finish.

MODEL AT-2000S STANDARD — 9mm Para. or .40 S&W (new 1993) cal., semi-auto in standard double action or double action only, 4.53 in. barrel, stainless steel fabrication, 10 (C/B 1994), 15* (9mm Para.), or 11* (.40 S&W) shot mag., checkered walnut grips, choice of two-tone or N/Pall (disc. 1994) finish, fixed sights, 35 oz. This model was originally derived from the Action Arms Model AT-88.

Mfg.'s Sug. Retail	$1,090	$965	$750	$625	$525	$450	$410	$375

Add $117 for .40 S&W cal.
Add $87 for N/Pall finish.

▲ **Model AT-2000PS Police Special** — similar to Model AT-2000S, except has compact slide and 3.66 in. barrel.

Mfg.'s Sug. Retail	$940	$850	$625	$525	$450	$410	$380	$350

Add $40 for .40 S&W cal.
Add $87 for N/Pall finish.

▲ **Model AT-2000P Compact** — similar to Model AT-2000 Standard, except has 3.66 in. barrel and 13 shot mag., 31 oz.

Mfg.'s Sug. Retail	$940	$850	$625	$525	$450	$410	$380	$350

Add $40 for .40 S&W cal.
Add $87 for N/Pall finish.

▲ **Model AT-2000H Sub-Compact** — similar to Model AT-2000 Compact, except has 3.34 in. barrel and 10 shot mag., 26 oz.

Mfg.'s Sug. Retail	$940	$850	$625	$525	$450	$410	$380	$350

Add $40 for .40 S&W cal.
Add $87 for N/Pall finish.

Model AT-2000MS Master — 9mm Para., 9x21mm, or .40 S&W cal., single action only, two-tone finish only, designed for Master's stock class competition. New 1995.

Mfg.'s Sug. Retail	$2,035	$1.795	$1,350	$1,100	$995	$895	$775	$650

Model AT-2000CS Competitor — 9mm Para., 9x21mm, or .40 S&W cal., single or double action, competition model featuring many shooting improvements including 5.3 in. compensated barrel, 10 (C/B 1994), 11* (.40 S&W), or 15* shot mag., Bo-Mar adj. sights, two-tone finish. Importation began 1993.

Mfg.'s Sug. Retail	$1,902	$1,725	$1,275	$1,050	$950	$850	$750	$675

Add $287 for Model AT-2000C (includes Sphinx scope mount).
Add $1,538 for AT-2000K conversion kit (new 1995).
Add $1,490 for Model AT-2000CKS (competition kit to convert AT-2000 to comp. pistol, disc. 1994).

Model AT-2000GMS Grand Master — similar to Model AT-2000 Competitor, except is SA only and includes more advanced competitive shooting features, Bo-Mar sights, top-of-the-line competition model. Importation began 1993.

Mfg.'s Sug. Retail	$2,894	$2,475	$1,925	$1,725	$1,500	$1,250	$1,050	$895

Add $78 for Model AT-2000GM (includes Sphinx scope mount).

SPITFIRE

See listing under JSL (Hereford) in this text.

SPRINGFIELD ARMORY

America's first federal armory located in Springfield, MA. Production began in 1795 and an Act of Congress made it an official federal arsenal in 1872. Not associated with the private firm of the same name located in Geneseo, IL.

In recent years, collectors have realized that military specimens in 98%-100% original condition are very rare and desirable in most cases. Since the supply of these guns is so limited, values listed below for these condition factors may not be indicative of current market conditions. As always, many collectors agree that it is hard to overpay for a mint, original, military specimen.

Grading	100%	98%	95%	90%	80%	70%	60%

MODEL 1870 ROLLING-BLOCK RIFLE, U.S.N. — .50 cal. centerfire, 32⅝ in. barrel, not serial numbered, 22,013 mfg.

	$1,600	$1,300	$1,050	$900	$775	$650	$600

MODEL 1871 ROLLING-BLOCK RIFLE, U.S.A. — .50 cal. centerfire, 36 in. barrel, not serial numbered, 10,001 mfg.

	$1,600	$1,300	$1,050	$900	$775	$650	$600

MODEL 1873 RIFLE "TRAPDOOR" — .45-70, 32⅝ in. barrel, 2 bands. Approx. 73,000 mfg. between 1873-1877. Deduct 20% if stock cartouche faint or absent.

	$1,500	$1,200	$900	$775	$650	$495	$395

MODEL 1884 RIFLE "TRAPDOOR" — .45-70, 32⅝ in. barrel, 2 bands. Approx. 232,000 mfg. between 1885-1890. Deduct 20% if stock cartouche faint or absent.

	$1,250	$950	$725	$625	$525	$425	$360

MODEL 1873 CARBINE — 22 in. barrel, half stock, single barrel band/stacking swivel, 20,000 made, but semi-scarce. Pre-Custer serial numbers made below 43,700, add up to 50%. (Pre-1876 mfg.).

	$2,350	$1,950	$1,750	$1,595	$1,400	$1,150	$900

MODEL 1873 CADET RIFLE — 29½ in. barrel, stacking swivel, no sling swivels. Deduct $100 for variation with sling-swivels.

	$1,600	$1,300	$1,050	$900	$775	$650	$600

Deduct 25-35% if restocked with butt plate and hole drilled for cleaning tools.

MODEL 1875 OFFICER'S RIFLE FIRST TYPE — mfg. 477 between 1875 and 1886, 26 in. barrel, single barrel band. Not serial numbered, some dated, non-issue.

	$7,750	$6,800	$5,750	$5,500	$5,000	$4,500	$4,000

Deduct 15-20% for types 2 and 3.
Approx. 25 rifles were mfg. prior to the standardization of this model.

MODEL 1877 RIFLE — mfg. 3943.

	$1,450	$1,200	$900	$800	$700	$600	$550

MODEL 1877 CARBINE — 22 in. barrel, "C" rear sight to 1,200 yards. Mfg. 2946.

	$2,750	$2,400	$2,000	$1,900	$1,800	$1,600	$1,300

MODEL 1877 CADET RIFLE — 29½ in. barrel. Mfg. 1,050.

	$1,475	$1,200	$1,000	$950	$900	$800	$700

MODEL 1879 RIFLE — mfg. approx. 140,000.

	$795	$650	$500	$450	$400	$350	$300

MODEL 1879 CARBINE — no stacking swivel. Approx. 15,000 mfg.

	$1,100	$900	$800	$700	$650	$550	$500

MODEL 1879 CADET RIFLE — stacking swivel but no sling swivels. Mfg. 5,000.

	$850	$775	$650	$550	$475	$425	$375

Grading	100%	98%	95%	90%	80%	70%	60%

MODEL 1880 — combination triangular, sliding type, bayonet-ramrod. Mfg. 1,001.

	$1,400	$1,200	$1,000	$895	$800	$700	$600

MODEL 1881 FORAGER — 20 ga., 1,376 mfg. 1881-1885. Be cautious when purchasing.

	$2,250	$1,950	$1,700	$1,500	$1,250	$1,000	$875

KRAG-JORGENSEN VARIATIONS MFG. BY SPRINGFIELD

M1892-DATED 1894, 1895, OR 1896 — Springfield Armory, with cleaning rod. Note: designated Type I, has wide, solid upper barrel band.

	$4,180	$3,960	$3,740	$3,575	$3,300	$3,000	$2,600

S

▲ **Dated 1894 or 1895** — designated Type II. Upper band has double strap instead of being solid as in Type I.

	$1,870	$1,705	$1,540	$1,210	$880	$720	$595

FACTORY — ALTERED TO M1896 STYLE

	$250	$220	$195	$165	$140	$125	$105

M1896 — Dated 1896, 1897, 1898, Springfield Armory.

	$470	$440	$330	$250	$220	$185	$155

M1896 CARBINE

	$660	$580	$495	$385	$360	$320	$280

M1895 CARBINE — This is a variant that was dated 1895 and 1896 and omits the word "Model".

	$880	$800	$660	$550	$440	$385	$330

M1896 CADET RIFLE

	$3,025	$2,750	$2,530	$2,200	$1,815	$1,500	$1,200

M1898 RIFLE

	$660	$575	$495	$440	$360	$330	$250

M1898 CARBINE

	$1,450	$1,225	$950	$800	$660	$580	$525

1898 KRAG NRA CARBINE — carbine stock and hardware, shortened rifle (22 in.) barreled action, identifiable by full band front sight.

	$850	$725	$600	$525	$450	$360	$330

M1899 CARBINE

	$750	$635	$525	$495	$470	$440	$395

M1899 CARBINE, PHILIPPINE CONSTABULARY

	$1,100	$990	$825	$715	$550	$480	$400

U.S. MODEL 1903 SPRINGFIELD — .30-06, bolt action, 24 in. barrel. Mfg. 1903-1930.

▲ **Pre-WWI Mfg.** — values below represent original rifles - deduct 80% if reworked.

	$1,750	$1,500	$1,250	$995	$750	$675	$600

▲ **Serialized 800,000 - 1,275,767** — double heat treated receiver.

	$395	$350	$275	$220	$195	$165	$140

▲ **Serialized 1,275,768+** — nickel steel receiver.

	$450	$395	$330	$275	$250	$220	$180

U.S. MODEL 1903 MARK I — similar to U.S. Model 1903 Springfield, except altered for the Pedersen device, a slot is milled into the left side of receiver to act as an ejection port for use of the semi-auto bolt insert, value without device.

	$450	$395	$330	$275	$250	$220	$180

Grading	100%	98%	95%	90%	80%	70%	60%

1903-A1 — similar to U.S. Model 1903 Springfield, except type C pistol grip stock. Mfg. 1930-1939. In 1941 Remington mfg. approx. 350,000.

	$450	$395	$350	$300	$260	$230	$195

▲ *Remington produced*

	$395	$350	$295	$250	$210	$180	$155

1903-A1 NATIONAL MATCH

	$1,200	$1,050	$895	$750	$625	$500	$395

1903-A3 — similar to 1903, with production modifications, aperture rear sight, no finger groove in forestock, lower quality finish, stamped floorplate and barrel band.   Mfg. WWII by Remington and Smith Corona.

	$450	$420	$390	$360	$330	$300	$275

1903-A3 NATIONAL MATCH — 200 mfg., known as the "unmatched" match rifle.

	$1,500	$1,300	$1,000	$850	$750	$675	$600

1903-A4 SNIPER — .30-06 with M73B1 or M84 scope in Redfield mount, no front sight.

	$1,250	$1,000	$775	$675	$575	$500	$450

1903 NRA SPORTING RIFLE — over 4,000 mfg.

	$695	$625	$550	$495	$450	$375	$295

1903 NRA NATIONAL MATCH — similar to 1903, with hand selected and custom fit parts, produced for target shooting. "NRA" and flaming bomb proofed on triggerguard. 1915 date.

	$1,250	$1,000	$775	$675	$575	$500	$450

1903 SPORTER — similar to National Match, with sporter stock and Lyman sight.

	$1,200	$1,000	$825	$750	$625	$525	$470

1903 MATCH STYLE T — similar to Sporter, with heavy barrel, globe sight, target bases, 26, 28, or 30 in. barrel.

	$1,500	$1,275	$1,000	$825	$725	$635	$580

1903 FREE RIFLE TYPE A — similar to Style T, with 28 in. barrel, and Swiss hook butt.

	$1,650	$1,475	$1,300	$1,150	$995	$895	$775

1903 FREE RIFLE TYPE B — similar to Type A, with double set triggers, cheekpiece stock, modified firing pin.

	$2,250	$1,900	$1,600	$1,300	$1,075	$950	$825

MODEL 1922-M1 — .22 Target Rifle or .22 LR, 5 shot mag., 24 in. barrel, modified 1903, Lyman receiver sight, sporter stock, issued 1927.

	$950	$875	$795	$695	$595	$540	$495

M2 .22 TARGET RIFLE — similar to 1922 M1, except improved lock time, adj. head space, bolt design.

	$1,000	$900	$800	$700	$600	$550	$500

SPRINGFIELD ARMORY (MFG. BY SPRINGFIELD INC.)

Private manufacturer/importer located in Geneseo, IL. Until 1992, this company was named Springfield Armory, Geneseo, IL.

The Springfield Armory manufactures commercial pistols and rifles, including reproductions of older military handguns and rifles. Prices shown below are for current manufactured models.

Grading	100%	98%	95%	90%	80%	70%	60%

COMBINATION GUNS

M6 SCOUT — .22 LR, .22 Mag. (disc.), or .22 Hornet/.410 O/U Survival Gun, 14 (legal transfer needed) or 18¼ in. barrels, matte or stainless (new 1995) steel, approx. 4 lbs.

Mfg.'s Sug. Retail	$160	$140	$115	$100	$85	$75	$70	$65

Add $30 for stainless steel.

Older mfg. does not incorporate a triggerguard while newer production has a triggerguard.

PISTOLS

M6 PISTOL — .22 cal. over .45 LC cal. (also shoots .410 ga. shotshells), 16 in. barrels. Mfg. Aug. 1991 - 1992.

		$200	$185	$165	$150	$135	$120	$110

Last Mfg.'s Sug. Retail was $226.

OMEGA PISTOL — .38 Super, 10mm Norma, or .45 ACP cal., single action, ported slide, 5 or 6 in. interchangeable ported or unported barrel with Polygon rifling, special lock-up system eliminates normal barrel link and bushing, Pachmayr grips, dual extractors, adj. rear sight. Mfg. 1987-90.

		$775	$650	$575	$495	$425	$360	$295

Last Mfg.'s Sug. Retail was $849.

Add $663 for interchangeable conversion units.

Each conversion unit includes an entire slide assembly, one mag., 5 or 6 in barrel, recoil spring guide mechanism assembly, and factory fitting.
Add $336 for interchangeable 5 or 6 in. barrel (including factory installation).

OMEGA MATCH — same cals. as Omega, except has low profile combat sights, 8 shot mag., and beveled mag. well. Mfg. 1991-1992.

		$925	$775	$660	$535	$460	$420	$385

Last Mfg.'s Sug. Retail was $1,103.

PISTOLS: P9 SERIES

MODEL P9 — 9mm Para., 9x21mm (new 1991) .40 S&W (new 1991), or .45 ACP cal., patterned after the Czech CZ-75, selective double action design, blue (standard beginning 1993), parkerized (standard until 1992), or duotone finish, various barrel lengths, checkered walnut grips. Mfg. in U.S. starting 1990.

▲ *P9 Standard* — 4.72 in. barrel, 15 shot (9mm Para.), 11 shot (.40 S&W), or 10 shot (.45 ACP) mag., parkerized finish standard until 1992 - blued finish beginning 1993, 32.16 oz. Disc. 1993.

		$430	$375	$335	$295	$275	$240	$215

Last Mfg.'s Sug. Retail was $518.

Add $61 for .45 ACP cal.
Add $182 for duotone finish (disc. 1992).
Subtract $40 for parkerized finish.

In 1992, Springfield added a redesigned stainless steel trigger, patented sear safety which disengages the trigger from the double action mechanism when the safety is on, lengthened the beavertail grip area offering less "pinch", and added a two piece slide stop design.

▲ *P9 Stainless* — similar to P9 Standard, except is constructed from stainless steel, 35.3 oz. Mfg. 1991-1993.

		$475	$425	$350				

Last Mfg.'s Sug. Retail was $589.

Add $50 for .45 ACP cal.

Grading	100%	98%	95%	90%	80%	70%	60%

▲ *P9 Compact* — 9mm Para. or .40 S&W cal., 3.66 in. barrel, 13 shot (9mm Para.) or 10 shot (.40 S&W) mag., shorter slide and frame, rounded triggerguard, 30 ½ oz. Disc. 1992.

	$395	$350	$300	$275	$250	$225	$200

Last Mfg.'s Sug. Retail was $499.

Add $20 for .40 S&W cal.
Add $20-$30 for blue finish depending on cal.
Add $78 for duotone finish.

▲ *P9 Sub-Compact* — 9mm Para. or .40 S&W cal., smaller frame than the P9 Compact, 3.66 in. barrel, 12 shot (9mm Para.) or 9 shot (.40 S&W) finger extension mag., squared off triggerguard, 30.1 oz. Disc. 1992.

	$395	$350	$300	$275	$250	$225	$200

Last Mfg.'s Sug. Retail was $499.

Add $20 for .40 S&W cal.
Add $20-$30 for blue finish depending on cal.

▲ *P9 Factory Comp* — 9mm Para., .40 S&W, or .45 ACP cal., 5 ½ in. barrel (with compensator attached), extended sear safety and mag. release, adj. rear sight, slim competition checkered wood grips, choice of all stainless (disc. 1992) or stainless bi-tone (matte black slide), dual port compensated, 15 shot (9mm Para.), 11 shot (.40 S&W), or 10 shot (.45 ACP) mag., 33.9 oz. Mfg. 1992-1993.

	$595	$525	$450	$420	$390	$360	$330

Last Mfg.'s Sug. Retail was $699.

Add $36 for .45 ACP cal.
Add $75-$100 for all stainless finish.

▲ *P9 Ultra IPSC (LSP)* — competition model with 5.03 in. barrel (long slide ported), adj. rear sight, choice of parkerized (standard finish until 1992 when disc.), blued (disc. 1992), bi-tone (became standard 1993), or stainless steel (disc. 1992) finish, extended thumb safety, and rubberized competition (9mm Para. and .40 S&W cals. only) or checkered walnut (.45 ACP cal. only) grips, 15 shot (9mm Para.), 11 shot (.40 S&W), or 10 shot (.45 ACP) mag., 34.6 oz. Disc. 1993.

		$555	$475	$415	$350	$300	$275	$250

Last Mfg.'s Sug. Retail was $694.

Add $30 for .45 ACP cal.

▲ *P9 Ultra LSP Stainless* — stainless steel variation of the P9 Ultra LSP. Mfg. 1991-92.

		$675	$525	$425

Last Mfg.'s Sug. Retail was $769.

Add $30 for .40 S&W cal.
Add $90 for .45 ACP cal.

▲ *P9 World Cup* — see listing under 1911-A1 Custom Models heading.

R-SERIES PISTOLS

PANTHER MODEL — 9mm Para., .40 S&W, or .45 ACP cal., semi-auto single or double action, 3.8 in. barrel, hammer drop or firing pin safety, 15 shot (9mm Para.), 11 shot (.40 S&W), or 9 shot (.45 ACP) mag., Commander hammer, frame mounted slide stop, narrow profile, non-glare blue finish only, walnut grips, squared off triggerguard, 29 oz. Mfg. 1992 only.

	$535	$450	$395	$350	$300	$275	$250

Last Mfg.'s Sug. Retail was $609.

FIRECAT MODEL — 9mm Para. or .40 S&W cal., single action, 3.5 in. barrel, 3 dot low profile sights, all steel mfg., firing pin block and frame mounted ambidextrous safety, 8 shot (9mm Para.) or 7 shot (.40 S&W) mag., checkered combat style triggerguard and front/rear grip straps, non-glare blue finish, 35 ¾ oz. Mfg. 1992-1993.

	$495	$425	$375	$330	$295	$275	$250

Last Mfg.'s Sug. Retail was $569.

BOBCAT MODEL — while advertised in 1992, this model was never mfg.

LINX MODEL — while advertised in 1992, this model was never mfg.

Grading	100%	98%	95%	90%	80%	70%	60%

1911-A2 S.A.S.S. SINGLE SHOT

Currently, Springfield is offering S.A.S.S. conversion kits at $299 each, S.A.S.S. barrel kits may be purchased for $149 each.

1911-A2 S.A.S.S. — various cals., single shot break open action featuring interchangeable barrels, Pachmayr grips, adj. front and rear sights, blue finish only, 61-66 oz. Mfg. 1990-1992.

▲ **10¾ in. barrel** — .22 LR, 7mm BR, .243 Win., .357 Mag., or .44 Mag. cal.

$650	$560	$495	$450	$420	$390	$360

Last Mfg.'s Sug. Retail was $749.

Add $399 per interchangeable conversion unit (includes barrel).

▲ **15 in. barrel** — .22 LR, .223 Rem., .243 Rem. (new 1991), 7mm BR, 7mm-08 Rem., .308 Win., or .358 Win. cal.

$650	$560	$495	$450	$420	$390	$360

Last Mfg.'s Sug. Retail was $749.

Add $399 per interchangeable conversion unit (includes barrel).

PISTOLS: DISC. 1911-A1 MODELS

MODEL 1911-A1 STANDARD MODEL — .38 Super, 9mm Para., 10mm (new 1990), or .45 ACP cal., patterned after the Colt M1911-A1, 5.04 (Standard) or 4.025 (Commander or Compact Model) in. barrel, 7 shot (Compact), 8 shot (.45 ACP), 9 shot (10mm), or 10 shot (9mm Para. and .38 Super) mag., walnut grips, parkerized, blue, or duotone finish. Mfg. 1985-1990.

$400	$360	$330	$300	$280	$260	$240

Last Mfg.'s Sug. Retail was $454.

Add $35 for blued finish.
Add $80 for duotone finish.
This model is also available with a .45 ACP to 9mm Para. conversion kit for $170 in parkerized finish, or $175 in blued finish.

▲ **Defender Model** — .45 ACP only, similar to Standard 1911-A1 Model, except has fixed combat sights, beveled mag. well, extended thumb safety, bobbed hammer, flared ejection port, walnut grips, factory serrated front strap and two stainless steel magazines, parkerized or blued finish. Mfg. 1988-90.

$485	$435	$375	$340	$300	$280	$260

Last Mfg.'s Sug. Retail was $567.

Add $35 for blued finish.

▲ **Commander Model** — .45 ACP cal. only, similar to Standard 1911-A1 Model, except has 3.63 in. barrel, shortened slide, Commander hammer, low profile 3-dot sights, walnut grips, parkerized, blued, or duotone finish. Mfg. in 1990 only.

$450	$415	$350	$325	$285	$260	$245

Last Mfg.'s Sug. Retail was $514.

Add $30 for blued finish.
Add $80 for duotone finish.

▲ **Combat Commander Model** — .45 ACP cal. only, 4¼ in. barrel, bobbed hammer, walnut grips. Mfg. 1988-89.

$435	$385	$325	$295	$275	$250	$230

Add $20 for blued finish.

▲ **Compact Model** — .45 ACP cal. only, compact variation featuring shortened Commander barrel and slide, reduced M1911 straight grip strap frame, checkered walnut grips, low profile 3-dot sights, extended slide stop, combat hammer, parkerized, blued, or duotone finish. Mfg. 1990 only.

$450	$415	$350	$325	$285	$260	$245

Last Mfg.'s Sug. Retail was $514.

Add $30 for blued finish.
Add $80 for duotone finish.

Grading	100%	98%	95%	90%	80%	70%	60%

▲ **Custom Carry Gun** — .38 Super (special order only), 9mm, 10mm (new 1990), or .45 ACP cal., similar to Defender Model, except has tuned trigger pull, heavy recoil spring, extended thumb safety, and other features. New 1988.

	$860	$725	$660	$535	$460	$420	$385

Last Mfg.'s Sug. Retail was $969.

Add $130 for .38 Super Ramped, 10mm was POR.

▲ **National Match Hardball Model** — .38 Super (disc.), 9mm (disc.), or .45 ACP cal., National Match barrel and bushing, specially fitted frame and slide, BoMar adj. rear sight, Herrett walnut grips, plastic cased. Mfg. 1988-90.

	$780	$650	$565	$515	$460	$415	$385

Last Mfg.'s Sug. Retail was $897.

This model is made specifically for DCM competition shooting.

▲ **Bullseye Wadcutter Model** — .45 ACP cal. only, designed for wadcutter loads only, 5 or 6 (ported or unported) in. barrel, BoMar rib mounted on slide, checkered grip straps, match trigger, beavertail grip safety, polished feed ramp and throated barrel. New 1989.

	$1,415	$1,200	$1,025	$925	$825	$750	$675

Last Mfg.'s Sug. Retail was $1,599.

Add $25 for 6 in. barrel.
Add $80 for 6 in. ported barrel.

▲ **Trophy Master Competition Pistol** — .38 Super, 9mm (disc.), 10mm (new 1990), or .45 ACP cal., competition model which includes low profile combat sights, ambidextrous safety, long match trigger, bobbed hammer, Pachmayr wraparound grips. Mfg. 1988-90.

	$1,300	$1,100	$950	$875	$800	$730	$660

Last Mfg.'s Sug. Retail was $1,443.

Add $130 for .38 Super with supported chamber, 10mm was POR.

▲ **Trophy Master Competition Expert Model** — .38 Super, 9mm (disc.), 10mm (new 1990), or .45 ACP cal., mfg. for IPSC competition shooting, dual chamber compensator system on match barrel, blued finish, ambidextrous thumb safety, beveled and polished mag. well, lowered and flared ejection port, wraparound Pachmayr grips, shock buffer, includes 2 mags. and plastic carrying case. Mfg. 1988-90.

	$1,664	$1,450	$1,225	$1,025	$950	$890	$850

Last Mfg.'s Sug. Retail was $1,664.

Add $130 for .38 Super with supported chamber, 10mm was POR.
This model is an improved variation of the Master Grade Competition Pistol "A".

▲ **Trophy Master Competition Distinguished Model** — similar to Expert Model, except has brushed hard chrome finish, checkered grip straps and triggerguard, top-of-the-line competition model. Mfg. 1988-90.

	$2,000	$1,675	$1,450	$1,225	$1,025	$950	$875

Last Mfg.'s Sug. Retail was $2,275.

Add $130 for .38 Super with supported chamber, 10mm was POR.
Subtract $130 for "B" Model.
This model is an improved variation of the Master Grade Competition Pistol "B-1".

MODEL 1911-A1 90s EDITION PISTOLS

The initials "PDP" refer to Springfield's Personal Defense Pistol series.

MODEL 1911-A1 90s EDITION — .38 Super (disc. 1995), 9mm Para., 10mm (disc. 1991), .40 S&W (disc. 1993), or .45 ACP cal., patterned after the Colt M1911-A1, except has linkless operating system, 5.04 (Standard) or 4 (Champion or Compact Model) in. barrel, 7 shot (Compact), 8 shot (.40 S&W or .45 ACP Standard), 9 shot (9mm Para. or 10mm), or 10 shot (.38 Super) mag., checkered walnut grips, parkerized (.38 Super beginning 1994 or .45 ACP beginning 1993), blue, or duotone (disc. 1992) finish. New 1991.

▲ **Mil-Spec Model 1911-A1** — 35.6 oz.

Mfg.'s Sug. Retail	$476	$415	$355	$325	$295	$275	$250	$225

Add $56 for .38 Super cal. (disc.).

Grading	100%	98%	95%	90%	80%	70%	60%

▲ *Standard/Lightweight Model* — Lightweight Model introduced 1995, matte finish, 28.6 or 35.6 oz.

Mfg.'s Sug. Retail	$527	$445	$395	$350	$325	$295	$275	$250

   Add $30 for 9mm Para. or .38 Super cal. (disc.) - blued finish only beginning 1993.

▲ *Stainless Standard Model* — 9mm Para. (new 1994) or .45 ACP cal., 8 shot mag., wraparound rubber grips, standard or Bomar type (new 1996) sights, beveled mag. well, 39.2 oz. New 1991.

Mfg.'s Sug. Retail	$572	$480	$410	$350

   Add $15 for 9mm Para. cal.
   Add $57 for Bomar type sights.

▲ *Trophy Match* — .45 ACP only, top-of-the-line pistol featuring improved trigger pull, adj. rear sight, match grade barrel and bushing, choice of stainless steel, bi-tone, or blue finish, 35.6 oz. New 1994.

Mfg.'s Sug. Retail	$954	$810	$675	$560	$495	$450	$420	$390

   Add $31 for stainless steel.
   Subtract $14 for bi-tone finish.

▲ *Standard High Capacity* — 9mm Para. or .45 ACP cal., 5 in. barrel, blue or matte parkerized (new 1996) finish with plastic grips, 3 dot fixed combat sights, 10 shot (except for law enforcement) mag. New 1995.

Mfg.'s Sug. Retail	$629	$555	$475	$435	$400	$360	$330	$295

   Add $30 for 9mm Para. cal.
   Add $30 for blue finish.

▲ *Stainless High Capacity* — similar to Standard High Capacity, except is stainless steel. New 1996.

Mfg.'s Sug. Retail	$696	$600	$500	$450

▲ *PDP Factory Comp* — .38 Super or .45 ACP cal. only, entry level IPSC gun, featuring $5\frac{5}{8}$ in. barrel with compensator attached, adj. rear sight, Videki speed trigger, checkered walnut grips, beveled mag. well, 10 shot (.38 Super) or 8 shot (.45 ACP) mag., blued finish only, 40 oz. New 1991.

Mfg.'s Sug. Retail	$947	$795	$665	$575	$495	$450	$420	$390

   Add $37 for .38 Super cal.

▲ *XM4 High Capacity Model* — 9mm or 45 ACP cal., features widened frame for high capacity mag., blued (mfg. 1993 only) or stainless finish only. Mfg. 1993-94.

	$595	$550	$500

Last Mfg.'s Sug. Retail was $689.

▲ *PDP High Capacity Factory Compensated* — .38 Super or .45 ACP cal. only, blued finish. New 1995.

Mfg.'s Sug. Retail	$1,075	$930	$785	$650	$575	$500	$450	$395

   Add $37 for .38 Super cal.

PDP DEFENDER MODEL — .40 S&W (disc. 1992) or .45 ACP cal., standard pistol with slide and barrel shortened to Champion height, tapered cone dual port compensator system, fully adj. sights, Videcki speed trigger, rubber grips, Commander style hammer, serrated front strap, parkerized (disc. 1992), duotone/bi-tone, or blued (disc. 1993) finish. Mfg. began 1991.

Mfg.'s Sug. Retail	$993	$850	$735	$630	$550	$495	$450	$425

1911-A1 COMMANDER MODEL — .45 ACP cal. only, similar to Standard 1911-A1 Model, except has 3.63 in. barrel, shortened slide, Commander hammer, low profile 3-dot sights, walnut grips, parkerized, blued, or duotone finish. Mfg. 1991-92.

	$425	$365	$330	$300	$275	$250	$225

▲ *Combat Commander Model* — .45 ACP cal. only, 4¼ in. barrel, bobbed hammer, walnut grips. Mfg. 1991 only.

	$425	$365	$330	$300	$275	$250	$225

1911-A1 CHAMPION MODEL — .380 ACP (Model MD-1, mfg. 1995 only) or .45 ACP cal., similar to Standard Model, except has 4 in. barrel and shortened slide, blue or parkerized (Mil-Spec Champion, new 1994) finish, Commander hammer, checkered walnut grips, 3 dot sights, 8 shot mag., 33½ oz. New 1992.

Mfg.'s Sug. Retail	$476	$415	$355	$300	$275	$250	$225	$200

   Add $67 for blue finish.
   Subtract $35 for .380 ACP cal. (Model MD-1, disc.).

Grading	100%	98%	95%	90%	80%	70%	60%

▲ *Stainless Champion Model* — .45 ACP cal. only, stainless steel variation of the Champion Model. New 1992.

Mfg.'s Sug. Retail	$582	$495	$420	$350			

▲ *PDP Champion Comp* — .45 ACP cal. only, compensated version of the Champion Model, blue. New 1993.

Mfg.'s Sug. Retail	$871	$780	$690	$600	$550	$500	$450	$395

▲ *Champion XM4 High Capacity* — 9mm or .45 ACP cal., high capacity variation. Mfg. 1994 only.

		$615	$555	$500			

Last Mfg.'s Sug. Retail was $699.

1911-A1 COMPACT MODEL — .45 ACP cal. only, compact variation featuring shortened 4 in. barrel and slide, reduced M1911-A1 curved grip strap frame, checkered walnut grips, low profile 3-dot sights, 6 or 7 shot mag., extended slide stop, standard or lightweight alloy (new 1994) frame, combat hammer, parkerized, blued, or duotone (disc. 1992) finish, standard or lightweight (new 1995) configuration, 27 or 32 oz. New 1991.

Mfg.'s Sug. Retail	$476	$415	$355	$300	$275	$250	$225	$200

Add $66 for blue finish.
Add $67 for Compact Lightweight Model (matte finish only).

▲ *Stainless Compact Model* — stainless steel variation of the Compact Model. New 1991.

Mfg.'s Sug. Retail	$582	$495	$420	$350			

▲ *Compact Comp Lightweight* — compensated version of the Compact Model, bi-tone or matte finish, regular or lightweight alloy (new 1994) frame. New 1993.

Mfg.'s Sug. Retail	$871	$775	$685	$600	$550	$500	$450	$395

▲ *High Capacity Compact* — blue or stainless steel, 3 dot fixed combat sights, black plastic grips, 10 shot (except for law enforcement) mag. New 1995.

Mfg.'s Sug. Retail	$609	$540	$465	$425	$395	$360	$330	$295

Add $39 for stainless steel.

▲ *PDP High Capacity Compact Comp* — .45 ACP cal. only, features compensated 3½ in. barrel, 10 shot (except law enforcement) mag., blue finish only. New 1995.

Mfg.'s Sug. Retail	$964	$830	$725	$625	$550	$495	$450	$425

ULTRA COMPACT — .380 ACP (Lightweight only, mfg. 1995 only) or .45 ACP cal., 3½ in. barrel, bi-tone (.45 ACP only), matte (.380 ACP, MD-1), or parkerized (Mil-Spec Ultra Compact) finish, 6 or 7 shot mag., 24 or 30 oz. New 1995.

Mfg.'s Sug. Retail	$499	$415	$365	$325	$295	$275	$250	$225

Add $70 for bi-tone finish.
Add $86 for stainless steel (RSR distributed - limited mfg.).
Subtract $50 for MD-1 variation (.380 ACP only).

▲ *High Capacity Ultra Compact* — parkerized (Mil-Spec) or blue finish, and stainless steel construction, 3 dot fixed combat sights, black plastic grips. New 1996.

Mfg.'s Sug. Retail	$629	$550	$475	$425	$395	$360	$330	$295

Add $30 for blue finish.
Add $67 for stainless steel.

▲ *V10 Ultra Compact Ported* — .45 ACP cal. only, 3½ in. specially compensated barrel/slide, bi-tone or parkerized (Mil-Spec Ultra Compact) finish, 3 dot combat sights, 30 oz. New 1995.

Mfg.'s Sug. Retail	$569	$470	$425	$365	$325	$295	$275	$250

Add $90 for bi-tone finish.
Add $130 for stainless steel (RSR distributed - limited mfg.).

GULF VICTORY SPECIAL EDITION — .45 ACP cal., special edition featuring presentation grade blued finish, gold etching on slide and other gold-plated small parts, includes specially padded and embroidered storage case with jacket patch, window decal, and cloisonne medallion honoring all U.S. Armed Forces. Mfg. 1991-1992.

			$750	$600	$475		

Last Mfg.'s Sug. Retail was $869.

Grading	100%	98%	95%	90%	80%	70%	60%

1911-A1 CUSTOM MODELS

In addition to the models listed below, Springfield also custom builds other configurations of Race Guns that are available through Springfield dealers. Prices range from $2,160-$3,322.

> Add $100 for all cals. other than .45 ACP.
> Add $449 for Aimpoint Competition Red Dot Scope for PDP variations only.

▲ *Custom Carry Gun* — .45 ACP (other cals. available upon request) cal., similar to Defender Model, except has tuned trigger pull, 7 shot mag., heavy recoil spring, extended thumb safety, available in blue or phosphate (disc.), finish. New 1991.

	100%	98%	95%	90%	80%	70%	60%
Mfg.'s Sug. Retail $1,388	$1,275	$1,000	$925	$750	$675	$550	$475

▲ *Basic Competition* — .45 ACP (other cals. available upon request) cal., BoMar adj. rear sight, blued finish, checkered walnut grips. New 1994.

Mfg.'s Sug. Retail $1,439	$1,325	$1,025	$925	$750	$675	$550	$475

▲ *NRA PPC* — .45 ACP (other cals. available upon request) cal., designed to comply with NRA PPC competitive rules/regulations, factory test target, custom carrying case. New 1995.

Mfg.'s Sug. Retail $1,632	$1,450	$1,175	$995	$850	$750	$650	$575

▲ *1911-A1 Custom Compact* — .45 ACP cal. only, carry or lady's model with shortened slide and frame, compensated, fixed 3 dot sights, Commander style hammer, Herrett walnut grips, other custom features, blue only.

$1,615	$1,325	$1,100	$950	$850	$750	$675

> Last Mfg.'s Sug. Retail was $1,815.

▲ *1911-A1 Custom Champion* — similar to Custom Compact, except is based on Champion model with full size frame and shortened slide.

$1,615	$1,325	$1,100	$950	$850	$750	$675

> Last Mfg.'s Sug. Retail was $1,815.

▲ *National Match Hardball* — .45 ACP cal. only, National Match barrel and bushing, specially fitted frame and slide, blue only, BoMar adj. rear sight, Herrett walnut grips, plastic cased.

Mfg.'s Sug. Retail $1,485	$1,375	$1,050	$950	$775	$700	$575	$500

> This model is made specifically for DCM competition shooting.

▲ *Bullseye Wadcutter* — .45 ACP (other cals. available upon request) cal., specifically designed for wadcutter loads, BoMar rib mounted on slide top, 5 or 6 in. barrel.

Mfg.'s Sug. Retail $1,665	$1,475	$1,200	$995	$850	$750	$650	$575

▲ *Entry Level Wadcutter* — .38 Super, .40 S&W, 10mm, or .45 ACP cal., 5 in. barrel, standard competition features.

$925	$800	$700	$600	$550	$475	$425

> Last Mfg.'s Sug. Retail was $1,049.

> Add $200 for .38 Super cal. Add $391 for 10mm or .40 S&W cal.
> This model features supported chamber in all cals. except .45 ACP.

▲ *Trophy Master "Competition"* — .45 ACP (other cals. available upon request) cal., competition model which includes low profile combat sights, ambidextrous safety, long match trigger, bobbed hammer, Pachmayr wraparound grips.

Mfg.'s Sug. Retail $1,598	$1,420	$1,125	$950	$875	$800	$725	$650

▲ *Trophy Master "Expert"* — .45 ACP (other cals. available upon request) cal., mfg. for IPSC competition shooting, dual chamber compensator system on match barrel, duotone finish.

Mfg.'s Sug. Retail $1,915	$1,695	$1,350	$1,125	$950	$850	$750	$675

> Subtract $111 for Limited Class variation.
> This model is an improved variation of the Trophy Master Competition Model.

▲ *Trophy Master "Distinguished"* — similar to Expert Model, except has brushed hard chrome finish, checkered grip straps and triggerguard, top-of-the-line competition model.

Mfg.'s Sug. Retail $2,717	$2,375	$1,925	$1,525	$1,200	$975	$850	$750

> Subtract $111 for Limited Class variation.

S

Grading	100%	98%	95%	90%	80%	70%	60%

▲ **P9 World Cup** — 9mmx21 or .40 S&W cal., state-of-the-art competition pistol, based on factory P9 Racegun, hard chrome finish only.

| | $2,550 | $2,100 | $1,775 | $1,500 | $1,250 | $975 | $795 |

Last Mfg.'s Sug. Retail was $2,935.

RIFLES: BOLT ACTION

CZ 98 HUNTER CLASSIC — .243 Win., .270 Win., .30-06, .308 Win., 6.5x55mm, 7x57 Mauser, 7x64mm, 7.29x57mm, .300 Win. Mag., or 7mm Rem. Mag. cal., features Mauser 98 Large Ring action, mfg. by CZ in the Czech Republic and Springfield Armory, controlled feeding, 24 in. hammer forged barrel, adj. trigger, choice of walnut or synthetic stock, 7.7 lbs. Limited mfg. 1995 only.

| | $345 | $315 | $285 | $260 | $240 | $220 | $195 |

Last Mfg.'s Sug. Retail was $411.

Add $38 for walnut stock.

RIFLES: SEMI-AUTO - MILITARY DESIGN

M1 GARAND AND VARIATIONS — .30-06 Springfield (disc.), .270 Win. (disc. 1987), or .308 Win. cal., semi-auto, 24 in. barrel, gas operated, 8 shot mag., adj. sights, 9½ lbs.

The M1 Garand and variations listed below were temporarily discontinued in 1985. The factory should be contacted directly for prices and availability of M1A parts and other rifle related accessories.

▲ **Standard Model** — supplied standard with camo GI fiberglass stock. Temporarily disc. in 1990.

| | $725 | $650 | $575 | $525 | $485 | $450 | $425 |

Last Mfg.'s Sug. Retail was $761.

Subtract $65 if with GI stock.

▲ **National Match** — walnut stock, match barrel and sights.

| | $850 | $775 | $700 | $650 | $600 | $550 | $495 |

Last Mfg.'s Sug. Retail was $897.

Add $240 for Kevlar stock (disc.).

▲ **Ultra Match** — match barrel and sights, glass bedded stock, walnut stock standard. Temporarily disc. in 1990.

| | $950 | $850 | $725 | $675 | $610 | $550 | $500 |

Last Mfg.'s Sug. Retail was $1,033.

Add $240 for Kevlar stock (disc.).

▲ **M1-D Sniper Rifle** — limited quantities, with original M84 scope, prong type flash suppressor, leather cheek pad and slings, .30-06 only.

| | $950 | $850 | $725 | $675 | $610 | $550 | $500 |

Last Mfg.'s Sug. Retail was $1,033.

▲ **Tanker Rifle** — similar to T-26 authorized by Gen. MacArthur at the end of WWII, 18¼ in. barrel, .30-06 or .308 Win. cal., GI stock standard.

| | $725 | $675 | $600 | $525 | $460 | $380 | $335 |

Last Mfg.'s Sug. Retail was $797.

Add $23 for walnut full stock.

BM 59 — .308 Win. cal., mfg. in Italy and machined and assembled in the Springfield Armory factory, 19.32 in. barrel, 20 shot box mag., 9½ lbs.

▲ **Standard Italian Rifle** — with grenade launcher, winter trigger, tri-compensator, and bipod.

| | $1,750 | $1,400 | $1,200 | $1,000 | $895 | $850 | $800 |

Last Mfg.'s Sug. Retail was $1,950.

▲ **Alpine Rifle** — with Beretta pistol grip type stock.

| | $2,025 | $1,625 | $1,350 | $1,150 | $1,000 | $925 | $850 |

Last Mfg.'s Sug. Retail was $2,275.

This model is also available in a Paratrooper configuration with folding stock at no extra charge.

Grading	100%	98%	95%	90%	80%	70%	60%

▲ **Nigerian Rifle** — similar to BM 59, except has Beretta pistol grip type stock.

	$2,075	$1,650	$1,375	$1,150	$1,000	$925	$850

Last Mfg.'s Sug. Retail was $2,340.

▲ **E Model Rifle**

	$1,975	$1,595	$1,325	$1,125	$975	$900	$825

Last Mfg.'s Sug. Retail was $2,210.

M1A RIFLES — .243 Win. (disc.), .308 Win., or 7mm-08 Rem. (1991 mfg. only) cal., patterned after the original Springfield M14 - except semi-auto, walnut or fiberglass stock, 22 in. barrel, fiberglass handguard, 9 lbs.

▲ **Standard/Basic Model** — above specifications, choice of Collector (original GI stock), new walnut (M1A Standard Model beginning 1993), black fiberglass (M1A Basic Model), camo fiberglass, GI wood (disc. 1992), and brown or black laminated (M1A Standard Model beginning 1996) stock, regular or National Match barrel.

Mfg.'s Sug. Retail	$1,249	$1,040	$825	$725	$625	$550	$495	$450

    Add $58 for GI Collector stock.
    Add $132 for new walnut stock.
    Add $191 for black or $217 for brown laminated stock.
    Add $117 for National Match barrel.
    Add $213 for National Match barrel and sights.
    Standard (entry level model) stock configuration for 1996 is black or camo fiberglass.

▲ **M1A E-2** — standard stock is birch. Disc.

	$975	$825	$745	$650	$590	$550	$495

Last Mfg.'s Sug. Retail was $842.

    Add $30 for walnut stock.
    Add $120 for Shaw stock with Harris bipod.

▲ **National Match** — National Match sights, barrel, mainspring guide, flash suppressor, and gas cylinder, special glass bedded oil finished match stock, tuned trigger, walnut stock became standard in 1991, 9 lbs.

Mfg.'s Sug. Retail	$1,729	$1,495	$1,060	$845	$725	$650	$575	$525

    Add $155 for heavy composition stock (disc.).
    Add $250 for either fiberglass or fancy burl wood stock (disc.).
    .243 Win. and 7mm-08 Rem. cals. are also available at extra charge.

▲ **Super Match** — similar to National Match, except has air-gauged Douglas or Hart heavy barrel, oversized walnut super match stock, and modified operating rod guide, rear lugged receiver beginning 1991, approx. 10 lbs.

Mfg.'s Sug. Retail	$2,050	$1,700	$1,125	$935	$800	$700	$625	$575

    Add approx. $200 for fiberglass or fancy burl walnut stock (disc.).
    .243 Win. and 7mm-08 Rem. cals. are also available at extra charge.

▲ **M21 Law Enforcement/Tactical Rifle** — .308 Win. cal., law enforcement variation of the Super Match mfg. with match grade parts giving superior accuracy, adj. cheekpiece stock. New 1990.

Mfg.'s Sug. Retail	$2,204	$1,875	$1,525	$1,325	$1,100	$925	$800	$700

M1A "GOLD SERIES" — .308 Win. cal., heavy walnut competition stock, gold medal grade heavy Douglas barrel. Add $126 for Kevlar stock, add $390 for special Hart stainless steel barrel, add $516 for Hart stainless steel barrel with Kevlar stock. Mfg. 1987 only.

	$1,944	$1,750	$1,375	$1,150	$975	$850	$740

Last Mfg.'s Sug. Retail was $1,944.

M1A-A1 RIFLE — .308 Win. cal., features new walnut stock. Mfg. 1993-94.

	$1,075	$865	$750	$625	$550	$495	$450

Last Mfg.'s Sug. Retail was $1,289.

    Add $200 for folding stock.

Grading	100%	98%	95%	90%	80%	70%	60%

▲ **M1A-A1 Bush Rifle** — .308 Win. cal., 18 in. shrouded barrel, 8 lbs. 12 oz., collector, walnut, black fiberglass folding (disc. 1994 per C/B), and black fiberglass or laminated black stock.

Mfg.'s Sug. Retail	$1,381	$1,195	$935	$800	$675	$575	$500	$450

Add $29 for walnut stock.
Add $15 for black fiberglass stock.
Add $86 for black laminated stock.
Add $235 for National Match variation (disc.).
Add $525 for Super Match variation (disc.).

SAR-8 — .308 Win. cal., patterned after the H & K Model 91, recoil operated delayed roller lock action, fluted chamber, rotary adj. rear aperture sight, 18 in. barrel, supplied with walnut (disc. 1994) or black fiberglass thumbhole sporter stock, 10 (C/B 1994) or 20 (disc. 1994) shot detachable mag., 8.7 lbs. Mfg. in U.S. starting 1990.

Mfg.'s Sug. Retail	$1,204	$1,015	$835	$750	$675	$600	$550	$500

SAR-8 parts are interchangeable with both SAR-3 and HK-91 parts.

▲ **SAR-8 Tactical Counter Sniper Rifle** — .308 Win. cal., tactical sniper variation of the SAR-8. New 1996.

Mfg.'s Sug. Retail	$1,610	$1,325	$1,000	$825	$725	$650	$575	$525

SAR-48/SAR-4800 SPORTER MODEL — .308 Win. cal., authentic model of the Belgian semi-auto FAL/LAR rifle, 21 in. barrel, adj. gas operation, 10 (C/B 1994) or 20 (disc.) shot mag., walnut (disc.) or black fiberglass thumbhole sporter stock, adj. sights, sling, and mag. loader. New 1985.

Mfg.'s Sug. Retail	$1,249	$1,080	$915	$785	$675	$625	$575	$525

Add $70 for Paratrooper model with folding stock (disc.).
Add $17 for Compact Sporter Model (disc.).

The SAR-48 was disc. in 1989 and reintroduced as the Model SAR-4800 in 1990. All SAR-4800 parts are interchangeable with both SAR-48 and FN/FAL parts. This model is an updated variation of the pre-WWII FN Model 49.

▲ **SAR-48/SAR-4800 Bush Rifle Sporter Model** — similar to standard model, except has 18 in. barrel.

		$1,085	$900	$795	$695	$640	$595	$550

Last Mfg.'s Sug. Retail was $1,216.

▲ **SAR-48 .22 Cal.** — .22 LR variation of the Sporter Model. Disc. 1989.

		$725	$660	$595	$540	$495	$450	$400

Last Mfg.'s Sug. Retail was $760.

DR-200 SPORTER RIFLE — while advertised, this model was never mfg. ($687 was planned MSR).

RIFLES: SPORTING

MAUSER M98 — 7x57mm, surplus rifles with standard military dimensions and features. Importation disc. 1989.

▲ **Hunting/Utility Grade**

		$70	$50	$45	$45	$40	$40	$35

Last Mfg.'s Sug. Retail was $75.

▲ **Collector Grade**

		$105	$90	$80	$70	$60	$50	$40

Last Mfg.'s Sug. Retail was $116.

▲ **Premium Grade**

		$170	$150	$130	$115	$100	$90	$80

Last Mfg.'s Sug. Retail was $194.

STALLARD ARMS

Manufacturer located in Mansfield, OH since 1991. Distributed by MKS Supply, Inc. located in Mansfield, OH.

Please refer to the Hi-Point listing in this text.

STANDARD ARMS COMPANY
Wilmington, DE.

Grading	100%	98%	95%	90%	80%	70%	60%

MODEL G AUTOLOADER — .25-35, .30-30, .25 Rem., .30 Rem., or .35 Rem. cal., bottom loading box mag., 22 in. barrel, open sight, straight stock. This was the first gas operated rifle in U.S.A. Gas port can be closed and gun will function as a slide action, mfg. 1910.

	$575	$475	$400	$300	$275	$250	$225

> A variation that was slide action only (Model M) also was mfg. — subtract 35% from values listed above.

STAR, BONIFACIO ECHEVERRIA
Manufactured in Eibar, Spain. Currently imported by Interarms located in Alexandria, VA.

PISTOLS: SEMI-AUTO

MODEL H — similar to Model HN, except 7.65mm, 7 shot.

	$350	$250	$170	$120	$100	$90	$75

MODEL HN — .380 auto, 6 shot, 2¾ in. barrel, blue, fixed sights, plastic grips. Mfg. 1934-1941.

	$375	$265	$180	$120	$100	$90	$75

MODEL I — .32 ACP, 9 shot, 4¾ in. barrel, blue, fixed sights, plastic grips. Mfg. 1934-1936.

	$350	$250	$170	$120	$100	$85	$70

MODEL IN — similar to Model I, except .380 ACP, 8 shot, 4¾ in. barrel, blue.

	$395	$265	$180	$125	$105	$90	$75

MODEL 1920 — 9mm BB or .38 Super cal., easily identified by unusual safety located on left rear slide.

	$475	$350	$295	$240	$185	$150	$120

MODEL 1921 — 9mm BB, this model was fitted with a grip safety that was later dropped when standardizing the Model A production.

	$450	$325	$240	$215	$180	$145	$115

MODEL 1922 — designation for the early Model A.

	$375	$285	$240	$215	$180	$145	$115

MODEL A — modified Government Colt, .38 Super, 5 in. barrel, no grip safety, blue, checkered wood grips. Mfg. 1934-present but not currently imported.

	$275	$230	$200	$165	$145	$130	$110

MODEL A CARBINE — usually 7.63mm, unusual variation, slotted with tangent rear sight and extended barrel.

	$1,750	$1,350	$1,050	$825	$700	$575	$450

> Add $500 for original stock (different from MB and MMS stock).

MODEL B — similar to Model A, but 9mm Luger. Mfg. 1934-1975.

	$295	$250	$205	$170	$150	$140	$115

> Add 150% if Waffenamt proofed.

MODEL M — similar to Model A, except has large frame, available in 9mm Bergmann, 9mm Luger, 8 shot, and .45 ACP, 7 shot, 5 in. barrel, blue, fixed sights, checkered wood or plastic grips.

	$295	$250	$200	$165	$150	$140	$120

Grading	100%	98%	95%	90%	80%	70%	60%

MODEL P — .45 ACP cal. only, similar to Model A, except has large frame, 7 shot mag. Mfg. 1934-1975.

	$325	$275	$210	$175	$155	$145	$120

MODELS SUPER A (9mm Largo), M (9mm Largo), & P (.45 ACP) — similar to Models A, M, & P, except has loaded chamber indicator, mag. safety, and easier takedown feature. Mfg. 1946-1989.

	$395	$325	$215	$180	$160	$145	$125

Last Mfg.'s Sug. Retail was $340.

Add 100% for Super M and Super P.

The Super A was a Spanish Service pistol. Recent imports in 80% condition are available in the $100 range.

MODEL SUPER B — 9mm Para., similar to Models B, except has loaded chamber indicator, mag. safety and easier takedown feature, choice of blue or Starvel finish on Model B. Importation disc. in 1990.

	$270	$240	$210	$185	$160	$140	$120

Last Mfg.'s Sug. Retail was $330.

Add $30 for Starvel finish.

SUPER TARGET MODEL — similar to Star Super, but target sights, extended trigger guard, modified trigger. Rare.

	$1,250	$950	$800	$700	$600	$500	$400

MODEL MB — 9mm Para., late production Model M cut for shoulder stock, mag. safety.

	$1,295	$975	$675	$565	$450	$365	$250

Add $300 for shoulder stock.

MODEL MMS — 7.63mm, late production Model M cut for shoulder stock, mag. safety.

	$1,000	$750	$460	$400	$325	$260	$200

Add $300 for shoulder stock.

MODEL SI — .32 ACP, 8 shot, 4 in. barrel, blue, without grip safety, small version of Government .45 in appearance, plastic grips. Mfg. 1941-1965.

	$200	$190	$160	$135	$115	$100	$80

MODEL S — similar to Model SI, except .380 ACP cal., 9 shot, mfg. 1941-1965. Importation of these Police contract models was disc. 1991.

	$195	$170	$145	$125	$110	$95	$85

Last Mfg.'s Sug. Retail was $237.

Add $30 for Starvel finish.

Beginning in 1989, Interarms started importing factory reconditioned used Spanish Police Contract Model S pistols - these guns are available in either blue or Starvel finish and are supplied with a plastic box with accessories.

MODELS SUPER SI AND S — similar to Model S, with Super Star improvements. Mfg. 1946-1972.

	$240	$230	$210	$195	$165	$140	$120

MODEL SUPER SM — similar to Model Super S, except adjustable sight and wood grips. Mfg. 1973-1981.

	$250	$235	$220	$200	$175	$145	$125

MODEL CO POCKET — .25 auto, 2¾ in. barrel, blue, fixed sights, plastic grips. Mfg. 1941-1957.

	$250	$190	$165	$145	$120	$110	$90

MODEL CU STARLET — .25 auto, 2⅜ in. barrel, alloy frame, fixed sights, plastic grips, blue, or chrome slide, frame anodized in black, blue, green, gray, or gold. Mfg. 1957-present, no longer imported as of 1968 due to Federal GCA legislation.

	$235	$200	$165	$145	$120	$110	$90

Grading	100%	98%	95%	90%	80%	70%	60%

MODEL DK (STARFIRE) — .380 auto, $3\frac{1}{8}$ in. barrel, fixed sights, plastic stocks, finished in same color availability as Model CU. Mfg. 1957-present, U.S. import ceased as of 1968 due to Federal GCA legislation.

	100%	98%	95%	90%	80%	70%	60%
	$400	$350	$295	$255	$225	$180	$155

Add 10% for unusual alloy colors.

MODEL HK LANCER — similar to Model Starfire, except .22 LR. Mfg. 1955-1968.

	100%	98%	95%	90%	80%	70%	60%
	$225	$200	$180	$160	$140	$120	$110

MODEL F — .22 LR, 10 shot, 4 in. barrel, fixed sights, blue, plastic grips. Mfg. 1942-1967.

	100%	98%	95%	90%	80%	70%	60%
	$325	$225	$140	$110	$95	$85	$55

MODEL FS — similar to Model F, except 6 in. barrel, adj. sights. Mfg. 1942-1967.

	100%	98%	95%	90%	80%	70%	60%
	$325	$225	$150	$120	$100	$90	$65

MODEL F OLYMPIC RAPID FIRE — .22 Short, 9 shot, 7 in. barrel, adj. sight, aluminum slide, barrel weights and muzzle brake, blue, plastic grips. Mfg. 1942-1967.

	100%	98%	95%	90%	80%	70%	60%
	$425	$325	$210	$175	$155	$140	$130

MODEL FR — restyled Model F, adj. sight and slide stop. Mfg. 1967-1972.

	100%	98%	95%	90%	80%	70%	60%
	$300	$225	$150	$120	$100	$90	$65

MODEL FRS — similar to Model FR, only 6 in. barrel, available in chrome. Mfg. 1967-present.

	100%	98%	95%	90%	80%	70%	60%
	$300	$225	$150	$120	$100	$90	$65

MODEL FM — similar to Model FR, except heavier frame, web ahead of trigger guard, $4\frac{1}{2}$ in. barrel. Mfg. 1972-present.

	100%	98%	95%	90%	80%	70%	60%
	$275	$180	$150	$120	$100	$90	$65

MODEL BKS STARLIGHT — 9mm Para., 8 shot, $4\frac{1}{4}$ in. barrel, plastic grips. Mfg. 1970-1981.

	100%	98%	95%	90%	80%	70%	60%
Blue	$265	$230	$210	$180	$160	$145	$130
Chrome	$295	$240	$220	$195	$170	$155	$145

MODEL BM SEMI-AUTO — 9mm, single action, 8 shot mag., 4 in. barrel, steel frame, Colt 1911 action, blue, chrome (disc. 1989), or Starvel (new 1990) finish, plastic grips, 35 oz. Importation disc. 1991.

	100%	98%	95%	90%	80%	70%	60%
	$285	$245	$205	$180	$165	$155	$145

Last Mfg.'s Sug. Retail was $415.

Add $30 for Starvel or chrome (disc. 1990) finish.
Add $150 for Navy issue with escutcheon grips.

MODEL BKM — similar to Model BM, except lightweight duraluminum frame, blued finish only, 26 oz. Importation disc. 1991.

	100%	98%	95%	90%	80%	70%	60%
	$285	$250	$215	$190	$170	$160	$150

Last Mfg.'s Sug. Retail was $415.

MODEL PD — .45 ACP, 6 shot mag., single action, 4 in. barrel, adj. rear sight, blue or Starvel (new 1990) finish only, walnut grips, alloy frame, 25 oz. Mfg. 1975-present. Importation disc. 1991.

	100%	98%	95%	90%	80%	70%	60%
	$345	$290	$250	$215	$195	$170	$160

Last Mfg.'s Sug. Retail was $475.

Add $20 for Starvel finish (new 1990).

MODEL 28 — 9mm, double action, 15 shot mag., $4\frac{1}{4}$ in. barrel, blue finish only, advanced design, 40 oz. Mfg. 1983 and 1984 only.

	100%	98%	95%	90%	80%	70%	60%
	$375	$310	$325	$275	$250	$225	$200

Note: Model 28 is interesting since no screws are used in its manufacture. Hammer assembly (including spring, cocking lever, sear, disconnector and ejector) is housed under removable backstrap.

Grading	100%	98%	95%	90%	80%	70%	60%

MODEL 30M — 9mm Para. only, successor to the Model 28, double action, 4.33 in. barrel, 15 shot mag., blued finish only, adj. rear sight, checkered wraparound plastic grips, steel frame, 40 oz. New 1985. Importation disc. 1991.

	100%	98%	95%	90%	80%	70%	60%
	$400	$340	$315	$295	$270	$250	$225

Last Mfg.'s Sug. Retail was $495.

MODEL 30/31 PK STARFIRE DURAL — similar to Model 30M, except duraluminum frame, 3.86 in. barrel, 30 oz.

	100%	98%	95%	90%	80%	70%	60%
	$455	$360	$315	$295	$270	$250	$225

Last Mfg.'s Sug. Retail was $580.

The Model 30 PK was discontinued in 1989 and the Model 31 PK was imported 1990-1993.

MODEL 31P STARFIRE — 9mm Para. (disc. 1993) or .40 S&W (new 1990) cal., compact variation utilizing double action, features Acculine barrel (3.86 in.) similar to Firestar Model, 14 shot mag., ambidextrous safety with decocking lever, blue or Starvel finish, all steel construction, 39.4 oz. Imported 1990-94.

	100%	98%	95%	90%	80%	70%	60%
	$350	$295	$270	$250	$225	$210	$195

Last Mfg.'s Sug. Retail was $398.

Add $30 for Starvel finish (disc. 1993).

MODEL M40 FIRESTAR — .40 S&W cal., single action, 6 shot mag., 3.39 in. Acculine barrel, checkered rubber grips, compact design utilizing all steel construction, 3 dot sighting system with adjustable rear sight, blue or Starvel finish, 30.35 oz. New 1990.

		100%	98%	95%	90%	80%	70%	60%
Mfg.'s Sug. Retail	$445	$325	$275	$230	$200	$180	$165	$150

Add $20 for Starvel finish.

▲ *Model M40 Firestar Plus* — similar to M40 Firestar, except incorporates alloy frame, new grip design, ambidextrous easy-view safety, and fast button release 10 shot mag. Mfg. 1995.

	100%	98%	95%	90%	80%	70%	60%
	$395	$330	$280	$250	$225	$200	$180

Last Mfg.'s Sug. Retail was $527.

Add $25 for Starvel finish.

MODEL M43 FIRESTAR — 9mm Para., 7 shot mag., otherwise similar to Model M40 Firestar.

		100%	98%	95%	90%	80%	70%	60%
Mfg.'s Sug. Retail	$430	$315	$275	$230	$200	$180	$165	$150

Add $20 for Starvel finish.

▲ *Model M43 Firestar Plus* — similar to M43 Firestar, except incorporates alloy frame, new grip design, ambidextrous easy-view safety, and fast button release 10 shot mag. New 1995.

		100%	98%	95%	90%	80%	70%	60%
Mfg.'s Sug. Retail	$460	$345	$290	$235	$200	$185	$170	$155

Add $27 for Starvel finish.

MODEL M45 FIRESTAR — .45 ACP, single action, ultra compact design featuring 4 barrel lugs, steel frame and slide, 3.6 in. reverse taper Acculine barrel, 6 shot mag., black synthetic grips, blue or Starvel finish, 35 oz. New 1992.

		100%	98%	95%	90%	80%	70%	60%
Mfg.'s Sug. Retail	$470	$355	$295	$240	$200	$185	$170	$155

Add $20 for Starvel finish.

▲ *Model M45 Firestar Plus* — similar to M45 Firestar, except incorporates alloy frame, new grip design, ambidextrous easy-view safety, and fast button release 10 shot mag. Mfg. 1995 only.

	100%	98%	95%	90%	80%	70%	60%
	$415	$345	$285	$250	$225	$200	$180

Last Mfg.'s Sug. Retail was $554.

Add $26 for Starvel finish.

MEGASTAR — 10mm or .45 ACP cal., larger variation of the Firestar featuring 4.6 in. barrel and 12 (.45 ACP) or 14 (10mm) shot mag., 47.6 oz. Imported 1992-94.

	100%	98%	95%	90%	80%	70%	60%
	$525	$375	$350	$325	$295	$275	$250

Last Mfg.'s Sug. Retail was $653.

Add $29 for Starvel finish.

Grading	100%	98%	95%	90%	80%	70%	60%

ULTRASTAR — 9mm Para. or .40 S&W (new 1996) cal., compact double action design, 3.57 in. barrel, 9 shot mag., blued steel metal, triple dot sights, steel internal mechanism, polymer exterior construction, 26 oz. New 1994.

Mfg.'s Sug. Retail	$490	$415	$360	$330	$295	$275	$250	$225

STEEL CITY ARMS, INC.

Manufacturer located in Pittsburgh, PA until 1990. In 1991, Desert Industries, Inc. acquired Steel City Arms, Inc. and moved the manufacture to Las Vegas, NV. To date, only the Steel City Arms, Inc. logo has appeared on newly mfg. Desert Industries, Inc. guns.

DOUBLE DEUCE — .22 LR only, double action semi-auto, matte finish stainless steel, 2½ in. barrel, 7 shot mag., uncheckered rosewood grips, 18 oz. Mfg. 1984-90.

			$265	$230	$200		

Last Mfg.'s Sug. Retail was $290.

Various select hardwood stocks were also available at extra cost ($20-100).

STERLING

Previous manufacturer located in Gasport, NY. Disc. 1983.

PISTOLS

Rather than list individual models, the following generalizations will help in ascertaining values for this trademark. Models 300, 302 and 402 will average between $75 and $150 if in 70%+ condition. Models 283, 284, 285 (Husky), and 286 (Trapper) arc semi-auto .22 cal. pistols with various barrel lengths — values will range between $90-$150. Models 400 (.380 ACP), PPL (.380 ACP short barrel), and 450 (.45 ACP) usually range in the $150-$275 range.

STERLING ARMAMENT, LTD.

Manufacturer located in England since 1900. Previously imported and distributed by Cassi Inc. located in Colorado Springs, CO until 1990.

CARBINES

AR-180 — .223 Rem. cal., side-folding stock. Disc.

		$850	$775	$695	$625	$550	$495	$450

STERLING MK 6 — 9mm Para., blowback semi-auto with floating firing pin, shrouded 16.1 in. barrel, side mounted mag., folding stock, 7½ lbs.

		$565	$495	$450	$410	$375	$340	$310

Last Mfg.'s Sug. Retail was $650.

PISTOLS

PARAPISTOL MK 7 C4 — 9mm Para., 4 in. barrel, semi-auto paramilitary design pistol, crinkle finish, same action as MK. 6 Carbine, fires from closed bolt, 10, 15, 20, 30, 34 or 68 shot mag., 5 lbs.

		$500	$435	$375	$350	$325	$295	$265

Last Mfg.'s Sug. Retail was $600.

PARAPISTOL MK 7 C8 — 9mm, similar to C4, except has 7.8 in. barrel, 5¼ lbs.

		$525	$450	$390	$365	$330	$300	$275

Last Mfg.'s Sug. Retail was $620.

STEVENS, J., ARMS COMPANY

J. Stevens Arms Company was founded in 1864 at Chicopee Falls, MA as J. Stevens & Co. In 1886 the name was changed to J. Stevens Arms and Tool Co. In 1916, the plant became New England Westinghouse, and tooled up for both Browning machine guns and Moisin-Nagant Rifles. In 1920, the plant was sold to the Savage Arms Corp. and manufactured guns were marked "J. Stevens Arms Co.". This designation was dropped in the late 1940s, and only the name "Stevens" has been used up to the present date.

In 1990, Savage Arms discontinued the manufacture of all firearms (rifles and shotguns) bearing the Stevens trademark. All guns manufactured by Savage Arms now bear the Savage trademark only.

Depending on the remaining Stevens factory data, a factory letter authenticating the configuration of a particular specimen may be obtained by contacting Mr. John Callahan (see Trademark Index for listings and address). The charge for this service is $10.00/gun - please allow 2-4 weeks for an adequate response.

Grading	100%	98%	95%	90%	80%	70%	60%

PISTOLS

NO. 10 TARGET SINGLE SHOT — .22 LR, 8 in. barrel, blue, adj. sights, rubber grips, squared off like an automatic pistol, tip up action. Mfg. 1919-1939.

	$220	$200	$185	$165	$140	$120	$100

NO. 35 TARGET SINGLE SHOT — .22 LR or .25 Rimfire cal., 6, 8, 10, or 12¼ in. barrel, blue, walnut grips. Mfg. 1907-1939.

	$350	$300	$265	$220	$200	$185	$165

NO. 35 "OFFHAND" AUTOSHOT — .22 LR or .410 (actually a pistol-length shotgun). Class Three — must be registered with BATF. Introduced 1931, disc. 1935.

	$350	$300	$250	$225	$200	$150	$125

RIFLES

Stevens made a wide variety of inexpensive, utilitarian rifles that to date have attracted mostly shooting interest, but little collector interest. A listing of these models may be found in the back of this text under "Serialization".

TIP-UP RIFLES — .22 S, .22 LR, .25 Stevens, .32, .38, or .44 Long RF or CF, variations No. 1- No. 15 feature various weights, wood styles, sights, and other differences, later series has full loop at rear triggerguard, circa 1870s-1895.

▲ *Basic Model No. 1 without forearm*

	$500	$475	$425	$375	$300	$250	$200

POCKET RIFLES — detachable serially numbered nickel-plated stock, variations found within each frame size.

▲ *Small Frame* — .22 cal. (various issues).

	$450	$400	$350	$300	$275	$235

▲ *Without Stock*

	$300	$250	$200	$150	$125	$100

▲ *Medium Frame* — .22, .32, .38, .44 cals. (various issues).

	$500	$450	$400	$350	$300	$250

▲ *Without Stock*

	$300	$250	$200	$150	$125	$100

▲ *Large Frame* — .22 to .44 cals.

	$600	$550	$500	$450	$400	$350

S

Grading	100%	98%	95%	90%	80%	70%	60%
▲ *Without Stock*	$425	$375	$325	$275	$225	$200	

MODEL 44 IDEAL SINGLE SHOT — .22 LR through .44-40 cals., rolling block, lever action, takedown, 24 or 26 in. barrels, straight grip stock and forearm. Mfg. 1894-1932.

	$600	$550	$500	$425	$325	$300	$275

Deduct 20% for Rimfire cals.

MODEL 44½ IDEAL SINGLE SHOT — similar to Model 44, except .22 LR through .44-40 cals., falling block, lever action, takedown, 24 or 26 in. barrels, straight grip stock and forearm, action redesigned 1903. Mfg. 1903-1916.

	$850	$775	$675	$575	$500	$425	$350

MODELS 45-54 SINGLE SHOTS — .22 LR through .44-40 cals., rolling and falling block receivers, lever action, takedown, deluxe versions of the Models 44 and 44½, many special order features, including double set triggers, types of finish, engraving, length and weight of barrels, stock configuration could be special ordered. The higher grade Schuetzens and Stevens-Pope are very collectible and command premiums. These models have to be taken one at a time for determining value. Therefore, no prices are shown. Mfg. 1896-1916.

NO. 325B — .30-30 cal., bolt action, 4 shot mag., circa 1940s.

	$350	$315	$260	$210	$175	$140	$125

NO. 414 ARMORY MODEL — .22 LR or .22 Short only, lever action, 26 in. barrel, single shot, Lyman aperture sight. Mfg. 1912-1932.

	$450	$400	$375	$330	$290	$250	$220

MODEL 416 — bolt action, .22 LR, 25 in. medium barrel, 5 shot mag. Disc.

	$140	$120	$110	$100	$90	$80	$70

This model was also mfg. as a U.S. military training rifle. Can be denoted by "U.S. Property" on rear of bolt housing. Healthy premiums exist for this variation.

NO. 417 WALNUT HILL MODEL — .22 LR, .22 Short, and .22 Hornet, lever action, 28 or 29 in. extra heavy barrel, target stock with full pistol grip, beavertail forend, made in 0-3 suffix variations (different sights). Mfg. 1932-1947.

	$875	$675	$525	$475	$440	$395	$360

NO. 417½ WALNUT HILL MODEL — similar to No. 417, except available in .25 rimfire also. Mfg. 1932-1940.

	$875	$675	$525	$475	$440	$395	$360

NO. 418 WALNUT HILL MODEL — .22 LR or .22 Short only, 26 in. barrel, pistol grip stock, semi beavertail forearm. Mfg. 1932-1940.

	$595	$400	$295	$260	$230	$200	$180

NO. 425 HIGH POWER LEVER ACTION RIFLE — .25, .30-30, .32, or .35 cal., 22 in. round barrel with ⅔ length mag. tube, side ejection, blue only, plain walnut stock and forearm. Approx. 26,000 mfg. 1910-1917.

	$650	$595	$535	$465	$400	$350	$295

Variations of the No. 425 include the No. 430 (deluxe checkered stock and forearm), No. 435 (extra fancy checkered stock and forearm with engraved designs on receiver borders and lever), or No. 440 (best quality checkered walnut with fully engraved game scenes, and engraved forearm tip and lever). Values range respectively from $450-$950, $650-$1,400, and $1,000-$2,950.

STEVENS' FAVORITE NO.'S 17-29 — .22 LR, .25 RF or .32 RF cal., 24 in. barrel most common, other lengths available, Rocky Mountain front sight, straight grip stock, small tapered forearm. Mfg. 1894-1935. Octagonal barrels command a 33% premium.

	$195	$165	$145	$125	$100	$80	$65

Grading	100%	98%	95%	90%	80%	70%	60%

STEVENS' MODEL 65 — bolt action, 20 in. barrel, open sights, 5 shot mag., checkered walnut stock. Mfg. 1969-disc.

	$90	$70	$55	$45	$35	$30	$30

NO. 70 "VISIBLE LOADING" SLIDE ACTION RIFLE — .22 LR-L-S, exposed hammer, 22 in. barrel, open sights, straight grip stock, tube mag., grooved slide handle. Other variations with different barrel lengths and sights will command slight premiums.

	$250	$175	$150	$130	$115	$100	$90

MODEL 71 "STEVENS' FAVORITE" COMMEMORATIVE — replica of original, .22 LR, 22 in. octagon barrel, plain straight stock, medallion inlaid, crescent butt. 1,000 mfg. in 1971.

	$250	$195	$150

Last Mfg.'s Sug. Retail was $75.

MODEL 72 CRACKSHOT — single shot falling block action, .22 cal., 22 in. octagon barrel, open sights, color case hardened frame, straight stock. Mfg. 1972-89.

	$145	$125	$110	$100	$90	$80	$70

Last Mfg.'s Sug. Retail was $165.

MODEL 987 — .22 LR only, semi-auto, 15 shot tube mag., 20 in. barrel, hardwood Monte Carlo stock, adj. rear sight, 6 lbs. Disc. 1989.

	$95	$80	$70	$60	$50	$40	$45

Last Mfg.'s Sug. Retail was $119.

MODEL 89 LEVER ACTION — .22 LR, single shot, 18½ in. barrel, Martini type action, Western style lever, straight stock. Mfg. 1976-disc.

	$85	$65	$60	$50	$45	$40	$35

SHOTGUNS

Stevens made a wide variety of inexpensive, utilitarian shotguns that to date have attracted mostly shooting interest, but little collector interest. A listing of these models may be found in the back of this text under "Serialization".

MODEL 520 PUMP

	$190	$180	$150	$125	$95	$85	$75

MODEL 520-30 TRENCH/RIOT MILITARY SHOTGUNS — see the "Trench/Riot Shotgun" category in the T section for more information and prices.

MODEL 620 — an improved version of the Model 520 with streamlined receiver.

	$325	$290	$250	$225	$175	$150	$100

MODEL 620 TRENCH/RIOT MILITARY SHOTGUNS — see the "Trench/Riot Shotgun" category in the T section for more information and prices.

MODEL 77 (F, M, & SC) SLIDE ACTION — 12, 16, or 20 ga., "M" suffix is 12 ga. Mag., "SC" designate Super Choke, "F" refers to 16 ga.

	$175	$160	$140	$120	$100	$80	$60

MODEL 67 SLIDE ACTION — 12, 20, or .410 ga., all are 3 in. chambered, steel receiver, 5 shot, upper receiver safety, 6¼ - 7½ lbs. Recent mfg. by Stevens. Disc. 1989.

	$200	$180	$170	$155	$145	$135	$125

Last Mfg.'s Sug. Retail was $229.

   Add $30 for choke tubes (with VR).
   Add $10 for VR only.

 ▲ *Model 67 VTR-K Camo* — 12 or 20 ga., 28 in. VR barrel with choke tubes, laminated camo stock. Mfg. 1986-1988.

	$250	$220	$190	$170	$155	$145	$135

Last Mfg.'s Sug. Retail was $295.

Grading	100%	98%	95%	90%	80%	70%	60%

▲ *Slug Model* — 12 ga. only, 21 in. barrel, rifle sights. Disc. 1989.

	$200	$165	$140	$110	$100	$90	$80

Last Mfg.'s Sug. Retail was $245.

▲ *Model 67 VRT-Y* — 20 ga. only, 22 in. VR barrel with choke tubes, youth model with smaller stock dimensions. Mfg. 1987-1988.

	$205	$170	$140	$110	$100	$90	$80

Last Mfg.'s Sug. Retail was $259.

MODEL 675 — 12 ga. only, 24 in. VR multi-choked barrel with iron sights (including removable rear ramp), hardwood stock with recoil pad, 6½ lbs. Mfg. 1987-1988.

	$250	$220	$190	$170	$155	$145	$135

Last Mfg.'s Sug. Retail was $295.

MODEL 240 O/U — .410 ga.

	$350	$300	$250	$220	$190	$170	$155

MODEL 69-RXL — 12 ga. only, slide action law enforcement version of the Model 67, 18¼ in. cylinder bore barrel with recoil pad, 6½ lbs. Disc. 1989.

	$200	$165	$140	$110	$100	$90	$80

Last Mfg.'s Sug. Retail was $245.

MODEL 311 SxS — 12, 16, 20, or .410 ga., 3 in. chambers, double triggers, extractors, VR. Disc. 1989.

	$245	$205	$185	$150	$140	$125	$115

Last Mfg.'s Sug. Retail was $309.

Add 10% for .410 ga.

▲ *Model 311-R* — 12 ga. only, similar to Model 311, except has 18¼ in. cylinder bore barrels for law enforcement use, 3 in. chambers, 6¾ lbs. Disc. 1989.

	$245	$205	$185	$150	$140	$125	$115

Last Mfg.'s Sug. Retail was $309.

FOX/STEVENS MODEL B — 12, 20 or .410 ga., double triggers, VR, extractors, 24, 26, 28, or 30 in. barrels, 7 lbs. Disc. 1986.

	$315	$280	$240	$220	$200	$180	$160

Last Mfg.'s Sug. Retail was $369.

Add 25% for BDE Model (with ejectors).

FOX/STEVENS MODEL B-SE — 12, 20, or .410 ga., single trigger, selective ejectors, VR, beavertail forend, select walnut. Disc. 1989.

	$415	$370	$325	$280	$240	$210	$180

Last Mfg.'s Sug. Retail was $525.

Add 20% for .410 ga.

MODEL 94 — 12, 16, 20, 28, or .410 ga., single shot breakopen, inertia firing pin design, open hammer, 6¼ lbs. Mfg. 1937-disc..

	$95	$85	$75	$60	$50	$45	$40

Last Mfg.'s Sug. Retail was $92.

STEYR AUSTRIAN MILITARY

Manufacturer located in Steyr, Austria.

MODEL 95 RIFLE — straight pull bolt action, 8x50R Mannlicher, 30 in. barrel, adj. sights, military full stock.

	$140	$110	$100	$85	$65	$55	$40

MODEL 90 CARBINE — similar to Model 95, except 19½ in. barrel.

	$155	$125	$110	$95	$85	$65	$45

STEYR DAIMLER PUCH A.G.

Steyr, Austria. 1911 to date.

Grading	100%	98%	95%	90%	80%	70%	60%

COMMERCIAL MODEL 1901

	$2,250	$1,750	$1,200	$900	$600	$500	$400

COMMERCIAL MODEL 1905

	$1,450	$1,000	$700	$500	$400	$350	$300

ARGENTINE MODEL 1905 — 7.65mm, Argentine crest on left panel is usually machined off. Values assume matching numbers but removed crest.

	$400	$350	$300	$255	$220	$185	$150

POCKET AUTO — .25 ACP or .32 cal., tip up barrel, mag. fed. Disc.

	$325	$265	$200	$150	$140	$130	$120

ROTH STEYR AUTO (MODEL 1907) — 8mm Steyr cal.

	$600	$500	$400	$350	$300	$250	$200

Add 30% for "Budapest" markings.

STEYR-HAHN MODEL 1911 AUTOMATIC — 9mm Steyr, 8 shot, 5.1 in. barrel, fixed magazine top loaded by stripper clip, blue, checkered wood grips. Mfg. 1911-1919. In 1938, the Germans confiscated and converted a quantity of these to 9mm Para., "08" was stamped on the left side of these guns.

	$425	$375	$325	$275	$225	$195	$175

Add 100% if marked "08" or with Rumanian Crest.

MODEL SP — .32 ACP, semi-auto, trigger cocking mechanism, very rare - mfg. in 1959 only.

	$650	$595	$540	$495	$450	$400	$350

STEYR MANNLICHER

Manufactured by Steyr-Daimler-Puch in Austria. Founded by Ferdinand Ritter Von Mannlicher and Otto Schoenauer in 1903. Currently imported and distributed by Gun South, Inc. located in Trussville, AL.

Note: also see Mannlicher Schoenauer in the M section for pre-WWII models.

PISTOLS

MODEL GB — 9mm, double action, 18 shot mag., gas delayed blowback action, non-glare checkered plastic grips, 5¼ in. barrel with Polygon rifling, matte finish, steel construction, 2 lbs. 6 oz. Importation disc. 1988.

	100%	98%	95%	90%	80%	70%	60%
Commercial	$525	$475	$425	$375	$335	$300	$280
Military	$450	$395	$350	$300	$280	$260	$240

Last Mfg.'s Sug. Retail was $514.

In 1987, Steyr mfg. a military variation of the Model GB featuring a phosphate finish - only 937 were imported into the U.S.

MODEL SPP — 9mm Para., single action semi-auto, delayed blow back system with rotating 5.9 in. barrel, 15 or 30 shot mag., utilizes synthetic materials and advanced ergonomics, adj. sights, grooved receiver for scope mounting, matte black finish, 44 oz. Limited importation 1992-93.

	$800	$675	$600	$550	$495	$450	$400

Last Mfg.'s Sug. Retail was $895.

RIFLES: BOLT ACTION - RECENT MFG.

Current production guns are now called Steyr-Mannlicher models. For models manufactured 1903-1971, please refer to the Mannlicher Schoenauer Sporting Rifles section in this text.

The below listed models have 4 different action lengths and model designations stand for the following: SL=Super Light, L=Light, M=Medium, S=Magnum,

Grading	100%	98%	95%	90%	80%	70%	60%

S/T=Magnum with heavy barrel. All sporting rifles are available with left-hand stock - add $109 and with either single set or double set triggers - add $125.

ZEPHYR 22 — .22 LR cal., features full length Mannlicher stock, single or double set triggers, open sights, checkered walnut stock with horn cap, sling swivels. Mfg. circa 1955-1971.

	$1,350	$1,200	$1,000	$850	$725	$600	$525

MODEL M72 L/M RIFLE — M72 bolt action, .243 Win., .308 Win., .270 Win., .30-06, 7x57mm, and 7x64mm cals., 23 in. barrel, single or double set triggers. Mfg. 1972-1980.

	$795	$725	$650	$575	$500	$460	$420

MODEL SL — .222 Rem.,.222 Rem. Mag. (disc.), .223 Rem., .22-250 Rem. (disc. 1992), or 5.6x50mm (disc. 1991) cal., bolt action, 23.6 in. barrel, double set triggers, rotary mag. Available in full-stock (Carbine), half stock (rifle), or varmint version (vent square forearm).

Mfg.'s Sug. Retail	$2,250	$1,875	$1,325	$950	$775	$675	$600	$540

▲ **Carbine Model (Full Stock)** — skipline checkered full stock, 20 in. barrel.

Mfg.'s Sug. Retail	$2,450	$1,995	$1,400	$995	$825	$700	$600	$540

▲ **Varmint Rifle** — .222 Rem. (disc.), .223 Rem. (new 1993), or .22-250 Rem. (disc. 1992) cal., 26 in. heavy barrel, stippled pistol grip, vent. forearm, no sights.

Mfg.'s Sug. Retail	$2,450	$1,995	$1,400	$995	$825	$700	$600	$540

MODEL L — 5.6x57mm (disc. 1991), .243 Win., or .308 Win. cals., available in .22-250 and 6mm Rem. on special order only, otherwise same general specifications as Model SL.

Mfg.'s Sug. Retail	$2,250	$1,875	$1,325	$950	$775	$675	$600	$540

▲ **Carbine Model (Full Stock)** — skip-line checkered full stock, 20 in. barrel.

Mfg.'s Sug. Retail	$2,450	$1,995	$1,400	$995	$825	$700	$600	$540

▲ **Varmint Rifle** — .222 Rem. (disc. 1991), .22-250 Rem., .243 Win. (disc.), or .308 Win. (disc.) cal., 26 in. heavy barrel, stippled pistol grip, vent. forearm, no sights.

Mfg.'s Sug. Retail	$2,450	$1,995	$1,400	$995	$825	$700	$600	$540

▲ **Model L Luxus** — 5.6x57mm, .243 Win., or .308 Win. cal., full or half stock only, .22-250 Rem. and 6mm Rem. available on special order, 3 shot mag.

Mfg.'s Sug. Retail	$2,950	$2,495	$1,750	$1,325	$1,000	$800	$700	$650

▲ **Model L Luxus Carbine (Full Stock)** — similar to L Luxus rifle, except has full stock and 20 in. barrel.

Mfg.'s Sug. Retail	$3,150	$2,625	$1,825	$1,350	$1,025	$800	$700	$650

MODEL M — 6.5x55mm, 6.5x57mm, 7x64mm, .270 Win., .30-06, or 9.3x62mm cal., bolt action, full stock or half stock, rotary mag., double set triggers.

Mfg.'s Sug. Retail	$2,250	$1,875	$1,325	$950	$775	$675	$600	$540

Add $400 for left-hand action.

▲ **Carbine Model (Full Stock)** — skipline checkered full stock, 20 in. barrel.

Mfg.'s Sug. Retail	$2,450	$1,995	$1,400	$995	$825	$700	$600	$540

Add $400 for left-hand action.

▲ **Professional Rifle** — .270 Win., 7x57mm (disc. 1991), 7x64mm, .30-06, or 9.3x62mm cal., 23.6 in. barrel, Cycolac synthetic stock, 7½ lbs. Disc. 1993.

	$1,500	$1,025	$850	$700	$600	$540	$495

Last Mfg.'s Sug. Retail was $1,710.

Add $469 for left hand action with half stock (rifle).
Add $625 for left hand action with full stock (carbine).
This variation is also available in .270 Win. or .30-06 cal. with half stock and 20 in. barrel (carbine).

▲ **Model M Luxus** — 6.5x55mm, 6.5x57mm (disc.), 7x64mm, .270 Win., or .30-06 cal., special order in 6.5x55mm and 7.5mm Swiss.

Mfg.'s Sug. Retail	$2,950	$2,495	$1,750	$1,325	$1,000	$800	$700	$650

Grading	100%	98%	95%	90%	80%	70%	60%

▲ *Model M Luxus Carbine (Full Stock)* — similar to Model M Luxus, except with full stock and 20 in. barrel.

Mfg.'s Sug. Retail	$3,150	$2,625	$1,825	$1,350	$1,025	$800	$700	$650

▲ *Carbine - 1000 Year Commemorative* — 1984 only, .30-06 cal.

		$4,200	$3,620	$2,835

M-III PROFESSIONAL — .25-06 (new 1996), .270 Win., .30-06, or 7x64mm cal., features black synthetic half stock, 23.6 in. barrel, no sights. Importation began 1994.

Mfg.'s Sug. Retail	$995	$900	$800	$700	$600	$525	$450	$375

Add $130 for stipled checkered European wood stock.

JAGD MATCH — .222 Rem., .243 Win., or .308 Win. cal., features shortened action, 23.6 in. heavy barrel with iron sights, 5 shot rotary mag., laminated checkered half-stock, recoil pad, designed for European Match events limited to hunting rifles, double set triggers, 8½ lbs. New 1995.

Mfg.'s Sug. Retail	$2,450	$2,025	$1,375	$1,025	$825	$675	$600	$540

MODEL S (MAGNUM) — 6.5x68mm, 8x68S, .300 Win. Mag., .338 Win. Mag. (disc. 1992), .375 H&H Mag., or 7mm Rem. Mag. cal., half-stock, 26 in. barrel, bolt action.

Mfg.'s Sug. Retail	$2,550	$2,075	$1,400	$1,050	$850	$725	$625	$550

MODEL S/T — available in 9.3x64 (disc. 1992), .375 H&H Mag., or .458 Win. Mag. cal., half-stock, 26 in. heavy barrel.

Mfg.'s Sug. Retail	$2,850	$2,325	$1,575	$1,125	$925	$775	$675	$595

▲ *Tropical Rifle* — .375 H&H and .458 Win. Mag. cals., 26 in. heavy barrel. Disc. 1985.

	$1,150	$900	$810	$730	$660	$600	$550

Last Mfg.'s Sug. Retail was $1,332.

▲ *Luxus S* — available in 6.5x68mm, 8x68S, 7mm Rem. Mag., or .300 Win. Mag. cal., 26 in. barrel, half-stock only, 3 shot mag., 8 lbs.

Mfg.'s Sug. Retail	$3,250	$2,700	$1,900	$1,475	$1,125	$875	$750	$675

MODEL SSG — .243 Win. (disc., PII Sniper only) or .308 Win cal., for competition or law-enforcement use. Marksman has regular sights, rotary mag., teflon coated bolt with heavy duty locking lugs, synthetic stock has removable spacers, parkerized finish. Match version has heavier target barrel and "match" bolt carrier, can be used as single shot. Extremely accurate.

▲ *PI Rifle* — 26 in. barrel, 3 shot mag., black or green ABS Cycolac synthetic stock.

Mfg.'s Sug. Retail	$2,195	$1,875	$1,300	$975	$795	$675	$600	$540

Add 15% for walnut stock (disc. 1992, retail was $448).

▲ *PII Sniper Rifle* — .243 Win. (disc.) or .308 Win. cal., 20 in. heavy (Model PIIK) or 26 in. heavy barrel, no sights, green or black synthetic Cycolac stock, modified bolt handle, choice of single or set triggers.

Mfg.'s Sug. Retail	$2,195	$1,875	$1,300	$975	$795	$675	$600	$540

Add 15% for walnut stock (disc. 1992, retail was $448).

▲ *PIII Rifle* — .308 Win. cal., 26 in. heavy barrel with diopter match sight bases, H-S Precision Pro-Series stock in black only. Importation 1991-93.

	$2,600	$1,875	$1,425	$1,050	$825	$700	$600

Last Mfg.'s Sug. Retail was $3,162.

▲ *PIV Urban Rifle* — .308 Win. cal., carbine variation with 16½ in. heavy barrel and flash hider, ABS Cycolac synthetic stock in green or black. Importation began 1991.

Mfg.'s Sug. Retail	$2,660	$2,285	$1,625	$1,275	$975	$775	$700	$650

▲ *Jagd Match* — .222 Rem., .243 Win., or .308 Win. cal., hunting rifle that features checkered wood laminate stock, 23.6 in. barrel, Mannlicher sights, double set triggers, supplied with test target. Mfg. 1991-92.

	$1,550	$1,050	$950	$800	$675	$600	$540

Last Mfg.'s Sug. Retail was $1,550.

Grading	100%	98%	95%	90%	80%	70%	60%

▲ **Match Rifle** — .308 Win. only, 26 in. heavy barrel, brown ABS Cycolac stock, Walther Diopter sights, 8.6 lbs. Mfg. disc. 1992.

	$2,000	**$1,500**	**$1,225**	**$925**	**$800**	**$700**	**$600**

Last Mfg.'s Sug. Retail was $2,306.

       Add $437 for walnut stock.

▲ **Model SPG-T** — .308 Win. cal., Target model. New 1993.

Mfg.'s Sug. Retail	**$3,695**	**$3,225**	**$2,850**	**$2,550**	**$2,200**	**$1,850**	**$1,500**	**$1,200**

▲ **Model SPG-CISM** — .308 Win. cal. New 1993.

Mfg.'s Sug. Retail	**$4,295**	**$3,850**	**$3,275**	**$2,850**	**$2,450**	**$2,050**	**$1,700**	**$1,400**

▲ **Match UIT** — .308 Win. only, 10 shot steel mag., special single set trigger, free floating barrel, Diopter sights, raked bolt handle, 10.8 lbs.

Mfg.'s Sug. Retail	**$3,995**	**$3,600**	**$3,150**	**$2,750**	**$2,400**	**$2,050**	**$1,700**	**$1,400**

       UIT stands for Union Internationale de Tir.

RIFLES: SEMI-AUTO

AUG S.A. — .223 Rem./5.56mm, semi-auto paramilitary design rifle, design incorporates use of advanced plastics, integral Swarovski scope, 16, 20, or 24 in. barrel, bullpup configuration, 7.9 lbs.

Mfg.'s Sug. Retail	**$1,575**	**$1,375**	**$975**	**$875**	**$750**	**$650**	**$575**	**$525**

       Add approx. $700 for special receiver mfg. using Stanag metallurgy.

       This model is now available in limited quantities only to law enforcement agencies due to 1989 Federal legislation banning the importation for commercial sales.

▲ **AUG S.A. Commercial** — similar to above, except values reflect price increases due to consumer demand after Federal legislation banned the commercial importation in 1989, green or black finish.

	$2,950	**$2,750**	**$2,500**	**$2,250**	**$1,975**	**$1,800**	**$1,675**

Last Mfg.'s Sug. Retail was $1,362 (1989).

STOCK, FRANZ

Germany.

SEMI-AUTO PISTOL — .22 LR. Mfg. in Germany 1920-1940.

	$275	**$250**	**$225**	**$175**	**$125**	**$100**	**$75**

SEMI-AUTO PISTOL — .25 ACP, .32 ACP. Mfg. in Germany 1920-1940.

	$275	**$225**	**$175**	**$150**	**$100**	**$90**	**$80**

STOEGER INDUSTRIES, INC.

Importer located in Wayne, NJ. Currently imported Stoeger Lugers may be found in the back of the Luger section in this text.

Stoeger has imported a wide variety of firearms during the past seven decades. Most of these guns were good quality and came from known makers in Europe (some were private labeled). Stoeger carried an extensive firearms inventory of both house brand and famous European trademarks - many of which were finely made with beautiful engraving, stock work, and other popular special order features. As a general rule, values for Stoeger rifles and shotguns may be ascertained by comparing them with a known trademark of equal quality and cal./ga. Certain configurations will be more desirable than others (i.e. a Stoeger .22 caliber Mannlicher with double set triggers and detachable mag. will be worth considerably more than a single shot target rifle).

Perhaps the best reference works available on these older Stoeger firearms (not to mention the other trademarks of that time) are the older Stoeger catalogs themselves - quite collectible in their own right. It is advised to purchase these older catalogs (some reprints are also available), if more information is needed on not only older Stoeger models, but the other firearms being sold at that time.

Grading	100%	98%	95%	90%	80%	70%	60%

PISTOLS: SEMI-AUTO

PRO SERIES 95 — .22 LR, target pistol with choice of either 5½ or 7¼ VR, fluted, or bull barrel, adj. rear sight, adj. trigger, push-button takedown, Pachmayr rubber grips, gold accents, 10 shot mag., 45-47 oz. New 1995.

➤ 5½ in. bull barrel

Mfg.'s Sug. Retail	$460	$415	$360	$330	$300	$275	$250	$225

➤ 5½ in. VR barrel

Mfg.'s Sug. Retail	$565	$495	$415	$355	$320	$285	$255	$225

➤ 7¼ in. fluted barrel

Mfg.'s Sug. Retail	$490	$435	$370	$335	$300	$275	$250	$225

STONER RIFLE

Please refer to the Knight's Manufacturing Company listing in this text.

STRAYER TRIPP INTERNATIONAL

Manufacturer located in Austin, TX since 1993. Dealer sales only.

In addition to manufacturing the pistols listed below, Strayer Tripp International also makes frame kits in steel, stainless steel, aluminum, or titanium - prices range between $441-$989.

PISTOLS: SEMI-AUTO

FALCON 3.9 — various cals., size comparable to Officer's Model. New 1995.

Mfg.'s Sug. Retail	$1,549	$1,375	$1,225	$995	$825	$700	$575	$475

HAWK 4.3 MATCH GRADE — similar cals. as the Eagle 5.1 Match, patterned after M-1911, choice of aluminum frame/steel slide or steel frame/steel slide, features many match grade components. New 1994.

Mfg.'s Sug. Retail	$1,549	$1,375	$1,225	$995	$825	$700	$575	$475

Add $108 for all-steel construction.

EAGLE 5.1 MATCH GRADE — .38 Super, 9x21mm, 10mm, .40 S&W, or .45 ACP cal., 14 (.45 ACP) features 17 (.40 S&W, 10mm, or 9x21mm), or 19 (9x21 or .38 Super) shot mag., match grade cone barrel, Bomar rear sight, threaded 2-piece guide rod, titanium claw hammer, stainless steel thumb safety and high grip beavertail, titanium strut and mainspring cap, alloy frame/steel slide or all-steel construction. New 1994.

Mfg.'s Sug. Retail	$1,549	$1,375	$1,225	$995	$825	$700	$575	$475

Add $108 for all-steel construction.

EAGLE 5.5 MATCH GRADE — similar to Eagle 5.1, except has compensated barrel, all-steel only. New 1994.

Mfg.'s Sug. Retail	$2,149	$1,900	$1,600	$1,300	$1,100	$975	$825	$700

Add $200 for Hybricomp variation.
Add $326 for scope and mounts on above variations.

STREET SWEEPER

Manufactured by Sales of Georgia, Inc. located in Atlanta, GA.

STREET SWEEPER — 12 ga. only, 12 shot rotary mag., paramilitary configuration with 18 in. barrel, double action, folding stock, 9¾ lbs. New 1989.

No Mfg.'s Retail		$550	$475	$425	$375	$350	$315	$275

STURM, RUGER, & COMPANY

Manufacturer with current production facilities located in Newport, NH (rifles and shotguns) beginning 1993 and Prescott, AZ (handguns) beginning 1986. Previously manufactured in Southport, CT 1949-1993 (office headquarters remain at this location).

NOTE: In 1976, Ruger stamped "Made in the 200th year of American Liberty" on the side of all of the guns they produced for this one year only. These Bicentennial or "Liberty Model" guns will bring a $50 - $75 premium from collectors interested in acquiring them. In most cases this is only true of 100% guns, unfired with the original box and papers.

Almost all the models in this section are factory variations, and non-factory limited or special editions are not included in this section because of the amount and price unpredictability.
ALL VALUES FOR 100% CONDITION RUGERS ASSUME NIB CONDITION — SUBTRACT 5% - 10% WITHOUT BOX AND ACCESSORIES.

Grading	100%	98%	95%	90%	80%	70%	60%

PISTOLS: SEMI-AUTO, RIMFIRE

Many distributors and customizers have produced special/limited editions on this popular series of .22 cal. pistols. Individual companies should be contacted for current pricing and special order features/prices.

STANDARD MODEL — .22 LR, 9 shot, 4¾ in. or 6 in. barrel, blue, fixed sights, checkered wood or rubber grips. Mfg. 1951-1982.

	100%	98%	95%	90%	80%	70%	60%
	$165	$140	$130	$110	$100	$90	$80

Variations marked "Hecho En Mexico" are rare. 98%+ condition specimens have sold for $750.

▲ *Stainless Steel 1 of 5,000*

	100%	98%	95%
	$425	$390	$325

"RED EAGLE" — approx. 29,000 mfg. 1949-1952, most production occurred prior to Alexander Sturm's death (1951).

	100%	98%	95%	90%	80%	70%	60%
Standard	$450	$400	$350	$300	$265	$235	$200
Target	$550	$500	$450	$375	$325	$275	$225

Distinguishable by recessed red enamel eagle in grips. Produced until early 1952. Serialized approx. 0001 - 35,000 with Mark I Auto occupying blocks from 15,000 - 17,000 and 25,000 - 25,300.

MARK I TARGET — similar to Standard, except has 5½ in. heavy barrel, 5¼ tapered (scarce) barrel, or 6⅞ heavy tapered barrel, adj. rear sights, target sight. Mfg. 1951-1982.

	100%	98%	95%	90%	80%	70%	60%
	$200	$185	$160	$150	$140	$130	$120

Add 200% if U.S. marked.
Add 175% for 5¼ in. tapered barrel.
Add $100 for Ruger addressed muzzle brake.

MARK II STANDARD — .22 LR, 4¾ or 6 in. barrel, checkered black Delrin synthetic grips, blue finish, 10 shot mag., approx. 2¼ lbs. Mfg. 1982 to date.

		100%	98%	95%	90%	80%	70%	60%
Mfg.'s Sug. Retail	$252	$195	$155	$125	$115	$110	$100	$95

▲ *Stainless Steel* — variation of the Mark II Standard.

		100%	98%	95%
Mfg.'s Sug. Retail	$330	$260	$195	$165

Serial numbers start approx. at 18-00001.

MARK II TARGET — .22 LR, 4 (new 1996) bull, 5¼ (disc. 1994), 5½ bull, 6⅞ standard, or 10 bull in. barrel, single action, 2⅝ - 3¼ lbs. depending on barrel.

		100%	98%	95%	90%	80%	70%	60%
Mfg.'s Sug. Retail	$311	$250	$225	$185	$160	$130	$120	$110

Subtract $16 for 10 in. bull barrel.

Grading	100%	98%	95%	90%	80%	70%	60%

▲ *Stainless Steel* — stainless variation of the Mark II Target, includes choice of 5¼ (disc. 1994), 5½ bull, 6⅞ standard, or 10 in. bull barrel.

Mfg.'s Sug. Retail	$389		$300	$245	$185		

Add $16 for 4 in. bull barrel.
Subtract $16 for 10 in. bull barrel.

GOVERNMENT TARGET MODEL (MK678G) — commercial variation of the government training model without "U.S." markings, 6⅞ in. bull barrel, adj. rear sight, blue finish, black plastic grips, 46 oz., individually test targeted. New 1987.

Mfg.'s Sug. Retail	$357	$285	$240	$190	$170	$155	$140	$125

▲ *Stainless Government Target Model* — 6⅞ in. bull barrel only. New 1993.

Mfg.'s Sug. Retail	$427	$340	$275	$215			

Add $14 for 6⅞ in. slab side bull barrel with scope rings and base.

MODEL 22/45 — .22 LR only, semi-auto single action, Zytel frame is patterned after the Model 1911 .45 ACP Gov't, stainless steel, 4¾, 5¼ regular (Target), or 5½ in. bull barrel, 10 shot mag. (push-button release), fixed or adj. sights, 28-35 oz. New 1993.

▲ *Stainless Steel Finish*

Mfg.'s Sug. Retail	$330		$265	$215	$185		

Subtract $50 for fixed sights (4¾ in. barrel only).

▲ *Blue Finish* — new 1994.

Mfg.'s Sug. Retail	$238	$195	$170	$150	$135	$125	$115	$100

PISTOLS: SEMI-AUTO, CENTERFIRE

P-85 MARK II — 9mm Para., double action, 4½ in. barrel, aluminum frame with steel slide, 3-dot fixed sights, 15 shot mag., ambidextrous safety or decocking levers, oversized trigger, synthetic Xenoy grips, matte black finish, 2 lbs. Mfg. 1987-92.

			$335	$295	$265	$235	$215	$200	$185

Last Mfg.'s Sug. Retail was $410.

Subtract $30 if without case and extra mag.
A variation (P-89DC) can be ordered in a decocking or double action only (P-89DAO) version at no extra charge.

▲ *KP-85 Mark II Stainless Steel* — stainless variation of the P-85. Mfg. 1990-92.

			$350	$315	$280				

Last Mfg.'s Sug. Retail was $452.

Subtract $30 if without case and extra mag.
A variation (P-89) can be ordered in a decocking or double action only version at no extra charge.

P-89 — 9mm Para., improved variation of the P-85 Mark II, 10 (C/B 1994) shot mag., ambidextrous safety or decocker, blued finish. New 1992.

Mfg.'s Sug. Retail	$410	$335	$295	$265	$235	$215	$200	$185

▲ *P-89 Stainless* — stainless variation of the P-89, also available in double action only. New 1992.

Mfg.'s Sug. Retail	$452	$375	$325	$295			

Add $45 for convertible .30 Luger cal. barrel (disc).

KP90 STAINLESS — .45 ACP cal., double action, 4½ in. barrel, oversized trigger, aluminum frame with stainless steel slide, 7 shot single column mag., ambidextrous safety (KP-90) or decocking (KP-90D), Xenoy grips, 3 dot fixed sights. New 1991.

Mfg.'s Sug. Retail	$489	$385	$335	$295			

This model was previously available in a double action only variation (K-P90C, disc. 1992).

S

Grading	100%	98%	95%	90%	80%	70%	60%

KP91 STAINLESS — .40 S&W cal., similar to Model K-P90 Stainless, except is not available with external safety and has 11 shot double column mag. Mfg. 1992-94.

	$385	$335	$295				

Last Mfg.'s Sug. Retail was $489.

This model was available in a decocking variation (K-P91D) or double action only (K-P91DAO).

KP93 STAINLESS — 9mm Para., compact variation with 3⁹⁄₁₀ in. tilting barrel - link actuated, matte blue or REM (new 1996) finish, 3 dot sights, 10 (C/B 1994) or 15* shot mag., available with ambidextrous decocking or double action only, 31 oz. New 1994.

Mfg.'s Sug. Retail	$520		$415	$350	$300		

KP94 STAINLESS — 9mm Para. or .40 S&W cal., available with ambidextrous safety, matte blue or REM (new 1996) finish, ambidextrous decocker, or double action only, 10 (C/B 1994), 11* (.40 S&W), or 15* (9mm Para.) shot mag., 33 oz. New 1994.

Mfg.'s Sug. Retail	$520		$415	$350	$300		

REVOLVERS: OLD MODELS - SINGLE ACTION

Note: Some of the following Rugers are known as "Old Models" (mfg. 1968 - early 1973) and are instantly recognized by the three screws through the frame and the four clicks emitted upon cocking. They are now actively sought by collectors and some shooters who desire the smoother operation they afford.

SINGLE SIX REVOLVER — .22 LR, 4⅝, 5½ (mfg. 1953-1972), 6½, or 9½ in. barrel, fixed sights, rubber or wood grips, blue. Mfg. 1953-1963.

	$265	$195	$175	$130	$120	$110	$100

This model will command a premium with either a 4⅝ in. or 9½ in. barrel.

▲ *Flat loading gate* — 5½ in. barrel only, approx. 61,000 mfg. from 1953-1957. Four variations.

	$350	$300	$250	$200	$175	$160	$150

Add 100% for non-serrated front sight (ser. no. 1-2,000)

▲ *.22 Mag.* — 6½ in. barrel only, mfg. only three years, serial numbered between 300,000 - 342,000. Frame stamped Mag. only.

	$300	$250	$200	$175	$165	$160	$150

Add 40% for extra .22 LR cylinder in Mag. only marked guns.

Approx. 250 factory cased, engraved Single Six models have been mfg. Seldom seen and among the rarest of Ruger revolvers, prices have been reported at over $2,500 - $3,500.

SINGLE SIX CONVERTIBLE — similar to Single Six, except .22 LR and .22 WMR interchangeable cylinders, 4⅝, 5½, 6½, or 9½ in. barrel with 4⅝ in. being the rarest. Mfg. 1960-1972.

	$275	$200	$175	$150	$140	$115	$100

LIGHTWEIGHT SINGLE SIX — similar to Single Six, except alloy frame, 4⅝ in. barrel, made 1956-1958. 200,000 - 212,000 serial range, can have alloy or steel cylinder.

	$395	$350	$300	$250	$200	$175	$150

Add 75% if all blue with blue alloy cyl.

SUPER SINGLE SIX CONVERTIBLE — similar to Single Six Convertible, except adj. sights. Mfg. 1964-1972.

	$275	$250	$200	$155	$140	$120	$105

This model in 4⅝ in. barrel is the rarest with prices ranging between $800-$1,500 in blue finish, nickel finish 6½ in. barrel specimens are trading for $1,500-$2,250.

Grading	100%	98%	95%	90%	80%	70%	60%

BLACKHAWK SINGLE ACTION "FLAT-TOP" — .357 Mag., 6 shot, $4\frac{5}{8}$, $6\frac{1}{2}$, and 10 in. barrel, flat top cylinder strap, adj. sight, blue, black rubber or walnut grips. Approx. 43,000 mfg. between 1955-1963.

	100%	98%	95%	90%	80%	70%	60%
	$495	$395	$300	$250	$210	$200	$175

Add 50% for $6\frac{1}{2}$ in. with 6-grooved barrel (mostly encountered under ser. no. 28,000).
Add 200% for 10 in. barrel.

BLACKHAWK SINGLE ACTION — .357 Mag., .41 Mag., or .45 LC cals., this model is the 1962 variation with hooded rear sight and $4\frac{5}{8}$ (.45 LC), $6\frac{1}{2}$ (.357 Mag. or .41 Mag.), or $7\frac{1}{2}$ (.45 LC) in. barrel.

	$350	$300	$250	$215	$180	$160	$140

Add 75% for factory installed brass grip frame (rare).

This model was also available in .30 Carbine cal. with a $7\frac{1}{2}$ in. barrel. Beware of non-factory brass grip frames on this model.

BLACKHAWK CONVERTIBLE — similar to Blackhawk, with extra cylinder, .357 and 9mm, and .45 Colt and .45 ACP cals.

	$400	$350	$295	$250	$225	$195	$175

Add 70% for NIB .357 Mag./9mm with non-prefix ser. no.
Add $100 for .45 LC/.45 ACP combination.

BLACKHAWK FLAT-TOP .44 MAGNUM — similar to Blackhawk Flat-Top, except heavier frame and cylinder, .44 Mag., $6\frac{1}{2}$, $7\frac{1}{2}$, and 10 in. barrels. Approx. 28,000 mfg. between 1956-1963.

	$595	$495	$415	$360	$305	$230	$210

Add 100% for $7\frac{1}{2}$ or 10 in. barrel.
Distinguishable by fluted cylinder and rounded triggerguard.

SUPER BLACKHAWK — .44 Mag., $6\frac{1}{2}$ (rare) or $7\frac{1}{2}$ in. barrel, larger frame and improved trigger-guard, unfluted cylinder, adj. sights, walnut grips. Mfg. 1959-1972.

	$350	$300	$250	$200	$190	$185	$175

Rare early models in wood case will command 100-300% premiums. White cardboard boxed Super Blackhawks will command a 300% premium. $6\frac{1}{2}$ in. barrel will command a 100%+ premium.

OLD MODEL BEARCAT — .22 cal., 6 shot, 4 in. barrel, alloy frame, brass trigger guard, blue, wood grips with medallion, 17 oz. Mfg. 1958-1973.

	$300	$265	$225	$195	$180	$165	$150

Add 100%+ for blued aluminum triggerguard variation (73,000-77,000 ser. no. range).
Numerous variations exist within this model incorporating production changes.

OLD MODEL SUPER BEARCAT — similar to Bearcat, except steel frame, made with brass trigger guard (early model), or blued steel guard, 25 oz. Mfg. 1971-1973.

	$330	$290	$250	$225	$200	$180	$165

HAWKEYE SINGLE SHOT — .256 Mag., single shot, round cylinder replaced by rectangular rotating breech block, $8\frac{1}{2}$ in. barrel, blue, walnut grips, adj. sight, very rare, 45 oz., approx. 3,300 mfg. Mfg. 1963-1964.

	$1,200	$1,000	$875	$700	$580	$475	$400

REVOLVERS: NEW MODELS - SINGLE ACTION

The following single actions are known as "New Models". They have 2 pins through the frame and cock without the clicks associated with the single action. The change over occurred as a result of desire for safety features. The "New Models" have a transfer bar similar to those found on modern double action revolvers and do not accidentally discharge if dropped. Manufacture started 1973.

During certain years of manufacture, Ruger's changes in production on certain models (cals., barrel markings, barrel lengths, etc.) have created rare variations that are

Grading	100%	98%	95%	90%	80%	70%	60%

now considered premium niches. These areas of low manufacture will add premiums to the values listed below on standard models.

Beginning 1996, Ruger started supplying all New Model revolvers with a case and lock.

SINGLE SIX CONVERTIBLE — .22 S, L, or LR cal., includes interchangeable .22 WMR cylinder, 5½ or 6½ in. barrel, fixed sights, blue finish, approx. 34 oz. New 1994.

Mfg.'s Sug. Retail	$313	$245	$190	$150	$130	$120	$110	$100

▲ *Single Six Convertible Stainless Steel* — similar to Single Six Convertible, except is stainless steel. New 1994.

Mfg.'s Sug. Retail	$393	$310	$250	$180

SUPER SINGLE SIX CONVERTIBLE — .22 LR, includes interchangeable .22 WMR cylinder, 4⅝, 5½, 6½, or 9½ in. barrel, 6 shot, similar to old Super Single Six, except has new interlocking safety mechanism previously described, adj. rear sight. Mfg. 1973-present.

Mfg.'s Sug. Retail	$313	$245	$190	$150	$130	$120	$110	$100

Subtract 15% if without extra .22 Mag. cylinder.

▲ *Super Single Six Stainless Steel* — similar to Super Single Six, except stainless steel construction, 4⅝ (disc. 1992), 5½, 6½, or 9½ (disc.-rare) in. barrel.

Mfg.'s Sug. Retail	$393	$310	$250	$180

Values for 4⅝ or 9½ in. barrel are approx. $575 if NIB.

▲ *Super Single Six High Gloss Stainless* — 5½ or 6½ in. barrel, features high gloss stainless steel finish. New 1994.

Mfg.'s Sug. Retail	$393	$310	$250	$180

▲ *Colorado Centennial Super Single Six* — 15,000 mfg. 1975 only, includes walnut case with medallion insert, stainless steel grip frame, 6½ in. barrel, issue price was $250.

	$295	$245	$200

This model also was a U.S. Bicentennial gun as well as the Colorado Centennial Pistol. Most specimens do not have the Bicentennial statement on the barrel and are rarer with that stamping.

SUPER SINGLE SIX SSM — .32 H&R Mag. cal., 4⅝, 5½, 6½ or 9½ in. barrel, blue only, adj. sights, 32 oz. with 5½ in. barrel.

Mfg.'s Sug. Retail	$313	$245	$190	$150	$130	$120	$110	$100

Add 50% if cylinder frame is marked "SSM".

BLACKHAWK — .30 Carbine, .357 Mag., .41 Mag., or .45 LC (disc. 1994) cal., similar to old Model Blackhawk, with new interlocking safety mechanism, 6 shot, 4⅝, 6½, or 7½ in. (.30 Carbine and .45 LC only) barrel. Mfg. 1973-present.

Mfg.'s Sug. Retail	$360	$275	$210	$170	$155	$145	$135	$125

▲ *Blackhawk Convertible* — similar to New Model Blackhawk, except interchangeable cylinders, .357 Mag./9mm (current), .44 Mag./.44-40 (disc.), or .45 LC/.45 ACP (disc. 1985), 4⅝ or 6½ in. barrel only.

Mfg.'s Sug. Retail	$380	$300	$250	$220	$190	$170	$160	$150

▲ *Buckeye Special* — .32-20/.32 H&R Mag., 6½ in. barrel. Mfg. 1989.

	$425	$350	$295	$250	$220	$200	$180

Buckeye Sports also offered a limited edition Buckeye Special in .38-40/10mm auto during 1990 - add 10%-15% on prices above.

▲ *Blackhawk Stainless Steel* — .357 Mag. or .45 LC (new 1993) cal., 4⅝, 6½, or 7½ in. barrel.

Mfg.'s Sug. Retail	$443	$395	$295	$250

300 .357 Mag./9mm Para. convertible pistols were made in this model - NIB prices have ranged $500-$750.

New Model .357 Mag. Blackhawks are serial numbered 32-00001 on up. New Model .45 LC Blackhawks are ser. numbered 46-00001 on up.

Grading	100%	98%	95%	90%	80%	70%	60%

▲ *Blackhawk High Gloss Stainless Steel* — .357 Mag. or .45 LC cal., $4\frac{5}{8}$, $6\frac{1}{2}$ (.357 Mag. only), or $7\frac{1}{2}$ (.45 LC only) in. barrel, features high gloss stainless steel finish. New 1994.

Mfg.'s Sug. Retail	$443	$360	$255	$210			

BLACKHAWK-SRM — similar to New Model Blackhawk, except is chambered for .357 Rem. MAXIMUM, $7\frac{1}{2}$ or $10\frac{1}{2}$ in. barrels available, target sights, 53 oz., 11,500 mfg. 1984 only - production suspended due to unresolvable engineering problems.

	$450	$360	$310	$275	$250	$225	$200

SUPER BLACKHAWK — .44 Mag., $4\frac{5}{8}$ (new 1994), $5\frac{1}{2}$ (new 1987), $7\frac{1}{2}$ or $10\frac{1}{2}$ bull in. barrel, 6 shot, blued finish, walnut grips, similar to old model in appearance, but has new action. Mfg. 1973-present. The new model started with serial number 81-00001.

Mfg.'s Sug. Retail	$413	$310	$245	$200	$180	$170	$160	$150

▲ *Super Blackhawk Stainless Steel* — stainless variation of the Super Blackhawk.

Mfg.'s Sug. Retail	$450	$365	$290	$220			

▲ *Super Blackhawk High Gloss Stainless Steel* — high gloss stainless steel finish, not available in $10\frac{1}{2}$ in. bull barrel. New 1994.

Mfg.'s Sug. Retail	$450	$365	$290	$220			

▲ *Super Blackhawk Stainless Hunter* — $7\frac{1}{2}$ in. ribbed barrel only, laminated wood grips, includes scope rings. Mfg. 1992-95.

	$410	$310	$250				

Last Mfg.'s Sug. Retail was $498.

VAQUERO — .44-40 (new 1994), .44 Mag. (new 1994), or .45 LC cal., 6 shot, $4\frac{5}{8}$ (.44-40 or .45 LC only), $5\frac{1}{2}$, or $7\frac{1}{2}$ in barrel, color case hardened frame, blued steel grip frame, barrel, and cylinder, transfer bar hammer safety, smooth rosewood grips, patterned after the Colt SAA, fixed sights. New 1993.

Mfg.'s Sug. Retail	$434	$350	$270	$235	$210	$190	$170	$160

Add $36 for simulated ivory grips (new 1996).

While uncataloged, Ruger offered a $4\frac{5}{8}$ in. barrel in .44 Mag. cal. only in both blue (33 mfg.) and stainless (150 mfg.) - healthy premiums exist.

▲ *Vaquero High Gloss Stainless Steel* — high gloss stainless steel finish. New 1994.

Mfg.'s Sug. Retail	$434	$350	$270	$235			

Add $36 for simulated ivory grips (new 1996).

BISLEY MODEL — .22 LR, .32 H&R Mag., .357 Mag., .41 Mag., .44 Mag., or .45 LC cal., incorporates Bisley features (flat-top frame, raked hammer, longer grip frame), $6\frac{1}{2}$ (.22 LR or .32 H&R Mag. only) or $7\frac{1}{2}$ in. barrel, fixed (disc. 1992, except for .32 H&R Mag.) or adj. sights, available with fluted/unfluted or roll-marked/unmarked (disc.) cylinders, satin blue finish only, Goncalo Alves smooth grips. New 1986.

▲ *.22 LR or .32 H&R Mag.*

Mfg.'s Sug. Retail	$360	$290	$225	$180	$170	$160	$150	$140

▲ *Other cals.*

Mfg.'s Sug. Retail	$430	$350	$295	$250	$225	$200	$180	$160

NEW BEARCAT — .22 LR cal., includes interchangeable .22 WMR cyl., frame slightly longer than old Bearcat, 4 in. barrel, transfer bar hammer safety, blue finish, smooth walnut grips, fixed sights. New 1994.

Mfg.'s Sug. Retail	$298	$235	$180	$150	$135	$125	$115	$105

▲ *New Bearcat Bright Stainless Steel* — similar to New Bearcat, except in bright stainless steel finish. Mfg. 1994-95 only.

	$250	$195	$160				

Last Mfg.'s Sug. Retail was $325.

Grading	100%	98%	95%	90%	80%	70%	60%

OLD ARMY PERCUSSION — .44 cal., black powder, 6 shot, 7½ in. barrel, single action, blued finish, fixed (new 1994) or adj. sights, walnut grips.

Mfg.'s Sug. Retail	$413	$320	$230	$175	$150	$135	$120	$110

Add $100 for brass frame (disc.).

▲ *Old Army Percussion Stainless Steel*

Mfg.'s Sug. Retail	$465	$365	$290	$215

REVOLVERS: DOUBLE ACTION

During certain years of manufacture, Ruger's changes in production on certain models (cals., barrel markings, barrel lengths, etc.) have created rare variations that are now considered premium niches. These areas of low manufacture will add premiums to the values listed below on standard models.

SPEED SIX (MODELS 207, 208 and 209) — .38 Spl., .357 Mag., or 9mm cals., 2¾ or 4 in. barrel, fixed sights, checkered walnut grips, round butt, blued finish, some guns have factory speed hammer (no hammer spur). Mfg. 1973-1988. Model 207 and 208 disc. 1988.

	$230	$205	$190	$170	$160	$150	$140

Last Mfg.'s Sug. Retail was $292.

Add $40 for 9mm (Model 209 disc. 1984).

▲ *Models 737 and 738* — stainless steel versions of Models 207 and 208, .357 Mag and .38 Spl. cals., 2¾ or 4 in. barrel. Disc. 1988.

	$280	$245	$220

Last Mfg.'s Sug. Retail was $320.

▲ *Model 739* — stainless steel, 9mm. Disc. 1984.

	$300	$250	$230

SECURITY SIX (MODEL 117) — .357 Mag. cal., 6 shot, 2¾, 4 (heavy), or 6 in. barrel, adj. sights, checkered walnut grips, square butt. Mfg. 1970-1985.

	$250	$225	$195	$185	$160	$150	$140

Last Mfg.'s Sug. Retail was $309.

Add $15 for target grips.

500 of this model were mfg. for the California Highway Patrol during 1983 (.38 Spl. cal.) in stainless steel only. They are distinguishable by a C.H.P. marking. Other Security Six Model 117 special editions have been made for various police organizations - premiums might exist in certain regions for these variations.

▲ *Model 717* — stainless steel version of Model 117. Disc. 1985.

	$295	$255	$230

Last Mfg.'s Sug. Retail was $338.

POLICE SERVICE SIX — .357 Mag, .38 Spl., and 9mm cals., blued finish only, square butt, fixed sights, checkered walnut grips.

▲ *Model 107* — .357 Mag, 2¾ or 4 in. barrel, fixed sights. Disc. 1988.

	$250	$220	$200	$190	$180	$170	$165

Last Mfg.'s Sug. Retail was $287.

▲ *Model 108* — .38 Spl., 4 in. barrel, fixed sights. Disc. 1988.

	$250	$220	$200	$190	$180	$170	$165

Last Mfg.'s Sug. Retail was $287.

▲ *Model 109* — 9mm, 4 in. barrel, fixed sights. Disc. 1984.

	$275	$230	$205	$195	$185	$180	$175

POLICE SERVICE SIX STAINLESS STEEL — stainless construction, 4 in. barrel only, fixed sights, checkered walnut grips.

▲ *Model 707* — .357 Mag., square butt. Disc. 1988.

	$270	$235	$210

Last Mfg.'s Sug. Retail was $310.

Grading	100%	98%	95%	90%	80%	70%	60%

▲ **Model 708** — .38 Spl., square butt. Disc. 1988.

	$270	$235	$210

Last Mfg.'s Sug. Retail was $310.

GP-100 — .357 Mag./.38 Spl. cal., 3 (new 1990, fixed sights only), 4, or 6 (.357 Mag. only) in. standard or heavy barrel, strengthened design intended for constant use with all .357 Mag. ammunition, rubber cushioned grip panels with polished Goncalo Alves wood inserts, fixed or adj. (.357 Mag. only) sights with white outlined rear and interchangeable front, 6 shot, 35-46 oz. depending on barrel configuration. New 1986.

Mfg.'s Sug. Retail $423 $355 $285 $245 $220 $200 $185 $170

Add $17 for adj. rear sight (.357 Mag. cal., 4 or 6 in. barrel only).

▲ **GP-100 Stainless Steel** — similar to GP-100, except is stainless steel. New 1987.

Mfg.'s Sug. Retail $457 $375 $295 $250

Add $17 for adj. rear sight (.357 Mag. cal. only).

▲ **GP-100 High Gloss Stainless Steel** — .357 Mag. only, high gloss stainless steel finish, 3 or 4 in. heavy barrel. New 1996.

Mfg.'s Sug. Retail $457 $375 $295 $250

SP-101 STAINLESS STEEL — .22 LR (6 shot - new 1990), .32 H&R (6 shot - new 1991), .38 Spl.(5 shot), 9mm Para. (5 shot - new 1991), or .357 Mag. (5 shot - new 1991) cal., 2¼, 3¹⁄₁₆, or 4 (new 1990) in. barrel, small frame variation of the GP-100 Stainless, fixed or adj. (new 1996) sights, approx. 27 oz. New 1989.

Mfg.'s Sug. Retail $443 $360 $280 $240

Ruger introduced adj. sights in 1996 available in .22 LR or .32 H&R cal. only.

Ruger introduced a .357 Mag./2¼ in. (new 1993) or .38 Spl./2¼ (new 1994) in. configuration featuring a spurless hammer, double action only.

SP-101 barrel lengths are as follows: .22 cal. is available in 2¼ or 4 standard or heavy in. barrel, .32 H&R is available in 3¹⁄₁₆ or 4 (new 1994) heavy in. barrel, .38 Spl. is available in 2¼ or 3¹⁄₁₆ in. length only, 9mm Para. is available in 2¼ (new 1992) or 3¹⁄₁₆ in. only, and .357 Mag. is available in 2¼ or 3¹⁄₁₆ in. only.

▲ **SP-101 High Gloss Stainless Steel** — similar to SP-101 Stainless Steel, except has high gloss stainless steel finish. New 1996.

Mfg.'s Sug. Retail $443 $360 $280 $240

Ruger introduced adj. sights in 1996 available in .22 LR or .32 H&R cal. only.

REDHAWK — .357 Mag. (disc. 1985), .41 Mag. (disc. 1992), or .44 Mag. cal., this is a redesigned large frame handgun, 5½ and 7½ in. barrel only, square butt, smooth hardwood grips, 52 oz.

Mfg.'s Sug. Retail $490 $410 $335 $290 $240 $215 $180 $165

Add $37 for scope rings.

.357 Mag. and .41 Mag. cals. will bring collector premiums if NIB.

▲ **Redhawk Stainless Steel** — stainless steel construction.

Mfg.'s Sug. Retail $547 $450 $370 $300

Add $42 for stainless scope rings.

SUPER REDHAWK STAINLESS — .44 Mag., 7½ or 9½ barrel, adj. rear sight, cushioned grip panels (GP-100 style), stainless steel scope rings, 53 oz. Delivery began in late 1987.

Mfg.'s Sug. Retail $589 $480 $370 $275

S

Grading	100%	98%	95%	90%	80%	70%	60%

RIFLES: LEVER ACTION

MODEL 96 CARBINE — .22 LR, .22 WMR, or .44 Mag. cal., 18½ in. barrel with single barrel band, uncheckered hardwood stock with curved butt plate, 10 (.22 LR), 9 (.22 WMR), or 4 (.44 Mag.) shot detachable rotary mag., sliding cross-button safety, adj. rear sight, rimfire receivers are drilled and tapped while the .44 Mag. has an integral base receiver with scope rings, approx. 5¼-5⅞ lbs. New 1996.

Mfg.'s Sug. Retail	$328	$265	$205	$180	$160	$145	$135	$125

  Add $17 for .22 WMR cal.
  Add $38 for .44 Mag. cal.

RIFLES: SEMI-AUTO

During certain years of manufacture, Ruger's changes in production on certain models (cals., barrel markings, barrel lengths, etc.) have created rare variations that are now considered premium niches. These areas of low manufacture will add premiums to the values listed below on standard models.

The Model 10/22 has been mfg. in a variety of limited production models including a multi-colored or green laminate wood stock variation (1986), a brown laminate stock (1988), a Kittery Trading Post Commemorative (1988), a smoke or tree bark laminate stock (1989), a Chief AJ Model, Wal-Mart (stainless with black laminated hardwood stock - 1990), etc. These limited editions will command premiums over the standard models listed below, depending on the desirability of the special edition.

Note: All Ruger Rifles, except Stainless Mini-14, all Mini-30s, and Model 77-22s were made during 1976 in a "Liberty" version. Add $50 - $75 when in 100% in the original box condition.

10/22 STANDARD CARBINE — .22 LR, 10 shot rotary mag., 18½ in. barrel, birch or deluxe hand checkered walnut stock, folding rear sight. Mfg. 1964-present.

Mfg.'s Sug. Retail	$213	$165	$140	$115	$95	$80	$60	$55

  Add $20 for uncheckered walnut stock (mfg. 1964-1980 and 1987-1989).
  Add $61 for deluxe checkered walnut sporter stock (Model 10/22 DSP).

▲ **10/22RB Standard Carbine Stainless** — similar to Standard Carbine, except has stainless barrel and birch stock. New 1992.

Mfg.'s Sug. Retail	$255	$190	$160	$120

10/22T TARGET MODEL — .22 LR, features brown laminated American hardwood stock, blued hammer-forge spiral finish barrel, w/o sights. New 1996.

Mfg.'s Sug. Retail	$393	$330	$265	$225

10/22 FINGERGROOVE SPORTER — similar to Standard, except Monte Carlo stock and beavertail forearm. Mfg. 1964-1971.

	$250	$225	$200	$175	$140	$120	$110

  Add 200% for checkered stock in NIB condition.

10/22 INTERNATIONAL (OLD MFG.) — similar to Standard, except walnut full stock Mannlicher style. Mfg. 1964-1971.

	$475	$425	$350	$330	$300	$250	$225

  Add 50% for checkered stock.

▲ **10/22RBI International (New mfg.)** — features Mannlicher style international birch full stock. New 1994.

Mfg.'s Sug. Retail	$262	$205	$170	$130

  Add $20 for stainless steel barrel.

Grading	100%	98%	95%	90%	80%	70%	60%

10/22 CANADIAN CENTENNIAL — 2,000 mfg. in 1967.

	$375	$295	$225				

Last Mfg.'s Sug. Retail was $100.

RUGER/REMINGTON CANADIAN CENTENNIAL MATCHED NO. 3 SET — includes a Remington Model 742 in .308 Win. cal. and a Ruger 10/22 Sporter with special commemorative appointments, cased. 1,000 sets mfg. 1967 only.

	$700	$525	$425				

▲ *Ruger Canadian Centennial Matched No. 2 Set* — 70 sets mfg. 1967 only.

	$950	$775	$550				

▲ *Ruger Canadian Centennial Matched No. 1 Special Deluxe Set* — 30 sets mfg. 1967 only.

	$1,150	$895	$675				

MODEL 44 STANDARD CARBINE — .44 Mag., 4 shot mag., 18½ in. barrel, gas operated, folding sight, curved butt. Mfg. 1961-1985.

	$395	$350	$325	$295	$275	$250	$225

Last Mfg.'s Sug. Retail was $332.

▲ *Deerstalker Model* — approx. 3,750 mfg. with "Deerstalker" marked on rifle until Ithaca lawsuit disc. manufacture (1962).

	$475	$425	$350	$285	$250	$220	$195

▲ *25th Year Anniversary Model* — mfg. 1985 only, limited production, engraved.

	$450	$395	$350				

Last Mfg.'s Sug. Retail was $495.

MODEL 44RS — similar to 44, but has aperture sight and swivels.

	$450	$395	$350	$295	$275	$250	$230

MODEL 44 FINGERGROOVE SPORTER — Monte Carlo stocked version of 44 Standard. Mfg. until 1971.

	$495	$425	$365	$300	$275	$250	$230

MODEL 44 INTERNATIONAL — similar to Standard, except full length Mannlicher style stock. Mfg. until 1971.

	$750	$625	$500	$400	$350	$300	$275

MINI-14 — .223 Rem. or .222 Rem. (disc.) cals., 5 (standard mag. starting in 1989), 10, or 20 shot detachable mag., 18½ in. barrel, gas operated, aperture rear sight, military style stock, 6½ lbs. Mfg. 1976-present.

Mfg.'s Sug. Retail	$516	$435	$375	$335	$300	$265	$240	$215

Add $85 for folding stock (disc. 1989).
Add 25% for Southport Model with gold bead front sight.
Due to 1989 Federal legislation and public sentiment, the Mini-14 is now being shipped with a 5 shot detachable mag. only.

▲ *Mini 14 Stainless* — mini stainless steel version.

Mfg.'s Sug. Retail	$569	$465	$395	$350			

Add $85 for folding stock (disc. 1990).

MINI-14 RANCH RIFLE — .223 Rem. cal., 18½ in. barrel, folding rear sight, receiver cut for factory rings, similar to Mini-14, supplied with scope rings, approx. 6 lbs. 5 oz.

Mfg.'s Sug. Retail	$556	$450	$395	$375	$355	$325	$300	$260

Due to 1989 Federal legislation and public sentiment, the Mini-14 Ranch Rifle is now being shipped with a 5 shot detachable mag. only.

▲ *Stainless Ranch Rifle* — stainless steel construction. New 1986.

Mfg.'s Sug. Retail	$609	$485	$425	$365			

Add $85 for folding stock (disc. 1990).

Grading	100%	98%	95%	90%	80%	70%	60%

MINI-THIRTY — 7.62x39mm Russian, 18½ in. barrel, 5 shot detachable mag., hardwood stock, includes scope rings, 7 lbs. 3 oz. New 1987.

Mfg.'s Sug. Retail	$556	$450	$395	$365	$325	$300	$275	$250

▲ *Mini-Thirty Stainless* — steel variation of the Mini-Thirty, new 1990.

Mfg.'s Sug. Retail	$609	$485	$425	$365				

XGI — While advertised, this model was never shipped commercially because it could not maintain Ruger accuracy standards.

Mfg.'s Sug. Retail was originally targeted at $425.

RIFLES: SINGLE SHOT

During certain years of manufacture, Ruger's changes in production on certain models (cals., barrel markings, barrel lengths, etc.) have created rare variations that are now considered premium niches. These areas of low manufacture will add premiums to the values listed below on standard models.

NO. 1-A LIGHT SPORTER — similar to Standard, .22 Hornet (disc., 355 mfg.), .243 Win., .270 Win., 7x57mm, or .30-06 cal., 22 in. barrel, folding sight on quarter rib, ramp front sight, no rings, Alexander Henry forearm, front swivel in barrel band, 7¼ lbs. Mfg. 1966-present.

Mfg.'s Sug. Retail	$665	$465	$395	$325	$300	$275	$245	$215

The "A" suffix designates an Alexander Henry classic forearm with light barrel.

NO. 1-B STANDARD — falling block action with curved Farquharson lever, popular cals. include .218 Bee (limited mfg. beginning 1993), .22 Hornet (new 1988), .22-250 Rem., .220 Swift, .223 Rem., .257 Roberts, .243 Win., 6mm, .25-06 Rem., .270 Win., .280 Rem., .30-06, 7mm Rem. Mag., .270 Wby. Mag. (new 1990), .300 Wby. Mag. (new in 1990), .300 Win. Mag., or .338 Win. Mag., 22 or 26 in. barrel, quarter rib with integral scope bases, supplied with rings and no sights, checkered stock and semi beavertail forearm. Mfg. 1966-present.

Mfg.'s Sug. Retail	$665	$485	$400	$335	$300	$275	$245	$215

The "B" suffix designates semi beavertail forearm with medium barrel and is available in all cals. under .375 H&H except 7x57mm.

NO. 1-RSI INTERNATIONAL — .243 Win., .270 Win., 7x57mm, or .30-06 cal., features 20 in. lightweight barrel with full length Mannlicher stock, includes swivels and open sights, 7¼ lbs.

Mfg.'s Sug. Retail	$688	$525	$425	$350	$300	$275	$245	$215

NO. 1-V VARMINT — similar to No. 1-B Standard, except .22 PPC (new 1993), .22-250 Rem., .220 Swift, .223 Rem., .243 Win. (disc.), .25-06 Rem., 6mm Rem., 6mm PPC (new 1993), or .280 (disc.) cal., 24 or 26 (.220 Swift only) in. heavy barrel, without rib, target scope blocks, 9 lbs. Mfg. 1966-present.

Mfg.'s Sug. Retail	$665	$485	$400	$335	$300	$275	$245	$215

NO. 1-S MEDIUM SPORTER — similar to Light Sporter, only .218 Bee (limited mfg. beginning 1993 only), 7mm Rem. Mag., .45-70, .300 Win. Mag. or .338 Win. Mag. cal., 22 (.45-70 cal. only) or 26 in. medium barrel, open sights, 7¼ - 8 lbs.

Mfg.'s Sug. Retail	$665	$485	$400	$335	$300	$275	$245	$215

NO. 1-H TROPICAL RIFLE — similar to Medium Sporter, except .375 H&H, .404 Jeffery (new 1993), .416 Rem. (new 1993), .416 Rigby (new 1991), or .458 Win. Mag. cal., 24 in. heavy barrel, open sights, approx. 9 lbs.

Mfg.'s Sug. Retail	$665	$500	$415	$345	$310	$275	$245	$215

Grading	100%	98%	95%	90%	80%	70%	60%

NO. 3 CARBINE — same basic action as No. 1, except simpler lever design, uncheckered stock, available in .22 Hornet, .30-40 Krag, .45-70 (only cal. available 1986), .223 Rem., .44 Mag., or .375 Win. cal., 22 in. barrel, folding sight. Mfg. 1972-1987.

	$295	$250	$200	$180	$165	$145	$130

Last Mfg.'s Sug. Retail was $284.

Add 25-35% for .223 Rem., .375 Win., or .44 Mag cal.

RIFLES: .22 CAL. BOLT ACTION

MODEL 77/22-R/RS — .22 LR only, 10 shot rotary mag., 20 in. barrel, all steel construction, 3 position safety, checkered walnut stock, blue finish, non-adj. trigger, available with either optional iron sights or plain barrel (no sights) with scope rings (included), 2.7 millisecond lock time on trigger, 6 lbs. 2 oz. New 1984.

Mfg.'s Sug. Retail	$473	$375	$320	$260	$235	$210	$190	$175

Add $8 for iron sights.
Add 125% if w/o 77/22 roll mark or with green laminated stock.

▲ *Model 77/22-RP/RSP All-Weather Stainless* — similar to Model 77/22 LR, except has stainless steel metal with matte black DuPont Zytel synthetic stock, 5 lbs. 14 oz. New 1989.

Mfg.'s Sug. Retail	$473	$375	$320	$260

Add $8 for iron sights.

▲ *Model 77/22-VBZ Varmint Stainless Laminated* — similar to Model 77/.22 LR, stainless steel, heavy stainless barrel with dull finish, laminated brown hardwood stock. New 1995.

Mfg.'s Sug. Retail	$499	$395	$330	$275

MODEL 77/22-RM/RSM MAG. — similar to Model 77/22-R/RS, except in .22 Win. Mag. cal., 9 shot rotary mag., blue finish, checkered walnut stock. New 1990.

Mfg.'s Sug. Retail	$473	$375	$320	$260	$235	$210	$190	$175

Add $8 for iron sights.

▲ *Model 77/22-RMP/RSMP Mag. All-Weather Stainless* — similar to Model 77/22-RM/RSM Mag., except has stainless steel metal with matte black Dupont Zytel synthetic stock. New 1990.

Mfg.'s Sug. Retail	$473	$375	$320	$260

Add $8 for iron sights.

▲ *Model 77/22-VMBZ Mag. Varmint Stainless Laminated* — similar to Model 77/.22 Mag., stainless steel, heavy stainless barrel with dull finish, laminated brown hardwood stock. New 1993.

Mfg.'s Sug. Retail	$499	$395	$330	$275

RIFLES: CENTERFIRE BOLT ACTION

During certain years of manufacture, Ruger's changes in production on certain models (cals., barrel markings, barrel lengths, etc.) have created rare variations that are now considered premium niches. These areas of low manufacture will add premiums to the values listed below on standard models.

Earlier flat-bolt models (pre-1972) are desirable in the rarer cals. and will command premiums if 98%+ condition.

MODEL 77/22-RH/RSH HORNET — .22 Hornet cal., features lengthened receiver, detachable 6 shot rotary mag. (not interchangeable with other 77/22 mags.), blued barrel, checkered American walnut stock, includes scope rings. New 1994.

Mfg.'s Sug. Retail	$489	$395	$335	$275

Add $10 for iron sights.

▲ *Model 77/22-VHZ Hornet Varmint Stainless Laminated* — similar to Model 77/.22 Hornet, stainless steel, heavy stainless barrel with dull finish, laminated brown hardwood stock. New 1995.

Mfg.'s Sug. Retail	$535	$425	$355	$290

Grading	100%	98%	95%	90%	80%	70%	60%

MODEL 77R — .22-250 Rem., .220 Swift, 6mm Rem. (disc.), .243 Win. (disc.), .257 Roberts, .25-06 Rem., .270 Win., 7x57mm, 7mm-08 (disc.), 6.5 Rem. Mag. (scarce), 7mm Rem. Mag., .280 Rem., .284 Win., .308 Win. (disc.), .30-06, .300 Win. Mag., .338 Win Mag., .350 Rem. Mag., cal., long or short action, blue finish, 5 shot mag., 3 shot in Mag. cals., 22 or 24 in. barrel, available with integral bases or round top, some models supplied with sights, stock is checkered walnut with red rubber butt plate, approx. 7 lbs. Mfg. 1968-1992.

	$420	$350	$295	$265	$245	$200	$200

Last Mfg.'s Sug. Retail was $558.

Add 10-15% for .284 cal.
Add 20%-30% for .350 Rem. Mag. cal.
This model is encountered with or without the "R" suffix.

▲ *Model 77 RL* — .22-250 Rem. (disc.), .257 Roberts, .270 Win., or .30-06 cal., ultra light variation weighing 6 lbs., black forearm tip. Disc. 1992.

	$445	$375	$300	$270	$250	$225	$205

Last Mfg.'s Sug. Retail was $592.

▲ *Model 77 RS* — .25-06 Rem. (disc.), 270 Win., .284 Win., .30-06, 7mm Rem. Mag., 300 Win. Mag., .338 Win. Mag., .35 Whelen, .350 Rem. Mag., .358 Win. cal., similar to Model 77R, except has open sights. Disc. 1992.

	$460	$395	$315	$285	$265	$230	$210

Last Mfg.'s Sug. Retail was $616.

Add 20%-30% for .284 Win. or .350 Rem. Mag. cal.

▲ *Model 77V Varmint* — .22-250 Rem., .220 Swift, .243 Win. (disc.), 6mm Rem. (disc.), .25-06 Rem., .280 Rem., or .308 Win. cal., 24 in. heavy barrel (26 in. on .220 Swift), drilled and tapped for target bases, approx. 9 lbs. Mfg. 1968-92.

	$430	$365	$300	$265	$245	$210	$200

Last Mfg.'s Sug. Retail was $574.

▲ *Model 77 RS African* — similar to Model 77R, except in .458 Win. Mag. cal. Disc. 1991.

	$550	$475	$400	$365	$335	$315	$300

Last Mfg.'s Sug. Retail was $680.

This model is supplied standard with a steel triggerguard and steel floor plate.

▲ *Model 77 RSC* — similar to Model 77 RS African, except has Circasian walnut stock (C suffix). Mfg. 1976-78.

	$675	$575	$500	$450	$400	$365	$335

▲ *Model 77 RLS* — .243 Win. (disc. 1989), .270 Win., .30-06, and .308 Win. cal. (disc. 1989), ultra light, 18½ in. barrel, open sights, 6 lbs. Mfg. 1987-93.

	$445	$375	$310	$280	$260	$230	$210

Last Mfg.'s Sug. Retail was $592.

▲ *Model 77 RSI* — .22-250 Rem. (disc. 1991), .250-3000 (reintroduced 1990), .270 Win., .30-06, .308 Win. (disc. 1991), or 7x57mm (rare), 7mm-08 Rem. cal., International Mannlicher (full length stock) with 18½ in. barrel and open sights (includes scope rings), approx. 7 lbs. Disc. 1993.

	$470	$400	$325	$295	$265	$230	$210

Last Mfg.'s Sug. Retail was $623.

Add 20% for 7mm-08 cal.

MODEL 77R MARK II SERIES — various cals. as listed below, evolutionary design of the Ruger Model 77R featuring slenderized proportioning, 3 position swing-back safety, new trigger, triggerguard and floor plate latch, stainless steel bolt with Mauser extractor design, 20 in. barrel, integral base receiver, hand checkered American walnut stock, approx. 6 lbs. 7 oz. New 1989.

▲ *Model 77R* — .220 Swift (mfg. 1995 only), .22-250 Rem. (mfg. 1993 only), .223 Rem. (new 1992), .243 Win., .25-06 Rem. (new 1993), .257 Roberts (new 1993), .270 Win. (new 1993), .280 Rem. (new 1993), 6mm Rem., 6.5x55 Swedish (new 1993), 7x57mm (new 1993), .30-06 (new 1993), .308 Win., 7mm Rem. Mag. (new 1993), .300 Win. Mag. (new 1993), or .338 Win. Mag. (new 1993) cal., standard model of the new Mark II Series.

Mfg.'s Sug. Retail	$574	$460	$350	$295	$265	$245	$200	$200

Grading	100%	98%	95%	90%	80%	70%	60%

▲ *Model 77 RL* — .223 Rem., .243 Win., .257 Roberts (new 1993), .270 Win. (new 1993), .30-06 (new 1993), or .308 Win. cal., ultra light variation weighing approx. 6 lbs., black forearm tip. New 1990.

Mfg.'s Sug. Retail	$610	$485	$400	$300	$270	$250	$225	$205

▲ *Model 77 RS* — 6mm Rem. (disc.), .243 Win., .25-06 Rem. (new 1993), .270 Win. (new 1993), .30-06 (new 1993), .308 Win., 7mm Rem. Mag. (new 1993), .300 Win. Mag. (new 1993), .338 Win Mag. (new 1993), or .458 Win. Mag. (new 1994) cal., similar to Model 77R, except has open sights. New 1990.

Mfg.'s Sug. Retail	$635	$510	$420	$325	$285	$265	$230	$210

▲ *Model 77 RSI* — .243 Win., .270 Win., .30-06, or .308 Win. cal., International Mannlicher (full length stock) with 18½ in. barrel and open sights (includes scope rings), approx. 7 lbs. New 1993.

Mfg.'s Sug. Retail	$642	$515	$425	$330	$285	$265	$230	$210

▲ *Model 77 RLS* — .243 Win. or .308 Win. cal., ultra light, 18½ in. barrel, open sights. Mfg. 1990 only.

		$460	$375	$310	$280	$260	$230	$210

Last Mfg.'s Sug. Retail was $564.

▲ *Model K77 RP All-Weather Stainless* — .22-250 (new 1996), .223 Rem., .243 Win., .270 Win., .280 Rem. (new 1993), .30-06, .308, 7mm Rem. Mag., .300 Win. Mag., or .338 Win. Mag. (new 1992) cal., similar to Model 77R Mark II except has stainless steel metal with matte black DuPont Zytel synthetic stock, no sights. New 1990.

Mfg.'s Sug. Retail	$574	$460	$370	$295

▲ *Model K77 RSP All-Weather Stainless* — .243 Win., .270 Win., .30-06, 7mm Rem. Mag., .300 Win. Mag., .338 Win. Mag., otherwise similar to Model K77 RP All-Weather Stainless, except has open sights.

Mfg.'s Sug. Retail	$635	$515	$425	$330

▲ *Model K77 VT* — .22 PPC, .220 Swift, .22-250 Rem., .223 Rem., .243 Win., .25-06 Rem., .308 Win., or 6mm PPC cal., features laminated stock and heavy steel barrel. New 1993.

Mfg.'s Sug. Retail	$684	$545	$430	$325

This model's nomenclature changed from VBZ to VTM during 1994.

▲ *Model 77 LR* — .270 Win., .30-06, .300 Win. Mag., or 7mm Rem. Mag. cal., left hand variation of the Model 77R. New 1991.

Mfg.'s Sug. Retail	$574	$460	$365	$295	$265	$245	$200	$200

▲ *Model 77 RSM* — .375 H&H, .404 Jeffery (mfg. 1994-95), or .416 Rigby cal., premium grade wood with hand cut checkering and ebony forend tip, integral barrel and sighting rib. New 1990.

Mfg.'s Sug. Retail	$1,550	$1,375	$1,100	$950	$825	$750	$675	$595

▲ *Model 77 RS Express* — .270 Win., .30-06, 7mm Rem. Mag., .300 Win. Mag., or .338 Win. Mag. (new 1994) cal., similar construction to Model 77RSM with premium grade wood and other materials. New 1991.

Mfg.'s Sug. Retail	$1,550	$1,375	$1,100	$950	$825	$750	$675	$595

SHOTGUNS

RED LABEL O/U — 12, 20, or 28 (new 1994) ga., 3 in. chambers, various barrel lengths and choke (including skeet) combinations, boxlock, SST, 26 or 28 in. VR barrels, auto ejectors, choice of checkered pistol grip or English straight grip (new 1992) stock, stainless steel frame became standard on 12 ga. 1985 (not available in 20 ga.). Choke tubes became optional in 1988, standard 1990. Mfg. 1977-present.

Mfg.'s Sug. Retail	$1,215	$925	$750	$675	$595	$550	$500	$450

Subtract 15%-20% without choke tubes.

During late 1994, some 12 and 20 ga. Red Label boxes were marked "EZ", indicating the new easy-opening feature (this is not mechanically spring-assisted, but rather works on tight machining tolerances). All Red Label shotguns will have the "EZ"-opening feature by mid-year 1995.

Earlier all-steel 12 ga. models (approx. 500 mfg.) with short field tubes could command 10%-15% premiums over values listed above to collectors interested in acquiring this variation. 20 ga. models w/o choke tubes are blue only.

▲ *Red Label English Field* — 12, 20, or 28 (new 1995) ga., similar to Red Label, except has English style straight grip stock. New 1992.

Mfg.'s Sug. Retail	$1,215	$925	$750	$675	$595	$550	$500	$450

Grading	100%	98%	95%	90%	80%	70%	60%

▲ *Red Label Sporting Clays* — 12 or 20 (new 1994) ga., features 30 in. separated barrels, Briley chokes with bores back bored to .744 in., ³⁄₈ in. VR with middle bead, sporting clays recoil pad. New 1992.

Mfg.'s Sug. Retail	$1,349	$1,000	$925	$725	$625	$550	$500	$450

RED LABEL "WOODSIDE" SPECIAL EDITION — 12 ga. only, 3 in. chambers, 28 in. barrels, straight or pistol grip stock, features premium checkered walnut, satin nickel finish, unique stock design permitting wood to fill-in where frame boxlock action would normally be, hand-engraving available at extra cost. New 1995.

Mfg.'s Sug. Retail	$1,675	$1,425	$1,150	$950	$775	$625	$550	$500

WILDLIFE FOREVER SPECIAL EDITION — 12 ga. only, limited edition to celebrate the 50th anniversary of Wildlife Forever, features Baron & Son engraving with gold pheasant and mallard inlays on receiver sides, 300 mfg. 1993 only.

	$1,595	$900	$775

Last Mfg.'s Sug. Retail was $1,595.

Add $125 for hard-fitted case.

SUNDANCE INDUSTRIES, INC.

Manufacturer located in Valencia, CA. Distributor sales only.

MODEL A-25 SEMI-AUTO PISTOL — .25 ACP cal., semi-auto single action design, 2⁷⁄₁₆ in. barrel, 7 shot mag., rotary safety, lower grip push button mag. release, satin nickel (disc.), bright chrome, or black teflon finish, choice of simulated pearl with different colors or grooved black grips, serrated slide. New 1989.

Mfg.'s Sug. Retail	$79	$65	$55	$45	$40	$35	$30	$25

LADY LASER/LASER 25 — .25 ACP cal., similar to Model A-25, except has factory installed and sighted 5mW Laser sight with no exposed wiring or switch, polished chrome or black finish (Laser 25 only), dual safety switch. New 1995.

Mfg.'s Sug. Retail	$220	$195	$160	$135	$115	$95	$80	$70

MODEL BOA — similar to Model A-25, except has patented squeeze grip safety. New in 1990.

Mfg.'s Sug. Retail	$95	$75	$60	$50	$45	$40	$35	$30

POINT BLANK DERRINGER — .22 LR cal., O/U design, double action, 3 in. barrels, black matte finish, 8 oz. Mfg. began mid-1994.

Mfg.'s Sug. Retail	$99	$80	$60	$50	$45	$40	$35	$30

SUPER SIX LIMITED

Previous manufacturer located in Brookfield, WI until 1992.

REVOLVERS

GOLDEN BISON SERIES — .45-70 Gov't, 6 shot revolver, 8 or 10½ in. octagon barrel, large size (overall length 15-17½ in.), manganese bronze frame, cross bolt manual safety, smooth hardwood grips, approx. 6 lbs. 177 total mfg. (including special/limited editions). Disc. approx. 1992.

	$1,675	$1,475	$1,275	$1,000	$875	$775	$675

Last Mfg.'s Sug. Retail was $1,895.

Low serialization specimens (ser. no.'s 1-15) have asking prices of $2,250-$2,950.

▲ *Centennial Limited Edition* — features special engraving and case. 20 total mfg.

	$2,950	$2,275	$1,675

Last Mfg.'s Sug. Retail was $3,995.

SURVIVAL ARMS, INC.

Manufacturer since 1990 located in Orange, CT. Previously located in Cocoa, FL until 1995. Distributor and dealer sales.

SURVIVAL ARMS, INC.

In 1990, Survival Arms, Inc. took over the manufacture of AR-7 Explorer rifles from Charter Arms located in Stratford, CT.

Grading	100%	98%	95%	90%	80%	70%	60%

RIFLES

AR-7 EXPLORER RIFLE — .22 LR cal., takedown or normal wood stock, takedown barreled action stores in Cycolac synthetic stock, 8 shot mag., adj. sights, 16 in. barrel, black matte finish on AR-7, silvertone on AR-7S, camouflage finish on AR-7C.

Mfg.'s Sug. Retail	$150	$120	$100	$85	$75	$65	$55	$50

AR-20 — similar to AR-22, except has vent style barrel, pistol grip stock, and two 10 shot mags. clipped together. New 1996.

Mfg.'s Sug. Retail	$200	$165	$140	$120	$105	$95	$80	$70

AR-22/AR-25 — .22 LR cal., 16 in. barrel, black rifle features pistol grip with choice of wood or metal folding* stock, includes 20 (1995 only) or 25 (disc. 1994) shot mag. Disc. 1995.

$155	$120	$95	$80	$70	$60	$55

Last Mfg.'s Sug. Retail was $200.

Subtract $50 for wood stock model.

SVENDSEN, ERL, F.A. MFG. CO.

Previous manufacturer located in Itasca, IL.

DERRINGERS

LITTLE ACE — .22 S cal., patterned after the Ethan Allen "HIDE-A-WAY", bronze frame, blued steel barrel with case hardened hammer and spur trigger.

$85	$75	$70	$65	$60	$55	$50

4-ACES — .22 S cal., 4 barrel derringer with rotating firing pin and spur trigger, bronze frame with blued rifled steel barrels and case hardened parts.

$175	$150	$135	$120	$105	$90	$75

SWING

Manufactured by Schutzen Bohme GmbH located in Rintein, Germany.

SWING BOLT ACTION — .308 Win., target bolt action rifle with thumbhole stock and vented forearm, target sights, 30 in. barrel, 12.1 lbs. New 1994.

Please contact the factory directly for more information and current pricing on this model (see Trademark Index).

SYMES & WRIGHT LTD.

Manufacturer located in London, England. Direct sales only.

Symes & Wright Ltd. manufactures approx. 25 best quality shotguns and double rifles annually. This manufacturer should be contacted directly (see listing in Trademark Index) for more information, including a price quotation based on an individual special order.

T section

TALON

While advertised, a presidential import ban and related government actions prohibited importation of the Talon MKI Model (suggested retail was planned at $495).

TANFOGLIO, F.LLI, Srl

Pistol manufacturer located in Gardone, Italy.

Tanfoglio manufactures good quality semi-auto pistols and single action revolvers. In addition to currently being imported by European American Armory Corp. (see individual listing), Tanfoglio also manufactures their own complete line which, to date, has been mostly distributed in Europe.

TANNER, ANDRE'

Manufacturer located in Switzerland. Currently imported and distributed by Mandall Shooting Supplies, Inc. located in Scottsdale, AZ. Previously imported by Osborne's located in Cheboygan, MI.

Tanner rifles are noted for their superior accuracy and limited production - less than 150 are mfg. each year.

Prices below reflect the recent devaluation of the U.S. dollar against some foreign currencies. While the manufacturer's suggested retails have gone up considerably, prices for used specimens (98% or less original condition) have not increased proportionately, and in some cases, have changed very little.

Grading	100%	98%	95%	90%	80%	70%	60%

300 METER MATCH RIFLE — 7.5 Swiss (special order) or 7.62mm cal. only, single shot, top-of-the-line 300 meter match rifle incorporating all match shooting features including deluxe palm rest, aperture sights.

Mfg.'s Sug. Retail	$4,900	$4,650	$3,995	$3,400	$2,775	$2,250	$1,900	$1,600

Add $100 for adj. cheekpiece.
Subtract $190 for repeating model with similar features.

▲ *300 Meter UIT Standard* — similar to Model 300, except is without palm rest and adj. Swiss butt plate, 10 shot mag., aperture sights.

Mfg.'s Sug. Retail	$4,700	$4,450	$3,850	$3,350	$2,750	$2,225	$1,925	$1,600

Add $100 for adj. cheekpiece.

SUPERMATCH MODEL 50 M — .22 LR only, 50 meter free rifle, deluxe palm rest, adj. butt plate, thumbhole stock.

Mfg.'s Sug. Retail	$3,900	$3,600	$3,200	$2,850	$2,450	$2,050	$1,800	$1,600

Add $100 for adj. cheekpiece.

TAR-HUNT CUSTOM RIFLES, INC.

Custom rifled shotgun manufacturer located in Bloomsburg, PA. Retail and dealer sales.

SHOTGUNS: BOLT ACTION

PROFESSIONAL MODEL RSG-12/20 — 12 (RSG-12) or 20 (RSG-20) ga., 2¾ in. chamber, bolt action shotgun featuring 21½ in. Shaw rifled slug barrel and 2 lug bolt, 2 shot box mag., matte black finish, McMillan fiberglass stock with Pachmayr Decelerator rifle pad, receiver drilled and tapped for standard Weaver bases (included), muzzle brake became standard 1994, various finish options, 7¾ lbs. New 1991.

Mfg.'s Sug. Retail	$1,395	$1,325	$1,100	$900	$800	$750	$700	$650

Grading	100%	98%	95%	90%	80%	70%	60%

MATCHLESS MODEL RSG-12/20 — upgraded variation featuring 400 grit polished gloss metal finish and the McMillan "Fiber" grain stock (wood grain finish). New 1995.

Mfg.'s Sug. Retail	$1,784	$1,625	$1,395	$1,100	$900	$800	$750	$700

PEERLESS MODEL RSG-12/20 — upgraded variation featuring NP-3 (nickel/Teflon) metal finish by Robar of Phoenix, AZ, McMillan "Fiber"-grain stock (wood grain finish). New 1995.

Mfg.'s Sug. Retail	$1,973	$1,775	$1,475	$1,175	$950	$800	$750	$700

RSG-TACTICAL (SNIPER) MODEL — 12 ga. only, similar to RSG-12, except has M-86 McMillan fiberglass black tactical stock with Pachmayr Decelerator pad.

Mfg.'s Sug. Retail	$1,595	$1,495	$1,250	$995	$875	$750	$700	$650

Add $150 for Bi-pod.

TAURUS INTERNATIONAL FIREARMS

Manufacturer located in Porto Alegre, Brazil. Currently imported by Taurus International Firearms located in Miami, FL since 1982. Distributor sales only.

Previous to 1990, this company's name was Taurus International Manufacturing, Inc. All Taurus products are backed by a lifetime repair policy.

REVOLVERS: RECENT MANUFACTURE

From 1990-1992, certain models became available with a Laser Aim LA1 sighting system that included mounts, rings (in matching finish), 110 volt AC recharging unit, 9 volt DC field charger, and high impact custom case.

MODEL 44 — .44 Mag. cal., 6 shot, integral compensator, adj. sights, 4, 6½ (VR), or 8⅜ (VR) in. barrel. New 1994.

Mfg.'s Sug. Retail	$425	$345	$295	$255	$215	$185	$155	$130

Add $18 for 6½ or 8 ⅜ in. barrel.

▲ *Model 44SS (Stainless Steel)* — similar to Model 44, except stainless steel. New 1994.

Mfg.'s Sug. Retail	$484	$400	$335	$285

Add $20 for 6½ or 8 ⅜ in. barrel.

MODEL 431 — .44 Spl. cal., 5 shot, 2 (new 1995), 3, or 4 in. barrel, blue only, fixed sights. New 1993.

Mfg.'s Sug. Retail	$286	$220	$170	$135	$125	$115	$100	$90

▲ *Model 431SS (Stainless Steel)* — similar to Model 431, except stainless steel. New 1993.

Mfg.'s Sug. Retail	$350	$280	$215	$180

MODEL 441 — similar to Model 431, except has 3, 4, or 6 in. barrel, adj. sights. New 1993.

Mfg.'s Sug. Retail	$298	$225	$170	$140	$125	$115	$100	$90

▲ *Model 441SS (Stainless Steel)* — similar to Model 441, except is stainless steel. New 1993.

Mfg.'s Sug. Retail	$374	$305	$225	$190

MODEL 65 — .357 Mag./.38 Spl. cal., double action, 6 shot, 2½ (new 1993), 3 (disc. 1992) or 4 in. barrel, blue finish, checkered walnut grips, 34 oz.

Mfg.'s Sug. Retail	$290	$225	$165	$125	$115	$100	$90	$85

Add $15 for satin nickel finish (disc.).

▲ *Model 65SS (Stainless Steel)* — similar to Model 65, except in stainless steel. New 1993.

Mfg.'s Sug. Retail	$357	$285	$220	$185

MODEL 66 — .357 Mag./.38 Spl. cal., double action, 6 shot, 2½ (new 1993), 3 (disc. 1992), 4, or 6 in. barrel, checkered walnut grips, blue finish, adj. sights, 35 oz.

Mfg.'s Sug. Retail	$318	$240	$175	$135	$125	$115	$100	$90

Add $15 for satin nickel finish (disc.).
Add $10 for 4 or 6 in. compensated (66CP) barrel (mfg. 1993-94).

Grading	100%	98%	95%	90%	80%	70%	60%

▲ **Model 66SS (Stainless Steel)** — similar to Model 66, but in stainless steel. New 1987.

Mfg.'s Sug. Retail	$392	$305	$225	$185			

Add $10 for 4 or 6 in. compensated (66CP) barrel (mfg. 1993-94).

MODEL 669 — similar to Model 66 except has fully shrouded barrel, 4 or 6 in. barrel, blue finish, 37 oz.

Mfg.'s Sug. Retail	$327	$250	$185	$145	$125	$115	$100	$90

Add $10 for VR barrel (mfg. 1989-1992).
Add $400 for Laser Aim Sight (offered 1990-1992).
Add $19 for compensated (669CP) barrel (new 1993).

▲ **Model 669SS (Stainless Steel)** — similar to Model 669, but in stainless steel.

Mfg.'s Sug. Retail	$401	$315	$240	$190			

Add $20 for compensated (669CP) barrel (new 1993).

MODEL 689 — similar to Model 669, except has VR.

Mfg.'s Sug. Retail	$341	$255	$190	$145	$125	$115	$100	$90

Add $390 for Laser Aim Sight (mfg. 1990-91 only).

▲ **Model 689SS (Stainless Steel)** — similar to Model 669, but in stainless steel.

Mfg.'s Sug. Retail	$415	$325	$245	$190			

MODEL 73 — .32 Long cal. only, double action, 6 shot, 3 in. heavy barrel only, checkered walnut grips, 20 oz. Disc. 1992.

	$175	$150	$125	$115	$105	$95	$85

Last Mfg.'s Sug. Retail was $223.

Add $20 for satin nickel finish.

MODEL 76 — .32 H&R Mag. cal., double action, 6 shot, 6 in. heavy barrel with solid rib, fully adj. rear sight, transfer bar safety, checkered hard wood grips, blue only, 34 oz. Mfg. 1991-94.

	$240	$190	$155	$130	$115	$100	$90

Last Mfg.'s Sug. Retail was $308.

MODEL 741 — .32 H&R Mag. cal., 6 shot, 3 or 4 in. barrel, blue only, adj. sights. Mfg. 1993-94.

	$205	$155	$125	$115	$100	$90	$85

Last Mfg.'s Sug. Retail was $254.

▲ **Model 741SS (Stainless Steel)** — similar to Model 741, except is stainless steel. Mfg. 1993-94.

	$275	$215	$185				

Last Mfg.'s Sug. Retail was $342.

MODEL 761 — .32 H&R Mag. cal., 6 shot, 6 in. barrel, blue only, adj. sights. Mfg. 1993-94.

	$250	$185	$145	$125	$115	$100	$90

Last Mfg.'s Sug. Retail was $326.

MODEL 80 — .38 Spl. cal. only, double action, 6 shot, 3 or 4 in. barrel, checkered walnut grips, fixed sights, 30 oz.

Mfg.'s Sug. Retail	$252	$190	$145	$115	$105	$95	$85	$80

Add $15 for satin nickel finish (disc. 1992).

▲ **Model 80SS (Stainless Steel)** — similar to Model 80, except stainless steel. New 1993.

Mfg.'s Sug. Retail	$299	$235	$175	$135			

MODEL 82 — .38 Spl. cal. only, double action, 6 shot, 3 or 4 in. heavy barrel, checkered walnut grips, fixed sights, 34 oz.

Mfg.'s Sug. Retail	$252	$190	$145	$115	$105	$95	$85	$80

Add $15 for satin nickel finish (disc.).

▲ **Model 82SS (Stainless Steel)** — similar to Model 82, except stainless steel. New 1993.

Mfg.'s Sug. Retail	$299	$235	$175	$135			

MODEL 83 — .38 Spl. cal. only, double action, 6 shot, 4 in. heavy barrel, checkered walnut grips, adj. sights, 34½ oz.

Mfg.'s Sug. Retail	$265	$205	$150	$125	$115	$105	$95	$80

Add $13 for satin nickel finish (disc.).

Grading	100%	98%	95%	90%	80%	70%	60%

▲ *Model 83SS (Stainless Steel)* — similar to Model 83, except stainless steel. New 1993.
Mfg.'s Sug. Retail $309 $240 $175 $135

MODEL 85 — .38 Spl. cal. only, double action, 5 shot, 2 or 3 in. heavy barrel, checkered walnut grips, fixed sights, 21 oz.

		100%	98%	95%	90%	80%	70%	60%
Mfg.'s Sug. Retail	$239	$185	$160	$130	$115	$105	$95	$85

Add $20 for satin nickel finish (3 in. barrel only, disc. 1992).

▲ *Model 85CH (Blue or Stainless)* — similar to Model 85, except has Brazilian hardwood combat grips and spurless hammer that fits flush with the frame, 2 in. barrel, double action only, 21 oz. New 1992.

		100%	98%	95%	90%	80%	70%	60%
Mfg.'s Sug. Retail	$239	$185	$160	$130	$115	$105	$95	$85

Add $48 for stainless steel.

▲ *Model 85SS (Stainless Steel)* — version of Model 85.
Mfg.'s Sug. Retail $287 $220 $175 $145

MODEL 86 CUSTOM TARGET — .38 Spl. cal. only, double action target model, 6 shot, 6 in. barrel, specially contoured smooth walnut grips, adj. rear sight, blue only, 34 oz. Disc. 1994.

			100%	98%	95%	90%	80%	70%	60%
			$270	$200	$160	$150	$140	$130	$120

Last Mfg.'s Sug. Retail was $352.

This model is available in either single or double action with adj. counterweight and interchangeable front sight inserts.

MODEL 94 — .22 LR cal., double action, 9 shot, 3 (new 1991), 4, or 5 (new 1996) in. barrel, blue finish, adj. rear sight, target features, 25 oz. New 1989.

		100%	98%	95%	90%	80%	70%	60%
Mfg.'s Sug. Retail	$293	$220	$165	$135	$120	$105	$95	$85

▲ *Model 94SS (Stainless Steel)* — version of Model 94. New 1990.
Mfg.'s Sug. Retail $339 $265 $195 $150

MODEL 941 — .22 Mag. cal., 8 shot, 3, 4, or 5 in. barrel, blue only, adj. sights. New 1993.

		100%	98%	95%	90%	80%	70%	60%
Mfg.'s Sug. Retail	$315	$240	$180	$140	$120	$105	$95	$85

▲ *Model 941SS (Stainless Steel)* — similar to Model 941, except is stainless steel. New 1993.
Mfg.'s Sug. Retail $366 $275 $210 $160

MODEL 96 TARGET SCOUT — .22 LR cal. only, double action, 6 shot, 6 in. barrel, checkered walnut grips, same features as Model 86, 34 oz.

		100%	98%	95%	90%	80%	70%	60%
Mfg.'s Sug. Retail	$358	$265	$195	$160	$150	$140	$130	$120

MODEL 605 — .357 Mag. cal., 5 shot, $2\frac{1}{4}$ or 3 (new 1996) in. barrel, blue or stainless, 4 port compensated barrel ($2\frac{1}{4}$ in. only) with fixed sights, full barrel shroud, oversized finger grooved rubber grips, $24\frac{1}{2}$ oz. New 1995.

		100%	98%	95%	90%	80%	70%	60%
Mfg.'s Sug. Retail	$262	$215	$170	$135	$120	$105	$95	$85

Add $50 for stainless steel.

MODEL 607 — .357 Mag. cal., 7 shot, 4 or $6\frac{1}{2}$ (VR) in. compensated barrel, adj. rear sight, Santoprene synthetic grips, 44 oz. New 1995.

		100%	98%	95%	90%	80%	70%	60%
Mfg.'s Sug. Retail	$425	$325	$275	$240	$205	$185	$160	$150

Add $18 for $6\frac{1}{2}$ in. VR barrel.

▲ *MODEL 607SS (Stainless Steel)* — stainless variation of the Model 607. New 1995.
Mfg.'s Sug. Retail $484 $365 $320 $265

Add $20 for $6\frac{1}{2}$ in. VR barrel.

MODEL 608 — .357 Mag. cal., 8 shot, 4 or $6\frac{1}{2}$ (VR) in. barrel with integral compensator, adj. sights. New 1996.

		100%	98%	95%	90%	80%	70%	60%
Mfg.'s Sug. Retail	$425	$325	$275	$240	$205	$185	$160	$150

Add $18 for $6\frac{1}{2}$ in. VR barrel.

Grading	100%	98%	95%	90%	80%	70%	60%

▲ **MODEL 608SS (Stainless Steel)** — stainless variation of the Model 608. New 1996.
Mfg.'s Sug. Retail $484 $365 $320 $265
   Add $20 for 6½ in. VR barrel.

PISTOLS: SEMI-AUTO

From 1990-1992, certain models became available with a Laser Aim LA1 sighting system that included mounts, rings (in matching finish), 110 volt AC recharging unit, 9 volt DC field charger, and high impact custom case.

   Add approx. $30 for the Deluxe Shooter's Pack option (includes extra mag. and custom case) on the 92, 99, 100, and 101 Series.

PT-22 — .22 LR cal., single or double action operation, tip-up 2¾ in. barrel, 9 shot mag., fixed sights, ambidextrous safety, blue or nickel (new 1995) finish, smooth hardwood grips, 12.3 oz. New 1992.
Mfg.'s Sug. Retail $187 $150 $125 $110 $100 $90 $80 $70
   Add $8 for nickel finish.

PT-25 — .25 ACP cal., similar to PT-22, except has 8 shot mag. New 1992.
Mfg.'s Sug. Retail $187 $150 $125 $110 $100 $90 $80 $70
   Add $8 for nickel finish.

PT-58 — .380 ACP cal., similar to PT-99AF, except in .380 ACP cal., 4 in. barrel, 10 (C/B 1994) or 12* shot mag. New 1988.
Mfg.'s Sug. Retail $429 $325 $275 $235 $215 $200 $190 $180
   Add $32 for satin nickel finish (disc. 1994).
   Beginning 1993, the PT-58 started incorporating the Taurus Tri-Position safety system which features a hammer-drop, "cocked-and-locked" option system.

▲ **PT-58SS (Stainless Steel)** — similar to PT-58, except is stainless steel. New 1992.
Mfg.'s Sug. Retail $470 $385 $310 $260

PT-91AF — .41 Action Express cal., action similar to PT-92AF, except is in .41 AE cal., 10 shot mag., 34 oz. Imported 1990 only.
                     $365 $300 $250 $225 $200 $190 $180
                     Last Mfg.'s Sug. Retail was $446.
   Add $36 for satin nickel finish.
   Add $25 for shooter's pack (includes custom case and extra mag.).

PT-92AF — 9mm Para., semi-auto double action, design similar to Beretta Model 92 SB-F, exposed hammer, 5 in. barrel, 10 (C/B 1994) or 15* shot mag., smooth Brazilian walnut grips, blue or nickel finish, fixed sights, 34 oz.
Mfg.'s Sug. Retail $449 $335 $285 $235 $215 $200 $190 $180
   Add $40 for satin nickel finish (disc. 1994).
   Add $415 for Laser Aim Sight (disc. 1991).

▲ **PT-92SS (Stainless Steel)** — similar to PT-92AF, except is fabricated from stainless steel. New 1992.
Mfg.'s Sug. Retail $493 $400 $310 $260

▲ **PT-92AFC** — compact variation of the Model PT-92AF, 4 in. barrel, 10 (C/B 1994) or 13* shot mag., fixed sights.
Mfg.'s Sug. Retail $449 $335 $285 $235 $225 $200 $190 $180
   Add $38 for satin nickel finish (disc. 1993).

▲ **PT-92AFC (Stainless Steel)** — similar to PT-92AFC, except stainless steel. New 1993.
Mfg.'s Sug. Retail $493 $400 $310 $260

▲ **PT-92AF Lew Horton Special Edition** — 9mm Para., matte satin finished frame with high polish stainless steel slide, blue barrel, hammer, trigger, mag. release, safety, and slide release. 250 mfg. in 1990 only.
                     $395 $350 $295 $250 $225 $210 $190
                     Last Mfg.'s Sug. Retail was $454.

Grading	100%	98%	95%	90%	80%	70%	60%

PT-99AF — similar to Model PT-92AF, except has adj. rear sight.

Mfg.'s Sug. Retail	$471	$380	$305	$260	$230	$210	$200	$190

Add $45 for satin nickel finish (disc. 1994).

This action is similar to the Beretta Model 92SB-F.

▲ *PT-99SS (Stainless Steel)* — similar to PT-99AF, except is fabricated from stainless steel. New 1992.

Mfg.'s Sug. Retail	$518	$415	$350	$275

PT-100 — .40 S&W cal., semi-auto, standard double action, 5 in. barrel, 10 (C/B 1994) or 11* shot mag., safeties include ambidextrous manual, hammer drop, inertia firing pin, and chamber loaded indicator, choice of blue, satin nickel or stainless steel finish, smooth Brazilian hard wood stocks, 34 oz. New 1992.

Mfg.'s Sug. Retail	$469	$370	$315	$250	$225	$200	$190	$180

Add $40 for satin nickel finish (disc. 1994).

▲ *PT-100SS (Stainless Steel)* — similar to PT-100, except is fabricated from stainless steel. New 1992.

Mfg.'s Sug. Retail	$514	$410	$350	$275

PT-101 — similar to PT-100, except has adj. sights. New 1992.

Mfg.'s Sug. Retail	$491	$395	$330	$270	$235	$200	$190	$180

Add $45 for satin nickel finish (disc. 1994).

▲ *PT-101SS (Stainless Steel)* — similar to PT-101, except is stainless steel. New 1992.

Mfg.'s Sug. Retail	$537	$415	$340	$280

PT-908 — 9mm Para., compact version of the PT-92 with 3.8 in. barrel and 8 shot mag., fixed sights, blue or nickel finish. New 1993.

Mfg.'s Sug. Retail	$435	$330	$285	$235	$215	$200	$190	$180

▲ *PT-908SS (Stainless Steel)* — similar to Model PT-908, except is stainless steel. New 1993.

Mfg.'s Sug. Retail	$473	$385	$310	$260

PT-940 — .40 S&W cal., compact version of the PT-100 with 3.8 in. barrel and 9 shot mag., fixed sights, 34 oz. New 1996.

Mfg.'s Sug. Retail	$453	$365	$315	$250	$225	$200	$190	$180

▲ *PT-940SS (Stainless Steel)* — similar to PT-940, except is stainless steel. New 1996.

Mfg.'s Sug. Retail	$497	$405	$310	$260

PT-945 — .45 ACP cal., compact double action, 3.8 in. barrel, 8 shot single stack mag., ambidextrous 3 position safety, chamber loaded indicator, 3 dot sights. New 1995.

Mfg.'s Sug. Retail	$453	$345	$295	$235	$215	$200	$190	$180

PT-945SS (Stainless Steel) — stainless steel variation of the PT-945. New 1995.

Mfg.'s Sug. Retail	$497	$405	$310	$260

TECHNO ARMS (PTY) LIMITED

Manufacturer located in Johannesburg, S. Africa since 1994. Currently imported by Vulcans Forge, Inc., Foxboro, MA.

MAG-7 SLIDE ACTION SHOTGUN — 12 ga. (60mm chamber length), 5 shot detachable mag. (in pistol grip), 14, 16, 18, or 20 in. barrel, stock or pistol grip, matte finish, 8 lbs. Importation began 1995.

Mfg.'s Sug. Retail	$875	$795	$675	$625	$550	$500	$450	$400

TERRIER ONE

Previously distributed by Serrifile located in Lancaster, CA.

Grading	100%	98%	95%	90%	80%	70%	60%

TERRIER ONE — .32 S&W cal. revolver, double action, 2¼ in. barrel, 5 shot, nickel-plated, 17 oz. Mfg. 1984-87.

	$45	$35	$30	$25	$25	$25	$25

Last Mfg.'s Sug. Retail was $55.

TEXAS ARMS

Manufacturer located in Waco, TX. Dealer sales only.

DERRINGERS: O/U

DEFENDER — .357 Mag., .38 Spl., 9mm Para., .44 Mag., .45 ACP, or .45 LC/.410 ga. shotshell, features 3 in. interchangeable SS octagon barrels, spur trigger, shell ejector for rimmed cartridges, rebounding hammer and retracting firing pins, cross bolt safety, bead blasted gray finish, 16-21 oz. New 1993.

Mfg.'s Sug. Retail	$310	$275	$235	$200	$175	$160	$145	$130

Add $100 per interchangeable set of barrels.

TEXAS GUNFIGHTERS

Previous importer located in Irving, TX circa 1988-1990.

SHOOTIST EDITION SINGLE ACTION — .45 LC cal., patterned after the Colt SAA, 4¾ in. barrel, nickel-plated black powder frame, one piece walnut grips, mfg. by A. Uberti of Italy. New 1988.

▲ *Standard Model* — 1,000 total mfg., cased.

$625	$525	$440

Last Mfg.'s Sug. Retail was $649.

▲ *1 of 100 Edition* — 100 total mfg., fully engraved, genuine mother-of-pearl one piece grips, cased.

$1,275	$1,050	$775

Last Mfg.'s Sug. Retail was $1,395.

This model is also supplied with an extra set of walnut grips.

TEXAS LONGHORN ARMS, INC.

Manufacturer located in Richmond, TX.

REVOLVERS

SINGLE-ACTION — various cals., patterned after Colt's SAA, except the ejection port has been moved to left side of frame enabling left-hand loading, mfg. from 4140 steel, 1-piece grip, adj. trigger, case-hardened and blued, entirely hand-made, supplied with lifetime warranty. Mfg. 1,000 of each model.

▲ *Texas Border Special* — .44 Spl., .44 Mag., or .45 LC cal., 3½ (disc.) or 4 in. barrel, 1-piece birdshead grip.

Mfg.'s Sug. Retail	$1,595		$1,595	$1,325	$1,000

▲ *South Texas Army* — .357 Mag., .44 Spl., .44 Mag., or .45 LC cal., 4¾ in. barrel, 1-piece regular walnut grip.

Mfg.'s Sug. Retail	$1,595		$1,595	$1,325	$1,000

▲ *Texas Flattop Target* — .32-20, .357 Mag., .44 Mag./Spl., or .45 LC cal., flat top frame, adj. rear sight, 7½ in. barrel.

Mfg.'s Sug. Retail	$1,595		$1,595	$1,325	$1,000

▲ *Grover's Northpaw* — .45 LC cal., 4 ¾ in. barrel, satin finish stainless steel, 6 shot, transfer bar safety, 2-piece grips, blade front sight and grooved receiver. New 1995.

Mfg.'s Sug. Retail	$685		$685	$550	$425

T

Grading	100%	98%	95%	90%	80%	70%	60%

▲ *Grover's Improved Number Five* — .44 Mag. or .45 LC cal., 5½ in. target barrel, 1,200 mfg. serial numbered K1-K1200. This variation incorporates Elmer Keith's 1926 designs including No. 5 lockwork, base pin and latch, and grip straps. New 1988.

Mfg.'s Sug. Retail $1,195 $1,195 $875 $675

SPECIAL EDITIONS — in addition to the models listed above, Texas Longhorn Arms also manufactures various special editions, including a Standard Model Set (3 guns, 1 of each above) retailing at $5,750, an Engraved Special Edition Set (3 gun set) retailing for $7,650, a Texas Sesquicentennial Commemorative retailing for $2,500, and a Mason Commemorative retailing for $1,500. For more information (including a color catalog) on these limited editions, please contact the manufacturer directly (see Trademark Index).

PISTOLS

JEZEBEL MODEL — while advertised, this gun has not been mfg. to date.

THOMAS
Manufactured by Alexander James Ordnance, Inc. located in Covina, CA.

Please refer to listing under A.J. Ordnance in this text.

THOMPSON CARBINES
See Auto Ordnance section of this book.

THOMPSON/CENTER ARMS
Manufacturer located in Rochester, NH from 1967 to date.

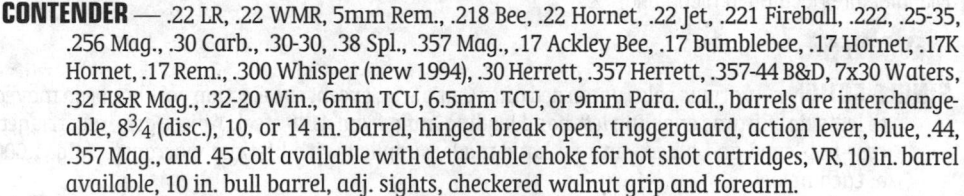

PISTOL: SINGLE SHOT

Caution: older and newer TC components do not interchange safely. Although parts will fit, they may not function properly. Special ordering of barrels, frames, and calibers started in 1988.

CONTENDER — .22 LR, .22 WMR, 5mm Rem., .218 Bee, .22 Hornet, .22 Jet, .221 Fireball, .222, .25-35, .256 Mag., .30 Carb., .30-30, .38 Spl., .357 Mag., .17 Ackley Bee, .17 Bumblebee, .17 Hornet, .17K Hornet, .17 Rem., .300 Whisper (new 1994), .30 Herrett, .357 Herrett, .357-44 B&D, 7x30 Waters, .32 H&R Mag., .32-20 Win., 6mm TCU, 6.5mm TCU, or 9mm Para. cal., barrels are interchangeable, 8¾ (disc.), 10, or 14 in. barrel, hinged break open, triggerguard, action lever, blue, .44, .357 Mag., and .45 Colt available with detachable choke for hot shot cartridges, VR, 10 in. barrel available, 10 in. bull barrel, adj. sights, checkered walnut grip and forearm.

The Contender action is in its third variation and a wide variety of changes have been made to grips, stocks, sights, etc. since 1967. These production variances do not necessarily add premiums to values listed below.

▲ *Bull Barrel* — available in 13 cals. between .17 Rem. and .45 Win. Mag., 10 in. round barrel only.

Mfg.'s Sug. Retail $464 $350 $270 $205 $185 $170 $160 $150

Add $5 for .45 Colt/.410 ga. with internal chokes.
Add $10 for .22 LR match grade chamber (new 1996).
Add approx. $230 per additional barrel.

▲ *Armour Alloy II Bull Barrel* — 7 cals. between .22 LR and .30-30, similar to regular Bull Barrel, except has Armour Alloy II satin finish which is harder than stainless steel. Mfg. 1986-89.

$320 $285 $230

Last Mfg.'s Sug. Retail was $415.

Add $5 for .45 Colt/.410 ga. internal choke.

Grading	100%	98%	95%	90%	80%	70%	60%

▲ **Vent. Rib** — .357 Mag. (disc.), .44 Mag. (disc.) or .45 Colt/.410 ga., 10 in. VR barrel only, adj. front and flip up rear sight, internal choke became standard in 1985.

Mfg.'s Sug. Retail	$484	$365	$270	$205	$180	$170	$160	$150

▲ **Armour Alloy Vent. Rib** — .45/.410 internal choke, has Armour Alloy II satin finish which is harder than stainless steel. Mfg. 1986-disc.

			$350	$295	$230

Last Mfg.'s Sug. Retail was $435.

▲ **Stainless Steel** — various cals., 10 in. bull barrel. New 1993.

Mfg.'s Sug. Retail	$495	$375	$280	$200

Add approx. $229 per additional barrel.
Add $5 for .45/.410 with adj. sights.
Add $20 for .45/.410 with VR.

▲ **Octagon Barrel** — .22 LR, .22 Mag. (disc.), .22 Hornet (disc.), .22K Hornet (disc.), .222 Rem. (disc.), or .357 Mag. (disc.) cal., 10 in. barrel.

Mfg.'s Sug. Retail	$474	$355	$260	$200	$180	$170	$160	$150

▲ **Match Grade Barrel** — .22 LR cal. only, choice of 10 or 14 in. match barrel. New 1992.

Mfg.'s Sug. Retail	$460	$350	$265	$200	$180	$170	$160	$150

Add $10 for 14 in. barrel.

CONTENDER SUPER — 13 cals. available from .17 Rem. - .45 Win. Mag. (disc.), 14 or 16 in. bull barrel only, special grips, beavertail forearm, adj. sight, 3½ lbs.

Mfg.'s Sug. Retail	$474	$360	$265	$200	$180	$170	$160	$150

Add $5 for 16 in. barrel.
Add $31 for .17 Rem. cal. (new 1992).
Add $10 for .45-70 cal. in 16 in. barrel only with muzzle brake (new 1992).
Add approx. $224 per additional barrel.
Add $31 for VR barrel (.45 LC/.410 ga. only).

Thompson Center will also make special order guns in different cals. other than those listed above. If factory work, these pistols will be worth a premium.

▲ **Stainless Contender Super** — various cals., choice of 14 or 16 in. barrel. New 1993.

Mfg.'s Sug. Retail	$505	$385	$275	$215

Add $5 for 16 in. barrel.
Add $25 for .45-70 bull barrel with muzzle tamer.
Add $30-$35 for .45 LC/.410 ga. with internal choke.
Add approx. $240 per additional barrel.

▲ **Armour Alloy II Super Contender** — 5 cals. between .22 LR and 7mm, similar to regular Super Contender, except has Armour Alloy II satin finish which is harder than stainless steel. Mfg. 1986-89.

			$355	$295	$240

Last Mfg.'s Sug. Retail was $425.

Extra Armour Alloy II Bull Barrels were available for $195+.

CONTENDER HUNTER PACKAGE — .223 Rem., .7-30 Waters, .30-30, .35 Rem., .357 Rem. Max. (disc. 1994), .375 Win. Mag. (new 1992), .44 Mag., or .45-70 cal., special 12 (disc.) or 14 (new 1992) in. barrel with muzzle brake, 2.5X power scope with lighted recticle, walnut grip has nonslip rubber insert to cushion recoil, includes studs, swivels, sling, and deluxe carrying case, approx. 4 lbs. New 1990.

Mfg.'s Sug. Retail	$798	$695	$575	$495	$430	$365	$315	$275

The Hunter Package became standard in 1993.

CONTENDER 25TH ANNIVERSARY — .22 LR cal. only, 10 in. octagon barrel, laser etched anniversary logo on receiver sides and barrel, checkered stock and forearm, limited mfg. in 1992 only.

	$610	$535	$465	$410	$360	$315	$275

Last Mfg.'s Sug. Retail was $700.

▲ **Contender 25th Anniversary Cased Set** — cased set with 5 barrels including .22 LR, .22 Mag., .22 Jet, .22 Hornet, and .38 Spl., 50 sets mfg. 1992 only.

	$1,850	$1,550	$1,225	$1,050	$900	$775	$650

Last Mfg.'s Sug. Retail was $1,975.

Grading	100%	98%	95%	90%	80%	70%	60%

RIFLES

CONTENDER CARBINE — available in 15 cals. between .17 Rem. and .44 Rem. Mag., also .410 ga. (3 in.), Contender action with pistol grip full stock and forearm, 21 in. interchangeable barrel, drilled for scope mounts, iron sights standard. New 1986.

Mfg.'s Sug. Retail	$515	$400	$300	$250	$215	$190	$175	$160

    Add $31 for .17 Rem. cal.
    Add $21 for .410 ga. barrel.
    Add approx. $234 per extra barrel.
    Add $10 for match grade .22 LR barrel.
    Subtract $36 for Youth Model (16¼ in. barrel w/o VR).
    Add $175 for Survival Carbine System (disc. - includes Rynite stock, 16¼ .223 Rem. barrel, extra .45 Colt/.410 barrel, and soft camo cordura case).

▲ *Rynite Contender Carbine* — similar to above, except has Rynite stock and forend. Mfg. 1990-1993.

	$335	$270	$220	$195	$180	$165	$155

Last Mfg.'s Sug. Retail was $425.

    Add $30 for .17 Rem. cal.
    Add $10 for match grade barrel.
    Add $25 for 21 in. VR smooth bore .410 ga. barrel.

▲ *Contender Carbine Stainless* — various cals., 21 in. barrel, choice of walnut (disc. 1993) or Rynite synthetic stock. New 1993.

Mfg.'s Sug. Retail	$510	$390	$295	$225

    Add $35 for walnut stock (disc.).
    Add $10 for .22 LR match barrel (new 1995).
    Add $26 for .410 smoothbore barrel with screw-in full choke.
    This model is also available in a Youth Model with walnut stock at no extra charge (disc. 1993).

HUNTER RIFLE MODEL — single shot, top lever break open action w/interchangeable barrels, .22 Hornet, .223, .22-250, .243, .270, 7mm, .30-06, .308 Win. .375 H&H (new 1992), or .416 Rem. Mag. (new 1992) cal., 23 in. barrel, 6 lbs. 14 oz., checkered walnut stock, choice of medium or light sporter weight barrel. New 1983 and improved in 1987. Available in left-hand at no extra charge. Disc. 1992.

	$500	$415	$350	$295	$265	$240	$220

Last Mfg.'s Sug. Retail was $595.

    Add $20 for .375 H&H or .416 Rem. Mag. cal.
    Add approx. $275 per extra rifle barrel.

▲ *Hunter Deluxe Rifle Model* — similar to Hunter Model, except features double triggers and up-graded walnut stock and forearm. Mfg. 1992 only.

	$550	$450	$375	$325	$285	$250	$225

Last Mfg.'s Sug. Retail was $675.

    Add $20 for .375 H&H or .416 Rem. Mag. cal.

▲ *Hunter Shotgun Model* — same action as Hunter Rifle, except is supplied with 12 ga. barrel (field choke with 3½ in. chamber or slug with 3 in. chamber and iron sights) or 10 ga. barrel (3½ in. chamber). Disc. 1992.

	$500	$415	$350	$295	$265	$240	$220

Last Mfg.'s Sug. Retail was $595.

    Add $275 per additional shotgun barrel.

TCR '83 ARISTOCRAT — similar to Hunter Model, except stock has cheekpiece and forearm is checkered, stainless steel double set triggers. Disc. 1986.

	$425	$370	$345	$320	$300	$280	$260

Last Mfg.'s Sug. Retail was $475.

    Add $175 for each additional barrel(s) (including 12 ga. slug).

THUNDER

Manufactured by Baford Arms, located in Bristol, TN, distributed by Sherman Yarbrough located in Smyrna, Georgia.

THUNDER — .44 Spl. or .410 ga., 2½ in. octagon barrel, spur-trigger, single shot derringer, interchangeable barrel sleeves, side pivot, blued steel, oversized walnut grips, 8½ oz.

    While advertised, this model has yet to be manufactured.

THUNDER-FIVE

Shotgun revolver manufactured by Mil, Inc. located in Piney Flats, TN. Distributed by C.L. Reedy & Associates, Inc. located in Jonesborough, TN. Dealer and direct consumer sales.

While previously advertised as the Spectre Five (not mfg.), this firearm has been re-named the Thunder Five.

Grading	100%	98%	95%	90%	80%	70%	60%

THUNDER-FIVE — .45 LC cal./.410 ga. with 3 in. chamber or .45-70 cal. (new 1994), unique 5 shot revolver design permits shooting .45 LC or .410 ga. shotshells interchangeably, 2 in. rifled barrel, phosphate finish, external ambidextrous hammer block safety, internal draw bar safety, combat sights, hammer, trigger, and triggerguard, Pachmayr grips, includes padded plastic carrying case, 48 oz., serialization starts at 1,101. New 1992.

Mfg.'s Sug. Retail	$550		$500	$450	$400	$375	$350	$325	$300

    Add $50 for .45-70 cal.

TIKKA

O/U shotguns are currently manufactured by Armi Marocchi located in Italy. Rifles are currently manufactured by Sako, Ltd. located in Riihimaki, Finland. Previously manufactured by Oy Tikkakoski Ab, of Tikkakoski, Finland (pre-1989). Currently imported by Stoeger Industries, Inc. located in Wayne, NJ.

Also see listings under Ithaca LSA for older models.

RIFLES: BOLT ACTION

NEW GENERATION RIFLE — .22-250 Rem., .223 Rem., .243 Win., .270 Win., .30-06, .308 Win., 7mm Rem. Mag., .300 Win. Mag., or .338 Win Mag. cal., 22½ (non-Mag.) or 24½ (Mag. cals.) in. barrel, detachable 3 (standard) or 5 (optional) shot mag., forged and milled action in two lengths, checkered walnut stock, 7-7 ½ lbs. Sako mfg. 1989-94.

	$725	$600	$550	$500	$450	$400	$360

    Last Mfg.'s Sug. Retail was $835.

    Add $25 for Mag. cals.

    Cals. .22-250 Rem., .308 Win., and .300 Win. Mag. were introduced in late 1989.

PREMIUM GRADE RIFLE — same cals. as New Generation Rifle, stock is select walnut with roll-over cheek-piece and rosewood pistol grip cap and forend tip, high polished barrel blue. Imported 1989-94.

	$860	$715	$600	$550	$500	$450	$400

    Last Mfg.'s Sug. Retail was $1,030.

    Add $40 for Mag. cals.

VARMINT RIFLE — .22-250, .223, .243 Win., or .308 Win. cal., 24½ in. heavy barrel, no sights. Mfg. 1991-94.

	$895	$750	$625	$550	$500	$450	$400

    Last Mfg.'s Sug. Retail was $1,090.

Grading	100%	98%	95%	90%	80%	70%	60%

WHITETAIL HUNTER/BATTUE RIFLE — .22-250 (new 1995), .223 Rem. (new 1995), .243 Win. (new 1995), .25-06 (new 1995), .270 Win., .30-06, .308 Win., 7mm Rem. Mag., .300 Win. Mag., or .338 Win. Mag. cal., 20½ (disc. 1994), 22½ (new 1995), or 24½ (new 1995) in. barrel, choice of wood or synthetic (new 1996) stock, open sights on raised rib. New in 1991.

Mfg.'s Sug. Retail	$559	$495	$435	$380	$350	$325	$300	$275

Add $30 for Mag. cals.
Add $60 for carved elk or deer game scene stock (new 1996).

CONTINENTAL VARMINT RIFLE — .22-250 Rem., .223 Rem., or .308 Win. cal., heavy 26 in. barrel, adj. trigger, quick release detachable mag., integral scope mount rails, recoil pad spacer system, 8⅝ lbs. New 1996.

Mfg.'s Sug. Retail	$644	$575	$495	$435	$380	$350	$325	$300

CONTINENTAL LONGRANGE HUNTING RIFLE — .25-06 Rem., .270 Win., 7mm Rem. Mag., or .300 Win. Mag. cal., heavy 26 in. barrel w/o sights, checkered walnut stock and forend, 8¾ lbs. New 1996.

Mfg.'s Sug. Retail	$644	$575	$495	$435	$380	$350	$325	$300

Add $30 for Mag. cals.

O/U COMBINATIONS (MODEL 512S)

Previously manufactured in Jyvaskyla, Finland. In 1989, under a joint venture agreement made in Italy, the 412 O/U shooting system is now being manufactured in Italy. Older models may be found in the Valmet trademark section of this text.

During 1993, the new models of the 512S series replaced the older 412S series. Separate listings have not been provided, since they are almost identical in most respects.

MODEL 512S O/U SHOOTING SYSTEM — interchangeable barrel assemblies permit a double rifle, shotgun/rifle, and O&U shotgun configuration, user installed interchangeable barrels, monobloc locking, rifle barrel positioning by adjustment, SST, extractors or ejectors, checkered walnut stock and forend, cocking indicators, blued finish.

The 412S Model nomenclature was changed to 512S in late 1993.

▲ *Model 512S Field Grade* — 12 ga. only, 3 in. chambers, auto ejectors, screw-in choke tubes (includes 5), 26 or 28 in. barrels, matte nickel finish. New 1986.

Mfg.'s Sug. Retail	$1,290	$1,035	$750	$595	$550	$475	$440	$400

Subtract 10% for Standard Grade.
The Premium Grade became standard issue beginning 1995.

▲ *Model 412ST Trap* — 12 ga., Monte Carlo stock, 30 in. barrels, screw-in chokes standard.

			$1,125	$925	$725	$650	$580	$540	$475

Last Mfg.'s Sug. Retail was $1,325.

This variation was made by Valmet in Finland and only small quantities remain.

▲ *Model 412ST Premium Grade Trap* — similar to Model 412ST Trap, except has better walnut and checkering.

		$1,425	$1,000	$875	$750	$625	$580	$515

Last Mfg.'s Sug. Retail was $1,665.

This variation was made by Valmet in Finland and only small quantities remain.

▲ *Model 512S Sporting Clays* — 12 ga. only, sporting clays configuration with 28 or 30 (new 1994) in. VR barrels and choke tubes. Importation began 1992.

Mfg.'s Sug. Retail	$1,325	$1,140	$945	$730	$650	$580	$540	$475

▲ *Model 512S Combination Gun* — combination rifle/shotgun, 12 ga, 3 in. chambers, 24 in. barrels, under rifle barrel has choice of .222, .30-06, or .308 cal., extractors.

Mfg.'s Sug. Retail	$1,400	$1,185	$965	$750	$650	$580	$540	$475

▲ *Model 512S Double Rifle* — .30-06 (new 1994), .308 Win. (new 1994), 9.3x74R cal., 24 in. barrels, extractors.

Mfg.'s Sug. Retail	$1,800	$1,450	$1,050	$795	$725	$625	$550	$475

Grading	100%	98%	95%	90%	80%	70%	60%

▲ *Extra Barrel Assemblies (Model 512S O/U)* — add $710-$730 each for shotgun (includes screw-in chokes), $775 each for shotgun/rifle combo, $990 each for double rifle.

TIMBERWOLF

Manufactured by I.M.I. (Israel Military Industries) located in Israel. Previously imported and distributed by Action Arms located in Philadelphia, PA until 1994.

RIFLE

TIMBERWOLF — .357 Mag. or .44 Mag. (disc.) cal., slide action, straight grip shotgun style stock with adj. drop, blue or satin chrome finish, takedown, 18½ in. barrel, 10 shot tube mag., sear locking and firing pin safeties, integral scope base, approx. 5½ lbs. Imported 1989-1993.

	100%	98%	95%	90%	80%	70%	60%
.357 Mag.	$260	$230	$195	$180	$160	$145	$130
.44 Mag. (blue only)	$425	$375	$335	$300	$275	$250	$225

Last Mfg.'s Sug. Retail was $299.

Add $80 for satin chrome finish.

This model was designed, imported, and distributed by Action Arms Ltd. Springfield Armory imported 1,000 .44 Mag. Timberwolf models during 1990-1991.

TIPPMAN ARMS CO.

Previous manufacturer located in Fort Wayne, IN.

Tippman Arms manufactured 1/2 scale semi-auto working models of famous machine guns. All models were available with an optional hardwood case, extra ammo cans, and other accessories. Mfg. 1986-1987 only.

MODEL 1919 A-4 — .22 LR cal. only, copy of Browning 1919 A-4 Model, belt fed, closed bolt operation, 11 in. barrel, includes tripod, 10 lbs.

	$2,200	$1,950	$1,675	$1,425	$1,200	$995	$775

Last Mfg.'s Sug. Retail was $1,325.

MODEL 1917 — .22 LR cal. only, copy of Browning M1917, watercooled, belt fed, closed bolt operation, 11 in. barrel, includes tripod, 10 lbs.

	$2,350	$2,050	$1,700	$1,425	$1,200	$995	$775

Last Mfg.'s Sug. Retail was $1,830.

MODEL .50 HB — .22 Mag. cal. only, copy of Browning .50 cal. machine gun, belt fed, closed bolt operation, 18¼ in. barrel, includes tripod, 13 lbs.

	$2,700	$2,350	$2,000	$1,675	$1,425	$1,200	$1,000

Last Mfg.'s Sug. Retail was $1,929.

TOKAREV

See Russian Service Pistols and Rifles section.

TOZ

Manufacturer located in Russia, mostly concentrating on competition pistols and longarms. Imported by Nygord Precision Products located in Prescott, AZ.

TOZ-35 FREE PISTOL — .22 LR, employs virtually every shooting refinement possible in a single shot target pistol, fully adj. target grips, limited mfg.

Mfg.'s Sug. Retail	$1,045	$925	$850	$775	$725	$675	$625	$575

Add $50 for "Vitarbo" adj. grips.

TRADEWINDS

Tacoma, WA Importers.

Grading	100%	98%	95%	90%	80%	70%	60%

HUSKY MODEL 5000 — .22-250, .243, .270, .308, or .30-06 cal., bolt action, 23¾ in. barrel, adj. sight, removable mag., hand-checkered walnut stock.

	$325	$310	$290	$250	$225	$200	$175

MODEL 311-A — .22 LR cal., bolt action, 5 shot, 22½ in. barrel, folding leaf rear sight, walnut checkered stock.

	$180	$170	$150	$130	$120	$100	$85

MODEL 260-A — .22 LR cal., semi-auto, 5 shot, 22½ in. barrel, 3 leaf folding sight, checkered walnut stock.

	$200	$190	$175	$150	$130	$120	$100

MODEL H-170 — 12 ga., auto shotgun, 2¾ in. chamber, 26 in. mod. or 28 in. full, recoil operated action, alloy receiver, 5 shot, tube mag., VR, checkered walnut stock.

	$275	$265	$250	$225	$200	$180	$150

TRENCH/RIOT SHOTGUNS

The following is a chronological listing beginning with WWI of the various U.S. commercial Riot and military Trench and Riot shotguns mfg. to date.

The publisher wishes to express thanks to Pat Redmond and Rick Crosier for the information in this section, much of which has been not been published previously.

Some 100% values have been intentionally omitted in this section as they are seldomly seen or sold.

MILITARY TRENCH SHOTGUNS - WWI

WINCHESTER MODEL 1897 MILITARY TRENCH GUN — high-polish commercial blue finish, solid frame with 6 row ventilated handguard for bayonet attachment. Serial range 650,000-690,000. Guns used by the U.S. Army for trench warfare in WWI, originally did not have military markings. A U.S. and ordnance bomb are stamped on the right side of the receiver on trench guns kept in Army's inventory after the war. Military markings were added in the 1920s to about 10% of the total production.

	100%	98%	95%	90%	80%	70%	60%
Trench Gun	N/A	$2,600	$1,200	$850	$750	$700	$600
Trench Gun with military markings	N/A	$3,200	$2,800	$1,500	$1,000	$800	$700

REMINGTON MODEL 10 MILITARY TRENCH GUN — high polish commercial blue finish with wood handguard on top of barrel, separate bayonet adaptor attaches to front of barrel for bayonet attachment. U.S. and ordnance bomb is marked on left side receiver, stock is unmarked. Serial 160,000-165,000. Extremely rare Trench gun and hard to find complete and in original condition. Trench gun barrel length is 22 in. as compared to 20 in. Riot gun. Prices quoted only for complete guns with wood handguard and bayonet adaptor.

	100%	98%	95%	90%	80%	70%	60%
Trench Gun	N/A	$4,250	$3,500	$2,500	$1,850	$1,250	$995
Riot Gun	N/A	$1,500	$1,200	$900	$500	$350	$300

MILITARY RIOT/TRENCH SHOTGUNS - WWII

ITHACA MODEL 37 MILITARY SHOTGUNS — rarest of all Trench shotguns, high polish commercial blue finish, RLB and ordnance bomb on left side of receiver, ordnance bomb on barrel, stocks not proofed, blue vent. handguard for bayonet attachment, only 1,420 Trench guns were ordered in 1941. Ithaca supplied mostly long barrel martially marked shotguns within serial range 49,000-62,000.

	100%	98%	95%	90%	80%	70%	60%
Trench Gun	N/A	$4,000	$3,500	$2,250	$1,750	$1,500	$1,200
Riot Gun	N/A	$1,800	$1,500	$1,250	$750	$600	$500
Long Barrel	N/A	$1,000	$750	$600	$500	$350	$300

Grading	100%	98%	95%	90%	80%	70%	60%

REMINGTON MODEL 31 RIOT GUN — commercial blue finish (high polish and flat blue finishes noted). Can be marked U.S. Property on receiver and/or barrel. Some examples noted with only ordnance mark on stock. Serial range 39,500-60,500.

Riot Gun	N/A	$1,200	$900	$750	$650	$550	$450

REMINGTON MODEL 11 RIOT GUNS — this is the most commonly found military shotgun. Examples of 5 shot and 3 shot Sportsman Model. Examples with plain or engraved receivers and plain or fancy checkered wood. Military marked with U.S. and ordnance bomb on receiver and barrel. Later models are marked military finish. These shotguns all have highly polished commercial blue finish and ordnance marked stocks. Serial range 450,000-500,000 and 700,000-711,000.

Riot Guns	N/A	$750	$500	$450	$400	$350	$300
Long Barrel	N/A	$500	$400	$350	$300	$250	$200

▲ *Riot Gun* — this configuration was sold by the government as surplus as late as the 1970s and can occasionally be found NIB with packing materials and instruction manual. Mint in factory box - $1,350.

SAVAGE MODEL 720 — appears identical to Remington Model 11. This was mfg. by Stevens/Savage in very limited quantities, plain and engraved receivers noted with high quality commercial blue finish. Stocks are unmarked and must have ramp sights to be original. Watch for altered guns made into Riots. Serial range 65,000-86,000.

Riot Gun	N/A	$1,500	$1,200	$1,000	$800	$650	$500
Long Barrel	N/A	$650	$600	$500	$400	$300	$250

STEVENS MODEL 620 MILITARY SHOTGUNS — this was the current model being sold by Stevens and has a commercial blue finish, but not of the same quality as the other companies. Trench guns are equipped with handguards that have a definite purple/reddish color to the front and dark blue vent. shaft. Model 620s are much rarer than 520s and have U.S. and ordnance bomb on receiver, ordnance bomb on barrel and unmarked stock. Serial range 3,000-36,000.

Trench Gun	N/A	$1,000	$750	$650	$550	$500	$450
Riot Gun	N/A	$750	$500	$450	$400	$350	$250
Long Barrels	N/A	$350	$300	$250	$200	$175	$150

STEVENS 520-30 MILITARY SHOTGUNS — this model was resurrected due to available machinery and is the most commonly found Trench gun. Riot guns in minty condition are hard to find. Same finish as Model 620, U.S. and ordnance bomb on receiver, ordnance bomb on barrel and no proofing on stocks, except for reworks. Trench gun has same style handguard as Model 620. Serial range 25,000-70,000.

Trench Gun	N/A	$900	$700	$600	$500	$450	$400
Riot Gun	N/A	$600	$400	$350	$300	$250	$200
Long Barrels	N/A	$300	$275	$225	$175	$150	$125

WINCHESTER MODEL 97 MILITARY SHOTGUNS — takedown model, high polish commercial blue finish with U.S. and/or ordnance bomb on left side of receiver. Barrels all have ordnance bomb and finger groove stocks are marked with ordnance mark and inspector's initials, with hard rubber buttplate, handguards on Trench guns can have 4 or 6 rows of vent. holes. The most sought after Trench gun by collectors. Serial range 924,000-980,000.

Trench Gun	N/A	$2,600	$2,000	$1,500	$1,000	$750	$600
Riot Gun	N/A	$1,000	$900	$750	$650	$500	$400

WINCHESTER MODEL 12 MILITARY SHOTGUNS — takedown model with improved hammerless receiver. These were made to supplement Model 97 production. Riot guns and Trench guns share same serial range. Finished in high polished commercial blue, until Trench guns (only) were the only WWII shotguns to have factory parkerized finishes. All Model 12s have U.S. and ordnance bomb on right side of receiver, ordnance bomb on barrel and ordnance mark and inspector initials on left side of stock. Trench guns have vent. handguards.

Grading	100%	98%	95%	90%	80%	70%	60%
▲ *Blue finish* — serial range 926,000-1,030,000.							
Trench Gun	N/A	$2,250	$1,650	$1,200	$975	$850	$575
Riot Gun	N/A	$1,400	$900	$750	$650	$500	$400
▲ *Parkerized finish* — serial range 1,030,000-1,040,000.							
Trench Gun	N/A	$2,450	$2,000	$1,400	$1,000	$900	$750

MILITARY RIOT/TRENCH SHOTGUNS - VIETNAM

ITHACA MODEL 37 — parkerized finish with U.S. marks on right side of receiver. Receiver and barrel are also marked "P." Serial range, applied on gun upside-down, is from S1,000-S23,500. Used in the Vietnam era. A very few original Trench guns with parkerized handguards have been noted.

Riot Gun	N/A	$750	$650	$500	$400	$350	$300
Trench Gun	N/A	$1,000	$900	$800	$600	$500	$400

SAVAGE 77E — parkerized finish with sling swivels and red rubber butt pad. U.S. marked on right side of receiver and military "P" proofmark on receiver and barrel. Hard to find in excellent condition.

Riot Gun	N/A	$750	$650	$400	$300	$250	$200

WINCHESTER MODEL 1200 — parkerized front barrel, mag. tube, and bayonet adapter with U.S. marking on barrel. Aluminum receiver with black or matte type finish, U.S. is marked under serial number. Very rare as few examples have been released by the government due to its continued use by military forces.

Trench Gun	N/A	$1,000	$900	$800	$600	$500	$400

RIOT/TRENCH GUN SHOTGUNS - COMMERCIAL SALES

WINCHESTER MODEL 12 RIOT — thousands mfg. between late '30s-'60s.

	N/A	$550	$450	$395	$350	$295	$240

WINCHESTER MODEL 97 — commercial high polish blue, changed from solid frame to takedown in 1935. Trench guns made thru 1945 and Riot gun mfg. continued until 1960s.

▲ *Solid Frame*							
Trench Gun	N/A	$2,000	$1,800	$1,500	$1,200	$1,000	$750
Riot Gun	N/A	$1,000	$900	$750	$600	$500	$300
▲ *Takedown*							
Trench Gun	N/A	$1,800	$1,500	$1,300	$1,100	$900	$600
Riot Gun	N/A	$800	$700	$600	$500	$400	$300

REMINGTON MODEL 10 — commercial high polish blue, sold in the 1920s to various government, banking agencies.

Riot Gun	N/A	$400	$350	$300	$275	$250	$200

REMINGTON MODEL 11 — made in 1930s for law enforcement use.

Riot Gun	N/A	$400	$350	$300	$275	$250	$200

MODEL 31R RIOT GUN — similar to 31A, with 20 in. barrel.

	N/A	$300	$200	$175	$150	$130	$110

ITHACA MODEL 37 — parkerized models made in 1960s for police agencies and commercial sales.

Trench Gun	N/A	$500	$400	$350	$300	$250	$200
Riot Gun	N/A	$275	$250	$225	$175	$150	$125

TRI-STAR SPORTING ARMS, LTD.
Importer located in N. Kansas City, MO since 1994.

Grading	100%	98%	95%	90%	80%	70%	60%

SHOTGUNS: O/U

MODEL 300 — 12 ga. only, 3 in. chambers, under-lug action, double triggers, extractors, etched engraving, standard checkered Turkish walnut stock and forearm, 26 or 28. in. VR barrels with fixed chokes. Importation began 1994.

Mfg.'s Sug. Retail	$429	$375	$330	$300	$275	$250	$225	$200

MODEL 333 FIELD GRADE — 12 or 20 ga., 3 in. chambers, engraved boxlock receiver with satin finish, SST, ejectors, fancy grade Turkish walnut with hand-cut checkering, 26 (12 ga. only), 28, or 30 in. VR barrels, supplied 5 choke-tubes, approx. 7½ lbs. Imported from Turkey beginning 1994.

Mfg.'s Sug. Retail	$800	$735	$625	$550	$500	$450	$400	$360

▲ *Model 333 Sporting Clays* — similar to Model 333 Field Grade, except has sporting recoil pad, elongated forcing cones, 28 or 30 in. ported barrels with extended stainless steel choke-tubes, 7¾ lbs. Importation began 1994.

Mfg.'s Sug. Retail	$900	$825	$725	$625	$550	$500	$450	$400

▲ *Model 333L Ladies Field* — similar to Model 333 Field Grade, except is fitted with special ladies stock, 26 or 28 in. barrels only.

Mfg.'s Sug. Retail	$800	$735	$625	$550	$500	$450	$400	$360

▲ *Model 333SCL Ladies Sporting Clays* — similar to Model 333 Sporting Clays, except is fitted with special ladies stock, 28 in. barrels only with four choke-tubes.

Mfg.'s Sug. Retail	$900	$825	$725	$625	$550	$500	$450	$400

MODEL 330 — 12 or 20 ga., 3 in. chambers, etched satin finished receiver, SST, extractors, fixed chokes, checkered standard Turkish walnut stock and forearm, approx. 7½ lbs. Importation began 1994.

Mfg.'s Sug. Retail	$549	$485	$425	$385	$350	$325	$300	$285

▲ *Model 330D* — similar to Model 330, except has ejectors, and three choke-tubes. Importation began 1994.

Mfg.'s Sug. Retail	$689	$625	$550	$500	$450	$400	$360	$330

SHOTGUNS: SxS

MODEL 311 — 12 or 20 ga., 3 in. chambers, Greener boxlock action, 26 or 28 in. barrels, standard checkered Turkish walnut stock and forearm, DTs, supplied with five choke-tubes, white chrome frame finish, extractors. Importation began 1994.

Mfg.'s Sug. Retail	$599	$535	$475	$435	$400	$360	$330	$295

▲ *Model 311R* — 12 or 20 ga., 20 in. cylinder bore barrels designed for cowboy reinactment shooting or home defense, other features similar to Model 311.

Mfg.'s Sug. Retail	$429	$375	$325	$300	$275	$250	$225	$200

TURKISH FIREARMS CORPORATION

Please refer to the HHF section in this text.

U section

USAS 12

Currently manufactured by International Ordnance Corporation located in Nashville, TN beginning 1992. Previously manufactured (1990-91) by Ramo Mfg., Inc. located in Nashville, TN because of BATF ruling. Previously distributed by Kiesler's Wholesale located in Jeffersonville, IN until 1994. Originally designed and previously distributed in the U.S by Gilbert Equipment Co., Inc. located in Mobile, AL. Previously manufactured under license by Daewoo Precision Industries, Ltd. located in South Korea.

Grading	100%	98%	95%	90%	80%	70%	60%

USAS 12 — 12 ga. only, gas operated action available in either semi or fully auto versions, 18¼ in. cylinder bore barrel, closed bolt, synthetic stock, pistol grip, and forearm, carrying handle, 10 round box or 20 drum (disc.) mag., 2¾ in. chamber only, parkerized finish, 12 lbs. New 1987.

Mfg.'s Sug. Retail	$995	$925	$850	$750	$650	$575	$500	$400

Add $150 for extra 20 shot drum magazine (banned by the BATF).

Values above are for a semi-auto model. This model is currently classified as a destructive device and necessary paperwork must accompany a sale.

U.S. ARMS COMPANY

Previous manufacturer located in Riverhead, NY.

REVOLVERS: SINGLE ACTION

ABILENE .357 MAG. — 6 shot, 4⅝, 5½, or 6½ in. barrel, adj. sights, transfer bar ignition, smooth walnut grips, blue finish only. Mfg. 1976-1983.

	$275	$240	$200	$185	$170	$155	$140

ABILENE .357 MAG. STAINLESS STEEL — similar to Abilene, only in stainless steel.

	$325	$275	$225

ABILENE .44 MAG. — 7½ and 8½ in. barrel, unfluted cylinder blue finish only, otherwise similar to .357 Mag.

	$325	$265	$240	$220	$200	$165	$150

ABILENE .44 MAG. STAINLESS STEEL — similar to Abilene .44 Mag., only stainless steel.

	$375	$330	$290

U.S. GENERAL TECHNOLOGIES, INC.

Manufacturer located in S. San Francisco, CA since 1994.

P-50 SEMI-AUTO — .50 BMG, semi-auto design, includes 10 shot detachable mag., folding bipod, muzzle brake, matte black finish. New 1995.

Mfg.'s Sug. Retail	$5,995	$5,600	$4,950	$4,475	$3,975	$3,500	$3,050	$2,600

UBERTI USA, INC.

Importer and distributor located in Lakeville, CT. Both Black Powder and Modern firearms are imported by Uberti USA, Inc. and are manufactured by Aldo Uberti of Ponte Zanano, Italy.

Other firms have imported Uberti guns under various names in the past.

REVOLVERS & CARBINES: SINGLE ACTION REPRODUCTIONS

These guns can be ordered with either black powder or modern configured frames. Factory engraving and other embellishments or finishes (including antique charcoal blue, white steel, nickel, etc.) can be special ordered by contacting the importer directly.

Grading	100%	98%	95%	90%	80%	70%	60%

Add $390 for standard hand-engraving pattern on Cattleman variations.
Add $25 for antique charcoal blue finish on all Cattleman variations.
Add $80 for silver-plating.
Add $25 for white finish or checkered grips.
Add $50 for select grade walnut one-piece fitted grips.
Add $50 for stag horn grips, $150 for black buffalo grips, or $225 for mother-of-pearl grips.

CATTLEMAN VARIATIONS — available in .22 LR (disc. 1990), .22 Mag. (disc. 1990), .357 Mag., .38 Spl., .38-40 (new 1989), .44 Spl., .44-40, or .45 LC cal., 4¾, 5½, and 7½ in. barrel lengths, brass or steel backstraps and triggerguard.

▲ *Quick Draw Model*
  ➤ **Steel backstrap and triggerguard**

	100%	98%	95%	90%	80%	70%	60%
Mfg.'s Sug. Retail	$410	$345	$265	$210	$175	$160	$150	$135

Add $25 for .357 Mag., .38-40, or .44 Spl. cal.
Add $65 for convertible cylinder (.45 LC/.45 ACP, .22 LR/.22 Mag. in 5½ in. barrel only).
Add $64 for stainless steel construction (disc. 1989).

  ➤ **Brass backstrap and triggerguard** — .357 Mag., .44-40, or .45 LC cal., 4¾, 5½, or 7½ in. barrel.

	100%	98%	95%	90%	80%	70%	60%
Mfg.'s Sug. Retail	$365	$310	$240	$190	$165	$150	$140	$130

Add $50 for convertible cylinder (.45 LC/.45 ACP).

▲ *Sheriff's Model* — .44-40 or .45 LC cal., 3 or 4 in. barrel, steel backstrap.

	100%	98%	95%	90%	80%	70%	60%
Mfg.'s Sug. Retail	$410	$345	$265	$210	$175	$160	$150	$135

▲ *Target Model* — similar to standard Cattleman model, only fully adj. rear blade sight, brass backstrap. Importation disc. 1990.

	95%	90%	80%	70%	60%
	$315	$245	$200	$185	$170	$150	$135

Last Mfg.'s Sug. Retail was $335.

Add $25 for steel backstrap and triggerguard.
Add $60 for stainless steel construction (disc.).

CATTLEMAN BUNTLINE — .357 Mag. (disc. 1995), .44-40 (disc.), or .45 LC cal., 18 in. barrel, steel backstrap cut for shoulder stock. Importation disc. 1989, re-introduced 1993.

	100%	98%	95%	90%	80%	70%	60%
Mfg.'s Sug. Retail	$475	$395	$310	$240	$195	$175	$160	$150

▲ *Buntline Carbine* — similar to Cattleman Buntline, 18 in. barrel, includes non-detachable shoulder stock with brass hardware and lanyard ring. Importation disc. 1989, re-introduced 1993-95.

	95%	90%	80%	70%	60%
	$390	$310	$245	$200	$175	$160	$150

Last Mfg.'s Sug. Retail was $475.

Add $34 for target sights.
Add $34 for .22 LR/.22 Mag. combo. (disc. 1989).
Add $175 for detachable shoulder stock.

BUCKHORN — .44 Mag., .44 Spl., or .44-40 cal., various barrel lengths, brass or steel backstrap, Buntline and revolving carbine models also available in the Buckhorn series — add approx. $65.

▲ *Quick Draw Model* — importation disc. 1989, re-introduced 1992-95.

	95%	90%	80%	70%	60%
	$375	$295	$235	$195	$175	$160	$150

Last Mfg.'s Sug. Retail was $445.

Add $50 for convertible cylinder.
Add $40 for Target Model.

▲ *Buckhorn Carbine* — .44-40 or .44 Mag. cal., 18 in. barrel, includes non-detachable shoulder stock with brass hardware and lanyard ring. Importation disc. 1989.

	95%	90%	80%	70%	60%
	$360	$285	$230	$200	$185	$180	$175

Last Mfg.'s Sug. Retail was $450.

Add $34 for target sights.
Add $40 for extra .44-40 cylinder combo.
Add $122 for detachable shoulder stock.

Grading	100%	98%	95%	90%	80%	70%	60%

STALLION 1873 COLT — .22 LR/.22 Mag. cal. combo only, 4¾, 5½, or 6½ in. barrel, case hardened frame, 1-piece walnut grip, 2.4 lbs. Importation disc. 1989.

		$300	$210	$195	$170	$155	$140	$120

Last Mfg.'s Sug. Retail was $325.

Add $27 for steel backstrap and triggerguard.
Add $26 for Target Model.

▲ *Stainless Stallion* — similar to standard Stallion, except is stainless steel. Importation disc. 1989.

		$370	$275	$225	$200	$185	$180	$175

Last Mfg.'s Sug. Retail was $425.

1875 "OUTLAW" REMINGTON — .357 Mag., .44-40, .45 ACP (new 1992), or .45 LC cal., 5½ (disc. 1995) or 7½ in. barrel, brass or steel (new 1993) triggerguard.

Mfg.'s Sug. Retail	$435	$365	$275	$215	$175	$160	$150	$135

Add $50 for nickel-plating (disc. 1995).
Add $40 for convertible cylinder (.45 LC/.45 ACP).

▲ *Model 1875 Carbine* — same cals. as Outlaw 1875, 18 in. barrel, includes non-detachable shoulder stock with brass hardware and lanyard ring. Importation disc. 1989.

		$425	$285	$230	$200	$185	$180	$175

Last Mfg.'s Sug. Retail was $440.

Add $110 for nickel plating.

1890 "POLICE" REMINGTON — .357 Mag., .44-40, .45 ACP (new 1993), or .45 LC cal., 5½ or 7½ (disc. 1995) in. barrel, brass or steel (new 1993) triggerguard.

Mfg.'s Sug. Retail	$435	$365	$275	$215	$175	$160	$150	$135

Add $50 for nickel-plating (disc. 1995).
Add $40 for convertible cylinder (.45 LC/.45 ACP).

PHANTOM MODEL — .357 or .44 Mag. cal. only, 10½ in. barrel for silhouette use. Imported 1985-89.

		$475	$395	$325	$290	$260	$230	$215

Last Mfg.'s Sug. Retail was $509.

REVOLVERS: DOUBLE ACTION

INSPECTOR MODEL — .32 S&W or .38 Spl. cal., 3, 4, or 6 in. barrels, double action, blued or chrome finish. Imported 1985-89.

		$390	$295	$245	$210	$170	$145	$125

Last Mfg.'s Sug. Retail was $406.

Add $35 for target sights.
Add $25 for chrome plating.

TARGET PISTOLS

1871 ROLLING BLOCK TARGET PISTOL/CARBINE — available in .22 LR, .22 Mag., .22 Hornet, .357 Mag. or .45 LC (Navy Model with open sights only, mfg. 1992-95) cal., 9½ in. barrel.

Mfg.'s Sug. Retail	$410	$335	$275	$230	$195	$175	$155	$135

Add $80 for carbine model (22 in. barrel - not available in .45 LC cal).

RIFLES: REPRODUCTIONS

Add approx. $400 for standard hand-engraving for most models listed below.

HENRY RIFLE/CARBINE — .44-40 or .45 LC (rifle only) cal., brass or steel (.44-40 only) frame, 24½ in. barrel on rifle, 22½ in. barrel on carbine, available in modern gun blue, charcoal blue, white, or chrome finish.

Mfg.'s Sug. Retail	$940	$840	$635	$525	$425	$360	$320	$260

Add $10 for carbine model.
Add $20 for steel frame on rifle only.

The carbine was disc. in 1989, re-introduced 1992.

Grading	100%	98%	95%	90%	80%	70%	60%

▲ *Henry Trapper* — similar to above, except has 16½ or 18½ in. barrel. Limited importation began 1990.

    Mfg.'s Sug. Retail $950 $850 $640 $525 $425 $360 $320 $260

▲ *Henry 1 of 1,000* — disc. several years ago.

    $1,450 $1,150 $975 $850 $700 $575 $425

1866 CARBINE — .22 LR (disc. 1989), .22 Mag. (disc. 1989), .38 Spl., .44-40 or .45 LC cal., brass receiver, 19 in. round barrel. Importation disc. 1995.

    $640 $525 $425 $360 $310 $275 $240

    Last Mfg.'s Sug. Retail was $587 for .22 Mag. or .22 LR (disc. 1989).

    Last Mfg.'s Sug. Retail was $720.

▲ *1866 Trapper Carbine* — .22 LR, .38 Spl., or .44-40 cal., 16 in. barrel. Importation disc. 1989.

    $650 $475 $395 $340 $285 $260 $235

    Last Mfg.'s Sug. Retail was $686.

▲ *1866 Yellowboy Indian Carbine* — .22 LR, .22 Mag., .38 Spl., .44-40, or .45 LC (new 1996) cal., 19 in. barrel. Limited importation.

    Mfg.'s Sug. Retail $760 $670 $535 $430 $360 $310 $275 $240

    Subtract $50 without brass tacks.

▲ *Red Cloud Commemorative Carbine* — same cals., special engraving and brass tacks in forearm and stock. Importation officially disc. 1989.

    $720 $600 $475 $400 $350 $330 $300

    Last Mfg.'s Sug. Retail was $850.

1866 SPORTING RIFLE — .38 Spl., .44-40, or .45 LC (new 1996) cal., brass receiver, 24¼ in. round (new 1993) or octagonal barrel.

    Mfg.'s Sug. Retail $840 $740 $575 $485 $385 $300 $260 $235

▲ *1866 Deluxe Uberti Model* — .44-40 cal., features high polished receiver with fire-blued small parts, latter rear sight, open edition beginning 1995.

    Mfg.'s Sug. Retail $895 $895 $675 $525

    This model is sold exclusively by Cherry's, located in Greensboro, NC.

▲ *1866 "L.D. Nimschke" Special Edition* — .44-40 cal., receiver, buttplate, and forend cap feature recreations of Nimschke scroll-engraving by Giovanelli of Italy, silver-plated, deluxe walnut, optional 2nd Edition of Nimschke pattern book by R. L. Wilson ($100), only 300 mfg. beginning 1995.

    Mfg.'s Sug. Retail $1,495 $1,495 $1,000 $650

    This model is sold exclusively by Cherry's, located in Greensboro, NC.

▲ *1866 Yellowboy Indian Rifle* — .22 LR (disc. 1989), .22 Mag. (disc. 1989), .38 Spl., or .44-40 cal., 24¼ in. barrel. Importation disc. 1989, reintroduced 1993-95.

    $700 $560 $475 $385 $300 $260 $235

    Last Mfg.'s Sug. Retail was $800.

1873 CARBINE — .22 LR (disc. 1991), .22 Mag. (disc. 1991), .357 Mag., .38 Spl. (disc. 1991) .44-40, or .45 LC (new 1992) cal., steel receiver, 19 in. round barrel.

    Mfg.'s Sug. Retail $900 $800 $600 $500 $425 $360 $320 $280

    Add $20 for .357 Mag. cal.

    Add $95 for nickel-plating (disc.).

▲ *1873 Trapper Carbine* — .357 Mag., .44-40, or .45 LC cal. only, 16⅛ in. barrel. Importation disc. 1990.

    $695 $550 $475 $400 $360 $320 $280

    Last Mfg.'s Sug. Retail was $750.

Grading	100%	98%	95%	90%	80%	70%	60%

1873 SPORTING RIFLE — .357 Mag. (new 1995), .44-40 (new 1995), or .45 LC cal., case hardened receiver, 20 in. octagon (new 1990), 24¼ in. octagon (.357 Mag. only) or half-round/half-octagon or 30 (new 1990) in. octagon barrel, can be drilled and tapped for Uberti rear tang aperture sight (new 1993).

Mfg.'s Sug. Retail	$940		$830	$640	$525	$425	$360	$320	$260

> Add $30 for .44-40 or .45 LC cal. in 24¼ octagon barrel only.
> Add $990 for "1 of 1,000" engraving pattern.
> Add $95 for hand-checkered pistol grip stock.

UGARTECHEA, ARMAS

Formerly known as Ugartechea, Ignacio. This manufacturer has recently undergone restructuring. Currently being distributed by Bill Hanus Birdguns of Newport, OR, and imported by Galaxy Imports of Victoria, TX.

SHOTGUNS: SIDE-BY-SIDE

BILL HANUS BIRDGUN — 16, 20, 28, or .410 ga., boxlock action, 26 in. barrels bored SK1/SK2, Churchill raised rib, SNT, ejectors, case colored receiver, checkered straight grip walnut stock and semi-beavertail forend, oil finish, lifetime operational warranty, 5¼-6½ lbs. Importation began 1995.

Mfg.'s Sug. Retail	$1,595		$1,355	$1,220	$1,035	$880	$750	$635	$540

> Add $100 for 28 ga.
> Add $150 for .410 ga.

BILL HANUS BIRDGUN CLASSIC — 20, 28, or .410 ga., similar to Birdgun Model, except has double triggers with hinged front trigger, 27 in. barrels, splinter forend and English leather handguard. Importation began 1996.

Mfg.'s Sug. Retail	$1,295		$1,100	$990	$840	$715	$610	$515	$440

> Add $100 for 28 ga.
> Add $200 for .410 ga.

UGARTECHEA, IGNACIO

Manufacturer located in Eibar, Spain. Bill Hanus Birdguns located in Newport, OR is the current U.S. agent beginning 1995. Currently imported by Galaxy Imports located in Victoria, TX.

Ignacio Urgartechea was founded in 1922 and is the oldest maker of side-by-side sidelock and boxlock shotguns in Spain. From 1970 until the Parker-Hale name was sold to Navy Arms, Ugartechea manufactured the popular line of Anson Deeley boxlocks imported by Precision Sports in Cortland, NY. Precision Sports continued to import these guns under the Classic "600" name until 1994. In 1995, Bill Hanus was appointed as U.S. agent for Ignacio Ugartechea. Previously imported by Precision Sports, Inc. located in Cortland, NY until 1994 as the Parker-Hale and the Bill Hanus Birdgun. Previously imported by Exel Arms in Gardener, MA until 1987 as the Exel Model 200 series.

SHOTGUNS: SIDELOCK

Ugartechea sidelocks are best quality guns, made to individual customer specifications in approx. 4-8 months.

MODEL 116 — 12, 16, or 20 ga., sidelock action, antique silver finish with elaborate floral engraving, deluxe oil finished walnut stock and forearm.

Mfg.'s Sug. Retail	$6,050		$5,500	$5,000	$4,400	$3,800	$3,200	$2,600	$2,000

MODEL 119 — 12, 16, 20, or 28 ga., sidelock action with case colored finish, English scroll engraving, deluxe oil finished walnut stock and forearm.

Mfg.'s Sug. Retail	$6,200		$5,650	$5,100	$4,450	$3,825	$3,200	$2,600	$2,000

> Add $450 for 28 ga.

Grading	100%	98%	95%	90%	80%	70%	60%

MODEL 1000 — 12, 16, or 20 ga., sidelock action with polished finish, Italianate style engraving, deluxe oil finished walnut stock and forearm.
Mfg.'s Sug. Retail $7,875 $7,150 $6,200 $5,650 $5,100 $4,450 $3,825 $3,200

MODEL 1042 — 12, 16, or 20 ga., sidelock action, antique silver finish, elaborate floral engraving, deluxe oil finished walnut stock and forearm.
Mfg.'s Sug. Retail $10,150 $9,400 $8,200 $7,000 $5,800 $4,600 $3,950 $3,350

SPECIAL MODELS — available in all gauges with game scene engraving and/or gold inlays to customer specifications. POR only.

SHOTGUNS: BOXLOCK

Included in this section are older Exel Series 200 shotguns (disc. 1986-87) in addition to the Parker-Hale 600 Series. The importation of Parker-Hale shotguns was disc. in 1993.

EXEL 200 SERIES — these side-by-sides are available in 12 or 20 ga. (3 in.) only. Model 201 is basic gun with 213 being the highest grade.

▲ *Model 201, 202, and 203* — double triggers, extractors, straight grip, matted rib, various chokes and barrel lengths.
$375 $325 $260 $240 $215 $180 $165
Last Mfg.'s Sug. Retail was $429.

Previously designated Model 30.

▲ *Model 281* — similar to 201 series, except 28 ga.
$420 $325 $275 $250 $235 $210 $195
Last Mfg.'s Sug. Retail was $472.

Previously designated Model 30.

▲ *Model 240* — similar to 201 series, except .410 ga.
$450 $355 $295 $270 $250 $235 $210
Last Mfg.'s Sug. Retail was $472.

Previously designated Model 30.

▲ *Models 204, 205, and 206* — single trigger optional, ejectors, straight grip, silver finish, various chokes and barrel lengths. Importation disc. 1986.
$550 $470 $415 $370 $340 $315 $280
Last Mfg.'s Sug. Retail was $627.

▲ *Models 207 and 207A* — 12 ga. only, sidelock, case hardened action. 207A is deluxe model with ejectors. Model 201 disc. 1986.
$725 $650 $580 $515 $465 $400 $345
Last Mfg.'s Sug. Retail was $836.

Deduct 33% without ejectors (Model 207).
This model was previously designated the Milano EX.

▲ *Models 208 and 208A* — similar to 207/207A, only engraved coin finished receiver. 208A is deluxe model with ejectors. Model 208 disc. 1986.
$775 $695 $625 $550 $485 $420 $360
Last Mfg.'s Sug. Retail was $925.

Deduct 33% without ejectors (Model 208).
This model was previously designated the Model 75 EX.

▲ *Models 209 and 210* — better engraving and walnut than 207/207A. Model 210 is 20 ga. Importation disc. 1986.
$580 $505 $450 $415 $375 $340 $310
Last Mfg.'s Sug. Retail was $672.

▲ *Models 211, 212, and 213* — top-of-the-line model, best quality engraving and walnut. Special order only.
$2,350 $2,000 $1,780 $1,475 $1,200 $1,000 $850
Last Mfg.'s Sug. Retail was $3,100.

Previously designated Model 110.

Grading	100%	98%	95%	90%	80%	70%	60%

MODEL 251 — .410-3 in. ga., folding design, 26 in. barrels only, DTs, extractors, walnut stock and forearm. Imported 1987 only.

| | $185 | $165 | $140 | $120 | $105 | $95 | $85 |

Last Mfg.'s Sug. Retail was $215.

MODEL 630 — 12 ga. only, 3 in. chambers, boxlock action with color case hardening, extractors, DTs, 26 or 28 in. barrels with fixed chokes, checkered English grip stock and forearm, includes deluxe shotgun case. Imported 1993 only.

| | $625 | $525 | $450 | $400 | $365 | $330 | $295 |

Last Mfg.'s Sug. Retail was $699.

MODEL 640E (ENGLISH) — 12, 16, 20, 28, or .410 ga., boxlock action, double triggers, straight grip stock, splinter forend, concave rib, extractors, silver finished receiver. Imported 1986-1993.

| | $750 | $595 | $540 | $475 | $415 | $350 | $295 |

Last Mfg.'s Sug. Retail was $850.

Add $90 for 28 or $120 for .410 ga.

The "E" suffix in this model designates English configuration.

▲ **Model 640A (AMERICAN)** — same ga.'s as 640E, except has non-selective single trigger, pistol grip, beavertail forend, and raised matted rib. Imported 1986-1993.

| | $840 | $700 | $630 | $560 | $475 | $400 | $350 |

Last Mfg.'s Sug. Retail was $970.

Add $110 for 28 or $130 for .410 ga.

The "A" suffix in this model designates American configuration (pistol grip stock and single trigger).

MODEL 640M (MAGNUM) — 10 ga., 3½ in. chambers, 26, 30, or 32 in. barrels bored full and full, DTs, recoil pad. Imported 1989-1993.

| | $860 | $725 | $650 | $575 | $495 | $415 | $365 |

Last Mfg.'s Sug. Retail was $1,000.

In this model, the 26 in. barrels are referred to as the Turkey Gun, the 30 in. is Big Ten, and the 32 in. is Goose Gun.

MODEL 640 SLUG GUN — 12 ga. only, 25 in. barrels bored IC/IC. Imported 1991-93.

| | $995 | $850 | $725 | $650 | $575 | $495 | $415 |

Last Mfg.'s Sug. Retail was $1,120.

MODEL 645E (ENGLISH) — 12, 16, 20, 28 or .410 ga., boxlock action, double triggers, straight grip stock, moderate engraving, splinter forend, concave rib, ejectors, silver finished receiver. Imported 1986-1993.

| | $940 | $775 | $675 | $595 | $500 | $415 | $365 |

Last Mfg.'s Sug. Retail was $1,090.

Add $60 for 28 or $110 for .410 ga.

▲ **Model 645E-XXV** — available in all ga.'s, 25 in. barrels only, ejectors, Churchill rib, moderately engraved, silver finished receiver. Imported 1986-1993.

| | $940 | $775 | $675 | $595 | $500 | $415 | $365 |

Last Mfg.'s Sug. Retail was $1,100.

Add $100 for 28 or $130 for .410 ga.

▲ **Model 645E Bi-Gauge** — 2 barrel set available in either 20/28 ga. or 28/.410 ga. combination. Mfg. 1988-1992.

| | $1,475 | $1,175 | $950 | $800 | $700 | $600 | $550 |

Last Mfg.'s Sug. Retail was $1,620.

Add $150 for 28/.410 ga. combo. (disc. 1991).

MODEL 645A (AMERICAN) — same ga.'s as 645E, except has non-selective single trigger, pistol grip, beavertail forend, and raised matted rib. Imported 1986-1993.

| | $1,025 | $825 | $700 | $615 | $515 | $440 | $400 |

Last Mfg.'s Sug. Retail was $1,200.

Add $110 for 28 or $150 for .410 ga.

Grading	100%	98%	95%	90%	80%	70%	60%

▲ *Model 645A Bi-Gauge* — 2 barrel set available in either 20/28 ga. or 28/.410 ga. combination. Mfg. 1988-92.

| | $1,600 | $1,325 | $995 | $850 | $750 | $625 | $575 |

Last Mfg.'s Sug. Retail was $1,750.

Add $150 for 28/.410 ga. combo. (disc. 1991).

MODEL 650 ENGLISH OR AMERICAN — 12 ga. only, 28 in. barrels with IC/M choke tubes, extractors, choice of English (DT and straight grip stock) or American (SNT, pistol grip stock, and beavertail forend), silver frame finish. Imported 1992-93.

| | $825 | $700 | $630 | $560 | $475 | $400 | $350 |

Last Mfg.'s Sug. Retail was $920.

Add $120 for Model 650 American option.

MODEL 655 ENGLISH OR AMERICAN — 12 ga. only, 28 in. barrels with IC/M choke tubes, ejectors, choice of English (DT and straight grip stock) or American (SNT, pistol grip stock, and beavertail forend), silver frame finish. Imported 1992-93.

| | $925 | $825 | $700 | $630 | $560 | $475 | $400 |

Last Mfg.'s Sug. Retail was $1,150.

Add $110 for Model 655 American option.

MODEL 670E (ENGLISH) — 12, 16, or 20 ga., sidelock action, 26, 27, or 28 in. barrels, ejectors, engraved silver finished receiver, double triggers, straight grip. Imported 1986-91.

| | $3,700 | $2,975 | $2,450 | $1,850 | $1,550 | $1,375 | $1,200 |

Last Mfg.'s Sug. Retail was $4,270.

Add $770 for 28 or .410 ga.
This model was available by custom order only.

MODEL 680E-XXV (ENGLISH) — similar to Model 670E, except has color case hardened sideplates and 25 in. barrels only.

| | $3,500 | $2,800 | $2,300 | $1,700 | $1,475 | $1,300 | $1,175 |

Last Mfg.'s Sug. Retail was $4,070.

Add $400 for 28 or .410 ga.
This model was available by custom order only.

BILL HANUS BIRDGUN — 16, 20, or 28 ga., boxlock action, 26 in. barrels bored SK1/SK2, Churchill raised rib, SNT, ejectors, case colored receiver, checkered straight grip walnut stock and semi-beavertail forend, oil finish, lifetime warranty, 5¼-6½ lbs. Imported 1989-93.

| | $1,100 | $835 | $700 | $615 | $515 | $440 | $400 |

Last Mfg.'s Sug. Retail was $1,270.

Add $130 for 28 ga.
Add $325 with hard case and accessories.

ULTIMATE

Please refer to Camex-Blaser USA in the C section of this text.

ULTRA LIGHT ARMS, INC.

Manufacturer located in Granville, WV. Dealer direct sales only.

RIFLES: BOLT ACTION

ULTRA LIGHT RIFLE — caliber to customer specs., various actions, 2-position 3-function safety in top of stock, Timney trigger, Douglas 22 or 24 in. barrel, no sights, graphite reinforced stock with recoil pad, matte finish standard, other finishes at extra cost. Many special order features and services are available on these models - contact the manufacturer for prices, 4¾-5¾ lbs. New 1985.

Grading	100%	98%	95%	90%	80%	70%	60%

MODEL 20 — 18 cals. available between .17 Rem. and .358 Win. Mag., short action, Kevlar stock.
Mfg.'s Sug. Retail $2,500 $2,225 $1,675 $1,225 $950 $800 $700 $640
 Add $100 for left-hand action.

▲ *Model 20 RF* — .22 LR cal., convertible from repeater to single shot, 22 in. Douglas premium barrel, DuPont composite stock with Imron paint (some color options available), no sights, drilled and tapped, 5¼ lbs. New 1983.
Mfg.'s Sug. Retail $800 $750 $650 $550 $475 $400 $350 $300
 Add $50 for repeater action.
 The first 100 pre-production rifles in this model are marked "1-of-100" consecutively, with owner's initials.

MODEL 24 — .25-06, .270 Win., .280 Rem. (mfg. 1992 only), .30-06, or 7mm Exp. cal., long action, Kevlar stock, 5¼ lbs.
Mfg.'s Sug. Retail $2,600 $2,325 $1,775 $1,300 $995 $825 $700 $640
 Add $100 for left-hand action.

MODEL 28 MAGNUM — .264 Win. Mag., .300 Win. Mag., .338 Win. Mag., 7mm Rem. Mag., or .416 Rigby (mfg. 1992 only) cal., Kevlar stock, 5¾ lbs.
Mfg.'s Sug. Retail $2,900 $2,625 $1,975 $1,550 $1,225 $950 $700 $600
 Add $100 for left-hand action.

MODEL 40 MAGNUM — .300 Wby. Mag. or .416 Rigby cal., otherwise similar to Model 28 Series. New 1993.
Mfg.'s Sug. Retail $2,900 $2,625 $1,975 $1,550 $1,225 $950 $700 $600
 Add $100 for left-hand action.

PISTOLS: BOLT-ACTION

MODEL 20 HUNTERS PISTOL — various cals., 14 in. Douglas heavy barrel, 5-shot mag., Kevlar graphite reinforced stock in choice of 4 colors, Timney trigger, left-hand or right-hand bolt, approx. 4 lbs. Mfg. 1987-89.

 $1,295 $1,150 $975 $850 $700 $640 $575
 Last Mfg.'s Sug. Retail was $1,600.

MODEL 20 REB — popular cals. from .22-250 Rem. through .308 Win. (other cals. on request), 14 in. Douglas #3 barrel, 5 shot mag., composite Kevlar graphite reinforced stock, green, brown, black, or camo Dupont Imron paint, Timney adj. trigger, includes hard case, 4 lbs. Mfg. 1994-95 only.

 $1,475 $1,200 $1,000 $875 $750 $625 $500
 Last Mfg.'s Sug. Retail was $1,600.

ULTRAMATIC
Manufacturer located in Enzesfeld, Austria. No current importer.

ULTRAMATIC PISTOL — 9mm Para. cal., double action semi-auto, various barrel lengths, competition model with muzzle brake.
 Please contact the factory directly (see Trademark Index listing) for more information on this model.

UNIQUE
Manufacturer located in Hendaye, France. Imported exclusively by Nygord Precision Products located in Prescott, AZ.

PISTOLS: SEMI-AUTO
 All currently manufactured Unique pistols are supplied with leatherette case, weights are additional.

Grading	100%	98%	95%	90%	80%	70%	60%

KREIGS MODEL L — 7.65mm, 9 shot, 3.2 in. barrel, blue, plastic grips, fixed sights. Mfg. 1940-1945, during German occupation of France, has German acceptance marks.

	$325	$250	$220	$200	$180	$160	$140

MODEL RR — post-war commercial version of Kreigsmodell, higher quality finish. Mfg. 1951-disc.

	$180	$170	$155	$130	$120	$110	$90

Add 15% for .22 LR.

MODEL B/CF — 7.65mm, 9 shot, or .380 auto cal., 8 shot, 4 in. barrel, blue, plastic thumbrest grips. Mfg. 1954-disc.

	$205	$195	$175	$155	$145	$130	$110

MODEL D6 — .22 LR cal., 10 shot, 6 in. barrel, adj. sights, blue, plastic grips. Mfg. 1954-disc.

	$300	$250	$200	$160	$145	$135	$120

MODEL D2 — similar to D6, except 4½ in. barrel.

	$300	$250	$200	$160	$145	$135	$120

MODEL L — .22 LR cal., 10 shot, 7.65mm cal., 7 shot, and .380 auto cal., 6 shot, 3.3 in. barrel, fixed sights, steel and alloy frame offered, plastic grips. Mfg. 1955-disc.

	$250	$200	$150	$130	$115	$100	$90

MODEL MIKROS POCKET — .22 Short and .25 auto cal., 6 shot, fixed sights, blue, plastic grips, steel or alloy frame. Mfg. 1957-disc.

	$200	$155	$140	$120	$100	$90	$75

MODEL DES/32U — .32 S&W L Wadcutter, 5.9 in. barrel, dry firing device, ergonomically designed French walnut grips with adj. hand rest, 5 or 6 shot mag., 40.2 oz.

Mfg.'s Sug. Retail	$1,350	$1,225	$1,025	$900	$775	$625	$500	$450

MODEL DES/69 MATCH — .22 LR cal. target pistol, wraparound grips, adj. features. Imported 1986-1988.

	$995	$850	$725	$625	$550	$490	$445

Last Mfg.'s Sug. Retail was $1,198.

Add $62 for left-hand model.

MODEL DES/69U STANDARD MATCH — .22 LR cal., 5 shot mag., 5.9 in. barrel, adj. rear sight, adj. target, stippled stocks, blue finish only. Importation began 1969.

Mfg.'s Sug. Retail	$1,250	$1,150	$995	$875	$750	$625	$500	$450

Add $30 for left-hand model.

MODEL DES/823-U RAPID FIRE MATCH — .22 Short, 5 shot, 6 in. barrel, adj. sight, adj. trigger, adj. walnut target grips, squared barrel assembly, dry fire mechanism. Imported 1974-1988.

	$1,100	$850	$725	$625	$550	$490	$445

Last Mfg.'s Sug. Retail was $1,300.

Add $60 for left-hand model.

MODEL 2000-U — .22 Short cal. only, specifically designed for rapid fire U.I.T. competition, 5.9 in. barrel, ergonomic styled grips with adj. hand rest, 5 shot mag. (inserted in top), 43.4 oz. Importation disc. 1995.

	$1,300	$1,050	$925	$775	$625	$500	$450

Last Mfg.'s Sug. Retail was $1,450.

Add $30 for left-hand model.

RIFLES

T66 MATCH RIFLE — .22 LR cal., single shot, bolt action, 25½ in. barrel, micro rear globe front, full target stock. Mfg. 1966-disc.

	$425	$410	$390	$350	$300	$280	$250

Grading	100%	98%	95%	90%	80%	70%	60%

MODEL F 11 — .22 LR cal., military trainer, adj. sights, target walnut stock. Limited importation.

| | $560 | $435 | $350 | $285 | $260 | $240 | $220 |

Last Mfg.'s Sug. Retail was $695.

MODEL T DIOPTRA — .22 LR or .22 Mag. cal., bolt action Sporter with 23.6 in. barrel and adj. rear sight, 5 (.22 Mag. only) or 10 shot mag., grooved receiver for scope, checkered French walnut Monte Carlo stock, approx. 6.4 lbs. Importation disc. 1995.

| | $795 | $700 | $600 | $525 | $450 | $375 | $300 |

Last Mfg.'s Sug. Retail was $890.

MODEL T/SM — .22 LR or .22 Mag cal., bolt action Target variation with 20½ in. barrel, no sights, 5 (.22 Mag. only) or 10 shot mag., stippled pistol grip stock and forend, right or left-hand action, 6.6 lbs. Importation disc. 1995.

| | $850 | $735 | $625 | $525 | $450 | $375 | $300 |

Last Mfg.'s Sug. Retail was $960.

Add $50 for left-hand action.

MODEL T/STANDARD UIT — .22 LR cal., designed for UIT competition, single shot, aperture sights, adj. cheekpiece and buttplate on stippled walnut stock, right or left hand action, 10.8 lbs. Importation disc. 1995.

| | $1,350 | $1,125 | $975 | $850 | $725 | $625 | $525 |

Last Mfg.'s Sug. Retail was $1,450.

Add $50 for left-hand action.

MODEL T/LIBRE UIT FREE RIFLE — .22 LR cal., Free Rifle variation of the Model T/Standard UIT.

Nygord Precision should be contacted directly for pricing on this model.

UNITED SPORTING ARMS, INC.

Previous manufacturer located in Tucson, AZ. Manufacture ceased in early 1986.

All the below models were disc. in early 1986.

SEVILLE — .357 Mag., .41 Mag., .44 Mag., or .45 Colt cal., single action revolver, 4⅝, 5½, 6½, or 7½ in. barrels, adj. sights, smooth walnut grips.

| | $395 | $350 | $315 | $280 | $260 | $240 | $220 |

Last Mfg.'s Sug. Retail was $435.

▲ *Stainless steel* — all stainless version of the Seville.

| | $395 | $350 | $315 |

Last Mfg.'s Sug. Retail was $435.

▲ *Silver Seville* — similar to Seville, except has blue barrel, and high polish stainless steel grip frame.

| | $425 | $370 | $330 |

Last Mfg.'s Sug. Retail was $460.

▲ *Stainless .357 Maxi* — available in 5½ or 7½ in. barrel only.

| | $575 | $475 | $395 |

Last Mfg.'s Sug. Retail was $465.

▲ *Stainless .375 USA* — only in 7½ in. barrel.

| | $625 | $525 | $425 |

Last Mfg.'s Sug. Retail was $490.

▲ *Stainless .454 Mag.* — only in 7½ in. barrel, 5 shot.

| | $700 | $600 | $500 |

Last Mfg.'s Sug. Retail was $595.

Note: In late 1986, some .454 Mags. were made up from parts purchased from the manufacturer. Unfortunately, while the exterior appearance might seem normal, they were not involved with any type of factory quality control program. As a result, shooting these non-factory revolvers could be dangerous, and careful inspection should be made before purchasing/shooting this particular specimen.

▲ *Eldorado Stainless* — .44 Mag., 10½ in. barrel, adj. sights.

| | $700 | $600 | $500 |

Grading	100%	98%	95%	90%	80%	70%	60%

SILVER SEVILLE SILHOUETTE — .357 Mag., .41 Mag., or .44 Mag. cal., single action revolver, 10½ in. barrel, adj. sights, Pachmayr grips, blued barrel finish with stainless grip frame.

	$445	$370	$330	$295	$270	$250	$230

Last Mfg.'s Sug. Retail was $485.

▲ *Stainless steel* — stainless version of the Silver Seville Silhouette.

	$425	$370	$330				

Last Mfg.'s Sug. Retail was $460.

▲ *Stainless .357 Maxi* — available in 10½ in. barrel only.

	$575	$475	$395

Last Mfg.'s Sug. Retail was $480.

▲ *Stainless .375 USA* — available in 10½ in. barrel only.

	$625	$525	$425

Last Mfg.'s Sug. Retail was $515.

▲ *Stainless .454 Mag.* — available in 10½ in. barrel only, 5 shot.

	$700	$600	$500

Last Mfg.'s Sug. Retail was $620.

> Note: In late 1986, some .454 Mags. were made up from parts purchased from the manufacturer. Unfortunately, while the exterior appearance might seem normal, they were not involved with any type of factory quality control program. As a result, shooting these non-factory revolvers could be dangerous, and careful inspection should be made before purchasing/shooting this particular specimen.

SHERIFF MODEL — .357 Mag., .38 Spl., .44 Spl., .44 Mag., or .45 Colt cal., single action revolver, 3½ in. barrel, adj. sights, smooth walnut grips.

	$395	$350	$315	$280	$260	$240	$220

Last Mfg.'s Sug. Retail was $435.

▲ *Stainless steel* — stainless version of the Sheriff Model.

	$395	$350	$315

Last Mfg.'s Sug. Retail was $435.

U.S. HISTORICAL SOCIETY

An organization which marketed historically significant firearms reproductions until April, 1994. Located in Richmond, VA. Most firearms are manufactured by the Williamsburg Firearms Manufactory and the Virginia Firearms Manufactory.

On April 1, 1994, the Antique Arms Divison of the U.S. Historical Society was acquired by America Remembers located in Mechanicsville, VA. America Remembers' affiliates include the Armed Forces Commemorative Society, American Heroes & Legends, and the United States Society of Arms and Armor. Issues that were not fully subscribed are now available through America Remembers.

The information listed below represents current information up until America Remembers acquired the Antique Arms Division of the U.S. Historical Society.

PISTOLS

ANDREW JACKSON

▲ *Silver Edition* — 2,500 mfg.

	$2,100	$1,750	$1,400

Issue price was $2,100.

▲ *Gold Edition* — 100 mfg.

	$5,500	$3,995	$2,750

Issue price was $5,500.

Grading	100%	98%	95%	90%	80%	70%	60%

PITCAIRN — 900 mfg.
$2,950 $2,300 $1,750
Issue price was $2,950.

THOMAS JEFFERSON — 1,000 mfg., issue price was $1,900.
$3,500 $2,750 $1,995

HAMILTON — BURR DUELING PISTOLS — 1,200 mfg., issue price was $2,995 in 1981.
$3,500 $2,750 $1,995

WASHINGTON AND LEE FLINTLOCK PISTOLS — .69 cal., flintlock pistols with $9^{15}/_{16}$ in. barrels, burl walnut stocks with sterling silver fittings, engraved silver plated lock plates, triggerguard, and sideplate, firing capability, cased with accessories, limited issue of 1,000 in 1989.
Mfg.'s Sug. Retail $2,700 $2,700 $2,150 $1,650

GEORGE WASHINGTON — includes pair of flintlocks, 975 mfg. 1976, cased, issue price was initially $3,000, and ended at $3,500.
$4,250 $3,400 $2,450

H. DERINGER PISTOL SET — .41 cal., percussion, reproduction of H. Deringer's famous pistol. Available with sterling silver mounts (1,000 pair manufactured — issue price $1,900), 14Kt. gold mounted (100 pair mfg.-$2,700 issue price), precious gem stone mounted (only 5 pair mfg. — $25,000 issue price). Mfg. 1978.

▲ *Silver mounted*
$2,500 $1,750 $1,000

▲ *14Kt. gold mounted*
$7,500 $5,000 $3,000

▲ *18Kt. jewel mounted* — too limited a supply for price evaluation.

TEXAS PATERSON EDITION — reproduction of the famous Colt folding trigger model mfg. in Paterson, NJ, engraved, cased. 1,000 mfg. starting in 1988. Cased with accessories.
Mfg.'s Sug. Retail $2,500 $2,500 $1,900 $1,450
This model is an exact reproduction of the original Colt Paterson ser. no. 755, Model 5

SAM HOUSTON WALKER — .44 cal., reproduction of the Colt Walker, 9 in. barrel, extensive gold etching on highly polished blued surface, smooth walnut stocks with S. Houston medallions, cased with accessories. 2,500 mfg.
$2,300 $2,000 $1,575
Issue price was $2,300.

TEXAS RANGER DRAGOON — .44 cal., features silver-plated cylinder, triggerguard, and gripstraps, color case hardened frame and loading lever, multiple 24 Kt. etchings on barrel and frame front, cased with accessories, 66 oz. 1,000 mfg. in 1990 only.
Mfg.'s Sug. Retail $1,585 $1,585 $1,050 $795

TOWER OF LONDON COL. SAM COLT DRAGOON — .44 cal., exact reproduction of the Second Model Dragoon, $7^{1}/_{2}$ in. barrel, hand engraved, Texas ranger cylinder scene, one piece walnut grip with inscribed sterling silver plaque, casehardened frame, hammer, loading lever and rammer, cased with accessories, limited issue of 1,000 in 1989.
Mfg.'s Sug. Retail $2,450 $2,450 $1,950 $1,500

ROBERT E. LEE MODEL 1851 NAVY — .36 cal. only, reproduction of the 1851 Navy Colt, extensive gold etching, cylinder scene portrays historical Civil War events, walnut stocks with Robert E. Lee medallion, cased with accessories, 41 oz. 2,500 mfg. during 1984.
$2,100 $1,900 $1,450
Issue price is $2,100.

U

Grading	100%	98%	95%	90%	80%	70%	60%

MONITOR AND VIRGINIA MODEL 1851 NAVY REVOLVER — .44 cal., issued to commemorate the Civil War naval battle between the USS Monitor and Confederate Virginia, features gold etchings on barrel, frame, and Monitor/Virginia battle scene on cylinder, cased, 41 oz. 1,000 mfg. in 1991.
Mfg.'s Sug. Retail $1,250 $1,250 $875 $500

STONEWALL JACKSON MODEL 1851 REVOLVER — .36 cal., reproduction of Colt's Model 1851 Navy, elaborate gold etching on frame and barrel, walnut grip with medallion, cased with sterling medallion and silver-plated powder flask. 1988 release. 2,500 total mfg.
Mfg.'s Sug. Retail $2,100 $2,100 $1,650 $1,250

JEFFERSON DAVIS 1851 NAVY REVOLVER — .36 cal., extensive Nimschke style engraving on barrel, loading lever, frame, and trigger, case hardened frame with silver plated brass backstrap and triggerguard, includes engraved, silver plated detachable shoulder stock, cased with accessories, 41 oz. 1,000 mfg. in 1990 only.
Mfg.'s Sug. Retail $2,750 $2,750 $1,850 $1,250

MODEL 1851 U.S. NAVY REVOLVER — .36 cal., 7½ in. octagon barrel, features gold etched cylinder and other embellishments, brass triggerguard and backstrap plated with 24 Kt. gold, 41 oz. 1,000 mfg. in 1988 only.
Mfg.'s Sug. Retail $1,250 $1,250 $875 $500

MODEL 1851 PONY EXPRESS REVOLVER — .36 cal., features gold-plated cylinder scene, other scroll work, and barrel address, walnut grips, cased. 1,000 mfg. beginning 1992.
Mfg.'s Sug. Retail $1,650 $1,650 $1,150 $850

U.S. CAVALRY MODEL 1860 ARMY — .44 cal., reproduction of the Colt Model 1860, stag grips, gold etched cylinder scene, cased with brass buckle. 975 manufactured starting in 1988.
Mfg.'s Sug. Retail $1,450 $1,450 $1,050 $800

FREDERIC REMINGTON MODEL 1860 ARMY REVOLVER — .44 cal., issued to commemorate Frederic Remington's 100th anniversary as an associate of the National Academy of Design, features gold etched barrel, cylinder (with 5 panels), trigger, frame, and gripstraps, cased with accessories, 42 oz. 1,000 mfg. in 1990 only.
Mfg.'s Sug. Retail $1,500 $1,500 $1,000 $775

BUFFALO BILL CENTENNIAL MODEL 1860 ARMY — .44 cal., reproduction of the Colt Model 1860, bonded ivory stocks, extensive gold etchings portraying various wild west scenes, bonded ivory powder flask, brass accessories, cased. 2,500 mfg. 1983.
                                       $1,950 $1,450 $1,100

   Issue price was $1,950.

BAT MASTERSON MODEL 1860 ARMY — .44 cal., original roll engraved pattern on cylinder, walnut grips, blued barrel decorated in 24 Kt. gold. 2,500 mfg. beginning 1991.
Mfg.'s Sug. Retail $1,250 $1,250 $875 $500

GETTYSBURG 1860 ARMY — .44 cal., blued steel with gold-plated cylinder scene, backstraps, and other small parts, walnut grips, cased with belt buckle. 1,863 mfg. beginning 1994.
Mfg.'s Sug. Retail $1,270 $1,270 $885 $500
   Add $145 for case.

SECRET SERVICE MUSEUM EDITION — 500 mfg. starting 1988.
Mfg.'s Sug. Retail $2,750 $2,750 $2,000 $1,600

   ▲ *Secret Service Investigator's Edition* — 1,000 mfg. starting 1988.
   Mfg.'s Sug. Retail $1,250 $1,250 $875 $500

Grading	100%	98%	95%	90%	80%	70%	60%

GEORGE JONES SAA — .45 LC cal., 5½ in. barrel, blued steel with multiple 24 Kt. gold decorations, including musical staff with notes and name on barrel, cased. 950 mfg. beginning 1993.

Mfg.'s Sug. Retail $1,675 $1,675 $1,150 $675

RICHARD PETTY SILVER EDITION SAA — .45 LC cal., 5½ in. barrel, blue steel with silver decoration, hand fitted faux ivory grips, Petty's signature carved on velvet lined cherry display case, comes with signed Richard Petty portrait and numbered to match gun. 1,000 mfg. starting 1992.

Mfg.'s Sug. Retail $1,675 $1,675 $1,150 $825

KING RICHARD HAND ENGRAVED COLT .45 SAA — .45 LC cal., 5½ in. barrel, mfg. by Colt, silver finished with multiple inlays and scroll engraving, scrimshawed ivory grips, cased. 100 mfg. beginning 1993.

Mfg.'s Sug. Retail $4,500 $4,500 $2,950 $1,750

CHARLTON HESTON SAA — .45 LC cal., 5½ in. barrel, blued steel finish with decorative gold and silver vine inlays, walnut grips with medallions. 500 mfg. beginning 1993.

Mfg.'s Sug. Retail $1,850 $1,850 $1,275 $925

HOPALONG CASSIDY COWBOY EDITION SAA — .45 LC cal., 5½ in. barrel, blue steel with silver decorations on cylinder, barrel, and frame, hand fitted genuine black horn grips, velvet lined cherry display case. 950 mfg. starting 1993.

Mfg.'s Sug. Retail $1,675 $1,675 $1,150 $825

HOPALONG PREMIER COLT EDITION SAA — .45 LC, 5½ in. barrel, silver-plated, deep hand engraving, 18 Kt. gold inlays, hand fitted genuine black buffalo horn inset with William Boyd's monogram in sterling silver, gold-embossed leather display case lined in velvet. 100 mfg. starting 1993.

Mfg.'s Sug. Retail $4,500 $4,500 $3,500 $2,450

MEL TORME COLT SAA — .45 LC cal., 5½ in. barrel, elaborate silver engraving with 24 Kt. gold highlights, mother-of-pearl grips, leather display case with Mel Torme's signature in gold. 100 mfg. starting 1992.

Mfg.'s Sug. Retail $4,500 $4,500 $3,500 $2,950

ROY ROGERS COWBOY EDITION SAA — .45 LC cal., SAA revolver, 4¾ in. barrel, features gold-plated cylinder and other 24 Kt. etchings on barrel, frame and gripstrap, hand fitted stag grips, made to commemorate Roy Rogers 50th Anniversary (1940-1990), cased. 2,500 mfg. in 1990 only.

Mfg.'s Sug. Retail $1,350 $1,350 $900 $550

▲ *Roy Premier Edition SAA* — similar to Cowboy Edition, except has elaborate inlays and engraving. 250 mfg. in 1990 only.

Mfg.'s Sug. Retail $4,500 $4,500 $2,950 $1,750

U.S. MARSHALS WYATT EARP SAA — .45 LC cal., 4¾ in. blued barrel, select walnut grips, case hardened frame and hammer, Marshal's etched 24 Kt. badge inset in grip. 2,500 mfg. beginning 1991.

Mfg.'s Sug. Retail $1,250 $1,250 $875 $500

NATIONAL COWBOY HALL OF FAME SAA — .45 LC cal., 4¾ in. barrel, 24 Kt. filigree on barrel and gold symbols of the American cowboy on cylinder, staghorn grips, velvet lined display case with glass lid. 1,000 mfg. beginning 1992.

Mfg.'s Sug. Retail $1,600 $1,600 $1,125 $825

Grading	100%	98%	95%	90%	80%	70%	60%

INTERPOL COLT SAA — .45 LC cal., 4¾ in. barrel, hand engraving based on Kornbrath Interpol Model, silver-plated faux ivory eagle grips, display cased in luxurious leather (designed like a book), 154 mfg. beginning 1991.

Mfg.'s Sug. Retail $4,500 $4,500 $2,950 $1,750

EISENHOWER .45 AUTO PISTOL — .45 ACP cal., 1911 Govt. Model mfg. by Springfield Armory, 7 shot mag., 5 in. barrel, checkered walnut grips inset with 2 bronze medallions, blued steel slide decorated in 24 Kt. gold, Eisenhower's signature etched on velvet-lined walnut display case, comes with framed portrait of D. Eisenhower, signed by his son, John Eisenhower. 1,000 mfg. beginning 1992.

Mfg.'s Sug. Retail $1,675 $1,675 $1,150 $825

"DON'T GIVE UP THE SHIP" MODEL .45 AUTO — .45 ACP cal., 1911 Colt Govt. Model, 7 shot mag., 5 in. barrel, rosewood grips, blue steel decorated with 24 Kt. gold, velvet-lined solid oak case with symbol of U.S. Navy carved into top of lid. 1,997 mfg. starting 1993.

Mfg.'s Sug. Retail $1,485 $1,485 $1,075 $825

AMERICAN EAGLE COLT .45 AUTO — .45 ACP cal., features large eagle with wing spread on sides of slide, other gold small parts, cased. 2,500 mfg. beginning 1993.

Mfg.'s Sug. Retail $1,950 $1,950 $1,375 $975

MINIATURE REVOLVER SERIES

1847 WALKER PRESIDENTIAL EDITION — miniature reproduction of 1847 Colt Walker, color case hardened receiver, all parts operational, sterling silver grips, full coverage engraving, cased. 1,500 mfg. starting 1990.

Mfg.'s Sug. Retail $1,575 $1,575 $1,100 $825

▲ *1847 Walker Classic Edition* — similar to Presidential Edition, except has walnut grips and frame is not engraved, cased. 1,500 mfg. starting 1990.

Mfg.'s Sug. Retail $625 $625 $450 $325

1851 NAVY PRESIDENTIAL EDITION — miniature reproduction of 1851 Navy Colt, color case hardened receiver, all parts operational, mother-of-pearl grips, full coverage engraving, cased. 1,500 mfg. starting 1988.

Mfg.'s Sug. Retail $1,575 $1,575 $1,100 $825

▲ *1851 Classic Edition* — similar to Presidential Edition, except has walnut grips and cylinder is roll-engraved, cased. 3,500 mfg. starting 1986.

Mfg.'s Sug. Retail $525 $525 $400 $295

1860 ARMY PRESIDENTIAL EDITION — miniature reproduction of 1860 Army Colt, color case hardened engraved receiver and barrel, roll-engraved cylinder scene, all parts operational, ivory grips, cherry cased. 1,500 mfg. starting 1988.

Mfg.'s Sug. Retail $1,575 $1,575 $1,200 $875

▲ *1860 Classic Edition* — similar to Presidential Edition without engraving, except has rosewood grips, cased. 3,500 mfg. starting 1988.

Mfg.'s Sug. Retail $525 $525 $400 $295

1861 NAVY PRESIDENTIAL EDITION — miniature reproduction of 1861 Navy Colt, color case hardened engraved receiver and barrel, roll-engraved cylinder scene, all parts operational, includes detachable shoulder stock, cased. 1,500 mfg. starting 1990.

Mfg.'s Sug. Retail $1,500 $1,500 $1,150 $850

Grading	100%	98%	95%	90%	80%	70%	60%

▲ *1861 Navy Classic Edition* — similar to Presidential Edition without engraving, cased. 1,500 mfg. starting 1990.

Mfg.'s Sug. Retail $750 $750 $550 $395

SA ARMY PRESIDENTIAL EDITION — miniature reproduction of 1873 SAA Colt, nickel-plated receiver and barrel with scroll engraving, gold-plated cylinder, hammer, trigger, and ejector rod housing, one piece ivory grips, cherry cased. 1,500 mfg. starting 1988.

Mfg.'s Sug. Retail $1,550 $1,550 $1,100 $825

> This miniature is an exact replica of Serial No. 114 SAA (earliest known gold engraved SAA). All features are the same, only on a miniature basis.

▲ *SA Army Classic Edition* — similar to Presidential Edition without engraving, except has color case hardened receiver and blued metal parts, one piece rosewood grips. 1,500 mfg. starting 1988.

Mfg.'s Sug. Retail $575 $575 $425 $300

> The Classic Edition is miniaturized, exact reproduction of Colt Serial No. 1 (includes pinched frame, slanted barrel address marking, donut ejector rod head, knurled hammer spur, etc.). All are serial numbered 1.

RIFLES

CONFEDERATE COMMEMORATIVE RIFLE — replicates Cook & Brother original 1861 Model Carbine, 1,500 mfg. during 1986, includes wood wall mount and velvet sleeved bag, 24 Kt. gold plating and accenting.

$1,750 $1,450 $995

> Issue price was $1,900.

SHOTGUNS

CHUCK YEAGER SHOTGUN — 12 ga. only, O/U boxlock action with engraved silver finished sideplates depicting Gen. Yeager and his P-51 Mustang, SST, 28 in. VR barrels with choke tubes, cased with accessories. 100 mfg. beginning 1989.

Mfg.'s Sug. Retail $12,500 $12,500 $9,000 $6,250

> This model was mfg. by Bertuzzi located in Brescia, Italy. Over 120 hours were required to engrave each gun.

ARNOLD PALMER SHOTGUN — 20 ga., SxS boxlock with engraved sideplates depicting Arnold Palmer in 24 Kt. gold as well as other inlays, 26 in. barrels, 6 lbs. 6 oz. 100 mfg. beginning 1990.

Mfg.'s Sug. Retail $9,750 $9,750 $6,250 $3,995

CHRISTOPHER COLUMBUS SHOTGUN — 20 ga., O/U boxlock action featuring engraved silver-plated sideplate depicting various scenes in 24 Kt. gold, 25.4 in. barrels with choke tubes, cased with accessories. 200 mfg. beginning 1991.

Mfg.'s Sug. Retail $12,500 $12,500 $9,000 $6,250

UNITED STATES PATENT FIRE ARMS MANUFACTURING COMPANY

Manufacturer located in Hartford, CT (at Colt's original old Armoury) beginning 1995.

Grading	100%	98%	95%	90%	80%	70%	60%

REVOLVERS

SINGLE ACTION ARMY — .22 LR (new 1996), .22 Mag. (new 1996), .357 Mag. (new 1996), .38-40, .44-40, .45 ACP, or .45 LC cal., 3 (no ejector), 4 (no ejector), $4\frac{3}{4}$, $5\frac{1}{2}$, or $7\frac{1}{2}$ in. barrel, original screw cylinder release, choice of Full Dome Blue, Dome Blue/Old Armoury Bone Case, or nickel finish.

Mfg.'s Sug. Retail	$655	$535	$460	$410	$365	$330	$300	$275

    Add $100 for Dome Blue/Old Armoury Bone Case finish.
    Add $162 for nickel finish.
    Subtract $9 for $5\frac{1}{2}$ in. barrel.
    Subtract $30 for 3 in. barrel w/o ejector rod.
    Subtract $21 for 4 in. barrel w/o ejector rod.

  ▲ *Henry Nettleton Cavalry Revolver* — .45 LC cal., faithful Cavalry Model reproduction following the original U.S. Government inspector specifications. New 1995.

Mfg.'s Sug. Retail	$950	$875	$725	$575

UNIVERSAL FIREARMS

Universal Firearms became a division of Iver Johnson's Arms, Inc. in 1982. Formerly imported out of Hialeah, FL. Currently manufactured in Jacksonville, AR.

RIFLES: SEMI-AUTO CARBINE

MODEL 440 VULCAN — .44 Mag. cal., slide action, $18\frac{1}{4}$ in. barrel with adj. rear and front ramp sight, 5 shot detachable mag.

	$325	$275	$230	$195	$175	$150	$135

1000 MILITARY — .30 cal., "G.I." copy, satin blue, birch stock, 18 in. barrel. Disc.

	$229	$180	$170	$160	$150	$135	$125

MODEL 1003 — 16, 18, or 20 in. barrel, .30 M1 copy, blued finish, adj. sight, birch stock, $5\frac{1}{2}$ lbs. Add $45 for 4X scope. See current listing under Iver Johnson. Disc.

	$180	$160	$140	$120	$110	$100	$85

Last Mfg.'s Sug. Retail was $203.

  ▲ *Model 1010* — nickel finish, disc.

	$299	$265	$240	$210	$180	$155	$120

  ▲ *Model 1015* — gold electroplated, disc.

	$325	$275	$250	$215	$185	$160	$130

1005 DELUXE — .30 cal., custom Monte Carlo walnut stock, high polish blue, oil finish on wood.

	$246	$200	$180	$170	$150	$140	$130

1006 STAINLESS — .30 cal., stainless steel construction, birch stock, 18 in. barrel, 6 lbs. Disc.

	$205	$190	$170

Last Mfg.'s Sug. Retail was $234.

1020 TEFLON — .30 cal., Dupont Teflon-S finish on metal parts, black or gray color, Monte Carlo stock.

	$279	$259	$240

1256 "FERRET" — .256 Win. Mag. cal., M1 Action, satin blue, birch stock, 18 in. barrel, $5\frac{1}{2}$ lbs. Disc.

	$200	$175	$165	$155	$145	$135	$125

Last Mfg.'s Sug. Retail was $219.

2200 LEATHERNECK — .22 cal., recoil operated action, birch stock, satin blue, 18 in. barrel, $5\frac{1}{2}$ lbs.

	$240	$190	$180	$170	$160	$145	$135

Grading	100%	98%	95%	90%	80%	70%	60%

MODEL 3000 ENFORCER PISTOL — .30 M1 Carbine cal., walnut stock, 11¼ in. barrel, 17¾ in. overall, 15, and 30 shot. Mfg. 1964-1983. Add $50 for Teflon-S finish. See current listing under Iver Johnson.

	100%	98%	95%	90%	80%	70%	60%
Blued finish	$235	$200	$185	$170	$160	$150	$140
Nickel-plated	$289	$235	$220	$200	$185	$165	$145
Gold-plated	$328	$235	$220	$200	$185	$165	$145
Stainless	$312	$280	$260				

5000 PARATROOPER — .30 cal., metal folding extension, walnut stock, 16 or 18 in. barrel. Disc. See current listing under Iver Johnson.

	100%	98%	95%	90%	80%	70%	60%
	$215	$185	$170	$160	$150	$140	$130

Last Mfg.'s Sug. Retail was $234.

5006 PARATROOPER STAINLESS — similar to 5000, only stainless with 18 in. barrel only. Disc.

	100%	98%	95%
	$255	$235	$205

Last Mfg.'s Sug. Retail was $281.

1981 COMMEMORATIVE CARBINE — .30 cal., "G.I Military" model, cased with accessories. Mfg. for 40th Anniversary 1941-1981.

	100%	98%	95%
	$650	$490	$400

SHOTGUNS

All Universal shotguns were disc. after 1982.

MODEL 7312 O/U — 12 ga., 30 in. full and mod., VR barrel, boxlock, vent. barrel spacer, SST, auto ejectors, barrels ported to reduce recoil, engraved, color case hardened receiver, trap or skeet style, checkered select stock.

100%	98%	95%	90%	80%	70%	60%
$1,650	$1,540	$1,485	$1,430	$1,320	$1,210	$1,045

MODEL 7412 O/U — similar to 7312, without ejectors, blue and silver receiver.

100%	98%	95%	90%	80%	70%	60%
$1,430	$1,210	$1,155	$1,100	$9,900	$880	$825

MODEL 7712 O/U — 12 ga., 26 or 28 in. barrel, VR, non-selective single trigger, extractors, light engraving, checkered pistol grip stock.

100%	98%	95%	90%	80%	70%	60%
$440	$415	$385	$360	$330	$275	$220

MODEL 7812 O/U — similar to 7712, with auto ejectors and more engraving.

100%	98%	95%	90%	80%	70%	60%
$605	$580	$550	$525	$470	$415	$385

MODEL 7912 O/U — similar to 7812, with selective single trigger and gold damascene engraving.

100%	98%	95%	90%	80%	70%	60%
$1,210	$1,155	$1,100	$1,045	$965	$880	$825

MODEL 7112 DOUBLE BARREL — 12 ga., 26 or 28 in. barrels, various chokes, boxlock, extractors, engraved case hardened frame, checkered pistol grip stock.

100%	98%	95%	90%	80%	70%	60%
$330	$305	$275	$250	$195	$165	$140

DOUBLE WING — 10, 12, 20, or .410 ga., 26, 28, or 30 in. barrels, various chokes, double triggers, boxlock, extractors, checkered pistol grip stock.

	100%	98%	95%	90%	80%	70%	60%
	$330	$305	$275	$250	$195	$165	$140
10 gauge.	$385	$360	$330	$305	$250	$220	$165

MODEL 7212 SINGLE BARREL TRAP — 12 ga., 30 in. full, Simmons type VR, engraved case colored frame, vent. barrel to reduce recoil, boxlock, auto ejector, select checkered trap style stock.

100%	98%	95%	90%	80%	70%	60%
$1,100	$990	$935	$880	$770	$715	$605

U.S. MILITARY

See listings under Colt, Springfield Armory, and Winchester. U.S. Military Trench and Riot guns may be found under the "Trench/Riot Shotguns" category in the T section of this text.

U.S. M1 CARBINE
Various makers.

Grading	100%	98%	95%	90%	80%	70%	60%

U.S. M1 CARBINE (MILITARY & COMMERCIAL) — semi-auto, .30 cal., 18 in. barrel, 15 or 30 shot box mag., wood stocked, two or four position aperture rear, blade front sight with protective ears, with or without bayonet lug. This weapon was designed by Winchester for the U.S. government, over 6 million were produced by 10 different companies. It is a gas operated lightweight carbine that was also used by other countries' armed forces. Makers and values as follows. Values are for original, unmodified carbines, with proper parts makers and stock cartouches. Some variations have the type III barrel band.

Values below are for original mfg. only, not recent imports (usually denoted by visible import markings and/or alterations to original finish).
Subtract 30% for original finish guns that have been changed back to the original configuration by switching parts.
Subtract 50% for modified guns with adj. sight and bayonet lug.

	100%	98%	95%	90%	80%	70%	60%
Underwood	$775	$625	$495	$400	$350	$300	$275
S.G. Saginaw	$750	$600	$475	$400	$350	$300	$275
Quality Hardware	$775	$625	$495	$415	$370	$325	$295
Nat'l Postal Meter	$850	$715	$525	$425	$375	$325	$295
IBM	$850	$715	$525	$425	$370	$325	$295
Standard Products	$750	$600	$495	$415	$370	$325	$295
Inland (round or square butt)	$775	$625	$495	$415	$370	$325	$295
SG Grand Rapids	$850	$715	$525	$425	$375	$325	$295
Winchester	$995	$875	$695	$525	$425	$350	$325
Irwin Pedersen	$1,500	$1,275	$975	$850	$775	$675	$580
Rockola	$925	$875	$675	$525	$425	$350	$325
Plainfield (Commercial only)	$195	$175	$160	$150	$140	$130	$120

M1 A1 PARATROOPER CARBINE — .30 cal., mfg. by Inland — WWII production, folding stock, crossed cannon proofed on bottom, 110,000 mfg. between 1942-1945. Stock folds to 26½ in. overall.

	100%	98%	95%	90%	80%	70%	60%
	$1,295	$950	$675	$500	$400	$350	$300

M1 GARAND — .30-06 cal., semi-auto, 8 shot en bloc clip fed, gas operated, adj. aperture sight, wooden stock. Made 1937-1957 by Springfield, Winchester, H&R, and International Harvester. Add 10% for WWII date, deduct 40% if rewelded, 20% if mismatched.

	100%	98%	95%	90%	80%	70%	60%
	$750	$635	$525	$475	$430	$400	$375

Add 100% for pre-WWII Winchester or Springfield mfg.

▲ *M1-C or M1-D Sniper* — with scope and mounts (be wary of fakes and rewelds).

	100%	98%	95%	90%	80%	70%	60%
M1-D	$1,650	$1,455	$1,200	$1,060	$900	$780	$650
M1-C	$2,450	$2,000	$1,850	$1,400	$1,100	$800	$700

M1 NATIONAL MATCH — target version of the Garand, using National Match barrel and sights, glass bedding, etc. Should have serialized N.M. paperwork for premium.

	100%	98%	95%	90%	80%	70%	60%
	$1,850	$1,475	$1,175	$950	$750	$525	$460

U.S. MODEL 1917 ENFIELD RIFLE — .30-06 cal., bolt action, 5 shot, 26 in. barrel, adj. sights, military stock, derived from English P14 Enfield, over two million produced in 1917 and 1918.

	100%	98%	95%	90%	80%	70%	60%
	$495	$450	$400	$350	$300	$275	$250

This model was manufactured primarily by Remington at the Eddystone plant in Eddystone, PA (Eddystone marked), the Ilion Remington plant, and by Winchester in New Haven, CT.

UZI

Manufactured by Israel Military Industries (IMI). Previously imported by Action Arms, Ltd., located in Philadelphia, PA until 1994.

Serial number prefixes used on Uzi Firearms are as follows: "SA" on all 9mm Para. semi-auto carbines Models A and B; "45 SA" on all .45 ACP Model B carbines; "41 SA" on all .41 AE Model B carbines; "MC" on all 9mm (only cal. made) semi-auto mini-carbines; "UP" on all 9mm Para. semi-auto Uzi pistols; "45 UP" on all .45 semi-auto Uzi pistols (disc. 1989). There are also prototypes or experimental Uzis with either "AA" or "AAL" prefixes - these are rare and will command premiums over values listed below.

Grading	100%	98%	95%	90%	80%	70%	60%

CARBINES: SEMI-AUTO

CARBINE MODEL A — 9mm Para., semi-auto, 16.1 in. barrel, parkerized finish, 25 shot mag., mfg. by IMI 1980-1983 and ser. range is SA01,001-SA037,000.

	$950	$825	$725	$650	$600	$550	$500

Approx. 100 Model As were mfg. with a nickel finish. These are rare and command considerable premiums over values listed above.

CARBINE MODEL B — 9mm, .41 Action Express (new 1987), or .45 ACP (new 1987) cal., semi-auto carbine, 16.1 in. barrel, baked enamel black finish over phosphated (parkerized) base finish, 16 (.45 ACP), 20 (.41 AE) or 25 (9mm Para.) shot mag., metal folding stock, includes molded case and carrying sling, 8.4 lbs. Mfg. 1983 - until Federal legislation disc. importation 1989 and ser. range is 037,001-SA073,544.

	$975	$875	$775	$675	$600	$550	$500

Last Mfg.'s Sug. Retail was $698.

Add $150 for .22 cal. conversion kit (new 1987).
Add $215 for .45 ACP to 9mm/.41 AE conversion kit.
Add $150 for 9mm to .41 AE (or vice-versa) conversion kit.
Add $215 for 9mm to .45 ACP conversion kit.

MINI CARBINE — 9mm Para. cal., similar to Carbine except has 19¾ in. barrel, 20 shot mag., swing-away metal stock, scaled down version of the regular carbine, 7.2 lbs. New 1987. Federal legislation disc. importation 1989.

	$2,250	$2,000	$1,775	$1,525	1,300	$1,100	$995

Last Mfg.'s Sug. Retail was $698.

PISTOLS: SEMI-AUTO

PISTOL — 9mm or .45 ACP cal. (disc.), semi-auto pistol, 4½ in. barrel, parkerized finish, 10 (.45 ACP) or 20 (9mm Para.) shot mag., supplied with molded carrying case, sight adj. key and mag. loading tool, 3.8 lbs. Importation disc. 1993.

	$975	$850	$795	$750	$700	$650	$600

Last Mfg.'s Sug. Retail was $695.

Add $285 for .45 ACP to 9mm/.41 AE conversion kit.
Add $100 for 9mm to .41 AE conversion kit.

U

U

V section

VALMET, INC.

Manufacturer located in Jyvaskyla, Finland. Previously imported by Stoeger Industries, Inc. located in South Hackensack, NJ.

The Valmet line was discontinued in 1989 and replaced by Tikka (please refer to the Tikka section in this text) in 1990.

Grading	100%	98%	95%	90%	80%	70%	60%

RIFLES

HUNTER MODEL — .223, .243, or .308 cal., gas operated semi-auto, Kalashnikov action, 20½ in. barrel, checkered walnut stock and forearm, matte finished metal, 5, 9, or 20 shot mag., 8 lbs. New 1986, Federal legislation disc. importation 1989.

	$795	$700	$625	$550	$500	$450	$420

Last Mfg.'s Sug. Retail was $795.

MODEL 76 — .223, 7.62x39mm, or .308 cal., gas operated semi-auto paramilitary design rifle, 16¾ in. or 20½ (.308 only) in. barrel, 15 or 30 (7.62x39mm only) shot mag., parkerized finish. Federal legislation disc. importation 1989.

	$750	$675	$600	$525	$475	$450	$420

Last Mfg.'s Sug. Retail was $740.

Add $95-$125 for synthetic or folding stock.

M-62S PARAMILITARY DESIGN RIFLE — semi-auto version of Finn M-62, 7.62x39 Russian, 15 or 30 shot mag., 16⅝ in. barrel, gas operated, rotary bolt, adj. rear sight, tube steel or wood stock. Mfg. 1962-disc.

	$1,395	$1,175	$975	$800	$700	$600	$550

Add $50 for wood stock.

M-71S — similar to M-62S, except .223 cal., reinforced resin or wood stock.

	$1,250	$1,100	$925	$750	$650	$550	$495

Add $50 for wood stock.

MODEL 76 — .223 Rem., .308 Win., or 7.62x39mm (rare) cal., paramilitary design, fixed wood or folding stock, sling, disc.

	$1,395	$1,175	$975	$800	$700	$600	$550

MODEL 78 — .308 Win. cal. only, similar to Model 76, except has 24½ in. barrel, wood stock and forearm, and barrel bipod, 11 lbs. New 1987. Federal legislation disc. importation 1989.

	$1,575	$1,325	$1,050	$850	$750	$650	$550

Last Mfg.'s Sug. Retail was $1,060.

MODEL 82 BULLPUP — .223 Rem. cal., limited importation, disc.

	$1,895	$1,625	$1,400	$1,200	$1,000	$825	$700

SHOTGUNS: O/U, DISC.

LION O/U SHOTGUN — 12 ga., 26, 28, or 30 in. barrels, various chokes, boxlock, SST, checkered stock. Mfg. 1947-1968.

	$415	$370	$340	$320	$305	$275	$240

Grading	100%	98%	95%	90%	80%	70%	60%

MODEL 412 O/U SHOOTING SYSTEM — interchangeable barrel assemblies permit a double rifle, shotgun/rifle, and O&U shotgun configuration, user installed interchangeable barrels, monobloc locking, rifle barrel positioning by adjustment, SST, extractors or ejectors, checkered walnut stock and forend, cocking indicators, blued finish. Importation on all models was disc. 1989.

> Add $100 for synthetic stock on all 412 models.

▲ *Model 412S Field Grade* — 12 ga. only, auto ejectors, screw-in choke tubes, matte nickel finish. Imported 1986-89.

	$855	$670	$580	$540	$475	$440	$400

Last Mfg.'s Sug. Retail was $999.

▲ *Model 412S Field and Target* — 12 ga. only, 2¾ and 3 in. chambers, ejectors. Disc. 1988.

	$775	$660	$580	$540	$475	$440	$400

Last Mfg.'s Sug. Retail was $874.

▲ *Model 412ST Trap and Skeet* — 12 ga., Monte Carlo stock on Trap model, 28 in. barrels on Skeet model, screw-in chokes standard.

	$1,040	$875	$695	$650	$580	$540	$475

Last Mfg.'s Sug. Retail was $1,215.

▲ *Model 412ST Premium Grade Target* — similar to Model 412ST Trap and Skeet, except has better walnut and checkering. Imported 1987-89.

	$1,355	$1,050	$865	$750	$640	$580	$515

Last Mfg.'s Sug. Retail was $1,550.

▲ *Model 412S Combination Gun* — combination, 12 ga, 3 in. chamber over choice of .222, .223, .243, .30-06, or .308 cal., extractors.

	$1,025	$850	$675	$600	$550	$475	$440

Last Mfg.'s Sug. Retail was $1,615.

▲ *Model 412S Double Rifle* — .243 (disc. 1987), .30-06, .308 (disc. 1987), .375 H&H (disc. 1987), or 9.3x73R cal., extractors, 24 in. barrels.

	$1,060	$895	$725	$650	$580	$540	$475

Last Mfg.'s Sug. Retail was $1,275.

> Add $100 for 9.3x74R cal. or .375 H&H cal.
> This model in .30-06 cal. has extractors only while in 9.3x74R cal. ejectors are standard.

▲ *Model 412K Double Rifle* — .30-06 or .308 cal. only, 24 in. separated barrels, extractors. Importation disc. 1986.

	$800	$660	$580	$540	$475	$440	$400

Last Mfg.'s Sug. Retail was $899.

▲ *Model 412 Engraved* — satin finish, receiver extensively bank note engraved in choice of 4 patterns, select Triple-X wood hand-checkered — choice of field or target, available in any Valmet model. Add $85 for shotgun rifle, $320 for double rifle.

> This model has limited availability and prices are on request from the manufacturer. Last Mfg.'s Sug. retail was $2,499.

▲ *Extra Barrel Assemblies (Model 412 O/U)* — $505 - $605 each for shotgun (includes screw-in chokes), $579 each for shotgun/rifle combo, $660 each for double rifle (add $100 for ejectors).

VALTRO

Manufacturer located in Brescia, Italy since 1988. Limited importation by American Arms located in N. Kansas City, MO.

Valtro manufactures a security slide action shotgun in addition to a variety of signal pistols. Please contact the importer or factory (see Trademark Index listings) directly for current pricing and more information.

VARBERGER

Rifle manufacturer located in Sweden. No current importer. Previously imported and distributed by the Paul & Associates, located in Wellsville, KS until late 1995.

Grading	100%	98%	95%	90%	80%	70%	60%

RIFLES: BOLT ACTION

MSRs listed below reflect the most recent retail prices - Varberger does not have any importation currently.

MODEL 711 GRADE 1 — available in 19 cals. between .22 PPC and .358 Norma, bolt action design featuring specially designed and manufactured receiver, rotary mag., 6 lug engine-turned bolt, and stock featuring metal retainer plate, individually test fired. Importation began 1994.

Mfg.'s Sug. Retail	$1,080	$950	$850	$750	$650	$550	$450	$375

MODEL 717 GRADE 1 MAGNUM — availabe in 11 Mag. cals. between .257 Wby. Mag. and .375 H&H. Importation began 1994.

Mfg.'s Sug. Retail	$1,130	$980	$875	$765	$650	$550	$450	$375

MODEL 757 GRADE 2 DELUXE — deluxe variation of the Model 711. Importation began 1994.

Mfg.'s Sug. Retail	$2,035	$1,775	$1,500	$1,250	$995	$895	$795	$695

Add $45 for Mag. cals.

MODEL 77 GRADE 3 PREMIER — top-of-the-line model. Importation began 1994.

Mfg.'s Sug. Retail	$2,375	$1,995	$1,675	$1,350	$1,050	$925	$795	$695

Add $65 for Mag. cals.

VARNER SPORTING ARMS, INC.

Manufacturer previously located in Marietta, GA until approximately 1989.

VARNER FAVORITE HUNTER — .22 LR cal., patterned after J. Stevens Favorite Model, ½ round - ½ octagon 21½ in. takedown barrel, blued frame, walnut stock and forearm, aperture rear sight, 5 lbs. Mfg. 1988-89.

	$325	$270	$220	$185	$150	$130	$110

Last Mfg.'s Sug. Retail was $369.

▲ *Hunter Deluxe* — similar to Favorite Hunter, except has case colored frame and lever, and deluxe walnut. Mfg. 1988-89.

	$450	$375	$285	$225	$175	$150	$135

Last Mfg.'s Sug. Retail was $500.

▲ *Presentation Grade* — includes target hammer and trigger, AAA quality checkered stock and forearm, includes takedown case. Mfg. 1988-89.

	$480	$400	$310	$250	$195	$170	$155

Last Mfg.'s Sug. Retail was $569.

PRESENTATION ENGRAVED — previously available in a No. 1 Grade for $649, a No. 2 for $779, or a No. 3 for $1,099.

VEKTOR

Handgun manufacturer located in South Africa.

Currently, Vektor has no importation into the U.S.

VERNEY-CARRON

Long gun manufacturer located in St. Etienne, France since 1820. No current importer for the U.S. Please contact the factory directly for more information regarding these firearms (see Trademark Index).

Verney-Carron manufactures a wide variety of quality bolt-action rifles, double rifles, O/U shotguns (boxlock action, with or without sideplates), SxS shotguns (boxlock action), semi-auto shotguns, and slide action shotguns.

VICKERS LIMITED

Manufacturer located in Crayford/Kent, England.

Grading	100%	98%	95%	90%	80%	70%	60%

JUBILEE SINGLE SHOT TARGET RIFLE — Martini type action, .22 LR cal., 28 in. heavy barrel, target sights, one piece pistol grip, target stock, pre-WWII.

	100%	98%	95%	90%	80%	70%	60%
	$440	$330	$305	$275	$250	$220	$165

EMPIRE MODEL — similar to Jubilee, with 27 or 30 in. barrel, straight grip stock.

	100%	98%	95%	90%	80%	70%	60%
	$415	$310	$285	$260	$220	$195	$150

VICTORY ARMS CO. LIMITED

Previously manufactured in prototype format only by Modern Manufacturing Company located in Phoenix, AZ.

PISTOL: SEMI-AUTO

MODEL MC5 — while a few prototypes were mfg. for trade shows (circa 1991-92), this model was never commercially manufactured. Last advertised retail was $465.

VIERLINGS

Four Barrel Long Arm Configuration mostly mfg. previously in Germany or Austria.

This configuration of long arm has four barrels, typically with a .22 caliber barrel incorporated in the center rib or stacked below two SxS shotgun barrels and a lower, larger caliber rifle barrel. Vierlings typically have two triggers, both single set. Barrel selectors are usually on the top tang. This unusual configuration is mostly of German mfg., although there are a few Austrian specimens also (the gunmakers of Ferlach still custom make this model). All Vierlings are mfg. one at a time, with fabrication being very complicated, lengthy, and expensive. As a result, every Vierling must be appraised individually - most specimens, however, are priced approx. $3,500 - $7,500.

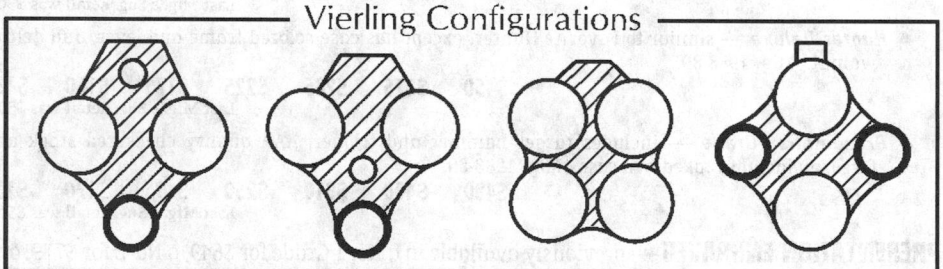

Vierling Configurations

VIRGINIAN

This trademark can be located under the Interarms section in this text.

VIS

F.B. Radom arsenal in Radom, Poland. Please refer to the Radom section in this text.

VOERE

Manufacturer located in Kufstein, Austria since 1965. No current importer. Previously imported by JagerSport, Ltd. located in Cranston, RI 1993-95. Mandall Shooting Supplies located in Scottsdale, AZ also retails the Voere line. To date, Voere has had little distribution in the U.S. Rahn Gun Works, Inc. located in Hastings, MI has imported this trademark on a limited basis in the past.

Grading	100%	98%	95%	90%	80%	70%	60%

Voere of Austria has nothing to do with the Voere trademark of Germany that was taken over by Mauser-Werke after going bankrupt.

Voere manufactures a complete line of quality rimfire semi-auto and centerfire bolt-action/semi-auto rifles. Their new caseless ammunition released in 1991 is a bold step and will have to hold up to the performance and reliability of its cased relatives. More information on this trademark can be obtained by writing/FAXing the factory directly (see Trademark Index for information).

RIFLES

While Voere rifles are currently not imported, MSRs listed below reflect the most recent pricing information.

MODEL VEC 91 BOLT ACTION — 5.7x26 UCC caseless ammo, unique ignition system requires electrical impulse to activate semi-conducting primer that ignites propellant (2 small batteries are housed in the pistol grip capable of igniting 5,000 shots), 5 shot detachable mag., 20 in. free floating barrel, twin forward locking lugs, 2-stage electrical trigger adj. from ½ oz. to 7 lbs, 55 grain bullet achieves 3,300 fps with no loss in accuracy over normal mechanical primer ignited cartridges, 6 lbs. New late 1992.

Mfg.'s Sug. Retail	$2,895		$2,525	$2,050	$1,850	$1,500	$1,225	$1,100	$995

MODEL 2185 MATCH SEMI-AUTO — .308 Win. cal., gas operated, free floating barrel, 3 or 5 shot detachable mag., manual safety, iron sights, laminate wood, 11 lbs.

Mfg.'s Sug. Retail	$3,995		$3,600	$3,175	$2,825	$2,500	$2,175	$1,800	$1,525

Add $1,000 for position style rifle (includes adj. cheekpiece, buttplate, and bottom sling rail, and Voere special scope base).

Other calibers are available on special order only.

MODEL 2185 HUNTING RIFLE — 9.3x62mm, other cals. available upon special request, checkered stock and forend, iron sights.

Mfg.'s Sug. Retail	$1,995		$1,775	$1,500	$1,350	$1,200	$1,050	$900	$700

Add $50 for Mannlicher full stock with 20 in. carbine barrel.

K-98 MAUSER — .243 Win., .270 Win., or .30-06 cal., 20 in. barrel, tang safety, no sights.

Mfg.'s Sug. Retail	$995		$875	$750	$625	$500	$400	$350	$300

Add $80 for Mag. cals. (7mm Rem. Mag. or .300 Win. Mag.).

▲ **K-98 Mauser Deluxe** — same cals. as K-98 Mauser, European traditional style bolt action, 22 in. barrel, detachable 5 shot mag., hand-checkered deluxe walnut.

Mfg.'s Sug. Retail	$1,495		$1,325	$1,100	$950	$825	$700	$600	$500

Add $50 for Mag. cals. (24 in. barrel).

AMERICAN CUSTOM CLASSIC K-98 MAUSER — .22-250 Rem., .243 Win., .270 Win., 7x57mm, 7x64mm, .30-06, or .308 Win. cal., 3 position safety, hinged floorplate, deluxe walnut with hand-rubbed oil finish and checkering.

Mfg.'s Sug. Retail	$1,795		$1,575	$1,450	$1,300	$1,150	$995	$850	$675

Add $50 for Mag. cals. (.300 Win. Mag., .338 Win. Mag., 7mm Rem. Mag., or 9.3x64mm).
Add $100 for .375 H&H or .458 Win. Mag. cal.

.22 SEMI-AUTO — .22 LR cal., open (disc.) or closed bolt design, 10 shot clip mag., checkered hardwood stock, adj. rear sight and trigger.

Mfg.'s Sug. Retail	$645		$585	$535	$460	$400	$350	$300	$250

Add $50 for Deluxe Model.

VOLUNTEER ENTERPRISES
Previous manufacturer located in Knoxville, TN.

Volunteer Enterprises became Commando Arms after 1978.

Grading	100%	98%	95%	90%	80%	70%	60%

COMMANDO MARK III CARBINE — semi-auto, blowback action, .45 ACP cal., 16½ in. barrel, aperture sight, stock styled after "Tommy Gun". Mfg. 1969-1976.

	$425	$365	$315	$280	$225	$195	$160

COMMANDO MARK III CARBINE
Vertical grip

	$440	$365	$320	$280	$225	$195	$160

COMMANDO MARK 9 — similar to Mark III in 9mm.

	$440	$375	$325	$285	$230	$195	$160
Vertical grip	$440	$365	$320	$280	$225	$195	$160

VOUZELAUD

Previous manufacturer located in France. Previously imported by Waverly Arms Co. located in Suffolk, VA.

SHOTGUNS: SxS

MODEL 315 E — 12, 16 or 20 ga., boxlock, 28 in. barrels, auto ejectors, straight grip French walnut stock, double triggers, case colored receiver, light engraving. Importation disc. 1987.

> Values generally range between $1,350-$2,000 for this model.

MODEL 315 EL — similar to Model 315 E, except has satin finish receiver engraved with bouquets of fine English scroll work, triggerguard and forearm also engraved. Importation disc. 1987.

> Values generally range between $1,475-$2,250 for this model.
>
> This model was also available by special order in 28 or .410 ga. (Model 315 EL-S) - add $600.

MODEL 315 EGL — 12, 16 or 20 ga., sidelock, 28 in. barrels, selective ejectors, double triggers, extensive scroll engraving on coin finish receiver, English style stock of extra fancy French walnut. Importation disc. 1987.

> Values generally range between $1,750-$2,750 for this model.

MODEL 315 EGL-S — same general features as the Model 315 EGL, except monobloc barrel construction, extensive game scene engraving, and grand deluxe walnut stock and forearm with extra fine hand-checkering. Importation disc. 1987.

> Values generally range between $1,950-$2,950 for this model.
>
> Last Mfg.'s Sug. Retail was $5,895.

W section

WAFFEN VERATSCHNIG
Manufacturer located in Ferlach, Austria.

Waffen Veratschnig manufactures a variety of high grade, made to individual special order, rifles, shotguns, combination guns, drillings, and vierlings. A wide variety of engraving scenes, wood carvings, and other special features are available at extra cost. Currently, they do not have a U.S. importer and for more information, please contact them directly (see Trademark Index).

Grading	100%	98%	95%	90%	80%	70%	60%

WALTHER
Previously manufactured in Zella-Mehlis (now Suhl, Germany) 1886 to 1945. Current production is in Ulm, Germany, 1953 to date. Currently imported and distributed by Interarms located in Alexandria, VA. Walther target pistols are currently being imported by Nygord Precision Products located in Prescott, AZ and Champions Choice located in La Vergne, TN.

The calibers listed in the Walther Pistol sections are listed in American caliber designations. The German metric conversion is as follows: .22 LR - same, .25 ACP - 6.35mm, .32 ACP - 7.65mm, .380 ACP - 9mm Kurz. The metric caliber designations in most cases will be indicated on the left slide legend for German mfg. pistols listed in the Walther section.

SEMI-AUTO PISTOLS, PRE-WAR

MODEL 1 — .25 ACP, 2.1 in. barrel, fixed sights, blue, checkered hard rubber grips, pre-WWI. Mfg. 1908.

	100%	98%	95%	90%	80%	70%	60%
	$550	$400	$350	$250	$200	$150	$125

MODEL 2 — .25 ACP, 2.1 in. barrel, fixed sights, blue, rubber grips, pop-up rear sight on early models, fixed on late models. Mfg. 1909.

	100%	98%	95%	90%	80%	70%	60%
	$425	$390	$325	$225	$175	$120	$100

This model can usually be distinguished by its knurled barrel ring.

▲ **Early Model** — differentiated by its pop-up rear sight.

	100%	98%	95%	90%	80%	70%	60%
	$1,350	$950	$875	$750	$675	$550	$400

MODEL 3 — .32 ACP, 2.6 in. barrel, blue, fixed sights, rubber grips, ejection port on left side. Mfg. 1910.

	100%	98%	95%	90%	80%	70%	60%
	$1,500	$1,250	$1,100	$800	$550	$500	$400

MODEL 4 — .32 ACP, 8 shot, 3½ in. barrel, blue, rubber grips, ejection port on left side. Mfg. 1910-1918.

	100%	98%	95%	90%	80%	70%	60%
	$375	$300	$250	$200	$125	$100	$80

Add 10% for WWI "Eagle" proofs.

MODEL 5 — better quality version of Model 2, fixed rear sight. Mfg. 1913.

	100%	98%	95%	90%	80%	70%	60%
	$350	$325	$275	$200	$145	$115	$100

MODEL 6 — 9mm Para., 4¾ in. barrel, blue, hard rubber grips, ejection port on right side. Mfg. 1915-1917. Some are Imperial proofed.

	100%	98%	95%	90%	80%	70%	60%
	$5,500	$4,500	$3,000	$2,300	$1,500	$1,050	$800

Grading	100%	98%	95%	90%	80%	70%	60%

MODEL 7 — .25 ACP, 3 in. barrel, blue, fixed sights, rubber grips, ejector port on right side. Mfg. 1917-1918.

	$625	$475	$425	$350	$250	$200	$125

MODEL 8 — .25 ACP, 2⅞ in. barrel, blue, fixed sights, plastic grips. Mfg. 1920-1945.

	$450	$400	$350	$265	$200	$150	$125

Add 10% for "Eagle N" proofing.
Add 25% for engraved slide.

MODEL 9 VEST POCKET — .25 ACP, engineering revision of Model 1, 2 in. barrel, blued finish standard, upward ejection, 6 shot bottom release mag., fixed sights, black checkered plastic grips with oval medallions, safety lever on left frame side behind trigger, 9 oz. Mfg. 1921-1945.

	$475	$425	$350	$275	$200	$160	$140

Add 40% for engraved slide, 20% for nickel.
Add 10% for "Allen" proofing.

MODEL PP DOUBLE ACTION AUTOMATIC "POLICE PISTOL" — .22 LR, .25 ACP, .32 ACP, or .380 ACP cal., 3⅞ in. barrel, blue, fixed sights, plastic grips. Mfg. 1929-1945. Crown N proof until 1939. Eagle N Nazi commercial proof until 1945.

	100%	98%	95%	90%	80%	70%	60%
.22 LR cal.	$895	$800	$700	$600	$525	$450	$375
.25 ACP cal.	$3,450	$3,100	$2,650	$2,000	$1,500	$1,200	$1,000
.32 ACP cal.	$450	$395	$375	$350	$275	$225	$200
.380 ACP cal.	$895	$825	$750	$675	$600	$550	$500

Add 15% for alloy frame.

Original nickel finished Model PPs are very rare; this precludes accurate price evaluation.

Values above assume original guns without import markings. Recently imported WWII/surplus Police used guns are stamped on the frame or receiver, indicating the current importer and address - deduct 20%-30% from values listed above for these recent imports.

▲ **.32 ACP Bottom Release Magazine** — 90 degree safety.

	$800	$700	$625	$600	$525	$425	$395

▲ **.380 ACP Bottom Release Magazine** — 90 degree safety.

	$1,050	$950	$875	$800	$700	$600	$500

▲ **Pre-War Persian proofed** — 9mm Kurz BMR.

	$2,000	$1,800	$1,600	$1,450	$1,250	$995	$825

▲ **Pre-War Verchromt .32 ACP cal.** — add 50% for .380 ACP cal.

	$1,450	$1,250	$800	$750	$675	$485	$395

▲ **Pre-War Stoeger** — .32 ACP cal. only.

	$1,200	$1,050	$925	$800	$600	$425	$325

▲ **Nairobi** — Chas. Heyer.

	$1,200	$1,000	$850	$725	$575	$400	$300

▲ **Aluminum frame** — 90 degree safety.

	$650	$600	$500	$400	$275	$235	$200

▲ **Allemagne** — French Comm.

	$1,050	$950	$825	$720	$600	$425	$325

MODEL PP WARTIME PRODUCTION — mfg. 1940-1945, "Eagle N" Proof (Nazi commercial nitro proof after April 1940) or "Crown N" (German commercial proof mark used to April, 1940) found on pre-WWII military production. Variations are listed either by proof marks or frame/slide markings.

Grading	100%	98%	95%	90%	80%	70%	60%

▲ **"Waffenamt" Proofed** — .32 ACP or .380 ACP cal., "Eagle N", military acceptance marking.

.32 ACP cal.	$525	$425	$375	$300	$250	$220	$200
.380 ACP cal.	$850	$750	$675	$600	$550	$500	$450

> Original nickel finished Model PPs are very rare; this precludes accurate price evaluation.
> Late war PPs are sometimes encountered with Walther marked walnut grips - add 20% if Waffenamt proofed.

▲ **Eagle N Proofed** — .22 LR or .32 ACP cal., with lanyard loop.

.32 ACP cal.	$475	$425	$375	$300	$250	$200	$150
.22 LR cal.	$775	$725	$650	$550	$495	$450	$395

> Add 25% to .32 ACP cal., Waffenamt proofed PP's that are hi-gloss finish (all .380's are hi-gloss).
> The .380 ACP cal. has the bottom mag. release.
> After WWII the French added a lanyard to the left side of the grip. Deduct 25% for this alteration.

▲ **Eagle C & F Marked (Nazi Police)** — .32 ACP cal., "Eagle N or C" proofed on left side of frame.

	100%	98%	95%	90%	80%	70%	60%
	$700	$650	$600	$500	$450	$380	$300

> Add 50% if Eagle C marked. All are hi-gloss early productions.

▲ **RFV Marked** — .32 ACP cal., "Crown N". Mfg. for Reich Finance Administration.

	$700	$650	$600	$500	$400	$325	$225

▲ **RJ Marked** — .32 ACP cal., "Crown N". Mfg. for Reich Justice Ministry.

	$750	$675	$600	$525	$450	$325	$225

▲ **SA Marked** — .22 LR or .32 ACP cal., "Crown N". Mfg. for SA (Sturm Abteilung - storm troops) of the Nazi party.

	$1,450	$1,350	$1,050	$925	$725	$600	$425

> Add 10% for .22 LR.
> Rare SA markings may bring as much as 50% more over values listed above.

▲ **NSKK Marked** — .32 ACP cal., "Crown N or Eagle N" proofed. Mfg. for Nazi Party Transport Corps, rare.

	$2,500	$2,000	$1,500	$1,025	$875	$700	$550

▲ **RRZ proofed** — .32 ACP cal., "Reich Rundfunk Zenhale", for German Radio Broadcasting - only 3 known.

	$3,500	$3,000	$2,500	

▲ **PDM Marked** — .32 ACP cal., "Crown N", Munich Police Department, all have bottom mag. release.

	$850	$775	$700	$625	$525	$450	$360

▲ **AC Marked** — .32 ACP cal., replaced Walther Banner during 1945, "Eagle N".

	$300	$275	$250	$225	$175	$150	$125

> Some are mismatched (assembled at factory by GI's after the factory was captured)

▲ **Czech. Contract** — stamped Rampant Lion.

	$950	$850	$825	$700	$600	$500	$400

▲ **Panagraphed**

	$825	$750	$695	$630	$550	$385	$275

▲ **Danish Rplt.**

	$975	$925	$825	$775	$700	$625	$400

MODEL PP LIGHTWEIGHT — aluminum alloy version.

> Add 20% to Standard Model prices.
> Add 20%-40% for original nickel finish (very rare).
> Add 25% for early hi-gloss finish.

Grading	100%	98%	95%	90%	80%	70%	60%

MODEL PPK PRE-WAR PRODUCTION — .22 LR, .25 ACP, .32 ACP, or .380 ACP cal., PPK designates Police Pistol Kriminal, 3¼ in. barrel, blue, fixed sights, plastic grips. Mfg. 1931-1940.

.22 LR cal.	$1,250	$925	$750	$700	$650	$525	$400
.25 ACP cal.	$5,000	$4,475	$3,800	$3,400	$2,800	$2,100	$1,475
.32 ACP cal.	$550	$500	$425	$350	$300	$250	$225
.380 ACP cal.	$2,000	$1,725	$1,500	$1,100	$800	$600	$500

Add 60% for bottom release Mag (.32 ACP cal.).

MODEL PPK WARTIME PRODUCTION — mfg. 1940-1945, "Eagle N" proofed after April 1940, "Crown N" proofs appear on pre-1940 production with frame/slide markings. Variations are listed either by proof marks, frame/slide markings, or type of finish.

▲ *Commercial "Eagle N" Proofed* — .22 LR, .32 ACP, or .380 ACP cal., Nazi Eagle over N (standard Nazi commercial acceptance proof).

.22 LR cal.	$1,100	$850	$675	$595	$525	$460	$420
.32 ACP cal.	$495	$425	$350	$300	$200	$180	$160
.380 ACP cal.	$1,100	$900	$800	$700	$600	$500	$400

This variation is normally encountered with semi-polished, exterior metal showing milling marks to various degrees.

▲ *Waffenamt Proofed With High Polish*

	$850	$650	$575	$500	$425	$330	$275

▲ *Eagle C Marked* — .32 ACP cal., "Crown N - Eagle C", mfg. for Nazi Police.

	$675	$550	$475	$400	$315	$260	$200

Add 25% for high polish finish.

▲ *Eagle F Marked* — .32 ACP cal., "Crown N - Eagle F", Nazi Police, all have the light weight aluminum frame.

	$800	$700	$600	$475	$375	$300	$250

▲ *RZM Marked* — .32 ACP cal., "Crown N", proof marking for Nazi Party Purchasing Office.

	$900	$825	$765	$600	$350	$275	$225

▲ *Party Leader* — .32 ACP cal., named because grips (brown or black plastic) have the German eagle holding a Swastika, "Crown N" or "Eagle N" proofed, honor weapon awarded 3rd Reich political leaders, rare. Be very wary of fake grips (especially black color) as reproductions have been made recently. Unfortunately, the grips on a Party Leader (mfg. 1936-1941) are the only distinguishing feature on this very desirable configuration.

	$2,650	$2,250	$1,800	$1,500	$1,200	$1,100	$1,000

▲ *RZM With Party Leader Grips* — .32 ACP cal., RZM marked, "Crown N" proofed.

	$3,200	$2,950	$2,650	$2,200	$1,300	$1,200	$1,100

▲ *RFV Marked* — .32 ACP cal., "Crown N". Mfg. for Reich Finance Administration.

	$975	$900	$825	$750	$800	$700	$675

▲ *PDM Marked* — .32 ACP cal., "Crown N". Mfg. for Police Dept. Munich. All have the bottom mag. release.

	$1,100	$900	$825	$750	$600	$500	$395

▲ *DRP Marked* — .32 ACP cal., "Crown N". Mfg. for Postal Service.

	$900	$750	$675	$525	$420	$350	$260

▲ *Panagraph Slide*

	$850	$750	$675	$525	$450	$375	$300

▲ *Verchromt* — .32 ACP or 380 ACP cal., differentiated by dull silver satin type finish.

	$2,000	$1,600	$1,300	$1,000	$800	$650	$500

Add 25% for .380 ACP cal.

▲ *"K" suffix* — "K" beneath ser. no.

	$625	$525	$475	$375	$300	$275	$250

▲ *"W" suffix* — .32 ACP cal., "Crown N" proofed, W-suffix ser. no.

	$625	$550	$475	$375	$300	$275	$250

Grading	100%	98%	95%	90%	80%	70%	60%
▲ **Early 90 degree safety**	$675	$600	$500	$425	$325	$260	$195
▲ **Early bottom release Mag.**	$950	$850	$750	$650	$500	$475	$375
▲ **PPK Marked PP**	$2,500	$2,150	$1,850	$1,600	$1,400	$1,180	$900
▲ **7-digit ser. no.**	$725	$700	$650	$600	$550	$400	$300
▲ **Dural frame** — .22 LR, .32 ACP, or .380 ACP cal., chrome finish (very rare), "Eagle N".	$650	$600	$575	$525	$400	$325	$275

Add 25% for .380 ACP or .22 LR cal.

	100%	98%	95%	90%	80%	70%	60%
▲ **Czech. Contract** — Rampant Lion stamped.	$950	$875	$750	$625	$550	$425	$325
▲ **Danish Rplt.**	$950	$875	$750	$625	$550	$425	$325
▲ **Allemagne** — French Commercial — rare.	$950	$875	$750	$625	$550	$425	$325

MODEL PPK LIGHTWEIGHT — aluminum alloy version.
Add 20% to commercial pricing.

SPORT MODEL 1926 — .22 S or LR (known as Standard Model in Germany) cal.

	100%	98%	95%	90%	80%	70%	60%
	$1,050	$900	$800	$675	$595	$550	$495

1932 OLYMPIA MODEL — .22 S or LR, 10 shot, 6 or 9 in. barrel, target sights, one-piece grip, introduced in 1928 and used in 1932 Olympics. Marketed by Stoeger and Chas. Heyer-Nairobi.

	100%	98%	95%	90%	80%	70%	60%
	$1,100	$900	$800	$625	$495	$440	$395

OLYMPIA SPORT MODEL — .22 LR, 4 in. barrel, adj. target sights, blue, wood grips, 4 barrel weights available. Mfg. 1936-1940.

	100%	98%	95%	90%	80%	70%	60%
	$925	$800	$700	$600	$475	$420	$375

Add 20% for weight set.

1936 OLYMPIA "JAGERSCHAFTS" HUNTING MODEL — similar to Sport, with 4 in. barrel. Mfg. 1936-1940. Also seen with Eagle N proofs.

	100%	98%	95%	90%	80%	70%	60%
	$875	$775	$700	$600	$495	$440	$360

OLYMPIA RAPID FIRE MODEL — .22 Short only, 7.4 in. barrel, blue, adj. sight, wood grip, has alloy slide. Mfg. 1936-1940.

	100%	98%	95%	90%	80%	70%	60%
	$950	$850	$785	$600	$520	$460	$380

1936 OLYMPIA FUNFKAMPF MODEL — .22 Short or LR, $9\frac{1}{4}$ in. barrel, blue, adj. sight, wood grips, barrel weights, circa 1936.

	100%	98%	95%	90%	80%	70%	60%
	$1,250	$1,000	$850	$775	$575	$500	$440

MODEL HP COMMERCIAL DOUBLE ACTION — pre-war version of P-38, 9mm, 5 in. barrel, fixed sight, blue, wood or plastic grips. Mfg. 1937-1944. Many variations, including several different finishes.
See German WWII Military Pistols for values on this model.

PISTOLS: SEMI-AUTO, POST-WAR

In 1983, Carl Walther from West Germany announced the discontinuance of models PP and PPK/S from the American market. These guns are attracting more collector interest as their production records are now complete. Manurhin of France no longer imports into the U.S. and guns imported between 1984-86 will not have the Interarms logo or Walther trademark.

W

Grading	100%	98%	95%	90%	80%	70%	60%

MODEL PP DOUBLE ACTION — .22 LR, .32 ACP, or .380 ACP cal., specifications similar to pre-war PP, 3⅞ in. barrel. Imported 1963-present. W. German manufacture.

▲ *.380 ACP cal.* — 6 shot mag.

Mfg.'s Sug. Retail	$999	$875	$550	$425	$330	$300	$275	$250

▲ *.32 ACP cal.* — 6 shot mag.

Mfg.'s Sug. Retail	$999	$875	$425	$350	$295	$275	$250	$225

▲ *.22 LR cal.* — 7 shot mag., disc. 1989, reintroduced 1992-94.

	$650	$500	$475	$350	$325	$300	$275

Last Mfg.'s Sug. Retail was $783.

▲ *Blue Engraved* — .22 LR (disc.) or .380 ACP (disc. 1991) cal.

	$1,350	$1,100	$950

Last Mfg.'s Sug. Retail was $1,650.

Add 5% for .22 LR cal.

▲ *Chrome Engraved* — .22 LR or .380 ACP cal. Disc. 1990.

	$1,350	$1,100	$950

Last Mfg.'s Sug. Retail was $1,600.

Add $50 for .22 LR cal.

▲ *Silver Engraved* — .22 LR or .380 ACP (disc. 1990) cal. Importation disc. 1993.

	$1,575	$1,150	$1,000

Last Mfg.'s Sug. Retail was $1,948.

▲ *Gold Engraved* — .22 LR or .380 ACP (disc. 1989) cal. Importation disc. 1993.

	$1,725	$1,350	$1,150

Last Mfg.'s Sug. Retail was $2,053.

▲ *Manurhin PP* — .22 LR, .32 ACP, or .380 ACP cal.

	$350	$310	$285	$225	$180	$165	$150

Add 10% for .380 ACP cal.

▲ *Model PP 100th Anniversary Commemorative* — .22 LR, .32 ACP, or .380 ACP cal., gold-plated parts, hand carved grips, presentation case. 500 imported to U.S. 1979.

	$1,000	$800	$600

Last Mfg.'s Sug. Retail was $1,700.

Add $100 for .22 LR cal.

PP SPORT — double action, thumbrest grips, round hammer with spur, adj. rear sight, long barrel. Mfg. 1953-1970.

Manurhin manufacture	$650	$625	$600	$525	$475	$400	$325
Mark II (mfg. 1955-1957)	$725	$680	$625	$575	$520	$480	$425
Walther manufacture	$775	$725	$700	$575	$520	$475	$400

Deduct 10% if not marked.

Note: Add $75 for barrel weight, $100 for factory case, 20% for factory nickel, 5% for single action.

▲ *PP Sport "C" Model C* — mfg. for competition shooting, single action, 7⅝ in. barrel, spur hammer.

	$750	$725	$675	$625	$525	$475	$400

MODEL PPK — similar to pre-war PPK, .22 LR, .32 ACP, or .380 ACP cal., 3.31 in. barrel. Mfg. post-war - present, U.S. import stopped by GCA 68 on W. German and French production.

.32 ACP cal.	$525	$450	$375	$325	$295	$270	$250
.22 LR cal.	$750	$650	$575	$500	$425	$350	$300
.380 ACP cal.	$700	$625	$550	$450	$400	$325	$275
Blue engraved	$1,600	$1,300	$950				
Silver engraved	$1,850	$1,400	$1,000				
Gold engraved	$2,200	$1,675	$1,250				

100% column assumes NIB condition - deduct 15% if not boxed.

MODEL PPK LIGHTWEIGHT — similar to Standard, with dural frame, .22 LR or .32 ACP cal.

	$500	$425	$390	$325	$295	$270	$250

Add 20% for .22 LR cal.

Grading	100%	98%	95%	90%	80%	70%	60%

MODEL PPK-1986 U.S. MFG. — .380 ACP cal. only, 3.35 in. barrel, similar specifications as previous W. German and French manufacture, 6 shot finger extension mag., black plastic grips, 21 oz. Made in the U.S. Introduced 1986.

Mfg.'s Sug. Retail	$540	$445	$375	$310	$285	$250	$225	$200

Manufacture in the U.S. is under an exclusive licensing agreement with Walther of W. Germany.

▲ *PPK Stainless* — stainless steel construction. New 1986.

Mfg.'s Sug. Retail	$540	$445	$375	$310

MODEL PPK/S — .22 LR, .32 ACP, or .380 ACP cal., similar to PPK, except has larger PP frame to meet import requirements of 1968, 3¼ in. barrel, production in W. Germany (now disc.), Manurhin of France (disc. 1986), and in the U.S. (mfg. under license from Walther by Interarms). 7 or 8 shot, double action, fixed sights.

▲ *American PPK/S* — .380 ACP cal. only, blue finish, 7 shot finger extension mag.

Mfg.'s Sug. Retail	$540	$445	$375	$310	$285	$250	$225	$200

▲ *Stainless PPK/S* — .380 ACP cal. only, American manufacture, introduced July of 1983.

Mfg.'s Sug. Retail	$540	$445	$375	$310

▲ *W. German PPK/S* — .22 LR, .32 ACP, or .380 ACP cal. Disc. 1982.

	100%	98%	95%	90%	80%	70%	60%
.32 ACP cal.	$495	$425	$350	$325	$295	$270	$250
.22 LR cal.	$675	$600	$525	$425	$350	$300	$275
.380 ACP cal.	$650	$550	$475	$375	$300	$275	$250

▲ *American PPK/S* — blue engraved. Disc. 1985.

	$875	$850	$800

Last Mfg.'s Sug. Retail was $990.

▲ *American PPK/S Gold-Engraved Commemorative* — 500 total mfg. Disc. 1987.

	$1,000	$850	$675

Last Mfg.'s Sug. Retail was $1,200.

▲ *American PPK/S Gold-Engraved* — disc. 1985.

	$975	$800	$675

Last Mfg.'s Sug. Retail was $1,070.

▲ *W. German PPK/S Blue Engraved* — all quantities became out of stock in 1990.

	$1,395	$1,050	$850

Last Mfg.'s Sug. Retail was $1,550.

▲ *W. German PPK/S Chrome Engraved* — importation disc. 1991.

	$1,450	$1,075	$950

Last Mfg.'s Sug. Retail was $1,700.

▲ *W. German PPK/S Silver Engraved* — disc. 1988.

	$1,595	$1,150	$975

Last Mfg.'s Sug. Retail was $1,700.

▲ *W. German PPK/S Gold Engraved* — disc. 1985.

	$1,850	$1,250	$1,000

Last Mfg.'s Sug. Retail was $1,800.

▲ *PPK/S Durgarde (Manurhin mfg.)* — similar to above, only with bonded brushed chrome finish.

Under Walther license	$395	$310	$290	$265	$245	$210	$195

Add $25 for .22 LR cal.

MANURHIN PPK/S — see listings under Manurhin section.

MODEL PP SUPER — 9x18mm, (Police) or .380 ACP cal., 3.6 in. barrel, fixed sights, plastic grips, blue. Mfg. 1975-1981.

	$700	$650	$525	$395	$285	$250	$235

Deduct 25% if in 9x18mm cal.

▲ *PP Super-Cutaway*

	$650	$600	$550

Grading	100%	98%	95%	90%	80%	70%	60%

MODEL TP — .22 LR or .25 ACP cal., updated version of Model 9, concealed hammer. Mfg. 1962-1970.

	100%	98%	95%	90%	80%	70%	60%
.22 LR cal.	$675	$600	$435	$350	$300	$260	$210
.25 ACP cal.	$495	$425	$360	$300	$250	$220	$185

MODEL TPH — .22 LR or .25 ACP cal., double action 2.8 in. barrel, alloy frame, blue, fixed sights, plastic grips. Mfg. 1969-present in W. Germany, U.S. import stopped by GCA of 1968.

	100%	98%	95%	90%	80%	70%	60%
.22 LR cal.	$600	$550	$495	$425	$300	$275	$220
.25 ACP cal.	$650	$600	$550	$475	$350	$300	$250

> Deduct 10% on the 100% values if not boxed with all accessories.
> 100% price assumes NIB condition.

AMERICAN MODEL TPH — .22 LR or .25 ACP (new 1992) cal., blued finish or stainless steel, double action, black plastic grips, 6 shot mag., 2¼ in. barrel, 14 oz. Introduced 1987.

Mfg.'s Sug. Retail	$440	$365	$300	$250

▲ **American Model TPH Stainless** — stainless steel fabrication.

Mfg.'s Sug. Retail	$440	$365	$300	$250

MODEL P.38 — Post-war version of P.38 Military, .22 LR, .30 Luger (disc.), or 9mm Para. cal., 5 in. barrel, alloy frame, matte black finish, 28 oz. W. German manufacture. Importation disc. 1995. See German WWII Military Pistols for wartime listings.

> Note: Due to the release of large numbers of W. German Police and Army trade-ins of P.38 9mm and PP .32 ACP cal. models recently, the actual value of these models has decreased somewhat. The two models most affected are the P-1 variation of the P.38, and the German PP in .32 ACP cal.

	100%	98%	95%	90%	80%	70%	60%
	$700	$575	$475	$350	$295	$245	$190

Last Mfg.'s Sug. Retail was $824.

▲ **Steel Frame P.38** — 9mm Para., similar to regular P.38, except has steel frame, 34 oz. Imported 1987-1989 only.

	100%	98%	95%	90%	80%	70%	60%
	$975	$850	$650	$550	$400	$295	$245

Last Mfg.'s Sug. Retail was $1,400.

▲ **P.38 in .22 LR cal.** — disc. 1989.

	100%	98%	95%	90%	80%	70%	60%
	$850	$750	$600	$450	$350	$300	$200

Last Mfg.'s Sug. Retail was $1,050.

MODEL P.38 SPECIAL EDITIONS/ENGRAVED

▲ **P.38 50th Year Commemorative** — alloy frame, carved grips, presentation engraved with deluxe walnut presentation case. Introduced 1987, inventory depleted 1992.

	$800	$690	$450

Last Mfg.'s Sug. Retail was $950.

▲ **Blue Engraved** — 9mm Para. cal. Importation disc. 1991.

	$1,850	$1,325	$1,125	$900

Last Mfg.'s Sug. Retail was $1,850.

▲ **Chrome Engraved** — 9mm Para. cal. Importation disc. 1991.

	$1,475	$1,175	$925

Last Mfg.'s Sug. Retail was $2,125.

▲ **Silver Engraved** — 9mm Para. cal. Importation disc. 1991.

	$1,450	$1,175	$925

Last Mfg.'s Sug. Retail was $2,100.

▲ **Gold Engraved** — 9mm Para. cal. Disc. 1987.

	$1,800	$1,500	$1,000

Last Mfg.'s Sug. Retail was $2,050.

MODEL P1 — 9mm Para., post-war commercial variation of the P.38 with steel slide and alloy frame, 5 in. barrel, 8 shot mag., black plastic grips, Disc.

	100%	98%	95%	90%	80%	70%	60%
	$600	$500	$350	$300	$250	$215	$165

W

Grading	100%	98%	95%	90%	80%	70%	60%

MODEL P4 — 9mm Para. cal., modernized variation of the original P.38, 4½ in. barrel, 8 shot mag., updates include reinforced steel slide and alloy frame, includes decocking lever and automatic safeties, adj. rear sight, 29 oz. Importation disc. 1982.

	$675	$575	$500	$350	$300	$250	$200

MODEL P.38K — 9mm Para. cal., shortened 2.8 in. barrel variation of P.38, front sight on slide. Mfg. 1974-1980.

	$900	$800	$650	$475	$300	$250	$200

MODEL P-5 — 9mm Para. cal., double action, alloy frame, frame mounted decocking lever, 3½ in. barrel, adj. rear sight, blue finish only, 8 shot mag., auto safeties, 28 oz.

Mfg.'s Sug. Retail	$900	$725	$675	$525	$475	$450	$425	$375

▲ *P-5 Compact* — compact variation of P-5 with 3.1 in. barrel, 26½ oz.

Mfg.'s Sug. Retail	$900	$750	$595	$525	$475	$450	$425	$375

▲ *P-5 100th Year Commemorative* — marked "1886-1986 100 Jahre" with Walther banner, elaborate grip carving, presentation walnut case. Imported 1986-91.

	$2,100	$1,425	$1,025

Last Mfg.'s Sug. Retail was $2,890.

MODEL P-88 — 9mm Para. cal., double action, alloy frame, 4 in. barrel, 15 shot side release mag., ambidextrous decocking lever, matte finish, adj. rear sight, internal safeties, loaded chamber indicator, black synthetic grips, 31½ oz. Imported 1987-94 - still available in Europe.

	$1,325	$1,175	$700	$575	$490	$450	$400

Last Mfg.'s Sug. Retail was $1,129.

▲ *P-88 Compact* — 3.8 in. barrel, 14 shot mag., 29 oz. Importation began 1993.

Mfg.'s Sug. Retail	$900	$825	$700	$600	$525	$475	$450	$425

This model had a substantial price decrease beginning 1996 (1994 retail price was $1,725).

TARGET PISTOLS

Walther target pistols are currently being imported by Nygord Precision Products located in Prescott, AZ and Champions Choice located in La Vergne, TN. Previously imported by Interarms until 1993.

Add 10% to the values listed below for left-hand stocks (available on most models).

MODEL GSP TARGET STANDARD — .22 LR cal., 4½ in. barrel, single action, 5 shot mag., adj. sights, blue finish, walnut target grips, 2-stage trigger became standard in 1995, supplied with carrying case, 49.4 oz.

Mfg.'s Sug. Retail	$1,450	$1,395	$1,100	$900	$650	$550	$475	$425

▲ *Model GSP Junior* — similar to GSP Target, except has slimmer barrel design, smaller walnut grips, less weight. Importation disc. 1992.

	$1,400	$1,100	$925	$750	$600	$500	$425

Last Mfg.'s Sug. Retail was $1,810.

▲ *Model GSP-C* — similar to Model GSP Target, except in .32 S&W Wadcutter, 42.3 oz.

Mfg.'s Sug. Retail	$1,550	$1,425	$1,025	$800	$650	$550	$475	$425

Add $1,495 for GSP-C .22 Short conversion unit.
Add $1,053 for GSP-C .22 LR cal. conversion unit.
Add $1,400 for GSP-C .32 S&W Wadcutter conversion unit.

MODEL OSP RAPID FIRE — similar to GSP, in .22 Short. Mfg. 1968-present, for international competition (meets ISU and NRA regs.), 4½ in. barrel, 44.4 oz., supplied with case.

Mfg.'s Sug. Retail	$1,530	$1,375	$1,000	$800	$650	$550	$475	$425

Add $145 for extended sight radius and semi-wraparound grip.

Grading	100%	98%	95%	90%	80%	70%	60%

FREE PISTOL — .22 LR cal., single shot, electronic trigger, 11.7 in. heavy barrel, advanced target design with fully adj. grips and sights, 48 oz. Importation disc. 1991.

| | $1,600 | $1,200 | $1,000 | $850 | $675 | $575 | $500 |

Last Mfg.'s Sug. Retail was $2,140.

P.38 WWII MILITARY MFG. — see German Military for breakdown.

HAMMERLI-WALTHER — see Hammerli.

RIFLES: DISC.

MODEL B — .30-06 bolt action, post-war mfg., 22 in. barrel. Add 20% for double set triggers. Disc.

| | $450 | $420 | $380 | $340 | $300 | $275 | $250 |

OLYMPIC SINGLE SHOT — .22 LR cal., bolt action, 26 in. heavy barrel, target sights, checkered pistol grip, full beavertail forearm, palm rest, adj. butt, pre-war.

| | $935 | $825 | $770 | $715 | $605 | $550 | $440 |

MODEL 1 — Carbine model, clip fed.

| | $395 | $350 | $310 | $295 | $270 | $250 | $200 |

MODEL 2 AUTOLOADING — may be used as bolt action, autoloader or single shot, .22 LR cal., 24½ in. barrel, tangent sight, checkered sporter stock, pre-war.

| | $495 | $440 | $385 | $330 | $275 | $220 | $165 |

MODEL 2 LIGHTWEIGHT — 20 in. barrel, lighter stock.

| | $495 | $440 | $385 | $330 | $275 | $220 | $165 |

MODEL V SINGLE SHOT — .22 LR cal., bolt action, 26 in. barrel, open sight, plain pistol grip stock, pre-war.

| | $385 | $360 | $330 | $305 | $275 | $250 | $195 |

MODEL V CHAMPION — similar to Model V Single Shot, with micrometer adj. sight and checkered pistol grip stock.

| | $470 | $440 | $415 | $385 | $330 | $305 | $250 |

MODEL KKM INTERNATIONAL MATCH — .22 LR cal., single shot bolt action, 28 in. heavy barrel, adj. aperture sight, adj. hook butt, thumbhole stock, accessory rail, post-war mfg.

| | $880 | $770 | $715 | $660 | $550 | $495 | $440 |

MODEL KKM-S — similar to KKM, with adj. cheekpiece.

| | $935 | $825 | $770 | $715 | $605 | $550 | $495 |

MODEL KKJ SPORTER — .22 LR cal., bolt action, 5 shot, 22½ in. barrel, open sight, checkered sporter stock, post-war.

| | $595 | $500 | $450 | $385 | $330 | $250 | $200 |

Add 20% for double set triggers.

MODEL KKW — .22 LR cal., single shot, military stock, tangent sight, pre-war mfg.

| | $540 | $490 | $420 | $300 | $260 | $220 | $195 |

MODEL KKJ-MA — .22 WMR cal.

| | $550 | $495 | $440 | $385 | $305 | $250 | $220 |

MODEL KKJ-HO — .22 Hornet cal.

| | $725 | $675 | $625 | $580 | $540 | $480 | $440 |

Add 20% for double set triggers.

MODEL SSV VARMINT — .22 LR cal., single shot bolt action, 25½ in. barrel, no sights, Monte Carlo pistol grip stock, post-war mfg.

| | $605 | $550 | $525 | $495 | $415 | $360 | $330 |
| .22 Hornet | $660 | $605 | $580 | $550 | $470 | $415 | $385 |

Grading	100%	98%	95%	90%	80%	70%	60%

MODEL PRONE 400 — similar to UIT Match, with Prone style competitive stock and no sights. Disc.

| | $750 | $635 | $580 | $525 | $415 | $360 | $305 |

RIFLES: RECENT MFG.

MODEL UIT BV UNIVERSAL — .22 LR cal., single shot bolt action, 25½ in. heavy barrel, adj. aperture sight, target stock with palm rest, adj. butt, meets ISU regs., 16 lbs. Disc. 1990.

| | $1,325 | $1,050 | $850 | $700 | $635 | $580 | $530 |

Last Mfg.'s Sug. Retail was $1,700.

This model was previously known as the Model UIT Special.

MODEL UIT MATCH — similar to Model UIT, except with improved stock design which includes fully stippled lower forearm and pistol grip, 13 lbs. Importation disc. 1993.

| | $1,125 | $925 | $800 | $660 | $610 | $555 | $510 |

Last Mfg.'s Sug. Retail was $1,400.

▲ *Model UIT-E* — electronic trigger, 25½ in. barrel, 9 lbs. Disc. 1986.

| | $1,350 | $940 | $860 | $770 | $670 | $630 | $560 |

Last Mfg.'s Sug. Retail was $1,250.

GX-1 — similar to UIT Match, 25½ in. barrel with fully adj. free rifle stock, all accessories included, 16½ lbs. Importation disc. 1991.

| | $1,895 | $1,375 | $1,125 | $985 | $860 | $775 | $680 |

Last Mfg.'s Sug. Retail was $2,350.

MODEL KK/MS SILHOUETTE — .22 LR cal. only, designed for silhouette shooting with no sights, thumbhole stock with adj. butt, fully stippled forend and stock grip, front barrel weight, 25½ in. barrel, 8¾ lbs. Imported 1984-91.

| | $975 | $795 | $625 | $560 | $495 | $435 | $395 |

Last Mfg.'s Sug. Retail was $1,175.

RUNNING BOAR MODEL 500 — similar to KK/MS, no sights, thumbhole stock with adj. butt and cheekpiece, 23½ in. barrel, 10¼ lbs. Disc. 1990.

| | $1,025 | $825 | $640 | $570 | $500 | $435 | $395 |

Last Mfg.'s Sug. Retail was $1,300.

MODEL WA-2000 — .300 Win. Mag. or .308 cal., ultra-deluxe semi-auto, includes aluminum case, two mags., integral bipod, adj. tools and leather sling, special order only. Disc. 1988.

| | $6,400 | $4,800 | $4,500 | $4,000 | $3,500 | $3,000 | $2,500 |

SHOTGUNS: SxS

MODEL SF — 12 or 16 ga., double barrel, checkered walnut stock, double triggers, boxlock, sling swivels. Disc.

| | $500 | $450 | $395 | $325 | $275 | $240 | $200 |

MODEL SFD — 12 or 16 ga., double barrel, cheekpiece, checkered walnut stock, double triggers, boxlock, sling swivels. Disc.

| | $625 | $575 | $500 | $425 | $375 | $340 | $300 |

WALTHER, FRENCH-MADE BY MANURHIN

Manufactured in Mulhouse, France. Previously imported 1984-86 by Matra-Manurhin International, Inc., Alexandria, VA.

PISTOLS: SEMI-AUTO

Manufacture of these Walther pistols commenced in France in 1951. They were marked MANURHIN on the slide until 1954. Since then they were designated Walther MKII. They were imported into the USA by Interarms up to 1983. In 1984, Manurhin was imported directly with no Interarms logo or Walther trademark appearing on Models PP and PPK/S. Importation was discontinued 1986.

Grading	100%	98%	95%	90%	80%	70%	60%

MODEL PP — .22 LR, .32 ACP, or .380 ACP cal., 3⅞ in. barrel, 10 shot mag.-.22 LR, 8 shot mag.-.32 ACP, 7 shot mag.-.380 ACP, blue only, all steel construction, double action with positive steel block safety, 24 oz.

	$400	$350	$300	$230	$205	$185	$170

Last Mfg.'s Sug. Retail was $419.

Add $10 for .22 LR cal.
Add $46 for Durgarde finish.

▲ *Collector Model* — blue finish, special engraving. New 1986.

	$465	$415	$350

Last Mfg.'s Sug. Retail was $529.

▲ *Presentation Model* — blue finish, special ornamentation. New 1986.

	$720	$650	$500

Last Mfg.'s Sug. Retail was $819.

Interarms import

	$350	$325	$285	$230	$205	$180	$160

Also available with various engraving options in either blue, nickel, or gold finish - prices range from $222 - $540.

PP SPORT — .22 LR cal. only, double action, 6.1 or 8.1 in. barrel, blue finish only, precision adj. sights, contoured plastic grips with thumb rest, 25 oz. New Manurhin design beginning 1985-disc.

	$545	$485	$430	$385	$325	$290	$270

Last Mfg.'s Sug. Retail was $635.

▲ *PP Sport-C* — similar to PP Sport, except is single action.

	$540	$475	$415	$370	$310	$280	$260

Last Mfg.'s Sug. Retail was $635.

MODEL PPK — .22 LR, .32 ACP, or .380 ACP cal., 3¼ in. barrel, 10 shot mag.-.22 LR, 8 shot mag.-.32 ACP, 7 shot mag.-.380 ACP, blue only, all steel construction, double action with positive steel block safety, 23 oz.

	$600	$495	$425	$375	$350	$325	$300

Add 10% for .22 LR cal.

MODEL PPK/S — .22 LR, .32 ACP, or .380 ACP cal., 3¼ in. barrel, 10 shot mag.-.22 LR, 8 shot mag.-.32 ACP, 7 shot mag.-.380 ACP, blue only, all steel construction, double action with positive steel block safety, 23 oz.

	$400	$350	$300	$230	$205	$185	$170

Last Mfg.'s Sug. Retail was $419.

Add 10% for .22 LR cal.

▲ *PPK/S Durgarde* — similar to above, only with bonded brushed chrome finish.

	$430	$380	$325	$290	$265	$250	$240

Last Mfg.'s Sug. Retail was $465.

Add 10% for .22 LR cal.

▲ *Collector Model* — blue finish, special engraving. New 1986.

	$465	$415	$350

Last Mfg.'s Sug. Retail was $529.

▲ *Presentation Model* — blue finish, special ornamentation. New 1986.

	$720	$650	$500

Last Mfg.'s Sug. Retail was $819.

Interarms import

	$395	$340	$300	$275	$250	$235	$210

Also available with various engraving options in either blue, nickel, or gold finish — prices range from $222 - $540.

WARNER ARMS CORPORATION

Norwich, CT.

INFALLIBLE POCKET AUTO PISTOL — .32 auto cal., 7 shot, 3 in. barrel, fixed sights, rubber grips. Mfg. 1917-1919.

	$450	$350	$250	$150	$125	$100	$90

WATSON BROS.

Long gun manufacturer located in London, England since 1875.

Watson Bros. manufactures distinct round body actions with self-opening locks in both SxS and O/U shotgun configurations. Please contact the factory directly (see Trademark Index) for more information including current pricing.

WEATHERBY

Manufacturer/importer located in Atascadero, CA since 1995. Previously located in South Gate, CA, 1945 - 1995. Weatherby began manufacturing rifles in the U.S. during early 1995.

Weatherby is an importer/manufacturer of long arms. Earlier production was from Germany and Italy, and German mfg. is usually what is collectible. Current rifle production is from the U.S., while shotguns are made in Japan. Workmanship in all instances is quite good. Weatherby is well known for their high-velocity proprietary rifle calibers.

Early Weatherby rifles used a Mathieu Arms action in the 1950s - primarily since it was available in left hand-action. Right-handed actions were normally mfg. from the FN Mauser type.

Grading	100%	98%	95%	90%	80%	70%	60%

SILHOUETTE PISTOL

WEATHERBY SILHOUETTE PISTOL — .22-250 or .308 cal., mfg. in Japan during late 1970s, 14½ in. barrel, Lyman or Williams sights, fitted case. Only 50 were mfg. in .22-250 and 150 in .308 cal.

	100%	98%	95%	90%	80%	70%	60%
	$3,750	$3,300	$2,750	$2,450	$2,100	$1,850	$1,650

RIFLES - MARK V BOLT ACTION

For German manufacture, add 15%-25% for calibers under .35 if condition is 95% or better. In 1992, 24 in. barrels were disc. on most calibers of .300 or greater (including Models Mark V Deluxe, Fibermark, Lazermark, and Euromark). Since 1957, the Mark V Action has been manufactured in Germany, Italy, Japan, and the U.S.

MARK V DELUXE — .240 Wby. Mag., .257 Wby. Mag., .270 Wby. Mag., 7mm Wby. Mag., .30-06, .300 Wby. Mag., .340 Wby. Mag., or .375 H&H (mfg. 1993 only) cal., bolt action, 3-5 shot mag., 24 or 26 in. barrel, deluxe skip line checkered pistol grip walnut stock with rosewood tipped forearm and pistol grip, no sights, 8 lbs. Left-hand actions (.270 Wby. Mag. and .300 Wby. Mag.) available at no extra charge.

	100%	98%	95%	90%	80%	70%	60%
Mfg.'s Sug. Retail $1,399	$1,115	$775	$625	$525	$475	$450	$410

Add $200 for .375 H&H Mag. cal. (disc. 1993).

▲ **.378 Wby. Mag.** — 26 in. barrel only, 8½ lbs.

	100%	98%	95%	90%	80%	70%	60%
Mfg.'s Sug. Retail $1,475	$1,215	$800	$700	$600	$525	$475	$425
German mfg.	$1,600	$1,400	$1,250	$1,000	$900	$825	$750

German mfg. in this model used the .375 Wby. Mag. cal.

▲ **.416 Wby. Mag.** — first new caliber (introduced 1989) since the .240 Mag. was released 1965.

	100%	98%	95%	90%	80%	70%	60%
Mfg.'s Sug. Retail $1,534	$1,235	$875	$710	$600	$525	$475	$425

▲ **.460 Wby. Mag.** — 24 or 26 in. barrel, includes custom stock, integral muzzle brake, 10 lbs. No extra charge for left-hand.

	100%	98%	95%	90%	80%	70%	60%
Mfg.'s Sug. Retail $1,892	$1,575	$1,175	$935	$775	$650	$600	$550
German mfg.	$1,675	$1,475	$1,295	$1,100	$1,000	$925	$850

Grading	100%	98%	95%	90%	80%	70%	60%

CLASSICMARK I — available in 9 Wby. Mag. cals. in addition to .270 Win., 7mm Rem. Mag., .30-06, or .375 H&H Mag. cal., oil finished American Claro walnut stock with no cheekpiece and ebony forend cap, 1 in. solid recoil pad, panel point checkering. Mfg. 1992-1993.

	$1,075	$750	$625	$525	$475	$450	$410

Last Mfg.'s Sug. Retail was $1,295.

> Add $15 for 26 in. barrel.
> Add $130 for .375 H&H Mag. cal.

▲ **.300 or .340 Wby. Mag.** — 26 in. barrel only, right or left-hand action, 8½ lbs.

	$1,095	$775	$625	$525	$475	$450	$410

Last Mfg.'s Sug. Retail was $1,323.

▲ **.378 Wby. Mag.** — 26 in. barrel only, right or left-hand action, 8½ lbs.

	$1,125	$795	$625	$525	$475	$450	$410

Last Mfg.'s Sug. Retail was $1,356.

▲ **.416 Wby. Mag.** — 26 in. barrel only, right or left-hand action.

	$1,150	$825	$650	$550	$495	$460	$430

Last Mfg.'s Sug. Retail was $1,411.

▲ **.460 Wby. Mag.** — 26 in. barrel only, includes custom stock, integral muzzle brake, 10 lbs. No extra charge for left-hand.

	$1,250	$900	$675	$575	$525	$475	$430

Last Mfg.'s Sug. Retail was $1,573.

CLASSICMARK II — available in 9 Wby. Mag. cals. in addition .270 Win., 7mm Rem. Mag., or .30-06, similar to Classicmark I, except has deluxe American walnut with 22 LPI multiple point checkering, steel grip cap, satin finished wood and metal, guaranteed 1½ in. or less 3 shot grouping at 100 yards, right hand action only. Mfg. 1992 only.

	$1,525	$1,175	$975	$800	$650	$600	$550

Last Mfg.'s Sug. Retail was $1,775.

> Add $28 for 26 in. barrel.

▲ **.300 or .340 Wby. Mag.** — 26 in. barrel only.

	$1,550	$1,175	$975	$800	$650	$600	$550

Last Mfg.'s Sug. Retail was $1,803.

▲ **.378 Wby. Mag.** — 26 in. barrel only.

	$1,700	$1,250	$1,000	$800	$650	$600	$550

Last Mfg.'s Sug. Retail was $1,976.

▲ **.416 Wby. Mag.** — 26 in. barrel only.

	$1,875	$1,375	$1,050	$825	$650	$600	$550

Last Mfg.'s Sug. Retail was $2,128.

▲ **.460 Wby. Mag.** — 26 in. barrel only, includes custom stock, integral muzzle brake, 10 lbs.

	$1,925	$1,400	$1,050	$825	$650	$600	$550

Last Mfg.'s Sug. Retail was $2,207.

▲ **Safari Classic** — .375 H&H cal., 24 in. barrel only, right-hand action, limited edition featuring custom action, quarter rib express and front ramp sights, barrel band swivel and engraved floor plate, stock similar to Classicmark II. Mfg. 1992 only.

	$2,300	$1,850	$1,650	$1,450	$1,300	$1,175	$995

Last Mfg.'s Sug. Retail was $2,693.

ULTRAMARK — .240 Wby. Mag., .257 Wby. Mag., .270 Wby. Mag., .30-06, 7mm Wby. Mag., .300 Wby. Mag., .378 Wby. Mag. (mfg. 1989 only), or .416 Wby. Mag. (mfg. 1989 only) cal., fancy American walnut, individually hand-bedded, high lustre finish, customized action, 24 or 26 in. barrel, basket weave checkering (including pistol grip). Imported 1989-90 only.

	$1,125	$925	$800	$700	$630	$590	$550

Last Mfg.'s Sug. Retail was $1,315.

> Add $25 for 26 in. barrel.
> Add $220 for .378 Wby. Mag. cal. (26 in. barrel only).
> Add $325 for .416 Wby. Mag. cal. (26 in. barrel only).

W

Grading	100%	98%	95%	90%	80%	70%	60%

SYNTHETIC WEATHERMARK — available in various Wby. Mag. cals. from .240 to .340 and .257 Roberts (disc. 1994), .270 Win., 7mm Rem. Mag., .300 Win. Mag., .30-06, .338 Win. Mag., or .375 H&H Mag. (disc.) cal., similar design as the Classicmark II, except is fitted with black checkered composite stock, satin finish black metal, 22 (disc. 1995, .270 Win. or .30-06 only), 24, or 26 in. barrel, right-hand only, 7½ lbs. Mfg. 1992-94.

Mfg.'s Sug. Retail	$749	$625	$500	$450	$400	$360	$330	$300

Add $100 for .375 H&H Mag. cal.

▲ ***Weathermark Alaskan Model*** — same cals. as Weathermark, similar to Weathermark, except has non-glare electroless nickel-plated metal parts, right or left-hand (mfg. 1992 only) action. Mfg. 1992-94.

		$750	$635	$560	$495	$450	$400	$360

Last Mfg.'s Sug. Retail was $875.

Add $37 for Wby. Mag. cals.
Add $164 for .375 H&H Mag. cal.
Add $375 for left-hand action (disc.).

STAINLESS MODEL — same cals. as Synthetic Weathermark, features bead blasted matte stainless construction, lightweight synthetic Monte Carlo stock, custom floorplate release. New 1995.

Mfg.'s Sug. Retail	$999	$855	$685	$495

Add $134 for .375 H&H Mag. cal. (disc.).

ACCUMARK — .257 Wby. Mag., .270 Wby. Mag., .300 Win. Mag., .300 Wby. Mag., 7mm Rem. Mag., 7mm Wby. Mag., or .340 Wby. Mag., features H-S Precision black synthetic stock, 26 in. stainless steel fluted barrel, aluminum bedding plate, custom trigger, approx. 8 lbs. New 1996.

Mfg.'s Sug. Retail	$1,199	$995	$855	$685

SPORTER — .240 Wby. Mag. (new 1996), .257 Wby. Mag., .270 Wby. Mag., 7mm Wby. Mag., 7mm Rem. Mag., .270 Win. (new 1996), .30-06, .300 Wby. Mag., .300 Win. Mag., .338 Win. Mag., .340 Wby. Mag., or .375 H&H Mag. cal., 24 or 26 in. barrel, similar features as the Mark V, except has checkered walnut stock without forearm or pistol grip caps, low luster metalwork, vent. recoil pad, no sights, approx. 8 lbs. New 1993.

Mfg.'s Sug. Retail	$899	$750	$610	$535	$475	$425	$395	$350

Add $59 for .375 H&H Mag. cal. (disc.).

WHITETAIL — .257 Savage cal., limited edition features deluxe high grade Claro walnut, hand checkered bolt knob and engraved floorplate, 22 in. #1 contoured barrel, 6 lbs. Mfg. 1993 only.

		$1,150	$925	$775

Last Mfg.'s Sug. Retail was $1,366.

VARMINTMASTER — .22-250 or .224 Varmintmaster (disc. 1994) cal., 24 (disc. 1991) or 26 in. barrel, 6½ lbs. Disc. 1995.

		$1,075	$775	$625	$525	$475	$450	$410

Last Mfg.'s Sug. Retail was $1,297.

Not available in left-hand action.

EUROMARK — available in most cals. as the Sporter Model, except also includes .378 Wby. Mag. and .416 Wby. Mag., differs from Mark V Deluxe in that it has an oil finished, hand checkered, deluxe American claro walnut pistol grip cap stock with ebony forend tip, low lustre bluing, and solid black recoil pad. Mfg. 1986-92, re-introduced 1995.

Mfg.'s Sug. Retail	$1,449	$1,150	$795	$640	$525	$475	$450	$410

Add $23 for .378 Wby. Mag. or $132 for .416 Wby. Mag. cal.

▲ ***.460 Wby. Mag.*** — 24 or 26 in. barrel, includes custom stock, internal muzzle brake, no extra charge for left-hand. Disc. 1992.

	$1,450	$1,100	$925	$775	$650	$600	$550

Last Mfg.'s Sug. Retail was $1,708.

EUROSPORT — same cals. as Sporter Model, features hand-rubbed satin finish stock with low-lustre blue metal work and iron sights. New 1995.

Mfg.'s Sug. Retail	$899	$750	$610	$535	$475	$425	$395	$350

W

Grading	100%	98%	95%	90%	80%	70%	60%

MARK V LAZERMARK — available in the same cals. and barrel lengths as the Mark V Deluxe, differs only in that stock and forearm have been laser carved, 24 or 26 in. barrel. New 1985.

Mfg.'s Sug. Retail $1,499 $1,275 $895 $715 $600 $525 $475 $450
Add $95 for .378 Wby. Mag. cal.

▲ **.416 Wby. Mag.** — first new caliber (introduced 1989) since the .240 Mag. was released 1965, includes muzzle brake.

Mfg.'s Sug. Retail $1,644 $1,395 $975 $860 $725 $625 $575 $525

▲ **.460 Wby. Mag.** — 24 or 26 in. barrel, includes custom stock, internal muzzle brake, no extra charge for left-hand.

Mfg.'s Sug. Retail $2,037 $1,715 $1,205 $1,000 $800 $650 $600 $550

▲ **Varmintmaster** — .22-250 or .224 Varmintmaster cal., 24 or 26 in. barrel. Disc. 1991.

$1,085 $815 $675 $575 $500 $460 $425
Last Mfg.'s Sug. Retail was $675.

Add $25 for 26 in. barrel.
Not available in left-hand action.

MARK V FIBERMARK — available in .240 Wby. Mag., .257 Wby. Mag., .270 Wby. Mag., .30-06, 7mm Wby. Mag., .300 Wby. Mag., or .340 Wby. Mag. cal., black non-glare fiberglass with wrinkle finish stock, metal has non-glare matte finish, 24 or 26 in. barrel, available in right (disc. 1991) or left-hand action, 7¼ lbs. Mfg. disc. 1992.

$1,195 $875 $725 $600 $525 $475 $450
Last Mfg.'s Sug. Retail was $1,376.

Add $118 for .300 or .340 Mag. cal.
This model was available in left-hand action (22 in. barrel) in .270 Win. or .30-06 cal. only.

1976 BICENTENNIAL MARK V — .257 Wby. Mag., .270 Wby. Mag., 7mm Wby. Mag., or .300 Wby Mag. cal., 1,000 mfg. in 1976 only.

$1,495 $1,150 $895
Last Mfg.'s Sug. Retail was $2,000.

1984 MARK V OLYMPIC COMMEMORATIVE — .257 Wby. Mag., .270 Wby. Mag., 7mm Wby. Mag., or .300 Wby. Mag. cal., special gold accenting, extra-fancy walnut stock with "star in motion" inlay. Mfg. 1,000 1984 only at $2,000 retail.

$1,000 $895 $700

MARK V 35TH ANNIVERSARY COMMEMORATIVE — .257 Wby. Mag., .270 Wby. Mag., 7mm Wby. Mag., or .300 Wby. Mag. cal., limited mfg. 1980, 1,000 produced total.

$1,000 $895 $700

CUSTOM GRADE — various cals. from .240 Wby. Mag. to .340 Wby. Mag., 24 or 26 in. barrel, super fancy walnut stock featuring No. 7 style inlays, floorplate is engraved "Weatherby Custom", 6-8 week delivery time.

Mfg.'s Sug. Retail $3,553 $3,000 $2,325 $1,900 $1,600 $1,450 $1,300 $1,175

SAFARI GRADE CUSTOM — .300 Wby. Mag., .340 Wby. Mag., .378 Wby. Mag., .416 Wby Mag., or .460 Wby. Mag. cal., custom order only, various options available, 12-18 month delivery.

Mfg.'s Sug. Retail $3,301 $2,875 $2,275 $1,875 $1,600 $1,450 $1,300 $1,175
Add approx. $180-$273 for .378 and larger cals.

CROWN CUSTOM MODEL — custom order only, engraved barrel receiver and scope mount, top-of-the-line model.

Mfg.'s Sug. Retail $4,953 $4,475 $3,450 $2,750 $2,300 $1,850 $1,550 $1,350
Subtract $1,400 without Crown engraving option.

Grading	100%	98%	95%	90%	80%	70%	60%

RIFLES - VANGUARD SERIES BOLT ACTION

VANGUARD — .243 Win., .25-06 Rem., .270 Win., .30-06, .308 Win., 7mm Rem. Mag., .264 Win. Mag., or .300 Win. Mag. cal., mfg. circa late 1960s-early 1970s.

	$450	$375	$325	$295	$260	$230	$200

Add 10% for .264 Win. Mag. cal.

VANGUARD CLASSIC I — .223 Rem., .243 Win., .270 Win., 7mm/08 Rem., 7mm Rem. Mag., .30-06 or .308 Win. cal., checkered walnut stock with satin finish, black butt pad, 24 in. barrel, 3 (7mm Rem. Mag.) or 5 shot mag., No. 1 barrel contour, approx. 7 lbs. 5 oz. Mfg. 1989-1993.

	$480	$375	$325	$295	$260	$230	$200

Last Mfg.'s Sug. Retail was $549.

This model is the replacement for the Vanguard VGS and VGL.

VANGUARD CLASSIC II — .22-250, .243 Win., .270 Wby. Mag., .270 Win., 7mm Rem. Mag., .30-06, .300 Win. Mag., .300 Wby. Mag., or .338 Win. Mag. cal., 24 in. No. 2 barrel contour, 3 or 5 shot mag., custom checkered deluxe walnut stock with pistol grip cap and black forend cap, solid black recoil pad, matte finished metal, approx. 7¾ lbs. Mfg. 1989-92.

	$675	$550	$475	$425	$395	$360	$330

Last Mfg.'s Sug. Retail was $750.

This model is also available in a No. 3 barrel contour in .22-250 Rem. cal. only.

VANGUARD VGX — .22-250, .243 Win., .25-06, .270 Win., 7mm Rem. Mag., .30-06, or .300 Win. Mag. cal., bolt action, checkered deluxe walnut stock with rosewood tip forearm and pistol grip, 24 in. barrel, no sights, 5 shot mag.(except 3 shot for .300 Win. Mag.), high luster bluing, about 8 lbs. Disc. 1988.

	$525	$425	$365	$330	$300	$275	$255

Last Mfg.'s Sug. Retail was $600.

Not available in left-hand action.

VANGUARD VGX DELUXE — .22-250, .243 Win., .270 Win., .270 Wby. Mag., .300 Win. Mag., .300 Wby. Mag., .30-06, .338 Win. Mag., or 7mm Rem. Mag. cal., 24 in. barrel, Monte Carlo stock with skipline checkering, high gloss wood and metal, rosewood forend cap. Mfg. 1989-1993.

	$625	$550	$475	$425	$395	$360	$330

Last Mfg.'s Sug. Retail was $699.

VANGUARD VGS — same cals. as Vanguard VGX, bolt action, checkered satin finished walnut stock, 24 in. barrel, no sights, approx. 8 lbs. Disc. 1988.

	$415	$355	$295	$265	$245	$220	$200

Last Mfg.'s Sug. Retail was $467.

Not available in left-hand action.

VANGUARD VGL — .223 Rem., .243 Win., .270 Win., 7mm Rem. Mag., .30-06, or .308 Win. cal., lightweight bolt action, checkered walnut stock, 5 shot mag.(6 on .223 Rem.), 20 in. barrel, no sights, 6½ lbs. Disc. 1988.

	$415	$355	$295	$265	$245	$220	$200

Last Mfg.'s Sug. Retail was $467.

Not available in left-hand action.

VANGUARD WEATHERGUARD — same cals. as Classic I, replacement for Fiberguard, wrinkle black finished synthetic stock, entry level Weatherby, similar specs. as Classic I, approx. 8 lbs. Mfg. 1989-1993.

	$440	$350	$320	$290	$260	$230	$200

Last Mfg.'s Sug. Retail was $499.

VANGUARD ALASKAN — same cals. as Classic I, features electroless nickel metal plating, no sights. Mfg. 1993-1994.

	$625	$550	$475	$425	$395	$360	$330

Last Mfg.'s Sug. Retail was $699.

Grading	100%	98%	95%	90%	80%	70%	60%

VANGUARD FIBERGUARD — .223 Rem., .243 Win., .270 Win., 7mm Rem. Mag., .30-06, or .308 Win. cal., 20 in. barrel, green fiberglass stock, 3 to 6 shot mags., no sights, blued metal parts, approx. 6½ lbs. Disc. 1988.

			$500	$450	$395	$355	$285	$255	$220

Last Mfg.'s Sug. Retail was $560.

Not available in left-hand action.

RIFLES - .22 LR BOLT ACTION

ACCUMARK CLASSIC & DELUXE — while these models were advertised in 1990 ($635 retail), they were never manufactured.

RIFLES - .22 LR SEMI-AUTO

MARK XXII CLIP MAG — .22 LR cal., mag. feed, skipline checkered walnut stock with rosewood forearm and pistol grip caps, 5 or 10 shot detachable mag., 24 in. barrel, open sights, 6 lbs. Disc. 1989.

	100%	98%	95%	90%	80%	70%	60%
Japanese mfg.	$395	$320	$265	$245	$215	$195	$180
Italian mfg.	$495	$440	$365	$325	$275	$240	$210

Last Mfg.'s Sug. Retail was $454.

The Mark XXII clip mag. was originally mfg. in Italy - a slight premium might be asked. This model featured a receiver slide-switch that allowed semi-auto operation to be converted to single shot mode.

MARK XXII TUBE MAG — .22 LR cal., same general specifications as above model, except tube-feed, 15 shot, 6 lbs. Disc. 1989.

	$395	$320	$265	$245	$215	$195	$180

Last Mfg.'s Sug. Retail was $454.

DRILLINGS

WEATHERBY DRILLING — mfg. by J. P. Sauer during the late 1960s-early 1970s for Weatherby importation (marked Weatherby on right barrel), identical to Sauer Model 3000, except was not available in all metric cals. Disc.

	$2,850	$2,450	$2,100	$1,800	$1,500	$1,250	$1,000

SHOTGUNS: O/U

Weatherby shotguns are currently mfg. by SKB located in Tokyo, Japan.

REGENCY FIELD GRADE — 20 ga. Mag. or 12 ga., checkered stock, VR, engraved side plates, SST, early importation beginning in 1972 was from Italy, later mfg. was switched to Japan.

	$1,250	$895	$800	$700	$600	$550	$500

Add 10-15% for early Italian mfg. (note proof marks).

REGENCY TRAP GRADE — 12 ga., checkered trap stock, engraved, VR, SST. Imported from Italy.

	$900	$800	$700	$600	$550	$500	$475

OLYMPIAN STANDARD — 12 and 20 ga., lightly engraved sideplates. Disc. 1980.

	$850	$775	$725	$625	$525	$450	$400

OLYMPIAN SKEET — 26 or 28 in. barrel.

	$885	$775	$725	$625	$525	$450	$400

OLYMPIAN TRAP — 30 or 32 in. barrel, VR.

	$850	$775	$725	$625	$525	$440	$400

Grading	100%	98%	95%	90%	80%	70%	60%

ATHENA GRADE IV — 12, 20, 28 (mfg. 1989-1993), or .410 (mfg. 1989-1993) ga., 3 in. chambers, 26 or 28 in. VR barrels with or without choke tubes, boxlock with Greener Crossbolt, SST, ejectors, high luster finish on hand checkered claro walnut, engraved sideplates with satin nickel finish, vent. barrels and rib, multi-chokes became standard (except .410 ga.) 1986 and 1992 (28 ga.), 6½-8 lbs. Introduced 1982.

Mfg.'s Sug. Retail	$2,200	$1,825	$1,350	$1,050	$875	$725	$600	$525

Subtract 10% if without choke tubes.

This model was redesignated the Grade IV in 1989.

▲ **Skeet & Trap Models** — 12 (Trap only) or 20 ga., special stock dimensions, target sights. Disc. 1992.

	$1,675	$1,275	$1,000	$875	$725	$600	$525

Last Mfg.'s Sug. Retail was $1,965.

Skeet models are available in fixed choke only.

▲ **Single Trap Model** — 12 ga., 32 or 34 in. barrel with multi-choke feature. Disc. 1992.

	$1,675	$1,275	$1,000	$875	$725	$600	$525

Last Mfg.'s Sug. Retail was $1,975.

▲ **Trap Combo** — 12 ga., includes a set of O/U barrels and oversingle barrel with multi-choke feature. Disc. 1992.

	$2,300	$1,900	$1,605	$1,300	$995	$800	$675

Last Mfg.'s Sug. Retail was $2,616.

▲ **Master Skeet Set** — 12 ga., includes 6 fitted full length Briley tubes with integral extractors (20, 28, and .410 ga.), cased. Imported 1988-91.

	$3,100	$2,650	$2,150	$1,900	$1,775	$1,625	$1,525

ATHENA GRADE V CLASSIC FIELD — 12 or 20 ga., 3 in. chambers, similar to Grade IV, except has more elaborate engraving and better walnut. New 1989.

Mfg.'s Sug. Retail	$2,527	$2,125	$1,750	$1,375	$1,150	$900	$775	$675

In 1993, Weatherby changed the styling of this gun to incorporate European shooting features including an oil finished, round knob stock and slim forearm, tight rose-and-scroll engraving, and matte VR.

ORION I FIELD — 12 or 20 ga., 3 in. chambers, 26, 28, or 30 (12 ga. only) in. VR barrels with multi-chokes, SST, ejectors, entry level O/U with no engraving, checkered walnut stock and forearm. New 1989.

Mfg.'s Sug. Retail	$1,289	$1,065	$875	$710	$550	$495	$450	$400

ORION II FIELD — 12, 20, 28, or .410 ga., 3 in. chambers (except 28 ga.), boxlock with Greener Crossbolt, SST, ejectors, walnut with high-gloss finish, blue only, light engraving. Multi-chokes became standard 1986. Field Grade disc. 1993.

	$1,075	$875	$750	$625	$550	$500	$450

Last Mfg.'s Sug. Retail was $1,207.

Subtract 10% without choke tubes on older models.
Subtract $14 for Skeet grade (12 and 20 ga., fixed chokes only).

This model was redesignated Grade II in 1989. In 1993, the Standard Field Models in this variation were discontinued (Classic Grade took its place) - only Trap, Skeet, and Sporting Clays variations are now available.

▲ **Orion II Classic Field** — 12, 20, or 28 ga., multi-choked barrels, features rounded pistol grip stock and oil finished Claro walnut stock and forearm, waterfowl scene on silver gray nitride finish, matted VR. New 1993.

Mfg.'s Sug. Retail	$1,363	$1,115	$885	$730	$625	$550	$500	$450

▲ **Orion II Sporting Clays** — 12 ga. only, Sporting Clays configuration, early mfg. was blue finish, current mfg. is silver nitride finish, acid etched engraving, rounded recoil pad, matte finish VR, lengthened forcing cones. New 1991.

Mfg.'s Sug. Retail	$1,460	$1,195	$950	$765	$625	$550	$500	$450

▲ **Ducks Unlimited Orion** — 12 ga. (sponsor gun in 1986) or 20 ga. (sponsor gun in 1987), deluxe walnut with gold duck scenes, blue receiver, multi-chokes, includes presentation case.

	$1,395	$1,100	$875

W

Grading	100%	98%	95%	90%	80%	70%	60%

ORION III FIELD — 12 or 20 ga. only, similar to Grade II, except has silver gray receiver with custom engraving including mallard and pheasant game scenes, multi-chokes standard. New 1989.

Mfg.'s Sug. Retail	$1,626	$1,325	$995	$815	$650	$575	$500	$450

▲ *Orion III Classic Field* — 12 or 20 ga., multi-choked barrels, features rounded pistol grip stock and oil finished Claro walnut stock and forearm, extensive engraving on silver gray nitride finish, matted VR. New 1993.

Mfg.'s Sug. Retail	$1,626	$1,325	$995	$815	$650	$575	$500	$450

SHOTGUNS: SEMI-AUTO

CENTURION FIELD GRADE — 12 ga., VR, checkered stock, gas operation, walnut full pistol grip stock. Mfg. 1972-1981.

	$300	$280	$250	$240	$230	$210	$190

CENTURION TRAP GRADE — 12 ga., checkered stock, VR.

	$335	$300	$250	$240	$230	$210	$190

CENTURION DE LUXE — 12 ga., VR, checkered stock, lightly engraved, fancy wood ($200-250).

	$375	$350	$310	$275	$250	$235	$210

▲ *Centurion DU* — mfg. 1980 for DU chapters.

	$550	$375	$325

MODEL 82 — 12 ga. only, 2¾ or 3 in. chamber, gas operation, alloy receiver, VR, deluxe walnut, multi-chokes became standard in 1985, Trap Grade was disc. 1984. Mfg. 1983-89.

	$395	$350	$315	$280	$250	$235	$210

Last Mfg.'s Sug. Retail was $500.

Subtract $30 without multi-chokes.
Subtract $35 for Trap Grade (disc. 1984).

▲ *Model 82 Buckmaster* — 22 in. barrel choked skeet, rifle sights, 7½ lbs. Disc. 1989.

	$395	$350	$315	$280	$250	$235	$210

Last Mfg.'s Sug. Retail was $500.

SHOTGUNS: SLIDE ACTION

PATRICIAN FIELD GRADE — 12 ga., checkered stock, VR. Mfg. 1972-1981.

	$275	$230	$210	$190	$180	$160	$140

PATRICIAN TRAP GRADE — 12 ga., checkered stock, VR.

	$295	$250	$225	$200	$185	$175	$165

PATRICIAN DE LUXE — 12 ga., checkered stock, lightly engraved, fancy wood, VR.

	$325	$275	$250	$215	$195	$175	$165

MODEL 92 — 12 ga. only, 2¾ and 3 in. chambers, ultra-short slide action w/twin rails, 26-30 in. VR barrels, engraved black alloy receiver, checkered pistol grip walnut stock and forearm. New 1983. Subtract $30 for Trap grade (disc. 1984), $20 if fixed choke (multi-chokes became standard 1985) barrel. Disc. 1987.

	$325	$275	$250	$225	$200	$185	$175

Last Mfg.'s Sug. Retail was $400.

▲ *Model 92 Buckmaster* — 22 in. skeet bore barrel, rifle sights, 7½ lbs. Disc. 1987.

	$345	$285	$260	$240	$220	$200	$185

Last Mfg.'s Sug. Retail was $400.

WEAVER ARMS CORPORATION

Previous manufacturer located in Escondido, CA from 1984-1990.

Grading	100%	98%	95%	90%	80%	70%	60%

NIGHTHAWK CARBINE — 9mm Para., closed bolt semi-auto paramilitary design carbine, fires from closed bolt, 16.1 in. barrel, retractable shoulder stock, 25, 32, 40, or 50 shot mag. (interchangeable with Uzi), ambidextrous safety, parkerized finish, 6½ lbs.

| | $495 | $440 | $360 | $330 | $300 | $275 | $250 |

Last Mfg.'s Sug. Retail was $575.

NIGHTHAWK PISTOL — 9mm Para., closed bolt semi-auto, 10 or 12 in. barrel, alloy upper receiver, ambidextrous safety, black finish, 5 lbs. Mfg. 1987-90.

| | $525 | $465 | $375 | $340 | $300 | $275 | $250 |

Last Mfg.'s Sug. Retail was $475.

WEBLEY & SCOTT, LIMITED

Firearms manufacturer located in Birmingham, England 1898 to 1979. Beginning 1980, Webley & Scott, Ltd. began manufacturing high quality weapons only. Currently, Webley & Scott manufactures airguns only (please refer to Airguns section or Trademark Index).

Webley & Scott, Ltd. had the shotgun business re-established as a separate company named W & C Scott (Gunmakers) Ltd. in 1979. Shortly after being acquired by Holland & Holland, firearms manufacture was discontinued while airgun production resumed.

PISTOLS

MARK III M&P REVOLVER — .32 S&W, .320 S&W, or .38 S&W cal., single/double action, 6 shot, 3 in. and 4 in. barrel, hinged top break, blue, fixed sights, wood service or competition grips. Mfg. 1896-1939.

| | $350 | $295 | $255 | $220 | $195 | $165 | $140 |

Some Mark III revolvers were fitted with a manual safety.

▲ **Mark III Target Model** — .38 S&W cal., similar to above, except was also available with 6 - 10 in. barrel with adj. sights.

| | $450 | $375 | $325 | $275 | $250 | $225 | $200 |

MARK IV M&P REVOLVER — similar to Mark III, except 3 in., 4 in., or 5 in. barrel, improved hammer and grip design. Mfg. 1929-1979.

| | $350 | $295 | $255 | $220 | $195 | $165 | $140 |

This was the last of the Webley series of revolvers.

MARK IV .22 TARGET REVOLVER — similar to Mark IV, except .22 LR, 6 in. barrel, target sights, mfg. 1931-1967.

| | $450 | $385 | $330 | $285 | $235 | $200 | $165 |

MARK IV SERVICE REVOLVER — .455 cal., single/double action, 4 or 6 in. barrel, top break, blue, fixed sights, known as the Boer War Model and is not to be confused with the smaller, later Mark IV introduced in 1929. Mfg. 1899-1914.

| | $375 | $325 | $275 | $225 | $175 | $140 | $110 |

NO. 1 MARK VI BRITISH SERVICE REVOLVER — .45 LC, .45 ACP, or .455 Webley cal., single/double action, 4, 6, or 7½ in. barrel, top break, blue, fixed sights, wood service or competition grips. Mfg. 1914-1939.

| | $300 | $250 | $225 | $195 | $165 | $135 | $110 |

MARK VI .22 TARGET REVOLVER — similar to Mark VI, except .22 LR, target sights, mfg. until 1945.

| | $300 | $250 | $225 | $195 | $165 | $135 | $110 |

Bayonet and shoulder stock attachments were also available for this model. These accessories are rare and command considerable premiums over values listed above.

MARK V REVOLVER — .455 cal., single/double action. Many were military-modified for .45 Colt or .45 ACP, many were civilian-modified, round butt, top break. Mfg. 1914-1915 only.

| | $375 | $325 | $275 | $225 | $175 | $150 | $125 |

W

Grading	100%	98%	95%	90%	80%	70%	60%

BULLDOG OR RIC MODEL — available in .320 - .476 cals. (.455 Webley most common), 5 shot, $2\frac{1}{8}$ - $4\frac{1}{2}$ in. barrel, solid frame, blue, fixed sights. Mfg. 1867-1939 for Royal Irish Constabulary.

	$295	$250	$225	$175	$140	$110	$90

WEBLEY-FOSBERY AUTOMATIC REVOLVER — .455 Webley cal., 6 shot, top break, recoil revolves cylinder and cocks hammer, walnut or hard rubber grips. Mfg. 1901-1939.

A small number of Webley-Fosbery pistols were chambered for .38 Colt Auto Cartridge, usually found in 13xx range, features 8 shot cylinder.
Add $1,000 for .38 cal.

▲ *1901 Model* — large frame, early features.

	$5,000	$4,000	$3,000	$2,250	$1,800	$1,350	$900

Add 20% for Target Model (adj. rear sight).

▲ *1902 Model* — large frame, late features.

	$3,500	$3,000	$2,300	$1,750	$1,500	$1,200	$900

Add 20% for Target Model (adj. rear sight).

▲ *1904 Model* — small frame, late features.

	$3,500	$3,000	$2,300	$1,750	$1,500	$1,200	$900

Add 20% for Target Model (adj. rear sight).

HAMMER MODEL .25 AUTOMATIC — .25 auto cal., 6 shot mag., 2 in. barrel, no sights, blue, composition grips. Mfg. 1906-1940.

	$350	$250	$175	$150	$135	$125	$115

HAMMERLESS MODEL .25 — .25 auto cal., similar to Hammer Model .25, except no exposed hammer and fixed sights. Mfg. 1909-1940.

	$295	$225	$175	$150	$135	$125	$115

SINGLE SHOT TARGET PISTOL — .22 LR, .32 (special order), or .38 (special order) cal., 10 in. barrel, top break, blue, fixed sights on early models. Mfg. 1909-1964.

	$375	$250	$120	$110	$100	$90	$75

METROPOLITAN POLICE AUTOMATIC — .32 auto or .380 auto cal., 7 or 8 shot, $3\frac{1}{2}$ in. barrel, blue, fixed sights, composition grips. Mfg. 1906-1940.

	$450	$300	$165	$120	$110	$100	$85

SEMI-AUTO SINGLE SHOT — .22 Long cal., $4\frac{1}{4}$ and 9 in. barrel, adj. sights, blue, composition grips, empty case is ejected and hammer cocked as in a semi-auto, then it is loaded singly and slide closed. Mfg. 1911-1927.

	$950	$750	$650	$600	$550	$475	$400

9MM M&P AUTOMATIC — 9mm Browning Long, 8 shot, 5 in. barrel, blue, fixed sights. Mfg. 1909-1930.

	$950	$850	$750	$650	$550	$475	$400

HAMMERLESS MODEL 1913 — .38 cal., high velocity, approx. 1,000 mfg.

	$1,650	$1,250	$1,000	$800	$700	$600	$500

MARK I .455 AUTO PISTOL — .455 Webley cal., 7 shot, 5 in. barrel, blue, fixed sights. Mfg. 1912-1945.

	$1,750	$1,300	$1,000	$750	$600	$500	$400

MARK I NO. 2 — similar to Mark I, except adj. sights, modified safety, and cut for shoulder stock.

	$4,500	$3,500	$3,000	$2,500	$2,000	$1,500	$1,000

The shoulder stock is an extremely rare accessory for this variation.

Grading	100%	98%	95%	90%	80%	70%	60%

SHOTGUNS

MODEL 700 SIDE-BY-SIDE DOUBLE BARREL — 12 or 20 ga., boxlock, case hardened receiver, minimum engraving, single trigger. Deduct $50 for double trigger. Mfg. 1949-1980.

	$1,700	$1,625	$1,500	$1,250	$1,000	$750	$600

MODEL 701 — similar to 700 but fanciest walnut, most engraving. Deduct $100 for double trigger. Mfg. 1949-1980.

	$3,150	$2,500	$2,100	$1,800	$1,400	$1,150	$925

MODEL 702 — similar to 700 but middle grade. Deduct $75 for double trigger. Mfg. 1949-1980.

	$2,650	$2,200	$1,800	$1,500	$1,250	$950	$750

MODEL 710 — same action as the Model 700, except is 28 ga. and designed specifically for the American market, only 40 were mfg. 1966-1968.

	$2,750	$2,400	$2,050	$1,775	$1,525	$1,300	$1,100

MODEL 712 — 12 ga., specifically designed for the American market.

	$1,700	$1,625	$1,500	$1,250	$1,000	$750	$600

MODEL 720 — 20 ga.

	$2,100	$1,700	$1,625	$1,500	$1,250	$1,000	$750

WEIHRAUCH, HANS-HERMANN

Manufacturer located in Mellrichstadt, Germany. Exclusive factory authorized U.S. distributor is European American Armory, located in Sharpes, FL.

MODEL HW 60 TARGET — .22 LR cal., target rifle featuring adj. sights, 26¾ in. barrel, single shot, match walnut stock, and other match features, aperture sights, 10.8 lbs. Importation disc. 1995.

	$625	$550	$450	$395	$350	$295	$275

Last Mfg.'s Sug. Retail was $705.

Add $220 for left-hand action (disc.).

MODEL HW 60J — .22 LR or .222 Rem. cal., sporter model with checkered walnut stock. Importation disc. 1992.

	$525	$465	$435	$395	$345	$300	$260

Last Mfg.'s Sug. Retail was $585.

Add $304 for .222 Rem. cal.

MODEL HW 66 RIFLE — .22 Hornet or .222 Rem. cal., match grade bolt action rifle. Imported 1989-90 only.

	$575	$495	$395	$325	$285	$250	$215

Last Mfg.'s Sug. Retail was $688.

Add $78 for double set triggers.
Add $55 for stainless steel barrel (.22 Hornet).

MODEL HW 660 MATCH — .22 LR cal., match rifle variation featuring adj. stock comb with vent. forend, aperture sights, 10.8 lbs. Importation began 1991.

Mfg.'s Sug. Retail	$875	$740	$640	$565	$475	$400	$350	$300

WESSON FIREARMS CO. INC.

Previous manufacturer located in Palmer, MA until 1995. In late 1990, ownership of Dan Wesson Arms changed (within the family), and the new company has been renamed Wesson Firearms Co., Inc.

Grading	100%	98%	95%	90%	80%	70%	60%

REVOLVERS: DOUBLE ACTION

MODEL 11 — .357 Mag. cal., 6 shot, 2½, 4, or 6 in. interchangeable barrels, fixed sights, blue, interchangeable grips, exposed barrel nut. Mfg. 1970-1971.

	$200	$175	$160	$150	$140	$130	$120

Add $60 per extra barrel.

MODEL 12 — similar to 11, with adj. sights. Mfg. 1970-1971.

	$245	$200	$175	$160	$150	$140	$130

MODEL 14 — similar to 11, with recessed barrel nut. Mfg. 1971-1975.

	$225	$185	$170	$160	$150	$140	$130

MODEL 8 — similar to 14, except .38 Spl. cal.

	$200	$170	$155	$145	$135	$125	$115

MODEL 15 — similar to 14, with adj. sights. Mfg. 1971-1975.

	$245	$200	$155	$145	$135	$125	$115

MODEL 9 — similar to 15, except .38 Spl. cal. Mfg. 1971-1975.

	$245	$200	$155	$145	$135	$125	$115

REVOLVERS: CURRENT MANUFACTURE

As a guideline, the following information is provided on Wesson Firearms frames. The smallest frames are Models 738P and 38P. Small frame models include 22, 722, 22M, 722M, 32, 732, 322, 7322, 8-2, 708, 9-2, 709, 14-2, 714, 15-2, and 715-2. Large frames include 41, 741, 44, 744, 45, and 745. SuperMag frame models include 40, 740, 375 (disc.), 414 (new 1995), 7414 (new 1995), 445, and 7445. Small frames are sideplate design, while large frames are solid frame construction. Current models listed below assume interchangeable barrels unless otherwise specified.

Dan Wesson revolvers are mfg. with solid rib barrels as standard equipment.

MODEL 22 — .22 LR cal., double action, 6 shot, adj. sights, 2½, 4, 6, 8, or 10 in. (disc. 1987) barrel, current production disc. 1995.

	$285	$225	$200	$190	$180	$170	$160

Last Mfg.'s Sug. Retail was $357.

Add approx. $9 for each additional barrel length, $21 for VR, $57 for vent. heavy rib shroud.

▲ **Model 22 Pistol Pac** — includes 2½, 4, 6, and 8 in. barrel assemblies, extra grip, 4 additional front sight blades, and aluminum case. Disc. 1995.

	$520	$400	$360	$330	$300	$275	$260

Last Mfg.'s Sug. Retail was $653.

Add $103 for full shroud VR barrels.
Add $227 for heavy full shroud VR barrels.

▲ **Model 22 Silhouette** — .22 LR cal., choice of 10 in. vent. or heavy vent. barrel, single action only, combat style grip, narrow rear sight blade and patridge front. Mfg. 1992-95.

	$395	$325	$295	$275	$260	$245	$230

Last Mfg.'s Sug. Retail was $474.

Add $18 for vent. heavy barrel.

MODEL 22M — .22 Mag. cal., otherwise similar to Model 22. Disc. 1994.

	$290	$230	$200	$190	$180	$170	$160

Last Mfg.'s Sug. Retail was $349.

▲ **Model 22M Pistol Pac** — includes 2½, 4, 6, and 8 in. barrel assemblies, extra grip, 4 additional front sight blades, and aluminum case. Disc. 1994.

	$500	$400	$360	$330	$300	$275	$260

Last Mfg.'s Sug. Retail was $637.

Add $101 for full shroud VR barrels.
Add $191 for heavy full shroud VR barrels.

Grading	100%	98%	95%	90%	80%	70%	60%

MODEL 32 — .32 H&R Mag. cal., 2½, 4, 6, or 8 in. barrel, adj. rear sight, interchangeable colored front sight blades, blue finish, checkered target grips. Mfg. 1986-95.

	$285	$225	$200	$190	$180	$170	$160

Last Mfg.'s Sug. Retail was $357.

Add $21 for VR barrel shroud (Model 32-V), add $57 for VR heavy barrel shroud (Model 32-VH), approx. $9 for each additional barrel length over 2½ in.

▲ *Model 32 Pistol Pac* — includes 2½, 4, 6, and 8 in. barrel assemblies, extra grip, 4 additional front sight blades, and aluminum case. Disc. 1995.

	$520	$400	$360	$330	$300	$275	$260

Last Mfg.'s Sug. Retail was $653.

Add $103 for full shroud VR barrels.
Add $227 for heavy full shroud VR barrels.

MODEL 38P — .38+P cal., 5 shot, 6½ in. barrel, fixed sights, wood or rubber grips, 24.6 oz. Mfg. 1992-93.

	$230	$190	$170	$150	$135	$120	$110

Last Mfg.'s Sug. Retail was $285.

MODEL 322 — .32-20 cal., 2½, 4, 6, or 8 in. barrel, adj. rear sight, interchangeable colored front sight blades, blue finish, checkered target grips. Mfg. 1991-95.

	$285	$225	$200	$190	$180	$170	$160

Last Mfg.'s Sug. Retail was $357.

Add $21 for VR barrel shroud (Model 322-V), add $57 for VR heavy barrel shroud (Model 322-VH), approx. $9-$30 for each additional barrel length over 2½ in.

▲ *Model 322 Pistol Pac* — includes 2½, 4, 6, and 8 in. barrel assemblies, extra grip, 4 additional front sight blades, and aluminum case. Disc. 1995.

	$520	$400	$360	$330	$300	$275	$260

Last Mfg.'s Sug. Retail was $653.

Add $103 for full shroud VR barrels.
Add $227 for heavy full shroud VR barrels.

MODEL 14 — .357 Mag. cal., 2½, 4, 6, or 8 (disc. 1994) in. interchangeable barrels, fixed sights, blue. Mfg. 1975-1995.

	$215	$170	$150	$140	$130	$120	$110

Last Mfg.'s Sug. Retail was $274.

Add approx. $7 for each additional barrel length.

▲ *Model 14 Fixed Barrel* — .357 Mag. cal., 2½ or 4 in. (fixed sight Service Model) barrel, satin blue finish. Mfg. 1993-95.

	$225	$175	$150	$140	$130	$120	$110

Last Mfg.'s Sug. Retail was $289.

Add $7 for 4 in. barrel.

▲ *Model 14 PPC* — .357 Mag. cal., extra heavy 6 in. bull shroud barrel with removable underweight, Hogue Gripper grips, Aristocrat sights. Mfg. 1992 only.

	$675	$550	$450	$375	$330	$300	$275

Last Mfg.'s Sug. Retail was $780.

▲ *Model 14 Pistol Pac* — includes 2½, 4, and 6 in. barrel assemblies, extra grip and aluminum case. Disc. 1994.

	$390	$325	$300	$275	$260	$245	$230

Last Mfg.'s Sug. Retail was $463.

MODEL 8 — similar to 14, except .38 Spl. cal. Disc. 1995.

	$220	$170	$150	$140	$130	$120	$110

Last Mfg.'s Sug. Retail was $274.

Add approx. $6 for each additional barrel length.

▲ *Model 8 PPC* — .38 Spl. cal., extra heavy 6 in. bull shroud barrel with removable underweight, Hogue Gripper grips, Aristocrat sights. Mfg. 1992 only.

	$675	$550	$450	$375	$330	$300	$275

Last Mfg.'s Sug. Retail was $780.

W

Grading	100%	98%	95%	90%	80%	70%	60%

MODEL 15 — similar to 14, except adj. sights, available with 2, 4, 6, 8, 10, 12, or 15 in. barrels. Disc. 1995.

▲ *2 in. barrel*

	$285	$225	$200	$190	$180	$170	$160

Last Mfg.'s Sug. Retail was $346.

Add approx. $8-$13 for each additional barrel length over 2 inches, $22 for VR barrel (Model 15V), or $60 for VR heavy barrel shroud (Model 15HV).

▲ *Model 15 Target Fixed Barrel* — .357 Mag. cal., 3, 4, 5, or 6 in. barrel, high bright blue finish. Mfg. 1993-95.

	$270	$220	$190	$175	$150	$125	$110

Last Mfg.'s Sug. Retail was $322.

Add approx. $9 for each barrel length over 3 in.
Add approx. $80 for compensated barrel (4, 5, or 6 in. - new 1994).

MODEL 15 GOLD SERIES — .357 Mag. cal., 6 or 8 in. VR heavy slotted barrel, "Gold" stamped shroud with Dan Wesson signature, smoother action (8 lb. double action pull), 18 kt. gold-plated trigger, white triangle rear sight with orange dot patridge front sight, exotic hardwood grips. Mfg. 1989-94.

	$425	$380	$340	$300	$260	$225	$185

Last Mfg.'s Sug. Retail was $544.

▲ *Model 15 Pistol Pac* — includes 2½, 4, 6, and 8 in. barrel assemblies, extra grip, 4 additional front sight blades, and aluminum case. Disc. 1995.

	$500	$395	$360	$330	$300	$275	$260

Last Mfg.'s Sug. Retail was $629.

Add $104 for full shroud VR barrels.
Add $214 for heavy full shroud VR barrels.

MODEL 9 — similar to 15, except .38 Spl. cal. Use same add-ons as in Model 15. Disc. 1995.

	$346	$285	$225	$200	$190	$180	$170

Last Mfg.'s Sug. Retail was $346.

This model was also available in a Pistol Pac - same specifications and values as the Model 15 Pistol Pac.

MODEL 375 SUPERMAG — .375 Super Mag. cal., 4, 6, 8, or 10 in. VR barrel, adj. rear sight, interchangeable front and rear sight blades, bright blue finish, smooth target grips. Mfg. 1986-94.

	$410	$335	$285	$260	$240	$230	$225

Last Mfg.'s Sug. Retail was $498.

Add approx. $15 for each barrel length after 6 in., $39 for slotted shroud (Model 375-V8S, 8 in. barrel only), $10-$12 for VR heavy shroud (Model 375-VH).

MODEL 40 (.357 SUPERMAG) — .357 Super Mag. cal. (.357 Max.), double action, 6 shot, 4, 6, 8, or 10 in. barrel VR. Disc. 1995.

	$410	$340	$285	$260	$240	$230	$225

Last Mfg.'s Sug. Retail was $502.

Add $87 for slotted barrel shroud (8 in. barrel only), $22-$129 for heavy VR barrel, approx. $33 for each additional barrel length.

MODEL 41 — .41 Mag. cal., double action, 6 shot, 4, 6, 8, or 10 in. barrel VR. Disc. 1995.

	$375	$305	$265	$250	$230	$215	$200

Last Mfg.'s Sug. Retail was $447.

Add approx. $20 for heavy barrel shroud, approx. $15 for each additional barrel length.

▲ *Model 41 Pistol Pac* — includes 6 and 8 in. VR barrel assemblies, extra grip, 2 additional front sight blades, and aluminum case. Disc. 1995.

	$555	$430	$380	$330	$300	$275	$260

Last Mfg.'s Sug. Retail was $678.

Add $53 for full shroud VR barrels.

Grading	100%	98%	95%	90%	80%	70%	60%

MODEL .414 SUPERMAG — .414 Super Mag. cal., 4, 6, 8, or 10 in. VR barrel, adj. rear sight, interchangeable front and rear sight blades (optional), bright blue finish, smooth target grips. Mfg. 1995 only.

	$425	$335	$290	$275	$250	$230	$225

Last Mfg.'s Sug. Retail $519.

Add approx. $14 for each barrel length after 4 in., $58 for slotted shroud (Model 414-V8S, 8 in. barrel only), approx. $23 for VR heavy rib shroud.

MODEL 44 — .44 Mag. cal., double action, similar to Model 41, adj. sights. Disc. 1995.

	$375	$305	$265	$250	$230	$215	$200

Last Mfg.'s Sug. Retail was $447.

Add approx. $20 for heavy barrel shroud, approx. $15 for each additional barrel length.

▲ *Model 44 Target Fixed Barrel* — .44 Mag. cal., 4, 5, 6, or 8 in. barrel, high bright blue finish. Mfg. 1994-95.

	$375	$305	$265	$250	$230	$215	$200

Last Mfg.'s Sug. Retail was $447.

Add approx. $4 for each barrel length over 3 in.

▲ *Model 44 Pistol Pac* — includes 6 and 8 in. VR barrel assemblies, extra grip, 4 additional front sight blades, and aluminum case. Disc. 1995.

	$555	$430	$380	$330	$300	$275	$260

Last Mfg.'s Sug. Retail was $678.

Add $53 for full shroud VR barrels.

MODEL 45 — .45 LC cal., 4, 6, 8, or 10 in. VR barrel, same frame as Model 44V, blued finish. Mfg. 1988-95.

	$375	$305	$265	$250	$230	$215	$200

Last Mfg.'s Sug. Retail was $447.

Add $20 for VR heavy barrel shroud, approx. $15 for each additional barrel length.

▲ *Model 45 Pistol Pac* — includes 6 and 8 in. VR barrel assemblies, extra grip, 2 additional front sight blades, and aluminum case. Disc. 1995.

	$555	$430	$380	$330	$300	$275	$260

Last Mfg.'s Sug. Retail was $678.

Add $53 for full shroud VR barrels.

MODEL .45 PIN GUN — .45 ACP cal., competition pin gun model with 5 in. vent. or heavy vent barrel configuration, blued steel, two stage Taylor forcing cone, 54 oz. Mfg. 1993-95.

	$575	$495	$440	$395	$350	$300	$250

Last Mfg.'s Sug. Retail was $654.

Add $9 for VR heavy shroud barrel.

MODEL .445 SUPERMAG — .445 Super Mag. cal., 4, 6, 8, or 10 in. VR barrel, adj. rear sight, interchangeable front and rear sight blades (optional), bright blue finish, smooth target grips. Mfg. 1991-95.

	$425	$335	$290	$275	$250	$230	$225

Last Mfg.'s Sug. Retail was $519.

Add approx. $14 for each barrel length after 4 in., $58 for slotted shroud (Model 445-V8S, 8 in. barrel only), approx. $23 for VR heavy rib shroud.

HUNTER SERIES — .357 Super Mag., .41 Mag., .44 Mag., or .445 Super Mag. cal., 7½ in. barrel with heavy shroud, Hogue rubber finger grooved and wood presentation grips, choice of Gunworks iron sights or w/o sights with Burris base and rings, non-fluted cylinder, with or w/o compensator, approx. 4 lbs. Mfg. 1994-95.

	$750	$575	$475	$400	$360	$330	$300

Last Mfg.'s Sug. Retail was $805.

Add $32 for compensated barrel.
Add $33 for scope mounts (w/o sights).

Grading	100%	98%	95%	90%	80%	70%	60%

REVOLVERS: STAINLESS STEEL

MODEL 722 — stainless version of Model 22, use same add-ons for various barrel options. Disc. 1995.

$335 $255 $205

Last Mfg.'s Sug. Retail was $400.

This model was also available in a Pistol Pac including 2½, 4, 6, and 8 in. solid rib barrel assemblies, extra grip, 4 additional sight blades, and fitted carrying case - Last Mfg.'s Suggested Retail was $712. Add $103 for VR barrels, $210 for full shroud heavy VR barrels.

▲ *Model 722 Silhouette* — .22 LR cal., choice of 10 in. vent. or heavy vent. barrel, single action only, combat style grip, narrow rear sight blade and patridge front. Mfg. 1992-95.

$410 $340 $295

Last Mfg.'s Sug. Retail was $504.

Add $28 for heavy vent. barrel.

MODEL 722M — .22 Mag cal., otherwise similar to Model 722, use same add-ons for various barrel options. Disc. 1994.

$320 $270 $230

Last Mfg.'s Sug. Retail was $391.

This model was also available in a Pistol Pac including 2½, 4, 6, and 8 in. solid rib barrel assemblies, extra grip, 4 additional sight blades, and fitted carrying case. Last Mfg.'s Suggested Retail was $724. Add $101 for VR barrels, $199 for full shroud heavy VR barrels.

MODEL 708 — .38 Spl. cal., similar to Model 8. Add approx. $6 for each additional barrel length. Disc. 1995.

$265 $200 $170

Last Mfg.'s Sug. Retail was $319.

This model was also available in a Pistol Pac including 2½, 4, and 6 in. solid rib barrel assemblies, extra grip and fitted carrying case. Disc. 1994. Last Mfg.'s Suggested Retail was $517.

▲ *Model 708 Action Cup/PPC* — .38 Spl. cal., extra heavy 6 in. bull shroud barrel with removable underweight, Hogue Gripper grips, mounted Tasco Pro Point II on Action Cup, Aristocrat sights on PPC. Mfg. 1992 only.

$725 $650 $550

Last Mfg.'s Sug. Retail was $857.

Add $56 for Action Cup Model with Tasco Scope.

MODEL 709 — .38 Spl. cal., target revolver, adj. sights. Also available in special order 10, 12 (disc.), or 15 (disc.) in. barrel lengths. Disc. 1995.

$310 $255 $205

Last Mfg.'s Sug. Retail was $376.

Add approx. $10 for each additional longer barrel length, approx. $19 for VR, approx. $56 for heavy VR.

This model was also available in a Pistol Pac including 2½, 4, 6, and 8 in. solid rib barrel assemblies, extra grip, 4 additional sight blades, and fitted carrying case. Last Mfg.'s Suggested Retail was $712. Add $103 for VR barrels, $210 for full shroud heavy VR barrels.

MODEL 714 (INTERCHANGEABLE OR FIXED) — .357 Mag. cal., fixed sight Service Model with 2½, 4, or 6 in. barrel, brushed stainless steel. Mfg. 1993-95.

$260 $200 $160

Last Mfg.'s Sug. Retail was $319.

Add approx. $6 for 4 or 6 in. barrel.
Subtract $6 for fixed barrel (2½ or 4 in. barrel only).

Grading	100%	98%	95%	90%	80%	70%	60%

▲ *Model 714 Action Cup/PPC* — .357 Mag. cal., extra heavy 6 in. bull shroud barrel with removable underweight, Hogue Gripper grips, mounted Tasco Pro Point II on Action Cup, Aristocrat sights on PPC. Mfg. 1992 only.

$725 $650 $550

Last Mfg.'s Sug. Retail was $857.

Add $56 for Action Cup Model with Tasco Scope.

MODEL 715 INTERCHANGEABLE — .357 Mag. cal., 2½, 4, 6, 8, or 10 in. with adj. rear sight, brushed stainless steel. Mfg. 1993-95.

$310 $255 $205

Last Mfg.'s Sug. Retail was $376.

Add approx. $10 for each additional longer barrel length, approx. $19 for VR, approx. $56 for heavy VR.

This model was also available in a Pistol Pac including 2½, 4, 6, and 8 in. solid rib barrel assemblies, extra grip, 4 additional sight blades, and fitted carrying case. Last Mfg.'s Suggested Retail was $712. Add $103 for VR barrels, $210 for full shroud heavy VR barrels.

▲ *Model 715 Fixed Target* — .357 Mag. cal., 3, 4, 5, or 6 in. fixed barrel, adj. rear sight. Mfg. 1993-95.

$280 $210 $170

Last Mfg.'s Sug. Retail was $345.

Add approx. $70 for compensated barrel (4, 5, or 6 in. - new 1994).

MODEL 732 — .32 H&R Mag. cal., similar to Model 32, except is stainless steel. Mfg. 1986-95.

$400 $335 $255 $205

Last Mfg.'s Sug. Retail was $400.

Add $22 for VR barrel shroud (Model 732-V), $53 for VR heavy barrel shroud (Model 732-VH), approx. $9 for each additional barrel length over 2½ in.

This model was also available in a Pistol Pac including 2½, 4, 6, and 8 in. solid rib barrel assemblies, extra grip, 4 additional sight blades, and fitted carrying case. Last Mfg.'s Suggested Retail was $712. Add $103 for VR barrels, $210 for full shroud heavy VR barrels.

MODEL 738P — .38+P cal., 5 shot, 6½ in. barrel, fixed sights, wood or rubber grips, 24.6 oz. Mfg. 1992-95.

$275 $210 $175

Last Mfg.'s Sug. Retail was $340.

MODEL 7322 — .32-20 cal., similar to Model 322, except is stainless steel. Mfg. 1991-95.

$335 $255 $205

Last Mfg.'s Sug. Retail was $400.

Add $22 for VR barrel shroud (Model 7322-V), $53 for VR heavy barrel shroud (Model 7322-VH), approx. $9 for each additional barrel length over 2½ in.

This model was also available in a Pistol Pac including 2½, 4, 6, and 8 in. solid rib barrel assemblies, extra grip, 4 additional sight blades, and fitted carrying case. Last Mfg.'s Suggested Retail was $712. Add $103 for VR barrels, $210 for full shroud heavy VR barrels.

MODEL 740V - .357 SUPERMAG — .357 Max. cal., 4, 6, 8, or 10 in. barrel, adj. rear sight with interchangeable front and rear blades, high polished finish, smooth target grips. Mfg. 1986-95.

$460 $350 $315

Last Mfg.'s Sug. Retail was $567.

Add approx. $20 for each additional barrel length after 4 in., $78 with vent. slotted shroud (only avail. with 8 in. barrel), $20 for VR heavy barrel shroud (Model 740-VH).

MODEL 741V — .41 Mag. cal., similar to Model 41V. Disc. 1995.

$420 $325 $270

Last Mfg.'s Sug. Retail was $524.

Add approx. $20 for heavy VR, approx. $13 for each barrel length over 4 in.

This model was also available in a Pistol Pac including 6 and 8 in. VR barrel assemblies, extra grip, 2 additional sight blades, and fitted carrying case. Last Mfg.'s Suggested Retail was $785. Add $54 for full shroud VR barrels.

W

Grading	100%	98%	95%	90%	80%	70%	60%

MODEL 744V — .44 Mag. cal., similar to Model 44V. Disc. 1995.

	$430	$345	$285				

Last Mfg.'s Sug. Retail was $524.

Add approx. $20 for heavy VR, $13 for each barrel length over 4 in.

This model was also available in a Pistol Pac including 6 and 8 in. VR barrel assemblies, extra grip, 2 additional sight blades, and fitted carrying case. Last Mfg.'s Suggested Retail was $785. Add $54 for full shroud VR barrels.

▲ *Model 744V Target Fixed Barrel* — .44 Mag. cal., 4, 5, 6, or 8 in. barrel, brushed stainless steel. Mfg. 1994-95.

	$395	$315	$265	$250	$230	$215	$200

Last Mfg.'s Sug. Retail was $493.

Add approx. $4 for each barrel length over 3 in.

▲ *Model 744 Commemorative* — limited mfg.

	$595	$475	$325				

MODEL 745V — .45 LC cal., similar to Model 45, except in stainless steel. Disc. 1995.

	$430	$345	$285				

Last Mfg.'s Sug. Retail was $524.

Add $20 for heavy full shroud VR barrels, $13 for each additional barrel length.

This model was also available in a Pistol Pac which included 6 and 8 in. VR barrel assemblies, extra grip, 2 additional sight blades, and fitted carrying case. Last Mfg.'s Suggested Retail was $785. Add $43 for full shroud VR barrels.

MODEL .45 PIN GUN — .45 ACP cal., similar to model described previously, except is stainless steel. Mfg. 1993-95.

	$625	$525	$425				

Last Mfg.'s Sug. Retail was $713.

Add $49 for VR heavy rib shroud.

MODEL 7414 SUPERMAG — .414 Super Mag. cal., 4, 6, 8, or 10 in. VR barrel, adj. rear sight, interchangeable front and rear sight blades (optional), bright blue finish, smooth target grips. Mfg. 1995 only.

	$475	$350	$295				

Last Mfg.'s Sug. Retail was $596.

Add approx. $14 for each barrel length after 4 in., $74 for slotted shroud (Model 7414-V8S, 8 in. barrel only), approx. $25 for VR heavy rib shroud.

MODEL 7445 SUPERMAG — .445 Super Mag. cal., 4, 6, 8, or 10 in. VR barrel, adj. rear sight, interchangeable front and rear sight blades (optional), high polished finish, smooth target grips. Mfg. 1991-95.

	$475	$350	$295				

Last Mfg.'s Sug. Retail was $596.

Add approx. $17 for each barrel length after 6 in., $74 for slotted shroud (Model 7445-VH8S, 8 in. barrel only), approx. $25 for VR heavy rib shroud, approx. $40 for VR heavy shroud and interchangeable sights (Model 7445-VH).

SUPER RAM SILHOUETTE — .357 Max., .414 Super Mag., or .44 Mag. cal., silhouette variation featuring modified Iron Sight Gun Works rear sight, Allen Taylor throated barrel, factory trigger job, 4 lbs. Mfg. 1995 only.

	$695	$550	$375				

Last Mfg.'s Sug. Retail was $807.

Add $43 for .414 Super Mag. cal.

HUNTER SERIES — .357 Super Mag., .41 Mag., .44 Mag., or .445 Super Mag. cal., 7½ in. barrel with heavy shroud, Hogue rubber finger grooved and wood presentation grips, choice of Gunworks iron sights or w/o sights with Burris base and rings, non-fluted cylinder, with or w/o compensator, approx. 4 lbs. Mfg. 1994-95.

	$780	$595	$475	$400	$360	$330	$300

Last Mfg.'s Sug. Retail was $849.

Add $32 for compensated barrel.
Add $32 for scope mounts (w/o sights).

WESSON, FRANK
Worcester, MA 1854 to 1865, Springfield, MA 1865-1875.

PISTOLS: SINGLE SHOT

100%	98%	95%	90%	80%	70%	60%	50%	40%	30%	20%	10%

SMALL FRAME FIRST MODEL — .22 cal., tip up action, 3½ in. ½ octagon barrel, brass frame, spur trigger, rosewood grips, round frame, irregular sideplate. Mfg. 2500, 1859-1862.

| $605 | $550 | $495 | $440 | $385 | $330 | $275 | $220 | $195 | $165 | $140 | $110 |

SMALL FRAME SECOND MODEL — similar to First Model, with flat sided frame and circular sideplate. Mfg. 12,000, 1862-1880.

| $550 | $495 | $440 | $385 | $330 | $305 | $250 | $195 | $165 | $110 | $105 | $85 |

MEDIUM FRAME FIRST MODEL — .30 S or L, .32 S rimfire cal., 4 in. ½ octagon barrel, iron frame, same as Small Frame in other respects, narrow hinge and short trigger. Mfg. 1000, 1859-1862.

| $525 | $470 | $415 | $360 | $305 | $275 | $220 | $195 | $165 | $110 | $105 | $85 |

MEDIUM FRAME SECOND MODEL — similar to First Model, with wider hinge and longer trigger. Mfg. 1000, 1862-1870.

| $495 | $440 | $385 | $330 | $275 | $250 | $220 | $195 | $165 | $110 | $105 | $85 |

RIFLES

NO. 1 LONG RANGE — side hammer, falling block lever actuated, .44-100 and .45-100 standard cal., 34 in. octagon barrel, tang. sight, select checkered pistol grip stock. Less than 50 mfg., circa 1870-1880.

| $4,950 | $4,675 | $4,400 | $3,850 | $3,575 | $3,080 | $2,860 | $2,475 | $2,200 | $2,035 | $1,760 | $1,540 |

NO. 2 HUNTING RIFLE — similar to No. 1, with finger loop lever. Less than 100 mfg.

| $4,400 | $4,180 | $3,850 | $3,520 | $3,025 | $2,750 | $2,420 | $2,255 | $2,035 | $1,925 | $1,760 | $1,540 |

NO. 1 SPORTING RIFLE — similar to No. 2, with center hammer, .38-100, .40-100, .45-100. Less than 25 mfg.

| $4,400 | $4,180 | $3,850 | $3,520 | $3,025 | $2,750 | $2,420 | $2,255 | $2,035 | $1,925 | $1,760 | $1,540 |

POCKET RIFLES

SMALL FRAME TIP UP — .22 rimfire cal., 6 in. ½ octagon barrel, brass frame, spur trigger, rosewood grips. Approx. 500 mfg., 1865-1875.

| $605 | $550 | $525 | $495 | $470 | $440 | $415 | $360 | $330 | $275 | $220 | $165 |

If without stock - deduct 25%.

MEDIUM FRAME TIP UP — .22, .30, or .32 rimfire cal.s, 10 or 12 in. barrel, same as small frame, with exceptions noted and larger frame. Approx. 1,000 mfg., 1862-1870.

| $605 | $550 | $525 | $495 | $470 | $440 | $415 | $360 | $330 | $275 | $220 | $165 |

If without stock - deduct 25%.

MODEL 1870 SMALL FRAME FIRST TYPE — similar to Small Frame Tip Up, except barrel rotates on its axis to load, detachable stock. Approx. 3,000 mfg., 1870-1890.

| $550 | $495 | $470 | $440 | $415 | $385 | $360 | $305 | $275 | $220 | $195 | $165 |

If without stock - deduct 25%.

MODEL 1870 SMALL FRAME SECOND TYPE — full octagon barrel.

| $525 | $470 | $440 | $415 | $385 | $360 | $330 | $275 | $250 | $195 | $165 | $140 |

MODEL 1870 SMALL FRAME THIRD TYPE — iron frame, push button ½ cock.

| $495 | $440 | $415 | $385 | $360 | $330 | $305 | $250 | $220 | $165 | $140 | $110 |

W

100%	98%	95%	90%	80%	70%	60%	50%	40%	30%	20%	10%

MODEL 1870 MEDIUM FRAME FIRST TYPE — similar to Small Frame, except in size and availability of .32 cal. Approx. 5,000 mfg., 1870-1893.

| $525 | $495 | $470 | $440 | $415 | $385 | $360 | $305 | $275 | $250 | $195 | $165 |

Deduct 25% if without stock.

MODEL 1870 MEDIUM FRAME SECOND TYPE — external push-button half cock and iron frame.

| $440 | $415 | $385 | $330 | $305 | $275 | $220 | $195 | $165 | $140 | $110 | $90 |

Deduct 25% if without stock.

MODEL 1870 MEDIUM FRAME THIRD TYPE — has three screws in frame, iron frame.

| $440 | $415 | $385 | $330 | $305 | $275 | $220 | $195 | $165 | $140 | $110 | $90 |

Deduct 25% if without stock.

MODEL 1870 LARGE FRAME FIRST TYPE — .32, .38, .42, or .44 rimfire cal., 15-24 in. barrels, similar to smaller frame models, auto extractor. Approx. 500 mfg., 1870-1880.

| $825 | $770 | $715 | $660 | $605 | $550 | $525 | $495 | $440 | $385 | $305 | $275 |

Deduct 25% if without stock.

MODEL 1870 LARGE FRAME SECOND TYPE — similar to First Type, with standard sliding extractor.

| $825 | $770 | $715 | $660 | $605 | $550 | $525 | $495 | $440 | $385 | $305 | $275 |

Deduct 25% if without stock.

WESTERN ARMS COMPANY
Ithaca, NY.

W

Grading	100%	98%	95%	90%	80%	70%	60%

WESTERN LONG RANGE DOUBLE BARREL SHOTGUN — 12, 16, 20, or .410 ga., 26-32 in. barrels, mod. and full choke, boxlock, extractors, double or single trigger, plain pistol grip stock, Western Arms Co. was a division of Ithaca Gun. Mfg. 1929-1946.

| $275 | $225 | $200 | $175 | $150 | $125 | $100 |

▲ *Single trigger*

| $325 | $275 | $250 | $225 | $200 | $150 | $125 |

WESTERN FIELD
Trademark used on Montgomery Ward rifles and shotguns.

The Western Field trademark has appeared literally on hundreds of various models (shotguns and rifles) sold through the Montgomery Ward retail network. Most of these models were manufactured through subcontracts with both domestic and international firearms manufacturers. Typically, they were "spec." guns made to sell at a specific price to undersell the competition. Most of these models were derivatives of existing factory models with less expensive wood and perhaps missing the features found on those models from which they were derived. To date, there has been very little interest in collecting Western Field guns, regardless of rarity. Rather than list J.C. Higgins models, a general guideline is that values generally are under those of their "1st generation relatives". As a result, prices are ascertained by the shooting value of the gun, rather than its collector value.

WESTLEY RICHARDS & CO. LTD.
Originally William Westley Richards was located in Birmingham, England. Currently manufactured by Westley Richards and Co., Ltd., Birmingham, England 1812 to date. In 1995, Westley Richards opened their own agency in the US located in Springfield, MO.

There seems to be a lot of confusion regarding W. Richards, W. R. Richards, William Richards, and other generic derivatives of the famous English gunmaker, Westley Richards. Part of the problem is that there are seventeen registered firms in England, including several in London, who have made guns by the name of Richards. A genuine Westley Richards gun never has the first name abbreviated, and the London address is usually found on the rib panel. Further compounding the problem, a previous Belgian gunmaker identifiable by W. Richards on the locks or rib, had many shotguns exported into the United States and are commonly confused with the real London maker. These Belgian guns are commonly hammer guns with damascus twist barrels most frequently encountered in either 10, 12, or 16 ga. The easiest way to determine this maker is to recognize the Liege proofmarks on the barrel flats and chamber length given in millimeters. Most of these Belgian guns sell in the $100-$400 range, depending on condition and configuration.

Note: Westley Richards guns are essentially custom ordered - only 25-30 guns are made annually. They make many weapons that are impossible to list and evaluate, except on an individual basis. Professional appraisal is necessary upon purchase or sale.

To obtain a quotation for a new Westley Richards shotgun, an inquiry should be submitted to the manufacturer or importer (see Trademark Index for addresses).

Grading	100%	98%	95%	90%	80%	70%	60%

SHOTGUNS: PRE-WWII MFG.

Add 20% for 20 ga.
Add 30% for 28 ga.
Add $1,500 for cased extra set of locks.

OVUNDO O/U — detachable lock boxlock, optional sideplates. Disc.

	100%	98%	95%	90%	80%	70%	60%
	$15,000	$13,000	$11,000	$9,750	$8,500	$7,250	$6,000

MODELE DE GRANDE LUXE - SxS — scalloped receiver, detachable locks, profuse scroll & game scene engraving. Disc.

	100%	98%	95%	90%	80%	70%	60%
	$15,000	$13,000	$11,000	$9,750	$8,500	$7,250	$6,000

MODEL DE LUXE - SxS — scalloped receiver, detachable locks, fine scroll & game scene engraving. Disc.

	100%	98%	95%	90%	80%	70%	60%
	$11,000	$9,500	$8,500	$7,500	$6,000	$5,500	$5,000

HAMMERLESS EJECTOR PLAIN QUALITY - SxS — scalloped receiver, Anson & Deeley fixed locks.

	100%	98%	95%	90%	80%	70%	60%
	$6,000	$5,000	$4,000	$3,500	$3,000	$2,500	$2,000

"B" QUALITY EJECTOR - SxS — boxlock with plain (unscalloped) receiver, light scroll engraving. Disc.

	100%	98%	95%	90%	80%	70%	60%
	$5,000	$4,000	$3,500	$3,000	$2,500	$2,250	$2,000

SHOTGUNS: CURRENT MFG.

CONNAUGHT MODEL SxS — 12, 20, or 28 ga., Anson & Deeley scalloped boxlock action, scroll engraving, 26 or 28 in. barrels, ejectors, about 6½ lbs. Disc.

	100%	98%	95%	90%	80%	70%	60%
	$9,250	$8,000	$6,600	$5,600	$4,800	$4,000	$3,400

Last Mfg.'s Sug. Retail was $10,900.

BEST QUALITY DROPLOCK SxS — 12, 16, 20, 28, or .410 ga., boxlock action, barrel lengths and chokes to order, detachable locks with hinged cover-plate, checkered straight or pistol grip stock, auto ejectors.

	Mfg.'s Sug. Retail		100%	98%	95%	90%	80%	70%	60%
	$27,000		$27,000	$19,450	$14,000	$10,750	$8,750	$7,600	$6,400

Add $1,000 for SST.

Only six .410 Best Quality Boxlocks have been mfg. to date.

W

Grading	100%	98%	95%	90%	80%	70%	60%

BEST QUALITY SIDELOCK — 12, 16, 20, 28, or .410 ga., barrel length and choke to order, hand detachable sidelocks, auto ejectors, checkered straight or pistol grip stock.

Mfg.'s Sug. Retail $25,000	$25,000	$18,950	$14,000	$10,750	$8,750	$7,600	$6,400

Add 20% for 20 ga.
Add 40% for 28 ga.
Add 60% for .410 ga.
Add $1,000 for SST.

Most specimens in this model were custom ordered, and as a result, each gun has to be evaluated individually.

WILLIAM BISHOP SIDELOCK MODEL — current mfg., best quality sidelock, made to individual customer specifications.

Mfg.'s Sug. Retail $29,000	$29,000	$23,500	$18,500	$15,000	$11,750	$9,500	$8,250

CARLTON DETACHABLE LOCK — 12 or 20 ga., current mfg., detachable sidelocks, top-of-the-line shotgun custom made per customer specifications, elaborate game scene engraving. Many options upon request - values below are for base gun only.

Mfg.'s Sug. Retail $34,075	$34,075	$26,500	$21,750	$17,250	$13,750	$10,500	$9,000

RIFLES

BEST QUALITY BOXLOCK DOUBLE RIFLE — .300, .375 H&H, .470 NE, .577 NE, or .600 NE cal., auto ejectors, boxlock, hammerless, folding leaf rear sight, hooded front sight, engraved with quality French walnut stock, horn forend tip.

Mfg.'s Sug. Retail $25,000	$25,000	$21,000	$18,750	$16,000	$13,750	$10,500	$9,250

Values will vary greatly on this model, depending on caliber.

DETACHABLE DROPLOCK DOUBLE RIFLE — available in most cals., boxlock with detachable locks and hinged cover-plate, ejectors, colored case hardened frame, cased.

Mfg.'s Sug. Retail $36,000	$36,000	$30,000	$25,000	$21,000	$18,750	$16,000	$13,000

STALKER MAGAZINE RIFLE — .243 Win., .270 Win., .30-06, .300 H&H, .375 H&H, or .458 Win. Mag. cal., bolt action, Mauser action, 22, 24, or 25 in. barrel, leaf rear and hooded front sight, engraved with French walnut stock, horn forend tip. Current mfg.

Mfg.'s Sug. Retail $9,000	$9,000	$7,850	$6,950	$5,750	$4,750	$4,000	$3,300

Add approx. $3,000 for Magnum Mauser action.

WHITNEY FIREARMS COMPANY

Manufactured between 1956-1959 in Hartford, CT.

PISTOL: SEMI-AUTO

WOLVERINE OR LIGHTNING — .22 auto cal., unique futuristic appearance, 10 shot, 4⅝ in. barrel, plastic grips, aluminum alloy frame and barrel shroud, blue model is more common (approx. 13,000 mfg.), nickel is rare (approx. 900 mfg.). Mfg. 1955-1962.

	100%	98%	95%	90%	80%	70%	60%
Blue finish	$425	$350	$300	$260	$230	$200	$175
Nickel finish	$550	$450	$375	$300	$260	$230	$200

WHITWORTH

This trademark can be found in the Interarms section of this text.

WICHITA ARMS, INC.

Manufacturer located in Wichita, KS.

Grading	100%	98%	95%	90%	80%	70%	60%

PISTOLS

WICHITA INTERNATIONAL PISTOL (WIP) — available in 8 cals. between .22 LR and .357 Mag., single shot, break open action, stainless steel, adj. sights, 10 or 14 in. barrel, adj. sights or scope mounts, smooth walnut stocks and forearm.

Mfg.'s Sug. Retail	$735		$660	$460	$350		

Add $79 for 14 in. barrel.

WICHITA CLASSIC PISTOL — assorted cals. to .308 Win., 11¼ in. barrel, action has left-hand bolt for shooting with right-hand, deluxe walnut, custom made, 3 lbs. 15 oz.

Mfg.'s Sug. Retail	$3,495		$3,280	$2,550	$2,150	$1,850	$1,575	$1,265	$1,000

▲ *Wichita Classic Engraved* — similar to Wichita Classic, except is extensively engraved.

Mfg.'s Sug. Retail	$5,250		$5,250	$3,750	$2,750				

WICHITA SILHOUETTE PISTOL (WSP) — .308 Win. or 7mm/IHMSA cal., adj. trigger and sights, 14¹⁵⁄₁₆ in. barrel, center grip walnut stock, rear grip, 4½ lbs. Left-hand action for shooting with right-hand.

Mfg.'s Sug. Retail	$1,418		$1,275	$925	$775	$600	$525	$460	$400

WICHITA MAGAZINE PISTOL — .308 Win. or 7mm/IHMSA cal., fiberthane (disc. 1987) or walnut (new 1988) stock, choice of MK-40, Silhouette, or Classic configuration, 13 in. barrel, adj. trigger, multi-range sights, 4½ lbs. Disc. 1994.

		$1,250	$875	$700	$600	$500	$450	$400

Last Mfg.'s Sug. Retail was $1,550.

▲ *Wichita Classic Pistol* — features octagon barrel, AAA walnut stock, 11¼ in. barrel, 3 lbs. 15 oz. Disc. 1994.

		$2,975	$2,450	$2,000	$1,650	$1,350	$1,150	$1,000

Last Mfg.'s Sug. Retail was $3,400.

WICHITA BENCH PISTOL — .222 Rem., 6 PPC, or .22 Cheetah cal., uses WBR 1200 action, rear grip, 18 in. stainless steel Douglas barrel. New 1994.

Mfg.'s Sug. Retail	$1,875		$1,875	$1,500	$1,250	$975	$850	$700	$600

RIFLES

WICHITA CLASSIC RIFLE (WCR) — .17-222, .17-222 Mag., .222 Rem., .222 Mag., 223 Rem., 6x47, and other cals. up to and including .308 cal., bolt action, single shot, select walnut, 21 in. octagon barrel, Canjar trigger, no sights, 7 lbs.

Mfg.'s Sug. Retail	$3,495		$3,275	$2,500	$2,150	$1,850	$1,575	$1,265	$1,000

Add $175 for left-hand action.

▲ *Wichita Varmint Rifle (WVR)* — similar to WCR, except available only in Varmint cals. (up to and including .308) and round barrel.

Mfg.'s Sug. Retail	$2,695		$2,500	$1,795	$1,375	$1,100	$950	$800	$750

Add $175 for left-hand action.

▲ *Wichita Silhouette Rifle (WSR)* — available in most cals., gray fiberthane stock, 24 in. match grade barrel, 2 oz. Canjar trigger, no sights, 9 lbs. Disc. 1995.

		$2,475	$1,775	$1,375	$1,100	$950	$800	$750

Last Mfg.'s Sug. Retail was $2,650.

Add $175 for left-hand action.

▲ *Wichita Magnum* — Mag. cals., stainless steel only. Disc. 1984.

		$1,725	$1,300	$1,175				

WICKLIFFE RIFLES

Previously manufactured by Triple S Development located in Wickliffe, OH.

Grading	100%	98%	95%	90%	80%	70%	60%

RIFLES - SINGLE SHOT

MODEL 76 STANDARD — falling block action, most popular cals., 22 or 26 in. barrel, no sights, select walnut pistol grip, 2 piece stock. Mfg. 1976-disc.

	$395	$350	$325	$300	$275	$250	$225

MODEL 76 DELUXE GRADE — similar to Standard, in .30-06 cal. only, 22 in. barrel, fancy wood, silver pistol grip cap.

	$460	$415	$385	$360	$320	$290	$250

MODEL 76 COMMEMORATIVE — similar to Deluxe, except etched receiver, U.S. silver dollar inlaid in stock, presentation case. Mfg. 100, 1976.

	$1,100	$825	$550	$495	$440	$330	$305

STINGER — similar to Model 76 Standard, in .22 Hornet or .223 cal., lightweight 22 in. barrel.

	$395	$350	$325	$300	$275	$250	$225

STINGER DELUXE — similar to 76 Deluxe, in .22 Hornet or .223 cal., lightweight 22 in. barrel.

	$460	$415	$385	$360	$325	$290	$250

TRADITIONALIST — similar to Standard 76, in .30-06 or .45-70 cal., 24 in. barrel.

	$395	$350	$325	$300	$275	$250	$225

KODIAK COMMEMORATIVE — similar to Model 76 Deluxe, .338 Mag. cal., 26 in. barrel, etched receiver.

	$650	$550	$475	$425	$375	$325	$275

WILDEY, INC.

Originally, the company was named Wildey Firearms Co., Inc. located in Cheshire, CT. At that time, serialization of pistols was 45-0000. When Wildey Inc. bought the company out of bankruptcy from the old shareholders, there had been approximately 800 pistols mfg. To distinguish the old company from the present company, the serial range was changed to 09-0000 (only 633 pistols with the 09 prefix were produced). These guns had the Cheshire, CT address. Pistols produced by Wildey Inc., New Milford, CT are serial numbered with 4 digits being used (no numerical prefix).

PISTOLS

Wildey has plans to introduce 4 new proprietary cartridges. They are the .30 WM, .357 WM, 10mm WM, and 11mm WM based on the .475 Wildey Mag. necked down to respective cartridge dimensions. Norma, located in Sweden, continues to produce the .475 WM brass.

WILDEY AUTO PISTOL — .45 Win. Mag., .357 Peterbilt (limited mfg.), or .475 Wildey Mag., gas operated, 5, 6, 7, 8, 10, or 14 in. VR barrel, selective single shot or semi-auto, 3 lug rotary bolt, fixed barrel (interchangeable), stainless steel construction, 7 shot, double action, adj. sights, smooth wood grips, designed to fire proprietary new cartridges specifically for this gun including the .45 Win. Mag. cal., 64 oz. with 5 in. barrel.
   Add $475-$590 per interchangeable barrel.

▲ *Survivor Model* — .45 Win. Mag., 11mm Wildey Mag., or .475 Wildey Mag. cal., 5, 6, 7, 8, 10, or 12 in. barrel only. New 1990.

Mfg.'s Sug. Retail	**$1,295**	**$1,125**	**$875**	**$725**

   Add $100 for 12 in. barrel.
   Add $21 for 8 or 10 in. barrel.
   Add $50 for new model VR (8, 10, or 12 in. barrel only).
   The .475 Wildey cal. is derived from the .284 Win. case. This cal. is available in 8 or 10 in. barrel only.

Grading	100%	98%	95%	90%	80%	70%	60%

▲ *Survivor Guardsman* — similar to Survivor Model, except has squared off trigger guard. New 1990.

Mfg.'s Sug. Retail	$1,295	$1,125	$885	$725

    Add $500 for 14 in. barrel.
    Add $100 for 12 in. barrel.
    Add $21 for 8 or 10 in. barrel.
    Add $46 for new model VR (8, 10, or 12 in. barrel only).

▲ *Hunter Model* — .45 Win. Mag. or .475 Wildey Mag. cal., 5, 6, 7, 8, 10, or 12 in. barrel, matte finish on all metal parts, adj. sights. New 1990.

Mfg.'s Sug. Retail	$1,413	$1,200	$975	$825

    Add $36 for 12 in. barrel.
    .475 Wildey Mag. is available in 8, 10, or 12 in. barrel only.

▲ *Hunter Guardsman* — similar to Hunter Model, except has squared off trigger guard. New 1990.

Mfg.'s Sug. Retail	$1,413	$1,200	$975	$850

    Add $36 for 12 in. barrel.

▲ *Presentation Model* — same specifications as above model, except is engraved with hand checkered stocks.

	$2,500	$2,000	$1,600

Last Mfg.'s Sug. Retail was $2,000.

▲ *Older Wildey Mfg.*
    Add $413-$513 per interchangeable barrel.

.475 Wildey Mag. cal. is available in 8 or 10 in. barrel only.

    ➤ SERIAL NOS. 1-200.

Mfg.'s Sug. Retail	$2,180	$1,900	$1,700	$1,550

    Add $20 for 8 or 10 in. barrel.
    ➤ SERIAL NOS. 201-400.

Mfg.'s Sug. Retail	$1,980	$1,750	$1,550	$1,400

    Add $20 for 8 or 10 in. barrel.
    ➤ SERIAL NOS. 401-600.

Mfg.'s Sug. Retail	$1,780	$1,650	$1,375	$1,250

    Add $20 for 8 or 10 in. barrel.
    ➤ SERIAL NOS. 601-800.

Mfg.'s Sug. Retail	$1,580	$1,450	$1,200	$1,000

    Add $20 for 8 or 10 in. barrel.
    ➤ SERIAL NOS. 801-1,000.

Mfg.'s Sug. Retail	$1,275	$1,100	$925	$800

    Add $25 for 8 or 10 in. barrel.
    ➤ SERIAL NOS. 1,001-2,489.

Mfg.'s Sug. Retail	$1,175	$1,025	$850	$750

    Add $20 for 8 or 10 in. barrel.

WILKINSON ARMS

Previous manufacturer located in Porma, ID.

DIANE AUTOMATIC PISTOL — .25 ACP cal., 6 shot, 2⅛ in. barrel, fixed sight, matte blue, plastic grips.

	$125	$110	$90	$80	$65	$55	$50

LINDA PISTOL — 9mm Para. cal., blowback action firing from closed bolt, 8.3 in. barrel, 31 shot mag., PVC pistol grip, maple forearm, Williams adj. rear sight.

	$325	$295	$260	$230	$200	$180	$165

    A conversion unit was also available enabling conversion of the Linda Pistol to the Terry Carbine.

Grading	100%	98%	95%	90%	80%	70%	60%

"TERRY" CARBINE — blowback action, 9mm Para., 30 shot mag., 16³⁄₁₆ in. barrel, closed breech, adj. sights.

With black P.V.C. stock	$325	$310	$300	$275	$230	$210	$180
With maple stock	$350	$340	$325	$300	$260	$230	$200

WILLIAM DOUGLAS & SONS

Manufacturer located in Staffordshire, England. Currently imported and distributed by Cape Outfitters located in Cape Girardeau, MO.

RIFLES: SIDE-BY-SIDE

EXPRESS RIFLE — .375 H&H cal., H&H type back action sidelock with bolster fences, DTs, ejectors, 24 in. regulated barrels, folding leaf rear sight, oil finished European walnut stock with 20 LPI checkering, light engraving, case hardened action.

Mfg.'s Sug. Retail	$11,295	$10,750	$8,900	$7,800	$6,700	$5,700	$4,900	$4,300

HUNTER BOXLOCK EXPRESS RIFLE — .470 NE cal., Anson & Deeley action with DT (front trigger is articulated), case colored action with deep blued small parts, 24 in. regulated barrels, checkered European walnut stock and forearm with oil finish, light border engraving.

Mfg.'s Sug. Retail	$7,536	$7,100	$6,500	$5,800	$5,150	$4,650	$4,100	$3,750

▲ *Hunter Boxlock Deluxe Express Rifle* — includes better walnut and fully engraved receiver.

Mfg.'s Sug. Retail	$11,131	$10,650	$8,900	$7,800	$6,700	$5,700	$4,900	$4,300

WILLIAM EVANS LIMITED

Manufacturer of long arms located in London, England since 1883.

William Evans, Gun & Rifle Makers, have been manufacturing high quality shotguns and rifles for over 100 years. Most William Evans shotguns and double rifles must be appraised individually since they were all custom ordered initially. All new guns must be ordered from the factory directly. Currently, the sidelock SxS shotgun starts at $42,390 w/o V.A.T. (value added tax), the sidelock O/U shotgun starts at $54,950 w/o V.A.T., the SxS double rifle starts at $62,800 (add $7,850 for cals. above 500), and the bolt action rifle starts at $10,990. All prices are FOB England. Please contact William Evans (refer to the Trademark Index) for more information, including any special orders.

WILLIAM POWELL & SON (GUNMAKERS) Ltd.

Manufacturer located in Birmingham, England since 1802. Currently imported by Bells Legendary Countrywear located in New York, NY. The Heritage Series was introduced into the U.S. in 1984.

SHOTGUNS: SxS

Values listed below do not include import duty or U.S. taxes.

Add $1,155 for 28 or .410 ga. in Heritage Series only.

NO. 1 SIDELOCK EJECTOR — 12, 16, 20, or .410 (disc.) ga., chopper lump barrels, extra choice French walnut, DTs, many special orders available. Gold inlays, deep relief carved action fences, can be obtained in self opener.

Mfg.'s Sug. Retail	$39,655	$39,655	$28,750	$23,250	$17,500	$14,750	$12,000	$10,000

Add $3,465 for assisted opening action.
Add $2,585 for SNT.

NO. 3 BOXLOCK EJECTOR — 12, 16, 20, or .410 (disc.) ga., chopper lump barrels, scalloped boxlock action, extra choice French walnut, many special orders available.

Mfg.'s Sug. Retail	$24,255	$24,255	$21,000	$16,000	$9,900	$7,500	$6,250	$5,000

Grading	100%	98%	95%	90%	80%	70%	60%

▲ **Model 4 Boxlock Ejector** — similar to Number 3, but has dovetail lump barrels and less engraving.
Mfg.'s Sug. Retail $21,100 $21,100 $16,500 $10,250 $7,950 $6,600 $5,400 $4,500
Add $2,235 for SNT.

▲ **Model 6 Boxlock Ejector** — disc. 1988.
$2,750 $2,450 $2,050 $1,700 $1,400 $1,150 $900

HERITAGE NO. 1 SIDELOCK EJECTOR MKII — 12 or 20 ga., 2¾ in. chambers, chopper lump barrels, choice of game scene or bouquet and scroll engraving, DTs. New 1984.
Mfg.'s Sug. Retail $13,215 $13,215 $10,750 $9,000 $7,800 $6,700 $5,500 $4,500

HERITAGE NO. 2 SIDELOCK MKII — similar to Heritage No. 1, except has less engraving and lesser grade walnut, easy opening action.
Mfg.'s Sug. Retail $5,620 $5,620 $5,200 $4,750 $4,375 $3,675 $3,100 $2,100

HERITAGE DE LUXE BOXLOCK DETACHABLE LOCK — features detachable locks, choice of traditional scroll or game scene engraving, ejectors.
Mfg.'s Sug. Retail $21,485 $21,485 $16,750 $13,750 $11,000 $8,500 $7,250 $5,950

HERITAGE ROUND ACTION EJECTOR — features unscalloped, rounded boxlock action with fine English scroll work throughout, DTs.
Mfg.'s Sug. Retail $15,785 $15,785 $12,000 $9,600 $7,800 $6,600 $5,400 $4,500

WILSON COMBAT

Pistol manufacturer, customizer, and supplier of 1911 style handgun accessories located in Berryville, AR since 1978.

Wilson Combat has an extensive line-up of competition handguns based on the 1911 Govt. Model. Please contact the company directly (see Trademark Index) for more information, including an extensive catalog which lists their guns, parts, and accessories.

WINCHESTER

Manufactured in New Haven, CT from 1866 to date. Also includes U.S. Repeating Arms formed in 1981 with licensing agreement from Olin Corp. to manufacture shotguns and rifles domestically using the Winchester Trademark. Olin Corp. previously  mfg. shotguns and rifles bearing the Winchester Hallmark at the Olin Kodensha Plant (closed 1989) located in Tochigi, Japan and also in European Countries. In 1992, U.S. Repeating Arms was acquired by Giat located in France.

WINCHESTER OVERVIEW

Note: Winchester Rifles are a field in themselves. Models Henry, 1866, 1873, 1876, 1885, 1886, 1892, 1894, and 1895 all were produced with a multitude of special order options. Special orders included front and rear special sights, half or ⅔ magazines, takedown, various barrel lengths, configurations, and weights, special metal finishes, deluxe wood (either checkered or carved) in a variety of finishes, an impressive range of engraving options, different butt plates, etc. All of these special orders act independently and interdependently to determine the correct value of a particular Winchester. Some of the finest rifles ever made are special order Winchesters engraved by the Ulrichs, G. Young, L.D. Nimschke, and others. For these reasons a Model 92 Winchester can range in price from $200 to over $250,000 - quite a price range for one model alone! When contemplating a purchase on the higher dollar range, qualified and professional opinions should be secured, preferably from at least 2 sources. Unfortunately many fakes and upgraded (non-original) guns have surfaced in the last 10 years with the sudden increase in prices. Winchesters shown in this section are priced assuming a standard model with no special orders. Any special orders will further add to the prices shown.   Caliber rarities must also be considered.   Many of the early Winchesters are broken down by year of manufacture.   Refer to the "Model Serialization" section in this book.

A factory letter specifying original shipping information by serial number will certainly help solidify values shown on older out of production Winchester rifles and shotguns. A listing has been provided below by model number with serialization range which can be historically researched by the Winchester Museum now located in Cody, WY. To use this outstanding service, make sure the model and its serial number fall within the ranges listed below. Simply mail in your request with serial number, model, and caliber. The charge for this service is $40 for non-members, or $25 for members - funds are payable to the Cody Firearms Museum, P.O. Box 1000 in Cody, WY, 82414. Information received back will include specimen caliber, barrel length, any special orders or finishes, return(s) to the factory, as well as any additional provenance contained by interpolating existing factory shipping ledgers. I would recommend a trip to the Buffalo Bill Historical Center as it contains the most comprehensive collection of projectile arms (including Chinese specimens that date back 2,000 years) and Americana housed under one roof in this country.

A NOTE ON WINCHESTER FINISHES: It is very important to understand that there is a big value difference between a Model 1873 with 90% bright blue as opposed to a gun that has 90% patina finish (turning brown). Even though it is true that both guns are 90%, the bright blue specimen might be worth 50%+ more because it is closer to the way it originally left the factory — with bright bluing. For this reason, the type of finish remaining becomes as important as the amount of finish. "Brown" guns are simply not as desirable as bright guns that show little discoloration, even though many surviving original specimens are typically encountered in either grayish patina or somewhat brown finish.   Because of this, much consideration must be given as to what type of finish a specimen has, and if shiny or mostly brown, value has to be taken away from prices listed below accordingly.

With the recent price appreciation on most upper condition Winchester rifles, excellent original condition has become so expensive that the many special order features Winchester offered do not cost that much more currently. However, on lesser condition guns that are much less expensive, these same special order features will cost more percentage-wise since the condition factor did not cost a premium.

PLEASE REFER TO THE 40-PAGE PHOTO PERCENTAGE GRADING SYSTEM IN THE FRONT OF THIS TEXT TO LEARN MORE ABOUT THE VARIOUS CONDITION FACTORS ENCOUNTERED ON WINCHESTER RIFLES AND SHOTGUNS (PAGES 60 - 68).

Model 1866 Lever Action Rifle — ser. no. range 124,995-170,101.

Model 1873 Lever Action Rifle — ser. no. range 1-720,496.

Model 1876 Lever Action Rifle — ser. no. range 1-63,871.

Model 1883 Bolt Action Rifle (Hotchkiss Repeater) — ser. no. range 1-84,555.

Model 1885 Single Shot Rifle or Shotgun — ser. no. range 1-109,999.

Model 1886 Lever Action Rifle — ser. no. range 1-156,599.

Model 1887 & 1901 Lever Action Shotguns — ser. no. range 1-72,999.

Model 1890 Slide Action Rifle — ser. no. range 1-329,999.

Model 1892 Lever Action Rifle — ser. no. range 1-379,999.

Model 1893 Slide Action Shotgun — ser. no. range 1-34,050.

Model 1894 Lever Action Rifle — ser. no. range 1-353,999.

Model 1895 Lever Action Rifle — ser. no. range 1-59,999.

Model "Lee" Bolt Action Rifle — ser. no. range 1-19,999.

Model 1897 Slide Action Shotgun — ser. no. range 34,051-377,999.

Model 1903 Semi-Auto .22 Cal. Rifle — ser. no. range 1-39,999.

Model 1905 Semi-Auto Rifle — ser. no. range 1-29,078.

Model 1906 Semi-Auto Rifle — ser. no. range 1-79,999.

Model 1907 Semi-Auto Rifle — ser. no. range 1-9,999.

Winchester factory data on models produced between approx. 1907-1961 is almost non-existent (except Custom Shop mfg.) since there was a fire at the Winchester factory in 1961.

GRADING EXPLANATION FOR WINCHESTER LEVER ACTIONS

A combination of grading systems is being used exclusively for this section to assist the reader in ascertaining the value of a particular specimen more accurately. They work as follows - the top line contains three value ranges (Above Average, Average, or Below Average) which have been created to encompass most of the specimens commonly encountered within this model. Please compare the specimen(s) in question for grading to Photos 59 - 64 of the Photo Percentage Grading System - Above Average would refer to Photos 59 - 61 (remember, No. 59 is 60%), Average refers to Photo 62, and Below Average refers to 63 - 64

Since there is a drastic value difference between 95% - 50% bright blue and 30% dull patina/fading finish on older Winchesters, another grading/pricing line has been included to give you an example of the top end of the marketplace. However, the condition of the gun(s) in question must appear similar to those guns pictured in Photos 53 - 59. Individual percentages of condition with corresponding values are listed here to give you a complete price range on older Winchester lever actions. While no grading system is perfect, it is hoped that this combination of pricing systems will be an advantage over previous attempts.

The three groupings include "Below Average Price Range", "Average Price Range", and "Above Average Price Range" (note the new grading line underneath specifying these condition factors). These ranges indicate the following:

W

BELOW AVERAGE PRICE RANGE - a specimen with no finish remaining, perhaps some parts have been replaced, deteriorated metal may be lightly pitted with faint barrel/frame markings, rounded edges of wood and metal, wood showing much wear with possible repairs or cracks, must be in working order. (Please refer to Photos No. 63 and 64 for visual identification).

AVERAGE PRICE RANGE - a specimen with all original parts, exhibits gun metal patina finish, metal mostly smooth (perhaps lightly pitted), principle lettering and markings legible throughout, wood showing honest wear with little finish remaining (may have small cracks and other imperfections), good working order. (Please refer to Photos No. 61 and 62 for visual identification).

ABOVE AVERAGE PRICE RANGE - a specimen featuring unpolished brass (on Henrys and Model 1866s) or plum brown patina with traces of bluing in protected areas (on all steel frame models), sharp corners, crisp barrel markings, traces of original finish remaining, metal should exhibit nice patina or older flaking finish, wood should have some original stock varnish remaining and minor handling marks and dings, good bore, perfect working order with no replacement parts. (Please refer to Photos No. 59 and 60 for visual identification).

VALUES FOR ABOVE AVERAGE CONDITION RANGE - this includes those specimens which are 50% bright blue or better condition - refer to Photos 53 - 59. When this type of condition is encountered, refer to the grading/price line listing individual percentage of condition prices located underneath the Above Average, Average, or Below Average pricing line. You may notice a gap in prices between the Above Average high price and 50% price. This is normal, because in some cases, a rare 50% bright blue/bright brass specimen will be worth considerably more than one in Above Average condition.

Above Average	•	Average	Below Average

RIFLES: LEVER ACTIONS — 1860-1964

HENRY RIFLE — .44 rimfire, 15 shot, 24 in. barrel with integral slotted tube mag. and loading lever, blued barrel, brass or iron frame. Approx. 13,000 total production, mfg. 1860-1866.

> Because almost all Henrys have little or no original finish left, values below are in ranges rather than in separate condition factors.
> Add 25%+ for engraving, depending on amount and condition (these specimens should have fancy wood).

▲ *Iron Frame Model* — frame made of iron, round type butt plate, without lever latch, adj. sporting type rear leaf sight, serial numbers are in three digits only. Total production is believed to be less than 300.

$36,500 - $20,000	$20,000 - $12,000	$12,000 - $9,000

▲ *First Model* — approx. 3,500 mfg., generally serialized below 3,500, with or without lever latch, perch belly stock and slotted receiver for rear sight.

$15,000 - $10,000	$10,000 - $7,500	$7,500 - 6,250

▲ *Martial Marked* — contracted by U.S. military for Civil War use, denoted by "C.G.C." inspector markings on upper barrel breech and stock, approx. 1,900 with serialization scattered.

$17,500 - $11,500	$11,500 - $8,250	$8,250 - $7,000

This rifle was the most revolutionary shoulder weapon introduced in the Civil War.

▲ *Late Model* — similar to first model, except butt plate heel has pointed profile, lever latch became standard and receiver is not slotted for rear sight, serial numbers over approx. 3,500, most commonly encountered Henry with approx. 8,000 mfg.

$12,500 - $9,500	$9,500 - $6,500	$6,500 - $4,500

MODEL 1866 LEVER ACTION — .44 rimfire or centerfire (4th Model only), 24 in. barrel, blued barrel with brass frame, differs from Henry in that it has a wood forearm, frame cartridge loading port (King's improvement), and separate tube mag. Total production reached 170,101 for all models, mfg. 1866-1898.

▲ *Model 1866 First Model Rifle* — "Improved Henry" action, .44 cal. rimfire, without forend cap, serialization is concealed on lower tang inside butt stock, serial range is from mid 12,000 to mid 15,000 (in Henry serial range sequence).

$9,000 - $7,000	$7,000 - $5,000	$5,000 - $3,000

95% = $18,000 90% = $15,000 80% = $13,000 70% = $12,000 60% = $11,000 50% = $10,000

▲ *Model 1866 Carbine First Model* — same action as Rifle, only with 20 in. barrel, 2 forearm bands and saddle ring.

$5,500 - $3,500	$3,500 - $2,500	$2,500 - $1,500

95% = $12,000 90% = $10,750 80% = $9,500 70% = $8,500 60% = $7,500 50% = $7,000

▲ *Model 1866 Rifle Second Model* — "New Model" with redesigned frame, with Henry barrel markings, serial number inside on the earlier guns after ser. no. 19,000, outside lower tang beneath lever (approx. after ser. no. 20,000).

$6,500 - $4,400	$4,500 - $3,000	$3,000 - $2,000

95% = $12,000 90% = $10,500 80% = $9,500 70% = $8,500 60% = $7,500 50% = $7,000

▲ *Model 1866 Carbine Second Model* — frame and other changes similar to Second Model Rifle.

$4,500 - $3,000	$3,000 - $2,000	$2,000 - $1,250

95% = $9,500 90% = $8,000 80% = $7,500 70% = $7,000 60% = $6,500 50% = $5,500

▲ *Model 1866 Rifle Third Model* — block style serial numbers usually located behind trigger, improved frame. Serial numbered approx. 25,000-149,000.

$4,750 - $3,500	$3,500 - $2,500	$2,500 - $1,500

95% = $10,000 90% = $8,500 80% = $8,000 70% = $7,500 60% = $7,000 50% = $6,500

Add 20% for brass forend cap and buttplate.

▲ *Model 1866 Carbine Third Model* — same changes as Model 1866 Third Model Rifle, 20 in. barrel with 2 bands.

$3,750 - $2,500	$2,500 - $1,750	$1,750 - $1,250

95% = $8,250 90% = $7,450 80% = $6,750 70% = $6,250 60% = $5,750 50% = $5,000

Above Average	Average	Below Average

▲ *Model 1866 Musket Third Model* — 27 in. round barrel, 24 in. magazine, 3 barrel bands.
$3,500 - $2,500 $2,500 - $1,750 $1,750 - $1,250
95% = $8,000   90% = $6,700   80% = $6,000   70% = $5,500   60% = $5,000   50% = $4,600

▲ *Model 1866 Rifle/Carbine/Musket Fourth Model* — .44 cal., twin rimfire and centerfire, script style serial number on lower tang near lever latch, improved frame, serial range approx. 149,000-170,101.
Values for these models are the same as for equivalent Third Model 1866s.

MODEL 1873 LEVER ACTION — .32-20, .38-40, or .44-40 centerfire cal., iron frame (changed to steel 1884) with sideplates, frame loading port, 24 in. round or octagon barrel, rifles have forearm caps and carbines have forearm bands, tube mag., blued finish with case hardened parts, oil finished stock, serial numbered on lower tang, 720,610 mfg. between 1873-1919, guns produced after serial number 525,923 are modern firearms.

Deluxe Models 1873 with color case hardened frames will add at least 50% to the values listed below for standard models.

▲ *Model 1873 First Model Rifle* — serial numbers approx. 1 - 30,000, sliding thumbprint dust cover on 2 guides that are integral part of upper frame, absence of any cal. marking.
$1,700 - $1,200 $1,200 - $800 $800 - $400
98% = $4,350   95% = $3,550   90% = $3,050   80% = $2,475   70% = $1,975   60% = $1,750

▲ *Model 1873 Carbine First Model* — 20 in. round barrel with carbine style forearm band. Distinctive curved butt plate, with saddle ring.
$2,000 - $1,400 $1,400 - $900 $900 - $500
98% = $4,750   95% = $4,250   90% = $3,900   80% = $3,650   70% = $3,275   60% = $2,800

▲ *Model 1873 Musket First Model* — 30 in. round barrel, 27 in. mag. with 3 barrel bands, approx. 500 mfg.
$2,050 - $1,600 $1,600 - $1,150 $1,150 - $750
98% = $4,250   95% = $3,500   90% = $3,050   80% = $2,675   70% = $2,300   60% = $2,050

▲ *Model 1873 Rifle Second Model* — improved dust cover featuring slides on center rail on rear section of frame top which is held in place by two screws, serial range 31,000 - 90,000.
$1,000 - $600 $600 - $400 $400 - $300
98% = $3,150   95% = $2,675   90% = $2,100   80% = $1,875   70% = $1,600   60% = $1,350

▲ *Model 1873 Carbine Second Model* — changes similar to 1873 Second Model Rifle, with 20 in. round barrel and 2 barrel bands.
$1,950 - $1,200 $1,200 - $600 $600 - $400
98% = $5,400   95% = $4,850   90% = $4,000   80% = $3,700   70% = $3,400   60% = $3,000

▲ *Model 1873 Musket Second Model* — changes similar to 1873 Second Model Rifle, with 30 in. barrel and 3 barrel bands.
$1,500 - $1,200 $1,200 - $800 $800 - $500
98% = $3,650   95% = $3,150   90% = $2,750   80% = $2,450   70% = $2,050   60% = $1,875

▲ *Model 1873 Rifle Third Model* — dust cover rail integral with frame, improved action with rear frame screws (2), serial 90,000-end of production.
$750 - $500 $500 - $400 $400 - $300
98% = $3,350   95% = $3,075   90% = $2,400   80% = $1,700   70% = $1,425   60% = $1,250
Add 20% for .44-40 cal.
Add 30% for octagon barrel for .44-40 cal. only.

▲ *Model 1873 Carbine Third Model* — changes similar to 1873 Rifle Third Model, with 20 in. barrel and 2 barrel bands.
$1,250 - $800 $800 - $600 $600 - $400
95% = $3,850   90% = $3,250   80% = $2,750   70% = $2,250   60% = $1,950   50% = $1,575
Add 30% for .32-20 cal.

▲ *Model 1873 Musket Third Model* — 30 in. round barrel and 3 barrel bands.
$1,000 - $800 $800 - $600 $600 - $400
98% = $4,000   90% = $3,650   80% = $2,700   70% = $2,200   60% = $1,925   50% = $1,600

	Above Average	Average	Below Average

▲ *Model 1873 .22 Rim Fire Rifle* — .22 S, L, or Extra L (very rare) cal., 24 in. barrel, no loading gate, the first .22 caliber repeater, 19,552 produced, mfg. 1884-1904. Made in rifle configuration only.

$1,200 - $900 $900 - $700 $700 - $500

95% = $2,750   90% = $2,350   80% = $1,900   70% = $1,700   60% = $1,500   50% = $1,350

▲ *Model 1873 "One of One Thousand"* — special care taken in manufacture to guarantee better accuracy, markings on top of breech designate model, deluxe walnut, extremely rare, barrel marked *"One of One Thousand"* in most cases, 136 mfg. Original cost was $100.

> Values can range from $30,000 - $200,000, depending on condition. A factory letter is a must for any "One of One Thousand" Winchester. Believe it or not, watch for fake letters.

> Note: Rarity of the "One of One Thousand" and the "One of Hundred" models makes upgrading to this model fairly common. Use extreme caution in purchasing.

▲ *Model 1873 "One of One Hundred"* — similar to "One of One Thousand" only rarer, 8 mfg. Sold new for $20 over the list price of a similarly equipped Model 1873.

> Values can range from $40,000 - $225,000, depending on condition. A factory letter is a must for any "One of One Hundred" Winchester. Believe it or not, watch for fake letters.

MODEL 1876 LEVER ACTION — .40-60, .45-60, .45-75 (first caliber offered), or .50-95 Express cal., 26 or 28 in. round or octagon barrel, similar but larger frame than Model 1873, tube mag., rifles have forearm caps while carbines have forearm bands, crescent butt, blued finish, straight grip stock, 63,871 mfg. between 1876-1897.

> The Model 1876 was also called the Centennial Model since its introduction coincided with the U.S. Centennial Exposition held in Philadelphia, PA in 1876. Popularity for this model decreased ten years later when the more powerful and advanced Model 1886 was introduced.

> Deluxe Model 1876s with color case hardened frames will add at least 50% to the values listed below for standard models. Deluxe Models 1876 with 90%+ original case colors are rare.

▲ *Model 1876 Rifle First Model* — serial numbered approx. 1-5,000, distinguishable by no dust cover on frame top.

$2,450 - $1,500 $1,500 - $800 $800 - $600

95% = $5,500   90% = $5,000   80% = $4,250   70% = $3,500   60% = $2,950   50% = $2,500

▲ *Model 1876 Carbine First Model* — 22 in. round barrel, one barrel band, saddle ring, full length forearm giving a musket appearance.

$3,000 - $2,000 $2,000 - $1,000 $1,000 - $700

95% = $7,250   90% = $6,500   80% = $5,700   70% = $5,000   60% = $4,150   50% = $3,250

▲ *Model 1876 Musket First Model* — 32 in. round barrel with 1 band, scarce model because no foreign military contracts.

$6,000 - $4,000 $4,000 - $2,500 $2,500 - $1,500

95% = $8,950   90% = $7,900   80% = $7,000   70% = $6,750   60% = $6,500   50% = $6,250

▲ *Model 1876 Rifle Second Model* — "Thumbprint" dust cover rail held on by screw, serial range 5,000-30,000.

$1,700 - $1,000 $1,000 - $700 $700 - $500

95% = $5,000   90% = $4,350   80% = $3,750   70% = $3,200   60% = $2,700   50% = $2,250

▲ *Model 1876 Carbine Second Model* — changes similar to Model 1876 Rifle Early Second Model, with 22 in. round barrel and full length forearm giving a musket appearance.

$2,950 - $1,800 $1,800 - $900 $900 - $600

95% = $6,000   90% = $5,500   80% = $5,150   70% = $4,700   60% = $4,200   50% = $3,675

▲ *Model 1876 Musket Second Model* — changes similar to Model 1876 Rifle Early Second Model, with 32 in. round barrel and carbine forend tip.

$5,000 - $3,000 $3,000 - $1,750 $1,750 - $1,250

95% = $8,250   90% = $7,500   80% = $7,000   70% = $6,750   60% = $6,500   50% = $6,250

▲ *Model 1876 Rifle Third Model* — dust cover rail integral with frame, serial range 30,000-end of production.

$1,500 - $1,000 $1,000 - $700 $700 - $500

98% = $4,750   95% = $4,000   90% = $3,500   80% = $3,000   70% = $2,750   60% = $2,350

W

Above Average	Average	Below Average

▲ *Model 1876 Carbine Third Model* — frame similar to Model 1876 Rifle Third Model, with 22 in. round barrel and full length forearm giving a musket appearance.

$2,275 - $1,475	$1,475 - $900	$900 - $600

98% = $6,000 95% = $5,500 90% = $5,000 80% = $4,650 70% = $4,250 60% = $3,775

▲ *Model 1876 Musket Third Model* — frame similar to Model 1876 Rifle Third Model, with 32 in. round barrel.

$5,000 - $3,000	$3,000 - $1,750	$1,750 - $1,250

95% = $7,250 90% = $6,500 80% = $6,000 70% = $5,500 60% = $5,250 50% = $5,000

▲ *Model 1876 "One of One Thousand"* — special care taken in manufacture to guarantee better accuracy, markings on top of breech designate model, deluxe walnut, extremely rare, 54 mfg. Original cost was $100.

Values can range from $35,000 - $250,000, depending on condition. A factory letter is a must for any "One of One Thousand" Winchester. Believe it or not, watch for fake letters.

Values are not listed because too few original specimens are bought or sold to accurately establish pricing. A factory letter is a must for any "One of One Thousand" Winchester.

Note: Rarity of the "One of One Thousand" and the "One of One Hundred" models makes unethical upgrading to this model fairly common. Use extreme caution in purchasing.

▲ *Model 1876 "One of One Hundred"* — similar to "One of One Thousand" only rarer, 8 mfg. Sold new for $20 over the list price of a similarly equipped Model 1876.

Values can range from $45,000 - $500,000, depending on condition. A factory letter is a must for any "One of One Hundred" Winchester. Believe it or not, watch for fake letters.

Values are not listed because too few original specimens are bought or sold to accurately establish pricing. A factory letter is a must for any "One of One Hundred" Winchester.

▲ *Model 1876 Northwest Mounted Police Carbine* — .45-75 cal. only, 22 in. barrel, "NWMP" lightly stamped on butt stock (with wear, this cartouche may not be visible) approx. 1,600 mfg.

$3,875 - $2,500	$2,500 - $1,500	$1,500 - $1,000

95% = $9,500 90% = $8,750 80% = $7,750 70% = $6,950 60% = $6,150 50% = $5,275

Above average specimens in this model should have traces of blue and a very good stock cartouche. Be very wary of the stock cartouche since these butt stocks were sold as surplus back in the 1920s. A letter of authenticity is a good idea on this model.

MODEL 1886 LEVER ACTION — .33 WCF, .38-56 WCF, .38-70 WCF (830 mfg.), .40-65 WCF, .40-70 WCF (629 mfg.), .40-82 WCF, .45-70, .45-90, .50-110 Express, or .50-100-450 (234 mfg.) cal. available, Browning's first high power lever action design distinguishable by vertical locking bars, .45-70 most popular cal., 26 in. round or octagon barrel, tube mag., steel forend cap, straight grip stock. Approx. 159,990 mfg. between 1886-1935.

The Model 1886 had case hardening standard on the frame, butt plate, and forend cap until 1901 (approx. 122,000 serial range) when the standard finish became blue.

On the Model 1886 variations listed below, add the following percentages for special order features.
Add 10% for octagon barrel.
Add 20% premium for Takedown Model.
Add 30% for .45-70 or .45-90 cal.
Add 100% for .50-110 or 125% for .50-100-450 cal.
Add 100% for Deluxe Model (pistol grip checkered walnut stock).

▲ *Model 1886 Rifle* — similar to above.

$1,250 - $900	$900 - $700	$700 - $500

98% = $3,500 95% = $3,000 90% = $2,850 80% = $1,850 70% = $1,600 60% = $1,400

▲ *Model 1886 Carbine* — same general specifications as Rifle, except 22 in. round barrel and saddle ring, solid frame only.

$2,500 - $1,600	$1,600 - $1,000	$1,000 - $700

98% = $9,250 95% = $8,000 90% = $6,750 80% = $4,750 70% = $3,750 60% = $2,750
Add 35% for full stock carbine (very rare).

	Above Average	Average	Below Average

▲ *Model 1886 Musket* — 30 in. round barrel, full length military style forearm, military sights, only 350 mfg., very rare.

	Above Average	Average	Below Average
	$6,000 - $4,450	$4,450 - $3,000	$3,000 - $2,250

95% = $13,750 90% = $11,250   80% = $9,000   70% = $8,000   60% = $7,000   50% = $6,000

Most specimens encountered in this variation are in very good condition - a pitted musket is almost never encountered.

▲ *Model 1886 Lightweight Rifle* — .45-70 or .33 WCF cal. only, 22 (.45-70 cal.) or 24 (.33 WCF cal.) in. round nickel steel tapered barrel, half mag., rubber shotgun butt plate.

▲ *.33 caliber*

	Above Average	Average	Below Average
	$700 - $600	$600 - $500	$500 - $400

98% = $1,750   95% = $1,350   90% = $1,200   80% = $1,100   70% = $1,000   60% = $900

▲ *.45-70 caliber*

	Above Average	Average	Below Average
	$1,500 - $1,250	$1,250 - $900	$900 - $700

98% = $3,750   95% = $3,250   90% = $2,850   80% = $2,350   70% = $1,975   60% = $1,725

Since lightweight rifles were fairly late production, all specimens are blue and in very good condition usually.

100%	98%	95%	90%	80%	70%	60%	50%	40%	30%	20%	10%

MODEL 1892 RIFLE — .218 Bee, .25-20, .32-20, .38-40, or .44-40 cal., 24 in. round or octagon barrel, blue, tube mag., forend cap, crescent butt. Mfg. 1,004,067 between 1892-1941.

100%	98%	95%	90%	80%	70%	60%	50%	40%	30%	20%	10%
N/A	N/A	$1,775	$1,300	$1,100	$995	$875	$775	$675	$550	$450	$350

Add 25% for .44-40 cal.
Add 15% for .38-40 cal.
Add 25% for Takedown Model.
Add 50% for fancy pistol grip checkered wood (Deluxe Model).
Add 10% for early mfg. featuring case colored lever and hammer.
.218 Bee is extremely rare in this model. Most specimens are re-barreled rather than being original.

MODEL 1892 CARBINE — 20 in. round barrel, forearm bands and saddle ring.

100%	98%	95%	90%	80%	70%	60%	50%	40%	30%	20%	10%
N/A	N/A	$1,775	$1,300	$1,100	$995	$875	$775	$675	$550	$450	$350

Add 15% for .44-40.

MODEL 1892 TRAPPER'S CARBINE — similar to Carbine, with 12, 14, 15, 16, or 18 in. barrel. So called because was handy for trappers who had to carry a powerful but lightweight repeating rifle.

100%	98%	95%	90%	80%	70%	60%	50%	40%	30%	20%	10%
N/A	N/A	$3,500	$3,100	$2,600	$2,200	$1,700	$1,400	$1,100	$900	$775	$650

Most 1892 Trapper's Carbines are in the 15 in., .44-40 cal. configuration. Most of the 1892 Trapper's Carbine were shipped to South America or Australia. This variation is almost never encountered over 30% condition - most are brown guns.

MODEL 1892 MUSKET — 30 in. round barrel, full length military style forearm with military style rear sight.

100%	98%	95%	90%	80%	70%	60%	50%	40%	30%	20%	10%
N/A	N/A	$14,250	$12,250	$9,950	$7,500	$6,000	$4,750	$3,500	$2,500	$1,750	$1,500

MODEL 1894 RIFLE — .25-35, .30-30 (.30 WCF), .32-40, .32 Spl., or .38-55 cal., most common (and popular) is .30-30 cal., tube mag., 26 in. octagon barrel, blue, straight grip stock. Over 5,000,000 produced to date, mfg. 1894-present, newer mfg. may be found in the RIFLES: 1894 LEVER ACTION - POST 1964 MFG. section.

▲ *1899-1936 Mfg.* — model 94s built post 1898-1936.

100%	98%	95%	90%	80%	70%	60%	50%	40%	30%	20%	10%
N/A	$1,675	$1,450	$1,150	$925	$850	$725	$650	$575	$500	$425	$350

Add 20% for Antique mfg. (pre-148,000 ser. no.).
Add 10% for early mfg. featuring case colored lever and hammer.
The Model 1894 Winchester has the distinction of being the world's most popular rifle. Deluxe models or takedown variations will command substantial premiums over values listed above.

100%	98%	95%	90%	80%	70%	60%	50%	40%	30%	20%	10%

▲ **Model 1894 Takedown Rifle** — magazine unscrews at frame allowing barrel/magazine takedown. Add 20%+ premium.

MODEL 1894 TRAPPER'S CARBINE — similar to Carbine, with 14, 15 (common), 16, 17 (rare) or 18 in. barrel.

100%	98%	95%	90%	80%	70%	60%	50%	40%	30%	20%	10%
N/A	N/A	N/A	$3,000	$2,700	$2,400	$2,150	$1,825	$1,625	$1,475	$1,250	$1,050

The large majority of this variation are encountered in .30-30 cal. with 15 in. barrel. Any other caliber or barrel length will constitute a premium. Most of these carbines are brown and rusty.

Note: Check federal laws on legality of 14 in. barrel. 70%-100% specimens are almost never encountered in this model. Shorter barrels than 14 in. have not been encountered on this model.

MODEL 1894 SADDLE RING CARBINE — 20 in. round barrel.

100%	98%	95%	90%	80%	70%	60%	50%	40%	30%	20%	10%
N/A	N/A	$1,300	$1,100	$995	$875	$775	$675	$550	$450	$350	$295

Add 30% for Antique Model.
Add 25% for any cal. other than .30-30 or .32 Spl.

▲ **Eastern Carbine** — features long forearm, early stock design, early style carbine post front sight, and without saddle ring, mfg. late '20s - mid-'40s.

100%	98%	95%	90%	80%	70%	60%	50%	40%	30%	20%	10%
N/A	N/A	$1,000	$900	$800	$700	$625	$550	$495	$450	$395	$350

MODEL 1894 1940-1964 MFG. CARBINE — 1940-1964 mfg. without saddle ring.

100%	98%	95%	90%	80%	70%	60%	50%	40%	30%	20%	10%
$395	$375	$350	$325	$300	$275	$250	$220	$195	$180	$165	$150

Add 40% for .25-35 cal.
Some WWII carbines with special U.S. markings will bring a premium over prices listed above.

MODEL 1895 RIFLE FLATSIDE — .30 US (most common), .38-72, or .40-72 cal., early model, distinguishable in that frame does not have fluting or ridge contouring, serial range approx. 1-5000.

100%	98%	95%	90%	80%	70%	60%	50%	40%	30%	20%	10%
N/A	N/A	$1,950	$1,725	$1,525	$1,275	$1,000	$825	$695	$575	$475	$425

Add 75% for .38-72 or .40-72 cal.

MODEL 1895 RIFLE — .30-03, .30-06, .30-40 Krag, .303 Brit., .35 Win., .38-72, .40-72, .405 Win., or 7.62mm Russian cal., 24-28 in. barrel, blued action, box mag., straight grip stock, 425,881 mfg. from 1896-1931.

100%	98%	95%	90%	80%	70%	60%	50%	40%	30%	20%	10%
$2,050	$1,375	$1,100	$935	$825	$675	$600	$525	$475	$450	$425	$375

Add 50% for Deluxe Models.
Add 25% for octagon barrel.
Add 50% for .405 Win. cal.
Add 15% for takedown model.

The Model 1895 was a Browning design incorporating the first box type mag. in a lever action repeating rifle. .30 US is the most commonly encountered cal. in this model. A large Russian military contract was secured in 1915 with chambering for the 7.62mm Russian cartridge (over 293,000 mfg. or over 66% of total production). A very few (3) were made with color case hardened frames (Winchester's last large frame rifle to have case colors) and are very rare and expensive.

MODEL 1895 CARBINE — .30 US (.30/40 Krag Army - most common cal.), .30-03, .30-06, or .303 Brit. cal., 22 in. round barrel, military style top handguard wood and military sights, with or without saddle ring, escalloped frame sides.

100%	98%	95%	90%	80%	70%	60%	50%	40%	30%	20%	10%
$2,500	$2,150	$1,850	$1,600	$1,400	$1,200	$1,000	$875	$750	$625	$500	$375

▲ **Model 1895 Government Carbine** — U.S. marked.

100%	98%	95%	90%	80%	70%	60%	50%	40%	30%	20%	10%
$4,000	$3,600	$3,200	$2,700	$2,300	$2,000	$1,700	$1,400	$1,100	$900	$700	$500

MODEL 1895 FLATSIDE MUSKET — early models have serial range under 5,000, no flutes on frame, .30-40 Krag only.

Rarity on this model means only a few specimens in several museums.

W

100%	98%	95%	90%	80%	70%	60%	50%	40%	30%	20%	10%

MODEL 1895 MUSKET — .30-03, .30-06, or .30-40 Krag cal., 24 (.30-03 or .30-06 cal.) or 28 (.30-40 Krag only) in. round barrel, two bands, hand guard over barrel, military sights.

N/A	N/A	$1,850	$1,600	$1,400	$1,200	$1,000	$875	$750	$625	$500	$375

Add 10%-15% if U.S. Govt. marked.

MODEL 1895 NRA MUSKET — similar to Standard, with 30 in. barrel, 1901 Krag, rear sight. NRA approved for official NRA competition.

N/A	N/A	$2,500	$2,150	$1,850	$1,600	$1,400	$1,200	$1,075	$975	$875	$750

Also available in Models 1903 and 1906 which designated .30-03 and .30-06 cals. respectively.

MODEL 1895 RUSSIAN MUSKET — 7.62mm Russian cal., over 293,000 mfg. for Imperial Russian Govt., mfg. 1915-1916, various Russian Ordnance stamps should be present.

N/A	N/A	$1,900	$1,600	$1,400	$1,200	$1,025	$900	$800	$700	$600	$500

MODEL 53 RIFLE — .25-20, .32-20, or .44-40 cal., 22 in. round barrel, ½ tube mag. holding 6 cartridges, solid frame or takedown, blued finish, pistol grip or straight grip stock, serial numbered both separately and within the Model 92 range. Mfg. 24,916 between 1924-1932.

N/A	N/A	$1,650	$1,375	$1,075	$950	$875	$800	$725	$650	$575	$525

Add 50% for .44-40 cal.
Add 15% for Takedown Model.

MODEL 55 RIFLE — .25-35, .30-30, or .32 Win. Spl. cal., lever action design, solid frame and takedown, 24 in. round barrel, shotgun style butt stock with checkered steel butt plate, tube mag., holds 3 cartridges. Approx. 20,500 mfg. between 1924-1932. Serial numbered independently to approx. 2,865, then serialized with Model 1894 production on underside of receiver. Simply could not compete with the Model 1894.

$1,325	$1,100	$900	$825	$750	$675	$600	$525	$475	$425	$375	$325

Add 50% for .25-35 cal.

MODEL 64 RIFLE — .219 Zipper, .25-35, .30-30, or .32 Win. Spl. cal., 20, 24, or 26 (standard with .219 Zipper cal.) in. round barrel, blued metal, pistol grip stock, revamped Model 55 action with increased mag. capacity, 66,783 mfg. between 1933-1957 and 1972-1973 (over 8,250 mfg. in .30-30 cal. only - these last two years with minor changes).

$600	$560	$530	$495	$470	$440	$410	$370	$340	$295	$260	$215

Add 60% for Deluxe Model.
Add 25% for 20 in. barrel (sometime referred to as Carbine).

▲ *.219 Zipper cal.* — mfg. 1938-1941 only.

$1,895	$1,650	$1,400	$1,300	$1,200	$1,100	$1,000	$925	$850	$775	$700	$650

Many of this variation now have extra holes drilled on the top of the receiver to accept scope mounts - deduct 50% for this alteration. The Model 64 is usually found in excellent condition.

Model 64 1972-1973 mfg. may be found in the post-'64 section.

▲ *.25-35 Cal.*

$1,100	$1,000	$925	$850	$775	$700	$650	$595	$550	$515	$475	$435

MODEL 65 RIFLE — .218 Bee (introduced 1939), .25-20, or .32-20 cal., 22 in. round barrel (except .218 Bee - 24 in.), ½ tube mag. holding 7 cartridges, blue with pistol grip stock. Mfg. 5704 between 1933-1947.

$2,500	$2,200	$1,875	$1,650	$1,475	$1,325	$1,150	$1,050	$950	$875	$800	$750

While the .25-20 cal. is the rarest, the .218 Bee has the most demand.

The Model 65 was a design evolved from the Model 53. The Model 65 was not tapped on receiver side for scope mounts. As a rule, most specimens are in either pretty nice or refinished condition.

100%	98%	95%	90%	80%	70%	60%	50%	40%	30%	20%	10%

MODEL 71 RIFLE STANDARD — .348 Win. cal., ⅔ tube mag. holding 4 cartridges, improved Model 1886 frame, blued metal with pistol grip stock, 20 or 24 in. barrel, short or long tang. Mfg. 47,254 between 1935-1957.

$950	$875	$795	$750	$700	$650	$600	$550	$515	$475	$425	$395

Add 25% for pre-war long tang.

▲ *Model 71 — 20 in. barrel* — disc. in 1938, earlier models had long tangs only.

N/A	$2,950	$2,650	$2,400	$2,200	$2,000	$1,800	$1,650	$1,475	$1,350	$1,250	$1,000

MODEL 71 RIFLE DELUXE — similar to Standard, with checkered stock and sling swivels, 20 in. barrel in this model is very rare.

$1,195	$950	$875	$800	$775	$750	$725	$700	$675	$650	$625	$585

Add 40% for pre-war long tang.

MODEL 88 RIFLE AND CARBINE — see listing under RIFLES: LEVER ACTION - POST-1964 MFG. section.

RIFLES: SINGLE SHOT

MODEL 1885 — most popular cals. available from .22-.50, falling block triggerguard activated action, John Browning's first high power single shot rifle design, many variations were made and we will list the standard types. Over 139,725 mfg. between 1885-1920.

This design was originally mfg. as the Model 1878 by the Browning Brothers in Ogden, UT in the early 1880s. Fewer than 600 were mfg. - see the Browning section for values.

▲ *Sporting Rifle Low Wall* — 28 in. round or octagon barrel, open sights, solid frame, standard trigger.

$1,250	$950	$875	$800	$750	$700	$650	$600	$550	$500	$450	$400

Add 20% for centerfire cal.

▲ *Sporting Rifle High Wall* — 30 in. barrel, standard trigger, open sights, solid frame. Available in various size and weight barrels numbered (in front of forearm) from numeric 1, 2, 3, 3½ (introduced 1910), 4, and 5, lightest to heaviest. Case hardened frames standard until 1901 when bluing became standard, three different frames depending on caliber. Heavier barrels in rare calibers will bring a premium.

▲ *Blued finish*

$1,875	$1,500	$1,350	$1,200	$1,075	$975	$900	$825	$750	$675	$595	$500

▲ *Case colored frame*

$2,475	$2,250	$1,900	$1,600	$1,400	$1,200	$1,050	$900	$800	$700	$600	$500

Add 30% for Takedown frame.
Add 25% for #5 barrel.
Add 25% for .45-70 or .45-90 cal.

▲ *20 ga. High Wall Shotgun* — chambered for 3 in., 26 in. full choke nickel steel barrel standard, receiver has matting on top. Also available with matted ribs (rare). Solid frame or takedown. Introduced 1914 - approx. 300 mfg.

N/A	N/A	$2,850	$2,475	$2,150	$1,800	$1,550	$1,350	$1,200	$1,050	$900	$775

▲ *Deluxe Grade High Wall* — similar to Standard, with fancy walnut and checkering.

$4,150	$3,350	$2,850	$2,550	$2,275	$2,000	$1,800	$1,650	$1,450	$1,300	$1,200	$1,125

▲ *Schuetzen Rifle* — high wall, 30 in. octagon barrel, double set triggers, spur lever, aperture sight, Schuetzen style stock, adj. palm rest and butt plate.

$5,100	$4,600	$4,250	$3,950	$3,750	$3,500	$3,250	$3,000	$2,750	$2,500	$2,250	$2,100

Add 20% for Takedown frame.

This model had many shooting alterations performed by various aftermarket suppliers of its time. Perhaps only 10% of remaining specimens are unaltered (or 100% factory).

▲ *High Wall Musket* — usually found in .22 LR cal.

$1,250	$1,100	$900	$775	$650	$575	$500	$450	$400	$365	$335	$300

Add 30% for .45-70 cal.

W

100%	98%	95%	90%	80%	70%	60%	50%	40%	30%	20%	10%

▲ **Winder Musket** — low wall, 3rd model, .22 Short or LR (most common), 28 in. barrel, standard trigger and lever, military style stock and sights, grooved forearm, one barrel band.

| $850 | $775 | $700 | $650 | $600 | $550 | $500 | $450 | $400 | $365 | $335 | $300 |

RIFLES: BOLT ACTION

MODEL 1883 (HOTCHKISS REPEATER) — .45-70 cal., designed by Benjamin D. Hotchkiss, unique tube mag. located in butt stock attached to receiver, up-turn/pull-back bolt action, 26 in. round or octagon barrel standard on rifle. Over 84,000 mfg. between 1879-1889. Also available in carbine configuration (24 in. round barrel with one band), and musket (32 in. round barrel with cleaning rod and two barrel bands) — subtract 25%. Carbine extremely rare in Third Model (20 in. barrel).

▲ **First Style** — approx. 6,419 mfg. with magazine cut off and safety control incorporated into one unit.

| $1,650 | $1,450 | $1,250 | $1,100 | $1,100 | $950 | $900 | $850 | $800 | $765 | $735 | $710 |

▲ **Second Style** — approx. 16,102 mfg., magazine cut off on right receiver top, safety on left side.

| $1,450 | $1,250 | $1,050 | $900 | $800 | $750 | $700 | $650 | $600 | $565 | $535 | $510 |

▲ **Third Style** — most commonly encountered Hotchkiss, 2-piece stock, approx. 62,034 mfg. 1883-1899.

| $1,650 | $1,425 | $1,250 | $1,100 | $900 | $825 | $750 | $675 | $625 | $565 | $525 | $480 |

The Model 1883 Hotchkiss was the first bolt action designed for the U.S. military .45-70 cartridge. On the First and Second models inspect wood directly below bolt and left frame side for cracks, breaks or older repairs as it is frequently encountered on these early models with thin wrists.

LEE STRAIGHT PULL RIFLE — 6mm Lee (.236 U.S.N. cal.), 5 shot non-detachable box mag., 24 (Sporting Rifle) or 28 (Musket) in. barrel, folding leaf sight, blue metal, military style full stock, mfg. 1897-1902, Navy Issue Model is the Musket with "236 U.S.N." on barrels. Approx. 20,000 mfg. (including 15,000 Muskets for the U.S. Navy military contract) between 1895-1902 with parts clean up occurring in 1916.

▲ **U.S.N. Military Musket**

| $1,475 | $1,300 | $1,150 | $1,000 | $900 | $800 | $700 | $625 | $550 | $500 | $450 | $425 |

▲ **Lee Sporting Rifle** — similar to Musket, with 24 in. barrel, sporter style stock. Approx. 1,700 mfg. 1897-1902.

| $1,475 | $1,300 | $1,150 | $1,000 | $900 | $800 | $700 | $625 | $550 | $500 | $450 | $425 |

This design was originally patented by James Paris Lee and assigned to the Lee Arms Company. Winchester obtained manufacturing rights to produce this model for the U.S Navy military contract 1895-1902.

MODEL 1900 SINGLE SHOT — .22 S and L cal., 18 in. round barrel, blued metal, open sights, one-piece straight grip gumwood stock without fitted butt plate, takedown, not serial numbered. Approx. 105,000 mfg. between 1899-1902.

| N/A | N/A | $350 | $330 | $310 | $290 | $270 | $250 | $220 | $185 | $140 | $110 |

This model is usually encountered with flaked frames.

MODEL 1902 SINGLE SHOT — similar to 1900, with minor improvements. Distinguishable by special shaped extended triggerguard. Not serial numbered. Approx. 640,299 mfg. between 1902-1931.

| N/A | $275 | $175 | $150 | $135 | $120 | $100 | $90 | $80 | $75 | $65 | $60 |

Chambering included .22 cal. Extra Long in 1914 (interchangeable with S&L).

THUMB TRIGGER MODEL 99 — similar to 1902, with button behind cocking piece used to fire with thumb instead of trigger, not serial numbered. Approx. 75,433 were mfg. between 1904-1923.

| N/A | $550 | $425 | $375 | $325 | $275 | $235 | $195 | $175 | $150 | $135 | $120 |

MODEL 1904 SINGLE SHOT — improved version of 1902, 21 in. round barrel, chambering included .22 Extra Long in 1914, not serial numbered. Approx. 302,859 mfg. between 1904-1931.

| $235 | $200 | $175 | $160 | $150 | $140 | $130 | $120 | $110 | $100 | $90 | $80 |

100%	98%	95%	90%	80%	70%	60%	50%	40%	30%	20%	10%

▲ *Model 1904-A* — introduced 1927 with new sear bar and chambered for .22 LR.

$250	$215	$190	$175	$165	$155	$145	$135	$125	$115	$105	$95

MODEL 43 — .218 Bee, .22 Hornet, .25-20, or .32-20 cal., dubbed "Poor Man's Model 70", 24 in. round tapered barrel, box type mag. Approx. 62,617 mfg. between 1949-1957.

$695	$595	$535	$475	$440	$400	$360	$320	$290	$260	$240	$220

Add 20% for Deluxe Model.
Add $50 for Special Grade.
Premiums exist (in order of rarity) for .32-20, .25-20, or .218 Bee cals.
Subtract 50% if non-factory drilled and tapped (early models).

Grading				100%	98%	95%	90%	80%	70%	60%

On Models 52, 54, 56, 57, 58, 59, 60, 60A, 67, 677, 68, 69, 69A, 697, and 70 values in 50% or less original condition have been omitted since values in those conditions will approximate the 60% price. This reflects the fact that while these lower condition specimens are not as desirable to collectors, they are still sought after as shooters.

MODEL 47 — .22 S, L, or LR cal., single shot bolt action, 25 in. round barrel, unique bolt design, unchecked walnut stock, 5¼ lbs., approx. 43,000 (not serial numbered) mfg. during 1948-1954.

									$300	$260	$210	$175	$150	$125	$100

MODEL 52 TARGET — .22 S (rare) or LR cal., 5 shot mag., 28 in. standard or heavy barrel (1st cataloged 1933), target sights and target style stock, speedlock trigger feature was introduced in 1929. Approx. 125,233 Model 52s in all variations were mfg. between 1919-1979.

			$440	$415	$375	$345	$315	$290	$265

With speedlock

			$495	$470	$415	$375	$335	$310	$290

Barrel drilling and tapping for scope blocks was not standard on the first Model 52s, but became more apparent approx. 1926.

▲ *Model 52A Target* — similar to Model 52, except all A-suffix Model 52s have a speedlock action. Values are similar to above. In scarcity, it seems the E suffix is probably the scarcest (also the most poorly mfg.), followed by the A suffix variation.

MODEL 52A HEAVY BARREL — similar to Standard Target, with heavy barrel.

$660	$605	$550	$525	$470	$415	$330

MODEL 52-B TARGET — extensively redesigned action, improved stock design, offered with a variety of sights. Approx. mfg. 1940-1947.

$605	$550	$495	$470	$415	$360	$305

MODEL 52-B HEAVY BARREL — similar to 52-B, with heavy barrel.

$660	$605	$550	$525	$470	$415	$330

MODEL 52-B BULL GUN — extra heavy weight barrel.

$690	$635	$580	$550	$495	$440	$360

MODEL 52 SPORTER (SPORTING RIFLE) — 24 in. round lightweight barrel with front sight cover, sporting type select walnut stock with cheekpiece, hard rubber pistol grip cap, black plastic tipped forearm, checkered steel butt plate, about 7¼ lbs. Mfg. 1934-1958. There is some controversy whether any of the Model 52 Sporters were drilled and tapped per factory workmanship. Be cautious of "factory" drilled and tapped receivers on all model 52s, as there are many "gunsmith" Sporters that have been made with turned down, shortened target barrels.

▲ *Model 52* — advertised approx. 1936.

$2,750	$2,350	$1,875	$1,500	$1,400	$1,275	$1,150

▲ *Model 52A* — introduced approx. 1937, receiver and locking lug were strengthened.

$2,950	$2,500	$2,000	$1,500	$1,400	$1,275	$1,150

W

Grading	100%	98%	95%	90%	80%	70%	60%

▲ *Model 52B* — introduced approx. 1940, 5 shot detachable mag., with adj. sling swivel assembly and single shot adapter.

	$2,950	$2,500	$2,000	$1,700	$1,500	$1,100	$1,000

▲ *Model 52B (1993 Re-issue)* — .22 LR cal., patterned after the original Model 52B and includes steel buttplate, forearm adjusting screw, and B-style stock with small cheekpiece, 6,250 mfg. beginning 1993.

Mfg.'s Sug. Retail $576 $500 $395 $325

▲ *Model 52C* — introduced 1947 with adj. Micro Motion trigger, less than 100 mfg., 2 screws in triggerguard.

	$3,150	$2,700	$2,450	$1,950	$1,650	$1,275	$1,150

A few Model 52 Sporters & Targets were mfg. with stainless steel barrels (17,XXX-27,XXX serial range) - these guns will command a premium over values shown above.

MODEL 52-C STANDARD TARGET — "Micro Motion" trigger and "Marksman" stock, single shot adaptor, 5 or 10 shot mag. was avail., standard barrel, otherwise similar to 52-B. Mfg. 1947-1961.

	$700	$625	$550	$525	$470	$415	$330

MODEL 52-C HEAVY TARGET — similar to Standard Target, with heavy barrel.

	$625	$550	$490	$470	$415	$360	$305

MODEL 52-C BULL TARGET — extra heavy (bull) barrel model of Heavy Target 52-C. Mfg. approx. 1947-1961.

	$775	$675	$580	$550	$495	$440	$360

MODEL 52-D TARGET — improved version of 52-C with free floating standard or heavy barrel and adj. bedding device, all 52-Ds were single shot. Mfg. 1961- approx. 1969.

	$625	$550	$495	$440	$385	$360	$275

MODEL 52-D & 52-E INTERNATIONAL MATCH — similar to 52-D, with free rifle stock, accessory rail. Mfg. 1969-disc.

	$750	$675	$605	$550	$495	$470	$385

Previous Model 52s with A, B, C, and D had serial suffixes following the ser. no., but after approx. 1969, rifles started appearing with an E serial prefix. Both Model 52 International and Prone could have factory stocks that were not Winchester mfg.

MODEL 52-D & 52-E PRONE — similar to International Match, with prone style stock. Mfg. 1975-disc.

	$750	$675	$605	$550	$495	$470	$385

MODEL 54 HIGH POWER SPORTER — .270, 7x57mm, .30-30, or .30-06 cal., 5 shot mag., 24 in. barrel, open sights, checkered pistol grip stock. Mfg. 1925-1930. Approx. 50,145 Model 54s were mfg. in all variations between 1925-1936.

	$675	$595	$525	$450	$385	$330	$305

Rare cals. will add premiums to the values listed above. This model was also mfg. with a stainless steel barrel during the late 1920s - early '30s with premiums also being asked.

MODEL 54 CARBINE — introduced 1927, similar to Rifle, with 20 in. barrel, plain stock.

	$750	$675	$595	$525	$475	$385	$360

MODEL 54 IMPROVED SPORTER — .22 Hornet, .220 Swift, .250-3000, .257 Robts., .270, 7 x 57mm, or .30-06 cal., 5 shot mag., 24 or 26 in. barrel, one piece firing pin, checkered pistol grip stock. Mfg. 1930-1936.

	$675	$595	$525	$450	$385	$330	$305

Rare cals. will add premiums to the values listed above.

MODEL 54 CARBINE IMPROVED — similar to Rifle, with 20 in. barrel.

	$750	$675	$595	$525	$475	$385	$360

Grading	100%	98%	95%	90%	80%	70%	60%

MODEL 54 SUPER GRADE— introduced 1934, similar to Sporter, with better wood and black forend tip and pistol grip cap.

	$950	$850	$775	$695	$625	$550	$525

> Rare calibers will command considerable premiums (i.e. this variation in 7x57mm cal. will sell for $2,500 in mint condition).

MODEL 54 SPORTING SNIPER'S RIFLE — introduced 1929, similar to Sporter, with 26 in. heavy barrel, .30-06 only, aperture sight.

	$1,000	$875	$775	$695	$625	$550	$525

MODEL 54 NATIONAL MATCH — introduced 1935, similar to Standard, with Lyman sights and Marksman stock.

	$1,000	$875	$775	$695	$625	$550	$525

MODEL 56 SPORTER — .22 S or LR cal., 5 or 10 shot box mag., 22 in. round barrel, open sights, plain pistol grip stock. Approx. 8,297 mfg. between 1926-1929.

	$600	$525	$460	$400	$350	$300	$250

> The .22 cal. Short was disc. 1929.

MODEL 57 SPORTER — .22 LR cal., 22 in. barrel, open sights, stock cutaway for aperture sight on left side, drilled and tapped receiver, pistol grip walnut stock with barrel band, 5 or 10 shot mag., left side push-button mag. release, approx. 5½ lbs.

	$550	$495	$450	$395	$350	$300	$250

▲ *Model 57 Target* — similar to Model 56, except with aperture sight and heavier target stock. Approx. 18,600 were mfg. between 1926-1936.

	$595	$525	$450	$375	$300	$260	$220

MODEL 58 SINGLE SHOT — similar to Models 1902 and 1904, .22 LR cal., 18 in. round barrel, open sights, takedown. Approx. 38,992 mfg. between 1928-1931.

	$375	$295	$240	$185	$160	$130	$120

MODEL 59 SINGLE SHOT — improved Model 58 with 23 in. round barrel and pistol grip stock with butt plate. Approx. 9,200 mfg. between 1930-1931.

	$450	$425	$400	$350	$300	$250	$200

> This model was disc. due to lack of sales.

MODEL 60 — improved Model 59, 23 in. round barrel increased to 27 in. 1933. Approx. 160,754 mfg. between 1930-1934.

	$295	$250	$200	$180	$160	$135	$110

MODEL 60A TARGET — similar to Model 60 with Lyman 55W aperture rear sight, heavier target stock, and 27 in. round tapered barrel. Approx. 6,118 mfg. between 1932-1939.

	$500	$425	$350	$325	$275	$235	$200

MODEL 67/67A — .22 LR or .22 WRF (authorized 1935) cal., 20 in. (Boys Rifle), 24 (miniature target boring), and 27 in. (sporting or smooth bore) round barrels, same basic action as the Model 60, not serial numbered. Approx. 383,000 mfg. between 1934-1963.

	$175	$130	$95	$80	$70	$60	$50

> Add 50% for Boys rifle.
> Add 200% for .22 WRF cal.

MODEL 677 — same basic specifications as Model 67, except no iron sights or sight cuts in barrel, not serial numbered, supplied with Win. 5-A scope. Approx. 2,240 mfg. between 1937-1939.

	$550	$475	$375	$275	$225	$150	$100
In .22 WRF cal. (rare)	$1,200	$1,000	$800	$600	$400	$300	$250

W

Grading	100%	98%	95%	90%	80%	70%	60%

MODEL 68 — .22 LR or .22 WRF cal., bolt action single shot, similar to Model 67, walnut stock, supplied with aperture sight (no rear sight), not serial numbered. Approx. 100,000 mfg. between 1934-1946.

	$175	$130	$95	$80	$70	$60	$50

MODEL 69 & 69A — .22 S, LR, or RF cal., 5 or 10 shot repeater, 25 in. barrel, aperture or open rear sight, not serial numbered. Approx. 355,000 mfg. between 1935-1963. Add $50 for Target version.

	$295	$275	$250	$150	$110	$100	$85

> The Model 69 was cocked by the closing motion of the bolt and had a non-swept back bolt handle, whereas the 69A was cocked by the opening motion of the bolt and had a swept back bolt handle. Number 97B rear aperture sight and 80A hooded front target sights and standard open sights were offered on both the Model 69 and 69A. Late 69As had "grooved" receiver for "tip-off" scope mounts - add 20%-25% for this feature.

MODEL 72/72A — .22 LR and Gallery Model (.22 short only), tube mag., bolt action, 25 in. round, tapered barrel, aperture or open rear sight, not serial numbered. Over 161,000 mfg. between 1938-1959.

	$295	$275	$250	$150	$110	$100	$85

> Add $50 for Target version.
> Add 70% for Gallery Model (mfg. 1939-1942) - rare.
> The Model 72 and 72A both cocked on opening. The Model 72A has a swept back bolt handle and some minor internal mechanical improvements. Same open sight options as Models 69/69A. Late 72As had "grooved" receiver for "tip-off" scope mounts - add 20%-25% for this feature.

MODEL 75 TARGET — .22 LR, 5 or 10 shot mag., 28 in. barrel, target sights, slight variation used by Government in WWII. Approx. 88,715 Model 75 Target and Model 75s were mfg. between 1938-1958.

	$500	$450 •	$400	$325	$275	$225	$175

> Add up to 25% for original Winchester leather sling.

MODEL 75 SPORTER — similar to Target, except 24 in. tapered barrel, clip feed, non-target sights and select checkered walnut.

	$700	$600	$500	$450	$425	$350	$275

> Late 75 Sporters had "grooved" receiver for "tip-off" scope mounts - add 10%-15% for this feature.

MODEL 697 — same general specifications as the Model 69, except no iron sights or sight cuts in barrel and no ramp or sight cover. Telescope bases attached to barrel were standard.

	$500	$450	$400	$300	$250	$200	$150
.22 WRF cal.	$600	$550	$450	$400	$350	$300	$250

MODEL 777 — .30-06 cal., bolt action, 4 shot mag., mfg. by Nikko in Japan during 1979-80 for sale to Winchester subsidiaries in Australia, Germany, Italy, and Scandinavia, only 3 were shipped to the U.S., checkered Monte Carlo stock with Wundhammer swell grip, lightweight barrel, engraved action, "Winchester" is cast on the left side of the receiver near the top, approx. 1,000 mfg. with 250 in .30-06 cal. - 750 mfg. in different cal. and sold elsewhere, 8½ lbs.

> Extreme rarity factor precludes accurate price evaluation. Some specimens have been reported as sold in the $1,850+ range.

RIFLES: MODEL 70 BOLT ACTION

The Pre-'64 Model 70 Bolt Action Rifle (advertised by Winchester throughout much of its production history as "The Rifleman's Rifle") was produced from 1936 through 1963. Collectors recognize three major manufacturing periods: "Pre-War" (1936-1941); "Transition" (1942-1948); and "Latter" (1949-1963). There were only eighteen (18) original chamberings, these are: .22 Hornet, .220 Swift, .243 Win., .250 Savage (.250-3000), .257 Roberts, .264 Win. Mag., .270 Win., 7x57mm Mauser, .300

Grading	100%	98%	95%	90%	80%	70%	60%

Savage, .300 H&H Mag., .300 Win. Mag., .30-06 (.30 Govt. '06 Springfield - approx. 80% of total mfg. by cal.,), .308 Win. (standard in Featherweight Style only), .338 Win. Mag., .35 Rem., .358 Win. (in Featherweight Style only), .375 H&H Mag., and .458 Win. Mag. (in Super Grade AFRICAN Style only). It is important to note that every caliber was not available during each manufacturing period. Any other caliber encountered (including 7.65mm Argentine and 9mm Mauser) may be regarded as either special ordered or non-original. Magazine capacities are as follows: "Standard Calibers" (including .22 Hornet) five (5) rounds; "H&H Magnums" (.300 & .375) four (4) rounds; and "Winchester Short Magnums" (.264, .300, .338, .458) three (3) rounds. The rifle was produced in a myriad of styles and variations — most of which are covered below individually. Unfortunately, a veritable "cottage industry" has developed involving the alteration, "upgrading" and/or outright faking of these guns. Be careful when contemplating a purchase of any rare Model 70 (and get a receipt describing the purchase accurately).

MODEL 70 PRE-WWII MFG. STANDARD GRADE — 12 standard cals., 5 shot mag., 4 shot mag. on Magnums, 24, 25, or 26 in. barrel, open sights, checkered walnut pistol grip stock, ser. range is 1-31,675. Mfg. 1937-1941.

Values listed below assume original, unaltered specimens — modifications/alterations to either the metal or wood surfaces can reduce prices by large amounts. All pre-war Model 70s have only 2 holes drilled in the front of the receiver (none in the back). An extra set of "holes" can decrease value as much as 50%. Some pre-WWII Model 70s have a "D" suffix indicating a doubled up serial number - this variation will command a premium because of its rarity. The Model 70 is one gun that caliber ranks before condition in terms of desirability. Specimens encountered in under 60% condition will not decrease in price substantially since almost any shooter is worth $450-$550.

	100%	98%	95%	90%	80%	70%	60%
Standard Cals.	$1,050	$875	$775	$595	$500	$450	$400
.22 Hornet	$1,650	$1,425	$1,075	$875	$725	$650	$550
.220 Swift	$1,200	$1,050	$950	$700	$595	$500	$450
.257 Roberts	$1,600	$1,225	$925	$700	$595	$500	$450
.270 Win.	$1,100	$975	$875	$695	$595	$500	$450
.300 H&H	$1,650	$1,100	$875	$700	$595	$500	$450
.375 H&H	$2,750	$2,300	$1,850	$1,400	$1,150	$875	$800
7x57mm Mauser	$2,500	$2,200	$1,900	$1,550	$1,300	$1,125	$895
.250-3000 Savage	$2,000	$1,750	$1,500	$1,100	$925	$775	$675

Add approx. 100% for Super Grades in common cals.

Add approx. 80% for carbine variations (mfg. 1936-1946 with 20 in. barrel in .22 Hornet, .250-3000 Savage, .257 Roberts, .270 Win., 7mm, or .30-06 cal.).

There are more fakes than legitimate specimens in cals. 7x57mm and .250-3000 Savage!

Rare cals. such as the .300 Savage, .35 Rem., 7.65mm, and 9mm are seldomly encountered and their scarcity precludes accurate price evaluation. Cals. 7.65mm and 9mm were special order only and made up from left-over Model 54 barrels. Also, the original factory box, papers, and hanging tag will add 25%-30% to the values listed above. Believe it or not, there are getting to be a lot of fake Model 70 boxes that have been intentionally aged. Carefully screen NIB (watch the hanging tag also) specimens in this model.

MODEL 70 CARBINE (MFG. 1936-1946) — available in most cals. during its period, 20 in. barrel, short rifle variation of the Pre-'64 Model 70 (Winchester never officially used the "Carbine" terminology). If original, front sight base will be an integral part of the barrel. All carbines were disc. shortly after WWII. Beware of fakes.

Model 70 Carbine values will bring an approximate 50% premium over Standard Rifles of identical chambering.

MODEL 70 TRANSITION (MFG. 1946-1948) — several of the post-war Model 70s mfg. between 1946-1948 exhibit the pre-war receiver characteristics and have a transition safety. This variation is more rare than normal models, with asking prices 10%-20% higher.

On this Transitional Model, the receiver bridge may or may not be factory drilled.

Grading	100%	98%	95%	90%	80%	70%	60%

MODEL 70 1946-1963 MFG. STANDARD GRADE — 18 standard cals. including .22 Hornet, .220 Swift, .243 Win., .250 Savage (.250-3000), .257 Roberts, .264 Win. Mag., .270 Win., 7x57mm Mauser, .300 Savage, .300 H&H Mag., .300 Win. Mag., .30-06, .308 Win., .338 Win. Mag., .35 Rem., .358 Win., and .375 H&H Mag., 5 shot mag., 4 shot mag. on Magnums, 24, 25, or 26 in. barrel, open sights, checkered walnut pistol grip stock, ser. range is 52,549-581,471. Mfg. 1946-1963.

Values listed below assume original, unaltered specimens — modifications/alterations to either the metal or wood surfaces can reduce prices by large amounts. Most post-war Model 70s are drilled on top of the receiver (2 holes in front and 2 holes in back) to accept scope mounts (except early .300 and .375 H&H cals.). Pre-1952 mfg. Model 70s are desirable since Winchester implemented manufacturing techniques that lowered the quality in 1953.

	100%	98%	95%	90%	80%	70%	60%
.22 Hornet	$1,395	$1,295	$1,195	$900	$750	$600	$500
.220 Swift	$1,195	$1,025	$900	$750	$650	$550	$500
.243 Win.	$995	$925	$800	$725	$625	$550	$500
.257 Roberts	$1,050	$925	$800	$675	$600	$525	$450
.264 Win. Mag.	$850	$695	$625	$595	$550	$495	$400
.270 Win.	$725	$650	$585	$550	$520	$475	$400
.30-06 cal.	$675	$575	$530	$495	$450	$415	$375
.300 H&H	$1,150	$925	$800	$725	$650	$575	$525
.300 Win. Mag.	$1,500	$1,295	$1,050	$900	$800	$700	$625
.338 Win. Mag.	$1,500	$1,350	$1,100	$950	$800	$725	$650
.375 H&H	$1,750	$1,550	$1,375	$1,000	$850	$775	$700

Rare cals. such as the .250-3000, .300 Savage, .308 Win. (extremely rare and watch for fakes), .35 Rem., and 7x57mm Mauser are seldomly seen or sold. Premiums depend on the rarity of the caliber and original condition.

Believe it or not, there are getting to be a lot of fake Model 70 boxes that have been intentionally aged. Carefully screen NIB (watch the hanging tag also) specimens in this model.

MODEL 70 FEATHERWEIGHT — lightened version of Standard, .243 Win., .264 Win. Mag. (Westerner), .270 Win., .308 Win., .30-06, or .358 Win. cal., 22 in. barrel, aluminum triggerguard and floorplate, ser. range is 206,626-581,471. Mfg. 1952-1963.

	100%	98%	95%	90%	80%	70%	60%
.243 W., .30-06	$825	$750	$675	$600	$550	$500	$450
.264 Win. Mag. (Westerner)	$1,200	$1,100	$1,000	$900	$800	$700	$600
.270 Win.,	$925	$850	$775	$700	$650	$600	$550
.308 Win.	$695	$575	$525	$475	$450	$425	$400
.358 Win.	$1,500	$1,450	$1,250	$975	$850	$725	$600

Add 400% for Super Grade Models.

The .358 Win. cal. is rare because Winchester had problems with this cal. Many of them were exchanged for other calibers, and the result is that original guns are rare in this cal.

MODEL 70 SUPER GRADE — similar to Standard Model, except has deluxe wood, black pistol grip cap and forend tip, all Super Grades have a raised cheekpiece with deluxe wraparound checkering, and Super Grade marked floorplate. Disc. 1960.

A general rule for Super Grades is that if you add 100% to the standard grade in similar cals., values should be rather close. For .375 H&H Mag. cal., values are listed below.

	100%	98%	95%	90%	80%	70%	60%
.375 H&H	$2,800	$2,350	$1,950	$1,675	$1,375	$950	$800

Later Model 70 Super Grades have jeweled action components.

W

Grading	100%	98%	95%	90%	80%	70%	60%

MODEL 70 SUPER GRADE FEATHERWEIGHT — .243 Win., .270 Win., .30-06, or .308 Win. cal. only, because of inconsistencies of Super Grade action component jeweling (i.e., engine turning), a simple stock and hinged floorplate change can create an "instant" Super Grade Featherweight (check stock carefully for wood filling near area of Standard Super Grade rear sight "boss" in barrel channel), all Super Grade Featherweights have a raised cheekpiece with wraparound "fish tail" checkering, less than 1,000 mfg.

Original S.G. Featherweights will command 4 times the value of a Standard Featherweight Model. This is perhaps the rarest variation of the Pre-'64 Model 70 - beware of fakes.

MODEL 70 SUPER GRADE AFRICAN — .458 Win. Mag. only, front swivel base relocated and attached to bottom of barrel, nearly all possess one or two visible stock crossbolts (usually covered with Bakelite). Most have all action components (bolt body, extractor, extractor ring and magazine follower) jeweled (i.e., engine turned). 1,226 mfg. 1956-1963.

	100%	98%	95%	90%	80%	70%	60%
	$3,750	$3,500	$3,250	$3,000	$2,750	$2,500	$2,250

While other Super Grades were disc. approx. 1960, the "AFRICAN" continued in that style until the end of all production. Normal attrition and collectors owning more than one contribute to extreme rarity. Retains considerable "shooter" value in lesser external conditions.

MODEL 70 NATIONAL MATCH — similar to Standard, with target stock and scope bases, .30-06 only. Disc. 1960.

	100%	98%	95%	90%	80%	70%	60%
	$1,450	$1,200	$995	$895	$775	$700	$660

MODEL 70 TARGET — similar to Model 70 Standard, in .243 or .30-06 cal. (mfg. 1955-1963), earlier pre-'51 Target guns were available in virtually any cal. (i.e., .22 Hornet, .220 Swift, etc.), 24 in. medium weight barrel and target stock. Disc. 1963.

Rather than list prices, add 80%-100% over standard values if condition is over 90%. 60% condition will be priced the same.

MODEL 70 BULL GUN — similar to Standard Model 70, with 28 in. heavy barrel, .300 H&H or .30-06 cal. only.

Add 300% to Standard Model values.

MODEL 70 VARMINT — similar to Standard Model 70, in .220 Swift or .243 cal., 26 in. heavy barrel, scope bases, varmint style stock. Mfg. 1956-1963.

	100%	98%	95%	90%	80%	70%	60%
	$1,100	$1,000	$850	$800	$750	$675	$600

Add 35% for .220 Swift cal.
Less than 900 were mfg. in .220 Swift cal. Stainless steel barrels are also encountered in this model with 3 different types of finishes.

MODEL 70 ALASKAN — similar to Standard Model 70, in .300 Win. Mag. (mfg. 1963 only with 24 in. barrel - known as Westerner-Alaskan), .338 Win. Mag., or .375 H&H Mag. cal., 25 in. barrel, recoil pad. Mfg. 1960-1963.

	100%	98%	95%	90%	80%	70%	60%
	$1,750	$1,500	$1,300	$1,000	$950	$825	$675

100%	98%	95%	90%	80%	70%	60%	50%	40%	30%	20%	10%

RIFLES: SEMI-AUTO, DISC.

MODEL 1903 — .22 Win. Auto rimfire, 10 shot tube mag., 20 in. round barrel, open sights, straight grip stock cut out for partial magazine filling. Approx. 126,000 mfg. between 1903-1932.

100%	98%	95%	90%	80%	70%	60%	50%	40%	30%	20%	10%
$365	$300	$260	$220	$180	$140	$120	$100	$85	$70	$60	$50

First U.S. semi-auto rifle designed for .22 rimfire cartridges.

MODEL 1905 — .32 Win. or .35 Win. cal., 5 or 10 shot box mag., 22 in. round barrel, open sights, plain pistol grip stock. Approx. 29,113 mfg. between 1905-1920.

100%	98%	95%	90%	80%	70%	60%	50%	40%	30%	20%	10%
$650	$575	$525	$465	$400	$365	$330	$300	$275	$250	$225	$195

W

100%	98%	95%	90%	80%	70%	60%	50%	40%	30%	20%	10%

MODEL 1907 — .351 Win., 5 or 10 shot box mag., 20 in. round barrel, open sights, plain pistol grip stock, an improved version of the Model 1905. Approx. 58,490 mfg. between 1907-1957.

$475	$425	$375	$330	$300	$275	$250	$225	$195	$175	$160	$145

MODEL 1910 — .401 Win., 4 shot box mag., 20 in. barrel, open sight, plain pistol grip stock. Mfg. 20,786 between 1910-1936.

$625	$550	$500	$450	$400	$365	$330	$300	$275	$250	$225	$195

Add 10-15% for Fancy Sporting Rifle (special checkered walnut).

MODEL 55 — .22 cal. only, top loading single shot, bottom ejection, 22 in. round barrel, open sporting sights, not serial numbered. Over 45,000 mfg. between 1958-1961.

$175	$135	$125	$115	$105	$95	$85	$75	$70	$65	$60	$60

MODEL 63 — .22 LR, styling similar to Model 1903, 10 shot tube mag., 20 (disc. 1936) or 23 in. barrel, open sights, plain pistol grip stock. Approx. 174,692 mfg. between 1933-1958.

$750	$625	$550	$500	$425	$350	$300	$265	$235	$215	$190	$175

Add 50%-100% for 20 in. barrel depending on condition.

The Model 63 was introduced to take advantage of the new .22 LR cartridge, which the older Model 1903 couldn't chamber. Add 20%-25% for grooved receiver variation.

MODEL 74 — .22 Short or LR, tubular mag. in stock, pop-out bolt assembly. Approx. 406,574 mfg. between 1939-1955. Distinguishable by squared off rear receiver.

$275	$235	$200	$175	$150	$125	$95	$90	$85	$80	$75	$70

Add 25% for .22 Short.
Add 25% for pre-WWII mfg.

W

MODEL 77 — .22 rimfire, detachable box mag. or tubular mag. under barrel. Over 217,000 mfg. between 1955-1962.

$195	$175	$150	$125	$110	$100	$95	$90	$85	$80	$75	$70

Add $40 for tube mag.

Grading	100%	98%	95%	90%	80%	70%	60%

MODEL 100 RIFLE — .243, .284, or .308 cal., 4 shot detachable mag., 22 in. round barrel with open sights, gas operated, basket weave pattern impressed on stock, pistol grip cap. Over 262,000 mfg. 1961-1973 with some production occurring in Japan.

		$400	$350	$300	$265	$240	$220	$200

▲ *Pre-1964 production*
Add $25 for .243 cal.
Add $50 for .284 cal.

MODEL 100 CARBINE — similar to rifle, with 19 in. barrel, plain pistol grip stock, barrel band. Mfg. 1967-1973.

		$475	$375	$300	$260	$235	$215	$200

Add $25 for .243 cal.
Add $50 for .284 cal.

MODEL 190 RIFLE — .22 S, L, or LR cal., semi-auto, 15 shot LR tube mag., alloy receiver, uncheckered walnut finished hardwood stock, 20½ (Carbine Model) or 24 (Rifle Model) in. barrel, approx. 2,150,000 (including the Model 290 listed below also) during 1967-1980.

		$150	$125	$100	$85	$75	$65	$55

MODEL 290 DELUXE RIFLE — similar to 190, with select Monte Carlo stock. Mfg. 1965-1973.

		$185	$160	$135	$115	$100	$90	$80

MODEL 490 RIFLE — .22 rimfire, 5 shot clip mag., 22 in. barrel, folding sight, checkered one piece stock. Mfg. 1975-1980.

		$250	$215	$185	$155	$145	$130	$110

100%	98%	95%	90%	80%	70%	60%	50%	40%	30%	20%	10%

RIFLES: SLIDE ACTION, DISC.

MODEL 1890 SLIDE ACTION — .22 S, L, LR, or WRF rimfire, cals. were non-interchangeable, visible hammer, solid-frame (first 15,000) or takedown, 24 in. octagonal barrel, case hardened receivers until 1901. Approx. 849,000 mfg. between 1890-1932.

▲ *Blued Finish* — post-1901 manufacture.

N/A	$850	$650	$600	$550	$495	$450	$395	$360	$320	$280	$235

Add 50% premium for .22 WRF cal.

▲ *Color casehardened receiver* — disc. 1901, takedown feature was added in 1892 after over 15,000 solid frames had been made.

$5,250	$4,650	$4,150	$3,650	$3,175	$2,700	$2,375	$1,950	$1,575	$1,100	$775	$450

Deluxe models or solid frames will bring premiums over values listed above. There were also a limited amount of guns mfg. with stainless steel barrels which will add to values of post-1901 mfg.

The Model 1890 was Winchester's first slide action repeating rifle. It replaced the Model 1873 .22 cal. It was an excellent and inexpensive .22 rifle that rapidly became the universal firearm used in shooting galleries. Even though production reached approx. 849,000 units, most guns were heavily used and specimens existing today in 98%+ condition are rare. Check carefully for rebarreling (notice proofmarks on barrel).

MODEL 1906 — .22 S, L, or LR, 20 in. round barrel, tube mag., visible hammer, open sights, straight stock with shotgun butt plate. Approx. 848,000 mfg. between 1906-1932.

N/A	$750	$600	$500	$400	$325	$250	$225	$175	$150	$125	$100

This model is seldom encountered in over 90% original condition.

▲ *Model 1906 Expert* — similar to Model 1906, except has a pistol grip stock and different shaped slide handle, finish choices included blue, nickel trimmed receiver, guard, and bolt, or full nickel trimmed, mfg. 1917-1925.

$1,650	$1,200	$1,000	$900	$850	$775	$700	$655	$600	$550	$515	$475

W

MODEL 61 HAMMERLESS — .22 S, L, LR, or WRF cal., 24 in. round or octagonal barrel (with rifling or smooth bore, i.e. Rutledge), tube mag., open sights, plain grip stock. Approx. 342,000 mfg. between 1932-1963.

$750	$650	$550	$450	$375	$325	$295	$250	$220	$190	$170	$150

Add 15% for single cal. barrel marking.
Add 100% for Rutledge bore.

Pre-war manufacture has small forearm. Pre-war octagon barrel in S or L cals. will command a 100% premium. "WRF" marked round barrel is rare - front of receiver must be marked "W.R.F.".

▲ *Model 61 Octagon* — .22 S, L, LR, or WRF cal., octagon barrel variation of the Model 61. Disc. approx. 1943.

N/A	$1,350	$1,050	$925	$800	$725	$675	$615	$550	$500	$450	$395

▲ *Model 61 Magnum* — similar to Standard 61, but chambered for .22 Win. Mag. Mfg. 1960-1963.

$895	$675	$575	$500	$450	$400	$365	$330	$300	$275	$250	$225

MODEL 62 — 62A VISIBLE HAMMER — modern version of 1890, 23 in. round tapered barrel. Over 409,000 mfg. between 1932-1958.

$550	$485	$425	$375	$325	$275	$235	$200	$185	$170	$155	$130

Add 30% for pre-war Model 62.

Pre-war model is 62, distinguishable by small forearm. The Model 62-A was introduced 1940 at serial number 99,200 with minor changes. Model 62A single cal. barrel markings do not add premiums. Gallery variations of these models will command a large premium.

Grading				100%	98%	95%	90%	80%	70%	60%

MODEL 270 SLIDE ACTION — .22 rimfire, tube mag., 20½ in. barrel, checkered pistol grip stock. Mfg. 1963-1973.

				$115	$90	$75	$60	$50	$40	$35

Grading	100%	98%	95%	90%	80%	70%	60%
▲ *Plastic stock version*							
	$85	$75	$50	$40	$30	$20	$20
▲ *Model 270 Deluxe* — similar to 270, with select wood, Monte Carlo stock. Mfg. 1965-1973.							
	$195	$150	$110	$80	$70	$60	$50

MODEL 275 — similar to 270, in .22 WMR.

	100%	98%	95%	90%	80%	70%	60%
	$135	$110	$100	$90	$80	$70	$65
▲ *Model 275 Deluxe* — similar to 270 Deluxe, in .22 WMR.							
	$210	$160	$130	$90	$80	$70	$60

RIFLES: LEVER ACTION - POST 1964 MFG.

Beginning in 1992, all Model 94s and variations (not including the 9422 models) received an engineering change utilizing a cross-bolt in the upper rear of the receiver that prevents the hammer from contacting the firing pin.

MODEL 64 1972-1974 MODEL — .30-30, lever action, 5 shot, $\frac{2}{3}$ tube mag., 24 in. barrel, open sight, plain pistol grip stock. Mfg. 1972-1974.

	100%	98%	95%	90%	80%	70%	60%
	$220	$195	$165	$140	$110	$90	$70

MODEL 88 LEVER ACTION CARBINE — .243 Win., .284 Win., .308 Win., or .358 Win. cal., 19 in. barrel, pistol gripped, one piece stock, barrel band. Mfg. 1955-1967.

	100%	98%	95%	90%	80%	70%	60%
.308 Win. cal.	$625	$500	$375	$275	$225	$200	$175
.243 Win. cal.	$750	$625	$475	$350	$275	$225	$200
.284 Win. cal.	$1,050	$825	$650	$525	$475	$425	$395
.358 Win. cal.	$975	$800	$700	$600	$400	$300	$250

The .358 Win. cal. was available between 1956-1962 only.

MODEL 88 RIFLE — .243 Win., .284 Win., .308 Win., or .358 Win. cal., 22 in. barrel, basket weave or diamond cut checkering, no barrel band. Approx. 284,000 mfg. 1968-1973.

	100%	98%	95%	90%	80%	70%	60%
.308 Win. cal.	$475	$395	$350	$250	$225	$200	$175
.243 Win. cal.	$495	$425	$375	$325	$275	$250	$225
.284 Win. cal.	$875	$700	$575	$500	$400	$300	$200

MODEL 150 LEVER ACTION — .22 rimfire, $20\frac{1}{2}$ in. barrel, tube mag., hammerless, uncheckered hardwood stock and forearm, sling swivels, approx. 47,400 mfg. 1967-1974.

	100%	98%	95%	90%	80%	70%	60%
	$125	$110	$95	$70	$60	$50	$40

MODEL 250 LEVER ACTION — .22 rimfire, $20\frac{1}{2}$ in. barrel, tube mag., hammerless, checkered pistol grip stock. Mfg. 1963-1973.

	100%	98%	95%	90%	80%	70%	60%
	$150	$125	$110	$95	$70	$60	$50
▲ *Model 250 Deluxe* — similar to Model 250, with select wood and sling swivels. Mfg. 1965-1971.							
	$195	$155	$110	$95	$70	$60	$50

MODEL 255 — .22 WMR, otherwise similar to Model 250. Mfg. 1964-1970.

	100%	98%	95%	90%	80%	70%	60%
	$185	$150	$135	$115	$90	$70	$60
▲ *Model 255 Deluxe* — .22 WMR, with select wood and swivels. Mfg. 1965-1973.							
	$240	$180	$150	$115	$90	$80	$70

MODEL 1895 LIMITED EDITION — .30-06, patterned after the Model 1895 Winchester, blued receiver, 24 in. round barrel, 4 shot mag.(box mag.), uncheckered woodstock and forearm, rear buckhorn sight, 2 piece cocking lever, 8 lbs. 4,000 mfg. beginning 1995.

	100%	98%	95%	90%	80%	70%	60%
Mfg.'s Sug. Retail	$853	$725	$550	$425			

▲ *Model 1895 High Grade* — same general specifications as the Model 1895 Limited Edition, features older No. 3 engraving pattern with double scenes, gold borders with multiple gold inlays, deluxe checkered walnut stock and forearm. 4,000 mfg. beginning 1995.

	100%	98%	95%	90%	80%	70%	60%
Mfg.'s Sug. Retail	$1,360	$1,175	$895	$795			

Grading	100%	98%	95%	90%	80%	70%	60%

RIFLES: 1894 LEVER ACTION - POST 1964 MFG.

100th Anniversary Model 1894s (mfg. 1994) are marked "1894-1994" on the receiver.

MODEL 94 STANDARD RIFLE — lever action, .30-30, .32 Win. Spl. (new 1992), 7-30 Waters (new 1989), or .44 Mag. (mfg. 1984 and 1985 only) cal., 6 or 7 (24 in. barrel only) shot tube mag., 20 or 24 (mfg. 1987-88 only) in. round barrel, open sights, straight walnut stock, barrel band on forearm. Mfg. 1964-present. Angled ejection became standard 1982, 6½ lbs.

Mfg.'s Sug. Retail	$363	$275	$215	$180	$165	$150	$140	$135

Add $15 for 24 in. barrel (disc. 1990).
Add $16 for .44 Mag. cal. (disc. 1986).

▲ **Model 94 Deluxe** — .30-30 only, similar to Standard Rifle, except has checkered walnut stock and forearm. New 1988.

Mfg.'s Sug. Retail	$393	$295	$225	$180	$165	$150	$140	$135

Add $50 for 1.5 - 4.5X scope with low mounts (disc.).

▲ **Model 94 Legacy** — .30-30 only, features pistol grip checkered walnut stock and forearm, 20 in. barrel. New 1995.

Mfg.'s Sug. Retail	$393	$295	$225	$180	$165	$150	$140	$135

▲ **Model 94 Ranger** — .30-30 only, 20 in. barrel, uncheckered hardwood stock and forearm, 5 shot mag., 6½ lbs. New for 1985.

Mfg.'s Sug. Retail	$320	$250	$195	$160	$150	$140	$130	$120

Add $56 for 4x32 scope with see-through mounts.

▲ **Model 94 Wrangler Large Loop** — .30-30 or .44 Rem. Mag. cal., 16 in. barrel, has large loop lever, uncheckered walnut stock and forearm, blued finish, open sights, 6 lbs. New 1992.

Mfg.'s Sug. Retail	$384	$290	$220	$175	$165	$150	$140	$135

Add $20 for .44 Rem. Mag. cal.

▲ **Win-Tuff Rifle** — .30-30 cal., similar to Model 94 Rifle, except has laminated hardwood stock and forearm with checkering. Drilled and tapped for scope mounts. New 1987.

Mfg.'s Sug. Retail	$404	$300	$230	$180	$165	$150	$140	$135

MODEL 94 TRAPPER — .30-30, .357 Mag. (mfg. beginning 1992), .44 Mag./.44 Spl., or .45 Colt (new 1985) cal., 16 in. barrel, side ejection, walnut stock, 5 or 9 shot tube mag., blue finish, dovetailed front sight, 6 lbs.

Mfg.'s Sug. Retail	$363	$290	$225	$180	$160	$150	$140	$130

Add $21 for .357 Mag., .45 Colt, or .44 Mag. cal.
The .44 Mag. cal. was introduced 1985.

MODEL 94 BIG BORE — .307 Win., .356 Win., or .375 (disc. 1987) Win. cal., angled ejection port provides scope mounting, checkered walnut Monte Carlo stock with recoil pad, 20 in. barrel, 6 shot mag., sling swivels, 6½ lbs. New 1983.

Mfg.'s Sug. Retail	$404	$315	$230	$195	$175	$160	$150	$140

Add 40% - 50% for .375 Win. cal.
Also mfg. in a top eject (pre-USRA). This model had an "XTR" suffix until 1989.

MODEL 94 LIMITED EDITION CENTENNIAL — .30-30 cal., cross-bolt safety, manufactured to commemorate the 100th anniversary of the Model 94 in 1994.

▲ **Grade I Limited Edition** — features No. 9 style Winchester engraving pattern (rolled) on both sides of receiver, 26 in. half-round half-octagonal barrel, pistol grip stock and forearm with cut checkering, half mag., open sights, crescent butt plate, 12,000 mfg. 1994.

$725 $550 $425

Last Mfg.'s Sug. Retail was $811.

Grading	100%	98%	95%	90%	80%	70%	60%

▲ *High Grade Limited Edition* — features No. 6 style Winchester engraving pattern (rolled) on both sides of receiver with gold outlines and 2 gold animals (mountain sheep and deer), Lyman No. 2 tang mounted rear sight, F-style checkering and carving, deluxe walnut, 26 in. half-round half-octagonal barrel, half-mag., crescent butt plate, 3,000 mfg. 1994.

$1,200 $875 $625

Last Mfg.'s Sug. Retail was $1,272.

▲ *Custom High Grade Limited Edition* — .30 WCF cal., features No. 5 style Winchester engraving pattern (hand-executed) on both sides of grayed receiver, gold outline panel scenes featuring caribou and pronghorns, Lyman No. 2 upper tang sight, F-style checkering and carving, 26 in. half-round half-octagonal barrel, half-mag., crescent butt plate, 94 mfg. in 1994.

$8,700 $7,750 $6,800

Last Mfg.'s Sug. Retail was $4,684.

Currently, a complete set of Model 94 Limited Edition Centennial rifles with the same serial number is selling in the $10,000+ range. Since there were only 94 Custom High Grade Limited Editions mfg., demand has escalated prices radically for this model.

MODEL 94 XTR — .30-30 or 7-30 Waters (new 1985) cal., 20 or 24 (7-30 Waters only) in. barrel, checkered select walnut, hooded front sight (except 7-30 Waters which has dovetailed front blade), 6½ lbs. Disc. 1988.

	$260	$225	$205	$185	$160	$150	$140

Last Mfg.'s Sug. Retail was $285.

Add $26 for 7-30 Waters cal. rifle.

▲ *Model 94 XTR Deluxe* — .30-30 cal. only, deluxe American walnut stock and lengthened forearm with fancy checkering, 20 in. barrel with deluxe script, rubber butt pad. Mfg. 1987-1988 only.

	$370	$310	$270	$235	$210	$190	$160

Last Mfg.'s Sug. Retail was $426.

MODEL 94 .44 MAG. S.R.C. — .44 Mag., top eject, 20 in. barrel, SRC. Mfg. 1967-72.

	$325	$275	$250	$225	$200	$175	$150

MODEL 94 CLASSIC SERIES — .30-30 cal., 20 or 26 in. octagon barrel. Approx. 47,000 mfg. 1967-70.

	$325	$285	$235	$200	$185	$160	$150

MODEL 94 ANTIQUE CARBINE — similar to Standard, with scroll on receiver, case hardened, gold-plated saddle ring. Mfg. 1964-1983.

	$250	$225	$200	$175	$160	$150	$140

MODEL 94 WRANGLER — .32 Win. Special, top ejection, only 7,947 mfg. Disc.

	$350	$310	$270	$235	$210	$190	$160

MODEL 94 WRANGLER II — .32 Win. Special (disc. 1984) or .38-55 Win. cal., angle ejection, 16 in. barrel, oversized hoop-shaped lever, roll-engraved receiver, 5 shot mag., 6⅛ lbs. Made 1983-1985 only.

	$245	$220	$200	$185	$165	$150	$140

Last Mfg.'s Sug. Retail was $275.

MODEL 9422 STANDARD — .22 LR or Mag., takedown, 20½ in. round barrel, 15 shot (LR) mag., grooved forged steel receiver, checkered straight grip, checkered high gloss (disc.) or satin weather resistant finish (new 1988) walnut stock and forearm, sights, 6¼ lbs. Mfg. 1972-present.

Mfg.'s Sug. Retail	$407	$315	$255	$210	$190	$175	$160	$145

This model had an "XTR" suffix until 1989. Earlier mfg. including pre-XTR and early XTR rifles had no checkering - these guns will command slight premiums over values listed above.

▲ *.22 Mag. cal.* — 11 shot mag., 6¼ lbs.

Mfg.'s Sug. Retail	$424	$330	$270	$225	$200	$185	$175	$165

▲ *Model 9422 High-Grade* — .22 LR cal., features engraved receiver with raccoon and coonhound, deluxe checkered walnut stock and forearm. New 1995.

Mfg.'s Sug. Retail	$489	$415	$340	$265	$225	$200	$185	$175

Grading	100%	98%	95%	90%	80%	70%	60%

▲ *Model 9422 Trapper* — .22 LR, 16 ½ in. barrel, checkered walnut stock and forearm. 11 shot tube mag., 5 ½ lbs. New 1996.

Mfg.'s Sug. Retail	$407	$315	$255	$210	$190	$175	$160	$145

▲ *Model 9422 Win-Cam* — .22 Win. Mag. only, similar to 9422 XTR Standard, except has checkered greenish laminated hardwood stock and forearm. New 1987.

Mfg.'s Sug. Retail	$424	$330	$270	$225	$200	$185	$175	$165

▲ *Model 9422 Win-Tuff* — .22 LR or .22 Mag., checkered laminated brown hardwood stock and forearm. New 1988.

Mfg.'s Sug. Retail	$407	$315	$255	$210	$190	$175	$160	$145

Add $17 for .22 Mag. cal.

MODEL 9422 XTR CLASSIC — same general specifications as Model 9422 XTR Standard, except has 22½ in. barrel and non-checkered, satin finished, pistol grip walnut stock and extended forearm, stock also has fluted comb with crescent steel butt plate, curved finger lever, 6½ lbs. Mfg. 1985-1987.

	$315	$285	$255	$230	$205	$185	$175

Last Mfg.'s Sug Retail was $301

RIFLES: BOLT ACTION - POST 1964 MFG.

MODEL 52D BOLT ACTION TARGET RIFLE — .22 LR, single shot, free floating standard or heavy barrel, scope bases, target stock with palm stop. Mfg. 1961-1980. Total production on all variations is approx. 125,233.

	$475	$435	$415	$385	$360	$305	$275

MODEL 52 INTERNATIONAL MATCH — similar to 52-D Heavy Barrel, with special free rifle stock, hooked butt.

	$495	$470	$440	$415	$330	$305	$250

MODEL 52 INTERNATIONAL PRONE — similar to 52-D, with prone stock, removable roll over cheekpiece. Mfg. 1975-1980.

	$495	$470	$440	$415	$330	$305	$250

RIFLES: BOLT ACTION - MODEL 70, 1964 - CURRENT MFG.

Beginning 1994, Winchester began using the Classic nomenclature to indicate those models featuring controlled round feeding.

MODEL 70 STANDARD — .22-250, .222, .225, .243, .270, .308, or .30-06 cal., 5 shot, 22 in. heavy barrel, open sight, Monte Carlo stock, swivels. Mfg. 1965-1980.

	$350	$330	$310	$285	$220	$200	$175

Add 25% for .225 Win. cal.

MODEL 70 MAGNUM — .264 Win. Mag., 7mm Rem. Mag., .300 H&H Mag., .300 Win. Mag., .338 Win. Mag., .375 H&H Mag., or .458 Win. Mag. cal., 24 in. barrel.

	$400	$350	$330	$310	$285	$220	$200

Add 25-35% for .375 H&H Mag. or .458 Win. Mag. (African Model) cal.

MODEL 70 FEATHERWEIGHT — .22-250, .223 Rem., .243 Win., .25-06 (disc. 1993), .257 Robts. (disc.), .270 Win., .280 Rem., 6.5x55mm Swedish (new 1991), 7mm Mauser (disc.), .30-06, .308, 7mm-08 Rem. (new 1992), 7mm Rem. Mag. (mfg. 1991-92 only), or .300 Win. Mag. (mfg. 1991-92 only) cal., bolt action, both short and medium action, 5 shot mag., 22 in. barrel (24 in. with .300 Win. Mag.), checkered walnut stock, no sights, approx. 6½ lbs. Mfg. 1981-94.

	$435	$380	$325	$300	$280	$260	$240

Last Mfg.'s Sug. Retail was $562.

In 1981, during U.S.R.A. takeover transition, guns were distinguishable by the U.S.R.A. trademark on the recoil pad. Some collectors will pay a premium for Win. marked pads. Cals. .257 Robts. and 7mm Mauser were disc. 1985.

This model had an "XTR" suffix until 1989.

Grading	100%	98%	95%	90%	80%	70%	60%

MODEL 70 CLASSIC FEATHERWEIGHT

— .22-250 Rem. (new 1994), .223 Rem. (mfg. 1994 only), .243 Win. (new 1994), .270 Win., .280 Rem., .30-06, .308 Win. (new 1994), or 7mm-08 Rem. (new 1994) cal., 22 in. barrel, features claw-controlled round feeding action bedded into standard grade walnut stock, jewelled bolt, knurled bolt handle, includes rings and bases, approx. 7 lbs. New 1992.

Mfg.'s Sug. Retail	$602	$460	$390	$330	$300	$280	$260	$240

▲ **Model 70 Classic Featherweight BOSS** — similar to Model 70 Classic Featherweight, except has 22 in. barrel with BOSS. New 1996.

Mfg.'s Sug. Retail	$735	$600	$500	$395	$350	$325	$295	$275

▲ **Model 70 Classic Featherweight All-Terrain** — .270 Win., 30-06, .300 Win. Mag., or 7mm Rem. Mag. cal., 22 or 24 in. matt finish stainless steel barrel/receiver, black fiberglass/graphite stock with checkering, with or without BOSS, 3 or 5 shot mag., 7 ¼ lbs. New 1996.

Mfg.'s Sug. Retail	$672	$565	$475	$375

Add $116 for BOSS.

▲ **Model 70 Win-Tuff Featherweight Rifle** — .22-250, .223 Rem., .243 Win., .270 Win., .30-06, or .308 Win. cal., features brown laminated, checkered stock with Schnabel forend, includes base and rings, pistol grip cap, 7 lbs., mfg. 1988-1990 - reintroduced 1992-1993.

	$445	$385	$325	$300	$280	$260	$240

Last Mfg.'s Sug. Retail was $572.

▲ **Model 70 Featherweight Special** — .243 cal., features custom fitted stock, hand-honed action, barrel, and bolt/follower, custom shop proofstamp, select American walnut with rounded pistol grips, no sights, only 50 mfg.

	$600	$525	$475	$425	$380	$340	$300

This model is distinguishable by the Super Grade floorplate marking.

MODEL 70 XTR EUROPEAN FEATHERWEIGHT

— 6.5x55 Swedish Mauser cal., 22 in. barrel, 5 shot mag., rifle sights, 6¾ lbs. Made 1986 only.

	$390	$365	$330	$305	$280	$260	$240

Last Mfg.'s Sug. Retail was $460.

MODEL 70 LIGHTWEIGHT RIFLE

— .22-250 (disc. 1992), .223 Rem., .243 Win., .270 Win., .280 Rem. (mfg. 1988-92), .30-06, or .308 Win. cal., 22 in. barrel, checkered walnut stock, no sights, 6½ lbs. Mfg. 1987-95.

	$420	$335	$290	$255	$230	$210	$190

Last Mfg.'s Sug. Retail was $513.

▲ **Model 70 Lightweight Carbine** — .22-250, .222 Rem. (scarce), .223 Rem., .243 Win., .250 Savage (new 1986), .308 Win., .270 Win., or .30-06 cal., bolt action, 5 shot mag., both short and medium action, 20 in. barrel, checkered walnut stock, no sights, approx. 6 lbs. Mfg. 1984-87.

	$355	$320	$285	$255	$230	$210	$190

Last Mfg.'s Sug. Retail was $395.

Add $15 for open sights.

▲ **Model 70 Win-Tuff Lightweight Rifle** — .22-250 (mfg. 1988-89), .223 (new 1989), .243 Win. (new 1988), .270 Win. .30-06 or .308 Win. (new 1989) cal., similar to Model 70 Lightweight Rifle, except has laminated brown hardwood stock with checkering. Mfg. 1987-92.

	$395	$330	$290	$255	$230	$210	$190

Last Mfg.'s Sug. Retail was $471.

▲ **Model 70 Win-Cam Lightweight Rifle** — .270 Win. or .30-06 cal., greenish laminated hardwood stock with checkering, 22 in. barrel. New 1987.

	$395	$330	$290	$255	$230	$210	$190

Last Mfg.'s Sug. Retail was $471.

This model was previously designated Featherweight before 1989.

Grading	100%	98%	95%	90%	80%	70%	60%

MODEL 70 SPORTER — .22-250 (mfg. 1989-1993), .223 (mfg. 1989-1993), .243 (mfg. 1989-1993), .25-06 Rem. (mfg. 1985-87 and reintroduced 1990), .264 Win. Mag., .270 Win., .270 Wby. Mag. (new 1988), .30-06, .300 Win. Mag., .300 Wby. Mag. (new 1989), .300 H&H (mfg. 1989-1992), .308 Win. (mfg. 1986-89), .338 Win. Mag., or 7mm Rem. Mag. cal., 24 in. barrel, 3 or 5 shot mag., custom Sporter styling, Monte Carlo cheek piece, detachable sling swivels, 7¾ lbs. Disc. 1994.

	$435	$375	$325	$300	$280	$260	$240

Last Mfg.'s Sug. Retail was $556.

Add $34 for iron sights (.270 Win., .30-06, .300 Win. Mag., or 7mm Rem. Mag. only).
This model had an "XTR" suffix until 1989.

▲ **Sporter Win-Tuff** — .270 Win., .30-06, 7mm Rem. Mag., .300 Win. Mag., .300 Wby. Mag., or .338 Win. Mag., similar to Model 70 Sporter, except has checkered brown laminate stock with sling swivels, solid recoil pad, 24 in. barrel, approx. 7¾ lbs. Mfg. 1992 only.

	$445	$380	$325	$300	$280	$260	$240

Last Mfg.'s Sug. Retail was $572.

MODEL 70 CLASSIC SPORTER — .25-06 Rem., .264 Win. Mag., .270 Win., .270 Wby. Mag., .30-06, .300 Win. Mag., .300 Wby. Mag., .338 Win. Mag., or 7mm Rem. Mag. cal., similar to Model 70 Sporter, except features controlled round feeding, 24 or 26 in. barrel, checkered walnut stock, blued finish, approx. 7½ lbs. New 1994.

Mfg.'s Sug. Retail	$613	$475	$395	$335	$300	$280	$260	$240

Add $38 for iron sights (.270 Win., .30-06, .300 Win. Mag., .338 Win. Mag., or 7mm Rem. Mag.).

▲ **Model 70 Classic Sporter BOSS** — .25-06 Rem., .270 Win., .30-06, .264 Win. Mag., 7mm Rem. Mag., .270 Wby. Mag. (new 1996), .300 Win. Mag., .300 Wby Mag. (new 1996), or .338 Win. Mag. cal., 24 or 26 in. barrel with BOSS, 3 or 5 shot mag., checkered walnut stock, approx. 7¾ lbs. New 1995.

Mfg.'s Sug. Retail	$728	$620	$535	$440	$350	$295	$275	$250

▲ **Model 70 Classic Laredo** — .300 Win Mag. or 7mm Rem. Mag. cal., features claw extraction and controlled round feeding, 26 in. barrel with or without BOSS. Non-catalog item. New 1996.

Mfg.'s Sug. Retail	$764	$645	$550	$445	$350	$295	$275	$250

Add $115 for BOSS on barrel.

▲ **Model 70 Classic Super Express Mag.** — .375 H&H, .416 Rem. Mag. (new 1994), or .458 Win. Mag. cal., 3 shot mag., claw extractor controlled round feeding (new 1993), open sights, 22 or 24 in. (.375 H&H or .416 Rem. Mag.) barrel, 8½ lbs.

Mfg.'s Sug. Retail	$865	$730	$585	$525	$495	$460	$430	$400

This model had an "XTR" suffix until 1989.

MODEL 70 DBM (DETACHABLE BOX MAGAZINE) — .22-250 Rem. (mfg. 1993 only), .223 Rem. (mfg. 1993 only), .243 Win. (new 1993), .270 Win., .30-06, .308 Win. (mfg. 1993 only), 7mm Rem. Mag., or .300 Win. Mag. cal., checkered walnut stock and forend, features 3 shot detachable box mag., 24 or 26 in. barrel with or without sights, includes bases and rings or iron sights (new 1993, optional) in .30-06, .300 Win. Mag., or 7mm Rem. Mag., 7¾ lbs. Mfg. 1992-94.

	$465	$390	$330	$300	$280	$260	$240

Last Mfg.'s Sug. Retail was $598.

Add $36 for iron sights.

MODEL 70 CLASSIC DBM — .22-250 Rem., .243 Win., .270 Win., .284 Win., .30-06, .308 Win., .300 Win. Mag., or 7mm Rem. Mag. cal., similar to Model 70 DBM, except has controlled round feeding, 24 or 26 in. barrel. Mfg. 1994 only.

Most cals.	$475	$395	$330	$300	$280	$260	$240
.284 Win. (less than 200 mfg.)	$625	$585	$475	$395	$330	$300	$280

Last Mfg.'s Sug. Retail was $619.

Add $52 for iron sights (.270 Win., .30-06, .300 Win. Mag., or 7mm Rem. Mag.).

▲ **Model 70 Classic DBM-S** — .270 Win., .30-06, .300 Win. Mag., or 7mm Rem. Mag. cal., similar to Model 70 DBM, except has black synthetic stock, this model became a Classic series in 1994 (featuring controlled round feeding). Mfg. 1993-94.

	$475	$395	$330	$300	$280	$260	$240

Last Mfg.'s Sug. Retail was $619.

W

Grading	100%	98%	95%	90%	80%	70%	60%

MODEL 70 STAINLESS — .270 Win., .30-06, 7mm Rem. Mag., .300 Win. Mag., or .338 Win. Mag., features matte finished stainless steel receiver barrel and bolt, black synthetic composite stock, 22 (.270 or .30-06 only, disc. 1992) or 24 in. barrel, approx. 6¾ lbs. Mfg. 1992-94.

				$475	$390	$330	

Last Mfg.'s Sug. Retail was $616.

MODEL 70 CLASSIC STAINLESS — .22-250 Rem., .223 Rem. (disc. 1994), .243 Win., .270 Win., .30-06, .308 Win., .300 Win. Mag., .300 Wby. Mag., .338 Win. Mag., .375 H&H (new 1995), or 7mm Rem. Mag. cal., features controlled round feeding, 22, 24, or 26 in. barrel, black synthetic composite stock, 3, 5, or 6 shot mag., without sights except for .375 H&H cal., 6¾-7½ lbs. New 1994.

Mfg.'s Sug. Retail $672 $515 $410 $340

Add $52 for .375 H&H cal.

▲ *Model 70 Classic Stainless BOSS* — .22-250 Rem., .243 Win., .270 Win., .30-06, .308 Win., .300 Win. Mag., .300 Wby. Mag. (new 1996), .338 Win. Mag., or 7mm Rem. Mag. cal., 22, 24, or 26 in. barrel with BOSS, black synthetic stock, 6¾-7½ lbs. New 1995.

Mfg.'s Sug. Retail $788 $645 $535 $430 $350 $295 $275 $250

MODEL 70 CLASSIC SM (SYNTHETIC MATTE) — .22-250 Rem. (mfg. 1993 only), .223 Rem. (mfg. 1993 only), .243 Win. (mfg. 1993 only), .270 Win., .30-06, .308 Win. (mfg. 1993 only), 7mm Rem. Mag., .300 Win. Mag., .338 Win. Mag., or .375 H&H Mag. (new 1993) cal., features black composite stock with checkering and sling swivels, 22 (.22-250, .223, .243, or .308 - mfg. 1993 only), 24, or 26 in. barrel with matte metal finish, 3 or 5 shot, approx. 7½ lbs. New 1992.

Mfg.'s Sug. Retail $620 $465 $395 $330 $300 $280 $260 $240

Add $52 for .375 H&H Mag. cal. (open sights only).

Until 1993, this model was called the Model 70 SSM. In 1994, this model became the Model 70 Classic SM featuring controlled round feeding.

▲ *Model 70 Classic SM BOSS* — .270 Win., .30-06, 7mm Rem. Mag., .300 Win. Mag., or .338 Win. Mag. cal., 24 or 26 in. barrel with BOSS, 3 or 5 shot, approx. 7¼ lbs. New 1995.

Mfg.'s Sug. Retail $735 $625 $525 $430 $350 $295 $275 $250

MODEL 70 VARMINT — same general specifications as standard Sporter, .22-250 Rem., .223 Rem., .225 Win., .243 Win., or .308 Win. cal., 26 in. heavy barrel with cold hammer forged rifling and counter-bored at muzzle, no sights, 5 shot mag., target scope bases, 7¾ lbs. Mfg. 1964-1993.

			$470	$375	$325	$295	$280	$260	$240

Last Mfg.'s Sug. Retail was $720.

Add 25% for .225 Win. cal.

This model had an "XTR" suffix 1978-89.

▲ *Model 70 Heavy Varmint* — .220 Swift (new 1994), .22-250 Rem., .223 Rem., .243 Win., or .308 Win. cal., push-feeding style, 26 in. heavy stainless barrel (countersunk muzzle) without sights, features black synthetic beavertail H&S precision stock with aluminum bedding block, 10¾ lbs. New 1993.

Mfg.'s Sug. Retail $764 $625 $515 $400 $350 $295 $275 $250

MODEL 70 SHB (SYNTHETIC HEAVY BARREL) — .308 Win. cal., features checkered black composite stock, 26 in. barrel with matte metal finish, jeweled bolt, 9 lbs. Mfg. 1992 only.

			$460	$375	$325	$300	$280	$260	$240

Last Mfg.'s Sug. Retail was $563.

MODEL 70 WINLIGHT — .25-06, .270, .280 Rem. (new 1987), .30-06, 7mm Rem. Mag., .300 Win. Mag., .300 Wby. Mag., or .338 Win. Mag. cal., McMillan fiberglass stock, thermoplastic receiver bedding, blued metal parts, 22 or 24 (Mag. cals. only) in. barrel, 3 or 4 shot mag., no sights, approx. 6½ lbs. Mfg. 1986-90.

			$555	$490	$440	$395	$350	$310	$280

Last Mfg.'s Sug. Retail was $637.

Grading	100%	98%	95%	90%	80%	70%	60%

MODEL 70 50TH ANNIVERSARY MODEL — .300 Win. Mag., 24 in. barrel, deluxe walnut stock, engraving and special motifs on metal surfaces, serial numbered 50 ANV 1 - 50 ANV 500, 7¾ lbs. 500 mfg. 1987 only.

$1,000 $840 $725

Last Mfg.'s Sug. Retail was $939.

MODEL 70 CUSTOM GRADE — various cals., old style Model 70 action, semi-fancy American walnut checkered stock, engine turned bolt and follower, hand honed internal parts. Mfg. 1988-89 only.

$1,100 $875 $700 $600 $525 $475 $425

Last Mfg.'s Sug. Retail was $1,172.

MODEL 70 CLASSIC SUPER GRADE — .270 Win. (new 1991), .30-06 (new 1991), 7mm Rem. Mag., .300 Win. Mag., or .338 Win. Mag. cal., 24 or 26 in. barrel, 3 shot mag., jeweled bolt, stainless steel extractor for true claw controlled round feeding and ejecting, three-position safety, checkered satin finish walnut stock with wood cheekpiece, black forend tip, bases and rings included, approx. 7¾ lbs. New 1990.

Mfg.'s Sug. Retail $840 $680 $510 $425 $375 $335 $300 $280

This model was designated the Model 70 Super Grade until 1995.

▲ **Model 70 Classic Super Grade BOSS** — similar to Model 70 Classic Super Grade, except has BOSS. New 1995.

Mfg.'s Sug. Retail $956 $810 $685 $555 $450 $375 $335 $300

MODEL 70 CLASSIC CUSTOM GRADE — .264 Win. Mag. (new 1994), .270 Win., .30-06, 7mm Rem. Mag., .300 Win. Mag., .300 Wby. Mag. (new 1994) or .338 Win. Mag. cal., 24 or 26 in. barrel, similar to Model 70 Super Grade, but must be special ordered through the Custom Gun Shop and includes many custom features including semi-fancy walnut with satin finish and hand-honed internal parts. Mfg. 1990-94.

$1,625 $1,250 $995 $875 $800 $725 $650

Last Mfg.'s Sug. Retail was $1,757.

A Model 70 Collector Grade is also a variation of this model that is mfg. in the Custom Gun Shop - this model is priced on request only.

▲ **Model 70 Classic Custom Grade Featherweight** — .22-250 Rem. (new 1994), .223 Rem. (new 1994), .243 Win. (new 1994), .270 Win., .280 Rem., .30 06, .308 (new 1994), 7mm-08 Rem. (new 1994) cal., 22 in. barrel, includes Featherweight features, controlled round feeding, higher grade wood. Mfg. 1992-94.

$1,625 $1,250 $995 $875 $800 $725 $650

Last Mfg.'s Sug. Retail was $1,757.

▲ **Model 70 Classic/Custom Sharpshooter I/II** — .22-250 Rem. (new 1993), .223 Rem. (mfg. 1993-94), .30-06, .308 Win., or .300 Win. Mag. cal., includes specially designed McMillan A-2 (disc. 1995) or H-S Precision heavy target stock, Schneider (disc. 1995) or H-S Precision (new 1996) 24 (.308 cal. only) or 26 in. stainless steel barrel, choice of blue or gray finish starting 1996. New 1992.

Mfg.'s Sug. Retail $1,994 $1,795 $1,375 $1,000 $875 $800 $725 $650

Subtract $100 if without stainless barrel (pre-1995).

This model was designated the Sharpshooter II in 1996 (features H-S Precision stock and stainless steel barrel).

▲ **Model 70 Classic/Custom Sporting Sharpshooter I/II** — .270 Win. (disc. 1994), 7mm STW (disc. 1995), or .300 Win. Mag. cal., ½-minute of angle sporting version of the Custom Sharpshooter, custom shop only, Sharpshooter II became standard in 1996. New 1993.

Mfg.'s Sug. Retail $1,875 $1,725 $1,295 $975 $850 $775 $700 $625

▲ **Model 70 Custom/Sporting Sharpshooter** — .220 Swift cal., 26 in. Schneider barrel, controlled round feeding, available with either McMillan A-2 or Sporting synthetic (disc. 1994) stock. Mfg. 1994-95 only.

$1,650 $1,250 $975 $850 $775 $700 $625

Last Mfg.'s Sug. Retail was $1,814.

Grading	100%	98%	95%	90%	80%	70%	60%

▲ *Model 70 Classic Custom Express* — .300 Petersen (mfg. 1995 only), .375 H&H Mag., .375 JRS (new 1992), 7mm STW (mfg. 1993-94), .416 Rem. Mag., .458 Win. Mag., or .470 Capstick (disc. 1995) cal., 24 in. (22 in. on .458 Win. Mag.) barrel, features claw controlled round feeding, deluxe walnut with satin finish and checkering, 3-leaf express (disc. 1995) or pre-64 style adj. rear sight (new 1996), high luster metal finish, bolt and follower are engine turned, available by special order through the custom gun shop only. New 1990.

Mfg.'s Sug. Retail $2,612 $2,375 $1,850 $1,575 $1,300 $1,125 $1,000 $895

> Subtract $200 for 7mm STW cal.
>
> In 1994, the model nomenclature was changed from Model 70 Custom Grade Express, and in 1996 it was changed from Model 70 Classic Express.

MODEL 70 ULTIMATE CLASSIC — .25-06 Rem., .270 Win., .280 Rem. (new 1996), .30-06, 7mm STW (disc. 1995), .264 Win. Mag., .270 Wby. Mag., 7mm Rem. Mag., .300 Win. Mag., .300 Wby. Mag., .300 H&H Mag. (new 1996), .338 Win. Mag., .375 H&H Mag. (1995 only), .416 Rem. Mag. (1995 only), or .458 Win. Mag. (1995 only) cal., controlled round feeding, checkered fancy walnut stock, choice of 22 (.458 Win. Mag. only), 24 or 26 in. tapered round full-fluted, ½ round/½ octagonal, or full octagonal tapered stainless barrel, choice blue or stainless barreled action, 3 or 5 shot mag., includes bases/rings except on some Mag. cals., approx. 7¾ lbs., except for large disc. cals., includes hard case. New 1995.

Mfg.'s Sug. Retail $2,386 $2,075 $1,675 $1,275 $1,025 $875 $775 $700

> Add $216 for .375 H&H Mag. and larger Mag. cals (disc. 1995).

MODEL 70 COLLECTOR GRADE — various cals., this variation must be special ordered through the Winchester Custom Shop and prices vary individually per quotation.

MODEL 70 CUSTOM BUILT — various cals., this variation must be special ordered through the Winchester Custom Shop and prices vary individually per quotation.

MODEL 70 EXHIBITION GRADE — various cals., fancy checkered American walnut stock with hardwood forend tip. Mfg. 1988-89 only.

                        $1,995 $1,575 $1,000

> Last Mfg.'s Sug. Retail was $2,192.

MODEL 70 XTR FEATHERWEIGHT ULTRA GRADE "1 OF 1,000" — .270 Win., bolt action, extensively engraved, finely checkered deluxe French walnut, with mahogany presentation case.

                        $1,800 $1,450 $950

> Last Mfg.'s Sug. Retail was $5,000.

RANGER RIFLE — .223 Rem. (new 1992), .243 Win. (new 1991), .270 Win., .30-06, or 7mm Rem. Mag. (disc. 1985) cal., push-feed action, 22 or 24 (disc. 1992) in. barrel, 3 (7mm Rem. Mag.) or 4 shot mag., plain hardwood stock without checkering, open sights, approx. 7 lbs.

Mfg.'s Sug. Retail $482 $360 $275 $215 $200 $180 $165 $155

RANGER LADIES/YOUTH CARBINE — .223 Rem. (disc. 1989), .243 Win., or .308 Win. (new 1991), cal., push-feed action, 20 (disc. 1992) or 22 (new 1993) in. barrel, 4 or 5 shot mag., shorter hardwood stock dimensions, open sights, 6½ lbs.

Mfg.'s Sug. Retail $482 $360 $285 $220 $200 $180 $165 $155

MODEL 70 DELUXE — .243, .270, .30-06, or .300 Win. Mag. cal., 22 in. barrel, open sight, hand checkered, black forend tip, became standard 1972. Mfg. 1964-1971.

                $475 $415 $360 $320 $285 $220 $180

MODEL 70 TARGET RIFLE 1964-1971 — .308 or .30-06 cal., 24 in. heavy barrel, no sights, target bases, heavy target style stock with hand stop. Mfg. 1972-disc.

                $630 $550 $495 $440 $360 $330 $275

MODEL 70 INTERNATIONAL ARMY MATCH 1971 — .308 cal., 5 shot, 24 in. heavy barrel, no sights, adj. trigger, ISU stock with forearm, accessory rail, adj. butt. Mfg. 1973-disc.

                $715 $660 $605 $550 $470 $440 $385

W

Grading	100%	98%	95%	90%	80%	70%	60%

MODEL 70 MANNLICHER 1969-1971 — .243, .270, .30-06, or .308 Win. cal., 19 in. barrel, open sight, full length Monte Carlo stock with steel forend cap. Disc. 1972.

	$550	$440	$385	$360	$305	$275	$250

MODEL 70A — economy version of 1972 type Model 70, same cals., no hinged floorplate or forend tip. Mfg. 1972-1978.

	$325	$285	$265	$230	$200	$165	$140

MODEL 70A MAGNUM — similar to Model 70A, except in Mag. cals. but not .375 H&H or .458. Mfg. 1972-1978.

	$340	$310	$275	$250	$220	$195	$165

MODEL 670 BOLT ACTION RIFLE — another economy version of the model 70, .225, .243, .270, .308, or .30-06 cal., 22 in. barrel, open sights, no hinged floorplate, pistol grip stock. Mfg. 1967-1973.

	$300	$250	$220	$195	$175	$165	$140

MODEL 670 CARBINE — similar to 670, with 19 in. barrel, not available in .308. Mfg. 1967-1970.

	$300	$250	$220	$195	$175	$165	$140

MODEL 670 MAGNUM — similar to 670, with reinforced stock, .264 Mag., 7mm Mag., or .300 Win. Mag. cal. Mfg. 1967-1970.

	$330	$275	$255	$220	$205	$195	$165

MODEL 770 BOLT ACTION — .22-250, .222, .243, .270, .30-06, or .308 cal., 22 in. barrel, open sights, no floorplate or forend tip. Mfg. 1969-1971.

	$325	$285	$275	$260	$250	$220	$195

MODEL 770 MAGNUM — similar to Standard, in .264 Mag., 7mm Mag., or .300 Win. Mag. cal., recoil pad. Mfg. 1969-1971.

	$350	$310	$285	$275	$265	$250	$220

MODEL 121 SINGLE SHOT RIFLE — .22 rimfire, bolt action, 20¾ in. barrel, open sights, plain pistol grip stock. Mfg. 1967-1973.

	$115	$85	$70	$55	$45	$35	$30

MODEL 121Y SINGLE SHOT RIFLE — similar to 121, with shorter stock.

	$115	$85	$70	$55	$45	$35	$30

MODEL 121 DELUXE — similar to 121, with ramp front sight and sling swivels.

	$125	$90	$75	$60	$50	$40	$35

MODEL 131 REPEATING RIFLE — .22 rimfire, bolt action, 7 shot, 20¾ in. barrel, plain Monte Carlo stock. Mfg. 1967-1973.

	$160	$135	$100	$85	$70	$60	$50

MODEL 141 REPEATER — similar to 131, with tube mag. in butt stock. Mfg. 1967-1973.

	$160	$135	$100	$90	$75	$65	$55

MODEL 310 SINGLE SHOT — .22 rimfire, bolt action, 22 in. barrel, open sights, checkered pistol grip stock, swivels. Mfg. 1972-1975.

	$200	$175	$140	$100	$80	$70	$60

MODEL 320 REPEATING RIFLE — similar to 310, with 5 shot clip. Mfg. 1972-1974.

	$300	$250	$200	$165	$140	$100	$85

MODEL 325 REPEATING RIFLE — .22 Mag. cal., otherwise similar to Model 320, limited mfg. 1972-74.

	$350	$300	$250	$200	$165	$140	$100

Grading	100%	98%	95%	90%	80%	70%	60%

RIFLES: O/U

DOUBLE EXPRESS RIFLE — .30-06, 7x65R, 9.3x74R, .257 Roberts, or .270 Win. cal., 23½ in. O/U barrels, iron sights with claw scope mounts, ejectors, fully engraved satin finish receiver with game scene engraving, walnut specially hand checkered, sling swivels, 8½ lbs. Mfg. 1984-1985 only.

	$2,500	$2,150	$1,850	$1,650	$1,450	$1,300	$1,200

Last Mfg.'s Sug. Retail was $2,995.

In 1984, Aero Marine located in Birmingham, AL special ordered 200 deluxe double rifles in 7x57mm Mauser cal. They featured better engraving and game scenes with bottom of receiver marked Jaeger. Of the 200, 100 were rifles with 90 being standard grade and 10 being deluxe. The other 100 were supplied with an extra set of O/U shotgun barrels. Sales were slow on these special guns and eventually they were liquidated to another wholesaler. Recently, prices are in the $2,250-$3,000 range for the rifle alone and $3,000-$3,750 for the Combo.

SHOTGUNS: 1879-1964

BREECH LOADING SxS — 10 or 12 ga., imported from England for sales through the Winchester New York City office only, exposed hammers, available in 5 grades ranging from Class D - Class A and Match gun (lowest to highest). Higher grades were mfg. by W.C. Scott & Sons, C.G. Bonehill, W.C. McEntree, Richard Redmond, and H. & E. Hammond Gun Mfg.'s. Approx. 10,000 were imported between 1879-1884. Prices vary greatly due to condition and grade. Prices can range from $300 (poor condition Class D) to over $4,000 (95%+ condition specimen in Class A or Match gun).

This side by side model was the first shotgun bearing the Winchester name sold in the U.S. Identifiable by "Winchester Repeating Arms Co., New Haven, Connecticut, U.S.A." marking on barrel rib top.

100%	98%	95%	90%	80%	70%	60%	50%	40%	30%	20%	10%

MODEL 1887 LEVER ACTION — 10 or 12 ga., 4 shot tube mag., 30 or 32 in. full choke fluid steel barrels, plain pistol grip stock, first Browning patent shotgun mfg. by Winchester. Mfg. 1887-1901. Approx. 64,855 mfg.

100%	98%	95%	90%	80%	70%	60%	50%	40%	30%	20%	10%
$2,250	$1,850	$1,550	$1,275	$1,000	$875	$775	$675	$575	$475	$375	$275

Standard frame finish on this model was color case hardening. Premiums exist for original bright case colored specimens. 10 ga. began production with serial number 22148. Also mfg. in Riot configuration (20 in. cylinder bore barrel). Gauges were chambered for 2⅝ in. (12 ga.) and 2⅞ in. (10 ga.). First lever action repeating shotgun domestically mfg.

▲ *Model 1887 Deluxe* — damascus barrel, checkered stock, and other special order features.

100%	98%	95%	90%	80%	70%	60%	50%	40%	30%	20%	10%
$3,000	$2,650	$2,300	$2,000	$1,750	$1,500	$1,275	$1,100	$950	$795	$650	$525

MODEL 1893 SLIDE ACTION — 12 ga., 30 (standard) and 32 in. barrel, black powder only. First Winchester shotgun with sliding forearm action, first Browning slide action patent, disc. 1897 after run of some 34,050. Note: chambered for 2⅝ shells only, damascus barrels were available at extra cost, as were fancy stocks.

100%	98%	95%	90%	80%	70%	60%	50%	40%	30%	20%	10%
$950	$850	$750	$675	$600	$525	$485	$425	$375	$325	$275	$225

This gun had limited sales because mechanical weaknesses developed when shooting smokeless powder.

MODEL 1897 SLIDE ACTION — 12 or 16 ga. (introduced 1900), improved Model 1893 action, 26-32 in. barrels, visible hammer, various chokes, takedown or solid frame, plain pistol grip stock. Over 1,024,700 mfg. between 1897-1957.

100%	98%	95%	90%	80%	70%	60%	50%	40%	30%	20%	10%
$595	$450	$350	$325	$295	$275	$250	$225	$195	$175	$150	$125

Add 10% for 16 ga.

Early 16 ga. Model 1897's were chambered for 2 9/16 in. shotshells and are worth less. The Model 1897 was the first Winchester shotgun chambered for 2¾ in. smokeless ammunition.

100%	98%	95%	90%	80%	70%	60%	50%	40%	30%	20%	10%

MODEL 1897 RIOT GUNS — see the "Trench/Riot Shotgun" category in the T section for more information and prices.

MODEL 1897 TRENCH GUNS — see the "Trench/Riot Shotgun" category in the T section for more information and prices.

This model changed its stock configuration after WWI.

MODEL 1897 TRAP — higher grade version of Standard, checkered stock, could have black diamond inlay in stock until 1919 (Black Diamond Trap), breech block marked Trap until approx. 1926. Mfg. 1897-1931.

| $1,100 | $900 | $700 | $550 | $450 | $375 | $325 | $295 | $275 | $250 | $225 | $200 |

▲ *Model 1897 Black Diamond Trap* — distinguishable by diamond ebony inlays in stock pistol grip.

| $1,750 | $1,500 | $1,250 | $1,075 | $975 | $850 | $700 | $575 | $465 | $385 | $325 | $295 |

MODEL 1897 PIGEON — higher grade version of Standard 97, should have engraved pigeon behind hammer on frame, breech block marked "Pigeon", most exhibit black diamond stock inlays until 1919. Mfg. 1897-1939.

| $3,500 | $2,750 | $2,200 | $1,950 | $1,650 | $1,450 | $1,225 | $1,000 | $875 | $725 | $600 | $525 |

MODEL 1901 — 10 ga. only, strengthened Model 1887 action to accept smokeless powder, lever action, standard barrel 32 in., blued barrel and frame, 5 shot mag. 13,500 mfg. between 1901-1920, starting with serial number 64,856.

| $1,750 | $1,500 | $1,225 | $1,000 | $875 | $775 | $675 | $575 | $475 | $375 | $275 | $225 |

Add 25% for Deluxe Grade (checkered wood).

This shotgun was chambered for 2⅞ in. smokeless powder ammunition.

MODEL 1911 SL AUTOLOADER — 12 ga., recoil operated, 26 or 28 in. barrel, various chokes, pistol grip laminated birch stock. Mfg. 1911-1925, 82,774 produced, action had design problems.

| $395 | $360 | $350 | $300 | $275 | $185 | $175 | $150 | $140 | $130 | $120 | $110 |

The Model 1911 was Winchester's first semi-auto shotgun. It did not prove to be satisfactory partly because the design had to be exclusive of the patents for Browning's famous A-5 model, interestingly enough a design which Winchester originally had helped Browning patent. Above values assume original wood without splitting or replacement.

MODEL 36 SINGLE SHOT — 9mm long shot, short shot, and ball, 18 in. round barrel, single shot bolt action, guns were not serial numbered, one-piece plain stock and forearm, special shaped triggerguard, 2¾ lbs. Approx. 20,000 mfg. between 1920-1927.

| $500 | $450 | $400 | $300 | $250 | $225 | $200 | $175 | $150 | $140 | $120 | $100 |

MODEL 12 SLIDE ACTION — 12, 16, 20 (2½ in. chamber mfg. until 1927), or 28 ga., 25 (20 ga. only, mfg. 1912-14), 26, 28, 30, or 32 in. standard, nickel, or stainless steel (scarce) barrel with or without rib (matted, solid, or VR), 2 9/16 (early 16 ga. only), 2 ¾ or 3 in. chamber, 6 shot, blued metal, various chokes, hammerless, plain pistol grip walnut stock. Mfg. 1912-1976.

Special order features on field guns have captured much collector interest in recent years. Combinations of these features can add a considerable percentage to the base values listed below. Rare special orders on rare variations are very desirable and prices can double and more if the combination is right. As is the case with most other collectible shotguns at this time, Model 12s with open choked barrels in shorter lengths are a lot more desirable (and expensive) than a specimen with a 30 in. full choke barrel (most common). Values listed below are for standard configuration (28 or 30 in. full choke barrel with no rib). For most Model 12s, values for condition factors less than 60% will approximate the 60% price, because of shooter demand. Premiums must be added for the rarer open choked barrels in shorter length on all gauges.

Original gauge can be determined by removing the butt stock and observing the gauge marking on the stock screw boss.

W

Grading	100%	98%	95%	90%	80%	70%	60%

The following add-ons DO NOT apply to 28 ga. values.
Add 20%-30% for Win. special VR (offset barrel proofmark).
Add 30%-40% for Win. solid rib.
Add 40%-50% for Win. milled VR.
Add 50% for each extra barrel(s).

	100%	98%	95%	90%	80%	70%	60%
12 ga.	$550	$450	$385	$295	$265	$235	$200
16 ga.	$625	$495	$395	$315	$275	$240	$215
20 ga.	$795	$675	$600	$525	$450	$395	$375
28 ga.	$3,500	$3,200	$2,750	$2,450	$2,000	$1,750	$1,500

Subtract 50% if with factory Cutts compensator.

Recently, some non-original, re-stamped 28 ga. barrels have been added to 16 or 20 ga. frames "creating" a more desirable (and expensive) gun to unsuspecting buyers. Roll die markings are getting better and better so be very cautious when considering a non-Cutts 28 ga. (as in get a receipt specifying originality). The last observed ser. no. for an original 28 ga. is 1,586,817. Believe it or not, there are getting to be a lot of fake Model 12 boxes that have been intentionally aged. Carefully screen NIB (watch the hanging tag also) specimens in this model.

Editor's Note: The Model 12 Winchester was produced continuously from 1912-1980. Over 2,027,500 were produced both in standard and deluxe (Pigeon) grades. Pigeon grades were first listed in 1914 and disc. during the war (1941). Reintroduced in 1948, they were disc. permanently in 1964, after which the Super Pigeon Grade became available only on a custom order basis from Winchester's Custom Gun Shop. These guns are worth 50-300% premiums depending on gauge, barrel lengths, stock options, engraving patterns, etc.

With an attrition rate of 33%, Model 12s with rare features 50 years ago will only be much rarer today (and expensive). 28 ga. guns were built between 1934 and 1960. Gauge rarity in increasing order is 12 ga, 16 ga, 20 ga, .410 (Model 42), and 28 ga. Serialization breakdown by year of manufacture is provided under the "Model Serialization" section of this book. When collecting Model 12s, ser. no.'s on the underside of receiver (forward end), should match ser. no. on bottom rear of Mag. tube. Stainless steel barrel Model 12s were mostly mfg. in the late 1920s - early 1930s (65X,XXX serial range). Values typically range between $1,000-$2,500.

"Y" prefix appears on Model 12s built 1964-1980 — see listing under Post-64 Models.

MODEL 12 FEATHERWEIGHT — similar to Standard, except with alloy guard and different takedown system. Mfg. 1959-1962. "F" suffix after ser. no.

	100%	98%	95%	90%	80%	70%	60%
	$425	$365	$325	$275	$250	$220	$190

MODEL 12 RIOT GUNS — see the "Trench/Riot Shotgun" category in the T section for more information and prices.

MODEL 12 MILITARY TRENCH GUNS — see the "Trench/Riot Shotgun" category in the T section for more information and prices.

MODEL 12 HEAVY DUCK GUN — 12 ga., 3 in. chamber, 30 or 32 in. barrel, solid rubber recoil pad, ½ in. shorter pull than regular Model 12. Mfg. 1935-1963.

	100%	98%	95%	90%	80%	70%	60%
	$650	$500	$450	$400	$350	$325	$300

Add 25% for solid rib.

▲ *Vent. rib* — 2 different styles mfg. by Simmons, notice barrel proof marking - rare.

	100%	98%	95%	90%	80%	70%	60%
	$1,600	$1,350	$1,250	$1,100	$850	$700	$600

Add 15% for 32 in. barrel.

Grading	100%	98%	95%	90%	80%	70%	60%

MODEL 12 SKEET GUN — 12, 16, 20, or 28 ga., 26 in. barrel, skeet choke, checkered pistol grip stock, pre-WWII. Mfg. 1933-1976.

	100%	98%	95%	90%	80%	70%	60%
	$800	$700	$500	$450	$400	$350	$300

Add 15% for solid rib.
Add 30% for Win. Special VR.
Add 40% for Win. milled VR.
Factory-Cutts compensator — subtract 50%.
16 gauge — rarity will command a premium.
Add 50% for 20 ga.
Add 400% for 28 ga.

MODEL 12 TRAP GUN — various ga.'s, full choke barrel, deluxe trap styled stock, solid recoil pad. Mfg. 1938-1964.

	100%	98%	95%	90%	80%	70%	60%
	$1,000	$850	$750	$650	$500	$435	$400

Add $100 for white or brown plastic Hydrocoil stock. While plain barreled variation is rare, it is not as desirable.

MODEL 12 SUPER FIELD GRADE — 12 or 20 ga. only, features 26, 28, or 30 in. matted rib barrel, deluxe walnut with checkered pistol grip stock and forearm, mfg. 1955-59.

	100%	98%	95%	90%	80%	70%	60%
	$1,100	$875	$775	$650	$500	$435	$400

Add 20% for 20 ga.

MODEL 12 PIGEON GRADE — finer and more deluxe version of Model 12, many variations. Mfg. 1914-1941 and 1948-1964, usually with engraved pigeon on bottom rear of mag. tube.

	100%	98%	95%	90%	80%	70%	60%
	$1,900	$1,500	$1,175	$850	$800	$775	$700

Add 15%-20% for VR.
Add 100% for 20 or 28 ga.
Add $700+ if NIB.
Above values are for 12 ga. - smaller gauges with desirable features will command healthy premiums.

MODEL 20 — .410 bore, single shot, hammer, boxlock, 26 in. full choke, 6 pounds. Mfg. 23,616 between 1919-1924.

	100%	98%	95%	90%	80%	70%	60%
	$495	$395	$350	$250	$200	$150	$125

▲ **Winchester Model 20 Junior Trap Shooting Outfit** — includes shotgun, midget hand trap, 150 .410 ga. shells, 100 clay targets and accessories, cased.

	100%	98%	95%	90%	80%	70%	60%
	$3,200	$3,000	$2,750	$2,600	$2,500	$2,200	$2,000

Prices for this model assume all accessories are included - if not, subtract substantially. Just the shotshell boxes and accessories from this outfit are worth $2,500+ in nice condition.

MODEL 21 — 12, 16, 20, 28, or .410 ga., boxlock action, after years in the design stage, production began in 1929 with guns being shipped to the warehouse in 1930 and first offered in Winchester's 1931 price list. Regular production continued for thirty years, through 1959. Approx. 32,500 mfg. 1931-1988. Approx. 2,000 were mfg. in Custom Grade. Current mfg. can be located in the Shotguns: Recent Mfg. SxS section of this chapter.

The early guns were plain, standard 12 gauge models with double triggers and extractors. Later in 1931, 16 and 20 gauge chamberings became available as did selective single triggers and automatic ejectors.

By the end of 1933 the Model 21 skeet gun had been introduced as had Tournament, Trap and Custom Built grades. By about this time options included fancier wood, beavertail or semi-beavertail fore-ends, checkered butts (standard on skeet guns) or skeleton steel butt plates, recoil pads and almost any variation the customers might desire. Metal finishes on a Model 21 are unusual in that they have salt blued frames and rust blued barrels — this explains the difference in coloration between these metal surfaces.

The Tournament Grade was dropped in 1936 and the Trap Grade in 1940. A Standard Grade Trap Gun was added in 1941. The early Custom Built Grade was dropped in 1942

Grading	100%	98%	95%	90%	80%	70%	60%

and the Deluxe Grade was added. This grade included as standard many of the previously available extra cost options.

Relatively few guns were produced in chamberings smaller than 20 gauge. 28 gauge first appeared in the 1936 catalog, although a few were probably produced before that. Winchester records are unclear as to the total but it is generally believed that fewer than 100 original factory guns were made. In addition, a number of original 20 gauge guns have been modified at the factory or elsewhere with factory 28 gauge barrels. These latter guns are just as valuable if the conversion was done at the Winchester Custom Gun Shop. Authenticity of the original guns should be established by factory letter.

.410 bore guns were first listed in 1955 but again some had been produced earlier, one having been built for John Olin in 1950. Throughout Winchester history all the rules seem to have had exceptions and nowhere is this more apparent than with respect to the Model 21 which, after all, has been pretty much a custom gun from the very beginning. Factory records and tallies among dealers indicate the existence of from 40 to 50 original factory guns. As in the case of the 28 gauge, extra barrels were available and at least some of those have been added to original 20 gauge guns.

The 3 inch Magnum 12 gauge Duck gun (stamped "Duck" on floor plate) was offered in Winchester catalogs from 1940 through 1952. Selective single triggers and automatic ejectors were standard as were the solid red Winchester recoil pads and 30 in. or 32 in. barrels. Some cases of non-factory upgrading of 2¾ or 3 inch Magnum guns have been reported. If authenticity is important to the buyer, a factory letter should be requested.

With respect to such letters, in cases where records may be missing or incomplete, the resultant letters may be less conclusive than desired. In some instances, consultation with, or a written appraisal from an authoritative collector arms dealer might be helpful.

Six standard patterns of engraving and several stock checkering and carving styles evolved during the production years. Values added by these and other embellishments such as precious metal inlays are beyond the scope of this work.

The following retail prices are for a standard field gun with average wood, beavertail forearm, ejectors, and single selective trigger with no alterations.

	100%	98%	95%	90%	80%	70%	60%
12 ga.	$3,000	$2,750	$2,400	$2,000	$1,800	$1,700	$1,500
16 ga.	$3,950	$3,500	$3,200	$2,900	$2,500	$2,100	$2,000
20 ga.	$4,950	$4,500	$3,750	$3,500	$3,000	$2,500	$2,250

Add $400-$550 for VR.

Double triggers w/extractors — deduct approx. 50%.

If double triggers with ejectors, subtract 10%-20%. Normally DT, extractor guns have splinter forearms.

▲ **Skeet Gun** — available in Standard, Tournament, and Trap grades. Introduced 1933. Add 10-20% depending on grade.

▲ **Trap Gun** — introduced 1940, Trap Grade disc. same year, unaltered specimens will bring premium — add 10-25%.

▲ **3 Inch Duck Gun** — introduced 1940, must be so stamped (observe the 3 in. marking very carefully — no premium exists for this variation.

As can be seen, values are partly based on a certain interdependence between options. Higher grade guns, of course, will bring somewhat higher prices although much of their increased value results from many "options" being included as standard features.

Buyers or sellers with limited experience should always seek expert advice or appraisals in dealing with a Model 21. This is especially true with regard to higher grade guns and those with extra ornamentation.

▲ **Model 21 .410 Ga.** — retail prices for original guns may be expected to range between $25,000 and $45,000 for mechanically sound guns depending on quality of finish. These prices take into consideration the reported sale of a plain standard gun in recent years for $37,000. Non-original guns with add-on factory barrels would probably be reduced by one-third.

▲ **Model 21 28 Ga.** — factory original guns will probably bring from $11,500 to $17,000 and, as with the 410s, 20 gauge guns modified to 28 gauge with factory barrels would be worth approx. the same if done at the factory.

Refinishing or Restoration: There is disagreement as to the effects of refinishing a Model 21. Many shooters and at least some collectors prefer a well refinished gun to a badly worn one. Higher grade guns restored by a master craftsman may approach factory original guns in value.

Grading	100%	98%	95%	90%	80%	70%	60%

MODEL 21: RECENT MFG. — refer to listing under SHOTGUNS: RECENT MFG. SxS

MODEL 24 DOUBLE-BARREL — 12, 16, or 20 ga., boxlock, hammerless, double triggers. Introduced 1940, disc. 1957 after approx. 116,280 mfg.

	$450	$400	$350	$300	$250	$200	$150

Add 10% for 16 ga.
Add 50% for 20 ga.

MODEL 25 SLIDE ACTION — 12 ga. only, non-takedown version of the Model 12, 26 or 28 in. barrel. 87,937 mfg. between 1949-1954.

	$375	$295	$240	$215	$185	$160	$135

MODEL 37 SINGLE-SHOT — 12, 16, 20, 28 or .410 ga., .410 bore, top-lever break-open action, all barrels are full choke. Note on pricing below that there is a big difference between a 100% gun without a box and NIB condition. Not serial-numbered. Over 1,015,000 mfg. between 1936-1963.

	100%	98%	95%	90%	80%	70%	60%
12 gauge	$215	$170	$140	$110	$100	$90	$75
16 gauge	$215	$170	$140	$110	$100	$90	$75
20 gauge	$245	$180	$145	$120	$100	$90	$75
28 gauge	$950	$850	$700	$600	$500	$400	$350
.410 gauge	$255	$225	$195	$175	$125	$100	$90

If above models are truly NIB, add $125-$175 to 100% condition values only, depending on gauge.
"Red Letter" models will bring 30% premiums.
All 28 ga. Model 37s have the "Red Letter".

▲ *Model 37 Youth/Boys/Red Dot* — 20 ga. only, 26 in. barrel marked Mod. Choke on barrel, solid red factory pad, identifiable by red dot inset into metal that is visible when hammer is cocked.

	N/A	$325	$285	$240	$195	$145	$110

MODEL 40 SEMI-AUTO — 12 ga. only, long recoil action, 28 or 30 in. barrel, walnut stock, skeet model also, poorly designed, many recalled by Winchester. Approx. 12,000 mfg. 1940-1941.

	$495	$450	$375	$300	$250	$200	$150

MODEL 41 BOLT ACTION — .410 ga., $2\frac{1}{2}$ in. chamber until 1933 when it changed to 3 in., bolt action, single shot, 24 in. round barrel bored F, one-piece plain walnut stock and forearm, not serialized, approx. 22,145 were mfg. 1920-1934.

	$450	$375	$300	$250	$200	$175	$150

This model is rarely encountered with over 80% original condition.

MODEL 42 SLIDE ACTION — the first pump specifically made for the .410 ga., hammerless, $2\frac{1}{2}$ (introduced 1935) or 3 in. chamber, 26 or 28 in. barrel, plain walnut pistol grip stock with circular grooved forearm (modified 1947). Approx. 160,000 mfg. between 1933-1963.

Special order features on field guns have captured much collector interest in recent years. Combinations of these features can add a considerable percentage to the base values listed below. Rare special orders on rare variations are very desirable and prices can double and more if the combination is right.

▲ *Standard Grade*

	$975	$850	$700	$600	$550	$500	$450

Add 50% for solid rib.
Add 70% for Win. special VR.

▲ *Skeet or Trap Grade* — has solid matted rib, fancy wood.

	$2,250	$1,850	$1,600	$1,500	$1,250	$1,100	$1,000

Add 10% for VR.

▲ *Diamond Deluxe Grade* — fanciest grade, value is affected by wood and finish. Factory special orders can bring prices up to $10,000.

	$2,650	$2,200	$2,000	$1,750	$1,600	$1,400	$1,200

Add 10% for VR.

Grading	100%	98%	95%	90%	80%	70%	60%

MODEL 42 HIGH GRADE LIMITED EDITION — .410 ga., 26 in. full choke VR barrel, features Grade V-VI wood with special scroll and gold border engraving, 850 mfg. 1993 only.

$1,400 $1,100 $895

Last Mfg.'s Sug. Retail was $1,617.

MODEL 50 SEMI-AUTO — 12 or 20 ga., 3 shot, recoil-operated (non-recoiling barrel), 26-30 in. barrels, VR optional, feather weight model introduced 1958, all steel construction. Over 196,000 mfg. between 1954-1961, starting with serial number 1,000.

$395 $335 $275 $240 $210 $180 $150

Add $50 for VR (Simmons installed).
Add $50 for 20 ga.
Add 15% for Trap & Skeet Model.
Add 200%-350% for Pigeon Grade.

MODEL 59 SEMI-AUTO — 12 ga. only, 3 shot, short recoil operation, Win-lite (steel and fiberglass) ribless barrels, 26-30 in. barrel lengths, alloy receiver inscribed with hunting scenes, Versalite (first interchangeable choke tubes) option introduced 1961, 6½ lbs. 82,085 mfg. between 1960-1965.

$500 $400 $350 $250 $225 $200 $175

Inspect carefully for either cracked receiver (by bolt handle cutout), or separating fiberglass on end of barrel.

▲ *Pigeon Grade* — mfg. 1962-1965, add 200-350% (rare).
Winchester also mfg. 20 and 14 ga.'s experimentally in this model, extremely rare and expensive.

SHOTGUNS: POST-1964

MODEL 370 SINGLE BARREL — 12, 16, 20, 28 or .410 ga., 28-32 in. full choke plain barrel, replaced the Model 37, top lever break open, exposed hammer, plain pistol grip stock. Approx. 221,578 mfg. between 1968-1973.

$120 $100 $90 $85 $80 $75 $70

Add 20-60%+ for .28 ga. and .410 ga.
The Model 370 was mfg. in Winchester's Canadian plant in Cobourg, Ontario.

MODEL 370 YOUTH — similar to 370, with 26 in. barrel, 12½ in. stock, with recoil pad.

$145 $110 $95 $85 $80 $75 $70

MODEL 37A SINGLE BARREL — replaced the Model 370, roll engraved receiver, gold trigger. Approx. 391,168 mfg. between 1973-1980 in the Winchester plant in Cobourg, Ontario.

$140 $110 $95 $85 $75 $65 $55

Add 10% for 36 in. goose barrel.
Add 30% for 28 ga. and 60% for .410 ga.

MODEL 37A YOUTH — similar to 37A, except 20 or .410 ga. with 12½ in. pull stock.

$175 $145 $100 $85 $70 $55 $40

MODEL 12 SUPER PIGEON GRADE — 12 ga., slide action, 26, 28, or 30 in. barrel, VR, any choke, hand honed action, engine turned breech block and loading flap, "B" checkering and No. 5 engraving, custom order grade walnut stock. Limited production between 1964-1972.

$2,995 $2,500 $2,250 $2,100 $1,750 $1,500 $1,300

An additional 380 Super Pigeon Grades were mfg. 1984-85.

MODEL 12 FIELD GRADE — 12 ga., slide action, 26, 28, or 30 in. VR barrel, various chokes, jeweled bolt, hand checkered, checkered select walnut stock. Mfg. 1972-1976, "Y" Serial No. Prefix.

$675 $550 $525 $495 $450 $400 $350

In 1984, Y series Model 12s were once again available through a private contract with U.S.R.A. Co. which included engraving on Grades 1A-1C, and 2-5. These guns were available in either Field, Trap, or Skeet configurations. Since there was no manufacturer's

Grading	100%	98%	95%	90%	80%	70%	60%

suggested retail, Model 12 values shown below are established by analyzing the sales of the two private contractors - no more of these variations are available.

▲ **Grades 1-A, 1-B, & 1-C** — light engraving depicting dogs or ducks. Disc.

	$1,300	$1,195	$1,000	$875	$785	$695	$600

Last Mfg.'s Sug. Retail was $1,375.

▲ **Grades 2 & 3** — engraving features large duck and dog game scenes on receiver flats. Disc.

	$1,600	$1,495	$1,295	$1,075	$950	$830	$725

Last Mfg.'s Sug. Retail was $1,695.

▲ **Grade 4** — more elaborate game scene engraving than Grades 2 & 3. Disc.

	$1,850	$1,695	$1,450	$1,225	$1,075	$950	$850

Last Mfg.'s Sug. Retail was $1,995.

▲ **Grade 5** — elaborate game scene engraving with style B checkering. Disc.

	$2,195	$1,995	$1,725	$1,500	$1,225	$1,095	$950

Last Mfg.'s Sug. Retail was $2,450.

Also available with gold inlays - add $1,000 to values shown above.

▲ **3 Barrel Set** — grade 5 engraving with gold inlays and two extra barrels. Disc.

	$5,500	$4,995	$4,350	$3,750	$3,325	$2,750	$2,300

Last Mfg.'s Sug. Retail was $6,000.

MODEL 12 SKEET GRADE — similar to Field Grade, with 26 in. VR skeet bore barrel, skeet style stock, with recoil pad. Mfg. 1972-1975.

	$950	$800	$625	$550	$495	$450	$425

See listings under Model 12 Field Grade for engraved values.

MODEL 12 TRAP GRADE — similar to Field grade, with 30 in. VR full choke barrel, trap style stock, straight or Monte Carlo, recoil pad. Mfg. 1972-1980.

	$750	$675	$575	$525	$495	$450	$425

See listings under Model 12 Field Grade for engraved values.

MODEL 12 DU — limited mfg. for Ducks Unlimited Chapters.

	$1,200	$995	$825

MODEL 12 LIMITED EDITION

▲ **Grade I 20 Ga.** — 20 ga. only, 2¾ in. chamber only, reproduction of the famous Winchester Model 12 with slight design improvements, 26 in. VR barrel bored modified, 5 shot mag., high post floating rib, walnut stock and forearm with semi-gloss finish, take down, 7 lbs. 4,000 mfg. by Miroku 1993-95.

	$795	$625	$450

Last Mfg.'s Sug. Retail was $879

▲ **Model 12 Grade V 20 Ga.** — similar specifications to Grade I, except has select walnut checkered 22 lines per inch with high gloss finish, extensive game scene engraving including multiple gold inlays. 1,000 mfg. 1993-95.

	$1,175	$850	$650

Last Mfg.'s Sug. Retail was $1,431.

MODEL 1200 SLIDE ACTION FIELD GRADE — 12, 16, or 20 ga., 26, 28, or 30 in. barrel, alloy receiver, various chokes, checkered pistol grip stock, pad. Mfg. 1964-1981.

	100%	98%	95%	90%	80%	70%	60%
	$220	$200	$180	$165	$140	$110	$100
Vent. rib	$240	$220	$205	$195	$165	$140	$110
Winchoke	$260	$240	$215	$200	$190	$180	$160

Add 33% for Hydro-coil recoil system.

MODEL 1200 MAGNUM — similar to 1200, chambered for 12 or 20 ga., 3 in. magnum shells. Mfg. 1964-1980.

	100%	98%	95%	90%	80%	70%	60%
	$230	$200	$175	$165	$140	$110	$100
Vent. rib	$275	$225	$200	$185	$150	$140	$110

W

Grading	100%	98%	95%	90%	80%	70%	60%

MODEL 1200 SKEET GUN — similar to 1200, 12 or 20 ga., 26 in. VR barrel, skeet bore, 2 shot mag. and select style stock. Mfg. 1965-1974.

	$300	$275	$250	$220	$195	$165	$140

MODEL 1200 TRAP GUN — similar to 1200, with 12 ga., VR, 30 in. full choke barrel, select trap style stock. Mfg. 1965-1974.

	$300	$275	$250	$220	$195	$165	$140
Winchoke	$360	$330	$305	$275	$250	$220	$165

MODEL 1200 DEER GUN — similar to 1200, with 22 in. barrel, rifle sights, 12 ga. only. Mfg. 1965-1974.

	$220	$195	$165	$140	$110	$100	$85

MODEL 1200 POLICE STAINLESS — 12 ga. only, 18 in. barrel, 7 shot mag. Disc.

	$275	$225	$195				

MODEL 1200 DEFENDER — 12 ga. only, 18 in. cylinder bore barrel, 7 shot mag., 6 lbs. Disc.

	$275	$225	$195	$170	$155	$140	$125

MODEL 1300 FEATHERWEIGHT SLIDE ACTION — 12 or 20 ga., 3 in. chamber, takedown, 26 (new 1991) or 28 in. barrel, 5 shot, plain or VR (became standard 1990), WinChoke tubes, checkered walnut stock and grooved forearm, alloy frame, recoil pad, 6¾ - 7⅛ lbs. Mfg. 1978-1993.

	$300	$260	$230	$195	$175	$160	$145

Last Mfg.'s Sug. Retail was $374.

Subtract $30 without VR.
This model had an "XTR" suffix until 1989. Older Model 1300 Featherweights had roll-engraving but no premiums are being asked at this time.

MODEL 1300 FIELD WALNUT — 12 or 20 (disc. 1994) ga., 26 or 28 in. VR barrel with WinChoke, checkered walnut stock and forearm, approx. 7¼ lbs. New 1994.

Mfg.'s Sug. Retail	$340	$275	$210	$180	$150	$135	$120	$110

▲ *Model 1300 Black Shadow Field* — 12 or 20 (new 1996) ga. , 3 in. chamber, 26 or 28 in. VR WinChoke barrel, black composite stock and forearm, 7 lbs. New 1995.

Mfg.'s Sug. Retail	$296	$235	$180	$150	$135	$120	$110	$95

MODEL 1300 CUSTOM HIGH GRADE — while advertised, this model was never mfg. Advertised retail was $1,395.

MODEL 1300 WATERFOWL — 12 ga. only, 3 in. chamber, 28 or 30 (disc.) in. VR barrel, matte finished metal, choice of low luster walnut finish or brown Win-Tuff wood, recoil pad, includes camo sling and swivels, Winchokes standard, 7 lbs. Mfg. 1984-91.

	$295	$260	$235	$200	$180	$165	$150

Last Mfg.'s Sug. Retail was $367.

MODEL 1300 TURKEY GUN — 12 ga. only, 3 in. chamber, 22 in. VR barrel, Winchoked, walnut stock and forearm with low luster finish, metal surfaces have matte finish, supplied with camouflaged fabric sling, 6⅜ lbs. Mfg. 1985-1988 only.

	$290	$265	$235	$200	$180	$165	$150

Last Mfg.'s Sug. Retail was $348.

▲ *Model 1300 Win-Cam Turkey Gun* — similar to Model 1300 Turkey Gun, except has greenish laminated hardwood stock and forearm. Mfg. 1987-1993.

	$350	$295	$250	$200	$180	$165	$150

Last Mfg.'s Sug. Retail was $435.

▲ *Model 1300 Ladies-Youth Win-Cam Turkey Gun* — 20 ga. only, 3 in. chamber, 22 in. VR barrel, green camo laminate shortened stock and forearm, includes sling and National Wild Turkey Federation engraving, 6 lbs. Mfg. 1992 only.

	$340	$295	$250	$200	$180	$165	$150

Last Mfg.'s Sug. Retail was $411.

W

Grading	100%	98%	95%	90%	80%	70%	60%

▲ *Model 1300 Win-Cam NWTF Series I-IV* — 12 or 20 ga., Series I was released 1989 (12 ga. only) and included special receiver engraving featuring National Wild Turkey Federation motifs, Series II was released 1990 with a choice of either 12 (disc.) or 20 ga. Ladies/Youth model, Series III was released 1991-92, Series IV was released 1993. Disc. 1994.

	$365	$300	$250	$200	$180	$165	$150

Last Mfg.'s Sug. Retail was $458.

MODEL 1300 SYNTHETIC TURKEY GUN
— 12 or 20 (new 1996, Black Shadow only) ga., 3 in. chamber, 22 in. VR barrel with choke tube, synthetic Realtree camo pattern on stock and forearm, full camo coverage available in Realtree or Advantage (new 1996), or non-glare black (Black Shadow) finish on all surfaces, approx. 7¼ lbs. New 1994.

▲ *Black Shadow Finish*

Mfg.'s Sug. Retail	$296		$235	$185	$150	$135	$120	$110	$95

▲ *Realtree/Advantage Camo Finish* — available with stock and forearm (Realtree only) camo or full coverage.

Mfg.'s Sug. Retail	$370		$290	$240	$180	$150	$130	$115	$100

> Add $62 for full coverage camo and sling.
> Add $40 for full coverage without sling.

MODEL 1300 COMBO PACK WIN-CAM
— 12 ga., supplied with 22 and 30 in. VR non-glare finished barrels, greenish laminated hardwood stock and forearm, camo sling, matte finished metal. Mfg. 1987-1988 only.

	$360	$320	$290	$260	$230	$200	$185

Last Mfg.'s Sug. Retail was $425.

MODEL 1300 LADIES-YOUTH
— 20 ga. only, 3 in. chamber, 22 in. VR barrel, shortened stock dimensions, walnut stock with recoil pad and rear positioned, grooved forearm, 6¼ lbs. Mfg. 1992 only.

	$315	$260	$220	$180	$165	$150	$135

Last Mfg.'s Sug. Retail was $355.

MODEL 1300 SLUG HUNTER
— 12 ga. only, 3 in. chamber, 22 in. rifled or smooth bore barrel with iron sights, checkered stock and forearm, satin walnut finish or brown laminate stock (Win-Tuff). Supplied with camo fabric sling and rings and bases. New 1988.

	$360	$300	$250	$200	$180	$165	$150

Last Mfg.'s Sug. Retail was $445.

> Add $10 for smooth bore barrel with Sabot rifled tubes (disc. 1992).
> Add $4 for "Whitetails Unlimited" Model (new 1991).

MODEL 1300 WALNUT DEER
— 12 ga. only, 3 in. chamber, 22 in. rifled barrel, non-glare metal surfaces, rifle sights, checkered walnut stock with recoil pad and forearm, 7¼ lbs. New 1994.

Mfg.'s Sug. Retail	$404		$335	$275	$250	$225	$200	$185	$170

▲ *Model 1300 Black Shadow Deer* — 12 ga. or 20 (new 1996), 3 in. chamber, 22 in. smooth bore or rifled (new 1996) barrel with IC Winchoke, matte black stock, forearm, and metal parts, rifle sights, drilled and tapped receiver, 7¼ lbs. New 1994.

Mfg.'s Sug. Retail	$296		$235	$180	$150	$135	$120	$110	$95

> Add $21 for rifled barrel (new 1996).
> Add $70 for deer combo package (includes 22 in. cyl. bore barrel and 28 in. VR WinChoke barrel).

▲ *Model 1300 Full Advantage Camo* — 12 ga. only, 3 in. chamber, choice of 22 in. rifled or smooth-bore barrel, entire gun is in Full Advantage camo pattern, drilled and tapped receiver, iron sights, 7 lbs. New 1995.

Mfg.'s Sug. Retail	$432		$350	$295	$260	$225	$200	$185	$170

Grading	100%	98%	95%	90%	80%	70%	60%

MODEL 1300 RANGER SLIDE ACTION — 12 or 20 ga., 3 in. chamber, 22 cyl. or rifled (deer only), 24⅛ cyl. (disc. deer barrel), 26 (new 1991), 28 or 30 (disc. 1992) in. plain or VR barrel, walnut finished hardwood stock, alloy receiver. New 1983.

Mfg.'s Sug. Retail	$309	$245	$185	$150	$135	$120	$110	$95

Subtract $40 without VR or WinChokes.
Add $34 for 22 in. rifled bore deer barrel.

This model is also available in a deer combination package which includes a deer and regular WinChoke barrel in either 12 or 20 ga. — add approx. 20% to values listed above.

▲ *Ranger Ladies/Youth Model* — 20 ga. only, 3 in. chamber, 22 in. VR barrel, shorter stock dimensions - 13 in. length of pull and rearward positioned forearm.

Mfg.'s Sug. Retail	$309	$250	$200	$170	$150	$125	$110	$100

Subtract $40 if without WinChoke and VR.

MODEL 1300 DEFENDER — 12 or 20 ga., 3 in. chamber, available in Police (disc. 1989), Marine, and Defender variations, 18 or 24 (new 1994) in. cyl. bore barrel, 5, 7 (disc), or 8 shot mag., wood (high gloss), synthetic (matte finish), or pistol grip (matte finish) stock, 5¾ - 7 lbs.

Mfg.'s Sug. Retail	$290	$230	$185	$150

Add $103 for Combo Package (includes extra 28 in. VR barrel).

▲ *Stainless Marine Defender* — 12 ga. only, 18 in. cyl. bore barrel, a new Sandstrom 9A phosphate coating was released late 1989 to give long lasting corrosion protection to all receiver and internal working parts, 7 shot mag., synthetic pistol grip or stock configuration, approx. 6 - 7 lbs.

Mfg.'s Sug. Retail	$460	$390	$330	$250

▲ *Model 1300 Lady Defender* — 20 ga. only, 3 in. chamber, choice of synthetic regular or pistol grip stock, 5 or 8 shot mag., 18 in. cyl. bore barrel (new 1996).

Mfg.'s Sug. Retail	$290	$235	$190	$150

MODEL 1400 SEMI-AUTO — 12, 16, or 20 ga., 26, 28, or 30 in. barrels, alloy receiver, various chokes, gas operated, checkered pistol grip stock. Mfg. 1964-1981.

	$275	$250	$220	$200	$175	$155	$140
Vent. rib	$315	$265	$240	$220	$195	$165	$150

Add 33% for Hydro-coil recoil system.

NEW MODEL 1400 WALNUT SEMI-AUTO — 12 or 20 ga., 2¾ in. chamber, 22 (disc.), 26 (mfg. 1991-1993), or 28 in. VR barrel, checkered walnut stock and forearm, Winchokes standard, 3 shot mag., rotary bolt system, 7-7½ lbs. Mfg. 1989-94.

	$350	$290	$260	$240	$220	$190	$165

Last Mfg.'s Sug. Retail was $419.

Add $15 for limited mfg. 1993 Quail Unlimited Model (2,500 mfg. 1993).

MODEL 1400 CUSTOM HIGH GRADE — 12 ga. only, 28 in. VR Winchoke barrel, special order only through the Custom Gun Shop, features deluxe hand checkered walnut and special engraving. Mfg. 1991-1992.

	$1,295	$995	$750

Last Mfg.'s Sug. Retail was $1,695.

MODEL 1400 SKEET GRADE — similar to 1400, 12 or 20 ga., with 26 in. VR barrel, skeet bore, select skeet style stock. Mfg. 1965-1973.

	$360	$330	$305	$275	$220	$195	$165

MODEL 1400 TRAP GRADE — similar to 1400, with 30 in. full choke VR barrel, select trap style stock. Mfg. 1965-1973.

	$360	$330	$305	$275	$220	$195	$165

MODEL 1400 DEER GUN — similar to 1400, with 22 in. barrel, rifle sights, 12 ga. only. Mfg. 1965-1974.

	$265	$240	$220	$200	$175	$165	$140

Note: In 1968 the model 1400 series was modified. The action release was improved and the checkering redesigned. From 1968-1972, they were designated MKII, which was

Grading	100%	98%	95%	90%	80%	70%	60%

then dropped. The values for the later guns mfg. from 1968-1973 may run approx. 10% higher - values shown are for guns mfg. from 1965-1968.

MODEL 1400 SLUG HUNTER — 12 ga. only, 22 in. smooth bore cyl. or rifled Sabot choke-tubed barrel, drilled and tapped for scope, includes bases or iron sights, 7¼ lbs. Mfg. 1990-92.

	$355	$310	$270	$250	$225	$195	$165

Last Mfg.'s Sug. Retail was $420.

MODEL 1500 XTR SEMI-AUTO — 12 or 20 ga., 2¾ inch only, 28 inch barrel, plain or VR, Winchoke tubes, gas operation. Mfg. 1978-1982.

	$300	$260	$240	$220	$200	$180	$160

MODEL 1400 RANGER SEMI-AUTO — 12 or 20 ga., gas operation, alloy receiver, 22 cyl. deer, 26 (mfg. 1991-1993), or 28 in. Winchoke barrel, checkered walnut finished hardwood stock and forearm, VR became standard 1985, 7¼ lbs. Disc. 1994.

	$285	$235	$200	$180	$160	$140	$120

Last Mfg.'s Sug. Retail was $377.

Add $53 for deer combo. (includes extra 22 in. cyl. bore barrel).
Subtract $40 without VR.

SUPER X MODEL 1 SEMI-AUTO — 12 ga., 26, 28, or 30 in. VR barrel, various chokes, steel receiver, gas operated - self compensating, checkered pistol grip stock and forearm. Mfg. 1974-1981.

	$425	$365	$345	$315	$295	$275	$240

SUPER X MODEL 1 SKEET — similar to Standard, with 26 in. skeet bore barrel, select skeet style stock. Mfg. 1974-1981.

	$595	$500	$475	$450	$425	$400	$350

Add 20% if NIB condition.

SUPER X MODEL 1 TRAP — similar to Standard, with 30 in. barrel, imp. mod. or full choke, select trap style stock.

	$550	$475	$425	$415	$395	$350	$300

Add 20% if NIB condition.

SUPER X MODEL 1 CUSTOM TRAP OR SKEET — 12 ga. only, limited production from the Custom Shop, deluxe checkered walnut stock and forearm, extensive scroll engraving on receiver, built to custom order. Limited mfg. 1987-1992.

	$1,100	$850	$650

▲ *Super X Model 1 Custom Engraved* — features number 5 engraving pattern with 7 gold inlays. Disc.

	$2,250	$1,800	$1,300

Last Mfg.'s Sug. Retail was $1,295.

Add $700 for factory gold inlays (8 flying ducks).

SHOTGUNS: O/U - RECENT MFG.

Model 101 dates of manufacture and serialization data can be found in the SERIALIZATION section in the back of this text.

In November of 1987 Olin/Winchester disc. the Model 101. Classic Doubles (listed separately in this text) imported this model under their own trademark until approx. 1990. With the discontinuance of the Model 101 and its many variations, both dealers and collectors have created a lot more demand for this model recently. As a result, prices have escalated and the scramble is on to try and pick off those rare and desirable variations. Since there have been a lot of limited editions and production changes in the 101 O/U series, it could very well be that this model might become very collectible in upcoming years (as in look what happened to the Model 12).

Note: Model 101 and Model 96 Xpert guns were made by Olin Kodensha located in Tochigi, Japan.

W

Grading	100%	98%	95%	90%	80%	70%	60%

Values listed below for Model 101s assume NIB condition - subtract 10%-15% if without box, warranty card, and original shipping container (with packing materials).

MODEL 91 O/U — 12 ga. only, mfg. by Laurona in Spain for international sales including Europe, SST, ejectors optional, VR, distinguishable by black chrome finish on metal parts. Disc.

Prices hard to evaluate because of limited importation domestically. In some regions they are bought as medium priced field guns ($550-$650), while in others they are sold as a rare Winchester O&U ($900-$1,100).

MODEL 96 XPERT O/U FIELD GRADE — similar action to Model 101, 12 or 20 ga., auto ejectors, SST, various barrel lengths and chokes, action similar to 101, no engraving, checkered pistol grip stock and forearm. Mfg. 1976-1982.

	$775	$650	$550	$475	$425	$375	$335

This model has become known as the "Poor Man's 101".

MODEL 96 XPERT SKEET GRADE — similar to Field Grade, with 27 in. skeet barrels, skeet style stock. Mfg. 1976-1982.

	$795	$675	$575	$500	$450	$410	$370

MODEL 96 XPERT TRAP GRADE — similar to Field, 12 ga. only, 30 in. imp. mod. and full or full and full choke, trap style stock. Mfg. 1976-1982.

	$750	$575	$525	$470	$430	$395	$360

MODEL 99 — 12 ga., DT, no engraving. Disc.

	$700	$575	$525	$470	$430	$395	$360

MODEL 101 FIELD GRADE O/U — 12, 20, or .410 ga., 26, 28, or 30 in. barrels, various chokes, boxlock, auto ejectors, SST, engraved receiver, checkered American walnut pistol grip stock. Mfg. 1963-1987. Values below assume Winchokes (standard since 1983) - subtract $60 if without.

▲ *Older production* — checkered walnut stock and forearm, ejectors, SST, blued metal with light engraving on receiver, various barrel lengths, w/o choke tubes.

	$925	$775	$675	$625	$585	$550	$500

Add 20% for 28 ga. or .410 ga.

▲ *Field Special* — 12 or 20 ga., 3 in. chambers, VR, 27 in. barrels with Winchokes, blued receiver with scroll engraving ejectors, 7 lbs. Disc. 1987.

	$1,150	$925	$850	$775	$695	$600	$500

Last Mfg.'s Sug. Retail was $1,185.

▲ *Lightweight Field* — 12 or 20 ga., similar to regular Field Grade, except has coin finished receiver, vent. barrels, and solid rubber recoil pad, 6½ - 7 lbs. Disc. 1987.

	$1,285	$1,030	$965	$895	$800	$700	$600

Last Mfg.'s Sug. Retail was $1,425.

▲ *Waterfowl Model* — 12 ga. only, 3 in. chambers, 30 or 32(disc.) in. Winchoked barrels, VR, matte blued receiver with moderate engraving, low gloss walnut stock with vent. recoil pad, 7¾ lbs. Disc. 1987.

	$1,410	$1,175	$995	$895	$800	$700	$600

Last Mfg.'s Sug. Retail was $1,570.

▲ *Model 101 Field Grade 2 Barrel Hunting Set* — 12 or 20 ga. barrels, both with Winchokes, 26 in. barrels - 20 ga., 28 in. barrels - 12 ga., scroll engraved, blued receiver with game scene engraving and borders, cased. Mfg. 1984-1987.

	$2,500	$2,050	$1,575	$1,375	$1,220	$1,050	$975

Last Mfg.'s Sug. Retail was $2,345.

▲ *Quail Special* — 12, 20 (disc.1984), 28 (new 1987) or .410 (new 1987) ga., 25½ in. Winchoke barrels, 6¾ lbs. - 12 ga., straight grip stock, vent. barrels and rib, coin finished receiver with game scene engraving, 500 of each ga. were mfg. Imported 1984-1986.

	100%	98%	95%	90%	80%	70%	60%
12 or .410 ga.	$1,995	$1,650	$1,475	$1,245	$1,050	$900	$775
20 ga.	$2,500	$2,100	$1,750	$1,500	$1,275	$1,100	$925
28 ga.	$3,350	$2,750	$2,150	$1,750	$1,450	$1,275	$1,025

Last Mfg.'s Sug. Retail was $1,950.

Grading	100%	98%	95%	90%	80%	70%	60%

▲ *National Wild Turkey Federation Commemorative* — features golden turkeys on receiver sides, 27 in. VR barrels with choke tubes, only 300 mfg.

$2,000 **$1,600** **$1,150**

Original issue price was $1,950.

▲ *American Flyer Live Bird* — 12 ga. only, 28 or 29½ (new 1988) in. separated barrels with special competition VR, blued frame with gold wire borders and pigeon inlay, 8 - 8½ lbs. Imported 1987 only.

$2,595 **$2,275** **$1,950** **$1,775** **$1,600** **$1,425** **$1,300**
Last Mfg.'s Sug. Retail was $2,910.

Add $925 for Combo Model (extra set of 29½ in. barrels - 45 mfg.).
Add $265 for 29½ in. barrel with WT4 choke tubes.
Approx. 200 of this model were mfg.

MODEL 101 MAGNUM O/U — similar to 101 Field, 12 or 20 ga., 3 in. Mag. chambering, recoil pad, 30 in. barrels, full and mod., or full and full choke. Mfg. 1966-1981.

$875 **$775** **$675** **$625** **$575** **$500** **$460**

MODEL 101 SKEET GRADE similar to 101 Field, with 26½ (12 or 20 ga.) or 28 (28 or .410 ga.) in. skeet bored barrels, skeet style stock. Mfg. 1966-1984.

$1,000 **$825** **$770** **$700** **$650** **$595** **$540**

Add 20% for 28 or .410 ga.

MODEL 101 THREE GAUGE SKEET SET — similar to Skeet 101, with 20, 28, and .410 ga. barrels, cased. Mfg. 1974-1984.

$2,695 **$2,300** **$2,000** **$1,750** **$1,500** **$1,300** **$1,100**

MODEL 101 TRAP GRADE — 12 ga. only, 30 or 32 in. barrels with normal or wide VR, imp. mod. and full or full and full chokes, trap style stock. Mfg. 1966-1984.

$1,320 **$1,100** **$935** **$825** **$715** **$660** **$605**

MODEL 101 SINGLE BARREL TRAP — similar to O/U Trap, with 32 or 34 in. full choke barrel, Monte Carlo trap style stock. Mfg. 1967-1971.

$880 **$660** **$550** **$495** **$385** **$360** **$330**

MODEL 101 PIGEON GRADE (XTR) — 12, 20, 28 or .410 (disc. 1986) ga., vent. O/U barrels, deluxe engraved silver receiver version of 101, select checkered wood. Mfg. 1974-1987.

▲ *Lightweight Field Model* — lightweight variation, Winchokes standard, 28 ga. baby frame has 27 in . barrels, 6½ - 7 lbs. Disc. 1987.

➤ **Lightweight current mfg.** — 20 ga. only, 27 in. barrels only with Winchokes, previously manufactured guns that have been photo-chemically engraved and gold-plated, 101 total mfg. currently being sold by Guns Unlimited Inc. located in Omaha, NE (see Trademark Index). Released 1995.

Mfg.'s Sug. Retail	$1,795	$1,695	$1,575	$1,350	$1,150	$975	$850	$750
12 or 20 ga.		$1,995	$1,650	$1,475	$1,245	$1,050	$900	$775
28 ga. standard		$2,400	$2,050	$1,700	$1,450	$1,250	$1,050	$925
28 ga. baby frame		$3,350	$2,750	$2,150	$1,750	$1,450	$1,275	$1,025

Last Mfg.'s Sug. Retail was $1,950.

Deduct 5% if without Winchokes (available in all gauges).

▲ *Lightweight two barrel set* — includes either 12/20 ga. with Winchokes (28 in. barrels on 12 ga. and 27 in. on 20 ga.) or 28/.410 ga. (27 in. barrels, 28 ga. has Winchokes; .410 ga. has fixed M/F chokes), 250 sets mfg. serial numbered HS1-HS250. Disc. 1986.

$3,395 **$3,050** **$2,675** **$2,350** **$2,025** **$1,800** **$1,575**
Last Mfg.'s Sug. Retail was $2,500.

▲ *Pigeon Grade 3 barrel set* — coin finished Pigeon Grade frame.

$3,750 **$3,250** **$2,750** **$2,300** **$2,000** **$1,850** **$1,700**

Grading	100%	98%	95%	90%	80%	70%	60%

▲ *Featherweight* — 12 or 20 ga., English straight stock, 25½ in. barrels bored IC/IM, 6½ - 6¾ lbs. Disc. 1987.

	$1,475	$1,225	$995	$850	$750	$675	$600

Last Mfg.'s Sug. Retail was $1,580.

Add 20% for Winchokes.

▲ *Skeet Grade* — 12, 20, 28, or .410 ga.

	$1,275	$1,100	$995	$880	$770	$715	$660

Add 10% for 20 ga.
Add 40% for 28 or .410 ga.

▲ *Trap Grade* — 12 ga. only, vent. barrels and rib, coin finish receiver with fine scroll engraving, engraved pigeon on floorplate, Winchoke standard, 8¼ lbs. Disc. 1985.

	$1,300	$1,180	$990	$880	$770	$715	$660

Last Mfg.'s Sug. Retail was $1,475.

Deduct 15% if w/o Winchokes.

▲ *Super Pigeon Grade* — 12 ga. only, blued receiver with elaborate engraving including multiple gold inlays, extra select walnut with fleur-de-lis checkering on stock and forearm, Winchoke standard, 7½ lbs. Imported 1985-1987 only.

	$4,025	$3,625	$3,225	$2,835	$2,500	$2,150	$1,920

Last Mfg.'s Sug. Retail was $4,590.

101 DIAMOND GRADE — Trap or Skeet O/U, 12 (Trap only), 20, 28, or .410 ga., vent. barrels and rib, Winchoke standard on Trap — add $75 on Skeet model (disc.1986), select hand checkered walnut, engraved satin-finish receiver. Trap model has extra high VR. Skeet model has raised rib and muzzle vents.

▲ *Standard Trap* — 12 ga. only, 30 or 32 in. vent. barrels, 8¾ - 9 lbs. Disc. 1987.

	$1,620	$1,440	$1,230	$1,075	$900	$780	$640

Last Mfg.'s Sug. Retail was $1,860.

▲ *Unsingle Trap* — 12 ga. only, lower single barrel, 32 or 34 in. barrel, extended rib. Add $60 for Winchoke. Disc. 1986.

	$1,575	$1,430	$1,200	$995	$895	$830	$740

Last Mfg.'s Sug. Retail was $1,760.

▲ *Oversingle Trap* — 12 ga. only, Winchokes, 34 in. upper barrel only, 8½ lbs. Imported 1986-1987 only.

	$1,985	$1,695	$1,545	$1,395	$1,200	$995	$895

Last Mfg.'s Sug. Retail was $2,145.

▲ *Oversingle Combo* — includes one set of O/U barrels and an oversingle barrel, cased. Imported 1987 only.

	$3,075	$2,750	$2,525	$2,300	$2,000	$1,750	$1,625

Last Mfg.'s Sug. Retail was $3,550.

▲ *Trap Combo* — 12 ga. only, includes a set of 30 or 32 in. vent. O/U barrels and a 32 or 34 in. high ribbed unsingle (lower) barrel, standard or Monte Carlo stock, approx. 9 lbs. Disc. 1987.

	$2,570	$2,320	$1,975	$1,800	$1,600	$1,400	$1,200

Last Mfg.'s Sug. Retail was $2,940.

Add $275 for ATA Trap set.

▲ *Standard Skeet* — 12, 20, 28, or .410 ga., 27½ in. vent. barrels and competition rib, 6½ - 7¼ lbs. Disc. 1987.

	$1,650	$1,465	$1,240	$1,075	$900	$780	$640

Last Mfg.'s Sug. Retail was $1,950.

Certain design features may increase/decrease the values of this model.

▲ *Four Gauge Skeet Set* — includes 12, 20, 28, and .410 ga. 27½ in. separated barrel assemblies, cased. Imported 1985-1987 only.

	$4,600	$3,975	$3,600	$3,200	$2,800	$2,500	$2,150

Last Mfg.'s Sug. Retail was $5,025.

▲ *Sporting Clays Grade* — 12 ga. only, marked Diamond Sporter, 28 in. barrels with Winchokes, designed for Sporting Clay competition. Disc. 1987.

	$1,875	$1,575	$1,325	$1,100	$925	$795	$650

Last Mfg.'s Sug. Retail was $1,965.

W

Grading	100%	98%	95%	90%	80%	70%	60%

501 GRAND EUROPEAN — Trap or Skeet, 12 or 20 (Skeet only) ga., 27, 30, or 32 in. barrels, extra select hand checkered walnut with oil finish, Schnabel forearm, entensive scroll engraving on satin-finished receiver, vent. barrels and rib. Mfg. 1981-86.

	$1,520	$1,385	$1,200	$1,050	$900	$780	$640

Last Mfg.'s Sug. Retail was $1,720.

Add 20% for 20 ga. Skeet.

▲ *Grand European Featherweight* — 20 ga. only, straight grip stock, 25½ in. VR barrels, 5¾ lbs. Disc. 1986.

	$1,950	$1,725	$1,450	$1,225	$1,075	$925	$800

Last Mfg.'s Sug. Retail was $1,720.

PRESENTATION GRADE — 12 ga. only, available in both Trap and Skeet models, blued action-extensively engraved with gold inlays, special crotch walnut, 27 (Skeet) or 30 in. vent. barrels, hand checkered, silver wire borders on perimeter of receiver. Imported 1984-1987 only.

	$3,675	$3,195	$2,995	$2,300	$2,000	$1,800	$1,600

Last Mfg.'s Sug. Retail was $3,840.

Subtract 10% for Trap Model.

SHOTGUN/RIFLE COMBINATION — combination 12 ga./.30-06 O/U, 25 in. barrels, top barrel is Winchoked, Grand European engraving and finish, 8½ lbs. Mfg. 1983-1985.

	$1,750	$1,495	$1,250	$1,125	$1,000	$875	$750

Last Mfg.'s Sug. Retail was $2,550.

This model was also available in limited quantities in .222 Rem., .223 Rem., 6.5x55mm, or 9.3x74R cal.

MODEL 1001 FIELD GRADE — 12 ga. only, 3 in. chambers, boxlock action, 28 in. VR (8mm) barrel with WinPlus chokes, blued metal featuring 40% engraving coverage, Grade I stock and forearm, high lustre finish, mfg. in Italy by Marocchi beginning 1993.

Mfg.'s Sug. Retail	$1,099	$975	$795	$725	$650	$595	$550	$495

▲ *Model 1001 Sporting Clays* — 12 ga. only, 2¾ in. chambers, 28 or 30 in. VR (10mm) vent. barrels with WinPlus chokes, full engraving (includes scroll and flying W with clay bird), silver nitrate receiver with remaining parts blue, Grade II-III stock and forearm, satin finish, mfg. in Italy by Marocchi beginning 1993.

Mfg.'s Sug. Retail	$1,253	$1,075	$925	$795	$725	$650	$595	$550

▲ *Model 1001 Sporting Clays Lite* — 12 ga. only, 3 in. chambers, blued finish, 28 in. VR barrels with WinPlus chokes, checkered walnut stock and forearm, gold SST, 7 lbs. New 1995.

Mfg.'s Sug. Retail	$1,153	$1,000	$795	$725	$650	$595	$550	$495

MODEL G5500 SPORTER — 12 ga. only, marked Sporter, 28 or 30 in. barrels with fixed chokes (bored IC/M, IM/F, or XF/F) or Winchokes.

	$1,550	$1,390	$1,200	$1,050	$900	$780	$640

Add 20% for Winchokes.

MODEL G6500 SPORTER — 12 ga. only, marked Sporter, barrels and chokes same as G5500.

	$1,850	$1,550	$1,390	$1,200	$1,050	$900	$780

Add 20% for Winchokes.

SHOTGUNS: RECENT MFG. SxS

Values for recently manufactured side-by-sides (including Models 96 and 101 with variations) assume NIB condition - subtract 10%-15% if without box, warranty card, and original shipping container (with packing materials).

MODEL 21: RECENT MFG. — since 1960 Model 21 production has been limited to high grade, built from special order, U.S.R.A. has disc. mfg. of the Model 21 beginning 1988. Values below are based on 1988 information, since it was the last year Winchester carried pricing in their catalog.

Standard Custom guns (12 ga.) are currently trading in the $6,500 - $7,000 range if NIB.

Grading	100%	98%	95%	90%	80%	70%	60%

▲ **Custom Built** — standard model with no engraving.
$6,500 $5,000 $3,750

Last Mfg.'s Sug. Retail was $8,100.

▲ **Custom Grade** — includes No. 6 engraved receiver and VR.
$9,250 $7,250 $5,500

Last Mfg.'s Sug. Retail was $11,080.

▲ **Grand American Grade** — includes 2 sets of barrels with forearms, No. 6 engraved with gold inlays, cased.
$18,500 $15,000 $11,500

Last Mfg.'s Sug. Retail was $22,745.

▲ **Grand American Small Gauge** — 28 or .410 ga.
$32,500 $25,000 $17,500

Last Mfg.'s Sug. Retail was $34,460.

Add 25% for 28/.410 ga. combo.

▲ **Grand American "1 of 8" set** — includes 20, 28, and .410 ga. VR barrels. Only 8 sets mfg.
$55,000 $39,500 $27,500

Last Mfg.'s Sug. Retail was $55,000.

MODEL 22 — 12 ga. only, subcontracted by Winchester and manufactured in Spain by Laurona circa 1975 for international sales including Europe, field configuration only with 28 in. barrels, DT, oil finished checkered walnut stock and semi-beavertail forearm, matted rib, black-chrome finish on metal parts, hand engraved receiver, limited mfg.
$1,200 $995 $825 $700 $600 $525 $475

MODEL 23 XTR — 12 or 20 ga., 3 in. chambers, 25½, 26, 28, or 30 in. barrels, various chokes, single trigger, VR, auto ejectors, scroll engraved, silver gray satin finish, blued barrel, checkered select walnut stock and forearm, first commercial gun to employ interchangeable chokes. Mfg. 1978-disc.

Grade 1 (disc.) $1,150 $895 $775 $650 $575 $500 $440
Deduct 20% for fixed chokes.

▲ **Pigeon Grade** — standard weight model, 6½ - 7 lbs, coin finished receiver with scroll engraving. Winchoke option became standard in 1986. Subtract $150 without Winchokes. Disc. 1986.
$1,650 $1,275 $1,050 $875 $750 $675 $600

Last Mfg.'s Sug. Retail was $1,460.

▲ **Pigeon Grade Lightweight** — 25½ in. barrels only bored IM/IC (12 ga.) or IC/M (20 ga.) or with Winchokes, 6¼ - 6¾ lbs., coin finished receiver with scroll engraving. English stock. Disc. 1986.
$1,300 $1,150 $995 $880 $760 $730 $680

Last Mfg.'s Sug. Retail was $1,420.

Add 30% for Winchokes.

▲ **Pigeon Grade Ducks Unlimited** — only 500 mfg. 1981, "SPO" serial no. suffix, cased.
$1,450 $1,200 $995 $880 $760 $730 $680

▲ **Golden Quail Model Series** — 12 ga. (1986), 20 ga. (1984), 28 ga. (1985), or .410 ga. (1987), 25½ in. solid rib barrels bored IC/M, mono-blocks are marked IC/M but the barrels are marked Q1/Q2, coin finished receiver with one gold inlay on floorplate, beavertail forearm, straight grip English stock with recoil pad, Only 500 mfg. each year per gauge. Disc. 1987.

	100%	98%	95%	90%	80%	70%	60%
12 ga.	$1,695	$1,325	$1,100	$950	$850	$750	$675
20 ga.	$2,200	$1,950	$1,575	$1,400	$1,225	$1,000	$875
28 ga.(20 ga. frame)	$2,650	$2,200	$1,850	$1,550	$1,325	$1,125	$975
410 ga.(small frame)	$2,895	$2,500	$2,175	$1,750	$1,500	$1,275	$1,050

Last Mfg.'s Sug. Retail was $1,950.

▲ **Model 23 Light Duck** — limited edition, 500 mfg., introduced 1985, blued receiver and barrels, select walnut, 20 ga., 28 in.- F&F, 8½ lbs.
$1,675 $1,375 $1,050 $925 $850 $775 $725

Last Mfg.'s Sug. Retail was $1,660.

▲ **Model 23 Heavy Duck** — limited edition, 500 mfg. 1984 only, blued receiver and barrels, select walnut, 12 ga., 30 in.- F&F, 8½ lbs.
$1,675 $1,375 $1,050 $925 $850 $775 $725

W

Grading	100%	98%	95%	90%	80%	70%	60%

▲ **Custom 2 Barrel Set** — interchangeable 20 and 28 ga. 26 in. barrels, blue engraved receiver with gold inlays, "B" checkering on stock and forearm, leather cased with accessories, only 500 sets mfg. 1986. Disc. 1987.

	$4,150	$3,550	$3,050	$2,800	$2,500	$2,150	$1,925

Last Mfg.'s Sug. Retail was $4,625.

MODEL 23 GRANDE CANADIAN— 12 or 20 ga., 25½ in. barrels with fixed chokes, coin finished receiver with oak leaf engraving and one gold leaf inlay on receiver bottom, English AAA select walnut stock with beavertail forearm, 51 mfg. in 12 ga., 450 mfg. in 20 ga., approx. 50 two-gun sets were also offered with cases (approx. ser. no.'s 1-51).

	$2,495	$2,150	$1,700	$1,500	$1,300	$1,050	$925
Cased set	$5,250	$4,750	$4,175	$3,750	$3,200	$2,750	$2,150

MODEL 23 CUSTOM — 12 ga. only, 27 in. Winchoke barrels, high lustre bluing, no engraving, SST, ejectors, solid red rubber recoil pad, 7 lbs. Imported 1987 only.

	$2,100	$1,700	$1,250	$1,050	$900	$775	$650

Last Mfg.'s Sug. Retail was $1,975.

MODEL 23 CLASSIC — 12, 20, 28, or .410 ga., 26 in. VR barrels, single trigger, deluxe hand checkered walnut stock and beavertail forearm, solid recoil pad, brass name plate, gold inlay on bottom of receiver, ebony inlay in forearm, 5¾ - 7 lbs. Imported 1986-1987 only.

	100%	98%	95%	90%	80%	70%	60%
12 ga.	$1,795	$1,550	$1,325	$1,100	$950	$850	$750
20 ga.	$1,950	$1,575	$1,400	$1,225	$1,000	$875	$775
28 ga.(small frame)	$2,250	$1,850	$1,550	$1,325	$1,125	$995	$875
.410 ga.(small frame)	$2,450	$1,975	$1,650	$1,400	$1,200	$995	$875

Last Mfg.'s Sug. Retail was $1,975.

100% values assume NIB for this model.

The 28 ga. on this model features a smaller frame.

W

WINCHESTER COMMEMORATIVES: U.S. MFG.

During the course of a year, I receive many phone calls and letters on Winchester special editions and limited editions that do not appear in this section. It should be noted that a factory commemorative issue is a gun that has been manufactured, marketed, and sold through the auspices of the specific trademark. There have literally been hundreds of special and limited editions which, although mostly made by Winchester (some were subcontracted), were not marketed or retailed by Winchester. These guns are NOT Winchester commemoratives and for the most part, do not have the desirability factor that the factory commemoratives have. Typically, special and limited editions are made for an organization, state, special event, personality, etc. and are sold and marketed through a company/individual to those people who want to purchase them. These special editions may or may not have a retail price and oftentimes, since demand is regional, values decrease rapidly in other areas of the country. Desirability is the key to determining values on these editions. More information on these special and limited editions not listed in the following pages can be obtained by contacting Cherry's in Greensboro, NC (see Trademark Index).

Until recently, the over-production of many factory commemoratives had created a "softness" in the commemorative marketplace. Commemorative production in some trademarks has totalled well over 250,000 units, and some collectors have weighed the "limited production" factor on each model before paying a premium over the standard production model of that particular commemorative. Approximately 3-5 years ago, Colt, Winchester and others decided to cut down on commemorative manufacture after perhaps too many years of over-production. Many commemorative consumers were starting to think that these "limited manufacture" guns had become more of a company marketing tool and sales gimmick rather than a legitimate vehicle for investment potential and collector support. During this 3-5 year period, both distributors and retailers saw their commemorative inventory levels gradually reach near zero - perhaps the first time in over two decades that they sold out of factory commemoratives. In other words, the commemorative "blow-out" sales were over. As this transition from distributor/dealer inventory to consumer purchases occurred, the commemorative marketplace became stronger and prices began to rise. Because the commemorative consumer is now more in charge (consumers now own most of the guns since distributor/dealer inventories are depleted) than during the 1980s, commemorative firearms are possibly as strong as they have ever been. When the supply side of commemorative economics has to be purchased from knowledgable collectors or savvy dealers and demand stays the same or increases slightly, prices have no choice but to go up. If and when the manufacturers crank up the commemorative production runs again (and it won't be like the good old days), then the old marketplace characteristics may reappear. Until then, however, the commemorative marketplace remains strong with values becoming more predictable.

As a reminder on commemoratives, I would like to repeat a few facts, especially for the beginning collector, applicable to all manufacturers of commemoratives. Commemoratives are current production guns designed as a reproduction of an historically famous gun model, or as a tie-in with historically famous persons or events. They are generally of very excellent quality and often embellished with select woods and finishes such as silver, nickel, or gold plating. Obviously, they are manufactured to be instant collectibles and to be pleasing to the eye. As with firearms in general, not all commemorative models have achieved collector status, although most enjoy an active market - especially during the past three years. Consecutive-numbered pairs as well as collections based on the same serial number will bring a premium. Remember that handguns usually are in some type of wood presentation case, and that rifles may be cased or in packaging with graphics styled to the particular theme of the collectible. The original factory packaging and papers should always accompany the firearm as they are necessary to realize full value at the time of sale. All commemorative firearms should be absolutely new, unfired, and as issued since any obvious use or wear removes it from collector status and lowers its value significantly. Many owners have allowed their commemoratives to sit in their boxes for years without inspecting them for corrosion or oxidation damage. Periodic inspection should be implemented to insure no damage occurs - this is important, since even light "freckling" created from touching the metal surfaces can reduce values significantly. A fired gun with obvious wear or without its original packaging can lose as much as 50% of its normal value - many used commemoratives get sold as "fancy shooters" with little, if any, premiums being asked.

The values below reflect actual prices paid recently in various areas of the U.S. In some regions it is possible to purchase a Winchester 94 commemorative made in substantial quantity for almost no premium over a standard production Winchester 94. Because of this, prices could fluctuate over 25% depending on the geographic location of purchase or sale.

A final note on commemoratives: One of the characteristics of commemoratives/special editions is that over the years of ownership, most of the original amount manufactured stays in the same NIB condition. Thus, if supply always is constant and in one condition, demand has to increase before price appreciation can occur. Many commemorative dealers have told me that recent changes in overseas currency rates have made domestic guns less expensive to own - for Europeans especially. For this reason, more commemoratives are being sold overseas resulting in less supply for the domestic market. Coupled with this increased foreign demand is the recent increase of domestic support and sales. After 29 years of special edition production, many models' performance records can be accurately analyzed and the appreciation (or depreciation) can be compared against other purchases of equal vintage. You be the judge.

U.S. Repeating Arms had announced in 1990 that they would once again resume the production of factory commemorative firearms.

Grading	100%	Issue Price	Qty. Made
1964 WYOMING DIAMOND JUBILEE 94 CARBINE			
	$1,295	$100	1,501
1966 CENTENNIAL '66 RIFLE			
	$450	$125	-
1966 CENTENNIAL '66 CARBINE — total mfg. of both the rifle and carbine was 102,309.			
	$425	$125	102,309
Add $50-$75 over individual prices for consecutively serial numbered rifle and carbine set.			
1966 NEBRASKA CENTENNIAL 94 RIFLE			
	$1,295	$100	2,500
1967 CANADIAN '67 CENTENNIAL RIFLE			
	$450	$125	-
1967 CANADIAN '67 CENTENNIAL CARBINE — total mfg. of both the rifle and carbine was 90,301.			
	$425	$125	90,301
Add $50-$75 over individual prices for consecutively serial numbered rifle and carbine set.			
1967 ALASKAN PURCHASE CENTENNIAL CARBINE			
	$1,495	$125	1,501
1968 ILLINOIS SESQUICENTENNIAL 94 CARBINE			
	$350	$110	37,468
1968 BUFFALO BILL RIFLE "1 OF 300" PRES.			
	$2,500	$1,000	300
1968 BUFFALO BILL RIFLE			
	$450	$130	-
1968 BUFFALO BILL CARBINE — total mfg. of both the rifle and carbine was 112,923.			
	$425	$130	112,923
Add $50-$75 over individual prices for consecutively serial numbered rifle and carbine set.			
1969 GOLDEN SPIKE CARBINE			
	$375	$120	69,996
1969 THEO. ROOSEVELT RIFLE			
	$450	$135	-
1969 THEO. ROOSEVELT CARBINE — total mfg. of both the rifle and carbine was 52,386.			
	$425	$135	52,386
1970 COWBOY COMMEMORATIVE CARBINE			
	$450	$125	27,549
1970 COWBOY CARBINE "1 OF 300"			
	$2,650	$1,000	300
1970 LONE STAR RIFLE			
	$450	$140	-
1970 LONE STAR CARBINE — total mfg. of both the rifle and carbine was 38,385.			
	$425	$140	38,385
1971 NRA CENTENNIAL MUSKET			
	$425	$150	23,400

Grading	100%	Issue Price	Qty. Made
1971 NRA CENTENNIAL RIFLE	$425	$150	21,000
1974 TEXAS RANGER CARBINE	$695	$135	4,850
1974 TEXAS RANGER PRESENTATION	$2,500	$1,000	150
1976 U.S. BICENTENNIAL CARBINE	$595	$325	19,999
1977 WELLS FARGO	$495	$350	19,999
1977 "LIMITED EDITION I"	$1,395	$1,500	1,500
1977 LEGENDARY LAWMEN	$495	$375	19,999
1978 ANTLERED GAME CARBINE	$495	$375	19,999
1979 LEGENDARY FRONTIERSMAN RIFLE	$495	$425	19,999
1979 "LIMITED EDITION II"	$1,395	$1,750	1,500
1979 MATCHED SET OF 1000	$2,250	$3,000	1,000
1980 BAT MASTERSON CARBINE	$795	$650	8,000
1980 "OLIVER WINCHESTER"	$695	$375	19,999
1981 U.S. BORDER PATROL	$595	$1,195	1,000
1981 U.S. BORDER PATROL — MEMBERS MODEL	$595	$695	800
1981 JOHN WAYNE	$895	$600	49,000

Optional accessories were also available for this model: the gun rack with leather insert is currently selling for approx. $40 and the leather scabbard is trading for $60.

Grading	100%	Issue Price	Qty. Made
1981 "DUKE"	$2,950	$2,250	1,000
1981 JOHN WAYNE "1 OF 300" SET	$6,500	$10,000	300
1982 GREAT WESTERN ARTIST I	$1,195	$2,200	999
1982 GREAT WESTERN ARTIST II	$1,195	$2,200	999

W

Grading	100%	Issue Price	Qty. Made

1982 ANNIE OAKLEY

	$695	$699	6,000

1982 OKLAHOMA DIAMOND JUBILEE

	$1,395	$2,250	1,001

1982 AMERICAN BALD EAGLE - SILVER

	$595	$895	2,800

1982 AMERICAN BALD EAGLE - GOLD

	$2,500	$2,950	200

1983 CHIEF CRAZY HORSE

	$495	$600	19,999

1984 WINCHESTER-COLT COMMEMORATIVE SET — 1 each of the Model 1894 Carbine and Colt Peacemaker, serial numbered 1 WC-4440 WC. .44-40 cal., elaborate gold etching, cased.

	$2,250	$3,995	2,300

Approx. 2,300 sets were actually put together in this combination. These sets have been split up with individual prices being discounted (Colt SAAs have been trading in the $700-$800 range).

1985 BOY SCOUTS 75TH ANNIVERSARY — Model 9422 action, .22 cal., rifle configuration, 6¼ lbs.

▲ *Boy Scout* — 15,000 mfg., serial numbered BSA 1 - BSA 15,000, roll engraved, antique pewter receiver, hooded front sight.

	$495	$495	15,000

▲ *Eagle Scout* — 1,000 mfg., serial numbered Eagle 1 - Eagle 1,000, receiver has triple level gold etching, select American walnut stock and forearm, gold-plated lever, hammer, and forearm cap.

	$2,500	$1,710	1,000

1985 MODEL 94 TEXAS SESQUICENTENNIAL — .38-55 cal., available in carbine or rifle.

▲ *Model 94 Rifle* — 24 in. round barrel, elaborate gold etching, includes Bowie knife, oak cased, 586 mfg.

	$2,400	$2,995	1,500

▲ *Model 94 Carbine* — 18½ in. round barrel, gold finished receiver and barrel bands, roll engraved receiver, 2,600 mfg., serial numbered TEX 1 and up.

	$695	$695	15,000

▲ *Rifle/Carbine Set* — includes one each of the Model 94 rifle and carbine, Bowie knife, 150 mfg.

	$6,250	$7,995	150

1986 120TH ANNIVERSARY MODEL 94 CARBINE — .44-40 cal. only, 20 in. barrel, hoop-type finger lever, crescent butt plate, deluxe checkered walnut stock and forearm, extensive gold etching on barrel and framesides, 1,000 mfg. ser. no. WRA001-WRA1000.

	$895	$995	1,000

1986 STATUE OF LIBERTY MODEL 94 — Model 94 rifle in .30-30 cal. with octagon barrel, extensive C. Giovanelli scroll engraving with multiple 22Kt. gold inlays, deluxe walnut with fine checkering, also includes 29 in. hand carved wooden statue of the Statue of Liberty, serial numbered SL1-SL62. This is not a USRAC factory commemorative.

	$7,000	$6,500	62

1986 MODEL 94 DU — .30-30 cal., approx. 2,800 rifles were mfg. in the U.S. Since each Model 94 DU was bid on for ownership, prices will vary from points of origin. An average bid price seems to be in the $700-$995 range with lower and completing set ser. no.'s selling at premiums. Serial numbered DU-86 0001 on up.

This model is not a factory commemorative, but rather a trade gun commissioned by Ducks Unlimited.

W

Grading	100%	Issue Price	Qty. Made

1987 U.S. CONSTITUTION 200TH ANNIVERSARY

| | $13,000 | $12,000 | 17 |

1988 WINCHESTER ARMS COLLECTOR'S ASSOCIATION CASED SET — includes Colt SAA and Winchester Model 1894 in cased set, features special embellishments and W.A.C.A. emblems and medallions. 100 sets were advertised, but only 22 were sold. This is not a USRAC factory commemorative.

| | $2,995 | $2,695 | 22 sets |

1990 WYOMING CENTENNIAL .30-30

| | $995 | $895 | 500 |

1991 125TH ANNIVERSARY .30-30

| | $5,250 | $4,995 | 61 |

1992 KENTUCKY BICENTENNIAL .30-30 — Winchester Model 94 with true charcoal case coloring, engraving depicts important KY graphics, serial numbered KY001-KY500.

| | $995 | $995 | 500 |

This model is distributed exclusively by Cherry's located in Greensboro, NC.

1992 ARAPAHO .30-30 — features gold-plated receiver with etched Indian scenes on both sides, checkered semi-fancy American walnut stock.

| | $995 | $895 | 500 |

This model is distributed exclusively by Cherry's located in Greensboro, NC.

1993 NEZ PERCE MODEL 94 CARBINE — features nickel finished receiver and barrel bands, extensively etched receiver, checkered semi-fancy American walnut stock and forearm, serial numbered NEZ 001 - NEZ 600.

| | $950 | $950 | 600 |

This model is distributed exclusively by Cherry's located in Greensboro, NC.

1995 FLORIDA SESQUICENTENNIAL 94 CARBINE — features motifs from Florida including alligator scene and space shuttle launch, 24 kt. gold-plated receiver, 500 mfg. ser. numbered FL001-FL500 during 1995 only.

| | $1,195 | $1,195 | 500 |

This model is distributed exclusively by Cherry's located in Greensboro, NC.

WINCHESTER COMMEMORATIVES: NON-DOMESTIC - 1970 TO DATE

1970 NORTH WEST TERRITORIES (CANADIAN)

| | $850 | $150 | 2,500 |

1970 NORTHWEST TERRITORIES DELUXE (CANADIAN)

| | $1,100 | $250 | 500 |

1973 YELLOW BOY (SOLD IN EUROPE ONLY)

| | $1,150 | $150 | 4,903 |

1973 M.P.X. (MADE ESPECIALLY FOR A MOVIE)

| | $9,995 | $78 | 32 |

1973 R.C.M.P. (CANADIAN)

| | $795 | $190 | 9,500 |

1973 R.C.M.P. MEMBERS ISSUE (CANADIAN)

| | $795 | $190 | 4,850 |

1973 R.C.M.P. PRESENTATION - (CANADIAN)

| | $9,995 | N/A | 100 |

Grading	100%	Issue Price	Qty. Made
1974 APACHE (CANADIAN)	$795	$150	8,600
1975 KLONDIKE GOLD RUSH (CANADIAN)	$795	$230	10,200
1975 K.G.R. (DAWSON CITY ISSUE) - (CANADIAN)	$8,500	N/A	25
1975 COMANCHE (CANADIAN)	$795	$230	11,511
1976 SIOUX (CANADIAN)	$795	$280	10,000
1976 LITTLE BIG HORN (CANADIAN)	$795	$230	11,000
1977 CHEYENNE (CANADIAN) — 44-40 Cal.	$795	$300	11,225
1977 CHEYENNE (CANADIAN) — .22 Cal.	$695	$320	5,000
1978 CHEROKEE (CANADIAN) — .30-30 Cal.	$795	$385	9,000
1978 CHEROKEE (CANADIAN) — .22 Cal.	$695	$385	3,950
1978 ONE OF ONE THOUSAND (SOLD IN EUROPE ONLY)	$7,995	$5,000	250
This model was not advertised in the U.S.			
1980 ALBERTA DIAMOND JUBILEE (CANADIAN)	$795	$650	2,700
1980 A.D.J. DELUXE PRESENTATION (CANADIAN)	$1,495	$1,900	300
1980 SASKATCHEWAN DIAMOND JUBILEE (CANADIAN)	$795	$695	2,700
1980 S.D.J. DELUXE PRESENTATION (CANADIAN)	$1,495	$1,995	300
1981 CALGARY STAMPEDE (CANADIAN)	$1,250	$2,200	1,000
1981 CANADIAN PACIFIC CENTENNIAL (CANADIAN)	$550	$800	2,700
1981 CANADIAN PACIFIC CENTENNIAL PRESENTATION (CANADIAN)	$1,100	$2,200	300
1981 CANADIAN PACIFIC (EMPL.) - (CANADIAN)	$550	$800	2,000
1981 JOHN WAYNE (CANADIAN)	$1,095	$995	1,000
1986 SECOND SERIES EUROPEAN 1 OF 1,000 — mfg. for European sales only 1986.	$6,500	$6,000	150

Grading	100%	Issue Price	Qty. Made

1992 ONTARIO CONSERVATION — this model was marketed in Canada only.

	$1,195	$1,195	400

WINSLOW ARMS COMPANY

Previous manufacturer located in Camden, SC.

WINSLOW BOLT ACTION SPORTING RIFLE — offered with various actions, FN Supreme, Mark X Mauser, Rem. 700 and 788, Sako and Win. 70, offered in all popular calibers from .17 Rem. to .458 Mag., standard calibers have 24 in. barrels and 3 shot magazines, magnum calibers have 26 in. barrels and 2 shot magazines, two style stocks, "Bushmaster Conventional", slender pistol grip and beavertail forearm, "Plainsmaster", full curl, hooked pistol grip and flat wide forearm, both are Monte Carlo with cheekpieces, recoil pads and swivels, walnut, maple, and myrtle are used with rosewood forend tip and pistol grip cap, rifle comes in 8 basic grades, custom embellishments can increase values greatly, discretion must be used, values are for basic models.

Grading	100%	98%	95%	90%	80%	70%	60%
COMMANDER GRADE	$495	$475	$440	$385	$360	$330	$305
REGAL GRADE	$605	$590	$560	$525	$470	$440	$415
REGENT GRADE	$725	$700	$670	$640	$605	$550	$495
REGIMENTAL GRADE	$935	$890	$855	$800	$745	$660	$605
CROWN GRADE	$1,375	$1,265	$1,155	$990	$910	$825	$715
ROYAL GRADE	$1,540	$1,375	$1,210	$1,100	$1,020	$965	$825
IMPERIAL GRADE	$3,520	$3,080	$2,860	$2,475	$2,200	$1,925	$1,320
EMPEROR GRADE	$6,215	$5,500	$4,950	$4,400	$3,300	$2,750	$2,200

WISEMAN, BILL AND CO.

Custom rifle manufacturer/retailer located in College Station, TX.

Wiseman/McMillan also manufactures rifle barrels and custom stocks.

RIFLES: BOLT ACTION

Add 11% excise tax to prices shown below for new manufacture.

HUNTER MODEL — available in various cals., Sako action, stainless steel barrel by Wiseman/McMillan, laminate stock, teflon finished metal parts, Pachmayr decelerator pad, sling swivels, glass bedded action.

Mfg.'s Sug. Retail	$1,995		$1,995	$1,625	$1,300	$1,100	$900	$775	$675

HUNTER DELUXE — similar to Hunter Model except has custom checkering.

Mfg.'s Sug. Retail	$2,195		$2,195	$1,825	$1,500	$1,225	$995	$875	$775

Grading		100%	98%	95%	90%	80%	70%	60%

MAVERICK — similar to Hunter but with black fiberglass stock.
Mfg.'s Sug. Retail $1,695 $1,695 $1,375 $1,100 $995 $875 $775 $675

VARMENTER — similar to Hunter but with thumbhole stock.
Mfg.'s Sug. Retail $2,095 $2,095 $1,725 $1,400 $1,225 $995 $875 $775

TEXAS SAFARI RIFLE — various cals., choice of hidden mag. (no floorplate), standard floorplate or 5 shot detachable mag., 2 or 3 position tang safety, stainless steel fluted barrel with integral muzzle brake, synthetic stock. New 1996.
Mfg.'s Sug. Retail $1,695 $1,695 $1,300 $995
    Add $100 for standard floorplate (TSR-II).
    Add $300 for 5 shot detachable mag. (TSR-I).
    Add $150 for 3 position tang safety.

TSR TACTICAL — .300 Win. mag., .308 Win., or .338 Lapua Mag., 5 shot inline, detachable mag., or standard floorplate, synthetic stock with adj. cheekpiece, stainless steel fluted barrel with integral muzzle brake, guaranteed $\frac{1}{2}$ minute of angle. New 1996.
Mfg.'s Sug. Retail $2,495 $2,495 $2,000 $1,600
    Add $195 for fluted barrel.
    Add $195 for muzzle brake.
    Add $150 for 3 position safety.

PISTOLS

SILHOUETTE PISTOL — various cals., Sako action, 14 in. Wiseman/McMillan fluted stainless barrel, 5 or 7 shot magazine, laminate pistol grip stock, no sights, $4\frac{1}{2}$-$5\frac{1}{2}$ lbs. New 1989.
Mfg.'s Sug. Retail $1,295 $1,295 $1,000 $900 $800 $750 $700 $650

WOODWARD, JAMES AND SONS

Previously mfg. in London, England. Acquired by James Purdey & Sons approx. 1935. In 1996, James Purdey & Sons once again started manufacturing new best quality Woodward side-by-side and over/under shotguns.

SHOTGUNS: DOUBLE AND SINGLE BARREL

Woodward made one of the world's finest shotguns. Prior to WWII, they were acquired by Purdey and Sons. Many of the weapons they made were custom built and grading and pricing should be done individually. We will list some of the general models with approximate values as a guideline, but strongly urge competent professional appraisal when contemplating purchase or sale.

BEST QUALITY SxS SHOTGUN — custom built in all gauges, barrel lengths and chokes, sidelock, auto ejectors, stocked to specifications, pre-WWII and new mfg. beginning 1996.
      $26,000 $23,000 $19,950 $17,000 $14,250 $12,000 $10,000
    Add 20% for 20 ga.
    Add 40% for 28 ga.
    Add 60% for .410 ga.
    Add $1,000 for SST

▲ **New Mfg.** — 20 ga. only beginning 1996.
Mfg.'s Sug. Retail $40,820 $40,820 $36,000 $31,500 $27,250 $22,450 $14,000 $10,000

BEST QUALITY O/U SHOTGUN — custom built in all gauges, barrel lengths, and chokes, VR, sidelock, auto ejectors, stocked to customer specifications, pre-WWII and new mfg. beginning 1996.
      $29,500 $25,500 $21,500 $18,500 $15,750 $13,800 $12,000
    Add 35% for 20 ga.
    Add 75% for 28 ga.
    .410 gauge — too rare to accurately predict.
    Add $1,000 for ST.

W

Grading	100%	98%	95%	90%	80%	70%	60%

▲ *New Mfg.* — 12, 16, 20, 28, or .410 ga.
Mfg.'s Sug. Retail   **$57,305** $57,305 $48,000 $40,000 $32,000 $24,000 $16,000 $10,000

BEST QUALITY SINGLE BARREL TRAP GUN — 12 ga. only, limited mfg. - pre-WWII only.
$12,750 $10,000 $8,950 $7,725 $6,500 $5,750 $4,900

WYOMING ARMS MFG. CORP.

Previous manufacturer located in Thermopolis, WY. Very small quantities of Parker pistols were mfg.

PARKER PISTOLS: STAINLESS STEEL

STANDARD PISTOL — 9mm Para., 10mm, .40 S&W, or .45 ACP cal., $3\frac{3}{8}$, 5, or 7 in. barrel, 7 (.45 ACP), 8 (10mm & .40 S&W), or 9 (9mm Para.) shot mag., Millett adj. sights, grooved synthetic grips, 29-39 oz. Disc. 1992.

$350 $300 $250

Last Mfg.'s Sug. Retail was $399.

Add $50 for 7 in. barrel.

.357 MAG. — .357 Mag. cal., single action semi-auto, 7 in. barrel, adj. sights, 8 shot mag., lifetime warranty, 44 oz. Disc. 1992.

$425 $350 $300

Last Mfg.'s Sug. Retail was $479.

Z section

Z-B RIFLE

Brno, Czechoslovakia.

Grading	100%	98%	95%	90%	80%	70%	60%

Z-B MAUSER VARMINT RIFLE — small Mauser bolt action, .22 Hornet, 23 in. barrel, double set triggers, 3 leaf sight, checkered pistol grip stock, (also known as Brno Hornet).

	100%	98%	95%	90%	80%	70%	60%
	$825	$745	$690	$605	$550	$470	$415

Z.D.F. IMPORT EXPORT INC.

Manufacturer located in Salt Lake City, UT since 1995.

RIFLES

SP 50 — .50 BMG cal., semi-auto bullpup configuration, 26 or 32 in. barrel with muzzle brake, 3 lug bolt, hardened aluminum parts, 17.2 lbs. New 1996.

		100%	98%	95%	90%	80%	70%	60%
Mfg.'s Sug. Retail	$2,500	$2,375	$2,100	$1,875	$1,600	$1,375	$1,150	$995

ZABALA HERMANOS, S.A.

Manufacturer located in Eibar, Spain. Z. Hermanos has had limited importation to date (American Arms located in Kansas City is private labeling a few models).

Zabala Hermanos manufactures quality boxlock SxS or O/U shotguns and sidelock SxS's. For more information regarding this trademark, (including current models and prices) please contact the manufacturer directly (see Trademark Index).

ZANARDINI

Manufacturer located in Brescia, Italy since 1946. Currently, Zanardini does not have a U.S. importer. Several U.S. firms have stocked a few Zanardini models in the past, but not the complete line. For current information and up-to-date pricing, please contact the factory directly (see Trademark Index).

The values below represent older importation as Zanardini has not been imported into the U.S. for the past several years.

COMBINATION GUNS O/U

Zanardini is currently offering the Model 2000 Deluxe Super Light (with or w/o new loading system), and the Boxer Model with H&H style sidelocks.

PRINCESS — super light variation.

$2,200	$1,925	$1,675	$1,400	$1,200	$1,000	$800

Last Mfg.'s Sug. Retail was $2,542.

BOXER MODEL — H&H styled sidelocks, top-quality engraving.

$5,750	$5,150	$4,600	$4,000	$3,550	$3,000	$2,650

Last Mfg.'s Sug. Retail was $6,246.

BOXER 4-LOCKS MODEL

$3,900	$3,400	$2,975	$2,625	$2,300	$2,050	$1,750

Last Mfg.'s Sug. Retail was $4,562.

402 STRAUSS — top-of-the-line combination gun with best quality engraving and wood.

$9,000	$8,000	$7,000	$6,000	$5,000	$4,000	$3,000

Last Mfg.'s Sug. Retail was $10,548.

Z

Grading	100%	98%	95%	90%	80%	70%	60%

RIFLES

Zanardini is currently offering the Fuchs folding single barrel, the New Prinz Model (single barrel tip-up), the O/U Express Koenig Models 403 A & B, and the SxS Oxford and Bristol Models (in various levels of grade).

403 OXFORD SxS — 9.3x74R and smaller cals.

	100%	98%	95%	90%	80%	70%	60%
	$3,400	$3,000	$2,700	$2,425	$2,150	$1,875	$1,575

Last Mfg.'s Sug. Retail was $3,835.

▲ *Larger cals.* .375 H&H, .458 Win. Mag., or .470 Nitro cal.

	100%	98%	95%	90%	80%	70%	60%
	$6,700	$6,000	$5,500	$5,000	$4,500	$3,950	$3,450

Last Mfg.'s Sug. Retail was $7,555.

Add approx. 135% for .470 Nitro cal.

EXPRESS RIFLE SxS — .470 NE cal., boxlock action, ST, checkered walnut stock (with cheekpiece), express sights. Other cals. available upon special order.

Mfg.'s Sug. Retail	$8,995	$8,400	$8,100	$7,450	$6,750	$6,000	$5,500	$5,000

This model is imported exclusively by Mandall Shooting Supplies, Inc. located in Scottsdale, AZ.

409 BRISTOL SxS — priced by individual request.

407 OXFORD SL SxS — sidelock action.

	$15,000	$13,250	$11,950	$10,000	$9,250	$8,500	$7,750

Last Mfg.'s Sug. Retail was $17,095.

MODEL 403 KOENIG O/U — 7.65R or 9.3x74R cal.

	$6,500	$5,850	$5,350	$4,850	$4,350	$3,800	$3,300

Last Mfg.'s Sug. Retail was $7,368.

MODEL 403 DELUXE O/U

	$3,650	$3,200	$2,875	$2,525	$2,250	$1,925	$1,600

Last Mfg.'s Sug. Retail was $4,188.

SHOTGUNS

Zanardini is currently offering the London Model with external hammers (standard and super deluxe models) and the Donau Model with H&H type sidelocks (standard and super deluxe models).

HAMMER LONDON MODEL SxS — features external hammers.

	$9,150	$8,125	$7,100	$6,100	$5,050	$4,000	$3,050

Last Mfg.'s Sug. Retail was $10,735.

HAMMERLESS LONDON MODEL SxS

	$4,200	$3,700	$3,175	$2,825	$2,500	$2,100	$1,700

Last Mfg.'s Sug. Retail was $4,936.

DONAU STANDARD MODEL SxS — boxlock action.

	$9,000	$8,000	$7,000	$6,000	$5,000	$4,000	$3,000

Last Mfg.'s Sug. Retail was $10,548.

DONAU SIDELOCK SxS — H&H style sidelock action.

	$16,500	$14,750	$12,950	$11,000	$9,950	$9,000	$8,000

Last Mfg.'s Sug. Retail was $18,966.

PRESTIGE TRAP AND SKEET SxS

	$2,250	$1,950	$1,675	$1,400	$1,200	$1,000	$800

Last Mfg.'s Sug. Retail was $2,598.

HASE CACCIA MONTECATINI SxS — boxlock action, double set triggers, extractors.

	$900	$800	$700	$600	$550	$495	$450

Last Mfg.'s Sug. Retail was $1,027.

Add 30% for ejectors.

Grading	100%	98%	95%	90%	80%	70%	60%

HORN MODEL SxS — boxlock action, double set triggers, extractors.

		$950	$850	$750	$625	$550	$495	$450

Last Mfg.'s Sug. Retail was $1,102.

Add 40% for ejectors.

ZANOTTI, FABIO

Manufacturer located in Brescia, Italy since 1625. Currently imported and distributed by New England Arms, Co. located in Kittery Point, ME. Fabio Zanotti became part of the Renato Gamba Group in 1985.

Fabio Zanotti is one of the world's oldest quality shotgun manufacturers. Current domestic importation is often times done on a custom order only basis. For more information on Zanotti models and their values, contact New England Arms Co.

SHOTGUNS: OVER/UNDER

MODEL 725 — 28 or .410 ga. only, scalloped case hardened shallow frame, DT or ST, ejectors, game scene and scroll engraving, custom built to individual specifications.

Mfg.'s Sug. Retail	$4,950		$4,550	$3,925	$3,450	$2,950	$2,450	$2,000	$1,875

CASSIANO — 12, 20, 28, or .410 ga., Boss style shallow action, best quality gun built to individual specifications. Prices start at $18,500 and go up accordingly.

SHOTGUNS: SIDE BY SIDE

Add $300 for ST.
Add $250 for beavertail forearm.
Add $450 for leather case.

MODEL 625 BOXLOCK

Mfg.'s Sug. Retail	$4,500		$3,900	$3,300	$2,850	$2,500	$2,200	$1,900	$1,800

MODEL 626 BOXLOCK — scroll, game scene, or combination engraving.

Mfg.'s Sug. Retail	$5,500		$5,100	$4,100	$3,650	$3,375	$3,100	$2,950	$2,600

MODEL GIACINTO — hammer gun.

Mfg.'s Sug. Retail	$4,950		$4,600	$3,850	$3,175	$2,450	$2,000	$1,825	$1,430

MODEL MAXIM SIDELOCK

Mfg.'s Sug. Retail	$8,000		$7,350	$6,100	$5,250	$4,600	$3,850	$3,175	$2,450

MODEL EDWARD SIDELOCK

Mfg.'s Sug. Retail	$10,500		$9,875	$8,250	$7,000	$6,150	$5,250	$4,000	$3,575

MODEL CASSIANO I SIDELOCK

Mfg.'s Sug. Retail	$12,000		$10,000	$8,750	$7,450	$6,450	$5,575	$4,700	$3,850

MODEL CASSIANO II

Mfg.'s Sug. Retail	$14,000		$12,250	$10,250	$9,350	$8,150	$6,700	$5,900	$5,100

CASSIANO EXECUTIVE — prices vary per individual order, top-of-the-line model. Prices start at $15,000 and go up.

ZASTAVA ARMS

Manufacturer located in Yugoslavia. Zastava Arms are not currently imported into the U.S. Previously imported by K.B.I., Inc. located in Harrisburg, PA and previously distributed by Nationwide Sports Distributors located in Southampton, PA.

Grading	100%	98%	95%	90%	80%	70%	60%

HANDGUNS: SEMI-AUTO

MODEL Z9 — 9mm Para., double action semi-auto, 15 shot, $4\frac{1}{4}$ in. barrel, short recoil, choice of mil. spec. black or commercial blue finish, SIG locking system, hammer drop safety, ambidextrous controls, 3-dot Tritium sighting system, alloy frame, firing pin block, chamber indicator, squared-off triggerguard, checkered dark gray polymer grips, 32 oz. While advertised, this model was never commercially imported c. 1991.

		100%	98%	95%	90%	80%	70%	60%
		$450	$395	$365	$330	$300	$285	$265

Last Mfg.'s Sug. Retail was $495.

Prior to 1991, this model was named the CZ-99 (only 100 mfg.).

MODEL Z40 — .40 S&W cal, although advertised, this model was never imported. Suggested retail was $495.

RIFLES

MODEL ZR 22 — .22 LR, .22 Mag., or .22 Hornet cal., although advertised, this model was never imported. Suggested retail was $275.

ZEPHYR

Manufacturer located in Spain, and imported by Stoegers 1930s-1972.

RIFLES

Stoeger's has imported a wide variety of bolt action rifles during the past 60 years. Rather than list the many models individually, each Zephyr rifle should be compared to a gun of equal caliber, quality, and features to ascertain an approximate value range.

SHOTGUNS: SxS OR SINGLE SHOT

WOODLANDER II DOUBLE BARREL SHOTGUN — 12 or 20 ga., various chokes, boxlock, double triggers, extractors, engraved, checkered pistol grip stock.

	$495	$440	$385	$360	$305	$275	$250

UPLANDER (4E) SxS — 12, 16, 20, 28, or .410 ga., sidelock action, double triggers, ejectors, engraved.

	$775	$695	$640	$585	$570	$480	$440

STERLINGWORTH II DOUBLE BARREL SHOTGUN — similar to Woodlander, with sidelock action.

	$825	$725	$660	$605	$580	$525	$495

UPLAND KING SxS — 12 or 16 ga., sidelock, single trigger, VR, ejectors, fully engraved.

	$1,000	$900	$800	$725	$650	$600	$550

THUNDERBIRD SxS — 10 ga. Mag, 32 in. barrels, double triggers, French walnut, engraved. Add $175 for ejectors.

	$850	$750	$625	$550	$510	$490	$475

HONKER — 10 ga. Mag, single shot, 36 in. VR barrel, lightly engraved.

	$500	$460	$420	$350	$310	$290	$270

VANDALIA — 12 ga. Trap Model, 32 in. barrel, engraved.

	$700	$620	$575	$525	$475	$425	$390

VICTOR SPECIAL DOUBLE BARREL SHOTGUN — 12 ga., 25, 28, or 30 in. barrels, various chokes, double triggers, extractors, checkered pistol grip stock.

	$440	$385	$330	$305	$250	$220	$195

ZOLI, ANGELO

Previous manufacturer located in Brescia, Italy. Previously imported and distributed exclusively by Angelo Zoli USA located in Addison, IL. Mfg. 1985-87.

Angelo Zoli went out of business in December, 1987 and was taken over by the Italian Bank of Brescia in 1989. Many people tend to confuse the shotguns of Angelo and Antonio Zoli (it is hard to determine which manufacturer made a gun marked "A. Zoli"). There is no correlation between these trademarks and Antonio Zoli DOES NOT have parts for these earlier Angelo Zoli long arms. Even though both trademarks may indicate "A. ZOLI" for a barrel address, they are mostly discernable by the model listings under both headings in this section.

Cape Outfitters (see Trademark Index under Angelo Zoli for address) has parts for most Angelo Zoli guns and should be contacted directly for availability and prices. All repairs are strictly non-warranty.

Grading	100%	98%	95%	90%	80%	70%	60%

SHOTGUNS: OVER AND UNDER

SNIPE — .410 ga., 3 in. chambers, 26 or 28 in. barrels, single trigger. Disc. 1987.

	$230	$200	$185	$170	$155	$145	$135

Last Mfg.'s Sug. Retail was $265.

TEXAS — all ga.'s, 26 or 28 in. barrels, double triggers, folding design, lever action. Disc. 1987.

	$250	$220	$200	$185	$170	$155	$145

Last Mfg.'s Sug. Retail was $291.

DOVE — .410 ga. only, 3 in. chambers, 26 or 28 in. barrels, single trigger. Disc. 1987.

	$260	$230	$200	$185	$170	$155	$145

Last Mfg.'s Sug. Retail was $306.

FIELD SPECIAL — 12, 20, or 28 ga., 3 in. chambers, various barrel lengths and chokings, single trigger. Disc. 1989.

	$450	$400	$360	$330	$300	$270	$240

Last Mfg.'s Sug. Retail was $699.

PIGEON MODEL — 12 or 20 ga., 3 in. chambers, various barrel lengths, single trigger. Disc. 1987.

	$350	$295	$270	$250	$220	$195	$175

Last Mfg.'s Sug. Retail was $394.

Add $60 for 20 ga.

STANDARD MODEL — 12 or 20 ga., 3 in. chambers, various barrel lengths and chokings, single trigger. Disc. 1987.

	$395	$345	$320	$300	$280	$260	$245

Last Mfg.'s Sug. Retail was $459.

SILVER SNIPE — 12 or 20 ga., 3 in. chambers on the 20 ga., single trigger, ejectors, light engraving. Disc. 1987.

	$675	$585	$530	$485	$440	$400	$375

Last Mfg.'s Sug. Retail was $739.

Add $50 for multi-chokes (12 ga. only).
This model was distributed by Euroarms of America, Inc.

CONDOR MODEL — 12 ga. skeet model, 28 in. barrels, SST, ejectors, wide VR, engraved silver finished receiver, recoil pad. Disc. 1987.

	$795	$700	$640	$585	$530	$485	$440

Last Mfg.'s Sug. Retail was $895.

This model was distributed by Mandall Shooting Supplies, Inc.

Z

Grading	100%	98%	95%	90%	80%	70%	60%

TARGET MODEL 208 — 12 ga. only, available in either Trap, Skeet, or Monotrap configuration. Disc. 1987.

	$895	$775	$695	$620	$575	$500	$450

Last Mfg.'s Sug. Retail was $996.

Add $494 for Monotrap II 208 Model.

TARGET MODEL 308 — 12 ga. only, available in either Trap, Skeet, or Monotrap configuration. Disc. 1987.

	$1,375	$1,125	$950	$875	$795	$725	$650

Last Mfg.'s Sug. Retail was $1,581.

Add $76 for multi-chokes.
Add $824 for Monotrap II 308 Model.

SPECIAL MODEL — 12 ga. only, 3 in. chambers, various barrel lengths and chokings, SST. Disc. 1987.

	$465	$395	$355	$325	$290	$270	$250

Last Mfg.'s Sug. Retail was $528.

Add $120 for multi-chokes.

DELUXE MODEL — similar to Special Model, except better wood and engraving. Disc. 1987.

	$645	$550	$495	$450	$400	$360	$320

Last Mfg.'s Sug. Retail was $730.

Add $80 for multi-chokes.

PRESENTATION MODEL — 12 ga. only, includes sideplates. Disc. 1987.

	$740	$630	$575	$495	$450	$395	$350

Last Mfg.'s Sug. Retail was $842.

Add $42 for multi-chokes.

ANGEL MODEL — 12 ga. only, field grade, SST, ejectors, wide VR, engraved receiver, recoil pad. Disc.

	$850	$775	$700	$640	$585	$530	$485

This model was distributed by Mandall Shooting Supplies, Inc.

ST. GEORGE'S TARGET — 12 ga. only, trap or skeet gun, SST, fixed choke. Disc. 1987.

	$900	$730	$645	$550	$495	$450	$400

Last Mfg.'s Sug. Retail was $1,024.

▲ *St. George's Competition* — 12 ga. only, includes 30 in. O/U barrels and single barrel multi-choke. Disc. 1989.

	$1,995	$1,750	$1,550	$1,250	$995	$875	$775

Last Mfg.'s Sug. Retail was $1,627.

PATRICIA MODEL — .410 ga. only, 3 in. chambers, 28 in. barrels, SST. Disc. 1987.

	$1,175	$1,010	$900	$895	$820	$740	$650

Last Mfg.'s Sug. Retail was $1,345.

Add $121 for case.

SHOTGUNS: SIDE-BY-SIDE

QUAIL SPECIAL — .410 ga., 3 in. chambers, single trigger, 28 in. barrels. Disc. 1987.

	$205	$185	$170	$150	$125	$110	$100

Last Mfg.'s Sug. Retail was $243.

FALCON II — .410 ga., 3 in. chambers, 26 or 28 in. barrels, double triggers. Disc. 1987.

	$205	$185	$170	$150	$125	$110	$100

Last Mfg.'s Sug. Retail was $246.

SILVER HAWK — 12 or 20 ga., double trigger, engraved.

	$420	$395	$360	$330	$300	$280	$260

SILVER SNIPE — 12 or 20 ga., various barrel lengths, VR, single trigger, engraved.

	$485	$440	$400	$360	$330	$300	$280

Grading	100%	98%	95%	90%	80%	70%	60%

PHEASANT — 12 ga. only, 3 in. chambers, 28 in. barrels only, single trigger. Disc. 1987.

	$370	$320	$300	$280	$260	$240	$220

Last Mfg.'s Sug. Retail was $428.

ALLEY CLEANER — 12 or 20 ga., 3 in. chambers, 20 in. barrels, riot configuration, SST. Disc. 1987.

	$575	$495	$460	$420	$390	$350	$310

Last Mfg.'s Sug. Retail was $649.

Add $65 for multi-chokes.

CLASSIC — 12 or 20 ga., 3 in. chambers, 26-30 in. barrels, ST. Disc. 1989.

	$995	$875	$750	$650	$550	$475	$400

Last Mfg.'s Sug. Retail was $706.

Add $80 for multi-chokes.

SHOTGUNS: SINGLE BARREL AND LEVER ACTION

DIANO I — 12, 20, or .410 ga., 3 in. chambers, top lever single barrel action, folding configuration, VR. Disc. 1987.

	$115	$95	$85	$80	$75	$70	$65

Last Mfg.'s Sug. Retail was $129.

DIANO II — similar to Diano I, except has bottom lever opening. Disc. 1987.

	$115	$95	$85	$80	$75	$70	$65

Last Mfg.'s Sug. Retail was $129.

LONER I — similar to Diano I. Disc. 1987.

	$95	$80	$75	$65	$55	$45	$35

Last Mfg.'s Sug. Retail was $109.

LONER II — similar to Diano II. Disc. 1987.

	$95	$80	$75	$65	$55	$45	$35

Last Mfg.'s Sug. Retail was $109.

APACHE — 12 ga. only, lever action, 3 in. chambers, 20 in. barrel, SST. Disc. 1987.

	$410	$355	$325	$300	$280	$260	$245

Last Mfg.'s Sug. Retail was $473.

Add $80 for multi-chokes.

SHOTGUNS: SLIDE ACTION

PUMP ACTION — 12 ga. only, available in riot, field, or deer (slug) barrel configurations, 3 in. chamber, hunter model has multi-chokes standard. Disc. 1987.

	$290	$245	$205	$185	$170	$150	$125

Last Mfg.'s Sug. Retail was $329.

COMBINATION GUNS

AIRONE — 12 ga./.30-06 or .308 Win. cal., boxlock with false sideplates, double triggers, checkered walnut stock and forearm, swivels. Disc. 1987.

	$1,450	$1,275	$1,050	$900	$800	$700	$600

CONDOR — similar to Airone, except does not have false sideplates. Disc. 1987.

	$1,295	$1,050	$900	$800	$700	$600	$500

DOUBLE RIFLES

LEOPARD EXPRESS — .30-06, .308 Win., .375 H&H, or 7x65R cal., boxlock action, double triggers, checkered walnut stock and forearm. Disc. 1987.

	$1,325	$1,150	$975	$900	$840	$775	$725

Last Mfg.'s Sug. Retail was $1,529.

Z

ZOLI, ANTONIO

Manufacturer located in Brescia, Italy. No current importation. Previously imported and distributed (1990-91 only) by European American Armory Corp. located in Hialeah, FL. Prior to 1990, A. Zoli was imported and distributed exclusively by Antonio Zoli U.S.A., Inc. located in Fort Wayne, IN.

Antonio Zoli firearms are totally unrelated to those guns of Angelo Zoli (guns marked "A. Zoli" make it hard to determine the correct manufacturer). Parts are not interchangeable and warranties from Antonio Zoli firearms DO NOT apply to Angelo Zoli guns.

Even though Antonio Zoli does not have a current importer, factory parts are available through Cape Outfitters, located in Cape Girardeau, MO (See Trademark Index for listing).

Grading	100%	98%	95%	90%	80%	70%	60%

RIFLES: O/U

The rifles listed below (including O/U, side by side, and bolt action) are imported exclusively by Euroarms of America.

EXPRESS — 7x65R, 7x57, .30-06, .308 Win. or 9.3x74R cal., 25.6 in. barrels, hand checkered walnut stock with cheekpiece, set trigger for bottom barrel, extractors. Importation disc. 1993.

	$3,875	$3,250	$2,900	$2,600	$2,200	$1,950	$1,650

Last Mfg.'s Sug. Retail was $4,400.

Add $600 for E Model (with ejectors).

EXPRESS EM — 7x65R, .30-06, .308 Win., or 9.3x74R cal., mechanical single trigger, ejectors. Importation disc. 1990, reintroduced 1992 only.

	$4,850	$3,975	$3,300	$2,900	$2,600	$2,200	$1,900

Last Mfg.'s Sug. Retail was $5,300.

Add $2,395 for De Luxe Model (disc.).
Add $7,200 for E3 De Luxe Model (disc.).
The Express E3 De Luxe Model includes 2 extra sets of barrels - 1 set is shotgun (20 ga. - 2¾ or 3 in. chambers).

RIFLES: S X S

SAVANA E — 7x65R, .30-06, .308 Win., or 9.3x74R cal., boxlock action, ejectors. Importation disc. 1990.

	$5,850	$4,850	$3,975	$3,300	$2,800	$2,350	$2,000

Last Mfg.'s Sug. Retail was $6,600.

Add $400 for Savana EM Model (single trigger).

▲ *Savana Deluxe* — similar to Savana E, except has elaborate game scene engraving. Importation disc. 1990.

	$7,750	$7,100	$6,500	$6,000	$5,500	$5,000	$4,600

Last Mfg.'s Sug. Retail was $8,295.

TROPHY MODEL — similar to Savana E, except is also available in .375 H&H cal., 25½ in. barrels, 8 lbs. Imported 1991 only.

	$5,275	$4,200	$3,600	$3,150	$2,750	$2,400	$2,050

Last Mfg.'s Sug. Retail was $5,895.

Grading	100%	98%	95%	90%	80%	70%	60%

RIFLES: BOLT ACTION

AZ 1900C — .243 Win., .270 Win., 6.5x55, .30-06, .308 Win., 7mm Rem. Mag., or .300 Win. Mag. cal., 21 or 24 (Mag. cals.) in. barrel, checkered walnut stock with weatherproof stock finish, sling swivels, iron sights, 7.4 lbs. Importation disc. 1993.

	$1,100	$850	$740	$660	$585	$500	$450

Last Mfg.'s Sug. Retail was $1,295.

> Add approx. 10% for AZ 1900 Deluxe (better walnut).
> Add 60% for AZ 1900 Super Deluxe (select walnut and moderate engraving).
> Add approx. 10% for Model AZ 1900 DL (photo engraved receiver and floorplate).

MODEL AZ 1900M — .243 Win., 6.5x55mm, .270 Win., .30-06, or .308 Win. cal., 21 in. barrel, composite stock is composed of fiberglass, Kevlar, and graphite and features baked on walnut wood grain finish with checkering, drilled and tapped receiver. Imported 1991 only.

	$725	$625	$550	$495	$450	$415	$375

Last Mfg.'s Sug. Retail was $840.

> Add approx. 10% for Model AZ 1900M DL (photo engraved receiver and floorplate).

SHOTGUNS: CURRENT MFG. O/U

SILVER FALCON — 12 or 20 ga., 3 in. chambers, boxlock action, SST, ejectors, 26 or 28 in. barrels with multi-chokes, coin finished receiver with engraving, checkered Turkish walnut stock and forearm with weatherproof finish. Importation disc. 1991.

	$1,450	$700	$575	$500	$450	$400	$365

Last Mfg.'s Sug. Retail was $1,695.

WOODSMAN — 12 ga. only, 3 in. chambers, 23 in. vent. barrels are designed to shoot rifle slugs at 55 yards and to accept 5 interchangeable choke tubes, SST, ejectors, quarter rib on barrels with pop-up rifle sights, checkered Circassian walnut stock and forearm with swivels (waterproof finish).

	$1,650	$1,150	$950	$800	$700	$600	$500

Last Mfg.'s Sug. Retail was $1,895.

▲ *Woodsman Combo* — includes 2 sets of barrels (3 in. chambers) with Zoli interchangeable choke system.

	$2,050	$1,700	$1,475	$1,200	$1,050	$925	$800

Last Mfg.'s Sug. Retail was $2,320.

MODEL Z-90 TARGET MODEL — 12 ga. only, boxlock action, adj. SST, black competition receiver, deluxe checkered Turkish walnut stock with recoil pad and forearm, vent. barrels and rib, SST, ejectors.

▲ *Trap Gun* — 29½ or 32 in. barrels with screw-in chokes and raised VR, Monte Carlo stock, blue finish. Importation disc. 1993.

	$2,150	$1,450	$1,200	$995	$850	$700	$600

Last Mfg.'s Sug. Retail was $2,495.

▲ *Mono Trap Gun* — 32 or 34 in. barrel with screw-in chokes and raised VR, Monte Carlo stock. Importation disc. 1993.

	$2,150	$1,450	$1,200	$995	$850	$700	$600

Last Mfg.'s Sug. Retail was $2,495.

▲ *Z-90 Combo Trap Set* — includes O/U trap barrels as well as Mono trap barrel on same receiver, available as 30/32 in. sets or 32/34 in. sets. Imported 1991-92.

	$2,350	$1,900	$1,650	$1,400	$1,150	$950	$825

Last Mfg.'s Sug. Retail was $2,700.

▲ *Skeet Gun* — 28 in. barrels only with screw-in chokes. Importation disc. 1993.

	$2,150	$1,450	$1,200	$995	$850	$700	$600

Last Mfg.'s Sug. Retail was $2,495.

Z

Grading	100%	98%	95%	90%	80%	70%	60%

▲ *Sporting Clays Gun* — 28 in. barrels with screw-in chokes, coin finished receiver with engraved sideplates, separated barrels, Schnabel forend, solid recoil pad. Importation disc. 1990.

	$2,150	$1,450	$1,200	$995	$850	$700	$600

Last Mfg.'s Sug. Retail was $2,495.

SHOTGUNS: DISC. MFG. O/U

GOLDEN SNIPE — 12 or 20 ga, various barrel lengths, VR, single trigger, ejectors, engraved.

	$560	$520	$475	$430	$395	$360	$330

DELFINO — 12 or 20 ga., 3 in. chambers, 26 or 28 in. barrels, ejectors, VR, single non-selective trigger, blued frame with delicate engraving, walnut pistol grip stock and forearm. Disc.

	$500	$425	$375	$325	$295	$280	$265

RITMO HUNTING — 12 ga. only, 3 in. chambers, 26 or 28 in. vent. barrels and rib, SST, ejectors, select checkered walnut, blued frame and barrels with moderate engraving, recoil pad, 7¼ lbs. Disc.

	$575	$510	$465	$410	$370	$350	$335

RITMO PIGEON GRADE IV — 12 ga. only, live pigeon gun, 28 in. barrels, SST, ejectors, superbly engraved silver finished receiver, extra fine checkering on deluxe walnut, vent. barrels and rib, cased, 7½ lbs. Disc.

	$1,600	$1,450	$1,200	$1,000	$875	$795	$725

M85 RITMO TRAP OR SKEET — 12 ga. only, 28 in. (Skeet only), 30, or 32 in. barrels, ejectors, SST, special stock dimensions, engraved blue receiver, select checkered walnut stock and forearm, cased, 7¾ lbs. Disc.

	$595	$500	$465	$440	$415	$395	$370

This model was also available in a single barrel trap model at no extra charge.

▲ *M85 Ritmo Trap Combination* — 12 ga. only, supplied with O/U and single barrel sets, various barrel lengths, cased. Disc.

	$995	$895	$800	$700	$620	$575	$500

SHOTGUNS: CURRENT MFG. SIDE-BY-SIDE

UPLANDER — 12 or 20 ga., 3 in. chambers, 25 in. barrels with fixed chokes (IC/M), ST, ejectors, color case hardened receiver, English style checkered Circassian walnut stock and forearm with oil or polyurethane finish. Importation disc. 1990.

	$750	$625	$560	$520	$485	$450	$425

Last Mfg.'s Sug. Retail was $1,295.

SILVER FOX — 12 or 20 ga., 3 in. chambers, 26 or 28 (12 ga. only) in. barrels with fixed chokes, ST, ejectors, hand engraved silver finished receiver with "AZ" in gold, straight grip checkered Circassian walnut stock and forearm. Importation disc. 1990.

	$1,650	$1,425	$1,200	$995	$875	$750	$625

Last Mfg.'s Sug. Retail was $2,995.

SHOTGUNS: DISC. MFG. SIDE-BY-SIDE

ARIETE M3 — 12 ga. only, 26 or 28 in. barrels, matted rib, single non-selective trigger, ejectors, blued receiver with fine scroll engraving, cased. Disc.

	$550	$475	$400	$360	$330	$310	$285

EMPIRE — 12 or 20 ga. Mag., 27 or 28 in. barrels, moderate engraving, coin finished receiver. Disc.

	$1,425	$1,175	$975	$875	$795	$725	$650

Add $100 for 3 in. Mag. chambers.

This model was distributed by Euroarms of America, Inc.

Grading	100%	98%	95%	90%	80%	70%	60%

VOLCANO RECORD — 12 ga. only, 28 in. barrels, H&H type sidelocks, ejectors, SST, treble Purdey locks, silver finished receiver with elaborate engraving, best quality fine checkered walnut, special order only. Disc.

	100%	98%	95%	90%	80%	70%	60%
	$5,300	$4,475	$3,950	$3,400	$2,950	$2,650	$2,300

▲ *Volcano Record ELM* — 12 ga. only, built to individual customer specifications, best quality H&H style sidelock. Discs.

	100%	98%	95%	90%	80%	70%	60%
	$13,250	$11,000	$9,750	$8,600	$7,400	$6,300	$5,450

This model was distributed by Euroarms of America, Inc.

CUSTOM SERIES — SxS, individual custom order only, every refinement is used in the construction of these extremely rare and expensive shotguns. The Volcano Extra Lusso shotgun is probably the most elaborate Antonio Zoli shotgun with the list price being $58,850. Also, the Tornado Extra begins at $45,000 with a mint 12 ga. currently bringing approx. $25,000.

COMBINATION GUNS

COMBINATO — 12 or 20 ga. over .243 or .222 cal., boxlock action, game scene engraved receiver with silver finish, double triggers, folding rear sight, skipline checkering, with sling swivels. Importation disc. 1993.

	100%	98%	95%	90%	80%	70%	60%
	$1,750	$1,500	$1,300	$1,100	$950	$775	$600

Last Mfg.'s Sug. Retail was $1,995.

▲ *Combinato Set* — includes one set of either 20 or 12 ga. barrels and an additional rifle/shotgun barrel set, same cals. as Combinato, cased. Importation disc. 1993.

	100%	98%	95%	90%	80%	70%	60%
	$2,400	$2,150	$1,850	$1,600	$1,400	$1,200	$995

Last Mfg.'s Sug. Retail was $2,700.

SAFARI DELUXE — similar to Combinato, except has sideplates with elaborate game scene engraving. Importation disc. 1993.

	100%	98%	95%	90%	80%	70%	60%
	$4,850	$4,400	$3,950	$3,550	$3,175	$2,800	$2,400

Last Mfg.'s Sug. Retail was $5,200.

Add approx. 50% for Safari Deluxe 2 (includes 2 sets of shotgun barrels).

EXPRESS E3 SET — includes one set of .30-06 O/U barrels, one set of 20 ga./.243 cal. barrels, one set of 20 ga./20 ga. barrels, special order, elaborate game scene engraving, includes German claw mount 4X scope and case. Disc.

	100%	98%	95%	90%	80%	70%	60%
	$2,750	$2,400	$2,100	$1,850	$1,650	$1,500	$1,375

Z

MODERN AIRGUNS

Dear Air Rifle Enthusiasts:

The air rifle industry appears to have a strong year going in 1996. Sales look promising, and most manufacturer's suggested retail prices stayed level or increased only at the rate of inflation.

Notable firms including Beeman, Diana and Crosman introduced a few new models oriented toward the medium priced market. Professional target models remained unchanged. Precharged pneumatic sales remain firm with several companies reporting considerable sales on certain models.

The Walther line, previously handled by InterArms in Alexandria, VA is now represented by Champion's Choice, Inc. of LaVergne, TN. This change should better position Walther in the retail marketplace.

After years of marketing the Anschutz line of fine quality target guns, Precision Sales of Westfield, MA has ceased its representation of this manufacturer. In their place, Precision Sales is now representing the BSA line. Unfortunately this has left Anshutz without a current representative. It is, however, hard to believe a new one isn't just around the corner.

The real news in the airgun industry is the old B.B. Guns! Although not covered in this section, many of the old, inexpensive, youth oriented guns have suddenly caught the eye of the collecting public instead of the select group of collectors who have specialized in these types of guns over the years.

Whether it be motivated by nostalgia, or people thinking they have found an untapped collector's niche, the prices of many older collectibles have increased dramatically. Many of these guns are now trading for 100% - 200% more than in 1994. Even with this type of windfall, keep in mind that many of these guns originally traded for well under $100.

But if you have enough of them...?

Sincerely,

Patrick M. Luckiny

Air Rifle Editor
Blue Book of Gun Values

A NOTE ABOUT AIRGUN PRICING

The prices listed in this section are reasonable RETAIL prices which you would expect to pay from an average dealer. Airguns purchased from factory importers or dealers with test facilities or factory authorized repair centers will COMMAND HIGHER PRICES. If you are using the prices in this section for WHOLESALE buying, you should REDUCE PRICES A MINIMUM OF 20% or more.

You will note throughout this section that pricing goes down to 95% grading - like Black Powder. Due to the mechanical complexity of airguns, and the fact that most sophisticated airguns are used solely for target practice (many have had several thousand rounds through them), guns under 95% condition retain very little of their original value. Most collector guns (e.g. old Benjamins, Crosman and Daisy) trade for under $100 with only a few 100% guns trading for more. "N/A" pricing for guns of 98% or less condition in this section reflect newly released models.

Medium priced airguns from large distributors, such as Marksman, RWS, Norica and Gamo may be discounted enough to the Distributor/Dealer that many "new-in-the-box" guns can be purchased by the consumer for the price of a 98% gun. Also, the lack of available parts for older collectibles and non-functioning airguns contribute to a reduced value. It should also be noted that prices in this section have to cover a broad range of vendors.

BECAUSE OF SPACE CONSIDERATIONS, AIRGUNS UNDER $100 ARE NOT IN-CLUDED. AIRGUNS THAT ARE ENGRAVED OR HAVE FANCY WOOD SHOULD BE DISCOUNTED A MINIMUM OF 50% IF UNDER 95% CONDITION.

ARS/FARCO

Manufactured in the Philippines. Imported by Air Rifle Specialists located in Elmira, NY. Guns available both through dealers or directly from the importer.

Grading	100%	98%	95%

AIR RIFLES

AR6 MAGNUM (REPEATING 6 SHOT) — .22 CO_2 or compressed air powered, 23¼ in. barrel, capable of delivering 18 shots at 50 ft./lbs. power (1,000 FPS) using compressed air or up to 80 shots at 19-22 ft./lbs. power using CO_2 (single fill), checkered walnut stock, 6 lbs. 12 oz.

Mfg.'s Sug. Retail	$580	$510	$450	$360

Add $20 for extra 6 shot cylinder.
Add $50 for charging unit.

CAREER 707 — .22 cal., 6 shot (or sideloading single shot) lever action repeater precharged pneumatic. 23 in. barrel, 1000 FPS, checkered walnut stock, 7 ¾ lbs. New 1995.

Mfg.'s Sug. Retail	$580	$510	$450	$360

FARCO FP SURVIVAL AIR RIFLE — .22 or .25 cal., footpump action, 22¾ in. barrel, single shot, hardwood stock, 5 ¾ lbs.

Mfg.'s Sug. Retail	$295	$260	$220	$175

FARCO STAINLESS STEEL — .22 or .25 cal., CO_2, charged by refillable (and removable) 10 oz. cylinder, hardwood stock, approx. 7 lbs.

Mfg.'s Sug. Retail	$460	$390	$340	$270

KING HUNTING MASTER (REPEATING 5 SHOT) — .22 cal., CO_2 or compressed air powerized, similar to above.

Mfg.'s Sug. Retail	$580	$510	$450	$360

MAGNUM 6 (REPEATING 6 SHOT) — .22 cal., CO_2 or compressed air powerized, similar to above.

Mfg.'s Sug. Retail	$500	$470	$410	$330

M 900 — 9mm precharged pneumatic, 26¾ in. barrel, 900 FPS, side-lever action (for inserting pellets) shoots 92 grain pellet, wood stock.

Mfg.'s Sug. Retail	$1,000	$1,000	$800	$640

QB 77 — .177 or .22 cal., CO_2 powered, 21½ in. barrel, hardwood stock, 5 ½ lbs., single shot.

Mfg.'s Sug. Retail	$195	$75	$65	$50

Grading	100%	98%	95%

AIR SHOTGUNS

FARCO AIR SHOTGUN — 28 ga., CO_2 powered, 30 in. barrel, 100 ft/lbs. of energy (standard airgun has 12-14 lbs.), charged by refillable (and removable) 10 oz. cylinder, hardwood stock, 7 lbs. Importation began in 1988.

Mfg.'s Sug. Retail	$460	$400	$350	$280

    Add $20 for extra CO_2 cylinder.
    Add $1 for extra brass shells (12 included w/gun).

AIR ARMS

Currently Imported by Dynamit Nobel-RWS, Inc. located in Closter, NJ. Previously imported by Air Rifle Specialists located in Elmira, NY. Available both through dealers and directly from the importer.

Editors note: These guns are filled from high pressure scuba tanks allowing many shots to be fired from one charge. This also allows one to adjust the power level of each shot. All guns are made with Walther barrels that float so that expansion or contraction of the air chamber will not affect its accuracy. Add $150 for Olympic trigger, $200 for regulator, and $50 for lever bolt.

SM100 — .177 or .22 cal. precharged pneumatic, 22 in. barrel, power can range from 12 to 19 ft./lbs. in .177 or 12 to 22 ft./lbs. in .22 cal, two stage trigger (adjustable), beech stock, 8 lbs. 8 oz. Disc. 1994.

	$750	$620	$500

       Last Mfg.'s Sug. Retail was $975.

    Add $60 for left-hand.

XM100 — same as above but with quick release tank connector, and walnut stock, 8 lbs. Disc. 1994.

	$875	$750	$590

       Last Mfg.'s Sug. Retail was $1,260.

    Add $60 for left-hand.

TM100 — same as above but with adj. cheekpiece and shoulder pad, (target style stock), 8 lbs. 12 oz.

	$1,100	$930	$740

       Last Mfg.'s Sug. Retail was $1,650.

    Add $60 for left-hand.

TX200/TX200SR — .177 or .22 cal., under-lever action, 15¾ in. barrel, 913/800 FPS, 9 lbs. 3 oz.

Mfg.'s Sug. Retail	$560	$460	$400	$310

    Add $80 for walnut stock, $75 for left-hand, $75 for recoiless S.R. model.

NJR100 — same as above but with hand picked barrel for accuracy, adj. cheekpiece, forearm and shoulder pad, designed by and named after Nick Jenkinson (one of England's top field target shooters), 10 lbs. 12 oz.

	$1,425	$1,210	$1,000

       Last Mfg.'s Sug. Retail was $2,600.

    Add $60 for left-hand.

AIR LOGIC

Manufacturer/distributor located in Forest Row, Sussex, England. Available through dealers and used market.

AIR-GUNS

Grading	100%	98%	95%

Air Logic has limited importation into the U.S. More information can be obtained by contacting Air Logic directly at: Air Logic Limited, 3 Medway Bldgs., Lower Road Forest Row, East Sussex ENGLAND RH18 5HE.

GENESIS — .22 cal., single stroke pneumatic, 630 FPS, unique bolt action sliding barrel (by L. Walther), recoilless, adj. trigger, side lever action, 9½ lbs. New for 1988.

$575 $450 $360

Last Mfg.'s Sug. Retail was $750.

AIR MATCH

Previously imported by Kendall International located in Paris, KY. No longer imported, used guns only.

AIR MATCH MODEL 600 PISTOL — .177 cal., side-lever action, adj. trigger, professional target model, 2 lbs.

$375 $280 $200

AMERICAN ARMS, INC.

Manufacturer/importer located in North Kansas City, MO.

Even though American Arms, Inc. imports Norica airguns, they are listed in this section because of their private label status. Importation began in late 1988 and was discontinued in 1989.

RIFLES

JET RIFLE — .177 cal., barrel break action, 855 FPS, adj. double set triggers, hardwood stock, 7 lbs.

$100 $85 $70

Last Mfg.'s Sug. Retail was $160.

Deduct $35 for Junior Model.

COMMANDO — .177 cal., barrel break action, 540 FPS, adj. sights, 5 lbs.

$75 $60 $40

Last Mfg.'s Sug. Retail was $115.

PISTOLS

IDEAL — .177 cal., barrel break action, 400 FPS, adj. sights, 3 lbs.

$75 $60 $40

Last Mfg.'s Sug. Retail was $105.

ANSCHUTZ

Manufactured in Ulm, Germany. Available through dealers and some models through Marksman direct. Models 2001 and 2002 previously imported by Precision Sales Intl. Inc., PO Box 1776, Westfield, MA 01086.

Models 333, 335, and 380 were previously imported by Crosman from 1986-1988. Model 380 was also previously imported by Marksman.

MODEL 333 — .177 cal., barrel-cocking action, 700 FPS, adj. trigger, 18 in. barrel, 6¾ lbs.

$175 $120 $90

Last Mfg.'s Sug. Retail was $175.

MODEL 335 — .177 cal., barrel-cocking, 700 FPS, adj. trigger, 18½ in. barrel, 7½ lbs. Add $10 for 335 Mag. (20% higher velocity).

$175 $130 $95

Last Mfg.'s Sug. Retail was $200.

Grading	100%	98%	95%

MODEL 380 — .177 cal., under-lever cocking, 600-640 FPS, professional match model, removable cheekpiece, adj. trigger, stippled walnut grips. Add $30 for left-hand, $60 for moving target. Disc. 1994.

	$1,005	**$875**	**$575**

Last Mfg.'s Sug. Retail was $1,250.

MODEL 2001 — .177 cal., single stroke pneumatic, side-lever action, exceptional target model, 10 lbs. 8 oz. Add $80 for left-hand.

	$1,250	**$920**	**$815**

Add $80 for Running Target Model.

Last Mfg.'s Sug. Retail was $1,800.

MODEL 2002 — .177 cal. single stroke pneumatic, side-lever action, 26 in. barrel, this gun incorporates some of the latest technology used in air rifles, 10½ lbs. New 1992. Add $60 for left-hand.

	$1,400	**$1,300**	**$1,050**

Add $20 for running target, $50 for laminated stock (colored).
Subtract $60 for non-walnut (blond) stock.

Last Mfg.'s Sug. Retail was $2,108.

B S A GUNS (U.K.), LTD.

Manufactured in Birmingham, England. Previously imported by Dynamit-Nobel RWS of Closter, NJ. Now imported by Precision Sales, Westfield, MA. Available both dealer and importer direct.

Add $100 for guns equipped with Theoben gas spring.

AIRSPORTER/AIRSPORTER SUPER: — .177, .22 or .25 cal., under-lever action, 1020-550 FPS/825-675 FPS, (Super), 8 lbs. Add $50 for Super, $25 for Monte Carlo stock Stutzen Model, $20 for Carbine.

Mfg.'s Sug. Retail	$375	$200	$170	$130

CENTENNIAL COMMEMORATIVE — .177 or .22 cal., designed to commemorate BSA's 100th year.

	$255	$205	$140

Last Mfg.'s Sug. Retail was $650.

GOLDSTAR — .177 or .22 cal., under-lever action, 1020 FPS, 800/625 FPS 18½ in. barrel, two-stage adjustable trigger, hardwood stock has 10 shot rotary magazine (developed from the VS2000), 8½ lbs.

Mfg.'s Sug. Retail	$690	$550	$475	$365

MERCURY/MERCURY SUPER — .177 or .22 cal., barrel-cocking action, 700-550 FPS/825-600 FPS (super), 7¼ lbs. Add $35 for Super.

	$150	$110	$80

MERCURY CHALLENGER — .177 or .22 cal., barrel-cocking action, 850-625 FPS, 7 lbs. 4 oz. Disc. 1988.

	$155	$115	$85

Last Mfg.'s Sug. Retail was $205.

METEOR/METEOR SUPER — .177 or .22 cal., barrel-cocking action, 650-500 FPS, 18½ in. barrel, 6 lbs. Add $15 for Super.

	$75	$60	$45

AIR-GUNS

Grading	100%	98%	95%

SUPER SPORT/SUPER SPORT CUSTOM/SUPERSPORT CARBINE — .177, .22 or .25 cal., barrel-cocking action, (850/625/530 FPS), 18½ in. barrel approx. 7 lbs. Add $115 for custom model, $120 for guns equipped with Theoben gas ram (spring). Add $25 for Carbine Model.

Mfg.'s Sug. Retail	$250	$210	$185	$160

SUPERSTAR/SUPERSTAR CARBINE — .177, .22, or .25 cal., under-lever action, (1020-850/800-625/675- 530 FPS), 18½ in. barrel, unique rotating breech for loading pellets directly into bore, checkered beech stock, maxi grip scope rail, two stage trigger, approx. 7¾ lbs. Prices equal for Carbine Model.

Mfg.'s Sug. Retail	$470	$375	$325	$260

Add $120 for guns equipped with Theoben gas ram (spring).

STUTZEN — same as above with shorter overall length (39 in.) (14 in. barrel) and Stutzen full length stock, 7 lbs. 4 oz.

Mfg.'s Sug. Retail	$540	$425	$360	$280

VS 2000 — .177 or .22 cal., 9 shot repeater, side-lever action, 850-625 FPS, 9 lbs. Add $65 for custom model. Disc. 1988.

	$450	$325	$230

Only 20 or so of this model ever made.

Last Mfg.'s Sug. Retail was $330.

PISTOLS

240 MAGNUM PISTOL — .177 or .22 cal., single stroke cocking system, 510/420 FPS, 6 in. barrel, two stage trigger, adjustable rear sight and integral scope rail, wt. 2 lbs.

Mfg.'s Sug. Retail	$235	$195	N/A	N/A

SCORPION PISTOL — .177 or .22 cal., barrel-cocking action 510-380 FPS, 3 lbs. 6 oz. Add $50 for carbine stock, Shadow Model.

	$170	$145	$90

Last Mfg.'s Sug. Retail was $190.

B.S.F. (BAYERISCHE SPORTWAFFENFABRIK)

Manufactured in Germany. Previously imported by Kendell International located in Paris, KY and Beeman Precision Arms under the Wischo label. Available only on the used market.

B.S.F. tooling and machinery have been purchased by Weihrauch and are being utilized to manufacture older versions of B.S.F. Models for Marksman (Marksman Models 28, 40, 55, 56, 58, 59, 70, 71, 72 and 75), and some models for Beeman.

RIFLES

BAVARIA MODEL 35 — .177 cal., barrel-cocking action, 500 FPS, 4½ lbs.

	$150	$120	$100

Last Mfg.'s Sug. Retail was $125.

BAVARIA MODEL 45 — .177 cal., barrel-cocking action, 700 FPS, 6 lbs.

	$165	$125	$105

Last Mfg.'s Sug. Retail was $125.

BAVARIA MODEL 50 — .177 cal., barrel-cocking action, 700 FPS, 6 lbs.

	$175	$130	$110

BAVARIA MODEL S54 — .177 or .22 cal., under-lever action, 685/500 FPS, 8 lbs. Add $15 for Sport Model (discontinued 1986), $30 for M Model.

	$235	$175	$110

AIR-GUNS

Grading	100%	98%	95%

BAVARIA MODEL 55 — .177 or .22 cal., barrel-cocking action, 800/570 FPS, 6½ lbs. Add $15 for Deluxe Model, $30 for Special Model (both discontinued 1986).

	$180	$140	$105

BAVARIA MODEL S60 — .177 or .22 cal., barrel-cocking action, 800/570 FPS, 6½ lbs.

	$180	$150	$110

BAVARIA MODEL S70 — .177 or .22 cal., barrel-cocking action, 800/570 FPS, 7 lbs.

	$185	$155	$110

BAVARIA MODEL S80 — .177 or .22 cal., barrel-cocking action, 800/570 FPS, 8¼ lbs.

	$210	$165	$135

Last Mfg.'s Sug. Retail was $185.

BEEMAN PRECISION AIRGUNS

Importers and distributors located in Huntington Beach, CA. Beeman has exclusive rights to any items marketed in the U.S. under the names Beeman, Feinwerkbau, Webley, and Weihrauch.

Beeman imported Feinwerkbau and Weihrauch Airguns will appear under their respective headings in this section. Webley airguns are incorporated into this section. Available through dealers and Beeman direct.

RIFLES

BEEMAN R1/R1 SUPER MAGNUM—.177, .20, .22 or .25 cal., barrel-cocking action, 1000-610 FPS, 8lbs. 8 oz. Add $300 for custom grade, $335 for custom fancy, $400 for X fancy, $60 for left-hand.

Mfg.'s Sug. Retail	$525	$400	$350	$275

Add $450 for Laser Model.
Add $160 for Field Target or Tyrolean Model.
Add $35 for blue/stainless steel version.
Add $150 for Tyrolean stock.
Add $95 for commemorative model.
Add $100 for AW Model with chrome finish and synthetic stock, available .20 cal. carbine only.
Chrome and gold plated variations of the R1 with RDB prefix serialization may exceed retail 50%-100% depending on region.

BEEMAN R6 — .177 cal., barrel cocking action, 815 FPS, two stage trigger, auto safety, beech stock, 7.1 lbs.

Mfg.'s Sug. Retail	$325	$270	N/A	N/A

BEEMAN R7 — .177, .20 cal., barrel-cocking action, 700 - 620 FPS, two stage adjustable trigger, beech stock, automatic safety, 6 lbs. 1 oz.

Mfg.'s Sug. Retail	$325	$270	$230	$185

BEEMAN R8 — .177 cal., barrel-cocking action, 720 FPS, two stage adjustable trigger, beech stock, automatic safety, 7 lbs. 2 oz.

Mfg.'s Sug. Retail	$380	$300	$260	$200

BEEMAN R9 — .177 or .20 cal., barrel cocking action, 1000/800 FPS, adjustable trigger, auto safety, beech stock, 7.3 lbs.

Mfg.'s Sug. Retail	$335	$265	N/A	N/A

Grading	100%	98%	95%

BEEMAN R10 — .177, .20, or .22 cal., barrel-cocking action, 1,000- 750 FPS, 7lbs 9 oz. Add $300 for custom grade, $335 for custom fancy, $400 for X fancy, $50 for left-hand, and $50 for deluxe.

Mfg.'s Sug. Retail	$400	$300	$250	$205

Add $400 for Laser Model.

BEEMAN R11 — .177 cal., barrel-cocking action, 925 FPS, 19⅝ barrel with sleeve, adj. cheekpiece and trigger, 8¾ lbs. New 1994.

Mfg.'s Sug. Retail	$530	$410	$350	$275

BEEMAN RX — .177, .20, .22, and .25 cal., Theoben gas spring, spring piston system (See Theoben), up to 1200 FPS/.177 cal., adj. velocity, (release delayed until summer 1991). Add $10 for .20 and .25 cal., $140 for Field Target, and $60 for left-hand. Add $125 for commemorative model. Disc. 1992.

	$350	$300	$220

Last Mfg.'s Sug. Retail was $470.

BEEMAN RX-1 — improved version of Model RX above.

Mfg.'s Sug. Retail	$575	$465	$400	$310

Add $45 for left-hand.
Add $85 for commemorative model.

BEEMAN S-1 — .177 cal., barrel cocking action, 900 FPS, two stage adjustable trigger, auto safety, beech stock, 7.1 lbs. (Manufactured for Beeman by Gamo).

Mfg.'s Sug. Retail	$210	$170	N/A	N/A

BEEMAN AIR WOLF — .177, .20, .22 and .25 cal. precharged pneumatic, 21 in. barrel, internal air chamber, manual safety, 5⅝ lbs. New in 1992. Disc. 1994.

	$575	$500	$400

Add $75 for charging adapter w/gauge - only 10-20 guns were ever imported.

Last Mfg.'s Sug. Retail was $680.

BEEMAN BEARCUB — .177 cal., barrel cocking action, 915 FPS, 13 in. barrel (approximately), single stage adjustable trigger, manual safety, beech stock, 7.2 lbs.

Mfg.'s Sug. Retail	$310	$245	N/A	N/A

BEEMAN CARBINE C1 — .177 or .22 cal., barrel-cocking action, 830-670 FPS, 6 lbs. 2 oz.- 6lbs 3 oz.

Mfg.'s Sug. Retail	$290	$210	$175	$140

BEEMAN CLASSIC MAGNUM — .177, .20, .22 and .25 cal., gas spring, barrel-cocking action, 15 in. barrel, manual button safety, checkered walnut stock, 8⅝ lbs. Mfg. 1992-93.

	$800	$700	$560

Add $80 for power adjustment pump.

Last Mfg.'s Sug. Retail was $895.

BEEMAN CROW MAGNUM II — .20, .22, and .25 cal., gas spring, barrel-cocking action, 32 ft./lbs., 16 in. barrel, manual button safety, Dampamount scope mounts included, 8¼ lbs. New 1993.

Mfg.'s Sug. Retail	$1,220	$1,155	$970	$780

Add $80 for power adjustment pump.

BEEMAN FALCON 1 & 2 — .177 cal., barrel-cocking action, 620-680 FPS/560-600 FPS, 5.9/6.7 lbs. Add $30 for Falcon 2. Disc. in 1984.

	$120	$90	$65

Last Mfg.'s Sug. Retail was $110.

Grading	100%	98%	95%

BEEMAN FX 1 & 2 — same as Beeman Falcon 1 & 2. Add $30 for FX 1. Disc. 1992.

| | **$125** | **$100** | **$85** |

Last Mfg.'s Sug. Retail was $140.

BEEMAN GAME KEEPER— .25 cal., precharged pneumatic, quick change gas cylinder (bottle), 15 in. barrel, manual lever safety, 7⅞-8¼ lbs. Only 5 imported domestically 1992-93.

| | **N/A** | **N/A** | **N/A** |

Model rarity precludes accurate price evaluation.

Last Mfg.'s Sug. Retail was $990.

BEEMAN/HARPER AIR CANE — .22 or .25 cal., pneumatic (reuseable gas cartridge), 650 FPS, reproduction of 19th century Walking Cane Gun, 1 lb. Add $60 for decorative head piece.

| | **$650** | **$540** | **$425** |

Only 50 of these models were ever imported into the U.S.

Last Mfg.'s Sug. Retail was $595.

BEEMAN MAKO — .177 cal., precharged pneumatic, 930 F.P.S., bolt action loading system, checkered beech stock, adjustable trigger, manual safety, 7 lbs. 5 oz. New 1995.

| **Mfg.'s Sug. Retail** | **$875** | **$725** | **$640** | **$520** |

Add $275 for FT Model with checkered thumbhole stock.

BEEMAN MANITOU FT — .177 cal. precharged pneumatic, internal air chamber, 21 in. barrel, 8¾ lbs. New 1992. Disc. 1994.

| | **$925** | **$840** | **$650** |

Add $100 for left-hand.
Add $75 for charge adapter with gauge.
Only 10-20 guns were ever imported.

Last Mfg.'s Sug. Retail was $995.

BEEMAN SUPER 7 — .22 or .25 (new 1994) cal., precharged pneumatic, 7 shot magazine, quick change gas cylinder (bottle), 19 in. barrel, 40 ft./lbs. in .25 cal., checkered walnut stock, manual button safety, 7¼ lbs. New 1992. .25 cal., disc. 1995.

| | **$1,430** | **$1,200** | **$950** |

Last Mfg.'s Sug. Retail was $1,575.

BEEMAN SUPER 12 — .25 cal., precharged pneumatic, 12 shot mag., 850 F.P.S., quick change gas cylinder (bottle), 40 ft./lbs. energy, checkered walnut stock, manual button safety. New 1995.

| **Mfg.'s Sug. Retail** | **$1,675** | **$1,550** | **$1,323** | **$1,000** |

BEEMAN UL-7 — .22 cal., under-lever action, gas spring, 12 in. barrel, manual button safety, 7 shot repeater with removable rotary magazine, checkered walnut stock, approx. 10 were imported 1992-93.

| | **$1,325** | **$1,120** | **$840** |

Add $80 for power adjustment pump.

Last Mfg.'s Sug. Retail was $1,560.

BEEMAN/WEBLEY OMEGA — .177 or .22 cal., barrel-cocking action, 830-675 FPS, 7lbs 8 oz. Disc. 1992.

| | **$240** | **$200** | **$160** |

Last Mfg.'s Sug. Retail was $430.

BEEMAN/WEBLEY ECLIPSE—.177, .22 or .25 cal., under-lever action, 990 FPS (in .177 cal.). New 1990.

| **Mfg.'s Sug. Retail** | **$510** | **$360** | **$300** | **$240** |

AIR-GUNS

Grading	100%	98%	95%

BEEMAN/WEBLEY KODIAK SUPER MAGNUM — .177, .22, or .25 cal., barrel-cocking action, 820 FPS/28-30 ft./lbs. (.25 cal.), 17½ in. barrel, 8.9 lbs. New 1993.

Mfg.'s Sug. Retail	$595	$500	$430	$350

BEEMAN/WEBLEY VULCAN III AND VULCAN III DELUXE — .177 or .22 cal., barrel-cocking action, 830-675 FPS, 7.6-7.7 lbs. Add $60 for Deluxe.

Mfg.'s Sug. Retail	$300	$210	$175	$140

BEEMAN WOLF PUP — .20, .22, and .25 precharged pneumatic, internal cylinder, 13½ in. barrel, manual safety. Disc. 1994.

		$575	$500	$400

Add $20 for .20 cal.
Add $75 for charging adaptor w/gauge.
Add $180 for Deluxe Model with thumbhole stock and match trigger.
Only 10-20 guns were ever imported.

Last Mfg.'s Sug. Retail was $680.

PISTOLS

BEEMAN ADDER — .20 and .25 cal. precharged pneumatic, internal air chamber, 7 in. barrel, manual safety, 2¾ lbs. New 1992. Disc. 1994.

$420	$365	$280

Only 10-20 guns were ever imported.

Last Mfg.'s Sug. Retail was $530.

BEEMAN/FAS 604 — .177 cal., top lever spring pneumatic action, 380 FPS, 2 lbs. 3 oz. Add $30 for left-hand. Disc. 1988.

$395	$340	$240

Last Mfg.'s Sug. Retail was $495.

BEEMAN/HARPER CLASSIC PISTOL — .22 or .25 cal., similar to Harper Air Cane rifle action, 300 FPS, 4 oz. Add $10 for .25 cal., $35 for deluxe. Disc. 1989.

$420	$350	$255

Add $210 if cased.
Only 6 ever imported into U.S.

Last Mfg.'s Sug. Retail was $285.
Last Retail for a cased pair was $700.

BEEMAN/HARPER PEPPERBOX PISTOL — .22 cal., pneumatic (like above), 9.8 oz. Disc. 1989.

$840	$700	$480

Only 3 of this model imported into U.S.

Last Mfg.'s Sug. Retail was $575.

BEEMAN P1 — .177, .20 or .22 cal. Mag., top cocking action, 600-350 FPS, dual power, walnut grips, Colt .45 look alike.

Mfg.'s Sug. Retail	$405	$300	$260	$200

Add $295 for gold plating.
Add $35 for stainless steel style or blue/stainless dual finish.
Add $100 for Commemorative Model (mfg. 1992 only).

BEEMAN P2 — .177 and .20 cal., single stroke pneumatic, similar to above but professional mid-priced match gun. New 1991.

Mfg.'s Sug. Retail	$435	$340	$300	$240

Add $25 for match grips.

Grading	100%	98%	95%

BEEMAN/WEBLEY HURRICANE — .177 or .22 cal., barrel-cocking action, 470-400 FPS, 2 lbs. 4 oz. Add $40 for M20 scope combo.

Mfg.'s Sug. Retail	$225	$190	$160	$125

BEEMAN/WEBLEY NEMESIS — .177 cal., single stroke pneumatic, 385 F.P.S. adjustable sight (rear) manual safety, 2 lbs. 3 oz.

Mfg.'s Sug. Retail	$190	$160	$130	$110

BEEMAN/WEBLEY TEMPEST — .177 or .22 cal., barrel-cocking action, 470-400 FPS, 2 lbs.

Mfg.'s Sug. Retail	$200	$165	$140	$105

BEEMAN WOLVERINE — .177, .20, .22, and .25 cal. precharged pneumatic, internal air chamber, 10½ in. barrel, manual safety, 3 lbs. Disc. 1994.

	$580	$510	$400

Only 10-20 gns were ever imported.

Last Mfg.'s Sug. Retail was $700.

BENJAMIN AIR RIFLE COMPANY

Manufacturer located in Racine, WI. Available both through dealers and factory direct. Purchased January 1992 by Crosman Air Guns located in E. Bloomfield, NY.

RIFLES

CENTENNIAL MODEL 87 — .177 or .22 cal., multi-stroke pneumatic, 750/650 FPS, polished brass barrel, all nickel trim, Williams aperture, built to commemorate the 100th anniversary, bronze medallion in stock, 6 lbs., 6,086 mfg.

	$205	$105	$70

Last Mfg.'s Sug. Retail was $250.

BENJAMIN MODEL 340, 342, AND 347 — BB, .177 or .22 cal., pneumatic pump action, 750-650 FPS, 4½ lbs., (340-BB), (342-.22), (347-.177). Add $15 for Williams sight, $30 for 4 x 15 scope.

	$90	$70	$55

Last Mfg.'s Sug. Retail was $110.

PISTOLS

BENJAMIN AIR PISTOL MODEL 130, 132, AND 137 — .177 cal., pneumatic pump action, 380 FPS, 2 lbs.

	$70	$50	$35

Last Mfg.'s Sug. Retail was $85.

BENJAMIN AIR PISTOL MODEL 242, 247 — .177 and .22 cal., pneumatic pump action, 418/315 FPS, 2 lbs. 8 oz.

	$75	$65	$50

Last Mfg.'s Sug. Retail was $90.

BENJAMIN SHERIDAN

E. Bloomfield, NY.

In 1994 thru 1995 after their purchase by Crosman air guns (some of) the separate lines of the Benjamin and Sheridan air gun companies were merged into one.

AIR-GUNS

Grading	100%	98%	95%

RIFLES

BENJAMIN SHERIDAN MODEL 392/397 — .177 and .22 cal. (392), CO_2 or pneumatic pump action, 685-800 FPS, $19\frac{3}{8}$ in. barrel, available in chrome or black matte finish, walnut stock, 5 lbs. 8 oz. New 1991.

No. Mfg.'s Retail	$115	$100	$80

    Add $5 for chrome.
    Add $25 for Williams peepsight.
    Subtract $10 for CO_2 (600-500 FPS). Denoted with "G"prefix, or"FB9"prefix on .20 cal.

▲ *Benjamin Model Carbine* — similar to above, except has shorter carbine barrel, new 1994.

No Mfg.'s Retail	$110	$95	$80

PISTOLS

BENJAMIN/SHERIDAN MODEL H/HB—.177, .20, and .22 cal., pneumatic pump action, 400 FPS, $9\frac{3}{8}$ in. barrel, available in chrome (H) or black matte finish (HB), walnut grips, 2 lbs. 8 oz. New in 1991. Add $5 for chrome.

No Mfg.'s Retail	$100	$85	$70

    Model E/EB is CO_2 version of above. Deduct $10 for CO_2.

BRNO AERON

Manufactured in Czechoslovakia and imported by Century International Arms, Inc. located in St. Albans, VT and Bohemia Arms, Fountain Valley, CA. Available through dealers.

RIFLES

TAU-200 — .177 cal., CO_2 powered professional target model, synthetic adj. stock.

No Mfg.'s Retail	$250	$200	$160

PISTOLS

TAU FREE PISTOL — .177 cal., CO_2 powered professional target model, attache case, extra seals and counter weight.

No Mfg.'s Retail	$295	$250	$200

CROSMAN AIR GUNS

East Bloomfield, NY.

Other than the continued sale of the Model 84 and Skanaker, Crosman has dropped adult precision Airguns. The Crosman/Anschutz models listed below should be watched for collectors value due to their limited U.S. distribution using Crosman model numbers. Available both through dealers and factory direct.

MODEL 84 AIR RIFLE — .177 cal., CO_2 powered, match rifle, 0-720 FPS (fully adj.), adj. sights, walnut stock with adj. cheekpiece and buttplate, 11 lbs. Disc. 1992.

	$800	$450	$360

    Crosman Model 84 was the first U.S. made air rifle designed to compete with established European models. Unlike its competitors, it is CO_2 powered with a digital gauge mounted on the forearm to show remaining pressure.

Last Mfg.'s Sug. Retail was $1,295.

6500 (ANSCHUTZ MODEL 335) — .177 cal., barrel break action, 700 FPS, $18\frac{1}{2}$ in. barrel, 7 lbs. $10\frac{1}{2}$ oz. Disc. in 1989.

	$175	$130	$95

Last Mfg.'s Sug. Retail was $200.

Grading	100%	98%	95%

6300 (ANSCHUTZ MODEL 333) — .177 cal., barrel break action, 700 FPS, 18½ in. barrel, 6 lbs. 13 oz. Disc. in 1989.

| | $175 | $120 | $90 |

Last Mfg.'s Sug. Retail was $175.

MODEL 6100 (MADE BY DIANAWERK) — .177 cal., barrel break action, 780/830 FPS, 20½ in. barrel, 8 lbs. 6 oz. Disc. in 1989.

| | $160 | $120 | $90 |

Last Mfg.'s Sug. Retail was $235.

PISTOLS

SKANAKER PISTOL MODEL 88 — .177 cal., CO_2 powered, 550 FPS, professional target model. New 1987.

| | $450 | $360 | $310 |

Add $65 for carrying case.

As of Dec. 31, 1991 Crosman liquidated its supply of Skanaker pistols. This was due to the expiration of a contract allowing them to use the Skanaker name. All remaining pistols were sold to Air Rifle Specialists, Elmira, NY.

Last Mfg.'s Sug. Retail was $795.

C Z

Manufacturer located in Czechoslovakia. Currently imported by Compasseco, Inc., Bradstown, KY.

RIFLES

CZ-77 (SALIVIA 630) — .177 cal., barrel-cocking action, 700 FPS, 21 in. barrel, adjustable sights, wood stock.

| Mfg.'s Sug. Retail | $150 | | $80 | $60 | $40 |

Add $20 for checkered stock on Lux or plastic stock on Lux B (Salivia 631).

CZ-BB — .177/BB cal., bolt action, military training gun, mfg. circa 1947 for Czech Army. New in box, collectors item.

| Mfg.'s Sug. Retail | $235 | | $120 | N/A | N/A |

PISTOLS

CZ-3 (TEX 3) — .177 cal., barrel-cocking action, 400 FPS, 7½ in. barrel. Adjustable sights, plastic stock.

| Mfg.'s Sug. Retail | $150 | | $80 | $60 | $40 |

DAISY MANUFACTURING CO., INC.

Manufactured and distributed in Rogers, AR.

Even though Daisy is one of the largest airgun manufacturers in the world, only 6 weapons fall into the category of adult precision airguns - these are the Daisy 126 El Gamo, Model 128 Gamo Olympic, Model 953, Model 753, and their 2 target pistols (Models 747 and 777). The Daisy 126 El Gamo rifle and Model 128 Gamo Olympic are manufactured in Spain and assembled in the U.S. All 6 airguns have barrels made by Lothar Walther. Available through dealers only.

Grading	100%	98%	95%

RIFLES

EL GAMO 126 SUPER MATCH TARGET RIFLE — .177 cal., single stroke pneumatic, 590 FPS, adj. sights, hardwood stock, 10 lbs. 9 oz. Disc. 1994.

	$470	$400	$300

Last Mfg.'s Sug. Retail was $765.

MODEL 128 GAMO OLYMPIC — same as above except with adj. cheekpiece and buttplate, high quality European diopter sight.

	$440	$375	$300

Last Mfg.'s Sug. Retail was $735.

MODEL 130 — .177 cal., barrel-cocking action, 800 FPS, adjustable micrometer sight, $5\frac{3}{4}$ lbs. Disc. 1993.

	$100	$80	$65

Last Mfg.'s Sug. Retail was $150.

MODEL 131 — .177 cal., barrel-cocking action, 630 FPS, adjustable micrometer sight 5 lbs. 6 oz.
No Mfg.'s Retail $90 $70 $55

MODEL 753 COMPETITION — .177 cal., single stroke pneumatic, 480 FPS, competition sights, 6 lbs. 8 oz.
No Mfg.'s Retail $245 $200 $145

MODEL 853 TARGET — .177 cal., single stroke pneumatic, 480 FPS, Lothar Walther barrel, adj. sights, 5 lbs. 8 oz.
No Mfg.'s Retail $140 $125 $100

MODEL 853C TARGET — .177 cal., similar to Model 853 Target, except has 5 shot mag.
No Mfg.'s Retail $185 $150 $120

MODEL 1170 — .177 cal., barrel-cocking action, 800 FPS, adjustable micrometer sight, $5\frac{1}{2}$ lbs.
No Mfg.'s Retail $100 $80 $65

PISTOLS

MODEL 747 TARGET PISTOL — .177 cal., side-lever action, single stroke pneumatic, 360 FPS, 3 lbs. 3 oz.
No Mfg.'s Retail $100 $85 $65

MODEL 777 TARGET PISTOL — .177 cal., side-lever action, single stroke pneumatic, 360 FPS, wood target style grips, 3 lbs. 3 oz.
No. Mfg.'s Retail $200 $165 $125

MODEL 91 — .177 cal., CO_2 powered, 425 FPS, $10\frac{1}{4}$ in. barrel, imported from Hungary, 2 lbs. 7 oz. New Spring 1991.
No Mfg.'s Retail $400 $350 $270

This is being imported by Daisy as an entry level professional target pistol, similar in design to Feinwerkbau or Crosman's Skanaker pistol.

DIANAWERK, MAYER AND GRAMMELSPACHER

Manufacturer located in Germany.

Dynamit Nobel RWS Inc. is the exclusive Dianawerk importer located in Closter, NJ. Available both from dealer and importer direct. Dynamit Nobel RWS, Inc. is also importing airguns manufactured by Air Arms, BSA, and Gamo. Please refer to their respective listings under this section for pricing.

AIR-GUNS

Grading	100%	98%	95%

RIFLES

MODEL 24 — .177 or .22 cal., barrel-cocking action, 700/400 FPS, 17¼ in. barrel, 6 lbs. Deduct $25 for Model 24J. New in 1987.

Mfg.'s Sug. Retail	$205	$140	$120	$90

MODEL 25D — .177 or .22 cal., barrel-cocking action, 525/380 FPS, 15¾ in. barrel, 5¾ lbs. (sport). Disc. in 1987.

	$115	$90	$65

Last Mfg.'s Sug. Retail was $120.

MODEL 26 — .177 or .22 cal., barrel-cocking action, 750/500 FPS, 17¼ in. barrel, 6 lbs. 1 oz. Disc. 1992.

	$175	$140	$90

Last Mfg.'s Sug. Retail was $195.

MODEL 27 — .177 or .22 cal., barrel-cocking action, 550/415 FPS, 17¼ in. barrel, 6 lbs. (sport). Disc. in 1987.

	$165	$120	$100

Last Mfg.'s Sug. Retail was $150.

MODEL 28 — .177 or .22 cal., barrel-cocking action, 750/500 FPS, 15¾ in. barrel, 6 lbs. 12 oz. Disc. 1992.

	$150	$125	$100

Last Mfg.'s Sug. Retail was $205.

MODEL 30 — 4.4mm (RWS #7) round ball, original European gallery gun action, 17 in. barrel, 7¼ lbs. New 1993, limited production piece.

Mfg.'s Sug. Retail	$1,025	$650	$550	$435

MODEL 34 — .177 or .22 cal., barrel-cocking action, 950/700 FPS, 19½ in. barrel, 7 lbs. 6 oz. Add $10 for 100 year Diana Commemorative Model (new in 1990), $40 for matte nickel finish, $135 for matte black finish and 4x32 airgun scope.

Mfg.'s Sug. Retail	$285	$160	$130	$95

MODEL 35 — .177 or .22 cal., barrel-cocking action, 665/540 FPS, 19 in. barrel, 8 lbs. (sport/target). Disc. in 1987.

	$130	$110	$75

Last Mfg.'s Sug. Retail was $160.

MODEL 36 AND 36 CARBINE — .177 or .22 cal., barrel cocking action, 1000/700 FPS, 19½ in. barrel, 8 lbs. Add $40 for new S Model w/scope, deduct $10 for muzzle brake model without factory sights.

Mfg.'s Sug. Retail	$415	$235	$170	$105

MODEL 38 — .177 or .22 cal., barrel break action, 1000/700 FPS, 19½ in. barrel, 8 lbs., walnut stock.

	$260	$185	$130

Model 38 is the deluxe version of the Model 36 listed above.

Last Mfg.'s Sug. Retail was $345.

MODEL 45 S/45 DELUXE — .177 or .22 cal., barrel-cocking action, 900/650 FPS, 20½ in. barrel, 7 lbs. 9 oz., S Model equipped w/factory sling and scope. Add $40 for deluxe, $70 for S model with scope.

Mfg.'s Sug. Retail	$330	$185	$165	$110

AIR-GUNS

Grading	100%	98%	95%

MODEL 48 — .177, .22 or .25 (new 1994) cal., side-lever action, 1,100/780 FPS, 17 in. barrel, 8½ lbs.

Mfg.'s Sug. Retail	$485	$265	$225	$155

Add $30 for .25 cal., add $30 for black matte finish (48B). New 1995.

MODEL 50T/T01 — .177, .22, or .25 cal., under-lever action, 745/600 FPS, 18½ in. barrel, 8 lbs., (sport/target), parkerized finish. Add $20 for blue finish, $100 for T01 Model. Disc. 1988.

	$250	$200	$155

Last Mfg.'s Sug. Retail was $210.

MODEL 52 — .177 or .25 cal., side-lever action, 1,100/780 FPS, 17 in. barrel, 8½ lbs.

Mfg.'s Sug. Retail	$535	$285	$255	$200

Add $160 for Deluxe version with handcrafted hardwood stock.

MODEL 54 — .177 or .22 cal., side-lever "recoilless" action, 1100/900 FPS, 17 in. barrel, 9 lbs.

Mfg.'s Sug. Retail	$750	$380	$340	$270

MODEL 70 — .177 cal., barrel-cocking action, 450 FPS, 13½ in. barrel. This is a junior sized adult air rifle.

	$130	$105	$85

Last Mfg.'s Sug. Retail was $190.

MODEL 72 — .177 cal., same as above but with recoilless action. Disc. 1994.

	$195	$155	$125

Last Mfg.'s Sug. Retail was $340.

MODEL 75, 75 HV, 75U, 75K, 75S — .177 cal., side-lever action, 580 FPS, 19 in. barrel (professional target), 11 lbs. Add $60 for left-hand, $165 for U, $100 for K, $90 for 75S with adj. cheek piece and micrometer sight. Model 75 HV and Model 75 U were disc. in 1989. Model K disc. 1990.

Mfg.'s Sug. Retail	$1,560	$810	$650	$450

MODEL 100 — .177 cal., single stroke pneumatic, 580 FPS, 19 in. barrel, adj. cheekpiece, professional target model, 11 lbs. New in 1989.

Mfg.'s Sug. Retail	$1,500	$950	$750	$600

MODEL CA 100 — .177 cal., precharged pneumatic, 22 in. barrel, diopter sight, match trigger, adjustable laminated stock, 11 lbs. 6 oz. Professional target model.

Mfg.'s Sug. Retail	$2,100	$1,570	$1,410	$1,130

Add $50 for left-hand.

MODEL 1000 — .177 cal., barrel-break action, unique colored plastic stocks (black, red, blue, white, and yellow). Disc. 1991.

	$160	$135	$100

Last Mfg.'s Sug. Retail was $215.

Model 1000 is the sport model of the standard Model 34.

PISTOLS

MODEL 5G/GS — .177 or .22 cal., barrel-cocking action, 450/300 FPS, 7 in. barrel, (sport) 2 lbs. 12 oz. GS Model equipped w/factory scope. Add $70 for GS, $10 for GN with matte nickel plating.

Mfg.'s Sug. Retail	$260	$155	$115	$85

MODEL 6G/6M/6GS — .177 cal., barrel-cocking action, 450 FPS , 7 in. barrel, (professional target), 3 lbs. GS Model equipped with factory scope. Add $70 for GS model, $30 for left-hand.

Grading		100%	98%	95%
▲ 6G				
Mfg.'s Sug. Retail	$450	$235	$210	$160
▲ 6M				
Mfg.'s Sug. Retail	$585	$300	$270	$200

MODEL 10 — .177 cal., barrel-cocking action, 450 FPS, 7 in. barrel, (professional target) 3 lbs. 4 oz. Add $50 for cased model, $40 for left-hand.

		$390	$310	$260

Last Mfg.'s Sug. Retail was $670.

ENSIGN ARMS CO., LTD.

Previous international distributors for Saxby Palmer Airguns located in Newbury, England. Available only on the used market.

Ensign Arms previously distributed the Saxby Palmer line of airguns into the U.S. Please refer to the Saxby Palmer section for these guns. "Ensign" designated models were trade - marked by Ensign Arms Co., Ltd. Marksman Products was the importer until 1988 located in Huntington Beach, CA.

F.A.S.

Previously imported by Beeman until 1988. Currently distributed by Nygord Products, located in Prescott, AZ. Manufactured in Italy. Available through dealers and importer direct.

FAS 604 — .177 cal., top lever single stroke, pneumatic action,

Mfg.'s Sug. Retail	$495	$430	$370	$270

FAS 606 — .177 cal., top lever single stroke, pneumatic action, 7½ in. barrel, professional target model, walnut grips, 2 lbs. 3 oz. Disc. 1994.

	$625	$510	$410

Last Mfg.'s Sug. Retail was $995.

F.E.G.

Formerly imported by K.B.I. INC. (formerly Kassnar Imports). (Model GPM also imported as Daisy Model 91). Manufactured in Hungary. Available through dealers and used market.

RIFLES

CLG-462 — .177 or .22 cal., CO_2 cartridge or cylinder charge, 490-410 FPS, 16½ in. barrel, (24 in. .22 cal.), 5 lbs. 8 oz.

	$400	$350	$270

Last Mfg.'s Sug. Retail was $550.

CLG-468 — .177 or .22 cal., CO_2 cartridge or cylinder charge, 705-525 FPS, 26¾ in. barrel, 5 lbs. 12 oz.

	$450	$380	$300

Last Mfg.'s Sug. Retail was $600.

PISTOLS

MODEL GPM-01.177 cal., CO_2 cartridge or cylinder charge, 425 FPS, 10¼ in. barrel, 2 lbs. 7 oz.

Mfg.'s Sug. Retail	$525	$400	$350	$270

AIR-GUNS

FAMAS

Imported by Century International Arms, Inc., St. Albans, VT.

Grading	100%	98%	95%

FAMAS AIR RIFLE — .177 cal., CO_2 action, copy of French made MAS .223 semi-automatic, used for military training, true semi-auto clip fed air rifle.

No Mfg.'s Sug. Retail	N/A	$220	$190	$160

FEINWERKBAU

Manufactured in Oberndorf, Germany. Imported and distributed by Beeman Precision Airguns located in Huntington Beach, CA. Available through dealers and Beeman direct.

> Feinwerkbau has been responsible for developing many of the current technical innovations used in fabricating target Air Pistols and Rifles. In 1992, Feinwerkbau Airguns swept the Olympic competition in this newly formed Olympic sport. Feinwerkbau has always been a leader in Airgun technology.

RIFLES

MODEL 124 — .177 cal., barrel-cocking action, 780-830 FPS, 7 lbs. 2 oz. Add $35 for deluxe, $20 for left-hand deluxe, $400 for custom select, $425 for custom fancy, $475 for custom extra fancy. Disc. 1989.

	$450	$400	$320

Add $350 for factory marked 5mm (only 3 mfg).

Last Mfg.'s Sug. Retail was $490.

MODEL 127 — .22 cal., barrel-cocking action, 620-680 FPS, 6 lbs./7 lbs. 1 oz. Additions same as above. Disc. 1989.

	$450	$400	$320

Last Mfg.'s Sug. Retail was $490.

MODEL 300S — .177 cal., side-lever action, 640 FPS, 8.8/10.8 lbs. Add $95 for left-hand (all styles), $60 for barrel sleeve.

Mfg.'s Sug. Retail	$1,270	$1,000	$900	$780

> Add $300 for Tyrolean stock. Add $75 for Running Boar stock configuration or Universal Model. Mini Model rifles are equal.

MODEL 600 — .177 cal., side-lever action, single stroke pneumatic operation, top of the line match rifle with aperture sights, unique hardwood laminate stock, 585 FPS, $10\frac{1}{2}$ lbs. Add $40 for left-hand. Disc. 1988.

	$980	$870	$760

> This model was also available in a Running Boar variation with extra-long barrel that unscrews for transporting.

Last Mfg.'s Sug. Retail was $900.

MODEL 601 — .177 cal., side-lever action single stroke, pneumatic operation, replaces Model 600 (see above), 10 lbs. 8 oz. Add $115 for left-hand. Running Target Model also available.

Mfg.'s Sug. Retail	$1,650	$1,350	$1,150	$920

Add $50 for 5454 diopter sight.

MODEL 602 — .177 cal., side-lever action, single stroke pneumatic operation. Replaces Model 601 above.

Mfg.'s Sug. Retail	$1,875	$1,525	$1,350	$1,070

Add $115 for left-hand.

AIR-GUNS

Grading	100%	98%	95%

MODEL C60 — .177 cal., CO$_2$ powered, 570 FPS, similar in style to Model 600/601 above, 9.2 lbs. to 10.6 lbs. Add $115 for left-hand, running target model also available.

Mfg.'s Sug. Retail	$1,675	$1,400	$1,200	$875

MODEL C62 — .177 cal., CO$_2$ powered, specifications same as above. Replaces Model C60 above.

Mfg.'s Sug. Retail	$1,750	$1,450	$1,325	$1,080

Add $115 for left-hand.

C60 MINI — .177 cal., CO$_2$ powered, quick change cylinder (bottle) smaller version of C60 Match Rifle, 7¾ lbs. New 1991.

Mfg.'s Sug. Retail	$1,675	$1,400	$1,200	$875

PISTOLS

MODEL 65 MK I AND II — .177 cal., side-lever action, 525 FPS, 2.6-2.9 lbs., short barrel Mark II only. Add $65 for left-hand or $25 for adj. grips.

Mfg.'s Sug. Retail	$1,170	$1,025	$850	$600

MODEL 80 — .177 cal., side-lever action, 475-525 FPS, 2.8-3.2 lbs. Disc. in 1983. (Like Model 65 with stacking barrel weights and fine mechanical trigger).

	$710	$600	$480

Last Mfg.'s Sug. Retail was $625.

MODEL 90 — specifications same as above but with electronic trigger. Add $45 for short barrel, $50 for left-hand. Disc. 1990.

	$800	$650	$515

Last Mfg.'s Sug. Retail was $1,155.

MODEL 100 — .177 cal., pneumatic action, 460 FPS, 2½ lbs. Disc. 1992.

	$725	$620	$495

Add $40 for left-hand variation.

Last Mfg.'s Sug. Retail was $1,100.

MODEL 102 — new version of Model 100 above (1992).

Mfg.'s Sug. Retail	$1,530	$1,250	$1,125	$900

Add $50 for left-hand variation.

MODEL C2 — .177 cal., CO$_2$ cylinder, 425-525 FPS, 2½ lbs. Add $40 for left-hand, deduct $20 for mini. Disc. 1989.

	$570	$465	$365

Last Mfg.'s Sug. Retail was $780.

MODEL C5 — .177 cal., CO$_2$ powered 5 shot rapid fire, 7⅓ in. barrel, 510 FPS, 2 lbs. 6 oz. Add $60 for left-hand. Disc. approx. 1993.

	$1,170	$970	$715

Last Mfg.'s Sug. Retail was $1,350.

MODEL C 10 — .177 cal., CO$_2$ cartridge, 510 FPS, 2½ lbs. Disc. 1990.

	$725	$620	$470

Add $60 for left-hand model.

Last Mfg.'s Sug. Retail was $965.

MODEL C20 — .177 cal., CO$_2$ powered, 510 FPS. Add $60 for left hand, 2 lbs. 8 oz. (replacement for the C2 and C10 new in 1991). Disc. 1995.

	$950	$825	$650

Add $50 for left-hand model.

Last Mfg.'s Sug. Retail was $1,160.

AIR-
GUNS

Grading	100%	98%	95%

MODEL C25 — .177 cal., CO_2 powered, 510 FPS, unique CO_2 ball placed directly below action (instead of standard long CO_2 cylinder), $2\frac{1}{2}$ lbs.

Mfg.'s Sug. Retail	$1,325	$1,200	$1,000	$800

Add $50 for left-hand.

MODEL C55 — .177 cal., CO_2 powered, single shot or 5 shot repeater, 510 FPS, unique CO_2 ball placed directly below action for vertical CO_2 feed, up to 225 shots/fill, $2\frac{1}{2}$ lbs. Add $75 for left-hand. New 1994.

Mfg.'s Sug. Retail	$1,705	$1,450	$1,300	$1,040

MODEL P30 — .177 cal., precharged pneumatic, 515 FPS, adjustable match trigger, stippled walnut match grip, wt. 2.4 lbs.

Mfg.'s Sug. Retail	$1,530	$1,250	N/A	N/A

Add $50 for left-hand.

GAMO

Previously imported by Stoeger Industries - importation discontinued in 1986. A few models are currently being imported by Daisy. Previously imported and distributed by Dynamit Nobel, RWS, Inc., located in Closter, NJ. Available through dealers. Most models now imported by Ruko, Buffalo, NY.

PISTOLS

AF-10 — .177 cal., pneumatic action, 430 FPS, 7 in. barrel, similar in style to Beeman P-1, $1\frac{1}{4}$ lbs. Importation disc. 1993.

	$75	$60	$45

Last Mfg.'s Sug. Retail was $115.

CENTER — .177 cal., under-barrel lever cocking, 400-435 FPS, 14 in. barrel, 2 lbs. 8 oz.

	$90	$75	$55

PR-45 — .177 cal., pneumatic, $9\frac{1}{4}$ in. barrel, 1 lb. 9 oz., looks similar to a Beeman P1.

	$100	$85	$70

Last Mfg.'s Sug. Retail was $135.

COMPACT — .177 cal., pneumatic, $9\frac{1}{4}$ in. barrel, two stage trigger, walnut grips, adj. sights, target model, 2 lbs. Add $30 for left-hand.

	$145	$120	$95

Last Mfg.'s Sug. Retail was $210.

FALCON — .177 cal., under-lever action, 430 FPS, 7 in. barrel. ABS plastic grips, $2\frac{7}{8}$ lbs. Importation disc. 1993.

	$70	$55	$40

Last Mfg.'s Sug. Retail was $105.

RIFLES

CF 20 — .177 and .22 cal., under-lever action, 790-625 FPS, $17\frac{3}{4}$ in. barrel, checkered stock, 6 lbs. 6 oz. Importation disc. 1993.

	$155	$125	$100

Last Mfg.'s Sug. Retail was $190.

CADET — .177 cal., barrel-cocking action, 570 FPS, beechwood stock, 5 lbs.

	$70	$60	$50

CONTEST — .177 cal., side-lever action, 543 FPS, beechwood stock, 10.1 lbs.

	$100	$80	$60

AIR-GUNS

Grading	100%	98%	95%

CUSTOM 600—.177 or .22 cal., barrel-cocking action, 690 FPS, 17$\frac{3}{4}$ in. barrel, two stage adj. trigger, checkered stock, 6 lbs. 3 oz.

$130 $105 $80

Last Mfg.'s Sug. Retail was $170.

DELTA — .177 cal., barrel-cocking action, 525 FPS, 15$\frac{3}{4}$ in. barrel, two stage trigger, automatic safety, adj. sights, plastic stock, 5 lbs. 5 oz. Disc. 1994.

$85 $70 $55

Last Mfg.'s Sug. Retail was $115.

EUROPIA — .177 cal., side-lever action, 625 FPS, adjustable sights, Monte Carlo stock.

$165 $145 $115

EXPO — .177 or .22 cal., barrel-cocking action, 625 FPS, adj. trigger, special sights, 5 lbs. 8 oz. Disc. 1994.

$80 $65 $50

Last Mfg.'s Sug. Retail was $135.

EXPOMATIC—.177 cal., repeating barrel-cocking action, 575 FPS, adj. trigger, 5 lbs. 5 oz.

$100 $85 $70

EXPO 2000 — .177 cal., barrel-cocking action, 625 FPS, 17 in. barrel, Monte Carlo style stock, 5$\frac{1}{2}$ lbs. New 1992. Disc. 1994.

$75 $60 $50

Last Mfg.'s Sug. Retail was $135.

GAMO 68 — .177 or .22 cal., barrel-cocking action, 600 FPS, 6 lbs. 8 oz.

$80 $65 $50

GAMATIC 85 — .177 cal., barrel-cocking action, 560 FPS, 17$\frac{3}{4}$ in. barrel, two stage trigger, unique loading system for up to 25 pellets, pistol grip stock, 6 lbs. 3 oz.

$75 $60 $50

Last Mfg.'s Sug. Retail was $160.

G-1200 — .177 cal., CO_2 cylinder, 560 FPS, 17$\frac{3}{4}$ in. barrel, unique pump action loading system for up to 12 pellets (styled like a pump centerfire rifle), 6 lbs. 6 oz.

$155 $125 $95

Last Mfg.'s Sug. Retail was $185.

HUNTER 440 — .177 cal., barrel-cocking action, 1000 FPS, 18 in. barrel, Monte Carlo style stock, 6$\frac{3}{4}$ lbs. New 1992. Disc. 1994.

$155 $120 $95

Last Mfg.'s Sug. Retail was $210.

MAGNUM 2000 — .177 and .22 cal., barrel-cocking action, 820-660 FPS, 17$\frac{3}{4}$ in. barrel, adj. two stage trigger, checkered stock, 7 lbs. 2 oz.

$155 $130 $100

Last Mfg.'s Sug. Retail was $200.

SUPER — .177 cal., side-lever action, 593 FPS, 10 lbs. 8 oz.

$140 $120 $100

TWIN — .177 and .22 cal., barrel-cocking action, 675 FPS. Adjustable sights, unique barrel insert tubes to change from .177 to .22 cal., hardwood stock.

No Mfg.'s Sug. Retail $155 $130 $100

HAENEL

Sold by Cape Outfitters, FL.

Unfortunately, no specifications were available at time of printing. The following models were old models imported by Cape Outfitters. Previously imported by G.S.I. located in Trussville, AL.

Grading	100%	98%	95%

KI 101 (MLG 550) — .177 cal., match rifle. Importation disc. 1993.
$400 $340 $270

Last Mfg.'s Sug. Retail was $695.

KI 102 (ML 311) — .177 cal. match rifle. Importation disc. 1993.
$220 $190 $150

Last Mfg.'s Sug. Retail was $395.

KI 103 (ML308-8) — .177 cal. match rifle. Importation disc. 1993.
$140 $120 $95

Last Mfg.'s Sug. Retail was $300.

KI 104 (310-4) — .177 cal. Importation disc. 1993.
$110 $95 $75

Last Mfg.'s Sug. Retail was $200.

KI 105 (303-4) — BB cal., BB clip fed. Importation disc. 1993.
$100 $85 $65

Last Mfg.'s Sug. Retail was $190.

KI 106 (85) — .177 cal. Importation disc. 1993.
$80 $70 $50

Last Mfg.'s Sug. Retail was $130.

HAMMERLI

Imported by Mandall Shooting Supplies, Inc. located in Scottsdale, AZ. Available through dealers and importer direct.

Hammerli Airguns are not mfg. by Sig in Switzerland, but rather subcontracted to other airgun manufacturers (including El Gamo), these models (403 and 420) are German made. Prices may increase or decrease based on the value of dollar on international markets.

RIFLES

MODEL 403 — .177 cal., side-lever action, 700 FPS, adj. sight target model, $9\frac{1}{4}$ lbs.
$280 $235 $160

Last Mfg.'s Sug. Retail was $400.

MODEL 420 — .177 cal., side-lever action, 700 FPS, military style plastic stock, $7\frac{1}{2}$ lbs.
$210 $175 $105

Last Mfg.'s Sug. Retail was $300.

MODEL 450 — .177 cal., top lever pneumatic action, adj. target sight and cheekpiece, professional target model. Importation began 1994.
Mfg.'s Sug. Retail $1,355 $1,200 $1,000 $780
Add $40 for walnut stock.

PISTOLS

MODEL 480 — .177 cal., precharged pneumatic or CO_2 (can use both systems), adj. grips, professional target sights and trigger, up to 320 shots per full compressed air tank, approx. $2\frac{1}{4}$ lbs. New 1994.
Mfg.'s Sug. Retail $1,155 $1,000 $900 $720
Add $145 for walnut grips.

IZH

Manufactured at Baikal/Izhevsk factory Russia. Imported by Big Bear Arms, Dallas, TX.

Grading	100%	98%	95%

PISTOLS

IZH-46 AIR PISTOL — .177 cal., single stroke pneumatic, 460 FPS, target sights, professional target model, 2 lbs. 8 oz.

Mfg.'s Sug. Retail	$650	$500	$425	$360

RIFLES

KATYA IZH-60 — .177 cal., barrel-cocking action, 460 FPS, 16 ½ in. barrel, telescoping stock, 5 lbs. 6 oz.

Mfg.'s Sug. Retail	$140	$100	$90	$70

INDUSTRY BRAND

Shanghai China, imported by Compasseco, Bradstown, KY.

Finish on these guns is much improved in 1996.

RIFLES

BS-4 OLYMPIC — .177 cal., side-lever action, diopter sight, stippled stock, professional target model, 11 lbs.

Mfg.'s Sug. Retail	$495	$300	$250	$200

QB-38 — .177 cal., under-lever cocking action, 900 FPS, 19½ in. barrel, Monte Carlo beech stock, 8½ lbs.

Mfg.'s Sug. Retail	$130	$55	N/A	N/A

QB-78 — .177 cal., CO_2 powered, 600 FPS, bolt action, 20½ in. barrel, wood stock, adjustable trigger. 5 lbs. 12 oz.

Mfg.'s Sug. Retail	$130	$55	$45	$35

QB-88 — .177 cal., side-lever action, 900 FPS, 19½ in. barrel, adjustable sights, safety. 7½ lbs.

Mfg.'s Sug. Retail	$130	$55	$45	$35

MARKSMAN

Division of S/R Industries, Huntington Beach, CA. Available both through dealers and Marksman direct.

JUNIOR MODEL 28 — .177 cal., barrel-cocking action, 600 FPS, 16¾ in. barrel, 6 lbs. Mfg. for Marksman by Weihrauch.

No Mfg.'s Retail	$180	$155	$120

MODEL 29/30 — .177 or .22 cal., barrel-cocking action, 800/625 FPS, 18½ in. barrel, 6 lbs. Mfg. for Marksman by BSA. Disc. 1991.

	$175	$135	$85

Last Mfg.'s Sug. Retail was $200.

MODEL 40 — .177 cal., barrel-cocking action, 720 FPS, 18⅜ in. barrel, 7 lbs. 5 oz.

No Mfg.'s Retail	$200	$175	$135

MODEL 45 — .177 cal., barrel-cocking action, 900-930 FPS, 19⅛ in. barrel, 7 lbs. 3 oz. New 1993.

No Mfg.'s Retail	$170	$135	$115

MODEL 55 (RIFLE) & 59 CARBINE — .177 cal., barrel-cocking action, 925 FPS, 19¾ (rifle) or 14 (carbine) in. barrel, 7 lbs. 8 oz. Mfg. for Marksman by Weihrauch.

No Mfg.'s Retail	$250	$215	$160

AIR-GUNS

Grading	100%	98%	95%

MODEL 56/56K — .177 cal., barrel-cocking action, 925 FPS, 19⅝ in. barrel, adj. cheekpiece and trigger, 8 lbs. 11 oz.

No Mfg.'s Retail $365 $315 $250

Add $180 for 56K Model with Marksman Model 6941 scope.

The Model 56/56K was manufactured for Marksman by Weihrauch.

MODEL 58/58K—.177 cal., barrel-cocking action, 925 FPS, 16 in. heavy bull barrel, adj. trigger, designed for silhouette shooting, 8 lbs. 8 oz. Importation disc. 1993.

         $300 $230 $180

Add $180 for 58K Model with Marksman Model 6941 scope.

The Model 58/58K was manufactured for Marksman by Weihrauch.

Last Mfg.'s Sug. Retail was $390.

MODEL 60/61 CARBINE — .177 cal., under-lever cocking action, 810-840 FPS, 8 lbs. 12 oz.

No Mfg.'s Retail $400 $350 $270

Modified version of HW77 by Weihrauch.

MODEL 70 — .177, .20, or .22 cal., barrel-cocking action, 925/760 FPS, 19¾ in. barrel, 8 lbs. Add $10 for .20 cal. Mfg. for Marksman by Weihrauch.

No Mfg.'s Retail $290 $255 $185

MAUSER

Mauser Airguns are subcontracted under license to use the Mauser trademark and are not manufactured by Mauser-Werke. Previously imported and distributed by Marksman located in Huntington Beach, CA. Available through dealers and used market.

RIFLES

MATCH 300SL/SLC—.177 cal., under-lever action, 550/450 FPS, adj. sights and hardwood stock, 8 lbs. 8 oz. Add $75 for SLC Model with diopter sights.

         $240 $200 $140

This model is mfg. in Hungary.

Last Mfg.'s Sug. Retail was $330.

PISTOLS

U90/U91 JUMBO AIR PISTOLS — .177 cal., barrel break action, 260 FPS, 2 lbs.

         $85 $70 $45

Add $15 for deluxe model U91 with adj. sights and checkered grips.

This model was mfg. by Record.

Last Mfg.'s Sug. Retail was $100.

MORINI

Manufacturer located in Switzerland. Imported and distributed since 1993 by Nygord Precision Products located in Prescott, AZ. Dealer direct.

PISTOLS

162E — .177 cal., precharged pneumatic, professional target pistol with target sights, adj. grips.

Mfg.'s Sug. Retail $1,050 $800 $610 $460

NORICA

Previously imported by KBI (Kassnar) Imports located in Harrisburg, PA and American Arms, Inc. located in North Kansas City, MO, and by S.A.E. located in Miami, FL.

Norica airguns imported by American Arms, Inc. will appear under the American Arms, Inc. heading in this text.

Even though the dollar has fallen on international markets, the current lack of an importer has caused prices to remain flat. Available on used market only.

Grading	100%	98%	95%

MODEL 47 — .177 cal., side-lever action, 600 FPS, unique black pistol grip handle, 5½ lbs.
| No Mfg.'s Retail | $125 | $85 | $65 |

MODEL 61C — .177 cal., barrel break action, 600 FPS, 5 lbs. 8 oz.
| No Mfg.'s Retail | $90 | $65 | $45 |

MODEL 73 — .177 or .22 cal., barrel break action, 580/525 FPS, 6 lbs. 4 oz.
| No Mfg.'s Retail | $110 | $80 | $50 |

MODEL 80G — .177 or .22 cal., barrel break action, 635/570 FPS, 7 lbs. 2 oz.
| No Mfg.'s Retail | $140 | $105 | $70 |

MODEL 90 — .177 cal., barrel break action, 650 FPS, factory equipped with scope.
| No Sug. Retail | $130 | $95 | $65 |

MODEL 92 — .177 cal., side-lever action, 650 FPS, 5¾ lbs.
| No Mfg.'s Retail | $125 | $90 | $65 |

NORICA YOUNG — .177 cal., barrel break action, 600 FPS, unique colored stock.
| No Mfg.'s Retail | $80 | $60 | $40 |

BLACK WIDOW — .177 or .22 cal., barrel break action, 500/450 FPS, unique black plastic stock, 5 lbs.
| No Mfg.'s Retail | $120 | $80 | $55 |

PARDINI PISTOLS
Previously imported by MCS. Inc., now imported by Nygord Precision Products, Prescott, AZ.

MODEL K58 — .177 cal., under-lever pneumatic, 9 in. barrel, 2 lbs. 6 oz., professional target model.
| Mfg.'s Sug. Retail | $795 | $650 | $550 | $440 |

MODEL K60 — .177 cal., CO_2 cylinder charge, 9½ in. barrel, 2 lbs. 4 oz.
| Mfg.'s Sug. Retail | $795 | $650 | $550 | $440 |

MODEL K90 — .177 cal. CO_2 powered junior model, 7¼ in. barrel, 1⅞ lbs.
| Mfg.'s Sug. Retail | $580 | $460 | $390 | $300 |

MODEL P10 — .177 cal., under-lever pneumatic, 7¾ in. barrel, 2 lbs. 3 oz., disc. 1990.
| | $425 | $355 | $295 |

Last Mfg.'s Sug. Retail was $560.

PARK RIFLE COMPANY
Kent, England

No current importer exists for these guns; however, enough guns have been sold directly to this market to warrant listing in this section. For more information contact Park Rifle Company at Unit 68A, Dartford Trade Park, Powder Mill Lane, Dartford, Kent DA 1 1NX.

AIR-
GUNS

Grading	100%	98%	95%

RIFLES

RH93 (93W & 93-800) — .177 or .22 cal., under-lever cocking action - 12ft./lbs power, 37 in. barrel (38 on Model 93-800). 9 lbs. 10 oz.

Mfg.'s Sug. Retail $500 $400 $350 $275

> Add $100 for thumbhole walnut stock, estimate $80 freight cost added to each gun purchased.

R W S

Importers located in Closter, NJ. See Dianawerk (earlier in this text).

S G S (SPORTING GUNS SELECTION)

Previously Imported by Kendell International. Available on used market only.

DUO 300AP — .177 or .22 cal., top cocking action, 455/430 FPS.

$150 $115 $70

DUO 300AR — .177 or .22 cal., top cocking action, 455/430 FPS, with extra stock and barrel assembly to create a 3-in-1 gun.

$200 $140 $85

SAXBY PALMER

Manufactured by Saxby Palmer located in Stratford-Upon-Avon, England. Previously imported/distributed by Marksman Products located in Huntington Beach, CA. Available on used market only.

Saxby Palmer has developed the world's first cartridge loading air rifle. This is not a CO_2 or other type of compressed gas gun. The cartridges are pressurized (2250 PSI) and reusable facilitating speed of loading and much greater velocities. New rifles are supplied with the table pump (for reloading brass or plastic cartridges) and 10 cartridges. You must have these accessories in order to operate air rifles or pistols. Deduct 50% for used guns witho ut these accessories.

RIFLES:

ENSIGN ELITE — .177 or .22 cal., bolt action cartridge, 1000-800 FPS auto safety.

$120 $95 $80

Last Mfg.'s Sug. Retail was $175.

ENSIGN ROYAL — .177 or .22 cal., bolt action cartridge, 1000-800 FPS auto safety, walnut stock.

$150 $120 $90

Last Mfg.'s Sug. Retail was $275.

GALAXY — .177 or .22 cal., bolt action cartridge, 1,000/800 FPS, auto safety, walnut stain, hardwood stock 6½ lbs.

$120 $95 $80

SATURN — .177 or .22 cal., bolt action cartridge, 1,000/800 FPS, auto safety, hi-strength black polymer stock 6½ lbs. Disc. in 1987.

$120 $95 $80

Last Mfg.'s Sug. Retail was $175.

AIR-GUNS

Grading	100%	98%	95%

REVOLVERS: DISCONTINUED

ORION AIR REVOLVER — .177 cal., 6 shot, compressed gas cartridges (reusable), 550 FPS, 6 in. barrel, 2 lbs. 3 oz. Disc. 1988.

$230 $175 $150

> This model is manufactured by Weihrauch of Germany and includes a Slim Jim pump and 12 reuseable cartridges. It also came with a 30 grain 38 cal. zinc pellet to allow cartridges to be used in a .38 Special pistol for practice.

MODEL 54 — .177 cal., 5 shot, compressed gas cartridges (reusable), 4 in. barrel, 1 lb. 5 oz. Disc. 1988.

$150 $110 $80

> This model is manufactured by Weihrauch of Germany and includes a Slim Jim pump and 12 reuseable cartridges.

SHARP

Japan (Imported By Beeman). Available on used market only.

SHARP INNOVA — .177 or .22 cal., pneumatic pump action, 920/720 FPS, 4 lbs. 6 oz. Disc. 1988.

$130 $110 $80

Last Mfg.'s Sug. Retail was $175.

SHARP ACE — .177 or .22 cal., pneumatic pump action, 920/750 FPS, 6 lbs. 4 oz. Disc. 1988.

$230 $195 $150

Last Mfg.'s Sug. Retail was $295.

SHERIDAN

Manufactured by Benjamin Air Rifle Co. located in East Bloomfield, NY. Available through dealers and Benjamin-Sheridan direct.

SHERIDAN BLUE STREAK/SILVER STREAK — .20 cal., pneumatic pump or CO_2 action, 700 FPS, 6 lbs. Add $5 for Silver Streak, $25 for Williams sight, $30 for 4 x 15 scope, $25 for paint pellet rifle. Deduct $15 for CO_2.

No Mfg.'s Retail $130 $110 $80

SHERIDAN AIR PISTOL

▲ *Model E* — .177, .20, or .22 cal., CO_2 cartridge, 400 FPS, $6^3/_8$ in. barrel, 2 lbs. 4 oz. Add $40 for paint pellet pistol.

No Mfg.'s Retail $90 $75 $60

SMITH & WESSON

Springfield, MA.

Smith & Wesson had a few air guns manufactured to their specifications for distribution in the U.S. Most guns trade for under $100 with a few models selling for $120 to $140.

STERLING

Manufactured by Benjamin Air Rifle Company located in East Bloomfield, NY. In 1994, after being purchased by Crosman Air Guns, manufacture of the Sterling line was discontinued.

AIR-
GUNS

Grading	100%	98%	95%

RIFLES

HR 81—.177, 20, .22 cal., under-lever cocking action, 700/660 FPS, adj. V type rear sight, 8½ lbs. Add $10 for .22 cal.

$250 $200 $135

Add $30 for original English markings.

Last Mfg.'s Sug. Retail was $250.

HR 83—.177, .20 or .22 cal., under-lever cocking action, 700/660 FPS, adj. Williams "FP" peep sight, walnut stock, 8½ lbs. Add $5 for .22 cal.

$300 $250 $180

Add $30 for original English markings.

Last Mfg.'s Sug. Retail was $300.

STEYR

Manufactured by Steyr located in Austria. Imported and distributed by Nygord Precision Products, located in Prescott, AZ. Available through dealers and importer direct.

RIFLES

MATCH 91 — .177 cal., CO_2 powered match rifle with precision receiver sight and adj. butt plate. New in 1988.

Mfg.'s Sug. Retail $1,400 $1,250 $1,000 $600

Add $50 for left-hand.
Add $100 for Running Target.

PISTOLS

LP-1   — .177 cal., CO_2 powered match pistol, 15 ⅓ in. overall, 2 lbs. 8 oz.

Mfg.'s Sug. Retail $1,250 $1,050 $875 $625

Add $30 for compensated version "LP-1C".
Add $80 for colored tank variations (red, blue, green, or silver - marked LP1-C).
Add $45 for precharged pneumatic version.

LP-5   — .177 cal., CO_2 powered match pistol, 5 shot semi-automatic.

Mfg.'s Sug. Retail $1,350 $1,200 $950 $650

THEOBEN ENGINEERING

Manufacturer located in England. Previously imported by Air Rifle Specialists located in Elmira, NY. Available both dealer and importer direct.

Beeman Precision Airguns, Inc. began importing Theoben manufactured rifles in 1992. These guns differ enough from standard Thoeben arms that they are listed in the Beeman section of this text.

Add $75 for Theoben pump applicable to some models listed below.

RIFLES

The importation of Theoben rifles was discontinued during 1993.

Grading	100%	98%	95%

SIROCCO COUNTRYMAN — .177 or .22 cal., Anschutz barrel break action, 1,100/800 FPS, unique precharged sealed gas spring replaces the metal main springs used in most spring piston air rifles, not to be confused with a gas powered (CO_2) air rifle, includes scope rings, barrel weight, walnut stained beechwood stock, $7\frac{1}{2}$ lbs. Importation disc. in 1987.

$350 $275 $220

Last Mfg.'s Sug. Retail was $585.

SIROCCO DELUXE — similar to Countryman, except has hand checkered walnut stock. Importation disc. in 1987.

$525 $385 $240

Last Mfg.'s Sug. Retail was $650.

SIROCCO CLASSIC — similar to Sirocco Deluxe, except has updated floating inertia system in piston chamber and auto safety, variable power, 900/1100 FPS. New in 1987. Add $60 for left-hand.

$550 $450 $375

This model was available with either a choked or unchoked Anschutz barrel as standard equipment.

Last Mfg.'s Sug. Retail was $830.

SIROCCO GRAND PRIX — similar specifications to the Sirocco Classic, except has checkered walnut thumbhole stock.

$635 $550 $420

Add $60 for left-hand.
Subtract 50% for older models without safety and new piston design.
In 1987, this model was updated with a floating inertia system in piston chamber and auto safety, variable power.
This model was available with either a choked or unchoked Anschutz barrel as standard equipment.

Last Mfg.'s Sug. Retail was $940.

ELIMINATOR — .177 or .22 cal., barrel break action, 1100/1400 FPS, variable power, deluxe checkered thumb hole stock with cheekpiece and pad $9\frac{1}{2}$ lbs.

$900 $475 $400

Add $60 for left-hand.
This model incorporated an improved barrel design featuring pronounced rifling for the higher velocity pellets.

Last Mfg.'s Sug. Retail was $1,500.

IMPERATOR — .22 cal., under-lever action, 750 FPS, variable power, walnut hand checkered stock, auto safety. New in 1989.

$900 $525 $420

Last Mfg.'s Sug. Retail was $1,500.

IMPERATOR SLR 88 — similar to above but with a 7 shot mag. Very limited importation.

$1,070 $850 $625

Last Mfg.'s Sug. Retail was $1,680.

RAPID 7 — .22 cal. precharged pneumatic, variable power, 19 in. Anschutz barrel, stippled walnut stock, unique 7 shot bolt action design, cylinder charge lasts 160 shots, $6\frac{3}{4}$ lbs.

$1,100 $850 $670

Add $60 for left-hand.
Add $120 for scuba tank adaptor.

Last Mfg.'s Sug. Retail was $1,300.

VENOM ARMS CUSTOM GUNS
Manufacturer/Customizer located in the United Kingdom.

Grading	100%	98%	95%

Venom Arms specializes in customizing Weihrauch firearms manufactured in Germany. A quick review of their latest pricing schedule for custom guns indicate prices may run nearly 100% over the initial cost of the uncustomized gun (see Weihrauch).

WALTHER

Manufacturer located in Ulm, Germany. Rifles previously imported by Interarms located in Alexandria, VA. Pistols and rifles are now imported by Nygord Precision Products located in La Crescenta, CA. Available through dealers or importer direct.

RIFLES

CG 90 — .177 cal., CO_2 powered, tilting block action, 18.9 in. barrel, 10 lbs. 2 oz. New in 1989.
$1,050 $925 $725

Last Mfg.'s Sug. Retail was $1,750.

CGM — .177, CO2 powered, professional target model, similar to LGM-2.
Mfg.'s Sug. Retail $1270 $1,150   N/A   N/A

LG 90 — side-lever action, single stroke pneumatic mechanism, professional target, 11 lbs.
$1,000 $900 $700

Last Mfg.'s Sug. Retail was $1,320.

LGM-1 — .177 cal., single stroke pneumatic, side-lever action, 19 in. barrel, wt. approx. 10 lbs. New 1992.
Mfg.'s Sug. Retail $1,890 $1,250 $1,100 $825

LGM-2 — .177 cal., single stroke pneumatic, side-lever action, new version of LGM-1 above, 10 lbs.
Mfg.'s Sug. Retail $1,335 $1,200   N/A   N/A

LGR RIFLE — .177 cal., side-lever action, single stroke pneumatic mechanism, 580 FPS (professional target) 10 lbs. 8 oz. Add $100 for universal, 10% for left-hand. Disc. 1991.
$1,075 $950 $640

Add $150 for Running Boar Model.

Last Mfg.'s Sug. Retail was $1,250.

PISTOLS

CPM-1 — .177 cal., CO_2 powered professional target model. New 1993.
Mfg.'s Sug. Retail $1,120 $1,000 $700 $550

CP 2 — .177 cal., CO_2 powered, 9 in. barrel, 2½ lbs, professional target model. Disc. 1990.
$670 $520 $420

Last Mfg.'s Sug. Retail was $850.

CP-3 — .177 cal., CO_2 powered, professional target model. Importation disc. 1993.
$720 $595 $475

Last Mfg.'s Sug. Retail was $1,360.

CP-5 — .177 cal., CO_2 powered, professional target model. Disc. 1992.
$800 $675 $550

Last Mfg.'s Sug. Retail was $1,650.

LP 3 — .177 cal., single stroke pneumatic action, 405 FPS, 2.8-3.0 lbs. Add $60 for match grade.
$520 $450 $340

Add $50 for shaped barrel rather than round.

LP 53 — .177 cal.
$395 $300 $200

Add $75 for blued receiver.

Grading	100%	98%	95%

LPM-1 — .177 cal. single stroke pneumatic, 10 in. barrel, 2¼ lbs. New 1992.

Mfg.'s Sug. Retail	$1,175	$1,000	$800	$650

WEIHRAUCH

Manufactured in Germany. Imported exclusively by Beeman Precision Airguns located in Huntington Beach, CA. Available through dealers or Beeman direct.

RIFLES

MODEL 30 — .177 or .20 cal., barrel-cocking action, 660 FPS/600 FPS, 17 in. barrel, 40 in. overall, 5 lbs. 5 oz. Add $5 for .20 cal.

Mfg.'s Sug. Retail	$230	$175	$135	$110

MODEL 35EB — .177 or .22 cal., barrel-cocking action, 755/660 FPS, 8 lbs. Add $50 for chrome, $10 for .22 cal. Deduct $20 for 35L. Disc. 1985.

	$295	$250	$180

Last Mfg.'s Sug. Retail was $450.

MODEL 50 — .177 cal., barrel-cocking action, 705 FPS, 17 in. barrel, 43.1 in. overall, 6 lbs. 9 oz. Disc. 1996.

	$190	$165	$120

Last Mfg.'s Sug. Retail was $245.

MODEL 55 — .177 cal., barrel-cocking action, 660-700 FPS, 7 lbs. 8 oz. Add $40 for left-hand, $105 for Match, or $145 for Tyrolean stock.

	$440	$375	$295

Last Mfg.'s Sug. Retail was $610.

MODEL 77/77 CARBINE — .177, .20, or .22 cal., under-lever cocking action, 830-710 FPS, 8 lbs. 9 oz. Add $40 for left-hand, $30 for Deluxe, or $100 for tyrolean stock.

	$385	$330	$250

Last Mfg.'s Sug. Retail was $530.

MODEL 97 — .177 or .20 cal., under-lever cocking action, 800-750 FPS, 9 lbs.

Mfg.'s Sug. Retail	$535	$415	$360	$280

PISTOLS

HW MODEL 70 — .177 cal., barrel-cocking action, 410 FPS, 2 lbs. 4 oz. Add $45 for chrome.

	$135	$115	$90

Last Mfg.'s Sug. Retail was $170.

▲ *HW Model 70-A* — similar to above, except has improved rear sight suitable for scope mount, also improved trigger. New 1993.

Mfg.'s Sug. Retail	$215	$170	$145	$105

WINCHESTER

Imported by Winchester from 1969 through 1974. Available through used market only.

Between 1969 and 1975 Winchester imported 8 rifle models and 2 pistols into the United States from a manufacturer in Germany. A total of 19,259 air guns were made and imported through 1973. Due to the $100 rule, only 6 guns will be listed in this section.

RIFLES

MODEL 427 — .22 cal., barrel-cocking action, 660 FPS, micrometer rear and hooded front sight, 42 in. overall, 6 lbs.

	$160	$115	$95

AIR-GUNS

Grading	100%	98%	95%

MODEL 435 — .177 cal. barrel-cocking action, 693 FPS, micrometer rear and interchangeable front sight, checkered stock and adjustable trigger, 44 in. overall, 6½ lbs.

$210 $160 $125

MODEL 450 — .177 cal., under-lever cocking action, 693 FPS, micrometer rear and interchangeable front sight, 44½ in. overall, dovetail base for scope, checkered Schutzen style stock, 7¾ lbs.

$270 $200 $155

MODEL 333 — .177 cal., barrel-cocking action, 576 FPS, diopter target sight, fully adjustable trigger, double piston recoilless action, walnut stock, checkered and stippled, 43½ in. overall, 9½ lbs.

$475 $400 $310

PISTOLS

MODEL 353 — .177 and .22 cal., barrel-cocking action, 378 FPS, plastic stock, 16 in. overall, 2¾ lbs.

$135 $100 $75

MODEL 363 — .177 cal., barrel-cocking action, 378 FPS, double piston recoilless design micrometer rear and interchangeable front sights, fully adjustable trigger, plastic stock, 16 in. overall, 3 lbs.

$175 $120 $85

WISCHO

Previously imported by Beeman Precision Arms, Inc. previously located in Santa Rosa, CA. Manufactured by B.S.F. Available through used market only.

WISCHO AIR PISTOL MODEL S-20 STANDARD — .177 cal., barrel-cocking action, 450 FPS, 2 lbs. 8 oz. Disc. 1988.

$110 $90 $50

Last Mfg.'s Sug. Retail was $130

MODEL CM — same as above but target style. Disc. in 1988.

$120 $105 $70

Last Mfg.'s Sug. Retail was $160.

BLACK POWDER

Dear Black Powder Enthusiast:

At the annual Shot Show held in Dallas, TX this January, there were lines of excited dealers three deep waiting at the booths of Flintlocks, Etc., Dixie, and Navy Arms to discuss the new full line of Pedersoli Sharps rifles.

It's beginning to look as if Sharps rifles are going to be as big in 1996 as they were in 1995. With black powder cartridge silhouette competitions growing by leaps and bounds, it is no wonder. Shiloh is still reporting a four year back order situation, but this hasn't dampened the manufacturer's spirits. They are still writing orders right and left.

Other big sellers this year are the Remington-style rolling block rifles produced by Uberti, Pedersoli, and Lone Star Rifle companies. Again this interest is fueled by the growth of black powder cartridge silhouette shooting.

Speaking of Remington, if you like in-line ignition, modern black powder guns - you are going to flip over Remington's new 700 black powder rifle! This short throw bolt action rifle has all the poise and balance of the well known 700 BDL, but in black powder percussion. The fact that a major manufacturer is now marketing a modern in-line black powder rifle indicates the industry has finally accepted this new technology (something Knight, White, and Gonic have known for years).

Colt Signature series introduced an 1860 Army in stainless steel, as well as an additional style of the 1861 musket. The United States Patent Arms Company is enjoying the rewards of their second full year in business. U.S. Patent is going to offer their black powder line both through dealer and retail direct. Any buyer will be welcome to stop by to actually watch the assembly of their own gun - sounds like fun.

A new rifle was introduced by the Peifer Rifle Company which uses a shotgun primer in lieu of a percussion cap. What makes this gun unique is the primer is mounted in a rotating cylinder pushed into the bottom of the receiver. At standby, the cylinder is rotated 90^{0} placing the primer safely away from the firing pin. You can also keep additional cylinders loaded in your pocket, enabling a very fast second shot.

Connecticut Valley Arms, Pedersoli, and Lyman have expanded their line of Apollo in-line black powder guns. Gonic Arms has introduced a new Safari series, essentially a one price all custom rifle built to your specifications.

Outside of this the market has remained stable with only modest price increases on new models. The manufacturers and distributors continue to increase sales steadily, without the roller coaster ride experienced by the center fire manufacturers due to previously passed legislation. In general, 1996 looks to be an exciting year for the black powder industry.

Sincerely,

Patrick M. Lucking

Patrick M. Lucking
Black Powder Editor
Blue Book of Gun Values

MODERN BLACK POWDER GUNS

A NOTE ABOUT BLACK POWDER PRICING

The following section differs from the rest of the book in the number of pricing lines contained. You will notice guns under 95% are not listed and should be heavily scrutinized by the buyer if one is presented to him (or her) at the trading table. Although many fine shooters exist under 95% condition, their value as collector pieces are negligible. This is due to limited demand for used guns and the relatively low price of many fine guns that are still in "new-in-the-box" condition.

Collectors and shooters wanting to enter the world of black powder guns would be far better off to buy a new gun that is being liquidated because of a blemish or overstock conditions than to invest in the unknown mechanical condition of a less than 95% gun. Of course, if you find a gun in excellent mechanical shape under 95% condition feel free to buy it for pleasure but not as an investment.

The guns listed in this section are factory assembled. Kit guns are also available from many of the below listed manufacturers at substantial savings. They are not included in this section, however. Also, most Black Powder guns under $100 in value are not listed, and all prices are rounded to the nearest $5.

ALL ADD-ON'S FOR PRICING LISTED IN THIS SECTION ARE RETAIL WITHOUT DEALER DISCOUNTING. ENGRAVING PRICES ON LESS THAN 100% GUNS SHOULD BE DISCOUNTED BY A MINIMUM OF 50%.

ALLEN FIREARMS

Previous importer located in Santa Fe, NM importing A. Uberti firearms until early in 1987. After Allen Firearms closed, Old-West Gun Co. (now called Cimarron Arms) located in Houston, TX purchased the remaining inventory. Since all guns sold by Allen Firearms were manufactured by A. Uberti (they even used the same catalog), please refer to the A. Uberti section at the end of this section.

Add the following amounts for engraving on handguns:
        Add $350 for "A" style engraving (30% coverage).
        Add $425 for "B" style engraving (50% coverage).
        Add $750 for "C" style engraving (100% coverage).
        Add $800 for "Texas Cattlebrands" engraving pattern.

AMERICAN ARMS, INC.

N. Kansas City, MO. Available through dealers. American Arms also imports a line of black powder revolvers manufactured by Armi San Marco, Pietta, and a line of lever action rifles by Uberti. Please refer to the following section for pricing.

Grading	100%	98%	95%

RIFLES

HAWKEYE — .50 and .54 cal. percussion, in-line ignition, 22 in. round blued or stainless steel barrel, dual safety contemporary styled design,stock has rubber recoil pad. Disc. 1993.

	$265	$220	$175

Add $120 for stainless steel.

Last Mfg.'s Sug. Retail was $275.

ARMI SAN MARCO

Mfg. in Italy, previously imported House of Muskets (formerly Denver Arms) located in Pagosa Springs, CO, Muzzle Loaders, Inc. located in Burke, VA. Currently imported by E.M.F., located in Santa Ana, CA, and Taylor's & Co. located in Winchester, VA. May be purchased through dealers and catalog houses. In 1993, the Hartford line was introduced by E.M.F. These guns have steel frames with German silver backstrap and triggerguard and cartouches on grip. Guns trade at approximately $20-$40 higher.

PISTOLS

CHARLEVILLE 1777 PISTOL — .69 cal. flintlock, 7½in. white steel smooth bore barrel, brass furniture, belt hook, walnut stock, wt. 2¾ lbs.

	$170	$150	$100

REVOLVERS: PERCUSSION

WALKER MODEL 1847 — .44 cal., percussion, 9 in. barrel, color case hardened frame, loading lever and hammer, brass triggerguard and steel backstrap, 4½ lbs.

	$250	$220	$165

BABY DRAGOON — .31 cal., percussion, 5 in. octagonal barrel, 5 shot cylinder, color case hardened frame, hammer and load lever, silver plated brass backstrap and triggerguard.

	$200	$180	$140

1ST MODEL DRAGOON — .44 cal., percussion, 8 in. barrel, color case hardened frame, loading lever and hammer, silver plated brass backstrap and triggerguard.

	$240	$210	$165

2ND MODEL DRAGOON — same as 1st Model Dragoon, except 7½ in. barrel.

	$240	$210	$165

3RD MODEL DRAGOON — .44 cal., percussion, 7½ in. barrel, Western Model has silver plated brass backstrap, Military Model has steel backstrap - cut for stock, Texas Model has brass backstrap. Add $15 for Western Model.

	$240	$210	$165

1849 WELLS FARGO — .31 cal., percussion, 3 in., 4 in., 5 in. octagonal barrel, 5 shot, color case hardened frame and hammer, no load lever, brass trim, 1½ lbs.

	$200	$180	$140

1851 NAVY — .36 or .44 cal., percussion, 7½ in. octagonal barrel, engraved (roll) cylinder, color case hardened frame and load lever, silver plated brass backstrap and square back triggerguard. Sheriff's Model has 5 in. barrel, brass triggerguard and backstrap. Deduct $20 for brass back strap and triggerguard, $25 for brass frame. Add $80 for engraved steel frame, $100 for shoulder stock.

	$135	$120	$100

Grading	100%	98%	95%

1860 ARMY — .44 cal., percussion 8 in. round barrel, color case hardened frame, hammer and load lever, Sheriff's Model has 5 in. barrel, 2¾ lbs. Add $5 for Sheriff's Model. Add $35 for fluted cylinder model. Add $10 for engraved brass, add $100 for engraved steel, add $100 for stock. Deduct $35 for brass frame.

	$170	$150	$120

1861 NAVY — .36 cal., percussion, 7½ in. round barrel, color case hardened frame, hammer and load lever, silver-plated brass backstrap and triggerguard (very similar to 1860 Army, except cal. and shorter Navy grips).

	$180	$165	$120

1862 POLICE POCKET — .36 cal., percussion, 4½, 5½, 6½ in. barrel, color case hardened steel frame, hammer and load lever or brass frame, cylinder semi-fluted or engraved, 1.6 lbs.

Brass	$145	$130	$100
Steel	$195	$175	$140

1858 REMINGTON ARMY — .44 cal percussion, 6 shot, 8 in. octagonal barrel, brass frame, triggerguard & backstrap, walnut grips, 2⅜ lbs.

	$135	$115	$100

Add $140 for stainless steel target model.
Add $70 for engraving on brass frame, add $25 for steel frame, Add $50 for 12 in. barrel Buffalo Target Model.

RIFLES

HAWKEN RIFLE — .45, .50, .54 or .58 cal., percussion, color case hardened hammer and lock, brass patch box.

	$230	$200	$160

HAWKENS — .50 cal., percussion, 30 in. octagonal chrome lined barrel, brass patchbox, target sights, double set triggers, 8 lbs.

	$230	$200	$160

ST. LOUIS HAWKEN — .50, .54, or .58 cal., percussion, color case hardened hammer and lock, 28 in. octagonal barrel, brass trim, 7 lbs. 15 oz. Add $65 for curly maple stock.

	$260	$230	$175

ROCKY MOUNTAIN SHORT RIFLE — .50 cal., percussion, 24 in. octagonal barrel, brass furniture.

	$225	$200	$140

BLACK POWDER

ARMI SAN PAOLO

Mfg. in Italy. Armi San Paolo is a wholly owned subsidiary of Euroarms of Europe which also owns Euroarms of America. See Euroarms section for pricing. Previously imported by Kendall International located in Paris, KY and Muzzle Loaders, Inc. located in Burke, VA. May be purchased through dealers and catalog houses.

ARMSPORT

Importers located in Miami, FL. Available through dealers.

PISTOLS

CORSAIR PISTOL — .44 cal., percussion, double barrel, blued finish, color case hardened hammer and lock, brass trim.

	$265	$210	$135

DUELING PISTOL — .45 cal., percussion, blued finish, color case hardened hammer and lock, brass trim.

	$200	$150	$110

Grading	100%	98%	95%

KENTUCKY PISTOL — .45 or .50 cal., percussion or flintlock, blued finish, color case hardened hammer and lock, brass trim. Add $10 for flint lock.

	$175	$140	$110

REVOLVERS

MODEL 1847 COLT WALKER REVOLVER — .44 cal., percussion, color case hardened frame, hammer, and load lever, brass triggerguard, steel backstrap, 6 shot, 4½ lbs.

Mfg.'s Sug. Retail	$305	$250	$220	$165

MODEL 1851 COLT NAVY — .36 or .44 cal., percussion, brass or color case hardened frame, brass triggerguard and backstrap, 6 shot. Add $40 for color case hardened steel with engraved cylinders. Add $100 for engraved gold and nickel.

Mfg.'s Sug. Retail	$160	$110	$95	$75

MODEL 1860 COLT ARMY — .44 cal., percussion, brass frame, triggerguard, and backstrap, color case hardened hammer and load lever, 6 shot. Add $35 for color case hardened steel, $30 for Steel Sheriff Model, $160 for stainless steel, $115 for engraved gold and silver.

Mfg.'s Sug. Retail	$165	$145	$115	$85

MODEL 1858 REMINGTON ARMY — .44 cal., percussion, blued frame, brass triggerguard, steel backstrap, 6 shot. Add $115 for stainless steel, $90 for engraved gold and silver, $25 for Target Model, $140 for stainless Target Model. Deduct $25 for brass frame, $30 for nickel plated brass.

Mfg.'s Sug. Retail	$230	$160	$145	$125

REMINGTON BUFFALO TARGET — .44 cal., percussion, 12 in. octagonal barrel, brass frame and triggerguard, adj. sights, based on 1858 Navy frame, 38 oz. Add $10 for nickel plated brass.

Mfg.'s Sug. Retail	$220	$195	$165	$120

REMINGTON POCKET — .31 cal. percussion, 5 shot 4 in. octagonal barrel, brass frame, 15 oz. Disc. 1994.

	$145	$130	$100

Last Mfg.'s Sug. Retail was $160.

RIFLES

BRISTOL KID RIFLE — .32 or .36 cal., percussion. Add $15 for standard version, $25 for deluxe. Discontinued in 1984.

	$220	$190	$140

HAWKEN RIFLE — .45, .50, .54, or .58 cal., percussion or flintlock, color case hardened hammer and lock, percussion cap holder in stock, chrome lined barrels. Add $25 for flintlock.

	$425	$375	$285

HAWKENTUCKY RIFLE — .36 or .50 cal., percussion or flintlock, color case hardened hammer and lock, percussion cap holder in stock, chrome lined barrels. Add $10 for flintlock.

	$360	$290	$200

KENTUCKY RIFLE — .36, .45, or .50, cal., percussion or flintlock, color case hardened hammer and lock, percussion cap holder in stock, chrome lined barrels, brass trim. Add $10 for flintlock, $55 for deluxe with engraved white steel hammer and lock.

	$345	$300	$225

SHARPS RIFLE/CARBINE — .45 and .54 cal., percussion, 28 in. barrel (22 in. carbine). (IAB) New 1992.

Mfg.'s Sug. Retail	$750	$575	$500	$400

Add $25 for 28 in. octagonal barrel.

TRYON TRAILBLAZER — .50 or .54 cal., percussion, color case hardened hammer and lock, cap holder in stock. Add $45 for deluxe engraved.

	$390	$360	$275

Grading	100%	98%	95%

TRYON BACK ACTION RIFLE — .50 and .54 cal., percussion, 28 and 30 in. barrel. New 1992. Disc. 1994.

$600 $550 $420

Add $55 for silver finish.

Last Mfg.'s Sug. Retail was $825.

BLACK POWDER CARTRIDGE

SHARPS RIFLE/CARBINE — .45/70 black powder cartridge, 28 in. round or octagonal barrel (22 in. on carbine). (IAB) New 1992.

Mfg.'s Sug. Retail $865 $670 $580 $460

Add $25 for octagonal barrel.
Deduct $20 for Carbine model.

SHOTGUNS

KENTUCKY RIFLE/SHOTGUN COMBO — .45 or .50 cal., 20 ga., percussion only, same as Kentucky Rifle above.

$360 $290 $200

DOUBLE BARREL SHOTGUN — 12 or 10 ga., percussion only, blued finish, color case hardened hammer and lock. Add $50 for 10 ga.

$380 $330 $260

CANNONS

BORDA CANNON — .50 cal. wick, nickel plated. Disc. 1994.

$200 $170 $135

Add $80 for gold plating.

Last Mfg.'s Sug. Retail was $195.

NAPOLEON CANNON — .45, .69 or .75 wick, nickel plated. Deduct $230 for .45 or .50 cal. Add for gold plating .75 cal. $150, .45 $70, .69 $120. Disc. 1994.

$450 $390 $310

Last Mfg.'s Sug. Retail was $525.

YORKTOWN CANNON — .50 cal. wick, nickel plated. Add $100 for gold plating. Disc. 1994.

$200 $170 $135

Last Mfg.'s Sug. Retail was $195.

ASSOCIATION FOR THE PRESERVATION OF WESTERN ANTIQUITY

Distributed by William Benjamin Ltd. located in Ashville, NC.

1862 COLT NAVY — .36 cal., percussion, standard construction, roll engraved cylinder with 24Kt. gold inlay, only 100 revolvers made, sold in custom cameo art presentation case depicting a miner panning for gold, some sets may come with the addition of a seated Liberty silver dollar and a Double Eagle gold piece, coins value should be based on current numismatic value, present retail for entire set including gold pieces is $2,395. Disc. 1994.

$825 $710 $570

Last Mfg.'s Sug. Retail was $995.

BENSON FIREARMS, LTD.

Previous importer/distributor of A. Uberti Firearms mfg. in Italy. Benson Firearms was located in Seattle, WA.

Grading	100%	98%	95%

Benson Firearms was a recent importer (1987-1988) and imported A. Uberti firearms that were marked "Benson Firearms Seattle, WA". In 1989 Benson Firearms, Ltd. combined with Uberti USA, Inc. located in New Milford, CT.

All guns were manufactured to the same exact specifications as the originals. Crafted with an unmistakable fire blue finish. A. Uberti is one of the largest manufacturers of black powder firearms. See A. Uberti at the end of this section for pricing.

BERETTA

Manufacturer located in Brescia, Italy 1680-present. Available on the used market only.

SHOTGUNS

COMMEMORATIVE O/U MODEL M1000 — 12 ga., percussion, 30 in. barrel, limited production. Disc. 1994.

$630 $535 $420

Last Mfg.'s Sug. Retail was $840.

BONDINI

Manufacturer located in Italy. Previously imported by Helmut Hofman, Inc. located in Placitas, NH, House Of Muskets located in Pagosa Lakes, CO, and Austin-Sheridan, USA Middlefield, CT. Available through dealers and catalog houses.

PISTOLS

ASHABELLA COOK UNDERHAMMER — .45 cal., unique underhammer design uses triggerguard as mainspring. Very accurate.

$200 $170 $120

WM. PARKER PISTOL — .45 cal., flintlock or percussion, 11 in. octagonal browned barrel, silver plated furniture, double set triggers. Add $10 for flintlock.

$205 $175 $140

F. ROCHATTE — .45 cal., percussion, round barrel, single set triggers, hand checkered stock.

$250 $210 $160

RIFLES

SANFTL SCHUETZEN RIFLE — .45 cal., percussion, 31 in. octagonal barrel, unique backward lock, both peep and open iron sights, Schuetzen style butt plate and triggerguard, brass furniture.

$800 $700 $600

SHOTGUNS

GALLYON SHOTGUN — 12 ga., percussion, blued barrel, single shot. Add $150 for extra 12 ga. barrel.

$330 $290 $230

BROWNING

Headquarters located in Morgan, UT. Available only on the used market.

BROWNING

Grading	100%	98%	95%

RIFLES

JONATHAN BROWNING MOUNTAIN RIFLE — 50 cal., percussion, 30 in. octagon barrel, single set trigger, engraved lock plate, select walnut stock, cased with medallion and powder horn, 1,000 mfg. in 1978. Issue price — $650.

$750 $595 $400

MOUNTAIN RIFLE — similar to Jonathan Browning Mountain Rifle, without Centennial embellishments, not cased. Also in .45 or .54 cal.

$450 $375 $275

CHARLES DALY

See "Daly, Charles".

CHENEY RIFLE WORKS

Cheney Rifle Works has changed its name to Wilderness Rifle Works, still located in Waldron, IN. All Cheney manufactured rifles will now appear in the Wilderness Rifle Works section in this text.

CIMARRON ARMS COMPANY

Importer/distributor of custom crafted A. Uberti Modern and **CIMARRON** F.A. C⁰. Blackpowder Firearms. Cimarron Arms is located in Houston, TX. Available direct or through dealers.

Cimarron Arms was previously named Old-West Gun Company.

> After years of research, Cimarron Arms Co. has contracted A. Uberti to manufacture the most authentic western firearms reproductions to date, including such exact modifications as changing the taper of the cylinder face to exactly match the original Colt's. Also, serial number location, cylinder scenes, stock configuration, etc. have all been carefully manufactured to duplicate the original. In 1992, Cimarron started bringing in guns in white steel and having the bluing and color case hardening done in the U.S. to match the original colors.

Add the following amounts for engraving on handguns:
    Add $350 for "A" style engraving (30% coverage).
    Add $425 for "B" style engraving (50% coverage).
    Add $750 for "C" style engraving (100% coverage).
    Add $800 for "Texas Cattlebrands" engraving pattern.
    Add $100 for old style case hardened frame.

REVOLVERS

1847 WALKER — .44 cal., percussion, charcoal finish, color case hardened frame, hammer, and load lever, brass trim, engraved cylinder, 4.4 lbs.

Mfg.'s Sug. Retail $310 $275 $240 $165
    Add $25 for charcoal or white finish.

1848 BABY DRAGOON — .31 cal., percussion, 3, 4, or 5 in. barrel, 5 shot, color case hardened frame, hammer, no load lever, engraved cylinder, 1.4 lbs. Add $15 for silver straps and triggerguard.

Mfg.'s Sug. Retail $270 $240 $210 $160
    Add $25 for charcoal or white finish.

Grading	100%	98%	95%

DRAGOON (1ST, 2ND, OR 3RD) — .44 cal., percussion, 6 shot, brass grip straps, color case hardened frame, hammer, and load lever, brass trim, 3.9 lbs. Add $20 for silver-plated straps, or cut for stock on 3rd Dragoon Model. Add $180 for stock. Add $25 for charcoal or white finish.

| Mfg.'s Sug. Retail | $300 | $260 | $230 | $170 |

1849 WELLS FARGO — .31 cal., percussion, 3, 4, or 5 in. octagonal barrel, 5 shot, color case hardened frame, hammer, no load lever, brass trim, 1½ lbs. Add $15 for silver straps.

| Mfg.'s Sug. Retail | $270 | $240 | $210 | $145 |

Add $25 for charcoal or white finish.

1849 POCKET — .31 cal., percussion, with loading lever, 3, 4, or 5 in. barrel, 5 shot, color case hardened frame, hammer, and load lever, brass trim, 1½ lbs. Add $15 for silver straps and triggerguard. Add $25 for charcoal or white finish.

| Mfg.'s Sug. Retail | $270 | $240 | $210 | $145 |

1851 NAVY — .36 cal., percussion, many styles, loading lever, 6 shot engraved cylinder, 2.8 lbs. Add $130 for stock, $45 for stainless steel, $15 for silver plated strap and triggerguard, or steel strap and triggerguard, for London model or cut for stock. Add $25 for charcoal or white finish.

| Mfg.'s Sug. Retail | $260 | $230 | $200 | $160 |

1860 ARMY — .44 cal., percussion, 8 in. barrel, 6 shot, loading lever, color case hardened frame, hammer, and load lever, all brass backstrap and triggerguard, or steel backstrap and brass triggerguard on fluted cylinder model, 2.6 lbs. Add $145 for stock, $15 for silver plated strap and triggerguard, $5 for cut for stock or $5 for fluted cylinder model, $5 for Civilian Model, $50 for stainless steel.

| Mfg.'s Sug. Retail | $265 | $225 | $205 | $150 |

Add $25 for charcoal or white finish.

1861 NAVY — .36 cal., percussion, 5 in. barrel, many styles, brass backstrap or triggerguard, color case hardened frame, hammer, and load lever, 2½ lbs. Add $15 for silver-plated strap and trigger guard, $50 for stainless steel, $145 for shoulder stock. Add $25 for charcoal or white finish.

| Mfg.'s Sug. Retail | $270 | $235 | $205 | $165 |

PATERSON — .36 cal., percussion, 7½ in. octagonal barrel, standard hidden trigger design, blued steel hardware, no loading lever, 2½ lbs. Add $25 for charcoal or white finish.

| Mfg.'s Sug. Retail | $345 | $310 | $270 | $210 |

Add $40 for loading lever.

1862 POLICE — .36 cal., percussion, 4½, 5½, or 6½ in. barrel, color case hardened frame, hammer, and load lever, cylinder, semi-fluted or engraved, 1.6 lbs. Add $15 for silver plated straps and triggerguard, $50 for stainless steel. Add $25 for charcoal or white finish.

| Mfg.'s Sug. Retail | $270 | $235 | $205 | $165 |

1862 POCKET NAVY — .36 cal., percussion, 4½, 5½, or 6½ in. barrel, color case hardened frame, hammer, and load lever, cylinder, semi-fluted or engraved, 1.6 lbs. Add $15 for silver plated straps and triggerguard, $50 for stainless steel. Add $25 for charcoal or white finish.

| Mfg.'s Sug. Retail | $270 | $220 | $200 | $160 |

AUGUSTA CONFEDERATE — .36 cal., percussion, 7½ in. octagonal barrel, color case hardened hammer and trigger, all brass frame, engraved cylinder, 2½-2¾ lbs.

| Mfg.'s Sug. Retail | $210 | $180 | $160 | $120 |

GRISWOLD AND GUNNISON CONFEDERATE — .36 or .44 cal., percussion, same as above except round barrel, forward of lug, does not have engraved cylinder. Disc. 1994.

| | $180 | $160 | $120 |

Last Mfg.'s Sug. Retail was $150.

BLACK POWDER

Grading	100%	98%	95%

LEECH AND RIGDON CONFEDERATE — .36 cal., percussion, same as above except all steel frame.
Mfg.'s Sug. Retail $280 $220 $200 $160

TEXAS CONFEDERATE DRAGOON — .44 cal., percussion, 7½ in. round barrel, color case hardened frame, hammer, and load lever, brass trim, "Tucker, Sherrard, and Co.", 4 lbs. Disc. 1994.

$260 $230 $155

Last Mfg.'s Sug. Retail was $210.

1858 REMINGTON — .44 cal., percussion, 7½ in. barrel, 6 shot, blued steel, brass triggerguard, 2.6 lbs. Add $40 for adj. sights.
Mfg.'s Sug. Retail $260 $230 $200 $160

1858 REMINGTON STAINLESS — same as above, has brass strap and triggerguard. Add $40 for adj. sights. Disc. 1994.

$305 $265 $210

Last Mfg.'s Sug. Retail was $260.

1858 REMINGTON NEW NAVY — .36 cal., percussion, 6½ in. octagonal barrel, 6 shot, blue frame, 2½ lbs. Add $40 for adj. sights. Disc. 1994.

$205 $180 $135

Last Mfg.'s Sug. Retail was $185.

1866 REVOLVING CARBINE — .44 cal., percussion, 18 in. barrel, 6 shot, blued steel, brass triggerguard, walnut stock, 4.6 lbs. Disc. 1994.

$345 $300 $200

Last Mfg.'s Sug. Retail was $320.

RIFLES: PERCUSSION

HAWKEN SANTA FE — .54 cal., single shot, 32 in. oct. barrel, damascened finish, double set triggers, 9½ lbs., walnut stock. Disc. 1994.

$385 $330 $265

Last Mfg.'s Sug. Retail was $350.

JEREDIAH SMITH SANTA FE HAWKENS — .50 and .54 cal. percussion, similar to above. Add $35 for Flintlock.
Mfg.'s Sug. Retail $445 $385 $330 $265

LEMAN TRADE RIFLE — .45, .50, .54, and .58 cal. percussion. Add $15 for .54 and .58 cal. Disc. 1994.

$250 $220 $160

Last Mfg.'s Sug. Retail was $250.

ST. LOUIS RIFLE — .45, .50, .54, or .58 cal., flintlock and percussion, color case hardened hammer lock and triggerguard, octagonal barrel. Add $15 for .54 and .58 cal. percussion, $15 for flintlock, $30 for 50 cal. flintlock. Disc. 1994.

$345 $280 $210

Last Mfg.'s Sug. Retail was $280.

BLACKPOWDER CARTRIDGE

ROLLING BLOCK SPORTING RIFLE — .45/.70 blackpowder cartridge, 30 in. barrel. Add $100 for deluxe sporting rifle. Disc. 1994.

$380 $330 $265

Last Mfg.'s Sug. Retail was $620.

COLT'S FIREARMS

Hartford, CT. Colt subcontracted the manufacture of these black powder pistols to Aldo Uberti in Italy from 1979-1982. Parts were shipped into the U.S. and assembled stateside.

Grading	100%	98%	95%

PERCUSSION REVOLVERS: 2ND GENERATION

See Colt Black Powder 2nd Generation Serialization section in the back of this text for more information. Last manufacturer's suggested retail values listed below are from the 1982 Colt factory catalog.

WALKER MODEL — .44 cal., 9 in. barrel, color case hardened frame, hammer, and loading lever, 73 oz., mfg. 1979-1982. Add $100 for cased Heritage Walker Commemorative Model. Disc. 1994.

$895 $675 $495

Last Mfg.'s Sug. Retail was $562.

BABY DRAGOON — .31 cal., 4 in. barrel, unfluted straight cylinder, color case hardened frame, short frame. Disc. 1994.

$450 $375 $275

Last Mfg.'s Sug. Retail was $405.

▲ *"1 of 500" cased set.*

$675 $525 $400

Last Mfg.'s Sug. Retail was $900.

1ST MODEL DRAGOON — .44 cal., 7½ in. barrel, oval bolt cuts in cylinder, color case hardened frame, loading lever, plunger, and hammer, one piece stocks, 66 oz. Disc. 1982.

$425 $325 $250

Last Mfg.'s Sug. Retail was $448.

2ND MODEL DRAGOON — .44 cal., 7½ in. barrel, rectangular bolt cuts in cylinder, color case hardened frame, loading lever, plunger, and hammer, one piece stocks, 66 oz. Disc. 1982.

$425 $325 $250

Last Mfg.'s Sug. Retail was $448.

3RD MODEL DRAGOON — .44 cal., 7½ in. barrel, rectangular bolt cuts in cylinder, color case hardened frame, loading lever, plunger, and hammer, round triggerguard, one piece stocks, 66 oz. Disc. 1982. Add $275 for cased Giuseppe Garibaldi Commemorative Model.

$425 $325 $250

Last Mfg.'s Sug. Retail was $448.

1851 NAVY — .36 cal., 7½ in. octagonal barrel, color case hardened frame, loading lever, plunger, and hammer, square triggerguard, one piece stocks, 42 oz. Disc. 1982.

$450 $350 $275

Last Mfg.'s Sug. Retail was $420.

▲ *1851 Stainless Navy* — stainless steel, only 498 mfg. Disc. 1994.

$695 $500 $395

Last Mfg.'s Sug. Retail was $473.

BLACK POWDER

1860 ARMY — .44 cal., 8 in. round barrel, color case hardened frame, loading lever, plunger, and hammer, round triggerguard, one piece stocks, 42 oz. Disc. 1981. Two versions made, one has an engraved rebated cylinder and the other has a blued fluted cylinder.

Fluted Cylinder	$550	$450	$300
Rebated Cylinder	$550	$450	$300

Last Mfg.'s Sug. Retail was $431 (non-fluted), $456 (fluted).

▲ *1860 Army Stainless Unfluted* — mfg. 1982. Disc. 1994.

$700 $550 $375

Last Mfg.'s Sug. Retail was $485.

1861 NAVY — .36 cal., 7½ in. round barrel, color case hardened frame, loading lever, plunger, and hammer, round triggerguard, one piece stocks, 42 oz. Disc. 1982.

$495 $375 $295

Last Mfg.'s Sug. Retail was $420.

Stainless variations of this model (only 3 or 4 are known to exist) are very desirable - 100% specimens would probably trade in the $2,000 range.

Last Mfg.'s Sug. Retail was $473.

Grading	100%	98%	95%

1862 POCKET NAVY — .36 cal., 5½ in. octagonal barrel, color case hardened frame, loading lever, plunger, and hammer, round triggerguard, one piece stocks, 27 oz. Disc. 1982.

                                  $395   **$300**   **$250**

                                                        Last Mfg.'s Sug. Retail was $394.

▲ *"1 of 500" cased set*

                                  $650   **$525**   **$350**

1862 POCKET POLICE — .36 cal., 5½ in. round barrel, color case hardened frame, loading lever, plunger, and hammer, round triggerguard, fluted cylinder, one piece stocks, 25 oz. Disc. 1982.

                                  $375   **$250**   **$200**

                                                        Last Mfg.'s Sug. Retail was $394.

▲ *"1 of 500" cased*

                                  $650   **$525**   **$350**

COLT REVOLVERS SIGNATURE SERIES

In 1994, Colt released a limited run of 4 Models in a new Signature Series, five more guns including the 1861 Musket were released in 1995. These guns are all manufactured under an authorized licensing agreement with Colt Firearms. Using the original subcontractors these guns are manufactured in Italy and assembled (by many of the same craftsmen responsible for the Colt 2nd Generation Revolvers) in New York, NY.

WALKER — .44 cal., 9 in. barrel, color case hardened frame, hammer, and loading lever, 73 oz. New 1994.

  Mfg.'s Sug. Retail   **$488**   **$440**   **$380**   **$310**

3RD MODEL DRAGOON — .44 Cal., 7½ in. barrel, rectangular bolt cuts in cylinder, color case hardened 3 screw frame, loading lever, plunger and hammer, round brass triggerguard and brass gripstrap, one piece walnut grip. Prices equal on Whitneyville Hartford Dragoon Model. New 1996.

  Mfg.'s Sug. Retail   **$488**   **$440**   **$380**   **$310**

    Add $15 for 4 screw model with blued steel backstrap (cut for optional stock) and folding rear leaf sight.

1849 POCKET DRAGOON — .31 cal., 4 in. barrel, unfluted straight cyl., color case hardened frame, short frame, walnut grips, 1½ lbs.

  Mfg.'s Sug. Retail   **$443**   **$365**   **$320**   **$260**

1851 NAVY — .36 cal., 7½ in. octagonal barrel, color case hardened frame, loading lever, plunger, and hammer, square triggerguard, one piece stocks, 42 oz. New 1994.

  Mfg.'s Sug. Retail   **$428**   **$370**   **$300**   **$240**

1860 ARMY — .44 cal., 8 in. round blued barrel, color case hardened, frame, loading lever, plunger and hammer, round brass triggerguard, walnut stock, 2¾ lbs. Four versions are currently mfg. - one with an engraved rebated cylinder and the other has a blued fluted cylinder, an Officer's Model is also available with handcrafted brilliant blue finish with traditional crossed sabers in 24 Kt. gold above the wedge pin, cut for shoulder stock, the backstrap is roll-engraved with Sam Colt's signature, a gold U.S. Calvary model completes the line.

▲ *Rebated Cylinder*
  Mfg.'s Sug. Retail   **$443**   **$320**   **$290**   **$230**

▲ *Fluted Cylinder*
  Mfg.'s Sug. Retail   **$465**   **$400**   **$360**   **$300**

▲ *Officer's Model*
  Mfg.'s Sug. Retail   **$690**   **$600**   **$540**   **$430**

Grading	100%	98%	95%

▲ *Gold U.S. Calvary Model*
Mfg.'s Sug. Retail $668 $600 $515 $410

▲ *Stainless Model*
Mfg.'s Sug. Retail $503 $430   N/A   N/A

1861 Navy Steel — .36 cal., $7\frac{1}{2}$ in. round barrel, color case hardened frame, loading lever, plunger, and hammer, steel backstrap and trigger guard, roll-engraved cylinder and barrel, one piece walnut grips. 42 oz.
Mfg.'s Sug. Retail $465 $400 $360 $300

1862 POCKET NAVY — .36 cal., $5\frac{1}{2}$ in. octagonal barrel, color case hardened frame, loading lever, plunger and hammer, round triggerguard (brass) rebated roll engraved cylinder. 25 oz.
Mfg.'s Sug. Retail $443 $400   N/A   N/A

1862 Trapper Model — .36 cal., $3\frac{1}{2}$ in. round barrel, color case hardened frame, and hammer, silver plated backstrap and triggerguard, no loading lever but supplied with $4\frac{5}{8}$ in. brass ramrod.
Mfg.'s Sug. Retail $443 $400 $360 $300

COLT RIFLES: SIGNATURE SERIES

1861 MUSKET — .58 cal. percussion, 40 in. round barrel with 3 barrel bands, all metal parts bright finished white steel, one-piece oil finished walnut stock. Artillery Model has $31\frac{1}{2}$ in. barrel with two barrel bands. New 1996.

▲ *Standard Model*
Mfg.'s Sug. Retail $700 $600 $510 $410

▲ *Artillery Model*
Mfg.'s Sug. Retail $700 $600   N/A   N/A

▲ *1 of 1,000*
Mfg.'s Sug. Retail $1,650 $1,490 $1,270 $1,140

CONNECTICUT VALLEY ARMS

Distributed in Norcross, GA. Available through dealers and catalog houses.

All pistols have color case hardened finishes with solid brass trim.

PISTOLS

COLONIAL PISTOL — .45 cal., percussion, $6\frac{3}{4}$ in. octagonal barrel, 31 oz. Mfg. 1989-1993. Disc. 1994.

$125 $105 $85

Last Mfg.'s Sug. Retail was $115.

"HAWKEN" PISTOL — .50 cal., percussion or flintlock, $9\frac{3}{4}$ in. octagonal barrel, 50 oz. Add $10 for flintlock.
Mfg.'s Sug. Retail $150 $135 $115 $90
Add $15 for laminated stock.

STANDARD KENTUCKY PISTOL — .45 or .50 cal., percussion, $10\frac{1}{4}$ in. octagonal barrel, brass blade front sight, 40 oz.
Mfg.'s Sug. Retail $150 $135 $115 $90

MOUNTAIN PISTOL — .45 or .50 cal., percussion, 9 in. octagonal barrel, German silver wedge plate with pewter cap, 40 oz.

$135 $115 $90

PHILADELPHIA DERRINGER — .45 cal., percussion, $3\frac{1}{4}$ in. octagonal barrel, 16 oz. Disc. 1994.

$95 $80 $60

Last Mfg.'s Sug. Retail was $90.

BLACK POWDER

Grading	100%	98%	95%

SIBER PISTOL — .45 cal., percussion, 10½ in. octagonal, white steel engraved barrel, lock also engraved white steel, checkered walnut grip, 38 oz. Disc. 1994.

$400 $345 $260

Last Mfg.'s Sug. Retail was $440.

TOWER PISTOL — .45 cal., percussion, 9 in. octagonal barrel at breech tapers to round, antique brass trigger, 36 oz.

$135 $115 $90

REVOLVERS

All revolvers have solid brass trim and walnut grips.

COLT WALKER MODEL — .44 cal., percussion, 9 in. barrel, color case hardened frame, hammer, and loading lever, 72 oz.

Mfg.'s Sug. Retail $280 $240 $205 $150

3RD MODEL DRAGOON — .44 cal., 7½ in. barrel, rectangular bolt cuts in cylinder, color case hardened frame, loading lever, plunger, and hammer, round triggerguard, one piece stocks, 66 oz. Disc. 1994.

$220 $190 $155

Last Mfg.'s Sug. Retail was $220.

WELLS FARGO — .31 cal., percussion, 3, 4, or 5 in. octagonal barrel, 5 shot, color case hardened frame, hammer, no load lever, brass trim, 1½ lbs. Add $65 for steel frame. Disc. 1994.

$105 $85 $65

Last Mfg.'s Sug. Retail was $130.

1851 NAVY — .36 or .44 cal., percussion, 7½ in. octagonal barrel, brass frame, 38 oz. Add $50 for steel frame.

Mfg.'s Sug. Retail $140 $110 $95 $75

CVA COLT POCKET POLICE — .36 cal., 5½ in. round barrel, color case hardened frame, loading lever, plunger, and hammer, round triggerguard, fluted cylinder, one piece stocks, 25 oz. Add $40 for steel frame.

Mfg.'s Sug. Retail $140 $115 $100 $80

Add $5 for Sheriff's Model.
Add $50 for engraved, nickel plated Sheriff's Model w/matching powder flask.

1860 ARMY — .44 cal., percussion, 8 in. round barrel, 6 shot engraved cylinder, color case hardened frame, trigger, and load lever, 44 oz. Deduct $40 for brass frame.

Mfg.'s Sug. Retail $195 $160 $145 $110

1861 NAVY — .36 or .44 cal., percussion, 7½ in. round barrel, 6 shot engraved cylinder, color case hardened frame, trigger, and load lever, or brass frame (.44 cal. only), 44 oz. Add $60 for color case hardened steel frame, $60 for presentation grade Sheriff's Model with matching powder flask (new in 1986).

Mfg.'s Sug. Retail $140 $115 $100 $80

Add $10 for brass frame on Standard Sheriff Model.
Add $25 for steel frame on Standard Sheriff Model.

WAR AND PEACE — .36 cal., 1851 Navy and 1851 Sheriff's Model, heavily engraved in rosewood presentation case. Disc. 1994.

$390 $330 $240

Last Mfg.'s Sug. Retail was $630.

1873 COLT SINGLE ACTION — .44 cal. percussion, 7 in. round barrel, brass backstrap and triggerguard, color case hardened frame and cylinder, new in 1991 (this is a ball and cap version of the 1873 Colt Cartridge gun). Disc. 1994.

$300 $260 $210

Last Mfg.'s Sug. Retail was $350.

Grading	100%	98%	95%

1858 REMINGTON ARMY — .44 cal., percussion, 8 in. octagonal barrel, color case hardened hammer, steel or brass frame, 38 oz. Add $35 for steel.

Mfg.'s Sug. Retail	$150	$125	$110	$90

REMINGTON BISON — .44 cal., percussion, 1858 Remington Army frame brass, $10\frac{1}{4}$ in. octagonal barrel, adj. sights, 3 lbs.

Mfg.'s Sug. Retail	$200	$170	$150	$120

REMINGTON POCKET — .31 cal., percussion, 5 shot, 4 in. octagonal barrel, brass frame, 15 oz. New in 1989.

Mfg.'s Sug. Retail	$150	$130	$110	$85

REMINGTON TARGET — .44 cal., percussion, 12 in. octagonal barrel, brass frame and trigger-guard, adj. sights, based on 1858 Navy frame, 38 oz.

	$185	$165	$135

Last Mfg.'s Sug. Retail was $205.

OFFICER AND THE GENTLEMAN —matched set .44 cal., 1858 Rem. Army and .31 cal. Pocket Rem., heavily engraved in rosewood presentation case. Disc. 1994.

	$500	$425	$300

Last Mfg.'s Sug. Retail was $650.

RIFLES

APOLLO RIFLE — .50 or .54 cal. percussion, straight line ignition, 22 in. (carbine), 24 in., 25 in. or 27 in. round tapered barrel with chrome bore, slide bolt design.

APOLLO 90 RIFLE

Mfg.'s Sug. Retail	$260	$240	$210	$170

APOLLO 90 SHADOW RIFLE — with duragrip synthetic stock.

Mfg.'s Sug. Retail	$230	$200	$170	$140

APOLLO BROWN BEAR — with hardwood stock and Williams Hunter sight.

Mfg.'s Sug. Retail	$230	$200	$170	$140

APOLLO BUCKMASTER — with camo duragrip synthetic stock.

Mfg.'s Sug. Retail	$240	$210	$175	$140

APOLLO CARBELITE — same as Apollo 90 above but with Carbelite stock.

	$200	$170	$140

Last Mfg.'s Sug. Retail was $350.

APOLLO COMET — with duragrip stock and adjustable trigger.

Mfg.'s Sug. Retail	$280	$225	$200	$160

APOLLO DOMINATOR — with Bell & Carlson synthetic stock, stainless steel barrel and modern adjustable trigger.

Mfg.'s Sug. Retail	$330	$275	$245	$180

APOLLO ECLIPSE — standard

Mfg.'s Sug. Retail	$200	$165	$150	$120

APOLLO SHADOW RIFLE — similar to 90 Shadow above.

Mfg.'s Sug. Retail	$230	$200	$170	$140

APOLLO SPORTER — with standard stock and 25 in. barrel.

	$200	$170	$140

Last Mfg.'s Sug. Retail was $225.

APOLLO STAG HORN — basic version of Apollo rifle with duragrip synthetic stock.

Mfg.'s Sug. Retail	$180	$155	$135	$110

APOLLO STARFIRE — with duragrip stock and stainless steel barrel.

Mfg.'s Sug. Retail	$250	$205	$185	$145

Grading	100%	98%	95%

BLAZER RIFLE — .50 cal., percussion, straight ignition (like Percussion Revolver), 28 in. octagonal barrel, stainless steel nipple, brass tipped ramrod, 6 lbs., 12 oz. Deduct $10 for Blazer II. Disc. 1994.

$130 $110 $90

Last Mfg.'s Sug. Retail was $210.

BLUNDERBUSS — .69 cal., flintlock, 16 in. tapered to flared muzzle barrel, brass trim, available right or left-hand, 5 lbs. 5 oz. Disc. 1994.

$240 $195 $155

Last Mfg.'s Sug. Retail was $255.

BOBCAT HUNTER RIFLE — .36, .50 & .54 cal., percussion, 26 in. octagonal barrel, (1:48 twist) matte black finish adjustable sights. New 1995.

Mfg.'s Sug. Retail $150 $130 $110 $90

Add $20 for .36 cal.

Deduct $20 for Bobcat Rifle with fixed sights.

BUSHWACKER RIFLE — .50 cal., percussion, 26 in. octagonal barrel, color case hardened hammer, lock and nipple, blued furniture, $7\frac{1}{2}$ lbs. Disc. 1994.

$140 $120 $95

Last Mfg.'s Sug. Retail was $160.

EXPRESS RIFLE —.50 or .54 cal., percussion, double barrel, 28 in. tapered round barrel, color case hardened plate, hammers and trim, adj. sights. Add $375 for presentation grade (new in 1986).

Mfg.'s Sug. Retail $430 $400 $350 $280

Add $160 for extra set of 12 ga. barrels.

FRONTIER RIFLE/CARBINE —.45, .50 & .54 cal., percussion or flintlock, 28 in. octagonal barrel, brass trim, right or left-hand, 7 lbs. 15 oz. Add $15 for flintlock, $10 for left-hand, add $10 for carbine model. Disc. 1994.

$175 $150 $110

Last Mfg.'s Sug. Retail was $190.

FRONTIER HUNTER CARBINE — .50 & .54 cal. percussion, 24 in. blued octagonal barrel, color case hardened hammer & lock, blued furniture, adj. sight (rear), wt. $7\frac{1}{2}$ lbs.

Mfg.'s Sug. Retail $220 $190 $170 $125

New in 1995 Frontier Hunter came with a laminated stock.

HAWKEN RIFLE/CARBINE —.50 or .54 cal., percussion or flintlock, 28 in. octagonal chrome bore barrel, brass trim, beaver tail select walnut stock, wt. 7 lbs. 15 oz. Add $10 for flintlock. Disc. 1994.

$335 $290 $240

Last Mfg.'s Sug. Retail was $440.

HAWKEN DEERSLAYER RIFLE/CARBINE — .50 cal., percussion, similar to above, $7\frac{1}{2}$ lbs. Mfg. 1992 only.

$220 $190 $160

Last Mfg.'s Sug. Retail was $250.

HUNTER HAWKEN RIFLE/CARBINE — .50 and .54 cal., percussion, 28 in. (24 in. carbine) octagonal barrel, color case hardened lock and nipple, sling swivels, adj. hunting sights. 8 lbs. Disc. 1994.

$230 $200 $160

Add $70 for premier grade (.50 cal. only).

Last Mfg.'s Sug. Retail was $330.

KENTUCKY RIFLE/HUNTER — .45 or .50 cal., percussion or flintlock, $33\frac{1}{2}$ in. octagonal barrel, color case hardened hammer and plate, antique brass trigger, 7 lbs. 4 oz. Add $10 for flintlock, or adj. hunting sights.

Mfg.'s Sug. Retail $280 $240 $210 $170

Grading	100%	98%	95%

LYNX RIFLE — .50 or .54 cal. percussion same as Bobcat Hunter above but with camo Realtree grey stock and 1:32 twist barrel. New 1995.

| Mfg.'s Sug. Retail | $180 | $160 | $130 | $105 |

MISSOURI HUNTER RIFLE — .50 cal. percussion, 28 in. octagonal barrel, adjustable hunting sights, color case hardened hammer and lock recoil pad, 9 lbs. 6 oz. New 1991. Disc. 1994.

| | $200 | $175 | $140 |

Last Mfg.'s Sug. Retail was $300.

MISSOURI RANGER — .50 cal., percussion, 28 in. octagonal barrel, color case hardened trim, right or left-hand, 7 lbs. 8 oz.

| | $190 | $170 | $130 |

MOUNTAIN RIFLE — .50 and .54 cal., percussion or flintlock, 32 in. octagonal barrel, German silver wedge plate and patch box, pewter or German silver nose cap, 7 lbs. 14 oz. Disc. 1993.

| | $240 | $210 | $170 |

Add $80 for premier grade (chrome bore and German silver trim). Disc. 1994.

Last Mfg.'s Sug. Retail was $260.

OVER/UNDER DOUBLE BARREL CARBINE — .50 cal., percussion, O/U 26 in. octagonal tapering to round barrels, color case hardened lock, hammers, and triggers, checkered walnut stock, 8½ lbs. Disc. 1994.

| | $575 | $500 | $400 |

Last Mfg.'s Sug. Retail was $800.

PANTHER CARBINE — .50 or .54 cal., percussion, 24 in. octagonal blued barrel, color case hardened hammer (45 degrees offset) and lock, modern trigger, adj. rear sight, available in left-hand (.50 cal. only), epoxy coated hardwood stock with recoil pad, 7½ lbs. Disc. 1994.

| | $140 | $120 | $100 |

Add $15 for left-hand.

Last Mfg.'s Sug. Retail was $190.

PENNSYLVANIA LONG RIFLE — .50 cal., percussion or flintlock, 40 in. octagonal barrel, color case hardened hammers and plate, brass trim, 8 lbs. 3 oz. Disc. 1993.

| | $385 | $335 | $255 |

Last Mfg.'s Sug. Retail was $455.

PLAINSHUNTER RIFLE — .50 cal. percussion, octagonal barrel (1:48 twist) color case hardened hammer and lock, brass nose cap and triggerguard. New 1995.

| Mfg.'s Sug. Retail | $175 | $160 | $120 | $95 |

PLAINSMAN RIFLE — .50 cal., flintlock or percussion, 26 in. octagonal barrel, color case hardened lock and nipple, 6 lbs. 9 oz.

| Mfg.'s Sug. Retail | $160 | $135 | $120 | $90 |

SIERRA STALKER RIFLE — .50 cal. percussion, 28 in. blued octagonal barrel, color case hardened hammer & lock, adj. sight (rear), wt. 7¼ lbs. Mfg. 1993 only. Disc. 1994.

| | $170 | $130 | $100 |

Last Mfg.'s Sug. Retail was $190.

SQUIRREL RIFLE — .32 cal., percussion or flintlock, 25 in. octagonal barrel, color case hardened hammer and plate, brass trim, stainless steel nipple, 5 lbs. 12 oz. Add $10 for flintlock, $10 for left-hand. Disc. 1994.

| | $230 | $200 | $160 |

Last Mfg.'s Sug. Retail was $250.

ST. LOUIS HAWKEN — .50, .54, or .58 cal., percussion or flintlock, 28 in. octagonal barrel, brass trim, 7 lbs. 13 oz. Add $25 for flintlock, $75 for 12 ga. combo. barrel, $70 for 1:48 twist extra .50 cal. barrel, $20 for left-hand, $40 for laminated stock, new 1995.

| Mfg.'s Sug. Retail | $210 | $195 | $170 | $135 |

BLACK
POWDER

Grading	100%	98%	95%

STALKER RIFLE — .50 cal. percussion, 28 in. octagonal barrel, hunting style sight (click adjustable) color case hardened hammer and lock recoil pad, 7 lbs. 4 oz. New 1991. Disc. 1994.

$190 $160 $130

    Add $100 for premier grade.
    Add $20 for left-hand.

Last Mfg.'s Sug. Retail was $220.

TRACKER CARBINE — .50 cal., percussion, 21 in. blued half round/half octagonal barrel, color case hardened nipple, hammer and lock, new laminated stock in 1994, 6½ lbs. Disc. 1994.

$195 $170 $135

Last Mfg.'s Sug. Retail was $230.

TROPHY CARBINE — .50 and .54 cal. percussion, 24 in. half round/half octagonal, similar to above with sling swivel mounts and dark stained Monte Carlo stock, 7½ lbs. Disc. 1994.

$230 $200 $140

Last Mfg.'s Sug. Retail was $260.

VARMINT RIFLE — .32 cal. percussion, 24 in. octagonal, blued barrel, color case hardened hammer and lock, brass triggerguard and furniture, adj. rear sight, wt. 6¾ lbs. New 1993.

Mfg.'s Sug. Retail $220 $200 $170 $135

WOLF SERIES RIFLES — .50 or .54 cal. percussion, 26 in. matte blued barrel, color case hardened hammer and lock, adj. sights, Tuff-Lite stock, 6½ lbs.

Mfg.'s Sug. Retail $170 $140 $125 $100

    Add $15 for Lone Wolf Rifle with better rear sight and vent. recoil pad (.50 cal. only).
    Add $25 for Timber Wolf Rifle with Real Tree all purpose camo stock (.50 cal. only).
    Add $25 for Silver Wolf Rifle with stainless steel barrel & nickeled hardware.
    Prices based on Grey Wolf Rifle.

WOODSMAN RIFLE — .50 or .54 percussion, 26 in. octagonal blued barrel, color case hardened hammer and lock, brass tip ramrod, adj. sights, laminated stock, 6½ lbs.

Mfg.'s Sug. Retail $190 $170 $150 $110

ZOUAVE RIFLE — .58 cal., percussion, 32½ in. tapered barrel with bayonet mount, brass trim and lands, adj. sight, 9¾ lbs. New in 1989. Disc. 1994.

$290 $250 $200

Last Mfg.'s Sug. Retail was $335.

SHOTGUNS

BRITTANY SHOTGUN — 12 ga., 28 in. double barrel, 7 lbs. 7 oz. Disc. after 1989.

$275 $230 $175

Last Mfg.'s Sug. Retail was $295.

BRITTANY SHOTGUN II — .410 ga., 24 in. double barrel, 6 lbs. 4 oz. Disc. after 1989.

$275 $180 $145

Last Mfg.'s Sug. Retail was $210.

SHOTGUN — 12 or .410 ga., percussion, 28 in. (24 in. on .410) double barrel, 6 lbs. 10 oz (6 lbs. 4 oz. on .410). Deduct $85 for .410 ga. New in 1987. Presentation grade side by side add $350. Disc. 1989.

$255 $220 $170

Last Mfg.'s Sug. Retail was $275.

TRAPPER SHOTGUN — 12 ga., 28 in. single barrel, color case hardened hammer and lock, blued barrel, 3 chokes, recoil pad, 5 lbs. 10 oz. New in 1988.

Mfg.'s Sug. Retail $240 $220 $190 $150

    Add $60 for extra 1:66 twist .50 cal. barrel combo.

CLASSIC TURKEY SxS — 12 ga., percussion, 28 in. round barrel, color case hardened lock, stainless steel nipple, recoil pad, 9 lbs.

Mfg.'s Sug. Retail $460 $380 $340 $270

CUMBERLAND MOUNTAIN ARMS, INC.

Manufacturer located in Winchester, TN.

Grading	100%	98%	95%

RIFLES

MOUNTAIN MUZZLE LOADER — .50 cal., percussion, falling block action, 22 or 28 in. heavy round barrel, manual safety, adj. rear sights, gold front (model uses a 209 shotgun primer instead of a percussion cap), walnut stock.

Mfg.'s Sug. Retail	$950	$895 $815 $650	

D.P. (DAVID PEDERSOLI and CO.)

Please refer to the Pedersoli listing in this section.

DALY, CHARLES

Previously distributed by Outdoor Sports, Hdqtrs., in Dayton, OH. Available only on the used market.

All rifles feature adj. sights, investment cast brass trim, patch boxes, color case hardened hammer and locks, octagonal rifle barrels, adj. double set triggers, and European hard wood stocks.

HAWKEN RIFLE — .45 cal., percussion, 28 in. barrel, right-hand only. Disc. 1994.

$400 $325 $250

Last Mfg.'s Sug. Retail was $240.

HAWKEN RIFLE — .50 cal., percussion, 28 in. barrel, right and left-hand. Add $20 for left-hand. Disc. 1994.

$400 $325 $250

Last Mfg.'s Sug. Retail was $240.

HAWKEN RIFLE — .50 cal., flintlock, 28 in. barrel, right and left-hand. Add $20 for left-hand. Disc. 1994.

$410 $330 $260

Last Mfg.'s Sug. Retail was $280.

HAWKEN CARBINE — .50 cal., flintlock, 22 in. barrel. Disc. 1994.

$400 $325 $250

Last Mfg.'s Sug. Retail was $240.

DEER CREEK MFG.

Manufacturer located in Waldron, IN. Sold exclusively by Mountain States Muzzle Loading in Williamstown, WV.

RIFLES

HIGHLANDER RIFLE — .50 or .54 cal. percussion, 32 in. browned octagonal barrel, browned furniture, hammer, lock & patchbox, maple half stock, wt. 7½ to 7¾ lbs. Disc. 1994.

$200 $180 $160

Last Mfg.'s Sug. Retail was $280.

ROUGHRIDER RIFLE — .45, .50 or .54 cal. percussion, 32 in. octagonal blued barrel, pewter nosecap, German silver, cap box and wedge plates, maple half stock, wt. 7½ to 7¾ lbs. Disc. 1994.

$200 $180 $160

Last Mfg.'s Sug. Retail was $280.

DIXIE GUN WORKS

Union City, TN — manufacturer and distributor. Available through dealers or from Dixie direct.

Short descriptions are for models of standard construction. Also, since 1986, many models are imported from Uberti (to eliminate duplications see Uberti, Aldo and Co.).

Grading	100%	98%	95%

REVOLVERS: PERCUSSION

WALKER — .44 cal., percussion, 9 in. barrel, 6 shot, color case hardened frame, hammer, and load lever, brass trim, 4½ lbs. (Armi San Marco). Add $70 for Deluxe Uberti version.
Mfg.'s Sug. Retail $225 $205 $180 $125

1ST MODEL DRAGOON — .44 cal., percussion, 6 shot, brass grip straps, color case hardened frame, hammer, and load lever, brass trim, 3.9 lbs. (Uberti).
Mfg.'s Sug. Retail $295 $260 $230 $180

2ND MODEL DRAGOON — .44 cal., percussion, 6 shot, brass grip straps, color case hardened frame, hammer, and load lever, brass trim, 3.9 lbs. (Uberti).
Mfg.'s Sug. Retail $295 $260 $230 $180

3RD MODEL DRAGOON — .45 cal., percussion, 7⅜ in. barrel, color case hardened frame, hammer, and load lever, brass triggerguard and back strap. Add $85 for Deluxe Uberti version.
Mfg.'s Sug. Retail $200 $175 $160 $120

BABY DRAGOON — .31 cal., 6 in. barrel, color case hardened frame (Armi San Marco). Add $75 for Deluxe Uberti version.
Mfg.'s Sug. Retail $185 $165 $145 $110

MODEL 1849 POCKET — .31 cal., percussion, with loading lever, 3, 4, or 5 in. barrel, 5 shot, color case hardened frame, hammer, and load lever, brass trim, 1½ lbs. (Uberti version).
Mfg.'s Sug. Retail $255 $240 $210 $145

1851 NAVY — .36 cal., brass frame. Add $5 for engraved model, $20 for steel, $110 for Deluxe or London marked (Uberti versions).
Mfg.'s Sug. Retail $135 $125 $110 $70

TEXAS PATERSON HOLSTER PISTOL — .36 cal., percussion, 7½ or 9 in. barrel, has hidden trigger and no loading lever (Uberti version). Add $20 for 9 in. barrel, deduct $20 for Pedersoli version. Deduct $60 for Pietta version.
Mfg.'s Sug. Retail $335 $310 $270 $220

1860 ARMY — .44 cal., percussion, half-fluted cylinder, 8 in. barrel, color case hardened hammer, frame, and load lever, and brass trigger guard (Pietta). Add $105 for Deluxe Uberti version. Add $105 for cut for stock Uberti version.
Mfg.'s Sug. Retail $170 $120 $105 $85

MODEL 1861 NAVY REVOLVER — .36 cal., percussion, 5 in. barrel, many styles, brass back strap or triggerguard, color case hardened frame, hammer, and load lever, 2½ lbs. (Uberti version). Add $15 for silver plated strap and triggerguard, $15 for fluted military cylinder, $50 for stainless steel. Add $100 for shoulder stock.
Mfg.'s Sug. Retail $255 $235 $205 $160

MODEL 1862 POLICE — .36 cal., percussion, 4½, 5½, or 6½ in. barrel, color case hardened frame, hammer, and load lever, cylinder, semi-fluted or engraved, 1.6 lbs. (Uberti version). Add $15 for silver plated straps and triggerguard, $50 for stainless steel.
Mfg.'s Sug. Retail $260 $235 $205 $160

Grading	100%	98%	95%

1858 REMINGTON — .44 cal., percussion, 8 in. octagonal barrel, blue finish (Pietta). Add $110 for Deluxe Uberti version, $100 for stainless steel, $180 for new "Shooters" Revolver, $30 for Target Model.
Mfg.'s Sug. Retail $170 $115 $100 $70

REMINGTON NAVY — .36 cal., percussion, 6¼ in. octagonal barrel, .36 cal. variation of the 1858 Remington, 2½ lbs. New in 1989. (Uberti version).
Mfg.'s Sug. Retail $230 $205 $180 $135

LEECH and RIGDON — .36 cal., percussion, 7 in. round barrel, Confederate copy of the Colt Navy, 2¾ lbs. New in 1989. (Uberti version).
Mfg.'s Sug. Retail $220 $220 $200 $160

ROGERS & SPENCER — .44 cal. percussion, 6 shot, 7½ octagonal barrel, walnut grips, 3 lbs. (Euroarms).
Mfg.'s Sug. Retail $300 $275 $250 $200

SPILLER and BURR — .36 cal., percussion, octagonal barrel, color case hardened hammer and load lever, brass frame and triggerguard (Pietta).
Mfg.'s Sug. Retail $150 $130 $115 $80

WYATT EARP — .44 cal., percussion, 6 shot, 12 in. oct. barrel, brass frame.
Mfg.'s Sug. Retail $130 $115 $100 $70

PISTOLS BLACK POWDER CARTRIDGE

CATTLEMAN S.A. REVOLVER — .44-40 cal., 4¾, 5½, 7½ in. barrel, color case hardened frame, brass triggerguard. Disc. 1994.
                       $340 $310 $250
Last Mfg.'s Sug. Retail was $375.

1875 ARMY S.A. — .44-40 cal. cartridge, 7½ in. barrel, fluted cylinder, color case hardened frame, brass triggerguard. Add $50 for nickel. Disc. 1994.
                       $340 $310 $250
Last Mfg.'s Sug. Retail was $395.

1890 ARMY — .44-40 cal., 6 shot, 5½ in. barrel, color case hardened frame. Add $40 for nickel. Disc. 1994.
                       $340 $310 $250
Last Mfg.'s Sug. Retail was $350.

PISTOLS

This is an alphabetized listing.

BLACK WATCH SCOTTISH PISTOL — .577 cal., flintlock, 7 in. smooth bore barrel.
                       $160 $140 $95
Last Mfg.'s Sug. Retail was $175.

CHARLES MOORE PISTOL — .36, .44, and .45 cal., flintlock (.44 or .45 cal.) or percussion (.36 or .45 cal.), 11 in. octagonal barrel, white steel hammer and lock (flintlock), color case hardened (percussion), brass furniture, adj. trigger, hand checkered walnut stock, 2½ lbs.
Mfg.'s Sug. Retail $365 $315 $275 $220

CHARLEVILLE PISTOL — .69 cal., flintlock, 7½ in. white steel barrel. Disc. 1994.
                       $170 $150 $100
Last Mfg.'s Sug. Retail was $195.

ENGLISH DUELING PISTOL — .45 cal. percussion, 11 in. octagonal barrel, silver thimble and nose cap., (Pedersoli).
Mfg.'s Sug. Retail $275 $240 $210 $165

HARPERS FERRY — .58 cal., flintlock, 10 in. barrel, color case hardened hammer and lock, (Pedersoli).
Mfg.'s Sug. Retail $275 $265 $220 $170

BLACK POWDER

Grading	100%	98%	95%

KENTUCKY PISTOL — .44 cal. flintlock or percussion, 10¼ in. blued barrel, color case hardened hammer and lock, brass furniture, 2¼ lbs. Disc. 1993.

| | $205 | $170 | $140 |

Last Mfg.'s Sug. Retail was $150.

LEPAGE DELUXE TARGET PISTOL — .45 cal., percussion, 9¼ in. white steel barrel, adj. sights, (Pedersoli).

| Mfg.'s Sug. Retail | $425 | $400 | $340 | $270 |

LEPAGE DUELING PISTOL — .45 cal., percussion, 10 in. barrel (Armi Sport).

| Mfg.'s Sug. Retail | $260 | $240 | $205 | $160 |

LINCOLN DERRINGER — .41 cal., percussion, 2 in. barrel, with case (Palmetto).

| Mfg.'s Sug. Retail | $285 | $260 | $225 | $150 |

MANG TARGET PISTOL — .38 cal. percussion, 10⁷⁄₁₆ in. octagonal browned barrel, white steel hammer and lock, (Pedersoli).

| Mfg.'s Sug. Retail | $750 | $700 | $600 | $400 |

MOORE AND PATRICK PISTOL — .45 cal., flintlock, 10 in. browned octagonal barrel, white steel hammer and lock, silver plated triggerguard checkered walnut grip.

| | $310 | $270 | $215 |

Last Mfg.'s Sug. Retail was $335.

MURDOCK SCOTTISH HIGHLANDERS PISTOL — .52 cal., flintlock, 7¾ in. white steel barrel, hammer, lock, and furniture, 4 lbs. Mfg. 1989-91 only. Disc. 1994.

| Mfg.'s Sug. Retail | $300 | $280 | $240 | $195 |

PENNSYLVANIA PISTOL — .44 cal., flintlock or percussion, 10 in. barrel, brass furniture, white steel hammer and lock. Add $5 for flintlock, (Pedersoli).

| Mfg.'s Sug. Retail | $150 | $135 | $120 | $90 |

QUEEN ANNE PISTOL — .50 cal., flintlock, 7½ in. bronzed steel barrel, (Pedersoli).

| Mfg.'s Sug. Retail | $190 | $175 | $150 | $120 |

TORNADO TARGET — .44 cal., percussion, 10 in. octagonal barrel. Built on Remington 1860 army frame.

| | $195 | $170 | $135 |

Last Mfg.'s Sug. Retail was $215.

WILLIAM PARKER PISTOL — .45 cal., flintlock, 11 in. barrel, hand checkered half stock, 2 lbs. 8 oz.

| | $205 | $175 | $140 |

Last Mfg.'s Sug. Retail was $335.

RIFLES

BROWN BESS MUSKET — .74 cal., flintlock, 41½ in. barrel, 9 lbs. 8 oz. Add $20 for 2nd Model (1762), $105 for Pedersoli version.

| Mfg.'s Sug. Retail | $495 | $480 | $425 | $340 |

BUFFALO HUNTER — .58 cal., percussion, 26 in. barrel.

| | $390 | $330 | $265 |

C.S. RICHMOND MUSKET — .58 cal., percussion, 40 in. round barrel, white steel hammer and lock, brass buttplate & nose cap, walnut stock, 10½ lbs.

| Mfg.'s Sug. Retail | $525 | $485 | $420 | $340 |

COOK & BROTHER CARBINE — .58 cal., percussion, 24 in. barrel, adj. front sight (windage only), 2 barrel bands, walnut stock, 7½ lbs. Add $30 for rifle.

| Mfg.'s Sug. Retail | $395 | $370 | $330 | $265 |

CHARLEVILLE MUSKET — .69 cal., flintlock, 44⅝ in. white steel barrel, hammer, lock, and furniture, 8¾ lbs. (Miroku). New in 1989. Add $65 for 1777 French Model, (Pedersoli).

| Mfg.'s Sug. Retail | $595 | $545 | $475 | $380 |

Grading	100%	98%	95%

DELUXE CUB RIFLE — .40 cal., flintlock or percussion, 28 in. octagonal barrel, color case hardened hammer, plate and triggers, brass trim and patch box, double set triggers. (Pedersoli).
Mfg.'s Sug. Retail $385 $345 $300 $240

1853 3-BAND ENFIELD — .58 cal., percussion, 3 barrel bands, 10 lbs. 8 oz. (Euroarms).
Mfg.'s Sug. Retail $495 $445 $390 $310

1858 2-BAND ENFIELD — .58 cal., percussion, 2 barrel bands, 9 lbs. 4 oz. (Euroarms).
Mfg.'s Sug. Retail $475 $410 $375 $300

ENFIELD MUSKETOON LONDON ARMORY — .58 cal., percussion, 24 in. round barrel, color case hardened hammer and lock, brass buttplate, triggerguard and nose cap (Euroarms).
Mfg.'s Sug. Retail $450 $395 $325 $220

ENGLISH MATCHLOCK — .72 cal., matchlock, 44 in. octagonal to round barrel (with cannon type muzzle), all white steel, walnut stock.
Mfg.'s Sug. Retail $895 $800 $680 $580

HAWKEN RIFLE — .45, .50, .54 or .58 cal., percussion, color case hardened hammer and lock, brass patch box (San Marco).
Mfg.'s Sug. Retail $250 $230 $200 $160

HARPERS FERRY RIFLE — .54 and .58 cal. flintlock, 35½ in. octagonal to round barrel, color case hardened hammer and lock, brass triggerguard and patchbox (EuroArms).
Mfg.'s Sug. Retail $645 $565 $480 $390
   Subtract $75 for .58 cal.

INDIAN GUN — same as Brown Bess Musket except 31 in. barrel, (Pedersoli).
Mfg.'s Sug. Retail $675 $600 $540 $425

JAPANESE TANEGASHIMA MATCHLOCK RIFLE — .50 cal. matchlock, smoothbore barrel, all brass furniture, triggerguard, trigger and matchlock, unique style, "buttstock" was held against shooter's cheek, cherry stock, OAL 54¾ in., wt. 8½ lbs. (Miruko)
Mfg.'s Sug. Retail $495 $445 $395 $340

J.P. MURRAY CARBINE — .58 cal. percussion, 23½ in. round barrel, color case hardened hammer and lock, brass buttplate triggerguard and barrel bands (2), factory sling swivels (EuroArms).
Mfg.'s Sug. Retail $425 $375 $340 $270

KENTUCKIAN RIFLE/CARBINE — .45 cal., flintlock or percussion, 33½ in. octagonal barrel, color case hardened hammer and lock, brass patchbox, trigger guard & furniture. (27½ in. barrel carbine). Add $10 for flintlock. Carbine disc. 1993 (Armi Sport).
Mfg.'s Sug. Retail $260 $235 $205 $165

KENTUCKY RIFLE — .45 cal., flintlock or percussion, 33½ in. barrel, brass patchbox and furniture. Add $10 for flintlock. Disc. 1994.
$275 $225 $180

Last Mfg.'s Sug. Retail was $270.

KODIAK DOUBLE RIFLE — .50, .54, and .58 (combo barrels .50x12 ga. and .58x12 ga.) cal. percussion, SxS, 28 in. barrels, hand checkered walnut stock, adjustable sights.
Mfg.'s Sug. Retail $650 $550 $500 $400

KODIAK MKIII RIFLE SHOTGUN COMBO — same as above but with one 12 ga. barrel, .50 and .58 cal. percussion.
Mfg.'s Sug. Retail $650 $550 $500 $400

LANCASTER COUNTY RIFLE — .45 cal., flintlock or percussion (same as Pennsylvania Rifle, except less ornate triggerguard and patch box). Add $5 for flintlock.
$240 $205 $165

BLACK
POWDER

Grading	100%	98%	95%

MISSISSIPPI RIFLE — U.S. rifle model 1841, .58 cal., percussion, 33½ in. barrel, color case hardened hammer and lock, solid brass furniture, similar to Zouave with nose cap replacing front barrel band (EuroArms).
Mfg.'s Sug. Retail $495 $420 $370 $290

MORTIMER RIFLE — .54 cal. flintlock, 36¼ in. octagonal to round barrel, color case hardened hammer, lock and triggerguard, waterproof pan, 8⅞ lbs., (Pedersoli).
$610 $555 $485
Last Mfg.'s Sug. Retail was $645.

MORTIMER WHITWORTH RIFLE — .45 cal. percussion, target version of standard Mortimer rifle with target sights and checkered stock.
Mfg.'s Sug. Retail $645 $630 $550 $440

PENNSYLVANIA RIFLE — .45 cal., flintlock or percussion, 41½ in. octagonal barrel, browned hammer, lock and barrel, brass patchbox and furniture walnut full stock, 8 lbs., (Pedersoli).
Mfg.'s Sug. Retail $460 $390 $340 $250

REVOLVING CARBINE — .36 or .44 cal., percussion, 18 in. tapered octagonal barrel, brass triggerguard and buttstock.
Mfg.'s Sug. Retail $375 $315 $275 $220

SANFTL SCHUETZEN TARGET RIFLE — .45 cal., percussion, 29 in. barrel, adj. sights. Disc. 1991.
$700 $600 $480
Last Mfg.'s Sug. Retail was $595.

SHARPS RIFLE/CARBINE — .54 cal., percussion. 28 in. barrel. (Pedersoli) Deduct $100 for carbine or sporting rifle (IAB).
Mfg.'s Sug. Retail $895 $700 $625 $450

1861 SPRINGFIELD MUSKET — .58 cal., percussion, 40 in. round tapered barrel, white steel furniture, 9 lbs. 8 oz. (Miroku).
Mfg.'s Sug. Retail $595 $545 $475 $380

1863 SPRINGFIELD MUSKET — .58 cal., percussion, 41½ in. barrel (Miroku).
Mfg.'s Sug. Retail $595 $545 $475 $380

TENNESSEE MOUNTAIN/SQUIRREL RIFLE — .32 or .50 cal., percussion or flintlock, 41½ in. browned barrel, browned furniture, cherry full stock, 8½ and 9½ lbs. respectively, (.32 cal. is a small cal. squirrel rifle), right or left-hand (Miroku).
Mfg.'s Sug. Retail $575 $525 $460 $370

TRYON CREEDMOOR RIFLE — .50 cal., percussion, 32 in. octagonal all black barrel, matte finish furniture and patchbox adjustable Creedmoor sights, 9½ lbs., (Pedersoli).
Mfg.'s Sug. Retail $625 $600 $550 $420

TRYON RIFLE — .50 cal. percussion, 32 in. octagonal barrel, color case hardened furniture and patchbox, chrome bore, 9½ lbs. (Pedersoli).
Mfg.'s Sug. Retail $450 $390 $360 $275

WAADTLANDER RIFLE — .44 cal. percussion, 31 in. octagonal browned barrel, color case hardened hammer, lock and triggerguard and heavy butt plate, adj. sights, professional target model, (Pedersoli).
Mfg.'s Sug. Retail $1,295 $1,245 $1,145 $950

VOLUNTEER TARGET RIFLE (2 BAND) — .451 cal., percussion, 33 in. round barrel, color case hardened hammer and lock, two barrel bands, brass furniture, adj. rear and hooded front sights, walnut stock, wt. 9½ lbs. New 1993.
Mfg.'s Sug. Retail $750 $620 $530 $420

WESSON RIFLE — .50 cal., percussion, 28 in. barrel, adj. sights. Disc. 1994.
$385 $335 $260
Last Mfg.'s Sug. Retail was $395.

BLACK POWDER

Grading	100%	98%	95%

YORK COUNTY RIFLE — .45 cal., flintlock or percussion, 36 in. barrel. Add $15 for flintlock. Disc. 1987.

				$270	$230	$175

Last Mfg.'s Sug. Retail was $210.

ZOUAVE RIFLE — .58 cal., percussion, 33½ in. blued barrel, color case hardened hammer and lock. (Armi Sport) Deduct $35 for carbine barrel. Add $115 for Deluxe (Euroarms) Range Model.

Mfg.'s Sug. Retail	$325		$290	$250	$200

BLACKPOWDER CARTRIDGE

HENRY RIFLE/HENRY TRAPPER — .44-40 cal., brass frame, lever action, 24½ in. barrel, (16¼ in. Trapper Model). Add $300 for engraving (Uberti).

Mfg.'s Sug. Retail	$850		$800	$700	$560

1866 CARBINE — .44-40 cal., brass receiver, lever action, 19 in. round barrel, (Uberti version).

Mfg.'s Sug. Retail	$645		$575	$500	$385

1873 SPORTING RIFLE — .44-40 cal., color case hardened steel receiver, lever action, 24¼ in. octagonal barrel. Also available with slight engraving. Add $115 for deluxe w/pistol grip stock, $400 for engraving (Uberti), add $200 for engraving (non-Uberti).

Mfg.'s Sug. Retail	$800		$730	$635	$510

1873 CARBINE — .44-40 cal., steel receiver, 19 in. round barrel (Uberti model). Add $120 for Deluxe, $100 for deluxe engraved with engraved blued receiver.

Mfg.'s Sug. Retail	$745		$690	$600	$475

REMINGTON REVOLVING CARBINE — .44-40 cal., 18 in. barrel, brass backstrap, with shoulder stock. (Uberti)

Mfg.'s Sug. Retail	$375		$315	$275	$220

REMINGTON ROLLING BLOCK LONG RANGE RIFLE — .45-70 cartridge, 30 in. octagonal blued barrel, (26 in. on Buffalo Model). Color case hardening on all exterior parts checkered pistol grip stock. Wt. 10¼ lbs. (Pedersoli)

Mfg.'s Sug. Retail	$750		$695	$630	$560

▲ *Buffalo Model*

Mfg.'s Sug. Retail	$500		$460	$400	$340

REMINGTON ROLLING BLOCK CREEDMOOR LONG RANGE RIFLE — .45/70 cartridge, 30 in. octagonal blued barrel, color case hardening on all other exterior parts, creedmoor sight, checkered stock, approx. 13 lbs. Disc. 1995.

				$750	$675	$575

Last Mfg.'s Sug. Retail was $750.

SHARPS 1874 NO. 3 SPORTING RIFLE — .45-70 and .40-65 cal., 30" matte blued octagonal barrel, color case hardened receiver and hammer, checkered walnut stock (pistol grip on silhouette model), 9 lbs. (Pedersoli).

Mfg.'s Sug. Retail	$895		$825	$750	$650

IN-LINE-IGNITION

IN-LINE CARBINE — .50 or .54 percussion, 28 in. round barrel, all sand blued except bolt (hammer), walnut stock, 6½ lbs. (.54 cal.) or 7¼ lbs. (.50 cal.). Disc. 1994.

Mfg.'s Sug. Retail	$350		$325	$295	$240

SHOTGUNS

MAGNUM SxS SHOTGUN — 10 and 12 ga., percussion, 28 in. barrels, chrome bore, color case hardened hammer and lock. (Engraved white steel on 10 ga.), checkered walnut stock. 7½ lbs. Add $20 for 10 ga., $1,500 for extra deluxe with gold inlays, (Pedersoli).

Mfg.'s Sug. Retail	$450		$420	$380	$300

BLACK POWDER

Grading	100%	98%	95%

MAGNUM CAPE SHOTGUN — 12 ga., percussion, 32 in. barrel, engraved with walnut stock, 5½ lbs.
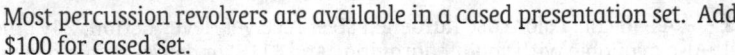

Mfg.'s Sug. Retail	$395	$365	$325	$260

MORTIMER SHOTGUN — 12 ga. Flintlock, similar to Mortimer Rifle listed in rifle section, 7 lbs., (Pedersoli).

Mfg.'s Sug. Retail	$625	$610	$540	$440

NORTHWEST TRADE — 20 ga., flintlock, 36 in. octagonal tapering to round barrel, browned barrel and lock assembly, 11 lbs. New in 1989. Disc. 1991.

$425 $370 $295

Last Mfg.'s Sug. Retail was $495.

E.M.F. COMPANY

Manufactured and distributed in Santa Ana, CA. Available through dealers and from E.M.F. direct.

Most percussion revolvers are available in a cased presentation set. Add $100 for cased set.

PISTOLS

1775 BLACK WATCH SCOTTISH PISTOL — .58 cal., flintlock, 7 in. smooth bore white steel barrel, brass frame, ram's horn grips with round ball trigger. Disc. 1994.

$160 $140 $95

Last Mfg.'s Sug. Retail was $260.

CHARLES MOORE — .45 cal. flintlock, 10 in. octagonal barrel, 2 lbs. Disc. 1994.

$345 $295 $230

Last Mfg.'s Sug. Retail was $400.

1777 CHARLEVILLE PISTOL — .69 cal., flintlock, 7½ in. white steel barrel, brass frame. Disc. 1994.

$170 $150 $100

Last Mfg.'s Sug. Retail was $315.

CORSAIR PISTOL — .36 or .44 cal., percussion, double barrel, color case hardened hammer and lock, brass trim. Disc. 1987.

$265 $210 $135

Last Mfg.'s Sug. Retail was $160.

HARPERS FERRY — .58 cal., flintlock, brass mounted brown barrel. Disc. 1994.

$265 $220 $170

Last Mfg.'s Sug. Retail was $405.

HAWKEN PISTOL — .54 cal. percussion, 9 in. octagonal barrel, adj. trigger, 2 lbs. 9 oz. Disc. 1994.

$230 $195 $150

Last Mfg.'s Sug. Retail was $370.

KENTUCKY PISTOL — .44 cal., flintlock or percussion, available engraved or with brass barrel. Add $30 for flintlock, $20 for brass barrel, $25 for engraved percussion. Disc. 1994.

$205 $170 $140

Last Mfg.'s Sug. Retail was $250.

LE PAGE PISTOL — .45 cal. percussion, 9 in. octagonal white steel barrel and trim, adj. sights, 2 lbs. 2 oz. Disc. 1994.

$240 $205 $160

Last Mfg.'s Sug. Retail was $400.

REMINGTON STYLE TARGET PISTOL — .44 cal., percussion, 9 in. octagonal barrel, factory engraved, adj. sights (windage only), based on Rem. frame, 43 oz. Disc. 1994.

$195 $170 $135

Last Mfg.'s Sug. Retail was $310.

Grading	100%	98%	95%

WM. PARKER PISTOL — .45 cal. percussion, 10 in. octagonal barrel, German silver lock and trim, adj. double set of triggers, 2 lbs. 8 oz. Disc. 1994.

	$280	$245	$200

Last Mfg.'s Sug. Retail was $400.

REVOLVERS

All percussion revolvers are available in cased sets. Add $80 for cased set. In 1993 the Hartford line was introduced w/German silver plated backstrap & triggerguard. Guns trade at approximately $40 higher than prices listed.

1847 WALKER — .44 cal., percussion, 9 in. barrel, color case hardened frame and load lever, brass trim, 4 lbs. 8 oz. Add $75 for nickel plate, $135 for engraving.

Mfg.'s Sug. Retail	$320	$225	$200	$160

1ST MODEL DRAGOON — .44 cal., percussion, 7½ in. barrel, color case hardened frame, brass trim, engraved cylinder, 4 lbs. 2 oz.

Mfg.'s Sug. Retail	$305	$240	$210	$165

2ND MODEL DRAGOON — .44 cal., percussion, 7½ in. barrel, color case hardened frame, brass trim, engraved cylinder, 4 lbs.

Mfg.'s Sug. Retail	$305	$240	$210	$165

3RD MODEL DRAGOON — .44 cal., percussion, 7½ in. barrel, color case hardened frame and loading lever, brass trim, engraved cylinder, 4 lbs. 2 oz., adj. target sights. Add $25 for buntline model. Add $10 for Texas Dragoon Model (Tucker and Sherrard and Co., Confederate States, Texas Star engraved on cylinder, square brass triggerguard).

Mfg.'s Sug. Retail	$310	$240	$210	$165

BABY DRAGOON — .31 cal., percussion, 5 shot, 4 and 6 in. barrel, color case hardened frame and loading lever, brass trim, Add $20 for engraving.

Mfg.'s Sug. Retail	$255	$200	$180	$140

WELLS FARGO MODEL 1849 — .31 cal., percussion, 5 shot, 5 in. barrel, no loading lever.

Mfg.'s Sug. Retail	$255	$200	$180	$140

1851 NAVY — .36 or .44 cal., percussion, 7½ in. barrel, brass frame, color case hardened hammer, and load lever, brass trim, engraved cylinder. Add $15 for engraving, brass, $110 for steel. Add $25 for steel frame, $25 for nickel plated brass (Mason Dixon Model), $70 for silver trimmed steel, $100 for 3 barrel set (.44 cal. only). Add $140 for commemorative issued with Eagle grip, $100 for shoulder stock.

Mfg.'s Sug. Retail	$145	$110	$95	$75

1851 NAVY BALLISTER — .44 cal., percussion, same as above, except with 12 in. barrel.

	$130	$100	$85

1851 NAVY SHERIFF'S MODEL — .36 or .44 cal., percussion, 5 in. round or octagonal barrel, (shorter barrel version of 1851 Navy), brass frame - add $35 for steel.

Mfg.'s Sug. Retail	$145	$110	$95	$75

The same add on's apply to this model as the 1851 Navy.

1851 GRISWOLD CONFEDERATE — .36 and .44 cal. percussion, 7½ in. round barrel, brass frame, 2 lbs. 12 oz.

Mfg.'s Sug. Retail	$145	$110	$95	$75

1860 ARMY — .44 cal., percussion, 8 in. barrel, brass frame, 2 lbs. 9 oz. Add $40 for steel frame, $150 for stainless steel, engraving, add $25 for brass, $150 for steel. Add $45 for steel Sheriff's Model, $80 for fluted cylinder (steel), $100 for shoulder stock, $145 for deluxe engraving.

Mfg.'s Sug. Retail	$160	$125	$115	$90

BLACK POWDER

Grading	100%	98%	95%

1861 NAVY — .36 cal., percussion, steel frame, 7½ round barrel, color case hardened frame, hammer and load lever.
Mfg.'s Sug. Retail $240 $180 $165 $120

1862 POLICE — .36 cal., percussion, 5 shot, color case hardened frame. Add $45 for steel frame, $100 for engraved steel.
Mfg.'s Sug. Retail $185 $145 $130 $100

1862 POCKET NAVY — .36 cal., percussion, 5 shot, color case hardened frame.
$160 $140 $95

Last Mfg.'s Sug. Retail was $200.

NAVY SQUAREBACK — .36 or .44 cal., percussion, 7½ in. barrel, color case hardened frame and load lever, Dragoon style square back trigger guard. Disc. 1994.
$110 $95 $75

Last Mfg.'s Sug. Retail was $130.

Additional features are priced similar to the Model 1851 Navy.

1858 REMINGTON ARMY — .36 and .44 cal., percussion, 8 in. barrel, brass frame, blue finish, 2 lbs. 8 oz. For engraving, add $100 brass, $140 steel. Add $35 for steel frame, $140 for stainless steel, $100 for 12 in. Buffalo Model, $55 for Target Model w/adj. sights.
Mfg.'s Sug. Retail $175 $135 $120 $100

RIFLES

BOSTONIAN — .45 cal., percussion. New in 1989.
$220 $190 $150

Last Mfg.'s Sug. Retail was $285.

ALAMO COMMEMORATIVE — .45 cal., percussion, embellished to commemorate the anniversary of the Alamo. New in 1989. Disc. 1994.
$405 $370 $300

Last Mfg.'s Sug. Retail was $435.

DELUXE BROWN BESS MUSKET — .75 cal., flintlock. Add $60 for bayonet. Disc. 1994.
$600 $540 $425

Last Mfg.'s Sug. Retail was $850.

HAWKEN RIFLE — .50 cal., percussion, brass trim, color case hardened lock and hammer, adj. sights, and stainless steel nipple.
Mfg.'s Sug. Retail $325 $245 $215 $160

KENTUCKY RIFLE —.36, .44, or .45 cal., percussion and flintlock, factory engraved, brass trim, color case hardened lock and hammer. Add $10 for flintlock, $30 for deluxe model, $50 for deluxe engraved.
$345 $300 $225

"LONDON ARMORY" ENFIELD — .58 cal., percussion. Deduct $20 for Musketoon Model.
$445 $390 $310

Last Mfg.'s Sug. Retail was $575.

MINUTEMAN KENTUCKY RIFLE — .45 cal., flintlock or percussion, 36 in. octagonal barrel, brass blade front sight, brass trim, color case hardened lock, hammer, and trigger. Add $15 for engraving, $15 for flintlock.
$345 $300 $225

PENNSYLVANIA KENTUCKY RIFLE — .50 cal., percussion, brass trim, color case hardened lock, hammer, and trigger. Disc. 1994.
$390 $340 $250

Last Mfg.'s Sug. Retail was $440.

PLAINSMAN KENTUCKY RIFLE — .44 cal., percussion, shorter forearm than Pennsylvania with more ornate finish. Disc. 1994.
$345 $300 $225

Last Mfg.'s Sug. Retail was $450.

Grading	100%	98%	95%

PURDEY DELUXE — .50 cal., percussion, half stock English style, select checkered walnut, color case hardened nose cap, lock, tang, butt plate and patch box, adj. sights, double set triggers. Carbine or rifles.

	$345	$300	$225

SAN FRANCISCO TO ST. LOUIS COMMEMORATIVE — .45 cal., Kentucky rifle, highly embellished, made to commemorate the 130th anniversary of the stage coach crossing "2,400 miles in 24 days". New in 1989. Disc. 1991.

	$380	$330	$240

Last Mfg.'s Sug. Retail was $395.

SHARPS RIFLE/CARBINE — .54 cal., percussion, 22 (carbine) or 28 (rifle) in. octagonal barrel, case hardened receiver, hammer and lever, standard falling block action, $9\frac{1}{2}$ (rifle) or $7\frac{3}{4}$ (carbine) lbs. (IAB)

Mfg.'s Sug. Retail	$860	$600	$525	$380

WESSON BERDAN RIFLE — .45 cal., percussion, engraved brass frame.

	$385	$335	$260

ZOUAVE RIFLE DELUXE — .58 cal., percussion, brass trim, color case hardened lock and hammer, blue finish, adj. "Sniper Sight".

Mfg.'s Sug. Retail	$625	$440	$400	$300

SHOTGUNS

SHOTGUN — 12 ga., SxS, percussion, based on early English design, brown barrel, color case hardened lock and hammer, imported from Italy. Disc. 1994.

	$420	$380	$300

Last Mfg.'s Sug. Retail was $535.

SHOTGUN O/U — 12 ga., percussion, O/U design. New in 1989. Disc. 1991.

	$470	$410	$310

Last Mfg.'s Sug. Retail was $640.

EASTERN MUZZLELOADERS SUPPLY

Importer/distributor located in Bear, Delaware. Available through dealers and catalog houses.

RIFLES

CRISTOFORO COLOMBO QUINCENTENARY MATCHLOCK — 1 of 500 made serial numbered CC1492-CC1992, classic matchlock styling of the period. The rear sight is a dolphin (a sign of good luck) the front sight, a stylized dolphin. The hammer is shaped like a sea monster (trigger being the tail), walnut stock, custom made by Pedersoli.

Mfg.'s Sug. Retail	$780	$745	$645	$515

We are not positive how many of these guns actually made it to market.

FRENCH M1777 NAVY MUSKET — .69 cal., flintlock, $42\frac{1}{2}$ in. white steel barrel, brass furniture, split ring iron center barrel band. non-corrosive brass priming pan, walnut stock, $8\frac{1}{2}$ - $9\frac{1}{2}$ lbs. (similar to Charleville Musket) custom manufactured by Pedersoli.

	$610	$530	$435

BLACKPOWDER CARTRIDGE

All models with the E.M.S. stamp are made by Uberti. See Uberti section at end of this section.

EUROARMS OF AMERICA

Manufacturer/importer, Winchester, VA. Available through dealers and catalog houses.

Grading		100%	98%	95%

REVOLVERS

1851 NAVY "SCHNEIDER and GLASSICK" — .36 or .44 cal., percussion, 5 or 7 in. octagonal barrel, brass frame, 38-40 oz.

Mfg.'s Sug. Retail	$120	$105	$90	$75

1851 NAVY "GRISWOLD and GUNNISON" — .36 or .44 cal., percussion, 7½ in. octagonal round barrel, brass frame, 39-41 oz. Disc. 1987.

		$105	$90	$75

Last Mfg.'s Sug. Retail was $100.

1851 NAVY — .36 or .44 cal., percussion, 7½ in. barrel, steel frame, 39-43 oz. Add $10 for square back trigger, $25 for silver strap. Deduct $40 for brass frame.

Mfg.'s Sug. Retail	$156	$130	$110	$90

1851 NAVY POLICE MODEL — .36 cal., percussion, 5 or 7½ in. octagonal barrel, steel frame, 5 shot fluted cylinder, 38-41 oz. Disc. 1994.

		$130	$110	$90

Last Mfg.'s Sug. Retail was $135.

1851 NAVY SHERIFF'S MODEL — .36 or .44 cal., percussion, 5 in. barrel, steel frame, 39 oz. Disc. 1994.

	$125	$105	$90	

Last Mfg.'s Sug. Retail was $105.

1860 ARMY — .44 cal., percussion, 5 or 8 in. barrel, steel frame, 41 oz. Add $50 for steel, $75 for stainless steel, $50 for engraving.

Mfg.'s Sug. Retail	$127	$110	$95	$75

1861 NAVY — .36 cal., percussion, 7½ in. barrel, steel frame, 42 oz.

		$160	$130	$100

Last Mfg.'s Sug. Retail was $245.

1862 POLICE — .36 cal., percussion, 7½ in. barrel, steel frame, 40 oz. Disc. 1987.

		$160	$130	$100

Last Mfg.'s Sug. Retail was $135.

REMINGTON REPLICAS

1858 ARMY — .36 or .44 cal., percussion, 6½ and 8 in. octagonal barrel, 40 oz. Add $50 for engraving, $30 for stainless steel, $10 for target adj. sights, deduct $50 for brass frame.

Mfg.'s Sug. Retail	$213	$185	$160	$130

1858 NAVY — .36 cal., percussion, 6½ in. octagonal barrel, 40 oz. Disc. 1991.

Mfg.'s Sug. Retail	$213	$185	$160	$130

ROGERS and SPENCER — .44 cal., percussion, 7½ in. octagonal barrel, 47 oz. Add $10 for target sights, $15 for London gray finish, $50 for engraving.

Mfg.'s Sug. Retail	$227	$200	$170	$135

RIFLES

BROWN BESS MUSKET "TOWER FLINTLOCK" — .75 cal., flintlock, 41¾ in. barrel, smooth bore. Disc. 1994.

	$520	$430	$335	

Last Mfg.'s Sug. Retail was $755.

BUFFALO CARBINE — .58 cal., percussion, 26 in. round barrel, color case hardened hammer and lock, brass patch box and furniture, 7¾ lbs. New in 1989.

Mfg.'s Sug. Retail	$440	$390	$330	$265

C.S. RICHMOND MUSKET — .58 cal., percussion, 40 in. round barrel, white steel hammer & lock, brass buttplate & nose cap, walnut stock, 10½ lbs.

Mfg.'s Sug. Retail	$564	$485	$420	$340

Grading	100%	98%	95%

CAPE GUN RIFLE — .50 cal., percussion, 32 in. barrel, engraved with walnut stock. New in 1989. Disc. 1991.

	$420	$360	$290

Last Mfg.'s Sug. Retail was $515.

CHARLIEVILLE MODEL 1777 MUSKET — .69 cal., flintlock, 44¾ in. white steel barrel, smooth bore. Disc. 1994.

	$660	$560	$450

Last Mfg.'s Sug. Retail was $835.

COOK and BROTHER RIFLE/CARBINE — .58 cal., percussion, 24 in. barrel, adj. front sight (windage only), 2 barrel bands, walnut stock, 7½ lbs. Add $30 for rifle.

Mfg.'s Sug. Retail	$440	$370	$330	$265

ENFIELD RIFLE MUSKET (LONDON ARMORY CO.), 1853 — .58 cal., percussion, 39 in. barrel, adj. rear sight (windage only), 3 barrel bands, walnut stock, 9½ lbs. Add $25 for white steel barrel.

Mfg.'s Sug. Retail	$484	$425	$360	$290

ENFIELD RIFLE MUSKET (LONDON ARMORY CO.), 1858 — .58 cal., percussion, 33 in. barrel, adj. rear sight (windage only), 2 barrel bands, walnut stock, 8 lbs.

Mfg.'s Sug. Retail	$467	$400	$350	$280

ENFIELD MUSKETOON (LONDON ARMORY CO.), 1861 — .58 cal., percussion, 24 in. barrel, adj. rear sight (windage only), 2 barrel bands, walnut stock, 8 lbs.

Mfg.'s Sug. Retail	$427	$370	$315	$250

HARPER'S FERRY MODEL 1803 — .54 and .58 cal., flintlock, 32½ in. browned barrel, walnut stock, 9 lbs.

Mfg.'s Sug. Retail	$567	$565	$480	$390

HAWKEN RIFLE — .58 cal., percussion, 28 in. octagonal barrel, double set triggers, target model, 9 lbs. 6 oz. Disc. 1989.

	$265	$225	$180

Last Mfg.'s Sug. Retail was $295.

J.P. MURRAY MODEL 1863 — .58 cal., percussion, 23 in. barrel, 7 lbs. 9 oz.

Mfg.'s Sug. Retail	$440	$375	$340	$270

MISSISSIPPI RIFLE MODEL 1841 — .54 or .58 cal., percussion, 33 in. barrel, 9 lbs. 8 oz.

Mfg.'s Sug. Retail	$487	$420	$370	$290

PENNSYLVANIA RIFLE — .45 or .50 cal., flintlock or percussion, 36 in. barrel, adj. rear sight (windage only), walnut stock, 7 lbs. Add $30 for flintlock. Disc. 1987.

	$330	$280	$220

Last Mfg.'s Sug. Retail was $285.

REMINGTON 1862 RIFLE — .58 cal., percussion, 33 in. barrel, 3 leaf folding rear sight, 3 barrel bands, beechwood stock, 9½ lbs. Disc. 1987.

	$325	$275	$220

Last Mfg.'s Sug. Retail was $285.

SPRINGFIELD RIFLE MUSKET — .58 cal., percussion, 40 in. barrel with 3 bands.

Mfg.'s Sug. Retail	$564	$480	$420	$340

VOLUNTEER TARGET RIFLE (2 BAND) — .451 cal., percussion, 33 in. round barrel, color case hardened hammer and lock, two barrel bands, brass furniture, adj. rear and hooded front sights, walnut stock, wt. 9½ lbs. New 1993.

Mfg.'s Sug. Retail	$720	$620	$530	$430

VOLUNTEER TARGET RIFLE (3 BAND) — .451 cal. percussion, same as above except with 3 bbl. bands and longer barrel.

Mfg.'s Sug. Retail	$773	$670	$570	$455

BLACK POWDER

Grading	100%	98%	95%

ZOUAVE RIFLE — .58 cal., percussion, brass trim, color case hardened lock and hammer, blue finish, adj. sniper sight.

Mfg.'s Sug. Retail	$340	$290	$250	$200

   Add $115 for "Range" grade Target Model.

SHOTGUNS

MAGNUM CAPE SHOTGUN — 12 ga., percussion, 32 in. barrel, engraved with walnut stock, 5½ lbs.

Mfg.'s Sug. Retail	$515	$365	$325	$260

DUCK SHOTGUN — 8, 10, or 12 ga., percussion, 33 in. round barrel, color case hardened hammer and lock, brass patchbox and furniture, 8½ lbs. New in 1989. Disc. 1992.

	$360	$300	$235

Last Mfg.'s Sug. Retail was $455.

DOUBLE BARREL SHOTGUN — 12 ga., percussion, 28 in. barrel, engraved with walnut stock, 6 lbs. Disc. 1994.

	$340	$285	$225

Last Mfg.'s Sug. Retail was $405.

FABER BROTHERS

Distributor located in Chicago, IL. Available through dealers.

Faber Brothers is currently marketing customized C.V.A. and InvestArms Hawken Rifles. These rifles come drilled and tapped for scope with offset hammers and chrome bores. Even though these rifles trade for prices equal to the C.V.A. Hawken, Faber Brothers could command a slight premium (see Connecticut Valley Arms).

FEDERAL ORDNANCE CORPORATION

Manufacturer/importer located in South El Monte, CA discontinued importation of Blackpowder Arms in 1990. Available only on the used market.

PISTOLS

DURS EGG SAW HANDLED PISTOL — .45 cal., flintlock or percussion, 9½ in. blued octagonal barrel, unique stock, hand checkered, German silver trim, white steel hammer and lock. Disc. 1994.

	$210	$175	$150

Last Mfg.'s Sug. Retail was $225.

F. ROCHATTE — .45 cal., percussion, single set triggers, hand checkered stock. Disc. 1994.

	$250	$210	$160

Last Mfg.'s Sug. Retail was $250.

KENTUCKY PISTOL — .45 cal., percussion, 10¼ in. octagonal barrel, brass blade front sight, 40 oz. Disc. 1994.

	$205	$170	$140

Last Mfg.'s Sug. Retail was $110.

WILLIAM MOORE PISTOL — .45 cal., flintlock or percussion, 10 in. octagonal barrel, white steel hammer and lock, silver plated trim, 2 lbs. Add $10 for flintlock. Disc. 1994.

	$310	$270	$215

Last Mfg.'s Sug. Retail was $230.

NAPOLEON LEPAGE PISTOL — .45 cal., percussion, 10 in. octagonal white steel barrel and lock, brass trim, adj. double set triggers, fluted grip, 2 lbs. 7 oz. Disc. 1994.

	$240	$205	$160

Last Mfg.'s Sug. Retail was $185.

Grading	100%	98%	95%

WILLIAM PARKER PISTOL — .45 cal., flintlock or percussion, 11 in. octagonal browned barrel, silver plated furniture, double set triggers. Add $10 for flintlock. Disc. 1994.

$270 $235 $190

Last Mfg.'s Sug. Retail was $200.

REVOLVERS

1858 REMINGTON — .44 cal., percussion, 7½ in. octagonal barrel, 6 shot, brass frame and triggerguard, 2 lbs. 10 oz. Add $30 for steel, $100 for stainless steel frame. Disc. 1994.

$85 $65 $50

Add $75 for target model.

Last Mfg.'s Sug. Retail was $110.

1860 ARMY — .44 cal., percussion, 8 in. barrel, 6 shot, color case hardened hammer, lock, and load lever, brass backstrap and trigger guard. Add $15 for Sheriff's Model, $75 for shoulder stock. Disc. 1994.

$155 $135 $100

Last Mfg.'s Sug. Retail was $125.

1862 POCKET NAVY — .36 cal., percussion, 6½ in. barrel, color case hardened frame, hammer and load lever, cylinder semi-fluted, or engraved. 1 lb. 9 oz. Disc. 1994.

$155 $135 $100

Last Mfg.'s Sug. Retail was $205.

ROGERS and SPENCER — .44 cal., percussion, 7½ in. octagonal barrel, blued steel, 3 lbs. Disc. 1994.

$275 $250 $200

Last Mfg.'s Sug. Retail was $200.

RIFLES

1853 3-BAND ENFIELD — .58 cal., percussion, 39 in. round barrel, color case hardened hammer and lock, brass trim, blued bands, adj. rear sight, 9½ lbs. Disc. 1994.

$445 $390 $310

Last Mfg.'s Sug. Retail was $400.

MODEL 1858 2-BAND ENFIELD — similar to 1853 3-Band Enfield except has 33 in. round barrel, 10 lbs. Disc. 1994.

$410 $375 $300

Last Mfg.'s Sug. Retail was $340.

ENFIELD MUSKETOON — .58 cal., percussion, 24 in. barrel, adj. rear sight (windage only), 2 barrel bands, walnut stock, 8 lbs. Disc. 1994.

$395 $325 $220

Last Mfg.'s Sug. Retail was $480

HARPERS FERRY — .58 cal., flintlock, 35 in. round barrel, color case hardened hammer and lock, brass trim, 8½ lbs. Disc. 1994.

$560 $480 $390

Last Mfg.'s Sug. Retail was $440.

HAWKENS RIFLE — .45 or .50 cal., flintlock or percussion, 28½ in. octagonal barrel, color case hardened hammer and lock, double set triggers, 7¾ lbs. Disc. 1994.

$265 $225 $180

Last Mfg.'s Sug. Retail was $220.

KENTUCKY RIFLE — .45 cal., percussion, color case hardened hammer and lock, percussion cap holder in stock, brass trim. Disc. 1994.

$275 $225 $180

Last Mfg.'s Sug. Retail was $210.

BLACK POWDER

Grading	100%	98%	95%

THE J.P. MURRAY CARBINE — .58 cal., percussion, 23½ in. browned round barrel, color case hardened hammer and lock, brass trim and bands, 7½ lbs. Disc. 1994.

$375 $340 $270

Last Mfg.'s Sug. Retail was $370.

MISSISSIPPI RIFLE — .58 cal., percussion, 33 in. browned round barrel, color case hardened hammer and lock, brass trim and bands, 9½ lbs. Disc. 1994.

$450 $390 $300

Last Mfg.'s Sug. Retail was $410.

SANFTL SCHUETZEN RIFLE — .45 cal., percussion, 31 in. octagonal barrel, both peep and iron sights, Schuetzen style butt plate and triggerguard, brass furniture. Disc. 1994.

$700 $600 $480

Last Mfg.'s Sug. Retail was $590.

ZOUAVE RIFLE — .58 cal., percussion, 32½ in. round barrel, color case hardened hammer, lock and trigger, brass trim, adj. rear sight, 9 lbs. Disc. 1994.

$320 $290 $230

Last Mfg.'s Sug. Retail was $360.

FREEDOM ARMS

Manufactured and distributed in Freedom, WY. Available only on the used market.

REVOLVERS

STAINLESS MINI-REVOLVER — .22 cal., percussion, 5 shot, 1, 1¾, or 3 in. barrel, stainless steel. Add $15 for 3 in. barrel, $40 for brass buckle. Disc. 1994.

$270 $230 $185

Due to an increase in demand for Freedom Arms .454 Casull, the .22 cal. percussion pistol is out of production. It is unknown if production of this gun will ever begin again.

Last Mfg.'s Sug. Retail was $205.

GIBBS RIFLE CO.

Manufacturer, Martinsburg, WV.

Founded in 1991, the Gibbs Rifle Company has purchased the rights to manufacture the Parker-Hale Enfield Black Powder replicas from Parker-Hale located in Birmingham, England. Navy Arms is still the only distributor of Parker-Hale Black Powder Replicas. See Navy Arms.

GONIC ARMS INC.

Manufacturer located in Gonic, NH. Available through dealers.

Gonic Arms has designed a true hunter's Magnum rifle. Equipped with an ambidextrous safety, it eliminates the noisy "click" often associated with bringing a hammer back from half cock or setting the first of double set triggers. A specially designed firing pin and housing allow spent caps to blow out the bottom of the rifle, thus eliminating the need to "dig out" the spent cap from the breech. This, combined with its modern appearance and newly designed loading system, makes it a true hunter's rifle without the problems associated with most Black Powder arms.

MODEL GA-87 RIFLE/CARBINE — .308 Spitfire, .38, .44, .458 Express, .50 cal., (rifle only), .54, and 20 ga., 26 in. round barrel, (24 in. carbine custom shop only) single stage trigger with left or right safety, cap is placed in breech, 6 lbs. New in 1987.

$505 $440 $360

Add $25 for sights, $20 for Deluxe, $70 for laminated stock, $250 for 1-1,000 limited edition.

Last Mfg.'s Sug. Retail was $570.

Grading	100%	98%	95%

MODEL GA-87 MAGNUM — .45 or .50 cal., in-line ignition, same features as GA-87 above. Deluxe Model, American walnut stock.

Mfg.'s Sug. Retail	$800	$675	N/A	N/A

MODEL GA-93 MAGNUM — .45 or .50 cal., 24 in. barrel, adj. trigger, tapped for scope bases, open hunting sights, hardwood stock.

Mfg.'s Sug. Retail	$485	$420	$365	$295

Add $25 for sights, $20 for Deluxe, $70 for laminated stock, $250 for 1-1,000 limited edition, $65 for stainless steel barrel (new 1994).

MODEL GA-93 MAGNUM SAFARI — .50 cal., in-line action. Same as above but available with any or all options (built to the purchasers specifications).

Mfg.'s Sug. Retail	$1,560	$1,300	N/A	N/A

MODEL GA-90 MAGNUM PISTOL BARREL — .30, .38, .44 and .45 cal., percussion, 16 or 24 in. barrels, uniquely designed to fit into a Thompson contender frame, using either a #11 percussion cap or a 209 shotgun shell primer, standard Thompson forearm must also be replaced. Add $10 for #11 percussion ignition, $40 for open or peep sights, $50 for required forearm assembly, $80 for thumbhole rifle stock (not required), $85 for laminated thumbhole stock.

Mfg.'s Sug. Retail	$220	$185	$160	$120

Deduct $15 for 16 in. barrel.

HATFIELD RIFLE WORKS

Previously manufactured in St. Joseph, MO. Sold by Mountain State Muzzleloading Supplies.

MOUNTAIN RIFLE — .50 and .54 cal., percussion, 32 in. octagonal barrel, browned furniture, ½ stock, 9 lbs. Disc. 1993.

	$575	$500	$360

During 1992/93, extensive work was done to all internal working parts to insure greater longevity for target or field use. All internal parts were U.S. made.

Last Mfg.'s Sug. Retail was $665.

SQUIRREL RIFLE — .32, .36, .45, or .50 cal., flintlock or percussion, 39 in. barrel, adj. sights, double set triggers, brass trim, 7½ lbs. Add $20 for flintlock. Disc. 1994.

	$520	$450	$360

Add $65 for extra fancy maple Grade II.

Add $175 for hand selected fancy Grade III.

Custom guns could easily run 200% over standard.

This gun is a one-of-a-kind model with exceptional craftsmanship in both wood and metal.

Last Mfg.'s Sug. Retail was $600.

HAWKEN SHOP

Manufacturer original Hawken rifles, located in Oak Harbor, Washington. Guns sold through dealers and factory direct.

The Hawken Shop (owned by the Dayton Traister Company) has purchased the rights and machinery to manufacture the original Hawken Rifle from Arthur Ressel. Mr. Ressel had previously purchased the rights to manufacture these rifles from the heirs of John Gemmer, who purchased S. Hawken Manufacturing directly from Samuel Hawken in 1860. These are truly original Hawken rifles. Standard Hawken rifles in new condition (100%) are selling for $2,000+, with the Hawken Commemorative Plains Rifle (1 of 50) selling in excess of $4,000.

HEGE

Uberlingen, Germany

Grading	100%	98%	95%

HEGE-MANTON — .44 cal., flintlock, 6 lbs. Add $100 for engraving. Disc. 1994.

$1,750 $1,480 $1,190

Last Mfg.'s Sug. Retail was $1,695.

HEGE-SIBER PISTOL — .33 or .44 cal., percussion, 10 in. blue octagonal barrel, exceptional finish, world class target model, color case hardened hammer and lock. Disc. 1994.

$1,025 $880 $700

Last Mfg.'s Sug. Retail was $1,000.

FRENCH STYLE HEGE-SIBER PISTOL — .33 or .44 cal., percussion, 10 in. blue octagonal barrel, exceptional finish, world class target model, London gray finish, 24 Kt. gold inlays, blue triggerguard. Disc. 1994.

$1,800 $1,530 $1,225

Last Mfg.'s Sug. Retail was $1,795.

▲ *Matched set* — same serial number. Disc. 1994.

$3,600 $3,050 $2,440

Last Mfg.'s Sug. Retail was $2,995.

J.P. GUN STOCK, INC.

Manufacturer located in Las Vegas, NV. Distributed by Mountain States Muzzleloading located in Williamstown, WV.

J.P. BECK RIFLE — .50 cal., flintlock, 42 in. octagonal barrel. Pennsylvania long rifle style, brass furniture, 9 lbs.

Mfg.'s Sug. Retail	$795	$795	$715	$650

J.P. HENRY TRADE RIFLE — .54 cal. flintlock, 35 in. octagonal browned barrel, brass triggerguard, buttplate and patchbox, curly maple stock. 10 lbs.

Mfg.'s Sug. Retail	$795	$795	$715	$650

J.P. MCCOY SQUIRREL RIFLE — .32 or .45 cal., flintlock or percussion, 42 in. browned barrel, browned hammer and lock, brass buttplate & triggerguard, full length select curly maple stock, 7½ lbs.

Mfg.'s Sug. Retail	$700	$690	$600	$480

Add $20 for flintlock.

IVER JOHNSON

Manufactured in Jackson, AR. Available only on the used market.

O/U DOUBLE RIFLE MODEL BP50HB — .50 cal., percussion, double barrel, separate hammers and triggers, color case hardened hammer and furniture.

$400 $300 $250

KBI

Harrisburg, PA. KBI ceased importing Black Powder arms in late 1994. Available through dealers.

PISTOLS

1851 NAVY — .44 cal., percussion, 7½ in. barrel, brass frame, 39-43 oz. Add $30 for engraving, or for Pony Express Sheriff Model. Disc. 1994.

$115 $100 $70

Last Mfg.'s Sug. Retail was $150.

1860 ARMY — .44 cal., percussion, 5 or 8 in. barrel, steel frame, 41 oz. Disc. 1994.

$170 $150 $120

Last Mfg.'s Sug. Retail was $240.

Grading	100%	98%	95%

1858 REMINGTON ARMY — .36 or .44 cal., percussion, 6½ and 8 in. octagonal barrel, 40 oz. Add $25 for steel frame, $140 for stainless steel. Add $20 for 12 in. Buffalo Model. Disc. 1994.

$135 $115 $100

Last Mfg.'s Sug. Retail was $170.

RIFLES

HAWKEN RIFLE — .45, .50, .54, or .58 cal., flintlock or percussion, 28 in. octagonal barrel, color case hardened hammer and lock, 9 lbs. Add $30 for flintlock and $10 for left-hand. Disc. 1994.

$230 $200 $160

Deduct $45 for Field Grade.

Last Mfg.'s Sug. Retail was $300.

KENTUCKY RIFLE — .50 cal., percussion, 35 in. octagonal barrel, color case hardened hammer and lock, brass furniture and triggerguard, 7 lbs. Disc. 1994.

$275 $225 $180

Last Mfg.'s Sug. Retail was $420.

KAHNKE GUNWORKS

Manufacturer/Markesbery located in Redwood Falls, MN. Kahnke Black Powder guns are now marketed by Markesbery Muzzle Loaders, Inc., Florence, KY.

In 1996 Kahnke/Markesbery dropped the Kahnke name and their guns are now sold only under the Markesbery name. The KM designation is still carried on the guns.

PISTOLS

KAHNKE .54 CAL. MODEL — .54 cal., percussion, single-shot hunting pistol, adj. sights, unusual combination of utilizing both old and new technologies, straight through ignition system, walnut grips. 3½ lbs. New in 1988.

$345 $315 $210

This model was available direct from the factory only.

Last Mfg.'s Sug. Retail was $295.

LONE STAR RIFLE CO.

Manufacturer located in Conroe, TX.

REMINGTON PATTERN ROLLING BLOCK RIFLES

ROLLING BLOCK RIFLES — .32-40, .38-55, .40-65, .40-70, 2 1/10 BN, .40-70SS, .40-90 BN, .45-70, .45-90, .45-100, .45-110, .45-120, .50-70, .50-90 Blackpowder cartridge, 28 in., 30 in., 32 in., 34 in. octagonal or ½ round ½ octagonal barrel, color case hardened action, hand checkered fancy walnut stock, sight options, custom made. Available as Creedmoor, Custer, Silhouette, Sporting or Deluxe Sporting Rifle.

Mfg.'s Sug. Retail   **$1,695 $1,695 $1,525 $1,400**

Add $800 for Custer Model in .50-70 cal., add for engraving Grade I $350, Grade II $490, add $50 for gold barrel bands (each), add $45 for silver barrel bands (each).

LOVEN-PIERSON INC.

Apalachin Arsenal - Apalachin, NY.

RIFLES: PERCUSSION

All rifles have a unique rotating over and under set of barrels to speed a 2nd shot. Available only through the used market.

BLACK POWDER

Grading	100%	98%	95%

LOVEN MODEL 10 — .45 cal., percussion swivel breech, 22 in. carbine or 28 in. rifle, octagonal or ½ in. round barrel, blued furniture, maple stock, 7¾ - 8½ lbs. Disc. 1994.

$300 $255 $200

Last Mfg.'s Sug. Retail was $330.

LOVEN MODEL 13 — .45, .50 or .54 cal., percussion, same as Loven Model 10, except brass furniture and walnut stock. Disc. 1994.

$400 $340 $270

Last Mfg.'s Sug. Retail was $440.

LOVEN MODEL 16 — .45, .50 or .54 cal., percussion, same as above except color case hardened lock and furniture, browned barrels and curly or birdseye maple or figured walnut stock. Disc. 1994.

$600 $540 $430

Last Mfg.'s Sug. Retail was $880.

LYMAN GUNS

Middlefield, CT.

Some discontinued models still sold by Dixie Gun Works, others available through Lyman or through dealers.

PISTOLS

REMINGTON .44 ARMY — .44 cal., 6 shot, percussion. Discontinued.

$125 $110 $90

Last Mfg.'s Sug. Retail was $170.

1851 NAVY — .36 cal., percussion. Discontinued.

$110 $95 $75

Last Mfg.'s Sug. Retail was $165.

1860 ARMY — .44 cal., percussion. Discontinued.

$160 $145 $110

Last Mfg.'s Sug. Retail was $170.

PLAINS PISTOL — .50 or .54 cal., percussion, color case hardened hammer and lock, brass triggerguard.

Mfg.'s Sug. Retail $225 $180 $160 $125

RIFLES

GREAT PLAINS RIFLE — .50 or .54 cal., flintlock or percussion, color case hardened hammer and lock, blackened steel furniture, 32 in. octagonal barrel, right or left-hand action, 11 lbs. 6 oz. Add $25 for flintlock.

Mfg.'s Sug. Retail $425 $325 $290 $230

TRADE RIFLE — .50 or .54 cal., percussion or flintlock, 28 in. octagonal barrel, color case hardened hammer and lock, right or left-hand action, 11 lbs. Add $15 for flintlock.

Mfg.'s Sug. Retail $300 $245 $220 $175

DEERSTALKER — .50 and .54 cal., flintlock or percussion, 24 in. octagonal barrel, color case hardened hammer and lock, sling swivels, adj. sights, available right or left-hand action, 10 lbs. 6 oz. Add $20 for flintlock.

Mfg.'s Sug. Retail $300 $245 $220 $175

Add $10 for Carbine Model w/21 in. stepped barrel.

IN-LINE ACTION

COUGAR RIFLE — .50 or .54 cal. percussion, in-line ignition, 22 in. blued barrel, dual safety, rubber recoil pad, walnut stock with swivels, wt. 7¼ lbs. New 1996.

Mfg.'s Sug. Retail $300 $260 $225 $180

BLACK POWDER

MANDALL SHOOTING SUPPLIES, INC.

Importer and distributor located in Scottsdale, AZ. Available through dealers or Mandall direct.

Grading	100%	98%	95%

FRENCH DUELING PISTOL — .44 cal., percussion, single trigger, classic fluted handle, sold with velvet lined display case and accessories. Disc. 1994.

	$450	$390	$310

Last Mfg.'s Sug. Retail was $295.

"NAPOLEON" CANNON — .69 ball, detailed scaled down model of the original used by both the Union and Confederacy during the Civil War, brass furniture, with carriage, 18 lbs. Disc. 1994.

	$450	$390	$310

Last Mfg.'s Sug. Retail was $290.

MARKESBERY MUZZLE LOADERS, INC.

Located in Florence, KY.

MARKESBERY MODEL KM82 — .36, .45, .50 & .54 cal., percussion $10\frac{1}{2}$ in, 12 in. & 14 in. blued or stainless barrel (.36 cal. $10\frac{1}{2}$ in. barrel only) same as above. New 1994.

Mfg.'s Sug. Retail	$400	$345	$315	$210

Add $30 for stainless steel, add $30 for Goncalo Alves grip.

RIFLES

MARKESBERY MODEL KM94 — .45, .50 & .54 cal., percussion 24 in. blued or stainless barrel, straight or pistol grip stock, rifle version of Model 82 above. Many styles, $6\frac{1}{2}$ lbs.

Mfg.'s Sug. Retail	$525	$490	$425	$360

Add $60 for Black Bear Series, add $80 for Grizzly Bear Series with two piece thumbhole stock.
Add $100 for Brown Bear Series with one piece thumbhole stock.

MICHIGAN ARMS CORPORATION

Manufactured in Troy, MI.

Michigan Arms made a long needed change for Black Powder enthusiasts. It is now possible with their 3 models — the Wolverine, the Friendship Special Match, and the Silver Wolf — to enjoy Black Powder shooting without the drawbacks commonly associated with it. Rather than using a percussion cap or flint, Michigan Arms designed an extremely accurate and reliable ignition system using a Model 209 Win. shotgun primer. It is unsure how many of these guns were produced. Because of this, any gun that could be acquired would have a unique collectors value. Available only through used market.

WOLVERINE RIFLE — .45, .50 or .54 cal., positive ignition Win. Model 209 centerfire primer, $25\frac{1}{4}$ in. octagonal barrel, adj. sights, Dayton Traister rifle trigger with adj. pull, 8 lbs. Disc. 1994.

	$400	$340	$250

Last Mfg.'s Sug. Retail was $400.

FRIENDSHIP SPECIAL MATCH — .45, .50 or .54 cal., positive ignition Win. Model 209 centerfire primer, $25\frac{1}{4}$ in. octagonal barrel, fully adj. target sights with custom Maple stock, Dayton Traister rifle trigger with adj. pull, 8 lbs. Disc. 1994.

	$470	$390	$310

Last Mfg.'s Sug. Retail was $600.

SILVERWOLF — same as Wolverine, only available in stainless steel. Disc. 1994.

	$500	$425	$330

Last Mfg.'s Sug. Retail was $600.

MITCHELL ARMS

Manufacturer/importer, located in Santa Ana, CA. Available through dealers.

In 1993, Mitchell Arms ceased the importation of black powder arms. (Pietta & Uberti)

Grading	100%	98%	95%

REVOLVERS

1851 NAVY — .36 and .44 cal., percussion, $7\frac{1}{2}$ in. round barrel, brass frame, 6 shot engraved cylinder, 2 lbs. 12 oz. Importation disc. 1993.

$100 $85 $70

Prices are equal on Sheriff's Model. Add $25 for steel frame.

Last Mfg.'s Sug. Retail was $225.

1860 ARMY — .44 cal., percussion, $7\frac{1}{2}$ in. barrel, 6 shot rebated cylinder, color case hardened frame, hammer and load lever, all brass backstrap and triggerguard, 2 lbs. 9 oz. Importation disc. 1993.

$120 $105 $85

Deduct $35 for brass frame.

Last Mfg.'s Sug. Retail was $225.

1861 NAVY — .36 and .44 cal., percussion, $7\frac{1}{2}$ in. barrel, brass backstrap and triggerguard, color case hardened frame, hammer, and load lever, 2 lbs. 8 oz. Importation disc. 1993.

$120 $105 $85

Last Mfg.'s Sug. Retail was $225.

1858 REMINGTON — .36 and .44 cal., percussion, 8 in. octagonal barrel, 6 shot, brass frame and triggerguard. Importation disc. 1993.

$85 $75 $60

Last Mfg.'s Sug. Retail was $225.

1858 REMINGTON — same as above, has steel frame with brass backstrap and triggerguard. Importation disc. 1993.

$115 $100 $70

Last Mfg.'s Sug. Retail was $225.

SPILLER and BURR — .36 cal., percussion, $7\frac{1}{2}$ in. barrel, brass frame, color case hardened hammer and loading lever, 2 lbs. 8 oz. Importation disc. 1993.

$130 $115 $90

Last Mfg.'s Sug. Retail was $225.

BLACKPOWDER CARTRIDGE

1858 HENRY RIFLE — .44-40 cal., $24\frac{1}{2}$ in. barrel, brass frame. Importation disc. 1993.

$780 $680 $530

Last Mfg.'s Sug. Retail was $1,000.

1866 WINCHESTER RIFLE/CARBINE — .44-40 cal., brass receiver, $24\frac{1}{4}$ in. octagonal barrel (19 in. round on carbine). Importation disc. 1993.

$575 $500 $400

Add $40 for rifle w/$24\frac{1}{4}$ in. barrel.

Last Mfg.'s Sug. Retail was $830.

1873 WINCHESTER RIFLE — .44-40 cal., color case hardened steel receiver, 24 $\frac{1}{4}$ in. octagonal barrel. Importation disc. 1993.

$730 $635 $510

Last Mfg.'s Sug. Retail was $950.

MODERN MUZZLE LOADING, INC.

Distributor located in Lancaster, MO. Available through dealers, catalog houses or Modern Muzzle Loading directly.

The Knight MK Series is the forerunner of the modern Black Powder rifle designed as a true hunting/sporting rifle. These Black Powder rifles feature a unique straight through sure-fire ignition system, double safety, in-line bolt assembly, and Timney deluxe trigger system. The Knight rifle is extremely accurate (especially with MMP Sabot bullets) and weighs under 7 lbs. New in 1988.

Grading	100%	98%	95%

PISTOLS

R-K 88 HAWK — .45, .50 and .54 cal., percussion, same action as MK rifles, modern (swept back) black composite stock. Mfg. 1991-1992 only. Disc. 1994.

$365   **$290**   **$230**

Last Mfg.'s Sug. Retail was $430.

HAWKEYE — .50 cal., percussion, 12 in. round barrel, adj. trigger, drilled and tapped for scope, synthetic stock, also available in stainless, 3¼ lbs.

Mfg.'s Sug. Retail	$375	$325	$275	$220

  Deduct $25 for black composite stock.
  Add $40 for stainless steel.

RIFLES

BK-92 BLACK KNIGHT — .50 or .54 cal., percussion, 24 in. blued barrel, Monte Carlo, wood, epoxy coated wood or composite stock, double safety, under 7 lbs. New 1991. (Composite stock standard in 1995).

Mfg.'s Sug. Retail	$400	$350	$320	$240

  Deduct $40 for standard wood stock.

MK-85 BACK COUNTRY CARBINE — .45, .50, and .54 cal., percussion, 20 in. round barrel, Monte Carlo stock, double safety, 6 lbs. 10 oz. Add $60 for stainless steel. Disc. 1992.

$430   **$365**   **$300**

Last Mfg.'s Sug. Retail was $520.

GRAND AMERICAN — .50 and .54 cal., percussion, hand selected deluxe model of MK-85 Hunter listed below. With thumbhole stock and gold inlaid barrel. New 1992. Disc. 1994.

$880   **$750**   **$600**

  Add $80 for stainless steel.

Last Mfg.'s Sug. Retail was $995.

MK85 KNIGHT HAWK — .50 and .54 cal., percussion, 24 in. blued barrel, synthetic thumbhole stock, tapped for scope, double safety system, wt. (6.75 lbs. stainless) 7.25 lbs. blued steel.

Mfg.'s Sug. Retail	$760	$600	$530	$425

  Add $70 for stainless.

MK-85 HUNTER — .45, .50 or .54 cal., percussion rifle, straight through ignition system, 24 in. round barrel drilled and tapped for scope, walnut stock, double safety system, under 7 lbs.

Mfg.'s Sug. Retail	$560	$470	$400	$340

LEGEND/BLACK LEGEND PLUS — .50 cal., 22 in. round blued barrel (24 in. on Black Legend Plus), double safety, fiber-tuff, walnut stained hardwood or black Prolight stock, 6¼ lbs. Disc. 1994.

$260   **$220**   **$175**

  Add $45 for stained hardwood stock or 24 in. barreled Black Legend Plus Model.

Last Mfg.'s Sug. Retail was $290.

Grading	100%	98%	95%

MAGNUM ELITE — .50 or .54 cal., percussion, unique new posi-fire system which uses a Magnum rifle primer, 24 in. round stainless steel barrel, all parts stainless steel, black composite or Realtree camo stock, 6¾ lbs. New 1994.

Mfg.'s Sug. Retail	$930	$780	$660	$530

  Add $60 for Realtree camo stock.

KNIGHT MK-85 STALKER — .45, .50 or .54 cal., percussion, 22 or 24 in. round barrel, Monte Carlo stock, double safety system, under 7 lbs.

Mfg.'s Sug. Retail	$650	$510	$435	$350

  Add $40 for camo composite stock.
  Add $25 for forest green or shadow black laminate.

KNIGHT MK-85 PREDATOR — .50 or .54 cal., percussion, 20 or 24 in. round barrel, black synthetic stock, double safety system, under 7 lbs.

Mfg.'s Sug. Retail	$730	$570	$485	$390

  Add $40 for camo composite stock.
  Add $25 for forest green or shadow black laminated stock.

LIGHT KNIGHT MK-85 — .50 or .54 cal., percussion, 20 in. round barrel, walnut or black composite stock, lightweight version of MK-85 Hunter listed above. Add $20 for composite stock. Disc. 1993.

	$445	$380	$310

  Last Mfg.'s Sug. Retail was $500.

BK-89 SQUIRREL — .36 cal., percussion, 24 in. barrel, Monte Carlo stock, double safety, 5 lbs. 8 oz. Disc. 1992.

	$445	$380	$310

  Last Mfg.'s Sug. Retail was $500.

T-5 WOODSMAN — .50 and .54 cal., percussion, 20 in. round barrel, hardwood stock, double safety, adj. sights, approx. 7 lbs. New in 1991. Disc. 1992.

	$230	$195	$160

  Last Mfg.'s Sug. Retail was $230.

MK-85 GRIZZLY "PLB" — .54 cal., percussion, brown laminate stock, double safety. New in 1991. Disc. 1992.

	$475	$410	$330

  Add $100 for stainless steel.

  Last Mfg.'s Sug. Retail was $650.

LK-93 WOLVERINE — .50 or .54 cal., percussion, 22 in. blued or stainless round barrel, double safety, composite stock in black or camo, 6 lbs.

Mfg.'s Sug. Retail	$270	$200	$170	$135

  Add $40 for camo stock, $70 for stainless steel barrel.

MOWREY GUN WORKS, INC.

Currently manufactured in Waldren, IN, previously manufactured in Saginaw, TX. Distributed exclusively by Mountain State Muzzle Loaders Supply, Williamstown, WV. Available through dealers and Mountain State direct.

Mowrey Gun Works has recreated the guns designed by Ethan Allen and marketed under the name Allen and Thurber in the early and mid 1800s. The guns themselves are beautifully hand crafted with "cut rifled" browned barrels (each groove cut individually using as many as 20 passes) and actions using only 5 moving parts creating exceptional accuracy and reliability. The 1 in 30 inch rifling was designed specifically to stabilize conical bullets. Each gun is available with a number of features and options (listed below).

Mowrey Gun Works is also now making reproductions of Hopkins & Allen underhammer rifles, new 1994.

Grading	100%	98%	95%

Standard: curly maple stocks and forearms, front blade-buckhorn rear and hand rubbed finish, brass or browned steel receivers.

Options: premium curly maple, cherry or walnut stock and forearm, barrel length from 22-40 in., primitive fixed sight, target sights, Scheutzen style butt plate. Add $38 for fancy Grade Curly Maple, $25 for other than standard barrel length or modern sights, $25 for brass forearm on Plains Rifle, $30 for fancy brass or steel Scheutzen butt plate.

RIFLES: PERCUSSION

1-N-30 CONICAL RIFLE — .45, .50 and .54 cal., percussion, 28 in. octagonal barrel, brass furniture, special 1-N-30 twist rifling for conical bullets, 8 lbs.

Mfg.'s Sug. Retail	$360	$325	$280	$200

PLAINS RIFLE — .50 or .54 cal., percussion, 28 or 32 in. full octagonal barrel, brass furniture, 10 lbs. Add $25 for brass forearm.

Mfg.'s Sug. Retail	$360	$325	$280	$200

ROCKY MOUNTAIN HUNTER — .50 or .54 cal., percussion, 28 in. full octagonal barrel, all browned steel furniture, 8 lbs.

Mfg.'s Sug. Retail	$360	$325	$280	$200

SILHOUETTE RIFLE — .40 cal., percussion, 28 or 32 in. octagonal barrel, brass furniture.

Mfg.'s Sug. Retail	$360	$325	$280	$200

SQUIRREL RIFLE — .32, .36 or .45 cal., percussion, 28 in. full octagonal barrel, brass furniture, 7 lbs., deduct $10 for all steel furniture.

Mfg.'s Sug. Retail	$360	$325	$280	$200

RIFLES: PERCUSSION - HOPKINS & ALLEN

HERITAGE RIFLE — .36, .45, or .50 cal., percussion, 32 in. octagonal barrel, all metal is browned, dark stained maple stock, unique underhammer design. New 1994.

Mfg.'s Sug. Retail	$250	$210	$180	$145

BUGGY RIFLE — .36, .45, or .50 cal., percussion, 26 in. octagonal barrel, all metal is browned, dark stained maple, unique underhammer design, approx. 6 lbs. New 1994.

Mfg.'s Sug. Retail	$250	$210	$180	$145

SHOTGUNS: PERCUSSION

12 GAUGE SHOTGUN — 12 ga., percussion, 32 in. full octagonal barrel, brass or steel furniture, 7½ lbs.

Mfg.'s Sug. Retail	$360	$325	$280	$200

28 GAUGE SHOTGUN — 28 ga., percussion, 28 in. full octagonal barrel, brass or steel furniture, built on squirrel frame, 7½ lbs. Disc. 1994.

	$320	$280	$200

Last Mfg.'s Sug. Retail was $350.

MUZZLE LOADERS, INC.

Previous importer/distributor located in Burke, VA. Available only on used market.

REVOLVERS

1847 WALKER — .44 cal., percussion, charcoal finish, color case hardened frame, hammer, and load lever, brass trim, engraved cylinder. 4.4 lbs.

$250	$220	$165

BLACK POWDER

Grading	100%	98%	95%

1848 1ST MODEL DRAGOON — .44 cal., percussion, 6 shot, brass grip straps, color case hardened frame, hammer, and load lever, brass trim, 3.9 lbs.

| | $240 | $210 | $165 |

1850 2ND MODEL DRAGOON — .44 cal., percussion, 6 shot, brass grip straps, color case hardened frame, hammer, and load lever, brass trim, 3.9 lbs.

| | $240 | $210 | $165 |

1851 3RD MODEL DRAGOON — .44 cal., percussion, 6 shot, brass grip straps, color case hardened frame, hammer, and load lever, brass trim, 3.9 lbs. Add $15 for silver-plated straps,or cut for stock, add $35 for Military Model.

| | $240 | $210 | $165 |

1851 NAVY — .36 or .44 cal., percussion, $7\frac{1}{2}$ in. octagonal barrel, engraved (roll) cylinder, color case hardened frame and load lever, silver plated brass backstrap and square back triggerguard. Sheriff's Model has 5 in. barrel, brass triggerguard and backstrap. Deduct $10 for Sheriff's Model, $20 for brass backstrap and triggerguard, $25 for brass frame.

| | $135 | $120 | $100 |

1860 ARMY — .44 cal., percussion, 8 in. round barrel, color case hardened frame, hammer and load lever, 2 lbs. 9 oz. Deduct $35 for brass frame.

| | $170 | $150 | $120 |

1862 POLICE — .36 cal., $5\frac{1}{2}$ in. round barrel, color case hardened frame, loading lever, plunger, and hammer, round triggerguard, fluted cylinder, one piece stocks, 25 oz.

| | $195 | $175 | $140 |

1858 REMINGTON — .36 or .44 cal., percussion, blued frame, brass trigger guard, steel backstrap, 6 shot, 2 lbs. 7 oz. Add $30 for stainless, deduct $50 for brass frame.

| | $135 | $115 | $100 |

ROGERS & SPENCER — .44 cal., percussion, $7\frac{1}{2}$ in. octagonal barrel, 2 lbs. 15 oz. Add $15 for target sights, $25 for engraved London grey finish.

| | $190 | $170 | $135 |

PISTOLS

DELUXE KENTUCKY PISTOL — .44 cal., percussion or flintlock, $10\frac{1}{4}$ in. octagonal barrel, brass blade front sight, 40 oz. Add $15 for flintlock.

| | $205 | $170 | $140 |

RIFLES

1858 2-BAND ENFIELD — .58 cal., percussion, 33 in. barrel, 2 barrel bands.

| | $410 | $375 | $300 |

DELUXE HAWKEN RIFLE — .45 or .50 cal., percussion or flintlock, color case hardened hammer and lock, percussion cap holder in stock, chrome lined barrels.

| | $425 | $375 | $300 |

DELUXE KENTUCKY RIFLE — .45 or .50 cal., percussion or flintlock, color case hardened hammer and lock, percussion cap holder in stock, chrome lined barrels, brass trim. Add $15 for flintlock.

| | $455 | $410 | $335 |

ST. LOUIS HAWKENS — .50 cal., percussion, color case hardened hammer and lock, 28 in. octagonal barrel, brass trim, 7 lbs. 15 oz.

| | $245 | $215 | $160 |

ZOUAVE RIFLE — .58 cal., percussion, brass trim, color case hardened hammer and lock, blue finish.

| | $290 | $250 | $200 |

NAVY ARMS CO.

Manufacturer/importer/distributor located in Ridgefield, NJ. Available through dealers, catalog houses and from Navy direct.

Grading	100%	98%	95%

PISTOLS: SINGLE SHOT

1775 BLACK WATCH SCOTTISH PISTOL — .58 cal., flintlock, 7 in. smooth bore white steel barrel, brass frame, ram's horn grip with round ball trigger. Disc. 1994.

	$160	$140	$95

Last Mfg.'s Sug. Retail was $200.

BRITISH DRAGOON PISTOL — .614 cal., flintlock, white steel with brass trim, first 240 production models were used in Governor's palace restoration, Colonial Williamsburg. Add $100 for official Williamsburg crest. Disc. 1994.

	$360	$300	$240

Last Mfg.'s Sug. Retail was $395.

CHARLEVILLE 1777 PISTOL — .69 cal., flintlock, 7½ in. white steel smooth bore barrel, brass furniture, belt hook, walnut stock, 2¾ lbs. Disc. 1994.

	$170	$150	$100

Last Mfg.'s Sug. Retail was $225.

DURS EGG SAW HANDLED PISTOL — .45 cal., flintlock, 9½ in. blued octagonal barrel, unique stock, hand checkered, German silver trim, white steel hammer and lock. Disc. 1994.

	$210	$175	$140

Last Mfg.'s Sug. Retail was $235.

HARPERS FERRY MODEL 1806 — .58 cal., flintlock or percussion, 11¾ in. barrel, color case hardened lock and hammer, brass trim, 3 lbs. 14 oz. (Pedersoli) Add $40 for cased gun. Deduct $25 for percussion.

Mfg.'s Sug. Retail	$310	$265	$220	$170

J.S. HAWKINS PISTOL — .50 or .54 cal., percussion, 9 in. octagonal barrel, German silver trim, blued barrel, adj. trigger, 2 lbs. 9 oz. Disc. 1994.

	$230	$195	$150

Last Mfg.'s Sug. Retail was $200.

KENTUCKY PISTOL — .44 cal., flintlock or percussion, 10⅛ in. barrel, color case hardened lock and hammer, brass trim, 2 lbs. (Pedersoli) Add $15 for brass barrel. Deduct $10 for percussion (each gun).

Mfg.'s Sug. Retail	$225	$205	$170	$140
▲ Cased				
Mfg.'s Sug. Retail	$350	$305	$270	$230
▲ Double cased set				
Mfg.'s Sug. Retail	$580	$510	$440	$340

LEPAGE PISTOL — .45 cal., flintlock or percussion, 9 in. octagonal white steel barrel and trim, adj. sights, engraved spur type triggerguard, 2 lbs. 2 oz. Deduct $100 for percussion, $100 for percussion cased set, $200 for percussion cased pair. Values also apply to smooth bore model (flintlock only).

Mfg.'s Sug. Retail	$625	$500	$440	$370
▲ Cased				
Mfg.'s Sug. Retail	$900	$725	$665	$595
▲ Cased pair				
Mfg.'s Sug. Retail	$1,575	$1,250	$1,130	$970

Grading	100%	98%	95%

▲ *1985 cased set* — custom order only, gold trim, consecutive serial number. Disc. 1994.

$1,800 $1,200 $1,000

Last Mfg.'s Sug. Retail was $1,975.

JOHN MANTON MATCH PISTOL — .45 cal., percussion, 10 in. white steel barrel and lock, brass trim, 2 lbs. 4 oz. Disc. 1994.

$215 $185 $135

Last Mfg.'s Sug. Retail was $225.

MOORE AND PATRICK PISTOL — .45 cal., flintlock or percussion, 10 in. octagonal barrel, white steel hammer and lock, German silver trim, 2 lbs. Disc. 1987.

$310 $270 $215

Last Mfg.'s Sug. Retail was $295.

MOUNTAIN PISTOL — .50 cal., flintlock or percussion, 10 in. octagonal barrel, color case hardened hammer and lock, brass furniture, 2 lbs. 4 oz. Add $10 for flintlock. Disc. 1994.

$220 $185 $140

Last Mfg.'s Sug. Retail was $215.

NAPOLEON LEPAGE PISTOL —.45 cal., percussion, 10 in. octagonal white steel barrel and lock, brass trim, adj. double set triggers, fluted grip, 2 lbs. 7 oz. Disc. 1994.

$240 $205 $160

Last Mfg.'s Sug. Retail was $175.

W. PARKER PISTOL — .45 cal., percussion, 10 in. blued octagonal barrel, German silver lock and trim, adj. double set triggers, 2 lbs. 8 oz. Disc. 1994.

$280 $245 $200

Last Mfg.'s Sug. Retail was $250.

QUEEN ANNE PISTOL — .50 cal., flintlock, $7\frac{1}{2}$ in. smooth bore, unique cannon style bronzed steel barrel, 2 lbs. 4 oz.

$170 $150 $110

Last Mfg.'s Sug. Retail was $200.

F. ROCHATTE PISTOL — .45 cal., percussion, 10 in. round barrel with flat top, white steel lock and trim, adj. double set triggers, 2 lbs. 8 oz. Disc. 1994.

$250 $210 $160

Last Mfg.'s Sug. Retail was $250.

PISTOLS: DERRINGER STYLE

ELGIN CUTLAS — .44 cal., percussion, combination knife pistol, white steel hammer and barrel, brass trim, 2 lbs. Disc. 1994.

$80 $65 $50

Last Mfg.'s Sug. Retail was $80.

PHILADELPHIA DERRINGER — .45 cal., percussion, 3 in. barrel, color case hardened lock and hammer, German silver trim, checkered stock, $\frac{3}{4}$ lb. Disc. 1994.

$120 $100 $80

Last Mfg.'s Sug. Retail was $130.

ENGRAVED "SNAKE EYES" PISTOL — .36 cal., percussion, $2\frac{5}{8}$ in. brass double barrel, double hammers, $1\frac{1}{2}$ lbs. Deduct $75 if not engraved. Disc. 1994.

$145 $120 $95

REVOLVERS

1847 WALKER — .44 cal., percussion, 9 in. round barrel, color case hardened hammer, frame, and load lever, brass trim, engraved barrel and cylinder, 4 lbs. 11 oz. Add $120 for cased set, $145 for deluxe Uberti cased set.

Mfg.'s Sug. Retail $275 $225 $200 $160

Grading	100%	98%	95%

COLT 1851 NAVY - YANK — .36 or .44 cal., percussion, 7½ in. octagonal barrel, color case hardened hammer, frame, and load lever, brass trim. (Pietta) Add $5 for silver plated back strap and triggerguard, $90 for shoulder stock.

Mfg.'s Sug. Retail	$155	$100	$85	$70

▲ *Cased set*

Mfg.'s Sug. Retail	$280	$200	$185	$160

▲ *Double cased set*

Mfg.'s Sug. Retail	$455	$380	$355	$250

AUGUSTA CONFEDERATE — .36 cal., percussion, 5 or 7½ in. barrel, brass frame (confederate copy of 1851 Navy), walnut grips. Disc. 1994.

	$100	$85	$70

Last Mfg.'s Sug. Retail was $200.

1861 NAVY —.36 cal., percussion, 7½ in. round barrel, cylinder engraved with navy scene, color case hardened hammer, frame, and load lever, brass trim, 2¾ lbs. Add $60 for shoulder stock. Also available in 5½ in. barrel Sheriff's model. Disc. 1994.

	$130	$105	$80

Last Mfg.'s Sug. Retail was $140.

▲ *Cased set. Disc. 1994.*

	$230	$205	$170

Last Mfg.'s Sug. Retail was $230.

▲ *Double cased set. Disc. 1994.*

	$385	$335	$280

Last Mfg.'s Sug. Retail was $385.

1860 ARMY — .44 cal., percussion, 8 in. round barrel, color case hardened hammer, frame, and load lever, roll engraved or fluted cylinder, 2 lbs. 12 oz. (Pietta) Add $100 for shoulder stock.

Mfg.'s Sug. Retail	$175	$120	$105	$85

▲ *Cased set*

Mfg.'s Sug. Retail	$300	$220	$205	$175

▲ *Double cased set*

Mfg.'s Sug. Retail	$490	$355	$325	$280

REB MODEL 1860 "GRISWOLD AND GUNNISON" — .36 or .44 cal., percussion, 7½ in. round barrel, brass frame, color case hardened hammer and load lever, 5½ in. barrel Sheriff's Model, (Pietta) 2 lbs. 12 oz. (Pricing on Sheriffs Model equal).

Mfg.'s Sug. Retail	$115	$105	$90	$70

▲ *Cased set*

Mfg.'s Sug. Retail	$235	$205	$180	$150

▲ *Double cased set*

Mfg.'s Sug. Retail	$365	$310	$270	$220

Due to overstock, several 1860 Reb revolvers were factory de-activated and cannot be re-activated. These guns can be used only as props — values currently are in the $55 range.

1862 POLICE — .36 cal., percussion, 5½ in. round to octagonal barrel, color case hardened hammer, frame, and load lever, brass trim, 1 lb. 10 oz. (Uberti) Add $70 for cased Law and Order set (book style presentation case).

Mfg.'s Sug. Retail	$290	$235	$205	$165

COLT PATERSON — .36 cal., percussion, 7½ in. octagonal barrel, standard "hidden trigger" design, blued steel hardware, no loading lever, 2 lbs. 9 oz. Add $135 for engraved version.

Mfg.'s Sug. Retail	$325	$250	$220	$180

LEECH and RIGDON — .36 cal., percussion, 7½ in. barrel, color case hardened hammer, frame, and load lever, brass trim, 2 lbs. 10 oz. (Add $100 for Uberti version).

	$120	$105	$80

BLACK POWDER

Grading	100%	98%	95%

LE MAT REVOLVER —.44 cal., percussion, 9 shot cylinder, plus 1 shot center barrel (maximum fire power for its day), $7\frac{5}{8}$ in. octagonal barrel, white steel frame, 3 lbs. 7 oz. (Pietta) Add $375 for engraved Beauregard model, $200 for 18th Georgia engraved model.

Mfg.'s Sug. Retail	$595	$570	$495	$380

Add $100 for single case, $125 for double case (not including guns).

REMINGTON 1858 NEW ARMY — .36. or .44 cal., percussion, $6\frac{1}{2}$ in. barrel, brass trim. (Pietta) Add $30 for nickel or target model, $70 for stainless steel, $115 for Deluxe Uberti Model. Deduct $30 for brass frame (each gun in a cased set).

Mfg.'s Sug. Retail	$170	$115	$100	$70

▲ *Cased set*

Mfg.'s Sug. Retail	$290	$215	$200	$170

▲ *Double cased set*

Mfg.'s Sug. Retail	$480	$355	$325	$260

ROGERS and SPENCER — .44 cal., percussion, $7\frac{1}{2}$ in. octagonal barrel, blued trim, 3 lbs. Add $15 for satin finish (London Grey Model), $25 for Target Model.

Mfg.'s Sug. Retail	$245	$200	$170	$135

SPILLER and BURR — .36. cal., percussion, 7 in. barrel, brass frame, color case hardened hammer and load lever, 2 lbs. 8 oz.

Mfg.'s Sug. Retail	$145	$130	$115	$90

▲ *Cased set*

Mfg.'s Sug. Retail	$270	$230	$205	$170

▲ *Double cased set*

Mfg.'s Sug. Retail	$430	$360	$320	$260

RIFLES

BROWN BESS MUSKET — .75 cal., flintlock, 42 in. white steel barrel, hammer, and lock, brass trim, $9\frac{1}{2}$ lbs. Add $100 for Colonial Williamsburg seal. Carbine model available in 30 in. barrel.

Mfg.'s Sug. Retail	$705	$600	$540	$425

BROWN BESS MUSKET (ECONOMY MODEL) — same as above, all brass hardware.

Mfg.'s Sug. Retail	$580	$480	$425	$340

BUFFALO HUNTER — .58 cal., percussion, 26 in. round barrel, color case hardened hammer and lock, brass trim, 8 lbs.

	$390	$330	$265

1763 CHARLEVILLE MUSKET — .69 cal., flintlock, $44\frac{5}{8}$ in. white steel barrel, hammer, and lock, brass trim, $8\frac{3}{4}$ lbs. Add $30 for 1777 model, or 1816 Mt. Wickman model with steel ramrod and brass flash pan.

Mfg.'s Sug. Retail	$705	$580	$500	$405

COUNTRY BOY — .32, .36, .45 or .50 cal., percussion, 26 in. octagonal barrel, matte black metal "no glare" finish on all parts, based on mule ear percussion lock, adj. sights, 6 lbs. Add $60 each for extra barrels. Disc. 1994.

	$225	$195	$160

Last Mfg.'s Sug. Retail was $165.

CUB RIFLE — .36 cal., percussion, 26 in. octagonal barrel, adj. sights, color case hardened lock, walnut stock, 5 lbs. 12 oz. Add $60 for extra barrel. Add $115 for Deluxe Pedersoli Model. Disc. 1994.

	$230	$190	$155

Last Mfg.'s Sug. Retail was $185.

Grading	100%	98%	95%

MODEL 1853 3 BAND ENFIELD — .58 cal., percussion, 39 in. round barrel, color case hardened hammer and lock, brass trim, blued bands, adj. rear sight, 9½ lbs. Add $80 for Parker Hale version.

Mfg.'s Sug. Retail	$480	$425	$360	$290

MODEL 1858 2 BAND ENFIELD — .58 cal., percussion, 33 in. round barrel, color case hardened hammer and lock, brass trim, blued bands, adj. rear sight, 10 lbs. Add $80 for Parker Hale version.

Mfg.'s Sug. Retail	$450	$400	$350	$280

MODEL 1861 ENFIELD MUSKETOON — .58 cal., percussion, 24 in. round barrel, color case hardened hammer and lock, brass trim, blued bands, adj. rear sight, 7 lbs. Add $50 for Parker Hale version.

Mfg.'s Sug. Retail	$405	$370	$315	$250

HARPERS FERRY 1803 RIFLE — .58 cal., flintlock, 35 in. round barrel, color case hardened hammer and lock, brass trim, 8 lbs. 8 oz.

Mfg.'s Sug. Retail	$615	$565	$480	$390

HAWKEN RIFLE — .50, .54, or .58 cal., flintlock and percussion, 28 in. octagonal barrel, double set triggers, brass trim, 8 lbs. 8 oz. Deduct $15 for percussion.

Mfg.'s Sug. Retail	$220	$200	$175	$140

HAWKEN MARK 1 RIFLE —.50 or .54 cal., flintlock or percussion. 26 in. octagonal barrel, adj. double set triggers and sights, brass trim, 9 lbs. Add $15 for flintlock, $140 for commemorative model. Disc. 1994.

		$220	$190	$150

Last Mfg.'s Sug. Retail was $260.

HAWKEN HUNTER RIFLE/CARBINE — .50, .54, or .58 cal., percussion, 28½ in. octagonal barrel, (22½ in. carbine), color case hardened hammer and lock, double set triggers, 7 lbs. 12 oz. (6 lbs. 12 oz. carbine).

Mfg.'s Sug. Retail	$240	$220	$190	$150

ITHACA-NAVY HAWKEN — .50 or .54 cal., flintlock or percussion, 26 in. octagonal barrel, adj. double set triggers and sights, brass trim, 9 lbs. Add $65 for flintlock. (Left hand version disc. in 1987).

Mfg.'s Sug. Retail	$445	$405	$355	$260

J.P. MURRAY ARTILLERY CARBINE — .58 cal., percussion, 23½ in. browned, round barrel, color case hardened hammer and lock, brass trim and bands, 7½ lbs.

Mfg.'s Sug. Retail	$405	$375	$340	$270

KENTUCKY RIFLE — .45 or .50 cal., percussion or flintlock, 35 in. barrel, color case hardened hammer and lock, brass trim, adj. brass rear sight (windage only), 6 lbs. 14 oz. Add $10 for flintlock or .45 cal. standard, $125 for .45 cal. deluxe.

Mfg.'s Sug. Retail	$400	$345	$300	$225

KODIAK DOUBLE RIFLE — .50, .54, or .58 cal., percussion, 28 in. double barrel, white steel furniture. New in 1989.

Mfg.'s Sug. Retail	$775	$550	$500	$400

MISSISSIPPI RIFLE 1841 — .54 or .58 cal., percussion, 33 in. browned round barrel, color case hardened hammer and lock, brass trim and bands, 9½ lbs.

Mfg.'s Sug. Retail	$465	$420	$370	$290

MORSE RIFLE — .50 cal., percussion, 26 in. octagonal barrel, brass trim and action, blued barrel and hammer, adj. rear sight, windage only, 6 lbs.

		$250	$215	$180

MORTIMER RIFLE — .54 cal., flintlock, 36 in. browned barrel, color case hardened furniture, waterproof flash pan, chrome lined bore, 9 lbs. Add $300 for extra 12 ga. barrel, $135 for flintlock match rifle.

Mfg.'s Sug. Retail	$780	$610	$555	$485

Grading	100%	98%	95%

MULE EAR MOUNTAIN MAN'S SQUIRREL RIFLE — .32, .36, or .45 cal., percussion, 26 in. octagonal barrel, brass trim, blued barrel, hammer, lock, and trigger, 5½ lbs. Disc. 1994.

	$210	$175	$140

Last Mfg.'s Sug. Retail was $185.

PARKER HALE VOLUNTEER RIFLE (IMPORTED) — .451 cal., percussion, 32 in. barrel, brass trim, blued band, color case hardened hammer and lock, adj. sights, 9½ lbs.

Mfg.'s Sug. Retail	$775	$700	$620	$500

PARKER HALE WHITWORTH VOLUNTEER RIFLE (IMPORTED) — .451 cal., percussion, 36 in. barrel, brass trim, blued barrel and bands, color case hardened hammer and lock, adj. sights, detented lock hammer, long range accuracy app. 1000 yds., comes with accessories, 9¼ lbs. (Pricing same for Parker-Hale 3 Band Volunteer rifle).

Mfg.'s Sug. Retail	$835	$770	$670	$535

PENNSYLVANIA HALF STOCK HUNTER — .50 cal., percussion, 30 in. octagonal barrel, white steel hammer and lock, brass patchbox and trim, walnut stock, 6 lbs. 4 oz. Disc. 1994.

	$220	$185	$150

Last Mfg.'s Sug. Retail was $220.

PENNSYLVANIA LONG RIFLE — .32 or .45 cal., flintlock or percussion, 40½ in. octagonal barrel, color case hardened hammer and lock, brass patchbox and trim, walnut stock, 7 lbs. 8 oz. Deduct $10 for percussion.

Mfg.'s Sug. Retail	$475	$390	$340	$260

PIONEER RIFLE — .45 or .50 cal., flintlock, 30 in. octagonal barrel, color case hardened hammer and lock, walnut stock, 6 lbs. 4 oz. Disc. 1994.

	$200	$185	$150

Last Mfg.'s Sug. Retail was $200.

RIGBY STYLE TARGET — .451 cal., 32 in. round blued barrel, color case hardened hammer and lock, hand checkered walnut stock, very similar to a modern day firearm, adj. vernier sights, 7 lbs. 12 oz. Disc. 1994.

	$750	$635	$500

Last Mfg.'s Sug. Retail was $645.

SHARPS RIFLE 1859 "BERDAN" MODEL — .54 cal., percussion, 30 in. round blued barrel, color case hardened hammer, lock, patch box, triggerguard, and furniture, 3 barrel bands, double set triggers, walnut stock, 8 lbs. 8 oz. New 1994.

Mfg.'s Sug. Retail	$1,095	$875	$800	$625

SHARPS 1859/1863 — .45 and .54 cal., percussion, 22, 28, 30 or 32 in. octagonal or round barrel, color case hardened hammer, frame and butt plate, 7¾ lbs.

Mfg.'s Sug. Retail–1859 Rifle	$1,030	$850	$775	$600
Mfg.'s Sug. Retail–1863 Carbine	$835	$700	$625	$450

1808/1835 SPRINGFIELD — .69 cal., flintlock, 44 in. round barrel, all white steel, walnut stock, 8 lbs. 12 oz.

Mfg.'s Sug. Retail	$810	$750	$650	$520

The Model 1835 Springfield is a more refined version of the Model 1808. This was the last flintlock issued by the U.S. Army.

1863 SPRINGFIELD — .58 cal., percussion, 40 in. barrel, all white steel, 3 barrel bands, 9½ lbs. (1861 Springfield and 1862 C.S. Richmond Musket are both earlier models of the 1863 Springfield, values are equal).

Mfg.'s Sug. Retail	$550	$450	$390	$310

SMITH ARTILLERY/CAVALRY CARBINE — .54 cal., percussion, 20½ in. octagonal tapering to round barrel, color case hardened hammer and receiver. New in 1989. (Pietta)

Mfg.'s Sug. Retail	$600	$535	$475	$370

Grading	100%	98%	95%

SWISS FEDERAL TARGET RIFLE — .45 cal., percussion, 32 in. octagonal barrel, color case hardened hammer, lock, and trim, double set triggers, classic Bristlen and Morges design, adj., sights, 13¼ lbs. Add $35 for palm rest. Imported from West Germany by Neumann Co. Disc. 1994.

$1,465 $1,275 $950

Last Mfg.'s Sug. Retail was $1,200.

TRYON RIFLE — .451 cal., percussion, 34 in octagonal barrel, white steel hammer and engraved lock and patchbox, double set triggers, walnut stock, 9 lbs. 12 oz. Add $35 for target sights.

$390 $360 $275

Last Mfg.'s Sug. Retail was $455.

TRYON CREEDMOOR RIFLE — .451 cal., percussion, Creedmoor target, version of above.
Mfg.'s Sug. Retail $780 $600 $550 $420

ZOUAVE RIFLE — .58 cal., percussion, 32½ in. round barrel, color case hardened hammer, lock, and trigger, brass trim, adj. rear sight, 9 lbs. (Armi Sport or EuroArms) Add $115 for deluxe. Range Model (EuroSport)
Mfg.'s Sug. Retail $465 $290 $250 $200

RIFLES: BLACK POWDER CARTRIDGE

CREEDMOOR TARGET — .45-70 cal., cartridge, 30 in. tapered barrel, color case hardened action, beautiful reproduction, adj. sights, 9 lbs.
Mfg.'s Sug. Retail $875 $750 $675 $555

IRON FRAME HENRY — .44-40, or .44 cal., cartridge, 24 in. barrel, cast iron action, color case hardened receiver, lever and hammer, beautiful reproduction, adj. sights, 9¼ lbs.
Mfg.'s Sug. Retail $945 $820 $720 $580

HENRY MILITARY/CARBINE RIFLE — .44-40 cal. cartridge, 24 in. barrel (22 in. carbine) brass frame and trim, color case hardened lever and hammer, beautiful reproduction, military version has sling swivels, mounted on left side, adj. sights, 9¼ lbs.
Mfg.'s Sug. Retail $875 $800 $700 $560

For engraving add $330 for 25%, $540 for 35%, $900 for 50%, add $15 for military w/24 in. barrel.

HENRY TRAPPER — .44-40 cal., cartridge or 16½ in. barrel, brass frame and trim, color case hardened lever and hammer, beautiful reproduction, adj. sights, 7¼ lbs.
Mfg.'s Sug. Retail $875 $800 $700 $560

For engraving add $330 for 25%, $540 for 35%, $900 for 50%.

KOKEAK MKIV DOUBLE RIFLE — .45-70 cal. cartridge, 24 in. SxS barrel, color case hardened lock and triggerguard, double leaf adjustable rear sight, hand checkered two piece walnut stock, 10 lbs. Add $1,100 for engraved with white steel engraved frame and hardware browned barrels.
Mfg.'s Sug. Retail $3,125 $2,050 $1,850 $1,520

ROLLING BLOCK BUFFALO RIFLE (REMINGTON STYLE) — .45-70 cal., cartridge, 26 or 30 in. barrel length, ½ round or octagonal, color case hardened action, brass triggerguard, beautiful reproduction, adj. sights, approx. 9 lbs. Add $180 for Creedmoor Model, $150 for telescopic sight.
Mfg.'s Sug. Retail $650 $570 $495 $395

SHARPS PLAINS RIFLE/CAVALRY CARBINE — .45-70 cal., cartridge, 28½ in. barrel, (22 in. barrel carbine), color case hardened hammer and receiver, walnut stock, 7 lbs. 12 oz.
Mfg.'s Sug. Retail $935 $825 $750 $650

Cavalry Model also available in .50 or .54 cal. percussion. Deduct $35 for .50 or .54 cal. percussion.

BLACK POWDER

Grading	100%	98%	95%

1874 SHARPS INFANTRY RIFLE — similar to "Berdan" Model on previous page, except single trigger & in .45-70 cal. New 1994.

Mfg.'s Sug. Retail	$1,060	$965	$845	$675

Add $50 for sniper rifle w/double set triggers.

WINCHESTER 1873 RIFLE/CARBINE — .44-40 cal. cartridge, 20 in. round barrel, 11 shot walnut stock, trapdoor buttplate for cleaning rod, 7 lbs. Add $20 for rifle, $115 for sporting rifle with 24 in. barrel, add $130 for sporting rifle 30 in. barrel.

Mfg.'s Sug. Retail	$820	$690	$600	$475

1866 YELLOW BOY RIFLE/CARBINE — .44-40 cal. cartridge, 19 in. round barrel, walnut stock, 7½ lbs. Add $10 for rifle.

Mfg.'s Sug. Retail	$670	$575	$500	$385

REVOLVERS BLACK POWDER CARTRIDGE

1873 SAA REVOLVER — .44-40 cal., cartridge, 3, 4¾, 5½ and 7½ in. barrel, color case hardened frame hammer and triggerguard (or brass backstrap and triggerguard), 2½ lbs.

Mfg.'s Sug. Retail	$390	$345	$300	$240

Add $65 for nickel finish.
Add $80 for U.S. Cavalry Model or Artillery Model.
Deduct $45 for brass backstrap and triggerguard. (Economy model).

1875 REMINGTON — .44-40 cartridge, 7½ in. barrel, color case hardened frame, brass trigger-guard, 2½ lbs.

Mfg.'s Sug. Retail	$435	$355	$310	$250

1890 REMINGTON — .44-40 cartridge, 5½ in. barrel, blued finish, brass triggerguard walnut grips w/lanyard loop, 2½ lbs.

Mfg.'s Sug. Retail	$445	$355	$310	$260

1875 SCHOFIELD — .44-40 cartridge, 7 in. barrel (5 in. on Wells-Fargo version), single action top break revolver, walnut grips, 2 lbs. 7 oz. New 1994.

Mfg.'s Sug. Retail	$795	$700	$595	$495

SHOTGUNS

CLASSIC SxS — 12 or 10 ga., percussion, 28 in. barrel, color case hardened hammer, lock, and trim, 7¾ lbs. Add $20 for .10 ga. (10 ga. disc. in 1987, 12 ga. disc. 1993).

	$315	$275	$220

Last Mfg.'s Sug. Retail was $395.

FOWLER SHOTGUN — 10 or 12 ga., SxS 28 in. barrel, color case hardened hammer and lock, 7 lbs. 6 oz. (Pietta)

Mfg.'s Sug. Retail	$340	$315	$275	$220

Add $150 for steel shot 10 ga. model.
Add $100 for extra 10 ga. barrel.

HUNTER SHOTGUN — 20 ga., 28½ in. barrel, round chrome lined color case hardened hammer and lock, double set triggers, 7 lbs. 12 oz. Disc. 1989.

	$300	$255	$200

Last Mfg.'s Sug. Retail was $190.

MORSE SHOTGUN — 12 ga., percussion, 26 in. barrel, brass receiver and trim, blued hammer and buttplate, 5¾ lbs. Disc. 1987.

	$300	$255	$200

Last Mfg.'s Sug. Retail was $165.

MORTIMER SHOTGUN — 12 ga., flintlock, 36 in. browned barrel, color case hardened furniture, walnut stock, waterproof pan and chrome bore. New in 1989.

Mfg.'s Sug. Retail	$735	$480	$420	$360

Grading	100%	98%	95%	

STEEL SHOT MAGNUM — 10 ga., percussion, SxS 28 in. barrel, engraved polished lock plates, chrome lined barrels, checkered walnut stock, 7 lbs. 9oz.

	$515	**$450**	**$360**

Last Mfg.'s Sug. Retail was $560.

TURKEY AND TRAP — 12 ga., percussion SxS, 28 in. blued barrels, color case hardened locks and furniture, walnut stock. (Pedersoli)

Mfg.'s Sug. Retail	**$540**	**$420**	**$380**	**$300**

OLD-WEST GUN CO.

Importer and distributor that took over the inventory of Allen Firearms after they went out of business in early 1987. Old-West Gun Co. became Cimarron Arms Co. in 1987. Older guns marked Old West have the same values as those of Cimarron Arms Co. (Please refer to the Cimarron heading in this text). Available only on used market.

PEDERSOLI, DAVIDE & C. s.n.c.

Imported by Navy, E.M.F., House of Muskets, and Sile Distributors, and Taylors, Inc. In 1992, entire Pedersoli line now being imported by Beauchamp and Son, Inc./Flintlocks, ETC. Available through dealers and catalog houses.

Add approximately 25% for engraving, 200% for extra luxury engraving.

PISTOLS

"BOUNTY" KENTUCKY — .44 or .50 cal., flintlock or percussion, 16½ in. octagonal barrel, white steel hammer and lock, brass furniture and triggerguard, walnut stock, 3 lbs.

Mfg.'s Sug. Retail	**$240**	**$215**	**$180**	**$140**

Add $10 for flintlock.
Add $40 for engraved model (hammer, lock and barrel).

ENGLISH DUELING PISTOL — .45 cal., percussion, 11 in. octagonal barrel, silver thimble and nosecap.

	$240	**$210**	**$165**

HARPERS FERRY 1806 — .58 cal., flintlock, 10 in. barrel, color case hardened lock, brass furniture, and inlaid butt cap, 2½ lbs. Add $90 for commemorative model with silver plated hardware and white steel barrel (stamped U.S. Army Commemorative).

Mfg.'s Sug. Retail	**$310**	**$265**	**$220**	**$170**

KENTUCKY PISTOL — .44, .45, .50 & .54 cal., flintlock or percussion, 10¼ octagonal barrel (steel or brass), walnut stock, brass furniture and triggerguard, 2¼ lbs. Add $10 for flintlock, $45 for deluxe engraved model w/German silver inlaid barrel, and color case hardened hammer and lock, $90 for silver star model with engraved white steel hammer and lock, German silver furniture, inlayed stock (star on forearm) and browned barrel, add $60 for maple stock version.

Mfg.'s Sug. Retail	**$215**	**$205**	**$170**	**$140**

KUCHEN REUTER — .38, .40, or .44 cal., 11¼ in. octagonal browned barrel, color case hardened, hammer lock, triggerguard, and furniture, walnut stock, 2 lbs. 10 oz. New 1994.

Mfg.'s Sug. Retail	**$1,120**	**$1,000**	**$890**	**$715**

LEPAGE PISTOL — .31, .36, .38, .44, and .45 cal., flintlock or percussion, 10½ in. browned octagonal barrel, white steel barrel percussion, white steel hammer, and lock, adj. triggers, 2 lbs. (cased set, gold trim, consecutive serial number).

Mfg.'s Sug. Retail	**$500**	**$400**	**$340**	**$270**

BLACK POWDER

Grading	100%	98%	95%

MANG TARGET PISTOL — .38 cal., percussion, 11½ in. octagonal browned barrel, color case hardened hammer and lock, fluted walnut stock, 2½ lbs.
Mfg.'s Sug. Retail $850 $700 $600 $400
   Add $2,000 for deluxe model with skin case.

CHARLES MOORE PISTOL — .36, .44, and .45 cal., flintlock (.44 or .45 cal.) or percussion (.36 or .45 cal.), 11 in. octagonal barrel, white steel hammer and lock (flintlock), color case hardened (percussion), brass furniture, adj. trigger, hand checkered walnut stock, 2½ lbs.
Mfg.'s Sug. Retail $365 $315 $275 $220
   Add $30 for smooth bore or rifled target Flintlock.
   Add $20 for percussion target.

"MOUNTAIN" KENTUCKY PISTOL — .44 or .50 cal., flintlock or percussion, 14½ in. octagonal barrel, color case hardened hammer and lock, brass furniture and triggerguard, hand checkered walnut stock, 2¼ lbs.
Mfg.'s Sug. Retail $245 $220 $185 $140
   Add $10 for flintlock.

PENNSYLVANIA PISTOL — .44 cal. flintlock or percussion, 10 in. octagonal barrel, brass furniture, locks left in white.
                                        $135 $120 $90

QUEEN ANN PISTOL — .50 cal., flintlock, 7½ in. cannon shaped brass or white steel barrel (smooth bore), white steel hammer and lock, grotesque mask under buttstock, 2¼ lbs.
Mfg.'s Sug. Retail $225 $175 $150 $120
   Add $40 for silver plated or deluxe model.

SALOON PISTOL — .36 cal., percussion, straight through ignition, 8 in. rounded barrel, color case hardened hammer and frame, walnut stock, 1¾ lbs.
Mfg.'s Sug. Retail $175 $155 $130 $105

UNDERHAMMER PISTOL — .36 cal. percussion, 8½ in. octagonal to round browned barrel, metal fittings are color case hardened, walnut stock, 2 lbs.
Mfg.'s Sug. Retail $725 $660 $575 $460

ZIMMER PISTOL — .36 and 4.3 cal., percussion, 8 in. octagonal blued barrel, white steel hammer and frame, fluted walnut stock, 1⅝ lbs.
Mfg.'s Sug. Retail $270 $230 $200 $155
   Add $20 for 4.3 cal. (designed to shoot with cap alone no powder).
   Add $35 for deluxe model either caliber.

REVOLVERS

PATERSON — .36 cal., percussion, 5 shot, 9 in. octagonal barrel, no loading lever, walnut stock, 2½ lbs.
                                        $275 $240 $190
   Add $450 for deluxe model with engraved cylinder, barrel, and frame with skin case.
   Last Mfg.'s Sug. Retail was $310.

ROGERS AND SPENCER FEINWERKBAU — .44 cal. percussion, 6 shot, 7½ in. octagonal barrel, walnut grips, 3 lbs.
Mfg.'s Sug. Retail $1,750 $1,550 $1,350 $1,080
   Manufactured by Feinwerkbau using the latest technology, molybdenum chrome steel frame, etc. Weight balanced for accurate firing.

ROGERS & SPENCER — same as above, but manufactured by Pedersoli.
Mfg.'s Sug. Retail $725 $685 $595 $470

Grading	100%	98%	95%

RIFLES

ALAMO — .38, .45. or .50 cal., percussion or flintlock, 36 in. octagonal barrel with double set triggers, white steel hammer and lock, brass furniture, patchbox engraved with scenes of the period, walnut stock, $6\frac{1}{2}$ lbs. Add $15 for flintlock.

Mfg.'s Sug. Retail	$475	$420	$380	$300

BRISTLEN MORGES — .44 cal. percussion, $29\frac{1}{2}$ in. octagonal barrel, color case hardened hammer and lock, walnut $\frac{1}{2}$ stock, palm rest professional target rifle, $16\frac{3}{4}$ lbs.

Mfg.'s Sug. Retail	$1,620	$1,280	$1,165	$950

Add $650 for deluxe version with engraved white steel hammer and lock.

BROWN BESS MUSKET/CARBINE — .75 cal., flintlock, $31\frac{1}{2}$ or 42 in. smooth bore barrel, white steel hammer and lock, brass furniture, $\frac{3}{4}$ stock (walnut), $8\frac{3}{4}$ lbs. ($7\frac{3}{4}$ carbine).

Mfg.'s Sug. Retail	$750	$600	$540	$425

Add $65 for bayonet.

1777 CHARLEVILLE MUSKET — .69 cal., flintlock or percussion, $44\frac{5}{8}$ in. white steel barrel, hammer, lock, and trim, $9\frac{3}{4}$ lbs. New in 1989.

Mfg.'s Sug. Retail	$800	$610	$530	$435

COUNTRY BOY — .32, .36, .45, and .50 cal., percussion, 26 in. octagonal barrel, color case hardened hammer and lock, unique mule ear hammer, blued furniture, adj. sights, walnut $\frac{1}{2}$ stock, $5\frac{1}{2}$ lbs. Disc. 1994.

	$225	$195	$160

Last Mfg.'s Retail was $240.

COUNTRY HUNTER — .50 cal., flintlock or percussion, $28\frac{1}{4}$ in. octagonal barrel, blued hardware, color case hardened hammer and lock, walnut $\frac{1}{2}$ stock, 6 lbs.

Mfg.'s Sug. Retail	$165	$160	$140	$110

Add $10 for flintlock.

DELUXE CUB RIFLE — .40 cal., flintlock or percussion, 28 in. octagonal barrel, color case hardened hammer, plate and triggers, brass trim and patch box, double set triggers.

Mfg.'s Sug. Retail	$385	$345	$300	$240

FREDERICKSBURG MUSKET — .75 cal., flintlock.

	$600	$540	$425

FRONTIER RIFLE/CARBINE — .32, .36, .45, .50, and .54 cal., flintlock (.54 cal. only) or percussion, 39 in. octagonal browned barrel, color case hardened hammer and lock, brass furniture, walnut or birdseye maple full stock, $7\frac{3}{4}$ lbs. ($7\frac{1}{4}$ lbs. .45 and .50 cal.).

Mfg.'s Sug. Retail	$465	$350	$315	$275

Add $15 for flintlock.
Add $120 for Grade I maple, $200 for Grade II maple, and $250 for Grade III maple.
Add $240 for birdseye maple stock w/patchbox.
Deduct $25 for carbine.
Also sold as Blue Ridge Rifle by Cabelas.

HAWKEN RIFLE — .54 cal. percussion, $32\frac{1}{4}$ in. octagonal browned barrel, color case hardened hammer, lock, and furniture, double set triggers, walnut or birdseye maple $\frac{1}{2}$ stock, $8\frac{3}{4}$ lbs. Disc. 1994.

	$425	$375	$300

Add $115 for birdseye maple stock.

Last Mfg.'s Sug. Retail was $450.

JAPANESE RIFLE — .492 cal., matchlock $41\frac{1}{2}$ in. octagonal browned barrel, brass matchlock and furniture, authentic reproduction of 16th century Tomonobu rifle.

Mfg.'s Sug. Retail	$1,095	$1,025	$895	$650

BLACK POWDER

Grading	100%	98%	95%

KENTUCKY — .32, .45, or .50 cal., percussion or flintlock, 35 in. barrel, color case hardened hammer and lock, brass furniture and patchbox, walnut full stock, 6½ lbs. Add $10 for flintlock, $110 for deluxe model with engraved white steel hammer, lock, and engraved brass patchbox and triggerguard, $305 for silver star model with engraved silver plated hammer, lock, triggerguard and patchbox, also has silver stars inlaid in stock.

Mfg.'s Sug. Retail	$400	$345	$300	$225

KODIAK — .50, .54, and .58 cal. percussion, double rifle (SxS), see Kodiak express combo below.

Mfg.'s Sug. Retail	$775	$550	$500	$400

MORTIMER/MORTIMER HUNTER RIFLE — .54 cal. flintlock or percussion, 36¼ in. octagonal to round browned barrel, color case hardened hammer, lock and trigger guard, waterproof pan, 8⅞ lbs. Prices based on Mortimer Hunter. Disc. 1994.

	$400	$345	$275

Add $345 for target model with target sights and checkered stock (flintlock), $1,180 for extra deluxe engraved with engraved white steel hammer, lock, and hardware with gold inlays (all models), add $210 for Std. Mortimer Rifle (flintlock), add $210 for .45 cal. percussion "Vetterli" 50MT Model, add $230 for .451 Whitworth 100MT Model.

Last Mfg.'s Sug. Retail was $425.

1816 MT. WICKHAM RIFLE — similar to Charleville rifle above but with slightly shorter barrel.

Mfg.'s Sug. Retail	$800	$720	$625	$500

PENNSYLVANIA RIFLE — .32 and .45 cal., flintlock or percussion, 41½ in. barrel, brass trim, color case hardened or white steel lock, hammer, and double set trigger, walnut full stock, 8¼ lbs. New in 1989.

Mfg.'s Sug. Retail	$460	$390	$340	$250

Add $10 for flintlock.

PLAINSMAN RIFLE — .38, .45. or .50 cal., flintlock or percussion, 37 in. octagonal barrel, white steel hammer and lock, brass furniture and patchbox, adj. sights and double set triggers, 6½ lbs. Disc. 1994.

	$400	$345	$240

Add $20 for flintlock
Add $65 for engraved model.

Last Mfg.'s Sug. Retail was $435.

1809 PRUSSIAN — .75 cal. flintlock, 41⅛ in. round white steel barrel, white steel hammer and lock, brass furniture, walnut stock (lock marked "Potsdam"), 9¼ lbs.

Mfg.'s Sug. Retail	$800	$720	$625	$500

ROLLING BLOCK MUZZLELOADER RIFLE/CARBINE — .50 or .54 cal., percussion, 26¼ in. octagonal barrel (22¼ in. carbine) color case hardened hammer, block & buttplate, brass triggerguard. Based on Remington rolling block frame adjustable sights, 8½ lbs. (7¾ lbs carbine.)

Mfg.'s Sug. Retail	$300	$260	$220	$190

SANFTL — .45 cal. percussion, 32¼ in. octagonal white steel barrel, white steel hammer and lock, brass triggerguard and buttplate (copy of Tyrolese Target Rifle), walnut stock, 10 lbs. New 1994.

Mfg.'s Sug. Retail	$1,725	$1,535	$1,395	$1,115

SCOUT RIFLE — .32, .45, and .50 cal., flintlock or percussion, carbine version of Pennsylvania rifle listed above with 28¼ in. barrel, 6 lbs.

Mfg.'s Sug. Retail	$400	$360	$320	$250

Add $10 for flintlock.

Grading	100%	98%	95%

SHARPS 1859/1863 — .45 and .54 cal., percussion, 22, 28, 30, or 32 in. octagonal or round barrel, color case hardened hammer, frame and butt plate, 7¾ lbs. Add $20 for octagonal barrel on civilian model, $80 for sporter model with hand-checkered walnut stock, $55 for patch box.

| Mfg.'s Sug. Retail | $885 | $700 | $625 | $450 |

Add $150 for 1859 Model w/3 barrel bands and patchbox, add $175 for "Berdan Military" Model, add $1,270 for engraved sporting model, add $2,000 for sporting model deluxe gold engraved.

1816 SPRINGFIELD/HARPERS FERRY — .69 cal. flintlock, 40 in. white steel round barrel, all white steel hardware, sling swivels, walnut stock, 9¾ lbs.

| Mfg.'s Sug. Retail | $800 | $715 | $625 | $500 |

1861 SPRINGFIELD RIFLE — .58 cal., percussion, 40 in. white steel barrel, white steel or color case hardened hammer and lock, white steel furniture, walnut full stock, (lock stamped "U.S. Springfield"), 9¾ lbs.

| Mfg.'s Sug. Retail | $800 | $715 | $625 | $500 |

SWIVEL BARREL — .50x.50 or .54x.54 percussion, 23⅝ in. double (O/U) octagonal barrel, blued barrel, hammer, lock and furniture (after 1st shot barrel simply needed to be rotated 180 degrees for second shot), checkered walnut stock, 9½ lbs. (9¾ on .54 cal.). New 1994.

| Mfg.'s Sug. Retail | $560 | $400 | $300 | $250 |

TRYON RIFLE — .45, .50, or .54 cal., percussion, 32¼ in. octagonal barrel, color case hardened hammer, lock, patchbox, and furniture, double set triggers, walnut ½ stock, 9½ lbs. Add $125 for engraved model with white steel hammer, lock, furniture and patchbox.

| Mfg.'s Sug. Retail | $560 | $390 | $360 | $275 |

TRYON CREEDMOOR — .451 cal., percussion, 32¾ in. barrel, all blued hardware, target version of above, 9½ lbs.

| Mfg.'s Sug. Retail | $780 | $600 | $550 | $420 |

WAADTLANDER RIFLE — .45 cal., percussion, 31 in. octagonal browned barrel, target sights, 14⅜ lbs. Target version of Bristlen Morges above. Add $500 for deluxe engraved model with white steel hardware and silver inlays.

| Mfg.'s Sug. Retail | $1,620 | $1,245 | $1,145 | $950 |

IN-LINE ACTION

GAMMA 901 — .50 or .54 cal. percussion, 28 in. round barrel, all sand blued except bolt (hammer), automatic safety, walnut stock, 6½ lbs. (.54 cal.) or 7¼ lbs. (.50 cal.).

| Mfg.'s Sug. Retail | $375 | $345 | $300 | $240 |

GAMMA 900 — same as above, except better sights, recoil pad, blued aluminum ramrod and better wood.

| Mfg.'s Sug. Retail | $425 | $390 | $340 | $270 |

GAMMA 9000 — same as above, except 32 in. barrel, better sights, and checkered walnut stock.

| Mfg.'s Sug. Retail | $525 | $500 | $420 | $360 |

BLACK POWDER CARTRIDGE

KODIAK MARK IV — .45-70 cartridge, 24 in. SxS barrel, color case hardened hammer lock and triggerguard, double leaf adj. rear sights, copy of 19th century "Colt Double Rifle", hand checkered walnut stock, 10 lbs. Add $800 for extra 12 ga. or 20 ga./.45-.70 barrel, $1,100 for engraved model with white steel engraved frame and hardware, browned barrels.

| Mfg.'s Sug. Retail | $2,750 | $2,050 | $1,850 | $1,520 |

BLACK POWDER

Grading	100%	98%	95%

REMINGTON ROLLING BLOCK REPRODUCTION — .45-70 cartridge, $19\frac{1}{2}$, $24\frac{1}{2}$, 26 and 30 in. octagonal blued barrel (octagonal to round on cavalry model), color case hardened frame and hammer, brass triggerguard and furniture, walnut stock, $9\frac{3}{4}$, $11\frac{1}{2}$, $11\frac{7}{8}$, and 13 lbs. respectively, ($9\frac{3}{8}$, 11, $11\frac{3}{8}$, $12\frac{3}{8}$ lbs. respectively on cavalry models). Add $55 for target model with adj. sights and white steel hammer and frame, $100 for Creedmoor sights, $180 for Creedmoor Target with Creedmoor adj. sights and color case hardened trigger-guard, $600 for engraved model with white steel engraved frame and brass triggerguard.

Mfg.'s Sug. Retail $650 $570 $495 $395

  Add $620 for engraved long range Creedmoor model.

SHARPS 1874 — .45-70 cartridge, 22, 24, 28, 30, or 32 in. octagonal or round barrel, color case hardened hammer, frame and buttplate, $7\frac{3}{4}$-9 lbs. Add $20 for octagonal barrel on civilian model. (Very improved 1993).

Mfg.'s Sug. Retail $1,050 $825 $750 $650

  Add $75 for target sights, $140 for patchbox, $175 for set triggers.
  Add $1320 for engraving on sporting rifle, add $2,000 for deluxe gold engraved.
  Deduct $100 for 22 in. Carbine model.

SHOTGUNS

CLASSIC TURKEY SxS — 12 ga., percussion, 28 in. round double barrel, color case hardened lock, stainless steel nipple, recoil pad, 9 lbs.

                             $420 $435 $300

KODIAK SxS SHOTGUN/EXPRESS/COMBO. — 10 ga. x.50 or x.58, 12 ga. x.50, x.54, or x.58, or .50x.58 cal. percussion, 28 in. double barrel, engraved white steel hammer and lock, blued furniture, checkered walnut $\frac{1}{2}$ stock, 9 lbs. Add $50 for .10 ga., $300 for rifle or comb. barrels (extra set).

Mfg.'s Sug. Retail $775 $640 $530 $410

SxS SHOTGUN — 10, 12, and 20 ga., percussion, 28 in. barrel, chrome bore, color case hardened hammer and lock, (engraved white steel on 10 ga.), checkered walnut stock, double triggers, $7\frac{1}{2}$ lbs. Add $20 for 10 or 12 ga., $20 for cavalry model, $900 for extra deluxe with gold inlays, $900 for case.

Mfg.'s Sug. Retail $540 $420 $380 $300

  Add $200 for extra 12 ga. barrels, $240 for extra 10 ga. barrels.

MORTIMER SHOTGUN — 12 ga. flintlock or percussion, version of Mortimer Rifle above.

Mfg.'s Sug. Retail $625 $420 $360 $300

  Add $60 for flintlock.
  Add $1,300 for deluxe engraving with gold.

PEIFER RIFLE CO.

Manufacturer located in Nokomis, IL.

RIFLES

TS-93 RIFLE — .45 or .50 cal. percussion, 24 in. blued chrome moly or stainless barrel, cocking action provided by moving triggerguard to right or left, primer holder rotates 90 degrees for added safety, tang safety, synthetic stock with recoil pad, uses #209 primer instead of percussion cap, 7 lbs.

Mfg.'s Sug. Retail $663 $625   N/A   N/A

  Add $50 for wood look synthetic stock, add $50 for stainless steel.

PIETTA, F. LLI

Manufacturer located in Brescia, Italy.

Grading	100%	98%	95%

1851 NAVY — .36 and .44 cal., percussion, 7½ in. round barrel, many styles, 6 shot engraved cylinder, 2 lbs. 12 oz.

$100 $85 $70

> Prices are equal on Sheriff's Model. Add $30 for steel frame. Deduct $30 for 1851 Confederate Model.

1860 ARMY — .44 cal., percussion, 7½ in. barrel, 6 shot rebated cylinder, color case hardened (or brass) frame, hammer and load lever, all brass backstrap and triggerguard, 2 lbs. 9 oz.

$120 $105 $85

> Deduct $35 for brass frame.

1861 NAVY — .36 and .44 cal., percussion, 7½ in. barrel, brass backstrap and triggerguard, color case hardened frame, hammer, and load lever, 2 lbs. 8 oz.

$120 $105 $85

1862 POLICE — .36 cal., percussion, 5½ in. round to octagonal barrel, color case hardened hammer, frame, and load lever, brass trim, 1 lb. 10 oz.

$130 $105 $80

COLT PATERSON — .36 cal., percussion, 7½ in. octagonal barrel, standard "hidden trigger" design, blued steel hardware, no loading lever, 2 lbs. 9 oz. Add $135 for engraved version.

$250 $220 $180

LE MAT REVOLVER —.44 cal., percussion, 9 shot cylinder plus 1 shot center barrel (maximum fire power for its day), 7⅝ in. octagonal barrel, white steel frame, 3 lbs. 7 oz. Add $375 for engraved Beauregard model, $160 for 18th Georgia engraved model.

$570 $495 $380

1858 REMINGTON — .36 and .44 cal., percussion, 8 in. octagonal barrel, 6 shot, brass frame and triggerguard.

$85 $75 $60

> Add $30 for Buffalo Model with 12 in. barrel.

1858 REMINGTON — same as above, has steel frame with brass backstrap and triggerguard.

$115 $100 $70

> Add $70 for stainless steel. $30 for Target Model.

SPILLER and BURR — .36 cal., percussion, 7½ in. barrel, brass frame, color case hardened hammer and loading lever, 2 lbs. 8 oz.

$130 $115 $90

RIFLES, PERCUSSION

SMITH ARTILLERY/CAVALRY CARBINE — .54 cal., percussion, 20½ in. octagonal tapering to round barrel, color case hardened hammer and receiver.

Mfg.'s Sug. Retail $600 $535 $475 $370

SHOTGUNS

FOWLER SHOTGUN — 10 or 12 ga., SxS 28 in. barrel, color case hardened hammer and lock, 7 lbs. 6 oz.

Mfg.'s Sug. Retail $340 $315 $275 $220

> Add $150 for steel shot 10 ga. model.
> Add $100 for extra 10 ga. barrel.

PRAIRIE RIVER ARMS

Princeton, IL

BLACK POWDER

Grading	100%	98%	95%

Prairie River Arms has developed a new percussion ignition system that contains the firing mechanism entirely within the gun stock. Advantages - more weather resistant, protection from percussion cap fragmentation, and better balance.

BULLPUP — .50 or .54 cal., percussion, 28 in round barrel (alloy or stainless steel), unique Bullpup design, hardwood or synthetic all weather thumbhole stock, 7½ lbs.

Mfg.'s Sug. Retail	$495	$455	$390	$310

Add $70 for stainless steel.

CLASSIC — .50 or .54 cal., percussion, 28 in. round barrel (alloy or stainless), hardwood or synthetic all weather stock.

Mfg.'s Sug. Retail	$375	$340	$290	$230

Add $15 for all weather stock, $50 for stainless steel.

REMINGTON ARMS CO., INC.
Manufacturer located in Wilmington, DE.

RIFLES

MODEL 700 ML/MLS — .50 or .54 cal., percussion, 24 in. barrel, in-line ignition, short throw bolt action, 3.0 millisecond lock time, synthetic stock with recoil pad, 7¾ lbs. New 1996.

▲ *700 ML Blued Steel*

Mfg.'s Sug. Retail	$360	$320	N/A	N/A

▲ *700 MLS Stainless*

Mfg.'s Sug. Retail	$452	$400	N/A	N/A

1816 COMMEMORATIVE FLINT-LOCK RIFLE — .50 cal., flintlock, 39 in. barrel, extra fancy curly maple stock, manufactured by Remington Custom Shop.

Mfg.'s Sug. Retail	$1,899	$1,750	$1,650	$1,500

RICHLAND ARMS
Previously distributed in Blissfield, MI. Available only on the used market.

PISTOLS

ANDREW TARGET — .32, .36. or .45 cal., percussion, 10 in. octagonal barrel, white steel hammer, barrel, frame, and sights, brass triggerguard, adj. trigger and sights, blued and engraved, 2 lbs. 10 oz. Add $55 for deluxe grade. Disc. 1994.

	$195	$170	$135

Last Mfg.'s Sug. Retail was $150.

REVOLVERS

WALKER — .44 cal., percussion, 9 in. round barrel, color case hardened hammer, frame, trigger and load lever, engraved cylinder, brass triggerguard, 73 oz. Disc. 1994.

	$250	$220	$165

Last Mfg.'s Sug. Retail was $185.

3rd MODEL DRAGOON — .44 cal., percussion, 7½ in. barrel, color case hardened hammer, frame, trigger and load lever, engraved cylinder, 66 oz. Disc. 1994.

	$240	$210	$165

Last Mfg.'s Sug. Retail was $165.

1851 NAVY — .36 cal., percussion, 7½ in. octagonal barrel, color case hardened load lever and hammer, brass frame and trigger guard, 44 oz. Add $25 for steel frame. Disc. 1994.

	$110	$95	$75

Last Mfg.'s Sug. Retail was $100.

Grading	100%	98%	95%

1860 ARMY — .44 cal., percussion, 8 in. barrel, color case hardened hammer, frame, trigger and load lever, brass triggerguard, engraved cylinder. Deduct $35 for brass frame. Disc. 1994.

$170 $150 $120

Last Mfg.'s Sug. Retail was $160.

REMINGTON REPLICAS

1858 ARMY — .44 cal., percussion, 8 in. octagonal barrel, brass frame and triggerguard, 44 oz. Add $35 for steel frame. Disc. 1994.

$135 $115 $100

Last Mfg.'s Sug. Retail was $125.

BUFFALO TARGET — .44 cal., percussion, 12 in. octagonal barrel, brass frame and triggerguard, adj. sights, based on 1858 Navy frame, 38 oz. Disc. 1994.

$185 $165 $150

Last Mfg.'s Sug. Retail was $150.

RIFLES

BRISTOL HUNTER — .50 or .54 cal., percussion, 28 in. octagonal barrel, color case hardened hammer and lock, rubber recoil pad, adj. rear sights, chrome plated bore, double set triggers. Disc. 1994.

$220 $190 $150

Last Mfg.'s Sug. Retail was $240.

HAWKEN RIFLE — .50 cal., percussion, 28 in. octagonal barrel, color case hardened hammer and lock, brass trim, adj. sights, double set triggers. Disc. 1994.

$230 $200 $160

Last Mfg.'s Sug. Retail was $225.

KODIAK DOUBLE BARREL RIFLE — .50 or .58 cal., percussion, 28 in. octagonal barrel. Add $280 for extra 12 ga. shotgun barrels. Disc. 1994.

$550 $500 $400

Last Mfg.'s Sug. Retail was $560.

SHOTGUNS

MUZZLE LOADING SHOTGUN — 10 or 12 ga., percussion. Add $20 for 10 ga. Disc. 1994.

$315 $275 $220

Last Mfg.'s Sug. Retail was $320.

BLACK POWDER

RUGER

Manufactured in Southport, CT. Available through dealers and catalog houses.

OLD ARMY — .44 cal., 6 shot, percussion, 7½ in. barrel, adj. rear sight, blue or stainless.

Mfg.'s Sug. Retail $413 $345 $300 $220

▲ *Stainless Old Army* — stainless steel variation of the Old Army.

Mfg.'s Sug. Retail $465 $390 $340 $250

SILE DISTRIBUTORS

Previous importer and distributor of Invest Arms brand and D. Pedersoli brand, located in New York, NY. Available through dealers.

Grading	100%	98%	95%

REVOLVERS

1860 COLT ARMY — .44 cal., percussion, 8 in. blued round barrel, brass or color case hardened steel frame, brass triggerguard and back strap, color case hardened hammer, trigger, and load lever, 2 lbs. 11 oz. Add $35 for steel frame.

$85 $70 $50

1858 REMINGTON ARMY — .44 cal., percussion, 8 in. white octagonal barrel, white steel frame, brass triggerguard, 2 lbs. 9 oz. Add $70 for stainless steel, $100 for stainless steel target.

$115 $100 $70

RIFLES

BROWN BESS MUSKET — .75 cal., flintlock, 41¾ in. smooth bore barrel, brass furniture, white steel barrel, hammer, and lock, engraved lock, 9 lbs. Disc. 1994.

$480 $425 $340

Last Mfg.'s Sug. Retail was $565.

HAWKEN RIFLE — .45, .50 or .54 cal., flintlock or percussion (.50 cal. only in flintlock), 29 in. octagonal barrel, solid brass furniture, color case hardened engraved lock, coil spring mechanism with adj. set triggers, stainless steel nipple, chrome bore, brass patch box, adj. sights, 8 lbs. 10 oz. Add $35 for flintlock. Disc. 1994.

$200 $175 $140

Last Mfg.'s Sug. Retail was $230.

HAWKEN RIFLE CARBINE — .45, .50 or .54 cal., flintlock or percussion (.50 cal. only in flintlock), 22 in. octagonal barrel, solid brass furniture, color case hardened engraved lock, coil spring mechanism with adj. set triggers, stainless steel nipple, chrome bore, brass patch box, adj. sights, 7 lbs. Add $10 for flintlock. Disc. 1994.

$160 $140 $110

Last Mfg.'s Sug. Retail was $250.

HAWKEN HUNTER CARBINE — .45, .50 or .54 cal., flintlock or percussion (.50 cal. only in flintlock), 22 in. octagonal barrel, solid brass furniture, color case hardened engraved lock, coil spring mechanism with adj. set triggers, stainless steel nipple, chrome bore, brass patch box, adj. sights, 7 lbs. Add $10 for flintlock. Disc. 1994.

$160 $140 $110

Last Mfg.'s Sug. Retail was $225.

KENTUCKY RIFLE — .45 or .50 cal., flintlock or percussion, 32 in. blued octagonal barrel, solid brass furniture, color case hardened hammer and engraved lock, brass patch box, adj. rear sight, 7 lbs. 2 oz. Add $10 for flintlock. Disc. 1994.

$345 $300 $225

PENNSYLVANIAN SQUIRREL RIFLE — .32 cal., flintlock, 40½ in. browned octagonal barrel, adj. double set triggers, polished white steel hammer and lock, 9 lbs.

$390 $340 $260

SHOTGUNS

SxS DOUBLE BARREL — 10 or 12 ga., percussion, 28 in. double blued barrels, engraved furniture, color case hardened hammer and engraved lock, chrome lined bores, 7 lbs. 12 oz. (8 lbs. 12 oz. for 10 ga.). Add $20 for 10 ga.

$420 $380 $300

SOUTHWEST MUZZLE LOADERS SUPPLY

Located in Angleton, TX.

Importer of Uberti, Italian replicas. See Uberti.

Grading	100%	98%	95%

DANCE REVOLVER — .36 or .44 cal., exact reproduction of the original J.H. Dance and Brothers revolver manufactured in Columbia, Texas, advertising listed 500 as total production - less than 50 were actually assembled and delivered, manufactured by Aldo Uberti and Co. from Brescia, Italy, cased. New in 1985. Disc. 1994.

$770 $655 $525

Last Mfg.'s Sug. Retail was $1,500.

STONE MOUNTAIN ARMS, INC.
Norcross, GA

Stone Mountain Arms is marketed exclusively by Connecticut Valley Arms.

REVOLVERS

1848 BABY DRAGOON — .31 cal., percussion 5 shot, 4 in. octagonal barrel, color case hardened steel frame, 1.4 lbs.

$140 $120 $95

Last Mfg. Sug. Retail was $240.

3RD MODEL DRAGOON — .44 cal., percussion, 6 shot, 7½ in. barrel, roll engraved cylinder, color case hardened steel frame, 3.9 lbs.

Mfg.'s Sug. Retail	$250	$225	$195	$150

1851 NAVY — .36 cal., percussion, 6 shot, 7½ in. barrel, (5½ in. on Sheriff model), color case hardened steel frame, brass backstrap & triggerguard, 2.8 lbs.

Mfg.'s Sug. Retail	$180	$140	$125	$100

1858 REMINGTON — .44 cal., percussion, 6 shot, 8 in. barrel, adjustable rear sight, steel frame or fixed sights w/color case hardened frame. Also offered in .31 cal. as "Pocket Model".

Mfg.'s Sug. Retail	$230	$160	$145	$120

Prices are equal for .31 cal. pocket Remington.

ROGERS & SPENCER — .44 cal., percussion, 6 shot, 7½ in. octagonal barrel, 3 lbs.

Mfg.'s Sug. Retail	$290	$225	$195	$150

REVOLVERS CARTRIDGE

1873 COLT — .44-40 cal., cartridge, 6 shot, 4½, 5½, 6½ in. Colorcase hardened steel frame & hammer.

Mfg.'s Sug. Retail	$395	$325	$280	$225

RIFLES

1803 HARPERS FERRY — .54 cal., Flintlock, 32½ in. browned barrel. Brass furniture, walnut stock, 9 lbs.

Mfg.'s Sug. Retail	$730	$560	$480	$380

1841 MISSISSIPPI RIFLE — .54 cal., percussion, 33½ in. barrel. Brass furniture, walnut stock, 9½ lbs.

Mfg.'s Sug. Retail	$575	$420	$370	$290

1853 3 BAND ENFIELD — .58 cal., percussion, 39 in. barrel, color case hardened hammer and lock, blued barrel bands, brass furniture, walnut stock, 9½ lbs.

Mfg.'s Sug. Retail	$550	$435	$375	$300

SILVER EAGLE RIFLE/HUNTER — .50 cal., percussion, 26 in. octagonal barrel, matte Weatherguard, nickel finish, synthetic stock.

Mfg.'s Sug. Retail	$140	$120	$100	$80

Add $20 for Hunter model w/adjustable hunting sights and sling swivels.

1861 SPRINGFIELD — .58 cal., percussion, 40 in. barrel. All white steel, walnut stock.

Mfg.'s Sug. Retail	$600	$425	$375	$300

Grading	100%	98%	95%

IN LINE IGNITION

PRO I IN-LINE RIFLE — .50 cal. percussion, 24 in. round barrel with weatherguard nickel finish, std. trigger, blade front sight, duragrip synthetic stock, chrome plated bolt, 6½ lbs.
Mfg.'s Sug. Retail $200 $170   N/A   N/A

PRO II RIFLE — .50 cal. percussion, similar to Pro I above but with adjustable sights, trigger and stainless steel bolt, 6½ lbs.
Mfg.'s Sug. Retail $220 $180   N/A   N/A

TAYLOR'S and CO., INC.

Importer/distributor located in Winchester, VA. Available through dealers or from Taylor's direct.

PISTOLS: SINGLE SHOT

KENTUCKY PISTOL — .45 cal., percussion, 10¼ in. octagonal barrel, brass blade front sight, 2½ lbs. (Armi Sport)
Mfg.'s Sug. Retail $180 $160 $140 $110

NAPOLEON LEPAGE PISTOL — .45 cal., percussion, 10 in. barrel, white steel barrel and lock, fixed sights with single barrel wedge, silver plated butt cap and triggerguard, double set triggers, 2 lbs. 7 oz. Disc. 1994.
$240 $205 $160

Last Mfg.'s Sug. Retail was $310.

F. ROCHATTE DUELING PISTOL — .45 cal., percussion, 10 in. round barrel with flat top, white steel lock and trim, adj. double set triggers, 2½ lbs. Disc. 1994.
$250 $210 $160

Last Mfg.'s Sug. Retail was $395.

REVOLVERS

1847 WALKER — .44 cal., percussion, 9 in. blued barrel, color case hardened frame, hammer, and loading lever, brass triggerguard and steel backstrap, 4 lbs. 6 oz.
Mfg.'s Sug. Retail $285 $250 $220 $165
    Add $20 for Uberti model.

DRAGOON (1ST, 2ND, OR 3RD) — .44 cal., percussion, 7½ in. barrel, roll engraved cylinder, brass backstrap.
Mfg.'s Sug. Retail $275 $240 $210 $165
    Add $20 for Uberti model.

1848 BABY DRAGOON — .31 cal., percussion, 4 in. octagonal barrel, 5 shot, color case hardened frame, hammer, no load lever, roll engraved cylinder, brass backstrap and triggerguard, 1.4 lbs. (Uberti version).
Mfg.'s Sug. Retail $260 $240 $210 $160

1851 NAVY — .36 or .44 cal., percussion, 7½ in. octagonal barrel, rolled cylinder scene, color case hardened frame, hammer, and loading lever, brass backstrap and triggerguard. Sheriff's Model has 5 in. barrel.
Mfg.'s Sug. Retail $140 $130 $115 $100
    Deduct $30 for brass frame.
    Add $100 for shoulder stock.

1860 ARMY — .44 cal., percussion, 8 in. round barrel, color case hardened frame, hammer, and loading lever, 2¾ lbs.
Mfg.'s Sug. Retail $196 $120 $105 $85
    Deduct $35 for brass frame.
    Add $100 for Uberti Sheriff model, add $100 for shoulder stock.

Grading	100%	98%	95%

1861 NAVY — .36 cal. percussion, 7½ in. barrel, brass backstrap and triggerguard, color case hardened frame, hammer and load lever, 2½ lbs.
Mfg.'s Sug. Retail $185 $120 $105 $85

1862 POLICE — .44 cal., 5½ in. barrel, fluted cylinder, color case hardened frame, hammer and loading lever, brass triggerguard. (Pietta)
Mfg.'s Sug. Retail $205 $130 $105 $80

1858 REMINGTON ARMY — .36 or .44 cal., percussion, 6½ and 8 in. octagonal barrel, color case hardened hammer, steel or brass frame, 2 lbs. 6 oz.
Mfg.'s Sug. Retail $196 $115 $100 $70
    Deduct $35 for brass frame.
    Add $100 for Uberti model.

RIFLES

BROWN BESS MUSKET — .75 cal. flintlock, 31½ in. or 42 in. smooth bore barrel, white steel barrel, hammer, lock and furniture, 8½ lbs. Disc. 1993.
    $600 $540 $425
        Last Mfg.'s Sug. Retail was $675.

C.S. RICHMOND MUSKET — .58 cal., percussion, white steel hammer and furniture, brass nosecap, similar to 1861 Springfield. (Armi Sport)
Mfg.'s Sug. Retail $465 $450 $395 $310

CHARLEVILLE 1777 MUSKET — .69 cal., flintlock, 44¾ in. smooth bore barrel, white steel lockplate, hammer, and ramrod, brass barrel bands, trigger guard, and buttplate, walnut stock. Disc. 1993.
    $470 $410 $330
        Last Mfg.'s Sug. Retail was $595.

ENFIELD 1853 "THREE BAND" — .58 cal. percussion, 39 in. round barrel, color case hardened hammer and lock, brass furniture, blued barrel bands, 9½ lbs. (Armi Sport)
Mfg.'s Sug. Retail $415 $400 $355 $285

DELUXE HAWKEN RIFLE — .50 cal., percussion, 30 in. octagonal chrome lined barrel, brass patchbox, target sights, double set triggers, 8 lbs. (Investarms)
Mfg.'s Sug. Retail $260 $200 $175 $140
    Deduct $40 for Trailsman Model.

HAWKEN HUNTER CARBINE — .50 cal., percussion, 24 in. octagonal chrome lined barrel, rubber recoil pad, sling swivels, double set triggers. (Investarms)
Mfg.'s Sug. Retail $285 $160 $140 $110

KENTUCKY RIFLE — .45 and .50 cal., percussion, 35 in. octagonal barrel, color case hardened lock, brass buttplate, triggerguard, patchbox, sideplates, thimbles and nosecap, walnut stock with large or small patchbox, rifle weighs 7½ lbs., carbine is 6 lbs. (Armi Sport)
Mfg.'s Sug. Retail $289 $270 $230 $180
    Add $10 for large patchbox.

  ▲ *Carbine Model* — .50 cal., percussion, chrome lined barrel. Disc. 1993.
    $255 $220 $180
    Add $10 for large patchbox.
        Last Mfg.'s Sug. Retail was $325.

MORTIMER HUNTER RIFLE — .50 or .54 cal. percussion, 25 in. blued (matte finish) ½ octagonal, ½ round barrel, adj. sights (rear), wt. 8⅞ lbs. Disc. 1993.
    $400 $345 $275
        Last Mfg.'s Sug. Retail was $485.

PENNSYLVANIA RIFLE — .45 cal., percussion, octagonal barrel, color case hardened hammer and lock, small brass patchbox, approx. 7 lbs. Add $185 for new Pedersoli model.
Mfg.'s Sug. Retail $215 $200 $175 $140

BLACK
POWDER

Grading	100%	98%	95%

1842 SPRINGFIELD — .69 Cal., percussion 42 in. round smooth bore barrel, white steel barrel, hammer, lock triggerguard and trigger, marked "US Springfield 1847", approx. 10 lbs. (Armi Sport).
Mfg.'s Sug. Retail $530 $465   N/A   N/A

1861 SPRINGFIELD — .58 cal., percussion, 40 in. round barrel, white steel barrel, hammer, lock, trigger, and trim, 10¼ lbs. (Armi Sport)
Mfg.'s Sug. Retail $450 $450 $390 $310

1863 SHARPS RIFLE/CARBINE — .54 cal. percussion, 28 in. round barrel (22 in. carbine), color case hardened hammer & receiver. (IAB)
Mfg.'s Sug. Retail $610 $600 $525 $380

ST. LOUIS HAWKEN RIFLE — .50 cal., percussion, 30 in. octagonal barrel, all black steel furniture, adj. rear sight, double set triggers, approx. 8 lbs. Disc. 1994.
$245 $215 $160
Last Mfg.'s Sug. Retail was $260.

TRYON RIFLE — .50 or .54 cal. percussion, 32¼ in. octagonal barrel, all white steel, engraved lock and hammer, 9½ lbs. Disc. 1994.
$390 $360 $275
Last Mfg.'s Sug. Retail was $595.

1863 ZOUAVE RIFLE — .58 cal., percussion, 32½ in. round barrel, color case hardened hammer, lock, and trigger, brass patchbox, triggerguard, and barrel bands, 9 lbs. (Armi Sport)
Mfg.'s Sug. Retail $407 $290 $250 $200

BLACKPOWDER CARTRIDGE

HENRY RIFLE — .44-40 cartridge, 24¼ half-octagonal barrel, tube mag., frame, elevator, butt plate is brass, walnut stock, 9¼ lbs. Mfg. by Uberti.
Mfg.'s Sug. Retail $1,050 $800 $700 $560
    Add $50 for steel frame.

SHARPS RIFLE MODEL 1866 — .45-70 cal., 28 in. octagonal browned barrel, color case hardened hammer & receiver, double set triggers. (IAB)
Mfg.'s Sug. Retail $720 $670 $500 $460

▲ *22 in. Carbine*
    Mfg.'s Sug. Retail $685 $610 $530 $420

THOMPSON/CENTER ARMS

U.S. manufacturer located in Rochester, NH. Available through dealers.

All Thompson/Center products are U.S. made.

PISTOLS

PATRIOT — .36 or .45 cal., percussion, 9 in. barrel, double set triggers, target stock, walnut, color case hardened hammer and lock. Disc. 1987.
$240 $200 $145
Last Mfg.'s Sug. Retail was $235.

SCOUT PISTOL — .45, .50, or .54 cal., percussion, 12 in. barrel, in-line ignition, walnut grips, 4 lbs. 6 oz.
Mfg.'s Sug. Retail $350 $280 $250 $200
    Similar in design to old style single shot Remington Target. Add $125 for extra barrel.

Grading	100%	98%	95%	

RIFLES

BIG BOAR — .58 cal. percussion, 26 in. octagonal barrel, color case hardened hammer and lock, single hunting style trigger, American walnut stock, recoil pad and swivels, 7 lbs. 12 oz.

Mfg.'s Sug. Retail	$355	$290	$245	$195

CHEROKEE — .32, .36 or .45 cal., percussion, 24 in. octagonal barrel, double set triggers, color case hardened hammer and lock, brass trim, American walnut. Add $105 for extra barrel. Disc. 1994.

	$300	$255	$200

Last Mfg.'s Sug. Retail was $320.

FIRE HAWK — .50 or .54 cal., cap lock percussion, in-line ignition, 24 in. round barrel (blued or stainless) adj, rear sight. Walnut or Rynite stock with recoil pad, 7 lbs.

Mfg.'s Sug. Retail	$365	$300	$255	$200

Add $15 for SST model with stainless steel barrel and Rynite stock.
Add $30 for SST model with stainless steel barrel and walnut stock.
Add $30 for stainless steel.
Add $100 for Deluxe.

GREY HAWK — .50 cal. percussion, 24 in. round barrel, all stainless steel construction, rynite stock, 7 lbs. New 1993.

Mfg.'s Sug. Retail	$330	$240	$205	$165

HAWKEN — .45, .50, or .54 cal., percussion or flintlock, 28 in. octagonal barrel, color case hardened hammer and lock, double set triggers, 8½ lbs. Add $10 for flintlock, add $105 for 12 ga. barrel, $60 for Hawken Custom. Add $70 for Silver Elite.

Mfg.'s Sug. Retail	$415	$325	$275	$220

HAWKEN COUGAR — .45 or .50 cal., stainless steel version of Hawken, percussion only, select hardwood stock.

	$360	$295	$235

HIGH PLAINS SPORTER — .50 cal. percussion, 24 in. round blued barrel, blued furniture, sling swivels, walnut stock w/recoil pad, 7 lbs. Mfg. 1992-1993. Disc. 1994.

	$300	$255	$200

Last Mfg.'s Sug. Retail was $340.

NEW ENGLANDER RIFLE — .50 and .54 cal., percussion, 24 and 28 in. barrel, brass furniture, walnut or rynite (new 1991) stock, 5 lbs. 2 oz. Add $105 for extra .50 cal. barrel, $15 for left-hand.

Mfg.'s Sug. Retail	$310	$235	$205	$165

Also available with Rynite stock, deduct $15.

PENNSYLVANIA HUNTER/CARBINE — .50 cal., flintlock or percussion, 31 in. octagonal to round barrel (21 in. on carbine), color case hardened hammer and lock, 7 lbs. 9 oz. Add $15 for left-hand, $15 for flintlock, $135 for 21 in. extra carbine barrel. Add $20 for Match Rifle (percussion).

Mfg.'s Sug. Retail	$375	$285	$250	$200

RENEGADE — .50 or .54 cal., percussion or flintlock, 26 in. octagonal barrel, color case hardened hammer and lock, double set triggers, 8 lbs. Also in .56 cal. — smooth bore. Add $10 for flintlock, add $105 for 12 ga. barrel. Deduct $25 for single trigger Hunter Model (new in 1987) and smooth bore model.

Mfg.'s Sug. Retail	$360	$290	$245	$195

Add $10 for left-hand.

SCOUT RIFLE/CARBINE — .50 and .54 cal., percussion, 24 in. round barrel (21 in. carbine), in-line ignition, 7 lbs. 4 oz.

Mfg.'s Sug. Retail	$435	$350	$300	$240

Deduct $80 for rynite stock model (new 1993).
Similar in design to old style single shot Remington Target. Add $135 for extra barrels.

BLACK POWDER

Grading	100%	98%	95%

SENECA — .36 or .45 cal., percussion, 27 in. octagonal barrel, color case hardened hammer and lock, double set triggers, American walnut, 6 lbs. Disc. 1987.

| | $300 | $255 | $200 |

Last Mfg.'s Sug. Retail was $300.

THUNDER HAWK — .50 cal. cap lock percussion, in-line ignition, 21 in. or 24 in. round blued barrel, adj. rear sight, walnut stock w/recoil pad, 6¾ lbs. (this is a modern style muzzleloader). New 1993.

| Mfg.'s Sug. Retail | $325 | $245 | $210 | $165 |

Add $15 for Thunder Hawk SST with stainless steel barrel and Rynnite stock.
Subtract $15 for composite stock.

TREE HAWK CARBINE — .50 cal. percussion, 21 in. round camo barrel, camo furniture, rynite camo stock, with swivels and sling, 6¾ lbs. Add $135 for extra 12 ga. barrel. New 1992. Disc. 1994.

| | $270 | $230 | $180 |

Last Mfg.'s Sug. Retail was $340.

WHITE MOUNTAIN CARBINE — .50 cal., flintlock or percussion, 21 in. octagonal tapering to a round barrel, color case hardened furniture, single hunting trigger, walnut stock, 6½ lbs. New in 1989. Add $20 for flintlock.

| | $285 | $255 | $200 |

Last Mfg.'s Sug. Retail was $350.

SHOTGUNS

NEW ENGLANDER SHOTGUN — 12 ga., percussion, 26 and 28 in. barrel, brass furniture, 5 lbs. 2 oz. Add $105 for extra .50 cal. barrel, $15 for left-hand, $20 for full choke. Also available with Rynite stock, deduct $15.

| Mfg.'s Sug. Retail | $330 | $280 | $240 | $190 |

TREE HAWK SHOTGUN — 12 ga., same as Tree Hawk above. Add $130 for extra .50 cal. revolver. Disc. 1994.

| | $270 | $230 | $180 |

Last Mfg.'s Sug. Retail was $345.

TRADITIONS, INC.

Deep River, CT. Available through dealers and catalog houses.

CANNONS

NAPOLEAN III — .72 or .50 cal., fuse ignition, finished in gold or nickel.

| Mfg.'s Sug. Retail | $496 | $435 | $370 | $295 |

Deduct $230 for .50 cal. mini version silver, deduct $170 for .50 cal. mini gold.
Add $100 for gold (large .72 cal.).

OLD IRONSIDES — .50 cal., fuse ignition, gold or nickel finish.

| Mfg.'s Sug. Retail | $156 | $135 | $115 | $95 |

Add $50 for gold finish.

YORKTOWN — .50 cal., fuse ignition, gold or nickel finish.

| Mfg.'s Sug. Retail | $165 | $145 | $125 | $100 |

Add $60 for gold finish.

PISTOLS

BUCKSKINNER PISTOL — .50 cal. percussion, 10 in. octagonal blued barrel, color case hardened hammer and lock, black furniture, beech or laminated stock, 2½ lbs. New 1993.

| Mfg.'s Sug. Retail | $165 | $150 | $120 | $90 |

Add $15 for laminated stock.

Grading	100%	98%	95%

KENTUCKY PISTOL — .50 cal., percussion, $9\frac{3}{4}$ in. octagonal barrel, color case hardened hammer and lock, brass triggerguard and nosecap. $2\frac{1}{2}$ lbs.

Mfg.'s Sug. Retail	$142	$120	$100	$80

PIONEER PISTOL — .45 or .50 cal. percussion, $9\frac{5}{8}$ octagonal barrel, German silver furniture, blackened hardware, 2 lbs. 4 oz. New in 1991.

Mfg.'s Sug. Retail	$160	$125	$105	$85

TRAPPER PISTOL — .45 or .50 cal., flintlock or percussion or 10 in. octagonal barrel, double set triggers, adj. sights, brass trim, 3 lbs. 4 oz.

Mfg.'s Sug. Retail	$190	$135	$115	$95

Add $15 for flintlock.

WILLIAM PARKER PISTOL — .45 or .50 cal., percussion, $10\frac{3}{8}$ in. barrel, all white steel, double set triggers, 2 lbs. 8 oz.

Mfg.'s Sug. Retail	$282	$205	$175	$140

REVOLVERS

1847 WALKER — .44 cal. percussion, 9 in. barrel, color case hardened hammer, frame and load lever, brass triggerguard, wt. 3.9 lbs.

Mfg.'s Sug. Retail	$265	$220	$190	$150

1851 NAVY — .44 cal. percussion, $7\frac{1}{2}$ octagonal barrel, color case hardened hammer and load lever, brass frame, cylinder has roll engraving.

Mfg.'s Sug. Retail	$140	$100	$85	$70

Add $30 for steel frame.

1860 ARMY — .44 cal. percussion, 8 in. barrel (round), color case hardened steel or brass frame, brass triggerguard.

Mfg.'s Sug. Retail	$149	$120	$105	$85

Add $50 for color case hardened steel frame.
Add $10 for laminated grip equipped steel frame model (not case hardened).

1858 Remington — .44 cal. percussion, 8 in. octagonal barrel, steel frame and brass triggerguard.

Mfg.'s Sug. Retail	$157	$115	$100	$70

Add $70 for stainless steel model w/adj. target sights.

RIFLES

BUCKSKINNER CARBINE — .50 cal. flintlock or percussion, 21 in. octagonal to round barrel, German silver furniture, blackened hardware, 6 lbs. (New 1991).

Mfg.'s Sug. Retail	$230	$200	$175	$140

Add $25 for flintlock.
Add $15 for left-hand, $50 for laminated stock.
Add $65 for Deluxe Model with nickeled barrel.

CREEDMOOR MATCH RIFLE — .451 cal. percussion, 32 in. octagonal to round blued barrel, color case hardened hammer, lock, and triggerguard, hooded front and adj. spindle diopter rear sight, checkered walnut stock, $8\frac{1}{2}$ lbs. New 1994.

	$940	$840	$680

Last Mfg.'s Sug. Retail was $1,150.

DEERHUNTER RIFLE — .32, .50, or .54 cal. flintlock or percussion, 26 in. octagonal bbl., color case hardened hammer & lock, single trigger, black furniture, beech or composite stock, approx. 6 lbs.

Mfg.'s Sug. Retail	$172	$145	$125	$100

Add $10 for beech stock.
Add $10 for flintlock.
Add $20 for all weather with nickel parts and epoxy coated stock.
Add $10 for .32 cal. Deerhunter small game rifle.

Grading	100%	98%	95%

1853 3 BAND ENFIELD — .58 cal., percussion, 39 in. round barrel, 3 barrel bands color case hardened hammer, lock and barrel bands, brass buttplate, triggerguard and nosecap. Full length walnut stock, 10 lbs.

Mfg.'s Sug. Retail $595 $505 $440 $350

FRONTIER RIFLE/FRONTIER CARBINE — .45 or .50 cal., percussion or flintlock, 28 in. octagonal barrel (24 in. carbine), double set triggers, adj. sights, brass trim, 6 lbs. 14 oz (6 lbs. 8 oz. carbine). Add $15 for flintlock (.50 cal. only). Disc. 1993.

$190 $160 $125

Last Mfg.'s Sug. Retail was $255.

FRONTIER SCOUT RIFLE — .36, .45 or .50 cal., flintlock or percussion, 26 in. octagonal barrel, double set triggers, adj. sights, brass trim, 5 lbs. 8 oz., lock has adj. sear. Add $10 for flintlock, $15 for carbine.

$150 $135 $110

Last Mfg.'s Sug. Retail was $215.

HAWKEN MATCH RIFLE — .451 cal., percussion, 32 in. octagonal blued barrel, engraved brass patchbox, color case hardened hammer and lock, brass triggerguard, buttplate, and furniture, checkered walnut stock, 10 lbs.

$505 $440 $350

Last Mfg.'s Sug. Retail was $605.

HAWKEN RIFLE — .50, .54, or .58 cal., percussion or flintlock, $32\frac{1}{4}$ in. octagonal barrel, double set triggers, adj. sights, brass trim, 8 lbs. 2 oz. Add $10 for flintlock (.50 and .54 cal. only). Disc. 1993.

$310 $265 $210

A fiberglass ramrod and deluxe rear sight were introduced in 1989.

Last Mfg.'s Sug. Retail was $415.

HAWKEN WOODSMAN RIFLE — .50 cal., percussion, 28 in. octagonal barrel, color case hardened hammer and lock, brass trim and patchbox, $7\frac{1}{2}$ lbs. Add $15 for left-hand.

Mfg.'s Sug. Retail $247 $215 $185 $155

HENRY TARGET RIFLE — .451 cal., percussion, 32 in. octagonal blued barrel, color case hardened hammer and lock, hooded front and spindle diopter rear sight, blued steel trim, checkered walnut stock, 11 lbs.

$1,000 $900 $750

Last Mfg.'s Sug. Retail was $1,325.

HUNTER RIFLE — .50 or .54 cal., percussion, 28 in. long octagonal barrel, double set triggers, adj. sights, black chrome brass trim with German silver wedge plates, lock has adj. sear, walnut stock, 8 lbs., 10 oz. Disc. 1994.

$310 $265 $210

A fiberglass ramrod and deluxe rear sight were introduced in 1989.

Last Mfg.'s Sug. Retail was $425.

KENTUCKY 2-PIECE RIFLE — .45 or .50 cal., percussion, $33\frac{1}{2}$ in. octagonal barrel, color case hardened hammer and lock, unique full length two piece stock is joined with brass plate, 7 lbs. 4 oz.

Mfg.'s Sug. Retail $247 $210 $185 $145

KENTUCKY SCOUT RIFLE — .45 or .50 cal., percussion or 26 in. octagonal barrel, double set triggers, adj. sights, brass trim, full length stock, lock has adj. sear, 5 lbs. 8 oz. Add $10 for flintlock. Disc. 1989.

$200 $160 $120

Last Mfg.'s Sug. Retail was $135.

PENNSYLVANIA RIFLE — .45 or .50 cal., flintlock or percussion, $40\frac{1}{2}$ in. octagonal barrel, double set triggers, adj. sights, brass trim, 9 lbs. 13 oz. Add $5 for flintlock.

Mfg.'s Sug. Retail $496 $400 $350 $280

Grading	100%	98%	95%

PIONEER CARBINE/RIFLE — .50 or .54 cal., percussion, 27¼ in. (24 in. carbine), octagonal barrel, color case hardened hammer, lock and furniture, German silver blade front sight, recoil pad, carbine style stock.

Mfg.'s Sug. Retail	$214	$175	$150	$110

SHENANDOAH RIFLE — .45 or .50 cal., flintlock or percussion, color case hardened hammer and lock, 33½ in. long octagonal barrel, brass furniture, 7 lbs. 4 oz. Add $10 for flintlock. Disc. 1994.

Mfg.'s Sug. Retail	$348	$250	$200	$160

1861 SPRINGFIELD — .58 cal., percussion, 40 in. round barrel, 3 barrel bands, full length walnut stock, all white steel. 10¼ lbs.

Mfg.'s Sug. Retail	$645	$565	$480	$380

TENNESSEE RIFLE — .50 cal., Flintlock or percussion, 24 in. octagonal barrel, color case hardened hammer and lock, brass buttplate, triggerguard and nosecap. Double set triggers. 6 lbs.

Mfg.'s Sug. Retail	$300	$260	$230	$200

add $15 for Flintlock.

TRAPPER RIFLE — .36, .45 and .50 cal., percussion, 25 in. octagonal barrel, color case hardened hammer and lock, brass trim, 5 lbs. Disc. 1989.

	$200	$160	$120

Last Mfg.'s Sug. Retail was $200.

TROPHY RIFLE — .50 or .54 cal., percussion, 27½ in. octagonal tapering to round barrel, adj. trigger, fiberglass ramrod, carbine style walnut stock, 7 lbs. Disc. 1994.

	$350	$300	$240

Last Mfg.'s Sug. Retail was $425.

WHITETAIL CARBINE/RIFLE — .50 or .54 flintlock or percussion, 26 in. (21 in. carbine) octagonal to round barrel, color case hardened hammer and lock, single trigger, adj. sights, 5¾ lbs. New 1993.

	$195	$170	$140

Add $10 for flintlock, $60 for synthetic stock and stainless steel barrel.

Last Mfg.'s Sug. Retail was $240.

IN-LINE IGNITION PISTOLS

BUCKHUNTER — .50 or .54 cal., percussion, 10 in. round barrel, walnut or all weather grip and forearm, blued or nickel finish, 3 lbs. New 1995.

Mfg.'s Sug. Retail	$230	$205	$170	$135

Add $15 for all weather grip & forearm and all weather nickel finish.

RIFLES

T93 CARBINE/RIFLE — .50 cal. percussion, in-line ignition, 28 in. (21 in. carbine) round barrel, adj. sights, black furniture, modern hunting rifle style, approx. 8 lbs. Disc. 1993.

	$250	$210	$170

Deduct $160 for Sporter Model.

Last Mfg.'s Sug. Retail was $430.

BUCKHUNTER IN-LINE RIFLE — .50 or .54 cal., percussion, in-line ignition, 24 in. tapered round blued barrel, 3-way safety, adj. sights, 7½ lbs. Add $25 for pro-line all styles.

Mfg.'s Sug. Retail	$220	$185	$160	$130

Add $25 for sights, $15 for all-weather version with nickel barrel and epoxy coated stock, $70 for brown laminated stock with blued barrel, $80 for black laminated stock with nickeled barrel, $70 for synthetic thumbholestock, $100 for synthetic thumbhold stock and nickel. Add $90 for "treestand" camo stock.

BLACK
POWDER

Grading	100%	98%	95%

SHOTGUNS

FOWLER SHOTGUN — 12 ga., percussion, 32 in. octagonal to round blued barrel, color case hardened hammer and lock, German silver furniture, checkered walnut stock, 5½ lbs.

$375 $310 $250

Last Mfg.'s Sug. Retail was $430.

SINGLE BARREL — 12 ga., percussion, 32 in. octagonal tapering to round barrel, German silver wedge plate, blued furniture, scroll engraving, and polished steel furniture on Deluxe version, 4 lbs. Add $85 for Deluxe. Disc. 1994.

$260 $225 $180

Last Mfg.'s Sug. Retail was $315.

IN-LINE IGNITION SHOTGUN

BUCKHUNTER IN-LINE SHOTGUN — 12 ga. percussion in-line ignition, 24 in. round barrel, bead sight, blackened furniture, composite black or camo stock, 6¼ lbs.

Mfg.'s Sug. Retail $313 $275   N/A   N/A

Add $40 for "treestand" or "advantage" camo stock.

TRAIL GUNS ARMORY

Conroe, TX (guns manufactured by D. Pedersoli Co. Italy). Available through flintlocks, etc. Navy & Dixie.

ALAMO LONG RIFLE — .45 or .50 cal., percussion or flintlock. Add $15 for flintlock. Disc. 1993.

$420 $380 $300

Last Mfg.'s Sug. Retail was $450.

KODIAK MK-I, MK-II and MK-III DOUBLE RIFLE — .50 and .58 cal., or 12 ga. percussion, 28 in. barrel, adj. sights. Add $300 for spare combo. barrels (.50 cal. x 12 ga.). $240 for 12 ga. barrels. Disc. 1993.

$550 $500 $400

Last Mfg.'s Sug. Retail was $650.

TRYON PLAINS RIFLE — .50 or .54 cal., percussion, 31 in. browned octagonal barrel, browned furniture, white steel hammer and lock, 9 lbs. 6 oz. Disc. 1993.

$390 $360 $275

Last Mfg.'s Sug. Retail was $490.

Deluxe $440 $450 $370

Last Mfg.'s Sug. Retail was $555.

RIFLES: BLACK POWDER CARTRIDGE

CREEDMOOR DELUXE ROLLING BLOCK — .45-70 cal., rimfire, 30 in. tapered barrel, color case hardened, w/double set triggers, adj. sights, 9 lbs. Disc. 1993.

$750 $675 $575

Last Mfg.'s Sug. Retail was $695.

REMINGTON SPORTING RIFLE — .45-70 cal. rimfire, same as above but without Creedmoor sight, straight stock. Disc. 1993.

$570 $495 $395

Last Mfg.'s Sug. Retail was $595.

KODIAK DOUBLE RIFLE —.45-70 cal. rimfire, 24 in. tapered round barrel, color case hardened hammer and lock, 2 piece high gloss walnut hand checkered stock, adj. twin sights, patterned after the very rare Colt SxS Double Rifle of the 1870's. Disc. 1993.

$2,050 $1,850 $1,520

Last Mfg.'s Sug. Retail was $1,895.

Grading	100%	98%	95%

SHARPS LONG RANGE RIFLE — .45-70 cal. rimfire, 28 in. octagonal barrel, color case hardened hammer and receiver, checkered walnut stock, 9 lbs. Disc. 1993.

$825 $750 $650

Last Mfg.'s Sug. Retail was $725.

SHARPS CARBINE — .45-70 cal. rimfire, 22 in. octagonal barrel, color case hardened receiver and hammer, 8 lbs. Disc. 1993.

$725 $650 $550

Last Mfg.'s Sug. Retail was $650.

SHOTGUNS

KODIAK 10 DOUBLE BARREL — 10 ga., percussion, goose gun barrels. Add $200 for spare barrel. Disc. 1994.

$690 $580 $460

Last Mfg.'s Sug. Retail was $495.

UBERTI, ALDO and CO.

Manufactured in Italy by Aldo Uberti and Co. Uberti guns are imported and distributed by various U.S. companies under both the Uberti trademark as well as a multitude of others (Uberti USA, Inc., Cimarron Arms Co., [formerly Old-West Gun Co.], Navy Arms, Dixie Gun Works, Etc.). Also previously imported by Allen Firearms and Benson Firearms Ltd. Available through dealers and catalog houses.

All guns are to the exact specifications of the original manufacturer. Crafted with an unmistakable fire blue finish. A. Uberti is one of the largest manufacturers of black powder firearms.

Add the following amounts for engraving on handguns:
    Add $325 for "A" style engraving (30% coverage).
    Add $425 for "B" style engraving (50% coverage).
    Add $750 for "C" style engraving (100% coverage).
    Add $800 for "Texas Cattlebrands" engraving pattern.
    Prices may fluctuate due to the recent devaluation of the U.S. dollar in international markets.

REVOLVERS

1847 WALKER — .44 cal., percussion, 9 in. barrel, charcoal finish, color case hardened frame, hammer, and load lever, brass trim, engraved cylinder, 4.4 lbs.

Mfg.'s Sug. Retail	$370	$275	$240	$165

1848 BABY DRAGOON — .31 cal., percussion, 3, 4, or 5 in. barrel, 5 shot, color case hardened frame, hammer, no load lever, engraved cylinder, 1.4 lbs. Add $15 for silver straps and triggerguard.

Mfg.'s Sug. Retail	$295	$240	$210	$160

DRAGOON (1ST, 2ND, OR 3RD) — .44 cal., percussion, 6 shot, brass grip straps, color case hardened frame, hammer, and load lever, brass trim, 3.9 lbs. Add $20 for silver-plated straps, $10 for cut stock on 3rd Model Dragoon, $170 for shoulder stock for 3rd Model Dragoon.

Mfg.'s Sug. Retail	$325	$260	$225	$180

1849 WELLS FARGO — .31 cal., percussion, 3, 4, or 5 in. octagonal barrel, 5 shot, color case hardened frame, hammer, no load lever, brass trim, 1½ lbs. Add $20 for silver straps.

Mfg.'s Sug. Retail	$295	$240	$210	$145

1849 POCKET — .31 cal., percussion, with loading lever, 3, 4, or 5 in. barrel, 5 shot, color case hardened frame, hammer, and load lever, brass trim, 1½ lbs. Add $15 for silver straps and triggerguard.

Mfg.'s Sug. Retail	$310	$240	$210	$145

BLACK POWDER

Grading	100%	98%	95%

1851 NAVY/NAVY SHERIFF — .36 cal., percussion, 5 (Sheriff's Model) or 7½ in. barrel, many styles, loading lever, 6 shot engraved cylinder, 2.8 lbs. Add $140 for stock, $50 for stainless steel, $15 for silver plated strap and triggerguard, or steel strap and triggerguard, $15 for "London" Model w/steel backstrap and triggerguard or if cut for stock (3rd Model Navy).

Mfg.'s Sug. Retail	$270	$230	$200	$160

1860 ARMY — .44 cal., percussion, 8 in. barrel, 6 shot, loading lever, color case hardened frame, hammer, and load lever, all brass back strap and triggerguard, or steel backstrap and brass triggerguard on fluted cylinder model, 2.6 lbs. Add $140 for stock, $15 for silver plated strap and triggerguard, $50 for stainless steel, $25 for steel backstrap.

Mfg.'s Sug. Retail	$270	$225	$205	$150

1861 NAVY — .36 cal., percussion, 7½ in. barrel, many styles, brass back strap and triggerguard, or color case hardened frame, hammer, and load lever, 2½ lbs. Add $15 for silver plated strap and triggerguard, $15 for fluted military cylinder, $25 for cut stock w/steel backstrap and triggerguard, $50 for stainless steel, $140 for shoulder stock.

Mfg.'s Sug. Retail	$270	$235	$205	$165

PATERSON MODEL — .36 cal., 7½ in. oct. barrel, hidden trigger design, without loading lever, 2 lbs. 9 oz. New in 1988.

Mfg.'s Sug. Retail	$399	$310	$265	$210

Add $30 for load lever.

1862 POCKET NAVY — .36 cal., percussion, 4½, 5½, or 6½ in. barrel, color case hardened frame, hammer, and load lever, cylinder, semi-fluted or engraved, 1.6 lbs. Add $15 for silver plated straps and triggerguard, $50 for stainless steel.

Mfg.'s Sug. Retail	$295	$220	$200	$160

1862 POLICE — .36 cal., percussion, 4½, 5½, or 6½ in. barrel, color case hardened frame, hammer, and load lever, cylinder, semi-fluted or engraved, 1.6 lbs. Add $15 for silver plated straps and triggerguard or fluted cylinder model, $50 for stainless steel.

Mfg.'s Sug. Retail	$295	$235	$205	$160

AUGUSTA CONFEDERATE — .36 cal., percussion, 7½ in. octagonal barrel, color case hardened hammer and trigger, all brass frame, engraved cylinder, 2½-2¾ lbs.

Mfg.'s Sug. Retail	$210	$180	$160	$120

GRISWOLD CONFEDERATE —.36 or .44 cal., 5½ or 7½ in. barrel, percussion, same as above except round barrel, forward of lug, does not have engraved cylinder. Disc. 1994.

	$180	$160	$120

Last Mfg.'s Sug. Retail was $220.

LEECH AND RIGDON CONFEDERATE — .36 cal., percussion, same as above except all steel frame.

Mfg.'s Sug. Retail	$280	$220	$200	$160

TEXAS CONFEDERATE DRAGOON — .44 cal., percussion, 7½ in. round barrel, color case hardened frame, hammer, and load lever, brass trim, "Tucker, Sherrard, and Co.", 4 lbs. Add $35 for stainless steel. Disc. 1994.

	$260	$230	$155

Last Mfg.'s Sug. Retail was $235.

1858 REMINGTON — .44 cal., percussion, 7½ in. barrel, 6 shot, blued steel, brass triggerguard, 2.6 lbs. Add $30 for adj. sights.

Mfg.'s Sug. Retail	$295	$230	$200	$160

1858 REMINGTON STAINLESS — same as above, has brass strap and triggerguard. Add $30 for adj. sights.

Mfg.'s Sug. Retail	$385	$305	$265	$210

1858 REMINGTON NEW NAVY — .36 cal., percussion, 6½ in. octagonal barrel, 6 shot, blue frame, 2½ lbs. Add $30 for adj. sights.

Mfg.'s Sug. Retail	$270	$205	$180	$135

Grading	100%	98%	95%

RIFLES: PERCUSSION

HAWKEN RIFLE — .50 and .54 cal., 32 in. octagonal barrel, double set triggers, approx. 9 lbs. Disc. 1994.

| | $405 | $355 | $270 |

Last Mfg.'s Sug. Retail was $535.

1866 REVOLVING CARBINE — .44 cal., percussion, 18 in. barrel, 6 shot, blued steel, brass triggerguard, walnut stock, 4.6 lbs.

| Mfg.'s Sug. Retail | $420 | $345 | $300 | $200 |

SANTA FE HAWKEN — .50 and .54 cal., percussion, single shot, 32 in. octagon barrel, damascened finish, double set triggers, 9½ lbs., walnut stock.

| Mfg.'s Sug. Retail | $445 | $385 | $330 | $265 |

ST. LOUIS RIFLE — .45, 50, .54, or .58 cal., flintlock and percussion, color case hardened hammer lock and triggerguard, octagonal barrel. Add $25 for .54 and .58 cal. percussion, $15 for flintlock, $30 for 54 cal. flintlock. Disc. 1994.

| | $345 | $280 | $210 |

Last Mfg.'s Sug. Retail was $265.

SQUIRREL RIFLE — .32 cal., percussion or flintlock, color case hardened hammer and lock, brass triggerguard, 28 in. octagonal barrel. Add $15 for flintlock.

| | $280 | $225 | $160 |

RIFLES: BLACK POWDER CARTRIDGE

HENRY RIFLE/CARBINE — .44-40 cal., brass frame, 24½ in. barrel on rifle, 22½ in. barrel on carbine.

| Mfg.'s Sug. Retail | $950 | $800 | $700 | $560 |

Add $50 for steel frame.

Can also be special ordered with Grade A engraving ($385 extra), Grade B engraving ($500 extra), and Grade 3 (C) engraving ($800 extra).

▲ *Henry 1 of 1,000* — discontinued several years ago, premiums are slightly higher than a C engraved gun.

1866 CARBINE — .44-40 cal., brass receiver, 19 in. round barrel.

| Mfg.'s Sug. Retail | $760 | $575 | $500 | $385 |

Add $40 for "Indian" Model.

▲ *1866 Trapper Carbine* — .44-40 cal., 16 or 18½ in. barrel. Disc. 1994.

| | $600 | $510 | $410 |

Last Mfg.'s Sug. Retail was $795.

▲ *1866 Yellowboy Indian Carbine* — .44-40 cal., 19 in. barrel.

| Mfg.'s Sug. Retail | $720 | $575 | $500 | $400 |

Subtract $20 without brass tacks.

▲ *Red Cloud Commemorative Carbine* — .44-40 cal., special engraving and brass tacks in forearm and stock. Disc. 1994.

| | $640 | $560 | $420 |

Last Mfg.'s Sug. Retail was $720.

1866 RIFLE — .44-40 cal., brass receiver, 24¼ in. octagonal barrel.

| Mfg.'s Sug. Retail | $840 | $575 | $500 | $440 |

▲ *Yellowboy Indian Rifle* — .44-40 cal., 19 in. rifle.

| Mfg.'s Sug. Retail | $760 | $575 | $510 | $410 |

This model comes without brass tacks.

1873 CARBINE — .44-40 cal., steel receiver, 19 in. round barrel.

| Mfg.'s Sug. Retail | $900 | $690 | $600 | $475 |

Add $95 for nickel plating.

Grading	100%	98%	95%

▲ *1873 Trapper Carbine* — .44-40 cal., 16 in. barrel.
 Mfg.'s Sug. Retail $900 $700 $620 $500

1873 RIFLE — .44-40 cal., case hardened receiver, 20 or 24¼ in. octagonal barrel. Add $30 for 24 in. barrel, deduct $25 for 30 in. barrel.
 Mfg.'s Sug. Retail $970 $710 $620 $495
  Add $100 for pistol grip checkered stock.

UFA INC.
Previous manufacturer located in Scottsdale, AZ.

RIFLES

TETON RIFLE — .45, .50, 12 ga. or 12 bore (.72 cal.) percussion, blued chrome moly steel or stainless steel barrel, straight thru ignition, style of a heavy Remington target action, interchangeable barrels, black or brown laminated stock. Walnut or maple upgrade available. Recoil pad.
                    $780 $660 $530
  Add $100 for walnut or maple stock, $150 for extra barrel.
                                    Last Mfg.'s Sug. Retail was $834.

TETON BLACKSTONE — .50 cal., percussion, 26 in. barrel. Same as above but in matte finish stainless steel with black epoxy coated wood stock.
                    $490 $415 $335
                                    Last Mfg.'s Sug. Retail was $534.

GRAND TETON — .45 or .50 cal., percussion, same as above but with 30 in. octagonal barrel.
                    $920 $760 $600
                                    Last Mfg.'s Sug. Retail was $995.

ULTRA LIGHT ARMS
Manufacturer located in Granville, WV.

MODEL 90 — .45 or .50 cal., 28 in. button rifled barrel, adj. Timney trigger, in-line action, Kevlar/graphite stock with colors optional, Williams rear sight, 6 lbs., includes hard case.
 Mfg.'s Sug. Retail $950 $900 $760 $610

U.S. HISTORICAL SOCIETY
Marketing organization which subcontracts special editions/commemoratives. Located in Richmond, VA. Available direct.

Please refer to listing in the Modern Firearms section of this text.

UNITED STATES PATENT FIRE ARMS, MFG. CO.
Manufacturer located in Hartford, CT.

United States Patent Fire Arms are manufacturing Colt reproductions in the original Colt plant at 25 Van Dyke Av., Hartford, CT. A sample of the quality of these original Patent Arms was shown to me at the 1995 SHOT show. Manufactured in Italy by Uberti, these guns are shipped in the white to U.S. Patent Arms for final polishing, blueing and color case hardeneing. The difference is a finished piece which truly shows the signs of an original Colt.

PISTOLS

All guns have color case hardened (bone) frames, hammers & loadlevers, dome blue barrels and cylinders, silver plated backstraps and trigger guards, exceptions will be noted.

BLACK
POWDER

Grading	100%	98%	95%

1847 WALKER — .44 cal., percussion, 9 in. barrel. Bright finish brass triggerguard, dome blue backstrap, 4.4 lbs.

Mfg.'s Sug. Retail	$420	$420	$375	$325

DRAGOON (1ST, 2ND, OR 3RD MODEL) — .44 cal., percussion, 6 shot, 7½ in. barrel, 3.9 lbs. Add $200 for carbine breech attachment.

Mfg.'s Sug. Retail	$400	$400	$355	$305

1848 BABY DRAGOON — .31 cal., percussion, 5 shot, 4 in. octagonal barrel, 1.4 lbs.

Mfg.'s Sug. Retail	$295	$295	$265	$225

1849 POCKET — .31 cal., percussion, 5 shot, 4 in. octagonal barrel, 1.5 lbs.

Mfg.'s Sug. Retail	$300	$300	$260	$225

1851 NAVY — .36 cal., percussion, 6 shot 7½ in. barrel, many styles including Squareback, London & Oval, 2.8 lbs.

Mfg.'s Sug. Retail	$360	$360	$320	$270

Add $10 for steel backstrap, $180 for carbine breech attachment.

1860 ARMY — .44 cal., percussion, 6 shot, 8 in. barrel, 2.6 lbs. Available with fluted or rebated cylinder.

Mfg.'s Sug. Retail	$370	$370	$330	$280

Add $180 for carbine breech attachment.

1861 NAVY — .36 cal., percussion, 6 shot, 7½ in. barrel.

Mfg.'s Sug. Retail	$350	$350	$310	$260

Add $180 for carbine breech attachment.

1862 POCKET NAVY — .36 cal., percussion, 4½, 5½ & 6½ in. barrel, 1.6 lbs.

Mfg.'s Sug. Retail	$320	$320	$285	$245

1862 POCKET POLICE — .36 cal., percussion, 4½, 5½ & 6½ in. barrel, 1.6 lbs.

Mfg.'s Sug. Retail	$320	$320	$280	$240

WHITE MUZZLELOADING SYSTEMS, INC.

Manufacturer located in Roosevelt, Utah. Available through dealers and catalog houses. Modern rifle styling.

PISTOLS

JAVELINA — .45 or .50 cal., percussion, 14 in. barrel, new G series, insta-fire in-line-ignition, double safeties, match grade trigger, adjustable sights, unique two handed black composite stock.

Mfg.'s Sug. Retail	P.O.R.	$375	$325	$280

RIFLES

BISON — .50 or .54 cal. percussion, 22 in. slightly tapered non-glare blued bull barrel, new G Series "Insta-Fire" in-line ignition action, fully adj. open hunting sights, drilled and tapped for scope, hardwood stock, 6½ lbs. New 1993.

Mfg.'s Sug. Retail	$400	$275	$225	$210

Add $50 for older model with black composite stock.

GRAND ALASKAN — .54 cal. percussion, 24 in. stainless bull barrel, W-Series in-line ignition, "Insta Fire" stainless hardened nipple, green laminate stock, 7¾ lbs.

Mfg.'s Sug. Retail	$700	$610	N/A	N/A

BLACK POWDER

Grading	100%	98%	95%

ORIGINAL 68 — .45 or .50 cal. percussion, 24 in. round tapered blued barrel, W series in-line ignition action, fully adjustable hunting sights, drilled & tapped for scope, black composite stock, 7¾ lbs. Mfg. 1993 only - very limited production. Disc. 1994.

$600 $500 $400

This model may have more value as a collectible due to its limited production. Please contact White Muzzleloaders (see Trademark Index) for more information.

Last Mfg.'s Sug. Retail was $600.

SPORTING RIFLE — .41, .45 (.451), or .50 (.504) cal., percussion, 26 in. straight tapered barrel, GR (Green River) Series sidelock with half-cock, super nipple "Insta-Fire" ignition, Manton style hooked breach, checkered crotchwood English styled composite stock, non-glare hunter's blue, 8¾ lbs. New 1994.

Mfg.'s Sug. Retail   P.O.R. $575 $500 $425

SUPER 91 — .410, .451 and .504 caliber, percussion, 24 in. barrel, W Series in-line ignition, blued steel or #416 stainless throughout, "Insta-Fire" stainless hardened nipple, cleans with soap and water, walnut or composite stock, approx. 7¾ lbs.

Mfg.'s Sug. Retail $600 $480 $410 $340

Add $50 for stainless steel, add $70 for stainless steel with black laminate stock.

▲ *Super 91 W/Side Swing Safety* — limited mfg., disc. Oct. 1993.

$700 $600 $500

Last Mfg.'s Sug. Retail was $700.

This model may have more value as a collectible due to its limited production. Please contact White Muzzleloaders (see Trademark Index) for more information.

SUPER SAFARI — .41, .45 (.451), or .50 (.504) cal., percussion, 24 in. Magnum tapered barrel, W. Series straight-line "Insta-Fire" ignition, straight pull cocking handle, double safety system, D&T for slope or receiver sight, full length Mannlicher style black composite stock, non-glare #416 stainless, 7¾ lbs.

Mfg.'s Sug. Retail $800 $615 $535 $450

WHITE LIGHTNING — .50 cal. percussion, 22 in. tapered stainless barrel "Insta Fire" in-line ignition, recoil pad, adjustable sights, black hardwood stock.

Mfg.'s Sug. Retail $300 $260 $220 $190

WHITETAIL RIFLE — .410, .451, .504 or .54 cal. percussion, 22 in. bull barrel (blued) tapered (stainless), new G series action, insta-fire in-line ignition, beech stock (blued), composite stock (stainless), 6½ lbs. New 1992.

Mfg.'s Sug. Retail $400 $310 $270 $215

Add $70 for stainless steel, add $100 for stainless steel with black laminate stock, add $160 for 1 of 1,000 Roger Ragun Signature Series with super sights and super sling factory installed.

The Whitetail Bull Barrel was disc. 1992.

SHOTGUNS

DOMINATOR — 12 ga., percussion, 26 in. blued barrel w/vent rib, new BG series action (larger version of G series), insta-fire, in-line-ignition, interchangeable chokes. Part of the new "Ray Eye" signature series - black laminate stock.

Mfg.'s Sug. Retail $550 $430 $390 $350

WHITE THUNDER — 12 ga., percussion, 26 in. blued barrel w/vent rib. New BG series action (larger version of G series), insta-fire, in-line-ignition. Interchangeable chokes - black hardwood stock.

Mfg.'s Sug. Retail $460 $360 $320 $280

WILDERNESS RIFLE WORKS/LEMAN RIFLES

Distributed by Mountain State Muzzle Loading Supplies, Williamstown, WV. Manufactured by Wilderness Rifle Works located in Waldron, IN. Available from Mountain State or through dealers.

Grading	100%	98%	95%

CLASSIC — .50 cal. flintlock or percussion copy of early Leman-Lancaster rifle, 35 in. browned octagonal barrel, high relief cheek on beautiful curly maple full stock brass furniture, browned hammer and lock, brass buttplate and triggerguard. Beautiful recreation.

Mfg.'s Sug. Retail	$695	$695	N/A	N/A

▲ *Silver Classic with nickel silver furniture*

Mfg.'s Sug. Retail	$995	$995	N/A	N/A

CUMBERLAND RIFLE — .32, .36, .40, .45, or .50 cal., flintlock or percussion 39½ in. octagonal browned barrel, browned hammer and lock, brass buttplate and triggerguard, 7¼ lbs. New 1994.

	$440	$375	$300

Add $20 for flintlock.

Last Mfg.'s Sug. Retail was $495.

ELKHUNTER RIFLE — .50 or .54 cal. percussion, 32 in. octagonal browned barrel, browned furniture, hammer and lock, curly maple stock, double set triggers, adjustable buckhorn rear sight, 9 lbs.

Mfg.'s Sug. Retail	$475	$425	$360	$290

MOUNTAINEER RIFLE — .36, .40, .45, or .50 cal., flintlock or percussion, 39 in. octagonal browned barrel, brass or browned furniture, hammer and lock, curly maple full stock, double set triggers, adjustable buckhorn rear sight, 7¼ to 8 lbs.

	$350	$300	$240

Add $20 for flintlock.

Last Mfg.'s Sug. Retail was $425.

PLAINS RIFLE — .50 or .54 percussion, 32 in. octagonal barrel, fancy maple stock, furniture is brass or browned steel, single set double action trigger, 9 lbs. Disc. 1993.

	$350	$300	$240

Last Mfg.'s Sug. Retail was $495.

PRAIRIE RIFLE — .36, .40, .45, or .50 cal., percussion, 32 in. barrel, furniture is brass or browned steel, double set triggers, fancy figure maple stock, 8 lbs.

Mfg.'s Sug. Retail	$425	$375	$315	$245

SUMMIT RIFLE — .50 and .54 cal. percussion, 30 in. octagonal barrel, furniture is brass or browned steel, single set double action trigger, fancy figure maple stock, 9 lbs. Disc. 1993.

	$350	$300	$240

Last Mfg.'s Sug. Retail was $495.

BLACK POWDER

BLACK
POWDER

TRADEMARK INDEX

The listings below represent manufacturers, trademarks, and related information (including importer and factory address for international makers) to assist you in obtaining additional firearms information from these companies. If parts are needed for older, discontinued makes and models (even though the manufacturer/trademark is current), it is recommended that you contact either the Gun Parts Corp. located in West Hurley, NY or Jack First, Inc. located in Rapid City, SD for domestic availability and prices - unless a company/trademark has an additional service/parts listing. In Canada, please refer to the Bomac Gunpar Ltd. listing. Remember, most of the people you come in contact with through the following information will probably be busy (especially this year) - have patience and respect their time.

As the 17th edition goes to press, we feel confident that the information listed below is the most up-to-date and accurate listing that has ever been published on current manufacturers and/or related trademarks. International FAX/phone numbers may require additional overseas and country/city coding (call 102880 for more information - this is an AT&T service). If you should require additional assistance in "tracking" any of the firearms manufacturers, distributors, or importers listed in this publication who are currently engaged in the business of selling newly manufactured goods, please call or FAX us and we will try to help you regarding these specific requests.

A.A. ARMS INC.
4811 Persimmon Court
Monroe, NC 28110
Phone No.: 704-289-5386
FAX No.: 704-289-5859

AMT
Arcadia Machine & Tool
6226 Santos Diaz Street
Irwindale, CA 91702
Phone No.: 818-334-6629
FAX No.: 818-969-5247

Custom Shop
5060 Pathfinder Trail
Placerville, CA 95667
Phone No.: 916-642-9333
FAX No.: 916-626-7333

ARS/FARCO (Airguns)
311 E. Water Street
Elmira, NY 14901

A-SQUARE
One Industrial Park
Bedford, KY 40006
Phone No.: 502-255-7456
FAX No.: 502-255-7657

AYA
Importer - See Armes De Chasse listing.

Factory - AYA
Edificio Aurrera
Urtzaile, 1-2
P.O. Box 45
20600 EIBAR (Guipuzcoa) SPAIN
FAX No.: 011-34-43100133

ABBIATICO & SALVINELLI
Importer - Southwest Shooter's Supply
P.O. Box 9987
Phoenix, AZ 85068
Phone No.: 602-943-8595
FAX No.: 602-943-1713

Factory
Via Valtrompia
25063 Gardone, V.T. ITALY
FAX No.: 011-39-30 8912894

ACCURACY INTERNATIONAL LTD.
U.S. Importer - Gunsite Training Center
P.O. Box 451
Paulden, AZ 86334
Phone No.: 520-636-4565
FAX No.: 204-748-1805

Factory - Accuracy International Ltd.
P.O. Box 81, Portsmouth
Hampshire, ENGLAND PO3 5SJ
Phone No.: 011-44-705-671-225
FAX No.: 011-44-705-691-852

ACCU-MATCH INTERNATIONAL INC.
952 East Baseline Road, Ste. 105
Mesa, AZ 85204
Phone No.: 602-507-9385
FAX No.: 602-507-0934

ACCU-TEK
4525 Carter Court
Chino, CA 91710
FAX No.: 909-627-7817

ACTION ARMS, LTD.
P.O. Box 9573
Philadelphia, PA 19124-0573
FAX No.: 215-533-2188

TRADE
MARKS

AIR RIFLE SPECIALISTS (Airguns)
P.O. Box 138
130 Holden Road
Pine City, NY 14871
FAX No.: 607-733-3261

ALESSANDRI, LOU, AND SON
P.O. Box 319
24 French Street
Rehoboth, MA 02769
Phone No.: 508-252-5590
U.S. and Canada: 800-248-5652
FAX No.: 508-252-3436

ALL AMERICA SALES, INC.
P.O. Box 22188
Memphis, TN 38122
Phone No.: 901-327-1721
FAX No.: 901-327-1889

AMERICA REMEMBERS
8428 Old Richfood Road
Mechanicsville, VA 23111
Phone No.: 804-746-3769
FAX No.: 804-746-4920

AMERICAN ARMS, INC.
715 Armour Road
N. Kansas City, MO 64116
Phone No.: 816-474-3161
FAX No.: 816-474-1225

AMERICAN DERRINGER CORPORATION
127 N. Lacy Dr.
Waco, TX 76705
Phone No.: 817-799-9111
FAX No.: 817-799-7935

AMERICAN FRONTIER FIREARMS CO.
40725 Brook Trails Way
Aguanga, CA 92536
Phone No.: 909-763-2209
FAX No.: 909-763-0014

AMERICAN HISTORICAL FOUNDATION, THE
1142 W. Grace St., #C175
Richmond, VA 23220
Phone No.: 804-353-1812
FAX No.: 804-359-4895

AMTEC 2000, INC.
P.O. Box 1191
Gardner, MA 01440
Phone No.: 508-632-9608

ANSCHUTZ
Importer - AcuSport Corporation
One Hunter Place
Bellfontaine, OH 43311-3001
Phone No.: 513-593-7010
FAX No.: 513-592-0843

Factory - Anschutz, J.G., GmbH
Postfact 1128
D-89001 Ulm, GERMANY
FAX No.: 011-49-731-4012-700

ARLINGTON ORDNANCE
728 Post Road East
Westport, CT 06880
Phone No.: 203-222-6700
FAX No.: 203-222-6704

ARMALITE, INC.
P.O. Box 299
Geneseo, IL 61254
Phone No.: 309-944-6939
FAX No.: 309-944-6949

ARMAS AZOR, S.A.
Importer - See Armes De Chasse listing.

ARMES DE CHASSE
P.O. Box No. 86
Hertford, NC 27944
Phone No.: 919-426-2245
FAX No.: 919-426-1557

ARMI SAN PAOLO (Black Powder)
3590 NW 49th Street
Miami, FL 33142
FAX No.: 305-633-2877

ARMI TECNICHE OF EMILIO RIZZINI
Armi Tecniche di Rizzini E. & C. S.N.C.
Via Localita Rovedolo
I-25060 Marcheno (Brescia) ITALY
Phone No.:011-39-30-861235
FAX No.: 011-39-30-861-367

ARMSCOR
Please refer to K.B.I. Listing

ARMS CORPORATION OF THE PHILIPPINES
Importer - please refer to the K.B.I., Inc. listing

Factory office - Arms Corp. of the Philippines
550 Epifanio De los Santos Avenue
Cubao, Quezon City, PHILIPPINES
FAX No.: 632-721-7093

ARMS TECH LTD.
5133 N. Central Ave.
Phoenix, AZ 85012
Phone No.: 602-264-2173

ARMSCORP USA, INC.
4424 John Avenue
Baltimore, MD 21227
Phone No.: 410-247-6200
FAX No.: 410-247-6205

ARMSPORT, INC.
3590 NW 49th St.
Miami, FL 33142
Phone No.: 305-635-7850
FAX No.: 305-633-2877

ARNOLD ARMS CO., INC.
P.O. Box 1011
6914 - 204th St. NE, Suite C
Arlington, WA 98223
Phone No.: 206-435-1011
FAX No.: 206-435-7304

ARRIETA, S.L.
Importer - Wingshooting Adventures
4320 Kalamazoo Ave.
Grand Rapids, MI 49508
Phone No.: 616-455-7810

Importer - See Griffin & Howe listing.

Importer - See New England Arms listing.

Importer - See Orvis listing.

Importer - See Quality Arms listing.

Factory - Arrieta, Manufacturas, S.L.
C/.Morkaiko, 5 Barrio Urasandi
E-20870 Elgoibar (Guipuzcoa) SPAIN
FAX No.: 011-34-43-74-3154

ARRIZABLAGA
Importer - See New England Arms Co. listing.
Factory - Arrizabalaga, Pedro, S.A.
Errekatxu, 5
E-20600 Eibar (Guipuzcoa) SPAIN
FAX No.: 011-3443-11-1743

ARSENAL
Importer - Sentinel Arms
P.O. Box 57
Detroit, MI 48231
FAX No.: 313-331-1456

ASPREY
165 - 169 New Bond Street
London, ENGLAND W1Y 0AR
Phone No.: 011-44-71-493 6767
FAX No.: 011-44-71-491 0384

ASTRA
Importer - See European American Armory
Factory - Astra Unceta Y Cia S.A.
Guernica Vizcaya S-48300 SPAIN
FAX No.: 011-344-6255186

AUTO-ORDNANCE CORP.
Williams Lane
West Hurley, NY 12491
FAX No.: 914-679-2698

BSA GUNS LTD. (Airguns)
Importer - see Precision Sales
Armoury Rd., Small Heath
Birmingham, W. Mids, B11 2PX, ENGLAND
FAX No.: 011-44-021-773-0845

B-WEST IMPORTS, INC.
Importer - Rifles and Pistols
2425 North Huachuca
Tucson, AZ 85745
Phone No.: 602-628-1990
FAX No.: 602-628-3602

BAIKAL
Importer - See K.B.I., Inc. listing.
Baikal Factory
Bogdan Khmelnitskij, 12
Moskau 107140/UdSSR
FAX No.: 011-95-230-2363

BAILONS GUNMAKERS LTD.
Correspondence and Repair - Guthrie Consulting
Attn: Sir Malcolm Guthrie
P.O. Box 134
Stourbridge, West Midlands, ENGLAND DY9 0YS
Phone/FAX No.: 011-44-562-730711

BANSNER'S
P.O. Box 839
261 East Main Street
Adamstown, PA 19501
Phone No.: 717-484-2370
FAX No.: 717-484-0523

BARRETT FIREARMS MANUFACTURING, INC.
P.O. Box 1077
Murfreesboro, TN 37133
FAX No.: 615-896-7313

BEAUCHAMP & SONS (dba FLINTLOCKS, ETC.)
160 Rossiter Rd.
Richmond, MA 01254

BEEMAN OUTDOOR SPORTS (Firearms)
Division of Robert's Precision Arms, Inc.
3440 Airway Dr.
Santa Rosa, CA 95403-2040
Phone No.: 707-578-7938
FAX No.: 707-578-7963

BEEMAN PRECISION AIRGUNS (Airguns only)

Division of S/R Industries (Maryland Corp.)
5454 Argosy Dr.
Huntington Beach, CA 92649-1039
Phone No.: 714-890-4800
Phone No.: 800-227-2744
FAX No.: 714-890-4808

BENELLI

Importer (Shotguns) - See Heckler & Koch listing.

Importer (Handguns) - See European American Armory listing.

Factory - Benelli Armi S.p.A.
Via della Stazione, 50
I-61029 Urbino (PS) ITALY
FAX No.: 011-39-722-327427

BENJAMIN AIR RIFLE COMPANY (Airguns)

Routes 5 & 20
East Bloomfield, NY 14443
FAX No.: 716-657-5405

BENTON & BROWN FIREARMS, INC.

411 First Street
Delhi, LA 71232-0326
Phone No.: 318-878-2499
FAX No.: 817-284-9300

BERETTA, PIETRO

Importer - Beretta U.S.A. Corp
17601 Beretta Drive
Accokeek, MD 20607
FAX No.: 301-283-0435

Beretta Premium Grades
c/o Beretta Gallery
317 South Washington Street
Old Town, Alexandria, VA 22314
Phone No.: 703-739-0596
FAX No.: 703-684-5754
c/o Beretta Gallery
718 Madison Avenue
New York, NY 10021
Phone No.: 212-319-3235

BERNARDELLI, VINCENZO

Importer - See Armsport, Inc. listing.

Factory - Bernardelli, Vincenzo, S.p.A.
Via G. Matteotti, 125
I-25063 Gardone V.T. (Brescia) ITALY
FAX No.: 011-39-30-8910249

BERSA

Importer - See Eagle Imports Inc. listing.

Factory - Bersa S.A.
Castillo 312
(1704) Ramos Mejia
ARGENTINA
FAX No.: 011-01-656-2093

BERTUZZI

Importer - See New England Arms Co. listing.

Factory - Bertuzzi, F.lli
Via Alessandro Volta, 65
I-25063 Gardone V.T. (BS) ITALY
FAX No.: 011-3930-837188

BIG BEAR ARMS (Various Russian Firearms)

2714 Fairmount Street
Dallas, TX 75201
Phone No.: 214-871-7061
FAX No.: 214-754-0449

BLAND, THOMAS & SONS GUNMAKERS LTD.

Woodcock Hill, Inc.
P.O. Box 363
Benton, PA 17814
Phone No.: 717-864-3242
FAX No.: 717-864-3232

London Agent - T. Thompson
Bushey Heath, Hertfordshire, ENGLAND
Phone No.: 011-4481-950-5236
FAX No.: 011-4481-950-9016

BLASER

Importer - Autumn Sales, Inc.
1320 Lake Street
Fort Worth, TX 76102
Phone No.: 817-335-1634
FAX No.: 817-338-0119

Factory - Blaser Jagdwaffen GmbH
Ziegelstadel 1
D-88316 Isny im Allgau, GERMANY
FAX No.: 011-4975-62702-43

BOHEMIA ARMS

17101 Los Modelos
Fountain Valley, CA 92708
Phone/FAX No.: 619-442-7005
Phone/FAX No.: 714-963-0809

BOHICA

P.O. Box 607
Sedalia, CO 80513
Phone/FAX No.: 303-532-0166

TRADE MARKS

BOMAC GUNPAR LTD.

Canadian parts supplier
Postal Bag 8090
Lakefield, Ontario
K0L 2H0 CANADA
Phone No.: 705-748-4004
FAX No.: 705-748-5916

BOSS & CO., LTD.

13 Dover St.
London, ENGLAND W1X 3PH
Phone No.: 011-44-171-493-1127
Phone/FAX No.: 011-44-171-493-0711

BOSWELL, CHARLES

Charles Boswell Gunmakers
Cape Horn International
9305-F Monroe Rd.
Greylyn Business Park
Charlotte, NC 28270
Phone No.: 704-845-5101
FAX No.: 704-841-7237

BREDA MECCANICA BRESCIANA

Via Lunga, 2
I-25126 Brescia
ITALY
FAX No.: 011-39-30-322115

BRETTON

Importer - See Mandall Shooting Supplies
listing.
19, Rue Victore
Grignard Z1
Montreynaud
St. Etienne, Cedex
F-42026 FRANCE
FAX No.: 011-39-77-790653

BRICKLEY TRADING CO.

1443 Potrero Ave.
South El Monte, CA 91733
Phone No.: 818-444-2745
FAX No.: 818-401-3299

BRITARMS

Importer - See Mandall Shooting Supplies
listing.

BRNO AERON (Airguns)

PO Box 714
St. Albans, VT 05478
FAX No.: 802-527-0470

BRNO ARMS

Importer - See Magnum Research listing.

Importer - Bohemia Arms (limited importa-
tion of some bolt action rifles, semi-auto &
O/U rifles, shotguns)
17101 Los Modelos Street
Fountain Valley, CA 92708
Phone/FAX No.: 714-963-0809

Importer (CANADA) - Pragotrade
307 Humberline Dr.
Rexdale, Ontario M9W 5V1 CANADA
FAX No.: 416-675-4567

Factory - BRNO Arms
BRNO 656 17
Lazaretni 7, CZECHOSLOVAKIA
FAX No.: 42-5571191

BROLIN ARMS

P.O. Box 698
La Verne, CA 91750-0698
Phone No.: 800-413-8766
FAX No.: 909-392-2354

DAVID MCKAY BROWN

32 Hamilton Road, Bothwell
Glasgow, SCOTLAND G71 8NA
Phone No.: 011-1698 853727
Fax No.: 011-1698 854207

BROWN PRECISION, INC.

P.O. Box 270W
7786 Molinos Avenue
Los Molinos, CA 96055
Phone No.: 800-543-2506
FAX No.: 916-384-1638

BROWNING

Administrative Headquarters
One Browning Place
Morgan, UT 84050
Sales Information: 800-234-2045
Product Service: 800-322-4626
FAX No.: 801-876-3331

Browning Parts and Service
3005 Arnold Tenbrook Rd.
Arnold, MO 63010
FAX No.: 314-287-9751

BRUCHET

See Darne listing.

BRYCO ARMS

Distributor - Jennings Firearms, Inc.
3680 Research Way
Carson City, NV 89706
FAX No.: 702-882-3129

BUL TRANSMARK LTD.

Importer - All America Sales, Inc.
P.O. Box 22188
Memphis, TN 38122
Phone No.: 901-327-1721
FAX No.: 901-327-1889

Factory - Bul Transmark Ltd.
10 Rival Street
Tel-Aviv 67778, ISRAEL
FAX No.: 972-3-6874853

BUSHMASTER FIREARMS

P.O. Box 1479
999 Roosevelt Trail Bldg. 3
Windham, ME 04062
FAX No.: 207-892-8068

C.L. REEDY & ASSOCIATES, INC.

See listing in R section.

C Z (CESKA ZBROJOVKA)

Firearms Importer - See Magnum Research, Inc. listing.

Airgun Importer - Compasseco, Inc.
151 Atkinson Hill Ave.
Bradstown, KY 40004
FAX No.: 502-349-0910

Factory - Ceska Zbrojovka
Svatopluka Cecha 1283
CZ-68827 Uhersky Brod
CZECHOSLOVAKIA
FAX No.: 011-42-633-3665

CABANAS

Importer - See Mandall Shooting Supplies listing.

Factory - Industrias Cabanas, S.A.
Calz. de las Aguilas 815
Col. Aguilas
01710 Mexico, D.F. MEXICO
FAX No.: 011-52-664-34-92

CABELA'S INC.

812 13th Ave.
Sidney, NE 69160
Phone No.: 308-254-5505
FAX No.: 308-254-7809

CALICO

405 East 19th Street
Bakersfield, CA 93305
Phone No.: 805-323-1327
FAX No.: 805-323-7844

CARL GUSTAF

Factory - Winscan AB, c/o Carl Gustaf
P.O. Box 545
S-631 07 Eskilstuna SWEDEN
FAX No.: 011-16-120054

CASARTELLI, CARLO

Importer - See New England Arms Co. listing.

CASPIAN ARMS, LTD.

14 North Main Street
Hardwick, VT 05843
Phone No.: 802-472-6454
FAX No.: 802-472-6709

CENTURY INTERNATIONAL ARMS, INC.

P.O. Box 714
St. Albans, VT 05478
Phone No.: 802-527-1252
FAX No.: 802-527-0470

CENTURY MFG., INC.

1467 Jason Road
Greenfield, IN 46140
Phone No.: 317-462-4524

CHAMPIONS CHOICE, INC.

201 International Blvd.
La Vergne, TN 37086
Phone/FAX No.: 615-793-4070

CHAMPLIN FIREARMS, INC.

P.O. Box 3191
Enid, OK 73702
Phone No.: 405-237-7388
FAX No.: 405-233-1724

CHAPUIS ARMES

Importer - Chadick's, Ltd.
P.O. Box 100
119 Moore Ave.
Terrell, Tx 75160
Phone No.: 214-563-7577
FAX No.: 214-563-1265

Factory - Chapuis Armes
Z.I. La Gravoux, B.P. 15
F-42380 St. Bonnet le Chateau, FRANCE
Phone No.: 011-3377/500696
FAX No.: 011-3377/501070

CHAPUIS, P. ARMES ET FILES

Factory
12, rue le Mont Mille
F-42380 St. Bonnet le Chateau FRANCE
FAX No.: 011-33-7750-1008

TRADE MARKS

CHARTER ARMS

Manufacturer - Charco, Inc.
26 Beaver St.
Ansonia, CT 06401
Phone No.: 203-735-4686
FAX No.: 203-735-6569

CHENEY RIFLE WORKS/LEMAN RIFLES (Black Powder)

Distributor - See Mountain States Muzzle-loading Supplies, Inc. listing.

CHERRY'S

Commemorative Research
3402-A West Wendover Avenue
P.O. Box 5307
Greensboro, NC 27435-0307
Phone No.: 919-854-4182
FAX No.: 919-854-4184

CHIPMUNK MANUFACTURING, INC.

Oregon Arms, Inc.
11 First St.
P.O. Box 20
Prospect, OR 97536
Phone No.: 503-560-4040
FAX No.: 503-560-4041

CHRISTENSEN ARMS

192 East 100 North
Fayette, UT 84630
Phone No.: 801-528-7999
FAX No.: 801-528-7494

CHURCHILL, E.J., (GUNMAKERS) LTD.

Ockley Road, Beare Green, Dorking
Surrey, ENGLAND RH5 4PU
Phone No.: 011-44306-711435

CHURCHILL

Ellett Brothers
P.O. Box 128
Chapin, SC 29036
FAX No.: 803-345-1820

CIMARRON, F.A. CO.

105 Winding Oak
Fredericksburg, TX 78624
Phone No.: 210-997-9090
FAX No.: 210-997-0802

CLARK CUSTOM GUNS, INC.

336 Shootout Lane
Princeton, LA 71067
Phone No.: 318-949-9884
FAX No.: 318-949-9829

CLIFTON ARMS

P.O. Box 1471
Medina, TX 78055
Phone No.: 210-589-2666
FAX No.: 210-589-2661

COLT'S MANUFACTURING CO., INC.

P.O. Box 1868
Hartford, CT 06144-1868
Phone No.: 203-236-6311
FAX No.: 203-244-1449
If research is needed, make sure the proper research fee is included (see Colt section for fee listings) and address the correspondence "Attn: Historical Dept."

COMPASSECO

151 Atkinson Hill
Bradstown, KY 40004
FAX No.: 502-349-0910

COMPETITOR CORPORATION

Appleton Business Center
30 Tricnit Rd., Unit 16
P.O. Box 508
New Ipswich, NH 03071
Phone No.: 603-878-3891
FAX No.: 603-878-3950

CONNECTICUT SHOTGUN MANUFACTURING COMPANY

P.O. Box 1692
35 Woodland St.
New Britain, CT 06501-1692
Phone No.: 203-225-6581
FAX No.: 203-832-8707

CONNECTICUT VALLEY ARMS, INC. (Black Powder)

5988 Peachtree Corners E.
P.O. Box 7225
Norcross, GA 30071
FAX No.: 404-242-8546

CONNECTICUT VALLEY CLASSICS, INC.

P.O. Box 2068
12 Taylor Lane
Westport, CT 06880
Phone No.: 203-254-3202
FAX No.: 203-256-1180

COONAN ARMS

JS Worldwide Distributing Co.
1745 Highway 36 E.
Maplewood, MN 55109
Phone No.: 612-777-3156
FAX No.: 612-777-3683

TRADE MARKS

COOPER ARMS
P.O. Box 114
Stevensville, MT 59870
Phone No.: 406-777-5534
FAX No.: 406-777-5228

COSMI, AMERICO & FIGLIO
Importer - See New England Arms Co. listing.

Factory - Cosmi Americo & Figlio S.n.c.
Via Flaminia, 307
I-60020 Torrette di Ancona, ITALY
FAX No.: 011-39-71-887008

CROSMAN AIR GUNS
Rts. 5 & 20
East Bloomfield, NY 14443
FAX No.: 716-657-5405

CUMBERLAND MOUNTAIN ARMS, INC.
P.O. Box 710
1045 Dinah Shore Blvd.
Winchester, TN 37398
Phone No.: 615-967-8414
FAX No.: 615-967-9199

DPMS, INC.
13983 Industry Avenue
Becker, MN 55308
Phone No.: 612-261-5600
FAX No.: 612-261-5599

DAEWOO
Exclusive U.S. distributor
Nationwide Sports Distributors, Inc. - Headquarters
70 James Way
Southampton, PA 18966
Phone No.: 800-355-3006
FAX No.: 215-322-5972

DAISY MANUFACTURING CO., INC. (Airguns)

P.O. Box 220
2111 S. 8th St.
Rodgers, AR 72756
FAX No.: 501-636-1601

DAKOTA ARMS, INC.
HC55 Box 326
Whitewood Rd.
Sturgis, SD 57785
Phone No.: 605-347-4686
FAX No.: 605-347-4459

DAKOTA SINGLE ACTION REVOLVERS
Importer - See E.M.F. Company listing.

DALY, CHARLES: CURRENT MFG.
Importer - Outdoor Sports Hdqtrs.
Attn: C. Daly Customer Service
967 Watertower Lane
Dayton, OH 45449
Phone No.: 800-444-6744
FAX No.: 513-865-5962

DAVID MILLER CO.
3131 E. Greenlee Rd.
Tucson, AZ 85716
FAX No.: 602-326-3117

DAVIS INDUSTRIES
15150 Sierra Bonita Lane
Chino, CA 91710
FAX No.: 909-393-9771

DEER CREEK RIFLE WORKS (Black Powder)
Distributor - See Mountain States Muzzle-loading Supply listing.

DESERT INDUSTRIES, INC.
3245 E. Patrick Lane, Suite H
P.O. Box 93443
Las Vegas, NV 89120
Phone No.: 702-597-1066
FAX No.: 702-434-9495

DIANAWERK, MAYER AND GRAMMELSPACHER (Airguns)
See Dynamit Nobel - RWS listing.

DIXIE GUN WORKS (Black Powder)
Hwy. 51 South
Union City, TN 38261
FAX No.: 901-885-0440

DOMINO
Importer - See Mandall Shooting Supplies listing.

DUCKS UNLIMITED, INC.
One Waterfowl Way
Memphis, TN 38120-2351
Phone No.: 901-758-3825
FAX No.: 901-758-3850

DUMOULIN, ERNEST
Factory
Rue Florent Boclinville, 8-10
B-4410 Votten-Herstal, BELGIUM
Phone No. 011-41-270890

DUMOULIN, HENRI & FILS

Importer - See New England Arms Co. listing.

Factory - Dumoulin, Henri & Fils
P.O. Box 30
Herstal 4400, BELGIUM
FAX No.: 011-31-49-3013255

DYNAMIT NOBEL - RWS, Inc. (Airguns)

81 Ruckman Road
Closter, NJ 07624
FAX No.: 201-767-1589
E-Mail: FTurner@AOL.COM

E.M.F. COMPANY

1900 E. Warner Ave., Suite 1-D
Santa Ana, CA 92705
FAX No.: 714-756-0133

EAGLE ARMS INC.

Division of ArmaLite, Inc.
Please refer to ArmaLite Listing.

EAGLE IMPORTS, INC.

1750 Brielle Ave., Unit B-1
Wanamassa, NJ 07712
Phone No.: 908-493-0333
FAX No.: 908-493-0301

EFFEBI SNC

Factory
Via Rossa, 4
I-25062 Concesio (BS) ITALY
FAX. No.: 011-3930-2180414

EGO ARMAS, S.A.

Victor Sarasqueta, 1
E-20600 Eibar (Guipuzcoa) SPAIN
FAX No.: 011-3443-120463

ERMA-WERKE

Importer - See Precision Sales Int'l listing.

Importer - See Nygord Precision Products listing.

Importer - See Mandall Shooting Supplies listing.

Factory - Erma-Werke GmbH
Johann-Ziegler-Strasse 13-15
D-85221 Dachau GERMANY
FAX No.: 011-49-8131/2803-59

EUROARMS OF AMERICA (Black Powder)

208 East Piccadilly Street
P.O. Box 3277
Winchester, VA 22604
FAX No.: 504-662-4464

EUROPEAN AMERICAN ARMORY CORP.

P.O. Box 1299
Sharpes, FL 32959
Phone No.: 407-639-4842
FAX No.: 407-639-7006

EVOLUTION USA

P.O. Box 154
White Bird, ID 83554
Phone No.: 208-983-9208
FAX No.: 208-983-9208

FAS

Importer - See Nygord Precision Products listing.

FEG

Importer - See K.B.I., Inc. listing.

Importer - See Century International Arms, Inc. listing.

F.I.E. FIREARMS CORP. (repairs only)

Please refer to Heritage Manufacturing, Inc.

FMJ

P.O. Box 759
Copperhill, TN 37317
Phone No.: 615-496-1600
FAX No.: 615-496-3622

FABARM S.p.A., FABRICA BRESCIANA ARMI

Importer - See Ithaca Acquisition Corp. listing.

Factory - Fabarm/S.N.P.E.
Via Averolda 31
I-25039 Travagliato, Brescia
ITALY
FAX No.: 011-39-30-6863684

FABBRI snc

Factory
Via Dante Alighieri, 29
I-25062 Concesio (BS) ITALY
FAX No.: 011-3930-275-2050

FABRIQUE NATIONALE

Factory - Browning S.A.

Fabrique Nationale Herstal SA
Parc Industriel des Hauts Sarts
3e Ave.
B-4040 Herstal, BELGIUM
FAX No.: 011-41-481490

FAMARS

Refer to listing under Abbiatico & Salvinelli

TRADE
MARKS

FAUSTI, CAV. STEFANO & FIGLIE SNC.

Factory
Via Martiri Dell'Indipendenza 70
I-25060 Marcheno (Brescia)
ITALY
FAX No.: 011-39-30-8610155

FEINWERKBAU

Airgun Importer - See Beeman Precision Airgun listing.

Factory - Feinwerkbau
Neckarstrasse 43
D-78727 Oberndorf/Neckar GERMANY
FAX No.: 011-49-7423/814-89

FERLACH GUNS

Exclusive Importer

Adler Arms ($10 for complete catalog)
268 Freeport Road, Suite 3006
Pittsburgh, PA 15238
Phone No.: 412-826-1232
FAX No.: 412-826-1232

Factory - Ferlach
Attn: Customer Service
Waagplatz, 6
A-9170 Ferlach, AUSTRIA
FAX No.: 011-434227/3714

FERLIB

Importer - See New England Arms Co. listing.
Importer - See Quality Arms, Inc. listing.
Importer - See Hi-Grade Imports listing.

Factory - Ferlib & Cs.d.f
Via Costa 46, Gardone 1-25063
ITALY
FAX No. 01139-3089-12586

FIAS

Fabrica Italiana Armi Sabatti
Via Volta 90
Gardone Val Trompia 1-25063
ITALY
FAX No.: 011-3930-831312

FIOCCHI OF AMERICA, INC.

Importer - Fiocchi of America, Inc.
Rt. 2, Box 90-8
Ozark, MO 65721
FAX No.: 417-725-1039

Factory - Fiocchi Munizioni S.P.A.
Via Santa Barbara, 4
I-22053 Lecco ITALY
FAX No.: 011-39-341/281-171

FORT WORTH FIREARMS

2006-B MLK Fwy.
Fort Worth, TX 76104-6303
Phone No.: 817-536-0718
FAX No.: 817-535-0290

A.H. FOX (Current mfg. only)

Manufacturer - Connecticut Shotgun Manufacturing Co.
P.O. Box 1692
35 Woodland St.
New Britain, CT 06051-1692
Phone No. 203-225-6682
FAX No.: 203-832-8707

Older A.H. Fox Historical Research
Mr. John Callahan
53 Old Quarry Rd.
Westfield, MA 01085
$10.00/gun research fee.

FRANCHI, LUIGI

Importer - See American Arms, Inc. listing.

Factory - Franchi, Luigi, S.p.A.
Via del Serpente, 12
I-25131 Fornaci (Brescia) ITALY
FAX No.: 011-39-30-3581554

FRANCOTTE, AUGUSTE & CIE. S.A.

Importer - See Armes De Chasse listing.

Factory - Auguste Francotte
Rue due Trois Juin, 109
B - 4040 Herstal BELGIUM
FAX No.: 011-3241-481179

FREEDOM ARMS

P.O. Box 1776
Freedom, WY 83120
Phone No.: 307-883-2468
FAX No.: 307-883-2005

FRIGON GUNS, INC.

627 West Crawford
Clay Center, KS 67432
Phone No.: 913-632-5607

GALIL

Service only - See Action Arms, Ltd. listing.

GAMBA, RENATO

Exclusive Importer - Gamba U.S.A.
P.O. Box 60452
Colorado Springs, CO 80960
Phone No.: 719-578-1145
FAX No.: 719-444-0731

Factory - Renato Gamba
Via Artigiani, 91/93
I-25063 Gardone V.T. (Brescia), ITALY
FAX No.: 011-39-30-8912-180

TRADE MARKS

GARBI

Importer - See W. L. Moore & Co. listing.

Factory - Armas Garbi
Urki, 12-14
E-20600 Eibar, SPAIN

GASTINNE RENETTE

39 Avenue Franklin D. Roosevelt
Paris, FRANCE 75008
FAX No.: 011-331-4256-2111

GATLING GUN COMPANY

Distributor - J & G Sales, Inc.
440 Miller Valley Rd.
Prescott, AZ 86304-0400
FAX No.: 602-445-9658
Phone No.: 602-445-9658

GAUCHER - Armes S.A.

*Importer - See Mandall Shooting Supplies
listing.*

Factory
46, rue Desjoyaux
F-42000 Saint-Etienne, FRANCE
FAX No.: 011-33-77419572

GENTRY, DAVID - CUSTOM GUNMAKER

314 N. Hoffman
Belgrade, MT 59714
Phone No.: 406-388-GUNS

GLOCK, INC.

P.O. Box 369
6000 Highlands Pkwy.
Smyrna, GA 30081-0369
FAX No.: 404-433-8719

GONIC ARMS INC. (Black Powder)

134 Flagg Rd
Gonic, NH 03839
Phone No.: 603-332-8456

GRANGER, G.

Factory
66, Cours Fauriel
F-42100 Saint-Etienne, FRANCE
Phone No.: 011-33-77/25-1473

GREENER, W. W.

Factory - W. W. Greener
One Belmont Row
GB-Birmingham, ENGLAND B4 7RE
FAX No.: 011-4421-359-4300

GRENDEL, INC.

P.O. Box 560909
Rockledge, FL 32956-0909
Phone No.: 407-636-1211
FAX No.: 407-633-6710

GRIFFIN & HOWE

36 West 44th Street, Suite 1011
New York, NY 10036
Phone No.: 212-921-0980
FAX No.: 212-921-2327
33 Claremont Road
Bernardsville, NJ 07924
Phone No.: 908-766-2287
FAX No.: 908-766-1068

GRULLA ARMAS, S.L.

Importer - Gun Sport, Ltd. Inc.
1803 West Crescent
Odessa, TX 79791
Phone No.: 915-367-9592

Factory - Grulla Armas
P.O. Box 453
Avda Otaola, 12
E-20600 Eibar (Guipuzcoa) SPAIN
Phone No.: 011-34-943-108756
FAX No.: 011-34-943-702133

GUN PARTS CORP.

Parts supplier only
Williams Lane
W. Hurley, NY 12491
Phone No.: 914-679-2417
FAX No.: 914-679-5849

GUN SOUTH, INC. (GSI)

P.O. Box 129
108 Morrow Avenue
Trussville, AL 35173
Phone No.: 205-655-8299
FAX No.: 205-655-7078

GUNS UNLIMITED, INC.

P.O. Box 37669
4325 S 120th Street
Omaha, NE 68137
Phone No.: 402-339-0771
FAX No.: 402-330-8029

GUSTAF, CARL

See Carl Gustaf listing.

HHF

Importer - Turkish Firearms Corp.
8487 Euclid Ave., Suite 1
Manassas Park, VA 22111
Phone No.: 703-369-6848
FAX No.: 703-257-7709

HJS ARMS, INC.

P.O. Box 3711
Brownsville, TX 78523-3711
Phone No.: 800-453-2767

H & R 1871, INC.

Harrington & Richardson (post-1991 mfg. only)
60 Industrial Rowe
Gardner, MA 01440
FAX No.: 508-632-2300

H-S PRECISION, INC.

1301 Turbine Dr.
Rapid City, SD 57701
Phone No.: 605-341-3006
FAX No.: 605-342-8964

HAENEL (Airguns)

Importer - See Gun South, Inc. listing.

HAMBRUSCH JAGDWAFFEN GmbH

Importer - CONCO Arms
P.O. Box 159
Emmaus, PA 18049
Phone No.: 215-967-5477

Factory - Hambrusch Jagdwaffen Gesellschaft
Gartengasse 4
A-9170 Ferlach, AUSTRIA
FAX No.: 011-4227/4106

HAMMERLI

Importer - Sigarms Inc.
Corporate Park
Exeter, NH 03833
Phone No.: 603-772-2302
FAX No.: 603-772-9082

Factory - Hammerli AG
Seoner Strasse
CH-5600 Lenzburg SWITZERLAND
FAX No.: 011-41-64/513827

HARRIS GUNWORKS

3840 N. 28th Ave.
Phoenix, AZ 85017-4733
Phone No.: 602-230-1414
FAX No.: 602-230-1422

HASKELL MFG. INC.

Refer to Hi-Point listing.

HATFIELD GUN CO., INC.

224 N 4th St.
St. Joseph, MO 64501
Phone No.: 816-279-8688
FAX No.: 816-279-2716

HATFIELD RIFLE WORKS (Black Powder)

Distributor - See Mountain States Muzzleloading Supply listing.

HECKLER & KOCH

Importer - Heckler & Koch
21480 Pacific Blvd.
Sterling, VA 20166-8903
FAX No.: 703-450-8160

Factory - Heckler & Koch GmbH
Postfach 1329
Oberndorf Neckar D-78722 GERMANY
FAX No.: 01149-7423-2539

HELWAN

Importer - See Navy Arms Co. listing.

HENDRY, RAMSAY & WILCOX

55/57 North Methven Street
Perth PH1 5PX, SCOTLAND
Phone No.: 011-44-1-738-623679
FAX No.: 011-44-1-738-443327

HERITAGE MANUFACTURING, INC.

4600 NW 135th St.
Opa Locka, FL 33054
Phone No.: 305-685-5966
FAX No.: 305-687-6721

HEYM, FRIEDRICH WILH.

Factory - F. W. Heym
Coburger Strasse 8
D-97702 Munnerstadt GERMANY
FAX No.: 011-49-9733/6349

HI-GRADE IMPORTS

8655 Monterey Road
Gilroy, CA 95020
Phone No.: 408-842-9301
FAX No.: 408-842-9323

HI-POINT FIREARMS

Distributor - MKS Supply, Inc.
5990 Philadelphia Drive
Dayton, OH 45415
Phone/FAX No.: 513-275-4991

HIGH STANDARD MANUFACTURING COMPANY, INC.

4601 South Pinemont, Ste. 148B
Houston, TX 77041
Phone No.: 713-462-4200
FAX No.: 713-462-6437

HOFER-JAGDWAFFEN, PETER

Kirchgasse 24
A-9170 Ferlach, AUSTRIA
FAX No.: 011-434227/3683/30

TRADE
MARKS

HOLLAND & HOLLAND LTD.

U.S. Store Location
50 East 57th Street
New York, NY 10022
Phone No.: 212-752-7755

Factory Address
Attn: Customer Service-BB
31-33 Bruton Street
London, ENGLAND W1X 8JS
Phone No.: 011-44-71-499 4411
FAX NO.: 011-44-71-499 4544

HOLLOWAY & NAUGHTON

Premier English Shotguns Ltd.
Turners Barn Farm
Kihworth Road, Three Gates
Ulston-on-the-Hill, Leicestershire
ENGLAND, LE7 9EQ

HORTON, LEW, DIST. CO.

See Lew Horton Dist. Co. listing.

I.A.B.

Factory - Industria Armi Brescaine
Via 1 Maggio, 39
Sarezzo Brescia 1-25068 ITALY
FAX No.: 01139-3080-0313

IAR

33171 Camino Capistrano
San Juan Capistrano, CA 92675
Phone No.: 714-443-3642
FAX No.: 714-443-3647

IGA SHOTGUNS

Importer - See Stoeger Industries, Inc. listing.

IZH

Importer - See Big Bear Listing.

IBERIA FIREARMS

Refer to Hi-Point listing.

IMPERIAL GUN CO. LTD.

1E, Threshold Way, Fairoaks Airport
Chobham, Surrey,
GREAT BRITAIN GU24 8HU
FAX No.: 011 44 276-856565

INFINITY

Manufacturer - Strayer-Voight Inc.
3435 Roy Orr Blvd., Ste. 200
Grand Prairie, TX 75050
Phone No.: 214-513-1911
FAX No.: 214-513-0575

INTERARMS

10 Prince Street
Box 208
Alexandria, VA 22313
FAX No.: 703-549-7826

INTRATEC

12405 SW 130th St.
Miami, FL 33186
FAX No.: 305-253-7207

IRWINDALE ARMS, INC.

See A M T listing.

ITHACA (50th Anniversary Pistol only)

See All America Sales, Inc. listing.

JP ENTERPRISES, INC.

P.O. Box 26324
Shoreview, MN 55126
Phone No.: 612-486-9064
FAX No.: 612-482-0970

J.O. ARMS

5709 Hartsdale
Houston, TX 77036
Phone No.: 713-789-0745
FAX No.: 713-789-7513

J.S.L. (HEREFORD) LTD.

No Current Importer

Factory
35 Church Street
Hereford, HR1 2LR, ENGLAND
FAX No.: 011-44432-355242

JAGD-UND SPORTWAFFEN SUHL GmbH

Importer - See Gun South, Inc. listing.
Factory - See Merkel listing.

JAGERSPORT, LTD.

1 Wholesale Way
Cranston, RI 02920
Phone No.: 401-944-9682
FAX No.: 401-946-2587

JACK FIRST, INC.

Gun Parts/Accessories/Service
1201 Turbine Dr.
Rapid City, SD 57701
Phone No.: 605-343-8481

JARRETT RIFLES, INC.

383 Brown Rd.
Jackson, SC 29831
Phone No.: 803-471-3616
FAX No.: 803-471-9246

TRADE
MARKS

K.B.I., INC.
P.O. Box 5440
Harrisburg, PA 17110-0440
Phone No.: 717-540-8518
FAX No.: 717-540-8567

KDF, INC.
2485 Highway 46 North
Seguin, TX 78155
Phone No.: 210-379-8141
FAX No.: 210-379-5420

KSN INDUSTRIES LTD.
Exclusive U.S. Agent - see All America Sales, Inc. listing above.

Exclusive Importer - J.O. Arms, Inc.
5709 Hartsdale
Houston, TX 77036
Phone No.: 713-789-0745
FAX No.: 713-789-7513

KAHNKE GUNWORKS (Black Powder)
206 West 11th
Redwood Falls, MN 56283
FAX No.: 507-637-2905

KAHR ARMS
P.O. Box 220
Blauvelt, NY 10913
Phone No.: 914-353-5996

KEL-TEC CNC INDUSTRIES, INC.
P.O. Box 3427
Cocoa, FL 32924-3427
Phone No.: 407-631-0068
Fax No.: 407-631-1169

KEMEN
Importer - Puglisi Gun Emporium
1336 Commonwealth Ave.
Duluth, MN 55808
Phone No.: 218-626-3618
FAX No.: 218-626-1904

Distributor - Kemen America
1336 Commonwealth Ave.
Duluth, MN 55808
Phone No.: 218-626-3618
FAX No.: 218-626-1904

Distributor - USA Sporting Inc.
1330 No. Glassell, Suite M
Orange, CA 92667
Phone No.: 714-538-3109
FAX No.: 714-538-1334

Factory - Kemen
Ermurarenbide, 14 - Apartado n. 60
20870 Elboibar (Guipuzcoa), SPAIN

KEPPELER + FRITZ GmbH
Aspachweg 4
D-74427 Fichtenberg, GERMANY
FAX No.: 011 49 7971/7971

KEPPLINGER, ING. HANNES
Carl-Wagner-Strasse 1
A-6330 Kufstein, AUSTRIA
FAX No.: 011 43 5372/71887

KIMBER OF AMERICA, INC.
Exclusive distributor - Nationwide Sports Distributors
70 Jamesway
South Hampton, PA 18966
Phone No.: 800-220-3006
FAX No.: 215-322-5972

Nationwide Sports Distributors
1460 Linda Way
Sparks, NV 89431
Phone No.: 800-927-3006
FAX No.: 702-358-2093

Factory - Kimber of America, Inc.
9039 SE Jannsen Road
Clackamas, OR 97015
FAX No.: 503-657-5357

KIMEL INDUSTRIES, INC.
Distributor
P.O. Box 335
3800 Old Monroe Road
Matthews, NC 28105
Phone No.: 704-821-7663
FAX No.: 704-821-6339

Factory - AAArms
4811 Persimmons Ct.
Monroe, NC 28110

KLEINGUENTHER FIREARMS
1604 N. Heideke St.
P.O. Box 2020
Seguin, TX 78155
Phone No.: 512-372-5050
FAX No.: 512-557-5310

KONGSBERG
Importer - Kongsberg America L.L.C.
2 Merwin's lane
Fairfield, CT 06430
Phone No.: 203-259-0938
FAX No.: 203-259-2566

KORTH

*Importer - See Mandall Shooting Supplies
listing.*

Factory - Korth
Robert Bosch Strasse 4
D-2418 Ratzeburg, GERMANY
FAX No.: 011-49451/4993230

KRICO

*Importer - See Mandall Shooting Supplies
listing.*

Factory - A. Kriegeskorte GmbH
Kronacher Str. 63
8510 Furth-Stadeln, GERMANY
FAX No.: 011-49-911-796074

KRIEGHOFF, H., GUN CO.

Importer - Krieghoff Intl., Inc.
P.O. Box 549
7528 Easton Rd.
Ottsville, PA 18942
Phone No.: 610-847-5173
FAX No.: 610-847-8691

Factory - H. Krieghoff GmbH
Boschstrasse 22
D-89079 Ulm, GERMANY
FAX No.: 011-49-731/40 18270

L.A.R. MANUFACTURING, INC.

4133 West Farm Road (8540 South)
West Jordan, UT 84088
Phone No.: 801-280-3505
FAX No.: 801-280-1972

LABANU, INC.

Importer - Labanu, Inc.
2201-F, Fifth Ave.
Ronkonkoma, NY 11779
FAX No.: 516-981-4112

LAKE FIELD ARMS LTD.

Factory
P.O. Box 129
Lakefield, Ontario
K0L 2H0 CANADA
Phone No.: 705-652-8000
FAX No.: 705-652-8431

LANBER

Lanber Armas, S.A.
Attn: Customer Service-BB
Zubiaurre, 5
E-Zaldibar, 48250 Vizcaya, SPAIN
FAX No.: 011-344-6827999

LASERAIM ARMS, INC.

Distributor - Emerging Technologies, Inc.
P.O. Box 3548
Little Rock, AR 72203
Phone No.: 501-375-2227
FAX No.: 501-372-1445

LAURONA ARMAS, S.A.

Importer - Galaxy Imports
P.O. Box 3661
Victoria, TX 77903
Phone No.: 512-573-4867
FAX No.: 512-576-9622

Factory
P.O. Box 260, Avda de Otaola, 25
Eibar (Guipuzcoa) SPAIN
Phone No.: 011-3443/700600
FAX No.: 011-3443/700616

LAZZERONI ARMS COMPANY

P.O. Box 26696
Tucson, AZ 85726-6696
Phone No.: 520-577-7500
FAX No.: 520-624-4250

LEBEAU-COURALLY

Importer - See New England Arms Co. listing.

Factory - Aug. Lebeau-Courally
386, rue Saint-Gilles
B-4000 Liege, BELGIUM
FAX No.: 011-3241-522008

LES BAER CUSTOM, INC.

29601 34th Avenue
Hillsdale, IL 61257
Phone No.: 309-658-2716
Fax No.: 309-658-2610

LEW HORTON DIST. CO.

Distributor Only
15 Walkup Dr.
Westboro, MA 01581
Phone No.: 508-366-7400
FAX No.: 508-366-5332

LIBERTY ARMS WORKS, INC.

823 Lincoln Ave.
West Chester, PA 19380
Phone No.: 610-429-1114

LJUTIC INDUSTRIES, INC.

P.O. Box 2117
732 North 16th Ave., Ste. 22
Yakima, WA 98907
Phone No.: 509-248-0476

TRADE
MARKS

LLAMA PISTOLS

Importer - Import Sports Inc.
1750 Brielle Ave., Unit B-1
Wanamassa, NJ 07712
Phone No.: 908-493-0302
FAX No.: 908-493-0301

LORCIN ENGINEERING CO., INC.

10427 San Sevaine Way, Unit A
Mira Loma, CA 91752
FAX No.: 909-360-0623

LUCCHINI, SANDRO

25060 Ponte Zanano V.T.
Via Petrarca, 47
Sarezzo (Brescia), ITALY

LUCIANO, BOSIS

Importer - See New England Arms, Co. listing.

LUGER (German Mfg.)

Mauser-Werke Oberndorf GmbH
Postfach 1360
D-7238 Oberndorf/Neckar GERMANY
FAX No.: 011-49-74-2370655

LUGER (STOEGER MFG.)

Stoeger Industries, Inc.
5 Mansard Court
Wayne, NJ 07606
201-872-9500
FAX No.: 201-872-2230

LYMAN GUNS (Black Powder)

Lyman Products Corporation
Rt 147
Middlefield, CT 06455
FAX No.: 203-349-3586

MKE

Importer - See Mandall Shooting Supplies, Inc. listing.

M.O.A. CORPORATION

2451 Old Camden Pike
Eaton, OH 45320
Phone No.: 513-456-3669

MAG-7

Importer - Techno Arms Inc.
Vulcans Forge, Inc.
11 Perry Drive, Unit G
Foxboro, MA 02035
Phone/FAX No.: 508-543-1422

Factory - Techno Arms Inc.
PO Box 1128
Johannesburg 2000
SOUTH AFRICA
FAX No.: 011 493-8283

MAGNUM RESEARCH, INC.

7110 University Ave. NE
Minneapolis, MN 55432
FAX No.: 612-574-0109

MAGTECH RECREATIONAL PRODUCTS, INC.

5030 Paradise Rd., Ste. A-104
Las Vegas, NV 89119
Phone No.: 702-736-2043
FAX No.: 702-736-2140

MAKAROV

Importer - See Century International Arms listing.

MANDALL SHOOTING SUPPLIES

3616 N. Scottsdale Rd.
Scottsdale, AZ 85252
Phone No.: 602-945-2553
FAX No.: 602-949-0734

MANUFRANCE

BP 139
St. Etienne Cedex
F-42012 FRANCE
FAX No.: 011-33-77-251166

MANURHIN HANDGUNS

Importer - ABO Industries
6046 Cornerstone Ct. W., Suite 206
San Diego, CA 92121
FAX No.: 619-453-2133

Factory - Manurhin Equipment
15, rue de Quimper
F-68060 Mulhouse Gedex FRANCE
FAX No.: 011-3389-536311

MARKSMAN (Airguns)

5482 Argosy Drive
Huntington Beach, CA 92649
FAX No.: 714-891-0782

MARLIN FIREARMS COMPANY

100 Kenna Drive
P.O. Box 248
North Haven, CT 06473-0905
FAX No.: 203-234-7991

TRADE
MARKS

MAROCCHI SHOTGUNS

Shotguns: Conquista and Model 92 Series

See Precision Sales Int.'l Inc. listing.

Factory - Marocchi di Stefano, F.lli, S.p.A.
Via Galileo Galilei, 6
I-25068 Sarezzo (Brescia) ITALY
FAX No.: 011-39-30-890-0370

MAUSER-WERKE

Importer - see GSI listing.

Factory - Mauser-Werke GmbH
78727 Werkstrabe 2
D-7238 Oberndorf am Neckar, GERMANY
FAX No.: 011-49-7423-70-655

MAVERICK ARMS, INC.

7 Grasso Ave., P.O. Box 497
North Haven, CT 06473
FAX No.: 203-230-5420

McBROS RIFLES

P.O. Box 86549
Phoenix, AZ 85080
Phone No.: 602-780-2115
FAX No.: 602-582-3930
E-Mail: mcbros@indirect.com

MERKEL & GEBRUDER

Importer - See Gun South, Inc. listing.

Factory - Jagd-und Sportwaffen
Auenstrasse 5
D-6000 Suhl, GERMANY
FAX No.: 011-49-66-24-562

MIL-SPEC INDUSTRIES CORP.

10 Mineola Avenue
Roslyn Heights, NY 11577
Phone No.: 516-625-5787
FAX No.: 516-625-0988

MILLER, DAVID

See David Miller Co. listing.

MIROKU FIREARMS MFG. CO.

537-1 Shinohara
Nangoku City
Kochi, JAPAN

MITCHELL ARMS, INC.

3433 W. Harvard St. #B
Santa Ana, CA 92704
FAX No.: 714-957-5732

MODERN MUZZLE LOADING, INC. (Black Powder)

PO Box 130-CAT
Centerville, IA 52544
FAX No.: 515-856-2628

MONTANA ARMORY, INC.

P.O. Box 885
Big Timber, MT 59011
Phone No.: 406-932-4353

MOORE, W.L. & CO.

see listing under W.L. Moore & Co.

MORINI

Importer - See Nygord Precision Products listing.

Importer - See Mandall Shooting Supplies, Inc. listing.

Factory - Morini Competition Arm SA
CH-6814 Lamone-Lugano, ITALY

MOSSBERG

O.F. Mossberg & Sons, Inc.
P.O. Box 497
7 Grasso Ave.
North Haven, CT 06473
FAX No.: 203-230-5420

Factory Service Center
Industrial Blvd.
Eagle Pass, TX 78853
Phone No.: 210-773-9007
FAX No.: 210-773-8862

MOUNTAIN RIFLES INC.

P.O. Box 2789
Palmer, AK 99645
Phone No.: 907-373-4194
FAX No.: 907-373-4195

MOUNTAIN STATES MUZZLELOADING SUPPLY (Black Powder)

RT 2 Box 154-1
Williamstown, WV 26187
FAX No.: 304-375-3737

MOWREY GUN WORKS (Black Powder)

See Cheney Rifle Works/Lehman Rifles

Distributor - See Mountain States Muzzleloading Supply listing.

MUSGRAVE

Musgrave Mfr.'s and Dist. Ltd.
Jagersfontein Road
PO Box 183
Bloemfontein 9300, REPUBLIC OF S. AFRICA
FAX No.: 051/212-903

NS FIREARMS CORP.

c/o KFS, Inc.
P.O. Box 44405
Atlanta, GA 30336-1405
FAX No.: 404-505-8445

TRADE MARKS

NATIONAL WILD TURKEY FEDERATION

National Organization
P.O. Box 530
Edgefield, SD 29824
Phone No.: 803-637-3106

NAVY ARMS CO.

689 Bergen Blvd.
Ridgefield, NJ 07657
FAX No.: 201-945-6859

NELSON, P.V., (GUNMAKERS)

Folly Meadow, Hammersley Lane
Penn, Bucks
HP10 8HF, ENGLAND
Phone/FAX No.: 011-49-4812836

NEW ENGLAND ARMS CO.

Lawrence Lane - Box 278
Kittery Point, ME 03905
Phone No.: 207-439-0593
FAX No.: 207-439-6726

NEW ENGLAND FIREARMS

60 Industrial Rowe
Gardner, MA 01440
Phone No.: 508-632-9393
FAX No.: 508-632-2300

NORINCO

Previous Importer - China Sports, Inc.

Previous Importer - See Interarms listing.

Previous Importer - See Century International Arms listing.

NORTH AMERICAN ARMS, INC.

2150 South, 950 East
Provo, UT 84606-6285
Phone No.: 801-374-9990
FAX No.: 801-344-9998

NYGORD PRECISION PRODUCTS

P.O. Box 12578
Prescott, AZ 86304
Phone No.: 520-717-2315
FAX No.: 520-717-2198

O.D.I.

Parts only
Essex Arms
Box 345
Island Pond, VT 05846
Phone No.: 802-723-4314

OLYMPIC ARMS, INC.

620-626 Old Pacific Hwy. S.E.
Olympia, WA 98513
Phone No.: 360-459-7940
FAX No.: 360-491-3447

OMEGA SYSTEM

Conversion units only - See Safari Arms listing.

OMNI

111 N. Main St., Bldg. B-3
Riverside, CA 92501
Phone No.: 909-684-5006
FAX No.: 909-684-9836.

ORVIS

Custom shotgun information only
Historic Route 7A
Manchester, VT 05254
Phone No.: 802-362-2580

P.A.W.S., INC.

Factory
8175 River Road N.E.
Salem, OR 97303
Phone No.: 503-393-0838
FAX No.: 503-393-0915

PARAMOUNT

Factory - Imperial Gun Co., Ltd.
Unite 1E, Threshold Way
Fairoaks Airport, Chobham
Surrey, GU24 8HU ENGLAND
FAX No.: 011 44 726 856565

PARA-ORDNANCE MFG. INC.

Factory
980 Tapscott Rd.
Scarborough, Ontario
M1X 1E7 CANADA
Phone No.: 416-297-7855
FAX No.: 416-297-1289

PARDINI

Importer - See Nygord Precision Products listing.

Importer - Mo's Competitor Supplies & Range, Inc.
34 Delmar Dr.
Brookfield, CT 06804
Phone No.: 203-775-1013
FAX No.: 203-775-9462

Factory - Pardini Armi Commerciale
55043 Lido di Camaiore
Lu, ITALY
FAX No.: 011-39584-90122

PARKER REPRODUCTIONS

Parker Reproduction Div.
124 River Road
Middlesex, NJ 08846
FAX No.: 908-469-9692

PASTUSEK INDUSTRIES

Distributor - Fort Worth Firearms
2006-B Martin L. King, Jr. Fwy.
Fort Worth, TX 76104-6303
Phone No.: 817-536-0718
FAX No.: 817-535-0290

PAUL & ASSOCIATES

27385 Pressonville Rd.
Wellsville, KS 66092
Phone No.: 913-883-4444
FAX No.: 913-883-2525

PAUZA SPECIALTIES

Distributor - U.S. General Technologies, Inc.
145 Mitchell Avenue
South San Francisco, CA 94080
Phone No.: 415-634-8440
FAX No.: 415-634-8452

Factory - Pauza Specialties Inc.
1023 Gou Hole Rd.
Baytown, TX 77520
Phone No.: 713-383-2420
FAX No.: 713-573-9817

PEDERSOLI, DAVIDE & C. s.n.c. (BLACK POWDER)

Importer - Flintlocks, Etc.
160 Rossiter Drive
Richmond, MA 01254
FAX No.: 413-698-3866

Factory
P.O. Box 11
Via Artigiani 57
25063 Gardone V.T. (BS), ITALY 25063
FAX No.: 011-39-30-8911019

PEIFER RIFLE CO.

P.O. Box 192
Nokomis, IL 62075
FAX No.: 217-563-7060

PENTHENY de PENTHENY, INC.

2352 Baggett Ct.
Santa Rosa, CA 95401
FAX No.: 707-573-1390

PERAZZI

Importer - Perazzi USA, Inc.
1207 South Shamrock Ave.
Monrovia, CA 91016
Phone No.: 818-303-0068
FAX No.: 818-303-2081

Factory - Manifattura Armi Perazzi
Via Fontanelle, 1-3
25080 Botticino M. Brescia ITALY
FAX No.: 011-3930-2692594

PEREGRINE INDUSTRIES, INC.

P.O. Box 1310
Huntington Beach, CA 92647-1310
Phone No.: 714-847-4700
FAX No.: 208-726-0957

PERUGINI-VISINI

Factory
Via Camprelle 126
Nuvolera, Brescia
1-25080 ITALY
FAX No.: 011-39-30-6897821

PETERS STAHL GmbH

Factory
Stettiner Strasse 42
D-33106 Paderborn, GERMANY
FAX No.: 011-49-5251-75611

PHELPS MFG. CO.

P.O. Box 2266
Evansville, IN 47714
Phone No.: 812-476-8791

PHILLIPS & ROGERS, INC.

100 Hilbig, Suite C
Conroe, TX 77301
Phone No.: 409-756-1001
FAX No.: 409-756-0976

PHOENIX ARMS

1420 S. Archibald Ave.
Ontario, CA 91761
FAX No.: 909-947-6798

PIETTA, Flli s.n.c. (Black Powder)

Via Mandolossa, 102
25064 Gussago (Brescia) ITALY
FAX No.: 011-3930-2529284

PIOTTI

Importer - See W.L. Moore & Co. listing.

Factory - Piotti, F.lli, S.n.c.
Via Cinelli, 10-12
I-25063 Gardone V.I. Brescia, ITALY
FAX No.: 011-39-30-358-0652

PIRANHA

Manufacturer - Ultima Technologies, Inc.
3432 W. Wilshire Dr. #11
Phoenix, AZ 85009
Phone No.: 602-278-8903
FAX No.: 602-272-5946

PRAIRIE RIVER ARMS

1220 North 6th St.
Princeton, IL 61356
FAX No.: 815-875-1402

TRADE MARKS

PRECISION SALES INT'I, INC.
P.O. Box 1770
Southwick Road
Westfield, MA 01086
Phone No.: 413-562-5055
FAX No.: 413-562-5056

PRECISION SMALL ARMS
Sales/Marketing
9777 Wilshire Blvd., Ste. 1005
Beverly Hills, CA 90212
Phone No.: 310-859-4867
FAX No.: 310-859-2868

PURDEY, JAMES, & SONS, LTD.
57-58 S Audley Street
London,
W1Y 6ED ENGLAND
Phone No.: 011 44 71 499 1801
FAX No.: 011 44 71 355 3297

QUAIL UNLIMITED, INC.
National Organization
Rt. 3 Box 47
PO Box 610
Edgefield, SC 29824
Phone No.: 803-637-5731
FAX No.: 803-637-0037

QUALITY ARMS, INC.
P.O. Box 19477
Houston, TX 77224
Phone No.: 713-870-8377
FAX No.: 713-870-8524

QUALITY PARTS CO.
Manufacturer of Bushmaster Firearms, Inc.
999 Roosevelt Trail Bldg. 3
Windham, ME 04062
FAX No.: 207-892-8068

RAF

103, rue Antoine Durafour
F-42100 Saint Etienne
FRANCE
FAX No.: 011 33 5 71 216 17

RND MANUFACTURING
Distributor - Mesa Sportsmen's Association, L.L.C.
250 Main Street
P.O. Box 854
Delta, CO 81416
Phone No.: 970-874-4571
FAX No.: 970-874-4571*51
Factory - RND Manufacturing
Longmont, CO

RPM
15481 N. Twin Lakes Dr.
Tucson, AZ 85737
Phone No.: 602-825-1233
FAX No.: 602-825-3333

RAM-LINE, INC.
545 Thirty One Road
Grand Junction, CO 81504
Phone No.: 303-434-4500
FAX No.: 303-434-4004

RAVELL LTD.
289 Diputacion Street
08009 Barcelona, SPAIN
FAX No.: 011-343-488-1394

C.L. REEDY & ASSOCIATES, INC.
314 Highland Road
Jonesborough, TN 37659
Phone No.: 615-753-7790
FAX No.: 615-753-7699

REMINGTON
Remington Arms Co., Inc.
Attn: Consumer Information
Brandywine Bldg. - 1007 Market Street
Wilmington, DE 19898
Phone No.: 302-773-5291
FAX No.: 302-774-5776
Remington Arms Co., Inc. (Repairs)
14 Hoefler Ave.
Ilion, NY 13357
Phone No.: 315-895-7791

RIFLES, INC.
873 West 5400 North
Cedar City, UT 84720
Phone No.: 801-586-5995
FAX No.: 801-586-5996

RIGBY, JOHN & CO. (GUNMAKERS), LTD.
Importer - See Griffin & Howe listing.
Factory
66 Great Suffolk Street
London, SE1 OBU ENGLAND
FAX No.: 011-4471-928-9205

RIZZINI B.
Importer - see New England Arms Co. listing.
Importer - see William Larkin Moore listing.
Factory
Via 2 Giugno, 7/7 bis
25060 Marcheno
Marcheno (Brescia), ITALY
FAX No.: 011-3930/861319

RIZZINI, F.LLI

Importer - See W. L. Moore & Co. listing.

Importer - See New England Arms Co. listing.

ROBAR COMPANIES, INC., THE

21438 N. 7th Avenue, Ste. B
Phoenix, AZ 85027
Phone No.: 602-581-2648
FAX No.: 602-582-0059

ROCKY MOUNTAIN ARMS, INC.

600 S. Sunset, Unit C
Longmont, CO 80501
Phone No: 303-678-8522
FAX No.: 303-678-8766
E-Mail: gunmkr@aol.com

ROCKY MOUNTAIN ELK FOUNDATION

2291 W. Broadway
Missoula, MT 59802
Phone No.: 406-523-4500
FAX No.: 406-523-4581

ROCHE, CHRISTIAN

12 Lotissement les Eglantiers
42 340 Veauche, France
Phone No.: 011-33-77-93-35-33
FAX No.: 011-33-77-94-35-33

ROSSI

Importer - See Interarms listing.

ROTTWEIL

Importer - See Dynamit Nobel of America listing.

RUKO SPORTING GOODS, INC.

2245 Kenmore Ave. Suite 102
Buffalo, NY 14207
Phone No.: 716-874-2707
FAX No.: 905-826-1353

RUTTEN HERSTAL

Importer - see Labanu, Inc. listing

Factory - Rutten Herstal
Parc Industriel des Hauts-Sarts
Premiere Avenue, 7-9
B-4040 Herstal, BELGIUM
FAX No.: 32(0)41/648589

SKB ARMS CO.

See Guns Unlimited, Inc. listing.

SSK INDUSTRIES

721 Woodvue Lane
Wintersville, OH 43952
Phone No. 614-264-0176
FAX No. 614-264-2257

STI INTERNATIONAL

12108-A Roxie Dr.
Austin, TX 78729
Phone: 512-250-0841
FAX No.: 512-250-0926
E-Mail: stint@aol.com

S.W.D., INC.

1872 Marietta Blvd.
Atlanta, GA 30318
Phone No. 404-355-2641
FAX No.: 404-350-9714

SABATTI S.r.l.

Importer - See European American Armory listing.

Factory - Sabatti S.r.l.
Via Dante No. 179
I-25068 Sarezzi, ITALY
FAX No.: 011-39-30-8900598

SAFARI ARMS

620-626 Old Pacific Hwy. S.E.
Olympia, WA 98513
Phone No.: 360-459-7940
FAX No.: 360-491-3447

SAKO

Importer - See Stoeger Industries, Inc. listing.

Factory - Sako, Ltd.
P.O. Box 149, Sakonkatu 2
SF-11101 Riihimaki, FINLAND
FAX No.: 014/720446

SAMCO GLOBAL ARMS, INC.

6995 N.W. 43rd St.
Miami, FL 33166
Phone No.: 305-593-9782
FAX No.: 305-477-1232

F. SARASQUETA

No current address available

SARSILMAZ SILAH SANAYII A.S.

Uzuncarsi Cad. No. 69/71 Mercan
Istanbul/TURKEY
FAX No.: 513 13 25/511 19 99

SAUER, J.P. & SOHN

Importer - See Sigarms listing.

Factory - Sauer, J.P. & Sohn GmbH
Postfach 1408, Sauerstrasse
D-24340 Eckernforde, GERMANY
FAX No.: 011-4943-511471-160

TRADE
MARKS

SAVAGE ARMS, INC

Attn: David Tolly
100 Springdale Road
P.O. Box 1110
Westfield, MA 01085
FAX No.: 413-562-7764

Older Savage Arms Historical Research
Mr. John Callahan
53 Old Quarry Rd.
Westfield, MA 01085
$10.00/gun research fee.

SCATTERGUN TECHNOLOGIES INC.

P.O. Box 24517
Nashville, TN 37202
Phone No.: 615-254-1441
FAX No.: 615-254-1449

SCHELLER - SPEZIALWAFFEN

Factory - Schiebsportzentrum
Postfach 405
Suhl, GERMANY O-6000

SCHUETZEN PISTOL WORKS, INC.

620-626 Old Pacific Hwy. S.E.
Olympia, WA 98513
Phone No.: 360-459-7940
FAX No.: 360-491-3447

SCHUTZEN BOHME GmbH

Muhlenstrabe 6-8
31737 Rintein, GERMANY
Phone No.: 011 49 57 51 4 47 70
FAX No.: 011 49 57 51 4 24 90

SCOTT, W. C., LTD.

Repair address
Holland & Holland, Ltd.
Attn: Mr. P. C. Chismon
31-33 Bruton St.
London W1X 8JS ENGLAND
FAX No.: 011-44-71/499-4544

SEECAMP, L.W. CO., INC.

301 Brewster Road
Milford, CT 06460
Phone No.: 203-877-3429

SEMMERLING

*Manufacturer - See American Derringer
Corp. listing.*

SHILOH RIFLE MFG. CO.

P.O. Box 279, Ind. Park
Big Timber, MT 59011
Phone No.: 406-932-4454
FAX No.: 406-932-5627

SIDEWINDER

Manufacturer - D-Max, Inc.
RR 1, Box 473
Bagley, MN 56621
Phone No.: 218-785-2278

SIGARMS, INC.

Corporation Park
Exeter, NH 03833
FAX No.: 603-772-9082

SIG SAUER

Importer - Sigarms, Inc.
Corporate Park Industrial Drive
Exeter, NH 03833
FAX No.: 603-772-9082

Factory - SIG - Schweizerische
CH-8212 Neuhausen am Rheinfall, SWITZER-
LAND
FAX No.: 011-41-153/216-601

SILE DISTRIBUTORS

7 Centre Market Place
New York, NY 10013
Phone No.: 212-925-4111
FAX No.: 212-925-3149

SILMA s.r.l.

Via 1- Maggio, nr. 74
25060 Zanano di Sarezzo, (BS) ITALY
Phone No.: 011-3930-8900505 (r.a.)
FAX No.: 011-3930-8900712

SMITH & WESSON

Customer Service
2100 Roosevelt Avenue
P.O. Box 2208
Springfield, MA 01102-2208
Phone No.: 800-331-0852, Ext. 2904
FAX No.: 413-731-8980

Smith & Wesson Research
Attn: Mr. Roy Jinks, S&W Historian
P.O. Box 2208
Springfield, MA 01102-2208
Phone No.: 413-781-8300
FAX No.: 413-731-8980

SNAKE CHARMER

Factory - Sporting Arms Mfg. Inc.
P.O. Box 191
Littlefield, TX 79339
FAX No.: 806-385-3394

SPHINX

Importer - Sphinx USA Inc.
998 N. Colony Rd.
Meriden, CT 06450
FAX No.: 203-238-1375

Factory - SPHINX ENGINEERING SA
Ch. des Grandes-Vies 2
CH-2900 Porrentruy
Phone No.: 011-41-66-667381
FAX No.: 011-41-66-667381
SWITZERLAND
FAX No.: 011 41 66 66 30 90

SPRINGFIELD ARMORY

Mfg. by Springfield Inc.
420 W. Main St.
Geneseo, IL 61254
Phone No.: 309-944-5631
FAX No.: 309-944-3676

STALLARD ARMS

Refer to Hi-Point listing.

STAR

Importer - See Interarms listing.

Factory - Star Bonifacio Echevarria S.A.
Torrekua 3
Eibar E-20600 SPAIN
FAX No.: 01134-4311-1524

STEVENS, J., ARMS COMPANY

Older Stevens Historical Research
Mr. John Callahan
53 Old Quarry Rd.
Westfield, MA 01085
$10.00/gun research fee.

STEYR (Airguns only)

PO Box 8394
La Crescenta, CA 91224

STEYR MANNLICHER

Importer - See Gun South, Inc. (GSI) listing.

Factory - Steyr Mannlicher A.G.
Box 1000, Mannlicher Str. 1
Steyr A-4400 AUSTRIA
FAX No.: 01143-7252-68621

STOEGER INDUSTRIES, INC.

5 Mansard Court
Wayne, NJ 07470
Phone No.: 201-872-9500
FAX No.: 201-872-2230

STONE MOUNTAIN ARMS, INC.

5988 Peachtree Corners East
Norcross, GA 30071
FAX No.: 404-242-8546

STONER RIFLE

Factory - Knight's Manufacturing Co.
7750 - 9th St. SW
Vero Beach, FL 32968
FAX No.: 407-569-2955

STRAYER TRIPP INTERNATIONAL

12108-A Roxie Drive
Austin, TX 78729
Phone No.: 512-250-0841
FAX No.: 512-250-0926

STREET SWEEPER

Sales of Georgia
P.O. Box 94168
Atlanta, GA 30318
FAX No.: 404-350-9714

STURM, RUGER & CO.

Lacey Place
Southport, CT 06490
FAX No.: 203-259-2167

SUNDANCE INDUSTRIES

25163 W. Ave. Stanford
Valencia, CA 91355
FAX No.: 805-257-4891

SUPER SIX LIMITED

Disc. Golden Bison Series
13105 W. Bluemound Road
Brookfield, WI 53005
Phone No.: 800-733-9325

SURVIVAL ARMS, INC.

P.O. Box 965
Orange, CT 06477
Phone No.: 203-924-6533
FAX No.: 203-924-2581

SYMES & WRIGHT LTD.

8 Monmouth Place
London, ENGLAND W2 5SA
FAX No.: 011-44-71-221-1424

TANNER, ANDRE

Importer - See Mandall Shooting Supplies listing.

TANFOGLIO, F.LLI, Srl

Importer - See European American Armory listing.

Factory - Tanfoglio, F.Lli, Srl
Via Vaitrompia 45
I-25063 Gardone V.T. (BS) ITALY
FAX No.: 011-39-30-8910183

TAR-HUNT CUSTOM RIFLES, INC.
R.R. 3 Box 572
Bloomsburg, PA 17815-9351
Phone or FAX No.: 717-784-6368

TAURUS INTERNATIONAL FIREARMS
16175 NW 49th Ave.
Miami, FL 33014-6314
Phone No.: 305-624-1115
FAX No.: 305-623-7506

TAYLOR'S & CO.(Black Powder)
304 Lenoir Dr.
Winchester, VA 22603
Phone No.: 540-722-2017
FAX No: 540-722-2018

TECHNI-MEC
Importer - See New England Arms Co. listing.

Importer - See Mandall Shooting Supplies listing.

Factory - Armi di Isidoro Rizzini
Via Gitti, Localita Rovedolo
I-25060 Marcheno (BS) ITALY
FAX No.: 011-3930-8610179

TEXAS ARMS
P.O. Box 154906
Waco, TX 76715
Phone No.: 817-867-6972

TEXAS LONGHORN ARMS, INC.
(Administrative Offices)
5959 West Loop South, Ste. 424
Bellaire, TX 77401
Phone No.: 713-660-6323
FAX No.: 713-660-0493

THOMPSON/CENTER ARMS
P.O. Box 5002
Rochester, NH 03866
FAX No.: 603-332-5133

THUNDER
Distributor - Sherman Yarbrough
2077 H. Lake Park Drive
Smyrna, GA 30080
Phone No.: 404-435-6842

THUNDER FIVE
Distributor - See C.L. Reedy & Associates, Inc. listing.

TIKKA
Importer - See Stoeger Industries, Inc. listing.

TRADITIONS, INC. (Black Powder)
PO Box 235
Deep River, CT 06417
FAX No.: 203-526-4564

TRAIL GUN ARMORY (Black Powder)
Route 22, Box 760
Conroe, TX 77303

UFA, INC.
7655 E. Evans Road, #2
Scottsdale, AZ 85260
FAX No.: 602-922-0148

U.S.A.S.
Factory - International Ordnance Corp.
412 Space Park South
Nashville, TN 37211
Phone No.: 615-831-9612
FAX No.: 615-832-9098

UBERTI, ALDO & C., S.r.l.
Importer - Uberti USA, Inc.
P.O. Box 509
362 Limerock Road
Lakeville, CT 06039
FAX No.: 203-435-2846

Factory - Aldo Uberti & C., S.r.l.
Via G. Carducci, 41
I-25068 Sarezzo (BS) ITALY
FAX No.: 011-39-30-8911061

UGARTECHEA, ARMAS
Distributor - Bill Hanus Birdguns
P.O. Box 533
Newport, OR 97365
Phone No.: 541-265-7433

UGARTECHEA, IGNACIO
U.S. Agent - Bill Hanus Birdguns
P.O. Box 533
Newport, OR 97365
Phone No.: 541-265-7433

Factory - Ugartechea, Ignacio
P.O. Box 21
Eibar, SPAIN
FAX No.: 011-3443-121669

ULTRA LIGHT ARMS
P.O. Box 1270
214 Prince Street
Granville, WV 26534
Phone/FAX No.: 304-599-5687

ULTRAMATIC PRODUCTIONS
Wiesengasse 6
A-2551 Enzesfeld
AUSTRIA
FAX No.: 011-43-22-568115218

TRADE
MARKS

UNIQUE

Importer - see Nygord Precision Products listing.

Factory - Unique Manufacture d'Armes
10, Avenue des Allees
F-64700 Hendaye, FRANCE
FAX No.: 011-33-5920/5085

U.S. GENERAL TECHNOLOGIES, INC.

145 Mitchell Avenue
South San Francisco, CA 94080
FAX No.: 415-634-8452

U.S. HISTORICAL SOCIETY

Also see America Remembers listing.
First & Main Streets
Richmond, VA 23219
FAX No.: 804-648-0002

UNITED STATES PATENT FIRE ARMS MANU-FACTURING COMPANY

No. 24 Van Dyke Ave.
Hartford, CT 06106
Phone No.: 800-877-2832

UZI (Not currently imported).

VALTRO

Importer - See American Arms, Inc. listing.

Factory
25060 Villa Carcina
Brescia, ITALY
FAX No.: 011-39-30-8980361

VARBERGER

Importer - See Paul & Associates listing.

VERNEY-CARRON

54, Boulevard Thiers
Boite Postale 72
42002 St. Etienne Cedex 1
FRANCE
FAX No.: 011-33-77-790702

VOERE

Factory - Voere Austria
Postfach 416
A-6333 Kufstein, AUSTRIA
FAX No.: 05372-5752

WAFFEN VERATSHNIG

Factory
Niederdorfl 30
A-9173 St. Margareten I. Rosental
Ferlach, AUSTRIA
FAX No.: 011-4226-397

WALTHER

Importer - See Interarms listing.

Importer (target pistols only) - See Nygord Precision Products listing.

Factory - Carl Walther, GmbH, Sportwaffenfabrik
Postfach 4325
D-89033 Ulm/Donau, GERMANY
FAX No.: 011-49-731-1539170

WATSON BROS.

39 Redcross Way
London Bridge
SE1 1HG ENGLAND
011-44-71-4033367

WEATHERBY, INC.

3100 El Camino Real
Atascadero, CA 93422
Phone No.: 805-466-1767
FAX No.: 805-466-2527

WEBLEY (Airguns only)

Exclusive Importer - See Beeman Precision Airguns listing.

WEBLEY & SCOTT LTD.

Factory (Airguns only)
Frankley Industrial Park
Tay Road, Rubery, Rednal
GB-Birmingham ENGLAND B45 0PA
Phone No.: 011-44-21-453-1864
FAX No.: 011-44-21-457-7846

WEIHRAUCH, HANS-HERMANN

Exclusive Airgun Importer - See Beeman Precision Airguns listing.

Firearms Importer - See European American Armory listing.

Factory - H. Weihrauch, Sportwaffenfabrik
Industriestrasse 11
D-97638 Mellrichstadt, GERMANY
FAX No.: 011-49-97-76-5532

WESSON FIREARMS CO., INC.

Maple Tree Industrial Ctr, Rt. 20
Wilbraham Road
Palmer, MA 01069
Phone No.: 413-267-4081
FAX No.: 413-267-3601

TRADE MARKS

WESTLEY RICHARDS & CO., Ltd.

U.S. Office
Chestnut Hall
4319 West Chestnut Expressway
Springfield, MO 65802
Phone No.: 417-869-8447

Factory - Westley Richards & Co., Ltd.
40 Grange Road
Birmingham, ENGLAND B29 6AR
FAX No.: 011-44-21-472-1701
Telex. No.: 334049 DETACH

WHITE MUZZLE LOADING SYSTEMS, INC. (Black Powder)

25 E. Hwy 40
Roosevelt, UT 84066
FAX No.: 801-722-3054

WICHITA ARMS, INC.

P.O. Box 11371
923 E. Gilbert
Wichita, KS 67211
Phone No.: 316-265-0661
FAX No.: 316-265-0760

WILDERNESS RIFLE WORKS (Black Powder)

Distributor - See Mountain States Muzzle-loading Supplies listing.

WILDEY, INC.

458 Danbury Rd., No. 6
New Milford, CT 06776
FAX No.: 203-354-7759

W. L. MOORE & CO.

8227 E. Via De Commercio, Suite A
Scottsdale, AZ 85258
Phone No.: 602-951-8913
FAX No.: 602-951-3677

WILLIAM DOUGLAS & SONS

Importer - Cape Outfitters
599 County Rd. 206
Cape Girardeau, MO 63701
Phone No.: 314-335-4103
FAX No.: 314-335-1555

WILLIAM EVANS LIMITED

67 St. James's Street
London SW1A 1PH
ENGLAND
FAX No.: 011-44-71-4991912

WILLIAM POWELL & SON (GUNMAKERS), Ltd.

Importer - Bells Legendary Countrywear
22 Circle Dr.
Bellmore, NY 11710

Factory
35-37 Carrs Lane
Birmingham B47SX ENGLAND
Phone No.: 011-44-21-6430689/8362
FAX No.: 011-44-21-6313504

WILSON COMBAT

Route 3
P.O. Box 578
Berryville, AR 72616-0578
FAX No.: 501-545-3310

WINCHESTER (U.S.REPEATING ARMS)

U.S. Repeating Arms Co.
275 Winchester Avenue, P.O. Box 30-300
New Haven, CT 06511-1970
Phone No.: 800-782-4440
Customer Service Phone No.: 800-945-1392
FAX No.: 801-876-3737
Product Service FAX No.: 203-789-5890

Custom Shop
same address as above
Phone No.: 203-789-5503
FAX No.: 203-789-5853

WINCHESTER/OLIN

Models 101 & 23 only (Disc.)
Attn: Shotgun Customer Service
427 N. Shamrock Street
East Alton, IL 62024
FAX No.: 618-258-3393

WISCHO JAGD-UND SPORTWAFFEN

Dresdener Strasse 30,
D-91058 Erlangen, GERMANY
FAX No.: 011-49-91-31-300930

WISEMAN, BILL & CO.

P.O. Box 3427
Bryan, TX 77805
Phone No.: 409-690-3456
FAX No.: 409-690-0156

WOODWARD, JAMES AND SONS

Factory - Purdey, James, & Sons, Ltd.
57-58 S Audley Street
London,
W1Y 6ED ENGLAND
Phone No.: 011 44 71 499 1801
FAX No.: 011 44 71 355 3297

ZDF IMPORT EXPORT INC.
2975 South 300 West
Salt Lake City, UT 84225
Phone No.: 801-485-1012
FAX No.: 801-484-4363

ZABALLA HERMANOS, S.A.
Apartado de Correos 97
20600 Eibar, SPAIN
FAX No.: 011-34-943 768201

ZANARDINI
Factory - Zanardini, P. & C., S.n.c.
Via C. Goldoni, 34
I-25063 Gardone V.T. (Brescia), ITALY
FAX No.: 011-39-30-8910590

ZANOTTI, FABIO
Importer - See New England Arms Co. listing.
Factory - R. Gamba c/o Zanotti
Via Artigiani, 93
I0-25063 Gardone Val Trompia
Brescia, ITALY
FAX No.: 011-39-30-837180

ZASTAVA ARMS
Factory - Zastava Arms
29 Novembra 12
YU-11000 Beograd, YUGOSLAVIA
011-184-007

ZOLI, ANGELO (discontinued)
Parts - Cape Outfitters
599 County Rd. 206
Cape Girardeau, MO 63701
Phone No.: 314-335-4103
FAX No.: 314-335-1555

ZOLI, ANTONIO
Not affiliated with Angelo Zoli.
Parts - Cape Outfitters
599 County Rd. 206
Cape Girardeau, MO 63701
Phone No.: 314-335-4103
FAX No.: 314-335-1555
Factory - Zoli Antonio S.p.A.
Via Zanardelli, 39
I-25063 Gardone V.T. (BS) ITALY
Phone No.: 011-39-30-891-2161/2
FAX No.: 011-39-30-891-1165

This section is included to identify year of manufacture dates on Brownings, Colts (including 3rd generation Colt S.A. model numbers), High Standard, Mauser broomhandles, Parker shotguns, Remington (manufacture dates), Savage/Stevens model information, Savage M-1899, and selected Winchesters. To use these tables, simply locate the Ser. No. of the above mentioned trademarks, locate the proper bracket it falls into by model, and refer to the adjacent year to determine the year of manufacture. In several cases, caliber rarity can also be determined.

BROWNING BELGIUM PRODUCTION

Year	Serial Number Beginning of Year	Serial Number at End of Year
A-5 (AUTOMATIC 5) SHOTGUN - approximate recapitulation - 12 ga.		
1924	1	3000
1925	3001	18000
1926	18001	33000
1927	33001	48000
1928	48001	63000
1929	63001	78000
1930	78001	93000
1931	93001	108000
1932	108001	123000
1933	123001	138000
1934	138001	153000
1935	153001	168000
1936	168001	183000
1937	183001	198000
1938	198001	213000
1939	213001	229000
1940 -		
1945	NO PRODUCTION	
1946	229001	237000
1947	237001	249000
1948	249001	270000
1949	270001	285000
1950	285001	315000
1952	346001	387000
1953	387001	438000
	Standard Model	
1954	H1	H39000
	Lightweight Model	
	L1	L42000
1955	**Standard Model**	
	H39001	H83000
	Lightweight Model	
	L42001	L83000
1956	**Standard Model**	
	H83001	H99000
	M1	M22000
	Lightweight Model	
	L83001	L99000
	G1	G23000
1957	**Standard Model**	
	M22001	M85000
	Lightweight Model	
	G23001	G85000
1958	**Standard Model**	
	M85001	M99000
	Lightweight Model	
	G85001	G99000

Year	Serial Number Beginning of Year	Serial Number at End of Year
1958-1976	Ser. No. sequence changed to include a one or two digit numeral followed by an alpha character. "M" prefix designates standard models, "G" includes lightweight models, and "V" shows magnum models. To illustrate, an A-5 with a Ser. No. of 8G19264 would indicate a lightweight model manufactured in 1958. Ser. No. 71V24690 would specify a 3 inch magnum gun built in 1971.	
SUPERPOSED MODEL - O & U - 12 GA.		
1931	1	2000
1932	2001	4000
1933	4001	6000
1934	6001	8000
1935	8001	10000
1936	10001	12000
1937	12001	14000
1938	14001	17000
1939 -		
1947	NO PRODUCTION	
1948	17001	17200
1949	17201	20000
1950	20001	21000
1951	21001	27000
1952	27001	33000
1953	33001	37000
1954	37001	43000
1955	43001	48000
1956	48001	54000
1957	54001	59000
1958	59001	68500
1959	68501	76500
1960	76501	86500
1961	86501	96500
1962	96501	99999
1963	S3 suffix after Ser. No.	
1964	S4 suffix after Ser. No.	
1965	S5 suffix after Ser. No.	
1966	S6 suffix after Ser. No.	
1967	S7 suffix after Ser. No.	
1968	S8 suffix after Ser. No.	
1969	S69 suffix after Ser. No.	
1970	S70 suffix after Ser. No.	
1971	S71 suffix after Ser. No.	
1972	S72 suffix after Ser. No.	
1973	S73 suffix after Ser. No.	
1974	S74 suffix after Ser. No.	

Year	Serial Number Beginning of Year	Serial Number at End of Year
1975	S75 suffix after Ser. No.	
1976	S76 suffix after Ser. No.	
1976 to 1984	"P" or Presentation Models only	

LIEGE O & U -
Approximately 10,000 produced

1973	73J prefix before Ser. No.	
1974	74J prefix before Ser. No.	
1975	75J prefix before Ser. No.	

DOUBLE AUTOMATIC SHOTGUN

1952 - 1959	N/A	
1960 - 1971	1st or both digits indicate last 2 digits in year of manufacture (i.e. - OA1947 - 1960 mfg., 70A245671 - 1970 mfg.)	

HI-POWER (9mm) PISTOL

1955 - 1956	No records available	
1957	70000	80000
1958	80001	85267
1959	85268	89687
1960	89688	93027
1961	93028	109145
1962	109146	113548
1963	113549	115822
1964	115823	T136538
1965	T136569	T146372
1966	T146373	T173285
1967	T173286	T213999
1968	T214000	T258000
1969	T258001	T261000+
	and 69C prefix before Ser. No.	
1970	70C prefix before Ser. No.	
1971	71C prefix before Ser. No.	
1972	72C prefix before Ser. No.	
1973	73C prefix before Ser. No.	
1974	74C prefix before Ser. No.	
1975	75C prefix before Ser. No.	
1976	76C prefix before Ser. No.	
1977 to date	New style serialization	

BROWNING .380

1955 - 1964	No records exist	
1965	500000	598804
1966	598805	603890
1967	603891	619474
1968	619475	N/A
1969 - 1970	Discontinued due to GCA of 1968. New model has longer barrel, adj. rear sight, modified grip.	
1971	71N prefix before Ser. No.	
1972	72N prefix before Ser. No.	
1973	73N prefix before Ser. No.	
1974	74N prefix before Ser. No.	
1975	75N prefix before Ser. No.	

Year	Serial Number Beginning of Year	Serial Number at End of Year
.25 CAL. BABY BROWNING PISTOL		
1955 - 1958	Records not available	
1959	181000	206349
1960	206350	230999
1961	231000	250999
1962	251000	278999
1963	279000	286099
1964	286100	308499
1965	308500	329999
1966	333000	367443
1967	367444	412999
1968	413000	479000
1969	Discontinued because of GCA of 1968	

.22 CAL. PISTOLS
(Nomad-Challenger-Medalist)

One or two digit suffix after single capital letter. "P" designates Nomad, "U" designates Challenger model, "T" designates Medalist model. "P5" suffix would indicate a Nomad built in 1965. "U71" suffix would indicate a Challenger built in 1971. Nomad models were manufactured from 1962 to 1973. Challenger and Medalist models were produced from 1962 to 1974.

BOLT ACTION RIFLES
(Safari, Medallion, & Olympian Models)

1959 - 1962	No prefix (numeral-letter) before Ser. No. (i.e., only digits)	
1963	3-single letter prefix or suffix by Ser. No.	
1964	4-single letter prefix or suffix by Ser. No.	
1965	5-single letter prefix or suffix by Ser. No.	
1966	6-single letter prefix or suffix by Ser. No.	
1967	7-single letter prefix or suffix by Ser. No.	
1968	8-single letter prefix or suffix by Ser. No.	
1969	Single letter (Y, Z, or L) followed by last 2 digits of year of mfg. Prefix only.	
1970	"Y70" prefix	
1971	"L71" prefix	
1972	"Z72" prefix	
1973	"Y73" prefix	
1974	"Z74" prefix	
1975	"L75" prefix	

B.A.R.

1967	"M7" suffix after Ser. No.	
1968	"M8" suffix after Ser. No.	
1969	"M69" suffix after Ser. No.	
1970	"M70" suffix after Ser. No.	
1971	"M71" suffix after Ser. No.	

Year	Serial Number Beginning of Year	Serial Number at End of Year
1972	"M72" suffix after Ser. No.	
1973	"M73" suffix after Ser. No.	
1974	"M74" suffix after Ser. No.	
1975	"M75" suffix after Ser. No.	
1976	"M76" suffix after Ser. No.	
1977 to date	New sequence with "RT" appearing in middle of Ser. No.	

.22 AUTO RIFLE (Grades I, II, and III)

Year	
1956 - 1964	Numeric only - 5 digits or less
1965	"5T" or "5E" prefix before Ser. No.
1966	"6T" or "6E" prefix before Ser. No.
1967	"7T" or "7E" prefix before Ser. No.
1968	"8T" or "8E" prefix before Ser. No.
1969	"69T" or "69E" prefix before Ser. No.

Year	Serial Number Beginning of Year	Serial Number at End of Year1970
1970	"70T" or "70E" prefix before Ser. No.	
1971	"71T" or "71E" prefix before Ser. No.	
1972	"72T" or "72E" prefix before Ser. No.	
1973	Japan production	

T-BOLT RIFLE (T1 and T2)

Year	
1965	"X5" suffix after Ser. No.
1966	"X6" suffix after Ser. No.
1967	"X7" suffix after Ser. No.
1968	"X8" suffix after Ser. No.
1969	"X69" suffix after Ser. No.
1970	"X70" suffix after Ser. No.
1971	"X71" suffix after Ser. No.
1972	"X72" suffix after Ser. No.
1973	"X73" suffix after Ser. No.
1974	"X74" suffix after Ser. No.
1975	"X75" suffix after Ser. No.

COLT'S FIREARMS

Year	Serial Number Beginning of Year	Serial Number at End of Year	Total Guns Produced in Year
MODEL 1849 POCKET REVOLVER			
1849	1	11999	11,999
1850	12000	15999	3,999
1851	16000	24999	8,999
1852	25000	54999	29,999
1853	55000	84999	29,999
1854	85000	99999	14,999
1855	100000	109999	9,999
1856	110000	129999	19,999
1857	130000	139999	9,999
1858	140000	149999	9,999
1859	150000	159999	9,999
1860	160000	183999	23,999
1861	184000	196999	12,999
1862	197000	222999	25,999
1863	223000	249999	26,999
1864	250000	269999	16,999
1865	270000	279999	9,999
1866	280000	289999	9,999
1867	290000	299999	9,999
1868	300000	309999	9,999
1869	310000	319999	9,999
1870	320000	324999	4,999
1871	325000	329999	4,999
1872	330000	330999	999
1873	331000	340000	9,000
MODEL 1849 POCKET REVOLVER - LONDON BARREL ADDRESS			
1853	1	999	999
1854	1000	4999	3999
1855	5000	8999	3999
1856	9000	11000	2000

Year	Serial Number Beginning of Year	Serial Number at End of Year	Total Guns Produced in Year
MODEL 1851 NAVY			
1850	1	2499	2499
1851	2500	9999	7499
1852	10000	19999	9999
1853	20000	34999	14,999
1854	35000	39999	4,999
1855	40000	44999	4,999
1856	45000	64999	19,999
1857	65000	84999	19,999
1858	85000	89999	4,999
1859	90000	92999	2,999
1860	93000	97999	4,999
1861	98000	117999	19,999
1862	118000	131999	13,999
1863	132000	174999	42,999
1864	175000	179999	4,999
1865	180000	184999	4,999
1866	185000	200000	14,999
1867	200000	203999	3,999
1868	204000	206999	2,999
1869	207000	209999	2,999
1870	210000	211999	1,999
1871	212000	213999	1,999
1872	214000	214999	999
1873	215000	215348	348
MODEL 1851 NAVY - LONDON BARREL ADDRESS			
1853	1	3999	3,999
1854	4000	14999	10,999
1855	15000	40999	25,999
1856	41000	42000	1,000

MODEL 1860 ARMY

Year	Serial Number Beginning of Year	Serial Number at End of Year	Total Guns Produced in Year
1860	1	1999	1,999
1861	2000	24999	22,999
1862	25000	84999	59,999
1863	85000	149999	64,999
1864	150000	152999	2,999
1865	153000	155999	2,999
1866	156000	161999	5,999
1867	162000	169999	7,999
1868	170000	176999	6,999
1869	177000	184999	7,999
1870	185000	189999	4,999
1871	190000	197999	7,999
1872	198000	198999	999
1873	199000	200500	1,500

MODEL 1861 NAVY

Year	Serial Number Beginning of Year	Serial Number at End of Year	Total Guns Produced in Year
1861	1	4599	4999
1862	4600	9999	53999
1863	1000	16999	6999
1864	17000	24999	7999
1865	25000	27999	2999
1866	28000	29999	1999
1867	30000	30999	999
1868	31000	32999	1,999
1869	33000	33999	999
1870	34000	34999	999
1871	35000	35999	999
1872	36000	36999	999
1873	37000	38843	1,843

MODEL 1862 POLICE

Year	Serial Number Beginning of Year	Serial Number at End of Year	Total Guns Produced in Year
1861	1	8499	84,999
1862	8500	14999	64,999
1863	15000	25999	10,999
1864	26000	28999	2,999
1865	29000	31999	2,999
1866	32000	34999	2,999
1867	35000	36999	1,999
1868	37000	39999	2,999
1869	40000	41999	1,999
1870	42000	43999	1,999
1871	44000	44999	999
1872	45000	45999	999
1873	46000	47000	1,000

MODEL 1873 - SINGLE ACTION ARMY (SAA) - PRE-WAR

Year	Caliber	Serial Number Beginning in Year
1873	.45 Colt Caliber, Standard	1
1874	.450 Boxer	200
1875	.44 Rimfire series (own serials, 1-1863 made through 1880)	1500
1876	.476 Eley introduced	22000
1877		
1878	.44-40 introduced in quantity	41000
1879		49000
1880		53000
1881		62000
1882	Sheriff's model introduced	73000
1883	.22 rimfire introduced	85000

Year	Caliber	Serial Number Beginning in Year
1884	.32-20 and .38-40 introduced	102000
1885	.41 Colt introduced	114000
1886	.38 Colt introduced	117000
1887	.32 Colt and .32 S&W introduced	119000
1888	Flattop Target S.A.A. began; no. 126530	125000
1889	.32 rimfire; .32-44 S&W, .38 S&W; and .44 Russian introduced	128000
1890	.44 Smoothbore; .380 and .450 Eley; and .44 S&W introduced	130000
1891	.38-44 introduced	136000
1892	Transverse cylinder latch introduced, screw lock at front of frame dropped	144000
1893		
1894	Beginning of Bisley models	154000
1895		159000
1896		163000
1897		168000
1898		175000
1899		182000
1900	Revolvers built to handle smokeless powder	192000
1901		203000
1902		220000
1903		238000
1904		250000
1905		261000
1906		273000
1907		288000
1908		304000
1909		308000
1910		312000
1911		316000
1912	Discontinue Bisley model	321000
1913	S&W Special introduced	325000
1914		328000
1915	Long flute cylinders; range no. 330001 to 331480	329500
1916		332000
1917		335000
1918		337000
1919		337200
1920		338000
1921		341000
1922		343000
1923		344500
1924	.45 ACP 33000 introduced, requiring special cylinders	346400
1925		347300
1926		348200
1927		349800
1928		351300
1929		352400

Year	Caliber	Serial Number Beginning in Year
1930	.38 Special introduced	353800
1931		354100
1932		354500
1933		354800
1934		355000
1935	.357 Magnum introduced	355200
1936		355300
1937		355400
1938		356100
1939		356600
1940	A few S.A.A. during and just after the war	357000 thru 357859

COLT SINGLE ACTION ARMY - POST-WAR PRODUCTION
"SA" suffix from 1956 to 1978, "SA" prefix 1978 to 1981

Year	Serial Number Beginning of Year	Serial Number at End of Year
1956	0001SA	8799SA
1957	8800SA	18499SA
1958	18500SA	23399SA
1959	23400SA	28499SA
1960	28500SA	33599SA
1961	33600SA	35649SA
1962	35650SA	37299SA
1963	37300SA	38499SA
1964	38500SA	39999SA
1965	40000SA	41499SA
1966	41500SA	43799SA
1967	43800SA	46299SA
1968	46300SA	48999SA
1969	49000SA	52599SA
1970	52600SA	59399SA
1971	59400SA	61699SA
1972	61700SA	64399SA
1973	64400SA	69399SA
1974	69400SA	73319SA
1975	NONE PRODUCED	
1976	80000SA (start of 3rd generation of production)	82000SA
1977	82001SA	95999SA
1978	96000SA	99999SA
1978	Start of "SA" prefix on front of Ser. No.	
Mid-1978	SA01000	SA12999
1979	SA13000	

NEW FRONTIER SINGLE ACTION ARMY

Year		
1961	3000NF	3005NF
1962	3006NF	3849NF
1963	4325NF	4699NF
1964	4700NF	4974NF
1965	4975NF	5399NF
1966	5400NF	5674NF
1967	5675NF	5699NF
1968	5700NF	

Year	Serial Number Beginning of Year	Serial Number at End of Year
1969	5701NF	5924NF
1970	5925NF	6874NF
1971	6875NF	7049NF
1972	7050NF	7074NF
1973	7075NF	7174NF
1974	7175NF	7264NF
1975	7265NF	7288NF
1978	7501NF	
	discontinuance in 1981	

COLT SINGLE ACTION ARMY - CALIBER BREAKDOWN

Caliber	S.A.A	Flattop Target	Bisley	Bisley Target
.22 Rimfire	107	93	0	0
.32 Rimfire	1	0	0	0
.32 Colt	192	24	160	44
.32 S&W	32	30	18	17
.32-44	2	9	14	17
.32-20	29,812	30	13,291	131
.38 Colt (through 1914)	1,011	122	412	96
.38 Colt (post-1922)	1,365	0	0	0
.38 S&W	9	39	10	5
.38 Colt Special	82	7	0	0
.38 S&W Special	25	0	2	0
.38-44	2	11	6	47
.357 Magnum	525	0	0	0
.380 Eley	1	3	0	0
.38-40	38,240	19	12,163	98
.41	16,402	91	3,159	24
.44 Smoothbore	15	0	1	0
.44 Rimfire	1,863	0	0	0
.44 German	59	0	0	0
.44 Russian	154	51	90	62
.44 S&W	24	51	29	64
.44 S&W Special	506	1	0	0
.44-40	64,489	21	6,803	78
.45	150,683	100	8,005	97
.45 Smoothbore	4	0	2	0
.45 ACP	44	0	0	0
.450 Boxer	729	89	0	0
.450 Eley	2,697	84	5	0
.455 Eley	1,150	37	180	196
.476 Eley	161	2	0	0
Total Quantities	310,386	914	44,350	976

MODEL 1911 AND 1911A1 -
Commercial production -
Capital "C" prefix - .45 cal.

Year	Serial Number Beginning of Year	Serial Number at End of Year
1912	**C1**	**C1899**
1913	C1900	C5399
1914	C5400	C16599
1915	C16600	C27599
1916	C27600	C74999
1917	C75000	C98999

Year	Serial Number Beginning of Year	Serial Number at End of Year
1918	C99000	C105999
1919	C106000	C120999
1920	C120000	C126999
1921	C127000	C128999
1922	C129000	C133999
1923	C134000	C144999
1924	C135000	C150999
1925	C140000	C154999
1926	C145000	C155999
1927	C151000	C158999
1928	C152000	C154999
1929	C155000	C155999
1930	C156000	C158999
1931	C159000	C160999
1932	C161000	C164799
1933	C164800	C174599
1934	C174600	C177999
1935	C178000	C179799
1936	C179800	C183199
1937	C183200	C188699
1938	C188700	C189599
1939	C189600	C198899
1940	C198900	C199299
1941	C199300	C208799
1942	C208800	C215018
1943-1945:	Commercial production interrupted by WWII	
1946	C221001	C222000
1947	C222001	C231999
1948	C232000	C238500
1949	C238501	C240000
1950	C240000	247701C
	"C" SUFFIX STARTED WITH SER. NO. 240228	
1951	247701C	253179C
1952	253180C	259549C
1953	259550C	266349C
1954	266350C	270549C
1955	270550C	272549C
1956	272550C	276699C
1957	276700C	281999C
1958	282000C	283799C
1959	283800C	285799C
1960	285800C	287999C
1961	288000C	289849C
1962	289850C	291299C
1963	291300C	293799C
1964	293800C	295999C
1965	296000C	300299C
1966	300300C	308499C
1967	308500C	315599C
1968	315600C	324499C
1969	324500C	332649C
1970	332650C	336169C
New Range	70G01001	70G05550
1971	70G05551	70G18000
1972	70G18001	70G34400
1973	70G34401	70G43000
1974	70G43001	70G73000
1975	70G73001	70G88900
1976	70G88901	70G99999
New Range	01001G70	13900G70
1977	13901G70	45199G70

Year	Serial Number Beginning of Year	Serial Number at End of Year
1978 TO DATE	45200G70	

MODEL 1911 AND 1911A1 MILITARY PRODUCTION

Year	Serial Number Beginning of Year	Serial Number at End of Year	Manufacturer
1912	1	500	COLT
	501	1000	COLT USN
	1001	1500	COLT
	1501	2000	COLT USN
	2001	2500	COLT
	2501	3500	COLT USN
	3501	3800	COLT USMC
	3801	4500	COLT
	4501	5500	COLT USN
	5501	6500	COLT
	6501	7500	COLT USN
	7501	8500	COLT
	8501	9500	COLT USN
	9501	10500	COLT
	10501	11500	COLT USN
	11501	12500	COLT
	12501	13500	COLT USN
	13501	17250	COLT USN
1913	17251	36400	COLT
	36401	37650	COLT USMC
	37651	38000	COLT
	38001	44000	COLT USN
	44001	60400	COLT
1914	60401	72570	COLT
	72571	83855	SPRINGFIELD -(THESE NUMBERS RESERVED SPRINGFIELD)
	83856	83900	COLT
	83901	84400	COLT USMC
	84401	96000	COLT
	96001	97537	COLT USN
	97538	102596	COLT
	102597	107596	SPRINGFIELD (RESERVED NO. RANGE)
1915	107597	109500	COLT
	109501	110000	COLT USN
	110001	113496	COLT
	113497	120566	SPRINGFIELD -(RESERVED FOR SPRINGFIELD)
	120567	125566	COLT
	125567	133186	SPRINGFIELD -(RESERVED FOR SPRINGFIELD)
1916	133187	137400	COLT
1917	137401	151186	COLT
	151187	151986	COLT USMC
	151987	185800	COLT
	185801	186200	COLT USMC
	186201	209586	COLT
	209587	210386	COLT USMC

Year	Serial Number Beginning of Year	Serial Number at End of Year	Manu-facturer	Year	Serial Number Beginning of Year	Serial Number at End of Year	Manu-facturer
	210387	215386	COLT FRAMES (RESERVED FOR RECEIVERS)		800501	801000	ASSIGNED TO H&R
					801001	856100	COLT
	215387	216186	COLT USMC	1943	856001	958100	COLT
	216187	216586	COLT		** 856101	856404	Replacement No
	216587	216986	COLT USMC		** 856405	916404	ITHACA
1918	216987	217386	COLT USMC		** 916405	1041404	REM. RAND
	217387	223952	COLT		1041405	1096404	US&S
	223953	223990	COLT USN		1088726	1208673	COLT
	223991	232000	COLT		1208674	1279673	ITHACA
	232001	233600	COLT USN		1279674	1279698	RE NO AA
	233601	580600	COLT		1279699	1441430	REM. RAND
	1	13152	REM. UMC		1441431	1471430	ITHACA
1919	13153	21676	REM. UMC		1471431	1609528	REM. RAND
	580601	629500	COLT	1944	1609529	1743846	COLT
	629501	717386	COLT		1743847	1816641	REM. RAND
1924	700001	710000	COLT		1816642	1890503	ITHACA
1937	710001	712349	COLT USN		1890504	2075103	REM. RAND
1938	712350	713645	COLT	1945	2075104	2134403	ITHACA
1939	713646	717281	COLT USN		2134404	2244803	REM. RAND
1940	717282	721977	COLT		2244804	2380013	COLT
1941	721978	756733	COLT		2380014	2619013	REM. RAND
1942	756734	793657	COLT		2619014	2693613	ITHACA
	793658	797639	COLT USN				
	797640	800000	COLT				
	S800001	S800500	SINGER				

** Denotes double issue ranges.

COLT SINGLE-ACTION MODEL NUMBERS

The author wishes to express thanks to Mr. Don Wilkerson for allowing the edited information published below from his 1986 **Post-War Single-Action Revolver, 1976-1986** publication.

A working knowledge of model numbers for the various Colt single-action revolvers is a must for even a novice collector. Since the mid-1970s Colt has placed the model number on the end label of the shipping cartons of virtually all their firearms. Many collectors and publications regularly use the model number to describe or differentiate between revolvers. Using the model number is an accurate and efficient method to dileneate a particular variation. Example: .45 caliber revolver with a 4³⁄₄ in. barrel, blue and casehardened finish and eagle stocks can be described as a simple "P-1840".

Each Colt model is specified by an alphabetical letter and 4 numerical digits. The basic model number as it pertains to single-action revolvers can be broken down as follows:

MODEL P — basic type of frame. The letter "P" is used to dileneate the single-action type of frame.

FIRST NUMERAL — "1" is the first model built on a particular type of frame. Numerals 2, 3, 4, etc. indicate later versions. These versions are not always numbered in numerical order and the same number has been used for different models at different times. A "1" denotes the basic standard single-action frame. A "2" denotes the new black powder frame available through the Colt Custom Gun Shop. A "3" has been used at various times to denote a non-standard frame or cylinder. The "4" is used to specify the New Frontier style of frame. Numbers such as "7" and "8" are frequently used to specify commemorative or special editions.

SECOND NUMERAL — specifies caliber. A "4" denotes .32-20, a "6" denotes .357 Magnum, a "7" denotes .44 Special, an "8" denotes .45 caliber, and a "9" specifies .44-40 caliber.*

THIRD NUMERAL — denotes barrel length. "3" is used to denote both a 3 inch and a 4 inch barrel. "4" is 4³⁄₄ inch or 5 inch, "5" is 5¹⁄₂ inch, "7" is 7¹⁄₂ inch, and "1" is 12 inch.*

FOURTH NUMERAL — is used to denote several different variations of the standard model. Some of the most common examples are: "1", "2", or "6" for nickel finish, "1" for full blue finish in the case of P-1871, and "2", "3", and "4" as used for the Sheriff's Model series to denote blue and casehardened finish, nickel finish, and Royal Blue and casehardened finish, respectively. The fourth numeral can also denote the type of stocks as in P- 1673. The fourth numeral in the basic model designation must be used in conjunction with the preceding three numerals to determine its exact meaning. The fourth numeral is kind of a "catch-all" number. Many times this number serves only to differentiate a later model from a similar model assembled years earlier.

*The .32-20 caliber and the 5 inch barrel length are listed in the 1984 *Colt Buyer's Guide*, but as of this date neither have been produced.

STANDARD MODEL P REVOLVER

The primary model numbers used by Colt for Model P revolvers produced since 1976 are as follows:

- P-1640 - .357 Magnum, 4¾ in. barrel, blue finish, eagle stocks.
- P-1641 - .357 Magnum, 4¾ in. barrel, nickel finish, wood stocks.
- P-1650 - .357 Magnum, 5½ in. barrel, blue finish, eagle stocks.
- P-1656 - .357 Magnum, 5½ in. barrel, nickel finish, wood stocks.
- P-1670 - .357 Magnum, 7½ in. barrel, blue finish, eagle stocks.
- P-1673 - .357 Magnum, 7½ in. barrel, blue finish, wood stocks.
- P-1676 - .357 Magnum, 7½ in. barrel, nickel finish, wood stocks.
- P-1740 - .44 Special, 4¾ in. barrel, blue finish, eagle stocks.
- P-1746 - .44 Special, 4¾ in. barrel, nickel finish, wood stocks.
- P-1750 - .44 Special, 5½ in. barrel, blue finish, eagle stocks.
- P-1756 - .44 Special, 5½ in. barrel, nickel finish, wood stocks.
- P-1770 - .44 Special, 7½ in. barrel, blue finish, eagle stocks.
- P-1776 - .44 Special, 7½ in. barrel, nickel finish, wood stocks.
- P-1716 - .44 Special, 12 in. barrel, nickel finish, wood stocks.
- P-1840 - .45 Colt, 4¾ in. barrel, blue finish, eagle stocks.
- P-1841 - .45 Colt, 4¾ in. barrel, nickel finish, wood stocks.
- P-1850 - .45 Colt, 5½ in. barrel, blue finish, eagle stocks.
- P-1856 - .45 Colt, 5½ in. barrel, nickel finish, wood stocks.
- P-1870 - .45 Colt, 7½ in. barrel, blue finish, eagle stocks.
- P-1876 - .45 Colt, 7½ in. barrel, nickel finish, wood stocks.
- P-1813 - .45 Colt, 12 in. barrel, blue finish, eagle stocks.
- P-1816 - .45 Colt, 12 in. barrel, nickel finish, wood stocks.
- P-1940 - .44-40 caliber, 4¾ in. barrel, blue finish, eagle stocks.
- P-1941* - .44-40 caliber, 4¾ in. barrel, nickel finish, wood stocks.
- P-1950 - .44-40 caliber, 5½ in. barrel, blue finish, eagle stocks.
- P-1970 - .44-40 caliber, 7½ in. barrel, blue finish, eagle stocks.
- P-1976* - .44-40 caliber, 7½ in. barrel, nickel finish, wood stocks.
- P-1911 - .44-40 caliber, 12 in. barrel, nickel finish, wood stocks.

*These model numbers were used primarily for engraved or special ordered revolvers as the two models indicated were never produced as a regular model. "Blue finish" in the above chart denotes the standard blue finish, i.e., blue with casehardened frame.

NEW FRONTIER MODEL

- P-4671 - .357 Magnum, 7½ in. barrel, nickel finish, wood stocks.
- P-4750 - .44 Special, 5½ in. barrel, Royal Blue finish, wood stocks.
- P-4770 - .44 Special , 7½ in. barrel, Royal Blue finish, wood stocks.
- P-4840 - .45 Colt, 4¾ in. barrel, Royal Blue finish, wood stocks.
- P-4850 - .45 Colt, 5½ in. barrel, Royal Blue finish, wood stocks.
- P-4870 - .45 Colt, 7½ in. barrel, Royal Blue finish, wood stocks.
- P-4940 - .44-40 caliber, 4¾ in. barrel, Royal Blue finish, wood stocks.
- P-4970 - .44-40 caliber, 7½ in. barrel, Royal Blue finish, wood stocks.

Note: The term "Royal Blue" in the New Frontier chart denotes a revolver with a casehardened frame and a Royal (high polish) Blue finish on the other major components.

SHERIFF'S MODELS

- P-1932 - .44-40 caliber, 3 in. barrel, blue finish, eagle stocks.
- P-1933* - .44-40/.44 Special, 3 in. barrel, nickel finish, wood stocks.
- P-1934* - .44-40/.44 Special, 3 in. barrel, Royal Blue finish, wood stocks.

*Circa 1984 all Sheriff's Models are listed as single calibers: .44-40 or .45 caliber.

REVOLVERS WITH FULL BLUE FRAMES

Some of the "full blue" models have had more than one model number assigned to the same variation. As a result, a particular model may have been identified by different model numbers at different times. Following the model numbers and descriptions in this chart will be an approximate time frame during which that particular model was in use. No date following the description indicates that only one model number for that particular variation is known to the author (Don Wilkerson).

P-1640 - FB - .357 Magnum, 4¾ in. barrel, fluted cylinder, eagle stocks.

P-1650 - FB - .357 Magnum, 5½ in. barrel, fluted cylinder, eagle stocks.

P-1740 - FB - .44 Special, 4¾ in. barrel, fluted cylinder, eagle stocks.

P-1750 - FB - .44 Special, 5½ in. barrel, fluted cylinder, eagle stocks.

P-1770 - FB - .44 Special, 7½ in. barrel, fluted cylinder, eagle stocks.

P-1770 - UB - .44 Special, 7½ in. barrel, unfluted cylinder, eagle stocks.

P-3840 - .45 Colt, 4¾ in. barrel, both fluted and unfluted cylinders, eagle stocks (early to mid-1982).

P-1840 - FB - .45 Colt, 4¾ in. barrel, fluted cylinder, eagle stocks (mid to late 1982 to date).

P-1840 - UB - .45 Colt, 4¾ in. barrel, unfluted cylinder, eagle stocks (mid to late 1982 to date).

P-1850 - FB - .45 Colt, 5½ in. barrel, fluted cylinder, eagle stocks.

P-1850 - UB - .45 Colt, 5½ in. barrel, unfluted cylinder, eagle stocks.

P-1871 - .45 Colt, 7½ in. barrel, fluted cylinder, wood stocks (1977 to 1979).

P-1870 - FB - .45 Colt, 7½ in. barrel, fluted cylinder, wood stocks (1982 to date).

P-1870 - UB - .45 Colt, 7½ in. barrel, unfluted cylinder, wood stocks (1982 to date).

P-1871 - FB - .45 Colt, 12 in. barrel, fluted cylinder, eagle stocks.

FULL BLUE NEW FRONTIERS

P-4770 - FB - .44 Special, 7½ in. barrel, fluted cylinder, wood stocks.

P-4870 - FB - .45 Colt, 7½ in. barrel, fluted cylinder, wood stocks.

P-4870 - UB - .45 Colt, 7½ in. barrel, unfluted cylinder, wood stocks.

MISCELLANEOUS MODEL NUMBERS

1750 - AA - .44 Special, 5½ in. barrel, blue finish with nickel cylinder, eagle stocks.

1750 - AB - .44 Special, 5½ in. barrel, blue finish with nickel cylinder with blue flutes, eagle stocks.

1840 - UC - .45 Colt, 4¾ in. barrel, blue finish, unfluted cylinder, eagle stocks.

1850 - UC - .45 Colt, 5½ in. barrel, blue finish, unfluted cylinder, eagle stocks.

1870 - UC - .45 Colt, 7½ in. barrel, blue finish, unfluted cylinder, eagle stocks.

Note: The term "blue finish" in this chart is the standard blue finish with a casehardened frame.

BLACK POWDER MODEL P REVOLVERS

P-2830 - .45 Colt, 3 in. barrel, blue finish.

P-2833 - .45 Colt, 3 in. barrel, nickel finish.

P-2834* - .45 Colt, 3 in. barrel, Royal Blue finish.

P-2836 - .45 Colt, 4 in. barrel, Royal Blue finish.

P-2837 - .45 Colt, 4 in. barrel, nickel finish.

P-2840 - .45 Colt, 4¾ in. barrel, blue finish.

P-2841 - .45 Colt, 4¾ in. barrel, nickel finish.

P-2847* - .45 Colt, 5 in. barrel, nickel finish.

P-2870 - .45 Colt, 7½ in. barrel, blue finish.

P-2871 - .45 Colt, 7½ in. barrel, nickel finish.

P-2940 - .44-40 caliber, 4¾ in. barrel, blue finish.

P-2941 - .44-40 caliber, 4¾ in. barrel, nickel finish.

P-2970 - .44-40 caliber, 7½ in. barrel, blue finish.

P-2971 - .44-40 caliber, 7½ in. barrel, nickel finish.

P-2437* - .32-20 caliber, 4 in. barrel, nickel finish.

P-2474* - .32-20 caliber, 7½ in. barrel, Royal Blue finish.

*As of this writing these calibers have not been produced. The terms "blue finish" and "Royal" in this chart refer to Colt's standard single-action finish, i.e., casehardened frame with all components finished in either standard blue or Royal Blue.

COLT BLACKPOWDER
2ND GENERATION SERIALIZATION

Model No.	Serial # Range		Total Prod.	Prod. Began	Prod. Ended
MODEL 1851 NAVY					
C-1121	4201	25100	20900	1971	1978
C-1122	As above but at higher range of numbers				
		Unk'n	—		1978
MODEL 1851 NAVY, R. E. LEE					
C-9001	251REL	5000 REL	4750	—	1971
MODEL 1851 NAVY, U. S. GRANT					
C-9002	251USG	5000 USG	4750	—	1971

Model No.	Serial # Range		Total Prod.	Prod. Began	Prod. Ended
MODEL 1851 GRANT-LEE PAIR					
C-9003	01 GLP	250 GLP	250	—	1971
3rd MODEL DRAGOON					
C-1770	20801	208	25	1974	1978
		Prototype			
	20901	24501	3601		
C-1770MN	S/N's As Above		20	1984	1984
MODEL 1851 NAVY					
F-1100	24900	29150	4250	5/80	10/81

Model No.	Serial # Range	Total Prod.	Prod. Began	Prod. Ended
F-1101	S/N's As Above	300	10/81	11/81
	W/Blank Cylinders			
F-1110	29151s 29640s	489	6/82	10/82
	Stainless Steel			
MODEL 1860 ARMY				
F-1200	201000 212835	7593	11/78	11/82
	Rebated Cylinder			
F-1200 EBO	S/N's As Above	500	1979	1979
	Butterfield			
F-1200 LNK	S/N's As Above	Unk'n	Unk'n	Unk'n
	Electroless Nickel			
F-1200MN	S/N's As Above	12	1984	1984
	Nickel/Ivory			
F-1202	S/N's As Above	500	1979	1979
	Limited Edition			
F-1203	207330 211250	2670	7/80	10/81
	Fluted Cylinder			
F-1210	211263s 212540s	1278	1/82	4/82
	Stainless Steel			
1861 NAVY				
F-1300	40000 43165	3166	9/80	10/81
1862 POCKET NAVY				
F-1400	48000 58850	5765	12/79	11/81
	and skip odd no's.			
F-1400MNS	/N's As Above	25	1984	1984
	Nickel/Ivory			
F-1401	S/N's As Above	500	1979	1980
	Limited Edition			

Model No.	Serial # Range	Total Prod.	Prod. Began	Prod. Ended
1862 POCKET POLICE				
F-1500	49000 57300	4801	1/80	9/81
	and skip even no's.			
F-1500MN	S/N's As Above	25	1984	1984
	Nickel/Ivory			
F-1501	S/N's As Above	500	1979	1980
	Limited Edition			
1847 WALKER				
F-1600	1200 4120	2573	6/80	4/82
	32256 32500	245	5/81	9/81
1st MODEL DRAGOON				
F-1700	25100 34500	3878	1/80	2/82
2nd MODEL DRAGOON				
F-172	S/N's As Above and Mix at Random for			
	1st, 2nd & 3rd	2676	1/80	2/82
3rd MODEL DRAGOON				
F-140	S/N's As Above and Mix at Random for			
	1st, 2nd & 3rd	2856	1/80	2/82
	31401 31450	50	10/81	11/81
F-1740EGA	Unk'n Unk'n	200	1982	1982
	(Garabaldi Model– "GCA" prefix)			
BABY DRAGOON				
F-1760	16000 17851	1852	2/81	4/81
F-1761	S/N's As Above	500	1979	1980
	Limited Edition			
1860 ARMY				
F-9005	US 001/001 US to			
	US 3025/3025 US	3025	9/77	1/80
	Cavalry Commemorative (Two Gun Set)			
HERITAGE WALKER				
F-9006	01 1853	1853	6/80	6/81

HARRINGTON & RICHARDSON SERIALIZATION
1940 - 1982

The following serial numbered prefixes are related to the corresponding year of manufacture:

Year Starting	S.N. Prefix
1940	A
1941	B
1942	C
1943	D
1944	E
1945	F
1946	G
1947	H
1948	I
1949	J
1950	K
1951	L
1952	M
1953	N
1954	P
1955	R
1956	S
1957	T
1958	U
1959	V

Year Starting	S.N. Prefix
1960	W
1961	X
1962	Y
1963	Z
1964	AA
1965	AB
1966	AC
1967	AD
1968	AE
1969	AF
1970	AG
1971	AH
(Snap on forecap)	
1972	AJ
1973	AL
1974	AM
1975	AN
1976	AP
1977	AR
(Striker Mech. Intr.)	
1978	AS
1979	AT
1980	AU
1981	AX
1982	AY

HIGH STANDARD SERIAL NUMBERS
1932 - 1957

Year Starting	Serial Number	Year Starting	Serial Number	Year Starting	Serial Number
1932	5,000	1941	70,600	1950	325,000
1933	5,050	1942	92,600	1951	330,000
1934	6,500	1943	103,600	1952	355,000
1935	8,300	1944	115,000	1953	400,000
1936	11,500	1945	134,700	1954	440,000
1937	18,500	1946	145,800	1955	480,000
1938	29,600	1947	174,200	1956	550,000
1939	39,200	1948	235,000	1957	640,000
1940	50,500	1949	299,000		

HIGH STANDARD AUTOMATIC PISTOL
1958 - 1984

Year Starting	Serial Number	Year Starting	Serial Number
1958	8192XX	1977	ML23XXX
1959	9854XX	Feb.1981	ML71000
1962	12606XX	Apr.1981	ML84000
1963	12954XX	May 1981	ML85000
1965	14204XX	June 1981	ML86000
1965	15709XX	June 1981	SH10000
1966	16078XX	Sept.1982	SH14000
1967	17509XX	Oct. 1982	SH15000
1967	18141XX	Nov. 1982	SH16000
1968	18891XX	Dec. 1982	SH17000
1968	19909XX	Jan. 1983	SH18000
1969	20485XX	Feb. 1983	SH19000
1969	21609XX	Apr. 1983	SH21000
1970	21971XX	May 1983	SH23000
1971	22662XX	Oct. 1983	SH24000
1972	22874XX	Feb. 1984	SH25000
1972	23337XX	Apr. 1984	SH26000
1973	23639XX	May 1984	SH27000
1973	24140XX	June 1984	SH29000
1974	24337XX	Sept 1984	SH34000
1975	ML15XXX		
1976	ML19XXX		

HOLLAND & HOLLAND

PARADOX SERIES

Year Starting	Serial Number	Year Starting	Serial Number
1885	11500	1900	15558
1886		1903	15655
1887		1905	15750
1888	11691	1906	15825
1889	11788	1907	15860
1890	11865	1911	15900
1891	11948	1914	15950
1895	15036	1919	19560
1892	15075	1922	15970
1895	15347	1930	15980
		1956	15979

HOLLAND AND HOLLAND RECORDED DATES

Year Starting	Serial Number	Year Starting	Serial Number
March 1856 (First Recorded Date)	565	A gap in records 1864	728-1059 1060
October 1868	580	1865	1101
February 1857	584	1868	1352
August 1859	700	1869	1439

Year Starting	Serial Number
1870	1578
1871	1769
1872	2002
1873	2401
1874	2759
1875	3174
1876	3649
1877	4179
1878	4774
1879	5274
1880	5819
1881	6382
1882	7009
1883	7473
1884	7904
1885	8406
1886	8809
1887	8999
Unused	9000-10000
Missing	10000-10849
Rook Rifles	10850-10999
Normal Series	11000-11499
Paradox Guns	11500-11999
Normal Series	12000-12999
Rook Rifles	13000-13999
Normal Series	14000-14999
Paradox Guns	15000-15999
Normal Series	16000-16999
Normal Series	17000-17399
Rifles and Rook Rifles	17400-17999
Believed Unused	18000-18999
Rifles	19000-19999
Misc. Guns and Rifles	20000-21999
See separate lists	22000+

ROOK RIFLES

Year Starting	Serial Number
1887	10850-10999
Assumed 1888	11000-11499
records missing	
1889	13106
1890	13465
1891	13566
1892	13674
1893	13885-13999
1894 Some rook rifles	17401
1899 among others	17999

MAGAZINE RIFLES

Year Starting	Serial Number
1910	28000
1911	28100
1913	28199
1913	28300
1919	28399
1920-29	1-581
1930-33	582-880
1920-32	881-1181
1935-49	1182-1782
1949-60	1783-2179
1951-58	2180-2577
1952-62	2578-2977
1958-65	2978-3377
1964-74	3378-3783
1975-80	3784-4000
1981-87	4001-4250
1988-92	4251-4330

PLAIN GUNS

Year Starting	Serial Number
1907	26200
1908	26300
1909	26400
1909	26500
1910	26600
1911	26700
1912	26800
1913	26900
1913	26999
1913	28600
1914	28700
1914	28800
1915	28900
1915	28999
1915	29500
1915	29600
1916	29700
1919	29800
1919	29900
1919	30000
1920	30100
1922	30200
1924	30300
1925	30334
1925	31100
1926	31200
1928	31300
1929	31399
1929	32200
1931	32300
1933	32400
1935	32499
1935	34000
1936	34100
1937	34200
1939	34300
1949	34400
1953	34500
1956	34600
1961	34700
1975	34800

ROYAL GUNS

Year Starting	Serial Number
1899	22000
1900	22500
1902	23000
1903	23500
1906	25000
1907	25500
1910	25599
1910	27000
1911	27250
1912	27500
1913	27750
1914	27999
1914	29000
1915	29100
1919	29200
1920	29300
1920	29400
1921	29499
1921	30500
1922	30600
1922	30700
1924	30800
1925	30900

Year Starting	Serial Number
1926	30999
1926	31500
1927	31600
1927	31700
1928	31800
1929	31900
1929	31999
1929	32500
1930	32600
1930	32700
1931	32800
1932	32900
1934	32999
1934	33000
1935	33100
1936	33200
1937	33300
1937	33400
1939	33500
1946	33600
1948	33700
1950	33800
1952	33900
1954	33999
1954	36251
1956	36300
1958	36400
1959	36500
1962	36600
1964	36700
1965	36800
1970	36900
1970	40006
1972	40100
1974	40200
1979	40300
1980	40400
1981	40500
1982	40530
1983	40560
1984	40590
1985	40650
1986	40770
1987	40820
1988	40880
1989	40920
1990	41000
1991	41075
1992	41150
1993	41210

ROYAL OVER & UNDER GUNS

Year Starting	Serial Number
1950	36000
1952	36010
1954	36020
1958	36029
1993	51001

SPORTING OVER & UNDER GUNS

Year Starting	Serial Number
1993	50500

CAVALIER GUNS

Year Starting	Serial Number
1986	50001
1989	50150
1992	50250

ROYAL DOUBLE RIFLES - .450 & .465

Year Starting	Serial Number
1910	28200
1914	28299
1914	28500
1919	28535
1921	30335
1921	30415
1925	31042
1925	31049
1927	32000
1941	32099

ROYAL DOUBLE RIFLES - .375

Year Starting	Serial Number
1911	28400
1920	28499
1920	30416
1925	30499
1925	31050
1927	31099
1927	32100
1933	32199

ROYAL DOUBLE RIFLES - .240 & Small Bores

Year Starting	Serial Number
1920	28566
1923	28599
1923	31000
1926	31041
1926	31400
1931	31450
1955	31499

ALL CALIBRES

Year Starting	Serial Number
1933	35000
1939	35100
1950	35200
1953	35250
1956	35300
1963	35350
1968	35450
1975	35495
1977	35498
1980	35500
1981	35505
1984	35524
1985	35527
1988	35540
1989	35542
1990	35552
1991	35590

MAUSER BROOMHANDLES
1896 - late 1930's

Serial # Range	Date	Nature of Changes
before #25	1896	— The cone hammer used in place of spur hammer.
#50	1896	— "SYSTEM MAUSER" marked on top of the chamber.
before #200	1897	— The locking system changed from one to two lugs. — The barrel contour at the chamber is tapered instead of stepped.
#390	1897	— "WAFFENFABRIK MAUSER OBERNDORF A/N" marked on top of the chamber.
#975	1897	— The center section of the rear panel on the left side of the frame is not milled out (this feature appears earlier on a few 20-shot pistols). This area is sometimes used for special markings on contract pieces such as the Turkish and Persian.
#12,200 to #14,999	1898	— The large ring hammer replaces the cone hammer.
#21,000	1899	— There is no panel milling on either side of the frame. — A single lug bayonet type mount adopted for retaining the firing pin instead of the dovetail plate. — The trigger is mounted directly to the frame by two integral lugs rather than attached to a removable block. — The position of the serial number moved from the rear of the frame above the stock slot to the left side of the chamber.
#22,000	1900	— Two integral lugs used to mount the rear sight instead of a pin.
#29,000	1902	— Very shallow panels milled into the frame on both sides.*
#31,200	1903	— "WAFFENFABRIK MAUSER OBERNDORF A NECKAR" added to the right rear frame panel.*
#34,000	1904	— The depth of the frame panel milling increased.*
#35,000	1904	— The barrel extension side rails lengthened about a half inch.* — An additional lug for mounting added to the firing pin.* — The hammer changed to the small ring pattern.* — The safety mechanism altered to require that the lever be pushed up to engaged it instead of down.* — The center of the safety lever knob is no longer milled out.*
#38,000	1905	— The short extractor with two ribs replaces the long thin extractor.*
#100,000 to #130,000	1910 1911	— The rifling changed from four groove to six groove.
#270,000	1915	— "NS" (Neues Sicherung or New Safety) appears on the back of the hammer. The hammer must be moved back beyond the cocked position to engage the safety.
#440,000	1921	— The lanyard ring stud is rotated 90 degrees.
#501,000	1923	— The Mauser "banner" appears on the left rear frame panel.
#800,000	1930	— The Mauser banner is enlarged. — A step is added to the barrel contour just ahead of the chamber. — The safety is changed to allow the hammer to be dropped from a cocked position, without danger, by pulling the trigger (called Universal Safety). — The front of the grip frame widened to equal the rear part where the stock slot is.
#850,000	1932	— "D.R.P.u.A.P." (Deutsches Reich Pattenten und Anderes Patenten) added below the inscription on the right rear frame panel.
#860,000	1932	— The lettering in the frame inscription is slanted forward.
#900,000	1934	— The serial number is moved to the rear of the barrel extension behind the sight. — The two grooves in each side of the barrel extension side rails are eliminated.

*These nine changes appear out of sequence (either early or late) on three small batches of guns (29,000 to 29,900, 40,000 to 41,000, and 42,600 to 43,900). Most of these pistols are of the "bolo" style, that is they have 3.9 inch barrels, small grips, six or 10-shot magazines and fixed or adjustable rear sights. A few of these pistols show non-standard barrel contours, barrel extension milling and hammer safety devices. Apparently the factory withheld these numbers from the regular production series and reissued them at later dates.

PARKER SHOTGUNS
1866 - 1942

Date	Number Serial	Date	Number Serial
1866-1868	0-6,800	1914	168,200
1868-1877	9,700	1915	171,500
1877-1879	15,700		*first year of Trojan grade*
1880	17,600	1916	173,450
1881	22,700	1917	175,650
1882	27,300		*first single barrel trap gun*
1883	34,900	1918	180,250
1884	36,000	1919	184,900
1885	46,450	1920	190,100
1886	48,125	1921	195,000
1887	56,650	1922	200,500
1889	59,500		*first Parker single trigger*
1890	61,350	1923	205,150
1891	66,800	1924	207,150
1892	71,600		*first beavertail forend*
1893	77,000	1925	214,400
1894	80,300	1926	218,050
1895	82,400		*first ventilated rib, first .410*
1896	85,200	1927	222,650
1897	86,450	1928	228,200
1898	89,350		*PH grade dropped*
1899	92,450	1929	230,700
1900	97,300	1930	234,200
1901	105,750	1931	235,950
1902	113,100	1932	236,100
1903	121,900	1933	236,300
1904	129,200	1934	236,650
1905	132,000		*first skeet guns,*
1906	138,300		*takeover of factory*
1907	144,250		*by Remington*
1908	148,250	1935	237,000
1910	153,000	1936	239,900
1911	157,050		*last regular catalog*
1912	157,800	1937	240,300
1913	165,000	1938-1942	242,385

REMINGTON
Firearms Serial Number Identification
(Code located on barrel, left side at frame)

Month of Manufacture
(Code letter corresponds to numeral underneath)

B	L	A	C	K	P	O	W	D	E	R	X
1	2	3	4	5	6	7	8	9	10	11	12

Year of Manufacture

1921	M	1932	A	1943	MM	1954	A	1965	M
1922	N	1933	B	1944	NN	1955	B	1966	N
1923	P	1934	C	1945	PP	1956	C	1967	P
1924	R	1935	D	1946	RR	1957	D	1968	R
1925	S	1936	E	1947	SS	1958	E	1969	S
1926	T	1937	F	1948	TT	1959	F	1970	T
1927	U	1938	G	1949	UU	1960	G	1971	U
1928	W	1939	H	1950	WW	1961	H	1972	W
1929	X	1940	J	1951	XX	1962	J		
1930	Y	1941	K	1952	YY	1963	K		
1931	Z	1942	L	1953	ZZ	1964	L		

SAVAGE/STEVENS PRODUCTION DATA

The information below represents a listing of most Savage/Stevens rifles and shotguns mfg. in the past (some data has been approximated). Rather than list these models separately, they have been provided in this section for quick reference. Values on many of the models listed below typically range between $50 - $175, depending on rarity and condition.

SAVAGE

MODEL	DATES	APPROX. GUNS
1903	1912-20	13,000
1904	1912-32	62,000
1905	1912-15	6,500
1909	1912-15	3,500
1911	1912-15	22,500
1912	1913-15	12,000
1914	1914-26	49,500
19	1933-45	16,000
1920	1920-32	12,000
1922	1922-25	16,000
'23A	1924-45	88,000
'23B	1924-45	16,500
'23C	1924-42	14,500
'23D	1932-45	15,000
3	1931-45	121,000
4	1933-45	38,000
5	1936-45	22,000
6	1938-45	45,500
7	1939-45	6,000
40	1928-42	16,000
45	1928-42	6,000
1925	1925-32	36,000
29	1933-45	23,500
CS22	1926-45	87,500
219	1938-45	12,500
220	1937-45	50,000
420	1937-42	13,500
430	1937-42	11.000
1921	1921-32	13,000
1928	1928-32	6,500
721	1930-32	12,000
FOX	1933-45	31,000
FX B	1940-45	20,000

STEVENS

MODEL	DATES	APPROX. GUNS
No. 12	1912-35	166,500
14-1/2	1912-41	592,500
Fav.	1912-42	462,000
No. 26	1912-45	501,500
44+414	1912-35	23,000
No. 70	1912-31	295,500
No. 71	1930-34	10,000
No. 75	1928-34	19,000
15+425	1912-17	11,500
No. 35	1912-19	12,500
No. 35	1923-42	43,000
41-43	1912-18	18,500
No. 10	1919-34	9,500
85-89	1912-42	38,500
No. 93	1912-19	12,500
No. 97	1912-19	16,000
No. 101	1914-20	5,000
No. 105	1912-45	221,500
No. 107	1912-45	443,500
106-08	1916-35	56,500
No. 115	1912-31	23,000

MODEL	DATES	APPROX. GUNS
No. 124	1949-55	– – – –
No. 125	1912-23	5,000
180-85	1912-23	16,000
No. 958	1925-33	5,000
116-17	1926-35	5,000
946-48	1928-34	7,000
No. 215	1913-32	61,000
No. 235	1912-32	61,500
No. 315	1914-36	192,000
No. 335	1912-31	67,500
No. 345	1916-31	3,500
No. 311	1926-45	145,500
No. 330	1926-35	33,500
No. 335	1926-35	2,000
No. 520	1912-32	191,000
No. 521	1930-32	5,000
60&61	1930-34	6,500
620-21	1926-45	66,500
Mod. 30	1933-34	26,000
Mod. 31	1933-34	2,000
No. 15	1936-45	224,000
No. 11	1923-33	141,500
No. 95	1926-35	55,000
No. 52	1933-37	88,000
No. 55	1935-36	3,500
No. 54	1933-42	23,500
No. 56	1933-45	97,500
No. 57	1939-42	500
No. 58	1933-45	29,500
No. 37	1936-42	29,000
No. 38	1936-45	33,500
No. 39	1938-45	64,000
No. 59	1938-45	21,000
No. 76	1938-45	6,000
65-66	1929-45	174,000
No. 82	1936-37	35,500
No. 83	1936-42	159,000
No. 84	1936-45	99,500
No. 85	1939-43	14,000
No. 86	1936-43	82,500
No. 87	1938-45	200,000
No. 872	1940-42	3,500
NO. 89	1926-37	12,000
No. 94	1926-45	934,000
No. 96	1926-33	3,500
No. 416	1937-42	2,000
No. 417	1932-42	1,000
No. 418	1932-42	1,500
No. 419	1932-36	1,000
No. 237	1936-43	16,000
No. 254	1936-42	1,000
No. 238	1936-45	40,000
No. 258	1936-45	11,000
102-04	1936-42	500
No. 116	1936-42	1,000
No. 944	1936-42	1,500
No. 600	1936-42	5,500
No. 900	1936-42	2,000
No. 515	1936-42	500
No. 5151	1936-42	95,000

MODEL	DATES	APPROX. GUNS	MODEL	DATES	APPROX. GUNS
No. 530	1936-42	8,000	22-410	1939-45	105,000
No. 500	1936-42	500	M.240	1940-45	20,500

THE NINETY-NINE

Serial Numbers At Year End:		Serial Numbers At Year End:	
10,000	1899	256,000	1923
13,400	1900	270,000	1924
19,500	1901	280,000	1925
25,000	1902	292,500	1926
35,000	1903	305,000	1927
45,000	1904	317,000	1928
53,000	1905	324,500	1929
67,500	1906	334,500	1930
73,500	1907	338,500	1931
81,000	1908	341,000	1932
95,000	1909	344,500	1933
110,000	1910	345,800	1934
119,000	1911	350,800	1935
131,000	1912	359,800	1936
146,500	1913	-	1937
162,000	1914	381,351	1938
175,500	1915	388,640	1939
187,500	1916	398,400	1940
193,000	1917	416,000	1941
-	1918	438,000	1946
212,500	1919	464,000	1947
229,000	1920	494,000	1948
237,500	1921	528,000	1949
244,500	1922	566,000	1950

WINCHESTER RIFLES

The following Winchester serial numbers appear courtesy of U.S. Repeating Arms, New Haven, CT. I would like to thank U.S. Repeating Arms and Mr. Pardee for making these production figures available.

Records at the factory indicate the following serial numbers were assigned to guns at the end of the calendar year.

MODEL 1866

Year	Serial
1866 -	12476 to 14813
67 -	15578
68 -	19768
69 -	29516
70 -	52527
71 -	88184
72 -	109784
73 -	118401
74 -	125038
75 -	125965
76 -	131907
77 -	148207
78 -	150493
79 -	152201
80 -	154379
81 -	156107
82 -	159513
83 -	162376
84 -	163649
85 -	163664
86 -	165071
87 -	165912
88 -	167155
89 -	167401
90 -	167702
91 -	169003
92 -	NONE
93 -	169007
94 -	169011
95 -	NONE
96 -	NONE
97 -	169015
98 -	170100
99 -	DISCONTINUED

MODEL 1873

Year	Serial
1873 -	1 to 126
74 -	2726
75 -	11325
76 -	23151
77 -	23628
78 -	27501
79 -	41525
80 -	63537
81 -	81620
82 -	109507
83 -	145503
84 -	175126
85 -	196221
86 -	222937
87 -	225922
88 -	284529
89 -	323220
90 -	363220
91 -	405026
92 -	441625
93 -	466641
94 -	481826
95 -	499308
96 -	507545
97 -	513421
98 -	525922
99 -	541328
1900 -	554128
01 -	557236
02 -	564557
03 -	573957
04 -	588953
05 -	602557
06 -	613780
07 -	NONE
08 -	NONE
09 -	630385
10 -	656101
11 -	669324
12 -	678527
13 -	684419
14 -	686510
15 -	688431
16 -	694020
17 -	698617
18 -	700734
19 -	702042
No last # available 20, 21, 22, 23,	720609

MODEL 1876

1876 -	1 to 1429
77 -	3579
78 -	7967
79 -	8971
80 -	14700
81 -	21759
82 -	32407
83 -	42410
84 -	54666
85 -	58714
86 -	60397
87 -	62420
88 -	63539
89 -	NONE
90 -	NONE
91 -	NONE
92 -	63561
93 -	63670
94 -	63678
95 -	NONE
96 -	63702
97 -	63869
98 -	63871

MODEL 1885 SINGLE SHOT

1885 -	1 to 375
86 -	6841
87 -	18328
88 -	30571
89 -	45019
90 -	NONE
91 -	53700
92 -	60371
93 -	69534
94 -	NONE
95 -	73771
96 -	78253
97 -	78815
98 -	84700
99 -	85086
1900 -	88501
01 -	90424
02 -	92031
03 -	92359
04 -	92785
05 -	93611
06 -	94208
07 -	95743
08 -	96819
09 -	98097
10 -	98506
11 -	99012
12 -	NONE
13 -	100352

No further serial numbers were recorded until the end of 1923. Last No. known was: 139700

MODEL 1886

1886 -	1 to 3211
87 -	14728
88 -	28577
89 -	38401
90 -	49723
91 -	63601
92 -	73816
93 -	83261
94 -	94543
95 -	103708

96 -	109670
97 -	113997
98 -	119192
99 -	120571
1900 -	122834
01 -	125630
02 -	128942
03 -	132213
04 -	135524
05 -	138838
06 -	142249
07 -	145119
08 -	147322
09 -	148237
10 -	150129
11 -	151622
12 -	152943
13 -	152947
14 -	153859
15 -	154452
16 -	154979
17 -	155387
18 -	156219
19 -	156930
20 -	158716
21 -	159108
22 -	159337

No further serial numbers were recorded until the discontinuance of the model which was in 1935 - at - 159994

MODEL 1887

1887 -	1 to 7431
88 -	22408
89 -	25673
90 -	29105
91 -	38541
92 -	49763
93 -	54367
94 -	56849
95 -	58289
96 -	60175
97 -	63952
98 -	64855

According to these records no guns were produced during the last few years of this model and it was therefore discontinued in 1901.

MODEL 1890

Records on the Model 1890 are somewhat incomplete. Our records indicate the following serial numbers were
assigned to guns at the end of the calendar year beginning with 1908. Actual records on the firearms which were manufactured between 1890 and 1907 will be available from the "Winchester Museum", located at the
"Buffalo Bill Historical Center"
Attn: Cody Firearms Museum
P.O. Box 1000,
Cody, WY 82414

1908 -	330000 to 363850
09 -	393427

10 -	423567
11 -	451264
12 -	478595
13 -	506936
14 -	531019
15 -	551290
16 -	570497
17 -	589204
18 -	603438
19 -	630801
20 -	NONE
21 -	634783
22 -	643304
23 -	654837
24 -	664613
25 -	675774
26 -	687049
27 -	698987
28 -	711354
29 -	722125
30 -	729015
31 -	733178
32 -	734454

The Model 1890 was discontinued in 1932, however, a clean up of the production run lasted another 8+ years and included another 14 to 15000 guns. Our figures indicate approximately 749,000 guns were made.

MODEL 1892

1892 -	1 to 23701
93 -	35987
94 -	73508
95 -	106721
96 -	144935
97 -	159312
98 -	165431
99 -	171820
1900 -	183411
01 -	191787
02 -	208871
03 -	253935
04 -	278546
05 -	315425
06 -	376496
07 -	437919
08 -	476540
09 -	522162
10 -	586996
11 -	643483
12 -	694752
13 -	742675
14 -	771444
15 -	804622
16 -	830031
17 -	853819
18 -	870942
19 -	903649
20 -	906754
21 -	910476
22 -	917300
23 -	926329
24 -	938641
25 -	954997
26 -	973896
27 -	990883
28 -	996517
29 -	999238
30 -	999730

31 -	1000727
32 -	1001324

MODEL 94

Records at the factory, and in some years, estimates, indicate the following serial numbers were assigned to guns at the end of the calendar year.

1894 -	1 to 14579
95 -	44359
96 -	76464
97 -	111453
98 -	147684
99 -	183371
1900 -	204427
01 -	233975
02 -	273854
03 -	291506
04 -	311363
05 -	337557
06 -	378878
07 -	430985
08 -	474241
09 -	505831
10 -	553062
11 -	599263
12 -	646114
13 -	703701
14 -	756066
15 -	784052
16 -	807741
17 -	821972
18 -	838175
19 -	870762
20 -	880627
21 -	908318
22 -	919583
23 -	938539
24 -	953198
25 -	978523
26 -	997603
27 -	1027571
28 -	1054465
29 -	1077097
30 -	1081755
31 -	1084156
32 -	1087836
33 -	1089270
34 -	1091190
35 -	1099605
36 -	1100065
37 -	1100679
38 -	1100915
39 -	1101051
40 -	1142423
41 -	1191307
42 -	1221289
43 -	No Record Available
44 -	No Record Available
45 -	No Record Available
46 -	No Record Available
47 -	No Record Available
48 -	1500000
49 -	1626100
50 -	1724295
51 -	1724295
52 -	1910000
53 -	2000000
54 -	2071100
55 -	2145296

56 -	2225000
57 -	2290296
58 -	2365887
59 -	2410555
60 -	2469821
61 -	2500000
62 -	2551921
63 -	2586000
*1964	2700000 - 2797428
65 -	2894428
66 -	2991927
67 -	3088458
68 -	3185691
69 -	3284570
70 -	3381299
71 -	3557385
72 -	3806499
73 -	3929364
74 -	4111426
75 -	4277926
75 -	4463553
76 -	4463553
77 -	4565925
78 -	4662210
79 -	4826596
80 -	4892951
81 -	5024957
82 -	5103248

* The post-64 Model 94 began with serial number 2,700,000.

Serial number 1,000,000 was presented to President Calvin Coolidge in 1927.

Serial number 1,500,000 was presented to President Harry S. Truman in 1948.

Serial number 2,500,000 and 3,000,000 were presented to the Winchester Gun Museum, now located in Cody, Wyoming.

Serial number 3,500,000 was not constructed until 1979 and was sold as auction in Las Vegas, Nevada.

Serial number 4,000,000 - whereabouts unknown at this time.

Serial number 4,500,000 - shipped to Italy by Olin in 1978. Whereabouts unknown.

Serial number 5,000,000 - in New Haven, not constructed as of March 1983.

Records at the factory indicate the following serial numbers were assigned to guns at the end of the calendar year.

MODEL 1895

1895 -	1 to 287
96 -	5715
97 -	7814
98 -	19871
99 -	26434
1900 -	29817
01 -	31584
02 -	35601
03 -	42514
04 -	47805
05 -	54783
06 -	55105
07 -	57351
08 -	60002
09 -	60951
10 -	63771
11 -	65017
12 -	67331
13 -	70823
14 -	72082
15 -	174233
16 -	377411
17 -	389106
18 -	392731
19 -	397250
20 -	400463
21 -	404075
22 -	407200
23 -	410289
24 -	413276
25 -	417402
26 -	419533
27 -	421584
28 -	422676
29 -	423680
30 -	424181
31 -	425132
32 -	425825

MODEL 1903

1903 -	# Not Available
04 -	6944
05 -	14865
06 -	23097
07 -	31852
08 -	39105
09 -	46496
10 -	54298
11 -	61679
12 -	69586
13 -	76732
14 -	81776
15 -	84563
16 -	87148
17 -	89501
18 -	92617
19 -	96565
20 -	# Not Available
21 -	97650
22 -	99011
23 -	100452
24 -	101688
25 -	103075
26 -	104230
27 -	105537
28 -	107157
29 -	109414
30 -	111276
31 -	112533

32 -	112992

This model was discontinued in 1932, however, a clean up of parts was used for further production of approximately 2000 guns. Total production was stopped at serial number 114962... in 1936.

MODEL 1905

1905 -	1 to 5659
06 -	15288
07 -	19194
08 -	20385
09 -	21280
10 -	22423
11 -	23503
12 -	24602
13 -	25559
14 -	26110
15 -	26561
16 -	26910
17 -	27297
18 -	27585
19 -	28287
20 -	29113

MODEL 1906

1906 -	1 to 52278
07 -	89147
08 -	114138
09 -	165068
10 -	221189
11 -	273355
12 -	327955
13 -	381922
14 -	422734
15 -	453880
16 -	483805
17 -	517743
18 -	535540
19 -	593917
20 -	NONE
21 -	598691
22 -	608011
23 -	622601
24 -	636163
25 -	649952
26 -	665484
27 -	679892
28 -	695915
29 -	711202
30 -	720116
31 -	725978
32 -	727353

A clean up of production took place for the next few years with a record of production reaching approximately 729305.

MODEL 1907

1907 -	1 to 8657
08 -	14486
09 -	19707
10 -	23230
11 -	25523
12 -	27724
13 -	29607
14 -	30872
15 -	32272
16 -	36215

17 -	38235
18 -	39172
19 -	40448
20 -	No # Available
21 -	40784
22 -	41289
23 -	41658
24 -	42029
25 -	42360
26 -	42688
27 -	43226
28 -	43685
29 -	44046
30 -	44357
31 -	44572
32 -	44683
33 -	44806
34 -	44990
35 -	45203
36 -	45482
37 -	45920
38 -	46419
39 -	46758
40 -	47296
1941 -	47957
42 -	48275
43 -	NONE
44 -	NONE
45 -	48281
46 -	48395
47 -	48996
48 -	49684
**49 -	50662
**50 -	51640
**51 -	52618
**52 -	53596
**53 -	54574
**54 -	55552
**55 -	56530
**56 -	57508
**57 -	58486

** Actual records on serial numbers stops in 1948. The serial numbers ending each year from 1948 to 1957 were derived at by taking the last serial number recorded (58486) and the last number from 1948, (49684) and dividing the years of production (9), which relates to 978 guns each year for the nine year period.

MODEL 1910

1910 -	1 to 4766
11 -	7695
12 -	9712
13 -	11487
14 -	12311
15 -	13233
16 -	13788
17 -	14255
18 -	14625
19 -	15665
20 -	No # Available
21 -	15845
22 -	16347
23 -	16637
24 -	17030

25 -	17281
26 -	17696
27 -	18182
28 -	18469
29 -	18893
30 -	19065
31 -	19172
32 -	19232
33 -	19281
34 -	19338
35 -	19388
36 -	19445

A cleanup of production continued into 1937 when the total of the guns was completed at approximately 20786

MODEL 1911 S.L.

1911 -	1 to 3819
12 -	27659
13 -	36677
14 -	40105
15 -	43284
16 -	45391
17 -	49893
18 -	52895
19 -	57337
20 -	60719
21 -	64109
22 -	69132
23 -	73186
24 -	76199
25 -	78611

The Model 1911 was discontinued in 1925. However, guns were produced for three years after that date to clean up production and excess parts. When this practice ceased there were approximately 82774 guns produced.

MODEL 52

1920 -	None indicated
21 -	397
22 -	745
23 -	1394
24 -	2361
25 -	3513
26 -	6383
27 -	9436
28 -	12082
29 -	14594
30 -	17253
31 -	21954
32 -	24951
33 -	26725
34 -	29030
35 -	32448
36 -	36632
37 -	40419
38 -	43632
39 -	45460
40 -	47519
41 -	50317
42 -	52129
43 -	52553
44 -	52560
45 -	52718
46 -	56080
47 -	60158

48 -	64265
49 -	68149
50 -	70766
51 -	73385
52 -	76000
53 -	79500
54 -	80693
55 -	81831
56 -	96869
57 -	97869
58 -	98599
59 -	98899
60 -	102200
61 -	106986
62 -	108718
63 -	113583
64 -	118447
65 -	120992
66 -	123537
67 -	123727
68 -	123917
69 -	E 124107
70 -	E 124297
71 -	E 124489
72 -	E 124574
73 -	E 124659
74 -	E 124744
75 -	E 124828
76 -	E 125019
77 -	E 125211
78 -	E 125315

This Model was discontinued in 1978. A small clean up of production was completed in 1979 with a total of - 125419.

MODEL 53

In the case of the Model 53 there is some confusion as to whether or not they were serially numbered concurrently with the MODEL 92 or whether the Model 53 had it's own serial number range.

This Model was discontinued in 1932, however, a clean up of production continued for 9 more years.

Total Production Approximately - 24,916

Records at the factory indicate the following serial numbers

were assigned to guns at the end of the calendar year.

MODEL 54

1925 -	1 to 3140
26 -	8051
27 -	14176
28 -	19587
29 -	29104
30 -	32499
31 -	36731
32 -	38543
33 -	40722
34 -	43466
35 -	47125
36 -	50145

MODEL 55 CENTERFIRE

1924 -	1 to 836
25 -	2783
26 -	4957
27 -	8021
28 -	10467
29 -	12258
30 -	17393
31 -	18198
32 -	19204
33 -	Clean up 20580

MODEL 61

1932 -	1 to 3532
33 -	6008
34 -	8554
35 -	12379
36 -	20615
37 -	30334
38 -	36326
39 -	42610
40 -	49270
41 -	57493
42 -	59871
43 -	59872
44 -	59879
45 -	60512
46 -	71629
47 -	92297
48 -	115281
49 -	125461
50 -	135461
51 -	145821
52 -	156000
53 -	171000
54 -	186000
55 -	200962
56 -	216923
57 -	229457
58 -	242992
59 -	262793
60 -	282594
61 -	302395
62 -	322196
63 -	342001

This Model was discontinued in 1963. For some unknown reason there are no actual records available from 1949 through 1963. The serial number figures for these years are arrived at by taking the total production figure of 342001, subtracting the last known # of 115281, and di-

viding the difference equally by the amount of remaining years available, (15).

MODEL 62

1932 -	1 to 7643
33 -	10695
34 -	14090
35 -	23924
36 -	42759
37 -	66059
38 -	80205
39 -	96534
40 -	116393
41 -	137379
42 -	155152
43 -	155422
44 -	155425
45 -	156073
46 -	183756
47 -	219085
48 -	252298
49 -	262473
50 -	272648
51 -	282823
52 -	293000
53 -	310500
54 -	328000
55 -	342776
56 -	357551
57 -	383513
58 -	409475

MODEL 63

1933 -	1 to 2667
34 -	5361
35 -	9830
36 -	16781
37 -	25435
38 -	30934
39 -	36055
40 -	41456
41 -	47708
42 -	51258
43 -	51631
44 -	51656
45 -	53853
46 -	61607
47 -	71714
48 -	80519
49 -	88889
50 -	97259
51 -	105629
52 -	114000
53 -	120500
54 -	127000
55 -	138000
56 -	150000
57 -	162345
58 -	174692

MODEL 70

1935 -	1 to 19
36 -	2238
37 -	11573
38 -	17844
39 -	23991
40 -	31675
41 -	41753
42 -	49206
43 -	49983
44 -	49997

45 -	50921
46 -	58382
47 -	75675
48 -	101680
49 -	131580
50 -	173150
51 -	206625
52 -	238820
53 -	282735
54 -	323530
55 -	361025
56 -	393595
57 -	425283
58 -	440792
59 -	465040
60 -	504257
61 -	545446
62 -	565592
63 -	581471

All post 64 Model 70s began
with the serial number 700,000.

64 -	740599
65 -	809177
66 -	833795
67 -	869000
68 -	925908
69 -	G941900
70 -	G957995
71 -	G1018991
72 -	G1099257
73 -	G1128731
74 -	G1175000
75 -	G1218700
76 -	G1266000
77 -	G1350000
78 -	G1410000
79 -	G1447000
80 -	G1490709
81 -	G1537134

MODEL 71

1935 -	1 to 4
36 -	7821
37 -	12988
38 -	14690
39 -	16155
40 -	18267
41 -	20810
42 -	21959
43 -	22048
44 -	22051
45 -	22224
46 -	23534
47 -	25728
48 -	27900
49 -	29675
50 -	31450
51 -	33225
52 -	35000
53 -	37500
54 -	40770
55 -	43306
56 -	45843
57 -	47254

MODEL 74

1939 -	1 to 30890
40 -	67085
41 -	114355
42 -	128293
43 -	NONE
44 -	128295
45 -	128878
46 -	145168
47 -	173524
48 -	223788
49 -	249900
50 -	276012
51 -	302124
52 -	328236

53 -	354348
54 -	380460
55 -	406574

MODEL 88

1955 -	1 to 18378
56 -	36756
57 -	55134
58 -	73512
59 -	91890
60 -	110268
61 -	128651
62 -	139838
63 -	148858
64 -	160307
65 -	162699
66 -	192595
67 -	212416
68 -	230199
69 -	H239899
70 -	H258229
71 -	H266784
72 -	H279014
73 -	H283718

MODEL 100

1961 -	1 to 32189
62 -	60760
63 -	78863
64 -	92016
65 -	135388
66 -	145239
67 -	209498
68 -	210053
69 -	A210999
70 -	A229995
71 -	A242999
72 -	A258001
73 -	A262833

WINCHESTER SHOTGUNS

Records at the factory indicate the following serial numbers were assigned to guns at the end of the calendar year.

MODEL 1897

1897 -	1 to 32335
98 -	64668
99 -	96999
1900 -	129332
01 -	161665
02 -	193998
03 -	226331
04 -	258664
05 -	296037
06 -	334059
07 -	377999
08 -	413618
09 -	446888
10 -	481062
11 -	512632
12 -	544313
13 -	575213
14 -	592732
15 -	607673
16 -	624537
17 -	646124
18 -	668383
19 -	691943
20 -	696183

21 -	700428
22 -	715902
23 -	732060
24 -	744942
25 -	757629
26 -	770527
27 -	783574
28 -	769806
1929 -	807321
30 -	812729
31 -	830721
32 -	833926
33 -	835637
34 -	837364
35 -	839728
36 -	848684
37 -	856729
38 -	860725
39 -	866938
40 -	875945
41 -	891190
42 -	910072
43 -	912205
44 -	912327
45 -	916472
46 -	926409

47 -	936682
48 -	944085
49 -	953042
50 -	961999
51 -	970956
52 -	979913
53 -	988860
54 -	997827
55 -	1006784
56 -	1015741
57 -	1024700

Records on this Model are incomplete. The above serial numbers are estimated from 1897 thru 1903 and again from 1949 thru 1957. The actual records are in existence from 1904 through 1949.

**MODEL 1901
SHOTGUN**

1904 -	64,856 to 64,860
05 -	66453
06 -	67486
07 -	68424

08 -	69197
09 -	70009
10 -	70753
11 -	71441
12 -	72167
13 -	72764
14 -	73202
15 -	73509
16 -	73770
17 -	74027
18 -	74311
19 -	74872
20 -	77000

MODEL 12

1912 -	5308
13 -	32418
14 -	79765
15 -	109515
16 -	136412
17 -	159391
18 -	183461
19 -	219457
20 -	247458
21 -	267253
22 -	304314
23 -	346319
24 -	385196
25 -	423056
26 -	464564
27 -	510693
28 -	557850
29 -	600834
30 -	626996
31 -	651255
32 -	660110
33 -	664544
34 -	673994
35 -	686978
36 -	720316
37 -	754250
38 -	779455
39 -	814121
40 -	856499
41 -	907431
42 -	958303
43 -	975640
44 -	975727
45 -	990004
1946 -	1029152
47 -	1102371
48 -	1176055
49 -	1214041
50 -	1252028
51 -	1290015
52 -	1328002
53 -	1399996
54 -	1471990
55 -	1541929
56 -	1611868
57 -	1651435
58 -	1690999
59 -	1795500
60 -	1800000
61 -	1930999
62 -	1956990
63 -	1962001

A clean up of production took place from 64 through 66 with the ending serial # 1970875.

NEW STYLE M/12

1972 -	Y200 011-
	Y2006396
73 -	Y2015662
74 -	Y2022061
75 -	Y2024478
76 -	Y2025482
77 -	Y2025874
78 -	Y2026156
79 -	Y2026399

MODEL 24

1939 -	1 to 8118
40 -	21382
41 -	27045
42 -	33670
43 -	NONE RECORDED
44 -	33683
45 -	34965
46 -	45250
47 -	58940
48 -	64417

There were no records kept on this model from 1949 until its discontinuance in 1958. The total production was approximately 116280.

MODEL 42

1933 -	1 to 9398
34 -	13963
35 -	17728
36 -	24849
37 -	30900
38 -	34659
39 -	38967
40 -	43348
41 -	48203
42 -	50818
43 -	50822
44 -	50828
45 -	51168
46 -	54256
47 -	64853
48 -	75142
49 -	81107
50 -	87071
51 -	93038
52 -	99000
53 -	108201
54 -	117200
55 -	121883
56 -	126566
57 -	131249
58 -	135932
59 -	140615
60 -	145298
61 -	149981
62 -	154664
63 -	159353

MODEL 50

1954 -	1 to 24550
55 -	49100
56 -	73650
57	98200
58 -	122750
59 -	147300
60 -	171850
61 -	196400

WINCHESTER MODEL 101 SERIALIZATION
12 gauge

Ser. No.	Mfg. Mo.	Year	Ser. No.	Mfg. Mo.	Year	Ser. No.	Mfg. Mo.	Year
50,000	10	1959	59,000	6	1963	69,000	6	1964
50,500	3	1960	59,500	6	1963	69,500	6	1964
51,000	5	1960	60,000	7	1963	70,000	7	1964
51,500	6	1960	60,500	8	1963	70,500	7	1964
52,000	9	1961	61,000	8	1963	71,000	8	1964
52,500	3	1962	61,500	11	1963	71,500	9	1964
53,000	4	1962	62,000	11	1963	72,000	9	1964
53,500	5	1962	62,500	11	1963	72,500	10	1964
54,000	8	1962	63,000	12	1963	73,000	10	1964
54,500	9	1962	63,500	1	1964	73,500	11	1964
55,000	10	1962	64,000	1	1964	74,000	11	1964
55,500	12	1962	64,500	2	1964	74,500	12	1964
56,000	1	1963	65,000	3	1964	75,000	12	1964
56,500	2	1963	65,500	3	1964	75,500	1	1965
57,000	3	1963	66,000	3	1964	76,000	2	1965
57,500	3	1963	66,500	3	1964	76,500	2	1965
58,000	4	1963	67,000	5	1964	77,000	3	1965
58,500	5	1963	67,500	5	1964	77,500	4	1965
			68,000	5	1964	78,000	4	1965
			68,500	5	1964	78,500	4	1965

Ser. No.	Mfg. Mo.	Year	Ser. No.	Mfg. Mo.	Year
79,000	4	1965	113,000	3	1968
79,500	4	1965	113,500	4	1968
80,000	5	1965	114,000	5	1968
80,500	6	1965	114,500	5	1968
81,000	6	1965	115,000	6	1968
81,500	6	1965	115,500	6	1968
82,000	6	1965	116,000	7	1968
82,500	8	1965	116,500	7	1968
83,000	8	1965	117,000	9	1968
83,500	8	1965	117,500	10	1968
84,000	9	1965	118,000	1	1969
84,500	9	1965	118,500	1	1969
85,000	10	1965	119,000	2	1969
85,500	10	1965	119,500	3	1969
86,000	10	1965	120,000	4	1969
86,500	10	1965	120,500	4	1969
87,000	10	1965	121,000	4	1969
87,500	10	1965	121,500	4	1969
88,000	11	1965	122,000	5	1969
88,500	11	1965	122,500	6	1969
89,000	11	1965	123,000	6	1969
90,000	12	1965	123,500	6	1969
90,500	12	1965	124,000	7	1969
91,000	12	1965	124,500	7	1969
91,500	1	1966	125,000	7	1969
92,000	1	1966	125,500	8	1969
92,500	2	1966	126,000	8	1969
93,000	2	1966	126,500	9	1969
93,500	2	1966	127,000	9	1969
94,000	3	1966	127,500	10	1969
94,500	3	1966	128,000	11	1969
95,000	5	1966	128,500	11	1969
95,500	5	1966	129,000	11	1969
96,000	6	1966	129,500	2	1970
96,500	7	1966	130,000	2	1970
97,000	7	1966	130,500	3	1970
97,500	7	1966	131,000	3	1970
98,000	8	1966	131,500	4	1970
98,500	8	1966	132,000	4	1970
99,000	9	1966	132,500	4	1970
99,500	9	1966	133,000	4	1970
100,000	10	1966	133,500	5	1970
100,500	10	1966	134,000	5	1970
101,000	10	1966	134,500	5	1970
101,500	11	1966	135,000	6	1970
102,000	11	1966	135,500	6	1970
102,500	12	1966	136,000	6	1970
103,000	1	1967	136,500	8	1970
103,500	1	1967	137,000	8	1970
104,000	2	1967	137,500	8	1970
104,500	3	1967	138,000	8	1970
105,000	4	1967	138,500	11	1970
105,500	5	1967	139,000	12	1970
106,000	5	1967	139,500	12	1970
106,500	5	1967	140,000	12	1970
107,000	9	1967	140,500	1	1971
107,500	10	1967	141,000	2	1971
108,000	10	1967	141,500	2	1971
108,500	11	1967	142,000	2	1971
109,000	11	1967	142,500	3	1971
109,500	11	1967	143,000	3	1971
110,000	12	1967	143,500	4	1971
110,500	1	1968	144,000	4	1971
111,000	2	1968	144,500	4	1971
111,500	3	1968	145,000	4	1971
112,000	3	1968	145,500	5	1971
112,500	3	1968			

20 gauge

Ser. No.	Mfg. Mo.	Year
200,000	3	1966
200,500	3	1966
201,000	3	1966
201,500	3	1966
202,000	4	1966
202,500	4	1966
203,000	4	1966
203,500	5	1966
204,000	6	1966
204,500	6	1966
205,000	7	1966
205,500	8	1966
206,000	8	1966
206,500	8	1966
207,000	9	1966
207,500	9	1966
208,000	9	1966
208,500	12	1966
209,000	2	1967
209,500	7	1967
210,000	10	1967
210,500	12	1967

28 ga. & .410 ga. added

Ser. No.	Mfg. Mo.	Year
211,000	1	1968
211,500	1	1968
212,000	10	1968
212,500	10	1968
213,000	10	1968
213,500	11	1968
214,000	12	1968
214,500	12	1968
215,000	1	1969
215,500	2	1969
216,000	5	1969
216,500	6	1969
217,000	9	1969
217,500	10	1969
218,000	11	1969
218,500	12	1969
219,000	12	1969
219,500	12	1969
220,000	12	1969
220,500	1	1970
221,000	1	1970
221,500	2	1970
222,000	3	1970
222,500	7	1970
223,000	9	1970
223,500	9	1970
224,000	9	1970
224,500	9	1970
225,000	10	1970
225,500	10	1970
226,000	11	1970
226,500	11	1970
227,000	11	1970
227,500	12	1970
228,000	12	1970
228,500	4	1971
229,000	4	1971
229,500	4	1971

"STORE BRAND" TO MANUFACTURER
CROSS OVER LIST

The following listing is provided as a cross reference of "Store Brands" to original manufacturer and model number. Although not exhaustive, this list covers most major stores and chains that have had their name put on guns by other manufacturers. The values for the firearms listed on these pages are approximately 15% - 40% less than the original manufacturers model(s).

Our thanks goes out to Gun Parts Corp., West Hurley, NY. They can be reached (914) 679-2417.

House Brand	Model No.	Orig. Mfgr.	Orig. Model	House Brand	Model No.	Orig. Mfgr.	Orig. Model
Aldens	670	Springfield	67	Cotter & Co	75-45	Glenfield	75
Aldens	670	Savage	67	Cotter & Co	842	Springfield	840
				Cotter & Co	911	Springfield	511
Belknap	964A	Stevens	87N	Cotter & Co	918	Springfield	18
Belknap	B63	Springfield	947	Cotter & Co	948	Stevens	940
Belknap	B63	Savage	947B	Cotter & Co	948E	Savage	948E
Belknap	B63E	Savage	940E	Cotter & Co	949	Springfield	944
Belknap	B64	Savage	67	Cotter & Co	949C	Savage	940
Belknap	B65C	Springfield	745	Cotter & Co	949Y	Savage	944Y
Belknap	865C	Savage	745				
Belknap	B68	Savage	94C	C.I.L.	125	Anschutz	184
Belknap	B68D	Savage	94D	C.I.L.	212	Savage	7J
Belknap	B963	Springfield	120	C.I.L.	221	Savage	7J
Belknap	B963	Savage	120	C.I.L.	227	Savage	871
Belknap	B964	Savage	87J	C.I.L.	233	Savage	85N
Belknap	B967	Savage	87N	C.I.L.	266	Savage	187
				C.I.L.	470	Anschutz	520/61
Coast to Coast	180	Savage	58	C.I.L.	607	Savage	67
Coast to Coast	1800	Savage	18D	C.I.L.	607 TD	Savage	30 FLD GR.
Coast to Coast	182	Savage	18S	C.I.L.	621	Savage	30
Coast to Coast	184	Savage	951	C.I.L.	621 TD	Savage	30D
Coast to Coast	267	Savage	77	C.I.L.	710	Savage	311
Coast to Coast	285	Savage	7J	C.I.L.	725	Savage	FOX BDE
Coast to Coast	286	Savage	46	C.I.L.	830	Savage	340
Coast to Coast	288	Savage	87J	C.I.L.	871	Savage	170
Coast to Coast	320	Savage	120	C.I.L.	950C.D	Savage	110C.D
Coast to Coast	367	Savage	30	C.I.L.	MKVII	H & R	865
Coast to Coast	40	Marlin	99C				
Coast to Coast	42	Marlin	70	Eastern Arms	101.1	Stevens	94B
Coast to Coast	650	Marlin	55	Eastern Arms	101.23	Savage	416
Coast to Coast	779	Mossberg	479				
Coast to Coast	843	Savage	340	Foremost See J.C.Penney			
Coast to Coast	843	Springfield	840				
Coast to Coast	843V2DS	Savage	340(.222)	Gamble Skogkmo, Hiawatha			
Coast to Coast	843V3DS	Savage	340(.30/30)				
Coast to Coast	946	Stevens	940	Gamble Skogkmo	130	Savage	30
Coast to Coast	946	Springfield	947	Gamble Skogkmo			
Coast to Coast	946E	Stevens	940E		1300-567 VR	Savage	67-VR
Coast to Coast	946Y	Stevens	940Y	Gamble Skogkmo	180N	Savage	87N
				Gamble Skogkmo	1 89J	Savage	87J
Cotter & Co	10-40	Glenfield	10	Gamble Skogkmo	189N	Stevens	87N
Cotter & Co	10-40	Marlin	101	Gamble Skogkmo	521	Savage	120
Cotter & Co	121	Stevens	120-15	Gamble Skogkmo	567	Savage	67
Cotter & Co	167	Springfield	67	Gamble Skogkmo	S87	Savage	187
Cotter & Co	167T	Savage	30	Gamble Skogkmo	594	Savage	944
Cotter & Co	168	Savage	30	Gamble Skogkmo	594Y	Savage	944Y
Cotter & Co	168	Springfield	67VR	Gamble Skogkmo			
Cotter & Co	287	Springfield	87J		GU12-5517A	J.C.Higgins	60 & 66
Cotter & Co	33	Marlin	336C				
Cotter & Co	410	Savage	110E	Glenfield	10	Marlin	101
Cotter & Co	424	Savage	24F	Glenfield	20	Marlin	80
Cotter & Co	434	Savage	34	Glenfield	25	Marlin	80 W/swivels
Cotter & Co	474	Savage	170	Glenfield	30A	Marlin	336
Cotter & Co	474	Springfield	174	Glenfield	35	Marlin	336 .35 cal
Cotter & Co	487T	Springfield	187	Glenfield	50	Marlin	55
Cotter & Co	489	Savage	89	Glenfield	60	Marlin	5
Cotter & Co	60-50	Glenfield	60	Glenfield	60	Marlin	99C
Cotter & Co	60-50	Marlin	99C	Glenfield	65	Marlin	99M1
Cotter & Co	645	Savage	745	Glenfield	70	Marlin	989M2
Cotter & Co	645C	Savage	745C	Glenfield	75	Marlin	989MI
Cotter & Co	75-46	Marlin	99M1				

House Brand	Model No.	Orig. Mfgr.	Orig. Model
Globco	Mohawk	Russian	Tokarev
Hawthorn See Wards			
Hercules	50	Stevens	5100
Hiawatha See Gambles			
J.C. Higgins See Sears			
J.C. Penney common name, F - Foremost			
J.C.Penney	2025	Marlin	80C
J.C.Penney	2035	Marlin	80
J.C.Penney	2035	Glenfield	20
J.C.Penney	2066	Marlin	49DL
J.C.Penney	2935	Marlin	336
J.C.Penney	3040	Marlin	336
J.C.Penney	3040	Glenfield	30A
J.C.Penney	4011	High Standard	FLIGHT KING
J.C.Penney	6400	Savage	340
J.C.Penney	6610	Savage	120
J.C.Penney	6630	Glenfield	50
J.C.Penney	6630	Marlin	66
J.C.Penney	6647	Savage	944
J.C.Penney	6647	Springfield	944
J.C.Penney	6660	Glenfield	60
J.C.Penney	6660	Marlin	99C
J.C.Penney	6670	Springfield	67H
J.C.Penney	6670	Savage	67
J.C.Penney	6870	Savage	30
J.C.Penney	6870H	Savage	30H
Katz	F-1282	Marlin	989M2
Katz	F-1282	Glenfield	70
Katz	F-1287	Marlin	55
Katz	F-1287	Glenfield	50
Kresge	151	Boito	CBC
K-Mart	151	Boito	CBC
Marlin/new	780	Marlin/old	80
Marlin/new	781	Marlin/old	81
Marlin/new	782	Marlin/old	980
New Haven	220K	Mossberg	320K-A
New Haven	240K	Mossberg	340K
New Haven	246K	Mossberg	346K-A
New Haven	250K	Mossberg	152K
New Haven	250K8	Mossberg	350K-A
New Haven	273	Mossberg	173
New Haven	273A	Mossberg	173A
New Haven	283.D	Mossberg	183D
New Haven	284	Mossberg	173
New Haven	285	Mossberg	185D-C
New Haven	290	Mossberg	190D-A
New Haven	453	Mossberg	353
New Haven	600AB	Mossberg	500AS
New Haven	600C	Mossberg	500C
New Haven	600E	Mossberg	500E
New Haven	679	Mossberg	472
New Haven	740	Mossberg	640
Otasco	30	Marlin	336
Otasco	30	Glenfield	30A
Otasco	65	Glenfield	60
Otasco	65	Marlin	99C
Palmetto	11	Stevens	85,89
Priemier	Trail Blazer	Stevens	29A
Revelation, see Western Auto			

House Brand	Model No.	Orig. Mfgr.	Orig. Model
Sears. Ranger. J.C. Higgins			
J.C.Higgins	101.1	Savage	94
J.C.Higgins	101.24	Savage	15-120
J.C.Higgins	20	High Standard	200
J.C.Higgins	42 DL	Marlin	80
J.C.Higgins	52	Sako	L46
J.C.Higgins	S4	Browning	FN-300
J.C.Higgins	583.13 to.23	High Standard	10
J.C.Higgins	583.2078-79	High Standard	20ga pump
J.C.Higgins	583.514-730	High Standard	20ga pump
J.C.Higgins	6670H	Stevens	67H
J.C.Higgins	80	High Standard	101
Ranger	101.2	Savage	238
Ranger	101.8	Stevens	83
Ranger	104.7	H&R	120
Ranger	105.20	H&R	120
Ranger	120	Winchester	1200
Ranger	30	Stevens	520A
Ranger	34A	Marlin	80.C,780
Ranger	34A	Marlin	50-50E
Ranger	35A	Stevens	66A
Ranger	36	Marlin	80 Adj. Trigger
Ranger	400	Stevens	311
Sears	101.1	Savage	94
Sears	101.100	Savage	96/96Y
Sears	101.10040	Savage	94
Sears	101.10041	Savage	94
Sears	101.10080	Stevens	940
Sears	101.1120	Savage	51 and 951
Sears	101.12	Stevens	39
Sears	101.13	Stevens	86-7
Sears	101.138	Savage	38A and 58A
Sears	101.138	Springfield	18.410
Sears	101.1380	Springfield	18,18C
Sears	101.1380	Stevens	58,C
Sears	101.1381	Springfield	18,951 E,F
Sears	101.1381	Stevens	58,51, E,F
Sears	101.16	Savage	6,87
Sears	101.1610	Savage	540 DL
Sears	101.1610	Savage	FOX BDL
Sears	101.1610	Fox BST	EC,BD,BE,B-F
Sears	101.1620-1670	Stevens	530,A; 311,A,C
Sears	101.1700	Savage	94
Sears	101.1701	Fox BSE	C,D,Ser F,H
Sears	101.1701-C	Savage	BSE
Sears	101.1710	Savage	FOX BDE
Sears	101.1710	Savage	540 BDE
Sears	101.1750	Savage	94
Sears	101.1760	Savage	94
Sears	101.19	Stevens	827-7
Sears	101.20	Stevens	15
Sears	101.22	Stevens	87M(MUSKET
Sears	101.25	Stevens	39A, 59A,BandC
Sears	101.2830	Savage	63-73
Sears	101.2830	Savage	73
Sears	101.3	Stevens	237
Sears	101.3538830	Stevens	89
Sears	101.4	Stevens	38
Sears	101.40	Springfield	947,D,Y
Sears	101.40	Stevens	940,D,Y,DY
Sears	101.451	Marlin	336
Sears	101.5	Stevens	37
Sears	101.51004	Savage	94
Sears	101.510070	Savage	94
Sears	101.51009	Springfield	944,Yseries A
Sears	101.51013	Springfield	944,Yseries A
Sears	101.51024	Savage	94
Sears	101.510270	Savage	94
Sears	101.51044	Savage	94

House Brand	Model No.	Orig. Mfgr.	Orig. Model	House Brand	Model No.	Orig. Mfgr.	Orig. Model
Sears	101.510660	Stevens	9478	Sears	103.350	Marlin	M90
Sears	101.510660	Springfield	944,Y series A	Sears	103.360	Marlin	90
Sears	101.510670	Stevens	9478	Sears	103.4	Marlin	A1
Sears	101.510680	Stevens	9478	Sears	103.450	Marlin	336
Sears	101.512220	Stevens	5100,530,311	Sears	103.451	Marlin	336
Sears	101.512230	Stevens	5100,530,311	Sears	103.720	Marlin	59
Sears	101.51451	Springfield	67	Sears	103.740	Marlin	59
Sears	101.51452	Springfield	67	Sears	103.8	Marlin	100
Sears	101.51454	Springfield	67	Sears	10.19790	Marlin	80
Sears	101.51472	Springfield	67 Series B	Sears	11.2	Stevens	238
Sears	101.52701	Stevens	71,74 S/S	Sears	153.512350	Laurona	S/S
Sears	101.52772	Savage	34,65,34M. 65M	Sears	153.512351	Laurona	S/S
				Sears	153.512360	Laurona	S/S
Sears	101.52773	Savage	34,65,34M, 65M	Sears	153.512361	Laurona	S/S
Sears	101.5350	Springfield	18.58	Sears	153.512740	Laurona	71 O/U
Sears	101.5350-D	Stevens	18D	Sears	18	Mossberg	183K
Sears	101.53521	Savage	340	Sears	18AC	Savage	18C
Sears	101.53527	Savage	340	Sears	2C	Winchester	131
Sears	101.5300	Savage	18/18AC.58	Sears	20	High Standard	? PUMP
Sears	101.5380	Springfield	18,12,16,20ga	Sears	200	Winchester	1200
Sears	101.5380D	Stevens	18ADC	Sears	200	Mossberg	G4
Sears	101.538840	Savage	34,65,34M, 65M	Sears	201	Mossberg	80
				Sears	202	Mossberg	80
				Sears	203	Mossberg	85
Sears	101.540	FOX	B-BST,BDL	Sears	204	Mossberg	83
Sears	101.5410	Springfield	18,58	Sears	205	Mossberg	73
Sears	101.5410D	Savage	18D	Sears	206	Mossberg	70
Sears	101.5410D	Springfield	18DS	Sears	207	Mossberg	75
Sears	101.54880	Stevens	80 Series A	Sears	209	Stevens	84-7
Sears	101.54880	Springfield	187 Series A	Sears	21	High Standard	K2011
Seem	101.64881	Marlin	980 DL,987	Sears	210	Mossberg	85B
Sears	101.600	Stevens	39A,59A,B,C	Sears	211	Mossberg	83B
Sears	101.7	Stevens	311	Sears	211	Stevens	86-7
Sears	101.750	SpringField	18.410	Sears	212	Mossberg	73B
Sears	101.750	Savage	38A and 58A	Sears	213	Mossberg	75B
Soars	101.7C	Stevens	311-C	Sears	215	Mossberg	85C
Sears	101.8	Stevens	83	Sears	216	Mossberg	83C
Sears	102	Stevens	240	Sears	217	Mossberg	75C
Sears	102.25	Stevens	520A	Sears	217	Stevens	87M (MUSKET)
Sears	102.35	Savage	M521				
Sears	102.35	Savage	M29-D2	Sears	218	Mossberg	73C
Sears	103.13	Marlin	81	Sears	218	Stevens	22/410
Sears	103.16	Marlin	80	Sears	231	Stevens	83
Sears	103.18	Marlin	100	Sears	232	Stevens	87-7
Sears	103.181	Marlin	101	Sears	233	Stevens	87 7
Sears	103.1977	Marlin	101	Sears	234	Savage	234
Sears	103.19770	Marlin	101	Sears	238	Stevens	827-7
Sears	103.19771	Marlin	101	Sears	25	High Standard	A1041 .22 auto
Sears	103.19780	Marlin	101				
Sears	103.19790	Marlin	80	Sears	273.2400	Winchester	190
Sears	103.19791	Marlin	80	Sears	273.27S10(2C)	Winchester	131
Sears	103.19800	Marlin	80	Sears	273.27520(2M)	Winchester	131
Sears	103.19801	Marlin	80	Sears	273.510770	Winchester	37A
Sears	103.1981	Marlin	81	Sears	273.510780	Winchester	37A
Sears	103.19810	Marlin	81	Sears	273.510790	Winchester	37A
Sears	103.19811	Marlin	81	Sears	273.53421	Winchester	100
Sears	103.1982	Marlin	81DL	Sears	277	Stevens	1S
Sears	103.19820	Marlin	81	Sears	278.28180	Cooey	64
Sears	103.19821	Marlin	81	Sears	281.512650	Antonio Zoli	O/U
Sears	103.19840	Marlin	56	Sears	281.512651	Antonio Zoli	O/U
Sears	103.19880	Marlin	57 LR-MAG.	Sears	281.512660	Antonio Zoli	O/U
Sears	103.19881	Marlin	57 LR-MAG.	Sears	281.512661	Antonio Zoli	O/U
Sears	103.19890	Marlin	57 LR-MAG.	Sears	281.512750	Antonio Zoli	O/U
Sears	103.2	Marlin	80	Sears	282.510821	Boito	ERA Single Bbl
Sears	103.228	Marlin	80				
Sears	103.229	Marlin	81	Sears	282.510831	Boito	ERA Single Bbl
Sears	103.273	Marlin	782				
Sears	103.273	Marlin	980	Sears	282.510841	Boito	ERA Single Bbi
Sears	103.274	Marlin	122				
Sears	103.275	Marlin	122	Sears	282.5227740	CBC	122
Sears	103.2751	Marlin	122	Sears	282.527740	FIE	122
Sears	103.2840	Marlin	80	Sears	2C	Winchester	131
Sears	103.2850	Marlin	81	Sears	2T	Winchester	121,131,141
Sears	103.2870	Marlin	56	Sears	2/57	Stevens	66

House Brand	Model No.	Orig. Mfgr.	Orig. Model	House Brand	Model No.	Orig. Mfgr.	Orig. Model
Sears	2/58	Stevens	66	Sears 200	273.2160	Winchester	1200
Sears	30	High Standard	22 PUMP	Sears 200	273.2250	Winchester	1200
Sears	300	Winchester	1400	Sears 200	273.2251	Winchester	1200
Sears	31	J.C. Higgins	31	Sears 200	273.2280	Winchester	1200
Sears	33	J.C. Higgins	33	Sears 200	273.4310	Winchester	1200
Sears	34	J.C. Higgins	34	Sears 200	273.4320	Winchester	1200
Sears	340.530430	Ithaca	49SS	Sears 200	273.4340	Winchester	1200
Sears	35A	Stevens	66A	Sears 200	273,4350	Winchester	1200
Sears	36	Marlin	80	Sears 200	273.4410	Winchester	1200
Sears	375	Mossberg	45B	Sears 200	273.4420	Winchester	1200
Sears	377	Mossberg	42C	Sears 200	273.4450	Winchester	1200
Sears	381	Mossberg	46B	Seem 200	273.514010	Winchester	1200
Sears	382	Mossberg	46B	Sears 200	273.614010	Winchester	1200
Sears	384	Mossberg	45A	Sears 200	273.514011	Winchester	1200
Sears	385	Mossberg	45B	Sears 200	273.514020	Winchester	1200
Sears	387	Mossberg	42C	Seem 200	273.514040	Winchester	1200
Sears	388	Mossberg	42C	Sears 200	273.514050	Winchester	1200
Sears	389	Mossberg	42A OR 26C	Sears 200	273.514051	Winchester	1200
Sears	390	Mossberg	26C	Sears 200	273.514210	Winchester	1200
Sears	3T	Winchester	190	Sears 200	273.514220	Winchester	1200
Sears	41	Marlin	101	Sears 200	273.514250	Winchester	1200
Sears	41 DLA	Marlin	122	Sears 200	273.514251	Winchester	1200
Sears	42	Marlin	80	Sears 200	273.514810	Winchester	1200
Sears	42DL	Marlin	80	Sears 200	273.614820	Winchester	1200
Sears	42DLM	Marlin	980	Sears 200	273.514830	Winchester	1200
Sears	43	Marlin	81	Sears 200	273.514840	Winchester	1200
Sears	43DL	Marlin	81	Sears 200	273.515010	Winchester	1200
Sears	44DL	Marlin	57	Sears 200	273.515020	Winchester	1200
Sears	44DLM	Marlin	57M	Sears 200	273.515050	Winchester	1200
Sears	45	Marlin	336C	Sears 200	273.515051	Winchester	1200
Sears	46	Marlin	56	Sears 200	273.515080	Winchester	1200
Sears	46DL	Marlin	56	Sears 200	273.515090	Winchester	1200
Sears	4980	Stevens	94-2 W/PAD	Sears 200	273.515220	Winchester	1200
Sears	49.11830/30	Savage	99 A	Sears 200	273.515221	Winchester	1200
Sears	53	Winchester	70	Sears 200	273.515250	Winchester	1200
Sears	54	Winchester	94	Sears 200	273.515251	Winchester	1200
Sears	583.1	High Standard	?	Sears 200	273.515280	Winchester	1200
Sears	583,126	Sako	L46	Sears 200	273.515290	Winchester	1200
Sears	583.13	High Standard	?	Sears 200	273.515410	Winchester	1200
Sears	583.14	H & R	120	Sears 200	273.515420	Winchester	1200
Sears	583.15	H&R	121	Sears 200	273.515470	Winchester	1200
Sears	583.16	High Standard	10	Sears 200	273.515710	Winchester	1200
Sears	583.17	High Standard	?	Sears 200	273.515720	Winchester	1200
Sears	583.18	H & R	120	Sears 200	273.515920	Winchester	1200
Sears	583.2	H & R	M120	Sears 200	273.5310	Winchester	1200
Sears	583.20	High Standard	Flight King	Sears 200	273.5350	Winchester	1200
Sears	583.2085-87	High Standard	20ga pump	Sears 2T	273.27530	Winchester	141
Sears	583.21	H&R	M1 20	Sears 300	273.1310	Winchester	1400
Sears	583.25	H&R	M1 21	Sears 300	273.1320	Winchester	1400
Sears	583.3	H&R	M121	Sears 300	273.1350	Winchester	1400
Sears	583.4	High Standard	10	Sears 300	273.21550	Winchester	1400
Sears	583.7	High Standard	10	Sears 300	273.2500	Winchester	1400
Sears	583.91	H & R	121	Sears 300	273.2540	Winchester	1400
Sears	6C (Canada)	Winchester	Cooy 64,64B	Sears 300	273.32060	Winchester	1400
Sears	6C(American)	Winchester	490	Sears 300	273.32070	Winchester	1400
Sears	66	J.C.Higgins	66	Sears 300	273.521050	Winchester	1400
Sears	73	Savage	73	Sears 300	273.521051	Winchester	1400
Sears	870.528140	Voere	Clip .22	Sears 300	273.521080	Winchester	1400
Sears	92	Stevens	39	Sears 300	273.521090	Winchester	1400
Sears	93	Stevens	38	Sears 300	273.521160	Winchester	1400
Sears	94	Stevens	237	Sears 300	273.521161	Winchester	1400
Sears	95	Stevens	238	Sears 300	273.521250	Winchester	1400
Sears	97	Savage	94	Sears 300	273.521251	Winchester	1400
Sears	97AC	Savage	94AC	Sears 300	273.521260	Winchester	1400
Sears	98	Stevens	37	Sears 300	273.521280	Winchester	1400
Sears	98	Springfield	944	Sears 300	273.521290	Winchester	1400
Sears	M30	Stevens	M520	Sears 300	273.521580	Winchester	1400
Sears	mzm	Savage	34	Sears 300	273.521680	Winchester	1400
Sears 100	273.532141	Winchester	NM 94	Sears 300	273.521710	Winchester	1400
Sears 200	2732.5320	Winchester	1200	Sears 300	273.521770	Winchester	1400
Sears 200	273.2011	Winchester	1200	Sears 300	273.521780	Winchester	1400
Sears 200	273.21010	Winchester	1200	Sears 300	273.523251	Winchester	1400
				Sears 300	273.52151	Winchester	1400
				Sears 3T-A	273.2390	Winchester	190-290

House Brand	Model No.	Orig. Mfgr.	Orig. Model	House Brand	Model No.	Orig. Mfgr.	Orig. Model
Sears 3T-A	273.2400	Winchester	190-290	Western Auto	103.13	Marlin	81
Sears 3T-A	273.528110	Winchester	190-290	Western Auto	103.16	Marlin	80
Sears 3T-A	273.528111	Winchester	190-290	Western Auto	103.18	Marlin	80
Sears 4T	273.2360	Winchester	270	Western Auto	103.181	Marlin	101
Sears 53A	273.532780	Winchester	70A	Western Auto	103.19780	Marlin	101
Sears 54	273.2120	Winchester	NM 94	Western Auto	103.19790	Marlin	80
Sears 54	273.532140	Winchester	NM 94	Western Auto	103.19800	Marlin	80
Sears 54	273.53419	Winchester	NM 94	Western Auto	103.1981	Marlin	81
Sears 54	273.810	Winchester	NM 94	Western Auto	103.1982	Marlin	81DL
Sears 54	273.811	Winchester	NM 94	Western Auto	103.19820	Marlin	81
Sears 6C	273.28130	Winchester	490	Western Auto	103.19840	Marlin	56
Sears 6C	273.528131	Winchester	490	Western Auto	103.19880	Marlin	57
Sears 6C	273.528132	Winchester	490	Western Auto	103.19890	Marlin	57M
Sears MI	273.27010	Winchester	121	Western Auto	103.1997	Marlin	101
Sears M5,M-5T	273.2340	Winchester	150-250	Western Auto	103.2	Marlin	80
Sears M5,M-5T	273.2341	Winchester	150-250	Western Auto	103.228	Marlin	80
Sears M5,M-5T	273.2350	Winchester	150-250	Western Auto	103.229	Marlin	81
Sears M5,M-5T	273.2351	Winchester	150-250	Western Auto	103.273	Marlin	980
Sears T.W. 73	273.532730	Winchester	670 Mag.	Western Auto	103.274	Marlin	122
Sears T.W. 73	23.31020	Winchester	New Mod 70	Western Auto	103.2751	Marlin	122
Sears T.W. 73	273.1390	Winchester	MN 30-06	Western Auto	103.2840	Marlin	80
Sears T.W. 73	273.1400	Winchester	MN 70 (.270)	Western Auto	103.2850	Marlin	81
Sears T.W. 73	273.1830	Winchester	New Mod 70	Western Auto	103.2870	Marlin	56
Sears T.W. 73	273.1840	Winchester	New Mod 70	Western Auto	103.360	Marlin	90
Sears T.W. 73	273.1850	Winchester	New Mod 70	Western Auto	103.450	Marlin	336
Sears T.W. 73	273.1860	Winchester	New Mod 70	Western Auto	103.451	Marlin	336
Sears T.W. 73	273.1870	Winchester	New Mod 70	Western Auto	103.720	Marlin	59
Sears T.W. 73	273.31010	Winchester	New Mod 70	Western Auto	103.740	Marlin	59
Sears T.W. 73	273.31060	Winchester	New Mod 70	Western Auto	105-2060	Marlin	780
Sears T.W. 73	273.32020	Winchester	New Mod 70	Western Auto	105-2060	Marlin	80
Sears T.W. 73	273.32030	Winchester	New Mod 70	Western Auto	107	Mossberg	640K
Sears T.W. 73	273.32040	Winchester	New Mod 70	Western Auto	107A	Mossberg	640
Sears T.W. 73	273.532061	Winchester	New Mod 70	Western Auto	110-2140	Marlin	81
Sears T.W. 73	273.532071	Winchester	New Mod 70	Western Auto	110-2140	Marlin	781
Sears T.W. 73	273.532081	Winchester	New Mod 70	Western Auto	115	Savage	46
Sears T.W. 73	273.53403	Winchester	New Mod 70	Western Auto	115-2277	Marlin	57
Sears T.W. 73	273.53406	Winchester	New Mod 70	Western Auto	116-2276	Marlin	57M
Sears T.W. 73	273.53409	Winchester	New Mod 70	Western Auto	117	Mossberg	402
Sears T.W. 73	273.32010	Winchester	Now Mod 70	Western Auto	120-2220	Marlin	99
				Western Auto	125	Mossberg	353
Ted Williams	340.530430	Ithaca	49SS	Western Auto	135	Savage	187
				Western Auto	135	Springfield	187A
Shapleigh's	KING NITRO	Savage	15	Western Auto	150m	Marlin	49
				Western Auto	150-2225	Marlin	49
Simmons	411	Savage	540DL	Western Auto	160	Springfield	187A
Simmons	411	Savage	Fox BDE 20ga	Western Auto	160	Savage	80
				Western Auto	200-2280	Marlin	39A
Simmons	411E	Savage	540 BDE	Western Auto	200-2282	Marlin	39A
Simmons	411E	Savage	Fox BDE 20ga	Western Auto	200-2550	Marlin	336
				Western Auto	200-2554	Marlin	336(.44MAG)
Talo	12DL	Stevens	120	Western Auto	205	Mossberg	472PCA
Talo	176 VR	Springfield	67 VR	Western Auto	210A	Mossberg	810AH
Talo	176DL	Springfield	67	Western Auto	220A	Mossberg	800A
				Western Auto	220AD	Mossberg	800AD
Western Auto,Revelation				Western Auto	220B	Mossberg	800B
				Western Auto	220BD	Mossberg	800BD
Revelation	300	Savage	30 D,E,F	Western Auto	220C	Mossberg	800C
Revelation	394 Series P	Stevens	94P	Western Auto	220CD	Mossberg	800CD
Revelation	76	High Standard	Double Nine	Western Auto	225	Savage	340
Revelation	R310	Mossberg	500AB	Western Auto	2280	Marlin	39A
				Western Auto	2282	Marlin	39A Mountie
Western Auto	100	Mossberg	321	Western Auto	230	Savage	340
Western Auto	101Y	Savage	73Y	Western Auto	250	Savage	110E
Western Auto	101.1701	Savage	540BS	Western Auto	250A	Savage	110D
Western Auto	101.171	Savage	540BD	Western Auto	250D	Savage	110
Western Auto	101.2830	Savage	73	Western Auto	260	Savage	170
Western Auto	101.52772	Savage	65M	Western Auto	260	Springfield	174
Western Auto	101.535D	Savage	18	Western Auto	300	Springfield	67
Western Auto	101.53500	Savage	18D	Western Auto	300	Stevens	30
Western Auto	101.53521	Savage	340	Western Auto	300A	Savage	30AC
Western Auto	101.5380	Savage	18AC	Western Auto	300F	Stevens	77C
Western Auto	101.5380D	Savage	18DAC	Western Auto	300H	Savage	30,HAC
Western Auto	101.5410	Savage	18DS,S	Western Auto	300-300AC	Springfield	67
Western Auto	103	Savage	89	Western Auto	310	Mossberg	500

House Brand	Model No.	Orig. Mfgr.	Orig. Model	House Brand	Model No.	Orig. Mfgr.	Orig. Model
Western Auto	310A	Mossberg	500A	Western Field	170	Mossberg	395K
Western Auto	310AB	Mossberg	500AB	Western Field	172	Mossberg	395K
Western Auto	310B	Mossberg	500B	Western Field	173	Mosaberg	395
Western Auto	310C	Mossberg	500C	Western Field	175	Mossberg	385K
Western Auto	310E	Mossberg	500E	Western Field	17A	Mossberg	73
Western Auto	312	Mossberg	395	Western Field	I8	Mossberg	75
Western Auto	312AK	Mossberg	395K	Western Field	20	Mossberg	9R
Western Auto	312SB	Mossberg	395T	Western Field	215A	Mossberg	85
Western Auto	316	Mossberg	390	Western Field	24M,488A	Mossberg	51
Western Auto	316BB	Mossberg	390T	Western Field	30	Savage	520
Western Auto	316BK	Mossberg	390K	Western Field	31A	Mossberg	44
Western Auto	325B	Mossberg	385T	Western Field	31A	Mossberg	40
Western Auto	325BK	Mossberg	385K	Western Field	32	Mossberg	21
Western Auto	330	Mossberg	183 & 183K	Western Field	32	Mossberg	20
Western Auto	330B	Mossberg	183T	Western Field	33	Marlin	336
Western Auto	335-3725	Marlin	59	Western Field	35A	Mossberg	30
Western Auto	336	Springfield	951	Western Field	36	Savage	521
Western Auto	350	Stevens	94	Western Field	36	Mossberg	10
Western Auto	350A	Savage	94D	Western Field	36B	Mossberg	25A
Western Auto	350M	Stevens	94	Western Field	36B	Mossberg	10
Western Auto	355	Stevens	947	Western Field	36C	Mossberg	25A
Western Auto	355Y	Savage	94Y	Western Field	360	Mossberg	26C
Western Auto	355YE	Springfield	947YE	Western Field	37	Mossberg	30
Western Auto	356Y	Springfield	944Y	Western Field	39	Mossberg	25
Western Auto	360	Savage	540	Western Field	390A	Mossberg	26C
Western Auto	360	Savage	FOX mod B	Western Field	40,D	Mossberg	44
Western Auto	360C	Savage	540C	Western Field	40	Marlin	101
Western Auto	400	Stevens	745	Western Field	40N	Noble	40NA
Western Auto	400C	Savage	745C	Western Field	40M-215A	Mossberg	185
Western Auto	420	High Standard	Supmatic C-011	Western Field	41	Mossberg	45
				Western Field	45	Marlin	989M2
Western Auto	425	High Standard	Supmatic C-120	Western Field	45	Mossberg	42
				Western Field	45B	Mossberg	26C
Western Auto	460	Springfield	511	Western Field	45C	Mossberg	25A
Western Auto	SD52A	Stevens	311	Western Field	46	Mossberg	42
				Western Field	466	Mossberg	RA1
West Point	45	Marlin	60	Western Field	469	Mossberg	RA1-Kit
				Western Field	46A	Mossberg	42
Wards, Western Field, and Hawthorn				Western Field	46C	Moseborg	42A
				Western Field	46D	Mossberg	42C
Hawthorn	110	Unknown	S shot SG	Western Field	47	Mossberg	45A
Hawthorn	580 EJN	Colt	Colteer/bolt	Western Field	472	Noble	50
Hawthorn	814 EJN	Colt	Colteer/SS	Western Field	47A,L	Mossberg	45A
Hawthorn	820B	Mossberg	340	Western Field	48	Mossberg	45A
Hawthorn	880	Colt	Colteer/semi	Western Field	488A	Mossberg	51
Hawthorn	880 EJN	Colt	Colteer/bolt	Western Field	48A	Mossberg	45B
				Western Field	48A	Mossberg	46MLB
Wards	24M 419A	Mossberg	9	Western Field	5-4	Mossberg	8-M4
Wards	472	Noble	50	Western Field	50	Glenfield	60
Wards	850	Mossberg	353	Western Field	502-26FR	Mossberg	500
Wards Triumph	52	Savage	315	Western Field	505	Mossberg	500
				Western Field	509	Mossberg	500
Western Field	04M-489A	Mossberg	50	Western Field	524	Mossberg	500
Western Field	04M-218A	Mossberg	73C	Western Field	534	Mossberg	500
Western Field	04M-2117A	Mossberg	9	Western Field	536	Mossberg	500
Western Field	04M-217A	Mossberg	75C	Western Field	539	Mossberg	500
Western Field	04M-214A	Mossberg	85C	Western Field	550A	Mossberg	500A
Western Field	04M-216A	Mossberg	83C	Western Field	550AS	Mossberg	500AB
Western Field	I	Mossberg	RF-1	Western Field	550B	Mossberg	500B
Western Field	10-SD247A	Stevens	94B (Tenite)	Western Field	550C	Mossberg	500B
Western Field	14	Savage	39A	Western Field	550E	Mossberg	500E
Western Field	14	Savage	59A	Western Field	550E	Mossberg	500E
Western Field	14M-215A	Mossberg	85	Western Field	60	Savage	620A
Western Field	14M-497B	Mossberg	M42	Western Field			
Western Field	14M-488A	Mossberg	50		600ERI 12 GA	Remington	SPT 58
Western Field	15	Mossberg	80	Western Field	60SB	Savage	620A
Western Field	150	Mossberg	183K	Western Field	679	Mossberg	472
Western Field	151X	Kessler	?	Western Field	710	Savage	110
Western Field	155	Mossberg	173	Western Field	72	Noble	50
Western Field	15A	Mossberg	83	Western Field	72C	Mossberg	472
Western Field	16	Mossberg	85	Western Field	730	Mossberg	8IOAH
Western Field	160	Mossberg	385K	Western Field	732	Mossberg	810AH
Western Field	16A	Mossberg	85	Western Field	734	Mossberg	810A
Western Field	17	Mossberg	73	Western Field	740	Marlin	336

House Brand	Model No.	Orig. Mfgr.	Orig. Model	House Brand	Model No.	Orig. Mfgr.	Orig. Model
Western Field	765	Mossberg	810A	Western Field	M10	Stevens	9.4
Western Field	766	Mossberg	810B				Short tang
Western Field	767	Mossberg	800A	Western Field	M150	Mossberg	183T
Western Field	768	Mossberg	800A	Western Field	M155	Mosaberg	183D
Western Field	771	Mossberg	472BA	Western Field	M160	Mossberg	385T
Western Field	772	Mossberg	472PCA	Western Field	M170	Mossberg	395S
Western Field	775	Mossberg	800AD	Western Field	M172	Mossberg	395K
Western Field	776	Mossberg	800BD	Western Field	M175	Mossberg	385K
Western Field	778	Mossberg	472BAS	Western Field			
Western Field	780	Mossberg	800A		KC3 NH402A	Stevens	820
Western Field	782	Mossberg	800B	Western Field	M35	Savage	520 POLY
Western Field	79	Mossberg	472 PRA	Western Field	M36	Savage	521
Western Field	50	Savage	29	Western Field	M60	Savage	620 DELUX
Western Field	807A ECH	CON	Colteer	Western Field	M61	Savage	621 DELUX
			S.S.	Western Field	M72	Mossberg	472 PRA
Western Field	808	Savage	87	Western Field	M734	Mossberg	810BH
Western Field	808C	Savage	87J	Western Field	M771	Moseberg	472SBA
Western Field	815	Mossberg	321	Western Field	M772	Mossberg	472PCA
Western Field	820B	Mossberg	340	Western Field	M7 75	Mossberg	800AD
Western Field	822	Mossberg	640K	Western Field	M776	Mossberg	800BD
Western Field	828	Mossberg	353	Western Field	M778	Mossberg	472BAS
Western Field	830	Mossberg	340K	Western Field	M780	Mossberg	800A
Western Field	832	Mossberg	341	Western Field	M782	Mossberg	800B
Western Field	836	Savage	187N	Western Field	M808.C	Stevens	87,C,J
Western Field	840	Mossberg	640	Western Field	M808N	Stevens	87N
Western Field	842	Mossberg	346K	Western Field	M80A	Savage	M29-D1
Western Field	846	Mossberg	351C	Western Field	M815	Mossberg	320
Western Field	850 855	Mossberg	353	Western Field	M822	Mossberg	640K
Western Field	852	Mossberg	341	Western Field	M85	Stevens	85
Western Field	865	Mossberg	402	Western Field	M-SD57	Stevens	87
Western Field	880	Colt	Colteer	Western Field	SS 94B	Stevens	94C
			Semi.	Western Field	SB033	Savage	520
Western Field	894	Mossberg	430-432				W/POLY
Western Field	895	Mossberg	402	Western Field	SB066	Savage	621
Western Field	9-2 3/4	Mossberg	9-2 1/2				DELX POLY
Western Field	93M	Mossberg	26C	Western Field	SB067	Savage	621
Western Field	93M-213A	Mossberg	75B				DELX COMP
Western Field	93M-2116A	Mossberg	9	Western Field	S5112C	Savage	540C
Western Field	93M-212A	Mossberg	738	Western Field	SB115	Savage	115
Western Field	93M-211A	Mossberg	83B	Western Field	SB300,C	Stevens	311,C
Western Field	93M-210A	Mossberg	85B	Western Field	SB30A	Savage	520
Western Field	93M-497A	Mossberg	42C	Western Field	SB311C	Savage	311C
Western Field	93M-491A	Mussberg	465	Western Field	SB312	Savage	540D
Western Field	93M-495A	Mossberg	45B	Western Field	SB312	Savage-Fox	BDL
Western Field	EMN 171	Marlin	50	Western Field	SB33	Savage	520 POLY
Western Field	EMN 176	Marlin	55	Western Field	SB60A	Savage	620 DFLUX
Western Field	M-SD57	Stevens	M87	Western Field	SB61A	Savage	621 DELUX
Western Field	M025	Savage	520A	Western Field	SB620A	Stevens	620A
Western Field	M040 0/U	Marlin	90	Western Field	SB66	Savage	621 DELX
Western Field	M040N	Stevens	820				POLY
Western Field	M051	Stevens	515	Western Field	SB712	Savage	840
Western Field	M059	Stevens	M87	Western Field	SB80A	Savage	29-DI
Western Field	M060	Stevens	620	Western Field	SB85TA	Stevens	85
Western Field	M080	Savage	29 & 75	Western Field	SB87,TA	Stevens	M87
Western Field	M087	Stevens	M87	Western Field	XNH 175	Marlin	55
				Western Field	XNH 565	Noble	60-66
				Widgeon	SA 650	Marlin	55 12 GA

PROOF MARKS

The proof marks shown below will assist in determining nationality of manufacturers when no other markings are evident. Since the U.S. has no proofing houses (as in England, France, Germany and other European countries), most U.S. manufacturers voluntarily proof their firearms with a specifed style of proofmark (i.e. the interlocked "WP" synonymous with the Winchester trademark can be fired using modern smokeless powder) shells. Pre-1850 European firearms oftentimes do not exhibit any commercial proof marks and with the exception of an occasional barrel address, they represent the single hardest bracket of firearms I can research properly. Captured weapons from major wars occasionally show 2 different nationalities of proofmarks. This is acceptable since the gun was proofed in a national proof house after original manufacture and again when the gun was "exported" to a different country as a military acquisition.

AUSTRIAN PROOF MARKS

PROOF MARK	CIRCA	PROOF HOUSE	TYPE OF PROOF and GUN
	since 1891	Vienna	provisional proof for multi barrel guns
	since 1891	Ferlach	provisional proof for multi barrel guns
	1829-1958	Vienna	black powder proof for multi barrel guns
	1829-1958	Ferlach	black powder proof for multi barrel guns
BH	since 1891	Bundesheer	preliminary proof for multi barrel guns
NPB	1891-1928	Budapest	smokeless powder proof for parabellum pistols
NPF	1891 to date	Ferlach	smokeless powder proof for parabellum pistols
NPP	1891-1931	Ferlach	smokeless powder proof for parabellum pistols
NPV	since 1891	Vienna	smokeless powder proof for parabellum pistols
NPW	1891-1931	Weipert	smokeless powder proof for parabellum pistols

BELGIAN PROOF MARKS

PROOF MARK	CIRCA	PROOF HOUSE	TYPE OF PROOF and GUN
	since 1852	Belgium	provisional black powder proof for breech loading guns & rifled barrels

	—	—	double proof marking for unfurnished barrels
	—	—	triple proof provisional marking for unfurnished barrels
	since 1893	—	definitive black powder proof for breech loading guns, small bore guns & handguns
	since 1853	Perron	View stamp & inspectors mark for parabellum pistols
P.V	since 1924	—	Nitro proof for rifled barrel & parabellum pistols
R	since 1852	—	rifled arms defense for smokeless proof parabellum pistols
PV	—	—	Superior nitro proof

BRITISH PROOF MARKS - ENGLAND

PROOF MARK	CIRCA	PROOF HOUSE	TYPE OF PROOF and GUN
	since 1856	London	provisional proof for barrels
	since 1856	Birmingham	provisional proof for barrels
	since 1637	London	definitive black powder proof for shotguns, muzzle loader barrels
NP	since 1904	London	definitive nitro proof for all guns - parabellum pistols
BNP	since 1954	Birmingham	definitive nitro proof for barrel & action
BP	since 1904	Birmingham	black powder proof only for parabellum pistols
SP	1868-1925	London	definitive special super power proof for parabellum pistols
SP	1868-1925	Birmingham	voluntary special black powder proof

	1868-1925	London	reproof marking for black powder rifles
	1868-1925	Birmingham	reproof marking for black powder rifles
	1868-1925	Birmingham	definitive black powder proof for shotguns
NP	since 1904	Birmingham	definitive nitro proof for all guns
V	since 1670	London	view mark
BV	since 1904	Birmingham	view mark

FRENCH PROOF MARKS

PARIS HOUSE	ST ETIENNE HOUSE	CIRCA	TYPE OF PROOF and GUN
		since 1897	provisional proof unfinished short barreled guns
	ST ETIENNE	1897	standard proof for finished guns
	ST ETIENNE	1897	double proof finished & joined barrels
N.A.	N.A. ST ETIENNE	1897	single barrel proof for non-assembled guns
	F	1897	finished black powder guns
	S	1897	special proof for finished guns
		1897	ordinary smokeless powder proof
	AR ST. ETIENNE	1897	superior smokeless powder proof

GERMAN PROOF MARKS

PROOF MARK	CIRCA	PROOF HOUSE	TYPE OF PROOF and GUN
	since 1952	Ulm	
	since 1968	Hannover	
	since 1968	Kiel (W. German)	
	since 1968	Munich	
	since 1968	Cologne (W. German)	
	since 1968	Berlin (W. German)	
FB	since 1952	W. German	voluntary proof for Flobert rifle
J	since 1952	W. German	repair proof for major gun parts
M	since 1952	W. German	provisional black powder for shotgun & multi barreled rifles
N	since 1952	W. German	definitive nitro proof for all guns
SP	since 1952	W. German	definitive black powder for smokeless ammo guns
	since 1952	W. German	Flobert for special purpose guns signal, flare, gas, & stun guns
N	since 1945	E. German, Suhl	smokeless powder proof
G	since 1950	E. German, Suhl	1st black powder proof for rifled barrels
N	since 1950	E. German, Suhl	nitro powder proof

	since 1950	E. German, Suhl repair proof
	since 1950	E. German, Suhl 1st black powder proof for smooth bored barrels
	since 1950	E. German, Suhl inspection mark
	since 1950	E. German, Suhl choke-bore barrel mark

ITALIAN PROOF MARKS

PROOF MARK	CIRCA	PROOF HOUSE	TYPE OF PROOF and GUN
	since 1951	Brescia	provisional proof for all guns
	since 1951	Gardone	provisional proof for all guns
	since 1951	Gardone & Brescia	definitive proof for guns with smokeless powder
	since 1951	Gardone & Brescia	finish proof for firearms non saleable
	since 1951	Gardone & Brescia	1st black powder proof

SPANISH PROOF MARKS

PROOF MARK	CIRCA	PROOF HOUSE	TYPE OF PROOF and GUN
	since 1910	Eibar	provisional black powder proof for shotguns
	since 1910	Eibar	temporary black powder proof for shotguns
	since 1910	Eibar	final black powder proof for breech loading shotguns
	since 1910	Eibar	final smokeless powder proof for breech loading shotguns
	since 1910	Eibar	re-enforced smokeless powder proof for breech loading shotguns
	since 1910	Eibar	provisional proof for shotguns

	since 1910	Eibar	final black powder proof for breech loading shotgun
	since 1923	Eibar	final & single black powder proof for double barreled muzzle loading shotun
	since 1923	Eibar	final & single black powder proof for single barrel smooth bored breechloading guns
	since 1923	Eibar	final black powder proof for double barreled breechloading rifles
	since 1923	Eibar	final black powder proof for single barrel breechloading rifles
E	since 1923	Eibar	re-enforced voluntary proof for single proof for single & double barrel shotguns
	since 1923	Eibar	Final proof of military-style rifle
	since 1923	Eibar	single & final proof of non-self loading pistols
	since 1923	Eibar	single & final proof for self loading pistols & revolvers
	since 1929	Eibar	admission proof for guns with old marks
	since 1929	Eibar	proof used in Barcelona for guns with old marks
R	since 1929	Eibar	final proof for revolver
P	since 1929	Eibar	proof for semi-automatic pistols
FE	since 1929	Eibar	special manufacturer's mark for guns made for foreign sales
AXIII	since 1929	Eibar	smokeless proof for shotgun barrels
CH	since 1929	Eibar	re-inforced smokeless proof for shotgun barrels

BATF Guide

A listing has been provided below of District/Technical offices for the U.S. and other territories. You are encouraged to contact them if you have any question(s) regarding the legality of any weapon(s) or their interpretation of existing laws and regulations. Remember, ignorance is no excuse when it involves Federal Firearms Regulations and Laws. Although these various regions may not be able to help you with state, city, county, or local firearms regulations and laws, their job is to assist you on a Federal level.

BATF REGULATORY ENFORCEMENT - DISTRICT/TECHNICAL SERVICES OFFICES
ADDRESSES AND PHONE NUMBERS

MIDWEST DISTRICT

IL, IN, KY, MI, MN, ND, OH, SD, WV, AND WI.
300 S. Riverside Plaza, Suite 310
Chicago, IL 60606-6616
Phone No.: 312-353-1967

CINCINNATI TECHNICAL SERVICES

6525 Federal Office Building
550 Main Street
Cincinnati, OH 45202-3263
Phone No.: 513-684-3334

NORTH ATLANTIC DISTRICT

CT, DE, ME, MD, MA, NH, NJ, NY, PA, RI, AND VT.
6 World Trade Center, 6th Fl.
New York, NY 10048
Phone No.: 212-264-2328

PHILADELPHIA TECHNICAL SERVICES

Independence Square West
Philadelphia, PA 19016
Phone No.: 215-597-4107

SOUTHEAST DISTRICT

AL, DC, FL, GA, MS, NC, PR, SC, TN, AND VA.
2600 Century Parkway, NE
Suite 300
Atlanta, GA 30345
Phone No.: 404-679-5010

SOUTHWEST DISTRICT

AR, AZ, CO, IA, KS, LA, MO, NE, NM, OK, AND TX.
1114 Commerce St, 7th Fl.
Dallas, TX 76242
Phone No.: 214-767-2280

WESTERN REGION

AK, CA, GU, HI, ID, MT, NV, OR, UT, WA, WY, AS, AND CAM.
221 Main St, 11th Fl.
San Francisco, CA 94105
Phone No.: 415-744-7013

Firearms Inventory Record

#___.**Type of Firearm:** Pistol _____Rifle _____Shotgun_____Other _____

Manufacturer _____Model _____

Ser. No._____Cal/ga._____Barrel Length _____in./cm.

Overall Condition_____Remarks _____

_____

Purchase: From _____Date_____Value $ _____

Appraisal: By _____Date_____Value $ _____

#___.**Type of Firearm:** Pistol _____Rifle _____Shotgun_____Other _____

Manufacturer _____Model _____

Ser. No._____Cal/ga._____Barrel Length _____in./cm.

Overall Condition_____Remarks _____

_____

Purchase: From _____Date_____Value $ _____

Appraisal: By _____Date_____Value $ _____

#___.**Type of Firearm:** Pistol _____Rifle _____Shotgun_____Other _____

Manufacturer _____Model _____

Ser. No._____Cal/ga._____Barrel Length _____in./cm.

Overall Condition_____Remarks _____

_____

Purchase: From _____Date_____Value $ _____

Appraisal: By _____Date_____Value $ _____

#___.**Type of Firearm:** Pistol _____Rifle _____Shotgun_____Other _____

Manufacturer _____Model _____

Ser. No._____Cal/ga._____Barrel Length _____in./cm.

Overall Condition_____Remarks _____

_____

Purchase: From _____Date_____Value $ _____

Appraisal: By _____Date_____Value $ _____

Firearms Inventory Record

#____.**Type of Firearm:** Pistol _____ Rifle _____ Shotgun _____ Other _____

Manufacturer _____ Model _____

Ser. No. _____ Cal/ga. _____ Barrel Length _____ in./cm.

Overall Condition _____ Remarks _____

_____

Purchase: From _____ Date _____ Value $ _____

Appraisal: By _____ Date _____ Value $ _____

#____.**Type of Firearm:** Pistol _____ Rifle _____ Shotgun _____ Other _____

Manufacturer _____ Model _____

Ser. No. _____ Cal/ga. _____ Barrel Length _____ in./cm.

Overall Condition _____ Remarks _____

_____

Purchase: From _____ Date _____ Value $ _____

Appraisal: By _____ Date _____ Value $ _____

#____.**Type of Firearm:** Pistol _____ Rifle _____ Shotgun _____ Other _____

Manufacturer _____ Model _____

Ser. No. _____ Cal/ga. _____ Barrel Length _____ in./cm.

Overall Condition _____ Remarks _____

_____

Purchase: From _____ Date _____ Value $ _____

Appraisal: By _____ Date _____ Value $ _____

#____.**Type of Firearm:** Pistol _____ Rifle _____ Shotgun _____ Other _____

Manufacturer _____ Model _____

Ser. No. _____ Cal/ga. _____ Barrel Length _____ in./cm.

Overall Condition _____ Remarks _____

_____

Purchase: From _____ Date _____ Value $ _____

Appraisal: By _____ Date _____ Value $ _____

References

Antaris, Leonardo, Dr., *Astra Automatic Pistols*. Sterling, Co: FIRAC Publishing Co., 1988.

Bady, Donald B., *Colt Automatic Pistols*. Los Angeles, Ca: Borden Publishing Co., 1973.

Baer, Larry L., *The Parker Book* North Hollywood, Ca: Beinfeld Publishing Co., 1974.

Barns, Frank C., *Cartridges of the World*. Northbrook, IL: DBI Books, Inc., 1989.

Belford, James N. and Dunlap, Jack, *Mauser Self Loading Pistol*. Alhambia, Ca: Borden Publishing Co., 1969.

Bender, Roy G. III, *Mauser*. Houston, Tx: Collector's Press, 1971.

Breathed and Schroeder, *System Mauser*. Chicago, Il: Handgun Press, 1967.

Brophy, William S., *L.C. Smith Shotguns*. North Hollywood, Ca: Beinfeld Publishing Co., 1977.

Brophy, William S., *Marlin Firearms*. Harrisburg, PA: Stackpole Books, 1989.

Butzer, David F., *The American Shotgun*. Middlefield, Ct: Lyman Publications, 1973.

Buxton, Warren H., *The P-38 Pistol: Volumes I,II & III*. Los Alamos, NM: U.C. Ross Books.

Costanza, Sam, *World of Lugers: Volume I*. Mayfield Heights, Oh: World of Lugers, 1977.

Dance, Tom, *High Standard; A Collector's Guide to the Hamden & Hartford Target Pistols*. Lincoln, RI.: Andrew Mobray Publishers, 1991.

Flayderman, Norm, *Flayderman's Guide (5th ed.)*. Northbrook, IL: DBI Books, Inc., 1990.

Hill and Anthony, *Confederate Long Arms and Pistols*. Charlotte, Nc: Confederate Arms, 1978.

Jinks, Roy G., *History of Smith & Wesson*. North Hollywood, Ca: Beinfeld Publishing Co., 1977.

Karr and Karr, Jr., *Remington Handgun*. Stackpole Co., Second Edition, 1951.

Kenyon, Charles Jr., *Lugers at Random*. Chicago, Il: Handgun Press, 1969.

Kimmel, J., *Savage & Stevens Arms*. Portland, OR: Corey/Stevens Pub., Inc., 1990.

Kopel, Graham, and Moore, *A Study of the Colt Single Action Army Revolver*. La Puente,CA: Kopel, Graham, and Moore Publishers, 1978.

Krasne, Jerry A. *Enyclopedia and Reference Catalog for Auto Loading Guns*. San Diego, CA: Triple K Manufacturing, 1989.

Leithe, Frederick, *Japanese Handguns*. California: Borden Publishing Co., 1968.

Madis, George, *The Model 12*. Lancaster, TX: Published by Author, 1981.

Madis, George, *The Winchester Book*. Lancaster, TX: Privately Published by Author, 1975.

Maxwell, Samuel L., Sr., *Lever Action Magazine Rifles*. Published by Author, 1978.

Murray, Douglas, *The Ninety-Nine*. Published by Author, 1985.

Nonte, Jr., George C. *Firearms Encyclopedia*. Outdoor Life: New York, NY, 1973.

Olson, Ludwig, *Mauser Bolt Action Rifles*. Montezuma, IA: F. Brownell & Son Publishers, Inc., 1976.

Rankin, James L., *Walther*, Vols. I, II, III. Coral Gables, FL: Published by Author, 1976.

Rule, Roger C., *The Rifleman's Rifle*. Northridge, CA: Alliance Books, Inc., 1982.

Sellers, Frank, *American Gunsmiths*. Highland Park, NJ: The Gun Room Press, 1983.

Sellers, Frank, *Sharp's Firearms*. North Hollywood, Ca: Beinfeld Publishing Co., 1978.

Serven, editor, *The Collecting of Guns*. Bonanza Books, 1964.

Sharpe, Phillip B., *The Rifle in America.* Funk and Wagnalls, 1947.

Shooter's Bible. S. Hackensack, NJ: Published annually by Stoeger Industries.

Steindler, *Steindler's New Firearms Dictionary.* Phoenix, AZ: Stackpole Books, 1985.

Still, Jan C. *Axis Pistols.* Marceline, MO: Walsworth Publishing Co., 1986.

Still, Jan C. *Imperial Lugers.* Marceline, MO: Walsworth Publishing Co., 1991.

Still, Jan C. *Third Reich Lugers.* Marceline, MO: Walsworth Publishing Co., 1988.

Tanner, Hans, *Guns of the World.* Bonanza Books, 1972, 1977.

Webster, Donald B. Jr., *Suicide Specials.* Harrisburg, PA: Stackpole, Co., 1958.

West, Bill, *Browning Arms & History.* Santa Fe Springs, Ca: Stockton Trade Press, Inc., 1972.

West, Bill, *Marlin and Ballard Firearms & History.* Norwalk, Ca: Stockton Trade Press, Inc., 1977.

West, Bill, *Remington Arms & History.* Whittier, Ca: Stockton Trade Press, Inc., 1970.

West, Bill, *Savage and Stevens Arms & History.* Whittier, Ca: Stockton Trade Press, Inc., 1971.

Whitaker, Dean H., *Model 70 Winchester 1937-1964.* Dallas, Tx: Taylor Publishing Co., 1978.

Wilkerson, Don, *Post War Colt Single Action Army.* Published by Author, 1978.

Wilkerson, Don, *Post-War Colt Single-Action Revolver, 1976-1986.* Dallas, TX: Taylor Publishing, 1986.

Wilson, R.L., *The Book of Colt Firearms.* Minneapolis, MN: Blue Book Publications, Inc., 1993.

Wilson, R.L., *Colt Commemorative Firearms.* Geneseo, Il: Robert E.P. Cherry Publishing Co., 1973.

Wilson, R.L., *The Colt Heritage.* New York, NY: Simon and Schuster.

Wirnsberger, Gerhard, *The Standard Dictionary of Proofmarks.* Jolex, Inc.

PERIODICALS LISTINGS

American Firearms Industry   2455 E. Sunrise Blvd. Ste. 916, Ft. Lauderdale, FL 33304. Phone No.: 305-561-3505. Membership is $35 per year. Trade publications and related material.

American Handgunner   Published by Publisher's Development. 591 Camino de la Reina, Suite 200, San Diego, CA 92108. Phone No.: 800-537-3006. Published monthly.

American Hunter   Published by the NRA, 11250 Waples Mill Rd., Fairfax, VA 22030. Phone No.: 800-672-3888. Published monthly.

American Rifleman   Published by the NRA, 11250 Waples Mill Rd., Fairfax, VA 22030. Phone No.: 800-672-3888. Subscription included in price of NRA Membership ($35). Published monthly.

Gun Journal   Published monthly by Blue Book Publications, 8009 - 34th Ave. So., Minneapolis, MN 55425. Phone No.: 800-368-2232. Subscription is $29.95 per year (12 issues). Trade Publication for buying & selling firearms.

The Double Gun Journal   5014 Rockery School Rd., East Jordan, MI 49727-9636. Phone No.: 616-536-7439. Published quarterly.

Field & Stream Magazine   P.O. Box 55652, Boulder, CO 80322. Phone No.: 800-289-0639 or 212-779-5000. Subscription rate $15.94 annually. Published monthly (12 issues).

Game & Gun   P.O. Box 968, Traverse City, MI 49685. FAX No.: 616-946-3289. Published bi-monthly.

Gray's Sporting Journal   Published by North American Publications, Inc., 735 Broad Street, Augusta, GA 30901. Phone No.: 706-722-6060. Published bimonthly.

Gun Dog   Published by The Stover Publishing Co., Inc. 1901 Bell Avenue, Des Moines, IA 50315. Phone No.: 515-243-2472. Published bimonthly.

Gun Report   P.O. Box 38, Aledo, IL 61231, Phone No.: 309-582-5311. $33.00 per year (USA), published monthly.

Guns and Ammo   Published by Petersen Publishing Co., 6420 Wilshire Blvd., Los Angeles, CA 90048. Phone No. 310-854-2222. $21.94 per year (USA), published monthly.

Gun Week   P.O. Box 488, Station C, Buffalo, NY 14209. Annual Subscription - $35. Published 3 times a month. Phone No.: 716- 885- 6408

Guns Magazine   Published by Publisher's Development. 591 Camino de la Reina, Suite 200, San Diego, CA 92108. Phone No.: 800-537-3006. Published monthly.

Hunting   Published by Petersen Publishing Co., 6420 Wilshire Blvd., Los Angeles, CA 90048. Phone No.: 213-782-2185. Published bimonthly.

Man at Arms   P.O. Box 460, Lincoln, RI 02865. Published bimonthly ($27 yearly). Phone No. 401-726-8011.

National Alliance of Stocking Gun Dealers   P.O. Box 187, Havelock, NC 28532. Phone No.: 919-447-1313. Members, dealers, and gun dealers - $25; others - $200. Published monthly.

North American Hunter   12301 Whitewater Dr., Minnetonka, MN 55343. Phone No.: 612-936-9333. Published bimonthly (included in membership).

Outdoor Life Magazine   Two Park Ave., New York, NY 10016. Phone No.: 800-365-1580 or 212-779-5000. $15.94 per year (USA).

Safari Club International   4800 W. Gates Pass Rd., Tucson, AZ 85745. Phone No.: 602-620-1220. Publications: Safari magazine, Safari Africa, Deer of the World, Sheep of the World, International Record Book of Trophy Animals, Record Book Field Edition.

Shooting Industry   591 Camino De la Reina #200, San Diego, CA 92108. Phone No.: 800-537-3006, $25 per year (USA). Published monthly.

Shotgun News   P.O. Box 669, Hastings, NE 68902. Subscription - $22 yearly (36 issues). 402-463-4589

Shotgun Sports   P.O. 669, Hastings, NE 68902. Subscription - $20 yearly (36 issues). Phone No.: 402-463-4589.

Skeet   5931 Roft Road, San Antonio, TX 78253. Phone No.: 210-688-3371. $20 per year. Published monthly.

Southern Outdoors   5845 Carmichael Rd., Montgomery, AL 36117. Phone No.: 205-277-3940. Published 9 times per year.

Sporting Clays Magazine   5211 S. Washington Ave., Titusville, FL 32780. Phone No.: 800-677-5212 or 803-681-2219. $23.95 per year (USA). Published bimonthly.

Sporting Goods Business   1 Penn Plaza, New York, NY 10119. Phone No.: 212-714-1300 or 800-933-3321. $65 per year.

The Sporting Goods Dealer   1212 N. Lindbergh Blvd., St. Louis, MO 63132. Phone No.: 314-997-7111.

Sports Afield Magazine   250 W. 55th St., New York, NY 10019. Phone No.: 212-649-4300. (12 issues) $13.97.

Trap & Field   Published by Curtis Magazine Group. 1200 Waterway Blvd., Indianapolis, IN 46202. Phone No.: 317-633-8802. Published monthly.

Turkey & Turkey Hunting   Published by Krause Publications, Inc. 700 E. State St., Iola, WI 54990. Phone No.: 715-445-2214. Published bimonthly

Waterfowl Magazine   P.O. Box 50, Edgefield, SC 29824. Phone No.: 803-637-5767. Published bimonthly.

Western Outdoors   3197 East Airport Dr., Costa Mesa, CA 92626. Phone No: 714-546-4370. Published 9 times per year.

Wildfowl   Published by Stover Publishing, Inc. 1901 Bell Ave., Ste. 4, Des Moines, IA 50315. Phone No.: 515-243-2472. Published bimonthly.

Wing and Clay   43 W. Front St., Ste. 11, Red Bank, NJ 07701. Phone No.: 908-224-8700. Published annually.

Wing & Shot   Published by Stover Publishing, Inc. 1901 Bell Ave., Ste. 4, Des Moines, IA 50315. Phone No.: 515-243-2472. Published bimonthly.

Women & Guns   Published by Second Amendment Foundation, P.O. Box 488, Station C, Buffalo, NY 14209. $24 annual subscription. Published weekly.

Show Time 1996-97!

During the course of a year, we get many requests about which upcoming trade shows we'll be attending. If you want to hook up with Steve, John and related troops up through early 1997, here's where to do it.

April 19-21, 1996
NRA 125th Anniversary - Annual
    Meetings & Exhibits
Dallas Convention Center
Dallas, TX
Booth #235 & #334
Contact: NRA
703-267-3785

May 31, June 1-2, 1996
Ducks Unlimited Great Outdoors
    Sporting & Wildlife Festival
Agricenter International
Memphis, TN
Booth # I-18

Contact: Petersen Publishing
6420 Wilshire Blvd
Los Angeles, CA 90048-5875
(800)395-0444
(213)782-2916

June 29-30, 1996
Duluth Gun Show
Duluth Entertainment Convention
    Center South
Pioneer Hall
Sat. 9-6pm. Sun. 9-3pm.
Contact: Bob White
1920 Greysolon Rd
Duluth, MN 55812
218-724-8387

July 26-28, 1995
Kansas City National Arms Show
26th Annual
at the K.C. Market Center
Exhibition Hall
Fri. 11-6, Sat. 9-6, Sun. 9-3
$4.00 admission
Contact: MVACA Show Committee
PO Box 33033
Kansas City, MO 64114
(913)642-2863

August 17-18, 1996
Minnesota Weapons Collectors Assn.
    Show
St. Paul Civic Center
Sat. 8-5, Sun. 9-3.
$4.00 admission
Contact: MWCA
PO Box 662
Hopkins, MN 55343
(612)721-8976

October 19-20, 1996
Tulsa Gun & Knife Show
at Expo Center - Expo Square
Tulsa Fairgrounds
Sat. 8-7pm, Sun. 8-5pm
Contact: Tulsa Gun Show, Inc.
PO Box 33201
Tulsa, OK 74153-1201
(918)492-0401

December 7-8, 1996
Collector Arms Dealers Assoc. Show
Rosemont Convention Center
Chicago, IL
Sat. 9-5, Sun. 9-2
Contact: CADA Association
P.O. Box 427
Thomson, IL 61285
(815)259-5445

January 30 - February 2, 1997
SHOT Show
Las Vegas Convention Center
Las Vegas, NV
Booth #6628 & #6630

January 31 - February 2, 1997
Antique Arms Show
Sahara Hotel
Las Vegas, NV
Contact: Antique Arms Shows, Inc.
PO Box 2231
Palm Springs, CA 92263
Wallace Beinfeld Show Director
(619)320-5389 FAX (619)320-5231

April 5-6, 1997
Tulsa Gun & Knife Show
at Expo Center - Expo Square
Tulsa Fairgrounds
Sat. 8-7pm, Sun. 8-5pm
Contact: Tulsa Gun Show, Inc.
PO Box 33201
Tulsa, OK 74153-1201
(918)492-0401

KRISPY KOMMENTS

Right when they don't need it is when you have to do it. After a billion phone calls, and a million "have you shipped my book yet?", the staff can usually be counted on for a few post-battle comments. Never have so few suffered so much in so little time.

Thomas J. Stock - "I can't think about this now, I got problems... I got problems..."

Barbara Knowles Olsen - "When I got to my neighbor's garage, there, in the back corner were the mummified bodies of our missing cats. Head-to-head, shoulder-to-shoulder, claw-to-claw, paw-to-paw, frozen in a deathlock for all eternity." — told to S.P. when he dared mention working another 58 day stretch.

Lisa M. Winkels - "Calgon, PLEASE.....take me away."

Jennifer Haugen - "Rilly, I fele jist as alurt as I did wen we startid. Honust, I due."

Walter Horishnyk - "What, me worry?"

Thomas Lundin - "I'm starving. I need some brain food. I could go for a pizza. And then some chocolate. Or maybe Taco Bell. But then again, White Castle sounds good, too. I'll be back after lunch..."

Beth Marthaler - "No...You have the wrong number. This isn't the Blue Book of Cowboy Boots...but hold on, I might find someone who can help you."

John Allen - "Wanted: One more gun, one more fishing pole, a new truck, and a girl-friend (call ext. 14)."

DJ Pallum - "When I started working here they told me it was the Blue Book of Gun Values, but now that I've been here for a month, I found I was really working with the Blue Book of Fruit Jars."

S.P. Fjestad - "No comment - after 1,359 pages of comments, who needs another one?"

Rebecca Glasser - "Always glad to see another book off to the press."

BACKWORD...

*...223 Rem., semi-auto action patterned after the AR-15, vented aluminum handguard with built-in...*TDI (telecommunications device interruption, usually in the form of the obnoxious telephone ring), "Brad, hi - no, we didn't get in the computer Intricacy Grading System disk yet. I know, but we haven't seen anything yet. We can probably generate it on Corel Draw, but it will probably take a lot more time than... Maybe we'll get it, but I kind of doubt it - gotta run, Brad." *...Harris bipod, 24 in. fluted barrel, TDI,* "Hi John. What? How many? Where's he located? Maybe you'd better give the boys out East a call and let them know they might have to do a little traveling real soon. Get a list first, and we'll go from there. Gotta run." *...with flat-top receiver and optional..,* TDI, "Hello, Hello?...beeeep!...beeeep! (start button activation silences this newest audible audacity)..." *...carrying handle, guaranteed less than 1..,* TDI, "Good morning, Victor. Yes, we got your tea - thank you very much! No problem, I got the latest copy of the contract right here. Paragraphs D & M, go ahead ...., Yes, me too, hope the weather gets a little bit better for you .... I know, but I really think we're getting close, (Ed. note: Barbara is now laughing) ....we'll make the changes and you'll have a FAX no later than another couple inches of snowfall. Thanks Victor, goodbye." *...MOA, non-glare parkerized finish, 10 - ...,* TDI, "No one wants us to get a book done, do they? Hi Steve, what's up? When? Next Tuesday? OK, for how long? I guess so, but we're trying to finish up the ... That's going to be tight, but maybe if Walter puts it on photo CD we can composite a B&W image into a foam-core panel and ... an original Gibson Flametop? Are you sure? Better call Dave, Jimmy Wallace, and maybe Mark at Charlie's and let them know that this Canuck is shopping around the lower 48 for the combination to Uncle Scrooge's money bin. You know, maybe two's enough at the forty grand level - whomever loses isn't going to send us an X-mas card. Gotta run, see you Tuesday." *...shot mag., 9.8 lbs. New 1996. V4 it, and give me $1,265, $1,100, $925, $800, $700,* TDI, "Hi Beth, yes, she is - just a second..." (Ed. note: weird form of verbal duck voice gargling occurs after which...) Hi Beth, what? OK, I'll call right away ...Marc! What's wrong now? A stomach ache? If you don't get your little butt into school right now ... I don't care - get to school...NOW! *$600, $550, $500 OK, now clone that and change it into an SN - OK, now make the SN an EA-71 Carbine, SD is, similar to EA-71 Rifle, ex...* TDI, "Who? How did you get this number? We're right in the final stages of trying to get this ... just a second - you need to talk to Barbara............." *...cept has 16 in. barrel with fiberglass shroud and* ...Wow! Look at this FAXed quotation on the Pool Cue book. How can 8½x11 cost $2 less than 9x12?*...integral rear sight assembly (non-detachable), 8. ...* Barbara, you've got to move your car so I... "Forget it. No one leaves until the Fat Lady Smells..." Well, you're the Boss! *...6 lbs. New 1996. Grab the V4 above and insert, insert first price of $1,475 and cut 'em ...* TDI, "Hi Tom, What? How could the Airgun and Blackpowder have almost no increase? I guess I just assumed both sections would be up 10% and I should have, figured out that ...that's fine - run them out at 11 pt. and probably no one will know the difference anyway. Yeh, I know, but we've bought the paper already and everybody is expecting 1,360...that's fine, I don't think we'll have any problems as long as you don't tell anybody. Gotta run!" *...off at the end, and put in an MT that ...* (Ed. note: doorbell chimes, after which we are greeted by the friendly traveling meatman who just happens to have some surplus cases leftover that have been discounted ...) "...OK, thank you sir, but my freezer won't hold that much and.." TDI, "Greg! You're kidding - when did it happen? Where is he now? How's mom doing? You think I should come up? OK, I'll..."